Collins

World
Encyclopedia

William Collins' dream of knowledge for all began with the publication of his first book in 1819. A self-educated mill worker, he not only enriched millions of lives, but also founded a flourishing publishing house. Today, staying true to this spirit, Collins books are packed with inspiration, innovation, and practical expertise. They place you at the centre of a world of possibility and give you exactly what you need to explore it.

Collins. Do more.

Collins

World
Encyclopedia

Collins

HarperCollins Publishers
Westerhill Road, Bishopbriggs,
Glasgow G64 2QT

www.collins.co.uk

First published 1995 as *Collins Paperback Encyclopedia*
Fourth edition 2003
Revised and updated 2005

© 2005 Research Machines plc
Maps and diagrams © 2005 Research Machines plc
Helicon Publishing is a division of Research Machines
Web links © 2005 HarperCollins Publishers

British Library Cataloguing in Publication Data

A catalogue record for this book is available from the British Library

ISBN 0 00 721191-0

Typeset by Davidson Pre-Press Graphics Ltd, Glasgow
Printed and bound in Great Britain by Clays Ltd, St Ives plc.

Preface

The *Collins World Encyclopedia* is an illustrated single-volume companion to world events, history, arts, science, medicine, and information technology for home, school, and library use. The aim throughout has been to provide up-to-date, readable entries, using clear and non-technical language.

Arrangements of entries

Entries are ordered alphabetically, as if there were no spaces between words. Thus, entries for words beginning 'national' follow the order:

national income
nationalism
nationalization
National Missile Defense

However, we have avoided a purely mechanical alphabetization in cases where a different order corresponds more with human logic. For example, sovereigns with the same name are grouped according to country before number, so that *King George II of England* is placed before *King George III of England*, and not next to *King George II of Greece*. Words beginning 'Mc' and 'Mac' are all treated as if they begin 'Mac'; 'St' is treated as if spelt out in full.

Foreign names

Names of foreign sovereigns and places are usually shown in their English form, except where the foreign name is more familiar, for example *Juan Carlos* and not *John Charles*, but *Florence* and not *Firenze*.

Titles

Entries for people with titles are under the name by which they are best known, for example the entry for *Anthony Eden* is under E for *Eden* and not under A for *Lord Avon*.

Cross references

These are indicated by an *asterisk. Cross referencing is selective; a cross reference is shown when another entry contains material directly relevant to the subject matter of an entry, and to where the reader may not otherwise think of looking.

Units

SI (metric) units are used throughout for scientific entries. Measurements of distances, temperatures, sizes and so on include an imperial conversion after the metric measurement.

Science, technology and medicine

Many scientific, technical, and medical terms also have common names that are more widely used. Both technical and common names are often listed, the main entry being given under the term the general reader is most likely to be familiar with. For example, the entry for *rubella* is a cross reference to the main entry under *German measles*.

Chinese names

Pinyin, the preferred system for transcribing Chinese names, is generally used: thus, there is an entry at *Mao Zedong* and not *Mao Tse-tung*. The former (Wade–Giles) forms, for example *Chiang Kai-shek* are given as cross references where appropriate.

Comments and suggestions

We welcome comments from readers on suggested improvements or alterations to the Encyclopedia.

Please send them to

Text Reference Department
HarperCollins Publishers
Westerhill Road
Bishopbriggs
Glasgow G64 2QT

a

A in physics, symbol for *ampere, a unit of electrical current.

Aalto, (Hugo) Alvar (Henrik) (1898–1976) Finnish architect and designer. He was a pioneer of the Modern Movement in his native Finland. Initially working within the confines of the International Style, he later developed a unique architectural style, characterized by asymmetry, curved walls, and contrast of natural materials. He invented a new form of laminated bent-plywood furniture in 1932 and won many design awards for household and industrial items. Aalto's buildings include Baker House, a Hall of Residence at the Massachusetts Institute of Technology 1947–49; Technical High School, Otaniemi, 1962–65; and Finlandia Hall, Helsinki, 1972.

aardvark (Afrikaans 'earth pig') nocturnal mammal *Orycteropus afer*, the only species in the order Tubulidentata, found in central and southern Africa. A timid, defenceless animal about the size of a pig, it has a long head, a piglike snout, large ears, sparse body hair, a thick tail, and short legs.

abacus ancient calculating device made up of a frame of parallel wires on which beads are strung. The method of calculating with a handful of stones on a 'flat surface' (Latin *abacus*) was familiar to the Greeks and Romans, and used by earlier peoples, possibly even in ancient Babylon; it survives in the more sophisticated bead-frame form of the Russian *schoty* and the Japanese *soroban*. The abacus has been superseded by the electronic calculator.

abalone edible marine snail of the worldwide genus *Haliotis*, family Haliotidae. Abalones have flattened, oval, spiralled shells, which have holes around the outer edge and a bluish mother-of-pearl lining. This lining is used in ornamental work.

Abba Swedish pop group 1973–81, one of the most successful groups in Europe during the 1970s. Their well-produced songs were characterized by the harmonies of the two female lead singers, and were aimed at a wide audience. Abba had a string of international hits beginning with 'Waterloo' (winner of the Eurovision Song Contest 1974) and including 'SOS' (1974), 'Fernando' (1976), 'Dancing Queen' (1976), and 'The Winner Takes It All' (1980).

Abbasid dynasty Family of rulers of the Islamic empire, whose *caliphs reigned in Baghdad 750–1258. They were descended from Abbas, the prophet Muhammad's uncle, and some of them, such as

Harun al-Rashid and Mamun (reigned 813–33), were outstanding patrons of cultural development. Later their power dwindled, and in 1258 Baghdad was burned by the Tatars.

abbey in the Christian church, a building or group of buildings housing a community of monks or of nuns, all dedicated to a life of celibacy and religious seclusion, governed by an abbot or abbess respectively. The word is also applied to a building that was once the church of an abbey; for example, Westminster Abbey, London.

Abbey Theatre playhouse in Dublin, Republic of Ireland, associated with the literary revival of the early 1900s, that was part of a general cultural Irish revival. The theatre opened in 1904 and staged the works of a number of Irish dramatists, including Lady Gregory, W B Yeats, J M Synge, and Seán O'Casey. Burned down in 1951, the Abbey Theatre was rebuilt in 1966.

Abd al-Hamid II (1842–1918) Last sultan of Turkey 1876–1909. In 1908 the *Young Turks under Enver Pasha forced Abd al-Hamid to restore the constitution of 1876 and in 1909 insisted on his deposition. He died in confinement. For his part in the *Armenian massacres suppressing the revolt of 1894–96 he was known as the 'Great Assassin'; his actions still motivate Armenian violence against the Turks.

abdication crisis in British history, the constitutional upheaval of the period 16 November 1936 to 10 December 1936, brought about by the British king *Edward VIII's decision to marry Wallis *Simpson, a US divorcee. The marriage of the 'Supreme Governor' of the Church of England to a divorced person was considered unsuitable and the king abdicated on 10 December and left for voluntary exile in France. He was created Duke of Windsor and married Mrs Simpson on 3 June 1937.

abdomen in vertebrates, the part of the body below the *thorax, containing the digestive organs; in insects and other arthropods, it is the hind part of the body. In mammals, the abdomen is separated from the thorax by the *diaphragm, a sheet of muscular tissue; in arthropods, commonly by a narrow constriction. In mammals, the female reproductive organs are in the abdomen. In insects and spiders, it is characterized by the absence of limbs.

Abdullah, Sheikh Muhammad (1905–1982) Indian politician, known as the 'Lion of Kashmir'. He headed the struggle for constitutional government against the Maharajah of Kashmir, and in 1948, following a coup, became prime minister. He agreed to the accession of the state to India, but was dismissed and imprisoned from 1953 (with brief intervals of freedom) until 1966, when he called for Kashmiri self-determination. He became chief minister of Jammu and Kashmir in 1975, accepting the sovereignty of India.

Abdullah ibn Hussein (1882–1951) King of Jordan 1946–51. In 1921, after the collapse of the Ottoman empire, he became emir of the British mandate of Transjordan, covering present-day Jordan, and became king when the mandate ended in May 1946. In May 1948 King Abdullah attacked the newly established state of Israel, capturing large areas. He retained the area called the West Bank (Arab Palestine) after a ceasefire in 1949 and renamed the country the Hashemite Kingdom of Jordan. He was assassinated in July 1951 by a Palestinian Arab fanatic.

Abdullah ibn Hussein (1962–) King of Jordan from 1999. Abdullah was crowned king of Jordan after his father, *Hussein ibn Talal, who had ruled the Hashemite Kingdom since 1952, died. Abdullah, who was an army major general, and untested in the affairs of state, became the fourth leader of this small but strategically vital state. He promised to maintain Hussein's legacy, continuing the course of moderation and commitment to Middle East peace.

Abelard, Peter (1079–1142) French **Pierre Abélard**, French scholastic philosopher who worked on logic and theology. His romantic liaison with his pupil *Héloïse caused a medieval scandal. Details of his life are contained in the autobiographical *Historia Calamitatum Mearum/The History of My Misfortunes*.

Aberdeen city in Aberdeen City unitary authority, Scotland, on the rivers Don and Dee, 120 km/75 mi north of Dundee; population (2001 est) 212,100. The third-largest city in Scotland, it is the administrative headquarters of both Aberdeen City and Aberdeenshire unitary authorities. The unitary authority was created in 1996 from the district of the same name that was part of Grampian region from 1975; before that it was part of Aberdeenshire. North Sea oil is the principal industry, and it is the main centre for offshore oil exploration in Europe. Other industries include oil and gas service industries, fishing, food processing, paper manufacture, textiles, engineering, chemicals, and tourism. Sited on a low-lying coastal area on the banks of the rivers Dee and Don, the city has 3 km/2 mi of sandy beaches.

Aberdeen, George Hamilton Gordon, 4th Earl of Aberdeen (1784–1860) British Tory politician, prime minister from 1852 until 1855, when he resigned because of criticism provoked by the miseries and mismanagement of the *Crimean War.

aberration of starlight apparent displacement of a star from its true position, due to the combined effects of the speed of light and the speed of the Earth in orbit around the Sun (about 30 kps/18.5 mps).

aberration, optical any of a number of defects that impair the image in an optical instrument. Aberration occurs because of minute variations in lenses and mirrors, and because different parts of the light *spectrum are reflected or refracted by varying amounts.

Abidjan port and former capital (until 1983) of the Republic of Côte d'Ivoire; population (1995 est) 2,722,000. There is an airport, communication by rail, as well as by sea, and the city has become increasingly important for its industries which include metallurgy, farm machinery, car and electrical assembly. Products include coffee, palm oil, cocoa, and timber (mahogany). There are tourist markets trading in handicrafts and traditional medicines.

Abkhazia (or Abkhaziya) autonomous republic in northwestern Georgia; area 8,600 sq km/3,320 sq mi; population (1993 est) 516,600. The region is located between the main range of the *Caucasus Mountains and the *Black Sea, with a subtropical climate on the latter's shores, and with densely wooded foothills. Most of the population, including that of the capital, Sokhumi, and the cities of Ochamchire and Gagra, is located in the lowland of the coastal area. Industries include the mining of tin and coal, and lumbering and sawmilling, but agriculture, including fruit, tobacco,

and tea cultivation, is still the leading occupation. Tourism and health resorts on the coast and on Lake Ritsa are also important.

abolitionism a movement culminating in the late 18th and early 19th centuries that aimed first to end the slave trade, and then to abolish the institution of *slavery and emancipate slaves. The movement took place in Europe, mainly in the UK, and in the USA.

Aboriginal art art of the Australian Aborigines. Traditionally almost entirely religious and ceremonial, it was directed towards portraying stories of the *Dreamtime, a creation mythology reflecting the Aboriginal hunter-gatherer lifestyle. Perishable materials were used, as in bark painting and carved trees and logs, and few early works of this type survive. A great deal of rock art remains intact, however, and forms one of the richest continuing traditions in the world. Abstract patterns and stylized figures predominate. Ground and body painting were also practised, chiefly as part of secret initiation rites.

aborigine (Latin *ab origine* 'from the beginning') any indigenous inhabitant of a region or country. The word often refers to the original peoples of areas colonized by Europeans, and especially to *Australian Aborigines.

abortion (Latin *aborire* 'to miscarry') ending of a pregnancy before the fetus is developed sufficiently to survive outside the uterus. Loss of a fetus at a later stage is termed premature stillbirth. Abortion may be natural (*miscarriage) or deliberate (termination of pregnancy).

Aboukir Bay, Battle of *or the* **Battle of the Nile** naval battle during the Napoleonic Wars between Great Britain and France, in which Admiral Horatio Nelson defeated Napoleon Bonaparte's fleet at the Egyptian seaport of Aboukir on 1 August 1798. The defeat put an end to French designs in the Middle East.

Abraham (lived c. 2300 BC) Arabic **Ibrahim**, (Hebrew 'father of many nations') in the Old Testament, the founder of the Jewish nation and one of the Jewish *patriarchs. In his early life he was called Abram. God promised him heirs and land for his people in Canaan (Israel), renamed him Abraham, and tested his faith by a command (later retracted) to sacrifice his son Isaac.

Abraham, Plains of plateau near Québec, Canada, where the British commander *Wolfe defeated the French under *Montcalm, on 13 September 1759, during the French and Indian War (1756–63). The outcome of the battle established British supremacy in Canada.

abrasive (Latin 'to scratch away') substance used for cutting and polishing or for removing small amounts of the surface of hard materials. There are two types: natural and artificial abrasives, and their hardness is measured using the *Mohs scale. Natural abrasives include quartz, sandstone, pumice, diamond, emery, and corundum; artificial abrasives include rouge, whiting, and carborundum.

Abruzzi *or* **Abruzzo** mountainous region of southern central Italy, comprising the provinces of L'Aquila, Chieti, Pescara, and Teramo; area 10,798 sq km/4,169 sq mi; population (2001 est) 1,244,200. The capital is L'Aquila, and other major towns include Pescara, Chieti, and Teramo. Gran Sasso d'Italia, 2,914 m/9,564 ft, is the highest point of the *Apennines. The region was opened up to the rest of Italy in the 1960s following motorway construction, but remains one of the least populated districted in the country.

abscissa in *coordinate geometry, the *x*-coordinate of a point – that is, the horizontal distance of that point from the vertical or *y*-axis. For example, a point with the coordinates (4, 3) has an abscissa of 4. The *y*-coordinate of a point is known as the ordinate.

abscission in botany, the controlled separation of part of a plant from the main plant body – most commonly, the falling of leaves or the dropping of fruit controlled by abscissin. In *deciduous plants the leaves are shed before the winter or dry season, whereas *evergreen plants drop their leaves continually throughout the year. Fruitdrop, the abscission of fruit while still immature, is a naturally occurring process.

absolute value *or* **modulus** in mathematics, the value, or magnitude, of a number irrespective of its sign. The absolute value of a number *n* is written $|n|$ (or sometimes as mod *n*), and is defined as the positive square root of n^2. For example, the numbers −5 and 5 have the same absolute value:

$$|5| = |-5| = 5$$

absolute zero lowest temperature theoretically possible according to kinetic theory, zero kelvin (0 K), equivalent to −273.15 °C/−459.67 °F, at which molecules are in their lowest energy state. Although the third law of *thermodynamics indicates the impossibility of reaching absolute zero, in practice temperatures of less than a billionth of a degree above absolute zero have been reached. Near absolute zero, the physical properties of some materials change substantially; for example, some metals lose their electrical resistance and become superconducting.

absolutism *or* **absolute monarchy** system of government in which the ruler or rulers have unlimited power and are subject to no constitutional safeguards or checks. The principle of an absolute monarch, given a right to rule by God (the *divine right of kings), was extensively used in Europe during the 17th and 18th centuries; it was based on an earlier theory of papal absolutism (absolute authority of the pope).

absorption in physics, taking up of matter or energy of one substance by another, such as a liquid by a solid (ink by blotting paper) or a gas by a liquid (ammonia by water). In physics, absorption is the phenomenon by which a substance retains the energy of radiation of particular wavelengths; for example, a piece of blue glass absorbs all visible light except the wavelengths in the blue part of the spectrum; it also refers to the partial loss of energy resulting from light and other electromagnetic waves passing through a medium. In nuclear physics, absorption is the capture by elements, such as boron, of neutrons produced by fission in a reactor.

abstract art nonrepresentational art. Ornamental art without figurative representation occurs in most cultures. The modern abstract movement in sculpture and painting emerged in Europe and North America between 1910 and 1920. Two approaches produce different abstract styles: images that have been 'abstracted' from nature to the point where they no longer reflect a conventional reality, and nonobjective, or 'pure', art forms, without any reference to reality.

abstract expressionism movement in US painting that was the dominant force in the country's art in the late 1940s and 1950s. It was characterized by the sensuous use of paint, often on very large canvases, to convey powerful emotions. Some of the artists involved painted pure abstract pictures, but others often retained figurative traces in their work. Most of the leading abstract expressionists were based in New York during the heyday of the movement (they are sometimes referred to as the New York School), and their critical and financial success (after initial opposition) helped New York to replace Paris as the world's leading centre of contemporary art, a position it has held ever since.

Absurd, Theatre of the avant-garde drama originating with a group of dramatists in the 1950s, including Samuel *Beckett, Eugène *Ionesco, Jean Genet, and Harold *Pinter. Their work expressed the belief that, in a godless universe, human existence has no meaning or purpose and all communication breaks down. Logical construction and argument gives way to irrational and illogical speech and to its ultimate conclusion, silence, as in Beckett's play *Breath* (1970).

Abu Bakr (*or* **Abu-Bekr**) **(573–634)** Muslim *caliph (civic and religious leader of Islam) from 632 to 34. Born Abd-al-Ka'aba, he adopted the name Abu Bakr ('Father of the virgin') about 618 when the prophet *Muhammad married his daughter Ayesha. He was a close adviser to Muhammad in 622–32 and succeeded the prophet as political leader at his death. As the first Muslim caliph he imposed Muslim authority over all the Arab tribes, added Mesopotamia to the Muslim world, and instigated expansion of Islam into Iraq and Syria.

Abu Dhabi Arabic **Abu Zabi**, sheikhdom in southwest Asia, on the Gulf, the largest of the seven *United Arab Emirates. Its capital, Abu Dhabi, is also the capital of the United Arab Emirates; area 67,350 sq km/26,000 sq mi; population (1999 est) 1,127,000. Formerly under British protection, it has been ruled since 1971 by Sheikh Sultan Zayed bin al-Nahayan, who is also president of the Supreme Council of Rulers of the United Arab Emirates. Abu Dhabi has rich oil reserves, both on- and off-shore, which have brought great prosperity in recent decades.

Abuja capital of Nigeria (formally designated as such 1982, although not officially recognized until 1992); population of Federal Capital District (1991 est) 378,700; population of city alone (1991 est) 107,100. Shaped like a crescent, the city was designed by Japanese architect Kenzo Tange; building of the city began in 1976 as a replacement for Lagos, and is still largely under construction. The city obtains electricity from the Shiroro Dam on the River Niger; the main functions of the city are administrative, with only light industry.

Abu Simbel site of two ancient temples cut into the rock on the banks of the Nile in southern Egypt during the reign of Rameses II, commemorating him and his wife Nefertari. The temples were moved in sections in 1966–67 and rebuilt 60 m/200 ft above their original location before the site was flooded by the waters of the Aswan High Dam.

abyssal plain broad, relatively flat expanse of sea floor lying 3–6 km/2–4 mi below sea level. Abyssal plains are found in all the major oceans, and they extend from bordering continental rises to mid-oceanic ridges. Abyssal plains are covered in a thick layer of sediment, and their flatness is punctuated by rugged low abyssal hills and high sea mounts.

abyssal zone dark ocean region 2,000–6,000 m/ 6,500–19,500 ft deep; temperature 4° C/39° F. Three-quarters of the area of the deep-ocean floor lies in the abyssal zone, which is too far from the surface for photosynthesis to take place. Some fish and crustaceans living there are blind or have their own light sources. The region above is the bathyal zone; the region below, the hadal zone.

abzyme in biotechnology, an artificially created antibody that can be used like an enzyme to accelerate reactions.

acacia any of a large group of shrubs and trees that includes the thorn trees of the African savannah and the gum arabic tree (*Acacia senegal*) of North Africa, and several North American species of the southwestern USA and Mexico. The hardy tree commonly known as acacia is the false acacia (*Robinia pseudacacia*, of the subfamily Papilionoideae). True acacias are found in warm regions of the world, particularly Australia. (Genus *Acacia*, family Leguminosae.)

Academy Award annual honour awarded since 1927 by the American Academy of Motion Picture Arts and Sciences in a number of categories that reflect the diversity and collaborative nature of film-making. The Academy Award is one of the highest accolades in the film industry, and a virtual guarantor of increased financial returns. The trophy itself is a gold-plated statuette, which since 1931 has been popularly nicknamed an 'Oscar'. The most prestigious awards are for Best Picture, Best Director, Best Actor, and Best Actress.

acanthus herbaceous plant with handsome lobed leaves. Twenty species are found in the Mediterranean region and Old World tropics, including bear's-breech (*Acanthus mollis*) whose leaves were used as a motif in classical architecture, especially on Corinthian columns. (Genus *Acanthus*, family Acanthaceae.)

a cappella (Italian 'in the style of the chapel') choral music sung without instrumental accompaniment. In modern music it is characteristic of *gospel music, doo-wop, and the evangelical Christian church movement.

acceleration rate of change of the velocity of a moving body. For example, an object falling towards the ground covers more distance in each successive time interval. Therefore, its velocity is changing with time and the object is accelerating. It is usually measured in metres per second per second (m s^{-2}) or feet per second per second (ft s^{-2}). Acceleration = change in velocity/time taken. Because velocity is a vector quantity (possessing both magnitude and direction), a body travelling at constant speed may be said to be accelerating if its direction of motion changes. According to Newton's second law of motion, a body will accelerate only if it is acted upon by an unbalanced, or resultant, *force. Acceleration of free fall is the acceleration of a body falling freely under the influence of the Earth's gravitational field; it varies slightly at different latitudes and altitudes. The value adopted internationally for gravitational acceleration is 9.806 m s^{-2}/32.174 ft s^{-2}.

accelerator in physics, a device to bring charged particles (such as protons and electrons) up to high speeds and energies, at which they can be of use in industry, medicine, and pure physics. At low energies, accelerated particles can be used to produce the image on a television screen and (by means of a *cathode-ray tube) generate X-rays, destroy tumour cells, or kill bacteria. When high-energy particles collide with other particles, the fragments formed reveal the nature of the fundamental forces.

acclimation *or* **acclimatization** physiological changes induced in an organism by exposure to new environmental conditions. When humans move to higher altitudes, for example, the number of red blood cells rises to increase the oxygen-carrying capacity of the blood in order to compensate for the lower levels of oxygen in the air.

accommodation in biology, the ability of the *eye to focus on near or far objects by changing the shape of the lens.

accordion musical instrument of the free-reed organ type, comprising left and right wind chests connected by flexible, pleated bellows. The accordionist's right hand plays the melody on the piano-style keyboard of 26–34 keys, while the left hand has a system of push buttons for selecting single notes or chord harmonies.

accounting the principles and practice of systematically recording, presenting, and interpreting financial accounts; financial record keeping and management of businesses and other organizations, from balance sheets to policy decisions, for tax or operating purposes. Forms of inflation accounting, such as CCA (current cost accounting) and CPP (current purchasing power), are aimed at providing valid financial comparisons over a period in which money values change.

Accra capital and port of Ghana; population (2002 est) 1,605,400. It is an important political, commercial, and administrative centre. The port trades in cacao, gold, diamonds, and timber; the leading industries are vehicle assembly, textiles, plastics, and pharmaceuticals; other industries include light engineering, brewing, and tobacco and food processing. Scrap metal is a major import and is the basis of local engineering businesses. Accra is connected by rail to Tema which serves as its deepwater port.

accumulator in electricity, a storage *battery – that is, a group of rechargeable secondary cells. A familiar example is the lead–acid car battery.

acetaldehyde common name for *ethanal.

acetate common name for *ethanoate.

acetic acid common name for *ethanoic acid.

acetone common name for *propanone.

acetylene common name for *ethyne.

Achaea (*or* **Achaia)** in ancient Greece, an area of the northern Peloponnese. The **Achaeans** were the predominant society during the Mycenaean period and are said by Homer to have taken part in the siege of Troy. The larger Roman province of Achaea was created after the defeat of the Achaean League in 146 BC; it included all mainland Greece south of a line drawn from the Ambracian to the Maliac Gulf.

Achebe, Chinua (1930–) born Albert Chinualumogu Achebe, Nigerian novelist. His themes include the social and political impact of European colonialism on African people, and the problems of newly independent African nations. His best-known work is the influential *Things Fall Apart* (1958), one of the first African novels to achieve a global reputation.

Achernar *or* **Alpha Eridani** brightest star in the constellation Eridanus, and the ninth-brightest star in the sky. It is a hot, luminous, blue star with a true luminosity 250 times that of the Sun. It is 144 light years away from the Sun.

Achilles Greek hero of Homer's *Iliad*. He was the son of Peleus, King of the Myrmidons in Thessaly, and of the sea nymph Thetis who, by dipping him in the River Styx, rendered him invulnerable, except for the heel by which she held him. Achilles killed *Hector at the climax of the *Iliad*, and according to subsequent Greek legends was himself killed by *Paris, who shot a poisoned arrow into Achilles' heel.

Achilles tendon tendon at the back of the ankle attaching the calf muscles to the heel bone. It is one of the largest tendons in the human body, and can resist great tensional strain, but is sometimes ruptured by contraction of the muscles in sudden extension of the foot. Ancient surgeons regarded wounds in this tendon as fatal, probably because of the Greek legend of *Achilles, which relates how the mother of the hero Achilles dipped him when an infant into the River Styx, so that he became invulnerable except for the heel by which she held him.

acid in chemistry, compound that releases hydrogen ions (H^+ or protons) in the presence of an ionizing solvent (usually water). Acids react with *bases to form salts, and they act as solvents. Strong acids are corrosive; dilute acids have a sour or sharp taste, although in some organic acids this may be partially masked by other flavour characteristics. The strength of an acid is measured by its hydrogen-ion concentration, indicated by the *pH value. All acids have a pH below 7.0.

acid rain acidic precipitation thought to be caused mainly by the release into the atmosphere of sulphur dioxide (SO_2) and oxides of nitrogen (NO_x), which dissolve in pure rainwater making it acidic. Sulphur dioxide is formed by the burning of fossil fuels, such as coal, that contain high quantities of sulphur; nitrogen oxides are produced by various industrial activities and are present in car exhaust fumes.

Ackroyd, Peter (1949–) English novelist, biographer, reviewer, and poet. His novel *Hawksmoor* (1985) won the Whitbread award, and *T S Eliot* (1984) won the Whitbread prize for biography. Ackroyd's other books include the novels *Chatterton* (1987), *The House of Doctor Dee* (1993), *Milton in America* (1996), and *The Clerkenwell Tales* (2003), and biographies of Ezra Pound (1987), Charles Dickens (1990), William Blake (1995), and Thomas More (1998). His work often blurs the distinction between biography and fiction.

aclinic line magnetic equator, an imaginary line near the Equator, where a compass needle balances horizontally, the attraction of the north and south magnetic poles being equal.

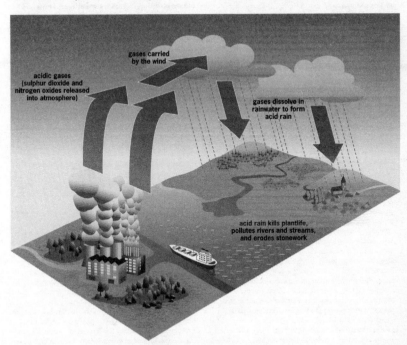

acidic gases
(sulphur dioxide and
nitrogen oxides released
into atmosphere)

gases carried
by the wind

gases dissolve in
rainwater to form
acid rain

acid rain kills plantlife,
pollutes rivers and streams,
and erodes stonework

acid rain How acid rain is formed in industrial areas and distributed over long distances, where it can kill trees and damage buildings and statues.

acne skin eruption, mainly occurring among adolescents and young adults, caused by inflammation of the sebaceous glands, which secrete an oily substance (sebum), the natural lubricant of the skin. Sometimes the openings of the glands become blocked, causing the formation of pus-filled swellings. Teenage acne is seen mainly on the face, back, and chest.

aconite *or* **monkshood** *or* **wolfsbane** herbaceous plant belonging to the buttercup family, with hooded blue–mauve flowers, native to Europe and Asia. It produces aconitine, a poison with pain-killing and sleep-inducing properties. (*Aconitum napellus*, family Ranunculaceae.)

acoustic term describing a musical instrument played without electrical amplification or assistance, for example an acoustic guitar or acoustic piano. It is also a term used by musicians to characterize room response, an important factor in performance. A so-called 'bright' acoustic provides a lively reverberation while a 'dry' or 'muddy' acoustic is lacking in response; see *acoustics.

acoustics in general, the experimental and theoretical science of sound and its transmission; in particular, that branch of the science that has to do with the phenomena of sound in a particular space such as a room or theatre. In architecture, the sound-reflecting character of an internal space.

acquired character feature of the body that develops during the lifetime of an individual, usually as a result of repeated use or disuse, such as the enlarged muscles of a weightlifter.

acre traditional English land measure equal to 4,840 square yards (4,047 sq m/0.405 ha). Originally meaning a field, it was the area that a yoke of oxen could plough in a day.

acronym word formed from the initial letters and/or syllables of other words, intended as a pronounceable abbreviation; for example, NATO (**N**orth **A**tlantic **T**reaty **O**rganization), radar (**ra**dio **d**etecting **a**nd **r**anging), RAM (**r**andom-**a**ccess **m**emory) and FORTRAN (**fo**rmula **tran**slation). There are other forms of abbreviation. Many acronyms are so successfully incorporated into everyday language that their origin as abbreviations is widely overlooked. Full stops are not normally used in acronyms.

acropolis (Greek 'high city') citadel of an ancient Greek town. The Acropolis of Athens contains the ruins of the *Parthenon and surrounding complexes, built there during the days of the Athenian empire. The term is also used for analogous structures.

acrostic (Greek 'at the extremity of a line or row') a number of lines of writing, usually verse, whose initial letters (read downwards) form a word, phrase, or sentence. A **single acrostic** is formed by the initial letters of lines only; a **double acrostic** is formed by the first and last letters.

Acrux *or* **Alpha Crucis** brightest star in the constellation of Crux, marking one of the four points of the *Southern Cross, and the 13th-brightest star in the night sky. It is a double star comprising two blue-white stars, and is 360 light years away from the Sun. Together with nearby Gacrux, it points towards the south celestial pole.

acrylic fibre synthetic fibre often used as a substitute for *wool. It was first developed in the mid-1940s but was not produced in large quantities until the 1950s. Strong and warm, acrylic fibre is often used for sweaters and tracksuits and as linings for boots and gloves, as well as in furnishing fabrics and carpets. It is manufactured as a filament, then cut into short staple lengths similar to wool hairs, and spun into yarn. **Modacrylic** is a modified acrylic yarn.

acrylic paint any of a range of synthetic substitutes for *oil paint, mostly soluble in water.

actinide any of a series of 15 radioactive metallic chemical elements with atomic numbers 89 (actinium) to 103 (lawrencium). Elements 89 to 95 occur in nature; the rest of the series are synthesized elements only. Actinides are grouped together because of their chemical similarities (for example, they are all bivalent), the properties differing only slightly with atomic number. The series is set out in a band in the *periodic table of the elements, as are the *lanthanides.

actinium chemical symbol Ac, (Greek *aktis* 'ray') white, radioactive, metallic element, the first of the actinide series, atomic number 89, relative atomic mass 227; it is a weak emitter of high-energy alpha particles. Actinium occurs with uranium and radium in pitchblende and other ores, and can be synthesized by bombarding radium with neutrons. The longest-lived isotope, Ac-227, has a half-life of 21.8 years (all the other isotopes have very short half-lives). Chemically, it is exclusively trivalent, resembling in its reactions the lanthanides and the other actinides. Actinium was discovered in 1899 by the French chemist André Debierne (1874–1949).

action painting *or* **gesture painting** *or* **tachisme** in abstract art, a form of abstract expressionism that emphasized the importance of the physical act of painting. It became widespread in the 1950s and 1960s. Jackson *Pollock, the leading exponent, threw, dripped, and dribbled paint onto canvases fastened to the floor. He was known to attack his canvas with knives and trowels and bicycle over it. Another principal action artist was Willem de Kooning.

action potential in biology, a change in the *potential difference (voltage) across the membrane of a nerve cell when an impulse passes along it. A change in potential (from about –60 to +45 millivolts) accompanies the passage of sodium and potassium ions across the membrane.

Actium, Battle of naval battle in which Octavian defeated the combined fleets of *Mark Antony and *Cleopatra on 2 September 31 BC to become the undisputed ruler of the Roman world (as the emperor *Augustus). The site of the battle is at Akri, a promontory in western Greece.

activation energy in chemistry, the minimum energy required in order to start a chemical reaction. Some elements and compounds will react together merely by bringing them into contact (spontaneous reaction). For others it is necessary to supply energy (heat, radiation, or electrical charge) in order to start the reaction, even if there is ultimately a net output of energy. This initial energy is the activation energy.

act of Congress in the USA, a bill or resolution passed by both houses of Congress, the Senate and the House of Representatives, which becomes law with the signature of the president. If vetoed by the president, it may still become law if it returns to Congress again and is passed by a majority of two-thirds in each house.

act of Parliament in Britain, a change in the law originating in Parliament and called a statute. Before an act receives the royal assent and becomes law it is a **bill**. The US equivalent is an *act of Congress.

acupuncture in alternative medicine, a system of inserting long, thin metal needles into the body at predetermined points to relieve pain, as an anaesthetic in surgery, and to assist healing. The needles are rotated manually or electrically. The method, developed in ancient China and increasingly popular in the West, is thought to work by stimulating the brain's own painkillers, the *endorphins.

acute angle angle between 0° and 90°; that is, an amount of turn that is less than a quarter of a circle.

AD in the Christian chronological system, abbreviation for *anno Domini.

Ada high-level computer-programming language, developed and owned by the US Department of Defense, designed for use in situations in which a computer directly controls a process or machine, such as a military aircraft. The language took more than five years to specify, and became commercially available only in the late 1980s. It is named after English mathematician Ada Augusta Byron, daughter of Lord Byron.

Adam family of Scottish architects and designers. **William Adam** (1689–1748) was the leading Scottish architect of his day, and his son **Robert Adam** (1728–1792) is considered one of the greatest British architects of the late 18th century, responsible for transforming the prevailing Palladian fashion in architecture to a neoclassical style.

Adam (Hebrew *adham* 'man') In the Old Testament (Genesis 2, 3), the first human. Formed by God from dust and given the breath of life, Adam was placed in the Garden of Eden, where Eve was created from his rib and given to him as a companion. Because she tempted him, he tasted the forbidden fruit of the tree of knowledge of good and evil, for which trespass they were expelled from the Garden.

Adams, Gerry (1948–) born Gerard Adams, Northern Irish politician, leader (president) of *Sinn Fein from 1983, member of Parliament for Belfast West 1983–92 and since 1997. He has been a key figure in Irish peace negotiations. In 1994 he was the main architect of the IRA ceasefire and in 1997 Adams entered into multiparty talks with the British government which, on Good Friday, 10 April 1998, resulted in an agreement accepted by all parties. He has since been a member of the Northern Ireland Assembly created by the peace process.

Adams, John (1735–1826) 2nd president of the USA 1797–1801, and vice-president 1789–97. He was a member of the Continental Congress 1774–78 and signed the Declaration of Independence. In 1779 he went to France and negotiated the treaty of 1783 that ended the American Revolution. In 1785 he became the first US ambassador in London.

Adams, John Couch (1819–1892) English astronomer. He mathematically deduced the existence of the planet Neptune in 1845 from the effects of its gravitational pull on the motion of Uranus, although it was not found until 1846 by J G Galle. Adams also studied the Moon's motion, the Leonid meteors, and terrestrial magnetism.

Adams, John Quincy (1767–1848) 6th president of the USA 1825–29, eldest son of President John *Adams. He negotiated the Treaty of Ghent (1814) to end the *War of 1812 (fought with Britain) on generous terms

for the USA. In 1817 he became President James Monroe's secretary of state, formulating the *Monroe Doctrine in 1823. As president, Adams was a *Federalist (an advocate of strong federal government), but was ultimately unable to accomplish many of his policies because of power struggles within his own Democratic-Republican party.

Adamson, Robert Scottish photographer. He collaborated with fellow Scottish photographer David Octavius Hill. See *Hill and Adamson.

adaptation (Latin *adaptare* 'to fit to') in biology, any feature in the structure or function of an organism that allows it to survive and reproduce more effectively in its environment. Much adaptation is inherited and is the result of many thousands of years of *evolution. It is thought to occur as a result of random variation in the genetic make-up of organisms coupled with *natural selection. Species become extinct when they are no longer adapted to their environment.

adaptive radiation in evolution, the formation of several species, with *adaptations to different ways of life, from a single ancestral type. Adaptive radiation is likely to occur whenever members of a species migrate to a new habitat with unoccupied ecological niches. It is thought that the lack of competition in such niches allows sections of the migrant population to develop new adaptations, and eventually to become new species. The colonization of newly formed volcanic islands has led to the development of many unique species. The 13 species of Darwin's finch on the Galapagos Islands, for example, are probably descended from a single species from the South American mainland. The parent stock evolved into different species that now occupy a range of diverse niches.

adder (Anglo-Saxon *naedre* 'serpent') European venomous snake, the common *viper *Vipera berus*. Growing on average to about 60 cm/24 in in length, it has a thick body, a triangular head, with a characteristic V-shaped mark and, often, zigzag markings along the back. It feeds on small mammals and lizards. The puff adder *Bitis arietans* is a large, yellowish, thick-bodied viper up to 1.6 m/5 ft long, living in Africa and Arabia.

addiction state of dependence caused by frequent and regular use of *drugs, *alcohol, or other substances. It is characterized by uncontrolled craving, tolerance, and symptoms of withdrawal when access is denied. Habitual use produces changes in body chemistry and treatment must be geared to a gradual reduction in dosage.

Addis Ababa (or **Adis Abeba)** (Amharic 'new flower') capital of Ethiopia; population (1992 est) 2,213,000. The city is at an altitude of 2,500 m/8,200 ft. It was founded in 1887 by Menelik II, chief of Shoa, who ascended the throne of Ethiopia in 1889. His former residence, Menelik Palace, is now occupied by the government. Industries include light engineering, food processing, brewing, livestock processing, chemicals, cement, textiles, footwear, clothing, and handicrafts.

Addison, Joseph (1672–1719) English poet and dramatist, and one of the most celebrated of English essayists. In 1704 he commemorated *Marlborough's victory at Blenheim in a poem commissioned by the government, 'The Campaign'. He subsequently held political appointments and was a Member of Parliament for Malmesbury from 1708 until his death.

From 1709 to 1711 he contributed to the *Tatler* magazine, begun by Richard *Steele, with whom he was cofounder in 1711–12 of the *Spectator*.

addition reaction chemical reaction in which the atoms of an element or compound react with a double bond or triple bond in an organic compound by opening up one of the bonds and becoming attached to it, for example:

$$CH_2=CH_2 + HCl \rightarrow CH_3CH_2Cl.$$

Another example is the addition of hydrogen atoms to *unsaturated compounds in vegetable oils to produce margarine. Addition reactions are used to make polymers from *alkenes.

additive in food, any natural or artificial chemical added to prolong the shelf life of processed foods (salt or nitrates), alter the colour, texture, or flavour of food, or improve its food value (vitamins or minerals). Many chemical additives are used and they are subject to regulation, since individuals may be affected by constant exposure even to traces of certain additives and may suffer side effects ranging from headaches and hyperactivity to cancer. However, it can be difficult to know how to test the safety of such substances; many natural foods contain toxic substances which could not pass the tests applied today to new products. Food companies in many countries are now required by law to list additives used in their products. Within the European Union, approved additives are given an official *E number.

Adelaide capital and chief port of *South Australia; population (2001 est) 1,072,600. Adelaide is situated on the River Torrens, 11 km/7 mi from the Gulf of St Vincent. The city is the economic and cultural centre of South Australia, and a major focus for rail, road, sea and air routes. This position, combined with the availability of many raw materials, has favoured considerable industrial development. Power sources include natural gas, piped into Adelaide from the Gidgealpa gas fields of the Cooper Basin. Industries include oil refining, shipbuilding, textiles, machinery, chemicals and electronics, and the manufacture of electrical goods, cars and motor components. Grain, wool, fruit, and wine, including much produce from the basin of the Murray River which has no port at its outlet to the sea, are exported from Port Adelaide, 11 km/7 mi northwest of the city and with facilities for both container and passenger traffic. Adelaide was founded in 1836 and named after the queen of William IV. The city's fine buildings include Parliament House, Government House, the Anglican cathedral of St Peter, and the Roman Catholic cathedral of St Francis Xavier (built 1856–1926).

Aden Arabic **'Adan**, main port and commercial centre of Yemen, on a rocky peninsula at the southwest corner of Arabia, commanding the entrance to the Red Sea; population (1995) 562,000. The city's economy is based on oil refining, fishing, shipping, and light industries, including boatbuilding. A British territory from 1839, Aden became part of independent South Yemen in 1967; it was the capital of South Yemen until 1990.

Adenauer, Konrad (1876–1967) German Christian Democrat politician, chancellor of West Germany 1949–63. With the French president Charles de Gaulle he achieved the post-war reconciliation of France and Germany and strongly supported all measures designed to strengthen the Western bloc in Europe.

adenoids masses of lymphoid tissue, similar to *tonsils, located in the upper part of the throat, behind the nose. They are part of a child's natural defences against the entry of germs but usually shrink and disappear by the age of ten.

adhesive substance that sticks two surfaces together. Natural adhesives (glues) include gelatin in its crude industrial form (made from bones, hide fragments, and fish offal) and vegetable gums. Synthetic adhesives include thermoplastic and thermosetting resins, which are often stronger than the substances they join; mixtures of *epoxy resin and hardener that set by chemical reaction; and elastomeric (stretching) adhesives for flexible joints. Superglues are fast-setting adhesives used in very small quantities.

adiabatic in biology and physics, describing a process that occurs without loss or gain of heat, especially the expansion or contraction of a gas in which a change takes place in the pressure or volume, although no heat is allowed to enter or leave. Adiabatic processes can be both non-reversible and approximately reversible.

Adi Granth the first volume of the Sikh scriptures. It was compiled by the Guru Arjan, and later became known as the *Guru Granth Sahib*, the holy book of Sikhism.

adipose tissue type of *connective tissue of vertebrates that serves as an energy reserve, and also pads some organs. It is commonly called fat tissue, and consists of large spherical cells filled with fat. In mammals, major layers are in the inner layer of skin and around the kidneys and heart.

Adirondacks mountainous area in northeast New York State, rising to 1,629 m/5,344ft at Mount Marcy; the source of the Hudson and Ausable rivers. The Adirondacks region is named after an American Indian people; it is now a summer resort area with good sports facilities, and is noted for its beautiful scenery.

Adler, Alfred (1870–1937) Austrian psychologist. He saw the 'will to power' as more influential in accounting for human behaviour than the sexual drive. A dispute over this theory led to the dissolution of his ten-year collaboration with psychiatry's founder Sigmund *Freud. The concepts of inferiority complex and overcompensation originated with Adler.

admiral butterfly any of several species of butterfly in the same family (Nymphalidae) as the tortoiseshells. The best-known is the **red admiral** (*Vanessa atalanta*), found worldwide in the northern hemisphere. It has black wings crossed by scarlet bands and marked with white and blue spots, and spanning 6 cm/2.5 in. It either hibernates, or migrates south each year from northern areas to subtropical zones. The spiny black caterpillar feeds on nettles.

Admiralty Islands group of small islands in the southwest Pacific, part of Papua New Guinea; area 2,071 sq km/800 sq mi; population (1995 est) 35,200. The islands form part of the *Bismarck Archipelago and with the North Western Islands constitute the Manus district of Papua New Guinea. The largest island (about 80 km/50 mi long) is Manus of which Lorengau is the chief town. Exports are copra and pearls. The islands became a German protectorate in 1884 and an Australian mandate in 1920.

adobe in architecture, a building method employing sun-dried earth bricks; also the individual bricks. The use of earth bricks and the construction of walls by enclosing earth within moulds (*pisé de terre*) are the two principal methods of raw-earth building. The techniques are commonly found in Spain, Latin America, and the southwestern USA.

adolescence in the human life cycle, the period between the beginning of *puberty and adulthood.

Adonis (Semitic *Adon* 'the Lord') in Greek mythology, a beautiful youth loved by the goddess *Aphrodite. He was killed while boar-hunting but was allowed to return from the underworld for a period every year to rejoin her. The anemone sprang from his blood.

adoption permanent legal transfer of parental rights and duties from one person to another, usually to provide care for children who would otherwise lack family upbringing.

ADP abbreviation for adenosine diphosphate, the chemical product formed in cells when *ATP breaks down to release energy.

adrenal gland *or* **suprarenal gland** triangular endocrine gland situated on top of the *kidney. The adrenals are soft and yellow, and consist of two parts: the cortex and medulla. The **cortex** (outer part) secretes various steroid hormones and other hormones that control salt and water metabolism and regulate the use of carbohydrates, proteins, and fats. The **medulla** (inner part) secretes the hormones adrenaline and noradrenaline which, during times of stress, cause the heart to beat faster and harder, increase blood flow to the heart and muscle cells, and dilate airways in the lungs, thereby delivering more oxygen to cells throughout the body and in general preparing the body for 'fight or flight'.

adrenaline *or* **epinephrine** hormone secreted by the medulla of the *adrenal glands. Adrenaline is synthesized from a closely related substance, noradrenaline, and the two hormones are released into the bloodstream in situations of fear or stress.

Adrian IV (c. 1100–1159) born Nicholas Breakspear, Pope 1154–59, the only English pope. He secured the execution of Arnold of Brescia and crowned Frederick I Barbarossa as German emperor. When he died, Adrian IV was at the height of a quarrel with Barbarossa over papal supremacy. He allegedly issued the controversial bull giving Ireland to Henry II of England in 1154. He was attacked for false representation, and the bull was subsequently refuted.

Adriatic Sea large arm of the Mediterranean Sea, lying northwest to southeast between the Italian and the Balkan peninsulas. The western shore is Italian; the eastern includes Croatia, Montenegro, and Albania, with two small strips of coastline owned by Slovenia and Bosnia Herzogovina. The Strait of Otranto, between Italy and Albania, links the Adriatic with the Ionian Sea to the south. The chief ports are Venice, Brindisi, Trieste, Ancona, and Bari in Italy, and Rijeka in Croatia. The sea is about 805 km/500 mi long; area 135,250 sq km/52,220 sq mi.

adsorption taking up of a gas or liquid at the surface of another substance, most commonly a solid (for example, activated charcoal adsorbs gases). It involves molecular attraction at the surface, and should be distinguished from *absorption (in which a uniform solution results from a gas or liquid being incorporated into the bulk structure of a liquid or solid).

Adventist person who believes that Jesus will return to make a second appearance on Earth. Expectation of the Second Coming of Christ is found in New Testament writings generally. Adventist views are held in particular by the *Seventh-Day Adventists church (with 4 million members in 200 countries), the Christadelphians, the *Jehovah's Witnesses, the Four Square Gospel Alliance, the Advent Christian church, and the Evangelical Adventist church.

Aegean Islands region of Greece comprising the Dodecanese islands, the Cyclades islands, Lesvos, Samos, and Chios; area 9,122 sq km/3,523 sq mi; population (2003 est) 320,000.

Aegean Sea branch of the Mediterranean between Greece and Turkey, extending as far south as Crete; the Dardanelles connect it with the Sea of Marmara, in turn linked with the Black Sea via the Bosporus. It is about 600 km/372 mi long and 290 km/180 mi wide, and covers some 214,000 sq km/82,625 sq mi, with a maximum depth of 3,540 m/11,600 ft. Tides are minimal, with a range of only about 40 cm/15 in. The numerous islands in the Aegean Sea include Crete, the Cyclades, the Sporades, and the Dodecanese. There is political tension between Greece and Turkey over sea limits claimed by Greece around such islands as Lesvos, Chios, Samos, and Kos.

Aelfric (c. 955–1020) English writer and abbot. Between 990 and 998 he wrote in vernacular *Old English prose two sets of sermons known as *Catholic Homilies*, and a further set known as *Lives of the Saints*, all of them largely translated from Latin. They are notable for their style and rhythm.

Aeneas in classical mythology, a Trojan prince who became the ancestral hero of the Romans. According to *Homer, he was the son of Anchises and the goddess Aphrodite. During the Trojan War he owed his life to the frequent intervention of the gods. The legend on which Virgil's epic poem the *Aeneid* is based describes his escape from Troy and his eventual settlement in Latium, on the Italian peninsula.

aerial *or* **antenna** in radio and television broadcasting, a conducting device that radiates or receives electromagnetic waves. The design of an aerial depends principally on the wavelength of the signal. Long waves (hundreds of metres in wavelength) may employ long wire aerials; short waves (several centimetres in wavelength) may employ rods and dipoles; microwaves may also use dipoles – often with reflectors arranged like a toast rack – or highly directional parabolic dish aerials. Because microwaves travel in straight lines, requiring line-of-sight communication, microwave aerials are usually located at the tops of tall masts or towers.

aerobic in biology, describing those organisms that require *oxygen in order to survive. Aerobic organisms include all plants and animals and many micro-organisms. They use oxygen (usually dissolved in water) to release the energy contained in food molecules such as glucose in a process called aerobic respiration. Oxygen is used to break down carbohydrates into *carbon dioxide and *water, releasing *energy, which is used to drive many processes within the cells.

aerodynamics branch of fluid physics that studies the forces exerted by air or other gases in motion. Examples include the airflow around bodies moving at speed through the atmosphere (such as land vehicles, bullets, rockets, and aircraft), the behaviour of gas in engines and furnaces, the air conditioning of buildings, the deposition of snow, the operation of air-cushion vehicles (hovercraft), wind loads on buildings and bridges, bird and insect flight, musical wind instruments, and meteorology. For maximum efficiency, the aim is usually to design the shape of an object to produce a streamlined flow, with a minimum of turbulence in the moving air. The behaviour of aerosols or the pollution of the atmosphere by foreign particles are other aspects of aerodynamics.

aeronautics science of travel through the Earth's atmosphere, including aerodynamics, aircraft structures, jet and rocket propulsion, and aerial navigation. It is distinguished from astronautics, which is the science of travel through space.

aeroplane US **airplane**, powered heavier-than-air craft supported in flight by fixed wings. Aeroplanes are propelled by the thrust of a jet engine, a rocket engine, or airscrew (propeller), as well as combinations of these. They must be designed aerodynamically, since streamlining ensures maximum flight efficiency. The Wright brothers flew the first powered plane (a biplane) in Kitty Hawk, North Carolina, USA, in 1903. For the history of aircraft and aviation, see *flight.

aerosol particles of liquid or solid suspended in a gas. Fog is a common natural example. Aerosol cans contain material packed under pressure with a device for releasing it as a fine spray. Most aerosols used *chlorofluorocarbons (CFCs) as propellants until these were found to cause destruction of the *ozone layer in the stratosphere.

Aeschylus (c. 525–c. 456 BC) Athenian dramatist. He developed Greek tragedy by introducing the second actor, thus enabling true dialogue and dramatic action to occur independently of the chorus. Ranked with *Euripides and *Sophocles as one of the three great tragedians, Aeschylus composed some 90 plays between 500 and 456 BC, of which seven complete tragedies survive in his name: *Persians* (472 BC), *Seven Against Thebes* (467 BC), *Suppliants* (463 BC), the *Oresteia* trilogy (*Agamemnon*, *Libation-Bearers*, and *Eumenides*) (458 BC), and *Prometheus Bound* (the last, although attributed to him, is of uncertain date and authorship).

Aesculapius in Roman mythology, the god of medicine, equivalent to the Greek *Asclepius.

Aesop by tradition, a writer of Greek fables. According to the historian Herodotus, he lived in the mid-6th

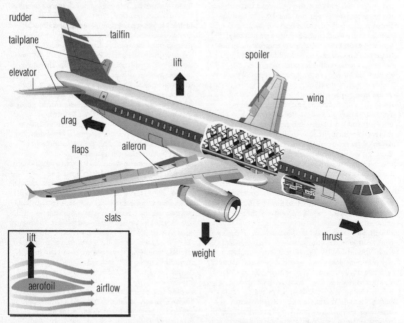

aeroplane In flight, the forces on an aeroplane are lift, weight, drag, and thrust. The lift is generated by the air flow over the wings, which have the shape of an aerofoil. The engine provides the thrust. The drag results from the resistance of the air to the aeroplane's passage through it. Various moveable flaps on the wings and tail allow the aeroplane to be controlled. The rudder is moved to turn the aeroplane. The elevators allow the craft to climb or dive. The ailerons are used to bank the aeroplane while turning. The flaps, slats, and spoilers are used to reduce lift and speed during landing.

century BC and was a slave. The fables that are ascribed to him were collected at a later date and are anecdotal stories using animal characters to illustrate moral or satirical points.

Aesthetic Movement English artistic movement of the late 19th century, dedicated to the doctrine of 'art for art's sake' – that is, art as a self-sufficient entity concerned solely with beauty and not with any moral or social purpose. Associated with the movement were the artists Aubrey *Beardsley and James McNeill *Whistler and writers Walter Pater and Oscar *Wilde.

aesthetics branch of philosophy that deals with the nature of beauty, especially in art. It emerged as a distinct branch of enquiry in the mid-18th century. Aesthetics attempts to explain the human reaction to beauty, and whether this reaction is objective or subjective; for instance, whether beauty is a universal concept, or whether environment – living conditions, class, gender, and race – affects a person's taste and what is considered beautiful.

aestivation in zoology, a state of inactivity and reduced metabolic activity, similar to *hibernation, that occurs during the dry season in species such as lungfish and snails. In botany, the term is used to describe the way in which flower petals and sepals are folded in the buds. It is an important feature in *plant classification.

affidavit legal document, used in court applications and proceedings, in which a person swears that certain facts are true.

affinity in chemistry, the force of attraction (see *bond) between atoms that helps to keep them in combination in a molecule. The term is also applied to attraction between molecules, such as those of biochemical significance (for example, between *enzymes and substrate molecules). This is the basis for affinity *chromatography, by which biologically important compounds are separated.

affinity in law, relationship by marriage not blood (for example, between a husband and his wife's blood relatives, between a wife and her husband's blood relatives, or between step-parent and stepchild), which may legally preclude their marriage. It is distinguished from consanguinity or blood relationship.

affirmative action policy of positive discrimination to increase opportunities for certain social groups in employment, business, government, and other areas. The policy is designed to counter the effects of long-term discrimination against groups such as women, disabled people, and minority ethnic groups. In Europe, Sweden, Belgium, the Netherlands, and Italy actively promote affirmative action through legal and financial incentives.

Afghan hound breed of fast hunting dog resembling the *saluki in build.

Afghanistan

National name: *Dowlat-e Eslāmi-ye Afghānestān/ Islamic State of Afghanistan*

Area: 652,225 sq km/251,825 sq mi

Capital: Kabul

Major towns/cities: Kandahar, Herat, Mazar-e Sharif, Jalalabad, Kondoz, Qal'eh-ye Now

Physical features: mountainous in centre and northeast (Hindu Kush mountain range; Khyber and Salang passes, Wakhan salient, and Panjshir Valley), plains in north and southwest, Amu Darya (Oxus) River, Helmand River, Lake Saberi

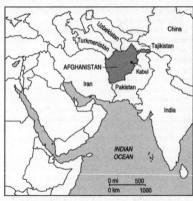

Head of state and government: Hamid Karzai from 2001

Political system: in transition

Political executive: in transition

Political parties: in transition

Currency: afgháni

GNI per capita (PPP): (US$) 800 (2000 est)

Exports: fruit and nuts, carpets, wool, karakul skins, cotton, natural gas, precious and semi-precious gems. Principal market: Pakistan (1999)

Population: 23,897,000 (2003 est)

Language: Pashto, Dari (both official), Uzbek, Turkmen, Balochi, Pashai

Religion: Muslim (84% Sunni, 15% Shiite), other 1%

Life expectancy: 43 (men); 43 (women) (2000–05)

Chronology

6th century BC: Part of Persian Empire under Cyrus II and Darius I.

329 BC: Conquered by Alexander the Great.

323 BC: Fell to the Seleucids, who ruled from Babylon.

304 BC: Ruled by Mauryan dynasty in south and independent Bactria in north.

135 BC: Central Asian tribes established Kusana dynasty.

3rd–7th centuries AD: Decline of Kusana dynasty. Emergence of Sassanids as ruling power with Hepthalites (central Asian nomads) and western Turks also fighting for control.

642–11th century: First Muslim invasion followed by a succession of Muslim dynasties, including Mahmud of Ghazni in 998.

1219–14th century: Mongol invasions led by Genghis Khan and Tamerlane.

16th–18th centuries: Much of Afghanistan came under the rule of the Mogul Empire under Babur (Zahir) and Nadir Shah.

1747: Afghanistan became an independent emirate under Dost Muhammad.

1838–42: First Afghan War, the first in a series of three wars between Britain and Afghanistan, instigated by Britain to counter the threat to British India from expanding Russian influence in Afghanistan.

1878–80: Second Afghan War.

1919: Afghanistan recovered full independence following the Third Afghan War.

1953: Lt-Gen Daud Khan became prime minister and introduced social and economic reform programme.

11

1963: Daud Khan forced to resign and constitutional monarchy established.
1973: Monarchy overthrown in coup by Daud Khan.
1978: Daud Khan assassinated in coup. Start of Muslim guerrilla (Mujahedin) resistance.
1979: The USSR invaded the country to prop up the pro-Soviet government.
1986: Partial Soviet troop withdrawal.
1988: New non-Marxist constitution adopted.
1989: Withdrawal of Soviet troops; Mujahedin continued resistance to communist People's Democratic Party of Afghanistan (PDPA) regime and civil war intensified.
1991: US and Soviet military aid withdrawn. Mujahedin began talks with the Russians and Kabul government.
1992: Mujahedin leader Burhanuddin Rabbani was elected president.
1993–94: There was fighting around Kabul.
1996: The Taliban controlled two-thirds of the country, including Kabul; the country was split between the Taliban-controlled fundamentalist south and the more liberal north; strict Islamic law was imposed.
1997: The Taliban was recognized as the legitimate government of Afghanistan by Pakistan and Saudi Arabia.
1998: Two earthquakes in the north killed over 8,000 people. The USA launched a missile attack on a suspected terrorist site in retaliation for bombings of US embassies in Nairobi and Dar es Salaam. Taliban extended its control in the north, massacring 6,000 people at Mazar-e Sharif.
1999: Fighting resumed in northern Afghanistan after a four-month lull. Intending to punish the Taliban regime for failing to expel suspected terrorist Osama bin Laden, the United Nations (UN) imposed sanctions on Afghanistan in November, which provoked mobs to attack UN offices in the capital, Kabul.
2000: Fighting continued between the Taliban and the opposing United Islamic Front for Salvation of Afghanistan (UIFSA), led by Ahmad Shah Masood, and the Taliban made further gains in the north. Pakistan closed its border with Afghanistan in November to prevent a further influx of refugees fleeing war and famine. The UN withdrew its aid workers and imposed tighter sanctions as bin Laden had still not been surrendered.
2001: The Taliban closed the UN political office in Kabul. The US named Osama bin Laden as the prime suspect in the terrorist attacks on the USA on 11 September 2001, and US and British forces launched a military offensive in October when the Taliban did not hand him over. By the end of November, the allied forces together with the Afghan opposition Northern Alliance had removed the Taliban from power, and an interim government was set up. However, the allied forces continued to search for Taliban and al-Qaeda fighters, and failed to capture bin Laden.
2002: A loya jirga (grand tribal council) of around 1,500 delegates from across the country convened in Kabul, to elect a new government. Hamid Karzai, an ethnic Pathan and leader of the UN-endorsed interim administration, was elected as president for 18 months. The former monarch Muhammad Zahir Shah, deposed in 1973, renounced any political role in the new administration. However, tribal divisions remained – Haji Abdul Qadir, vice-president and minister of public works in Afghanistan's fledgling government, was assassinated, Karzai narrowly survived an assassination attempt, and a car bomb exploded in the capital, Kabul, killing at least 25 people.
2003: The international peacekeeping force in Kabul was placed under the strategic command of NATO (North Atlantic Treaty Organization). It was the Western alliance's first ground mission outside Europe.
2004: A new constitution was signed in January and the first direct presidential elections were held in October. Hamid Karzai won with 55.4% of the vote.
2005: Elections for the country's National Assembly were scheduled for spring 2005.

Afghan Wars three wars waged between Britain and Afghanistan to counter the threat to British India from expanding Russian influence in Afghanistan.
First Afghan War (1838–42): the British invaded Afghanistan to protect their own interests after Persia, encouraged by Russia, became involved in the region. Although successful at first, a later Afghan rising drove them out of Afghanistan, and of the 4,000 British who formed the garrison of Kabul only one arrived safely at Jalalabad. Another British expedition was dispatched, which captured Kabul, released British prisoners there, and then evacuated the country.
Second Afghan War (1878–80): General Roberts captured Kabul in 1789 and relieved Kandahar.
Third Afghan War (1919): peace followed the dispatch by the UK of the first aeroplane ever seen in Kabul.

Africa second largest of the seven continents. Africa is connected with Asia by the isthmus of Suez, and separated from Europe by the Mediterranean Sea. The name Africa was first given by the Romans to their African provinces with the city of Carthage, and it has since been extended to the whole continent. **area:** 30,097,000 sq km/11,620,451 sq mi (three times the area of Europe) **largest cities:** (population over 2 million; population given in millions) Abidjan (2.9), Addis Ababa (2.6), Alexandria (3.7), Algiers (3.8), Cairo (9.9), Casablanca (3.2), Johannesburg (2.2), Khartoum (2.3), Kinshasa (4.4), Lagos (10.9), Luanda (2.2), Maputo (2.4) **features:** Great Rift Valley, containing most of the great lakes of East Africa (except Lake Victoria); Atlas Mountains in the northwest; Drakensberg mountain range in the southeast; Sahara Desert (world's largest desert) in the north; Namib, Kalahari, and Great Karoo deserts in the south; Nile, Congo, Niger, Zambezi, Limpopo, Volta, and Orange rivers **physical:** dominated by a uniform central plateau comprising a southern tableland with a mean altitude of 1,070 m/3,000 ft that falls northwards to a lower elevated plain with a mean altitude of 400 m/1,300 ft. Although there are no great alpine regions or extensive coastal plains, Africa has a mean altitude of 610 m/2,000 ft, two times greater than Europe. The highest points are Mount Kilimanjaro 5,900 m/19,364 ft, and Mount Kenya 5,200 m/17,058 ft; the lowest point is Lac Assal in Djibouti –144 m/–471 ft. Compared with other continents, Africa has few broad estuaries or inlets and therefore has proportionately the shortest coastline (24,000 km/15,000 mi). The geographical extremities of the continental mainland are Cape Hafun in the east, Cape Almadies in the west, Ras Ben Sekka in the north, and Cape Agulhas in the south. The Sahel is a narrow belt of savannah and scrub forest which covers 700 million hectares/1.7 billion acres of west and central Africa; 75% of the continent lies within the tropics **population:** (2000 est) 793.6 million; more than double the 1970 population of 364 million, and rising to an estimated 1 billion by 2010; annual growth rate 3% (10 times greater than Europe); 27% of the world's undernourished people live in sub-Saharan Africa, where an estimated 25 million are facing famine.

Africa, Horn of projection on the east coast of Africa constituted by Somalia and adjacent territories.

African art art of black African origin, in particular the sculpture and carving of the sub-Saharan domain, from prehistory to the art of ancient civilizations and post-imperialist Africa. Covering a vast range of art forms and styles, it also incorporates two distinct categories: the historic courtly art of Ife and Benin (13th–16th-century Nigeria), noted for its naturalistic bronze and terracotta sculptures; and the more traditional African art forms, which are in the first instance functional, and are more conceptual and abstract in form, reflecting local religious beliefs and values. Knowledge of African art history south of the Sahara is sketchy, partly because of the limited amount of archaeological work that has been carried out in such a huge area, and partly because humidity and termites quickly destroy perishable materials.

African National Congress (ANC) South African political party, founded in 1912 as a multiracial nationalist organization with the aim of extending the franchise to the whole population and ending all racial discrimination. Its president from 1997 is Thabo *Mbeki. The ANC was banned by the government from 1960 to January 1990. Talks between the ANC and the South African government began in December 1991 and culminated in the adoption of a non-racial constitution in 1993 and the ANC's agreement to participate in a power-sharing administration, as a prelude to full majority rule. In the country's first universal suffrage elections in April 1994, the ANC won a sweeping victory, capturing 62% of the vote, and Nelson Mandela was elected president. The ANC also won a majority in South Africa's first democratic local government elections in November 1995, when it won 66.3% of the vote. The ANC won 66% of the vote in the country's second non-racial election in June 1999, but fell just short of a two-thirds majority in parliament. The ANC government secured the coveted two-thirds majority needed to change aspects of the South African constitution by making a deal with a small Indian-led party. Through a coalition agreement with the Minority Front, the ANC secured the single extra seat it needed after the national election, taking it to 267 seats out of 400.

African nationalism political movement for the unification of Africa (Pan-Africanism) and for national self-determination. Early African political organizations included the Aborigines Rights Protection Society in the Gold Coast in 1897, the African National Congress in South Africa in 1912, and the National Congress of West Africa in 1920.

African violet herbaceous plant from tropical central and East Africa, with velvety green leaves and scentless purple flowers. Different colours and double-flowered varieties have been bred. (*Saintpaulia ionantha*, family Gesneriaceae.)

Africa, the scramble for drive by European nations to establish colonies in Africa. It began in the 1880s and by 1914 only two African countries remained completely independent. They were Ethiopia, which had been a kingdom for about 2,000 years, and Liberia, established in 1822 as a homeland for freed black slaves. The rest were under the control of seven European powers: Belgium, Britain, France, Germany, Italy, Portugal, and Spain. Britain and France had the most colonies. All these colonies were short-lived, and the majority attained their independence in the 1960s and 1970s.

Afrikaans language an official language (with English) of the Republic of South Africa and Namibia. Spoken mainly by the *Afrikaners – descendants of Dutch and other 17th-century colonists – it is a variety of the Dutch language, modified by circumstance and the influence of German, French, and other immigrant as well as local languages. It became a standardized written language about 1875.

Afrikaner formerly **Boer**, inhabitant of South Africa descended from the original Dutch, Flemish, and *Huguenot settlers of the 17th century. Comprising approximately 60% of the white population in South Africa, Afrikaners were originally farmers but have now become mainly urbanized. Their language is Afrikaans.

Afro-Asiatic language any of a family of languages spoken throughout the world. There are two main branches, the languages of North Africa and the languages originating in Syria, Mesopotamia, Palestine, and Arabia, but now found from Morocco in the west to the Gulf in the east.

Afro-Caribbean West Indian people of African descent. Afro-Caribbeans are the descendants of West Africans captured or obtained in trade from African procurers. European slave traders then shipped them to the West Indies to English, French, Dutch, Spanish, and Portuguese colonies founded from the 16th century. Since World War II many Afro-Caribbeans have migrated to North America and to Europe, especially to the USA, the UK, and the Netherlands.

afterbirth in mammals, the placenta, umbilical cord, and ruptured membranes that become detached from the uterus and expelled soon after birth.

afterimage persistence of an image on the retina of the eye after the object producing it has been removed. This leads to persistence of vision, a necessary phenomenon for the illusion of continuous movement in films and television. The term is also used for the persistence of sensations other than vision.

Agamemnon in Greek mythology, a Greek hero of the Trojan wars, son of Atreus, king of Mycenae, and brother of *Menelaus. He sacrificed his daughter Iphigenia in order to secure favourable winds for the Greek expedition against Troy and after a ten-year siege sacked the city, receiving Priam's daughter *Cassandra as a prize. On his return home, he and Cassandra were murdered by his wife *Clytemnestra and her lover Aegisthus.

agamid lizard in the family Agamidae, containing about 300 species.

agar jellylike carbohydrate, obtained from seaweeds. It is used mainly in microbiological experiments as a culture medium for growing bacteria and other micro-organisms. The agar is resistant to breakdown by micro-organisms, remaining a solid jelly throughout the course of the experiment.

agaric any of a group of fungi (see *fungus) of typical mushroom shape. Agarics include the field mushroom *Agaricus campestris* and the cultivated edible mushroom *A. brunnensiens*. Closely related is the often poisonous *Amanita*, which includes the fly agaric *A. muscaria*. (Genus *Agaricus*, family Agaricaceae.)

Agassiz, (Jean) Louis Rodolphe (1807–1873) Swiss-born US palaeontologist and geologist who developed the idea of the ice age. He established his name through his work on the classification of fossil fishes. Unlike Charles Darwin, he did not believe that individual species themselves changed, but that new species were created from time to time.

agate cryptocrystalline (with crystals too small to be seen with an optical microscope) silica, SiO_2, composed of cloudy and banded *chalcedony, sometimes mixed with *opal, that forms in rock cavities.

agave any of several related plants with stiff, sword-shaped, spiny leaves arranged in a rosette. All species come from the warmer parts of the New World. They include *Agave sisalana*, whose fibres are used for rope making, and the Mexican century plant *A. americana*, which may take many years to mature (hence its common name). Alcoholic drinks such as tequila and pulque are made from the sap of agave plants. (Genus *Agave*, family Agavaceae.)

Agent Orange selective *weedkiller, notorious for its use by US forces during the Vietnam War to eliminate ground cover that could protect enemy forces. It was subsequently discovered to contain highly poisonous *dioxin.

Agincourt, Battle of battle fought on 25 October 1415 at Agincourt during the Hundred Years' War, between Henry V of England and a much larger force of French under a divided command. Henry completely defeated the French, hastening the English conquest of Normandy. Some 6,000 French died and hundreds, including the richest nobles, were taken prisoner. Henry gained France and the French princess Catherine of Valois as his wife. The village of Agincourt (modern **Azincourt**) is 48 km/30 mi south of Calais, in northern France.

agitprop (Russian 'agitation propaganda') Soviet government bureau established in September 1920 in charge of communist agitation and propaganda. The idea was later developed by left-wing groups in the West for the use of theatre and other arts to convey political messages.

agnosticism belief that the existence of God cannot be proven; that in the nature of things the individual cannot know anything of what lies behind or beyond the world of natural phenomena. The term was coined in 1869 by T H *Huxley.

agoraphobia *phobia involving fear of open spaces and public places. The anxiety produced can be so severe that some sufferers are unable to leave their homes for many years.

agouti small rodent of the genus *Dasyprocta*, family Dasyproctidae. It is found in the forests of Central and South America. The agouti is herbivorous, swift-running, and about the size of a rabbit.

Agra city in Uttar Pradesh, northern India, on the River Jumna (or Yamuna), 160 km/100 mi southeast of Delhi; population (2001 est) 1,321,400. It is a centre for commerce, tourism and industry. There are many small-scale engineering plants and grain mills, and cotton textiles, carpets, leather goods, gold and silver embroidery, and engraved marble are produced. The capital of the Mogul empire from 1566–69 and 1601–58, it is the site of the *Taj Mahal, built during the latter period. Other notable buildings include the Moti Masjid (Pearl Mosque), the Jama Masjid (Great Mosque), and the Red Fort, with red sandstone walls over 20 m/65 ft high and 2.5 km/1.5 mi long. The tomb of the emperor *Akbar lies to the northwest at Sikandra. The city is home to Agra University (1927) and six affiliated colleges.

agrarian revolution until the 1960s historians believed that there had been an 18th-century revolution in *agriculture, similar to the revolution that occurred in industry. They claimed that there had been sweeping changes, possibly in response to the increased demand for food from a rapidly expanding population. Major events included the *enclosure of open fields; the development of improved breeds of livestock; the introduction of four-course crop rotation; and the use of new crops such as turnips as animal fodder. Recent research, however, has shown that these changes were only part of a much larger, slower, ongoing process of development: many were in fact underway before 1750, and other breakthroughs, such as farm mechanization, did not become common until after 1945.

agribusiness commercial farming on an industrial scale, often financed by companies whose main interests lie outside agriculture, for example *multinational corporations. Agribusiness farms are mechanized, large, highly structured, and reliant on chemicals.

Agricola, Gnaeus Julius (40—93) Roman general and politician. Born at Forum Julii (Fréjus) in Provence, he became consul in 77, and then governor of Britain 78–85. He extended Roman rule to the Firth of Forth in Scotland and in 84 won the Battle of Mons Graupius. His fleet sailed round the north of Scotland and proved Britain an island.

agricultural revolution see *agrarian revolution.

agriculture (Latin *ager* 'field', *colere* 'to cultivate') the practice of farming, including the cultivation of the soil (for raising crops) and the raising of domesticated animals. The units for managing agricultural production vary from smallholdings and individually owned farms to corporate-run farms and collective farms run by entire communities or by the government. **Crops** are cultivated for human or animal food, or as industrial crops such as cotton and sisal. For successful production, the land must be prepared (ploughed, cultivated, harrowed, and rolled), seed must be planted and the growing plants nurtured. This may involve fertilizers, irrigation, pest control by chemicals, and monitoring of acidity or nutrients. When the crop has grown, it must be harvested and, depending on the crop, processed in a variety of ways before it is stored or sold. Greenhouses allow cultivation of plants in cold climates. Hydroponics allows commercial cultivation of crops using nutrient-enriched water instead of soil. Special methods, such as terracing, may be adopted to allow cultivation in steep regions and to retain topsoil in mountainous areas with heavy rainfall. **Animals** are raised for wool, milk, leather, dung (as fuel), or meat. They may be semidomesticated, such as reindeer, or fully domesticated but nomadic (where naturally growing or cultivated food supplies are sparse), or kept on a farm. Animal farming involves rearing, feeding, breeding, gathering the produce (eggs, milk, or wool), slaughtering, and further processing such as tanning.

agronomy study of crops and soils, a branch of agricultural science. Agronomy includes such topics as selective breeding (of plants and animals), irrigation, pest control, and soil analysis and modification.

AH in the Muslim calendar, abbreviation for *anno hegirae.

Ahern, Bertie (1951–) Irish politician, Taoiseach (prime minister) from 1997, leader of Fianna Fáil from 1994. After the May 1997 election he formed a minority government as Ireland's youngest Taoiseach. His promotion of peace negotiations culminated in the 1998 Good Friday Agreement between Northern Ireland's contending parties, which received 94% backing in a referendum in the Irish Republic in May 1998.

ahimsa in Hinduism, Buddhism, and Jainism, the doctrine of respect for all life (including the lowest forms and even the elements themselves) and consequently an extreme form of non-violence. It arises in part from the concept of *karma, which holds that a person's actions (and thus any injury caused to any form of life) determine his or her experience and condition in this and future lives.

Ahmadabad or **Ahmedabad** city in Gujarat, India, situated on the Sabarmati River, 430 km/260 mi north of Mumbai (formerly Bombay); population (2001 est) 4,519,300. The former state capital and Gujarat's largest city, it is a major industrial centre specializing in cotton manufacturing, and other industries include pharmaceuticals, flour milling, and the manufacture of soap, glass, carpets, and tobacco products. It has many sacred buildings of the Hindu, Muslim, and Jain faiths, as well as buildings designed by 20th-century architects, such as Le Corbusier, reflecting commercial success.

Ahmad Shah Durrani (1724–1773) founder and first ruler of Afghanistan. Elected shah in 1745, he had conquered the Punjab by 1751 and defeated the *Maratha people's confederacy at Panipat, Punjab, in 1761.

AI abbreviation for *artificial intelligence and *artifical insemination.

aid financial or other assistance given or lent, on favourable terms, by richer, usually industrialized, countries to war-damaged or developing states. It may be given for political, commercial, or humanitarian reasons, or a combination of all three. A distinction may be made between **short-term aid** (usually food and medicine), which is given to relieve conditions in emergencies such as famine, and **long-term aid**, or **development aid**, which is intended to promote economic activity and improve the quality of life – for example, by funding irrigation, education, and communications programmes.

Aidan, St (c. 600–651) Irish monk who converted Northumbria to Christianity and founded Lindisfarne monastery on Holy Island off the northeast coast of England. His feast day is 31 August.

AIDS acronym for **acquired immune deficiency syndrome**, most serious of all the *sexually transmitted diseases (STDs). It is caused by the *retrovirus human immunodeficiency virus (*HIV),

and is transmitted in body fluids, such as blood, saliva, semen, and vaginal secretions. AIDS is the world's most deadly STD and the fourth leading global cause of death. Unlike other diseases, which typically claim most lives among young children and the elderly, AIDS particularly hits those of working age. This has resulted in huge demographic changes in the countries most severely affected by AIDS, causing widespread social and economic hardship.

ailanthus any of several trees or shrubs with compound leaves made up of pointed leaflets and clusters of small greenish flowers with an unpleasant smell. The tree of heaven (*Ailanthus altissima*), native to East Asia, is grown worldwide as an ornamental; it can grow to 30 m/100 ft in height and the trunk can reach 1 m/3 ft in diameter. (Genus *Ailanthus*, family Simaroubaceae.)

Ainu aboriginal people of Japan, driven north in the 4th century AD by ancestors of the Japanese. They now number about 25,000, inhabiting Japanese and Russian territory on Sakhalin, Hokkaido, and the Kuril Islands. Their language has no written form, and is unrelated to any other. The Ainu were recognized by the Japanese government as a minority people in 1991.

air the mixture of gases making up the Earth's *atmosphere.

aircraft any aeronautical vehicle capable of flying through the air. It may be lighter than air (supported by buoyancy) or heavier than air (supported by the dynamic action of air on its surfaces. *Balloons and *airships are lighter-than-air craft. Heavier-than-air craft include the *aeroplane, glider, autogiro, and helicopter.

Airedale terrier breed of large terrier, about 60 cm/ 24 in tall, with a wiry red-brown coat and black saddle patch. It originated about 1850 in England, as a cross between the otterhound and Irish and Welsh terriers.

airlock airtight chamber that allows people to pass between areas of different pressure; also an air bubble in a pipe that impedes fluid flow. An airlock may connect an environment at ordinary pressure and an environment that has high air pressure (such as a submerged caisson used for tunnelling or building dams or bridge foundations).

air pollution contamination of the atmosphere caused by the discharge, accidental or deliberate, of a wide range of toxic airborne substances. Often the amount of the released substance is relatively high in a certain locality, so the harmful effects become more noticeable. The cost of preventing any discharge of pollutants into the air is prohibitive, so attempts are more usually made to reduce the amount of discharge gradually and to disperse it as quickly as possible by using a very tall chimney, or by intermittent release.

air sac in birds, a thin-walled extension of the lungs. There are nine of these and they extend into the abdomen and bones, effectively increasing lung capacity.

airship or **dirigible** any aircraft that is lighter than air and power-driven, consisting of an ellipsoidal balloon that forms the streamlined envelope or hull and has below it the propulsion system (propellers), steering mechanism, and space for crew, passengers, and/or cargo. The balloon section is filled with lighter-than-air gas, either the nonflammable helium or, before helium was industrially available in large enough quantities, the easily ignited and flammable hydrogen. The envelope's form is maintained by internal pressure in the nonrigid (blimp) and semirigid (in which the nose and tail sections have a metal framework connected by a rigid keel) types. The rigid type (zeppelin) maintains its form using an internal metal framework. Airships have been used for luxury travel, polar exploration, warfare, and advertising.

Ajax Greek hero in Homer's *Iliad*. Son of Telamon, King of Salamis, he was second only to Achilles among the Greek heroes in the Trojan War. He fought *Hector single-handed, defended the ships, and killed many Trojans. According to subsequent Greek legends, Ajax went mad with jealousy when *Agamemnon awarded the armour of the dead Achilles to *Odysseus. He later committed suicide in shame.

Ajman smallest of the seven states making up the United Arab Emirates; area 250 sq km/96 sq mi; population (1999 est) 161,000.

ajolote Mexican reptile of the genus *Bipes*. It and several other tropical burrowing species are placed in the Amphisbaenia, a group separate from lizards and snakes among the Squamata. Unlike the others, however, which have no legs, it has a pair of short but well-developed front legs. In line with its burrowing habits, the skull is very solid, the eyes small, and external ears absent. The scales are arranged in rings, giving the body a wormlike appearance.

Akbar, Jalal ud-Din Muhammad (1542–1605) Third Mogul emperor of North India from 1556, when he succeeded his father Humayun. He gradually established his rule throughout North India. He is considered the greatest of the Mogul emperors, and the firmness and wisdom of his rule won him the title 'Guardian of Mankind'; he was a patron of the arts.

à Kempis, Thomas German religious writer; see *Thomas à Kempis.

Akhenaton (or Ikhnaton) King (pharaoh) of ancient Egypt of the 18th dynasty (c. 1353–1335 BC), who may have ruled jointly for a time with his father Amenhotep III. He developed the cult of the Sun, Aton, rather than the rival cult of Amen, and removed his capital to Akhetaton.

Akihito (1933–) Emperor of Japan from 1989, succeeding his father Hirohito (Showa). His reign is called the Heisei ('achievement of universal peace') era.

Akkad northern Semitic people who conquered the Sumerians 2350 BC and ruled Mesopotamia. Their language was Semitic (old Akkadian). Akkad was also the northern of the two provinces into which Babylonia was divided. The ancient city of Akkad in central Mesopotamia, founded by Sargon I, was an imperial centre in the late third millennium BC; the site is unidentified, but it was on the River Euphrates somewhere near Babylon.

Aksum or Axum ancient Greek-influenced Semitic kingdom that flourished in the 1st–6th centuries AD and covered a large part of modern Ethiopia as well as the Sudan. The ruins of its capital, also called Aksum, lie northwest of Adwa, but the site has been developed as a modern city.

al- for Arabic names beginning *al-*, see rest of name; for example, for 'al-Fatah', see *Fatah, al-.

Alabama (American Indian Creek 'thicket clearers') called **Heart of Dixie** or the **Yellowhammer State**, state in southeastern USA, bordered to the east by *Georgia, to the north by *Tennessee, to the west by *Mississippi, and to the south by *Florida and the Gulf of Mexico; area 131,426 sq km/50,744 sq mi; population (2000) 4,447,100; capital *Montgomery. The nickname 'Heart of Dixie' refers to Alabama's leading role in the *Confederacy and 'Yellowhammer State' to the colourful uniforms of Confederate soldiers. Alabama is two-thirds low-lying coastal plain, with an 85 km-/53 mi-long stretch of coast on the Gulf of Mexico, intersected by Mobile Bay. Service industries form a major part of its economy, but oil, natural gas, marble, wood, iron, steel, aluminium, chemical, paper, and textile manufactures are also important. Livestock, poultry, peanuts, pecans, soft fruit, soybeans, and cotton are produced, and fishing is a key industry. The city of Birmingham has the largest population; other major cities include the port of Mobile, the missile and aerospace centre Huntsville, and former state capital Tuscaloosa, home to the University of Alabama. There are also large urban conurbations in Anniston, Decatur, Dothan, Florence, and Gadsden. Historically Alabama was a plantation state associated with slavery and, in the 20th century, the civil-rights movement. Alabama was admitted to the Union in 1819 as the 22nd US state.

alabaster naturally occurring fine-grained white or light-coloured translucent form of gypsum, often streaked or mottled. A soft material, it is easily carved, but seldom used for outdoor sculpture.

Alamein, El, battles of two decisive battles of World War II in the western desert of northern Egypt. In the first (1–22 July 1942), the British 8th Army under Auchinleck held off the German and Italian forces under *Rommel; in the second (23 October–4 November 1942), *Montgomery defeated Rommel.

Alamo, the mission fortress in San Antonio, Texas, USA. During the War of Texan Independence from Mexico, it was besieged 23 February–6 March 1836 by *Santa Anna and 4,000 Mexicans. They killed the garrison of about 180 Texans, including Davy Crockett and Jim Bowie.

Alanbrooke, Alan Francis Brooke (1883–1963) 1st Viscount Alanbrooke, British army officer. He was Chief of Staff in World War II and largely responsible for the strategy that led to the German defeat.

Åland Islands Finnish **Ahvenanmaa** 'land of waters', group of some 6,000 islands in the Baltic Sea, at the southern extremity of the Gulf of Bothnia; area 1,481 sq km/572 sq mi; population (1992) 25,000. Only 80 are inhabited; the largest island, Åland, has a small town, Mariehamn. The main sectors of the island economy are tourism, agriculture, and shipping.

Alania formerly **North Ossetia**, autonomous republic in the south of the Russian Federation, on the border with Georgia; area 8,000 sq km/3,088 sq mi; population (1992) 695,000. A new constitution was adopted in 1994 and the republic took its former name of Alania. The capital is Vladikavkaz (formerly Ordzhonikidze). Alania lies on the northern slopes of the central Caucasus, and its main rivers are the Terek, the Gizeldon, and the Ardon. Its industries include mining and metallurgy (lead, zinc, silver), maize processing, timber and woodwork, textiles, building materials, distilleries, food processing, and hydroelectric power generation.

Alaric (c. 370–410) Visigothic king 395–410 who campaigned against the Romans in the Balkans and Italy. On 24 August 410 he captured and sacked Rome. After three days he led the Goths south, intending to invade Sicily and then Africa, but died of a sudden illness.

Alaska (American Indian Aleut *alaxsxaq* 'the mainland') called the **Last Frontier**, state of the USA, separated from the lower, continental US states by Canada and bordered to the south by *British Columbia, to the east by the *Yukon Territory, to the north by the *Beaufort Sea on the Arctic Ocean, to the northwest by the Chukchi Sea and *Bering Sea, and to the west by the Gulf of Alaska on the North Pacific Ocean; area 1,481,346 sq km/571,951 sq mi; population (2000) 626,900; capital Juneau. Alaska is the largest state in the USA and one of the least populated. Situated on the northwest extremity of North America, it is separated from Russian East Asia by the 80 km-/50 mi-wide Bering Strait. Alaska's *Aleutian Island chain extends in a long east–west arc across the North Pacific from the Alaska Peninsula. Historically and commercially the state has been associated with mineral exploitation, and Alaska continues to produce oil, natural gas, coal, copper, iron, gold, and tin. The lumber, fur, and tourist industries are also important; tourists outnumber the resident population each year. Fishing and canning, particularly salmon, are key activities. The port of *Anchorage on the Gulf of Alaska is the most populous city. American Indian peoples, including Aleut and *Inuit, make up about 15% of Alaska's population. Alaska was admitted to the Union in 1959 as the 49th US state.

Alba Gaelic name for *Scotland; also an alternative spelling for *Alva, Ferdinand Alvarez de Toledo, Duke of Alva, Spanish politician and general.

Alban, St (lived 3rd century) First Christian martyr in England. In 793 King Offa founded a monastery on the site of Alban's martyrdom, around which the city of St Albans grew up. His feast day is 20 June.

Albania
National name: *Republika e Shqipërisë/ Republic of Albania*

Area: 28,748 sq km/11,099 sq mi
Capital: Tirana
Major towns/cities: Durrës, Shkodër, Elbasan, Vlorë, Korçë

Major ports: Durrës
Physical features: mainly mountainous, with rivers flowing east–west, and a narrow coastal plain
Head of state: Alfred Moisiu from 2002
Head of government: Fatos Nano from 2002
Political system: emergent democracy
Political executive: limited presidency
Political parties: Democratic Party of Albania (PDS; formerly the Democratic Party: DP), moderate, market-oriented; Socialist Party of Albania (PSS), ex-communist; Human Rights Union (HMU), Greek minority party; Agrarian Party (AP); Christian Democratic Party (CDP); Democratic Alliance Party (DAP), centrist; Democratic Party
Currency: lek
GNI per capita (PPP): (US$) 4,040 (2002 est)
Exports: textiles and footwear, mineral products, base metals, food and live animals, beverages and tobacco, vegetable products. Principal market: Italy 70.3% (2000)
Population: 3,166,000 (2003 est)
Language: Albanian (official), Greek
Religion: Muslim, Albanian Orthodox, Roman Catholic
Life expectancy: 71 (men); 77 (women) (2000–05)
Chronology
2000 BC: Albania was part of Illyria.
168 BC: Illyria was conquered by the Romans.
AD 395: Became part of Byzantine Empire.
6th–14th centuries: Byzantine decline exploited by Serbs, Normans, Slavs, Bulgarians, and Venetians.
1381: Ottoman invasion of Albania followed by years of resistance to Turkish rule.
1468: Resistance led by national hero Skanderbeg (George Kastrioti) largely collapsed, and Albania passed to Ottoman Empire.
15th–16th centuries: Thousands fled to southern Italy to escape Ottoman rule; over half of the rest of the population converted to Islam.
1878: Foundation of Albanian League promoted emergence of nationalism.
1912: Achieved independence from Turkey as a result of First Balkan War and end of Ottoman Empire in Europe.
1914–20: Occupied by Italy.
1925: Declared itself a republic.
1928–39: Monarchy of King Zog.
1939: Italian occupation led by Benito Mussolini.
1943–44: Under German rule following Italian surrender.
1946: Proclaimed Communist People's Republic of Albania, with Enver Hoxha as premier.
1949: Developed close links with Joseph Stalin in USSR and entered Comecon (Council for Mutual Economic Assistance).
1961: Broke with USSR in wake of Nikita Khrushchev's denunciation of Stalin, and withdrew from Comecon. In 1978 Albania also severed diplomatic links with China.
1987: Normal diplomatic relations restored with Canada, Greece, and West Germany.
1990–91: The one-party system was abandoned in the face of popular protest; the first opposition party was formed, and the first multiparty elections were held.
1992: Former communist officials were charged with corruption and abuse of power. Totalitarian and communist parties were banned.
1993: Conflict began between ethnic Greeks and Albanians, followed by a purge of ethnic Greeks from the civil service and army.

1997: Antigovernment riots; police killed demonstrators in the southern port of Vlorë. Southern Albania fell under rebel control. The government signed a World Bank and IMF rescue package to salvage the economy.

1998: A new constitution came into effect.

1999: Ilir Meta, a socialist, became prime minister.

2002: Fatos Nano of the Socialist Party became prime minister (for the fourth time) and Alfred Moisin president. The royal family returned from exile.

2003: Albania and the European Union (EU) held initial talks towards Albania's possible EU membership.

2004: Demonstrations in Tirana called for the resignation of the prime minister Fatos Nano, appointed in 2002. The protestors were angry at the government's failure to improve living standards.

albatross large seabird, genus *Diomedea*, with long narrow wings adapted for gliding and a wingspan of up to 3.4 m/11 ft, mainly found in the southern hemisphere. It belongs to the family Diomedeidae, order Procellariiformes, the same group as petrels and shearwaters. The nostrils of birds in this order are tubular, and the bills are hooked.

Albee, Edward (Franklin) (1928–) US dramatist. Associated with the Theatre of the *Absurd, he is best known for his play *Who's Afraid of Virginia Woolf?* (1962, filmed 1966), a grim depiction of a miserable marriage. His other internationally-performed plays include *The Zoo Story* (1960), *The American Dream* (1961), and *Tiny Alice* (1965). *A Delicate Balance* (1966) and *Seascape* (1975) both won Pulitzer Prizes, and *Three Tall Women* (1994) marked his return to critical acclaim.

Albert, Prince Consort (1819–1861) Husband of British Queen *Victoria from 1840. A patron of the arts, science, and industry, Albert was the second son of the Duke of Saxe Coburg-Gotha and first cousin to Queen Victoria, whose chief adviser he became. He planned the Great Exhibition of 1851, the profits from which were used to buy the sites in London of all the South Kensington museums and colleges and the Royal Albert Hall, built in 1871. He died of typhoid. The Queen never fully recovered from his premature death, and remained in mourning for him for the rest of her life.

Alberta province of western Canada; area 661,200 sq km/255,223 sq mi; population (2001 est) 2,974,800. Its capital is *Edmonton, and the main towns and cities include Calgary, Lethbridge, Medicine Hat, and Red Deer. Oil extraction is the most important economic activity in Alberta, with the province accounting for most of the country's oil production. It became a province in 1905.

Alberti, Leon Battista (1404–1472) Italian Renaissance architect and theorist. He set out the principles of classical architecture, and covered their modification for Renaissance practice, in *De re aedificatoria/On Architecture*, which he started in 1452 and worked on until his death (published in 1485; translated as *Ten Books on Architecture* in 1955).

Albert, Lake lake on the border of Uganda and the Democratic Republic of Congo in the Great *Rift Valley; area 5,600 sq km/2,162 sq mi. The first European to see it was the British explorer Samuel Baker, who named it Lake Albert after the Prince Consort. From 1973 to 1997 it was called Lake Mobutu after President Mobutu of Zaire (now Democratic Republic of Congo).

Albigenses heretical sect of Christians (also known as the Cathars) who flourished in southern France near Albi and Toulouse during the 11th–13th centuries. They adopted the Manichean belief in the duality of good and evil and pictured Jesus as being a rebel against the cruelty of an omnipotent God.

albinism rare hereditary condition in which the body has no tyrosinase, one of the enzymes that form the pigment *melanin, normally found in the skin, hair, and eyes. As a result, the hair is white and the skin and eyes are pink. The skin and eyes are abnormally sensitive to light, and vision is often impaired. The condition occurs among all human and animal groups.

Albion name for Britain used by the ancient Greeks and Romans. It was mentioned by Pytheas of Massilia (4th century BC), and is probably of Celtic origin, but the Romans, having in mind the white cliffs of Dover, assumed it to be derived from the word *albus* (white).

albumin any of a group of sulphur-containing *proteins. The best known is in the form of egg white (albumen); others occur in milk, and as a major component of serum. Many vegetables and fluids also contain albumins. They are soluble in water and dilute salt solutions, and are coagulated by heat.

alchemy (Arabic *al-Kimya*) supposed technique of transmuting base metals, such as lead and mercury, into silver and gold by the philosopher's stone, a hypothetical substance, to which was also attributed the power to give eternal life.

Alcibiades (451/0–404/3 BC) Athenian politician and general during the Peloponnesian War. In 415 BC Alcibiades was appointed one of the commanders of an Athenian expedition against Sicily, but was recalled to answer charges of sacrilege and fled to Sparta. Further scandal led to his flight to Persia, but he rehabilitated himself with the Athenians and played a leading part at Cyzicus in 410 BC. He was given command of Athenian forces in Asia Minor but was replaced after his lieutenant's defeat off Notium in 407 BC. He was murdered shortly after the war.

Alcock, John William (1892–1919) English aviator. On 14 June 1919, he and Arthur Whitten-Brown made the first non-stop transatlantic flight, from Newfoundland to Ireland. He was awarded the KBE in 1919.

alcohol in chemistry, any member of a group of organic chemical compounds characterized by the presence of one or more aliphatic OH (hydroxyl) groups in the molecule, and which form *esters with acids. The main uses of alcohols are as solvents for gums, resins, lacquers, and varnishes; in the making of dyes; for essential oils in perfumery; and for medical substances in pharmacy. The alcohol produced naturally in the *fermentation process and consumed as part of alcoholic beverages is called *ethanol. When consumed the effects of alcohol include poisoning at high concentrations, and changes in the functioning of human nerve cells.

alcoholic beverage any drink containing alcohol, often used for its intoxicating effects. *Ethanol (ethyl alcohol), a colourless liquid (C_2H_5OH) is the basis of all common intoxicants. Foods rich in sugars, such as grapes, produce this alcohol as a natural product of decay, called *fermentation.

alcoholism dependence on alcohol. It is characterized as an illness when consumption of alcohol interferes with normal physical or emotional health. Excessive alcohol consumption, whether through sustained ingestion or irregular drinking bouts or binges, may produce physical and psychological addiction and lead to nutritional and emotional disorders. Long-term heavy consumption of alcohol leads to diseases of the heart, liver, and peripheral nerves. Support groups such as Alcoholics Anonymous are helpful.

Alcott, Louisa May (1832–1888) US author. Her children's classic *Little Women* (1869) drew on her own home circumstances; the principal character Jo was a partial self-portrait. Sequels to *Little Women* were *Good Wives* (1869), *Little Men* (1871), and *Jo's Boys* (1886).

Alcuin (735–804) born Flaccus Albinus Alcuinus, English scholar. Born in York, he went to Rome in 780, and in 782 took up residence at Charlemagne's court in Aachen. From 796 he was abbot at St Martin's in Tours. He disseminated Anglo-Saxon scholarship. Alcuin organized education and learning in the Frankish empire and was a prominent member of Charlemagne's academy, providing a strong impulse to the Carolingian Renaissance.

Aldebaran *or* **Alpha Tauri** brightest star in the constellation Taurus and the 14th-brightest star in the night sky; it marks the eye of the 'bull'. Aldebaran is a red giant 65 light years away from the Sun, shining with a true luminosity of about 100 times that of the Sun.

aldehyde any of a group of organic chemical compounds prepared by oxidation of primary alcohols, so that the OH (hydroxyl) group loses its hydrogen to give an oxygen joined by a double bond to a carbon atom (the aldehyde group, with the formula CHO).

alder any of a group of trees or shrubs belonging to the birch family, found mainly in cooler parts of the northern hemisphere and characterized by toothed leaves and catkins. (Genus *Alnus*, family Betulaceae.)

Alderney third largest of the *Channel Islands, with its capital at St Anne's; area 8 sq km/3 sq mi; population (2001 est) 2,400. Tourism flourished on Alderney from the early 20th century. The main employers are now tourist-related businesses and services providing building and maintenance work for locals and immigrants. There is also a small finance industry.

aleatory music (Latin *alea* 'dice') method of composition practised by post-war avant-garde composers in which the performer or conductor chooses the order of succession of the composed pieces. Examples of aleatory music include Pierre Boulez's *Piano Sonata No 3* (1956–57), Earle Brown's *Available Forms I* (1961), and Stockhausen's *Momente/Moments* (1961–72). Another term for aleatory music is 'mobile form'. Aleatory music is distantly related to the 18th-century 'musical dice game' and to the freely assembled music for silent movies using theme catalogues by Giuseppe Becce and others. The use by John *Cage of dice and the I Ching differs in that it intervenes in the actual process of composition.

Aletsch most extensive glacier in Europe, 23.6 km/ 14.7 mi long, beginning on the southern slopes of the Jungfrau in the Bernese Alps, Switzerland.

Aleutian Islands volcanic island chain in the North Pacific, stretching 1,900 km/1,200 mi southwest of Alaska, of which it forms part, towards Kamchatka; population in Aleutians East Borough (2000 est) 2,700; in Aleutians West Census Area (2000 est) 5,500. There are 14 large and more than 100 small islands running along the Aleutian Trench; the largest island is Unimak

(with an area of 3,500 sq km/1,360 sq mi), which contains two active volcanoes. They are mountainous, barren, and almost treeless; they are ice-free all year but are often foggy, with only about 25 days of sunshine recorded annually. Unalaska is the chief island for trade as it has a good harbour. Most of the islands lie within the Aleutians National Wildlife Reserve.

A level abbreviation for Advanced level, in England, Wales, and Northern Ireland, examinations taken by students usually at the age of 17 or 18. AS levels are taken after one year's study and A2 levels after two. Scottish students sit Highers and Advanced Highers.

Alexander eight popes, including:
Alexander III (died 1181) born Orlando Bandinelli, Pope 1159–81. His authority was opposed by Frederick I Barbarossa, but Alexander eventually compelled him to render homage in 1178. He held the third Lateran Council in 1179. He supported Henry II of England in his invasion of Ireland, but imposed penance on him after the murder of Thomas à *Becket.
Alexander VI (1430 *or* **1432–1503)** born Rodrigo Borgia or Rodrigo Borja, Pope 1492–1503. Of Spanish origin, he bribed his way to the papacy, where he furthered the advancement of his illegitimate children, who included Cesare and Lucrezia *Borgia. When *Savonarola preached against his corrupt practices Alexander had him executed.

Alexander three tsars of Russia:
Alexander I (1777–1825) Tsar of Russia from 1801. Defeated by Napoleon at Austerlitz in 1805, he made peace at Tilsit in 1807, but economic crisis led to a break with Napoleon's *Continental System and the opening of Russian ports to British trade; this led to Napoleon's ill-fated invasion of Russia in 1812. After the Congress of Vienna in 1815, Alexander hoped through the Holy Alliance with Austria and Prussia to establish a new Christian order in Europe.
Alexander II (1818–1881) Tsar of Russia from 1855. He embarked on reforms of the army, the government, and education, and is remembered as 'the Liberator' for his emancipation of the serfs in 1861, but he lacked the personnel to implement his reforms. However, the revolutionary element remained unsatisfied, and Alexander became increasingly autocratic and reactionary. He was assassinated by an anarchistic terrorist group, the *Nihilists.
Alexander III (1845–1894) Tsar of Russia from 1881, when he succeeded his father, Alexander II. He pursued a reactionary policy, promoting Russification and persecuting the Jews. He married Dagmar (1847–1928), daughter of Christian IX of Denmark and sister of Queen Alexandra of Britain, in 1866.

Alexander three kings of Scotland:
Alexander I (c. 1078–1124) King of Scotland from 1107, known as 'the Fierce'. He ruled over the area to the north of the rivers Forth and Clyde, while his brother and successor *David ruled over the area to the south. He assisted Henry I of England in his campaign against Wales in 1114, but defended the independence of the church in Scotland. Several monasteries, including the abbeys of Inchcolm and Scone, were established by him.
Alexander II (1198–1249) King of Scotland from 1214, when he succeeded his father, William the Lion. Alexander supported the English barons in their struggle with King John after *Magna Carta.

The accession of Henry III of England allowed a *rapprochement* between the two countries, and the boundaries between England and Scotland were agreed by the Treaty of York in 1237. By the Treaty of Newcastle in 1244 he pledged allegiance to Henry III. Alexander consolidated royal authority in Scotland and was a generous patron of the church.

Alexander III (1241–1286) King of Scotland from 1249, son of Alexander II. After defeating the Norwegian forces in 1263, he was able to extend his authority over the Western Isles, which had been dependent on Norway. The later period of his reign was devoted to administrative reforms, which limited the power of the barons and brought a period of peace and prosperity to Scotland.

Alexander I, Karageorgevich (1888–1934) Regent of Serbia 1912–21 and king of Yugoslavia 1921–34, as dictator from 1929. The second son of Peter I, King of Serbia, he was declared regent for his father in 1912 and on his father's death became king of the state of South Slavs – Yugoslavia – that had come into being in 1918.

Alexander Nevski, St (1220–1263) Russian military leader, ruler of Novgorod in 1236, and Grand Prince of Vladimir in 1252. He survived Mongol attacks in 1237–40, which enabled him to defeat the Swedes in 1240 and the Germans in 1242.

Alexander Severus (AD 208–235) born Marcus Aurelius Severus Alexander, Roman emperor from 222, when he succeeded his cousin Heliogabalus. He attempted to involve the Senate more closely in administration, and was the patron of the jurists Ulpian and Paulus, and the historian Cassius Dio. His campaign against the Persians in 232 achieved some success, but in 235, on his way to defend Gaul against German invaders, he was killed in a mutiny.

Alexander technique in alternative medicine, a method of correcting bad habits of posture, breathing, and muscular tension, which Australian therapist F M Alexander maintained cause many ailments. The technique is also used to promote general health and relaxation and enhance vitality.

Alexander (III) the Great (356–323 BC) King of Macedon 336–323 BC and conqueror of the Persian Empire. As commander of the powerful Macedonian army he conquered Greece in 336 BC, defeated the Persian king Darius III in Asia Minor in 333 BC, then moved on to Egypt where he founded Alexandria. He defeated the Persians again in Assyria in 331 BC, then advanced further east, invading India in 327 BC. He conquered the Punjab before mutinous troops forced his retreat.

Alexandria or **El Iskandarīya** city, chief port, and second-largest city of Egypt, situated between the Mediterranean and Lake Maryut; population (1996 est) 3,328,200. It is linked by canal with the Nile. There is oil refining, gas processing, and trade in cotton and grain. Founded in 332 BC by Alexander the Great, Alexandria was the capital of Egypt for over 1,000 years.

Alexandria, Library of the world's first state-funded scientific institution, founded in 330 BC in Alexandria, Egypt, by Ptolemy I and further expanded by Ptolemy II. It comprised a museum, teaching facilities, and a library that contained up to 700,000 scrolls, including much ancient Greek literature. It sustained significant damage in AD 391, when the Roman emperor Theodosius I ordered its destruction. It was burned down in 640 AD at the time of the Arab conquest.

Alexandria, school of group of writers and scholars of Alexandria, Egypt, who made the city the chief centre of culture in the Western world from about 331 BC to AD 642. They include the poets Callimachus, Apollonius of Rhodes, and Theocritus; *Euclid, pioneer of geometry; *Eratosthenes, a geographer; Hipparchus, who developed a system of trigonometry; Ptolemy, whose system of astronomy endured for over 1,000 years; and the Jewish philosopher Philo. The Gnostics and Neo-Platonists also flourished in Alexandria.

Alexius five emperors of Byzantium, including:

Alexius I, Comnenus (1048–1118) Byzantine emperor 1081–1118. With meagre resources, he dealt successfully with internal dissent and a series of external threats from the Turks and Normans. He managed the difficult passage of the First Crusade through Byzantine territory on its way to Jerusalem, and by the end of his reign he had, with the help of the Crusaders, restored much of Byzantine control over Anatolia. His daughter Anna Comnena chronicled his reign.

Alexius III, Angelos (died 1210) Byzantine emperor 1195–1203. He gained power by deposing and blinding his brother Isaac II, but Isaac's Venetian allies enabled him and his son Alexius IV to regain power as coemperors.

Alexius IV, Angelos (1182–1204) Byzantine emperor from 1203, when, with the aid of the army of the Fourth Crusade, he deposed his uncle Alexius III. He soon lost the support of the Crusaders (by that time occupying Constantinople), and was overthrown and murdered by another Alexius, Alexius Mourtzouphlus (son-in-law of Alexius III) in 1204, an act which the Crusaders used as a pretext to sack the city the same year.

alfalfa or **lucerne** perennial tall herbaceous plant belonging to the pea family. It is native to Europe and Asia and has spikes of small purple flowers in late summer. It is now a major fodder crop, commonly processed into hay, meal, or silage. Alfalfa sprouts, the sprouted seeds, have become a popular salad ingredient. (*Medicago sativa*, family Leguminosae.)

Alfonso thirteen kings of León, Castile, and Spain, including:

Alfonso (X), the Wise (1221–1284) King of Castile from 1252. His reign was politically unsuccessful but he contributed to learning: he made *Castilian the official language of the country and commissioned a history of Spain and an encyclopedia, as well as several translations from Arabic concerning, among other subjects, astronomy and games.

Alfonso XIII (1886–1941) King of Spain 1886–1931. He assumed power in 1906 and married Princess Ena, granddaughter of Queen Victoria of Great Britain, in the same year. He abdicated in 1931 soon after the fall of the Primo de Rivera dictatorship 1923–30 (which he supported), and Spain became a republic. His assassination was attempted several times.

Alfred the Great (c. 849–c. 901) Anglo-Saxon king 871–899 who defended England against Danish invasion and founded the first English navy. He succeeded his brother Aethelred to the throne of Wessex in 871, and a new legal code came into force during his reign. He encouraged the translation of scholarly works from Latin (some he translated himself), and promoted the development of the *Anglo-Saxon Chronicle.

algae singular **alga**, highly varied group of plants, ranging from single-celled forms to large and complex seaweeds. They live in both fresh and salt water, and in damp soil. Algae do not have true roots, stems, or leaves. Marine algae help combat *global warming by removing carbon dioxide from the atmosphere during *photosynthesis.

Algarve (Arabic *al-gharb* 'the west') ancient kingdom in southern Portugal, bordered on the east by Spain, and on the west and south by the Atlantic Ocean; it is co-extensive with the modern district of Faro, the provincial capital of the Algarve; area 5,071 sq km/1,958 sq mi; population (1995 est) 346,000. The population increased during the 1980s and 1990s as a result of inward migration. Tourism is the largest employer in the area. It is based mainly on beach resorts although there has been a shift towards cultural and golfing tourism. Regional agriculture is mainly citrus fruits, due to the use of modern irrigation methods, although traditional crops of grapes, figs, olives, almonds, and carobs are still grown. The hilly areas are heavily forested with pine and eucalyptus trees.

algebra branch of mathematics in which the general properties of numbers are studied by using symbols, usually letters, to represent variables and unknown quantities. For example, the algebraic statement: $(x + y)^2 = x^2 + 2xy + y^2$ is true for all values of x and y. For instance, the substitution $x = 7$ and $y = 3$ gives:

$$(7 + 3)^2 = 7^2 + 2(7 + 3) + 3^2 = 100$$

An algebraic expression that has one or more variables (denoted by letters) is a *polynomial equation. A polynomial equation has the form:

$$f(x) = a_n x^n + a_{n-1} x^{n-1} + \ldots + a_2 x^2 + a_1 x + a_0$$

where $a_n, a_{n-1}, \ldots, a_0$ are all constants, n is a positive integer, and $a_n \neq 0$. Examples of polynomials are: $f(x) = 3x^4 + 2x^2 + 1$ or $f(x) = x^5 - 18x + 71$ or $f(x) = 2x + 3$ Algebra is used in many areas of mathematics – for example, *arithmetic progressions, or number sequences, and Boolean algebra (the latter is used in working out the logic for computers).

Algeria

National name: *Al-Jumhuriyyat al-Jaza'iriyya ad-Dimuqratiyya ash-Sha'biyya/Democratic People's Republic of Algeria*

Area: 2,381,741 sq km/919,590 sq mi
Capital: Algiers (Arabic al-Jaza'ir)
Major towns/cities: Oran, Annaba, Blida, Sétif, Constantine
Major ports: Oran (Ouahran), Annaba (Bône)
Physical features: coastal plains backed by mountains in north, Sahara desert in south; Atlas mountains, Barbary Coast, Chott Melrhir depression, Hoggar mountains
Head of state: Abdelaziz Bouteflika from 1999
Head of government: Ahmed Ouyahia from 2003
Political system: military
Political executive: military
Political parties: National Democratic Rally (RND), left of centre; National Liberation Front (FLN), nationalist, socialist; Socialist Forces Front (FSS), Berber-based, left of centre; Islamic Front for Salvation (FIS), Islamic fundamentalist (banned from 1992); Movement for a Peacetime Society (MSP), formerly Hamas, fundamentalist
Currency: Algerian dinar
GNI per capita (PPP): (US$) 5,330 (2002 est)
Exports: crude oil, gas, vegetables, tobacco, hides, dates. Principal market: Italy 22.8% (2001)
Population: 31,800,000 (2003 est)
Language: Arabic (official), Berber, French
Religion: Sunni Muslim (state religion) 99%, Christian and Jewish 1%
Life expectancy: 68 (men); 71 (women) (2000–05)
Chronology
9th century BC: Part of Carthaginian Empire.
146 BC: Conquered by Romans, who called the area Numidia.
6th century: Part of the Byzantine Empire.
late 7th century: Conquered by Muslim Arabs, who spread Islam as the basis of a new Berberized Arab-Islamic civilization.
1516: Ottoman Turks expelled recent Christian Spanish invaders.
1816: Anglo-Dutch forces bombarded Algiers as a reprisal against the Barbary pirates' attacks on Mediterranean shipping.
1830–47: French occupation of Algiers, followed by extension of control to the north, overcoming fierce resistance from Amir Abd al-Qadir, a champion of Arab Algerian nationalism, and from Morocco.
1850–70: The mountainous inland region, inhabited by the Kabyles, was occupied by the French.
1871: There was a major rebellion against French rule as French settlers began to take over the best agricultural land.
1900–09: The Sahara region was subdued by France, who kept it under military rule.
1940: Following France's defeat by Nazi Germany, Algeria became allied to the pro-Nazi Vichy regime during World War II.
1945: 8,000 died following the ruthless suppression of an abortive uprising against French rule.
1954–62: Battle of Algiers: bitter war of independence fought between the National Liberation Front (FLN) and the French colonial army.
1958: French inability to resolve the civil war in Algeria, toppled the Fourth Republic and brought to power, in Paris, Gen Charles de Gaulle, who accepted the principle of national self-determination.

1962: Independence from France was achieved and a republic declared. Many French settlers fled.

1963: A one-party state was established.

1976: New Islamic-socialist constitution approved.

1988: Riots took place in protest at austerity policies; 170 people were killed. A reform programme was introduced. Diplomatic relations were restored with Morocco after a 12-year break.

1989: Constitutional changes introduced limited political pluralism.

1992: The military took control of the government and a state of emergency was declared.

1993: The civil strife worsened, with assassinations of politicians and other public figures.

1994: The fundamentalists' campaign of violence intensified.

1996: The constitution was amended to increase the president's powers and counter religious fundamentalism. Arabic was declared the official public language.

1998: The violence continued.

1999: Abdel Aziz Bouteflika was elected president.

2000: Ali Benflis was appointed prime minister. The violence continued, averaging 200 deaths a month.

2002: Tamazight (a Berber dialect) was included in the constitution as a national language.

2003: A major earthquake, measuring 6.7 on the Richter scale, in the north of the country killed at least 2,200 people and injured thousands more.

2004: Adbel Aziz Bouteflika was re-elected as president with an overwhelming majority.

2005: The government signed an agreement with Berber leaders, promising economic aid and recognition of Berber language and culture. A government-commissioned enquiry reported that the security forces had been responsible for the disappearance of more than 6,000 people during the 1990s.

Algiers Arabic *al-Jaza'ir*; French *Alger*, capital of Algeria, situated on the narrow coastal plain between the Atlas Mountains and the Mediterranean; population (1995) 2,168,000. It distributes grain, iron, phosphates, wines, and oil from central Algeria. The main industries are oil refining, petrochemicals, and metal working. The city is a popular winter resort.

Algiers, Battle of bitter conflict in Algiers 1954–62 between the Algerian nationalist population and the French colonial army and French settlers. The conflict ended with Algerian independence in 1962.

ALGOL contraction of algorithmic language, in computing, an early high-level programming language, developed in the 1950s and 1960s for scientific applications. A general-purpose language, ALGOL is best suited to mathematical work and has an algebraic style. Although no longer in common use, it has greatly influenced more recent languages, such as Ada and Pascal.

Algol *or* **Beta Persei** *eclipsing binary, a pair of orbiting stars in the constellation Perseus, one of which eclipses the other every 69 hours, causing its brightness to drop by two-thirds.

Algonquin the Algonquian-speaking hunting and fishing people who once lived around the Ottawa River in eastern Canada. Many now live on reservations in northeastern USA, eastern Ontario, and western Québec; others have chosen to live among the general populations of Canada and the USA.

algorithm procedure or series of steps that can be used to solve a problem. In computer science, it describes the logical sequence of operations to be performed by a program. A *flow chart is a visual representation of an algorithm.

Ali (c. 598–661) Fourth *caliph of *Islam. He was born in Mecca, the son of Abu Talib, and was the cousin and close friend and supporter of the prophet Muhammad, who gave him his daughter Fatima in marriage. He was one of the first to believe in Islam. On Muhammad's death in 632, Ali had a claim to succeed him, but this was not conceded until 656, following the murder of the third caliph, Uthman. After a brief and stormy reign, Ali was assassinated. Controversy has raged around Ali's name between the Sunni Muslims and the Shiites, the former denying his right to the caliphate and the latter supporting it.

Ali, Muhammad (1942–) adopted name of Cassius Marcellus Clay, Jr, US boxer. Olympic light-heavyweight champion in 1960, he went on to become world professional heavyweight champion in 1964, and was the only man to regain the title twice. He was known for his fast footwork and extrovert nature. In December 1999 he was voted the British Broadcasting Corporation (BBC) Sports Personality of the Century and the US magazine *Sports Illustrated* and the US newspaper *USA Today* both named him Sportsman of the Century.

alienation sense of isolation, powerlessness, and therefore frustration; a feeling of loss of control over one's life; a sense of estrangement from society or even from oneself. As a concept it was developed by German philosophers G W F Hegel and Karl Marx; the latter used it as a description and criticism of the condition that developed among workers in capitalist society.

alimentary canal tube through which food passes in animals – it extends from the mouth to the anus and forms a large part of the digestive system. In human adults, it is about 9 m/30 ft long, consisting of the mouth cavity, pharynx, oesophagus, stomach, and the small and large intestines. It is also known as the gut. It is a complex organ, specifically adapted for *digestion and the absorption of food. Enzymes from the wall of the canal and from other associated organs, such as the pancreas, speed up the digestive process.

alimony in the USA, money allowance given by court order to a former spouse after separation or *divorce. The right has been extended to relationships outside marriage and is colloquially termed palimony. Alimony is separate and distinct from court orders for child support.

aliphatic compound any organic chemical compound in which the carbon atoms are joined in straight chains, as in hexane (C_6H_{14}), or in branched chains, as in 2-methylpentane ($CH_3CH(CH_3)CH_2CH_2CH_3$).

alkali in chemistry, a *base that is soluble in water. Alkalis neutralize acids, and solutions of alkalis are soapy to the touch. The strength of an alkali is measured by its hydrogen-ion concentration, indicated by the *pH value. They may be divided into strong and weak alkalis: a strong alkali (for example, potassium hydroxide, KOH) ionizes completely when dissolved in water, whereas a weak alkali (for example, ammonium hydroxide, NH_4OH) exists in a partially ionized state in solution. All alkalis have a pH above 7.0. The hydroxides of metals are alkalis. Those of sodium and potassium are corrosive; both were historically derived from the ashes of plants.

alkali metal any of a group of six metallic elements with similar chemical properties: *lithium, *sodium, *potassium, *rubidium, *caesium, and *francium. They form a linked group (Group 1) in the *periodic table of the elements. They each have a valency of one and have very low densities (lithium, sodium, and potassium float on water); in general they are reactive, soft, low-melting-point metals. Because of their reactivity they are only found as compounds in nature.

alkaline-earth metal any of a group of six metallic elements with similar bonding properties: beryllium, magnesium, calcium, strontium, barium, and radium. They form a linked group in the *periodic table of the elements. They are strongly basic, bivalent (have a valency of two), and occur in nature only in compounds.

alkaloid any of a number of physiologically active and frequently poisonous substances contained in some plants. They are usually organic bases and contain nitrogen. They form salts with acids and, when soluble, give alkaline solutions.

alkane member of a group of *hydrocarbons having the general formula C_nH_{2n+2}, commonly known as **paraffins**. As they contain only single *covalent bonds, alkanes are said to be saturated. Lighter alkanes, such as methane, ethane, propane, and butane, are colourless gases; heavier ones are liquids or solids. In nature they are found in natural gas and petroleum.

alkene member of the group of *hydrocarbons having the general formula C_nH_{2n}, formerly known as **olefins**. Alkenes are unsaturated compounds, characterized by one or more double bonds between adjacent carbon atoms. Lighter alkenes, such as *ethene and propene, are gases, obtained from the cracking of oil fractions. Alkenes react by addition, and many useful compounds, such as *polythene and bromoethane, are made from them.

alkyne member of the group of *hydrocarbons with the general formula C_nH_{2n-2}, formerly known as the **acetylenes**. They are unsaturated compounds, characterized by one or more triple bonds between adjacent carbon atoms. Lighter alkynes, such as ethyne, are gases; heavier ones are liquids or solids.

Allah (Arabic *al-Ilah* 'the God') Islamic name for God. Muslims believe that Allah is *tauhid*, that is 'absolute' or 'One', and the supreme creator and power behind the universe. Muhammad's concept of Allah lays stress on his uniqueness and his role as the all-powerful ruler and judge of humans. Equally, however, he is merciful and compassionate. He is omniscient and all things depend on him for their being. Uncreated and eternal, he is the creator of all things, not least of the *Koran, of which Muhammad was merely the voice and messenger. Humans are entrusted with the care of his creation on earth. Evidence for the worship of Allah in pre-Islamic times is found as early as the 3rd century BC, where he ranks alongside other tribal and local deities as a special god. It was probably contact with Christians and Jews that led the prophet Muhammad to formulate his belief in Allah as the one, supreme God.

Allahabad ('city of god') historic city in Uttar Pradesh state, India, 580 km/360 mi southeast of Delhi, on the Yamuna River where it meets the Ganges and the mythical underground Seraswati River; population (2001 est) 1,049,600. A growing commercial centre,

its main industries are textiles and food processing. A Hindu religious event, the festival of the jar of nectar of immortality (Kumbh Mela), is held here every 12 years with the participants washing away sin and sickness by bathing in the rivers; in 1989 15 million pilgrims attended. It is also the site of the Asoka Pillar, dating from 232 BC in the Buddhist period of Indian history, on which are carved edicts of the Emperor *Asoka.

Allegheny Mountains *or* **the Alleghenies** mountain range over 800 km/500 mi long extending from Pennsylvania to Virginia, rising to more than 1,500 m/4,900 ft and averaging 750 m/2,500 ft. Part of the *Appalachian Mountains system, the Alleghenies are rich in hardwood timber and bituminous coal, and also contain iron ore, natural gas, clay, and petroleum. The mountains initially hindered western migration, with the first settlement to the west being Marietta in 1788.

allegory in literature, the description or illustration of one thing in terms of another, or the personification of abstract ideas. The term is also used for a work of poetry or prose in the form of an extended metaphor or parable that makes use of symbolic fictional characters.

allegro (Italian 'merry, lively') in music, a tempo marking indicating lively or quick. It can be used as the title for a movement or composition.

allele one of two or more alternative forms of a *gene at a given position (locus) on a *chromosome, caused by a difference in the sequence of *DNA. This is best explained with examples. A gene which controls eye colour in humans may have two alternative forms – an allele that can produce blue eyes, and an allele that produces brown eyes. In a plant that occurs in tall and short forms, there may be an allele that tends to produce tall plants and an alternative allele that produces short plants.

Allen, Woody (1935–) adopted name of Allen Stewart Konigsberg, US film writer, director, and actor. One of the true auteurs of contemporary US cinema, Allen has written, directed, and frequently acted in a number of comic and dramatic works which are informed by his personal aesthetic, religious, and sexual preoccupations. One of his most successful and critically acclaimed works is *Annie Hall* (1977), which won Academy Awards for Best Picture, Best Screenplay, Best Director, and Best Actress.

Allenby, Edmund Henry Hynman (1861–1936) 1st Viscount Allenby, British field marshal. In World War I he served in France before taking command 1917–19 of the British forces in the Middle East. After preparations in Egypt, he captured Gaza, Beersheba and, in 1917, Jerusalem. His defeat of the Turkish forces at Megiddo in Palestine in September 1918 was followed almost at once by the capitulation of Turkey. He was high commissioner in Egypt 1919–35. KCB 1915, Viscount 1919.

Allende (Gossens), Salvador (1908–1973) Chilean left-wing politician, president 1970–73. Elected president as the candidate of the Popular Front alliance, Allende never succeeded in keeping the electoral alliance together in government. His failure to solve the country's economic problems or to deal with political subversion allowed the army, backed by the Central Intelligence Agency (CIA), to stage the 1973 coup that brought about the death of Allende and many of his supporters.

allergy special sensitivity of the body that makes it react with an exaggerated response of the natural immune defence mechanism to the introduction of an otherwise harmless foreign substance (**allergen**).

Allies, the in World War I, the 27 Allied and Associated powers aligned against the Central Powers (Germany, Austro-Hungary, Turkey, and Bulgaria) and represented at the Treaty of Versailles (1919); they included France, Italy, Russia, the UK, Australia and other Commonwealth nations, and, in the latter part of the war, the USA. In World War II they were some 49 countries allied against the *Axis Powers (Germany, Italy, and Japan), including France, the UK, Australia and other Commonwealth nations, the USA, and the former Soviet Union.

alligator (Spanish *el lagarto* 'the lizard') reptile of the genus *Alligator*, related to the crocodile. There are only two living species: *A. mississipiensis*, the Mississippi alligator of the southern states of the USA, and *A. sinensis* from the swamps of the lower Chang Jiang in China. The former grows to about 4 m/12 ft, but the latter only to 1.5 m/5 ft. Alligators lay their eggs in waterside nests of mud and vegetation and are good mothers. They swim well with lashing movements of the tail and feed on fish and mammals but seldom attack people.

alliteration in poetry and prose, the use, within a line or phrase, of words beginning with the same sound, as in Two tired toads trotting to Tewkesbury. It was a common device in Old English literature, and its use survives in many traditional phrases, such as dead as a doornail and pretty as a picture. Alliteration is used in modern poetry more sparingly than in Old English, as an emphasis for certain imagery or words. While alliteration focuses on repetition of consonants, *assonance is repetition upon vowel sounds.

allium any of a group of plants of the lily family, usually strong-smelling with a sharp taste; they form bulbs in which sugar is stored. Cultivated species include onion, garlic, chive, and leek. Some species are grown in gardens for their decorative globular heads of white, pink, or purple flowers. (Genus *Allium*, family Liliaceae.)

allopathy (Greek *allos* 'other', *pathos* 'suffering') in *homeopathy, a term used for orthodox medicine, using therapies designed to counteract the manifestations of the disease. In strict usage, allopathy is the opposite of homeopathy.

allotropy property whereby an element can exist in two or more forms (allotropes), each possessing different physical properties but the same state of matter (gas, liquid, or solid). The allotropes of carbon are diamond, fullerene, and graphite. Sulphur has several allotropes (flowers of sulphur, plastic, rhombic, and monoclinic). These solids have different crystal structures, as do the white and grey forms of tin and the black, red, and white forms of phosphorus.

alloy metal blended with some other metallic or non-metallic substance to give it special qualities, such as resistance to corrosion, greater hardness, or tensile strength. The atoms in a *metal are held together by the *metallic bond. In a pure metal the atoms are all the same size and can slip over each other if a force is applied. In an alloy, the presence of different sized atoms prevents such dislocations from weakening the metal. Useful alloys include bronze, brass, cupronickel, duralumin, German silver, gunmetal, pewter, solder, steel, and stainless steel.

All Saints' Day *or* **All-Hallows** *or* **Hallowmas** festival on 1 November for all Christian saints and martyrs who have no special day of their own. It was instituted in 835.

All Souls' Day festival in the Roman Catholic Church, held on 2 November (following All Saints' Day) in the conviction that through prayer and self-denial the faithful can hasten the deliverance of souls expiating their sins in purgatory.

allspice spice prepared from the dried berries of the evergreen pimento tree, also known as the West Indian pepper tree, (*Pimenta dioica*) of the myrtle family, cultivated chiefly in Jamaica. It has an aroma similar to that of a mixture of cinnamon, cloves, and nutmeg.

alluvial deposit layer of broken rocky matter, or sediment, formed from material that has been carried in suspension by a river or stream and dropped as the velocity of the current decreases. River plains and deltas are made entirely of alluvial deposits, but smaller pockets can be found in the beds of upland torrents.

Al Manamah capital and free trade port of Bahrain, on Bahrain Island; population (1991 est) 120,900. With a deepwater harbour, major refrigeration facilities and docks for the repair of large oceangoing ships, it is a leading port of the Persian Gulf, handling especially oil and entrepôt trade.

Alma-Tadema, Lawrence (1836–1912) Dutch artist who worked in England from 1870. He painted romantic, idealized scenes from ancient Greek, Roman, and Egyptian life, which combined Victorian sentiment with detailed historical accuracy.

Almaty formerly **Vernyi** (1854–1921), **Alma-Ata** (1921–94), former capital (to 1998) of Kazakhstan, in the southeast of the country on the Almaatinka River, and capital of Almaty oblast; population (1999 est) 1,129,400. Its industries include engineering, printing, tobacco processing, textile manufacturing, and the production of leather goods. The city is at the centre of a large fruit-growing region, and food processing (meat packing, flour milling, wine bottling) is also a major source of employment in the city. Since Kazakhstan's independence in 1991, Almaty has experienced a boom as a commercial and financial centre.

Almohad Berber dynasty 1130–1269 founded by the Berber prophet Muhammad ibn Tumart (c. 1080–1130). The Almohads ruled much of Morocco and Spain, which they took by defeating the *Almoravids; they later took the area that today forms Algeria and Tunis. Their policy of religious 'purity' involved the forced conversion and massacre of the Jewish population of Spain. The Almohads were themselves defeated by the Christian kings of Spain in 1212, and in Morocco in 1269.

almond tree related to the peach and apricot. Dessert almonds, which can be eaten whole, are the kernels of the fruit of the sweet variety *Prunus amygdalus dulcis*, which is also used to produce a low-cholesterol cooking oil. Oil of bitter almonds, from the variety *P. amygdalus amara*, is used in flavouring. Bitter almonds contain hydrocyanic acid, which is poisonous and must be extracted before the oil can be processed. Almond oil is also used for cosmetics, perfumes, and fine lubricants. (*Prunus amygdalus*, family Rosaceae.)

Almoravid Berber dynasty 1056–1147 founded by the prophet Abdullah ibn Tashfin, ruling much of Morocco and Spain in the 11th–12th centuries. The Almoravids came from the Sahara and in the 11th century began laying the foundations of an empire covering the whole of Morocco and parts of Algeria; their capital was the newly founded Marrakesh. In 1086 they defeated Alfonso VI of Castile to gain much of Spain. They were later overthrown by the *Almohads.

aloe one of a group of plants native to southern Africa, with long, fleshy, spiny-edged leaves. The drug usually referred to as 'bitter aloes' is a powerful purgative (agent that causes the body to expel impurities) prepared from the juice of the leaves of several of the species. (Genus *Aloe*, family Liliaceae.)

alpaca domesticated South American hoofed mammal Lama pacos of the camel family, found in Chile, Peru, and Bolivia, and herded at high elevations in the Andes. It is bred mainly for its long, fine, silky wool, and stands about 1 m/3 ft tall at the shoulder with neck and head another 60 cm/2 ft.

alphabet set of conventional symbols used for writing, based on a correlation between individual symbols and spoken sounds, so called from alpha (α) and beta (β), the names of the first two letters of the classical Greek alphabet. The earliest known alphabet is from Palestine, about 1700 BC. Alphabetic writing now takes many forms – for example, the Hebrew aleph-beth and the Arabic script, both written from right to left; the Devanagari script of the Hindus, in which the symbols 'hang' from a line common to all the symbols; and the Greek alphabet, with the first clearly delineated vowel symbols.

Alpha Centauri brightest star in the constellation Centaurus; see *Rigil Kent.

alpha particle *or* **alpha ray** positively charged (2+), high-energy particle emitted from the nucleus of a radioactive atom. It is one of the products of the spontaneous disintegration of radioactive elements (see *radioactivity) such as radium and thorium, and is identical to the nucleus of a helium atom (^{4}He) – that is, it consists of two protons and two neutrons. The process of emission, **alpha decay**, transforms one element into another, decreasing the atomic number by two and the atomic mass by four. Plutonium-239 (^{239}Pu) is an example of a material that emits alpha particles.

Alps the highest and most extensive mountain range in Europe. The Alps run in an arc from the Mediterranean coast of France in the west through northern Italy, Switzerland, southern Germany, and Austria to the outskirts of Vienna and the River Danube in the east – a total distance of some 960 km/597 mi. Alpine ranges also extend down the Adriatic coast into Slovenia and Croatia. The Alps form a natural frontier between several countries in south-central Europe. The highest peak, at 4,808 m/15,774 ft, is *Mont Blanc, on the Franco-Italian border. The Alps are the source of many of Europe's major rivers – or their tributaries – including the Rhine, the Rhône, the Po, and the Danube. As well as agriculture, an important economic activity in the Alps is tourism: winter visitors come for the skiing offered at numerous resorts; summer tourism centres on sightseeing and walking in this area of outstanding natural beauty. The Alps are also a widely exploited source of hydroelectric power. Much Alpine woodland has been severely damaged by acid rain.

Alps, Australian see *Australian Alps.

Alps, Southern see *Southern Alps.

Alsace region and former province of France; area 8,280 sq km/3,197 sq mi; population (1999 est) 1,734,100. It consists of the départements of Bas-Rhin and Haut-Rhin; its administrative centre is *Strasbourg, which is the seat of the European Parliament and the Council of Europe. Alsace has much rich agricultural land, particularly between the River Rhine and the Vosges mountains. Vineyards dot the low-lying areas that rise up from the Rhine, and Alsace is noted for its white wines. The region also produces about half the beer consumed in France.

Alsace-Lorraine area of northeast France, lying west of the River Rhine. It forms the French regions of *Alsace and *Lorraine, and corresponds to the three French départements of Bas-Rhin, Haut-Rhin, and Moselle. As a political entity, Alsace-Lorraine was created by the Treaty of Frankfurt, which ended the Franco-Prussian War in 1871. The former iron and steel industries are being replaced by electronics, chemicals, and precision engineering. Although the official language is French and most place names have been gallicized, much of Alsace's population and part of Lorraine's are still German-speaking. The German dialect spoken there is not considered on a par with French, and there is autonomist sentiment.

Alsatian another name for the *German shepherd dog.

Altai *or* **Altay** formerly **Oirot Autonomous Oblast** (1922–48), republic of the Russian Federation, within the Altai krai (territory) of southern Siberia; area 92,600 sq km/35,752 sq mi; population (1996) 202,000 (24% urban). The oblast was formed in 1922, and Altai was formed after the break-up of the Soviet Union in 1992. Its capital is Gorno-Altaisk.

Altai Mountains *or* **Altay Mountains** mountain system running through Kazakhstan, the *Altai Republic of the Russian Federation, western Mongolia, and northern China. It is divided into two parts: the Russian Altai, which includes the highest peak, Mount Belukha, 4,506 m/14,783 ft, on the border with Kazakhstan; and the Mongolian or Great Altai. Alpine pastureland is found on the upper slopes below the snowline, while the lower slopes are heavily wooded with a variety of conifer and birch trees.

Altair *or* **Alpha Aquilae** brightest star in the constellation Aquila and the 13th-brightest star in the night sky. It is a white star about 16 light years away from the Sun and forms the Summer Triangle with the stars Deneb (in the constellation Cygnus) and Vega (in Lyra).

Altamira cave decorated with Palaeolithic wall paintings, the first such to be discovered, in 1879. The paintings are realistic depictions of bison, deer, and horses in polychrome (several colours). The cave is near the village of Santillana del Mar in Santander province, northern Spain; other well-known Palaeolithic cave paintings are in *Lascaux, southwestern France.

altarpiece a painting (more rarely a sculpture) placed on, behind, or above an altar in a Christian church. Altarpieces vary greatly in size, construction, and number of images (diptych, triptych, and polyptych). Some are small and portable; some (known as a **retable** or **reredos** – there is no clear distinction) are fixed.

Altdorfer, Albrecht (c. 1480–1538) German painter, architect, and printmaker. He was active in Regensburg, Bavaria. He is best known for his vast panoramic battle scenes in which his use of light creates movement and drama. On a smaller scale, he also painted some of the first true landscapes.

alternating current (AC) electric current that flows for an interval of time in one direction and then in the opposite direction; that is, a current that flows in alternately reversed directions through or around a circuit. Electric energy is usually generated as alternating current in a power station, and alternating currents may be used for both power and lighting.

alternation of generations typical life cycle of terrestrial plants and some seaweeds, in which there are two distinct forms occurring alternately: **diploid** (having two sets of chromosomes) and **haploid** (one set of chromosomes). The diploid generation produces haploid spores by *meiosis, and is called the sporophyte, while the haploid generation produces gametes (sex cells), and is called the gametophyte. The gametes fuse to form a diploid zygote which develops into a new sporophyte; thus the sporophyte and gametophyte alternate.

alternative medicine see *medicine, alternative.

alternator electricity *generator that produces an alternating current.

Althing parliament of Iceland, established in about 930, the oldest in the world. It was dissolved in 1800, revived in 1843 as an advisory body, and became a legislative body again in 1874. It has 63 members who serve a four-year term.

altimeter instrument used in aircraft that measures altitude, or height above sea level. The common type is a form of aneroid *barometer, which works by sensing the differences in air pressure at different altitudes. This must continually be recalibrated because of the change in air pressure with changing weather conditions. The *radar altimeter measures the height of the aircraft above the ground, measuring the time it takes for radio pulses emitted by the aircraft to be reflected. Radar altimeters are essential features of automatic and blind-landing systems.

altiplano sparsely populated upland plateau of the Andes of South America, stretching from southern Peru and southwest Bolivia to northwestern Argentina. It lies between the eastern and western cordilleras (ranges) of the Andes, and has an elevation of 3,000–4,000 m/10,000–13,000 ft.

Altman, Robert (1925–) US film director and producer. His films vary in tone from the comic to the elegiac, but are frequently ambitious in both content and form, utilizing a complex and sometimes fragmentary style. His antiwar comedy *M*A*S*H* (1970) was a critical and commercial success, as were *Nashville* (1975), *The Player* (1992), and *Gosford Park* (2002).

alto (Italian 'high') voice or musical instrument between tenor and soprano, of approximate range G3–D5. It is also used before the name of an instrument, for example alto saxophone, and indicates a size larger than soprano.

altruism in biology, helping another individual of the same species to reproduce more effectively, as a direct result of which the altruist may leave fewer offspring itself. Female honey bees (workers) behave altruistically by rearing sisters in order to help their mother, the queen bee, reproduce, and forgo any possibility of reproducing themselves.

alumina or **corundum** Al_2O_3, oxide of aluminium, widely distributed in clays, slates, and shales. It is

formed by the decomposition of the feldspars in granite and used as an abrasive. Typically it is a white powder, soluble in most strong acids or caustic alkalis but not in water. Impure alumina is called 'emery'. Rubies, sapphires, and topaz are corundum gemstones. It is the chief component of *bauxite.

aluminium chemical symbol Al, lightweight, silver-white, ductile and malleable, metallic element, atomic number 13, relative atomic mass 26.9815, melting point 658 °C/1,216 °F. It is the third most abundant element (and the most abundant metal) in the Earth's crust, of which it makes up about 8.1% by mass. It is non-magnetic, an excellent conductor of electricity, and oxidizes easily, the layer of oxide on its surface making it highly resistant to tarnish.

Alva, Ferdinand Alvarez de Toledo (1508–1582) Duke of Alva or Alba, Spanish politician and general. He successfully commanded the Spanish armies of the Holy Roman Emperor Charles V and his son Philip II of Spain. In 1567 he was appointed governor of the Netherlands, where he set up a reign of terror to suppress Protestantism and the revolt of the Netherlands. In 1573 he was recalled at his own request. He later led a successful expedition against Portugal 1580–81.

Alzheimer's disease common manifestation of *dementia, thought to afflict 1 in 20 people over 65. After heart disease, cancer, and strokes it is the most common cause of death in the Western world. Attacking the brain's 'grey matter', it is a disease of mental processes rather than physical function, characterized by memory loss and progressive intellectual impairment. It was first described by Alois Alzheimer in 1906. Dementia affects nearly 18 million people worldwide, 66% of whom live in developed countries; this includes some 4 million people in the USA, and over 750,000 in Britain (2001). Numbers are expected to rise with the world's ageing population, reaching an estimated 34 million worldwide by 2025.

Amalfi seaport and resort in Campania, Italy, situated at the foot of Monte Cerrato, on the Gulf of Salerno, 39 km/24 mi southeast of Naples; population (1990) 5,900. For 700 years it was an independent republic. It is an ancient archiepiscopal see (seat of an archbishop) and has a Romanesque cathedral.

amalgam any alloy of mercury with other metals. Most metals will form amalgams, except iron and platinum. Amalgam is used in dentistry for filling teeth, and usually contains copper, silver, and zinc as the main alloying ingredients. This amalgam is pliable when first mixed and then sets hard, but the mercury leaches out and may cause a type of heavy-metal poisoning.

Amazon Portuguese and Spanish **Rio Amazonas**, (Indian Amossona 'destroyer of boats') river in South America, the second longest in the world, after the *Nile; length 6,516 km/4,050 mi. The Amazon ranks as the largest river in the world in terms of the volume of water it discharges (around 95,000 cu m/3.3 million cu ft every second), its number of tributaries (over 500), and the total basin area that it drains (7 million sq km/2.7 million sq mi – almost half the landmass of South America). It has 48,280 km/30,000 mi of navigable waterways. The river empties into the Atlantic Ocean on the Equator, through an estuary 80 km/50 mi wide. Over 5 million sq km/2 million sq mi of the Amazon basin is virgin rainforest, containing 30% of all known plant and animal species. This is the wettest region on Earth, with an average annual rainfall of 2.54 m/8.3 ft.

Amazon in Greek mythology, a member of a group of female warriors living near the Black Sea, who cut off their right breasts to use the bow more easily. Their queen Penthesilea was killed by *Achilles at the siege of Troy. The term Amazon has come to mean a large, strong woman.

Amazonian Indian indigenous inhabitants of the Amazon River Basin in South America. The majority of the societies are kin-based; traditional livelihood includes hunting and gathering, fishing, and shifting cultivation. A wide range of indigenous languages are spoken. Numbering perhaps 2.5 million in the 16th century, they had been reduced to perhaps one-tenth of that number by the 1820s. Their rainforests are being destroyed for mining and ranching, and they are being killed, transported, or assimilated. In June 1998 a previously unknown tribe of about 200 hunters and gatherers was discovered in Brazil's Amazon rainforest.

amber fossilized *resin from coniferous trees of the Middle *Tertiary period. It is often washed ashore on the Baltic coast with plant and animal specimens preserved in it; many extinct species have been found preserved in this way. It ranges in colour from red to yellow, and is used to make jewellery.

ambergris fatty substance, resembling wax, found in the stomach and intestines of the sperm *whale. It is found floating in warm seas, and is used in perfumery as a fixative.

Amenhotep III (1391–1353 BC) King (pharaoh) of ancient Egypt. He built great monuments at Thebes, including the temples at Luxor. Two portrait statues at his mortuary temple were known to the Greeks as the colossi of Memnon; one was cracked, and when the temperature changed at dawn it gave out an eerie sound, then thought supernatural. His son **Amenhotep IV** changed his name to *Akhenaton.

America landmass in the Western hemisphere of the Earth, comprising the continents of *North America and *South America, with *Central America in between. This great landmass extends from the Arctic to the Antarctic, from beyond 75° N to past 55° S. The area is about 42,000,000 sq km/16,000,000 sq mi, and the estimated population is over 832 million (2000 est). Politically, it consists of 36 nations and US, British, French, and Dutch dependencies.

American Civil War 1861–65; see *Civil War, American.

American football see *football, American.

American Independence, War of alternative name of the *American Revolution, the revolt 1775–83 of the British North American colonies that resulted in the establishment of the United States of America.

American Indian or **Native American** member of one of the aboriginal peoples of the Americas; the Arctic peoples (*Inuit and Aleut) are often included, especially by the Bureau of Indian Affairs (BIA) of the US Department of the Interior, responsible for overseeing policy on US American Indian life, their reservations, education, and social welfare. The first American Indians arrived during the last ice age, approximately 20,000–30,000 years ago, passing from northeastern Siberia into Alaska over a land-bridge across the Bering Strait. The earliest reliably dated archaeological sites in North America are about 13,000–14,000 years old.

In South America they are generally dated at about 12,000–13,000 years old, but discoveries made in 1989 suggest an even earlier date, perhaps 35,000–40,000 years ago. There are about 1.9 million (1995) American Indians in the USA and Canada.

American Revolution or **War of American Independence** revolt 1775–83 of the British North American colonies, resulting in the establishment of the USA. It was caused by opposition in the colonies to British economic exploitation and by the unwillingness of the colonists to pay for a British army garrisoned in America. It was also fuelled by the colonists' antimonarchist sentiment and their desire to participate in the policies affecting them.

American Samoa see *Samoa, American.

America's Cup international yacht-racing trophy named after the US schooner *America*, owned by J L Stevens, who won a race around the Isle of Wight in 1851.

americium chemical symbol Am, radioactive metallic element of the *actinide series, atomic number 95, relative atomic mass 243.13; it was first synthesized in 1944. It occurs in nature in minute quantities in *pitchblende and other uranium ores, where it is produced from the decay of neutron-bombarded plutonium, and is the element with the highest atomic number that occurs in nature. It is synthesized in quantity only in nuclear reactors by the bombardment of plutonium with neutrons. Its longest-lived isotope is Am-243, with a half-life of 7,650 years.

amethyst variety of *quartz, SiO_2, coloured violet by the presence of small quantities of impurities such as manganese or iron; used as a semi-precious stone. Amethysts are found chiefly in the Ural Mountains, India, the USA, Uruguay, and Brazil.

Amhara an ethnic group comprising approximately 25% of the population of Ethiopia; 13 million (1987). The Amhara are traditionally farmers. They speak Amharic, a language of the Semitic branch of the Hamito-Semitic (Afro-Asiatic) family. Most are members of the Ethiopian Christian Church.

amide any organic chemical derived from a fatty acid by the replacement of the hydroxyl group (–OH) by an amino group (–NH$_2$). One of the simplest amides is ethanamide (acetamide, CH_3CONH_2), which has a strong odour.

Amin (Dada), Idi (1925–2003) Ugandan politician, president 1971–79. He led the coup that deposed Milton Obote in 1971, expelled the Asian community in 1972, and exercised a reign of terror over his people during which an estimated 300,000 people were killed. After he invaded Tanzania in 1978, the Tanzanian army combined with dissident Ugandans to counter-attack. Despite assistance from Libya, Amin's forces collapsed and he fled in 1979. He now lives in Saudi Arabia.

amine any of a class of organic chemical compounds in which one or more of the hydrogen atoms of ammonia (NH$_3$) have been replaced by other groups of atoms.

amino acid water-soluble organic *molecule, mainly composed of carbon, oxygen, hydrogen, and nitrogen, containing both a basic amino group (NH$_2$) and an acidic carboxyl (COOH) group. They are small molecules able to pass through membranes. When two or more amino acids are joined together, they are known as *peptides; *proteins are made up of peptide chains folded or twisted in characteristic shapes. (See diagram, p. 28.)

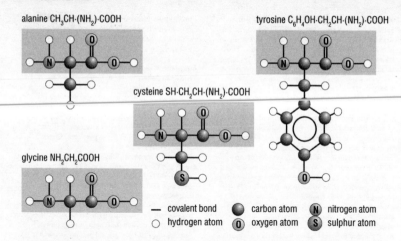

alanine CH₃CH·(NH₂)·COOH

tyrosine C₆H₄OH·CH₂CH·(NH₂)·COOH

cysteine SH·CH₂CH·(NH₂)·COOH

glycine NH₂CH₂COOH

— covalent bond   ● carbon atom   Ⓝ nitrogen atom
◯ hydrogen atom   ⑩ oxygen atom   Ⓢ sulphur atom

amino acid Amino acids are natural organic compounds that make up proteins and can thus be considered the basic molecules of life. There are 20 different common amino acids. They consist mainly of carbon, oxygen, hydrogen, and nitrogen. Each amino acid has a common core structure (consisting of two carbon atoms, two oxygen atoms, a nitrogen atom, and four hydrogen atoms) to which is attached a variable group, known as the R group. In glycine, the R group is a single hydrogen atom; in alanine, the R group consists of a carbon and three hydrogen atoms (methyl group).

Amis, Kingsley (William) (1922–1995) English novelist and poet. He was associated early on with the *Angry Young Men group of writers. His sharply ironic works include his first novel, the best-selling *Lucky Jim* (1954), a comic portrayal of life at a provincial university. His later novels include the satiric comedy *The Old Devils* (1986), for which he won the Booker Prize.

Amis, Martin Louis (1949–) English novelist and journalist. His works are characterized by their sharp black humour and include *The Rachel Papers* (1973), a memoir of adolescence told through flashbacks, *Dead Babies* (1975), which addresses decadence and sadism, *Money* (1984), *London Fields* (1989), and *Time's Arrow* (1991). Later works include *The Information* (1995), *Night Train* (1997), *Heavy Water and Other Stories* (1998), *Yellow Dog* (2003), and his memoir *Experience* (2000).

Amman capital and chief industrial and commercial centre of Jordan, 80 km/50 mi northeast of Jerusalem; population (1994 est) 969,600. It is a major communications centre, linking historic trade routes across the Middle East, and is served by major roads to the west and by Jordan's main north-south highway which links the city to the port of Aqaba. Industries include food processing, textiles, plastic and aluminium goods, cement, and electrical batteries.

ammeter instrument that measures electric current (flow of charge per unit time), usually in *amperes, through a conductor. It should not to be confused with a voltmeter, which measures potential difference between two points in a circuit. The ammeter is placed in series (see *series circuit) with the component through which current is to be measured, and is constructed with a low internal resistance in order to prevent the reduction of that current as it flows through the instrument itself. A common type is the moving-coil meter, which measures direct current (DC), but can, in the presence of a rectifier (a device which converts alternating current to direct current), measure alternating current (AC) also. Hot-wire, moving-iron, and dynamometer ammeters can be used for both DC and AC.

Ammon or **Amen** or **Amun** in Egyptian mythology, king of the gods; the equivalent of the Greek Zeus (Roman Jupiter). The Egyptian pharaohs identified themselves with his supremacy, adopting his name as in Tutankhamen. In art he is represented as a ram or goose, as a man with a ram's head, or as a man crowned with two tall feathers. He had temples at Siwa oasis, Libya, and at Napata and *Thebes, Egypt; his oracle at Siwa was patronized by the classical Greeks.

ammonia NH₃, colourless pungent-smelling gas, lighter than air and very soluble in water. It is made on an industrial scale by the *Haber (or Haber–Bosch) process, and used mainly to produce nitrogenous fertilizers, nitric acid, and some explosives.

ammonite extinct marine *cephalopod mollusc of the order Ammonoidea, related to the modern nautilus. The shell was curled in a plane spiral and made up of numerous gas-filled chambers, the outermost containing the body of the animal. Many species flourished between 200 million and 65 million years ago, ranging in size from that of a small coin to 2 m/6 ft across.

amnesia loss or impairment of memory. As a clinical condition it may be caused by disease or injury to the brain, by some drugs, or by shock; in some cases it may be a symptom of an emotional disorder.

amniocentesis sampling the amniotic fluid surrounding a fetus in the womb for diagnostic purposes. It is used to detect Down's syndrome and other genetic abnormalities. The procedure carries a 1 in 200 risk of miscarriage.

amoeba plural **amoebae**, one of the simplest living animals, consisting of a single cell and belonging to the *protozoa group. The body consists of colourless protoplasm. Its activities are controlled by the nucleus, and it feeds by flowing round and engulfing organic debris. It reproduces by *binary fission. Some species of amoeba are harmful parasites.

ampere symbol A, SI unit of electrical current. Electrical current (a flow of negative charge) is measured in a similar way to water current, in terms of an amount per unit time; one ampere (amp) represents a flow of one coulomb per second, which is about 6.28×10^{18} *electrons per second.

amphetamine *or* **speed** powerful synthetic *stimulant. Benzedrine was the earliest amphetamine marketed, used as a 'pep pill' in World War II to help soldiers to overcome fatigue, and until the 1970s amphetamines were prescribed by doctors as an appetite suppressant for weight loss; as an antidepressant, to induce euphoria; and as a stimulant, to increase alertness. Indications for its use today are very restricted because of severe side effects, including addiction. It is a sulphate or phosphate form of $C_9H_{13}N$.

amphibian (Greek 'double life') member of the vertebrate class Amphibia, which generally spend their larval (tadpole) stage in fresh water, transferring to land at maturity (after *metamorphosis) and generally returning to water to breed. Like fish and reptiles, they continue to grow throughout life, and cannot maintain a temperature greatly differing from that of their environment. The class contains about 4,500 known species, 4,000 of which are frogs and toads, 390 salamanders, and 160 caecilians (wormlike in appearance).

amphitheatre (Greek *amphi* 'around') large oval or circular building used by the Romans for gladiatorial contests, fights of wild animals, and other similar events. It is an open structure with a central arena surrounded by rising rows of seats. The *Colosseum in Rome, completed in AD 80, held 50,000 spectators.

amplifier electronic device that increases the strength of a signal, such as a radio signal. The ratio of output signal strength to input signal strength is called the gain of the amplifier. As well as achieving high gain, an amplifier should be free from distortion and able to operate over a range of frequencies. Practical amplifiers are usually complex circuits, although simple amplifiers can be built from single transistors or valves.

amplitude in physics, maximum displacement of an oscillation from the equilibrium position. For a transverse wave motion, as in electromagnetic waves, it is the height of a crest (or the depth of a trough). For a longitudinal wave, such as a sound wave, amplitude is the maximum distance a particle is pushed (due to compression) or pulled (due to rarefaction) from its resting position. A quiet sound has a lower amplitude and a loud sound has a higher amplitude. For a louder sound, more sound energy enters the ear every second. Amplitude is generally denoted by a.

amplitude modulation (AM) method by which radio waves are altered for the transmission of broadcasting signals. AM waves are constant in frequency, but the *amplitude of the transmitting wave varies in accordance with the signal being broadcast.

Amritsar formerly **Ramdaspur**, ('pool of nectar') holy city of *Sikhism and industrial centre in the Punjab,

India; population (2001 est) 1,011,300. The centre of the Sikh faith, it contains the Golden Temple, surrounded by the sacred pool Amrit Saras; and the Guru Nanak Dev University (1969; named after the first Sikh guru), which was established as the main Sikh educational centre. There are also medical, dental, arts, and technical colleges. Industries include textiles, chemicals, four milling, silk weaving, tanning, food processing, and machinery manufacture.

Amritsar Massacre *or* **Jallianwalah Bagh massacre** the killing of 379 Indians (and wounding of 1,200) in *Amritsar, at the site of a Sikh religious shrine in the Punjab in 1919. British troops under General Edward Dyer opened fire without warning on a crowd of some 10,000, assembled to protest against the arrest of two Indian National Congress leaders (see *Congress Party).

Amsterdam constitutional capital and largest city of the Netherlands; population (2003 est) 737,900. The Netherlands' second most important port after Rotterdam, Amsterdam is connected to the North Sea by the North Sea Canal, completed in 1876. A new canal leading to the River Waal, south of Utrecht, was completed in 1952 to improve the connection between Amsterdam and the River Rhine. Industries include diamond cutting and polishing, sugar refining, clothing, printing, chemicals, shipbuilding, brewing, and tourism. Amsterdam, the seat of one of the world's chief stock exchanges, is also an international centre of banking and insurance. It is one of the great intellectual and artistic cities of Europe.

Amu Darya *or* **Amudar'ya** formerly **Oxus**, river in central Asia, flowing 2,530 km/1,578 mi from the *Pamirs to the *Aral Sea.

Amundsen, Roald Engelbrecht Gravning (1872–1928) Norwegian explorer who in 1903–06 became the first person to navigate the *Northwest Passage. Beaten to the North Pole by US explorer Robert Peary in 1910, he reached the South Pole ahead of Captain Scott in 1911.

Amur river in east Asia, which with its tributary, the Ussuri, forms the boundary between Russia and China for much of its course. Formed by the Argun and Shilka rivers, the Amur flows for over 4,400 km/2,730 mi and enters the Sea of Okhotsk. At its mouth at Nikolevsk it is 16 km/10 mi wide.

amylase *enzyme that breaks down starch into a complex sugar that can be used in the body. It occurs widely in both plants and animals. In humans it is found in saliva and in the pancreatic digestive juices that drain into the *alimentary canal.

Anabaptist (Greek 'baptize again') member of any of various 16th-century radical Protestant sects. They believed in adult rather than child baptism, and sought to establish utopian communities. Anabaptist groups spread rapidly in northern Europe, particularly in Germany, and were widely persecuted.

anabolic steroid any *hormone of the *steroid group that stimulates musuclar tissue growth. Its use in medicine is limited to the treatment of some anaemias and breast cancers; it may help to break up blood clots. Side effects include aggressive behaviour, masculinization in women, and, in children, reduced height.

anaconda South American snake Eunectes murinus, a member of the python and boa family, the Boidae. One of the largest snakes, growing to 9 m/30 ft or more, it is found in and near water, where it lies in wait for the birds and animals on which it feeds. The anaconda is not venomous, but kills its prey by coiling round it and squeezing until the creature suffocates.

anaemia condition caused by a shortage of haemoglobin, the oxygen-carrying component of red blood cells. The main symptoms are fatigue, pallor, breathlessness, palpitations, and poor resistance to infection. Treatment depends on the cause.

anaerobic not requiring oxygen for the release of energy from food molecules such as glucose. An organism is described as anaerobic if it does not require *oxygen in order to survive. Instead, anaerobic organisms use anaerobic respiration to obtain energy from food. Most anaerobic organisms are micro-organisms such as bacteria, yeasts, and internal parasites that live in places where there is never much oxygen, such as in the mud at the bottom of a lake or pond, or in the alimentary canal. Anaerobic organisms release much less of the available energy from their food than do *aerobic organisms.

anaesthetic drug that produces loss of sensation or consciousness; the resulting state is **anaesthesia**, in which the patient is insensitive to stimuli. Anaesthesia may also happen as a result of nerve disorder.

analgesic agent for relieving *pain. *Opiates alter the perception or appreciation of pain and are effective in controlling 'deep' visceral (internal) pain. Non-opiates, such as *aspirin, *paracetamol, and NSAIDs (nonsteroidal anti-inflammatory drugs), relieve musculoskeletal pain and reduce inflammation in soft tissues.

analogous in biology, term describing a structure that has a similar function to a structure in another organism, but not a similar evolutionary path. For example, the wings of bees and of birds have the same purpose – to give powered flight – but have different origins. Compare *homologous.

analogue (of a quantity or device) changing continuously; by contrast, a *digital quantity or device varies in series of distinct steps. For example, an analogue clock measures time by means of a continuous movement of hands around a dial, whereas a digital clock measures time with a numerical display that changes in a series of discrete steps.

analogue computer computing device that performs calculations through the interaction of continuously varying physical quantities, such as voltages (as distinct from the more common digital computer, which works with discrete quantities). An analogue computer is said to operate in real time (corresponding to time in the real world), and can therefore be used to monitor and control other events as they happen.

analogue signal in electronics, current or voltage that conveys or stores information, and varies continuously in the same way as the information it represents (compare *digital signal). Analogue signals are prone to interference and distortion.

analytical chemistry branch of chemistry that deals with the determination of the chemical composition of substances. **Qualitative analysis** determines the identities of the substances in a given sample; **quantitative analysis** determines how much of a particular substance is present.

Anatolia Turkish **Anadolu**, Asian part of Turkey, consisting of a mountainous peninsula with the Black Sea to the north, the Aegean Sea to the west, and the Mediterranean Sea to the south.

anatomy study of the structure of the body and its component parts, especially the *human body, as distinguished from physiology, which is the study of bodily functions.

ANC abbreviation for *African National Congress, a South African political party and former nationalist organisation.

ancestor worship religious rituals and beliefs oriented towards deceased members of a family or group as a symbolic expression of values or in the belief that the souls of the dead remain involved in this world and are capable of influencing current events.

Anchorage port and largest city in Alaska, at the head of Cook Inlet; population (2000 est) 260,300. It is an important centre of administration, communication, and commerce for much of central and western Alaska. Local industries include oil and gas extraction, tourism, and fish canning.

anchovy small fish *Engraulis encrasicholus* of the *herring family. It is fished extensively, being abundant in the Mediterranean, and is also found on the Atlantic coast of Europe and in the Black Sea. It grows to 20 cm/8 in.

ancien régime the old order; the feudal, absolute monarchy in France before the French Revolution of 1789.

Andalusia Spanish **Andalucía**, (Arabic *Al Andalus* 'country of the Vandals') autonomous community of southern Spain, including the provinces of Almería, Cádiz, Córdoba, Granada, Huelva, Jaén, Málaga, and Seville; area 87,268 sq km/33,694 sq mi; population (2001 est) 7,404,000. The Guadalquivir River flows through Andalusia, which is bounded on the north by the Sierra Morena mountain range. Spain's largest and most populous region, it is fertile, and produces cereals, sugarcane, oranges and other fruits, olives, and wine (especially sherry); cattle, bulls (for the bullring), and fine horses are bred here, and copper is mined at Río Tinto. Seville, an inland port, is the administrative capital and the largest industrial centre; Málaga, Cádiz, and Algeciras are the chief ports and also important industrial centres. The Costa del Sol on the south coast has many tourist resorts, including Marbella and Torremolinos; the *Sierra Nevada mountain range in the southeast is a winter ski destination.

Andaman and Nicobar Islands two groups of islands in the Bay of Bengal, 1,200 km/745 mi off the east coast of India, forming a Union Territory of the Republic of India; capital Port Blair; area 8,293 sq km/3,202 sq mi; population (2001 est) 356,300. Many of the islands are densely forested but the economy is based mainly on agriculture, with rice, maize, coconuts, betel nuts, cassava, and chillies as leading crops; timber production and copra manufacture are also significant.

andante (Italian 'going, walking') in music, a tempo marking indicating the music to be performed at a walking pace; that is, at a moderately slow tempo.

Andersen, Hans Christian (1805–1875) Danish writer of fairy tales. Examples include 'The Ugly Duckling', 'The Snow Queen', 'The Little Mermaid', and 'The Emperor's New Clothes'. Their inventiveness, sensitivity, and strong sense of wonder have given these stories perennial and universal appeal; they have been translated into many languages. He also wrote adult novels and travel books.

Anderson, Elizabeth Garrett (1836–1917) English physician, the first English woman to qualify in medicine. In 1859 Anderson met the US doctor Elizabeth Blackwell, who inspired her to become a doctor. Unable to attend medical school because of the legal bar on women entering university, Anderson studied privately and was licensed by the Society of Apothecaries in London in 1865. She set up St Mary's Dispensary in 1866 to treat women and children; this later became the Marylebone Dispensary for Women and Children, and was renamed the Elizabeth Garrett Anderson Hospital in 1918.

Andes great mountain system or cordillera that forms the western fringe of South America, extending through some 67° of latitude and the republics of Colombia, Venezuela, Ecuador, Peru, Bolivia, Chile, and Argentina. It is the longest mountain range in the world, 8,000 km/5,000 mi, and its peaks exceed 3,600 m/ 12,000 ft in height for half that length. It has an average breadth of 241 km/150 mi.

andesite volcanic igneous rock, intermediate in silica content between rhyolite and basalt. It is characterized by a large quantity of feldspar *minerals, giving it a light colour. Andesite erupts from volcanoes at destructive plate margins (where one plate of the Earth's surface moves beneath another; see *plate tectonics), including the Andes, from which it gets its name.

Andhra Pradesh state in east central India;area 276,814 sq km/106,878 sq mi; population (2001 est) 75,727,500. The main cities and towns are Hyderabad (capital), Secunderabad, Visakhapatnam, Vijayawada, Kakinda, Guntur, and Nellore. The state is situated on coastal plains with extensive river valleys (Krishna and Godavari) reaching into the Eastern Ghats; smaller rivers are the Pennar and Cheyyar; the Deccan plateau lies inland. During the second half of the 20th century, with government support and a massive increase in hydroelectric and thermal power production, the state became highly industrialized, with industries including iron and steel, oil refining, shipbuilding, chemicals, and fertilizers. The main agricultural products are rice, millet, sugar cane, tobacco, groundnuts, sorghum, and cotton. The languages spoken are Telugu, Urdu, and Tamil.

Andorra

National name: *Principat d'Andorra/Principality of Andorra*
Area: 468 sq km/181 sq mi
Capital: Andorra la Vella
Major towns/cities: Les Escaldes, Escaldes-Engordany (a suburb of the capital)
Physical features: mountainous, with narrow valleys; the eastern Pyrenees, Valira River
Heads of state: Joan Enric Vivez i Sicilia (bishop of Urgel, Spain; from 2003) and Jacques Chirac (president of France; from 1995)
Head of government: Marc Forné Molné from 1994
Political system: emergent democracy
Political executive: parliamentary
Political parties: National Democratic Grouping (AND; formerly the Democratic Party of Andorra: PDA) moderate, centrist; National Democratic Initiative (IND), left of centre; New Democracy Party (ND), centrist; New Andorran Coalition (CNA), centrist; Liberal Union (UL), right of centre
Currency: euro

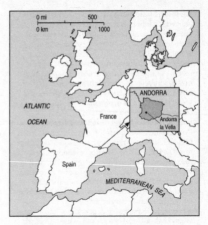

GNI per capita (PPP): (US$) 19,370 (2000)
Exports: cigars and cigarettes, furniture, electricity. Principal market: Spain 60.9% (2000)
Population: 71,000 (2003 est)
Language: Catalan (official), Spanish, French
Religion: Roman Catholic (92%)
Life expectancy: 81 (men); 87 (women) (2001 est)
Chronology
AD 803: Holy Roman Emperor Charlemagne liberated Andorra from Muslim control.
819: Louis I 'the Pious' the son of Charlemagne, granted control over the area to the Spanish bishop of Urgel.
1278: A treaty was signed making Spanish bishop and French count joint rulers of Andorra. Through marriage the king of France later inherited the count's right.
1806: After a temporary suspension during the French Revolution, from 1789 the feudal arrangement of dual allegiance to the French and Spanish rulers was re-established by the French emperor Napoleon Bonaparte.
1976: The first political organization, the Democratic Party of Andorra, was formed.
1981: The first prime minister was appointed by the General Council.
1991: Links with the European Community (EC) were formalized.
1993: A new constitution legalized political parties and introduced the first direct elections. Andorra became a member of the United Nations (UN).
1994: Andorra joined the Council of Europe.
1997: The Partit Liberal d'Andorra (PLA; Liberal Party of Andorra) won an assembly majority in a general election.
2001: In general elections, the PLA retained power.
2005: The PLA again won the general election. Albert Pintat became prime minister.

Andrea del Sarto (1486–1530) born Andrea d'Agnolo di Francesco, Italian Renaissance painter. Active in Florence, he was one of the finest portraitists and religious painters of his time. His frescoes in Florence, such as the Birth of the Virgin (1514; Sta Annunziata), rank among the greatest of the Renaissance. His style is serene and noble, characteristic of High Renaissance art.

Andreotti, Giulio (1919–) Italian Christian Democrat politician, a fervent Eurosceptic. He headed seven postwar governments: 1972–73, 1976–79 (four successive terms), and 1989–92 (two terms). In addition he was defence minister eight times, and foreign minister five times. In 1993 Andreotti was among several high-ranking politicians accused of possible involvement in Italy's corruption network; he went on trial in September 1995 charged with using his influence to protect Mafia leaders in exchange for political support. He was acquitted in October 1999.

Andrew, Andrew Albert Christian Edward (1960–) Prince of the UK, Duke of York, second son of Queen Elizabeth II. He married Sarah Ferguson in 1986; their first daughter, Princess Beatrice, was born in 1988, and their second daughter, Princess Eugenie, was born in 1990. The couple separated in 1992 and were officially divorced in May 1996. Prince Andrew was a naval helicopter pilot and served during the Falklands War. He retired from the navy in 2001.

Andrews, Julie (1935–) stage name of Julia Elizabeth Wells, English-born US actor and singer. She was the original Eliza Doolittle in the Broadway production of Lerner and Loewe's musical *My Fair Lady* (1956), and also appeared in their *Camelot* (1960). She is particularly associated with the hit film *The Sound of Music* (1965).

Andrew, St (lived 1st century AD) New Testament apostle and patron saint of Scotland and Greece. According to tradition, he went with John to Ephesus, preached in Scythia, and was martyred at Patrai in Greece on an X-shaped cross (St Andrew's cross). His feast day is 30 November.

androecium male part of a flower, comprising a number of *stamens.

androgen general name for any male sex hormone, of which *testosterone is the most important. They are all *steroids and are principally involved in the production of male *secondary sexual characteristics (such as beard growth).

Andromache in Greek mythology, the loyal wife of *Hector and mother of Astyanax. After the fall of Troy she was awarded to Neoptolemus, Achilles' son; she later married a Trojan seer called Helenus. Andromache is the heroine of Homer's Iliad and the subject of a play by *Euripides.

Andromeda major constellation of the northern hemisphere, visible in autumn. Its main feature is the *Andromeda galaxy. The star Alpha Andromedae forms one corner of the Square of Pegasus. It is named after the princess of Greek mythology.

Andromeda galaxy galaxy 2.2 million light years away from Earth in the constellation Andromeda, and the most distant object visible to the naked eye. It is the largest member of the Local Group of galaxies. Like the Milky Way, it is a spiral orbited by several companion galaxies but contains about twice as many stars as the Milky Way. It is about 200,000 light years across.

Andropov, Yuri (1914–1984) Soviet communist politician, president of the USSR 1983–84. As chief of the KGB 1967–82, he established a reputation for efficiently suppressing dissent.

anemometer device for measuring wind speed and liquid flow. The most basic form, the **cup-type anemometer**, consists of cups at the ends of arms, which rotate when the wind blows. The speed of rotation indicates the wind speed.

anemone flowering plant belonging to the buttercup family, found in northern temperate regions, mainly in woodland. It has *sepals which are coloured to attract insects. (Genus *Anemone*, family Ranunculaceae.)

aneroid barometer kind of *barometer.

aneurysm weakening in the wall of an artery, causing it to balloon outwards with the risk of rupture and serious, often fatal, blood loss. If detected in time, some accessible aneurysms can be repaired by bypass surgery, but such major surgery carries a high risk for patients in poor health.

angel (Greek angelos 'messenger') in Jewish, Christian, and Muslim belief, a supernatural being intermediate between God and humans. The Christian hierarchy has nine orders, from the top down: Seraphim, Cherubim, Thrones (who contemplate God and reflect his glory), Dominations, Virtues, Powers (who regulate the stars and the universe), Principalities, Archangels, and Angels (who minister to humanity). In traditional Catholic belief, every human being has a guardian angel.

Angel Falls *or* **Salto Angel** waterfall on the River Caroní, a tributary of the *Orinoco in the tropical rainforest of Bolívar Region, southeast Venezuela. It is the highest continuous cataract in the world with a total height of 978 m/3,210 ft. The falls plunge from the lip of the Auyán–Tepúplateau (Guinana Highlands). They were named after the aviator and prospector James Angel who flew over the falls and crash-landed nearby in 1935.

angelfish any of a number of unrelated fishes. The freshwater angelfish, genus *Pterophyllum*, of South America, is a tall, side-to-side flattened fish with a striped body, up to 26 cm/10 in long, but usually smaller in captivity. The angelfish or monkfish of the genus *Squatina* is a bottom-living shark up to 1.8 m/6 ft long with a body flattened from top to bottom. The marine angelfishes, *Pomacanthus* and others, are long narrow-bodied fish with spiny fins, often brilliantly coloured, up to 60 cm/2 ft long, living around coral reefs in the tropics.

angelica any of a group of tall, perennial herbs with divided leaves and clusters of white or greenish flowers, belonging to the carrot family. Most are found in Europe and Asia. The roots and fruits have long been used in cooking and in medicine. (Genus *Angelica*, family Umbelliferae.)

Angelico, Fra (c. 1400–1455) born Guido di Pietro, Italian painter. He was a monk, active in Florence, and painted religious scenes. His series of frescoes at the monastery of San Marco, Florence, was begun after 1436. He also produced several altarpieces in a style characterized by a delicacy of line and colour.

Angelou, Maya (1928–) born Marguerite Annie Johnson, US writer and black activist. She became noted for her powerful autobiographical works, *I Know Why the Caged Bird Sings* (1970) and its five sequels up to *A Song Flung Up to Heaven* (2002). Based on her traumatic childhood, they tell of the struggles towards physical and spiritual liberation of a black woman from growing up in the US South to emigrating to Ghana.

Angevin term used to describe the English kings Henry II and Richard I (also known, with the later English kings up to Richard III, as the Plantagenets). Angevin derives from Anjou, a region in northwestern France. The Angevin Empire comprised the territories (including England) that belonged to the Anjou dynasty.

angina *or* **angina pectoris** severe pain in the chest due to impaired blood supply to the heart muscle because a coronary artery is narrowed. Faintness and difficulty in breathing accompany the pain. Treatment is by drugs or bypass surgery.

angiosperm flowering plant in which the seeds are enclosed within an ovary, which ripens into a fruit. Angiosperms are divided into *monocotyledons (single seed leaf in the embryo) and *dicotyledons (two seed leaves in the embryo). They include the majority of flowers, herbs, grasses, and trees except conifers.

Angkor site of the ancient capital of the Khmer Empire in northwestern Cambodia, north of Tonle Sap. The remains date mainly from the 10th to 12th centuries, and comprise temples originally dedicated to the Hindu gods, shrines associated with Theravada Buddhism, and royal palaces. Many are grouped within the enclosure called Angkor Thom, but the great temple of Angkor Wat (early 12th century) lies outside.

Angle member of the Germanic tribe that occupied the Schleswig-Holstein district of North Germany known as Angeln. The Angles, or Angli, invaded Britain after the Roman withdrawal in the 5th century and settled in East Anglia, Mercia, and Northumbria. The name 'England' (Angleland) is derived from this tribe. See *Anglo-Saxon.

angle in mathematics, the amount of turn or rotation; it may be defined by a pair of rays (half-lines) that share a common endpoint (vertex) but do not lie on the same line. Angles are measured in *degrees (°) or *radians (rads or ^{c}) – a complete turn or circle being 360° or 2π rads. All angles around a point on a straight line add up to 180°. All angles around a point add up to 360°. Angles are classified generally by their degree measures: **acute angles** are less than 90°; **right angles** are exactly 90° (a quarter turn) and are created by two *perpendicular lines crossing; **obtuse angles** are greater than 90° but less than 180° (a straight line); **reflex angles** are greater than 180° but less than 360°; **supplementary angles** add up to 180°.

angle of declination angle at a particular point on the Earth's surface between the direction of the true or geographic North Pole and the magnetic north pole. The angle of declination has varied over time because of the slow drift in the position of the magnetic north pole.

angler any of an order of fishes Lophiiformes, with flattened body and broad head and jaws. Many species have small, plantlike tufts on their skin. These act as camouflage for the fish as it waits, either floating among seaweed or lying on the sea bottom, twitching the enlarged tip of the threadlike first ray of its dorsal fin to entice prey.

Anglesey Welsh Ynys Môn (island); **Sir Ynys Môn** (authority), island and unitary authority off the northwest coast of Wales. **area:** 720 sq km/278 sq mi (34 km/21 mi long and 31 km/19 mi broad) **towns:** Llangefni (administrative headquarters), Holyhead, Beaumaris, Amlwch **physical:** coastline 201 km/125 mi in length; highest point Holyhead Mountain (219 m/719 ft) **features:** separated from the mainland by the Menai Strait, which is spanned by the Britannia tubular railway bridge and Telford's suspension bridge, originally built between 1819 and 1826 but since rebuilt; rich fauna, notably bird life, and flora; many buildings

and relics of historic interest including Beaumaris Castle (1295) **population:** (1998) 65,400.

Anglican communion family of Christian churches including the *Church of England, the US Episcopal Church, and those holding the same essential doctrines, that is the Lambeth Quadrilateral 1888 Holy Scripture as the basis of all doctrine, the Nicene and Apostles' Creeds, Holy Baptism and Holy Communion, and the historic episcopate.

angling fishing with rod and line. It is widespread and ancient in origin, fish hooks having been found in prehistoric cave dwellings. Competition angling exists and world championships take place for most branches of the sport. The oldest is the World Freshwater Championship, inaugurated in 1957.

Anglo-American War war between the USA and Britain 1812–1814; see *War of 1812.

Anglo-Catholicism in the Anglican Church, the Catholic heritage of faith and liturgical practice which was stressed by the founders of the *Oxford Movement. The term was first used in 1838 to describe the movement, which began in the wake of pressure from the more Protestant wing of the Church of England. Since the Church of England voted in 1992 to ordain women as priests, some Anglo-Catholics have found it difficult to remain within the Church of England.

Anglo-Irish Agreement *or* **Hillsborough Agreement** concord reached in 1985 between the UK prime minister Margaret Thatcher and Irish prime minister Garret FitzGerald. One sign of the improved relations between the two countries was increased cooperation between police and security forces across the border between Northern Ireland and the Republic of Ireland.

Anglo-Saxon one of several groups of Germanic invaders (including Angles, Saxons, and Jutes) that conquered much of Britain between the 5th and 7th centuries. Initially they established conquest kingdoms, commonly referred to as the Heptarchy; these were united in the early 9th century under the overlordship of Wessex. The Norman invasion in 1066 brought Anglo-Saxon rule to an end.

Anglo-Saxon art English art from the late 5th century to the 11th century. Sculpted crosses and ivories, manuscript painting, and gold and enamel jewellery survive, demonstrating a love of intricate, interwoven designs. The relics of the *Sutton Hoo ship burial (7th century) and the Lindisfarne Gospels (about 690; British Museum, London) have typical Celtic ornamental patterns. In the manuscripts of southern England, in particular those produced at Winchester and Canterbury, a different style emerged in the 9th century, with delicate, lively pen-and-ink figures and heavily decorative foliage borders.

Anglo-Saxon Chronicle a history of England from the Roman invasion to the 11th century, consisting of a series of chronicles written in Old English by monks, begun in the 9th century (during the reign of King Alfred), and continuing until 1154.

Anglo-Saxon language group of dialects, also known as Old English, spoken between the 5th and 12th centuries by peoples of Saxon origin who invaded and settled in central and southern England in the 5th–7th centuries; thus the term properly does not include the language of the Angles who settled in the areas to the north. See *Old English and *English language.

Angola

Angola
National name: *República de Angola/Republic of Angola*

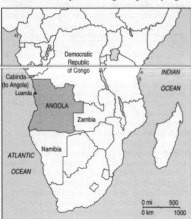

Area: 1,246,700 sq km/481,350 sq mi
Capital: Luanda (and chief port)
Major towns/cities: Lobito, Benguela, Huambo, Lubango, Malanje, Namibe, Kuito
Major ports: Huambo, Lubango, Malanje
Physical features: narrow coastal plain rises to vast interior plateau with rainforest in northwest; desert in south; Cuanza, Cuito, Cubango, and Cunene rivers
Head of state: José Eduardo dos Santos from 1979
Head of government: Fernando da Piedade Dias dos Santos from 2002
Political system: emergent democracy
Political executive: limited presidency
Political parties: People's Movement for the Liberation of Angola–Workers' Party (MPLA–PT), Marxist-Leninist; National Union for the Total Independence of Angola (UNITA), conservative; National Front for the Liberation of Angola (FNLA), conservative
Currency: kwanza
GNI per capita (PPP): (US$) 1,730 (2002 est)
Exports: petroleum and petroleum products, diamonds, gas. Principal market: USA 60% (1999)
Population: 13,625,000 (2003 est)
Language: Portuguese (official), Bantu, other native dialects
Religion: Roman Catholic 38%, Protestant 15%, animist 47%
Life expectancy: 37 (men); 42 (women) (2000–05)
Chronology
14th century: The powerful Kongo kingdom controlled much of northern Angola.
early 16th century: The Kongo ruler King Afonso I adopted Christianity and sought relations with Portuguese traders.
1575 and 1617: Portugal secured control over the ports of Luanda and Benguela and began to penetrate inland, meeting resistance from Queen Nzinga, the Ndonga ruler.
17th–18th centuries: Inland, the Lunda peoples established powerful kingdoms that stretched into

southern Congo. The Portuguese made Angola a key centre for the export of slaves; over 1 million were shipped to Brazil 1580–1680.
1836: The slave trade was officially abolished.
1885–1915: Military campaigns were waged by Portugal to conquer the interior.
1951: Angola became an overseas territory of Portugal.
1956: The People's Movement for the Liberation of Angola (MPLA), a socialist guerrilla independence movement based in the Congo, was formed.
1961: 50,000 people were massacred in rebellions on coffee plantations. Forced labour was abolished. There was an armed struggle for independence.
1962: The National Front for the Liberation of Angola (FNLA), a nationalist guerrilla movement, was formed.
1966: The National Union for the Total Independence of Angola (UNITA) was formed in southeastern Angola as a breakaway from the FNLA.
1975: Independence from Portugal was achieved. The MPLA (backed by Cuba) proclaimed the People's Republic of Angola. The FNLA and UNITA (backed by South Africa and the USA) proclaimed the People's Democratic Republic of Angola.
1976: The MPLA gained control of most of the country. South African troops withdrew, but Cuban units remained as the civil war continued.
1980: UNITA guerrillas, aided by South Africa, continued raids against the government and bases of the Namibian South West Africa People's Organization (SWAPO) in Angola.
1988: A peace treaty providing for the withdrawal of all foreign troops was signed with South Africa and Cuba.
1989: A ceasefire agreed with UNITA broke down and guerrilla activity resumed.
1991: A peace agreement ended the civil war. An amnesty was declared for all political prisoners, and there was a new multiparty constitution.
1992: A MPLA general election victory was fiercely disputed by UNITA, and plunged the country into renewed civil war.
1993: The MPLA government was recognized by the USA. United Nations (UN) sanctions were imposed against UNITA.
1994: A peace treaty was signed by the government and UNITA representatives.
1995: UN peacekeepers were drafted in.
1996: UNITA leader Jonas Savimbi rejected an offer of the vice presidency. President dos Santos appointed Fernando Franca van Dunem as his new prime minister.
1997: After some delay a national unity government was eventually sworn in but was boycotted by Savimbi.
1998: UNITA was demilitarized and transformed into a political party, but after UNITA was accused of massacres, UNITA ministers were suspended and the peace process threatened.
2000: Fighting between government forces and UNITA rebels continued in the south and east, with government troops making significant gains in the east.
2001: UNITA shot down an Angolan Armed Forces airliner, killing 22 people.
2002: UNITA leader Jonas Savimbi was killed in combat. The government signed a ceasefire agreement with UNITA, parliament approved an amnesty for guerrillas who surrendered, and UNITA re-organized itself as a political party.

2003: President dos Santos appointed Fernando da Piedade Dias dos Santos as his prime minister.

2004: The government announced that it had expelled 300,000 illegal foreign diamond miners and dealers from the country.

2005: The highly infectious Marburg virus killed more than 240 people in the north of Angola.

Angry Young Men journalistic term applied to a loose group of British writers who emerged in the 1950s after the creative hiatus that followed World War II. They revolted against the prevailing social mores, class distinction, and 'good taste'. Their dissatisfaction was expressed in works such as Kingsley Amis's *Lucky Jim* (1954), John *Osborne's *Look Back in Anger* (1956), Colin Wilson's *The Outsider* (1956), John Braine's *Room at the Top* (1957), and John Wain's *Hurry on Down* (1953).

angstrom symbol Å, unit of length equal to 10^{-10} metres or one-ten-millionth of a millimetre, used for atomic measurements and the wavelengths of electromagnetic radiation. It is named after the Swedish scientist Anders *Ångström.

Ångström, Anders Jonas (1814–1874) Swedish astrophysicist who worked in spectroscopy and solar physics. In 1861 he identified the presence of hydrogen in the Sun. His outstanding Recherches sur le spectre solaire (1868) presented an atlas of the solar spectrum with measurements of 1,000 spectral lines expressed in units of one-ten-millionth of a millimetre, the unit which later became the angstrom.

Anguilla island in the eastern Caribbean; area 160 sq km/ 62 sq mi; population (2000) 11,800. Anguilla is a popular tourist destination because of its white coral-sand beaches. However, 80% of its coral reef has been lost through tourism (pollution and souvenir sales). Its main exports include lobster and salt. The currency used is the East Caribbean dollar. It has been a separate dependency of the UK since 1980, with its capital being The Valley. Both English and Creole languages are spoken.

Anhui or **Anhwei** province of eastern China, bounded to the north by Shandong, to the east by Jiangsu, to the southeast by Zhejiang, to the south by Jiangxi, to the southwest by Hubei, and to the northwest by Henan provinces; area 139,900 sq km/54,000 sq mi; population (2000 est) 62,370,000. The province consists mainly of alluvial lowlands, both of the Huai River in the north and the *Chang Jiang in the south. It is intensively cultivated, with grain the most important crop. Its capital is Hefei, while important towns and cities include Anqing, Bengbu, Huainan, and Wuhu.

anhydride chemical compound obtained by the removal of water from another compound; usually a dehydrated acid. For example, sulphur(VI) oxide (sulphur trioxide, SO_3) is the anhydride of sulphuric acid (H_2SO_4).

aniline or **phenylamine** $C_6H_5NH_2$, (Portuguese anil 'indigo') one of the simplest aromatic chemicals (a substance related to benzene, with its carbon atoms joined in a ring). When pure, it is a colourless oily liquid; it has a characteristic odour, and turns brown on contact with air. It occurs in coal tar, and is used in the rubber industry and to make drugs and dyes. It is highly poisonous.

animal or **metazoan** (Latin *anima* 'breath', 'life') member of the *kingdom Animalia, one of the major

categories of living things, the science of which is zoology. Animals are all multicellular *heterotrophs (they obtain their energy from organic substances produced by other organisms); they have eukaryotic cells (the genetic material is contained within a distinct nucleus) which are bounded by a thin cell membrane rather than the thick cell wall of plants. Most animals are capable of moving around for at least part of their life cycle.

animism in anthropology, the belief that everything, whether animate or inanimate, possesses a soul or spirit. It is a fundamental system of belief in certain religions, particularly those of some pre-industrial societies. Linked with this is the worship of natural objects such as stones and trees, thought to harbour spirits (naturism); fetishism; and ancestor worship.

anion *ion carrying a negative charge. An anion is formed from an *atom by the gain of electrons, a process known as **ionic bonding**. *Non-metallic elements form anions. During *electrolysis, anions in the electrolyte move towards the anode (positive electrode).

anise Mediterranean plant belonging to the carrot family, with small creamy-white flowers in clusters; its fragrant seeds, similar to liquorice in taste, are used to flavour foods. Aniseed oil is used in cough medicines. (*Pimpinella anisum*, family Umbelliferae.)

Ankara formerly **Angora**, capital of Turkey; population (1990) 2,559,500. Industries include cement, textiles, and leather products. It replaced Istanbul (then in Allied occupation) as capital in 1923.

Annapurna mountain 8,075 m/26,502 ft in the Himalayas, Nepal. The north face was first climbed by a French expedition (Maurice Herzog) in 1950 and the south by a British team in 1970.

Anne (1665–1714) Queen of Great Britain and Ireland 1702–14. She was the second daughter of James, Duke of York, who became James II, and his first wife, Anne Hyde, daughter of Edward Hyde, Earl of Clarendon. She succeeded William III in 1702. Events of her reign include the War of the *Spanish Succession, Marlborough's victories at Blenheim, Ramillies, Oudenarde, and Malplaquet, and the union of the English and Scottish parliaments in the 1707 Act of *Union.

Anne, Anne Elizabeth Alice Louise (1950–) Princess of the UK, second child of Queen Elizabeth II, declared Princess Royal in 1987. She is actively involved in global charity work, especially for children. An excellent horse rider, she won silver medals in both individual and team events in the 1975 European Championships, and competed in the 1976 Olympics.

annealing controlled cooling of a material to increase ductility and strength. The process involves first heating a material (usually glass or metal) for a given time at a given temperature, followed by slow cooling. It is a common form of *heat treatment.

annelid any segmented worm of the phylum Annelida. Annelids include earthworms, leeches, and marine worms such as lugworms.

Anne of Austria (1601–1666) Queen of France from 1615 and regent 1643–61. Daughter of Philip III of Spain, she married Louis XIII of France (whose chief minister, Cardinal Richelieu, worked against her). On her husband's death she became regent for their son, Louis XIV, until his majority.

Anne of Cleves (1515–1557) Fourth wife of *Henry VIII of England, whom she married in 1540. She was the daughter of the Duke of Cleves, and was recommended to Henry as a wife by Thomas *Cromwell, who wanted an alliance with German Protestantism against the Holy Roman Empire. Henry did not like her looks, had the marriage declared void after six months, pensioned her, and had Cromwell beheaded.

anno Domini (Latin 'in the year of our Lord') in the Christian chronological system, refers to dates since the birth of Jesus, denoted by the letters AD. There is no year 0, so AD 1 follows immediately after the year 1 BC (before Christ). The system became the standard reckoning in the Western world after being adopted by English historian Bede in the 8th century. The abbreviations CE (Common Era) and BCE (before Common Era) are often used instead by scholars and writers as objective, rather than religious, terms.

anno hegirae (Latin 'year of the flight') first year of the Muslim calendar, the year of the flight of Muhammad from Mecca to Medina in 622. In dates it is often abbreviated to AH.

annual plant plant that completes its life cycle within one year, during which time it germinates, grows to maturity, bears flowers, produces seed, and then dies.

annual rings *or* **growth rings** concentric rings visible on the wood of a cut tree trunk or other woody stem. Each ring represents a period of growth when new *xylem is laid down to replace tissue being converted into wood (secondary xylem). The wood formed from xylem produced in the spring and early summer has larger and more numerous vessels than the wood formed from xylem produced in autumn when growth is slowing down. The result is a clear boundary between the pale spring wood and the denser, darker autumn wood. Annual rings may be used to estimate the age of the plant (see *dendrochronology), although occasionally more than one growth ring is produced in a given year.

anode positive electrode of an electrolytic cell, towards which negative particles (anions), usually in solution, are attracted. See *electrolysis.

anodizing process that increases the resistance to *corrosion of a metal, such as aluminium, by building up a protective oxide layer on the surface. The natural corrosion resistance of aluminium is provided by a thin film of aluminium oxide; anodizing increases the thickness of this film and thus the corrosion protection.

anorexia lack of desire to eat, or refusal to eat, especially the pathological condition of **anorexia nervosa**, most often found in adolescent girls and young women. Compulsive eating, or *bulimia, distortions of body image, and depression often accompany anorexia.

Anouilh, Jean (1910–1987) French dramatist. His plays, which are often studies in the contrast between purity and cynical worldliness, include Antigone (1944), *L'Invitation au château/Ring Round the Moon* (1947), *Colombe* (1950), and *Becket* (1959), about St Thomas à Becket and Henry II.

Anselm, St (c. 1033–1109) Italian priest and philosopher. He was born in Piedmont and educated at the abbey of Bec in Normandy, which, as abbot from 1078, he made a centre of scholarship in Europe. He was appointed archbishop of Canterbury by William II of England in 1093, but was later forced into exile.

He holds an important place in the development of *scholasticism. Feast day 21 April.

ant insect belonging to the family Formicidae, and to the same order (Hymenoptera) as bees and wasps. Ants are characterized by a conspicuous waist and elbowed antennae. About 10,000 different species are known; all are social in habit, and all construct nests of various kinds. Ants are found in all parts of the world, except the polar regions. It is estimated that there are about 10 million billion ants.

antacid any substance that neutralizes stomach acid, such as sodium hydrogencarbonate (sodium bicarbonate) or magnesium hydroxide ('milk of magnesia'). Antacids are weak *bases, swallowed as solids or emulsions. They may be taken between meals to relieve symptoms of hyperacidity, such as pain, bloating, nausea, and 'heartburn'. Excessive or prolonged need for antacids should be investigated medically.

Antall, József (1932–1993) Hungarian politician, prime minister 1990–93. He led the centre-right Hungarian Democratic Forum (MDF) to electoral victory in April 1990, becoming Hungary's first post-communist prime minister. He promoted gradual, and successful, privatization and encouraged inward foreign investment.

Antananarivo formerly Tananarive, capital and administrative centre of Madagascar, on the interior plateau at a height of 1,250 m/4,100 ft, with a rail link to Toamasina (Tamatave), the chief port of the island; population (1993 est) 1,103,300. Industries include food processing, leather goods, clothing, wood pulp and paper manufacturing, and brewing.

Antarctica region lying south of the Antarctic Circle that includes the Antarctic continent surrounding the South Pole. Occupying 10% of the world's surface, in summer it is almost one-and-a-half times the size of the USA. Antarctica contains 90% of the world's ice, representing nearly three-quarters of its fresh water. It is thought that if all the ice suddenly melted, the world sea level would rise by 60 m/197 ft. **area:** 13,000,000 sq km/5,019,300 sq mi; in winter Antarctica virtually doubles in area because of the increase in surrounding sea ice **features:** Mount Erebus on Ross Island is the world's most southern active volcano, and reaches a height of 3,794 m/12,448 ft above sea level; the Ross Ice Shelf is formed by several glaciers coalescing in the Ross Sea **physical:** Antarctica can be divided into two regions, separated by the Transantarctic Mountains, which extend for 3,500 km/2,175 mi and whose peaks, many of them exceeding 3,000 m/9,850 ft in height, protrude through the ice. The larger region, known as Greater or East Antarctica, is comprised of ancient rocks lying mostly at sea level, which are approximately 3,800 million years old. In contrast, Lesser or West Antarctica is 150–200 million years old and has mountain ranges buried under the ice. These include the Antarctic Peninsular and the Ellsworth Mountains, in which the highest peak in Antarctica, the Vinson Massif, is located; height 5,140 m/16,863 ft. The few peaks that are visible above the ice are known as nunataks. Two vast seas, the Ross Sea and the Weddell Sea, cut into the continent. Between them lies the mountainous Antarctic Peninsula, which was originally connected to South America before continental drift. **population:** no permanent residents and no indigenous inhabitants; settlement is limited to scientific research stations with maximum population of 10,000 (including 3,000 tourists) during the summer months. Sectors of Antarctica are claimed by Argentina, Australia, Chile, France, the UK, Norway, and New Zealand.

Antarctic Circle imaginary line that encircles the South Pole at latitude 66° 32′ S. The line encompasses the continent of Antarctica and the Antarctic Ocean.

Antarctic Ocean popular name for the reaches of the Atlantic, Indian, and Pacific oceans extending south of the Antarctic Circle (66° 32′ S). The term is not used by the International Hydrographic Bureau.

Antarctic Territory, Australian islands and territories south of 60° south, between 160° and 45° east longitude, excluding Adélie Land; area 6,044,000 sq km/ 2,333,600 sq mi of land and 75,800 sq km/29,259 sq mi of ice shelf. The population on the Antarctic continent is limited to scientific personnel.

Antarctic Territory, British British dependent territory created in 1961 and comprising all British territories south of latitude 60° south and between 20° and 80° west longitude, including the South Orkney Islands, the South Shetland Islands, the Antarctic Peninsula and all adjacent lands, and Coats Land, extending to the South Pole; total land area 1,810,000 sq km/700,000 sq mi; population (exclusively scientific personnel) c. 300.

Antarctic Treaty international agreement between 13 nations aiming to promote scientific research and keep Antarctica free from conflict, dating from 1961. In 1991 a 50-year ban on mining activity was secured. An environmental protection protocol, addressing the issues of wildlife conservation, mineral exploitation, and marine pollution, came into effect in January 1998 after it was ratified by Japan. Antarctica is now a designated 'natural reserve devoted to peace and science'.

Antares or **Alpha Scorpii** brightest star in the constellation Scorpius and the 15th-brightest star in the night sky. It is a red supergiant several hundred times larger than the Sun and perhaps 10,000 times as luminous. It lies about 420 light years away from the Sun, and varies in brightness.

anteater mammal of the family Myrmecophagidae, order Edentata, native to Mexico, Central America, and tropical South America. The anteater lives almost entirely on ants and termites. It has toothless jaws, an extensile tongue, and claws for breaking into the nests of its prey.

antelope any of numerous kinds of even-toed, hoofed mammals belonging to the cow family, Bovidae. Most antelopes are lightly built and good runners. They are grazers or browsers, and chew the cud. They range in size from the dik-diks and duikers, only 30 cm/1 ft high, to the eland, which can be 1.8 m/6 ft at the shoulder.

antenatal in medicine, before birth. Antenatal care refers to health services provided to ensure the health of pregnant women and their babies.

antenna in zoology, an appendage ('feeler') on the head. Insects, centipedes, and millipedes each have one pair of antennae but there are two pairs in crustaceans, such as shrimps. In insects, the antennae are involved with the senses of smell and touch; they are frequently complex structures with large surface areas that increase the ability to detect scents.

anthem in music, a short, usually elaborate, religious choral composition, sometimes accompanied by the organ; also a song of loyalty or devotion.

anther in a flower, the terminal part of a stamen in which the *pollen grains are produced. It is usually borne on a slender stalk or filament, and has two lobes, each containing two chambers, or pollen sacs, within which the pollen is formed.

Anthony, St (c. 251–356) also known as **Anthony of Thebes**, Egyptian founder of Christian monasticism. At the age of 20, he renounced all his possessions and began a hermetic life of study and prayer, later seeking further solitude in a cave in the desert.

anthracite (from Greek *anthrax* 'coal') hard, dense, shiny variety of *coal, containing over 90% carbon and a low percentage of ash and impurities, which causes it to burn without flame, smoke, or smell. Because of its purity, anthracite gives off relatively little sulphur dioxide when burnt.

anthrax disease of livestock, occasionally transmitted to humans, usually via infected hides and fleeces. It may also be used as a weapon in *biological warfare. It develops as black skin pustules or severe pneumonia. Treatment is possible with antibiotics, and vaccination is effective.

anthropoid (Greek *anthropos* 'man', *eidos* 'resemblance') any primate belonging to the suborder Anthropoidea, including monkeys, apes, and humans.

anthropology (Greek *anthropos* 'man', *logos* 'discourse') the study of humankind. It investigates the cultural, social, and physical diversity of the human species, both past and present. It is divided into two broad categories: biological or physical anthropology, which attempts to explain human biological variation from an evolutionary perspective; and the larger field of social or cultural anthropology, which attempts to explain the variety of human cultures. This differs from sociology in that anthropologists are concerned with cultures and societies other than their own.

anthropomorphism (Greek *anthropos* 'man', morphe 'shape') the attribution of human characteristics to animals, inanimate objects, or deities. It appears in the mythologies of many cultures and as a literary device in fables and allegories. See also *personification.

antibiotic drug that kills or inhibits the growth of bacteria and fungi.

antibody protein molecule produced in the blood by *lymphocytes in response to the presence of foreign or invading substances (*antigens); such substances include the proteins carried on the surface of infecting micro-organisms. Antibody production is only one aspect of *immunity in vertebrates.

Antichrist in Christian theology, the opponent of Christ. The appearance of the Antichrist was believed to signal the Second Coming, at which Christ would conquer his opponent. The concept may stem from the idea of conflict between Light and Darkness, present in Persian, Babylonian, and Jewish literature, which influenced early Christian thought.

anticoagulant substance that inhibits the formation of blood clots. Common anticoagulants are heparin, produced by the liver and some white blood cells, and derivatives of coumarin, such as warfarin. Anticoagulants are used medically in the prevention and treatment of thrombosis and heart attacks. Anticoagulant substances are also produced by blood-feeding animals, such as mosquitoes, leeches, and vampire bats, to keep the victim's blood flowing.

Anti-Corn Law League an extra-parliamentary pressure group formed in the UK in September 1838 by Manchester industrialists, and led by Liberals Richard *Cobden and John *Bright. It argued for free trade and campaigned successfully against duties on the import of foreign corn to Britain imposed by the *Corn Laws, which were repealed in 1846.

anticyclone area of high atmospheric pressure caused by descending air, which becomes warm and dry. Winds radiate from a calm centre, taking a clockwise direction in the northern hemisphere and an anticlockwise direction in the southern hemisphere. Anticyclones are characterized by clear weather and the absence of rain and violent winds. In summer they bring hot, sunny days and in winter they bring fine, frosty spells, although fog and low cloud are not uncommon in the UK. Blocking anticyclones, which prevent the normal air circulation of an area, can cause summer droughts and severe winters.

antidepressant any drug used to relieve symptoms in depressive illness. The main groups are the selective serotonin-reuptake inhibitors (SSRIs), the tricyclic antidepressants (TCADs), and the monoamine oxidase inhibitors (MAOIs). They all act by altering chemicals available to the central nervous system. All may produce serious side effects.

anti-emetic any substance that counteracts nausea or vomiting.

antifreeze substance added to a water-cooling system (for example, that of a car) to prevent it freezing in cold weather.

antigen any substance that causes the production of *antibodies by the body's immune system. Common antigens include the proteins carried on the surface of bacteria, viruses, and pollen grains. The proteins of incompatible blood groups or tissues also act as antigens, which has to be taken into account in medical procedures such as blood transfusions and organ transplants.

Antigone in Greek mythology, the daughter of Jocasta by her son *Oedipus. She is the subject of a tragedy by *Sophocles.

Antigua and Barbuda

Area: 440 sq km/169 sq mi (Antigua 280 sq km/108 sq mi, Barbuda 161 sq km/62 sq mi, plus Redonda 1 sq km/0.4 sq mi)

Capital: St John's (on Antigua) (and chief port)

Major towns/cities: Codrington (on Barbuda)

Physical features: low-lying tropical islands of limestone and coral with some higher volcanic outcrops; no rivers and low rainfall result in frequent droughts and deforestation. Antigua is the largest of the Leeward Islands; Redonda is an uninhabited island of volcanic rock rising to 305 m/1,000 ft

Head of state: Queen Elizabeth II from 1981, represented by Governor General James B Carlisle from 1993

Head of government: Baldwin Spencer from 2004

Political system: liberal democracy

Political executive: parliamentary

Political parties: Antigua Labour Party (ALP), moderate left of centre; United Progressive Party (UPP), centrist; Barbuda People's Movement (BPM), left of centre

Currency: East Caribbean dollar

GNI per capita (PPP): (US$) 9,960 (2002 est)

Exports: petroleum products, food, manufactures, machinery and transport equipment. Principal market: Barbados 15% (1999 est)

Population: 73,000 (2003 est)

Language: English (official), local dialects

Religion: Christian (mostly Anglican)

Life expectancy: 69 (men); 74 (women) (2000–05)

Chronology

1493: Antigua, peopled by American Indian Caribs, was visited by Christopher Columbus.

1632: Antigua was colonized by British settlers from St Kitts.

1667: The Treaty of Breda ceded Antigua to Britain.

1674: Christopher Codrington, a sugar planter from Barbados, established sugar plantations and acquired Barbuda island on lease from the British monarch in 1685; Africans were brought in as slaves.

1834: Antigua's slaves were freed.

1860: Barbuda was annexed.

1871–1956: Antigua and Barbuda were administered as part of the Leeward Islands federation.

1958–62: Antigua and Barbuda became part of the West Indies Federation.

1967: Antigua and Barbuda became an associated state within the Commonwealth.

1969: A separatist movement developed on Barbuda.

1981: Independence from Britain was achieved.

1983: Antigua and Barbuda assisted in the US invasion of Grenada.

1994: General elections were won by the ALP, with Lester Bird becoming prime minister.

1995: Hurricane Luis damaged 75% of all homes.

1999: Lester Bird and the ALP won general election.

2000: Agreement was reached to set standards for offshore banking to avoid money laundering.

2004: General elections were won by the United Progressive Party. Baldwin Spencer became prime minister.

2005: Personal income tax was implemented for the first time since 1975.

antihistamine any substance that counteracts the effects of *histamine. Antihistamines may occur naturally or they may be synthesized.

Antilles group of West Indian islands, divided north–south into the **Greater Antilles** (Cuba, Jamaica, Haiti–Dominican Republic, Puerto Rico) and **Lesser Antilles**, subdivided into the Leeward Islands (Virgin

Islands, St Kitts and Nevis, Antigua and Barbuda, Anguilla, Montserrat, and Guadeloupe) and the Windward Islands (Dominica, Martinique, St Lucia, St Vincent and the Grenadines, Barbados, and Grenada). Total population (2001 est) 29,544,000.

antimatter in physics, form of matter in which most of the attributes (such as electrical charge, magnetic moment, and spin) of *elementary particles are reversed. These *antiparticles can be created in particle accelerators, such as those at CERN in Geneva, Switzerland, and at Fermilab in the USA. In 1996 physicists at CERN created the first atoms of antimatter: nine atoms of antihydrogen survived for 40 nanoseconds (40 billionths of a second).

antimony chemical symbol Sb, silver-white, brittle, semimetallic element (a metalloid), atomic number 51, relative atomic mass 121.75. Its chemical symbol comes from Latin stibium. It occurs chiefly as the ore stibnite, and is used to make alloys harder; it is also used in photosensitive substances in colour photography, optical electronics, fireproofing, pigments, and medicine. It was employed by the ancient Egyptians in a mixture to protect the eyes from flies.

Antioch ancient capital of the Greek kingdom of Syria, founded 300 BC by Seleucus I in memory of his father Antiochus, and famed for its splendour and luxury. Under the Romans it was an early centre of Christianity. St Paul set off on his missionary journeys from here. It was captured by the Arabs in AD 637. After a five-month siege in 1098 Antioch was taken by the crusaders, who held it until 1268. The site is now occupied by the Turkish town of Antakya.

Antiochus thirteen kings of Syria of the Seleucid dynasty, including:

Antiochus I (c. 324–c. 261 BC) King of Syria from 281 BC, son of Seleucus I, one of the generals of Alexander the Great. He earned the title of Antiochus Soter, or Saviour, by his defeat of the Gauls in Galatia in 276 BC.

Antiochus (III) the Great (c. 241–187 BC) King of Syria 223–187 BC. He earned his title 'the Great' by restoring the Seleucid empire in 25 years of continuous campaigning from western Asia Minor to Afghanistan. He also finally wrested the Lebanon and Palestine from Egypt, despite defeat at Raphia in 201 BC.

Antiochus IV (c. 215–164 BC) King of Syria from 175 BC, known as Antiochus Epiphanes, the Illustrious, son of Antiochus III. He occupied Jerusalem about 170 BC, seizing much of the Temple treasure, and instituted worship of the Greek type in the Temple in an attempt to eradicate Judaism. This produced the revolt of the Hebrews under the Maccabees; Antiochus died before he could suppress it.

Antiochus VII (c. 159–129 BC) King of Syria from 138 BC. The last strong ruler of the Seleucid dynasty, he took Jerusalem in 134 BC, reducing the Maccabees to subjection. He was defeated and killed in battle against the *Parthians.

Antiochus XIII (lived 1st century BC) King of Syria 69–65 BC, the last of the Seleucid dynasty. During his reign Syria was made a Roman province by Pompey the Great.

anti-oxidant any substance that prevents deterioration of fats, oils, paints, plastics, and rubbers by oxidation. When used as food *additives, anti-oxidants prevent

fats and oils from becoming rancid when exposed to air, and thus extend their shelf life.

antiparticle in nuclear physics, a particle corresponding in mass and properties to a given *elementary particle but with the opposite electrical charge, magnetic properties, or coupling to other fundamental forces. For example, an electron carries a negative charge whereas its antiparticle, the positron, carries a positive one. When a particle and its antiparticle collide, they destroy each other, in the process called 'annihilation', their total energy being converted to lighter particles and/or photons. A substance consisting entirely of antiparticles is known as *antimatter.

antiphony music exploiting directional and canonic opposition of widely spaced choirs or groups of instruments to create perspectives in sound. It was developed in 17th-century Venice by Giovanni Gabrieli and in Germany by his pupil Heinrich Schütz and Roland de Lassus; an example is the double-choir motet Alma Redemptoris Mater (1604). The practice was revived in the 20th century by Béla Bartók, Karlheinz Stockhausen, and Luciano Berio.

antipodes (Greek 'opposite feet') places at opposite points on the globe.

anti-Semitism prejudice or discrimination against, and persecution of, the Jews as an ethnic group. Historically, this has been practised for many different reasons, by the ancient Egyptians before the Exodus, under the *Babylonian Captivity in 586 BC, and for almost 2,000 years by European Christians. Anti-Semitism was a tenet of Nazi Germany, and in the *Holocaust (Hebrew Shoah) 1933–45 about 6 million Jews died in concentration camps and in local extermination *pogroms, such as the siege of the Warsaw ghetto. In Eastern Europe, as well as in Islamic nations, anti-Semitism exists and is promoted by neo-fascist groups. It is a form of *racism.

antiseptic any substance that kills or inhibits the growth of micro-organisms. The use of antiseptics was pioneered by Joseph *Lister. He used carbolic acid (*phenol), which is a weak antiseptic; antiseptics such as TCP are derived from this.

antivivisection opposition to vivisection, that is, experiments on living animals, which is practised in the pharmaceutical and cosmetics industries on the grounds that it may result in discoveries of importance to medical science. Antivivisectionists argue that it is immoral to inflict pain on helpless creatures, and that it is unscientific because results achieved with animals may not be paralleled with human beings.

antler 'horn' of a deer, often branched, and made of bone rather than horn. Antlers, unlike true horns, are shed and regrown each year. Reindeer of both sexes grow them, but in all other types of deer, only the males have antlers.

Antonine Wall Roman line of fortification built in Scotland in 142 in the reign of Antoninus Pius (ruled 138–61). It was the Roman empire's furthest northwest frontier, between the Clyde and Forth rivers in Scotland. It was defended until about 200, after which the frontier returned to *Hadrian's Wall.

Antoninus Pius, Titus Aurelius Fulvus (AD 86–161) Roman emperor. He was adopted in 138 as Hadrian's heir, and succeeded him later that year. He enjoyed a prosperous reign, during which the *Antonine Wall was built. His daughter Faustina the Younger married his successor *Marcus Aurelius.

Antonioni, Michelangelo (1912–) Italian film director. He specialized in subtle presentations of neuroses and personal relationships among the leisured classes, with an elliptical approach to film narrative. His directorial credits include *L'avventura* (1959), *L'eclisse/Eclipse* (1962), *Il Deserto Rosso/Red Desert* (1964), and *Blow-Up* (1966).

Antrim historic county of Northern Ireland, occupying the northeastern corner of Northern Ireland, with a coastal eastern boundary; area 2,830 sq km/1,092 sq mi. The principal towns and cities are *Belfast, Larne (port), Antrim, Ballymena, Ballymoney, Lisburn, and Carrickfergus. The county borders Lough *Neagh, and is separated from Scotland by the North Channel, which is only 21 km/13 mi wide at Torr Head, the narrowest point. The Antrim Mountains (highest point 554 m/1,817 ft) run parallel to the coastline. The main rivers are the Bann and the Lagan, and there are peat bogs. Administrative responsibility for the county is held by the councils of Belfast, Larne, Antrim, Ballymena, Ballymoney, Lisburn, Moyle, Carrickfergus, and Newtownabbey.

Antwerp Flemish Antwerpen; French Anvers, port in Belgium on the River Schelde, capital of the province of Antwerp, 43 km/27 mi north of Brussels; population (2003 est) 450,000, urban agglomeration 952,600. A commercial and financial centre, it is Belgium's second city and the largest town in Flanders, the Flemish-speaking part of Belgium. One of the world's busiest ports, it is a major international centre of the diamond industry, and is the seat of the world's first stock exchange (founded 1406). Other industries include shipbuilding, oil refining, petrochemicals, dyes, photographic supplies, motor vehicles, food processing, and textiles. The home of the 17th-century Flemish artist *Rubens is preserved, and several of his works are in the Gothic cathedral.

Anubis in Egyptian mythology, the jackal-headed god of the dead, son of Osiris. Anubis presided over the funeral cult, including the weighing of the heart and embalming, and led the dead to judgement.

anus *or* **anal canal** opening at the end of the *alimentary canal which allows undigested foods and other waste materials to pass out of the body in the form of faeces. In humans the term is also used to describe the last 4 cm/1.5 in of the alimentary canal. It is normally kept closed by a ring of muscle called a sphincter. A common medical condition in humans associated with the anus is haemorrhoids (piles).

anxiety unpleasant, distressing emotion usually to be distinguished from fear. Fear is aroused by the perception of actual or threatened danger; anxiety arises when the danger is imagined or cannot be identified or clearly perceived. It is a normal response in stressful situations, but is frequently experienced in many mental disorders.

Anyang ancient Yin; later Changteh or Zhangde, city in Henan province, east China; population (1994) 1,038,000. It lies on the Beijing–Guangzhou railway. Iron- and steel-smelting are the principal industries, using local coal and iron ore from the nearby Hanxing mining area, and the Hebi coalmining complex.

Engineering and the manufacture of textiles are also important. The city was a capital of the Shang dynasty (16th–11th centuries BC). Rich archaeological remains have been uncovered since the 1920s.

Anzac acronym for Australian and New Zealand Army Corps, general term for all troops of both countries serving in World War I, particularly one who fought at *Gallipoli, and to some extent in World War II. It began as a code name based on the initials of the Corps in January 1915. The term may also be used generally of any Australian or New Zealand soldier, though 'digger' is more usual.

Aoraki formerly **Mount Cook**, highest point, 3,764 m/12,349 ft, of the *Southern Alps, a range of mountains running through New Zealand.

aorta the body's main *artery, arising from the left ventricle of the heart in birds and mammals. Carrying freshly oxygenated blood, it arches over the top of the heart and descends through the trunk, finally splitting in the lower abdomen to form the two iliac arteries. Arteries branching off the arch of the aorta carry blood to the upper body. Loss of elasticity in the aorta provides evidence of *atherosclerosis, which may lead to heart disease.

Aouita, Said (1959–) Moroccan runner. Outstanding at middle and long distances, he won the 1984 Olympic and 1987 World Championship 5,000-metre titles, and has set many world records. In Rome, Italy, in 1987, he became the first person to run the 5,000 metres in under 13 minutes.

Apache (Apache 'fighting men') member of an *American Indian people who migrated from Canada to Arizona, and parts of Colorado, New Mexico, Texas, and north Mexico, between AD 850 and 1400. The Apache language belongs to the Athabaskan linguistic group, through which they are related to the neighbouring *Navajo. Buffalo hunting and raiding were traditional. Known as fierce horse warriors from the 18th century, the Apache fought prominently against US settlement, Cochise and *Geronimo being notable 19th-century leaders. The Apache now live on reservations in Arizona, southwest Oklahoma, and New Mexico. Government agencies, tourism, and ranching form the basis of their modern economy. Their population numbers about 57,000 (2000).

apartheid (Afrikaans 'apartness') racial-segregation policy of the government of South Africa from 1948 to 1994. Under the apartheid system, non-whites – classified as Bantu (black), coloured (mixed), or Indian – did not share full rights of citizenship with the white minority. For example, black people could not vote in parliamentary elections, and until 1990 many public facilities and institutions were restricted to the use of one race only. The establishment of *Black National States was another manifestation of apartheid. In 1991, after years of internal dissent and violence and the boycott of South Africa, including the imposition of international trade sanctions by the United Nations (UN) and other organizations, President F W de Klerk repealed the key elements of apartheid legislation and by 1994 apartheid had ceased to exist. The term apartheid has also been loosely applied to similar movements and other forms of racial separation, for example social or educational, in other parts of the world.

apatosaurus large plant-eating dinosaur, formerly called brontosaurus, which flourished about 145 million years ago. Up to 21 m/69 ft long and 30 tonnes in weight, it stood on four elephantlike legs and had a long tail, long neck, and small head. It probably snipped off low-growing vegetation with peglike front teeth, and swallowed it whole to be ground by pebbles in the stomach.

ape *primate of the family Pongidae, closely related to humans, including gibbon, orang-utan, chimpanzee, and gorilla.

Apennines *or* **Appennino** chain of mountains stretching the length of the Italian peninsula. It extends around 840 mi/1,350 km south from the Cadibona pass in the northwestern *Liguria region. An older and more weathered continuation of the Maritime Alps, from Genoa the Apennines swing across the peninsula to Ancona on the east coast, and then back to the west coast and into the 'toe' of Italy. The system is continued over the Strait of Messina along the north Sicilian coast, then across the Mediterranean Sea in a series of islands to the Atlas Mountains of North Africa. The highest peak is Monte Corno in Gran Sasso d'Italia at 2,914 m/9,560 ft.

aperture in photography, an opening in the camera that allows light to pass through the lens to strike the film. Controlled by the iris diaphragm, it can be set mechanically or electronically at various diameters.

aphelion point at which an object, travelling in an elliptical orbit around the Sun, is at its farthest from the Sun. This is a solar-orbit apoapsis. The Earth is at its aphelion on 5 July.

aphid any of the family of small insects, Aphididae, in the order Hemiptera, suborder Homoptera, that live by sucking sap from plants. There are many species, often adapted to particular plants; some are agricultural pests.

aphorism (Greek *apo* 'from', *horos* 'limit') short, sharp, witty saying, usually making a general observation. 'Experience is the name everyone gives to their mistakes' is one of many aphorisms by Irish playwright Oscar Wilde. The term derives from the Aphorisms ascribed to Greek writer Hippocrates. An aphorism which has become universally accepted is a proverb.

Aphrodite in Greek mythology, the goddess of love (Roman Venus, Phoenician Astarte, Babylonian Ishtar). She is said to be either a daughter of *Zeus (in Homer) or sprung from the foam of the sea (in Hesiod). She was the unfaithful wife of Hephaestus, the god of fire, and the mother of Eros.

Apis ancient Egyptian deity, a manifestation of the creator god Ptah of Memphis, in the form of a black bull with a small white triangle on the forehead, often bearing a Sun-disc between its horns.

Apocrypha (Greek *apokryptein* 'to hide away') appendix to the Old Testament of the Bible, 14 books not included in the final Hebrew canon but recognized by Roman Catholics. There are also disputed New Testament texts known as Apocrypha.

apogee point at which a spacecraft, or other object, travelling in an elliptical orbit around the Earth is at its farthest from the Earth. This is an Earth-orbit apoapsis.

Apollinaire, Guillaume (1880–1918) pen-name of Guillaume Apollinaire de Kostrowitsky, French poet of aristocratic Polish descent. He was a leader of the avant-garde in Parisian literary and artistic circles.

His novel *Le Poète assassiné/The Poet Assassinated* (1916), followed by the experimental poems *Alcools/Alcohols* (1913) and *Calligrammes/Word Pictures* (1918), show him as a representative of the Cubist and Futurist movements.

Apollo in Greek and Roman mythology, the god of sun, music, poetry, prophecy, agriculture, and pastoral life, and leader of the Muses. He was the twin child (with *Artemis) of Zeus and Leto. Ancient statues show Apollo as the embodiment of the Greek ideal of male beauty. His chief cult centres were his supposed birthplace on the island of Delos, in the Cyclades, and Delphi.

Apollo asteroid member of a group of *asteroids whose orbits cross that of the Earth. They are named after the first of their kind, Apollo, discovered in 1932 by German astronomer Karl Reinmuth and then lost until 1973. Apollo asteroids are so small and faint that they are difficult to see except when close to the Earth (Apollo is about 2 km/1.2 mi across).

Apollonius of Rhodes (*or* Apollonius Rhodius) (lived 3rd century BC) Greek poet. He was the author of the epic Argonautica, which tells the story of Jason and the Argonauts and their quest for the Golden Fleece. A pupil of Callimachus, he was for a time head of the library at Alexandria.

Apollo project US space project to land a person on the Moon, achieved on 20 July 1969, when Neil *Armstrong was the first to set foot there. He was accompanied on the Moon's surface by Buzz Aldrin; Michael Collins remained in the orbiting command module.

apostolic succession doctrine in the Christian church that certain spiritual powers were received by the first apostles directly from Jesus, and have been handed down in the ceremony of 'laying on of hands' from generation to generation of bishops.

Appalachian Mountains mountain system in eastern North America, stretching about 2,400 km/1,500 mi from Alabama to Québec. The chain, composed of ancient eroded rocks and rounded peaks, includes the Allegheny, Catskill, and Blue Ridge mountains. Its width in some parts reaches 500 km/311 mi. Mount Mitchell, in the Blue Ridge Mountains of North Carolina, is the highest peak at 2,037 m/6,684 ft, and is the highest point in North America east of the Mississippi River. The eastern edge of the system has a fall line to the Coastal Plain where Philadelphia, Baltimore, and Washington stand. The Appalachians are heavily forested and have deposits of coal and other minerals.

appeasement historically, the conciliatory policy adopted by the British government, in particular under Neville Chamberlain, towards the Nazi and fascist dictators in Europe in the 1930s in an effort to maintain peace. It was strongly opposed by Winston Churchill, but the *Munich Agreement of 1938 was almost universally hailed as its justification. Appeasement ended when Germany occupied Bohemia–Moravia in March 1939.

appendicitis inflammation of the appendix, a small, blind extension of the bowel in the lower right abdomen. In an acute attack, the pus-filled appendix may burst, causing a potentially lethal spread of infection. Treatment is by removal (appendicectomy).

appendix short, blind-ended tube attached to the caecum. It has no known function in humans, but in herbivores it may be large, containing millions of bacteria that secrete enzymes to digest grass (as no vertebrate can secrete enzymes that will digest cellulose, the main constituent of plant cell walls).

apple fruit of several species of apple tree. There are several hundred varieties of cultivated apples, grown all over the world, which may be divided into eating, cooking, and cider apples. All are derived from the wild *crab apple (Genus Malus, family Rosaceae.)

Appleton layer or **F-layer** band containing ionized gases in the Earth's upper atmosphere, at a height of 150–1,000 km/94–625 mi, above the *E-layer (formerly the Kennelly–Heaviside layer). It acts as a dependable reflector of radio signals as it is not affected by atmospheric conditions, although its ionic composition varies with the sunspot cycle.

application in computing, program or job designed for the benefit of the end user. Examples of **general-purpose** application programs include word processors, desktop publishing programs, databases, spreadsheet packages, and graphics programs. **Application-specific** programs include payroll and stock control systems. Applications may also be **custom designed** to solve a specific problem, not catered for in other types of application. The term is used to distinguish such programs from those that control the computer (systems programs) or assist the programmer, such as a compiler.

Appomattox Court House former town in Virginia, USA, scene of the surrender on 9 April 1865 of the Confederate army under Robert E Lee to the Union army under Ulysses S Grant, which ended the American Civil War.

apricot yellow-fleshed fruit of the apricot tree, which is closely related to the almond, peach, plum, and cherry. Although native to the Far East, it has long been cultivated in Armenia, from where it was introduced into Europe and the USA. (Genus *Prunus armeniaca*, family Rosaceae.)

Apuleius, Lucius (lived 2nd century AD) Roman lawyer, philosopher, and writer. He was the author of The Golden Ass, or Metamorphoses, a prose fantasy.

Apulia Italian **Puglia**, region of Italy, in the southeast 'heel', comprising the provinces of Bari, Brindisi, Foggia, Lecce, and Taranto; area 19,362 sq km/7,476 sq mi; population (2001 est) 3,983,500. Apulia borders the Adriatic Sea in the east and the Strait of Otranto in the south; the capital is Bari, and the main industrial centre is Taranto.

Aqaba, Gulf of gulf extending northwards from the Red Sea for 160 km/100 mi to the Negev; its coastline is uninhabited except at its head, where the frontiers of Israel, Egypt, Jordan, and Saudi Arabia converge. The two ports of Elat and Aqaba, Jordan's only port, are situated here.

aquaculture the cultivation of fish and shellfish for human consumption; see *fish farming.

aqualung or **scuba** underwater breathing apparatus worn by divers, developed in the early 1940s by French diver Jacques Cousteau. Compressed-air cylinders strapped to the diver's back are regulated by a valve system and by a mouth tube to provide air to the diver at the same pressure as that of the surrounding water (which increases with the depth).

aquamarine blue variety of the mineral *beryl. A semi-precious gemstone, it is used in jewellery.

aquaplaning phenomenon in which the tyres of a road vehicle cease to make direct contact with the road surface, owing to the presence of a thin film of water. As a result, the vehicle can go out of control, particularly if the steered wheels are involved.

Aquarius zodiacal constellation a little south of the celestial equator near Pegasus. Aquarius is represented as a man pouring water from a jar. The Sun passes through Aquarius from late February to early March. In astrology, the dates for Aquarius, the 11th sign of the zodiac, are between about 20 January and 18 February (see *precession).

aquatint printmaking technique. When combined with *etching it produces areas of subtle tone as well as more precisely etched lines. Aquatint became common in the late 18th century.

aqueduct any artificial channel or conduit for water, originally applied to water supply tunnels, but later used to refer to elevated structures of stone, wood, or iron carrying navigable canals across valleys. One of the first great aqueducts was built in 691 BC, carrying water for 80 km/50 mi to Ninevah, capital of the ancient Assyrian Empire. Many Roman aqueducts are still standing, for example the one carried by the Pont du Gard at Nîmes in southern France, built about 8 BC (48 m/160 ft high).

aqueous humour watery fluid found in the chamber between the cornea and lens of the vertebrate eye. Similar to blood serum in composition, it is constantly renewed.

aquifer a body of rock through which appreciable amounts of water can flow. The rock of an aquifer must be porous and permeable (full of interconnected holes) so that it can conduct water. Aquifers are an important source of fresh water, for example for drinking and irrigation, in many arid areas of the world, and are exploited by the use of *artesian wells.

Aquila constellation on the celestial equator (see *celestial sphere). Its brightest star is first-magnitude *Altair, flanked by the stars Beta and Gamma Aquilae. It is represented by an eagle.

Aquinas, St Thomas (1225–1274) Italian philosopher and theologian, the greatest figure of the school of *scholasticism. He was a Dominican monk, known as the 'Angelic Doctor'. In 1879 his works were recognized as the basis of Catholic theology. His *Summa contra Gentiles/Against the Errors of the Infidels* (1259–64) argues that reason and faith are compatible. He assimilated the philosophy of Aristotle into Christian doctrine. He was canonized in 1323.

Aquino, (Maria) Corazon (1933–) called 'Cory'; born Maria Corazon Cojuangco, Filipino centrist politician, president 1986–92. She was instrumental in the nonviolent overthrow of President Ferdinand *Marcos in 1986. As president, she sought to rule in a conciliatory manner, but encountered opposition from the left (communist guerrillas) and the right (army coup attempts), and her land reforms were seen as inadequate.

Aquitaine region of southwest France; administrative capital Bordeaux; area 41,308 sq km/15,949 sq mi; population (1999 est) 2,908,400. It comprises the départements of Dordogne, Gironde, Landes, Lot-et-Garonne, and Pyrénées-Atlantiques. The climate is extremely wet. Red wines (Margaux, St Julien) are produced in the *Médoc district, bordering the Gironde. Fishing and tourism are important industries.

Arab any of the Semitic (see *Semite) people native to the Arabian peninsula, but now settled throughout North Africa and the nations of the Middle East.

Arab Emirates see *United Arab Emirates.

arabesque in ballet, a pose in which the dancer stands on one leg, straight or bent, with the other leg raised behind, fully extended. The arms are held in a harmonious position to give the longest possible line from fingertips to toes. It is one of the fundamental positions in ballet.

arabesque in the visual arts and architectural design, a linear decoration based on plant forms. Arabesque motifs are complicated, intertwined, flowing designs first found in ancient Arabic art – hence the term. They are a feature of ancient Greek and Roman art, and are particularly common in *Islamic art.

Arabia *or* **Arabian Peninsula** (Arabic Jazirat al-Arab, the 'peninsula of the Arabs') peninsula between the Gulf and the Red Sea, in southwest Asia; area 2,600,000 sq km/1,000,000 sq mi. The length from north to south is about 2,400 km/1,490 mi and the greatest width about 1,600 km/994 mi. The peninsula contains the world's richest gas reserves and half the world's oil reserves. It comprises the states of Bahrain, Kuwait, Oman, Qatar, Saudi Arabia, the United Arab Emirates, and Yemen.

Arabian Nights tales in oral circulation among Arab storytellers from the 10th century, probably having their roots in India. They are also known as *The Thousand and One Nights* and include 'Ali Baba', 'Aladdin', 'Sinbad the Sailor', and 'The Old Man of the Sea'.

Arabian Sea northwestern branch of the *Indian Ocean, covering 3,859,000 sq km/1,489,970 sq mi, with India to the east, Pakistan and Iran to the north, and the Arabian Peninsula and Somalia to the west. It is linked with the Red Sea via the Gulf of Aden, and with the Gulf via the Gulf of Oman. Its mean depth is 2,730 m/8,956 ft. The chief river flowing into the Arabian Sea is the Indus, which is linked with a large submarine canyon in the continental shelf. The sea is rich in fish.

Arabic language major Semitic language of the Hamito-Semitic family of West Asia and North Africa, originating among the Arabs of the Arabian peninsula. It is spoken today by about 120 million people in the Middle East and North Africa. Arabic script is written from right to left.

Arab–Israeli Wars series of wars and territorial conflicts between Israel and various Arab states in the Middle East since the founding of the state of Israel in May 1948. These include the war of 1948–49; the 1956 Suez War between Israel and Egypt; the Six-Day War of 1967, in which Israel captured territory from Syria and Jordan; the October War of 1973; and the 1982–85 war between Israel and Lebanon. In the times between the wars tension has remained high in the area, and has resulted in skirmishes and terrorist activity taking place on both sides.

Arab League *or* **League of Arab States** organization of Arab states established in Cairo in 1945 to promote Arab unity, primarily in opposition to Israel. The original members were Egypt, Syria, Iraq, Lebanon, Transjordan (Jordan 1949), Saudi Arabia, and Yemen. They were later joined by Algeria, Bahrain, Comoros, Djibouti, Kuwait, Libya, Mauritania, Morocco, Oman, Palestine, the PLO, Qatar, Somalia, Sudan, Tunisia, and the United Arab Emirates. In 1979 Egypt was suspended and the league's headquarters transferred to Tunis in protest against the Egypt–Israeli peace, but Egypt was readmitted as a full member in May 1989, and in March 1990 its headquarters returned to Cairo. Despite the strains imposed on it by the 1990–91 Gulf War, the alliance survived. The secretary general is Amr Mohammed Musa, a former Egyptian foreign minister, from 2001.

arable farming cultivation of crops, as opposed to the keeping of animals. Crops may be *cereals, vegetables, or plants for producing oils or cloth. Arable farming generally requires less attention than livestock farming. In a *mixed farming system, crops may therefore be found farther from the farm centre than animals.

arachnid *or* **arachnoid** type of arthropod of the class Arachnida, including spiders, scorpions, ticks, and mites. They differ from insects in possessing only two main body regions, the cephalothorax and the abdomen, and in having eight legs.

Arafat, Yassir (1929–2004) born Muhammad Yassir Abdul-Ra'ouf Arafat As Qudwa al-Husseini, Palestinian nationalist politician, cofounder of the al-*Fatah (Movement for the National Liberation of Palestine) resistance group in 1958, leader of the *Palestine Liberation Organization (PLO) from 1969, and president of the Palestinian National Authority (PNA) from 1994. He was a key player in peace talks with Israel regarding the status of the Palestinian territories of the Gaza Strip and the West Bank within Israel. His power as president of the PNA was diminished by his failure to control Palestinian extremists during the intifada (uprising) against Israel that began in September 2000, and the appointment in 2003 of a prime minister to run day-to-day government in the PNA. In 1994, he shared the Nobel Prize for Peace with Israeli prime minister Yitzhak Rabin and foreign minister Shimon *Peres for their agreement of an accord on Palestinian self-rule.

Arafura Sea area of the Pacific Ocean between northern Australia and Indonesia, bounded by the Timor Sea in the west and the Coral Sea, via the Torres Strait, in the east; 1,290 km/800 mi long and 560 km/350 mi wide. It lies on the Arafura Shelf, and is 50–80 m/165–265 ft deep. The Indonesian Aru islands lie to the north. To the northwest, the Aru Trough (3,650 m/12,000 ft deep) separates the Arafura Sea from the Banda Sea.

Aragón autonomous community and former kingdom of northeast Spain, including the provinces of Huesca, Teruel, and Zaragoza (Saragossa); area 47,669 sq km/18,405 sq mi; population (2001 est) 1,199,800. Agriculture is centred at the oases and irrigated areas; products include cereals, rice, olive oil, almonds, figs, grapes, and olives. Industries include the manufacturing of machinery, industrial vehicles, and electrical appliances; iron, sulphur, and lignite are mined; merino wool is a major export. The principal river of Aragón is the Ebro, which receives numerous tributaries both from the mountains of the south and from the Pyrenees in the north. Aragón was an independent kingdom from 1035 to 1479. The capital of modern Aragón is Zaragoza.

Aral Sea Russian **Aralskoye More**, inland sea divided between Kazakhstan and Uzbekistan, the world's fourth-largest lake; former area 62,000 sq km/24,000 sq mi, but decreasing. Since the 1960s water from its tributaries, the Amu Darya and Syr Darya, has been diverted for irrigation and city use, and the sea is disappearing, with long-term consequences for the climate. It has also become increasingly saline, with the salinity having tripled since the mid-20th century.

Aramaic language Semitic language of the Hamito-Semitic family of western Asia, the everyday language of Palestine 2,000 years ago, during the Roman occupation and the time of Jesus.

Aran Islands group of three limestone islands in the mouth of Galway Bay, which is about 32 km/20 mi wide. They lie 48 km/30 mi from Galway, on the west coast of the Republic of Ireland; the principal town is Kilronan on Inishmore. The islands form a natural breakwater, and comprise Inishmore (Irish Inis Mór), area 3,092 ha/7,637 acres, population (1996) 838; Inishmaan (Irish Inis Meáin), area 912 ha/2,253 acres, population (1996) 191; and Inisheer (Irish Inis Óirr), area 567 ha/1,400 acres, population (1996) 274. The chief industries are tourism, fishing, and agriculture.

Arapaho (Arapaho 'trader') member of an *American Indian people who moved from Minnesota and North Dakota to the upper Missouri River area in the 17th century, where they became close allies of the Cheyenne. Their language belongs to the Algonquian family. Originally a farming people in the eastern woodlands, they acquired horses and adopted the nomadic existence of the *Plains Indians, hunting buffalo, and raiding other peoples and Anglo-American settlers. They also became known as great traders. The Arapaho now live on reservations in Wyoming and Oklahoma, and number about 5,000 (1990).

Ararat, Mount double-peaked mountain in Turkey near the Iranian border; Great Ararat, at 5,137 m/16,854 ft, is the highest mountain in Turkey. According to the Old Testament, it was the resting place of Noah's Ark after the Flood.

araucaria coniferous tree related to the firs, with flat, scalelike needles. Once widespread, it is now native only to the southern hemisphere. Some grow to gigantic size. Araucarias include the monkey-puzzle tree (*Araucaria araucana*), the Australian bunya bunya pine (*A. bidwillii*), and the Norfolk Island pine (*A. heterophylla*). (Genus *Araucaria*, family Araucariaceae.)

Arawak indigenous American people of the Caribbean and northeastern Amazon Basin. Arawaks lived mainly by shifting cultivation in tropical forests. They were driven out of many West Indian islands by another American Indian people, the Caribs, shortly before the arrival of the Spanish in the 16th century. their numbers on *Hispaniola declined from some 4 million in 1492 to a few thousand after their exploitation by the Spanish in their search for gold; the remaining few were eradicated by disease (smallpox was introduced in 1518). Arawakan languages belong to the Andean-Equatorial group.

arbitrageur in finance, a person who buys securities (such as currency or commodities) in one country or market for immediate resale in another market, to take advantage of different prices.

arbor vitae any of several coniferous trees or shrubs belonging to the cypress family, with flattened branchlets covered in overlapping aromatic green scales. The northern white cedar (*Thuja occidentalis*) and the western red cedar (*T. plicata*) are found in North America. The Chinese or oriental species *T. orientalis*, reaching 18 m/60 ft in height, is widely grown as an ornamental. (Genus *Thuja*, family Cupressaceae.)

arc in geometry, a section of a curved line or circle. A circle has three types of arc: a **semicircle**, which is exactly half of the circle; **minor arcs**, which are less than the semicircle; and **major arcs**, which are greater than the semicircle.

Arcadia Greek **Arkadhia**, central plateau and department of southern Greece; area 4,419 sq km/1,706 sq mi; population (1991) 103,800. Tripolis is the capital town.

arch in masonry, a curved structure that supports the weight of material over an open space, as in a bridge or doorway. The first arches consisted of several wedge-shaped stones supported by their mutual pressure. The term is also applied to any curved structure that is an arch in form only, such as the Arc de Triomphe, Paris, 1806–36.

Archaea group of micro-organisms that are without a nucleus and have a single chromosome. Most taxonomists now classify these bacteria in their own kingdom, separate from other bacteria. All are strict anaerobes, that is, they are killed by oxygen. This is thought to be a primitive condition and to indicate that Archaea are related to the earliest life forms, which appeared about 4 billion years ago, when there was little

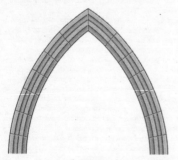
Gothic arch

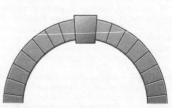
Roman arch

arch A Gothic arch and a Roman arch.

oxygen in the Earth's atmosphere. They are found in undersea vents, hot springs, the Dead Sea, and salt pans, and have even adapted to refuse tips.

Archaean or **Archaeozoic** widely used term for the earliest era of geological time; the first part of the Precambrian **Eon**, spanning the interval from the formation of Earth to about 2,500 million years ago.

archaeology (Greek *archaia* 'ancient things', *logos* 'study') study of prehistory and history, based on the examination of physical remains. Principal activities include preliminary field (or site) surveys, *excavation (where necessary), and the classification, *dating, and interpretation of finds.

archaeopteryx (Greek *archaios* 'ancient', *pterux* 'wing') extinct primitive bird, known from fossilized remains, about 160 million years old, found in limestone deposits in Bavaria, Germany. It is popularly known as 'the first bird', although some earlier bird ancestors are now known. It was about the size of a crow and had feathers and wings, with three clawlike digits at the endof each wing, but in many respects its skeleton is reptilian (teeth and a long, bony tail) and very like some small meat-eating dinosaurs of the time.

archery use of the bow and arrow, originally in hunting and warfare, now as a competitive sport. The world governing body is the Fédération Internationale de Tir à l'Arc (FITA) founded in 1931. In Olympic competition, archers shoot at targets 70 m/230 ft away in four events - men's and women's individual and team competitions. The target is 1.22 m/4 ft in diameter and marked with ten concentric rings, scoring ten points for the centre ring, or bullseye, down to one point for the outermost ring. Archers, or teams, compete in head-to-head elimination matches after being ranked in the qualifying round Archery was reintroduced to the Olympic Games in 1972.

Archimedes (c. 287–212 BC) Greek mathematician and philosopher who made major discoveries in geometry, hydrostatics, and mechanics, and established the sciences of statics and hydrostatics. He formulated a law of fluid displacement (Archimedes' principle), and is credited with the invention of the Archimedes screw, a cylindrical device for raising water. His method of finding mathematical proof to substantiate experiment and observation became the method of modern science in the High Renaissance.

Archimedes' principle in physics, the principle that the weight of the liquid displaced by a floating body is equal to the weight of the body. The principle is often stated in the form: 'an object totally or partially submerged in a fluid displaces a volume of fluid that weighs the same as the apparent loss in weight of the object (which, in turn, equals the upwards force, or upthrust, experienced by that object).' It was discovered by the Greek mathematician Archimedes.

Archimedes screw one of the earliest kinds of pump, associated with the Greek mathematician Archimedes. It consists of an enormous spiral screw revolving inside a close-fitting cylinder. It is used, for example, to raise water for irrigation.

archipelago group of islands, or an area of sea containing a group of islands. The islands of an archipelago are usually volcanic in origin, and they sometimes represent the tops of peaks in areas around continental margins flooded by the sea.

architecture art of designing structures. The term covers the design of the visual appearance of structures; their internal arrangements of space; selection of external and internal building materials; design or selection of natural and artificial lighting systems, as well as mechanical, electrical, and plumbing systems; and design or selection of decorations and furnishings. Architectural style may emerge from evolution of techniques and styles particular to a culture in a given time period with or without identifiable individuals as architects, or may be attributed to specific individuals or groups of architects working together on a project.

arc lamp or **arc light** electric light that uses the illumination of an electric arc maintained between two electrodes. The English chemist Humphry Davy demonstrated the electric arc in 1802 and electric arc lighting was first introduced by English electrical engineer W E Staite in 1846. The lamp consists of two carbon electrodes, between which a very high voltage is maintained. Electric current arcs (jumps) between the two electrodes, creating a brilliant light. Its main use in recent years has been in cinema projectors.

arc minute symbol ´, unit for measuring small angles, used in geometry, surveying, map-making, and astronomy. An arc minute is one-sixtieth of a degree and is divided into 60 arc seconds (symbol ˝). Small distances in the sky, as between two close stars or the apparent width of a planet's disc, are expressed in minutes and seconds of arc.

Arctic, the that part of the northern hemisphere surrounding the North Pole; generally defined as the region lying either north of the Arctic Circle (66° 30´ north) or north of the treeline; area 36 million sq km/ 14 million sq mi; population around 1 million.

Arctic Circle imaginary line that encircles the North Pole at latitude 66° 30´ north. Within this line there is at least one day in the summer during which the Sun never sets, and at least one day in the winter during which the Sun never rises.

Arctic Ocean ocean surrounding the North Pole; area 14,000,000 sq km/5,405,400 sq mi. Because of the Siberian and North American rivers flowing into it, it has comparatively low salinity and freezes readily.

Arcturus or **Alpha Boötis** brightest star in the constellation Boötes and the fourth-brightest star in the night sky. Arcturus is a red giant about 28 times larger than the Sun and 70 times more luminous, 36 light years away from the Sun.

Ardennes hilly, wooded plateau in northeast France, southeast Belgium, and northern Luxembourg, cut through by the River Meuse. The area gives its name to the region of *Champagne-Ardenne and the département of the Ardennes in France. The highest hills are about 590 m/1,936 ft. Cattle and sheep are raised and the area is rich in timber and minerals, but relatively sparsely populated. There was heavy fighting here in both world wars, notably in the Battle of the *Bulge (1944–1945, also known as the Ardennes offensive). In World War I it was the route of the main German advance in 1914.

are metric unit of area, equal to 100 square metres (119.6 sq yd); 100 ares make one *hectare.

area size of a surface. It is measured in square units, usually square centimetres (cm^2), square metres (m^2), or square kilometres (km^2). **Surface area** is the area of the outer surface of a solid. *Integration may be used to determine the area of shapes enclosed by curves.

areca any of a group of palm trees native to Asia and Australia. The *betel nut comes from the species *Areca catechu*. (Genus *Areca*.)

Ares in Greek mythology, the god of war, equivalent to the Roman *Mars. The son of Zeus and Hera, he was worshipped chiefly in Thrace.

arête German **grat**; North American **combe-ridge**, sharp narrow ridge separating two glacial troughs (U-shaped valleys), or corries. They are formed by intense *freeze–thaw weathering on the sides of mountains. The typical U-shaped cross-sections of glacial troughs give arêtes very steep sides. Arêtes are common in glaciated mountain regions such as the Rockies, the Himalayas, and the Alps. There are also several in the UK, for example Striding Edge and Swirral Edge in the English Lake District.

Argentina

National name: *República Argentina/Argentine Republic*

Area: 2,780,400 sq km/1,073,518 sq mi
Capital: Buenos Aires
Major towns/cities: Rosario, Córdoba, San Miguel de Tucumán, Mendoza, Santa Fé, La Plata
Major ports: La Plata and Bahía Blanca
Physical features: mountains in west, forest and savannah in north, pampas (treeless plains) in east-central area, Patagonian plateau in south; rivers Colorado, Salado, Paraná, Uruguay, Río de La Plata estuary; Andes mountains, with Aconcagua the highest peak in western hemisphere; Iguaçu Falls
Territories: disputed claim to the Falkland Islands (*Islas Malvinas*), and part of Antarctica
Head of state and government: Néstor Kirchner Ostoic from 2003
Political system: liberal democracy
Political executive: limited presidency
Political parties: Radical Civic Union Party (UCR), moderate centrist; Justicialist Party (PJ), right-wing Perónist; Movement for Dignity and Independence (Modin), right wing; Front for a Country in Solidarity (Frepaso), left of centre

Currency: peso (= 10,000 australs, which it replaced in 1992)
GNI per capita (PPP): (US$) 9,930 (2002 est)
Exports: meat and meat products, prepared animal fodder, cereals, petroleum and petroleum products, soybeans, vegetable oils and fats. Principal market: Brazil 27% (2000)
Population: 38,428,000 (2003 est)
Language: Spanish (official) (95%), Italian (3%), English, German, French
Religion: predominantly Roman Catholic (state-supported), 2% protestant, 2% Jewish
Life expectancy: 71 (men); 78 (women) (2000–05)
Chronology
1516: The Spanish navigator Juan Diaz de Solis discovered Río de La Plata.
1536: Buenos Aires was founded, but was soon abandoned because of attacks by American Indians.
1580: Buenos Aires was re-established as part of the Spanish province of Asunción.
1617: Buenos Aires became a separate province within the Spanish viceroyalty of Lima.
1776: The Spanish South American Empire was reorganized: Atlantic regions became viceroyalty of La Plata, with Buenos Aires as capital.
1810: After the French conquest of Spain, Buenos Aires junta took over government of viceroyalty.
1816: Independence was proclaimed, as the United Provinces of Río de La Plata, but Bolivia and Uruguay soon seceded; civil war followed between federalists and those who wanted a unitary state.
1835–52: Dictatorship of Gen Juan Manuel Rosas.
1853: Adoption of federal constitution based on US model; Buenos Aires refused to join confederation.
1861: Buenos Aires was incorporated into the Argentine confederation by force.
1865–70: Argentina took part in the War of Triple Alliance against Paraguay.
late 19th century: Large-scale European immigration and economic development.
1880: Buenos Aires became the national capital.
1880–1916: The government was dominated by an oligarchy of conservative landowners.
1916: The secret ballot was introduced and the Radical Party of Hipólito Irigoyen won elections, beginning a period of 14 years in government.
1930: A military coup ushered in a series of conservative governments sustained by violence and fraud.
1946: Col Juan Perón won presidential elections; he secured working-class support through welfare measures, trade unionism, and the popularity of his wife, Eva Perón (Evita).
1949: A new constitution abolished federalism and increased powers of president.
1952: Death of Evita. Support for Perón began to decline.
1955: Perón was overthrown; the constitution of 1853 was restored.
1966–70: Dictatorship of Gen Juan Carlos Ongania.
1973: Perónist Party won free elections; Perón returned from exile in Spain to become president.
1974: Perón died and was succeeded by his third wife, Isabel Perón.
1976: A coup resulted in rule by a military junta.
1976–83: The military regime conducted murderous campaign ('Dirty War') against left-wing elements. More than 8,000 people disappeared.

1982: Argentina invaded the Falkland Islands but was defeated by the UK.

1983: Return to civilian rule; an investigation into the 'Dirty War' was launched.

1989: Annual inflation reached 12,000%. Carlos Menem won the presidential elections.

1990: Full diplomatic relations with the UK were restored.

1991: The government introduced the peso to replace the austral.

1995: Carlos Menem was elected for a second term as president.

1999: Falkland Islanders held their first talks with Argentina since 1982. Fernando de la Rua won the presidential elections.

2000: There were protests against spending cuts that aimed to bring the economy into line with targets set by the International Monetary Fund (IMF).

2001: Congress granted President de la Rua emergency powers to implement his economic programme. Amnesty laws protecting members of the armed forces from human rights prosecutions were overturned.

2002: Eduardo Duhalde, a Peronist senator and former vice-president, took office in January as Argentina's fifth president in two weeks. In the wake of continuing financial upheaval the government devalued the peso, ending a ten-year policy of pegging the currency to the US dollar.

2003: Former president Carlos Menem withdrew from a run-off poll in presidential elections. His nearest rival Néstor Kirchner, a fellow member of the ruling, but divided, Peronist Partido Justicialista (Justicialist Party), took power. Congress voted to remove laws protecting former members of the military from prosecution for human rights abuses. Argentina and the International Monetary Fund (IMF) agreed on a restructuring of the country's debt.

2004: An international arrest warrant was issued for former President Carlos Menem over allegations of fraud. He returned to Argentina from Chile after two arrest warrants were cancelled.

2005: President Néstor Kirchner announced that the restructuring of the country's debt had been successful.

argon chemical symbol Ar, (Greek *argos* 'idle') colourless, odourless, non-metallic, gaseous element, atomic number 18, relative atomic mass 39.948. It is grouped with the *noble gases (rare gases) in Group 0 of the *periodic table of the elements. It was long believed not to react with other substances, but observations now indicate that it can be made to combine with boron fluoride to form compounds. It constitutes almost 1% of the Earth's atmosphere, and was discovered in 1894 by British chemists John Rayleigh and William Ramsay after all oxygen and nitrogen had been removed chemically from a sample of air. It is used in electric discharge tubes and argon lasers.

Argonauts in Greek mythology, the band of heroes who accompanied *Jason when he set sail in the Argo to find the *Golden Fleece.

Argus in Greek mythology, a giant with 100 eyes. When he was killed by Hermes, Hera transplanted his eyes into the tail of her favourite bird, the peacock.

Argyll and Bute unitary authority in western Scotland, created in 1996 from the district of the same name and part of Dumbarton district, which were both parts of Strathclyde region; it includes the islands of Gigha,

Bute, Mull, Islay, Jura, Tiree, Coll, Colonsay, Iona, and Staffa. **area:** 7,016 sq km/2,709 sq mi **towns:** Campbeltown, Dunoon, Helensburgh, Inveraray, Lochgilphead (administrative headquarters), Oban, Rothesay **physical:** rural area consisting of mainland and islands; the coast is heavily indented. Inland the area is mountainous; highest peak, Ben Cruachan (1,126 m/3,693 ft). Lochs Fyne and Long are the largest sea lochs; freshwater lochs include Loch Awe and Loch Lomond; Fingal's Cave (Staffa); Corryvrekan Whirlpool (Jura-Scarba); Ben Arthur (The Cobbler), 884 m/2,900 ft **features:** Bronze, Stone, and Iron Age remains **population:** (2001 est) 91,300.

aria (Italian 'air') melodic solo song of reflective character, often with a contrasting middle section. It is used to express a moment of importance in the action of an opera or oratorio. Already to be found in Jacopo Peri's Euridice (1600) and Claudio *Monteverdi's Orfeo (1607), it reached its more elaborate form in the work of Alessandro *Scarlatti and George Frideric *Handel, becoming a set piece for virtuoso opera singers. An example is Handel's 'Where'er you walk' from the secular oratorio Semele (1744) to words by William Congreve. In instrumental music, an aria may be the title of a songlike piece, or a theme suitable for variations.

Ariadne in Greek mythology, the daughter of Minos, King of Crete. When *Theseus came from Athens as one of the sacrificial victims offered to the *Minotaur, she fell in love with him and gave him a ball of thread, which enabled him to find his way out of the labyrinth. When Theseus abandoned her on the island of Naxos, she married *Dionysus.

Arianism system of Christian theology that denied the complete divinity of Jesus, giving God the Father primacy over the created son Jesus. It was founded about 310 by Arius, and condemned as heretical at the Council of Nicaea in 325.

arid region in earth science, a region that is very dry and has little vegetation. Aridity depends on temperature, rainfall, and evaporation, and so is difficult to quantify, but an arid area is usually defined as one that receives less than 250 mm/10 in of rainfall each year. (By comparison, New York City receives 1,120 mm/44 in per year.) There are arid regions in North Africa, Pakistan, Australia, the USA, and elsewhere. Very arid regions are *deserts.

Aries zodiacal constellation in the northern hemisphere between Pisces and Taurus, near Auriga, represented as the legendary ram whose golden fleece was sought by Jason and the Argonauts. Its most distinctive feature is a curve of three stars of decreasing brightness. The brightest of these is Hamal or Alpha Arietis, 65 light years from Earth.

Ariosto, Ludovico (1474–1533) Italian poet. He wrote Latin poems and comedies on classical lines. His major work is the poem *Orlando furioso* (1516, published in 1532), an epic treatment of the *Roland story, the perfect poetic expression of the Italian Renaissance.

Aristarchus of Samos (c. 320–c. 250 BC) Greek astronomer. The first to argue that the Earth moves around the Sun, he was ridiculed for his beliefs. He was also the first astronomer to estimate (quite inaccurately) the sizes of the Sun and Moon and their distances from the Earth.

Aristides (c. 530–468 BC) Athenian politician. He was one of the ten Athenian generals at the Battle of *Marathon in 490 BC and was elected chief archon, or magistrate. Later he came into conflict with the democratic leader Themistocles, and was exiled in about 483 BC. He returned to fight against the Persians at Salamis in 480 BC and in the following year commanded the Athenians at Plataea. As commander of the Athenian fleet he established the alliance of Ionian states known as the Delian League.

aristocracy (Greek *aristos* 'best', *kratos* 'power') social elite or system of political power associated with landed wealth, as in Western Europe; with monetary wealth, as in Carthage and Venice; or with religious superiority, as were the Brahmans in India. Aristocracies are also usually associated with monarchy but have frequently been in conflict with the sovereign over their respective rights and privileges. In Europe, their economic base was undermined during the 19th century by inflation and falling agricultural prices, leading to their demise as a political force after 1914.

Aristophanes (c. 445–c. 380 BC) Greek comedy dramatist. Of his 11 extant plays (of a total of over 40), the early comedies are remarkable for the violent satire with which he ridiculed the democratic war leaders. He also satirized contemporary issues such as the new learning of Socrates in *The Clouds* (423 BC) and the obsession with war, with the sex-strike of women in *Lysistrata* (411 BC). The chorus plays a prominent role, frequently giving the play its title, as in *The Wasps* (422 BC), *The Birds* (414 BC), and *The Frogs* (405 BC).

Aristotle (384–322 BC) Greek philosopher who advocated reason and moderation. He maintained that sense experience is our only source of knowledge, and that by reasoning we can discover the essences of things, that is, their distinguishing qualities. In his works on ethics and politics, he suggested that human happiness consists in living in conformity with nature. He derived his political theory from the recognition that mutual aid is natural to humankind, and refused to set up any one constitution as universally ideal. Of Aristotle's works, around 22 treatises survive, dealing with logic, metaphysics, physics, astronomy, meteorology, biology, psychology, ethics, politics, and literary criticism.

arithmetic branch of mathematics concerned with the study of numbers and their properties. The fundamental operations of arithmetic are addition, subtraction, multiplication, and division. Raising to powers (for example, squaring or cubing a number), the extraction of roots (for example, square roots), percentages, fractions, and ratios are developed from these operations.

arithmetic and logic unit (ALU) in a computer, the part of the *central processing unit (CPU) that performs the basic arithmetic and logic operations on data.

arithmetic mean average of a set of n numbers, obtained by adding the numbers and dividing by n. For example, the arithmetic mean of the set of 5 numbers 1, 3, 6, 8, and 12 is $(1 + 3 + 6 + 8 + 12) \div 5 = 30 \div 5 = 6$.

arithmetic progression *or* **arithmetic sequence** sequence of numbers or terms that have a common difference between any one term and the next in the sequence. For example, 2, 7, 12, 17, 22, 27, ... is an arithmetic sequence with a common difference of 5.

Arizona called the **Grand Canyon State**, (Aztec *arizuma* 'silver bearing' or *Pima arizonac* 'little spring place' or Spanish *árida-zona* 'dry belt') state in southwestern USA, bordered to the east by *New Mexico,

to the south by the Mexican state of Sonora, to the west by the Mexican state of Baja California and the US states of *California and *Nevada, and to the north by *Utah and, at the 'Four Corners' to the northeast, *Colorado; area 294,313 sq km/113,635 sq mi; population (2000) 5,130,600; capital and largest city Phoenix. A desert state of mountains, plateaux, and dry basins, Arizona is renowned for its natural wonders, such as Monument Valley and the *Grand Canyon. The *Colorado River marks the state's boundary between Nevada and California. Service industries, including tourism, provide the main source of revenue, and copper, silver, and uranium mining, and aeronautics and electronics are also important. Cotton is grown under irrigation, and ranching is widespread. Tucson is the second largest city; other major conurbations include Mesa, Tempe, Scottsdale, Glendale, and Flagstaff in the north, and Yuma on the Californian border. Arizona has the third largest *American Indian population in the USA, with 21 federally-recognized peoples (including the *Navajo, *Apache, and *Hopi) owning over 5.8 million ha/14.7 million acres, or 28%, of Arizona's land. Arizona was admitted to the Union in 1912 as the 48th US state.

Arkansas called the **Natural State** or the **Land of Opportunity**, (Sioux *acansa* 'downstream place') state in southern central USA, bordered to the south by *Louisiana, to the southwest by *Texas, to the west by *Oklahoma, to the north by *Missouri, and to the east by *Tennessee and *Mississippi; area 134,856 sq km/ 52,068 sq mi; population (2000) 2,673,400; capital and largest city *Little Rock. The state's nicknames come from its abundance of natural resources. Arkansas is physically divided into two areas: the Highlands, a mountain region; and the Lowlands, a coastal plain. The Red, St Francis, and Mississippi rivers form part of the state's natural borders. Major cities include Fort Smith on the Oklahoma border, an important manufacturing centre, North Little Rock, Pine Bluff, Jonesboro, Fayetteville, Hot Springs, Springdale, Jacksonville, and West Memphis. Arkansas's economy is centred on the service industry, but manufacturing is also important, with products including processed foods, electronics, and paper; it is the leading US producer of broilers (chickens reared for meat) and rice. Historically Arkansas was a cotton plantation state, dependent on slavery. Arkansas was admitted to the Union in 1836 as the 25th US state but was governed by federal troops during the *Reconstruction period 1865–77 because it refused to permit African Americans to vote. Arkansas only achieved independent statehood when it permitted the black vote in the state constitution of 1874, still in force today. The state was the site of civil-rights struggles in the 1950s and 1960s, and was closely associated with the Whitewater scandal that dogged the presidency of Bill Clinton during the 1990s.

Arkwright, Richard (1732–1792) English inventor and manufacturing pioneer who in 1768 developed a machine for spinning cotton (he called it a 'water frame'). In 1771 he set up a water-powered spinning factory and in 1790 he installed steam power in a Nottingham factory. He was knighted in 1786.

Armada fleet sent by Philip II of Spain against England in 1588. See *Spanish Armada.

armadillo mammal of the family Dasypodidae, with an armour of bony plates along its back or, in some species, almost covering the entire body. Around 20 species live between Texas and Patagonia and range in size from the fairy armadillo, or pichiciego, *Chlamyphorus truncatus*, at 13 cm/5 in, to the giant armadillo *Priodontes giganteus*, 1.5 m/4.5 ft long. Armadillos feed on insects, snakes, fruit, and carrion. Some can roll into an armoured ball if attacked; others defend themselves with their claws or rely on rapid burrowing for protection.

Armageddon in the New Testament (Revelation 16:16), the site of the final battle between the nations that will end the world; it has been identified with *Megiddo in Israel.

Armagh Irish **Ard Macha**, ('the height of Macha' (a legendary queen) historic county of Northern Ireland, bordering Lough *Neagh to the north and the Republic of Ireland to the south; area 1,250 sq km/483 sq mi. The principal towns and cities are Armagh, Craigavon, and Keady. The county is flat in the north, with many bogs and mounds formed from glacial deposits, and has low hills in the south, the highest of which is Slieve Gullion (577 m/1,893 ft). The principal rivers are the Bann, the Blackwater, and its tributary, the Callan. Administrative responsibility for the county is held by the councils of Craigavon and Armagh.

armature in a motor or generator, the wire-wound coil that carries the current and rotates in a magnetic field. (In alternating-current machines, the armature is sometimes stationary.) The pole piece of a permanent magnet or electromagnet and the moving, iron part of a *solenoid, especially if the latter acts as a switch, may also be referred to as armatures.

Armenia

National name: *Hayastani Hanrapetoutioun/ Republic of Armenia*

Area: 29,800 sq km/11,505 sq mi
Capital: Yerevan
Major towns/cities: Gyumri (formerly Leninakan), Vanadzor (formerly Kirovakan), Hrazdan, Aboyvan
Physical features: mainly mountainous (including Mount Ararat), wooded
Head of state: Robert Kocharian from 1998
Head of government: Andranik Markaryan from 2000
Political system: authoritarian nationalist
Political executive: unlimited presidency
Political parties: Armenian Pan-National Movement (APM), nationalist, left of centre; Armenian Revolutionary Federation (ARF), centrist (banned in 1994); Communist Party of Armenia (banned 1991–92); National Unity, opposition coalition; Armenian Christian Democratic Union (CDU), moderately right wing; Huchak Armenian Social Democratic Party
Currency: dram (replaced Russian rouble in 1993)
GNI per capita (PPP): (US$) 2,880 (2001)
Exports: precious or semi-precious metals and stones, machinery and metalworking products, chemical and petroleum products, base metals, equipment. Principal market: Russia 17.7% (2001)
Population: 3,061,000 (2003 est)
Language: Armenian (official)
Religion: Armenian Orthodox
Life expectancy: 69 (men); 76 (women) (2000–05)
Chronology
6th century BC: Armenian peoples moved into the area, which was then part of the Persian Empire.
***c.* 94–56 BC:** Under King Tigranes II 'the Great', Armenia reached the height of its power, becoming the strongest state in the eastern Roman empire.
***c.* AD 300:** Christianity became the state religion when the local ruler was converted by St Gregory the Illuminator.
***c.* AD 390:** Armenia was divided between Byzantine Armenia, which became part of the Byzantine Empire, and Persarmenia, under Persian control.
886–1045: Became independent under the Bagratid monarchy.
13th century: After being overrun by the Mongols, a substantially independent Little Armenia survived until 1375.
early 16th century: Conquered by Muslim Ottoman Turks.
1813–28: Russia took control of eastern Armenia.
late 19th century: Revival in Armenian culture and national spirit, provoking Ottoman backlash in western Armenia and international concern at Armenian maltreatment: the 'Armenian Question'.
1894–96: Armenians were massacred by Turkish soldiers in an attempt to suppress unrest.
1915: Suspected of pro-Russian sympathies, two-thirds of Armenia's population of 2 million were deported to Syria and Palestine. Around 600,000 to 1 million died en route: the survivors contributed towards an Armenian diaspora in Europe and North America.
1916: Armenia was conquered by tsarist Russia and became part of a brief 'Transcaucasian Alliance' with Georgia and Azerbaijan.
1918: Armenia became an independent republic.
1920: Occupied by Red Army of Soviet Union (USSR), but western Armenia remained part of Turkey and northwest Iran.
1936: Became constituent republic of USSR; rapid industrial development.
late 1980s: Armenian 'national reawakening', encouraged by *glasnost* (openness) initiative of Soviet leader Mikhail Gorbachev.
1988: Around 20,000 people died in an earthquake.
1989: Strife-torn Nagorno-Karabakh was placed under direct rule from Moscow; civil war erupted with Azerbaijan over Nagorno-Karabakh and Nakhichevan, an Azerbaijani-peopled enclave in Armenia.
1990: Independence was declared, but ignored by Moscow and the international community.

1991: After the collapse of the USSR, Armenia joined the new Commonwealth of Independent States. Nagorno-Karabakh declared its independence.

1992: Armenia was recognized as an independent state by the USA and admitted into the United Nations (UN).

1993: Armenian forces gained control of more than a fifth of Azerbaijan, including much of Nagorno-Karabakh.

1994: A Nagorno-Karabakh ceasefire ended the conflict.

1997: There was border fighting with Azerbaijan.

1999: Prime Minister Vazgen Sarkisian was assassinated in October when gunmen burst into parliament and shot him and seven other officials. He was replaced by his brother, Amen Sarkisian.

2000: President Robert Kocharian dismissed Amen Sarkisian as prime minister and replaced him with Andranik Markarya.

2001: Armenia was admitted to the Council of Europe.

2003: President Kocharian was re-elected despite competition from anti-corruption challenger Stepan Demirchyan in a run-off poll. International observers said the vote-counting process fell short of international standards. The death penalty was abolished.

2004: Demonstrations were held by thousands of opposition supporters, calling for President Kocharian's resignation.

Armenian member of the largest ethnic group inhabiting Armenia. There are Armenian minorities in Azerbaijan (see *Nagorno-Karabakh), as well as in Syria, Lebanon, Turkey, and Iran. Christianity was introduced to the ancient Armenian kingdom in the 3rd century. There are 4–5 million speakers of Armenian, which belongs to the Indo-European family of languages.

Armenian massacres series of massacres of Armenians by Turkish soldiers between 1895 and 1915. In 1894–96 demands for better treatment led to massacres of Armenians in eastern Asia Minor. Over 50,000 Armenians were killed by Kurdish irregulars and Ottoman troops. The killing was stopped by the major European powers, but in 1915 Ottoman suspicions of Armenian loyalty led to further massacres and deportations. The Turks deported 1.75 million Armenians to Syria and Palestine; 600,000 to 1 million were either killed or died of starvation during the journey.

armistice cessation of hostilities while awaiting a peace settlement. The Armistice refers specifically to the end of World War I between Germany and the Allies on 11 November 1918. On 22 June 1940, following the German invasion of France, French representatives signed an armistice with Germany in the same railway carriage at Compiègne as in 1918. No armistice was signed with either Germany or Japan in 1945; both nations surrendered and there was no provision for the suspension of fighting. The Korean armistice, signed at Panmunjom on 27 July 1953, terminated the Korean War 1950–53.

Armistice Day anniversary of the armistice signed 11 November 1918, ending World War I.

armour body protection worn in battle. Body armour is depicted in Greek and Roman art. Chain mail was developed in the Middle Ages but the craft of the armourer in Europe reached its height in design in the 15th century, when knights were completely encased in plate armour that still allowed freedom of movement. Medieval Japanese armour was articulated, made of iron, gilded metal, leather, and silk. Contemporary bulletproof vests and riot gear are forms of armour.

The term is used in a modern context to refer to a mechanized armoured vehicle, such as a tank.

arms control attempts to limit the arms race between the superpowers by reaching agreements to restrict the production of certain weapons; see *disarmament.

arms trade sale of conventional weapons, such as tanks, combat aircraft, and related technology, from a manufacturing country to another nation. Arms exports are known in the trade as 'arms transfers'. Most transfers take place between governments and can be accompanied by training and maintenance agreements. International agreements, such as the Nuclear Non-Proliferation Treaty, outlaw the transfer of nuclear weapons and weapons of biological or chemical warfare. There are also agreements not to supply certain countries with conventional weapons, such as Iraq and Libya which may use weapons for internal repression or neighbour disputes. However, an active black market means that these arms embargoes are typically overcome. Around a half of the world's arms exports end up in countries of the developing world. Iraq, for instance, was armed in the years leading up to the 1991 Gulf War mainly by the USSR but also by France, Brazil, and South Africa.

Armstrong, Louis (1901–1971) called 'Satchmo', US jazz cornet and trumpet player and singer, considered one of the most influential jazz musicians. His Chicago recordings in the 1920s with the Hot Five and Hot Seven brought him recognition for his warm and pure trumpet tone, his skill at improvisation, and his quirky, gravelly voice. In 1947 he formed the Louis Armstrong All-Stars, with whom he produced his most popular hits, including 'Mack the Knife' and 'Hello, Dolly!'.

Armstrong, Neil Alden (1930–) US astronaut. On 20 July 1969, he became the first person to set foot on the Moon and made his now famous remark, 'That's one small step for man, one giant leap for mankind.' The Moon landing was part of the *Apollo project.

Arnhem, Battle of in World War II, airborne operation by the Allies, 17–26 September 1944, to secure a bridgehead over the Rhine, thereby opening the way for a thrust towards the Ruhr and a possible early end to the war. It was only partially successful, with 7,600 casualties.

Arnhem Land plateau of the central peninsula in northeast Northern Territory, Australia, west of the Gulf of Carpentaria; approximate area 80,776 sq km/ 31,188 sq mi. Arnhem Land was named after a Dutch ship which dropped anchor here in 1618. The chief town is Nhulunbuy; population (1996) 3,695. It is the largest of the Aboriginal reserves, and was declared Aboriginal land in 1976. Many of the inhabitants live in small settlements and maintain a traditional way of life. Bauxite and uranium mining and the supporting industries provide the main economic base of the area.

Arnold, Malcolm Henry (1921–) English composer. His work is tonal and includes a large amount of orchestral, chamber, ballet, and vocal music. His best-known overtures include Beckus the Dandipratt (1948), A Sussex Overture (1951), and Tam O'Shanter (1955). His operas include The Dancing Master (1951), and he has written music for more than 80 films, including The Bridge on the River Kwai (1957), for which he won an Academy Award.

Arnold, Matthew (1822–1888) English poet and critic. His poem 'Dover Beach' (1867) was widely regarded as one of the most eloquent expressions of the spiritual anxieties of Victorian England. In his highly influential critical essays collected in *Culture and Anarchy* (1869), he attacked the smugness and ignorance of the Victorian middle classes, and argued for a new culture based on the pursuit of artistic and intellectual values.

aromatherapy in alternative medicine, use of oils and essences derived from plants, flowers, and wood resins. Bactericidal properties and beneficial effects upon physiological functions are attributed to the oils, which are sometimes ingested but generally massaged into the skin.

aromatic compound organic chemical compound in which some of the bonding electrons are delocalized (shared among several atoms within the molecule and not localized in the vicinity of the atoms involved in bonding). The commonest aromatic compounds have ring structures, the atoms comprising the ring being either all carbon or mostly carbon with one or more different atoms (usually nitrogen, sulphur, or oxygen). Typical examples are benzene (C_6H_6) and pyridine (C_5H_5N).

Arran large island in the Firth of Clyde, lying between the Kintyre peninsula and the mainland of North Ayrshire, Scotland; area 427 sq km/165 sq mi; population (2001 est) 4,900. The economy is largely based on tourism and craft industries, though other industries include whisky distilling and food processing. The island, which is mountainous to the north and undulating to the south, is a popular holiday resort. The chief town is Brodick. Arran villages include Lamlash, which possesses a fine natural harbour, and Whiting Bay.

Arrhenius, Svante August (1859–1927) Swedish scientist, the founder of physical chemistry. He was awarded the Nobel Prize for Chemistry in 1903 for his study of electrolysis. In 1905 he predicted global warming as a result of carbon dioxide emission from burning fossil fuels.

arrhythmia disturbance of the normal rhythm of the heart. There are various kinds of arrhythmia, some benign, some indicative of heart disease. In extreme cases, the heart may beat so fast as to be potentially lethal and surgery may be used to correct the condition.

arsenic chemical symbol As, brittle, greyish-white, semimetallic element (a metalloid), atomic number 33, relative atomic mass 74.92. It occurs in many ores and occasionally in its elemental state, and is widely distributed, being present in minute quantities in the soil, the sea, and the human body. In larger quantities, it is poisonous. The chief source of arsenic compounds is as a by-product from metallurgical processes. It is used in making semiconductors, alloys, and solders.

art in the broadest sense, all the processes and products of human skill, imagination, and invention. In contemporary usage, definitions of art usually reflect art theory, and the term may encompass literature, music, drama, painting, and sculpture. Popularly, the term is most commonly used to refer to the visual arts. In Western culture, artistic thought and theories introduced by the ancient Greeks still influence our perceptions and judgements of art.

art deco style in the decorative arts that influenced design and architecture, and is particularly associated with mass-produced domestic goods. It emerged in Europe in the 1920s and continued through the 1930s, achieving greatest popularity in the USA and France. Art deco pulls together aspects of abstraction and cubism to create a deliberately modern style, which was originally called 'Jazz Modern'. Its features include angular, geometrical patterns and bright colours, and the use of materials such as enamel, chrome, glass, and plastic. The graphic designer Erté became fashionable for his art deco work.

Artemis in Greek mythology, the goddess of chastity, all young creatures, the Moon, and the hunt (Roman Diana). She was the daughter of Zeus and the Titaness Leto, and the twin sister of *Apollo. She was worshipped

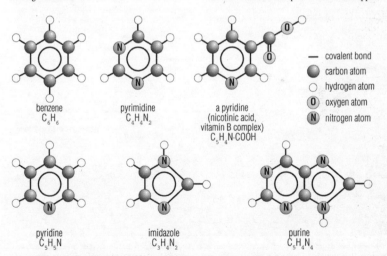

benzene
C_6H_6

pyrimidine
$C_4H_4N_2$

a pyridine
(nicotinic acid,
vitamin B complex)
$C_5H_4N \cdot COOH$

— covalent bond
⬤ carbon atom
○ hydrogen atom
Ⓞ oxygen atom
Ⓝ nitrogen atom

pyridine
C_5H_5N

imidazole
$C_3H_4N_2$

purine
$C_5H_4N_4$

aromatic compound Compounds whose molecules contain the benzene ring, or variations of it, are called aromatic. The term was originally used to distinguish sweet-smelling compounds from others.

at cult centres throughout the Greek world; one of the largest was at Ephesus where her great temple, reconstructed several times in antiquity, was one of the *Seven Wonders of the World.

arteriosclerosis hardening of the arteries, with thickening and loss of elasticity. It is associated with smoking, ageing, and a diet high in saturated fats. The term is used loosely as a synonym for *atherosclerosis.

artery blood vessel that carries *blood from the *heart to any part of the body. It is built to withstand considerable pressure, having thick walls that contain *muscle and elastic fibres. As blood pulses out of the heart, arteries expand to allow for the increase in pressure – this elasticity helps the blood to flow evenly. The *pulse or pressure wave generated can be felt at the wrist. Not all arteries carry oxygenated (oxygen-rich) blood – the pulmonary arteries convey deoxygenated (oxygen-poor) blood from the heart to the lungs.

artesian well well that is supplied with water rising naturally from an underground water-saturated rock layer (*aquifer). The water rises from the aquifer under its own pressure. Such a well may be drilled into an aquifer that is confined by impermeable rocks both above and below. If the water table (the top of the region of water saturation) in that aquifer is above the level of the well head, hydrostatic pressure will force the water to the surface.

arthritis inflammation of the joints, with pain, swelling, and restricted motion. Many conditions may cause arthritis, including gout, infection, and trauma to the joint. There are three main forms of arthritis: *rheumatoid arthritis; osteoarthritis; and septic arthritis.

arthropod member of the phylum Arthropoda; an invertebrate animal with jointed legs and a segmented body with a horny or chitinous casing (exoskeleton), which is shed periodically and replaced as the animal grows. Included are arachnids such as spiders and mites, as well as crustaceans, millipedes, centipedes, and insects.

Arthur (lived 6th century) semi-legendary Romano-British warleader who led British resistance against the Saxons, Picts, and Scots in the first half of the 6th century. He was probably a warlord rather than a king. He operated throughout Britain, commanding a small force of mobile warriors, reminiscent of the late Roman comitatenses (line units). Arthur is credited with a great victory over the Saxons at Mount Badon, possibly in Dorset.

artichoke either of two plants belonging to the sunflower family, parts of which are eaten as vegetables. The common or globe artichoke (*Cynara scolymus*) is a form of thistle native to the Mediterranean. It is tall, with purplish-blue flowers; the leaflike structures (bracts) around the unopened flower are eaten. The Jerusalem artichoke (*Helianthus tuberosus*), which has edible tubers, is a native of North America (its common name is a corruption of the Italian for sunflower, girasole). (Family Compositae.)

artificial insemination (AI) introduction by instrument of semen from a sperm bank or donor into the female reproductive tract to bring about fertilization. Originally used by animal breeders to improve stock with sperm from high-quality males, in the 20th century it was developed for use in humans, to help the infertile. See *in vitro fertilization.

artificial intelligence (AI) branch of science concerned with creating computer programs that can perform actions comparable with those of an intelligent human. AI research covers such areas as planning (for robot behaviour), language understanding, pattern recognition, and knowledge representation.

artificial respiration emergency procedure to restart breathing once it has stopped; in cases of electric shock or apparent drowning, for example, the first choice is the expired-air method, the kiss of life by mouth-to-mouth breathing until natural breathing is restored.

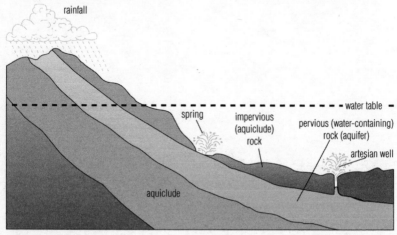

rainfall

water table

spring

impervious (aquiclude) rock

pervious (water-containing) rock (aquifer)

artesian well

aquiclude

artesian well In an artesian well, water rises from an underground water-containing rock layer under its own pressure. Rain falls at one end of the water-bearing layer, or aquifer, and percolates through the layer. The layer fills with water up to the level of the water table. Water will flow from a well under its own pressure if the well head is below the level of the water table.

artificial selection in biology, selective breeding of individuals that exhibit the particular characteristics that a plant or animal breeder wishes to develop. In plants, desirable features might include resistance to disease, high yield (in crop plants), or attractive appearance. In animal breeding, selection has led to the development of particular breeds of cattle for improved meat production (such as the Aberdeen Angus) or milk production (such as Jersey cows).

artillery collective term for military *firearms too heavy to be carried. Artillery can be mounted on tracks, wheels, ships, or aeroplanes and includes cannons and rocket launchers.

art nouveau (French 'new art') decorative style in the visual arts, interior design, and architecture that flourished from 1890 to 1910. It is characterized by organic, sinuous patterns and ornamentations based usually on twisting plant forms. In England, it appears in the illustrations of Aubrey *Beardsley; in Scotland, in the interior and exterior designs of Charles Rennie *Mackintosh; in France, in the glass of René Lalique and the posters of Alphonse *Mucha; and in the USA, in the lamps and metalwork of Louis Comfort *Tiffany. Art nouveau took its name from a shop in Paris, which opened in 1895 to sell products in the new style. It was known as Jugendstil ('youth style') in Germany and Stile Liberty in Italy, after the Liberty department store, London, which sold art nouveau fabrics and wallpaper.

Arts and Crafts Movement English social and aesthetic movement of the late 19th century that stressed the importance of manual skills and the dignity of labour. It expressed a rejection of Victorian industrialization and mass production, and a nostalgic desire to return to a medieval way of life. The movement influenced art nouveau and, less directly, the Bauhaus school of design.

Aruba island in the Caribbean, the westernmost of the Lesser Antilles, 30 km/19 mi north of the Paraguana Peninsula in Venezuela; area 193 sq km/75 sq mi; population (1996) 66,687 (half of Indian descent). The chief town is Oranjestad. Aruba is an overseas territory of the Netherlands. Languages spoken are Dutch (official) and Papiamento (a Creole language). Tourism is a mainstay of the economy.

arum any of a group of mainly European plants with narrow leaves and a single, usually white, special leaf (spathe) surrounding the spike of tiny flowers. The ornamental arum called the trumpet lily (*Zantedeschia aethiopica*) is a native of South Africa. (Genus *Arum*, family Araceae.)

Arunachal Pradesh state of India, in the Himalayas on the borders of Tibet and Myanmar; area 83,578 km/33,270 sq mi; population (2001 est) 1,091,100 (including over 80 ethnic groups). Formerly part of the state of Assam, Arunachal Pradesh became a state of India in 1987. The main towns include Bomdila and Ziro, while its capital is Itanagar.

Aryan the hypothetical parent language of an ancient people believed to have lived between Central Asia and Eastern Europe and to have reached Persia and India in one direction and Europe in another, some time in the 2nd century BC, diversifying into the various *Indo-European language speakers of later times.

asbestos any of several related minerals of fibrous structure that offer great heat resistance because of their nonflammability and poor conductivity. Commercial asbestos is generally either made from serpentine ('white' asbestos) or from sodium iron silicate ('blue' asbestos). The fibres are woven together or bound by an inert material. Over time the fibres can work loose and, because they are small enough to float freely in the air or be inhaled, asbestos usage is now strictly controlled; exposure to its dust can cause cancer.

Ascension British island of volcanic origin in the South Atlantic, a dependency of *St Helena since 1922; area 88 sq km/34 sq mi; population (2001 est) 1,100 (excluding military personnel). The chief settlement is Georgetown.

ASCII acronym for American Standard Code for Information Interchange, in computing, coding system in which numbers are assigned to letters, di..s, and punctuation symbols. Although computers work in code based on the *binary number system, ASCII numbers are usually quoted as decimal hexadecimal numbers. For example, the decimal number 45 (binary 0101101) represents phen, and 65 (binary 1000001) a capital A. The first 32 codes are used for control functions as carriage return and backspace.

Asclep. in Greek mythology, the god of medicine (Roman Aesculapius); son of *Apollo; father of Panacea and Hygieia, goddess of health. His emblem was the caduceus, a winged staff encoiled by two snakes; the creatures appear to renew life by shedding their skin. His worship originated in Thessaly in northern Greece, but the major sanctuary of the classical period was at Epidaurus. Patients slept in his temple overnight, and treatment was based on their dreams. The cult spread to Rome in 293 BC.

ascorbic acid or **vitamin C** $C_6H_8O_6$, relatively simple organic acid found in citrus fruits and vegetables. It is soluble in water and destroyed by prolonged boiling, so soaking or overcooking of vegetables reduces their vitamin C content. Lack of ascorbic acid results in scurvy.

Ascot small town in Windsor and Maidenhead unitary authority, southern England, about 10 km/6 mi southwest of Windsor; population (1991) 6,200. The Royal Ascot race meeting, established by Queen Anne in 1711, is held annually in June. It is a social as well as a sporting event.

ASEAN acronym for *Association of South East Asian Nations.

asepsis practice of ensuring that bacteria are excluded from open sites during surgery, wound dressing, blood sampling, and other medical procedures. Aseptic technique is a first line of defence against infection.

asexual reproduction reproduction that does not involve the manufacture and fusion of sex cells (gametes) from two parents. Asexual reproduction has advantages in that there is no need to search for a mate; every asexual organism can reproduce on its own. Asexual reproduction can therefore lead to a rapid population build-up. However, every new organism produced by asexual reproduction is genetically identical to the parent – a *clone.

ash any tree of a worldwide group belonging to the olive family, generally with a compound leaf with leaflets arranged on either side of a steam and a winged fruit. Ash is the name given to a few northern European trees and shrubs of the *Fraxinus* genus. Other members of the family include the olive, lilac, and jasmine. The *mountain ash or rowan, which resembles the ash, belongs to the family Rosaceae. (Genus *Fraxinus*, family Oleaceae.)

Ashanti *or* **Asante** region of Ghana, western Africa; area 25,100 sq km/9,700 sq mi; population (1990 est) 2,487,300. Kumasi is the capital. It is the most densely populated region in Ghana, and most of the people are Ashanti. Most are cultivators and the main crop is cocoa, but the region is also noted for its forestry, mining of gold and bauxite, metalwork, and textiles. For more than 200 years Ashanti was an independent kingdom.

Ashe, Arthur (Robert, Jr) (1943–1993) US tennis player and coach. He won the US national men's singles title at Forest Hills and the first US Open in 1968. Known for his exceptionally strong serve, Ashe turned professional in 1969. Playing in an environment that was initially hostile to black participation in a traditionally white sport, he won the Australian Open men's title in 1970 and Wimbledon in 1975. He also topped the world rankings twice, in 1968 and 1975. Cardiac problems ended his playing career in 1979, but he continued his involvement with the sport as captain of the US Davis Cup team, leading them to victory in 1981 and 1982. In 1992 he launched a fund-raising campaign to combat AIDS.

Ashes, the cricket trophy held by the winning team in the England–Australia Test series.

Ashgabat formerly **Poltoratsk** (1919–27); **Ashkhabad** (1927–92), capital of Turkmenistan; population (1999 est) 605,000. Industries include the manufacture of glass, carpets (handwoven 'Bukhara' carpets and rugs are made here), cotton goods, and metalworking. The city is in a spectacular natural setting, between the *Kara-Kum Desert and the Kopet-Dag mountain range.

Ashkenazi plural **Ashkenazim**, any Jew of German or Eastern European descent, as opposed to a Sephardi, of Spanish, Portuguese, or North African descent.

Ashmore and Cartier Islands group of uninhabited Australian islands comprising Middle, East, and West Islands (the Ashmores), and Cartier Island, in the Indian Ocean, about 190 km/120 mi off the northwest coast of Australia; area 5 sq km/2 sq mi. They were transferred to the authority of Australia by Britain in 1931. Formerly administered as part of the Northern Territory, they became a separate territory in 1978. West Ashmore has an automated weather station. Ashmore reef was declared a national nature reserve in 1983.

ashram Indian community whose members lead a simple life of discipline and self-denial and devote themselves to social service. Noted ashrams are those founded by Mahatma Gandhi at Wardha (near Nagpur, Maharashtra state) and poet Rabindranath Tagore at Santiniketan.

Ashton, Frederick William Mallandaine (1904–1988) English choreographer and dancer. He was director of the Royal Ballet, London 1963–70. He studied with Marie Rambert before joining the Sadler's Wells (now Royal) Ballet in 1935 as chief choreographer. His choreography is marked by a soft, pliant, classical lyricism. His many works and long association with Margot Fonteyn, for whom he created her most famous roles, contributed to the worldwide reputation of British ballet and to the popularity of ballet in the mid-20th century. He was knighted in 1962.

Asia largest of the continents, occupying one-third of the total land surface of the world. The origin of the name is unknown, though it seems probable that it was at first used with a restricted local application, gradually extended to the whole continent.

area: 44,000,000 sq km/17,000,000 sq mi **largest cities:** (population over 5 million) Bangkok, Beijing, Chennai (formerly Madras), Delhi, Dhaka, Hong Kong, Hyderabad, Istanbul, Jakarta, Kolkata (formerly Calcutta), Karachi, Lahore, Manila, Mumbai (formerly Bombay), Osaka, Seoul, Shanghai, Shenyang, Tehran, Tianjin, Tokyo **features:** Mount Everest, at 8,872 m/ 29,118 ft is the world's highest mountain; the Dead Sea at –394 m/–1,293 ft is the world's lowest point below sea level; rivers (over 3,200 km/2,000 mi) include Chang Jiang (Yangtze), Huang He (Yellow River), Ob-Irtysh, Amur, Lena, Mekong, Yenisey; lakes (over 18,000 sq km/7,000 sq mi) include the Caspian Sea (the largest lake in the world), the Aral Sea, Lake Baikal (largest freshwater lake in Eurasia), Balkhash; deserts include the Gobi, Takla Makan, Syrian Desert, Arabian Desert, Negev **physical:** lying in the eastern hemisphere, Asia extends from the Arctic Circle to just over 10° south of the Equator. The Asian mainland, which forms the greater part of the Eurasian continent, lies entirely in the northern hemisphere and stretches from Cape Chelyubinsk at its northern extremity to Cape Piai at the southern tip of the Malay Peninsula. From Dezhneva Cape in the east, the mainland extends west over more than 165° longitude to Cape Baba in Turkey **climate:** showing great extremes and contrasts, the heart of the continent becomes bitterly cold in winter and extremely hot in summer. When the heated air over land rises, moisture-laden air from the surrounding seas flows in, bringing heavy monsoon rains to all Southeast Asia, China, and Japan between May and October **industries:** 62% of the population are employed in agriculture; Asia produces 46% of the world's cereal crops (91% of the world's rice); other crops include mangoes (India), groundnuts (India, China), 84% of the world's copra (Philippines, Indonesia), 93% of the world's rubber (Indonesia, Malaysia, Thailand), tobacco (China), flax (China, Russia), 95% of the world's jute (India, Bangladesh, China), cotton (China, India, Pakistan), silk (China, India), fish (Japan, China, Korea, Thailand); China produces 55% of the world's tungsten; 45% of the world's tin is produced by Malaysia, China, and Indonesia; Saudi Arabia is the world's largest producer of oil **population:** (2000 est) 3,672 million; the world's largest population, amounting to more than half the total number of people in the world; between 1950 and 1990 the death rate and infant mortality were reduced by more than 60%; annual growth rate 1.6% (exceeded only by Africa) **language:** predominantly tonal languages (Chinese) and Japanese in the east, Indo-Iranian languages (Hindi, Urdu, Persian) in South Asia, Altaic languages (Mongolian, Turkish) in West and Central Asia, Semitic languages (Arabic, Hebrew) in the southwest **religion:** the major religions of the world had their origins in Asia – Judaism and Christianity in the Middle East; Islam in Arabia; Buddhism, Hinduism, and Sikhism in India; Confucianism in China; and Shintoism in Japan.

Asia Minor historical name for *Anatolia, the Asian part of Turkey.

Asimov, Isaac (1920–1992) Russian-born US author and editor of science fiction and nonfiction. He published more than 400 books, including his science fiction novels *I, Robot* (1950) and the *Foundation trilogy* (1951–53), continued in *Foundation's Edge* (1983). His two-volume work *The Intelligent Man's Guide to Science* (1960) gained critical acclaim.

AS level abbreviation for Advanced Supplementary level, examinations introduced in the UK in 1988 as the equivalent to 'half an *A level' as a means of broadening the sixth-form (age 16–18) curriculum and including more students in the examination system.

Asmara *or* **Asmera** capital of* Eritrea, 64 km/40 mi southwest of the port of Massawa on the Red Sea and 2,300 m/7,546 ft above sea level; population (2002 est) 392,500. Products include beer, clothes, leather goods, cement, and textiles. The University of Asmara is here, together with a naval school, a cathedral and many modern buildings. The population is half Christian and half Muslim.

Asoka (*or* **Ashoka) (lived c. 272–228 BC)** *Mauryan emperor of India c. 268–232 BC, the greatest of the Mauryan rulers. He inherited an empire covering most of north and south-central India which, at its height, had a population of at least 30 million, with its capital at Pataliputra. A devout Buddhist, he renounced militarism and concentrated on establishing an efficient administration with a large standing army and a secret police.

asp any of several venomous snakes, including *Vipera aspis* of southern Europe, allied to the adder, and the Egyptian cobra *Naja haje*, reputed to have been used by the Egyptian queen Cleopatra for her suicide.

asparagus any of a group of plants with small scalelike leaves and many fine, feathery branches. Native to Europe and Asia, *Asparagus officinalis* is cultivated and the tender young shoots (spears) are greatly prized as a vegetable. (Genus *Asparagus*, family Liliaceae.)

aspen any of several species of *poplar tree. The European quaking aspen (*Populus tremula*) has flattened leafstalks that cause the leaves to flutter in the slightest breeze. The soft, light-coloured wood is used for matches and paper pulp. (Genus *Populus*.)

asphalt mineral mixture containing semisolid brown or black *bitumen, used in the construction industry. Asphalt is mixed with rock chips to form paving material, and the purer varieties are used for insulating material and for waterproofing masonry. It can be produced artificially by the distillation of *petroleum.

asphodel either of two related Old World plants of the lily family. The white asphodel or king's spear (*Asphodelus albus*) is found in Italy and Greece, sometimes covering large areas, and providing grazing for sheep. The other asphodel is the yellow asphodel (*Asphodeline lutea*). (Genera *Asphodelus* and *Asphodeline*, family Liliaceae.)

asphyxia suffocation; a lack of oxygen that produces a potentially lethal build-up of carbon dioxide waste in the tissues.

aspidistra any of several Asiatic plants of the lily family. The Chinese *Aspidistra elatior* has broad leaves which taper to a point and, like all aspidistras, grows well in warm indoor conditions. (Genus *Aspidistra*, family Liliaceae.)

aspirin acetylsalicylic acid, a popular pain-relieving drug (*analgesic) developed in the late 19th century as a household remedy for aches and pains. It relieves pain and reduces inflammation and fever. It is the world's most widely used drug.

Asquith, Herbert Henry (1852–1928) 1st Earl of Oxford and Asquith, British Liberal politician, prime

minister 1908–16. As chancellor of the Exchequer, he introduced old-age pensions in 1908. He limited the powers of the House of Lords and attempted to give Ireland *home rule.

ass any of several horselike, odd-toed, hoofed mammals of the genus *Equus*, family Equidae. Species include the African wild ass *E. asinus*, and the Asian wild ass *E. hemionus*. They differ from horses in their smaller size, larger ears, tufted tail, and characteristic bray. Donkeys and burros are domesticated asses.

Assad, Hafez al (1930–2000) Syrian Ba'athist politician, president 1971–2000. He became prime minister after a bloodless military coup in 1970. The following year he became the first president to be elected by popular vote. Having suppressed dissent, he was re-elected in 1978, 1985, 1991, and 1999. He was a Shia (Alawite) Muslim.

Assam state of northeast India; area 78,523 sq km/30,318 sq mi; population (2001 est) 26,638,400. The state includes 12 million Assamese (Hindus), 5 million Bengalis (chiefly Muslim immigrants from Bangladesh), Nepalis, and 2 million indigenous people (Christian and traditional religions). Assamese is the official language. Half of India's oil is produced here, while coal, petrochemicals, paper, and cement are the other main industries. Two-thirds of the population, however, depend on agriculture for their living. Half of India's tea is grown here, but most of the land is devoted to rice cultivation, with jute, sugar, and cotton also being popular crops. Its main towns and cities are Guwahati, Dibrugarh, Silchar, while the capital is Dispur, a suburb of Guwahati.

assassination murder, usually of a political, royal, or public person. The term derives from the order of the Assassins, a Muslim sect that, in the 11th and 12th centuries, murdered officials to further its political ends.

assassin bug member of a family of blood-sucking bugs that contains about 4,000 species. Assassin bugs are mainly predators, feeding on other insects, but some species feed on birds and mammals, including humans. They are found, mainly in tropical regions, although some have established themselves in Europe and North America. Assassin bugs are in the family Reduviidae, suborder Heteroptera, order Hemiptera (true bugs), class Insecta, phylum Arthropoda.

assay in chemistry, the determination of the quantity of a given substance present in a sample. Usually it refers to determining the purity of precious metals.

assembly language low-level computer-programming language closely related to a computer's internal codes. It consists chiefly of a set of short sequences of letters (mnemonics), which are translated, by a program called an assembler, into *machine code for the computer's *central processing unit (CPU) to follow directly. In assembly language, for example, 'JMP' means 'jump' and 'LDA' means 'load accumulator'. Assembly code is used by programmers who need to write very fast or efficient programs.

asset in accounting, anything owned by or owed to the company that is either cash or can be turned into cash. The term covers physical assets such as land or property of a company or individual, as well as financial assets such as cash, payments due from bills, and investments. Assets are divided into fixed assets – assets that are expected to be used in the business for some time such as land, plant, machinery, buildings – and current assets – assets which are frequently turnover in the course of business, such as stock. On a company's balance sheet, total assets mustbe equal to total liabilities (money and services owed).

assimilation in animals, the process by which absorbed food molecules, circulating in the blood, pass into the cells and are used for growth, tissue repair, and other metabolic activities. The actual destiny of each food molecule depends not only on its type, but also on the body requirements at that time.

assize in medieval Europe, the passing of laws, either by the king with the consent of nobles, as in the Constitutions of Clarendon passed by Henry II of England in 1164; or as a complete system, such as the Assizes of Jerusalem, a compilation of the law of the feudal kingdom of Jerusalem in the 13th century.

Association of Caribbean States (ACS) association of 25 states in the Caribbean region, formed in 1994 in Colombia to promote social, political, and economic cooperation and eventual integration. Its members include the states of the Caribbean and Central America plus Colombia, Suriname, and Venezuela. Associate membership has been adopted by 12 dependent territories in the region. Its creation was seen largely as a reaction to the *North American Free Trade Agreement between the USA, Canada, and Mexico, although its far smaller market raised doubts about its vitality.

Association of South East Asian Nations (ASEAN) regional alliance formed in Bangkok in 1967; it took over the non-military role of the Southeast Asia Treaty Organization in 1975. Its members are Indonesia, Malaysia, the Philippines, Singapore, Thailand, (from 1984) Brunei, (from 1995) Vietnam, (from 1997) Laos and Myanmar, and (from 1999) Cambodia; its headquarters are in Jakarta, Indonesia. North Korea took part in the organization for the first time at the 2000 annual meeting of foreign ministers.

assonance the matching of vowel sounds in a line (and sometimes, consonants with differing vowels), generally used in poetry. 'Load' and 'moat', 'farther' and 'harder' are examples of assonance, since they match in vowel sounds and stress pattern, but do not *rhyme. The device is used to emphasize particular words or imagery, and is similar to *alliteration, which involves the repetition of consonants.

assortative mating in population genetics, selective mating in a population between individuals that are genetically related or have similar characteristics. If sufficiently consistent, assortative mating can theoretically result in the evolution of new species without geographical isolation (see *speciation).

Assyria empire in the Middle East c. 2500–612 BC, in northern Mesopotamia (now Iraq); early capital Ashur, later Nineveh. It was initially subject to Sumer and intermittently to Babylon. The Assyrians adopted largely the Sumerian religion and structure of society. At its greatest extent the empire included Egypt and stretched from the eastern Mediterranean coast to the head of the Gulf.

Astaire, Fred (1899–1987) adopted name of Frederick Austerlitz, US dancer, actor, singer, and choreographer. The greatest popular dancer of his time, he starred in numerous films, including Top Hat (1935), Easter Parade (1948), and Funny Face (1957), many containing inventive sequences that he designed and choreographed himself. He made ten classic films with the most popular of his dancing partners, Ginger *Rogers.

Astana formerly Russian Akmolinsk (1824–1961), Tselinograd (1961–93), Akmola (1993–98), commercial and industrial city in northern Kazakhstan, capital of Akmola oblast (region), and from 1998 the capital of Kazakhstan; population (1999 est) 313,000. Astana is situated on the River Ishim, 190 km/118 mi northwest of Qaraghandy, and stands at the centre of a major wheat-farming area of steppe. Agricultural machinery, textiles, and chemicals are produced here. Astana is also located at an important railway junction, and is the site of rolling-stock repair depots. The city replaced *Almaty as the republic's capital in 1998.

astatine chemical symbol At, (Greek astatos 'unstable') non-metallic, radioactive element, atomic number 85, relative atomic mass 210. It is a member of the *halogen group, and is found at the bottom of Group 7 of the *periodic table of the elements. It is very rare in nature. Astatine is highly unstable, with at least 19 isotopes; the longest lived has a *half-life of about eight hours.

aster any plant of a large group belonging to the same subfamily as the daisy. All asters have starlike flowers with yellow centres and outer rays (not petals) varying from blue and purple to white. Asters come in many sizes. Many are cultivated as garden flowers, including the Michaelmas daisy (Aster nova-belgii). (Genus Aster, family Compositae.)

asteroid any of many thousands of small bodies, made of rock and minerals, that orbit the Sun. Most lie in a region called the **asteroid belt** between the orbits of Mars and Jupiter, and are thought to be fragments left over from the formation of the Solar System. About 100,000 asteroids may exist, but their total mass is only a few hundredths of the mass of the Moon. These rocky fragments range in size from 1 km/0.6 mi to 900 km/560 mi in diameter.

asthenosphere layer within Earth's *mantle lying beneath the *lithosphere, typically beginning at a depth of approximately 100 km/63 mi and extending to depths of approximately 260 km/160 mi. Sometimes referred to as the 'weak sphere', it is characterized by being weaker and more elastic than the surrounding mantle. The asthenosphere's elastic behaviour and low viscosity allow the overlying, more rigid plates of lithosphere to move laterally in a process known as *plate tectonics. Its elasticity and viscosity also allow overlying crust and mantle to move vertically in response to gravity to achieve isostatic equilibrium (see *isostasy).

asthma chronic condition characterized by difficulty in breathing due to spasm of the bronchi (air passages) in the lungs. Attacks may be provoked by allergy, infection, and stress. The incidence of asthma may be increasing as a result of air pollution and occupational hazard. Treatment is with bronchodilators to relax the bronchial muscles and thereby ease the breathing, and in severe cases by inhaled *steroids that reduce inflammation of the bronchi.

astigmatism aberration occurring in the lens of the eye. It results when the curvature of the lens differs in two perpendicular planes, so that rays in one plane may be in focus while rays in the other are not. With astigmatic eyesight, the vertical and horizontal cannot be in focus at the same time; correction is by the use of a cylindrical lens that reduces the overall focal length of one plane so that both planes are seen in sharp focus.

Astor Prominent US and British family. **John Jacob Astor** (1763–1848) emigrated from Germany to the USA in 1884, and became a millionaire. His great-grandson **Waldorf Astor**, 2nd Viscount Astor (1879–1952), was a British politician, and served as Conservative member of Parliament for Plymouth from 1910 to 1919, when he succeeded to the peerage. His US-born wife Nancy Witcher Langhorne, **Lady Astor** (1879–1964), was the first woman member of Parliament to take a seat in the House of Commons, when she succeeded her husband in the constituency of Plymouth in November 1919. She remained in parliament until 1945, as an active champion of women's rights, educational issues, and temperance.

astrolabe ancient navigational instrument, forerunner of the sextant. Astrolabes usually consisted of a flat disc with a sighting rod that could be pivoted to point at the Sun or bright stars. From the altitude of the Sun or star above the horizon, the local time could be estimated.

astrology (Greek *astron* 'star', *legein* 'speak') study of the relative position of the planets and stars in the belief that they influence events on Earth. The astrologer casts a horoscope based on the time and place of the subject's birth. Astrology has no proven scientific basis, but has been widespread since ancient times. Western astrology is based on the 12 signs of the zodiac; Chinese astrology is based on a 60-year cycle and lunar calendar.

astrometry measurement of the precise positions of stars, planets, and other bodies in space. Such information is needed for practical purposes including accurate timekeeping, surveying and navigation, and calculating orbits and measuring distances in space. Astrometry is not concerned with the surface features or the physical nature of the body under study.

astronomical unit (AU) unit equal to the mean distance of the Earth from the Sun: 149.6 million km/92.96 million mi. It is used to describe planetary distances. Light travels this distance in approximately 8.3 minutes.

astronomy science of the celestial bodies: the Sun, the Moon, and the planets; the stars and galaxies; and all other objects in the universe. It is concerned with their positions, motions, distances, and physical conditions and with their origins and evolution. Astronomy thus divides into fields such as astrophysics, celestial mechanics, and *cosmology. See also *gamma-ray astronomy, *infrared astronomy, *radio astronomy, *ultraviolet astronomy, and *X-ray astronomy.

astrophysics study of the physical nature of stars, galaxies, and the universe. It began with the development of spectroscopy in the 19th century, which allowed astronomers to analyse the composition of stars from their light. Astrophysicists view the universe as a vast natural laboratory in which they can study matter under conditions of temperature, pressure, and density that are unattainable on Earth.

Asturias autonomous community and province of northern Spain; area 10,565 sq km/4,079 sq mi; population (2001 est) 1,075,300. The region is crossed by the well-forested Cantabrian Mountains and drained by numerous swift rivers. The mountain climate favours a large dairy industry, while along the coast, apple orchards produce the areaouths world-famous cider; corn is an important crop, and sheep and other livestock are reared. In the past Asturias produced half of Spain's coal; most of the coal mines have since closed down. Oviedo (the capital) and Gijón are the main industrial towns. Gijón is also the chief port, and fishing is a major occupation.

Asunción capital and chief port of Paraguay, situated on the east bank of the Paraguay River, near its confluence with the River Pilcomayo; population (2002 est) 513,400 (metropolitan area 1,620,500); there are textile, footwear, furniture, tobacco, and food-processing industries. The climate is subtropical, and cattle are raised in the surrounding area; maize, cotton, sugar, fruit, and tobacco are grown, and meat, timber, and cotton are the leading exports.

asylum, political in international law, refuge granted in another country to a person who, for political reasons, cannot return to his or her own country without putting himself or herself in danger. A person seeking asylum is a type of *refugee, someone who has fled their own country because of a well-founded fear of persecution for reasons of race, religion, nationality, political opinion, or membership in a particular social group, and who cannot or does not want to return.

asymptote in *coordinate geometry, a straight line that a curve approaches progressively more closely but never reaches. The x and y axes are asymptotes to the graph of xy = constant (a rectangular *hyperbola).

Atacama Desert arid coastal region of northern Chile, with an area of about 80,000 sq km/31,000 sq mi, and extending south from the Peruvian border for 965 km/600 mi. It consists of a series of salt pans within a plateau region. Its rainless condition is caused by the *Peru Current offshore; any moist airstreams from the Amazon basin are blocked by the Andean Mountains. The desert has silver and copper mines, and extensive nitrate and iodine deposits. The main population centres are the ports of Antofagasta and Iquique.

Atahualpa (c. 1502–1533) Last emperor of the Incas of Peru. He was taken prisoner in 1532 when the Spaniards arrived and agreed to pay a substantial ransom, but he was accused of plotting against the conquistador Pizarro and was sentenced to be burned. On his consenting to Christian baptism, the sentence was commuted to strangulation.

Atatürk, Kemal (1881–1938) born Mustafa Kemal Pasha, (Turkish 'Father of the Turks') Turkish politician and general, first president of Turkey from 1923. After World War I he established a provisional rebel government and in 1921–22 the Turkish armies under his leadership expelled the Greeks who were occupying Turkey. He was the founder of the modern republic, which he ruled as a virtual dictator, with a policy of consistent and radical Westernization.

atavism (Latin *atavus* 'ancestor') in genetics, the reappearance of a characteristic not apparent in the immediately preceding generations; in psychology, the manifestation of primitive forms of behaviour.

ataxia loss of muscular coordination due to neurological damage or disease.

Athanasian creed one of the three ancient *creeds of the Christian church. Mainly a definition of the Trinity and Incarnation, it was written many years after the death of Athanasius, but was attributed to him as the chief upholder of Trinitarian doctrine.

atheism nonbelief in, or the positive denial of, the existence of a God or gods. A related concept is *agnosticism. Like theism, its opposite, atheism cannot be proved or disproved conclusively.

Athelstan (895–939) King of England 924–39. The son of *Edward the Elder, Athelstan brought about English unity by ruling both Mercia and Wessex. He defeated an invasion by Scots, Irish, and the men of Strathclyde at Brunanburh in 937. He overcame the Scandinavian kingdom based in York and increased English power on the Welsh and Scottish borders.

Athena *or* **Athene** *or* **Pallas Athena** in Greek mythology, the goddess of war, wisdom, and the arts and crafts (Roman **Minerva**). She was reputed to have sprung fully-armed and grown from the head of Zeus, after he had swallowed her mother Metis, the Titaness of wisdom. In Homer's Odyssey, Athena is the protector of *Odysseus and his son Telemachus. Her chief cult centre was the *Parthenon in Athens, and her principal festival was the Panathenaea, held every fourth year in August.

Athens Greek **Athinai**, capital city of Greece and of ancient Attica; population (2003 est) 747,300, urban agglomeration 3,247,000. Situated 8 km/5 mi northeast of its port of Piraeus on the Gulf of Aegina, it is built around the rocky hills of the Acropolis (around 150 m/ 492 ft) and the Areopagus (112 m/367 ft), and is overlooked from the northeast by the hill of Lycabettus (277 m/909 ft). It lies in the south of the central plain of Attica, between the Kifissos and Eilissos rivers. Athens is Greece's largest city and its administrative, economic and cultural centre; it is also an important tourist centre. It has less green space than any other European capital (4%) and severe air and noise pollution. Athens hosted the Olympic Games in 2004.

atherosclerosis thickening and hardening of the walls of the arteries, associated with atheroma.

athletics competitive track and field events consisting of running, throwing, and jumping disciplines. Running events range from sprint races (100 metres) and hurdles to cross-country running and the *marathon (26 miles 385 yards). Jumping events are the high jump, long jump, triple jump, and pole vault. Throwing events are javelin, discus, shot put, and hammer throw.

Athos mountainous peninsula on the Macedonian coast of Greece. Its peak is 2,033 m/6,672 ft high. The promontory is occupied by a group of 20 Orthodox monasteries, inhabited by some 3,000 monks and lay brothers. A council of representatives from the monasteries runs the affairs of the peninsula as a self-governing republic under the protection of the Greek government.

Atlanta capital and largest city of *Georgia, situated 300 m/984 ft above sea level in the foothills of the Blue Ridge Mountains; seat of Fulton County; population (2000 est) 416,500. It is the headquarters of Coca-Cola and also since 1994 EarthLink, an Internet service provider second only to AOL in the USA. Ford and Lockheed motor-vehicle and aircraft assembly plants are located in the city. Atlanta hosted the 1996 Olympic Games. The area was named Marthasville in 1843, it was renamed Atlanta in 1843 and was incorporated as a city in 1847; it became state capital in 1868.

Atlantic, Battle of the German campaign during World War I to prevent merchant shipping from delivering food supplies from the USA to the Allies, chiefly the UK. By 1917, some 875,000 tons of shipping had been lost. The odds were only turned by the belated use of naval convoys and depth charges to deter submarine attack.

Atlantic, Battle of the during World War II, continuous battle fought in the Atlantic Ocean by the sea and air forces of the Allies and Germany, to control the supply routes to the UK. It is estimated that the Allies destroyed nearly 800 U-boats, and at least 2,200 convoys (75,000 merchant ships) crossed the Atlantic, protected by Allied naval forces.

Atlantic City seaside resort on Absecon Island, Atlantic County, southeastern New Jersey, USA; population (2000 est) 40,500. Formerly a family resort, Atlantic City is now a centre for casino gambling, which was legalized here in 1978 to help revive the flagging tourist trade. Other industries include shell fishing.

Atlantic Ocean ocean lying between Europe and Africa to the east and the Americas to the west; area of basin 81,500,000 sq km/31,500,000 sq mi; including the Arctic Ocean and Antarctic seas, 106,200,000 sq km/ 41,000,000 sq mi. It is generally divided by the Equator into the North Atlantic and South Atlantic. It was probably named after the legendary island continent of *Atlantis. The average depth is 3 km/2 mi; greatest depth is at the Milwaukee Depth in the Puerto Rico Trench 8,648 m/ 28,374 ft. The Mid-Atlantic Ridge, of which the Azores, Ascension, St Helena, and Tristan da Cunha form part, divides it from north to south. Lava welling up from this central area annually increases the distance between South America and Africa. The North Atlantic is the saltiest of the main oceans and has the largest tidal range.

Atlantis in Greek mythology, an island continent west of the Straits of Gibraltar, said to have sunk following an earthquake. Although the Atlantic Ocean is probably named after it, the structure of the sea bed rules out its former existence in the Atlantic region. Derived from an Egyptian priest's account, the Greek philosopher Plato created an imaginary early history for the island in Timaeus and Critias, describing it as a utopia (perfect place) submerged 9,000 years previously as punishment for waging war against Athens; an act deemed impious.

Atlas in Greek mythology, one of the *Titans who revolted against the gods; as punishment, he was compelled to support the heavens on his head and shoulders. Growing weary, he asked *Perseus to turn him into stone by showing him the *Medusa's head, and was transformed into Mount Atlas.

Atlas Mountains mountain system of northwest Africa, stretching 2,400 km/1,500 mi from the Atlantic coast of Morocco to the Gulf of Gabes, Tunisia, and lying between the Mediterranean on the north and the Sahara on the south. The highest peak is Mount Toubkal 4,165 m/13,665 ft.

atmosphere mixture of gases surrounding a planet. Planetary atmospheres are prevented from escaping by the pull of gravity. On Earth, atmospheric pressure decreases with altitude. In its lowest layer, the atmosphere consists of nitrogen (78%) and oxygen (21%), both in molecular form (two atoms bonded together) and argon (1%). Small quantities of other gases are important to the chemistry and physics of the Earth's atmosphere, including water, carbon dioxide, and traces of other noble gases (rare gases), as well as ozone. The atmosphere plays a major part in the various cycles of nature (the *water cycle, the *carbon cycle, and the *nitrogen cycle). It is the principal industrial source of nitrogen, oxygen, and argon, which are obtained by the *fractional distillation of liquid air.

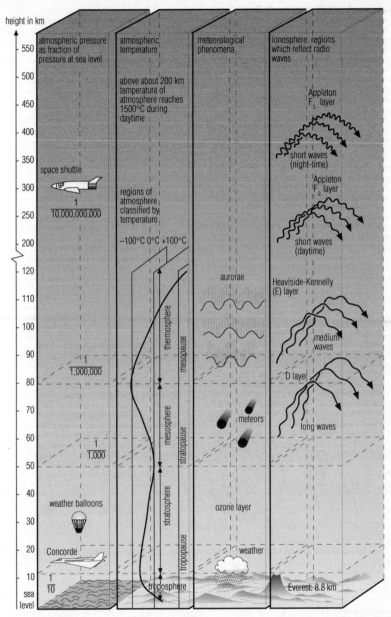

height in km

- 550 — atmospheric pressure as fraction of pressure at sea level | atmospheric temperature | meteorological phenomena | ionosphere: regions which reflect radio waves

above about 200 km temperature of atmosphere reaches 1500°C during daytime

Appleton F₁ layer

short waves (night-time)

space shuttle

$\frac{1}{10,000,000,000}$

regions of atmosphere classified by temperature

Appleton F₂ layer

short waves (daytime)

−100°C 0°C +100°C

aurorae

Heaviside-Kennelly (E) layer

thermosphere

mesopause

medium waves

$\frac{1}{1,000,000}$

D layer

meteors

long waves

mesosphere

stratopause

$\frac{1}{1,000}$

weather balloons

stratosphere

ozone layer

Concorde

tropopause

weather

$\frac{1}{10}$

troposphere

Everest: 8.8 km

atmosphere All but 1% of the Earth's atmosphere lies in a layer 30 km/19 mi above the ground. At a height of 5,500 m/18,000 ft, air pressure is half that at sea level. The temperature of the atmosphere varies greatly with height; this produces a series of layers, called the troposphere, stratosphere, mesosphere, and thermosphere.

atmosphere symbol atm; or **standard atmosphere**, in physics, a unit of pressure equal to 760 mmHg, 1013.25 millibars, or 1.01325×10^5 pascals, or newtons per square metre. The actual pressure exerted by the atmosphere fluctuates around this value, which is assumed to be standard at sea level and 0 °C/32 °F, and is used when dealing with very high pressures. (See diagram, p. 59.)

atmospheric pressure pressure at any point on the Earth's surface that is due to the weight of the column of air above it; it therefore decreases as altitude increases, because there is less air above. Particles in the air exert a force (pressure) against surfaces; when large numbers of particles press against a surface, the overall effect is known as air pressure. At sea level the average pressure is 101 kilopascals (1,013 millibars, or 760 mm Hg, or 14.7 lb per sq in, or 1 atmosphere). Changes in atmospheric pressure, measured with a barometer, are used in weather forecasting. Areas of relatively high pressure are called *anticyclones; areas of low pressure are called *depressions.

atoll continuous or broken circle of *coral reef and low coral islands surrounding a lagoon.

atom (Greek *atomos* 'undivided') smallest unit of matter that can take part in a chemical reaction, and which cannot be broken down chemically into anything simpler. An atom is made up of protons and neutrons in a central nucleus (except for hydrogen, which has a single proton in its nucleus) surrounded by electrons (see *atomic structure). The atoms of the various elements differ in atomic number, relative atomic mass, and chemical behaviour.

atom, electronic structure of arrangement of electrons around the nucleus of an atom, in distinct energy levels, also called atomic orbitals, or shells. These shells can be regarded as a series of concentric spheres, each of which can contain a certain maximum number of electrons; the noble gases (rare gases) have an arrangement in which every shell contains this number. The energy levels are usually numbered beginning with the shell nearest to the nucleus. The outermost shell is known as the *valency shell as it contains the valence electrons.

sodium 2.8.1   sulphur 2.8.6

atom, electronic structure The arrangement of electrons in a sodium atom and a sulphur atom. The number of electrons in a neutral atom gives that atom its atomic number: sodium has an atomic number of 11 and sulphur has an atomic number of 16.

atomic bomb or **atom bomb** bomb deriving its explosive force from nuclear fission (see *nuclear energy) as a result of a neutron chain reaction, developed in the 1940s in the USA into a usable weapon.

atomic clock timekeeping device regulated by various periodic processes occurring in atoms and molecules, such as atomic vibration or the frequency of absorbed or emitted radiation.

atomic mass see *relative atomic mass.

atomic mass unit or **dalton** symbol u, unit of mass that is used to measure the relative mass of atoms and molecules. It is equal to one-twelfth of the mass of a carbon-12 atom, which is approximately the mass of a proton or 1.66×10^{-27} kg. The *relative atomic mass of an atom has no units; thus oxygen-16 has an atomic mass of 16 daltons and a relative atomic mass of 16.

atomic number or **proton number** symbol Z, number of protons in the nucleus of an atom. It is equal to the positive charge on the nucleus. In a neutral atom, it is also equal to the number of electrons surrounding the nucleus. The chemical elements are arranged in the *periodic table of the elements according to their atomic number. Nuclear notation is used to label an atom according to the composition of its nucleus.

atomic radiation energy given out by disintegrating atoms during *radioactive decay, whether natural or synthesized. The energy may be in the form of fast-moving particles, known as *alpha particles and *beta particles, or in the form of high-energy electromagnetic waves known as *gamma radiation. Overlong exposure to atomic radiation can lead to *radiation sickness.

atomic structure internal structure of an *atom.

the nucleus The core of the atom is the **nucleus**, a dense body only one ten-thousandth the diameter of the atom itself. The simplest nucleus, that of hydrogen, comprises a single stable positively charged particle, the **proton**. Nuclei of other elements contain more protons and additional particles, called **neutrons**, of about the same mass as the proton but with no electrical charge. Each element has its own characteristic nucleus with a unique number of protons, the atomic number. The number of neutrons may vary. Where atoms of a single element have different numbers of neutrons, they are called *isotopes. Although some isotopes tend to be unstable and exhibit *radioactivity, all those of a single element have identical chemical properties.

electrons The nucleus is surrounded by a number of moving electrons, each of which has a negative charge equal to the positive charge on a proton, but which has a mass of only $\frac{1}{1,836}$ times as much. In a neutral atom, the nucleus is surrounded by the same number of electrons as it contains protons. According to *quantum theory, the position of an electron is uncertain; it may be found at any point. However, it is more likely to be found in some places than others. The region of space in which an electron is most likely to be found is called an atomic orbital. The chemical properties of an element are determined by the ease with which its atoms can gain or lose electrons.

atomic weight another name for *relative atomic mass.

atonality music that has no sense of *tonality and no obvious key. Atonal music uses the notes of the chromatic scale and, depending on the system employed, uses all twelve pitch classes in hierarchies other than triadic harmony. This means that there is no pull towards any particular tonic note.

atonement in Christian theology, the doctrine that Jesus suffered on the cross to bring about reconciliation and forgiveness between God and humanity.

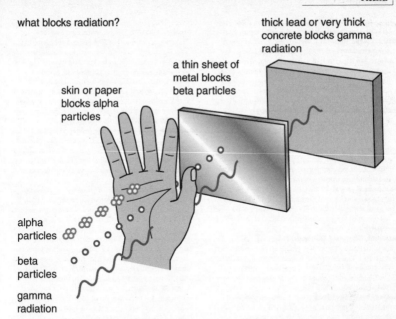

what blocks radiation?

skin or paper blocks alpha particles

a thin sheet of metal blocks beta particles

thick lead or very thick concrete blocks gamma radiation

alpha particles

beta particles

gamma radiation

atomic radiation Atomic radiation may be in the form of alpha particles, beta particles, or gamma radiation. Alpha particles are fast-moving and consist of two protons and two neutrons. Because they have a relatively large mass, alpha particles have a range of up to 10 cm in air and can be stopped by skin or thin paper. Beta particles are electrons created and then instantly ejected from a radioactive atom. They have a greater range in air than alpha particles and can be stopped by a thin sheet of metal, such as aluminium. Gamma radiation is high-frequency, high-energy electromagnetic radiation. It is very penetrating and can only be blocked by thick lead or very thick concrete.

Atonement, Day of Jewish holy day of *Yom Kippur.

ATP abbreviation for **adenosine triphosphate**, nucleotide molecule found in all cells. It can yield large amounts of energy, and is used to drive the thousands of biological processes needed to sustain life, growth, movement, and reproduction. Green plants use light energy to manufacture ATP as part of the process of *photosynthesis. In animals, ATP is formed by the breakdown of glucose molecules, usually obtained from the carbohydrate component of a diet, in a series of reactions termed *respiration. It is the driving force behind muscle contraction and the synthesis of complex molecules needed by individual cells.

atrium in architecture, an open inner courtyard. An atrium was originally the central court or main room of an ancient Roman house, open to the sky, often with a shallow pool to catch rainwater.

atropine alkaloid derived from *belladonna, a plant with toxic properties. It acts as an anticholinergic, inhibiting the passage of certain nerve impulses. It is used in premedication, to reduce bronchial and gastric secretions. It is also administered as a mild antispasmodic drug, and to dilate the pupil of the eye.

Attenborough, Richard (Samuel) (1923–) Baron Attenborough, English director, actor, and producer. He appeared in such films as *Brighton Rock* (1947) and *10 Rillington Place* (1971), and directed *Oh! What a*

Lovely War (1969), and such biopics as *Gandhi* (which won eight Academy Awards including Best Picture and Best Director) (1982) and *Cry Freedom* (1987).

attention-deficit hyperactivity disorder (ADHD) psychiatric condition occurring in young children characterized by impaired attention and hyperactivity. The disorder, associated with disruptive behaviour, learning difficulties, and under-achievement, is more common in boys. It is treated with methylphenidate (Ritalin). There was a 50% increase in the use of the drug in the USA 1994–96, with an estimated 5% of school-age boys diagnosed as suffering from ADHD. In 1998 the number of children and adults in the USA taking medication for ADHD (mostly Ritalin) was approximately 4 million. In the UK the prescription of Ritalin doubles each year.

Attica Greek *Attiki*, region of Greece comprising Athens and the district around it; area 3,381 sq km/1,305 sq mi; population (2003 est) 3,812,000. It is renowned for its language, art, and philosophical thought in Classical times, when Athens, Piraeus, and Eleusis were its major towns. It is a prefecture of modern Greece, with Athens as its capital.

Attila (c. 406–453) King of the Huns in an area from the Alps to the Caspian Sea from 434, known to later Christian history as the 'Scourge of God'. He twice attacked the Eastern Roman Empire to increase the quantity of tribute paid to him, 441–443 and 447–449, and then attacked the Western Roman Empire 450–452.

Attis *or* **Atys** in classical mythology, a Phrygian god whose death and resurrection symbolized the end of winter and the arrival of spring; also regarded as a vegetation god. Beloved by the earth goddess Cybele, who drove him mad as punishment for his infidelity, he castrated himself and bled to death. Violets sprang from his blood, and Zeus turned him into a pine tree.

Attlee, Clement (Richard) (1883–1967) 1st Earl Attlee, British Labour politician. In the coalition government during World War II he was Lord Privy Seal 1940–42, dominions secretary 1942–43, and Lord President of the Council 1943–45, as well as deputy prime minister from 1942. As prime minister 1945–51 he introduced a sweeping programme of nationalization and a whole new system of social services.

Attorney General in the UK, principal law officer of the crown and head of the English Bar; the post is one of great political importance. In the USA, it is the chief law officer of the government and head of the Department of Justice.

Atwood, Margaret (Eleanor) (1939–) Canadian novelist, short-story writer, and poet. Her novels often treat feminist themes with wit and irony, and include *The Handmaid's Tale* (1986, filmed 1990, opera 2003), *The Blind Assassin* (2000, Booker Prize), and *Oryx and Crake* (2003).

aubergine *or* **eggplant** plant belonging to the nightshade family, native to tropical Asia. Its purple-skinned, sometimes white, fruits are eaten as a vegetable. (Solanum melongena, family Solanaceae.)

Aubrey, John (1626–1697) English biographer and antiquary. He was the first to claim Stonehenge as a Druid temple. His *Lives*, begun in 1667, contains gossip, anecdotes, and valuable insights into the celebrities of his time. It was published as *Brief Lives* in 1898. *Miscellanies* (1696), a work on folklore and ghost stories, was the only work to be published during his lifetime.

aubrieta any of a group of spring-flowering dwarf perennial plants native to the Middle East. All are trailing plants with showy, purple flowers. They are widely cultivated in rock gardens. (Genus *Aubrieta*, family Cruciferae.)

Auckland largest city in New Zealand, in the north of North Island, in an area of impressive volcanic scenery; population (2001 est) 367,700. It fills the isthmus that separates its two harbours (Waitemata and Manukau), and is part of the largest conurbation in the country which includes the cities of Manukau, North Shore, and Waitakere. It is the country's chief port and leading industrial centre, with iron and steel plants, engineering, car assembly, textiles, food processing, sugar refining, and brewing. Exports include the products of pastoral farming such as dairy products, meat, and leather. Auckland was officially founded as New Zealand's capital in 1840, remaining so until 1865.

Auden, W(ystan) H(ugh) (1907–1973) English-born US poet. He wrote some of his most original poetry, such as *Look, Stranger!* (1936), in the 1930s when he led the influential left-wing literary group that included the writers Louis MacNeice, Stephen *Spender, and Cecil *Day-Lewis. Auden moved to the USA in 1939, became a US citizen in 1946, and adopted a more conservative and Christian viewpoint, for

example in *The Age of Anxiety* (1947). He also wrote verse dramas with English writer Christopher *Isherwood, such as *The Dog Beneath the Skin* (1935) and *The Ascent of F6* (1936), and opera librettos, notably for Russian-born composer Igor Stravinsky's *The Rake's Progress* (1951). Auden was professor of poetry at Oxford 1956–61. His last works, including *Academic Graffiti* (1971) and *Thank You, Fog* (1973), are light and mocking in style and tone, but are dazzling virtuoso performances by a poet who recognized his position as the leading writer in verse of his time.

Audubon, John James (1785–1851) US naturalist and artist. In 1827, after extensive travels and observations of birds, he published the first part of his *Birds of North America*, with a remarkable series of colour plates. Later he produced a similar work on North American quadrupeds.

Augean stables in Greek mythology, the stables of Augeas, king of Elis in southern Greece. The yards, containing 3,000 cattle, had not been swept for 30 years. *Heracles had to clean them as one of 12 labours set by Eurystheus, king of Argos; a feat accomplished in one day by diverting the rivers Peneius and Alpheus.

Augsburg, Confession of statement of the Lutheran faith composed by Philip *Melanchthon. Presented to the Holy Roman Emperor Charles V, at the Diet of Augsburg in 1530, it was intended originally as a working document for the negotiations at the Diet aiming at reconciliation between Lutherans and Catholics. It came, however, to be seen as the crucial expression of Lutheran beliefs.

augur member of a college of Roman priests who interpreted the will of the gods from signs or 'auspices' such as the flight, song, or feeding of birds, the condition of the entrails of sacrificed animals, and the direction of thunder and lightning. Their advice was sought before battle and on other important occasions. Consuls and other high officials had the right to consult the auspices themselves, and a campaign was said to be conducted 'under the auspices' of the general who had consulted the gods.

Augustan Age age of the Roman emperor *Augustus (31 BC–AD 14), during which art and literature flourished. It is also used to characterize the work of 18th-century writers who adopted the style, themes, and structure of classical texts.

Augustine of Hippo, St (354–430) born Aurelius Augustinus, One of the early Christian leaders and writers known as the Fathers of the Church. He was converted to Christianity by Ambrose in Milan and became bishop of Hippo (modern Annaba, Algeria) in 396. Among Augustine's many writings are his *Confessions*, a spiritual autobiography, and *De Civitate Dei/The City of God*, vindicating the Christian church and divine providence in 22 books.

Augustine, St (died 605) First archbishop of Canterbury, England. He was sent from Rome to convert England to Christianity by Pope Gregory I. He landed at Ebbsfleet in Kent in 597 and soon after baptized Ethelbert, King of Kent, along with many of his subjects. He was consecrated bishop of the English at Arles in the same year, and appointed archbishop in 601, establishing his see at Canterbury. Feast day is 26 May.

Augustinian member of a religious community that follows the Rule of St *Augustine of Hippo. It includes the Canons of St Augustine, Augustinian Friars and Hermits, Premonstratensians, Gilbertines, and Trinitarians.

Augustus (63 BC–AD 14) Title of Octavian (born Gaius Octavius), first Roman emperor 31 BC–AD 14. He joined forces with *Mark Antony and Lepidus in the Second Triumvirate. Following Mark Antony's liaison with the Egyptian queen *Cleopatra, Augustus defeated her troops at Actium in 31 BC. As emperor he reformed the government of the empire, the army, and Rome's public services, and was a patron of the arts. The period of his rule is known as the *Augustan Age.

auk oceanic bird belonging to the family Alcidae, order Charadriiformes, consisting of 22 species of marine diving birds including razorbills, puffins, murres, and guillemots. Confined to the northern hemisphere, their range extends from well inside the Arctic Circle to the lower temperate regions. They feed on fish, and use their wings to 'fly' underwater in pursuit.

Aung San (1916–1947) Burmese (Myanmar) politician. He was a founder and leader of the Anti-Fascist People's Freedom League, which led Burma's fight for independence from the UK. During World War II he collaborated first with Japan and then with the UK. In 1947 he became head of Burma's provisional government but was assassinated the same year by political opponents. His daughter *Suu Kyi spearheaded a nonviolent pro-democracy movement in Myanmar from 1988.

Aung San Suu Kyi Burmese (Myanmar) politician; see *Suu Kyi.

Aurangzeb (or Aurungzebe) (1618–1707) Mogul emperor of northern India from 1658. Third son of *Shah Jahan, he made himself master of the court by a palace revolution. His reign was the most brilliant period of the Mogul dynasty, but his despotic tendencies and Muslim fanaticism aroused much opposition. His latter years were spent in war with the princes of Rajputana and the Marathas and Sikhs. His drive south into the Deccan overextended Mogul resources.

Aurelian (c. AD 215–275) born Lucius Domitius Aurelianus, Roman emperor 270–75. A successful soldier, he was proclaimed emperor by his troops on the death of Claudius II. He campaigned on the Danube and then defeated a large raid into Italy mounted by the Alamanni and Juthungi. He moved east and captured Queen Zenobia of Palmyra (now Tadmur, Syria) by the end of 272, destroying Palmyra itself in 273. He was planning a campaign against the Persians when he was murdered by a group of his own officers.

Aurelius, Marcus Roman emperor; see *Marcus Aurelius Antoninus.

Auriga constellation of the northern hemisphere, represented as a charioteer. Its brightest star is the first-magnitude *Capella, about 42 light years from the Sun; Epsilon Aurigae is an *eclipsing binary star with a period of 27 years, the longest of its kind (last eclipse in 1983).

aurochs plural **aurochs**, extinct species of long-horned wild cattle *Bos primigenius* that formerly roamed Europe, southwestern Asia, and North Africa. It survived in Poland until 1627. Black to reddish or grey, it was up to 1.8 m/6 ft at the shoulder. It is depicted in many cave paintings, and is considered the ancestor of domestic cattle.

aurora coloured light in the night sky near the Earth's magnetic poles, called **aurora borealis** ('northern lights') in the northern hemisphere and **aurora australis** ('southern lights') in the southern hemisphere. Although auroras are usually restricted to the polar skies, fluctuations in the *solar wind occasionally cause them to be visible at lower latitudes. An aurora is usually in the form of a luminous arch with its apex towards the magnetic pole, followed by arcs, bands, rays, curtains, and coronae, usually green but often showing shades of blue and red, and sometimes yellow or white. Auroras are caused at heights of over 100 km/60 mi by a fast stream of charged particles from solar flares and low-density 'holes' in the Sun's corona. These are guided by the Earth's magnetic field towards the north and south magnetic poles, where they enter the upper atmosphere and bombard the gases in the atmosphere, causing them to emit visible light.

Aurora in Roman mythology, goddess of the dawn (Greek *Eos*). Preceded by her sons, the fresh morning winds, she would fly or drive a chariot across the sky to announce the approach of *Apollo's chariot bearing the sun.

Auschwitz Polish Oswiecim, town near Kraków in Poland; the site of the notorious Auschwitz-Birkenau *concentration camp used by the Nazis in World War II to exterminate Jews and other political and social minorities, as part of the 'final solution'; population (1992 est) 45,100. The camp's four gas chambers, disguised as bathhouses and with crematoria attached, had a combined capacity to kill over 12,000 people a day.

Austen, Jane (1775–1817) English novelist. She described her raw material as 'three or four families in a Country Village'. *Sense and Sensibility* was published in 1811, *Pride and Prejudice* in 1813, *Mansfield Park* in 1814, *Emma* in 1816, and *Northanger Abbey* and *Persuasion* together in 1818, all anonymously. She observed speech and manners with wit and precision, and her penetrating observation of human behaviour results in insights that go beyond the limitations of the historical period. Many of her works have been successfully adapted for film and television.

Austerlitz, Battle of battle on 2 December 1805, in which the French forces of Emperor Napoleon Bonaparte defeated those of Alexander I of Russia and Francis II of Austria at a small town in the Czech Republic (formerly in Austria), 19 km/12 mi east of Brno. The battle was one of Napoleon's greatest victories, resulting in the end of the coalition against France – the Austrians signed the Treaty of Pressburg and the Russians retired to their own territory.

Australia
National name: *Commonwealth of Australia*
Area: 7,682,850 sq km/2,966,136 sq mi
Capital: Canberra
Major towns/cities: Adelaide, Alice Springs, Brisbane, Darwin, Melbourne, Perth, Sydney, Hobart, Newcastle, Wollongong
Physical features: Ayers Rock; Arnhem Land; Gulf of Carpentaria; Cape York Peninsula; Great Australian Bight; Great Sandy Desert; Gibson Desert; Great Victoria Desert; Simpson Desert; the Great Barrier Reef; Great Dividing Range and Australian Alps in the east (Mount Kosciusko, 2,229 m/7,136 ft, Australia's highest peak). The fertile southeast region is watered by the Darling, Lachlan, Murrumbridgee, and Murray rivers. Lake Eyre basin and Nullarbor Plain in the south

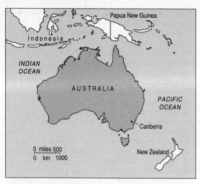

Territories: Norfolk Island, Christmas Island, Cocos (Keeling) Islands, Ashmore and Cartier Islands, Coral Sea Islands, Heard Island and McDonald Islands, Australian Antarctic Territory

Head of state: Queen Elizabeth II from 1952, represented by Governor General Michael Jeffery from 2003

Head of government: John Howard from 1996

Political system: liberal democracy

Political executive: parliamentary

Political parties: Australian Labor Party, moderate left of centre; Liberal Party of Australia, moderate, liberal, free enterprise; National Party of Australia (formerly Country Party), centrist non-metropolitan; Australian Democratic Party (AD), liberal, moderately left wing; One Nation (ON), right-wing racist and anti-immigrant

Currency: Australian dollar

GNI per capita (PPP): (US$) 26,960 (2002 est)

Exports: major world producer of raw materials: iron ore, aluminium, coal, nickel, zinc, lead, gold, tin, tungsten, uranium, crude oil; wool, meat, cereals, fruit, sugar, wine. Principal market: Japan 19.3% (2000)

Population: 19,731,000 (2003 est)

Language: English (official), Aboriginal languages

Religion: Anglican 26%, Roman Catholic 26%, other Christian 24%

Life expectancy: 76 (men); 82 (women) (2000–05)

Chronology

c. **40,000 BC:** Aboriginal immigration from southern India, Sri Lanka, and Southeast Asia.

AD 1606: First recorded sightings of Australia by Europeans including discovery of Cape York by Dutch explorer Willem Jansz in *Duyfken*.

1770: Capt James Cook claimed New South Wales for Britain.

1788: Sydney founded as British penal colony.

late 18th–19th centuries: Great age of exploration.

1804: Castle Hill Rising by Irish convicts in New South Wales.

1813: Crossing of Blue Mountains removed major barrier to exploration of interior.

1825: Tasmania seceded from New South Wales.

1829: Western Australia colonized.

1836: South Australia colonized.

1840–68: End of convict transportation.

1850: British Act of Parliament permitted Australian colonies to draft their own constitutions and achieve virtual self-government.

1851–61: Gold rushes contributed to exploration and economic growth.

1851: Victoria seceded from New South Wales.

1855: Victoria achieved self-government.

1856: New South Wales, South Australia, and Tasmania achieved self-government.

1859: Queensland was formed from New South Wales and achieved self-government.

1890: Western Australia achieved self-government.

1891: Depression gave rise to the Australian Labor Party.

1901: The Commonwealth of Australia was created.

1919: Australia was given mandates over Papua New Guinea and the Solomon Islands.

1927: The seat of federal government moved to Canberra.

1931: Statute of Westminster confirmed Australian independence.

1933: Western Australia's vote to secede was overruled.

1948–75: Influx of around 2 million new immigrants, chiefly from continental Europe.

1967: A referendum gave Australian Aborigines full citizenship rights.

1970s: Japan became Australia's chief trading partner.

1974: 'White Australia' immigration restrictions were abolished.

1975: Papua New Guinea became independent.

1978: Northern Territory achieved self-government.

1986: The Australia Act was passed by British Parliament, eliminating the last vestiges of British legal authority in Australia.

1988: A Free Trade Agreement was signed with New Zealand.

1992: The Citizenship Act removed the oath of allegiance to the British crown.

1998: John Howard's Liberal–National coalition government was re-elected.

1999: Australians voted to keep the British queen as head of state, rather than become a republic.

2000: Torrential rains in much of eastern Australia during November caused widespread flooding in rural areas.

2001: The ruling Liberal Party lost two state elections as the economy suffered a sharp slowdown.

2002: Over 90 Australians were killed in terrorist bombing of a nightclub in Bali, Indonesia.

2003: Devastating bushfires threatened the major cities of Canberra and Sydney. The Senate passed a motion of no confidence against Prime Minister John Howard over his handling of the Iraq crisis.

2004: The government was cleared of manipulating military intelligence during the Iraq crisis. John Howard's Liberal–National coalition government was re-elected. The Australian embassy in Jakarta, Indonesia was bombed.

2005: Australia experienced the worst bush fires for over 20 years.

Australian Aborigine member of any of the 500 groups of indigenous inhabitants of the continent of Australia, who migrated to this region from South Asia about 40,000 years ago. Traditionally hunters and gatherers, they are found throughout the continent and their languages probably belong to more than one linguistic family. They are dark-skinned, with fair hair in childhood and heavy dark beards and body hair in adult males. There are about 228,000 Aborigines in

Australia, making up about 1.5% of the population of
16 million. The Aborigine rights movement campaigns
against racial discrimination in housing, education,
wages, and medical facilities.

Australian Alps southeastern and highest area of the
Eastern Highlands of Australia, extending for about
433 km/269 mi through Victoria and New South Wales
in a northeasterly direction, and forming a continuation
of the *Great Dividing Range. They include the
*Snowy Mountains and Mount *Kosciusko, Australia's
highest mountain, 2,229 m/7,316 ft. The Alps are
popular for winter sports.

Australian art art in Australia appears to date back
at least 40,000 years, judging by radiocarbon dates
obtained from organic material trapped in varnish
covering apparently abstract rock engravings in South
Australia, but may be even older, since worn crayons of
ochre have been found in occupation layers of more
than 50,000 years ago. *Aboriginal art is closely linked
with religion and mythology, notably the *Dreamtime
creation stories. In the pre-colonial era pictures and
decorated objects, including rock and bark paintings,
were produced in nearly all settled areas. Subjects
included humans, animals, and geometric ornament.
The 'X-ray style', showing the inner organs in an animal
portrait, is unique to Australian Aboriginal art. True
Aboriginal art is now rare.

Australian Capital Territory federal territory of
southeastern Australia, an enclave in the state of
New South Wales; it includes Jervis Bay Territory (the
site of Canberra's port on the coast) for administrative
purposes; area 2,400 sq km/926 sq mi (Jervis Bay
73 sq km/28 sq mi); population (2001 est) 311,500.
Government administration and defence employs
almost half of the population of Australian Capital
Territory; retail, property, and business services are also
important. *Canberra is the main city in the territory.

Austria
National name: *Republik Österreich/Republic of Austria*

Area: 83,859 sq km/32,367 sq mi
Capital: Vienna
Major towns/cities: Graz, Linz, Salzburg, Innsbruck,
Klagenfurt

Physical features: landlocked mountainous state,
with Alps in west and south (Austrian Alps, including
Grossglockner and Brenner and Semmering passes,
Lechtaler and Allgauer Alps north of River Inn, Carnic
Alps on Italian border) and low relief in east where
most of the population is concentrated; River Danube
Head of state: Heinz Fischer from 2004
Head of government: Wolfgang Schüssel from 2000
Political system: liberal democracy
Political executive: parliamentary
Political parties: Social Democratic Party of Austria
(SPÖ), democratic socialist; Austrian People's Party
(ÖVP), progressive centrist; Freedom (formerly
Freedom Party of Austria: FPÖ), right wing; United Green
Party of Austria (VGÖ), conservative ecological; Green
Alternative Party (ALV), radical ecological; Liberal Forum,
moderately left wing; Communist Party of Austria
Currency: euro (schilling until 2002)
GNI per capita (PPP): (US$) 28,240 (2002 est)
Exports: dairy products, food products, wood and
paper products, machinery and transport equipment,
metal and metal products, chemical products.
Principal market for exports: Germany 33% (2000)
Population: 8,116,000 (2003 est)
Language: German (official)
Religion: Roman Catholic 78%, Protestant 5%
Life expectancy: 75 (men); 82 (women) (2000–05)
Chronology
14 BC: Country south of River Danube conquered by
Romans.
5th century AD: The region was occupied by Vandals,
Huns, Goths, Lombards, and Avars.
791: Charlemagne conquered the Avars and established
East Mark, the nucleus of the future Austrian Empire.
976: Holy Roman Emperor Otto II granted East Mark
to House of Babenburg, which ruled until 1246.
1282: Holy Roman Emperor Rudolf of Habsburg seized
Austria and invested his son as its duke; for over 500 years
most rulers of Austria were elected Holy Roman Emperor.
1453: Austria became an archduchy.
1519–56: Emperor Charles V was both archduke of
Austria and king of Spain; the Habsburgs were
dominant in Europe.
1526: Bohemia came under Habsburg rule.
1529: Vienna was besieged by the Ottoman Turks.
1618–48: Thirty Years' War: Habsburgs weakened by
failure to secure control over Germany.
1683: Polish-Austrian force led by Jan Sobieski defeated
the Turks at Vienna.
1699: Treaty of Karlowitz: Austrians expelled the Turks
from Hungary, which came under Habsburg rule.
1713: By the Treaty of Utrecht, Austria obtained the
Spanish Netherlands (Belgium) and political control
over most of Italy.
1740–48: War of Austrian Succession: Prussia (supported
by France and Spain) attacked Austria (supported by
Holland and England) on the pretext of disputing
rights of Maria Theresa; Austria lost Silesia to Prussia.
1772: Austria joined in partition of Poland, annexing
Galicia.
1780–90: 'Enlightened despotism': Joseph II tried to
impose radical reforms.
1792: Austria went to war with revolutionary France.
1804: Francis II took the title Emperor of Austria.
1806: The Holy Roman Empire was abolished.

1809–48: Austria took a leading role in resisting liberalism and nationalism throughout Europe.
1815: After the Napoleonic Wars, Austria lost its Netherlands but received Lombardy and Venetia.
1848: Outbreak of liberal-nationalist revolts throughout the Austrian Empire; Ferdinand I abdicated in favour of Franz Joseph; revolutions suppressed with difficulty.
1859: France and Sardinia expelled Austrians from Lombardy by force.
1866: Seven Weeks' War: Prussia defeated Austria, which ceded Venetia to Italy.
1867: Austria conceded equality to Hungary within the dual monarchy of Austria-Hungary.
1878: Treaty of Berlin: Austria-Hungary occupied Bosnia-Herzegovina; annexed in 1908.
1914: Archduke Franz Ferdinand, the heir to the throne, was assassinated by a Serbian nationalist; Austria-Hungary invaded Serbia, precipitating World War I.
1916: Death of Franz Joseph; succeeded by Karl I.
1918: Austria-Hungary collapsed in military defeat; empire dissolved; republic proclaimed.
1919: Treaty of St Germain reduced Austria to its present boundaries and prohibited union with Germany.
1934: Political instability culminated in brief civil war; right-wingers defeated socialists.
1938: The *Anschluss*: Nazi Germany incorporated Austria into the Third Reich.
1945: Following World War II, the victorious Allies divided Austria into four zones of occupation (US, British, French, and Soviet); the Second Republic was established under Karl Renner.
1955: Austrian State Treaty ended occupation; Austria regained independence on condition of neutrality.
1960–70s: Austria experienced rapid industrialization and prosperity.
1986: Kurt Waldheim was elected president, despite allegations of war crimes during World War II. This led to some diplomatic isolation until Waldheim's replacement by Thomas Klestil in 1992.
1995: Austria became a full member of the European Union (EU).
1998: NATO membership was ruled out.
2000: A new coalition government was elected, made up of the conservative People's Party, led by Wolfgang Schüssel, and the far-right Freiheitliche Partei Österreichs (FPÖ; Freedom Party of Austria), led by Jörg Haider. This was met with protests from across Europe and the imposition of diplomatic sanctions. Haider resigned in May, but his party remained part of the coalition. In September, sanctions were lifted after a favourable report on the country's human rights record.
2002: The right-wing coalition government collapsed when members of the populist FPÖ resigned from the cabinet led by Chancellor Schëssel.
2003: Schëssel again allied with the FPÖ to form a government. The government introduced new asylum laws.
2004: Heinze Fischer was elected president.
2005: The FPÖ broke up when Jörg Haider left to set up the Alliance for Austria's Future.

Austrian Succession, War of the war 1740–48 between Austria (supported by England and Holland) and Prussia (supported by France and Spain). The Holy Roman Emperor Charles VI died in 1740 and the succession of his daughter Maria Theresa was disputed by a number of European powers. Frederick the Great of Prussia seized Silesia from Austria. At Dettingen in 1743 an army of British, Austrians, and Hanoverians under the command of George II was victorious over the French. In 1745 an Austro-English army was defeated at Fontenoy but British naval superiority was confirmed, and there were gains in the Americas and India. The war was ended in 1748 by the Treaty of Aix-la-Chapelle.

Austro-Hungarian Empire the Dual Monarchy established by the Habsburg Franz Joseph in 1867 between his empire of Austria and his kingdom of Hungary (including territory that became Czechoslovakia as well as parts of Poland, the Ukraine, Romania, Yugoslavia, and Italy). It collapsed in the autumn of 1918 with the end of World War I. Only two king-emperors ruled: Franz Joseph and Karl.

Austronesian languages *or* **Malayo-Polynesian** family of languages spoken in Malaysia, the Indonesian archipelago, parts of the region that was formerly Indochina, Taiwan, Madagascar, Melanesia, and Polynesia (excluding Australia and most of New Guinea). The group contains some 500 distinct languages, including Malay in Malaysia, Bahasa in Indonesia, Fijian, Hawaiian, and Maori.

autarchy national economic policy that aims at achieving self-sufficiency and eliminating the need for imports (by imposing tariffs, for example). Such a goal may be difficult, if not impossible, for a small country. Countries that take protectionist measures and try to prevent free trade are sometimes described as autarchical.

authoritarianism rule of a country by a dominant elite who repress opponents and the press to maintain their own wealth and power. They are frequently indifferent to activities not affecting their security, and rival power centres, such as trade unions and political parties, are often allowed to exist, although under tight control. An extreme form is *totalitarianism.

autism rare disorder, generally present from birth, characterized by a withdrawn state and a failure to develop normally in language or social behaviour. Although the autistic child may, rarely, show signs of high intelligence (in music or with numbers, for example), many have impaired intellect. The cause is unknown, but is thought to involve a number of factors, possibly including an inherent abnormality of the child's brain. Special education may bring about some improvement.

autochrome in photography, a single-plate additive colour process devised by the *Lumière brothers in 1903. It was the first commercially available process, in use 1907–35.

autocracy form of government in which one person holds absolute power. The autocrat has uncontrolled and undisputed authority. Russian government under the tsars was an autocracy extending from the mid-16th century to the early 20th century. The title Autocratix (a female autocrat) was assumed by Catherine II of Russia in the 18th century.

auto-da-fé (Portuguese 'act of faith') religious ceremony, including a procession, solemn mass, and sermon, which accompanied the sentencing of heretics by the Spanish *Inquisition before they were handed over to the secular authorities for punishment, usually burning.

autoimmunity in medicine, condition in which the body's immune responses are mobilized not against 'foreign' matter, such as invading germs, but against the body itself. Diseases considered to be of autoimmune origin include myasthenia gravis, *rheumatoid arthritis, and *lupus erythematosus.

automation widespread use of self-regulating machines in industry. Automation involves the addition of control devices, using electronic sensing and computing techniques, which often follow the pattern of human nervous and brain functions, to already mechanized physical processes of production and distribution; for example, steel processing, mining, chemical production, and road, rail, and air control.

automatism performance of actions without awareness or conscious intent. It is seen in sleepwalking and in some (relatively rare) psychotic states.

autonomic nervous system in mammals, the part of the nervous system that controls those functions not controlled voluntarily, including the heart rate, activity of the intestines, and the production of sweat. There are two divisions of the autonomic nervous system. The **sympathetic** system responds to stress, when it speeds the heart rate, increases blood pressure, and generally prepares the body for action. The **parasympathetic** system is more important when the body is at rest, since it slows the heart rate, decreases blood pressure, and stimulates the digestive system.

autonomy in politics, a term used to describe political self-government of a state or, more commonly, a subdivision of a state. Autonomy may be based upon cultural or ethnic differences and often leads eventually to independence.

autopsy or **postmortem** examination of the internal organs and tissues of a dead body, performed to try to establish the cause of death.

autosome any *chromosome in the cell other than a sex chromosome. Autosomes are of the same number and kind in both males and females of a given species.

autosuggestion conscious or unconscious acceptance of an idea as true, without demanding rational proof, but with potential subsequent effect for good or ill. Pioneered by French psychotherapist Emile Coué in healing, it is sometimes used in modern psychotherapy to conquer nervous habits and dependence on addictive substances such as tobacco and alcohol.

autotroph any living organism that synthesizes organic substances from inorganic molecules by using light or chemical energy. Autotrophs are the primary producers in all food chains since the materials they synthesize and store are the energy sources of all other organisms. All green plants and many planktonic organisms are autotrophs, using sunlight to convert carbon dioxide and water into sugars by *photosynthesis.

autumn crocus any of a group of late-flowering plants belonging to the lily family. The mauve meadow saffron (*Colchicum autumnale*) yields colchicine, which is used in treating gout and in plant breeding. (Genus *Colchicum*, family Liliaceae.)

Auvergne ancient province of central France and modern region comprising the départements of Allier, Cantal, Haute-Loire, and Puy-de-Dôme; administrative centre Clermont-Ferrand; area 26,013 sq km/10,044 sq mi; population (1999 est) 1,308,900. It is a mountainous area, composed chiefly of volcanic rocks in several masses, and there are places with hot mineral springs (including the Vichy and Mont-Dore spas). The region

is largely agricultural (cattle, sheep, wheat), and its main output includes wine and dairy products. Manufacturing is centred at the main towns of Clermont-Ferrand, Aurillac, Riom, and Thiers, and includes tyres and metal goods. The region hosts many folk festivals and is rich in examples of Romanesque architecture. There are also two large regional parks, and the growth of tourism has contributed increasingly to the economy.

auxin plant *hormone that regulates stem and root growth in plants. Auxins influence many aspects of plant growth and development, including cell enlargement, inhibition of development of axillary buds, *tropisms, and the initiation of roots. Auxin affects cell division mainly at the tip, because it is here that cell division in a stem or root mainly occurs. Just behind the tip the cells grow in size under the influence of auxins, causing the stem or root to grow longer. Auxin therefore affects the amount of elongation here too.

Avalokitesvara in Mahayana Buddhism, one of the most important *bodhisattvas, seen as embodying compassion. He is an emanation of Amida Buddha. In China, as **Kuan Yin**, and in Japan, as **Kannon**, he is confused with his female consort, becoming the popular goddess of mercy.

Avalon or **Isle of Apples** in Celtic mythology, the island of the blessed or paradise; one of the names of the Welsh **Otherworld**. In the legend of King Arthur, it is the land of heroes, a fruitful land of youth and health ruled over by *Morgan le Fay; Arthur is conveyed here to be healed of his wounds after his final battle with *Mordred. It has been identified since the Middle Ages with *Glastonbury in Somerset, southwest England.

avant-garde (French 'forward guard') in the arts, those artists or works that are in the forefront of new developments in their media. The term was introduced (as was 'reactionary') after the French Revolution, when it was used to describe any socialist political movement.

avatar or **avatara** in Hindu mythology, the descent of a deity to earth in a visible form, for example the ten avatars of *Vishnu.

Avebury Europe's largest stone circle (diameter 412 m/1,350 ft), in Wiltshire, England. This megalithic henge monument is thought to be part of a ritual complex, and contains 650 massive blocks of stone arranged in circles and avenues. It was probably constructed around 3,500 years ago, and is linked with nearby *Silbury Hill.

avens any of several low-growing plants found throughout Europe, Asia, and North Africa. (Genus *Geum*, family Rosaceae.)

average in statistics, a term used inexactly to indicate the typical member of a set of *data. It usually refers to the *arithmetic mean. The term is also used to refer to the middle member of the set when it is sorted in ascending or descending order (the *median), and the most commonly occurring item of data (the *mode), as in 'the average family'.

Averroës (1126–1198) Arabic **Ibn Rushd**, Arabian philosopher who argued for the eternity of matter and against the immortality of the individual soul. His philosophical writings, including commentaries on Aristotle and on Plato's *Republic*, became known to the West through Latin translations. He influenced Christian and Jewish writers into the Renaissance, and reconciled Islamic and Greek thought in asserting that philosophic truth comes through reason. St Thomas Aquinas opposed this position.

Avicenna (979–1037) Arabic **Ibn Sina**, Iranian philosopher and physician. He was the most renowned philosopher of medieval Islam. His Canon Medicinae was a standard work for many centuries. His philosophical writings were influenced by al-Farabi, Aristotle, and the neo-Platonists, and in turn influenced the scholastics of the 13th century.

Avignon city in Provence, France, administrative centre of Vaucluse *département*, on the River Rhône, 80 km/ 50 mi northwest of Marseille; population (2002 est) 86,600. Tourism and food processing are important; other industries include the manufacture of leather, textiles, paper, machinery, and chemicals. Avignon has a significant trade in wine (Côtes du Rhone) and fruit. An important Gallic and Roman city, it has a 12th-century bridge (only half of which still stands), a 13th-century cathedral, 14th-century walls, and the Palais des Papes, the enormous fortress-palace of the popes, one of the most magnificent Gothic buildings of the 14th-century. The city is also famous for its annual summer festival of cinema, theatre, and dance.

avocado tree belonging to the laurel family, native to Central America. Its dark-green, thick-skinned, pear-shaped fruit has buttery-textured flesh and is used in salads. (*Persea americana*, family Lauraceae.)

avocet wading bird, with a characteristic long, narrow, upturned bill, which it uses to sift water as it feeds in the shallows. It is about 45 cm/18 in long, has long legs, partly webbed feet, and black and white plumage. There are four species of avocet, genus *Recurvirostra*, family Recurvirostridae, order Charadriiformes. They are found in Europe, Africa, and central and southern Asia. Stilts belong to the same family.

Avogadro's hypothesis in chemistry, the law stating that equal volumes of all gases, when at the same temperature and pressure, have the same numbers of molecules. One *mole of any gas contains 6.023×10^{23} particles and occupies 24 dm^3 at room temperature and pressure. The type of gas does not make any difference. The law was first put forward by Italian chemist Amedeo Avogadro.

Avogadro's number *or* **Avogadro's constant** number of carbon atoms in 12 g of the carbon-12 isotope (6.022045×10^{23}). It is named after Italian chemist Amedeo Avogadro. The *relative atomic mass of any element, expressed in grams, contains this number of atoms and is called a *mole. For example, one mole of any substance contains 6.022×10^{23} particles. One mole of carbon has a mass of 12 g.

avoirdupois system of units of mass based on the pound (0.45 kg), which consists of 16 ounces (each of 16 drams) or 7,000 grains (each equal to 65 mg).

Avon *or* **Warwickshire Avon** (Celtic *afon* 'river') river in southern England; length 154 km/96 mi. It rises in the Northamptonshire uplands near Naseby and flows southwest through Warwick, Stratford-upon-Avon, and Evesham, before joining the River Severn near Tewkesbury, Gloucestershire.

AWACS acronym for Airborne Warning And Control System, surveillance system that incorporates a long-range surveillance and detection radar mounted on a Boeing E-3 Sentry aircraft. It was used with great success in the 1991 Gulf War.

Axel, Richard (1946–) US neuroscientist. With US neuroscientist Linda Buck he shared the Nobel Prize for Physiology or Medicine in 2004 for his contributions in determining how the olfactory system recognizes and differentiates between different smells.

axiom in mathematics, a statement that is assumed to be true and upon which theorems are proved by using logical deduction; for example, two straight lines cannot enclose a space. The Greek mathematician Euclid used a series of axioms that he considered could not be demonstrated in terms of simpler concepts to prove his geometrical theorems.

axis plural **axes**, in geometry, one of the reference lines by which a point on a graph may be located. The horizontal axis is usually referred to as the x-axis, and the vertical axis as the y-axis. The term is also used to refer to the imaginary line about which an object may be said to be symmetrical (**axis of symmetry**) – for example, the diagonal of a square – or the line about which an object may revolve (**axis of rotation**).

Axis alliance of Nazi Germany and fascist Italy before and during World War II. The **Rome–Berlin Axis** was formed in 1936, when Italy was being threatened with sanctions because of its invasion of Ethiopia (Abyssinia). It became a full military and political alliance in May 1939. A ten-year alliance between Germany, Italy, and Japan (**Rome–Berlin–Tokyo Axis**) was signed in September 1940 and was subsequently joined by Hungary, Bulgaria, Romania, and the puppet states of Slovakia and Croatia. The Axis collapsed with the fall of Mussolini and the surrender of Italy in 1943 and Germany and Japan in 1945.

axolotl (Aztec 'water monster') aquatic larval form ('tadpole') of the Mexican salamander *Ambystoma mexicanum*, belonging to the family Ambystomatidae. Axolotls may be up to 30 cm/12 in long. They are remarkable because they can breed without changing to the adult form, and will metamorphose into adults only in response to the drying-up of their ponds. The adults then migrate to another pond.

axon long threadlike extension of a *nerve cell that conducts electrochemical impulses away from the cell body towards other nerve cells, or towards an effector organ such as a muscle. Axons terminate in *synapses, junctions with other nerve cells, muscles, or glands.

ayatollah (Arabic 'sign of God') honorific title awarded to Shiite Muslims in Iran by popular consent, as, for example, to Ayatollah Ruhollah *Khomeini (1900–1989).

Ayckbourn, Alan (1939–) English playwright and artistic director of the Stephen Joseph Theatre, Scarborough, England, from 1970. His abundant output, characterized by comic dialogue and teasing experiments in dramatic structure, includes *Relatively Speaking* (1967), *Absurd Person Singular* (1973), *The Norman Conquests* (1974; a trilogy), *Joking Apart* (1979), *Intimate Exchanges* (1982), *A Woman in Mind* (1986), *Haunting Julia* (1994), and *Things We Do For Love* (1998).

aye-aye nocturnal tree-climbing prosimian *Daubentonia madagascariensis* of Madagascar, related to the lemurs. It is just over 1 m/3 ft long, including a tail 50 cm/20 in long.

Ayer, A(lfred) J(ules) (1910–1989) English philosopher. He wrote *Language, Truth and Logic* (1936), an exposition of the theory of 'logical positivism', presenting a criterion by which meaningful statements ('essentially truths of logic, as well as statements derived from experience) could be distinguished from meaningless metaphysical utterances (for example, claims that there is a God or that the world external to our own minds is illusory). He was knighted in 1970.

Ayers Rock Aboriginal **Uluru**, vast ovate mass of pinkish sandstone rock in Northern Territory, Australia; 335 m/1,110 ft high and 9 km/6 mi around. It lies within the Ayers Rock–Mount Olga National Park and is famed for its stark rise from the surrounding land and for the striking orange-red colour which it assumes at sunset. For the Aboriginals, who have officially owned the Rock since 1985 and whose paintings decorate its caves, Ayers Rock has magical significance.

Aymara the American Indian people of Bolivia and Peru, builders of a great culture, who were conquered first by the Incas and then by the Spaniards. Today 1.4 million Aymara farm and herd llamas and alpacas in the highlands; their language, belonging to the Andean-Equatorial language family, survives, and their Roman Catholicism incorporates elements of their old beliefs.

Ayurveda basically naturopathic system of medicine widely practised in India and based on principles derived from the ancient Hindu scriptures, the *Vedas. Hospital treatments and remedial prescriptions tend to be nonspecific and to coordinate holistic therapies for body, mind, and spirit.

azalea any of a group of deciduous flowering shrubs belonging to the heath family. Several species are native to Asia and North America, and many cultivated varieties have been derived from these. Azaleas are closely related to the mostly evergreen *rhododendrons. (Genus *Rhododendron*, family Ericaceae.)

Azerbaijan

National name: *Azärbaycan Respublikasi/ Republic of Azerbaijan*

Area: 86,600 sq km/33,436 sq mi
Capital: Baku
Major towns/cities: Gäncä, Sumqayit, Nakhichevan, Xankändi, Mingechaur
Physical features: Caspian Sea with rich oil reserves; the country ranges from semidesert to the Caucasus Mountains
Head of state: Ilham Aliyev from 2003
Head of government: Artur Rasizade from 2003
Political system: authoritarian nationalist
Political executive: unlimited presidency

Political parties: Popular Front of Azerbaijan (FPA), democratic nationalist; New Azerbaijan, ex-communist; Communist Party of Azerbaijan (banned 1991–93); Muslim Democratic Party (Musavat), Islamic, pro-Turkic unity
Currency: manat (replaced Russian rouble in 1993)
GNI per capita (PPP): (US$) 2,920 (2002 est)
Exports: refined petroleum products, machinery, food products, textiles, chemicals. Principal market: Italy 57.2% (2001)
Population: 8,370,000 (2003 est)
Language: Azeri (official), Russian
Religion: Shiite Muslim 68%, Sunni Muslim 27%, Russian Orthodox 3%, Armenian Orthodox 2%
Life expectancy: 69 (men); 76 (women) (2000–05)
Chronology
4th century BC: Established as an independent state for the first time by Atrophates, a vassal of Alexander III of Macedon.
7th century AD: Spread of Islam.
11th century: Immigration by Oghuz Seljuk peoples, from the steppes to the northeast.
13th–14th centuries: Incorporated within Mongol Empire; the Mongol ruler Tamerlane had his capital at Samarkand.
16th century: Baku besieged and incorporated within Ottoman Empire, before falling under Persian dominance.
1805: Khanates (chieftaincies), including Karabakh and Shirvan, which had won independence from Persia, gradually became Russian protectorates, being confirmed by the Treaty of Gulistan, which concluded the 1804–13 First Russo-Iranian War.
1828: Under the Treaty of Turkmenchai, which concluded the Second Russo-Iranian War begun in 1826, Persia was granted control over southern and Russia over northern Azerbaijan.
late 19th century: The petroleum industry developed, resulting in a large influx of Slav immigrants to Baku.
1917–18: Member of anti-Bolshevik Transcaucasian Federation.
1918: Became an independent republic.
1920: Occupied by Red Army and subsequently forcibly secularized.
1922–36: Became part of the Transcaucasian Federal Republic with Georgia and Armenia.
early 1930s: Peasant uprisings against agricultural collectivization and Stalinist purges of the local Communist Party.
1936: Became a constituent republic of the USSR.
late 1980s: Growth in nationalist sentiment, taking advantage of the *glasnost* initiative of the reformist Soviet leader Mikhail Gorbachev.
1988: Riots followed the request of Nagorno-Karabakh, an Armenian-peopled enclave within Azerbaijan, for transfer to Armenia.
1989: Nagorno-Karabakh was placed under direct rule from Moscow; civil war broke out with Armenia over Nagorno-Karabakh.
1990: Soviet troops were dispatched to Baku to restore order amid calls for secession from the USSR.
1991: Independence was declared after the collapse of an anti-Gorbachev coup in Moscow, which had been supported by the Azeri communist leadership. Azerbaijan joined the new Commonwealth of Independent States (CIS); Nagorno-Karabakh declared independence.

69

1992: Azerbaijan was admitted into the United Nations (UN).

1993: Nagorno-Karabakh was overtaken by Armenian forces.

1995: An attempted coup was foiled. A market-centred economic reform programme was introduced.

1997: There was border fighting with Armenia. The extraction of oil from oilfields in the Caspian Sea began, operated by a consortium of 11 international oil companies.

1998: A new pro-government grouping, Democratic Azerbaijan, was formed. Heidar Aliyev was re-elected president in a disputed poll. A Nagorno-Karabakh peace plan was rejected.

2000: Heidar Aliyev was re-elected, although foreign observers denounced the election as deeply flawed.

2001: Azerbaijan was admitted to the Council of Europe. A declaration was signed with Russia, agreeing on political, economic, and military cooperation.

2002: Pope John Paul II made his first visit.

2003: President Geidar Aliyev died. His son, Ilham Aliyev, took over the presidency following elections blighted by violence.

2005: Thousands of people publicly mourned the death of Elmar Huseynov, a journalist who had been highly critical of the authorities and was shot dead in Baku.

Azerbaijan, Iranian ancient Greek **Atropatene**, two provinces of northwest Iran: **Eastern Azerbaijan** (population (1996 est) 3,325,500, capital Tabriz); and **Western Azerbaijan** (population (1996 est) 2,496,300, capital Orumiyeh). Azerbaijanis in Iran, as in the Republic of Azerbaijan, are mainly Shiite Muslim ethnic Turks, descendants of followers of the Khans from the Mongol Empire.

Azeri *or* **Azerbaijani** native of the Azerbaijan region of Iran (population 5,500,000) or of the Republic of Azerbaijan (formerly a Soviet republic) (population 7,145,600). Azeri is a Turkic language belonging to the Altaic family. Of the total population of Azeris, 70% are Shiite Muslims and 30% Sunni Muslims.

azimuth in astronomy, angular distance of an object eastwards along the horizon, measured from due north, between the astronomical *meridian (the vertical circle passing through the centre of the sky and the north and south points on the horizon) and the vertical circle containing the celestial body whose position is to be measured.

Azores *or* **Açores** group of nine islands in the North Atlantic, forming an autonomous region belonging to Portugal; area 2,247 sq km/867 sq mi; population (1991) 237,800. The islands are outlying peaks of the Mid-Atlantic Ridge and are volcanic in origin. Products include sugar cane, coffee, tobacco, fruit, and wine. There are many hot springs, and the countryside is mountainous and rugged; the coastline is largely volcanic and there are few sandy beaches. The climate is moist but mild, and some of the islands are used as winter resorts. There are three administrative centres: Ponta Delgada which serves the islands of São Miguel and Santa Maria; Angra do Heroísmo serves the islands of Terceira, Graciosa, and São Jorge; and Horta serves the islands of Pico, Faial, Flores, and Corvo.

Azov, Sea of Russian **Azovskoye More**, Latin **Palus Maeotis**, inland sea between Ukraine and Russia, forming a gulf in the northeast of the Black Sea, to which it is connected by the narrow Kerch Strait. It has an area of 37,555 sq km/14,500 sq mi, and is extremely shallow, with an average depth of only 8 m/26 ft, and nowhere exceeding 16 m/52 ft. The sea is frozen for four to six months every year. Principal ports include Rostov-na-Donu, Mariupol, Kerch', and Taganrog. The main rivers flowing into the Sea of Azov are the *Don, and the Kuban.

AZT drug used in the treatment of AIDS; see *zidovudine.

Aztec member of an *American Indian people who migrated south into the valley of Mexico in about 1168. They belonged to the *Nahuatl, a Mesoamerican people who remain the largest ethnic group in Mexico today; their language was from the Uto-Aztecan family. The Aztec developed a highly structured civilization, known for its architecture and precious artefacts, and centred on a complex ritual calendar that included large-scale human sacrifice. From 1325 they built their capital *Tenochtitlán on the site now occupied by *Mexico City. Under Montezuma I (reigned 1437–64), they created an empire in central Mexico which lasted until the arrival of the Spanish conquistador Hernán *Cortés in 1519. The Aztec subsequently became subjects of Spain, but their lineage continues and some Mexicans still use the Uto-Aztecan language.

b

BA in education, abbreviation for the degree of **Bachelor of Arts**.

Baader–Meinhof gang popular name for the West German left-wing guerrilla group the *Rote Armee Fraktion/Red Army Faction*, active from 1968 against what it perceived as US imperialism. The three main founding members were Andreas Baader, Gudrun Ensslin, and Ulrike Meinhof.

Baal (Semitic 'lord' or 'owner') divine title given to their chief male gods by the Phoenicians, or Canaanites, of the eastern Mediterranean coast about 1200–332 BC. Their worship as fertility gods, often orgiastic and of a phallic character, was strongly denounced by the Hebrew prophets.

Ba'ath Party Party of Arab Renaissance, ruling political party in Iraq and Syria. Despite public support of pan-Arab unity and its foundation in 1943 as a party of Arab nationalism, its ideology has been so vague that it has fostered widely differing (and often opposing) parties in Syria and Iraq.

Babbage, Charles (1792–1871) English mathematician who devised a precursor of the computer. He designed an analytical engine, a general-purpose mechanical computing device for performing different calculations according to a program input on punched cards (an idea borrowed from the *Jacquard loom). This device was never built, but it embodied many of the principles on which digital computers are based.

Babbitt, Milton (Byron) (1916–) US composer and theorist. A leading proponent of *serialism, he pioneered the application of information theory to music in the 1950s, introducing set theory to series manipulations and the term 'pitch class' to define every octave identity of a note name. His works include four string quartets, works for orchestra, *Philomel* for soprano and electronic tape (1963–64), and *Ensembles for Synthesizer* (1967), both composed using the 1960 RCA Princeton-Columbia Mark II Synthesizer, which he helped to design.

babbler bird of the thrush family Muscicapidae with a loud babbling cry. Babblers, subfamily Timaliinae, are found in the Old World, and there are some 250 species in the group.

Babel Hebrew name for the city of *Babylon, chiefly associated with the **Tower of Babel** which, in the Genesis story in the Old Testament, was erected in the plain of Shinar by the descendants of Noah. It was a ziggurat, or staged temple, seven storeys high (100 m/328 ft) with

a shrine of Marduk on the summit. It was built by Nabopolassar, father of Nebuchadnezzar, and was destroyed when Sennacherib sacked the city in 689 BC.

Babism religious movement founded during the 1840s by Mirza Ali Muhammad ('the Bab'). An offshoot of Islam, it differs mainly in the belief that Muhammad was not the last of the prophets. The movement split into two groups after the death of the Bab; Baha'u'llah, the leader of one of these groups, founded the *Baha'i faith.

Babi Yar ravine near Kiev, Ukraine, where more than 100,000 people (80,000 of whom were Jews, the remainder being Poles, Russians, and Ukrainians) were murdered by the Nazis in 1941. The site was ignored until the Soviet poet Yevgeny *Yevtushenko wrote a poem called 'Babi Yar' (1961) in protest at plans for a sports centre on the site.

baboon large monkey of the genus *Papio*, with a long doglike muzzle and large canine teeth, spending much of its time on the ground in open country. Males, with head and body up to 1.1 m/3.5 ft long, are larger than females, and dominant males rule the 'troops' in which baboons live. They inhabit Africa and southwestern Arabia.

Babur (1483–1530) born Zahir ud-Din Muhammad, (Arabic 'lion') First Great Mogul of India from 1526. He was the great-grandson of the Mogul conqueror Tamerlane and, at the age of 11, succeeded his father, Omar Sheikh Mirza, as ruler of Fergana (Turkestan). In 1526 he defeated the emperor of Delhi at Panipat in the Punjab, captured Delhi and *Agra (the site of the Taj Mahal), and established a dynasty that lasted until 1858.

Babylon capital of ancient Babylonia, on the bank of the lower Euphrates River. The site is now in Iraq, 88 km/55 mi south of Baghdad and 8 km/5 mi north of Hillah, which is built chiefly of bricks from the ruins of Babylon. The Hanging Gardens of Babylon, one of the *Seven Wonders of the World, were probably erected on a vaulted stone base, the only stone construction in the mud-brick city. They formed a series of terraces, irrigated by a hydraulic system.

Babylonian Captivity *or* **Babylonian exile** exile of Jewish deportees to Babylon after *Nebuchadnezzar II's capture of Jerusalem in 586 BC; it was the first *diaspora of the Jewish people. According to tradition, the Captivity lasted 70 years, but Cyrus of Persia, who conquered Babylon, actually allowed them to go home in 536 BC. By analogy, the name has also been applied to the papal exile to Avignon, France, AD 1309–77.

Bacall, Lauren (1924–) stage name of Betty Joan Perske, US actor. She became an overnight star when cast by Howard Hawks opposite Humphrey Bogart in *To Have and Have Not* (1944). She and Bogart went on to star together in *The Big Sleep* (1946), *The Dark Passage* (1947), and *Key Largo* (1948). They married in 1945.

Bacchus in Greek and Roman mythology, the god of fertility (see *Dionysus) and of wine; his rites (the **Bacchanalia**) were orgiastic.

Bach, Carl Philip Emanuel (1714–1788) German composer. He was the third son of Johann Sebastian Bach. He introduced a new 'homophonic' style, light and easy to follow, which influenced Mozart, Haydn, and Beethoven.

Bach, Johann Christian (1735–1782) German composer. The eleventh son of Johann Sebastian Bach, he became celebrated in Italy as a composer of operas. In 1762 he was invited to London, where he became music master to the royal family. He remained in England until his death; his great popularity both as a composer and a performer declined in his last years for political and medical reasons.

Bach, Johann Sebastian (1685–1750) German composer. A master of *counterpoint, his music represents the final stage of the *baroque polyphonic style. His orchestral music includes the six *Brandenburg Concertos* (1721), other concertos for keyboard instrument and violin, four orchestral suites, sonatas for various instruments, three partitas and three sonatas for violin solo, and six unaccompanied cello suites. Bach's keyboard music, for clavier and organ, his fugues, and his choral music are of equal importance.

bacille Calmette-Guérin tuberculosis vaccine *BCG.

bacillus genus of rod-shaped *bacteria that occur everywhere in the soil and air. Some are responsible for diseases such as *anthrax, or for causing food spoilage.

backgammon board game for two players, often used in gambling. It was known in Mesopotamia, Greece, Rome, and in medieval England.

background radiation radiation that is always present in the environment. By far the greater proportion (87%) of it is emitted from natural sources. *Alpha particles, *beta particles, and *gamma radiation are emitted by the traces of radioactive minerals that occur naturally in the environment and even in the human body (for example, by breathing in ^{14}C). Radioactive gases such as *radon and thoron are found in soil and may seep upwards into buildings. Radiation from space (*cosmic radiation) also contributes to the background level.

backswimmer *or* **water boatman** aquatic predatory bug living mostly in fresh water. The adults are about 15 mm/0.5 in long and rest upside down at the water surface to breathe. When disturbed they dive, carrying with them a supply of air trapped under the wings. They have piercing beaks, used in feeding on tadpoles and small fish. Backswimmers belong to the genus *Notonecta*, family Notonectidae in suborder Heteroptera, order Hemiptera (true bugs), class Insecta, phylum Arthropoda.

Bacon, Francis (1909–1992) Irish painter. Self-taught, he practised abstract art, then developed a stark Expressionist style characterized by distorted, blurred figures enclosed in loosely defined space. He aimed to 'bring the figurative thing up onto the nervous system more violently and more poignantly'. One of his best-known works is *Study after Velázquez's Portrait of Pope Innocent X* (1953; Museum of Modern Art, New York).

Bacon, Francis (1561–1626) 1st Baron Verulam and Viscount St Albans, English philosopher, politician, and writer, a founder of modern scientific research. His works include *Essays* (1597, revised and augmented 1612 and 1625), characterized by pith and brevity; *The Advancement of Learning* (1605), a seminal work discussing scientific method; *Novum Organum* (1620), in which he redefined the task of natural science, seeing it as a means of empirical discovery and a method of increasing human power over nature; and *The New Atlantis* (1626), describing a utopian state in which scientific knowledge is systematically sought and exploited. He was briefly Lord Chancellor in 1618 but lost his post through corruption.

Bacon, Roger (c. 1214–1294) English philosopher and scientist. He was interested in alchemy, the biological and physical sciences, and magic. Many discoveries have been credited to him, including the magnifying lens. He foresaw the extensive use of gunpowder and mechanical cars, boats, and planes. Bacon was known as *Doctor Mirabilis* (Wonderful Teacher).

bacteria singular **bacterium**, microscopic single-celled organisms lacking a membrane-bound nucleus. Bacteria, like fungi and *viruses, are micro-organisms – organisms that are so small they can only be seen using a microscope. They are organisms that are more simple than the cells of animals, plants, and fungi in that they lack a nucleus. Bacteria are widespread, being present in soil, air, and water, and as parasites on and in other living things. In fact, they occur anywhere life can exist. Some parasitic bacteria cause disease by producing toxins, but others are harmless and can even benefit their hosts. Bacteria usually reproduce by *binary fission (dividing into two equal parts), and, on average, this occurs every 20 minutes. Only 4,000 species of bacteria are known (1998), although bacteriologists believe that around 3 million species may actually exist. Certain types of bacteria are vital in many food and industrial processes, while others play an essential role in the *nitrogen cycle, which maintains soil fertility. They can be the first organism of a food chain, by acting as decomposers of dead plant and animal remains. This helps to recycle nutrients.

bacteriophage virus that attacks *bacteria, commonly called a phage. Such viruses are now useful vectors in genetic engineering to introduce genetically modified DNA.

bactrian species of *camel, *Camelus bactrianus*, found in the Gobi Desert in central Asia. Body fat is stored in two humps on the back. It has very long winter fur which is shed in ragged lumps. The bactrian has a head and body length of about 3 m/10 ft, and is about 2.1 m/6.8 ft tall at the shoulder. Most bactrian camels are domesticated and are used as beasts of burden in central Asia.

Baden former state of southwestern Germany, which had Karlsruhe as its capital. Baden was captured from the Romans in 282 by the Alemanni; later it became a margravate and, in 1806, a grand duchy. A state of the German empire 1871–1918, then a republic, and under Hitler a *Gau* (province), it was divided between the *Länder* of Württemberg-Baden and Baden in 1945 and in 1952 made part of *Baden-Württemberg.

Baden-Powell, Robert Stephenson Smyth (1857–1941) 1st Baron Baden-Powell, British general, founder of the *Scout Association. He was commander of the garrison during the 217-day siege of Mafeking (now Mafikeng) in the Second South African War (1899–1900). After 1907 he devoted his time to developing the Scout movement, which rapidly spread throughout the world.

Baden-Württemberg administrative region (German *Land*) in southwest Germany, bordered to the west by France, to the south by Switzerland, to the east by Bavaria, and to the west by the Rhine valley; area 35,752 sq km/13,804 sq mi; population (2003 est) 10,546,800. It is the third-largest and the most industrialized of the

16 federal states of Germany. The capital is Stuttgart, and other major towns include Mannheim, Karlsruhe, Freiburg im Breisgau, Heidelberg, Heilbronn, Pforzheim, and Ulm.

badger large mammal of the weasel family with molar teeth of a crushing type adapted to a partly vegetable diet, and short strong legs with long claws suitable for digging. The Eurasian **common badger** *Meles meles* is about 1 m/3 ft long, with long, coarse, greyish hair on the back, and a white face with a broad black stripe along each side. Mainly a woodland animal, it is harmless and nocturnal, and spends the day in a system of burrows called a 'sett'. Earthworms make up 90% of the badger's diet but it also feeds on roots, a variety of fruits and nuts, insects, mice, and young rabbits.

badlands barren landscape cut by erosion into a maze of ravines, pinnacles, gullies, and sharp-edged ridges. Areas in South Dakota and Nebraska, USA, are examples.

badminton racket game similar to lawn *tennis but played on a smaller court and with a shuttlecock (a half sphere of cork or plastic with a feather or nylon skirt) instead of a ball. The object of the game is to prevent the opponent from being able to return the shuttlecock.

Baffin, William (1584–1622) English explorer and navigator. In 1616 he and Robert Bylot explored Baffin Bay, northeastern Canada, and reached latitude 77° 45′ N, which for 236 years remained the 'furthest north'.

Baffin Island island in the Canadian territory of Nunavut, situated across the entrance to *Hudson Bay; area 507,451 sq km/195,927 sq mi; population (2001 est) 14,400. The island's principal town is Iqaluit. Baffin Island is the largest island in Canadia, and the fifth-largest in the world. Its mountains rise 2,156 m/7,074 ft at Tête Blanche and 2,011 m/6,598 ft at Mount Asgard, and there are several large lakes. The northernmost part of the strait separating Baffin Island from Greenland forms Baffin Bay; the southern end is Davis Strait. The predominantly Inuit population is settled mainly around Iqaluit and Kimmirut (formerly Lake Harbour) in the south.

bagatelle (French 'trifle') in music, a short character piece, often for piano.

Bagehot, Walter (1826–1877) British writer and economist. His *English Constitution* published in 1867, a classic analysis of the British political system, is still a standard work.

Baghdad capital city and largest city of Iraq, and capital of the governorate of Baghdad, on the River Tigris; population (2002 est) 5,605,000 (urban area 6,508,200). The city is the home of most of the industrial, commercial, and financial activities of the country. Industries include oil refining, distilling, tanning, tobacco processing, and the manufacture of petrochemicals, iron and steel, textiles, clothing, electrical goods, and cement. Founded in 762, it became Iraq's capital in 1921. During the Gulf War of 1991, the UN coalition forces bombed it in repeated air raids, and in 2003 it was bombed and then occupied by US forces.

bagpipes any of an ancient family of double-reed folk woodwind instruments employing a bladder, filled by the player through a mouthpiece, or bellows as an air reservoir to a 'chanter' or fingered melody pipe, and

two or three optional drone pipes providing a continuous accompanying harmony.

Bahadur Shah II (1775–1862) Last of the Mogul emperors of India. He reigned, though in name only, as king of Delhi 1837–57, when he was hailed by the mutineers of the *Indian Mutiny as an independent emperor at Delhi. After the rebellion he was exiled to Burma (now Myanmar) with his family.

Baha'i Faith religion founded in the 19th century from a Muslim splinter group, *Babism, by the Persian Baha'u'llah. His message in essence was that all great religious leaders are manifestations of the unknowable God and all scriptures are sacred. There is no priesthood: all Baha'is are expected to teach, and to work towards world unification. There are about 6 million Baha'is worldwide.

Bahamas
National name: *Commonwealth of the Bahamas*

Area: 13,880 sq km/5,383 sq mi
Capital: Nassau (on New Providence island)
Major towns/cities: Freeport (on Grand Bahama)
Physical features: comprises 700 tropical coral islands and about 1,000 cays; the Exumas are a narrow spine of 365 islands; only 30 of the desert islands are inhabited; Blue Holes of Andros, the world's longest and deepest submarine caves
Principal islands: Andros, Grand Bahama, Abaco, Eleuthera, New Providence, Berry Islands, Bimini Islands, Great Inagua, Acklins Island, Exuma Islands, Mayguana, Crooked Island, Long Island, Cat Islands, Rum Cay, Watling (San Salvador) Island, Inagua Islands
Head of state: Queen Elizabeth II from 1973, represented by Governor General Ivy Dumont from 2001
Head of government: Perry Christie from 2002
Political system: liberal democracy
Political executive: parliamentary
Political parties: Progressive Liberal Party (PLP), centrist; Free National Movement (FNM), left of centre
Currency: Bahamian dollar
GNI per capita (PPP): (US$) 16,500 (2001)
Exports: fish and crawfish, oil products and transhipments, chemicals, rum, aragonite, fruit and vegetables. Principal market: USA 28.2% (2000)
Population: 314,000 (2003 est)

Language: English (official), Creole
Religion: Christian 94% (Baptist 32%, Roman Catholic 19%, Anglican 20%, other Protestant 23%)
Life expectancy: 64 (men); 70 (women) (2000–05)
Chronology
8th–9th centuries AD: Arawak Indians driven northwards to the islands by the Caribs.
1492: Visited by Christopher Columbus; Arawaks deported to provide cheap labour for the gold and silver mines of Cuba and Hispaniola (Haiti).
1629: King Charles I of England granted the islands to Robert Heath.
1666: The colonization of New Providence island began.
1783: Recovered after brief Spanish occupation and became a British colony, being settled during the American War of Independence by American loyalists, who brought with them black slaves.
1838: Slaves were emancipated.
from 1950s: Major development of the tourist trade.
1964: Became internally self-governing.
1967: First national assembly elections.
1973: Full independence was achieved within the British Commonwealth.
1992: A centre-left Free National Movement (FNM) led by Hubert Ingraham won an absolute majority in elections.
2002: The Progressive Liberal Party under Perry Christie wins a landslide election victory.
2004: The Bahamas were hit by two hurricanes, Hurricane Frances and Hurricane Jeanne.

Bahrain

National name: *Mamlakat al-Bahrayn/ Kingdom of Bahrain*

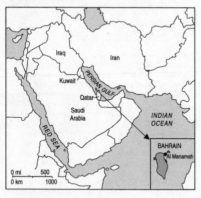

Area: 688 sq km/266 sq mi
Capital: Al Manamah (on Bahrain island)
Major towns/cities: Al Muharraq, Jidd Hafs, Isa Town, Rifa'a, Sitra
Major ports: Mina Sulman
Physical features: archipelago of 35 islands in Arabian Gulf, composed largely of sand-covered limestone; generally poor and infertile soil; flat and hot; causeway linking Bahrain to mainland Saudi Arabia
Head of state: Sheikh Hamad bin Isa al-Khalifa from 1999

Head of government: Sheikh Khalifa bin Salman al-Khalifa from 1970
Political system: monarchy
Political executive: absolute
Political parties: not permitted
Currency: Bahraini dinar
GNI per capita (PPP): (US$) 15,900 (2002 est)
Exports: petroleum and petroleum products, aluminium, chemicals, textiles. Principal market: India 8.4% (2000)
Population: 724,000 (2003 est)
Language: Arabic (official), Farsi, English, Urdu
Religion: 85% Muslim (Shiite 60%, Sunni 40%), Christian; Islam is the state religion
Life expectancy: 72 (men); 76 (women) (2000–05)
Chronology
4th century AD: Became part of Persian (Iranian) Sassanian Empire.
7th century: Adopted Islam.
8th century: Came under Arab Abbasid control.
1521: Seized by Portugal and held for eight decades, despite local unrest.
1602: Fell under the control of a Persian Shiite dynasty.
1783: Persian rule was overthrown and Bahrain became a sheikdom under the Sunni Muslim al-Khalifa dynasty, which originated from the same tribal federation, the Anaza, as the al-Saud family who now rule Saudi Arabia.
1816–20: Friendship and peace treaties were signed with Britain, which sought to end piracy in the Gulf.
1861: Became British protectorate; government shared between the ruling sheikh (Arab leader) and a British adviser.
1923: British influence increased when Sheikh Isa al-Khalifa was deposed and Charles Belgrave was appointed as the dominating 'adviser' to the new ruler.
1928: Sovereignty was claimed by Persia (Iran).
1930s: Oil was discovered, providing the backbone for the country's wealth.
1953–56: Council for National Unity was formed by Arab nationalists, but was suppressed after large demonstrations against British participation in the Suez War.
1968: Britain announced its intention to withdraw its forces. Bahrain formed, with Qatar and the Trucial States of the United Arab Emirates, the Federation of Arab Emirates.
1970: Iran accepted a United Nations (UN) report showing that Bahrain's inhabitants preferred independence to Iranian control.
1971: Qatar and the Trucial States withdrew from the federation; Bahrain became an independent state under Sheikh Isa bin Sulman al-Khalifa, who assumed the title of emir.
1973: A new constitution was adopted.
1975: The national assembly was dissolved and political activists driven underground. The emir and his family assumed virtually absolute power.
early 1980s: Tensions between the Sunni and Shiite Muslim communities were heightened by the Iranian Shiite Revolution of 1979.
1986: A causeway opened linking the island with Saudi Arabia.
1991: Bahrain joined a UN coalition that ousted Iraq from its occupation of Kuwait, and signed a defence cooperation agreement with the USA.
1995: Pro-democracy demonstrations were violently suppressed, with 11 deaths.

1999: Sheikh Hamad became Emir and head of state.
2000: A new Shura (consultative council) included women and non-Muslims for the first time.
2001: Women were given the vote for the first time in a referendum that approved the creation of a new constitution. Bahrain accepted the ruling of the International Court of Justice on a long-standing territorial dispute with Qatar.
2002: Sheikh Hamad bin Isa al-Khalifa proclaimed himself king of a constitutional kingdom after constitutional reforms were implemented. There were municipal and parliamentary elections for the first time in nearly 30 years, and for the first time women were allowed to run for national office in a Gulf State, although none were elected.
2003: The king was petitioned by thousands of alleged torture victims to repeal the law which protected suspected torturers from legal action.
2004: Nada Haffadh was appointed health minister, the first woman to head a government ministry. Bahrain and the US signed a free trade pact.

Baikal, Lake Russian **Ozero Baykal**, freshwater lake in southern Siberia, Russia, the largest in Asia, and the eighth largest in the world (area 31,500 sq km/12,150 sq mi). Lake Baikal is also the world's deepest lake (up to 1,640 m/5,700 ft) and its oldest, having existed for over 25 million years. It extends for some 636 km/395 mi, and has an average width of 48 km/30 mi. Fed by more than 300 rivers, the main one of which is the Selenga, it is drained only by the Lower Angara. Lake Baikal is famous for its great clarity and the diversity of its fauna.

bail the temporary setting at liberty of a person in legal custody on an undertaking (usually backed by some security, bonds or money, given either by that person or by someone else) to attend at a court at a stated time and place. If the person does not attend, the bail may be forfeited.

Baile Átha Cliath (Irish 'the town of the ford of the hurdles') official Irish name of *Dublin, capital of the Republic of Ireland, from 1922.

Baird, John Logie (1888–1946) Scottish electrical engineer who pioneered television. In 1925 he gave the first public demonstration of television, transmitting an image of a recognizable human face. The following year, he gave the world's first demonstration of true television before an audience of about 50 scientists at the Royal Institution, London. By 1928 Baird had succeeded in demonstrating colour television.

Bairiki port and capital of Kiribati on Tarawa atoll; population (2002 est) 25,900. Mother-of-pearl and copra are exported.

Baja California mountainous peninsula that forms the twin northwestern states of Lower (Spanish *baja*) California, Mexico; Baja California in the north, and Baja California Sur in the south.

Bakelite first synthetic *plastic, created by Belgian-born US chemist Leo Baekeland in 1909. Bakelite is hard, tough, and heatproof, and is used as an electrical insulator. It is made by the reaction of phenol with methanal (formaldehyde), producing a powdery resin that sets solid when heated. Objects are made by subjecting the resin to compression moulding (simultaneous heat and pressure in a mould).

Baker, Josephine (1906–1975) born Freda Josephine McDonald, US-born dancer and entertainer. Baker achieved international fame for her daring stage act which involved lively dancing, scat singing, and scanty costume. After appearing in the Paris Folies Bergère in 1925, she became enormously successful in France, becoming a French citizen in 1937. Baker boycotted the USA for many years, refusing to accept the secondary status afforded to African-American citizens. On her return to the USA in the 1950s, she campaigned for racial equality, forcing the integration of several theatres and night-clubs. She addressed the crowds before the Lincoln Memorial at the 1963 march on Washington.

baking powder mixture of *bicarbonate of soda, an acidic compound, and a nonreactive filler (usually starch or calcium sulphate), used in baking as a raising agent. It gives a light open texture to cakes and scones, and is used as a substitute for yeast in making soda bread.

Bakst, Leon (1866–1924) adopted name of Leon Rosenberg, Russian painter and theatrical designer. He combined intense colours and fantastic images adapted from Oriental and folk art with an art nouveau tendency toward graceful surface pattern. His designs for Diaghilev's touring Ballets Russes made a deep impression in Paris from 1909 to 1914.

Baku (or Baki) capital city of the republic of Azerbaijan, located on the Apsheron Peninsula on the western shore of the Caspian Sea; population of the city (1997 est) 1,066,800; population of the metropolitan area (1997 est) 1,727,200. Baku is an important industrial city and port. It has been a major centre of oil extraction and refining since the 1870s; the oilfields here are linked by pipelines with the Georgian Black Sea port of Batumi, while petroleum exports to Russia are shipped across the Caspian to Astrakhan and along the Volga River. Heavy engineering enterprises in the city produce equipment for the oil industry and ships; other industries include electrical machinery, chemicals, cement, textiles, leather tanning, footwear, and food processing. Baku has a hot climate and is subject to strong northwest winds.

Bakunin, Mikhail (1814–1876) Russian anarchist, active in Europe. In 1848 he was expelled from France as a revolutionary agitator. In Switzerland in the 1860s he became recognized as the leader of the anarchist movement. In 1869 he joined the First International (a coordinating socialist body) but, after stormy conflicts with Karl Marx, was expelled in 1872.

Balaclava, Battle of a Russian attack on 25 October 1854, during the Crimean War, on British positions, near a town in Ukraine, 10 km/6 mi southeast of Sevastopol. It was the scene of the ill-timed **Charge of the Light Brigade** of British cavalry against the Russian entrenched artillery. Of the 673 soldiers who took part, there were 272 casualties. **Balaclava helmets** were knitted hoods worn here by soldiers in the bitter weather.

Balakirev, Mily Alexeyevich (1837–1910) Russian composer. He wrote piano music, including the fantasy *Islamey* (1869), orchestral works, songs, and a symphonic poem *Tamara* (1867–82), all imbued with the Russian national character and spirit. He was the leader of the group known as 'The Five' and taught its members, Modest Mussorgsky, César Cui, Nikolai Rimsky-Korsakov, and Aleksandr Borodin.

balalaika Russian musical instrument, resembling a guitar. It has a triangular soundbox, frets, and two, three, or four strings played by strumming with the fingers. A range of instruments is made, from treble to bass, and orchestras of balalaikas are popular in Russia.

balance apparatus for weighing or measuring mass. The various types include the **beam balance**, consisting of a centrally pivoted lever with pans hanging from each end, and the **spring balance**, in which the object to be weighed stretches (or compresses) a vertical coil spring fitted with a pointer that indicates the weight on a scale. Kitchen and bathroom scales are balances.

balance of nature in ecology, the idea that there is an inherent equilibrium in most *ecosystems, with plants and animals interacting so as to produce a stable, continuing system of life on Earth. The activities of human beings can, and frequently do, disrupt the balance of nature.

balance of payments in economics, an account of a country's debit and credit transactions with other countries. Items are divided into the current account, which includes both visible trade (imports and exports of goods) and invisible trade (services such as transport, tourism, interest, and dividends), and the capital account, which includes investment in and out of the country, international grants, and loans. Deficits or surpluses on these accounts are brought into balance by buying and selling reserves of foreign currencies.

balance of power in politics, the theory that the best way of ensuring international order is to have power so distributed among states that no single state is able to achieve a dominant position. The term, which may also refer more simply to the actual distribution of power, is one of the most enduring concepts in international relations. Since the development of nuclear weapons, it has been asserted that the balance of power has been replaced by a 'balance of terror'.

Balanchine, George (1904–1983) born Georgi Melitonovich Balanchivadze, Russian-born US choreographer. After leaving the USSR in 1924, he worked with *Diaghilev in France. Moving to the USA in 1933, he became a major influence on dance, starting the New York City Ballet in 1948. He was the most influential 20th-century choreographer of ballet in the USA. He developed an 'American Neoclassic' dance style and made the New York City Ballet one of the world's great companies. His ballets are usually plotless and are performed in practice clothes to modern music. He also choreographed dances for five Hollywood films.

Balboa, Vasco Núñez de (1475–1519) Spanish *conquistador. He founded a settlement at Darien (now Panama) in 1511 and crossed the Isthmus in search of gold, reaching the Pacific Ocean (which he called the South Sea) on 25 September 1513, after a 25-day expedition. He was made admiral of the Pacific and governor of Panama but was removed by Spanish court intrigue, imprisoned, and executed.

Balder called 'the Good', in Norse mythology, the best, wisest, and most loved of all the gods; son of Odin and Frigga; husband of Nanna. He was one of the Aesir (principal gods), but was killed unwittingly with a twig of mistletoe shot by Hodur, his blind brother; the tragedy was engineered by the god-giant *Loki.

Baldwin, James Arthur (1924–1987) US writer and civil-rights activist. He portrayed with vivid intensity the suffering and despair of African-Americans in contemporary society. After his first novel, *Go Tell It on the Mountain* (1953), set in Harlem, and *Giovanni's Room* (1956), about a homosexual relationship in Paris, his writing became more politically indignant with *Another Country* (1962) and *The Fire Next Time* (1963), a collection of essays.

Baldwin, Stanley (1867–1947) 1st Earl Baldwin of Bewdley, British Conservative politician, prime minister 1923–24, 1924–29, and 1935–37. He weathered the general strike of 1926, secured complete adult suffrage in 1928, and handled the *abdication crisis of Edward VIII in 1936, but failed to prepare Britain for World War II.

Balearic Islands Spanish **Islas Baleares**, group of Mediterranean islands forming an autonomous region (since 1983) and province of Spain, comprising *Mallorca, *Menorca, *Ibiza, Cabrera, and *Formentera; area 5,014 sq km/1,936 sq mi; population (2001 est) 878,600. The capital is *Palma de Mallorca. Noted for their scenery and mild climate, the islands attract many visitors, making tourism a mainstay of the economy; agriculture and fishing are the chief economic activities, while limited quantities of coal, iron, and slate are mined. Exports include oranges, figs and other fruits, olive oil, wine, brandy, majolica ware, leather goods, and silver filigree. Both Castilian and Catalan are spoken.

Balfour, Arthur James (1848–1930) 1st Earl of Balfour, British Conservative politician, born in Scotland, prime minister 1902–05, and foreign secretary 1916–19. He issued the Balfour Declaration in 1917 and was involved in peace negotiations after World War I, signing the Treaty of Versailles.

Balfour Declaration letter, dated 2 November 1917, from British foreign secretary A J Balfour to Lord Rothschild (chair, British Zionist Federation) stating: 'HM government view with favour the establishment in Palestine of a national home for the Jewish people.' It helped form the basis for the foundation of Israel in 1948.

Bali island of Indonesia, east of Java, one of the Lesser Sunda Islands; area 5,800 sq km/2,240 sq mi; population (2000 est) 3,151,200. The capital is Denpasar. The island has many volcanic mountains, and the highest peak is Gunung Agung (3,142 m/10,308 ft). Tourism is a major source of revenue, and other industries include gold and silver work, woodcarving, weaving, copra, salt, and coffee. Arts include Balinese dancing, music (the Gamelan), and drama. Bali's Hindu culture dates back to the 7th century, but the island became a Dutch colony in 1908.

Baliol (or Balliol), John de (c. 1249–1315) King of Scotland 1292–96. As an heir to the Scottish throne on the death of Margaret, the Maid of Norway, he had the support of the English king, Edward I, against 12 other claimants. Baliol was proclaimed king, having paid homage to Edward. When English forces attacked Scotland, Baliol rebelled against England and gave up the kingdom.

Balkans (Turkish 'mountains') peninsula of southeastern Europe, stretching into Slovenia between the Adriatic and Aegean seas, comprising Albania, Bosnia-Herzegovina, Bulgaria, Croatia, Macedonia, Greece, Romania, the part of Turkey in Europe, and Serbia and Montenegro. It is joined to the rest of

Europe by an isthmus 1,200 km/750 mi wide between Rijeka, Croatia, on the west and the mouth of the Danube on the Black Sea to the east. The great ethnic diversity resulting from successive waves of invasion has made the Balkans a byword for political dissension, and the 1990s saw the break-up of Yugoslavia along ethnic lines. To '**Balkanize**' is to divide into small warring states.

Balkan Wars two wars 1912–13 and 1913 (preceding World War I) which resulted in the expulsion by the Balkan states of Ottoman Turkey from Europe, except for a small area around Istanbul.

Ball, John (died c. 1381) English priest. He was one of the leaders of the *Peasants' Revolt of 1381, known as 'the mad priest of Kent'. A follower of John Wycliffe and a believer in social equality, he was imprisoned for disagreeing with the archbishop of Canterbury. During the revolt he was released from prison, and when in Blackheath, London, incited people against the ruling classes by preaching from the text 'When Adam delved and Eve span, who was then the gentleman?' When the revolt collapsed he escaped but was captured near Coventry and executed.

ballad (Latin *ballare* 'to dance') literary *genre of traditional narrative poetry, widespread in Europe and the USA. Ballads are simple in metre, sometimes (as in Russia) without regular lines and *rhymes or (as in Denmark) dependent on *assonance. Concerned with some strongly emotional event, the ballad is halfway between the *lyric poem and the *epic. Most English ballads date from the 15th century but may describe earlier events. Poets involved in *Romanticism both in England and in Germany were greatly influenced by the ballad revival, as seen in, for example, the *Lyrical Ballads* (1798) of English poets *Wordsworth and *Coleridge. *Des Knaben Wunderhorn/The Boy's Magic Horn* (1805–08), a collection edited by German writers Klemens Brentano and Achim von Arnim, was a major influence on 19th-century German poetry. The ballad form was adapted in 'broadsheets' (so called because they were printed on large sheets of paper), with a satirical or political motive, and in the 'hanging' ballads purporting to come from condemned criminals.

ballade in literature, a poetic form developed in France in the later Middle Ages from the ballad, generally consisting of one or more groups of three stanzas of seven or eight lines each, followed by a shorter stanza or envoy, the last line being repeated as a chorus. In music, a ballade is an instrumental piece based on a story; a form used in piano works by Chopin and Liszt.

Ballard, J(ames) G(raham) (1930–) English novelist. He became prominent in the 1960s for his science fiction works on the theme of catastrophe and collapse of the urban landscape. His fundamentally moral vision is expressed with an unrestrained imagination and a pessimistic irony.

ballet (Italian *balletto* 'a little dance') theatrical representation in *dance form in which music also plays a major part in telling a story or conveying a mood. Some such form of entertainment existed in ancient Greece, but Western ballet as we know it today first appeared in Renaissance Italy, where it was a court entertainment. From there it was brought by Catherine de' Medici to France in the form of a spectacle combining singing, dancing, and declamation. During the 18th century there were major developments in

technique and ballet gradually became divorced from opera, emerging as an art form in its own right. In the 20th century Russian ballet had a vital influence on the classical tradition in the West, and ballet developed further in the USA through the work of George Balanchine and the American Ballet Theater, and in the UK through the influence of Marie Rambert. *Modern dance is a separate development.

ballistics study of the motion and impact of projectiles such as bullets, bombs, and missiles. For projectiles from a gun, relevant exterior factors include temperature, barometric pressure, and wind strength; and for nuclear missiles these extend to such factors as the speed at which the Earth turns.

balloon lighter-than-air craft that consists of a gasbag filled with gas lighter than the surrounding air and an attached basket, or gondola, for carrying passengers and/or instruments. In 1783, the first successful human ascent was in Paris, in a hot-air balloon designed by the *Montgolfier brothers Joseph Michel and Jacques Etienne. In 1785, a hydrogen-filled balloon designed by French physicist Jacques Charles travelled across the English Channel.

ballot (Italian *ballotta*, diminutive of *balla*, 'a ball') the process of voting in an election. In political elections in democracies ballots are usually secret: voters indicate their choice of candidate on a voting slip which is then placed in a sealed ballot box. **Ballot rigging** is a term used to describe elections that are fraudulent because of interference with the voting process or the counting of *votes.

ball valve valve that works by the action of external pressure raising a ball and thereby opening a hole.

balsam any of various garden plants belonging to the balsam family. They are usually annuals with spurred red or white flowers and pods that burst and scatter their seeds when ripe. (Genus *Impatiens*, family Balsaminaceae.) In medicine and perfumery, balsam refers to various oily or gummy aromatic plant *resins, such as balsam of Peru from the Central American tree *Myroxylon pereirae*.

Baltic Sea shallow sea, extending northeast from the narrow Skagerrak arm of the North Sea and the Kattegat strait, between Sweden and Denmark, to the Gulf of Bothnia between Sweden and Finland. Its coastline is 8,000 km/5,000 mi long; the sea is 1,500 km/930 mi long and 650 km/404 mi wide, and its area, including the gulfs of Riga, Finland, and Bothnia, is 422,300 sq km/163,000 sq mi. Its average depth is 65 m/213 ft, but it is 460 m/1,500 ft at its deepest. Its shoreline is shared by Denmark, Germany, Poland, the Baltic States, Russia, Finland, and Sweden.

Baltic States collective name for the states of Estonia, Latvia, and Lithuania. They were formed as independent states after World War I out of former territories of the Russian Empire. The government of the USSR recognized their independence in peace treaties signed in 1920, but in 1939 forced them to allow occupation of important military bases by Soviet troops. In the following year, the Baltic states were absorbed into the Soviet Union as constituent republics. They regained their independence in September 1991 after the collapse of the Soviet Union.

Baltimore industrial port and largest city in Maryland, on the western shore of Chesapeake Bay, 50 km/31 mi northeast of Washington, DC; population (2000 est) 651,200. Industries include shipbuilding, oil refining, food processing, and the manufacture of steel, chemicals, and aerospace equipment. The city was named after George Calvert, 1st Lord Baltimore, the founder of Maryland. It dates from 1729 and was incorporated as a city in 1797.

Baltistan region in the *Karakoram range of northeast Kashmir, western Ladakh, held by Pakistan since 1949. The region lies to the south of K2, the world's second highest mountain (8,611 m/28,2161 ft); the average elevation is 3,350 m/11,000 ft. It contains the upper reaches of the Indus River. It is the home of Balti Muslims of Tibetan origin.

Baluchistan mountainous desert area, comprising a province of Pakistan, part of the Iranian province of Sistán and Balúchestan, and a small area of Afghanistan. The Pakistani province has an area of 347,200 sq km/134,050 sq mi and a population (2002 est) of 7,215,700; its capital is Quetta. Sistán and Balúchestan has an area of 181,600 sq km/70,098 sq mi and a population (2002 est) of 2,093,600; its capital is Zahedan. The Quetta region has become important for fruit-growing. Coal, natural gas, chrome and other minerals have been discovered and exploited. The 1,600 km/1,000 mi rail network has strategic as well as economic significance. Much of Baluchistan consists of dry and rocky plateau areas with a rainfall of less than 13 cm/5 in a year and therefore little plant life.

Balzac, Honoré de (1799–1850) French writer. He was one of the major novelists of the 19th century. His first success was *Les Chouans/The Chouans*, inspired by Walter Scott. This was the beginning of the long series of novels *La Comédie humaine/The Human Comedy* which includes *Eugénie Grandet* (1833), *Le Père Goriot* (1834), and *Cousine Bette* (1846). He also wrote the Rabelaisian *Contes drolatiques/Ribald Tales* (1833).

Bamako or **Bamaku** or **Bammaco** capital and port of Mali, lying on the upper Niger River, in the southwest of the country; population (2001 est) 947,100. As a major river port, it is vital to the economy of a landlocked country. It also has an international airport and is linked by rail to the port of Dakar in Senegal on the Atlantic coast. Industries include ceramics, pharmaceuticals, chemicals, textiles, farm machinery, batteries, river fishing, and food and tobacco processing.

bamboo any of a large group of giant grass plants, found mainly in tropical and subtropical regions. Some species grow as tall as 36 m/120 ft. The stems are hollow and jointed and can be used in furniture, house, and boat construction. he young shoots are edible; paper is made from the stems. (Genus *Bambusa*, family Gramineae.)

banana any of several treelike tropical plants which grow up to 8 m/25 ft high. The edible banana is the fruit of a sterile hybrid form. (Genus *Musa*, family Musaceae.). The banana plant grows as a series of suckers from a rhizome. Each stem gradually droops downwards and produces at its tip the male flowers, which are sterile. The female flowers, which produce the edible fruit without fertilization, are found further along the stem. After a stem has produced a crop of fruit, it dies and is replaced by a new stem from a bud further along the rhizome. A banana plant may live for over 60 years.

Banda, Hastings Kamuzu (1905–1997) Malawi politician, physician, and president (1966–94). He led his country's independence movement and was prime minister of Nyasaland (the former name of Malawi) from 1964. He became Malawi's first president in 1966 and was named president for life in 1971; his rule was authoritarian. Having bowed to opposition pressure and opened the way for a pluralist system, Banda stood in the first free presidential elections for 30 years in 1994, but was defeated by Bakili Muluzi. In January 1996 he and his former aide, John Tembo, were acquitted of the murders of three senior politicians and a lawyer in 1983.

Bandaranaike, Sirimavo (1916–2000) born Sirimavo Ratwatte Dias Bandaranaike, Sri Lankan politician, prime minister 1994–2000. She succeeded her husband Solomon Bandaranaike to become the world's first female prime minister, 1960–65 and 1970–77, but was expelled from parliament in 1980 for abuse of her powers while in office. Her daughter Chandrika Bandaranaike Kumaratunga was elected president in 1994. She resigned her position on 10 August 2000 because of poor health, and was replaced by Ratnasiri Wickremanayake.

Bandar Seri Begawan formerly **Brunei Town** (until 1970), capital and largest town of *Brunei, 14 km/9 mi from the mouth of the Brunei River; population (1995 est) 50,000. The port serves ocean-going vessels; industries include oil refining and construction.

bandicoot small marsupial mammal inhabiting Australia and New Guinea. There are about 11 species, family Peramelidae. Bandicoots are rat- or rabbit-sized and live in burrows. They have long snouts, eat insects, and are nocturnal. A related group, the rabbit bandicoots or bilbies, is reduced to a single species that is now endangered and protected by law.

Bandung or **Bandoeng** commercial city and capital of Jawa Barat province on the island of Java, Indonesia, 180 km/112 mi southeast of Jakarta; population (1997 est) 2,429,000. Bandung is the third-largest city in Indonesia. Industries include textiles, chemicals, and plastics.

Bandung Conference first conference, in 1955, of the Afro-Asian nations, proclaiming anticolonialism and neutrality between East and West. It was organized by Indonesia, Myanmar, Sri Lanka, India, and Pakistan.

Bangalore capital of *Karnataka state, southern India, lying 950 m/3,000 ft above sea level; population (2001 est) 4,292,200. Industries include electronics, aircraft, railway-carriage, and machine-tools construction, as well as the manufacture of electrical goods and the processing of coffee. Bangalore University and the University of Agriculture Sciences were founded in 1964, and the National Aeronautical Institute in 1960.

Banghazi alternative spelling of Benghazi, an industrial port in northern Libya.

Bangkok Thai **Krung Thep**, (Thai 'City of Angels') capital and port of Thailand, on the east bank of the River Chao Phraya, 40 km/24 mi from the Gulf of Thailand; population (2000 est) 6,320,200; the population of the whole metropolitan area, including the industrial centre of Thon Buri across the river, is 10,068,000 (2000 est). It is the economic centre of the country and the hub of the transport system. The port is accessible to smaller ocean-going ships, but much of its trade now passes through outports, such as Samut

Prakan. Industries such as the manufacture of automobile parts, computers, and textiles have largely overtaken agricultural output. Banking and tourism are particularly important economically, while other industries include paper, ceramics, cement, silk, tobacco, and rice. The city has been the headquarters of the Southeast Asia Treaty Organization (SEATO) since 1955, and hosted the 13th Asian Games in 1998.

Bangladesh
formerly **East Bengal (until 1955)**, **East Pakistan (1955–71)**
National name: *Gana Prajatantri Bangladesh/People's Republic of Bangladesh*

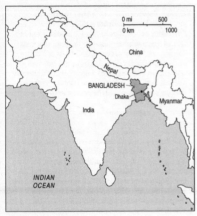

Area: 144,000 sq km/55,598 sq mi
Capital: Dhaka
Major towns/cities: Rajshahi, Khulna, Chittagong, Sylhet, Rangpur, Narayanganj
Major ports: Chittagong, Khulna
Physical features: flat delta of rivers Ganges (Padma) and Brahmaputra (Jamuna), the largest estuarine delta in the world; annual rainfall of 2,540 mm/100 in; some 75% of the land is less than 3 m/10 ft above sea level; hilly in extreme southeast and northeast
Head of state: Iajuddin Ahmed from 2002
Head of government: Khaleda Zia from 2001
Political system: emergent democracy
Political executive: parliamentary
Political parties: Bangladesh Nationalist Party (BNP), Islamic, right of centre; Awami League (AL), secular, moderate socialist; Jatiya Dal (National Party), Islamic nationalist
Currency: taka
GNI per capita (PPP): (US$) 1,720 (2002 est)
Exports: clothing, raw jute and jute goods, tea, leather and leather products, shrimps and frogs' legs. Principal market: USA 29.6% (2001)
Population: 146,736,000 (2003 est)
Language: Bengali (official), English
Religion: Muslim 88%, Hindu 11%; Islam is the state religion
Life expectancy: 61 (men); 62 (women) (2000–05)
Chronology
c. **1000 BC:** Arrival of Bang tribe in lower Ganges valley, establishing the kingdom of Banga (Bengal).

8th–12th centuries AD: Bengal was ruled successively by the Buddhist Pala and Hindu Senha dynasties.
1199: Bengal was invaded and briefly ruled by the Muslim Khiljis from Central Asia.
1576: Bengal was conquered by the Muslim Mogul emperor Akbar.
1651: The British East India Company established a commercial factory in Bengal.
1757: Bengal came under de facto British rule after Robert Clive defeated the nawab (ruler) of Bengal at Battle of Plassey.
1905–12: Bengal was briefly partitioned by the British Raj into a Muslim-dominated east and Hindu-dominated west.
1906: The Muslim League (ML) was founded in Dhaka.
1947: Bengal was formed into an eastern province of Pakistan on the partition of British India, with the ML administration in power.
1954: The opposition United Front, dominated by the Awami League (AL) and campaigning for East Bengal's autonomy, trounced the ML in elections.
1955: East Bengal was renamed East Pakistan.
1966: Sheikh Mujibur Rahman of AL announced a Six-Point Programme of autonomy for East Pakistan.
1970: 500,000 people were killed in a cyclone. The pro-autonomy AL secured an electoral victory in East Pakistan.
1971: Bangladesh ('land of the Bangla speakers') emerged as an independent nation after a bloody civil war with Indian military intervention on the side of East Pakistan; 10 million refugees fled to India.
1974: Hundreds of thousands died in a famine; a state of emergency was declared.
1975: Martial law was imposed.
1978–79: Elections were held and civilian rule restored.
1982: Martial law was reimposed after a military coup.
1986: Elections were held but disputed. Martial law ended.
1987: A state of emergency was declared in response to demonstrations and violent strikes.
1988: Assembly elections were boycotted by the main opposition parties. The state of emergency was lifted. Islam was made the state religion. Monsoon floods left 30 million people homeless and thousands dead.
1991: A cyclone killed around 139,000 people and left up to 10 million homeless. Parliamentary government was restored.
1996: Power was handed to a neutral caretaker government. A general election was won by the AL, led by Sheikh Hasina Wazed, and Shahabuddin Ahmed was appointed president. The BNP boycotted parliament. An agreement was made with India on the sharing of River Ganges water.
1998: The BNP ended its boycott of parliament. Two-thirds of Bangladesh was devastated by floods; 1,300 people were killed. Opposition-supported general strikes sought the removal of Sheikh Hasina's government.
2000: Ex-president Hussain Mohammad Ershad was fined US$1 million and sentenced to five years' imprisonment for corruption by the Dhaka high court.
2001: Khaleda Zia of the BNP became prime minister after an election victory.
2002: President Chowdhury resigned, replaced by Iajuddin Ahmed. Bombings killed 17 and injured thousands of people.

2004: Twenty-one general strikes were called as part of a campaign to bring down the government. Parliament amended the constitution to reserve seats for female MPs. Bombings killed and injured people in the northeast of the country. The Awami League leader Sheikh Hasina survived a grenade atttack in Dhaka. Flooding killed almost 800 people and left millions homeless and stranded.

2005: An Awami League politician, Shah AMS Kibria, was killed by a grenade attack during a political rally.

Bangui capital and main river port of the Central African Republic, on the River Ubangi; population (1995 est) 698,000. The city is the centre for the country's light industries, including beer, cigarettes, office machinery, and timber and metal products. Bangui has an airport and contains the main depot for the storage and transportation of imported petroleum products. The city, which also serves as an outlet for the Republic of Chad, has a considerable trade in cotton and coffee.

banjo resonant stringed musical instrument with a long fretted neck and circular drum-type soundbox covered on the topside only by stretched skin (now usually plastic). It is played with a plectrum. Modern banjos normally have five strings.

Banjul capital and chief port of Gambia, on an island at the mouth of the River Gambia; population of urban area (1995 est) 186,000; city (1995 est) 58,700. It is located 195 km/121 mi southeast of Dakar (capital of Senegal). Established in 1816 as a settlement for freed slaves, it was known as Bathurst until 1973. The city has an airport and industries include peanut processing and exporting, brewing, and tourism (centred at the nearby resorts of Bakau, Fajara, Kotu, and Kololi).

bank financial institution that uses funds deposited with it to lend money to companies or individuals, and also provides financial services to its customers. The first banks opened in Italy and Cataluña around 1400.

bank holiday in the UK, a public holiday, when banks are closed by law. Bank holidays were instituted by the Bank Holiday Acts 1871 and 1875.

Bank of England UK central bank founded by act of Parliament in 1694. It was entrusted with issuing bank notes in 1844 and nationalized in 1946. It is banker to the clearing banks and the UK government.

bank rate interest rate fixed by the Bank of England as a guide to mortgage, hire purchase rates, and so on, which was replaced in 1972 by the **minimum lending rate** (lowest rate at which the Bank acts as lender of ast resort to the money market), which from 1978 was again a 'bank rate' set by the Bank.

bankruptcy process by which the property of a person (in legal terms, an individual or corporation) unable to pay debts is taken away under a court order and divided fairly among the person's creditors, after preferential payments such as taxes and wages. Proceedings may be instituted either by the debtor (voluntary bankruptcy) or by any creditor for a substantial sum (involuntary bankruptcy). Until 'discharged', a bankrupt is severely restricted in financial activities.

banksia any shrub or tree of a group native to Australia, including the honeysuckle tree. They are named after the English naturalist and explorer Joseph Banks. (Genus *Banksia*, family Proteaceae.)

Bannister, Roger Gilbert (1929–) English track and field athlete. He was the first person to run a mile in under four minutes. He achieved this feat at Iffley Road, Oxford, England, on 6 May 1954, in a time of 3 min 59.4 sec.

Bannockburn, Battle of battle fought on 23–24 June 1314 at Bannockburn, near Stirling, Scotland, between Robert (I) the Bruce, King of Scotland, and Edward II of England. The defeat of the English led to the independence of Scotland.

bantam small ornamental variety of domestic chicken weighing about 0.5–1 kg/1–2 lb. Bantams can either be a small version of one of the larger breeds, or a separate type. Some are prolific egg layers. Bantam cocks have a reputation as spirited fighters.

Banting, Frederick Grant (1891–1941) Canadian physician who was awarded a Nobel Prize for Physiology or Medicine in 1923 for his discovery, in 1921, of a technique for isolating the hormone insulin. Banting and his colleague Charles *Best tied off the ducts of the *pancreas to determine the function of the cells known as the islets of Langerhans and thus made possible the treatment of diabetes. John J R Macleod, Banting's mentor, shared the prize, and Banting divided his prize with Best.

Bantu languages group of related languages belonging to the Niger-Congo family, spoken widely over the greater part of Africa south of the Sahara, including Swahili, Xhosa, and Zulu. Meaning 'people' in Zulu, the word Bantu itself illustrates a characteristic use of prefixes: *mu-ntu* 'man', *ba-ntu* 'people'.

banyan tropical Asian fig tree. It produces aerial roots that grow down from its spreading branches, forming supporting pillars that look like separate trunks. (*Ficus benghalensis*, family Moraceae.)

baobab tree with rootlike branches, hence the nickname 'upside-down tree', and a disproportionately thick girth, up to 9 m/30 ft in diameter. The pulp of its fruit is edible and is known as monkey bread. (Genus *Adansonia*, family Bombacaceae.)

baptism (Greek 'to dip') immersion in or sprinkling with water as a religious rite of initiation. It was practised long before the beginning of Christianity. In Christian infant baptism, the ceremony welcomes the child into the church community. Sponsors or godparents make vows on behalf of the child, which are renewed by the child at confirmation; some denominations only practise baptism of believers, performed in adulthood when its significance may be understood. Baptism is one of the seven sacraments. The Amrit Sanskar ceremony in Sikhism is sometimes referred to as baptism.

Baptist member of any of several Protestant and evangelical Christian sects that practise baptism by immersion only upon profession of faith. Baptists seek their authority in the Bible. They originated among English Dissenters who took refuge in the Netherlands in the early 17th century, and spread by emigration and, later, missionary activity. Of the world total of approximately 31 million, some 26.5 million are in the USA and 265,000 in the UK.

bar modular segment of music incorporating a fixed number of beats, as in the phrase 'two/three/four beats to the bar'. It is shown in notation by vertical 'barring' of the musical continuum. The US term is **measure**.

barb general name for fish of the genus *Barbus* and some related genera of the family Cyprinidae. As well as the *barbel, barbs include many small tropical Old World species, some of which are familiar aquarium species. They are active egg-laying species, usually of 'typical' fish shape and with barbels at the corner of the mouth.

Barbados

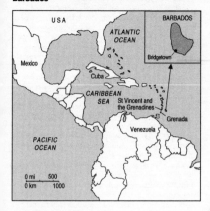

Area: 430 sq km/166 sq mi
Capital: Bridgetown
Major towns/cities: Speightstown, Holetown, Oistins
Physical features: most easterly island of the West Indies; surrounded by coral reefs; subject to hurricanes June–November; highest point Mount Hillaby 340 m/1,115 ft
Head of state: Queen Elizabeth II from 1966, represented by Governor General Sir Clifford Straughn Husbands from 1996
Head of government: Owen Arthur from 1994
Political system: liberal democracy
Political executive: parliamentary
Political parties: Barbados Labour Party (BLP), moderate left of centre; Democratic Labour Party (DLP), moderate left of centre; National Democratic Party (NDP), centrist
Currency: Barbados dollar
GNI per capita (PPP): (US$) 15,560 (2002 est)
Exports: sugar, molasses, syrup-rum, chemicals, electrical components. Principal market: USA 15.3% (2000)
Population: 270,000 (2003 est)
Language: English (official), Bajan (a Barbadian English dialect)
Religion: 40% Anglican, 8% Pentecostal, 6% Methodist, 4% Roman Catholic
Life expectancy: 75 (men); 80 (women) (2000–05)
Chronology
1536: Visited by Portuguese explorer Pedro a Campos and the name Los Barbados ('The Bearded Ones') given in reference to its 'bearded' fig trees. Indigenous Arawak people were virtually wiped out, via epidemics, after contact with Europeans.
1627: British colony established; developed as a sugar-plantation economy, initially on basis of black slaves brought in from West Africa.
1639: The island's first parliament, the House of Assembly, was established.

1834: The island's slaves were freed.
1937: There was an outbreak of riots, followed by establishment of the Barbados Labour Party (BLP) by Grantley Adams, and moves towards a more independent political system.
1951: Universal adult suffrage was introduced. The BLP won a general election.
1954: Ministerial government was established, with BLP leader Adams as the first prime minister.
1955: A group broke away from the BLP and formed the Democratic Labour Party (DLP).
1961: Independence was achieved from Britain.
1966: Barbados achieved full independence within the Commonwealth.
1967: Barbados became a member of the United Nations (UN).
1972: Diplomatic relations with Cuba were established.
1983: Barbados supported the US invasion of Grenada.
1999: The BLP gained a landslide victory in general elections, securing 26 of the 28 House of Assembly seats.
2003: The BLP, led by Prime Minister Owen Arthur, retained power in parliamentary elections, winning 23 of the 30 seats in the House of Assembly.
2004: A sea border dispute between Barbados and Trinidad and Tobago was taken to a United Nations-backed tribunal.

Barbary ape tailless, yellowish-brown macaque monkey *Macaca sylvanus*, 55–75 cm/20–30 in long. Barbary apes are found in the mountains and wilds of Algeria and Morocco, especially in the forests of the Atlas Mountains. They were introduced to Gibraltar, where legend has it that the British will leave if the ape colony dies out.

barbastelle insect-eating bat *Barbastella barbastellus* with hairy cheeks and lips, 'frosted' black fur, and a wingspan of about 25 cm/10 in. It lives in hollow trees and under roofs, and is occasionally found in the UK but more commonly in Europe.

barbel freshwater fish *Barbus barbus* found in fast-flowing rivers with sand or gravel bottoms in Britain and Europe. Long-bodied, and up to 1 m/3 ft long in total, the barbel has four **barbels** ('little beards' – sensory fleshy filaments) near the mouth.

barbet (Latin *barbatus*, 'bearded') small, tropical bird, often brightly coloured. There are about 78 species of barbet in the family Capitonidae, order Piciformes, common to tropical Africa, Asia, and America. Barbets eat insects and fruit and, being distant relations of woodpeckers, drill nest holes with their beaks. The name comes from the 'little beard' of bristles about the mouth that assists them in catching insects.

Barbie, Klaus (1913–1991) German Nazi, a member of the *SS paramilitary organization from 1936. During World War II he was involved in the deportation of Jews from the occupied Netherlands from 1940 to 1942 and in tracking down Jews and Resistance workers in France from 1942 to 1945. He was arrested in 1983 and convicted of crimes against humanity in France in 1987.

barbiturate hypnosedative drug, commonly known as a 'sleeping pill', consisting of any salt or ester of barbituric acid $C_4H_4O_3N_2$. It works by depressing brain activity. Most barbiturates, being highly addictive, are no longer prescribed and are listed as controlled substances.

Barbizon School French school of landscape painters of the mid-19th century, based at Barbizon in the forest of Fontainebleau. They aimed to paint fresh, realistic scenes, sketching and painting their subjects in the open air. Members included Jean François Millet, Théodore Rousseau, and Charles Daubigny.

Barbour, John (c. 1320–1395) Scottish poet. His epic 13,000-line poem *The Brus* (written 1374–75, printed 1571) chronicles the war of Scottish independence and includes a vivid account of Robert Bruce's victory over the English at Bannockburn in 1314. It is among the earliest known works of Scottish poetry.

Barcelona port and capital of Barcelona province and of the autonomous community of *Cataluña, northeast Spain; population (2001 est) 1,505,300; conurbation (2003 est) 3,889,200. Barcelona is Spainouths second-largest city, its largest port, and its chief commercial centre. Industries include textiles, engineering, motor vehicles, electrical equipment, and chemicals. As the chief centre of Catalan nationalism, Barcelona was prominent in the overthrow of the monarchy in 1931 and was the last city of the republic to surrender to General Francisco Franco in 1939. The city hosted the Summer Olympics in 1992.

bard Celtic minstrel who, in addition to composing songs, usually at a court, often held important political posts. Originating in the pre-Christian era, bards were persecuted in Wales during the 13th century on political grounds. Since the 19th century annual meetings and competitions in Wales – known as *eisteddfod – have attempted to revive the musical tradition of the bard.

Bardeen, John (1908–1991) US physicist. He was awarded the Nobel Prize for Physics in 1956, with Walter Brattain and William Shockley, for the development of the *transistor in 1948 and he became the first double winner of the Nobel Prize for Physics in 1972 (with Leon Cooper and Robert Schrieffer) for his work on *superconductivity.

Bardot, Brigitte (1934–) adopted name of Camille Javal, French film actor. A celebrated sex symbol of the 1950s and 1960s, she did much to popularize French cinema internationally. Her films include *Et Dieu créa la femme/And God Created Woman* (1956) directed by Roger Vadim (1928–), Jean-Luc Godard's *Le Mépris/Contempt* (1963), and Louis Malle's *Viva Maria!* (1965).

Barebones Parliament English assembly called by Oliver *Cromwell to replace the *Rump Parliament in July 1653. Although its members attempted to pass sensible legislation (civil marriage; registration of births, deaths, and marriages; custody of lunatics), their attempts to abolish tithes, patronage, and the court of chancery, and to codify the law, led to the resignation of the moderates and its dissolution in December 1653.

Barents, Willem (c. 1550–1597) Dutch explorer and navigator. He made three expeditions to seek the *Northeast Passage; he died on the last voyage. The Barents Sea, part of the Arctic Ocean north of Norway, is named after him.

baritone male voice pitched between bass and tenor, of approximate range G2–F4. It is also used before the name of an instrument, for example baritone saxophone, and indicates that the instrument sounds in approximately the same range.

barium chemical symbol Ba, (Greek *barytes* 'heavy') soft, silver-white, metallic element, atomic number 56, relative atomic mass 137.33. It is one of the alkaline-earth metals, found in nature as barium carbonate and barium sulphate. As the sulphate it is used in medicine: taken as a suspension (a 'barium meal'), its movement along the gut is followed using X-rays. The barium sulphate, which is opaque to X-rays, shows the shape of the gut, revealing any abnormalities of the alimentary canal. Barium is also used in alloys, pigments, and safety matches and, with strontium, forms the emissive surface in cathode-ray tubes. It was first discovered in baryte or heavy spar.

bark protective outer layer on the stems and roots of woody plants, composed mainly of dead cells. To allow for expansion of the stem, the bark is continually added to from within, and the outer surface often becomes cracked or is shed as scales. Trees deposit a variety of chemicals in their bark, including poisons. Many of these chemical substances have economic value because they can be used in the manufacture of drugs. Quinine, derived from the bark of the *Cinchona* tree, is used to fight malarial infections; curare, an anaesthetic used in medicine, comes from the *Strychnus toxifera* tree in the Amazonian rainforest.

bark beetle any one of a number of species of mainly wood-boring beetles. Bark beetles are cylindrical, brown or black, and 1–9 mm/0.04–0.4 in long. Some live just under the bark and others bore deeper into the hardwood. The detailed tunnelling pattern that they make within the trunk varies with the species concerned, and is used for identification.

barley cereal belonging to a family of grasses. It resembles wheat but is more tolerant of cold and draughts. Cultivated barley (*Hordeum vulgare*) comes in three main varieties – six-rowed, four-rowed, and two-rowed. (Family Gramineae.)

bar mitzvah (Hebrew 'son of the commandment') in Judaism, initiation of a boy, which takes place at the age of 13, into the adult Jewish community; less common is the **bat mitzvah** for girls, an identical ceremony conducted mainly in Reform and Liberal congregations. The child is called up to the bimah to read a passage from the Torah in the synagogue on the Sabbath, and is subsequently regarded as a full member of the congregation.

barnacle marine crustacean of the subclass Cirripedia. The larval form is free-swimming, but when mature, it fixes itself by the head to rock or floating wood. The animal then remains attached, enclosed in a shell through which the cirri (modified legs) protrude to sweep food into the mouth. Barnacles include the stalked **goose barnacle** *Lepas anatifera* found on ships' bottoms, and the **acorn barnacles**, such as *Balanus balanoides*, common on rocks.

Barnardo, Thomas John (1845–1905) British philanthropist. He was known as Dr Barnardo, although he was not medically qualified. He opened the first of a series of homes for destitute children in 1867 in Stepney, East London.

Barnard's star star, 6 light years away from the Sun, in the constellation Ophiuchus. It is the second-closest star to the Sun, after Alpha Centauri, a triple star, the closest component of which, Proxima Centauri, is 4.2 light years away from the Sun. It is a faint red dwarf of 10th magnitude, visible only through a telescope. It is named after the US astronomer Edward E Barnard (1857–1923), who discovered in 1916 that it has the fastest proper motion of any star, 10.3 arc seconds per year.

Barnet, Battle of in the Wars of the *Roses, the defeat of Lancaster by York on 14 April 1471 in Barnet (now in northwest London).

barometer instrument that measures atmospheric pressure as an indication of weather. Most often used are the mercury barometer and the aneroid barometer.

baron rank in the *peerage of the UK, above a baronet and below a viscount. Historically, any member of the higher nobility, a direct vassal (feudal servant) of the king, not bearing other titles such as duke or count. The term originally meant the vassal of a lord, but acquired its present meaning in the 12th century.

baronet British order of chivalry below the rank of baron, but above that of knight, created in 1611 by James I to finance the settlement of Ulster. It is a hereditary honour, although women cannot succeed to a baronetcy. A baronet does not have a seat in the House of Lords but is entitled to the style *Sir* before his name. The sale of baronetcies was made illegal in 1937.

Barons' Wars civil wars in England: **1215–17** between King *John and his barons, over his failure to honour *Magna Carta; **1264–67** between *Henry III (and the future Edward I) and his barons (led by Simon de *Montfort); **1264** 14 May Battle of Lewes at which Henry III was defeated and captured; **1265** 4 August Simon de Montfort was defeated by Edward at Evesham and killed.

baroque in the visual arts, architecture, and music, a style characterized by expressive, flamboyant, and dynamic design. It flourished in Europe between 1600 and 1750, particularly in Catholic countries, where it played a central role in the crusading work of the Catholic Counter-Reformation. To inspire its viewers, the style used elaborate effects to appeal directly to the emotions. In some of its most characteristic works – such as Giovanni Bernini's Cornaro Chapel (Sta Maria della Vittoria, Rome), containing his sculpture *Ecstasy of St Theresa* (1645–52) – painting, sculpture, decoration, and architecture were designed to create a single, dramatic effect. Many masterpieces of the baroque emerged in churches and palaces in Rome, but the style soon spread throughout Europe, changing in character as it did so. The term baroque has also by extension been used to describe the music and literature of the period, but it has a much less clear meaning in these fields, and is more a convenient label than a stylistic description.

Barra southern island of the larger Outer *Hebrides, Scotland, part of the Western Isles unitary council area; area 90 sq km/35 sq mi; population (1991) 1,280. It is separated from South Uist by the Sound of Barra. The principal town is Castlebay. The main industries are fishing and tourism.

barracuda large predatory fish *Sphyraena barracuda* found in the warmer seas of the world. It can grow over 2 m/6 ft long and has a superficial resemblance to a pike. Young fish shoal, but the older ones are solitary. The barracuda has very sharp shearing teeth and may attack people.

Barras, Paul François Jean Nicolas, Count (1755–1829) French revolutionary. He was elected to the National Convention in 1792 and helped to overthrow Robespierre in 1794. In 1795 he became a member of the ruling Directory (see *French Revolution). In 1796 he

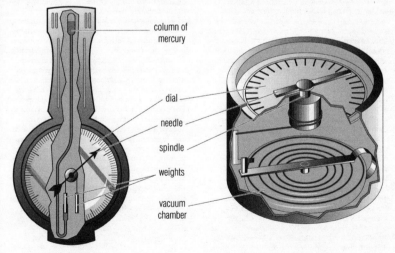

column of mercury

dial

needle

spindle

weights

vacuum chamber

mercury barometer

aneroid barometer

barometer The mercury barometer (left) and the aneroid barometer (right). In the mercury barometer, the weight of the column of mercury is balanced by the pressure of the atmosphere on the lower end. A change in height of the column indicates a change in atmospheric pressure. In the aneroid barometer, any change of atmospheric pressure causes the metal box which contains the vacuum to be squeezed or to expand slightly. The movements of the box sides are transferred to a pointer and scale via a chain of levers.

brought about the marriage of his former mistress, Joséphine de Beauharnais, with Napoleon and assumed dictatorial powers. After Napoleon's coup d'état on 19 November 1799, Barras fell into disgrace.

barrel organ portable pipe organ, played by turning a handle, or occasionally by a clockwork mechanism. The handle works a pump and drives a replaceable cylinder upon which music is embossed as a pattern of ridges controlling the passage of air to the pipes. It is often confused with the barrel or street piano used by buskers, which employed a barrel-and-pin mechanism to control a piano hammer action.

Barrett Browning, Elizabeth English poet; see *Browning, Elizabeth Barrett.

Barrie, J(ames) M(atthew) (1860–1937) Scottish dramatist and novelist. His work includes *The Admirable Crichton* (1902) and the children's fantasy *Peter Pan* (1904).

barrier island long island of sand, lying offshore and parallel to the coast. Some are over 100 km/60 mi in length. Most barrier islands are derived from marine sands piled up by shallow longshore currents that sweep sand parallel to the seashore. Others are derived from former spits, connected to land and built up by drifted sand, that were later severed from the mainland.

barrier reef *coral reef that lies offshore, separated from the mainland by a shallow lagoon.

barrister in the UK, a lawyer qualified by study at the *Inns of Court to plead for a client in court. In Scotland such lawyers are called advocates. Barristers also undertake the writing of opinions on the prospects of a case before trial. They act for clients through the intermediary of *solicitors. In the USA an attorney may serve the functions of barrister and solicitor.

barrow (Old English *beorgh* 'hill or mound') burial mound, usually composed of earth but sometimes of stones. Examples are found in many parts of the world. The two main types are **long**, dating from the Neolithic period (New Stone Age), and **round**, dating from the Mesolithic period (early Bronze Age). Barrows made entirely of stones are known as cairns.

Barry, Charles (1795–1860) English architect. He designed the neo-Gothic new Palace of Westminster, London (the Houses of Parliament; 1840–60), in collaboration with A W N *Pugin. His early designs for the Travellers Club (1829–32) and for the Reform Club (1837), both in London, were in Renaissance style.

Barthes, Roland (1915–1980) French critic and theorist of *semiology, the science of signs and symbols. One of the French 'new critics' and an exponent of *structuralism, he attacked traditional literary criticism in his first collection of essays, *Le Degré zéro de l'écriture/Writing Degree Zero* (1953).

Bartók, Béla (1881–1945) Hungarian composer. His works are influenced by folk music and often use modality. His music is highly dissonant and contrapuntal, but not atonal(see *atonality). His large output includes six string quartets, a *Divertimento* for string orchestra (1939), concertos for piano, violin, and viola, the *Concerto for Orchestra* (1943–44), a one-act opera *Duke Bluebeard's Castle* (1911), and graded teaching pieces for piano.

Bartolommeo, Fra (c. 1472–1517) also known as **Baccio della Porta**, Italian religious painter of the High Renaissance, active in Florence. He introduced Venetian artists to the Florentine High Renaissance style during

a visit to Venice in 1508, and took back with him to Florence a Venetian sense of colour. His style is one of classic simplicity and order, as in *The Mystical Marriage of St Catherine* (1511; Louvre, Paris).

Barton, Edmund (1849–1920) Australian politician. He was leader of the Federation Movement from 1896 and first prime minister of Australia 1901–03.

baryon in nuclear physics, a heavy subatomic particle made up of three indivisible elementary particles called quarks. The baryons form a subclass of the *hadrons and comprise the nucleons (protons and neutrons) and hyperons.

Baryshnikov, Mikhail (Nikolayevich) (1948–) Latvian-born dancer, now based in the USA.

He joined the Kirov Ballet in 1966 and, after defecting from the USSR in 1974, joined the American Ballet Theater (ABT) as principal dancer, partnering Gelsey Kirkland. He left to join the New York City Ballet (1978–80), but rejoined ABT as director 1980–90. From 1990 he has danced for various companies including his own modern dance company, White Oak Project. His physical prowess and amazing aerial feats have combined with an impish sense of humour and dash to make him one of the most accessible of dancers.

basal metabolic rate (BMR) minimum amount of energy needed by the body to maintain life. It is measured when the subject is awake but resting, and includes the energy required to keep the heart beating, sustain breathing, repair tissues, and keep the brain and nerves functioning. The rate varies depending on the height, weight, age, and activity of the person. Measuring the subject's consumption of oxygen gives an accurate value for BMR, because oxygen is needed to release energy from food.

basalt commonest volcanic *igneous rock in the Solar System. Basalt is an *extrusive rock, created by the outpouring of volcanic magma. The magma cools quickly, allowing only small crystals to form. Much of the surfaces of the terrestrial planets Mercury, Venus, Earth, and Mars, as well as the Moon, are composed of basalt. Earth's ocean floor is virtually entirely made of basalt. Basalt is mafic, that is, it contains relatively little *silica: about 50% by weight. It is usually dark grey but can also be green, brown, or black. Its essential constituent minerals are calcium-rich *feldspar, and calcium- and magnesium-rich pyroxene.

base in chemistry, a substance that accepts hydrogen ions, or protons. A base reacts with an *acid, neutralizing it to form a *salt: acid + base → salt + water. Metal oxides and metal hydroxides are bases; examples include copper oxide and sodium hydroxide. Bases can contain negative ions such as the hydroxide ion (OH^-), which is the strongest base, or be molecules such as ammonia (NH_3). Ammonia is a weak base, as only some of its molecules accept protons.

$$OH^- + H^+_{(aq)} \rightarrow H_2O_{(l)}$$
$$NH_3 + H_2O \rightleftharpoons NH_4^+ + OH^-$$

Bases that dissolve in water are called *alkalis.

base in mathematics, the number of different single-digit symbols used in a particular number system. In our usual (decimal) counting system of numbers (with symbols 0, 1, 2, 3, 4, 5, 6, 7, 8, 9) the base is 10. In the *binary number system, which has only the symbols 1 and 0, the base is two. A base is also a number that, when raised to a particular power (that is, when multiplied by itself a particular number of times as in $10^2 = 10 \times 10 = 100$), has a *logarithm equal to the power. For example, the logarithm of 100 to the base ten is 2. In geometry, the term is used to denote the line or area on which a polygon or solid stands.

baseball national summer game of the USA, derived in the 19th century from the English game of *rounders. Baseball is a bat-and-ball game played between two teams, each of nine players, on a pitch ('field') marked out in the form of a diamond, with a base at each corner. The ball is struck with a cylindrical bat, and the players try to score ('make a run') by circuiting the bases. A 'home run' is a circuit on one hit.

basenji breed of dog originating in Central Africa, where it is used for hunting. About 41 cm/16 in tall, it has pointed ears, curled tail, and short glossy coat of black or red, often with white markings. It is remarkable because it has no true bark.

base pair in biochemistry, the linkage of two base (purine or pyrimidine) molecules that join the complementary strands of *DNA. Adenine forms a base pair with thymine (or uracil in RNA) and cytosine pairs with guanine in a double-stranded nucleic acid molecule.

base rate in economics, interest rate set by banks to determine the cost of borrowing. In the UK the base rate is the rate at which the Bank of England lends to other financial institutions. The base rate is set by the Monetary Policy Committee according to economic conditions. Retails banks usually follow the lead of the Bank of England by adopting the base rate although they are under no obligation to do so. Similarly mortgage lenders may or may not pass on the base rate to their borrowers. In the USA the Federal Reserve System sets the discount interest rate governing the rate of interest banks pay the Federal Reserve Banks for short term borrowing of reserves.

Bashkortostan formerly **Bashkiria** or **Bashkir Autonomous SSR**, autonomous republic of the Russian Federation; area 143,600 sq km/55,444 sq mi; population (1990) 3,964,000 (40% Russian, 30% Tatar, 25% Bashkir). The capital is Ufa. The Ural Mountains are in the east and River Kama in the northwest; other rivers are Belaya, Ufa, Dema, and Zilim. Chief industries are oil, natural gas, minerals (gold and iron ore), chemicals, engineering, timber, and paper. The languages Russian and Bashkir are spoken.

Basho (1644–1694) pen-name of Matsuo Munefusa, Japanese poet. He was a master of the **haiku**, a 17-syllable poetic form with lines of 5, 7, and 5 syllables, which he infused with subtle allusiveness. His *Oku-no-hosomichi/The Narrow Road to the Deep North* (1694), an account of a visit to northern and western Honshu, consists of haiku interspersed with prose passages.

BASIC acronym for Beginner's All-purpose Symbolic Instruction Code, high-level computer-programming language, developed in 1964, originally designed to take advantage of multiuser systems (which can be used by many people at the same time). The language is relatively easy to learn and has been popular among microcomputer users.

basic–oxygen process most widely used method of steelmaking, involving the blasting of oxygen at high pressure into molten pig iron and scrap steel in a converter lined with basic refractory materials. The

impurities, principally carbon, quickly burn out, producing steel.

Basie, Count (1904–1984) born William Basie, US jazz band leader and pianist. He developed the *big-band jazz sound and a simplified, swinging style of music. He led impressive groups of musicians in a career spanning more than 50 years. Basie's compositions include 'One O'Clock Jump' (1937) and 'Jumpin' at the Woodside' (1938).

basil or **sweet basil** plant with aromatic leaves, belonging to the mint family. A native of the tropics, it is cultivated in Europe as a herb and used to flavour food. Its small white flowers appear on spikes. (Genus *Ocimum basilicum*, family Labiatae.)

Basil II (c. 958–1025) Byzantine emperor 976–1025. He completed the work of his predecessors Nicephorus (II) Phocas and John Zimisces and expanded the borders of the Byzantine Empire to their greatest extent since the 5th century. He eliminated political rivals, drove the Muslims from Syria, and destroyed the power of the Bulgars.

basilica Roman public building; a large, roofed hall flanked by columns, generally with an aisle on each side, used for judicial or other public business. The earliest known basilica, at Pompeii, dates from the 2nd century BC. This architectural form was adopted by the early Christians for their churches.

Basilicata Roman **Lucania**, mountainous region of southern Italy, forming the instep of the Italian 'boot'. Bordering on the Tyrrhenian Sea in the southwest and the Gulf of Taranto in the southeast, it comprises the provinces of Potenza and Matera; area 9,992 sq km/3,858 sq mi; population (2001 est) 595,700. The capital is Potenza.

basilisk Central and South American lizard, genus *Basiliscus*. It is about 50 cm/20 in long and weighs about 90 g/o.2 lb. Its rapid speed (more than 2 m/6.6 ft per second) and the formation of air pockets around the feet enable it to run short distances across the surface of water. The male has a well-developed crest on the head, body, and tail.

basketball ball game between two teams of five players on an indoor enclosed court. The object is, via a series of passing moves, to throw the large inflated ball through a circular hoop and net positioned at each end of the court, 3.05 m/10 ft above the in ground. The first world championship for men was held in 1950, and 1953 for women. They are now held every four years.

Basque the people inhabiting the *Basque Country of central northern Spain and the extreme southwest of France. The Basques are a pre-Indo-European people whose language (**Euskara**) is unrelated to any other language. Although both the Romans and, later, the Visigoths conquered them, they largely maintained their independence until the 19th century. During the Spanish Civil War (1936–39), they were on the republican side defeated by Franco. The Basque separatist movement Euskadi ta Askatasuna (ETA; 'Basque Nation and Liberty') and the French organization Iparretarrak ('ETA fighters from the North Side') have engaged in guerrilla activity from 1968 in an attempt to secure a united Basque state.

Basque Country Basque **Euskal Herria**, cultural homeland of the *Basque people in the western Pyrenees, divided by the Franco-Spanish border, and covering an area of 20,742 sq km/8,009 sq mi. The Spanish *Basque Country (País Vasco) is an autonomous community of central northern Spain; it has a much stronger separatist movement than the French Basque Country to the north. The French Basque Country (Pays Basque) is the area occupied by Basques in the *département* of Pyrénées-Atlantiques, made up of the small districts of Soule and Labourd (which joined France in 1451) and Lower Navarre (annexed in 1620 by Louis XIII). The total Basque population is approximately 3 million, with about 92% being Spanish citizens.

Basque Country Spanish **País Vasco**; Basque **Euskal Herria**, autonomous community of central northern Spain, created in 1979, including the provinces of Vizcaya, Álava, and Guipúzcoa; area 7,261 sq km/2,803 sq mi; population (2002 est) 2,067,600. The region is bordered by the Bay of Biscay to the north and separated from the French part of the *Basque Country cultural region by the Pyrenees. *Bilbao, the capital of Vizcaya province, is the region's largest city and one of Spain's main industrial centres. Other important cities include San Sebastián, the capital of Guipúzcoa province; Vitoria, capital of Álava province, and historic Guernica.

Basque language language of Western Europe known to its speakers, the Basques, as *Euskara*, and apparently unrelated to any other language on Earth. It is spoken by some half a million people in central northern Spain and southwestern France, around the Bay of Biscay, as well as by emigrants in both Europe and the Americas. The language is of central importance to the Basque nationalist movement.

bas relief see *relief.

bass long-bodied scaly sea fish *Morone labrax* found in the North Atlantic and Mediterranean. They grow to 1 m/3 ft, and are often seen in shoals.

bass lowest male voice, of approximate range C2–D4. It is also used before the name of an instrument and indicates that the instrument sounds in approximately the same range.

Basse-Normandie English **Lower Normandy**, coastal region of northwest France lying between Haute-Normandie and Brittany (Bretagne). It includes the *départements* of Calvados, Manche, and Orne; area 17,589 sq km/6,791 sq mi; population (1999 est) 1,422,200. Its administrative centre is Caen. Apart from stock farming, dairy farming (including the production of Camembert cheese), and textiles, the area produces apples, cider, and Calvados apple brandy. Tourism is important.

basset any of several breeds of hound with a long low body and long pendulous ears, of a type originally bred in France for hunting hares by scent.

Basseterre capital and port of St Kitts and Nevis, in the Leeward Islands; population (1995 est) 18,000. Industries include data processing, rum, clothes, and electrical components; chief exports are sugar, salt, cotton, and copra.

basset horn musical woodwind instrument, a wide-bore alto clarinet pitched in F, invented about 1765 and used by Mozart in his *Masonic Funeral Music* (1785), for example, and by Richard Strauss. It was revived in 1981 by Karlheinz Stockhausen and features prominently as a solo in his opera cycle *LICHT*. Performers include Alan Hacker and Suzanne Stephens.

bassoon double-reed woodwind instrument in C. It is the bass of the oboe family and lowest sounding of the four main orchestral woodwinds (the flute, clarinet, oboe, and bassoon). It doubles back on itself in a conical tube about 2.5 m/7.5 ft long and has a rich, deep tone. The bassoon concert repertoire extends from the early Baroque via Antonio Vivaldi, Wolfgang Amadeus Mozart, and Paul Dukas, to Karlheinz Stockhausen.

Bass Strait sea channel separating the mainland of Australia from Tasmania. The strait is 322 km/200 mi long, with an average width of 255 km/158 mi. Oil was discovered here in 1965 and first extracted in 1969. The region now has 18 oil and gas fields.

Bastille castle of St Antoine, built about 1370 as part of the fortifications of Paris. It was made a state prison by Cardinal *Richelieu and was stormed by the mob that set the French Revolution in motion on 14 July 1789. Only seven prisoners were found in the castle when it was stormed; the governor and most of the garrison were killed, and the Bastille was razed.

bat any mammal of the order Chiroptera, related to the Insectivora (hedgehogs and shrews), but differing from them in being able to fly. Bats are the only true flying mammals. Their forelimbs are developed as wings capable of rapid and sustained flight. There are two main groups of bats: **megabats**, which eat fruit, and **microbats**, which mainly eat insects. Bats are nocturnal, and those native to temperate countries hibernate in winter. There are about 977 species forming the order Chiroptera, making this the second-largest mammalian order; bats make up nearly one-quarter of the world's mammals. Although bats are widely distributed, populations have declined alarmingly and many species are now endangered.

Bates, H(enry) W(alter) (1825–1892) English naturalist and explorer. He spent 11 years collecting animals and plants in South America and identified 8,000 new species of insects. He made a special study of *camouflage in animals, and his observation of insect imitation of species that are unpleasant to predators is known as 'Batesian mimicry'.

Bates, H(erbert) E(rnest) (1905–1974) English writer. Of his many novels and short stories, *The Jacaranda Tree* (1949) and *The Darling Buds of May* (1958) particularly demonstrate the fineness of his natural observation and compassionate portrayal of character. His work captures the feeling of life in the changing countryside of England in a simple, direct manner.

Bath historic city and administrative headquarters of *Bath and North East Somerset unitary authority, southwest England, 171 km/106 mi west of London; population (1996 est) 85,000. Industries include printing, plastics, engineering, and tourism. Bath was the site of the Roman town of Aquae Sulis, and in the 18th century flourished as a fashionable spa, with the only naturally occurring hot mineral springs in Britain. Although the baths were closed to the public in 1977, the Bath Spa Project, due to open in 2003, is intended to bring back public bathing to Bath's hot springs.

Bath and North East Somerset unitary authority in southwest England created in 1996 from part of the former county of Avon. **area:** 351 sq km/136 sq mi **towns and cities:** *Bath (administrative headquarters), Keynsham, Chew Magna, Paulton, Radstock, Peasedown St John, Midsomer Norton **features:** River

Avon and tributaries; Chew Valley Lake; Beckford's Tower (Bath) built in 1827 for William Beckford; Roman baths with hot springs (Bath); Regency architecture including Royal Crescent, The Circus, and Assembly Rooms designed by John Wood (1700–1854) and his son John Wood; Pulteney Bridge, 18th century shop-lined Italianate bridge designed by Robert Adam; Stanton Drew bronze age stone circles including second largest in Great Britain. **population:** (2001 est) 169,000.

batholith large, irregular, deep-seated mass of intrusive *igneous rock, usually granite, with an exposed surface of more than 100 sq km/40 sq mi. The mass forms by the intrusion or upwelling of magma (molten rock) through the surrounding rock. Batholiths form the core of some large mountain ranges like the Sierra Nevada of western North America.

Bath, Order of the British order of knighthood (see *knighthood, orders of), believed to have been founded in 1399 by Henry IV. The order now consists of three classes: Knights of the Grand Cross (GCB), Knights Commanders (KCB), and Knights Companions (CB).

bathyscaph *or* **bathyscaphe** *or* **bathyscape** deep-sea diving apparatus used for exploration at great depths in the ocean. In 1960, Jacques Piccard and Don Walsh took the bathyscaph *Trieste* to a depth of 10,917 m/35,820 ft in the Challenger Deep in the *Mariana Trench off the island of Guam in the Pacific Ocean.

batik Javanese technique used to dye fabrics. Areas of material are sealed with wax, which resists *dye.

battery any energy-storage device allowing release of electricity on demand. It is made up of one or more electrical *cells. Electricity is produced by a chemical reaction in the cells. There are two types of battery: primary-cell batteries, which are disposable; and secondary-cell batteries, or *accumulators, which are rechargeable. Primary-cell batteries are an extremely uneconomical form of energy, since they produce only 2% of the power used in their manufacture. It is dangerous to try to recharge a primary-cell battery.

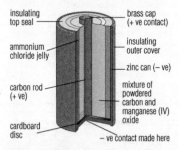

battery The common dry cell relies on chemical changes occurring between the electrodes – the central carbon rod and the outer zinc casing – and the ammonium chloride electrolyte to produce electricity. The mixture of carbon and manganese is used to increase the life of the cell.

baud in engineering, a unit of electrical signalling speed equal to one pulse per second, measuring the rate at which signals are sent between electronic devices such as telegraphs and computers.

Baudelaire, Charles Pierre (1821–1867) French poet. His immensely influential work combined rhythmical and musical perfection with a morbid romanticism and eroticism, finding beauty in decadence and evil. His first and best-known book of verse was *Les Fleurs du mal/Flowers of Evil* (1857). He was one of the main figures in the development of *Symbolism.

Bauhaus (German 'building house') German school of art, design, and architecture founded in 1919 in Weimar by the architect Walter *Gropius, who aimed to fuse art, design, architecture, and crafts into a unified whole. By 1923, as Germany's economy deteriorated, handcrafts were dropped in favour of a more functionalist approach, combining craft design with industrial production. The adoption of industrial technology had previously been criticized by other craft and design movements. In 1925, under political and financial pressure, the Bauhaus moved to Dessau, where it was housed in a building designed by Gropius, and formalized a new statement of beliefs: 'Art and Technology, a new unity'. In 1932 it made another forced move to Berlin, where it was closed by the Nazis the following year. In spite of its short life and troubled existence, the Bauhaus is regarded as the most important art school of the 20th century, and it exercised a huge influence on the world of design: its art education system was adopted by the rest of the art world. The teachers at the school included some of the outstanding artists of the time, among them the painters Paul *Klee and Vasily *Kandinsky and the architect Ludwig *Mies van der Rohe.

Baum, L(yman) Frank (1856–1919) US writer. He was the author of the children's fantasy *The Wonderful Wizard of Oz* (1900) and its 13 sequels. The series was continued by another author after his death. The film *The Wizard of Oz* (1939) with Judy *Garland became a US classic.

bauxite principal ore of *aluminium, consisting of a mixture of hydrated aluminium oxides and hydroxides, generally contaminated with compounds of iron, which give it a red colour. It is formed by the chemical weathering of rocks in tropical climates. Chief producers of bauxite are Australia, Guinea, Jamaica, Russia, Kazakhstan, Suriname, and Brazil.

Bavaria German **Bayern**, administrative region (German *Land*) in southeast Germany, bordered to the west by Hesse and Baden-Württemberg, to the north by Thuringia and Saxony, to the northeast by the Czech Republic, and to the south and southeast by Austria; area 70,549 sq km/27,239 sq mi; population (2003 est) 12,209,900. Bavaria is the largest of the German *Länder*. The capital is *Munich, and other major towns include Nuremberg, Augsburg, Würzburg, Regensburg, Passau, Fürth, and Ingolstadt.

Bax, Arnold Edward Trevor (1883–1953) English composer. His works, often based on Celtic legends, include seven symphonies, *The Garden of Fand* (1913–16), and *Tintagel* (1917–19) (both tone poems). He was Master of the King's Musick 1942–53.

bay any of various species of *laurel tree. The aromatic evergreen leaves are used for flavouring in cookery. There is also a golden-leaved variety. (Genus *Laurus*, family Lauraceae.)

Bayeux Tapestry linen hanging made about 1067–70 that gives a vivid pictorial record of the invasion of

England by William I (the Conqueror) in 1066. It is an embroidery rather than a true tapestry, sewn with woollen threads in eight visibly different colours. The hanging is 70 m/231 ft long and 50 cm/20 in wide, and contains 72 separate scenes with descriptive wording in Latin. It is exhibited at the museum of Bayeux in Normandy, France.

Bayliss, William Maddock (1860–1924) English physiologist who discovered the digestive hormone secretin, the first hormone to be found, with Ernest Starling in 1902. During World War I, Bayliss introduced the use of saline (salt water) injections to help the injured recover from *shock. Knighted in 1922.

bayonet short sword attached to the muzzle of a firearm. The bayonet was placed inside the barrel of the muzzleloading muskets of the late 17th century. The **sock** or ring bayonet, invented in 1700, allowed a weapon to be fired without interruption, leading to the demise of the pike.

Bayreuth town in Bavaria, south Germany, on the Red Main River, 65 km/40 mi northeast of Nuremberg; population (1995) 72,700. There are cotton textile, porcelain, cigarette, and optical industries. Bayreuth was the home of the composer Richard Wagner, and the Wagner theatre was established in 1876 as a performing centre for his operas. Opera festivals are held here every summer.

BBC abbreviation for *British Broadcasting Corporation.

BC in the Christian calendar, abbreviation for **before Christ**, used with dates.

BCG abbreviation for **bacille Calmette-Guérin**, bacillus injected as a vaccine to confer active immunity to *tuberculosis (TB).

Beach Boys, the US pop group. Known for their vocal-harmony surf music, their first hit was 'Surfin' USA' (1963); this was followed by 'I Get Around' (1964), and 'California Girls' (1965). Their albums include the complex and influential *Pet Sounds* (1966).

Beachy Head (French *beau chef*, 'beautiful head') chalk headland on the south coast of England, between Seaford and Eastbourne in East Sussex. Rising to 163 m/ 535 ft, it is the eastern end of the South Downs. The lighthouse at the foot of the cliff is 38 m/125 ft high.

beagle short-haired hound with pendant ears, sickle tail, and a bell-like voice for hunting hares on foot ('beagling').

beak horn-covered projecting jaws of a bird (see *bill), or other horny jaws such as those of the octopus, platypus, or tortoise.

Beaker people prehistoric people thought to have been of Iberian origin, who spread out over Europe from the 3rd millennium BC. They were skilled in metalworking, and are associated with distinctive earthenware drinking vessels with various designs, in particular, a type of beaker with a bell-shaped profile, widely distributed throughout Europe.

bean seed of a large number of leguminous plants (see *legume). Beans are rich in nitrogen compounds and proteins and are grown both for human consumption and as food for cattle and horses. Varieties of bean are grown throughout Europe, the USA, South America, China, Japan, Southeast Asia, and Australia.

bear in business, trader in financial market who believes the market is going to fall. Such negative sentiments are said to be bearish. A bear is the opposite of a *bull. In a bear market, prices fall and bears prosper.

bear large mammal with a heavily built body, short powerful limbs, and a very short tail. Bears breed once a year, producing one to four cubs. In northern regions they hibernate, and the young are born in the winter den. They are found mainly in North America and northern Asia. Bears walk on the soles of the feet and have long, nonretractable claws. The bear family, Ursidae, is related to carnivores such as dogs and weasels, and all bears are capable of killing prey.

bearberry any of a group of evergreen trailing shrubs belonging to the heath family, found in high and rocky places. Most bearberries are North American but *Arctostaphylos uva-ursi* is also found in Asia and Europe in northern mountainous regions. It has small pink flowers in spring, followed by red berries that are dry but edible. (Genus *Arctostaphylos*, family Ericaceae.)

Beardsley, Aubrey Vincent (1872–1898) English illustrator and leading member of the *Aesthetic Movement. His meticulously executed black-and-white drawings show the influence of Japanese prints and French rococo, and also display the sinuous line, asymmetry, and decorative mannerisms of art nouveau. His work was often charged with being grotesque and decadent.

Bear, Great and Little common names (and translations of the Latin) for the constellations *Ursa Major and *Ursa Minor respectively.

bearing device used in a machine to allow free movement between two parts, typically the rotation of a shaft in a housing. **Ball bearings** consist of two rings, one fixed to a housing, one to the rotating shaft. Between them is a set, or race, of steel balls. They are widely used to support shafts, as in the spindle in the hub of a bicycle wheel.

bearing direction of a fixed point, or the path of a moving object, from a point of observation. Bearings are angles measured in degrees (°) from the north line in a clockwise direction. A bearing must always have three figures. For instance, north is 000°, northeast is 045°, south is 180°, and southwest is 225°.

beat frequency in musical acoustics, fluctuation produced when two notes of nearly equal pitch or *frequency are heard together. Beats result from the *interference between the sound waves of the notes. The frequency of the beats equals the difference in frequency of the notes.

Beat Generation *or* **Beat movement** US social and literary movement of the 1950s and early 1960s. Members of the Beat Generation, called **beatniks**, responded to the conformist materialism of the period by adopting lifestyles derived from Henry David Thoreau's social disobedience and Walt Whitman's poetry of the open road. The most influential writers were Jack *Kerouac (who is credited with coining the term), Allen *Ginsberg, and William Burroughs.

beatification in the Catholic Church, the first step towards *canonization. Persons who have been beatified can be prayed to, and the title 'Blessed' can be put before their names.

Beatitudes (Latin 'happy') in the New Testament, the sayings of Jesus reported in Matthew 5:3–11 and Luke 6:20–22, describing the spiritual qualities of character that should characterize those influenced by the kingdom of God, and are the way to true happiness. They form part of the Sermon on the Mount.

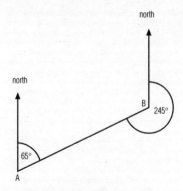

north

the bearing of B from A is 065°
the backbearing, or bearing of A from B, is 245°

bearing A bearing is the direction of a fixed point, or the path of a moving object, from a point of observation on the Earth's surface, expressed as an angle from the north. In the diagram, the bearing of a point A from an observer at B is the angle between the line BA and the north line through B, measured in a clockwise direction from the north line.

Beatles, the English pop group with a career spanning 1960–70. The members, all born in Liverpool, England, were John *Lennon (rhythm guitar, vocals), Paul *McCartney (bass, vocals), George *Harrison (lead guitar, vocals), and Ringo *Starr (drums). Using songs written largely by Lennon and McCartney, the Beatles dominated rock music and pop culture in the 1960s.

beat music pop music that evolved in the UK in the early 1960s, known in its purest form as Mersey beat, and as British Invasion in the USA. The beat groups characteristically had a simple, guitar-dominated line-up, vocal harmonies, and catchy tunes. They included the Beatles (1960–70), the Hollies (1962–), and the Zombies (1962–67).

Beaton, Cecil Walter Hardy (1904–1980) English photographer. His elegant and sophisticated fashion pictures and society portraits often employed exotic props and settings. He adopted a more simple style for his wartime photographs of bomb-damaged London. He also worked as a stage and film designer, notably for the musicals *Gigi* (1959) and *My Fair Lady* (1965). He was knighted in 1972.

Beatrix, (Wilhelmina Armgard) (1938–) Queen of the Netherlands. The eldest daughter of Queen Juliana, she succeeded to the throne on her mother's abdication in 1980. In 1966 she married West German diplomat Claus von Amsberg, who was created Prince of the Netherlands. Her heir is Prince Willem Alexander.

Beaufort scale system of recording wind velocity, devised by Francis Beaufort in 1806. It is a numerical scale ranging from 0 to 17, calm being indicated by 0 and a hurricane by 12; 13–17 indicate degrees of hurricane force.

Beaufort Sea section of the Arctic Ocean off Alaska and Canada, named after the British admiral Francis Beaufort. Oil drilling is allowed only in the winter

months because the sea is the breeding and migration route of bowhead whales, the staple diet of the local Inuit people.

Beaumarchais, Pierre Augustin Caron de (1732–1799) French dramatist. His great comedies, *Le Barbier de Seville/The Barber of Seville* (1775) and *Le Mariage de Figaro/The Marriage of Figaro* (1778, but prohibited until 1784), form the basis of operas by *Rossini and *Mozart, with their blend of social criticism and sharp humour.

Beauvoir, Simone de (1908–1986) French socialist, feminist, and writer. She played a large role in French intellectual life from the 1940s to the 1980s. Her book *Le Deuxième Sexe/The Second Sex* (1949), one of the first major feminist texts, is an encyclopedic study of the role of women in society, drawing on literature, myth, and history. In this work she argues that the subservient position of women is the result of their systematic repression by a male-dominated society that denies their independence, identity, and sexuality.

beaver aquatic rodent with webbed hind feet, a broad flat scaly tail, and thick waterproof fur. It has very large incisor teeth and fells trees to feed on the bark and to use the logs to construct the 'lodge', in which the young are reared, food is stored, and much of the winter is spent. There are two species, the Canadian *Castor canadensis* and the European *C. fiber*. They grow up to 1.4 m/4.6 ft in length and weigh about 20 kg/44 lb.

Beaverbrook, (William) Max(well) Aitken (1879–1964) 1st Baron Beaverbrook, Canadian-born British financier, proprietor and publisher of the *Daily Express* group of newspapers, and a UK government minister in cabinets during both world wars. He bought a majority interest in the *Daily Express* in 1916, founded the *Sunday Express* in 1918, and bought the London *Evening Standard* in 1923. He served in David Lloyd George's World War I cabinet and Winston Churchill's World War II cabinet.

bebop *or* **bop** hot jazz style with complicated melody lines improvised against often dissonant harmonies and complex rhythms. It was developed in New York in the 1940s and 1950s by Charlie 'Bird' *Parker, Dizzy *Gillespie, Thelonius Monk, and other black musicians reacting against swing music.

Bechet, Sidney Joseph (1897–1959) US jazz musician. He played clarinet and was the first to forge an individual style on soprano saxophone. He developed a jazz-swing improvisational style during the mid-1920s that established his reputation, and was known for his use of a pronounced *vibrato. Bechet was based in Paris from 1951, where he was greatly esteemed.

Bechuanaland former name (to 1966) of Botswana.

Becket, St Thomas à (1118–1170) English archbishop and politician. He was chancellor to Henry II from 1155 to 1162, when he was appointed Archbishop of Canterbury. The interests of the Roman Catholic medieval church soon conflicted with those of the crown and Becket was assassinated; he was canonized (made into a saint) in 1172.

Beckett, Samuel Barclay (1906–1989) Irish dramatist, novelist, and poet, who wrote in both French and English. He won international acclaim for his work, which includes the play *En attendant Godot* – first performed in Paris in 1952, and then in his own translation as *Waiting for Godot* in London in 1955 and

New York in 1956 – and for his later dramas, such as *Fin de partie/Endgame* (1957–58) and *Happy Days* (1961). He was awarded the Nobel Prize for Literature in 1969. Grappling with fundamental problems of identity, choice, purpose, knowledge, and narration, his characters demonstrate a distinctive compound of despair, endurance, and wit.

Beckham, David Robert Joseph (1975–) English footballer. A midfielder with great passing ability and an effective free-kick taker, he played for Manchester United and, from 2003, for Real Madrid, and has been regarded as one of the world's best players. He became captain of England in November 2000.

Beckmann, Max (1884–1950) German expressionist painter and graphic artist. He was influenced both by medieval art and by the *Neue Sachlichkeit* movement and after World War I his art concentrated on themes of cruelty in human society, as in *Night* (1918–19; Kunstsammlung Nardrheim-Westfalen, Düsseldorf).

becquerel symbol Bq, SI unit of *radioactivity, equal to one radioactive disintegration (change in the nucleus of an atom when a particle or ray is given off) per second.

Becquerel, (Antoine) Henri (1852–1908) French physicist. He was awarded the Nobel Prize for Physics in 1903 for his discovery of penetrating radiation coming from uranium salts, the first indication of spontaneous *radioactivity. He shared the award with Marie and Pierre *Curie.

bed in geology, a single *sedimentary rock unit with a distinct set of physical characteristics or contained fossils, readily distinguishable from those of beds above and below. Well-defined partings called **bedding planes** separate successive beds or strata.

Bede (c. 673–735) English theologian and historian, known as the Venerable Bede. Active in Durham and Northumbria, he wrote many scientific, theological, and historical works. His *Historia Ecclesiastica Gentis Anglorum* (*Ecclesiastical History of the English People*) of 731 is a primary source for early English history, and was translated into the vernacular by King Alfred.

Bedfordshire county of south central England (since April 1997 Luton has been a separate unitary authority). **area:** 1,192 sq km/460 sq mi **towns and cities:** Bedford (administrative headquarters), Dunstable **physical:** the Great Ouse River and its tributary, the Ivel; the county is low lying with the Chiltern Hills in the southwest **features:** Whipsnade Wild Animal Park, near Dunstable (200 ha/494 acres), belonging to the London Zoological Society; Woburn Abbey(18th century), seat of the duke of Bedford; Cranfield Institute of Technology **population:** (2001 est) 384,400.

Bedlam popular name for Bethlem Royal Hospital, the earliest mental hospital in Europe. The Priory of St Mary of Bethlehem was founded in Bishopsgate, London, in 1247 and was used as a hospice by the 14th century. It has been sited in West Wickham, Kent, since 1930. It is now used as a slang word meaning chaos.

Bedlington breed of *terrier with a short body, long legs, and curly hair, usually grey, named after a district of Northumberland, England.

Bedouin (Arabic 'desert dweller') member of any of the nomadic, Arabic-speaking peoples occupying the desert regions of Arabia and North Africa. Originating in Arabia, they spread to Syria and Mesopotamia, and later to Egypt and Tunisia.

bee four-winged insect of the superfamily Apoidea in the order Hymenoptera, usually with a sting. There are over 12,000 species, of which fewer than 1 in 20 are social in habit. The **hive bee** or **honeybee** *Apis mellifera* establishes perennial colonies of about 80,000, the majority being infertile females (workers), with a few larger fertile males (drones), and a single very large fertile female (the queen). Worker bees live for no more than a few weeks, while a drone may live a few months, and a queen several years. Queen honeybees lay two kinds of eggs: fertilized, female eggs, which have two sets of chromosomes and develop into workers or queens, and unfertilized, male eggs, which have only one set of chromosomes and develop into drones.

beech one of several European hardwood trees or related trees growing in Australasia and South America. The common beech (*Fagus sylvaticus*), found in European forests, has a smooth grey trunk and edible nuts, or 'mast', which are used as animal feed or processed for oil. In the southern hemisphere there are 36 species of the genus *Nothofagus*, both deciduous and evergreen. The timber is used in furniture. (Genera *Fagus* and *Nothofagus*, family Fagaceae.)

Beecham, Thomas (1879–1961) English conductor and impresario. He established the Royal Philharmonic Orchestra in 1946 and fostered the works of composers such as Delius, Sibelius, and Richard Strauss. He was knighted and succeeded to the baronetcy in 1916.

Beecher, Harriet unmarried name of US author Harriet Beecher *Stowe who wrote *Uncle Tom's Cabin*.

Beeching Report official report, published in 1963, on the railway network of Britain, which recommended the closure of loss-making lines and the improvement of money-making routes. Hundreds of lines and several thousand stations were closed as a result.

bee-eater brightly-coloured bird *Merops apiaster*, family Meropidae, order Coraciiformes, found in Africa, southern Europe, and Asia. Bee-eaters are slender, with chestnut, yellow, and blue-green plumage, a long bill and pointed wings, and a flight like that of the swallow, which they resemble in shape. They feed on bees, wasps, and other insects, and nest in colonies in holes dug out with their long bills in sandy river banks.

Beelzebub (Hebrew 'lord of the flies') in the New Testament, the leader of the devils, sometimes identified with Satan and sometimes with his chief assistant (see *devil). In the Old Testament Beelzebub was a fertility god worshipped by the Philistines and other Semitic groups (*Baal).

beer alcoholic drink made from water and malt (fermented barley or other grain), flavoured with hops. Beer contains between 1% and 6% alcohol. One of the oldest alcoholic drinks, it was brewed in ancient China, Egypt, and Babylon.

beet any of several plants belonging to the goosefoot family, used as food crops. One variety of the common beet (*Beta vulgaris*) is used to produce sugar and another, the mangelwurzel, is grown as a cattle feed. The beetroot, or red beet (*B. rubra*), is a salad plant. (Genus *Beta*, family Chenopodiaceae.)

Beethoven, Ludwig van (1770–1827) German composer. His mastery of musical expression in every type of music made him the dominant influence on 19th-century music. Beethoven's repertoire includes concert overtures; the opera *Fidelio* (1805, revised 1806 and 1814); 5 piano concertos and 1 for violin; 32 piano sonatas, including the *Moonlight* (1801) and *Appassionata* (1804–05); 17 string quartets; the Mass in D (*Missa solemnis*) (1819–22); and 9 symphonies, as well as many youthful works. He usually played his own piano pieces and conducted his orchestral works until he became deaf in 1801; nevertheless he continued to compose.

beetle common name of insects in the order Coleoptera (Greek 'sheath-winged') with leathery forewings folding down in a protective sheath over the membranous hindwings, which are those used for flight. They pass through a complete metamorphosis. They include some of the largest and smallest of all insects: the largest is the **Hercules beetle** *Dynastes hercules* of the South American rainforests, 15 cm/6 in long; the smallest is only 0.05 cm/0.02 in long. Comprising more than 50% of the animal kingdom, beetles number some 370,000 named species, with many not yet described.

Beeton, Mrs (1836–1865) born Isabella Mary Mayson, British writer on cookery and domestic management. She produced *Mrs Beeton's Book of Household Management* (1861), the first comprehensive work on domestic science.

Begin, Menachem (1913–1992) Israeli politician. He was leader of the extremist Irgun Zvai Leumi organization in Palestine from 1942 and prime minister of Israel 1977–83, as head of the right-wing Likud party. Following strong encouragement from US president Jimmy *Carter, he entered into negotiations with President Anwar *Sadat of Egypt, which resulted in the Camp David Agreements. He shared the Nobel Prize for Peace in 1978 with Anwar Sadat for their efforts towards the Israel-Egypt peace treaty of 1979. In 1981 Begin won a new term of office but his health was failing. The death of his wife in 1982 was a grave blow, resulting in his retirement in September 1983. For the rest of his life he was a virtual recluse.

begonia any of a group of tropical and subtropical plants. They have fleshy and succulent leaves, and some have large, brilliant flowers. There are numerous species in the tropics, especially in South America and India. (Genus *Begonia*, family Begoniaceae.)

Behan, Brendan Francis (1923–1964) Irish writer and dramatist, born in Dublin and educated by the Christian Brothers until the age of 14. Behan's extended family included many talented musicians and writers as well as Republican activists. An important figure of both controversy and literary brilliance, Behan is best known for his autobiography *Borstal Boy* (1958), based on his experiences of prison and knowledge of the workings of the *IRA. These themes are revisited in his play *The Quare Fellow* (1954), and tragicomedy *The Hostage* (1958), first written in Gaelic as *An Giall*. Behan's other output included poetry in Gaelic, radio plays, and some late volumes of reminiscence and anecdote, notably *Brendan Behan's New York* (1964).

behaviourism school of psychology originating in the USA, of which the leading exponent was John B Watson. Behaviourists maintain that all human activity can ultimately be explained in terms of conditioned reactions or reflexes and habits formed in consequence. Leading behaviourists include Ivan *Pavlov and B F *Skinner.

behaviour therapy in psychology, the application of behavioural principles, derived from learning theories,

to the treatment of clinical conditions such as *phobias, *obsessions, and sexual and interpersonal problems.

behemoth (Hebrew 'beasts') in the Old Testament (Job 40), an animal cited by God as evidence of his power; usually thought to refer to the hippopotamus. It is used proverbially to mean any giant and powerful creature.

Behn, Aphra (1640–1689) English novelist and dramatist. She was the first woman in England to earn her living as a writer. Her works were criticized for their explicitness; they frequently present events from a woman's point of view. Her novel *Oroonoko* (1688), based on her visit to Suriname, is an attack on slavery.

Behrens, Peter (1868–1940) German architect. A pioneer of the *Modern Movement and of the adaptation of architecture to industry. He designed the AEG turbine factory in Berlin (1909), a landmark in industrial architecture, and taught Le Corbusier, Walter Gropius, and Mies van der Rohe.

Behring, Emil (Adolph von) (1854–1917) German physician who was awarded the first Nobel Prize for Physiology or Medicine, in 1901, for his discovery that the body produces antitoxins, substances able to counteract poisons released by bacteria. Using this knowledge, he developed new treatments for diseases such as *diphtheria.

Beiderbecke, Bix (1903–1931) born Leon Bismarck Beiderbecke, US jazz cornetist, composer, and pianist. A romantic soloist with the bands of King Oliver, Louis *Armstrong, and Paul Whiteman, Beiderbecke was the first accepted white jazz innovator. He was influenced by the classical composers Claude Debussy, Maurice Ravel, and Igor Stravinsky. His recordings include 'I'm Coming, Virginia' (1927) and 'Singin' the Blues' (1927).

Beijing formerly **Peking**, ('northern capital') capital of China; parts of the northeast municipal boundary coincide with sections of the *Great Wall of China; population (2001 est) 6,995,500. The municipality of Beijing has an area of 17,800 sq km/6,871 sq mi and a population (1996) of 12,590,000. Industries include engineering and the production of steel, motor vehicles, textiles, and petrochemicals; the city is also a major centre of printing and publishing.

Beirut or **Beyrouth** capital and port of Lebanon, 90 km/60 mi northwest of Damascus, situated on a promontory into the eastern Mediterranean with the Lebanon Mountains behind it; population (2002 est) 1,147,800, conurbation 1,878,200. The city dates back to at least 1400 BC. It was devastated by civil war in the 1970s and 1980s and by the conflict between the Palestine Liberation Organization (PLO) and the Israeli forces which invaded in 1982 with the intention of securing the northern border territory of Israel.

Bekaa, the or **El Beqa'a** valley in central Lebanon, situated between the Lebanon and Anti-Lebanon mountain ranges; length 130 km/80 mi, width 20 km/12 mi. It is also a governorate (estimated population in 2002: 516,900), its main population centres being the city of Zahle and the ancient town of Baalbek. The Orontes and Litani rivers rise in the Bekaa. The southern part of the valley is particularly fertile with significant production of wheat, maize, cotton, fruit, and, in recent years, hashish and opium. Of strategic importance, the Bekaa was occupied by Syrian troops following the outbreak of the Lebanese civil war in the mid-1970s and has been a centre of operations for the radical Islamic Hezbollah organization.

Belarus

Belarus
or **Byelorussia** *or* **Belorussia**
National name: *Respublika Belarus/Republic of Belarus*

Area: 207,600 sq km/80,154 sq mi
Capital: Minsk (Belorussian Mensk)
Major towns/cities: Gomel, Vitsyebsk, Mahilyow, Bobruisk, Hrodna, Brest
Physical features: more than 25% forested; rivers Dvina, Dnieper and its tributaries, including the Pripet and Beresina; the Pripet Marshes in the east; mild and damp climate
Head of state: Alexandr Lukashenko from 1994
Head of government: Sjarhej Sidorski from 2003
Political system: authoritarian nationalist
Political executive: unlimited presidency
Political parties: Belarus Communist Party (BCP, banned 1991–92); Belarus Patriotic Movement (BPM), populist; Belorussian Popular Front (BPF; Adradzhenne), moderate nationalist; Christian Democratic Union of Belarus, centrist; Socialist Party of Belarus, left of centre
Currency: Belarus rouble, or zaichik
GNI per capita (PPP): (US$) 5,330 (2002 est)
Exports: machinery, petroleum and gas, chemicals and petrochemicals, iron and steel, light industrial goods, textiles. Principal market: Russia 53.7% (2001)
Population: 9,895,000 (2003 est)
Language: Belorussian (official), Russian, Polish
Religion: 80% Eastern Orthodox; Baptist, Roman Catholic Muslim, and Jewish minorities
Life expectancy: 65 (men); 75 (women) (2000–05)
Chronology
5th–8th centuries: Settled by East Slavic tribes, ancestors of present-day Belorussians.
11th century: Minsk was founded.
12th century: Part of Kievan Russia, to the south, with independent Belarus state developing around Polotsk, on River Dvina.
14th century: Incorporated within Slavonic Grand Duchy of Lithuania, to the west.
1569: Union with Poland.
late 18th century: Came under control of tsarist Russia as Belarussia ('White Russia'), following three partitions of Poland in 1772, 1793, and 1795.

1812: Minsk was destroyed by French emperor Napoleon Bonaparte during his campaign against Russia.
1839: The Belorussian Catholic Church was abolished.
1914–18: Belarus was the site of fierce fighting between Germany and Russia during World War I.
1918–19: Belarus was briefly independent from Russia.
1919–20: Wars between Poland and Soviet Russia over control of Belarus.
1921: West Belarus was ruled by Poland; East Belarus became a Soviet republic.
1930s: Agriculture was collectivized despite peasant resistance; over 100,000 people, chiefly writers and intellectuals, shot in mass executions ordered by the Soviet dictator Joseph Stalin.
1939: West Belarus was occupied by Soviet troops.
1941–44: The Nazi occupation resulted in the death of 1.3 million people, including many Jews; Minsk was destroyed.
1945: Belarus became a founding member of the United Nations (UN); much of West Belarus was incorporated into Soviet republic.
1950s–60s: Large-scale immigration of ethnic Russians and 'Russification'.
1986: Fallout from the nearby Chernobyl nuclear reactor in Ukraine rendered 20% of agricultural land unusable.
1989: The Belorussian Popular Front was established as national identity was revived under the *glasnost* initiative of Soviet leader Mikhail Gorbachev.
1990: Belorussian was established as the state language and republican sovereignty declared.
1991: Independence was recognized by the USA; the Commonwealth of Independent States (CIS) was formed in Minsk.
1996: An agreement on economic union was signed with Russia. Syargey Ling became prime minister.
1997: There were pro-democracy demonstrations.
1998: The Belarus rouble was devalued. A new left-wing and centrist political coalition was created. Food rationing was imposed as the economy deteriorated. Belarus signed a common policy with Russia on economic, foreign, and military matters.
2000: President Lukashenko dismissed Prime Minister Syargey Ling and appointed Uladzimir Yarmoshyn. Lukashenko was re-elected in October, although western observers described the election as undemocratic, and opposition leaders led popular protests. Lukashenko and Vladimir Putin, the President of Russia, agreed to introduce a single common currency by 2008.
2001: Elections were re-run in some areas. Belarus officials declared the votes valid but thousands demonstrated against the president. Lukashenko was re-elected in September, although the elections were criticised as neither free nor fair by western observers.
2002: President Lukashenko rejected Russian proposals for union under a Russian constitution with a single government and parliament. Fourteen European Union (EU) countries imposed a travel ban on senior officials, including President Lukashenko, in protest at their poor human rights record.
2003: Opposition members were briefly jailed after calling for the president's resignation. The travel ban against Lukashenko and his officials was lifted.

2004: The Council of Europe condemned reports of human rights abuses and the EU imposed travel restrictions on senior ministers. Demonstrations were held against President Lukashenko on the occasion of his tenth year in power. A referendum vote allowed Lukashenko to serve more then the previous limit of two terms in office. Parliamentary elections were held in which opposition parties failed to win a single seat; western observers described the election as corrupt; violent demonstrations followed. The EU extended the travel restrictions on senior ministers. Mikhail Marinich, an opposition politician, was jailed, a charge he described as being politically motivated.

Belau former name for the Republic of Palau.

bel canto (Italian 'beautiful song') in music, an 18th-century Italian style of singing with emphasis on perfect technique and beautiful tone. The style reached its peak in the operas of Gioacchino *Rossini, Gaetano *Donizetti, and Vincenzo *Bellini.

Belfast (Irish *Béal Feirste* 'the mouth of the Farset') capital city and industrial port of *Northern Ireland, situated in County Antrim and County Down, at the mouth of the River Lagan on Belfast Lough; population (2001 est) 277,170. It is the county town of County Antrim, and has been the capital of Northern Ireland since 1920. Industries include air-craft components, engineering, electronics, fertilizers, food processing, and textiles; linen and shipbuilding declined in importance after the 19th century. From the 1990s the city underwent considerable redevelopment, in terms of its physical infrastructure and industrial investment and regeneration, particularly in the service industries.

Belgian Congo former name (1908–60) of the Democratic Republic of Congo; known 1960–97 as Zaire.

Belgium

National name: *Royaume de Belgique* (French), *Koninkrijk België* (Flemish)/*Kingdom of Belgium*

Area: 30,510 sq km/11,779 sq mi
Capital: Brussels
Major towns/cities: Antwerp, Ghent, Liège, Charleroi, Bruges, Mons, Namur, Louvain
Major ports: Antwerp, Ostend, Zeebrugge
Physical features: fertile coastal plain in northwest, central rolling hills rise eastwards, hills and forest in southeast; Ardennes Forest; rivers Schelde and Meuse
Head of state: King Albert II from 1993
Head of government: Guy Verhofstadt from 1999
Political system: liberal democracy
Political executive: parliamentary
Political parties: Flemish Christian Social Party (CVP), left of centre; French Social Christian Party (PSC), left of centre; Flemish Socialist Party (SP), left of centre; French Socialist Party (PS), left of centre; Flemish Liberal Party (PVV), moderate centrist; French Liberal Reform Party (PRL), moderate centrist; Flemish People's Party (VU), federalist; Flemish Vlaams Blok, right wing; Flemish Green Party (Agalev); French Green Party (Ecolo), ecological
Currency: euro (Belgian franc until 2002)
GNI per capita (PPP): (US$) 27,350 (2002 est)
Exports: food, livestock and livestock products, gem diamonds, iron and steel manufacturers, machinery and transport equipment, chemicals and related products. Principal market: France 17.6% (2000)
Population: 10,318,000 (2003 est)
Language: Flemish (a Dutch dialect, known as *Vlaams*; official) (spoken by 56%, mainly in Flanders, in the north), French (especially the dialect Walloon; official) (spoken by 32%, mainly in Wallonia, in the south), German (0.6%; mainly near the eastern border)
Religion: Roman Catholic 75%, various Protestant denominations
Life expectancy: 76 (men); 82 (women) (2000–05)
Chronology
57 BC: Romans conquered the Belgae (the indigenous Celtic people), and formed the province of Belgica.
3rd–4th centuries AD: The region was overrun by Franks and Saxons.
8th–9th centuries: Part of Frankish Empire; peace and order fostered growth of Ghent, Bruges, and Brussels.
843: Division of Holy Roman Empire; became part of Lotharingia, but frequent repartitioning followed.
10th–11th centuries: Several feudal states emerged: Flanders, Hainaut, Namur, Brabant, Limburg, and Luxembourg, all nominally subject to French king or Holy Roman Emperor, but in practice independent.
12th century: The economy began to flourish.
15th century: One by one, the states came under rule of the dukes of Burgundy.
1477: Passed into Habsburg dominions through the marriage of Mary of Burgundy to Maximilian, archduke of Austria.
1555: Division of Habsburg dominions; Low Countries allotted to Spain.
1648: Independence of Dutch Republic recognized; south retained by Spain.
1713: Treaty of Utrecht transferred Spanish Netherlands to Austrian rule.
1792–97: Austrian Netherlands invaded by revolutionary France and finally annexed.
1815: The Congress of Vienna reunited north and south Netherlands as one kingdom under the House of Orange.
1830: The largely French-speaking people in south rebelled against union with Holland and declared Belgian independence.
1831: Leopold of Saxe-Coburg-Gotha became the first king of Belgium.

93

1839: The Treaty of London recognized the independence of Belgium and guaranteed its neutrality.
1914–18: Belgium was invaded and occupied by Germany. Belgian forces under King Albert I fought in conjunction with the Allies.
1919: Belgium acquired the Eupen-Malmédy region from Germany.
1940: Second invasion by Germany; King Leopold III ordered the Belgian army to capitulate.
1944–45: Belgium was liberated.
1948: Belgium formed the Benelux customs union with Luxembourg and the Netherlands.
1949: Belgium was a founding member of the North Atlantic Treaty Organization (NATO). Brussels became its headquarters in 1967.
1958: Belgium was a founding member of the European Economic Community (EEC), which made Brussels its headquarters.
1971: The constitution was amended to safeguard cultural rights of Flemish- (Flanders in north) and French-speaking communities (Walloons in southeast).
1974: Separate regional councils and ministerial committees were established for Flemings and Walloons.
1980: There was violence over language divisions; regional assemblies for Flanders and Wallonia and a three-member executive for Brussels were created.
1999: In the general election, Guy Verhofstadt became liberal prime minister of a coalition government together with socialists and Greens.
2000: Local elections were marked by the rise of the far-right party Vlaams Blok, which campaigned against immigration.
2003: The Vlaamse Liberalen en Democraten (VLD; Flemish Liberals and Democrats), part of the governing coalition led by VLD prime minister Guy Verhofstadt, won the largest vote share in the Chamber of Representatives.
2004: A massive gas explosion in an industrial area southwest of Brussels killed 18 people and injured more than 100. The high court ruled that the far-right party Vlaams Blok was racist, forcing it to disband. It was re-established under a new name, Vlaams Belang (Flemish Interest).

Belgrade Serbo-Croat Beograd, port and capital of Serbia and Montenegro, and of its constituent republic of Serbia, at the confluence of the Danube and Sava rivers: population (1991 est) 1,168,500. It is linked to the port of Bar on the Adriatic Sea. Industries include light engineering, food processing, textiles, pharmaceuticals, and electrical goods.

Belisarius (c. 505–565) East Roman general who led Rome's reconquest of the West. Though given inadequate resources by the jealous emperor Justinian I, Belisarius achieved notable victories against the Persians, Huns, Vandals, and Goths.

Belize
formerly **British Honduras (until 1973)**
Area: 22,963 sq km/8,866 sq mi
Capital: Belmopan
Major towns/cities: Belize City, Dangriga, Orange Walk, Corozal, San Ignacio de Agana
Major ports: Belize City, Dangriga, Punta Gorda
Physical features: tropical swampy coastal plain, Maya Mountains in south; over 90% forested

Head of state: Queen Elizabeth II from 1981, represented by Governor General Dr Colville Young from 1993
Head of government: Said Musa from 1998
Political system: liberal democracy
Political executive: parliamentary
Political parties: People's United Party (PUP), left of centre; United Democratic Party (UDP), moderate conservative; National Alliance for Belizean Rights (NABR), dissolved
Currency: Belize dollar
GNI per capita (PPP): (US$) 5,340 (2002 est)
Exports: sugar, clothes, citrus products, forestry and fish products, bananas. Principal market: USA 53.8% (2001)
Population: 256,000 (2003 est)
Language: English (official), Spanish (widely spoken), Creole dialects
Religion: Roman Catholic 62%, Protestant 30%
Life expectancy: 70 (men); 73 (women) (2000–05)
Chronology
325–925 AD: Part of American Indian Maya civilization.
1600s: Colonized by British buccaneers and log-cutters
1862: Formally declared a British colony, known as British Honduras.
1893: Mexico renounced its longstanding claim to the territory.
1954: Constitution adopted, providing for limited internal self-government.
1964: Self-government was achieved. Universal adult suffrage and a two-chamber legislature were introduced.
1970: The capital was moved from Belize City to the new town of Belmopan.
1973: Name changed to Belize.
1975: British troops sent to defend the long-disputed frontier with Guatemala.
1980: The United Nations (UN) called for full independence.
1981: Full independence was achieved.
1991: Diplomatic relations were re-established with Guatemala, which finally recognized Belize's sovereignty.
1993: The UK announced its intention to withdraw troops following the resolution of the border dispute with Guatemala.
1998: The PUP won a sweeping victory in assembly elections, with Said Musa as prime minister.

2002: Belize and Guatemala agreed a draft settlement of border dispute.

2003: The PUP retained power in elections, although with a reduced majority.

2004: The UK Privy Council dismissed an appeal against the Belize government's approval of the proposed Chalillo dam.

2005: Strikes were called in protest at the government's budget measures. Rioters in Belmopan demonstrated against the government.

Belize City former capital (until 1970) and chief port of Belize, situated at the mouth of the Belize River on the Caribbean coast; population (2000 est) 49,100. It is Belize's largest city and capital of Belize district. Exports include sugar, timber, citrus fruits, coconuts, and maize. The port also serves parts of Mexico. The city was severely damaged by hurricanes in September 1931 and in October 1961, after which it was decided to move the capital inland, to Belmopan.

bell musical instrument, made in many sizes, comprising a suspended resonating vessel swung by a handle or from a pivoted frame to make contact with a beater which hangs inside the bell. Church bells are among the most massive structures to be cast in bronze in one piece; from high up in a steeple they can be heard for many miles. Their shape, a flared bowl with a thickened rim, is engineered to produce a clangorous mixture of tones. Miniature **handbells** are tuned to resonate harmoniously. Orchestral **tubular bells**, of brass or steel, are tuned to a chromatic scale of pitches and are played by striking with a wooden mallet. A set of steeple bells played from a keyboard is called a **carillon**.

Bell, Alexander Graham (1847–1922) Scottish-born US scientist and inventor. He was the first person ever to transmit speech from one point to another by electrical means. This invention – the telephone – was made in 1876, when Bell transmitted speech from Paris, Ontario, to Brantford, Ontario (a distance of 13 km/8 mi). Later Bell experimented with a type of phonograph and, in aeronautics, invented the tricycle undercarriage.

belladonna *or* **deadly nightshade** poisonous plant belonging to the nightshade family, found in Europe and Asia. It grows to 1.5 m/5 ft in height, with dull green leaves growing in unequal pairs, up to 20 cm/8 in long, and single purplish flowers that produce deadly black berries. Drugs are made from the leaves. (*Atropa belladonna*, family Solanaceae.)

belles lettres (French 'fine letters') literature that is appreciated more for its aesthetic qualities than for its content.

bellflower general name for many plants with bell-shaped flowers. The *harebell (Campanula rotundifolia)* is a wild bellflower. The Canterbury bell (*C. medium*) is the garden variety, originally from southern Europe. (Genus *Campanula*, family Campanulaceae.)

Bellini Venetian family of artists, founders of the Venetian School in the 15th and early 16th centuries. **Jacopo Bellini** (*c.* 1400–1470/71) worked in Venice, Padua, Verona, and Ferrara. **Gentile Bellini** (*c.* 1429–1507) was probably the elder son of Jacopo and was trained by him. Although now overshadowed by his brother, he was no less famous in his own day. **Giovanni Bellini** (*c.* 1430–1516) contributed more than any other painter of his time to the creation of the great Venetian School.

Bellini, Vincenzo (1801–1835) Italian composer of operas. He worked with the tenor Giovanni Battista Rubini (1794–1854) to develop lyrical melodic lines, and his operas contain superbly crafted dramatic tension often with potentially tragic themes, as in *La sonnambula/ The Sleepwalker* and *Norma* (both 1831). In *I puritani/ The Puritans* (1835), his last work, he discovered a new boldness and vigour of orchestral effect.

Belloc, (Joseph) Hilaire (René Pierre) (1870–1953) French-born British writer. He wrote nonsense verse for children, including *The Bad Child's Book of Beasts* (1896) and *Cautionary Tales for Children* (1907). Belloc also wrote historical, biographical, travel, and religious books (he was a devout Catholic). With G K *Chesterton, he advocated a return to the late medieval *guild system of commercial association in place of capitalism or socialism.

Bellow, Saul (1915–2005) Canadian-born US novelist. From his first novel, *Dangling Man* (1944), Bellow typically set his naturalistic narratives in Chicago and made his central character an anxious, Jewish-American intellectual. Other works, known for their skilled characterization, include *The Adventures of Augie March* (1953), *Herzog* (1964), *Mr Sammler's Planet* (1970), and *Humboldt's Gift* (1975). He was awarded the Nobel Prize for Literature in 1976.

belly dancing dance of the Middle East. It is characterized by the use of the hips, spine, shoulders, and stomach muscles rather than the legs. The dance is performed by women and is accompanied by varying rhythms. Traditionally, belly dance was performed only among women as a celebration of birth.

Belmopan capital of Belize from 1970; situated in central Belize, 80 km/50 mi inland in Central America, between the Belize and Sibun Rivers; population (2000 est) 8,100. It is 80 km/50 mi southwest of Belize City, near the junction of the Western Highway and the Hummingbird Highway to Dangriga. Principal exports from the region are sugar cane, citrus fruits, bananas, and coconuts. Belmopan was established in 1970 in the mountainous interior to replace Belize City as the administrative centre of the country following hurricane damage to the latter in 1961. The traditional Maya-style architecture prevails.

Belorussian *or* **Byelorussian** 'White Russian', member of an eastern Slav people closely related to the Russians (Great Russians) and Ukrainians, who live in Belarus and the surrounding area. Belorussian, a Balto-Slavic language belonging to the Indo-European family, is spoken by about 10 million people, including some in Poland. It is written in the Cyrillic script. Belorussian literature dates from the 11th century.

Belshazzar In the Old Testament, the last king of Babylon, son of Nebuchadnezzar. During a feast (known as **Belshazzar's Feast**) he saw a message, interpreted by Daniel as prophesying the fall of Babylon and death of Belshazzar.

Benares alternative transliteration of *Varanasi, a holy Hindu city in Uttar Pradesh, India.

Ben Bella, Muhammad Ahmed (1916–) Algerian politician. He was among the leaders of the Front de Libération Nationale (FLN), the first prime minister of independent Algeria 1962–63, and its first president 1963–65. His centralization of power and systematic purges were among the reasons behind his overthrow in 1965 by Houari Boumédienne. He was detained until 1979. In 1985 he founded a new party, Mouvement pour la Démocratie en Algérie (MDA), and returned to Algeria in 1990 after nine years in exile. The cancellation of the 1991 legislative elections led to his exile for the second time, and his party was banned in 1997.

bends or **compressed-air sickness** or **caisson disease** popular name for a syndrome seen in deep-sea divers, arising from too rapid a release of nitrogen from solution in their blood. If a diver surfaces too quickly, nitrogen that had dissolved in the blood under increasing water pressure is suddenly released, forming bubbles in the bloodstream and causing pain (the 'bends') and paralysis. Immediate treatment is gradual decompression in a decompression chamber, whilst breathing pure oxygen.

Benedictine order religious order of monks and nuns in the Roman Catholic Church, founded by St *Benedict at Subiaco, Italy, in the 6th century. It had a strong influence on medieval learning and reached the height of its prosperity early in the 14th century.

Benedict, St (c. 480–c. 547) founder of Christian monasticism in the West and of the *Benedictine order. He founded the monastery of Monte Cassino and others in Italy. His feast day is 11 July.

Benelux acronym for BElgium, the NEtherlands, and LUXembourg, customs union of Belgium, the Netherlands, and Luxembourg, an agreement for which was signed in London by the three governments in exile in 1944, and ratified in 1947. It came into force in 1948 and was further extended and strengthened by the Benelux Economic Union Treaty in 1958. The full economic union between the three countries came into operation in 1960. The three Benelux countries were founder-members of the European Economic Community (now the *European Union), for which the Benelux union was an important stimulus.

Beneš, Edvard (1884–1948) Czechoslovak politician. He worked with Tomáš *Masaryk towards Czechoslovak nationalism from 1918 and was foreign minister and representative at the League of Nations. He was president of the republic from 1935 until forced to resign by the Germans and headed a government in exile in London during World War II. He personally gave the order for the assassination of Reinhard *Heydrich in Prague in 1942. Having signed an agreement with Joseph Stalin, he returned home as president in 1945 but resigned again after the communist coup in 1948.

Bengal former province of British India, in the northeast of the subcontinent. It was the first major part of India to come under the control of the British *East India Company (the 'Bengal Presidency'). When India gained independence in 1947, Bengal was divided into *West Bengal, a state of India, and East Bengal, which from 1972 onwards became part of the newly independent state of Bangladesh.

Bengal, Bay of part of the Indian Ocean lying between the east coast of India and the west coast of Myanmar (Burma) and the Malay Peninsula. The Irrawaddy, Ganges, and Brahmaputra rivers flow into the bay. The principal islands are to be found in the Andaman and Nicobar groups.

Bengali people of Bengali culture from Bangladesh and India (West Bengal, Tripura). There are 80–150 million speakers of Bengali, an Indo-Iranian language

belonging to the Indo-European family. It is the official language of Bangladesh and of the state of Bengal and is also used by emigrant Bangladeshi and Bengali communities in such countries as the UK and the USA. Bengalis in Bangladesh are predominantly Muslim, whereas those in India are mainly Hindu.

Ben-Gurion, David (1886–1973) adopted name of David Gruen, Israeli statesman and socialist politician. He was one of the founders of the state of Israel, the country's first prime minister 1948–53, and again 1955–63. He retired from politics in 1970, but remained a lasting symbol of the Israeli state.

Benin former African kingdom 1200–1897, now a province of Nigeria. It reached the height of its power in the 14th–17th centuries when it ruled the area between the Niger Delta and Lagos. The province trades in timber and rubber.

Benin

formerly **Dahomey (1899–75)**

National name: *République du Bénin/Republic of Benin*

Area: 112,622 sq km/43,483 sq mi

Capital: Porto-Novo (official), Cotonou (de facto)

Major towns/cities: Abomey, Natitingou, Parakou, Kandi, Ouidah, Djougou, Bohicon, Cotonou

Major ports: Cotonou

Physical features: flat to undulating terrain; hot and humid in south; semiarid in north; coastal lagoons with fishing villages on stilts; Niger River in northeast

Head of state and government: Mathieu Kerekou from 1996

Political system: emergent democracy

Political executive: limited presidency

Political parties: Union for the Triumph of Democratic Renewal (UTDR); National Party for Democracy and Development (PNDD); Party for Democratic Renewal (PRD); Social Democratic Party (PSD); National Union for Solidarity and Progress (UNSP); National Democratic Rally (RND). The general orientation of most parties is left of centre

Currency: franc CFA

GNI per capita (PPP): (US$) 1,020 (2002 est)

Exports: cotton and textiles, crude petroleum, palm oil and other palm products. Principal market: India 21% (2001)

Population: 6,736,000 (2003 est)

Language: French (official), Fon (47%), Yoruba (9%) (both in the south), six major tribal languages in the north

Religion: animist 70%, Muslim 15%, Christian 15%
Life expectancy: 48 (men); 53 (women) (2000–05)
Chronology
12th–13th centuries: The area was settled by a Ewe-speaking people called the Aja, who mixed with local peoples and gradually formed the Fon ethnic group.
16th century: The Aja kingdom, called Great Ardha, was at its peak.
early 17th century: The Kingdom of Dahomey was established in the south by Fon peoples, who defeated the neighbouring Dan; following contact with European traders, the kingdom became an intermediary in the slave trade.
1800–50: King Dezo of Dahomey raised regiments of female soldiers to attack the Yoruba ('land of the big cities') kingdom of eastern Benin and southwest Nigeria in order to obtain slaves.
1857: A French base was established at Grand-Popo.
1892–94: War broke out between the French and Dahomey, after which the victorious French established a protectorate.
1899: Incorporated in federation of French West Africa as Dahomey.
1914: During World War I French troops from Dahomey participated in conquest of German-ruled Togoland to the west.
1940–44: During World War II, along with the rest of French West Africa, the country supported the 'Free French' anti-Nazi resistance cause.
1960: Independence achieved from France.
1960–77: Acute political instability, with frequent switches from civilian to military rule, and regional ethnic disputes.
1975: The name of the country was changed from Dahomey to Benin.
1989: The army was deployed against antigovernment strikers and protesters, inspired by Eastern European revolutions; Marxist-Leninism was dropped as the official ideology and a market-centred economic reform programme adopted.
1990: A referendum backed the establishment of multiparty politics.
1991: In multiparty elections, the leader of the new Benin Renaissance Party (PRB), Nicéphore Soglo, became president and formed a ten-party coalition government.
1996: Major Mathieu Kerekou became president.
1998: Prime Minister Adrien Houngbedji resigned; no immediate successor was appointed.
2001: President Kerekou was re-elected amidst allegations of electoral fraud.
2002: Benin joined the Community of Sahel-Saharan States. Benin and Niger requested that the International Court of Justice mediate in their border dispute. Local elections were held for the first time in over 10 years.
2003: Parties supporting President Kerekou won the majority of seats in legislative elections.
2004: Benin and Nigeria agreed to redraw their border. A US telecommunications company admitted to giving millions of dollars to President Kerekou's 2001 election campaign.

Bennett, (Enoch) Arnold (1867–1931) English novelist, playwright, and journalist. His major works are set in the industrial 'five towns' of the Potteries in Staffordshire (now Stoke-on-Trent) and are concerned with the manner in which the environment dictates the pattern of his characters' lives. They include *Anna of the Five Towns* (1902), *The Old Wives' Tale* (1908), and the trilogy *Clayhanger, Hilda Lessways*, and *These Twain* (1910–15).

Bennett, Alan (1934–) English dramatist and screenwriter. His works (often set in his native north of England) treat, with macabre, gruesome comedy, such subjects as class, senility, illness, and death. They include the series of monologues for television *Talking Heads* (1987) and *Talking Heads 2* (1998), and the play *The Madness of George III* (1991), made into the critically acclaimed film *The Madness of King George* (1995; Academy Award for Best Adapted Screenplay).

Ben Nevis highest mountain in the British Isles (1,344 m/4,409 ft), 7 km/4 mi southeast of Fort William, Scotland.

bent *or* **bent grass** any of a group of grasses. Creeping bent grass (*Agrostis stolonifera*), also known as fiorin, is common in northern North America, Europe, and Asia, including lowland Britain. It spreads by *runners and has large attractive clusters (panicles) of yellow or purple flowers on thin stalks, like oats. It is often used on lawns and golf courses. (Genus *Agrostris*, family Gramineae.)

Bentham, Jeremy (1748–1832) English philosopher, legal and social reformer, and founder of *utilitarianism. He believed that every individual action could be submitted to a 'felicific calculus', a quantitative comparison of pleasures and pains, the product of which could be used for the purposes of arriving at legislation that would achieve 'the greatest happiness of the greatest number'. The essence of his moral philosophy is found in *Principles of Morals and Legislation* (1789).

Benz, Karl (Friedrich) (1844–1929) German automobile engineer. He produced the world's first petrol-driven motor vehicle. He built his first model engine in 1878 and the petrol-driven car in 1885.

benzene C_6H_6, clear liquid hydrocarbon of characteristic odour, occurring in coal tar. It is used as a solvent and in the synthesis of many chemicals.

Beowulf Old English poem of 3,182 lines, thought to have been composed in the first half of the 8th century. It is the only complete surviving example of Germanic folk epic and exists in a single manuscript copied in England about 1000 and now housed in the Cottonian collection of the British Museum, London.

Berber the non-Semitic Caucasoid people of North Africa who since prehistoric times have inhabited Barbary – the Mediterranean coastlands from Egypt to the Atlantic. Their language, present-day Berber (a member of the Hamito-Semitic or Afro-Asiatic language family), is written in both Arabic and Berber characters and is spoken by about 10 million people: about one-third of Algerians and nearly two-thirds of Moroccans. Berbers are mainly agricultural, but some are still nomadic.

Berbera seaport in Somalia, with the only sheltered harbour on the south side of the Gulf of Aden; population (1990) 70,000. It is in a strategic position on the oil route and has a deep-sea port, completed in 1969. The port, which was the capital of *British Somaliland until 1941, is the terminus of roads from Hargeysa and Burko, and an airport now adds to its accessibility. Berbera exports sheep, gum arabic, frankincense, and myrrh. Its seaborne trade is chiefly with Aden which lies in Yemen 240 km/150 mi to the north.

Berengaria of Navarre (1165–c. 1230) Queen of England. The only English queen never to set foot in England, she was the daughter of King Sancho VI of Navarre. She married Richard I of England in Cyprus 1191, and accompanied him on his crusade to the Holy Land.

Berg, Alban (1885–1935) Austrian composer. He studied under Arnold Schoenberg and developed a personal 12-tone idiom of great emotional and stylistic versatility. His relatively small output includes two operas – *Wozzeck* (1914–20), a grim story of working-class life, and the unfinished *Lulu* (1929–35) – and chamber music incorporating coded references to friends and family.

Berg, Paul (1926–) US molecular biologist who, in 1972, spliced and combined into a single hybrid the *DNA from an animal tumour virus (SV40) and the DNA from a bacterial virus, using gene-splicing techniques developed by others. He shared the Nobel Prize for Chemistry in 1980 for his work on the biochemistry of nucleic acids, especially recombinant DNA.

bergamot small evergreen tree belonging to the rue family. A fragrant citrus-scented essence is obtained from the rind of its fruit and used as a perfume and food flavouring, for example in Earl Grey tea. The sole source of supply is southern Calabria, Italy, but the name comes from the town of Bergamo, in Lombardy. (*Citrus bergamia*, family Rutaceae.)

Bergius, Friedrich Karl Rudolf (1884–1949) German chemist who invented processes for converting coal into oil and wood into sugar. He shared the Nobel Prize for Chemistry in 1931 with Carl Bosch for his part in inventing and developing high-pressure industrial methods.

Bergman, (Ernst) Ingmar (1918–) Swedish stage and film director. He is regarded by many as a unique auteur and one of the masters of modern cinema. His work deals with complex moral, psychological, and metaphysical problems and is often strongly pessimistic. Bergman gained an international reputation with *Det sjunde inseglet/The Seventh Seal* (1957) and *Smultronstället/Wild Strawberries* (1957).

Bergman, Ingrid (1915–1982) Swedish-born actor. Having moved to the USA in 1939 to appear in David O Selznick's remake of the Swedish film *Intermezzo* (1936) in which she had first come to prominence, she went on to appear in such Hollywood classics as *Casablanca* (1942), *For Whom the Bell Tolls* (1943), *Gaslight* (1944; for which she won an Academy Award), and *Notorious* (1946). On screen she projected a combination of radiance, refined beauty, and fortitude.

Bergson, Henri Louis (1859–1941) French philosopher. He believed that time, change, and development were the essence of reality. He thought that time was a continuous process in which one period merged imperceptibly into the next. In *Creative Evolution* (1907) he attempted to prove that all evolution and progress are due to the working of the *élan vital*, or life force. He was awarded the Nobel Prize for Literature in 1927.

beriberi nutritional disorder occurring mostly in the tropics and resulting from a deficiency of vitamin B_1 (*thiamine). The disease takes two forms: in one *oedema (waterlogging of the tissues) occurs; in the other there is severe emaciation. There is nerve

degeneration in both forms and many victims succumb to heart failure.

Bering, Vitus Jonassen (1681–1741) Danish explorer. He was the first European to sight Alaska. He died on Bering Island in the Bering Sea, both named after him, as is the Bering Strait, which separates Asia (Russia) from North America (Alaska).

Bering Sea section of the Pacific Ocean north of the Aleutian Islands, between Siberia and Alaska; area 2.28 million sq km/880,000 sq mi. It connects with the Chukchi Sea, to the north, via the Bering Strait, extending for 87 km/54 mi from east–west, between the Chukchi Peninsula of Siberia and the Seward Peninsula of Alaska. It is named after the Danish explorer Vitus *Bering, who explored the Bering Strait in 1728.

Bering Strait strait between Alaska and Siberia, linking the North Pacific and Arctic oceans.

Berio, Luciano (1925–) Italian composer. His work, usually involving electronic sound, combines serial techniques with commedia dell'arte and antiphonal practices, as in *Alleluiah II* (1958) for five instrumental groups. His large output includes 11 *Sequenzas/Sequences* (1958–85) for various solo instruments or voice, *Sinfonia* (1968) for voices and orchestra, *Formazioni/Formations* (1987) for orchestra, and the opera *Un re in ascolto/A King Listens* (1984).

Berkeley, George (1685–1753) Irish philosopher and cleric who believed that nothing exists apart from perception, and that the all-seeing mind of God makes possible the continued apparent existence of things. For Berkeley, everyday objects are collections of ideas or sensations, hence the dictum *esse est percipi* ('to exist is to be perceived'). He became bishop of Cloyne in 1734.

berkelium chemical symbol Bk, synthesized, radioactive, metallic element of the actinide series, atomic number 97, relative atomic mass 247. It was first produced in 1949 by US nuclear chemist Glenn Seaborg and his team, at the University of California at Berkeley, California, after which it is named.

Berkshire or **Royal Berkshire** former county of south-central England; from April 1998 split into six unitary authorities: *West Berkshire, *Reading, *Slough, *Windsor and Maidenhead, *Wokingham and *Bracknell Forest.

Berlin administrative region (German *Land*) of northeast Germany, coextensive with *Berlin, city and capital of the country; area 891 sq km/344 sq mi. It is an enclave within the *Land* of *Brandenburg.

Berlin industrial city, administrative region (German *Land*) and capital of Germany, lying on the River Spree; population (2003 est) 3,274,500, urban agglomeration 3,933,300. Products include machine tools, electronics, textiles and garments, engineering goods (including cars), electrical goods, paper, food and drink, and printed works. After the division of Germany in 1949, East Berlin became the capital of East Germany and Bonn was made the provisional capital of West Germany. The *Berlin Wall divided the city from 1961 until it was opened in November 1989. Following the reunification of Germany on 3 October 1990, East and West Berlin were once more reunited as the 16th *Land* (administrative region) of the Federal Republic, and Berlin became once again the national capital.

Berlin, Irving (1888–1989) adopted name of Israel Baline, Belorussian-born US songwriter. His songs include hits such as 'Alexander's Ragtime Band' (1911), 'Always' (1925), 'God Bless America' (1917, published 1939), and 'White Christmas' (1942), and the musicals *Top Hat* (1935), *Annie Get Your Gun* (1946), and *Call Me Madam* (1950). He also provided songs for films like *Blue Skies* (1946) and *Easter Parade* (1948). 'White Christmas' has been the most performed Christmas song in history, with more than 500 versions recorded.

Berlin blockade the closing of entry to Berlin from the west by Soviet Forces from June 1948 to May 1949. It was an attempt to prevent the other Allies (the USA, France, and the UK) unifying the western part of Germany. The British and US forces responded by sending supplies to the city by air for over a year (the **Berlin airlift**). In May 1949 the blockade was lifted; the airlift continued until September. The blockade marked the formal division of the city into Eastern and Western sectors. In 1961 East Berlin was sealed off with the construction of the *Berlin Wall.

Berlin Wall dividing barrier between East and West Berlin from 1961 to 1989, erected by East Germany to prevent East Germans from leaving for West Germany. Escapers were shot on sight. It became an icon of the division of Europe during the Cold War.

Berlioz, (Louis) Hector (1803–1869) French Romantic composer. He is regarded as the founder of modern orchestration. Much of his music was inspired by drama and literature and has a theatrical quality. He wrote symphonic works, such as *Symphonie fantastique/Fantasy Symphony* (1830) and *Roméo et Juliette/Romeo and Juliet* (1839); dramatic cantatas including *La Damnation de Faust/The Damnation of Faust* (1846) and *L'Enfance du Christ/The Childhood of Christ* (1850–54); sacred music; and three operas: *Benvenuto Cellini* (1838), *Les Troyens/The Trojans* (1856–58), and *Béatrice et Bénédict/Beatrice and Benedict* (1860–62).

Bermuda British overseas territory in the Northwest Atlantic Ocean; area 54 sq km/21 sq mi; population (1994 est) 60,500. The colony consists of 138 small islands, of which 20 are inhabited; the 6 principal islands are linked by bridges and causeways. The capital and chief port is Hamilton. Bermuda is Britain's oldest colony, officially taken by the crown in 1684. Under the constitution of 1968, it is fully self-governing, with a governor (John Vereker from 2002), senate, and elected House of Assembly (premier from 1998 Jennifer Smith, Progressive Labour Party). The principal economic activities are tourism and finance, especially insurance. Industries include pharmaceuticals and growing Easter lilies. The currency used in the colony is the Bermuda dollar, the main language spoken is English, and the main religion is Christianity.

Bermuda Triangle sea area bounded by Bermuda, Florida, and Puerto Rico, which gained the nickname 'Deadly Bermuda Triangle' in 1964 when it was suggested that unexplained disappearances of ships and aircraft were exceptionally frequent there. Analysis of the data has not confirmed the idea.

Bern French **Berne**, capital of Switzerland and of Bern canton, in the west of the country on the River Aare; population (2003 est) 122,700. Industries include the manufacture of textiles, precision instruments, chocolate, pharmaceuticals, and light metal and electronic goods. There is a magnificent Gothic cathedral, dating from the 15th century. Bern joined

the Swiss confederation in 1353 as its eighth member, and became the capital in 1848.

Bernadette, St, of Lourdes (originally Maries Bernard Soubirous) (1844–1879) French saint, born in Lourdes in the French Pyrenees. In February 1858 she had a vision of the Virgin Mary in a grotto, and it became a centre of pilgrimage. Many sick people who were dipped in the water of a spring there were said to have been cured. Canonized in 1933. Her feast day is 16 April.

Bernard, Claude (1813–1878) French physiologist and founder of experimental medicine. Bernard first demonstrated that digestion is not restricted to the stomach, but takes place throughout the small intestine. He discovered the digestive input of the pancreas, several functions of the liver, and the vasomotor nerves which dilate and contract the blood vessels and thus regulate body temperature. This led him to the concept of the *milieu intérieur* ('internal environment') whose stability is essential to good health.

Bernard of Clairvaux, St (1090–1153) Christian founder in 1115 of Clairvaux monastery in Champagne, France. He reinvigorated the *Cistercian order, preached in support of the Second Crusade in 1146, and had the scholastic philosopher Abelard condemned for heresy. He is often depicted with a beehive. Canonized in 1174. His feast day is 20 August.

Bernese Alps or **Berner Alpen** mountainous area in the south of Bern canton, Switzerland. It includes the Jungfrau, Eiger, and Finsteraarhorn peaks. Interlaken is the chief town.

Bernhardt, Sarah (1844–1923) stage name of Henriette Rosine Bernard, French actor. She dominated the stage in her day, frequently performing at the Comédie Française in Paris. She excelled in tragic roles, including Cordelia in Shakespeare's *King Lear*, the title role in Racine's *Phèdre*, and the male roles of Hamlet and of Napoleon's son in Edmond Rostand's *L'Aiglon*.

Bernini, Gianlorenzo (Giovanni Lorenzo) (1598–1680) Italian sculptor, architect, and painter. He was a leading figure in the development of the *baroque style. His work in Rome includes the colonnaded piazza in front of St Peter's Basilica (1656), fountains (as in the Piazza Navona), and papal monuments. His sculpture includes *The Ecstasy of St Theresa* (1645–52; Santa Maria della Vittoria, Rome), and numerous portrait busts.

Bernoulli's principle law stating that the pressure of a fluid varies inversely with speed, an increase in speed producing a decrease in pressure (such as a drop in hydraulic pressure as the fluid speeds up flowing through a constriction in a pipe) and vice versa. The principle also explains the pressure differences on each surface of an aerofoil, which gives lift to the wing of an aircraft. The principle is named after Swiss mathematician and physicist Daniel Bernoulli.

Bernstein, Leonard (1918–1990) US composer, conductor, and pianist. He was one of the most energetic and versatile 20th-century US musicians. His works, which established a vogue for realistic, contemporary themes, include symphonies such as *The Age of Anxiety* (1949), ballets such as *Fancy Free* (1944), and scores for musicals, including *Wonderful Town* (1953), *West Side Story* (1957), and *Mass* (1971) in memory of President J F Kennedy.

berry fleshy, many-seeded *fruit that does not split open to release the seeds. The outer layer of tissue, the exocarp, forms an outer skin that is often brightly coloured to attract birds to eat the fruit and thus disperse the seeds. Examples of berries are the tomato and the grape.

Berry, Chuck (1926–) born Charles Edward Anderson Berry, US singer, songwriter, and guitarist. Considered one of the most influential performers in *rock-and-roll music, his characteristic guitar riffs and humorous storytelling lyrics have been widely imitated. He had a string of hits in the 1950s and 1960s beginning with 'Maybellene' (1955), which became an early rock-and-roll classic. He enjoyed a revival of popularity in the 1970s and 1980s. In 1986 he was the first member of the Rock 'n' Roll Hall of Fame.

Berthollet, Claude Louis (1748–1822) Count, French chemist who carried out research into dyes and bleaches (introducing the use of *chlorine as a bleach) and determined the composition of *ammonia. Modern chemical nomenclature is based on a system worked out by Berthollet and Antoine *Lavoisier.

beryl in full **beryllium aluminium silicate**, $3BeO.Al_2O_3.6SiO_2$, mineral that forms crystals chiefly in granite. It is the chief ore of beryllium. Two of its gem forms are aquamarine (light-blue crystals) and emerald (dark-green crystals).

beryllium chemical symbol Be, hard, lightweight, silver-white, metallic element, atomic number 4, relative atomic mass 9.012. It is one of the *alkaline-earth metals, with chemical properties similar to those of magnesium. In nature it is found only in combination with other elements and occurs mainly as beryl ($3BeO.Al_2O_3.6SiO_2$). It is used to make sturdy, light alloys and to control the speed of neutrons in nuclear reactors. Beryllium oxide was discovered in 1798 by French chemist Louis-Nicolas Vauquelin (1763–1829), but the element was not isolated until 1828, by Friedrich Wöhler and Antoine-Alexandre-Brutus Bussy independently.

Berzelius, Jöns Jakob (1779–1848) Swedish chemist. He accurately determined more than 2,000 relative atomic and molecular masses. In 1813–14, he devised the system of chemical symbols and formulae now in use and proposed oxygen as a reference standard for atomic masses. His discoveries include the elements cerium in 1804, selenium in 1817, and thorium in 1828; he was the first to prepare silicon in its amorphous form and to isolate zirconium. The words 'isomerism', 'allotropy', and 'protein' were coined by him.

Bessarabia former region in southeastern Europe, bordering on the Black Sea and standing between the Prut and Dniester rivers. Its capital was at Kishinev. The region is now divided between the states of Moldova and Ukraine.

Bessemer process first cheap method of making *steel, invented by Henry Bessemer in England in 1856. It has since been superseded by more efficient steel-making processes, such as the *basic–oxygen process. In the Bessemer process compressed air is blown into the bottom of a converter, a furnace shaped like a cement mixer, containing molten pig iron. The excess carbon in the iron burns out, other impurities form a slag, and the furnace is emptied by tilting.

Best, Charles H(erbert) (1899–1978) Canadian physiologist. He was one of the team of Canadian scientists including Frederick *Banting whose research resulted in 1922 in the discovery of insulin as a treatment for diabetes.

Best, George (1946–) Northern Irish footballer. One of football's greatest talents, he was a vital member of the Manchester United side that won the league championship in 1965 and 1967, and the European Cup in 1968, when he was voted both English and European Footballer of the Year. A goal provider as much as a goal scorer, he scored 178 goals in his 466 appearances for the club from 1963 to 1973.

bestiary in medieval times, a book with stories and illustrations which depicted real and mythical animals or plants to illustrate a (usually Christian) moral. The stories were initially derived from the Greek *Physiologus*, a collection of 48 such stories, written in Alexandria around the 2nd century.

beta-blocker any of a class of drugs that block impulses that stimulate certain nerve endings (beta receptors) serving the heart muscle. This reduces the heart rate and the force of contraction, which in turn reduces the amount of oxygen (and therefore the blood supply) required by the heart. Beta-blockers may be useful in the treatment of angina, arrhythmia (abnormal heart rhythms), and raised blood pressure, and following heart attacks. They must be withdrawn from use gradually.

beta decay disintegration of the nucleus of an atom to produce a beta particle, or high-speed electron, and an electron antineutrino. During beta decay, a neutron in the nucleus changes into a proton, thereby increasing the atomic number by one while the mass number stays the same. The mass lost in the change is converted into kinetic (movement) energy of the beta particle. Beta decay is caused by the weak nuclear force, one of the fundamental *forces of nature operating inside the nucleus.

beta particle or **beta ray** electron ejected with great velocity from a radioactive atom that is undergoing spontaneous disintegration. Beta particles are created in the nucleus on disintegration, beta decay, when a neutron converts to a proton (the atomic number increases by one while the atomic mass stays the same) by emitting an electron. The mass lost in the change is converted into *kinetic energy of the beta particle. Strontium-90 (^{90}Sr) is an example of a material that emits beta particles.

Betelgeuse or **Alpha Orionis** red supergiant star in the constellation of *Orion. It is the tenth-brightest star in the night sky, although its brightness varies. It is 1,100 million km/700 million mi across, about 800 times larger than the Sun, roughly the same size as the orbit of Mars. It is over 10,000 times as luminous as the Sun, and lies 310 light years from the Sun. Light takes 60 minutes to travel across the giant star.

betel nut fruit of the areca palm (*Areca catechu*), which is chewed together with lime and betel pepper as a stimulant by peoples of the East and Papua New Guinea. Chewing it blackens the teeth and stains the mouth deep red.

Bethlehem Arabic **Beit-Lahm**, city on the west bank of the River Jordan, 8 km/5 mi south of Jerusalem; population (1997 est) 136,400. It was occupied by Israel in 1967 and came under control of the Palestine National Authority in December 1995. In the Bible it is mentioned as the birthplace of King David and *Jesus, and in 326 the Church of the Nativity was built over the grotto said to be the birthplace of Jesus. The modern city is an agricultural marketing centre, and has particular importance as a centre for pilgrims and tourists. Its industries are still largely associated with the pilgrim and tourist trade, and include the manufacture of religious articles.

Betjeman, John (1906–1984) English poet and essayist. He was the originator of a peculiarly English light verse, nostalgic, and delighting in Victorian and Edwardian architecture. He also wrote prose works on architecture and social history which reflect his interest in the *Gothic Revival. His *Collected Poems* appeared in 1958 and a verse autobiography, *Summoned by Bells*, in 1960. Betjeman's verse, seen by some as facile, has been much enjoyed for its compassion and wit, and its evocation of places and situations. He was knighted in 1969 and became poet laureate in 1972.

betony plant belonging to the mint family, formerly used in medicine and dyeing. It has a hairy stem and leaves, and dense heads of reddish-purple flowers. (*Stachys* (formerly *Betonica*) *officinalis*, family Labiatae.)

Beuys, Joseph (1921–1986) German sculptor and performance artist. He was one of the leaders of the European avant-garde during the 1970s and 1980s. An exponent of Arte Povera, he made use of so-called 'worthless', unusual materials such as felt and fat. His best-known performance was *How to Explain Pictures to a Dead Hare* (1965). He was also an influential exponent of video art, for example, *Felt TV* (1968).

Bevan, Aneurin (Nye) (1897–1960) British Labour politician. Son of a Welsh miner, and himself a miner at 13, he was member of Parliament for Ebbw Vale 1929–60. As minister of health 1945–51, he inaugurated the National Health Service (NHS); he was minister of labour from Januaryto April 1951, when he resigned (with Harold Wilson) on the introduction of NHS charges and led a Bevanite faction against the government. In 1956 he became chief Labour spokesperson on foreign affairs, and deputy leader of the Labour party in 1959. He was an outstanding speaker.

Beveridge, William Henry (1879–1963) 1st Baron Beveridge, British economist. A civil servant, he acted as Lloyd George's lieutenant in the social legislation of the Liberal government before World War I. His *Report on Social Insurance and Allied Services* (1942), known as the **Beveridge Report**, formed the basis of the welfare state in Britain.

Beveridge Report, the in Britain, popular name of *Social Insurance and Allied Services*, a report written by William Beveridge in 1942 that formed the basis for the social-reform legislation of the Labour government of 1945–50.

Bevin, Ernest (1881–1951) British Labour politician. Chief creator of the Transport and General Workers' Union, he was its general secretary 1921–40. He served as minister of labour and national service 1940–45 in Winston Churchill's wartime coalition government, and organized the 'Bevin boys', chosen by ballot to work in the coalmines as war service. As foreign secretary in the Labour government 1945–51, he played a leading part in the creation of NATO.

Bhagavad-Gita (Hindi 'the Song of the Blessed') religious and philosophical Sanskrit poem, dating from around 300 BC, forming an episode in the sixth book of

the *Mahabharata*, one of the two great Hindu epics. It is the supreme religious work of Hinduism, regarded as one of the smriti (sacred tradition).

bhakti (Sanskrit 'devotion') in Hinduism, a tradition of worship that emphasizes devotion to a personal god as the sole necessary means for achieving salvation. It developed in southern India in the 6th–8th centuries and in northern India from the 14th century.

Bhopal industrial city and capital of *Madhya Pradesh, central India, 525 km/326 mi southwest of Allahabad; population (2001 est) 1,433,900. Textiles, chemicals, and heavy electrical goods such as motors and transformers are manufactured. Nearby Bhimbetka Caves, discovered in 1973, have the world's largest collection of prehistoric paintings, about 10,000 years old. In 1984 some 2,600 people died from an escape of the poisonous gas methyl isocyanate from a factory owned by US company Union Carbide; another 300,000 suffer from long-term health problems.

Bhutan

National name: *Druk-yul/Kingdom of Bhutan*

Area: 47,500 sq km/18,147 sq mi
Capital: Thimphu
Major towns/cities: Paro, Punakha, Mongar, Phuntsholing, Wangdiphodrang, Tashigang
Physical features: occupies southern slopes of the Himalayas; Gangkar Punsum (7,529 m/24,700 ft) is one of the world's highest unclimbed peaks; cut by valleys formed by tributaries of the Brahmaputra; thick forests in south
Head of state: Jigme Singye Wangchuk from 1972
Head of government: Yeshey Zimba from 2004
Political system: absolutist
Political executive: absolute
Political parties: none officially; illegal Bhutan People's Party (BPP) and Bhutan National Democratic Party (BNDP), both ethnic Nepali
Currency: ngultrum, although the Indian rupee is also accepted
GNI per capita (PPP): (US$) 1,530 (2002 est)
Exports: cardamon, cement, timber, fruit, electricity, precious stones, spices. Principal market: India 94% (1998)

Population: 2,257,000 (2003 est)
Language: Dzongkha (a Tibetan dialect; official),
Tibetan, Sharchop, Bumthap, Nepali, English
Religion: 70% Mahayana Buddhist (state religion),
25% Hindu
Life expectancy: 62 (men); 65 (women) (2000–05)
Chronology
to 8th century: Under effective Indian control.
16th century: Came under Tibetan rule.
1616–51: Unified by Ngawang Namgyal, leader of the
Drukpa Kagyu (Thunder Dragon) Tibetan Buddhist
branch.
1720: Came under Chinese rule.
1774: Treaty signed with East India Company.
1865: Trade treaty with Britain signed after invasion.
1907: Ugyen Wangchuk, governor of Tongsa, became
Bhutan's first hereditary monarch.
1910: Anglo-Bhutanese Treaty signed, placing foreign
relations under the 'guidance' of the British government
in India.
1949: Indo-Bhutan Treaty of Friendship signed, giving
India continued influence over Bhutan's foreign
relations, but returning territory annexed in 1865.
1953: The national assembly (Tshogdu) was established.
1958: Slavery was abolished.
1959: 4,000 Tibetan refugees were given asylum after
Chinese annexation of Tibet.
1968: The first cabinet was established.
1973: Bhutan joined the nonaligned movement.
1979: Tibetan refugees were told to take Bhutanese
citizenship or leave; most stayed.
1983: Bhutan became a founding member of the
South Asian Regional Association for Cooperation.
1988: The Buddhist Dzongkha king imposed a 'code
of conduct' suppressing the customs of the large
Hindu-Nepali community in the south.
1990: Hundreds of people were allegedly killed during
pro-democracy demonstrations.
1998: Political powers were ceded from the monarchy
to the National Assembly. Lyonpo Jigme Thimley
became prime minister.
2002: A draft constitution was proposed for
parliamentary democracy.
2005: The new constitution proposed a parliamentary
democracy, to be approved or rejected by referendum.
Bhutto, Benazir (1953–) Pakistani politician. She
was leader of the Pakistan People's Party (PPP) from
1984, a position she held in exile until 1986. Bhutto
became prime minister of Pakistan from 1988 until
1990, when the opposition manoeuvred her from office
and charged her with corruption. She again rose to the
office of prime minister (1993–96), only to be removed
for a second time under suspicion of corruption.
In 1999, while living in self-imposed exile in London,
Bhutto was found guilty of corruption and given a
five-year prison sentence.
Biafra, Bight of or **Bonny, Bight of** area of sea off
the coasts of Nigeria and Cameroon.
Biafra, Republic of African state proclaimed 1967
when fears that Nigerian central government was
increasingly in the hands of the rival Hausa tribe led
the predominantly Ibo Eastern Region of Nigeria to
secede under Lt-Col Odumegwu Ojukwu. On the
proclamation of Biafra, civil war ensued with the rest
of the federation. In a bitterly fought campaign federal

forces confined the Biafrans to a shrinking area of the
interior by 1968, and by 1970 Biafra ceased to exist.
Around 1 million Biafrans died in the famine caused
by the civil war.
Bible (Greek *ta biblia* 'the books') the sacred book of
*Judaism and *Christianity, containing a collection
of sacred writings (scriptures). The ***Old Testament**,
recognized by both Jews and Christians, is called the
Hebrew Bible in Judaism. The ***New Testament**
comprises books recognized by the Christian church
as sacred doctrine from the 4th century. The Roman
Catholic Bible also includes the ***Apocrypha**.
bicarbonate of soda or **baking soda** technical name
sodium hydrogencarbonate, $NaHCO_3$, white
crystalline solid that neutralizes acids and is used
in medicine to treat acid indigestion. It is also used
in baking powders and effervescent drinks.
bicycle pedal-driven two-wheeled vehicle used in
*cycling. It consists of a metal frame mounted on two
large wire-spoked wheels, with handlebars in front and
a seat between the front and back wheels. The bicycle
is an energy-efficient, nonpolluting form of transport,
and it is estimated that 800 million bicycles are in use
throughout the world – outnumbering cars three to
one. China, India, Denmark, and the Netherlands are
countries with a high use of bicycles. More than 10%
of road spending in the Netherlands is on cycleways
and bicycle parking.
Biedermeier early- to mid-19th-century Germanic
style of art and furniture design, derogatorily named
after Gottlieb Biedermeier, a humorous pseudonym used
by several German poets, embodying bourgeois taste.
biennial plant plant that completes its life cycle in two
years. During the first year it grows vegetatively and the
surplus food produced is stored in its *perennating
organ, usually the root. In the following year these food
reserves are used for the production of leaves, flowers,
and seeds, after which the plant dies. Many root
vegetables are biennials, including the carrot *Daucus
carota* and parsnip *Pastinaca sativa*. Some garden plants
that are grown as biennials are actually perennials, for
example, the wallflower *Cheiranthus cheiri*.
bigamy in law, the offence of marrying a person while
already lawfully married to another. In some countries
marriage to more than one wife or husband is lawful;
see also *polygamy.
big-band jazz swing music created in the late 1930s
and 1940s by bands of 13 or more players, such as those
of Duke *Ellington and Benny Goodman. Big-band
jazz relied on fixed arrangements, where there is more
than one instrument to some of the parts, rather than
improvisation. Big bands were mainly dance bands,
and they ceased to be economically viable in the 1950s.
Big Bang in astronomy, the hypothetical 'explosive'
event that marked the origin of the universe as we
know it. At the time of the Big Bang, the entire universe
was squeezed into a hot, superdense state. The Big Bang
explosion threw this compact material outwards,
producing the expanding universe seen today (see *red
shift). The cause of the Big Bang is unknown; observations
of the current rate of expansion of the universe suggest
that it took place about 10–20 billion years ago. The Big
Bang theory began modern *cosmology.
Big Bang in economics, popular term for the changes
instituted in late 1986 to the organization and practices

of the City of London as Britain's financial centre, including the liberalization of the London *stock exchange. This involved merging the functions of jobber (dealer in stocks and shares) and broker (who mediates between the jobber and the public), introducing negotiated commission rates, and allowing foreign banks and financial companies to own British brokers/jobbers, or themselves to join the London Stock Exchange.

Big Ben popular name for the bell in the clock tower of the Houses of Parliament in London, cast at the Whitechapel Bell Foundry in 1858, and known as 'Big Ben' after Benjamin Hall, First Commissioner of Works at the time. It weighs 13.7 tonnes. The name is often used to mean the tower as well.

Bihar or **Behar** state of northeast India; area 99,199 sq km/38,301 sq mi; population (2001 est) 82,878,800. The capital is Patna. The River Ganges runs west–east in the north of the state, through intensely cultivated alluvial plains which are prone to drought and floods. The chief industries are copper, iron, and coal; Bihar accounts for 15% of India's mineral production. Three-quarters of the population live in the northern plains, and the majority are involved in agriculture, producing rice, jute, sugar cane, cereals, oilseed, tobacco, and potatoes. The languages spoken are Hindi and Bihari. As part of the Bihar Reorganization Act, the region was split in November 2000 to form the new state of *Jharkhand.

Bihari a northern Indian people, also living in Bangladesh, Nepal, and Pakistan, and numbering over 40 million. The Bihari are mainly Muslim. The Bihari language is related to Hindi and has several widely varying dialects. It belongs to the Indic branch of the Indo-European family. Many Bihari were massacred during the formation of Bangladesh, which they opposed.

Bikini Atoll atoll in the Marshall Islands, western Pacific, where the USA carried out 23 atomic- and hydrogen-bomb tests (some underwater) from 1946 to 1958.

Biko, Steve (1946–1977) born Bantu Stephen Biko, South African civil-rights leader. An active opponent of *apartheid, he was arrested in August 1977, and died in detention on 12 September. Following his death in the custody of South African police, he became a symbol of the anti-apartheid movement. An inquest in the late 1980s found no one was to blame for Biko's death. Five former security policemen confessed to being involved in Biko's murder in January 1997. They applied for an amnesty to the Truth and Reconciliation Commission (TRC), the body charged with healing South Africa by exposing its past and laying foundations for a more peaceful future. The amnesty application angered Biko's family, and his widow challenged the legitimacy of the TRC in the Constitutional Court.

bilateralism in economics, a trade agreement between two countries or groups of countries in which they give each other preferential treatment. Usually the terms agreed result in balanced trade and are favoured by countries with limited foreign exchange reserves. Bilateralism is incompatible with free trade.

Bilbao industrial port and capital of Vizcaya province in the Basque Country, northern Spain; it is surrounded by mountains, and situated on an inlet of the Bay of Biscay, and on the Nervion River; population (2003 est) 342,800. Bilbao is a commercial centre and one of the chief ports in Spain; industries include iron and steel production, shipbuilding, chemicals, cement, and food-processing. Much of the city's heavy industries declined during the 1980s and 1990s, causing it to take steps to modernize its infrastructure and attract more tourism.

bilberry any of several shrubs belonging to the heath family, closely related to North American blueberries. Bilberries are sometimes referred to as blaeberries, whortleberries, or huckleberries. They have blue or black edible berries. (Genus *Vaccinium*, family Ericaceae.)

Bildungsroman (German 'education novel') novel that deals with the psychological and emotional development of its protagonist, tracing his or her life from inexperienced youth to maturity. The first example of the type is generally considered to be C M Wieland's *Agathon* (1765–66), but it was *Goethe's *Wilhelm Meisters Lehrjahre/Wilhelm Meister's Apprenticeship* (1795–96) that established the genre. Although taken up by writers in other languages, it remained chiefly a German form; later examples include Thomas *Mann's *Der Zauberberg/The Magic Mountain* (1924).

bile brownish alkaline fluid produced by the *liver. Bile is stored in the gall bladder and is intermittently released into the small intestine (the duodenum), which is part of the *gut, in order to help *digestion. Bile contains chemicals that emulsify fats. In other words it acts to disperse fat globules into tiny droplets, which speeds up their digestion.

bilharzia or **schistosomiasis** disease that causes anaemia, inflammation, formation of scar tissue, dysentery, enlargement of the spleen and liver, cancer of the bladder, and cirrhosis of the liver. It is contracted by bathing in water contaminated with human sewage. Some 200 million people are thought to suffer from this disease in the tropics, and 750,000 people a year die.

bill in birds, the projection of the skull bones covered with a horny sheath. It is not normally sensitive, except in some aquatic birds, rooks, and woodpeckers, where the bill is used to locate food that is not visible. The bills of birds are adapted by shape and size to specific diets, for example, shovellers use their bills to sieve mud in order to extract food; birds of prey have hooked bills adapted to tearing flesh; the bills of the avocet and the curlew are long and narrow for picking tiny invertebrates out of the mud; and those of woodpeckers are sharp for pecking holes in trees and plucking out insects. The bill is also used by birds for preening, fighting, display, and nest-building.

billiards indoor game played, normally by two players, with tapered poles (cues) and composition balls (one red, two white) on a rectangular table covered with a green, felt-like cloth (baize). The table has six pockets, one at each corner and in each of the long sides at the middle. Scoring strokes are made by potting the red ball, potting the opponent's ball, or potting another ball off one of these two. The cannon (when the cue ball hits the two other balls on the table) is another scoring stroke. In 1998 billiards received recognition from the International Olympic Committee as an Olympic sport, along with snooker, pool, and carom (or French) billiards.

bill of exchange form of commercial credit instrument, or IOU, used in international trade. In Britain, a bill of exchange is defined by the Bills of Exchange Act 1882 as an unconditional order in writing addressed by one person to another, signed by the person giving it, requiring the person to whom it is addressed to pay on demand or at a fixed or determinable future time a certain sum in money to or to the order of a specified person, or to the bearer.

bill of lading document giving proof of particular goods having been loaded on a ship. The person to whom the goods are being sent normally needs to show the bill of lading in order to obtain the release of the goods. For air freight, there is an **airway bill**.

Bill of Rights in the USA, the first ten amendments to the US Constitution, incorporated in 1791:
1 guarantees freedom of worship, of speech, of the press, of assembly, and to petition the government;
2 grants the right to keep and bear arms;
3 prohibits billeting of soldiers in private homes in peacetime;
4 forbids unreasonable search and seizure;
5 guarantees none be 'deprived of life, liberty or property without due process of law' or compelled in any criminal case to be a witness against himself or herself;
6 grants the right to speedy trial, to call witnesses, and to have defence counsel;
7 grants the right to trial by jury of one's peers;
8 prevents the infliction of excessive bail or fines, or 'cruel and unusual punishment';
9, 10 provide a safeguard to the states and people for all rights not specifically delegated to the central government.

Bill of Rights in Britain, an act of Parliament of 1689 that established Parliament as the primary governing body of the country. It made provisions limiting *royal prerogative (the right to act independently of Parliament) with respect to legislation, executive power, money levies, courts, and the army, and stipulated Parliament's consent to many government functions.

Billy the Kid (1859–1881) born William H Bonney, US outlaw. A leader in the 1878 Lincoln County cattle war in New Mexico, he allegedly killed his first victim at age 12 and was reputed to have killed 21 men by age 18.

binary fission in biology, a form of *asexual reproduction, whereby a single-celled organism, such as a bacterium or amoeba, divides into two smaller 'daughter' cells.

binary number system system of numbers to *base two, using combinations of the digits 1 and 0. Codes based on binary numbers are used to represent instructions and data in all modern digital computers, the values of the binary digits (contracted to 'bits') being stored or transmitted as, for example, open/closed switches, magnetized/unmagnetized disks and tapes, and high/low voltages in circuits.

binary star pair of stars moving in orbit around their common centre of mass. Observations show that most stars are binary, or even multiple – for example, the nearest star system to the Sun, *Rigil Kent (Alpha Centauri).

binary weapon in chemical warfare, weapon consisting of two substances that in isolation are harmless but when mixed together form a poisonous nerve gas. They are loaded into the delivery system separately and combine after launch.

binding energy in physics, the amount of energy needed to break the nucleus of an atom into the neutrons and protons of which it is made.

bind over in law, a UK court order that requires a person to carry out some act, usually by an order given in a magistrates' court. A person may be bound over to appear in court at a particular time if bail has been granted or, most commonly, be bound over not to commit some offence; for example, causing a breach of the peace.

bin Laden, Osama (1957–) Saudi-born Islamic fundamentalist terrorist leader who is believed to have masterminded a number of terrorist attacks directed at US targets since the early 1990s. The 11 September 2001 destruction of the World Trade Center in New York, by suicide hijackers of two commercial airliners, and two other aircraft hijackings, claimed around 3,000 lives. It was the worst act of terrorism on record. US president George W Bush responded by launching a 'War on Terrorism', with a US-led international coalition mounting military strikes on Afghanistan in an attempt to force its Taliban government to give bin Laden up, but he escaped, possibly to Pakistan. Earlier, bin Laden was thought to have engineered attacks including the February 1993 bombing of the World Trade Center in which 6 people died, the June 1996 bombing of the US military complex in Saudi Arabia, killing 19, the August 1998 bombings of US embassies in Kenya and Tanzania, killing 224, and an October 2000 suicide bomb attack on the USS *Cole* in Yemen, which killed 17 US sailors. Bin Laden promotes jihad (holy war) against the USA with the aim of 'liberating' Islam's three holiest places – Mecca, Medina, and Jerusalem.

binoculars optical instrument for viewing an object in magnification with both eyes; for example, field glasses and opera glasses. Binoculars consist of two telescopes containing lenses and prisms, which produce a stereoscopic effect as well as magnifying the image. Use of prisms has the effect of 'folding' the light path, allowing for a compact design.

binomial in mathematics, an expression consisting of two terms, such as $a + b$ or $a - b$.

binomial system of nomenclature in biology, the system in which all organisms are identified by a two-part Latinized name. Devised by the biologist *Linnaeus, it is also known as the Linnaean system. The first name is capitalized and identifies the *genus; the second identifies the *species within that genus, for example the bear genus *Ursus* includes *Ursus arctos*, the grizzly bear, and *Ursus maritimus*, the polar bear.

binturong shaggy-coated mammal *Arctitis binturong*, the largest member of the mongoose family, nearly 1 m/3 ft long excluding a long muscular tail with a prehensile tip. Mainly nocturnal and tree-dwelling, the binturong is found in the forests of Southeast Asia, feeding on fruit, eggs, and small animals.

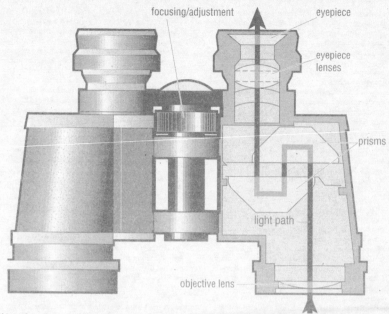

focusing/adjustment

eyepiece

eyepiece lenses

prisms

light path

objective lens

binoculars The essential components of binoculars are objective lenses, eyepieces, and a system of prisms to invert and reverse the image. A focusing system provides a sharp image by adjusting the relative positions of these components.

biochemical oxygen demand (BOD) amount of dissolved oxygen taken up by micro-organisms in a sample of water. Since these micro-organisms live by decomposing organic matter, and the amount of oxygen used is proportional to their number and metabolic rate, BOD can be used as a measure of the extent to which the water is polluted with organic compounds.

biochemistry science concerned with the chemistry of living organisms: the structure and reactions of proteins (such as enzymes), nucleic acids, carbohydrates, and lipids.

biodegradable capable of being broken down by living organisms, principally bacteria and fungi. In biodegradable substances, such as food and sewage, the natural processes of decay lead to compaction and liquefaction, and to the release of nutrients that are then recycled by the ecosystem.

biodiversity contraction of biological diversity, measure of the variety of the Earth's animal, plant, and microbial species, of genetic differences within species, and of the *ecosystems that support those species. High biodiversity means there are lots of different species in an area. The maintenance of biodiversity is important for ecological stability and as a resource for research into, for example, new drugs and crops.

biodynamic farming agricultural practice based on the principle of *homeopathy: tiny quantities of a substance are applied to transmit vital qualities to the soil. It is a form of *organic farming, and was developed by the Austrian holistic mystic Rudolf *Steiner and Ehrenfried Pfiffer.

bioengineering application of engineering to biology and medicine. Common applications include the design and use of artificial limbs, joints, and organs, including hip joints and heart valves.

biofuel any solid, liquid, or gaseous fuel produced from organic (once living) matter, either directly from plants or indirectly from industrial, commercial, domestic, or agricultural wastes. There are three main methods for the development of biofuels: the burning of dry organic wastes (such as household refuse, industrial and agricultural wastes, straw, wood, and peat); the fermentation of wet wastes (such as animal dung) in the absence of oxygen to produce biogas (containing up to 60% methane), or the fermentation of sugar cane or maize to produce alcohol and esters; and energy forestry (producing fast-growing wood for fuel).

biological clock regular internal rhythm of activity, produced by unknown mechanisms, and not dependent on external time signals. Such clocks are known to exist in almost all animals, and also in many plants, fungi, and unicellular organisms; the first biological clock gene in plants was isolated in 1995 by a US team of researchers. In higher organisms, there appears to be a series of clocks of graded importance. For example, although body temperature and activity cycles in human beings are normally 'set' to 24 hours, the two cycles may vary independently, showing that two clock mechanisms are involved.

biological control control of pests such as insects and fungi through biological means, rather than the use of chemicals. This can include breeding resistant crop strains; inducing sterility in the pest; infecting the pest species with disease organisms; or introducing the pest's natural predator. Biological control tends to be naturally self-regulating, but as ecosystems are so complex, it is difficult to predict all the consequences of introducing a biological controlling agent.

biological warfare the use of living organisms, or of infectious material derived from them, to bring about death or disease in humans, animals, or plants. At least ten countries have this capability. Advances in *genetic engineering make the development of new varieties of potentially offensive biological weapons more likely.

biology (Greek *bios* 'life', *logos* 'discourse') science of life. Biology includes all the life sciences – for example, anatomy and physiology (the study of the structure of living things), cytology (the study of cells), zoology (the study of animals), botany (the study of plants), ecology (the study of habitats and the interaction of living species), animal behaviour, embryology, and taxonomy (classification), and plant breeding. Increasingly biologists have concentrated on molecular structures: biochemistry, biophysics, and genetics (the study of inheritance and variation).

bioluminescence production of light by living organisms. It is a feature of many deep-sea fishes, crustaceans, and other marine animals. On land, bioluminescence is seen in some nocturnal insects such as glow-worms and fireflies, and in certain bacteria and fungi. Light is usually produced by the oxidation of luciferin, a reaction catalysed by the *enzyme luciferase. This reaction is unique, being the only known biological oxidation that does not produce heat. Animal luminescence is involved in communication, camouflage, or the luring of prey, but its function in some organisms is unclear.

biomass total mass of living organisms present in a given area. It may be used to describe the mass of a particular species (such as earthworm biomass), for a general category (such as herbivore biomass – animals that eat plants), or for everything in a *habitat. Estimates also exist for the entire global plant biomass. Biomass can be the mass of the organisms as they are – wet biomass – or the mass of the organisms after they have been dried to remove all the water – dry biomass. Measurements of biomass can be used to study interactions between organisms, the stability of those interactions, and variations in population numbers. Growth results in an increase in biomass, so biomass is a good measure of the extent to which organisms thrive in particular habitats. For a plant, biomass increase occurs as a result of the process of *photosynthesis. For a herbivore, biomass increase depends on the availability of plant food. Studying biomass in a habitat is a useful way to see how food is passed from organism to organism along *food chains and through food webs.

biome broad natural assemblage of plants and animals shaped by common patterns of vegetation and climate. Examples include the *tundra biome, the *rainforest biome, and the *desert biome.

bionics (from 'biological electronics') design and development of electronic or mechanical artificial systems that imitate those of living things. The bionic arm, for example, is an artificial limb (*prosthesis) that uses electronics to amplify minute electrical signals generated in body muscles to work electric motors, which operate the joints of the fingers and wrist.

biopsy removal of a living tissue sample from the body for diagnostic examination.

biosphere narrow zone that supports life on our planet. It is limited to the waters of the Earth, a fraction of its crust, and the lower regions of the atmosphere. The biosphere is made up of all the Earth's *ecosystems. It is affected by external forces such as the Sun's rays, which provide energy, the gravitational effects of the Sun and Moon, and cosmic radiations.

biosynthesis synthesis of organic chemicals from simple inorganic ones by living cells – for example, the conversion of carbon dioxide and water to glucose by plants during *photosynthesis. Other biosynthetic reactions produce cell constituents including proteins and fats.

biotechnology industrial use of living organisms. Examples of its uses include fermentation, *genetic engineering (gene technology), and the manipulation of reproduction. The brewing and baking industries have long relied on the yeast micro-organism for *fermentation purposes, while the dairy industry employs a range of bacteria and fungi to convert milk into cheeses and yoghurts. *Enzymes, whether extracted from cells or produced artificially, are central to most biotechnological applications. Recent advances include genetic engineering, in which single-celled organisms with modified *DNA are used to produce insulin and other drugs.

biotin *or* **vitamin H** vitamin of the B complex, found in many different kinds of food; egg yolk, liver, legumes, and yeast contain large amounts. Biotin is essential to the metabolism of fats. Its absence from the diet may lead to dermatitis.

birch any of a group of slender trees with small leaves and fine, peeling bark. About 40 species are found in cool temperate parts of the northern hemisphere. Birches grow rapidly, and their hard, beautiful wood is used for veneers and cabinet work. (Genus *Betula*, family Betulaceae.)

bird backboned animal of the class Aves, the biggest group of land vertebrates, characterized by warm blood, feathers, wings, breathing through lungs, and egg-laying by the female. Birds are bipedal; feet are usually adapted for perching and never have more than four toes. Hearing and eyesight are well developed, but the sense of smell is usually poor. No existing species of bird possesses teeth. Most birds fly, but some groups (such as ostriches) are flightless, and others include flightless members. Many communicate by sounds (nearly half of all known species are songbirds) or by visual displays, in connection with which many species are brightly coloured, usually the males. Birds have highly developed patterns of instinctive behaviour. There are nearly 8,500 species of birds.

bird of paradise one of 40 species of crowlike birds in the family Paradiseidae, native to New Guinea and neighbouring islands. Females are generally drably coloured, but the males have bright and elaborate plumage used in courtship display. Hunted almost to extinction for their plumage, they are now subject to conservation.

Birmingham industrial city and administrative headquarters of *West Midlands metropolitan county,

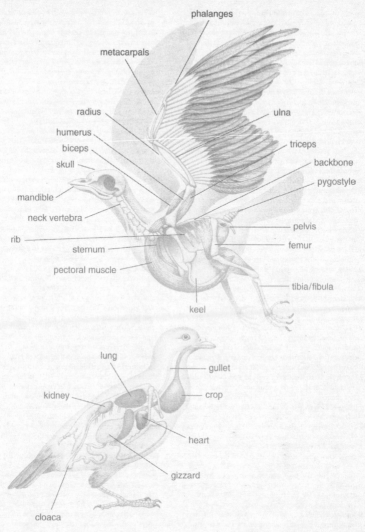

bird Cross sections of a bird (a pigeon) showing skeleton, muscles, feathers, and major organs. Many of a bird's bones are hollow and the weight of its skeleton may be as little as 5% of its total body weight.

central England, second-largest city in the UK, 177 km/ 110 mi northwest of London; population (2001 est) 977,100. It is a major manufacturing, engineering, commercial, and service centre. The city's concert halls, theatres, and three universities also make it an important cultural and educational centre. Its chief products are motor vehicles, vehicle components and accessories, machine tools, aerospace control systems, weapons, electrical equipment, plastics, chemicals, food, chocolate (Cadbury), jewellery, and glass.

Biró, Lazlo (1900–1985) Hungarian-born Argentine who invented a ballpoint pen in 1944. His name became generic for ballpoint pens in the UK.

birth act of producing live young from within the body of female animals. Both viviparous and ovoviviparous animals give birth to young. In viviparous animals, embryos obtain nourishment from the mother via a *placenta or other means. In ovoviviparous animals, fertilized eggs develop and hatch in the oviduct of the mother and gain little or no nourishment from maternal tissues. See also *pregnancy.

birth control the use of *contraceptives prevent pregnancy. It is part of the general practice of *family planning.

birth rate the number of live births per 1,000 of the population over a period of time, usually a year (sometimes it is also expressed as a percentage). For example, a birth rate of 20/1,000 (or 2%) would mean that 20 babies were being born per 1,000 of the population. It is sometimes called **crude birth rate** because it takes in the whole population, including men and women who are too old to bear children.

Birtwistle, Harrison (1934–) English avant-garde composer. In his early career he wrote much for chamber ensemble, for example, his chamber opera *Punch and Judy* (1967) and *Down by the Greenwood Side* (1969). Birtwistle's early music was influenced by the Russian-born composer Igor *Stravinsky, by the medieval and Renaissance masters, and particularly by the book *On Growth and Form* by the biologist D'Arcy Wentworth Thompson (1860–1948). For many years he worked alongside Peter Maxwell *Davies.

Biscay, Bay of bay of the Atlantic Ocean between northern Spain and western France, known for rough seas and high tides. It is traditionally a rich fishing area.

Bishkek formerly Pishpek (1878–1926); **Frunze** (1926–92), capital of Kyrgyzstan; population (1996) 670,000. Bishkek is situated in the valley of the River Chu north of the Kyrgyz Alatau mountain range, 180 km/112 mi west of Almaty in Kazakhstan. Among the goods produced here are textiles, agricultural machinery, and electrical and electronic goods. Food industries include meat-packing and tobacco production.

Bismarck, Otto Eduard Leopold von (1815–1898) German politician, prime minister of Prussia 1862–90 and chancellor of the German Empire 1871–90. He pursued an aggressively expansionist policy, waging wars against Denmark (1863–64), Austria (1866), and France (1870–71), which brought about the unification of Germany. He became Prince in 1871.

Bismarck Archipelago group of over 200 islands in the southwest Pacific Ocean, part of Papua New Guinea; area 49,660 sq km/19,200 sq mi. The largest island is New Britain. Coconut fibre, copra, cotton, rubber, coffee, tortoiseshell, trepang (sea cucumbers), mother-of-pearl, and fruit are the chief products. The population is mostly Papuan.

bismuth chemical symbol Bi, hard, brittle, pinkish-white, metallic element, atomic number 83, relative atomic mass 208.98. It has the highest atomic number of all the stable elements (the elements from atomic number 84 up are radioactive). Bismuth occurs in ores and occasionally as a free metal (*native metal). It is a poor conductor of heat and electricity, and is used in alloys of low melting point and in medical compounds to soothe gastric ulcers. The name comes from the Latin *besemutum*, from the earlier German *Wismut*.

bison large, hoofed mammal of the bovine family. There are two species, both brown. The **European bison** or **wisent** *Bison bonasus*, of which only a few protected herds survive, is about 2 m/7 ft high and weighs up to 1,100 kg/2,500 lb. The **North American bison** (also known historically as the North American buffalo) *Bison bison* is slightly smaller, with a heavier mane and more sloping hindquarters. Formerly roaming the prairies in vast numbers, it was almost exterminated in the 19th century, but survives in protected areas. There were about 14,000 bison in North American reserves in 1994.

Bissau capital and chief port of *Guinea-Bissau, on an island at the mouth of the Geba River; population (2002 est) 288,300. Originally a Portuguese fortified slave-trading centre (1687), Bissau became a free port in 1869. Industries include agricultural processing, fishing, textiles, and crafts; exports include nuts, rice, wax, and hides. There are refrigeration units at the port, and there is an international airport and a university. Bissau replaced Bolama as the capital in 1941.

bit contraction of binary digit, in computing, a single binary digit, either 0 or 1. A bit is the smallest unit of data stored in a computer; all other data must be coded into a pattern of individual bits. A *byte represents sufficient computer memory to store a single character of data, and usually contains eight bits. For example, in the *ASCII code system used by most microcomputers the capital letter A would be stored in a single byte of memory as the bit pattern 01000001.

bittern any of several species of small herons, in particular the common bittern *Botaurus stellaris* of Europe and Asia. It is shy, stoutly built, buff-coloured, speckled with black and tawny brown, with a long bill and a loud, booming call. Its habit of holding its neck and bill in a vertical position conceals it among the reeds, where it rests by day, hunting for frogs, reptiles, and fish towards nightfall. An inhabitant of marshy country, it is now extremely rare in Britain. In 2000 there were only an estimated 20 pairs of bitterns breeding in the British Isles.

bitumen involatile, tarry material, containing a mixture of *hydrocarbons (mainly *alkanes), that is the residue from the *fractional distillation of crude oil (unrefined *petroleum). Sometimes the term is restricted to a soft kind of pitch resembling asphalt.

bivalve marine or freshwater mollusc whose body is enclosed between two shells hinged together by a ligament on the dorsal side of the body.

Bizet, Georges (Alexandre César Léopold) (1838–1875) French composer of operas. Among his works are *Les Pêcheurs de perles/The Pearl Fishers* (1863) and *La Jolie Fille de Perth/The Fair Maid of Perth* (1866). He also wrote the concert overture *Patrie* and incidental music to Alphonse Daudet's play *L'Arlésienne* (1872), which has remained a standard work in the form of two suites for orchestra. His operatic masterpiece *Carmen* was produced a few months before his death. His Symphony in C, written when he was 17, is now frequently performed.

Black and Tans nickname of a special auxiliary force of the Royal Irish Constabulary formed from British ex-soldiers on 2 January 1920 and in action in Ireland March 1920–December 1921. They were employed by the British government to combat the killing of policemen by the Irish Republican Army (IRA), the military wing of the Irish nationalist *Sinn Fein government, during the Anglo-Irish War, or War of Independence (1919–21). The name derives from the colours of their improvised khaki and black uniforms, and was also the name of a famous pack of hounds.

black beetle another name for *cockroach, although cockroaches belong to an entirely different order of insects (Dictyoptera) from the beetles (Coleoptera).

blackberry prickly shrub, closely related to raspberries and dewberries. Native to northern parts of Europe, it produces pink or white blossom and edible black compound fruits. (*Rubus fruticosus*, family Rosaceae.)

blackbird bird *Turdus merula* of the thrush family, Muscicapidae, order Passeriformes, about 25 cm/10 in long. The male is black with a yellow bill and eyelids, the female dark brown with a dark beak. It lays three to five blue-green eggs with brown spots in a nest of grass and moss, plastered with mud, built in thickets or creeper-clad trees. The blackbird feeds on fruit, seeds, worms, grubs, and snails. Its song is rich and flutelike.

black box popular name for the unit containing an aeroplane's flight and voice recorders. These monitor the plane's behaviour and the crew's conversation, thus providing valuable clues to the cause of a disaster. The box is nearly indestructible and usually painted orange for easy recovery. The name also refers to any compact electronic device that can be quickly connected or disconnected as a unit.

blackbuck antelope *Antilope cervicapra* found in central and northwestern India. It is related to the gazelle, from which it differs in having spirally-twisted horns. The male is black above and white beneath, whereas the female and young are fawn-coloured above. It is about 76 cm/2.5 ft in height.

Blackburn with Darwen unitary authority (borough status) in northwest England created in 1998, formerly part of Lancashire. **area:** 136 sq km/53 sq mi **towns and cities:** Blackburn (administrative headquarters), Darwen **features:** Leeds–Liverpool canal; River Darwen; Darwen Hill and Tower (372 m/1,220 ft); western foothills of Rossendale uplands; Lewis Textile Museum (Blackburn) includes working model of spinning jenny; Blackburn Museum and Art Gallery has largest display of European icons in Britain **population:** (2001 est) 137,500.

blackcap *warbler *Sylvia atricapilla*, family Muscicapidae, order Passeriformes. The male has a black cap, the female a reddish-brown one. The general colour of the bird is an ashen-grey, turning to an olive-brown above and pale or whitish-grey below. About 14 cm/5.5 in long, the blackcap likes wooded areas, and is a summer visitor to northern Europe, wintering in Africa.

Black Country central area of England, to the west and north of Birmingham, incorporating the towns of Dudley, Walsall, Wolverhampton, and Sandwell. Heavily industrialized, it gained its name in the 19th century from its belching chimneys and mining spoil. Anti-pollution laws and the decline of heavy industry have changed the region's landscape. Coalmining in the area ceased in 1968.

blackcurrant variety of *currant.

Black Death great epidemic of *plague, mainly the bubonic variant, that ravaged Europe in the mid-14th century. Contemporary estimates that it killed between one-third and half of the population (about 75 million people) are probably accurate. The cause of the plague was the bacterium *Yersinia pestis*, transmitted by fleas that infested migrating Asian black rats. Originating in

China, the disease followed the trade routes through India into Europe. The name Black Death was first used in England in the early 19th century.

blackfly plant-sucking insect, a type of *aphid.

Black Forest German **Schwarzwald**, mountainous region of coniferous forest in Baden-Württemberg, western Germany; length 160 km/100 mi, greatest breadth 57 km/35 mi. Bounded to the west and south by the Rhine, which separates it from the Vosges, it rises to 1,493 m/4,898 ft in the Feldberg. It extends to the Swiss border in the south and to the Neckar valley in the north. Parts of the forest have recently been affected by *acid rain. The region is a popular year-round tourist destination, known for its winter sports an mineral springs; lumbering and woodworking are important industries.

Black Hills mountains in western South Dakota and northeastern Wyoming. They rise out of the Great Plains, 300–400 km/186–248 mi east of the Rocky Mountains front. The Black Hills occupy about 15,500 sq km/6,000 sq mi and rise to 2,207 m/7,242 ft at Harney Peak, South Dakota. The region includes a national forest (area 4,921 sq km/1,900 sq mi) and Mount Rushmore, which has the faces of four former presidents (George Washington, Thomas Jefferson, Abraham Lincoln, and Theodore Roosevelt) carved into a granite cliff (height 1,745 m/5,725 ft).

black hole object in space whose gravity is so great that nothing can escape from it, not even light. It is thought to form when a massive star shrinks at the end of its life. A black hole sucks in more matter, including other stars, from the space around it. Matter that falls into a black hole is squeezed to infinite density at the centre of the hole. Black holes can be detected because gas falling towards them becomes so hot that it emits X-rays.

Black Hole of Calcutta incident in Anglo-Indian history: according to tradition, the nawab (ruler) of Bengal confined 146 British prisoners on the night of 20 June 1756 in one small room, of whom only 23 allegedly survived. Later research reduced the death count to 43, assigning negligence rather than intention.

black humour humour based on the grotesque, morbid, or macabre. It is often an element of satire. A classic example is Irish writer Jonathan *Swift's 'A Modest Proposal' (1729), in which he argues that eating Irish children would help to alleviate Ireland's poverty. 20th-century examples can be found in the works of Samuel *Beckett, the routines of the US comic Lenny Bruce, the work of US film-maker Quentin Tarantino, and the drawings of the English caricaturist Gerald Scarfe. It is also an important element of Theatre of the *Absurd.

Black Monday worldwide stockmarket crash that began 19 October 1987, prompted by the announcement of worse-than-expected US trade figures and the response by US Secretary of the Treasury, James Baker, who indicated that the sliding dollar needed to decline further. This caused a world panic as fears of the likely impact of a US recession were voiced by the major industrialized countries. Between 19 and 23 October, the New York Stock Exchange fell by 33%, the London Stock Exchange Financial Times 100 Index by 25%, the European index by 17%, and Tokyo by 12%. The expected world recession did not occur; by the end of 1988 it was clear that the main effect had been a steadying in stock market activity and only a slight slowdown in world economic growth.

Black Muslims religious group founded in 1930 in the USA. Members adhere to Muslim values and believe in economic independence for black Americans. Under the leadership of Louis Farrakhan and the group's original name of the Nation of Islam, the movement has undergone a resurgence of popularity in recent years. In October 1995 more than 400,000 black males attended a 'Million Man March' to Washington DC. Organized by the Nation of Islam, it was the largest ever civil-rights demonstration in US history.

Black National State area in the Republic of South Africa set aside from 1971 to 1994 for development towards self-government by black Africans, in accordance with *apartheid. Before 1980 these areas were known as **black homelands** or **bantustans**. Making up less than 14% of the country, they tended to be situated in arid areas (though some had mineral wealth), often in scattered blocks. This meant that they were unsuitable for agriculture and unlikely to be profitable economic units. Those that achieved nominal independence were Transkei in 1976, Bophuthatswana in 1977, Venda in 1979, and Ciskei in 1981. They were not recognized outside South Africa because of their racial basis.

Blackpool seaside resort and administrative centre of Blackpool unitary authority, in northwest England, 28 mi/45 km north of Liverpool; population (2001 est) 142,300. The economy is based on tourism, with the service and tourism industries providing over 86% of local employment. There is some light industry. Known for its 11 km/7 mi of promenades, the resort is also famous for its 'illuminations' of coloured lights.

Black Power movement towards black separatism in the USA during the 1960s, embodied in the **Black Panther Party** founded in 1966 by Huey Newton and Bobby Seale. Its declared aim was the creation of a separate black state in the USA to be established by a black plebiscite under the aegis of the United Nations. Following a National Black Political Convention in 1972, a National Black Assembly was established to exercise pressure on the Democratic and Republican parties.

Black Prince nickname of *Edward, Prince of Wales, eldest son of Edward III of England.

Black Sea Russian **Chernoye More**, inland sea in southeast Europe, linked with the seas of Azov and Marmara, and via the Dardanelles strait with the Mediterranean; area 423,000 sq km/163,320 sq mi; maximum depth 2,245 m/7,365 ft, decreasing in the Sea of Azov to only 13.5 m/44 ft. It is bounded by Ukraine, Russia, Georgia, Turkey, Bulgaria, and Romania, and the rivers Danube, Volga, Bug, Dniester and Dnieper flow into it, keeping salinity levels low. Uranium deposits beneath it are among the world's largest. About 90% of the water is polluted, mainly by agricultural fertilizers.

Blackshirts term widely used to describe fascist paramilitary organizations. Originating with Mussolini's fascist Squadristi in the 1920s, it was also applied to the Nazi SS (*Schutzstaffel*) and to the followers of Oswald Mosley's British Union of Fascists.

blacksnake any of several species of snake. The blacksnake *Pseudechis porphyriacus* is a venomous snake of the cobra family found in damp forests and swamps in eastern Australia. The blacksnake, *Coluber constrictor* from the eastern USA, is a relative of the European grass snake, growing up to 1.2 m/4 ft long, and without venom.

blackthorn densely branched spiny European bush. It produces white blossom on bare black branches in early spring. Its sour plumlike blue-black fruit, the sloe, is used to make sloe gin. (*Prunus spinosa*, family Rosaceae.)

Black Thursday day of the Wall Street stock market crash on 24 October 1929, which precipitated the *depression in the USA and throughout the world.

Black Volta one of the two main upper branches of the River *Volta, running through Burkina Faso and Ghana.

black widow North American spider *Latrodectus mactans*. The male is small and harmless, but the female is 1.3 cm/0.5 in long with a red patch below the abdomen and a powerful venomous bite. The bite causes pain and fever in human victims, but they usually recover.

bladder hollow elastic-walled organ which stores the urine produced in the kidneys. It is present in the *urinary systems of some fishes, most amphibians, some reptiles, and all mammals. Urine enters the bladder through two ureters, one leading from each kidney, and leaves it through the urethra.

bladderwort any of a large group of carnivorous aquatic plants. They have leaves with bladders (hollow sacs) that trap small animals living in the water. (Genus *Utricularia*, family Lentibulariaceae.)

Blaenau Gwent unitary authority in south Wales, created in 1996 from part of the former county of Gwent. **area:** 109 sq km/42 sq mi **towns:** Ebbw Vale (administrative headquarters), Tredegar, Abertillery **features:** Mynydd Carn-y-Cefn (550 m/1,800 ft); rivers Sirhowy and Ebbw; part of the Brecon Beacons National Park is here; Silent Valley Nature Reserve is a 392 ha/969 acre-site of special scientific interest **population:** (2000 est) 71,200.

Blair, Tony (1953–) born Anthony Charles Lynton Blair, British Labour politician, leader of the Labour Party from 1994, prime minister from 1997. A centrist in the manner of his predecessor John Smith, he became *Labour's youngest leader by a large majority in the first fully democratic elections to the post in July 1994. He moved the party away from its traditional socialist base towards the 'social democratic' political centre, under the slogan 'New Labour', securing approval in 1995 of a new Labour Party charter, which removed the commitment to public ownership. During the 2003 US-led Iraq War, he was a firm ally of US president George W Bush, despite strong opposition from within sections of the Labour Party and the public. This damaged his public standing, amid accusations that his government had overstated the military threat posed by Iraqi president Saddam Hussein. Blair and his party secured landslide victories in the 1997 and 2001 general elections, with 179-seat and 167-seat majorities respectively. During his first term as prime minister, Blair retained high public approval ratings and achieved a number of significant reforms, including Scottish and Welsh devolution, reform of the House of Lords, ceding control over interest rates to the Bank of England, a national minimum wage, the creation of an elected mayor for London, and a peace agreement in Northern Ireland. His government pursued a cautious economic programme, similar to that of the preceding Conservative administrations, involving tight control over public expenditure and the promotion, in the Private Finance Initiative, of 'public–private partnerships'. This achieved steady economic growth and higher levels of employment, providing funds for greater investment in public services during Blair's second term, from 2001. In 2003, public support for Blair fell, both because of concerns that investment in public services had not delivered clear improvements, and because of criticism of his stance on the Iraq War. Blair's presidential style of governing involves delegating much to individual ministers, but intervening in key areas in an effort to build up public support. He was supported by a large team of political advisers and media 'spin doctors', who emphasized the importance of image and presentation. In his second term, Blair spent more time on international diplomacy, trying to act as a bridge between the USA and European Union countries in the run-up to the Iraq War.

Blake, William (1757–1827) English poet, artist, engraver, and visionary, and one of the most important figures of English *Romanticism. His lyrics, often written with a childlike simplicity, as in *Songs of Innocence* (1789) and *Songs of Experience* (1794), express a unique spiritual vision. In his 'prophetic books', including *The Marriage of Heaven and Hell* (1790), he created a vast personal mythology. He illustrated his own works with hand-coloured engravings.

blank verse in literature, the unrhymed iambic pentameter or ten-syllable line of five stresses. First used by the Italian Gian Giorgio Trissino in his tragedy *Sofonisba* (1514–15), it was introduced to England in about 1540 by the Earl of Surrey, who used it in his translation of Virgil's *Aeneid*. It was developed by Christopher Marlowe and Shakespeare, quickly becoming the distinctive verse form of Elizabethan and Jacobean drama. It was later used by Milton in *Paradise Lost* (1667) and by Wordsworth in *The Prelude* (1805). More recent exponents of blank verse in English include Thomas Hardy, T S Eliot, and Robert Frost.

Blanqui, (Louis) Auguste (1805–1881) French revolutionary politician. He formulated the theory of the 'dictatorship of the proletariat', used by Karl Marx, and spent a total of 33 years in prison for insurrection. Although in prison, he was elected president of the Commune of Paris in 1871. His followers, the Blanquists, joined with the Marxists in 1881.

blasphemy (Greek 'evil-speaking') written or spoken insult directed against religious belief or sacred things with deliberate intent to outrage believers.

blast furnace smelting furnace used to extract iron from a mixture of iron ore, coke, and limestone. The temperature is raised by the injection of an air blast. The molten iron sinks to the bottom of the furnace and is tapped off into moulds referred to as pigs. The iron extracted this way is also known as pig iron.

blastocyst in mammals, the hollow ball of cells which is an early stage in the development of the *embryo, roughly equivalent to the *blastula of other animal groups.

blastomere in biology, a cell formed in the first stages of embryonic development, after the splitting of the

fertilized ovum, but before the formation of the *blastula or blastocyst.

blastula early stage in the development of a fertilized egg, when the egg changes from a solid mass of cells (the morula) to a hollow ball of cells (the blastula), containing a fluid-filled cavity (the blastocoel). See also *embryology.

Blaue Reiter, der German **the Blue Rider**, loose association of German expressionist painters formed in 1911 in Munich. They were united by an interest in the expressive qualities of colour, in primitive and folk art, and in the necessity of painting 'the inner, spiritual side of nature', though their individual styles varied greatly. Two central figures were *Kandinsky and Franz *Marc.

bleaching decolorization of coloured materials. The two main types of bleaching agent are **oxidizing bleaches**, which bring about the *oxidation of pigments and include the ultraviolet rays in sunshine, hydrogen peroxide, and chlorine in household bleaches; and **reducing bleaches**, which bring about *reduction and include sulphur dioxide.

bleak freshwater fish *Alburnus alburnus* of the carp family. It is up to to 20 cm/8 in long, and lives in still or slow-running clear water in Britain and Europe.

bleeding loss of blood from the circulation; see *haemorrhage.

blenny any fish of the family Blenniidae, mostly small fishes found near rocky shores, with elongated slimy bodies tapering from head to tail, no scales, and long pelvic fins set far forward.

Blériot, Louis (1872–1936) French aviator. In a 24-horsepower monoplane of his own construction, he made the first flight across the English Channel on 25 July 1909.

blesbok African antelope *Damaliscus albifrons*, about 1 m/3 ft high, with curved horns, brownish body, and a white blaze on the face. It was seriously depleted in the wild at the end of the 19th century. A few protected herds survive in South Africa. It is farmed for meat.

Bligh, William (1754–1817) English sailor. He accompanied Captain James *Cook on his second voyage around the world (1772–74), and in 1787 commanded HMS *Bounty* on an expedition to the Pacific. On the return voyage, in protest against harsh treatment, the crew mutinied. Bligh was sent to Australia as governor of New South Wales in 1805, where his discipline again provoked a mutiny in 1808 (the Rum Rebellion).

blight any of a number of plant diseases caused mainly by parasitic species of *fungus, which produce a whitish appearance on leaf and stem surfaces; for example, **potato blight** *Phytophthora infestans*. General damage caused by aphids or pollution is sometimes known as blight.

blindness complete absence or impairment of sight. It may be caused by heredity, accident, disease, or deterioration with age.

blind spot area where the optic nerve and blood vessels pass through the retina of the *eye. No visual image can be formed as there are no light-sensitive cells in this part of the retina. Thus the organism is blind to objects that fall in this part of the visual field.

Bliss, Arthur Edward Drummond (1891–1975) English composer and conductor. He became Master of the Queen's Musick in 1953. Among his works are

A Colour Symphony (1922); music for the ballets *Checkmate* (1937), *Miracle in the Gorbals* (1944), and *Adam Zero* (1946); an opera *The Olympians* (1949); and dramatic film music, including *Things to Come* (1935). He conducted the first performance of US composer Igor Stravinsky's *Ragtime* for 11 instruments in 1918.

Blitzkrieg (German 'lightning war') swift military campaign, as used by Germany at the beginning of World War II (1939–41). It was characterized by rapid movement by mechanized forces, supported by tactical air forces acting as 'flying artillery' and is best exemplified by the campaigns in Poland in 1939 and France in 1940.

Blixen, Karen (1885–1962) Baroness Blixen; born Karen Christentze Dinesen, Danish writer. She wrote mainly in English and is best known for her short stories, Gothic fantasies with a haunting, often mythic quality, published in such collections as *Seven Gothic Tales* (1934) and *Winter's Tales* (1942) under the pen-name **Isak Dinesen**. Her autobiography *Out of Africa* (1937; filmed 1985) is based on her experience of running a coffee plantation in Kenya.

blockade cutting-off of a place by hostile forces by land, sea, or air so as to prevent any movement to or fro, in order to compel a surrender without attack or to achieve some other political aim (for example, the *Berlin blockade (1948) and Union blockade of Confederate ports during the American Civil War). Economic sanctions are sometimes used in an attempt to achieve the same effect.

Bloemfontein (Afrikaans 'fountain of flowers') capital of the *Free State (formerly Orange Free State) and judicial capital of the Republic of South Africa; population (1996 est) 333,800. Founded in 1846 and declared a municipality in 1880, the city produces canned fruit, glassware, furniture, plastics, and railway engineering. The economic growth of the city was was stimulated from the mid-20th century by the

development of the Free State goldfields (160 km/100 mi to the northeast), as well as by the Orange River project which is a major source both of hydroelectricity and of water for irrigation and domestic supply. The city's climate makes it a popular health resort.

blood fluid pumped by the *heart, that circulates in the *arteries, *veins, and *capillaries of vertebrate animals forming the bloodstream. The term also refers to the corresponding fluid in those invertebrates that possess a closed *circulatory system. Blood carries nutrients and oxygen to each body cell and removes waste products such as carbon dioxide. It is also important in the immune response and, in many animals, in the distribution of heat throughout the body.

Blood, Thomas (1618–1680) Irish adventurer, known as Colonel Blood. In 1663 he tried to seize the Lord Lieutenant of Ireland at Dublin Castle, and in 1670 he attempted to assassinate the Duke of Ormond in 1670, possibly on instructions from the Duke of *Buckingham. In 1671 he and three accomplices succeeded in stealing the crown and orb from the Tower of London, but were captured soon afterwards.

blood clotting complex series of events (known as the blood clotting cascade) resulting from a series of enzymatic reactions in the blood that prevents excessive bleeding after injury. The result is the formation of a meshwork of protein fibres (fibrin) and trapped blood cells over the cut blood vessels.

blood group any of the types into which blood is classified according to the presence or otherwise of certain *antigens on the surface of its red cells. Red blood cells of one individual may carry molecules on their surface that act as antigens in another individual whose red blood cells lack these molecules. The two main antigens are designated A and B. These give rise to four blood groups: having A only (A), having B only (B), having both (AB), and having neither (O). Each of these groups may or may not contain the *rhesus

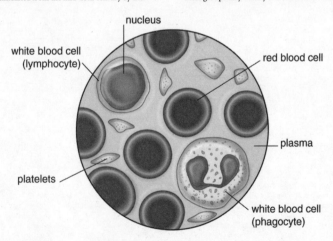

blood Composition of blood. Human blood contains red blood cells, white blood cells (phagocytes and lymphocytes), and platelets, suspended in plasma.

factor. Correct typing of blood groups is vital in transfusion, since incompatible types of donor and recipient blood will result in coagulation, with possible death of the recipient.

bloodhound breed of dog that originated as a hunting dog in Belgium in the Middle Ages. Black and tan in colour, it has long, pendulous ears and distinctive wrinkled head and face. It grows to a height of about 65 cm/26 in. Its excellent powers of scent have been employed in tracking and criminal detection from very early times.

blood poisoning presence in the bloodstream of quantities of bacteria or bacterial toxins sufficient to cause serious illness.

blood pressure pressure, or tension, of the blood against the inner walls of blood vessels, especially the arteries, due to the muscular pumping activity of the heart. Abnormally high blood pressure (*hypertension) may be associated with various conditions or arise with no obvious cause; abnormally low blood pressure (hypotension) occurs in *shock and after excessive fluid or blood loss from any cause.

blood test laboratory evaluation of a blood sample. There are numerous blood tests, from simple typing to establish the *blood group to sophisticated biochemical assays of substances, such as hormones, present in the blood only in minute quantities.

blood transfusion see *transfusion.

Bloomsbury Group intellectual circle of writers and artists based in Bloomsbury, London, which flourished in the 1920s. It centred on the house of publisher Leonard Woolf and his wife, novelist Virginia *Woolf. Typically modernist, their innovative artistic contributions represented an important section of the English avant-garde.

blowfly any fly of the genus *Calliphora*, also known as bluebottle, or of the related genus *Lucilia*, when it is greenbottle. It lays its eggs in dead flesh, on which the maggots feed.

Blücher, Gebhard Leberecht von (1742–1819) Prussian general and field marshal, popularly known as 'Marshal Forward'. He took an active part in the patriotic movement, and in the War of German Liberation defeated the French as commander-in-chief at Leipzig in 1813, crossed the Rhine to Paris in 1814, and was made prince of Wahlstadt (Silesia). In 1815 he was defeated by Napoleon at Ligny but came to the aid of British commander Wellington at Waterloo.

bluebell name given in Scotland to the *harebell (*Campanula rotundifolia*), and in England to the wild hyacinth (*Endymion nonscriptus*), belonging to the lily family (Liliaceae).

blueberry any of various North American shrubs belonging to the heath family, growing in acid soil. The genus also includes huckleberries, bilberries, deerberries, and cranberries, many of which resemble each other and are difficult to tell apart from blueberries. All have small oval short-stalked leaves, slender green or reddish twigs, and whitish bell-like blossoms. Only true blueberries, however, have tiny granular speckles on their twigs. Blueberries have black or blue edible fruits, often covered with a white bloom. (Genus *Vaccinium*, family Ericaceae.)

bluebird *or* **blue robin** *or* **blue warbler** three species of a North American bird, genus *Sialia*, belonging to the thrush subfamily, Turdinae, order Passeriformes. The eastern bluebird *Sialia sialis* is regarded as the herald of spring as it returns from migration. About 18 cm/7 in long, it has a reddish breast, the upper plumage being sky-blue, and a distinctive song. It lays about six pale-blue eggs.

bluebottle another name for *blowfly.

bluebuck any of several species of antelope, including the blue *duiker *Cephalophus monticola* of South Africa, about 33 cm/13 in high. The male of the Indian nilgai antelope is also known as the bluebuck.

blue chip in business and finance, a stock that is considered strong and reliable in terms of the dividend yield and capital value. Blue-chip companies are favoured by stock-market investors more interested in security than risk taking.

bluegrass dense spreading grass, which is blue-tinted and grows in clumps. Various species are known from the northern hemisphere. Kentucky bluegrass (*Poa pratensis*), introduced to the USA from Europe, provides pasture for horses. (Genus *Poa*, family Gramineae.)

blue-green algae *or* **cyanobacteria** single-celled, primitive organisms that resemble bacteria in their internal cell organization, sometimes joined together in colonies or filaments. Blue-green algae are among the oldest known living organisms and, with bacteria, belong to the kingdom Monera; remains have been found in rocks up to 3.5 billion years old. They are widely distributed in aquatic habitats, on the damp surfaces of rocks and trees, and in the soil.

blue gum either of two Australian trees: Tasmanian blue gum (*Eucalyptus globulus*) of the myrtle family, with bluish bark, a chief source of eucalyptus oil; or the tall, straight Sydney blue gum (*E. saligna*). The former is widely cultivated in California and has also been planted in South America, India, parts of Africa, and southern Europe.

Blue Mountains part of the *Great Dividing Range, New South Wales, Australia. The Blue Mountains consist of a sandstone plateau running almost parallel with the coast, 80–100 km/50–62 mi west of Sydney. The highest peak is Mount Beemarang (1,247 m/4,091 ft). The mountains are popular with tourists, notably many Sydney residents, attracted by the fine scenery, including the spectacular limestone caverns of Jenolan, and the cooler summer weather.

Blue Nile Arabic **Bahr el-Azraq**, river rising at a spring site upstream of Lake Tana in Ethiopia, 2,150 m/7,054 ft above sea level. Flowing west then north for 1,460 km/ 907 mi, it eventually meets the White Nile at Khartoum. A length of 800 km/500 mi is navigable at high water. Some 80% of Sudan's electricity is provided by hydroelectric schemes at Roseires and Sennar, and these dams provide irrigation water for over 10,000 sq km/3,860 sq mi of the Gezira Plain.

blue riband *or* **blue ribbon** the highest distinction in any sphere.

Blue Ridge Mountains mountain range in southeastern USA, and part of the *Appalachian Mountains system. The Blue Ridge Mountains run from northwest Georgia to West Virginia. The highest summit (and also the highest point in eastern USA) is Mount Mitchell; height 2,037 m/6,684 ft.

blues African-American music that originated in the work songs and Negro spirituals of the rural American

South in the late 19th century. It is usually of a slow to moderate speed and characteristic features include a 12-bar (sometimes 8-bar or 16-bar) construction and a syncopated melody line that often includes 'blue notes' (quarter tones lying between the minor and major third of the scale – as found on some African five-note xylophones – or between the minor and major seventh). The lyrics are melancholy and tell tales of woe or unhappy love. The guitar is the main instrument, although the harmonica and piano are also common. Blues guitar and vocal styles have played a vital part in the development of jazz, rock, and pop music in general.

blue shift in astronomy, manifestation of the *Doppler effect in which an object appears bluer when it is moving towards the observer or the observer is moving towards it (blue light is of a higher frequency than other colours in the spectrum). The blue shift is the opposite of the *red shift.

Blunkett, David (1947–) British Labour politician, home secretary 2001–04. He was leader of Sheffield city council from 1980 before becoming member of Parliament for Sheffield Brightside in 1987. A member of Labour's shadow cabinet from 1992, he was responsible for health and then, from 1994, for education and employment. After Labour's 1997 general election victory he became secretary of state for education and employment. As home secretary he took a firm line on asylum control and law and order, and was an advocate of identity cards. He was forced to resign after a series of allegations over the fast-tracking of a visa application for a personal acquaintance.

Blunt, Anthony Frederick (1907–1983) English art historian and double agent. As a Cambridge lecturer, he recruited for the Soviet secret service and, as a member of the British Secret Service 1940–45, passed information to the USSR. In 1951 he assisted the defection to the USSR of the British agents Guy Burgess and Donald Maclean (1913–1983). He was the author of many respected works on Italian and French art, including a study of Poussin 1966–67. Unmasked in 1964, he was given immunity after his confession.

Blyton, Enid Mary (1897–1968) English writer of children's books. She used her abilities as a trained teacher of young children and a journalist, coupled with her ability to think like a child, to produce books at all levels which, though criticized for their predictability and lack of characterization, and more recently for social, racial, and sexual stereotyping, satisfy the reader's need for security. Her best-selling series were, the *Famous Five* series, the 'Secret Seven', and 'Noddy'.

boa any of various nonvenomous snakes of the family Boidae, found mainly in tropical and subtropical parts of the New World. Boas feed mainly on small mammals and birds. They catch these in their teeth or kill them by constriction (crushing the creature within their coils until it suffocates). The boa constrictor *Constrictor constrictor* can grow up to 5.5 m/18.5 ft long, but rarely reaches more than 4 m/12 ft. Other boas include the anaconda and the emerald tree boa *Boa canina*, about 2 m/6 ft long and bright green.

Boadicea alternative (Latin) spelling of British queen *Boudicca.

boar wild member of the pig family, such as the Eurasian wild boar *Sus scrofa*, from which domestic pig

breeds derive. The wild boar is sturdily built, being 1.5 m/4.5 ft long and 1 m/3 ft high, and possesses formidable tusks. Of gregarious nature and mainly woodland-dwelling, it feeds on roots, nuts, insects, and some carrion.

Boat Race, the annual UK *rowing race between the crews of Oxford and Cambridge universities. It is held during the Easter vacation over a 6.8 km/4.25 mi course on the River Thames between Putney and Mortlake, southwest London.

bobcat wild cat *Lynx rufus* living in a variety of habitats from southern Canada through to southern Mexico. It is similar to the lynx, but only 75 cm/2.5 ft long, with reddish fur and less well-developed ear tufts.

bobsleighing or **bobsledding** sport of racing steel-bodied, steerable toboggans, crewed by two or four people, down mountain ice-chutes at speeds of up to 80 mph/130 kph. It was introduced as an Olympic event for men in 1924 and for women in 2002. The World Championships have been held every year since 1931, and in Olympic years winners automatically become world champions.

Boccaccio, Giovanni (1313–1375) Italian writer and poet. He is chiefly known for the collection of tales called the *Decameron* (1348–53). Equally at home with tragic and comic narrative, he laid the foundations for the humanism of the Renaissance and raised vernacular literature to the status enjoyed by the ancient classics.

Bode's law or **Titius-Bode law** numerical sequence that gives the approximate distances, in astronomical units (distance between Earth and Sun = one astronomical unit), of the planets from the Sun by adding 4 to each term of the series 0, 3, 6, 12, 24, ... and then dividing by 10. Bode's law predicted the existence of a planet between Mars and Jupiter, which led to the discovery of the asteroid belt.

Bodhidharma (lived 6th century) Indian Buddhist and teacher. He entered China from southern India about 520 and was the founder of the Ch'an school. Ch'an focuses on contemplation leading to intuitive meditation, a direct pointing to and stilling of the human mind. In the 20th century, the Japanese variation, *Zen, has attracted many followers in the West.

bodhisattva in Mahayana Buddhism, someone who has reached *enlightenment but has chosen to remain on the human plane in order to help other living beings. A bodhisattva is free to enter *nirvana but voluntarily chooses to be reborn until all other beings have attained that state. Bodhisattvas are seen as intercessors to whom believers may pray for help.

Boeotia ancient and modern district of central Greece, of which *Thebes was and remains the chief city. The Boeotian League (formed by ten city-states in the 6th century BC) was brought under strong central Theban control in the later 5th century BC. It superseded *Sparta as the leading military power in Greece in the 4th century BC until the rise of *Philip II of Macedon.

Boer Dutch settler or descendant of Dutch and Huguenot settlers in South Africa; see also *Afrikaner.

Boer War the second of the *South African Wars 1899–1902, waged between Dutch settlers in South Africa and the British.

Boethius, Anicius Manlius Severinus (AD 480–524) Roman philosopher. He wrote treatises on music and mathematics and *De Consolatione Philosophiae/The*

Consolation of Philosophy, a dialogue in prose. It was translated into European languages during the Middle Ages.

bog type of wetland where decomposition is slowed down and dead plant matter accumulates as *peat. Bogs develop under conditions of low temperature, high acidity, low nutrient supply, stagnant water, and oxygen deficiency. Typical bog plants are sphagnum moss, rushes, and cotton grass; insectivorous plants such as sundews and bladderworts are common in bogs (insect prey make up for the lack of nutrients).

Bogarde, Dirk (1921–1999) stage name of Derek Niven van den Bogaerde, English actor and writer. He appeared in comedies and adventure films such as *Doctor in the House* (1954) and *Campbell's Kingdom* (1957), before acquiring international recognition for complex roles in Joseph Losey's *The Servant* (1963) and *Accident* (1967), and Luchino Visconti's *Death in Venice* (1971). As a writer he was best known for his several volumes of autobiography, including *A Postillion Struck by Lightning* (1977).

Bogart, Humphrey (DeForest) (1899–1957) US film actor. He became an international cult figure through roles as a tough, romantic loner in such films as *High Sierra* (1941), *The Maltese Falcon* (1941), *Casablanca* (1942), *To Have and Have Not* (1944), *The Big Sleep* (1946), and *In a Lonely Place* (1950). He won an Academy Award for his role in *The African Queen* (1952).

bogbean *or* **buckbean** aquatic or bog plant belonging to the gentian family, with a creeping rhizome (underground stem) and leaves and pink flower spikes held above water. It is found over much of the northern hemisphere. (*Menyanthes trifoliata*, family Gentianaceae.)

Bogotá officially **Santa Fé de Bogotá**, capital of Colombia, and of Cundinamarca department, situated at 2,640 m/8,660 ft above sea level, on the edge of the Eastern Cordillera plateau of the Andes; population (1999 est) 6,260,900. Main industries include textiles, chemicals, food processing, and tobacco. Bogotá is Colombia's largest city, and the financial, commercial, and cultural centre of the country.

Bohemia area of the Czech Republic, a fertile plateau drained by the Elbe and Vltava rivers. It is rich in mineral resources, including uranium, coal, lignite, iron ore, silver, and graphite. The main cities are Prague and Plzen. The name Bohemia derives from the Celtic Boii, its earliest known inhabitants.

Bohr, Niels Henrik David (1885–1962) Danish physicist who was awarded the Nobel Prize for Physics in 1922 for his discovery of the structure of atoms and the radiation emanating from them. He pioneered *quantum theory by showing that the nuclei of atoms are surrounded by shells of electrons, each assigned particular sets of quantum numbers according to their orbits. He explained the structure and behaviour of the nucleus, as well as the process of nuclear *fission. Bohr also proposed the doctrine of **complementarity**, the theory that a fundamental particle is neither a wave nor a particle, because these are complementary modes of description.

bohrium chemical symbol Bh, synthesized, radioactive element of the *transactinide series, atomic number 107, relative atomic mass 262. It was first synthesized by the Joint Institute for Nuclear Research in Dubna,

Russia, in 1976; in 1981 the Laboratory for Heavy-Ion Research in Darmstadt, Germany, confirmed its existence. It was named in 1997 after Danish physicist Niels *Bohr.

boiler any vessel that converts water into steam. Boilers are used in conventional power stations to generate steam to feed steam *turbines, which drive the electricity generators. They are also used in steamships, which are propelled by steam turbines, and in steam locomotives. Every boiler has a furnace in which fuel (mainly coal, oil, or gas) is burned to produce hot gases, and a system of tubes in which heat is transferred from the gases to the water.

boiling point for any given liquid, the temperature at which the application of heat raises the temperature of the liquid no further, but converts it into vapour. The boiling point of water under normal pressure is 100 °C/212 °F. The lower the pressure, the lower the boiling point and vice versa.

bolero Spanish dance in moderate triple time (3/4), invented in the late 18th century. It is performed by a solo dancer or a couple, usually with castanet accompaniment, and is still a contemporary form of dance in Caribbean countries. In music, Maurice Ravel's one-act ballet score *Boléro* (1928) is the most famous example.

boletus any of several fleshy fungi (see *fungus) with thick stems and caps of various colours. The European *Boletus edulis* is edible, but some species are poisonous. (Genus *Boletus*, class Basidiomycetes.)

Boleyn, Anne (c. 1507–1536) Queen of England 1533–36 as the second wife of Henry VIII. She gave birth to the future Queen Elizabeth I in 1533, but was unable to produce a male heir to the throne, and was executed on a false charge.

Bolingbroke title of Henry of Bolingbroke, *Henry IV of England.

Bolingbroke, Henry St John, 1st Viscount Bolingbroke (1678–1751) British Tory politician and political philosopher. He was foreign secretary 1710–14 and a Jacobite conspirator. His books, such as *Idea of a Patriot King* (1738) and *The Dissertation upon Parties* (1735), laid the foundations for 19th-century Toryism.

Bolívar, Simón (1783–1830) South American nationalist, leader of revolutionary armies, known as the Liberator. He fought the Spanish colonial forces in several uprisings and eventually liberated Colombia in 1819, his native Venezuela in 1821, Ecuador in 1822, Peru in 1824, and Bolivia (a new state named after him, formerly Upper Peru) in 1825.

Bolivia

National name: *República de Bolivia/Republic of Bolivia*

Area: 1,098,581 sq km/424,162 sq mi

Capital: La Paz (seat of government), Sucre (legal capital and seat of the judiciary)

Major towns/cities: Santa Cruz, Cochabamba, Oruro, El Alto, Potosí, Tarija

Physical features: high plateau (Altiplano) between mountain ridges (cordilleras); forest and lowlands (llano) in east; Andes; lakes Titicaca (the world's highest navigable lake, 3,800 m/12,500 ft) and Poopó

Head of state and government: Carlos Mesa Gisbert from 2003

Political system: liberal democracy

115

Political executive: limited presidency
Political parties: National Revolutionary Movement (MNR), right of centre; Movement of the Revolutionary Left (MIR), left of centre; Nationalist Democratic Action Party (ADN), right wing; Solidarity and Civic Union (UCS), populist, free market; Patriotic Conscience Party, populist
Currency: boliviano
GNI per capita (PPP): (US$) 2,300 (2002 est)
Exports: metallic minerals, natural gas, jewellery, soybeans, wood. Principal market: USA 24.2% (2000). Illegal trade in coca and its derivatives (mainly cocaine) constituted more than 50% of Bolivia's export earnings in 1997 according to the UN.
Population: 8,808,000 (2003 est)
Language: Spanish (official) (4%), Aymara, Quechua
Religion: Roman Catholic 90% (state-recognized)
Life expectancy: 62 (men); 66 (women) (2000–05)
Chronology
c. **AD 600:** Development of sophisticated civilization at Tiahuanaco, south of Lake Titicaca.
c. **1200:** Tiahuanaco culture was succeeded by smaller Aymara-speaking kingdoms.
16th century: Became incorporated within westerly Quechua-speaking Inca civilization, centred in Peru.
1538: Conquered by Spanish and, known as 'Upper Peru', became part of the Viceroyalty of Peru, whose capital was at Lima (Peru); Charcas (now Sucre) became the local capital.
1545: Silver was discovered at Potosí in the southwest, which developed into chief silver-mining town and most important city in South America in the 17th and 18th centuries.
1776: Transferred to the Viceroyalty of La Plata, with its capital in Buenos Aires.
late 18th century: Increasing resistance of American Indians and mestizos to Spanish rule; silver production slumped.
1825: Liberated from Spanish rule by the Venezuelan freedom fighter Simón Bolívar, after whom the country was named, and his general, Antonio José de Sucre; Sucre became Bolivia's first president.

1836–39: Bolivia became part of a federation with Peru, headed by Bolivian president Andres Santa Cruz, but it dissolved following defeat in war with Chile.
1879–84: Coastal territory in the Atacama, containing valuable minerals, was lost after defeat in war with Chile.
1903: Territory was lost to Brazil.
1932–35: Further territory was lost after defeat by Paraguay in the Chaco War, fought over control of the Chaco Boreal.
1952: After the military regime was overthrown in the Bolivian National Revolution, Dr Victor Paz Estenssoro of the centrist National Revolutionary Movement (MNR) became president and introduced social reforms.
1964: An army coup was led by Vice-President Gen René Barrientos.
1967: There was a peasant uprising, led by Ernesto 'Che' Guevara. The uprising was put down with US help, and Guevara was killed.
1969: Barrientos was killed in a plane crash, and replaced by Siles Salinas, who was soon deposed in an army coup.
1971: Col Hugo Bánzer Suárez came to power after a military coup.
1974: An attempted coup prompted Bánzer to postpone promised elections and ban political and trade-union activity.
1980: Inconclusive elections were followed by the country's 189th coup. Allegations of corruption and drug trafficking led to the cancellation of US and European Community (EC) aid.
1982: With the economy worsening, the military junta handed power over to a civilian administration headed by Siles Zuazo.
1983: US and EC economic aid resumed as austerity measures were introduced.
1985: The inflation rate was 23,000%.
1993: Foreign investment was encouraged as inflation fell to single figures.
1997: Hugo Bánzer was elected president.
2000: The government lost support due to widespread poverty and the stagnation of the economy. There were violent clashes between security forces and protesters, who called for the resignation of President Bánzer.
2001: Bánzer's 1970s government was linked to a cross-border 'dirty war'.
2003: In two days of rioting in La Paz demonstrators protested against planned tax rises and clashed with army soldiers – 27 people were killed and over 100 injured. President Gonzalo Sanchez de Lozada suspended the tax increases and ordered the withdrawal of troops. He resigned and was replaced by Carlos Mesa.
2004: A referendum supported the export of gas and the first deal was signed, allowing Bolivia to export gas via a Peruvian port.
2005: There were anti-government protests at fuel price rises. President Mesa's resignation and his request for early elections were rejected by congress and he remained in office.
Böll, Heinrich (Theodor) (1917–1985) German novelist. A radical Catholic and anti-Nazi, he attacked Germany's political past and the materialism of its contemporary society. His many publications include poems, short stories, and novels which satirized West German society, for example *Billard um Halbzehn/Billiards at Half-Past Nine* (1959) and *Gruppenbild mit Dame/Group Portrait with Lady* (1971). He was awarded the Nobel Prize for Literature in 1972.

boll weevil small American beetle *Anthonomus grandis* of the weevil group. The female lays her eggs in the unripe pods or 'bolls' of the cotton plant, and on these the larvae feed, causing great destruction.

Bolshevik (from Russian *bolshinstvo* 'a majority') member of the majority of the Russian Social Democratic Party who split from the *Mensheviks in 1903. The Bolsheviks, under *Lenin, advocated the destruction of capitalist political and economic institutions, and the setting up of a socialist state with power in the hands of the workers. The Bolsheviks set the *Russian Revolution of 1917 in motion. They changed their name to the Russian Communist Party in 1918.

Boltzmann constant symbol k, in physics, the constant that relates the kinetic energy (energy of motion) of a gas atom or molecule to temperature. Its value is 1.38066×10^{-23} joules per kelvin. It is equal to the gas constant R, divided by *Avogadro's number.

bomb container filled with explosive or chemical material and generally used in warfare. There are also *incendiary bombs and nuclear bombs and missiles (see *nuclear warfare). Any object designed to cause damage by explosion can be called a bomb (car bombs, letter bombs). Initially dropped from aeroplanes (from World War I), bombs were in World War II also launched by rocket (V1, V2). The 1960s saw the development of missiles that could be launched from aircraft, land sites, or submarines. In the 1970s laser guidance systems were developed to hit small targets with accuracy.

bombardier beetle beetle that emits an evil-smelling fluid from its abdomen, as a defence mechanism. This fluid rapidly evaporates into a gas, which appears like a minute jet of smoke when in contact with air, and blinds the predator about to attack. Bombardier beetles are classified in genus *Brachinus*, family Carabidae, order Coleoptera, class Insecta, phylum Arthropoda.

Bombay former name (until 1995) of *Mumbai, capital of Maharashtra state in west central India. The city's name was officially changed in July 1995, and was renamed Mumbai after the goddess Mumba, the name in the local Marathi language for Parvati, the wife of the Hindu god Shiva.

Bombay duck or **bummalow** small fish *Harpodon nehereus* found in the Indian Ocean. It has a thin body, up to 40 cm/16 in long, and sharp, pointed teeth. It feeds on shellfish and other small fish. It is valuable as a food fish, and is eaten, salted and dried, with dishes such as curry.

bona fide (Latin 'in good faith') legal phrase used to signify that a contract is undertaken without intentional misrepresentation.

Bonaparte Corsican family of Italian origin that gave rise to the Napoleonic dynasty: see *Napoleon I, *Napoleon II, and *Napoleon III. Others were the brothers and sister of Napoleon I: **Joseph** (1768–1844) whom Napoleon made king of Naples in 1806 and of Spain in 1808; **Lucien** (1775–1840) whose handling of the Council of Five Hundred on 10 November 1799 ensured Napoleon's future; **Louis** (1778–1846) the father of Napoleon III, who was made king of Holland 1806–10; also called (from 1810) comte de Saint Leu; **Caroline** (1782–1839) who married Joachim Murat in 1800; full name Maria Annunciata Caroline; **Jerome** (1784–1860) made king of Westphalia in 1807.

Bonar Law British Conservative politician; see *Law, Andrew Bonar.

bond in chemistry, the result of the forces of attraction that hold together atoms in an element or compound. The principal types of bonding are *ionic, *covalent, *metallic, and intermolecular (such as hydrogen bonding).

bond in commerce, a security issued by a government, local authority, company, bank, or other institution on fixed interest. Usually a long-term security, a bond may be irredeemable (with no date of redemption), secured (giving the investor a claim on the company's property or on a part of its assets), or unsecured (not protected by a lien). Bonds are generally issued for a fixed period, at a fixed (nominal) value, are repayable on a fixed date (the maturity date), and pay a fixed rate of interest during that period. Property bonds are nonfixed securities with the yield fixed to property investment. Bonds are bought and sold in a similar way to equities. Financial institutions often consider the prevailing interest rates when setting the price of bonds in an attempt to make them attractive to purchasers.

Bond, Edward (1934–) English dramatist. His early work aroused controversy because of the savagery of some of his imagery, for example, the brutal stoning of a baby by bored youths in *Saved* (1965). Other works include *Early Morning* (1968); *Narrow Road to the Deep North* (1968); *Lear* (1972), a reworking of Shakespeare's play; *Bingo* (1973), an account of Shakespeare's last days; *The War Plays* (1985); and *Jackets 2/Sugawara* and *In the Company of Men* (both 1990).

bone hard connective tissue comprising the skeleton of most vertebrate animals. Bone is composed of a network of collagen fibres impregnated with mineral salts (largely calcium phosphate and calcium carbonate), a combination that gives it great density and strength, comparable in some cases with that of reinforced concrete. Enclosed within this solid matrix are bone cells, blood vessels, and nerves. The interior of the long bones of the limbs consists of a spongy matrix filled with a soft marrow that produces blood cells. There are two types of bone: those that develop by replacing cartilage and those that form directly from connective tissue. The latter, which includes the bones of the cranium, are usually platelike in shape and form in the skin of the developing embryo. Humans have 206 distinct bones in the skeleton, of which the smallest are the three ossicles in the middle ear. However, a different total is sometimes given, because of a number of fused pairs of bones in the skull that may be counted as one or two bones.

bone china or **softpaste** semiporcelain made of 5% bone ash added to 95% kaolin. It was first made in the West in imitation of Chinese porcelain, whose formula was kept secret by the Chinese.

bone marrow substance found inside the cavity of bones. In early life it produces red blood cells but later on lipids (fat) accumulate and its colour changes from red to yellow.

bongo Central African antelope *Boocercus eurycerus*, living in dense humid forests. Up to 1.4 m/4.5 ft at the shoulder, it has spiral horns which may be 80 cm/2.6 ft or more in length. The body is rich chestnut, with narrow white stripes running vertically down the sides, and a black belly.

Boniface, St (680–754) English Benedictine monk, known as the 'Apostle of Germany'; originally named Wynfrith. After a missionary journey to Frisia in 716, he was given the task of bringing Christianity to Germany

section through a long bone (the femur)

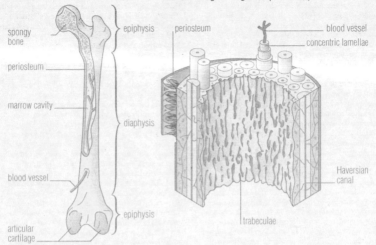

spongy bone

epiphysis

periosteum

blood vessel

concentric lamellae

periosteum

marrow cavity

diaphysis

blood vessel

Haversian canal

epiphysis

trabeculae

articular cartilage

bone The upper end of the thighbone or femur is made up of spongy bone, which has a fine lacework structure designed to transmit the weight of the body. The shaft of the femur consists of hard compact bone designed to resist bending. Fine channels carrying blood vessels, nerves, and lymphatics interweave even the densest bone.

in 718 by Pope Gregory II, and was appointed archbishop of Mainz in 746. He returned to Frisia in 754 and was martyred near Dockum. His feast day is 5 June.

bonito any of various species of medium-sized tuna, predatory fish of the genus *Sarda*, in the mackerel family. The ocean bonito *Katsuwonus pelamis* grows to 1 m/3 ft and is common in tropical seas. The Atlantic bonito *Sarda sarda* is found in the Mediterranean and tropical Atlantic and grows to the same length but has a narrower body.

Bonnard, Pierre (1867–1947) French painter, designer, and graphic artist. Influenced by Gauguin and Japanese prints, he specialized in intimate domestic scenes and landscapes, his paintings shimmering with colour and light. With other members of *les *Nabis*, he explored the decorative arts (posters, stained glass, furniture), but is most widely known for his series of nudes, for example, *Nude in the Bath* (1938; Petit Palais, Paris).

Bonnie Prince Charlie Scottish name for *Charles Edward Stuart, pretender to the throne.

bonsai (Japanese 'bowl cultivation') art of producing miniature trees by selective pruning. It originated in China many centuries ago and later spread to Japan.

bony fish fish of the class Osteichthyes, the largest and most important class of fish. The head covering and the scales are based on bone. Bony fish have a swimbladder, which may be modified into lungs and the gills are covered by a flap, the operculum.

booby tropical seabird of the genus *Sula*, in the same family, Sulidae, as the northern *gannet, order Pelicaniformes. There are six species, including the circumtropical brown booby S. *leucogaster*. Plumage is

white and black or brown, with no feathers on the throat and lower jaw. They inhabit coastal waters, and dive to catch fish. The name was given by sailors who saw the bird's tameness as stupidity.

boogie-woogie jazz played on the piano, using a repeated motif for the left hand. It was common in the USA from around 1900 to the 1950s. Boogie-woogie players included Pinetop Smith, Meade 'Lux' Lewis, and Jimmy Yancey. Rock-and-roll pianist Jerry Lee *Lewis adapted the style.

booklouse any of numerous species of tiny wingless insects of the order Psocoptera, especially *Atropus pulsatoria*, which lives in books and papers, feeding on starches and moulds.

Boole, George (1815–1864) English mathematician. His work *The Mathematical Analysis of Logic* (1847) established the basis of modern mathematical logic, and his **Boolean algebra** can be used in designing computers.

boomslang rear-fanged venomous African snake *Dispholidus typus*, often green but sometimes brown or blackish, and growing to a length of 2 m/6 ft. It lives in trees, and feeds on tree-dwelling lizards such as chameleons. Its venom can be fatal to humans; however, boomslangs rarely attack people.

Boone, Daniel (1734–1820) US pioneer. He cleared a forest path called the Wilderness Road (East Virginia–Kentucky) in 1775 and for the first westward migration of settlers.

boot *or* **bootstrap** in computing, the process of starting up a computer. Most computers have a small, built-in boot program that starts automatically when the computer is switched on – its only task is to load a slightly larger program, usually from a hard disk, which in turn loads the main *operating system.

Boötes constellation of the northern hemisphere represented by a herdsman driving a bear (*Ursa Major) around the pole. Its brightest star is *Arcturus (or Alpha Boötis), which is 36 light years from Earth. The herdsman is assisted by the neighbouring *Canes Venatici, 'the Hunting Dogs'.

Booth, William (1829–1912) English founder of the *Salvation Army (1878), and its first 'general'.

bootlegging illegal manufacture, distribution, or sale of a product. The term originated in the USA, when the sale of alcohol to American Indians was illegal and bottles were hidden for sale in the legs of the jackboots of unscrupulous traders. The term was later used for all illegal liquor sales during the period of *Prohibition in the USA 1919–33. More recently it has been applied to unauthorized commercial tape recordings and the copying of computer software.

Bophuthatswana, Republic of former *Black National State within South Africa, independent from 1977 (although not recognized by the United Nations) until 1994 when it was re-integrated into South Africa (in North West Province, Free State (formerly Orange Free State), and Mpumalanga (formerly Eastern Transvaal)) after rioting broke out in the run-up to the first multiracial elections.

borage plant native to southern Europe, used in salads and in medicine. It has small blue flowers and hairy leaves. (*Borago officinalis,* family Boraginaceae.)

borax hydrous sodium borate, $Na_2B_4O_7.10H_2O$, found as soft, whitish crystals or encrustations on the shores of hot springs and in the dry beds of salt lakes in arid regions, where it occurs with other borates, halite, and gypsum. It is used in bleaches and washing powders.

border terrier small, hardy, short-tailed dog with an otterlike head, moderately broad skull and short, strong muzzle. Its small, V-shaped ears drop forward. The coat is hard and dense with a close undercoat and is red, beige, and tan, or blue and tan. Dogs weigh 6–7 kg/13–15.5 lb; bitches 5–6.5 kg/ 11–14.5 lb.

Bordet, Jules Jean Baptiste Vincent (1870–1961) Belgian bacteriologist and immunologist who was awarded a Nobel Prize for Physiology or Medicine in 1919 for his work on immunity. He researched the role of blood serum in the human immune response, and was the first to isolate the whooping-cough bacillus, in 1906.

bore surge of tidal water up an estuary or a river, caused by the funnelling of the rising tide by a narrowing river mouth. A very high tide, possibly fanned by wind, may build up when it is held back by a river current in the river mouth. The result is a broken wave, a metre or a few feet high, that rushes upstream.

Borg, Björn Rune (1956–) Swedish tennis player. A left-handed player, he was known for his fitness and athleticism, an his accurate and reliable groundstrokes. He won the men's singles title at Wimbledon five times 1976–80, a record since the abolition of the challenge system in 1922. He also won six French Open singles titles 1974–75 and 1978–81. In 1990 Borg attempted a return to professional tennis, but he enjoyed little competitive success.

Borges, Jorge Luis (1899–1986) Argentine poet and short-story writer. He was an exponent of *magic realism. In 1961 he became director of the National Library, Buenos Aires, and was professor of English literature at the university there. He is known for his fantastic and paradoxical work *Ficciones/Fictions* (1944). He became blind in later life, but continued to write.

Borgia, Cesare (c. 1475–1507) Italian general, illegitimate son of Pope *Alexander VI. Made a cardinal at 17 by his father, he resigned to become captain-general of the papacy, campaigning successfully against the city republics of Italy. Ruthless and treacherous in war, he was an able ruler (a model for Machiavelli's *The Prince*), but his power crumbled on the death of his father. He was a patron of artists, including Leonardo da Vinci.

Borgia, Lucrezia (1480–1519) Duchess of Ferrara from 1501. She was the illegitimate daughter of Pope *Alexander VI and sister of Cesare *Borgia. She was married at 12 and again at 13 to further her father's ambitions, both marriages being annulled by him. At 18 she was married again, but her husband was murdered in 1500 on the order of her brother, with whom (as well as with her father) she was said to have committed incest. Her final marriage was to the Alfonso d'Este, the heir to the duchy of Ferrara. She made the court a centre of culture and was a patron of authors and artists such as Ariosto and Titian.

boric acid *or* **boracic acid** $B(OH)_3$, acid formed by the combination of hydrogen and oxygen with non-metallic boron. It is a weak antiseptic and is used in the manufacture of glass and enamels. It is also an efficient insecticide against ants and cockroaches.

Boris Godunov tsar of Russia from 1598; see Boris *Godunov.

Borlaug, Norman Ernest (1914–) US microbiologist and agronomist. He developed high-yielding varieties of wheat and other grain crops to be grown in developing countries, and was the first to use the term 'Green Revolution'. He was awarded the Nobel Prize for Peace in 1970 for his development of agricultural technology.

Born, Max (1882–1970) German-born British physicist. He was awarded the Nobel Prize for Physics in 1954 for fundamental work on the *quantum theory, especially his 1926 discovery that the wave function of an electron is linked to the probability that the electron is to be found at any point.

Borneo third-largest island in the world, one of the Sunda Islands in the West Pacific; area 754,000 sq km/ 290,000 sq mi; population (2000 est) 15,969,500. It comprises the country of Brunei; the Malaysian territories of *Sabah and *Sarawak; and, occupying by far the largest part, the Indonesian territory of *Kalimantan. It is mountainous and densely forested. A forest fire in early 1998 destroyed 30,000 sq km/11,583 sq mi of forest. In coastal areas the people of Borneo are mainly of Malaysian origin, with a few Chinese, and the interior is inhabited by the indigenous Dyaks. It was formerly under both Dutch and British colonial influence until Sarawak was formed in 1841.

Bornu kingdom of the 9th–19th centuries to the west and south of Lake Chad, western central Africa. Converted to Islam in the 11th century, Bornu reached its greatest strength in the 15th–18th centuries. From 1901 it was absorbed into the British, French, and German colonies in this area, which became the states of Niger, Cameroon, and Nigeria. The largest section of ancient Bornu is now the **state of Bornu** in Nigeria.

Borodin, Aleksandr Porfirevich (1833–1887)
Russian composer. Born in St Petersburg, the illegitimate son of a Russian prince, he became an expert in medical chemistry, but enjoyed music and wrote it in his spare time. His main work is the opera *Prince Igor*, left unfinished; it was completed by Nikolai Rimsky-Korsakov and Aleksandr Glazunov and includes the Polovtsian Dances. His other works include symphonies, songs, and chamber music, using traditional Russian themes.

Borodino, Battle of French victory over Russian forces under Kutusov on 7 September 1812 near the village of Borodino, 110km/70 mi northwest of Moscow, during Napoleon Bonaparte's invasion of Russia. This was one of the bloodiest battles of the Napoleonic years: the Russians lost 15,000 dead and 25,000 wounded; the French lost about 28,000, including 12 generals.

boron chemical symbol B, non-metallic element, atomic number 5, relative atomic mass 10.811. In nature it is found only in compounds, as with sodium and oxygen in borax. It exists in two allotropic forms (see *allotropy): brown amorphous powder and very hard, brilliant crystals. Its compounds are used in the preparation of boric acid, water softeners, soaps, enamels, glass, and pottery glazes. In alloys it is used to harden steel. Because it absorbs slow neutrons, it is used to make boron carbide control rods for nuclear reactors. It is a necessary trace element in the human diet. The element was named by Humphry Davy, who isolated it in 1808, from *bor*ax + -on, as in carb*on*.

borough (Old English burg, 'a walled or fortified place') urban-based unit of local government in the UK and USA. It existed in the UK from the 8th century until 1974, when it continued as an honorary status granted by royal charter to a district council, entitling its leader to the title of mayor. In England in 1998 there were 32 London borough councils and 36 metropolitan borough councils. The name is sometimes encountered in the USA: New York City has five administrative boroughs, Alaska has local government boroughs,
and in other states some smaller towns use the name.

Borromini, Francesco, originally Francesco Castelli (1599–1667) Swiss-born Italian baroque architect. He was one of the two most important architects (with *Bernini, his main rival) in 17th-century Rome. Whereas Bernini designed in a florid, expansive style, his pupil Borromini developed a highly idiosyncratic and austere use of the classical language of architecture. His genius may be seen in the cathedrals of San Carlo alle Quattro Fontane (1637–41), Sant' Ivo della Sapienza (1643–60), and the Oratory of San Filippo Neri (1638–50).

borzoi (Russian 'swift') breed of large dog originating in Russia. It is of the greyhound type, white with darker markings, with a thick, silky coat, and stands 75 cm/30 in or more at the shoulder.

Bosch, Hieronymus (c. 1460–1516) born Jeroen van Aken, Early Dutch painter. His fantastic visions, often filled with bizarre and cruel images, depict a sinful world in which people are tormented by demons and weird creatures, as in *Hell*, a panel from the triptych *The Garden of Earthly Delights* (c. 1505–10; Prado, Madrid). In their richness, complexity, and sheer strangeness, his pictures foreshadow surrealism.

Bosnia-Herzegovina
National name: *Bosna i Hercegovina/Bosnia-Herzegovina*

Area: 51,129 sq km/19,740 sq mi
Capital: Sarajevo
Major towns/cities: Banja Luka, Mostar, Prijedor, Tuzla, Zenica, Bihac, Gorazde
Physical features: barren, mountainous country, part of the Dinaric Alps; limestone gorges; 20 km/12 mi of coastline with no harbour
Head of state: Borislav Paravac, Sulejman Tihic, and Dragan Covic from 2003
Head of government: Adnan Terzic from 2003
Political system: emergent democracy
Political executive: limited presidency
Political parties: Party of Democratic Action (PDA), Muslim-oriented; Serbian Renaissance Movement (SPO), Serbian nationalist; Croatian Christian Democratic Union of Bosnia-Herzegovina (CDU), Croatian nationalist; League of Communists (LC) and Socialist Alliance (SA), left wing
Currency: konvertable mark
GNI per capita (PPP): (US$) 5,800 (2002 est)
Exports: coal, base metals, domestic appliances (industrial production and mining remain low). Principal market: Italy 27% (2000)
Population: 4,161,000 (2003 est)
Language: Serbian, Croat, Bosnian
Religion: 40% Muslim, 31% Serbian Orthodox, 15% Roman Catholic
Life expectancy: 71 (men); 77 (women) (2000–05)
Chronology
1st century AD: Part of Roman province of Illyricum.
395: On division of Roman Empire, stayed in west, along with Croatia and Slovenia, while Serbia to the east became part of the Byzantine Empire.
7th century: Settled by Slav tribes.
12–15th centuries: Independent state.
1463 and 1482: Bosnia and Herzegovina, in south, successively conquered by Ottoman Turks; many Slavs were converted to Sunni Islam.
1878: Became an Austrian protectorate, following Bosnian revolt against Turkish rule in 1875–76.
1908: Annexed by Austrian Habsburgs in wake of Turkish Revolution.

1914: Archduke Franz Ferdinand, the Habsburg heir, was assassinated in Sarajevo by a Bosnian-Serb extremist, precipitating World War I.

1918: On the collapse of the Habsburg Empire, the region became part of the Serb-dominated 'Kingdom of Serbs, Croats, and Slovenes', known as Yugoslavia from 1929.

1941: The region was occupied by Nazi Germany and became 'Greater Croatia' fascist puppet state and the scene of fierce fighting.

1943–44: Bosnia was liberated by communist Partisans, led by Marshal Tito.

1945: The region became a republic within the Yugoslav Socialist Federation.

1980: There was an upsurge in Islamic nationalism.

1990: Ethnic violence erupted between Muslims and Serbs. Communists were defeated in multiparty elections; a coalition was formed by Serb, Muslim, and Croatian parties.

1991: The Serb–Croat civil war in Croatia spread unrest into Bosnia. Fears that Serbia planned to annex Serb-dominated parts of the republic led to a declaration of sovereignty by parliament. Serbs within Bosnia established autonomous enclaves.

1992: Bosnia was admitted into the United Nations (UN). Violent civil war broke out, as an independent 'Serbian Republic of Bosnia-Herzegovina', comprising parts of the east and the west, was proclaimed by Bosnian-Serb militia leader Radovan Karadzic, with Serbian backing. UN forces were drafted into Sarajevo to break the Serb siege of the city; Bosnian Serbs were accused of 'ethnic cleansing', particularly of Muslims.

1993: A UN–EC peace plan failed. The USA began airdrops of food and medical supplies. Six UN 'safe areas' were created, intended as havens for Muslim civilians. A Croat–Serb partition plan was rejected by Muslims.

1994: The Serb siege of Sarajevo was lifted after a UN–NATO ultimatum and Russian diplomatic intervention. A Croat–Muslim federation was formed.

1995: Hostilities resumed. A US-sponsored peace accord, providing for two sovereign states (a Muslim–Croat federation and a Bosnian Serb Republic, the Republika Srpska) as well as a central legislature (House of Representatives, House of Peoples, and three-person presidency), was agreed at Dayton, Ohio. A 60,000-strong NATO peacekeeping force was deployed.

1996: An International Criminal Tribunal for Former Yugoslavia began in the Hague and an arms-control accord was signed. Full diplomatic relations were established with the Federal Republic of Yugoslavia. The collective rotating presidency was elected, with Alija Izetbegovic (Muslim), Momcilo Krajisnik (Serb), and Kresimir Zubak (Croat); Izetbegovic was elected overall president. Biljana Plavsic was elected president of the Serb Republic and Gojko Klickovic its prime minister. Edhem Bicakcic became prime minister of the Muslim–Croat Federation.

1997: Vladimir Soljic was elected president of the Muslim–Croat Federation. The Serb part of Bosnia signed a customs agreement with the Federal Republic of Yugoslavia.

1998: A moderate, pro-western government was formed in the Bosnian Serb republic, headed by Milorad Dodik; Nikola Poplasen became president. The first

Muslims and Croats were convicted in The Hague for war crimes during 1992. Zivko Radisic and Ante Jelavic replaced Krajisnik and Zubak respectively on the rotating presidency.

2000: In January, Ejup Ganic became president of the Muslim–Croat federation. Hardline nationalist Mirko Sarovic became president of the Bosnian Serb republic. Izetbegovic was replaced by Halid Genjac as the Muslim member of the rotating presidency. The northeastern town of Brcko, the only territorial dispute outstanding from the Dayton peace accord, was established as a self-governing neutral district in March, to be ruled by an elected alliance. The year saw three changes of prime minister, with Martin Raguz elected in October.

2001: Biljana Plavsic gave herself up to the war crimes tribunal, but pleaded 'not guilty' to nine counts of war crimes. Dario Kordic was the first senior politician to be convicted of war crimes at the tribunal. The Bosnian Serb nationalist party (SDS) voted to expel all war crimes suspects, including Radovan Karadzic.

2002: The nationalist party gained the majority in federation presidential, parliamentary and local elections. Biljana Plavsic changed her plea to guilty and was sentenced to 11 years in prison.

2003: Adnan Terzic was installed as leader of the new government. Mirko Sarovic, a Serb member of the presidency, resigned and was replaced by Borislav Paravac of the SDS. Naser Oric, a Muslim wartime commander in Srebrenica, was arrested for war crimes against Serbs.

2004: The 16th-century bridge at Mostar, destroyed during fighting in 1993, was reopened. NATO handed over peace-keeping duties to a European Union-led force, Eufor.

2005: Dragan Covic, the Croat member of the presidency, was sacked for alleged corruption.

boson in physics, an elementary particle whose spin can only take values that are whole numbers or zero. Bosons may be classified as *gauge bosons (carriers of the four fundamental forces) or *mesons. All elementary particles are either bosons or *fermions.

Bosporus Turkish **Istanbul Bogazi** or **Karadeniz Bogazi**, strait 27 km/17 mi long, joining the Black Sea with the Sea of Marmara and forming part of the water division between Europe and Asia; its name may be derived from the Greek legend of Io. Istanbul stands on its west side. The **Bosporus Bridge** (1973), 1,621 m/5,320 ft, links Istanbul and Anatolia (the Asian part of Turkey). In 1988 a second bridge across the straits was opened, linking Asia and Europe.

bossa nova (Portuguese *bossa nova* 'new trend') Brazilian dance rhythm of the 1950s, combining *samba and cool jazz. It became internationally popular in songs like 'The Girl From Ipanema' (1964), and developed into a dance very similar to the samba.

Boston industrial port and commercial centre, capital of Massachusetts, on Massachusetts Bay; population (2000 est) 589,100. Its economy is dominated by financial and health services and government. It is also a publishing and academic centre. The subway system, begun in 1897, was the first in the USA. Boston's baseball team, the Red Sox, is based at Fenway Park. Boston was founded by Puritans in 1630 and has played an important role in American history.

Boston Tea Party protest in 1773 by colonists in Massachusetts, USA, against the tea tax imposed on them by the British government before the *American Revolution.

Boswell, James (1740–1795) Scottish biographer and diarist. He was a member of Samuel *Johnson's Literary Club and the two men travelled to Scotland together in 1773, as recorded in Boswell's *Journal of a Tour to the Hebrides* (1785). His *Life of Samuel Johnson* was published in 1791. Boswell's ability to record Johnson's pithy conversation verbatim makes this a classic of English biography.

Bosworth, Battle of battle fought on 22 August 1485, during the English Wars of the Roses (see *Roses, Wars of the). Richard III, the Yorkist king, was defeated and killed by Henry Tudor, who became Henry VII. The battlefield is near the village of Market Bosworth, 19 km/12 mi west of Leicester, England.

botany (Greek *botane* 'herb') study of living and fossil *plants, including form, function, interaction with the environment, and classification.

Botany Bay inlet from the Tasman Sea on the east coast of New South Wales, Australia, 8 km/5 mi south of Sydney. It is the outlet of the rivers Georges and Cooks. The English explorer Captain James *Cook landed here in 1770. In 1787 the bay was chosen as the site for a British penal colony, but proved unsuitable, and the colony was located at Port Jackson.

botfly any fly of the family Oestridae. The larvae are parasites that feed on the skin (warblefly of cattle) or in the nasal cavity (nostrilflies of sheep and deer). The horse botfly belongs to another family, the Gasterophilidae. It has a parasitic larva that feeds in the horse's stomach.

Botha, Louis (1862–1919) South African soldier and politician. He was a commander in the Second South African War (Boer War). In 1907 he became premier of the Transvaal and in 1910 of the first Union South African government. On the outbreak of World War I in 1914 he rallied South Africa to the Commonwealth, suppressed a Boer revolt, and conquered German South West Africa.

Botha, P(ieter) W(illem) (1916–) South African politician, prime minister 1978–89. He initiated a modification of *apartheid, which later slowed down in the face of *Afrikaner (Boer) opposition, and made use of force both inside and outside South Africa to stifle *African National Congress (ANC) party activity. In 1984 he became the first executive state president. After suffering a stroke in 1989, he unwillingly resigned both party leadership and presidency and was succeeded by F W de Klerk.

Botham, Ian Terence (1955–) English cricketer. One of the world's greatest all-rounders, in 102 Tests for England between 1977 and 1992 he became the first player in Test cricket to score over 5,000 runs as well as take over 300 wickets. He played county cricket for Somerset, Worcestershire, and Durham, and briefly represented Queensland in the Sheffield Shield.

Bothwell, James Hepburn, 4th Earl of Bothwell (c. 1536–1578) Scottish nobleman. The third husband of *Mary Queen of Scots, 1567–70, he was alleged to have arranged the explosion that killed Darnley, her previous husband, in 1567. He succeeded as Earl in 1556 and became Duke in 1567.

bo tree *or* **peepul** Indian *fig tree, said to be the tree under which the Buddha became enlightened. (*Ficus religiosa*, family Moraceae.)

Botswana
formerly Bechuanaland (until 1966)
National name: *Republic of Botswana*

Area: 582,000 sq km/224,710 sq mi
Capital: Gaborone
Major towns/cities: Mahalapye, Serowe, Francistown, Selebi-Phikwe, Molepoloe, Kange, Maun
Physical features: Kalahari Desert in southwest (70–80% of national territory is desert), plains (Makgadikgadi salt pans) in east, fertile lands and Okavango Delta in north
Head of state and government: Festus Mogae from 1998
Political system: liberal democracy
Political executive: limited presidency
Political parties: Botswana Democratic Party (BDP), moderate centrist; Botswana National Front (BNF), moderate left of centre; Botswana Freedom Party (BFP)
Currency: pula
GNI per capita (PPP): (US$) 7,770 (2002 est)
Exports: diamonds, copper and nickel, beef. Principal market: UK 70% (2000)
Population: 1,785,000 (2003 est)
Language: English (official), Setswana (national)
Religion: Christian 50%, animist 50%
Life expectancy: 39 (men); 41 (women) (2000–05)
Chronology
18th century: Formerly inhabited by nomadic hunter-gatherer groups, including the Kung, the area was settled by the Tswana people, from whose eight branches the majority of the people are descended.
1872: Khama III the Great, a converted Christian, became chief of the Bamangwato, the largest Tswana group. He developed a strong army and greater unity among the Botswana peoples.
1885: Became the British protectorate of Bechuanaland at the request of Chief Khama, who feared invasion by Boers from the Transvaal (South Africa) following the discovery of gold.

1895: The southern part of the Bechuanaland Protectorate was annexed by Cape Colony (South Africa).
1960: A new constitution created a legislative council controlled (until 1963) by a British High Commissioner.
1965: The capital was transferred from Mafeking to Gaborone. Internal self-government was achieved.
1966: Independence was achieved from Britain. Name changed to Botswana.
mid-1970s: The economy grew rapidly as diamond mining expanded.
1985: South African raid on Gaborone, allegedly in search of African National Congress (ANC) guerrillas.
1993: Relations with South Africa were fully normalized following the end of apartheid and the establishment of a multiracial government.
1997: Major constitutional changes reduced the voting age to 18.
1998: Festus Mogae of the Botswana Democratic Party (BDP) became president. The Botswana Congress Parth (BCP) was declared the official opposition party.
1999: The BDP won the general elections and Festus Mogae was confirmed as president.
2000: Devastating floods made more than 60,000 people homeless. President Mogae announced that Aids drugs would be available free of charge from 2001.
2002: Kalahari bushmen challenged their forced eviction by the government. The case was dismissed on a technicality.
2004: Botswana's HIV infection rate fell to 37.5%. President Mogae and the BDP won the general election with a large majority.

Botticelli, Sandro (1445–1510) born Alessandro Filipepi, Florentine painter. He depicted religious and mythological subjects. He was patronized by the ruling *Medici family and was deeply influenced by their neo-Platonic circle. It was for the Medicis that he painted *Primavera* (1478) and *The Birth of Venus* (c. 1482–84). From the 1490s he was influenced by the religious fanatic *Savonarola, and developed a harshly expressive and emotional style, as seen in his *Mystic Nativity* (1500).

botulism rare, often fatal type of *food poisoning. Symptoms include vomiting, diarrhoea, muscular paralysis, breathing difficulties and disturbed vision. It is caused by a toxin produced by the bacterium *Clostridium botulinum*, found in soil and sometimes in improperly canned foods.

Boudicca (died AD 61) Queen of the Iceni (native Britons), often referred to by the Latin form of her name, **Boadicea**. Her husband, King Prasutagus, had been a tributary of the Romans, but on his death in AD 60 the territory of the Iceni was violently annexed. Boudicca was scourged and her daughters raped. Boudicca raised the whole of southeastern England in revolt, and before the main Roman armies could return from campaigning in Wales she burned Londinium (London), Verulamium (St Albans), and Camulodunum (Colchester). Later the Romans under governor Suetonius Paulinus defeated the British between London and Chester; they were virtually annihilated and Boudicca poisoned herself.

Bougainville autonomous island, formerly of Papua New Guinea, which with Buka Island and other smaller islands forms the province of North Solomon; area 10,620 sq km/4,100 sq mi; population (1994) 160,000. It is the largest of the Solomon Islands archipelago.

The capital is Arawa. The land is volcanic and mountainous, with the Emperor Range in the north and Crown Prince Range in the south; the highest peak is the active volcano Mount Balbi, 3,110 m/10,205 ft. The chief industries are copper, gold, and silver; copra, ivory nuts, and tortoiseshell are exported.

bougainvillea any plant of a group of South American tropical vines of the four o'clock family, now cultivated in warm countries around the world for the colourful red and purple bracts (leaflike structures) that cover the flowers. They are named after the French navigator Louis de Bougainville. (Genus *Bougainvillea*, family Nyctaginaceae.)

Boulanger, Nadia Juliette (1887–1979) French music teacher and conductor. She studied under Gabriel Fauré at the Paris Conservatory, where she later taught, as well as at the École Normale de Musique and the American Conservatory at Fontainebleau. Many distinguished composers were her pupils, including her sister, Lili Boulanger, Lennox Berkeley, Aaron Copland, Jean Françaix, Roy Harris, Walter Piston, and Philip Glass.

boules (French 'balls') French game (also called *boccie* and *pétanque*) between two players or teams; it is similar to bowls. While boules remains the quintessential French game, it has become increasingly popular elsewhere both as a recreation and as a competitive sport. In 1998 the international governing body, the Confédération Mondiale Sports Boules, had over 70 member countries.

Boulez, Pierre (1925–) French composer and conductor. He is the founder and director of IRCAM, a music research studio at the Pompidou Centre in Paris, France, that opened in 1977. His music, strictly adhering to ideas of *serialism and expressionistic in style, includes the cantatas *Le Visage nuptial* (1946–52) and *Le Marteau sans maître* (1953–55), both to texts by René Char; *Pli selon pli* (1962) for soprano and orchestra; and *Répons* (1981) for soloists, orchestra, tapes, and computer-generated sounds.

Boulogne-sur-Mer port on the English Channel in the *département* of Pas-de-Calais, northern France, situated at the mouth of the River Liane; population (1990) 44,200, conurbation 95,000. The city is a ferry port (connecting with the English ports of Dover and Folkestone) and seaside resort. Industries include oil refining, food processing, boatbuilding and the manufacture of textiles, It is the chief fishing port of France and carries an important import/export trade. Boulogne was a medieval countship, but was united with the French crown by Louis XI in 1477.

Bourbon dynasty French royal house (succeeding that of *Valois), beginning with Henry IV and ending with Louis XVI, with a brief revival under Louis XVIII, Charles X, and Louis Philippe. The Bourbons also ruled Spain almost uninterruptedly from Philip V to Alfonso XIII and were restored in 1975 (*Juan Carlos); at one point they also ruled Naples and several Italian duchies. The Grand Duke of Luxembourg is also a Bourbon by male descent.

Bourdon gauge instrument for measuring pressure, patented by French watchmaker Eugène Bourdon in 1849. The gauge contains a C-shaped tube, closed at one end. When the pressure inside the tube increases, the tube uncurls slightly causing a small movement at its closed end. A system of levers and gears magnifies this movement and turns a pointer, which indicates the pressure on a circular scale. Bourdon gauges are often fitted to cylinders of compressed gas used in industry and hospitals.

Bourgeois, Léon Victor Auguste (1851–1925) French politician. Entering politics as a Radical, he was prime minister in 1895, and later served in many cabinets. He was awarded the Nobel Prize for Peace in 1920 for his pioneering advocacy of the League of Nations and international cooperation.

bourgeoisie (French 'the freemen of a borough') the social class above the workers and peasants, and below the nobility; the middle class. 'Bourgeoisie' (and **bourgeois**) has also acquired a contemptuous sense, implying commonplace, philistine respectability. By socialists it is applied to the whole propertied class, as distinct from the proletariat.

Bourgogne French name of *Burgundy, a region of eastern France.

Bournemouth seaside resort and administrative centre of Bournemouth unitary authority in southern England, on Poole Bay, 40 km/25 mi southwest of Southampton; population (2001 est) 163,400. The tourist industry is important to the local economy, and in 2000 the town won the national 'Resort of the Year Award'. Other industries include insurance provision, banking, and the manufacturing of communications systems.

Boutros-Ghali, Boutros (1922–) Egyptian diplomat and politician, deputy prime minister 1991–92, secretary general of the *United Nations (UN) 1992–96. He worked towards peace in the Middle East in the foreign ministry posts he held from 1977 to 1991. The first Arab and African to become UN secretary-general, his term saw lengthy and difficult peacekeeping operations in Bosnia, Somalia, and Rwanda, and other challenges in Haiti and the post-Cold War world. The USA, a permanent member of the UN security council, was dissatisfied with his independent leadership and ensured he did not get a second term. In December 1996 he was replaced by Kofi Annan. In 1997–2002, Boutros-Ghali was secretary general of La Francophonie, a 49-member grouping of French-speaking nations.

bovine somatotropin (BST) hormone that increases an injected cow's milk yield by 10–40%. It is a protein naturally occurring in milk and breaks down within the human digestive tract into harmless amino acids. However, doubts have arisen as to whether such a degree of protein addition could in the long term be guaranteed harmless either to cattle or to humans.

bovine spongiform encephalopathy (BSE) *or* **mad cow disease** disease of cattle, related to *scrapie in sheep, that attacks the nervous system, causing aggression, lack of coordination, and collapse. It was formally identified in the UK in November 1986, and between 1986 and 2002 there were 181,376 cases of BSE identified in British cattle, which were all slaughtered to contain the spread of the disease. After safety measures were put in place for the selection and processing of cattle, British beef was declared safe (by the UK government) in 1999. Following outbreaks of BSE in French, German, and Spanish cattle in late 2000, European Union (EU) agriculture ministers agreed to ban, as of 1 January 2001, the use of meat-and-bone meal from animal feed and to ban all cattle over 30 months old from the food chain unless tested for BSE.

Bow Bells the bells of St Mary-le-Bow church, Cheapside, London; a person born within the sound of Bow Bells is traditionally considered a true Cockney. The bells also feature in the legend of Dick Whittington.

Bowdler, Thomas (1754–1825) English editor. His expurgated versions of Shakespeare and other authors gave rise to the verb **bowdlerize**.

bower bird New Guinean and northern Australian bird of the family Ptilonorhynchidae, order Passeriformes, related to the *bird of paradise. The males are dull-coloured, and build elaborate bowers of sticks and grass, decorated with shells, feathers, or flowers, and even painted with the juice of berries, to attract the females. There are 17 species.

bowfin North American fish *Amia calva* with a swim bladder highly developed as an air sac, enabling it to breathe air. It is the only surviving member of a primitive group of bony fishes.

bowhead Arctic whale *Balaena mysticetus* with strongly curving upper jawbones supporting the plates of baleen with which it sifts planktonic crustaceans from the water. Averaging 15 m/50 ft long and 90 tonnes/100 tons in weight, these slow-moving, placid whales were once extremely common, but by the 17th century were already becoming scarce through hunting. In 2000 it was believed that only 700–1,000 bowhead whales remained in existence.

Bowie, David (1947–) stage name of David Robert Jones, English pop singer, songwriter, and actor. His career has been a series of image changes. His hits include 'Jean Genie' (1973), 'Rebel, Rebel' (1974), 'Golden Years' (1975), and 'Underground' (1986). He has acted in plays and films, including Nicolas Roeg's *The Man Who Fell to Earth* (1976).

bowls outdoor and indoor game popular in Commonwealth countries. The outdoor game is played on a finely cut grassed area called a rink, with bowls (called 'woods') 13 cm/5 in in diameter. It is played as either singles, pairs, triples, or fours. The object is to get one's bowl (or bowls) as near as possible to the jack (target).

box any of several small evergreen trees and shrubs, with small, leathery leaves. Some species are used as hedging plants and for shaping into garden ornaments. (Genus *Buxus*, family Buxaceae.)

boxer breed of dog, about 60 cm/24 in tall, with a smooth coat and a set-back nose. The tail is usually docked. A boxer is usually brown, often with white markings, but may be fawn or brindled.

Boxer member of the *I ho ch'üan* ('Righteous Harmonious Fists'), a society of Chinese nationalists dedicated to fighting Western influence in China. They were known as Boxers by Westerners as they practised boxing training which they believed made them impervious to bullets. In 1898 the Chinese government persuaded the Boxers to join forces to oppose foreigners. In 1900 the *Boxer Rebellion was instigated by the empress *Zi Xi and thousands of Chinese Christian converts and missionaries were murdered.

Boxer Rebellion *or* **Boxer Uprising** rebellion of 1900 by the Chinese nationalist *Boxer society against Western influence. European and US legations in Beijing (Peking) were besieged and many missionaries and Europeans were killed. An international punitive force was dispatched and Beijing was captured on

14 August 1900. In September 1901 China agreed to pay reperations.

boxfish *or* **trunkfish** any fish of the family Ostraciodontidae, with scales that are hexagonal bony plates fused to form a box covering the body, only the mouth and fins being free of the armour. Boxfishes swim slowly. The cowfish, genus *Lactophrys*, with two 'horns' above the eyes, is a member of this group.

boxing fighting with gloved fists, almost entirely a male sport. The sport dates from the 18th century, when fights were fought with bare knuckles and untimed rounds. Each round ended with a knockdown. Fighting with gloves became the accepted form in the latter part of the 19th century after the formulation of the Queensberry Rules in 1867.

Boycott, Charles Cunningham (1832–1897) English ex-serviceman and land agent in County Mayo, Ireland, 1873–86. He strongly opposed the demands for agrarian reform by the Irish Land League, 1879–81, with the result that the peasants refused to work for him; hence the word **boycott**, meaning to isolate an individual, organization, or country, socially or commercially.

Boycott, Geoffrey (1940–) English cricketer. A prolific right-handed opening batsman for Yorkshire and England, he is one of only six players to have hit over 150 first-class centuries, and has scored the fourth most Test runs for England. In 1981 he overtook Gary Sobers's world record total of Test runs. He made 108 Test appearances, with an average of 47.72.

Boyle's law law stating that the volume of a given mass of gas at a constant temperature is inversely proportional to its pressure. For example, if the pressure on a gas doubles, its volume will be reduced by a half, and vice versa. The law was discovered in 1662 by Irish physicist and chemist Robert Boyle. See also *gas laws.

Boyne river in the Republic of Ireland, rising in the Bog of Allen in County Kildare, and flowing 110 km/69 mi northeastwards through Trim, Navan, and Drogheda to the Irish Sea. An obelisk marks the site of the Battle of the *Boyne, fought at Oldbridge near the mouth of the river on 1 July 1690.

Boyne, Battle of the battle fought on 1 July 1690 in eastern Ireland, in which the exiled King James II was defeated by William III and fled to France. It was the decisive battle of the War of English Succession, confirming a Protestant monarch, and has become the most commemorated battle in modern Irish history. It took its name from the River Boyne which rises in County Kildare and flows 110 km/69 mi northeast to the Irish Sea.

brachiopod *or* **lamp shell** any member of the phylum Brachiopoda, marine invertebrates with two shells, resembling but totally unrelated to bivalves. There are about 300 living species; they were much more numerous in past geological ages. They are suspension feeders, ingesting minute food particles from water. A single internal organ, the lophophore, handles feeding, aspiration, and excretion.

bracken any of several large ferns (especially *Pteridium aquilinum*) which grow abundantly in the northern hemisphere. The rootstock produces coarse fronds each year, which die down in autumn.

brackets pairs of signs that show which part of a calculation should be worked out first. For example, $4(7 + 3)$ indicates that 4 is to be multiplied by the result

obtained from adding 7 and 3. The mnemonic BODMAS can help one to remember the order in which an arithmetical expression should be calculated. Brackets may be nested, for example, $4(20 − (7 + 3))$, in which case the expression $7 + 3$ within the innermost pair of brackets is evaluated first, the result subtracted from 20 and that result multiplied by 4.

Bracknell Forest unitary authority (borough status) in central south England, created in 1998 from part of the former county of Berkshire. **area:** 109 sq km/42 sq mi **towns:** Bracknell (administrative headquarters), Sandhurst, Crowthorne **features:** Royal Military Academy at Sandhurst (established in 1799 for officer training); Transport Research Laboratory; Broadmoor Hospital **population:** (2001 est) 109,600.

bract leaflike structure in whose axil a flower or inflorescence develops. Bracts are generally green and smaller than the true leaves. However, in some plants they may be brightly coloured and conspicuous, taking over the role of attracting pollinating insects to the flowers, whose own petals are small; examples include poinsettia *Euphorbia pulcherrima* and bougainvillea.

Bradbury, Malcolm (Stanley) (1932–2000) English novelist and critic. His fiction includes comic and satiric portrayals of provincial British and US campus life: *Eating People is Wrong* (1959) (his first novel), *Stepping Westward* (1965), and *The History Man* (1975). *Dr Criminale* (1992) is an academic satire with a 1990s setting. His critical works include *The Modern American Novel* (1983) and *The Modern British Novel* (1993). He was knighted in 1999.

Bradford industrial city and metropolitan borough in West Yorkshire, England, 14 km/9 mi west of Leeds; population (2001 est) 467,700. The manufacture of textiles, traditionally the base of Bradford's prosperity, declined in the 1970s but remains important. Other principal industries include printing, precision and construction engineering, and the manufacture of chemicals and electronics.

Bradley, Omar Nelson (1893–1981) US general in World War II. In 1943 he commanded the 2nd US Corps in their victories in Tunisia and Sicily, leading to the surrender of 250,000 Axis troops, and in 1944 led the US troops in the invasion of France. His command, as the 12th Army Group, grew to 1.3 million troops, the largest US force ever assembled.

Bradman, Don(ald George) (1908–2001) Australian cricketer. From 52 Test matches he averaged 99.94 runs per innings, the highest average in Test history. He only needed four runs from his final Test innings to average 100 but was dismissed second ball. In April 2000, he was voted to be the greatest cricketer of the 20th century by the Wisden Cricketers' Almanack.

Braganza the royal house of Portugal whose members reigned from 1640 until 1910; members of another branch were emperors of Brazil from 1822 to 1889.

Brahe, Tycho (1546–1601) Danish astronomer. His accurate observations of the planets enabled German astronomer and mathematician Johannes *Kepler to prove that planets orbit the Sun in ellipses. Brahe's discovery and report of the 1572 supernova brought him recognition, and his observations of the comet of 1577 proved that it moved in an orbit among the planets, thus disproving Aristotle's view that comets were in the Earth's atmosphere.

Brahma in Hinduism, the creator god. Brahma combines with *Vishnu, the preserver, and *Shiva, the destroyer of evil, to make up the Trimurti, the three aspects of *Brahman, the supreme being, acting in the world.

Brahman in Hinduism, the supreme being, an impersonal and infinite creator of the universe. Brahman exists in everything, and is the spirit, or atman, of every living thing. Achieving union with Brahman and ceasing to be reborn is the goal of every Hindu. All the images of gods, such as Vishnu or Durga, are aspects of Brahman, the one indivisible god. Brahman acts in the world through three major forms: *Brahma, *Shiva, and *Vishnu, known collectively as the Trimurti.

Brahmanism earliest stage in the development of *Hinduism. Its sacred scriptures are the *Vedas, with their accompanying literature of comment and explanation known as Brahmanas, Aranyakas, and Upanishads.

Brahmaputra river in Asia 2,900 km/1,800 mi long, a tributary of the *Ganges, rising in the *Himalayas range, and flowing through Tibet, India, and Bangladesh.

Brahms, Johannes (1833–1897) German composer, pianist, and conductor. He is considered one of the greatest composers of symphonic music and songs. His works include four symphonies, lieder (songs), concertos for piano and for violin, chamber music, sonatas, and the choral *Ein Deutsches Requiem/ A German Requiem* (1868). He performed and conducted his own works.

Braille system of writing for the blind. Letters are represented by a combination of raised dots on paper or other materials, which are then read by touch. It was invented in 1829 by **Louis Braille**, who became blind at the age of three.

brain in higher animals, a mass of interconnected *nerve cells forming the anterior part of the *central nervous system, whose activities it coordinates and controls. In *vertebrates, the brain is contained by the skull. It is composed of three main regions. At the base of the *brainstem, the **medulla oblongata** contains centres for the control of respiration, heartbeat rate and strength, blood pressure, and thermoregulatory control (the control of body temperature). Overlying this is the **cerebellum**, which is concerned with coordinating complex muscular processes such as maintaining posture and moving limbs, and the control of balance. The **cerebrum** (cerebral hemispheres) are paired outgrowths of the front end of the forebrain, in early vertebrates mainly concerned with the senses, but in higher vertebrates greatly developed and involved in the integration of all sensory input and motor output, and in thought, emotions, memory, and behaviour. Sensory information arrives in the cerebrum in the form of nerve impulses that come from receptors – these may be found in sense organs, such as cones (light sensitive cells) in the retina of the eye, which send impulses to the brain along the optic nerve. The cerebrum processes the information received and can cause impulses to be sent out to the body to produce a response, such as moving towards an object that has been seen. Because a decision is made whether to make this kind of movement it is said to be voluntary.

brainstem region where the top of the spinal cord merges with the undersurface of the brain, consisting largely of the medulla oblongata and midbrain.

brake device used to slow down or stop the movement of a moving body or vehicle. The mechanically applied calliper brake used on bicycles uses a scissor action to press hard rubber blocks against the wheel rim. The main braking system of a car works hydraulically: when the driver depresses the brake pedal, liquid pressure forces pistons to apply brakes on each wheel.

Bramante (1444–1514) adopted name of Donato di Pascuccio, Italian High Renaissance architect and artist. Inspired by classical designs and by the work of Leonardo da Vinci, he was employed by Pope Julius II in rebuilding part of the Vatican and St Peter's in Rome. The circular Tempietto of San Pietro in Montorio, Rome (commissioned in 1502, built about 1510), is possibly his most important completed work. Though small in size, this circular colonnaded building possesses much of the grandeur of ancient Roman buildings.

bramble any of a group of prickly bushes belonging to the rose family. Examples are *blackberry, raspberry, and dewberry. (Genus *Rubus*, family Rosaceae.)

Brancusi, Constantin (1876–1957) Romanian sculptor. One of the main figures of 20th-century art, he revolutionized modern sculpture. Active in Paris from 1904, he was a pioneer of abstract sculpture, reducing a few basic themes such as birds, fishes, and the human head to simple essential forms appropriate to the special quality of his material, whether stone, bronze, or wood. His works include *Sleeping Muse* (1910; Musée National d'Art Moderne, Paris) and *Bird in Space* (1928; Museum of Modern Art, New York).

Brandenburg administrative region (German *Land*) of northeast Germany; area 29,476 sq km/11,381 sq mi; population (2003 est) 2,651,200. The capital is Potsdam, and other major towns include Cottbus, Brandenburg, and Frankfurt-an-der-Oder. Drained by the Havel, Spree, and Oder rivers, the region has many lakes and pine forests. The German capital Berlin is situated within Brandenburg but is an autonomous administrative unit. The main industries are iron and steel, paper, pulp, metal products, and semiconductors.

Brando, Marlon (1924–2004) US actor. One of the great exponents of method acting, he had a powerful presence on both stage and screen, and was one of the most influential actors of his generation. He won Best Actor Academy Awards for *On the Waterfront* (1954) and *The Godfather* (1972), although he declined the second award to protest against Hollywood's portrayal of American Indians. Brando directed one film, the psychological Western *One Eyed Jacks* (1961).

Brandt, Willy (1913–1992) adopted name of Karl Herbert Frahm, German socialist politician, federal chancellor (premier) of West Germany 1969–74. He played a key role in the remoulding of the Social Democratic Party (SPD) as a moderate socialist force (leader 1964–87). As mayor of West Berlin 1957–66, Brandt became internationally known during the Berlin Wall crisis of 1961. He was awarded the Nobel Prize for Peace in 1971 for his contribution towards reconciliation between West and East Germany.

brandy (Dutch *brandewijn*, 'burnt wine') alcoholic drink distilled from fermented grape juice (wine). The best-known examples are produced in France, notably

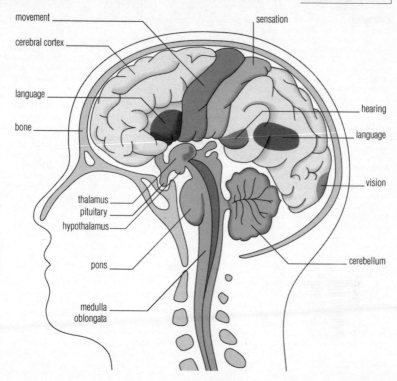

brain The structure of the human brain. At the back of the skull lies the cerebellum, which coordinates reflex actions that control muscular activity. The medulla controls respiration, heartbeat, and blood pressure. The hypothalamus is concerned with instinctive drives and emotions. The thalamus relays signals to and from various parts of the brain. The pituitary gland controls the body's hormones. Distinct areas of the large convoluted cerebral hemispheres that fill most of the skull are linked to sensations, such as hearing and sight, and voluntary activities, such as movement.

Armagnac and Cognac. Brandy can also be prepared from other fruits, for example, apples (Calvados) and cherries (Kirschwasser). Brandies contain up to 55% alcohol.

Braque, Georges (1882–1963) French painter. With Picasso, he played a decisive role in the development of cubism (1907–1910). It was during this period that he began to experiment with collage and invented the technique of gluing paper, wood, and other materials to canvas.

Brasília capital of Brazil from 1960, situated on the central plateau, 1,150 m/3,773 ft above sea level; population (2000 est) 2,043,200. The main area of employment is in government service; only light industry is allowed within the city. Brasília is also capital of the Federal District, which has an area of 5,794 sq km/2,317 sq mi. The city was originally designed to accommodate up to 500,000 people, which has now been considerably exceeded, and many people live in shanty towns located outside the main city.

brass metal *alloy of copper and zinc, with not more than 5% or 6% of other metals. The zinc content ranges from 20% to 45%, and the colour of brass varies accordingly from coppery to whitish yellow. Brasses are characterized by the ease with which they may be shaped and machined; they are strong and ductile, resist many forms of corrosion, and are used for electrical fittings, ammunition cases, screws, household fittings, and ornaments.

brassica any of a group of plants, many of which are cultivated as vegetables. The most familiar is the common cabbage (*Brassica oleracea*), with its varieties broccoli, cauliflower, kale, and Brussels sprouts. (Genus *Brassica*, family Cruciferae.)

brass instrument any of a group of musical instruments made of brass or other metal. It does not include woodwind instruments made of metal, such as the saxophone or flute. The sound is produced when the column of air inside the instrument is made to vibrate by the player's lips vibrating against the

127

mouthpiece. Orchestral brass instruments are descended from signalling instruments (the 'natural horn', 'natural trumpet') consisting of a single tube with no extra mechanism. These instruments could only produce notes in their own harmonic series – the higher notes of the series being produced by the player increasing the lip tension. To achieve a variety of notes, a player used a set of crooks (several pieces of tubing of differing lengths). Early in the 19th century, the invention of the valve system meant that brass instruments could now play all the notes throughout their pitch range. They are powerful and efficient generators of sound, and produce tones of great depth and resonance.

Bratislava German **Pressburg**, city and capital of the Slovak Republic, and a leading port on the River Danube; population (2003 est) 428,800. A well-diversified industrial centre, its manufacturing includes textiles, chemicals, and metal goods. During the Communist period, heavy industry was focused on the production of armaments. The city is surrounded by forests, large farms, and vineyards, and has an active trade in agricultural products. It was the capital of Hungary from 1541 to 1784 and capital of the province of Slovakia (within Czechoslovakia) from 1919 until 1949, when the city became the capital of the newly created Bratislava Region. The region was abolished in 1960, and in 1993 it became the capital of the newly independent Slovak Republic.

Braun, Eva (1912–1945) German mistress of Adolf Hitler. Secretary to Hitler's photographer and personal friend, Heinrich Hoffmann, she became Hitler's mistress in the 1930s and married him in the air-raid shelter of the Chancellery in Berlin on 29 April 1945. The next day they committed suicide together.

Brazil

National name: *República Federativa do Brasil/ Federative Republic of Brazil*

Area: 8,511,965 sq km/3,286,469 sq mi
Capital: Brasília
Major towns/cities: São Paulo, Belo Horizonte, Nova Iguaçu, Rio de Janeiro, Belém, Recife, Porto Alegre, Salvador, Curitiba, Manaus, Fortaleza

Major ports: Rio de Janeiro, Belém, Recife, Porto Alegre, Salvador
Physical features: the densely forested Amazon basin covers the northern half of the country with a network of rivers; south is fertile; enormous energy resources, both hydroelectric (Itaipú Reservoir on the Paraná, and Tucuruí on the Tocantins) and nuclear (uranium ores); mostly tropical climate
Head of state and government: Luiz Inácio da Silva from 2003
Political system: liberal democracy
Political executive: limited presidency
Political parties: Workers' Party (PT), left of centre; Social Democratic Party (PSDB), moderate, left of centre; Brazilian Democratic Movement Party (PMDB), left of centre; Liberal Front Party (PFL), right wing; National Reconstruction Party (PRN), right of centre
Currency: real
GNI per capita (PPP): (US\$) 7,250 (2002)
Exports: steel products, transport equipment, coffee, iron ore and concentrates, aluminium, iron, tin, soybeans, meal and oils, orange juice (85% of world's concentrates), tobacco, leather footwear, sugar, beef, textiles. Principal market: USA 24.2% (2001)
Population: 178,470,000 (2003 est)
Language: Portuguese (official), Spanish, English, French, 120 Indian languages
Religion: Roman Catholic 70%; Indian faiths
Life expectancy: 64 (men); 73 (women) (2000–05)
Chronology
1500: Originally inhabited by South American Indians. Portuguese explorer Pedro Alvares Cabral sighted and claimed Brazil for Portugal.
1530: Start of Portuguese colonization; Portugal monopolized trade but colonial government was decentralized.
1580–1640: Brazil came under Spanish rule along with Portugal.
17th century: Sugar-cane plantations were established with slave labour in coastal regions, making Brazil the world's largest supplier of sugar; cattle ranching was developed inland.
1695: Gold was discovered in the central highlands.
1763: The colonial capital moved from Bahia to Rio de Janeiro.
1770: Brazil's first coffee plantations were established in Rio de Janeiro.
18th century: Population in 1798 totalled 3.3 million, of which around 1.9 million were slaves, mainly of African origin; significant growth of gold-mining industry.
1808: The Portuguese regent, Prince John, arrived in Brazil and established his court at Rio de Janeiro; Brazilian trade opened to foreign merchants.
1815: The United Kingdom of Portugal, Brazil, and Algarve made Brazil co-equal with Portugal.
1821: Crown Prince Pedro took over the government of Brazil.
1822: Pedro defied orders to return to Portugal; he declared Brazil's independence and avoided reversion to colonial status.
1825: King John VI recognized his son as Emperor Pedro I of Brazil.
1831: Pedro I abdicated in favour of his infant son, Pedro II.
1847: The first prime minister was appointed, but the emperor retained many powers.

1865–70: Brazilian efforts to control Uruguay led to the War of the Triple Alliance with Paraguay.

1888: Slavery was abolished in Brazil.

1889: The monarch was overthrown by a liberal revolt; a federal republic was established, with a central government controlled by the coffee planters.

1902: Brazil produced 65% of the world's coffee.

1915–19: Lack of European imports during World War I led to rapid industrialization.

1930: A revolution against the coffee planter oligarchy placed Getúlio Vargas in power; he introduced social reforms.

1937: Vargas established an authoritarian corporate state.

1942: Brazil entered World War II as an ally of the USA.

1945–54: Vargas was ousted by a military coup. In 1951 he was elected president and continued to extend the state control of the economy. In 1954 he committed suicide.

1960: The capital moved to Brasília.

1964: A bloodless coup established a technocratic military regime; free political parties were abolished; intense concentration on industrial growth was aided by foreign investment and loans.

1970s: Economic recession and inflation undermined public support for the military regime.

1985: After gradual democratization from 1979, Tancredo Neves became the first civilian president in 21 years.

1988: A new constitution reduced the powers of the president.

1989: Fernando Collor (PRN) was elected president. Brazil suspended its foreign debt payments.

1992: Collor was charged with corruption and replaced by Vice-President Itamar Franco.

1994: A new currency was introduced, the third in eight years. Fernando Henrique Cardoso (PSDB) won presidential elections. Collor was cleared of corruption charges.

1997: The constitution was amended to allow the president to seek a second term of office.

1998: President Cardoso was re-elected. A stock market crash weakened Brazil's currency, and although an International Monetary Fund (IMF) rescue package was announced, the government had to devalue the real as foreign capital was withdrawn from the economy.

1999: The economy began to recover and economic reforms were put in place.

2001: Prison riots in São Paulo state involving 28,000 prisoners left 20 people dead.

2002: The IMF granted the government a US$30 billion loan, the IMF's largest-ever financial rescue package. With a comprehensive victory in presidential elections, Luiz Inacio Lula da Silva ('Lula') of the left-wing Partido dos Trabalhadores (PT; Workers' Party) was able to put a left-wing government in power for the first time in 40 years.

2004: Brazil applied for a permanent seat on the UN Security Council. The country sucessfully launched its first space rocket.

2005: The government announced plans to protect part of the Amazon region. In Rio de Janeiro at least 30 people were killed by a death squad, the city's worst massacre for over 10 years.

Brazil nut gigantic South American tree; also its seed, which is rich in oil and highly nutritious. The seeds (nuts) are enclosed in a hard outer casing, each fruit containing 10–20 seeds arranged like the segments of an orange. The timber of the tree is also valuable. (*Bertholletia excelsa*, family Lecythidaceae.)

Brazzaville capital, river port, and largest city of the Republic of the Congo (Congo-Brazzaville), on the west bank of the Congo River, opposite Kinshasa; population (2002 est) 1,133,800. It is the leading commercial centre of the Republic and industries include foundries, railway repairs, shipbuilding, beverages, textiles, food processing, shoes, soap, furniture, and bricks. Tourism is important, with arts and crafts markets in the Plateau district of the city.

breadfruit fruit of two tropical trees belonging to the mulberry family. It is highly nutritious and when baked is said to taste like bread. It is native to many South Pacific islands. (*Artocarpus communis* and *A. altilis*, family Moraceae.)

Breakspear, Nicholas original name of *Adrian IV, the only English pope.

bream deep-bodied, flattened fish *Abramis brama* of the carp family, growing to about 50 cm/1.6 ft, typically found in lowland rivers across Europe.

breast one of a pair of organs on the chest of the adult human female, also known as a *mammary gland. Each of the two breasts contains milk-producing cells and a network of tubes or ducts that lead to openings in the nipple.

breast cancer in medicine, *cancer of the *breast. It is usually diagnosed following the detection of a painless lump in the breast (either through self-examination or *mammography). Other, less common symptoms, include changes in the shape or texture of the breast and discharge from the nipple. It is the commonest cancer amongst women: there are 28,000 new cases of breast cancer in Britain each year and 185,700 in the USA.

breast screening in medicine, examination of the breast to detect the presence of breast cancer at an early stage. Screening methods include self-screening by monthly examination of the breasts and formal programmes of screening by palpation (physical examination) and mammography in special clinics. Screening may be offered to older women on a routine basis and it is important in women with a family history of breast cancer.

breathing *or* **ventilation** movement of air into and out of the air passages of an animal, brought about by muscle contraction. It is a form of gas exchange. Breathing is sometimes referred to as external respiration, for true respiration is a cellular (internal) process. In a mammal, breathing involves the action of the muscles of the diaphragm and the intercostal muscles (between the ribs). When a mammal breathes in, the diaphragm muscles contract, which lowers the diaphragm. The external intercostal muscles contract, which raises the ribs. Lowering the diaphragm and raising the ribs increases the volume of the *thorax. This lowers the pressure of the air inside the lungs in the thorax. The pressure is now lower than atmospheric pressure so air flows into the air passages and the lungs inflate.

Brecht, Bertolt (Eugen Berthold Friedrich) (1898–1956) German dramatist and poet. He was one of the most influential figures in 20th-century theatre. A committed Marxist, he sought to develop an 'epic theatre' which aimed to destroy the 'suspension of disbelief' usual in the theatre and so encourage audiences to develop an active and critical attitude to a play's subject. He adapted John Gay's *The Beggar's Opera* as *Die Dreigroschenoper/The Threepenny Opera* (1928), set to music by Kurt Weill. Later plays include *Mutter Courage und ihre Kinder/Mother Courage and her Children* (1941), set during the Thirty Years' War, and *Der kaukasische Kreidekreis/The Caucasian Chalk Circle* (1945).

breed recognizable group of domestic animals, within a species, with distinctive characteristics that have been produced by *artificial selection.

breeder reactor *or* **fast breeder** alternative name for *fast reactor, a type of nuclear reactor.

breeding in biology, the crossing and selection of animals and plants to change the characteristics of an existing *breed or cultivar (variety), or to produce a new one. Selective breeding is breeding in which humans choose the parent plants or parent animals.

Bremen administrative region (German *Land*) in northern Germany, formed in 1947, consisting of the cities of Bremen (the administrative capital) and Bremerhaven; area 404 sq km/156 sq mi; population (2003 est) 643,700. It is an enclave within the *Land* of Lower Saxony, bounded on the west by the River Weser. Fishing and farming are the main economic activities; the main industries are shipping, shipbuilding, and steel processing. The first regular ship service between continental Europe and the USA was started in Bremerhaven in 1847.

Brest-Litovsk, Treaty of bilateral treaty signed on 3 March 1918 between Russia and Germany, Austria-Hungary, and their allies. Under its terms, Russia agreed to recognize the independence of Georgia, Ukraine, Poland, and the Baltic States, and to pay heavy compensation. Under the November 1918 armistice that ended World War I, it was annulled, since Russia was one of the winning allies.

Breton, André (1896–1966) French writer and poet. He was among the leaders of the *Dada art movement and was also a founder of surrealism, publishing *Le Manifeste du surréalisme/Surrealist Manifesto* (1924).

Bretton Woods township in New Hampshire, USA, where the United Nations Monetary and Financial Conference was held in 1944 to discuss post-war international payments problems. The agreements reached on financial assistance and measures to stabilize exchange rates led to the creation of the International Bank for Reconstruction and Development in 1945 and the International Monetary Fund (IMF).

Breuer, Marcel (Lajos) (1902–1981) Hungarian-born US architect and designer. He studied and taught at the *Bauhaus school in Germany. His tubular steel chair, known as the Wassily chair (1925), was the first of its kind. He moved to England, then to the USA, where he was in partnership with Walter *Gropius (1937–40). His buildings show an affinity with natural materials, as exemplified in the Bijenkorf, Rotterdam, the Netherlands (with Elzas; 1953).

brewing making of beer, ale, or other alcoholic beverage, from *malt and *barley by steeping (mashing), boiling, and fermenting. Mashing the barley releases its sugars. Yeast is then added, which contains the enzymes needed to convert the sugars into ethanol (alcohol) and carbon dioxide. Hops are added to give a bitter taste.

Brezhnev, Leonid Ilyich (1906–1982) Soviet leader. A protégé of Joseph Stalin and Nikita Khrushchev, he came to power (after he and Aleksei *Kosygin forced Khrushchev to resign) as general secretary of the Communist Party of the Soviet Union (CPSU) 1964–82 and was president 1977–82. Domestically he was conservative; abroad the USSR was established as a military and political superpower during the Brezhnev era, extending its influence in Africa and Asia.

Brian Bóruma (*or* Brian Boru) (*c.* 941–1014) King of Munster from 976 and high king of Ireland from 999. His campaigns represent the rise of Munster as a power in Ireland, symbolized by his victory over Leinster and the Dublin Norse at Glen Mama in 999. He was renowned as a builder of forts, and this may have been his most significant military legacy. He died in victory over the Vikings at Clontarf in Dublin.

Briand, Aristide (1862–1932) French republican politician, 11 times prime minister 1909–29. A skilful parliamentary tactician and orator, he was seldom out of ministerial office between 1906 and 1932. As foreign minister 1925–32, he was the architect, with the German chancellor Gustav Stresemann, of the 1925 Locarno Pact (settling Germany's western frontier) and the 1928 Kellogg–Briand Pact (renouncing war). In 1930 he outlined an early scheme for the political and economic unification of Europe. He shared the Nobel Prize for Peace in 1926 with Stresemann for their work for European reconciliation.

brick common block-shaped building material, with all opposite sides parallel. It is made of clay that has been fired in a kiln. Bricks are made by kneading a mixture of crushed clay and other materials into a stiff mud and extruding it into a ribbon. The ribbon is cut into individual bricks, which are fired at a temperature of up to about 1,000 °C/1,800 °F. Bricks may alternatively be pressed into shape in moulds.

bridewealth *or* **bride price** goods or property presented by a man's family to his prospective wife's family as part of the marriage agreement. It is common practice among many societies in Africa, Asia, and the Pacific, and some American Indian groups. In most European and South Asian countries the alternative custom is *dowry.

bridge structure that provides a continuous path or road over water, valleys, ravines, or above other roads. The basic designs and composites of these are based on the way they bear the weight of the structure and its load. Beam, or **girder**, bridges are supported at each end by the ground with the weight thrusting downwards. **Cantilever** bridges are a complex form of girder in which only one end is supported. **Arch** bridges thrust outwards and downwards at their ends. **Suspension** bridges use cables under tension to pull inwards against anchorages on either side of the span, so that the span hangs from the main cables by a network of vertical cables. The **cable-stayed** bridge relies on diagonal cables connected directly between the bridge deck and supporting towers at each end. Some bridges are too low to allow traffic to pass beneath easily, so they are designed with movable parts, like swing and draw bridges.

Bridgend unitary authority in south Wales created in 1996 from part of the former county of Mid Glamorgan. **area:** 40 sq km/15 sq mi **towns:** Bridgend (administrative headquarters), Porthcawl (resort and residential area), Maesteg **physical:** most of the authority consists of the western end of a lowland plateau, Bro Morgannwg, a rich agricultural area of mixed farming and large villages; in the north is the Cymer Forest and Mynydd Caerau (556 m/1,824 ft) **features:** Ewenny Priory and Church (1141); Ewenny Pottery (1610), one of the oldest working potteries in Wales; Cefn Cribwr, a well-preserved 18th-century industrial ironworks; Bryngarw Country Park, with 46 ha/113 acres of woodland, wetland, and gardens **population:** (2000 est) 131,500.

Bridges, Robert Seymour (1844–1930) English poet and critic. He was poet laureate from 1913 to 1930. His topographical poems and lyrics, which he began to publish in 1873, demonstrate a great command of rhythm and melody. He wrote *The Testament of Beauty* (1929), a long philosophical poem. In 1918 he edited and published posthumously the poems of Gerard Manley *Hopkins.

Bridgetown port, capital, and leading commercial centre of Barbados; population (2000 est) 7,000 (town), 97,500 (urban area). It lies in the southwest of the island on Carlisle Bay, and to the northwest includes a deep-water harbour, through which the products of traditional sugar manufacturing are exported. Tourism is also an important industry, and to the north of Bridgetown is the resort of Paradise Beach. Bridgetown was founded in 1628; it became the capital of Barbados at independence in 1966.

Bridgewater, Francis Egerton, 3rd Duke of Bridgewater (1736–1803) Pioneer of British inland navigation. With James Brindley as his engineer, he constructed (1762–72) the Bridgewater Canal from Worsley to Manchester and on to the Mersey, a distance of 67.5 km/42 mi. Initially built to carry coal, the canal crosses the Irwell Valley on an aqueduct. He succeeded as duke in 1748.

Bright, John (1811–1889) British Liberal politician. He was a campaigner for free trade, peace, and social reform. A Quaker mill-owner, he was among the founders of the Anti-Corn Law League in 1839, and was largely instrumental in securing the passage of the Reform Bill of 1867. He sat in Gladstone's cabinets as president of the Board of Trade 1868–70 and chancellor of the Duchy of Lancaster 1873–74 and 1880–82, but broke with him over the Irish Home Rule Bill.

Brighton seaside resort in *Brighton and Hove unitary authority, on the south coast of England; population (1994 est) 155,000. The city was part of the county of East Sussex until 1997. It is an education and service centre with two universities, language schools, and tourist and conference business facilities.

Brighton and Hove unitary authority in southern England, created in 1997. **area:** 84 sq km/32 sq mi **towns:** Brighton, Hove (administrative headquarters), Woodingdean, Rottingdean, Portslade-by-Sea **features:** English Channel; South Downs; Royal Pavilion (Brighton) redesigned and enlarged by English architect John Nash in the 19th century; Palace Pier and West Pier (Brighton); Hollingbury Castle fort; Booth Museum of Natural History (Brighton); British Engineerium (Hove); 400 registered pubs and restaurants, the largest number of places to eat per head outside central London **population:** (2001 est) 248,100.

brill flatfish *Scophthalmus laevis*, living in shallow water over sandy bottoms in the northeastern Atlantic and Mediterranean. It is a freckled sandy brown, and grows to 60 cm/2 ft.

Brisbane capital and chief port of the state of *Queensland, Australia; population (2001 est) 1,627,500. Brisbane is situated on the east coast of Australia, 14 km/9 mi inland of the mouth of the River Brisbane, about 29 km/18 mi south of Moreton Bay. It is the third-largest city in Australia, and the financial and commercial centre for Queensland; it is also the major manufacturing centre of the state, with diverse industries including shipbuilding, engineering, oil refining, brewing, food processing, tobacco production, tanning, the manufacture of motor vehicles, agricultural machinery, fertilizers, shoes, and clothing. As well as industrial products, including processed foods, the port exports large quantities of wool and cereals. Tourism is also important. A pipeline from Moonie carries oil for refining. Brisbane has three universities, Queensland University (1909), Griffith University (1975), and Queensland University of Technology (1989).

bristlecone pine the oldest living species of *pine tree.

bristletail primitive wingless insect of the order Thysanura. Up to 2 cm/0.8 in long, bristletails have a body tapering from front to back, two long antennae, and three 'tails' at the rear end. They include the silverfish *Lepisma saccharina* and the firebrat *Thermobia domestica*. Two-tailed bristletails constitute another insect order, the Diplura. They live under stones and fallen branches, feeding on decaying material.

Bristol industrial port and administrative centre of Bristol City unitary authority, in southwest England, situated at the junction of the rivers Avon and Frome, 48 km/30 mi east of Cardiff; population (2001 est) 380,600. Industries include engineering, microelectronics, tobacco, printing, metal refining, and banking.

Britain island off the northwest coast of Europe, one of the British Isles. It comprises England, Scotland, and Wales (together officially known as *Great Britain), and is part of the United Kingdom. The name is also sometimes used loosely to denote the United Kingdom. It is derived from the Roman name for the island Britannia, which in turn is derived from the ancient Celtic name for the inhabitants, *Bryttas*.

Britain, Battle of World War II air battle between German and British air forces over Britain from 10 July to 31 October 1940. The height of the battle occurred 30–31 August.

British Broadcasting Corporation (BBC) the UK state-owned broadcasting network. It operates television and national and local radio stations, and is financed by the sale of television (originally radio) licences. It is not permitted to carry advertisements but it has an additional source of income through its publishing interests and the sales of its programmes. The BBC is controlled by a board of governors, each appointed by the government for five years. The BBC was converted from a private company (established in 1922) to a public corporation under royal charter in 1927. Under the charter, news programmes were required to be politically impartial. The first director-general was John Reith from 1922 to 1938.

British Columbia most westerly, and only Pacific, province of Canada, area 947,800 sq km/365,851 sq mi; population (2001 est) 3,907,700. It is bordered on the east by Alberta, with the Continental Divide in the Rocky Mountains forming its southeastern boundary. To the south, it has a frontier along the 49th Parallel with the US states of Montana, Idaho, and Washington. To the north, along the 60th Parallel, lie the Northwest Territories and Yukon Territory. In the northwest, the province borders the panhandle of Alaska for about half its length. The province also includes a number of islands to the west, including Vancouver Islands and the Queen Charlotte Islands. The capital is *Victoria on Vancouver Island; other main cities and towns are Vancouver, Prince George, Kamloops, Kelowna, Surrey, Richmond, and Nanaimo. British Columbia is mostly mountainous and over half the land is forested; it has a deeply indented coastline, over 80 major lakes, and numerous rivers, including the Fraser and Columbia. Chief industries are lumbering and the manufacture of finished wood products, fishing, mining (coal, copper, iron, lead), extraction of oil and natural gas, and hydroelectric power generation; there is also fruit and vegetable growing. Newer industries include ecotourism and film – the province ranks in importance behind only Los Angeles, California, and New York City in the North American film industry.

British East India Company commercial company (1600–1873) chartered by Queen Elizabeth I and given a monopoly of trade between England and the Far East. In the 18th century, the company became, in effect, the ruler of a large part of India, and a form of dual control by the company and a committee responsible to Parliament in London was introduced by Pitt's India Act 1784. The end of the monopoly of China trade came in 1834, and after the *Indian Mutiny 1857–58 the crown took complete control of the government of British India. The India Act 1858 transferred all the company's powers to the British government.

British Empire empire covering, at its height in the 1920s, about a sixth of the landmass of the Earth, all of its lands recognizing the United Kingdom (UK) as their leader. It consisted of the Empire of India, four self-governing countries known as dominions, and dozens of colonies and territories. The Empire was a source of great pride to the British, who believed that it was an institution for civilizing the world, and for many years Empire Day (24 May) saw celebration throughout the UK. After World War II it began to dissolve as colony after colony became independent, and in 2001 the UK had only 13 small dependent territories. With 53 other independent countries, it forms the British *Commonwealth. Although Britain's monarch is accepted as head of the Commonwealth, most of its member states are republics.

British Empire, Order of the British order of knighthood (see *knighthood, orders of) instituted in 1917 by George V. There are military and civil divisions, and the ranks are GBE, Knight Grand Cross or Dame Grand Cross; KBE, Knight Commander; DBE, Dame Commander; CBE, Commander; OBE, Officer; MBE, Member.

British Expeditionary Force (BEF) during World War I (1914–18) the term commonly referred to the British army serving in France and Flanders, although strictly speaking it referred only to the forces sent to France in 1914; during World War II it was also the army in Europe, which was evacuated from Dunkirk, France in 1940.

British Honduras former name (to 1973) of Belize.

British Indian Ocean Territory British colony in the Indian Ocean directly administered by the Foreign and Commonwealth Office, consisting of the Chagos Archipelago some 1,900 km/1,200 mi northeast of Mauritius; area 60 sq km/23 sq mi. Copra, salted fish, and tortoiseshell are produced. There is a US naval and air base on Diego Garcia. In 2000 a number of Ilois, British subjects who had lived on the Chagos islands, claimed that the British government had unlawfully removed them from the islands during the period 1967–73 to allow the US military base to be built. The High Court ruled that they had been unlawfully ejected, and the remaining Ilois, many in exile in Mauritius, began planning to return to the islands.

British Isles archipelago off the northwest coast of Europe, consisting of *Great Britain (England, Wales, and Scotland), Ireland, the Orkney and Shetland islands, the Isle of Man, and many other islands that are included in various counties, such as the Isle of Wight, Scilly Isles, Lundy Island, and the Inner and Outer Hebrides. The Channel Islands are often included in the definition, but are geographically closer to France. The British Isles are divided from Europe by the North Sea, Strait of Dover, and the English Channel, and face the Atlantic to the west.

British Somaliland British protectorate 1884–1960 comprising over 176,000 sq km/67,980 sq mi of territory on the north Somali coast of East Africa, opposite its base at Aden. In 1960 British Somaliland united with *Italian Somaliland to form the independent state of Somalia. British authorities were harassed from 1899 by Somali nationalists, led by the Muslim leader Muhammad bin Abdullah Hassan (Sayyid Maxamed Cabdulle Xasan), who held the interior until his death in 1920.

British Virgin Islands part of the *Virgin Islands group in the West Indies.

Brittany French **Bretagne**; Breton **Breiz**, modern region of northwest France and former province, on the Breton peninsula between the Bay of Biscay and the English Channel; area 27,208 sq km/10,505 sq mi; population (1999 est) 2,906,200. It includes the *départements* of Côtes-d'Armor, Finistère, Ille-et-Vilaine, and Morbihan. The administrative centre is Rennes, and other towns include Brest, Lorient, Nantes, St-Brieuc, Vannes, and Quimper. One of the major occupations is animal husbandry, and the region is the country's leading milk producer.

Britten, (Edward) Benjamin, Baron Britten (1913–1976) English composer. He often wrote for individual singers; for example, the role in the opera *Peter Grimes* (1945), based on verses by George Crabbe, was written for his life companion, the tenor Peter Pears. Among his many works are the *Young Person's Guide to the Orchestra* (1946); the chamber opera *The Rape of Lucretia* (1946); *Billy Budd* (1951); *A Midsummer Night's Dream* (Shakespeare; 1960); and *Death in Venice* (after Thomas Mann; 1973).

brittle-star any member of the echinoderm class Ophiuroidea. A brittle-star resembles a starfish, and has a small, central, rounded body and long, flexible, spiny arms used for walking. The small brittle-star *Amphipholis squamata* is greyish, about 4.5 cm/2 in across, and found on sea bottoms worldwide. It broods its young, and its arms can be luminous.

broadbill primitive perching bird of the family Eurylaimidae, found in Africa and South Asia. Broadbills are forest birds and are often found near water. They are gregarious and noisy, have brilliant coloration and wide bills, and feed largely on insects.

broadcasting the transmission of sound and vision programmes by *radio and *television. Broadcasting may be organized under private enterprise, as in the USA, or may operate under a dual system, as in Britain, where a television and radio service controlled by the state-regulated *British Broadcasting Corporation (BBC) operates alongside commercial channels operating under franchises granted by the Independent Television Commission (known as the Independent Broadcasting Authority before 1991) and the Radio Authority.

broad-leaved tree another name for a tree belonging to the *angiosperms, such as ash, beech, oak, maple, or birch. The leaves are generally broad and flat, in contrast to the needlelike leaves of most *conifers. See also *deciduous tree.

Broads, Norfolk area of navigable lakes and rivers in England; see *Norfolk Broads.

Broadway major avenue in New York running northwest from the tip of Manhattan and crossing Times Square at 42nd Street, at the heart of the theatre district, where Broadway is known as 'the Great White Way'. New York theatres situated outside this area are described as **off-Broadway**; those even smaller and farther away are **off-off-Broadway**, the home of avant-garde and experimental works.

brocade rich woven fabric, produced on a Jacquard loom. It is patterned, normally with more than two colours. Today brocade may be produced from artificial fibres, but it was traditionally made from silk, sometimes with highlights in metal thread.

broccoli variety of *cabbage. It contains high levels of the glucosinolate compound glucoraphanin. A breakdown product of this was found to neutralize damage to cells and so help to prevent cancer.

Brodsky, Joseph Alexandrovich (1940–1996) Russian poet. He emigrated to the USA in 1972. His work, often dealing with themes of exile, is admired for its wit and economy of language, particularly in its use of understatement. Many of his poems, written in Russian, have been translated into English (*A Part of Speech* (1980)). Later in his career he also wrote in English. He was awarded the Nobel Prize for Literature in 1987 and became US poet laureate in 1991.

Broglie, Louis Victor Pierre Raymond de (1892–1987) 7th duc de Broglie, French theoretical physicist. He established that all subatomic particles can be described either by particle equations or by wave equations, thus laying the foundations of wave mechanics. He was awarded the Nobel Prize for Physics in 1929 for his discovery of the wavelike nature of electrons. Succeeded as Duke in 1960.

brome grass any of several annual grasses found in temperate regions; some are used as food for horses and cattle, but many are weeds. (Genus *Bromus*, family Gramineae.)

bromeliad any tropical or subtropical plant belonging to the pineapple family, usually with stiff leathery leaves, which are often coloured and patterned, and bright, attractive flower spikes. There are about 1,400 species in tropical America; several are cultivated as greenhouse plants. (Family Bromeliaceae.)

bromine chemical symbol Br, (Greek *bromos* 'stench') dark, reddish-brown, non-metallic element, a volatile liquid at room temperature, atomic number 35, relative atomic mass 79.904. It is a member of the *halogen group, has an unpleasant odour, and is very irritating to mucous membranes. Its salts are known as bromides.

bronchitis inflammation of the bronchi (air passages) of the lungs, usually caused initially by a viral infection, such as a cold or flu. It is aggravated by environmental pollutants, especially smoking, and results in a persistent cough, irritated mucus-secreting glands, and large amounts of sputum.

Brontë three English novelists, daughters of a Yorkshire parson. Charlotte Brontë (1816–1855), notably with *Jane Eyre* (1847) and *Villette* (1853), reshaped autobiographical material into vivid narrative. Emily Brontë (1818–1848) in *Wuthering Heights* (1847) expressed the intensity and nature mysticism which also pervades her poetry (*Poems*, 1846). The more modest talent of Anne Brontë (1820–1849) produced *Agnes Grey* (1847) and *The Tenant of Wildfell Hall* (1848).

brontosaurus former name of a type of large, plant-eating dinosaur, now better known as *apatosaurus.

bronze alloy of copper and tin, yellow or brown in colour. It is harder than pure copper, more suitable for casting, and also resists *corrosion. Bronze may contain as much as 25% tin, together with small amounts of other metals, mainly lead.

Bronze Age stage of prehistory and early history when copper and bronze (an alloy of tin and copper) became the first metals worked extensively and used for tools and weapons. One of the classifications of the Danish archaeologist Christian Thomsen's Three Age System, it developed out of the Stone Age and generally preceded the Iron Age. It first began in the Far East and may be dated 5000–1200 BC in the Middle East and about 2000–500 BC in Europe.

Brooke, Rupert (Chawner) (1887–1915) English poet. He stands as a symbol of the World War I 'lost generation'. His five war sonnets, including '*The Soldier*', were published after his death. Other notable poems are '*Grantchester*' (1912) and '*The Great Lover*', written in 1914. Brooke's war sonnets were published in *1914 and Other Poems* (1915); they caught the prevailing early wartime spirit of selfless patriotism.

Brookeborough, Basil Stanlake Brooke (1888–1973) Viscount Brookeborough, Northern Irish Unionist politician and prime minister 1943–63. He was born in Colebrook, County Fermanagh, and educated at Winchester and Sandhurst. A conservative unionist and staunch advocate of strong links with Britain, he entered the Northern Ireland House of Commons in 1929 and held ministerial posts 1933–45. His regime, particularly in the 1950s and 1960s, saw moderate improvements in economic prosperity and community relations but maintained an illiberal stance towards Northern Ireland's Catholic minority, and made no real attempt at significant political or economic reform.

Brooks, Louise (1906–1985) US actor. Her dark, enigmatic beauty can be seen in silent films such as *A Girl in Every Port* (1928), *Die Büchse der Pandora/Pandora's Box*, and *Das Tagebuch einer Verlorenen/The Diary of a Lost Girl* (both 1929), both directed by G W Pabst. At 25 she had appeared in 17 films. She retired from the screen in 1938.

broom any of a group of shrubs (especially species of *Cytisus* and *Spartium*), often cultivated for their bright yellow flowers. (Family Leguminosae.)

Brown, 'Capability' (Lancelot) (1716–1783) English landscape gardener and architect. He acquired his nickname because of his continual enthusiasm for the 'capabilities' of natural landscapes. He worked on or improved the gardens of many great houses and estates, including Hampton Court; Kew; Blenheim, Oxfordshire; Stowe, Buckinghamshire; and Petworth, West Sussex, occasionally contributing to the architectural designs.

Brown, Ford Madox (1821–1893) English painter, associated with the *Pre-Raphaelite Brotherhood through his pupil Dante Gabriel Rossetti. His pictures, which include *The Last of England* (1855; City Art Gallery, Birmingham) and *Work* (1852–65; City Art Gallery, Manchester), are characterized by elaborate symbolism and abundance of realistic detail.

Brown, (James) Gordon (1951–) British Labour politician, born in Scotland, chancellor of the Exchequer from 1997. He entered Parliament in 1993, rising quickly to the opposition front bench, with a reputation as an outstanding debater. His cautious economic policies as chancellor has led to a period of economic stability.

Brown, John (1800–1859) US slavery abolitionist. With 18 men, on the night of 16 October 1859, he seized the government arsenal at *Harpers Ferry in West Virginia, apparently intending to distribute weapons to runaway slaves who would then defend a mountain stronghold, which Brown hoped would become a republic of former slaves. On 18 October the arsenal was stormed by US Marines under Col Robert E *Lee. Brown was tried and hanged at Charlestown on 2 December, becoming a martyr and the hero of the popular song 'John Brown's Body'.

brown dwarf in astronomy, object less massive than a star but denser than a planet. Brown dwarfs do not have enough mass to ignite nuclear reactions at their centres, but shine by heat released during their contraction from a gas cloud. Groups of brown dwarfs have been discovered, and some astronomers believe that vast numbers of them exist throughout the Galaxy.

Browne, Thomas (1605–1682) English writer and physician. His works display a richness of style and an enquiring mind. They include *Religio medici/ The Religion of a Doctor* (1643), a justification of his profession; 'Vulgar Errors' (1646), an examination of popular legend and superstition; and *Urn Burial* and *The Garden of Cyrus* (both 1658).

Browning, Elizabeth (Moulton) Barrett (1806–1861) English poet. In 1844 she published *Poems* (including 'The Cry of the Children'), which led to her friendship with and secret marriage to Robert *Browning in 1846. She wrote *Sonnets from the Portuguese* (1850), a collection of love lyrics, during their courtship. She wrote strong verse about social injustice and oppression in Victorian England, and she was a learned, fiery, and metrically experimental poet.

Browning, Robert (1812–1889) English poet. His work is characterized by the accomplished use of dramatic monologue (in which a single imaginary speaker reveals his or her character, thoughts, and situation) and an interest in obscure literary and historical figures. It includes *Pippa Passes* (1841) (written in dramatic form) and the poems 'The Pied Piper of Hamelin' (1842), 'My Last Duchess' (1842), 'Home Thoughts from Abroad' (1845), and 'Rabbi Ben Ezra' (1864). He was married to Elizabeth Barrett *Browning.

Brownshirts the SA (*Sturmabteilung*) or Storm Troops, the private army of the German Nazi party, who derived their name from the colour of their uniform.

Bruce one of the chief Scottish noble houses. *Robert (I) the Bruce and his son, David II, were both kings of Scotland descended from Robert de Bruis (died 1094), a Norman knight who arrived in England with William the Conqueror in 1066.

Bruce, James (1730–1794) Scottish explorer who, in 1770, was the first European to reach the source of the Blue Nile and, in 1773, to follow the river downstream to Cairo.

Bruce, Robert King of Scotland; see *Robert (I) the Bruce.

brucellosis disease of cattle, goats, and pigs, also known when transmitted to humans as **undulant fever** since it remains in the body and recurs. It was named after Australian doctor David Bruce (1855–1931), and is caused by bacteria (genus *Brucella*). It is transmitted by contact with an infected animal or by drinking contaminated milk.

Bruckner, (Josef) Anton (1824–1896) Austrian Romantic composer. He was cathedral organist at Linz 1856–68, and professor at the Vienna Conservatory from 1868. His works include many choral pieces and 11 symphonies, the last unfinished. His compositions were influenced by Richard Wagner and Ludwig van Beethoven.

Brueghel (or Bruegel) family of Flemish painters. **Pieter Brueghel the Elder** (*c.* 1525–1569) was one of the greatest artists of his time. His pictures of peasant life helped to establish genre painting, and he also popularized works illustrating proverbs, such as *The Blind Leading the Blind* (1568; Museo di Capodimonte, Naples). A contemporary taste for the macabre can be seen in *The Triumph of Death* (1562; Prado, Madrid), which clearly shows the influence of Hieronymus Bosch. One of his best-known works is *Hunters in the Snow* (1565; Kunsthistorisches Museum, Vienna).

Brundtland, Gro Harlem (1939–) Norwegian Labour politician, prime minister 1981, 1986–89 and 1990–96 and director-general (head) of the World Health Organization (WHO) 1998–2003. She entered politics in 1974, when invited to become environment minister (to 1976), and became the country's first female major party leader and prime minister in 1981. She held office as prime minister for 7 months in 1981 and returned to office in 1986. Her government was forced to push through austerity measures, after the collapse of world petroleum prices. She resigned as leader of the Norwegian Labour Party in 1992 but continued as prime minister. From 1993, she led a' minority Labour government committed to European Union membership, but failed to secure backing for the membership application in a 1994 national referendum and resigned as prime minister in 1996.

Brunei

National name: *Negara Brunei Darussalam/State of Brunei*

Area: 5,765 sq km/2,225 sq mi
Capital: Bandar Seri Begawan (and chief port)
Major towns/cities: Seria, Kuala Belait
Physical features: flat coastal plain with hilly lowland in west and mountains in east (Mount Pagon 1,850 m/6,070 ft); 75% of the area is forested; the Limbang valley splits Brunei in two, and its cession to Sarawak in 1890 is disputed by Brunei; tropical climate; Temburong, Tutong, and Belait rivers
Head of state and government: Sultan Muda Hassanal Bolkiah from 1967
Political system: absolutist
Political executive: absolute
Political parties: Brunei National Democratic Party (BNDP) and Brunei People's Party (BPP) (both banned); Brunei National United Party (BNUP) (inactive)
Currency: Bruneian dollar, although the Singapore dollar is also accepted
GNI per capita (PPP): (US$) 25,320 (2000 est)
Exports: crude petroleum, natural gas and refined products, textiles. Principal market: Japan 43.6% (2001)
Population: 358,000 (2003 est)
Language: Malay (official), Chinese (Hokkien), English
Religion: Muslim 66%, Buddhist 14%, Christian 10%
Life expectancy: 74 (men); 79 (women) (2000–05)
Chronology
15th century: An Islamic monarchy was established, ruling Brunei and north Borneo, including the Sabah and Sarawak states of Malaysia.
1841: Control of Sarawak was lost.
1888: Brunei became a British protectorate.
1906: Brunei became a British dependency.
1929: Oil was discovered.
1941–45: Brunei was occupied by Japan.
1959: A written constitution made Britain responsible for defence and external affairs.

1962: The sultan began rule by decree after a plan to join the Federation of Malaysia was opposed by a rebellion organized by the Brunei People's Party (BPP).
1967: Hassanal Bolkiah became sultan.
1971: Brunei was given full internal self-government.
1975: A United Nations (UN) resolution called for independence for Brunei.
1984: Independence from Britain was achieved, with Britain maintaining a small force to protect the oil and gas fields.
1985: The Brunei National Democratic Party (BNDP) was legalized.
1986: The multiethnic Brunei National United Party (BNUP) was formed; nonroyals were given key cabinet posts for the first time.
1988: The BNDP and the BNUP were banned.
1991: Brunei joined the nonaligned movement.
1998: Prince Billah was proclaimed heir to the throne.
2000: The government announced plans to retrain as much as a quarter of the workforce to develop alternative industries to oil.
2004: After more than 20 years, a new parliament was created, with 21 appointed members. The constitution was amended to allow the direct election of 15 members for the next parliament.

Brunel, Isambard Kingdom (1806–1859) English engineer and inventor. In 1833 he became engineer to the Great Western Railway, which adopted the 2.1-m/7-ft gauge on his advice. He built the Clifton Suspension Bridge over the River Avon at Bristol and the Saltash Bridge over the River Tamar near Plymouth. His shipbuilding designs include the *Great Western* (1837), the first steamship to cross the Atlantic regularly; the *Great Britain* (1843), the first large iron ship to have a screw propeller; and the *Great Eastern* (1858), which laid the first transatlantic telegraph cable.

Brunel, Marc Isambard (1769–1849) French-born British engineer and inventor, father of Isambard Kingdom Brunel. He constructed the tunnel under the River Thames in London from Wapping to Rotherhithe (1825–43). He was knighted in 1841.

Brunelleschi, Filippo (1377–1446) Italian Renaissance architect. The first and one of the greatest of the Renaissance architects, he pioneered the scientific use of perspective. He was responsible for the construction of the dome of Florence Cathedral (completed 1436), a feat deemed impossible by many of his contemporaries.

Bruno, Giordano (1548–1600) born Filippo Bruno, Italian philosopher. He entered the Dominican order of monks in 1563, but his sceptical attitude to Catholic doctrines forced him to flee Italy in 1577. He was arrested by the *Inquisition in 1593 in Venice and burned at the stake for his adoption of Copernican astronomy and his heretical religious views.

Bruno, St (c. 1030–1101) German founder of the monastic Catholic *Carthusian order. He was born in Cologne, became a priest, and controlled the cathedral school of Rheims from 1057 to 1076. Withdrawing to the mountains near Grenoble after an ecclesiastical controversy, he founded the monastery at Chartreuse in 1084. He was canonized in 1514. His feast day is 6 October.

Brussels Flemish **Brussel**; French **Bruxelles**, city and capital of Belgium, and of Brabant province, situated almost in the centre of the country in the Senne river valley at the junction of the Charleroi-Brussels and Willebroek canals; city population (2003 est) 981,200, urban agglomeration 1,750,600. Industries include lace, textiles, pharmaceuticals, electronics, processed food, machinery, and chemicals. It is the headquarters of the European Union (EU) and, since 1967, of the international secretariat of NATO. It contains the Belgian royal seat, the chief courts, the chamber of commerce, and is the centre of the principal banks of the country. Founded on an island in the River Senne *c.* 580, Brussels became a city in 1312, and was declared capital of the Spanish Netherlands in 1530 and of Belgium in 1830. The city is officially bilingual (French and Flemish).

Brussels sprout one of the small edible buds along the stem of a variety of *cabbage. (*Brassica oleracea* var. *gemmifera*.) They are high in the glucosinolate compound sinigrin. Sinigrin was found to destroy precancerous cells in laboratory rats in 1996.

Brussels, Treaty of pact of an economic, political, cultural, and military alliance established in 17 March 1948, for 50 years, by the UK, France, and the Benelux countries, joined by West Germany and Italy in 1955. It was the forerunner of the North Atlantic Treaty Organization and the European Community (now the European Union).

brutalism architectural style of the 1950s and 1960s that evolved from the work of Le Corbusier and Mies van der Rohe. It is uncompromising in its approach, believing that practicality and user-friendliness should be the first and foremost aims of architectural design. Materials such as steel and concrete are favoured.

Brutus, Marcus Junius (*c.* 85 BC–42 BC) Roman senator and general who conspired with *Cassius to assassinate Julius *Caesar in order to restore the purity of the Republic. He and Cassius were defeated by the united forces of *Mark Antony and Octavian at Philippi in 42 BC, and Brutus committed suicide.

bryony either of two climbing hedgerow plants found in Britain: **white bryony** (*Bryonia dioca*) belonging to the gourd family (Cucurbitaceae), and **black bryony** (*Tamus communis*) of the yam family (Dioscoreaceae).

bryophyte member of the Bryophyta, a division of the plant kingdom containing three classes: the Hepaticae (*liverwort), Musci (*moss), and Anthocerotae (*hornwort). Bryophytes are generally small, low-growing, terrestrial plants with no vascular (water-conducting) system as in higher plants. Their life cycle shows a marked *alternation of generations. Bryophytes chiefly occur in damp habitats and require water for the dispersal of the male gametes (antherozoids).

bubble chamber in physics, a device for observing the nature and movement of atomic particles, and their interaction with radiation. It is a vessel filled with a superheated liquid through which ionizing particles move and collide. The paths of these particles are shown by strings of bubbles, which can be photographed and studied. By using a pressurized liquid medium instead of a gas, it overcomes drawbacks inherent in the earlier *cloud chamber. It was invented by US physicist Donald Glaser in 1952. See *particle detector.

bubonic plague epidemic disease of the Middle Ages; see *plague and *Black Death.

buccaneer member of any of various groups of seafarers who plundered Spanish ships and colonies on the Spanish American coast in the 17th century. Unlike true pirates, they were acting on (sometimes spurious) commission.

Buchan, John (1875–1940) 1st Baron Tweedsmuir, Scottish writer and politician. His popular adventure stories, today sometimes criticized for their alleged snobbery, sexism, and anti-Semitism, include *The Thirty-Nine Steps*, a tale of espionage published in 1915, *Greenmantle* (1916), and *The Three Hostages* (1924).

Bucharest Romanian **Bucuresti**, capital and largest city of Romania; population (1993) 2,343,800. The conurbation of Bucharest district has an area of 1,520 sq km/587 sq mi. It was originally a citadel built by Vlad the Impaler (see *Dracula) to stop the advance of the Ottoman invasion in the 14th century. Bucharest became the capital of the princes of Wallachia in 1698 and of Romania in 1861. Savage fighting took place in the city during Romania's 1989 revolution.

Buchenwald site of a Nazi *concentration camp from 1937 to 1945 at a village northeast of Weimar, eastern Germany.

Buck, Linda (1947–) US neuroscientist. With US neuroscientist Richard Axel she shared the Nobel Prize for Physiology or Medicine in 2004 for her contributions to understanding how the olfactory system is able to recognize and differentiate between different smells.

Buck, Pearl S(ydenstricker) (1892–1973) US novelist. Daughter of missionaries to China, she spent much of her life there and wrote novels about Chinese life, such as *East Wind–West Wind* (1930) and *The Good Earth* (1931), for which she received a Pulitzer Prize in 1932. She was awarded the Nobel Prize for Literature in 1938.

Buckingham, George Villiers, 1st Duke of Buckingham (1592–1628) English courtier, adviser to James I and later Charles I. After Charles's accession, Buckingham attempted to form a Protestant coalition in Europe, which led to war with France; however, he failed to relieve the Protestants (*Huguenots) besieged in La Rochelle in 1627. His policy on the French Protestants was attacked in Parliament, and when about to sail for La Rochelle for a second time, he was assassinated in Portsmouth.

Buckingham, George Villiers, 2nd Duke of Buckingham (1628–1687) English politician, a member of the *Cabal under Charles II. A dissolute son of the first duke, he was brought up with the royal children. His play *The Rehearsal* satirized the style of the poet Dryden, who portrayed him as Zimri in *Absalom and Achitophel*. He succeeded to the dukedom in 1628.

Buckinghamshire county of southeast central England. **area:** 1,565 sq km/604 sq mi **towns:** Aylesbury (administrative headquarters), Beaconsfield, Buckingham, High Wycombe, Olney **physical:** Chiltern Hills; Vale of Aylesbury **features:** *Chequers (country seat of the prime minister); the church of the poet Thomas Gray's 'Elegy' at Stoke Poges; Bletchley Park, home of World War II code-breaking activities, formerly used as a training post for GCHQ (Britain's electronic surveillance centre); homes of the poets William Cowper at Olney and John Milton at Chalfont

St Giles, and of the Tory prime minister Disraeli at Hughenden Valley; grave of William Penn, Quaker founder of Pennsylvania, at Jordans near Chalfont St Giles. **population:** (2001 est) 479,000.

buckminsterfullerene form of carbon, made up of molecules (buckyballs) consisting of 60 carbon atoms arranged in 12 pentagons and 20 hexagons to form a perfect sphere. It was named after the US architect and engineer Richard Buckminster Fuller because of its structural similarity to the geodesic dome that he designed. See *fullerene.

buckthorn any of several thorny shrubs. The buckthorn (*Rhamnus catharticus*) is native to Britain, but is also found throughout Europe, West Asia, and North Africa. Its berries were formerly used in medicine as a purgative, to clean out the bowels. (Genus *Rhamnus*, family Rhamnaceae.)

buckwheat any of a group of cereal plants. The name usually refers to *Fagopyrum esculentum*, which reaches about 1 m/3 ft in height and can grow on poor soil in a short summer. The highly nutritious black triangular seeds (groats) are eaten by both animals and humans. They can be cooked and eaten whole or as a cracked meal (kasha), or ground into flour, often made into pancakes. (Genus *Fagopyrum*, family Polygonaceae.)

bud undeveloped shoot usually enclosed by protective scales; inside is a very short stem and numerous undeveloped leaves, or flower parts, or both. Terminal buds are found at the tips of shoots, while axillary buds develop in the axils of the leaves, often remaining dormant unless the terminal bud is removed or damaged. Adventitious buds may be produced anywhere on the plant, their formation sometimes stimulated by an injury, such as that caused by pruning.

Budapest capital of Hungary, industrial city (chemicals, textiles) on the River Danube; population (1993 est) 2,009,000. Buda, on the right bank of the Danube, became the Hungarian capital in 1867 and was joined with Pest, on the left bank, in 1872.

Buddha (c. 563–483 BC) born Prince Siddartha Gautama, (Sanskrit 'enlightened one') Religious leader, founder of *Buddhism, born at Lumbini in Nepal, and raised in his father's palace at Kapilavastu. At the age of 29 he left his wife and son and a life of luxury, to resolve the problems of existence. After six years of austerity he realized that asceticism, like overindulgence, was futile, and chose the Middle Way of meditation. He became enlightened under a bo, or bodhi, tree near Bodhgaya in Bihar, India. He began teaching at Varanasi, Uttar Pradesh, and founded the *Sangha, or order of monks. He spent the rest of his life travelling around northern India, and died at Kusinagara. He is not a god.

Buddhism one of the great world religions, which originated in India in the 5th century BC. It derives from the teaching of the *Buddha, who is regarded as one of a series of such enlightened beings. The chief doctrine is that all phenomena share three characteristics: they are impermanent, unsatisfactory, and lack a permanent essence (such as a soul). All beings, including gods, are subject to these characteristics, but can achieve freedom through enlightenment. The main forms of Buddhism are *Theravada (or Hinayana) in Southeast Asia and *Mahayana in North and East Asia; *Lamaism in Tibet and *Zen in Japan are among the many Mahayana

forms of Buddhism. There are over 350 million Buddhists worldwide (2000).

buddleia any of a group of ornamental shrubs or trees with spikes of fragrant flowers. The purple or white flower heads of the butterfly bush (*Buddleia davidii*) attract large numbers of butterflies. (Genus *Buddleia*, family Buddleiaceae.)

budgerigar small Australian parakeet *Melopsittacus undulatus* of the parrot family, Psittacidae, order Psittaciformes, that feeds mainly on grass seeds. In the wild, it has a bright green body and a blue tail with yellow flares; yellow, white, blue, and mauve varieties have been bred for the pet market. Budgerigars breed freely in captivity.

Buenos Aires industrial city, chief port, and capital of Argentina, situated in the 'Capital Federal' – a separate federal district, on the south bank of the Río de la Plata, at its estuary; population (2001 est) 13,756,000. Industries include motor vehicles, engineering, oil, chemicals, textiles, paper, and food processing. Main exports are grain, beef, and wool, which are produced in the surrounding pampas. The administrative Federal District of Buenos Aires has an area of 200 sq km/77 sq mi and a population of (2001 est) 2,729,500. Buenos Aires is the financial and cultural centre of Argentina, and has many museums and libraries. It is a major railway terminus, and has an international airport 35 km/22 mi southwest of the city centre.

buffalo either of two species of wild cattle. The Asiatic water buffalo *Bubalis bubalis* is found domesticated throughout South Asia and wild in parts of India and Nepal. It likes moist conditions. Usually grey or black, up to 1.8 m/6 ft tall, both sexes carry large horns. The African buffalo *Syncerus caffer* is found in Africa, south of the Sahara, where there is grass, water, and cover in which to retreat. There are a number of subspecies, the biggest up to 1.6 m/5 ft tall, and black, with massive horns set close together over the head. The name is also commonly applied to the North American *bison.

bug in computing, an *error in a program. It can be an error in the logical structure of a program or a syntax error, such as a spelling mistake. Some bugs cause a program to fail immediately; others remain dormant, causing problems only when a particular combination of events occurs. The process of finding and removing errors from a program is called **debugging**.

bug in entomology, an insect belonging to the order Hemiptera. All these have two pairs of wings with forewings partly thickened. They also have piercing mouthparts adapted for sucking the juices of plants or animals, the 'beak' being tucked under the body when not in use.

bugle compact valveless treble brass instrument with a shorter tube and less flared bell than the trumpet. Constructed of copper plated with brass, it has long been used as a military instrument for giving a range of signals based on the tones of a harmonic series. The bugle has a conical bore whereas the trumpet is cylindrical.

bugle any of a group of low-growing plants belonging to the mint family, with spikes of white, pink, or blue flowers. The leaves may be smooth-edged or slightly toothed, the lower ones with a long stalk. They are often grown as ground cover. (Genus *Ajuga*, family Labiatae.)

bugloss any of several plants native to Europe and Asia, distinguished by their rough, bristly leaves and small blue flowers. (Genera *Anchusa*, *Lycopsis*, and *Echium*, family Boraginaceae.)

Bujumbura formerly **Usumbura** (until 1962), capital of Burundi, located at the northeastern end of Lake Tanganyika; population (1996 est) 300,000. Bujumbura is the main banking and financial centre of Burundi; industries include food processing and paint manufacture. It was founded in 1899 by German colonists, and a university was established in 1960.

Bukhara or **Bokhara** or **Bukhoro** city in south-central Uzbekistan, on the Zerevshan River 220 km/137 mi east of Samarkand; population (1999 est) 237,900. A historic city with over 140 protected buildings, it was once the heart of Muslim Central Asia, and second only to Mecca as an Islamic holy site. It is the capital of the Bukhara province of Uzbekistan, which has given its name to a type of handwoven carpet. Textiles, including rugs and carpets, are manufactured here (though 'Bukhara' carpets are now principally made in *Ashgabat, in Turkmenistan). Natural gas is extracted in the surrounding region, and cotton is grown extensively.

Bukharin, Nikolai Ivanovich (1888–1938) Soviet politician and theorist. A moderate, he was the chief Bolshevik thinker after Lenin. Executed on Stalin's orders for treason in 1938, he was posthumously rehabilitated in 1988.

bulb underground bud with fleshy leaves containing a reserve food supply and with roots growing from its base. Bulbs function in vegetative reproduction and are characteristic of many monocotyledonous plants such as the daffodil, snowdrop, and onion. Bulbs are grown on a commercial scale in temperate countries, such as England and the Netherlands.

bulbul fruit-eating bird of the family Pycnonotidae, order Passeriformes, that ranges in size from that of a sparrow to a blackbird. They are mostly rather dull coloured and very secretive, living in dense forests. They are widely distributed throughout Africa and Asia; there are about 120 species.

Bulganin, Nikolai Aleksandrovich (1895–1975) Soviet politician and military leader. His career began in 1918 when he joined the Cheka, the Soviet secret police. He helped to organize Moscow's defences in World War II, became a marshal of the USSR in 1947, and was minister of defence 1947–49 and 1953–55. On the fall of Georgi Malenkov he became prime minister (chair of the council of ministers) 1955–58 until ousted by Nikita Khrushchev.

Bulgaria
National name: *Republika Bulgaria/Republic of Bulgaria*
Area: 110,912 sq km/42,823 sq mi
Capital: Sofia
Major towns/cities: Plovdiv, Varna, Ruse, Burgas, Stara Zagora, Pleven
Major ports: Burgas, Varna
Physical features: lowland plains in north and southeast separated by mountains (Balkan and Rhodope) that cover three-quarters of the country; River Danube in north
Head of state: Georgi Parvanov from 2001
Head of government: Simeon Koburgotski from 2001
Political system: emergent democracy
Political executive: parliamentary

Political parties: Union of Democratic Forces (UDF), right of centre; Bulgarian Socialist Party (BSP), left wing, ex-communist; Movement for Rights and Freedoms (MRF), Turkish-oriented, centrist; Civic Alliances for the Republic (CAR), left of centre; Real Reform Movement (DESIR)
Currency: lev
GNI per capita (PPP): (US$) 6,840 (2002 est)
Exports: base metals, chemical and rubber products, processed food, beverages, tobacco, chemicals, textiles, footwear. Principal market: Italy 15% (2001)
Population: 7,897,000 (2003 est)
Language: Bulgarian (official), Turkish
Religion: Eastern Orthodox Christian, Muslim, Jewish, Roman Catholic, Protestant
Life expectancy: 67 (men); 75 (women) (2000–05)
Chronology
c. **3500 BC onwards:** Semi-nomadic pastoralists from the central Asian steppes settled in the area and formed the Thracian community.
mid-5th century BC: The Thracian state was formed; it was to extend over Bulgaria, northern Greece, and northern Turkey.
4th century BC: Phillip II and Alexander the Great of Macedonia waged largely unsuccessful campaigns against the Thracian Empire.
AD 50: The Thracians were subdued and incorporated within the Roman Empire as the province of Moesia Inferior.
3rd–6th centuries: The Thracian Empire was successively invaded and devastated by the Goths, Huns, Bulgars, and Avars.
681: The Bulgars, an originally Turkic group that had merged with earlier Slav settlers, revolted against the Avars and established, south of the River Danube, the first Bulgarian kingdom, with its capital at Pliska.
864: Orthodox Christianity was adopted by Boris I.
1018: Subjugated by the Byzantines, whose empire had its capital at Constantinople; led to Bulgarian Church breaking with Rome in 1054.
1185: Second independent Bulgarian Kingdom formed.
mid-13th century: Bulgarian state destroyed by Mongol incursions.

1396: Bulgaria became the first European state to be absorbed into the Turkish Ottoman Empire; the imposition of a harsh feudal system and the sacking of the monasteries followed.

1859: The Bulgarian Catholic Church re-established links with Rome.

1876: A Bulgarian nationalist revolt against Ottoman rule was crushed brutally by Ottomans, with 15,000 massacred at Plovdiv ('Bulgarian Atrocities').

1878: At the Congress of Berlin, concluding a Russo-Turkish war in which Bulgarian volunteers had fought alongside the Russians, the area south of the Balkans, Eastern Rumelia, remained an Ottoman province, but the area to the north became the autonomous Principality of Bulgaria, with a liberal constitution and Alexander Battenberg as prince.

1885: Eastern Rumelia annexed by the Principality; Serbia defeated in war.

1908: Full independence proclaimed from Turkish rule, with Ferdinand I as tsar.

1913: Following defeat in the Second Balkan War, King Ferdinand I abdicated and was replaced by his son Boris III.

1919: Bulgarian Agrarian Union government, led by Alexander Stamboliiski, came to power and redistributed land to poor peasants.

1923: Agrarian government was overthrown in right-wing coup and Stamboliiski murdered.

1934: A semifascist dictatorship was established by King Boris III.

1944: Soviet invasion of German-occupied Bulgaria.

1946: The monarchy was abolished and a communist-dominated people's republic proclaimed following a plebiscite.

1947: Gained South Dobruja in the northeast, along the Black Sea, from Romania; Soviet-style constitution established a one-party state; industries and financial institutions were nationalized and cooperative farming introduced.

1954: Bulgaria became a loyal and cautious satellite of the USSR.

1968: Bulgaria participated in the Soviet-led invasion of Czechoslovakia.

1971: A new constitution was introduced.

1985–89: Haphazard administrative and economic reforms, known as *preustroistvo* ('restructuring'), were introduced under the stimulus of the reformist Soviet leader Mikhail Gorbachev.

1989: A programme of enforced 'Bulgarianization' resulted in a mass exodus of ethnic Turks to Turkey. Opposition parties were tolerated.

1991: A new liberal-democratic constitution was adopted. The first noncommunist government was formed.

1993: A voucher-based 'mass privatization' programme was launched.

1996: Radical economic and industrial reforms were imposed. There was mounting inflation and public protest at the state of the economy.

1997: There was a general strike. The UDF leader Ivan Kostov became prime minister. The Bulgarian currency was pegged to the Deutschmark in return for support from the International Monetary Fund. A new political group, the Real Reform Movement (DESIR), was formed.

1999: Bulgaria joined the Central European Free Trade Agreement (CEFTA).

2002: Bulgaria was invited to join NATO.

2004: Bulgaria was admitted to Nato.

2005: Bulgaria signed the Treaty of Accession to the European Union (EU), for planned admission to the EU in 2007.

Bulgarian an ethnic group living mainly in Bulgaria. There are 8–8.5 million speakers of Bulgarian, a Slavic language belonging to the Indo-European family. The Bulgarians use the Cyrillic alphabet.

Bulge, Battle of the *or* **Ardennes offensive** in World War II, Hitler's plan (code-named 'Watch on the Rhine') for a breakthrough by his field marshal Gerd von *Rundstedt, aimed at the US line in the Ardennes from 16 December 1944 to 28 January 1945. Hitler aimed to isolate the Allied forces north of the corridor which would be created by a drive through the Ardennes, creating a German salient (prominent part of a line of attack, also known as a 'bulge'). There were 77,000 Allied casualties and 130,000 German, including Hitler's last powerful reserve of elite Panzer units. Although US troops were encircled for some weeks at Bastogne, the German counter-offensive failed.

bulgur wheat *or* **bulgar** *or* **burghul** cracked whole wheat, made by cooking the grains, then drying and cracking them. It is widely eaten in the Middle East. Coarse bulgur may be cooked in the same way as rice; more finely ground bulgur is mixed with minced meat to make a paste that may be eaten as a dip with salad, or shaped and stuffed before being grilled or fried.

bulimia (Greek 'ox hunger') eating disorder in which large amounts of food are consumed in a short time ('binge'), usually followed by depression and self-criticism. The term is often used for **bulimia nervosa**, an emotional disorder in which eating is followed by deliberate vomiting and purging. This may be a chronic stage in *anorexia nervosa.

bull in business, trader in financial market who believes the market is going to rise. Such positive sentiments are said to be bullish. A bull is the opposite of a *bear. In a bull market, prices fall and bears prosper.

bull *or* **papal bull** document or edict issued by the pope; so called from the circular seals (medieval Latin *bulla*) attached to them. Some of the most celebrated bulls include Leo X's condemnation of Luther in 1520 and Pius IX's proclamation of papal infallibility in 1870.

Bull, John imaginary figure personifying England; see *John Bull.

bulldog British breed of dog of ancient but uncertain origin, formerly bred for bull-baiting. The head is broad and square, with deeply wrinkled cheeks, small folded ears, very short muzzle, and massive jaws, the peculiar set of the lower jaw making it difficult for the dog to release its grip. Thickset in build, the bulldog grows to about 45 cm/18 in and has a smooth beige, tawny, or brindle coat. The French bulldog is much lighter in build and has large upright ears.

bull fighting the national sport of Spain (where there are more than 400 bullrings), which is also popular in Mexico, Portugal, and much of Latin America. It involves the ritualized taunting of a bull in a circular ring, until its eventual death at the hands of the matador (bullfighter). Originally popular in Greece and Rome, it was introduced into Spain by the Moors in the 11th century.

bullfinch Eurasian finch with a thick head and neck, and short heavy bill, genus *Pyrrhula pyrrhula*, family Fringillidae, order Passeriformes. It is small and blue-grey or black in colour, the males being reddish and the females brown on the breast. Bullfinches are 15 cm/6 in long, and usually seen in pairs. They feed on tree buds as well as seeds and berries, and are usually seen in woodland. They also live in the Aleutians and on the Alaska mainland.

bullroarer *or* **whizzer** *or* **whizzing stick** *or* **lightning stick** musical instrument used by Australian Aborigines for communication and during religious rites. It consists of a weighted aerofoil (a rectangular slat of wood about 15 cm/6 in to 60 cm/24 in long and about 1.25 cm/0.5 in to 5 cm/2 in wide) whirled rapidly about the head on a long cord to make a deep whirring noise. It is also used in many other parts of the world, including Britain.

Bull Run, battles of in the American Civil War, two victories for the Confederate army under General Robert E Lee at **Manassas** Junction, northeastern Virginia, named after the stream where they took place: **First Battle of Bull Run** 21 July 1861; **Second Battle of Bull Run** 29–30 August 1862. The battles are known as the Battle of Manassas in the southern states.

bull terrier breed of dog, originating as a cross between a terrier and a bulldog. Very powerfully built, it grows to about 40 cm/16 in tall, and has a short, usually white, coat, narrow eyes, and distinctive egg-shaped head. It was formerly used in bull-baiting. Pit bull terriers are used in illegal dog fights. The Staffordshire bull terrier is a distinct breed.

bulrush either of two plants: the great reed mace or cat's tail (*Typha latifolia*) with velvety chocolate-brown spikes of tightly packed flowers reaching up to 15 cm/6 in long; and a type of sedge (*Scirpus lacustris*) with tufts of reddish-brown flowers at the top of a rounded, rushlike stem.

bumblebee any large *bee, 2–5 cm/1–2 in, usually dark-coloured but banded with yellow, orange, or white, belonging to the genus *Bombus*.

Bunker Hill, Battle of the first significant engagement in the *American Revolution, on 17 June 1775, near a small hill in Charlestown (now part of Boston), Massachusetts; the battle actually took place on Breed's Hill, but is named after Bunker Hill as this was the more significant of the two. Although the colonists were defeated, they were able to retreat to Boston in good order.

Bunsen burner gas burner used in laboratories, consisting of a vertical metal tube through which a fine jet of fuel gas is directed. Air is drawn in through airholes near the base of the tube and the mixture is ignited and burns at the tube's upper opening.

Buñuel, Luis (1900–1983) Spanish-born film director. He is widely considered one of the giants of European art cinema, responsible for such enduring classics as *Los olvidados/The Young and the Damned* (1950), *Viridiana* (1961), *Belle de jour* (1966), and *Le Charme discret de la bourgeoisie/The Discreet Charm of the Bourgeoisie* (1972).

Bunyan, John (1628–1688) English writer, author of *The *Pilgrim's Progress* (first part 1678, second part 1684), one of the best-known English religious allegories (a symbolic story with meaning beyond its literal reading).

bur *or* **burr** in botany, a type of 'false fruit' or *pseudocarp, surrounded by numerous hooks; for instance, that of burdock *Arctium*, where the hooks are formed from bracts surrounding the flowerhead. Burs catch in the feathers or fur of passing animals, and thus may be dispersed over considerable distances.

burbot *or* **eelpout** long, rounded fish *Lota lota* of the cod family, the only one living entirely in fresh water. Up to 1 m/3 ft long, it lives on the bottom of clear lakes and rivers, often in holes or under rocks, throughout Europe, Asia, and North America.

burdock any of several bushy herbs characterized by hairy leaves and ripe fruit enclosed in *burs with strong hooks. (Genus *Arctium*, family Compositae.)

bureaucracy organization whose structure and operations are governed to a high degree by written rules and a hierarchy of offices; in its broadest sense, all forms of administration, and in its narrowest, rule by officials.

Burgenland federal state of southeast Austria, extending south from the Danube along the western border of the Hungarian plain, bordering Lower Austria in the northwest and Styria in the southwest; area 3,965 sq km/1,531 sq mi; population (2001 est) 278,600. Its capital is Eisenstadt.

Burgess, Anthony (1917–1993) pen-name of John Anthony Burgess Wilson, English novelist, critic, and composer. A prolific and versatile writer, Burgess wrote about 60 books as well as screenplays, television scripts, and reviews. His work includes *A Clockwork Orange* (1962) (made into a film by Stanley Kubrick in 1971), a despairing depiction of high technology and violence set in a future London terrorized by teenage gangs, and the panoramic *Earthly Powers* (1980).

burgh *or* **burh** *or* **borough** archaic form of *borough.

burgh former unit of Scottish local government, referring to a town enjoying a degree of self-government. Burghs were abolished in 1975; the terms **burgh** and **royal burgh** once gave mercantile privilege but are now only an honorary distinction.

Burghley, William Cecil, 1st Baron Burghley (1520–1598) English politician, chief adviser to Elizabeth I as secretary of state from 1558 and Lord High Treasurer from 1572. He was largely responsible for the religious settlement of 1559, and took a leading role in the events preceding the execution of Mary Queen of Scots in 1587.

burglary offence committed when a trespasser enters a building intending to steal, do damage to property, grievously harm any person, or rape a woman. Entry needs only be effective so, for example, a person who puts their hand through a broken shop window to steal something may be guilty of burglary.

Burgundy ancient kingdom in the valleys of the rivers Rhône and Saône in eastern France and southwestern Germany, partly corresponding with modern-day Burgundy. Settled by the Teutonic Burgundi around AD 443, and brought under Frankish control in AD 534, Burgundy played a central role in the medieval history of northwestern Europe.

Burgundy French **Bourgogne**, modern region and former duchy of east-central France that includes the *départements* of Ain, Côte-d'Or, Nièvre, Saône-et-Loire, and Yonne; area 31,582 sq km/12,194 sq mi; population (1999 est) 1,610,100. Its administrative centre is Dijon.

Burke, Edmund (1729–1797) British Whig politician and political theorist, born in Dublin, Ireland. During a parliamentary career spanning more than 30 years, he was famous for opposing the government's attempts to coerce the American colonists, for example in *Thoughts on the Present Discontents* (1770), and for supporting the emancipation of Ireland. However, he was a vehement opponent of the French Revolution, which he denounced in *Reflections on the Revolution in France* (1790), and attacked the suggestion of peace with France in *Letters on a Regicide Peace* (1795–97).

Burke, Robert O'Hara (1821–1861) Irish-born Australian explorer who in 1860–61 made the first south–north crossing of Australia (from Victoria to the Gulf of Carpentaria), with William Wills (1834–1861). Both died on the return journey, and only one of their party survived.

Burkina Faso

formerly **Upper Volta** (until 1984)

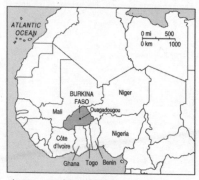

Area: 274,122 sq km/105,838 sq mi
Capital: Ouagadougou
Major towns/cities: Bobo-Dioulasso, Koudougou, Banfora, Ouahigouya, Tenkodogo
Physical features: landlocked plateau with hills in west and southeast; headwaters of the River Volta; semiarid in north, forest and farmland in south; linked by rail to Abidjan in Côte d'Ivoire, Burkina Faso's only outlet to the sea
Head of state: Blaise Compaoré from 1987
Head of government: Paramanga Ernest Yonli from 2000
Political system: emergent democracy
Political executive: limited presidency
Political parties: Popular Front (FP), centre-left coalition grouping; National Convention of Progressive Patriots–Democratic Socialist Party (CNPP–PSD), left of centre
Currency: franc CFA
GNI per capita (PPP): (US$) 1,010 (2002 est)
Exports: cotton, gold, livestock and livestock products. Principal market: Singapore 14.9% (2001)
Population: 13,002,000 (2003 est)
Language: French (official), 50 Sudanic languages (90%)
Religion: animist 40%, Sunni Muslim 50%, Christian (mainly Roman Catholic) 10%
Life expectancy: 45 (men); 46 (women) (2000–05)

Chronology

13th–14th centuries: Formerly settled by Bobo, Lobi, and Gurunsi peoples, east and centre were conquered by Mossi and Gurma peoples, who established powerful warrior kingdoms, some of which survived until late 19th century.
1895–1903: France secured protectorates over the Mossi kingdom of Yatenga and the Gurma region, and annexed the Bobo and Lobi lands, meeting armed resistance.
1904: The French-controlled region, known as Upper Volta, was attached administratively to French Sudan; tribal chiefs were maintained in their traditional seats and the region was to serve as a labour reservoir for more developed colonies to the south.
1919: Made a separate French colony.
1932: Partitioned between French Sudan, the Côte d'Ivoire, and Niger.
1947: Became a French overseas territory.
1960: Independence was achieved, with Maurice Yaméogo as the first president.
1966: A military coup was led by Lt-Col Sangoulé Lamizana, and a supreme council of the armed forces established.
1977: The ban on political activities was removed. A referendum approved a new constitution based on civilian rule.
1978–80: Lamizana was elected president. In 1980 he was overthrown in a bloodless coup led by Col Saye Zerbo, as the economy deteriorated.
1982–83: Maj Jean-Baptiste Ouedraogo became president and Capt Thomas Sankara prime minister. In 1983 Sankara seized complete power.
1984: Upper Volta was renamed Burkina Faso ('land of upright men') to signify a break with the colonial past; literacy and afforestation campaigns were instigated by Sankara, who established links with Libya, Benin, and Ghana.
1987: Capt Blaise Compaoré became president.
1991: A new constitution was approved.
1992: Multiparty elections were won by the pro-Compaoré Popular Front (FP).
1996: Kadre Desire Ouedraogo was appointed prime minister.
1997: The CDP won assembly elections. Ouedraogo was reappointed prime minister.
1998: President Blaise Compaoré was re-elected with an overwhelming majority.
2000: Prime Minister Ouedraogo resigned and was replaced by Paramanga Ernest Yonli. The government agreed to UN-supervised monitoring of weapons imports.
2001: The country suffered an outbreak of meningitis which killed more than 1,500 people. The HIV infection rate was one of the highest in West Africa.
2004: A military tribunal tried 13 people accused of plotting a coup against President Blaise Compaoré in 2003. An army captain, Luther Ouali, was jailed for 10 years.

burlesque in the 17th and 18th centuries, a form of satirical comedy parodying a particular play or dramatic genre. For example, John *Gay's *The Beggar's Opera* (1728) is a burlesque of 18th-century opera, and Richard Brinsley *Sheridan's *The Critic* (1777) satirizes the sentimentality in contemporary drama. In the USA from the mid-19th century, 'burlesque' referred to a sex-and-comedy show invented by Michael Bennett

141

Leavitt in 1866 with acts including acrobats, singers, and comedians. During the 1920s striptease was introduced in order to counteract the growing popularity of the movies; Gypsy Rose Lee was the most famous stripper. Burlesque was frequently banned in the USA.

Burlington, Richard Boyle, 3rd Earl of Burlington (1695–1753) Anglo-Irish architectural patron and architect. He was one of the premier exponents of the Palladian style in Britain. His buildings are characterized by absolute adherence to the classical rules. William *Kent was his major protégé.

burn in medicine, destruction of body tissue by extremes of temperature, corrosive chemicals, electricity, or radiation. **First-degree burns** may cause reddening; **second-degree burns** cause blistering and irritation but usually heal spontaneously; **third-degree burns** are disfiguring and may be life-threatening.

Burne-Jones, Edward Coley (1833–1898) English painter. In 1856 he was apprenticed to the Pre-Raphaelite painter and poet Dante Gabriel *Rossetti, who remained a dominant influence. His paintings, inspired by legend and myth, were characterized by elongated forms and subdued tones, as in *King Cophetua and the Beggar Maid* (1880–84; Tate Gallery, London). He also collaborated with William *Morris in designing stained-glass windows, tapestries, and book decorations for the Kelmscott Press. His work influenced both *Symbolism and *art nouveau. He was created a baronet in 1894.

burnet herb belonging to the rose family, also known as **salad burnet**. It smells of cucumber and can be used in salads. The name is also used for other members of the genus. (*Sanguisorba minor*, family Rosaceae.)

Burnett, Frances Eliza Hodgson (1849–1924) English writer. She emigrated with her family to the USA in 1865. Her novels for children include the rags-to-riches tale *Little Lord Fauntleroy* (1886) and *The Secret Garden* (1911), which has its values anchored in nature mysticism.

Burney, Fanny (Frances) (1752–1840) English novelist and diarist. She achieved success with *Evelina*, an epistolary novel published in 1778, became a member of Samuel *Johnson's circle, and received a post at court from Queen Charlotte. She published three further novels, *Cecilia* (1782), *Camilla* (1796), and *The Wanderer* (1814).

Burns, Robert (1759–1796) Scottish poet. He used a form of Scots dialect at a time when it was not considered suitably 'elevated' for literature. Burns's first volume, *Poems, Chiefly in the Scottish Dialect*, appeared in 1786. In addition to his poetry (such as 'To a Mouse'), Burns wrote or adapted many songs, including 'Auld Lang Syne'. **Burns Night** is celebrated on 25 January, his birthday. His strength lies in his essential sincerity to his own experience and the extraordinary vitality of its expression.

Burroughs, Edgar Rice (1875–1950) US novelist. He wrote *Tarzan of the Apes* (1914; filmed 1918), the story of an aristocratic child lost in the jungle and reared by apes, and followed it with over 20 more books about the Tarzan character. He also wrote a series of novels about life on Mars, including *A Princess of Mars* (1917) and *Synthetic Men of Mars* (1940).

Burton, Richard (1925–1984) stage name of Richard Walter Jenkins, Jr, Welsh stage and screen actor. He was best known for his rich, dramatic voice, commanding stage presence, and collaborations with the actor Elizabeth *Taylor, to whom he was married twice. He starred in 11 films with Taylor, including *Cleopatra* (1963) and *Who's Afraid of Virginia Woolf?* (1966). Among his later films are *Equus* (1977) and *Nineteen Eighty-Four* (1984).

Burton, Richard Francis (1821–1890) English explorer and translator (he knew 35 oriental languages). He travelled mainly in the Middle East and northeast Africa, often disguised as a Muslim. He made two attempts to find the source of the White Nile, in 1855 and 1857–58 (on the second, with John Speke, he reached Lake Tanganyika), and wrote many travel books. He translated oriental erotica and the *Arabian Nights* (1885–88).

Burundi
formerly **Urundi** (until 1962)
National name: *Republika y'Uburundi/ République du Burundi/Republic of Burundi*

Area: 27,834 sq km/10,746 sq mi
Capital: Bujumbura
Major towns/cities: Gitega, Bururi, Ngozi, Muyinga, Ruyigi, Kayanza
Physical features: landlocked grassy highland straddling watershed of Nile and Congo; Lake Tanganyika, Great Rift Valley
Head of state and government: Domitien Ndayizeye from 2003
Political system: military
Political executive: military
Political parties: Front for Democracy in Burundi (FRODEBU), left of centre; Union for National Progress (UPRONA), nationalist socialist; Socialist Party of Burundi (PSB); People's Reconciliation Party (PRP)
Currency: Burundi franc
GNI per capita (PPP): (US$) 610 (2002 est)
Exports: coffee, tea, glass products, hides and skins. Principal market: Switzerland 32.6% (2001)
Population: 6,825,000 (2003 est)
Language: Kirundi, French (both official), Kiswahili
Religion: Roman Catholic 62%, Pentecostalist 5%, Anglican 1%, Muslim 1%, animist
Life expectancy: 40 (men); 41 (women) (2000–05)
Chronology
10th century: Originally inhabited by the hunter-gatherer Twa Pygmies. Hutu peoples settled in the region and became peasant farmers.

13th century: Taken over by Banu Hutus.

15th–17th centuries: The majority Hutu community came under the dominance of the cattle-owning Tutsi peoples, immigrants from the east, who became a semi-aristocracy; the minority Tutsis developed a feudalistic political system, organized around a nominal king, with royal princes in control of local areas.

1890: Known as Urundi, the Tutsi kingdom, along with neighbouring Rwanda, came under nominal German control as Ruanda-Urundi.

1916: Occupied by Belgium during World War I.

1923: Belgium was granted a League of Nations mandate to administer Ruanda-Urundi; it was to rule 'indirectly' through the Tutsi chiefs.

1962: Burundi was separated from Ruanda-Urundi, and given independence as a monarchy under Tutsi King Mwambutsa IV.

1965: The king refused to appoint a Hutu prime minister after an election in which Hutu candidates were victorious; an attempted coup by Hutus was brutally suppressed.

1966: The king was deposed by his teenage son Charles, who became Ntare V; he was in turn deposed by his Tutsi prime minister Col Michel Micombero, who declared Burundi a republic; the Tutsi-dominated Union for National Progress (UPRONA) was declared the only legal political party.

1972: Ntare V was killed, allegedly by Hutus, provoking a massacre of 150,000 Hutus by Tutsi soldiers; 100,000 Hutus fled to Tanzania.

1976: An army coup deposed Micombero and appointed the Tutsi Col Jean-Baptiste Bagaza as president. He launched a drive against corruption and a programme of land reforms and economic development.

1987: Bagaza was deposed in a coup by the Tutsi Maj Pierre Buyoya.

1988: About 24,000 Hutus were killed by Tutsis and 60,000 fled to Rwanda.

1992: A new multiparty constitution was adopted following a referendum.

1993: Melchior Ndadaye, a Hutu, was elected president in the first-ever democratic contest, but was killed in a coup by the Tutsi-dominated army; 100,000 people died in the massacres that followed.

1994: Cyprien Ntaryamira, a Hutu, became president but was later killed in an air crash along with the Rwandan president Juvenal Habyarimana. There was an eruption of ethnic violence; 750,000 Hutus fled to Rwanda. Hutu Sylvestre Ntibantunganya became head of state, serving with a Tutsi prime minister, as part of a four-year power-sharing agreement.

1995: Renewed ethnic violence erupted in the capital, Bujumbura, following a massacre of Hutu refugees.

1996: The former Tutsi president Pierre Buyoya seized power amid renewed ethnic violence; the coup provoked economic sanctions by other African countries. A 'government of national unity' was appointed, with Pascal-Firmin Ndimira as premier. Bujumbura was shelled by Hutu rebels.

1998: There was renewed fighting between Tutsi-led army and Hutu rebels. A ceasefire was agreed between the warring political factions. The position of head of government was abolished, with President Buyoya assuming the position's authority.

2000: With the civil war worsening, Nelson Mandela, former president of South Africa, and the new mediator for Burundi, met government, opposition, and rebel leaders in Tanzania. A power-sharing peace agreement was reached by most political factions, though three Tutsi parties declined to sign. Despite the agreement, the war continued.

2001: A regional summit chaired by Nelson Mandela failed to bring peace. The violence escalated in battles south of Bujumbura.

2002: A ceasefire was signed between government and Hutu rebels, but some fighting continued.

2003: Domitien Ndayizeye, a Hutu, took over as president from Buyoya, a Tutsi, under the terms of the power-sharing agreement. Ndayizeye was the first state leader from the Hutu majority in seven years. However, the ceasefire later broke down and renewed fighting erupted in Bujumbura. President Ndayizeye and Pierre Nkurunziza of the Forces for Defence of Democracy (FDD, the largest former rebel group) signed an agreement to end the civil war.

2004: African Union peacekeeping troops were replaced by United Nations (UN) troops. The UN and the government began to demobilize soldiers and former rebel fighters.

2005: President Ndayizeye signed a decree establishing a national army. A new power-sharing constitution was approved by voters. Regional leaders extended the transitional government's mandate and demanded government elections.

Buryat *or* **Buryatiya** formerly (1923–58) **Buryat–Mongol Autonomous Soviet Socialist Republic,** republic in the eastern Siberian region of the Russian Federation; area 351,300 sq km/135,637 sq mi; population (1996) 1,053,000 (70% Russian, 24% Buryat). The main cities are Ulan-Ude (capital), Kyakhta, and Gusinoozersk. Buryat is bordered on the south by Mongolia, and occupies the eastern and northern shores of Lake *Baikal. The land is largely mountainous and covered by coniferous forests; the Sayan Mountains are in the far west. Mineral deposits include rare metals (tungsten, molybdenum, gold), together with lignite (brown coal), iron ore, and graphite. The chief industries are aerospace engineering, mining, food processing, fishing, lumbering, and the breeding of sheep and cattle. The republic is crossed by the Trans-Siberian Railway.

bus in computing, the electrical pathway through which a computer processor communicates with some of its parts and/or peripherals. Physically, a bus is a set of parallel tracks that can carry digital signals; it may take the form of copper tracks laid down on the computer's *printed circuit boards (PCBs), or of an external cable or connection.

Bush, George Herbert Walker (1924–) 41st president of the USA 1989–93, a Republican. He was director of the Central Intelligence Agency (CIA) 1976–81 and US vice-president 1981–89. As president, his response to the Soviet leader Mikhail Gorbachev's diplomatic initiatives were initially criticized as inadequate, but his sending of US troops to depose his former ally, General Manuel *Noriega of Panama, proved a popular move at home. Success in the 1991 Gulf War against Iraq further raised his standing. Domestic economic problems 1991–92 were followed by his defeat in the 1992 presidential elections by the Democrat Bill Clinton. His son, George W *Bush, became president of the USA in 2001.

Bush, George W(alker), Jr (1946–) 43rd president of the USA from 2001. Republican governor of Texas 1994–2000 and son of former US president George *Bush, he was elected president after defeating Democrat Al Gore in a hotly disputed contest and with a smaller share (48.1%) of the popular vote than his Democrat rival (48.3%). The presidency was conceded to Bush 36 days after the election, following a narrow decision by the divided US Supreme Court. Inexperienced in foreign affairs, Bush is supported in his administration by his father's former defense secretary, Dick *Cheney, who is vice-president. Condoleezza Rice was appointed secretary of state in 2004, the first black female to hold this position. In 2003 Bush instigated the US-led Iraq War, as part of his broader 'war against terrorism' and to overthrow Iraqi president Saddam Hussein. However, this action, along with decisions to withdraw from the antiballistic missile agreement and not to adopt the Kyoto Protocol on the environment, led to concerns of increasing US unilateralism in international affairs. He was narrowly re-elected in 2004 after a bitter and often personal election battle with Democrat challenger John Kerry.

bushbaby small nocturnal African prosimian with long feet, long, bushy tail, and large ears. Bushbabies are active tree dwellers and feed on fruit, insects, eggs, and small birds.

bushbuck antelope *Tragelaphus scriptus* found over most of Africa south of the Sahara. Up to 1 m/3 ft tall, the males have keeled horns twisted into spirals, and are brown to blackish. The females are generally hornless, lighter, and redder. All have white markings, including stripes or vertical rows of dots down the sides. Rarely far from water, bushbuck live in woods and thick brush.

bushel dry or liquid measure equal to eight gallons or four pecks (36.37 l/2,219.36 cu in) in the UK; some US states have different standards according to the goods measured.

bushman's rabbit *or* **riverine rabbit** a wild rodent *Bunolagus monticularis* found in dense riverine bush in South Africa. It lives in small populations, and individuals are only seen very occasionally; it is now at extreme risk of extinction owing to loss of habitat to agriculture. Very little is known about its life or habits.

bushmaster large snake *Lachesis muta*. It is a type of pit viper, and is related to the rattlesnakes. Up to 4 m/ 12 ft long, it is found in wooded areas of South and Central America, and is the largest venomous snake in the New World. When alarmed, it produces a noise by vibrating its tail among dry leaves.

Bushmen former name for the *Kung, San, and other hunting and gathering groups (for example, the Gikwe, Heikom, and Sekhoin) living in and around the Kalahari Desert in southern Africa. They number approximately 50,000 and speak San and other click languages of the Khoisan family. They are characteristically small-statured.

bushranger Australian armed robber of the 19th century. The first bushrangers were escaped convicts. The last gang was led by Ned Kelly and his brother Dan in 1878–80. They form the subject of many Australian ballads.

Busoni, Ferruccio Dante Benvenuto (1866–1924) Italian pianist, composer, and music critic. Much of his music was for the piano, but he also composed several operas including *Doktor Faust*, completed by Philipp Jarnach after Busoni's death. His work shows the influence of Liszt and his ballet score for *Doktor Faust* shows his debt to Bizet. Specimens of his style at its best are to be found in his later sonatinas, *Sarabande und Cortège* from *Faust*, and the monumental *Fantasia contrappuntistica* for piano. An apostle of Futurism, he encouraged the French composer Edgard Varèse.

bustard bird of the family Otididae, order Gruiformes, related to *cranes but with a rounder body, thicker neck, and a relatively short beak. Bustards are found on the ground on open plains and fields.

butane C_4H_{10}, *alkane (saturated hydrocarbon) derived from *natural gas and as a product of the *fractional distillation of crude oil (unrefined *petroleum). Liquefied under pressure, it is used as a *fuel for industrial and domestic purposes (for example, in portable cookers).

Bute, John Stuart, 3rd Earl of Bute (1713–1792) British Tory politician, prime minister 1762–63. On the accession of George III in 1760, he became the chief instrument in the king's policy for breaking the power of the Whigs and establishing the personal rule of the monarch through Parliament.

Buthelezi, Chief Mangosuthu Gatsha (1928–) South African Zulu leader and politician, president of the Zulu-based *Inkatha Freedom Party (IFP), which he founded as a paramilitary organization for attaining a nonracial democratic society in 1975. Buthelezi's threatened boycott of South Africa's first multiracial elections led to a dramatic escalation in politically motivated violence, but he eventually agreed to register his party and in May 1994 was appointed home affairs minister in the country's first post-apartheid government. In December 1995 there were unsubstantiated claims that he had colluded with the security service during the apartheid period. In June 1999 Buthelezi was offered the post of deputy president of South Africa by the new president Thabo Mbeki. Buthelezi refused the post.

Butler, Samuel (1835–1902) English writer. He made his name in 1872 with a satiric attack on contemporary utopianism, *Erewhon* (an anagram of *nowhere*). He is now remembered for his unfinished, semi-autobiographical discursive novel, *The Way of All Flesh*, a study of Victorian conventions, the causes and effects of the clash between generations, and religious hypocrisy (written and frequently revised 1873–84 and posthumously published in 1903).

buttercup any plant of the buttercup family with divided leaves and yellow flowers. (Genus *Ranunculus*, family Ranunculaceae.)

butterfly fish any of several fishes, not all related. They include the freshwater butterfly fish *Pantodon buchholzi* of western Africa and the tropical marine butterfly fishes in family Chaetodontidae.

butterwort insectivorous plant belonging to the bladderwort family, with purplish flowers and a rosette of flat leaves covered with a sticky substance that traps insects. (Genus *Pinguicula*, family Lentibulariaceae.)

Buxtehude, Dietrich (1637–1707) Danish composer. In 1668 he was appointed organist at the Marienkirche,

Lübeck, Germany, where his fame attracted Johann Sebastian Bach and Handel. He is remembered for his organ works and cantatas, written for his evening concerts (*Abendmusiken*); he also wrote numerous trio sonatas for two violins, viola da gamba, and harpsichord.

buzzard species of medium-sized hawk with broad wings, often seen soaring. Buzzards are in the falcon family, Falconidae, order Falconiformes. The **common buzzard** *Buteo buteo* of Europe and Asia is about 55 cm/ 1.8 ft long with a wingspan of over 1.2 m/4 ft. It preys on a variety of small animals up to the size of a rabbit.

Byelorussia alternative name for *Belarus.

Byrd, Richard Evelyn (1888–1957) US aviator and explorer. The first to fly over the North Pole (1926), he also flew over the South Pole (1929) and led five overland expeditions in Antarctica.

Byrd, William (1543–1623) English composer. His sacred and secular choral music, including over 200 motets and Masses for three, four, and five voices, is typical of the English polyphonic style.

Byron, George Gordon, 6th Baron Byron (1788–1824) English poet. He became the symbol of *Romanticism and political liberalism throughout Europe in the 19th century. His reputation was established with the first two cantos (divisions within a poem) of *Childe Harold* (1812). Later works include *The Prisoner of Chillon* (1816), *Beppo* (1818), *Mazeppa* (1819), and, most notably, the satirical *Don Juan* (1819–24). He left England in 1816 and spent most of his later life in Italy.

byte sufficient computer memory to store a single character of data, such as a letter of the alphabet. The character is stored in the byte of memory as a pattern of *bits (binary digits), using a code such as *ASCII. A byte usually contains eight bits – for example, the capital letter F can be stored as the bit pattern 01000110.

Byzantine style in the visual arts and architecture that originated in the 4th–5th centuries in Byzantium (capital of the Eastern Roman Empire; renamed Constantinople in 330; now Istanbul). It spread to Italy, throughout the Balkans, and to Russia, where it survived for many centuries. The term Byzantine refers now to a specific style rather than a geographic place. It is characterized by rich use of colour such as gold, rigid artistic stereotypes, and stylized figures composed of strong lines, giving a flat appearance. Byzantine artists excelled in mosaic work, manuscript painting, and religious *icon painting. The simplicity and stylization of such religious works made them useful teaching aids, and Byzantine art is often called Christian art. In Byzantine architecture, the dome supported on pendentives (supportive structures at the intersection of arch and dome) was in widespread use.

Byzantine Empire the **Eastern Roman Empire** 395–1453, with its capital at Constantinople (formerly Byzantium, modern Istanbul). It was the direct continuation of the Roman Empire in the East, and inherited many of its traditions and institutions.

Byzantium modern **Istanbul**, ancient Greek city on the Bosporus, founded as a colony of the Greek city of Megara on an important strategic site at the entrance to the Black Sea about 660 BC. In AD 330 the capital of the Roman Empire was transferred there by Constantine the Great, who renamed it Constantinople and it became the capital of the *Byzantine Empire to which it gave its name.

C

c. abbreviation for **circa** (Latin 'about'), used with dates that are uncertain.

°C symbol for degrees *Celsius, sometimes called centigrade.

C in computing, a high-level, general-purpose programming language popular on minicomputers and microcomputers. Developed in the early 1970s from an earlier language called BCPL, C was first used as the language of the operating system Unix, though it has since become widespread beyond Unix. It is useful for writing fast and efficient systems programs, such as operating systems (which control the operations of the computer).

Cabal, the (from *Kabbalah*) group of politicians, the English king Charles II's counsellors 1667–73, whose initials made up the word by coincidence – Clifford (Thomas Clifford 1630–1673), Ashley (Anthony Ashley Cooper, 1st Earl of *Shaftesbury), *Buckingham (George Villiers, 2nd Duke of Buckingham), Arlington (Henry Bennett, 1st Earl of Arlington 1618–1685), and *Lauderdale (John Maitland, Duke of Lauderdale). The word cabal, meaning 'association of intriguers', is now applied to any faction that works in secret for private or political ends.

cabbage vegetable plant related to the turnip and wild mustard, or charlock. It was cultivated as early as 2000 BC, and the many commercial varieties include kale, Brussels sprouts, common cabbage, savoy, cauliflower, sprouting broccoli, and kohlrabi. (*Brassica oleracea*, family Cruciferae.)

Cabbala alternative spelling of *Kabbalah.

Cabinda *or* **Kabinda** coastal exclave, a province of Angola, bounded on the east and south by the Democratic Republic of Congo, on the north by the Republic of the Congo, and on the west by the Atlantic Ocean; area 7,770 sq km/3,000 sq mi; population (1992) 152,100. The capital is Cabinda. There are oil reserves. Products include timber and phosphates. Attached to Angola in 1886, the exclave has made claims to independence.

cabinet ('a small room, implying secrecy') in politics, the group of ministers holding a country's highest executive positions who decide government policy. In Britain the cabinet system originated under the Stuarts in the 17th century. Under William III it became customary for the king to select his ministers from the party with a parliamentary majority (having the most members of Parliament). The US cabinet, unlike the British, does not initiate legislation, and its members,

appointed by the president, must not be members of Congress. The term was used in the USA from 1793.

cable unit of length, used on ships, originally the length of a ship's anchor cable or 120 fathoms (219 m/720 ft), but now taken as one-tenth of a *nautical mile (185.3 m/608 ft).

cable television distribution of broadcast signals through cable relay systems. Narrow-band systems were originally used to deliver services to areas with poor regular reception; systems with wider bands, using coaxial and fibreoptic cable, are increasingly used for distribution and development of home-based interactive services, typically telephones.

Caboto, Giovanni (*c.* **1450–***c.* **1498**) English **John Cabot**, Italian navigator. Commissioned, with his three sons, by Henry VII of England to discover unknown lands, he arrived at Cape Breton Island on 24 June 1497, thus becoming the first European to reach the North American mainland (he thought he was in northeast Asia). In 1498 he sailed again, touching Greenland, and probably died on the voyage.

cacao tropical American evergreen tree, now also cultivated in West Africa and Sri Lanka. Its seeds are cocoa beans, from which *cocoa and chocolate are prepared. (*Theobroma cacao*, family Sterculiaceae.)

cactus plural **cacti**, strictly, any plant of the family Cactaceae, although the word is commonly used to describe many different succulent and prickly plants. True cacti have a woody axis (central core) surrounded by a large fleshy stem, which takes various forms and is usually covered with spines (actually reduced leaves). They are all specially adapted to growing in dry areas.

CAD acronym for **computer-aided design**, use of computers in creating and editing design drawings. CAD also allows such things as automatic testing of designs and multiple or animated three-dimensional views of designs. CAD systems are widely used in architecture, electronics, and engineering, for example in the motor-vehicle industry, where cars designed with the assistance of computers are now commonplace. With a CAD system, picture components are accurately positioned using grid lines. Pictures can be resized, rotated, or mirrored without loss of quality or proportion.

caddis fly insect of the order Trichoptera. Adults are generally dull brown, mothlike, with wings covered in tiny hairs. Mouthparts are poorly developed, and many caddis flies do not feed as adults. They are usually found near water.

cadmium chemical symbol Cd, soft, silver-white, ductile, and malleable metallic element, atomic number 48, relative atomic mass 112.40. Cadmium occurs in nature as a sulphide or carbonate in zinc ores. It is a toxic metal that, because of industrial dumping, has become an environmental pollutant. It is used in batteries, electroplating, and as a constituent of alloys used for bearings with low coefficients of friction; it is also a constituent of an alloy with a very low melting point.

caecilian tropical amphibian of wormlike appearance. There are about 170 species known in the family Caeciliidae, forming the amphibian order Apoda (also known as Caecilia or Gymnophiona). Caecilians have a grooved skin that gives a 'segmented' appearance; they have no trace of limbs or pelvis. The body is 20–130 cm/8–50 in long, beige to black in colour. The eyes are very small and weak or blind. They eat insects and small worms. Some species bear live young, others lay eggs. Caecilians live in burrows in damp ground in the tropical Americas, Africa, Asia, and the Seychelles.

Caedmon (lived seventh century) Earliest known English Christian poet. According to the Northumbrian historian Bede, when Caedmon was a cowherd at the monastery of Whitby, he was commanded to sing by a stranger in a dream, and on waking produced a hymn on the Creation. The poem is preserved in some manuscripts. Caedmon became a monk and may have composed other religious poems.

Caerphilly unitary authority in south *Wales, created in 1996 from parts of the former counties of Mid Glamorgan and Gwent. **area:** 270 sq km/104 sq mi **towns:** Hengoed (administrative headquarters), Caerphilly, Bargoed, Newbridge, Rhymney **physical:** rivers Rhymney and Sirhowy; highest point Twyn Ceilog (552 m/181 ft) **features:** Caerphilly Castle (1268) **population:** (2000 est) 170,500.

Caesar family name of Julius Caesar and later an imperial title. Julius Caesar's grand-nephew and adopted son Octavian became Gaius Julius Caesar Octavianus (the future emperor *Augustus). From his day onwards, 'Caesar' became the family name of the reigning emperor and his heirs. When the emperor *Nero, the last of the Julio-Claudian line, died, all his successors from Galba onwards were called 'Caesar'. What had been a family name thus became a title.

Caesar, Gaius Julius (100–44 BC) Roman general and dictator, considered Rome's most successful military commander. He formed with Pompey the Great and Marcus Licinius *Crassus (the Elder) the First Triumvirate in 60 BC. He conquered Gaul 58–50 BC and invaded Britain 55–54 BC. By leading his army across the river Rubicon in 49 BC, an act of treason, he provoked a civil war which ended in 45 BC with the defeat of Pompey and his supporters. He was voted dictator for life, but was assassinated by conspirators on 15 March 44 BC. Caesar was a skilled historian whose *Commentarii*, recounting his campaigns, has had a major impact on the way military history is written up to the present day.

Caesarean section surgical operation to deliver a baby by way of an incision in the mother's abdominal and uterine walls. It may be recommended for almost any obstetric complication implying a threat to mother or baby.

caesium chemical symbol Cs, (Latin *caesius* 'bluish-grey') soft, silvery-white, ductile metallic element, atomic number 55, relative atomic mass 132.905. It is one of the *alkali metals that form Group 1 of the periodic table of the elements. The alkali metals increase in reactivity down the group, and caesium, with only the short-lived radioactive francium below it, is the most reactive of them all. In air it ignites spontaneously, and it reacts violently with water. It is the most electropositive of all the elements. It is used in the manufacture of photocells.

caffeine *alkaloid organic substance found in tea, coffee, and kola nuts; it stimulates the heart and central nervous system. When isolated, it is a bitter crystalline compound, $C_8H_{10}N_4O_2$. Too much caffeine (more than six average cups of tea or coffee a day) can be detrimental to health.

Cage, John (1912–1992) US composer. His interest in Indian classical music led him to the view that the

purpose of new music was to change the way people listen. From 1948 he experimented with instruments, graphics, and methods of random selection in an effort to generate a music of pure incident. For example, he used a number of radios, tuned to random stations, in *Imaginary Landscape IV* (1951). His ideas greatly influenced late 20th-century aesthetics.

Cagney, James (Francis, Jr) (1899–1986) US actor. His physical dynamism and staccato vocal delivery made him one of the first stars of talking pictures. Often associated with gangster roles, as in *The Public Enemy* (1931) and *White Heat* (1949), he was equally adept at playing comedy, singing, and dancing, as in *Blonde Crazy* (1931), *Footlight Parade* (1933), *A Midsummer Night's Dream* (1935), and *Yankee Doodle Dandy* (1942).

caiman or **cayman** large reptile, related to the *alligator.

Caine, Michael (1933–) stage name of Maurice Joseph Micklewhite, English screen actor. He is a prolific and versatile performer with an enduring Cockney streak. His first major success was in *Alfie* (1966). He has played historical roles in *Zulu* (1964) and *The Man Who Would Be King* (1975), hardboiled psychopaths in *Get Carter* (1971) and *Mona Lisa* (1986), and comic buffoons in *Educating Rita* (1983) and *Sweet Liberty* (1986). He won the Academy Award for Best Supporting Actor for both *Hannah and Her Sisters* (1986) and *The Cider House Rules* (1999), and the Golden Globe for Best Actor for *Little Voice* (1998).

cairn Scottish breed of *terrier. Shaggy, short-legged, and compact, it can be sandy, greyish brindle, or red. It was formerly used for flushing out foxes and badgers.

Cairngorm Mountains granite mountain group in Scotland, northern part of the *Grampian Mountains, between the River Dee and the upper Spey. The central range includes four out of five of Britain's highest mountains: Ben Macdhui (1,309 m/4,296 ft), Braeriach (1,296 m/4,251 ft), Cairn Toul (1,291 m/4,235 ft), and Cairn Gorm (1,245 m/4,084 ft). Cairn Gorm can be accessed by chair-lift.

Cairo Arabic **El Qahira**, ('the victorious') capital of Egypt, and the largest city in Africa and in the Middle East, situated on the east bank of the River Nile 13 km/8 mi above the apex of the delta and 160 km/100 mi from the Mediterranean; population (1996 est) 6,789,500 (city), 9,900,000 (urban agglomeration). The city is the leading commercial and industrial centre of Egypt; its industries include the manufacture of textiles, chemicals, leather, cement, processed foods, vegetable oils, and steel. At Helwan, 24 km/15 mi to the south, an industrial centre is powered by electricity from the Aswan High Dam. With the attractions of the pyramids and sphinx at Giza and the Egyptian museum, which has one of the world's leading archaeological collections, there is also a very substantial tourist industry, while the film and publishing industries serve most of the Middle East.

Cajun member of a French-speaking community of *Louisiana, USA, descended from French Canadians. In the 18th century these people were driven to Louisiana from Nova Scotia (then known as Acadia, from which the name Cajun comes). The modern Cajun people are known for their music, which has a lively rhythm and features steel guitar, fiddle, and accordion, and for their spicy cuisine.

CAL acronym for **computer-assisted learning**, use of computers in education and training: the computer displays instructional material to a student and asks questions about the information given; the student's answers determine the sequence of the lessons.

calabash tropical South American evergreen tree with gourds (fruits) 50 cm/20 in across, whose dried skins are used as water containers. The Old World tropical-vine bottle gourd (*Lagenaria siceraria*, of the gourd family Cucurbitaceae) is sometimes also called a calabash, and it produces equally large gourds. (*Crescentia cujete*, family Bignoniaceae.)

Calabria mountainous region occupying the 'toe' of Italy, comprising the provinces of Catanzaro, Cosenza, Crotone, Reggio di Calabria, and Vibo Valenzia; area 15,080 sq km/5,822 sq mi; population (2001 est) 1,993,300. A peninsula lying between the Tyrrhenian and Ionian seas, Calabria is separated from Sicily by the Strait of Messina, and has a narrow, fertile coastal strip. Its capital is Catanzaro, and other major towns include Crotone and Reggio di Calabria.

calceolaria plant with brilliantly coloured slipper-shaped flowers. Native to South America, calceolarias were introduced to Europe and the USA in the 1830s. (Genus *Calceolaria*, family Scrophulariaceae.)

calcite colourless, white, or light-coloured common rock-forming mineral, calcium carbonate, $CaCO_3$. It is the main constituent of *limestone and marble and forms many types of invertebrate shell.

calcium chemical symbol Ca, (Latin *calcis* 'lime') soft, silvery-white metallic element, atomic number 20, relative atomic mass 40.08. It is one of the *alkaline-earth metals. It is the fifth most abundant element (the third most abundant metal) in the Earth's crust. It is found mainly as its carbonate $CaCO_3$, which occurs in a fairly pure condition as chalk and limestone (see *calcite). Calcium is an essential component of bones, teeth, shells, milk, and leaves, and it forms 1.5% of the human body by mass.

calcium carbonate $CaCO_3$, white solid, found in nature as limestone, marble, and chalk. It is a valuable resource, used in the making of iron, steel, cement, glass, slaked lime, bleaching powder, sodium carbonate and bicarbonate, and many other industrially useful substances.

calcium hydroxide *or* **slaked lime** $Ca(OH)_2$, white solid, slightly soluble in water. A solution of calcium hydroxide is called limewater and is used in the laboratory to test for the presence of carbon dioxide.

calculus (Latin 'pebble') branch of mathematics which uses the concept of a derivative to analyse the way in which the values of a *function vary. Calculus is probably the most widely used part of mathematics. Many real-life problems are analysed by expressing one quantity as a function of another – position of a moving object as a function of time, temperature of an object as a function of distance from a heat source, force on an object as a function of distance from the source of the force, and so on – and calculus is concerned with such functions.

Calcutta former name (until 2000) of Kolkata, city in India.

Caledonia Roman term for the Scottish Highlands, inhabited by the Caledoni. The tribes of the area remained outside Roman control – they were defeated but not conquered by Agricola in AD 83 to 84 and again by Septimius Severus who reached beyond modern Aberdeen in 208. Since the 18th century, the name has been revived as a romantic alternative for the whole of Scotland.

Caledonian Canal waterway in northwest Scotland, 98 km/61 mi long, linking the Atlantic and the North Sea. Situated between the Moray Firth and Loch Linnhe, the canal was constructed as a transport route to save the long sail around Scotland. Of its total length, only a 37 km/22 mi stretch is artificial, the rest being composed of lochs Lochy, Oich, and Ness.

calendar division of the *year into months, weeks, and days and the method of ordering the years. From year one, an assumed date of the birth of Jesus, dates are calculated backwards (BC 'before Christ' or BCE 'before common era') and forwards (AD, Latin *anno Domini* 'in the year of the Lord', or CE 'common era'). The **lunar month** (period between one new moon and the next) naturally averages 29.5 days, but the Western calendar uses for convenience a **calendar month** with a complete number of days, 30 or 31 (February has 28). For adjustments, since there are slightly fewer than six extra hours a year left over, they are added to February as a 29th day every fourth year (**leap year**), century years being excepted unless they are divisible by 400. For example, 1896 was a leap year; 1900 was not.

California called the **Golden State**, the **Land of Milk and Honey**, the **El Dorado State**, or the **Grape State**, western state of the USA, bordered to the south by the Mexican state of Baja California, to the east by *Arizona and *Nevada, to the north by *Oregon, and to the west by the *Pacific Ocean; area 403,932 sq km/155,959 sq mi; population (2000 est) 33,871,600; capital Sacramento. Its nicknames refer to the gold that led to the California gold rush of 1849–56, and to the state's sunshine, orange groves, vineyards, and abundant resources. Geographically the state is diverse, with features including the *Sierra Nevada mountains, desert areas, and a fertile central plains region. The *San Andreas Fault extends from northwest California southward, causing tremors and occasional earthquakes from San Francisco to the southeast part of the state. The state's economy is the largest in the USA, and very significant to the country as whole. California is a leader in both agriculture, producing fruit, vegetables, cotton, beef cattle, and fish; and manufacturing, concentrated on engineering and technology. *Silicon Valley is known for its electronics industries, while *Hollywood is the centre of the US film industry. Tourism, the property market, and mining, including petroleum and boron, are also important to the state's economy. The largest city is *Los Angeles (LA); other major cities are *San Diego, *San Francisco, *San José, and Fresno. California is the most populous state of the USA, with over a quarter of the population being Hispanic American. Formerly a Spanish and Mexican territory, California passed to the USA following the Mexican War (1846–48). California was admitted to the Union in 1850 as the 31st US state and is governed under a constitution dating from 1879.

californium chemical symbol Cf, synthesized, radioactive, metallic element of the actinide series, atomic number 98, relative atomic mass 251. It is produced in very small quantities and used in nuclear reactors as a neutron source. The longest-lived isotope, Cf-251, has a half-life of 800 years.

Caligula (AD 12–41) born Gaius Julius Caesar Germanicus, Roman emperor (AD 37–41), son of Germanicus and Agrippina the Elder, and successor to *Tiberius. Caligula was a cruel tyrant and was assassinated by an officer of his guard. He appears to have been mentally unstable.

caliph title of civic and religious heads of the world of Islam. The first caliph was *Abu Bakr. Nominally elective, the office became hereditary, held by the Umayyad dynasty 661–750 and then by the *Abbasid dynasty. After the death of the last Abbasid (1258), the title was claimed by a number of Muslim chieftains in Egypt, Turkey, and India. The most powerful of these were the Turkish sultans of the Ottoman Empire.

Callaghan, (Leonard) James (1912–2005) Baron Callaghan of Cardiff, British Labour politician, prime minister and party leader 1976–79. He became prime minister in April 1976 after the unexpected retirement of Harold Wilson and he headed a minority government, which stayed in power from 1977 through a pact with the Liberal Party. A Labour moderate, he held power at a time when trade unions and the party's left wing had increasing influence, and he was forced to implement austerity measures agreed with the International Monetary Fund (IMF). Callaghan was previously chancellor of the Exchequer 1964–67, home secretary 1967–70, and foreign secretary 1974–76.

Callas, Maria (1923–1977) adopted name of Maria Kalogeropoulos, US lyric soprano. She was born in New York of Greek parents. With a voice of fine range and a gift for dramatic expression, she excelled in operas including *Norma, La sonnambula, Madame Butterfly, Aïda, Tosca,* and *Medea.*

calligraphy art of handwriting, regarded in China and Japan as the greatest of the visual arts, and playing a large part in Islamic art because the depiction of the human and animal form is forbidden.

calorie c.g.s. unit of heat, now replaced by the *joule (one calorie is approximately 4.2 joules). It is the heat required to raise the temperature of one gram of water by 1 °C. In dietetics, the Calorie or kilocalorie is equal to 1,000 calories.

calorific value amount of heat generated by a given mass of fuel when it is completely burned. It is measured in joules per kilogram. Calorific values are measured experimentally with a bomb calorimeter.

calorimeter instrument used in physics to measure various thermal properties, such as heat capacity or the heat produced by fuel. A simple calorimeter consists of a heavy copper vessel that is polished (to reduce heat losses by radiation) and covered with insulating material (to reduce losses by convection and conduction).

calotype paper-based photograph using a wax paper negative, the first example of the *negative/positive process invented by the English photographer Fox *Talbot around 1834.

Calvin (or Cauvin or Chauvin), John (1509–1564) French-born Swiss Protestant church reformer and theologian. He was a leader of the Reformation in Geneva and set up a strict religious community there. His theological system is known as Calvinism, and his church government as *Presbyterianism. Calvin wrote (in Latin) *Institutes of the Christian Religion* (1536) and commentaries on the New Testament and much of the Old Testament.

Calvin, Melvin (1911–1997) US chemist who was awarded the Nobel Prize for Chemistry in 1961 for his study of the assimilation of carbon dioxide by plants. Using radioactive carbon-14 as a tracer, he determined the biochemical processes of *photosynthesis, in which green plants use *chlorophyll to convert carbon dioxide and water into sugar and oxygen.

Calvinism Christian doctrine as interpreted by John *Calvin and adopted in Scotland, parts of Switzerland, and the Netherlands; by the *Puritans in England and New England, USA; and by the subsequent Congregational and Presbyterian churches in the USA. Its central doctrine is predestination, under which certain souls (the elect) are predestined by God through the sacrifice of Jesus to salvation, and the rest to damnation. Although Calvinism is rarely accepted today in its strictest interpretation, the 20th century has seen a neo-Calvinist revival through the work of Karl Barth.

calyx collective term for the *sepals of a flower, forming the outermost whorl of the perianth. It surrounds the other flower parts and protects them while in bud. In some flowers, for example, the campions *Silene,* the sepals are fused along their sides, forming a tubular calyx.

CAM acronym for **computer-aided manufacturing,** use of computers to control production processes; in particular, the control of machine tools and *robots in factories. In some factories, the whole design and production system is automated by linking *CAD (computer-aided design) to CAM.

cam part of a machine that converts circular motion to linear motion or vice versa. The **edge cam** in a car engine is in the form of a rounded projection on a shaft, the camshaft. When the camshaft turns, the cams press against linkages (plungers or followers) that open the valves in the cylinders.

Camargue area of the *Rhône delta enclosed by the two principal arms of the river, south of Arles, France; area about 780 sq km/300 sq mi. One-third of the area is lake or marshland and dykes have been constructed to prevent widespread flooding. Black bulls and white horses are bred, and rice and vines are grown. A nature reserve, known for its bird life, forms the southern part.

cambium in botany, a layer of actively dividing cells (lateral *meristem), found within stems and roots, that gives rise to *secondary growth in perennial plants, causing an increase in girth. There are two main types of cambium: **vascular cambium,** which gives rise to secondary *xylem and *phloem tissues, and **cork cambium** (or phellogen), which gives rise to secondary cortex and cork tissues (see *bark).

Cambodia
formerly **Khmer Republic (1970–76), Kampuchea (1976–89)**
National name: *Preah Réaché'anachâkr Kâmpuchéa/ Kingdom of Cambodia*
Area: 181,035 sq km/69,897 sq mi
Capital: Phnom Penh
Major towns/cities: Battambang, Kompong Cham, Siem Reap, Prey Vêng, Preah Seihânu
Major ports: Kompong Cham
Physical features: mostly flat, forested plains with mountains in southwest and north; Mekong River runs north–south; Lake Tonle Sap

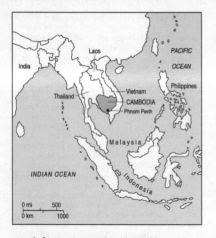

Head of state: King Norodom Sihanouk from 1991
Head of government: Hun Sen from 1998
Political system: emergent democracy
Political executive: dual executive
Political parties: United Front for an Independent, Neutral, Peaceful, and Cooperative Cambodia (FUNCINPEC), nationalist, monarchist; Liberal Democratic Party (BLDP), republican, anticommunist (formerly the Khmer People's National Liberation Front (KPNLF)); Cambodian People's Party (CPP), reform socialist (formerly the communist Kampuchean People's Revolutionary Party (KPRP)); Cambodian National Unity Party (CNUP) (political wing of the Khmer Rouge), ultranationalist communist
Currency: Cambodian riel
GNI per capita (PPP): (US$) 1,590 (2002 est)
Exports: garments, timber, rubber, fishery products. Principal market: USA 57.9% (2001)
Population: 14,144,000 (2003 est)
Language: Khmer (official), French
Religion: Theravada Buddhist 95%, Muslim, Roman Catholic
Life expectancy: 55 (men); 60 (women) (2000–05)
Chronology
1st century AD: Part of the kingdom of Hindu-Buddhist Funan (Fou Nan), centred on Mekong delta region.
6th century: Conquered by the Chenla kingdom.
9th century: Establishment by Jayavarman II of extensive and sophisticated Khmer Empire, supported by an advanced irrigation system and architectural achievements.
14th century: Theravada Buddhism replaced Hinduism.
15th century: Came under the control of Siam (Thailand), which made Phnom Penh the capital and, later, Champa (Vietnam).
1863: Became a French protectorate.
1887: Became part of French Indo-China Union, which included Laos and Vietnam.
1941: Prince Norodom Sihanouk was elected king.
1941–45: Occupied by Japan during World War II.

1946: Recaptured by France; parliamentary constitution adopted.
1949: Guerrilla war for independence secured semi-autonomy within the French Union.
1953: Independence was achieved from France as the Kingdom of Cambodia.
1955: Norodom Sihanouk abdicated as king and became prime minister, representing the Popular Socialist Community mass movement. His father, Norodom Suramarit, became king.
1960: On the death of his father, Norodom Sihanouk became head of state.
later 1960s: There was mounting guerrilla insurgency, led by the communist Khmer Rouge, and civil war in neighbouring Vietnam.
1970: Sihanouk was overthrown by US-backed Lt-Gen Lon Nol in a right-wing coup; the new name of Khmer Republic was adopted; Sihanouk, exiled in China, formed his own guerrilla movement.
1975: Lon Nol was overthrown by the Khmer Rouge, which was backed by North Vietnam and China; Sihanouk became head of state.
1976: The Khmer Republic was renamed Democratic Kampuchea.
1976–78: The Khmer Rouge, led by Pol Pot, introduced an extreme Maoist communist programme, forcing urban groups into rural areas and resulting in over 2.5 million deaths from famine, disease, and maltreatment; Sihanouk was removed from power.
1978–79: Vietnam invaded and installed a government headed by Heng Samrin, an anti-Pol Pot communist.
1979: Democratic Kampuchea was renamed the People's Republic of Kampuchea.
1980–82: Faced by guerrilla resistance from Pol Pot's Chinese-backed Khmer Rouge and Sihanouk's Association of South East Asian Nations (ASEAN) and US-backed nationalists, more than 300,000 Cambodians fled to refugee camps in Thailand and thousands of soldiers were killed.
1985: The reformist Hun Sen was appointed prime minister and more moderate economic and cultural policies were pursued.
1987–89: Vietnamese troops were withdrawn.
1989: The People's Republic of Kampuchea was renamed the State of Cambodia and Buddhism was re-established as the state religion.
1991: There was a ceasefire, and a United Nations Transitional Authority in Cambodia (UNTAC) agreed to administer the country in conjunction with an all-party Supreme National Council; communism was abandoned. Sihanouk returned as head of state.
1992: Political prisoners were released, refugees resettled, and freedom of speech restored. However, the Khmer Rouge refused to disarm.
1993: FUNCINPEC won general elections (boycotted by the Khmer Rouge, who continued fighting); a new constitution was adopted. Sihanouk was reinstated as constitutional monarch; his son Prince Norodom Ranariddh, FUNCINPEC leader, was appointed prime minister, with CPP leader Hun Sen as deputy premier.
1994: An antigovernment coup was foiled. Seven thousand Khmer Rouge guerrillas surrendered in response to an amnesty.
1995: Prince Norodom Sirivudh, FUNCINPEC leader and half-brother of King Sihanouk, was exiled for

allegedly plotting to assassinate Hun Sen and topple the government.

1996: There were heightened tensions between Hun Sen's CPP and the royalist FUNCINPEC.

1997: Pol Pot was sentenced to life imprisonment. FUNCINPEC troops were routed by the CPP, led by Hun Sen. Prime Minister Prince Norodom Ranariddh was deposed and replaced by Ung Huot. There was fighting between supporters of Hun Sen and Ranariddh.

1998: Ranariddh was found guilty of arms smuggling and colluding with the Khmer Rouge, but was pardoned by the king. Pol Pot died and thousands of Khmer Rouge guerrillas defected. The CPP won elections, and political unrest followed. A new CPP–FUNCINPEC coalition was formed, with Hun Sen as prime minister and Prince Norodom Ranariddh as president. Cambodia re-occupied its UN seat.

2001: The Senate approved the creation of an international tribunal to prosecute former leaders of the Khmer Rouge.

2002: The UN withdrew its participation from an international tribunal to try former leaders of the Khmer Rouge regime for genocide and crimes against humanity because of concerns about the independence and objectivity of the tribunal.

2003: The Thai embassy in the Cambodian capital of Phnom Penh was set on fire by rioters and Thai-owned businesses were attacked after claims by a Thai actress that Cambodia's Angkor Wat ancient temple complex belonged to the Thai people. The ruling Kanakpak Pracheachon Kampuchea (KPK; Cambodian People's Party) won the parliamentary elections but did not secure a sufficient majority to govern alone.

2004: The KPK formed a coalition government with the FUNCINPEC party. Cambodia joined the World Trade Organization (WTO). King Sihanouk abdicated in favour of his son Norodom Sihamoni.

2005: Parliament stripped the opposition leader Sam Rainsy of immunity from prosecution and he left the country. The UN received sufficient donations to fund its share of the costs of a tribunal to try surviving leaders of the Khmer Rouge.

Cambrian Mountains region of hills, plateaux, and deep valleys in Wales, 175 km/110 mi long, linking Snowdonia in the northwest and the Brecon Beacons and Black Mountains in the south.

Cambrian period period of geological time roughly 570–510 million years ago; the first period of the Palaeozoic Era. All invertebrate animal life appeared, and marine algae were widespread. The **Cambrian Explosion** 530–520 million years ago saw the first appearance in the fossil record of modern animal phyla; the earliest fossils with hard shells, such as trilobites, date from this period.

Cambridge city and administrative headquarters of *Cambridgeshire, eastern England, on the River Cam, 80 km/50 mi north of London; population (1998 est) 120,650. It is the seat of Cambridge University (founded in the 13th century). Industries include the manufacture of computers and electronic products, scientific instruments, and paper, printing, publishing, financial services, and insurance, as well as technological, medical, and telecommunications research. Tourism is also an important industry; there are about 4.1 million visitors each year.

Cambridgeshire county of eastern England, which has contained the unitary authority Peterborough since April 1998. **area:** 3,410 sq km/1,316 sq mi **towns and cities:** *Cambridge (administrative headquarters), Ely, Huntingdon, March, Wisbech, St Neots, Whittlesey **physical:** county is flat with fens, whose soil is very fertile; Bedford Level (a peaty area of the fens); rivers: Nene, Ouse (with tributaries Cam, Lark, and Little Ouse), Welland **features:** Cambridge University; Ely Cathedral (1083, with 16th-, 18th- and 20th-century refurbishments); the Imperial War Museum at Duxford, which is Britain's foremost aviation museum; the 17th-century Grantchester vicarage, former home of English poet Rupert *Brooke; the Rupert Brooke Museum in Grantchester **population:** (1997 est) 537,600.

Camden Town Group school of British painters (1911–13), based in Camden, London, led by Walter *Sickert. The work of Spencer Gore (1878–1914) and Harold Gilman (1876–1919) is typical of the group, rendering everyday town scenes in post-Impressionist style. In 1913 they merged with another group to form the London Group.

camel large cud-chewing mammal with two toes which have broad soft soles for walking on sand, and hooves resembling nails. Part of the even-toed hoofed order Artiodactyla, it is a *ruminant, although it differs from most ruminants in having, only a three-chambered stomach. There are two species, the single-humped **Arabian camel**, or *dromedary, *Camelus dromedarius* and the twin-humped **bactrian camel** *C. bactrianus* from Asia. They carry a food reserve of fatty tissue in the hump, can go without drinking for long periods, can feed on salty vegetation, and withstand extremes of heat and cold, thus being well adapted to desert conditions.

camellia any oriental evergreen shrub with roselike flowers belonging to the tea family. Many species, including *Camellia japonica* and *C. reticulata*, have been introduced into Europe, the USA, and Australia; they are widely cultivated as ornamental shrubs. (Genus *Camellia*, family Theaceae.)

Camelot in medieval romance, legendary seat of King Arthur.

cameo small relief carving of semi-precious stone, shell, or glass, in which a pale-coloured surface layer is carved to reveal a darker ground. Fine cameos were produced in ancient Greece and Rome, during the Renaissance, and in the Victorian era. They were used for decorating goblets and vases, and as jewellery.

camera apparatus used in *photography, consisting of a lens system set in a light-proof box inside of which a sensitized film or plate can be placed. The lens collects rays of light reflected from the subject and brings them together as a sharp image on the film. The opening or hole at the front of the camera, through which light enters, is called an *aperture. The aperture size controls the amount of light that can enter. A shutter controls the amount of time light has to affect the film. There are small-, medium-, and large-format cameras; the format refers to the size of recorded image and the dimensions of the image obtained.

camera obscura ('dark room') darkened box with a tiny hole for projecting the inverted image of the scene outside on to a screen inside. For its development as a device for producing photographs, see *photography.

Cameroon
formerly **Kamerun** (until 1916)
  National name: *République du Cameroun/ Republic of Cameroon*

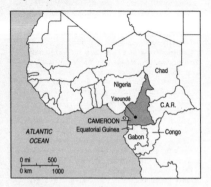

Area: 475,440 sq km/183,567 sq mi
Capital: Yaoundé
Major towns/cities: Garoua, Douala, Nkongsamba, Maroua, Bamenda, Bafoussam, Ngaoundéré
Major ports: Douala
Physical features: desert in far north in the Lake Chad basin, mountains in west, dry savannah plateau in the intermediate area, and dense tropical rainforest in south; Mount Cameroon 4,070 m/13,358 ft, an active volcano on the coast, west of the Adamawa Mountains
Head of state: Paul Biya from 1982
Head of government: Ephraim Inoni from 2004
Political system: emergent democracy
Political executive: limited presidency
Political parties: Cameroon People's Democratic Movement (RDPC), nationalist, left of centre; Front of Allies for Change (FAC), left of centre (There are 47 parties in Cameroon and seven parties in parliament)
Currency: franc CFA
GNI per capita (PPP): (US$) 1,640 (2002 est)
Exports: crude petroleum and petroleum products, timber and timber products, cocoa, coffee, aluminium, cotton, bananas. Principal market: Italy 21.7% (2000)
Population: 16,018,000 (2003 est)
Language: French, English (both official; often spoken in pidgin), Sudanic languages (in the north), Bantu languages (elsewhere); there has been some discontent with the emphasis on French – there are 163 indigenous peoples with their own African languages
Religion: animist 50%, Christian 33%, Muslim 16%
Life expectancy: 45 (men); 47 (women) (2000–05)
Chronology
1472: First visited by the Portuguese, who named it the Rio dos Camaroes ('River of Prawns') after the giant shrimps they found in the Wouri River estuary, and later introduced slave trading.
early 17th century: The Douala people migrated to the coastal region from the east and came to serve as intermediaries between Portuguese, Dutch, and English traders and interior tribes.
1809–48: The northern savannahs were conquered by the Fulani, Muslim pastoral nomads from the southern Sahara.

1856: Douala chiefs signed a commercial treaty with Britain and invited British protection.
1884: A treaty was signed establishing German rule as the protectorate of Kamerun; cocoa, coffee, and banana plantations were developed.
1916: Captured by Allied forces in World War I.
1919: Divided under League of Nations' mandates between Britain, which administered the southwest and north (adjoining Nigeria), and France, which administered the east and south.
1946: The French Cameroon and British Cameroons were made UN trust territories.
1955: The French crushed a revolt by the Union of the Cameroon Peoples (UPC), southern-based radical nationalists.
1960: French Cameroon became the independent Republic of Cameroon, with the Muslim Ahmadou Ahidjo as president; a UPC rebellion in the southwest was crushed, and a state of emergency declared.
1961: Following a UN plebiscite, the northern part of the British Cameroons merged with Nigeria, and the southern part joined the Republic of Cameroon to become the Federal Republic of Cameroon.
1966: An autocratic one-party regime was introduced; government and opposition parties merged to form the Cameroon National Union (UNC).
1970s: Petroleum exports made successful investment in education and agriculture possible.
1972: A new constitution made Cameroon a unitary state.
1982: President Ahidjo resigned; he was succeeded by his prime minister Paul Biya, a Christian.
1983–84: Biya began to remove the northern Muslim political 'barons' close to Ahidjo, who went into exile in France. Biya defeated a plot by Muslim officers from the north to overthrow him.
1985: The UNC adopted the name RDPC.
1990: There was widespread public disorder as living standards declined; Biya granted an amnesty to political prisoners.
1992: The ruling RDPC won the first multiparty elections in 28 years, with Biya as president.
1995: Cameroon was admitted to the Commonwealth.
1996: Peter Musonge Mafani became prime minister.
1997: RDPC won assembly elections; Biya was re-elected.
2002: RDPC won election amidst some allegations of fraud from the opposition. The International Court of Justice (ICJ) ruled in favour of Cameroon on the sovereignty of the oil-rich Bakassi peninsula, occupied by Nigerian troops.
2003: Nigeria relinquished control of 32 villages as part of the ICJ ruling.
2004: Cameroon and Nigeria agreed on joint security patrols along their disputed border, but Nigeria failed to meet the deadline for the handover of the Bakassi peninsula. Biya won a further seven-year term as president.

Camoëns (*or* Camões), Luis Vaz de (1524–1580)
Portuguese poet and soldier. He went on various military expeditions, and was shipwrecked in 1558. His poem *Os Lusiades/The Lusiads* (1572) tells the story of the explorer Vasco da Gama and incorporates much Portuguese history; it was immediately acclaimed and has become the country's national epic. His posthumously published lyric poetry is also now valued.

Camorra Italian secret society formed about 1820 by criminals in the dungeons of Naples and continued once they were freed. It dominated politics from 1848, was suppressed in 1911, but many members eventually surfaced in the US *Mafia. The Camorra still operates in the Naples area.

camouflage colours or structures that allow an animal to blend with its surroundings to avoid detection by other animals. Camouflage can take the form of matching the background colour, of countershading (darker on top, lighter below, to counteract natural shadows), or of irregular patterns that break up the outline of the animal's body. More elaborate camouflage involves closely resembling a feature of the natural environment, as with the stick insect; this is closely akin to *mimicry. Camouflage is also important as a military technique, disguising either equipment, troops, or a position in order to conceal them from an enemy.

Campaign for Nuclear Disarmament (CND) non-party-political British organization advocating the abolition of nuclear weapons worldwide. Since its foundation in 1958, CND has sought unilateral British initiatives to help start, and subsequently to accelerate, the multilateral process and end the arms race.

Campania region of southern Italy, comprising the provinces of Avellino, Benevento, Caserta, Naples, and Salerno; area 13,595 sq km/5,249 sq mi; population (1998 est) 5,792,600. The administrative capital is *Naples; industrial centres include Benevento, Caserta, and Salerno. Agriculture is important; wheat, citrus fruits, wine, vegetables, tobacco, and hemp are produced. The volcano *Vesuvius is near Naples, and there are ancient sites at Pompeii, Herculaneumm, and Paestum.

Campbell, Donald Malcolm (1921–1967) British car and speedboat enthusiast, son of Malcolm Campbell, who simultaneously held the land-speed and water-speed records. In 1964 he set the world water-speed record of 444.57 kph/276.3 mph on Lake Dumbleyung, Australia, with the turbojet hydroplane *Bluebird*, and achieved the land-speed record of 648.7 kph/403.1 mph at Lake Eyre salt flats, Australia. He was killed in an attempt to raise his water-speed record on Coniston Water, England.

Campbell, Malcolm (1885–1948) British racing driver who once held both land- and water-speed records. He set the land-speed record nine times, pushing it up to 484.8 kph/301.1 mph at Bonneville Flats, Utah, USA, in 1935, and broke the water-speed record three times, the best being 228.2 kph/141.74 mph on Coniston Water, England, in 1939. His car and boat were both called *Bluebird*.

Campbell-Bannerman, Henry (1836–1908) British Liberal politician, prime minister 1905–08, leader of the Liberal party 1898–1908. The Entente Cordiale was broadened to embrace Russia during his premiership, which also saw the granting of 'responsible government' to the Boer republics in southern Africa. He was succeeded as prime minister and Liberal leader by H H *Asquith, who had effectively led the House during Campbell-Bannermann's premiership, as the latter was dogged by ill health.

Camp David Agreements two framework accords agreed in 1978 and officially signed in March 1979 by Israeli prime minister *Begin and Egyptian president *Sadat at Camp David, Maryland, USA, under the guidance of US president *Carter. They cover an Egypt–Israel peace treaty and phased withdrawal of Israel from Sinai, which was completed in 1982, and an overall Middle East settlement including the election by the *West Bank and *Gaza Strip Palestinians of a 'self-governing authority'. The latter issue has stalled repeatedly over questions of who should represent the Palestinians and what form the self-governing body should take.

Campese, David (1962–) Australian rugby union player, one of the outstanding entertainers of the game. He holds the world record for the most tries scored in international rugby, is the most-capped Australian international (101 caps), and was a key element in Australia's 1991 World Cup victory. He retired from international 15-a-side rugby in 1996, and from competitive rugby in 1998. In August 1999 he announced his retirement as a player.

camphor $C_{10}H_{16}O$, volatile, aromatic *ketone substance obtained from the camphor tree *Cinnamomum camphora*. It is distilled from chips of the wood, and is used in insect repellents and medicinal inhalants and liniments, and in the manufacture of celluloid.

campion any of several plants belonging to the pink family. They include the garden campion (*Lychnis coronaria*), the wild white and red campions (*Silene alba* and *S. dioica*), and the bladder campion (*S. vulgaris*). (Genera *Lychnis* and *Silene*, family Caryophyllaceae.)

Campylobacter genus of bacteria that cause serious outbreaks of gastroenteritis. The bacteria grow best at 43 °C, and so are well suited to the digestive tract of birds. Poultry is therefore the most likely source of a *Campylobacter* outbreak, although the bacteria can also be transmitted via beef or milk. *Campylobacter* can survive in water for up to 15 days, so may be present in drinking water if supplies are contaminated by sewage or reservoirs are polluted by seagulls.

Camus, Albert (1913–1960) Algerian-born French writer. His works, such as the novels *L'Étranger/ The Outsider* (1942) and *La Peste/The Plague* (1948), owe much to *existentialism in their emphasis on the absurdity and arbitrariness of life. Other works include *Le Mythe de Sisyphe/The Myth of Sisyphus* (1943) and *L'Homme révolté/The Rebel* (1951). Camus's criticism of communism in the latter book led to a protracted quarrel with the philosopher Jean-Paul Sartre. He was awarded the Nobel Prize for Literature in 1957.

Canaan ancient region between the Mediterranean and the Dead Sea, called in the Bible the 'Promised Land' of the Israelites. It was occupied as early as the 3rd millennium BC by the Canaanites, a Semitic-speaking people who were known to the Greeks of the 1st millennium BC as Phoenicians. The capital was Ebla (now Tell Mardikh, Syria).

Canada
Area: 9,970,610 sq km/3,849,652 sq mi
Capital: Ottawa
Major towns/cities: Toronto, Montréal, Vancouver, Edmonton, Calgary, Winnipeg, Québec, Hamilton, Saskatoon, Halifax, London, Kitchener, Mississauga, Laval, Surrey
Physical features: mountains in west, with low-lying plains in interior and rolling hills in east; St Lawrence Seaway, Mackenzie River; Great Lakes; Arctic Archipelago; Rocky Mountains; Great Plains or Prairies;

Canada

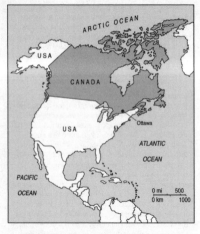

Canadian Shield; Niagara Falls; climate varies from temperate in south to arctic in north; 45% of country forested

Head of state: Queen Elizabeth II from 1952, represented by Governor General Adrienne Clarkson from 1999

Head of government: Paul Martin from 2003

Political system: liberal democracy

Political executive: parliamentary

Political parties: Liberal Party, nationalist, centrist; Bloc Québécois, Québec-based, separatist; Reform Party, populist, right wing; New Democratic Party (NDP), moderate left of centre; Progressive Conservative Party (PCP), free enterprise, right of centre; Confederation of Regions (COR); Party of New Brunswick; Green Party of Canada

Currency: Canadian dollar

GNI per capita (PPP): (US$) 28,070 (2002 est)

Exports: motor vehicles and parts, lumber, wood pulp, paper and newsprint, crude petroleum, natural gas, aluminium and alloys, petroleum and coal products. Principal market: USA 85% (2001)

Population: 31,510,000 (2003 est)

Language: English (60%), French (24%) (both official), American Indian languages, Inuktitut (Inuit)

Religion: Roman Catholic 45%, various Protestant denominations

Life expectancy: 76 (men); 82 (women) (2000–05)

Chronology

35,000 BC: First evidence of people reaching North America from Asia by way of Beringia.

c. 2000 BC: Inuit (Eskimos) began settling the Arctic coast from Siberia eastwards to Greenland.

c. AD 1000: Vikings, including Leif Ericsson, established Vinland, a settlement in northeast America that did not survive.

1497: John Cabot, an Italian navigator in the service of English king Henry VII, landed on Cape Breton Island and claimed the area for England.

1534: French navigator Jacques Cartier reached the Gulf of St Lawrence and claimed the region for France.

1608: Samuel de Champlain, a French explorer, founded Québec; French settlers developed fur trade and fisheries.

1663: French settlements in Canada formed the colony of New France, which expanded southwards.

1670: Hudson's Bay Company established trading posts north of New France, leading to Anglo-French rivalry.

1689–97: King William's War: Anglo-French conflict in North America arising from the 'Glorious Revolution' in Europe.

1702–13: Queen Anne's War: Anglo-French conflict in North America arising from the War of the Spanish Succession in Europe; Britain gained Newfoundland.

1744–48: King George's War: Anglo-French conflict in North America arising from the War of Austrian Succession in Europe.

1756–63: Seven Years' War: James Wolfe captured Québec in 1759; France ceded Canada to Britain by the Treaty of Paris.

1775–83: American Revolution caused an influx of 40,000 United Empire Loyalists, who formed New Brunswick in 1784.

1791: Canada was divided into Upper Canada (much of modern Ontario) and Lower Canada (much of modern Québec).

1793: British explorer Alexander Mackenzie crossed the Rocky Mountains to reach the Pacific coast.

1812–14: War of 1812 between Britain and USA; US invasions repelled by both provinces.

1820s: Start of large-scale immigration from British Isles caused resentment among French Canadians.

1837: Rebellions were led by Louis Joseph Papineau in Lower Canada and William Lyon Mackenzie in Upper Canada.

1841: Upper and Lower Canada united as Province of Canada; achieved internal self-government in 1848.

1867: British North America Act united Ontario, Québec, Nova Scotia, and New Brunswick in Dominion of Canada.

1869: Red River Rebellion of Métis (people of mixed French and American Indian descent), led by Louis Riel, against British settlers in Rupert's Land.

1870: Manitoba (part of Rupert's Land) formed the fifth province of Canada; British Columbia became the sixth in 1871, and Prince Edward Island became the seventh in 1873.

1885: The Northwest Rebellion was crushed and Riel hanged. The Canadian Pacific Railway was completed.

1905: Alberta and Saskatchewan were formed from the Northwest Territories and became provinces of Canada.

1914–18: Half a million Canadian troops fought for the British Empire on the western front in World War I.

1931: The Statute of Westminster affirmed equality of status between Britain and the Dominions.

1939–45: World War II: Canadian participation in all theatres.

1949: Newfoundland became the tenth province of Canada; Canada was a founding member of the North Atlantic Treaty Organization (NATO).

1960: The Québec Liberal Party of Jean Lesage launched a 'Quiet Revolution' to re-assert French-Canadian identity.

1970: Pierre Trudeau invoked the War Measures Act to suppress separatist terrorists of the Front de Libération du Québec.

1976: The Parti Québécois won control of the Québec provincial government; a referendum rejected independence in 1980.

1982: 'Patriation' of the constitution removed Britain's last legal control over Canada.

1987: Meech Lake Accord: a constitutional amendment was proposed to increase provincial powers (to satisfy Québec); failed to be ratified in 1990.

1992: A self-governing homeland for the Inuit was approved.

1994: Canada formed the North American Free Trade Area with USA and Mexico.

1995: A Québec referendum narrowly rejected a sovereignty proposal.

1997: The Liberals were re-elected by a narrow margin.

1999: The government passed a bill making secession by Québec more difficult to achieve.

2000: The Liberals were elected for a third term.

2001: Bernard Landry replaced Lucien Bouchard as prime minister of Québec.

2003: Jean Chrétien steped down as prime minister and was replaced as premier and leader of the Liberal Party by former finance minister Paul Martin.

2004: The prime minister ordered an enquiry into allegations of misuse of government money. In spite of protests by environmentalists and animal rights groups, the largest seal cull for 50 years took place. The Liberals won the election, but lost their majority. Paul Martin returned as prime minister.

2005: Paul Martin and his predecessor Jean Chrétien appeared before a commission investigating allegations of misspent government money.

canal artificial waterway constructed for drainage, irrigation, or navigation. Irrigation canals carry water for irrigation from rivers, reservoirs, or wells, and are designed to maintain an even flow of water over the whole length. Navigation and ship canals are constructed at one level between *locks, and frequently link with rivers or sea inlets to form a waterway system. The Suez Canal in 1869 and the Panama Canal in 1914 eliminated long trips around continents and dramatically shortened shipping routes.

Canaletto, Antonio (1697–1768) adopted name of Giovanni Antonio Canal, Italian painter. He painted highly detailed views (*vedute*) of Venice (his native city), and of London and the River Thames (1746–56). Typical of his Venetian works is *Venice: Regatta on the Grand Canal* (*c.* 1735; National Gallery, London).

canary bird (*Serinus canaria*) of the finch family Fringillidae, found wild in the Canary Islands and Madeira. In its wild state the plumage is green, sometimes streaked with brown. The wild canary builds its nest of moss, feathers, and hair in thick high shrubs or trees, and produces two to four broods in a season. Canaries have been bred as cage birds in Europe since the 15th century, and many domestic varieties are yellow or orange as a result of artificial selection.

Canary Islands Spanish **Islas Canarias**, group of volcanic islands and autonomous Spanish community 100 km/60 mi off the northwest coast of Africa, comprising the provinces of Las Palmas and Santa Cruz de Tenerife; area 7,273 sq km/2,808 sq mi; population (1996 est) 1,606,500. Products include bananas and tomatoes, both grown for export. Tourism is the major industry.

Canberra capital of Australia and seat of the federal government, situated in the *Australian Capital Territory in southeast Australia; population (2001 est) 311,500. Canberra lies on a plain adjoining the Australian Alps and is enclosed within the state of New South Wales; it is 289 km/180 mi southwest of Sydney and 655 km/407 mi northeast of Melbourne, on the River Molonglo, a tributary of the Murrumbidgee. It succeeded Melbourne as capital of Australia in 1927. It is an administrative, cultural, and tourist centre. The new Parliament House (1988) is located here, as well as government offices, foreign embassies, and many buildings of national importance.

cancan high-kicking stage dance in fast duple time (2/4) for women (solo or line of dancers), originating in Paris, France, about 1830. The music usually associated with the cancan is the *galop* from Jacques Offenbach's *Orphée aux enfers/Orpheus in the Underworld* (1858).

cancer group of diseases characterized by abnormal proliferation of cells. Cancer (malignant) cells are usually degenerate, capable only of reproducing themselves (tumour formation). Malignant cells tend to spread from their site of origin by travelling through the bloodstream or lymphatic system. Cancer kills about 6 million people a year worldwide.

Cancer faintest of the zodiacal constellations (its brightest stars are fourth magnitude). It lies in the northern hemisphere between *Leo and *Gemini, and is represented as a crab. The Sun passes through the constellation during late July and early August. In astrology, the dates for Cancer are between about 22 June and 22 July (see *precession).

candela symbol cd, SI unit of luminous intensity, which replaced the former units of candle and standard candle. It measures the brightness of a light itself rather than the amount of light falling on an object, which is called **illuminance** and measured in *lux. *Candida albicans* yeastlike fungus present in the human digestive tract and in the vagina, which causes no harm in most healthy people. However, it can cause problems if it multiplies excessively, as in vaginal candidiasis or *thrush, the main symptom of which is intense itching. The most common form of thrush is oral, which often occurs in those taking steroids or prolonged courses of antibiotics.

cane reedlike stem of various plants such as the sugar cane, bamboo, and, in particular, the group of palms called rattans, consisting of the genus *Calamus* and its allies. Their slender stems are dried and used for making walking sticks, baskets, and furniture.

Canes Venatici constellation of the northern hemisphere near *Ursa Major, identified with the hunting dogs of *Boötes, the herder. Its stars are faint, and it contains the Whirlpool galaxy (M51), the first spiral galaxy to be recognized.

cane toad toad of the genus *Bufo marinus*, family Bufonidae. Also known as the giant or marine toad, the cane toad is the largest in the world. It acquired its name after being introduced to Australia from South America in 1935 to eradicate the cane beetle, which had become a serious pest there. However, having few natural enemies, the cane toad itself has now become a pest in Australia.

Canetti, Elias (1905–1994) Bulgarian-born writer. He was exiled from Austria in 1937 and settled in

England in 1939. His books, written in German, include *Die Blendung/Auto da Fé* (1935). He was concerned with crowd behaviour and the psychology of power, and wrote the anthropological study *Masse und Macht/Crowds and Power* (1960). He was awarded the Nobel Prize for Literature in 1981.

Canis Major brilliant constellation of the southern hemisphere, represented (with Canis Minor) as one of the two dogs following at the heel of *Orion. Its main star, *Sirius, is the brightest star in the night sky.

Canis Minor small constellation along the celestial equator (see *celestial sphere), represented as the smaller of the two dogs of *Orion (the other dog being *Canis Major). Its brightest star is the first magnitude *Procyon.

cannabis dried leaves and female flowers (marijuana) and *resin (hashish) of certain varieties of *hemp, which are smoked or swallowed to produce a range of effects, including feelings of happiness and altered perception. (*Cannabis sativa*, family Cannabaceae.)

canning food preservation in hermetically sealed containers by the application of heat. Originated by Nicolas Appert in France in 1809 with glass containers, it was developed by Peter Durand in England in 1810 with cans made of sheet steel thinly coated with tin to delay corrosion. Cans for beer and soft drinks are now generally made of aluminium.

Canning, Charles John (1812–1862) 1st Earl Canning, British administrator, son of George *Canning and first viceroy of India from 1858. As governor general of India from 1856, he suppressed the Indian Mutiny with a fair but firm hand which earned him the nickname 'Clemency Canning'. Viscount (1837), Earl (1859).

Canning, George (1770–1827) British Tory politician, foreign secretary 1807–10 and 1822–27, and prime minister in 1827 in coalition with the Whigs. He was largely responsible, during the *Napoleonic Wars, for the seizure of the Danish fleet and British intervention in the Spanish peninsula.

canoeing sport of propelling a lightweight, shallow boat, pointed at both ends, by paddles or sails. Present-day canoes are made from fibreglass, but original boats were of wooden construction covered in bark or skin. Canoeing was popularized as a sport in the 19th century, although canoes have been in use for thousands of years.

canon piece or passage of contrapuntal music in which one voice repeats the part of another, like an echo. The first vocal or instrumental part begins with the melody and is followed soon after by the second part imitating that melody note for note (though often starting on a different note and keeping the intervallic distance throughout). This can go on up to five or six voices. The second part may follow at half a bar, one bar, two bars, or any other distance the composer chooses. Many examples of canon can be found in the fugues of Johann Sebastian Bach. Canon is called 'stretto' when used in a *fugue.

canonical hours in the Catholic Church, seven set periods of devotion: **matins** and **lauds**, **prime**, **terce**, **sext**, **nones**, **evensong** or **vespers**, and **compline**.

canonization in the Catholic Church, the admission of one of its members to the Calendar of *Saints. The evidence of the candidate's exceptional piety is contested before the Congregation for the Causes of Saints by the Promotor Fidei, popularly known as the

Devil's advocate. Papal ratification of a favourable verdict results in *beatification, and full sainthood (conferred in St Peter's Basilica, the Vatican) follows after further proof.

canon law rules and regulations of the Christian church, especially the Greek Orthodox, Roman Catholic, and Anglican churches. Its origin is sought in the declarations of Jesus and the apostles. In 1983 Pope John Paul II issued a new canon law code reducing offences carrying automatic excommunication, extending the grounds for annulment of marriage, removing the ban on marriage with non-Catholics, and banning trade-union and political activity by priests.

Canopus or **Alpha Carinae** second-brightest star in the night sky (after Sirius), lying in the southern constellation *Carina. It is a yellow-white supergiant about 100 light years from the Sun, and thousands of times more luminous than the Sun.

Canova, Antonio, Marquese d'Ischia (1757–1822) Italian neoclassical sculptor. He was based in Rome from 1781. He received commissions from popes, kings, and emperors for his highly finished marble portrait busts and groups of figures. He made several portraits of Napoleon.

Cantabria autonomous community and province of northern Spain; area 5,289 sq km/2,042 sq mi; population (2001 est) 537,600. From the coastline on the Bay of Biscay it rises to the Cantabrian Mountains. There is some mining (iron, zinc, and some lead) here, as well as engineering and food industries, particularly dairy products. Along the coast, chief occupations are fishing, fish-processing, and ship-building. The capital is Santander; other chief towns are Reinosa, Torrelavega, Castro Urdiales, and Santoña.

Cantabrian Mountains Spanish **Cordillera Cantábrica**, mountain range running along the north coast of Spain, continuing the line of the Pyrenees westwards for about 480 km/300 mi, parallel to the coast of the Bay of Biscay. They rise to 2,648 m/8,688 ft in the Picos de Europa massif. The mountains contain coal and iron deposits, but they are of poor quality; little is mined today.

cantata in music, a work in three or more movements, using one or more vocal soloists, and sometimes a chorus. It is usually accompanied by an ensemble or small orchestra, and can be sacred or secular. The word comes from the Italian, meaning 'sung', as opposed to *sonata ('sounded', 'played') for instruments. The first printed collection of sacred cantata texts dates from 1670. The most well-known composer of sacred cantatas was Johann Sebastian Bach, with Alessandro Scarlatti being a major master of the secular form.

Canterbury, archbishop of archbishop of the Church of England (Anglican), the primate (archbishop) of all England, and first peer of the realm, ranking next to royalty. He crowns the sovereign, has a seat in the House of Lords, and is a member of the Privy Council. He is appointed by the prime minister.

cantilever beam or structure that is fixed at one end only, though it may be supported at some point along its length; for example, a diving board. The cantilever principle, widely used in construction engineering, eliminates the need for a second main support at the free end of the beam, allowing for more elegant structures and reducing the amount of materials required. Many large-span bridges have been built on the cantilever principle.

canton in France, an administrative district, a subdivision of the *arrondissement*; in Switzerland, one of the 23 subdivisions forming the Confederation.

cantor Hebrew **chazan**, (Latin *cantare*, 'to sing') in Judaism and Roman Catholicism, the prayer leader and choirmaster, responsible for singing solo parts of the chant. The position can be held by any lay person. In Protestant churches, the music director is known as the cantor.

Canute (or **Cnut** or **Knut) (c. 995–1035)** also known as **Canute the Great**, King of England from 1016, Denmark from 1018, and Norway from 1028. Having invaded England in 1013 with his father, Sweyn, king of Denmark, he was acclaimed king on Sweyn's death in 1014 by his *Viking army. Canute defeated Edmund (II) Ironside at Assandun, Essex, in 1016, and became king of all England on Edmund's death. He succeeded his brother Harold as king of Denmark in 1018, compelled King Malcolm to pay homage by invading Scotland in about 1027, and conquered Norway in 1028. He was succeeded by his illegitimate son Harold I.

canyon (Spanish *cañon* 'tube') deep, narrow valley or gorge running through mountains. Canyons are formed by stream down-cutting, usually in arid areas, where the rate of down-cutting is greater than the rate of weathering, and where the stream or river receives water from outside the area.

cap another name for a *diaphragm contraceptive.

capacitance, electrical property of a capacitor that determines how much charge can be stored in it for a given potential difference between its terminals. It is equal to the ratio of the electrical charge stored to the potential difference. The SI unit of capacitance is the *farad, but most capacitors have much smaller capacitances, and the microfarad (a millionth of a farad) is the commonly used practical unit.

capacitor or **condenser** device for storing electric charge, used in electronic circuits; it consists of two or more metal plates separated by an insulating layer called a dielectric (see *capacitance).

Cape Cod hook-shaped peninsula in southeastern Massachusetts, USA, separated from the rest of the state by the Cape Cod Canal; length 100 km/62 mi; width 1.6–32 km/1–20 mi. Its beaches and woods make it a popular tourist area. The islands of Martha's Vineyard and Nantucket are just south of the cape.

Capella or **Alpha Aurigae** brightest star in the constellation *Auriga and the sixth-brightest star in the night sky. It is a visual and spectroscopic binary that consists of a pair of yellow-giant stars 42 light years from the Sun, orbiting each other every 104 days.

Cape Province Afrikaans **Kaapprovinsie**, former province of the Republic of South Africa to 1994, now divided into Western, Eastern, and Northern Cape Provinces. It was named after the Cape of Good Hope. Dutch traders (the Dutch East India Company) established the first European settlement on the Cape in 1652, but it was taken by the British in 1795, after the French Revolutionary armies had occupied the Netherlands, and was sold to Britain for £6 million in 1814. The Cape achieved self-government in 1872. It was an original province of the Union of 1910.

caper trailing shrub native to the Mediterranean. Its flower buds are preserved in vinegar as a condiment. (*Capparis spinosa*, family Capparidaceae.)

Capet, Hugh (938–996) King of France from 987, when he claimed the throne on the death of Louis V. He founded the **Capetian dynasty**, of which various branches continued to reign until the French Revolution, for example, *Valois and *Bourbon.

Cape Town Afrikaans **Kaapstad**, port and oldest city (founded in 1652) in South Africa, situated at the northern end of the Cape Peninsula, on Table Bay; population (urban area, 1996 est) 878,000, (peninsula, 1996 est) 2,415,400. Industries include oil-refining, shipbuilding, diamond-cutting, food processing, and the manufacture of plastics and clothing. The port is the second-largest in the country after Durban and there is considerable trade in wool, wine, fruit, grain, and oil. Tourism is important. It is the legislative capital of the Republic of South Africa and capital of Western Cape province.

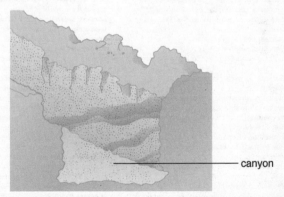

canyon

canyon Cross section of a canyon. Canyons are formed in dry regions where rivers maintain a constant flow of water over long periods of time. The Grand Canyon, for example, was first cut around 26 million years ago, in Miocene times.

Cape Verde

National name: *República de Cabo Verde/ Republic of Cape Verde*

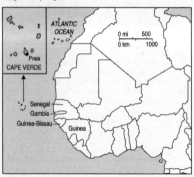

Area: 4,033 sq km/1,557 sq mi
Capital: Praia
Major towns/cities: Mindelo, Santa Maria
Major ports: Mindelo
Physical features: archipelago of ten volcanic islands 565 km/350 mi west of Senegal; the windward (Barlavento) group includes Santo Antão, São Vicente, Santa Luzia, São Nicolau, Sal, and Boa Vista; the leeward (Sotovento) group comprises Maio, São Tiago, Fogo, and Brava; all but Santa Luzia are inhabited
Head of state: Pedro Pires from 2001
Head of government: José Maria Neves from 2001
Political system: emergent democracy
Political executive: limited presidency
Political parties: African Party for the Independence of Cape Verde (PAICV), African nationalist; Movement for Democracy (MPD), moderate, centrist; Party for Democratic Convergence (PCD), centrist; Party of Work and Solidarity (PTS)
Currency: Cape Verde escudo
GNI per capita (PPP): (US$) 4,720 (2002 est)
Exports: footwear and clothing, fish, shellfish and fish products, salt, bananas. Principal market: Portugal 89.1% (2000)
Population: 463,000 (2003 est)
Language: Portuguese (official), Creole
Religion: Roman Catholic 93%, Protestant (Nazarene Church)
Life expectancy: 67 (men); 73 (women) (2000–05)
Chronology
1462: Originally uninhabited; settled by Portuguese, who brought in slave labour from West Africa.
later 19th century: There was a decline in prosperity as slave trade ended.
1950s: A liberation movement developed on the islands and the Portuguese African mainland colony of Guinea-Bissau.
1951: Cape Verde became an overseas territory of Portugal.
1975: Independence was achieved and a national people's assembly elected, with Aristides of the PAICV as the first executive president; a policy of nonalignment followed.
1981: The goal of union with Guinea-Bissau was abandoned; Cape Verde became a one-party state.

1988: There was rising unrest and demand for political reforms.
1991: In the first multiparty elections, the new Movement for Democracy party (MPD) won a majority and Antonio Mascarenhas Monteiro became president; market-centred economic reforms were introduced.
2000: Gualberto do Rosário became prime minister.
2001: José Maria Neves became prime minister, and Pedro Pires was elected president.

capillarity spontaneous movement of liquids up or down narrow tubes, or capillaries. The movement is due to unbalanced molecular attraction at the boundary between the liquid and the tube. If liquid molecules near the boundary are more strongly attracted to molecules in the material of the tube than to other nearby liquid molecules, the liquid will rise in the tube. If liquid molecules are less attracted to the material of the tube than to other liquid molecules, the liquid will fall.

capillary in biology, narrowest blood vessel in vertebrates measuring 0.008–0.02 mm in diameter, barely wider than a *red blood cell. Capillaries are distributed as **beds**, complex networks connecting *arteries and *veins. The function of capillaries is to exchange materials with their surroundings. For this reason, capillary walls are extremely thin, consisting of a single layer of cells through which nutrients, dissolved gases, and waste products can easily pass. This makes the capillaries the main area of exchange between the fluid (*lymph) bathing body tissues and the blood. They provide a large surface area in order to maximize *diffusion.

capital in architecture, a stone placed on the top of a column, pier, or pilaster, and usually wider on the upper surface than the diameter of the supporting shaft. It comes directly below the entablature (architrave, frieze, and cornice) and/or the lintel (top of a door or window frame). A capital consists of three parts: the top member, called the **abacus**, a block that acts as the supporting surface to the superstructure; the middle portion, known as the bell or **echinus**; and the lower part, called the necking or **astragal**.

capital in economics, the stock of goods used in the production of other goods. Classical economics regards capital as a factor of production, distinguishing between **financial capital** and **physical capital**. Financial capital is accumulated or inherited wealth held in the form of assets, such as stocks and shares, property, and bank deposits, while physical capital is wealth in the form of physical assets such as machinery and plant. The term is also used to describe investment in a company as either share capital or debt (called loan capital).

capitalism economic system in which the principal means of production, distribution, and exchange are in private (individual or corporate) hands and competitively operated for profit. A **mixed economy** combines the private enterprise of capitalism and a degree of state monopoly, as in nationalized industries and welfare services.

capital punishment punishment by death. Capital punishment is retained in 87 countries and territories (2001), including the USA (38 states), China, and Islamic countries. Methods of execution include electrocution, lethal gas, hanging, shooting, lethal injection, garrotting, and decapitation. It was abolished in the UK in 1965 for all crimes except treason and piracy, and in 1998 it was entirely abolished in the UK.

Capone, Al(phonse) (1899–1947) called 'Scarface', US gangster. During the *Prohibition period, he built a formidable criminal organization in Chicago. He was brutal in his pursuit of dominance, killing seven members of a rival gang in the St Valentine's Day Massacre of 1929. He was imprisoned from 1931 to 1939 for income-tax evasion, the only charge that could be sustained against him.

Capote, Truman (1924–1984) pen-name of Truman Streckfus Persons, US novelist, journalist, and playwright. After achieving early success as a writer of sparkling prose in the stories of *Other Voices, Other Rooms* (1948) and the novel *Breakfast at Tiffany's* (1958), Capote's career flagged until the sensational 'non-fiction novel' *In Cold Blood* (1965) made him a celebrity.

Cappadocia ancient region of Asia Minor, in eastern central Turkey. It was conquered by the Persians in 584 BC but in the 3rd century BC became an independent kingdom. The region was annexed as a province of the Roman empire in AD 17.

Capra, Frank (1897–1991) Italian-born US film director. His satirical comedies, which often have the common man pitted against corrupt institutions, were hugely successful in the Depression years of the 1930s. He won Academy Awards for the *It Happened One Night* (1934), *Mr Deeds Goes to Town* (1936), and *You Can't Take It with You* (1938). Among his other classic films are *Mr Smith Goes to Washington* (1939), and *It's a Wonderful Life* (1946).

Capri Italian island at the southern entrance of the Bay of Naples; 32 km/20 mi south of Naples; area 13 sq km/5 sq mi; population (1987 est) 7,800. It has two towns, Capri and Anacapri, a profusion of flowers, beautiful scenery, and an ideal climate. The Blue Grotto on the north coast is an important tourist attraction.

Capricornus zodiacal constellation in the southern hemisphere next to *Sagittarius. It is represented as a sea-goat, and its brightest stars are third magnitude. The Sun passes through it from late January to mid-February. In astrology, the dates for Capricornus (popularly known as Capricorn) are between about 22 December and 19 January (see *precession).

capsicum any of a group of pepper plants belonging to the nightshade family, native to Central and South America. The different species produce green to red fruits that vary in size. The small ones are used whole to give the hot flavour of chilli, or ground to produce cayenne or red pepper; the large pointed or squarish pods, known as sweet peppers or pimientos (green, red, or yellow peppers), are mild-flavoured and used as a vegetable. (Genus *Capsicum*, family Solanaceae.)

capsule in botany, a dry, usually many-seeded fruit formed from an ovary composed of two or more fused *carpels, which splits open to release the seeds. The same term is used for the spore-containing structure of mosses and liverworts; this is borne at the top of a long stalk or seta.

capuchin monkey of the genus *Cebus* found in Central and South America, so called because the hairs on the head resemble the cowl of a Capuchin monk. Capuchins live in small groups, feed on fruit and insects, and have a long tail that is semiprehensile and can give support when climbing through the trees.

capybara world's largest rodent *Hydrochoerus hydrochaeris*, up to 1.3 m/4 ft long and 50 kg/110 lb in weight. It is found in South America, and belongs to the guinea-pig family. The capybara inhabits marshes and dense vegetation around water. It has thin, yellowish hair, swims well, and can rest underwater with just eyes, ears, and nose above the surface.

car small, driver-guided, passenger-carrying motor vehicle; originally the automated version of the horse-drawn carriage, meant to convey people and their goods over streets and roads. Over 50 million motor cars are produced each year worldwide. The number of cars in the world in 1997 exceeded 500 million. Most are four-wheeled and have water-cooled, piston-type internal-combustion engines fuelled by petrol or diesel. Variations have existed for decades that use ingenious and often nonpolluting power plants, but the motor industry long ago settled on this general formula for the consumer market. Experimental and sports models are streamlined, energy-efficient, and hand-built.

caracal cat *Felis caracal* related to the *lynx. It has long black ear tufts, a short tail, and short reddish-fawn fur. It lives in bush and desert country in Africa, Arabia, and India, hunting birds and small mammals at night. Head and body length is about 75 cm/2.5 ft.

Caracalla (AD *c.* 186–217) also known as **Marcus Aurelius Severus Antoninus Augustus**; born **Septimius Bassianus**, Roman emperor from 211, son and successor of *Septimius Severus. He accompanied his father to Britain (208–211) and when Severus died in 211 Caracalla became joint emperor with his younger brother Geta. With the support of the army he murdered Geta in 212 and became sole ruler of the empire. During his reign in 212, Roman citizenship was extended to all the free inhabitants of the empire. He was assassinated at the instigation of his praetorian prefect Macrinus who succeeded him.

Caracas chief city and capital of Venezuela, situated in the Central Highlands of the Andes Mountains 900 m/2,950 ft above sea level, 13 km/8 mi south of its port La Guaira on the Caribbean coast; population (2000 est) 1,975,800; Federal District, including Vargas state (2000 est) 2,284,900. Main industries include oil refining, textiles, chemicals, and food processing. During the oil boom of the 1950s Caracas developed rapidly, its rate of growth greater than that of any other South American capital; much of the old colonial town was largely effaced during this period. It is now a large modern industrial and commercial centre, notably for oil companies, developed since the 1950s.

carambola small evergreen tree of Southeast Asia. The fruits, called **star fruit**, are yellowish, about 12 cm/4 in long, with a five-pointed star-shaped cross-section. They can be eaten raw, cooked, or pickled, and are juicily acidic. The juice is also used to remove stains from hands and clothes. (*Averrhoa carambola*, family Averrhoaceae.)

carat (Arabic *quirrat* 'seed') unit for measuring the mass of precious stones; it is equal to 0.2 g/0.00705 oz, and is part of the troy system of weights. It is also the unit of purity in gold (US 'karat'). Pure gold is 24-carat; 22-carat (the purest used in jewellery) is 22 parts gold and two parts alloy (to give greater strength); 18-carat is 75% gold.

Caravaggio, Michelangelo Merisi da (1573–1610) Italian early baroque painter. He was active in Rome between 1592 and 1606, then in Naples, and finally in

Malta. He created a forceful style, using contrasts of light and shade, dramatic foreshortening, and a meticulous attention to detail. His life was as dramatic as his art: he had to leave Rome after killing a man in a brawl.

caraway herb belonging to the carrot family. Native to northern temperate regions of Europe and Asia, it is grown for its spicy, aromatic seeds, which are used in cookery, medicine, and perfumery. (*Carum carvi*, family Umbelliferae.)

carbide compound of carbon and one other chemical element, usually a metal, silicon, or boron.

carbohydrate chemical compounds composed of carbon, hydrogen, and oxygen, with the basic formula $C_m(H_2O)_n$, and related compounds with the same basic structure but modified *functional groups. They are important to living organisms and, as sugar and starch, are an important part of a balanced human diet, providing energy for life processes including growth and movement. Excess carbohydrate intake can be converted into fat and stored in the body.

carbolic acid common name for the aromatic compound *phenol.

carbon chemical symbol C, (Latin *carbo, carbonaris* 'coal') non-metallic element, atomic number 6, relative atomic mass 12.011. It occurs on its own as diamond, graphite, and as fullerenes (the allotropes), as compounds in carbonaceous rocks such as chalk and limestone, as carbon dioxide in the atmosphere, as hydrocarbons in petroleum, coal, and natural gas, and as a constituent of all organic substances.

carbonate CO_3^{2-}, ion formed when carbon dioxide dissolves in water; any salt formed by this ion and another chemical element, usually a metal.

carbon cycle sequence by which *carbon circulates and is recycled through the natural world. Carbon is usually found in a carbon compound of one sort or another and so the carbon cycle is really about the cycling of carbon compounds. Carbon dioxide is released into the atmosphere by most living organisms as a result of *respiration. The CO_2 is taken up and converted into high-energy chemicals – *glucose and other *carbohydrates – during *photosynthesis by plants; the oxygen component is released back into the atmosphere. Some glucose is used by the plant and some is converted into other carbon compounds,

making new tissues. However, some of these compounds can be transferred to other organisms. An animal may eat the plant and that animal may be eaten and so on down the food chain. Carbon is also released through the *decomposition of dead plant and animal matter, and the burning of *fossil fuels such as *coal and *oil, which produce carbon dioxide that is released into the atmosphere. The oceans absorb 25–40% of all carbon dioxide released into the atmosphere.

carbon dating alternative name for *radiocarbon dating.

carbon dioxide CO_2, colourless, odourless gas, slightly soluble in *water, and denser than air. It is formed by the complete oxidation of carbon. Carbon dioxide is produced by living things during the processes of *respiration and the *decomposition of organic matter, and it is used up during *photosynthesis. It therefore plays a vital role in the *carbon cycle.

carbon fibre fine, black, silky, continuous filament of pure carbon produced by heating organic fibres, such as cellulose, in an inert atmosphere, and used for reinforcing plastics, epoxy, and polyester resins. The resulting composite is very stiff and, weight for weight, has four times the strength of high-tensile steel. It is used in the aerospace industry, cars, and electrical and sports equipment.

Carboniferous period period of geological time roughly 362.5 to 290 million years ago, the fifth period of the Palaeozoic Era. In the USA it is divided into two periods: the Mississippian (lower) and the Pennsylvanian (upper). Typical of the lower-Carboniferous rocks are shallow-water *limestones, while upper-Carboniferous rocks have *delta deposits with *coal (hence the name). Amphibians were abundant, and reptiles evolved during this period.

carbon monoxide CO, colourless, odourless gas formed when carbon is oxidized in a limited supply of air. It is a poisonous constituent of car exhaust fumes, forming a stable compound with haemoglobin in the blood, thus preventing the haemoglobin from transporting oxygen to the body tissues.

carburation any process involving chemical combination with carbon, especially the mixing or charging of a gas, such as air, with volatile compounds of carbon (petrol, kerosene, or fuel oil) in order to increase potential heat energy during combustion. Carburation applies to

graphite

diamond

buckminsterfullerene

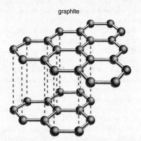  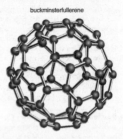

carbon Carbon has three allotropes: diamond, graphite, and the fullerenes. Diamond is strong because each carbon atom is linked to four other carbon atoms. Graphite is made up of layers that slide across one another (giving graphite its qualities as a lubricator); each layer is a giant molecule. In the fullerenes, the carbon atoms form spherical cages. Buckminsterfullerene (shown here) has 60 atoms. Other fullerenes, with 28, 32, 50, 70, and 76 carbon atoms, have also been identified.

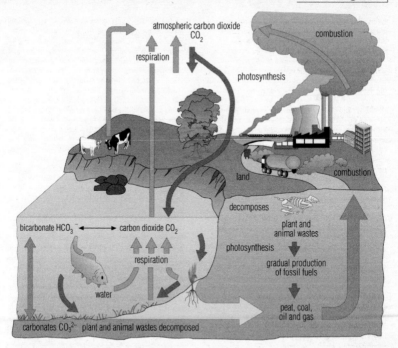

atmospheric carbon dioxide
CO_2

combustion

respiration

photosynthesis

land

combustion

decomposes

plant and
animal wastes

bicarbonate HCO_3^- ⟷ carbon dioxide CO_2

photosynthesis

gradual production
of fossil fuels

respiration

water

peat, coal,
oil and gas

carbonates CO_3^{2-} plant and animal wastes decomposed

carbon cycle The carbon cycle is necessary for the continuation of life. Since there is only a limited amount of carbon in the Earth and its atmosphere, carbon must be continuously recycled if life is to continue. Other chemicals necessary for life – nitrogen, sulphur, and phosphorus, for example – also circulate in natural cycles.

combustion in the cylinders of reciprocating petrol engines of the types used in aircraft, road vehicles, or marine vessels. The device by which the liquid fuel is atomized and mixed with air is called a **carburettor**.

carcinogen any agent that increases the chance of a cell becoming cancerous (see *cancer), including various chemical compounds, some viruses, X-rays, and other forms of ionizing radiation. The term is often used more narrowly to mean chemical carcinogens only.

carcinoma malignant *tumour arising from the skin, the glandular tissues, or the mucous membranes that line the gut and lungs.

Cardiff unitary authority in south Wales, created in 1996 from part of the former county of South Glamorgan; administrative headquarters is *Cardiff. **area:** 139 sq km/ 54 sq mi **towns:** Cardiff **physical:** highest point Garth Hill (307 m/1,007 ft) **features:** Llandaff cathedral (1120, restored in 20th century), Millennium Stadium, University of Wales, Cardiff; National Assembly for Wales **population:** (2001 est) 305,300.

Cardiff Welsh **Caerdydd**, seaport, capital of Wales (from 1955), and administrative centre of *Cardiff unitary authority, situated at the mouth of the Taff, Rhymney, and Ely rivers; population (2001 est) 305,300. It is the seat of government for the *National Assembly for Wales, which was established in 1998 following

the Government of Wales Act passed by the British parliament. Industries are predominantly in the service sector, with 82% of the workforce employed in services, the largest of which are education, business services, health, and consumer services. Manufacturing has declined in importance, although electronics and motor components remain important industries.

Cardin, Pierre (1922–) French pioneering fashion designer. He was the first to launch menswear (1960) and designer ready-to-wear collections (1963) and has given his name to a perfume. Cardin has franchised his name for labelling many different accessories and household products.

cardinal number in mathematics, one of the series of numbers 0, 1, 2, 3, 4, ... Cardinal numbers relate to quantity, whereas ordinal numbers (first, second, third, fourth, ...) relate to order.

Carey, Peter Philip (1943–) Australian novelist. Noted for his imaginative use of *magic realism, he won the Booker Prize for his novels *Oscar and Lucinda* (1988, filmed 1997) and *True History of the Kelly Gang* (2001). His other works include *Bliss* (1981, filmed 1985), *Illywhacker* (1985), and *Jack Maggs* (1998, Commonwealth Writers' Prize).

cargo cult one of a number of religious movements, chiefly in Melanesia, that first appeared in the late 19th

161

century but were particularly prevalent during and after World War II with the apparently miraculous dropping of supplies from aeroplanes. Adherents believe in the imminent arrival of European material goods, or 'cargo', by supernatural agents such as tribal gods or ancestral spirits. In anticipation, landing strips, wharves, warehouses, and other elaborate preparations for receiving the cargo are often made, and normal activities such as gardening cease, stocks of food are destroyed, and current customs abandoned. These preparations herald the end of the old order and the arrival of a new age of freedom and plenty.

Carib member of a group of *American Indian people of the north coast of South America and the islands of the southern West Indies in the Caribbean. Those who moved north to take the islands from the Arawak Indians were alleged by the conquering Spaniards to be fierce cannibals. In 1796, the English in the West Indies deported most of them to Roatan Island, off Honduras. Carib languages belong to the Ge-Pano-Carib family.

Caribbean Sea western part of the Atlantic Ocean between Cuba to the north and the northern coasts of South America to the south. Central America is to the west and to the east are the West Indies. The sea is about 2,740 km/1,700 mi long and 650–1,500 km/400–900 mi wide; area 2,640,000 sq km/1,019,304 sq mi. It is linked with the Gulf of Mexico via the Yucatan Strait. It is from here that the *Gulf Stream turns towards Europe.

caribou the *reindeer of North America.

caricature in the arts or literature, an exaggerated portrayal of an individual or type, aiming to ridicule or otherwise expose the subject; in art, features are often made comical or grotesque. Classical and medieval examples of pictorial caricatures survive. Artists of the 18th, 19th, and 20th centuries have often used caricature as a way of satirizing society and politics. Notable exponents include the French artist Honoré *Daumier and the German George *Grosz. In literature, caricatures have appeared since the comedies of Aristophanes in ancient Greece. Shakespeare and Dickens were adept at creating caricatures.

CARICOM acronym for Caribbean Community and Common Market.

caries decay and disintegration, usually of the substance of teeth (cavity) or bone, caused by acids produced when the bacteria that live in the mouth break down sugars in the food. Fluoride, a low sugar intake, and regular brushing are all protective. Caries form mainly in the 45 minutes following consumption of sugary food.

Carina constellation of the southern hemisphere, represented as a ship's keel. Its brightest star is *Canopus, the second brightest in the night sky; it also contains Eta Carinae, a massive and highly luminous star embedded in a gas cloud, perhaps 8,000 light years away from the Sun.

Carinthia German **Kärnten**, federal state of alpine southeast Austria, bordering Italy and Slovenia in the south; area 9,533 sq km/3,681 sq mi; population (2001 est) 561,100. Its capital is Klagenfurt.

Carlist supporter of the claims of the Spanish pretender Don Carlos de Bourbon (1788–1855), and his descendants, to the Spanish crown. The Carlist revolt continued, primarily in the Basque provinces, until 1839. In 1977 the Carlist political party was legalized and

Carlos Hugo de Bourbon Parma (1930–) renounced his claim as pretender and became reconciled with King Juan Carlos. See also *Bourbon.

Carlow (Irish 'four lakes') second-smallest county in the Republic of Ireland, in the province of Leinster; county town Carlow; area 900 sq km/347 sq mi; population (2002 est) 45,800. The land is mostly flat except for the Blackstairs mountains in the south (rising to 796 m/2,612 ft in Mount Leinster). The land in the west is fertile and well suited to dairy farming. Products include barley, wheat, and sugar beet.

Carlyle, Thomas (1795–1881) Scottish essayist and social historian. His works include the partly autobiographical *Sartor Resartus/The Tailor Retailored* (1833–34), reflecting his loss of Christian belief; *The French Revolution* (1837); and the long essay 'Chartism' (1839), attacking the doctrine of *laissez faire*. His prose style was idiosyncratic, encompassing grand, thunderous rhetoric and deliberate obscurity.

Carmarthenshire Welsh **Sir Gaerfyrddin**, unitary authority in south *Wales; a former county, it was part of Dyfed between 1975 and 1996. **area:** 2,390 sq km/923 sq mi **towns:** Carmarthen (administrative headquarters), Llanelli **physical:** rivers Tywi, Taf, Teifi; Black Mountain range in the east, southern spur of the Cambrian Mountains in the north, including Mynydd Mallaen (459 m/1,1,506 ft); along the coast are extensive sands and marshes. Carmarthenshire is dominated by the Vale of Tywi, but there are numerous grassy hills, mostly under 300 m/1,000 ft; the valleys are fertile and the hillsides afford good pasturage **features:** Brecon Beacons National Park; the largest Iron Age Hillfort in Wales at Garn Goch; the National Coracle Centre at Cenarth; home of Welsh poet Dylan *Thomas in the village of Laugharne, the National Botanic Garden of Wales, in the Regency park of Middleton Hall, was established in 2000 as a Millennium project and contains the Great Glasshouse, the largest single-span glasshouse in the world **population:** (2000 est) 169,100.

Carmelite order mendicant order of friars in the Roman Catholic Church. The order was founded on Mount Carmel in Palestine by Berthold, a crusader from Calabria, about 1155, and spread to Europe in the 13th century. The Carmelites have devoted themselves largely to missionary work and mystical theology. They are known as **White Friars** because of the white overmantle they wear (over a brown habit).

Carnac site of prehistoric *megaliths in Brittany, France, where remains of tombs and stone alignments of the period 2000 to 1500 BC (Neolithic and early Bronze Age) are found. Stones removed for local building have left some gaps in the alignments.

carnation any of a large number of double-flowered cultivated varieties of a plant belonging to the *pink family. The flowers smell like cloves; they are divided into flake, bizarre, and picotees, according to whether the petals have one or more colours on their white base, have the colour appearing in strips, or have a coloured border to the petals. (*Dianthus caryophyllus*, family Carophyllaceae.)

Carnegie, Andrew (1835–1919) Scottish-born US industrialist and philanthropist, who used his personal fortune from the creation of his Pittsburgh iron and steel industries to fund educational, cultural, and peace institutions, many of which bear his name. After his death, the Carnegie trusts continued his philanthropic activities. Carnegie Hall in New York, which opened in 1891 as the Music Hall, was renamed to honour his large donations in 1898.

carnivore organism that eats other animals. In zoology, a mammal of the order Carnivora.

Carnot, Lazare Nicolas Marguérite (1753–1823) French general and politician. A member of the National Convention in the French Revolution, he organized the armies of the republic. He was war minister 1800–01 and minister of the interior in 1815 under Napoleon. His work on fortification, *De la défense des places fortes* (1810), became a military textbook. Minister of the interior during the *hundred days, he was proscribed at the restoration of the monarchy and retired to Germany.

Carnot cycle series of changes in the physical condition of a gas in a reversible heat engine, necessarily in the following order: (1) isothermal expansion (without change of temperature), (2) adiabatic expansion (without change of heat content), (3) isothermal compression, and (4) adiabatic compression.

carob small Mediterranean tree belonging to the *legume family. Its pods, 20 cm/8 in long, are used as an animal feed; they are also the source of a chocolate substitute. (*Ceratonia siliqua*, family Leguminosae.)

Caroline Islands scattered archipelago in Micronesia, Pacific Ocean, consisting of over 500 coral islets; area 1,200 sq km/463 sq mi. The chief islands are Ponape, Kusai, and Truk in the eastern group, and Yap and Palau in the western group. Products include coconuts, cassava, copra, sugar cane, and fish, especially bonito.

Caroline of Anspach (1683–1737) Queen of George II of Great Britain and Ireland. The daughter of the Margrave of Brandenburg-Anspach, she married George, Electoral Prince of Hannover, in 1705, and followed him to England in 1714 when his father became King George I.

Caroline of Brunswick (1768–1821) Queen consort of George IV of Great Britain. King George attempted to divorce her, unsuccessfully, on his accession to the throne in 1820.

Carolingian art the art of the reign of Charlemagne, the first Holy Roman Emperor (800–814), and his descendants until about 900. In line with his revival of learning and Roman culture, Charlemagne greatly encouraged the arts, which had been in eclipse. Illuminated manuscripts, metalwork, and small-scale sculpture survive from this period. See also *medieval art.

Carolingian dynasty Frankish dynasty descending from *Pepin the Short (died 768) and named after his son Charlemagne; its last ruler was Louis V of France (reigned 966–87), who was followed by Hugh *Capet, first ruler of the Capetian dynasty.

carp fish *Cyprinus carpio* found all over the world. It commonly grows to 50 cm/1.8 ft and 3 kg/7 lb, but may be even larger. It lives in lakes, ponds, and slow rivers. The wild form is drab, but cultivated forms may be golden, or may have few large scales (mirror carp) or be scaleless (leather carp). **Koi** carp are highly prized and can grow up to 1 m/3 ft long with a distinctive pink, red, white, or black colouring.

Carpaccio, Vittore (1450/60–1525/26) Italian painter. He is famous for scenes of his native Venice, for example, the series *The Legend of St Ursula* (1490–98;

Accademia, Venice). His paintings are a graceful blend of fantasy and closely observed details from everyday life.

Carpathian Mountains central European mountain system, forming a semicircle through Slovakia–Poland–Ukraine–Moldova–Romania, 1,450 km/900 mi long. The central **Tatra Mountains** on the Slovak–Polish frontier include the highest peak, Gerlachovka, 2,663 m/8,737 ft.

carpel female reproductive unit in flowering plants (*angiosperms). It usually comprises an *ovary containing one or more ovules, the stalk or style, and a *stigma at its top which receives the pollen. A flower may have one or more carpels, and they may be separate or fused together. Collectively the carpels of a flower are known as the *gynoecium.

Carpentaria, Gulf of shallow gulf opening out of the Arafura Sea, between the capes of Arnhem and York, north of Australia; 600 km/373 mi long, 490 km/304 mi wide. The first European to reach it was the Dutch navigator Abel Tasman in 1606 and it was named in 1623 in honour of Pieter Carpentier, governor general of the Dutch East Indies.

carpetbagger in US history, derogatory name for any of the entrepreneurs and politicians from the North who moved to the Southern states during *Reconstruction (1865–77) after the Civil War, to exploit the chaotic conditions for their own benefit.

carpet beetle small black or brown beetle. The larvae are covered with hairs and often known as **woolly bears**; they feed on carpets, fabrics, and hides causing damage.

carragheen species of deep-reddish branched seaweed. Named after Carragheen, near Waterford, in the Republic of Ireland, it is found on rocky shores on both sides of the Atlantic. It is exploited commercially in food and medicines and as cattle feed. (*Chondrus crispus*.)

Carrel, Alexis (1873–1944) French-born US surgeon who was awarded a Nobel Prize for Physiology or Medicine in 1912 for his work on the techniques for connecting severed blood vessels and for transplanting organs. Working at the Rockefeller Institute, New York City, he devised a way of joining blood vessels end to end (anastomosing). This was a key move in the development of transplant surgery, as was his work on keeping organs viable outside the body.

carrier in medicine, anyone who harbours an infectious organism without ill effects but can pass the infection to others. The term is also applied to those who carry a recessive gene for a disease or defect without manifesting the condition.

Carroll, Lewis (1832–1898) pen-name of Charles Lutwidge Dodgson, English author of the children's classics *Alice's Adventures in Wonderland* (1865) and its sequel *Through the Looking-Glass, and What Alice Found There* (1872). Among later works was the mock-heroic narrative poem *The Hunting of the Snark* (1876). He was a lecturer in mathematics at Oxford University from 1855 until 1881 and also published mathematical works.

carrot hardy European biennial plant with feathery leaves and an orange tapering root that is eaten as a vegetable. It has been cultivated since the 16th century. The root has a high sugar content and also contains carotene, which is converted into vitamin A by the human liver. (*Daucus carota*, family Umbelliferae.)

cartel (German *Kartell* 'a group') agreement among national or international firms not to compete with one another. Cartels can be formed to fix prices by maintaining the price of a product at an artificially low level, to deter new competitors, or to restrict production of a commodity in order to maintain prices at an artificially high level to boost profits. The members of a cartel may also agree on which member should win a contract, known as bid rigging, or which customers they will supply. Cartels therefore represent a form of *oligopoly. *OPEC, for example, is an example of a transnational cartel restricting the output of a commodity, in this case oil. In many countries, including the USA and the UK, companies operating a cartel may be breaching legislation designed to abolish anticompetitive practices.

Carter, Jimmy (1924–) born James Earl Carter, 39th president of the USA 1977–81, a Democrat. Features of his presidency were the return of the Panama Canal Zone to Panama, the introduction of an amnesty programme for deserters and draft dodgers of the Vietnam War, and the Camp David Agreements for peace in the Middle East. During the 1990s he emerged as a mediator and peace negotiator, securing President Jean-Bertrand Aristide's safe return to Haiti in October 1994. He was awarded the Presidential Medal of Freedom in 1999 and the Nobel Prize for Peace in 2002.

Cartesian coordinates in *coordinate geometry, components used to define the position of a point by its perpendicular distance from a set of two or more axes, or reference lines. For a two-dimensional area defined by two axes at right angles (a horizontal x-axis and a vertical y-axis), the coordinates of a point are given by its perpendicular distances from the y-axis and x-axis, written in the form (x, y). For example, a point P that lies three units from the y-axis and four units from the x-axis has Cartesian coordinates $(3, 4)$ (see *abscissa).

Carthage ancient Phoenician port in North Africa founded by colonists from Tyre in the late 9th century BC; it lay 16 km/10 mi north of Tunis, Tunisia. A leading trading centre, it was in conflict with Greece from the 6th century BC, and then with Rome, and was destroyed by Roman forces in 146 BC at the end of the *Punic Wars. About 45 BC, Roman colonists settled in Carthage, and it became the wealthy capital of the province of Africa. After its capture by the Vandals in AD 439 it was little more than a pirate stronghold. From 533 it formed part of the Byzantine Empire until its final destruction by Arabs in 698, during their conquest in the name of Islam.

Carthusian order Roman Catholic order of monks and, later, nuns, founded by St Bruno in 1084 at Chartreuse, near Grenoble, France. Living chiefly in unbroken silence, they ate one vegetarian meal a day and supported themselves by their own labours; the rule is still one of severe austerity.

Cartier, Jacques (1491–1557) French navigator who, while seeking a northwest passage to China and Japan in 1535, was the first European to sail up the St Lawrence River, Canada. On this expedition, he named the site of Montréal.

Cartier-Bresson, Henri (1908–2004) French photographer. He is considered one of the greatest photographic artists and photojournalists. His

documentary work was shot in black and white, using a small-format Leica camera. His work is remarkable for its tightly structured composition and his ability to capture the decisive moment. He was a founder member of Magnum Photos Inc, a cooperative photographic agency that supplied leading photojournalists to cover world events.

cartilage flexible bluish-white *connective tissue made up of the protein collagen. In cartilaginous fish it forms the skeleton; in other vertebrates it forms the greater part of the embryonic skeleton, and is replaced by *bone in the course of development, except in areas of wear such as bone endings, and the discs between the backbones. It also forms structural tissue in the larynx, nose, and external ear of mammals.

cartilaginous fish fish in which the skeleton is made of cartilage. Sharks, rays, and skates are cartilaginous. Their scales are placoid (isolated structures made of dentine resembling simple teeth) and are present all over the body surface. The scales do not continue to grow once fully formed, but are replaced by new scales as they wear out. The notochord (primitive skeletal rod) is reduced and replaced to varying degrees by cartilage.

cartography art and practice of drawing *maps, originally with pens and drawing boards, but now mostly with computer-aided drafting programs.

cartoon humorous or satirical drawing or *caricature; a strip cartoon or comic strip; traditionally, the base design for a large fresco, mosaic, or tapestry, transferred to a wall or canvas by tracing or pricking out the design on the cartoon and then dabbing with powdered charcoal to create a faint reproduction. Surviving examples include Leonardo da Vinci's *Virgin and St Anne* (National Gallery, London).

Cartwright, Edmund (1743–1823) English inventor. He patented the power loom (1785), built a weaving mill (1787), and patented a wool-combing machine (1789).

Caruso, Enrico (1873–1921) Italian operatic tenor. His voice was dark, with full-bodied tone and remarkable dynamic range. In 1902 he starred, with the Australian soprano Nellie Melba, in Puccini's *La Bohème/ Bohemian Life*. He was among the first opera singers to achieve lasting fame through gramophone recordings.

caryatid building support or pillar in the shape of a female figure, the name deriving from the Karyatides, who were priestesses at the temple of Artemis at Karyai; the male equivalent is a **telamon** or **atlas**.

Casablanca Arabic **Dar el-Beida**, port, commercial, and industrial centre on the Atlantic coast of Morocco; population (1994 est) 2,770,600. Casablanca is one of the major ports of Africa, and the industrial and commercial centre of Morocco. Industries include textiles, leather, electronic goods, and processed food; it trades in fish, phosphates, and manganese. The Great Hassan II Mosque, completed in 1989, is the world's largest; it is built on a platform (40,000 sq m/430,000 sq ft) jutting out over the Atlantic, with walls 60 m/ 200 ft high, topped by a hydraulic sliding roof, and a minaret 175 m/574 ft high.

Casals, Pablo (Pau) (1876–1973) Catalan cellist, composer, and conductor. He was largely self-taught. As a cellist, he was celebrated for his interpretations of Johann Sebastian Bach's unaccompanied suites. He wrote instrumental and choral works, including the Christmas oratorio *The Manger*. He was an outspoken critic of fascism who openly defied Franco, and a tireless crusader for peace.

Casanova de Seingalt, Giovanni Giacomo (1725–1798) Italian adventurer, spy, violinist, librarian, and, according to his *Memoires* (published 1826–38, although the complete text did not appear until 1960–61), one of the world's great lovers. From 1774 he was a spy in the Venetian police service. In 1782 a libel got him into trouble, and after more wanderings he was in 1785 appointed librarian to Count Waldstein at his castle of Dûx in Bohemia. It was here that Casanova wrote his *Memoires*.

casein main protein of milk, from which it can be separated by the action of acid, the enzyme rennin, or bacteria (souring); it is also the main protein in cheese. Casein is used as a protein supplement in the treatment of malnutrition. It is used commercially in cosmetics, glues, and as a sizing for coating paper.

cash crop crop grown solely for sale rather than for the farmer's own use, for example, coffee, cotton, or sugar beet. Many developing world countries grow cash crops to meet their debt repayments rather than grow food for their own people.

cashew tropical American tree. Widely cultivated in India and Africa, it produces poisonous kidney-shaped nuts that become edible after being roasted. (*Anacardium occidentale*, family Anacardiaceae.)

cash flow input of cash required to cover all expenses of a business, whether revenue or capital. Alternatively, the actual or prospective balance between the various outgoing and incoming movements which are designated in total. Cash flow is positive if receipts are greater than payments; negative if payments are greater than receipts. Money may be received through cash sales of products or assets, and receipts of debts. Money may flow out through purchase of raw materials, the settlement of debts, and the payment of salaries.

cashmere natural fibre originating from the wool of the goats of Kashmir, India, used for shawls, scarves, sweaters, and coats. It can also be made artificially.

Caspian Sea world's largest inland sea, on the border between Europe and Asia east of the Black Sea, divided between Iran, Azerbaijan, Russia, Kazakhstan, and Turkmenistan. It extends north–south for 1,200 km/745 mi, and its average width is 300 km/186 mi; area about 400,000 sq km/155,000 sq mi, with a maximum depth of 1,000 m/3,250 ft. An underwater ridge divides it into two halves, of which the shallow northern half is almost salt-free. There are no tides, but violent storms make navigation hazardous. The chief ports are Astrakhan (Russia), Baku (Azerbaijan), and Bandar Shah (Iran). The River Volga supplies 80% of freshwater inflow; the Ural, Emba, Terek, Kura, and Atrek rivers also flow into the Caspian Sea. Prolonged drought, drainage in the north, and regulation of the Volga and Kura rivers reduced the area from 430,000 sq km/166,000 sq mi in 1930 to 382,000 sq km/147,000 sq mi in 1957, and left the sea approximately 28 m/90 ft below sea level. This turned much of the shallow northeastern part of the sea into dry land or marsh. In June 1991 opening of sluices in river dams caused the water level to rise dramatically to its former level, threatening towns and industrial areas.

Cassandra in Greek mythology, Trojan daughter of Priam and Hecuba. Loved by the god *Apollo, she was promised the gift of prophecy in return for her favours, but rejected his advances after receiving her powers. Her thwarted lover cursed her prophecies with disbelief, including that of the fall of Troy.

cassava *or* **manioc** plant belonging to the spurge family. Native to South America, it is now widely grown throughout the tropics for its starch-containing roots, from which tapioca and bread are made. (*Manihot utilissima*, family Euphorbiaceae.)

Cassiopeia prominent constellation of the northern hemisphere, named after the mother of Andromeda (who was the wife of Perseus). It has a distinctive W-shape, and contains one of the most powerful radio sources in the sky, Cassiopeia A. This is the remains of a *supernova (star explosion) that occurred *c.* AD 1702, too far away to be seen from Earth.

Cassius (*c.* 85 BC–42 BC) born Gaius Cassius Longinus, Roman general and politician, one of Julius *Caesar's assassins. He fought with Marcus Licinius *Crassus (the Elder) against the Parthians in 53 BC and distinguished himself after Carrhae by defending the province of Syria. He sided with Pompey against Julius Caesar on the outbreak of the civil war in 49 BC, but was pardoned after the battle of Pharsalus in 48 BC. Nevertheless, he became a leader in the conspiracy against Caesar which resulted in the latter's murder in 44 BC.

cassowary large flightless bird, genus *Casuarius*, of the family Casuariidae, order Casuariiformes, found in New Guinea and northern Australia, usually in forests. Related to the emu, the cassowary has a bare head with a horny casque, or helmet, on top, and brightly-coloured skin on the neck. Its loose plumage is black and its wings tiny, but it can run and leap well and defends itself by kicking. Cassowaries stand up to 1.5 m/ 5 ft tall. They live in pairs and the male usually incubates the eggs, about six in number, which the female lays in a nest of leaves and grass.

castanets Spanish percussion instrument made of two hollowed wooden shells, originally chestnut wood (Spanish *castaña*). They are held in the palm and drummed together by the fingers to produce a rhythmic accompaniment to dance.

caste (Portuguese *casta* 'race') a system of stratifying a society into ranked groups defined by marriage, descent, and occupation. Most common in South Asia, caste systems are also found in other societies. such as in Mali and Rwanda. In the past, such systems could be found in Japan, in South Africa under apartheid, and among the *Natchez – an American Indian people. The caste system in Hindu society dates from ancient times. Traditional society is loosely ranked into four varnas (social classes): Brahmin (priests), Kshatriyas (nobles and warriors), Vaisyas (traders and farmers), and Sudras (servants), plus a fifth group, Harijan (untouchables). Their subdivisions, jati, number over 3,000, each with its own occupation. A Hindu's *dharma, or holy path in life, depends not only on the stage of life (ashrama) that he or she is currently in, but also on caste; it is a duty to follow the caste into which one is born by the laws of rebirth. Traditionally, Hindus would only mix with and marry people of their own caste.

Castile kingdom founded in the 10th century, occupying the central plateau of Spain. Its union with *Aragón in 1479, based on the marriage of Ferdinand

and Isabella, effected the foundation of the Spanish state, which at the time was occupied and ruled by the *Moors. Castile comprised the two great basins separated by the Sierra de Gredos and the Sierra de Guadarrama, known traditionally as Old and New Castile. The area now forms the autonomous communities of *Castilla-León and *Castilla-La Mancha.

Castilian language member of the Romance branch of the Indo-European language family, originating in northwestern Spain, in the provinces of Old and New Castile. It is the basis of present-day standard Spanish (see *Spanish language) and is often seen as the same language, the terms *castellano* and *español* being used interchangeably in both Spain and the Spanish-speaking countries of the Americas.

Castilla-La Mancha autonomous community of central Spain; area 79,226 sq km/30,589 sq mi; population (2001 est) 1,755,100. It includes the provinces of Albacete, Ciudad Real, Cuenca, Guadalajara, and Toledo. Irrigated land produces mainly cereals, sunflowers, cotton, and vines, especially in the Valdepeñas region, and merino sheep are raised. The capital is Toledo. It was established as an autonomous region in 1982.

Castilla-León *or* **Castilla y León** autonomous community of central Spain; area 94,147 sq km/36,350 sq mi; population (2001 est) 2,479,400. It includes the provinces of Burgos, León, Palencia, Salamanca, Segovia, Soria, Valladolid, and Zamora. Irrigated land produces wheat, sugarbeets, and potatoes; cattle, sheep, and fighting bulls are bred in the uplands. There are important food industries in Burgos, Palencia, and Segovia provinces. The capital is Valladolid, which is the main manufacturing centre, particularly for engineering and the production of motor vehicles. Castilla-León was established as an autonomous region in 1983.

cast iron cheap but invaluable constructional material, most commonly used for car engine blocks. Cast iron is partly refined pig (crude) *iron, which is very fluid when molten and highly suitable for shaping by casting; it contains too many impurities (for example, carbon) to be readily shaped in any other way. Solid cast iron is heavy and can absorb great shock but is very brittle.

castle fortified building or group of buildings, characteristic of medieval Europe. The castle was originally designed as a defensive fortification, but it also functioned as a residence for the royalty and nobility, an administrative centre, and a place of safety for local people in times of invasion. In England castles were always designed as a fortified home. In 13th-century Wales, Edward I built a string of castles as military centres to keep control of the country. The castle underwent many changes, its size, design, and construction being largely determined by changes in siege tactics and the development of artillery. Outstanding examples are the 12th-century Krak des Chevaliers, Syria (built by crusaders); the 13th-century Caernarfon Castle, Wales; and the 15th-century Manzanares el Real, Spain.

Castlereagh, Robert Stewart (1769–1822) Viscount Castlereagh, British Tory politician. As chief secretary for Ireland 1797–1801, he suppressed the rebellion of 1798 and helped the younger Pitt secure the union of England, Scotland, and Ireland in 1801.

As foreign secretary 1812–22, he coordinated European opposition to Napoleon and represented Britain at the Congress of Vienna (1814–15).

Castor and Pollux/Polydeuces *or the* **Dioscuri** in Greek mythology, the inseparable twins or sons of *Leda; brothers of *Helen and *Clytemnestra; protectors of sailors. Their brotherly love was symbolized in the constellation *Gemini. Many versions of their birth exist; in one tradition, the boys were fathered by Zeus in the form of a swan, and born from an egg.

castor-oil plant tall tropical and subtropical shrub belonging to the spurge family. The seeds, called 'castor beans' in North America, yield the purgative castor oil (which cleans out the bowels) and also ricin, one of the most powerful poisons known. Ricin can be used to destroy cancer cells, leaving normal cells untouched. (*Ricinus communis*, family Euphorbiaceae.)

castration removal of the sex glands (either ovaries or testes). Male domestic animals may be castrated to prevent reproduction, to make them larger or more docile, or to eradicate disease.

Castries *or* **Port Castries** capital and port of St Lucia, on the northwest coast of the island; population (2001 est) 59,600. From its almost enclosed harbour, it exports sugar cane, bananas, limes, coconuts, cacao, and rum. The town processes foodstuffs and drinks, and manufacturing industries include tobacco, textiles, wood, rubber and metal products, chemicals, and printing. The nearby Vigie airport has helped the rise of a significant tourist industry.

Castro (Ruz), Fidel (1927–) Cuban communist politician, prime minister 1959–76, and president from 1976. He led the revolution that overthrew the right-wing regime of the dictator Fulgencio Batista in 1959. He raised the standard of living for most Cubans but dealt harshly with dissenters. From 1991, deprived of the support of the USSR and experiencing the long-term effects of a US trade embargo, Castro began to make reforms limiting state control over the economy; foreign ownership was permitted in major areas of commerce and industry from 1995 (the USA continued its economic embargo). In February 1998 Castro was elected president.

cat small, domesticated, carnivorous mammal *Felis catus*, often kept as a pet or for catching small pests such as rodents. Found in many colour variants, it may have short, long, or no hair, but the general shape and size is constant – fully-grown cats range from about 51 cm/21 in to about 71 cm/28 in in length. Cats have short muzzles, strong limbs, and flexible spines that enable them to jump and climb. All walk on the pads of their toes (digitigrade) and have retractile claws, so are able to stalk their prey silently. They have large eyes and an acute sense of hearing. The canine teeth are long and well-developed, as are the shearing teeth in the side of the mouth.

catabolism in biology, the destructive part of *metabolism where living tissue is changed into energy and waste products. It is the opposite of anabolism. It occurs continuously in the body, but is accelerated during many disease processes, such as fever, and in starvation.

catacomb (Greek *kata* 'down'; *kumbe* 'a hollow') underground burial chambers, such as the catacombs of the early Christians. Examples include those beneath the basilica of St Sebastian in Rome, where bodies were buried in niches in the walls of the tunnels.

Catalan language member of the Romance branch of the Indo-European language family, an Iberian language closely related to Provençal in France. It is spoken in Cataluña in northeastern Spain, the Balearic Islands, Andorra, and a corner of southwestern France.

Catalonia alternative spelling for *Cataluña.

catalpa any of a group of trees belonging to the trumpet creeper family, found in North America, China, and the West Indies. The northern catalpa (*Catalpa speciosa*) of North America grows to 20 m/65 ft and has heart-shaped deciduous leaves and tubular white flowers with purple borders. (Genus *Catalpa*, family Bignoniaceae.)

Cataluña *or* **Catalonia** Catalan **Catalunya**, autonomous community of northeast Spain; area 31,930 sq km/12,328 sq mi; population (2001 est) 6,361,400. It includes the provinces of Barcelona, Girona, Lleida, and Tarragona. Olives, vines, cereals, and nuts are grown, and some livestock is raised. Cataluña is the main industrial region of Spain. Originally based on the textile industry, the region has diversified into engineering, chemicals, paper, publishing, and many service industries; hydroelectric power is also produced. The capital is *Barcelona, which contains more than one-third of the regionouths residents.

catalyst substance that alters the speed of, or makes possible, a chemical or biochemical reaction but remains unchanged at the end of the reaction. *Enzymes are natural biochemical catalysts. In practice most catalysts are used to speed up reactions.

catalytic converter device fitted to the exhaust system of a motor vehicle in order to reduce toxic emissions from the engine. It converts the harmful exhaust products that cause *air pollution to relatively harmless ones.

catamaran (Tamil 'tied log') twin-hulled sailing vessel, based on the native craft of South America and the Indies, made of logs lashed together, with an outrigger. A similar vessel with three hulls is known as a trimaran. Car ferries with a wave-piercing catamaran design are also in use in parts of Europe and North America. They have a pointed main hull and two outriggers and travel at a speed of 35 knots (84.5 kph/52.5 mph).

cataract eye disease in which the crystalline lens or its capsule becomes cloudy, causing blindness. Fluid accumulates between the fibres of the lens and gives place to deposits of *albumin. These coalesce into rounded bodies, the lens fibres break down, and areas of the lens or the lens capsule become filled with opaque products of degeneration. The condition is estimated to have blinded more than 25 million people worldwide, and 150,000 in the UK.

catarrh inflammation of any mucous membrane, especially of the nose and throat, with increased production of mucus.

catastrophe theory mathematical theory developed by René Thom in 1972, in which he showed that the growth of an organism proceeds by a series of gradual changes that are triggered by, and in turn trigger, large-scale changes or 'catastrophic' jumps. It also has applications in engineering – for example, the gradual strain on the structure of a bridge that can eventually result in a sudden collapse – and has been extended to economic and psychological events.

category in philosophy, a fundamental concept applied to being that cannot be reduced to anything more elementary. Aristotle listed ten categories: substance, quantity, quality, relation, place, time, position, state, action, and passion.

caterpillar larval stage of a *butterfly or *moth. Wormlike in form, the body is segmented, may be hairy, and often has scent glands. The head has strong biting mandibles, silk glands, and a spinneret.

catfish fish belonging to the order Siluriformes, in which barbels (feelers) on the head are well-developed, so giving a resemblance to the whiskers of a cat. Catfishes are found worldwide, mainly but not exclusively in fresh water, and are plentiful in South America.

cathedral (Latin *cathedra* 'seat' or 'throne') principal Christian church of a bishop or archbishop, containing his throne, which is usually situated on the south side of the choir. In the Middle Ages, cathedrals were used for state occasions, such as parliaments, and they are still used for royal coronations and weddings, and state funerals. Many cathedrals also house the relics of the saints, and so in the Middle Ages were centres of *pilgrimage. Until modern times, only a town with a cathedral could be called a city.

Catherine (II) the Great (1729–1796) Empress of Russia from 1762, and daughter of the German prince of Anhalt-Zerbst. In 1745 she married the Russian grand duke Peter. Catherine dominated her husband; six months after he became Tsar Peter III in 1762, he was murdered in a coup and Catherine ruled alone. During her reign Russia extended its boundaries to include territory from wars with the Turks (1768–74), (1787–92), and from the partitions of Poland in 1772, 1793, and 1795, as well as establishing hegemony over the Black Sea.

Catherine de' Medici (1519–1589) French queen consort of Henry II, whom she married in 1533; daughter of Lorenzo de' Medici, Duke of Urbino; and mother of Francis II, Charles IX, and Henry III. At first outshone by Henry's mistress Diane de Poitiers (1490–1566), she became regent for Charles IX (1560–63) and remained in power until his death in 1574.

Catherine of Alexandria, St (lived early 4th century) Christian martyr. According to legend she disputed with 50 scholars, refusing to give up her faith and marry Emperor Maxentius. Her emblem is a wheel, on which her persecutors tried to kill her (the wheel broke and she was beheaded). Her feast day is 25 November; removed from the church calendar in 1969.

Catherine of Aragón (1485–1536) First queen of Henry VIII of England, 1509–33, and mother of Mary I. Catherine had married Henry's elder brother Prince Arthur in 1501 and on his death in 1502 was betrothed to Henry, marrying him on his accession. She failed to produce a male heir and Henry divorced her without papal approval, thus creating the basis for the English *Reformation.

Catherine of Valois (1401–1437) Queen of Henry V of England, whom she married in 1420; the mother of Henry VI. After the death of Henry V, she secretly married Owen Tudor (*c.* 1400–1461) about 1425, and their son Edmund Tudor was the father of Henry VII.

cathode in chemistry, the negative electrode of an electrolytic cell, towards which positive particles (cations), usually in solution, are attracted. See *electrolysis. A cathode is given its negative charge by connecting it to the negative side of an external electrical supply.

cathode in electronics, the part of an electronic device in which electrons are generated. In a thermionic valve, electrons are produced by the heating effect of an applied current; in a photocell, they are produced by the interaction of light and a semiconducting material. The cathode is kept at a negative potential relative to the device's other electrodes (anodes) in order to ensure that the liberated electrons stream away from the cathode and towards the anodes.

cathode ray stream of fast-moving electrons that travel from a cathode (negative electrode) towards an anode (positive electrode) in a vacuum tube. They carry a negative charge and can be deflected by electric and magnetic fields. Cathode rays focused into fine beams of fast electrons are used in cathode-ray tubes, the electrons' *kinetic energy being converted into light energy as they collide with the tube's fluorescent screen.

cathode-ray oscilloscope (CRO) instrument used to measure electrical potentials or voltages that vary over time and to display the waveforms of electrical oscillations or signals. Readings are displayed graphically on the screen of a *cathode-ray tube.

cathode-ray tube (CRT) vacuum tube in which a beam of electrons is produced and focused onto a fluorescent screen. The electrons' kinetic energy is converted into light energy as they collide with the screen. It is an essential component of television receivers, computer visual display units, and *oscilloscopes.

Catholic Church the whole body of the Christian church, though usually referring to the Roman Catholic Church (see *Roman Catholicism).

Catholic Emancipation in British history, acts of Parliament passed between 1780 and 1829 to relieve Roman Catholics of civil and political restrictions imposed from the time of Henry VIII and the Reformation.

cation *ion carrying a positive charge. During *electrolysis, cations in the electrolyte move to the cathode (negative electrode). Cations are formed from *atoms by loss of electrons during *ionic bonding. *Metals form cations.

catkin in flowering plants (*angiosperms), a pendulous inflorescence, bearing numerous small, usually unisexual flowers. The tiny flowers are stalkless and the petals and sepals are usually absent or much reduced in size. Many types of trees bear catkins, including willows, poplars, and birches. Most plants with catkins are wind-pollinated, so the male catkins produce large quantities of pollen. Some *gymnosperms also have catkin-like structures that produce pollen, for example, the swamp cypress *Taxodium*.

CAT scan *or* **CT scan** acronym for **computerized axial tomography scan**, sophisticated method of X-ray imaging. Quick and noninvasive, CAT scanning is used in medicine as an aid to diagnosis, helping to pinpoint problem areas without the need for exploratory surgery. It is also used in archaeology to investigate mummies.

Catskill Mountains mountain range in southeastern New York State, USA, forming part of the *Appalachian Mountains west of the Hudson River; drained by headwaters of the Delaware River; the highest peaks are Slide Mountain (1,281 m/4,204 ft) and Hunter

Mountain (1,227 m/4,026 ft). The Catskill Mountains have long been a vacation and resort centre for residents of New York City, offering hiking, skiing, hunting and fishing. The valleys, which have been carved out by glaciation, are the chief scenic attractions; much of the mountain area is included in the Catskill Forest Preserve.

cattle any large, ruminant, even-toed, hoofed mammal of the genus *Bos*, family Bovidae, including wild species such as the yak, gaur, gayal, banteng, and kouprey, as well as domestic breeds. Asiatic water buffaloes *Bubalus*, African buffaloes *Syncerus*, and American bison *Bison* are not considered true cattle. Cattle are bred for meat (beef cattle) or milk (dairy cattle).

Catullus, Gaius Valerius (c. 84–54 BC) Roman lyric poet. He wrote in a variety of metres and forms, from short narratives and hymns to epigrams. He moved with ease through the literary and political society of late republican Rome. His love affair with the woman he called 'Lesbia' provided the inspiration for many of his poems.

Caucasus mountain range extending from the Taman Peninsula on the Black Sea to the Apsheron Peninsula on the Caspian Sea, a total length of 1,200 km/750 mi. The Caucasus, which form the boundary between Europe and Asia, is divided into the **Greater Caucasus** (northern) and **Little Caucasus** (southern) chains. The range crosses the territory of the Russian Federation, Georgia, Armenia, and Azerbaijan. At 5,642 m/18,510 ft, Elbrus (in the Greater Caucasus) is the highest peak in Europe.

cauliflower variety of *cabbage, with a large edible head of fleshy, cream-coloured flowers which do not fully mature. It is similar to broccoli but less hardy. (*Brassica oleracea botrytis*, family Cruciferae.)

causality in philosophy, a consideration of the connection between cause and effect, usually referred to as the 'causal relationship'.

cauterization in medicine, the use of special instruments to burn or fuse small areas of body tissue to destroy dead cells, prevent the spread of infection, or seal tiny blood vessels to minimize blood loss during surgery.

cavalier horseman of noble birth, but mainly used as a derogatory nickname to describe a male supporter of Charles I in the English Civil War (Cavalier), typically with courtly dress and long hair (as distinct from a Roundhead); also a supporter of Charles II after the Restoration.

Cavalli, (Pietro) Francesco (1602–1676) Italian composer. He was organist at St Mark's, Venice, and the first to make opera a popular entertainment with such works as *Equisto* (1643) and *Xerxes* (1654), later performed in honour of Louis XIV's wedding in Paris. Twenty-seven of his operas survive.

Cavan county of the Republic of Ireland, on the border with Northern Ireland, in the province of Ulster; county town Cavan; area 1,890 sq km/730 sq mi; population (2002 est) 56,400. The chief rivers are the Woodford, the Shannon (rising on the south slopes of Cuilcagh mountain; 667 m/2,188 ft), and the Erne, which divides Cavan into two parts: a narrow, mostly low-lying stretch of ground, 30 km/19 mi long, between Leitrim and Fermanagh; and an eastern section of wild and bare hill country. The chief towns are Cavan and Kilmore, seat of Roman Catholic and Protestant bishoprics. Agriculture is the chief industry; mushrooms and oats are major crops; dairying and pig- and beef-farming are also important.

cave passage or tunnel – or series of tunnels – formed underground by water or by waves on a coast. Caves of the former type commonly occur in areas underlain by limestone, such as Kentucky, USA, and many Balkan regions, where the rocks are soluble in water. A **pothole** is a vertical hole in rock caused by water descending a crack; it is thus open to the sky.

Cavendish, Henry (1731–1810) English physicist and chemist. He discovered hydrogen (which he called 'inflammable air') in 1766, and determined the compositions of water and of nitric acid. The Cavendish experiment (1798) enabled him to discover the mass and density of the Earth.

caviar salted roe (eggs) of sturgeon, salmon, and other fishes. Caviar is prepared by beating and straining the egg sacs until the eggs are free from fats and then adding salt. Russia and Iran are the main exporters of the most prized variety of caviar, derived from Caspian Sea sturgeon. Iceland produces various high-quality, lower-priced caviars.

Cavour, Camillo Benso di, Count (1810–1861) Italian nationalist politician, a leading figure in the Italian *Risorgimento*. As prime minister of Piedmont 1852–59 and 1860–61, he enlisted the support of Britain and France for the concept of a united Italy, achieved in 1861; after expelling the Austrians in 1859, he assisted Garibaldi in liberating southern Italy in 1860.

cavy short-tailed South American rodent, family Caviidae, of which the guinea-pig *Cavia porcellus* is an example. Wild cavies are greyish or brownish with rather coarse hair. They live in small groups in burrows, and have been kept for food since ancient times.

Caxton, William (c. 1422–1491) English printer. He learned the art of *printing in Cologne, Germany, in 1471 and set up a press in Belgium where he produced the first book printed in English, his own version of a French romance, *Recuyell of the Historyes of Troye* (1474). Returning to England in 1476, he established himself in London, where he produced the first book printed in England, *Dictes or Sayengis of the Philosophres* (1477).

Cayenne capital and chief port of the overseas *département* of *French Guiana in South America; situated on Cayenne Island on the Atlantic coast at the mouth of the River Cayenne; population (1999 est) 50,600. The main occupation is fishing, of which fresh and processed shrimp constitute nearly 75% of total exports by value. Rum, pineapples, hardwoods, and cayenne pepper – a main constituent of hot curries – are also exported. Many imports pass through the port as the country is very much import-dependent.

cayenne pepper *or* **red pepper** spice produced from the dried fruits of several species of *capsicum (especially *Capsicum frutescens*), a tropical American group of plants. Its origins are completely different from black or white pepper, which comes from an East Indian plant (*Piper nigrum*).

cayman another name for *caiman.

Cayman Islands British island group in the West Indies; area 260 sq km/100 sq mi; population (2001 est) 35,500 (mostly on Grand Cayman). The Caymans lie 160 km/100 mi south of Cuba and comprise three low-lying coral islands: Grand Cayman, Cayman Brac, and Little Cayman. The capital is George Town (on Grand Cayman), which has an international airport to serve the tourist industry. The islands export seawhip coral (a source of prostaglandins), lobsters, shrimps, honey, and jewellery.

CD abbreviation for *compact disc; **Corps Diplomatique** (French 'Diplomatic Corps'); **certificate of deposit**.

CD-ROM acronym for **Compact-Disc Read-Only Memory**, computer storage device developed from the technology of the audio *compact disc. It consists of a plastic-coated metal disk, on which binary digital information is etched in the form of microscopic pits. This can then be read optically by passing a laser beam over the disk. CD-ROMs typically hold over 600 megabytes of data, and are used in distributing large amounts of text, graphics, audio, and video, such as encyclopedias, catalogues, technical manuals, and games.

Ceausescu, Nicolae (1918–1989) Romanian politician, leader of the Romanian Communist Party (RCP), in power from 1965 to 1989. He pursued a policy line independent of and critical of the USSR. He appointed family members, including his wife Elena Ceausescu (1919–1989), to senior state and party posts, and governed in an increasingly repressive manner, zealously implementing schemes that impoverished the nation. The Ceausescus were overthrown in a bloody revolutionary coup in December 1989 and executed on Christmas Day that year.

Cecil, Robert (1563–1612) 1st Earl of Salisbury, Secretary of state to Elizabeth I of England, succeeding his father, Lord Burghley; he was afterwards chief minister to James I (James VI of Scotland) whose accession to the English throne he secured. He discovered the *Gunpowder Plot, the conspiracy to blow up the king and Parliament in 1605. James I created him Earl of Salisbury in 1605. He was knighted in 1591, and made a baron in 1603 and viscount in 1604.

cedar any of an Old World group of coniferous trees belonging to the pine family. The cedar of Lebanon (*Cedrus libani*) grows to great height and age in the mountains of Syria and Asia Minor. Of the historic forests on Mount Lebanon itself, only a few groups of trees remain. (Genus *Cedrus*, family Pinaceae.)

celandine either of two plants belonging to different families, the only similarity being their bright yellow flowers. The **greater celandine** (*Chelidonium majus*) belongs to the poppy family and is common in hedgerows. The **lesser celandine** (*Ranunculus ficaria*) is a member of the buttercup family and is a common wayside and meadow plant in Europe.

celeriac variety of garden celery belonging to the carrot family, with an edible turniplike root and small bitter stems. (*Apium graveolens* var. *rapaceum*, family Umbelliferae.)

celery Old World plant belonging to the carrot family. It grows wild in ditches and salt marshes and has a coarse texture and sharp taste. Cultivated varieties of celery are grown under cover to make the edible stalks less bitter. (*Apium graveolens*, family Umbelliferae.)

celesta musical instrument, a keyboard *glockenspiel producing high-pitched sounds of glistening purity. It was invented by Auguste Mustel of Paris in 1886 and first used to effect by Tchaikovsky in *The Nutcracker* ballet (1890).

celestial mechanics branch of astronomy that deals with the calculation of the orbits of celestial bodies, their gravitational attractions (such as those that produce the Earth's tides), and also the orbits of artificial satellites and space probes. It is based on the laws of motion and gravity laid down by 17th-century English physicist and mathematician Isaac *Newton.

celestial sphere imaginary sphere surrounding the Earth, on which the celestial bodies seem to lie. The positions of bodies such as stars, planets, and galaxies are specified by their coordinates on the celestial sphere. The equivalents of latitude and longitude on the celestial sphere are called declination and right ascension (which is measured in hours from 0 to 24). The **celestial poles** lie directly above the Earth's poles, and the **celestial equator** lies over the Earth's Equator. The celestial sphere appears to rotate once around the Earth each day, actually a result of the rotation of the Earth on its axis.

cell in biology, the basic unit of a living organism. It is the smallest unit capable of independent existence.

In organisms, other than the smallest ones, the body of the organism is made up of several cells or many cells. A single cell, therefore, is the smallest unit that shows characteristic features of life, such as *reproduction, growth, *respiration, response to environmental stimuli, and the ability to take in mineral salts. *Viruses are particles that are not cells. A virus can only reproduce by 'taking over' a cell from another organism. This cell often dies as a result of making many new virus particles.

cell, electrical or **voltaic cell** or **galvanic cell** device in which chemical energy is converted into electrical energy; the popular name is *'battery', but this strictly refers to a collection of cells in one unit. The reactive chemicals of a **primary cell** cannot be replenished, whereas **secondary cells** – such as storage batteries – are rechargeable: their chemical reactions can be reversed and the original condition restored by applying an electric current. It is dangerous to attempt to recharge a primary cell.

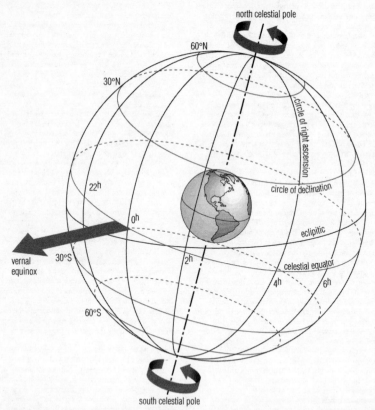

celestial sphere The main features of the celestial sphere. Declination runs from 0° at the celestial equator to 90° at the celestial poles. Right ascension is measured in hours eastwards from the vernal equinox, one hour corresponding to 15° of longitude.

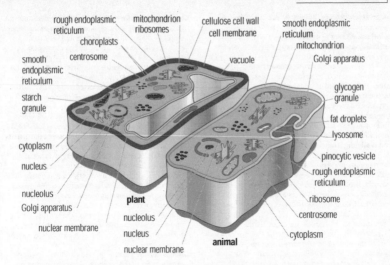

rough endoplasmic reticulum
mitochondrion
ribosomes
cellulose cell wall
cell membrane
smooth endoplasmic reticulum
choroplasts
centrosome
mitochondrion
smooth endoplasmic reticulum
Golgi apparatus
vacuole
starch granule
glycogen granule
fat droplets
lysosome
cytoplasm
nucleus
pinocytic vesicle
rough endoplasmic reticulum
nucleolus
Golgi apparatus
plant
ribosome
nuclear membrane
nucleolus
centrosome
nucleus
cytoplasm
animal
nuclear membrane

cell Typical plant and animal cell. Plant and animal cells share many structures, such as ribosomes, mitochondria, and chromosomes, but they also have notable differences: plant cells have chloroplasts, a large vacuole, and a cellulose cell wall. Animal cells do not have a rigid cell wall but have an outside cell membrane only.

cell, electrolytic device to which electrical energy is applied in order to bring about a chemical reaction; see *electrolysis.

Cellini, Benvenuto (1500–1571) Italian Mannerist sculptor and goldsmith. Among his works are a graceful bronze *Perseus* (1545–54; Loggia dei Lanzi, Florence) and a gold salt cellar made for Francis I of France (1540–43; Kunsthistorisches Museum, Vienna), topped by nude reclining figures. He wrote a frank autobiography (begun in 1558), which gives a vivid picture both of him and his age.

cell membrane *or* **plasma membrane** thin layer of protein and fat surrounding cells that keeps the cells together and controls substances passing between the cytoplasm and the intercellular space. The cell membrane is semipermeable, allowing some substances to pass through and some not. Generally, small molecules s uch as water, glucose, and amino acids can penetrate the membrane, while large molecules, such as starch, cannot. Substances often cross the membrane by *diffusion, a spontaneous passage of molecules. Water movement across the membrane is a special case of diffusion known as *osmosis.

cello bowed, string instrument that is the third largest member of the violin family and one of the four instruments that make up the string quartet. Its full name is **violoncello** but the abbreviation cello is more commonly used today. Although similar in shape to the violin, it is more than twice the size and is played resting on the ground on an adjustable spike, being held in place lightly between the knees. It has a range of well over four octaves, with its four strings being tuned in fifths at C2, G2, D3, and A4. The solo potential of the cello was recognized by Johann Sebastian Bach (his five

cello suites are still the instrument's most important repertoire), and its concerto repertoire extends from Joseph Haydn (who also gave the cello a leading role in his string quartets) and Luigi Boccherini to Antonín Dvořák, Edward Elgar, Benjamin Britten, György Ligeti, and Witold Lutoslawski. The *Bachianas Brasilieras 1* (1930–44) by Heitor Villa-Lobos is scored for eight cellos, and Pierre Boulez's *Messagesquisse* (1977) for seven cellos. One of the best-known pieces for solo cello is 'The Swan' from Charles Saint-Saëns's *Carnival of Animals* (1887).

cellophane transparent wrapping film made from wood *cellulose, widely used for packaging, first produced by Swiss chemist Jacques Edwin Brandenberger in 1908.

cellular phone *or* **cellphone** see *mobile phone.

cellulite fatty compound alleged by some dietitians to be produced in the body by liver disorder and to cause lumpy deposits on the hips and thighs. Medical opinion generally denies its existence, attributing the lumpy appearance to a type of subcutaneous fat deposit.

celluloid transparent or translucent, highly flammable, plastic material (a thermoplastic) made from cellulose nitrate and camphor. It was once used for toilet articles, novelties, and photographic film, but has now been replaced by the nonflammable substance cellulose acetate.

cellulose complex *carbohydrate composed of long chains of glucose units, joined by chemical bonds called glycosidic links. It is the principal constituent of the cell wall of higher plants, and a vital ingredient in the diet of many *herbivores. Molecules of cellulose are organized into long, unbranched microfibrils that give support to the cell wall. No mammal produces the enzyme cellulase, necessary for digesting cellulose; mammals such as rabbits and cows are only able to digest grass because the bacteria present in their gut can manufacture it.

cellulose nitrate *or* **nitrocellulose** series of esters of cellulose with up to three nitrate (NO_3) groups per monosaccharide unit. It is made by the action of concentrated nitric acid on cellulose (for example, cotton waste) in the presence of concentrated sulphuric acid. Fully nitrated cellulose (gun cotton) is explosive, but esters with fewer nitrate groups were once used in making lacquers, rayon, and plastics, such as coloured and photographic film, until replaced by the nonflammable cellulose acetate. *Celluloid is based on cellulose nitrate.

cell wall tough outer surface of the cell in plants. It is constructed from a mesh of *cellulose and is very strong and only very slightly elastic so that it protects the cell and holds it in shape. Most living cells are turgid (swollen with water). Water is absorbed by osmosis causing the cell to expand and develop an internal hydrostatic pressure (wall pressure) that acts against the cellulose wall. The result of this turgor pressure is to give the cell, and therefore the plant, rigidity. Plants, or sections of plants, that are not woody are particularly reliant on this form of support.

Celsius scale of temperature, previously called centigrade, in which the range from freezing to boiling of water is divided into 100 degrees, freezing point being 0 degrees and boiling point 100 degrees.

Celt (Greek *Keltoi*) Indo-European people that originated in Alpine Europe and spread to the Iberian peninsula and beyond. They were ironworkers and farmers. In the 1st century BC they were defeated by the Roman Empire and by Germanic tribes and confined largely to Britain, Ireland, and northern France.

Celtic art art of the Celtic peoples of Western Europe, emerging about 500 BC, probably on the Rhine. It spread to most parts of Europe, but after the 1st century BC flourished only in Britain and Ireland, its influence being felt well into the 10th century AD. Pottery, woodwork, jewellery, and weapons are among its finest products, with manuscript illumination and stone crosses featuring in late Celtic art. Typically, Celtic art is richly decorated with flowing curves which, though based on animal and plant motifs, often form semi-abstract designs.

Celtic languages branch of the Indo-European family, divided into two groups: the **Brythonic** or **P-Celtic** (*Welsh language, Cornish, and Breton) and the **Goidelic** or **Q-Celtic** (Irish, Scottish, and Manx (*Gaelic) languages). Celtic languages once stretched from the Black Sea to Britain, but have been in decline for centuries, limited to the so-called 'Celtic fringe' of western Europe.

Celtic Sea sea area bounded by Wales, Ireland, and southwest England; the name is commonly used by workers in the oil industry to avoid nationalist significance. The Celtic Sea is separated from the Irish Sea by St George's Channel.

cement any bonding agent used to unite particles in a single mass or to cause one surface to adhere to another. **Portland cement** is a powder which when mixed with water and sand or gravel turns into mortar or concrete. In geology, cement refers to a chemically precipitated material such as carbonate that occupies the interstices of clastic rocks.

Cenozoic Era *or* **Caenozoic** era of geological time that began 65 million years ago and continues to the present day. It is divided into the Tertiary and Quaternary periods. The Cenozoic marks the emergence of mammals as a dominant group, and the rearrangement of continental masses towards their present positions.

censor in ancient Rome, either of two senior magistrates, high officials elected every five years to hold office for 18 months. They were responsible for regulating public morality, carrying out a census of the citizens, and revising the senatorial list. The Roman censorship was instituted in 443 BC, and was last held as an independent office in 22 BC. Thereafter, the various censorial powers came to be exercised by the emperor.

censorship suppression by authority of material considered immoral, heretical, subversive, libellous, damaging to state security, or otherwise offensive. It is generally more strict under *totalitarian (one-party) or strongly-religious regimes, and in wartime. Concerns over the ready availability of material such as bomb recipes and pornography have led a number of countries to pass laws attempting to censor the Internet, such as the US Communications Decency Act of 1996.

census official count of the population of a country, originally for military call-up and taxation, later for assessment of social trends as other information regarding age, sex, and occupation of each individual was included. The data collected are used by government departments in planning for the future in such areas as health, education, transport, and housing.

centaur in Greek mythology, a creature half human and half horse, wild and lawless. Chiron, the mentor of the hero Heracles and tutor of the god of medicine Asclepius, was an exception. Their home was said to be on Mount Pelion, Thessaly.

Centaurus large, bright constellation of the southern hemisphere, represented as a centaur. Its brightest star, *Rigil Kent, is a triple star, and contains the closest star to the Sun, Proxima Centauri, which is only 4.2 light years away from the Sun, and 0.1 light years closer than its companions, Alpha Centauri A and B. Omega Centauri, which is just visible to the naked eye as a hazy patch, is the largest and brightest *globular cluster of stars in the sky, 16,000 light years away from the Sun.

centigrade former name for the *Celsius temperature scale.

centipede jointed-legged animal of the group Chilopoda, members of which have a distinct head and a single pair of long antennae. Their bodies are composed of segments (which may number nearly 200), each of similar form and bearing a single pair of legs. Most are small, but the tropical *Scolopendra gigantea* may reach 30 cm/1 ft in length. **Millipedes**, class Diplopoda, have fewer segments (up to 100), but have two pairs of legs on each.

Central African Republic
formerly **Ubangi-Shari** (until 1958), **Central African Empire** (1976–79)
National name: *République Centrafricaine/ Central African Republic*
Area: 622,436 sq km/240,322 sq mi
Capital: Bangui
Major towns/cities: Berbérati, Bouar, Bambari, Bossangoa, Carnot, Kaga Bandoro

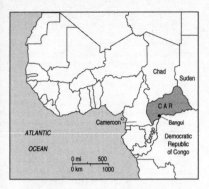

Physical features: landlocked flat plateau, with rivers flowing north and south, and hills in northeast and southwest; dry in north, rainforest in southwest; mostly wooded; Kotto and Mbari river falls; the Ubangi River rises 6 m/20 ft at Bangui during the wet season (June–November)
Head of state: François Bozizé from 2003
Head of government: Abel Goumba from 2003
Political system: emergent democracy
Political executive: limited presidency
Political parties: Central African People's Liberation Party (MPLC), left of centre; Central African Democratic Rally (RDC), nationalist, right of centre
Currency: franc CFA
GNI per capita (PPP): (US$) 1,190 (2002 est)
Exports: timber, diamonds, coffee, cotton. Principal market: Belgium 53% (2001)
Population: 3,865,000 (2003 est)
Language: French (official), Sangho (national), Arabic, Hunsa, Swahili
Religion: Protestant 25%, Roman Catholic 25%, animist 24%, Muslim 15%
Life expectancy: 39 (men); 41 (women) (2000–05)
Chronology
10th century: Immigration by peoples from Sudan to the east and Cameroon to the west.
16th century: Part of the Gaoga Empire.
16th–18th centuries: Population reduced greatly by slave raids both by coastal traders and Arab empires in Sudan and Chad.
19th century: The Zande nation of the Bandia peoples became powerful in the east. Bantu speakers immigrated from Zaire and the Baya from northern Cameroon.
1889–1903: The French established control over the area, quelling insurrections; a French colony known as Ubangi-Shari was formed and partitioned among commercial concessionaries.
1920–30: A series of rebellions against forced labour on coffee and cotton plantations were savagely repressed by the French.
1946: Given a territorial assembly and representation in French parliament.
1958: Achieved self-government within French Equatorial Africa, with Barthélémy Boganda, founder of the pro-independence Movement for the Social Evolution of Black Africa (MESAN), as prime minister.

1960: Achieved independence as Central African Republic; David Dacko, the nephew of the late Boganda, was elected president.
1962: The republic became a one-party state, dominated by MESAN and loyal to the French interest.
1965: Dacko was ousted in a military coup led by Col Jean-Bedel Bokassa, as the economy deteriorated.
1972: Bokassa, a violent and eccentric autocrat, declared himself president for life. In 1977 he made himself emperor of the 'Central African Empire'.
1979: Bokassa was deposed by Dacko in a French-backed bloodless coup, following violent repressive measures including the massacre of 100 children. Bokassa went into exile and the country became known as the Central African Republic again.
1981: Dacko was deposed in a bloodless coup, led by Gen André Kolingba, and a military government was established.
1983: A clandestine opposition movement was formed.
1984: Amnesty for all political party leaders was announced.
1988: Bokassa, who had returned from exile, was found guilty of murder and embezzlement; he received a death sentence, later commuted to life imprisonment.
1991: Opposition parties were allowed to form.
1992: Multiparty elections were promised, but cancelled with Kolingba in last place.
1993: Kolingba released thousands of prisoners, including Bokassa. Ange-Félix Patasse of the leftist African People's Labour Party (MLPC) was elected president, ending 12 years of military dictatorship.
1996: There was an army revolt over pay; Patasse was forced into hiding.
1999: Anicet Georges Dologuélé was appointed prime minister.
2002: Troops loyal to General Bozize attempted to overthrow President Patasse.
2003: President Patasse was deposed in a coup led by former army chief François Bozize. The takeover sparked widespread looting.
2004: A new constitution was approved by referendum.
2005: Presidential and parliamentary elections were held. François Bozize and his main rival Martin Ziguele, a former prime minister, failed to win an outright victory and faced a run-off vote.

Central America the part of the Americas that links Mexico with the Isthmus of Panama, comprising Belize and the republics of Costa Rica, El Salvador, Guatemala, Honduras, Nicaragua, and Panama. It is also an isthmus, crossed by mountains that form part of the Cordilleras, rising to a maximum height of 4,220 m/13,845 ft. There are numerous active volcanoes. The principal river is the Usumacinta, which rises in Guatemala and flows north for 965 km/600 mi, crossing Mexico, and empties into the Bay of Campeche in the Gulf of Mexico. Central America has an area of about 523,000 sq km/200,000 sq mi, and a population (2001 est) of 28,764,000, comprising mostly Indians or mestizos (of mixed white–Indian ancestry), with the exception of Costa Rica, which has a predominantly white population. Tropical agricultural products, raw materials, and other basic commodities are exported.

Central American Common Market (CACM)
Spanish **Mercado Común Centroamericana (MCCA)**, economic alliance established in 1961 by El Salvador,

Guatemala, Honduras (seceded in 1970), and Nicaragua; Costa Rica joined in 1962. Formed to encourage economic development and cooperation between the smaller Central American nations and to attract industrial capital, CACM failed to live up to early expectations: nationalist interests remained strong and by the mid-1980s political instability in the region and border conflicts between members were hindering its activities. Its offices are in Guatemala City, Guatemala.

Central Asian Republics geographical region covering the territory of five nation-states: Kazakhstan, Kyrgyzstan, Tajikistan, Turkmenistan, and Uzbekistan. These republics were part of the Soviet Union before gaining their independence in 1991. Central Asia is bordered on the north by the Russian Federation, on the south by Iran and Afghanistan, and on the east by the Chinese region of Xinjiang Uygur. The western boundary of Central Asia is marked by the Caspian Sea. The topography of the region is characterized by several major mountain ranges, including the Tien Shan range and the *Pamirs, and extensive deserts, principally the *Kara-Kum and Kyzyl-Kum. The people of Central Asia are predominantly Muslim.

central dogma in genetics and evolution, the fundamental belief that *genes can affect the nature of the physical body, but that changes in the body (*acquired character, for example, through use or accident) cannot be translated into changes in the genes.

Central Intelligence Agency (CIA) US intelligence organization established in 1947. It has actively intervened overseas, generally to undermine left-wing regimes or to protect US financial interests; for example, in the Democratic Republic of Congo (formerly Zaire) and Nicaragua. From 1980 all covert activity by the CIA had by law to be reported to Congress, preferably beforehand, and to be authorized by the president. In 1994 the CIA's estimated budget was around US$3.1 billion. John M Deutsch became CIA director in 1995 after the Agency's standing was diminished by a scandal involving Aldrich Ames, a CIA agent who had been a longtime mole for the KGB. George Tenet was director 1997–2004.

Central Lowlands one of the three geographical divisions of Scotland, being the fertile and densely populated plain that lies between two geological fault lines, which run nearly parallel northeast–southwest across Scotland from Stonehaven to Dumbarton and from Dunbar to Girvan.

central nervous system (CNS) brain and spinal cord, as distinct from other components of the *nervous system. The CNS integrates all nervous function.

central processing unit (CPU) older name for the main component of a computer, the part that executes individual program instructions and controls the operation of other parts. It is now known simply as the processor or, when contained on a single integrated circuit, microprocessor.

Centre region of north-central France; area 39,151 sq km/15,116 sq mi; population (1999 est) 2,440,300. Centre includes the *départements* of Cher, Eure-et-Loir, Indre, Indre-et-Loire, Loire-et-Cher, and Loiret. The administrative centre is Orléans.

centre of mass point in or near an object at which the whole mass of the object may be considered to be concentrated. A symmetrical homogeneous object such as a sphere or cube has its centre of mass at its geometrical centre; a hollow object (such as a cup) may have its centre of mass in space inside the hollow.

centrifugal force in physics, apparent force arising for an observer moving with a rotating system. For an object of mass m moving with a velocity v in a circle of radius r, the centrifugal force F equals mv^2/r (outwards).

centrifuge apparatus that rotates containers at high speeds, creating centrifugal forces. One use is for separating mixtures of substances of different densities.

centripetal force force that acts radially inwards on an object moving in a curved path. For example, with a weight whirled in a circle at the end of a length of string, the centripetal force is the tension in the string. For an object of mass m moving with a velocity v in a circle of radius r, the centripetal force F equals mv^2/r (inwards). The reaction to this force is the *centrifugal force.

cephalopod any predatory marine mollusc of the class Cephalopoda, with the mouth and head surrounded by tentacles. Cephalopods are the most intelligent, the fastest-moving, and the largest of all animals without backbones, and there are remarkable luminescent forms that swim or drift at great depths. They have the most highly developed nervous and sensory systems of all invertebrates, the eye in some closely paralleling that found in vertebrates. Examples include squid, *octopus, and *cuttlefish. Shells are rudimentary or absent in most cephalopods.

Cepheid variable yellow supergiant star that varies regularly in brightness every few days or weeks as a result of pulsations. The time that a Cepheid variable takes to pulsate is directly related to its average brightness; the longer the pulsation period, the brighter the star.

Cepheus constellation of the north polar region, named after King Cepheus of Greek mythology, husband of Cassiopeia and father of Andromeda. It contains the Garnet Star (Mu Cephei), a red supergiant of variable brightness that is one of the reddest-coloured stars known, and Delta Cephei, prototype of the *Cepheid variables, which are important both as distance indicators and for the information they give about stellar evolution.

ceramic object made from clay, hardened into a permanent form by baking (firing) at very high temperatures in a kiln. Once clay has been turned into ceramic, it can no longer be recycled in water. Ceramics are very versatile. They are used not only for dishes, vessels, and other decorative or functional household objects, but also for building construction and decoration (bricks, tiles), for specialist industrial uses (linings for furnaces used to manufacture steel, fuel elements in nuclear reactors, and so on). Different types of clay and different methods and temperatures of firing create a variety of results. Ceramics may be cast in a mould or hand-built, using the pinch, coil, or slab methods. Alternatively shapes and vessels can be formed by 'throwing' on a potter's, or pottery, wheel. Technically, the main categories are *earthenware (including *terracotta), stoneware, and hard- and softpaste porcelain (see *pottery and porcelain).

Cerberus in Greek mythology, the three-headed dog which guarded the entrance to *Hades, the underworld.

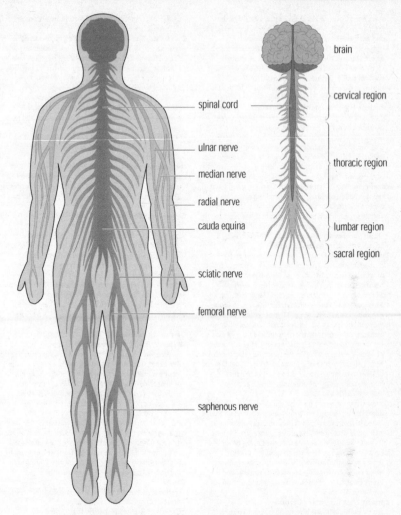

central nervous system The central nervous system (CNS) with its associated nerves.

cereal grass grown for its edible, nutrient-rich, starchy seeds. The term refers primarily to wheat, oats, rye, and barley, but may also refer to maize (corn), millet, and rice. Cereals contain about 75% complex carbohydrates and 10% protein, plus fats and fibre (roughage). They store well. If all the world's cereal crop were consumed as whole-grain products directly by humans, everyone could obtain adequate protein and carbohydrate; however, a large proportion of cereal production in affluent nations is used as animal feed to boost the production of meat, dairy products, and eggs.

cerebellum part of the brain of *vertebrate animals which controls muscle tone, movement, balance, and coordination. It is relatively small in lower animals such as newts and lizards, but large in birds since flight demands precise coordination. The human cerebellum is also well developed, because of the need for balance when walking or running, and for finely coordinated hand movements.

cerebral haemorrhage *or* **apoplectic fit** in medicine, a form of *stroke in which there is bleeding from a cerebral blood vessel into the surrounding brain tissue.

It is generally caused by degenerative disease of the arteries and high blood pressure. Depending on the site and extent of bleeding, the symptoms vary from transient weakness and numbness to deep coma and death. Damage to the brain is permanent, though some recovery can be made. Strokes are likely to recur.

cerebral palsy any nonprogressive abnormality of the brain occurring during or shortly after birth. It is caused by oxygen deprivation, injury during birth, haemorrhage, meningitis, viral infection, or faulty development. Premature babies are at greater risk of being born with cerebral palsy, and in 1996 US researchers linked this to low levels of the thyroid hormone thyroxine. The condition is characterized by muscle spasm, weakness, lack of coordination, and impaired movement; or there may be spastic paralysis, with fixed deformities of the limbs. Intelligence is not always affected.

cerebrum part of the vertebrate *brain, formed from the two paired cerebral hemispheres, separated by a central fissure. In birds and mammals it is the largest and most developed part of the brain. It is covered with an infolded layer of grey matter, the cerebral cortex, which integrates brain functions. The cerebrum coordinates all voluntary activity.

Ceredigion unitary authority in southwest Wales, created in 1996 from part of the former county of Dyfed, of which it was a district. **area:** 1,793 sq km/692 sq mi **towns:** Aberaeron (administrative headquarters), Aberystwyth, Cardigan, Lampeter, Llandyssul, Tregaron **physical:** part of the Cambrian Mountains, including Plynlimon Fawr (752 m/2,468 ft); rivers Teifi, Rheidol, Ystwyth, Aeron, and Tywi **features:** remains of Roman camps, roads, and military stations, and inscribed stones; ruins of Strata Florida Abbey (1164) southeast of Aberystwyth; Devil's Bridge (spanning the Rheidol Falls); Aberystwyth is the home of the National Library of Wales, the Welsh Books Council, and Britain's longest cliff railway **population:** (1998 est) 70,700; 52% are Welsh speaking.

Ceres largest asteroid, 940 km/584 mi in diameter, and the first to be discovered (by Italian astronomer Giuseppe Piazzi in 1801). Ceres orbits the Sun every 4.6 years at an average distance of 414 million km/257 million mi. Its mass is about 0.014 of that of the Earth's Moon.

Ceres in Roman mythology, the goddess of corn, representing the fertility of the earth as its producer; patron of the corn trade. Her cult was established in Rome by 496 BC, and showed early identification with the Greek *Demeter.

cerium chemical symbol Ce, malleable and ductile, grey, metallic element, atomic number 58, relative atomic mass 140.12. It is the most abundant member of the lanthanide series, and is used in alloys, electronic components, nuclear fuels, and lighter flints. It was discovered in 1804 by the Swedish chemists Jöns *Berzelius and Wilhelm Hisinger (1766–1852), and, independently, by German chemist Martin Klaproth. The element was named after the then recently discovered asteroid Ceres.

cermet contraction of ceramics and metal, bonded material containing ceramics and metal, widely used in jet engines and nuclear reactors. Cermets behave much like metals but have the great heat resistance of ceramics. Tungsten carbide, titanium, zirconium bromide, and aluminium oxide are among the ceramics

used; iron, cobalt, nickel, and chromium are among the metals.

Cervantes, Saavedra, Miguel de (1547–1616) Spanish novelist, dramatist, and poet. His masterpiece *Don Quixote de la Mancha (in full El ingenioso hidalgo Don Quixote de la Mancha) was published in 1605. In 1613 his Novelas ejemplares/Exemplary Novels appeared, followed by Viaje del Parnaso/The Voyage to Parnassus (1614). A spurious second part of Don Quixote prompted Cervantes to bring out his own second part in 1615, often considered superior to the first in construction and characterization.

cervical cancer *cancer of the cervix (neck of the womb). It can be detected at an early stage through screening by cervical smear.

cervical smear in medicine, removal of a small sample of tissue from the cervix (neck of the womb) to screen for changes implying a likelihood of cancer. The procedure is also known as the **Pap test** after its originator, George Papanicolaou.

Cetewayo, (Cetshwayo) (c. 1826–1884) King of Zululand, South Africa, 1873–83, whose rule was threatened by British annexation of the Transvaal in 1877. Although he defeated the British at Isandhlwana in 1879, he was later that year defeated by them at Ulundi. Restored to his throne in 1883, he was then expelled by his subjects.

Cetus (Latin 'whale') large constellation on the celestial equator (see *celestial sphere), represented as a sea monster or a whale. Cetus contains the long-period variable star *Mira, and Tau Ceti, one of the nearest stars, which is visible with the naked eye.

Ceylon former name (to 1972) of Sri Lanka.

Cézanne, Paul (1839–1906) French post-Impressionist painter. He was a leading figure in the development of modern art. He broke away from the Impressionists' concern with the ever-changing effects of light to develop a style that tried to capture the structure of natural forms, whether in landscapes, still lifes, or portraits. Joueurs de Cartes/Cardplayers (c. 1890–95; Louvre, Paris) is typical of his work.

CFC abbreviation for *chlorofluorocarbon.

c.g.s. system system of units based on the centimetre, gram, and second, as units of length, mass, and time, respectively. It has been replaced for scientific work by the *SI units to avoid inconsistencies in definition of the thermal calorie and electrical quantities.

Chad

National name: *République du Tchad/Republic of Chad*
Area: 1,284,000 sq km/495,752 sq mi
Capital: Ndjamena (formerly Fort Lamy)
Major towns/cities: Sarh, Moundou, Abéché, Bongor, Doba, Kélo, Koumra
Physical features: landlocked state with mountains (Tibetsi) and part of Sahara Desert in north; moist savannah in south; rivers in south flow northwest to Lake Chad
Head of state: Idriss Deby from 1990
Head of government: Moussa Faki Mahamat from 2003
Political system: emergent democracy
Political executive: limited presidency
Political parties: Patriotic Salvation Movement (MPS), left of centre; Alliance for Democracy and Progress (RDP), left of centre; Union for Democracy and Progress (UPDT), left of centre; Action for Unity and

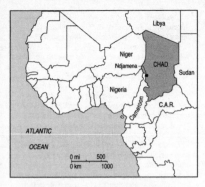

Libya

Niger

Njamena · CHAD · Sudan

Nigeria

C.A.R.

ATLANTIC

OCEAN

0 mi 500
0 km 1000

Socialism (ACTUS), left of centre; Union for Democracy and the Republic (UDR), left of centre

Currency: franc CFA

GNI per capita (PPP): (US$) 1,000 (2002 est)

Exports: livestock, cotton, meat, hides and skins. Principal market: Portugal 17% (2001)

Population: 8,598,000 (2003 est)

Language: French, Arabic (both official), over 100 African languages

Religion: Muslim 50%, Christian 25%, animist 25%

Life expectancy: 44 (men); 46 (women) (2000–05)

Chronology

7th–9th centuries: Berber pastoral nomads, the Zaghawa, immigrated from the north and became a ruling aristocracy, dominating the Sao people, sedentary black farmers, and establishing the Kanem state.

9th–19th centuries: The Zaghawa's Saifi dynasty formed the kingdom of Bornu, which stretched to the west and south of Lake Chad, and converted to Islam in the 11th century. At its height between the 15th and 18th centuries, it raided the south for slaves, and faced rivalry from the 16th century from the Baguirmi and Ouadai Arab kingdoms.

1820s: Visited by British explorers.

1890s–1901: Conquered by France, who ended slave raiding by Arab kingdoms.

1910: Became a colony in French Equatorial Africa. Cotton production expanded in the south.

1944: The pro-Nazi Vichy government signed an agreement giving Libya rights to the Aouzou Strip in northern Chad.

1946: Became an overseas territory of the French Republic, with its own territorial assembly and representation in the French parliament.

1960: Independence was achieved, with François Tombalbaye of the Chadian Progressive Party (CPT), dominated by Sara Christians from the south, as president.

1963: Violent opposition in the Muslim north, led by the Chadian National Liberation Front (Frolinat), backed by Libya following the banning of opposition parties.

1968: A revolt of northern militias was quelled with France's help.

1973: An Africanization campaign was launched by Tombalbaye, who changed his first name to Ngarta.

1975: Tombalbaye was killed in a military coup led by southerner Gen Félix Malloum. Frolinat continued its resistance.

1978: Malloum formed a coalition government with former Frolinat leader Hissène Habré, but it soon broke down.

1979: Malloum was forced to leave the country; an interim government was set up under Gen Goukouni Oueddei (Frolinat). Habré continued his opposition with his Army of the North (FAN), and Libya provided support for Goukouni.

1981–82: Habré gained control of half the country. Goukouni fled and set up a 'government in exile'.

1983: Habré's regime was recognized by the Organization of African Unity (OAU; later African Union) and France, but in the north, Goukouni's supporters, with Libya's help, fought on. Eventually a ceasefire was agreed, with latitude 16° north dividing the country.

1987: Chad, France, and Libya agreed on an OAU ceasefire to end the civil war between the Muslim Arab north and Christian and animist black African south.

1988: Libya relinquished its claims to the Aozou Strip.

1990: President Habré was ousted after the army was defeated by Libyan-backed Patriotic Salvation Movement (MPS) rebel troops based in the Sudan and led by Habré's former ally Idriss Deby.

1991–92: Several antigovernment coups were foiled.

1993: A transitional charter was adopted, as a prelude to full democracy at a later date.

1997: A reconciliation agreement was signed with rebel forces.

1998: A new rebel force, the Movement for Democracy and Justice in Chad (MDJC), led by a former defence minster, began armed rebellion.

1999: Nagoum Yamassoum was appointed prime minister.

2000: Former president Hissene Habré was freed after having been charged with torture and murder.

2001: Idriss Deby won the presidential elections. Alleged irregularities meant that results from 25% of polling stations were cancelled but Deby was confirmed president and sworn in for a second five-year term.

2002: A Libyan brokered peace deal was signed between the government and the MDJC; fighting broke out again during the year. Thousands of refugees arrived in Chad, fleeing fighting in Darfur, Sudan.

2003: The government and the National Resistance Army (ANR) sign a peace agreement. An oil pipeline was opened between Chad and Cameroon, allowing the first oil exports. The government and the MDJC signed a further peace agreement.

2004: Refugees fleeing fighting in Darfur were moved deeper into Chad to avoid attacks by Sudanese militias. Amendments to the constitution were approved, allowing Deby to stand for a third term as president in 2006.

2005: Chad accused Sudan of aiding Chadian rebels.

Chad, Lake lake on the northeastern boundary of Nigeria and the eastern boundary of Chad. It once varied in extent between rainy and dry seasons from 50,000 sq km/19,000 sq mi to 20,000 sq km/7,000 sq mi, but a series of droughts between 1979 and 1989 reduced its area to 2,500 sq km/965 sq mi in 1993. It is a shallow lake (depth does not exceed 5–8 m/16–26 ft), with the northern part being completely dry and the southern area being densely vegetated, with swamps and open pools. The lake was first seen by European explorers in 1823.

chafer beetle of the family Scarabeidae. The adults eat foliage or flowers, and the underground larvae feed on roots, chiefly those of grasses and cereals, and can be very destructive. Examples are the **cockchafer** and the **rose chafer** *Cetonia aurata*, about 2 cm/0.8 in long and bright green.

chaffinch bird *Fringilla coelebs* of the finch family, common throughout much of Europe and West Asia. About 15 cm/6 in long, the male is olive-brown above, with a bright chestnut breast, a bluish-grey cap, and two white bands on the upper part of the wing; the female is duller. During winter they form single-sex flocks.

Chagall, Marc (1887–1985) Belorussian-born French painter and designer. Much of his highly coloured, fantastic imagery was inspired by the village life of his boyhood and by Jewish and Belorussian folk traditions. He was an original figure, often seen as a precursor of surrealism. *I and the Village* (1911; Museum of Modern Art, New York) is characteristic.

Chagas's disease disease common in Central and South America, infecting approximately 18 million people worldwide. It is caused by a trypanosome parasite, *Trypanosoma cruzi*, transmitted by several species of blood-sucking insect; it results in incurable damage to the heart, intestines, and brain. It is named after Brazilian doctor Carlos Chagas (1879–1934).

Chain, Ernst Boris (1906–1979) German-born British biochemist who was awarded a Nobel Prize for Physiology or Medicine in 1945, together with Alexander *Fleming and Howard *Florey (Fleming for his discovery of the bactericidal effect of penicillin, and Chain and Florey for their isolation of penicillin and its development as an antibiotic drug). Chain also discovered penicillinase, an enzyme that destroys penicillin. Chain was knighted in 1969.

chain reaction in chemistry, a succession of reactions, usually involving *free radicals, where the products of one stage are the reactants of the next. A chain reaction is characterized by the continual generation of reactive substances.

chain reaction in nuclear physics, a fission reaction that is maintained because neutrons released by the splitting of some atomic nuclei themselves go on to split others, releasing even more neutrons. Such a reaction can be controlled (as in a nuclear reactor) by using moderators to absorb excess neutrons. Uncontrolled, a chain reaction produces a nuclear explosion (as in an atom bomb).

chalcedony form of the mineral quartz, SiO_2, in which the crystals are so fine-grained that they are impossible to distinguish with a microscope (cryptocrystalline). Agate, onyx, and carnelian are *gem varieties of chalcedony.

chalk soft, fine-grained, whitish sedimentary rock composed of calcium carbonate, $CaCO_3$, extensively quarried for use in cement, lime, and mortar, and in the manufacture of cosmetics and toothpaste. **Blackboard chalk** in fact consists of gypsum (calcium sulphate, $CaSO_4.2H_2O$).

Chalmers, Thomas (1780–1847) Scottish theologian. At the Disruption of the *Church of Scotland in 1843, Chalmers withdrew from the church along with a large number of other priests, and became principal of the Free Church college, thus founding the *Free Church of Scotland.

Chamberlain, (Arthur) Neville (1869–1940) British Conservative politician, son of Joseph *Chamberlain. He was prime minister 1937–40;

his policy of appeasement toward the Italian fascist dictator Benito Mussolini and German Nazi Adolf Hitler (with whom he concluded the *Munich Agreement in 1938) failed to prevent the outbreak of World War II. He resigned in 1940 following the defeat of the British forces in Norway.

Chamberlain, (Joseph) Austen (1863–1937) British Conservative politician, elder son of Joseph *Chamberlain; foreign secretary 1924–29. He shared the Nobel Prize for Peace in 1925 with Charles G Dawes for his work in negotiating and signing the Pact of *Locarno, which fixed the boundaries of Germany. In 1928 he also signed the *Kellogg–Briand pact to outlaw war and provide for peaceful settlement of disputes.

Chamberlain, Joseph (1836–1914) British politician, reformist mayor of and member of Parliament for Birmingham. In 1886 he resigned from the cabinet over William Gladstone's policy of home rule for Ireland, and led the revolt of the Liberal-Unionists that saw them merge with the Conservative Party.

chamber music music intended for performance in a small room or chamber, rather than in the concert hall, and usually written for instrumental combinations, played with one instrument to a part, as in the *string quartet.

chameleon any of 80 or so species of lizard of the family Chameleontidae. Some species have highly developed colour-changing abilities, caused by stress and changes in the intensity of light and temperature, which alter the dispersal of pigment granules in the layers of cells beneath the outer skin.

chamois goatlike mammal *Rupicapra rupicapra* found in mountain ranges of southern Europe and Asia Minor. It is brown, with dark patches running through the eyes, and can be up to 80 cm/2.6 ft high. Chamois are very sure-footed, and live in herds of up to 30 members.

champagne sparkling white wine invented by Dom Pérignon, a Benedictine monk, in 1668. It is made from a blend of grapes (*pinot noir* and *chardonnay*) grown in the Marne River region around Reims and Epernay, in Champagne, northeastern France. After a first fermentation, sugar and yeast are added to the still wine, which, when bottled, undergoes a second fermentation to produce the sparkle. Sugar syrup may be added to make the wine sweet (*sec*) or dry (*brut*).

Champagne-Ardenne region of northeast France; area 25,606 sq km/9,887 sq mi; population (1999 est) 1,342,400. Its largest town is Reims, but its administrative centre is Châlons-sur-Marne. It comprises the *départements* of Ardennes, Aube, Marne, and Haute-Marne. The land is fertile in the west and supports sheep and dairy farming; its vineyards in the Reims-Épernay area produce the famous *champagne sparkling wines. The region also includes part of the *Ardennes forest.

champignon any of a number of edible fungi (see *fungus). The fairy ring champignon (*Marasmius oreades*) has this name because its fruiting bodies (mushrooms) grow in rings around the outer edge of the underground mycelium (threadlike body) of the fungus. (Family Agaricaceae.)

Champlain, Samuel de (1567–1635) French pioneer, soldier, and explorer in Canada. Having served in the army of Henry IV and on an expedition to the West Indies, he began his exploration of Canada in 1603. In a third expedition in 1608 he founded and named Québec, and was appointed lieutenant governor of French Canada in 1612.

Champlain, Lake lake in northeastern USA (extending some 10 km/6 mi into Canada) on the New York–Vermont border, west of the Green Mountains and east of the Adirondacks; length 201 km/125 mi; area 1,116 sq km/430 sq mi. Lake Champlain is linked to the St Lawrence River via the Richelieu River, and to the Hudson River by canal; it is the fourth-largest freshwater lake in the USA.

chancel (from Late Latin *cancellus* 'a screen') in architecture, the eastern part of a Christian church where the choir and clergy sit, formerly kept separate from the nave by an open-work screen or rail. In some medieval churches the screen is very high, so that the congregation is completely shut off. The choir stalls and the rector's pew are in the chancel, and the altar or communion table on a raised platform at the far end.

Chancellor, Lord UK state official; see *Lord Chancellor.

chancellor of the Exchequer in the UK, senior cabinet minister responsible for the national economy. The office, established under Henry III, originally entailed keeping the Exchequer seal. The current chancellor of the Exchequer, from 1997, is Gordon Brown.

Chancery in the UK, a division of the High Court that deals with such matters as the administration of the estates of deceased persons, the execution of trusts, the enforcement of sales of land, and foreclosure of mortgages. Before reorganization of the court system in 1875, it administered the rules of equity as distinct from *common law.

chancroid *or* **soft sore** acute localized, sexually transmitted ulcer on or about the genitals, caused by the bacterium *Haemophilus ducreyi*. It causes painful enlargement and suppuration of lymph nodes in the groin area.

Chandler, Raymond Thornton (1888–1959) US novelist. He turned the pulp detective mystery form into a successful genre of literature and created the quintessential private eye in the tough but chivalric loner, Philip Marlowe. Marlowe is the narrator of such books as *The Big Sleep* (1939; filmed 1946), *Farewell My Lovely* (1940; filmed 1944), *The Lady in the Lake* (1943; filmed 1947), and *The Long Goodbye* (1954; filmed 1975). He also wrote numerous screenplays, notably *Double Indemnity* (1944), *Blue Dahlia* (1946), and *Strangers on a Train* (1951).

Chandragupta Maurya (died c. 297 BC) Ruler of northern India and first Indian emperor c. 325–296 BC, founder of the Mauryan dynasty. He overthrew the Nanda dynasty of Magadha in 325 BC and then conquered the Punjab in 322 BC after the death of *Alexander (III) the Great, expanding his empire west to Iran. He is credited with having united most of India.

Chandrasekhar, Subrahmanyan (1910–1995) Indian-born US astrophysicist who was awarded the Nobel Prize for Physics in 1983 for his theoretical studies of the physical processes in connection with the structure and evolution of stars. The Chandrasekhar limit is the maximum mass of a *white dwarf before it turns into a *neutron star.

Chanel, Coco (Gabrielle) (1883–1971) French fashion designer. She was renowned as a trendsetter. She created the 'little black dress', the informal cardigan suit, costume jewellery, and perfumes.

change of state in science, change in the physical state (solid, liquid, or gas) of a material. For instance, melting, boiling, and evaporation and their opposites, solidification and condensation, are changes of state. The former set of changes are brought about by heating or decreased pressure; the latter by cooling or increased pressure.

Chang Jiang *or* **Yangtze Kiang** ('long river') longest river of China and Asia, and third longest in the world, flowing about 6,300 km/3,900 mi from Qinghai on the

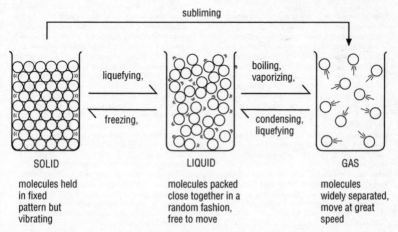

change of state The state (solid, liquid, or gas) of a substance is not fixed but varies with changes in temperature and pressure.

Tibetan Plateau to the Yellow Sea. It is a major commercial waterway and, with its tributaries, is navigable for 30,000 km/18,640 mi; Yichang is considered the head of navigation, but ocean-going vessels can reach inland as far as Wuhan. The whole drainage basin covers a vast area of over 1,827,000 sq km/705,400 sq mi, and produces about 70% of China's rice crop. The Three Gorges Dam on the river, begun in 1994 and nearing completion, will help control flooding and generate about 10% of the country's electricity supply.

Channel 5 Britain's fifth television channel. Launched on 30 March 1997, it was set up by the 1990 Broadcasting Act, under which the Independent Television Commission (ITC) was required to create a fifth national channel. It was awarded by competitive tender in 1995 to Channel 5 Broadcasting Ltd, a consortium of companies including Pearson, owners of the *Financial Times*, and United News and Media, owners of the *Daily Express* and Anglia Television.

Channel 4 Britain's fourth national television channel, launched on 2 November 1982 as a wholly-owned subsidiary of the IBA (Independent Broadcasting Authority; now known as the ITC or Independent Television Commission). Its brief was to serve minority interests, encourage innovation through the use of independent producers, and develop a character distinct from the other channels.

Channel Islands group of islands in the English Channel, off the northwest coast of France; they are a possession of the British crown. They comprise the islands of Jersey, Guernsey, Alderney, Great and Little Sark, with the lesser Herm, Brechou, Jethou, and Lihou; area 194 sq km/75 sq mi; population (1999 est) 149,000. Chief industries are farming, fishing, and tourism; flowers, early potatoes, tomatoes, butterflies, and dairy cattle are exported. It has a very mild climate and productive soil. The official language is French (*Norman French) but English is more widely used. The islands are a tax haven. The currency is the English pound, as well as local coinage.

Channel Tunnel tunnel built beneath the English Channel, linking Britain with mainland Europe. It comprises twin rail tunnels, 50 km/31 mi long and 7.3 m/24 ft in diameter, located 40 m/130 ft beneath the seabed. Construction began in 1987, and the French and English sections were linked in December 1990. It was officially opened on 6 May 1994. The shuttle train service, Le Shuttle, opened to lorries in May 1994 and to cars in December 1994. The tunnel's high-speed train service, Eurostar, linking London to Paris and Brussels, opened in November 1994. The final cost of the tunnel was £12 billion.

chanson song type common in France and Italy, often based on a folk tune that originated with the *troubadours. Josquin *Desprez was a chanson composer.

chant ritual incantation by an individual or group, for confidence or mutual support. Chants can be secular (as, for example, sports supporters' chants) or religious, both Eastern and Western. Ambrosian and *Gregorian chants are forms of *plainsong.

chanterelle edible *fungus that is bright yellow and funnel-shaped. It grows in deciduous woodland. (*Cantharellus cibarius*, family Cantharellaceae.) It is looked for in autumn, being most likely to appear when

a period of warm weather is accompanied by abundant rainfall. It has the colour and smell of apricots

chantry (from Old French *chanterie*; Latin *cantare* 'to sing') in medieval Europe, a religious foundation in which, in return for an endowment of land, the souls of the donor and the donor's family and friends would be prayed for. A chantry could be held at an existing altar, or in a specially constructed **chantry chapel** in which the donor's body was usually buried. Chantry chapels are often built off the aisle or nave of a church, and have the tomb of the founder placed in the centre. The word is also applied to the endowment intended by the founder as a perpetual stipend for masses in such a chapel.

chaos theory *or* **chaology** *or* **complexity theory** branch of mathematics that attempts to describe irregular, unpredictable systems – that is, systems whose behaviour is difficult to predict because there are so many variable or unknown factors. Weather is an example of a chaotic system.

chapel (from Latin *capella*, diminutive of *cappa* 'a cloak') a small or subordinate place of Christian worship other than a parish or cathedral church; also a church subordinate to and dependent on the principal parish church, to which it is in some way supplementary. The term can also refer to a building or part of a building or institution (for example, a palace, college, convent, hospital, or prison) erected for private devotion and often for private or semi-public religious services; also a recess in a church containing an altar that has been separately dedicated. In England the word 'chapel' is commonly applied to places of Nonconformist worship, as distinct from those of the Anglican and Roman Catholic churches.

Chaplin, Charlie (1889–1977) born Charles Spencer Chaplin, English film actor, director, producer, and composer. One of cinema's most popular stars, he made his reputation as a tramp with a smudge moustache, bowler hat, and twirling cane in silent comedies, including *The Rink* (1916), *The Kid* (1921), and *The Gold Rush* (1925). His work combines buffoonery with pathos, as in *The Great Dictator* (1940) and *Limelight* (1952).

chapterhouse in church architecture, a building in which the canonical chapter of a monastery, cathedral, or collegiate church meets for the discussion of its affairs. It is often elaborately designed and ornamented, and usually polygonal, or octagonal, as at Lichfield and York. The position of the chapterhouse is usually to the west of the transepts of the church, to which it is connected either directly or by a passage from the cloister. Crypts are occasionally found beneath the floor.

char *or* **charr** fish *Salvelinus alpinus* related to the trout, living in the Arctic coastal waters, and also in Europe and North America in some upland lakes. It is one of Britain's rarest fish, and is at risk from growing acidification.

characin freshwater fish belonging to the family Characidae. There are over 1,300 species, mostly in South and Central America, but also in Africa. Most are carnivores. In typical characins, unlike the somewhat similar carp family, the mouth is toothed, and there is a small dorsal adipose fin just in front of the tail.

charcoal black, porous form of *carbon, produced by heating wood or other organic materials in the absence of air. It is used as a fuel in the smelting of metals such as copper and zinc, and by artists for making black line drawings. **Activated charcoal** has been powdered and dried so that it presents a much increased surface area for adsorption; it is used for filtering and purifying liquids and gases – for example, in drinking-water filters and gas masks.

Chardin, Jean-Baptiste-Siméon (1699–1779) French painter. He took as his subjects naturalistic still lifes and quiet domestic scenes that recall the Dutch tradition. His work is a complete contrast to that of his contemporaries, the rococo painters. He developed his own technique, using successive layers of paint to achieve depth of tone, and is generally considered one of the finest exponents of genre painting.

charge see *electric charge.

charge-coupled device (CCD) device for forming images electronically, using a layer of silicon that releases electrons when struck by incoming light. The electrons are stored in *pixels and read off into a computer at the end of the exposure. CCDs are used in digital cameras, and have now almost entirely replaced photographic film for applications such as astrophotography, where extreme sensitivity to light is paramount.

Charge of the Light Brigade disastrous attack by the British Light Brigade of cavalry against the Russian entrenched artillery on 25 October 1854 during the Crimean War at the Battle of *Balaclava. Of the 673 soldiers who took part, there were 272 casualties.

chariot ancient two-wheeled carriage, used both in peace and war by the Egyptians, Assyrians, Babylonians, Greeks, Romans, ancient Britons, and others.

Charlemagne, Charles I the Great (742–814) King of the *Franks from 768 and *Holy Roman Emperor from 800. By inheritance (his father was *Pepin the Short) and extensive campaigns of conquest, he united most of Western Europe by 804, when after 30 years of war the *Saxons came under his control.

Charles, Jacques Alexandre César (1746–1823) French physicist who studied gases and made the first ascent in a hydrogen-filled balloon in 1783. His work on the expansion of gases led to the formulation of *Charles's law.

Charles two kings of Great Britain and Ireland:

Charles I (1600–1649) King of Great Britain and Ireland from 1625, son of James I of England (James VI of Scotland). He accepted the petition of right in 1628 but then dissolved Parliament and ruled without a parliament from 1629 to 1640, a period known as the Eleven Years' Tyranny. His advisers were *Strafford and *Laud, who persecuted the *Puritans and provoked the Scots to revolt. The *Short Parliament, summoned in 1640, refused funds, and the *Long Parliament later that year rebelled. Charles declared war on Parliament in 1642 but surrendered in 1646 and was beheaded in 1649. He was the father of Charles II.

Charles II (1630–1685) King of Great Britain and Ireland from 1660, when Parliament accepted the restoration of the monarchy after the collapse of Oliver Cromwell's Commonwealth. He was the son of Charles I. His chief minister Edward *Clarendon, who arranged Charles's marriage in 1662 to Catherine of Braganza, was replaced in 1667 with the *Cabal of advisers. His plans to restore Catholicism in Britain led to war with the Netherlands (1672–74) in support of Louis XIV of France and a break with Parliament, which he dissolved in 1681. He was succeeded by James II.

Charles, (Charles Philip Arthur George) (1948–) Prince of the UK, heir to the British throne, and Prince of Wales since 1958 (invested 1969). He is the first-born child of Queen Elizabeth II and the Duke of Edinburgh. He studied at Trinity College, Cambridge, (1967–70), before serving in the Royal Air Force and Royal Navy. The first royal heir since 1660 to have an English wife, he married Diana, Princess of Wales (then Lady Diana Spencer), daughter of the 8th Earl Spencer, in 1981. There are two sons and heirs, William (1982–) and Henry (1984–). Amid much publicity, Charles and Diana separated in 1992 and were divorced in 1996. His long-standing relationship with Camilla Parker Bowles (later the Duchess of Cornwall) was formally recognized when they married in 2005.

Charles ten kings of France including:

Charles I King of France, better known as the Holy Roman Emperor *Charlemagne.

Charles (V) the Wise (1337–1380) king of France (1364–80). He was regent during the captivity of his father John II in England from 1356 to 1360, and became king upon John's death. During the *Hundred Years' War he reconquered nearly all of France from England between 1369 and 1380, and diminished the power of the medieval mercenary companies in France.

Charles (VI) the Mad (1368–1422) also known as **Charles the Well-Beloved**, King of France from 1380, succeeding his father Charles V; he was under the regency of his uncles until 1388. He became mentally unstable in 1392, and civil war broke out between the dukes of Orléans and Burgundy. *Henry V of England invaded France in 1415, conquering Normandy, and in 1420 forced Charles to sign the Treaty of Troyes, recognizing Henry as his successor.

Charles VII (1403–1461) King of France from 1422. Son of Charles VI, he was excluded from the succession by the Treaty of Troyes, but recognized by the south of France. In 1429 Joan of Arc raised the siege of Orléans and had him crowned at Reims. He organized France's first standing army and by 1453 had expelled the English from all of France except Calais.

Charles VIII (1470–1498) King of France from 1483, when he succeeded his father, Louis XI. In 1494 he unsuccessfully tried to claim the Neapolitan crown, and when he entered Naples in 1495 he was forced to withdraw by a coalition of Milan, Venice, Spain, and the Holy Roman Empire. He defeated them at Fornovo, but lost Naples. He died while preparing a second expedition.

Charles IX (1550–1574) King of France from 1560. Second son of Henry II and Catherine de' Medici, he succeeded his brother Francis II at the age of ten but remained under the domination of his mother's regency for ten years while France was torn by religious wars. In 1570 he fell under the influence of the *Huguenot leader Gaspard de Coligny; alarmed by this, Catherine instigated his order for the Massacre of *St Bartholomew, which led to a new religious war.

Charles X (1757–1836) King of France from 1824. Grandson of Louis XV and brother of Louis XVI and Louis XVIII, he was known as the comte d'Artois before his accession. As comte d'Artois, Charles enjoyed a notoriously dissolute life at court, and became involved in reactionary politics. Returning to France after the French Revolution, he became leader of the ultra-royalist group that put his brother Louis XVIII on the throne in 1814. He fled to England at the beginning of the French Revolution, and when he came to the throne on the death of Louis XVIII, he attempted to reverse the achievements of the Revolution. A revolt ensued in 1830, and he again fled to England.

Charles seven rulers of the Holy Roman Empire including:

Charles (II) the Bald (823–877) Holy Roman Emperor from 875 and (as Charles II) king of West Francia from 843. He was the younger son of Louis (I) 'the Pious' (778–840) and warred against his brother the emperor Lothair I (c. 795–855). The Treaty of Verdun in 843 made him king of the West Frankish Kingdom (now France and the Spanish Marches). He entered Italy in 875 and was crowned emperor.

Charles (III) the Fat (839–888) Holy Roman Emperor (881–87); he became king of the West Franks in 885, thus uniting for the last time the whole of Charlemagne's dominions, but was deposed.

Charles IV (1316–1378) Holy Roman Emperor from 1355 and king of Bohemia from 1346. Son of John of Luxembourg, King of Bohemia, he was elected king of Germany in 1346 and ruled all Germany from 1347. He was the founder of the first German university in Prague in 1348.

Charles V (1500–1558) Holy Roman Emperor (1519–56). Son of Philip of Burgundy and Joanna of Castile, he inherited vast possessions, which led to rivalry from Francis I of France, whose alliance with the Ottoman Empire brought Vienna under siege in 1529 and 1532. Charles was also in conflict with the Protestants in Germany until the Treaty of Passau of 1552, which allowed the Lutherans religious liberty.

Charles VI (1685–1740) Holy Roman Emperor from 1711, father of *Maria Theresa, whose succession to his Austrian dominions he tried to ensure, and himself claimant to the Spanish throne in 1700, thus causing the War of the *Spanish Succession.

Charles, (Karl Franz Josef) (1887–1922) Emperor of Austria and king of Hungary from 1916, the last of the Habsburg emperors. He succeeded his great-uncle Franz Josef in 1916 but was forced to withdraw to Switzerland in 1918, although he refused to abdicate. In 1921 he attempted unsuccessfully to regain the crown of Hungary and was deported to Madeira, where he died.

Charles Spanish **Carlos**, four kings of Spain including:

Charles II (1661–1700) King of Spain from 1665. The second son of Philip IV, he was the last of the Spanish Habsburg kings. Mentally disabled from birth, he bequeathed his dominions to Philip of Anjou, grandson of Louis XIV, which led to the War of the *Spanish Succession.

Charles III (1716–1788) King of Spain from 1759. Son of Philip V, he became duke of Parma in 1732 and conquered Naples and Sicily in 1734. On the death of his half-brother Ferdinand VI (1713–1759), he became king of Spain, handing over Naples and Sicily to his son Ferdinand (1751–1825). At home, he reformed state finances, strengthened the armed forces, and expelled the Jesuits. During his reign, Spain was involved in the Seven Years' War with France against England. This led to the loss of Florida in 1763, which was only regained when Spain and France supported the colonists during the American Revolution.

Charles IV (1748–1819) King of Spain from 1788, when he succeeded his father, Charles III; he left the

government in the hands of his wife and her lover, the minister Manuel de Godoy (1767–1851). In 1808 Charles was induced to abdicate by Napoleon's machinations in favour of his son Ferdinand VII (1784–1833), who was subsequently deposed by Napoleon's brother Joseph. Charles was awarded a pension by Napoleon and died in Rome.

Charles Swedish **Carl**, fifteen kings of Sweden (the first six were local chieftains), including:

Charles IX (1550–1611) King of Sweden from 1604, the youngest son of Gustavus Vasa. In 1568 he and his brother John led the rebellion against Eric XIV (1533–1577); John became king as John III and attempted to catholicize Sweden, and Charles led the opposition. John's son Sigismund, King of Poland and a Catholic, succeeded to the Swedish throne in 1592, and Charles led the Protestants. He was made regent in 1595 and deposed Sigismund in 1599. Charles was elected king of Sweden in 1604 and was involved in unsuccessful wars with Russia, Poland, and Denmark. He was the father of Gustavus Adolphus.

Charles X (1622–1660) King of Sweden from 1654, when he succeeded his cousin Christina. He waged war with Poland and Denmark and in 1657 invaded Denmark by leading his army over the frozen sea.

Charles XII (1682–1718) King of Sweden from 1697, when he succeeded his father, Charles XI. From 1700 he was involved in wars with Denmark, Poland, and Russia. He won a succession of victories until, in 1709 while invading Russia, he was defeated at Poltava in the Ukraine, and forced to take refuge in Turkey until 1714. He was killed while besieging Fredrikshall, Norway, although it was not known whether he was murdered by his own side or by the enemy.

Charles XIV (1763–1844) born Jean Baptiste Jules Bernadotte, King of Sweden and Norway from 1818. A former marshal in the French army, in 1810 he was elected crown prince of Sweden under the name of Charles John (Carl Johan). Loyal to his adopted country, he brought Sweden into the alliance against Napoleon in 1813, as a reward for which Sweden received Norway. He was the founder of the present dynasty.

Charles Albert (1798–1849) King of Sardinia from 1831. He showed liberal sympathies in early life, and after his accession introduced some reforms. On the outbreak of the 1848 revolution he granted a constitution and declared war on Austria. His troops were defeated at Custozza and Novara. In 1849 he abdicated in favour of his son Victor Emmanuel and retired to a monastery, where he died.

Charles Edward Stuart (1720–1788) also known as **the Young Pretender** or **Bonnie Prince Charlie**, British prince, grandson of James II and son of James, the Old Pretender. In the *Jacobite rebellion of 1745 (the *Forty-Five) Charles won the support of the Scottish Highlanders; his army invaded England to claim the throne but was beaten back by the Duke of *Cumberland and routed at *Culloden on 16 April 1746. Charles fled; for five months he wandered through the Highlands with a price of £30,000 on his head before escaping to France. He visited England secretly in 1750, and may have made other visits. In later life he degenerated into a friendless drunkard. He settled in Italy in 1766.

Charles Martel (c. 688–741) Frankish ruler (Mayor of the Palace) of the eastern Frankish kingdom from

717 and the whole kingdom from 731. His victory against the Moors at Moussais-la-Bataille near Tours in 732 earned him his nickname of Martel, 'the Hammer', because he halted the Islamic advance by the *Moors into Europe.

Charles's law law stating that the volume of a given mass of gas at constant pressure is directly proportional to its absolute temperature (temperature in kelvin). It was discovered by French physicist Jacques *Charles in 1787, and independently by French chemist Joseph Gay-Lussac in 1802.

Charles the Bold, Duke of Burgundy (1433–1477) Duke of Burgundy from 1463 who fought in the French civil war at Montlhéry in 1465, then crushed Liège (1464–68). He reformed his army before engaging in an ambitious campaign for conquest, unsuccessfully besieging the imperial town of Neuss (1474–75), before being defeated in his attack on the Swiss Federation (1476–77). He died in battle near Nancy, in Lorraine.

Charleston back-kicking dance of the 1920s that originated in Charleston, South Carolina, and became a US craze following the musical *Runnin' Wild* (1923).

charlock or **wild mustard** annual plant belonging to the cress family, found in Europe and Asia. It has hairy stems and leaves and yellow flowers. (*Sinapis arvensis*, family Cruciferae.)

Charlotte Amalie formerly St Thomas (1921–37), capital, tourist resort, and free port of the US Virgin Islands, on the island of St Thomas; population (2000 est) 11,000 (town), 18,900 (urban area). Boat-building, rum distillation, and tourism are among the economic activities.

Charlotte Sophia (1744–1818) British queen consort. The daughter of the German duke of Mecklenburg-Strelitz, she married George III of Great Britain and Ireland in 1761, and they had nine sons and six daughters.

Charlton, Bobby (1937–) born Robert Charlton, English footballer who between 1958 and 1970 scored a record 49 goals for England in 105 appearances. An elegant attacking midfield player who specialized in fierce long-range shots, he spent most of his playing career with Manchester United and played in the England team that won the World Cup in 1966. He is the younger brother of Jack *Charlton and the nephew of the Newcastle and England forward Jackie Milburn.

Charlton, Jack (1935–) born John Charlton, English footballer. A tall commanding centre-half he spent all his playing career with Leeds United and played a record 773 games for them. He appeared in the England team that won the World Cup in 1966. He is the older brother of Bobby *Charlton and the nephew of the Newcastle and England forward Jackie Milburn.

charm in physics, a property possessed by one type of *quark (very small particles found inside protons and neutrons), called the charm quark. The effects of charm are only seen in experiments with particle *accelerators. See *elementary particles.

Charon in Greek mythology, the boatman who ferried the dead (shades) over the rivers Acheron and Styx to *Hades, the underworld. An *obolus* (coin) placed on the tongue of the dead paid for their passage.

Chartism radical British democratic movement, mainly of the working classes, which flourished around 1838 to 1848. It derived its name from the People's Charter, a

six-point programme comprising universal male suffrage, equal electoral districts, secret ballot, annual parliaments, and abolition of the property qualification for, and payment of, members of Parliament.

Charybdis in Greek mythology, a monster and the whirlpool it forms, on the Sicilian side of the northern end of the narrow Straits of Messina, opposite the sea monster Scylla.

château country house or important residence in France. The term originally applied to a French medieval castle. The château was first used as a domestic building in the late 15th century. By the reign of Louis XIII (1610–43) fortifications such as moats and keeps were no longer used for defensive purposes, but merely as decorative features. The Loire valley contains some fine examples of châteaux.

Chateaubriand, François Auguste René, Vicomte de (1768–1848) French writer. He was a founder of Romanticism. Having lived in exile from the French Revolution between 1794 and 1800, he wrote *Atala* (1801; based on his encounters with North American Indians), *Le Génie du christianisme/The Genius of Christianity* (1802) – a defence of the Christian faith in terms of social, cultural, and spiritual benefits – and the autobiographical *René* (1805).

Chatterton, Thomas (1752–1770) English poet. His medieval-style poems and brief life were to inspire English Romanticism. Having studied ancient documents, he composed poems he ascribed to a 15th-century monk, 'Thomas Rowley', and these were at first accepted as genuine. He committed suicide after becoming destitute.

Chaucer, Geoffrey (c. 1340–1400) English poet. *The Canterbury Tales*, a collection of stories told by a group of pilgrims on their way to Canterbury, reveals his knowledge of human nature and his stylistic variety, from the sophisticated and subtly humorous to the simple and bawdy. His early work shows formal French influence, as in the dream-poem *The Book of the Duchess* and his adaptation of the French allegorical poem on courtly love, *The Romaunt of the Rose*, in which the meaning is conveyed in symbols. More mature works reflect the influence of Italian realism, as in *Troilus and Criseyde*, a substantial narrative poem about the tragic betrayal of an idealized courtly love, adapted from the Italian writer *Boccaccio. In *The Canterbury Tales* he shows his own genius for metre (rhythm) and characterization. Chaucer was the most influential English poet of the Middle Ages.

Chechnya or **Chechenia** or **Chechen Republic** breakaway part of the former Russian autonomous republic of Checheno-Ingush, on the northern slopes of the *Caucasus Mountains; official name **Noxcijn Republika Ickeriy** from 1994; area 17,300 sq km/6,680 sq mi; population (1990 est) 1,290,000 (Chechen 90%). The capital is *Grozny. Chief industries are oil extraction (at one of the largest Russian oilfields), engineering, chemicals, building materials, and timber. Most of the inhabitants are Sunni Muslim.

cheese food made from the **curds** (solids) of soured milk from cows, sheep, or goats, separated from the **whey** (liquid), then salted, put into moulds, and pressed into firm blocks. Cheese is ripened with bacteria or surface fungi, and kept for a time to mature before eating.

cheetah large wild cat *Acinonyx jubatus* native to Africa, Arabia, and southwestern Asia, but now rare in some areas. Yellowish with black spots, it has a slim lithe build. It is up to 1 m/3 ft tall at the shoulder, and up to 1.5 m/5 ft long. It can reach 103 kph/64 mph, but tires after about 400 yards. Cheetahs live in open country where they hunt small antelopes, hares, and birds.

Chekhov, Anton Pavlovich (1860–1904) Russian dramatist and writer of short stories. His plays concentrate on the creation of atmosphere and delineation of internal development, rather than external action. His first play, *Ivanov* (1887), was a failure, as was *The Seagull* (1896) until revived by Stanislavsky in 1898 at the Moscow Art Theatre, for which Chekhov went on to write his finest plays: *Uncle Vanya* (1897), *The Three Sisters* (1901), and *The Cherry Orchard* (1904).

chelate chemical compound whose molecules consist of one or more metal atoms or charged ions joined to chains of organic residues by coordinate (or dative covalent) chemical *bonds.

chemical change change that occurs when two or more substances (reactants) interact with each other, resulting in the production of different substances (products) with different chemical compositions. A simple example of chemical change is the burning of carbon in oxygen to produce carbon dioxide (*combustion). Other types of chemical change include *decomposition, *oxidation, and *reduction.

chemical element alternative name for *element.

chemical equation method of indicating the reactants and products of a chemical reaction by using chemical symbols and formulae. A chemical equation gives two basic pieces of information: (1) the reactants (on the left-hand side) and products (right-hand side); and (2) the reacting proportions (stoichiometry) – that is, how many units of each reactant and product are involved. The equation must balance; that is, the total number of atoms of a particular element on the left-hand side must be the same as the number of atoms of that element on the right-hand side.

chemical equilibrium condition in which the products of a chemical reaction are formed at the same rate at which they decompose back into the reactants, so that the concentration of each reactant and product remains constant. It is a *reversible reaction; the reaction can happen in both directions.

chemical warfare use in *war of gaseous, liquid, or solid substances intended to have a toxic effect on humans, animals, or plants. Together with *biological warfare, it was banned by the Geneva Protocol in 1925, and the United Nations, in 1989, also voted for a ban. In June 1990 the USA and USSR agreed bilaterally to reduce their stockpile to 5,000 tonnes each by 2002. The USA began replacing its stocks with new nerve-gas *binary weapons. In 1993 over 120 nations, including the USA and Russian Federation, signed a treaty outlawing the manufacture, stockpiling, and use of chemical weapons. The Russian parliament ratified the treaty in 1997.

chemisorption attachment, by chemical means, of a single layer of molecules, atoms, or ions of gas to the surface of a solid or, less frequently, a liquid. It is the basis of catalysis (see *catalyst) and is of great industrial importance.

chemistry branch of science concerned with the study of the structure and composition of the different kinds of matter, the changes that matter may undergo, and the phenomena which occur in the course of these changes. **Organic chemistry** is the branch of chemistry that deals with carbon compounds. **Inorganic chemistry** deals with the description, properties, reactions, and preparation of all the elements and their compounds, with the exception of carbon compounds. **Physical chemistry** is concerned with the quantitative explanation of chemical phenomena and reactions, and the measurement of data required for such explanations. This branch studies in particular the movement of molecules and the effects of temperature and pressure, often with regard to gases and liquids.

chemosynthesis method of making *protoplasm (contents of a cell) using the energy from chemical reactions, in contrast to the use of light energy employed for the same purpose in *photosynthesis. The process is used by certain bacteria, which can synthesize organic compounds from carbon dioxide and water using the energy from special methods of *respiration.

chemotherapy any medical treatment with chemicals. It usually refers to treatment of cancer with cytotoxic and other drugs. The term was coined by the German bacteriologist Paul Ehrlich for the use of synthetic chemicals against infectious diseases.

chemotropism movement by part of a plant in response to a chemical stimulus. The response by the plant is termed 'positive' if the growth is towards the stimulus or 'negative' if the growth is away from the stimulus.

Cheney, Dick (1941–) born Richard Bruce Cheney, US Republican politician, vice-president from 2001. He was the youngest-ever chief-of-staff 1975–77 under President Gerald Ford, a congressman 1979–89, and defence secretary 1989–93 under President George Bush. He was selected in 2000 as the running-mate of Bush's son, George W *Bush, to bring experience in federal matters and foreign policy to the electoral ticket.

Chengdu *or* **Chengtu** ancient city and capital of *Sichuan province, China; population (2001 est) 1,909,400. It is a busy rail junction and has railway workshops. Industries include food-processing, engineering (especially precision machinery), electronics, and the manufacture of textiles and petrochemicals. There are well-preserved temples of the 8th-century poet Tu Fu and other historical figures.

Chennai formerly **Madras** (to 1996), industrial port and capital of Tamil Nadu, India, on the Bay of Bengal; population (2001 est) 4,216,300. An all-weather artificial harbour handles cotton goods, oilseeds, hides and skins, and industrial raw materials. Main industries include cotton, cement, chemicals, railway, car and bicycle manufacture, electrical-engineering, rubber, fertilizers, oil refining, iron, and steel. Fort St George (1639) remains from the East India Company when Chennai was the chief port on the east coast; the fort now contains government offices and St Mary's Church, the first English church built in India (1680). Chennai was occupied by the French from 1746 to 1748 and shelled by the German ship *Emden* in 1914, the only place in India attacked in World War I. The University of Madras was founded in 1857, and there is a technical institute (1959).

Chequers *or* **Chequers Court** country home of the prime minister of the UK. It is an Elizabethan mansion in the Chiltern hills near Princes Risborough, Buckinghamshire, and was given to the nation by Lord Lee of Fareham under the Chequers Estate Act 1917, which came into effect in 1921. Its estate contains about 500 ha/1235 acres of farmlands and woods.

Cherenkov, Pavel Alexeevich (1904–1990) Soviet physicist. He was awarded the Nobel Prize for Physics in 1958 for his discovery in 1934 of Cherenkov radiation; this occurs as a bluish light when charged atomic particles pass through water or other media at a speed in excess of that of light. He shared the award with his colleagues Ilya Frank and Igor Tamm for work resulting in a cosmic-ray counter.

Chernobyl town in northern Ukraine, 100 km/62 mi north of Kiev; site of a former nuclear power station. The town is now abandoned. On 26 April 1986, two huge explosions occurred at the plant, destroying a central reactor and breaching its 1,000-tonne roof. In the immediate vicinity of Chernobyl, 31 people died (all firemen or workers at the plant) and 135,000 were permanently evacuated. It has been estimated that there will be an additional 20,000–40,000 deaths from cancer over 60 years; 600,000 people are officially classified as at risk. According to World Health Organization (WHO) figures from 1995, the incidence of thyroid cancer in children increased 200-fold in Belarus as a result of fallout from the disaster. The last remaining nuclear reactor at Chernobyl was shut down in December 2000.

Cherokee member of an *American Indian people who moved from the Great Lakes region to the southern Appalachian Mountains (Virginia, North and South Carolina, Alabama, Georgia, Tennessee, and possibly Kentucky); by the 16th century they occupied some 64,000 sq km/40,000 sq mi. Their language belonged to the Iroquoian family. They lived in log cabins in permanent farming settlements. Known as one of the Five Civilized Tribes, they assimilated many white customs. In 1838 they were ousted to Indian Territory (Oklahoma) in a bloody removal known as the Trail of Tears. They are now the largest American Indian group, numbering 281,000 (2000); many live in Oklahoma and North Carolina.

cherry any of a group of fruit-bearing trees distinguished from plums and apricots by their fruits, which are round and smooth and not covered with a bloom. They are cultivated in temperate regions with warm summers and grow best in deep fertile soil. (Genus *Prunus*, family Rosaceae.)

chervil any of several plants belonging to the carrot family. The garden chervil (*Anthriscus cerefolium*) has leaves with a sweetish smell, similar to parsley. It is used as a garnish and in soups. Chervil originated on the borders of Europe and Asia and was introduced to Western Europe by the Romans. (Genus *Anthriscus*, family Umbelliferae.)

Chesapeake Bay largest of the inlets on the Atlantic coast of the USA, bordered by eastern Maryland and eastern Virginia. Chesapeake Bay extends southwards from Havre de Grace in northeast Maryland, and enters the Atlantic between Cape Charles and Cape Henry in Virginia; it is about 320 km/200 mi in length and 6–64 km/4–40 mi in width. There are several deep-water ports located on the bay: Newport News, Norfolk, Portsmouth, and Baltimore.

Cheshire county of northwest England, which has contained the unitary authorities Halton and Warrington since April 1998. **area:** 2,320 sq km/896 sq mi. **towns and cities:** Chester (administrative headquarters), Crewe, Congleton, Macclesfield **physical:** chiefly a fertile plain, with the Pennines in the east; rivers: Mersey, Dee, Weaver; a sandstone ridge extending south through central Cheshire together with Delamere Forest constitute a woodland and heath landscape **features:** salt mines at Alderley Edge (in use from Roman times until the 1920s); Little Moreton Hall (15th century); Tatton Park Mansion (1790); Old Hall (1520); Chester Roman Amphitheatre (the largest in the UK); Chester Cathedral (1092), Chester Zoo (1930), Chester Races (16th-century; the oldest in the UK); discovery of Lindow Man, the first 'bogman' to be found in mainland Britain, dating from around 500 BC; Quarry Bank Mill (1784) at Styal is a cotton-industry museum.

chess board game originating as early as the 2nd century. Two players use 16 pieces each, on a board of 64 squares of alternating colour (usually black and white), to try to force the opponent into a position ('checkmate') where the main piece (the king) is threatened and cannot move to another position without remaining threatened.

the way each piece can move

arrangement of the chessmen

chess The names of chess pieces reflect the game's long history. Behind the eight pawns (foot-soldiers) on the board stand the king and queen, two bishops, two knights and two rooks (or castles). The queen is the most powerful piece, being able to move any number of squares vertically or diagonally.

Chesterton, G(ilbert) K(eith) (1874–1936) English novelist, essayist, and poet. He wrote numerous short stories featuring a Catholic priest, Father Brown, who solves crimes by drawing on his knowledge of human nature. Other novels include the fantasy *The Napoleon of Notting Hill* (1904) and *The Man Who Was Thursday* (1908), a deeply emotional allegory about the problem of evil.

chestnut any of a group of trees belonging to the beech family. The Spanish or sweet chestnut (*Castanea sativa*) produces edible nuts inside husks; its timber is also valuable. *Horse chestnuts are quite distinct, belonging to the genus *Aesculus*, family Hippocastanaceae. (True chestnut genus *Castanea*, family Fagaceae.)

Chetnik member of a Serbian nationalist group that operated underground during the German occupation of Yugoslavia in World War II. Led by Col Draza Mihailovic, the Chetniks initially received aid from the Allies, but this was later transferred to the communist partisans led by Tito. The term was also popularly applied to Serb militia forces in the 1991–92 Yugoslav civil war.

Chhattisgarh state of central India, bordered by Maharashtra, Andhra Pradesh, Orissa, Jharkhand, Uttar Pradesh, and Madhya Pradesh; area 146,361 sq km/ 56,510 sq mi; population (2001 est) 20,796,000. It is a rural and economically impoverished area, and was separated from Madhya Pradesh in 2000 in an effort to promote greater stability and prosperity for both states. The capital is Raipur. The state touches the northern-most part of the Deccan Plateau, and is crossed by the Mahandi River. Over 80% of the population is involved in agricultural activities and, nicknamed the 'Rice Bowl of India', Chhattisgarh provides rice to 600 rice mills within the state and Madhya Pradesh. Industries also include forest production and the mining of bauxite, limestone, iron ore, diamonds, gold, and china clay. One-third of the population is tribal, and the principal languages are Hindu and Chhattisgarhi.

Chiang Kai-shek Wade–Giles transliteration of *Jiang Jie Shi*.

chiaroscuro (Italian 'light-dark') in painting and graphic art, the use of strong contrasts of light and shade for dramatic impact. This is made particularly effective where contrasting materials are represented, for example, transparent glass, shining metal, rich velvets, and glossy wood. Masters of chiaroscuro include *Rembrandt, *Leonardo da Vinci, and *Caravaggio. The term is also used to describe a monochromatic painting employing light and dark shades only.

Chicago (Chippewa 'wild onion place') financial and industrial city in Illinois, USA, on Lake Michigan. It is the third-largest US city; population (2000 est) 2,896,000. Industries include iron, steel, chemicals, electrical goods, machinery, meatpacking and food processing, publishing, and fabricated metals. The once famous stockyards closed in 1971. Chicago grew from a village in the mid-19th century. The world's first skyscraper was built here in 1885 and some of the world's tallest skyscrapers, including the Sears Tower (442 m/1,450 ft high), are in Chicago.

Chicano citizens or residents of the USA who are of Mexican descent. The term was originally used for those who became US citizens after the *Mexican War. The word probably derives from the Spanish word *Mexicanos*.

chicken domestic fowl; see under *poultry.

chickenpox *or* **varicella** common, usually mild disease, caused by a virus of the *herpes group and

transmitted by airborne droplets. Chickenpox chiefly attacks children under the age of ten. The incubation period is two to three weeks. One attack normally gives immunity for life.

chickpea annual leguminous plant (see *legume), grown for food in India and the Middle East. Its short hairy pods contain edible seeds similar to peas. (*Cicer arietinum*, family Leguminosae.)

chicory plant native to Europe and West Asia, with large, usually blue, flowers. Its long taproot is used dried and roasted as a coffee substitute. As a garden vegetable, grown under cover, its blanched leaves are used in salads. It is related to *endive. (*Cichorium intybus*, family Compositae.)

chiffchaff small songbird *Phylloscopus collybita* of the warbler family, Muscicapidae, order Passeriformes. It is found in woodlands and thickets in Europe and northern Asia during the summer, migrating south for winter. About 11 cm/4.3 in long, olive above, greyish below, with yellow-white nether parts, an eyestripe, and usually dark legs, it looks similar to a willow warbler but has a distinctive song.

chigger *or* **harvest mite** scarlet or rusty brown *mite genus *Trombicula*, family Trombiculidae, in the order Acarina, common in summer and autumn. Chiggers are parasitic, and their tiny red larvae cause intensely irritating bites in places where the skin is thin, such as behind the knees or between the toes. After a time they leave their host and drop to the ground where they feed upon minute insects.

chihuahua smallest breed of dog, 15 cm/10 in high, developed in the USA from Mexican origins. It may weigh only 1 kg/2.2 lb. The domed head and wide-set ears are characteristic, and the skull is large compared to the body. It can be almost any colour, and occurs in both smooth (or even hairless) and long-coated varieties.

Chihuahua capital of Chihuahua state, Mexico, 1,285 km/800 mi northwest of Mexico City; population (2000 est) 671,800. It lies in the north of Mexico at an altitude of 1,402 m/4,600 ft, and was founded in 1707. It is the centre of both a mining district and a cattle raising area and has textile mills and smelting industries. The area is noted for breeding the small, short-haired dogs named after the town and state.

chilblain painful inflammation of the skin of the feet, hands, or ears, due to cold. The parts turn red, swell, itch violently, and are very tender. In bad cases, the skin cracks, blisters, or ulcerates.

Childers, (Robert) Erskine (1870–1922) English civil servant and writer, Irish republican, author of the spy novel *The Riddle of the Sands* (1903).

Chile

National name: *República de Chile/Republic of Chile*
Area: 756,950 sq km/292,258 sq mi
Capital: Santiago
Major towns/cities: Concepción, Viña del Mar, Valparaíso, Talcahuano, Puente Alto, Temuco, Antofagasta
Major ports: Valparaíso, Antofagasta, Arica, Iquique, Punta Arenas
Physical features: Andes mountains along eastern border, Atacama Desert in north, fertile central valley, grazing land and forest in south
Territories: Easter Island, Juan Fernández Islands, part of Tierra del Fuego, claim to part of Antarctica

Head of state and government: Ricardo Lagos Escobar from 2000
Political system: emergent democracy
Political executive: limited presidency
Political parties: Christian Democratic Party (PDC), moderate centrist; National Renewal Party (RN), right wing; Socialist Party of Chile (PS), left wing; Independent Democratic Union (UDI), right wing; Party for Democracy (PPD), left of centre; Union of the Centre-Centre (UCC), right wing; Radical Party (PR), left of centre
Currency: Chilean peso
GNI per capita (PPP): (US$) 9,180 (2002 est)
Exports: copper, fruits, timber products, fishmeal, vegetables, manufactured foodstuffs and beverages. Principal market: USA 19.2% (2001)
Population: 15,805,000 (2003 est)
Language: Spanish (official)
Religion: Roman Catholic 80%, Protestant 13%, atheist and nonreligious 6%
Life expectancy: 73 (men); 79 (women) (2000–05)
Chronology
1535: The first Spanish invasion of Chile was abandoned in the face of fierce resistance from indigenous Araucanian Indians.
1541: Pedro de Valdivia began the Spanish conquest and founded Santiago.
1553: Valdivia was captured and killed by Araucanian Indians, led by Chief Lautaro.
17th century: The Spanish developed small agricultural settlements ruled by a government subordinate to the viceroy in Lima, Peru.
1778: The king of Spain appointed a captain-general to govern Chile.
1810: A Santiago junta proclaimed Chilean autonomy after Napoleon dethroned the king of Spain.
1814: The Spanish viceroy regained control of Chile.
1817: The Army of the Andes, led by José de San Martín and Bernardo O'Higgins, defeated the Spanish.
1818: Chile achieved independence from Spain with O'Higgins as supreme director.

1823–30: O'Higgins was forced to resign; a civil war between conservative centralists and liberal federalists ended with conservative victory.
1833: An autocratic republican constitution created a unitary Roman Catholic state with a strong president and limited franchise.
1851–61: President Manuel Montt bowed to pressure to liberalize the constitution and reduce privileges of landowners and the church.
1879–84: Chile defeated Peru and Bolivia in the War of the Pacific and increased its territory by a third.
late 19th century: Mining of nitrate and copper became a major industry; large-scale European immigration followed the 'pacification' of Araucanian Indians.
1891: A constitutional dispute between president and congress led to civil war; congressional victory reduced the president to figurehead status.
1925: A new constitution increased presidential powers, separated church and state, and made primary education compulsory.
1927: A military coup led to the dictatorship of Gen Carlos Ibáñez del Campo.
1931: A sharp fall in price of copper and nitrate caused dramatic economic and political collapse.
1938: A Popular Front of Radicals, Socialists, and Communists took power under Pedro Aguirre Cedra, who introduced economic policies based on the US New Deal.
1948–58: The Communist Party was banned.
1970: Salvador Allende, leader of the Popular Unity coalition, became the world's first democratically elected Marxist president; he embarked on an extensive programme of nationalization and radical social reform.
1973: Allende was killed in a CIA-backed military coup; Gen Augusto Pinochet established a dictatorship combining severe political repression with free-market economics.
1981: Pinochet began an eight-year term as president under a new constitution described as a 'transition to democracy'.
1983: Economic recession provoked growing opposition to the governing regime.
1988: A referendum on whether Pinochet should serve a further term resulted in a clear 'No' vote.
1990: The military regime ended, with a Christian Democrat (Patricio Aylwin) as president, with Pinochet as commander in chief of the army. An investigation was launched into over 2,000 political executions during the military regime.
1995: Dante Cordova was appointed prime minister.
1998: Pinochet retired from the army and was made life senator. Pinochet was placed under arrest in the UK; proceedings began to extradite him to Spain on murder charges.
1999: The ruling on the extradition of Pinochet to Spain was left to the British government.
2000: Ricardo Lagos was elected president. Pinochet was found unfit for trial by British doctors and allowed to return to Chile. However, in Chile, Pinochet was stripped of immunity from prosecution.
2001: Pinochet was arrested and charged with organizing the killings of left-wing activists and union leaders during his time in power. The charges were later dropped after a court ruling that Pinochet was unfit to stand trial.

2003: An application to remove Pinochet's immunity from prosecution was twice blocked by the courts.
2004: Chileans were given the legal right to divorce. The courts lifted Pinochet's immunity from prosecution.
2005: Pinochet was put under house arrest following his indictment for alleged human rights abuses.

chilli pod, or powder made from the pod, of a variety of *capsicum (*Capsicum frutescens*), a small, hot, red pepper. It is widely used in cooking. The hot ingredient of chilli is capsaicin. It causes a burning sensation in the mouth by triggering nerve branches in the eyes, nose, tongue, and mouth. Capsaicin does not activate the taste buds and therefore has no flavour. It is claimed that people can become physically addicted to it.

Chiltern Hills range of chalk hills extending for some 72 km/45 mi in a curve from a point north of Reading to the Suffolk border. Coombe Hill, near Wendover, 260 m/852 ft high, is the highest point.

chimaera fish of the group Holocephali. Chimaeras have thick bodies that taper to a long thin tail, large fins, smooth skin, and a cartilaginous skeleton. They can grow to 1.5 m/4.5 ft. Most chimaeras are deep-water fish, and even *Chimaera monstrosa*, a relatively shallow-living form caught around European coasts, lives at a depth of 300–500 m/1,000–1,600 ft.

chimera *or* **chimaera** in Greek mythology, a fire-breathing animal with a lion's head and foreparts, a goat's middle, a dragon's rear, and a tail in the form of a snake; hence any apparent hybrid of two or more creatures. The chimera was killed by the hero Bellerophon on the winged horse Pegasus.

chimpanzee highly intelligent African ape *Pan troglodytes* that lives mainly in rainforests but sometimes in wooded savannah. Chimpanzees are covered in thin but long black body hair, except for the face, hands, and feet, which may have pink or black skin. They normally walk on all fours, supporting the front of the body on the knuckles of the fingers, but can stand or walk upright for a short distance. They can grow to 1.4 m/4.5 ft tall, and weigh up to 50 kg/110 lb. They are strong and climb well, but spend time on the ground, living in loose social groups. The bulk of the diet is fruit, with some leaves, insects, and occasional meat. Females reach sexual maturity at 8–12 years of age, males at 17–18. Chimpanzees give birth to a single infant approximately every five years. Chimpanzees can use 'tools', fashioning twigs to extract termites from their nests. According to a 1998 estimate by the Worldwide Fund for Nature, the world population of chimpanzees stands at 200,000.

China
National name: *Zhonghua Renmin Gongheguo (Zhongguo)/People's Republic of China*
Area: 9,572,900 sq km/3,696,000 sq mi
Capital: Beijing (or Peking)
Major towns/cities: Shanghai, Hong Kong, Chongqing, Tianjin, Guangzhou (English Canton), Shenyang (formerly Mukden), Wuhan, Nanjing, Harbin, Chengdu, Xi'an
Major ports: Tianjin, Shanghai, Hong Kong, Qingdao, Guangzhou
Physical features: two-thirds of China is mountains or desert (north and west); the low-lying east is irrigated by rivers Huang He (Yellow River), Chang Jiang (Yangtze-Kiang), Xi Jiang (Si Kiang)

Territories: Paracel Islands
Head of state: Hu Jintao from 2003
Head of government: Wen Jiabao from 2003
Political system: communist
Political executive: communist
Political party Chinese Communist Party (CCP), Marxist-Leninist-Maoist; eight registered small parties controlled by the CCP
Currency: yuan
GNI per capita (PPP): (US$) 4,390 (2002 est)
Exports: basic manufactures, miscellaneous manufactured articles (particularly clothing and toys), crude petroleum, machinery and transport equipment, fishery products, cereals, canned food, tea, raw silk, cotton cloth. Principal market: USA 20.4% (2001)
Population: 1,304,196,000 (2003 est)
Language: Chinese (dialects include Mandarin (official), Yue (Cantonese), Wu (Shanghaiese), Minbai, Minnah, Xiang, Gan, and Hakka)
Religion: Taoist, Confucianist, and Buddhist; Muslim 2–3%; Christian about 1% (divided between the 'patriotic' church established in 1958 and the 'loyal' church subject to Rome); Protestant 3 million
Life expectancy: 69 (men); 73 (women) (2000–05)
Chronology
c. 3000 BC: Yangshao culture reached its peak in the Huang He Valley; displaced by Longshan culture in eastern China.
c. 1766–*c.* 1122 BC: First major dynasty, the Shang, arose from Longshan culture; writing and calendar developed.
c. 1122–256 BC: Zhou people of western China overthrew Shang and set up new dynasty; development of money and written laws.
c. 500 BC: Confucius expounded the philosophy that guided Chinese government and society for the next 2,000 years.
403–221 BC: 'Warring States Period': Zhou Empire broke up into small kingdoms.
221–206 BC: Qin defeated all rivals and established first empire with strong central government; emperor Shi Huangdi built the Great Wall of China.

202 BC–AD 220: Han dynasty expanded empire into central Asia; first overland trade with Europe; art and literature flourished; Buddhism introduced from India.

AD 220–581: Large-scale rebellion destroyed the Han dynasty; the empire split into three competing kingdoms; several short-lived dynasties ruled parts of China.

581–618: Sui dynasty reunified China and repelled Tatar invaders.

618–907: Tang dynasty enlarged and strengthened the empire; great revival of culture; major rebellion (875–84).

907–60: 'Five Dynasties and Ten Kingdoms': disintegration of the empire amid war and economic decline; development of printing.

960–1279: Song dynasty reunified China and restored order; civil service examinations introduced; population reached 100 million; Manchurians occupied northern China in 1127.

1279: Mongols conquered all China, which became part of the vast empire of Kublai Khan, founder of the Yuan dynasty; the Venetian traveller Marco Polo visited China (1275–92).

1279–1368: Yuan dynasty.

1368: Rebellions drove out the Mongols; Ming dynasty expanded the empire; architecture flourished in the new capital of Beijing.

1368–1644: Ming dynasty.

1516: Portuguese explorers reached Macau. Other European traders followed, with the first Chinese porcelain arriving in Europe in 1580.

1644: Manchurian invasion established the Qing (or Manchu) dynasty; Manchurians were assimilated and Chinese trade and culture continued to thrive.

1644–1911: Qing dynasty.

1796–1804: Anti-Manchu revolt weakened the Qing dynasty; a population increase in excess of food supplies led to falling living standards and cultural decline.

1839–42: First Opium War; Britain forced China to cede Hong Kong and open five ports to European trade; Second Opium War extracted further trade concessions (1856–60).

1850–64: Millions died in the Taiping Rebellion; Taipings combined Christian and Chinese beliefs and demanded land reform.

1894–95: Sino–Japanese War: Chinese driven out of Korea.

1897–98: Germany, Russia, France, and Britain leased ports in China.

1898: Land around Hong Kong was secured by Britain on a 99-year lease.

1900: Anti-Western Boxer Rebellion crushed by foreign intervention; jealousy between the Great Powers prevented partition.

1911: Revolution broke out; Republic of China proclaimed by Sun Zhong Shan (Sun Yat-sen) of Guomindang (National People's Party).

1912: Abdication of infant emperor Pu-i; Gen Yuan Shih-K'ai became dictator.

1916: The power of the central government collapsed on the death of Yuan Shih-K'ai; northern China dominated by local warlords.

1919: Beijing students formed the 4th May movement to protest at the transfer of German possessions in China to Japan.

1921: Sun Zhong Shan elected president of nominal national government; Chinese Communist Party

founded; communists worked with Guomindang to reunite China from 1923.

1925: Death of Sun Zhong Shan; leadership of Guomindang gradually passed to military commander Jiang Jie Shi (Chiang Kai-shek).

1926–28: Revolutionary Army of Jiang Jie Shi reunified China; Guomindang broke with communists and tried to suppress them in civil war.

1932: Japan invaded Manchuria and established the puppet state of Manchukuo.

1934–35: Communists undertook Long March from Jiangxi and Fujian in south to Yan'an in north to escape encirclement by Guomindang.

1937–45: Japan renewed invasion of China; Jiang Jie Shi received help from USA and Britain from 1941.

1946: Civil war resumed between Guomindang and communists led by Mao Zedong.

1949: Victorious communists proclaimed People's Republic of China under Chairman Mao; Guomindang fled to Taiwan.

1950–53: China intervened heavily in Korean War.

1958: 'Great Leap Forward': extremist five-year plan to accelerate output severely weakened the economy.

1960: Sino-Soviet split: China accused USSR of betraying communism.

1962: Economic recovery programme under Liu Shaoqi caused divisions between 'rightists' and 'leftists'; brief border war with India.

1966–69: 'Great Proletarian Cultural Revolution'; leftists overthrew Liu Shaoqi with support of Mao; Red Guards disrupted education, government, and daily life in attempt to enforce revolutionary principles.

1970: Mao supported the efforts of Prime Minister Zhou Enlai to restore order.

1971: People's Republic of China admitted to United Nations.

1976: Deaths of Zhou Enlai and Mao Zedong led to a power struggle between rightists and leftists; Hua Guofeng became leader.

1977–81: Rightist Deng Xiaoping emerged as supreme leader; pragmatic economic policies introduced market incentives and encouraged foreign trade.

1979: Full diplomatic relations with USA established

1987: Deng Xiaoping retired from Politburo but remained a dominant figure.

1989: Over 2,000 people were killed when the army crushed pro-democracy student demonstrations in Tiananmen Square, Beijing; international sanctions were imposed.

1991: China and the USSR reached an agreement on their disputed border.

1993: Jiang Zemin became head of state

1996: Reunification with Taiwan was declared a priority.

1997: A border agreement was signed with Russia. Hong Kong was returned to Chinese sovereignty.

1998: Zhu Rongji became prime minister. The Yangtze in Hubei province flooded, causing widespread devastation. Dissident Xu Wenli was jailed for trying to set up an opposition party.

1999: The USA and China announced a deal to allow for China's entry into the World Trade Organization (WTO), in exchange for opening China's markets to foreign firms. Macau was returned to China, with the promise that it would have an independent political system for fifty years. The religious sect Falun Gong was banned and its leaders arrested.

2000: A drive against corruption convicted a number of high-ranking government officials, including a former deputy chairman of the National People's Congress. The first verdicts in trials of at least 200 officials accused of evading tariffs on the importing of US$6.6 billion worth of goods resulted in 14 people being sentenced to death.

2001: Five members of the Falun Gong set themselves alight in Tiananmen Square, Beijing, in protest at the continued government crackdown on the sect. The mid-air collision of a US spy plane and a Chinese fighter jet provoked a diplomatic crisis.

2002: The country became a member of the World Trade Organization (WTO). Contact was re-established between the Dalai Lama and the Chinese government over the issue of Tibet for the first time since 1993.

2003: Having previously assumed the chair of the Chinese Communist Party at the 16th congress in November 2002, Hu Jintao became state president of China. The killer pneumonia-like virus identified as severe acute respiratory syndrome (SARS) originated in Guangdong province and spread worldwide. Yang Liwei became the first Chinese astronaut after a 21-hour orbital mission.

2004: The former president Jiang Zemin resigned as army chief, three years ahead of schedule. China signed a trade agreement with ten southeast Asian countries.

2005: The first direct flights since 1949 took place between China and Taiwan. Tung Chee-hwa resigned as Chief Executive of Hong Kong. Taiwan brought in a new law calling for the use of force if Taipei declared independence from mainland China; the Taiwanese National Party leader, Lien Chan, visited China for the first meeting between nationalist and communist party leaders since 1949. Anti-Japanese protests were held after a Japanese school book allegedly minimized Japan's war-crimes against China.

china clay commercial name for *kaolin.

China Sea area of the Pacific Ocean bordered by China, Vietnam, Borneo, the Philippines, and Japan. Various groups of small islands and shoals, including the Paracels, 500 km/300 mi east of Vietnam, have been disputed by China and other powers because they lie in oil-rich areas. The chief rivers which flow into the South China Sea are the Red River and Mekong; the main ports include Canton, Hong Kong, Manila, Bangkok, Singapore, and Ho Chi Minh City.

chinchilla South American rodent *Chinchilla laniger* found in high, rather barren areas of the Andes in Bolivia and Chile. About the size of a small rabbit, it has long ears and a long bushy tail, and shelters in rock crevices. These gregarious animals have thick, soft, silver-grey fur, and were hunted almost to extinction for it. They are now farmed and protected in the wild.

Chinese the native groups or inhabitants of China and Taiwan, and those people of Chinese descent. The Chinese comprise more than 25% of the world's population, and the Chinese language (Mandarin) is the largest member of the Sino-Tibetan family.

Chinese art the painting and sculpture of China. From the Bronze Age to the Cultural Revolution, Chinese art shows a stylistic unity unparalleled in any other culture. From about the 1st century AD Buddhism inspired much sculpture and painting. The **Han dynasty** (206 BC–AD 220) produced outstanding metalwork, ceramics, and sculpture. The **Song dynasty** (960–1278) established standards of idyllic landscape and nature painting in a delicate calligraphic style.

Chinese language language or group of languages of the Sino-Tibetan family, spoken in China, Taiwan, Hong Kong, Singapore, and Chinese communities throughout the world. Varieties of spoken Chinese differ greatly, but all share a written form using thousands of ideographic symbols – characters – which have changed little in 2,000 years. Nowadays, *putonghua* ('common speech'), based on the educated Beijing dialect known as Mandarin Chinese, is promoted throughout China as the national spoken and written language.

Chinese Revolution series of great political upheavals in China between 1911 and 1949 which eventually led to Communist Party rule and the establishment of the People's Republic of China. In 1912 a nationalist revolt overthrew the imperial Manchu dynasty. Under the leaders *Sun Zhong Shan (Sun Yat-sen) (1923–25) and *Jiang Jie Shi (Chiang Kai-shek) (1925–49), the Nationalists, or *Guomindang, were increasingly challenged by the growing communist movement. The 10,000 km/6,000 mi *Long March to the northwest, undertaken by the communists from 1934 to 1935 to escape Guomindang harassment, resulted in the emergence of *Mao Zedong as a communist leader. During World War II the various Chinese political groups pooled military resources against the Japanese invaders, but in 1946 the conflict reignited into open civil war. In 1949 the Guomindang were defeated at Nanjing and forced to flee to Taiwan. Communist rule was established in the People's Republic of China under the leadership of Mao Zedong.

chip *or* **silicon chip** another name for an *integrated circuit, a complete electronic circuit on a slice of silicon (or other semiconductor) crystal only a few millimetres square.

chipmunk any of several species of small ground squirrel with characteristic stripes along its side. Chipmunks live in North America and East Asia, in a variety of habitats, usually wooded, and take shelter in burrows. They have pouches in their cheeks for carrying food. They climb well but spend most of their time on or near the ground.

Chippendale, Thomas (1718–1779) English furniture designer. He set up his workshop in St Martin's Lane, London, in 1753. His trade catalogue *The Gentleman and Cabinet Maker's Director* (1754), was a significant contribution to furniture design, and the first of its type to be published. Although many of his most characteristic designs are *rococo, he also employed Louis XVI, Chinese, Gothic, and neoclassical styles. He worked mainly in mahogany, newly introduced from South America.

Chirac, Jacques René (1932–) French right-of-centre Gaullist politician and head of state, president from 1995 and prime minister 1974–76 and 1986–88, 'co-habiting' on the second occasion with the socialist president François *Mitterrand. Chirac led the Gaullist party 1974–95, refounding it in 1976 as the Rally for the Republic (RPR), now part of the Union for a Popular Movement (UMP). He also served as the first elected mayor of Paris 1977–95. In 2003 Chirac fell out with US president George W Bush over the US-led war against Iraq, which France refused to support, preferring a UN solution.

Chirico, Giorgio de (1888–1978) Greek-born Italian painter. He founded the school of *metaphysical painting, which in its enigmatic imagery and haunted, dreamlike settings presaged surrealism, as in *Nostalgia of the Infinite* (1911; Museum of Modern Art, New York).

Chiron unusual object orbiting between Saturn and Uranus, discovered in 1977 by US astronomer Charles Kowal. Initially classified as an asteroid, it is now believed to be a giant cometary nucleus at least 200 km/120 mi across, composed of ice with a dark crust of carbon dust. It has a 51-year orbit and a coma (cloud of gas and dust) caused by evaporation from its surface, resembling that of a comet. It is classified as a centaur.

chiropractic in alternative medicine, technique of manipulation of the spine and other parts of the body, based on the principle that physical disorders are attributable to aberrations in the functioning of the nervous system, which manipulation can correct.

Chisinau Russian **Kishinev**, capital of Moldova, situated in a rich agricultural area; population (1990) 676,000. It is a commercial and cultural centre; industries include cement, food processing, tobacco, and textiles.

chitin complex long-chain compound, or *polymer; a nitrogenous derivative of glucose. Chitin is widely found in invertebrates. It forms the *exoskeleton of insects and other arthropods. It combines with protein to form a covering that can be hard and tough, as in beetles, or soft and flexible, as in caterpillars and other insect larvae. It is insoluble in water and resistant to acids, alkalis, and many organic solvents. In crustaceans such as crabs, it is impregnated with calcium carbonate for extra strength.

chivalry code of gallantry and honour that medieval knights were pledged to observe. Its principal virtues were piety, honour, valour, courtesy, chastity, and loyalty. The word originally meant the knightly class of the feudal Middle Ages. Modern orders of chivalry such as the Order of the *Garter are awarded as a mark of royal favour or as a reward for public services; see *knighthood, order of.

chive *or* **chives** perennial European plant belonging to the lily family, related to onions and leeks. It has an underground bulb, long hollow tubular leaves, and globe-shaped purple flower heads. The leaves are used as a garnish for salads. (*Allium schoenoprasum*, family Liliaceae.)

chlamydia viruslike bacteria which live parasitically in animal cells, and cause disease in humans and birds. Chlamydiae are thought to be descendants of bacteria that have lost certain metabolic processes. In humans, a strain of chlamydia causes *trachoma, a disease found mainly in the tropics (a leading cause of blindness); venereally transmitted chlamydiae cause genital and urinary infections.

chloride (Cl⁻) negative ion formed when hydrogen chloride dissolves in water, and any salt containing this ion, commonly formed by the action of hydrochloric acid (HCl) on various metals or by direct combination of a metal and chlorine. Sodium chloride (NaCl) is common table salt.

chlorination treatment of water with chlorine in order to disinfect it; also, any chemical reaction in which a chlorine atom is introduced into a chemical compound.

chlorine chemical symbol Cl, (Greek *chloros* 'green') greenish-yellow, gaseous, non-metallic element with a pungent odour, atomic number 17, relative atomic mass 35.453. It is a member of the *halogen group and is widely distributed, in combination with the *alkali metals, as chlorides.

chlorofluorocarbon (CFC) a class of **synthetic chemicals** that are odourless, non-toxic, non-flammable, and chemically inert. The first CFC was synthesized in 1892, but no use was found for it until the 1920s. Their stability and apparently harmless properties made CFCs popular as propellants in *aerosol cans, as refrigerants in refrigerators and air conditioners, as degreasing agents, and in the manufacture of foam packaging. They are now known to be partly responsible for the destruction of the *ozone layer. In 1987, an international agreement called the Montréal Protocol was established; it was one of the first global environmental treaties and it banned the use of chemicals responsible for ozone damage, such as CFCs in aerosols and refrigerants.

chloroform *or* **trichloromethane (CHCl₃)** clear, colourless, toxic, carcinogenic liquid with a characteristic pungent, sickly sweet smell and taste, formerly used as an anaesthetic (now superseded by less harmful substances). It is used as a solvent and in the synthesis of organic chemical compounds.

chlorophyll group of pigments including chlorophyll a and chlorophyll b, the green pigments present in *chloroplasts in most plants; it is responsible for the absorption of *light energy during *photosynthesis. The pigment absorbs the red and blue-violet parts of sunlight but reflects the green, thus giving plants their characteristic colour. Other chlorophylls include chlorophyll c (in brown algae) and chlorophyll d (found in red algae).

chloroplast structure (*organelle) within a plant cell containing the green pigment *chlorophyll. Chloroplasts occur in most cells of green plants that are exposed to light, often in large numbers. Typically, they are shaped like a flattened disc, with a double membrane enclosing the stroma, a gel-like matrix. Within the stroma are stacks of fluid-containing cavities, or vesicles, where *photosynthesis occurs, creating *glucose from carbon dioxide and water to be used in the plant's life processes. Sunlight is absorbed by chlorophyll, providing energy which is transferred to the glucose. The glucose may be converted to starch and stored. Starch can then be converted back to glucose to provide energy for the plant at a later stage.

chlorosis abnormal condition of green plants in which the stems and leaves turn pale green or yellow. The yellowing is due to a reduction in the levels of the green chlorophyll pigments. It may be caused by a deficiency in essential elements (such as magnesium, iron, or manganese), a lack of light, genetic factors, or viral infection.

chocolate powder, syrup, confectionery, or beverage derived from cacao seeds. See *cocoa and chocolate.

choir group of singers with several performers or voices to a part. A **mixed voice choir** contains parts for both women and men; a **male voice choir** is usually men only, but may be boys and men; a **double choir** is two equal choirs often used in antiphonal singing (where the choirs sing alternately, one answering the other, creating a 'stereo' effect, heightened by their placement on either side of the church).

cholecalciferol or **vitamin D** fat-soluble chemical important in the uptake of calcium and phosphorous for bones. It is found in liver, fish oils, and margarine. It can be produced in the skin, provided that the skin is adequately exposed to sunlight. Lack of vitamin D leads to rickets and other bone diseases.

cholera disease caused by infection with various strains of the bacillus *Vibrio cholerae*, transmitted in contaminated water and characterized by violent diarrhoea and vomiting. It is prevalent in many tropical areas.

cholesterol white, crystalline *sterol found throughout the body, especially in fats, blood, nerve tissue, and bile; it is also provided in the diet by foods such as eggs, meat, and butter. A high level of cholesterol in the blood is thought to contribute to atherosclerosis (hardening of the arteries).

Chomsky, (Avram) Noam (1928–) US professor of linguistics and political commentator. He proposed a theory of transformational generative grammar, which attracted widespread interest because of the claims it made about the relationship between language and the mind and the universality of an underlying language structure. He has been a leading critic of the imperialist tendencies of the US government.

Chongqing or **Chungking** or **Pahsien** city, formerly in Sichuan province, China, at the confluence of the Chang Jiang and Jialing Jiang rivers; population (1999 est) 3,193,900. From the time of the 1990 census it has been included directly under the central government in the capital district of Chongqing, the largest of China's four capital districts, with an area of 82,000 sq km/ 31,700 sq mi and a total population (2000) of 30,900,000. Industries include coalmining, food-processing, and the manufacture of iron, steel, chemicals, synthetic rubber, automobiles, electrical equipment, and textiles.

Chopin, Frédéric (1810–1849) Polish composer and pianist. He made his debut as a pianist at the age of eight. As a performer, Chopin revolutionized the technique of pianoforte-playing, turning the hands outward and favouring a light, responsive touch. His compositions, which include two piano concertos and other orchestral works, have great changes of mood, and flowing rhythms.

chord in geometry, a straight line joining any two points on a curve. The chord that passes through the centre of a circle (its longest chord) is the diameter. The longest and shortest chords of an ellipse (a regular oval) are called the major and minor axes, respectively.

chord in music, a group of three or more notes sounded together. This 'vertical' combination of notes (of any number) is almost infinite in possibility, and yet is fundamental in determining a style of music. This goes some way to explaining the enormous variation of music in existence.

chordate animal belonging to the phylum Chordata, which includes vertebrates, sea squirts, amphioxi, and others. All these animals, at some stage of their lives, have a supporting rod of tissue (notochord or backbone) running down their bodies.

chorea condition featuring involuntary movements of the face muscles and limbs. It is seen in a number of neurological diseases, including *Huntington's chorea.

choreography the art of creating and arranging ballet and dance for performance; originally, in the 18th century, dance notation.

chorionic villus sampling (CVS) *biopsy of a small sample of placental tissue, carried out in early pregnancy at 10–12 weeks' gestation. Since the placenta forms from embryonic cells, the tissue obtained can be tested to reveal genetic abnormality in the fetus. The advantage of CVS over *amniocentesis is that it provides an earlier diagnosis, so that if any abnormality is discovered, and the parents opt for an abortion, it can be carried out more safely.

chorus in classical Greek drama, the group of actors who jointly comment on the main action or advise the main characters. The action in Greek plays took place offstage; the chorus provided a link in the drama when the principals were offstage. The chorus did not always speak in unison; it was common for members of the chorus to show some individuality. The device of a chorus has also been used by later dramatists.

Chou En-lai alternative transliteration of *Zhou Enlai.

chough bird *Pyrrhocorax pyrrhocorax* of the crow family, Corvidae, order Passeriformes, about 38 cm/ 15 in long, black-feathered, with red bill and legs, and long hooked claws. Choughs are frugivorous and insectivorous. They make mud-walled nests and live on sea cliffs and mountains from Europe to East Asia, but are now rare.

chow chow breed of dog originating in China in ancient times. About 45 cm/1.5 ft tall, it has a broad neck and head, round catlike feet, a soft woolly undercoat with a coarse outer coat, and a mane. Its coat should be of one colour, and it has an unusual blue-black tongue.

Chrétien, (Joseph Jacques) Jean (1934–) French-Canadian politician, prime minister of Canada 1993–2003. He won the leadership of the Liberal Party in 1990 and defeated Kim Campbell of the governing Progressive Conservative Party by a landslide margin in the October 1993 election. Although himself a Québécois, he has been consistently opposed Québéc's separatist ambitions, advocating instead national unity within a federal structure. His Liberal Party was re-elected in the 1997 and 2000 general elections. He retired as prime minister in December 2003, being replaced by Paul Martin.

Chrétien de Troyes (died c. 1183) French poet. His epics, which introduced the concept of the *Holy Grail, include *Lancelot, ou le chevalier de la charrette* (c. 1178), written for Marie, Countess of Champagne; *Perceval, ou le conte du Graal* (c. 1182), written for Philip, Count of Flanders; *Erec* (c. 1170); *Yvain, ou le chevalier au Lion* (c. 1178); and other Arthurian romances.

Christ (Greek *Khristos* 'anointed one') the *Messiah as prophesied in the Hebrew Bible, or Old Testament. See *Jesus.

Christchurch city on South Island, New Zealand, 11 km/ 7 mi from the mouth of the Avon River; population (2001 est) 316,200. The second largest city in New Zealand, it is the principal commercial and industrial centre of the Canterbury Plains. Traditional industries such as farming, meat-packing, tanning, and the manufacture of woollen goods are still important, and other industries include the manufacture of carpets, clothing, tyres, fertilizers, glass, and footwear. The city derives its name from Christ Church College in Oxford, England, where some of the Anglican founders of the city had studied.

Christian ten kings of Denmark and Norway, including:

Christian I (1426–1481) King of Denmark from 1448, and founder of the Oldenburg dynasty. In 1450 he established the union of Denmark and Norway that lasted until 1814. He was king of Sweden 1457–64 and 1465–67.

Christian IV (1577–1648) King of Denmark and Norway from 1588. He sided with the Protestants in the Thirty Years' War (1618–48), and founded Christiania (now Oslo, capital of Norway). He was succeeded by Frederick II in 1648.

Christian Democracy ideology of a number of parties active in Western Europe since World War II, especially in Italy, the Federal Republic of Germany, and France, and (since 1989) in central and Eastern Europe. Christian Democrats are essentially moderate conservatives who believe in a mixed economy and in the provision of social welfare. They are opposed to both communism and fascism but are largely in favour of European integration.

Christianity world religion derived from the teaching of *Jesus, as found in the *New Testament, during the first third of the 1st century. It has a present-day membership of about a billion, and is divided into groups or denominations that differ in some areas of belief and practice. Its main divisions are the *Roman Catholic, Eastern *Orthodox, and *Protestant churches.

Christian Science or **the Church of Christ, Scientist** sect established in the USA by Mary Baker Eddy in 1879. Christian Scientists believe that since God is good and is a spirit, matter and evil are not ultimately real. Consequently they refuse all medical treatment. The church publishes a daily newspaper, the *Christian Science Monitor*, which reports on international news.

Christie, Agatha (Mary Clarissa) (1890–1976) born Agatha (Mary Clarissa) Miller, English detective novelist. She is best known for her ingenious plots and for the creation of the characters Hercule Poirot and Miss Jane Marple. She wrote more than 70 novels, including *The Murder of Roger Ackroyd* (1926) and *The Body in the Library* (1942). Her play *The Mousetrap*, which opened in London in 1952, is the longest continuously running show in the world.

Christie, Linford (1960–) Jamaican-born English sprinter who, with his win in the 1993 World Championships, became the first track athlete ever to hold World, Olympic, European, and Commonwealth 100-metre titles simultaneously.

Christina (1626–1689) Queen of Sweden (1632–54). Succeeding her father Gustavus Adolphus at the age of six, she assumed power in 1644, but disagreed with the former regent Oxenstjerna. Refusing to marry, she eventually nominated her cousin Charles Gustavus (Charles X) as her successor. As a secret convert to Roman Catholicism, which was then illegal in Sweden, she had to abdicate in 1654, and went to live in Rome, twice returning to Sweden unsuccessfully to claim the throne.

Christmas ('Christ's Mass') Christian religious holiday, the second most important Christian festival after *Easter. Observed throughout the Western world on 25 December, it is traditionally marked by feasting and gift-giving. In the Christian church, it is the day on which the birth of *Jesus is celebrated, although his actual birth date is unknown. Many of its customs have a non-Christian origin and were adapted from celebrations of the winter *solstice (the turning point of winter).

Christmas Island (officially Kiritimati – pronounced 'kirisimas') island in the Indian Ocean, 360 km/224 mi south of Java; area 140 sq km/54 sq mi; population (1994 est) 2,500. Found to be uninhabited when reached by English explorer Captain W Mynars on Christmas Day 1643, it was annexed by Britain in 1888, occupied by Japan between 1942 and 1945, and transferred to Australia in 1958. After a referendum in 1984, it was included in Northern Territory. Its phosphate mine was closed in 1987. Tourism and casinos are being developed.

Christopher, St Patron saint of travellers. His feast day, 25 July, was dropped from the Roman Catholic liturgical calendar in 1969.

chromatic scale musical scale consisting entirely of semitones. All the notes on a keyboard, black and white, are used for this scale. Dividing the octave into 12 equal steps of one semitone each makes this a neutral scale without a definite key.

chromatography (Greek *chromos* 'colour') technique for separating or analysing a mixture of gases, liquids, or dissolved substances. This is brought about by means of two immiscible substances, one of which (**the mobile phase**) transports the sample mixture through the other (**the stationary phase**). The mobile phase may be a gas or a liquid; the stationary phase may be a liquid or a solid, and may be in a column, on paper, or in a thin layer on a glass or plastic support. The components of the mixture are adsorbed or impeded by the stationary phase to different extents and therefore become separated. The technique is used for both qualitative and quantitive analyses in biology and chemistry.

chromite $FeCr_2O_4$, iron chromium oxide, the main chromium ore. It is one of the spinel group of minerals, and crystallizes in dark-coloured octahedra of the cubic system. Chromite is usually found in association with ultrabasic and basic rocks; in Cyprus, for example, it occurs with *serpentine, and in South Africa it forms continuous layers in a layered *intrusion.

chromium chemical symbol Cr, (Greek *chromos* 'colour') hard, brittle, grey-white, metallic element, atomic number 24, relative atomic mass 51.996. It takes a high polish, has a high melting point, and is very resistant to corrosion. It is used in chromium electroplating, in the manufacture of stainless steel and other alloys, and as a catalyst. Its compounds are used for tanning leather and for alums. In human nutrition it is a vital trace element. In nature, it occurs chiefly as chrome iron ore or chromite ($FeCr_2O_4$). Kazakhstan, Zimbabwe, and Brazil are sources.

chromosome structures in a cell *nucleus that carry the many thousands of *genes, in sequence, that determine the characteristics of an organism. There are 46 chromosomes in a normal human cell. Each chromosome normally consists of one very long strand (or molecule) of DNA, coiled and folded to produce a compact structure. The exception is just before cell division when each chromosome contains two strands of DNA, a result of the copying of each molecule of

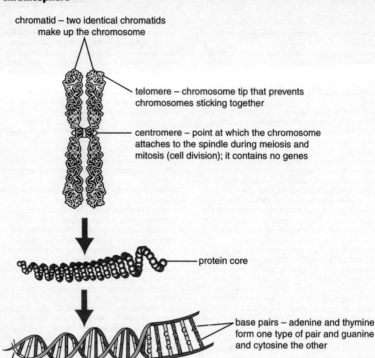

chromatid – two identical chromatids make up the chromosome

telomere – chromosome tip that prevents chromosomes sticking together

centromere – point at which the chromosome attaches to the spindle during meiosis and mitosis (cell division); it contains no genes

protein core

base pairs – adenine and thymine form one type of pair and guanine and cytosine the other

DNA molecule – the double helix is connected by base pairs

chromosome The structure of a chromosome. The chromosome is made up of two identical chromatids joined by a centromere. Each chromatid is made up of coiled DNA.

DNA. The point on a chromosome where a particular gene occurs is known as its locus. Most higher organisms have two copies of each chromosome, together known as a **homologous pair** (they are *diploid) but some have only one (they are *haploid). See also *mitosis and *meiosis.

chromosphere (Greek *chromos* 'colour', *sphaira* 'sphere') layer of mostly hydrogen gas about 10,000 km/ 6,000 mi deep above the visible surface of the Sun (the photosphere). It appears pinkish red during *eclipses of the Sun.

chronic in medicine, term used to describe a condition that is of slow onset and then runs a prolonged course, such as rheumatoid arthritis or chronic bronchitis. In contrast, an **acute** condition develops quickly and may be of relatively short duration.

chronic fatigue syndrome (CFS) *or* **myalgic encephalomyelitis (ME)** *or* **postviral fatigue syndrome** common debilitating condition characterized by a diffuse range of symptoms present for at least six months including extreme fatigue, muscular pain, weakness, depression, poor balance and coordination, joint pains, and gastric upset. It is usually diagnosed after exclusion of other diseases and frequently follows a flulike illness.

chronometer instrument for measuring time precisely, originally used at sea. It is designed to remain accurate through all conditions of temperature and pressure. The first accurate marine chronometer, capable of an accuracy of half a minute a year, was made in 1761 by John Harrison in England.

chrysalis pupa of an insect, but especially that of a *butterfly or *moth. It is essentially a static stage of the creature's life, when the adult insect, benefiting from the large amounts of food laid down by the actively feeding larva, is built up from the disintegrating larval tissues. The chrysalis may be exposed or within a cocoon.

chrysanthemum any of a large group of plants with colourful, showy flowers, containing about 200 species. There are hundreds of cultivated varieties, whose exact wild ancestry is uncertain. In the Far East the common chrysanthemum has been cultivated for more than 2,000 years and is the imperial emblem of Japan. Chrysanthemums can be grown from seed, but new plants are more commonly produced from cuttings or by dividing up established plants. (Genus *Chrysanthemum*, family Compositae.)

Chuang the largest minority group in China, numbering about 15 million. They live in southern China, where they cultivate rice fields. Their religion includes elements of ancestor worship. The Chuang language belongs to the Tai family.

chub freshwater fish *Leuciscus cephalus* of the carp family. Thickset and cylindrical, it grows up to 60 cm/ 2 ft, is dark greenish or grey on the back, silvery yellow below, with metallic flashes on the flanks. It lives generally in clean rivers throughout Europe.

church in architecture, a building designed as a place of worship for the Christian church community. Churches were first built in the 3rd century, when persecution of Christians ceased under the Roman emperor Constantine. The term also refers to the community of people who attend the church. (See diagram, p. 196.)

Churchill, Lord Randolph Henry Spencer (1849–1895) British Conservative politician, chancellor of the Exchequer and leader of the House of Commons in 1886; father of Winston Churchill.

Churchill, Winston (Leonard Spencer) (1874–1965) British Conservative politician, prime minister 1940–45 and 1951–55. In Parliament from 1900, as a Liberal until 1924, he held a number of ministerial offices, including First Lord of the Admiralty 1911–15 and chancellor of the Exchequer 1924–29. Absent from the cabinet in the 1930s, he returned in September 1939 to lead a coalition government from 1940 to 1945, negotiating with Allied leaders in World War II to achieve the unconditional surrender of Germany in 1945. He led a Conservative government between 1951 and 1955. His books include a six-volume history of World War II (1948–54) and a four-volume *History of the English-Speaking Peoples* (1956–58). *War Speeches 1940–45* (1946) contains his most memorable orations. He was awarded the Nobel Prize for Literature in 1953.

Church of England or **Anglican Church** established form of Christianity in England, a member of the *Anglican communion. It was dissociated from the Roman Catholic Church in 1534 under Henry VIII; the British monarch is still the supreme head of the Church of England today. The service book until November 2000 was the Book of Common Prayer. It is now *Common Worship*.

Church of Scotland established form of Christianity in Scotland, first recognized by the state in 1560. It is based on the Protestant doctrines of the reformer *Calvin and governed on Presbyterian lines. The church went through several periods of episcopacy (government by bishops) in the 17th century, and those who adhered to episcopacy after 1690 formed the Episcopal Church of Scotland, an autonomous church in communion with the Church of England. In 1843 there was a split in the Church of Scotland (the Disruption), in which almost a third of its ministers and members left and formed the *Free Church of Scotland. By an Act of Union of 3 October 1929 the Church of Scotland was

united with the United Free Church of Scotland to form the United Church of Scotland. There are over 680,000 members of the Church of Scotland (1998).

Chu Teh Chinese Red Army leader; see *Zhu De.

Chuvash or **Chuvashiya** autonomous republic in the western Russian Federation; area 18,300 sq km/7,066 sq mi; population (1990) 1,340,000 (68% Chuvash, 25% Russian). The main cities are Cheboksary (capital), Alatyr, and Shumerla. Chuvash lies south of the Volga River, 560 km/350 mi east of Moscow. The main industries are textiles, lumbering, electrical and engineering industries, phosphates, and limestone; there is grain and fruit farming.

chyme general term for the stomach contents. Chyme resembles a thick creamy fluid and is made up of partly digested food, hydrochloric acid, and a range of enzymes.

CIA abbreviation for the US *Central Intelligence Agency.

cicada any of several insects of the family Cicadidae. Most species are tropical, but a few occur in Europe and North America. The adults live on trees, whose juices they suck. The males produce a loud, almost continuous, chirping by vibrating membranes in resonating cavities in the abdomen. Cicadas with a periodic life cycle, such as the 13-year cicada and the 17-year cicada, are found only in the USA. These species spend most of their lives as larvae underground, synchronizing their emergence every 13 or 17 years depending on species.

Cicero, Marcus Tullius (106–43 BC) Roman orator, writer, and politician. His speeches and philosophical and rhetorical works are models of Latin prose, and his letters provide a picture of contemporary Roman life. As consul in 63 BC he exposed the Roman politician Catiline's conspiracy in four major orations.

cichlid any freshwater fish of the family Cichlidae. Cichlids are somewhat perchlike, but have a single nostril on each side instead of two. They are mostly predatory, and have deep, colourful bodies, flattened from side to side so that some are almost disc-shaped. Many are territorial in the breeding season and may show care of the young. There are more than 1,000 species found in South and Central America, Africa, and India.

Cid, El, Rodrigo Díaz de Vivar (c. 1040–1099) Spanish soldier, nicknamed El Cid ('the lord') by the *Moors. Born in Castile of a noble family, he fought against the king of Navarre and won his nickname *el Campeador* ('the Champion') by killing the Navarrese champion in single combat. Essentially a mercenary, fighting both with and against the Moors, he died while defending Valencia against them, and in subsequent romances became Spain's national hero.

cider in the UK, a fermented drink made from the juice of the apple; in the USA, the term cider usually refers to unfermented (non-alcoholic) apple juice. Cider has been made for more than 2,000 years, and for many centuries has been a popular drink in France and England, which are now its main centres of production.

Ciechanover, Aaron (1947–) Israeli scientist. With Hungarian-born Israeli scientist Avram Hershko and US scientist Irwin Rose he shared the Nobel Prize for Chemistry in 2004 for his contributions to the discovery of how cells can regulate protein levels by controlled selection and degradation processes.

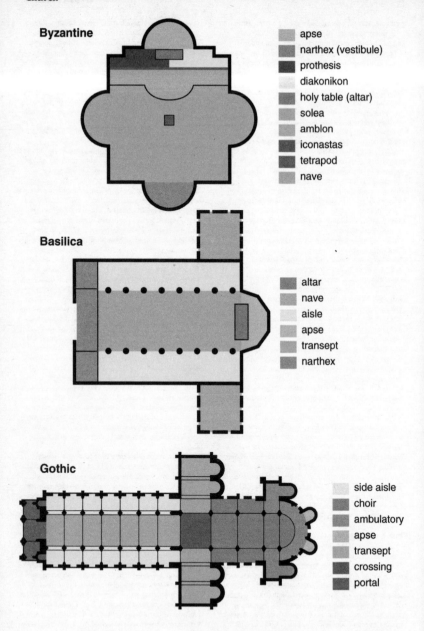

Byzantine

- apse
- narthex (vestibule)
- prothesis
- diakonikon
- holy table (altar)
- solea
- amblon
- iconastas
- tetrapod
- nave

Basilica

- altar
- nave
- aisle
- apse
- transept
- narthex

Gothic

- side aisle
- choir
- ambulatory
- apse
- transept
- crossing
- portal

church The basic layouts of Byzantine, Basilica, and Gothic churches.

c.i.f. *or* **CIF** abbreviation for cost, insurance, and freight, or charged in full, way to value a commodity. Many countries value their imports on this basis, whereas exports are usually valued f.o.b. (**free-on-board**). For balance of payments purposes, figures are usually adjusted to include the freight and insurance costs.

cilia singular **cilium**, small hairlike organs on the surface of some cells, particularly the cells lining the upper respiratory tract. Their wavelike movements waft particles of dust and debris towards the exterior. Some single-celled organisms move by means of cilia. In multicellular animals, they keep lubricated surfaces clear of debris. They also move food in the digestive tracts of some invertebrates.

Cilicia ancient region of Asia Minor, now forming part of Turkey, situated between the Taurus Mountains and the Mediterranean. Access from the north across the Taurus range is through the **Cilician Gates**, a strategic pass that has been used for centuries as part of a trade route linking Europe and the Middle East.

Cimabue, Giovanni (*c.* **1240–1302**) also known as **Cenni di Peppi**, Italian painter. Active in Florence, he is traditionally styled the 'father of Italian painting'. His paintings retain the golden background of Byzantine art but the figures have a new naturalism. Among the works attributed to him are *Maestà* (*c.* 1280; Uffizi, Florence), a huge Gothic image of the Virgin, with a novel softness and solidity that points forwards to Giotto.

cinchona any of a group of tropical American shrubs or trees belonging to the madder family. The drug *quinine is produced from the bark of some species, and these are now cultivated in India, Sri Lanka, the Philippines, and Indonesia. (Genus *Chinchona*, family Rubiaceae.)

Cincinnati city and port in southwestern Ohio, on the northern bank of the Ohio River; seat of Hamilton County; population (2000 est) 331,300. The city is an important inland port on the Ohio–Mississippi system, and a major manufacturing centre; its chief industries include aircraft and car machinery, clothing, furniture making, wine, chemicals, and meatpacking. Founded in 1788 as Losantiville, Cincinnati was incorporated as a city in 1819. It attracted large numbers of European immigrants, particularly Germans, during the 19th century.

cine camera camera that takes a rapid sequence of still photographs called frames. When the frames are projected one after the other on to a screen, they appear to show movement, because our eyes hold on to the image of one picture until the next one appears.

cinema (Greek *kinema* 'movement') form of art and entertainment consisting of moving pictures, in either black and white or colour, projected on a screen. Cinema draws on other arts, such as literature, drama, and music. Its development, beginning in the 1890s, has been closely linked to technological advances, including action and colour *photography, sound reproduction, and film processing and printing. The first sound feature film was released in 1927.

cinnabar mercuric sulphide mineral, HgS, the only commercially useful ore of mercury. It is deposited in veins and impregnations near recent volcanic rocks and hot springs. The mineral itself is used as a red pigment, commonly known as **vermilion**. Cinnabar is found in the USA (California), Spain (Almadén), Peru, Italy, and Slovenia.

cinnamon dried inner bark of a tree belonging to the laurel family, grown in India and Sri Lanka. The bark is ground to make the spice used in curries and confectionery. Oil of cinnamon is obtained from waste bark and is used as flavouring in food and medicine. (*Cinnamomum zeylanicum*, family Lauraceae.)

cinquefoil any of a group of plants that usually have five-lobed leaves and brightly coloured flowers. They are widespread in northern temperate regions. (Genus *Potentilla*, family Rosaceae.)

Cinque Ports group of ports in southern England, originally five, Sandwich, Dover, Hythe, Romney, and Hastings, later including Rye, Winchelsea, and others. Probably founded in Roman times, they rose to importance after the Norman conquest and until the end of the 15th century were bound to supply the ships and men necessary against invasion. Their importance declined in the 16th and 17th centuries with the development of a standing navy.

circadian rhythm metabolic rhythm found in most organisms, which generally coincides with the 24-hour day. Its most obvious manifestation is the regular cycle of sleeping and waking, but body temperature and the concentration of *hormones that influence mood and behaviour also vary over the day. In humans, alteration of habits (such as rapid air travel round the world) may result in the circadian rhythm being out of phase with actual activity patterns, causing malaise until it has had time to adjust.

Circe in Greek mythology, an enchantress living on the island of Aeaea. In Homer's *Odyssey*, she turned the followers of *Odysseus into pigs. Odysseus, protected by the herb moly provided by Hermes, messenger of the gods, forced her to release his men.

circle perfectly round shape, the path of a point that moves so as to keep a constant distance from a fixed point (the centre). A circle has a *radius (the distance from any point on the circle to the centre), a *circumference (the boundary of the circle, part of which is called an *arc), *diameters (straight lines crossing the circle through the centre), *chords (lines joining two points on the circumference), tangents (lines that touch the circumference at one point only), *sectors (regions inside the circle between two radii), and segments (regions between a chord and the circumference).

circuit in physics or electrical engineering, an arrangement of electrical components connected by a conducting material through which a current can flow. There are two basic circuits, series and parallel. In a *series circuit, the components are connected end to end so that the current flows through all components one after the other. In a parallel circuit, components are connected side by side so that part of the current passes through each component. A circuit diagram shows in graphical form how components are connected together, using standard symbols for the components. If the circuit is unbroken, it is a closed circuit and current flows. If the circuit is broken, it becomes an open circuit and no current flows.

circuit breaker switching device designed to protect an electric circuit from overloads such as excessive current flows and voltage failures. It has the same action as a *fuse, and many houses now have a circuit breaker between the incoming mains supply and the domestic circuits. Circuit breakers usually work by means of magnetic-type relays or *solenoids. Those at electricity-generating stations have to be specially designed to prevent dangerous arcing (the release of luminous discharge) when the high-voltage supply is switched off. They may use an air blast or oil immersion to quench the arc.

circulatory system system of vessels in an animal's body that transports essential substances (*blood or other circulatory fluid) to and from the different parts of the body. It was first discovered and described by English physician William *Harvey. All animals except for the most simple – such as sponges, jellyfish, sea anemones, and corals – have some type of circulatory system. Some invertebrates (animals without a backbone), such as insects, spiders, and most shellfish, have an 'open' circulatory system which consists of a simple network of tubes and hollow spaces. Other invertebrates have pump-like structures that send blood through a system of blood vessels. All vertebrates (animals with a backbone), including humans, have a 'closed' circulatory system which principally consists of a pumping organ – the *heart – and a network of blood vessels.

circumcision surgical removal of all or part of the foreskin (prepuce) of the penis, usually performed on the newborn; it is practised among Jews (*b'rit milah*) and Muslims as a sign of God's covenant with the prophet *Abraham. In some societies in Africa and the Middle East, female circumcision or clitoridectomy (removal of the labia minora and/or clitoris; see *female genital mutilation) is practised on adolescents as well as babies; it is illegal in the West.

circumference in geometry, the curved line that encloses a curved plane figure, for example a *circle or an ellipse. Its length varies according to the nature of the curve, and may be ascertained by the appropriate formula. The circumference of a circle is πd or $2\pi r$, where d is the diameter of the circle, r is its radius, and π is the constant pi, approximately equal to 3.1416.

cire perdue or **lost-wax technique** bronze-casting method. A model is made of wax and enclosed in an envelope of clay and plaster, with a small hole in the bottom. When heat is applied, the wax melts and runs away through the hole, and the clay and plaster becomes a hard mould. Molten bronze is poured in and allowed to cool; then the clay envelope is cut away.

cirque French name for a corrie, a steep-sided armchair-shaped hollow in a mountainside.

cirrhosis any degenerative disease in an organ of the body, especially the liver, characterized by excessive development of connective tissue, causing scarring and painful swelling. Cirrhosis of the liver may be caused by an infection such as viral hepatitis, chronic obstruction of the common bile duct, chronic alcoholism or drug use, blood disorder, heart failure, or malnutrition. However, often no cause is apparent. If cirrhosis is diagnosed early, it can be arrested by treating the cause; otherwise it will progress to coma and death.

CIS abbreviation for *Commonwealth of Independent States, established in 1992 by 11 former Soviet republics.

Ciskei part of the former independent *Black National State within South Africa, independent from 1981 (but not recognized by the United Nations) until 1994 when it was re-integrated into South Africa, in Eastern Cape

Province. The region covered an area of 7,700 sq km/ 2,970 sq mi. It was one of two homelands of the Xhosa people created by South Africa, the other being Transkei.

Cistercian order Roman Catholic monastic order established at Cîteaux in 1098 by St Robert de Champagne, abbot of Molesmes, as a stricter form of the Benedictine order. Living mainly by agricultural labour, the Cistercians made many advances in farming methods in the Middle Ages. The *Trappists, so called after the original house at La Trappe in Normandy (founded by Dominique de Rancé in 1664), followed a particularly strict version of the rule.

cistron in genetics, the segment of *DNA that is required to synthesize a complete polypeptide chain. It is the molecular equivalent of a *gene.

cithara ancient musical instrument resembling a *lyre but with a flat back. It was strung with wire and plucked with a plectrum or (after the 16th century) with the fingers. The bandurria and laúd, still popular in Spain, are instruments of the same type.

Citizen's Charter series of proposals aimed at improving public services in the UK, unveiled by prime minister John Major in 1991. Major's 'programme for a decade' covered the activities of a range of public-sector bodies, including the police, the health service, schools, local authorities, and public and private utility companies. It promised better quality for consumers through the publication of service standards, the right of redress, performance monitoring, penalties for public services, tighter regulation of privatized utilities, and the increased pressures resulting from competition and privatization.

citizenship status as a member of a state. In most countries citizenship may be acquired either by birth or by naturalization. The status confers rights such as voting and the protection of the law and also imposes responsibilities such as military service, in some countries.

citric acid $HOOCCH_2C(OH)(COOH)CH_2COOH$, organic acid widely distributed in the plant kingdom; it is found in high concentrations in citrus fruits and has a sharp, sour taste. At one time it was commercially prepared from concentrated lemon juice, but now the main source is the fermentation of sugar with certain moulds.

citrus any of a group of evergreen and aromatic trees or shrubs, found in warm parts of the world. Several species – the orange, lemon, lime, citron, and grapefruit – are cultivated for their fruit. (Genus *Citrus*, family Rutaceae.)

civet small to medium-sized carnivorous mammal found in Africa and Asia, belonging to the family Viverridae, which also includes *mongooses and *genets. Distant relations of cats, they generally have longer jaws and more teeth. All have a scent gland in the inguinal (groin) region. Extracts from this gland are taken from the **African civet** *Civettictis civetta* and used in perfumery.

civil aviation operation of passenger and freight transport by air. With increasing traffic, control of air space is a major problem. In the USA, the Federal Aviation Agency (FAA) is responsible for regulating development of aircraft, air navigation, traffic control, and communications and the Civil Aeronautics Board prescribes safety regulations and investigates accidents. In Europe, Eurocontrol was established in 1963 by

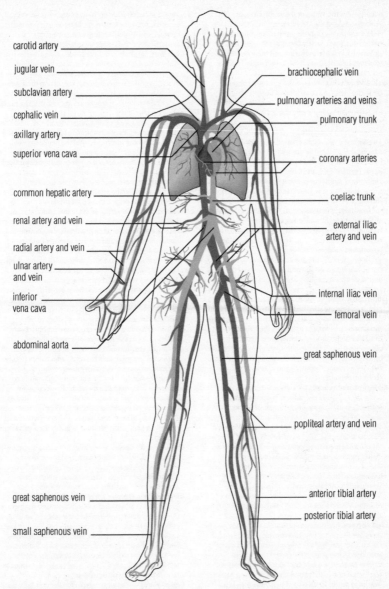

carotid artery

jugular vein

subclavian artery

cephalic vein

axillary artery

superior vena cava

common hepatic artery

renal artery and vein

radial artery and vein

ulnar artery and vein

inferior vena cava

abdominal aorta

great saphenous vein

small saphenous vein

brachiocephalic vein

pulmonary arteries and veins

pulmonary trunk

coronary arteries

coeliac trunk

external iliac artery and vein

internal iliac vein

femoral vein

great saphenous vein

popliteal artery and vein

anterior tibial artery

posterior tibial artery

circulatory system Blood flows through 96,500 km/60,000 mi of arteries and veins, supplying oxygen and nutrients to organs and limbs. Oxygen-poor blood circulates from the heart to the lungs where oxygen is absorbed. Oxygen-rich blood flows back to the heart and is then pumped round the body through the aorta, the largest artery, to smaller arteries and capillaries. Here oxygen and nutrients are exchanged with carbon dioxide and waste products and the blood returns to the heart via the veins. Waste products are filtered by the liver, spleen, and kidneys, and nutrients are absorbed from the stomach and small intestine.

Belgium, France, West Germany, Luxembourg, the Netherlands, and the UK to supervise both military and civil movement in the air space over member countries. Close cooperation is maintained with authorities in other countries, and there is also a tendency to coordinate services and other facilities between national airlines.

civil engineering branch of engineering that is concerned with the construction of roads, bridges, airports, aqueducts, waterworks, tunnels, canals, irrigation works, and harbours.

civilization (Latin *civis* 'citizen') highly developed human society with structured division of labour. The earliest civilizations evolved in the Old World from advanced *Neolithic farming societies in the Middle East (Sumer in 3500 BC; Egypt in 3000 BC), the Indus Valley (in 2500 BC), and China (in 2200 BC). In the New World, similar communities evolved civilizations in Mesoamerica (the Olmec in 1200 BC) and Peru (the Chavin in 800 BC).

civil law legal system based on *Roman law. It is one of the two main European legal systems, *English (common) law being the other. Civil law may also mean the law relating to matters other than criminal law, such as *contract and *tort.

civil list in the UK, the annual sum provided from public funds to meet the official expenses of the sovereign and immediate dependents; private expenses are met by the *privy purse.

civil rights rights of the individual citizen. In many countries they are specified (as in the Bill of Rights of the US constitution) and guaranteed by law to ensure equal treatment for all citizens. In the USA, the struggle to obtain civil rights for former slaves and their descendants, both through legislation and in practice, has been a major theme since the Civil War. See *civil-rights movement, *women's movement, and *gay rights movement.

civil-rights movement US movement especially active during the 1950s and 60s that aimed to end segregation and discrimination against blacks, as well as affirm their constitutional rights and improve their status in society. Organizations such as the National Association for the Advancement of Colored People (NAACP) helped bring about important legislation, including the 1954 *Brown* v. *Board of Education* decision, desegregating schools. Further legislation followed, such as the Civil Rights Acts 1964 and the Voting Rights Act 1965, under President Lyndon Johnson. Prominent civil-rights activists such as Martin Luther *King inspired nonviolent protest and helped effect these changes.

civil service body of administrative staff employed to carry out the policy of a government. Members of the UK civil service may not take any active part in politics, and do not change with the government. In the USA, federal employees are restricted in the role they may play in political activity, and also retain their posts (except at senior levels) when there is a change in administration.

Civil War, American *or* **the War Between the States** war (1861–65) between the Southern or Confederate States of America (see *Confederacy) and the Northern or Union states. The former wished to maintain certain 'states' rights', in particular the right to determine state law on the institution of *slavery, and claimed the right to secede from the Union; the latter fought primarily to maintain the Union, with slave emancipation (proclaimed in 1863) a secondary issue.

Civil War, English conflict between King Charles I and the Royalists (also called Cavaliers) on one side and the Parliamentarians (also called Roundheads) on the other. Their differences centred initially on the king's unconstitutional acts, but later became a struggle over the relative powers of crown and Parliament. Hostilities began in 1642 and a series of Royalist defeats (at Marston Moor in 1644, and then at Naseby in 1645) culminated in Charles's capture in 1647, and execution in 1649. The war continued until the final defeat of Royalist forces at Worcester in 1651. Oliver *Cromwell then became Protector (ruler) from 1653 until his death in 1658.

Civil War, Spanish war (1936–39) precipitated by a military revolt led by General Franco against the Republican government. Inferior military capability led to the gradual defeat of the Republicans by 1939, and the establishment of Franco's dictatorship.

Clackmannanshire unitary authority in central Scotland, bordering the north side of the Firth of Forth. A former county (until 1974), it was a district of Central region (1975–96). **area:** 161 sq km/62 sq mi **towns:** Alloa (administrative headquarters), Tillicoultry **physical:** compact geographical area comprising the extensive flat flood plain of the River Devon, which rises dramatically at the Ochil Hills to Ben Cleuch (721 m/2,365 ft) **population:** (1996) 47,700.

cladistics method of biological classification that uses a formal step-by-step procedure for objectively assessing the extent to which organisms share particular characteristics, and for assigning them to taxonomic groups called **clades**. Clades comprise all the species descended from a known or inferred common ancestor plus the ancestor itself, and may be large – consisting of a hierarchy of other clades.

clam common name for a *bivalve mollusc. The giant clam *Tridacna gigas* of the Indopacific can grow to 1 m/3 ft across in 50 years and weigh, with the shell, 500 kg/1,000 lb. A giant clam produces a billion eggs in a single spawning.

clan (Scottish Gaelic *clann* 'children') social grouping based on *kinship. Some traditional societies are organized by clans, which are either matrilineal or patrilineal, and whose members must marry into another clan in order to avoid in-breeding.

Clapton, Eric (1945–) born Eric Patrick Clapp, English blues and rock guitarist, singer, and songwriter. Originally a blues purist, he became one of the pioneers of heavy rock with Cream (1966–68), but then returned to the blues after making the landmark album *Layla and Other Assorted Love Songs* (1970) with Derek and the Dominos. His solo albums include *Journeyman* (1989) and the acoustic *Unplugged* (1992), for which he received six Grammy awards (1993).

Clare county on the west coast of the Republic of Ireland, in the province of Munster, situated between Galway Bay in the north and the Shannon estuary in the south; county town Ennis; area 3,190 sq km/1,231 sq mi; population (2002 est) 103,300. Other towns include Kilrush, Kilkee, and Shannon, an important 'new' town noted for its light industry, and electronics and aerospace industries. Dairying and cattle rearing are the principal farming activities; there are also important salmon fisheries and extensive oyster beds. Slate and black marble are quarried and worked; lead is also found. The Shannon is a source of hydroelectricity: there is a power station at Ardnacrusha, 5 km/3 mi north of Limerick.

Clarendon, Edward Hyde (1609–1674) 1st Earl of Clarendon, English politician and historian, chief adviser to Charles II from 1651 to 1667. A member of Parliament in 1640, he joined the Royalist side in 1641. The **Clarendon Code** (1661–65), a series of acts passed by the government, was directed at Nonconformists (or Dissenters) and was designed to secure the supremacy of the Church of England.

clarinet any of a family of single-reed woodwind instruments of cylindrical bore. It is one of the four main orchestral woodwinds, but did not join the orchestra until after the middle of the 18th century. In their concertos for clarinet, Wolfgang Amadeus Mozart and Carl Maria von Weber made good use of the instrument's wide range of tone from the rich, dark notes of the low register rising to brilliance in the high register, and its capacity for sustained dynamic control. The ability of the clarinet both to blend and to contrast with other instruments makes it popular for chamber music and as a solo instrument. It is also used in military and concert bands and widely as a jazz instrument.

Clarke, Arthur C(harles) (1917–) English science fiction and non-fiction writer. He originated the plan for a system of communications satellites in geostationary orbit in 1945. His works include the short story 'The Sentinel' (1951; filmed in 1968 by Stanley Kubrick as *2001: A Space Odyssey*), and the novels *Childhood's End* (1953), *2010: Odyssey Two* (1982), *3001: The Final Odyssey* (1997), *Rendezvous with Rama* (1997), and *A Fall of Moondust* (1998).

class in biological classification, a subdivision of *phylum and forms a group of related *orders. For example, all mammals belong to the class Mammalia and all birds to the class Aves. Among plants, all class names end in 'idae' (such as Asteridae) and among fungi in 'mycetes'; there are no equivalent conventions among animals. Related classes are grouped together in a phylum.

class in sociology, the main grouping of social stratification in industrial societies, based primarily on economic and occupational factors, but also referring to people's style of living or sense of group identity.

class action in law, a court procedure where one or more claimants represent a larger group of people who are all making the same kind of claim against the same defendant. The court's decision is binding on all the members of the group.

classical economics school of economic thought that dominated 19th-century thinking. It originated with Adam *Smith's *The Wealth of Nations* (1776), which embodied many of the basic concepts and principles of the classical school. Smith's theories were further developed in the writings of John Stuart Mill and David Ricardo. Central to the theory were economic freedom, competition, and *laissez-faire* government. The idea that economic growth could best be promoted by free trade, unassisted by government, was in conflict with *mercantilism.

classicism term used in art, music, and literature, to characterize work that emphasizes the qualities traditionally associated with ancient Greek and Roman art, that is, reason, balance, objectivity, and restraint, as opposed to the individuality of expression typical of Romanticism. Classicism and Romanticism are often considered as opposite poles of art, but in fact many artists show elements of both in their work. At certain times, however, classicism has been a dominant trend, notably during the Renaissance and the neoclassical periods. At both these times ancient art exercised a strong direct influence, but this is not an essential component of classicism. The word is often used imprecisely and sometimes conveys no more than an idea of clarity or conservatism.

classification in biology, the arrangement of organisms into a hierarchy of groups on the basis of their similarities. The basic grouping is a *species, several of which may constitute a *genus, which in turn are grouped into families, and so on up through orders, classes, phyla (in plants, sometimes called divisions), and finally to kingdoms. The system that is used is one that reflects the evolutionary origin of the organisms. In other words, organisms belonging one group are thought to have evolved from a common ancestor at some time in the past. (See diagram, p. 202.)

Claude Lorrain (1600–1682) born Claude Gelée, French painter who worked in Rome. One of the leading classical painters of the 17th century, he painted landscapes in a distinctive, luminous style that had a great impact on late 17th- and 18th-century taste. In his paintings insignificant figures (mostly mythological or historical) are typically lost in great expanses of poetic scenery, as in *The Enchanted Castle* (1664; National Gallery, London).

Claudius I (10 BC–AD 54) born Tiberius Claudius Drusus Nero Germanicus, nephew of *Tiberius, and son of Drusus Nero, made Roman emperor by the Praetorian Guard in AD 41, after the murder of his nephew *Caligula. Claudius was a scholar and historian. During his reign the Roman empire was considerably extended, and in 43 he took part in the invasion of Britain.

Clausewitz, Carl Philipp Gottlieb von (1780–1831) Prussian officer and military theorist whose major work *Vom Kriege/On War* (posthumously published in 1832) revolutionized military, and later business, strategists. His famous theory of conflict is that war is an extension of political policy *by other means* and therefore not an end in itself. Clausewitz's ideas have been enthusiastically adopted by modern business strategists. In Clausewitz's terms, business is a civilized version of war in which companies, not nations, compete against each other.

claustrophobia *phobia involving fear of enclosed spaces.

Claverhouse, John Graham (c. 1649–1689) Viscount Dundee, Scottish soldier. Appointed by *Charles II to suppress the *Covenanters from 1677, he was routed at Drumclog in 1679, but three weeks later won the battle of Bothwell Bridge, by which the rebellion was crushed. Until 1688 he was engaged in continued persecution and became known as 'Bloody Clavers', regarded by the Scottish people as a figure of evil. His army then joined the first *Jacobite rebellion

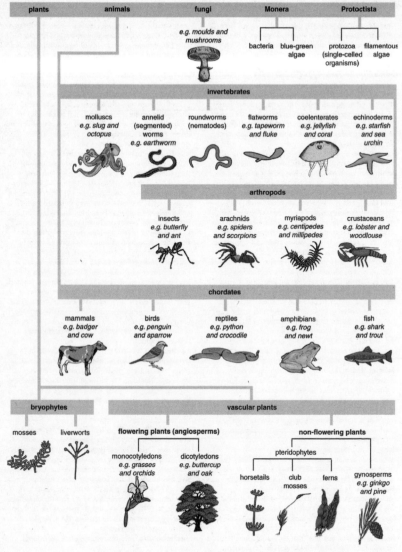

plants	animals	fungi	Monera	Protoctista

e.g. moulds and mushrooms

bacteria · blue-green algae

protozoa (single-celled organisms) · filamentous algae

invertebrates

molluscs e.g. slug and octopus

annelid (segmented) worms e.g. earthworm

roundworms (nematodes)

flatworms e.g. tapeworm and fluke

coelenterates e.g. jellyfish and coral

echinoderms e.g. starfish and sea urchin

arthropods

insects e.g. butterfly and ant

arachnids e.g. spiders and scorpions

myriapods e.g. centipedes and millipedes

crustaceans e.g. lobster and woodlouse

chordates

mammals e.g. badger and cow

birds e.g. penguin and sparrow

reptiles e.g. python and crocodile

amphibians e.g. frog and newt

fish e.g. shark and trout

bryophytes

mosses · liverworts

vascular plants

flowering plants (angiosperms)

monocotyledons e.g. grasses and orchids

dicotyledons e.g. buttercup and oak

non-flowering plants

pteridophytes

horsetails · club mosses · ferns

gynosperms e.g. ginkgo and pine

classification The classification of the plant and animal kingdoms.

and defeated the loyalist forces at the Battle of Killiecrankie, where he was mortally wounded.

clavichord small domestic keyboard instrument developed in the 16th century from the monochord. Its tone is soft and delicate and it is best suited for playing in small rooms. The notes are sounded by a metal blade striking the string, and a form of vibrato (bebung) is possible by varying the finger pressure on the key. It dropped in popularity in the 18th century due to the arrival of the *fortepiano.

clavicle (Latin *clavis* 'key') the collar bone of many vertebrates. In humans it is vulnerable to fracture, since falls involving a sudden force on the arm may result in very high stresses passing into the chest region by way of the clavicle and other bones. It is connected at one end with the sternum (breastbone), and at the other end with the shoulder-blade, together with which it forms the arm socket. The wishbone of a chicken is composed of its two fused clavicles.

claw hard, hooked, pointed outgrowth of the digits of mammals, birds, and most reptiles. Claws are composed of the protein keratin, and grow continuously from a bundle of cells in the lower skin layer. Hooves and nails are modified structures with the same origin as claws.

clay very fine-grained *sedimentary deposit that has undergone a greater or lesser degree of consolidation. When moistened it is plastic, and it hardens on heating, which renders it impermeable. It may be white, grey, red, yellow, blue, or black, depending on its composition. Clay minerals consist largely of hydrous silicates of aluminium and magnesium together with iron, potassium, sodium, and organic substances. The crystals of clay minerals have a layered structure, capable of holding water, and are responsible for its plastic properties. According to international classification, in mechanical analysis of soil, clay has a grain size of less than 0.002 mm/0.00008 in.

Clay, Cassius Marcellus, Jr original name of boxer Muhammad *Ali.

clef in music, a sign placed at the beginning of a stave to indicate the pitch of the written notes. It was introduced as a visual aid in plainchant notation, and takes the form of a stylized letter centred on a particular line to show the pitch of that line.

cleg another name for *horsefly.

Cleisthenes (born c. 570) Athenian statesman, later celebrated as the founder of Athenian democracy. Although an early collaborator of the Pisistratids, the Athenian tyrants, he was later exiled with his family, the Alcmaeonidae, and intrigued and campaigned against Hippias and Hipparchus. After their removal in 510 BC, in 508 to 507 BC he won over the people by offering to place the constitution on a more democratic basis. His democracy was established by his reforms over the next few years.

clematis any of a group of temperate woody climbing plants with colourful showy flowers. They belong to the buttercup family. (Genus *Clematis*, family Ranunculaceae.)

Clémenceau, Georges Eugène Benjamin (1841–1929) French radical politician, prime minister 1906–09 and 1917–20 when he chaired the Versailles peace conference but failed to secure the Rhine as a frontier for France in the treaty.

Clement of Rome, St (lived late 1st century) one of the early Christian leaders and writers known as the fathers of the church. According to tradition he was the third or fourth bishop of Rome, and a disciple of St Peter. He was pope AD 88–97 or 92–101. He wrote a letter addressed to the church at Corinth (First Epistle of Clement), and many other writings have been attributed to him.

Cleopatra (c. 68–30 BC) Queen of Egypt 51–48 and 47–30 BC. When the Roman general Julius Caesar

arrived in Egypt, he restored Cleopatra to the throne from which she had been ousted. Cleopatra and Caesar became lovers and she went with him to Rome. After Caesar's assassination in 44 BC she returned to Alexandria and resumed her position as queen of Egypt. In 41 BC she was joined there by Mark Antony, one of Rome's rulers. In 31 BC Rome declared war on Egypt and scored a decisive victory in the naval Battle of Actium off the west coast of Greece. Cleopatra fled with her 60 ships to Egypt; Antony abandoned the struggle and followed her. Both he and Cleopatra committed suicide.

Cleveland port and city in northeastern Ohio, USA, on Lake Erie, at the mouth of the Cuyahoga River; seat of Cuyahoga County; population (2000 est) 478,400. Cleveland is the centre of a seven-county (including Cuyahoga, Portage, Summit, Lake, Medina, and Lorain) metropolitan area (CMSA) with a population (1990) of 2,759,800. An industrial, commercial, and transportation centre, and formerly one of the leading iron and steel producers in the USA, the city has also figured prominently in petroleum, chemicals, automobile manufacturing, and electric power. Cleveland's current industries include chemical and food processing, steel (although not on the scale seen previously), and the manufacture of electrical products and auto parts. Printing and publishing and international and Great Lakes ore shipping also figure prominently. It is also the location of dozens of corporate headquarters.

click beetle *beetle that can regain its feet from lying on its back by jumping into the air and turning over, clicking as it does so.

client–server architecture in computing, a system in which the mechanics of looking after data are separated from the programs that use the data. For example, the 'server' might be a central database, typically located on a large computer that is reserved for this purpose. The 'client' would be an ordinary program that requests data from the server as needed.

climate combination of weather conditions at a particular place over a period of time – usually a minimum of 30 years. A climate classification encompasses the averages, extremes, and frequencies of all meteorological elements such as temperature, atmospheric pressure, precipitation, wind, humidity, and sunshine, together with the factors that influence them.

climax community group of plants and animals that is best able to exploit the environment in which it exists. It is brought about by *succession (a change in the species present) and represents the point at which succession ceases to occur.

clinical psychology branch of psychology dealing with the understanding and treatment of health problems, particularly mental disorders. The main problems dealt with include anxiety, phobias, depression, obsessions, sexual and marital problems, drug and alcohol dependence, childhood behavioural problems, psychoses (such as schizophrenia), mental disability, and brain disease (such as dementia) and damage. Other areas of work include forensic psychology (concerned with criminal behaviour) and health psychology.

Clinton, Bill (1946–) born William Jefferson Clinton, 42nd president of the USA 1993–2001. A Democrat, he served as governor of Arkansas 1979–81 and 1983–93, establishing a liberal and progressive reputation. As president, he sought to implement a New Democrat programme, combining social reform with economic conservatism as a means of bringing the country out of recession. He introduced legislation to reduce the federal deficit and cut crime. Clinton presided over a period of unchecked expansion for the US economy, which regained global pre-eminence, and he sought, with mixed success, to promote peace and stability in the Balkans, Middle East, and Northern Ireland. He was the first Democrat since Franklin Roosevelt to be elected for a second term. Following accusations of perjury and obstruction of justice Clinton underwent an impeachment trial (the second such trial in US history) in early 1999 but was acquitted.

clitoris (Greek *kleitoris* 'little hill') in anatomy, part of the female reproductive system. The glans of the clitoris is visible externally. It connects to a pyramid-shaped pad of erectile tissue. Attached to this are two 'arms' that extend backwards into the body towards the anus and are approximately 9 cm/3.5 in in length. Between these arms are the clitoral bulbs, lying one on each side of the vaginal cavity.

Clive, Robert (1725–1774) 1st Baron Clive, British soldier and administrator who established British rule in India by victories over French troops at Arcot and over the nawab (prince) of Bengal at Plassey in 1757. This victory secured Bengal for the East India Company, and Clive was appointed governor of the province from 1757. He returned to Britain on account of ill health in 1760, but was sent out to Bengal again in 1764, where he held the post of governor and commander-in-chief 1765–66. On his return to Britain in 1767, his wealth led to allegations that he had abused his power. Although acquitted by a Parliamentary enquiry, he committed suicide.

cloaca the common posterior chamber of most vertebrates into which the digestive, urinary, and reproductive tracts all enter; a cloaca is found in most reptiles, birds, and amphibians; many fishes; and, to a reduced degree, marsupial mammals. Placental mammals, however, have a separate digestive opening (the anus) and urinogenital opening. The cloaca forms a chamber in which products can be stored before being voided from the body via a muscular opening, the cloacal aperture.

clock rate frequency of a computer's internal electronic clock. Every computer contains an electronic clock, which produces a sequence of regular electrical pulses used by the control unit to synchronize the components of the computer and regulate the fetch–execute cycle by which program instructions are processed. A fixed number of time pulses is required in order to execute each particular instruction. The speed at which a computer can process instructions therefore depends on the clock rate: increasing the clock rate will decrease the time required to complete each particular instruction.

clone exact replica – in genetics, any one of a group of genetically identical cells or organisms. An identical *twin is a clone; so too are bacteria living in the same colony. 'Clone' also describes genetically engineered replicas of DNA sequences.

clothes moth moth whose larvae feed on clothes, upholstery, and carpets. The adults are small golden or silvery moths. The natural habitat of the larvae is in the nests of animals, feeding on remains of hair and feathers, but they have adapted to human households and can cause considerable damage, for example, the common clothes moth *Tineola bisselliella*.

cloud water vapour condensed into minute water particles that float in masses in the atmosphere. Clouds, like fogs or mists, that occur at lower levels, are formed by the cooling of air containing water vapour, which generally condenses around tiny dust particles. The height and nature of a cloud can be deduced from its name. Cirrus clouds are at high levels and have a wispy appearance. Stratus clouds form at low level and are layered. Middle-level clouds have names beginning with 'alto'. Cumulus clouds, ball or cottonwool clouds, occur over a range of height.

cloud chamber apparatus, now obsolete, for tracking ionized particles. It consists of a vessel fitted with a piston and filled with air or other gas, saturated with water vapour. When the volume of the vessel is suddenly expanded by moving the piston outwards, the vapour cools and a cloud of tiny droplets forms on any nuclei, dust, or ions present. As fast-moving ionizing particles collide with the air or gas molecules, they show as visible tracks.

clove dried, unopened flower bud of the clove tree. A member of the myrtle family, the tree is a native of the Maluku Islands, Indonesia. Cloves are used for flavouring in cookery and confectionery. Oil of cloves, which has tonic qualities and relieves wind, is used in medicine. The aroma of cloves is also shared by the leaves, bark, and fruit of the tree. (*Eugenia caryophyllus*, family Myrtaceae.)

clover any of an Old World group of low-growing leguminous plants (see *legume), usually with leaves consisting of three leaflets and small flowers in dense heads. Sweet clover refers to various species belonging to the related genus *Melilotus*. (True clover genus *Trifolium*, family Leguminosae.)

Clovis (465–511) also known as **Chlodovech**, Merovingian king of the Franks (481–511), who extended his realm from a small area around Tournai to encompass most of modern France and parts of modern Germany. He succeeded his father Childeric I as king of the Salian (western) Franks; defeated the Gallo-Romans (Romanized Gauls) near Soissons; and defeated the Alemanni, a confederation of Germanic tribes, near Cologne. He embraced Christianity and subsequently proved a powerful defender of orthodoxy against the Arian Visigoths, whom he defeated at Poitiers. He made Paris his capital.

club moss *or* **lycopod** any of a group of mosslike plants that do not produce seeds but reproduce by *spores. They are related to the ferns and horsetails. (Order Lycopodiales, family Pteridophyta.)

cluster in music, the effect of playing simultaneously and without emphasis all the notes within a chosen interval. It was introduced by the US composer Henry Cowell in the piano piece *The Banshee* (1925), for which using a ruler on the keys is recommended. Its use in film and radio incidental music symbolizes a hallucinatory or dreaming state, presumably because it resembles an internalized disturbance of normal hearing.

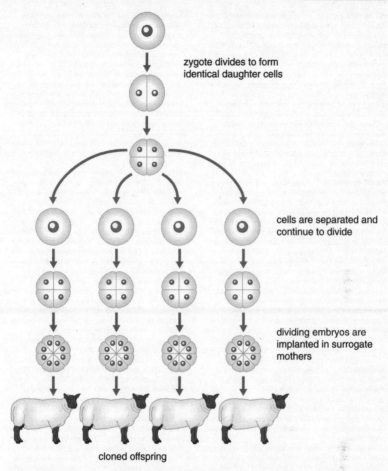

zygote divides to form
identical daughter cells

cells are separated and
continue to divide

dividing embryos are
implanted in surrogate
mothers

cloned offspring

clone The production of a clone (an exact replica) happens naturally when a zygote undergoes division. This is the process that brings about multiple births such as identical twins and triplets. Zygote division can be induced in vitro with the resulting embryos then implanted into surrogate mothers. The offspring are all clones of each other but not of their parents.

clutch any device for disconnecting rotating shafts, used especially in a car's transmission system. In a car with a manual gearbox, the driver depresses the clutch when changing gear, thus disconnecting the engine from the gearbox.

Clwyd former county of north Wales, created in 1974 and, in 1996, divided between *Conwy, *Denbighshire, *Flintshire, *Powys, and *Wrexham unitary authorities.

Clyde third-longest river and firth in Scotland, and longest in southern Scotland; 171 km/106 mi long. Formerly one of the world's great industrial waterways, and famed for its shipbuilding, its industrial base has declined in recent years and the capacity of the ports

on the Clyde has reduced. A decline in pollution has led to the return of salmon and sea trout.

Clytemnestra in Greek mythology, the daughter of King Tyndareus of Sparta and *Leda, half-sister of *Helen, and wife of *Agamemnon, king of Mycenae. After killing her first husband in battle, Agamemnon had married her by force, and later sacrificed their daugher Iphegenia to secure fair winds for the Greek expedition to Troy. With the help of her lover Aegisthus, she murdered her husband and the seer *Cassandra, whom he brought back from the Trojan War, but was killed in turn by her son *Orestes, aided by her daughter Electra.

coal black or blackish mineral substance formed from the compaction of ancient plant matter in tropical swamp conditions. It is used as a fuel and in the chemical industry. Coal is classified according to the proportion of carbon it contains. The main types are *anthracite (shiny, with about 90% carbon), **bituminous coal** (shiny and dull patches, about 75% carbon), and **lignite** (woody, grading into peat, about 50% carbon). Coal can be burned to produce heat energy, for example in power stations to produce electricity. Coal burning is one of the main causes of *acid rain, which damages buildings and can be detrimental to aquatic and plant life.

coal mining extraction of coal from the Earth's crust. Coal mines may be opencast, adit, or deepcast. The least expensive is opencast but this may result in scars on the landscape.

coastal erosion the erosion of the land by the constant battering of the sea, primarily by the processes of hydraulic action, corrasion, attrition, and corrosion. Hydraulic action occurs when the force of the waves compresses air pockets in coastal rocks and cliffs. The air expands explosively, breaking the rocks apart. It is also the force of the water on the cliff. During severe gales this can be as high as 6 tonnes/cm^3 – the force of a bulldozer. Rocks and pebbles flung by waves against the cliff face wear it away by the process of corrasion, or abrasion as it is also known. Chalk and limestone coasts are often broken down by *solution (also called *corrosion). Attrition is the process by which the eroded rock particles themselves are worn down, becoming smaller and more rounded.

coati *or* **coatimundi** any of several species of carnivores of the genus *Nasua*, in the same family, Procyonidae, as the raccoons. A coati is a good climber and has long claws, a long tail, a good sense of smell, and a long, flexible piglike snout used for digging. Coatis live in packs in the forests of South and Central America.

coaxial cable electric cable that consists of a solid or stranded central conductor insulated from and surrounded by a solid or braided conducting tube or sheath. It can transmit the high-frequency signals used in television, telephone, and other telecommunications transmissions.

cobalt chemical symbol Co, (German *Kobalt* 'evil spirit') hard, lustrous, grey, metallic element, atomic number 27, relative atomic mass 58.933. It is found in various ores and occasionally as a free metal, sometimes in metallic meteorite fragments. It is used in the preparation of magnetic, wear-resistant, and high-strength alloys; its compounds are used in inks, paints, and varnishes.

Cobbett, William (1763–1835) English Radical politician and journalist, who published the weekly *Political Register* 1802–35. He spent much of his life in North America. His crusading essays on the conditions of the rural poor were collected as 'Rural Rides' (1830).

Cobden, Richard (1804–1865) British Liberal politician and economist, cofounder with John Bright of the Anti-Corn Law League in 1838. A member of Parliament from 1841, he opposed class and religious privileges and believed in disarmament and free trade.

COBOL acronym for **common business-oriented language**, high-level computer-programming language, designed in the late 1950s for commercial data-processing problems; it has become the major language in this field. COBOL features powerful facilities for file handling and business arithmetic. Program instructions written in this language make extensive use of words and look very much like English sentences. This makes COBOL one of the easiest languages to learn and understand.

cobra any of several poisonous snakes, especially the genus *Naja*, of the family Elapidae, found in Africa and southern Asia, species of which can grow from 1 m/3 ft to over 4.3 m/14 ft. The neck stretches into a hood when the snake is alarmed. Cobra venom contains nerve toxins powerful enough to kill humans.

coca South American shrub belonging to the coca family, whose dried leaves are the source of the drug cocaine. It was used as a holy drug by the Andean Indians. (*Erythroxylon coca*, family Erythroxylaceae.)

cocaine $C_{17}H_{21}NO_4$, alkaloid extracted from the leaves of the coca tree. It has limited medical application, mainly as a local anaesthetic agent that is readily absorbed by mucous membranes (lining tissues) of the nose and throat. It is both toxic and addictive. Its use as a stimulant is illegal. *crack is a derivative of cocaine.

coccus plural **cocci**, member of a group of globular bacteria, some of which are harmful to humans. The cocci contain the subgroups **streptococci**, where the bacteria associate in straight chains, and **staphylococci**, where the bacteria associate in branched chains.

Cochin-China region of Southeast Asia. With Cambodia it formed part of the ancient Khmer empire. In the 17th–18th centuries it was conquered by Annam. Together with Cambodia it became, from 1863 to 1867, the first part of the Indochinese peninsula to be occupied by France. Since 1949 it has been part of Vietnam.

cochlea part of the inner *ear. It is equipped with approximately 10,000 hair cells, which move in response to sound waves and thus stimulate nerve cells to send messages to the brain. In this way they turn vibrations of the air into electrical signals.

cockatiel Australian parrot *Nymphicus hollandicus*, about 20 cm/8 in long, with greyish or yellow plumage, yellow cheeks, a long tail, and a crest like a cockatoo. Cockatiels are popular as pets and aviary birds.

cockatoo any of several crested parrots, especially of the genus *Cacatua*, family Psittacidae, of the order Psittaciformes. They usually have light-coloured plumage with tinges of red, yellow, or orange on the face, and an erectile crest on the head. They are native to Australia, New Guinea, and nearby islands.

cockchafer *or* **maybug** European beetle *Melolontha melolontha*, of the scarab family, up to 3 cm/1.2 in long, with clumsy, buzzing flight, seen on early summer evenings. Cockchafers damage trees by feeding on the foliage and flowers.

cockle any of over 200 species of bivalve mollusc with ribbed, heart-shaped shells. Some are edible and are sold in Western European markets.

cockroach any of numerous insects of the family Blattidae, distantly related to mantises and grasshoppers. There are 3,500 species, mainly in the tropics. They have long antennae and biting mouthparts. They can fly, but rarely do so.

cocoa and chocolate (Aztec *xocolatl*) food products made from the *cacao (or cocoa) bean, fruit of a tropical tree *Theobroma cacao*, now cultivated mainly in Africa. Chocolate as a drink was introduced to

Europe from the New World by the Spanish in the 16th century; eating-chocolate was first produced in the late 18th century. Cocoa and chocolate are widely used in confectionery and drinks. More than 30 different pesticides are commonly used on cocoa crops, and traces of some have been detected in chocolate.

coconut fruit of the coconut palm, which grows throughout the lowland tropics. The fruit has a large outer husk of fibres, which is removed and used to make coconut matting and ropes. Inside this is the nut which is exported to temperate countries. Its hard shell contains white flesh and clear coconut milk, both of which are tasty and nourishing. (*Cocos nucifera*, family Arecaceae.)

cocoon pupa-case of many insects, especially of *moths and *silkworms. This outer web or ball is spun from the mouth by caterpillars before they pass into the *chrysalis state.

Cocos Islands *or* **Keeling Islands** group of 27 small coral islands in the Indian Ocean, about 2,700 km/ 1,678 mi northwest of Perth, Australia; area 14 sq km/ 5.5 sq mi; population (2001 est) 620. An Australian external territory since 1955, the islanders voted to become part of Australia in 1984, and in 1992 they became subject to the laws of Western Australia. The main commercial product is copra (dried kernels of coconut, used to make coconut oil), but fishing is important for subsistence and for local trade, and the islands are a site for ecotourism. West Island and Home Island are the only inhabited islands, the population being mainly of Malay origin.

Cocteau, Jean (1889–1963) French poet, dramatist, and film director. A leading figure in European modernism, he worked with the artist *Picasso, the choreographer *Diaghilev, and the composer *Stravinsky. He produced many volumes of poetry, ballets such as *Le Boeuf sur le toit/The Ox on the Roof* (1920), plays like *Orphée/Orpheus* (1926), and a mature novel of bourgeois French life, *Les Enfants terribles* (1929), which he filmed in 1948.

cod any fish of the family Gadidae, especially the Atlantic cod *Gadus morhua*, found in the North Atlantic and Baltic. It is brown to grey with spots, with a white underbelly, and can grow to 1.5 m/5 ft in length.

coda (Italian 'tail') in music, a concluding section of a movement added to emphasize the destination key.

codeine opium derivative that provides *analgesia in mild to moderate pain. It also suppresses the cough centre of the brain. It is an alkaloid, derived from morphine but less toxic and addictive.

codex plural **codices**, book from before the invention of printing: in ancient times wax-coated wooden tablets; later, folded sheets of parchment were attached to the boards, then bound together. The name 'codex' was used for all large works, collections of history, philosophy, poetry, and during the Roman empire designated collections of laws. During the 2nd century AD codices began to replace the earlier rolls in the West. They were widely used by the medieval Christian church to keep records, from about 1200 onwards.

Cody, William Frederick (1846–1917) called 'Buffalo Bill', US scout and performer. From 1883 he toured the USA and Europe with a Wild West show which featured the recreation of Indian attacks and, for a time, the cast included Chief *Sitting Bull as well as Annie Oakley. His nickname derives from a time when he had a contract to supply buffalo carcasses to railway labourers (over 4,000 in 18 months).

Coe, Sebastian Newbold (1956–) English middle-distance runner, Olympic 1,500-metre champion in 1980 and 1984. He became UK's most prolific world-record breaker with eight outdoor world records and three indoor world records (1979–81).

coefficient number part in front of an algebraic term, signifying multiplication. For example, in the expression $4x^2 + 2xy - x$, the coefficient of x^2 is 4 (because $4x^2$ means $4 \times x^2$), that of xy is 2, and that of x is -1 (because $-1 \times x = -x$).

coelacanth large dark brown to blue-grey fish that can grow to about 2 m/6 ft in length, and weigh up to 73 kg/ 160 lb. It has bony, overlapping scales, and muscular lobe (limblike) fins sometimes used like oars when swimming and for balance while resting on the sea floor. They feed on other fish, and give birth to live young rather than shedding eggs as most fish do. Coelacanth fossils exist dating back over 400 million years and coelacanth were believed to be extinct until one was caught in 1938 off the coast of South Africa. For this reason they are sometimes referred to as 'living fossils'. Populations have since been discovered off the Comoros Islands in the Indian Ocean, the island of Sulawesi in Indonesia, and Sodwana Bay on the northeast coast of South Africa.

coelenterate any freshwater or marine organism of the phylum Coelenterata, having a body wall composed of two layers of cells. They also possess stinging cells. Examples are jellyfish, hydra, and coral.

coeliac disease disease in which the small intestine fails to digest and absorb food. The disease can appear at any age but has a peak incidence in the 30–50 age group; it is more common in women. It is caused by an intolerance to gluten (a constituent of wheat, rye and barley) and characterized by diarrhoea and malnutrition. Treatment is by a gluten-free diet.

coffee drink made from the roasted and ground beanlike seeds found inside the red berries of any of several species of shrubs, originally native to Ethiopia and now cultivated throughout the tropics. It contains a stimulant, *caffeine. (Genus *Coffea*, family Rubiaceae.)

cognition in psychology, a general term covering the functions involved in synthesizing information – for example, perception (seeing, hearing, and so on), attention, memory, and reasoning.

cognitive therapy *or* **cognitive behaviour therapy** treatment for emotional disorders such as *depression and *anxiety states. It encourages the patient to challenge the distorted and unhelpful thinking that is characteristic of depression, for example. The treatment may include *behaviour therapy.

coil in medicine, another name for an *intrauterine device.

coke clean, light fuel produced, along with town gas, when coal is strongly heated in an airtight oven. Coke contains 90% carbon and makes a useful domestic and industrial fuel (used, for example, in the iron and steel industries).

Coke, Edward (1552–1634) Lord Chief Justice of England 1613–17. He was a defender of common law against royal prerogative; against Charles I he drew up the petition of right in 1628, which defines and protects Parliament's liberties.

cola or **kola** any of several tropical trees, especially *Cola acuminata*. In West Africa the nuts are chewed for their high *caffeine content, and in the West they are used to flavour soft drinks. (Genus *Cola*, family Sterculiaceae.)

cold, common minor disease of the upper respiratory tract, caused by a variety of viruses. Symptoms are headache, chill, nasal discharge, sore throat, and occasionally cough. Research indicates that the virulence of a cold depends on psychological factors and either a reduction or an increase of social or work activity, as a result of stress, in the previous six months.

cold-blooded of animals, dependent on the surrounding temperature; see *poikilothermy.

cold fusion in nuclear physics, the fusion of atomic nuclei at room temperature. If cold fusion were possible it would provide a limitless, cheap, and pollution-free source of energy, and it has therefore been the subject of research around the world.

Colditz castle in eastern Germany, near Leipzig, used as a high-security prisoner-of-war camp (Oflag IVC) in World War II. Among daring escapes was that of British Captain Patrick Reid (1910–1990) and others in October 1942, whose story contributed much to its fame. It became a museum in 1989. A highly successful British TV drama series called *Colditz* (1972) was based on prisoners' experiences.

Cold War ideological, political, and economic tensions from 1945 to 1989 between the USSR and Eastern Europe on the one hand and the USA and Western Europe on the other. The Cold War was fuelled by propaganda, undercover activity by intelligence agencies, and economic sanctions; and was intensified by signs of conflict anywhere in the world. Arms-reduction agreements between the USA and USSR in the late 1980s, and a reduction of Soviet influence in Eastern Europe, led to a reassessment of positions, and the 'war' was officially ended in December 1989. The term 'Cold War' was first used by Bernard Baruch, advisor to US President Truman, in a speech made in April 1947. He spoke about Truman's intent for the USA to 'support free peoples who are resisting attempted subjugation by armed minorities or by outside pressures' (see *Truman Doctrine).

coleoptile the protective sheath that surrounds the young shoot tip of a grass during its passage through the soil to the surface. Although of relatively simple structure, most coleoptiles are very sensitive to light, ensuring that seedlings grow upwards.

Coleridge, Samuel Taylor (1772–1834) English poet, critic, and philosopher. A friend of the poets Robert Southey and William *Wordsworth, he collaborated with the latter on the highly influential collection *Lyrical Ballads* (1798), which expressed their theory of poetic sensation and was the spearhead of English *Romanticism. His poems include 'The Rime of the Ancient Mariner', 'Christabel', and 'Kubla Khan' (all written 1797–98); his critical works include *Biographia Literaria* (1817).

Colette, Sidonie-Gabrielle (1873–1954) French writer. Her best novels reveal an exquisite sensitivity, largely centred on the joys and sorrows of love, and include *Chéri* (1920), *La Fin de Chéri/The End of Chéri* (1926), and *Gigi* (1944).

colic spasmodic attack of pain in the abdomen, usually coming in waves. Colicky pains are caused by the painful muscular contraction and subsequent distension of a hollow organ; for example, the bowels, gall bladder (biliary colic), or ureter (renal colic).

colitis inflammation of the colon (large intestine) with diarrhoea (often bloody). It is usually due to infection or some types of bacterial dysentery.

collage (French 'sticking', 'pasting', or 'paper-hanging') in art, the use of various materials, such as pieces of newspaper, fabric, and wallpaper, to create a picture or design by sticking them on canvas or another suitable surface, often in combination with painted or drawn features.

collagen protein that is the main constituent of *connective tissue. Collagen is present in skin, cartilage, tendons, and ligaments. Bones are made up of collagen, with the mineral calcium phosphate providing increased rigidity.

collateral security available in return for a loan. Usually stocks, shares, property, or life insurance policies will be accepted as collateral.

collective bargaining process whereby management, representing an employer, and a trade union, representing employees, agree to negotiate jointly terms and conditions of employment. Agreements can be company-based or industry-wide.

collective responsibility doctrine found in governments modelled on the British system of cabinet government. It is based on convention, or usage, rather than law, and requires that once a decision has been taken by the cabinet, all members of the government are bound by it and must support it or resign their posts.

collective security system for achieving international stability by an agreement among all states to unite against any aggressor. Such a commitment was embodied in the post-World War I *League of Nations and also in the *United Nations (UN), although the League was not able to live up to the ideals of its founders, nor has the UN been able to do so.

collective unconscious in psychology, a shared pool of memories, ideas, modes of thought, and so on, which, according to the Swiss psychiatrist Carl Jung, comes from the life experience of one's ancestors, indeed from the entire human race. It coexists with the personal *unconscious, which contains the material of individual experience, and may be regarded as an immense depository of ancient wisdom.

collectivism in politics, a position in which the collective (such as the state) has priority over its individual members. It is the opposite of *individualism, which is itself a variant of anarchy.

College of Arms or **Heralds' College** English heraldic body formed in 1484. There are three kings-of-arms, six heralds, and four pursuivants, who specialize in genealogical and heraldic work. The college establishes the right to a coat of arms, and the kings-of-arms grant arms by letters patent. The office of king-of-arms for Ulster was transferred to the College of Arms in London in 1943.

collie any of several breeds of sheepdog originally bred in Britain. They include the border collie, the bearded collie, and the rough collie and its smooth-haired counterpart.

Collins, (William) Wilkie (1824–1889) English author of mystery and suspense novels. He wrote *The Woman in White* (1860), often called the first English detective fiction novel, and *The Moonstone* (1868) (with Sergeant Cuff, one of the first detectives in English literature). Both novels have been successfully dramatized for television.

Collins, Michael (1890–1922) Irish nationalist. He was a *Sinn Fein leader, a founder and director of intelligence of the *Irish Republican Army (IRA) in 1919, a minister in the provisional government of the Irish Free State in 1922, commander of the Free State forces in the civil war, and for ten days head of state before being killed by Irish republicans.

collision theory theory that explains how chemical reactions take place and why rates of reaction alter. For a reaction to occur the reactant particles must collide. Only a certain fraction of the total collisions cause chemical change; these are called **successful collisions**. The successful collisions have sufficient energy (activation energy) at the moment of impact to break the existing bonds and form new bonds, resulting in the products of the reaction. Increasing the concentration of the reactants and raising the temperature bring about more collisions and therefore more successful collisions, increasing the rate of reaction.

colloid substance composed of extremely small particles of one material (the dispersed phase) evenly and stably distributed in another material (the continuous phase). The size of the dispersed particles (1–1,000 nanometres across) is less than that of particles in suspension but greater than that of molecules in true solution. Colloids involving gases include **aerosols** (dispersions of liquid or solid particles in a gas, as in fog or smoke) and **foams** (dispersions of gases in liquids). Those involving liquids include **emulsions** (in which both the dispersed and the continuous phases are liquids) and **sols** (solid particles dispersed in a liquid). Sols in which both phases contribute to a molecular three-dimensional network have a jellylike form and are known as **gels**; gelatin, starch 'solution', and silica gel are common examples. Steel is a solid colloid.

Colombia

National name: *República de Colombia/ Republic of Colombia*

Area: 1,141,748 sq km/440,828 sq mi

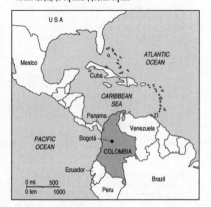

Capital: Bogotá

Major towns/cities: Medellín, Cali, Barranquilla, Cartagena, Bucaramanga, Cúcuta, Ibagué

Major ports: Barranquilla, Cartagena, Buenaventura

Physical features: the Andes mountains run north–south; flat coastland in west and plains (llanos) in east; Magdalena River runs north to Caribbean Sea; includes islands of Providencia, San Andrés, and Mapelo; almost half the country is forested

Head of state and government: Alvaro Uribe Vélez from 2002

Political system: liberal democracy

Political executive: limited presidency

Political parties: Liberal Party (PL), centrist; Conservative Party (PSC), right of centre; M-19 Democratic Alliance (ADM-19), left of centre; National Salvation Movement (MSN), right-of-centre coalition grouping

Currency: Colombian peso

GNI per capita (PPP): (US$) 5,870 (2002 est)

Exports: petroleum and petroleum products, coal, coffee, gold, bananas, cut flowers, cotton, chemicals, textiles, paper. Principal market: USA 42.8% (2001). Illegal trade in cocaine; Colombia is one of the world's main producers of coca, the raw material for cocaine; it is estimated that drug money accounted for about 2% of GDP in 2000; still the main source of illegal cocaine in the USA

Population: 44,222,000 (2003 est)

Language: Spanish (official) (95%)

Religion: Roman Catholic

Life expectancy: 69 (men); 75 (women) (2000–05)

Chronology

late 15th century: Southern Colombia became part of Inca Empire, whose core lay in Peru.

1522: Spanish conquistador Pascual de Andagoya reached the San Juan River.

1536–38: Spanish conquest by Jimenez de Quesada overcame powerful Chibcha Indian chiefdom, which had its capital in the uplands at Bogotá and was renowned for its gold crafts; became part of Spanish Viceroyalty of Peru, which covered much of South America.

1717: Bogotá became capital of the new Spanish Viceroyalty of Nueva (New) Granada, which also ruled Ecuador and Venezuela.

1809: Struggle for independence from Spain began.

1819: Venezuelan freedom fighter Simón Bolívar, 'the Liberator', who had withdrawn to Colombia in 1814, raised a force of 5,000 British mercenaries and defeated the Spanish at the battle of Boyacá, establishing Colombia's independence; Gran Colombia formed, also comprising Ecuador, Panama, and Venezuela.

1830: Became a separate state, which included Panama, on the dissolution of the Republic of Gran Colombia.

1863: Became major coffee exporter. Federalizing, anti-clerical Liberals came to power, with the country divided into nine largely autonomous 'sovereign' states; the church was disestablished.

1885: Conservatives came to power, beginning 45 years of political dominance; power was recentralized and the church restored to influence.

1899–1903: Civil war between Liberals and Conservatives, ending with Panama's separation as an independent state.

1930: Liberals returned to power at the time of the economic depression; social legislation introduced and a labour movement encouraged.

1946: Conservatives returned to power.

1948: The left-wing mayor of Bogotá was assassinated to a widespread outcry.

1949–57: Civil war, 'La Violencia', during which over 250,000 people died.

1957: Hoping to halt violence, Conservatives and Liberals agreed to form National Front, sharing the presidency.

1970: National Popular Alliance (ANAPO) formed as left-wing opposition to National Front.

1974: National Front accord temporarily ended.

1975: Civil unrest due to disillusionment with government.

1978: Liberals, under Julio Turbay, revived the accord and began an intensive fight against drug dealers.

1982: The Liberals maintained their control of congress but lost the presidency. Conservative president Belisario Betancur granted guerrillas an amnesty and freed political prisoners.

1984: The minister of justice was assassinated by drug dealers; the campaign against them was stepped up.

1989: A drug cartel assassinated the leading presidential candidate and an antidrug war was declared by the president; a bombing campaign by drug traffickers killed hundreds; the police killed José Rodriguez Gacha, one of the most wanted cartel leaders.

1991: A new constitution prohibited the extradition of Colombians wanted for trial in other countries. Several leading drug traffickers were arrested. Many guerrillas abandoned the armed struggle, but the Colombian Revolutionary Armed Forces (FARC) and the National Liberation Army remained active.

1993: Medellín drug-cartel leader Pablo Escobar was shot while attempting to avoid arrest.

1995: President Samper came under pressure to resign over corruption allegations; a state of emergency was declared. Leaders of the Cali drug cartel were imprisoned.

1998: There were clashes between the army and left-wing guerrillas. The conservative Andres Pastrana won presidential elections. Peace talks were held with rebels.

1999: Formal peace talks were broken off after violence, but later resumed.

2000: US president Clinton announced US$1.3 billion in aid for Colombia in January and a further US$1.3 billion in August, most of which was to go to the armed forces. Pastrana's government sank to just 20% public support. Talks with one rebel group secured the release of 42 hostages in December.

2001: A deal was signed by Pastrana and Manuel Marulanda, the FARC leader, paving the way for a ceasefire.

2002: An upsurge of violence by the FARC guerrilla group brought an end to three years of peace talks with the Colombian government, which retaliated by launching military strikes against rebel positions. President Alvaro Uribe declared a limited state of emergency for 90 days and decreed a wealth tax to raise funds for a military build-up against terrorism.

2003: A FARC car bomb in Bogotá killed 35 people and injured about 160 – the worst terrorist incident in the capital for more than a decade. President Alvaro Uribe suffered defeat in a sweeping 15-point referendum on proposed political and fiscal reforms to fight terrorism

and boost the country's faltering economy. Around 800 members of the right-wing United Self Defence Forces of Colombia (AUC) demobilized and the AUC announced that all its paramilitaries would disarm by the end of 2005.

2004: Ricardo Palmera, of FARC, was jailed for 35 years. Formal peace talks between the government and the AUC began and a further 450 AUC fighters were demobilized.

2005: A senior member of FARC, Rodrigo Granda, was arrested. Relations between Colombia and Venezuela were strained when it was alleged that Granda was captured on Venezuelan soil.

Colombo chief commercial city and seaport, and former capital, of Sri Lanka, on the west coast near the mouth of the Kelani River; population (2001 est) 642,000. It trades in the export of tea, rubber, and cacao, and its industries include iron- and steelworks, an oil refinery, and motor vehicle assembly. Colombo is the hub of the road and rail network of Sri Lanka, is served by an international airport at Katunayake, and is the main commercial centre of the island. It was succeeded as capital by nearby Sri Jayewardenepura Kotte in 1982.

colon in anatomy, the main part of the large intestine, between the caecum and rectum. Water and mineral salts are absorbed from undigested food in the colon, and the residue passes as faeces towards the rectum.

colonialism another name for *imperialism.

colonization in ecology, the spread of species into a new habitat, such as a freshly cleared field, a new motorway verge, or a recently flooded valley. The first species to move in are called **pioneers**, and may establish conditions that allow other animals and plants to move in (for example, by improving the condition of the soil or by providing shade). Over time a range of species arrives and the habitat matures; early colonizers will probably be replaced, so that the variety of animal and plant life present changes. This is known as *succession.

Colorado river in southwestern USA and northwestern Mexico, rising in the Rocky Mountains and flowing 2,333 km/1,447 mi to the Gulf of California through Colorado, Utah, Arizona (including the Grand Canyon), and extending into northern Mexico. The many dams along its course, including Hoover Dam and Glen Canyon Dam, provide hydroelectric power and irrigation water, but have destroyed wildlife and scenery; they have also created a series of lakes including Lake Powell, Lake Mead, and Lake Havasu. Around 20 million people depend on the Colorado for food, power, or water.

Colorado called the **Centennial State**, (Spanish 'coloured red') state of the western central USA in the heart of the 'Mountain States', bordered to the west by *Utah, to the north by *Nebraska and *Wyoming, to the east by *Kansas and *Nebraska, to the southeast by *Oklahoma, to the south by *New Mexico, and meeting Utah, *Arizona, and New Mexico at the 'Four Corners' to the southwest; area 268,628 sq km/103,718 sq mi; population (2000) 4,301,300; capital and largest city *Denver. The economy is led by the service industry, and tourism is important in the central and western parts of the states; information technology and engineering are also significant industries. Other major cities in Colorado include Colorado Springs, Aurora, Lakewood, Fort Collins, Greeley, Pueblo, Boulder, and

Arvada. The state's expansion from World War II onwards has been closely associated with the USA's military-industrial surge. One third of Colorado is owned by the US federal government; the US Air Force has its academy close to Colorado Springs, and has defence headquarters in Cheyenne Mountain, with its finance centre based in Denver. Colorado joined the Union in 1876, the 100th anniversary of the signing of the *Declaration of Independence, as the 38th US state.

Colorado beetle *or* **potato beetle** North American black and yellow striped beetle that is a pest on potato crops. Although it was once a serious pest, it can now usually be controlled by using insecticides. It has also colonized many European countries. Colarado beetles *Leptinotarsa decemlineata* are in the family Chrysomelidae, order Coleoptera, class Insecta, phylum Arthropoda.

coloratura in music, a rapid ornamental vocal passage with runs and trills. A **coloratura soprano** is a light, high voice suited to such music.

Colosseum amphitheatre in ancient Rome, begun by the emperor Vespasian to replace the one destroyed by fire during the reign of Nero, and completed by his son Titus in AD 80. It was 187 m/615 ft long and 49 m/160 ft high, and seated 50,000 people. Early Christians were martyred there by lions and gladiators. It could be flooded for mock sea battles.

Colossus of Rhodes bronze statue of Apollo erected at the entrance to the harbour at Rhodes between 292 BC and 280 BC. Said to have been about 30 m/100 ft high, it was counted as one of the *Seven Wonders of the World, but in 224 BC fell as a result of an earthquake.

colour in art, one of the most powerful of the visual or formal art elements, and a property of light. Specifically, colour is the quality or *wavelength of light emitted or reflected from an object. Colours may be produced by the use of pigment (paint or dye), by the choice of naturally coloured objects, or (in installation art) by the use of lights or television screens.

colour in physics, quality or wavelength of light emitted or reflected from an object. Visible white light consists of electromagnetic radiation of various wavelengths, and if a beam is refracted through a prism, it can be spread out into the visible spectrum (that can be detected by the human eye), in which the various colours correspond to different wavelengths. From long to short wavelengths (from about 700 to 400 nanometres) the colours are red, orange, yellow, green, blue, indigo, and violet. The colour of grass is green because grass absorbs all the colours from the spectrum and only transmits or reflects the wavelength corresponding to green. A sheet of white paper reflects all the colours of the spectrum from its surface; black objects absorb all the colours of the spectrum.

colour blindness hereditary defect of vision that reduces the ability to discriminate certain colours, usually red and green. The condition is sex-linked, affecting men more than women.

Coltrane, John (William) (1926–1967) US jazz saxophonist. He first came to fame in 1955 with the Miles *Davis quintet, later playing with Thelonious Monk in 1957. He was a powerful and individual artist, whose performances featured much experimentation. His 1960s quartet was highly regarded for its innovations in melody and harmony.

colugo *or* **flying lemur** Southeast Asian climbing mammal of the genus *Cynocephalus*, order Dermoptera, about 60 cm/2 ft long including the tail. It glides between forest trees using a flap of skin that extends from head to forelimb to hindlimb to tail. It may glide 130 m/425 ft or more, losing little height. It feeds largely on buds and leaves, and rests hanging upside down under branches.

Columba, St (521–597) (Latin form of *Colum-cille*, 'Colum of the cell') Irish Christian abbot, missionary to Scotland. He was born in County Donegal of royal descent, and founded monasteries and churches in Ireland. In 563 he sailed with 12 companions to Iona, and built a monastery there that was to play a leading part in the conversion of Britain. Feast day 9 June.

Columbia river in western North America; length over 2,005 km/1,245 mi. It rises in Columbia Lake on the western slope of the Rocky Mountains in British Columbia, Canada, 130 km/81 mi north of the USA border. It flows through Washington State along the northern border of Oregon, until it reaches the Pacific below Astoria; its estuary is about 55 km/34 mi long and from 5–11 km/3–7 mi wide, and its mouth is the only deep-water harbour between San Francisco and Cape Flattery.

Columbia, District of federal district of the USA, see *District of Columbia and *Washington, DC.

columbine any of a group of plants belonging to the buttercup family. All are perennial herbs with divided leaves and hanging flower heads with spurred petals. (Genus *Aquilegia*, family Ranunculaceae.)

columbium symbol Cb, former name for the chemical element *niobium. The name is still used occasionally in metallurgy.

Columbus, Christopher (1451–1506) Spanish Cristóbal Colón, Italian Cristoforo Colombo, Italian navigator and explorer who made four voyages to the New World: in 1492 to San Salvador Island, Cuba, and Haiti; from 1493 to 1496 to Guadaloupe, Montserrat, Antigua, Puerto Rico, and Jamaica; in 1498 to Trinidad and the mainland of South America; from 1502 to 1504 to Honduras and Nicaragua. Believing that Asia could be reached by sailing westwards, he eventually won the support of King Ferdinand and Queen Isabella of Spain and set off on his first voyage from Palos on 3 August 1492 with three small ships, the *Niña*, the *Pinta*, and his flagship the *Santa María*. Land was sighted on 12 October, probably Watling Island (now San Salvador Island), and within a few weeks he reached Cuba and Haiti, returning to Spain in March 1493.

column in architecture, a structure, round or polygonal in plan, erected vertically as a support for some part of a building. Cretan paintings reveal the existence of wooden columns in Aegean architecture in about 1500 BC. The Hittites, Assyrians, and Egyptians also used wooden columns, and they are a feature of the monumental architecture of China and Japan. In classical architecture there are five principal types of column; see *order. (See diagram, p. 212.)

coma in medicine, a state of deep unconsciousness from which the subject cannot be roused. Possible causes include head injury, brain disease, liver failure, cerebral haemorrhage, and drug overdose.

Combination Acts laws passed in Britain in 1799 and 1800 making trade unionism illegal. They were

Doric

Ionic

Corinthian

Tuscan

Composite

column The five orders of column in classical architecture: Doric, Ionic, Corinthian, Tuscan, and Composite. The Doric is the earliest, being used before the 5th century BC, and the Composite is the latest, appearing in AD 82.

introduced after the French Revolution for fear that the *trade unions would become centres of political agitation. The unions continued to exist, but claimed to be friendly societies or went underground, until the acts were repealed in 1824, largely owing to the radical Francis Place.

combine harvester machine used for harvesting cereals and other crops, so called because it combines the actions of reaping (cutting the crop) and threshing (beating the ears so that the grain separates).

combustion burning, defined in chemical terms as the rapid combination of a substance with oxygen, accompanied by the evolution of heat and usually light. A slow-burning candle flame and the explosion of a mixture of petrol vapour and air are extreme examples of combustion. Combustion is an exothermic reaction as heat energy is given out.

Comecon acronym for COuncil for Mutual ECONomic Assistance; or **CMEA**, economic organization from 1949 to 1991, linking the USSR with Bulgaria, Czechoslovakia, Hungary, Poland, Romania, East Germany (1950–90), Mongolia (from 1962), Cuba (from 1972), and Vietnam (from 1978), with Yugoslavia as an associated member. Albania also belonged between 1949 and 1961. Its establishment was prompted by the *Marshall Plan. Comecon was formally disbanded in June 1991.

Comédie Française French national theatre (for both comedy and tragedy) in Paris, founded in 1680 by Louis XIV. Its base is the Salle Richelieu on the right bank of the River Seine, and the Théâtre de l'Odéon, on the left bank, is a testing ground for avant-garde ideas.

comedy literary *genre that aims to make its audience laugh. *Drama, *verse, and *prose can all have a comic aim. Stereotypically, comedy has a happy or amusing ending, as opposed to tragedy, but it can also embody a far subtler structure and purpose. Traditional comedy, like tragedy, has human weakness as its primary focus but, instead of being destroyed, in comedy the characters are mostly rescued from their faults and often learn from them. The laughter is typically provided by 'licensed fools', whose role is to expose and develop the flaws of the characters who take themselves too seriously, are silly, or are mistaken. The fool may ironically prove to be the saviour of the other characters. The final act in a comedy resolves all conflict, with the common exception of a single bitter character, who provides dramatic contrast.

comet small, icy body orbiting the Sun, usually on a highly elliptical path that takes it beyond the planet Pluto. A comet consists of a central nucleus a few kilometres across and is made mostly of ice mixed with gas and dust. As a comet approaches the Sun its nucleus heats up, releasing gas and dust, which form a coma (comet head) up to 100,000 km/60,000 mi wide. Gas and dust stream away from the coma to form one or more tails, which may extend for millions of kilometres. Some comets, such as Halley's comet, stay within Pluto's orbit for most of the time. Comets are normally visible during sunset or sunrise.

comfrey any of a group of plants belonging to the borage family, with rough, hairy leaves and small bell-shaped flowers (blue, purple-pink, or white). They are found in Europe and western Asia. (Genus *Symphytum*, family Boraginaceae.)

Comintern acronym for Communist *International.

command economy or **planned economy** economy planned and directed by government, where resources are allocated to factories by the state through central planning. This system is unresponsive to the needs and whims of consumers and to sudden changes in conditions (for example, crop failure or fluctuations in the world price of raw materials).

command language in computing, a set of commands and the rules governing their use, by which users control a program. For example, an *operating system may have commands such as SAVE and DELETE, or a payroll program may have commands for adding and amending staff records.

commando member of a specially trained, highly mobile military unit. The term originated in South Africa in the 19th century, where it referred to Boer military reprisal raids against Africans and, in the South African Wars, against the British. Commando units have often carried out operations behind enemy lines.

commedia dell'arte popular form of Italian improvised comic drama in the 16th and 17th centuries, performed by trained troupes of actors and involving stock characters and situations. It exerted considerable influence on writers such as Carlo Goldoni, and *Molière, and on the genres of *pantomime, harlequinade, and the Punch and Judy show. It laid the foundation for a tradition of mime, strong in France, that continued with the modern mime of Jean-Louis Barrault and Marcel Marceau. Overtly subversive in plot, commedia deals with servants tricking and swindling their foolish masters.

commensalism in biology, a relationship between two *species whereby one (the commensal) benefits from the association, whereas the other neither benefits nor suffers. For example, certain species of millipede and silverfish inhabit the nests of army ants and live by scavenging on the refuse of their hosts, but without affecting the ants.

commodity something produced for sale. Commodities may be consumer goods, such as radios, or producer goods, such as copper bars.

Commodity markets deal in raw or semi-raw materials that are amenable to grading and that can be stored for considerable periods without deterioration.

Commodus, Lucius Aelius Aurelius (AD 161–192) Roman emperor from 177 (jointly with his father), sole emperor from 180, son of Marcus Aurelius. He was a tyrant, spending lavishly on gladiatorial combats, confiscating the property of the wealthy, persecuting the Senate, and renaming Rome 'Colonia Commodiana'. There were many attempts against his life, and he was finally strangled at the instigation of his mistress, Marcia, and advisers, who had discovered themselves on the emperor's death list.

Common Agricultural Policy (CAP) system of financial support for farmers in *European Union (EU) countries, a central aspect of which is the guarantee of minimum prices for part of what they produce. The objectives of the CAP were outlined in the *Treaties of Rome (1957): to increase agricultural productivity, to provide a fair standard of living for farmers and their employees, to stabilize markets, and to assure the availability of supply at a price that was reasonable to the consumer. The CAP has been criticized for its role in creating overproduction, and consequent environmental damage, and for the high price of food subsidies.

common land unenclosed wasteland, forest, and pasture used in common by the community at large. Poor people have throughout history gathered fruit, nuts, wood, reeds, roots, game, and so on from common land; in dry regions of India, for example, the landless derive 20% of their annual income in this way, together with much of their food and fuel. Codes of conduct evolved to ensure that common resources were not depleted. But in the 20th century, in the developing world as elsewhere, much common land has been privatized or appropriated by the state, and what remains is overburdened by those who depend upon it.

common law that part of the English law not embodied in legislation. It consists of rules of law based on common custom and usage and on judicial (court) decisions. English common law became the basis of law in the USA and many other English-speaking countries.

Common Market popular name for the **European Economic Community**; see *European Union.

Commons, House of lower chamber of the UK *Parliament. It consists of 659 elected members of Parliament, each of whom represents a constituency. Its functions are to debate, legislate (pass laws), and to oversee the activities of government. Constituencies are kept under continuous review by the Parliamentary Boundary Commissions (1944). The House of Commons is presided over by the Speaker. Proceedings in the House of Commons began to be televised from November 1989. After the 1997 election, the Commons

included a record 120 women members, including 101 female Labour MPs; this fell to 118 after the 2001 election.

commonwealth body politic founded on law for the common 'weal' or good. Political philosophers of the 17th century, such as Thomas Hobbes and John Locke, used the term to mean an organized political community. In Britain it is specifically applied to the period between 1649 and 1660 when, after the execution of Charles I in the English *Civil War, England was a republic.

Commonwealth Games multisport gathering of competitors from British Commonwealth countries, held every four years. The first meeting (known as the British Empire Games) was in Hamilton, Canada, in August 1930. It has been held in Britain on five occasions: London in 1934, Cardiff in 1958, Edinburgh in 1970 and 1986, and Manchester in 2002.

Commonwealth of Independent States (CIS) successor body to the Union of Soviet Socialist Republics, initially formed as a new commonwealth of Slav republics on 8 December 1991 by the presidents of the Russian Federation, Belarus, and Ukraine. On 21 December, eight of the nine remaining non-Slav republics – Moldova, Tajikistan, Armenia, Azerbaijan, Turkmenistan, Kazakhstan, Kyrgyzstan, and Uzbekistan – joined the CIS at a meeting held in Kazakhstan's former capital, Alma-Ata (now Almaty). Georgia joined in 1994. The CIS formally came into existence in January 1992 when President Gorbachev resigned and the Soviet government voted itself out of existence. It has no formal political institutions and its role is uncertain.

Commonwealth, the (British) voluntary association of 54 sovereign (self-ruling) countries and their dependencies, the majority of which once formed part of the *British Empire and are now independent sovereign states. They are all regarded as 'full members of the Commonwealth'; the newest member being Mozambique, which was admitted in November 1995. Additionally, there are 13 territories that are not completely sovereign and remain dependencies of the UK or one of the other fully sovereign members, and are regarded as 'Commonwealth countries'. Heads of government meet every two years, apart from those of Nauru and Tuvalu; however, Nauru and Tuvalu have the right to take part in all functional activities. The Commonwealth, which was founded in 1931, has no charter or constitution, and is founded more on tradition and sentiment than on political or economic factors. However, it can make political statements by withdrawing membership; for example Nigeria's suspension between November 1995 and May 1999 because of human-rights abuses. Fiji was readmitted in October 1997, ten years after its membership had been suspended as a result of discrimination against its ethnic Indian community.

commune group of people or families living together, sharing resources and responsibilities. There have been various kinds of commune through the ages, including a body of burghers or burgesses in medieval times, a religious community in America, and a communal division in communist China.

Commune, Paris two separate periods in the history of Paris (between 1789 and 1794 and from March to May 1871); see *Paris Commune.

communication in biology, the signalling of information by one organism to another, usually with the intention of altering the recipient's behaviour. Signals used in communication may be **visual** (such as the human smile or the display of colourful plumage in birds), **auditory** (for example, the whines or barks of a dog), **olfactory** (such as the odours released by the scent glands of a deer), **electrical** (as in the pulses emitted by electric fish), or **tactile** (for example, the nuzzling of male and female elephants).

communication the sending and receiving of messages. The messages can be verbal or nonverbal; verbal messages can be transmitted by *written communication or by speaking, as well as by a variety of *telecommunications. Most nonverbal messages between human beings are in the form of body language. Vocal devices, such as intonation, evade capture in written form. Communication can in this way involve a mixture of verbal and nonverbal messages, and also a blend of written and spoken communication. For example, a politician's speech is often published as a written transcript and actors speak a playwright's script. The development of telecommunications, including television, radio and the Internet, has led to increasingly sophisticated combinations of visual, spoken, and written 'texts'.

communications satellite relay station in space for sending telephone, television, telex, and other messages around the world. Messages are sent to and from the satellites via ground stations. Most communications satellites are in *geostationary orbit, appearing to hang fixed over one point on the Earth's surface.

communism (French *commun* 'common, general') revolutionary socialism based on the theories of the political philosophers Karl *Marx and Friedrich *Engels, emphasizing common ownership of the means of production and a planned, or *command economy. The principle held is that each should work according to his or her capacity and receive according to his or her needs. Politically, it seeks the overthrow of capitalism through a proletarian (working-class) revolution. The first communist state was the Union of Soviet Socialist Republics (USSR) after the revolution of 1917. Revolutionary socialist parties and groups united to form communist parties in other countries during the inter-war years. After World War II, communism was enforced in those countries that came under Soviet occupation. Communism as the ideology of a nation state survives in only a few countries in the 21st century, notably China, Cuba, North Korea, Laos, and Vietnam, where market forces are being encouraged in the economic sphere. China emerged after 1961 as a rival to the USSR in world communist leadership, and other countries attempted to adapt communism to their own needs. The late 1980s saw a movement for more individual freedom in many communist countries, ending in the abolition or overthrow of communist rule in Eastern European countries and Mongolia, and further state repression in China. The failed hard-line coup in the USSR against President Gorbachev in 1991 resulted in the abandonment of communism there. However, in December 1995 the reform-socialist Communist Party of the Russian Federation (CPRF) did well in Russian parliamentary elections, with the party's leader,

Gennady Zyuganov, running high in the opinion polls. Reform communist parties have also recovered some strength in other states in central and Eastern Europe, forming governments.

Communism Peak alternative form of Pik Kommunizma, the highest mountain in the *Pamirs.

community in ecology, an assemblage (group) of plants, animals, and other organisms living within a defined area. Communities are usually named by reference to a dominant feature, such as characteristic plant species (for example, a beech-wood community), or a prominent physical feature (for example, a freshwater-pond community).

community in the social sciences, the sense of identity, purpose, and companionship that comes from belonging to a particular place, organization, or social group. The idea dominated sociological thinking in the first half of the 20th century, and inspired academic courses in **community studies**.

Community law law of the member states of the *European Union, as adopted by the Council of Ministers. The *European Court of Justice interprets and applies EU law. Community law forms part of the law of states and prevails over national law. In the UK, community law became effective after enactment of the European Communities Act 1972.

commutator device in a DC (direct-current) electric motor that reverses the current flowing in the armature coils as the armature rotates. A DC generator, or *dynamo, uses a commutator to convert the AC (alternating current) generated in the armature coils into DC. A commutator consists of opposite pairs of conductors insulated from one another, and contact to an external circuit is provided by carbon or metal brushes.

Comoros

National name: *Jumhuriyyat al-Qumur al-Itthadiyah al-Islamiyah* (Arabic), *République fédérale islamique des Comores* (French)/*Federal Islamic Republic of the Comoros*

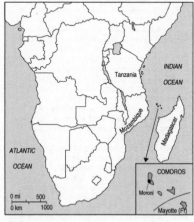

Area: 1,862 sq km/718 sq mi
Capital: Moroni
Major towns/cities: Mutsamudu, Domoni, Fomboni, Mitsamiouli

Physical features: comprises the volcanic islands of Njazídja, Nzwani, and Mwali (formerly Grande Comore, Anjouan, Moheli); at northern end of Mozambique Channel in Indian Ocean between Madagascar and coast of Africa
Head of state and government: Azali Assoumani from 1999
Political system: military
Political executive: military
Political parties: National Union for Democracy in the Comoros (UNDC), Islamic, nationalist; Rally for Democracy and Renewal (RDR), left of centre
Currency: Comorian franc
GNI per capita (PPP): (US$) 1,640 (2002 est)
Exports: vanilla, cloves, ylang-ylang, essences, copra, coffee. Principal market: France 38.6% (2000)
Population: 768,000 (2003 est)
Language: Arabic, French (both official), Comorian (a Swahili and Arabic dialect), Makua
Religion: Muslim; Islam is the state religion
Life expectancy: 59 (men); 62 (women) (2000–05)
Chronology
5th century AD: First settled by Malay-Polynesian immigrants.
7th century: Converted to Islam by Arab seafarers and fell under the rule of local sultans.
late 16th century: First visited by European navigators.
1886: Moheli island in south became a French protectorate.
1904: Slave trade abolished, ending influx of Africans.
1912: Grande Comore and Anjouan, the main islands, joined Moheli to become a French colony, which was attached to Madagascar from 1914.
1947: Became a French Overseas Territory separate from Madagascar.
1961: Internal self-government achieved.
1975: Independence achieved from France, but island of Mayotte to the southeast voted to remain part of France. Joined the United Nations.
1976: President Ahmed Abdallah was overthrown in a coup by Ali Soilih; relations deteriorated with France as a Maoist-Islamic socialist programme was pursued.
1978: Soilih was killed by French mercenaries. A federal Islamic republic was proclaimed, with exiled Abdallah restored as president; diplomatic relations re-established with France.
1979: The Comoros became a one-party state; powers of the federal government increased.
1989: Abdallah killed by French mercenaries who, under French and South African pressure, turned authority over to French administration; Said Muhammad Djohar became president in a multiparty democracy.
1995: Djohar was overthrown in a coup led by Denard, who was persuaded to withdraw by French troops.
1997: Secessionist rebels took control of the island of Anjouan.
1999: The government was overthrown by an army coup, after granting greater autonomy to the islands of Anjouan and Moheli. The new president was Colonel Azali Assoumani.
2000: A coup against the military government was foiled. Hamada Madi was appointed prime minister.
2001: The Organization of African Unity (OAU; later African Union) brokered a deal between the government and the secessionist islands of Anjouan and Moheli.
2002: The presidential election for the Union of Comoros was marred by violence. It was held on Grand Comore, which was granted first turn for the rotating presidency of the Union under the December 2001 constitution. The military ruler, Azali Assoumani, won more than 80% of the vote. Although the electoral commission cancelled the results due to an opposition boycott, Assoumani took up the position of president.
2003: An agreement on power-sharing was signed by the leaders of the three semi-autonomous islands.
2004: Elections were held for the assemblies on the semi-autonomous islands and for the national assembly. The first federal government was named.
2005: President Assoumani visited France, the first visit by a Comoran leader for 30 years.

compact disc *or* **CD** disk for storing digital information, about 12 cm/4.5 in across, mainly used for music, when it can have over an hour's playing time. A laser beam etches the compact disc with microscopic pits that carry a digital code representing the sounds; the pitted surface is then coated with aluminium. During playback, a laser beam reads the code and produces signals that are changed into near-exact replicas of the original sounds.

company in economics, a number of people grouped together as a business enterprise. Types of company include public limited companies, partnerships, joint ventures, sole proprietorships, and branches of foreign companies. Most companies are private and, unlike public companies, cannot offer their shares to the general public.

compass any instrument for finding direction. The most commonly used is a *magnetic compass, consisting of a thin piece of magnetic material with the north-seeking pole indicated, free to rotate on a pivot and mounted on a compass card on which the points of the compass are marked. When the compass is properly adjusted and used, the north-seeking pole will point to the magnetic north, from which true north can be found from tables of magnetic corrections.

compensation point in biology, the point at which there is just enough light for a plant to survive. At this point all the food produced by *photosynthesis is used up by *respiration. For aquatic plants, the compensation point is the depth of water at which there is just enough light to sustain life (deeper water = less light = less photosynthesis).

competition in ecology, the interaction between two or more organisms, or groups of organisms, that use a common resource in short supply. There can be competition between members of the same species and competition between members of different species. Competition invariably results in a reduction in the numbers of one or both competitors, and in *evolution contributes both to the decline of certain species and to the evolution of *adaptations.

compiler computer program that translates programs written in a *high-level language into machine code (the form in which they can be run by the computer). The compiler translates each high-level instruction into several machine-code instructions – in a process called **compilation** – and produces a complete independent program that can be run by the computer as often as required, without the original source program being present.

complementary medicine in medicine, systems of care based on methods of treatment or theories of disease that differ from those taught in most western medical schools. See *medicine, alternative.

complex in psychology, a group of ideas and feelings that have become repressed because they are distasteful to the person in whose mind they arose, but are still active in the depths of the person's unconscious mind, continuing to affect his or her life and actions, even though he or she is no longer fully aware of their existence. Typical examples include the *Oedipus complex and the *inferiority complex.

complex number in mathematics, a number written in the form $a + ib$, where a and b are *real numbers and i is the square root of -1 (that is, $i^2 = -1$); i used to be known as the 'imaginary' part of the complex number. Some equations in algebra, such as those of the form $x^2 + 5 = 0$ cannot be solved without recourse to complex numbers, because the real numbers do not include square roots of negative numbers.

Compositae daisy family, comprising dicotyledonous flowering plants characterized by flowers borne in composite heads. It is the largest family of flowering plants, the majority being herbaceous. Birds seem to favour the family for use in nest 'decoration', possibly because many species either repel or kill insects (see *pyrethrum). Species include the daisy and dandelion; food plants such as the artichoke, lettuce, and safflower; and the garden varieties of chrysanthemum, dahlia, and zinnia.

compost organic material decomposed by bacteria under controlled conditions to make a nutrient-rich natural fertilizer for use in gardening or farming. A well-made compost heap reaches a high temperature during the composting process, killing most weed seeds that might be present.

compound chemical substance made up of two or more *elements bonded together, so that they cannot be separated by physical means. Compounds are held together by ionic or covalent bonds.

compound interest interest calculated by computing the rate against the original capital plus reinvested interest each time the interest becomes due. When simple interest is calculated, only the interest on the original capital is added.

comprehensive school secondary school that admits pupils of all abilities, and therefore without any academic selection procedure. In England 86.8% of all pupils attend a comprehensive school. Other state secondary schools are middle, deemed secondary (5.2%), secondary modern (2.6%), secondary grammar (4.2%), and technical (0.1%). There were 4,462 state secondary schools in 1995 to 1996, with 3,675,600 pupils.

Compton, Denis Charles Scott (1918–1997) English cricketer and football player. He played cricket for Middlesex and England, and was a right-handed batsman of prodigious talent and great style. In the 1947 English season he scored 3,816 runs (at an average of 90.85) and 18 hundreds, records that are unlikely ever to be surpassed. As a footballer he won Football League and FA Cup winners' medals with Arsenal and played in 12 wartime internationals for England.

Compton-Burnett, Ivy (1884–1969) English novelist. She used dialogue to show reactions of small groups of characters dominated by the tyranny of family relationships. Her novels, set at the turn of the century, include *Pastors and Masters* (1925), *More Women than Men* (1933), and *Mother and Son* (1955).

computer programmable electronic device that processes data and performs calculations and other symbol-manipulation tasks. There are three types: the digital computer, which manipulates information coded as binary numbers (see *binary number system); the *analogue computer, which works with continuously varying quantities; and the **hybrid computer**, which has characteristics of both analogue and digital computers. In common usage, when someone refers to a 'computer', they tend to mean a digital computer.

computer-aided design use of computers to create and modify design drawings; see *CAD.

computer-aided manufacturing use of computers to regulate production processes in industry; see *CAM.

computer-assisted learning use of computers in education and training; see *CAL.

computer graphics use of computers to display and manipulate information in pictorial form. Input may be achieved by scanning an image, by drawing with a mouse or stylus on a graphics tablet, or by drawing directly on the screen with a light pen.

computerized axial tomography medical technique, usually known as *CAT scan, for noninvasive investigation of disease or injury.

computer program coded instructions for a computer; see *program.

Comte, (Isidore) Auguste (Marie François Xavier) (1798–1857) French philosopher regarded as the founder of sociology, a term he coined in 1830. He sought to establish sociology as an intellectual discipline, using a scientific approach ('positivism') as the basis of a new science of social order and social development.

Conakry capital, largest city, and chief port of the Republic of Guinea; population (2002 est) 1,142,500 (city), 1,587,600 (urban agglomeration). It is on the island of Tumbo, and is linked with the Kaloum Peninsula by a causeway and (from 1914) by rail with Kankan, 480 km/300 mi to the northeast. Conakry is the leading commercial and industrial centre of Guinea and one of the major exports is alumina (treated bauxite), which is mined at Fria; iron ore is mined on the nearby Kaloum Peninsula. Other industries include plastics, motor vehicle assembly, printed materials, fisheries, and tourism. Agricultural products include bananas, oranges, pineapples, palm products, and coffee.

concave of a surface, curving inwards, or away from the eye. For example, a bowl appears concave when viewed from above. In geometry, a concave polygon is one that has an interior angle greater than 180°. Concave is the opposite of *convex.

concave lens lens that possesses at least one surface that curves inwards. It is a diverging lens, spreading out those light rays that have been refracted through it. A concave lens is thinner at its centre than at its edges, and is used to correct short-sightedness (myopia).

concentration in chemistry, the amount of a substance (*solute) present in a specified amount of a solution. Either amount may be specified as a mass or a volume (liquids only). Common units used are *moles per cubic decimetre, grams per cubic decimetre, grams per 100 cubic centimetres, and grams per 100 grams.

concentration camp prison camp for civilians in wartime or under totalitarian rule. Concentration camps called *reconcentrados* were used by the Spanish in Cuba in 1896, to 'reconcentrate' Cubans in urban areas (and in which 200,000 were believed to have died), and by the British during the Second Boer War in South Africa in 1899 for the detention of Afrikaner women and children (with the subsequent deaths of more than 20,000 people). A system of hundreds of concentration camps was developed by the Nazis in Germany and occupied Europe (1933–45) to imprison Jews and political and ideological opponents after Adolf *Hitler became chancellor in January 1933. The most infamous camps in World War II were the extermination camps of *Auschwitz, Belsen, *Dachau, Maidanek, Sobibor, and Treblinka. The total number of people who died at the camps exceeded 6 million, and some inmates were subjected to medical experimentation before being killed.

Concepción industrial city in south-central Chile, 350 km/217 mi southwest of Santiago; situated on the north bank of the Bió-Bió River, near its mouth; population (1992) 330,400. It is Chile's third-largest city and capital of Concepción province and of Bió-Bió region. The city is a tourist resort and lies in a rich agricultural district. Industries include coal (from the pits on the Península de Lebú), steel, glass, cement, paper, and textiles. Most of Chile's coal is mined in the vicinity. Its port, Talcahuano, 15 km/9 mi to the north, is Chile's most important naval base.

conceptual art *or* **concept art** *or* **conceptualism** type of modern art in which the idea or ideas that a work expresses are considered its essential point, with its visual appearance being of secondary (often negligible) importance. Conceptual art challenges the validity of traditional art, and claims that the materials used and the product of the process are unnecessary. As the idea or ideas are of prime significance, conceptual art is made up of information, including perhaps a written proposal, photographs, documents, and maps. The term has come to encompass all art forms outside traditional painting or sculpture, such as video art and *performance art.

concertina musical instrument, a portable reed organ related to the *accordion but smaller in size and hexagonal in shape, with buttons for keys. Metal reeds are blown by wind from pleated bellows which are opened and closed by the player's hands. It was invented in England in the 19th century.

concerto composition, traditionally in three movements, for solo instrument (or instruments) and orchestra. It developed during the 18th century from the concerto grosso form for orchestra, in which a group of solo instruments (concerto) is contrasted with a full orchestra (ripieno).

concordance book containing an alphabetical list of the important words in a major work, with reference to the places in which they occur. The first concordance was one for the Latin Vulgate Bible compiled by a Dominican monk in the 13th century.

concordat agreement regulating relations between the papacy and a secular government, for example, that for France between Pius VII and the emperor Napoleon, which lasted from 1801 to 1905; Mussolini's concordat, which lasted from 1929 to 1978 and safeguarded the position of the church in Italy; and one of 1984 in Italy in which Roman Catholicism ceased to be the Italian state religion.

concrete building material composed of cement, stone, sand, and water. It has been used since Roman times. Since the late 19th century, it has been increasingly employed as an economical alternative to materials such as brick and wood, and has been combined with steel to increase its tension capacity.

concrete music see *musique concrète.

concussion temporary unconsciousness resulting from a blow to the head. It is often followed by amnesia for events immediately preceding the blow.

condensation conversion of a vapour to a liquid. This is frequently achieved by letting the vapour come into contact with a cold surface. It is the process by which water vapour turns into fine water droplets to form a *cloud.

condensation polymerization *polymerization reaction in which one or more monomers, with more than one reactive functional group, combine to form a polymer with the elimination of water or another small molecule.

condenser laboratory apparatus used to condense vapours back to liquid so that the liquid can be recovered. It is used in *distillation and in reactions where the liquid mixture can be kept boiling without the loss of solvent.

conditioning in psychology, two major principles of behaviour modification. In **classical conditioning**, described by Russian psychologist Ivan Pavlov, a new stimulus can evoke an automatic response by being repeatedly associated with a stimulus that naturally provokes that response. For example, the sound of a bell repeatedly associated with food will eventually trigger salivation, even if sounded without food being presented. In **operant conditioning**, described by US psychologists Edward Lee Thorndike (1874–1949) and B F Skinner, the frequency of a voluntary response can be increased by following it with a reinforcer or reward.

condom *or* **sheath** *or* **prophylactic** barrier contraceptive, made of rubber, which fits over an erect penis and holds in the sperm produced by ejaculation. It is an effective means of preventing pregnancy if used carefully, preferably with a *spermicide. A condom with spermicide is 97% effective; one without spermicide is 85% effective as a contraceptive. Condoms can also give some protection against sexually transmitted diseases, including AIDS.

condor name given to two species of birds in separate genera. The **Andean condor** *Vultur gryphus*, has a wingspan up to 3 m/10 ft, weighs up to 13 kg/28 lb, and can reach up to 1.2 m/3.8 ft in length. It is black, with some white on the wings and a white frill at the base of the neck. It lives in the Andes at heights of up to 4,500 m/14,760 ft, and along the South American coast, and feeds mainly on carrion. The **Californian condor** *Gymnogyps californianus* is a similar bird, with a wingspan of about 3 m/10 ft. It feeds entirely on carrion, and is on the verge of extinction.

conductance ability of a material to carry an electrical current, usually given the symbol G. For a direct current, it is the reciprocal of *resistance: a conductor of resistance R has a conductance of $1/R$. For an alternating current, conductance is the resistance R divided by the *impedance Z: $G = R/Z$. Conductance was formerly expressed in reciprocal ohms (or mhos); the SI unit is the *siemens (S).

conduction, electrical flow of charged particles through a material giving rise to electric current. Conduction in metals involves the flow of negatively charged free *electrons. Conduction in gases and some liquids involves the flow of *ions that carry positive charges in one direction and negative charges in the other. Conduction in a *semiconductor such as silicon involves the flow of electrons and positive holes.

conduction, heat flow of heat energy through a material without the movement of any part of the material itself (compare *conduction, electrical). Heat energy is present in all materials in the form of the *kinetic energy of their constituent vibrating particles, and may be conducted from one particle to the next in the form of this vibration.

conductor any material that conducts heat or electricity (as opposed to an insulator, or nonconductor). A good conductor has a high electrical or heat conductivity, and is generally a substance rich in loosely-held free electrons, such as a metal. Copper and aluminium are good conductors. A poor conductor (such as the non-metals glass, porcelain, and rubber) has few free electrons and resists the flow of electricity or heat. *Carbon is exceptional in being non-metallic and yet (in some of its forms) a relatively good conductor of heat and electricity. Substances such as *silicon and *germanium, with intermediate conductivities that are improved by heat, light, or impurities, are known as *semiconductors.

cone in botany, the reproductive structure of the conifers and cycads; also known as a strobilus. It consists of a central axis surrounded by numerous, overlapping, scalelike, modified leaves (sporophylls) that bear the reproductive organs. Usually there are separate male and female cones, the former bearing pollen sacs containing pollen grains, and the larger female cones bearing the ovules that contain the ova or egg cells. The pollen is carried from male to female cones by the wind (anemophily). The seeds develop within the female cone and are released as the scales open in dry atmospheric conditions, which favour seed dispersal.

cone in geometry, a pyramid with a circular base. If the point (vertex) is directly above the centre of the circle, it is known as a **right circular cone**. The *volume (V) of this cone is given by the formula

$$V = \tfrac{1}{3}\pi r^2 h$$

where h is the perpendicular height and r is the base radius.

Confederacy in US history, popular name for the **Confederate States of America**, the government established by 7 (later 11) Southern states in February 1861 when they seceded from the Union, precipitating the American *Civil War. Richmond, Virginia, was the capital, and Jefferson Davis the president. The Confederacy fell after its army was defeated in 1865 and General Robert E *Lee surrendered.

Confederation, Articles of in US history, the initial means by which the 13 former British colonies created

a form of national government based on a loose confederation of states. Ratified in 1781, the articles established a unicameral legislature, Congress, with limited powers of raising revenue, regulating currency, and conducting foreign affairs. Fearing the consequences of a powerful central government, the articles recognized state sovereignty. However, because the individual states retained significant autonomy, the confederation was unmanageable. The articles were superseded by the US Constitution, ratified in 1788.

confidence vote in politics, a test of support for the government in the legislature. In political systems modelled on that of the UK, the survival of a government depends on assembly support. The opposition may move a vote of 'no confidence'; if the vote is carried, it requires the government, by convention, to resign.

Confucianism body of beliefs and practices based on the Chinese classics and supported by the authority of the philosopher Confucius. The origin of things is seen in the union of **yin** and **yang**, the passive and active principles. Human relationships follow the patriarchal pattern. For more than 2,000 years Chinese political government, social organization, and individual conduct was shaped by Confucian principles. In 1912, Confucian philosophy, as a basis for government, was dropped by the state.

Confucius (551–479 BC) Chinese **Kong Fu Zi** or **K'ung Fu Tzu**; born Kong Qiu or K'ung Ch'iu, (Chinese *Kong Fu Zi*, 'Kong the master') Chinese sage whose name is given to the ethical system of Confucianism. He placed emphasis on moral order and observance of the established patriarchal family and social relationships of authority, obedience, and mutual respect. His emphasis on tradition and ethics attracted a growing number of pupils during his lifetime. *The Analects of Confucius*, a compilation of his teachings, was published after his death.

conga Latin American dance, originally from Cuba, in which the participants form a winding line, take three steps forwards or backwards, and then kick.

congenital disease in medicine, a disease that is present at birth. It is not necessarily genetic in origin; for example, congenital herpes may be acquired by the baby as it passes through the mother's birth canal.

conger any large marine eel of the family Congridae, especially the genus *Conger*. Conger eels live in shallow water, hiding in crevices during the day and active by night, feeding on fish and crabs. They are valued for food and angling.

Congo, Democratic Republic of
or **Congo (Kinshasa)**; formerly **Republic of Congo** (1960–64), **Zaire** (1971–97)
National name: *République Démocratique du Congo/Democratic Republic of Congo*
Area: 2,344,900 sq km/905,366 sq mi
Capital: Kinshasa
Major towns/cities: Lubumbashi, Kananga, Mbuji-Mayi, Kisangani, Kolwezi, Likasi, Boma
Major ports: Matadi, Kalemie
Physical features: Congo River basin has tropical rainforest (second-largest remaining in world) and savannah; mountains in east and west; lakes Tanganyika, Albert, Edward; Ruwenzori Range
Head of state and government: Joseph Kabila from 2001

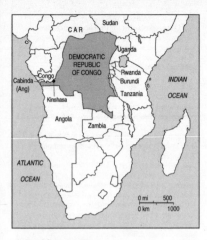

Political system: military
Political executive: military
Political parties: Popular Movement of the Revolution (MPR), African socialist; Democratic Forces of Congo–Kinshasa (formerly Sacred Union, an alliance of some 130 opposition groups), moderate, centrist; Union for Democracy and Social Progress (UPDS), left of centre; Congolese National Movement–Lumumba (MNC), left of centre
Currency: congolese franc
GNI per capita (PPP): (US$) 580 (2002 est)
Exports: mineral products (mainly copper, cobalt, industrial diamonds, and petroleum), agricultural products (chiefly coffee). Principal market: Belgium–Luxembourg 62.2% (2001)
Population: 52,771,000 (2003 est)
Language: French (official), Swahili, Lingala, Kikongo, Tshiluba (all national languages), over 200 other languages
Religion: Roman Catholic 41%, Protestant 32%, Kimbanguist 13%, animist 10%, Muslim 1–5%
Life expectancy: 41 (men); 43 (women) (2000–05)
Chronology
13th century: Rise of Kongo Empire, centred on banks of the Congo River.
1483: First visited by the Portuguese, who named the area Zaire (from Zadi, 'big water') and converted local rulers to Christianity.
16th–17th centuries: Great development of slave trade by Portuguese, Dutch, British, and French merchants, initially supplied by Kongo intermediaries.
18th century: Rise of Luba state, in southern copper belt of north Katanga, and Lunda, in Kasai region in central south.
mid-19th century: Eastern Zaire invaded by Arab slave traders from East Africa.
1874–77: Welsh-born US explorer Henry Morton Stanley navigated Congo River to Atlantic Ocean.
1879–87: Stanley engaged by King Leopold II of Belgium to sign protection treaties with local chiefs and the 'Congo Free State' was awarded to Leopold by 1884–85 Berlin Conference; great expansion in rubber export, using forced labour.

1908: Leopold was forced to relinquish personal control of Congo Free State, after international condemnation of human-rights abuses. Became a colony of the Belgian Congo and important exporter of minerals.
1959: Riots in Kinshasa (Léopoldville) persuaded Belgium to decolonize rapidly.
1960: Independence achieved as Republic of the Congo. Civil war broke out between central government based in Kinshasa (Léopoldville) with Joseph Kasavubu as president, and rich mining province of Katanga.
1961: Former prime minister Patrice Lumumba was murdered in Katanga; fighting between mercenaries engaged by Katanga secessionist leader Moise Tshombe, and United Nations (UN) troops; Kasai and Kivu provinces also sought (briefly) to secede.
1963: Katanga secessionist war ended; Tshombe forced into exile.
1964: Tshombe returned from exile to become prime minister; pro-Marxist groups took control of eastern Zaire. The country was renamed the Democratic Republic of Congo.
1965: Western-backed Col Sese Seko Mobutu seized power in coup, ousting Kasavubu and Tshombe.
1971: Country renamed Republic of Zaire, with Mobutu as president and *authenticité* (Africanization) policy launched.
1972: Mobutu's Popular Movement of the Revolution (MPR) became the only legal political party. Katanga province was renamed Shaba.
1974: Foreign-owned businesses and plantations seized by Mobutu and given to his political allies.
1977: Zairean guerrillas invaded Shaba province from Angola, but were repulsed by Moroccan, French, and Belgian paratroopers.
1980s: The collapse in world copper prices increased foreign debts, and international creditors forced a series of austerity programmes.
1991: After antigovernment riots, Mobutu agreed to end the ban on multiparty politics and share power with the opposition.
1993: Rival pro- and anti-Mobutu governments were created.
1994: There was an influx of Rwandan refugees.
1995: There was secessionist activity in Shaba and Kasai provinces and interethnic warfare in Kivu, adjoining Rwanda in the east.
1996: Thousands of refugees were allowed to return to Rwanda.
1997: Mobutu was ousted by the rebel forces of Laurent Kabila, who declared himself president and changed the name of Zaire back to the Democratic Republic of the Congo. There was fighting between army factions.
1998: There was a rebellion by Tutsi-led forces, backed by Rwanda and Uganda, against President Kabila; government troops aided by Angola and Zimbabwe put down the rebellion. A constituent assembly was appointed prior to a general election. UN-urged peace talks and a ceasefire agreed by rebel forces failed.
1999: A peace deal, signed by both the government and rebel factions, was broken in November with fighting in the north of the country, and a reported bombing by the government of the centre in an attempt to free 700 Zimbabwean troops besieged by rebels.
2000: The war between government and rebel soldiers intensified. President Kabila walked out of a peace

conference held in Lusaka, Zambia and called for a summit with Uganda, Rwanda, and Burundi. Ugandan-backed rebels made gains in the northwest of the country. Kabila allowed some United Nations (UN) troops into the country, but hindered the operation.

2001: In January President Kabila was assassinated in suspicious circumstances, allegedly by a bodyguard. He was succeeded by his son, Joseph. Peace talks with rebel factions took place in Zambia. More armed UN peacekeeping troops were deployed.

2002: Belgium apologized, for the first time, for the 1961 murder of Patrice Lumumba. President Joseph Kabila and Ugandan president Yoweri Museveni signed a peace agreement providing for the withdrawal of Ugandan troops from the country, and Rwanda completed its troop withdrawal. The government signed a peace deal with the country's two main rebel groups, providing for the establishment of a democracy.

2003: Despite the signing of a power-sharing agreement between the government of President Joseph Kabila and rebel groups, a European-led 1,400-strong rapid reaction force began to deploy to Ituri province in an attempt to deter further tribal massacres of civilians in the ongoing civil war. An interim parliament was launched.

2004: There were reports of an attempted coup in Kinshasa and rebel soldiers occupied Bukavu, an eastern town. There was fighting in the east between the Congolese army and militia from a former pro-Rwanda rebel group.

Congo, Republic of
or Congo (Brazzaville)

National name: *République du Congo/Republic of Congo*

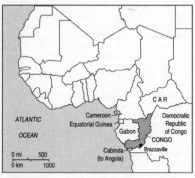

Area: 342,000 sq km/132,046 sq mi
Capital: Brazzaville
Major towns/cities: Pointe-Noire, Nkayi, Loubomo, Bouenza, Mossendjo, Ouesso, Owando
Major ports: Pointe-Noire
Physical features: narrow coastal plain rises to central plateau, then falls into northern basin; Congo River on the border with the Democratic Republic of Congo; half the country is rainforest
Head of state and government: Denis Sassou-Nguessou from 1997
Political system: nationalistic socialist
Political executive: unlimited presidency
Political parties: Pan-African Union for Social

Democracy (UPADS), moderate, left of centre; Congolese Movement for Democracy and Integral Development (MCDDI), moderate, left of centre; Congolese Labour Party (PCT), left wing
Currency: franc CFA
GNI per capita (PPP): (US$) 700 (2002 est)
Exports: petroleum and petroleum products, saw logs and veneer logs, veneer sheets, sugar. Principal market: USA 17.2% (2001)
Population: 3,724,000 (2003 est)
Language: French (official), Kongo, Monokutuba and Lingala (both patois), and other dialects
Religion: Christian 50%, animist 48%, Muslim 2%
Life expectancy: 47 (men); 50 (women) (2000–05)

Chronology
late 15th century: First visited by Portuguese explorers, at which time the Bakongo (a six-state confederation centred south of the Congo River in Angola) and Bateke, both Bantu groups, were the chief kingdoms.
16th century: The Portuguese, in collaboration with coastal peoples, exported slaves from the interior to plantations in Brazil and São Tomé; missionaries spread Roman Catholicism.
1880: French explorer Pierre Savorgnan de Brazza established French claims to coastal region, with the makoko (king) of the Bateke accepting French protection.
1905: There was international outrage at revelations of the brutalities of forced labour as ivory and rubber resources were ruthlessly exploited by private concessionaries.
1910: As Moyen-Congo became part of French Equatorial Africa, which also comprised Gabon and the Central African Republic, with the capital at Brazzaville.
1920s: More than 17,000 were killed as forced labour was used to build the Congo-Ocean railway; first Bakongo political organization founded.
1940–44: Supported the 'Free French' anti-Nazi resistance cause during World War II, Brazzaville serving as capital for Gen Charles de Gaulle's forces.
1946: Became autonomous, with a territorial assembly and representation in French parliament.
1960: Achieved independence from France, with Abbé Fulbert Youlou, a moderate Catholic Bakongo priest, as the first president.
1963: Alphonse Massamba-Débat became president and a single-party state was established under the socialist National Revolutionary Movement (MNR).
1968: A military coup, led by Capt Marien Ngouabi, ousted Massamba-Débat.
1970: A Marxist People's Republic declared, with Ngouabi's PCT the only legal party.
1977: Ngouabi was assassinated in a plot by Massamba-Débat, who was executed.
early 1980s: Petroleum production increased fivefold.
1990: The PCT abandoned Marxist-Leninism and promised multiparty politics and market-centred reforms in an economy crippled by foreign debt.
1992: Multiparty elections gave the coalition dominated by the Pan-African Union for Social Democracy (UPADS) an assembly majority, with Pascal Lissouba elected president.
1995: A new broad-based government was formed, including opposition groups; market-centred economic reforms were instigated, including privatization.
1997: Violence between factions continued despite

the unity government. Sassou-Nguesso took over the presidency.

2002: Sassou-Nguesso was re-elected. Fighting continued against rebels.

2003: The government signed a peace agreement with rebels.

2004: Congo was removed from the Kimberley Process, a list of countries dealing legitimately in diamonds.

Congo River *or* **Zaire River** second-longest river in Africa, rising near the Zambia–Democratic Republic of Congo border (and known as the **Lualaba River** in the upper reaches) and flowing 4,500 km/2,800 mi to the Atlantic Ocean, running in a great curve that crosses the Equator twice, and discharging a volume of water second only to the River Amazon. The chief tributaries are the Ubangi, Sangha, and Kasai.

Congregationalism form of church government adopted by those Protestant Christians known as Congregationalists, who let each congregation manage its own affairs. The first Congregationalists established themselves in London, England, and were called the Brownists after Robert Browne, who defined the congregational principle in 1580. They opposed King James I and were supporters of Oliver *Cromwell. They became one of the most important forces in the founding of New England.

Congress national legislature of the USA, consisting of the House of Representatives (435 members, apportioned to the states of the Union on the basis of population, and elected for two-year terms) and the Senate (100 senators, two for each state, elected for six years, one-third elected every two years). Both representatives and senators are elected by direct popular vote. Congress meets in Washington DC, in the Capitol Building. An *act of Congress is a bill passed by both houses.

Congress Party Indian political party, founded in 1885 as the Indian National Congress. It led the movement to end British rule and was the governing party from independence in 1947 until 1977, when Indira Gandhi lost the leadership she had held since 1966. Congress also held power from 1980 to 1989 and from 1991 to 1996. Heading a splinter group, known as **Congress (I)** ('I' for Indira), she achieved an overwhelming victory in the elections of 1980, and reduced the main Congress Party to a minority. The 'I' was dropped from the name in 1993 following the assassination of Rajiv *Gandhi in 1991, and a small split occurred in the party in 1995.

Congreve, William (1670–1729) English dramatist and poet. His first success was the comedy *The Old Bachelor* (1693), followed by *The Double Dealer* (1694), *Love for Love* (1695), the tragedy *The Mourning Bride* (1697), and *The Way of the World* (1700). His plays, which satirize and criticize the social affectations (show of manners) of the time, are characterized by elegant wit and wordplay, and complex plots.

congruent in geometry, having the same shape and size (and area), as applied to two-dimensional or solid figures. With plane congruent figures, one figure will fit on top of the other exactly, though this may first require rotation, translation, or reflection of one of the figures.

conic section curve obtained when a conical surface is intersected by a plane. If the intersecting plane cuts both extensions of the cone, it yields a *hyperbola; if it is parallel to the side of the cone, it produces a *parabola. Other intersecting planes produce *circles or *ellipses.

conifer any of a large number of cone-bearing trees or shrubs. They are often pyramid-shaped, with leaves that are either scaled or needle-shaped; most are evergreen. Conifers include pines, spruces, firs, yews, junipers, monkey puzzles, and larches. (Order Coniferales.)

conjugation in biology, temporary union of two single cells (or hyphae in fungi) with at least one of them receiving genetic material from the other: the bacterial equivalent of sexual reproduction. A fragment of the *DNA from one bacterium is passed along a thin tube, the pilus, into another bacterium.

conjunction in astronomy, alignment of two celestial bodies as seen from Earth. A superior planet (or other object) is in conjunction when it lies behind the Sun. An inferior planet (or other object) comes to **inferior conjunction** when it passes between the Earth and the Sun; it is at **superior conjunction** when it passes behind the Sun. **Planetary conjunction** takes place when a planet is closely aligned with another celestial object, such as the Moon, a star, or another planet.

conjunctivitis inflammation of the conjunctiva, the delicate membrane that lines the inside of the eyelids and covers the front of the eye. Symptoms include redness, swelling, and a watery or pus-filled discharge. It may be caused by infection, allergy, or other irritant.

Connacht *or* **Connaught** historic province of the Republic of Ireland, comprising the counties of Galway, Leitrim, Mayo, Roscommon, and Sligo; area 17,130 sq km/6,612 sq mi; population (2002 est) 469,100. The chief towns are Galway, Roscommon, Castlebar, Sligo, and Carrick-on-Shannon. Mainly lowland, it is agricultural and stock-raising country, with poor land in the west.

Connecticut called the **Constitution State** or the **Nutmeg State**, (American Indian *Quinnehtukqut* 'beside the long tidal river') state in *New England, USA, bordered to the north by *Massachusetts, to the east by *Rhode Island, to the west and southwest by *New York State, and to the south by Long Island Sound on the Atlantic Ocean; area 12,548 sq km/4,845 sq mi; population (2000) 3,405,600; capital Hartford. It was nicknamed the Constitution State after the Fundamental Orders of 1638 under which it was originally governed, regarded as a forerunner of American constitutionalism. Connecticut is the third smallest state in the USA, roughly rectangular in shape, with a narrow strip of land in the southwest projecting westwards to within 19 km/12 mi of New York City; New York's Long and Fishers islands lie opposite Connecticut in Long Island Sound. The Connecticut River crosses the centre of the state, and the Pawcatuck River forms part of the state boundary with Rhode Island. The state is the centre of the US insurance industry, and is also a manufacturer of military technology. Its largest city is Bridgeport; other major cities and metropolitan areas are Danbury, New Haven, New London, Norwich, Stamford, Waterbury, and Worcester. One of the original *Thirteen Colonies, Connecticut ratified the US Constitution in 1788, becoming the fifth state in the Union.

connective tissue in animals, tissue made up of a noncellular substance, the extracellular matrix, in which some cells are embedded. Skin, bones, tendons, cartilage, and adipose tissue (fat) are the main connective tissues. There are also small amounts of connective tissue in organs such as the brain and liver, where they maintain shape and structure.

Connery, Sean (1930–) born Thomas Sean Connery, Scottish film actor. He was the first interpreter of James Bond in several films based on the spy thrillers of Ian Fleming, including *Dr No* (1962), *From Russia with Love* (1963), and *Goldfinger* (1964). He enjoyed success as a mature actor in such films as *The Name of the Rose* (1986), *Highlander* (1986), and *Indiana Jones and the Last Crusade* (1989). He won an Academy Award for his supporting performance in the crime thriller *The Untouchables* (1987). In 1998 he won the BAFTA Lifetime Achievement Award.

Connors, Jimmy (1952–) born James Scott Connors, US tennis player who won the Wimbledon title in 1974 and 1982, and subsequently won ten Grand Slam events. He was one of the first players to popularize the two-handed backhand, and won 78 career titles.

conquistador (Spanish 'conqueror') any of the early Spanish conquerors in the Americas. The title is applied in particular to those leaders who overthrew the indigenous empires of Peru and Mexico, and other parts of Central and South America. They include Hernán *Cortés, who subjugated Mexico; Francisco *Pizarro, conqueror of Peru with Diego de Almagro; and Juan *Ponce de León.

Conrad, Joseph (1857–1924) pen-name of Teodor Józef Konrad Nalecz Korzeniowski, British novelist, born in Ukraine of Polish parents. His greatest works include the novels *Lord Jim* (1900), *Nostromo* (1904), *The Secret Agent* (1907), and *Under Western Eyes* (1911), also the short novels *Heart of Darkness* (1902) and *The Shadow Line* (1917). These combine a vivid and sensuous evocation of various lands and seas with a rigorous, humane scrutiny of moral dilemmas, pitfalls, and desperation.

conscientious objector person refusing compulsory service, usually military, on moral, religious, or political grounds.

conscription legislation for all able-bodied male citizens (and female in some countries, such as Israel) to serve with the armed forces. It originated in France in 1792, and in the 19th and 20th centuries became the established practice in almost all European states. Modern conscription systems often permit alternative national service for conscientious objectors.

conservation in the life sciences, action taken to protect and preserve the natural world, usually from pollution, overexploitation, and other harmful features of human activity. The late 1980s saw a great increase in public concern for the environment, with membership of conservation groups, such as Friends of the Earth, Greenpeace, and the US Sierra Club, rising sharply and making the *green movement an increasingly-powerful political force. Globally the most important issues include the depletion of atmospheric ozone by the action of *chlorofluorocarbons (CFCs), the build-up of carbon dioxide in the atmosphere (thought to contribute to the *greenhouse effect), and *deforestation.

conservation of energy principle that states that in a chemical reaction, the total amount of energy in the system remains unchanged. Energy can be transferred from one form into another but cannot be created or destroyed.

conservation of mass in chemistry, the principle that states that in a chemical reaction the sum of all the masses of the substances involved in the reaction (reactants) is equal to the sum of all of the masses of the substances produced by the reaction (products) – that is, no matter is gained or lost.

conservatism approach to government favouring the preservation of existing institutions and identified with a number of Western political parties, such as the British Conservative, US Republican, German Christian Democratic, and Australian Liberal parties. It tends to favour a 'practical' rather than a theoretical approach but generally emphasizes free-enterprise capitalism, minimal government intervention in the economy, strict law and order, and the importance of national traditions. In the UK, modern conservatism, under the ideological influence of *Thatcherism, has become increasingly extremist, attacking established institutions and promoting free-market economies.

Conservative Party UK political party, one of the two historic British parties; the name replaced **Tory** in general use from 1830 onwards. Traditionally the party of landed interests (those owning substantial land or property), it broadened its political base under Benjamin *Disraeli's leadership in the 19th century. In recent history, the Conservative Party was in power under Margaret *Thatcher (1979–90) and John *Major (1990–97). After the party's defeat in the 1997 general election, John Major resigned as party leader and was succeeded by William Hague, who in turn resigned following defeat in the 2001 general election. He was replaced by Iain *Duncan Smith. The party's Central Office is located in Smith Square, London. In 2001, the party had 325,000 members.

Constable, John (1776–1837) English artist; one of the greatest landscape painters of the 19th century. He painted scenes of his native Suffolk, including *The Haywain* (1821; National Gallery, London), as well as castles, cathedrals, landscapes, and coastal scenes in other parts of Britain. Constable inherited the Dutch tradition of sombre realism, in particular the style of Jacob *Ruisdael. He aimed to capture the momentary changes of the weather as well as to create monumental images of British scenery, as in *The White Horse* (1819; Frick Collection, New York) and *Salisbury Cathedral from the Bishop's Grounds* (1827; Victoria and Albert Museum, London).

Constance, Lake German **Bodensee**, lake bounded by Germany, Austria, and Switzerland, through which the River Rhine flows; area 539 sq km/208 sq mi. It is about 72 km/45 mi long, 13 km/8 mi wide, and lies 396 m/1,300 ft above sea level. At its northwestern end it divides into two lakes, the northern being the Überlingen, and the southern – joined to Lake Constance by a short stretch of the River Rhine – the Untersee. The main part of the lake is known as the Obersee.

constant in mathematics, a fixed quantity or one that does not change its value in relation to *variables. For example, in the algebraic expression $y^2 = 5x - 3$, the numbers 3 and 5 are constants. In physics, certain quantities are regarded as universal constants, such as the speed of light in a vacuum.

constant composition, law of in chemistry, the law that states that the proportions of the amounts of the elements in a pure compound are always the same and are independent of the method by which the compound was produced.

Constantine the Great (c. AD 285–337) First Christian emperor of Rome and founder of Constantinople. He defeated Maxentius, joint emperor of Rome in AD 312, and in 313 formally recognized Christianity. As sole emperor of the west of the empire, he defeated Licinius, emperor of the east, to become ruler of the Roman world in 324. He presided over the church's first council at Nicaea in 325. Constantine moved his capital to Byzantium on the Bosporus in 330, renaming it Constantinople (now Istanbul).

Constantinople ancient city founded by the Greeks as Byzantium in about 660 BC and refounded by the Roman emperor Constantine (I) the Great in AD 330 as the capital of the Eastern Roman Empire. Constantinople (modern Istanbul, Turkey) was the impregnable bastion of the Eastern Roman Empire and the Byzantine Empire, its successor, until it fell to the Turks on 29 May 1453 after a nearly two-month siege and became the capital of the Ottoman Empire.

constellation one of the 88 areas into which the sky is divided for the purposes of identifying and naming celestial objects. The first constellations were simple, arbitrary patterns of stars in which early civilizations visualized gods, sacred beasts, and mythical heroes.

constipation in medicine, the infrequent emptying of the bowel. The intestinal contents are propelled by peristaltic contractions of the intestine in the digestive process. The faecal residue collects in the rectum, distending it and promoting defecation. Constipation may be due to illness, alterations in food consumption, stress, or as an adverse effect of certain drugs. An increased intake of dietary fibre (see *fibre, dietary) can alleviate constipation. Laxatives may be used to relieve temporary constipation but they should not be used routinely.

constitution body of fundamental (basic) laws of a state, laying down the system of government and defining the relations of the executive (administration), legislature (law-making body), and judiciary (courts) to each other and to the citizens. Since the French Revolution (1789–1799) almost all countries (the UK is an exception) have adopted written constitutions; that of the USA (1787) is the oldest. Of all the world's states, 69 have adopted their current constitutions in the period since 1989.

constitutional law that part of the law relating to the constitution. It sets out the rules defining the powers, limits, and rights of government. In countries without a written constitution, such as the United Kingdom, constitutional law is a mixture of legislation, judicial precedent, and accepted conventional behaviour. Agencies that maintain constitutional law include, in Britain, the law courts and House of Lords; and, in the USA, the Supreme Court.

constructivism abstract art movement that originated in Russia in about 1914 and subsequently had great influence on Western art. Constructivism usually involves industrial materials such as glass, steel, and plastic in clearly defined arrangements, but the term is difficult to define precisely, as the meaning attached to it has varied according to place and time. Some art historians distinguish between Russian (or Soviet) constructivism and the more diffuse European (or international) constructivism.

consul chief magistrate of the ancient Roman Republic, after the expulsion of the last king in 510 BC. Two consuls were elected annually by the *comitia centuriata* (assembly of the Roman people), and their names were used to date the year. With equal power they shared the full civil authority in Rome and the chief military command in the field. After the establishment of the Roman empire the office became far less important.

consumption in economics, the purchase of goods and services for final use, as opposed to spending by firms on capital goods, known as capital formation.

contact lens lens, made of soft or hard plastic, that is worn in contact with the cornea and conjunctiva of the eye, beneath the eyelid, to correct defective vision. In special circumstances, contact lenses may be used as protective shells or for cosmetic purposes, such as changing eye colour.

contempt of court behaviour that shows lack of respect for the authority of a court of law, such as disobeying a court order, breach of an injunction, or improper use of legal documents. Behaviour that disrupts, prejudices, or interferes with court proceedings either inside or outside the courtroom may also be contempt. The court may punish contempt with a fine or imprisonment.

continent any one of the seven large land masses of the Earth, as distinct from the oceans. They are Asia, Africa, North America, South America, Europe, Australia, and Antarctica. Continents are constantly moving and evolving (see *plate tectonics). A continent does not end at the coastline; its boundary is the edge of the shallow continental shelf, which may extend several hundred kilometres out to sea. Continental crust, as opposed to the crust that underlies the deep oceans, is composed of a wide variety of igneous, sedimentary, and metamorphic rocks. The rocks vary in age from recent (currently forming) to almost 4,000 million years old. Unlike the ocean crust, the continents are not only high standing, but extend to depths as great at 70 km/45 mi under high mountain ranges. Continents, as high, dry masses of rock, are present on Earth because of the density contrast between them and the rock that underlies the oceans. Continental crust is both thick and light, whereas ocean crust is thin and dense. If the crust were the same thickness and density everywhere, the entire Earth would be covered in water.

Continental Congress in US history, the federal legislature of the original 13 states, acting as a provisional government before the *American Revolution. It convened in Philadelphia from 1774 to 1789, when the US Constitution was adopted. The Second Continental Congress, convened in May 1775, was responsible for drawing up the *Declaration of Independence (1776) and, in 1777, the *Articles of Confederation.

continental drift in geology, the theory that, about 250–200 million years ago, the Earth consisted of a single large continent (*Pangaea), which subsequently broke apart to form the continents known today. The theory was first proposed in 1912 by German meteorologist Alfred Wegener, but such vast continental movements could not be satisfactorily explained or even accepted by geologists until the 1960s. (See diagram, p. 224.)

continental shelf submerged edge of a continent, a gently sloping plain that extends into the ocean. It typically has a gradient of less than 1°. When the angle of the sea bed increases to 1°–5° (usually several hundred kilometres away from land), it becomes known as the continental slope.

Continental System

200 million years ago	140 million years ago	today

continental drift The changing positions of the Earth's continents. Millions of years ago, there was a single large continent, Pangaea. This split 200 million years ago: the continents had started to move apart, to form Gondwanaland in the south and Laurasia in the north. By 50 million years ago the continents were almost in their present positions.

Continental System system of economic preference and protection within Europe from 1806 to 1813 created by the French emperor Napoleon in order to exclude British trade. Apart from its function as economic warfare, the system also reinforced the French economy at the expense of other European states. It failed owing to British naval superiority.

continuo (Italian, *basso continuo* 'continuous bass') in music, the bass line on which a keyboard player, accompanied by a bass stringed instrument, builds up a harmonic accompaniment. In 17th-century baroque music, composers wrote figures under a bass part to indicate the chords to be played (also called figured bass) rather than write out each chord in detail. This continuo part was played as a single bass line by a bass stringed instrument, such as a cello or double bass. At the same time, another continuo player filled in the harmonies by playing the chords (broken into patterns) on lute or a keyboard instrument, such as a harpsichord or organ. The role of continuo is similar to the traditional role of the bass and piano or guitar in jazz music.

continuous data in mathematics, *data that can take any of an infinite number of values between whole numbers and so may not be measured completely accurately. This type of data contrasts with *discrete data, in which the variable can only take one of a finite set of values. For example, the sizes of apples on a tree form continuous data, whereas the numbers of apples form discrete data.

Contra member of a Central American right-wing guerrilla force attempting to overthrow the democratically elected Nicaraguan Sandinista government between 1979 and 1990. The Contras, many of them mercenaries or former members of the deposed dictator Somoza's guard (see *Nicaraguan Revolution), operated mainly from bases outside Nicaragua, mostly in Honduras, with covert US funding, as revealed by the *Irangate hearings of 1986–87.

contrabassoon double-reed woodwind instrument, also known as the **double bassoon**. It is a larger version of the *bassoon, sounding an octave lower.

contraceptive any drug, device, or technique that prevents pregnancy. The contraceptive pill (the *Pill) contains female hormones that interfere with egg production or the first stage of pregnancy. The

'morning-after' pill can be taken up to 72 hours after unprotected intercourse. Barrier contraceptives include *condoms (sheaths), femidoms (a female condom), and *diaphragms, also called caps or Dutch caps; they prevent the sperm entering the cervix (neck of the womb). *Intrauterine devices, also known as IUDs or coils, cause a slight inflammation of the lining of the womb; this prevents the fertilized egg from becoming implanted. See also *family planning.

contract legal agreement between two or more parties, where each party agrees to do something. For example, a contract of employment is a legal agreement between an employer and an employee and lays out the conditions of employment. Contracts need not necessarily be written; they can be verbal contracts. In consumer law, for example, a contract is established when a good is sold.

contract bridge card game first played in 1925. From 1930 it quickly outgrew auction bridge in popularity. It is based on auction bridge, but used a different scoring system.

contractile root in botany, a thickened root at the base of a corm, bulb, or other organ that helps position it at an appropriate level in the ground. Contractile roots are found, for example, on the corms of plants of the genus *Crocus*. After they have become anchored in the soil, the upper portion contracts, pulling the plant deeper into the ground.

contralto low-register female voice, a high (falsetto) male voice, or a low-register boy's voice; also called an *alto.

control experiment essential part of a scientifically valid experiment, designed to show that the factor being tested is actually responsible for the effect observed. In the control experiment all factors, apart from the one under test, are exactly the same as in the test experiments, and all the same measurements are carried out. In drug trials, a placebo (a harmless substance) is given alongside the substance being tested in order to compare effects.

convection transfer of heat energy that involves the movement of a fluid (gas or liquid). Fluid in contact with the source of heat expands and tends to rise within the bulk of the fluid. Cooler fluid sinks to take its place, setting up a convection current. This is the principle of natural convection in many domestic hot-water systems and space heaters.

convection current current caused by the expansion of a liquid, solid, or gas as its temperature rises. The expanded material, being less dense, rises, while colder, denser material sinks. Material of neutral buoyancy moves laterally. Convection currents arise in the atmosphere above warm land masses or seas, giving rise to sea breezes and land breezes, respectively. In some heating systems, convection currents are used to carry hot water upwards in pipes.

convergent evolution *or* **convergence** in biology, the independent evolution of similar structures in species (or other taxonomic groups) that are not closely related, as a result of living in a similar way. Thus, birds and bees have wings, not because they are descended from a common winged ancestor, but because their respective ancestors independently evolved flight.

convex of a surface, curving outwards, or towards the eye. For example, the outer surface of a ball appears convex. In geometry, the term is used to describe any polygon possessing no interior angle greater than 180°. Convex is the opposite of *concave.

convex lens lens that possesses at least one surface that curves outwards. It causes light to deviate inward, bringing the rays of light to a focus, and is thus called a converging lens. A convex lens is thicker at its centre than at its edges, and is used to correct long-sightedness (hypermetropism).

conveyancing administrative process involved in transferring title to land, usually on its sale or purchase.

convolvulus *or* **bindweed** any of a group of plants belonging to the morning-glory family. They are characterized by their twining stems and by their petals, which are joined into a funnel-shaped tube. (Genus *Convolvulus*, family Convolvulaceae.)

convulsion series of violent contractions of the muscles over which the patient has no control. It may be associated with loss of consciousness. Convulsions may arise from any one of a number of causes, including brain disease (such as *epilepsy), injury, high fever, poisoning, and electrocution.

Conwy unitary authority in north Wales, created in 1996 from parts of the former counties of Clwyd and Gwynedd. **area:** 1,107 sq km/427 sq mi **towns:** Conwy (administrative headquarters), Abergele, Llandudno, Llanrwst **physical:** rivers Conwy and Elwy **features:** Snowdonia National Park; coastline of sandy beaches, including the seaside resort of Colwyn Bay; Orme's Head limestone promontories at Llandudno; Conwy Castle (1287) **population:** (2000 est) 112,700.

Cook, James (1728–1779) English naval explorer. After surveying the St Lawrence River in North America in 1759, he made three voyages: 1768–71 to Tahiti, New Zealand, and Australia; 1772–75 to the South Pacific; and 1776–79 to the South and North Pacific, attempting to find the Northwest Passage and charting the Siberian coast. He was largely responsible for Britain's initial interest in acquiring colonies in Australasia. He was killed in Hawaii early in 1779 in a scuffle with islanders.

Cook Islands group of six large and a number of smaller Polynesian islands 2,600 km/1,600 mi northeast of Auckland, New Zealand; area 290 sq km/112 sq mi; population (2001 est) 14,300. Their main products include citrus fruit, copra, bananas, pearl-shell, cultivated (black) pearls, and crafts. The islands became a self-governing overseas territory of New Zealand in 1965.

Cook Strait strait dividing North Island and South Island, New Zealand, about 30 km/19 mi in width at its narrowest point. A submarine cable carries electricity from South to North Island.

Coolidge, (John) Calvin (1872–1933) 30th president of the USA 1923–29, a Republican. As governor of Massachusetts in 1919, he was responsible for crushing a Boston police strike. As Warren *Harding's vice-president 1921–23, he succeeded to the presidency on Harding's death. He won the 1924 presidential election, and his period of office was marked by economic growth.

Cooper, Gary (Frank James) (1901–1961) US film actor. One of the great stars of the classical Hollywood era, who created a screen persona of quiet dignity, moral rectitude, and powerful action. He won Academy Awards for his performances in *Sergeant York* (1941) and *High Noon* (1952).

Cooper, Henry (1934–) English heavyweight boxer, the only man to win three Lonsdale Belts outright (1961, 1965, and 1970). He held the British heavyweight title 1959–71 and lost it to Joe Bugner. He fought for the world heavyweight title but lost in the sixth round to Muhammad Ali in 1966. He received a knighthood in the New Year's Honours list of 2000.

Cooper, James Fenimore (1789–1851) US writer, considered the first great US novelist. He wrote some 50 novels, mostly about the frontier, wilderness life, and the sea, first becoming popular with *The Spy* (1821). He is best remembered for his series of *Leatherstocking Tales*, focusing on the frontier hero Natty Bumppo and the American Indians before and after the American Revolution; they include *The Last of the Mohicans* (1826). Still popular as adventures, his novels have been reappraised for their treatment of social and moral issues in the settling of the American frontier.

cooperative business organization with limited liability where each shareholder has only one vote however many shares they own. In a worker cooperative, it is the workers who are the shareholders and own the company. The workers decide on how the company is to be run. In a consumer cooperative, consumers control the company.

cooperative movement the banding together of groups of people for mutual assistance in trade, manufacture, the supply of credit, housing, or other services. The original principles of the cooperative movement were laid down in 1844 by the Rochdale Pioneers, under the influence of Robert *Owen, and by Charles Fourier in France.

Cooperative Party former political party founded in Britain in 1917 by the cooperative movement to maintain its principles in parliamentary and local government. A written constitution was adopted in 1938. The party had strong links with the Labour Party; from 1946 Cooperative Party candidates stood in elections as Cooperative and Labour Candidates and, after the 1959 general election, agreement was reached to limit the party's candidates to 30.

coordinate in geometry, a number that defines the position of a point relative to a point or axis (reference line). *Cartesian coordinates define a point by its perpendicular distances from two or more axes drawn through a fixed point mutually at right angles to each other. *Polar coordinates define a point in a plane by its distance from a fixed point and direction from a fixed line.

coordinate geometry *or* **analytical geometry** system of geometry in which points, lines, shapes, and surfaces are represented by algebraic expressions. In plane (two-dimensional) coordinate geometry, the plane is usually defined by two axes at right angles to each other, the horizontal *x*-axis and the vertical *y*-axis, meeting at O, the origin. A point on the plane can be represented by a pair of *Cartesian coordinates, which define its position in terms of its distance along the *x*-axis and along the *y*-axis from O. These distances are, respectively, the *x* and *y* coordinates of the point.

coot freshwater bird of the genus *Fulica* in the rail family, order Gruiformes. Coots are about 38 cm/1.2 ft long, and mainly black. They have a white bill, extending up the forehead in a plate, and big feet with four lobed toes. Coots are omnivores, but feed mainly on water weed, except as chicks, when they feed on insects and other invertebrates.

Copenhagen Danish København, capital of Denmark, on the islands of Zealand and Amager; population (1995) 1,353,300 (including suburbs).

Copenhagen, Battle of naval victory on 2 April 1801 by a British fleet under Sir Hyde Parker (1739–1807) and *Nelson over the Danish fleet. Nelson put his telescope to his blind eye and refused to see Parker's signal for withdrawal.

Copernicus, Nicolaus (1473–1543) Polish **Mikolaj Kopernik**, Polish astronomer who believed that the Sun, not the Earth, is at the centre of the Solar System, thus defying the Christian church doctrine of the time. For 30 years, he worked on the hypothesis that the rotation and the orbital motion of the Earth are responsible for the apparent movement of the heavenly bodies. His great work *De Revolutionibus Orbium Coelestium/On the Revolutions of the Heavenly Spheres* was the important first step to the more accurate picture of the Solar System built up by Tycho *Brahe, *Kepler, *Galileo, and later astronomers.

Copland, Aaron (1900–1990) US composer. His early works, such as his piano concerto (1926), were in the jazz style but he gradually developed a gentler style with a regional flavour drawn from American folk music. Among his works are the ballet scores *Billy the Kid* (1938), *Rodeo* (1942), and *Appalachian Spring* (1944; based on a poem by Hart Crane). Among his orchestral works is *Inscape* (1967).

copper chemical symbol Cu, red-brown, very malleable and ductile, metallic element, atomic number 29, relative atomic mass 63.546. Its symbol comes from the Latin *cuprum*. It is one of the *transition metals in the *periodic table. Copper is used for its durability, pliability, high thermal and electrical conductivity, and resistance to corrosion. It is used in electrical wires and cables, and water pipes and tanks.

coppicing woodland management practice of severe pruning where trees are cut down to near ground level at regular intervals, typically every 3–20 years, to promote the growth of numerous shoots from the base.

Coppola, Francis Ford (1939–) US film director and screenwriter. He directed *The Godfather* (1972), which became one of the biggest moneymaking films of all time, and its sequels *The Godfather Part II* (1974), which won seven Academy Awards, and *The Godfather Part III* (1990). His other films include the influential *Apocalypse Now* (1979) and *Rumblefish* (1983).

copra dried meat from the kernel of the *coconut, used to make coconut oil.

Copt descendant of those ancient Egyptians who adopted Christianity in the 1st century and refused to convert to Islam after the Arab conquest. They now form a small minority (about 5%) of Egypt's population. **Coptic** is a member of the Hamito-Semitic language family. It is descended from the language of the ancient Egyptians and is the ritual language of the Coptic Christian church. It is written in the Greek alphabet with some additional characters derived from *demotic script.

Coptic art the art of the indigenous Christian community of 5th–8th-century Egypt. Flat and colourful in style, with strong outlines and stylized forms, it shows the influence of Byzantine, late Roman, and ancient Egyptian art. Wall paintings, textiles, stone and ivory carvings, and manuscript illuminations remain, the most noted examples of which are in the Coptic Museum, Cairo. The influence of Coptic art was widespread in the Christian world, and Coptic interlacing patterns may have been the source for the designs of Irish and Northumbrian illuminated gospels. For the later period of Fatimid art (10th–11th centuries), see *Islamic art.

copulation act of mating in animals with internal *fertilization. Male mammals have a *penis or other organ that is used to introduce spermatozoa into the reproductive tract of the female. Most birds transfer sperm by pressing their cloacas (the openings of their reproductive tracts) together.

copyright law applying to literary, musical, and artistic works (including plays, recordings, films, photographs, radio and television broadcasts, and, in the USA and the UK, computer programs), which prevents the reproduction of the work, in whole or in part, without the author's consent. It is the exclusive right to reproduce, distribute, display, license, or perform a work. Copyright is a form of intellectual property.

coral marine invertebrate of the class Anthozoa in the phylum Cnidaria, which also includes sea anemones and jellyfish. It has a skeleton of lime (calcium carbonate) extracted from the surrounding water. Corals exist in warm seas, at moderate depths with sufficient light. Some coral is valued for decoration or jewellery, for example, Mediterranean red coral *Corallum rubrum*.

Coral Sea *or* **Solomon Sea** part of the *Pacific Ocean bounded by northeastern Australia, New Guinea, the Solomon Islands, Vanuatu, and New Caledonia; area 4,790,000 sq km/1,849,000 sq mi, with an average depth of 2,400 m/7,870 ft, with three deep trenches on its eastern edge. It contains numerous coral islands and reefs. The Coral Sea Islands are a territory of Australia; they comprise scattered reefs and islands over an area of about 1,000,000 sq km/386,000 sq mi. They are uninhabited except for a meteorological station on Willis Island. The *Great Barrier Reef lies along its western edge, just off the east coast of Australia.

cor anglais *or* **English horn** musical instrument, an alto *oboe, pitched a fifth lower (in F) than the oboe.

It has a distinctive tulip-shaped bell and produces a warm nasal tone. It is heard in Rossini's overture to *William Tell* (1829), and portrays a plaintive Sasha the duck in Prokofiev's *Peter and the Wolf* (1936).

Corbusier, Le French architect; see *Le Corbusier.

Cordilleras, The mountainous western section of North America, including the Rocky Mountains and the coastal ranges parallel to the contact between the North American and the Pacific plates.

core in earth science, the innermost part of the Earth. It is divided into an outer core, which begins at a depth of 2,900 km/1,800 mi, and an inner core, which begins at a depth of 4,980 km/3,100 mi. Both parts are thought to consist of iron-nickel alloy. The outer core is liquid and the inner core is solid.

Corelli, Arcangelo (1653–1713) Italian composer and violinist. Living at a time when the viol was being replaced by the violin, he was one of the first virtuoso players of the baroque violin, and his music, marked by graceful melody, includes a set of *concerti grossi* and five sets of chamber sonatas.

Corfu Greek *Kérkyra*, northernmost and second largest of the Ionian islands of Greece, off the coast of Epirus in the Ionian Sea; area 1,072 sq km/414 sq mi; population (2003 est) 115,200. Its businesses include tourism, fruit, olive oil, and textiles; livestock raising and fishing are important sources of livelihood. Its largest town is the port of Corfu (Kérkyra), population (2003 est) 36,900. Corfu was colonized by the Corinthians about 700 BC. Venice held it 1386–1797, and Britain 1815–64.

corgi breed of dog. See *Welsh corgi.

coriander pungent fresh herb belonging to the parsley family, native to Europe and Asia; also a spice made from its dried ripe seeds. The spice is used commercially as a flavouring in meat products, bakery goods, tobacco, gin, liqueurs, chilli, and curry powder. Both are commonly used in cooking in the Middle East, India, Mexico, and China. (*Coriandrum sativum*, family Umbelliferae.)

Coriolis effect effect of the Earth's rotation on the atmosphere, oceans, and theoretically all objects moving over the Earth's surface. In the northern hemisphere it causes moving objects and currents to be deflected to the right; in the southern hemisphere it causes deflection to the left. The effect is named after its discoverer, French mathematician Gaspard de Coriolis (1792–1843).

cork light, waterproof outer layers of the bark covering the branches and roots of almost all trees and shrubs. The cork oak (*Quercus suber*), a native of southern Europe and North Africa, is cultivated in Spain and Portugal; the exceptionally thick outer layers of its bark provide the cork that is used commercially.

Cork largest county of the Republic of Ireland, in the province of Munster; county town Cork; area 7,460 sq km/2,880 sq mi; population (2002 est) 448,200. Cork is mainly agricultural, but there is some copper and manganese mining, marble quarrying, salmon farming, and river and sea fishing; industries include chemical, and computer hardware and software. There are natural gas and oil fields off the south coast at Kinsale. Angling is a popular sport, and tourism is concentrated in Kinsale, Bantry, Glengarriff, and Youghal; one of the most popular visitor attractions is the 17th-century Charles Fort, Kinsale. Cork is rich in Christian and pre-Christian antiquities.

corm short, swollen, underground plant stem, surrounded by protective scale leaves, as seen in the genus *Crocus*. It stores food, provides a means of *vegetative reproduction, and acts as a *perennating organ.

cormorant any of various diving seabirds, mainly of the genus *Phalacrocorax*, order Pelecaniformes, about 90 cm/3 ft long, with webbed feet, a long neck, hooked beak, and glossy black plumage. Cormorants generally feed on fish and shellfish, which they catch by swimming and diving under water, sometimes to a considerable depth. They collect the food in a pouch formed by the dilatable skin at the front of the throat. Some species breed on inland lakes and rivers.

corn general term for the main *cereal crop of a region – for example, wheat in the UK, oats in Scotland and Ireland, maize in the USA. Also, another word for *maize.

corncrake or **landrail** bird *Crex crex* of the rail family Rallidae, order Gruiformes. About 25 cm/10 in long, the bill and tail are short, the legs long and powerful, and the toes have sharp claws. It is drably coloured, shy, and has a persistent rasping call. The corncrake can swim and run easily, but its flight is heavy. It lives in meadows and crops in temperate regions, but has become rare where mechanical methods of cutting corn are used.

cornea transparent front section of the vertebrate *eye. The cornea is curved and behaves as a fixed lens, so that light entering the eye is partly focused before it reaches the lens.

Corneille, Pierre (1606–1684) French dramatist. His tragedies, such as *Horace* (1640), *Cinna* (1641), and *Oedipe* (1659), glorify the strength of will governed by reason, and established the French classical dramatic tradition. His first comedy, *Mélite*, was performed in 1629, followed by others that gained him a brief period of favour with Cardinal Richelieu. His early masterpiece, *Le Cid* (1636), was attacked by the Academicians, although it received public acclaim, and was produced in the same year as *L'Illusion comique/The Comic Illusion*.

cornet soprano three-valved brass instrument, usually in B flat. It is similar in size to the *trumpet but squatter in shape, and developed from the coiled post-horn in Austria and Germany between about 1820 and 1850 for military band use. Its cylindrical bore, compact shape, and deeper conical bell, give it greater speed and agility of intonation than the trumpet, at the expense of less tonal precision and brilliance. A small E flat cornet is standard in brass bands alongside a B flat cornet section.

cornflower native European and Asian plant belonging to the same genus as the *knapweeds but distinguished from them by its deep azure-blue flowers. Formerly a common weed in northern European wheat fields, it is now widely grown in gardens as a herbaceous plant with flower colours ranging from blue through shades of pink and purple to white. (*Centaurea cyanus*, family Compositae.)

Cornforth, John Warcup (1917–) Australian chemist. Using *radioisotopes as markers, he found out how cholesterol is manufactured in the living cell and how enzymes synthesize chemicals that are mirror images of each other (optical *isomers). He shared the

Nobel Prize for Chemistry in 1975 with Swiss chemist Vladimir Prelog for his work in the stereochemistry of enzyme-catalysed reactions. He was knighted in 1977.

Cornish language extinct member of the *Celtic languages, a branch of the Indo-European language family, spoken in Cornwall, England, until 1777. In recent years the language has been revived in a somewhat reconstructed form by people interested in their Cornish heritage.

Corn Laws in Britain until 1846, laws used to regulate the export or import of cereals in order to maintain an adequate supply for consumers and a secure price for producers. For centuries the Corn Laws formed an integral part of the mercantile system in England; they were repealed because they became an unwarranted tax on food and a hindrance to British exports.

cornucopia (Latin 'horn of plenty') in Greek mythology, one of the horns of the goat Amalthaea, which Zeus caused to refill perpetually with food and drink. As an artistic symbol it denotes prosperity. In paintings, the cornucopia is depicted as a horn-shaped container spilling over with fruit and flowers.

Cornwall county in southwest England including the Isles of *Scilly (Scillies). **area:** (excluding Scillies) 3,550 sq km/1,370 sq mi **towns and cities:** Truro (administrative headquarters), Camborne, Launceston; Bude, Falmouth, Newquay, Penzance, St Ives (resorts) **physical:** Bodmin Moor (including Brown Willy 419 m/1,375 ft); Land's End peninsula; rivers Camel, Fal, Fowey, Tamar **features:** St Michael's Mount; the Stannary or Tinners' Parliament; Tate St Ives art gallery; Eden Project, two 'biomes' (tropical rainforest and Mediterranean) built in a disused china-clay pit near St Austell; the 'Lost' Gardens of Heligan; the Minack Theatre, carved from the cliff face at Porthcuno **population:** (1996) 483,300.

Cornwallis, Charles, 1st Marquis and 2nd Earl (1738–1805) British general in the *American Revolution until 1781, when his defeat at Yorktown led to final surrender and ended the war. He then served twice as governor-general of India and once as viceroy of Ireland. He succeeded to the earldom in 1762, and was made a marquis in 1792.

corona faint halo of hot (about 2,000,000 °C/3,600,000 °F) and tenuous gas around the Sun, which boils from the surface. It is visible at solar *eclipses or through a **coronagraph**, an instrument that blocks light from the Sun's brilliant disc. Gas flows away from the corona to form the *solar wind. NASA's High-Energy Solar Spectroscopic Imager mission, launched in 2001, was to study the evolution of energy in the corona.

coronary artery disease (Latin corona 'crown', from the arteries encircling the heart) condition in which the fatty deposits of *atherosclerosis form in the coronary arteries that supply the heart muscle, narrowing them and restricting the blood flow.

coronation ceremony of investing a sovereign with the emblems of royalty, as a symbol of inauguration in office. Since the coronation of Harold in 1066, English sovereigns have been crowned in Westminster Abbey, London.

coroner official who investigates the deaths of persons who have died suddenly by acts of violence or under suspicious circumstances, by holding an inquest or ordering a postmortem examination (autopsy).

Corot, Jean-Baptiste Camille (1796–1875) French painter. He created a distinctive landscape style using a soft focus and a low-key palette of browns, ochres, and greens. His early work, including Italian scenes of the 1820s, influenced the *Barbizon School of painters. Like them, Corot worked outdoors, but he also continued a conventional academic tradition with his romanticized paintings of women.

corporal punishment physical punishment of wrongdoers – for example, by whipping. It is still used as a punishment for criminals in many countries, especially under Islamic law. Corporal punishment of children by parents is illegal in some countries, including Sweden, Finland, Denmark, and Norway.

corporatism belief that the state in capitalist democracies should intervene to a large extent in the economy to ensure social harmony. In Austria, for example, corporatism results in political decisions often being taken after discussions between chambers of commerce, trade unions, and the government.

corporative state state in which the members are organized and represented not on a local basis as citizens, but as producers working in a particular trade, industry, or profession. Originating with the syndicalist workers' movement (see *syndicalism), the idea was superficially adopted by the fascists during the 1920s and 1930s. Catholic social theory, as expounded in some papal encyclicals, also favours the corporative state as a means of eliminating class conflict.

corpus luteum glandular tissue formed in the mammalian *ovary after ovulation from the Graafian follicle, a group of cells associated with bringing the egg to maturity. It secretes the hormone progesterone in anticipation of pregnancy.

Correggio (c. 1494–1534) adopted name of Antonio Allegri, Italian painter of the High Renaissance. His style followed the classical grandeur of *Leonardo da Vinci and *Titian, but anticipated the *baroque in its emphasis on movement, softer forms, and contrasts of light and shade.

correlation degree of relationship between two sets of information. If one set of data increases at the same time as the other, the relationship is said to be **positive** or direct. If one set of data increases as the other decreases, the relationship is **negative** or inverse. If there is no relationship between the two sets of data the relationship is said to be **zero linear correlation**. Correlation can be shown by plotting a line of best fit on a scatter diagram. The steeper the line drawn, whether positive or negative, the stronger the correlation.

corrosion in earth science, an alternative name for *solution, the process by which water dissolves rocks such as limestone.

corrosion eating away and eventual destruction of metals and alloys by chemical attack. The rusting of ordinary iron and steel is the most common form of corrosion. Rusting takes place in moist air, when the iron combines with oxygen and water to form a brown-orange deposit of *rust (hydrated iron oxide). The rate of corrosion is increased where the atmosphere is polluted with sulphur dioxide. Salty road and air conditions accelerate the rusting of car bodies.

Corsica French Corse, island region of France, in the Mediterranean off the west coast of Italy, north of Sardinia; it comprises the départements of Haute Corse and Corse du Sud; area 8,680 sq km/3,351 sq mi; population (1999 est) 260,200 (including just under 50% native Corsicans). The capital, Ajaccio, and Bastia (at the island's northern tip) are the chief towns and ports. The island is largely mountainous and characterized by maquis vegetation (drought-tolerant shrubs such as cork oak and myrtle). The main products are wine and olive oil; tourism is the island's economic mainstay. The languages spoken are French (official) and Corsican, an Italian dialect. The French emperor Napoleon was born in Ajaccio in 1769, the same year that Corsica became a province of France. The island's characteristic maquis has long provided ideal hideouts for bandits, and banditry remained a problem on the island until the 1930s. Vendettas, or blood feuds, between clans remained common until recent times. This practice was similar to that in Sicily and parts of southern Italy, and indicates the close ties that have continued to exist between the island and Italy.

Cortés, Hernán (1485–1547) Spanish conquistador. He conquered the Aztec empire 1519–21, and secured Mexico for Spain.

cortex in biology, the outer part of a structure such as the brain, kidney, or adrenal gland. In botany the cortex includes nonspecialized cells lying just beneath the surface cells of the root and stem.

corticosteroid any of several steroid hormones secreted by the cortex of the *adrenal glands; also synthetic forms with similar properties. Corticosteroids have anti-inflammatory and immunosuppressive effects and may be used to treat a number of conditions, including rheumatoid arthritis, severe allergies, asthma, some skin diseases, and some cancers. Side effects can be serious, and therapy must be withdrawn very gradually.

cortisone natural corticosteroid produced by the *adrenal gland, now synthesized for its anti-inflammatory qualities and used in the treatment of rheumatoid arthritis.

Cortona, Pietro da Italian baroque painter; see *Pietro da Cortona.

corundum Al₂O₃, native aluminium oxide and the hardest naturally occurring mineral known, apart from diamond (corundum rates 9 on the Mohs scale of hardness); lack of cleavage also increases its durability. Its crystals are barrel-shaped prisms of the trigonal system. Varieties of gem-quality corundum are **ruby** (red) and **sapphire** (any colour other than red, usually blue). Poorer-quality and synthetic corundum is used in industry, for example as an *abrasive.

Cosgrave, William Thomas (1880–1965) Irish revolutionary and politician; president of the executive council (prime minister) of the Irish Free State 1922–32, leader of Cumann na nGaedheal 1923–33, and leader of Fine Gael 1935–44. He was born in Dublin and educated by the Christian Brothers. A founding member of *Sinn Fein, he fought in the *Easter Rising of 1916 but his death sentence was commuted. He supported the Anglo-Irish Treaty (1921) and oversaw the ruthless crushing of Irregular IRA forces during the Irish Civil War (1922–23), executing far more IRA members than his British predecessors.

cosine cos, in trigonometry, a *function of an angle in a right-angled *triangle found by dividing the length of the side adjacent to the angle by the length of the hypotenuse (the longest side). This function can be used to find either angles or sides in a right-angled triangle.

cosmic background radiation *or* **3° radiation** electromagnetic radiation left over from the original formation of the universe in the *Big Bang between 10 and 20 billion years ago. It corresponds to an overall background temperature of 2.73 K (−270.4 °C/−454.7 °F), or 3 °C above absolute zero. In 1992 the US Cosmic Background Explorer satellite detected slight 'ripples' in the strength of cosmic background radiation that are believed to mark the first stage in the formation of galaxies.

cosmic radiation streams of high-energy particles and electromagnetic radiation from outer space, consisting of electrons, protons, alpha particles, light nuclei, and gamma rays, which collide with atomic nuclei in the Earth's atmosphere and produce secondary nuclear particles (chiefly *mesons, such as pions and muons) that shower the Earth. Space shuttles carry dosimeter instruments to measure the levels of cosmic radiation.

cosmology branch of astronomy that deals with the structure and evolution of the universe as an ordered whole. Cosmologists construct 'model universes' mathematically and compare their large-scale properties with those of the observed universe.

Cossack people of southern and southwestern Russia, Ukraine, and Poland, predominantly of Russian or Ukrainian origin, who took in escaped serfs and lived in independent communal settlements (military brotherhoods) from the 15th to the 19th century. Later they held land in return for military service in the cavalry under Russian and Polish rulers. After 1917, the various Cossack communities were incorporated into the Soviet administrative and collective system.

Costa Brava (Spanish 'Wild Coast') Mediterranean coastline of northeast Spain, stretching from Port-Bou on the French border southwards to Blanes, northeast of Barcelona. It is noted for its irregular rocky coastline, small fishing villages, and resorts such as Puerto de la Selva, Palafrugell, Playa de Aro, and Lloret del Mar.

Costa del Sol (Spanish 'Coast of the Sun') Mediterranean coastline of Andalusia, southern Spain, stretching for nearly 300 km/190 mi from Gibraltar to Almería. Málaga is the principal port and Marbella, Torremolinos, and Nerja are the chief tourist resorts.

Costa Rica
National name: *República de Costa Rica/ Republic of Costa Rica*
Area: 51,100 sq km/19,729 sq mi
Capital: San José
Major towns/cities: Alajuela, Cartago, Limón, Puntarenas, San Isidro, Desamparados
Major ports: Limón, Puntarenas
Physical features: high central plateau and tropical coasts; Costa Rica was once entirely forested, containing an estimated 5% of the Earth's flora and fauna
Head of state and government: Abel Pacheco de la Espriella from 2002
Political system: liberal democracy
Political executive: limited presidency
Political parties: National Liberation Party (PLN), left of centre; Christian Socialist Unity Party (PUSC), centrist coalition; ten minor parties
Currency: colón

GNI per capita (PPP): (US$) 8,260 (2002 est)

Exports: manufactured products, bananas, coffee, sugar, cocoa, textiles, seafood, meat, tropical fruit. Principal market: USA 51.8% (2001)

Population: 4,173,000 (2003 est)

Language: Spanish (official)

Religion: Roman Catholic 95% (state religion)

Life expectancy: 76 (men); 81 (women) (2000–05)

Chronology

1502: Visited by Christopher Columbus, who named the area Costa Rica (the rich coast), observing the gold decorations worn by the Guaymi American Indians.

1506: Colonized by Spain, but there was fierce guerrilla resistance by the indigenous population. Many later died from exposure to European diseases.

18th century: Settlements began to be established in the fertile central highlands, including San José and Alajuela.

1808: Coffee was introduced from Cuba and soon became the staple crop.

1821: Independence achieved from Spain, and was joined initially with Mexico.

1824: Became part of United Provinces (Federation) of Central America, also embracing El Salvador, Guatemala, Honduras, and Nicaragua.

1838: Became fully independent when it seceded from the Federation.

later 19th century: Immigration by Europeans to run and work small coffee farms.

1940–44: Liberal reforms, including recognition of workers' rights and minimum wages, were introduced by President Rafael Angel Calderón Guradia, founder of the United Christian Socialist Party (PUSC).

1949: New constitution adopted, giving women and blacks the vote. National army abolished and replaced by civil guard. José Figueres Ferrer, cofounder of the PLN, elected president; he embarked on an ambitious socialist programme, nationalizing the banks and introducing a social security system.

1958–73: Mainly conservative administrations.

1978: Sharp deterioration in the state of the economy.

1982: A harsh austerity programme was introduced.

1985: Following border clashes with Nicaraguan Sandinista forces, a US-trained antiguerrilla guard was formed.

1986: Oscar Arias Sanchez (PLN) won the presidency on a neutralist platform.

1987: Arias won the Nobel Prize for Peace for devising a Central American peace plan signed by the leaders of Nicaragua, El Salvador, Guatemala, and Honduras.

1998: Miguel Angel Rodriguez Echeverria (PUSC) was elected president.

2000: The long-standing dispute with Nicaragua over navigation along the San Juan river, the border between the two countries, was resolved.

2002: Abel Pacheco of the PUSC won the presidential elections.

2004: Investigations were begun into allegations of corruption against three former presidents (Jose Maria Figueres, Miguel Angel Rodriguez and Rafael Angel Calderon).

2005: Heavy rain causes serious flooding along the Caribbean coast and a national emergency is declared.

cot death *or* **sudden infant death syndrome (SIDS)** death of an apparently healthy baby, almost always during sleep. It is most common in the winter months, and strikes more boys than girls. The cause is not known but risk factors that have been identified include prematurity, respiratory infection, overheating, and sleeping position. In August 2001, it was announced that smoking during pregnancy can increase the risk of cot death by a factor of 15.

Côte d'Azur Mediterranean coast from Menton to St-Tropez in the *départements* of Alpes-Maritimes and Var, France, renowned for its beaches; it is part of the region *Provence-Alpes-Côte d'Azur. The chief resorts are Antibes, Cannes, Nice, Juan-Les-Pins, and Monte Carlo in Monaco.

Côte d'Ivoire

National name: *République de la Côte d'Ivoire/ Republic of the Ivory Coast*

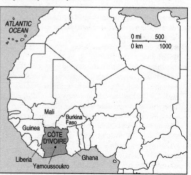

Area: 322,463 sq km/124,502 sq mi

Capital: Yamoussoukro

Major towns/cities: Abidjan, Bouaké, Daloa, Man, Korhogo, Gagnoa

Major ports: Abidjan, San Pedro

Physical features: tropical rainforest (diminishing as exploited) in south; savannah and low mountains in north; coastal plain; Vridi canal, Kossou dam, Monts du Toura

Head of state: Laurent Gbagbo from 2000

Head of government: Seydou Diarra from 2003

Political system: emergent democracy

Political executive: limited presidency

Political parties: Democratic Party of Côte d'Ivoire (PDCI), nationalist, free enterprise; Rally of Republicans (RDR), nationalist; Ivorian Popular Front (FPI), left of centre; Ivorian Labour Party (PIT), left of centre; over 20 smaller parties

Currency: franc CFA

GNI per capita (PPP): (US$) 1,430 (2002 est)

Exports: cocoa beans and products, petroleum products, timber, coffee, cotton, tinned tuna. Principal market: France 15.3% (2000)

Population: 16,631,000 (2003 est)

Language: French (official), over 60 ethnic languages

Religion: animist 17%, Muslim 39% (mainly in north), Christian 26% (mainly Roman Catholic in south)

Life expectancy: 41 (men); 41 (women) (2000–05)

Chronology

1460s: Portuguese navigators arrived.

16th century: Ivory export trade developed by Europeans and slave trade, though to a lesser extent than neighbouring areas; Krou people migrated from Liberia to the west and Senoufo and Lubi from the north.

late 17th century: French coastal trading posts established at Assini and Grand Bassam.

18th–19th centuries: Akan peoples, including the Baoulé, immigrated from the east and Malinke from the northwest.

1840s: French began to conclude commercial treaties with local rulers.

1893: Colony of Côte d'Ivoire created by French, after war with Mandinkas; Baoulé resistance continued until 1917.

1904: Became part of French West Africa; cocoa production encouraged.

1940–42: Under pro-Nazi French Vichy regime.

1946: Became overseas territory in French Union, with own territorial assembly and representation in French parliament: Felix Houphouët-Boigny, a Western-educated Baoulé chief who had formed the Democratic Party (PDCI) to campaign for autonomy, was elected to the French assembly.

1947: A French-controlled area to the north, which had been added to Côte d'Ivoire in 1932, separated to create new state of Upper Volta (now Burkina Faso).

1950–54: Port of Abidjan constructed.

1958: Achieved internal self-government.

1960: Independence secured, with Houphouët-Boigny as president of a one-party state.

1960s–1980s: Political stability, close links maintained with France and economic expansion of 10% per annum, as the country became one of the world's largest coffee producers.

1986: The country's name was officially changed from Ivory Coast to Côte d'Ivoire.

1987–93: Per capita incomes fell by 25% owing to an austerity programme promoted by the International Monetary Fund.

1990: There were strikes and student unrest. Houphouët-Boigny was re-elected as president as multiparty politics were re-established.

1993: Houphouët-Boigny died and was succeeded by parliamentary speaker and Baoulé Henri Konan Bedie.

1999: After a largely bloodless coup over Christmas 1999 Bedie was replaced by a new military leader, General Robert Guei.

2000: Guei announced suspension of the country's foreign debt repayments in January. A new constitution

for the return of civilian rule was approved by referendum. Mutinous soldiers launched three unsuccessful coups against Guei, and a state of emergency was imposed. Guei attempted to sabotage the presidential elections held in October, but was forced to flee. The elections were won by Laurent Gbagbo, and marked by violence against supporters of Alassane Outtara, who had been excluded from standing in the contest. Violence also surrounded the parliamentary elections held in December.

2001: The government foiled an armed coup by rebel soldiers.

2002: A coup attempt was launched by mutinous soldiers against Laurent Gbagbo's government, leading to heavy fighting and hundreds of casualties, including the deaths of the interior minister and of former military ruler Robert Guei.

2003: A power-sharing coalition government was formed between leading political parties and rebel groups as part of a French-brokered peace accord, aiming to end nearly six months of civil war.

2004: Fighting continued as government forces attacked the rebel-held north of the country.

cotoneaster any of a group of shrubs or trees found in Europe and Asia, belonging to the rose family and closely related to the hawthorn and medlar. The fruits, though small and unpalatable, are usually bright red and conspicuous, often surviving through the winter. Some of the shrubs are cultivated for their attractive appearance. (Genus *Cotoneaster*, family Rosaceae.)

Cotonou chief port and largest city of Benin, on the Bight of Benin; population (1994) 537,000. Palm products and timber are exported, and textiles are manufactured. Although not the official capital, it is the seat of the president, and the main centre of commerce and politics.

Cotopaxi active Andean volcano in north-central Ecuador on the border of the Cotopaxi, Napo, and Pichincha provinces. It is located 48 km/30 mi south of *Quito at an altitude of 5,897 m/19,347 ft above sea level. It one of the highest volcanoes in the world. It is now contained within a 340 sq km/131 sq mi national park, established in 1975.

Cotswold Hills or **Cotswolds** range of limestone hills in Gloucestershire, South Gloucestershire, and Bath and North East Somerset, England, 80 km/50 mi long, between Bath and Chipping Camden. They rise to 333 m/1,086 ft at Cleeve Cloud, near Cheltenham, but average about 200 m/600 ft. The area is known for its picturesque villages, built with the local honey-coloured stone. Tourism is important.

cotton tropical and subtropical herbaceous plant belonging to the mallow family. (Genus *Gossypium*, family Malvaceae). Fibres surround the seeds inside the ripened fruits, or bolls, and these are spun into yarn for cloth. Cotton fabric is cool and comfortable to wear, resilient, absorbs moisture, is light, washes easily, and dyes well, but can crease quite badly.

cottonwood any of several North American *poplar trees with seeds topped by a thick tuft of silky hairs. The eastern cottonwood (*Populus deltoides*), growing to 30 m/100 ft, is native to the eastern USA. The name 'cottonwood' is also given to the downy-leaved Australian tree *Bedfordia salaoina*. (True cottonwood genus *Populus*, family Salicaceae.)

cotyledon structure in the embryo of a seed plant that may form a 'leaf' after germination and is commonly known as a seed leaf. The number of cotyledons present in an embryo is an important character in the classification of flowering plants (*angiosperms).

couch grass European grass that spreads rapidly by underground stems. It is considered a troublesome weed in North America, where it has been introduced. (*Agropyron repens*, family Gramineae.)

cougar another name for the *puma, a large North American cat.

coulomb symbol C, SI unit of electrical charge. One coulomb is the amount of charge transferred by a current of one *ampere in one second. The unit is named after French scientist Charles Augustin de Coulomb.

council in local government in England and Wales, a popularly elected local assembly charged with the government of the area within its boundaries. Under the Local Government Act 1972, they comprise three types: *county councils, *district councils, and *parish councils. Many city councils exist in the USA.

Council of Europe body constituted in 1949 to achieve greater unity between European countries, to help with their economic and social progress, and to uphold the principles of parliamentary democracy and respect for human rights. It has a **Committee** of foreign ministers, a **Parliamentary Assembly** (with members from national parliaments), and a **European Commission on Human Rights**, established by the 1950 European Convention on Human Rights.

Council of the European Union formerly **Council of Ministers**, chief decision-making and legislative body of the* European Union (EU). Member states are represented at council meetings by the ministers appropriate to the subject under discussion (for example, ministers of agriculture, environment, education, and so on). The presidency of the Council changes every six months and rotates in turn among the 25 EU member countries. The Council sets the EU's objectives, coordinates the national policies of the member states, resolves differences with the *European Commission and the *European Parliament, and concludes international agreements on behalf of the EU. European Community law is adopted by the Council, or by the Council and the European Parliament through the co-decision procedure, and may take the form of binding 'regulations', 'directives', and 'decisions'.

council tax method of raising revenue (income) for local government in Britain. It replaced the community charge, or *poll tax, from April 1993. The tax is based on property values at April 1991, but takes some account of the number of people occupying each property.

counterfeiting fraudulent imitation, usually of banknotes. It is countered by special papers, elaborate watermarks, skilled printing, and sometimes the insertion of a metallic strip. Forgery is also a form of counterfeiting.

counterpoint in music, two or more lines that are arranged so that they fit well together. Even though the combination of the melodies is the main aim, they must make a satisfactory harmony. Another word for this is *polyphony. Giovanni Palestrina and Johann Sebastian Bach were masters of counterpoint.

Counter-Reformation movement initiated by the Catholic Church at the Council of Trent (1545–63) to counter the spread of the *Reformation. Extending into the 17th century, its dominant forces included the rise of the *Jesuits as an educating and missionary group and the deployment of the Spanish *Inquisition in Europe and the Americas.

countertenor the highest natural male voice, as opposed to the falsetto of the male *alto. It was favoured by the Elizabethans for its heroic brilliance of tone.

country *or* **country and western** popular music of the white US South and West; it originated in the 20th century and evolved from the folk music of the English, Irish, and Scottish settlers, and contains some blues influence. Instruments commonly used are slide guitar, mandolin, and fiddle. Lyrics typically extol family values and traditional sex roles, and often have a strong narrative element. Country music includes a variety of regional styles, and ranges from mournful ballads to fast and intricate dance music.

county (Latin *comitatus* through French *comté*) administrative unit of a country or state. It was the name given by the Normans to Anglo-Saxon 'shires', and the boundaries of many present-day English counties date back to Saxon times. There are currently 34 English administrative non-metropolitan counties and 6 metropolitan counties, in addition to 34 unitary authorities. Welsh and Scottish counties were abolished in 1996 in a reorganization of local government throughout the UK, and replaced by 22 and 33 unitary authorities respectively. Northern Ireland has 6 geographical counties, although administration is through 26 district councils. In the USA a county is a subdivision of a state; the power of counties differs widely among states.

county council in England, a unit of local government whose responsibilities include broad planning policy, highways, education, personal social services, and libraries; police, fire, and traffic control; and refuse disposal. The tier below the county council has traditionally been the district council, but with local government reorganization from 1996, there has been a shift towards unitary authorities (based on a unit smaller than the county) replacing both. By 1998 there were 34 two-tier non-metropolitan county councils under which there were 274 district councils.

county palatine in medieval England, a county whose lord held particular rights, in lieu of the king, such as pardoning treasons and murders. Under William I there were four counties palatine: Chester, Durham, Kent, and Shropshire.

coup d'état *or* **coup** (French 'stroke of state') forcible takeover of the government of a country by elements from within that country, generally carried out by violent or illegal means. It differs from a revolution in typically being carried out by a small group (for example, of army officers or opposition politicians) to install its leader as head of government, rather than being a mass uprising by the people.

Couperin, François le Grand (1668–1733) French composer. He is the best-known member of a musical family that included his uncle Louis Couperin (*c.* 1626–1661), composer for harpsichord and organ. He was a favourite composer of Louis XIV, and composed numerous chamber concertos and harpsichord suites, and published a standard keyboard tutor *L'Art de* *toucher le clavecin/The Art of Playing the Harpsichord* (1716) in which he laid down guidelines for fingering, phrasing, and ornamentation.

Courbet, Gustave (1819–1877) French artist. He was a portrait, genre, and landscape painter. Reacting against academic trends, both classicist and Romantic, he became a major exponent of *realism, depicting contemporary life with an unflattering frankness. His *Burial at Ornans* (1850; Musée d'Orsay, Paris), showing ordinary working people gathered around a village grave, shocked the public and the critics with its 'vulgarity'.

courgette small variety of *marrow, belonging to the gourd family. It is cultivated as a vegetable and harvested before it is fully mature, at 15–20 cm/6–8 in. In the USA and Canada it is known as a zucchini. (*Cucurbita pepo*, family Cucurbitaceae.)

coursing chasing of hares by greyhounds, not by scent but by sight, as a sport and as a test of the greyhound's speed. It is one of the most ancient of field sports. Since the 1880s it has been practised in the UK on enclosed or park courses.

Court, Margaret (1942–) Australian tennis player. The most prolific winner in the women's game, she won a record 62 Grand Slam titles, including 24 at singles.

Cousteau, Jacques-Yves (1910–1997) French oceanographer. He pioneered the invention of the aqualung in 1943, as well as techniques in underwater filming. In 1951 he began the first of many research voyages in the ship *Calypso*. His film and television documentaries and books established him as a household name.

covalent bond chemical *bond produced when two atoms share one or more pairs of electrons (usually each atom contributes an electron). The bond is often represented by a single line drawn between the two atoms. Covalently bonded substances include hydrogen (H_2), water (H_2O), and most organic substances.

Covenanter in Scottish history, one of the Presbyterian Christians who swore to uphold their forms of worship in a National Covenant, signed on 28 February 1638, when *Charles I attempted to introduce a liturgy on the English model into Scotland.

Coventry industrial city in the West Midlands, England, on the River Sherbourne, 29 km/18 mi southeast of Birmingham; population (2001 est) 300,800.

Coward, Noël (Peirce) (1899–1973) English dramatist, actor, revue-writer, director, and composer. He epitomized the witty and sophisticated man of the theatre. From his first success with *The Young Idea* (1923), he wrote and appeared in plays and comedies on both sides of the Atlantic such as *Hay Fever* (1925), *Private Lives* (1930) with Gertrude Lawrence, *Design for Living* (1933), *Blithe Spirit* (1941), and *A Song at Twilight* (1966). His revues and musicals included *On With the Dance* (1925) and *Bitter Sweet* (1929).

cow parsley or **keck** tall perennial plant belonging to the carrot family, found in Europe, northern Asia, and North Africa. It grows up to 1 m/3 ft tall and has pinnate leaves (leaflets growing either side of a stem), hollow furrowed stems, and heads of delicate white flowers. (*Anthriscus sylvestris*, family Umbelliferae.)

cowrie marine snail of the family Cypreidae, in which the interior spiral form is concealed by a double outer lip. The shells are hard, shiny, and often coloured. Most cowries are shallow-water forms, and are found in many parts of the world, particularly the tropical

Indo-Pacific. Cowries have been used as ornaments and fertility charms, and also as currency, for example the Pacific money cowrie *Cypraea moneta*.

cowslip European plant related to the primrose, with several small deep-yellow fragrant flowers growing from a single stem. It is native to temperate regions of the Old World. The oxlip (*Primula elatior*) is also closely related. (*Primula veris*, family Primulaceae.)

two hydrogen atoms

or H×̈H, H–H
a molecule of hydrogen
sharing an electron pair

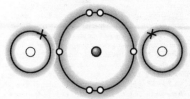

two hydrogen atoms and one
oxygen atom

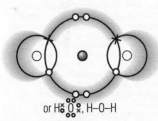

or H×̈O×̈, H–O–H
a molecule of water
showing the two covalent bonds

covalent bond The formation of a covalent bond between two hydrogen atoms to form a hydrogen molecule (H_2), and between two hydrogen atoms and an oxygen atom to form a molecule of water (H_2O). The sharing means that each atom has a more stable arrangement of electrons (its outer electron shells are full).

coyote wild dog *Canis latrans*, in appearance like a small wolf, living in North and Central America. Its head and body are about 90 cm/3 ft long and brown, flecked with grey or black. Coyotes live in open country and can run at 65 kph/40 mph. Their main foods are rabbits and rodents. Although persecuted by humans for over a century, the species is very successful.

coypu South American water rodent *Myocastor coypus*, about 60 cm/2 ft long and weighing up to 9 kg/20 lb. It has a scaly, ratlike tail, webbed hind feet, a blunt-muzzled head, and large orange incisors. The fur ('nutria') is reddish brown. It feeds on vegetation, and lives in burrows in rivers and lake banks.

CPU in computing, abbreviation for *central processing unit.

crab any decapod (ten-legged) crustacean of the division Brachyura, with a broad, rather round, upper body shell (carapace) and a small *abdomen tucked beneath the body. Crabs are related to lobsters and crayfish. Mainly marine, some crabs live in fresh water or on land. They are alert carnivores and scavengers. They have a typical sideways walk, and strong pincers on the first pair of legs, the other four pairs being used for walking. Periodically, the outer shell is cast to allow for growth. The name 'crab' is sometimes used for similar arthropods, such as the horseshoe crab, which is neither a true crab nor a crustacean.

crab apple any of 25 species of wild apple trees, native to temperate regions of the northern hemisphere. Numerous varieties of cultivated apples have been derived from *Malus pumila*, the common native crab apple of southeastern Europe and central Asia. The fruit of native species is smaller and more bitter than that of cultivated varieties and is used in crab-apple jelly. (Genus *Malus*, family Rosaceae.)

Crab Nebula cloud of gas 6,000 light years from Earth, in the constellation *Taurus. It is the remains of a star that, according to Chinese records, exploded as a *supernova observed as a brilliant point of light on 4 July 1054. At its centre is a *pulsar that flashes 30 times a second. It was named by Lord Rosse after its crablike shape.

crack street name for a chemical derivative (bicarbonate) of *cocaine in hard, crystalline lumps; it is heated and inhaled (smoked) as a stimulant. Crack was first used in San Francisco in the early 1980s, and is highly addictive.

crag in previously glaciated areas, a large lump of rock that a glacier has been unable to wear away. As the glacier passed on and over the crag, weaker rock on the far side was largely protected from erosion and formed a tapering ridge, or **tail**, of debris.

Craig, James (1871–1940) 1st Viscount Craigavon, Ulster Unionist politician; first prime minister of Northern Ireland 1921–40. Elected to Westminster as MP for East Down 1906–18 (Mid-Down 1918–21), he was a highly effective organizer of the Ulster Volunteers and unionist resistance to home rule before World War I. In 1921 he succeeded Edward Carson as leader of the Ulster Unionist Party, and was appointed prime minister later that year. As leader of the Northern Ireland government he carried out systematic discrimination against the Catholic minority, abolishing proportional representation in 1929 and redrawing constituency boundaries to ensure Protestant majorities.

crake any of several small birds of the family Rallidae, order Gruiformes, related to the *corncrake.

Cram, Steve (1960–) born Stephen Cram, English middle distance runner who won the 1,500 metres at the inaugural World Championships in 1983, and between 1982 and 1990 also won two European and two Commonwealth gold medals and an Olympic silver medal at the same distance. In 1985, within the space of 19 days he broke world records in the mile, 1,500 metres, and 2,000 metres, with times of 3:46.32, 3:29.67, and 4:51.39 respectively. Having retired as an athlete, he became a commentator and broadcaster for the British Broadcasting Corporation (BBC).

Cranach, Lucas the Elder (1472–1553) adopted name of Lucas Müller, German painter, etcher, and woodcut artist. A leading figure in the German Renaissance, he painted religious scenes, allegories (many featuring full-length nudes), and precise and polished portraits, such as *Martin Luther* (1521; Uffizi, Florence).

cranberry any of several trailing evergreen plants belonging to the heath family, related to bilberries and blueberries. They grow in marshy places and bear small, acid, crimson berries, high in vitamin C content, used for making sauce and jelly. (Genus *Vaccinium*, family Ericaceae.)

crane in zoology, a large, wading bird of the family Gruidae, order Gruiformes, with long legs and neck, short powerful wings, a naked or tufted head, and unwebbed feet. The hind toe is greatly elevated, and has a sharp claw. Cranes are marsh- and plains-dwelling birds, feeding on plants as well as insects and small animals. They fly well and are usually migratory. Their courtship includes frenzied, leaping dances. They are found in all parts of the world except South America.

crane fly *or* **daddy-long-legs** any fly of the family Tipulidae, with long, slender, fragile legs. They look like giant mosquitoes, but the adults are quite harmless. The larvae live in soil or water. Females have a pointed abdomen; males have a club-shaped one.

cranesbill any of a group of plants containing about 400 species. The plants are named after the long beaklike protrusion attached to the seed vessels. When ripe, this splits into coiling spirals which jerk the seeds out, helping to scatter them. (Genus *Geranium*, family Geraniaceae.)

cranium the dome-shaped area of the vertebrate skull that protects the brain. It consists of eight bony plates fused together by sutures (immovable joints). Fossil remains of the human cranium have aided the development of theories concerning human evolution.

crankshaft essential component of piston engines that converts the up-and-down (reciprocating) motion of the pistons into useful rotary motion. The car crankshaft carries a number of cranks. The pistons are connected to the cranks by connecting rods and *bearings; when the pistons move up and down, the connecting rods force the offset crank pins to describe a circle, thereby rotating the crankshaft.

Cranmer, Thomas (1489–1556) English cleric, archbishop of Canterbury from 1533. A Protestant convert, he helped to shape the doctrines of the Church of England under *Edward VI. He was responsible for the issue of the Book of Common Prayer of 1549 and 1552. He was tried for treason and heresy and burnt at the stake in 1556 for supporting the succession of Lady Jane Grey in 1553.

crevasse

Crassus the Elder, Marcus Licinius (115–53 BC)
Roman general who crushed the Spartacus Revolt in
71 BC and became consul in 70 BC. In 60 BC he joined
with Julius Caesar and Pompey the Great in the First
Triumvirate and obtained a command in the east in
55 BC. Eager to gain his own reputation for military
glory, he invaded Parthia (Mesopotamia and Persia),
but was defeated by the Parthians at Carrhae, captured,
and put to death.

Crassus the Younger, Marcus Licinius Roman
general, grandson of the triumvir Marcus Licinius
Crassus the Elder. He fought first with Sextus Pompeius
and Mark Antony before defecting to Octavian (later
the emperor Augustus). In 29 BC he defeated the
Bastarnae of modern Romania and Bulgaria, killing
their king, Deldo, in single combat.

crater bowl-shaped depression in the ground, usually
round and with steep sides. Craters are formed by
explosive events such as the eruption of a volcano or
the impact of a meteorite.

Crawford, Joan (1908–1977) stage name of Lucille
Fay Le Sueur, US film actor. She became a star with her
performance as a flapper in *Our Dancing Daughters*
(1928). Later she appeared as a sultry, often suffering,
mature woman. She won an Academy Award for
Mildred Pierce (1945).

crayfish freshwater decapod (ten-limbed) crustacean
belonging to several families structurally similar to, but
smaller than, the *lobster. Crayfish are brownish-green
scavengers and are found in all parts of the world
except Africa. They are edible, and some species are
farmed. There are 300–400 species worldwide.

Crazy Horse (1849–1877) Sioux Ta-Sunko-Witko,
American Indian Sioux chief, one of the leaders at the
massacre of Little Bighorn. He was killed when
captured.

creationism theory concerned with the origins of
matter and life, claiming, as does the Bible in Genesis,
that the world and humanity were created by a
supernatural Creator, not more than 6,000 years ago.
It was developed in response to Darwin's theory of
*evolution; it is not recognized by most scientists as
having a factual basis.

Crécy, Battle of first major battle of the *Hundred
Years' War, fought on 26 August 1346. Philip VI of
France was defeated by *Edward III of England at
the village of Crécy-en-Ponthieu, now in Somme
département, France, 18 km/11 mi northeast of
Abbeville. The English archers played a crucial role
in Edward's victory, which allowed him to besiege
and take Calais.

credit in economics, a means by which goods or
services are obtained without immediate payment,
usually by agreeing to pay interest. The three main
forms are **consumer credit** (usually given to
individuals by retailers), **bank credit** (such as
overdrafts or personal loans), and **trade credit**
(common in the commercial world both within
countries and internationally).

creed in general, any system of belief; in the Christian
church the verbal confessions of faith expressing the
accepted doctrines of the church. The different forms
are the Apostles' Creed, the *Nicene Creed, and the
*Athanasian Creed. The only creed recognized by the
Orthodox Church is the Nicene Creed.

creep in civil and mechanical engineering, the property
of a solid, typically a metal, under continuous stress
that causes it to deform below its yield point (the point
at which any elastic solid normally stretches without
any increase in load or stress). Lead, tin, and zinc, for
example, exhibit creep at ordinary temperatures, as
seen in the movement of the lead sheeting on the roofs
of old buildings.

creeper any small, short-legged passerine bird of the
family Certhidae. They spiral with a mouselike
movement up tree trunks, searching for insects and
larvae with their thin, down-curved beaks.

cremation disposal of the dead by burning. The
custom was universal among ancient Indo-European
peoples, for example, the Greeks, Romans, and Teutons.
It was discontinued among Christians until the late
19th century because of their belief in the bodily
resurrection of the dead. Overcrowded urban
cemeteries gave rise to its revival in the West. It has
remained the usual method of disposal in the East.

Creole (Spanish *criar* 'to create') in the West Indies
and Spanish America, originally someone of European
descent born in the New World; later someone of
mixed European and African descent. In Louisiana and
other states on the Gulf of Mexico, it applies either to
someone of French or Spanish descent or (popularly)
to someone of mixed French or Spanish and African
descent.

creole language any *pidgin language that has ceased
to be simply a trade jargon in ports and markets and
has become the mother tongue of a particular community,
such as the French dialects of the New Orleans area.
Many creoles have developed into distinct languages
with literatures of their own; for example, Jamaican
Creole, Haitian Creole, Krio in Sierra Leone, and Tok
Pisin, now the official language of Papua New Guinea.

cress any of several plants of the cress family,
characterized by a pungent taste. The common
European garden cress (*Lepidium sativum*) is cultivated
worldwide. (Genera include *Lepidium*, *Cardamine*, and
Arabis; family Cruciferae.)

Cretaceous period of geological time approximately
143–65 million years ago. It is the last period of the
Mesozoic era, during which angiosperm (seed-bearing)
plants evolved, and dinosaurs reached a peak. The end
of the Cretaceous period is marked by a mass
extinction of many lifeforms, most notably the
dinosaurs. The north European chalk, which forms
the white cliffs of Dover, was deposited during the
latter half of the Cretaceous, hence the name
Cretaceous, which comes from the Latin *creta*, 'chalk'.

Crete Greek **Kriti**, largest Greek island in the eastern
Mediterranean Sea, 100 km/62 mi southeast of
mainland Greece; area 8,378 sq km/3,234 sq mi;
population (2003 est) 603,000. The capital is Iraklion
(Heraklion); other major towns are Khaniá (Canea),
Rethymnon, and Aghios Nikolaos. The island produces
citrus fruit, olives, and wine; tourism is vital to the
economy. A Cretan dialect of Greek is spoken.

crevasse deep crack in the surface of a glacier; it can
reach several metres in depth. Crevasses often occur
where a glacier flows over the break of a slope, because
the upper layers of ice are unable to stretch and cracks
result. Crevasses may also form at the edges of glaciers
owing to friction with the bedrock.

Crick, Francis Harry Compton (1916–) English molecular biologist who was awarded a Nobel Prize for Physiology or Medicine in 1962, together with Maurice *Wilkins and James *Watson, for the discovery of the double-helical structure of *DNA and of the significance of this structure in the replication and transfer of genetic information.

cricket in zoology, an insect belonging to any of various families, especially the Gryllidae, of the order Orthoptera. Crickets are related to grasshoppers. They have somewhat flattened bodies and long antennae. The males make a chirping noise by rubbing together special areas on the forewings. The females have a long needlelike egglaying organ (ovipositor). There are around 900 species known worldwide.

cricket bat-and-ball game between two teams of 11 players each. It is played with a small solid ball and long flat-sided wooden bats, on a round or oval field, at the centre of which is a finely mown pitch, 20 m/22 yd long. At each end of the pitch is a wicket made up of three upright wooden sticks (stumps), surmounted by two smaller sticks (bails). The object of the game is to score more runs than the opposing team. A run is normally scored by the batsman striking the ball and exchanging ends with his or her partner until the ball is returned by a fielder, or by hitting the ball to the boundary line for an automatic four or six runs.

Crimea Ukrainian **Krym'**, northern peninsula on the Black Sea, an autonomous republic of Ukraine; formerly an oblast (region) of the Soviet Union (1954–91); area 27,000 sq km/10,425 sq mi; population (1995) 2,632,400. The capital is Simferopol; other main towns are Sevastopol and Yalta. The region produces iron, steel, and oil, and there is fruit- and vine-growing. The land is mainly steppe, but the south coast is a holiday resort.

Crimean War war (1853–56) between Russia and the allied powers of England, France, Turkey, and Sardinia. The war arose from British and French mistrust of Russia's ambitions in the Balkans. It began with an allied Anglo-French expedition to the Crimea to attack the Russian Black Sea city of Sevastopol. The battles of the River Alma, Balaclava (including the charge of the Light Brigade), and Inkerman in 1854 led to a siege which, owing to military mismanagement, lasted for a year until September 1855. The war was ended by the Treaty of Paris in 1856. The scandal surrounding French and British losses through disease led to the organization of proper military nursing services by Florence Nightingale.

criminal law body of law that defines the public wrongs (crimes) that are punishable by the state and establishes methods of prosecution and punishment. It is distinct from *civil law, which deals with legal relationships between individuals (including organizations), such as contract law.

critical mass in nuclear physics, the minimum mass of fissile material that can undergo a continuous *chain reaction. Below this mass, too many *neutrons escape from the surface for a chain reaction to carry on; above the critical mass, the reaction may accelerate into a nuclear explosion.

Croagh Patrick holy mountain rising to 765 m/2,510 ft in County Mayo, Republic of Ireland, a national place of pilgrimage. An annual pilgrimage on the last Sunday

of July commemorates St Patrick, who fasted there for the 40 days of Lent in 441 AD.

Croat the majority ethnic group in Croatia. Their language is generally considered to be identical to that of the Serbs, hence *Serbo-Croat.

Croatia

National name: *Republika Hrvatska/Republic of Croatia*

Area: 56,538 sq km/21,829 sq mi
Capital: Zagreb
Major towns/cities: Osijek, Split, Dubrovnik, Rijeka, Zadar, Pula
Major ports: chief port: Rijeka (Fiume); other ports: Zadar, Sibenik, Split, Dubrovnik
Physical features: Adriatic coastline with large islands; very mountainous, with part of the Karst region and the Julian and Styrian Alps; some marshland
Head of state: Stjepan Mesic from 2000
Head of government: Ivo Sanader from 2003
Political system: emergent democracy
Political executive: limited presidency
Political parties: Croatian Democratic Union (CDU), Christian Democrat, right of centre, nationalist; Croatian Social-Liberal Party (CSLP), centrist; Social Democratic Party of Change (SDP), reform socialist; Croatian Party of Rights (HSP), Croat-oriented, ultranationalist; Croatian Peasant Party (HSS), rural-based; Serbian National Party (SNS), Serb-oriented
Currency: kuna
GNI per capita (PPP): (US$) 9,760 (2002 est)
Exports: machinery and transport equipment, chemicals, foodstuffs, miscellaneous manufactured items (mainly clothing). Principal market: Italy 23.7% (2001)
Population: 4,428,000 (2003 est)
Language: Croat (official), Serbian
Religion: Roman Catholic (Croats) 76.5%; Orthodox Christian (Serbs) 11%, Protestant 1.4%, Muslim 1.2%
Life expectancy: 70 (men); 78 (women) (2000–05)
Chronology
early centuries AD: Part of Roman region of Pannonia.
AD 395: On division of Roman Empire, stayed in western half, along with Slovenia and Bosnia.
7th century: Settled by Carpathian Croats, from northeast; Christianity adopted.

924: Formed by Tomislav into independent kingdom, which incorporated Bosnia from 10th century.

12th–19th centuries: Autonomy under Hungarian crown, following dynastic union in 1102.

1526–1699: Slavonia, in east, held by Ottoman Turks, while Serbs were invited by Austria to settle along the border with Ottoman-ruled Bosnia, in Vojna Krajina (military frontier).

1797–1815: Dalmatia, in west, ruled by France.

19th century: Part of Austro-Hungarian Habsburg Empire.

1918: On dissolution of Habsburg Empire, joined Serbia, Slovenia, and Montenegro in 'Kingdom of Serbs, Croats, and Slovenes', under Serbian Karageorgevic dynasty.

1929: The Kingdom became Yugoslavia. Croatia continued its campaign for autonomy.

1930s: Ustasa, a Croat terrorist organization, began a campaign against dominance of Yugoslavia by the non-Catholic Serbs.

1941–44: Following German invasion, a 'Greater Croatia' Nazi puppet state, including most of Bosnia and western Serbia, formed under Ustasa leader, Ante Pavelic; more than half a million Serbs, Jews, and members of the Romany community were massacred in extermination camps.

1945: Became constituent republic of Yugoslavia Socialist Federation after communist partisans, led by Croat Marshal Tito, overthrew Pavelic.

1970s: Separatist demands resurfaced, provoking a crackdown.

late 1980s: Spiralling inflation and a deterioration in living standards sparked industrial unrest and a rise in nationalist sentiment, which affected the local communist party.

1989: The formation of opposition parties was permitted.

1990: The communists were defeated by the conservative nationalist CDU led by ex-Partisan Franjo Tudjman in the first free election since 1938. Sovereignty was declared.

1991: The Serb-dominated region of Krajina in the southwest announced its secession from Croatia. Croatia declared independence, leading to military conflict with Serbia, and civil war ensued.

1992: A United Nations (UN) peace accord was accepted; independence was recognized by the European Community (EC) and the USA; Croatia joined the UN. A UN peacekeeping force was stationed in Croatia. Tudjman was elected president.

1993: A government offensive was launched to retake parts of Serb-held Krajina, violating the 1992 UN peace accord.

1994: There was an accord with Muslims and ethnic Croats within Bosnia, to the east, to link the recently formed Muslim–Croat federation with Croatia.

1995: Serb-held western Slavonia and Krajina were captured by government forces; there was an exodus of Croatian Serbs. The offensive extended into Bosnia-Herzegovina to halt a Bosnian Serb assault on Bihac in western Bosnia. Serbia agreed to cede control of eastern Slavonia to Croatia over a two-year period. Zlatko Matesa was appointed prime minister.

1996: Diplomatic relations between Croatia and the Federal Republic of Yugoslavia (Serbia and Montenegro from 2003) were restored. Croatia entered the Council of Europe.

1997: The opposition was successful in local elections. The constitution was amended to prevent the weakening of Croatia's national sovereignty.

1998: Croatia resumed control over East Slavonia.

2000: In parliamentary elections, the ruling Croatian Democratic Union (HDZ) lost heavily to a centre-left coalition. The reformist Stipe Mesic was elected president. The Social Democrat leader, Ivica Rajan, became prime minister. Constitutional changes reduced the powers of the president and turned Croatia into a parliamentary democracy.

2003: Croatia submitted an application to join EU. The HDZ became the largest party with 66 seats in the 151-member legislature, ousting the centre-left governing coalition headed by the Social Democrats.

2005: President Mesic was re-elected for a further five-year term. Talks were expected to begin for Croatia's admission to the European Union.

crocodile large scaly-skinned *reptile with a long, low body and short legs. Crocodiles can grow up to 7 m/23 ft in length, and have long, powerful tails that propel them when swimming. They are found near swamps, lakes, and rivers in Asia, Africa, Australia, and Central America. They are fierce hunters and active mainly at night. Young crocodiles eat worms and insects, but as they mature they add frogs and small fish to their diet. Adult crocodiles will attack animals the size of antelopes and, occasionally, people. They can live up to 100 years and are related to the *alligator and the smaller cayman.

crocus any of a group of plants belonging to the iris family, with single yellow, purple, or white flowers and narrow, pointed leaves. They are native to northern parts of the Old World, especially southern Europe and Asia Minor. (Genus *Crocus*, family Iridaceae.)

Croesus (died 547 BC) Last king of Lydia (in western Asia Minor) 560–547 BC. Famed for his wealth, he expanded Lydian power to its greatest extent, conquering all Anatolia west of the river Halys and entering alliances with Media, Egypt, and Sparta. He invaded Persia but was defeated by *Cyrus (II) the Great. Lydia was subsequently absorbed into the Persian Empire.

croft small farm in the Highlands of Scotland, traditionally farmed cooperatively with other crofters; the 1886 Crofters Act gave security of tenure to crofters. Today, although grazing land is still shared, arable land is typically enclosed. Crofting is the only form of subsistence farming found in the UK.

Crohn's disease *or* **regional ileitis** chronic inflammatory bowel disease. It tends to flare up for a few days at a time, causing diarrhoea, abdominal cramps, loss of appetite, weight loss, and mild fever. The cause of Crohn's disease is unknown. However, research teams in Europe and the USA found that a number of cases of Crohn's disease can be attributed to a fault in the gene *Nod2*, which partly controls the way the immune system responds to gut microbes. Stress may also be a factor.

Cro-Magnon prehistoric human *Homo sapiens sapiens* believed to be ancestral to Europeans, the first skeletons of which were found in 1868 in the Cro-Magnon cave near Les Eyzies, in the Dordogne region of France. They are thought to have superseded the Neanderthals in the Middle East, Africa, Europe, and Asia about

40,000 years ago. Although modern in skeletal form, they were more robust in build than some present-day humans. They hunted bison, reindeer, and horses, and are associated with Upper Palaeolithic cultures, which produced fine flint and bone tools, jewellery, and naturalistic cave paintings.

Crompton, Samuel (1753–1827) English inventor at the time of the Industrial Revolution. He developed the 'spinning mule' in 1779, combining the ideas of Richard *Arkwright and James *Hargreaves. This span a fine, continuous yarn and revolutionized the production of high-quality cotton textiles.

Cromwell, Oliver (1599–1658) English general and politician, Puritan leader of the Parliamentary side in the English *Civil War. He raised cavalry forces (later called 'Ironsides'), which aided the victory at *Marston Moor in 1644, and organized the New Model Army, which he led (with General Fairfax) to victory at *Naseby in 1645. He declared Britain a republic (the *Commonwealth) in 1649, following the execution of Charles I. As Lord Protector (ruler) from 1653, Cromwell established religious toleration and raised Britain's prestige in Europe on the basis of an alliance with France against Spain.

Cromwell, Richard (1626–1712) Son of Oliver Cromwell, he succeeded his father as Lord Protector but resigned in May 1659, having been forced to abdicate by the army. He lived in exile after the Restoration until 1680, when he returned.

Cromwell, Thomas (c. 1485–1540) Earl of Essex, English politician who drafted the legislation that made the Church of England independent of Rome. Originally in Lord Chancellor Wolsey's service, he became secretary to *Henry VIII in 1534 and the real director of government policy; he was executed for treason. He was created a baron in 1536.

Cronus or **Kronos** in Greek mythology, the youngest of the *Titans; ruler of the world under his father *Uranus, the sky; and son of *Gaia, mother of the Earth. He was eventually overthrown by his son *Zeus.

crop in birds, the thin-walled enlargement of the digestive tract between the oesophagus and stomach. It is an effective storage organ especially in seed-eating birds; a pigeon's crop can hold about 500 cereal grains. Digestion begins in the crop, by the moisturizing of food. A crop also occurs in insects and annelid worms.

crop rotation system of regularly changing the crops grown on a piece of land. The crops are grown in a particular order to utilize and add to the nutrients in the soil and to prevent the build-up of insect and fungal pests. Including a legume crop, such as peas or beans, in the rotation helps build up nitrate in the soil, because the roots contain bacteria capable of fixing nitrogen from the air.

croquet outdoor game played with mallets and balls on a level hooped lawn measuring 27 m/90 ft by 18 m/60 ft. Played in France in the 16th and 17th centuries, it gained popularity in the USA and England in the 1850s.

Crosby, Bing (1904–1977) born Harry Lillis Crosby, US film actor and singer. He achieved world success with his distinctive style of crooning in such songs as 'Pennies from Heaven' (1936) (featured in a film of the same name) and 'White Christmas' (1942). He won an Academy Award for Best Actor for *Going My Way* (1944).

crossbill species of *finch, genus *Loxia*, family Fringillidae, order Passeriformes, in which the hooked tips of the upper and lower beak cross one another, an adaptation for extracting the seeds from conifer cones. The red or common crossbill *Loxia curvirostra* is found in parts of Eurasia and North America, living chiefly in pine forests.

croup inflammation of the larynx in small children, with harsh, difficult breathing and hoarse coughing. Croup is most often associated with viral infection of the respiratory tract.

crow any of 35 species of omnivorous birds in the genus *Corvus*, family Corvidae, order Passeriformes, which also includes choughs, jays, and magpies. Crows are usually about 45 cm/1.5 ft long, black, with a strong bill feathered at the base. The tail is long and graduated, and the wings are long and pointed, except in the jays and magpies, where they are shorter. Crows are considered to be very intelligent. The family is distributed throughout the world, though there are very few species in eastern Australia or South America. The common crows are *C. brachyrhynchos* in North America, and *C. corone* in Europe and Asia.

Crown colony any British colony that is under the direct legislative control of the Crown and does not possess its own system of representative government. Crown colonies are administered by a crown-appointed governor or by elected or nominated legislative and executive councils with an official majority. Usually the Crown retains rights of veto and of direct legislation by orders in council.

Crown jewels or **regalia** symbols of royal authority. The British set (except for the Ampulla and the Anointing Spoon) were broken up at the time of Oliver Cromwell, and the current set dates from the Restoration. In 1671 Colonel *Blood attempted to steal them, but was captured, then pardoned and pensioned by Charles II. The Crown Jewels are kept in the Tower of London in the Crown Jewel House.

Crown Prosecution Service body established by the Prosecution of Offences Act 1985, responsible for prosecuting all criminal offences in England and Wales. It is headed by the Director of Public Prosecutions (DPP), and brought England and Wales in line with Scotland (which has a procurator fiscal) in having a prosecution service independent of the police.

crucifixion death by fastening to a cross, a form of capital punishment used by the ancient Romans, Persians, and Carthaginians, and abolished by the Roman emperor Constantine. Specifically, the Crucifixion refers to the execution by the Romans of *Jesus in this manner.

crude oil unrefined form of *petroleum.

Cruelty, Theatre of theory advanced by Antonin Artaud in his book *Le Théâtre et son double/Theatre and its Double* (1938) and adopted by a number of writers and directors. It aims to substitute gesture and sound for spoken dialogue, and to shock the audience into awareness through the release of feelings usually repressed by conventional behaviour.

cruise missile long-range guided missile that has a terrain-seeking radar system and flies at moderate speed and low altitude. It is descended from the German V1 of World War II. Initial trials in the 1950s demonstrated the limitations of cruise missiles, which included high fuel consumption and relatively slow speeds (when compared to intercontinental ballistic missiles – ICBMs) as well as inaccuracy and a small warhead. Improvements to guidance systems by the use of terrain-contour matching (TERCOM) ensured pinpoint accuracy on low-level flights after launch from a mobile ground launcher (ground-launched cruise missile – GLCM), from an aircraft (air-launched cruise missile – ALCM), or from a submarine or ship (sea-launched cruise missile – SLCM).

crusade (French *croisade*) any one of a series of wars 1096–1291 undertaken by Christian Europeans to take control of Palestine, the Holy Land, from the Muslim rulers of the Middle East. Sanctioned by the *pope, leader of the Roman Catholic Church, the aims and effects of the crusades were varied. The crusaders were motivated by religious zeal and a desire for land and wealth, and the trading ambitions of the major Italian cities were also significant. The term came to embrace any war or campaign for alleged religious, political, or social ends.

crust rocky outer layer of the Earth, consisting of two distinct parts – the oceanic crust and the continental crust. The **oceanic** crust is on average about 10 km/6 mi thick and consists mostly of basaltic rock overlain by muddy sediments. By contrast, the **continental** crust is largely of granitic composition and has a more complex structure. Because it is continually recycled back into the mantle by the process of subduction, the oceanic crust is in no place older than about 200 million years. However, parts of the continental crust are over 3.5 billion years old.

crustacean one of the class of arthropods that includes crabs, lobsters, shrimps, woodlice, and barnacles. The external skeleton is made of protein and chitin hardened with lime. Each segment bears a pair of appendages that may be modified as sensory feelers (antennae), as mouthparts, or as swimming, walking, or grasping structures.

cryogenics science of very low temperatures (approaching *absolute zero), including the production of very low temperatures and the exploitation of special properties associated with them, such as the disappearance of electrical resistance (*superconductivity).

cryptosporidium waterborne parasite that causes disease in humans and other animals. It has been found in drinking water in the UK and USA, causing diarrhoea, abdominal cramps, vomiting, and fever, and can be fatal in people with damaged immune systems, such as AIDS sufferers or those with leukaemia. Just 30 cryptosporidia are enough to cause prolonged diarrhoea.

crystal regular-shaped solid that reflects light. Examples include diamonds, grains of salt, and sugar. Particles forming a crystal are packed in an exact and ordered pattern. When this pattern is repeated many millions of times, the crystal is formed. Such an arrangement of particles, that is regular and repeating, is called a giant molecular structure.

crystallography scientific study of crystals. In 1912 it was found that the shape and size of the repeating atomic patterns (unit cells) in a crystal could be determined by passing X-rays through a sample. This method, known as *X-ray diffraction, opened up an

sodium chloride

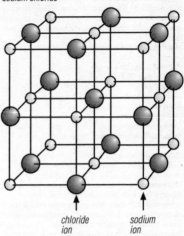

chloride | sodium
ion | ion

crystal The sodium chloride, or common salt, crystal is a regular cubic array of charged atoms (ions) – positive sodium ions and negative chloride ions. Repetition of this structure builds up into cubic salt crystals.

entirely new way of 'seeing' atoms. It has been found that many substances have a unit cell that exhibits all the symmetry of the whole crystal; in table salt (sodium chloride, NaCl), for instance, the unit cell is an exact cube.

CT scanner medical device used to obtain detailed X-ray pictures of the inside of a patient's body. See *CAT scan.

Cuba

National name: *República de Cuba/Republic of Cuba*

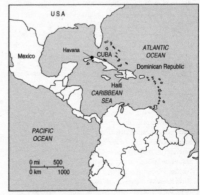

Area: 110,860 sq km/42,803 sq mi
Capital: Havana
Major towns/cities: Santiago de Cuba, Camagüey, Holguín, Guantánamo, Santa Clara, Bayamo, Cienfuegos

Physical features: comprises Cuba and smaller islands including Isle of Youth; low hills; Sierra Maestra mountains in southeast; Cuba has 3,380 km/2,100 mi of coastline, with deep bays, sandy beaches, coral islands and reefs

Head of state and government: Fidel Castro Ruz from 1959

Political system: communist

Political executive: communist

Political party Communist Party of Cuba (PCC), Marxist-Leninist

Currency: Cuban peso

GNI per capita (PPP): (US$) 2,300 (2002 est)

Exports: minerals, sugar, tobacco, citrus fruits, fish products. Principal market: Russia 22.4% (2001)

Population: 11,300,000 (2003 est)

Language: Spanish (official)

Religion: Roman Catholic; also Episcopalians and Methodists

Life expectancy: 75 (men); 79 (women) (2000–05)

Chronology

3rd century AD: The Ciboney, Cuba's earliest known inhabitants, were dislodged by the immigration of Taino, Arawak Indians from Venezuela.

1492: Christopher Columbus landed in Cuba and claimed it for Spain.

1511: Spanish settlement established at Baracoa by Diego Velazquez.

1523: Decline of American Indian population and rise of sugar plantations led to import of slaves from Africa.

mid-19th century: Cuba produced one-third of the world's sugar.

1868–78: Unsuccessful first war for independence from Spain.

1886: Slavery was abolished.

1895–98: Further uprising against Spanish rule, led by José Martí, who died in combat; 200,000 soldiers deployed by Spain.

1898: USA defeated Spain in Spanish-American War; Spain gave up all claims to Cuba, which was ceded to the USA.

1901: Cuba achieved independence; Tomás Estrada Palma became first president of the Republic of Cuba.

1906–09: Brief period of US administration after Estrada resigned in the face of an armed rebellion by political opponents.

1924–33: Gerado Machado established a brutal dictatorship.

1925: Socialist Party founded, from which the Communist Party later developed.

1933: Army sergeant Fulgencio Batista seized power.

1934: USA abandoned its right to intervene in Cuba's internal affairs.

1944: Batista retired and was succeeded by the civilian Ramon Gray San Martin.

1952: Batista seized power again to begin an oppressive and corrupt regime.

1953: Fidel Castro Ruz led an unsuccessful coup against Batista.

1956: Second unsuccessful coup by Castro.

1959: Batista overthrown by Castro and his 9,000-strong guerrilla army. Constitution was replaced by a 'Fundamental Law', making Castro prime minister, his brother Raúl Castro his deputy, and Argentine-born Ernesto 'Che' Guevara third in command.

1960: All US businesses in Cuba appropriated without compensation; USA broke off diplomatic relations.

1961: USA sponsored an unsuccessful invasion by Cuban exiles at the Bay of Pigs. Castro announced that Cuba had become a communist state, with a Marxist-Leninist programme of economic development, and became allied with the USSR.

1962: Cuban missile crisis: Cuba was expelled from the Organization of American States. Castro responded by tightening relations with the USSR, which installed nuclear missiles in Cuba (subsequently removed at US insistence). US trade embargo imposed.

1965: Cuba's sole political party renamed Cuban Communist Party (PCC). With Soviet help, Cuba began to make considerable economic and social progress.

1972: Cuba became a full member of the Moscow-based Council for Mutual Economic Assistance (COMECON).

1976: New socialist constitution approved; Castro elected president.

1976–81: Castro became involved in extensive international commitments, sending troops as Soviet surrogates, particularly to Africa.

1982: Cuba joined other Latin American countries in giving moral support to Argentina in its dispute with Britain over the Falklands.

1984: Castro tried to improve US–Cuban relations by discussing exchange of US prisoners in Cuba for Cuban 'undesirables' in the USA.

1988: A peace accord with South Africa was signed, agreeing to the withdrawal of Cuban troops from Angola, as part of a reduction in Cuba's overseas military activities.

1991: Soviet troops were withdrawn with the collapse of the USSR.

1993: The US trade embargo was tightened; market-oriented reforms were introduced in the face of a deteriorating economy.

1994: There was a refugee exodus; US policy on Cuban asylum seekers was revised.

1998: Castro was confirmed as president for a further five-year term.

1999: In an immigration dispute with the US, which focused on one child, Cuba demanded the return of illegal immigrants, and condemned the use of the US justice system on such matters.

2000: Trade talks were cancelled with European Union (EU) officials after EU countries voted in a UN committee to condemn Cuba's human rights record. The USA eased its 40-year-old economic embargo of Cuba, allowing exports of food and medicine.

2003: Government cracked down on dissidents. In elections, all 601 candidates nominated by the Partido Comunista Cubano (PCC; Communist Party of Cuba) were elected unopposed and Castro was re-elected unchallenged as leader for a sixth term of office.

2004: Cuba's human rights record continued to attract international condemnation.

Cuban missile crisis confrontation in international relations in October 1962 when Soviet rockets were installed in Cuba and US president John F *Kennedy compelled Soviet leader Nikita *Khrushchev, by military threats and negotiation, to remove them. This event prompted an unsuccessful drive by the USSR to match the USA in nuclear weaponry.

cube in geometry, a solid shape whose faces are all *squares. It has 6 equal-area faces and 12 equal-length edges.

cube in arithmetic, to multiply a number by itself and then by itself again. For example, 5 cubed = $5^3 = 5 \times 5 \times 5 = 125$. Alternatively, the *cube root of 125 is 5. The term also refers to a number formed by cubing; for example, 1, 8, 27, 64 are the first four cubes.

cube root number that, multiplied by itself, and then by the product, produces the *cube. For example, $3 \times 3 \times 3 = 27$, 3 being the cube root of 27, which is the cube of 3.

cubism revolutionary style of painting created by Georges *Braque and Pablo *Picasso in Paris between 1907 and 1914. It was the most radical of the developments that revolutionized art in the years of unprecedented experimentation leading up to World War I, and it changed the course of painting by introducing a new way of seeing and depicting the world. To the cubists, a painting was first and foremost a flat object that existed in its own right, rather than a kind of window through which a representation of the world is seen. Cubism also had a marked, though less fundamental, effect on sculpture, and even influenced architecture and the decorative arts.

Cuchulain (*or* **Cú Chulainn**) (lived 1st century AD) Legendary Celtic hero. A stupendous fighter in Irish hero-tales, he was the chief figure in a cycle associated with his uncle Conchobar mac Nessa, King of Ulster. While still a little boy, he performed his first great feat by slaying a ferocious hound. As a young man, he single-handedly kept a whole army at bay, and won battles in both the real world and the otherworld, but was slain through a combination of magic and treachery. His most famous exploits were recorded in *Tain Bó Cuailnge/The Cattle Raid of Cooley*. Cuchulain became a symbolic figure for the Irish cultural revival in the late 19th century, and a bronze statue of him stands in Dublin General Post Office, commemorating the Easter Rising.

cuckoo species of bird, any of about 200 members of the family Cuculidae, order Cuculiformes, especially the Eurasian cuckoo *Cuculus canorus*, whose name derives from its characteristic call. Somewhat hawklike, it is about 33 cm/1.1 ft long, bluish-grey and barred beneath (females are sometimes reddish), and typically has a long, rounded tail. Cuckoos feed on insects, including hairy caterpillars that are distasteful to most birds. It is a 'brood parasite', laying its eggs singly, at intervals of about 48 hours, in the nests of small insectivorous birds. As soon as the young cuckoo hatches, it ejects all other young birds or eggs from the nest and is tended by its 'foster parents' until fledging. American species of cuckoo hatch and rear their own young.

cucumber trailing annual plant belonging to the gourd family, producing long, green-skinned fruit with crisp, translucent, edible flesh. Small cucumbers, called gherkins, usually the fruit of *Cucumis anguria*, are often pickled. (*Cucumis sativus*, family Cucurbitaceae.)

Cugnot, Nicolas-Joseph (1725–1804) French engineer who produced the first high-pressure steam engine and, in 1769, the first self-propelled road vehicle. Although it proved the viability of steam-powered traction, the problems of water supply and pressure maintenance severely handicapped the vehicle.

Culloden, Battle of defeat in 1746 of the *Jacobite rebel army of the British prince *Charles Edward Stuart (the 'Young Pretender') by the Duke of Cumberland on a stretch of moorland in Inverness-shire, Scotland. This battle effectively ended the military challenge of the Jacobite rebellion.

Cultural Revolution Chinese mass movement from 1966 to 1969 begun by Communist Party leader *Mao Zedong, directed against the upper middle class – bureaucrats, artists, and academics – who were killed, imprisoned, humiliated, or 'resettled'. Intended to 'purify' Chinese communism, it was also an attempt by Mao to renew his political and ideological pre-eminence inside China. Half a million people are estimated to have been killed.

culture in biology, the growing of living cells and tissues in laboratory conditions.

culture in sociology and anthropology, the way of life of a particular society or group of people, including patterns of thought, beliefs, behaviour, customs, traditions, rituals, dress, and language, as well as art, music, and literature. Archaeologists use the word to mean the surviving objects or artefacts that provide evidence of a social grouping.

Cumberland, William Augustus (1721–1765) Duke of Cumberland, British general who ended the *Jacobite rising in Scotland with the Battle of *Culloden in 1746; his brutal repression of the Highlanders earned him the nickname of 'Butcher'.

Cumbria county of northwest England, created in 1974 from Cumberland, Westmorland, the Furness district of northwest Lancashire, and the Sedbergh district of northwest Yorkshire. **area:** 6,810 sq km/2,629 sq mi **towns and cities:** Carlisle (administrative headquarters), Barrow, Kendal, Penrith, Whitehaven, Workington **physical:** Scafell Pike (978 m/3,210 ft), the highest mountain in England; Helvellyn (950 m/3,118 ft); Lake Windermere, the largest lake in England (17 km/10.5 mi long, 1.6 km/1 mi wide), and other lakes (Derwentwater, Grasmere, Haweswater, Ullswater); the rivers Eden and Derwent **features:** Lake District National Park; Grizedale Forest sculpture project; Furness peninsula; western part of Hadrian's Wall **population:** (2001 est) 487,800.

cumin seedlike fruit of the herb cumin, which belongs to the carrot family. It has a bitter flavour and is used as a spice in cooking. (*Cuminum cyminum*, family Umbelliferae.)

Cummings, E(dward) E(stlin) (1894–1962) US poet and novelist. His work is marked by idiosyncratic punctuation and typography (often using only lower case letters in his verse, for example), and a subtle, lyric celebration of life. Before his first collection *Tulips and Chimneys* (1923), Cummings published an avant-garde novel, *The Enormous Room* (1922), based on his internment in a French concentration camp during World War I.

cuneiform ancient writing system formed of combinations of wedge-shaped strokes, usually impressed on clay. It was probably invented by the Sumerians, and was in use in Mesopotamia as early as the middle of the 4th millennium BC.

Cupid *or* **Amor** (Latin *cupido* 'desire') in Roman mythology, the god of love (Greek Eros); son of the goddess of love, *Venus, and either *Mars, *Jupiter, or *Mercury. Joyous and mischievous, he is generally represented as a winged, naked boy with a bow and arrow, sometimes with a blindfold, torch, or quiver.

According to the Roman poet Ovid, his golden arrows inspired love, while those of lead put love to flight.

cupronickel copper alloy (75% copper and 25% nickel), used in hardware products and for coinage.

curare black, resinous poison extracted from the bark and juices of various South American trees and plants. Originally used on arrowheads by Amazonian hunters to paralyse prey, it blocks nerve stimulation of the muscles. Alkaloid derivatives (called curarines) are used in medicine as muscle relaxants during surgery.

Curie, Marie (1867–1934) born Maria Sklodowska, Polish scientist who, with husband Pierre Curie, discovered in 1898 two new radioactive elements in pitchblende ores: polonium and radium. They isolated the pure elements in 1902. Both scientists refused to take out a patent on their discovery and were jointly awarded the Nobel Prize for Physics in 1903, with Henri *Becquerel, for their research on radiation phenomena. Marie Curie was also awarded the Nobel Prize for Chemistry in 1911 for the discovery of radium and polonium, and the isolation and study of radium.

curium chemical symbol Cm, synthesized, radioactive, metallic element of the *actinide* series, atomic number 96, relative atomic mass 247. It is produced by bombarding plutonium or americium with neutrons. Its longest-lived isotope has a half-life of 1.7×10^7 years.

curlew wading bird of the genus *Numenius* of the sandpiper family, Scolopacidae, order Charadriiformes. The curlew is between 36 cm/14 in and 55 cm/1.8 ft long, and has pale brown plumage with dark bars and mainly white underparts, long legs, and a long, thin, downcurved bill. It feeds on a variety of insects and other invertebrates. Several species live in northern Europe, Asia, and North America. The name derives from its haunting flutelike call.

curling game played on ice with stones; sometimes described as 'bowls on ice'. One of the national games of Scotland, it has spread to many countries. It can also be played on artificial (cement or tarmacadam) ponds. At the 1998 Winter Olympics in Nagano, Japan, curling was included as a medal event for the first time. In 1998 and 1992 it had been a demonstration event. At Nagano, the inaugural men's and women's titles were won by Switzerland and Canada respectively.

currant berry of a small seedless variety of cultivated grape (*Vitis vinifera*). Currants are grown on a large scale in Greece and California and are dried for use in cooking and baking. Because of the similarity of the fruit, the name 'currant' is also given to several species of shrubs (genus *Ribes*, family Grossulariaceae).

current in earth science, flow of a body of water or air, or of heat, moving in a definite direction. Ocean currents are fast-flowing bodies of seawater moved by the wind or by variations in water density between two areas. They are partly responsible for transferring heat from the Equator to the poles and thereby evening out the global heat imbalance. There are three basic types of ocean current: **drift currents** are broad and slow-moving; **stream currents** are narrow and swift-moving; and **upwelling currents** bring cold, nutrient-rich water from the ocean bottom.

current, electric see *electric current.

curve in geometry, the *locus of a point moving according to specified conditions. The circle is the locus of all points equidistant from a given point (the

centre). Other common geometrical curves are the *ellipse, *parabola, and *hyperbola, which are also produced when a cone is cut by a plane at different angles.

custard apple any of several large edible heart-shaped fruits produced by a group of tropical trees and shrubs which are often cultivated. Bullock's heart (*Annona reticulata*) produces a large dark-brown fruit containing a sweet reddish-yellow pulp; it is a native of the West Indies. (Family Annonaceae.)

Custer, George Armstrong (1839–1876) US Civil War general, who became the Union's youngest brigadier general in 1863 as a result of a brilliant war record. He was made a major general in 1865 but, following the end of the American Civil War, his rank was reduced to captain. He later rose to the rank of lieutenant colonel. He took part in an expedition against the Cheyennes in 1868, and several times defeated other American Indian groups in the West during the *Plains Wars. Custer campaigned against the Sioux from 1874, and was killed with a detachment of his troops by the forces of Hunkpapa Sioux chief Sitting Bull in the Battle of *Little Bighorn, Montana, also known as **Custer's last stand**, on 25 June 1876.

customs union organization of autonomous countries where trade between member states is free of restrictions, but where a tariff or other restriction is placed on products entering the customs union from nonmember states. Examples include the *European Union (EU), the Caribbean Community (CARICOM), the Central American Common Market, and the Central African Economic Community.

cuttlefish any of a family, Sepiidae, of squidlike cephalopods with an internal calcareous shell (cuttlebone). The common cuttle *Sepia officinalis* of the Atlantic and Mediterranean is up to 30 cm/1 ft long. It swims actively by means of the fins into which the sides of its oval, flattened body are expanded, and jerks itself backwards by shooting a jet of water from its 'siphon'.

Cuzco *or* **Cusco** capital of Cuzco department, south-central Peru, 560 km/350 mi southeast of Lima; situated in a small valley in the Andes at a height of over 3,350 m/11,000 ft above sea level; population (1993) 255,600. The city is a commercial centre, the hub of the South American travel network, and a tourist resort. Manufactures include woollen and leather goods, beer, and fertilizers. Cuzco was founded *c.* 1200 as the ancient capital of the *Inca empire and was captured by the Spanish conquistador Francisco Pizarro in 1533. It is the archaeological capital of the Americas and the oldest continually inhabited city on the continent.

cyanide CN⁻, ion derived from hydrogen cyanide (HCN), and any salt containing this ion (produced when hydrogen cyanide is neutralized by alkalis), such as potassium cyanide (KCN). The principal cyanides are potassium, sodium, calcium, mercury, gold, and copper. Most cyanides are poisons. Organic compounds containing a CN group are sometimes called cyanides but are more properly known as nitrites.

cyanobacteria singular **cyanobacterium**, alternative name for *blue-green algae. These organisms are actually not algae but bacteria. The ancestors of modern cyanobacteria generated the oxygen that caused a transformation some 2 billion years ago of the Earth's atmosphere.

cyanocobalamin chemical name for vitamin B_{12}, which is normally produced by micro-organisms in the gut. The richest sources are liver, fish, and eggs. It is essential to the replacement of cells, the maintenance of the myelin sheath which insulates nerve fibres, and the efficient use of folic acid, another vitamin in the B complex. Deficiency can result in pernicious anaemia (defective production of red blood cells), and possible degeneration of the nervous system.

cybernetics (Greek *kubernan* 'to steer') science concerned with how systems organize, regulate, and reproduce themselves, and also how they evolve and learn. In the laboratory, inanimate objects are created that behave like living systems. Applications range from the creation of electronic artificial limbs to the running of the fully automated factory where decision-making machines operate up to managerial level.

cyberspace imaginary, interactive 'worlds' created by networked computers; often used interchangeably with 'virtual world'. The invention of the word 'cyberspace' is generally credited to US science fiction writer William Gibson in his novel *Neuromancer* (1984).

cycad any of a group of plants belonging to the *gymnosperms, whose seeds develop in cones. Some are superficially similar to palms, others to ferns. Their large cones (up to 0.5 m/1.6 ft in length) contain fleshy seeds. There are ten genera and about 80–100 species, native to tropical and subtropical countries. Cycads were widespread during the Mesozoic era (245–65 million years ago). (Order Cycadales.)

Cyclades Greek **Kyklades**, group of about 200 Greek islands in the Aegean Sea, lying between mainland Greece and Turkey; area 2,579 sq km/996 sq mi; population (1991 est) 95,100. They include Andros, Melos, Paros, Naxos, and Siros, on which is the capital Hermoupoli.

cyclamen any of a group of perennial plants belonging to the primrose family, with heart-shaped leaves and petals that are twisted at the base and bent back, away from the centre of the downward-facing flower. The flowers are usually white or pink, and several species are cultivated. (Genus *Cyclamen*, family Primulaceae.)

cycle in physics, a sequence of changes that moves a system away from, and then back to, its original state. An example is a vibration that moves a particle first in one direction and then in the opposite direction, with the particle returning to its original position at the end of the vibration.

cycling riding a *bicycle for sport, pleasure, or transport. Cycle racing can take place on oval artificial tracks, on the road, or across country (cyclocross and mountain biking).

cyclone alternative name for a *depression, an area of low atmospheric pressure with winds blowing in a anticlockwise direction in the northern hemisphere and in a clockwise direction in the southern hemisphere. A severe cyclone that forms in the tropics is called a tropical cyclone or *hurricane.

Cyclops (Greek 'circle-eyed') in Greek mythology, one of a race of Sicilian giants with one eye in the middle of their foreheads. According to Homer, they lived as shepherds. *Odysseus blinded the Cyclops Polyphemus in Homer's *Odyssey*.

Cygnus large prominent constellation of the northern hemisphere, represented as a swan. Its brightest star is first-magnitude Alpha Cygni or *Deneb.

cylinder in geometry, a prism with a circular cross-section. In everyday use, the term applies to a **right cylinder**, in which the curved surface is perpendicular to the base.

cymbal ancient percussion instrument of indefinite pitch. It consists of a shallow, circular brass dish suspended from the centre. They are either used in pairs clashed together or singly, struck with a beater. Crashed cymbals can be heard in Dvorak's first and eighth *Slavonic Dances*. Extensive use of cymbals is found in much 20th-century orchestral music, often in conjunction with gongs and tam tams, such as in the *The Triumph of Time* (1972) by Harrison Birtwistle. Smaller finger cymbals or **crotala**, of ancient origin but used in the 20th century by Claude Debussy and Karlheinz Stockhausen, are precise in pitch. Rivet or 'buzz' cymbals incorporate loose rivets to add a sizzle to the sound. This effect can also be achieved by draping small chains over the cymbal.

Cymbeline (*or* **Cunobelin**) (**lived 1st century AD**) King of the Catuvellauni (AD 5–40), who fought unsuccessfully against the Roman invasion of Britain. His capital was at Colchester.

Cymru Welsh name for *Wales.

cynic member of a school of Greek philosophy (cynicism), founded in Athens about 400 BC by Antisthenes, a disciple of Socrates, who advocated a stern and simple morality and a complete disregard of pleasure and comfort.

cypress any of a group of coniferous trees or shrubs containing about 20 species, originating from temperate regions of the northern hemisphere. They have tiny scalelike leaves and cones made up of woody, wedge-shaped scales containing an aromatic *resin. (Genera *Cupressus* and *Chamaecyparis*, family Cupressaceae.)

Cyprus
National name: *Kipriakí Dimokratía/Greek Republic of Cyprus* (south); *Kibris Cumhuriyeti/Turkish Republic of Northern Cyprus* (north)

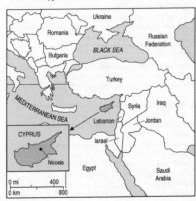

Area: 9,251 sq km/3,571 sq mi (3,335 sq km/1,287 sq mi is Turkish-occupied)
Capital: Nicosia (divided between Greek and Turkish Cypriots)
Major towns/cities: Limassol, Larnaca, Paphos, Lefkosia, Gazimagusa

Major ports: Limassol, Larnaca, and Paphos (Greek); Kyrenia and Famagusta (Turkish)
Physical features: central plain between two east–west mountain ranges
Head of state and government: Tassos Papadopoulos (Greek) from 2003 and Rauf Denktas (Turkish) from 1976
Political system: liberal democracy
Political executive: limited presidency
Political parties: *Greek zone*: Democratic Party (DEKO), federalist, centre left; Progressive Party of the Working People (AKEL), socialist; Democratic Rally (DISY), centrist; Socialist Party–National Democratic Union of Cyprus (SK–EDEK), socialist; *Turkish zone*: National Unity Party (NUP); Communal Liberation Party (CLP); Republican Turkish Party (RTP); New British Party (NBP)
Currency: Cyprus pound and Turkish lira
GNI per capita (PPP): (US$) 18,040 (2002 est)
Exports: pharmaceutical products, clothing, potatoes, manufactured foods, cigarettes, minerals, citrus fruits, industrial products. Principal market: UK 20.5% (2001)
Population: 802,000 (2003 est)
Language: Greek, Turkish (both official), English
Religion: Greek Orthodox 78%, Sunni Muslim 18%, Maronite, Armenian Apostolic
Life expectancy: 76 (men); 81 (women) (2000–05)
Chronology
14th–11th centuries BC: Colonized by Myceneans and Achaeans from Greece.
9th century BC: Phoenicans settled in Cyprus.
7th century BC: Several Cypriot kingdoms flourished under Assyrian influence.
414–374 BC: Under Evagoras of Salamis (in eastern Cyprus) the island's ten city kingdoms were united into one state and Greek culture, including the Greek alphabet, was promoted.
333–58 BC: Became part of the Greek Hellenistic and then, from 294 BC, the Egypt-based Ptolemaic empire.
58 BC: Cyprus was annexed by the Roman Empire.
AD 45: Christianity introduced.
AD 395: When the Roman Empire divided, Cyprus was allotted to the Byzantine Empire.
7th–10th centuries: Byzantines and Muslim Arabs fought for control of Cyprus.
1191: Richard the Lionheart of England conquered Cyprus as a base for Crusades; he later sold it to a French noble, Guy de Lusignan, who established a feudal monarchy which ruled for three centuries.
1498: The Venetian Republic took control of Cyprus.
1571: Conquered by Ottoman Turks, who introduced Turkish Muslim settlers, but permitted Christianity to continue in rural areas.
1821–33: Period of unrest, following execution of popular Greek Orthodox Archbishop Kyprianos.
1878: Anglo-Turkish Convention: Turkey ceded Cyprus to British administration in return for defensive alliance.
1914: Formally annexed by Britain after Turkey entered World War I as a Central Power.
1915: Greece rejected an offer of Cyprus in return for entry into World War I on Allied side.
1925: Cyprus became a crown colony.
1931: Greek Cypriots rioted in support of demand for union with Greece (*enosis*); legislative council suspended.

1948: Greek Cypriots rejected new constitution because it did not offer links with Greece.
1955: The National Organization of Cypriot Fighters (EOKA) began a terrorist campaign for *enosis*.
1958: Britain proposed autonomy for Greek and Turkish Cypriot communities under British sovereignty; plan accepted by Turks, rejected by Greeks; violence increased.
1959: Britain, Greece, and Turkey agreed to Cypriot independence, with partition and *enosis* both ruled out.
1960: Cyprus became an independent republic with Archbishop Makarios as president; Britain retained two military bases.
1963: Makarios proposed major constitutional reforms; Turkish Cypriots withdrew from government and formed separate enclaves; communal fighting broke out.
1964: United Nations (UN) peacekeeping force installed.
1968: Intercommunal talks made no progress; Turkish Cypriots demanded federalism; Greek Cypriots insisted on unitary state.
1974: Coup by Greek officers in Cypriot National Guard installed Nikos Sampson as president; Turkey, fearing *enosis*, invaded northern Cyprus; Greek Cypriot military regime collapsed; President Makarios restored.
1975: Northern Cyprus declared itself the Turkish Federated State of Cyprus, with Rauf Denktas as president.
1977: Makarios died; succeeded by Spyros Kyprianou.
1983: Denktas proclaimed independent Turkish Republic of Cyprus; recognized only by Turkey.
1985: Summit meeting between Kyprianou and Denktas failed to reach agreement; further peace talks failed in 1989 and 1992.
1988: Kyprianou was succeeded as Greek Cypriot president by Georgios Vassiliou.
1993: Glafkos Clerides (DISY) replaced Vassiliou.
1994: The European Court of Justice declared trade with northern Cyprus illegal.
1996: Further peace talks were jeopardized by the boundary killing of a Turkish Cypriot soldier; there was mounting tension between north and south.
1997: UN-mediated peace talks between Clerides and Denktas collapsed.
1998: President Clerides was re-elected. Denktas refused to meet a British envoy. US mediation failed. Full EU membership negotiations commenced. Greek Cyprus rejected Denktas's confederation proposals.
2000: Turkish Cypriot President Denktas was re-elected for a fourth five-year term.
2003: Denktas rejected a federal unity deal with the Greek part of the island, affecting Cyprus' proposed accession to the European Union (EU) in 2004.
2004: Turkish Cypriots endorsed a UN reunification plan, but in a simultaneous referendum the Greek community rejected it. A still-divided Cyprus was admitted to the EU in May.
2005: Turkey recognized Cyprus as a member of the EU, prior to its own accession talks, but stopped short of full diplomatic recognition.

Cyrano de Bergerac, Savinien (1619–1655) French writer. Joining a corps of guards at the age of 19, he performed heroic feats. He is the hero of a classic play by Edmond *Rostand, in which his excessively long nose is used as a counterpoint to his chivalrous character.

Cyrenaic member of a school of Greek *hedonistic philosophy founded in about 400 BC by Aristippus of Cyrene. He regarded pleasure as the only absolutely

worthwhile thing in life but taught that self-control and
intelligence were necessary to choose the best pleasures.

Cyril and Methodius, Sts Two brothers, both
Christian saints: Cyril (826–869) and Methodius
(815–885). Born in Thessalonica, they were sent as
missionaries to what is today Moravia. They invented
a Slavonic alphabet, and translated the Bible and the
liturgy from Greek to Slavonic. The language (known
as **Old Church Slavonic**) remained in use in churches
and for literature among Bulgars, Serbs, and Russians
up to the 17th century. The **cyrillic alphabet** is named
after Cyril and may also have been invented by him.
Their feast day is 14 February.

Cyrus (II) the Great (died 530 BC) King of Persia
559–530 BC and founder of the Achaemenid Persian
Empire. The son of the vassal king of Persia and of a
daughter of his Median overlord Astyages, Cyrus
rebelled in about 550 BC with the help of mutiny in the
Median army and replaced the Median Empire with a
Persian one. In 547 BC he defeated *Croesus of Lydia
at Pteria and Sardis, conquering Asia Minor. In 539 BC
he captured Babylon from Nabu-naid (Nabonidus) the
Chaldaean, formerly his ally against the Medes, and
extended his frontiers to the borders of Egypt. He was
killed while campaigning in Central Asia, and was
succeeded by his son Cambyses II.

cystic fibrosis hereditary disease involving defects of
various tissues, including the sweat glands, the mucous
glands of the bronchi (air passages), and the pancreas.
The sufferer experiences repeated chest infections and
digestive disorders and generally fails to thrive. In 1989
a gene for cystic fibrosis was identified by teams of
researchers in Michigan, USA, and Toronto, Canada.
This discovery enabled the development of a screening
test for carriers; the disease can also be detected in the
unborn child.

cystitis inflammation of the bladder, usually caused
by bacterial infection, and resulting in frequent and
painful urination. It is more common in women.
Treatment is by antibiotics and copious fluids with
vitamin C.

cytology study of the structure of *cells and their
functions. Major advances have been made possible in
this field by the development of *electron microscopes.

cytoplasm part of plant and animal cells outside the
*nucleus (and outside the large vacuole of plant cells).
Strictly speaking, this includes all the *organelles
(mitochondria, chloroplasts, and so on) and is the area
in which most cell activities take place. However,
cytoplasm is often used to refer to the jellylike matter in
which the organelles are embedded (correctly termed
the cytosol). Most of the activities in the cytoplasm are
chemical reactions (metabolism), for example, protein
synthesis.

cytotoxic drug any drug used to kill the cells of a
malignant tumour; it may also damage healthy cells.
Side effects include nausea, vomiting, hair loss, and
bone-marrow damage. Some cytotoxic drugs are also
used to treat other diseases and to suppress rejection
in transplant patients.

czar alternative spelling of *tsar, an emperor of Russia.

Czech Republic
formerly **Czechoslovakia (with Slovakia) (1918–93)**
National name: *Ceská Republika/Czech Republic*
Area: 78,864 sq km/30,449 sq mi

Capital: Prague
Major towns/cities: Brno, Ostrava, Olomouc, Liberec,
Plzen, Hradec Králové, Ceské Budejovice
Physical features: mountainous; rivers: Morava, Labe
(Elbe), Vltava (Moldau)
Head of state: Václav Klaus from 2003
Head of government: Stanislav Gross from 2004
Political system: liberal democracy
Political executive: parliamentary
Political parties: Civic Democratic Party (CDP), right
of centre, free-market; Civic Democratic Alliance
(CDA), right of centre, free-market; Civic Movement
(CM), liberal, left of centre; Communist Party of
Bohemia and Moravia (KSCM), reform socialist;
Agrarian Party, centrist, rural-based; Liberal National
Social Party (LNSP; formerly the Czech Socialist Party
(SP)), reform socialist; Czech Social Democratic Party
(CSDP), moderate left of centre; Christian Democratic
Union–Czech People's Party (CDU–CPP), right of
centre; Movement for Autonomous Democracy of
Moravia and Silesia (MADMS), Moravian and Silesian-
based, separatist; Czech Republican Party, far right
Currency: koruna (based on the Czechoslovak koruna)
GNI per capita (PPP): (US$) 14,500 (2002 est)
Exports: machinery and transport equipment, basic
manufactures, miscellaneous manufactured articles,
chemicals, beer. Principal market: Germany 38.1% (2001)
Population: 10,236,000 (2003 est)
Language: Czech (official), Slovak
Religion: Roman Catholic 39%, atheist 30%, Protestant
5%, Orthodox 3%
Life expectancy: 72 (men); 79 (women) (2000–05)
Chronology
5th century: Settled by West Slavs.
8th century: Part of Charlemagne's Holy Roman Empire.
9th century: Kingdom of Greater Moravia, centred
around the eastern part of what is now the Czech
Republic, founded by the Slavic prince Sviatopluk;
Christianity adopted.
906: Moravia conquered by the Magyars (Hungarians).
995: Independent state of Bohemia in the northwest,
centred around Prague, formed under the Premysl rulers,
who had broken away from Moravia; became kingdom
in 12th century.

1029: Moravia became a fief of Bohemia.

1355: King Charles IV of Bohemia became Holy Roman Emperor.

early 15th century: Nationalistic Hussite religion, opposed to German and papal influence, founded in Bohemia by John Huss.

1526: Bohemia came under the control of the Austrian Catholic Habsburgs.

1618: Hussite revolt precipitated the Thirty Years' War, which resulted in the Bohemians' defeat, more direct rule by the Habsburgs, and re-Catholicization.

1867: With creation of dual Austro-Hungarian monarchy, Bohemia was reduced to a province of Austria, leading to a growth in national consciousness.

1918: Austro-Hungarian Empire dismembered; Czechs joined Slovaks in forming Czechoslovakia as independent democratic nation, with Tomas Masaryk president.

1938: Under the Munich Agreement, Czechoslovakia was forced to surrender the Sudeten German districts in the north to Germany.

1939: The remainder of Czechoslovakia annexed by Germany, Bohemia-Moravia being administered as a 'protectorate'; President Eduard Beneš set up a government-in-exile in London; liquidation campaigns against intelligentsia.

1945: Liberated by Soviet and US troops; communist-dominated government of national unity formed under Beneš; 2 million Sudeten Germans expelled.

1948: Beneš ousted; communists assumed full control under a Soviet-style single-party constitution.

1950s: Political opponents purged; nationalization of industries.

1968: 'Prague Spring' political liberalization programme, instituted by Communist Party leader Alexander *Dubček, crushed by invasion of Warsaw Pact forces to restore the 'orthodox line'.

1969: New federal constitution, creating a separate Czech Socialist Republic; Gustáv Husák became Communist Party leader.

1977: The formation of the 'Charter '77' human-rights group by intellectuals encouraged a crackdown against dissidents.

1987: Reformist Miloš Jakeš replaced Husák as communist leader, and introduced a *prestvaba* ('restructuring') reform programme on the Soviet leader Mikhail Gorbachev's *perestroika* model.

1989: Pro-democracy demonstrations in Prague; new political parties formed and legalized, including Czech-based Civic Forum under Havel; Communist Party stripped of powers. New 'grand coalition' government formed; Havel appointed state president. Amnesty granted to 22,000 prisoners.

1991: The Civic Forum split into the centre-right Civic Democratic Party (CDP) and the centre-left Civic Movement (CM), evidence of increasing Czech and Slovak separatism.

1992: Václav Klaus, leader of the Czech-based CDP, became prime minister; Havel resigned as president following nationalist Slovak gains in assembly elections. The creation of separate Czech and Slovak states and a customs union were agreed. A market-centred economic-reform programme was launched, including mass privatization.

1993: The Czech Republic became a sovereign state within the United Nations (UN), with Klaus as prime minister. Havel was elected president.

1994: The Czech Republic joined NATO's 'partnership for peace' programme. Strong economic growth was registered.

1996: The Czech Republic applied for European Union (EU) membership.

1997: The former communist leader Miloš Jakeš was charged with treason. The ruling coalition survived a currency crisis. The Czech Republic was invited to begin EU membership negotiations. Klaus resigned after allegations of misconduct.

1998: Havel was re-elected president. The centre-left Social Democrats won a general election and a minority government was formed by Miloš Zeman, including communist ministers and supported from outside by Václav Klaus, who became parliamentary speaker. Full EU membership negotiations commenced.

1999: The Czech Republic became a full member of NATO.

2000: In December, television journalists went on strike, and thousands of protesters demonstrated in Prague, in response to the appointment of a new director general of television who was widely believed to be politically biased. The situation was resolved by the appointment of a new director general in January 2001.

2003: President Havel stepped down and was replaced by Václav Klaus. In a referendum 77% of voters supported accession to the European Union (EU) in 2004.

2004: The Czech Republic joined the EU.

2005: Jiri Paroubek, of the Social Democratic Party, became prime minister of a coalition government.

d

d abbreviation for **day**; **diameter**; **died**; in the UK, d was the symbol for a **penny** (Latin *denarius*) until decimalization of the currency in 1971.

D abbreviation for **500**, in the Roman numeral system.

dab small marine flatfish of the flounder family, especially the genus *Limanda*. Dabs live in the North Atlantic and around the coasts of Britain and Scandinavia.

dace freshwater fish *Leuciscus leuciscus* of the carp family. Common in England and mainland Europe, it is silvery and grows up to 30 cm/1 ft.

Dachau site of a Nazi *concentration camp during World War II, in Bavaria, Germany. The first such camp to be set up, it opened early in 1933 and functioned as a detention and forced labour camp until liberated in 1945.

dachshund (German 'badger-dog') small dog of German origin, bred originally for digging out badgers. It has a long body and short legs. Several varieties are bred: standard size (up to 10 kg/22 lb), miniature (5 kg/ 11 lb or less), long-haired, smooth-haired, and wire-haired.

Dacia ancient region covering much of modern Romania. The various Dacian tribes were united around 60 BC, and for many years posed a threat to the Roman empire; they were finally conquered by the Roman emperor Trajan AD 101–07, and the region became a province of the same name. It was abandoned by the emperor Aurelian to the invading Goths about 270.

Dada *or* **Dadaism** artistic and literary movement founded in 1915 in a spirit of rebellion and disillusionment during World War I and lasting until about 1922. Although the movement had a fairly short life and was concentrated in only a few centres (New York being the only non-European one), Dada was highly influential, allowing for new and more modern art movements to question and challenge traditional artistic and cultural conventions and values; indeed this was its aim. The intention of Dada art – often called anti-art – was to expose the ridiculous pretensions of a society that countenanced World War I by producing nihilistic and antirational art; for example, Marcel *Duchamp's *Fountain* (1917; Paris), a ceramic urinal signed R Mutt (the US manufacturer).

daddy-long-legs popular name for a *crane fly.

Dadra and Nagar Haveli since 1961, a Union Territory of west India, between Gujarat and Maharashtra states; area 491 sq km/190 sq mi; population (2001 est) 220,500. The capital is Silvassa. Four-fifths of the population belong to the Adivasi ethnic group, which includes the Varli, Dhodia, and Kondkan peoples. The predominant religion is Hinduism, with Christian and Muslim minorities. Until 1954 the territory was part of Portuguese Daman. Most of the population depends on agriculture, producing rice, wheat, and millet, although there are some industrial estates manufacturing plastics, chemicals, and fertilizers largely with the aid of migrant workers. 40% of the total area is forest, and felling of the valuable teak timber is regulated.

Daedalus in Greek mythology, a talented Athenian artisan. He made a wooden cow to disguise Pasiphae, wife of King Minos of Crete, when she wished to mate with a bull, and then constructed a *Labyrinth to house the creature of their union, the *Minotaur. Having incurred the displeasure of Minos, Daedalus fled from Crete with his son *Icarus, using wings made from feathers fastened with wax.

daffodil any of several Old World species of bulbous plants belonging to the amaryllis family, characterized by their trumpet-shaped yellow flowers which appear in spring. The common daffodil of northern Europe (*Narcissus pseudonarcissus*) has large yellow flowers and grows from a large bulb. There are numerous cultivated forms in which the colours range from white to deep orange. (Genus *Narcissus*, family Amaryllidaceae.)

Dagestan *or* **Daghestan** ('mountain kingdom') autonomous republic in the southwestern Russian Federation, in northern Caucasia; area 50,300 sq km/ 19,421 sq mi; population (1996) 2,098,000 (42% urban). The main cities are Makhachkala (capital) and Derbent. Situated mainly on the northeastern slopes of the main Caucasus Mountains, Dagestan is bounded on the east by the northwestern shore of the Caspian Sea; the Nogay steppe lowland is in the north, and the principal river is the Terek. There are plentiful oil and natural-gas deposits. Chief industries are oil and gas extraction, metalworking, and traditional crafts (carpet weaving); agricultural activities centre on the raising of livestock, the cultivation of grain and grapevines, and horticulture.

Daguerre, Louis Jacques Mandé (1787–1851) French pioneer of photography. Together with Joseph Niépce, he is credited with the invention of photography (though others were reaching the same point simultaneously). In 1837 he invented the *daguerreotype, a single image process superseded by *Fox Talbot's negative/positive process.

daguerreotype in photography, a single-image process using mercury vapour and an iodine-sensitized silvered plate; it was invented by Louis Daguerre in 1838.

Dahl, Roald (1916–1990) British writer, of Norwegian ancestry. He is celebrated for short stories with a twist, such as *Tales of the Unexpected* (1979), and for his children's books, including *James and the Giant Peach* (1961), *Charlie and the Chocolate Factory* (1964), *The BFG* (1982), and *Matilda* (1988). Many of his works have been successfully adapted for television or film. He also wrote the screenplay for the James Bond film *You Only Live Twice* (1967), and the script for *Chitty Chitty Bang Bang* (1968).

dahlia any of a group of perennial plants belonging to the daisy family, comprising 20 species and many cultivated forms. Dahlias are stocky plants with tuberous roots and showy flowers that come in a wide

247

range of colours. They are native to Mexico and Central America. (Genus *Dahlia*, family Compositae.)

Dahomey former name (until 1975) of the People's Republic of Benin.

Dáil Éireann lower house of the legislature of the Republic of Ireland (Oireachtas). It consists of 166 members elected by adult suffrage through the single transferable vote system of proportional representation from 41 constituencies for a five-year term.

Daimler, Gottlieb Wilhelm (1834–1900) German engineer who pioneered the car and the internal-combustion engine together with Wilhelm Maybach. In 1885 he produced a motor bicycle and in 1889 his first four-wheeled motor vehicle. He combined the vaporization of fuel with the high-speed four-stroke petrol engine.

daisy any of numerous species of perennial plants belonging to the daisy family, especially the field daisy of Europe and North America (*Chrysanthemum leucanthemum*) and the English common daisy (*Bellis perennis*), with a single white or pink flower rising from a rosette of leaves. (Family Compositae.)

Dakar capital, chief port (with artificial harbour), and administrative centre of Senegal; population (urban area, 1998 est) 1,905,000. It is situated at the tip of the Cape Verde peninsula, the westernmost point of Africa. It is a major industrial centre, with industries including mineral-oil and groundnut-oil refining, engineering, vehicle assembly, chemicals, brewing, and tobacco- and food-processing. Dakar contains the Grand Mosque, National Museum, and a university (established in 1949).

Dakota subgroup of the American Indian *Sioux people and dialect of the Siouan language.

Daladier, Edouard (1884–1970) French Radical politician, prime minister in 1933, 1934, and 1938–40, when he signed the Munich Agreement in 1938 (ceding the Sudeten districts of Czechoslovakia to Germany). After declaring war on Germany in September 1939, his government failed to aid Poland and, at home, imprisoned pacificists and communists. After his government resigned in March 1940, Daladier was arrested by the Vichy authorities, tried with Léon Blum at Riom in 1942, then deported to Germany, 1943–45. He was re-elected as a deputy 1946–58.

Dalai Lama (1935–) title of Tenzin Gyatso, (Tibetan 'oceanic guru') Tibetan Buddhist monk, political ruler of Tibet 1940–59, when he went into exile in protest against Chinese annexation and oppression. He has continued to campaign for self-government, and was awarded the Nobel Prize for Peace in 1989 for his work as spiritual and temporal leader of Tibet. Tibetan Buddhists believe that each Dalai Lama is a reincarnation of his predecessor and also of *Avalokitesvara. His deputy is called the Panchen Lama.

Dalap-Uliga-Darrit *or* **D-U-D** capital of the Marshall Islands; population (1999 est) 15,500. It is formed from Dalap (or Delap), Uliga, and Darrit (or Rita), three of the inhabited islands of the Majuro Atoll, on whose 57 islands and islets over half the total population of the Marshall Islands lives. The local economy is based on fishing and the cultivation of coconuts (copra is the chief export), cassava, and sweet potatoes.

Dales *or* **Yorkshire Dales** series of river valleys in northern England, running east from the Pennines in West Yorkshire; a National Park was established in 1954.

The principal valleys are Airedale, Nidderdale, Swaledale, Teesdale, Wensleydale, and Wharfedale. The three main peaks are Ingleborough, Whernside, and Pen-y-Ghent.

Dalglish, Kenny (Kenneth Mathieson) (1951–) Scottish footballer and football manager. A prolific goalscorer for Glasgow Celtic and then Liverpool, he was the first player to score 100 goals in both the English and Scottish first divisions. He won nine trophies as a player with Celtic and twelve with Liverpool including three European Cups. Overall, Dalglish made a record 102 international appearances for Scotland and equalled Denis Law's record of 30 goals. As a manager he won the league championship with Liverpool in 1986, 1988, and 1990, and with Blackburn Rovers in 1995.

Dalí, Salvador Felippe Jacinto (1904–1989) Spanish painter, designer, and writer. Originally drawn to many modern movements, in 1929 he joined the *surrealists and became one of their most notorious members, renowned for his flamboyant eccentricity. Influenced by the psychoanalytic theories and dream studies of Sigmund *Freud, he developed a repertoire of striking, dreamlike, hallucinatory images – distorted human figures, limp pocket watches, and burning giraffes – in superbly executed works, which he termed 'hand-painted dream photographs'. *The Persistence of Memory* (1931; Museum of Modern Art, New York) is typical. By the late 1930s he had developed a more conventional style – this, and his apparent fascist sympathies, led to his expulsion from the surrealist movement in 1938. It was in this more traditional though still highly inventive and idiosyncratic style that he painted such celebrated religious works as *The Crucifixion* (1951; Glasgow Museums). He also painted portraits of his wife Gala.

Dallas commercial city in northeastern Texas, USA, on the Trinity River; seat of Dallas County; population (2000 est) 1,188,600. The second-largest city in Texas (Houston is the largest), Dallas is the hub of a rich cotton-farming and oil-producing region, and is one of the leading cultural and manufacturing centres in the Southwest; its industries include banking, insurance, oil, aviation, aerospace, and electronics. Dallas was founded in 1841, and was incorporated as a city in 1871.

Dalmatia region divided between Croatia, Serbia and Montenegro, and Bosnia-Herzegovina. The capital is Split. It lies along the eastern shore of the Adriatic Sea and includes a number of islands. The interior is mountainous. Important products are wine, olives, and fish. Notable towns in addition to the capital are Zadar, Sibenik, and Dubrovnik. Dalmatia became Austrian in 1815 and by the treaty of Rapallo in 1920 became part of the kingdom of the Serbs, Croats, and Slovenes (Yugoslavia from 1931), except for the town of Zadar (Zara) and the island of Lastovo (Lagosta), which, with neighbouring islets, were given to Italy until transferred to Yugoslavia in 1947.

Dalmatian breed of dog, about 60 cm/24 in tall, with a distinctive smooth white coat with spots that are black or brown. Dalmatians are born white; the spots appear later. They were formerly used as coach dogs, running beside horse-drawn carriages to fend off highwaymen.

Dalton, John (1766–1844) English chemist who proposed the theory of atoms, which he considered to be the smallest parts of matter. He produced the first list of relative atomic masses in 'Absorption of Gases' in 1805 and put forward the law of partial pressures of gases (**Dalton's law**).

dam *or* **barrage** structure built across a river to hold back a body of water (called a reservoir) in order to prevent flooding, provide water for irrigation and storage, and provide *hydroelectric power. The biggest dams are of the earth- and rock-fill type, also called embankment dams. Such dams are generally built on broad valley sites. Deep, narrow gorges dictate a concrete dam, where the strength of reinforced concrete can withstand the water pressures involved.

Dam, Carl Peter Henrik (1895–1976) Danish biochemist who was awarded a Nobel Prize for Physiology or Medicine in 1943 for his discovery of vitamin K. He shared the prize with US biochemist Edward Doisy, who received the award for determining the chemical nature of vitamin K.

damages in law, compensation for a *tort (such as personal injuries caused by negligence) or breach of contract. In the case of breach of contract the complainant can claim all the financial loss he or she has suffered. Damages for personal injuries include compensation for loss of earnings, as well as for the injury itself. The court might reduce the damages if the claimant was partly to blame. In the majority of cases, the parties involved reach an out-of-court settlement (a compromise without going to court).

Daman and Diu Union Territory of west India; area 110 sq km/43 sq mi; capital Daman; population (2001 est) 158,000. **Daman** has an area of 72 sq km/28 sq mi. The port and capital, Daman, is on the west coast, 160 km/100 mi north of Mumbai (formerly Bombay), on the estuary of the Daman Ganga River flowing in the Gulf of Khambhat. The economy is based on tourism and fishing. **Diu** is an island off the Kathiawar peninsula with an area of 40 sq km/15 sq mi. The main town is also called Diu. The economy is based on tourism, coconuts, pearl millet, and salt.

Damascus Arabic **Dimashq** or **ash-Sham**, capital of Syria, on the River Barada, 100 km/62 mi southeast of Beirut; population (1994 est) 1,394,300. It produces silk, wood products, textiles, brass, and copperware. Said to be the oldest continuously inhabited city in the world, Damascus was an ancient city even in Old Testament times.

Dame in the UK honours system, the title of a woman who has been awarded the Order of the Bath, Order of St Michael and St George, Royal Victorian Order, or Order of the British Empire. It is also the legal title of the wife or widow of a knight or baronet, placed before her name.

Damocles (lived 4th century BC) in classical legend, a courtier of the elder Dionysius, ruler of Syracuse, Sicily. When Damocles made too much of his sovereign's good fortune, Dionysius invited him to a feast where he symbolically hung a sword over Damocles' head by a single horse-hair to demonstrate the precariousness of the happiness of kings.

damper any device that deadens or lessens vibrations or oscillations; for example, one used to check vibrations in the strings of a piano. The term is also used for the movable plate in the flue of a stove or furnace for controlling the draught.

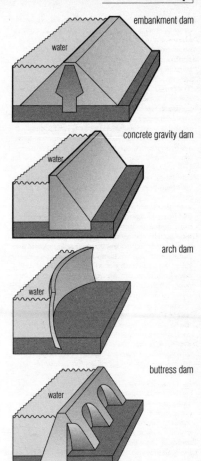

dam There are two basic types of dam: the gravity dam and the arch dam. The gravity dam relies upon the weight of its material to resist the forces imposed upon it; the arch dam uses an arch shape to take the forces in a horizontal direction into the sides of the river valley. The largest dams are usually embankment dams. Buttress dams are used to hold back very wide rivers or lakes.

Dampier, William (1651–1715) English explorer and hydrographic surveyor who circumnavigated the world three times.

damselfly long, slender, colourful *dragonfly of the suborder Zygoptera, with two pairs of similar wings that are generally held vertically over the body when at rest, unlike those of other dragonflies.

damson cultivated variety of plum tree, distinguished by its small oval edible fruits, which are dark purple or blue-black in colour. (*Prunus domestica* var. *institia*.)

dance rhythmic movement of the body, usually performed in time to music. Its primary purpose may be religious, magical, martial, social, or artistic – the last two being characteristic of nontraditional societies. The pre-Christian era had a strong tradition of ritual dance, and ancient Greek dance still exerts an influence on dance movement today. Although Western folk and social dances have a long history, the Eastern dance tradition long predates the Western. The European classical tradition dates from the 15th century in Italy, the first printed dance text from 16th-century France, and the first dance school in Paris from the 17th century. The 18th century saw the development of European classical *ballet as we know it today, and the 19th century saw the rise of Romantic ballet. In the 20th century *modern dance firmly established itself as a separate dance idiom, not based on classical ballet, and many divergent styles and ideas have grown from a willingness to explore a variety of techniques and amalgamate different traditions.

dandelion common plant throughout Europe and Asia, belonging to the same family as the daisy. The stalk rises from a rosette of leaves that are deeply indented like a lion's teeth, hence the name (from French *dent de lion*). The flower heads are bright yellow, and the fruit is covered with fine hairs, known as the dandelion 'clock'. (*Taraxacum officinale*, family Compositae.)

Dandie Dinmont breed of *terrier that originated in the Scottish border country. It is about 25 cm/10 in tall, short-legged and long-bodied, with drooping ears and a long tail. Its hair, about 5 cm/2 in long, can be greyish or yellowish. It is named after the character Dandie Dinmont in Walter Scott's novel *Guy Mannering* (1815).

Dane people of Danish culture from Denmark and northern Germany. There are approximately 5 million speakers of Danish (including some in the USA), a Germanic language belonging to the Indo-European family. The Danes are known for their seafaring culture, which dates back to the Viking age of expansion between the 8th and 10th centuries.

danegeld in English history, a tax imposed from 991 onwards by Anglo-Saxon kings to pay tribute to the Vikings. After the Norman Conquest (1066), the tax was revived and was levied until 1162; the Normans used it to finance military operations.

Danelaw 11th-century name for the area of northern and eastern England settled by the Vikings in the 9th century. It occupied about half of England, from the River Tees to the River Thames. Within its bounds, Danish law, customs, and language prevailed, rather than West Saxon or Mercian law. Its linguistic influence is still apparent in place names in this area.

Danish language member of the North Germanic group of the Indo-European language family, spoken in Denmark and Greenland and related to Icelandic, Faroese, Norwegian, and Swedish. It has had a particularly strong influence on Norwegian. As one of the languages of the Vikings, who invaded and settled in parts of Britain during the 9th to 11th centuries, Old Danish had a strong influence on English.

Dante Alighieri (1265–1321) Italian poet. His masterpiece *La divina commedia/The Divine Comedy* (1307–21) is an epic account in three parts of his journey through Hell, Purgatory, and Paradise, during which he is guided part of the way by the poet Virgil; on a metaphorical level, the journey is also one of Dante's own spiritual development. Other works include *De vulgari eloquentia/Concerning the Vulgar Tongue* (1304–06), an original Latin work on Italian, its dialects, and kindred languages; the philosophical prose treatise *Convivio/The Banquet* (1306–08), the first major work of its kind to be written in Italian rather than Latin; *De monarchia/On World Government* (1310–13), expounding his political theories; and *Canzoniere/Lyrics*.

Danton, Georges Jacques (1759–1794) French revolutionary. Originally a lawyer, during the early years of the Revolution he was one of the most influential people in Paris. He organized the uprising 10 August 1792 that overthrew Louis XVI and the monarchy, roused the country to expel the Prussian invaders, and in April 1793 formed the revolutionary tribunal and the **Committee of Public Safety**, of which he was the leader until July of that year. Thereafter he lost power to the *Jacobins, and, when he attempted to recover it, was arrested and guillotined.

Danube German *Donau*, second longest of European rivers, rising on the eastern slopes of the Black Forest, and flowing 2,858 km/1,776 mi across Europe to enter the Black Sea in Romania by a swampy delta.

Danzig German name for the Polish port of Gdansk.

Daphne in Greek mythology, a river *nymph who was changed by her mother, the earth goddess *Gaia, into a laurel tree to escape *Apollo's amorous pursuit. Determined to possess her, Apollo fashioned her branches and leaves into a crown and decorated his lyre and quiver with her foliage.

Dardanelles Turkish Çanakkale Bogazi; ancient **Hellespont**, Turkish strait connecting the Sea of Marmara with the Aegean Sea; its shores are formed by the *Gallipoli peninsula on the northwest and the mainland of Anatolia on the southeast. It is 75 km/47 mi long and 5–6 km/3–4 mi wide.

Dar es Salaam (Arabic 'haven of peace') chief city and seaport of Tanzania, on the Indian Ocean, administrative capital, pending the transfer of government functions to Dodoma, which was designated the official capital in 1974; population (2002 est) 2,212,700. Industries include food processing, textiles, clothing, footwear, petroleum refining, glass, printing, timber, aluminium, steel, polystyrene, machinery, and car components. Exports include copper, coffee, sisal, and cotton. As well as being the chief port and largest city, it is also the main industrial, commercial, and financial centre of Tanzania, and site of the main international airport.

Darius I the Great (c. 558–486 BC) King of Persia 521–486 BC. A member of a younger branch of the Achaemenid dynasty, he won the throne from the usurper Gaumata (died 522 BC) and reorganized the government. In 512 BC he marched against the Scythians, a people north of the Black Sea, and subjugated Thrace and Macedonia.

dark matter theoretical matter that, according to certain modern theories of *cosmology, is thought to make up over 90% of the mass of the universe but so far remains undetected. Measurements of the mass of galaxies using modern theories showed large discrepancies in the expected values, which led scientists to the conclusion that a theoretical substance that cannot be seen had to account for a significant proportion of the universe. Dark matter, if shown to exist, would account for many currently unexplained gravitational effects in the movement of galaxies.

Darling river in southeast Australia, a tributary of the River Murray; length 2,736 km/1,700 mi. The Darling is formed about 40 km/25 mi northeast of Bourke, at the union of the Culgoa and Bogan rivers (which rise in central Queensland to the west of the Great Dividing range); it flows southwest before joining the Murray at Wentworth. Its waters are conserved in Menindee Lake (155 sq km/60 sq mi) and others nearby. The river is usually navigable as far as Bourke during August to March.

Darlington unitary authority (borough status) in northeast England, created in 1997. **area:** 197 sq km/ 76 sq mi **towns and cities:** Darlington (administrative headquarters); villages of Hurworth on Tees, Middleton St George, Heighington, Hurworth Place **features:** River Tees forms southern boundary of authority; Darlington Railway Centre and Museum houses English engineer George Stephenson's Locomotion engine, which first ran from here to Stockton in 1825; St Cuthbert's church (1180) **population:** (2001 est) 97,900.

Darnley, Henry Stewart or **Stuart, Lord Darnley (1545–1567)** English aristocrat, second husband of Mary Queen of Scots from 1565, and father of James I of England (James VI of Scotland). On the advice of her secretary, David Rizzio, Mary refused Darnley the crown matrimonial; in revenge, Darnley led a band of nobles who murdered Rizzio in Mary's presence. Darnley was assassinated in 1567. He was knighted and became Earl of Ross and Duke of Albany in 1565.

Dartmoor plateau of southwest Devon, England; mostly a national park, 956 sq km/369 sq mi in area. Over half the region is around 300 m/1,000 ft above sea level, making it the highest and largest of the moorland areas in southwest England. The moor is noted for its wild aspect and the tors, rugged blocks of bare granite, which crown its loftier points. The highest are Yes Tor, rising to 619 m/2,030 ft, and High Willhays, which climbs to 621 m/2,039 ft.

darts indoor game played on a circular board. Darts (like small arrow shafts) about 13 cm/5 in long are thrown at segmented targets and score points according to their landing place.

Darwin, Charles Robert (1809–1882) English naturalist who developed the modern theory of *evolution and proposed, with Welsh naturalist Alfred Russel *Wallace, the principle of *natural selection. After research in South America and the Galapagos Islands as naturalist on HMS *Beagle* (1831–36), Darwin published *On the Origin of Species by Means of Natural Selection or the Preservation of Favoured Races in the Struggle for Life* (1859). This book explained the evolutionary process through the principles of natural selection and aroused widespread argument and debate among scientists and religious leaders because it disagreed with the literal interpretation of the Book of Genesis in the Bible.

dasyure any *marsupial of the family Dasyuridae, also known as a 'native cat', found in Australia and New Guinea. Various species have body lengths from 25 cm/10 in to 75 cm/2.5 ft. Dasyures have long, bushy tails and dark coats with white spots. They are agile, nocturnal carnivores, able to move fast and climb.

DAT abbreviation for *digital audio tape.

data singular *datum*, facts, figures, and symbols, especially as stored in computers. The term is often used to mean raw, unprocessed facts, as distinct from information, to which a meaning or interpretation has been applied.

database in computing, a structured collection of data, which may be manipulated to select and sort desired items of information. For example, an accounting system might be built around a database containing details of customers and suppliers. In larger computers, the database makes data available to the various programs that need it, without the need for those programs to be aware of how the data are stored. The term is also sometimes used for simple record-keeping systems, such as mailing lists, in which there are facilities for searching, sorting, and producing records. Examples of database software include Oracle, Sybase, and Microsoft Access.

data communications sending and receiving data via any communications medium, such as a telephone line. The term usually implies that the data are digital (such as computer data) rather than analogue (such as voice messages). However, in the ISDN (*Integrated Services Digital Network) system, all data – including voices and video images – are transmitted digitally. See also *telecommunications.

data compression in computing, techniques for reducing the amount of storage needed for a given amount of data. They include word tokenization (in which frequently used words are stored as shorter codes), variable bit lengths (in which common characters are represented by fewer *bits than less common ones), and run-length encoding (in which a repeated value is stored once along with a count).

data processing DP or **electronic data processing (EDP)** use of computers for performing clerical tasks such as stock control, payroll, and dealing with orders. DP systems are typically batch systems, running on mainframe computers.

date palm tree, also known as the date palm. The female tree produces the brown oblong fruit, dates, in bunches weighing 9–11 kg/20–25 lb. Dates are an important source of food in the Middle East, being rich in sugar; they are dried for export. The tree also supplies timber and materials for baskets, rope, and animal feed. (Genus *Phoenix*.)

dating in geology, the process of determining the age of minerals, rocks, fossils, and geological formations. There are two types of dating: relative and absolute. **Relative dating** involves determining the relative ages of materials, that is determining the chronological order of formation of particular rocks, fossils, or formations, by means of careful field work. **Absolute dating** is the process of determining the absolute age (that is the age in years) of a mineral, rock, or fossil. Absolute dating is accomplished using methods such as *radiometric dating (measuring the abundances of particular isotopes in a mineral), fission track dating, and even counting annual layers of sediment.

datura any of a group of plants belonging to the nightshade family, such as the *thorn apple. They have handsome trumpet-shaped blooms. They have narcotic (pain-killing and sleep-inducing) properties. (Genus *Datura*, family Solanaceae.)

Daumier, Honoré Victorin (1808–1879) French artist. His sharply dramatic and satirical cartoons dissected Parisian society. He produced over 4,000 lithographs and, mainly after 1860, powerful, sardonic oil paintings that were little appreciated in his lifetime.

dauphin title of the eldest son of the kings of France, derived from the personal name of a count, whose lands, known as the **Dauphiné**, traditionally passed to the heir to the throne from 1349 to 1830.

David king of the Hebrews 1004–965 BC. He became king of Judah on the death of King Saul at Mount Gilboa in 1004 BC, then king of Israel in 997 BC. He united the tribes against the Philistines, conquering their cities (such as Ekron), and extending his kingdom over Moab and other surrounding lands. He captured Jerusalem to make it the city of David, capital of the united tribes of Israel and Judah. He was succeeded by his son Solomon, and the Davidic line ruled in Jerusalem until 586 BC when the city was destroyed by *Nebuchadnezzar.

David statue in marble by *Michelangelo (1501–04; Accademia, Florence). The subject of David, biblical boy hero who killed the giant Goliath, was a popular symbol of the small republic of Florence; that Michelangelo portrayed the diminutive hero as a giant was seen as a grand statement of civic confidence. The sculpture's size (about 5.5 m/18 ft), combined with the mastery of its execution, has made it a symbol of the Renaissance itself.

David, Jacques-Louis (1748–1825) French painter. One of the greatest of the neoclassicists, he sought to give his art a direct political significance. He was an active supporter of the republic during the French Revolution, and was imprisoned 1794–95. In his *Death of Marat* (1793; Musées Royaux, Brussels), he turned political murder into classical tragedy. Later he devoted himself to the newly created empire in grandiose paintings such as *The Coronation of Napoleon* (1805–07; Louvre, Paris).

David two kings of Scotland:
David I (1084–1153) King of Scotland from 1124. The youngest son of Malcolm III Canmore and St *Margaret, he was brought up in the English court of *Henry I, and in 1113 married *Matilda, widow of the 1st earl of Northampton. He invaded England in 1138 in support of Queen Matilda, but was defeated at Northallerton in the Battle of the Standard, and again in 1141.
David II (1324–1371) King of Scotland from 1329, son of *Robert (I) the Bruce. David was married at the age of four to Joanna, daughter of Edward II of England. In 1346 David invaded England, was captured at the battle of Neville's Cross, and imprisoned for 11 years.

David, St (*or* St Dewi) (lived 5th–6th century) Patron saint of Wales, Christian abbot and bishop. According to legend he was the son of a prince of Dyfed and uncle of King Arthur. He was responsible for the adoption of the leek as the national emblem of Wales, but his own emblem is a dove. Feast day 1 March.

Davies, Peter Maxwell (1934–) English composer and conductor. His music combines medieval and serial techniques with a heightened expressionism as in his opera *Taverner* (1970), based on the life and works of the 16th-century composer John Taverner. Other works include the chamber opera *The Lighthouse* (1980), the music-theatre piece *Miss Donnithorne's Maggot* (1974), and the orchestral piece *Mavis in Las Vegas* (1997).

da Vinci Italian painter, sculptor, architect, engineer, and scientist; see *Leonardo da Vinci.

Davis, Bette (Ruth Elizabeth) (1908–1989) US actor. She established a reputation as a forceful dramatic actor with *Of Human Bondage* (1934). Other films include *Jezebel* (1938, Academy Award), *Now, Voyager* (1942), and *All About Eve* (1950). Her screen trademarks were a clipped, precise diction and a flamboyant use of cigarettes.

Davis, Jefferson (1808–1889) US politician, president of the short-lived Confederate States of America 1861–65. He was a leader of the Southern Democrats in the US Senate from 1857, and a defender of 'humane' slavery; in 1860 he issued a declaration in favour of secession from the USA. During the Civil War he assumed strong political leadership, but often disagreed with military policy. He was imprisoned for two years after the war, one of the few cases of judicial retribution against Confederate leaders.

Davis, Miles (Dewey, Jr) (1926–1991) US jazz trumpeter, composer, and bandleader. He was one of the most influential and innovative figures in jazz. He pioneered *bebop with Charlie *Parker in 1945, cool jazz in the 1950s, and jazz-rock *fusion from the late 1960s. His albums include *Birth of the Cool* (1957; recorded 1949 and 1950), *Milestones* (1958), *Sketches of Spain* (1960), *Bitches Brew* (1969), and *Tutu* (1985).

Davis, Steve (1957–) English snooker player who won every major honour in the game after turning professional in 1978. He was world champion six times and the number one ranked player from 1981 to 1989.

Davis Cup annual lawn tennis tournament for men's international teams, first held in 1900 after Dwight Filley Davis (1879–1945) donated the trophy.

Davison, Emily Wilding (1872–1913) English militant *suffragette who died after throwing herself under the king's horse at the Derby at Epsom (she was trampled by the horse). She joined the Women's Social and Political Union in 1906 and served several prison sentences for militant action such as stone throwing, setting fire to pillar boxes, and bombing Lloyd George's country house.

Davy, Humphry (1778–1829) English chemist. He discovered, by electrolysis, the metallic elements *sodium and *potassium in 1807, and *calcium, *boron, *magnesium, *strontium, and *barium in 1808. In addition, he established that *chlorine is an element and proposed that hydrogen is present in all acids. He invented the safety lamp for use in mines where *methane was present, enabling miners to work in previously unsafe conditions. He was knighted for his work in 1812 and made baronet in 1818.

Dawkins, (Clinton) Richard (1941–) English zoologist, born in Kenya, whose book *The Selfish Gene* (1976) popularized the theories of sociobiology (social behaviour in humans and animals in the context of evolution). In *The Blind Watchmaker* (1986) he explained the modern theory of evolution.

day time taken for the Earth to rotate once on its axis. That part of the Earth's surface at any one time facing the Sun experiences day. As the Earth rotates, these parts move to face away from the Sun, receiving no direct sunlight, and experience night.

Dayan, Moshe (1915–1981) Israeli general and politician. As minister of defence 1967 and 1969–74, he was largely responsible for the victory over neighbouring Arab states in the 1967 Six-Day War, but he was criticized for Israel's alleged unpreparedness in the 1973 October War and resigned along with Prime Minister Golda *Meir.

Day-Lewis, C(ecil) (1904–1972) Irish poet. With W H Auden and Stephen Spender, he was one of the influential left-wing poets of the 1930s. His later poetry moved from political concerns to a more traditional personal lyricism. He also wrote detective novels under the pseudonym **Nicholas Blake**. He was British poet laureate 1968–72.

D-day 6 June 1944, the day of the Allied invasion of Normandy under the command of General Eisenhower to commence Operation Overlord, the liberation of Western Europe from German occupation. The Anglo-US invasion fleet landed on the Normandy beaches on the stretch of coast between the Orne River and St Marcouf. Artificial harbours known as 'Mulberries' were constructed and towed across the Channel so that equipment and armaments could be unloaded on to the beaches. After overcoming fierce resistance the allies broke through the German defences; Paris was liberated on 25 August, and Brussels on 3 September. D-day is also military jargon for any day on which a crucial operation is planned. D+1 indicates the day after the start of the operation.

DDT abbreviation for dichloro-diphenyl-trichloroethane; $(ClC_6H_5)_2CHC(HCl_3)$, insecticide discovered in 1939 by Swiss chemist Paul Müller. It is useful in the control of insects that spread malaria, but resistant strains develop. DDT is highly toxic and persists in the environment and in living tissue. Despite this and its subsequent danger to wildlife, it has evaded a worldwide ban because it remains one of the most effective ways of controlling malaria. China and India were the biggest DDT users in 1999.

deadly nightshade another name for *belladonna, a poisonous plant.

Dead Sea large lake, partly in Israel and partly in Jordan, lying 394 m/1,293 ft below sea level; it is the lowest surface point on earth; area 1,020 sq km/394 sq mi. The chief river entering it is the Jordan; it has no outlet and the water is very salty (340 g of salt per litre of water). The sea is not, however, completely dead. *Dunaliella parva*, a single-celled green alga, and a group of halophilic (salt-loving) *Archaea are found here, and in 1998, three species of fungi were recorded.

Dead Sea Scrolls collection of ancient scrolls (rolls of writing) and fragments of scrolls found 1947–56 in caves on the western side of the Jordan, at *Qumran. They include copies of Old Testament books a thousand years older than those previously known to be extant. The documents date mainly about 150 BC–AD 68, when the monastic community that owned them, the Essenes, was destroyed by the Romans because of its support for a revolt against their rule.

deafness partial or total deficit of hearing in either ear.

Of assistance are hearing aids, lip-reading, a cochlear implant in the ear in combination with a special electronic processor, sign language, and 'cued speech' (manual clarification of ambiguous lip movement during speech). Approximately 10% of people worldwide experience some hearing difficulties. This amounts to approximately 28 million people in the USA alone.

Deakin, Alfred (1856–1919) Australian politician, prime minister 1903–04, 1905–08, and 1909–10. In his second administration, he enacted legislation on defence and pensions.

Dean, James (Byron) (1931–1955) US actor. A stage performer who had appeared in a small number of minor film roles, Dean was killed in a car accident soon after the public showing of the first film in which he starred, Elia Kazan's *East of Eden* (1955). He posthumously became a cult hero with *Rebel Without a Cause* (1955) and *Giant* (1956). Since his death, his image has endured as the classic icon of teenage rebellion.

death cessation of all life functions, so that the molecules and structures associated with living things become disorganized and indistinguishable from similar molecules found in nonliving things. In medicine, a person is pronounced dead when the brain ceases to control the vital functions, even if breathing and heartbeat are maintained artificially.

death cap fungus of the amanita group, the most poisonous mushroom known. The fruiting body, or mushroom, has a scaly white cap and a collarlike structure (volva) near the base of the stalk. (*Amanita phalloides*, family Agaricaceae.)

death's-head moth largest British *hawk moth with downy wings measuring 13 cm/5 in from tip to tip, and its thorax is marked as though with a skull.

Death Valley desert depression in southeastern California, USA; 225 km/140 mi long and 6–26 km/4–16 mi wide; area 8,368 sq km/3,231 sq mi. At 85 m/280 ft below sea level, Death Valley is the lowest point in North America. It is one of the world's hottest and driest places, with summer temperatures sometimes exceeding 51.7 °C/125 °F and an annual rainfall of less than 5 cm/2 in. Borax, iron ore, tungsten, gypsum, and salts are extracted here.

deathwatch beetle any wood-boring beetle of the family Anobiidae, especially *Xestobium rufovillosum*. The larvae live in oaks and willows, and sometimes cause damage by boring in old furniture or structural timbers. To attract the female, the male beetle produces a ticking sound by striking his head on a wooden surface, and this is taken by the superstitious as a warning of approaching death.

debt something that is owed by a person, organization, or country, usually money, goods, or services. Debt usually occurs as a result of borrowing *credit. **Debt servicing** is the payment of interest on a debt. The **national debt** of a country is the total money owed by the national government to private individuals, banks, and so on; **international debt**, the money owed by one country to another, began on a large scale with the investment in foreign countries by *newly industrialized countries in the late 19th to early 20th centuries. By the end of the 20th century, the two main types of debt in developing countries were **multilateral debt** (owed to international financial institutions such as the *World Bank) and **bilateral debt** owed to governments, either for aid loans or export credit guarantee department (ECGD) loans (made to underwrite exports). International debt became a global problem as a result of the oil crisis of the 1970s. Debtor countries paid an ever-increasing share of their national output in **debt servicing** (paying off the interest on a debt, rather than paying off the debt itself). In 1996 the World Bank and International Monetary Fund (IMF) introduced the Heavily Indebted Poor Countries (HIPC) debt-relief initiative, a debt-relief programme. The Cologne Debt Initiative (or HIPC2), launched by the Group of Eight (G8) industrialized nations in 1999, sought to speed up this process and release funding for poverty reduction.

debt-for-environment swap *or* **debt-for-nature swap** agreement under which a proportion of a country's debts are written off in exchange for a commitment by the debtor country to undertake projects for environmental protection. Debt-for-environment swaps were set up by environment groups in the 1980s in an attempt to reduce the debt problem of poor countries, while simultaneously promoting conservation. From its introduction until 2001, over fifty countries had taken part in some sort of debt-for-environment scheme.

Debussy, (Achille-) Claude (1862–1918) French composer. He broke with German Romanticism and introduced new qualities of melody and harmony based on the whole-tone scale. His work includes *Prélude à l'après-midi d'un faune/Prelude to the Afternoon of a Faun* (1894), illustrating a poem by Stéphane Mallarmé, and the opera *Pelléas et Mélisande* (1902).

Decameron, The collection of tales by the Italian writer Giovanni Boccaccio, brought together 1348–53. Ten young people, fleeing plague-stricken Florence, amuse their fellow travellers by each telling a story on the ten days they spend together. The work had a great influence on English literature, particularly on Chaucer's *Canterbury Tales*.

decathlon two-day athletic competition for men consisting of ten events: 100 metres, long jump, shot put, high jump, 400 metres (day one); 110-metre hurdles, discus, pole vault, javelin, 1,500 metres (day two). Points are awarded for performances, and the winner is the athlete with the greatest aggregate score. The decathlon is an Olympic event.

decay, radioactive see *radioactive decay.

decibel symbol dB, unit of measure used originally to compare sound intensities and subsequently electrical or electronic power outputs; now also used to compare voltages. A whisper has a sound intensity of 20 dB; 140 dB (a jet aircraft taking off nearby) is the threshold of pain.

deciduous describing trees and shrubs, that shed their leaves at the end of the growing season or during a dry season to reduce *transpiration (the loss of water by evaporation).

decimal fraction in mathematics, *fraction in which the denominator is any higher power of 10. Thus $^3/_{10}$, $^{51}/_{100}$, and $^{23}/_{1,000}$ are decimal fractions and are normally expressed as 0.3, 0.51, and 0.023. The use of *decimals greatly simplifies addition and multiplication of fractions, though not all fractions can be expressed exactly as decimal fractions.

decimal number system *or* **denary number system** most commonly used number system, to the base ten. Decimal numbers do not necessarily contain a decimal point; 563, 5.63, and –563 are all decimal numbers. Other systems are mainly used in computing and include the *binary number system, octal number system, and *hexadecimal number system.

Declaration of Independence historic US document stating the theory of government on which the USA was founded, based on the right 'to life, liberty, and the pursuit of happiness'. The statement was issued by the *Continental Congress on 4 July 1776, renouncing all allegiance to the British crown and ending the political connection with Britain.

Declaration of Rights in Britain, the statement issued by the Convention Parliament in February 1689, laying down the conditions under which the crown was to be offered to William III and Mary. Its clauses were later incorporated in the *Bill of Rights.

decolonization gradual achievement of independence by former colonies of the European imperial powers, which began after World War I. The process of decolonization accelerated after World War II with 43 states achieving independence between 1956 and 1960, 51 between 1961 and 1980, and 23 from 1981. The movement affected every continent: India and Pakistan gained independence from Britain in 1947; Algeria gained independence from France in 1962, the 'Soviet empire' broke up 1989–91.

decomposer in biology, any organism that breaks down dead matter. Decomposers play a vital role in the *ecosystem by freeing important chemical substances, such as nitrogen compounds, locked up in dead organisms or excrement. They feed on some of the released organic matter, but leave the rest to filter back into the soil as dissolved nutrients, or pass in gas form into the atmosphere, for example as nitrogen and carbon dioxide. The principal decomposers are bacteria and fungi, but earthworms and many other invertebrates are often included in this group. The *nitrogen cycle relies on the actions of decomposers.

decomposition chemical change in which one substance is broken down into two or more simpler substances. In biology, decomposition is the result of the action of decomposer organisms, such as bacteria and fungi. The decomposer organisms obtain food from dead organisms, such as carbon compounds, which are energy-rich. These organisms have an important role in the cycling of carbon compounds as part of the *carbon cycle. The *respiration of the organisms releases *carbon dioxide back into the atmosphere. Other organisms feed on the decomposers and they are part of the decomposer food chain. The decomposition of dead plants and animals allows chemicals to be washed out of the decaying remains into the soil. Many of these are important nutrients that plants can use.

decompression sickness illness brought about by a sudden and substantial change in atmospheric pressure. It is caused by a too rapid release of nitrogen that has been dissolved into the bloodstream under pressure; when the nitrogen forms bubbles it causes the *bends. The condition causes breathing difficulties, joint and muscle pain, and cramps, and is experienced mostly by deep-sea divers who surface too quickly.

deconstruction in literary theory, a radical form of *structuralism, pioneered by the French philosopher Jacques Derrida, which views text as a 'decentred' play of structures, lacking any ultimately determinable meaning.

Deconstructionism in architecture, a style that fragments forms and space by taking the usual building elements of floors, walls, and ceilings and sliding them apart to create a sense of disorientation and movement.

Decorated in architecture, the second period of English Gothic, covering the latter part of the 13th century and the 14th century. Chief characteristics include ornate window tracery, the window being divided into several lights by vertical bars called mullions; sharp spires ornamented with crockets and pinnacles; complex church vaulting; and slender arcade piers.

decretal in medieval Europe, a papal ruling on a disputed point, sent to a bishop or abbot in reply to a request or appeal. The earliest dates from Siricius 385. Later decretals were collected to form a decretum.

deduction in philosophy, a form of argument in which the conclusion necessarily follows from the premises. It would be inconsistent *logic to accept the premises but deny the conclusion.

Dee river which flows through Aberdeenshire, Scotland and the city of Aberdeen; length 137 km/85 mi. From its source in the Cairngorm Mountains, it flows east into the North Sea at Aberdeen (by an artificial channel in this latter stage). Near Braemar the river passes through a rock gorge, the **Linn of Dee**. Balmoral Castle is on its banks. It is noted for salmon fishing and is the fifth-longest river in Scotland.

Dee river that flows through Wales and England; length 112 km/70 mi. Rising in Bala Lake, Gwynedd, it flows into the Irish Sea west of Chester. There is another River Dee (61 km/38 mi) in Aberdeenshire, Scotland.

deed legal document that passes an interest in property or binds a person to perform or abstain from some action. Deeds are of two kinds: indenture and deed poll. **Indentures** bind two or more parties in mutual obligations. A **deed poll** is made by one party only, such as when a person changes his or her name.

deep-sea trench another term for *ocean trench.

deer any of various ruminant, even-toed, hoofed mammals belonging to the family Cervidae. The male typically has a pair of antlers, shed and regrown each year. Most species of deer are forest-dwellers and are distributed throughout Eurasia and North America, but are absent from Australia and Africa south of the Sahara.

deerhound breed of large, rough-coated dog, formerly used in Scotland for hunting and killing deer. Slim and long-legged, it grows to 75 cm/30 in or more, usually with a bluish-grey coat.

de Falla, Manuel Spanish composer; see *Falla, Manuel de.

defamation in law, an attack on a person's reputation by *libel or *slander.

Defender of the Faith one of the titles of the English sovereign, conferred on Henry VIII in 1521 by Pope Leo X in recognition of the king's treatise against the Protestant Martin Luther. It appears on coins in the abbreviated form **F.D.** (Latin *Fidei Defensor*).

defibrillation use of electrical stimulation to restore a chaotic heartbeat to a rhythmical pattern. In fibrillation, which may occur in most kinds of heart disease, the heart muscle contracts irregularly; the heart is no longer working as an efficient pump. Paddles are applied to the chest wall, and one or more electric shocks are delivered to normalize the beat.

deflation in economics, a reduction in the level of economic activity, usually caused by an increase in interest rates and reduction in the money supply, increased taxation, or a decline in government expenditure.

Defoe, Daniel (1660–1731) English writer. His *Robinson Crusoe* (1719), though claiming to be a factual account of shipwreck and solitary survival, was influential in the development of the novel. The fictional *Moll Flanders* (1722) and the partly factual *A Journal of the Plague Year* (1722) are still read for their concrete realism. A highly productive journalist and pamphleteer, he was imprisoned in 1703 for the ironic *The Shortest Way with Dissenters* (1702).

deforestation destruction of forest for timber, fuel, charcoal burning, and clearing for agriculture and extractive industries, such as mining, without planting new trees to replace those lost (reforestation) or working on a cycle that allows the natural forest to regenerate. The rate of deforestation is of major environmental concern as irreversible damage is being done to the habitats of plants and animals. Deforestation ultimately leads to famine, and is thought to be partially responsible for the flooding of lowland areas, since trees are needed to help slow down water movement.

Degas, (Hilaire Germain) Edgar (1834–1917) French painter and sculptor. Known for his ability to capture movement, he devoted himself to lively, informal situations (often using pastels) of ballet, horse racing, and young women working. From the 1890s he turned increasingly to sculpture, modelling figures in wax in a fluent, naturalistic style. Although he had links with *Impressionism, his work was in many ways quite distinct from the movement, favouring carefully draughted compositions executed in a studio environment.

de Gaulle, Charles André Joseph Marie (1890–1970) French general and first president of the Fifth Republic 1958–69. He organized the Free French troops fighting the Nazis 1940–44, was head of the provisional French government 1944–46, and leader of his own Gaullist party. In 1958 the national assembly asked him to form a government during France's economic recovery and to solve the crisis in Algeria. He became president at the end of 1958, having changed the constitution to provide for a presidential system, and served until 1969.

Degenerate Art German **Entartete Kunst**, art condemned by the Nazi regime in Germany from 1933. The name was taken from a travelling exhibition mounted by the Nazi Party in 1937 to show modern art as 'sick' and 'decadent' – a view that fitted with Nazi racial theories. The exhibition was paralleled by the official Great German Art Exhibition to display officially approved artists. However, five times as many people (more than 3 million) saw the former as the latter. Artists condemned included Max Beckmann, Emil Nolde, Wassily Kandinsky, Henri Matisse, Ernst Barlach, and Pablo Picasso.

degree symbol °, in mathematics, a unit of measurement of an angle or arc. A circle or complete rotation is divided into 360°. A degree may be subdivided into 60 minutes (symbol ´), and each minute may be subdivided in turn into 60 seconds (symbol ″). **Temperature** is also measured in degrees, which are divided on a decimal scale. See also *Celsius, and *Fahrenheit.

De Havilland, Geoffrey (1882–1965) English aircraft designer who designed and whose company produced the Moth biplane, the Mosquito fighter-bomber of World War II, and in 1949 the Comet, the world's first jet-driven airliner to enter commercial service. He was knighted in 1944.

dehydration process to preserve food. Moisture content is reduced to 10–20% in fresh produce, and this provides good protection against moulds. Bacteria are not inhibited by drying, so the quality of raw materials is vital.

Deimos one of the two moons of the planet Mars. It is irregularly shaped, 15 × 12 × 11 km/9 × 7.5 × 7 mi, orbits at a height of 24,000 km/15,000 mi every 1.26 days, and is not as heavily cratered as Mars's other moon, Phobos. Deimos was discovered in 1877 by US astronomer Asaph Hall, and is thought to be an asteroid captured by Mars's gravity.

Deirdre in Celtic mythology, the beautiful intended bride of Conchobar, king of Ulster. She eloped with Noísí, and died of sorrow when Conchobar killed him and his two brothers.

deism (Latin *deus* 'god') belief in a supreme being. The term usually refers to a movement in the 17th and 18th centuries characterized by the belief in a rational 'religion of nature' as opposed to the orthodox beliefs of Christianity. Deists believed that God is the source of natural law but does not intervene directly in the affairs of the world, and that the only religious duty of humanity is to be virtuous.

de Kooning, Willem (1904–1997) Dutch-born US painter. He emigrated to the USA in 1926 and worked as a commercial artist. After World War II he became, together with Jackson Pollock, one of the leaders of the abstract expressionist movement, although he retained figural images, painted with quick, violent brushstrokes. His *Women* series, exhibited in 1953, was criticized for its grotesque depictions of women.

Delacroix, (Ferdinand Victor) Eugène (1798–1863) French Romantic painter. His prolific output included religious and historical subjects and portraits of friends, among them the musicians Paganini and Chopin. Antagonistic to the French academic tradition, he evolved a highly coloured, fluid style, as in *The Death of Sardanapalus* (1829; Louvre, Paris).

de la Mare, Walter John (1873–1956) English poet and writer. His works include verse for children, such as *Peacock Pie* (1913), and the novels *The Three Royal Monkeys* (1910) (for children) and *The Memoirs of a Midget* (1921) (for adults). He excelled at creating a sense of eeriness and supernatural mystery. *The Listeners* (1912) established his reputation as a writer of delicately imaginative verse in the twin domains of childhood and dreamland.

Delaunay, Robert (1885–1941) French painter. He was a pioneer of abstract art. With his wife Sonia Delaunay-Terk, he developed a style known as *Orphism, an early variation of cubism, focusing on the effects of pure colour contrasts.

Delaware called the **First State** or the **Diamond State**, state in northeastern USA bordered to the north by *Pennsylvania, to the west and south by *Maryland, with which it shares the upper part of the Delmarva Peninsula, and to the east by the Atlantic Ocean; area 5,061 sq km/1,954 sq mi; population (2000) 783,600; capital Dover. The name Delaware originates from Thomas West de la Warr, the governor of Virginia from 1609. Physically, the land is divided into two regions, one hilly and wooded, the other undulating farmland. The most important sources of revenue are the finance, insurance, and property industries, and important products include dairy produce, poultry, market-garden produce, fish, and chemicals. The largest city is Wilmington, with the Wilmington–Newark area, extending into Maryland, forming the state's third major metropolitan area. The state was one of the original *Thirteen Colonies and on 7 December 1787 it became the first of the original 13 states to ratify the US Constitution.

de Lesseps, Ferdinand, Vicomte French engineer; see *Lesseps, Ferdinand, Vicomte de Lesseps.

Delhi *or* **Old Delhi** city of India, and administrative capital of the Union Territory of *Delhi (state); population (2001 est) 9,817,400. It borders on *New Delhi, capital of India, to the south. Manufactured goods include electronic goods, chemicals, motor-vehicle parts, and precision instruments, as well as traditional handicrafts such as hand-woven textiles, decorative copper and brass goods, gold and silver embroidery, and jewellery. Delhi is the hub of many national roads and railways, as well as being the major air terminal of northern India, with Indira Gandhi International Airport handling most international flights, while Palam Airport handles mainly domestic flights.

Delhi Union Territory of India from 1956, capital *Delhi; area 1,422 sq km/557 sq mi; population (2001 est) 13,660,000. It produces grain, sugar cane, fruit, and vegetables.

Delibes, (Clément Philibert) Léo (1836–1891) French composer. His lightweight, perfectly judged works include the ballet scores *Coppélia* (1870) and *Sylvia* (1876), and the opera *Lakmé* (1883).

delirium in medicine, a state of acute confusion in which the subject is incoherent, frenzied, and out of touch with reality. It is often accompanied by delusions or hallucinations.

Delius, Frederick Theodore Albert (1862–1934) English composer. His haunting, richly harmonious works include the opera *A Village Romeo and Juliet* (1901); the choral pieces *Appalachia* (1903), *Sea Drift* (1904), and *A Mass of Life* (1905); orchestral works such as *In a Summer Garden* (1908) and *A Song of the High Hills* (1911); chamber music; and songs.

della Robbia Italian family of artists; see *Robbia, della.

Delors, Jacques Lucien Jean (1925–) French socialist politician, economy and finance minister 1981–84 under François *Mitterrand's presidency, and president of the European Commission, 1985–94, when he oversaw significant budgetary reform, the introduction of the single European market, and the negotiation and ratification of the 1992 Maastricht Treaty on European Union.

Delphi city of ancient Greece, situated in a rocky valley north of the gulf of Corinth, on the southern slopes of Mount Parnassus, site of a famous *oracle in the temple of Apollo. The site was supposed to be the centre of the Earth and was marked by a conical stone, the *omphalos*. Towards the end of the 6th century BC the Athenian family of the Alcmaeonidae helped to rebuild the temple. The oracle was interpreted by priests from the inspired utterances of the Pythian priestess until it was closed down by the Roman emperor Theodosius I AD 390.

delphinium any of a group of plants containing about 250 species, including the butterfly or Chinese delphinium (*Delphinium grandiflorum*), an Asian form and one of the ancestors of the garden delphinium. Most species have blue, purple, or white flowers on a long spike. (Genus *Delphinium*, family Ranunculaceae.)

del Sarto, Andrea Italian Renaissance painter; see *Andrea del Sarto.

delta river sediments deposited when a river flows into a standing body of water with no strong currents, such as a lake, lagoon, sea, or ocean. A delta is the result of fluvial and marine processes. Deposition is enhanced when water is saline because salty water causes small clay particles to adhere together. Other factors influencing deposition include the type of sediment, local geology, sea-level changes, plant growth, and human impact. Some examples of large deltas are those of the Mississippi, Ganges and Brahmaputra, Rhône, Po, Danube, and Nile rivers. The shape of the Nile delta is like the Greek letter *delta* or Δ, and gave rise to the name.

dementia mental deterioration as a result of physical changes in the brain. It may be due to degenerative change, circulatory disease, infection, injury, or chronic poisoning. **Senile dementia**, a progressive loss of mental faculties such as memory and orientation, is typically a disease process of old age, and can be accompanied by *depression.

demesne in the Middle Ages in Europe, land kept in the lord's possession, not leased out but, under the *feudal system, worked by villeins to supply the lord's household.

Demeter in Greek mythology, the goddess of agriculture, especially corn (Roman **Ceres**); daughter of the Titans Kronos and Rhea; and mother of *Persephone by Zeus. Demeter and her daughter were worshipped in a sanctuary at Eleusis, where the Eleusinian Mysteries, one of the foremost *mystery religions of Greece, were celebrated.

DeMille, Agnes George (1909–1993) US dancer and choreographer. She introduced popular dance idioms into ballet with such works as *Rodeo* (1942). One of the most significant contributors to the American Ballet Theater, with dramatic ballets like *Fall River Legend* (1948), based on the Lizzie Borden murder case, she also led the change on Broadway to new-style musicals with her choreography of *Oklahoma!* (1943), *Carousel* (1945), and others.

De Mille, Cecil B(lount) (1881–1959) US film director and producer. He entered films in 1913 with Jesse L Lasky (with whom he later established Paramount Pictures), and was one of the founders of Hollywood. He specialized in lavish biblical epics, such as *The Sign of the Cross* (1932) and *The Ten Commandments* (1923), which he remade in 1956. His other films include *The King of Kings* (1927), *Cleopatra* (1934), *The Plainsman* (1936), *Samson and Delilah* (1949), and the 1952 Academy Award-winning *The Greatest Show on Earth*.

democracy (Greek *demos* 'the community', *kratos* 'sovereign power') government by the people, usually through elected representatives, such as local councillors or members of a parliamentary government. In the modern world, democracy has developed from the American and French revolutions.

Democratic Party older of the two main political parties of the USA, founded in 1792. It tends to be the party of the working person, as opposed to the Republicans, the party of big business, but the divisions between the two are not clear cut. Its stronghold since the Civil War has traditionally been industrial urban centres and the southern states, but conservative southern Democrats were largely supportive of Republican positions in the 1980s and helped elect President Reagan. Bill Clinton became the first Democrat president for 13 years in 1993. The party lost control of both chambers of Congress to the Republicans in November 1994, and increasing numbers of southern Democrat politicians later defected. However, in November 1996 Clinton became the first Democrat president since Franklin D Roosevelt to be elected for a second term, winning 31 states, chiefly in the northeast and west. Al Gore, who was vice president under Clinton, lost the 2000 presidential election to Republican George Bush, Jr.

Democritus (c. 460–c. 370 BC) Greek philosopher and speculative scientist who made a significant contribution to metaphysics with his atomic theory of the universe: all things originate from a vortex of tiny, indivisible particles, which he called atoms, and differ according to the shape and arrangement of their atoms.

demography study of the size, structure, dispersement, and development of human *populations to establish reliable statistics on such factors as birth and death rates, marriages and divorces, life expectancy, and migration. Demography is used to calculate life tables, which give the life expectancy of members of the population by sex and age.

Demosthenes (c. 384–322 BC) Athenian politician, famed for his oratory. From 351 BC he led the party that advocated resistance to the growing power of *Philip of Macedon, and in his *Philippics*, a series of speeches, incited the Athenians to war. This policy resulted in the defeat of Chaeronea in 338 BC, and the establishment of Macedonian supremacy. After the death of Alexander he organized a revolt; when it failed, he took poison to avoid capture by the Macedonians.

Demotic Greek common or vernacular variety of the modern *Greek language.

demotic script cursive (joined) writing derived from Egyptian hieratic script, itself a cursive form of *hieroglyphic.It was written horizontally, from right to left. Demotic documents are known from the 6th century BC to about AD 470.

Denbighshire Welsh **Sir Ddinbych**, unitary authority in north Wales. A former county, between 1974 and 1996 it was largely merged, together with Flint and part of

Merioneth, into Clwyd; a small area along the western border was included in Gwynedd. **area:** 844 sq km/ 326 sq mi **towns:** Ruthin (administrative headquarters), Denbigh, Llangollen **physical:** Clwydian range of mountains rises to a height of 555 m/1,820 ft, with *Offa's Dyke along the main ridge; rivers Clwyd, Dee, Elwy **features:** Denbigh and Rhuddlan castles (both 13th century); seaside resorts of Rhyl and Prestatyn **population:** (1998 est) 90,500.

Dench, Judi(th Olivia) (1934–) English actor. She made her professional debut as Ophelia in *Hamlet* (1957) with the Old Vic Company. Her Shakespearean roles include Viola (1969), Lady Macbeth (1976), and Cleopatra (1987). Her films include *A Room with a View* (1986), *A Handful of Dust* (1988), *Mrs Brown* (1997), and *Shakespeare in Love* (1998) for which she won an Academy Award for Best Supporting Actress. Her performance in the film *Chocolat* (2000) earned her a nomination for the same award in 2001.

dendrite part of a *nerve cell or neuron. The dendrites are slender filaments projecting from the cell body. They receive incoming messages from many other nerve cells and pass them on to the cell body. If the combined effect of these messages is strong enough, the cell body will send an electrical impulse along the axon (the threadlike extension of a nerve cell). The tip of the axon passes its message to the dendrites of other nerve cells.

dendrochronology *or* **tree-ring dating** analysis of the *annual rings of trees to date past events by determining the age of timber. Since annual rings are formed by variations in the water-conducting cells produced by the plant during different seasons of the year, they also provide a means of establishing past climatic conditions in a given area.

Deneb *or* **Alpha Cygni** brightest star in the constellation *Cygnus, and the 20th-brightest star in the night sky. It is one of the greatest supergiant stars known, with a true luminosity of about 60,000 times that of the Sun. Deneb is 1,800 light years from the Sun.

Deneuve, Catherine (1943–) born Catherine Dorléac, French actor. Graceful and elegant, she is one of the most famous French stars. Her breakthrough came with Jacques Demy's *Les Parapluies de Cherbourg/ Umbrellas of Cherbourg* (1964); since then she has worked with a number of leading film-makers, including Luis *Buñuel, Roman Polanski, and François *Truffaut.

Deng Xiaoping (*or* **Teng Hsiao-ping) (1904–1997)** Chinese political leader. A member of the Chinese Communist Party (CCP) from the 1920s, he took part in the *Long March (1934–36). He was in the Politburo from 1955 until ousted in the *Cultural Revolution (1966–69). Reinstated in the 1970s, he gradually took power and introduced a radical economic modernization programme. He retired from the Politburo in 1987 and from his last official position (as chair of the State Military Commission) in March 1990. He was last seen in public in February 1994. He appointed Jiang Zemin to succeed him on his death in 1997.

denier unit used in measuring the fineness of yarns, equal to the mass in grams of 9,000 metres of yarn. Thus 9,000 metres of 15 denier nylon, used in nylon stockings, weighs 15 g/0.5 oz, and in this case the thickness of thread would be 0.00425 mm/0.0017 in.

The term is derived from the French silk industry; the *denier* was an old French silver coin.

De Niro, Robert (1943–) US actor. He has frequently appeared in the works of the film-maker Martin Scorsese; for example, *Taxi Driver* (1976). He won Academy Awards for his performances in *The Godfather Part II* (1974) and *Raging Bull* (1980), in which he played a boxer struggling to control his emotional aggression. He is known for his portrayal of violent characters and total immersion in his roles.

denitrification process occurring naturally in soil, where bacteria break down *nitrates to give nitrogen gas, which returns to the atmosphere.

Denmark

National name: *Kongeriget Danmark/Kingdom of Denmark*

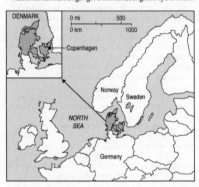

Area: 43,075 sq km/16,631 sq mi
Capital: Copenhagen
Major towns/cities: Århus, Odense, Ålborg, Esbjerg, Randers, Kolding, Horsens
Major ports: Århus, Odense, Ålborg, Esbjerg
Physical features: comprises the Jutland peninsula and about 500 islands (100 inhabited) including Bornholm in the Baltic Sea; the land is flat and cultivated; sand dunes and lagoons on the west coast and long inlets on the east; the main island is Sjælland (Zealand), where most of Copenhagen is located (the rest is on the island of Amager)
Territories: the dependencies of Faroe Islands and Greenland
Head of state: Queen Margrethe II from 1972
Head of government: Anders Fogh Rasmussen from 2001
Political system: liberal democracy
Political executive: parliamentary
Political parties: Social Democrats (SD), left of centre; Conservative People's Party (KF), moderate right-of-centre; Liberal Party (V), left of centre; Socialist People's Party (SF), moderate left wing; Radical Liberals (RV), radical internationalist, left of centre; Centre Democrats (CD), moderate centrist; Progress Party (FP), radical antibureaucratic; Christian People's Party (KrF), interdenominational, family values
Currency: Danish krone
GNI per capita (PPP): (US$) 29,450 (2002 est)
Exports: machinery and parts, pig meat and pork products, other food products, fish, industrial

258

machinery, chemicals, transport equipment. Principal market: Germany 18.9% (2000)
Population: 5,384,000 (2003 est)
Language: Danish (official), German
Religion: Evangelical Lutheran 87% (national church), other Protestant and Roman Catholic 3%
Life expectancy: 74 (men); 79 (women) (2000–05)
Chronology
5th–6th centuries: Danes migrated from Sweden.
8th–10th centuries: Viking raids throughout Europe.
c. 940–85: Harald Bluetooth unified Kingdom of Denmark and established Christianity.
1014–35: King Canute I created an empire embracing Denmark, Norway, and England; the empire collapsed after his death.
12th century: Denmark re-emerged as dominant Baltic power.
1340–75: Valdemar IV restored order after a period of civil war and anarchy.
1397: Union of Kalmar: Denmark, Sweden, and Norway (with Iceland) united under a single monarch.
1449: Sweden broke away from union.
1536: Lutheranism established as official religion of Denmark.
1563–70: Unsuccessful war to recover Sweden. There were two further unsuccessful attempts to reclaim Sweden, 1643–45 and 1657–60.
1625–29: Denmark sided with Protestants in Thirty Years' War.
1665: Frederick III made himself absolute monarch.
1729: Greenland became a Danish province.
1780–81: Denmark, Russia, and Sweden formed 'Armed Neutrality' coalition to protect neutral shipping during the American revolution.
1788: Serfdom abolished.
1800: France persuaded Denmark to revive Armed Neutrality against British blockade.
1801: First Battle of Copenhagen: much of Danish fleet destroyed by British navy.
1807: Second Battle of Copenhagen: British seized rebuilt fleet to pre-empt Danish entry into Napoleonic War on French side.
1814: Treaty of Kiel: Denmark ceded Norway to Sweden as penalty for supporting France in Napoleonic War; Denmark retained Iceland.
1849: Liberal pressure compelled Frederick VII to grant a democratic constitution.
1914–1919: Denmark neutral during World War I.
1918: Iceland achieved full self-government.
1929–40: Welfare state established under left-wing coalition government dominated by Social Democrat Party.
1940–45: German occupation.
1944: Iceland declared independence.
1949: Denmark became a founding member of the North Atlantic Treaty Organization (NATO).
1960: Denmark joined the European Free Trade Association (EFTA).
1973: Denmark withdrew from EFTA and joined the European Economic Community (EEC).
1981: Greenland achieved full self-government.
1992: A referendum rejected the Maastricht Treaty on European union; it was approved in 1993 after the government negotiated a series of 'opt-out' clauses
1993: Conservative leader Poul Schlüter resigned as prime minister due to a legal scandal.

1994: Schlüter was succeeded as prime minister by Poul Rasmussen, who, leading a Social Democrat-led coalition, won the general election.
1998: The government won a slim majority in assembly elections. A referendum endorsed the Amsterdam European Union (EU) treaty.
2000: A referendum rejected joining Europe's single currency and adopting the euro.
2003: Danish forces took part in the US-led invasion of Iraq.
2005: Anders Fogh Rasmussen (Liberal) became prime minister for the second time.

density measure of the compactness of a substance; it is equal to its mass per unit volume and is measured, for example, in kg per cubic metre or lb per cubic foot. Density is a scalar quantity. The average density D of a mass m occupying a volume V is given by the formula: $D = m/V$. Relative density is the ratio of the density of a substance to that of water at 4 °C/39.2 °F.

dental caries in medicine, another name for *caries.

dental formula way of showing the number of teeth in an animal's mouth. The dental formula consists of eight numbers separated by a line into two rows. The four above the line represent the teeth on one side of the upper jaw, starting at the front. If this reads 2 1 2 3 (as for humans) it means two incisors, one canine, two premolars, and three molars (see *tooth). The numbers below the line represent the lower jaw. The total number of teeth can be calculated by adding up all the numbers and multiplying by two.

dentistry care and treatment of the teeth and gums. Orthodontics deals with the straightening of the teeth for aesthetic and clinical reasons, and **periodontics** with care of the supporting tissue (bone and gums).

dentition type and number of teeth in a species. Different kinds of teeth have different functions; a grass-eating animal will have large molars for grinding its food, whereas a meat-eater will need powerful canines for catching and killing its prey. The teeth that are less useful to an animal's lifestyle may be reduced in size or missing altogether. An animal's dentition is represented diagramatically by a *dental formula.

Denver city and capital of *Colorado, in Denver County, on the South Platte River; population (2000 est) 554,600. At 1,609 m/5,280 ft above sea level, it is known as 'Mile High City' and is situated on the western edge of the Great Plains, 24 km/15 mi from the foothills of the Rocky Mountains. Denver is the commercial, manufacturing, and transportation centre for the central west region of the USA. It has major sheep and cattle markets, and is the headquarters for several US government agencies; industries include aerospace, the manufacture of rubber products, processed food, electronics, and building materials. Mining and tourism are also important to the economy. Denver was incorporated in 1861 and was made capital of Colorado Territory in 1867, and capital of the new state of Colorado in 1876. It became a city in 1902.

deoxyribonucleic acid full name of *DNA.

deposition in Christian art, a depiction of the body of Christ being taken down from the cross. Notable examples include van der Weyden's *Deposition* (c. 1430; Prado, Madrid) and Ruben's *Descent from the Cross* (1612–14; Notre Dame Cathedral, Antwerp).

depreciation in economics, the decline of a currency's value in relation to other currencies. Depreciation is also an accounting procedure applied to tangible assets. It describes the decrease in value of the asset (such as factory machinery) resulting from usage, obsolescence, or time. Amortization is used for intangible assets and depletion for wasting assets. Depreciation is applied to assets yearly, each time reducing the net book value of the asset. It is an important factor in assessing company profits and tax liabilities.

depression in economics, a period of low output and investment, with high unemployment. Specifically, the term describes two periods of crisis in world economy: 1873–96 and 1929 to the mid-1930s.

depression in medicine, an emotional state characterized by sadness, unhappy thoughts, apathy, and dejection. Sadness is a normal response to major losses such as bereavement or unemployment. After childbirth, *postnatal depression is common. Clinical depression, which is prolonged or unduly severe, often requires treatment, such as *antidepressant medication, *cognitive therapy, or, in very rare cases, *electroconvulsive therapy (ECT), in which an electrical current is passed through the brain.

depression or **cyclone** or **low** in meteorology, a region of relatively low atmospheric pressure. In mid-latitudes a depression forms as warm, moist air from the tropics mixes with cold, dry polar air, producing warm and cold boundaries (*fronts) and unstable weather – low cloud and drizzle, showers, or fierce storms. The warm air, being less dense, rises above the cold air to produce the area of low pressure on the ground. Air spirals in towards the centre of the depression in an anticlockwise direction in the northern hemisphere, clockwise in the southern hemisphere, generating winds up to gale force. Depressions tend to travel eastwards and can remain active for several days.

De Quincey, Thomas (1785–1859) English writer. His works include *Confessions of an English Opium-Eater* (1821) and the essays 'On the Knocking at the Gate in Macbeth' (1825) and 'On Murder Considered as One of the Fine Arts' (in three parts, 1827, 1839, and 1854). He was a friend of the poets William *Wordsworth and Samuel Taylor *Coleridge, and his work had a powerful influence on Charles Baudelaire and Edgar Allan Poe, among others.

Derain, André (1880–1954) French painter. He experimented with the strong, almost primary colours associated with *fauvism but later developed a more sombre landscape and figurative style. *Pool of London* (1906; Tate Gallery, London) is a typical work. He also produced costumes and scenery for Diaghilev's Ballets Russes.

Derby industrial city and administrative centre of Derby City unitary authority in north-central England, on the River Derwent, 51 km/32 mi northeast of Birmingham; population (2001 est) 221,700. Derby was granted city status in 1977 as part of the Queen's Silver Jubilee celebrations. Industries include engineering, chemicals, paper, textiles, plastics, and financial services.

Derby English horse-racing event, run over 2.4 km/1.5 mi at Epsom Downs, Surrey, every June. It was established in 1780 and named after the 12th Earl of Derby. The USA has an equivalent horse race, the Kentucky Derby.

Derby, Edward (George Geoffrey Smith) Stanley (1799–1869) 14th Earl of Derby, British politician. He was leader of the Conservative Party 1846–68 and prime minister 1852, 1858–59, and 1866–68, each time as head of a minority government. Originally a Whig, he became secretary for the colonies in 1830, and introduced the bill for the abolition of slavery. He joined the Tories in 1834, serving as secretary for war and the colonies in Peel's government. Derby was a protectionist and the split the Tory party over Peel's free-trade policy gave him the leadership for 20 years. During his third adminstration, the second Reform Act (1867) was passed. He inherited the title of Lord Stanley in 1834, became a peer in 1844, and succeeded to the earldom in 1851.

Derbyshire county of north central England (since April 1997 Derby City has been a separate unitary authority). **area:** 2,550 sq km/984 sq mi **towns and cities:** Matlock (administrative headquarters), Buxton, Chesterfield, Glossop, Ilkeston, Long Eaton **physical:** Peak District National Park (including Kinder Scout 636 m/2,088 ft); rivers Dane, Derwent, Dove, Goyt, Rother, Trent, Wye; Dove Dale **features:** Chatsworth House (seat of the Duke of Devonshire); Bakewell, home to the eponymous tart; Haddon Hall (1170 and 1370); Hardwick Hall (1597); Kedleston Hall (1759, designed by Robert Adam); well-dressing at Tissington, Wirksworth, Eyam, and other villages; Castleton Caverns **population:** (2001 est) 734,900.

dermatology medical speciality concerned with diagnosis and treatment of skin disorders.

derris climbing leguminous plant (see *legume) of southeast Asia. Its roots contain rotenone, a strong insecticide. (*Derris elliptica*, family Fabaceae.)

dervish in Iran and Turkey, a religious mendicant; throughout the rest of Islam a member of an Islamic religious brotherhood, not necessarily mendicant in character. The Arabic equivalent is **fakir**. There are various orders of dervishes, each with its rule and special ritual. The 'whirling dervishes' claim close communion with the deity through ecstatic dancing, reaching spiritual awareness with a trancelike state created by continual whirling. The spinning symbolizes the Earth's orbit of the Sun. 'Howling dervishes' gash themselves with knives to demonstrate the miraculous feats possible to those who trust in Allah.

desalination removal of salt, usually from sea water, to produce fresh water for irrigation or drinking. Distillation has usually been the method adopted, but in the 1970s a cheaper process, using certain polymer materials that filter the molecules of salt from the water by reverse osmosis, was developed.

Descartes, René (1596–1650) French philosopher and mathematician. He believed that commonly accepted knowledge was doubtful because of the subjective nature of the senses, and attempted to rebuild human knowledge using as his foundation the dictum *cogito ergo sum* ('I think, therefore I am'). He also believed that the entire material universe could be explained in terms of mathematical physics, and founded coordinate geometry as a way of defining and manipulating geometrical shapes by means of algebraic expressions. *Cartesian coordinates, the means by which points are represented in this system, are named after him. Descartes also established the science of optics, and helped to shape contemporary theories of astronomy and animal behaviour.

desert arid area with sparse vegetation (or, in rare cases, almost no vegetation). Soils are poor, and many deserts include areas of shifting sands. Deserts can be either hot or cold. Almost 33% of the Earth's land surface is desert, and this proportion is increasing. Arid land is defined as receiving less than 250 mm/9.75 in rain per year.

desertification spread of deserts by changes in climate, or by human-aided processes. Desertification can sometimes be reversed by special planting (marram grass, trees) and by the use of water-absorbent plastic grains, which, added to the soil, enable crops to be grown. About 30% of land worldwide is affected by desertification (1998), including 1 million hectares in Africa and 1.4 million hectares in Asia. The most rapid desertification is in developed countries such as the USA, Australia, and Spain.

Desert Storm, Operation code-name of the military action to eject the Iraqi army from Kuwait during 1991. The build-up phase was code-named **Operation Desert Shield** and lasted from August 1990, when Kuwait was first invaded by Iraq, to January 1991 when Operation Desert Storm was unleashed, starting the *Gulf War. Desert Storm ended with the defeat of the Iraqi army in the Kuwaiti theatre of operations in late February 1991. The cost of the operation was $53 billion.

desktop publishing (DTP) use of microcomputers for small-scale typesetting and page makeup. DTP systems are capable of producing camera-ready pages (pages ready for photographing and printing), made up of text and graphics, with text set in different typefaces and sizes. The page can be previewed on the screen before final printing on a laser printer.

Desmoulins, (Lucie Simplice) Camille (Benoist) (1760–1794) French revolutionary who summoned the mob to arms on 12 July 1789, so precipitating the revolt that culminated in the storming of the Bastille. A prominent left-wing *Jacobin, he was elected to the National Convention in 1792. His *Histoire des Brissotins* was largely responsible for the overthrow of the right-wing *Girondins, but shortly after he was sent to the guillotine as too moderate.

Desprez, Josquin Franco-Flemish composer; see *Josquin Desprez.

Dessalines, Jean Jacques (c. 1758–1806) Emperor of Haiti 1804–06. Born in Guinea, he was taken to Haiti as a slave, where in 1802 he succeeded *Toussaint L'Ouverture as leader of the black revolt against the French. After defeating the French, he proclaimed Haiti's independence and made himself emperor. He was killed when trying to suppress an uprising provoked by his cruelty.

détente (French) reduction of political tension and the easing of strained relations between nations, as seen in the ending of the *Cold War 1989–90. The term was first used in the 1970s to describe the new easing of relations between the world's two major superpowers, the USA and the USSR. This resulted in increased contact between East and West in the form of trade agreements and cultural exchanges, and even saw restored relation between the USA and communist China.

detergent surface-active cleansing agent. The common detergents are made from *fats (hydrocarbons) and sulphuric acid, and their long-chain molecules have a type of structure similar to that of *soap molecules: a salt group at one end attached to a long hydrocarbon 'tail'. They have the advantage over soap in that they do not produce scum by forming insoluble salts with the calcium and magnesium ions present in hard water.

determinant in mathematics, an array of elements written as a square, and denoted by two vertical lines enclosing the array. For a 2×2 matrix, the determinant is given by the difference between the products of the diagonal terms. Determinants are used to solve sets of *simultaneous equations by matrix methods.

determinism in philosophy, the view that every event is an instance of some scientific law of nature; or that every event has at least one cause; or that nature is uniform. The thesis cannot be proved or disproved. Determinism is also the theory that we do not have free will, because our choices and actions are caused.

deterrence underlying conception of the nuclear arms race: the belief that a potential aggressor will be discouraged from launching a 'first strike' nuclear attack by the knowledge that the adversary is capable of inflicting 'unacceptable damage' in a retaliatory strike. This doctrine is widely known as that of **mutual assured destruction (MAD)**. Three essential characteristics of deterrence are: the 'capability to act', 'credibility', and the 'will to act'.

de Tocqueville, Alexis French politician; see *Tocqueville, Alexis de.

Detroit industrial city and port in southeastern Michigan, USA, 788 km/489 mi west of New York and 395 km/245 mi east of Chicago, situated on the Detroit River opposite the city of Windsor in Ontario, Canada; seat of Wayne County; area 370 sq km/143 sq mi (excluding neighbouring cities); metropolitan area 10,093 sq km/3,897 sq mi; population (2000 est) 951,300. Detroit is the headquarters of the automobile manufacturers Ford, Chrysler (merged with Daimler in 1991), and General Motors, hence its nickname Motown (from 'motor town'). Other manufactured products include steel, machine tools, chemicals, and pharmaceuticals. It is the tenth-largest city in the USA.

deuterium *or* **heavy hydrogen** naturally occurring heavy isotope of hydrogen, mass number 2 (one proton and one neutron), discovered by US chemist Harold Urey in 1932. It is sometimes given the symbol D. In nature, about one in every 6,500 hydrogen atoms is deuterium. Combined with oxygen, it produces 'heavy water' (D_2O), used in the nuclear industry.

de Valera, Éamon (1882–1975) Irish nationalist politician, president/Taoiseach (prime minister) of the Irish Free State/Eire/Republic of Ireland 1932–48, 1951–54, and 1957–59, and president 1959–73. Repeatedly imprisoned, de Valera participated in the *Easter Rising of 1916 and was leader of the nationalist *Sinn Fein party 1917–26, when he formed the republican *Fianna Fáil party. He opposed the Anglo-Irish Treaty (1921) but formulated a constitutional relationship with Britain in the 1930s that achieved greater Irish sovereignty.

de Valois, Ninette (1898–2001) stage name of Edris Stannus, Irish choreographer, dancer, and teacher. In setting up the Vic-Wells Ballet in 1931 (later the Royal Ballet and Royal Ballet School) she was, along with choreographer Frederick *Ashton, one of the architects of British ballet. Among her works are *Job* (1931), *The Rake's Progress* (1935), *Checkmate* (1937), and *The Prospect Before Us* (1940), revived by the Birmingham Royal Ballet in honour of her 100th birthday in June 1998. She was reverentially and affectionately known as 'Madam' in the ballet world.

devaluation in economics, the lowering of the official value of a currency against other currencies, so that exports become cheaper and imports more expensive. Used when a country is badly in deficit in its balance of trade, it results in the goods the country produces being cheaper abroad, so that the economy is stimulated by increased foreign demand.

developing world *or* **Third World** *or* **the South** those countries that are less developed than the industrialized free-market countries of the West and the industrialized former communist countries. Countries of the developing world are the poorest, as measured by their income per head of population, and are concentrated in Asia, Africa, and Latin America. The early 1970s saw the beginnings of attempts by countries in the developing world to act together in confronting the powerful industrialized countries over such matters as the level of prices of primary products, with the nations regarding themselves as a group that had been exploited in the past by the developed nations and that had a right to catch up with them. Countries that adopted a position of political neutrality towards the major powers, whether poor or wealthy, are known as *non-aligned movement.

development in biology, the process whereby a living thing transforms itself from a single cell into a vastly complicated multicellular organism, with structures, such as limbs, and functions, such as respiration, all able to work correctly in relation to each other. Most of the details of this process remain unknown, although some of the central features are becoming understood.

development in the social sciences, the acquisition by a society of industrial techniques and technology; hence the use of the term 'developed' to refer to the nations of the Western capitalist countries and the Eastern communist countries, and the term 'underdeveloped' or '*developing world' to refer to poorer, non-aligned nations. The terms 'more economically-developed countries' (MEDC) and 'less economically-developed countries' (LEDC) are now used.

developmental psychology study of development of cognition and behaviour from birth to adulthood.

devil in Jewish, Christian, and Muslim theology, the supreme spirit of evil (**Beelzebub, Lucifer, Iblis**), or an evil spirit generally.

devil ray any of several large rays of the genera *Manta* and *Mobula*, in which two 'horns' project forwards from the sides of the huge mouth. These flaps of skin guide the plankton, on which the fish feed, into the mouth. The largest of these rays can be 7 m/23 ft across, and weigh 1,000 kg/2,200 lb. They live in warm seas.

devil's coach horse large, black, long-bodied, omnivorous beetle *Ocypus olens*, about 3 cm/1.2 in long. It has powerful jaws and is capable of giving a painful bite. It emits an unpleasant smell when threatened.

Devil's Island French Ile du Diable, smallest of the Iles du Salut (Salvation isles), off the northeast coast of French Guiana, 43 km/27 mi northwest of Cayenne.

The group of islands was collectively and popularly known by the name Devil's Island and formed a penal colony notorious for its terrible conditions.

devolution delegation of authority and duties; in the later 20th century, the movement to decentralize governmental power.

Devon *or* **Devonshire** county of southwest England; Plymouth and Torbay have been separate unitary authorities since April 1998. **area:** 6,720 sq km/2,594 sq mi **towns and cities:** Exeter (administrative headquarters); resorts: Barnstaple, Bideford, Exmouth, Ilfracombe, Sidmouth, Teignmouth, Tiverton **physical:** rivers: Dart, Exe, Plym, Tamar (94 km/58 mi), Taw, Teign, Torridge; National Parks: Dartmoor, Exmoor **features:** Lundy bird sanctuary and marine nature reserve in the Bristol Channel **population:** (1996) 1,059,300.

Devonian period period of geological time 408–360 million years ago, the fourth period of the Palaeozoic era. Many desert sandstones from North America and Europe date from this time. The first land plants flourished in the Devonian period, corals were abundant in the seas, amphibians evolved from air-breathing fish, and insects developed on land.

Devonshire, 8th Duke of British politician; see Spencer Compton Cavendish *Hartington.

dew precipitation in the form of moisture that collects on plants and on the ground. It forms after the temperature of the ground has fallen below the *dew point of the air in contact with it. As the temperature falls during the night, the air and its water vapour become chilled, and condensation takes place on the cooled surfaces.

Dewar, James (1842–1923) Scottish chemist and physicist who invented the *vacuum flask (Thermos) in 1872 during his research into the properties of matter at extremely low temperatures. He was knighted in 1904.

Dewey, Melvil (1851–1931) US librarian. In 1876, he devised the Dewey decimal system of classification for accessing, storing, and retrieving books, widely used in libraries. The system uses the numbers 000 to 999 to designate the major fields of knowledge, then breaks these down into more specific subjects by the use of decimals.

dew point temperature at which the air becomes saturated with water vapour. At temperatures below the dew point, the water vapour condenses out of the air as droplets. If the droplets are large they become deposited on plants and the ground as dew; if small they remain in suspension in the air and form mist or fog.

Dhaka formerly **Dacca**, capital of Bangladesh since 1971 following the war of independence from Pakistan, in Dhaka region, west of the River Meghna on the *Ganges delta; population (2001 est) 4,255,000. It is served by the river port of Narayanganj which lies 16 km/10 mi to the south, and trades in rice, oilseed, sugar, and tea. The area between Dhaka and Narayanganj is the leading industrial zone of Bangladesh and industries include jute-processing, tanning, and the production of textiles, chemicals, glass, and metal products, as well as the more traditional craft trades of embroidery, jewelry, and silk and muslin goods.

dharma (Sanskrit 'justice, order') in Hinduism, the consciousness of forming part of an ordered universe, and hence the moral duty of accepting one's station in life.

dhole wild dog *Cuon alpinus* found in Asia from Siberia to Java. With head and body up to 1 m/39 in long, variable in colour but often reddish above and lighter below, the dhole lives in groups of from 3 to 30 individuals. The species is becoming rare and is protected in some areas.

diabetes disease that can be caused by reduced production of the *hormone *insulin, or a reduced response of the liver, muscle, and fat cells to insulin. This affects the body's ability to use and regulate sugars effectively. Diabetes mellitus is a disorder of the islets of Langerhans in the *pancreas that prevents the production of insulin. Treatment is by strict dietary control and oral or injected insulin, depending on the type of diabetes.

Diaghilev, Sergei Pavlovich (1872–1929) Russian ballet impresario. In 1909 he founded the Ballets Russes/Russian Ballet (headquarters in Monaco), which he directed for 20 years. Through this company he brought Russian ballet to the West, introducing and encouraging a dazzling array of dancers, choreographers, composers, and artists, such as Anna Pavlova, Vaslav Nijinsky, Bronislava Nijinksa, Mikhail Fokine, Léonide Massine, George Balanchine, Igor Stravinsky, Sergey Prokofiev, Pablo Picasso, and Henri Matisse. Many of the works he commissioned are now firmly established in the concert repertory, including Stravinsky's *Le Sacre du Printemps/The Rite of Spring*.

dialectic Greek term, originally associated with the philosopher Socrates' method of argument through dialogue and conversation. **Hegelian dialectic**, named after the German philosopher *Hegel, refers to an interpretive method in which the contradiction between a thesis and its antithesis is resolved through synthesis.

dialectical materialism political, philosophical, and economic theory of the 19th-century German thinkers Karl Marx and Friedrich Engels, also known as *Marxism.

dialysis technique for removing waste products from the blood suffering chronic or acute kidney failure. There are two main methods, haemodialysis and peritoneal dialysis.

diameter straight line joining two points on the circumference of a circle that passes through the centre of that circle. It divides a circle into two equal halves.

diamond generally colourless, transparent mineral, an *allotrope of carbon. It is regarded as a precious gemstone, and is the hardest substance known (10 on the *Mohs scale). Industrial diamonds, which may be natural or synthetic, are used for cutting, grinding, and polishing.

Diana in Roman mythology, the goddess of chastity, hunting, and the Moon; daughter of Jupiter and twin of *Apollo. Her Greek equivalent is the goddess *Artemis.

Diana, Princess of Wales (1961–1997) born Diana Frances Spencer, Daughter of the 8th Earl Spencer, Diana married Prince Charles in St Paul's Cathedral, London, in 1981. She had two sons, William and Henry, before her separation from Charles in 1992. In February 1996, she agreed to a divorce, after which she became known as Diana, Princess of Wales. Her worldwide prominence for charity work contributed to a massive outpouring of public grief after her death in a car crash in Paris on 31 August 1997.

diaphragm in mammals, a thin muscular sheet separating the thorax from the abdomen. It is attached by way of the ribs at either side and the breastbone and backbone, and a central tendon. Arching upwards against the heart and lungs, the diaphragm is important in the mechanics of breathing. It contracts at each inhalation, moving downwards to increase the volume of the chest cavity, and relaxes at exhalation.

diaphragm or **cap** or **Dutch cap** barrier *contraceptive that is passed into the vagina to fit over the cervix (neck of the uterus), preventing sperm from entering the uterus. For a cap to be effective, a *spermicide must be used and the diaphragm left in place for six to eight hours after intercourse. This method is 97% effective if practised correctly.

diarrhoea frequent or excessive action of the bowels so that the faeces are liquid or semiliquid. It is caused by intestinal irritants (including some drugs and poisons), infection with harmful organisms (as in dysentery, salmonella, or cholera), or allergies.

diary informal record of day-to-day events, observations, or reflections, usually not intended for a general readership. One of the earliest diaries still in existence is that of a Japanese noblewoman, the *Kagero Nikki* (954–974), and the earliest known diary in English is that of Edward VI (ruled 1547–53). Notable diaries include those of English writer Samuel *Pepys and German Jewish girl Anne *Frank.

diaspora (Greek 'dispersion') dispersal of the Jews, initially from Israel and Judah 586–538 BC after the Babylonian conquest (the *Babylonian Captivity, or exile); and then the major diaspora following the Roman sacking of Jerusalem in AD 70 and their crushing of the Jewish revolt of 135. The term has come to refer to all the Jews living outside Israel.

diatom microscopic *alga found in all parts of the world in either fresh or marine waters. Diatoms consist of single cells that secrete a hard cell wall made of *silica. There are approximately 10,000 species of diatom. (Division Bacillariophyta.)

diatonic scale in music, a scale consisting of the seven notes of any major or minor *key.

Diaz, Bartholomeu (c. 1450–1500) Portuguese explorer, the first European to reach the Cape of Good Hope, in 1488, and to establish a route around Africa. He drowned during an expedition with Pedro Cabral.

dichloro-diphenyl-trichloroethane full name of the insecticide *DDT.

Dickens, Charles (John Huffam) (1812–1870) English novelist. He is enduringly popular for his memorable characters and his portrayal of the social evils of Victorian England. In 1836 he published the first number of the *Pickwick Papers*, followed by *Oliver Twist* (1837), the first of his 'reforming' novels; *Nicholas Nickleby* (1838), *The Old Curiosity Shop* (1840), *Barnaby Rudge* (1841); and *David Copperfield* (1850). Among his later books are *A Tale of Two Cities* (1859) and *Great Expectations* (1861). All his novels were written as serials.

Dickinson, Emily Elizabeth (1830–1886) US poet. She wrote most of her poetry between 1850 and the late 1860s and was particularly prolific during the Civil War years. She experimented with poetic rhythms, rhymes, and forms, as well as language and syntax. Her work is characterized by a wit and boldness that seem to contrast sharply with the reclusive life she led. Very few of her many short, mystical poems were published during her lifetime, and her work became well known only in the 20th century. The first collection of her poetry, *Poems by Emily Dickinson*, was published in 1890.

dicotyledon major subdivision of the *angiosperms, containing the great majority of flowering plants. Dicotyledons are characterized by the presence of two seed leaves, or *cotyledons, in the embryo, which is usually surrounded by the endosperm. They generally have broad leaves with netlike veins.

dictatorship term or office of an absolute ruler, overriding the constitution. (In ancient Rome a dictator was a magistrate invested with emergency powers for six months.) Although dictatorships were common in Latin America during the 19th century, the only European example during this period was the rule of Napoleon III. The crises following World War I produced many dictatorships, including the regimes of Atatürk and Pilsudski (nationalist); Mussolini, Hitler, Primo de Rivera, Franco, and Salazar (all right-wing); and Stalin (communist). The most notable contemporary dictatorship was that of Saddam *Hussein in Iraq.

Diderot, Denis (1713–1784) French philosopher. He is closely associated with the Enlightenment, the European intellectual movement for social and scientific progress, and was editor of the enormously influential *Encyclopédie* (1751–80).

didgeridoo *or* **didjeridu** musical lip-reed wind instrument, made from a hollow eucalyptus branch 1.5 m/4 ft long and blown to produce rhythmic, booming notes of relatively constant pitch. It was first developed and played by Australian Aborigines.

Dido *or* **Elissa** in Greek mythology, a Phoenician princess and legendary founder of *Carthage, northern Africa, in 853 BC. She was the sister of *Pygmalion, king of Tyre. According to Carthaginian tradition, Dido committed suicide to avoid a marriage, but in the Latin epic *Aeneid*, Virgil places her 300 years earlier, attributing the suicide to her desertion by *Aeneas at the fall of Troy (traditionally 1184 BC).

Dien Bien Phu, Battle of decisive battle in the *Indochina War at a French fortress in North Vietnam, near the Laotian border. French troops were besieged 13 March–7 May 1954 by the communist Vietminh, and the eventual fall of Dien Bien Phu resulted in the end of French control of Indochina.

diesel engine *internal-combustion engine that burns a lightweight fuel oil. The diesel engine operates by compressing air until it becomes sufficiently hot to ignite the fuel. It is a piston-in-cylinder engine, like the *petrol engine, but only air (rather than an air-and-fuel mixture) is taken into the cylinder on the first piston stroke (down). The piston moves up and compresses the air until it is at a very high temperature. The fuel oil is then injected into the hot air, where it burns, driving the piston down on its power stroke. For this reason the engine is called a compression-ignition engine.

diesel oil lightweight fuel oil used in diesel engines. Like petrol, it is a petroleum product. When used in vehicle engines, it is also known as **derv** (diesel-engine road vehicle).

diet range of foods eaten by an animal each day; it is also a particular selection of food, or the total amount and choice of food for a specific person or group of people. Most animals require seven kinds of food in their diet: proteins, carbohydrates, fats, vitamins, minerals, water, and roughage. A diet that contains all of these things in the correct amounts and proportions is termed a balanced diet. The amounts and proportions required varies with different animals, according to their size, age, and lifestyle. The *digestive systems of animals have evolved to meet particular needs; they have also adapted to cope with the foods available in the surroundings in which they live. The necessity of finding and processing an appropriate diet is a very basic drive in animal evolution. **Dietetics** is the science of feeding individuals or groups; a dietician is a specialist in this science.

diet meeting or convention of the princes and other dignitaries of the Holy Roman (German) Empire, for example, the **Diet of Worms** of 1521 which met to consider the question of Luther's doctrines and the governance of the empire under Charles V.

Dietrich, Marlene (1901–1992) born Maria Magdalene Dietrich, German-born US actor and singer known for her femme fatale film roles and sophisticated style. She became a star in *Der Blaue Engel/The Blue Angel* (1930), directed by Josef von Sternberg, with whom she would collaborate throughout the 1930s. Her films include *Morocco* (1930), *Blonde Venus* (1932), *The Devil is a Woman* (1935), *Destry Rides Again* (1939), and *Touch of Evil* (1958). In the 1960s she stopped acting and began a career as a concert singer.

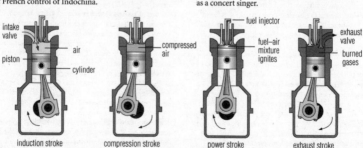

intake valve · air · piston · cylinder

induction stroke

compressed air

compression stroke

fuel injector · fuel–air mixture ignites

power stroke

exhaust valve · burned gases

exhaust stroke

diesel engine In a diesel engine, fuel is injected on the power stroke into hot compressed air at the top of the cylinder, where it ignites spontaneously. The four stages are exactly the same as those of the four-stroke or Otto cycle.

difference engine mechanical calculating machine designed (and partly built in 1822) by the English mathematician Charles *Babbage to produce reliable tables of life expectancy. A precursor of the analytical engine, it was to calculate mathematical functions by solving the differences between values given to *variables within equations. Babbage designed the calculator so that once the initial values for the variables were set it would produce the next few thousand values without error.

differential calculus branch of *calculus involving applications such as the determination of maximum and minimum points and rates of change.

differentiation in embryology, the process by which cells become increasingly different and specialized, giving rise to more complex structures that have particular functions in the adult organism. For instance, embryonic cells may develop into nerve, muscle, or bone cells.

diffraction the spreading out of waves when they pass through a small gap or around a small object, resulting in some change in the direction of the waves. In order for this effect to be observed, the size of the object or

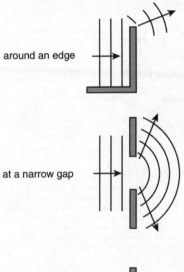

around an edge

at a narrow gap

at a wide gap

diffraction When waves pass around a barrier or through a gap, they spread out. The effect, known as diffraction, will be more pronounced at a narrow gap than at a wider gap.

gap must be comparable to or smaller than the *wavelength of the waves. Diffraction occurs with all forms of progressive waves – electromagnetic, sound, and water waves – and explains such phenomena as the ability of long-wave radio waves to bend around hills more easily than short-wave radio waves.

diffusion net spontaneous and random movement of molecules or particles in a fluid (gas or liquid) from a region in which they are at a high concentration to a region of lower concentration, until a uniform concentration is achieved throughout. The difference in concentration between two such regions is called the **concentration gradient**. No mechanical mixing or stirring is involved. For instance, a drop of ink added to water will diffuse down the concentration gradient until evenly mixed.

digestion process by which food eaten by an animal is broken down mechanically, and chemically by *enzymes, mostly in the *stomach and *intestines, to make the nutrients available for absorption and cell metabolism. In digestion large molecules of food are broken into smaller, soluble molecules, which are absorbed through the wall of the *gut into the bloodstream and carried to individual cells. The first stage of this may involve just the mixing of the food with water and the crushing and chopping of pieces of food by teeth or the mixing of food as it is squeezed along the gut. The second stage is the breakdown of large molecules by enzymes. The uptake of digested foods is mainly by absorption.

digestive system in the body, all the organs and tissues involved in the digestion of food. In animals, these consist of the mouth, stomach, intestines, and their associated glands. The process of digestion breaks down the food by physical and chemical means into the different elements that are needed by the body for energy and tissue building and repair. Digestion begins in the mouth and continues in the *stomach; from there most nutrients enter the small intestine from where they pass through the intestinal wall into the bloodstream; what remains is stored and concentrated into faeces in the large intestine. Birds have two additional digestive organs – the *crop and *gizzard. In smaller, simpler animals such as jellyfish, the digestive system is simply a cavity (coelenteron or enteric cavity) with a 'mouth' into which food is taken; the digestible portion is dissolved and absorbed in this cavity, and the remains are ejected back through the mouth. (See diagram, p. 266.)

Digger *or* **True Leveller** member of an English 17th-century radical sect that attempted to seize and share out common land. The Diggers became prominent in April 1649 when, headed by Gerrard Winstanley, they set up communal colonies near Cobham, Surrey, and elsewhere. The Diggers wanted to return to what they claimed was a 'golden age' before the Norman Conquest, when they believed that all land was held in common and its fruits were shared fairly between the people, and when men and women were equal. They did not allow private property or possessions; it is sometimes claimed that they were the first communist society. The Diggers' colonies were attacked by mobs and, being pacifists, they made no resistance. The support they attracted alarmed the government and they were dispersed in 1650. Their ideas influenced the early Quakers (called the Society of *Friends).

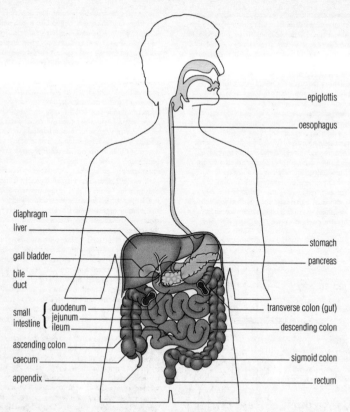

epiglottis

oesophagus

diaphragm
liver

stomach

gall bladder

pancreas

bile
duct

small intestine { duodenum
jejunum
ileum

transverse colon (gut)

descending colon

ascending colon

caecum

sigmoid colon

appendix

rectum

digestive system The human digestive system. When food is swallowed, it is moved down the oesophagus by the action of muscles (peristalsis) into the stomach. Digestion starts in the mouth and continues in the stomach as the food is mixed with enzymes and strong acid. After several hours, the food passes to the small intestine. Here more enzymes are added and digestion is completed. After all nutrients have been absorbed, the indigestible parts pass into the large intestine and thence to the rectum. The liver has many functions, such as storing minerals and vitamins and making bile, which is stored in the gall bladder until needed for the digestion of fats. The pancreas supplies enzymes. The appendix appears to have no function in human beings.

digit any of the numbers from 0 to 9 in the decimal system. Different bases have different ranges of digits. For example, the *hexadecimal system has digits 0 to 9 and A to F, whereas the binary system has two digits (or *bits), 0 and 1.

digital in electronics and computing, a term meaning 'coded as numbers'. A digital system uses two-state, either on/off or high/low voltage pulses, to encode, receive, and transmit information. A **digital display** shows discrete values as numbers (as opposed to an analogue signal, such as the continuous sweep of a pointer on a dial).

digital audio tape (DAT) digitally recorded audio tape produced in cassettes that can carry up to two hours of sound on each side and are about half the

size of standard cassettes. DAT players/recorders were developed in 1987. Pre-recorded cassettes are copy-protected.

The first DAT for computer data was introduced in 1988.

digital compact cassette (DCC) digitally recorded audio cassette that is roughly the same size as a standard cassette. It cannot be played on a normal tape recorder, though standard tapes can be played on a DCC machine; this is known as 'backwards compatibility'. The playing time is 90 minutes.

digital data transmission in computing, a way of sending data by converting all signals (whether pictures, sounds, or words) into numeric (normally binary) codes before transmission, then reconverting them on receipt. This virtually eliminates any distortion or degradation of the signal during transmission, storage, or processing.

digitalis drug that increases the efficiency of the heart by strengthening its muscle contractions and slowing its rate. It is derived from the leaves of the common European woodland plant *Digitalis purpurea* (foxglove).

digitalis any of a group of plants belonging to the figwort family, which includes the *foxgloves. The leaves of the common foxglove (*Digitalis purpurea*) are the source of the drug **digitalis** used in the treatment of heart disease. (Genus *Digitalis*, family Scrophulariaceae.)

digital recording technique whereby the pressure of sound waves is sampled more than 30,000 times a second and the values converted by computer into precise numerical values. These are recorded and, during playback, are reconverted to sound waves.

digital sampling electronic process used in *telecommunications for transforming a constantly varying (analogue) signal into one composed of discrete units, a digital signal. In the creation of recorded music, sampling enables the composer, producer, or remix engineer to borrow discrete vocal or instrumental parts from other recorded work (it is also possible to sample live sound).

digital-to-analogue converter electronic circuit that converts a digital signal into an *analogue (continuously varying) signal. Such a circuit is used to convert the digital output from a computer into the analogue voltage required to produce sound from a conventional loudspeaker.

dik-dik any of several species of tiny antelope, genus *Madoqua*, found in Africa south of the Sahara in dry areas with scattered brush. Dik-diks are about 60 cm/ 2 ft long and 35 cm/1.1 ft tall, and are often seen in pairs. Males have short, pointed horns. The dik-dik is so named because of its alarm call.

dilatation and curettage (D and C) common gynaecological procedure in which the cervix (neck of the womb) is widened, or dilated, giving access so that the lining of the womb can be scraped away (curettage). It may be carried out to terminate a pregnancy, treat an incomplete miscarriage, discover the cause of heavy menstrual bleeding, or for biopsy.

Dili *or* **Dilli** *or* **Dilly** capital, chief port, and main commercial centre of East Timor, situated on the Ombai Strait on the northern coast; population (2002 est) 49,900. Coffee, cotton, rice, sandalwood, copra, and hides are the chief exports, while industries include soap, perfume, pottery, and textiles, as well as crafts such as basketry and sandalwood carving.

dill herb belonging to the carrot family, whose bitter seeds and aromatic leaves are used in cooking and in medicine. (*Anethum graveolens*, family Umbelliferae.)

dilution process of reducing the concentration of a solution by the addition of a solvent.

DiMaggio, Joe (Joseph Paul) (1914–1999) US baseball player with the New York Yankees 1936–51, with whom he won the World Series ten times between 1936 and 1951. In 1941 he set a record – yet to be surpassed – by getting hits in 56 consecutive games. He was an outstanding fielder, played centre field, hit 361 home runs, and had a career average of .325. DiMaggio was married to the actor Marilyn Monroe between January and October 1954. He was elected to the Baseball Hall of Fame in 1955.

dimension in science, any directly measurable physical quantity such as mass (M), length (L), and time (T), and the derived units obtainable by multiplication or division from such quantities. For example, acceleration (the rate of change of velocity) has dimensions (LT^{-2}), and is expressed in such units as km s^{-2}. A quantity that is a ratio, such as relative density or humidity, is dimensionless.

diminishing returns, law of in economics, the principle that additional application of one factor of production, such as an extra machine or employee, at first results in rapidly increasing output but eventually yields declining returns, unless other factors are modified to sustain the increase.

Dingaan (1795–c. 1843) Zulu chief who obtained the throne in 1828 by murdering his predecessor, Shaka, and became notorious for his cruelty. In warfare with the Boer immigrants into Natal he was defeated on 16 December 1838 – 'Dingaan's Day'. He escaped to Swaziland, where he was deposed by his brother Mpande and subsequently assassinated.

dingo wild dog of Australia. Descended from domestic dogs brought from Asia by Aborigines thousands of years ago, it belongs to the same species *Canis familiaris* as other domestic dogs. It is reddish brown with a bushy tail, and often hunts at night. It cannot bark.

dinitrogen oxide alternative name for *nitrous oxide, or 'laughing gas', one of the nitrogen oxides.

dinosaur (Greek *deinos* 'terrible', *sauros* 'lizard') any of a group (sometimes considered as two separate orders) of extinct reptiles living between 205 million and 65 million years ago. Their closest living relations are crocodiles and birds. Many species of dinosaur evolved during the millions of years they were the dominant large land animals. Most were large (up to 27 m/90 ft), but some were as small as chickens. They disappeared 65 million years ago for reasons not fully understood, although many theories exist, perhaps the most widely accepted being that the Earth was struck by a comet.

Diocletian (AD 245–313) born Gaius Aurelius Valerius Diocletianus, Roman emperor 284–305 who initiated severe persecution of Christians in 303. He was commander of the *protectores domestici* (Roman staff officers) under the emperor Numerian, and proclaimed emperor by his troops following Numerian's death. He defeated his rival Carinus in 285. In 293 he appointed Maximian (*c.* 240–*c.* 310) as co-ruler and reorganized and subdivided the empire, with two joint and two subordinate emperors. This was known as the Tetrarchic system. In 305 he abdicated in favour of Galerius, living in retirement until his death.

diode combination of a cold anode and a heated cathode, or the semiconductor equivalent, which incorporates a *p–n* junction. Either device allows the passage of direct current in one direction only, and so is commonly used in a *rectifier to convert alternating current (AC) to direct current (DC).

Diogenes (c. 412–c. 323 BC) Ascetic Greek philosopher of the *cynic school. He believed in freedom and self-sufficiency for the individual, and that the virtuous life was the simple life; he did not believe in social mores. His own writings do not survive.

Dionysius Two tyrants of the ancient Greek city of Syracuse in Sicily. **Dionysius the Elder** (*c.* 430–367 BC) seized power in 405 BC. His first two wars with Carthage further extended the power of Syracuse, but in a third (383–378 BC) he was defeated. He was a patron of *Plato. He was succeeded by his son, **Dionysius the Younger**, who was driven out of Syracuse by Dion in 356 BC; he was tyrant again in 353 BC, but in 343 BC returned to Corinth.

Dionysus in Greek mythology, the god of wine, mystic ecstasy, and orgiastic excess; son of princess *Semele and Zeus. In his original savage form he was attended by *satyrs, lustful, drunken creatures; and **maenads**, women considered capable of tearing animals to pieces with their bare hands when under his influence. Later, as a more benign deity, his rites became less extreme; the Roman *Bacchus embodied this form.

Dior, Christian (1905–1957) French couturier. He established his own Paris salon in 1947 and made an impact with the 'New Look' – long, cinch-waisted, and full-skirted – after wartime austerity.

dioxin any of a family of over 200 organic chemicals, all of which are heterocyclic hydrocarbons. The term is commonly applied, however, to only one member of the family, 2,3,7,8-tetrachlorodibenzo-*p*-dioxin (2,3,7,8-TCDD), a highly toxic chemical that occurs, for example, as an impurity in the defoliant Agent Orange, used in the Vietnam War, and sometimes in the weedkiller 2,4,5-T. It has been associated with chloracne (a disfiguring skin complaint), birth defects, miscarriages, and cancer.

diphtheria acute infectious disease in which a membrane forms in the throat (threatening death by *asphyxia), along with the production of a powerful toxin that damages the heart and nerves. The organism responsible is a bacterium (*Corynebacterium diphtheriae*). It is treated with antitoxin and antibiotics.

diplodocus plant-eating sauropod dinosaur that lived about 145 million years ago, the fossils of which have been found in the western USA. Up to 27 m/88 ft long, most of which was neck and tail, it weighed about 11 tonnes. It walked on four elephantine legs, had nostrils on top of the skull, and peglike teeth at the front of the mouth.

diploid having paired *chromosomes in each cell. In sexually reproducing species, one set is derived from each parent, the *gametes, or sex cells, of each parent being *haploid (having only one set of chromosomes) due to *meiosis (reduction cell division).

diplomacy process by which states attempt to settle their differences through peaceful means such as negotiation or arbitration.

dipper *or* **water ouzel** any of various birds of the genus *Cinclus*, family Cinclidae, order Passeriformes, found in hilly and mountainous regions across Eurasia and North America, where there are clear, fast-flowing streams. It can swim, dive, or walk along the bottom, using the pressure of water on its wings and tail to keep it down, while it searches for insect larvae and other small animals. Both wings and tail are short, the beak is fairly short and straight, and the general colour of the bird is brown, the throat and part of the breast being white.

Dirac, Paul Adrien Maurice (1902–1984) English physicist who worked out a version of quantum mechanics consistent with special *relativity. The existence of antiparticles, such as the positron (positive electron), was one of its predictions. He shared the

Nobel Prize for Physics in 1933 (with Austrian physicist Erwin *Schrödinger) for his work on the development of quantum mechanics.

direct access *or* **random access** type of file access. A direct-access file contains records that can be accessed by the computer directly because each record has its own address on the storage disk. Direct access storage media include CD-ROMs and magnetic disks (such as floppy disks).

direct current (DC) electric current where the electrons (negative charge) flow in one direction, and that does not reverse its flow as *alternating current does. The electricity produced by a battery is direct current. Electromagnets and electric trains use direct current.

directory in computing, a list of file names, together with information that enables a computer to retrieve those files from backing storage. The computer operating system will usually store and update a directory on the backing storage to which it refers. So, for example, on each *disk used by a computer a directory file will be created listing the disk's contents. The term is also used to refer to the area on a disk where files are stored; the main area, the **root** directory, is at the top-most level, and may contain several separate **sub-directories**.

Directory the five-man ruling executive in France 1795–99. Established by the constitution of 1795, it failed to deal with the political and social tensions in the country and became increasingly unpopular after military defeats. It was overthrown by a military coup 9 November 1799 that brought Napoleon Bonaparte to power.

dirigible another name for *airship.

Dis in Roman mythology, the god of the underworld, also known as Orcus; he is equivalent to the Greek god *Pluto, ruler of Hades. Dis is also a synonym for the underworld itself.

disaccharide *sugar made up of two monosaccharides or simple sugars. Sucrose, $C_{12}H_{22}O_{11}$, or table sugar, is a disaccharide.

disarmament reduction of a country's weapons of war. Most disarmament talks since World War II have been concerned with nuclear-arms verification and reduction, but biological, chemical, and conventional weapons have also come under discussion at the United Nations and in other forums. Attempts to limit the arms race (initially between the USA and the USSR and since 1992 between the USA and Russia) have included the *Strategic Arms Limitation Talks (SALT) of the 1970s and the *Strategic Arms Reduction Talks (START) of the 1980s–90s.

disciple follower, especially of a religious leader. The word is used in the Bible for the early followers of Jesus. The 12 disciples closest to him are known as the apostles.

disco music international style of dance music of the 1970s with a heavily emphasized beat, descended from *funk. It was designed to be played in discotheques rather than performed live; hence the production was often more important than the performer, and drum machines came to dominate.

discrete data in mathematics, *data that can take only whole-number or fractional values, that is, distinct values. The opposite is *continuous data, which can take all in-between values. Examples of discrete data

distributor

include *frequency and population data. However, measurements of time and other dimensions can give rise to continuous data.

discrimination distinction made (social, economic, political, or legal) between individuals or groups such that one has the power to treat the other unfavourably. **Negative discrimination**, often based on *stereotype, includes anti-Semitism, caste, *racism, *sexism, and slavery. **Positive discrimination**, or *affirmative action, is sometimes practised in an attempt to counteract the effects of previous long-term negative discrimination. Minorities and, in some cases, majorities have been targets for discrimination.

discus circular disc thrown by athletes who rotate the body to gain momentum from within a circle 2.5 m/8 ft in diameter. The men's discus weighs 2 kg/4.4 lb and the women's 1 kg/2.2 lb. Discus throwing was a competition in ancient Greece at gymnastic contests, such as those of the Olympic Games. It is an event in the modern Olympics and athletics meetings.

disease condition that disturbs or impairs the normal state of an organism. Diseases can occur in all living things, and normally affect the functioning of cells, tissues, organs, or systems. Diseases are usually characterized by specific symptoms and signs, and can be mild and short-lasting – such as the common cold – or severe enough to decimate a whole species – such as *Dutch elm disease. Diseases can be classified as infectious or noninfectious. Infectious diseases are caused by micro-organisms, such as bacteria and viruses, invading the body; they can be spread across a species, or transmitted between one or more species. All other diseases can be grouped together as noninfectious diseases. These can have many causes: they may be inherited (*congenital diseases); they may be caused by the ingestion or absorption of harmful substances, such as toxins; they can result from poor nutrition or hygiene; or they may arise from injury or ageing. The causes of some diseases are still unknown.

disinfectant agent that kills, or prevents the growth of, bacteria and other micro-organisms. Chemical disinfectants include carbolic acid (phenol, used by Joseph *Lister in surgery in the 1870s), ethanol, methanol, chlorine, and iodine.

disk in computing, a common medium for storing large volumes of data. A **magnetic disk** is rotated at high speed in a disk-drive unit as a read/write (playback or record) head passes over its surfaces to record or read the magnetic variations that encode the data. **Optical disks**, such as *CD-ROM (compact-disc read-only memory) and *WORM (write once, read many times), are also used to store computer data. Data are recorded on the disk surface as etched microscopic pits and are read by a laser-scanning device.

disk drive mechanical device that reads data from a *disk. Many types can also write data to the disk. When a floppy disk is inserted into the drive, its surface is exposed to the read-write head, which moves over the spinning disk surface to locate a specific track.

Disney, Walt(er Elias) (1901–1966) US film producer, animator, and pioneer of family entertainment, whose career spanned the development of the motion picture medium. Disney created many world-famous cartoon characters, including Mickey Mouse and Donald Duck, made phenomenally successful feature-length animated films, including *Snow White and the Seven Dwarfs* (1937), and opened Disneyland, his first theme park, in 1955. The first person to add music and effects to cartoons, he was also the originator of the modern multimedia corporation, the Walt Disney Company.

dispersion in physics, a particular property of *refraction in which the angle and velocity of waves passing through a dispersive medium depends upon their frequency. When visible white light passes through a prism it is split into a spectrum (see *electromagnetic waves). This occurs because each component frequency of light, which corresponds to a colour, is refracted by a slightly different angle, and so the light is split into its component frequencies (colours). A rainbow is formed when sunlight is dispersed by raindrops.

Disraeli, Benjamin (1804–1881) 1st Earl of Beaconsfield, British Conservative politician and novelist. Elected to Parliament in 1837, he was chancellor of the Exchequer under Lord *Derby in 1852, 1858–59, and 1866–68, and prime minister in 1868 and 1874–80. His imperialist policies brought India directly under the crown, and he was personally responsible for purchasing control of the Suez Canal. The central Conservative Party organization is his creation. His popular, political novels reflect an interest in social reform and include *Coningsby* (1844) and *Sybil* (1845).

dissection cutting apart of bodies to study their organization, or tissues to gain access to a site in surgery. Postmortem dissection was considered a sin in the Middle Ages. In the UK before 1832, hanged murderers were the only legal source of bodies, supplemented by graverobbing (Burke and Hare were the most notorious grave robbers). The Anatomy Act of 1832 authorized the use of deceased institutionalized paupers unclaimed by next of kin, and by the 1940s bequests of bodies had been introduced.

Dissenter in Britain, former name for a Protestant refusing to conform to the established Christian church. For example, Baptists, Presbyterians, and Independents (now known as Congregationalists) were Dissenters.

dissociation in chemistry, the process whereby a single compound splits into two or more smaller products, which may be capable of recombining to form the reactant.

distemper any of several infectious diseases of animals characterized by catarrh, cough, and general weakness. Specifically, it refers to a virus disease in young dogs, also found in wild animals, which can now be prevented by vaccination. In 1988 an allied virus killed over 10,000 common seals in the Baltic and North seas.

distillation technique used to purify liquids or to separate mixtures of liquids possessing different boiling points. **Simple distillation** is used in the purification of liquids or the separation of substances in solution from their solvents – for example, in the production of pure water from a salt solution or the recovery of sodium chloride (table salt) from sea water.

distributor device in the ignition system of a piston engine that distributes pulses of high-voltage electricity to the *spark plugs in the cylinders. The electricity is passed to the plug leads by the tip of a rotor arm, driven by the engine camshaft, and current is fed to the rotor arm from the ignition coil. The distributor also houses

269

the contact point or breaker, which opens and closes to interrupt the battery current to the coil, thus triggering the high-voltage pulses. With electronic ignition the distributor is absent.

district council lower unit of local government in England. In 1998 there were 274 district councils under 34 (two-tier) non-metropolitan county councils, and 36 single-tier metropolitan district councils. Their responsibilities cover housing, local planning and development, roads (excluding trunk and classified), bus services, environmental health (refuse collection, clean air, food safety and hygiene, and enforcement of the Offices, Shops and Railway Premises Act 1963), council tax, museums and art galleries, parks and playing fields, swimming baths, cemeteries, and so on.

District of Columbia (DC) federal district and seat of the federal government of the USA, coextensive with the capital city, *Washington, DC, situated on the Potomac and Anacostia rivers; area 158 sq km/61 sq mi; population (2000 est) 572,100. The area was selected by President George *Washington and approved by Congress in 1790, and the government moved from the previous capital, Philadelphia, in 1800. The area was chosen as a politically neutral area midway between the North and South of the country, and was formed from parts of Maryland and Virginia, although the Virginia part was returned to that state in 1846.

diuretic any drug that increases the output of urine by the kidneys. It may be used in the treatment of high blood pressure and to relieve *oedema associated with heart, lung, kidney or liver disease, and some endocrine disorders.

diver *or* **loon** any of four species of marine bird of the order Gaviiformes, specialized for swimming and diving, found in northern regions of the northern hemisphere. The legs are set so far back that walking is almost impossible, but they are powerful swimmers and good flyers, and only come ashore to nest. They have straight bills, short tail-feathers, webbed feet, and long bodies; they feed on fish, crustaceans, and some water plants. During the breeding period they live inland and the female lays two eggs which hatch into down-covered chicks. Of the four species, the largest is the white-billed diver *Gavia adamsii*, an Arctic species 75 cm/2.5 ft long.

divertissement (French 'entertainment') dance, or suite of dances, within a ballet or opera, where the plot comes to a halt for a display of technical virtuosity, such as the character dances in the last act of *Coppélia* by Delibes, or the last acts of *Sleeping Beauty* and *A Midsummer Night's Dream*.

dividend in business, the amount of money that company directors decide should be taken out of net profits for distribution to shareholders. It is usually declared as a percentage or fixed amount per *share. The dividend, in the form of cash or shares, is recommended by the board and approved by the shareholders at the annual general meeting. A dividend payment is not guaranteed and may be withheld for many reasons including poor performance. Shares bought with the right to receive a declared dividend payment are said to be cum-dividend and those without the right are ex-dividend.

divination art of ascertaining future events or eliciting other hidden knowledge by supernatural or nonrational means. Divination played a large part in the ancient civilizations of the Egyptians, Greeks (see *oracle), Romans, and Chinese (using the *I Ching*), and is still practised throughout the world.

Divine Comedy, The epic poem by *Dante 1307–21, describing a journey through Hell, Purgatory, and Paradise. The poet Virgil is Dante's guide through Hell and Purgatory; to each of the three realms, or circles, Dante assigns historical and contemporary personages according to their moral (and also political) worth. In Paradise Dante finds his lifelong love, Beatrice. The poem makes great use of symbolism and allegory, and influenced many English writers including Milton, Byron, Shelley, and T S Eliot.

divine right of kings Christian political doctrine that hereditary monarchy is the system approved by God, hereditary right cannot be forfeited, monarchs are accountable to God alone for their actions, and rebellion against the lawful sovereign is therefore blasphemous.

diving sport of entering water either from a springboard 1 m/3 ft or 3 m/10 ft above the water, or from a platform, or highboard, 10 m/33 ft above the water. Various differing starts are adopted, facing forwards or backwards, and somersaults, twists, and combinations thereof are performed in midair before entering the water. Points are awarded by judges and the level of difficulty of each dive is used as a multiplying factor.

divorce legal dissolution of a lawful marriage. It is distinct from an annulment, which is a legal declaration that the marriage was invalid. The ease with which a divorce can be obtained in different countries varies considerably and is also affected by different religious practices.

Diwali *or* **Divali** ('garland of lamps') in Hinduism, festival in October/November celebrating Lakshmi, goddess of light and wealth, as well as the New Year and the story of the *Ramayana*. It is marked by the lighting of lamps and candles (inviting the goddess into the house), feasting, and the exchange of gifts.

Dix, Otto (1891–1969) German painter. He was a major exponent of the harsh realism current in Germany in the 1920s and closely associated with the *Neue Sachlichkeit* group. He is known chiefly for his unsettling 1920s paintings of prostitutes and sex murders and for his powerful series of works depicting the hell of trench warfare, for example *Flanders: After Henri Barbusse 'Le Feu'* (1934–36; Nationalgalerie, Berlin).

Dixieland jazz jazz style that originated in New Orleans, Louisiana, in the early 20th century and worked its way up the Mississippi River. It is characterized by improvisation and the playing back and forth of the cornet, trumpet, clarinet, and trombone. The steady background beat is supplied by the piano, bass, and percussion instrument players, who also have their turns to solo. It is usually played by bands of four to eight members. Noted Dixieland musicians were King Oliver, Jelly Roll Morton, and Louis *Armstrong.

Djibouti *or* **Jibuti** chief port and capital of the Republic of Djibouti, on a peninsula 240 km/149 mi southwest of Aden, Yemen, and 565 km/351 mi northeast of Addis Ababa, Ethiopia; population (2002 est) 534,700. Industries include petroleum refining, textiles, and rail freighting. The city is an important regional bunkering and supply centre for the export trade in petroleum, and is the main export route for Ethiopian coffee; other exports include hides and salt.

Djibouti

formerly **French Somaliland (1888–1967)**,
French Territory of the Afars and Issas (1966–77)
  National name: *Jumhouriyya Djibouti/ Republic of Djibouti*

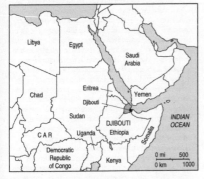

Area: 23,200 sq km/8,957 sq mi
Capital: Djibouti (and chief port)
Major towns/cities: Tadjoura, Obock, Dikhil, Ali-Sabieh
Physical features: mountains divide an inland plateau from a coastal plain; hot and arid
Head of state: Ismail Omar Guelleh from 1999
Head of government: Dileita Mohamed Dileita from 2001
Political system: authoritarian nationalist
Political executive: unlimited presidency
Political parties: People's Progress Assembly (RPP), nationalist; Democratic Renewal Party (PRD), moderate left-of-centre; Democratic National Party (DND)
Currency: Djibouti franc
GNI per capita (PPP): (US$) 2,070 (2002 est)
Exports: hides, cattle, coffee (exports are largely re-exports). Principal market: Somalia 56% (2000)
Population: 703,000 (2003 est)
Language: French (official), Issa (Somali), Afar, Arabic
Religion: Sunni Muslim
Life expectancy: 45 (men); 47 (women) (2000–05)
Chronology
3rd century BC: The north settled by Able immigrants from Arabia, whose descendants are the Afars (Danakil).
early Christian era: Somali Issas settled in coastal areas and south, ousting Afars.
825: Islam introduced by missionaries.
16th century: Portuguese arrived to challenge trading monopoly of Arabs.
1862: French acquired a port at Obock.
1888: Annexed by France as part of French Somaliland.
1900s: Railroad linked Djibouti port with the Ethiopian hinterland.
1946: Became overseas territory within French Union, with own assembly and representation in French parliament.

1958: Voted to become overseas territorial member of French Community.
1967: French Somaliland renamed the French Territory of the Afars and the Issas.
early 1970s: Issas (Somali) peoples campaigned for independence, but the minority Afars, of Ethiopian descent, and Europeans sought to remain French.
1977: Independence was achieved as Djibouti, with Hassan Gouled Aptidon, the leader of the independence movement, elected president.
1981: A new constitution made the People's Progress Assembly (RPP) the only legal party. Treaties of friendship were signed with Ethiopia, Somalia, Kenya, and Sudan.
1984: The policy of neutrality was reaffirmed. The economy was undermined by severe drought.
1992: A new multiparty constitution was adopted; fighting erupted between government forces and Afar Front for Restoration of Unity and Democracy (FRUD) guerrilla movement in the northeast.
1993: Opposition parties were allowed to operate, but Gouled was re-elected president.
1994: A peace agreement was reached with Afar FRUD militants, ending the civil war.
1999: Ismail Omar Guelleh was elected president.
2001: Dileita Mohamed Dileita replaced Barkat Gourad Hamdaou as prime minister.
2002: Full multi-party democracy was implemented. Hitherto, only four political parties had been allowed.
2003: The first multi-party elections took place. A bloc of four pro-government parties supporting President Guelleh, known as the Union pour la Majorité Présidentielle (UMP; Union for the Presidential Majority), took all 65 parliamentary seats.
2005: President Guelleh won an uncontested presidential election.

DNA abbreviation for deoxyribonucleic acid, molecular basis of heredity. It is a complex giant molecule that contains, in chemically coded form, the information needed for a cell to make *proteins. In other words it determines the order in which amino acids are joined to make a specific protein in a cell. DNA is a ladder-like double-stranded *nucleic acid, which forms the basis of genetic inheritance in all organisms, except for a few viruses that have only *RNA. DNA is organized into *chromosomes and, in organisms other than bacteria, it is found only in the cell nucleus.

DNA fingerprinting *or* **DNA profiling** another name for *genetic fingerprinting.

Dnieper *or* **Dnepr** Greek **Borysthenes**, river rising in the Valdai Hills west of Moscow, in the Smolensk region of the Russian Federation, and flowing south through Belarus and Ukraine to enter the Black Sea near Kherson; total length 2,250 km/1,400 mi. The Dnieper is the third longest European river (after the Volga and Danube).

Dobermann *or* **Dobermann pinscher** breed of smooth-coated dog with a docked tail, much used as a guard dog. It stands up to 70 cm/27.5 in tall, has a long head with a flat, smooth skull, and is often black with brown markings. It takes its name from the man who bred it in 19th-century Germany.

dock *or* **sorrel** in botany, any of a number of plants belonging to the buckwheat family. They are tall, annual or perennial herbs, often with lance-shaped leaves and small greenish flowers. Native to temperate regions, there are 30 North American and several British species. (Genus *Rumex*, family Polygonaceae.)

Docklands urban development area east of St Katherine's Dock, London, occupying the site of the former Wapping and Limehouse docks, the Isle of Dogs, and Royal Docks. It comprises 2,226 hectares/5,550 acres of former wharves, warehouses, and wasteland. Plans for its redevelopment were set in motion in 1981. The tallest building is the Canary Wharf tower. Docklands is served by the London City airport (Stolport) and the Docklands Light Railway (DLR). The London Underground Jubilee Line was extended to Canary Wharf in 1999.

dodder parasitic plant belonging to the morning-glory family, without leaves or roots. The thin stem twines around the host plant, and penetrating suckers withdraw nourishment. (Genus *Cuscuta*, family Convolvulaceae.)

dodecahedron regular solid with 12 pentagonal faces and 12 vertices. It is one of the five regular *polyhedra, or Platonic solids.

Dodecanese Greek **Dodekanisos**, ('twelve islands') group of islands in the Aegean Sea; area 2,663 sq km/1,028 sq mi; population (1991 est) 162,400. Once Turkish, the islands were Italian from 1912 to 1947, when they were ceded to Greece. They include *Rhodes and *Kos. Chief products include fruit, olives, and sponges.

dodecaphony music composed according to the *twelve-tone system of composition.

Dodgson, Charles Lutwidge real name of English author Lewis *Carroll.

dodo extinct flightless bird *Raphus cucullatus*, order Columbiformes, formerly found on the island of Mauritius, but exterminated by early settlers around 1681. Although related to the pigeons, it was larger than a turkey, with a bulky body, rudimentary wings, and short curly tail-feathers. The bill was blackish in colour, forming a horny hook at the end.

Dodoma official capital (replacing Dar es Salaam in 1974) of Tanzania; 1,132 m/3,713 ft above sea level; population (1995 est) 189,000. Dar es Salaam remains the administrative capital, pending the transfer of government functions to Dodoma, a move intended to be completed by 2005. Dodoma is a centre of communications, linked by rail with Dar es Salaam, and Kigoma on Lake Tanganyika, and by road with Kenya to the north and Zambia and Malawi to the south. There is an airport. Dodoma is a marketplace for locally-grown coffee and peanuts, but has a limited industrial base, which includes the manufacture of bricks.

dog any carnivorous mammal of the family Canidae, including wild dogs, wolves, jackals, coyotes, and foxes. Specifically, the domestic dog *Canis familiaris*, the earliest animal descended from the wolf. Dogs were first domesticated around 14,000 years ago, and migrated with humans to all the continents. They have been selectively bred into many different varieties for use as working animals and pets.

doge chief magistrate in the ancient constitutions of Venice and Genoa. The first doge of Venice was appointed in 697 with absolute power (modified in 1297), and from his accession dates Venice's prominence in history. The last Venetian doge, Lodovico Manin, retired in 1797 and the last Genoese doge in 1804.

dogfish any of several small sharks found in the northeast Atlantic, Pacific, and Mediterranean.

dogwood any of a group of trees and shrubs belonging to the dogwood family, native to temperate regions of North America, Europe, and Asia. The flowering dogwood (*Cornus florida*) of the eastern USA is often cultivated as an ornamental for its beautiful blooms consisting of clusters of small greenish flowers surrounded by four large white or pink petal-like bracts (specialized leaves). (Genus *Cornus*, family Cornaceae.)

Doha Arabic **Ad Dawhah**, capital and chief port of Qatar, on the east coast of the peninsula; population (2001 est) 299,300. As well as being the chief commercial and communications centre of Qatar, Doha also has a considerable trade in cargo for other countries of the Gulf, and serves as their centre for vocational training. The exploitation of Qatar's large oil reserves in the second half of the 20th century boosted the prosperity of Doha; industries include oil refining, engineering, refrigeration and construction equipment, as well as shrimp fishing and processing. Over half the population of the country resides in Doha, and the city has an international airport.

Dohnányi, Ernst (Ernö) von (1877–1960) Hungarian pianist, conductor, composer, and teacher. As a pianist his powers were prodigious, while as a composer he drew upon the classical German tradition, especially Brahms. His compositions include *Variations on a Nursery Song* (1913) and *Second Symphony for Orchestra* (1948).

doldrums area of low atmospheric pressure along the Equator, in the intertropical convergence zone where the northeast and southeast trade winds converge. The doldrums are characterized by calm or very light winds, during which there may be sudden squalls and stormy weather. For this reason the areas are avoided as far as possible by sailing ships.

dolerite igneous rock formed below the Earth's surface, a form of basalt, containing relatively little silica (mafic in composition).

Dollfuss, Engelbert (1892–1934) Austrian Christian Socialist politician. He was appointed chancellor in 1932, and in 1933 suppressed parliament and ruled by decree. In February 1934 he crushed a protest by the socialist workers by force, and in May Austria was declared a 'corporative' state. The Nazis attempted a coup on 25 July; the Chancellery was seized and Dollfuss murdered.

dolmen prehistoric *megalith in the form of a chamber built of three or more large upright stone slabs, capped by a horizontal flat stone. Dolmens are the burial chambers of Neolithic (New Stone Age) chambered tombs and passage graves, revealed by the removal of the covering burial mound. They are found in Europe and Africa, and occasionally in Asia as far east as Japan.

dolomite in mineralogy, white mineral with a rhombohedral structure, calcium magnesium carbonate ($CaMg(CO_3)_2$). Dolomites are common in geological successions of all ages and are often formed when *limestone is changed by the replacement of the mineral calcite with the mineral dolomite.

dolphin any of various highly intelligent aquatic mammals of the family Delphinidae, which also includes porpoises. There are about 60 species. Most inhabit tropical and temperate oceans, but there are some freshwater forms in rivers in Asia, Africa, and South America. The name 'dolphin' is generally applied to species having a beaklike snout and slender body, whereas the name 'porpoise' is reserved for the smaller species with a blunt snout and stocky body. Dolphins use sound (*echolocation) to navigate, to find prey, and for communication. The common dolphin *Delphinus delphis* is found in all temperate and tropical seas. It is up to 2.5 m/8 ft long, and is dark above and white below, with bands of grey, white, and yellow on the sides. It has up to 100 teeth in its jaws, which make the 15 cm/6 in 'beak' protrude forward from the rounded head. The corners of its mouth are permanently upturned, giving the appearance of a smile, though dolphins cannot actually smile. Dolphins feed on fish and squid.

Domagk, Gerhard (1895–1964) German pathologist who was awarded a Nobel Prize for Physiology or Medicine in 1939 for his discovery of the first antibacterial *sulphonamide drug. In 1932 he found that a coal-tar dye called Prontosil red contains chemicals with powerful antibacterial properties. Sulphanilamide became the first of the sulphonamide drugs, used – before antibiotics were discovered – to treat a wide range of conditions, including pneumonia and septic wounds.

Domenichino (1581–1641) adopted name of Domenico Zampieri, Italian *baroque painter and architect, active in Bologna, Naples, and Rome. He began as an assistant to the Carracci family of painters and continued the early baroque style in, for example, frescoes 1624–28 in the choir of the church of S Andrea della Valle, Rome. He is considered one of the pioneers of landscape painting in the baroque period.

Domesday Book record of the survey of England carried out in 1086 by officials of *William the Conqueror in order to assess land tax and other dues, find out the value of the crown lands, and enable the king to estimate the power of his vassal barons. The name is derived from the belief that its judgement was as final as that of Doomsday.

dominance in genetics, the masking of one *allele (an alternative form of a gene) by another allele. For example, if a *heterozygous person has one allele for blue eyes and one for brown eyes, his or her eye colour will be brown. The allele for blue eyes is described as *recessive and the allele for brown eyes as dominant.

dominant in tonal music, the fifth note of a major or minor scale; for example, G in the C major scale. It is next in importance to the tonic and can be said to dominate because of its special relationship to the tonic (brass players will know it as the 'third harmonic' – the first being the 'fundamental' note produced by a length of tubing and the second being the octave above that).

Domingo, Placido (1941–) Spanish lyric tenor. He specializes in Italian and French 19th-century operatic roles to which he brings a finely-tuned dramatic temperament. Since his New York debut in 1965 he has established a world reputation as a sympathetic leading tenor.

Dominica
National name: *Commonwealth of Dominica*
Area: 751 sq km/290 sq mi
Capital: Roseau
Major towns/cities: Portsmouth, Marigot, Mahaut, Atkinson, Grand Bay

Major ports: Roseau, Portsmouth, Berekua, Marigot, Rosalie
Physical features: second-largest of the Windward Islands, mountainous central ridge with tropical rainforest
Head of state: Nicholas Liverpool from 2003
Head of government: Roosevelt Skerrit from 2004
Political system: liberal democracy
Political executive: parliamentary
Political parties: Dominica Freedom Party (DFP), centrist; Labour Party of Dominica (LPD), left-of-centre coalition (before 1985 the DLP); Dominica United Workers' Party (DUWP), left of centre
Currency: East Caribbean dollar, although the pound sterling is also accepted
GNI per capita (PPP): (US$) 4,840 (2002 est)
Exports: bananas, soap, coconuts, grapefruit, galvanized sheets. Principal market: Jamaica 26.5% (1999)
Population: 79,000 (2003 est)
Language: English (official), a Dominican patois (which reflects earlier periods of French rule)
Religion: Roman Catholic 80%
Life expectancy: 72 (men); 77 (women) (2000–05)
Chronology
1493: Visited by the explorer Christopher Columbus, who named the island Dominica ('Sunday Island').
1627: Presented by the English King Charles I to the Earl of Carlisle, but initial European attempts at colonization were fiercely resisted by the indigenous Carib community.
later 18th century: Succession of local British and French conflicts over control of the fertile island.
1763: British given possession of the island by the Treaty of Paris, but France continued to challenge militarily until 1805, when there was formal cession in return for the sum of £12,000.
1834: Slaves, who had been brought in from Africa, were emancipated.
1870: Became part of the British Leeward Islands federation.
1940: Transferred to British Windward Islands federation.
1951: Universal adult suffrage established.
1958–62: Part of the West Indies Federation.

1960: Granted separate, semi-independent status, with a legislative council and chief minister.

1961: Edward le Blanc, leader of the newly formed DLP, became chief minister.

1978: Independence was achieved as a republic within the Commonwealth, with Patrick John (DLP) as prime minister.

1980: The DFP won a convincing victory in a general election, and Eugenia Charles became the Caribbean's first woman prime minister.

1983: A small force participated in the US-backed invasion of Grenada.

1985: The regrouping of left-of-centre parties resulted in the new Labour Party of Dominica (LPD).

1991: A Windward Islands confederation comprising St Lucia, St Vincent, Grenada, and Dominica was proposed.

1993: Charles resigned the DFP leadership, but continued as prime minister.

1995: DUWP won a general election; Edison James was appointed prime minister and Eugenia Charles retired from politics.

1998: Vernon Shaw elected president.

2000: Rosie Douglas was elected prime minister, leading a DLP-DFP coalition, but died in October. He was replaced by Pierre Charles.

2004: Roosevelt Skerrit became prime minister in January after the death of Pierre Charles. Dominica established diplomatic links with China (cutting those with Taiwan) and received Chinese financial aid.

2005: Prime Minister Skerrit's government won a general election in May.

Dominican order Roman Catholic order of friars founded in 1215 by St Dominic. The Dominicans are also known as Friars Preachers, Black Friars, or Jacobins. The order is worldwide and there is also an order of contemplative nuns; the habit is black and white.

Dominican Republic

formerly **Hispaniola (with Haiti) (until 1844)**

National name: *República Dominicana/ Dominican Republic*

Area: 48,442 sq km/18,703 sq mi

Capital: Santo Domingo

Major towns/cities: Santiago, La Romana, San Pedro de Macoris, San Francisco de Macoris, La Vega, San Juan, San Cristóbal

Physical features: comprises eastern two-thirds of island of Hispaniola; central mountain range with fertile valleys; Pico Duarte 3,174 m/10,417 ft, highest point in Caribbean islands

Head of state and government: Leonel Fernández Reyna from 2004

Political system: liberal democracy

Political executive: limited presidency

Political parties: Dominican Revolutionary Party (PRD), moderate, left of centre; Christian Social Reform Party (PRSC), independent socialist; Dominican Liberation Party (PLD), nationalist

Currency: Dominican Republic peso

GNI per capita (PPP): (US$) 5,870 (2002 est)

Exports: ferro-nickel, raw sugar and derivatives, molasses, coffee, cocoa, tobacco, gold, silver. Principal market: USA 87.3% (2000)

Population: 8,745,000 (2003 est)

Language: Spanish (official)

Religion: Roman Catholic

Life expectancy: 69 (men); 70 (women) (2000–05)

Chronology

14th century: Settled by Carib Indians, who followed an earlier wave of Arawak Indian immigration.

1492: Visited by Christopher Columbus, who named it Hispaniola ('Little Spain').

1496: At Santo Domingo the Spanish established the first European settlement in the western hemisphere, which became capital of all Spanish colonies in America.

first half of 16th century: One-third of a million Arawaks and Caribs died, as a result of enslavement and exposure to European diseases; black African slaves were consequently brought in to work the island's gold and silver mines, which were swiftly exhausted.

1697: Divided between France, which held the western third (Haiti), and Spain, which held the east (Dominican Republic, or Santo Domingo).

1795: Santo Domingo was ceded to France.

1808: Following a revolt by Spanish Creoles, with British support, Santo Domingo was retaken by Spain.

1821: Became briefly independent after uprising against Spanish rule, and then fell under the control of Haiti.

1844: Separated from Haiti to form Dominican Republic.

1861–65: Under Spanish protection.

1904: The USA took over the near-bankrupt republic's debts.

1916–24: Temporarily occupied by US forces.

1930: Military coup established personal dictatorship of Gen Rafael Trujillo Molina.

1937: Army massacred 19,000–20,000 Haitians living in the Dominican provinces adjoining the frontier.

1961: Trujillo assassinated.

1962: First democratic elections resulted in Juan Bosch, founder of the left-wing Dominican Revolutionary Party (PRD), becoming president.

1963: Bosch overthrown in military coup.

1965: 30,000 US marines intervened to restore order and protect foreign nationals after Bosch had attempted to seize power.

1966: New constitution adopted. Joaquín Balaguer, protégé of Trujillo and leader of the centre-right Christian Social Reform Party (PRSC), became president.

1978: PRD returned to power.

1985: PRD president Jorge Blanco was forced by the International Monetary Fund to adopt austerity measures to save the economy.

1986: The PRSC returned to power.

1996: Leonel Fernandez of the left-wing PLD was elected president.

2000: Presidential elections were won by Hipólito Mejía, a social democrat.

2004: Leonel Fernandez was elected president for the second time.

Dominions term formerly used to describe those countries of the *British Empire and Commonwealth enjoying complete autonomy in internal and external affairs. In this context the term was first applied to Canada, the formal title of which is the **Dominion of Canada**. It was subsequently applied as a generic term, though not as a formal title (except in the case of New Zealand, which has since ceased to use it), to describe Australia, South Africa, and, in 1922, the Irish Free State.

Domitian, (Titus Flavius Domitianus) (AD 51–96) Roman emperor from AD 81. He finalized the conquest of Britain (see *Agricola), strengthened the Rhine–Danube frontier, and suppressed immorality as well as freedom of thought in philosophy and religion. His reign of terror led to his assassination.

Don ancient Greek **Tanais**, navigable river in the western Russian Federation; length 1,870 km/1,162 mi; basin covers 422,000 sq km/163,000 sq mi. The Don rises in the central Russian uplands near the city of Tula, flows southeast towards the Volga near Volgograd, then turns southwest to empty into the northeast of the Sea of Azov. In its lower reaches the Don is 1.5 km/1 mi wide, and for about four months of the year it is closed by ice. It has long been a major traffic artery linking inland European Russia with the Black Sea. Its chief tributaries are the Donets, Voronezh, Khoper, and Medveditsa, and it is linked to the Volga by the Volga–Don Canal. The main port is Rostov-on-Don, which lies near the river's mouth.

Donatello (c. 1386–1466) born Donato di Niccolo Bardi, Italian sculptor of the early Renaissance. He was instrumental in reviving the classical style, as in his graceful bronze statue of the youthful *David* (about 1433; Bargello, Florence) and his equestrian statue of the general *Gattamelata* (1447–50; Piazza del Santo, Padua). The course of Florentine art in the 15th century was strongly influenced by his work.

Donegal mountainous county in the northwest of the Republic of Ireland, surrounded on three sides by the Atlantic Ocean, and bordering the counties of Londonderry, Tyrone, and Fermanagh (Northern Ireland), and Leitrim (Republic of Ireland); area 4,830 sq km/1,864 sq mi; county town Lifford; population (2002 est) 137,400. Ballyshannon is the largest town, and the market town and port of **Donegal** is at the head of **Donegal Bay** in the southwest. The severe climate renders much of the county barren, although the soil is suitable for potatoes, oats, and barley (in places). Commercial activities include sheep and cattle raising, tweed, linen, and carpet manufacture, and some salmon and deep-sea fishing. Tourism is also very important; the county is noted for dramatic scenery and geology as well as archaeological and historic remains, and the castles of Donegal and Glenveagh as well as Glenveagh National Park are among the top

visitor attractions in the county. The River Erne hydroelectric project (1952) involved the building of a large artificial lake (405 ha/1,000 acres) and a power station at Ballyshannon.

Dongola town in Northern State, northern Sudan; population (2001 est) 16,900. It has palm groves and produces dates; there is some light engineering and livestock rearing. There are road and river links to Khartoum. The town was founded in about 1811 to replace Old Dongola, 120 km/75 mi upriver, which was destroyed by the *Mamelukes. Old Dongola, a trading centre on a caravan route, was the capital of the Christian kingdom of Nubia between the 6th and 14th centuries.

Dönitz, Karl (1891–1980) German admiral, originator of the wolf-pack submarine technique, which sank Allied shipping in World War II. He succeeded Hitler in 1945, capitulated, and was imprisoned 1946–56.

Donizetti, (Domenico) Gaetano (Maria) (1797–1848) Italian composer. He wrote more than 70 operas, including *Lucrezia Borgia* (1833), *Lucia di Lammermoor* (1835), *La Fille du régiment* (1840), *La Favorite* (1840), and *Don Pasquale* (1843). They show the influence of Gioacchino Rossini and Vincenzo Bellini, and his ability to create a good tune is heard in his expressive melodies.

Don Juan Italian **Don Giovanni**, character of Spanish legend, Don Juan Tenorio, supposed to have lived in the 14th century and notorious for his debauchery. Tirso de Molina, Molière, Mozart, Byron, and George Bernard Shaw have featured the legend in their works.

donkey another name for *ass.

Donne, John (1572–1631) English poet, one of the *metaphysical poets. His work consists of love poems, religious poems, verse satires, and sermons. His sermons rank him with the century's greatest orators, and his fervent poems of love and hate, violent, tender, or abusive, give him a unique position among English poets. A Roman Catholic in his youth, he converted to the Church of England and finally became dean of St Paul's Cathedral, London.

Don Quixote de la Mancha satirical romance by the Spanish novelist Miguel de Cervantes, published in two parts (1605 and 1615). Don Quixote, a self-styled knight, embarks on a series of chivalric adventures accompanied by his servant Sancho Panza. Quixote's imagination leads him to see harmless objects as enemies to be fought, as in his tilting at windmills. English translators include Tobias Smollett (1775).

Doomsday Book variant spelling of *Domesday Book, the English survey of 1086.

Doors, the US psychedelic rock group formed in 1965 in Los Angeles, California, by Jim Morrison (1943–1971, vocals), Ray Manzarek (1935– , keyboards), Robby Krieger (1946– , guitar), and John Densmore (1944– , drums). Their first hit was 'Light My Fire' from their debut album *The Doors* (1967). They were noted for Morrison's poetic lyrics and flamboyant performance.

dopamine neurotransmitter, hydroxytyramine $C_8H_{11}NO_2$, an intermediate in the formation of adrenaline. There are special nerve cells (neurons) in the brain that use dopamine for the transmission of nervous impulses. One such area of dopamine neurons lies in the basal ganglia, a region that controls movement. Patients suffering from the tremors of

Parkinson's disease show nerve degeneration in this region. Another dopamine area lies in the limbic system, a region closely involved with emotional responses. It has been found that schizophrenic patients respond well to drugs that limit dopamine excess in this area.

doppelgänger (German 'double-goer') apparition of a living person, a person's double, or a guardian spirit. The German composer and writer E T A Hoffman wrote a short story called 'Die Doppelgänger' in 1821. English novelist Charles Williams (1886–1945) used the idea to great effect in his novel *Descent into Hell* (1937).

Doppler effect change in the observed frequency (or wavelength) of waves due to relative motion between the wave source and the observer. The Doppler effect is responsible for the perceived change in pitch of a siren as it approaches and then recedes, and for the *red shift of light from distant galaxies. It is named after the Austrian physicist Christian Doppler.

Doré, (Paul) Gustave (1832–1883) French artist. Chiefly known as a prolific illustrator, he was also active as a painter, etcher, and sculptor. He produced closely worked engravings of scenes from, for example, Rabelais, Dante, Cervantes, the Bible, Milton, and Edgar Allan Poe.

Dorian people of ancient Greece. They entered Greece from the north and took most of the Peloponnese from the Achaeans, perhaps destroying the *Mycenaean civilization; this invasion appears to have been completed before 1000 BC. Their chief cities were Sparta, Argos, and Corinth.

dormancy in botany, a phase of reduced physiological activity exhibited by certain buds, seeds, and spores. Dormancy can help a plant to survive unfavourable conditions, as in annual plants that pass the cold winter season as dormant seeds, and plants that form dormant buds.

dormitory town rural settlement that has a high proportion of commuters in its population. The original population may have been displaced by these commuters and the settlements enlarged by housing estates. Dormitory towns have increased in the UK since 1960 as a result of counter-urbanization.

dormouse small rodent, of the family Gliridae, with a hairy tail. There are about ten species, living in Europe, Asia, and Africa. They are arboreal (live in trees) and nocturnal, hibernating during winter in cold regions. They eat berries, nuts, pollen, and insects.

dorsal in vertebrates, the surface of the animal closest to the backbone. For most vertebrates and invertebrates this is the upper surface, or the surface furthest from the ground. For bipedal primates such as humans, where the dorsal surface faces backwards, then the word is 'back'.

Dorset county of southwest England (since April 1997 Bournemouth and Poole have been separate unitary authorities). **area:** 2,541 sq km/981 sq mi **towns and cities:** Dorchester (administrative headquarters), Shaftesbury, Sherborne; Lyme Regis, Weymouth, Poole, Swanage (resorts) **physical:** Chesil Beach, a shingle bank along the coast 19 km/11 mi long, connecting Isle of Portland to the mainland; Dorset Downs (chalk); River Stour, and rivers Frome and Piddle (which flow into Poole Harbour); clay beds in the north and west; Canford Heath, the home of some of Britain's rarest

breeding birds and reptiles (including the nightjar, Dartford warbler, sand lizard, and smooth snake) **features:** Isle of Purbeck, a peninsula where china clay and Purbeck 'marble' are quarried, and which includes 11th-century Corfe Castle and the holiday resort of Swanage; Cranborne Chase; Maiden Castle (prehistoric earthwork); Tank Museum at Royal Armoured Corps Centre, Bovington, where the cottage of the soldier and writer T E *Lawrence is a museum; Wimborne Minster; abbey church of Sherborne (rebuilt in 12, 15th, and 19th centuries) **population:** (2001 est) 391,500.

dory marine fish *Zeus faber* found in the Mediterranean and Atlantic. It grows up to 60 cm/2 ft, and has nine or ten long spines at the front of the dorsal fin, and four at the front of the anal fin. It is considered to be an excellent food fish and is also known as **John Dory**.

DOS acronym for Disk Operating System, computer *operating system specifically designed for use with disk storage; also used as an alternative name for a particular operating system, MS-DOS.

Dos Santos, José Eduardo (1942–) Angolan left-wing politician, president from 1979, a member of the People's Movement for the Liberation of Angola (MPLA). By 1989, he had negotiated the withdrawal of South African and Cuban forces, and in 1991 a peace agreement to end the civil war. In 1992 his victory in multiparty elections was disputed by Jonas Savimbi, leader of the rebel group National Union for the Total Independence of Angola (UNITA), and fighting resumed, escalating into full-scale civil war in 1993. Representatives of the two leaders signed a peace agreement in 1994. Dos Santos' proposal to make Savimbi vice-president was declined by the latter in 1996.

Dostoevsky, Fyodor Mihailovich (1821–1881) Russian novelist. Remarkable for their profound psychological insight, Dostoevsky's novels have greatly influenced Russian writers, and since the beginning of the 20th century have been increasingly influential abroad. In 1849 he was sentenced to four years' hard labour in Siberia, followed by army service, for printing socialist propaganda. *The House of the Dead* (1861) recalls his prison experiences, followed by his major works *Crime and Punishment* (1866), *The Idiot* (1868–69), and *The Brothers Karamazov* (1879–80).

dotterel bird *Eudromias morinellus* of the plover family, in order Charadriiformes, nesting on high moors and tundra in Europe and Asia, and migrating south for the winter. About 23 cm/9 in long, its plumage is patterned with black, brown, and white in summer, duller in winter, but always with white eyebrows and breastband. The female is larger than the male, and mates up to five times with different partners, each time laying her eggs and leaving them in the sole care of the male, who incubates and rears the brood. Three pale-green eggs with brown markings are laid in hollows in the ground.

double bass largest and lowest-sounding instrument of the violin family. It is 1.85 m/6 ft high and is played resting on the ground with the performer either standing or sitting on a high stool. Its sloping shoulders and flatter back link it to the viol family, where it is descended from the bass viol or violone. Until 1950, after which it was increasingly replaced by the electric bass, it also provided bass support (plucked) in popular music, although it is still the main bass instrument used in jazz. Performers include Domenico Dragonetti, composer of eight concertos, the Russian-born US conductor Serge Koussevitsky (1874–1951), and the jazz player and composer Charles Mingus. The double bass features as a solo in 'The Elephants' from Charles Camille *Saint-Saëns's *Carnival of the Animals* (1897).

double coconut treelike *palm plant, also known as **coco de mer**, of the Seychelles. It produces a two-lobed edible nut, one of the largest known fruits. (*Lodoicea maldivica*.)

double decomposition reaction between two chemical substances (usually *salts in solution) that results in the exchange of a constituent from each compound to create two different compounds.

double star pair of stars that appear close together. Many stars that appear single to the naked eye appear double when viewed through a telescope. Some double stars attract each other due to gravity, and orbit each other, forming a genuine *binary star, but other double stars are at different distances from Earth, and lie in the same line of sight only by chance. Through a telescope both types look the same.

Douglas, Kirk (1916–) born Issur Danielovitch Demsky, US film actor. Usually cast as a dynamic though ill-fated hero, as in *Spartacus* (1960), he was a major star of the 1950s and 1960s, appearing in such films as *Ace in the Hole* (1951), *The Bad and the Beautiful* (1953), *Paths of Glory* (1957), *The Vikings* (1958), and *The War Wagon* (1967). He received lifetime achievement awards from the American Film Institute in 1991, the Academy Awards in 1995, and the Screen Actors Guild in 1999.

Douglas, Michael (Kirk) (1944–) US film actor and producer. Known for his portrayal of ordinary men in situations out of their control, in films such as *Fatal Attraction* (1987) and *Falling Down* (1993), he has maintained a consistent career in the Hollywood mainstream. He won an Academy Award for his portrayal of a ruthless entrepreneur in *Wall Street* (1987). His credits as producer include *One Flew Over the Cuckoo's Nest* (1975), which earned him, with co-producer Saul Zaentz, a 1976 Academy Award for Best Picture.

Douglas fir any of some six species of coniferous evergreen tree belonging to the pine family. The most common is *Pseudotsuga menziesii*, native to western North America and east Asia. It grows up to 60–90 m/200–300 ft in height, has long, flat, spirally-arranged needles and hanging cones, and produces hard, strong timber. *P. glauca* has shorter, bluish needles and grows to 30 m/100 ft in mountainous areas. (Genus *Pseudotsuga*, family Pinaceae.)

Douglas-Home, Alec (1903–1995) Baron Home of the Hirsel; born Alexander Frederick Douglas-Home, British Conservative politician. He was foreign secretary 1960–63, and succeeded Harold Macmillan as prime minister in 1963. He renounced his peerage (as 14th Earl of Home) and re-entered the Commons after successfully contesting a by-election, but failed to win the 1964 general election, and resigned as party leader in 1965. He was again foreign secretary 1970–74, when he received a life peerage. The playwright William Douglas-Home was his brother. He was knighted in 1962.

Doulton, Henry (1820–1897) English ceramicist. He developed special wares for the chemical, electrical, and building industries, and established the world's

first stoneware-drainpipe factory in 1846. From 1870 he created art pottery and domestic tablewares in Lambeth, South London, and Burslem, near Stoke-on-Trent. He was knighted in 1887.

Dounreay site of the world's first fast nuclear reactor on the north coast of Scotland, in the Highland unitary authority, 13 km/8 mi west of Thurso. The first nuclear reactor, the Dounreay Fast Reactor (DFR), was active from 1959 until 1977. A second nuclear reactor, the Prototype Fast Reactor (PFR), was active between 1974 and 1994. The site became a nuclear reprocessing plant after the closure of the second reactor. In 2001 the UK government decided to end reprocessing at Dounreay, and the UK Atomic Energy Authority (UKAEA) began the process of decommissioning the site. Environmental campaigners welcomed the move, as they had raised concerns over the site's possible detrimental impact on the environment.

Douro Spanish **Duero**, river in Spain and Portugal, the third-largest in the Iberian peninsula; length 775 km/482 mi. It rises in Spain, on the south side of the Peña de Urbión in the province of Soria, and flows west across the plateau of Castile. It follows the Spanish-Portuguese frontier for 105 km/65 mi, and reaches the Atlantic Ocean at São João de Foz, 5 km/3 mi south of Porto. Navigation at the river mouth is hindered by sand bars. There are hydroelectric installations along its course.

dove person who takes a moderate, sometimes pacifist, view on political issues. The term originated in the US during the Vietnam War. Its counterpart is a *hawk. In more general usage today, a dove is equated with liberal policies, and a hawk with conservative ones.

dove another name for *pigeon.

Dover, Strait of French **Pas-de-Calais**, stretch of water separating England from France, and connecting the English Channel with the North Sea. It is about 35 km/22 mi long and 34 km/21 mi wide at its narrowest part (from Dover pier to Cap Griz-Nez); its greatest depth is 55 m/180 ft. It is one of the world's busiest sea lanes. The main ports are Dover and Folkestone (England), and Calais and Boulogne (France). There are regular ferry services between Folkestone and Boulogne-sur-Mer, and Dover and Calais, as well as hydrofoil services between British ports and Ostende (Belgium) and rail ferries to Dunkerque. The ferry traffic continued after the Channel Tunnel began providing regular rail and car-on-rail services in 1994–95.

dowager the style given to the widow of a British peer or baronet.

Dowding, Hugh Caswall Tremenheere, 1st Baron Dowding (1882–1970) British air chief marshal. He was chief of Fighter Command at the outbreak of World War II in 1939, a post he held through the Battle of Britain 10 July–12 October 1940.

Dowell, Anthony James (1943–) English classical ballet dancer. He is known for his elegant poise, accurate finish, and exemplary classical style. He was principal dancer with the Royal Ballet 1966–86, and was artistic director 1986–2001.

Dow Jones average New York Stock Exchange index, the most widely used indicator of US stock market prices. The average (no longer simply an average but today calculated to take into account changes in the constituent companies) is based on prices of 30 major companies, such as IBM and Walt Disney. It was first compiled in 1884 by Charles Henry Dow, cofounder of Dow Jones & Co., publishers of the *Wall Street Journal*.

Dowland, John (c. 1563–c. 1626) English composer of lute songs. He become known as the greatest composer and finest performer of these 'ayres' and is considered the main pioneer in the development of the art song. For the first time the 'top' part became more important than the others and the lute was used to provide a real accompaniment. This was different to the previous style of the madrigal, where all voices are equally important. His work includes *Lachrymae* (1605).

Down historic county of southeastern Northern Ireland; area 2,448 sq km/945 sq mi. The principal towns and cities are Downpatrick, Bangor, Newtownards, Newry, and Banbridge. The northern part of the county lies within the commuter belt for Belfast, and includes part of the city of Belfast, east of the River Lagan. Down is a largely lowland county, although the south is dominated by the Mourne Mountains, the highest point of which is Slieve Donard (852 m/2,796 ft), the highest point in Northern Ireland. Administrative responsibility for the county is held by the councils of Down, Castlereagh, North Down, Banbridge, Ards, and Newry and Mourne.

Downing Street street in Westminster, London, leading from Whitehall to St James's Park, named after Sir George Downing (died 1684), a diplomat under Cromwell and Charles II. **Number 10** is the official residence of the prime minister and **Number 11** is the residence of the chancellor of the Exchequer. After his appointment as prime minister in May 1997, Tony Blair chose to use Number 11 to accommodate his family, using Number 10 as his office and for Cabinet meetings. The chancellor of the Exchequer, Gordon Brown, retained his office in Number 11 but used the flat above Number 10 as his residence.

Down's syndrome condition caused by a chromosomal abnormality (the presence of an extra copy of chromosome 21), which in humans produces mental retardation; a flattened face; coarse, straight hair; and a fold of skin at the inner edge of the eye (hence the former name 'mongolism'). The condition can be detected by prenatal testing.

dowry property or money given by the bride's family to the groom or his family as part of the marriage agreement; the opposite of *bridewealth (property or money given by the groom's to the bride's family). In 1961, dowries were made illegal in India; however, in 1992, the Indian government reported more than 15,000 murders or suicides between 1988 and 1991 that were a direct result of insufficient dowries.

dowsing ascertaining the presence of water or minerals beneath the ground with a forked twig or a pendulum. Unconscious muscular action by the dowser is thought to move the twig, usually held with one fork in each hand, possibly in response to a local change in the pattern of electrical forces. The ability has been known since at least the 16th century and, though not widely recognized by science, it has been used commercially and in archaeology.

Doyle, Arthur Conan (1859–1930) Scottish writer. He created the detective Sherlock *Holmes and his assistant Dr Watson, who first appeared in *A Study in Scarlet* (1887) and featured in a number of subsequent stories, including *The Hound of the Baskervilles* (1902). Among Doyle's other works is the fantasy adventure *The Lost World* (1912). In his later years he became a spiritualist and wrote a *History of Spiritualism* (1926).

D'Oyly Carte, Richard (1844–1901) English producer of the Gilbert and Sullivan operas. They were performed at the Savoy Theatre, London, which he built. The D'Oyly Carte Opera Company, founded in 1876, was disbanded in 1982 following the ending of its monopoly on the Gilbert and Sullivan operas. The present company, founded in 1988, moved to the Alexandra Theatre, Birmingham, in 1991.

Drabble, Margaret (1939–) English writer. Her novels portray contemporary life with toughness and sensitivity, often through the eyes of intelligent modern women. They include *The Millstone* (1965), *The Ice Age* (1977), *The Middle Ground* (1980), the trilogy *The Radiant Way* (1987), *A Natural Curiosity* (1989), and *The Gates of Ivory* (1991), and *The Witch of Exmoor* (1996).

Draco large but faint constellation represented as a dragon coiled around the north celestial pole. Due to *precession (Earth's axial wobble), the star Alpha Draconis (Thuban) was the pole star 4,700 years ago.

Draco (lived 7th century BC) Athenian politician, the first to codify the laws of the Athenian city-state. These were notorious for their severity; hence **draconian**, meaning particularly harsh.

Dracula in the novel *Dracula* (1897) by Bram Stoker, the caped count who, as a *vampire, drinks the blood of beautiful women. The original of Dracula is thought to have been Vlad Tepes, or Vlad the Impaler, ruler of medieval Wallachia, who used to impale his victims and then mock them.

dragon name popularly given to various sorts of lizard. These include the *flying dragon *Draco volans* of southeast Asia; the komodo dragon *Varanus komodoensis* of Indonesia, at over 3 m/10 ft the largest living lizard; and some Australian lizards with bizarre spines or frills.

dragonfly any of numerous insects of the order Odonata, including the *damselfly. They all have long narrow bodies, two pairs of almost equal-sized, glassy wings with a network of veins; short, bristlelike antennae; powerful, 'toothed' mouthparts; and very large compound eyes which may have up to 30,000 facets. They can fly at speeds of up to 64–96 kph/40–60 mph.

Drake, Francis (c. 1540–1596) English buccaneer and explorer. After enriching himself as a pirate against Spanish interests in the Caribbean between 1567 and 1572, as well as in the slave trade, he was sponsored by *Elizabeth I for an expedition to the Pacific, sailing round the world from 1577 to 1580 in the *Golden Hind*, robbing Spanish ships as he went. This was the second circumnavigation of the globe (the first was by the Portuguese explorer Ferdinand Magellan). Drake also helped to defeat the *Spanish Armada in 1588 as a vice admiral in the *Revenge*.

drama (Greek 'action') literary *genre of scripted work. A theatrical drama is intended to be performed by actors for an audience. *Verse and *prose drama can both be performed (often in the same work), although dramas are also sometimes written to be read and not performed. The term is used collectively to group plays into historical or stylistic periods – for example, Greek drama, Restoration drama – as well as referring to the whole body of work written by a dramatist for performance.

draughts board game (known as **checkers** in the USA and Canada because of the chequered board of 64 squares) with elements of a simplified form of chess. Each of the two players has 12 men (disc-shaped pieces), and attempts either to capture all the opponent's men or to block their movements.

Dravidian (Sanskrit *Dravida* or *Dramida*) member of a group of non-Indo-European peoples of the Deccan region of India and northern Sri Lanka. The Dravidian language family is large, with about 20 languages spoken in southern India; the main ones are *Tamil,which has a literary tradition 2,000 years old; Kanarese; *Telugu; *Malayalam; and Tulu.

dream series of events or images perceived through the mind during sleep. Their function is unknown, but Sigmund *Freud saw them as wish fulfilment (nightmares being failed dreams prompted by fears of 'repressed' impulses). Dreams occur in periods of rapid eye movement (REM) by the sleeper, when the cortex of the brain is approximately as active as in waking hours. Dreams occupy about a fifth of sleeping time.

Dreamtime *or* **Dreaming** mythical past of the Australian Aborigines, the basis of their religious beliefs and creation stories. In the Dreamtime, spiritual beings shaped the land, the first people were brought into being and set in their proper territories, and laws and rituals were established. Belief in a creative spirit in the form of a huge snake, the Rainbow Serpent, occurs over much of Aboriginal Australia, usually associated with waterholes, rain, and thunder. A common feature of religions across the continent is the Aborigines' bond with the land.

Drenthe low-lying northern province of the Netherlands, south of Groningen and Friesland; area 2,660 sq km/1,027 sq mi; population (2003 est) 483,500. The main cities are Assen (capital), Emmen (the chief industrial centre), and Hoogeveen. The terrain is fenland and moors, with well-drained clay and peat soils. The chief industry is petroleum, and the main agricultural activities are livestock, arable crops, and horticulture.

Dresden capital of the *Land* (administrative region) of *Saxony, Germany, lying in a wide basin in the upper Elbe Valley; population (2001 est) 570,700. Dresden was a district capital within the former state of East Germany, the German Democratic Republic, and became a state capital within the Federal Republic of Germany. Products include chemicals, machinery, glassware, and musical instruments; engineering, agri-business, refrigeration, and telecommunications and high-tech industries are also important. One of the most beautiful German cities, with a rich architectural and cultural heritage, it was devastated by Allied bombing in 1945; much rebuilding has since taken place, and the city has become an important tourist destination.

dressage (French 'preparation') method of training a horse to carry out a predetermined routine of specified movements. Points are awarded for discipline and style.

Dreyfus, Alfred (1859–1935) French army officer, victim of miscarriage of justice, anti-Semitism, and cover-up. Employed in the War Ministry, in 1894 he was accused of betraying military secrets to Germany, court-martialled, and sent to the penal colony on *Devil's Island, French Guiana. When his innocence was discovered in 1896 the military establishment tried to conceal it, and the implications of the Dreyfus affair were passionately discussed in the press until he was exonerated in 1906.

driver in computing, a program that controls a peripheral device. Every device connected to the computer needs a driver program. The driver ensures that communication between the computer and the device is successful.

dromedary variety of Arabian *camel. The dromedary or one-humped camel has been domesticated since 400 BC. During a long period without water, it can lose up to one-quarter of its body weight without ill effects.

drug any of a range of substances, natural or synthetic, administered to humans and animals as therapeutic agents: to diagnose, prevent, or treat disease, or to assist recovery from injury. Traditionally many drugs were obtained from plants or animals; some minerals also had medicinal value. Today, increasing numbers of drugs are synthesized in the laboratory. It is useful to categorize drugs used by humans into three groups: over-the-counter and prescription drugs (*medicines) such as paracetamol and penicillin; recreational drugs such as alcohol and nicotine; and the drugs which are taken illegally if they are not prescribed, such as amphetamines, cannabis, and cocaine.

drug misuse illegal use of drugs for nontherapeutic purposes. Under the 1971 UK Misuse of Drugs regulations, illegal drugs include: Class A substances, such as heroin, LSD (acid), cocaine, ecstasy, heroin, magic mushrooms prepared for use, and amphetamines (speed) prepared for injection; Class B substances, such as amphetamines (speed) not prepared for injection, and barbiturates; and Class C substances, such as tranquillizers, anabolic steroids, and, from 2001 when it was moved in from Class B, cannabis. **Designer drugs** (for example, ecstasy) are usually modifications of the amphetamine molecule, altered in order to evade the law as well as for different effects, and may be many times more powerful and dangerous. Crack, a highly toxic derivative of cocaine, became available to drug users in the 1980s. Some athletes misuse drugs such as ephedrine and *anabolic steroids. In 1998 there were an estimated 100,000 problem drug users in the UK.

Druidism religion of the Celtic peoples of the pre-Christian British Isles and Gaul. The word is derived from the Greek *drus* ('oak'), a tree regarded by the Druids as sacred. One of the Druids' chief rites was the cutting of mistletoe from the oak with a golden sickle. They taught the immortality of the soul and a reincarnation doctrine, and were expert in astronomy. The Druids are thought to have offered human sacrifices.

drum any of a class of percussion instruments consisting of a frame or hollow vessel of wood, metal, or earthenware with a membrane of hide or plastic stretched across one or both ends. Drums are usually sounded by striking the membrane with the hands, a stick, or pair of sticks. They are among the oldest instruments known and exist in a wide variety of shapes and sizes. They include **slit drums** made of wood, **steel drums** made from oil containers, and a majority group of **skin drums**.

drupe fleshy *fruit containing one or more seeds which are surrounded by a hard, protective layer – for example cherry, almond, and plum. The wall of the fruit (*pericarp) is differentiated into the outer skin (exocarp), the fleshy layer of tissues (mesocarp), and the hard layer surrounding the seed (endocarp).

Druze or **Druse** religious sect in the Middle East of some 300,000 people. It began as a branch of Shiite Islam, based on a belief in the divinity of the Fatimid caliph al-Hakim (996–1021) and that he will return at the end of time. Their particular doctrines are kept secret, even from the majority of members. They refer to themselves as the Mowahhidoon, meaning monotheistic. The religion is exclusive, with conversion forbidden, either to or from the sect.

dryad (Greek *drys* '(oak) tree') in Greek mythology, a forest *nymph or tree spirit, especially of the oak. Each tree had a **hamadryad** who lived and died with it, from the Greek *hama* meaning 'together'.

Dryden, John (1631–1700) English poet and dramatist. He is noted for his satirical verse and for his use of the heroic couplet. His poetry includes the verse satire *Absalom and Achitophel* (1681), *Annus Mirabilis* (1667), and 'A Song for St Cecilia's Day' (1687). Plays include the heroic drama *The Conquest of Granada* (1672), the comedy *Marriage à la Mode* (1673), and *All for Love* (1678), a reworking of Shakespeare's *Antony and Cleopatra*.

dry ice solid carbon dioxide (CO_2), used as a refrigerant. At temperatures above –79 °C/–110.2 °F, it sublimes (turns into vapour without passing through a liquid stage) to gaseous carbon dioxide.

dry point in printmaking, a technique of engraving on copper, using a hard, sharp tool. The resulting lines tend to be fine and angular, with a strong furry edge created by the metal shavings. Dürer, Rembrandt, and Max Beckmann were outstanding exponents.

dry rot infection of timber in damp conditions by fungi (see *fungus), such as *Merulius lacrymans*, that form a threadlike surface. Whitish at first, the fungus later reddens as reproductive spores are formed. Tentacles from the fungus also work their way into the timber, making it dry-looking and brittle. Dry rot spreads rapidly through a building.

DTP abbreviation for *desktop publishing.

dualism in philosophy, the belief that reality is essentially dual in nature. The French philosopher René *Descartes, for example, referred to thinking and material substance. These entities interact but are fundamentally separate and distinct. Dualism is contrasted with monism, the theory that reality is made up of only one substance.

Dubai also known as Dubayy, one of the United Arab Emirates; population (1999 est) 858,000. Following the discovery of substantial oil reserves offshore in 1966, Dubai became very prosperous; developments included the building of modern hotels, an international airport, a new deepwater harbour, and a dry dock for supertankers.

Dubček, Alexander (1921–1992) Czechoslovak politician, chair of the federal assembly 1989–92. He was a member of the Slovak *resistance movement during World War II, and became first secretary of the Communist Party 1967–69. He launched a liberalization campaign (called the *Prague Spring) that was opposed by the USSR and led to the Soviet invasion of Czechoslovakia in 1968. He was arrested by Soviet troops and expelled from the party in 1970. In 1989 he gave speeches at pro-democracy rallies, and after the fall of the hardline regime, he was elected speaker of the National Assembly in Prague, a position to which he was re-elected in 1990. He was fatally injured in a car crash in September 1992.

Dublin county in the Republic of Ireland, in Leinster province, facing the Irish Sea and bounded by the counties of Meath, Kildare, and Wicklow; county town Dublin; area 920 sq km/355 sq mi; population (2002 est) 1,122,600. The county is mostly level and low-lying, but rises in the south to 753 m/2,471 ft in Kippure, part of the Wicklow Mountains. The River Liffey enters Dublin Bay. The county is dominated by Ireland's capital city of Dublin and its suburbs, but also contains pastoral and agricultural land. Dún Laoghaire is the other major town and large port.

Dublin official Irish name **Baile Átha Cliath**, 'the town of the ford of the hurdles', (Irish *dubh linn* 'dark pool') city and port on the east coast of Ireland, at the mouth of the River Liffey, facing the Irish Sea; capital of the Republic of Ireland, and county town of County Dublin; population (2002 est) 495,100 (city); 1,122,600 (Greater Dublin, including Dún Laoghaire). Around a quarter of the Republic's population lives in the Dublin conurbation, with a high density of young, professional workers. In the 1990s the city underwent a renaissance, with the restoration of many old city-centre buildings, notably in the Temple Bar area. Dublin is the site of one of the world's largest breweries (Guinness); other industries include information technology, financial services, textiles, pharmaceuticals, electrical goods, whiskey distilling, glass, food processing, and machine tools. Dublin is a major centre for culture and tourism, known particularly for its Georgian architecture and plethora of bars.

dubnium chemical symbol Db, synthesized, radioactive, metallic element of the *transactinide series, atomic number 105, relative atomic mass 261. Six isotopes have been synthesized, each with very short (fractions of a second) half-lives. Two institutions claim to have been the first to produce it: the Joint Institute for Nuclear Research in Dubna, Russia, in 1967; and the University of California at Berkeley, USA, who disputed the Soviet claim in 1970.

Duccio di Buoninsegna (before 1278–1318/19) Italian painter. As the first major figure in the Sienese school, his influence on the development of painting was profound. His works include his altarpiece for Siena Cathedral, the *Maestà* (1308–11, Cathedral Museum, Siena). In this the figure of the Virgin is essentially Byzantine in style, with much gold detail, but depicted with a new warmth and tenderness.

Duce (Italian 'leader') title bestowed on the fascist dictator Benito *Mussolini by his followers and later adopted as his official title.

Duchamp, Marcel (1887–1968) French-born US artist. He achieved notoriety with his *Nude Descending a Staircase No 2* (1912; Philadelphia Museum of Art), influenced by cubism and Futurism. An active exponent of *Dada, he invented ready-mades, everyday items (for example, a bicycle wheel mounted on a kitchen stool) which he displayed as works of art.

duck any of about 50 species of short-legged waterbirds with webbed feet and flattened bills, of the family Anatidae, order Anseriformes, which also includes the larger geese and swans. Ducks were domesticated for eggs, meat, and feathers by the ancient Chinese and the ancient Maya (see *poultry). Most ducks live in fresh water, feeding on worms and insects as well as vegetable matter. They are generally divided into dabbling ducks and diving ducks.

duckweed any of a family of tiny plants found floating on the surface of still water throughout most of the world, except the polar regions and tropics. Each plant consists of a flat, circular, leaflike structure 0.4 cm/0.15 in or less across, with a single thin root up to 15 cm/6 in long below. (Genus chiefly *Lemna*, family Lemnaceae.)

ductless gland alternative name for an *endocrine gland.

Dufay, Guillaume (c. 1400–1474) Flemish composer. He wrote secular songs and sacred music, including 84 songs and 8 masses. His work marks a transition from the style of the Middle Ages to the expressive melodies and rich harmonies of the Renaissance.

Dufy, Raoul (1877–1953) French painter and designer. Inspired by *fauvism he developed a fluent, brightly coloured style in watercolour and oils, painting scenes of gaiety and leisure, such as horse racing, yachting, and life on the beach. He also designed tapestries, textiles, and ceramics.

dugong marine mammal *Dugong dugong* of the order Sirenia (sea cows), found in the Red Sea, the Indian Ocean, and western Pacific Ocean. It can grow to 3.6 m/11 ft long, and has a tapering body with a notched tail and two fore-flippers. All dugongs are listed on the Convention on International Trade in Endangered Species (CITES) Appendix 1, which bans all trade in the species.

duiker (Afrikaans *diver*) any of several antelopes of the family Bovidae, common in Africa. Duikers are shy and nocturnal, and grow to 30–70 cm/12–28 in tall. The grey duiker *Cephalopus Sylvicapra grimmia* is the commonest species of duiker. It occurs over most of sub-Saharan Africa, surviving in every kind of habitat – except deserts and rainforests – up to an altitude of 4,600 m/15,090 ft.

Dukas, Paul Abraham (1865–1935) French composer and teacher. His scrupulous orchestration and chromatically enriched harmonies were admired by Debussy. He wrote very little, composing slowly and with extreme care. His small output includes the opera *Ariane et Barbe-Bleue/Ariane and Bluebeard* (1907), the ballet *La Péri/The Peri* (1912), and the animated orchestral scherzo *L'Apprenti sorcier/The Sorcerer's Apprentice* (1897).

duke highest title in the English peerage. It originated in England in 1337, when Edward III created his son Edward, Duke of Cornwall.

dulcimer musical instrument, a form of *zither, consisting of a shallow open trapezoidal soundbox across which strings are stretched laterally; they are horizontally struck by lightweight hammers or beaters. It produces clearly differentiated pitches of consistent quality and is more agile and wide-ranging in pitch than the harp or lyre. In Hungary the dulcimer is known as a cimbalom, and is a national instrument.

Dulong, Pierre Louis (1785–1838) French chemist and physicist. In 1819 he formulated, together with physicist Alexis Petit, the Dulong and Petit law, which states that, for many elements solid at room temperature, the product of *relative atomic mass and *specific heat capacity is approximately constant. He also discovered the explosive nitrogen trichloride in 1811.

dulse any of several edible red seaweeds, especially *Rhodymenia palmata*, found on middle and lower shores of the north Atlantic. They may have a single broad blade up to 30 cm/12 in long rising directly from the holdfast which attaches them to the sea floor, or may be palmate (with five lobes) or fan-shaped. The frond is tough and dark red, sometimes with additional small leaflets at the edge.

Dumas, Alexandre (1824–1895) French author, known as Dumas *fils* (the son of Dumas *père*). He is remembered for the play *La Dame aux camélias/The Lady of the Camellias* (1852), based on his own novel, and the source of Verdi's opera *La Traviata*.

Dumas, Alexandre (1802–1870) French writer, known as Dumas *père* (the father). His popular historical romances were the reworked output of a 'fiction-factory' of collaborators. They include *Les Trois Mousquetaires/The Three Musketeers* (1844) and its sequels. He is best known for *Le Comte de Monte Cristo/The Count of Monte Cristo*, which appeared in 12 volumes (1845). His play *Henri III et sa cour/Henry III and His Court* (1829) established French romantic historical drama. Dumas *fils* was his son.

Du Maurier, Daphne (1907–1989) English novelist. Her romantic fiction includes *Jamaica Inn* (1936), *Rebecca* (1938), *Frenchman's Creek* (1942), and *My Cousin Rachel* (1951), and is set in Cornwall. Her work, though lacking in depth and original insights, is made compelling by her storytelling gift.

Dumbarton Oaks 18th-century mansion in Washington, DC, USA, used for conferences and seminars. It was the scene of a conference held in 1944 that led to the foundation of the United Nations.

Dumfries and Galloway unitary authority in southern Scotland, formed in 1996 from the regional council of the same name (1975–96). **area:** 6,421 sq km/2,479 sq mi **towns:** Annan, Dumfries (administrative headquarters), Kirkcudbright, Stranraer, Castle Douglas, Newton Stewart **physical:** area characterized by an indented coastline, including Luce Bay and Wigtown Bay, backed by a low-lying coastal strip of varying width; intensively forested in the Galloways. Much of the inland area is upland: east to west this includes Eskdalemuir (Hart Fell 808 m/2,651 ft), the Lowther Hills (Green Lowther 732 m/2,402 ft) and the Galloway Hills (the Merrick 843 m/2,766 ft) **features:** Wanlockhead (the highest village in Scotland); the oldest working post office in the world at Sanquhar; Galloway Forest Park incorporating Glen Trool; the Ruthwell Cross, Whithorn archaeological dig **population:** (2001 est) 147,800.

dump in computing, the process of rapidly transferring data to external memory or to a printer. It is usually done to help with debugging (see *bug) or as part of an error-recovery procedure designed to provide data security. A screen dump makes a printed copy of the current screen display.

Duncan, Isadora (1878–1927) born Angela Duncan, US dancer. A pioneer of modern dance, she adopted an emotionally expressive free form, dancing barefoot and wearing a loose tunic, inspired by the ideal of Hellenic beauty. She danced solos accompanied to music by Beethoven and other great composers, believing that the music should fit the grandeur of the dance. Having made her base in Paris in 1908, she toured extensively, often returning to Russia after her initial success there in 1904.

Duncan Smith, Iain (1954–) British Conservative politician, party leader 2001–03. The candidate of the party's Eurosceptic and socially conservative right wing, he was selected in September 2001 by the party's members to replace leader William Hague, who stood down after the party suffered a second successive general election defeat. Duncan Smith sought to unite the party around a programme of opposition to the UK joining the European single currency, and of reforms in domestic policies, including greater citizen choice in education and health. He was replaced as party leader by Michael Howard.

Dundee city and administrative centre of Dundee City unitary authority, in eastern Scotland, on the north side of the firth of Tay; 96 km/60 mi east of Edinburgh; population (2001 est) 147,000. Dundee developed around the jute, jam, and journalism industries in the 19th century. In the 20th century, Dundee has diversified into biomedical research, oil-industry support, and high-technology manufacturing.

Dundee, John Graham Claverhouse, Viscount Dundee see John Graham *Claverhouse.

dune mound or ridge of wind-drifted sand, common on coasts and in deserts. Loose sand is blown and bounced along by the wind, up the windward side of a dune (saltation). The sand particles then fall to rest on the lee side, while more are blown up from the windward side. In this way a dune moves gradually downwind. Dunes occur in areas where there is a large supply of sand, strong winds, low rainfall, and some vegetation or obstructions to trap the sand.

Dunfermline industrial town north of the Firth of Forth in Fife, Scotland; population (2001 est) 127,900. Industries include engineering, electronics, and textiles. It was the ancient capital of Scotland, with many sites of royal historical significance. Many Scottish kings, including Robert the Bruce, Malcolm Canmore and his queen Margaret, and Elizabeth I, are buried in **Dunfermline Abbey**.

Dún Laoghaire formerly **Kingstown**, major port, residential town, and borough in County Dublin, Republic of Ireland, 10 km/6 mi south of the centre of Dublin; population (1996) 190,000 (Dún Laoghaire – Rathdown). It is a terminal for ferries to Britain, and there are fishing industries. The National Maritime Museum is located here, and it is an important yachting centre and popular tourist resort. The James Joyce museum is located in a Martello tower at Sandycove, 3 km/2 mi south of the town, where the Irish author once stayed.

dunlin small gregarious shore bird *Calidris alpina* of the sandpiper family Scolopacidae, order Charadriiformes, about 18 cm/7 in long, nesting on moors and marshes in the far northern regions of Eurasia and North America. Chestnut above and black below in summer, it is greyish in winter; the bill and feet are black.

Dunlop, John Boyd (1840–1921) Scottish inventor who founded the rubber company that bears his name.

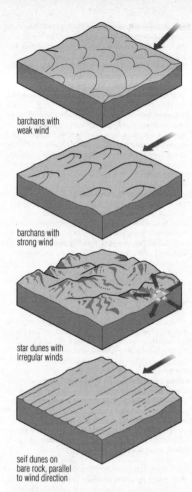

barchans with weak wind

barchans with strong wind

star dunes with irregular winds

seif dunes on bare rock, parallel to wind direction

dune The shape of a dune indicates the prevailing wind pattern. Crescent-shaped dunes form in sandy desert with winds from a constant direction. Seif dunes form on bare rocks, parallel to the wind direction. Irregular star dunes are formed by variable winds.

In 1888, to help his child win a tricycle race, he bound an inflated rubber hose to the wheels. The same year he developed commercially practical pneumatic tyres, first patented by Robert William Thomson (1822–1873) in 1845 for bicycles and cars.

dunnock *or* **hedge sparrow** European bird *Prunella modularis* family Prunellidae, similar in size and colouring to the sparrow, but with a slate-grey head and breast, and more slender bill. It is characterized in the field by a hopping gait, with continual twitches of the wings whilst feeding. It nests in bushes and hedges.

Duns Scotus, John (c. 1265–c. 1308) Scottish monk, a leading figure in the theological and philosophical system of medieval *scholasticism, which attempted to show that Christian doctrine was compatible with the ideas of the Greek philosophers Aristotle and Plato. The church rejected his ideas, and the word **dunce** is derived from Dunses, a term of ridicule applied to his followers. In the medieval controversy over universals he advocated nominalism, maintaining that classes of things have no independent reality. He belonged to the Franciscan order, and was known as *Doctor Subtilis* (the Subtle Teacher).

duodecimal system system of arithmetic notation using 12 as a base, at one time considered superior to the decimal number system in that 12 has more factors (2, 3, 4, 6) than 10 (2, 5).

duodenum in vertebrates, a short length of *alimentary canal found between the stomach and the small intestine. Its role is in digesting carbohydrates, fats, and proteins. The smaller molecules formed are then absorbed, either by the duodenum or the ileum.

Dürer, Albrecht (1471–1528) German artist. He was the leading figure of the northern Renaissance. He was born in Nürnberg and travelled widely in Europe. Highly skilled in drawing and a keen student of nature, he perfected the technique of woodcut and engraving, producing woodcut series such as the *Apocalypse* (1498) and copperplate engravings such as *The Knight, Death, and the Devil* (1513) and *Melancholia* (1514). His paintings include altarpieces and meticulously observed portraits, including many self-portraits.

Durham city and administrative headquarters of the county of Durham, northeast England, on the River Wear, 19 km/12 mi south of Newcastle-upon-Tyne; population (1991) 36,900. Formerly a centre for the coalmining industry (the last pit closed in 1993), the city now has light engineering industries and manufactures textiles, carpets, and clothing.

Durham county of northeast England (since April 1997 Darlington has been a separate unitary authority). **area:** 2,232 sq km/862 sq mi **towns and cities:** Durham (administrative headquarters), Newton Aycliffe, Peterlee, Chester-le-Street **physical:** Pennine Hills; rivers Wear and Tees **features:** Beamish open-air industrial museum; site of one of Britain's richest coalfields (pits now closed); Bowes Museum; Barnard Castle; Durham Cathedral (1133); University of Durham (1832), partly housed in Durham Castle; dales in the west of the county **population:** (2001 est) 493,700.

Durkheim, Emile (1858–1917) French sociologist, one of the founders of modern sociology, who also influenced social anthropology. He worked to establish sociology as a respectable and scientific discipline, capable of diagnosing social ills and recommending possible cures.

durra *or* **doura** grass, also known as Indian millet, grown as a cereal in parts of Asia and Africa. *Sorghum vulgare* is the chief cereal in many parts of Africa. See also *sorghum. (Genus *Sorghum.*)

Durrell, Gerald (Malcolm) (1925–1995) English naturalist, writer, and zoo curator. He became director of Jersey Zoological Park in 1958, and wrote 37 books, including the humorous memoir *My Family and Other Animals* (1956). He was the brother of the writer Lawrence *Durrell.

Durrell, Lawrence (George) (1912–1990) English novelist and poet. He lived mainly in the eastern Mediterranean, the setting of his novels, including the Alexandria Quartet: *Justine, Balthazar, Mountolive*, and *Clea* (1957–60). He also wrote travel books, including *Bitter Lemons* (1957) about Cyprus. His heady prose and bizarre characters reflect his exotic sources of inspiration. He was the brother of the naturalist Gerald Durrell.

Dushanbe formerly **Stalinabad** (1929–61), capital of Tajikistan, situated in the Gissar Valley 160 km/100 mi north of the Afghan frontier; population (1999 est) 582,400. Dushanbe is a road, rail, and air centre. Long-established industries include cotton and silk mills, tanneries, meat-packing factories, and printing works, while factories producing refrigerators, electric cables and automatic looms have been established relatively recently. It is the seat of Tajik State university (1948) and the Takik Academy of Sciences (1951), and has medical, agricultural and teacher-training colleges.

dust bowl area in the Great Plains region of North America (Texas to Kansas) that suffered extensive wind erosion as the result of drought and poor farming practice in once-fertile soil. Much of the topsoil was blown away in the droughts of the 1930s and the 1980s.

Dutch art painting and sculpture of the Netherlands. The country became effectively independent, with approximately the boundaries it has today, in the early 17th century, although its independence was not officially recognized by Spain – previously its overlord – until 1648. The 17th century was the great age of Dutch painting. Among the many artists of this period were *Rembrandt; Willem Kalf, who excelled at still lifes; Adriaen van Ostade, who painted Flemish peasant scenes; Gerard Terborch the Younger, the first painter of characteristic Dutch interiors; Albert Cuyp; Jakob van *Ruisdael, who specialized in landscapes; Jan Steen; Pieter de Hooch; Jan *Vermeer; Willem van de Velde, sea painter to Charles II of England; and Meindert Hobbema. Despite the quality and abundance of art produced in the Netherlands in the 17th century, there was a marked decline in Dutch art during the 18th and 19th centuries. This was reversed with the arrival of the expressionist genius, Vincent *van Gogh in the late 19th century, and the abstract painter Piet *Mondrian in the 20th century.

Dutch cap common name for a barrier method of contraception; see *diaphragm.

Dutch East India Company (VOC, or Vereenigde Oost-Indische Compagnie) trading company chartered by the States General (parliament) of the Netherlands, and established in the northern Netherlands in 1602. It was given a monopoly on Dutch trade in the Indonesian archipelago, and certain sovereign rights such as the creation of an army and a fleet.

Dutch East Indies former Dutch colony, which in 1945 became independent as Indonesia.

Dutch elm disease disease of elm trees *Ulmus*, principally Dutch, English, and American elm, caused by the fungus *Certocystis ulmi*. The fungus is usually spread from tree to tree by the elm-bark beetle, which lays its eggs beneath the bark. The disease has no cure, and control methods involve injecting insecticide into the trees annually to prevent infection, or the destruction of all elms in a broad band around an infected area, to keep the beetles out.

Dutch Guiana former Dutch colony, which in 1975 became independent as Suriname.

Dutch language member of the Germanic branch of the Indo-European language family, often referred to by scholars as Netherlandic and taken to include the standard language and dialects of the Netherlands (excluding Frisian) as well as Flemish (in Belgium and northern France) and, more remotely, its offshoot Afrikaans in South Africa.

Duvalier, François (1907–1971) Right-wing president of Haiti 1957–71. Known as **Papa Doc**, he ruled as a dictator, organizing the Tontons Macoutes ('bogeymen') as a private security force to intimidate and assassinate opponents of his regime. He rigged the 1961 elections in order to have his term of office extended until 1967, and in 1964 declared himself president for life. He was excommunicated by the Vatican for harassing the church, and was succeeded on his death by his son Jean-Claude Duvalier.

Dvořák, Antonín Leopold (1841–1904) Czech composer. His Romantic music extends the classical tradition of Ludwig van Beethoven and Johannes Brahms and displays the influence of Czech folk music. He wrote nine symphonies; tone poems; operas, including *Rusalka* (1900); large-scale choral works; the *Carnival* (1891–92) and other overtures; violin and cello concertos; chamber music; piano pieces; and songs. International recognition came with two sets of *Slavonic Dances* (1878 and 1886). Works such as his *New World Symphony* (1893) reflect his interest in American folk themes, including black and American Indian music. He was director of the National Conservatory, New York, in 1892–95.

Dyck, Anthony van (1599–1641) Flemish painter. He was an assistant to Rubens from 1618 to 1620, then worked briefly in England at the court of James I before moving to Italy in 1622. In 1627 he returned to his native Antwerp, where he continued to paint religious works and portraits. From 1632 he lived in England and produced numerous portraits of royalty and aristocrats, such as *Charles I on Horseback* (about 1638; National Gallery, London).

dye substance that, applied in solution to fabrics, stains with a permanent colour. Different types of dye are needed for different types of fibres. **Direct dyes** combine with cellulose-based fabrics like cotton, linen, and rayon, to colour the fibres. **Indirect dyes** require the presence of another substance (a mordant), with which the fabric must first be treated, to ensure that the dye will remain 'fast' during washing. **Vat dyes** are colourless soluble substances that on exposure to air yield an insoluble coloured compound that is resistant to water.

Dyfed former county of southwest Wales, created in 1974 and, in 1996, divided between the unitary authorities of *Carmarthenshire, *Ceredigion, and *Pembrokeshire.

dyke in earth science, a sheet of *igneous rock created by the intrusion of magma (molten rock) across layers of pre-existing rock. (By contrast, a sill is intruded *between* layers of rock.) It may form a ridge when exposed on the surface if it is more resistant than the rock into which it intruded. A dyke is also a human-made embankment built along a coastline (for example, in the Netherlands) to prevent the flooding of lowland coastal regions.

Dylan, Bob (1941–) adopted name of Robert Allen Zimmerman, US singer and songwriter. His lyrics provided catchphrases for a generation and influenced innumerable songwriters. He began in the folk-music tradition. His early songs, as on his albums *The Freewheelin' Bob Dylan* (1963) and *The Times They Are A-Changin'* (1964), were associated with the US civil-rights movement and anti-war protest. From 1965 he worked in his own unique rock style, as on the albums *Highway 61 Revisited* (1965) and *Blonde on Blonde* (1966). His prolific folk-rock output continued into the 21st century.

Dynamic HTML in computing, the fourth version of hypertext markup language (HTML), the language used to create Web pages. It is called Dynamic HTML because it enables dynamic effects to be incorporated in pages without the delays involved in downloading Java applets and without referring back to the server.

dynamics in music, markings added to show the varying degrees or changes in volume or loudness. They are written as words, abbreviations, letters, or signs. For example: dynamics for volume include **f** for forte (loud), **mf** for mezzo forte (medium loud), **mp** for mezzo piano (medium soft), and **p** for piano (soft); changes in volume include **crescendo** (becoming gradually louder), and **diminuendo** (becoming gradually softer); accents include **sf** for sforzando (meaning a sudden accent on a note or chord).

dynamics *or* **kinetics** in mechanics, the mathematical and physical study of the behaviour of bodies under the action of forces that produce changes of motion in them.

dynamite explosive consisting of a mixture of nitroglycerine and diatomaceous earth (diatomite, an absorbent, chalklike material). It was first devised by Alfred Nobel.

dynamo in physics, a simple *generator or machine for transforming mechanical energy into electrical energy. A dynamo in basic form consists of a powerful field magnet between the poles of which a suitable conductor, usually in the form of a coil (armature), is rotated. The magnetic lines of force are cut by the rotating wire coil, which induces a current to flow through the wire. The mechanical energy of rotation is thus converted into an electric current in the armature.

dysentery infection of the large intestine causing abdominal cramps and painful *diarrhoea with blood. There are two kinds of dysentery: **amoebic** (caused by a protozoan), common in the tropics, which may lead to liver damage; and **bacterial**, the kind most often seen in the temperate zones.

dyslexia (Greek 'bad', 'pertaining to words') malfunction in the brain's synthesis and interpretation of written information, popularly known as 'word blindness'.

dysprosium chemical symbol Dy, (Greek *dusprositos* 'difficult to get near') silver-white, metallic element of the *lanthanide series, atomic number 66, relative atomic mass 162.50. It is among the most magnetic of all known substances and has a great capacity to absorb neutrons.

dystopia imaginary society whose evil qualities are meant to serve as a moral or political warning. The term was coined in 1868 by the English philosopher John Stuart *Mill, and is the opposite of a Utopia. George Orwell's *1984*, published in 1949 and Aldous Huxley's *Brave New World* (1932) are examples of novels about dystopias. Dystopias are common in science fiction.

e

eagle any of several genera of large birds of prey of the family Accipitridae, order Falconiformes, including the golden eagle *Aquila chrysaetos* of Eurasia and North America, which has a 2 m/6 ft wingspan. Eagles occur worldwide, usually building eyries or nests in forests or mountains, and all are fierce and powerful birds of prey. The harpy eagle is the largest eagle.

Eames Charles (1907–1978) and Ray (born Ray Kaiser, 1916–1988), US designers. A husband-and-wife team, they worked together in California 1941–78. They created some of the most highly acclaimed furniture designs of the 20th century: a moulded plywood chair 1945–46; the Lounge Chair, a black leather-upholstered chair, 1956; and a fibreglass armchair 1950–53.

ear organ of hearing in animals. It responds to the vibrations that constitute sound, which are translated into nerve signals and passed to the brain. A mammal's ear consists of three parts: outer ear, middle ear, and inner ear. The **outer ear** is a funnel that collects sound, directing it down a tube to the **eardrum** (tympanic membrane), which separates the outer and **middle ear**. Sounds vibrate this membrane, the mechanical movement of which is transferred to a smaller membrane leading to the **inner ear** by three small bones, the auditory ossicles. Vibrations of the inner ear membrane move fluid contained in the spiral-shaped cochlea, which vibrates hair cells that stimulate the auditory nerve connected to the brain. There are approximately 30,000 sensory hair cells (**stereocilia**). Exposure to loud noise and the process of ageing damages the stereocilia, resulting in hearing loss. Three fluid-filled canals of the inner ear detect changes of position; this mechanism, with other sensory inputs, is responsible for the sense of balance.

Earhart, Amelia (1898–1937) US aviation pioneer and author, who in 1928 became the first woman to fly across the Atlantic. With copilot Frederick Noonan, she attempted a round-the-world flight in 1937. Somewhere over the Pacific their plane disappeared.

earl in the British peerage, the third title in order of rank, coming between marquess and viscount; it is the oldest of British titles, deriving from the Anglo-Saxon post of ealdorman. For some time earls were called counts, and their wives are still called countesses.

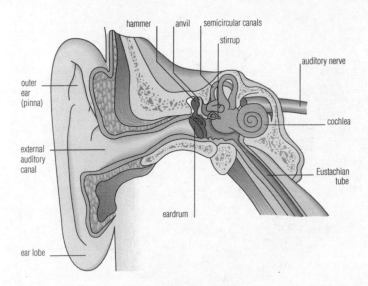

ear The structure of the ear. The three bones of the middle ear – hammer, anvil, and stirrup – vibrate in unison and magnify sounds about 20 times. The spiral-shaped cochlea is the organ of hearing. As sound waves pass down the spiral tube, they vibrate fine hairs lining the tube, which activate the auditory nerve connected to the brain. The semicircular canals are the organs of balance, detecting movements of the head.

Early English

Early English in architecture, the first of the three periods of the English Gothic style, late 12th century to late 13th century. It is characterized by tall, elongated windows (lancets) without mullions (horizontal bars), often grouped in threes, fives, or sevens; the pointed arch; pillars of stone centres surrounded by shafts of black Purbeck marble; and dog-tooth (zig-zag) ornament. Salisbury Cathedral (begun in 1220) is almost entirely Early English.

Earth third planet from the Sun. It is almost spherical, flattened slightly at the poles, and is composed of five concentric layers: inner *core, outer core, *mantle, *crust, and atmosphere. About 70% of the surface (including the north and south polar ice caps) is covered with water. The Earth is surrounded by a life-supporting atmosphere and is the only planet on which life is known to exist. **mean distance from the Sun:** 149,500,000 km/92,860,000 mi **equatorial diameter:** 12,755 km/7,920 mi **circumference:** 40,070 km/24,900 mi **rotation period:** 23 hours 56 minutes 4.1 seconds **year:** (complete orbit, or sidereal period) 365 days 5 hours 48 minutes 46 seconds. The Earth's average speed

around the Sun is 30 kps/18.5 mps. The plane of its orbit is inclined to its equatorial plane at an angle of 23.5°; this is the reason for the changing seasons **atmosphere:** nitrogen 78.09%; oxygen 20.95%; argon 0.93%; carbon dioxide 0.03%; and less than 0.0001% neon, helium, krypton, hydrogen, xenon, ozone, and radon **surface:** land surface 150,000,000 sq km/ 57,500,000 sq mi (greatest height above sea level 8,872 m/ 29,118 ft Mount Everest); water surface 361,000,000 sq km/139,400,000 sq mi (greatest depth 11,034 m/ 36,201 ft *Mariana Trench in the Pacific). The interior is thought to be an inner core about 2,600 km/1,600 mi in diameter, of solid iron and nickel; an outer core about 2,250 km/1,400 mi thick, of molten iron and nickel; and a mantle of mostly solid rock about 2,900 km/1,800 mi thick. The crust and the uppermost layer of the mantle form about twelve major moving plates, some of which carry the continents. The plates are in constant, slow motion, called tectonic drift **satellite:** the *Moon **age:** 4.6 billion years. The Earth was formed with the rest of the *Solar System by consolidation of interstellar dust. Life began 3.5–4 billion years ago.

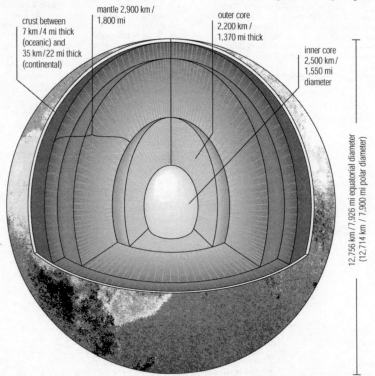

mantle 2,900 km / 1,800 mi

crust between 7 km / 4 mi thick (oceanic) and 35 km / 22 mi thick (continental)

outer core 2,200 km / 1,370 mi thick

inner core 2,500 km / 1,550 mi diameter

12,756 km / 7,926 mi equatorial diameter (12,714 km / 7,900 mi polar diameter)

Earth Inside the Earth. The surface of the Earth is a thin crust about 7 km/4 mi thick under the sea and 35 km/ 22 mi thick under the continents. Under the crust lies the mantle, about 2,900 km/1,800 mi thick and with a temperature of 1,500–3,000 °C/2,700–5,400 °F. The outer core is about 2,200 km/1,370 mi thick, of molten iron and nickel. The inner core is probably solid iron and nickel, at about 5,000 °C/9,000 °F.

earth electrical connection between an appliance and the ground. In the event of a fault in an electrical appliance, for example, involving connection between the live part of the circuit and the outer casing, the current flows to earth, causing no harm to the user.

earthenware pottery made of porous clay and fired at relatively low temperatures of up to 1,200 °C/2,200 °F. It does not vitrify but remains porous, so will continue to absorb fluids. Earthenware may be unglazed (terracotta flowerpots, wine-coolers) or glazed to give a smooth, shiny, waterproof surface (most tableware); the glaze and body characteristically form quite separate layers.

earthquake abrupt motion of the Earth's surface. Earthquakes are caused by the sudden release in rocks of strain accumulated over time as a result of *plate tectonics. The study of earthquakes is called *seismology. Most earthquakes occur along *faults (fractures or breaks) and Benioff zones. As two plates move past each other they can become jammed. When sufficient strain has accumulated, the rock breaks, releasing a series of elastic waves (*seismic waves) as the plates spring free. The force of earthquakes (magnitude) is measured on the *Richter scale, and their effect (intensity) on the *Mercalli scale. The point at which an earthquake originates is the **focus** or **hypocentre**; the point on the Earth's surface directly above this is the *epicentre.

earth science scientific study of the planet Earth as a whole. The mining and extraction of minerals and gems, the prediction of weather and earthquakes, the pollution of the atmosphere, and the forces that shape the physical world all fall within its scope of study. The emergence of the discipline reflects scientists' concern that an understanding of the global aspects of the Earth's structure and its past will hold the key to how humans affect its future, ensuring that its resources are used in a sustainable way. It is a synthesis of several traditional subjects such as *geology, *meteorology, *oceanography, geophysics, geochemistry, and *palaeontology.

Earth Summit *or* **World Development** *or* **United Nations Conference on Environment and Development** international meetings aiming at drawing up measures for the environmental protection of the world. The first summit took place in Rio de Janeiro, Brazil, in June 1992. Treaties were made to combat global warming and protect biodiversity (the latter was not signed by the USA). The second Earth Summit was held in New York in June 1997 to review progress. The meeting agreed to work towards a global forest convention with the aim of halting the destruction of tropical and old-growth forests. The last Earth Summit took place on 17 March 2004 in Johannesburg, South Africa. Russia backed the *Kyoto treaty on global warming, ensuring that it would still go ahead despite US non-participation.

earthworm *annelid worm of the class Oligochaeta. Earthworms are hermaphroditic and deposit their eggs in cocoons. They live by burrowing in the soil, feeding on the organic matter it contains. They are vital to the formation of humus, aerating the soil and levelling it by transferring earth from the deeper levels to the surface as castings.

earwig nocturnal insect of the order Dermaptera. The forewings are short and leathery and serve to protect the hindwings, which are large and are folded like a fan when at rest. Earwigs seldom fly. They have a pincerlike appendage in the rear. The male is distinguished by curved pincers; those of the female are straight. Earwigs are regarded as pests because they feed on flowers and fruit, but they also eat other insects, dead or alive. Eggs are laid beneath the soil, and the female cares for the young even after they have hatched. The male dies before the eggs have hatched.

East Anglia region of eastern England, formerly a Saxon kingdom, including Norfolk, Suffolk, and parts of Essex and Cambridgeshire. Norwich is the principal city of East Anglia. East Anglian ports such as Harwich and Felixstowe have greatly developed as trade with the rest of Europe has increased.

East Ayrshire unitary authority in southwest Scotland, created in 1996 from two districts of Strathclyde region. **area:** 1,269 sq km/490 sq mi **towns:** Kilmarnock (administrative headquarters), Cumnock, Stewarton, Galston, Crosshouse **physical:** predominantly low-lying and undulating in the north, mountainous toward the south; Loch Doon; rivers Ayr, Irvine; Blackcraig Hill (700 m/2,298 ft); Loudoun Hill **features:** Burns' House Museum, Mauchline; Loudoun Castle Theme Park; Dunaskin Heritage Museum **population:** (2001 est) 120,300.

East China Sea see *China Sea.

East Dunbartonshire unitary authority in central Scotland, created in 1996 from two districts of Strathclyde region. **area:** 175 sq km/67 sq mi. **towns:** Kirkintilloch (administrative headquarters), Bearsden, Milngavie **physical:** low-lying lands to the south give way dramatically to the Campsie Fells in the north; Earl's Seat (578 m/1,896 ft); River Kelvin **features:** Forth and Clyde Canal; Antonine Wall **population:** (2001 est) 108,300.

Easter spring feast of the Christian church, commemorating the *resurrection of Jesus. It is a moveable feast, falling on the first Sunday following the full moon after the vernal equinox (21 March); that is, between 22 March and 25 April.

Easter Island *or* **Rapa Nui** Spanish Isla de Pascua, Chilean island in the south Pacific Ocean, part of the Polynesian group, about 3,500 km/2,200 mi west of Chile; area about 166 sq km/64 sq mi; population (1998 est) 2,000. The island consists of three extinct volcanoes, reaching a maximum altitude of 538 m/1,765 ft. It was first reached by Europeans on Easter Sunday 1722. On it stand over 800 huge carved statues (*moai*) and the remains of boat-shaped stone houses, the work of Neolithic peoples from Polynesia. The chief centre is Hanga-Roa.

Eastern Cape province of the Republic of South Africa from 1994, formerly part of Cape Province; area 170,616 sq km/65,875 sq mi; population (2000 est) 6,811,400. The capital is Bisho; the other main towns are East London, Port Elizabeth, and Grahamstown. Much of the terrain is elevated, with the interior plateau of the Highveld and the southern part of the Drakensberg mountains falling southwards and eastwards to a narrow coastal plain bordering the Indian Ocean. In agriculture the drier western areas are important for merino sheep, angora goats, and beef cattle, while irrigated areas of the interior produce good crops of wheat, maize, and sorghum. The coastlands are noted for citrus fruit, pineapple, and tobacco cultivation. Industries include motor manufacturing, textiles, and dairy and meat products. The languages spoken are Xhosa (85%), Afrikaans (9%), and English (3%).

Eastern Orthodox Church see *Orthodox Church.

Easter Rising *or* **Easter Rebellion** in Irish history, a republican insurrection against the British government that began on Easter Monday, April 1916, in Dublin. The rising was organized by the Irish Republican Brotherhood (IRB), led by Patrick *Pearse, along with sections of the Irish Volunteers and James Connolly's socialist Irish Citizen Army. Although a military failure, it played a central role in shifting nationalist opinion from allegiance to the constitutional Irish Parliamentary Party (IPP) to separatist republicanism.

East India Company, British commercial company (1600–1858) that had a monopoly on trade between England and the Far East; see *British East India Company.

East India Company (Dutch) trading monopoly of the 17th and 18th centuries; see *Dutch East India Company.

East Lothian unitary authority in southeast Scotland which was previously a district within Lothian region (1975–96) and a county until 1974. **area:** 677 sq km/ 261 sq mi **towns:** Haddington (administrative headquarters), North Berwick, Dunbar **physical:** area of contrasts, with coastal plains of cliffs, beaches and estuarine marines, broad river valley of the Tyne, volcanic outcrops (Bass Rock, Traprain Law) and gentle slopes of the Lammermuir Hills **features:** Tantallon Castle (14th century); Muirfield golf course; Traprain Law fort **population:** (2001 est) 90,200.

Eastman, George (1854–1932) US entrepreneur and inventor who founded the Eastman Kodak photographic company in 1892. He patented flexible film in 1884, invented the Kodak box camera in 1888, and introduced daylight-loading film in 1892. By 1900 his company was selling a pocket camera for as little as one dollar.

East Renfrewshire unitary authority in central Scotland, created in 1996 from part of Renfrew district in Strathclyde region. **area:** 174 sq km/67 sq mi **towns:** Barrhead, Giffnock (administrative headquarters), Newton Mearns, Clarkston **physical:** low-lying plateau rising from the plain of the River Clyde **population:** (2001 est) 89,400.

East Riding of Yorkshire unitary authority in northern England created in 1996 from part of the former county of Humberside. **area:** 2,416 sq km/933 sq mi **towns:** Beverley (administrative headquarters), Driffield, Goole, Hornsea, Bridlington **features:** Humber Estuary to south of authority spanned by Humber Bridge (1981), the longest single-span suspension bridge when built; North Sea to east; Flamborough Head chalk cliffs; Spurn Head – dynamic spit at mouth of estuary; River Hull; River Ouse; Holderness Peninsula; The Wolds; Hornsea Mere; Beverley Minster (13th century); the 15th-century All Saints Tower (34 m/110 ft) at Driffield; Sledmere House – 18th-century mansion with grounds laid out by English landscape gardener Capability Brown; Rudstone has Britain's tallest standing stone (8 m/25 ft); Sewerby Hall (Bridlington) – Georgian mansion including museum dedicated to the aviator Amy Johnson; Hornsea Pottery; Withernsea Lighthouse (1892; with a height of 39 m/127 ft) including museum; site of the Battle of Stamford Bridge (1066) **population:** (1996) 310,000.

East Sussex county of southeast England, created in 1974, formerly part of Sussex (since April 1997 Brighton and Hove has been a separate unitary authority). **area:** 1,725 sq km/666 sq mi **towns:** Lewes (administrative headquarters), Newhaven (cross-channel port), Eastbourne, Rye, Winchelsea; Bexhill-on-Sea, Hastings, St Leonards, Seaford (all coastal resorts) **physical:** Beachy Head, highest headland on the south coast (180 m/590 ft), the eastern end of the South Downs; the Weald (including Ashdown Forest); Friston Forest; rivers Cuckmere, Ouse, and East Rother (which flows into the sea near Rye); Romney Marsh **features:** the 'Long Man' chalk hill figure at Wilmington, near Eastbourne; prehistoric earthworks; Iron Age hill fort at Mount Caburn, near Lewes; Roman villas; Herstmonceux, with a 15th-century castle (conference and exhibition centre) and adjacent modern buildings, site of the Greenwich Royal Observatory (1958–90); other castles at Hastings, Lewes (1066), Pevensey (Roman walls and medieval castle), and Bodiam (1385); Bayham Abbey (13th century); Battle Abbey (1090) and the site of the Battle of Hastings; Michelham Priory (1229); Sheffield Park garden; University of Sussex (1961) and University of Brighton (1992, formerly Brighton Polytechnic), both at Falmer, near Brighton **population:** (2001 est) 493,100.

East Timor

National name: *Repúblika Demokrátika de Timor Leste/ Democratic Republic of East Timor*

Area: 14,874 sq km/5,743 sq mi
Capital: Dili
Major towns/cities: Ainaro, Bacau, Maliana, Suai, Viqueque
Major ports: Dili, Carabela, Com
Physical features: comprises the largely mountainous eastern half of the island of Timor in the Malay Archipelago, together with two islands, Atauro and Jaco, and an enclave around Ocusse on the northwest coast
Head of state: Xanana Gusmão from 2002

Head of government: Mari Alkatiri from 2002
Political system: emergent democracy
Political executive: parliamentary
Political parties: Frente Revolucionária do Timor Leste Independente (Fretilin; Revolutionary Front of an Independent East Timor), nationalist; Partido Democrático (PD; Democratic Party), left-wing; União Democrática Timorense (UDT; Timorese Democratic Union), centrist
Currency: US dollar
GNI per capita (US$) 520 (2002 est)
Exports: coffee, marble, potential for oil exports
Population: 778,000 (2003 est)
Language: Tetum (national language), Portuguese (official language)
Religion: Roman Catholic (86%), Islam, Animism
Life expectancy: 49 (men); 50 (women) (2000–05)
Chronology
1520: Portuguese traders first landed in Timor looking for the sandalwood tree.
1860: The Dutch secured control of West Timor, leaving the Portuguese in control of East Timor.
1974: Nicolau Lobato formed the Timorese Social Democratic Association, which became the communist Frente Revolucionária do Timor Leste Independente (Fretilin; Revolutionary Front of an Independent East Timor) in September 1975, to fight for independence.
1975: Fretilin seized control of East Timor and declared independence, pre-empting a planned Portuguese withdrawal. Indonesia reacted by invading in early December. An estimated 100,000–200,000 Timorese, out of a total population of around 650,000, were killed in the military crackdown and the subsequent spread of famine and disease. However, resistance, led by Fretilin, continued.
1976: The Indonesian president, T N J Suharto, signed the Bill of Integration incorporating East Timor as Indonesia's 27th province, Timor Timur. The United Nations (UN) refused to recognize the annexation and called for Indonesia's withdrawal.
1990: The Indonesian government rejected proposals for unconditional peace negotiations by Xanana Gusmão, commander-in-chief of Fretilin's army, the Falintil.
1991: The Indonesian army killed between 100 and 180 peaceful pro-independence demonstrators during the funeral ceremony for a separatist sympathizer at Santa Cruz cemetery in Dili, and subsequently executed a further 60–100 'subversives'.
1992: Fretilin leader Gusmão was arrested and taken to Jakarta, where he was tried and, in 1993, found guilty of conspiracy and rebellion and sentenced to 20 years' imprisonment.
1994: Under UN auspices, Fretilin Secretary for International Relations, José Ramos-Horta, met Indonesia's foreign minister, Ali Alatas, for the first time in inaugural official talks on the island's status.
1995: Serious rioting in Dili, involving Timorese Roman Catholics and Muslim immigrants from Indonesia, was defused through the intervention of the Roman Catholic Bishop of Dili, Carlos Belo.
1996: Ramos-Horta and Belo were jointly awarded the Nobel Prize for Peace for their efforts to achieve a peaceful resolution to the East Timor conflict.
1998: The Indonesian president, B J Habibie, who on 21 May had replaced the autocratic and unpopular

T N J Suharto, ending his 32 years in power, offered partial autonomy to East Timor, but ruled out independence.
1999: Following UN-brokered talks, Indonesia agreed to hold a referendum in August, offering the East Timorese voters the choice between 'special autonomy' within Indonesia or independence. The East Timorese voted overwhelmingly (79%) for independence. Pro-Indonesian militias, opposed to the vote, embarked on weeks of violence. An Australian-led peacekeeping force, the International Force for East Timor (INTERFET), arrived to liberate East Timor from Indonesia and restore order. The Indonesian government eventually conceded.
2000: INTERFET was replaced by the UN Transitional Administration in East Timor (UNTAET), the handover being completed on 28 February. However, 150,000 East Timorese remained in refugee camps in West Timor. An eight-member power-sharing provisional government, composed half of UNTAET officials and half of East Timorese was formed.
2001: A large voter turnout marked East Timor's first democratic elections. Fretilin won 55 of the 88 seats in East Timor's constituent assembly.
2002: East Timor's assembly approved a draft constitution envisaging a government run along parliamentary lines. East Timor and Indonesia signed two agreements aimed at easing relations. Xanana Gusmão was elected as president, and on 20 May, East Timor celebrated its formal independence. The country became the 191st member of the United Nations (UN).
2005: UN representatives completed their scheduled pull-out of East Timor.

Eastwood, Clint(on) (1930–) US film actor and director. His breakthrough came in the Western *A Fistful of Dollars* (1964), after which he proved himself a box-office attraction in such films as *Dirty Harry* (1973), directed by his regular collaborator Don Siegel. In 1971 he started an accomplished directing career with *Play Misty for Me*, and his latter-day Western *Unforgiven* (1992) won Academy Awards for Best Film and Best Director.

ebony any of a group of hardwood trees belonging to the ebony family, especially some tropical *persimmons native to Africa and Asia. (Genus chiefly *Diospyros*, family Ebenaceae.)

EC abbreviation for European Community, former name (to 1993) of the *European Union.

ecclesiastical law church law. In England, the Church of England has special ecclesiastical courts to administer church law. Each diocese has a consistory court with a right of appeal to the Court of Arches (in the archbishop of Canterbury's jurisdiction) or the Chancery Court of York (in the archbishop of York's jurisdiction). They deal with the constitution of the Church of England, church property, the clergy, services, doctrine, and practice. These courts have no influence on churches of other denominations, which are governed by the usual laws of contract and trust.

ecdysis periodic shedding of the *exoskeleton by insects and other arthropods to allow growth. Prior to shedding, a new soft and expandable layer is laid down underneath the existing one. The old layer then splits, the animal moves free of it, and the new layer expands and hardens.

ECG abbreviation for *electrocardiogram.

echidna *or* **spiny anteater** toothless, egg-laying, spiny mammal of the order Monotremata, found in Australia and New Guinea. There are two species: *Tachyglossus aculeatus*, the short-nosed echidna, and the rarer *Zaglossus bruijni*, the long-nosed echidna. They feed entirely upon ants and termites, which they dig out with their powerful claws and lick up with their prehensile tongues. When attacked, an echidna rolls itself into a ball, or tries to hide by burrowing in the earth.

echinoderm marine invertebrate of the phylum Echinodermata ('spiny-skinned'), characterized by a five-radial symmetry. Echinoderms have a water-vascular system which transports substances around the body. They include starfishes (or sea stars), brittle-stars, sea lilies, sea urchins, and sea cucumbers. The skeleton is external, made of a series of limy plates. Echinoderms generally move by using tube-feet, small water-filled sacs that can be protruded or pulled back to the body.

echo repetition of a sound wave, or of a *radar or *sonar signal, by reflection from a hard surface such as a wall or building. By accurately measuring the time taken for an echo to return to the transmitter, and by knowing the speed of a radar signal (the speed of light) or a sonar signal (the speed of sound in water), it is possible to calculate the range of the object causing the echo (*echolocation).

Echo in Greek mythology, a mountain *nymph personifying disembodied sound. According to Ovid's *Metamorphoses*, Hera deprived Echo of her speech, except for the repetition of another's last words, after her chatter had kept the goddess from catching faithless Zeus with the nymphs. After being rejected by *Narcissus, she wasted away until only her voice remained.

echolocation *or* **biosonar** method used by certain animals, notably bats, whales, and dolphins, to detect the positions of objects by using sound. The animal emits a stream of high-pitched sounds, generally at ultrasonic frequencies (beyond the range of human hearing), and listens for the returning echoes reflected off objects to determine their exact location.

eclecticism in artistic theory, the use of motifs and elements from various styles, periods, and geographical areas. This selection and recombination of features from different sources is a characteristic of Victorian architecture; for example, J F Bentley's design for Westminster Cathedral, London, 1895–1903, in Byzantine style.

eclipse passage of one astronomical body through the shadow of another. The term is usually used for solar and lunar eclipses. A **solar eclipse** occurs when the Moon is between the Earth and the Sun (which can happen only at new Moon), the Moon blocking the Sun's rays and casting a shadow on the Earth's surface. A **lunar eclipse** occurs when the Earth is between the Moon and the Sun (which can happen only at full Moon), the Earth blocking the Sun's rays and casting a shadow on the Moon's surface.

eclipsing binary binary (double) star in which the two stars periodically pass in front of each other as seen from Earth.

ecliptic path, against the background of stars, that the Sun appears to follow each year as it is orbited by the Earth. It can be thought of as the plane of the Earth's orbit projected onto the *celestial sphere.

Eco, Umberto (1932–) Italian writer and literary critic. His works include *The Role of the Reader* (1979), the 'philosophical thriller' *The Name of the Rose* (1981; filmed 1986), *Foucault's Pendulum* (1988), *The Island of the Day Before* (1994), and *Kant and the Platypus: Essays on Language and Cognition* (1999). He has taught semiology, the study of signs and symbols, at the University of Bologna, Italy.

E. coli abbreviation for *Escherichia coli.

ecology (Greek *oikos* 'house') study of the relationship among organisms and the environments in which they live, including all living and nonliving components. The chief environmental factors governing the distribution of plants and animals are temperature, humidity, soil, light intensity, day length, food supply, and interaction with other organisms. The term ecology was coined by the biologist Ernst Haeckel in 1866.

Economic and Monetary Union (EMU) development of a unitary economy across the member states of *European Union (EU) with a single currency, single market, and harmonized interest and taxation rates. In June 1989, the *European Council decided to initiate moves towards EMU from 1 July 1990, on the basis of a report by Jacques Delors, the then president of the *European Commission. The *Maastricht Treaty then set out a timetable and criteria for the achievement of EMU and agreed to the future establishment of a single European currency, the *euro.

economic community *or* **common market** organization of autonomous countries formed to promote trade. Examples include the European Union, which was formed as the European Community in 1957, Caribbean Community (CARICOM) 1973, Latin American Economic System 1975, and Central African Economic Community 1985.

Economic Community of Central African States *or* **Communauté Economique des Etats de l'Afrique Centrale (CEEAC)** organization formed in 1983 to foster economic cooperation between member states, which include Burundi, Cameroon, Central African Republic, Chad, the Republic of the Congo, Equatorial Guinea, Gabon, Rwanda, São Tomé and Principe, and the Democratic Republic of Congo (formerly Zaire). Angola has observer status.

Economic Community of West African States ECOWAS *or* **Communauté Economique des Etats de l'Afrique de l'Ouest** organization promoting economic cooperation and development, established in 1975 by the Treaty of Lagos. Its members include Benin, Burkina Faso, Cape Verde, Gambia, Ghana, Guinea, Guinea-Bissau, Côte d'Ivoire, Liberia, Mali, Mauritania, Niger, Nigeria, Senegal, Sierra Leone, and Togo. Its headquarters are in Abuja, Nigeria.

Economic Cooperation Organization (ECO) Islamic regional grouping formed in 1985 by Iran, Pakistan, and Turkey to reduce customs tariffs and promote commerce, with the aim of eventual customs union. In 1992 the newly independent republics of Azerbaijan, Kyrgyzstan, Tajikistan, Turkmenistan, and Uzbekistan were admitted into ECO.

economics (from Greek for 'household management') social science devoted to studying the production,

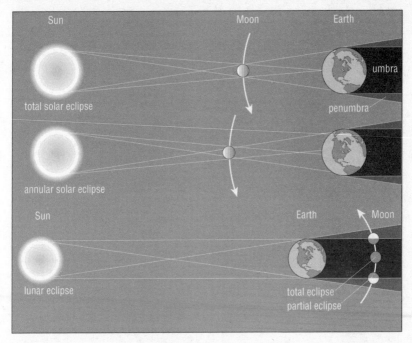

eclipse The two types of eclipse: solar and lunar. A solar eclipse occurs when the Moon passes between the Sun and the Earth, blocking out the Sun's light. During a total solar eclipse, when the Moon completely covers the Sun, the Moon's shadow sweeps across the Earth's surface from west to east at a speed of 3,200 kph/2,000 mph. A lunar eclipse occurs when the Moon passes through the shadow of the Earth.

distribution, and consumption of wealth. It consists of the disciplines of *microeconomics (the study of individual producers, consumers, or markets), and *macroeconomics, (the study of whole economies or systems – in particular, areas such as taxation and public spending).

economy set of interconnected activities concerned with the production, distribution, and consumption of goods and services. The contemporary economy is very complex and includes transactions ranging from the distribution and spending of children's pocket money to global-scale financial deals being conducted by *multinational corporations.

ecosystem in ecology, a unit consisting of living organisms and the environment that they live in. A simple example of an ecosystem is a pond. The pond ecosystem includes all the pond plants and animals and also the water and other substances that make up the pond itself. Individual organisms interact with each other and with their environment in a variety of relationships, such as two organisms in competition, predator and prey, or as a food source for other organisms in a *food chain. These relationships are usually complex and finely balanced, and in natural ecosystems should be self-sustaining. However, major changes to an ecosystem, such as climate change,

overpopulation, or the removal of a species, may threaten the system's sustainability and result in its eventual destruction. For instance, the removal of a major carnivore predator can result in the destruction of an ecosystem through overgrazing by herbivores. Ecosystems can be large, such as the global ecosystem (the ecosphere) or small, such as the pools that collect water in the branch of a tree, and they can contain smaller systems.

ECOWAS acronym for *Economic Community of West African States.

ecstasy *or* **MDMA** (3,4-methylenedioxymeth-amphetamine) illegal recreational drug in increasing use since the 1980s. It is a modified *amphetamine with mild psychedelic effects, and works by depleting serotonin (a neurotransmitter) in the brain. The effects of the drug are to intensify the perception of colour, sound, and even emotion in a user, which can last up to six hours, depending on the dose taken. The comedown from the drug causes lethargy and depression that can persist for several weeks. It has been found that ecstasy permanently reduces serotonin levels, but most of its other long-term effects are unknown.

ECT abbreviation for *electroconvulsive therapy.

ectoparasite *parasite that lives on the outer surface of its host.

291

ectopic in medicine, term applied to an anatomical feature that is displaced or found in an abnormal position. An ectopic pregnancy is one occurring outside the womb, usually in a Fallopian tube.

ectotherm 'cold-blooded' animal (see *poikilothermy), such as a lizard, that relies on external warmth (ultimately from the Sun) to raise its body temperature so that it can become active. To cool the body, ectotherms seek out a cooler environment.

ECU abbreviation for European Currency Unit, a unit of account the value of which depended on the underlying value of the constituent currencies of participating *European Union states. The ECU, which converted into the *euro on 1 January 1999, was not legal tender and was not represented by official banknotes and coins – unlike the euro which is a true currency in its own right.

Ecuador

National name: *República del Ecuador/ Republic of Ecuador*

Area: 270,670 sq km/104,505 sq mi
Capital: Quito
Major towns/cities: Guayaquil, Cuenca, Machala, Portoviejo, Manta, Ambato, Santo Domingo
Major ports: Guayaquil
Physical features: coastal plain rises sharply to Andes Mountains, which are divided into a series of cultivated valleys; flat, low-lying rainforest in the east; Galapagos Islands; Cotopaxi, the world's highest active volcano. Ecuador is crossed by the Equator, from which it derives its name
Head of state and government: Lucio Edwin Gutierrez Borbua from 2003
Political system: liberal democracy
Political executive: limited presidency
Political parties: Social Christian Party (PSC), right wing; Ecuadorean Roldosist Party (PRE), populist, centre left; Popular Democracy (DP), centre right; Democratic Left (ID), moderate socialist; Conservative Party (PCE), right wing; Popular Democratic Movement (MPD), far-left

Currency: US dollar
GNI per capita (PPP): (US$) 3,130 (2002 est)
Exports: petroleum and petroleum products, bananas, shrimps (a major exporter), coffee, seafood products, cocoa beans and products, cut flowers. Principal market: USA 36.6% (2001)
Population: 13,003,000 (2003 est)
Language: Spanish (official), Quechua, Jivaro, other indigenous languages
Religion: Roman Catholic
Life expectancy: 68 (men); 74 (women) (2000–05)
Chronology
1450s: The Caras people, whose kingdom had its capital at Quito, conquered by Incas of Peru.
1531: Spanish conquistador Francisco Pizarro landed on Ecuadorean coast, en route to Peru, where Incas were defeated.
1534: Conquered by Spanish. Quito, which had been destroyed by American Indians, was refounded by Sebastian de Belalcazar; the area became part of the Spanish Viceroyalty of Peru, which covered much of South America, with its capital at Lima (Peru).
later 16th century: Spanish established large agrarian estates, owned by Europeans and worked by American Indian labourers.
1739: Became part of new Spanish Viceroyalty of Nueva Granada, which included Colombia and Venezuela, with its capital in Bogotá (Colombia).
1809: With the Spanish monarchy having been overthrown by Napoleon Bonaparte, the Creole middle class began to press for independence.
1822: Spanish Royalists defeated by Field Marshal Antonio José de Sucre, fighting for Simón Bolívar, 'The Liberator', at battle of Pichincha, near Quito; became part of independent Gran Colombia, which also comprised Colombia, Panama, and Venezuela.
1830: Became fully independent state, after leaving Gran Colombia.
1845–60: Political instability, with five presidents holding power, increasing tension between conservative Quito and liberal Guayaquil on the coast, and minor wars with Peru and Colombia.
1860–75: Power held by Gabriel García Moreno, an autocratic theocrat-Conservative who launched education and public-works programmes.
1895–1912: Dominated by Gen Eloy Alfaro, a radical, anticlerical Liberal from the coastal region, who reduced the power of the church.
1925–48: Great political instability; no president completed his term of office.
1941: Lost territory in Amazonia after defeat in war with Peru.
1948–55: Liberals in power.
1956: Camilo Ponce became first conservative president in 60 years.
1960: Liberals in power, with José María Velasco Ibarra as president.
1962: Military junta installed.
1968: Velasco returned as president.
1970s: Ecuador emerged as significant oil producer.
1972: Coup put military back in power.
1979: New democratic constitution; Liberals in power but opposed by right- and left-wing parties.
1981: Border dispute with Peru flared up again.
1982: The deteriorating economy and austerity

measures provoked strikes, demonstrations, and a state of emergency.

1988: Unpopular austerity measures were introduced.

1992: PUR leader Sixto Duran Ballen was elected president; PSC became the largest party in congress. Ecuador withdrew from OPEC to enable it to increase its oil exports.

1994: There was mounting opposition to Duran's economic liberalization and privatization programme.

1998: A 157-year border dispute was settled with Peru.

2000: After the currency lost 65% of its value in 1999, President Mahuad declared a state of emergency, froze all bank accounts valued at over £100, and said that he would introduce the dollar in favour of the sucre. After a bloodless coup in protest to the measures, Gustavo Noboa was sworn in as president. He nevertheless continued with the introduction of the dollar after positive international response to the plans.

2001: President Noboa imposed a five-day state of emergency, to deal with the large-scale protests prompted by economic austerity measures.

2002: Lucio Gutierrez a left-winger was elected president, promising to fight corruption.

2003: Lucio Gutierrez was installed as president.

2005: President Gutierrez was forced out of office by congress and replaced by his vice-president Alfredo Palacio.

ecumenical movement movement for reunification of the various branches, or denominations, of the Christian church. It began in the 19th century with the extension of missionary work to Africa and Asia, where the divisions created in Europe were incomprehensible and hindered the work of spreading the gospel. The movement gathered momentum in the 20th century, mainly from the need for unity in the face of growing secularism (lack of religious faith) in Christian countries and of the challenge posed by such faiths as Islam. The **World Council of Churches** was founded in 1948.

eczema inflammatory skin condition, a form of dermatitis, marked by dryness, rashes, itching, formation of blisters, and the exudation of fluid. It may be allergic in origin and is sometimes complicated by infection.

Edda two collections of early Icelandic literature that together constitute our chief source for Old Norse mythology. The term strictly applies to the **Younger** or **Prose Edda**, compiled by Snorri Sturluson, a priest, in about AD 1230.

Eddery, Pat(rick James John) (1952–) Irish-born flat-racing jockey who has ridden 14 English classic winners, including the Derby winner on three occasions. He won the jockey's championship in Britain 11 times. He has ridden 100 winners in a British flat racing season a record 28 times, and finished his career with 4,632 winners overall. Only Gordon Richards has ridden more winners than Eddery.

edelweiss perennial alpine plant belonging to the daisy family, with a white, woolly, star-shaped flower, found in the high mountains of Europe and Asia. (*Leontopodium alpinum*, family Compositae.)

Eden, (Robert) Anthony (1897–1977) 1st Earl of Avon, British Conservative politician, foreign secretary 1935–38, 1940–45, and 1951–55; prime minister 1955–57, when he resigned after the failure of the Anglo-French military intervention in the *Suez Crisis.

Eden, Garden of in the Old Testament book of Genesis and in the Koran, the 'garden' in which Adam and Eve lived after their creation, and from which they were expelled for disobedience.

Edgar the Peaceful (944–975) King of all England from 959. He was the younger son of Edmund I, and strove successfully to unite English and Danes as fellow subjects.

Edgehill, Battle of first battle of the English Civil War. It took place in 1642, on a ridge in south Warwickshire, between Royalists under *Charles I and Parliamentarians under the Earl of Essex. Both sides claimed victory.

Edinburgh capital and administrative centre of Scotland and Edinburgh City unitary authority, near the southern shores of the Firth of Forth, 67 km/42 mi east of Glasgow; population (2001 est) 449,400. Since devolution in 1998, Edinburgh has been the seat of the *Scottish Parliament. The city is a cultural centre and hosts the annual **Edinburgh Festival** (1947), an international arts festival, and the **Edinburgh Fringe Festival**. The city was made a World Heritage City in 1995. Industries include brewing, whisky distilling, electronics, printing and publishing, and banking and finance.

Edinburgh, Duke of title of Prince *Philip of the UK.

Edison, Thomas Alva (1847–1931) US scientist and inventor, whose work in the fields of communications and electrical power greatly influenced the world in which we live. With more than 1,000 patents, Edison produced his most important inventions in Menlo Park, New Jersey 1876–87, including the phonograph. He obtained a US patent for the electric light bulb in 1879. He also constructed a system of electric power distribution for consumers, the telephone transmitter, and the megaphone.

Edmonton capital of *Alberta, Canada, on the North Saskatchewan River at an altitude of 665 m/2,182 ft; population (2001 est) 666,100. It is the centre of an oil and mining area to the north and is also an agricultural and dairying region. Manufactured goods include processed foods, petrochemicals, plastic and metal products, lumber, and clothing. Edmonton is known as the 'gateway to the north': it is situated on the Alaska Highway, and petroleum pipelines link the city with Superior in Wisconsin, and Vancouver in British Columbia. The city was incorporated in 1892.

Edmund I (921–946) King of England from 939. The son of Edward the Elder, he succeeded his half-brother, Athelstan, as king in 939. He succeeded in regaining control of Mercia, which on his accession had fallen to the Norse inhabitants of Northumbria, and of the Five Boroughs, an independent confederation within the Danelaw. He then moved on to subdue the Norsemen in Cumbria and finally extended his rule as far as southern Scotland. As well as uniting England, he bolstered his authority by allowing St Dunstan to reform the Benedictine order. He was killed in 946 at Pucklechurch, Gloucestershire, by an outlawed robber.

Edmund (II) Ironside (c. 981–1016) King of England in 1016, the son of Ethelred II 'the Unready' (c. 968–1016). He led the resistance to Canute's invasion in 1015, and on Ethelred's death in 1016 was chosen king by the citizens of London. Meanwhile, the Witan (the king's council) elected Canute. In the struggle for the throne, Canute defeated Edmund at Ashingdon (or

Assandun), and they divided the kingdom between them. When Edmund died the same year, Canute ruled the whole kingdom.

Edmund, St (c. 840–870) King of East Anglia from 855. In 870 he was defeated and captured by the Danes at Hoxne, Suffolk, and martyred on refusing to renounce Christianity. He was canonized and his shrine at Bury St Edmunds became a place of pilgrimage.

education process, beginning at birth, of developing intellectual capacity, skills, and social awareness, especially by instruction. In its more restricted sense, the term refers to the process of imparting literacy, numeracy, and a generally accepted body of knowledge.

Edward (1964–) full name Edward Antony Richard Louis, Prince of the UK, third son of Queen Elizabeth II. He is seventh in line to the throne after Charles, Charles's two sons, Andrew, and Andrew's two daughters. In 1999 he married Miss Sophie Rhys-Jones at Windsor Castle and the couple became the Earl and Countess of Wessex.

Edward (1330–1376) called 'the Black Prince', Prince of Wales, eldest son of Edward III of England. The epithet (probably posthumous) may refer to his black armour. During the *Hundred Years' War he fought at the Battle of Crécy in 1346 and captured the French king at Poitiers in 1356. He ruled Aquitaine from 1360 to 1371. In 1367 he invaded Castile and restored to the throne the deposed king, Pedro the Cruel (1334–69). During the revolt that eventually ousted him, he caused the massacre of Limoges in 1370.

Edward eight kings of England or Great Britain:

Edward I (1239–1307) King of England from 1272, son of Henry III. He led the royal forces against Simon de Montfort (the Younger) in the Barons' War of 1264–67, and was on a crusade when he succeeded to the throne. He established English rule over all of Wales in 1282–84, and secured recognition of his overlordship from the Scottish king, although the Scots under Sir William Wallace and Robert (I) the Bruce fiercely resisted actual conquest. His reign saw Parliament move towards its modern form with the *Model Parliament of 1295. He married Eleanor of Castile (1245–1290) in 1254 and in 1299 married Margaret, daughter of Philip III of France. He was succeeded by his son Edward II (1284–1327).

Edward II (1284–1327) King of England from 1307, son of Edward I. Born at Caernarfon Castle, he was created the first Prince of Wales in 1301. Edward was incompetent, with a weak personality, and was over-influenced by his unpopular friend Piers Gaveston. He struggled throughout his reign with discontented barons, who attempted to restrict his power through the Ordinances of 1311. His invasion of Scotland in 1314 to suppress revolt resulted in defeat at Bannockburn. When he fell under the influence of a new favourite, Hugh le Despenser, he was deposed in 1327 by his wife Isabella (1292–1358), daughter of Philip IV of France, and her lover Roger de *Mortimer, and murdered in Berkeley Castle, Gloucestershire. He was succeeded by his son, Edward III.

Edward III (1312–1377) King of England from 1327, son of Edward II. He assumed the government in 1330 from his mother, through whom in 1337 he laid claim to the French throne and thus began the Hundred Years' War. Edward was the victor of Halidon Hill in 1333,

Sluys in 1340, Crécy in 1346, and at the siege of Calais 1346–47, and created the Order of the Garter. He was succeeded by his grandson Richard II.

Edward IV (1442–1483) King of England 1461–70 and from 1471. He was the son of Richard, Duke of York, and succeeded Henry VI in the Wars of the Roses, temporarily losing his throne to Henry when Edward fell out with his adviser Richard Neville, Earl of Warwick. Edward was a fine warrior and intelligent strategist, with victories at Mortimer's Cross and Towton in 1461, Empingham in 1470, and Barnet and Tewkesbury in 1471. He was succeeded by his son Edward V.

Edward V (1470–1483) King of England in 1483. Son of Edward IV, he was deposed three months after his accession in favour of his uncle (*Richard III), and is traditionally believed to have been murdered (with his brother) in the Tower of London on Richard's orders.

Edward VI (1537–1553) King of England from 1547, only son of Henry VIII and his third wife, Jane Seymour. The government was entrusted to his uncle, Edward Seymour, 1st Duke of *Somerset (who fell from power in 1549), and then to the Earl of Warwick, John Dudley, later created Duke of Northumberland. He was succeeded by his half-sister Mary I.

Edward VII (1841–1910) King of Great Britain and Ireland from 1901. As Prince of Wales he was a prominent social figure, but his mother Queen Victoria considered him too frivolous to take part in political life. In 1860 he made the first tour of Canada and the USA ever undertaken by a British prince.

Edward VIII (1894–1972) King of Great Britain and Northern Ireland January–December 1936, when he renounced the throne to marry Wallis Warfield *Simpson (see *abdication crisis). He was created Duke of Windsor and was governor of the Bahamas 1940–45.

Edward the Confessor (c. 1003–1066) King of England from 1042, the son of Ethelred II. He lived in Normandy until shortly before his accession. During his reign power was held by Earl Godwin and his son *Harold, while the king devoted himself to religion, including the rebuilding of Westminster Abbey (consecrated in 1065), where he is buried. His childlessness left four claimants to the English throne on his death and led ultimately to the Norman Conquest in 1066. He was canonized in 1161.

Edward the Elder (c. 870–924) King of the West Saxons. He succeeded his father Alfred the Great in 899. He reconquered southeast England and the Midlands from the Danes, uniting Wessex and Mercia with the help of his sister Aethelflaed. By the time of his death his kingdom was the most powerful in the British Isles. He was succeeded by his son *Athelstan.

Edward the Martyr (c. 963–978) King of England from 975. Son of King Edgar, he was murdered at Corfe Castle, Dorset, probably at his stepmother Aelfthryth's instigation (she wished to secure the crown for her son, Ethelred). He was canonized in 1001.

EEC abbreviation for European Economic Community.

eel any fish of the order Anguilliformes. Eels are snakelike, with elongated dorsal and anal fins. They include the freshwater eels of Europe and North America (which breed in the Atlantic), the marine conger eels, and the morays of tropical coral reefs.

Egypt

Section through a fertilized egg

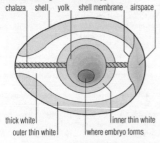

chalaza, shell, yolk, shell membrane, airspace

thick white | inner thin white
outer thin white | where embryo forms

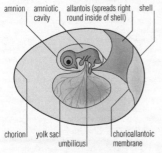

amnion, amniotic cavity, allantois (spreads right round inside of shell), shell

chorion, yolk sac, umbilicus, chorioallantoic membrane

egg Section through a fertilized bird egg. Inside a bird's egg is a complex structure of liquids and membranes designed to meet the needs of the growing embryo. The yolk, which is rich in fat, is gradually absorbed by the embryo. The white of the egg provides protein and water. The chalaza is a twisted band of protein which holds the yolk in place and acts as a shock absorber. The airspace allows gases to be exchanged through the shell. The allantois contains many blood vessels which carry gases between the embryo and the outside.

efficiency in physics, a general term indicating the degree to which a process or device can convert energy from one form to another without loss, or how effectively energy is used, and wasted energy, such as heat and sound, minimized. It is normally expressed as a fraction or a percentage, where 100% indicates conversion with no loss. The efficiency of a machine, for example, is the ratio of the energy output to the energy input; in practice it is always less than 100% because of frictional heat losses.

EFTA acronym for *European Free Trade Association.

egalitarianism belief that all citizens in a state should have equal rights and privileges. Interpretations of this can vary, from the notion of equality of opportunity to equality in material welfare and political decision-making. Some states reject egalitarianism; most accept the concept of equal opportunities but recognize that people's abilities vary widely. Even those states which claim to be socialist find it necessary to have hierarchical structures in the political, social, and economic spheres. Egalitarianism was one of the principles of the French Revolution.

Egbert (died 839) King of the West Saxons from 802, the son of Ealhmund, an under-king of Kent. By 829 he had united England for the first time under one king.

egg in animals, the ovum, or female *gamete (reproductive cell). After fertilization by a sperm cell, it begins to divide to form an embryo. Eggs may be deposited by the female (*ovipary) or they may develop within her body (*vivipary and *ovovivipary). In the oviparous reptiles and birds, the egg is protected by a shell, and well supplied with nutrients in the form of yolk.

eggplant another name for *aubergine.

ego (Latin 'I') in psychology, the processes concerned with the self and a person's conception of himself or herself, encompassing values and attitudes. In Freudian psychology, the term refers specifically to the element of the human mind that represents the conscious processes concerned with reality, in conflict with the *id (the instinctual element) and the *superego (the ethically aware element).

egret any of several *herons with long tufts of feathers on the head or neck. They belong to the order Ciconiiformes.

Egypt

National name: *Jumhuriyyat Misr al-'Arabiyya/ Arab Republic of Egypt*
Area: 1,001,450 sq km/386,659 sq mi
Capital: Cairo
Major towns/cities: El Gíza, Shubra Al Khayma, Alexandria, Port Said, El-Mahalla el-Koubra, Tanta, El Mansûra, Suez
Major ports: Alexandria, Port Said, Suez, Damietta, Shubra Al Khayma
Physical features: mostly desert; hills in east; fertile land along Nile valley and delta; cultivated and settled area is about 35,500 sq km/13,700 sq mi; Aswan High Dam and Lake Nasser; Sinai
Head of state: Hosni Mubarak from 1981
Head of government: Ahmed Nazif from 2004
Political system: liberal democracy
Political executive: limited presidency
Political parties: National Democratic Party (NDP), moderate, left of centre; Socialist Labour Party (SLP), right of centre; Liberal Socialist Party, free enterprise; New Wafd Party, nationalist; National Progressive Unionist Party, left wing

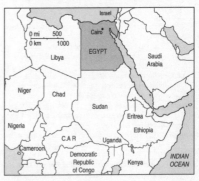

295

Egypt, ancient

Currency: Egyptian pound
GNI per capita (PPP): (US$) 3,710 (2002 est)
Exports: petroleum and petroleum products, cotton, textiles, clothing, food, live animals. Principal market: USA 14.4% (2001)
Population: 71,931,000 (2003 est)
Language: Arabic (official), Coptic (derived from ancient Egyptian), English, French
Religion: Sunni Muslim 90%, Coptic Christian and other Christian 6%
Life expectancy: 67 (men); 71 (women) (2000–05)
Chronology
1st century BC–7th century AD: Conquered by Augustus in AD 30, Egypt passed under rule of Roman, and later Byzantine, governors.
AD 639–42: Arabs conquered Egypt, introducing Islam and Arabic; succession of Arab dynasties followed.
1250: Mamelukes seized power.
1517: Became part of Turkish Ottoman Empire.
1798–1801: Invasion by Napoleon followed by period of French occupation.
1801: Control regained by Turks.
1869: Opening of Suez Canal made Egypt strategically important.
1881–82: Nationalist revolt resulted in British occupation.
1914: Egypt became a British protectorate.
1922: Achieved nominal independence under King Fuad I.
1936: Full independence from Britain achieved. King Fuad succeeded by his son Farouk.
1946: Withdrawal of British troops except from Suez Canal zone.
1952: Farouk overthrown by army in bloodless coup.
1953: Egypt declared a republic, with Gen Neguib as president.
1956: Neguib replaced by Col Gamal Nasser. Nasser announced nationalization of Suez Canal; Egypt attacked by Britain, France, and Israel. Ceasefire agreed following US intervention.
1958: Short-lived merger of Egypt and Syria as United Arab Republic (UAR).
1967: Six-Day War with Israel ended in Egypt's defeat and Israeli occupation of Sinai and Gaza Strip.
1970: Nasser died suddenly; succeeded by Anwar Sadat.
1973: An attempt to regain territory lost to Israel led to the Yom Kippur War; ceasefire arranged by US secretary of state Henry Kissinger.
1978–79: Camp David talks in USA resulted in a peace treaty between Egypt and Israel. Egypt expelled from Arab League.
1981: Sadat was assassinated by Muslim fundamentalists and succeeded by Hosni Mubarak.
1983: Relations between Egypt and the Arab world improved; only Libya and Syria maintained a trade boycott.
1987: Egypt was readmitted to the Arab League.
1989: Relations with Libya improved; diplomatic relations with Syria were restored.
1991: Egypt participated in the Gulf War on the US-led side and was a major force in convening a Middle East peace conference in Spain.
1994: The government cracked down on Islamic militants.
1997: Islamic extremists killed and injured tourists at Luxor.
1999: President Mubarak was awarded a fourth term as president, and Atef Obeid was appointed as prime minister.
2000: At least 20 people were killed in clashes between Christians and Muslims in southern Egypt. In parliamentary elections, opposition parties did much better than usual and the banned Muslim Brotherhood won 17 seats, re-establishing their presence in parliament for the first time in a decade.
2005: Parliament approved a change in the constitution to allow multiple candidacy in presidential elections, as opposed to the practice of having a single, parliament-approved, candidate.

Egypt, ancient ancient civilization, based around the River Nile in Egypt, which emerged 5,000 years ago and reached its peak in the 16th century BC. Ancient Egypt was famed for its great power and wealth, due to the highly fertile lands of the Nile delta, which were rich sources of grain for the whole Mediterranean region. Egyptians were advanced in agriculture, engineering, and applied sciences. Many of their monuments, such as the *pyramids and the sphinx, survive today.

Egyptian art, ancient the art of ancient Egypt falls into three main periods – the Old, Middle, and New Kingdoms – beginning about 3000 BC and spanning 2,000 years overall. During this time, despite some stylistic development, there is remarkable continuity, representing a deeply religious and traditionalist society. Sculpture and painting are highly stylized, following strict conventions and using symbols of a religion centred on the afterlife and idealization of the dead, their servants, families, and possessions. Depictions of the human form show the face and legs in profile, the upper torso facing forwards, the hips three quarters turned, and the eye enlarged and enhanced. During Egypt's slow decline in power, the style of art remained conservative and subservient to religion, but the level of technical expertise continued to be high, with an almost constant and prolific production of artefacts. Major collections of Egyptian art are to be found in the National Museum, Cairo, and in the British Museum, London.

the early dynastic period and the Old Kingdom (2920–2134 BC) is exemplified by the monumental statue of the Great Sphinx at El Gîza, about 2530 BC. A gigantic lion figure with a human head, the sphinx is carved from an outcrop of natural rock, 56.4 m/185 ft long and 19.2 m/63 ft high, and guards the path to the pyramid of Khafre. A rich collection of grave goods survive from the period, including clothes, ornaments, jewellery, and weapons, as well as statues in stone and precious metals. The stylistic conventions of painting – such as showing the human figure with head, legs, and feet in profile, the eyes and shoulders frontally – are established. Vivid wall paintings, such as *Geese of Medum* (National Museum, Cairo) about 2530, show a variety of scenes from the life of the time.

Middle Kingdom (2040–1640 BC), a period when Egypt was reunited under one ruler, is typified by tombs hewn from rock, attempts at realism in frescoes, and deepened perception in portrait sculpture, for example the head of Sesostris III (National Museum, Cairo). Typical of the period are sculptures of figures wrapped in mantles, with only head, hands, and feet showing.

New Kingdom (1550–1070 BC) is represented by a softer and more refined style of painting and a new sophistication in jewellery and furnishings. The golden age of the 18th dynasty, 1550–1070 BC, saw the building of the temples of Karnak and Luxor and the maze of tombs in the Valley of the Kings. The pharaohs of the period, Akhenaton and Tutankhamen, inspired a most extravagant style, as exemplified in the carved images of these godlike creatures, the statues of Akhenaton, the golden coffins of Tutankhamen's mummified body (National Museum, Cairo) about 1361–1352 BC, and the head of Akhenaton's queen, Nefertiti (Museo Archaeologico, Florence) about 1360 BC. The monumental statues of Ramses II in Abu Simbel date from the 13th century BC.

Egyptology the study of ancient Egypt. Interest in the subject was aroused by the Napoleonic expedition's discovery of the *Rosetta Stone in 1799. Various excavations continued throughout the 19th century and gradually assumed a more scientific character, largely as a result of the work of the British archaeologist Flinders Petrie from 1880 onwards and the formation of the Egyptian Exploration Fund in 1882. In 1922 another British archaeologist, Howard Carter, discovered the tomb of Tutankhamen, the only royal tomb with all its treasures intact.

Ehrlich, Paul (1854–1915) German bacteriologist and immunologist who was awarded a Nobel Prize for Physiology or Medicine in 1908 with Ilya Mechnikov for their work on immunity. He produced the first cure for *syphilis, developing the arsenic compounds, in particular Salvarsan, that were used in the treatment of syphilis before the discovery of antibiotics.

eider large marine *duck of the genus *Somateria*, family Anatidae, order Anseriformes. They are found on the northern coasts of the Atlantic and Pacific oceans. The **common eider** *S. molissima* is highly valued for its soft down, which is used in quilts and cushions for warmth. The adult male has a black cap and belly and a green nape. The rest of the plumage is white with a pink breast and throat, while the female is a mottled brown. The bill is large and flattened and both bill and feet are olive green.

Eid ul-Adha Muslim festival that takes place during the *hajj, or pilgrimage to Mecca, and commemorates the willingness of Ibrahim (Abraham) to sacrifice his son Ishmael at the command of Allah.

Eid ul-Fitr Muslim festival celebrating the end of Ramadan, the month of sawm (fasting).

Eiffel, (Alexandre) Gustave (1832–1923) French engineer who constructed the Eiffel Tower for the 1889 Paris Exhibition. The tower, made of iron, is 320 m/1,050 ft high and stands in the Champ de Mars, Paris. Sightseers may ride to the top for a view.

Einstein, Albert (1879–1955) German-born US physicist whose theories of *relativity revolutionized our understanding of matter, space, and time. Einstein established that light may have a particle nature. He was awarded the Nobel Prize for Physics in 1921 for his work on theoretical physics, especially the **photoelectric law**. He also investigated Brownian motion, confirming the existence of atoms. His last conception of the basic laws governing the universe was outlined in his *unified field theory, made public in 1953.

einsteinium chemical symbol Es, synthesized, radioactive, metallic element of the actinide series, atomic number 99, relative atomic mass 254.09.

Eire name of southern Ireland as prescribed in the 1937 Constitution.

Eisenhower, Dwight David ('Ike') (1890–1969) 34th president of the USA 1953–60, a Republican. A general in World War II, he commanded the Allied forces in Italy in 1943, then the Allied invasion of Europe, and from October 1944 all the Allied armies in the West. As president he promoted business interests at home and conducted the *Cold War abroad. His vice-president was Richard Nixon.

eisteddfod (Welsh 'sitting') traditional Welsh gathering lasting up to a week and dedicated to the encouragement of the bardic arts of music, poetry, and literature. The custom dates from pre-Christian times.

eland largest species of *antelope, *Taurotragus oryx*. Pale fawn in colour, it is about 2 m/6 ft high, and both sexes have spiral horns about 45 cm/18 in long. It is found in central and southern Africa.

elasticity in economics, the measure of response of one variable to changes in another. Such measures are used to test the effects of changes in prices and incomes on demand and supply.

elasticity in physics, the ability of a solid to recover its shape once deforming forces are removed. An elastic material obeys *Hooke's law, which states that its deformation is proportional to the applied stress up to a certain point, called the **elastic limit**; beyond this point additional stresses will deform it permanently. Elastic materials include metals and rubber; however, all materials have some degree of elasticity.

E-layer formerly **Kennelly-Heaviside layer**, lower regions (90–120 km/56–75 mi) of the *ionosphere, which reflect radio waves, allowing their reception around the surface of the Earth. The E-layer approaches the Earth by day and recedes from it at night.

Elba Greek **Aethalia**; Roman **Ilva**, island in the Mediterranean Sea, 10 km/6 mi off the west coast of Italy; area 223 sq km/86 sq mi; population (1981) 35,000. Iron ore is exported from the island's capital, Portoferraio, to the Italian mainland. There is a fishing industry, olives are grown, and tourism is important. Elba was French emperor Napoleon's place of exile (1814–15).

Elbe Czech **Labe**; ancient **Albis**, one of the principal rivers of Germany; length 1,166 km/725 mi. It rises on the southern slopes of the Riesengebirge, Czech Republic, and flows northwest across the German plain to the North Sea. It is navigable for ocean-going vessels as far as Hamburg (101 km/62 mi from the mouth), and for smaller boats as far as its junction with the Vltava (845 km/525 mi). The river basin is approximately 145,039 sq km/56,000 sq mi.

Elbrus or **Elbruz** (Persian 'two heads') highest peak in Europe; located in the Caucasus Mountains, Caucasia, in the Russian Federation. Its western summit reaches a height of 5,642 m/18,510 ft, while the eastern summit stands at 5,595 m/18,356 ft.

elder in botany, any of a group of small trees or shrubs belonging to the honeysuckle family, native to North America, Europe, Asia, and North Africa. Some are grown as ornamentals for their showy yellow or white flower clusters and their colourful black or scarlet berries. (Genus *Sambucus*, family Caprifoliaceae.)

El Dorado fabled city of gold believed by the 16th-century Spanish and other Europeans to exist somewhere in the area of the Orinoco and Amazon rivers.

Eleanor of Aquitaine (c. 1122–1204) Queen of France 1137–51 as wife of Louis VII, and of England from 1154 as wife of *Henry II. Henry imprisoned her 1174–89 for supporting their sons, the future Richard I and King John, in revolt against him.

Eleanor of Castile (c. 1245–1290) Queen of Edward I of England, the daughter of Ferdinand III of Castile. She married Prince Edward in 1254, and accompanied him on his crusade in 1270. She died at Harby, Nottinghamshire, and Edward erected stone crosses in towns where her body rested on the funeral journey to London. Several **Eleanor Crosses** are still standing, for example, at Northampton.

election process of appointing a person to public office or a political party to government by voting. Elections were occasionally held in ancient Greek democracies; Roman tribunes were regularly elected.

elector German **Kurfürst**, any of originally seven (later ten) princes of the Holy Roman Empire who had the prerogative of electing the emperor (in effect, the king of Germany). The electors were the archbishops of Mainz, Trier, and Cologne, the court palatine of the Rhine, the Duke of Saxony, the Margrave of Brandenburg, and the king of Bohemia (in force to 1806). Their constitutional status was formalized in 1356 in the document known as the **Golden Bull**, which granted them extensive powers within their own domains, to act as judges, issue coins, and impose tolls.

electoral college in the US government, the indirect system of voting for the president and vice-president. The people of each state officially vote not for the presidential candidate, but for a list of electors nominated by each party. The whole electoral-college vote of the state then goes to the winning party (and candidate). A majority is required for election.

electoral system see *vote and *proportional representation.

electric arc a continuous electric discharge of high current between two electrodes, giving out a brilliant light and heat. The phenomenon is exploited in the carbon-arc lamp, once widely used in film projectors. In the electric-arc furnace an arc struck between very large carbon electrodes and the metal charge provides the heating. In arc *welding an electric arc provides the heat to fuse the metal. The discharges in low-pressure gases, as in neon and sodium lights, can also be broadly considered as electric arcs.

electric charge property of some bodies that causes them to exert forces on each other. Two bodies both with positive or both with negative charges repel each other, whereas bodies with opposite or 'unlike' charges attract each other. *Electrons possess a negative charge, and *protons an equal positive charge. The *SI unit of electric charge is the coulomb (symbol C).

electric current flow of electrically charged particles through a conducting circuit due to the presence of a *potential difference. The current at any point in a circuit is the amount of charge flowing per second; its SI unit is the ampere (coulomb per second).

electric eel South American freshwater bony fish. It grows to almost 3 m/10 ft and the electric shock produced, normally for immobilizing prey, is enough to stun an adult human. Electric eels are not true eels. *Electrophorus electricus* is in the order Cypriniformes, class Osteichthyes.

electric field in physics, a region in which a particle possessing electric charge experiences a force owing to the presence of another electric charge. The strength of an electric field, E, is measured in volts per metre (V m^{-1}). It is a type of *electromagnetic field.

electricity all phenomena caused by *electric charge. There are two types of electricity: static and current. Electric charge is caused by an excess or deficit of electrons in a substance, and an electric current is the movement of charge through a material. Materials having equal numbers of positive and negative charges are termed neutral, as the charges balance out. Substances may be electrical conductors, such as metals, which allow the passage of electricity through them readily, or insulators, such as rubber, which are extremely poor conductors. Substances with relatively poor conductivities that increase with a rise in temperature or when light falls on the material are known as *semiconductors. Electric currents also flow through the nerves of organisms. For example, the optic nerve in humans carries electric signals from the eye to the brain. Electricity cannot be seen, but the effects it produces can be clearly seen; for example, a flash of lightning, or the small sparks produced by rubbing a nylon garment.

electric ray another name for the *torpedo.

electrocardiogram (ECG) graphic recording of the electrical activity of the heart, as detected by electrodes placed on the skin. Electrocardiography is used in the diagnosis of heart disease.

electrochemistry branch of science that studies chemical reactions involving electricity. The use of electricity to produce chemical effects, *electrolysis, is employed in many industrial processes, such as electroplating, the manufacture of chlorine, and the extraction of aluminium. The use of chemical reactions to produce electricity is the basis of electrical *cells, such as the dry cell and the Leclanché cell.

electroconvulsive therapy (ECT) *or* **electroshock therapy** treatment mainly for severe *depression, given under anaesthesia and with a muscle relaxant. An electric current is passed through one or both sides of the brain to induce alterations in its electrical activity. The treatment can cause distress and loss of concentration and memory, and so there is much controversy about its use and effectiveness.

electrocution death caused by electric current. It is used as a method of execution in some US states. The condemned person is strapped into a special chair and a shock of 1,800–2,000 volts is administered. See *capital punishment.

electrode any terminal by which an electric current passes in or out of a conducting substance; for example, the anode or *cathode in an electrolytic cell. The anode is the positive electrode and the cathode is the negative electrode.

electroencephalogram (EEG) graphic record of the electrical discharges of the brain, as detected by electrodes placed on the scalp. The pattern of electrical activity revealed by electroencephalography is helpful in the diagnosis of some brain disorders, in particular epilepsy.

electrolysis in chemistry, the production of chemical changes by passing an electric current through a solution or molten salt (the electrolyte), resulting in the migration of ions to the electrodes: positive ions (*cations) to the negative electrode (*cathode) and negative ions (*anions) to the positive electrode (*anode).

electrolyte solution or molten substance in which an electric current is made to flow by the movement and discharge of ions in accordance with Faraday's laws of *electrolysis.

electromagnet coil of wire wound around a soft iron core that acts as a magnet when an electric current flows through the wire. Electromagnets have many uses: in switches, electric bells, *solenoids, and metal-lifting cranes.

electromagnetic field in physics, region in which a particle with an *electric charge experiences a force. If it does so only when moving, it is in a pure **magnetic field**; if it does so when stationary, it is in an **electric field**. Both can be present simultaneously. For example, a light wave consists of an electric field and a magnetic field travelling simultaneously at right angles to each other.

electromagnetic force one of the four fundamental *forces of nature, the other three being the gravitational force (gravity), the weak nuclear force, and the strong nuclear force. The particle that is the carrier for the electromagnetic force is the *photon.

electromagnetic induction in electronics, the production of an *electromotive force (emf) in a circuit by a change of magnetic flux through the circuit or by relative motion of the circuit and the magnetic flux. As a magnet is moved in and out of a coil of wire in a closed circuit an induced current will be produced. All dynamos and generators produce electricity using this effect. When magnetic tape is driven past the playback head (a small coil) of a tape recorder, the moving magnetic field induces an emf in the head, which is then amplified to reproduce the recorded sounds.

electromagnetic spectrum complete range, over all wavelengths and frequencies, of *electromagnetic waves. These include (in order of decreasing wavelength) radio and television waves, microwaves, infrared radiation, visible light, ultraviolet light, X-rays, and gamma radiation.

electromagnetic waves oscillating electric and magnetic fields travelling together through space at a speed of nearly 300,000 kps/186,000 mps. Visible light is composed of electromagnetic waves. The **electromagnetic spectrum** is a family of waves that includes radio waves, infrared radiation, visible light, ultraviolet radiation, X-rays, and gamma rays. All electromagnetic waves are transverse waves. They can be reflected, refracted, diffracted, and polarized. (See diagram, p. 300.)

electromotive force emf, loosely, the voltage produced by an electric battery or generator in an electrical circuit or, more precisely, the energy supplied by a source of electric power in driving a unit charge around the circuit. The unit is the *volt.

electron negatively-charged particle with negligible mass. Electrons form the outer portion of all atoms, orbiting the nucleus in groupings called shells. The first shell can hold up to two electrons; the second and third shells can hold up to eight electrons each. The electron arrangement of an element is called its **electronic configuration**; for example, the electronic configuration

of the sodium atom is $Na_{(2,8,1)}$. In a neutral atom the number of electrons is equal to the number of protons in the nucleus. This electron structure is responsible for the chemical properties of the atom (see *atomic structure). Electrons are a member of the class of elementary particles known as *leptons.

electronic funds transfer (EFT) method of transferring funds automatically from one account to another by electronic means, for example **electronic funds transfer at point of sale** (EFTPOS), which provides for the automatic transfer of money from buyer to seller at the time of sale. For example, a customer inserts a plastic card into a point-of-sale computer terminal in a supermarket, and telephone lines are used to make an automatic debit from the customer's bank account to settle the bill.

electronic mail see *e-mail.

electronic music music composed completely or partly of electronically generated and/or modified sounds. The term was first used in 1954 to describe music made up of synthesized sounds recorded on tape, to distinguish it from *musique concrète ('concrete music'), but later included music for electronic sounds with traditional instruments or voices.

electronic point of sale (EPOS) system used in retailing in which a bar code on a product is scanned at the cash till and the information relayed to the store computer. The computer will then relay back the price of the item to the cash till. The customer can then be given an itemized receipt while the computer removes the item from stock figures.

electronic publishing distribution of information using computer-based media such as *multimedia and *hypertext in the creation of electronic 'books'. Critical technologies in the development of electronic publishing were *CD-ROM, with its massive yet compact storage capabilities, and the advent of computer networking with its ability to deliver information instantaneously anywhere in the world.

electronics branch of science that deals with the emission of *electrons from conductors and *semiconductors, with the subsequent manipulation of these electrons, and with the construction of electronic devices. The first electronic device was the thermionic valve, or vacuum tube, in which electrons moved in a vacuum, and led to such inventions as *radio, *television, *radar, and the digital *computer. Replacement of valves with the comparatively tiny and reliable *transistor from 1948 revolutionized electronic development. Modern electronic devices are based on minute *integrated circuits (silicon chips), wafer-thin crystal slices holding tens of thousands of electronic components.

electronic tagging see *tagging, electronic.

electron microscope instrument that produces a magnified image by using a beam of *electrons instead of light rays, as in an optical *microscope. An **electron lens** is an arrangement of electromagnetic coils that control and focus the beam. Electrons are not visible to the eye, so instead of an eyepiece there is a fluorescent screen or a photographic plate on which the electrons form an image. The wavelength of the electron beam is much shorter than that of light, so much greater magnification and resolution (ability to distinguish detail) can be achieved. The development of the

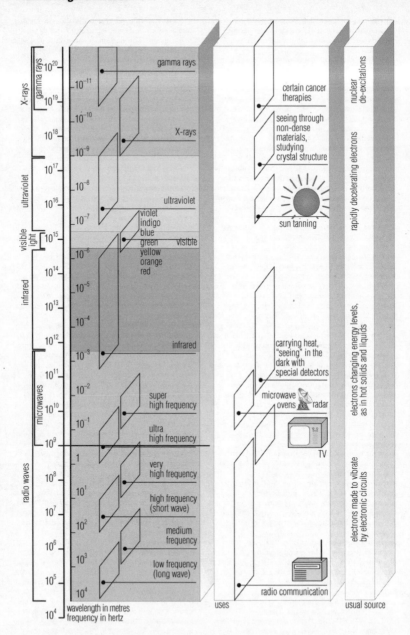

electromagnetic waves Radio waves have the lowest frequency. Infrared radiation, visible light, ultraviolet radiation, X-rays, and gamma rays have progressively higher frequencies.

electron microscope has made possible the observation of very minute organisms, viruses, and even large molecules.

electron volt symbol eV, unit for measuring the energy of a charged particle (*ion or *electron) in terms of the energy of motion an electron would gain from a potential difference of one volt. Because it is so small, more usual units are mega-(million) and giga- (billion) electron volts (MeV and GeV).

electrophoresis the *diffusion of charged particles through a fluid under the influence of an electric field. It can be used in the biological sciences to separate *molecules of different sizes, which diffuse at different rates. In industry, electrophoresis is used in paint-dipping operations to ensure that paint reaches awkward corners.

electroplating deposition of metals upon metallic surfaces by *electrolysis for decorative and/or protective purposes. It is used in the preparation of printing plates, 'master' audio discs, and in many other processes.

electroscope apparatus for detecting *electric charge. The simple gold-leaf electroscope consists of a vertical conducting (metal) rod ending in a pair of rectangular pieces of gold foil, mounted inside and insulated from an earthed metal case or glass jar. An electric charge applied to the end of the metal rod makes the gold leaves diverge, because they each receive a similar charge (positive or negative) via the rod and so repel each other.

electrovalent bond another name for an *ionic bond, a chemical bond in which the combining atoms lose or gain electrons to form ions.

electrum naturally occurring alloy of gold and silver used by early civilizations to make the first coins, about the 6th century BC.

element substance that cannot be split chemically into simpler substances. The atoms of a particular element all have the same number of protons in their nuclei (their proton or *atomic number). Elements are classified in the *periodic table of the elements. Of the known elements, 92 are known to occur naturally on Earth (those with atomic numbers 1–92). Those elements with atomic numbers above 96 do not occur in nature and must be synthesized in particle accelerators. Of the elements, 81 are stable; all the others, which include atomic numbers 43, 61, and from 84 up, are radioactive.

elementary particle in physics, a subatomic particle that is not known to be made up of smaller particles, and so can be considered one of the fundamental units of matter. There are three groups of elementary particles: quarks, leptons, and gauge bosons.

elements, the four earth, air, fire, and water. The Greek philosopher Empedocles believed that these four elements made up the fundamental components of all matter and that they were destroyed and renewed through the action of love and discord.

elephant large grazing mammal with thick, grey wrinkled skin, large ears, a long flexible trunk, and huge curving tusks. There are fingerlike projections at the end of the trunk used for grasping food and carrying it to the mouth. The trunk is also used for carrying water to the mouth. The elephant is herbivorous and, because of its huge size, much of its time must be spent feeding on leaves, shoots, bamboo, reeds, grasses, and fruits, and, where possible, cultivated crops such as maize and bananas. Elephants are the largest living land animal and usually live in herds containing between 20 and 40 females (cows), led by a mature, experienced cow. Most male (bull) elephants live alone or in small groups; young bulls remain with the herd until they reach sexual maturity. Elephants have the longest gestation period of any animal (18–23 months between conception and birth) and usually produce one calf , which takes 10–15 years to reach maturity. Their tusks, which are initially tipped with enamel but later consist entirely of ivory, continue growing throughout life. They are preceded by milk tusks, which are shed at an early age. Elephants can live up to 60 years in the wild, but those in captivity have been known to reach over 65.

Elgar, Edward (William) (1857–1934) English composer. Although his celebrated oratorio *The Dream of Gerontius* (1900), based on the written work by the theologian John Henry Newman, was initially unpopular in Britain, its good reception in Düsseldorf, Germany, in 1902 led to a surge of interest in his earlier works, including the *Pomp and Circumstance Marches* (1901). His *Enigma Variations* (1899) brought him lasting fame.

Elgin marbles collection of ancient Greek sculptures, including the famous frieze and other sculptures from the Parthenon at Athens, assembled by the 7th Earl of Elgin. Sent to England 1803–1812, and bought for the nation in 1816 for £35,000, they are now in the British Museum. Greece has repeatedly asked for them to be returned to Athens.

Eliot, George (1819–1880) pen-name of Mary Ann (later Marian) Evans, English novelist. Her works include the pastoral *Adam Bede* (1859); *The Mill on the Floss* (1860), with its autobiographical elements; *Silas Marner* (1861), containing elements of the folk tale; and *Daniel Deronda* (1876). *Middlemarch*, published serially (1871–72), is considered her greatest novel for its confident handling of numerous characters and central social and moral issues. She developed a subtle psychological presentation of character, and her work is pervaded by a penetrating and compassionate intelligence.

Eliot, T(homas) S(tearns) (1888–1965) US-born poet, playwright, and critic, who lived in England from 1915. His first volume of poetry, *Prufrock and Other Observations* (1917), introduced new verse forms and rhythms; subsequent major poems were *The Waste Land* (1922), a long symbolic poem of disillusionment, and *The Hollow Men* (1925). For children he published *Old Possum's Book of Practical Cats* (1939). Eliot's plays include *Murder in the Cathedral* (1935) and *The Cocktail Party* (1950). His critical works include *The Sacred Wood* (1920), setting out his views on poetic tradition. He makes considerable demands on his readers, and is regarded as the founder of *modernism in poetry. As a critic he profoundly influenced the ways in which literature was appreciated. He was awarded the Nobel Prize for Literature in 1948.

Elizabeth, the Queen Mother (1900–2002) Wife of King George VI of Great Britain. She was born Lady Elizabeth Angela Marguerite Bowes-Lyon, and on 26 April 1923 she married Albert, Duke of York, who became King George VI in 1936. Their children are Queen Elizabeth II and Princess Margaret (died 2002).

Elizabeth two queens of England or the UK:

Elizabeth I (1533–1603) called 'the Virgin Queen', Queen of England from 1558; the daughter of Henry VIII and Anne Boleyn. Through her Religious Settlement of 1559 she enforced the Protestant religion by law. She had *Mary Queen of Scots executed in 1587. Her conflict with Roman Catholic Spain led to the defeat of the *Spanish Armada in 1588. The Elizabethan age was expansionist in commerce and geographical exploration, and arts and literature flourished. The rulers of many European states made unsuccessful bids to marry Elizabeth, and she manipulated her suitors to strengthen England's position in Europe. She was succeeded by James I.

Elizabeth II (1926–) born Elizabeth Alexandra Mary Windsor, Queen of Great Britain and Northern Ireland from 1952, the elder daughter of George VI. She married her third cousin, Philip, the Duke of Edinburgh, in 1947. They have four children: Charles, Anne, Andrew, and Edward. She celebrated her Golden Jubilee as Queen in 2002.

elk large deer *Alces alces* inhabiting northern Europe, Asia, Scandinavia, and North America, where it is known as the moose. It is brown in colour, stands about 2 m/6 ft at the shoulders, has very large palmate antlers, a fleshy muzzle, short neck, and long legs. It feeds on leaves and shoots. In North America, the *wapiti is called an elk.

elkhound Norwegian dog resembling the *husky but much smaller. Its coat is thick, with a full undercoat and the tail is bushy. Elkhounds are grey, with a darker shade on the back, and are about 50 cm/20 in high, weighing approximately 22 kg/48 lb.

Ellesmere Island island in the extreme northeast of the Arctic Archipelago, in the Canadian territory of Nunavut; area 196,236 sq km/75,767 sq mi; population (1996 est) 100. It is the second-largest island in the archipelago and is part of the Queen Elizabeth island group, at the northern end of Baffin Bay. Its northern tip, Cape Columbia, is the most northerly point of the North American continent. The island is, for the most part, barren or glacier-covered. Industries include oil and gas exploration, and tourism. The island is also a base for scientific and military operations.

Ellice Islands former name of *Tuvalu, a group of islands in the western Pacific Ocean.

Ellington, Duke (Edward Kennedy) (1899–1974) US pianist. He had an outstanding career as a composer and arranger of *jazz. He wrote numerous pieces for his own jazz orchestra, emphasizing the strengths of individual virtuoso instrumentalists, and became one of the leading figures in jazz over a 55-year period. Some of his most popular compositions include 'Mood Indigo' (1930), 'It Don't Mean a Thing' (1932), 'Sophisticated Lady' (1932), 'Solitude' (1934), and 'Black and Tan Fantasy' (1938). He was one of the founders of *big-band jazz.

ellipse curve joining all points (loci) around two fixed points (foci) such that the sum of the distances from those points is always constant. The diameter passing through the foci is the major axis, and the diameter bisecting this at right angles is the minor axis. An ellipse is one of a series of curves known as *conic

sections. A slice across a cone that is not made parallel to, and does not pass through, the base will produce an ellipse.

Ellis Island island in New York harbour, USA, 1.5 km/1 mi from Manhattan Island; area 0.1 sq km/0.04 sq mi. A former reception centre for immigrants during the immigration waves between 1892 and 1943 (12 million people passed through it from 1892 to 1924), it was later used (until 1954) as a detention centre for nonresidents without documentation, or for those who were being deported. Ellis Island is now a national historic site (1964) and contains the Museum of Immigration (1989).

elm any of a group of trees found in temperate regions of the northern hemisphere and in mountainous parts of the tropics. All have doubly-toothed leaf margins and clusters of small flowers. (Genus *Ulmus*, family Ulmaceae.)

El Niño (Spanish 'the child') marked warming of the eastern Pacific Ocean that occurs when a warm current of water moves from the western Pacific, temporarily replacing the cold Peru Current along the west coast of South America. This results in a reduction in marine plankton, the main food source in the ocean, and fish numbers decline. The atmospheric circulation in the region is also seriously disturbed, and may result in unusual climatic events, for example floods in Peru, and drought in Australia. El Niño events occur at irregular intervals of between two and seven years. It is understood that there might be a link between El Niño and global warming.

El Paso city and administrative headquarters of El Paso County, Texas, at the base of the Franklin Mountains, on the Rio Grande, opposite the Mexican city of Ciudad Juárez; population (2000 est) 563,700. It is the centre of an agricultural and cattle-raising area, and there are electronics, food processing, packing, textile, and leather industries, as well as oil refineries and industries based on local iron and copper mines. With strong links to Mexico the economy particularly benefited from the *North American Free Trade Agreement of 1992. There are several military installations in the area. The city is home to the University of Texas at El Paso (formerly Texas Western; founded in 1913).

El Salvador

National name: *República de El Salvador/ Republic of El Salvador*

Area: 21,393 sq km/8,259 sq mi

Capital: San Salvador

Major towns/cities: Soyapango, Santa Ana, San Miguel, Nueva San Salvador, Mejicanos, Apopa, Delgado

Physical features: narrow coastal plain, rising to mountains in north with central plateau

Head of state and government: Elias Antonio Saca from 2004

Political system: emergent democracy

Political executive: limited presidency

Political parties: Christian Democrats (PDC), anti-imperialist; Farabundo Martí Liberation Front (FMLN), left wing; National Republican Alliance (ARENA), extreme right wing; National Conciliation Party (PCN), right wing

Currency: US dollar (replaced Salvadorean colón in 2001)

GNI per capita (PPP): (US$) 4,570 (2002 est)
Exports: coffee, textiles and garments, sugar, shrimp, footwear, pharmaceuticals. Principal market: USA 65.4% (2001)
Population: 6,515,000 (2003 est)
Language: Spanish (official), Nahuatl
Religion: about 75% Roman Catholic, Protestant
Life expectancy: 68 (men); 74 (women) (2000–05)
Chronology
11th century: Pipils, descendants of the Nahuatl-speaking Toltec and Aztec peoples of Mexico, settled in the country and came to dominate El Salvador until the Spanish conquest.
1524: Conquered by the Spanish adventurer Pedro de Alvarado and made a Spanish colony, with resistance being crushed by 1540.
1821: Independence achieved from Spain; briefly joined with Mexico.
1823: Became part of United Provinces (Federation) of Central America, also embracing Costa Rica, Guatemala, Honduras, and Nicaragua.
1833: Unsuccessful rebellion against Spanish control of land led by Anastasio Aquino.
1840: Became fully independent when the Federation was dissolved.
1859–63: Coffee growing introduced by President Gerardo Barrios.
1932: Peasant uprising, led by Augustín Farabundo Martí, suppressed by military at a cost of the lives of 30,000, virtually eliminating American Indian Salvadoreans.
1961: Following a coup, the right-wing National Conciliation Party (PCN) established and in power.
1969: Brief 'Football War' with Honduras, which El Salvador attacked, at the time of a football competition between the two states, following evictions of thousands of Salvadoran illegal immigrants from Honduras.
1977: Allegations of human-rights violations; growth of left-wing Farabundo Martí National Liberation Front (FMLN) guerrilla activities. Gen Carlos Romero elected president.
1979: A coup replaced Romero with a military-civilian junta.
1980: The archbishop of San Salvador and human-rights champion, Oscar Romero, was assassinated; the country was on the verge of civil war. José Napoleón

Duarte (PDC) became the first civilian president since 1931.
1979–81: 30,000 people were killed by right-wing death squads.
1981: Mexico and France recognized the FMLN guerrillas as a legitimate political force, but the USA actively assisted the government in its battle against them.
1982: Assembly elections were boycotted by left-wing parties. Held amid considerable violence, they were won by far-right National Republican Alliance (ARENA).
1986: Duarte sought a negotiated settlement with the guerrillas.
1989: Alfredo Cristiani (ARENA) became president in rigged elections; rebel attacks intensified.
1991: A peace accord sponsored by the United Nations (UN) was signed by representatives of the government and the socialist guerrilla group, the FMLN, which became a political party.
1993: A UN-sponsored commission published a report on war atrocities; there was a government amnesty for those implicated; top military leaders officially retired.
1999: Francisco Guillermo Flores Pérez was elected president.
2000: The FMLN displaced the ruling ARENA as the largest party in Congress, but did not win an overall majority. The government signed a free-trade agreement with Mexico.
2001: El Salvador adopted the US dollar as its currency, phasing out the colon. Two powerful earthquakes killed over 1,500 people and left 1 million homeless.
2003: In congressional and country-wide mayoral elections the opposition FMLN won 31 congressional seats and claimed victory in more than 100 mayorships, including San Salvador – far more than the ruling ARENA party.
2004: Elias Antonio (Tony) Saca, of the ARENA party, was elected as president, advocating closer ties with the USA.

Elysium *or the* **Elysian Fields** in Greek mythology, an afterworld or paradise, originally identified with the Islands of the Blessed, for those who found favour with the gods. Later poets depicted Elysium as a region in *Hades, the underworld. It was ruled over by Rhadamanthys, a judge of the dead.

e-mail contraction of electronic mail, messages sent electronically from computer to computer via network connections such as Ethernet or the *Internet, or via telephone lines to a host system. Messages once sent are stored on the network or by the host system until the recipient picks them up. As well as text, messages may contain enclosed text files, artwork, or multimedia clips.

emancipation being liberated, being set free from servitude or subjection of any kind. The changing role of women in social, economic, and particularly in political terms, in the 19th and 20th centuries is sometimes referred to as the 'emancipation of women' (see also *women's movement).

Emancipation Proclamation official order made by US president Abraham *Lincoln on 22 September 1862, during the American *Civil War, that freed slaves in Confederate (southern) states. The order stated that from 1 January 1863 all slaves in states that were still rebelling against the Union would be forever free.

Border states that remained loyal to the Union were excluded. Parts of the South that were then under Union control were also exempt.

embolism blockage of a blood vessel by an obstruction called an embolus (usually a blood clot, fat particle, or bubble of air).

embryo early developmental stage of an animal or a plant following fertilization of an ovum (egg cell), or activation of an ovum by *parthenogenesis. In humans, the term embryo describes the fertilized egg during its first seven weeks of existence; from the eighth week onwards it is referred to as a fetus.

embryology study of the changes undergone by an organism from its conception as a fertilized ovum (egg) to its emergence into the world at hatching or birth. It is mainly concerned with the changes in cell organization in the embryo and the way in which these lead to the structures and organs of the adult (the process of *differentiation).

emerald clear, green gemstone variety of the mineral *beryl. It occurs naturally in Colombia, the Ural Mountains in Russia, Zimbabwe, and Australia. The green colour is caused by the presence of the element chromium in the beryl.

Emerson, Ralph Waldo (1803–1882) US philosopher, essayist, and poet. He settled in Concord, Massachusetts, which he made a centre of *transcendentalism, and wrote *Nature* (1836), which states the movement's main principles emphasizing the value of self-reliance and the godlike nature of human souls. His two volumes of *Essays* (1841, 1844) made his reputation: 'Self-Reliance' and 'Compensation' in the earlier volume are among the best known.

emery black to greyish form of impure *corundum that also contains the minerals magnetite and haematite. It is used as an *abrasive.

Emilia-Romagna region of northern central Italy, comprising the provinces of Bologna, Ferrara, Forlì, Modena, Parma, Piacenza, Reggio nell'Emilia, and Rimini; area 22,124 sq km/8,542 sq mi; population (2001 est) 3,960,600. The capital is Bologna; other towns include Reggio nell'Emilia, Rimini, Parma, Ferrara, and Ravenna. An economically prosperous region, agricultural produce includes fruit, wine, sugar beet, beef, dairy products, rice, and wheat. Oil and natural-gas resources have been developed in the Po Valley.

emotion in psychology, a powerful feeling; a complex state of body and mind involving, in its bodily aspect, changes in the viscera (main internal organs) and in facial expression and posture, and in its mental aspect, heightened perception, excitement and, sometimes, disturbance of thought and judgement. The urge to action is felt and impulsive behaviour may result.

emphysema incurable lung condition characterized by disabling breathlessness. Progressive loss of the thin walls dividing the air spaces (alveoli) in the lungs reduces the area available for the exchange of oxygen and carbon dioxide, causing the lung tissue to expand. The term 'emphysema' can also refer to the presence of air in other body tissues.

empire collective name for a group of countries under the control of a single country or dynasty. Major empires in Europe have included the *Roman Empire and the *British Empire, and in Asia the *Ottoman Empire and Mogul Empire (see *Mogul dynasty).

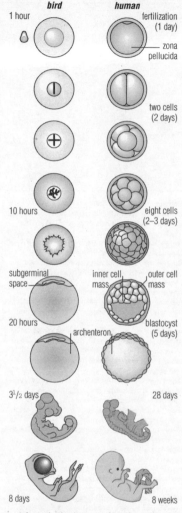

embryo The development of a bird and a human embryo. In the human, division of the fertilized egg, or ovum, begins within hours of conception. Within a week, a hollow, fluid-containing ball – a blastocyte – with a mass of cells at one end has developed. After the third week, the embryo has changed from a mass of cells into a recognizable shape. At four weeks, the embryo is 3 mm/0.1 in long, with a large bulge for the heart and small pits for the ears. At six weeks, the embryo is 1.5 cm/0.6 in long with a pulsating heart and ear flaps. By the eighth week, the embryo (now technically a fetus) is 2.5 cm/1 in long and recognizably human, with eyelids and small fingers and toes.

Empire State Building landmark building in New York, USA. It is 443 m/1,454 ft high with 102 floors, and was the highest building in the world until 1972, when it was superseded by the World Trade Center, New York (which was destroyed in 2001 by a terrorist attack). It was built in 1930 at a cost of over US$40,000,000.

Empire style French decorative arts style prevalent during the rule of the emperor Napoleon Bonaparte (1804–14). A late form of *neoclassicism, it featured motifs drawn from ancient Egyptian as well as Greek and Roman art. Dark woods and draperies were also frequently used. The influence of the style extended through Europe and North America.

empiricism (Greek *empeiria* 'experience' or 'experiment') in philosophy, the belief that all knowledge is ultimately derived from sense experience. It is suspicious of metaphysical schemes based on a priori propositions, which are claimed to be true irrespective of experience. It is frequently contrasted with *rationalism.

EMS abbreviation for *European Monetary System.

emu flightless bird *Dromaius novaehollandiae*, family Dromaiidae, order Casuariidae, native to Australia. It stands about 1.8 m/6 ft high and has coarse brown plumage, small rudimentary wings, short feathers on the head and neck, and powerful legs, which are well adapted for running and kicking. The female has a curious bag or pouch in the windpipe that enables her to emit a characteristic loud booming note. Emus are monogamous, and the male wholly or partially incubates the eggs.

EMU abbreviation for *Economic and Monetary Union, the proposed *European Union (EU) policy for a single currency and common economic policies.

emulsion stable dispersion of a liquid in another liquid – for example, oil and water in some cosmetic lotions.

enamel vitrified (glasslike) coating of various colours used for decorative purposes on a metallic or porcelain surface. In cloisonné the various sections of the design are separated by thin metal wires or strips. In champlevé the enamel is poured into engraved cavities in the metal surface.

encaustic painting ancient technique of painting, commonly used by the Egyptians, Greeks, and Romans, in which coloured pigments were mixed with molten wax and painted on panels. In the 20th century the technique was used by the US artist Jasper Johns.

encephalitis inflammation of the brain, nearly always due to viral infection but it may also occur in bacterial and other infections. It varies widely in severity, from shortlived, relatively slight effects of headache, drowsiness, and fever to paralysis, coma, and death.

Encke's Comet comet with the shortest known orbital period, 3.3 years. It is named after German astronomer Johann Encke, who calculated its orbit in 1819 from earlier sightings.

enclosure in Britain, seizure of *common land and change to private property, or the changing of open-field systems (farming in strips apportioned over two or three large fields) to enclosed fields owned by individual farmers. The enclosed fields were often used for sheep. This process began in the 14th century and became widespread in the 15th and 16th centuries. It caused poverty, homelessness, and rural depopulation, and resulted in revolts in 1549 and 1607. A further wave of enclosures occurred between about 1760 and 1820 during the *agrarian revolution.

encyclical letter addressed by the pope to Roman Catholic bishops for the benefit of the people. The first was issued by Benedict XIV in 1740, but encyclicals became common only in the 19th century. They may be doctrinal (condemning errors), exhortative (recommending devotional activities), or commemorative.

Encyclopédie encyclopedia in 35 volumes written 1751–77 by a group of French scholars (*Encyclopédistes*) including D'Alembert and Diderot, inspired by the English encyclopedia produced by Ephraim Chambers in 1728. Religious scepticism and *Enlightenment social and political views were a feature of the work.

endangered species plant or animal species whose numbers are so few that it is at risk of becoming extinct. Officially designated endangered species are listed by the World Conservation Union (or IUCN).

endive cultivated annual plant, the leaves of which are used in salads and cooking. One variety has narrow, curled leaves; another has wide, smooth leaves. It is related to *chicory. (*Cichorium endivia*, family Compositae.)

endocrine gland gland that secretes hormones into the bloodstream to regulate body processes. Endocrine glands are most highly developed in vertebrates, but are also found in other animals, notably insects. In humans the main endocrine glands are the pituitary, thyroid, parathyroid, adrenal, pancreas, ovary, and testis. (See diagram, p. 306.)

endorphin natural substance (a polypeptide) that modifies the action of nerve cells. Endorphins are produced by the pituitary gland and hypothalamus of vertebrates. They lower the perception of pain by reducing the transmission of signals between nerve cells.

endoscopy examination of internal organs or tissues by an instrument allowing direct vision. An endoscope is equipped with an eyepiece, lenses, and its own light source to illuminate the field of vision. The endoscope used to examine the digestive tract is a flexible fibreoptic instrument swallowed by the patient.

endoskeleton internal supporting structure of vertebrates, made up of cartilage or bone. It provides support, and acts as a system of levers to which muscles are attached to provide movement. Certain parts of the skeleton (the skull and ribs) give protection to vital body organs.

endotherm 'warm-blooded', or homeothermic, animal. Endotherms have internal mechanisms for regulating their body temperatures to levels different from the environmental temperature.

Endymion in Greek mythology, a beautiful young shepherd or hunter visited each night by *Selene, the Moon goddess. She kissed him as he slept in a cave on Mount Latmos in Caria, sending him into an eternal sleep in which he became ageless.

energy capacity for doing *work. This work may be as simple as reading a book, using a computer, or driving a car. Without energy no activity is possible. Energy can exist in many different forms. For example, potential energy (PE) is energy deriving from position; thus a stretched spring has elastic PE, and an object raised to a height above the Earth's surface, or the water in an elevated reservoir, has gravitational PE. Moving bodies possess kinetic energy (KE). Energy can be converted

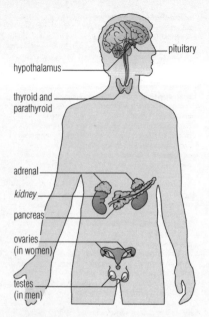

pituitary

hypothalamus

thyroid and
parathyroid

adrenal

kidney

pancreas

ovaries
(in women)

testes
(in men)

endocrine gland The main human endocrine glands.
These glands produce hormones – chemical
messengers – which travel in the bloodstream
to stimulate certain cells.

from one form to another, but the total quantity in
a system stays the same (in accordance with the
*conservation of energy principle). Energy cannot be
created or destroyed. For example, as an apple falls it
loses gravitational PE but gains KE. Although energy
is never lost, after a number of conversions it tends to
finish up as the kinetic energy of random motion of
molecules (of the air, for example) at relatively low
temperatures. This is 'degraded' energy that is difficult
to convert back to other forms.

energy in biology, the basis for conducting living
processes. Much of life involves energy transfer. Energy
is transferred from the surroundings of an organism
into its body, and is also transferred within an
organism's body. Energy is used by organisms to do
things, such as growing or moving. When they do these
things energy is transferred from one substance to
another or from one place to another.

energy, alternative energy from sources that are
renewable and ecologically safe, as opposed to sources
that are non-renewable with toxic by-products, such as
coal, oil, or gas (fossil fuels), and uranium (for nuclear
power). The most important alternative energy source
is flowing water, harnessed as *hydroelectric power.
Other sources include the oceans' tides and waves (see
*wave power), *wind power (harnessed by windmills
and wind turbines), the Sun (*solar energy), and the
heat trapped in the Earth's crust (*geothermal energy)
(see also *cold fusion).

energy conservation the practice and methods used
to reduce* energy resource consumption, usually by
identification of those processes that are energy-
inefficient and providing alternative solutions. The
term can also used to describe the conservation of non-
renewable resources such as coal, oil, and natural gas by
increasing the efficiency of related processes, or finding
alternatives so that existing stocks are depleted at a
slower rate. Common conservation methods are
insulation, optimization of processes to use minimum
energy, increasing the efficiency of a process by
changing the methods and/or components used, and
finding alternatives that do not use non-renewable
resources. Profligate energy use by industrialized
countries contributes greatly to air pollution and the
*greenhouse effect when it draws on non-renewable
energy sources.

energy of reaction or **enthalpy of reaction** or
heat of reaction energy released or absorbed during
a chemical reaction, part of the energy transfer that
takes place. In a chemical equation it may be
represented by the symbol ΔH. In a chemical reaction,
the energy stored in the reacting molecules is rarely
the same as that stored in the product molecules.
Depending on which is the greater, energy is either
released (an exothermic reaction) or absorbed
(an endothermic reaction) from the surroundings. The
amount of energy released or absorbed by the
quantities of substances represented by the chemical
equation is the energy of reaction. The principle that
the total amount of energy in a given chemical
reaction stays the same is known as *conservation
of energy.

Engels, Friedrich (1820–1895) German social and
political philosopher, a friend of, and collaborator with,
Karl *Marx on *The Communist Manifesto* (1848) and
other key works. His later interpretations of Marxism,
and his own interpretations and historical studies such
as *Origins of the Family, Private Property, and the State*
(1884) (which linked patriarchy with the development
of private property), developed such concepts as
historical materialism. His use of positivism and
Darwinian ideas gave Marxism a scientific and
deterministic flavour which was to influence Soviet
thinking.

engine device for converting stored energy into useful
work or movement. Most engines use a fuel as their
energy store. The fuel is burnt to produce heat energy –
hence the name 'heat engine' – which is then converted
into movement. Heat engines can be classified
according to the fuel they use (*petrol engine or
*diesel engine), or according to whether the fuel is
burnt inside (*internal combustion engine) or outside
(*steam engine) the engine, or according to whether
they produce a reciprocating or a rotary motion
(*turbine or Wankel engine).

engineering the application of science to the design,
construction, and maintenance of works, machinery,
roads, railways, bridges, harbour installations, engines,
ships, aircraft and airports, spacecraft and space
stations, and the generation, transmission, and use of
electrical power. The main divisions of engineering are
aerospace, chemical, civil, computer, electrical,
electronic, gas, marine, materials, mechanical, mining,
production, radio, and structural.

England largest constituent part of the United Kingdom; area 130,357 sq km/50,331 sq mi; population (2001 est) 49,181,300. The capital is *London, and other main towns and cities include Birmingham, Cambridge, Coventry, Leeds, Leicester, Manchester, Newcastle upon Tyne, Nottingham, Oxford, Sheffield, and York. The main ports are Bristol, Dover, Felixstowe, Harwich, Liverpool, Portsmouth, and Southampton. Important industries include agriculture (cereals, rape, sugar beet, potatoes, meat, and meat products), electronic and telecommunications equipment, computer software, scientific instruments, textiles and fashion goods, North Sea oil and gas, petrochemicals, pharmaceuticals, fertilizers, beer, china clay, pottery, porcelain, and glass. Tourism is important, and there are worldwide banking and insurance interests. England also exports films and radio and television programmes, and has a large music industry.

English horn alternative name for the *cor anglais, a musical instrument of the oboe family.

English language member of the Germanic branch of the Indo-European language family. It is traditionally described as having passed through four major stages over about 1,500 years: **Old English** or **Anglo-Saxon** (c. 500–1050), rooted in the dialects of invading settlers (Jutes, Saxons, Angles, and Frisians); **Middle English** (c. 1050–1550), influenced by Norman French after the Conquest of 1066 and by ecclesiastical Latin; **Early Modern English** (c. 1550–1700), including a standardization of the diverse influences of Middle English; and **Late Modern English** (c. 1700 onwards), including in particular the development and spread of current Standard English. Through extensive exploration, colonization, and trade, English spread worldwide from the 17th century onwards and remains the most important international language of trade and technology. It is used in many variations, for example, British, American, Canadian, West Indian, Indian, Singaporean, and Nigerian English, and many pidgins and creoles.

English law one of the major European legal systems, *Roman law being the other. English law has spread to many other countries, including former English colonies such as the USA, Canada, Australia, and New Zealand.

English toy terrier or **black-and-tan terrier** breed of toy dog closely resembling the *Manchester terrier but smaller and with erect ears. It weighs no more than 3.5 kg/8 lb and is 25–30 cm/10–12 in high.

engraving art of creating a design by means of inscribing blocks of metal, wood, or some other hard material with a point. With **intaglio printing** the design is cut into the surface of a plate, usually metal. It is these cuts, often very fine, which hold the ink. In **relief printing**, by contrast, it is the areas left when the rest has been cut away which are inked for printing. See *printmaking.

enlightenment in Buddhism, the term used to translate the Sanskrit *bodhi* 'awakening': the transcendence of worldy values to perceive the true nature of the world and the unreality of the self, and the liberation from suffering (dukkha). By experience of *bodhi*, *nirvana is attained.

Enlightenment European intellectual movement that reached its high point in the 18th century.

Enlightenment thinkers were believers in social progress and in the liberating possibilities of rational and scientific knowledge. They were often critical of existing society and were hostile to religion, which they saw as keeping the human mind chained down by superstition.

Entente Cordiale (French 'friendly understanding') agreement reached by Britain and France in 1904 recognizing British interests in Egypt and French interests in Morocco. It was expressly designed to check the colonial ambitions of the German Second Empire under *William II. Though not a formal alliance, the Entente generated tripartite cooperation between Britain, France, and Russia from 1907 (the Triple Entente), and formed the basis for Anglo-French military collaboration before the outbreak of World War I in 1914.

enthalpy alternative term for *energy of reaction, the heat energy associated with a chemical change.

entomology study of *insects.

entropy in *thermodynamics, a parameter representing the state of disorder of a system at the atomic, ionic, or molecular level; the greater the disorder, the higher the entropy. Thus the fast-moving disordered molecules of water vapour have higher entropy than those of more ordered liquid water, which in turn have more entropy than the molecules in solid crystalline ice.

E number code number for additives that have been approved for use by the European Commission (EC). The E written before the number stands for European. E numbers do not have to be displayed on lists of ingredients, and the manufacturer may choose to list *additives by their name instead. E numbers cover all categories of additives apart from flavourings. Additives, other than flavourings, that are not approved by the European Commission, but are still used in Britain, are represented by a code number without an E.

Enver Pasha (1881–1922) Turkish politician and soldier. He led the military revolt of 1908 that resulted in the Young Turks' revolution. He was killed fighting the Bolsheviks in Turkestan.

environmental issues matters relating to the damaging effects of human activity on the biosphere, their causes, and the search for possible solutions. The political movement that supports protection of the environment is the green movement. Since the Industrial Revolution, the demands made by both the industrialized and developing nations on the Earth's natural resources are increasingly affecting the balance of the Earth's resources. Over a period of time, some of these resources are renewable – trees can be replanted, soil nutrients can be replenished – but many resources, such as minerals and fossil fuels (coal, oil, and natural gas), are *non-renewable and in danger of eventual exhaustion. In addition, humans are creating many other problems that may endanger not only their own survival, but also that of other species. For instance, *deforestation and *air pollution are not only damaging and radically altering many natural environments, they are also affecting the Earth's climate by adding to the *greenhouse effect and *global warming, while *water pollution is seriously affecting aquatic life, including fish populations, as well as human health.

environment–heredity controversy see *nature–nurture controversy.

enzyme biological *catalyst produced in cells, and capable of speeding up the chemical reactions necessary for life. They are large, complex *proteins, usually soluble, and are highly specific, each chemical reaction requiring its own particular enzyme. The enzyme's specificity arises from its active site, an area with a shape corresponding to part of the molecule with which it reacts (the substrate). The shape of the enzyme where the chemical binds only allows the binding of that particular chemical, rather like a specific key only working a specific lock (the lock and key hypothesis). The enzyme and the substrate slot together forming an enzyme–substrate complex that allows the reaction to take place, after which the enzyme falls away unaltered.

Eocene epoch second epoch of the Tertiary period of geological time, roughly 56.5–35.5 million years ago. Originally considered the earliest division of the Tertiary, the name means 'early recent', referring to the early forms of mammals evolving at the time, following the extinction of the dinosaurs.

Eos in Greek mythology, the goddess of the dawn (Roman **Aurora**); daughter of the Titans Hyperion and Theia; herald of *Helios's chariot bearing the sun. She was cursed to fall in love with many youths by *Aphrodite after they quarrelled over Ares, god of war. When distracted by love, Eos would neglect her responsibilities, and the sun could not rise.

Ephesus ancient Greek seaport in Asia Minor, a centre of the *Ionian Greeks, with a temple of Artemis destroyed by the Goths in AD 262. Now in Turkey, it is one of the world's largest archaeological sites. St Paul visited the city and addressed a letter (*epistle) to the Christians there.

epic *genre of narrative poem or cycle of poems dealing with some great deed – often the founding of a nation or the forging of national unity – and often using religious or cosmological themes. The two main epic poems in the Western tradition are *The Iliad* and *The Odyssey*, attributed to the Ancient Greek *Homer, which were probably intended to be chanted in sections at feasts. Sometimes called 'heroic poetry', an epic poem may employ the metre (formal structure) termed heroic verse.

epicentre point on the Earth's surface immediately above the seismic focus of an *earthquake. Most building damage takes place at an earthquake's epicentre. The term is also sometimes used to refer to a point directly above or below a nuclear explosion ('at ground zero').

Epicureanism system of moral philosophy named after the Greek philosopher Epicurus. He argued that pleasure is the basis of the ethical life, and that the most satisfying form of pleasure is achieved by avoiding pain, mental or physical. This is done by limiting desire as far as possible, and by choosing pleasures of the mind over those of the body.

epicyclic gear or **sun-and-planet gear** gear system that consists of one or more gear wheels moving around another. Epicyclic gears are found in bicycle hub gears and in automatic gearboxes.

epidemic outbreak of infectious disease affecting large numbers of people at the same time. A widespread epidemic that sweeps across many countries (such as the *Black Death in the late Middle Ages) is known as a **pandemic**.

epidermis outermost layer of *cells on an organism's body. In plants and many invertebrates such as insects, it consists of a single layer of cells. In vertebrates, it consists of several layers of cells.

epiglottis small flap located behind the root of the tongue in mammals. It closes off the end of the windpipe during swallowing to prevent food from passing into it and causing choking.

epigram short, witty, and pithy saying or short poem. The poem form was common among writers of ancient Rome, including *Catullus and *Martial. The epigram has been used by English poets Ben *Jonson, John *Donne, and Alexander *Pope, Irish writers Jonathan *Swift and W B *Yeats, and US writer Ogden Nash. An epigram was originally a religious inscription, such as that on a tomb.

epilepsy medical disorder characterized by a tendency to develop fits, which are convulsions or abnormal feelings caused by abnormal electrical discharges in the cerebral hemispheres of the *brain. Epilepsy can be controlled with a number of anticonvulsant drugs.

epiphyte any plant that grows on another plant or object above the surface of the ground, and has no roots in the soil. An epiphyte does not parasitize the plant it grows on but merely uses it for support. Its nutrients are obtained from rainwater, organic debris such as leaf litter, or from the air.

epistemology branch of philosophy that examines the nature of knowledge and attempts to determine the limits of human understanding. Central issues include how knowledge is derived and how it is to be validated and tested.

epistle (Greek *epistellein* 'to send to'; Latin *epistola* 'letter') letter, particularly an open literary letter or letter in the form of a poem. In the New Testament, the Epistles are 21 letters to individuals or to the members of various churches written by Christian leaders, including the 13 written by St *Paul, known as the Pauline Epistles, which include the books Romans, Ephesians, and Corinthians. These epistles are intended to instruct the members of the early church during the first days of Christianity. The epistles of Roman writer *Horace were widely imitated in later literature, particularly during the *Renaissance period. The English poet Alexander *Pope wrote many poetical *Epistles*, addressing them both to famous figures and to personal friends.

epoch subdivision of a geological period in the geological time scale. Epochs are sometimes given their own names (such as the Palaeocene, Eocene, Oligocene, Miocene, and Pliocene epochs comprising the Tertiary period), or they are referred to as the late, early, or middle portions of a given period (as the Late Cretaceous or the Middle Triassic epoch).

epoxy resin synthetic *resin used as an *adhesive and as an ingredient in paints. Household epoxy resin adhesives come in component form as two separate tubes of chemical, one tube containing resin, the other a curing agent (hardener). The two chemicals are mixed just before application, and the mix soon sets hard.

Epsom salts $MgSO_4.7H_2O$, hydrated magnesium sulphate, used as a relaxant and laxative and added to baths to soothe the skin. The name is derived from a bitter saline spring at Epsom, Surrey, England, which contains the salt in solution.

Epstein, Jacob (1880–1959) US-born British sculptor. Initially influenced by Rodin, he turned to primitive forms after Brancusi and is chiefly known for his controversial muscular nude figures, such as *Genesis* (1931; Whitworth Art Gallery, Manchester). He was better appreciated as a portraitist; his bust of Albert Einstein (1933) demonstrating a characteristic vigorous modelling in clay. In later years he executed several monumental figures, notably the bronze *St Michael and the Devil* (1959; Coventry Cathedral) and *Social Consciousness* (1953; Fairmount Park, Philadelphia).

Equal Opportunities Commission commission established by the UK government in 1975 (1976 in Northern Ireland) to implement the Sex Discrimination Act 1975. Its aim is to prevent discrimination, particularly on sexual or marital grounds. The US equivalent is the Equal Employment Opportunity Commission (EEOC) established by the Civil Rights Act of 1964. It investigates possible employment discrimination based on race, sex, age, religion, or national origin. The EEOC has the power to initiate law suits in the federal district courts.

equation in chemistry, representation of a chemical reaction by symbols and numbers; see *chemical equation. For example, the reaction of sodium hydroxide (NaOH) with hydrochloric acid (HCl) to give sodium chloride and water may be represented by:

$$NaOH + HCl \rightarrow NaCl + H_2O.$$

equation in mathematics, an expression that represents the equality of two expressions involving constants and/or variables, and thus usually includes an equals (=) sign. For example, the equation $A = \pi r^2$ equates the area A of a circle of radius r to the product πr^2. This is also known as the *formula for the area of a circle. The algebraic equation $y = mx + c$ is the general one in coordinate geometry for a straight line and is known as a *linear equation. See also *algebra, *quadratic equations, *simultaneous equations, inequations or inequalities, and *graphs.

Equator *or* **terrestrial equator** *great circle whose plane is perpendicular to the Earth's axis (the line joining the poles). Its length is 40,092 km/24,902 mi, divided into 360 degrees of longitude. The Equator encircles the broadest part of the Earth, and represents 0° latitude. It divides the Earth into two halves, called the northern and the southern hemispheres.

Equatorial Guinea

National name: *República de Guinea Ecuatorial/ Republic of Equatorial Guinea*
Area: 28,051 sq km/10,830 sq mi
Capital: Malabo
Major towns/cities: Bata, Mongomo, Ela Nguema, Mbini, Campo Yaunde, Los Angeles
Physical features: comprises mainland Río Muni, plus the small islands of Corisco, Elobey Grande and Elobey Chico, and Bioko (formerly Fernando Po) together with Annobón (formerly Pagalu); nearly half the land is forested; volcanic mountains on Bioko
Head of state: Teodoro Obiang Nguema Mbasogo from 2004
Head of government: Miguel Abia Biteo Borico from 2001

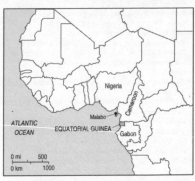

Political system: authoritarian nationalist
Political executive: unlimited presidency
Political parties: Democratic Party of Equatorial Guinea (PDGE), nationalist, right of centre, militarily controlled; People's Social Democratic Convention (CSDP), left of centre; Democratic Socialist Union of Equatorial Guinea (UDS), left of centre; Liberal Democratic Convention (CLD)
Currency: franc CFA
GNI per capita (PPP): (US$) 5,590 (2002 est)
Exports: petroleum, methanol, timber, re-exported ships and boats, textile fibres and waste, cocoa, coffee. Principal market: Spain 53% (2001)
Population: 494,000 (2003 est)
Language: Spanish (official), pidgin English, a Portuguese patois (on Annobón, whose people were formerly slaves of the Portuguese), Fang and other African patois (on Río Muni)
Religion: Roman Catholic, Protestant, animist
Life expectancy: 48 (men); 51 (women) (2000–05)
Chronology
1472: First visited by Portuguese explorers.
1778: Bioko (formerly known as Fernando Po) Island ceded to Spain, which established cocoa plantations there in the late 19th century, importing labour from West Africa.
1885: Mainland territory of Mbini (formerly Rio Muni) came under Spanish rule, the whole colony being known as Spanish Guinea, with the capital at Malabu on Bioko Island.
1920s: League of Nations special mission sent to investigate the forced, quasi-slave labour conditions on the Bioko cocoa plantations, then the largest in the world.
1959: Became a Spanish Overseas Province; African population finally granted full citizenship.
early 1960s: On the mainland, the Fang people spearheaded a nationalist movement directed against Spanish favouritism towards Bioko Island and its controlling Bubi tribe.
1963: Achieved internal autonomy.
1968: Independence achieved from Spain. Macias Nguema, a nationalist Fang, became first president, discriminating against the Bubi community.
1970s: The economy collapsed as Spanish settlers and other minorities fled in the face of intimidation by Nguema's brutal, dictatorial regime, which was marked

309

by the murder, torture, and imprisonment of tens of thousands of political opponents and rivals.

1979: Nguema was overthrown, tried, and executed. He was replaced by his nephew, Teodoro Obiang Nguema Mbasogo, who established a military regime, but released political prisoners and imposed restrictions on the Catholic Church.

1992: A new pluralist constitution was approved by referendum.

1993: Obiang's PDGE won the first multiparty elections on low turnout.

1996: Obiang was re-elected amid claims of fraud by opponents. Angel Serafin Seriche Dougan became prime minister, and was reappointed in 1998.

2001: Dougan resigned following allegations of corruption, and was replaced by Cándido Muatetema Rivas.

2002: Obiang was again re-elected as president.

2004: A party of alleged mercenaries was arrested in Zimbabwe and accused of being en route to stage a coup in Equatorial Guinea.

equestrianism skill in horse riding, as practised under Fédération Equestre Internationale (FEI; International Equestrian Federation) rules. An Olympic sport, there are three main branches of equestrianism: showjumping, dressage, and three-day eventing. Three other disciplines are under the authority of the FEI: carriage driving, endurance riding, and vaulting.

Equidae horse family in the order Perissodactyla, which includes the odd-toed hoofed animals. Besides the domestic horse, wild asses, wild horses, onagers, and zebras, there are numerous extinct species known from fossils.

equilateral describing a geometrical figure, having all sides of equal length.

equilibrium in physics, an unchanging condition in which an undisturbed system can remain indefinitely in a state of balance. In a **static equilibrium**, such as an object resting on the floor, there is no motion. In a **dynamic equilibrium**, in contrast, a steady state is maintained by constant, though opposing, changes. For example, in a sealed bottle half-full of water, the constancy of the water level is a result of molecules evaporating from the surface and condensing on to it at the same time.

equinox time when the Sun is directly overhead at the Earth's *Equator and consequently day and night are of equal length at all latitudes. This happens twice a year: 21 March is the spring, or vernal, equinox and 23 September is the autumn equinox.

era any of the major divisions of geological time that includes several periods but is part of an eon. The eras of the current Phanerozoic in chronological order are the Palaeozoic, Mesozoic, and Cenozoic. We are living in the Recent epoch of the Quaternary period of the Cenozoic era.

Erasmus, Desiderius (c. 1469–1536) Dutch scholar and leading humanist of the Renaissance era, who taught and studied all over Europe and was a prolific writer. His pioneer translation of the Greek New Testament (with parallel Latin text, 1516) exposed the Vulgate as a second-hand document. Although opposed to dogmatism and abuse of church power, he remained impartial during Martin *Luther's conflict with the pope.

Eratosthenes (c. 276–c. 194 BC) Greek geographer and mathematician whose map of the ancient world was the first to contain lines of latitude and longitude, and who calculated the Earth's circumference with an error of about 10%. His mathematical achievements include a method for duplicating the cube, and for finding *prime numbers (Eratosthenes' sieve).

erbium chemical symbol Er, soft, lustrous, greyish, metallic element of the *lanthanide series, atomic number 68, relative atomic mass 167.26. It occurs with the element yttrium or as a minute part of various minerals. It was discovered in 1843 by Carl Mosander (1797–1858), and named after the town of Ytterby, Sweden, near which the lanthanides (rare-earth elements) were first found. Erbium has been used since 1987 to amplify data pulses in optical fibres, enabling faster transmission. Erbium ions in the fibreglass, charged with infrared light, emit energy by amplifying the data pulse as it moves along the fibre.

Erebus in Greek mythology, the god of darkness; also the intermediate subterranean region between upper Earth and *Hades through which the spirits (shades) passed.

Erebus, Mount the world's southernmost active volcano, located on Ross Island, Antarctica; height 4,072 m/13,359 ft.

ergonomics study of the relationship between people and the furniture, tools, and machinery they use at work. The object is to improve work performance by removing sources of muscular stress and general fatigue: for example, by presenting data and control panels in easy-to-view form, making office furniture comfortable, and creating a generally pleasant environment.

ergot any of a group of parasitic fungi (especially of the genus *Claviceps*), whose brown or black grainlike masses replace the kernels of rye or other cereals. *C. purpurea* attacks the rye plant. Ergot poisoning is caused by eating infected bread, resulting in burning pains, gangrene, and convulsions.

Erhard, Ludwig (1897–1977) German economist and Christian Democrat politician, chancellor of the Federal Republic 1963–66. He became known as the 'father of the German economic miracle'. As economics minister 1949–63 he instituted policies driven by his vision of a 'social market economy', in which a capitalist free market would be tempered by an active role for the state in providing a market-friendly social welfare system. His period as chancellor was less distinguished.

erica any plant of a large group that includes the heathers. There are about 500 species, distributed mainly in South Africa with some in Europe. (Genus *Erica*, family Ericaceae.)

Eric the Red (c. 950–1010) Allegedly the first European to find Greenland. According to a 13th-century saga, he was the son of a Norwegian chieftain, and was banished from Iceland in about 982 for murder. He then sailed westward and discovered a land that he called Greenland.

Eridanus sixth-largest constellation, which meanders from the celestial equator (see *celestial sphere) deep into the southern hemisphere of the sky. Eridanus is represented as a river. Its brightest star is *Achernar, a corruption of the Arabic for 'the end of the river'.

Erie, Lake fourth largest of the Great Lakes of North America, connected to Lake Ontario by the Niagara

River and bypassed by the Welland Canal; length 388 km/
241 mi; width 48–91 km/30–56 mi; area 25,720 sq km/
9,930 sq mi. The most southerly of the Great Lakes,
it is bounded on the north by Ontario, Canada; on
the south and southeast by Ohio, Pennsylvania, and
New York State; and on the west by Michigan. Lake Erie
is an important link in the St Lawrence Seaway.

Eritrea
National name: *Hagere Eretra al-Dawla al-Iritra/
State of Eritrea*

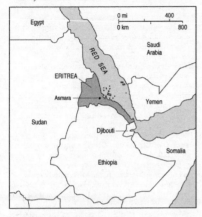

Area: 125,000 sq km/48,262 sq mi
Capital: Asmara
Major towns/cities: Assab, Keren, Massawa, Adi Ugri, Ed
Major ports: Assab, Massawa
Physical features: coastline along the Red Sea 1,000
km/620 mi; narrow coastal plain that rises to an inland
plateau; Dahlak Islands
Head of state and government: Issaias Afwerki from
1993
Political system: nationalistic socialist
Political executive: unlimited presidency
Political parties: People's Front for Democracy and
Justice (PFDJ) (formerly Eritrean People's Liberation
Front: EPLF), left of centre, the only party recognised
by the government; Eritrean National Pact Alliance
(ENPA), moderate, centrist
Currency: nakfa
GNI per capita (PPP): (US$) 950 (2002 est)
Exports: textiles, leather and leather products,
beverages, petroleum products, basic household goods.
Principal market: Sudan 27.2% (1998)
Population: 4,141,000 (2003 est)
Language: Tigre, Tigrinya, Arabic, English, Afar,
Amharic, Kunama, Italian
Religion: mainly Sunni Muslim and Coptic Christian,
some Roman Catholic, Protestant, and animist
Life expectancy: 51 (men); 54 (women) (2000–05)
Chronology
4th–7th centuries AD: Part of Ethiopian Aksum
kingdom.
8th century: Islam introduced to coastal areas by Arabs.
12th–16th centuries: Under influence of Ethiopian
Abyssinian kingdoms.

mid-16th century: Came under control of Turkish
Ottoman Empire.
1882: Occupied by Italy.
1889: Italian colony of Eritrea created out of Ottoman
areas and coastal districts of Ethiopia.
1920s: Massawa developed into the largest port in
East Africa.
1935–36: Used as base for Italy's conquest of Ethiopia
and became part of Italian East Africa.
1941: Became British protectorate after Italy removed
from North Africa.
1952: Federation formed with Ethiopia by United
Nations (UN).
1958: Eritrean People's Liberation Front (EPLF) was
formed to fight for independence after a general strike
was brutally suppressed by Ethiopian rulers.
1962: Annexed by Ethiopia, sparking a secessionist
rebellion which was to last 30 years and claim 150,000
lives.
1974: Ethiopian emperor Haile Selassie was deposed
by the military; the EPLF continued the struggle for
independence.
1977–78: The EPLF cleared the territory of Ethiopian
forces, but the position was soon reversed by the
Soviet-backed Marxist Ethiopian government of
Col Mengistu Haile Mariam.
mid-1980s: There was severe famine in Eritrea and
a refugee crisis as the Ethiopian government sought
forcible resettlement.
1990: The strategic port of Massawa was captured by
Eritrean rebel forces.
1991: Ethiopian president Mengistu was overthrown.
The EPLF secured the whole of Eritrea and a
provisional government was formed under Issaias
Afwerki.
1993: Independence was approved in a regional
referendum and recognized by Ethiopia. A transitional
government was established, with Afwerki elected
president; 500,000 refugees outside Eritrea began to
return.
1998: Border disputes with Ethiopia escalated, with
bombing raids from both sides.
1999: The border dispute with Ethiopia erupted into
war in February. Peace was agreed the following
month, but fighting was renewed.
2000: An Ethiopian military offensive caused Eritrea
to pull its forces back to the line it held before the
escalation of violence in 1998. A ceasefire was agreed in
June and a peace agreement signed in December that
provided for UN troops to keep the peace along the
border.
2003: Ethiopia rejected the UN-sponsored ruling on
the border issue.

ERM abbreviation for *Exchange Rate Mechanism.

ermine the *stoat during winter, when its coat becomes
white. In northern latitudes the coat becomes
completely white, except for a black tip on the tail, but
in warmer regions the back may remain brownish.
The fur is used commercially.

Ernst, Max (1891–1976) German artist, a major
figure in *Dada and then *surrealism. He worked in
France 1922–38 and in the USA from 1941. He
experimented with collage, photomontage, and surreal
images, creating some of the most haunting and
distinctive images of 20th-century art. His works

include *The Elephant Celebes* (1921; Tate Gallery, London) and *The Temptation of St Anthony* (1945; Lehmbruck Museum, Duisburg).

Eros in astronomy, asteroid discovered in 1898 by German astronomer Gustav Witt. It was the first asteroid to be discovered that has an orbit coming within that of Mars. It passes within 22 million km/ 14 million mi of the Earth. It is elongated, measures $33 \times 13 \times 13$ km/$21 \times 8 \times 8$ mi, rotates around its shortest axis every 5.3 hours, and orbits the Sun every 1.8 years.

erosion wearing away of the Earth's surface by a moving agent, caused by the breakdown and transport of particles of rock or soil. Agents of erosion include the sea, rivers, glaciers, and wind. By contrast, *weathering does not involve transportation.

erratic in geology, a displaced rock that has been transported by a glacier or some other natural force to a site of different geological composition.

error in computing, a fault or mistake, either in the software or on the part of the user, that causes a program to stop running (crash) or produce unexpected results. Program errors, or bugs, are largely eliminated in the course of the programmer's initial testing procedure, but some will remain in most programs. All computer operating systems are designed to produce an **error message** (on the display screen, or in an error file or printout) whenever an error is detected, reporting that an error has taken place and, wherever possible, diagnosing its cause.

ESA abbreviation for *European Space Agency.

escape velocity minimum velocity required for a spacecraft or other object to escape from the gravitational pull of a planetary body. In the case of the Earth, the escape velocity is 11.2 kps/6.9 mps; the Moon, 2.4 kps/1.5 mps; Mars, 5 kps/3.1 mps; and Jupiter, 59.6 kps/37 mps.

escarpment *or* **cuesta** large ridge created by the erosion of dipping sedimentary rocks. It has one steep side (scarp) and one gently sloping side (dip). Escarpments are common features of chalk landscapes, such as the Chiltern Hills and the North Downs in England. Certain features are associated with chalk escarpments, including dry valleys (formed on the dip slope), combes (steep-sided valleys on the scarp slope), and springs.

Escher, M(aurits) C(ornelis) (1898–1972) Dutch graphic artist. His prints are often based on mathematical concepts and contain paradoxes and illusions. The lithograph *Ascending and Descending* (1960), with interlocking staircases creating a perspective puzzle, is a typical work. His work has continued to fascinate artists, mathematicians, psychologists, and the general public.

Escherichia coli *or* **colon bacillus** rod-shaped Gram-negative bacterium (see *bacteria) that lives, usually harmlessly, in the colon of most warm-blooded animals. It is the commonest cause of urinary tract infections in humans. It is sometimes found in water or meat where faecal contamination has occurred and can cause severe gastric problems. The mapping of the genome of *E. coli*, consisting of 4,403 genes, was completed in 1997. It is probably the organism about which most molecular genetics is known, and is of pre-eminent importance in recombinant DNA research. It is the only species in the bacterial family Enterobacteriaceae.

Eskimo Algonquian term for Arctic peoples meaning 'eater of raw meat', now considered offensive. See *Inuit.

ESP abbreviation for *extrasensory perception.

esparto species of grass native to southern Spain, southern Portugal, and the Balearics, but now widely grown in dry, sandy locations throughout the world. The plant is just over 1 m/3 ft high, producing greyish-green leaves, which are used for making paper, ropes, baskets, mats, and cables. (*Stipa tenacissima*.)

Esperanto language devised in 1887 by Polish philologist Ludwig L Zamenhof as an international auxiliary language. For its structure and vocabulary it draws on Latin, the Romance languages, English, and German. At its centenary in 1987, Esperantists claimed 10–15 million users worldwide.

essay short piece of non-fiction writing, often dealing with a particular subject from a personal point of view. The essay became a recognized form with the publication of *Essais* (1580) by French writer *Montaigne and *Essays* (1597) by English politician, philosopher, and writer Francis *Bacon. Today the essay is a part of journalism; articles in the broadsheet newspapers are in the essay tradition.

Essex (Old English East-Seaxe) county of southeast England, which has contained the unitary authorities of Southend and Thurrock since April 1998.
area: 3,670 sq km/1,417 sq mi **towns and cities:** Chelmsford (administrative headquarters), Basildon, Colchester, Harlow, Harwich (port), Clacton-on-Sea (resort) **physical:** flat and marshy near the coast; richly wooded in the southwest; rivers: the Blackwater, Crouch, Colne, Lee, Stour, and Thames **features:** former royal hunting ground of Epping Forest (2300 ha/5680 acres, controlled from 1882 by the City of London); since 1111 at Little Dunmow (and later at Great Dunmow) the Dunmow flitch (side of cured pork) can be claimed every four years by any couple proving to a jury they have not regretted their marriage within the year (winners are few); Stansted, London's third airport; new Roman Catholic cathedral at Brentwood (designed by Quinlan Terry), dedicated in 1991. **population:** (2001 est) 1,312,700.

Essex, Robert Devereux, 2nd Earl of Essex (1566–1601) English soldier and politician. Having taken part in the Dutch fight against Spain, he became a favourite with Queen *Elizabeth I in 1587, but fell from grace because of his policies in Ireland, where he was Lieutenant from 1599, and was executed.

Establishment, the a perceived elite of the professional and governing classes (judges, civil servants, politicians, and so on) who collectively symbolize authority and the status quo.

estate in European history, an order of society that enjoyed a specified share in government. In medieval theory, there were usually three estates – the **nobility**, the **clergy**, and the **commons** – with the functions of, respectively, defending society from foreign aggression and internal disorder, attending to its spiritual needs, and working to produce the base with which to support the other two orders.

ester organic compound formed by the reaction between an alcohol and an acid, with the elimination of water. Unlike *salts, esters are covalent compounds.

Estonia
National name: *Eesti Vabariik/Republic of Estonia*

Area: 45,000 sq km/17,374 sq mi
Capital: Tallinn
Major towns/cities: Tartu, Narva, Kohtla-Järve, Pärnu
Physical features: lakes and marshes in a partly
forested plain; 774 km/481 mi of coastline; mild climate;
Lake Peipus and Narva River forming boundary with
Russian Federation; Baltic islands, the largest of which
is Saaremaa
Head of state: Arnold Rüütl from 2001
Head of government: Juhan Parts from 2003
Political system: emergent democracy
Political executive: dual executive
Political parties: Coalition Party (KMU), ex-communist,
left of centre, 'social market'; Isamaa (National
Fatherland Party, or Pro Patria), right wing, nationalist,
free market; Estonian Reform Party (ERP), free market;
Centre Party (CP), moderate nationalist (formerly the
Estonian Popular Front (EPF; Rahvarinne); Estonian
National Independence Party (ENIP), radical nationalist;
Communist Party of Estonia (CPE); Our Home is Estonia;
Estonian Social Democratic Party (ESDP) (last three draw
much of their support from ethnic Russian community)
Currency: kroon
GNI per capita (PPP): (US$) 11,120 (2002 est)
Exports: foodstuffs, animal products, textiles, timber
products, base metals, mineral products, machinery.
Principal market: Finland 33.8% (2001)
Population: 1,323,000 (2003 est)
Language: Estonian (official), Russian
Religion: Eastern Orthodox, Evangelical Lutheran,
Russian Orthodox, Muslim, Judaism
Life expectancy: 67 (men); 77 (women) (2000–05)
Chronology
1st century AD: First independent state formed.
9th century: Invaded by Vikings.
13th century: Tallinn, in the Danish-controlled north,
joined Hanseatic League, a northern European union
of commercial towns; Livonia, comprising southern
Estonia and Latvia, came under control of German
Teutonic Knights and was converted to Christianity.
1561: Sweden took control of northern Estonia.
1629: Sweden took control of southern Estonia from
Poland.
1721: Sweden ceded the country to tsarist Russia.

late 19th century: Estonian nationalist movement
developed in opposition to Russian political and
cultural repression and German economic control.
1914: Occupied by German troops.
1918–19: Estonian nationalists, led by Konstantin Pats,
proclaimed and achieved independence, despite efforts
by the Russian Red Army to regain control.
1920s: Land reforms and cultural advances under
democratic regime.
1934: Pats overthrew parliamentary democracy in a
quasi-fascist coup at a time of economic depression;
Baltic Entente mutual defence pact signed with Latvia
and Lithuania.
1940: Estonia incorporated into Soviet Union (USSR);
100,000 Estonians deported to Siberia or killed.
1941–44: German occupation during World War II.
1944: USSR regained control; 'Sovietization' followed,
including agricultural collectivization and immigration
of ethnic Russians.
late 1980s: Beginnings of nationalist dissent,
encouraged by *glasnost* initiative of reformist Soviet
leader Mikhail Gorbachev.
1988: Popular Front (EPF) established to campaign
for democracy. Sovereignty declaration issued by state
assembly rejected by USSR as unconstitutional.
1989: Estonian replaced Russian as the main language.
1990: The CPE monopoly of power was abolished;
pro-independence candidates secured a majority after
multiparty elections; a coalition government was
formed with EPF leader Edgar Savisaar as prime
minister; Arnold Rüütel became president. The prewar
constitution was partially restored.
1991: Independence was achieved after an attempted
anti-Gorbachev coup in Moscow; the CPE was
outlawed. Estonia joined the United Nations (UN).
1992: Savisaar resigned over food and energy shortages;
Isamaa leader Lennart Meri became president and free-
marketer Mart Laar prime minister.
1993: Estonia joined the Council of Europe and signed
a free-trade agreement with Latvia and Lithuania.
1994: The last Russian troops were withdrawn. A radical
economic reform programme was introduced; a
controversial law on 'aliens' was passed, requiring non-
ethnic Estonians to apply for residency. Laar resigned.
1995: Former communists won the largest number of
seats in a general election; a left-of-centre coalition
was formed under Tiit Vahi.
1996: President Meri was re-elected. The ruling
coalition collapsed; Prime Minister Tiit Vahi continued
with a minority government.
1997: Vahi, accused of corruption, resigned and was
replaced by Mart Siimann. Estonia was invited to begin
European Union (EU) membership negotiations.
1998: The legislature voted to ban electoral alliances
in future elections.
1999: Mart Laar became prime minister.
2002: EU accepted Estonia for membership in 2004,
subject to a referendum.
2003: In a referendum, 67% of voters supported
accession to the European Union (EU) in 2004.
2004: Estonia joined the EU and, later in the year, NATO.
Estonian the largest ethnic group in Estonia. There are
1 million speakers of the Estonian language, a member
of the Finno-Ugric branch of the Uralic family. Most
live in Estonia.

etching printmaking technique in which a metal plate (usually copper or zinc) is covered with a waxy overlayer (ground) and then drawn on with an etching needle. The exposed areas are then 'etched', or bitten into, by a corrosive agent (acid), so that they will hold ink for printing.

ethanal common name **acetaldehyde**; CH_3CHO, one of the chief members of the group of organic compounds known as *aldehydes. It is a colourless flammable liquid boiling at 20.8 °C/69.6 °F. Ethanal is formed by the oxidation of ethanol or ethene and is used to make many other organic chemical compounds.

ethanoate common name **acetate**; $CH_3CO_2^-$, negative ion derived from ethanoic (acetic) acid; any salt containing this ion. In photography, acetate film is a non-flammable film made of cellulose ethanoate. In textiles, it is known as acetate, and is most commonly known in the form of a *synthetic fibre which can be woven or knitted to produce a variety of different fabrics including satin, moire, and taffeta. Fabrics made from acetate absorb moisture, do not shrink, and are cheaper to produce than natural fibres, but they also tend to attract dirt and can be damaged by heat. Acetate filaments are also used to make filters for cigarettes.

ethanoic acid common name **acetic acid**; CH_3CO_2H, one of the simplest carboxylic acids (fatty acids). In the pure state it is a colourless liquid with an unpleasant pungent odour; it solidifies to an icelike mass of crystals at 16.7 °C/62.4 °F, and hence is often called glacial ethanoic acid. In a dilute form, mixed with water, it is the acid found in vinegar. Vinegar contains 5% or more ethanoic acid, produced by fermentation.

ethanol *or* **ethyl alcohol** C_2H_5OH, alcohol found in beer, wine, cider, spirits, and other alcoholic drinks. When pure, it is a colourless liquid with a pleasant odour, miscible with water or ether; it burns in air with a pale blue flame. The vapour forms an explosive mixture with air and may be used in high-compression internal combustion engines. It is produced naturally by the fermentation of carbohydrates by yeast cells. Industrially, it can be made by absorption of *ethene and subsequent reaction with water, or by the reduction of ethanal (acetaldehyde) in the presence of a catalyst, and is widely used as a solvent.

Ethelbert (*c.* 552–616) King of Kent 560–616. He was defeated by the West Saxons in 568 but later became ruler of England south of the River Humber. Ethelbert received the Christian missionary Augustine in 597 and later converted to become the first Christian ruler of Anglo-Saxon England. He issued the first written code of laws known in England.

Ethelred (II) the Unready (968–1016) King of England from 978, following the murder of his half-brother, Edward the Martyr. He was son of King Edgar. Ethelred tried to buy off the Danish raiders by paying Danegeld. In 1002 he ordered the massacre of the Danish settlers, provoking an invasion by Sweyn I of Denmark. War with Sweyn and Sweyn's son, Canute, occupied the rest of Ethelred's reign. His nickname is a corruption of the Old English 'unreed', meaning badly counselled or poorly advised.

ethene common name **ethylene**; C_2H_4, colourless, flammable gas, the first member of the *alkene series of hydrocarbons. It is the most widely used synthetic organic chemical and is used to produce the plastics *polythene (polyethene), polychloroethene, and polyvinyl chloride (PVC). It is obtained from natural gas or coal gas, or by the dehydration of ethanol.

ether any of a series of organic chemical compounds having an oxygen atom linking the carbon atoms of two hydrocarbon radical groups (general formula R-O-R′); also the common name for ethoxyethane $C_2H_5OC_2H_5$ (also called diethyl ether). This is used as an anaesthetic and as an external cleansing agent before surgical operations. It is also used as a solvent, and in the extraction of oils, fats, waxes, resins, and alkaloids.

ethics *or* **moral philosophy** branch of *philosophy concerned with the systematic study of human values. It involves the study of theories of conduct and goodness, and of the meanings of moral terms.

Ethiopia
formerly **Abyssinia** (until the 1920s)
National name: *Ya'Ityopya Federalawi Dimokrasiyawi Repeblik/Federal Democratic Republic of Ethiopia*

Area: 1,096,900 sq km/423,513 sq mi
Capital: Addis Ababa
Major towns/cities: Jimma, Dire Dawa, Harar, Nazret, Dese, Gonder, Mek'ele, Bahir Dar
Physical features: a high plateau with central mountain range divided by Rift Valley; plains in east; source of Blue Nile River; Danakil and Ogaden deserts
Head of state: Girma Woldegiorgis from 2001
Head of government: Meles Zenawi from 1995
Political system: emergent democracy
Political executive: limited presidency
Political parties: Ethiopian People's Revolutionary Democratic Front (EPRDF), nationalist, left of centre; Tigré People's Liberation Front (TPLF); Ethiopian People's Democratic Movement (EPDM); United Oromo Liberation Front, Islamic nationalist
Currency: Ethiopian birr
GNI per capita (PPP): (US$) 720 (2002 est)
Exports: coffee, hides and skins, petroleum products, oilseeds, fruit and vegetables. Principal market: Djibouti 13.2% (2001)
Population: 70,678,000 (2003 est)
Language: Amharic (official), Arabic, Tigrinya, Orominga, about 100 other local languages
Religion: Muslim 45%, Ethiopian Orthodox Church (which has had its own patriarch since 1976) 35%, animist 12%, other Christian 8%

Life expectancy: 45 (men); 46 (women) (2000–05)

Chronology

1st–7th centuries AD: Founded by Semitic immigrants from Saudi Arabia, the kingdom of Aksum and its capital, northwest of Adwa, flourished. It reached its peak in the 4th century when Coptic Christianity was introduced from Egypt.

7th century onwards: Islam was spread by Arab conquerors.

11th century: Emergence of independent Ethiopian kingdom of Abyssinia, which was to remain dominant for nine centuries.

late 15th century: Abyssinia visited by Portuguese explorers.

1889: Abyssinia reunited by Menelik II.

1896: Invasion by Italy defeated by Menelik at Adwa, who went on to annex Ogaden in the southeast and areas to the west.

1916: Haile Selassie became regent.

1930: Haile Selassie became emperor.

1936: Conquered by Italy and incorporated in Italian East Africa.

1941: Return of Emperor Selassie after liberation by the British.

1952: Ethiopia federated with Eritrea.

1962: Eritrea annexed by Selassie; Eritrean People's Liberation front (EPLF) resistance movement began, a rebellion that was to continue for 30 years.

1963: First conference of Selassie-promoted Organization of African Unity (OAU; later African Union) held in Addis Ababa.

1973–74: Severe famine in northern Ethiopia; 200,000 died in Wallo province.

1974: Haile Selassie deposed and replaced by a military government.

1977: Col Mengistu Haile Mariam took over the government. Somali forces ejected from the Somali-peopled Ogaden in the southeast.

1977–79: 'Red Terror' period in which Mengistu's single-party Marxist regime killed thousands of people and promoted collective farming; Tigré People's Liberation Front guerrillas began fighting for regional autonomy in the northern highlands.

1984: The Workers' Party of Ethiopia (WPE) was declared the only legal political party.

1985: The worst famine in more than a decade; Western aid was sent and forcible internal resettlement programmes undertaken in Eritrea and Tigré in the north.

1987: Mengistu Mariam was elected president under a new constitution. There was another famine; food aid was hindered by guerrillas.

1989: Peace talks with Eritrean rebels were mediated by the former US president Jimmy Carter.

1991: Mengistu was overthrown; a transitional government was set up by the opposing Ethiopian People's Revolutionary Democratic Front (EPRDF), headed by Meles Zenawi. The EPLF took control of Eritrea. Famine again gripped the country.

1993: Eritrean independence was recognized after a referendum; private farming and market sector were encouraged by the EPRDF government.

1994: A new federal constitution was adopted.

1995: The ruling EPRDF won a majority in the first multiparty elections to an interim parliament. Negasso

Ghidada was chosen as president; Zenawi was appointed premier.

1998: There was a border dispute with Eritrea.

1999: The border dispute with Eritrea erupted into war. Peace proposals were agreed by Eritrea but fighting continued.

2000: A ceasefire with Eritrea was agreed in June and a peace agreement signed in December that provided for UN troops to keep the peace along the border. Haile Selassie was ceremoniously reburied in Addis Ababa.

2001: Prime Minister Zenawi survived an attempt by his own party, the Tigrayan People's Liberation Front (TPLF), to remove him from office.

2003: Ethiopia rejected the UN-sponsored ruling on the border with Eritrea.

2004: In an effort to avoid recurrent drought and famine problems the government began a massive relocation of the population of the arid eastern highlands.

ethnic cleansing the forced expulsion of one ethnic group by another to create a homogenous population, for example, of more than 2 million Muslims by Serbs in Bosnia-Herzegovina 1992–95. The term has also been used to describe the killing of Hutus and Tutsis in Rwanda and Burundi in 1994, and for earlier mass exiles, as far back as the book of Exodus.

ethnography study of living cultures, using anthropological techniques like participant observation (where the anthropologist lives in the society being studied) and a reliance on informants. Ethnography has provided much data of use to archaeologists as analogies.

ethnology study of contemporary peoples, concentrating on their geography and culture, as distinct from their social systems. Ethnologists make a comparative analysis of data from different cultures to understand how cultures work and why they change, with a view to deriving general principles about human society.

ethology comparative study of animal behaviour in its natural setting. Ethology is concerned with the causal mechanisms (both the stimuli that elicit behaviour and the physiological mechanisms controlling it), as well as the development of behaviour, its function, and its evolutionary history.

ethyl alcohol common name for *ethanol.

ethylene common name for *ethene.

ethyne common name **acetylene**; CHCH, colourless inflammable gas produced by mixing calcium carbide and water. It is the simplest member of the *alkyne series of hydrocarbons. It is used in the manufacture of the synthetic rubber neoprene, and in oxyacetylene welding and cutting.

etiolation in botany, a form of growth seen in plants receiving insufficient light. It is characterized by long, weak stems, small leaves, and a pale yellowish colour (*chlorosis) due to a lack of chlorophyll. The rapid increase in height enables a plant that is surrounded by others to quickly reach a source of light, after which a return to normal growth usually occurs.

Etna, Mount volcano on the east coast of the Italian island of Sicily, 3,323 m/10,906 ft, the highest active volcano in Europe. About 90 eruptions have been recorded since 1800 BC, yet the lower slopes are densely populated because of the rich soil. This cultivated zone includes the coastal town of Catania.

Etruscan member of an ancient people inhabiting Etruria, Italy (modern-day Tuscany and part of Umbria) from the 8th to 2nd centuries BC. The Etruscan dynasty of the Tarquins ruled Rome 616–509 BC. At the height of their civilization, in the 6th century BC, the Etruscans achieved great wealth and power from their maritime strength. They were driven out of Rome in 509 BC and eventually dominated by the Romans.

Etruscan art the art of the inhabitants of Etruria, central Italy, a civilization that flourished 8th–2nd centuries BC. The Etruscans produced sculpture, painting, pottery, metalwork, and jewellery. Etruscan terracotta coffins (sarcophagi), carved with reliefs and topped with portraits of the dead reclining on one elbow, were to influence the later Romans and early Christians.

étude (French 'study') in music, an exercise designed to develop technique. Although originally intended for practice only, some composers, notably Frédéric Chopin, wrote études of such virtuosity that they are now used as concert showpieces.

etymology study of the origin and history of words within and across languages. It has two major aspects: the study of the phonetic and written forms of words, and of the semantics or meanings of those words.

EU abbreviation for *European Union.

eucalyptus any tree of a group belonging to the myrtle family, native to Australia, where they are commonly known as gumtrees. About 90% of Australian timber belongs to the eucalyptus genus, which contains about 500 species. The trees have dark hardwood timber which is used for heavy construction work such as railway and bridge building. They are mostly tall, aromatic, evergreen trees with pendant leaves and white, pink, or red flowers. (Genus *Eucalyptus*, family Myrtaceae.)

Euclid (*c.* 330–*c.* 260 BC) Greek mathematician who wrote the *Stoicheia/Elements* in 13 books, nine of which deal with plane and solid geometry and four with number theory. His great achievement lay in the systematic arrangement of previous mathematical discoveries and a methodology based on axioms, definitions, and theorems.

eugenics (Greek *eugenes* 'well-born') study of ways in which the physical and mental characteristics of the human race may be improved. The eugenic principle was abused by the Nazi Party in Germany during the 1930s and early 1940s to justify the attempted extermination of entire social and ethnic groups and the establishment of selective breeding programmes. Modern eugenics is concerned mainly with the elimination of genetic disease.

eukaryote in biology, one of the two major groupings (superkingdoms) into which all organisms are divided. Included are all organisms, except bacteria and cyanobacteria (*blue-green algae), which belong to the *prokaryote grouping.

Eumenides *or* **Semnai** (Greek 'kindly ones') in Greek mythology, an appeasing name for the *Furies, used by 458 BC in *Eumenides* by the Greek dramatist *Aeschylus. Originally they were worshipped at the foot of the Areopagus in Athens, in Colonus, and outside Attica; their cult was similar to that of *Gaia, mother of the Earth.

eunuch (Greek *eunoukhos* 'one in charge of a bed') castrated man. Originally eunuchs were bedchamber attendants in harems in the East, but as they were usually castrated to keep them from taking too great an interest in their charges, the term became applied more generally. In China, eunuchs were employed within the imperial harem from some 4,000 years ago and by medieval times wielded considerable political power. Eunuchs often filled high offices of state in India and Persia.

euphemism figure of speech that substitutes a direct or offensive statement with one that is suitably mild or evasive. Thus, 'he passed away' is used in place of 'he died'; 'sleep with someone' substitutes for 'have sex with someone'; and 'liquidate the opposition' has a softer impact than 'kill one's enemies'.

euphonium tenor four-valved brass band instrument of the bugle type, often mistaken for a tuba. It is used chiefly in brass and military bands.

Euphrates Turkish **Firat**; Arabic **Al Furat**, river rising in east Turkey and flowing through Syria and Iraq, joining the River Tigris above Basra to form the River *Shatt-al-Arab at the head of the Gulf; length 3,600 km/ 2,240 mi. The ancient cities of Babylon, Eridu, and Ur were situated along its course and depended largely for their prosperity on irrigation from its waters.

Eurasia the combined land areas of *Europe and *Asia.

Eurasian a person of mixed European and Asian parentage; also, native to or an inhabitant of both Europe and Asia.

Eureka Stockade incident at Ballarat, Australia, when about 150 goldminers, or 'diggers', rebelled against the Victorian state police and military authorities. They took refuge behind a wooden stockade, which was taken in a few minutes by the military on 3 December 1854. Some 30 gold diggers were killed, and a few soldiers killed or wounded, but the majority of the rebels were taken prisoner. Among those who escaped was Peter Lalor, their leader. Of the 13 tried for treason, all were acquitted, thus marking the emergence of Australian democracy.

eurhythmics practice of coordinated bodily movement as an aid to musical development. It was founded about 1900 by the Swiss musician Emile Jaques-Dalcroze, professor of harmony at the Geneva conservatoire. He devised a series of 'gesture' songs, to be sung simultaneously with certain bodily actions.

Euripides (*c.* 485–*c.* 406 BC) Athenian tragic dramatist. He is ranked with Aeschylus and Sophocles as one of the three great tragedians. His plays deal with the emotions and reactions of ordinary people and social issues rather than with deities and the grandiose themes of his contemporaries. He wrote about 90 plays, of which 18 and some long fragments survive. These include *Alcestis* (438 BC), *Medea* (431 BC), *Andromache* (about 430 BC), *Hippolytus* (428 BC), the satyr-drama *Cyclops* (about 424–423 BC), *Electra* (417 BC), *Trojan Women* (415 BC), *Iphigenia in Tauris* (413 BC), *Iphigenia in Aulis* (about 414–412 BC), and *The Bacchae* (about 405 BC) (the last two were produced shortly after his death).

euro single currency of the *European Union (EU), which was officially launched on 1 January 1999 in 11 of the 15 EU member states (Austria, Belgium, Finland, France, Germany, Republic of Ireland, Italy,

Luxembourg, the Netherlands, Portugal, and Spain). Greece adopted the euro on 1 January 2001. Euro notes and coins were introduced from 1 January 2002, circulating in parallel with national currencies for two months. Thereafter the national currencies was abolished.

Europa in astronomy, fourth-largest moon of the planet Jupiter, diameter 3,140 km/1,950 mi, orbiting 671,000 km/417,000 mi from the planet every 3.55 days. It is covered by ice and was originally thought to be criss-crossed by thousands of thin cracks some 50,000 km/30,000 mi long. These are now known to be low ridges.

Europa in Greek mythology, a princess carried off by Zeus under the guise of a white bull. She was the daughter of the Phoenician king Agenor of Tyre; sister of Cadmus, founder of Thebes; and the personification of the continent of Europe.

Europe the second-smallest continent, occupying 8% of the Earth's surface. It is bounded on the north by the Arctic Ocean, on the west by the Atlantic Ocean, and on the south by the Mediterranean Sea; its eastern border conventionally runs along the Ural Mountains and Ural River, swinging south to include the trans-Caucasian republics. Europe can be divided into six composite regions, which are not all equally homogeneous: Scandinavia, Western Europe, Central Europe, Eastern Europe, Mediterranean Europe, and the Balkans. **area:** 10,400,000 sq km/4,000,000 sq mi **population:** (2000 est) 728 million (excluding European Turkey); annual growth rate -0.1% (2000–2005); projected population of 705 million by the year 2020. Of the continents, Europe ranks third in total population and first in population density **language:** mostly Indo-European, with a few exceptions, including Finno-Ugric (Finnish and Hungarian), Basque, and Altaic (Turkish); apart from a fringe of Celtic, the northwest is Germanic; Letto-Lithuanian languages separate the Germanic from the Slavonic tongues of Eastern Europe; Romance languages spread east–west from Romania through Italy and France to Spain and Portugal **religion:** Christian (Protestant, Roman Catholic, Eastern Orthodox), Muslim (Turkey, Albania, Bosnia-Herzegovina, Bulgaria), Jewish **largest cities:** (population over 1.5 million) Ankara, Athens, Barcelona, Berlin, Birmingham, Bucharest, Budapest, Hamburg, Istanbul, Kharkov, Kiev, Lisbon, London, Madrid, Manchester, Milan, Minsk, Moscow, Paris, Rome, St Petersburg, Vienna, Warsaw **features:** Mount Elbrus 5,642 m/18,517 ft in the Caucasus Mountains is the highest peak in Europe; Mont Blanc 4,807 m/15,772 ft is the highest peak in the Alps; lakes (over 5,100 sq km/ 2,000 sq mi) include Ladoga, Onega, Vänern; rivers (over 800 km/500 mi) include the Volga, Danube, Dnieper Ural, Don, Pechora, Dniester, Rhine, Loire, Tagus, Vistula, Elbe, Weser, Ebro, Oder, Prut, Rhône **physical:** conventionally occupying that part of Eurasia to the west of the Ural Mountains, north of the Caucasus Mountains, and north of the Sea of Marmara, Europe lies entirely in the northern hemisphere between 36° N and the Arctic Ocean. About two-thirds of the continent is a great plain which covers the whole of European Russia and spreads westwards through Poland to the Low Countries and the Bay of Biscay. To the north lie the Scandinavian highlands, rising to 2,472 m/8,110 ft at Glittertind in the Jotenheim range of Norway. To the south, a series of mountain ranges stretch east–west (Caucasus, Balkans, Carpathians, Apennines, Alps, Pyrenees, and Sierra Nevada). The most westerly point of the mainland is Cape Roca in Portugal; the most southerly location is Tarifa Point in Spain; the most northerly point on the mainland is Nordkynn in Norway.

European the natives and inhabitants of the continent of Europe and their descendants. Europe is multicultural and, although most of its languages belong to the Indo-European family, there are also speakers of Uralic (such as Hungarian) and Altaic (such as Turkish) languages, as well as Basque.

European Commission executive body that proposes legislation on which the *Council of the European Union and the *European Parliament decide, and implements the decisions made in the *European Union (EU). The European Commission is the biggest of the European institutions, and must work in close partnership with the governments of the member states and with the other European institutions. The aim of the Commission is to ensure the close union of EU member states, and to defend the interests of Europe's citizens. As well as having responsibility for policy and legislative proposals, the European Commission ensures that legislation passed by the EU is applied correctly; if it is not, the Commission can take action against the public or private sector. The Commission also manages policies and negotiates international trade and cooperation agreements. The president of the Commission is José Manuel Durão Barroso, from 2004.

European Community (EC) collective term for the European Economic Community (EEC), the European Coal and Steel Community (ECSC), and the European Atomic Energy Community (Euratom). The EC is now a separate legal entity with the *European Union (EU), which was established under the *Maastricht Treaty (1992) and includes intergovernmental cooperation on security and judicial affairs.

European Council name given to the meetings or summits between the heads of state and government of the *European Union (EU) member states and the president of the *European Commission. The council meets at least twice a year, usually towards the end of each country's rotating six-month presidency, and gives overall direction to the work of the EU. Foreign ministers and other ministers attend by invitation. The member state holding the presidency hosts the European Council.

European Court of Human Rights court established under the European Convention on Human Rights (1950), whereby cases of alleged human rights violations were referred to the Court by the then **European Commission of Human Rights**, or by a member state of the *Council of Europe following a report by the Commission. Under organizational and supervisory reforms, a revised Court came into operation in November 1998.

European Court of Justice court of the *European Union (EU) responsible for interpreting *Community law and ruling on breaches of such law. It sits in Luxembourg, with a judge from each of the 15 member states.

European Free Trade Association (EFTA) organization established in 1960 and consisting of

Iceland, Norway, Switzerland, and (from 1991) Liechtenstein, previously a non-voting associate member. There are no import duties between members. Of the original EFTA members, Britain and Denmark left in 1972 to join the *European Community (EC), as did Portugal in 1985; Austria, Finland, and Sweden joined the *European Union (EU) in 1995.

European Monetary System (EMS) arrangement to promote monetary stability and closer economic cooperation in the countries of the *European Community, launched in March 1979. The *Exchange Rate Mechanism (ERM) was at the core of the system. With the advent of the *euro, the ERM was revised.

European Parliament parliament of the* European Union (EU), which meets in Strasbourg, France, and Brussels, Belgium. Members are elected for a five-year term. The number of seats in the parliament is related to the number of EU members – after the accession of ten new countries to the EU in 2004 the number of seats rose from 626 to 732. The president of the European Parliament is Pat Cox (from 1999).

European Space Agency (ESA) organization of 15 European countries that engages in space research and technology. It was founded in 1975, with headquarters in Paris, France. The participating countries are Austria, Belgium, Denmark, Finland, France, Germany, Ireland, Italy, the Netherlands, Norway, Portugal, Spain, Sweden, Switzerland, and the UK.

European Union (EU) political and economic grouping, comprising 25 countries (in 2004). The six original members – Belgium, France, (West) Germany, Italy, Luxembourg, and the Netherlands – were joined by the United Kingdom, Denmark, and the Republic of Ireland in 1973, Greece in 1981, Spain and Portugal in 1986, Austria, Finland, and Sweden in 1995, and Cyprus, the Czech Republic, Estonia, Hungary, Latvia, Lithuania, Malta, Poland, the Slovak Republic, and Slovenia in 2004. East Germany was incorporated on German reunification in 1990. The *European Community (EC) preceded the EU, and comprised the European Coal and Steel Community (set up by the 1951 Treaty of Paris), the European Economic Community, and the European Atomic Energy Community (both set up by the 1957 Treaties of *Rome). The EU superseded the EC in 1993, following intergovernmental arrangements for a common foreign and security policy and for increased cooperation on justice and home affairs policy issues set up by the *Maastricht Treaty (1992). Other important agreements have been the *Single European Act (1986), the Amsterdam Treaty (1997), and the Treaty of Nice (2000). The basic aims of these treaties have been the expansion of trade, the abolition of restrictive economic practices, the encouragement of free movement of capital and labour, and establishment of a closer union among European peoples.

europium chemical symbol Eu, soft, greyish, metallic element of the *lanthanide series, atomic number 63, relative atomic mass 151.96. It is used in lasers and as the red phosphor in colour televisions; its compounds are used to make control rods for nuclear reactors. It was named in 1901 by French chemist Eugène Demarçay (1852–1904) after the continent of Europe, where it was first found.

Eustachian tube small air-filled canal connecting the middle *ear with the back of the throat. It is found in all land vertebrates and equalizes the pressure on both sides of the eardrum.

euthanasia in medicine, mercy killing of someone with a severe and incurable condition or illness. Euthanasia is an issue that creates much controversy on medical and ethical grounds. A patient's right to refuse life-prolonging treatment is recognized in several countries.

eutrophication excessive enrichment of rivers, lakes, and shallow sea areas, primarily by municipal sewage, by sewage itself, and by the nitrates and phosphates from *fertilizers used in agriculture. These encourage the growth of algae and bacteria which use up the oxygen in the water, making it uninhabitable for fish and other animal life. In this way eutrophication is responsible for a particular type of *water pollution.

evangelicalism the beliefs of some Protestant Christian movements that stress biblical authority, faith, and the personal commitment of the 'born again' experience.

Evans, Arthur John (1851–1941) English archaeologist. His excavations at *Knossos on Crete uncovered a vast palace complex, and resulted in the discovery of various Minoan scripts. He proved the existence of a Bronze Age civilization that predated the Mycenean, and named it Minoan after Minos, the legendary king of Knossos.

evaporation process in which a liquid turns to a vapour without its temperature reaching boiling point. Evaporation is the *change of state that occurs when a *liquid turns into a *gas. In a liquid the particles are close together, with forces holding them together, yet able to move about. Some particles in a liquid have more energy than others. Even when a liquid is below its boiling point, some particles have enough energy to escape and form a gas. Evaporation is greater when temperatures and wind speeds are high, and the air is dry. It is why puddles dry up in the sun, and clothes dry faster in dry, windy weather.

Evelyn, John (1620–1706) English diarist and author. He was a friend of the diarist Samuel Pepys, and like him remained in London during the Plague and the Great Fire of London. His fascinating diary, covering the years 1641–1706, and first published in 1818, is an important source of information about 17th-century England. He also wrote some 30 books on a wide variety of subjects, including horticulture and the cultivation of trees, history, religion, and the arts. He was one of the founders of the Royal Society.

evening primrose any of a group of plants that typically have pale yellow flowers which open in the evening. About 50 species are native to North America, several of which now also grow in Europe. Some are cultivated for their oil, which is rich in gamma-linoleic acid (GLA). The body converts GLA into substances which resemble hormones, and **evening primrose oil** is beneficial in relieving the symptoms of *premenstrual tension. It is also used in treating such ailments as eczema and chronic fatigue syndrome. (Genus *Oenothera*, family Onagraceae.)

eventing see **three-day eventing** under *equestrianism.

Everest, Mount (Tibetan *Qomolungma* 'goddess mother of the world'; Nepalese *Sagarmatha* 'head of the earth') world's highest mountain above sea level, in the *Himalayas range, on the China–Nepal frontier; height 8,848 m/29,028 ft. It was first climbed by New Zealand mountaineer Edmund *Hillary and Sherpa Tenzing Norgay in 1953. More than 700 climbers have reached the summit; over 100 have died attempting the ascent, 55 of those in the period 1990–98.

Everglades subtropical area of swamps, marsh, and lakes in southern Florida, USA; area 7,000 sq km/2,700 sq mi. Formed by the overflow of Lake Okeechobee after heavy rains, it is one of the wildest areas in the USA, with distinctive plant and animal life, including alligators. The natural vegetation of the swamplands is sawgrass and rushes, with trees such as cypress, palm, and hardwoods where the conditions are slightly drier. Several hundred Seminole, an American Indian people, live here. A national park (established in 1947) covers the southern tip of the Everglades, making up about one-fifth of the Everglades' original area. The Everglades were declared an International Biosphere Reserve in 1976, a World Heritage site in 1979, and a Wetland of International Importance in 1987.

evergreen in botany, a plant such as pine, spruce, or holly, that bears its leaves all year round. Most *conifers are evergreen. Plants that shed their leaves in autumn or during a dry season are described as *deciduous.

evolution slow gradual process of change from one form to another, as in the evolution of the universe from its formation to its present state, or in the evolution of life on Earth. In biology, it is the process by which life has developed by stages from single-celled organisms into the multiplicity of animal and plant life, extinct and existing, that inhabits the Earth. The development of the concept of evolution is usually associated with the English naturalist Charles *Darwin who attributed the main role in evolutionary change to *natural selection acting on randomly occurring variations. These variations in species are now known to be *adaptations produced by spontaneous changes or *mutations in the genetic material of organisms. In short, evolution is the change in the genetic makeup of a population of organisms from one generation to another. Evidence shows that many species of organisms do not stay the same over generations. The most dramatic evidence of this comes from fossils.

evolutionary stable strategy (ESS) in *sociobiology, an assemblage of behavioural or physical characters (collectively termed a 'strategy') of a population that is resistant to replacement by any forms bearing new traits, because the new traits will not be capable of successful reproduction.

ex cathedra (Latin 'from the throne') term describing a statement by the pope, taken to be indisputably true, and which must be accepted by Catholics.

excavation *or* **dig** in archaeology, the systematic recovery of data through the exposure of buried sites and artefacts. Excavation is destructive, and is therefore accompanied by a comprehensive recording of all material found and its three-dimensional locations (its context). As much material and information as possible must be recovered from any dig. A full record of all the techniques employed in the excavation itself must also be made, so that future archaeologists will be able to evaluate the results of the work accurately.

exchange rate price at which one currency is bought or sold in terms of other currencies, gold, or accounting units such as the special drawing right (SDR) of the *International Monetary Fund. Exchange rates may be fixed by international agreement or by government policy; or they may be wholly or partly allowed to 'float' (that is, find their own level) in world currency markets.

Exchange Rate Mechanism (ERM) system established in 1979 for controlling exchange rates within the *European Monetary System of the *European Union (EU). It has now been replaced by the *euro. The member currencies of the ERM were fixed against each other within a narrow band of fluctuation based on a central European Currency Unit (ECU) rate, but floating against non-member countries. If a currency deviated significantly from the central ECU rate, the European Monetary Cooperation Fund and the central banks concerned stepped in to stabilize the currency.

excise duty indirect tax levied on certain goods produced within a country, such as petrol, alcohol, and tobacco. It is collected by the British government's Customs and Excise department.

excommunication in religion, exclusion of an offender from the rights and privileges of the Roman Catholic Church. The English monarchs King John, Henry VIII, and Elizabeth I were all excommunicated.

excretion in biology, the removal of the waste products of metabolism from living organisms. In plants and simple animals, waste products are removed by *diffusion. Plants, for example, excrete O_2, a product of photosynthesis. In mammals, waste products are removed by specialized excretory organs, principally the *kidneys, which excrete urea. Water and metabolic wastes are also excreted in the faeces and, in humans, through the sweat glands in the skin; carbon dioxide and water are removed via the lungs. The liver excretes bile pigments.

existentialism branch of philosophy based on the situation of the individual in an absurd or meaningless universe where humans have free will. Existentialists argue that people are responsible for and the sole judge of their actions as they affect others. The origin of existentialism is usually traced back to the Danish philosopher *Kierkegaard; among its proponents were Martin Heidegger in Germany and Jean-Paul *Sartre in France.

Exmoor moorland district in north Devon and west Somerset, southwest England, forming (with the coast from Minehead to Combe Martin) a national park since 1954. The park covers an area of around 7,700 ha/ 19,000 acres, and includes Dunkery Beacon, its highest point at 519 m/1,705 ft; and the Doone Valley.

exocrine gland gland that discharges secretions, usually through a tube or a duct, onto a surface. Examples include sweat glands which release sweat on to the skin, and digestive glands which release digestive juices onto the walls of the intestine. Some animals also have *endocrine glands (ductless glands) that release hormones directly into the bloodstream.

exorcism rite used in a number of religions for the expulsion of evil spirits and ghosts. In Christianity it is employed, for example, in the Roman Catholic and Pentecostal churches.

exoskeleton hardened external skeleton of insects, spiders, crabs, and other arthropods. It provides attachment for muscles and protection for the internal organs, as well as support. To permit growth it is periodically shed in a process called *ecdysis.

exosphere uppermost layer of the *atmosphere. It is an ill-defined zone above the thermosphere, beginning at about 700 km/435 mi and fading off into the vacuum of space. The gases are extremely thin, with hydrogen as the main constituent.

expansion in physics, the increase in size of a constant mass of substance caused by, for example, increasing its temperature (thermal expansion) or its internal pressure. The **expansivity**, or coefficient of thermal expansion, of a material is its expansion (per unit volume, area, or length) per degree rise in temperature.

experimental psychology application of scientific methods to the study of mental processes and behaviour.

exponent *or* **index** in mathematics, a superscript number that indicates the number of times a term is multiplied by itself; for example $x^2 = x \times x$, $4^3 = 4 \times 4 \times 4$.

exponential in mathematics, descriptive of a *function in which the variable quantity is an exponent (a number indicating the power to which another number or expression is raised).

export goods or service produced in one country and sold to another. Exports may be visible (goods such as cars physically exported) or invisible (services such as banking and tourism, that are provided in the exporting country but paid for by residents of another country).

expressionism in music, use of melodic or harmonic distortion for expressive effect, associated with Arnold *Schoenberg, Paul *Hindemith, Ernst Krenek, and others.

expressionism style of painting and sculpture that expresses inner emotions; in particular, a movement in early 20th-century art in northern and central Europe. Expressionist artists tended to distort or exaggerate natural colour and appearance in order to describe an inner vision or emotion; the Norwegian painter Edvard *Munch's *Skriket/The Scream* (1893; National Gallery, Oslo) is perhaps the most celebrated example.

extinction in biology, the complete disappearance of a species from the planet. Extinctions occur when a species becomes unfit for survival in its natural habitat usually to be replaced by another, better-suited species. An organism becomes ill-suited for survival because its environment is changed or because its relationship to other organisms is altered. For example, a predator's fitness for survival depends upon the availability of its prey.

extradition surrender, by one state or country to another, of a person accused of a criminal offence in the state or country to which that person is extradited.

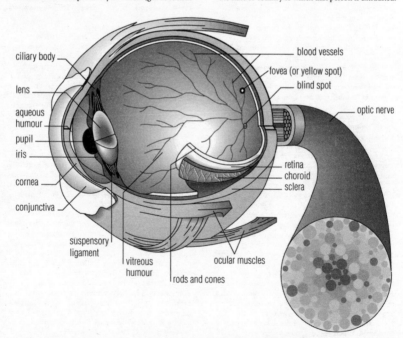

eye The human eye. The retina of the eye contains about 137 million light-sensitive cells in an area of about 650 sq mm/ 1 sq in. There are 130 million rod cells for black and white vision and 7 million cone cells for colour vision. The optic nerve contains about 1 million nerve fibres. The focusing muscles of the eye adjust about 100,000 times a day. To exercise the leg muscles to the same extent would need an 80 km/50 mi walk.

extrasensory perception (ESP) any form of perception beyond and distinct from the known sensory processes. The main forms of ESP are clairvoyance (intuitive perception or vision of events and situations without using the senses); precognition (the ability to foresee events); and telepathy or thought transference (communication between people without using any known visible, tangible, or audible medium). Verification by scientific study has yet to be achieved.

Extremadura autonomous community of western Spain, on the border with Portugal, comprising the provinces of Badajoz and Cáceres; area 41,602 sq km/16,063 sq mi; population (2001 est) 1,073,400. Irrigated land is used for growing wheat, wine grapes, and olives; the remainder is either oak forest or used for pig or sheep grazing. There are also food industries. Much of the region is not prosperous, and has suffered from steady emigration. The capital is Mérida.

extroversion *or* **extraversion** personality dimension described by the psychologists Carl *Jung and, later, Hans Eysenck. The typical extrovert is sociable, impulsive, and carefree. The opposite of extroversion is *introversion.

extrusive rock *or* **volcanic rock** *igneous rock formed on the surface of the Earth by volcanic activity (as opposed to intrusive, or plutonic, rocks that solidify below the Earth's surface). Magma (molten rock) erupted from volcanoes cools and solidifies quickly on the surface. The crystals that form do not have time to grow very large, so most extrusive rocks are finely grained. The term includes fine-grained crystalline or glassy rocks formed from hot lava quenched at or near Earth's surface, and those made of welded fragments of ash and glass ejected into the air during a volcanic eruption. The formation of extrusive igneous rock is part of the rock cycle.

Eyck, Jan van (c. 1390–1441) Flemish painter, who gained in his lifetime a Europe-wide reputation. One of the first painters to use oil paint effectively, he is noted for his meticulous detail and his brilliance of colour and finish. He painted religious scenes like the altarpiece *The Adoration of the Lamb* (1432; St Bavo Cathedral, Ghent), and portraits, including *The Arnolfini Wedding* (1434; National Gallery, London), which records the betrothal of the Bruges-based Lucchese cloth merchant Giovanni Arnolfini to Giovanna Cenami.

eye organ of vision. In the human eye, the light is focused by the combined action of the curved cornea, the internal fluids, and the lens. The insect eye is compound – made up of many separate facets, known as ommatidia, each of which collects light and directs it separately to a receptor to build up an image. Invertebrates have much simpler eyes, with no lenses. Among molluscs, cephalopods have complex eyes similar to those of vertebrates. The mantis shrimp's eyes contain ten colour pigments with which to perceive colour; some flies and fish have five, while the human eye has only three.

eyebright any of a group of annual plants belonging to the figwort family. They are 2–30 cm/1–12 in high and have whitish flowers streaked with purple. The name indicates their traditional use as an eye-medicine. (Genus *Euphrasia*, family Scrophulariaceae.)

Eyre, Lake lake in northeast South Australia; area up to 9,000 sq km/3,500 sq mi. It is the largest lake in Australia, and includes Lake Eyre North and Lake Eyre South. Much of the lake remains a dry salt crust, while parts form a salt marsh in dry seasons. It is filled only when the rivers which drain into it (such as the Diamantina) flood. It lies in a basin of inland drainage and is the continent's lowest point, 16 m/52 ft below sea level.

°F symbol for degrees *Fahrenheit.

F in physics, symbol for *farad, the SI unit of capacitance equal to that of a capacitor with a potential difference of 1 volt between plates carrying a charge of 1 coulomb.

Fabergé, Peter Carl (1846–1920) born Karl Gustavovich, Russian goldsmith and jeweller. Among his masterpieces was a series of jewelled Easter eggs, the first of which was commissioned by Alexander III for the tsarina in 1884.

Fabian Society UK socialist organization for research, discussion, and publication, founded in London in 1884. Its name is derived from the Roman commander Fabius Maximus, and refers to the evolutionary methods by which it hopes to attain socialism by a succession of gradual reforms. Early members included the playwright George Bernard Shaw and Beatrice and Sidney Webb. The society helped to found the Labour Representation Committee in 1900, which became the Labour Party in 1906.

fable *genre of story, in either verse or prose, in which animals or inanimate objects are given the mentality and speech of human beings to point out a moral. Fables are common in folklore and children's literature, and range from the short fables of the ancient Greek writer *Aesop to the modern novel *Animal Farm* (1945) by English writer George Orwell.

facsimile transmission full name for *fax or telefax.

factor in algebra, certain kinds of *polynomials (expressions consisting of several or many terms) can be factorized using their common *factors. Brackets are put into an expression, and the common factor is sought. For example, the factors of $2a^2 + 6ab$ are $2a$ and $a + 3b$, since $2a^2 + 6ab = 2a(a + 3b)$. This rearrangement is called **factorization**.

factor number that divides into another *number exactly. It is also known as a divisor. For example, the factors of 24 are 1, 2, 4, 8, 12, and 24; and the factors of 64 are 1, 2, 4, 8, 16, 32, and 64. The highest factor of both 24 and 64 is 8. This is known as the highest common factor (HCF) of the two numbers.

factory farming intensive rearing of poultry or other animals for food. These are usually fed on high-protein foodstuffs in confined quarters. Chickens for eggs and meat, and calves for veal are commonly factory farmed. Some countries restrict the use of antibiotics and growth hormones as aids to factory farming because they can persist in the flesh of the animals after they are slaughtered. The emphasis is on productive yield rather than animal welfare, so conditions for the animals are often very poor. For this reason, many people object to factory farming on moral as well as health grounds.

FA Cup abbreviation for **Football Association Challenge Cup**, the major annual soccer knockout competition in England and Wales, open to all member clubs of the English Football Association. First held in 1871–72, it is the oldest football knockout competition.

faeces remains of food and other waste material eliminated from the digestive tract of animals by way of the anus. Faeces consist of quantities of fibrous material, bacteria and other micro-organisms, rubbed-off lining of the digestive tract, bile fluids, undigested food, minerals, and water.

Fagatogo seat of government of American Samoa, situated on Pago Pago Harbour, next to the dependency capital Pago Pago, on Tutuila Island; population (2000 est) 2,100.

Fahd (1923–) in full **Fahd ibn Abdul Aziz al-Saud**, King of Saudi Arabia from 1982. He encouraged the investment of the country's enormous oil wealth in infrastructure and new activities – such as petrochemical industries – in order to diversify the economy, and also built up the country's military forces. When Iraq invaded neighbouring Kuwait in August 1990, King Fahd joined with the USA and other international forces in 'Operation Desert Storm' in the course of the 1990–91 Gulf War, in which Saudi Arabia was used as the base from which Kuwait was liberated in February 1991. From the early 1990s King Fahd's absolutist regime faced twin pressures from liberals, campaigning for democratic elections, and from fundamentalist Islamic groups, which opposed the monarchy and sought the full imposition of Islamic *sharia* law. In November 1995 King Fahd suffered a stroke, and since then power has effectively rested with his half-brother, Crown Prince Abdullah, his legal successor.

Fahrenheit, Gabriel Daniel (1686–1736) Polish-born Dutch physicist who invented the first accurate thermometer in 1724 and devised the Fahrenheit temperature scale. Using his thermometer, Fahrenheit was able to determine the boiling points of liquids and found that they vary with atmospheric pressure.

Fahrenheit scale temperature scale invented in 1714 by Gabriel Fahrenheit that was commonly used in English-speaking countries until the 1970s, after which the *Celsius scale was generally adopted, in line with the rest of the world. In the Fahrenheit scale, intervals are measured in degrees (°F); $°F = (°C \times 9/5) + 32$.

fainting sudden, temporary loss of consciousness caused by reduced blood supply to the brain. It may be due to emotional shock or physical factors, such as pooling of blood in the legs from standing still for long periods.

Fairbanks, Douglas Elton Ulman, Sr (1883–1939) US actor. He played acrobatic, swashbuckling heroes in silent films such as *The Mark of Zorro* (1920), *The Three Musketeers* (1921), *Robin Hood* (1922), *The Thief of Bagdad* (1924), and *Don Quixote* (1925). He was married to the film star Mary Pickford 1920–35. In 1919 they founded United Artists with Charlie Chaplin and D W Griffith.

Fairbanks, Douglas (Elton Ulman), Jr (1909–2000)
US actor. He initially appeared in the same type of
swashbuckling film roles – *Catherine the Great* (1934),
The Prisoner of Zenda (1937), and *Sinbad the Sailor*
(1947) – as his father, Douglas Fairbanks Sr. Later he
produced TV films and acted in a variety of productions.

Fairfax, Thomas (1612–1671) 3rd Baron Fairfax,
English general, commander-in-chief of the
Parliamentary army in the English *Civil War.
With Oliver *Cromwell he formed the *New Model
Army and defeated Charles I at the Battle of *Naseby.
He opposed the king's execution, resigned in protest
against the invasion of Scotland in 1650, and
participated in the restoration of Charles II after
Cromwell's death. Knighted in 1640, he succeeded
to the barony in 1648.

Faisal Ibn Abd al-Aziz (1905–1975) King of Saudi
Arabia from 1964. Ruling without a prime minister,
he instituted a successful programme of economic
modernization, using Saudi Arabia's vast annual oil
revenues, which grew from $334 million in 1960 to $22.5
billion in 1974, after the quadrupling of world oil prices
in 1973–74. A generous welfare system was established,
including free medical care and education to
postgraduate level, and subsidized food, water, fuel,
electricity, and rents; slavery was outlawed; and
financial support was given to other Arab states in
their struggle with Israel. In March 1975 Faisal was
assassinated by a mentally unstable nephew, Prince
Museid, and his half-brother Khalid became king.

Falange (Spanish 'phalanx') also known as Falange
Española. Former Spanish Fascist Party, founded in
1933 by José Antonio Primo de Rivera (1903–1936), son
of military ruler Miguel Primo de Rivera. It was closely
modelled in programme and organization on the
Italian fascists and on the Nazis. In 1937, when *Franco
assumed leadership, it was declared the only legal party,
and altered its name to Traditionalist Spanish Phalanx.

falcon any bird of prey of the genus *Falco*, family
Falconidae, order Falconiformes. Falcons are the
smallest of the hawks (15–60 cm/6–24 in). They have
short curved beaks with one tooth in the upper
mandible; the wings are long and pointed, and the toes
elongated. They nest in high places and kill their prey
on the wing by 'stooping' (swooping down at high
speed). They include the peregrine and kestrel.

falconry the use of specially trained falcons and hawks
to capture birds or small mammals. Practised since
ancient times in the Middle East, falconry was
introduced from continental Europe to Britain in
Saxon times.

Falkirk unitary authority in central Scotland, created
from the former district of the same name in 1996 from
part of the former Central region. **area:** 297 sq km/
115 sq mi **towns:** Falkirk (administrative headquarters),
Grangemouth **physical:** centrally located between
Edinburgh and Glasgow, this low-lying area borders
the southern side of the Firth of Forth; River Avon
flows through **features:** Forth and Clyde and Union
canals; Roman Rough Castle fort and Antonine Wall
population: (2001 est) 145,300.

Falkland Islands Argentine **Islas Malvinas**, British
crown colony in the South Atlantic, 480 km/300 mi east
of the Straits of Magellan; area 12,173 sq km/4,700 sq mi,
made up of two main islands: East Falkland (6,760 sq km/

2,610 sq mi) and West Falkland (5,413 sq km/2,090 sq mi);
population (2001 est) 2,400. The capital is Stanley, the
main port, which was extended and modernized in
1984. The main economic activities are sheep farming
and wool processing, fishing and the production of
alginates (used as dyes and as a food additive) from
seaweed beds, and fishing. The islands are heavily
dependent on imports, especially fuels, foodstuffs,
textiles, hardware, and machinery. The accessibility
of the islands was greatly improved by the completion
of Mount Pleasant Airport in 1985.

Falklands War war between Argentina and Britain over
disputed sovereignty of the Falkland Islands initiated
when Argentina invaded and occupied the islands on
2 April 1982. On the following day, the United Nations
Security Council passed a resolution calling for
Argentina to withdraw. A British task force was
immediately dispatched and, after a fierce conflict in
which more than 1,000 Argentine and British lives were
lost, 12,000 Argentine troops surrendered and the
islands were returned to British rule on 14–15 June 1982.

Falla, Manuel de (1876–1946) born Manuel Maria
de Falla y Matheu, Spanish composer. The folk music
(flamenco) of southern Spain is a major part of his
compositions. His opera *La vida breve/Brief Life* (1905;
first performed 1913) was followed by the ballets
El amor brujo/Love the Magician (first performed 1915)
and *El sombrero de tres picos/The Three-Cornered Hat*
(1919), and his most ambitious concert work, *Noches
en los jardines de España/Nights in the Gardens of Spain*
(1916). He also wrote songs and pieces for piano and
guitar.

Fall of Man, the myth that explains the existence of
evil as the result of some primeval wrongdoing by
humanity. It occurs independently in many cultures.
The biblical version, recorded in the Old Testament
(Genesis 3), provided the inspiration for the epic poem
Paradise Lost (1667) by John *Milton.

Fallopian tube *or* **oviduct** in mammals, one of two
tubes that carry eggs from the ovary to the uterus. An
egg is fertilized by sperm in the Fallopian tubes, which
are lined with cells whose *cilia move the egg towards
the uterus.

fallout harmful radioactive material released into the
atmosphere in the debris of a nuclear explosion (see
*nuclear warfare) and descending to the surface of the
Earth. Such material can enter the food chain, cause
*radiation sickness, and last for hundreds of thousands
of years (see *half-life).

false-colour imagery graphic technique that displays
images in false (not true-to-life) colours so as to
enhance certain features. It is widely used in displaying
electronic images taken by spacecraft; for example,
Earth-survey satellites such as *Landsat*. Any colours can
be selected by a computer processing the received data.

family in biological classification, a group of related
genera (see *genus). Family names are not printed in
italic (unlike genus and species names), and by
convention they all have the ending -idae (animals) or
-aceae (plants and fungi). For example, the genera of
hummingbirds are grouped in the hummingbird
family, Trochilidae. Related families are grouped
together in an *order.

family group of people related to each other by blood
or by marriage. Families are usually described as either

extended (a large group of relations living together or in close contact with each other) or nuclear (a family consisting of two parents and their children).

family planning deliberate control of human population growth by various means (*contraceptives, sterilization, and abortion), in order to reduce the *birth rate. The majority of developing nations now have governments that support some sort of family planning programme.

famine severe shortage of food affecting a large number of people. A report made by the United Nations (UN) Food and Agriculture Organization (FAO), published in October 1999, showed that although the number of people in the developing world without sufficient food declined by 40 million during the first half of the 1990s, there were still, in 1999, 790 million hungry people in poor countries and 34 million in richer ones. The food availability deficit (FAD) theory explains famines as being caused by insufficient food supplies. A more recent theory is that famines arise when one group in a society loses its opportunity to exchange its labour or possessions for food.

Fang Lizhi (1936–) Chinese political dissident and astrophysicist. He advocated human rights and political pluralism and encouraged his students to campaign for democracy. After the Red Army massacred the student demonstrators in Tiananmen Square, Beijing, in June 1989, Fang and his wife took refuge in the US embassy in Beijing until June 1990, when they received official permission to leave China.

fantasia or **fantasy** or **phantasy** or **fancy** in music, a free-form instrumental composition for keyboard or chamber ensemble, originating in the late Renaissance, and much favoured by the English composers John Dowland, Orlando Gibbons, and William Byrd. It implies the free manipulation of musical figures without regard to models of form. Later composers include Georg Telemann, Johann Sebastian Bach, and Mozart.

Fantin-Latour, (Ignace) Henri (Jean Théodore) (1836–1904) French painter. He excelled in delicate still lifes, flower paintings, and portraits. *Homage à Delacroix* (1864; Musée d'Orsay, Paris) is a portrait group featuring several poets, authors, and painters, including Charles Baudelaire and James McNeill Whistler.

FAO abbreviation for *Food and Agriculture Organization.

farad symbol F, SI unit of electrical capacitance (how much electric charge a *capacitor can store for a given voltage). One farad is a capacitance of one *coulomb per volt. For practical purposes the microfarad (one millionth of a farad, symbol μF) is more commonly used.

faraday unit of electrical charge equal to the charge on one mole of electrons. Its value is 9.648×10^4 coulombs.

Faraday, Michael (1791–1867) English chemist and physicist. In 1821 he began experimenting with *electromagnetism, and discovered electromagnetic induction (the production of a continuous supply of electricity using magnetic fields). He made the first dynamo, the first electric motor, the first transformer, and developed the first electric generator. He also pointed out that the energy of a magnet is in the field around it and not in the magnet itself. In chemistry, Faraday isolated *benzene from gas oils, demonstrated

the use of *platinum as a catalyst, and developed the laws of *electrolysis in 1834.

Faraday's constant symbol F, constant representing the electric charge carried on one mole of electrons. It is found by multiplying Avogadro's constant by the charge carried on a single electron, and is equal to 9.648×10^4 coulombs per mole. One **faraday** is this constant used as a unit. The constant is used to calculate the electric charge needed to discharge a particular quantity of ions during *electrolysis.

Faraday's laws three laws of electromagnetic induction, and two laws of electrolysis, all proposed originally by English physicist Michael Faraday. The laws of induction are: (1) a changing magnetic field induces an electromagnetic force in a conductor; (2) the electromagnetic force is proportional to the rate of change of the field; and (3) the direction of the induced electromagnetic force depends on the orientation of the field. The laws of electrolysis are: (1) the amount of chemical change during electrolysis is proportional to the charge passing through the liquid; and (2) the amount of chemical change produced in a substance by a given amount of electricity is proportional to the electrochemical equivalent of that substance.

Far East geographical term for all Asia east of the Indian subcontinent. The term is considered by many to have ethnocentric connotations, and has tended to be replaced by **East Asia**.

farming business of cultivating land. Different approaches to farming can be classified in several ways: according to crop or animal combinations, for example *arable farming or pastoral farming; according to the dominant product group, for example dairy farming or *market gardening; or according to the overall approach or techniques used, for example *organic farming or *shifting cultivation.

Faroe Islands or **Faeroe Islands** or **Faeroes** (Danish *Faerøerne* 'Sheep Islands') island group (18 out of 22 inhabited) in the North Atlantic, between the Shetland Islands and Iceland, forming an outlying part of Denmark; area 1,399 sq km/540 sq mi; population (1992 est) 46,800. The largest islands are Strømø, Østerø, Vagø, Suderø, Sandø, and Bordø. The capital is Thorshavn on Strømø. The main industries are fishing and crafted goods. Faeroese and Danish are spoken.

Farouk (1920–1965) King of Egypt. He succeeded the throne on the death of his father Fuad I. His early popularity was later overshadowed by his somewhat unsuccessful private life, and more importantly by the humiliating defeat of the Egyptian army in 1948. In 1952 a group called the 'Free Officers', led by Muhammad Neguib and Gamal Abdel Nasser, forced him to abdicate, and he was temporarily replaced by his son Ahmad Fuad II. Exiled for the remainder of his life, he died in Rome in 1965.

Farquhar, George (c. 1677–1707) Irish dramatist. His most notable plays are *The Recruiting Officer* (1706) and *The Beaux Stratagem* (1707). Although typical of the Restoration tradition of comedy of manners, the good-humoured realism of his drama transcends the artificiality and cynicism of the genre.

Farsi or **Persian** language belonging to the Indo-Iranian branch of the Indo-European family, and the official language of Iran (formerly Persia). It is also spoken in Afghanistan, Iraq, and Tajikistan.

fascism political ideology that denies all rights to individuals in their relations with the state; specifically, the *totalitarian nationalist movement founded in Italy in 1919 by *Mussolini and followed by Hitler's Germany in 1933. Fascism came about essentially as a result of the economic and political crisis of the years after World War I. Units called *fasci di combattimento* (combat groups), from the Latin *fasces*, were originally established to oppose communism. The fascist party, the *Partitio Nazionale Fascista*, controlled Italy 1922–43. Fascism protected the existing social order by suppressing the working-class movement by force and by providing scapegoats for popular anger such as minority groups: Jews, foreigners, or blacks; it also prepared the citizenry for the economic and psychological mobilization of war.

Fassbinder, Rainer Werner (1946–1982) German film director. He began as a fringe actor and founded his own 'anti-theatre' before moving into films. His works are mainly stylized indictments of contemporary German society. He made more than 40 films, including *Die bitteren Tränen der Petra von Kant/ The Bitter Tears of Petra von Kant* (1972), *Angst essen Seele auf/Fear Eats the Soul* (1974), and *Die Ehe von Maria Braun/The Marriage of Maria Braun* (1979).

fast breeder *or* **breeder reactor** alternative name for *fast reactor, a type of nuclear reactor.

fasting the practice of voluntarily going without food. It can be undertaken as a religious observance, a sign of mourning, a political protest (hunger strike), or for slimming purposes.

fast reactor *or* **fast breeder reactor** *nuclear reactor that makes use of fast neutrons to bring about fission. Unlike other reactors used by the nuclear-power industry, it has little or no *moderator, to slow down neutrons. The reactor core is surrounded by a 'blanket' of uranium carbide. During operation, some of this uranium is converted into plutonium, which can be extracted and later used as fuel.

fat in the broadest sense, a mixture of *lipids – chiefly triglycerides (lipids containing three *fatty acid molecules linked to a molecule of glycerol). More specifically, the term refers to a lipid mixture that is solid at room temperature (20 °C/68 °F); lipid mixtures that are liquid at room temperature are called oils. The higher the proportion of saturated fatty acids in a mixture, the harder the fat. Fats and oils (lipids) are compounds made up of glycerol and fatty acids. Fats are insoluble in *water. Boiling fats in strong alkali forms soaps (saponification).

Fatah, al- Palestinian nationalist organization, founded in 1957 to bring about an independent state of Palestine. Also called Tahir al-Hatani al Falastani (Movement for the National Liberation of Palestine), it is the main component of the *Palestine Liberation Organization (PLO).

Fates *or* **Moirai** in Greek mythology, three female figures who determined the destiny of human lives; later, the duration of human life. They were envisaged as spinners: Clotho spun the thread of life, Lachesis apportioned the thread, and Atropos cut it off. They are analogous to the Roman Parcae or Fata and Norse Norns.

Father Christmas *or* **Santa Claus** popular personification of the spirit of Christmas, derived from the Christian legend of St *Nicholas and elements of Scandinavian mythology. He is depicted as a fat, jolly old man with a long white beard, dressed in boots and a red hat and suit trimmed with white fur. He lives with his toy-making elves at the North Pole, and on Christmas Eve he travels in an airborne sleigh, drawn by eight reindeer, to deliver presents to good children, who are fast asleep when he arrives. The most popular legends claim that Father Christmas lands his sleigh on rooftops, secretly entering homes through the chimney.

fathom (Anglo-Saxon *faethm* 'to embrace') in mining, seafaring, and handling timber, a unit of depth measurement (1.83 m/6 ft) used prior to metrication; it approximates to the distance between an adult man's hands when the arms are outstretched.

Fatimid dynasty of Muslim Shiite caliphs founded in 909 by Obaidallah, who claimed to be a descendant of Fatima (the prophet Muhammad's daughter) and her husband Ali, in North Africa. In 969 the Fatimids conquered Egypt, and the dynasty continued until overthrown by Saladin in 1171.

fatty acid *or* **carboxylic acid** organic compound consisting of a hydrocarbon chain of an even number of carbon atoms, with a carboxyl group (–COOH) at one end. The covalent bonds between the carbon atoms may be single or double; where a double bond occurs the carbon atoms concerned carry one instead of two hydrogen atoms. Chains with only single bonds have all the hydrogen they can carry, so they are said to be saturated with hydrogen. Chains with one or more double bonds are said to be unsaturated (see *polyunsaturate). Fatty acids are produced in the small intestine when fat is digested.

fatwa in Islamic law, an authoritative legal opinion on a point of doctrine. In 1989, a fatwa calling for the death of British novelist Salman *Rushdie was made by the Ayatollah *Khomeini of Iran, following publication of Rushdie's controversial and allegedly blasphemous book *The Satanic Verses* (1988).

Faulkner, William (Cuthbert) (1897–1962) US novelist. His works employ difficult narrative styles in their epic mapping of a quasi-imaginary region of the American South. His third novel, *The Sound and the Fury* (1929), deals with the decline of a Southern family, told in four voices, beginning with an especially complex stream-of-consciousness narrative. He was awarded the Nobel Prize for Literature in 1949.

fault fracture in the Earth's crust, on either side of which rocks have moved past each other. Faults may occur where rocks are being pushed together (compression) or pulled apart (tension) by *plate tectonics, movements of the *plates of the Earth's crust. When large forces build up quickly in rocks, they become brittle and break; *folds result from a more gradual compression. Faults involve displacements, or offsets, ranging from the microscopic scale to hundreds of kilometres. Large offsets along a fault are the result of the accumulation of many small movements (metres or less) over long periods of time. Large movements cause detectable *earthquakes, such as those experienced along the *San Andreas Fault in California, USA. (See diagram, p. 326.)

Faunus in Roman mythology, one of the oldest Italian deities; god of fertility and prophecy; protector of agriculturists and shepherds. He was later identified with the Greek *Pan and represented with goat's ears, horns, tail, and hind legs.

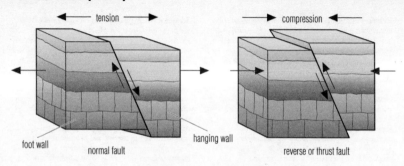

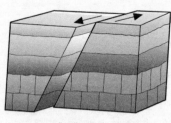

tension

compression

foot wall

normal fault

hanging wall

reverse or thrust fault

strike-slip or
transverse fault

fault Faults are caused by the movement of rock layers, producing such features as block mountains and rift valleys. A normal fault is caused by a tension or stretching force acting in the rock layers. A reverse fault is caused by compression forces. Faults can continue to move for thousands or millions of years.

Fauré, Gabriel (Urbain) (1845–1924) French composer. He wrote songs, chamber music, and a choral *Requiem* (1887–89). He was a pupil of Saint-Saëns, became professor of composition at the Paris Conservatoire in 1896, and was its director 1905–20.

Faust legendary magician who sold his soul to the devil. The historical Georg (or Johann) Faust appears to have been a wandering scholar and conjurer in Germany at the start of the 16th century. Christopher Marlowe, J W Goethe, Heinrich Heine, and Thomas Mann all used the legend, and it inspired musical works by Franz Liszt, Hector Berlioz, Charles Gounod, and Richard Wagner.

fauvism (French *fauve* 'wild beast') movement in modern French painting characterized by the use of very bold, vivid, pure colours. The name is a reference to the fact that the works seemed crude and untamed to many people at the time. The Fauves believed that colour and a strong linear pattern were more important than realistic representation; André *Derain's *London Bridge* (1906; Museum of Modern Art, New York) is an example. Although short-lived, lasting only about three years (1905–08), the movement was highly influential. It was the first specific artistic movement of the 20th century, that would transform European art between the turn of the century and World War I. The key figure of fauvism was Henri *Matisse, other important members being Maurice de Vlaminck, Georges *Braque, Georges *Rouault, Raoul *Dufy, and Derain.

Fawkes, Guy (1570–1606) English conspirator in the *Gunpowder Plot to blow up King James I and the members of both Houses of Parliament. Fawkes, a Roman Catholic convert, was arrested in the cellar underneath the House of Lords on 4 November 1605, tortured, and executed. The event is still commemorated in Britain and elsewhere every 5 November with bonfires, fireworks, and the burning of the 'guy', an effigy.

fax *or* **facsimile transmission** *or* **telefax** transmission of images over a *telecommunications link, usually the telephone network. When placed on a fax machine, the original image is scanned by a transmitting device and converted into coded signals, which travel via the telephone lines to the receiving fax machine, where an image is created that is a copy of the original. Photographs as well as printed text and drawings can be sent. The standard transmission takes place at 4,800 or 9,600 bits of information per second.

FBI abbreviation for *Federal Bureau of Investigation, agency of the US Department of Justice.

fealty in feudalism, the loyalty and duties owed by a vassal to a lord. In the 9th century fealty obliged the vassal not to take part in any action that would endanger the lord or his property, but by the 11th century the specific duties of fealty were established and included financial obligations and military service. Following an oath of fealty, an act of allegiance and respect (homage) was made by the vassal; when a fief was granted by the lord, it was formalized in the process of investiture.

feather rigid outgrowth of the outer layer of the skin of birds, made of the protein keratin. Feathers provide insulation and facilitate flight. There are several types, including long quill feathers on the wings and tail, fluffy down feathers for retaining body heat, and contour feathers covering the body. The colouring of feathers is often important in camouflage or in courtship and other displays. Feathers are normally replaced at least once a year. There is an enormous variation between species in the number of feathers; for example a whistling swan has over 25,000 contour feathers, whereas a ruby-throated hummingbird has less than 950.

feather star any of an unattached, free-swimming group of sea lilies, order Comatulida. The arms are branched into numerous projections (hence 'feather' star), and grow from a small cup-shaped body. Below the body are appendages that can hold on to a surface, but the feather star is not permanently attached.

Federal Bureau of Investigation (FBI) agency of the US Department of Justice that investigates violations of federal law not specifically assigned to other agencies, and is particularly concerned with internal security. The FBI was established in 1908 and built up a position of powerful autonomy during the autocratic directorship of J Edgar Hoover 1924–72. The director is Robert Mueller, a former federal prosecutor, from 2001.

federalism system of government in which two or more separate states unite into a *federation under a common central government. A federation should be distinguished from a **confederation**, a looser union of states for mutual assistance. The USA is an example of federal government.

Federalist in US history, one who advocated the ratification of the US Constitution 1787–88 in place of the Articles of *Confederation. The Federalists became in effect the ruling political party under the first two presidents, George Washington and John Adams, 1789–1801, legislating to strengthen the authority of the newly created federal government.

federation political entity made up from a number of smaller units or states where the central government has powers over national issues such as foreign policy and defence, while the individual states retain a high degree of regional and local autonomy. A federation should be distinguished from a **confederation**, a looser union of states for mutual assistance. Contemporary examples of federated states established since 1750 include the USA, Canada, Australia, India, the Federal Republic of Germany, Malaysia, and Micronesia.

feedback general principle whereby the results produced in an ongoing reaction become factors in modifying or changing the reaction; it is the principle used in self-regulating control systems, from a simple *thermostat and steam-engine *governor to automatic computer-controlled machine tools. A fully computerized control system, in which there is no operator intervention, is called a **closed-loop feedback** system. A system that also responds to control signals from an operator is called an **open-loop feedback** system.

feldspar any of a group of *silicate minerals. Feldspars are the most abundant mineral type in the Earth's crust. They are the chief constituents of *igneous rock and are present in most metamorphic and sedimentary rocks. All feldspars contain silicon, aluminium, and oxygen, linked together to form a framework. Spaces within this framework structure are occupied by sodium, potassium, calcium, or occasionally barium, in various proportions. Feldspars form white, grey, or pink crystals and rank 6 on the *Mohs scale of hardness.

feldspathoid any of a group of silicate minerals resembling feldspars but containing less silica. Examples are nepheline ($NaAlSiO_4$ with a little potassium) and leucite ($KAlSi_2O_6$). Feldspathoids occur in igneous rocks that have relatively high proportions of sodium and potassium. Such rocks may also contain alkali feldspar, but they do not generally contain quartz because any free silica would have combined with the feldspathoid to produce more feldspar instead.

Fellini, Federico (1920–1993) Italian film director and screenwriter. His work has been a major influence on modern cinema. Many of his films combine dream and fantasy sequences with satire and autobiographical detail. They include *I vitelloni/The Young and the Passionate* (1953), *La strada/The Road* (1954), *Le notti di Cabiria/Nights of Cabiria* (1956), *La dolce vita/The Sweet Life* (1960), *8½* (1963), *Giulietta degli spiriti/Juliet of the Spirits* (1965), *Amarcord* (1973), and *Ginger e Fred/Ginger and Fred* (1986).

female circumcision see *female genital mutilation.

female genital mutilation (FGM) the partial or total removal of female external genitalia for cultural, religious, or other non-medical reasons. There are three types: **sunna**, which involves cutting off the hood, and sometimes the tip, of the clitoris; **clitoridectomy**, the excision of the clitoris and sometimes parts of the inner and outer labia; **infibulation** (most widely practised in Sudan and Somalia), the removal of the clitoris, the inner and outer labia, and the stitching of the scraped sides of the vulva across the vagina leaving a small hole to allow passage of urine and menstrual blood.

feminism active belief in equal rights and opportunities for women; see *women's movement.

femur *or* **thigh-bone** also the upper bone in the hind limb of a four-limbed vertebrate.

fencing sport of fighting with swords including the **foil**, derived from the light weapon used for practising duels; the **épée**, a heavier weapon derived from the duelling sword proper; and the **sabre**, with a curved handle and narrow V-shaped blade. In sabre fighting, cuts count as well as thrusts. Masks and protective jackets are worn, and hits are registered electronically in competitions. Men's fencing has been part of every Olympic programme since 1896. Women's fencing was included from 1924, but only using the foil; the épée was not added until in 1996. The sport's governing body is the Fédération Internationale d'Escrime (FIE; International Fencing Federation).

Fenian movement Irish-American republican secret society, founded in the USA in 1858 to campaign for Irish-American support for armed rebellion following the death of the Irish nationalist leader Daniel O'Connell and the break-up of Young Ireland. Its name, a reference to the ancient Irish legendary warrior band of the **Fianna**, became synonymous with underground Irish republicanism in the 19th century. The collapse of the movement began when an attempt to establish an independent Irish republic by an uprising in Ireland in 1867 failed, as did raids into Canada in 1866 and 1870, and England in 1867. In the 1880s the US-based Fenian society Clan-Na-Gael conducted assassinations and bombings through its agents in England and Ireland in an attempt to force Irish home rule.

fennec small nocturnal desert *fox *Fennecus zerda* found in North Africa and Arabia. It has a head and body only 40 cm/1.3 ft long, and its enormous ears act as radiators to lose excess heat. It eats insects and small animals.

fennel any of several varieties of a perennial plant with feathery green leaves, belonging to the carrot family. Fennels have an aniseed (liquorice) flavour, and the leaves and seeds are used in seasoning. The thickened leafstalks of sweet fennel (*F. vulgare dulce*) are eaten as a vegetable. (*Foeniculum vulgare*, family Umbelliferae.)

Fens, the level, low-lying tracts of reclaimed marsh in eastern England, west and south of the Wash, covering an area of around 40,000 sq km/15,500 sq mi, about 115 km/70 mi north–south and 55 km/34 mi east–west. They fall within the counties of Lincolnshire, Cambridgeshire, and Norfolk. Formerly a bay of the North Sea, they are now crossed by numerous drainage canals and form some of the most fertile and productive agricultural land in Britain. The southern peat portion of the Fens is known as the Bedford Level.

Ferdinand Spanish **Fernando**, five kings of Castile including:
Ferdinand (I) the Great (c. 1016–1065) King of Castile from 1035. He began the reconquest of Spain from the Moors and united all northwestern Spain under his and his brothers' rule.
Ferdinand II (1452–1516) King-consort of Castile from 1474 (as **Ferdinand V**), King of Aragon from 1479, and **Ferdinand III** of Naples from 1504. In 1469 he married his cousin *Isabella I, who succeeded to the throne of Castile in 1474; they were known as **the Catholic Monarchs** because they completed the *reconquista* (reconquest) of the Spanish peninsula from the Muslims by taking the last Moorish kingdom, Granada, in 1492. To celebrate this success they expelled the Jews and financed Christopher *Columbus's expedition to the Americas in 1492.

Ferdinand three Holy Roman emperors including:
Ferdinand II (1578–1637) Holy Roman Emperor from 1619, when he succeeded his uncle Matthias; king of Bohemia from 1617 and of Hungary from 1618. A zealous Catholic, he provoked the Bohemian revolt that led to the Thirty Years' War. He was a grandson of Ferdinand I.
Ferdinand III (1608–1657) Holy Roman Emperor from 1637 when he succeeded his father Ferdinand II; king of Hungary from 1625. Although anxious to conclude the Thirty Years' War, he did not give religious liberty to Protestants.

Ferdinand, Franz (*or* Francis) (1863–1914) Archduke of Austria. He became heir to Emperor Franz Joseph, his uncle, in 1884 but while visiting Sarajevo on 28 June 1914, he and his wife were assassinated by a Serbian nationalist. Austria used the episode to make unreasonable demands on Serbia that ultimately precipitated World War I.

Ferguson, Alex(ander) (1941–) Scottish football manager. One of British football's most successful managers, he has won 15 trophies with Manchester United since 1986, including seven league championship titles and four FA Cups. In 1999 Manchester United became the first club to achieve the league championship and FA Cup double three times. The club also won the European Cup the same year, thus achieving a unique treble in English football. As manager of Aberdeen from 1978 to 1986, he won ten trophies including three Scottish championships and the European Cup Winners' Cup. He was manager of the Scottish national side 1985–86.

Fermanagh historic county of Northern Ireland; area 1,680 sq km/648 sq mi. It occupies the southwestern corner of Northern Ireland is characterized by hills in the west and Lough Erne, which has many wooded islands and is used for fishing and sailing. The principal towns are Enniskillen, Lisnaskea, and Irvinestown. Administrative responsibility for the county is held by Fermanagh council.

Fermat, Pierre de (1601–1665) French mathematician who, with Blaise *Pascal, founded the theory of *probability and the modern theory of numbers. Fermat also made contributions to analytical geometry. In 1657 Fermat published a series of problems as challenges to other mathematicians, in the form of theorems to be proved.

fermentation breakdown of sugars by bacteria and yeasts using a method of respiration without oxygen (*anaerobic). The enzymes in yeast break down glucose to give two products: *ethanol (alcohol) and *carbon dioxide. Fermentation processes have long been utilized in baking bread, making beer and wine, and producing cheese, yogurt, soy sauce, and many other foodstuffs.

Fermi, Enrico (1901–1954) Italian-born US physicist who was awarded the Nobel Prize for Physics in 1938 for his proof of the existence of new radioactive elements produced by bombardment with neutrons, and his discovery of nuclear reactions produced by low-energy neutrons. This research was the basis for studies leading to the atomic bomb and nuclear energy. Fermi built the first nuclear reactor in 1942 at Chicago University and later took part in the Manhattan Project to construct an atom bomb. His theoretical work included the study of the weak nuclear force, one of the fundamental forces of nature, and beta decay.

fermion in physics, a subatomic particle whose spin can only take values that are half-odd-integers, such as $\frac{1}{2}$ or $\frac{3}{2}$. Fermions may be classified as leptons, such as the electron, and hadrons, such as the proton, neutron, mesons, and so on. All elementary particles are either fermions or *bosons.

fermium chemical symbol Fm, synthesized, radioactive, metallic element of the *actinide series, atomic number 100, relative atomic mass 257.10. Ten isotopes are known, the longest-lived of which, Fm-257, has a half-life of 80 days. Fermium has been produced only in minute quantities in particle accelerators.

fern any of a group of plants related to horsetails and clubmosses. Ferns are spore-bearing, not flowering,

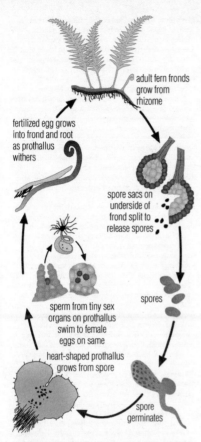

adult fern fronds grow from rhizome

fertilized egg grows into frond and root as prothallus withers

spore sacs on underside of frond split to release spores

spores

sperm from tiny sex organs on prothallus swim to female eggs on same

heart-shaped prothallus grows from spore

spore germinates

fern The life cycle of a fern. Ferns have two distinct forms that alternate during their life cycle. For the main part of its life, a fern consists of a short stem (or rhizome) from which roots and leaves grow. The other part of its life is spent as a small heart-shaped plant called a prothallus.

plants and most are perennial, spreading by slow-growing roots. The leaves, known as fronds, vary widely in size and shape. Some taller types, such as tree ferns, grow in the tropics. There are over 7,000 species.

Ferrari, Enzo (1898–1988) Italian founder of the Ferrari car-manufacturing company, which specializes in Grand Prix racing cars and high-quality sports cars. He was a racing driver for Alfa Romeo in the 1920s, went on to become one of their designers, and took over their racing division in 1929. In 1947 the first 'true' Ferrari was seen. Ferrari have won more world championship Grand Prix than any other team. In 2000 Michael *Schumacher brought Ferrari their first Drivers' Championship since 1979.

ferret domesticated variety of the Old World *polecat. About 35 cm/1.2 ft long, it usually has yellowish-white fur and pink eyes, but may be the dark brown colour of a wild polecat. Ferrets may breed with wild polecats. They have been used since ancient times to hunt rabbits and rats.

ferromagnetism form of *magnetism that can be acquired in an external magnetic field and usually retained in its absence, so that ferromagnetic materials are used to make permanent magnets. A ferromagnetic material may therefore be said to have a high magnetic permeability and susceptibility (which depends upon temperature). Examples are iron, cobalt, nickel, and their alloys.

fertility organism's ability to reproduce, as distinct from the rate at which it reproduces (fecundity). Individuals that can reproduce are fertile. Individuals that cannot reproduce are infertile. Individuals become infertile (unable to reproduce) when they cannot generate gametes (eggs or sperm) or when their gametes cannot yield a viable *embryo after fertilization. Common causes of infertility are: low sperm numbers in the male; blocked oviducts; infrequent ovulation (release of gamete) in the female; consequence of infections in the female reproductive tract; and genetic makeup.

fertilization in *sexual reproduction, the union of two *gametes (sex cells, often called egg or ovum, and sperm) to produce a zygote, which combines the genetic material contributed by each parent. In self-fertilization the male and female gametes come from the same plant; in cross-fertilization they come from different plants. Self-fertilization rarely occurs in animals; usually even *hermaphrodite animals cross-fertilize each other.

fertilizer substance containing some or all of a range of about 20 chemical elements necessary for healthy plant growth, used to compensate for the deficiencies of poor or depleted *soil. Fertilizers may be organic, for example farmyard manure, composts, bonemeal, blood, and fishmeal; or inorganic (synthetic or artificial), in the form of simple compounds, mainly of nitrogen, phosphate, and potash, which have been used on a very much increased scale since 1945. Compounds of nitrogen and phosphorus are of particular importance.

Fès *or* **Fez** Arabic **Fas**, former capital of Morocco 808–1062, 1296–1548, and 1662–1912, in the Fès valley north of the Great Atlas Mountains, 160 km/100 mi east of Rabat; population (1994 est) 769,000. Textiles, carpets, and leather are manufactured, in many cases on a craft basis, and the *fez*, a brimless hat worn in southern and eastern Mediterranean countries, is traditionally said to have originated here.

fescue any grass of a widely distributed group. Many are used in temperate regions for lawns and pasture. Many upland species are viviparous, producing young plantlets instead of flowers. (Genus *Festuca*, family Gramineae.)

fetishism in anthropology, belief in the supernormal power of some inanimate object that is known as a fetish. Fetishism in some form is common to most cultures, and often has religious or magical significance.

fetishism in psychology, the transfer of erotic interest to an object, such as an item of clothing, whose real or fantasized presence is necessary for sexual gratification. The fetish may also be a part of the body not normally considered erogenous, such as the feet.

fetus or **foetus** stage in mammalian *embryo development after fusion of gametes produces a zygote cell. The human embryo is usually termed a fetus after the eighth week of development, when the limbs and external features of the head are recognizable. The stage ends at birth.

feudalism or the **feudal system** (Latin feudem 'fief') the main form of social organization in medieval Europe; the term was first used in 1839. A system based primarily on land, feudalism involved a hierarchy of authority, rights, and power that extended from the monarchy downwards. At the head of the system the crown owned all the land. Beneath the crown, an intricate network of duties and obligations linked royalty, tenants-in-chief (such as the barons), under-tenants (knights), and villeins (serfs). Feudalism was reinforced by personal oaths of allegiance and a complex legal system and supported by the Christian medieval church.

fever condition of raised body temperature, usually due to infection.

Feynman, Richard P(hillips) (1918–1988) US physicist whose work laid the foundations of quantum electrodynamics. He was awarded the Nobel Prize for Physics in 1965 for his work on the theory of radiation. He shared the award with Julian Schwinger and Sin-Itiro Tomonaga. He also contributed to many aspects of particle physics, including quark theory and the nature of the weak nuclear force.

Fianna Fáil (Irish 'Soldiers of Destiny') Republic of Ireland political party, founded by the Irish nationalist Éamon *de Valera in 1926, and led since 1994 by Bertie *Ahern. A broad-based party, it is conservative socially and economically, and generally right of centre. It was the governing party in the Republic of Ireland 1932–48, 1951–54, 1957–73, 1977–81, 1982, 1987–94 (from 1993 in coalition with Labour), and from 1997. Its official aims include the establishment of a united and completely independent all-Ireland republic.

Fibonacci, Leonardo (c. 1170–c. 1250) also known as Leonardo of Pisa, Italian mathematician. He published Liber abaci/The Book of the Calculator in Pisa in 1202, which was instrumental in the introduction of Arabic notation to Europe. From 1960, interest increased in **Fibonacci numbers**, in their simplest form a sequence in which each number is the sum of its two predecessors (1, 1, 2, 3, 5, 8, 13, ...). They have unusual characteristics with possible applications in botany, psychology, and astronomy (for example, a more exact correspondence than is given by *Bode's law to the distances between the planets and the Sun).

fibre, dietary or **roughage** plant material (outer husks and peel) that cannot be digested by human digestive enzymes. It consists largely of cellulose, a carbohydrate found in plant cell walls. Fibre adds bulk to the gut contents because it can absorb water, assisting the muscular contractions that force food along the intestine. A diet low in fibre causes constipation and is believed to increase the risk of developing diverticulitis, diabetes, gall-bladder disease, and cancer of the large bowel – conditions that are rare in non-industrialized countries, where the diet contains a high proportion of unrefined cereals. It is also known as NSP (non-starch polysaccharide).

fibreglass glass that has been formed into fine fibres, either as long continuous filaments or as a fluffy, short-fibred glass wool. Fibreglass is heat- and fire-resistant and a good electrical insulator. It has applications in the field of fibre optics and as a strengthener for plastics in GRP (glass-reinforced plastics).

fibre optics branch of physics dealing with the transmission of light and images through glass or plastic fibres known as *optical fibres. Such fibres are now commonly used in both communications technology and medicine.

fibrin insoluble protein involved in blood clotting. When an injury occurs fibrin is deposited around the wound in the form of a mesh, which dries and hardens, so that bleeding stops. Fibrin is developed in the blood from a soluble protein, fibrinogen.

fibula rear lower bone in the hind leg of a vertebrate. It is paired and often fused with a smaller front bone, the tibia.

fiction in literature, any work in which the content is completely or largely invented. The term describes imaginative works of narrative *prose (such as the novel or the short story), and is distinguished from non-fiction writing (such as history, biography, or works on practical subjects) and from *poetry.

Fidei Defensor Latin for the title of 'Defender of the Faith' (still retained by British sovereigns) conferred by Pope Leo X on Henry VIII of England in 1521 to reward his writing of a treatise against the Protestant Martin Luther.

field in physics, region of space in which an object exerts a force on a separate object because of certain properties they both possess. For example, there is a force of attraction between any two objects that have mass when one is within the gravitational field of the other.

Fielding, Henry (1707–1754) English novelist. His greatest work, The History of Tom Jones, a Foundling (1749), which he described as 'a comic epic poem in prose', was an early landmark in the development of the English novel, realizing for the first time in English the form's potential for memorable characterization, coherent plotting, and perceptive analysis. The vigour of its comic impetus, descriptions of high and low life in town and country, and its variety of characters made it immediately popular. Fielding gave a new prominence to dialogue in his work.

Fields, W C (1880–1946) stage name of William Claude Dukenfield, US actor and screenwriter. His distinctive speech and professed attitudes such as hatred of children and dogs gained him enormous popularity in such films as David Copperfield (1935), My Little Chickadee (1940; co-written with Mae West), The Bank Dick (1940), and Never Give a Sucker an Even Break (1941).

Fife unitary authority in eastern Scotland, which was formerly a region of three districts (1975–96) and a county until 1974. **area:** 1,321 sq km/510 sq mi **towns:** Cupar, Dunfermline, Glenrothes (administrative headquarters), Kirkcaldy, St Andrews **physical:** coastal area, predominantly low lying, undulating interior with dramatic escarpment at Lomond Hills; rivers Eden and Leven flow through **features:** University of St Andrews, Old Course, St Andrews, former Rosyth naval base **population:** (2001 est) 350,000.

fifth column group within a country secretly aiding an enemy attacking from without. The term originated in 1936 during the Spanish Civil War, when General Mola boasted that Franco supporters were attacking Madrid with four columns and that they had a 'fifth column' inside the city.

fifth-generation computer anticipated new type of computer based on emerging microelectronic technologies with high computing speeds and *parallel processing. The development of very large-scale integration (VLSI) technology, which can put many more circuits onto an integrated circuit (chip) than is currently possible, and developments in computer hardware and software design may produce computers far more powerful than those in current use.

fig any of a group of trees belonging to the mulberry family, including the many cultivated varieties of *F. carica*, originally from western Asia. They produce two or three crops of fruit a year. Eaten fresh or dried, figs have a high sugar content and laxative properties. (Genus *Ficus*, family Moraceae.)

fighting fish any of a southeast Asian genus *Betta* of fishes of the gourami family, especially *B. splendens*, about 6 cm/2 in long and a popular aquarium fish. It can breathe air, using an accessory breathing organ above the gill, and can live in poorly oxygenated water. The male has large fins and various colours, including shining greens, reds, and blues. The female is yellowish brown with short fins.

figwort any of a group of Old World plants belonging to the figwort family, which also includes foxgloves and snapdragons. Members of the genus have square stems, opposite leaves, and open two-lipped flowers in a cluster at the top of the stem. (Genus *Scrophularia*, family Scrophulariaceae.)

Fiji Islands

National name: *Matanitu Ko Viti/Republic of the Fiji Islands*

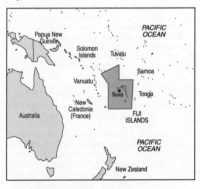

Area: 18,333 sq km/7,078 sq mi
Capital: Suva
Major towns/cities: Lautoka, Nadi, Ba, Labasa, Nausori, Lami
Major ports: Lautoka, Levuka
Physical features: comprises about 844 Melanesian and Polynesian islands and islets (about 100 inhabited), the largest being Viti Levu (10,429 sq km/4,028 sq mi) and

Vanua Levu (5,556 sq km/2,146 sq mi); mountainous, volcanic, with tropical rainforest and grasslands; almost all islands surrounded by coral reefs; high volcanic peaks
Head of state: Ratu Josefa Iloilo from 2000
Head of government: Laisenia Qarase from 2000
Political system: military
Political executive: military
Political parties: National Federation Party (NFP), moderate left of centre, Indian; Fijian Labour Party (FLP), left of centre, Indian; United Front, Fijian; Fijian Political Party (FPP), Fijian centrist
Currency: Fiji dollar
GNI per capita (PPP): (US$) 5,310 (2002 est)
Exports: clothing, sugar, gold, fish and fish products, re-exported petroleum products, timber, ginger, molasses. Principal market: Australia 25.6% (2001)
Population: 839,000 (2003 est)
Language: English (official), Fijian, Hindi
Religion: Methodist 37%, Hindu 38%, Muslim 8%, Roman Catholic 8%, Sikh
Life expectancy: 68 (men); 72 (women) (2000–05)
Chronology
c. **1500 BC:** Peopled by Polynesian and, later, by Melanesian settlers.
1643: The islands were visited for the first time by a European, the Dutch navigator Abel Tasman.
1830s: Arrival of Western Christian missionaries.
1840s–50s: Western Fiji came under dominance of a Christian convert prince, Cakobau, ruler of Bau islet, who proclaimed himself Tui Viti (King of Fiji), while the east was controlled by Ma'afu, a Christian prince from Tonga.
1857: British consul appointed, encouraging settlers from Australia and New Zealand to set up cotton farms in Fiji.
1874: Fiji became a British crown colony after a deed of cession was signed by King Cakobau.
1875–76: A third of the Fijian population were wiped out by a measles epidemic; a rebellion against the British was suppressed with the assistance of Fijian chiefs.
1877: Fiji became the headquarters of the British Western Pacific High Commission (WPHC), which controlled other British protectorates in the Pacific region.
1879–1916: Indian labourers brought in, on ten-year indentured contracts, to work sugar plantations.
1904: Legislative Council formed, with elected Europeans and nominated Fijians, to advise the British governor.
1963: Legislative Council enlarged; women and Fijians were enfranchised. The predominantly Fijian Alliance Party (AP) formed.
1970: Independence was achieved from Britain; Ratu Sir Kamisese Mara of the AP was elected as the first prime minister.
1973: Ratu Sir George Cakobau, the great-grandson of the chief who had sworn allegiance to the British in 1874, became governor general.
1985: The FLP was formed by Timoci Bavadra, with trade-union backing.
1987: After a general election had brought to power an Indian-dominated coalition led by Bavadra, Lt-Col Sitiveni Rabuka seized power in a military coup, and proclaimed a Fijian-dominated republic outside the Commonwealth.

1990: A new constitution, favouring indigenous (Melanese) Fijians, was introduced. Civilian rule was re-established, with resignations from the cabinet of military officers, but Rabuka remained as home affairs minister, with Mara as prime minister.

1992: A general election produced a coalition government with Rabuka of the FPP as prime minister.

1994: Ratu Sir Kamisese Mara became president.

1997: A nondiscriminatory constitution was introduced. Fiji was re-admitted to the Commonwealth.

1999: President Mara's term in office was renewed for an additional five years. Mahendra Chaudhry became Fiji's first prime minister of Indian descent.

2000: A coup led by George Speight took cabinet members hostage and ended Mara's presidency. The head of Fiji's armed forces, Commodore Frank Bainimarama, announced that he was taking power, proclaimed martial law, and revoked the 1997 non-discriminatory constitution (the aim of Speight's coup). When the hostages were released in July, the military handed over executive power to the new president, Ratu Josefa Iloilo, and installed Laisenia Qarase as prime minister. Speight was arrested and charged with treason. The high court later ruled that Chaudhry's deposed government should be reinstated.

2001: President Iloilo appointed an interim government with Ratu Tevita Momoedonu as prime minister, and announced elections for later in the year.

2002: Coup leader George Speight was sentenced to death. However the sentence was commuted by President Iloilo to life imprisonment.

2004: The ethnic Indian Fijian Labour Party withdrew from the governing coalition to go into opposition.

file in computing, a collection of data or a program stored in a computer's external memory (for example, on *disk). It might include anything from information on a company's employees to a program for an adventure game. Serial (or sequential) access files hold information as a sequence of characters, so that, to read any particular item of data, the program must read all those that precede it. Random-access (or direct access) files allow the required data to be reached directly. Files are usually located via a *directory.

film noir (French 'dark film') genre of dark, cynical crime film. Thematically indebted to the 'hard-boiled' school of fiction, and stylistically to German expressionism, French poetic realism, and the constraints imposed by B film-making, *film noir* first appeared in Hollywood in the 1940s and 1950s. Examples are *Double Indemnity* (1944) by Billy Wilder and *In a Lonely Place* (1950) by Nicholas Ray.

film, photographic strip of transparent material (usually cellulose acetate) coated with a light-sensitive emulsion, used in cameras to take pictures. The emulsion contains a mixture of light-sensitive silver halide salts (for example, bromide or iodide) in gelatin. When the emulsion is exposed to light, the silver salts are invisibly altered, giving a latent image, which is then made visible by the process of developing. Films differ in their sensitivities to light, this being indicated by their speeds. Colour film consists of several layers of emulsion, each of which records a different colour in the light falling on it.

filter in chemistry, a porous substance, such as blotting paper, through which a mixture can be passed to separate out its solid constituents.

filter in electronics, a circuit that transmits a signal of some frequencies better than others. A low-pass filter transmits signals of low frequency and also direct current; a high-pass filter transmits high-frequency signals; a band-pass filter transmits signals in a band of frequencies.

filter in optics, a device that absorbs some parts of the visible *spectrum and transmits others. A beam of white light can be made into a beam of coloured light by placing a transparent colour filter in the path of the beam. For example, a green filter will absorb or block all colours of the spectrum except green, which it allows to pass through. A yellow filter absorbs only light at the blue and violet end of the spectrum, transmitting red, orange, green, and yellow light.

filtration process by which suspended solid particles in a fluid are removed by passing the mixture through a filter, usually porous paper, plastic, or cloth. The particles are retained by the filter to form a residue and the fluid passes through to make up the filtrate. For example, soot may be filtered from air, and suspended solids from water.

fin in aquatic animals, flattened extension from the body that aids balance and propulsion through the water.

final solution (to the Jewish question; German *Endlosung der Judenfrage*) euphemism used by the Nazis to describe the extermination of Jews (and other racial groups and opponents of the regime) before and during World War II in the *Holocaust.

Financial Times Index FT Index, indicator measuring the daily movement of 30 major industrial share prices on the London Stock Exchange, issued by the UK *Financial Times* newspaper. Other FT indices cover government securities, fixed-interest securities, gold mine shares, and Stock Exchange activity.

finch any of various songbirds of the family Fringillidae, in the order Passeriformes (perching birds). They are seed-eaters with stout conical beaks. The name may also be applied to members of the Emberizidae (buntings), and Estrildidae (weaver-finches).

fin de siècle (French 'end of century') the art and literature of the 1890s; decadent.

fine arts *or* **beaux arts** *or* **non-functional art** arts judged predominantly in aesthetic rather than functional terms, for example painting, sculpture, and print making. Architecture is also classified as one of the fine arts, though here the functional element is also important. Music and poetry are also sometimes called fine arts. The fine arts are traditionally contrasted with the applied arts.

Fine Gael (Irish 'family of the gael') Republic of Ireland political party founded in 1933 by William *Cosgrave and led by John Bruton from 1990. It has been socially liberal in recent years but fiscally conservative. Though it formed a coalition government with the Labour and Democratic Left parties 1994–97, it has typically been the main opposition party.

Fingal's Cave cave on the island of Staffa, Inner Hebrides, Argyll and Bute, Scotland. It is lined with volcanic basalt columns, and is 70 m/230 ft long and 20 m/65 ft high. Visited by the German Romantic composer Felix Mendelssohn in 1829, the cave was the inspiration of his *Hebridean* overture, otherwise known as *Fingal's Cave*.

Finland

National name: *Suomen Tasavalta* (Finnish)/
Republiken Finland (Swedish)/*Republic of Finland*

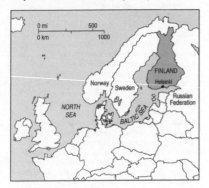

Area: 338,145 sq km/130,557 sq mi
Capital: Helsinki (Swedish Helsingfors)
Major towns/cities: Tampere, Turku, Espoo, Vantaa,
Oulu
Major ports: Turku, Oulu
Physical features: most of the country is forest, with
low hills and about 60,000 lakes; one-third is within
the Arctic Circle; archipelago in south includes Åland
Islands; Helsinki is the most northerly national capital
on the European continent. At the 70th parallel there is
constant daylight for 73 days in summer and 51 days of
uninterrupted night in winter.
Head of state: Tarja Halonen from 2000
Head of government: Matti Taneli Vanhanen from 2003
Political system: liberal democracy
Political executive: dual executive
Political parties: Finnish Social Democratic Party
(SSDP), moderate left of centre; National Coalition
Party (KOK), moderate right of centre; Finnish Centre
Party (KESK), radical centrist, rural-oriented; Swedish
People's Party (SFP), independent Swedish-oriented;
Finnish Rural Party (SMP), farmers and small
businesses; Left-Wing Alliance (VL), left wing; Finnish
Christian League (SKL), centre-right
Currency: euro (markka until 2002)
GNI per capita (PPP): (US$) 25,440 (2002 est)
Exports: metal and engineering products, gold, paper
and paper products, machinery, ships, wood and pulp,
clothing and footwear, chemicals. Principal market:
Germany 12.5% (2000)
Population: 5,207,000 (2003 est)
Language: Finnish (93%), Swedish (6%) (both
official), Saami (Lapp), Russian
Religion: Evangelical Lutheran 87%, Greek Orthodox
1%
Life expectancy: 74 (men); 82 (women) (2000–05)
Chronology
1st century: Occupied by Finnic nomads from Asia
who drove out native Saami (Lapps) to the far north.
12th–13th centuries: A series of Swedish crusades
conquered Finns and converted them to Christianity.
16th–17th centuries: Finland was a semi-autonomous
Swedish duchy with Swedish landowners ruling Finnish

peasants; Finland was allowed relative autonomy,
becoming a grand duchy in 1581.
1634: Finland fully incorporated into Swedish kingdom.
1700–21: Great Northern War between Sweden and
Russia; half of Finnish population died in famine and
epidemics.
1741–43 and 1788–90: Further Russo-Swedish wars;
much of the fighting took place in Finland.
1808: Russia invaded Sweden (with support of
Napoleon).
1809: Finland ceded to Russia as grand duchy with
Russian tsar as grand duke; Finns retained their own
legal system and Lutheran religion and were exempt
from Russian military service.
1812: Helsinki became capital of grand duchy.
19th century: Growing prosperity was followed by rise
of national feeling among new Finnish middle class.
1904–05: Policies promoting Russification of Finland
provoked a national uprising; Russians imposed
military rule.
1917: Finland declared independence.
1918: Bitter civil war between Reds (supported by
Russian Bolsheviks) and Whites (supported by
Germany); Baron Carl Gustaf Mannerheim led the
Whites to victory.
1919: Republican constitution adopted with Kaarlo
Juho Ståhlberg as first president.
1927: Land reform broke up big estates and created
many small peasant farms.
1939–40: Winter War: USSR invaded Finland after a
demand for military bases was refused.
1940: Treaty of Moscow: Finland ceded territory to USSR.
1941: Finland joined the German attack on USSR in the
hope of regaining lost territory.
1944: Finland agreed separate armistice with USSR;
German troops withdrawn.
1947: Finno-Soviet peace treaty: Finland forced to cede
12% of its total area and to pay $300 million in
reparations.
1948: Finno-Soviet Pact of Friendship, Cooperation,
and Mutual Assistance (YYA treaty): Finland pledged
to repel any attack on USSR through its territories.
1950s: Unstable centre-left coalitions excluded
communists from government and adopted strict
neutrality in foreign affairs.
1955: Finland joined the United Nations (UN) and the
Nordic Council.
1956: There was a general strike as a result of
unemployment and inflation.
1973: Trade agreements were signed with the European
Economic Community (EEC) and Comecon.
1991: There was a swing towards the Centre Party in a
general election.
1995: Finland joined the European Union (EU); the
Social Democrats won a general election, with Paavo
Lipponen becoming prime minister.
2000: Tarja Halonen was elected president. A former
foreign minister, she became the first woman president
of Finland.
2003: Only two months after becoming Finland's first
woman prime minister, Anneli Jaatteenmaki resigned
from office amid claims that she lied about a leak of
sensitive political information during the election
campaign. Former defence minister Matti Vanhanen
replaced her.

Finland, Gulf of eastern arm of the *Baltic Sea, separating Finland from Estonia. It is 420 km/260 mi long and 40–150 km/25–90 mi wide. Helsinki and St Petersburg are the main ports.

Finnish language member of the Finno-Ugric language family, the national language of Finland and closely related to neighbouring Estonian, Livonian, Karelian, and Ingrian languages. At the beginning of the 19th century Finnish had no official status, since Swedish was the language of education, government, and literature in Finland. The publication of the *Kalevala*, a national epic poem, in 1835, contributed greatly to the arousal of Finnish national and linguistic feeling.

Finn Mac Cumhaill (*or* Fionn *or* Finn McCool) ('the fair-haired son of Cumhall') Legendary Irish hero, the best-known character in the hero-tales of Ireland, identified with a general who organized an Irish regular army in the 3rd century. The word 'Fionn' (from Celtic *Vindos*) also has connotations of illumination and wisdom, and his most typical act was the gaining of knowledge through chewing his thumb. The Scottish writer James *Macpherson featured him (as Fingal) and his followers in the verse of his popular epics 1762–63, which were supposedly written by a 3rd-century bard called *Ossian.

Finno-Ugric group or family of more than 20 languages spoken by some 22 million people in scattered communities from Norway in the west to Siberia in the east and to the Carpathian mountains in the south. Members of the family include Finnish, Lapp, and Hungarian.

fir any of a group of *conifer trees belonging to the pine family. The true firs include the balsam fir (*A. balsamea*) of northern North America and the silver fir (*A. alba*) of Europe and Asia. Douglas firs of the genus *Pseudotsuga* are native to western North America and the Far East. (True fir genus *Abies*, family Pinaceae.)

firearm weapon from which projectiles are discharged by the combustion of an explosive. Firearms are generally divided into two main sections: *artillery (ordnance or cannon), with a bore greater than 2.54 cm/ 1 in, and *small arms, with a bore of less than 2.54 cm/ 1 in. Although gunpowder was known in Europe 60 years previously, the invention of guns dates from 1300 to 1325, and is attributed to Berthold Schwartz, a German monk.

firedamp gas that occurs in coal mines and is explosive when mixed with air in certain proportions. It consists chiefly of methane (CH_4, natural gas or marsh gas) but always contains small quantities of other gases, such as nitrogen, carbon dioxide, and hydrogen, and sometimes ethane and carbon monoxide.

firefly any winged nocturnal beetle of the family Lampyridae. They all emit light through the process of *bioluminescence.

Fire of London fire 2–5 September 1666 that destroyed four-fifths of the City of London. It broke out in a bakery in Pudding Lane and spread as far west as the Temple. It destroyed 87 churches, including St Paul's Cathedral, and 13,200 houses, although fewer than 20 people lost their lives.

First World War another name for *World War I, 1914–18.

fiscal policy that part of government policy concerning *taxation and other revenues, *public spending, and government borrowing (the *public sector borrowing requirement).

fiscal year a year as defined by a company or government for financial accounting purposes. A company can choose any 12-month period for its accounting year and in exceptional circumstances may determine a longer or shorter period as its fiscal year. It does not necessarily coincide with the calendar year.

Fischer, Bobby (Robert James) (1943–) US chess player who was world champion from 1972 to 1975. In 1958, after proving himself in international competition, he became the youngest grand master in history at the age of 15. He was the author of *Games of Chess* (1959), and was also celebrated for his unorthodox psychological tactics.

Fischer, Emil Hermann (1852–1919) German chemist who produced synthetic sugars and, from these, various enzymes. His descriptions of the chemistry of the carbohydrates and peptides laid the foundations for the science of biochemistry. He was awarded the Nobel Prize for Chemistry in 1902 for his work on the synthesis of sugars and purine compounds.

Fischer, Hans (1881–1945) German chemist awarded the Nobel Prize for Chemistry in 1930 for his work on haemoglobin, the oxygen-carrying, red colouring matter in blood. He determined the molecular structures of three important biological pigments: haemoglobin, chlorophyll, and bilirubin.

Fischer-Dieskau, Dietrich (1925–) German baritone singer. His intelligently focused and subtly understated interpretations of opera and lieder introduced a new depth and intimacy to a wide-ranging repertoire extending in opera from Christoph Willibald von Gluck to Alban Berg's Wozzeck, Hans Werner Henze, and Benjamin Britten, and from Bach arias to lieder of Schubert, Hugo Wolf, and Arnold Schoenberg. Since 1973 he has also conducted.

fish aquatic vertebrate that uses gills to obtain oxygen from fresh or sea water. There are three main groups: the bony fishes or Osteichthyes (goldfish, cod, tuna); the cartilaginous fishes or Chondrichthyes (sharks, rays); and the jawless fishes or Agnatha (hagfishes, lampreys). Fishes of some form are found in virtually every body of water in the world except for the very salty water of the Dead Sea and some of the hot larval springs. Of the 30,000 fish species, approximately 2,500 are freshwater.

fish farming *or* aquaculture raising fish (including molluscs and crustaceans) under controlled conditions in tanks and ponds, sometimes in offshore pens. It has been practised for centuries in the Far East, where Japan today produces some 100,000 tonnes of fish a year; the USA, Norway, and Canada are also big producers. Fish farms are environmentally controversial because of the risk of escapees that could spread disease and alter the genetic balance of wild populations.

fission in physics, the splitting of a heavy atomic nucleus into two or more major fragments. It is accompanied by the emission of two or three neutrons and the release of large amounts of *nuclear energy.

fit in medicine, popular term for *convulsion.

Fitzgerald, Ella (1917–1996) US jazz singer. She is recognized as one of the finest, most lyrical voices in

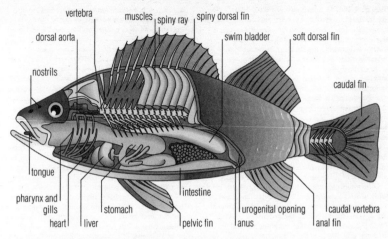

vertebra muscles spiny ray spiny dorsal fin

dorsal aorta

swim bladder soft dorsal fin

nostrils

caudal fin

tongue

pharynx and gills

heart liver

stomach

pelvic fin

intestine

anus

urogenital opening

caudal vertebra

anal fin

fish The anatomy of a fish. All fishes move through water using their fins for propulsion. The bony fishes, like the specimen shown here, constitute the largest group of fishes with about 20,000 species.

jazz, both in solo work and with big bands. She is celebrated for her smooth interpretations of George *Gershwin and Cole *Porter songs.

Fitzgerald, F(rancis) Scott (Key) (1896–1940) US novelist and short-story writer. His early autobiographical novel *This Side of Paradise* (1920) made him known in the post-war society of the East Coast, and *The Great Gatsby* (1925) epitomizes the Jazz Age.

Five Pillars of Islam the five duties required of every Muslim. **Shahadah:** to affirm that there is only one God, Allah, and that Muhammad was his messenger. **Salat:** to pray five times a day. **Zakah:** to give alms (money) in a 'tithe' system. **Sawm:** to fast during the month of Ramadan. ***Hajj;** to go on a pilgrimage to Mecca (Makkah) at least once in a lifetime, unless prevented by ill health or poverty.

fixed point temperature that can be accurately reproduced and used as the basis of a temperature scale. In the Celsius scale, the fixed points are the temperature of melting ice, defined to be 0 °C (32 °F), and the temperature of boiling water (at standard atmospheric pressure), defined to be 100 °C (212 °F).

fjord *or* **fiord** narrow sea inlet enclosed by high cliffs. Fjords are found in Norway, New Zealand, Southern Chile, and western parts of Scotland. They are formed when an overdeepened U-shaped glacial valley is drowned by a rise in sea-level. At the mouth of the fjord there is a characteristic lip causing a shallowing of the water. This is due to reduced glacial erosion and the deposition of *moraine at this point.

flame test in chemistry, the use of a flame to identify metal *cations present in a solid.

flame tree any of various trees with brilliant red flowers, including the smooth-stemmed semi-deciduous *Brachychiton acerifolium* with scarlet bell-shaped flowers, native to Australia, but spread throughout the tropics.

flamingo long-legged and long-necked wading bird, family Phoenicopteridae, of the stork order Ciconiiformes. Largest of the family is the greater or roseate flamingo *Phoenicopterus ruber,* found in Africa, the Caribbean, and South America, with delicate pink plumage and 1.25 m/4 ft tall. They sift the mud for food with their downbent bills, and build colonies of high, conelike mud nests, with a little hollow for the eggs at the top.

flat symbol ♭, in music, a sign that tells a player to lower the pitch of a note by one semitone. It can also describe the inaccurate intonation of players when they are playing lower in pitch than they should be.

flatfish bony fishes of the order Pleuronectiformes, having a characteristically flat, asymmetrical body with both eyes (in adults) on the upper side. Species include flounders, turbots, halibuts, plaice, and the European soles.

flatworm invertebrate of the phylum Platyhelminthes. Some are free-living, but many are parasitic (for example, tapeworms and flukes). The body is simple and bilaterally symmetrical, with one opening to the intestine. Many are hermaphroditic (with both male and female sex organs) and practise self-fertilization.

Flaubert, Gustave (1821–1880) French writer. One of the major novelists of the 19th century, he was the author of *Madame Bovary* (1857), *Salammbô* (1862), *L'Education sentimentale/Sentimental Education* (1869), and *La Tentation de Saint Antoine/The Temptation of St Anthony* (1874). Flaubert also wrote the short stories *Trois Contes/Three Tales* (1877). His dedication to art resulted in a meticulous prose style, realistic detail, and psychological depth, which is often revealed through interior monologue.

flax any of a group of plants including the cultivated *L. usitatissimum;* **linen** is produced from the fibre in its stems. The seeds yield **linseed oil,** used in paints and varnishes. The plant, of almost worldwide distribution, has a stem up to 60 cm/24 in high, small leaves, and bright blue flowers. (Genus *Linum*, family Linaceae.)

flea wingless insect of the order Siphonaptera, with blood-sucking mouthparts. Fleas are parasitic on warm-blooded animals. Some fleas can jump 130 times their own height.

fleabane any of several plants of two related groups, belonging to the daisy family. Common fleabane (*P. dysenterica*) has golden-yellow flower heads and grows in wet and marshy places throughout Europe. (Genera *Pulicaria* and *Erigeron*, family Compositae.)

Fleming, Alexander (1881–1955) Scottish bacteriologist who was awarded a Nobel Prize for Physiology or Medicine in 1945 for his discovery of the bactericidal effect of *penicillin in 1928. In 1922 he had discovered lysozyme, an antibacterial enzyme present in saliva, nasal secretions, and tears. While studying this, he found an unusual mould growing on a culture dish, which he isolated and grew into a pure culture. This led to his discovery of penicillin, which came into use in 1941. He shared the award with Howard W *Florey and Ernst B *Chain, whose research had brought widespread realization of the value of penicillin with its isolation and its development as an antibiotic drug.

Fleming, Ian Lancaster (1908–1964) English author. His suspense novels feature the ruthless, laconic James Bond, British Secret Service agent 007. The first novel in the series was *Casino Royale* (1953); others include *From Russia with Love* (1957), *Goldfinger* (1959), and *The Man with the Golden Gun* (1965). Most of the novels were made into a successful series of Bond films.

Fleming's rules memory aids used to recall the relative directions of the magnetic field, current, and motion in an electric generator or motor, using one's fingers. The three directions are represented by the thu*m*b (for *m*otion), fore*f*inger (for *f*ield), and second finger (for conventional *c*urrent), all held at right angles to each other. The right hand is used for generators and the left for motors. The rules were devised by the English physicist John Fleming.

Flemish member of the West Germanic branch of the Indo-European language family, spoken in north Belgium and the Nord *département* of France. It is closely related to Dutch.

Flemish art painting and sculpture of Flanders (now divided between Belgium, the Netherlands, and France). A distinctive Flemish style emerged in the early 15th century based on manuscript illumination and the art of the Burgundian court. It is distinguished by keen observation, minute attention to detail, bright colours, and superb technique – oil painting was a Flemish invention. Apart from portraits, Flemish art is chiefly religious and often set in contemporary landscapes, townscapes, and interiors.

Flemish Brabant Flemish **Vlaams-Brabant**, province of Belgium, part of the Dutch-speaking Flemish community and region, bounded by Antwerp to the north, Limbourg and Liège to the east, Walloon Brabant and Hainaut to the south, and East Flanders to the west; area 2,106 sq km/813 sq mi; population (2003 est) 1,025,800. Contained within its borders is the Brussels-Capital Region, an autonomous administrative division created in 1995 at the same time

as the province of Brabant was bisected into Flemish Brabant and Walloon Brabant. Its capital is the city of Louvain, and other major towns include Halle, Tienen, and Vilvoorde.

flight *or* **aviation** method of transport in which aircraft carry people and goods through the air. People first took to the air in *balloons in 1783 and began powered flight in 1852 in *airships, but the history of flying, both for civilian and military use, is dominated by the *aeroplane. The earliest planes were designed for *gliding; the advent of the petrol engine saw the first powered flight by the *Wright brothers in 1903 in the USA. This inspired the development of aircraft throughout Europe. Biplanes were succeeded by monoplanes in the 1930s. The first jet plane (see *jet propulsion) was produced in 1939, and after the end of World War II the development of jetliners brought about a continuous expansion in passenger air travel. In 1969 came the supersonic aircraft Concorde. Concorde ceased service in 2003 and aircraft development has focused on economy and passenger numbers.

flint compact, hard, brittle mineral (a variety of chert), brown, black, or grey in colour, found as nodules in limestone or shale deposits. It consists of cryptocrystalline (grains too small to be visible even under a light microscope) *silica, SiO_2, principally in the crystalline form of *quartz. Implements fashioned from flint were widely used in prehistory.

Flintshire Welsh **Sir y Fflint**, unitary authority in north Wales. A former county, it was part of Clwyd between 1974 and 1996. **area:** 437 sq km/169 sq mi **towns:** Mold (administrative headquarters), Flint, Holywell, Buckley, Connah's Quay **physical:** bounded by the Irish Sea in the north, the Dee estuary in the east, and the Clwydian Range, which rises to 555 m/1,820 ft, in the southwest; rivers Dee, Alyn **features:** St Winifride's Holy Well (646), ruins of Basingwerk Abbey (1132), ruins of Fflint Castle (1284) **population:** (1998 est) 147,000.

Flodden, Battle of defeat of the Scots by the English under the Earl of Surrey on 9 September 1513, on a site 5 km/3 mi southeast of Coldstream, in Northumberland, England. *James IV of Scotland, declaring himself the active ally of France, crossed the border to England with an invading army of 30,000. The Scots were defeated, suffering heavy losses, and James himself was killed.

Flood, the in the Old Testament, the Koran, and *The Epic of Gilgamesh* (an ancient Sumerian legend), a deluge lasting 40 days and nights, a disaster alleged to have obliterated all humanity except a chosen few (in the Old Testament, the survivors were the family of Noah and the pairs of animals sheltered on his ark).

floppy disk in computing, a storage device consisting of a light, flexible disk enclosed in a plastic jacket. The disk is placed in a disk drive, where it rotates at high speed. Data are recorded magnetically on one or both surfaces.

Florence Italian **Firenze**; Roman **Florentia**, capital of *Tuscany, northern Italy, on the River Arno, 88 km/ 55 mi from the river's mouth; population (1992) 397,400. It has printing, engineering, and optical industries; many crafts, including leather, gold and silver work, and embroidery; and its art and architecture attract large numbers of tourists. Notable medieval and Renaissance citizens included the writers Dante and

Boccaccio, and the artists Giotto, Leonardo da Vinci, and Michelangelo.

Florey, Howard Walter (1898–1968) Baron Florey, Australian pathologist who was awarded the Nobel Prize for Physiology or Medicine in 1945 with Ernst *Chain for the isolation of penicillin and its development as an antibiotic drug. His research into lysozyme, an antibacterial enzyme discovered by Alexander *Fleming (who shared the prize), led him to study penicillin (another of Fleming's discoveries), which he and Chain isolated and prepared for widespread use.

Florida called the **Sunshine State**, (Spanish *Pascua Florida* 'Easter of Flowers') southeasternmost state of the USA, bordered to the north by *Georgia and by *Alabama; area 139,670 sq km/53,927 sq mi; population (2000) 15,982,400; capital Tallahassee. Florida is a low-lying tropical peninsula, and has large areas of swampland, such as the *Everglades, as well as large bays, lagoons, and beaches along the coastline. The *Florida Keys island chain extends to the southwest. Florida produces almost 75% of the citrus fruit crop in the USA, and the fishing industry is also important, with about 10% of the total shrimp catch in the USA. Tourism and finance are significant industries, and there is manufacturing based around the NASA space programme at Cape Canaveral. The largest city and urban area is Jacksonville, and other major cities include *Miami, Tampa, St Petersburg, Hialeah, Orlando, Fort Lauderdale, and Hollywood. Florida was admitted to the Union in 1845 as the 27th US state and is governed under the 1969 state constitution.

Florida Keys series of small coral islands that curve over 240 km/150 mi southwest from the southern tip of Florida, USA, between the Straits of Florida and Florida Bay. The most important are Key Largo (the largest settlement) and Key West (which has a US naval and air station); economically they depend on fishing and tourism. A causeway links the keys to each other and to the mainland.

flotation, law of law stating that a floating object displaces its own weight of the fluid in which it floats. See *Archimedes principle.

flounder small flatfish *Platychthys flesus* of the northeastern Atlantic and Mediterranean, although it sometimes lives in estuaries. It is dull in colour and grows to 50 cm/1.6 ft.

flour beetle beetle that is a major pest of stored agricultural products, such as flour. They are found worldwide in granaries and stores where both the adult beetles and the larvae feed on damaged grain or flour. Neither adults nor larvae can eat intact grains. Flour beetles are in the genus *Tribolium*, family Tenebrionidae, class Insecta, phylum Arthropoda.

flow chart diagram, often used in computing, to show the possible paths that data can take through a system or program.

flower reproductive unit of an angiosperm (flowering plant), typically consisting of four whorls of modified leaves: *sepals, *petals, *stamens, and *carpels. These are borne on a central axis or *receptacle. The many variations in size, colour, number, and arrangement of parts are closely related to the method of pollination. Flowers adapted for wind pollination typically have reduced or absent petals and sepals and long, feathery

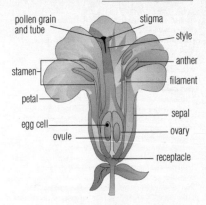

flower Cross section of a typical flower showing its basic components: sepals, petals, stamens (anthers and filaments), and carpel (ovary and stigma). Flowers vary greatly in the size, shape, colour, and arrangement of these components.

stigmas that hang outside the flower to trap airborne pollen. In contrast, the petals of insect-pollinated flowers are usually conspicuous and brightly coloured.

flowering plant term generally used for *angiosperms, which bear flowers with various parts, including sepals, petals, stamens, and carpels. Sometimes the term is used more broadly, to include both angiosperms and *gymnosperms, in which case the *cones of conifers and cycads are referred to as 'flowers'. Usually, however, the angiosperms and gymnosperms are referred to collectively as *seed plants, or spermatophytes.

flugelhorn valved brass instrument of the *bugle type. It is made in three sizes: soprano, alto, and tenor, and is used in military and brass bands. In Britain only the alto instrument, in B flat, is used, normally only in brass bands. The alto flugelhorn has a similar range to the *cornet but is of mellower tone.

fluke any of various parasitic flatworms of the classes Monogenea and Digenea, that as adults live in and destroy the livers of sheep, cattle, horses, dogs, and humans. Monogenetic flukes can complete their life cycle in one host; digenetic flukes require two or more hosts, for example a snail and a human being, to complete their life cycle.

fluorescence short-lived *luminescence (a glow not caused by high temperature). *Phosphorescence lasts a little longer.

fluoridation addition of small amounts of fluoride salts to drinking water by certain water authorities to help prevent tooth decay. Experiments in Britain, the USA, and elsewhere have indicated that a concentration of fluoride of 1 part per million in tap water retards the decay of children's teeth by more than 50%.

fluoride F⁻, negative ion formed when hydrogen fluoride dissolves in water; compound formed between fluorine and another element in which the fluorine is the more electronegative element.

fluorine chemical symbol F, pale yellow, gaseous, non-metallic element, atomic number 9, relative atomic mass 19. It is the first member of the halogen group of elements, and is pungent, poisonous, and highly reactive, uniting directly with nearly all the elements. It occurs naturally as the minerals fluorite (CaF_2) and cryolite (Na_3AlF_6). Hydrogen fluoride is used in etching glass, and the freons, which all contain fluorine, are widely used as refrigerants.

fluorocarbon compound formed by replacing the hydrogen atoms of a hydrocarbon with fluorine. Fluorocarbons are used as inert coatings, refrigerants, synthetic resins, and as propellants in aerosols.

flute *or* **transverse flute** side-blown woodwind instrument with a long history, capable of intricate melodies and a wide range of expression. The player holds the flute horizontally, and to the right, and blows across an end hole. The air current is split by the opposite edge of the hole, causing the air column inside the instrument to vibrate and produce a sound. The fingers operate a system of keys to open and close holes in the side of the flute to create different notes. The standard soprano flute has a range of three octaves.

fly any insect of the order Diptera. A fly has a single pair of wings, antennae, and compound eyes; the hind wings have become modified into knoblike projections (halteres) used to maintain equilibrium in flight. There are over 90,000 species.

flying dragon lizard *Draco volans* of the family Agamidae. It lives in southeast Asia, and can glide on flaps of skin spread and supported by its ribs. This small (7.5 cm/3 in head and body) arboreal lizard can glide between trees for 6 m/20 ft or more.

flying fish any marine bony fishes of the family Exocoetidae, order Beloniformes, best represented in tropical waters. They have winglike pectoral fins that can be spread to glide over the water.

flying fox another name for the fruit bat, a fruit-eating *bat of the suborder Megachiroptera.

flying squirrel any of 43 known species of squirrel, not closely related to the true squirrels. They are characterized by a membrane along the side of the body from forelimb to hindlimb (in some species running to neck and tail) which allows them to glide through the air. Several genera of flying squirrel are found in the Old World; the New World has the genus *Glaucomys*. Most species are eastern Asian.

Flynn, Errol (1909–1959) stage name of Leslie Thomson Flynn, Australian-born US film actor. He portrayed swashbuckling heroes in such films as *Captain Blood* (1935), *Robin Hood* (1938), *The Charge of the Light Brigade* (1938), *The Private Lives of Elizabeth and Essex* (1939), *The Sea Hawk* (1940), and *The Master of Ballantrae* (1953).

Fo, Dario (1926–) Italian dramatist and actor. His plays are predominantly political satires combining black humour with slapstick. They include *Morte accidentale di un anarchico/Accidental Death of an Anarchist* (1970), *Non si paga non si paga/Can't Pay? Won't Pay!* (1974) and *L'Anomalo Bicefalo/The Abnormal Two-brainer* (2003). Fo was awarded the Nobel Prize for Literature in 1997.

focal length *or* **focal distance** distance from the centre of a lens or curved mirror to the focal point. For a concave mirror or convex lens, it is the distance at which rays of light parallel to the principal axis of the mirror or lens are brought to a focus (for a mirror, this

is half the radius of curvature). For a convex mirror or concave lens, it is the distance from the centre to the point from which rays of light originally parallel to the principal axis of the mirror or lens diverge after being reflected or refracted.

Foch, Ferdinand (1851–1929) Marshal of France during World War I. He was largely responsible for the Allied victory at the first battle of the *Marne in September 1914, and commanded on the northwestern front October 1914–September 1916. He was appointed commander-in-chief of the Allied armies in the spring of 1918, and launched the Allied counter-offensive in July that brought about the negotiation of an armistice to end the war.

focus *or* **focal point** in optics, the point at which light rays converge, or from which they appear to diverge. Other electromagnetic rays, such as microwaves, and sound waves may also be brought together at a focus. Rays parallel to the principal axis of a lens or mirror are converged at, or appear to diverge from, the principal focus.

foetus stage in mammalian embryo development; see *fetus.

fog cloud that collects at the surface of the Earth, composed of water vapour that has condensed on particles of dust in the atmosphere. Cloud and fog are both caused by the air temperature falling below *dew point. The thickness of fog depends on the number of water particles it contains. Officially, fog refers to a condition when visibility is reduced to 1 km/0.6 mi or less, and mist or haze to that giving a visibility of 1–2 km/0.6–1.2 mi.

Fokine, Mikhail (1880–1942) Russian choreographer and dancer. He was chief choreographer to the Ballets Russes 1909–14, and with *Diaghilev revitalized and reformed the art of ballet, promoting the idea of artistic unity among dramatic, musical, and stylistic elements.

fold in geology, a deformation (bend) in *beds or layers of rock. Folds are caused by pressures within the Earth's crust resulting from *plate-tectonic activity. Rocks are slowly pushed and compressed together, forming folds. Such deformation usually occurs in *sedimentary layers that are softer and more flexible. If the force is more sudden, and the rock more brittle, then a *fault forms instead of a fold.

folic acid *vitamin of the B complex. It is found in liver, legumes and green leafy vegetables, and whole grain foods, and is also synthesized by the intestinal bacteria. It is essential for growth, and plays many other roles in the body. Lack of folic acid causes anaemia because it is necessary for the synthesis of nucleic acids and the formation of red blood cells.

folklore oral traditions and culture of a people, expressed in legends, riddles, songs, tales, and proverbs.

folk music traditional music, especially from rural areas, which is passed on by listening and repeating, and is usually performed by amateurs. The term is used to distinguish it from the classical music of a country, and from urban popular or commercial music. Most folk music exists in the form of songs, or instrumental music to accompany folk dancing, and is usually melodic and rhythmic rather than harmonic in style.

follicle in zoology, a small group of cells that surround and nourish a structure such as a hair (hair follicle) or a cell such as an egg (Graafian follicle; see *menstrual cycle).

Fomalhaut *or* **Alpha Piscis Austrini** brightest star in the southern constellation *Piscis Austrinus and the 18th-brightest star in the night sky. It is 25 light years from the Sun, with a true luminosity 13 times that of the Sun.

Fongafale capital of Tuvalu, on Funafuti atoll; population (2001 est) 5,000.

font *or* **fount** complete set of printed or display characters of the same typeface, size, and style (bold, italic, underlined, and so on).

Fontainebleau (Latin *Fons Bellaqueus*) town in Seine-et-Marne *département*, France, situated 60 km/ 37 mi southeast of Paris near the River Seine; population (1990) 35,500. Its royal palace was founded by Philip the Good, but, as it exists today, was built by Francis I in the 16th century. Louis XIV's mistress, Mme de Montespan, lived here, as did Louis XV's mistress, Mme du Barry. The French emperor Napoleon signed his abdication here in 1814. Nearby is the village of Barbizon, the haunt of several 19th-century painters (known as the *Barbizon School).

Fontainebleau School French school of Mannerist painting and sculpture. It was established at the court of François I, who brought Italian artists to Fontainebleau, near Paris, to decorate his hunting lodge: Rosso Fiorentino arrived in 1530, Francesco Primaticcio came in 1532. They evolved a distinctive decorative style using a combination of stucco relief and painting. Their work, with its exuberant ornamental and figurative style, had a lasting impact on French art in the 16th century.

Fonteyn, Margot (1919–1991) stage name of Peggy (Margaret) Hookham, English ballet dancer. She made her debut with the Vic-Wells Ballet in *Nutcracker* (1934) and first appeared as Giselle in 1937, eventually becoming prima ballerina of the Royal Ballet, London. Renowned for her perfect physique, clear line, musicality, and interpretive powers, she created many roles in Frederick *Ashton's ballets and formed a legendary partnership with Rudolf *Nureyev. She retired from dancing in 1979.

food anything eaten by human beings and other animals, or absorbed by plants, to sustain life and health. The building blocks of food are nutrients, and humans can utilize the following nutrients: **carbohydrates** as starches found in bread, potatoes, and pasta; as simple sugars in sucrose and honey; and as fibres in cereals, fruit, and vegetables; **proteins** from nuts, fish, meat, eggs, milk, and some vegetables; **fats** as found in most animal products (meat, lard, dairy products, fish), also in margarine, nuts and seeds, olives, and edible oils; **vitamins**, found in a wide variety of foods, except for vitamin B_{12} which is found mainly in foods of animal origin; and **minerals**, found in a wide variety of foods (for example, calcium from milk and broccoli, iodine from seafood, and iron from liver and green vegetables).

Food and Agriculture Organization (FAO) United Nations specialized agency that coordinates activities to improve food and timber production and levels of nutrition throughout the world. It is also concerned with investment in agriculture and dispersal of emergency food supplies. It has headquarters in Rome and was founded in 1945.

food chain in ecology, a sequence showing the feeding relationships between organisms in a *habitat or *ecosystem. It shows who eats whom. An organism in one food chain can belong to other food chains. This can be shown in a diagram called a **food web**. (See diagram, p. 340.)

food poisoning any acute illness characterized by vomiting and diarrhoea and caused by eating food contaminated with harmful bacteria (for example, *listeriosis), poisonous food (for example, certain mushrooms or puffer fish), or poisoned food (such as lead or arsenic introduced accidentally during processing). A frequent cause of food poisoning is *Salmonella bacteria. Salmonella comes in many forms, and strains are found in cattle, pigs, poultry, and eggs. Some people are more susceptible to food poisoning than others, and extra care is taken with food products designed for babies, pregnant women, or elderly people. Many types of bacteria can cause food poisoning and the incubation periods, symptoms, and methods of control vary.

foot symbol ft, imperial unit of length, equivalent to 0.3048 m, in use in Britain since Anglo-Saxon times. It originally represented the length of a human foot. One foot contains 12 inches and is one-third of a yard.

foot unit of metrical pattern in poetry. The five most common types of foot in English poetry are iamb (v –), trochee (– v), dactyl (– vv), spondee (—), and anapaest (vv –); the symbol v stands for an unstressed syllable and – for a stressed one.

foot-and-mouth disease contagious eruptive viral disease of cloven-hoofed mammals, characterized by blisters in the mouth and around the hooves. In cattle it causes deterioration of milk yield and abortions. It is an airborne virus, which makes its eradication extremely difficult.

football, American contact sport similar to the English game of rugby, played between two teams of 11 players, with an inflated oval ball. Players are well padded for protection and wear protective helmets. The **Super Bowl**, first held in 1967, is now an annual meeting between the winners of the National and American Football Conferences.

football, association *or* **soccer** form of football originating in the UK, popular throughout the world. The modern game is played in the UK according to the rules laid down by the home countries' football associations. Slight amendments to the rules take effect in certain competitions and international matches as laid down by the sport's world governing body, Fédération Internationale de Football Association (FIFA, 1904). FIFA organizes the competitions for the World Cup, held every four years since 1930.

football, Australian rules game that combines aspects of Gaelic football, rugby, and association football; it is played between two teams of 18 players each, with an inflated oval ball. It is unique to Australia.

football, Gaelic kicking and catching game played mainly in Ireland. The two teams have 15 players each. The game is played on a field with an inflated spherical ball. The goalposts have a crossbar and a net across the lower half. Goals are scored by kicking the ball into the net (three points) or over the crossbar (one point).

forage crop plant that is grown to feed livestock; for example, grass, clover, and kale (a form of cabbage).

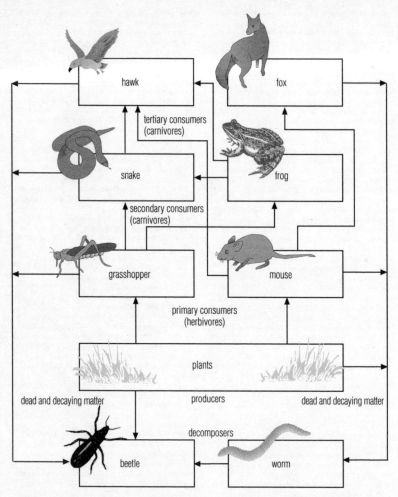

food web The complex interrelationships between animals and plants in a food web. A food web shows how different food chains are linked in an ecosystem. Note that the arrows indicate movement of energy through the web. For example, an arrow shows that energy moves from plants to the grasshopper, which eats the plants.

Forage crops cover a greater area of the world than food crops, and grass, which dominates this group, is the world's most abundant crop, though much of it is still in an unimproved state.

force any influence that tends to change the state of rest of a body its uniform motion in a straight line. The action of an unbalanced or resultant force results in the acceleration of a body in the direction of action of the force, or it may, if the body is unable to move freely, result in its deformation (see *Hooke's law). A force is a

push or a pull on an object. A force will cause an object to move if it is stationary, change direction, slow down, or speed up. Force is a vector quantity, possessing both magnitude and direction; its SI unit is the newton.

forces, fundamental in physics, four fundamental interactions currently known to be at work in the physical universe. There are two long-range forces: the **gravitational force**, or gravity, which keeps the planets in orbit around the Sun and acts between all particles that have mass; and the **electromagnetic force**, which stops solids from falling apart and acts between all particles with *electric charge. There are two very short-range forces, which operate over distances comparable with the size of the atomic nucleus: the **weak nuclear force**, responsible for the reactions that fuel the Sun and for the emission of *beta particles by some particles; and the **strong nuclear force**, which binds together the protons and neutrons in the nuclei of atoms. The relative strengths of the four forces are: strong, 1; electromagnetic, 10^{-2}; weak, 10^{-6}; gravitational, 10^{-40}.

Ford, Gerald R(udolph) (1913–) 38th president of the USA 1974–77, a Republican. He was elected to the House of Representatives in 1948, was nominated to the vice-presidency by Richard Nixon in 1973 on the resignation of Spiro Agnew, and became president in 1974, when Nixon was forced to resign following the *Watergate scandal. He granted Nixon a full pardon in September 1974.

Ford, Henry (1863–1947) US car manufacturer. He built his first car in 1896 and founded the Ford Motor Company in 1903 with 11 investors. Ford held 25.5% of the stock, and it was three years before he took a controlling interest and was named president. His first car, the Model A, was sold in 1903. He was a pioneer of large-scale manufacture and his Model T (1908–27) was the first car to be constructed solely by assembly-line methods; 15 million had been sold by the time production ceased. Ford's innovative policies, such as a daily minimum wage and a five-day working week, revolutionized employment practices, but he staunchly opposed and impeded the introduction of trade unions.

Ford, John (1895–1973) adopted name of Sean Aloysius O'Feeney, US film director. Active from the silent film era, he became one of the most acclaimed figures of classical Hollywood cinema, winning four Academy Awards for best director. Responsible for a number of impressive Westerns such as *The Iron Horse* (1924), *Stagecoach* (1939), *My Darling Clementine* (1946), *She Wore a Yellow Ribbon* (1949), *The Searchers* (1956), and *The Man Who Shot Liberty Valance* (1962), he also directed a range of comedies and dramas, including *The Grapes of Wrath* (1940).

foreign aid see *aid.

Foreign and Commonwealth Office (FCO) UK government department established in 1782 as the Foreign Office. It is responsible for the conduct of the UK's overseas relations, including advising on policy, negotiating with overseas governments, and conducting business in international organizations. It promotes British business overseas (jointly with the Department of Trade and Industry through British Trade International), and is also responsible for protecting UK interests and citizens abroad, and (together with the Home Office) for entry clearance.

Foreign Legion volunteer corps of foreigners within a country's army. The French **Légion Etrangère**, founded in 1831, is one of a number of such forces. Enlisted volunteers are of any nationality (about half are now French), but the officers are usually French. Headquarters until 1962 was in Sidi Bel Abbés, Algeria; the main base is now Corsica, with reception headquarters at Aubagne, near Marseille, France.

forensic medicine in medicine, branch of medicine concerned with the resolution of crimes. Examples of forensic medicine include the determination of the cause of death in suspicious circumstances or the identification of a criminal by examining tissue found at the scene of a crime. Forensic psychology involves the establishment of a psychological profile of a criminal that can assist in identification.

forensic science use of scientific techniques to solve criminal cases. A multidisciplinary field embracing chemistry, physics, botany, zoology, and medicine, forensic science includes the identification of human bodies or traces. Ballistics (the study of projectiles, such as bullets), another traditional forensic field, makes use of such tools as the comparison microscope and the electron microscope.

forestry science of forest management. Recommended forestry practice aims at multipurpose crops, allowing the preservation of varied plant and animal species as well as human uses (lumbering, recreation). Forestry has often been confined to the planting of a single species, such as a rapid-growing conifer providing softwood for paper pulp and construction timber, for which world demand is greatest. In tropical countries, logging contributes to the destruction of *rainforests, causing global environmental problems. Small unplanned forests are *woodland.

forget-me-not any of a group of plants belonging to the borage family, including *M. sylvatica* and *M. scorpioides*, with small bright blue flowers. (Genus *Myosotis*, family Boraginaceae.)

forging one of the main methods of shaping metals, which involves hammering or a more gradual application of pressure. A blacksmith hammers red-hot metal into shape on an anvil, and the traditional place of work is called a forge. The blacksmith's mechanical equivalent is the drop forge. The metal is shaped by the blows from a falling hammer or ram, which is usually accelerated by steam or air pressure. Hydraulic presses forge by applying pressure gradually in a squeezing action.

formaldehyde common name for *methanal.

formatting in computing, short for disk formatting (laying down a structure for organizing, saving, and retrieving data), or text formatting (changing its appearance). Modern office programs and *desktop publishing packages also allow the formatting of objects such as pictures and frames.

Formentera smallest inhabited island in the Spanish Balearic Islands, lying south of Ibiza; area 93 sq km/ 36 sq mi; population (1990) 5,200. The chief town is San Francisco Javier and the main port is La Sabina. The main industry is tourism.

formic acid common name for *methanoic acid.

formula in chemistry, a representation of a molecule, radical, or ion, in which the component chemical elements are represented by their symbols. For example, the formula for carbon dioxide is CO_2, showing that a molecule of carbon dioxide consists of one atom of carbon (C) and two atoms of oxygen (O_2). An **empirical formula** indicates the simplest ratio of the elements in a compound, without indicating how many of them there are or how they are combined. A **molecular formula** gives the number of each type of element present in one molecule. A **structural formula** shows the relative positions of the atoms and the bonds between them. For example, for ethanoic (acetic) acid, the empirical formula is CH_2O, the molecular formula is $C_2H_4O_2$, and the structural formula is CH_3COOH.

formula in mathematics, a set of symbols and numbers that expresses a fact or rule. For example, $A = \pi r^2$ is the formula for calculating the area of a circle. $E = mc^2$ is Einstein's famous formula relating energy and mass. Other common formulae exist for *density, *mass, *volume, and *area.

Formula 1 form of *motor racing. Formula 1 Grand Prix racing first began in 1906. A world championship for drivers has been in existence since 1950 and for constructors since 1958. The first eight drivers and cars in each race are awarded 10, 8, 6, 5, 4, 3, 2 and 1 point respectively, and the cumulative total at the end of a season decides the winners.

Forster, E(dward) M(organ) (1879–1970) English novelist, short-story writer, and critic. He was concerned with the interplay of personality and the conflict between convention and instinct. His novels include *A Room with a View* (1908), *Howards End* (1910), and *A Passage to India* (1924). Other works include the collections of stories *The Celestial Omnibus* (1911) and *Collected Short Stories* (1948), and the collection of essays and reviews 'Abinger Harvest' (1936). His most lasting critical work is *Aspects of the Novel* (1927). The integrity with which Forster approached life in his novels has also enhanced the value of his miscellaneous and critical writings. Many of his works have been successfully adapted for film.

forsythia any of a group of temperate eastern Asian shrubs, which bear yellow bell-shaped flowers in early spring before the leaves appear. (Genus *Forsythia*, family Oleaceae.)

Fort-de-France capital, chief commercial centre, and port of Martinique, West Indies, on the west coast at the mouth of the Madame River; population (1999 est) 94,000 (city), 134,700 (commune). It exports sugar, rum, tinned fruit, and cacao. There is an airport and the tourist industry is a source of much local revenue.

fortepiano early 18th-century piano invented by Italian instrument maker Bartolommeo Cristofori in 1709. It has small, leather-bound hammers and harpsichord strings. Unlike the harpsichord, it can produce a varying intensity of tone, depending on the pressure of the player's touch, hence the name, which means 'loud-soft' in Italian.

Forth river in central Scotland, with its headstreams, Duchray Water and Avondhu, rising on the northeast slopes of Ben Lomond. It flows east approximately 105 km/65 mi to Kincardine where the **Firth of Forth** begins. The Firth is approximately 80 km/50 mi long, and is 26 km/16 mi wide where it joins the North Sea.

FORTRAN *or* **fortran** contraction of formula translation, high-level computer-programming language suited to mathematical and scientific computations. Developed by John Backus at IBM in 1956, it is one of the earliest computer languages still in use. A recent version, Fortran 90, is now being used on advanced parallel computers. *BASIC was strongly influenced by FORTRAN and is similar in many ways.

Forty-Five, the *Jacobite rebellion of 1745, led by Prince *Charles Edward Stuart. With his army of Highlanders 'Bonnie Prince Charlie' occupied Edinburgh and advanced into England as far as Derby, but then turned back. The rising was crushed by the Duke of Cumberland at Culloden in 1746.

forum (Latin 'market') in an ancient Roman town, the meeting place and market, like the Greek *agora*. In Rome the Forum Romanum contained the Senate House, the public speaking platform, covered halls for trading, temples of Saturn, Concord, and the Divine Augustus, and memorial arches. Later constructions included the Forum of Caesar (temple of Venus), the Forum of *Augustus (temple of Mars), and the colonnaded Forum of *Trajan, containing Trajan's Column.

fossil (Latin *fossilis* 'dug up') cast, impression, or the actual remains of an animal or plant preserved in rock. Dead animals and plant remains that fell to the bottom of the sea bed or an inland lake were gradually buried under the accumulation of layers of sediment. Over millions of years, the sediment became *sedimentary rock and the remains preserved within the rock became fossilized. Fossils may include footprints, an internal cast, or external impression. A few fossils are preserved intact, as with *mammoths fossilized in Siberian ice, or insects trapped in tree resin that is today amber. The study of fossils is called *palaeontology. Palaeontologists are able to deduce much of the geological history of a region from fossil remains. The existence of fossils is key evidence that organisms have changed with time, that is, evolved (see *evolution).

fossil fuel combustible material, such as coal, lignite, oil, *peat, and *natural gas, formed from the fossilized remains of plants that lived hundreds of millions of years ago. Such fuels are *non-renewable resources – once they are burnt, they cannot be replaced.

Foster, Norman Robert (1935–) English architect of the high-tech school. His buildings in England include the Willis Faber & Dumas insurance offices, Ipswich (1975); the Sainsbury Centre for the Visual Arts, Norwich (1977); and Stansted Airport, Essex, England (1991). His works abroad include the headquarters of the Hong Kong and Shanghai Bank (1986) in Hong Kong. In 1999 he won the Pritzker Architecture Prize. He designed the Millennium Bridge (2000) in London, England.

Foucault, (Jean Bernard) Léon (1819–1868) French physicist who used a pendulum to demonstrate the rotation of the Earth on its axis, and invented the *gyroscope in 1852. In 1862 he made the first accurate determination of the velocity of light.

Foucault, Michel Paul (1926–1984) French philosopher who argued that human knowledge and subjectivity are dependent upon specific institutions and practices, and that they change through history. In particular, he was concerned to subvert conventional assumptions about 'social deviants' – the mentally ill, the sick, and the criminal – who, he believed, are oppressed by the approved knowledge of the period in which they live.

four-colour process colour *printing using four printing plates, based on the principle that any colour is made up of differing proportions of the primary colours blue, red, and yellow. Ink colours complementary to those represented on the plates are used for printing – cyan for the blue plate, magenta for the red, and yellow for the yellow. The first stage in preparing a colour picture for printing is to produce separate films, one each for the cyan, magenta, and yellow respectively in the picture (colour separations). From these separations three printing plates are made, with a fourth plate for black. The black is used for shading or outlines and type, and also to darken colour without making the ink too dense.

Four Noble Truths in Buddhism, the central teaching of the Buddha, comprising of four basic concepts. Firstly, there is the reality of suffering (Pali dukkha). In the Four Noble Truths, dukkha also carries the meaning of impermanence and imperfection. Secondly, suffering is caused. Human attachments, cravings, and desires lead to the suffering described in the first Noble Truth. Such a desire or thirst for things can be understood by the concept of tanha (in Sanskrit, samudaya or trishna). Thirdly, suffering can be ended. Suffering can be extinguished by breaking our attachment to desires and this is known by the Sanskrit term nirodha. Fourthly, there is the path to the ending of suffering. The Buddha taught that the way to end suffering is by following the Eightfold Path – magga – eight ways to regulate and discipline behaviour. It is through following this path that desires will be extinguished and *nirvana will be achieved.

four-stroke cycle engine-operating cycle of most petrol and *diesel engines. The 'stroke' is an upward or downward movement of a piston in a cylinder. In a petrol engine the cycle begins with the induction of a fuel mixture as the piston goes down on its first stroke. On the second stroke (up) the piston compresses the mixture in the top of the cylinder. An electric spark then ignites the mixture, and the gases produced force the piston down on its third, power, stroke. On the fourth stroke (up) the piston expels the burned gases from the cylinder into the exhaust.

fourth estate another name for the press. The term was coined by the British politician Edmund Burke in analogy with the traditional three *estates.

fourth-generation language in computing, a type of programming language designed for the rapid programming of *applications but often lacking the ability to control the individual parts of the computer. Such a language typically provides easy ways of designing screens and reports, and of using databases. Other 'generations' (the term implies a class of language rather than a chronological sequence) are *machine code (first generation); *assembly languages, or low-level languages (second); and conventional high-level languages such as *BASIC and *Pascal (third).

fowl chicken or chickenlike bird. Sometimes the term is also used for ducks and geese. The red jungle fowl *Gallus gallus* is the ancestor of all domestic chickens. It is a forest bird of Asia, without the size or egg-laying ability of many domestic strains. *Guinea fowl are of African origin.

Fowler, Henry Watson (1858–1933) and Francis George (1870–1918) English brothers who were scholars and authors of a number of English dictionaries. *Modern English Usage* (1926), the work of Henry Fowler, has become a classic reference work for matters of style and disputed usage.

fox one of the smaller species of wild dog of the family Canidae, which live in Africa, Asia, Europe, North America, and South America. Foxes feed on a wide range of animals from worms to rabbits, scavenge for food, and also eat berries. They are very adaptable, maintaining high populations close to urban areas.

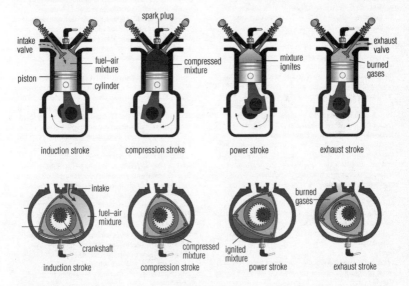

four-stroke cycle Two different types of engine that function on exactly the same principle of four clearly definable strokes. The Otto engine uses a mixture of fuel and air ignited by a spark; and the Wankel uses a fuel-air mixture, but has a rotary arm rather than a two-way piston.

Fox, Charles James (1749–1806) English Whig politician, son of the 1st Baron Holland. He entered Parliament in 1769 as a supporter of the court, but went over to the opposition in 1774. As secretary of state in 1782, leader of the opposition to William Pitt the Younger, and foreign secretary in 1806, he welcomed the French Revolution and brought about the abolition of the slave trade.

foxglove any of a group of flowering plants found in Europe and the Mediterranean region. They have showy spikes of bell-like flowers, and grow up to 1.5 m/ 5 ft high. (Genus *Digitalis*, family Scrophulariaceae.)

foxhound small, keen-nosed hound, up to 60 cm/2 ft tall and black, tan, and white in colour. There are two recognized breeds: the English foxhound, bred for some 300 years to hunt foxes, and the American foxhound, not quite as stocky, used for foxes and other game.

foxtrot ballroom dance originating in the USA about 1914. It is believed to be named after Harry Fox, a US vaudeville comedian who did a distinctive trotting dance to ragtime music.

f.p.s. system system of units based on the foot, pound, and second as units of length, mass, and time, respectively. It has now been replaced for scientific work by the *SI system.

fractal (from Latin *fractus* 'broken') irregular shape or surface produced by a procedure of repeated subdivision. Generated on a computer screen, fractals are used in creating models of geographical or biological processes (for example, the creation of a coastline by erosion or accretion, or the growth of plants).

fraction in chemistry, a group of similar compounds, the boiling points of which fall within a particular range and which are separated during *fractional distillation (fractionation).

fraction (from Latin *fractus* 'broken') in mathematics, a number that indicates one or more equal parts of a whole. Usually, the number of equal parts into which the unit is divided (denominator) is written below a horizontal or diagonal line, and the number of parts comprising the fraction (numerator) is written above; for example, $\frac{2}{3}$ has numerator 2 and denominator 3. Such fractions are called vulgar fractions or **simple fractions**. The denominator can never be zero.

fractional distillation *or* **fractionation** process used to split complex mixtures (such as *petroleum) into their components, usually by repeated heating, boiling, and condensation; see *distillation. In the laboratory it is carried out using a fractionating column.

Fragonard, Jean-Honoré (1732–1806) French painter. He was the leading exponent of the rococo style (along with his teacher François Boucher). His light-hearted subjects, often erotic, include *Les heureux Hazards de l'escarpolette/The Swing* (c. 1766; Wallace Collection, London). Madame de Pompadour was one of his patrons.

France

National name: *République Française/French Republic*
Area: (including Corsica) 543,965 sq km/210,024 sq mi
Capital: Paris
Major towns/cities: Lyon, Lille, Bordeaux, Toulouse, Nantes, Marseille, Nice, Strasbourg, Montpellier, Rennes, Le Havre

Major ports: Marseille, Nice, Le Havre
Physical features: rivers Seine, Loire, Garonne, Rhône; mountain ranges Alps, Massif Central, Pyrenees, Jura, Vosges, Cévennes; Auvergne mountain region; Mont Blanc (4,810 m/15,781 ft); Ardennes forest; Riviera; caves of Dordogne with relics of early humans; the island of Corsica
Territories: Guadeloupe, French Guiana, Martinique, Réunion, St Pierre and Miquelon, Southern and Antarctic Territories, New Caledonia, French Polynesia, Wallis and Futuna, Mayotte, Bassas da India, Clipperton Island, Europa Island, Glorioso Islands, Juan de Nova Island, Tromelin Island
Head of state: Jacques Chirac from 1995
Head of government: Jean-Pierre Raffarin from 2002
Political system: liberal democracy
Political executive: dual executive
Political parties: Rally for the Republic (RPR), neo-Gaullist conservative; Union for French Democracy (UDF), centre right; Socialist Party (PS), left of centre; Left Radical Movement (MRG), left of centre; French Communist Party (PCF), Marxist-Leninist; National Front, far right; Greens, fundamentalist-ecologist; Génération Ecologie, pragmatic ecologist; Movement for France, right wing, anti-Maastricht
Currency: euro (franc until 2002)
GNI per capita (PPP): (US$) 26,180 (2002 est)
Exports: machinery and transport equipment, food and live animals, chemicals, beverages and tobacco, textile yarn, fabrics and other basic manufactures, clothing and accessories, perfumery and cosmetics. Principal market: Germany 14.4% (2001)
Population: 60,144,000 (2003 est)
Language: French (official; regional languages include Basque, Breton, Catalan, Corsican, and Provençal)
Religion: Roman Catholic, about 90%; also Muslim, Protestant, and Jewish minorities
Life expectancy: 75 (men); 83 (women) (2000–05)
Chronology
5th century BC: Celtic peoples invaded the region.
58–51 BC: Romans conquered Celts and formed province of Gaul.

5th century AD: Gaul overrun by Franks and other Germanic tribes.

481–511: Frankish chief Clovis accepted Christianity and formed a kingdom based at Paris; under his successors, the Merovingian dynasty, the kingdom disintegrated.

751–68: Pepin the Short usurped the Frankish throne, reunified the kingdom, and founded the Carolingian dynasty.

768–814: Charlemagne conquered much of Western Europe and created the Holy Roman Empire.

843: Treaty of Verdun divided the Holy Roman Empire into three, with the western portion corresponding to modern France.

9th–10th centuries: Weak central government allowed the great nobles to become virtually independent.

987: Frankish crown passed to House of Capet; the Capets ruled the district around Paris, but were surrounded by vassals more powerful than themselves.

1180–1223: Philip II doubled the royal domain and tightened control over the nobles; the power of the Capets gradually extended with support of church and towns.

1328: When Charles IV died without an heir, Philip VI established the House of Valois.

1337: Start of the Hundred Years' War: Edward III of England disputed the Valois succession and claimed the throne. English won victories at Crécy in 1346 and Agincourt in 1415.

1429: Joan of Arc raised the siege of Orléans; Hundred Years' War ended with Charles VII expelling the English in 1453.

1483: France annexed Burgundy and Brittany after Louis XI had restored royal power.

16th–17th centuries: French kings fought the Habsburgs (of Holy Roman Empire and Spain) for supremacy in Western Europe.

1562–98: Civil wars between nobles were fought under religious slogans, Catholic versus Protestant (or Huguenot).

1589–1610: Henry IV, first king of Bourbon dynasty, established peace, religious tolerance, and absolute monarchy.

1634–48: The ministers Richelieu and Mazarin, by intervening in the Thirty Years' War, secured Alsace and made France the leading power in Europe.

1701–14: War of the Spanish Succession: England, Austria, and allies checked expansionism of France under Louis XIV.

1756–63: Seven Years' War: France lost most of its colonies in India and Canada to Britain.

1789: French Revolution abolished absolute monarchy and feudalism; First Republic proclaimed and revolutionary wars began in 1792.

1799: Napoleon Bonaparte seized power in coup; crowned himself emperor in 1804; France conquered much of Europe.

1814: Defeat of France; restoration of Bourbon monarchy; comeback by Napoleon defeated at Waterloo in 1815.

1830: Liberal revolution deposed Charles X in favour of his cousin Louis Philippe, the 'Citizen King'.

1848: Revolution established Second Republic; conflict between liberals and socialists; Louis Napoleon, nephew of Napoleon I, elected president.

1852: Louis Napoleon proclaimed Second Empire, taking title Napoleon III.

1870–71: Franco-Prussian War: France lost Alsace-Lorraine; Second Empire abolished; Paris Commune crushed; Third Republic founded.

late 19th century: France colonized Indo-China, much of North Africa, and South Pacific.

1914–18: France resisted German invasion in World War I; Alsace-Lorraine recovered in 1919.

1936–37: Left-wing 'Popular Front' government introduced many social reforms.

1939: France entered World War II.

1940: Germany invaded and occupied northern France; Marshal Pétain formed right-wing puppet regime at Vichy; resistance maintained by Maquis and Free French; Germans occupied all France in 1942.

1944: Allies liberated France; provisional government formed by Gen Charles de Gaulle, leader of Free French.

1946: Fourth Republic proclaimed.

1949: Became a member of NATO; withdrew from military command structure in 1966.

1954: French withdrew from Indo-China after eight years of war; start of guerrilla war against French rule in Algeria.

1957: France was a founder member of the European Economic Community.

1958: Algerian crisis caused collapse of Fourth Republic; de Gaulle took power, becoming president of the Fifth Republic in 1959.

1962: Algeria achieved independence.

1968: Revolutionary students rioted in Paris; there was a general strike throughout France.

1981: François Mitterrand was elected the Fifth Republic's first socialist president.

1995: Jacques Chirac (RPR) was elected president. There was widespread condemnation of the government's decision to resume nuclear tests in the South Pacific, and this was stopped in 1996.

1996: Spending cuts were agreed to meet European Monetary Union entry criteria. Unemployment was at a post-war high.

1997: A general election was called by President Chirac, with victory for Socialists; Lionel Jospin (PS) was appointed prime minister.

1998: There were protests by the unemployed.

1999: Two-thirds of France was declared a disaster zone after powerful storms struck Europe and caused widespread damage.

2000: An Air France Concorde aircraft crash killed 113 people. Disruptive protests over fuel prices forced the government to make tax concessions on fuel. Fears over BSE in French cattle rose and President Chirac called for an immediate ban on cattle remains in all French animal feed.

2001: A high-profile corruption scandal, relating to the state-owned oil company Elf Aquitaine, led to the trial of former foreign minister Roland Dumas. Bertand Delanoi became the first socialist mayor of Paris since 1871.

2002: In the first round of the presidential election in France, Jean-Marie Le Pen, the leader of the far-right Front National (FN; National Front), came second. Le Pen's unexpected success sparked anti-fascist street demonstrations across the country. However, in the second round, centre-right incumbent Jacques Chirac won with 82.2% of the vote (the highest ever margin of victory in the Fifth Republic). President Chirac later escaped an apparent assassination attempt by a far-right extremist.

2003: France's opposition to the US-led invasion of Iraq jeopardized relations with the United States and the United Kingdom.

2004: Tensions arose within France's Muslim population with the enactment of a law banning the wearing of conspicuous religious symbols by school students. This was seen by many as being directed at girls wearing the Islamic veil.

France, Anatole (1844–1924) pen-name of Jacques Anatole François Thibault, French writer. His works are marked by wit, urbanity, and style. His earliest novel was *Le Crime de Sylvestre Bonnard/The Crime of Sylvester Bonnard* (1881); later books include the satiric *L'Ile des pingouins/Penguin Island* (1908). He was awarded the Nobel Prize for Literature in 1921.

Francesca, Piero della Italian painter; see *Piero della Francesca.

Franche-Comté region of eastern France; area 16,202 sq km/6,256 sq mi; population (1999 est) 1,117,100. Its administrative centre is Besançon, and it includes the *départements* of Doubs, Jura, Haute-Saône, and Territoire de Belfort. About 40% of the land is forested, especially in the mountainous Jura, where there is dairying, farming, and forestry; elsewhere there are engineering, automobile, and plastics industries. Besançon is the region's largest city and traditional centre for manufacturing (watches and precision instruments). Other chief towns include Montbéliard, the site of an automobile production complex, Lons-le-Saulier, Vesoul, Pontarlier, and Dôle, which had been capital of the historic region until 1676.

franchise in politics, the eligibility, right, or privilege to vote at public elections, especially for the members of a legislative body, or parliament. In the UK adult citizens are eligible to vote from the age of 18, with the exclusion of peers, the insane, and criminals. The voting age for adults in the USA was lowered from 21 to 18 by the Twenty-Sixth Amendment in 1971, and the Voting Rights Act of 1965 eliminated local laws that restricted full participation by minorities.

Francis (*or* François) two kings of France:
Francis I (1494–1547) King of France from 1515. He succeeded his cousin Louis XII, and from 1519 European politics turned on the rivalry between him and the Holy Roman emperor Charles V, which led to war in 1521–29, 1536–38, and 1542–44. In 1525 Francis was defeated and captured at Pavia and released only after signing a humiliating treaty. At home, he developed absolute monarchy.

Francis II (1544–1560) King of France from 1559 when he succeeded his father, Henri II. He married Mary Queen of Scots in 1558. He was completely under the influence of his mother, *Catherine de' Medici.

Francis II (1768–1835) Holy Roman Emperor 1792–1806. He became Francis I, Emperor of Austria in 1804, and abandoned the title of Holy Roman Emperor in 1806. During his reign Austria was five times involved in war with France, 1792–97, 1798–1801, 1805, 1809, and 1813–14. He succeeded his father, Leopold II.

Franciscan order Catholic order of friars, **Friars Minor** or **Grey Friars**, founded in 1209 by Francis of

Assisi. Subdivisions were the strict Observants; the Conventuals, who were allowed to own property corporately; and the Capuchins, founded in 1529.

Francis of Assisi, St (1182–1226) born Giovanni Bernadone, Italian founder of the Roman Catholic *Franciscan order of friars in 1209 and, with St Clare, of the Poor Clares in 1212. In 1224 he is said to have undergone a mystical experience during which he received the stigmata (five wounds of Jesus). Many stories are told of his ability to charm wild animals, and he is the patron saint of ecologists. His feast day is 4 October. He was canonized in 1228.

francium chemical symbol Fr, radioactive metallic element, atomic number 87, relative atomic mass 223. It is one of the alkali metals and occurs in nature in small amounts as a decay product of actinium. Its longest-lived isotope has a half-life of only 21 minutes. Francium was discovered and named in 1939 by Marguérite Perey, to honour her country.

Franco (Bahamonde), Francisco (Paulino Hermenegildo Teódulo) (1892–1975) Spanish dictator from 1939. As a general, he led the insurgent Nationalists to victory in the Spanish *Civil War 1936–39, supported by fascist Italy and Nazi Germany, and established a dictatorship. In 1942 Franco reinstated a Cortes (Spanish parliament), which in 1947 passed an act by which he became head of state for life. After his death, Spain returned to democracy.

Franco-Prussian War 1870–71 The Prussian chancellor Otto von Bismarck put forward a German candidate for the vacant Spanish throne with the deliberate, and successful, intention of provoking the French emperor Napoleon III into declaring war. The Prussians defeated the French at Sedan, then besieged Paris. The Treaty of Frankfurt of May 1871 gave Alsace, Lorraine, and a large French indemnity to Prussia. The war established Prussia, at the head of a newly established German empire, as Europe's leading power.

frangipani any of a group of tropical American trees, especially the species *P. rubra*, belonging to the dogbane family. Perfume is made from the strongly scented waxy flowers. (Genus *Plumeria*, family Apocynaceae.)

Frank member of a group of Germanic peoples prominent in Europe in the 3rd to 9th centuries. Believed to have originated in Pomerania on the Baltic Sea, they had settled on the Rhine by the 3rd century, spread into the Roman Empire by the 4th century, and gradually conquered most of Gaul, Italy, and Germany under the *Merovingian and *Carolingian dynasties. The kingdom of the western Franks became France; the kingdom of the eastern Franks became Germany.

Frank, Anne(lies Marie) (1929–1945) German Jewish diarist. She fled to the Netherlands with her family in 1933 to escape Nazi anti-Semitism (the *Holocaust). During the German occupation of Amsterdam, they and two other families remained in a sealed-off room, protected by Dutch sympathizers 1942–44, when betrayal resulted in their deportation and Anne's death in Belsen concentration camp. Her diary of her time in hiding was published in 1947.

Frankenstein* or *The Modern Prometheus Gothic horror story by Mary *Shelley, published in England in 1818. It is considered to be the origin of modern science fiction, and there have been many film versions. Frankenstein, a scientist, discovers how to bring inanimate matter to life, and creates a man-monster. When Frankenstein fails to provide a mate to satisfy the creature's human emotions, it seeks revenge by killing Frankenstein's brother and bride. Frankenstein dies in an attempt to destroy his creation.

Frankfurt am Main (German 'ford of the Franks') city in Hessen, Germany, 72 km/45 mi northeast of Mannheim; population (1995) 651,200. It is a commercial and banking centre, with electrical and machine industries, and an inland port on the River Main. The International Book Fair is held here annually in the autumn. It is the site of the Bundesbank (German Central Bank), and the European Central Bank (from 1999).

frankincense resin of various African and Asian trees, burned as incense. Costly in ancient times, it is traditionally believed to be one of the three gifts brought by the Magi to the infant Jesus. (Genus *Boswellia*, family Burseraceae.)

Franklin, Benjamin (1706–1790) US scientist, inventor, statesman, diplomat, writer, printer, and publisher. He proved that lightning is a form of electricity, distinguished between positive and negative electricity, and invented the lightning conductor. He was the first US ambassador to France 1776–85, and negotiated peace with Britain in 1783. As a delegate to the *Continental Congress from Pennsylvania 1785–88, he helped to draft the *Declaration of Independence and the US Constitution. He was president of the first US abolitionist society in 1775 and was responsible for many improvements in American life, including a modernized postal system, and the first US fire and police departments, hospital, and insurance company.

Franz Josef Land Russian **Zemlya Frantsa Iosifa**, archipelago of over 85 islands in the Arctic Ocean, east of Svalbord and northwest of Novaya Zemlya, Russia; area 20,720 sq km/8,000 sq mi. There are scientific stations on the islands.

Franz Joseph (or Francis Joseph) (1830–1916) Emperor of Austria-Hungary from 1848, when his uncle Ferdinand I abdicated. After the suppression of the 1848 revolution, Franz Joseph tried to establish an absolute monarchy but had to grant Austria a parliamentary constitution in 1861 and Hungary equality with Austria in 1867. He was defeated in the Italian War in 1859 and the Prussian War in 1866. In 1914 he made the assassination of his heir and nephew Franz Ferdinand the excuse for attacking Serbia, thus precipitating World War I.

Fraser river in southern British Columbia, Canada; length 1,375 km/855 mi. It rises in the Yellowhead Pass of the Rocky Mountains and flows northwest into the interior plateau of British Columbia. It then flows south through its lower valley at Hope, then west where it enters the Strait of Georgia, near Vancouver. The Fraser River has acted as the focus of economic life in the southern part of the province: as a salmon fishery, as a means of transportation for the rich lumber reserves of its upper valley, and as a source of irrigation and hydroelectric power. It was named for Canadian explorer Simon Fraser, who led expeditions in the area in 1808.

Fraser, (John) Malcolm (1930–) Australian Liberal politician, prime minister 1975–83; nicknamed 'the Prefect' because of a supposed disregard of subordinates.

fraud in law, an act of deception resulting in injury to another. To establish fraud it has to be demonstrated that (1) a false representation (for example, a factually untrue statement) has been made, with the intention that it should be acted upon; (2) the person making the representation knows it is false or does not attempt to find out whether it is true or not; and (3) the person to whom the representation is made acts upon it to his or her detriment.

Frazer, James (George) (1854–1941) Scottish anthropologist. Frazer's book *The Golden Bough* (12 volumes, 1890–1915), a pioneer study of the origins of religion and sociology on a comparative basis, exerted considerable influence on subsequent anthropologists and writers such as T S Eliot and D H Lawrence. By the standards of modern anthropology, many of its methods and findings are unsound.

Frederick V (1596–1632) called 'the Winter King', Elector palatine of the Rhine 1610–23 and king of Bohemia 1619–20 (for one winter, hence the name), having been chosen by the Protestant Bohemians as ruler after the deposition of Catholic emperor *Ferdinand II. His selection was the cause of the Thirty Years' War. Frederick was defeated at the Battle of the White Mountain, near Prague, in November 1620, by the army of the Catholic League and fled to Holland.

Frederick two Holy Roman emperors:

Frederick (I) Barbarossa (c. 1123–1190) called 'red-beard', Holy Roman Emperor from 1152. Originally duke of Swabia, he was elected emperor in 1152, and was engaged in a struggle with Pope Alexander III 1159–77, which ended in his submission; the Lombard cities, headed by Milan, took advantage of this to establish their independence of imperial control. Frederick joined the Third Crusade, and was drowned while crossing a river in Anatolia.

Frederick II (1194–1250) Holy Roman Emperor from 1212, called 'the Wonder of the World'. He was the son of Holy Roman Emperor *Henry VI. He led a crusade in 1228–29 that recovered Jerusalem by treaty without fighting. Frederick quarrelled with the pope, who excommunicated him three times, and a feud began that lasted with intervals until the end of his reign. Frederick, who was a religious sceptic, is often considered the most cultured person of his age. His later years were marred by the rebellions of his chief minister and his son.

Frederick three kings of Prussia, including:

Frederick (II) the Great (1712–1786) King of Prussia from 1740, when he succeeded his father Frederick William I. In that year he started the War of the *Austrian Succession by his attack on Austria. In the peace of 1745 he secured Silesia. The struggle was renewed in the *Seven Years' War 1756–63. He acquired West Prussia in the first partition of Poland in 1772 and left Prussia as Germany's foremost state. He was an efficient and just ruler in the spirit of the Enlightenment and a patron of the arts.

Frederick William four kings of Prussia, including:

Frederick William III (1770–1840) King of Prussia from 1797. He was defeated by Napoleon in 1806, but contributed to his final overthrow 1813–15 and profited by being allotted territory at the Congress of Vienna.

Free Church or Nonconformist Church Protestant denominations of England and Wales that became members of the Free Church Federal Council from 1940. They include the *Methodist Church, *Baptist Union, United Reformed Church, Society of *Friends (Quakers), *Salvation Army, and *Pentecostalist churches. The denominations were founded by those who did not wish to conform to the traditional forms of worship laid down by the established Church of England, but united for common action.

Free Church of Scotland body of Scottish Presbyterians who seceded from the Established Church of Scotland in the Disruption of 1843. In 1900 all but a small section that retains the old name (known as the **Wee Frees**) combined with the United Presbyterian Church to form the United Free Church of Scotland. Most of this reunited with the Church of Scotland in 1929, although there remains a continuing United Free Church of Scotland. It has 6,000 members, 110 ministers, and 140 churches.

freehold in England and Wales, ownership of land for an indefinite period. It is contrasted with a **leasehold**, which is always for a fixed period. In practical effect, a freehold is absolute ownership.

freemasonry beliefs and practices of a group of linked national organizations open to men over the age of 21, united by a common code of morals and certain traditional 'secrets'. Modern freemasonry began in 18th-century Europe. Freemasons do much charitable work, but have been criticized in recent years for their secrecy, their male exclusivity, and their alleged use of influence within and between organizations (for example, the police or local government) to further each other's interests.

free radical in chemistry, an atom or molecule that has an unpaired electron and is therefore highly reactive. Most free radicals are very short-lived. They are by-products of normal cell chemistry and rapidly oxidize other molecules they encounter. Free radicals are thought to do considerable damage. They are neutralized by protective enzymes.

freesia any of a South African group of plants belonging to the iris family, commercially grown for their scented, funnel-shaped flowers. (Genus *Freesia*, family Iridaceae.)

Free State formerly **Orange Free State** (until 1995), province of the Republic of South Africa; area 127,993 sq km/49,418 sq mi; population (2000 est) 2,762,700. Lesotho forms an enclave on the KwaZulu-Natal and Eastern Cape Province border. The capital is *Bloemfontein, which is also the judicial capital of the republic; other main towns are Springfontein, Kroonstad, Bethlehem, Harrismith, and Koffiefontein. The province is located on the Highveld plateau and slopes downwards from heights of around 1,800 m/6,000 ft in the east to about 1,200 m/4,000 ft in the west. The main industries are gold, oil from coal, cement, and pharmaceuticals; agricultural production is centred on grain, wool, and cattle.

Freetown capital of Sierra Leone; population (1992) 505,000. It has a naval station and a harbour. Industries include cement, plastics, footwear, oil refining, food production, and tobacco processing. Platinum, chromite, rutile, diamonds, and gold are traded. Freetown was founded as a settlement for freed slaves in 1787. It was made capital of the independent Sierra Leone in 1961. The beaches of Freetown peninsula attract tourists.

free trade economic system where governments do not interfere in the movement of goods between countries; there are thus no taxes on imports. In the modern economy, free trade tends to hold within economic groups such as the European Union (EU), but not generally, despite such treaties as the *General Agreement on Tariffs and Trade (GATT) of 1948 and subsequent agreements to reduce tariffs. The opposite of free trade is *protectionism.

free verse poetry without metrical form. At the beginning of the 20th century, many poets believed that the 19th century had accomplished most of what could be done with regular metre, and rejected it, in much the same spirit as John Milton in the 17th century had rejected rhyme, preferring irregular metres that made it possible to express thought clearly and without distortion.

free will the doctrine that human beings are free to control their own actions, and that these actions are not fixed in advance by God or fate. Some Jewish and Christian theologians assert that God gave humanity free will to choose between good and evil; others that God has decided in advance the outcome of all human choices (*predestination), as in Calvinism.

freeze–thaw form of physical *weathering, common in mountains and glacial environments, caused by the expansion of water as it freezes. Water in a crack freezes and expands in volume by 9% as it turns to ice. This expansion exerts great pressure on the rock, causing the crack to enlarge. After many cycles of freeze–thaw, rock fragments may break off to form *scree slopes.

freezing *change of state from liquid to solid, as when water becomes ice. For a given substance, freezing occurs at a definite temperature, known as the **freezing point**, that is invariable under similar conditions of pressure, and the temperature remains at this point until all the liquid is frozen; the freezing point and melting point of the substance are the same temperature. By measuring the temperature of a liquid against time as it cools a cooling curve can be plotted; on the cooling curve the temperature levels out at the freezing point.

French Antarctic Territories *or* **French Southern and Antarctic Territories** territory created in 1955; population approximately 200 research scientists. It includes Adélie Land (area 432,000 sq km/165,500 sq mi) on the Antarctic continent, the Kerguelen and Crozet archipelagos (7,515 sq km/2,901 sq mi), and St Paul and Nouvelle Amsterdam islands (67 sq km/26 sq mi) in the southern seas. It is administered from Paris, France.

French art painting, sculpture, and decorative arts of France. As the birthplace of the Gothic style, France was a centre for sculpture and manuscript illumination in the Middle Ages, and of tapestry from the 15th century. 17th-century French painting is particularly rich, dominated by the Italianate Classicism of *Claude Lorrain and Nicolas *Poussin. Subsequent light-hearted rococo scenes of upper-class leisure gave way with the French Revolution to the neoclassicism of Jacques-Louis *David and Jean *Ingres. In the 19th century, Romanticism was superseded first by *realism and then by *Impressionism, led by such painters as Claude *Monet and Auguste *Renoir, which in turn fragmented, via the work of Georges *Seurat, Paul *Cézanne, and others, into the modern art of the

20th century. Georges *Braque (cubism) and Henri *Matisse (fauvism) were among the pioneers. In sculpture the towering figure was that of Auguste *Rodin. From the mid-19th to the mid-20th century, Paris was the hotbed of Western art.

French Guiana French **Guyane Française**, French overseas *département* from 1946, and administrative region from 1974, on the north coast of South America, bounded west by Suriname and east and south by Brazil; area 83,500 sq km/32,230 sq mi; population (1999 est) 157,200. The main towns are *Cayenne and St Laurent. The main economic activity is fishing; other resources include bauxite, tropical hardwood timber, gold, cinnabar, and kaolin. Agricultural products include rice, maize, cocoa, bananas, and sugar, though the country depends largely on imported food. Unemployment is high, particularly among the young, with as much as a quarter of the population without work at one time. The second-largest town, Kourou, is the site of a European Space Agency launch site.

French horn brass instrument descended from the natural hunting horn. It is valved and curved into a circular loop, with a funnel-shaped mouthpiece and wide bell.

French language member of the Romance branch of the Indo-European language family, spoken in France, Belgium, Luxembourg, Monaco, and Switzerland in Europe; also in Canada (principally in the province of Québec), various Caribbean and Pacific Islands (including overseas territories such as Martinique and French Guiana), and certain North and West African countries (for example, Mali and Senegal).

French Polynesia French Overseas Territory in the South Pacific, consisting of five archipelagos: Windward Islands, Leeward Islands (the two island groups comprising the Society Islands), Tuamotu Archipelago (including Gambier Islands), Tubuai Islands, and Marquesas Islands; total area 3,940 sq km/1,521 sq mi; population (2001 est) 235,000. The capital is Papeete on Tahiti, the main island. Tourism is the mainstay of the economy; other industries are cultivated pearls, copra, coconut oil, and vanilla, all of which provide significant exports.

French Revolution the period 1789–1799 that saw the end of the monarchy in France. The revolution began as an attempt to create a constitutional monarchy, where the powers of the king would be limited by a *parliament. By late 1792, however, demands for long-overdue reforms resulted in the proclamation of the First Republic and the execution of King *Louis XVI in January 1973. The violence of the revolution, attacks by other nations, and bitter factional struggles, riots, and counter-revolutionary uprisings across France severely weakened the republic. This helped bring the extremists to power, and the bloody Reign of *Terror followed. French armies then succeeded in holding off their foreign enemies and one of the generals, *Napoleon Bonaparte, seized power in 1799.

French West Africa group of French colonies administered from Dakar 1895–1958. They are now Senegal, Mauritania, Sudan, Burkina Faso, Guinea, Niger, Côte d'Ivoire, and Benin.

frequency in physics, number of periodic oscillations, vibrations, or waves occurring per unit of time. The SI unit of frequency is the hertz (Hz), one hertz being equivalent to one cycle per second. Frequency is related to wavelength and velocity by the equation:

$$f = \frac{v}{\lambda}$$

where f is frequency, v is velocity, and λ is wavelength. Frequency is the reciprocal of the period T:

$$f = \frac{1}{T}.$$

frequency in statistics, the number of times an event occurs. For example, in a survey carried out to find out a group of children's favourite colour of the rainbow, the colour red is chosen 26 times. This gives the colour red a frequency of 26. A table of the raw data collected, including the frequencies, is called a **frequency distribution**. It is usually presented in a **frequency table** or tally chart. The frequencies can also be shown diagrammatically using a **frequency polygon**.

frequency modulation (FM) method by which radio waves are altered for the transmission of broadcasting signals. FM varies the frequency of the carrier wave in accordance with the signal being transmitted. Its advantage over AM (*amplitude modulation) is its better signal-to-noise ratio. It was invented by the US engineer Edwin Armstrong.

fresco (Italian 'fresh') mural painting technique using water-based paint on wet plaster that has been freshly applied to the wall. The technique is ancient and widespread; some of the earliest examples (c. 1750–1400 BC) were found in Knossos, Crete (now preserved in the Archaeological Museum in Heraklion). However, fresco reached its finest expression in Italy from the 13th to the 17th centuries. One of the finest examples of fresco is the ceiling of the Sistine Chapel (1508–12) by *Michelangelo, in the Vatican, Rome.

Freud, Lucian (1922–) German-born British painter. One of the greatest contemporary figurative artists, he combines meticulous accuracy with a disquieting intensity, painting from unusual angles and emphasizing the physicality of his subjects, whether nudes, still lifes, or interiors. His *Portrait of Francis Bacon* (1952; Tate Gallery, London) is one of his best-known works. He is a grandson of Sigmund *Freud.

Freud, Sigmund (1856–1939) Austrian physician who pioneered the study of the *unconscious mind. He developed the methods of free association and interpretation of dreams that are basic techniques of *psychoanalysis. The influence of unconscious forces on people's thoughts and actions was Freud's discovery, as was his controversial theory of the repression of infantile sexuality as the root of neuroses in the adult. His books include *Die Traumdeutung/The Interpretation of Dreams* (1900), *Jenseits des Lustprinzips/Beyond the Pleasure Principle* (1920), *Das Ich und das Es/The Ego and the Id* (1923), and *Das Unbehagen in der Kultur/Civilization and its Discontents* (1930). His influence has permeated the world to such an extent that it may be discerned today in almost every branch of thought.

Freya or **Freyja** in Norse mythology, goddess of married love and the hearth. She was also the goddess of death, Odin's punishment after her dalliance with four dwarfs to gain the necklace Brisingamen. In this capacity, she caused war between mortals and flew over their battlefields in a chariot drawn by two cats. Half the heroes slain were banqueted in Sessrumnir, her hall in Asgard; the others were feasted by Odin.

friction in physics, the force that opposes the movement of two bodies in contact as they move relative to each other. The **coefficient of friction** is the ratio of the force required to achieve this relative motion to the force pressing the two bodies together.

Friedan, Betty (Elizabeth) (1921–) born Elizabeth Goldstein, US liberal feminist. Her book *The Feminine Mystique* (1963) started the contemporary women's movement in the USA and the UK. She was a founder of the National Organization for Women (NOW) in 1966 (and its president 1966–70), the National Women's Political Caucus in 1971, and the First Women's Bank in 1973.

Friedman, Milton (1912–) US economist, best known for his advocacy of *monetarism – the control of aggregate demand solely by control of the money supply – and his unflinching support of the market in virtually all areas of economic life. He was awarded the Nobel Prize for Economics in 1976.

Friedrich, Caspar David (1774–1840) German Romantic landscape painter. He was active mainly in Dresden. He imbued his subjects – mountain scenes and moonlit seas – with poetic melancholy and was later admired by Symbolist painters. *The Cross in the Mountains* (1808; Gemäldegalerie, Dresden) and *Moonrise over the Sea* (1822; Nationalgalerie, Berlin) are among his best-known works.

friendly society association that makes provisions for the needs of sickness and old age by money payments. In 1995 there were 1,013 orders and branches (17 orders, 996 branches), 18 collecting societies, 294 other centralized societies, 72 benevolent societies, 2,271 working men's clubs, and 131 specially authorized societies in the UK. Among the largest are the National Deposit, Odd Fellows, Foresters, and Hearts of Oak. In the USA similar 'fraternal insurance' bodies are known as **benefit societies**; they include the Modern Woodmen of America (1883) and the Fraternal Order of Eagles (1898).

Friends, Society of *or* **Quakers** Christian Protestant sect founded by George Fox in England in the 1660s. They were persecuted for their nonviolent activism, and many emigrated to form communities elsewhere; for example, in Pennsylvania and New England. The worldwide movement had about 219,800 members in 1997. Their faith is based on the belief that God speaks individually to everyone. They have no sacraments or formal creed, and rely on the Holy Spirit for guidance. Worship is simple and stresses *meditation. Services (called meetings) are held in a meeting house and have no set form; all are free to take an active part. There are no clergy, but elders are elected. The Friends are *pacifists.

Friesland maritime province on the northeast side of the IJsselmeer, north Netherlands, which includes the Frisian Islands and land reclaimed from the former Zuider Zee; area 3,400 sq km/1,313 sq mi; population (1997) 615,000 (the inhabitants of the province are called Frisians). The capital is Leeuwarden; other main towns are Drachten, Harlingen, Sneek, and Heerenveen.

Small boats are made; agriculture centres on livestock (Friesian cattle, which originated here, and black Friesian horses), dairy products, and arable farming.

Frigga *or* **Frigg** in Norse mythology, queen of the gods; wife of Odin. Her sons were *Balder, the beloved god; Bragi, god of poetry and wisdom; and *Thor, god of thunder. She was one of the Aesir, the principal warrior gods who lived in Asgard. Friday was named after her.

fritillary in botany, any of a group of plants belonging to the lily family. The snake's head fritillary (*F. meleagris*) has bell-shaped flowers with purple-chequered markings. (Genus *Fritillaria*, family Liliaceae.)

fritillary in zoology, any of a large grouping of butterflies of the family Nymphalidae. Mostly medium-sized, fritillaries are usually orange and reddish with a black criss-cross pattern or spots above and with silvery spots on the underside of the hindwings.

Friuli-Venezia Giulia province and autonomous agricultural and wine-producing region of northeast Italy, bordered to the east by Slovenia and to the north by Austria, comprising the provinces of Pordenone, Gorizia, Trieste, and Udine; area 7,855 sq km/3,033 sq mi; population (2001 est) 1,180,400. The most important industrial centres are Udine, Gorizia, the ports of Trieste (which is the region's capital) and Monfalcone (which has dockyards and chemical industries), and Pordenone. Maize, soybeans, wine, and fruit are produced on the plain, and cattle and pigs are raised on the hills.

Frobisher, Martin (c. 1535–1594) English navigator. He made his first voyage to Guinea, West Africa, in 1554. In 1576 he set out in search of the Northwest Passage, and visited Labrador and Frobisher Bay, Baffin Island. Second and third expeditions sailed in 1577 and 1578. Knighted in 1588.

Froebel, Friedrich Wilhelm August (1782–1852) German educationist. He evolved a new system of education using instructive play, described in *Education of Man* (1826) and other works. In 1836 he founded the first kindergarten (German 'garden for children') in Blankenburg, Germany. He was influenced by the Swiss Johann Pestalozzi.

frog any amphibian of the order Anura (Greek 'tailless'). There are about 24 different families of frog, containing more than 3,800 species. There are no clear rules for distinguishing between frogs and *toads. Frogs usually have squat bodies, with hind legs specialized for jumping, and webbed feet for swimming. Most live in or near water, though as adults they are air-breathing. A few live on land or even in trees. Their colour is usually greenish in the genus *Rana*, but other Ranidae are brightly coloured, for instance black and orange or yellow and white. Many use their long, extensible tongues to capture insects. The eyes are large and bulging. Frogs vary in size from the North American little grass frog *Limnaoedus ocularis*, 12 mm/0.5 in long, to the giant aquatic frog *Telmatobius culeus*, 50 cm/20 in long, of Lake Titicaca, South America. Frogs are widespread, inhabiting all continents except Antarctica, and they have adapted to a range of environments including deserts, forests, grasslands, and even high altitudes, with some species in the Andes and Himalayas existing above 5,000 m/19,600 ft.

Fronde French revolts 1648–53 against the administration of the chief minister *Mazarin during Louis XIV's minority. In 1648–49 the Paris parlement attempted to limit the royal power, its leaders were arrested, Paris revolted, and the rising was suppressed by the royal army under Louis II Condé. In 1650 Condé led a new revolt of the nobility, but this was suppressed by 1653. The defeat of the Fronde enabled Louis to establish an absolutist monarchy in the later 17th century.

front in meteorology, the boundary between two air masses of different temperature or humidity. A **cold front** marks the line of advance of a cold air mass from below, as it displaces a warm air mass; a **warm front** marks the advance of a warm air mass as it rises up over a cold one. Frontal systems define the weather of the mid-latitudes, where warm tropical air is continually meeting cold air from the poles.

frost condition of the weather that occurs when the air temperature is below freezing, 0 °C/32 °F. Water in the atmosphere is deposited as ice crystals on the ground or on exposed objects. As cold air is heavier than warm air and sinks to the ground, ground frost is more common than hoar (air) frost, which is formed by the condensation of water particles in the air.

Frost, Robert (Lee) (1874–1963) US poet. His accessible, colloquial (written in local, informal dialect) blank verse, often flavoured with New England speech patterns, is written with an individual voice and penetrating vision. His poems include 'Mending Wall' ('Something there is that does not love a wall'), 'The Road Not Taken', and 'Stopping by Woods on a Snowy Evening'. They are collected in *Complete Poems* (1951).

frostbite the freezing of skin or flesh, with formation of ice crystals leading to tissue damage. The treatment is slow warming of the affected area; for example, by skin-to-skin contact or with lukewarm water. Frostbitten parts are extremely vulnerable to infection, with the risk of gangrene.

fructose $C_6H_{12}O_6$, sugar that occurs naturally in honey, the nectar of flowers, and many sweet fruits; it is commercially prepared from glucose.

fruit (from Latin *frui* 'to enjoy') in botany, the ripened ovary in flowering plants that develops from one or more seeds or carpels and encloses one or more seeds. Its function is to protect the seeds during their development and to aid in their dispersal. Fruits are often edible, sweet, juicy, and colourful. When eaten they provide vitamins, minerals, and enzymes, but little protein. Most fruits are borne by perennial plants. (See diagram, p. 352.)

Fry, Elizabeth (1780–1845) born Elizabeth Gurney, English Quaker philanthropist. From 1813 she began to visit and teach the women in Newgate Prison in London who lived with their children in terrible conditions. She formed an association for the improvement of conditions for female prisoners in 1817, and worked with her brother, **Joseph Gurney** (1788–1847), on an 1819 report on prison reform. She was a pioneer for higher nursing standards and the education of working women.

FT Index abbreviation for *Financial Times Index, a list of leading share prices.

fuchsia any shrub or herbaceous plant of a group belonging to the evening-primrose family. Species are native to South and Central America and New Zealand, and bear red, purple, or pink bell-shaped flowers that hang downwards. (Genus *Fuchsia*, family Onagraceae.)

fuel any source of heat or energy, embracing the entire range of materials that burn in air (combustibles). A fuel is a substance that gives out energy when it burns. A **nuclear fuel** is any material that produces energy by nuclear fission in a nuclear reactor. *Fossil fuels are formed from the fossilized remains of plants and animals.

fuel cell cell converting chemical energy directly to electrical energy. It works on the same principle as a battery but is continually fed with fuel, usually hydrogen and oxygen. Fuel cells are silent and reliable (no moving parts) but expensive to produce. They are an example of a renewable energy source.

fuel injection injecting fuel directly into the cylinders of an internal combustion engine, instead of by way of a carburettor. It is the standard method used in *diesel engines, and is now becoming standard for petrol engines. In the diesel engine, oil is injected into the hot compressed air at the top of the second piston stroke and explodes to drive the piston down on its power stroke. In the petrol engine, fuel is injected into the cylinder at the start of the first induction stroke of the *four-stroke cycle.

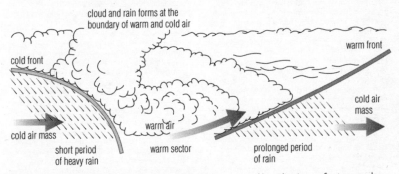

cloud and rain forms at the boundary of warm and cold air

warm front

cold front

cold air mass

cold air mass

warm air

short period of heavy rain

warm sector

prolonged period of rain

front The boundaries between two air masses of different temperature and humidity. A warm front occurs when warm air displaces cold air; if cold air replaces warm air, it is a cold front.

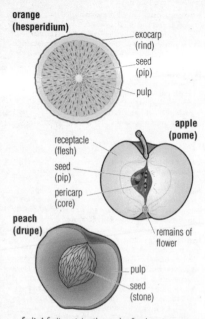

orange (hesperidium)
- exocarp (rind)
- seed (pip)
- pulp

apple (pome)
- receptacle (flesh)
- seed (pip)
- pericarp (core)
- remains of flower

peach (drupe)
- pulp
- seed (stone)

fruit A fruit contains the seeds of a plant. Its outer wall is the exocarp, or epicarp; its inner layers are the mesocarp and endocarp. The orange is a hesperidium, a berry having a leathery rind and containing many seeds. The apple is a pome, a fruit with a fleshy outer layer and a core containing the seeds. The peach is a drupe, a fleshy fruit with a hard seed, or 'stone', at the centre.

Fugard, Athol (Harold Lanigan) (1932–) South African dramatist, director, and actor. He has written more than 20 plays, many of which deal with the effects of apartheid, the former official government policy of racial discrimination in South Africa. Among his most explicitly political plays are a trilogy published as *Statements* in 1974. Other plays include *Boesman and Lena* (1969; filmed in 1974), the autobiographical '*Master Harold'... and the Boys* (1982), and *My Children! My Africa!* (1989). Fugard's film roles include *Gandhi* (1982). He has also published one novel, *Tsotsi* (1980).

fugue (Latin 'flight'; Italian 'chase') in music, a contrapuntal form where two or more (usually four) parts or voices (principal melodies for voices or instruments) are woven together. The voices enter one after the other in strict imitation of each other. They may be transposed to a higher or lower key, or combined in augmented form (larger note values). The fugue is the highest form of contrapuntal composition as heard in works such as Johann Sebastian Bach's *Das musikalische Opfer/The Musical Offering* (1747), on a theme of Frederick II of Prussia, and *Die Kunst der Fuge/The Art of the Fugue* published in 1751, and Ludwig van Beethoven's *Grosse Fuge/Great Fugue* for string quartet (1825–26).

Führer (or Fuehrer) (German 'leader') title adopted by Adolf *Hitler as leader of the Nazi Party.

Fujian or Fukien maritime province of southeast China, lying opposite Taiwan, bounded to the southwest by Guangdong, to the west and northwest by Jiangxi, to the northeast by Zhejiang, and to the southeast by the Taiwan Strait on the China Sea; area 123,100 sq km/47,500 sq mi; population (2000 est) 34,710,000. The main cities are Fuzhou (capital), Xiamen, Zhangzhou, and Nanping. The main industries are steel-rolling, electrical goods, tourism, handicrafts, and leather goods. Agricultural products are rice, sweet potatoes, sugar, special aromatic teas, tobacco, timber, and citrus fruit.

Fuji, Mount Japanese Fuji-san, Japanese volcano and highest peak, on Honshu Island, near Tokyo; height 3,778 m/12,400 ft. Dormant since 1707, it has a *Shinto shrine and a weather station on its summit. Fuji has long been revered for its picturesque cone-shaped crater peak, and figures prominently in Japanese art, literature, and religion.

Fulani member of a West African people from the southern Sahara and Sahel. The Fulani language is divided into four dialects and belongs to the West Atlantic branch of the Niger-Congo family; it has more than 10 million speakers. Traditionally they are nomadic pastoralists and traders; many are now settled agriculturalists or live in cites. Fulani groups are found in Senegal, Guinea, Mali, Burkina Faso, Niger, Nigeria, Chad, and Cameroon.

Fuller, (Richard) Buckminster (1895–1983) US architect, engineer, and social philosopher. He embarked on an unorthodox career in an attempt to maximize energy resources through improved technology. In 1947 he invented the lightweight geodesic dome, a hemispherical space-frame of triangular components linked by rods, independent of buttress or vault and capable of covering large-span areas. Within 30 years over 50,000 had been built.

fullerene form of carbon, discovered in 1985, based on closed cages of carbon atoms. The molecules of the most symmetrical of the fullerenes are called *buckminsterfullerenes (or buckyballs). They are perfect spheres made up of 60 carbon atoms linked together in 12 pentagons and 20 hexagons fitted together like those of a spherical football. Other fullerenes with 28, 32, 50, 70, and 76 carbon atoms, have also been identified.

fuller's earth soft, greenish-grey rock resembling clay, but without clay's plasticity. It is formed largely of clay minerals, rich in montmorillonite, but a great deal of silica is also present. Its absorbent properties make it suitable for removing oil and grease, and it was formerly used for cleaning fleeces ('fulling'). It is still used in the textile industry, but its chief application is in the purification of oils. Beds of fuller's earth are found in the southern USA, Germany, Japan, and the UK.

fulmar any of several species of petrels of the family Procellariidae, which are similar in size and colour to herring gulls. The northern fulmar *Fulmarus glacialis* is found in the North Atlantic and visits land only to nest, laying a single egg.

fumitory any of a group of plants native to Europe and Asia. The common fumitory (*F. officinalis*) grows to 50 cm/20 in and produces pink flowers tipped with blackish red; it has been used in medicine for stomach and liver complaints. (Genus *Fumeria*, family Fumariaceae.)

function in computing, a small part of a program that supplies a specific value – for example, the square root of a specified number, or the current date. Most programming languages incorporate a number of built-in functions; some allow programmers to write their own. A function may have one or more arguments (the values on which the function operates). A **function key** on a keyboard is one that, when pressed, performs a designated task, such as ending a program.

function in mathematics, a function f is a non-empty set of ordered pairs $(x, f(x))$ of which no two can have the same first element. Hence, if $f(x) = x^2$ two ordered pairs are $(-2, 4)$ and $(2, 4)$. The set of all first elements in a function's ordered pairs is called the **domain**; the set of all second elements is the **range**. Functions are used in all branches of mathematics, physics, and science generally. For example, in the *equation $y = 2x + 1$, y is a function of the symbol x. This can be written as $-y = f(x)$.

functional group in chemistry, a small number of atoms in an arrangement that determines the chemical properties of the group and of the molecule to which it is attached (for example, the carboxyl group COOH, or the amine group NH_2). Organic compounds can be considered as structural skeletons, with a high carbon content, with functional groups attached.

Functionalism in architecture and design, the principle of excluding everything that serves no practical purpose. Central to 20th-century *modernism, the Functionalist ethic developed as a reaction against the 19th-century practice of imitating and combining earlier styles. Its finest achievements are in the realms of industrial architecture and office furnishings.

fundamental constant physical quantity that is constant in all circumstances throughout the whole universe. Examples are the electric charge of an electron, the speed of light, Planck's constant, and the gravitational constant.

fundamental forces see *forces, fundamental.

fundamentalism in religion, an emphasis on basic principles or articles of faith. **Christian fundamentalism** emerged in the USA just after World War I (as a reaction to theological modernism and the historical criticism of the Bible) and insisted on belief in the literal truth of everything in the Bible. **Islamic fundamentalism** insists on strict observance of Muslim Shari'a law.

fungus plural **fungi**, any of a unique group of organisms that includes moulds, yeasts, rusts, smuts, mildews, mushrooms, and toadstools. There are around 70,000 species of fungi known to science, although there may be as many as 1.5 million actually in existence. They are not considered to be plants for three main reasons: they have no leaves or roots; they contain no chlorophyll (green colouring) and are therefore unable to make their own food by *photosynthesis; and they reproduce by *spores. Some fungi are edible but many are highly poisonous; they often cause damage and sometimes disease to the organic matter on which they live and feed, but some fungi are exploited in the production of food and drink (for example, yeasts in baking and brewing) and in medicine (for example, penicillin).

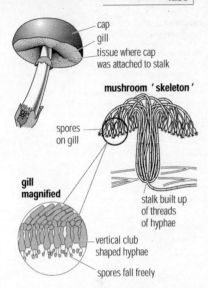

cap
gill
tissue where cap was attached to stalk

mushroom 'skeleton'

spores on gill

stalk built up of threads of hyphae

gill magnified

vertical club shaped hyphae

spores fall freely

fungus Fungi grow from spores as fine threads, or hyphae. These have no distinct cellular structure. Mushrooms and toadstools are the fruiting bodies formed by the hyphae. Gills beneath the caps of these aerial structures produce masses of spores.

funk dance music of black US origin, relying on heavy percussion in polyrhythmic patterns. Leading exponents include James Brown and George Clinton.

fur the *hair of certain animals. Fur is an excellent insulating material and so has been used as clothing. This is, however, vociferously criticized by many groups on humane grounds, as the methods of breeding or trapping animals are often cruel. Mink, chinchilla, and sable are among the most valuable, the wild furs being finer than the farmed. Fur such as mink is made up of a soft, thick, insulating layer called underfur and a top layer of longer, lustrous guard hairs.

Furies *or* **Erinyes** in Greek mythology, spirits of vengeance, principally of murder within the family but also of other breaches of natural order such as filial disobedience, inhospitality, and oath-breaking; they may have been considered the personifications of curses. The Furies were also associated with fertility, and were appeasingly called the *Eumenides 'kindly ones'. Represented as winged maidens with serpents twisted in their hair, they inhabited Hades, the underworld.

furlong unit of measurement, originating in Anglo-Saxon England, equivalent to 220 yd (201.168 m).

fuse in electricity, a wire or strip of metal designed to melt (thus breaking the circuit) when excessive current passes through. It is a safety device that halts surges of current that would otherwise damage equipment and cause fires. In explosives, a fuse is a cord impregnated with chemicals so that it burns slowly at a

353

predetermined rate. It is used to set off a main explosive charge, sufficient length of fuse being left to allow the person lighting it to get away to safety.

fusion in music, a combination of styles; the term usually refers to jazz-rock fusion. Jazz trumpeter Miles Davis began to draw on rock music in the late 1960s, and jazz-rock fusion flourished in the 1970s with bands like Weather Report (formed in 1970 in the USA) and musicians like English guitarist John McLaughlin.

fusion in physics, the fusing of the nuclei of light elements, such as hydrogen, into those of a heavier element, such as helium. The resultant loss in their combined mass is converted into energy. Stars and thermonuclear weapons are powered by nuclear fusion.

futures trading buying and selling futures. The notional value of the futures contracts traded annually worldwide is $140,000 billion (1994). The volume of crude oil futures and options traded on the New York Mercantile Exchange amounts to 200 million barrels a day, almost four times the amount actually produced.

Futurism avant-garde art movement founded in 1909 that celebrated the dynamism of the modern world. It was chiefly an Italian movement and was mainly expressed in painting, but it also embraced other arts, including literature and music, and it had extensive influence outside Italy, particularly in Russia. In Italy the movement virtually died out during World War I, but in Russia it continued to flourish into the 1920s.

fuzzy logic in mathematics and computing, a form of knowledge representation suitable for notions (such as 'hot' or 'loud') that cannot be defined precisely but depend on their context. For example, a jug of water may be described as too hot or too cold, depending on whether it is to be used to wash one's face or to make tea.

g

gabbro mafic (consisting primarily of dark-coloured crystals) igneous rock formed deep in the Earth's crust. It contains pyroxene and calcium-rich feldspar, and may contain small amounts of olivine and amphibole. Its coarse crystals of dull minerals give it a speckled appearance.

Gable, (William) Clark (1901–1960) US actor. A star for more than 30 years, he played a range of hard-boiled, comic, and romantic roles. He won an Academy Award for his performance in Frank Capra's *It Happened One Night* (1934), and starred as Rhett Butler in *Gone With the Wind* (1939).

Gabon

National name: *République Gabonaise/Gabonese Republic*

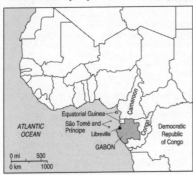

Area: 267,667 sq km/103,346 sq mi
Capital: Libreville
Major towns/cities: Port-Gentil, Franceville (or Masuku), Lambaréné, Mouanda, Oyem, Mouila
Major ports: Port-Gentil and Owendo
Physical features: virtually the whole country is tropical rainforest; narrow coastal plain rising to hilly interior with savannah in east and south; Ogooué River flows north–west
Head of state: Omar Bongo Odimba from 1967
Head of government: Jean-François Ntoutoume-Emane from 1999
Political system: emergent democracy
Political executive: limited presidency
Political parties: Gabonese Democratic Party (PDG), nationalist; Gabone Progress Party (PGP), left of centre; National Lumberjacks Rally (RNB), left of centre

Currency: franc CFA
GNI per capita (PPP): (US$) 5,320 (2002 est)
Exports: petroleum and petroleum products, manganese, timber and wood products, uranium. Principal market: USA 50% (2000)
Population: 1,329,000 (2003 est)
Language: French (official), Fang (in the north), Bantu languages, and other local dialects
Religion: Christian 60% (mostly Roman Catholic), animist about 4%, Muslim 1%
Life expectancy: 56 (men); 58 (women) (2000–05)
Chronology
12th century: Immigration of Bantu speakers into an area previously peopled by Pygmies.
1472: Gabon Estuary first visited by Portuguese navigators, who named it Gabao ('hooded cloak'), after the shape of the coastal area.
17th–18th centuries: Fang, from Cameroon in the north, and Omiene peoples colonized the area, attracted by the presence in coastal areas of European traders, who developed the ivory and slave trades, which lasted until the mid-19th century.
1839–42: Mpongwe coastal chiefs agreed to transfer sovereignty to France; Catholic and Protestant missionaries attracted to the area.
1849: Libreville ('Free Town') formed by slaves from a slave ship liberated by the French.
1889: Became part of French Congo, with Congo.
1910: Became part of French Equatorial Africa, which also comprised Congo, Chad, and Central African Republic.
1890s–1920s: Human and natural resources exploited by private concessionary companies.
1940–44: Supported the 'Free French' anti-Nazi cause during World War II.
1946: Became overseas territory within the French Community, with its own assembly.
1960: Independence achieved; Léon M'ba, a Fang of the pro-French Gabonese Democratic Block (BDG), became the first president.
1967: M'ba died and was succeeded by his protégé Albert Bernard Bongo, drawn from the Teke community.
1968: A One-party state established, with the BDG dissolved and replaced by Gabonese Democratic Party (PDG).
1973: Bongo converted to Islam and changed his first name to Omar, but continued to follow a pro-Western policy course and exploit rich mineral resources to increase prosperity.
1989: A coup attempt against Bongo was defeated; the economy deteriorated.
1990: The PDG won the first multiparty elections since 1964. French troops were sent in to maintain order following antigovernment riots.
1993: A national unity government was formed, including some opposition members.
1998: A new party, Rassemblement des Gaullois, was recognized. President Bongo was re-elected.
1999: Jean-François Ntoutoume-Emane was appointed prime minister.
2002: PDG kept its majority in parliamentary elections.
2003: The constitution was altered to remove limitations on the number of times an individual may serve as president, allowing President Bongo to run indefinitely.

355

Gaborone capital of Botswana, mainly an administrative and government-service centre; population (1995 est) 158,000. The city lies at altitude 1000 m/3300 ft and has an airport. Light industries include motor vehicle assembly, textiles, brewing, printing and publishing, and construction. The city developed after 1962 when it replaced Mafikeng as capital in preparation for the country's independence in 1966.

Gaddafi alternative form of *Khaddhafi, Libyan leader.

gadolinium chemical symbol Gd, silvery-white metallic element of the lanthanide series, atomic number 64, relative atomic mass 157.25. It is found in the products of nuclear fission and used in electronic components, alloys, and products needing to withstand high temperatures.

Gaelic football see *football, Gaelic.

Gaelic languages members of the Celtic branch of the Indo-European language family, spoken in Ireland, Scotland, and (until 1974) the Isle of Man. Scottish Gaelic has been in decline for several centuries, though efforts are being made to keep it alive, for example by means of the government's Gaelic Broadcasting Fund, established in 1993, which subsidises television and radio programmes in Gaelic for transmission in Scotland.

Gagarin, Yuri Alexeyevich (1934–1968) Soviet cosmonaut who on 12 April 1961 became the first human in space, aboard the spacecraft *Vostok 1* (see *Vostok). He completed one orbit of the Earth, taking 108 minutes from launch to landing. He died in a plane crash while training for the *Soyuz 3* mission.

Gaia *or* **Ge** in Greek mythology, the goddess of the Earth. She sprang from primordial Chaos and herself produced Uranus, by whom she was the mother of the Cyclopes and *Titans.

Gaia hypothesis theory that the Earth's living and nonliving systems form an inseparable whole that is regulated and kept adapted for life by living organisms themselves. The planet therefore functions as a single organism, or a giant cell. The hypothesis was elaborated by British scientist James Lovelock and first published in 1968.

gain in electronics, the ratio of the amplitude of the output signal produced by an amplifier to that of the input signal. In a voltage amplifier the voltage gain is the ratio of the output voltage to the input voltage; in an inverting operational amplifier (op-amp) it is equal to the ratio of the resistance of the feedback resistor to that of the input resistor.

Gainsborough, Thomas (1727–1788) English landscape and portrait painter. In 1760 he settled in Bath, where his elegant and subtly characterized society portraits brought great success. In 1774 he went to London, becoming one of the original members of the Royal Academy and the principal rival of Joshua Reynolds. He was one of the first British artists to follow the Dutch example in painting realistic landscapes rather than imaginative Italianate scenery, as in *Mr and Mrs Andrews* (about 1750; National Gallery, London).

Galahad in Arthurian legend, one of the knights of the Round Table. His virtue allowed him to succeed in the quest for the *Holy Grail, and he died in ecstasy, having seen its mystery. He was the son of *Lancelot of the Lake and Elaine, daughter of the Fisher King, whom Lancelot believed to be his beloved *Guinevere.

Galapagos Islands officially **Archipiélago de Colón**, (Spanish *galápagos* 'terrapins') group of 12 large and several hundred smaller islands in the Pacific lying 800 km/500 mi off the coast of Ecuador, of which they form a province; area 7,800 sq km/3,000 sq mi; population (1999 est) 16,900. This island group, of volcanic origin, includes the six main islands of San Cristóbal (where the capital of the same name is situated), Santa Cruz, Isabela, Floreana, Santiago, and Fernandina, as well as 12 smaller islands, with other islets. Volcán Wolf, at 1707 m/5600 ft, on Isabela I is the highest peak. The Galapagos National Park was established in 1934 and, because of the unique fauna, the islands have been established as a UNESCO World Heritage Site. They were uninhabited when discovered by Spanish explorers in 1535; no colony was established. They were annexed by Ecuador in 1832.

galaxy grouping of millions or billions of stars, held together by gravity. It is believed that there are billions of galaxies in the *universe. There are different types, including spiral, barred spiral, and elliptical galaxies. Our own Galaxy, the *Milky Way, is about 100,000 light years across (a light year is the distance light travels in a year, about 9.5 billion km/6 billion mi), and contains at least 100 billion stars.

Galbraith, John Kenneth (1908–) Canadian-born US economist who never ceased to criticize mainstream neo-classical economics. Author of *American Capitalism: The Concept of Countervailing Power* (1952) and *The Affluent Society* (1958), Galbraith was seen as a renegade by many of his fellow economists. They voted him president of the American Economic Association in 1972, but they never stopped criticizing his racy style, his belief in planning and more state control, his contempt for rigorous analysis, and his insistence that most economics is simple 'conventional wisdom'.

Galen (c. 129–c. 200) Greek physician and anatomist whose ideas dominated Western medicine for almost 1,500 years. Central to his thinking were the threefold circulation of the blood and the theory of *humours (blood, phlegm, choler/yellow bile, and melancholy/black bile) that contributed to mental and physical state. His *On Anatomical Procedures*, a detailed description of animal dissections when work on human corpses was forbidden, became a standard text on anatomy when rediscovered in Western Europe in the 16th century. He remained the highest medical authority until Andreas *Vesalius and William *Harvey exposed the fundamental errors of his system.

galena mineral consisting of lead sulphide, PbS, the chief ore of lead. It is lead-grey in colour, has a high metallic lustre and breaks into cubes because of its perfect cubic cleavage. It may contain up to 1% silver, and so the ore is sometimes mined for both metals. Galena occurs mainly among limestone deposits in Australia, Mexico, Russia, Kazakhstan, the UK, and the USA.

Galicia mountainous but fertile autonomous community of northwest Spain, comprising the provinces of La Coruña, Lugo, Orense, and Pontevedra; area 29,434 sq km/11,365 sq mi; population (2001 est) 2,733,000. Industries include fishing (Galicia has the largest fishing fleet in the European Union), cattle and hog raising, food processing, and tungsten and tin mining. The climate is very wet, and the region is traversed northeast to southwest by the River Miño. The chief harbours are La Coruña, Vigo, and El Ferrol (a major naval base). The Galician language (Gallego) is similar to Portuguese. The capital is *Santiago de Compostela, the site of an important Christian shrine (since the 9th century) which continues to attract great numbers of pilgrims.

Galilee region of northern Israel (once a Roman province in Palestine) that includes Nazareth and Tiberias, frequently mentioned in the Gospels of the New Testament.

Galilee, Sea of alternative name for Lake *Tiberias in northern Israel.

Galileo (1564–1642) born Galileo Galilei, Italian mathematician, astronomer, and physicist. He developed the astronomical telescope and was the first to see sunspots, the four main satellites of Jupiter, and the appearance of Venus going through phases, thus proving it was orbiting the Sun. Galileo discovered that freely falling bodies, heavy or light, have the same, constant acceleration and that this acceleration is due to gravity. He also determined that a body moving on a perfectly smooth horizontal surface would neither speed up nor slow down. He invented a thermometer, a hydrostatic balance, and a compass, and discovered that the path of a projectile is a parabola.

Galileo spacecraft launched from the space shuttle *Atlantis* on 18 October 1989 to explore the planet Jupiter. Galileo's probe entered the atmosphere of Jupiter in December 1995. It radioed information back to the orbiter for 57 minutes before the craft was destroyed by atmospheric pressure. The first pictures of Jupiter were transmitted in 1996. In 1997 Galileo completed two fly-bys of Jupiter's fourth-largest and icy moon *Europa, and in February 2000 it passed within 200 km/125 mi of Jupiter's third-largest moon *Io.

gall abnormal outgrowth on a plant that develops as a result of attack by insects or, less commonly, by bacteria, fungi, mites, or nematodes. The attack causes an increase in the number of cells or an enlargement of existing cells in the plant. Gall-forming insects generally pass the early stages of their life inside the gall. Gall wasps are responsible for the conspicuous bud galls forming on oak trees, 2.5–4 cm/1–1.5 in across, known as 'oak apples'. The organisms that cause galls are host-specific. Thus, for example, gall wasps tend to parasitize oaks, and *sawflies willows.

gall bladder small muscular sac, part of the digestive system of most, but not all, vertebrates. In humans, it is situated on the underside of the liver and connected to the small intestine by the bile duct. It stores bile from the liver.

galley ship powered by oars, and usually also equipped with sails. Galleys typically had a crew of hundreds of rowers arranged in banks. They were used in warfare in the Mediterranean from antiquity until the 18th century.

Gallic Wars series of military campaigns 58–51 BC in which Julius Caesar, as proconsul of Gaul, annexed Transalpine Gaul (the territory that formed the geographical basis of modern-day France). His final victory over the Gauls led by Vercingetorix 52 BC left him in control of the land area from the Rhine to the

Pyrenees and from the Alps to the Atlantic. The final organization of the provinces followed under Augustus.

Gallipoli port in European Turkey, giving its name to the peninsula (ancient name **Chersonesus**) on which it stands. In World War I, at the instigation of Winston Churchill, an unsuccessful attempt was made between February 1915 and January 1916 by Allied troops to force their way through the Dardanelles and link up with Russia. The campaign was fought mainly by Australian and New Zealand (*Anzac) forces, who suffered heavy losses. An estimated 36,000 Commonwealth troops died during the nine-month campaign.

gallium chemical symbol Ga, grey metallic element, atomic number 31, relative atomic mass 69.72. It is liquid at room temperature. Gallium arsenide (GaAs) crystals are used for semiconductors in microelectronics, since electrons travel a thousand times faster through them than through silicon. The element was discovered in 1875 by Lecoq de Boisbaudran (1838–1912).

Gallo, Robert Charles (1937–) US scientist credited with identifying the virus responsible for *AIDS. Gallo discovered the virus, now known as human immunodeficiency virus (HIV), in 1984; the French scientist Luc Montagnier of the Pasteur Institute, Paris, discovered the virus, independently, in 1983.

gallon symbol gal, imperial liquid or dry measure, equal to 4.546 litres, and subdivided into four quarts or eight pints. The US gallon is equivalent to 3.785 litres.

gallstone pebblelike, insoluble accretion formed in the human gall bladder or bile ducts from cholesterol or calcium salts present in bile. Gallstones may be symptomless or they may cause pain, indigestion, or jaundice. They can be dissolved with medication or removed, either by means of an endoscope or, along with the gall bladder, in an operation known as cholecystectomy.

Galsworthy, John (1867–1933) English novelist and dramatist. His work examines the social issues of the Victorian period. He wrote *The Forsyte Saga* (1906–22) and its sequel, the novels collectively entitled *A Modern Comedy* (1929). His plays include *The Silver Box* (1906). He was awarded the Nobel Prize for Literature in 1932.

Galton, Francis (1822–1911) English scientist, inventor, and explorer who studied the inheritance of physical and mental attributes with the aim of improving the human species. He was the first to use twins to try to assess the influence of environment on development, and is considered the founder of *eugenics (a term he coined).

Galvani, Luigi (1737–1798) Italian physiologist who discovered galvanic, or voltaic, electricity in 1762, when investigating the contractions produced in the muscles of dead frogs by contact with pairs of different metals. His work led quickly to Alessandro *Volta's invention of the electrical *cell, and later to an understanding of how nerves control muscles.

galvanizing process for rendering iron rust-proof, by plunging it into molten zinc (the dipping method), or by electroplating it with zinc.

Galway county on the west coast of the Republic of Ireland, in the province of Connacht; county town Galway; area 5,940 sq km/2,293 sq mi; population (2002 est) 208,800. Lead and zinc are found at Tynagh, and marble is quarried and processed at several sites. The main farming activity is cattle and sheep grazing. The

Connemara National Park is in Galway. Towns include Salthill, a suburb of Galway city and seaside resort, Ballinasloe, Clifden, and Tuam.

Gama, Vasco da (c. 1469–1524) Portuguese navigator. He commanded an expedition in 1497 to discover the route to India around the Cape of Good Hope (in modern South Africa). On Christmas Day 1497 he reached land, which he named Natal. He then crossed the Indian Ocean, arriving at Calicut (now Kozhikode in Kerala) in May 1498, and returned to Portugal in September 1499.

Gambia river in western Africa, 1,000 km/620 mi long, which gives its name to The Gambia. It rises in Guinea and flows west through Senegal and The Gambia to the Atlantic Ocean.

Gambia, The
National name: *Republic of the Gambia*

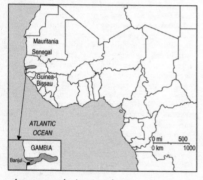

Area: 10,402 sq km/4,016 sq mi
Capital: Banjul
Major towns/cities: Serekunda, Brikama, Bakau, Farafenni, Sukuta, Gunjur, Basse
Physical features: consists of narrow strip of land along the River Gambia; river flanked by low hills
Head of state and government: Yahya Jammeh from 1994
Political system: transitional
Political executive: transitional
Political parties: Alliance for Patriotic Reorientation and Construction (APRC), authoritarian, anti-democratic; National Reconciliation Party (NRP), reformist, pro-democratic; People's Democratic Organization for Independence and Socialism (PDOIS), socialist; United Democratic Party (UDP), reformist. The Progressive People's Party (PPP), moderate centrist; National Convention Party (NCP), left of centre; and the Gambian People's Party (GPP) were all banned in 1996
Currency: dalasi
GNI per capita (PPP): (US$) 1,680 (2002 est)
Exports: groundnuts and related products, cotton lint, fish and fish preparations, hides and skins. Principal market: UK 53% (2001)
Population: 1,425,000 (2003 est)
Language: English (official), Mandinka, Fula, Wolof, other indigenous dialects
Religion: Muslim 85%, with animist and Christian minorities

Life expectancy: 53 (men); 56 (women) (2000–05)
Chronology
13th century: Wolof, Malinke (Mandingo), and Fulani tribes settled in the region from east and north.
14th century: Became part of the great Muslim Mali Empire, which, centred to northeast, also extended across Senegal, Mali, and southern Mauritania.
1455: The Gambia River was first sighted by the Portuguese.
1663 and 1681: The British and French established small settlements on the river at Fort James and Albreda.
1843: The Gambia became a British crown colony, administered with Sierra Leone until 1888.
1965: Independence was achieved as a constitutional monarchy within the Commonwealth, with Dawda K Jawara of the People's Progressive Party (PPP) as prime minister at the head of a multiparty democracy.
1970: The Gambia became a republic, with Jawara as president.
1982: The Gambia formed the Confederation of Senegambia with Senegal, which involved the integration of military forces, economic and monetary union, and coordinated foreign policy.
1994: Jawara was ousted in a military coup, and fled to Senegal; Yahya Jammeh was named acting head of state.
1996: A civilian constitution was adopted.
2002: The ruling Alliance for Patriotic Reorientation and Construction (APRC) retained power overwhelmingly in parliamentary elections.
2004: The government announced the discovery of extensive oil reserves.

gamelan percussion ensemble of 15 to 20 players using mainly tuned knobbed gongs and keyed metallophones found in Indonesia (especially Java and Bali) and Malaysia. Most modern gamelan are tuned to a five-note or seven-note scale. Gamelan music is performed as an accompaniment for dance and theatre.

gamete cell that functions in sexual reproduction by merging with another gamete to form a zygote. Examples of gametes include sperm and egg cells. In most organisms, the gametes are haploid (they contain half the number of chromosomes of the parent), owing to reduction division or *meiosis.

gametophyte the *haploid generation in the life cycle of a plant that produces gametes; see *alternation of generations.

gamma radiation very high-frequency, high-energy electromagnetic radiation, similar in nature to X-rays but of shorter wavelength, emitted by the nuclei of radioactive substances during decay or by the interactions of high-energy electrons with matter. Cosmic gamma rays have been identified as coming from pulsars, radio galaxies, and quasars, although they cannot penetrate the Earth's atmosphere.

gamma-ray astronomy study of celestial objects that emit gamma rays (energetic photons with very short wavelengths). Much of the radiation detected comes from collisions between hydrogen gas and cosmic rays in our Galaxy. Some sources have been identified, including the Crab Nebula and the Vela pulsar (the most powerful gamma-ray source detected).

Gance, Abel (1889–1981) French film director. His films were grandiose melodramas. *Napoléon* 1927 was one of the most ambitious silent epic films. It features colour tinting and triple-screen sequences, as well as multiple-exposure shots, and helped further the technological and aesthetic development of the film medium.

Gandhi, Indira Priyadarshani (1917–1984) born Indira Priyadarshani Nehru, Indian politician, prime minister of India 1966–77 and 1980–84, and leader of the *Congress Party 1966–77 and subsequently of the Congress (I) party. She was assassinated in 1984 by members of her Sikh bodyguard, resentful of her use of troops to clear malcontents from the Sikh temple at *Amritsar.

Gandhi, Mahatma (1869–1948) honorific name of Mohandas Karamchand Gandhi, (Sanskrit *Mahatma* 'Great Soul') Indian nationalist leader. A pacifist, he led the struggle for Indian independence from the UK by advocating non-violent non-cooperation (*satyagraha* 'truth and firmness') from 1915. He was imprisoned several times by the British authorities. He was influential in the nationalist Congress Party and in the independence negotiations in 1947. He was assassinated by a Hindu nationalist in the violence that followed the partition of British India into India and Pakistan in 1948. Religious violence in India and Pakistan soon waned, and his teachings came to inspire non-violent movements in other parts of the world, notably in the USA under civil-rights leader Martin Luther King Jr, and in South Africa under Nelson Mandela.

Gandhi, Rajiv (1944–1991) Indian politician, prime minister from 1984 (following his mother Indira Gandhi's assassination) to November 1989. As prime minister, he faced growing discontent with his party's elitism and lack of concern for social issues. He was assassinated at an election rally.

Ganesh *or* **Ganesha** Hindu god of prophecy, son of *Shiva and Parvati; he is represented as elephant-headed and is worshipped as a remover of obstacles. Hindus seek his aid before difficult undertakings, such as an examination or job interview.

Ganges Hindi Ganga, major river of India and Bangladesh; length 2,510 km/1,560 mi. It drains a fertile and densely populated basin, approximately a quarter of the total area of India, and is the most sacred river for Hindus.

ganglion plural **ganglia**, solid cluster of nervous tissue containing many cell bodies and *synapses, usually enclosed in a tissue sheath; found in invertebrates and vertebrates.

Gang of Four in Chinese history, the chief members of the radical faction that played a key role in directing the *Cultural Revolution and tried to seize power after the death of the communist leader *Mao Zedong in 1976. It included his widow *Jiang Qing; the other members were three young Shanghai politicians: Zhang Chunqiao, Wang Hongwen, and Yao Wenyuan. The coup failed and the Gang of Four were arrested. Publicly tried in 1980, they were found guilty of treason.

gangrene death and decay of body tissue (often of a limb) due to bacterial action; the affected part gradually turns black and causes blood poisoning.

gannet any of three species of North Atlantic seabirds; the largest is *Sula bassana*. When fully grown, it is white with buff colouring on the head and neck; the beak is long and thick and compressed at the point; the wings are black-tipped with a span of 1.7 m/5.6 ft. It breeds on cliffs in nests made of grass and seaweed, laying a single white egg. Gannets feed on fish that swim near the surface, such as herrings and pilchards. (Family Sulidae, order Pelecaniformaes.)

Gansu *or* **Kansu** province of northwest China, bounded to the north by Mongolia and Inner Mongolia, to the east by Ningxia Hui Autonomous Region and Shaanxi, to the south by Sichuan, and to the west by Qinghai and Xinjiang Uygur Autonomous Region; area 530,000 sq km/205,000 sq mi; population (2000 est) 25,620,000. The main cities are Lanzhou (capital), Yumen, Tianshui, Dunhuang, and Jiayuguan. Chief industries are coal, oil, iron and steel, and petrochemicals. Hydroelectric power from the Huang He River has been important in industrial development, and other industries include mining, metal-processing, and tourism. Agriculture is based on the cultivation of spring wheat, millet, sorghum, flax, and fruit, and animal rearing.

Ganymede in astronomy, largest moon of the planet Jupiter, orbiting every 7.2 days at a distance of 1.1 million km/700,000 mi. It is the largest moon in the Solar System, 5,260 km/3,270 mi in diameter (larger than the planet Mercury). Its surface is a mixture of extensively cratered and grooved terrain. Molecular oxygen was identified on Ganymede's surface in 1994. It is thought that Ganymede has a water ice crust and possibly a buried water ocean.

Ganymede in Greek mythology according to Homer, a youth so beautiful he was taken as cupbearer to Zeus, king of the gods. He was deemed responsible for the annual flooding of the Nile, and was later identified with the constellation *Aquarius.

Garbo, Greta (1905–1990) stage name of Greta Lovisa Gustafsson, Swedish-born US film actor. She went to the USA in 1925, and her captivating beauty and leading role in *Flesh and the Devil* (1927) made her one of Hollywood's greatest stars. Her later films include *Mata Hari* (1931), *Grand Hotel* (1932), *Queen Christina* (1933), *Anna Karenina* (1935), *Camille* (1936), and *Ninotchka* (1939). Her ethereal qualities and romantic mystery on the screen intermingled with her seclusion in private life. She retired in 1941.

García Lorca, Federico Spanish poet. See *Lorca, Federico García.

García Márquez, Gabriel (Gabo) (1928–) Colombian novelist. His sweeping novel *Cien años de soledad/One Hundred Years of Solitude* (1967) (which tells the story of a family over a period of six generations) is an example of magic realism, a technique used to heighten the intensity of realistic portrayal of social and political issues by introducing grotesque or fanciful material. He was awarded the Nobel Prize for Literature in 1982.

Garda, Lake Italian **Lago di Garda**; ancient **Lacus Benacus**, largest lake in Italy; situated on the border between the regions of Lombardy and Veneto; area 370 sq km/143 sq mi.

garden city in the UK, a town built in a rural area and designed to combine town and country advantages, with its own industries, controlled developments, private and public gardens, and cultural centre. The idea was proposed by Ebenezer *Howard, who in 1899 founded the Garden City Association, which established the first garden city: Letchworth in Hertfordshire.

gardenia any of a group of subtropical and tropical trees and shrubs found in Africa and Asia, belonging to the madder family, with evergreen foliage and flattened rosettes of fragrant waxen-looking flowers, often white in colour. (Genus *Gardenia*, family Rubiaceae.)

Garfield, James A(bram) (1831–1881) 20th president of the USA 1881, a Republican. A compromise candidate for the presidency, he held office for only four months before being assassinated in a Washington, DC, railway station by a disappointed office-seeker. His short tenure was marked primarily by struggles within the Republican Party over influence and cabinet posts.

Garibaldi, Giuseppe (1807–1882) Italian soldier who played a central role in the unification of Italy by conquering Sicily and Naples in 1860. From 1834 a member of the nationalist Mazzini's Young Italy society, he was forced into exile until 1848 and again 1849–54. He fought against Austria 1848–49, in 1859, and in 1866, and led two unsuccessful expeditions to liberate Rome from papal rule in 1862 and 1867.

Garland, Judy (1922–1969) stage name of Frances Gumm, US singer and actor. Her performances are marked by a compelling intensity. Her films include *The Wizard of Oz* (1939) (which featured the tune that was to become her theme song, 'Over the Rainbow'), *Babes in Arms* (1939), *Strike Up the Band* (1940), *Meet Me in St Louis* (1944), *Easter Parade* (1948), *A Star is Born* (1954), and *Judgment at Nuremberg* (1961).

garlic perennial Asian plant belonging to the lily family, whose strong-smelling and sharp-tasting bulb, made up of several small segments, or cloves, is used in cooking. The plant has white flowers. It is widely cultivated and has been used successfully as a fungicide in the cereal grass *sorghum. It also has antibacterial properties. (*Allium sativum*, family Liliaceae.)

garnet group of *silicate minerals with the formula $X_3Y_3(SiO_4)_3$, where X is calcium, magnesium, iron, or manganese, and Y is usually aluminium or sometimes iron or chromium. Garnets are used as semi-precious gems (usually pink to deep red) and as abrasives. They occur in metamorphic rocks such as gneiss and schist.

Garrick, David (1717–1779) English actor and theatre manager. From 1747 he became joint licensee of the Drury Lane Theatre, London, with his own company, and instituted a number of significant theatrical conventions including concealed stage lighting and banishing spectators from the stage. He played Shakespearean characters such as Richard III, King Lear, Hamlet, and Benedick, and collaborated with George Colman (1732–1794) in writing the play *The Clandestine Marriage* (1766). He retired from the stage in 1766, but continued as a manager.

Garter, Order of the senior British order of knighthood (see *knighthood, order of), founded by Edward III in about 1347. Its distinctive badge is a garter of dark-blue velvet, with the motto of the order – *Honi soit qui mal y pense* ('Shame be to him who thinks evil of it') – in gold letters. Knights of the Garter write KG after their names.

Garvey, Marcus (Moziah) (1887–1940) Jamaican political thinker and activist, an early advocate of black nationalism. He led a Back to Africa movement for black Americans to establish a black-governed country in Africa. The Jamaican politico-religious movement of *Rastafarianism is based largely on his ideas.

gas form of matter, such as air, in which the molecules move randomly in otherwise empty space, filling any size or shape of container into which the gas is put.

Gascony ancient province of southwest France. With Guienne it formed the duchy of Aquitaine in the 12th century. Henry II of England gained possession of it through his marriage to Eleanor of Aquitaine in 1152, and it was often in English hands until 1451. Thereafter it was ruled by the king of France until it was united with the French royal domain in 1607 under Henry IV.

Gaskell, Elizabeth Cleghorn (1810–1865) born Elizabeth Cleghorn Stevenson, English novelist. Her most popular book, *Cranford* (1853), is the study of a small, close-knit circle in a small town, modelled on Knutsford, Cheshire, where she was brought up. Her other books, which often deal with social concerns, include *Mary Barton* (1848), *North and South* (1855), *Sylvia's Lovers* (1863–64), and the unfinished *Wives and Daughters* (1866). She wrote a frank and sympathetic biography of her friend Charlotte Brontë (1857).

gas laws physical laws concerning the behaviour of gases. They include *Boyle's law and *Charles's law, which are concerned with the relationships between the pressure (P), temperature (T), and volume (V) of an ideal (hypothetical) gas. These two laws can be combined to give the general or universal gas law, which may be expressed as: PV/T = constant.

gastroenteritis inflammation of the stomach and intestines, giving rise to abdominal pain, vomiting, and diarrhoea. It may be caused by food or other poisoning, allergy, or infection. Dehydration may be severe and it is a particular risk in infants.

gastrolith stone that was once part of the digestive system of a dinosaur or other extinct animal. Rock fragments were swallowed to assist in the grinding process in the dinosaur digestive tract, much as some birds now swallow grit and pebbles to grind food in their crop. Once the animal has decayed, smooth round stones remain – often the only clue to their past use is the fact that they are geologically different from their surrounding strata.

gastropod any member of a very large group of *molluscs (soft-bodied invertebrate animals). Gastropods have a single shell (in a spiral or modified spiral form) and eyes on stalks, and they move on a flattened, muscular foot. They have well-developed heads and rough, scraping tongues called radulae. Some are marine, some freshwater, and others land creatures, but they all tend to live in damp places. (Class Gastropoda.)

gas turbine engine in which burning fuel supplies hot gas to spin a *turbine. The most widespread application of gas turbines has been in aviation. All jet engines (see under *jet propulsion) are modified gas turbines, and some locomotives and ships also use gas turbines as a power source. They are also used in industry for generating and pumping purposes.

Gates, Bill (1955–) born William Henry Gates, III, US computer entrepreneur. He co-founded Microsoft Corporation in 1975, with school friend and fellow entrepreneur Paul Allen, and has succeeded in converting a passion for computers into a globally dominant software business. Gates and Allen adapted a version of BASIC, an early computer language, and licensed the operating system MS-DOS to IBM for its first personal computer (PC) in 1981. US magazine *Forbes* estimated his net worth at US$90 billion in 1999 and, despite a reduction in his wealth due to a slump in technology shares, he remains the world's richest person. In 2003, the magazine put Gates's net worth at US$40.7 billion.

GATT acronym for *General Agreement on Tariffs and Trade.

Gaudí, Antonio (1852–1926) Spanish architect. Known for his flamboyant *art nouveau style, his work also shows the influence of *cubism and *surrealism. Gaudí worked mainly in Barcelona, designing both domestic and industrial buildings. He introduced colour, unusual materials, and audacious technical innovations. His Church of the Holy Family, Barcelona (begun 1883 and still under construction) is a spectacular edifice of rough stone, mosaic, and undulating line.

Gaudier-Brzeska, Henri (1891–1915) born Henri Gaudier, French sculptor, active in London from 1911. He is regarded as one of the outstanding sculptors of his generation. He studied art in Bristol, Nuremberg, and Munich, and became a member of the English Vorticist movement, which sought to reflect the energy of the industrial age through an angular, semi-abstract style. His works include the portrait *Horace Brodsky* (1913; Tate Gallery, London); and *Birds Erect* (1914; Museum of Modern Art, New York).

gauge boson *or* **field particle** any of the particles that carry the four fundamental forces of nature (see *forces, fundamental). Gauge bosons are *elementary particles that cannot be subdivided, and include the photon, the graviton, the gluons, and the W^+, W^-, and Z particles.

Gauguin, (Eugène Henri) Paul (1848–1903) French post-Impressionist painter. Going beyond the Impressionists' concern with ever-changing appearances, he developed a heavily symbolic and decorative style characterized by his sensuous use of pure colours. In his search for a more direct and intense experience of life, he moved to islands in the South Pacific, where he created many of his finest works. Among his paintings is *The Yellow Christ* (1889; Albright-Knox Art Gallery, Buffalo, New York State).

Gaul the Celtic-speaking peoples who inhabited France and Belgium in Roman times; also their territory. Certain Gauls invaded Italy around 400 BC, sacked Rome 387 BC, and settled between the Alps and the Apennines; this district, known as Cisalpine Gaul, was conquered by Rome in about 225 BC.

Gaulle, Charles de French politician, see Charles *de Gaulle.

gauss symbol Gs, centimetre-gram-second (*c.g.s.*) unit of magnetic induction or magnetic flux density, replaced by the SI unit, the *tesla, but still commonly used. It is equal to one line of magnetic flux per square centimetre. The Earth's magnetic field is about 0.5 Gs, and changes to it over time are measured in gammas (one gamma equals 10^{-5} gauss).

Gautama family name of the historical *Buddha, Siddhartha Gautama.

Gauteng (Sotho 'Place of Gold') province of the Republic of South Africa from 1994, known as Pretoria-Witwatersrand-Vereeniging before 1995, and historically part of the Transvaal; area 18,760 sq km/7,243 sq mi;

population (2000 est) 7,780,600. It lies on the Highveld plateau at an average elevation of 1,740 m/5,710 ft, and the Vaal River and Magaliesberg Mountains pass through the province. The main cities are *Johannesburg (capital), Pretoria (administrative capital of the republic), Vereeniging, Krugersdorp, Benoni, and Germiston. The most important industries are gold mining, coal, iron and steel, uranium, and chemicals; tobacco, maize, sorghum and groundnuts are cultivated.

Gawain in Arthurian legend, one of the knights of the Round Table who participated in the quest for the *Holy Grail. He is the hero of the 14th-century epic poem *Sir Gawayne and the Greene Knight*.

Gay, John (1685–1732) English poet and dramatist. He wrote *Trivia* (1716), a verse picture of 18th-century London. His *The Beggar's Opera* (1728), a 'Newgate pastoral' using traditional songs and telling of the love of Polly for highwayman Captain Macheath, was an extraordinarily popular success. Its satiric political touches led to the banning of *Polly*, a sequel. Bertolt Brecht (1898–1956) based his *Threepenny Opera* (1928) on the story of *The Beggar's Opera*.

gay rights movement political activity by homosexuals in pursuit of equal rights and an end to discrimination. Strongly active since the 1960s, the gay rights movement also seeks to educate the public about gay issues, promote tolerance of gay relationships and lifestyles, and encourage pride and solidarity among homosexuals.

Gaza Strip strip of land on the Mediterranean Sea, 10 km/6 mi wide and 40 km/25 mi long, stretching northeast from the Egyptian border; area 363 sq km/ 140 sq mi; population (2001 est) 1,022,200, mainly Palestinians, plus about 6,000 Israeli settlers, most of whom arrived during the 1990s and who occupy a fifth of the territory. The Gaza Strip was captured by Israel from Egypt in 1967 during the Six-Day War and occupied by Israel until 1994, when responsibility for its administration was transferred to the Palestine National Authority (PNA). The capital is Gaza; other main centres of population are Khan Yunis and Rafah. Prior to the great influx of Palestinian refugees in 1948 the area was rural, and is geographically part of the *Negev. The area is dependent on Israel for the supply of electricity. Agriculture is the main activity and occupies three-quarters of the area; citrus fruit (much of which is exported to Europe), wheat, and olives are farmed. Industry is on a small scale, including handmade goods, such as olive wood carvings, for Israel's tourist industry. Living standards in the area are low, with limited water supplies, inadequate sewage systems, and a very high level of unemployment; about a tenth of the population commutes daily to work in Israel. International relief agencies provide important support for the economy. An international airport was opened at Daniyeh, in the south of the Gaza Strip, in November 1998.

gazelle any of a number of lightly built, fast-running antelopes found on the open plains of Africa and southern Asia. (Especially species of the genus *Gazella*.)

GCSE abbreviation for **General Certificate of Secondary Education**, in the UK, from 1988, the examination for 16-year-old pupils, superseding both GCE O level and CSE, and offering qualifications for up to 60% of school leavers in any particular subject.

GDP abbreviation for *gross domestic product.

gear toothed wheel that transmits the turning movement of one shaft to another shaft. Gear wheels may be used in pairs, or in threes if both shafts are to turn in the same direction. The gear ratio – the ratio of the number of teeth on the two wheels – determines the torque ratio, the turning force on the output shaft compared with the turning force on the input shaft. The ratio of the angular velocities of the shafts is the inverse of the gear ratio.

gearing relationship between company funding that bears a fixed interest charge, such as debentures, and preference shares to its equity or ordinary share capital. When the proportion of long-term fixed interest capital is greater, the company is said to be highly geared. Highly geared companies are considered speculative investments for ordinary shareholders as the fixed interest is paid before funds become available for other purposes such as paying a dividend.

Gebrselassie, Haile (1973–) Ethiopian long-distance runner. Between 1994 and 1998 he broke the 5,000-metre world record four times and the 10,000-metre record three times, and has broken more than 15 world records in indoor and outdoor competition. From 1993 to 2000 he won every Olympic and world title in the 10,000 metres.

gecko any lizard of the family Gekkonidae. Geckos are common worldwide in warm climates, and have large heads and short, stout bodies. Many have no eyelids. They are able to climb vertically and walk upside down on smooth surfaces in their search for flies, spiders, and other prey.

Geddes, Patrick (1854–1932) Scottish town planner. He established the importance of surveys, research work, and properly planned 'diagnoses before treatment'. His major work is *City Development* (1904). His protégé was Lewis Mumford.

Gehry, Frank Owen (1929–) US architect based in Los Angeles. His architecture approaches abstract art in its use of collage and montage techniques. He is best known for designing the Guggenheim Art Museum in Bilbao, Spain, which was completed in 1997. He was awarded the 1998 National Medal of Arts.

Geiger counter any of a number of devices used for detecting nuclear radiation and measuring its intensity by counting the number of ionizing particles produced (see *radioactivity). It detects the momentary current that passes between *electrodes (anode and cathode) in a suitable gas (such as argon) when radiation causes the ionization of the gas. The electrodes are connected to electronic devices that enable the number of particles passing to be measured. The increased frequency of measured particles indicates the intensity of radiation. The device is named after the German physicist Hans Geiger.

gel solid produced by the formation of a three-dimensional cage structure, commonly of linked large-molecular-mass polymers, in which a liquid is trapped. It is a form of *colloid. A gel may be a jellylike mass (pectin, gelatin) or have a more rigid structure (silica gel).

gelatin water-soluble protein prepared from boiled hide and bone, used in cookery to set jellies, and in glues and photographic emulsions.

Gelderland English **Guelders**, province of the east Netherlands, bounded on the southeast by Germany, on the southwest by the River Maas, and on the northwest by the Ijsselmeer; area 5,020 sq km/1,938 sq mi; population (2003 est) 1,968,000. The capital is Arnhem; other main cities are Apeldoorn, Nijmegen, and Ede. Textiles, electrical goods, and paper are produced; agriculture is based on livestock and dairying, wheat, fruit, flowers, and vegetables.

Geldof, Bob (1954–) born Robert Frederick Xenon, Irish rock singer, born in Dun Laoghaire. He was the leader of the group the Boomtown Rats 1975–86. In the mid-1980s he instigated the charity Band Aid, which raised some £60 million for famine relief, primarily for Ethiopia.

gem mineral valuable by virtue of its durability (hardness), rarity, and beauty, cut and polished for ornamental use, or engraved. Of 120 minerals known to have been used as gemstones, only about 25 are in common use in jewellery today; of these, the diamond, emerald, ruby, and sapphire are classified as precious, and all the others semi-precious; for example, the topaz, amethyst, opal, and aquamarine.

Gemeinschaft* and *Gesellschaft German terms (roughly, 'community' and 'association') coined by Ferdinand Tönnies in 1887 to contrast social relationships in traditional rural societies with those in modern industrial societies. He saw *Gemeinschaft* (traditional) as intimate and positive, and *Gesellschaft* (modern) as impersonal and negative.

Gemini prominent zodiacal constellation in the northern hemisphere represented as the twins Castor and Pollux. Its brightest star is *Pollux; Castor is a system of six stars. The Sun passes through Gemini from late June to late July. Each December, the Geminid meteors radiate from Gemini. In astrology, the dates for Gemini are between about 21 May and 21 June (see *precession).

***Gemini* project** US space programme (1965–66) in which astronauts practised rendezvous and docking of spacecraft, and working outside their spacecraft, in preparation for the *Apollo* project Moon landings.

gemsbok species of antelope that inhabits the desert regions of southern Africa. It stands about 1.2 m/4 ft in height, and its general colour is greyish. Its horns are just over 1 m/3.3 ft long. The gemsbok *Oryx gazella* is in family Bovidae, order Artiodactyla.

gender in grammar, one of the categories into which nouns are divided in many languages, such as masculine, feminine, and neuter (as in Latin, German, and Russian), masculine and feminine (as in French, Italian, and Spanish), or animate and inanimate (as in some American Indian languages).

gene basic unit of inherited material, encoded by a strand of *DNA and transcribed by *RNA. In higher organisms, genes are located on the *chromosomes. A gene consistently affects a particular character in an individual – for example, the gene for eye colour. Also termed a Mendelian gene, after Austrian biologist Gregor *Mendel, it occurs at a particular point, or locus, on a particular chromosome and may have several variants, or *alleles, each specifying a particular form of that character – for example, the alleles for blue or brown eyes. Some alleles show *dominance. These mask the effect of other alleles, known as *recessive.

Genes can be manipulated using the techniques of *genetic engineering (gene technology).

gene amplification technique by which selected DNA from a single cell can be duplicated indefinitely until there is a sufficient amount to analyse by conventional genetic techniques.

gene bank collection of seeds or other forms of genetic material, such as tubers, spores, bacterial or yeast cultures, live animals and plants, frozen sperm and eggs, or frozen embryos. These are stored for possible future use in agriculture, plant and animal breeding, or in medicine, genetic engineering, or the restocking of wild habitats where species have become extinct. Gene banks may be increasingly used as the rate of extinction increases, depleting the Earth's genetic variety (biodiversity).

gene pool total sum of *alleles (variants of *genes) possessed by all the members of a given population or species alive at a particular time.

General Agreement on Tariffs and Trade (GATT) agreement designed to provide an international forum to encourage regulation of international trade. The original agreement was signed in 1947, shortly after World War II. It was followed in 1948 by the creation of an international organization, within the United Nations, to support the agreement and to encourage *free trade between nations by reducing tariffs, subsidies, quotas, and regulations that discriminate against imported products. The agency GATT was effectively replaced by the *World Trade Organization (WTO) in January 1995, following the Uruguay Round. The legal agreement still exists although it was updated in 1994 to reflect a shift from trade in goods to trade in goods, services, and intellectual property. The new GATT agreements are administered by the WTO.

general strike refusal to work by employees in several key industries, with the intention of paralysing the economic life of a country. In British history, the General Strike was a nationwide strike called by the Trade Union Congress (TUC) on 3 May 1926 in support of striking miners. Elsewhere, the general strike was used as a political weapon by anarchists and others (see *syndicalism), especially in Spain and Italy.

generator machine that produces electrical energy from mechanical energy, as opposed to an electric motor, which does the opposite. A simple generator (known as a dynamo in the UK) consists of a wire-wound coil (*armature) that is rotated between the poles of a permanent magnet. As the coil rotates it cuts across the magnetic field lines and a current is generated. A dynamo on a bicycle is an example of a simple generator.

genet any of several small, nocturnal, carnivorous mammals belonging to the mongoose and civet family. Most species live in Africa, but the common genet *G. genetta* is also found in Europe and the Middle East. It is about 50 cm/1.6 ft long with a 45 cm/1.5 ft tail, weighs up to 2 kg/4.4 lb, with the male slightly larger than the female, and is greyish yellow in colour with rows of black spots. It is a good climber. Females have up to four young that begin to fend for themselves after about the age of four months. (Genus *Genetta*, family Viverridae.)

gene therapy medical technique for curing or alleviating inherited diseases or defects that are due to a gene malfunction; certain infections, and several kinds of cancer in which affected cells from a sufferer are removed from the body, the *DNA repaired in the laboratory (*genetic engineering), and the normal functioning cells reintroduced. In 1990 a genetically engineered gene was used for the first time to treat a patient.

genetically-modified foods *or* **GM foods** foods produced using genetic engineering technology. Individual genes can be copied or transferred from one living organism to another, to incorporate particular characteristics into the organism or remove undesirable characteristics. The technology, developed in the 1980s, may be used, for example, to produce crops with higher yields, improved taste, resistance to pests, or a longer growing season. The first genetically-modified (GM) food, the 'Flavr Savr' tomato, went on sale in the USA in 1994. GM ingredients appearing in foods on the market today include tomatoes, soya, and maize. However, there remain some doubts and reservations about GM products, and some companies and countries, including the UK, have taken steps to delay the growing of GM crops until risks have been assessed, and to introduce legislation forcing GM products to be declared as such.

genetic code way in which instructions for building proteins, the basic structural molecules of living matter, are 'written' in the genetic material *DNA. This relationship between the sequence of bases (the subunits in a DNA molecule) and the sequence of *amino acids (the subunits of a protein molecule) is the basis of heredity. The code employs codons of three bases each; it is the same in almost all organisms, except for a few minor differences recently discovered in some protozoa.

genetic disease any disorder caused at least partly by defective genes or chromosomes. In humans there are some 3,000 genetic diseases, including cystic fibrosis, Down's syndrome, haemophilia, Huntington's chorea, some forms of anaemia, spina bifida, and Tay-Sachs disease.

genetic engineering all-inclusive term that describes the deliberate manipulation of genetic material by biochemical techniques. It is often achieved by the introduction of new *DNA, usually by means of a virus or *plasmid. This can be for pure research, *gene therapy, or to breed functionally specific plants, animals, or bacteria. These organisms with a foreign gene added are said to be transgenic and the new DNA formed by this process is said to be recombinant. In most current cases the transgenic organism is a micro-organism or a plant, because ethical and safety issues are limiting its use in mammals. (See diagram, p. 364.)

genetic fingerprinting *or* **genetic profiling** technique developed in the UK by Professor Alec Jeffreys (1950–), and now allowed as a means of legal identification. It determines the pattern of certain parts of the genetic material *DNA that is unique to each individual. Like conventional fingerprinting, it can accurately distinguish humans from one another, with the exception of identical siblings from multiple births. It can be applied to as little material as a single cell.

genetics branch of biology concerned with the study of *heredity and variation – inheritance. It attempts to explain how characteristics of living organisms are

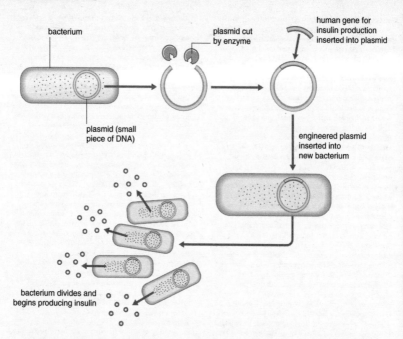

genetic engineering The genetic modification of a bacterium to produce insulin. The human gene for the production of insulin is collected from a donor chromosome and spliced into a vector plasmid (DNA found in bacteria but separate from the bacterial chromosomes). The plasmids and recipient bacteria are mixed together, during which process the bacteria absorb the plasmids. The plasmids replicate as the bacteria divide asexually (producing clones) and begin to produce insulin.

passed on from one generation to the next. The science of genetics is based on the work of Austrian biologist Gregor *Mendel whose experiments with the cross-breeding (hybridization) of peas showed that the inheritance of characteristics and traits takes place by means of discrete 'particles', now known as *genes. These are present in the cells of all organisms, and are now recognized as being the basic units of heredity. All organisms possess *genotypes (sets of variable genes) and *phenotypes (characteristics produced by certain genes). Modern geneticists investigate the structure, function, and transmission of genes.

genetic screening in medicine, the determination of the genetic make-up of an individual to determine if he or she is at risk of developing a hereditary disease later in life. Genetic screening can also be used to determine if an individual is a carrier for a particular genetic disease and, hence, can pass the disease on to any children. Genetic counselling should be undertaken at the same time as genetic screening of affected individuals. Diseases that can be screened for include cystic fibrosis, Huntington's chorea, and certain forms of cancer.

Geneva French **Genève**; German **Genf**, city in Switzerland, capital of Geneva canton, on the southwestern shore of Lake Geneva; population

(2003 est) 178,900. It is a point of convergence of natural routes and is a cultural, financial, and administrative centre. Industries include trade, banking, insurance, and the manufacture of watches, scientific and optical instruments, foodstuffs, jewellery, and musical boxes. CERN, the particle physics research organization, is here, as are the headquarters of the International Red Cross and the World Health Organization. The United Nations has its second-largest office (after the New York City headquarters) in Geneva.

Geneva Convention international agreement of 1864 regulating the treatment of those wounded in war, and later extended to cover the types of weapons allowed, the treatment of prisoners and the sick, and the protection of civilians in wartime. The rules were revised at conventions held in 1906, 1929, and 1949, and by the 1977 Additional Protocols.

Geneva, Lake French **Lac Léman**; German **Genfersee**, largest of the central European lakes, between the Alps and the Jura mountains on the Swiss-French border; area 580 sq km/225 sq mi. The main part of the lake (about 347 sq km/134 sq mi) lies in western Switzerland; the remainder is French. It is in the shape of a crescent 72 km/45 mi long and 13 km/8 mi wide; it has a maximum depth of 391 m/1,283 ft.

Geneva Protocol international agreement of 1925 designed to prohibit the use of poisonous gases, chemical weapons, and bacteriological methods of warfare. It came into force in 1928 but was not ratified by the USA until 1974.

Genghis Khan (or Chingiz Khan) (c. 1155–1227) (Greek 'World Conqueror') Mongol conqueror, ruler of all Mongol peoples from 1206. He conquered the empires of northern China 1211–15 and Khwarazm 1219–21, and invaded northern India in 1221, while his lieutenants advanced as far as the Crimea. When he died, his empire ranged from the Yellow Sea to the Black Sea; it continued to expand after his death to extend from Hungary to Korea. Genghis Khan controlled probably a larger area than any other individual in history. He was not only a great military leader, but the creator of a stable political system.

genocide deliberate and systematic destruction of a national, racial, religious, or ethnic group defined by the exterminators as undesirable. The term is commonly applied to the policies of the Nazis during World War II (what they called the 'final solution' – the extermination of all 'undesirables' in occupied Europe, particularly the Jews, in the *Holocaust).

genome full complement of *genes carried by a single (haploid) set of *chromosomes. The term may be applied to the genetic information carried by an individual or to the range of genes found in a given species. The human genome is made up of between 27,000 and 40,000 genes, according to a rough draft of the sequenced genome completed by the *Human Genome Project in June 2000. Final sequencing of the complete human genome was announced in April 2003, although scientists still did not have a definitive figure for the total number of genes in the human genome. The sequence for human chromosome 20 was completed in December 2001 and those for human chromosomes Y, 7, and 6 in 2003.

genotype particular set of *alleles (variants of genes) possessed by a given organism. The term is usually used in conjunction with *phenotype, which is the product of the genotype and all environmental effects.

genre particular kind of work within an art form, differentiated by its structure, content, or style. For instance, the novel is a literary genre and the historical novel is a genre of the novel. The Western is a genre of film, and the symphonic poem is a musical genre. In the visual arts, genre refers to paintings that depict common incidents in the lives of ordinary people.

Gentile da Fabriano (c. 1370–c. 1427) born Niccolò di Giovanni di Massio, Italian painter of frescoes and altarpieces who worked in a Gothic style uninfluenced by the fashions of contemporary Florence. Gentile was active in Venice, Florence, Siena, Orvieto, and Rome and collaborated with the artists Pisanello and Jacopo Bellini. His *Adoration of the Magi* (1423; Uffizi, Florence), painted for the church of Santa Trinità in Florence, is typically rich in detail and colour.

gentry the lesser nobility, particularly in England and Wales, not entitled to sit in the House of Lords. By the later Middle Ages, it included knights, esquires, and gentlemen, and after the 17th century, baronets.

genus plural **genera**, group of one or more *species with many characteristics in common. Thus all doglike species (including dogs, wolves, and jackals) belong to the genus *Canis* (Latin 'dog'). Species of the same genus are thought to be descended from a common ancestor species. Related genera are grouped into *families.

geochronology branch of geology that deals with the dating of rocks, minerals, and fossils in order to create an accurate and precise geological history of the Earth. The *geological time scale is a result of these studies. It puts stratigraphic units in chronological order and assigns actual dates, in millions of years, to those units.

geodesic dome hemispherical dome, a type of space-frame, whose surface is formed out of short rods arranged in triangles. The rods lie on geodesics (the shortest lines joining two points on a curved surface). This type of dome allows large spaces to be enclosed using the minimum of materials, and was patented by US engineer Buckminster Fuller in 1954.

geodesy science of measuring and mapping Earth's surface for making maps and correlating geological, gravitational, and magnetic measurements. Geodetic surveys, formerly carried out by means of various measuring techniques on the surface, are now commonly made by using radio signals and laser beams from orbiting satellites.

Geoffrey of Monmouth (c. 1100–1154) Welsh writer and chronicler. While a canon at Oxford, he wrote *Historia Regum Britanniae/History of the Kings of Britain* (c. 1139), which included accounts of the semi-legendary kings Lear, Cymbeline, and Arthur. He is also thought by some to be the author of *Vita Merlini*, a life of the legendary wizard. He was bishop-elect of St Asaph, North Wales, in 1151 and ordained a priest in 1152.

geography study of the Earth's surface; its topography, climate, and physical conditions, and how these factors affect people and society. It is usually divided into **physical geography**, dealing with landforms and climates, and **human geography**, dealing with the distribution and activities of peoples on Earth.

geological time time scale embracing the history of the Earth from its physical origin to the present day. Geological time is traditionally divided into eons (Archaean or Archaeozoic, Proterozoic, and Phanerozoic in ascending chronological order), which in turn are subdivided into eras, periods, epochs, ages, and finally chrons. (See diagram, p. 366.)

geology science of the Earth, its origin, composition, structure, and history. It is divided into several branches, inlcuding mineralogy (the minerals of Earth), petrology (rocks), stratigraphy (the deposition of successive beds of sedimentary rocks), palaeontology (fossils) and tectonics (the deformation and movement of the Earth's crust), geophysics (using physics to study the Earth's surface, interior, and atmosphere), and geochemistry.

geometry branch of mathematics concerned with the properties of space, usually in terms of plane (two-dimensional, or 2D) and solid (three-dimensional, or 3D) figures. The subject is usually divided into pure geometry, which embraces roughly the plane and solid geometry dealt with in Greek mathematician *Euclid's *Stoicheia/Elements*, and analytical or *coordinate geometry, in which problems are solved using algebraic methods. A third, quite distinct, type includes the non-Euclidean geometries.

EON	ERA	PERIOD	EPOCH	TIME (my)
PHANEROZOIC	CENOZOIC *Age of mammals*	QUATERNARY *Age of man*	HOLOCENE	0.01
			PLEISTOCENE	1.64
		TERTIARY	PLIOCENE	5.20
			MIOCENE	23.5
			OLIGOCENE	35.5
			EOCENE	56.6
			PALAEOCENE	65.0
	MESOZOIC	CRETACEOUS		146
		JURASSIC *Age of Cycads*		208
		TRIASSIC		245
	PALAEOZOIC	PERMIAN *Age of Amphibians*		290
		CARBONIFEROUS *Age of Coal* *Age of Amphibians*		363
		DEVONIAN *Age of Fishes*		409
		SILURIAN *Age of Fishes*		439
		ORDOVICIAN *Age of Marine Invertebrates*		510
		CAMBRIAN *Age of Marine Invertebrates*		570
PROTEROZOIC				2500
ARCHAEOZOIC				4600

geological timescale The time column shows millions of years ago.

George six kings of Great Britain:

George I (1660–1727) King of Great Britain and Ireland from 1714. He was the son of the first elector of Hannover, Ernest Augustus (1629–1698), and his wife *Sophia, and a great-grandson of James I. He succeeded to the electorate in 1698, and became king on the death of Queen Anne. He attached himself to the Whigs, and spent most of his reign in Hannover, never having learned English.

George II (1683–1760) King of Great Britain and Ireland from 1727, when he succeeded his father, George I. He was accused, with his minister John Carteret, of favouring Hannover at the expense of Britain's interest in the War of the Austrian Succession; his victory at Dettingen in 1743 was the last battle to be commanded by a British king. He married Caroline of Anspach in 1705, and was succeeded by his grandson, George III.

George III (1738–1820) King of Great Britain and Ireland from 1760, when he succeeded his grandfather George II. His rule was marked by intransigence resulting in the loss of the American colonies, for which he shared the blame with his chief minister Lord North, and the emancipation of Catholics in England. Possibly suffering from *porphyria, he was believed to be insane. His condition deteriorated dramatically after 1811. He was succeeded by his son George IV.

George IV (1762–1830) King of Great Britain and Ireland from 1820, when he succeeded his father George III, for whom he had been regent during the king's period of insanity 1811–20. In 1785 he secretly married a Catholic widow, Maria Fitzherbert, but in 1795 also married Princess *Caroline of Brunswick, in return for payment of his debts. He was a patron of the arts. His prestige was undermined by his treatment of Caroline (they separated in 1796), his dissipation, and his extravagance. He was succeeded by his brother, the duke of Clarence, who became William IV.

George V (1865–1936) King of Great Britain and Northern Ireland from 1910, when he succeeded his father Edward VII. He was the second son, and became heir in 1892 on the death of his elder brother Albert, Duke of Clarence. In 1893, he married Princess Victoria Mary of Teck (Queen Mary), formerly engaged to his brother. During World War I he made several visits to the front. In 1917, he abandoned all German titles for himself and his family. The name of the royal house was changed from Saxe-Coburg-Gotha to Windsor.

George VI (1895–1952) King of Great Britain and Northern Ireland from 1936, when he succeeded after the abdication of his brother Edward VIII, who had succeeded their father George V. Created Duke of York in 1920, he married in 1923 Lady Elizabeth Bowes-Lyon (1900–), and their children are Elizabeth II and Princess Margaret. During World War II, he visited the Normandy and Italian battlefields.

George two kings of Greece, including:

George II (1890–1947) King of Greece 1922–23 and 1935–47. He became king on the expulsion of his father Constantine I in 1922 but was himself overthrown in 1923. Restored by the military in 1935, he set up a dictatorship under Joannis Metaxas, and went into exile during the German occupation 1941–45.

George, St (died c. 303) patron saint of England. The story of St George rescuing a woman by slaying a dragon, evidently derived from the Greek *Perseus legend, first appears in the 6th century. The cult of St George was introduced into Western Europe by the *Crusaders. His feast day is 23 April.

Georgetown capital and main port of Guyana, situated on the east bank of the Demerara River at its mouth on the Atlantic coast; population (2002 est) 225,800. There are food processing and shrimp fishing industries. Principal exports include sugar, bauxite, rice, and diamonds.

Georgia called the **Empire State** or the **Peach State**, state in southeastern USA bordered to the northeast by *South Carolina, to the north by *North Carolina and *Tennessee, to the west by *Alabama, and to the south by *Florida; area 149,976 sq km/57,906 sq mi; population (2000) 8,186,500; capital *Atlanta. Georgia was named after King George II. The state is approximately 60% forested, and ranges from the *Blue Ridge Mountains in the north, to the light, sandy, fertile soils of the coastal plains. Its many forests and swamplands give the state a wide range of wildlife, particularly birds. Service industries are Georgia's chief source of income. Atlanta has leading finance, trade, and transport centres, with major corporations having headquarters there. Savannah is home to many shipping companies. Agriculture is still central to the economy of Georgia, a former slave and cotton state, and pecans, peaches, and peanut production are especially important. The film epic *Gone With The Wind*, set against the background of the Civil War, was set in Atlanta and was written by Margaret Mitchell who was born in Georgia. Major cities include Columbus, Savannah, Macon, and Albany. One of the original *Thirteen Colonies, Georgia seceded from the Union in 1861, and was not readmitted until 1870 after a two-year delay prompted by the state's initial refusal to ratify the Fifteenth Amendment to the US Constitution. Georgia had originally ratified the US Constitution in 1788, becoming the fourth state to join the Union.

Georgia

National name: *Sak'art'velo/Georgia*

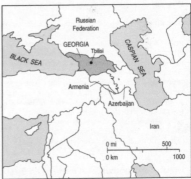

Area: 69,700 sq km/26,911 sq mi

Capital: Tbilisi

Major towns/cities: Kutaisi, Rustavi, Batumi, Zugdidi, Gori

Physical features: largely mountainous with a variety of landscape from the subtropical Black Sea shores to the ice and snow of the crest line of the Caucasus; chief rivers are Kura and Rioni

Head of state: Mikhail Saakashvili from 2004

Head of government: Zurab Zhvania from 2004

Political system: emergent democracy

Political executive: limited presidency

Political parties: Citizens' Union of Georgia (CUG), nationalist, pro-Shevardnadze; National Democratic Party of Georgia (NDPG), nationalist; Round Table/Free Georgia Bloc, nationalist; Georgian Popular Front (GPF), moderate nationalist, prodemocratization; Georgian Communist Party (GCP); National Independence Party (NIP), ultranationalist; Front for the Reinstatement of Legitimate Power in Georgia, strong nationalist

Currency: lari

GNI per capita (PPP): (US$) 2,210 (2002 est)

Exports: aluminium and metal products, machinery, wine, tea, food and tobacco products. Principal market: Russia 23% (2001)

Population: 5,126,000 (2003 est)

Language: Georgian (official), Russian, Abkazian, Armenian, Azeri

Religion: Georgian Orthodox, also Muslim

Life expectancy: 70 (men); 78 (women) (2000–05)

Chronology

4th century BC: Georgian kingdom founded.

1st century BC: Part of Roman Empire.

AD 337: Christianity adopted.

458: Tbilisi founded by King Vakhtang Gorgasal.

mid-7th century: Tbilisi brought under Arab rule and renamed Tiflis.

1121: Tbilisi liberated by King David II the Builder, of the Gagrationi dynasty. An empire was established across the Caucasus region, remaining powerful until Mongol onslaughts in the 13th and 14th centuries.

1555: Western Georgia fell to Turkey and Eastern Georgia to Persia (Iran).

1783: Treaty of Georgievsk established Russian dominance over Georgia.

1804–13: First Russo-Iranian war fought largely over Georgia.

late 19th century: Abolition of serfdom and beginnings of industrialization, but Georgian church suppressed.

1918: Independence established after Russian Revolution.

1921: Invaded by Red Army; Soviet republic established.

1922–36: Linked with Armenia and Azerbaijan as the Transcaucasian Federation.

1930s: Rapid industrial development, but resistance to agricultural collectivization and violent political purges instituted by the Georgian Soviet dictator Joseph Stalin.

1936: Became separate republic within the USSR.

early 1940s: 200,000 Meskhetians deported from southern Georgia to Central Asia on Stalin's orders.

1972: Drive against endemic corruption launched by new Georgian Communist Party (GCP) leader Eduard Shevardnadze.

1978: Violent demonstrations by nationalists in Tbilisi.

1981–88: Increasing demands for autonomy were encouraged from 1986 by the *glasnost* initiative of the reformist Soviet leader Mikhail Gorbachev.

1989: The formation of the nationalist Georgian Popular Front led the minority Abkhazian and Ossetian communities in northwest and central-north Georgia to demand secession, provoking interethnic clashes. A state of emergency was imposed in Abkhazia; 20 pro-independence demonstrators were killed in Tbilisi by Soviet troops; Georgian sovereignty was declared by parliament.

1990: A nationalist coalition triumphed in elections and Gamsakhurdia became president. The GCP seceded from the Communist Party of the USSR.

1991: Independence was declared. The GCP was outlawed and all relations with the USSR severed. Demonstrations were held against the increasingly dictatorial Gamsakhurdia; a state of emergency was declared.

1992: Gamsakhurdia fled to Armenia; Shevardnadze, with military backing, was appointed interim president. Georgia was admitted into the United Nations (UN). Clashes continued in South Ossetia and Abkhazia, where independence had been declared.

1993: The conflict with Abkhazi separatists intensified, forcing Shevardnadze to seek Russian military help. Otar Patsatsia was appointed prime minister.

1994: Georgia joined the Commonwealth of Independent States (CIS). A military cooperation pact was signed with Russia. A ceasefire was agreed with the Abkhazi separatists; 2,500 Russian peacekeeping troops were deployed in the region and paramilitary groups disarmed. Inflation exceeded 5,000% per annum.

1996: A cooperation pact with the European Union (EU) was signed as economic growth resumed. Elections to the secessionist Abkhazi parliament were declared illegal by the Georgian government.

1997: A new opposition party, Front for the Reinstatement of Legitimate Power in Georgia, was formed. There were talks between the government and the breakaway Abkhazi government.

1998: There was another outbreak of fighting in Abkhazia.

2000: President Shevardnadze won a second term as president in elections. Giorgi Arsenishvili became secretary of state (prime minister). The government signed a pact with the Abkhazian prime minister, Vyacheslav Tsugba, both sides repudiating the use of force to settle the conflict.

2003: Political protest following legislative elections dismissed by opposition parties as fraudulent led eventually to the resignation of President Shevardnadze in a bloodless transfer of power. Mikhail Saakashvili, leader of the takeover, became president.

2005: Prime minister Zurab Zhvania died suddenly and was replaced by Zurab Noghaideli, an ally of President Saakashvili.

Georgian period of English architecture, furniture making, and decorative art between 1714 and 1830. The architecture is mainly classical in style, although external details and interiors were often rich in *rococo carving. Furniture was frequently made of mahogany and satinwood, and mass production became increasingly common; designers included Thomas Chippendale, George Hepplewhite, and Thomas Sheraton. The silver of this period is particularly fine, and ranges from the earlier, simple forms to the ornate, and from the neoclassical style of Robert Adam to the later, more decorated pre-Victorian taste.

geostationary orbit or **geostationary Earth orbit** circular path 35,900 km/22,300 mi above the Earth's Equator on which a *satellite takes 24 hours, moving from west to east, to complete an orbit, thus appearing to hang stationary over one place on the Earth's surface. Geostationary orbits are used particularly for communications satellites and weather satellites.

geothermal energy energy extracted for heating and electricity generation from natural steam, hot water, or hot dry rocks in the Earth's crust. It is a form of *renewable energy. Water is pumped down through an injection well where it passes through joints in the hot rocks. It rises to the surface through a recovery well and may be converted to steam or run through a heat exchanger. Steam may be directed through *turbines to produce electrical energy. It is an important source of energy in volcanically-active areas such as Iceland and New Zealand.

geranium any of a group of plants either having divided leaves and white, pink, or purple flowers (geraniums), or having a hairy stem, and white, pink, red, or black-purple flowers (*pelargoniums). Some geraniums are also called *cranesbill. (Genera *Geranium* and *Pelargonium*, family Geraniaceae.)

gerbil any of numerous rodents with elongated back legs, good at hopping or jumping. Gerbils range from mouse- to rat-size, and have hairy tails. Many of the 13 genera live in dry, sandy, or sparsely vegetated areas of Africa and Asia. (Family Cricetidae.)

geriatrics medical speciality concerned with diseases and problems of the elderly.

Géricault, (Jean Louis André) Théodore (1791–1824) French painter and graphic artist. One of the main figures of the Romantic movement, he brought a new energy and emotional intensity to painting. His subjects included spirited horses, Napoleonic cavalry officers, and portraits, including remarkable studies of the insane, such as *A Kleptomaniac* (1822–23; Musée des Beaux Arts, Ghent). His *The Raft of the Medusa* (1819; Louvre, Paris), a vast history piece, was notorious in its day for its grim depiction of a recent scandal in which shipwrecked sailors had turned to murder and cannibalism in order to survive.

germ colloquial term for a micro-organism that causes disease, such as certain *bacteria and *viruses. Formerly, it was also used to mean something capable of developing into a complete organism (such as a fertilized egg, or the *embryo of a seed).

German the native people or inhabitants of Germany, or a person of German descent, as well as their culture and language. In eastern Germany the Sorbs (or Wends) comprise a minority population who speak a Slavic language. The Austrians and Swiss Germans speak German, although they are ethnically distinct. German-speaking minorities are found in France (Alsace-Lorraine), Romania (Transylvania), the Czech Republic, Siberian Russia, Central Asia, Poland, and Italy (Tyrol).

German art painting and sculpture in the Germanic north of Europe from the 8th century AD to the present. This includes Germany, Austria, and Switzerland. The Gothic style is represented by a wealth of woodcarvings and paintings for churches. Influences came from first the Low Countries and then Renaissance Italy, shown in the work of such painters as Albrecht *Dürer and Hans Holbein. The baroque and neoclassical periods, though important in Germany, had no individual artists of that stature; the Romantic movement produced the nature mysticism of Caspar David Friedrich. In the 20th century, expressionism began as an almost entirely German movement; *Dada was founded in Switzerland; and the *Bauhaus school of art and design was influential worldwide. Recent German art includes the multimedia work of Joseph Beuys, dealing with wartime experiences.

Germanic languages branch of the Indo-European language family, divided into East Germanic (Gothic, now extinct), North Germanic (Danish, Faroese, Icelandic, Norwegian, Swedish), and West Germanic (Afrikaans, Dutch, English, Flemish, Frisian, German, Yiddish).

germanium chemical symbol Ge, brittle, grey-white, weakly metallic (*metalloid) element, atomic number 32, relative atomic mass 72.6. It belongs to the silicon group, and has chemical and physical properties between those of silicon and tin. Germanium is a semiconductor material and is used in the manufacture of transistors and integrated circuits. The oxide is transparent to infrared radiation, and is used in military applications. It was discovered in 1886 by German chemist Clemens Winkler (1838–1904).

German language member of the Germanic group of the Indo-European language family, the national language of Germany and Austria, and an official language of Switzerland. There are many spoken varieties of German, including High German (*Hochdeutsch*) and Low German (*Plattdeutsch*).

German measles or **rubella** mild, communicable virus disease, usually caught by children. It is marked by a sore throat, pinkish rash, and slight fever, and has an incubation period of two to three weeks. If a woman contracts it in the first three months of pregnancy, it may cause serious damage to the unborn child.

German shepherd or **Alsatian** breed of dog. It is about 63 cm/25 in tall and has a wolflike appearance, a thick coat with many varieties of colouring, and a distinctive way of moving. German shepherds are used as police dogs because of their courage and intelligence.

Germany

National name: *Bundesrepublik Deutschland/ Federal Republic of Germany*
Area: 357,041 sq km/137,853 sq mi
Capital: Berlin
Major towns/cities: Cologne, Hamburg, Munich, Essen, Frankfurt am Main, Dortmund, Stuttgart, Düsseldorf, Leipzig, Dresden, Hannover
Major ports: Hamburg, Kiel, Bremerhaven, Rostock
Physical features: flat in north, mountainous in south with Alps; rivers Rhine, Weser, Elbe flow north, Danube flows southeast, Oder and Neisse flow north along Polish frontier; many lakes, including Müritz; Black Forest, Harz Mountains, Erzgebirge (Ore Mountains), Bavarian Alps, Fichtelgebirge, Thüringer Forest
Head of state: Horst Köhler from 2004
Head of government: Gerhard Schroeder from 1998
Political system: liberal democracy
Political executive: parliamentary
Political parties: Christian Democratic Union (CDU), right of centre, 'social market'; Christian Social Union (CSU), right of centre; Social Democratic Party (SPD),

Germany

left of centre; Free Democratic Party (FDP), liberal; Greens, environmentalist; Party of Democratic Socialism (PDS), reform-socialist (formerly Socialist Unity Party: SED); German People's Union (DVU), far-right; German Communist Party (DKP)

Currency: euro (Deutschmark until 2002)

GNI per capita (PPP): (US$) 26,220 (2002 est)

Exports: road vehicles, electrical machinery, metals and metal products, textiles, chemicals. Principal market: France 11.1% (2001)

Population: 82,476,000 (2003 est)

Language: German (official)

Religion: Protestant (mainly Lutheran) 38%, Roman Catholic 34%

Life expectancy: 75 (men); 81 (women) (2000–05)

Chronology

c. 1000 BC: Germanic tribes from Scandinavia began to settle the region between the rivers Rhine, Elbe, and Danube.

AD 9: Romans tried and failed to conquer Germanic tribes.

5th century: Germanic tribes plundered Rome, overran Western Europe, and divided it into tribal kingdoms.

496: Clovis, King of the Franks, conquered the Alemanni tribe of western Germany.

772–804: After series of fierce wars, Charlemagne extended Frankish authority over Germany, subjugated Saxons, imposed Christianity, and took title of Holy Roman Emperor.

843: Treaty of Verdun divided the Holy Roman Empire into three, with eastern portion corresponding to modern Germany; local princes became virtually independent.

919: Henry the Fowler restored central authority and founded Saxon dynasty.

962: Otto the Great enlarged the kingdom and revived title of Holy Roman Emperor.

1024–1254: Emperors of Salian and Hohenstaufen dynasties came into conflict with popes; frequent civil wars allowed German princes to regain independence.

12th century: German expansion eastwards into lands between rivers Elbe and Oder.

13th–14th centuries: Hanseatic League of Allied German cities became a great commercial and naval power.

1438: Title of Holy Roman Emperor became virtually hereditary in the Habsburg family of Austria.

1517: Martin Luther began the Reformation; Emperor Charles V tried to suppress Protestantism; civil war ensued.

1555: Peace of Augsburg: Charles V forced to accept that each German prince could choose the religion of his own lands.

1618–48: Thirty Years' War: bitter conflict, partly religious, between certain German princes and emperor, with foreign intervention; the war wrecked the German economy and reduced the Holy Roman Empire to a name.

1701: Frederick I, Elector of Brandenburg, promoted to King of Prussia.

1740: Frederick the Great of Prussia seized Silesia from Austria and retained it through war of Austrian Succession (1740–48) and Seven Years' War (1756–63).

1772–95: Prussia joined Russia and Austria in the partition of Poland.

1792: Start of French Revolutionary Wars, involving many German states, with much fighting on German soil.

1806: Holy Roman Empire abolished; France formed puppet Confederation of the Rhine in western Germany and defeated Prussia at Battle of Jena.

1813–15: National revival enabled Prussia to take part in the defeat of Napoleon at Battles of Leipzig and Waterloo.

1814–15: Congress of Vienna rewarded Prussia with Rhineland, Westphalia, and much of Saxony; loose German Confederation formed by 39 independent states.

1848–49: Liberal revolutions in many German states; Frankfurt Assembly sought German unity; revolutions suppressed.

1862: Otto von Bismarck became prime minister of Prussia.

1866: Seven Weeks' War: Prussia defeated Austria, dissolved German Confederation, and established North German Confederation under Prussian leadership.

1870–71: Franco-Prussian War; southern German states agreed to German unification; German Empire proclaimed, with King of Prussia as emperor and Bismarck as chancellor.

1890: Wilhelm II dismissed Bismarck and sought to make Germany a leading power in world politics.

1914: Germany encouraged the Austrian attack on Serbia that started World War I; Germany invaded Belgium and France.

1918: Germany defeated; a revolution overthrew the monarchy.

1919: Treaty of Versailles: Germany lost land to France, Denmark, and Poland; demilitarization and reparations imposed; Weimar Republic proclaimed.

1922–23: Hyperinflation: in 1922, one dollar was worth 50 marks; in 1923, one dollar was worth 2.5 trillion marks.

1929: Start of economic slump caused mass unemployment and brought Germany close to revolution.

1933: Adolf Hitler, leader of Nazi Party, became chancellor.

1934: Hitler took title of Führer (leader), murdered rivals, and created one-party state with militaristic and racist ideology; rearmament reduced unemployment.

1938: Germany annexed Austria and Sudeten; occupied remainder of Czechoslovakia in 1939.

1939: German invasion of Poland started World War II; Germany defeated France in 1940, attacked USSR in 1941, and pursued extermination of Jews.

1945: Germany defeated and deprived of its conquests; eastern lands transferred to Poland; USA, USSR, UK, and France established zones of occupation.

1948–49: Disputes between Western allies and USSR led to Soviet blockade of West Berlin.

1949: Partition of Germany: US, French, and British zones in West Germany became Federal Republic of Germany with Konrad Adenauer as chancellor; Soviet zone in East Germany became communist German Democratic Republic led by Walter Ulbricht.

1953: Uprising in East Berlin suppressed by Soviet troops.

1955: West Germany became a member of NATO; East Germany joined the Warsaw Pact.

1957: West Germany was a founder member of the European Economic Community.

1960s: West Germany achieved rapid growth and great prosperity.

1961: East Germany constructed Berlin Wall to prevent emigration to West Berlin (part of West Germany).

1969: Willy Brandt, Social Democratic Party chancellor of West Germany, sought better relations with USSR and East Germany.

1971: Erich Honecker succeeded Ulbricht as Communist Party leader, and became head of state in 1976.

1972: The Basic Treaty established relations between West Germany and East Germany as between foreign states.

1982: Helmut Kohl (Christian Democratic Union) became the West German chancellor.

1989: There was a mass exodus of East Germans to West Germany via Hungary; East Germany opened its frontiers, including the Berlin Wall.

1990: The communist regime in East Germany collapsed; Germany was reunified with Kohl as chancellor.

1991: Germany took the lead in pressing for closer European integration in the Maastricht Treaty.

1995: Unemployment reached 3.8 million.

1996: There was a public-sector labour dispute over welfare reform plans and the worsening economy. Spending cuts were agreed to meet European Monetary Union entry criteria.

1998: Unemployment reached a post-war high of 12.6%. The CDU–CSU–FDP coalition was defeated in a general election and a 'Red–Green' coalition government was formed by the SPD and the Greens, with Gerhard Schroeder as chancellor. Kohl was replaced as CDU leader by Wolfgang Schäuble.

1999: A delay was announced in the planned phasing out of nuclear power. Social Democrat Johannes Rau was elected president.

2000: Former chancellor Helmut Kohl admitted accepting secret, and therefore illegal, donations to his party, and a criminal investigation was launched as he resigned his honorary leadership of the CDU. Leader Wolfgang Schäuble was also forced to resign, and was replaced by Angela Merkel. The first cases of BSE were discovered in German cattle.

2001: Kohl was heavily fined for accepting illegal donations to his party, but spared a criminal trial. Foreign minister Joschka Fischer faced a perjury charge relating to his account of far-left revolutionary activities in the 1970s. Two ministers resigned following criticism of the handling of the BSE crisis.

2002: Chancellor Gerhard Schroeder was re-elected in general elections, but by a close margin. Germany became the first European Union country to enshrine animal rights in the constitution.

2004: Chancellor Schroeder resigned as leader of the Social Democrats.

Germany, East formerly **German Democratic Republic (GDR)**, country 1949–90, formed from the Soviet zone of occupation in the partition of Germany following World War II. East Germany became a sovereign state in 1954, and was reunified with West Germany in October 1990.

Germany, West formerly **Federal Republic of Germany, FRG**, country 1949–90, formed from the British, US, and French occupation zones in the partition of Germany following World War II; reunified with East Germany in October 1990.

germination in botany, the initial stages of growth in a seed, spore, or pollen grain. Seeds germinate when they are exposed to favourable external conditions of moisture, light, and temperature, and when any factors causing dormancy have been removed. (See diagram, p. 372.)

Geronimo (1829–1909) Apache **Goyahkla**, Chief of the Chiricahua Apache Indians and war leader. From 1875 to 1885, he fought US federal troops, as well as settlers encroaching on tribal reservations in the Southwest, especially in southeastern Arizona and New Mexico.

Gershwin, George (1898–1937) born Jacob Gershvin, US composer. His musical comedies, mostly to lyrics by his brother **Ira Gershwin** (1896–1983), were among Broadway's most successful in the 1920s and 1930s, including *Strike up the Band* (1927), *Funny Face* (1927), and *Girl Crazy* (1930). He also wrote concert works including the tone poems *Rhapsody in Blue* (1924) and *An American in Paris* (1928). His opera *Porgy and Bess* (1935) used jazz rhythms and popular song styles in an operatic format.

Gestalt (German 'form') concept of a unified whole that is greater than, or different from, the sum of its parts; that is, a complete structure whose nature is not explained simply by analysing its constituent elements. A chair, for example, will generally be recognized as a chair despite great variations between individual chairs in such attributes as size, shape, and colour.

Gestapo (contraction of **Geheime Staatspolizei**) Nazi Germany's secret police, formed in 1933, and under the direction of Heinrich *Himmler from 1934.

gestation in all mammals except the *monotremes (platypus and spiny anteaters), the period from the time of implantation of the embryo in the uterus to birth. This period varies among species; in humans it is about 266 days, in elephants 18–22 months, in cats about 60 days, and in some species of marsupial (such as opossum) as short as 12 days.

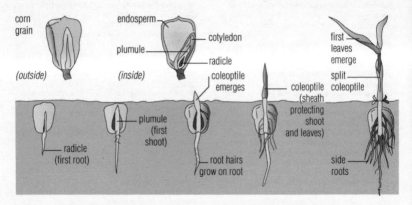

corn grain

(outside)

endosperm

plumule

cotyledon

radicle

(inside)

coleoptile emerges

coleoptile (sheath protecting shoot and leaves)

first leaves emerge

split coleoptile

plumule (first shoot)

radicle (first root)

root hairs grow on root

side roots

germination The germination of a corn grain. The plumule and radicle emerge from the seed coat and begin to grow into a new plant. The coleoptile protects the emerging bud and the first leaves.

Gethsemane site of the garden where Judas Iscariot, according to the New Testament, betrayed Jesus. It is on the Mount of Olives, in east Jerusalem.

Getty, J(ean) Paul (1892–1976) US oil billionaire and art collector. He was president and general manager of George F Getty Inc., his father's oil prospecting company, from 1930. The firm was reorganized as the Getty Oil Company in 1956 and Getty became the firm's director and principal owner. He was also the founder of the Getty Museum (housing the world's highest-funded art collections) in Malibu, California. Getty's publications include *Europe In The Eighteenth Century* (1941), *My Life And Fortunes* (1953), and *How To Be Rich* (1965).

Gettysburg site of one of the decisive battles of the American *Civil War: a Confederate defeat by Union forces 1–3 July 1863, at Gettysburg, Pennsylvania, 80 km/ 50 mi northwest of Baltimore. The site is now a national cemetery, at the dedication of which President Abraham Lincoln delivered the **Gettysburg Address** on 19 November 1863, a speech in which he reiterated the principles of freedom, equality, and democracy embodied in the US Constitution. The site is part of Gettysburg National Military Park (1895).

geyser natural spring that intermittently discharges an explosive column of steam and hot water into the air due to the build-up of steam in underground chambers. One of the most remarkable geysers is Old Faithful, in Yellowstone National Park, Wyoming, USA. Geysers also occur in New Zealand and Iceland.

g-force force experienced by a pilot or astronaut when the craft in which he or she is travelling accelerates or decelerates rapidly. The unit *g* denotes the acceleration due to gravity, where 1 *g* is the ordinary pull of gravity. Early astronauts were subjected to launch and re-entry forces of up to 6 *g* or more; in the space shuttle, more than 3 *g* is experienced on lift-off. Pilots and astronauts wear *g*-suits that prevent their blood pooling too much under severe *g*-forces, which can lead to unconsciousness.

Ghana
formerly **the Gold Coast** (until 1957)
National name: *Republic of Ghana*
Area: 238,540 sq km/92,100 sq mi
Capital: Accra
Major towns/cities: Kumasi, Tamale, Tema, Sekondi-Takoradi, Cape Coast, Koforidua, Bolgatanga, Obuasi
Major ports: Sekondi, Tema
Physical features: mostly tropical lowland plains; bisected by River Volta
Head of state and government: John Agyekum Kufuor from 2001
Political system: emergent democracy
Political executive: limited presidency
Political parties: National Democratic Congress (NDC), centrist, progovernment; New Patriotic Party (NPP), left of centre
Currency: cedi
GNI per capita (PPP): (US$) 2,000 (2002 est)
Exports: gold, cocoa and related products, timber, manganese (one of the world's largest exporters). Principal market: the Netherlands 14% (2001)

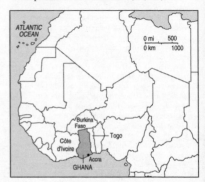

Population: 20,922,000 (2003 est)
Language: English (official), Ga, other African languages
Religion: Christian 40%, animist 32%, Muslim 16%
Life expectancy: 57 (men); 59 (women) (2000–05)

Chronology

5th–12th century: Ghana Empire (from which present-day country's name derives) flourished, with its centre 500 mi/800 km to the northwest, in Mali.

13th century: In coastal and forest areas Akan peoples founded the first states.

15th century: Gold-seeking Mande traders entered northern Ghana from the northeast, founding Dagomba and Mamprussi states; Portuguese navigators visited coastal region, naming it the 'Gold Coast', building a fort at Elmina, and slave trading began.

17th century: Gonja kingdom founded in north by Mande speakers; Ga and Ewe states founded in southeast by immigrants from Nigeria; in central Ghana, controlling gold reserves around Kumasi, the Ashanti, a branch of the Akans, founded what became the most powerful state in precolonial Ghana.

1618: British trading settlement established on Gold Coast.

18th–19th centuries: Centralized Ashanti kingdom at its height, dominating between Komoe River in the west and Togo Mountains in the east and active in slave trade; Fante state powerful along coast in the south.

1874: Britain, after ousting the Danes and Dutch and defeating the Ashanti, made the Gold Coast (the southern provinces) a crown colony.

1898–1901: After three further military campaigns, Britain finally subdued and established protectorates over Ashanti and the northern territories.

early 20th century: The colony developed into a major cocoa-exporting region.

1917: West Togoland, formerly German-ruled, was administered with the Gold Coast as British Togoland.

1949: Campaign for independence launched by Kwame Nkrumah, who formed the Convention People's Party (CPP) and became prime minister in 1952.

1957: Independence achieved, within the Commonwealth, as Ghana, which included British Togoland; Nkrumah became prime minister. Policy of 'African socialism' and nonalignment pursued.

1960: Became a republic, with Nkrumah as president.

1964: Ghana became a one-party state, dominated by the CCP, and developed links with communist bloc.

1972: A coup placed Col Ignatius Acheampong at the head of a military government as the economy deteriorated.

1978: Acheampong was deposed in a bloodless coup. Flight-Lt Jerry Rawlings, a populist soldier who launched a drive against corruption, came to power.

1979: There was a return to civilian rule.

1981: Rawlings seized power again. All political parties were banned.

1992: A pluralist constitution was approved in a referendum, lifting the ban on political parties. Rawlings won presidential elections.

1993: The fourth republic of Ghana was formally inaugurated.

1994: Ethnic clashes in the north left more than 6,000 people dead.

1996: The New Democratic Congress (NDC) won an assembly majority. Rawlings was re-elected as president.

2001: John Kufuor, leader of the liberal New Patriotic Party, was elected president.

2004: President Kufuor was elected for a second term.

Ghana, ancient trading empire that flourished in northwestern Africa between the 5th and 13th centuries. Founded by the Soninke people, the Ghana Empire was based, like the Mali Empire that superseded it, on the Saharan gold trade. Trade consisted mainly of the exchange of gold from inland deposits for salt from the coast. At its peak in the 11th century, it occupied an area that includes parts of present-day Mali, Senegal, and Mauritania. Wars with the Berber tribes of the Sahara led to its fragmentation and collapse in the 13th century, when much of its territory was absorbed into Mali.

Ghats, Eastern and Western twin mountain ranges in south India, east and west of the central plateau; a few peaks reach about 3,000 m/9,800 ft. The name is a European misnomer, the Indian word *ghat* meaning 'pass', not 'mountain'.

ghetto (Old Venetian *gèto* 'foundry') any deprived area occupied by a minority group, whether voluntarily or not. Originally a ghetto was the area of a town where Jews were compelled to live, decreed by a law enforced by papal bull 1555. The term came into use 1516 when the Jews of Venice were expelled to an island within the city which contained an iron foundry. Ghettos were abolished, except in Eastern Europe, in the 19th century, but the concept and practice were revived by the Germans and Italians 1940–45.

Ghiberti, Lorenzo (1378–1455) Italian sculptor and goldsmith. In 1402 he won the commission for a pair of gilded bronze doors for the baptistry of Florence's cathedral. He produced a second pair 1425–52, the *Gates of Paradise*, one of the masterpieces of the early Italian Renaissance. They show a sophisticated use of composition and perspective, and the influence of classical models. Around 1450 he wrote *Commentarii/Commentaries*, the earliest surviving autobiography of an artist and an important source of information on the art of his time.

Ghirlandaio, Domenico (c. 1449–1494) adopted name of Domenico di Tommaso Bigordi, Italian fresco painter. He was the head of a large and prosperous workshop in Florence. His fresco cycle (1486–90) in Sta Maria Novella, Florence, includes portraits of many Florentines and much contemporary domestic detail. He also worked in Pisa, Rome, and San Gimignano, and painted many portraits.

Giacometti, Alberto (1901–1966) Swiss sculptor and painter. In the 1940s, he developed a highly original style, creating thin, rough-textured single figures in bronze. These emaciated figures have often been seen as an expression of the acute sense of alienation of people in the modern world. *Man Pointing* (1947) is one of many examples in the Tate Gallery, London.

Giant's Causeway stretch of basalt columns forming a headland on the north coast of Antrim, Northern Ireland. It was formed by an outflow of lava in Tertiary times which has solidified in polygonal columns. The Giant's Causeway and Causeway Coast became a World Heritage Site in 1986.

gibberellin plant growth substance (see also *auxin) that promotes stem growth and may also affect the breaking of dormancy in certain buds and seeds, and the induction of flowering. Application of gibberellin can stimulate the stems of dwarf plants to additional growth, delay the ageing process in leaves, and promote the production of seedless fruit.

gibbon any of a group of several small southern Asian apes. The **common** or **lar gibbon** (*H. lar*) is about 60 cm/2 ft tall, with a body that is hairy except for the buttocks, which distinguishes it from other types of apes. Gibbons have long arms and no tail. They spend most of their time in trees and are very agile when swinging from branch to branch. On the ground they walk upright, and are more easily caught by predators. (Genus *Hylobates*, including the subgenus *Symphalangus*.)

Gibbon, Edward (1737–1794) English historian. He wrote one major work, arranged in three parts, *The History of the Decline and Fall of the Roman Empire* (1776–88), a continuous narrative from the 2nd century AD to the fall of Constantinople in 1453.

Gibraltar (Arabic Jabal-al-Tariq, 'Mountain of Tariq') British dependency, situated on a narrow rocky promontory at the southern tip of Spain; the **Rock of Gibraltar** formed one of the Pillars of Hercules with Mount Acho, near Ceuta, across the Strait of Gibraltar on the north African coast; area 6.5 sq km/2.5 sq mi; population (2003 est) 29,000. Gibraltar is mainly a trading centre for the import and re-export of goods. The climate is mild and pleasant, and tourism is an important industry. Since the colony is a fortress, most of the area is taken up by military installations and the population is kept small.

Gibraltar, Strait of strait between north Africa and Spain, forming the entrance from the Atlantic Ocean to the Mediterranean Sea, with the Rock of Gibraltar to the north side and Mount Acho to the south, the so-called Pillars of *Hercules.

Gibson Desert desert in central Western Australia, between the Great Sandy Desert to the north and the Great Victoria Desert in the south; area 220,000 sq km/ 85,000 sq mi.

Gide, André (Paul Guillaume) (1869–1951) French novelist. His work is largely autobiographical and concerned with the conflict between desire and conventional morality. It includes *Les Nourritures terrestres/Fruits of the Earth* (1897), *L'Immoraliste/ The Immoralist* (1902), *La Porte étroite/Strait is the Gate* (1909), *Les Caves du Vatican/The Vatican Cellars* (1914), and *Les Faux-monnayeurs/The Counterfeiters* (1926). He was a cofounder of the influential literary periodical *Nouvelle Revue française* (1908), and kept an almost lifelong *Journal*. He was awarded the Nobel Prize for Literature in 1947.

Gielgud, (Arthur) John (1904–2000) English actor and director. One of the greatest Shakespearean actors of his time, he made his debut at the Old Vic in 1921 and played Hamlet in 1929. His stage appearances ranged from roles in works by Anton Chekhov and Richard Sheridan to those of Alan Bennett, Harold Pinter, and David Storey. He won an Academy Award for his role as a butler in the film *Arthur* (1981).

giga- prefix signifying multiplication by 10^9 (1,000,000,000 or 1 billion), as in **gigahertz**, a unit of frequency equivalent to 1 billion hertz.

gigabyte in computing, a measure of *memory capacity, equal to 1,024 *megabytes. It is also used, less precisely, to mean 1,000 billion *bytes.

gila monster lizard native to the southwestern USA and Mexico. It is one of the only two existing venomous lizards, the other being the Mexican beaded lizard of the same genus. It has poison glands in its lower jaw, but its bite is not usually fatal to humans. (Species *Heloderma suspectum*.)

Gilbert, W(illiam) S(chwenck) (1836–1911) English humorist and dramatist. He collaborated with composer Arthur *Sullivan, providing the libretti for their series of light comic operas from 1871 performed by the *D'Oyly Carte Opera Company; they include *HMS Pinafore* (1878), *The Pirates of Penzance* (1879), and *The Mikado* (1885).

Gilbert, Walter (1932–) US molecular biologist who studied genetic control, seeking the mechanisms that switch genes on and off. By 1966 he had established the existence of the lac repressor, a molecule that suppresses lactose production. He was awarded the Nobel Prize for Chemistry in 1980 for his work on the sequencing of *DNA nucleotides. He shared the award with Frederick *Sanger and Paul *Berg.

Gilbert and Ellice Islands former British colony in the Pacific, known since independence (1978) as the countries of Tuvalu and Kiribati.

Gilgamesh hero of Sumerian, Hittite, Akkadian, and Assyrian legend, and lord of the Sumerian city of Uruk. The 12 verse books of the *Epic of Gilgamesh* were recorded in a standard version on 12 cuneiform tablets by the Assyrian king Ashurbanipal's scholars in the 7th century BC, and the epic itself is older than Homer's *Iliad* by at least 1,500 years.

gill in biology, the main respiratory organ of most fishes and immature amphibians, and of many aquatic invertebrates. In all types, water passes over the gills, and oxygen diffuses across the gill membranes into the circulatory system, while carbon dioxide passes from the system out into the water.

gill imperial unit of volume for liquid measure, equal to one-quarter of a pint or five fluid ounces (0.142 litre), traditionally used in selling alcoholic drinks.

Gill, (Arthur) Eric (Rowton) (1882–1940) English sculptor, graphic designer, engraver, and writer. He designed the typefaces Perpetua in 1925 and Gill Sans (without serifs) in 1927, and created monumental stone sculptures with clean, simplified outlines, such as *Prospero and Ariel* (1929–31) on Broadcasting House, London.

Gillespie, Dizzy (John Birks) (1917–1993) US jazz trumpeter and composer. With Charlie *Parker, he was the chief creator and representative of the *bebop style. Gillespie influenced many modern jazz trumpeters, including Miles *Davis.

gilt-edged securities stocks and shares issued and guaranteed by the British government to raise funds and traded on the Stock Exchange. A relatively risk-free investment, gilts bear fixed interest and are usually redeemable on a specified date. The term is now used generally to describe securities of the highest value.

gin (Dutch *jenever* 'juniper') alcoholic drink made by distilling a mash of maize, malt, or rye, with juniper flavouring. It was first made in the Netherlands.

ginger southeast Asian reedlike perennial plant; the hot-tasting spicy underground root is used as a food flavouring and in preserves. (*Zingiber officinale*, family Zingiberaceae.)

ginkgo or **maidenhair tree** tree belonging to the *gymnosperm (or naked-seed-bearing) division of plants. It may reach a height of 30 m/100 ft by the time it is 200 years old. (*Ginkgo biloba*.)

Ginsberg, (Irwin) Allen (1926–1997) US poet and political activist. His reputation as a visionary, overtly political poet was established by *Howl* (1956), which expressed and shaped the spirit of the *Beat Generation and criticized the materialism of contemporary US society. Ginsberg, like many of his generation of poets, found his authorial voice via experimentation with drugs, alternative religion, and the hippie culture; his poetry drew, for example, on Oriental philosophies and utilized mantric breath meditations.

ginseng plant with a thick forked aromatic root used in alternative medicine as a tonic. (*Panax ginseng*, family Araliaceae.)

Giorgione, da Castelfranco (1475–1510) born Giorgio Barbarelli, Italian Renaissance painter. Active in Venice, he created the Renaissance poetic landscape, with its rich colours, soft forms, and gentle sense of intimacy. An example is his *Sleeping Venus* (about 1510; Gemäldegalerie, Dresden), a work that was probably completed by *Titian.

Giotto (c. 1267/77–1337) born Giotto di Bondone, Italian painter and architect. Widely considered the founder of modern painting, he had a profound influence on the development of European art. He broke away from the conventions of the Byzantine style and introduced a new naturalism, painting saints as real people, solid, lifelike, and expressive. His style gave a greater narrative coherence, dramatic power, and dignity to the depiction of biblical incidents. His main works are cycles of frescoes in churches in Florence and Padua.

Giotto space probe built by the European Space Agency to study *Halley's Comet. Launched by an Ariane rocket in July 1985, Giotto passed within 600 km/375 mi of the comet's nucleus on 13 March 1986. On 2 July 1990, it flew within 23,000 km/14,000 mi of the Earth, which diverted its path to encounter another comet, Grigg-Skjellerup, on 10 July 1992.

giraffe world's tallest mammal. It stands over 5.5 m/18 ft tall, the neck accounting for nearly half this amount. The giraffe has two to four small, skin-covered, hornlike structures on its head and a long, tufted tail. The fur has a mottled appearance and is reddish brown and cream. Giraffes are found only in Africa, south of the Sahara Desert. They eat leaves and vegetation that is out of reach of smaller mammals, and are ruminants; that is, they chew the cud. (Species *Giraffa camelopardalis*, family Giraffidae.)

Girl Guides female equivalent of the *Scout organization, founded in 1910 in the UK by Robert Baden-Powell and his sister Agnes. There are three branches: Brownie Guides (age 7–11); Guides (10–16); Ranger Guides (14–20); they are led by Guiders (adult leaders). The World Association of Girl Guides and Girl Scouts (as they are known in the USA) has some 9 million members (1998).

Gironde navigable estuary 75 km/46 mi long on the southwest coast of France between Bordeaux and the sea, formed by the mouths of the Garonne and Dordogne rivers. It flows into the Bay of Biscay between the Médoc and Côtes vineyards. The estuary has sand banks and strong tides, but is used by ocean-going vessels. The passenger port is Le Verdon-sur-Mer. There are oil refineries at Pauillac and Bec d'Ambès.

Girondin or **Girondist** Brissotin member of the moderate republican party in the French Revolution, so called because a number of its leaders came from the Gironde region of southwestern France. The Girondins controlled the Legislative Assembly from late 1791 to late 1792, but were ousted by the radical Montagnards under Jean Paul *Marat in 1793. Many Girondin leaders were executed during the *Reign of Terror.

Giscard d'Estaing, Valéry (1926–) French centre-right politician and head of state, president of France 1974–81. At home he secured divorce and abortion law reforms early on, reduced the voting age to 18, and amended the constitution to enable the parliamentary opposition to refer legislation to the Constitutional Council. In Europe, he helped initiate the new Exchange Rate Mechanism in 1978 and direct elections to the European Parliament from 1979. Faced with increasingly difficult economic circumstances, he brought in Raymond Barre as prime minister to manage a deflationary programme from 1976. Defeated by Mitterrand in 1981, he was re-elected to the National Assembly in 1984, resigning in 1989 in order to sit in the European Parliament. He led the creation of a new European constition (draft 2003).

gizzard muscular grinding organ of the digestive tract, below the *crop of birds, earthworms, and some insects, and forming part of the *stomach. The gizzard of birds is lined with a hardened horny layer of the protein keratin, preventing damage to the muscle layer during the grinding process. Most birds swallow sharp grit which aids maceration of food in the gizzard.

glacier body of ice, originating in mountains in snowfields above the snowline, that moves slowly downhill and is constantly built up from its source. The geographic features produced by the erosive action of glaciers (*erosion) are characteristic and include glacial troughs (U-shaped valleys), corries, and *arêtes. In lowlands, the laying down of debris carried by glaciers (glacial deposition) produces a variety of landscape features, such as *moraines and drumlins.

gladiator in ancient Rome, a trained fighter, recruited mainly from slaves, criminals, and prisoners of war, who fought to the death in arenas for the entertainment of spectators. The custom was introduced into Rome from Etruria in 264 BC and continued until the 5th century AD.

gladiolus any plant of a group of southern European and African cultivated perennials belonging to the iris family, with brightly coloured funnel-shaped flowers borne on a spike; the swordlike leaves spring from a corm (swollen underground stem). (Genus *Gladiolus*, family Iridaceae.)

Gladstone, William Ewart (1809–1898) British Liberal politician, four times prime minister. He entered Parliament as a Tory in 1833 and held ministerial office, but left the party in 1846 and after 1859 identified himself with the Liberals. He was chancellor of the Exchequer 1852–55 and 1859–66, and prime minister 1868–74, 1880–85, 1886, and 1892–94. He introduced elementary education in 1870 and vote by secret ballot in 1872 and many reforms in Ireland, although he failed in his efforts to get a Home Rule Bill passed.

Glamorgan Welsh **Morgannwg**, three counties of south Wales – *Mid Glamorgan, *South Glamorgan, and *West Glamorgan – created in 1974 from the former county of Glamorganshire. All are on the Bristol Channel. In 1996 Mid Glamorgan was divided amongst Rhondda Cynon Taff, Merthyr Tydfil, Bridgend, and Vale of Glamorgan; South Glamorgan was divided amongst Cardiff and Vale of Glamorgan; and West Glamorgan was divided into Neath Port Talbot and Swansea.

gland specialized organ of the body that manufactures and secretes enzymes, hormones, or other chemicals. In animals, glands vary in size from small (for example, tear glands) to large (for example, the pancreas), but in plants they are always small, and may consist of a single cell. Some glands discharge their products internally, *endocrine glands, and others externally, *exocrine glands. Lymph nodes are sometimes wrongly called glands.

glandular fever *or* **infectious mononucleosis** viral disease characterized at onset by fever and painfully swollen lymph nodes (in the neck); there may also be digestive upset, sore throat, and skin rashes. Lassitude persists for months and even years, and recovery can be slow. It is caused by the Epstein–Barr virus.

Glasgow city and administrative headquarters of Glasgow City unitary authority, situated on the river Clyde in southwest Scotland, 67 km/42 mi west of Edinburgh; population (2001 est) 578,700. The city is the administrative, social, and service centre for the Glasgow conurbation, which extends from Gourock on the west to Carluke on the east; it is thus one of the largest continuously built-up areas in Britain. The largest city in Scotland, Glasgow used to be one of the world's great shipbuilding areas, but the industry is in decline. Despite this, the city is still the UK's fourth-largest manufacturing centre. The service sector has become increasingly important, and Glasgow was the third-most visited city in the UK in 2000.

glasnost (Russian 'openness') Soviet leader Mikhail *Gorbachev's policy of liberalizing various aspects of Soviet life, such as introducing greater freedom of expression and information and opening up relations with Western countries. *Glasnost* was introduced and adopted by the Soviet government in 1986.

glass transparent or translucent substance that is physically neither a solid nor a liquid. Although glass is easily shattered, it is one of the strongest substances known. It is made by fusing certain types of sand (silica); this fusion occurs naturally in volcanic glass (see *obsidian).

Glass, Philip (1937–) US composer. While a student of French music teacher Nadia *Boulanger he became strongly influenced by Indian music; his work is characterized by repeated rhythmic figures that are continually expanded and modified. His compositions include the operas *Einstein on the Beach* (1976), *Akhnaten* (1984), *The Making of the Representative for Planet 8* (1988), and the *'Low' Symphony* (1992) on themes from English pop singer David Bowie's *Low* album.

glasses pair of lenses fitted in a frame and worn in front of the *eyes to correct or assist defective vision. Common defects of the eye corrected by lenses are short sight (myopia) by using concave (spherical) lenses, long sight (hypermetropia) by using convex (spherical) lenses, and astigmatism by using cylindrical lenses.

glass snake *or* **glass lizard** any of a worldwide group of legless lizards. Their tails are up to three times the head–body length and are easily broken off. (Genus *Ophisaurus*, family Anguidae.)

Glastonbury market town in Somerset, southwest England, on the River Brue, 8 km/5 mi southwest of Wells; population (1996 est) 8,100. King Arthur founded an abbey here and by legend it is the site of the first Christian church in Britain, founded by Joseph of Arimathea. **Glastonbury Tor**, a hill crowned by a ruined 14th-century church tower, rises to 159 m/522 ft. Glastonbury lake village, occupied from around 150 BC to AD 50, lies 5 km/3 mi to the northwest.

glaucoma condition in which pressure inside the eye (intraocular pressure) is raised abnormally as excess fluid accumulates. It occurs when the normal outflow of fluid within the chamber of the eye (aqueous humour) is interrupted. As pressure rises, the optic nerve suffers irreversible damage, leading to a reduction in the field of vision and, ultimately, loss of eyesight.

Glen Coe valley in the Highland unitary authority, Scotland, extending 16 km/10 mi east from Rannoch Moor to Loch Leven. The mountains rise steeply on either side to over 1,000 m/3,300 ft, and the River Coe flows through the valley. Thirty-eight members of the Macdonald clan were massacred in Glen Coe on 13 February 1692 by government troops led by Robert Campbell of Glen Lyon; 300 escaped.

Glendower, Owen (c. 1350–1416) also known as **Owain Glyndw'r**, Welsh nationalist leader. He led a rebellion against Henry IV of England, taking the title 'Prince of Wales' in 1400, and successfully led the Welsh defence against English invasions in 1400–02, though Wales was reconquered by the English in 1405–13. He gained control of most of the country and established an independent Welsh parliament, but from 1405 onwards suffered repeated defeats at the hands of Prince Henry, later *Henry V.

gliding the art of using air currents to fly unpowered aircraft. Technically, gliding involves the gradual loss of altitude; gliders designed for soaring flight (utilizing air rising up a cliff face or hill, warm air rising as a thermal above sun-heated ground, and so on) are known as sailplanes.

globalization process by which different parts of the globe become interconnected by economic, social, cultural, and political means. Globalization has become increasingly rapid since the 1970s and 1980s as a result of developments in technology, communications, and trade liberalization. Critics of globalization fear the increasing power of unelected multinational corporations, financial markets, and non-government organizations (NGOs), whose decisions can have direct and rapid effects on ordinary citizens' lives. This has led to growing antiglobalization and anticapitalist protests in the 1990s and early 21st century, which have disrupted international trade talks and meetings of international finance ministers. Supporters of globalization point to the economic benefits of growing international trade and specialization.

global warming increase in average global temperature of approximately 0.5 °C/0.9 °F over the past century. Much of this is thought to be related to human activity. Global temperature has been highly variable in Earth history and many fluctuations in global temperature have occurred in historical times, but this most recent episode of warming coincides with the spread of industrialization, prompting the suggestion that it is the result of an accelerated *greenhouse effect caused by atmospheric pollutants, especially *carbon dioxide gas. The melting and collapse of the Larsen Ice Shelf, Antarctica, since 1995, is a consequence of global warming. Melting of ice is expected to raise the sea level in the coming decades.

globefish another name for the *puffer fish.

globular cluster spherical or near-spherical star cluster containing from approximately 10,000 stars to many millions. About 120 globular clusters are distributed in a spherical halo around our Galaxy. They consist of old stars, formed early in the Galaxy's history. Globular clusters are also found around other galaxies.

glockenspiel tuned percussion instrument of light metal bars mounted on a carrying frame for use in military bands or on a standing frame for use in an orchestra (in which form it resembles a small xylophone or celesta). It is played with hammers or via a piano keyboard attachment.

Glorious Revolution in British history, the events surrounding the removal of *James II from the throne and his replacement in 1689 by his daughter Mary and William of Orange as joint sovereigns (*Mary II and *William III), bound by the *Bill of Rights.

glottis in medicine, narrow opening at the upper end of the larynx that contains the vocal cords.

Gloucestershire county of southwest England. **area:** 2,640 sq km/1,019 sq mi **towns and cities:** Gloucester (administrative headquarters), Cheltenham, Cirencester, Stroud, Tewkesbury **physical:** Cotswold Hills; River Severn and tributaries **features:** Berkeley Castle (1153), where Edward II was murdered; Prinknash Abbey (1520), where pottery is made; Cotswold Farm Park, near Stow-on-the-Wold, which has rare and ancient breeds of farm animals; pre-Norman churches at Cheltenham and Cleeve; Gloucester Cathedral (Norman remains and 14th century redevelopment); Tewkesbury Abbey, Saxon site with early 12th-century nave **population:** (2001 est) 565,000.

glow-worm wingless female of any of a large number of luminous beetles (fireflies). The luminous organs, situated under the abdomen, at the end of the body, give off a greenish glow at night and attract winged males for mating. There are about 2,000 species of glow-worms, distributed worldwide. (Family Lampyridae.)

Gluck, Christoph Willibald von (1714–1787) Bohemian-German composer. His series of 'reform' operas moved music away from the usual practices of the day, in which the interests of singers were the most important considerations. He felt that music should serve poetry by means of expression and follow the situations of the story without interrupting the action. He therefore replaced the endless recitatives with orchestral accompaniments, which helped improve the dramatic flow. In 1762 his *Orfeo ed Euridice/Orpheus*

and Eurydice revolutionized the 18th-century idea of opera by paying more attention to the dramatic aspects of opera and less attention to the formal musical aspects. It was followed by *Alceste/Alcestis* (1767) and *Paride ed Elena/Paris and Helen* (1770).

glucose or **dextrose** or **grape sugar** $C_6H_{12}O_6$, simple sugar present in the blood and manufactured by green plants during *photosynthesis. It belongs to the group of chemicals known as *carbohydrates. The *respiration reactions inside cells involves the oxidation of glucose to produce *ATP, the 'energy molecule' used to drive many of the body's biochemical reactions.

glue ear or **secretory otitis media** condition commonly affecting small children, in which the Eustachian tube, which normally drains and ventilates the middle *ear, becomes blocked with mucus. The resulting accumulation of mucus in the middle ear muffles hearing. It is the leading cause of deafness (usually transient) in children.

glue-sniffing or **solvent abuse** inhalation of the fumes from organic solvents of the type found in paints, lighter fuel, and glue, for their hallucinatory effects. As well as being addictive, solvents are dangerous for their effects on the user's liver, heart, and lungs. It is believed that solvents produce hallucinations by dissolving the cell membrane of brain cells, thus altering the way the cells conduct electrical impulses.

gluon in physics, a *gauge boson that carries the *strong nuclear force, responsible for binding quarks together to form the strongly interacting subatomic particles known as *hadrons. There are eight kinds of gluon.

gluten protein found in cereal grains, especially wheat and rye. Gluten enables dough to expand during rising. Sensitivity to gliadin, a type of gluten, gives rise to *coeliac disease.

glycerol or **glycerine** or **propan-1,2,3-triol** $HOCH_2CH(OH)CH_2OH$, thick, colourless, odourless, sweetish liquid. It is obtained from vegetable and animal oils and fats (by treatment with acid, alkali, superheated steam, or an enzyme), or by fermentation of glucose, and is used in the manufacture of high explosives, in antifreeze solutions, to maintain moist conditions in fruits and tobacco, and in cosmetics.

glycine or **aminoethanoic acid** $CH_2(NH_2)COOH$, simplest amino acid, and one of the main components of proteins. When purified, it is a sweet, colourless crystalline compound.

glycol or **ethylene glycol** or **ethane-1,2-diol** $HOCH_2CH_2OH$, thick, colourless, odourless, sweetish liquid. It is used in antifreeze solutions, in the preparation of ethers and esters (used for explosives), as a solvent, and as a substitute for glycerol.

gnat any of a group of small two-winged biting insects belonging to the mosquito family. The eggs are laid in water, where they hatch into wormlike larvae, which pass through a pupal stage (see *pupa) to emerge as adults. (Family Culicidae.)

gneiss coarse-grained *metamorphic rock, formed under conditions of high temperature and pressure, and often occurring in association with schists and granites. It has a foliated, or layered, structure consisting of thin bands of micas and/or amphiboles dark in colour alternating with bands of granular quartz and feldspar that are light in colour. Gneisses are formed during regional *metamorphism; **paragneisses** are derived from metamorphism of sedimentary rocks and **orthogneisses** from metamorphism of granite or similar igneous rocks.

Gnosticism esoteric cult of divine knowledge (a synthesis of Christianity, Greek philosophy, Hinduism, Buddhism, and the mystery cults of the Mediterranean), which flourished during the 2nd and 3rd centuries and was a rival to, and influence on, early Christianity. The medieval French Cathar heresy and the modern Mandean sect (in southern Iraq) descend from Gnosticism.

GNP abbreviation for *gross national product.

gnu another name for *wildebeest.

Goa state on the west coast of India, lying 400 km/250 mi south of Mumbai (formerly Bombay); area 3,702 sq km/ 1,429 sq mi; population (2001 est) 1,344,000. The capital is Panaji. Tourism is very important to the economy; local industries include clothing, footwear, pesticides, manganese, and fishing nets. Agriculture is based on the cultivation of rice, pulses, cashew nuts, coconuts, and ragi (a cereal). Iron ore is mined in the state, and exported from the port of Marmagoa, while the tropical climate and picturesque Indian Ocean beaches contributed to the rise of Goa as a major tourist resort in the late 20th century.

goat ruminant mammal (it chews the cud), closely related to sheep. Both male and female goats have horns and beards. They are sure-footed animals, and feed on shoots and leaves more than on grass. (Genus *Capra*, family Bovidae.)

Gobi vast desert region of Central Asia in the independent state of Mongolia, and Inner Mongolia, China. It covers an area of 1,280,000 sq km/490,000 sq mi (800 km/500 mi north–south and 1,600 km/ 1,000 mi east–west), and lies on a high plateau 900–1,500 m/2,950–4,920 ft above sea level. It is mainly rocky, with shifting sands and salt marshes at lower levels. The desert is sparsely populated, mainly by nomadic herders. It is rich in the fossil remains of extinct species and Stone Age implements.

Gobind Singh (1666–1708) born Gobind Rai, Indian religious leader, the tenth and last guru (teacher) of Sikhism, 1675–1708, and founder of the Sikh brotherhood known as the *Khalsa. Following his death, and at his request, the *Guru Granth Sahib (Sikh holy book), replaced the line of human gurus as the teacher and guide of the Sikh community.

god the concept of a supreme being, a unique creative entity, basic to several monotheistic religions (for example Judaism, Christianity, Islam); in many polytheistic cultures (for example Norse, Roman, Greek), the term refers to a supernatural being who personifies the force behind an aspect of life (for example Neptune, Roman god of the sea).

Godard, Jean-Luc (1930–) French film director. A politically motivated, neo-modernist film-maker, he was one of the leaders of *New Wave cinema. He made his name with the highly influential *A bout de souffle/Breathless* (1959), in which his subversive approach to conventional narrative, in this case US gangster films, was evident.

Goddard, Robert Hutchings (1882–1945) US rocket pioneer. He launched the first liquid-fuelled

rocket at Auburn, Massachusetts, in 1926. By 1932 his rockets had gyroscopic control and could carry cameras to record instrument readings. Two years later a Goddard rocket achieved the world altitude record with an ascent of 3 km/1.9 mi.

Godiva, *or* **Godgifu, Lady (c. 1040–1080)** Wife of Leofric, Earl of Mercia (died 1057). Legend has it that her husband promised to reduce the heavy taxes on the people of Coventry if she rode naked through the streets at noon. The grateful citizens remained indoors as she did so, but 'Peeping Tom' bored a hole in his shutters and was struck blind.

Godthåb Greenlandic **Nuuk**, capital and largest town of Greenland, on the Godthåbsfjord; population (2003 est) 14,100. Godthåb is the seat of the national council and of the supreme court. It is a storage centre for oil and gas, and the chief industry is fish processing. The surrounding region has fine pastures and supports reindeer herds. The town was founded in 1728 by Hans Egede, a Norwegian missionary.

Godunov, Boris Fyodorovich (1552–1605) Tsar of Russia from 1598, elected after the death of Fyodor I, son of Ivan the Terrible. He was assassinated by a pretender to the throne who professed to be Dmitri, a brother of Fyodor and the rightful heir. The legend that has grown up around this forms the basis of Pushkin's play *Boris Godunov* (1831) and Mussorgsky's opera of the same name (1874).

Goebbels, (Paul) Joseph (1897–1945) German Nazi leader. As minister of propaganda from 1933, he brought all cultural and educational activities under Nazi control and built up sympathetic movements abroad to carry on the 'war of nerves' against Hitler's intended victims. On the capture of Berlin by the Allies, he committed suicide.

Goering, Hermann Wilhelm (1893–1946) Nazi leader, German field marshal from 1938. He was part of Hitler's inner circle, and with Hitler's rise to power was appointed commissioner for aviation from 1933 and built up the Luftwaffe (airforce). He built a vast economic empire in occupied Europe, but later lost favour and was expelled from the party in 1945. Tried at Nürnberg for war crimes, he poisoned himself before he could be executed.

Goethe, Johann Wolfgang von (1749–1832) German poet, novelist, dramatist, and scholar. He is generally considered the founder of modern German literature, and was the leader of the Romantic *Sturm und Drang movement. His masterpiece is the poetic play *Faust* (1808 and 1832). His other works include the partly autobiographical *Die Leiden des Jungen Werthers/The Sorrows of the Young Werther* (1774); the classical dramas *Iphigenie auf Tauris/Iphigenia in Tauris* (1787), *Egmont* (1788), and *Torquato Tasso* (1790); the *Wilhelm Meister* novels (1795–1829); the short novel *Die Wahlverwandschaften/Elective Affinities* (1809); and scientific treatises including *Farbenlehre/Treatise on Colour* (1810).

Gogh, Vincent (Willem) van (1853–1890) Dutch post-Impressionist painter. He began painting in the 1880s, his early works often being sombre depictions of peasant life, such as *The Potato Eaters* (1885; Van Gogh Museum, Amsterdam). Influenced by the Impressionists and by Japanese prints, he developed a freer style characterized by intense colour and expressive brushwork, as seen in his *Sunflowers* series (1888). His influence on modern art, particularly on expressionism, has been immense.

Gogol, Nicolai Vasilyevich (1809–1852) Russian writer. His first success was a collection of stories, *Evenings on a Farm near Dikanka* (1831–32), followed by *Mirgorod* (1835). Later works include *Arabesques* (1835), the comedy play *The Inspector General* (1836), and the picaresque novel *Dead Souls* (1842), which satirizes Russian provincial society.

Goh Chok Tong (1941–) Singaporean politician, prime minister 1990–2004. A trained economist, Goh became a member of parliament for the ruling People's Action Party in 1976. Under Lee Kuan Yew, who was the country's prime minister for more than 30 years, he served as trade and industry minister (1979–81), health minister (1981–82) and defence minister from 1982. He was appointed deputy prime minister in 1985, and subsequently chosen by the cabinet as Lee Kuan Yew's successor, first as prime minister and from 1992 also as party leader.

goitre enlargement of the thyroid gland seen as a swelling on the neck. It is most pronounced in simple goitre, which is caused by iodine deficiency. More common is toxic goitre or hyperthyroidism, caused by overactivity of the thyroid gland.

Golan Heights Arabic **Jawlan**, plateau on the Syrian border with Israel, bitterly contested in the *Arab–Israeli Wars due to its strategic importance. Having been used by Syria to bombard Israeli settlements in the valley below, the Golan Heights were captured by Israel in the 1967 Six-Day War. Nearly all of the Syrian population of 148,000 were expelled. Israel withdrew from 30% of the area in 1974. Despite opposition from the United Nations, Israeli 'law, jurisdiction, and administration' were extended to the territory in 1981. Syrian–Israeli peace talks have focused on the territory. In talks held in 1999–2000, Syria called for a full Israeli withdrawal, but Israel sought to link the issue with the activities in Lebanon of Hezbollah guerrillas, whom Israel wanted Syria to disarm.

gold chemical symbol Au, heavy, precious, yellow, metallic element, atomic number 79, relative atomic mass 197.0. Its symbol comes from the Latin *aurum* meaning 'gold'. It occurs in nature frequently as a free metal (see *native metal) and is highly resistant to acids, tarnishing, and corrosion. Pure gold is the most malleable of all metals and is used as gold leaf or powder, where small amounts cover vast surfaces, such as gilded domes and statues. The elemental form is so soft that it is alloyed for strength with a number of other metals, such as silver, copper, and platinum. Its purity is then measured in *carats on a scale of 24 (24 carats is pure gold). It is used mainly for decorative purposes (jewellery, gilding) but also for coinage, dentistry, and conductivity in electronic devices.

Gold Coast former name for Ghana, but historically the west coast of Africa from Cape Three Points to the Volta River, where alluvial gold is washed down. Portuguese and French navigators visited this coast in the 14th century, and a British trading settlement developed into the colony of the Gold Coast in 1618. With its dependencies of Ashanti and Northern Territories plus the trusteeship territory of Togoland, it became Ghana in 1957. The name is also used for many coastal resort areas – for example, in Florida, USA.

goldcrest smallest European bird, about 9 cm/3.5 in long and weighing 5 g/0.011 lb; a *warbler. It is olive green, with a bright orange-yellow streak running from the beak to the back of the head and a black border above the eye. The tail is brown, marked with black and white, and the cheeks, throat, and breast are a greyish white. (Species *Regulus regulus*, family Muscicapidae, order Passeriformes.)

Golden Fleece in Greek legend, the fleece of the winged ram Chrysomallus, which hung on an oak tree at Colchis and was guarded by a dragon. It was stolen by *Jason and the Argonauts.

Golden Horde the invading Mongol-Tatar army that first terrorized Europe from 1237 under the leadership of Batu Khan, a grandson of Genghis Khan. *Tamerlane broke their power in 1395, and *Ivan III ended Russia's payment of tribute to them in 1480.

goldenrod one of several tall and leafy North American perennial plants, belonging to the daisy family. Flower heads are mostly composed of many small yellow flowers, or florets. (Genus *Solidago*, family Compositae.)

golden section *or* **golden mean** mathematical relationship between three points, A, B, C, in a straight line, in which the ratio AC:BC equals the ratio BC:AB (about 8:13 or 1:1.618). The area of a rectangle produced by the whole line and one of the segments is equal to the square drawn on the other segment. A **golden rectangle** has sides in the golden mean. Considered a visually satisfying ratio, it was first constructed by the Greek mathematician *Euclid and used in art and architecture, where it was given almost mystical significance by some Renaissance theorists.

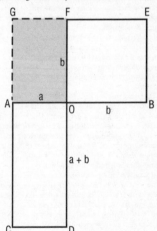

golden section The golden section is the ratio a:b, equal to 8:13. A golden rectangle is one, like that shaded in the picture, that has its length and breadth in this ratio. These rectangles are said to be pleasant to look at and have been used instinctively by artists in their pictures.

goldfinch songbird found in Eurasia, North Africa, and North America. (Species *Carduelis carduelis*, family Fringillidae, order Passeriformes.)

goldfish fish belonging to the *carp family, found in East Asia. It is greenish-brown in its natural state, but has been bred by the Chinese for centuries, taking on highly coloured and sometimes freakishly shaped forms. Goldfish can occur in a greater range of colours than any other animal tested. (Species *Carassius auratus*, family Cyprinidae.)

Golding, William (Gerald) (1911–1993) English novelist. His work is often principally concerned with the fundamental corruption and evil inherent in human nature. His first book, *Lord of the Flies* (1954; filmed in 1962), concerns the degeneration into savagery of a group of English schoolboys marooned on a Pacific island after their plane crashes; it is a chilling allegory (story with a meaning beyond its literal sense) about the savagery lurking beneath the thin veneer of modern 'civilized' life. Later novels include *The Spire* (1964). He was awarded the Nobel Prize for Literature in 1983 and knighted in 1988.

Goldsmith, Oliver (1728–1774) Irish playwright, novelist, poet, and essayist. His works include the novel *The Vicar of Wakefield* (1766), an outwardly artless and gentle story which is also a social and political satire, and in which rural honesty, kindness, and patience triumph over urban values; it became one of the most popular works of fiction in English. Other works include the poem 'The Deserted Village' (1770) and the play *She Stoops to Conquer* (1773). In 1761 Goldsmith met English writer Samuel *Johnson and became a member of his circle.

gold standard system under which a country's currency is exchangeable for a fixed weight of gold on demand at the central bank. It was almost universally applied 1870–1914, but by 1937 no single country was on the full gold standard. Britain abandoned the gold standard in 1931; the USA abandoned it in 1971. Holdings of gold are still retained because it is an internationally recognized commodity, which cannot be legislated upon or manipulated by interested countries.

golf outdoor game in which a small rubber-cored ball is hit with a wooden- or iron-faced club into a series of holes using the least number of shots. On the first shot for each hole, the ball is hit from a tee, which elevates the ball slightly off the ground; subsequent strokes are played off the ground. Most courses have 18 holes and are approximately 5,500 m/6,000 yd in length. Golf developed in Scotland in the 15th century.

Golgi, Camillo (1843–1926) Italian cell biologist who was awarded a Nobel Prize for Physiology or Medicine in 1906 with Santiago Ramón y Cajal for their discovery of the fine structure of the nervous system.

gonad the part of an animal's body that produces the sperm or egg cells (ova) required for sexual reproduction. The sperm-producing gonad is called a *testis, and the egg-producing gonad is called an *ovary.

Goncourt, de Edmond (1822–1896) and Jules (1830–1870), French writers. The brothers collaborated in producing a compendium, *L'Art du XVIIIème siècle/18th-Century Art* 1859–75, historical studies, and a *Journal* published 1887–96 that depicts French literary life of their day. Edmond de Goncourt founded the Académie Goncourt, opened in 1903, which awards an annual prize, the Prix Goncourt, to the author of the best French novel of the year.

Gondwanaland *or* **Gondwana** southern landmass formed 200 million years ago by the splitting of the single world continent *Pangaea. (The northern landmass was *Laurasia.) It later fragmented into the continents of South America, Africa, Australia, and Antarctica, which then drifted slowly to their present positions. The baobab tree found in both Africa and Australia is a relic of this ancient land mass.

gonorrhoea common sexually transmitted disease arising from infection with the bacterium *Neisseria gonorrhoeae*, which causes inflammation of the genito-urinary tract. After an incubation period of two to ten days, infected men experience pain while urinating and a discharge from the penis; infected women often have no external symptoms.

Good Hope, Cape of South African headland forming a peninsula between Table Bay and False Bay, Cape Town. The first European to sail around it was Bartolomeu *Diaz in 1488. Formerly named Cape of Storms, it was given its present name by King John II of Portugal.

Goodman, Benny (1909–1986) US clarinettist, composer, and band-leader, nicknamed the 'King of Swing'. He played in various jazz and dance bands from 1921. In 1934 he founded a 12-piece band, which combined the expressive improvisation of black jazz with disciplined precision ensemble playing. He is associated with such numbers as 'Blue Skies' and 'Let's Dance'.

Goodyear, Charles (1800–1860) US inventor who developed rubber coating in 1837 and vulcanized rubber in 1839, a method of curing raw rubber to make it strong and elastic.

goose any of several large aquatic birds belonging to the same family as ducks and swans. There are about 12 species, found in North America, Greenland, Europe, North Africa, and Asia north of the Himalayas. Both sexes are similar in appearance: they have short, webbed feet, placed nearer the front of the body than in other members of the family, and a slightly hooked beak. Geese feed entirely on grass and plants, build nests of grass and twigs on the ground, and lay 5–9 eggs, white or cream-coloured, according to the species. (Genera mainly *Anser* and *Branta*, family Anatidae, order Anseriformes.)

gooseberry edible fruit of a low-growing bush (*Ribes uva-crispa*) found in Europe and Asia, related to the *currant. It is straggling in its growth, and has straight sharp spines in groups of three and rounded, lobed leaves. The flowers are green and hang on short stalks. The sharp-tasting fruits are round, hairy, and generally green, but there are reddish and white varieties.

goosefoot any of a group of plants belonging to the goosefoot family, closely related to spinach and beets. The seeds of white goosefoot (*C. album*) were used as food in Europe from Neolithic times, and also from early times in the Americas. White goosefoot grows to 1 m/3 ft tall and has lance- or diamond-shaped leaves and packed heads of small inconspicuous flowers. The green part is eaten as a spinach substitute. (Genus *Chenopodium*, family Chenopodiaceae.)

gopher any of a group of burrowing rodents. Gophers are a kind of ground squirrel represented by some 20 species distributed across western North America, Europe, and Asia. Length ranges from 15 cm/6 in to 90 cm/16 in, excluding the furry tail; colouring ranges from plain yellowish to striped and spotted species. (Genus *Citellus*, family Sciuridae.)

Gorbachev, Mikhail Sergeyevich (1931–) Soviet president, in power 1985–91. He was a member of the Politburo from 1980. As general secretary of the Communist Party (CPSU) 1985–91 and president of the Supreme Soviet 1988–91, he introduced liberal reforms at home (**perestroika* and **glasnost*), proposed the introduction of multiparty democracy, and attempted to halt the arms race abroad. He became head of state in 1989. He was awarded the Nobel Prize for Peace in 1990 for promoting greater openness in the USSR and helping to end the Cold War.

Gordian knot in Greek mythology, the knot tied by King Gordius of Phrygia that – so an oracle revealed – could be unravelled only by the future conqueror of Asia. According to tradition, Alexander the Great, unable to untie it, cut it with his sword in 334 BC.

Gordimer, Nadine (1923–) South African novelist and short-story writer. Internationally acclaimed for her fiction and regarded by many as South Africa's conscience, Gordimer was for many years one of the most prominent opponents of **apartheid and censorship. Her novel *The Conservationist* (1974) won the Booker Prize, and she was awarded the Nobel Prize for Literature in 1991.

Gordon, Charles George (1833–1885) British general sent to Khartoum in the Sudan in 1884 to rescue English garrisons that were under attack by the **Mahdi, Muhammad Ahmed; he was himself besieged for ten months by the Mahdi's army. A relief expedition arrived on 28 January 1885 to find that Khartoum had been captured and Gordon killed two days before.

Gorgon in Greek mythology according to the Greek poet Hesiod, any of three monsters; the sisters **Stheno** and **Euryale**, daughters of the sea god Phorcys and Ceto, and the mortal **Medusa. They had wings, claws, enormous teeth, and snakes for hair; direct sight of them turned living creatures to stone. Medusa was slain by **Perseus who watched her reflection in his shield, although her head retained its power to transform.

gorilla largest of the apes, found in the dense forests of West Africa and mountains of central Africa. The male stands about 1.8 m/6 ft high and weighs about 200 kg/450 lb. Females are about half this size. The body is covered with blackish hair, silvered on the back in older males. Gorillas live in family groups; they are vegetarian, highly intelligent, and will attack only in self-defence. They are dwindling in numbers, being shot for food by some local people, or by poachers taking young for zoos, but protective measures are having some effect. (Species *Gorilla gorilla*.)

Gorky, Maxim (1868–1936) pen-name of Alexei Maximovich Peshkov, Russian writer. Born in Nizhniy-Novgorod (named Gorky 1932–90 in his honour), he was exiled 1906–13 for his revolutionary principles. His works, which include the play *The Lower Depths* (1902) and the memoir *My Childhood* (1913–14), combine realism with optimistic faith in the potential of the industrial proletariat.

gorse *or* **furze** *or* **whin** any of a group of plants native to Europe and Asia, consisting of thorny shrubs with spine-shaped leaves growing thickly along the stems and bright-yellow coconut-scented flowers. (Genus *Ulex*, family Leguminosae.)

goshawk *or* **northern goshawk** woodland hawk similar in appearance to the peregrine falcon, but with shorter wings and legs. It is native to most of Europe, Asia, and North America, and is used in falconry. The male is much smaller than the female. It is ash grey on the upper part of the body and whitish underneath with brown horizontal stripes; it has a dark head and cheeks with a white stripe above the eye. The tail has dark bands across it. (Species *Accipiter gentilis*, order Falconiformes.)

Gospel (Middle English 'good news') in the **New Testament generally, the message of Christian salvation; in particular the four written accounts of the life of Jesus in the books of **Matthew, **Mark, **Luke, and **John. Although the first three give approximately the same account or synopsis (giving rise to the name 'Synoptic Gospels'), their differences from John have raised problems for theologians.

gospel music vocal music developed in the 1920s in the African-American Baptist churches of the US South from spirituals. It has an enthusiastic and emotional style and is often accompanied by rhythmical hand-clapping and foot-stamping. Outstanding among the early gospel singers was Mahalia Jackson, but from the 1930s to the mid-1950s male harmony groups took the lead, among them the Dixie Hummingbirds, the Swan Silvertones, and the Five Blind Boys of Mississippi.

Goth East Germanic people who settled near the Black Sea around AD 2nd century. There are two branches, the eastern Ostrogoths and the western Visigoths. The **Ostrogoths** were conquered by the Huns in 372. They regained their independence in 454 and under Theodoric the Great conquered Italy 488–93; they disappeared as a nation after the Byzantine emperor Justinian I reconquered Italy 535–55. The **Visigoths** migrated to Thrace. Under **Alaric they raided Greece and Italy 395–410, sacked Rome, and established a kingdom in southern France. Expelled from there by the Franks, they established a Spanish kingdom which lasted until the Moorish conquest of 711.

Gothic architecture style of architecture that flourished in Europe from the mid-12th century to the end of the 15th century. It is characterized by the vertical lines of tall pillars and spires, greater height in interior spaces, the pointed arch, rib vaulting, and the flying buttress.

Gothic art style that succeeded Romanesque as the most popular force in European art and prevailed in most countries, particularly in northern Europe, from the middle of the 12th century to the 16th century, when it gave way to **Renaissance influence. The term 'Gothic' was first used with reference to architecture, and it is only in **Gothic architecture that it has a clear meaning, with pointed arches being the most obvious characteristic. The term is used as a convenient label for other visual arts of the period, but its meaning in these contexts is rarely precise.

gothic novel literary **genre established by Horace **Walpole's *The Castle of Otranto* (1764) and marked by mystery, violence, and horror; other pre-20th century practitioners were the English writers Ann Radcliffe, Matthew 'Monk' Lewis, Mary *Shelley, the Irish writer Bram Stoker, and the US writer Edgar Allen *Poe. The late 20th century has seen a huge revival in interest in the genre, particularly in film, and the novels of the US writer Stephen King are carefully crafted examples.

Gothic Revival the resurgence of interest in Gothic architecture, as displayed in the late 18th and 19th centuries, notably in Britain and the USA. Gothic Revival buildings include Charles Barry and Augustus Pugin's Houses of Parliament (1836–65) and Gilbert Scott's St Pancras Station Hotel (1868–74) in London; the Town Hall, Vienna (1872–83), by Friedrich von Schmidt (1825–1891); and Trinity Church, New York (1846), by Richard Upjohn (1802–1878).

gouache *or* **body colour** painting medium in which watercolour is mixed with opaque white pigment. Applied in the same way as watercolour, gouache gives a chalky finish similar to that of *tempera painting. It has long been popular in continental Europe, where Dürer and Boucher were both masters of the technique. Poster paints are usually a form of gouache.

Gounod, Charles (François) (1818–1893) French composer and organist. His operas, notably *Faust* (1859) and *Roméo et Juliette* (1867), and church music, including *Messe solennelle/Solemn Mass* (1849), combine graceful melody and elegant harmonization. His *Méditation sur le prélude de Bach/Meditation on Bach's 'Prelude'* (1889) for soprano and instruments, based on Prelude No. 1 of Bach's *Well-Tempered Clavier*, achieved popularity as 'Gounod's *Ave Maria*'.

gourd any of a group of plants that includes melons and pumpkins. In a narrower sense, the name applies only to the genus *Lagenaria*, of which the bottle gourd or *calabash (*L. siceraria*) is best known. (Family Cucurbitaceae.)

gout hereditary form of *arthritis, marked by an excess of uric acid crystals in the tissues, causing pain and inflammation in one or more joints (usually of the feet or hands). Acute attacks are treated with anti-inflammatories.

government any system whereby political authority is exercised. Modern systems of government distinguish between liberal democracies, totalitarian (one-party) states, and autocracies (authoritarian, relying on force rather than ideology). The Greek philosopher Aristotle was the first to attempt a systematic classification of governments. His main distinctions were between government by one person, by few, and by many (monarchy, oligarchy, and democracy), although the characteristics of each may vary between states and each may degenerate into tyranny (rule by an oppressive elite in the case of oligarchy or by the mob in the case of democracy).

governor in engineering, any device that controls the speed of a machine or engine, usually by regulating the intake of fuel or steam.

Gower, David (Ivon) (1957–) English cricketer. An elegant left-handed batsman who was England's record run scorer in Test cricket from 1992, when he surpassed Geoffrey Boycott's record, until 1993, when his total was overtaken by Graham Gooch. He played county cricket for Leicestershire 1975–89 and for Hampshire 1990–93. He retired in 1993.

Goya, Francisco José de Goya y Lucientes (1746–1828) Spanish painter and engraver. One of the major figures of European art, Goya depicted all aspects of Spanish life – portraits, including those of the royal family, religious works, scenes of war and of everyday life. Towards the end of his life, he created strange, nightmarish works, the 'Black Paintings', with such horrific images as *Saturn Devouring One of His Sons* (c. 1822; Prado, Madrid). His series of etchings include *The Disasters of War* (1810–14), depicting the horrors of the French invasion of Spain.

Graafian follicle fluid-filled capsule that surrounds and protects the developing egg cell inside the ovary during the *menstrual cycle. After the egg cell has been released, the follicle remains and is known as a corpus luteum.

Gracchus Tiberius Sempronius (c. 163–133 BC) and Gaius Sempronius (c. 153–121 BC), In ancient Rome, two brothers who worked for agrarian reform. As *tribune (magistrate) 133 BC, Tiberius tried to redistribute land away from the large slave-labour farms in order to benefit the poor as well as increase the number of those eligible for military service by providing them with the miniumum property requirement. He was murdered by a mob of senators. Gaius, tribune 123–122 BC, revived his brother's legislation, and introduced other reforms, but was outlawed by the Senate and killed in a riot.

Grace, W(illiam) G(ilbert) (1848–1915) English cricketer. By profession a doctor, he became the most famous sportsman in Victorian England. A right-handed batsman, he began playing first-class cricket at the age of 16, scored 152 runs in his first Test match, and scored the first triple century in 1876. He appeared in 22 Tests and 870 first-class cricket matches.

Graces in Greek mythology, three goddesses (Aglaia, Euphrosyne, Thalia), daughters of Zeus and Hera, personifications of pleasure, charm, and beauty; the inspirers of the arts and the sciences.

Graf, Steffi (1969–) German lawn-tennis player who brought Martina *Navratilova's long reign as the world's number-one female player to an end. Graf reached the semi-final of the US Open in 1985 at the age of 16, and won five consecutive *Grand Slam singles titles 1988–89. In 1994 she became the first defending Wimbledon ladies' singles champion to lose her title in the first round. In June 1999 she won her sixth French Open singles title, and her 22nd Grand Slam singles in total. Only Chris Evert, with seven victories, has won the women's French Open more times, and only Margaret Court has won more Grand Slam singles titles. In August 1999 Graf announced her retirement from competitive tennis.

grafting in medicine, the operation by which an organ or other living tissue is removed from one organism and transplanted into the same or a different organism. In horticulture, it is a technique widely used for propagating plants, especially woody species. A bud or shoot on one plant, termed the **scion**, is inserted into another, the **stock**, so that they continue growing together, the tissues combining at the point of union. In this way some of the advantages of both plants are obtained.

Graham, Martha (1894–1991) US dancer, choreographer, teacher, and director. The greatest exponent of modern dance in the USA, she developed a distinctive vocabulary of movement, the **Graham Technique**, now taught worldwide. Her pioneering technique, designed to express inner emotion and intention through dance forms, represented the first real alternative to classical ballet.

Graham, Thomas (1805–1869) Scottish chemist who laid the foundations of physical chemistry (the branch of chemistry concerned with changes in energy during a chemical transformation) by his work on the diffusion of gases and liquids. **Graham's law** (1829) states that the diffusion rate of a gas is inversely proportional to the square root of its density.

Grahame, Kenneth (1859–1932) Scottish-born writer. The early volumes of sketches of childhood, *The Golden Age* (1895) and *Dream Days* (1898), were followed by his masterpiece *The Wind in the Willows* (1908) which became a children's classic. Begun as a bedtime story for his son, it is a charming tale of life on the river bank, with its blend of naturalistic style and fantasy, and its memorable animal characters, the practical Rat, Mole, Badger, and conceited, bombastic Toad. It was dramatized by A A Milne as *Toad of Toad Hall* (1929) and by Alan Bennett (1990).

grain the smallest unit of mass in the three English systems (avoirdupois, troy, and apothecaries' weights) used in the UK and USA, equal to 0.0648 g. It was reputedly the weight of a grain of wheat. One pound avoirdupois equals 7,000 grains; one pound troy or apothecaries' weight equals 5,760 grains.

gram symbol g, metric unit of mass; one-thousandth of a kilogram.

grammar (Greek *grammatike tekhne* 'art of letters') the rules for combining words into phrases, clauses, sentences, and paragraphs. The standardizing impact of print has meant that spoken or colloquial language is often perceived as less grammatical than written language, but all forms of a language, standard or otherwise, have their own grammatical systems. People often acquire several overlapping grammatical systems within one language; for example, a formal system for writing and standard communication and a less formal system for everyday and peer-group communication.

grammar school in the UK, secondary school catering for children of high academic ability, about 20% of the total, usually measured by the Eleven Plus examination. Most grammar schools have now been replaced by *comprehensive schools.

Grampian Mountains mountain range in north central Scotland that includes **Ben Nevis**, the highest mountain in the British Isles at 1,343 m/4,406 ft, and the Cairngorm Mountains, which include the second highest mountain, **Ben Macdhui** 1,309 m/4,295 ft. The region includes Aviemore, a winter holiday and sports centre.

Gramsci, Antonio (1891–1937) Italian Marxist who attempted to unify social theory and political practice. He helped to found the Italian Communist Party in 1921 and was elected to parliament in 1924, but was imprisoned by the Fascist leader Mussolini from 1926; his *Quaderni di carcere/Prison Notebooks* were published posthumously in 1947.

Granada capital of Granada province in Andalusia, southern Spain, situated to the north of the *Sierra Nevada mountain range on the confluence of the rivers Genil and Darro; population (2001 est) 243,300.

Products include textiles, soap, and paper; there are also food industries and tourism. Granada has many palaces and monuments, including the Alhambra, a fortified hilltop palace built in the 13th and 14th centuries by the Moorish kings; a Gothic and Renaissance cathedral (1523–1703); and a university (1533).

Grand Canal *or* **Imperial Canal** Chinese **Da Yunhe**, the world's longest canal, running north from Hangzhou to near Beijing, China; 1,600 km/1,000 mi long and 30–61 m/100–200 ft wide. The earliest section was completed in 486 BC; the central section linking the Chang Jiang and Huang He rivers was built from AD 605 to 610; and the northern section was built between 1282 and 1292 during the reign of Kublai Khan.

Grand Canyon gorge in northwestern Arizona, USA, containing the *Colorado River. It is 350 km/217 mi long, 6–29 km/4–18 mi wide, and reaches depths of over 1.7 km/1.1 mi. The gorge cuts through a multicoloured series of rocks – mainly limestones, sandstones, and shales, and ranging in age from the Precambrian to the Cretaceous – and various harder strata stand out as steps on its slopes. It is one of the country's most popular national parks and around 5 million tourists visit it each year.

Grand Guignol genre of short horror play originally produced at the Grand Guignol theatre in Montmartre, Paris (named after the bloodthirsty character Guignol in late 18th-century marionette plays).

Grand National horse-race held in March or April at Aintree, Liverpool, England. The most famous steeplechase race in the world, it was inaugurated in 1839 as the Grand Liverpool Steeple Chase, adopting its present name in 1847. The current course is 7,242 m/4.5 mi long, with 30 formidable jumps. The highest jump is the Chair at 156 cm/5 ft 2in. Grand National steeplechases based on the Aintree race are held in Scotland, Wales, and Ireland at Ayr, Chepstow, and Fairyhouse respectively.

grand opera type of opera without any spoken dialogue (unlike the *opéra-comique*), as performed at the Paris Opéra, France, in the 1820s to 1880s. Grand operas were extremely long (five acts), and included incidental music and a ballet.

Grand Remonstrance petition passed by the English Parliament in November 1641 that listed all the alleged misdeeds of *Charles I – 'the evils under which we have now many years suffered'. It then went on to blame those it thought responsible – the 'Jesuited papists', the bishops and Charles's councillors and courtiers. It demanded parliamentary approval for the king's ministers and the reform of the church. Charles refused to accept the Grand Remonstrance and countered by trying to arrest five leading members of the House of Commons. The worsening of relations between king and Parliament led to the outbreak of the English Civil War in 1642.

grand slam in tennis, the winning of four major tournaments in one season: the Australian Open, the French Open, Wimbledon, and the US Open. In golf, it is also winning the four major tournaments in one season: the Masters, the US Open, the British Open, and the US PGA Championship. In baseball, a grand slam is a home run with runners on all the bases. A grand slam in bridge is when all 13 tricks are won by one team.

grand unified theory in physics, sought-for theory that would combine the theory of the strong nuclear force (called quantum chromodynamics) with the theory of the weak nuclear and electromagnetic forces (see *forces, fundamental). The search for the grand unified theory is part of a larger programme seeking a *unified field theory, which would combine all the forces of nature (including gravity) within one framework.

granite coarse-grained intrusive *igneous rock, typically consisting of the minerals quartz, feldspar, and biotite mica. It may be pink or grey, depending on the composition of the feldspar. Granites are chiefly used as building materials.

Grant, Cary (1904–1986) stage name of Archibald Alexander Leach, English-born actor, a US citizen from 1942. His witty, debonair personality and good looks made him a screen favourite for more than three decades. Among his many films are *She Done Him Wrong* (1933), *Bringing Up Baby* (1938), *The Philadelphia Story* (1940), *Notorious* (1946), *To Catch a Thief* (1955), *North by Northwest* (1959), and *Charade* (1963).

Grant, Ulysses S(impson) (1822–1885) born Hiram Ulysses Grant, US Civil War general in chief for the Union and 18th president of the USA 1869–77. As a Republican president, he carried through a liberal *Reconstruction policy in the South. He failed to suppress extensive political corruption within his own party and cabinet, which tarnished the reputation of his second term.

grape fruit of any grape *vine, especially *V. vinifera*. (Genus *Vitis*, family Vitaceae.)

grapefruit round, yellow, juicy, sharp-tasting fruit of the evergreen grapefruit tree. The tree grows up to 10 m/more than 30 ft and has dark shiny leaves and large white flowers. The large fruits grow in grapelike clusters (hence the name). Grapefruits were first established in the West Indies and subsequently cultivated in Florida by the 1880s; they are now also grown in Israel and South Africa. Some varieties have pink flesh. (*Citrus paradisi*, family Rutaceae.)

graph pictorial representation of numerical *data, such as statistical data, or a method of showing the mathematical relationship between two or more variables by drawing a diagram.

graphical user interface (GUI) in computing, a type of *user interface in which programs and files appear as icons (small pictures), user options are selected from pull-down menus, and data are displayed in windows (rectangular areas), which the operator can manipulate in various ways. The operator uses a pointing device, typically a *mouse, to make selections and initiate actions. It is also known as **WIMP** (Windows, Icons, Menus, Pointing device).

graphite blackish-grey, soft, flaky, crystalline form of *carbon. It is used as a lubricant and as the active component of pencil lead.

graphology the study of the writing systems of a language, including the number and formation of letters, spelling patterns, accents, and punctuation. In the 19th century it was believed that analysis of a person's handwriting could give an indication of his or her personality, a belief still held in a more limited fashion today.

grass any of a very large family of plants, many of which are economically important because they provide grazing for animals and food for humans in the form of cereals. There are about 9,000 species distributed worldwide except in the Arctic regions. Most are perennial, with long, narrow leaves and jointed, hollow stems; flowers with both male and female reproductive organs are borne on spikelets; the fruits are grainlike. Included in the family are bluegrass, wheat, rye, maize, sugarcane, and bamboo. (Family Gramineae.)

Grass, Günter (Wilhelm) (1927–) German writer. The grotesque humour and socialist feeling of his novels *Die Blechtrommel/The Tin Drum* (1959) and *Der Butt/The Flounder* (1977) are also characteristic of many of his poems. Deeply committed politically, Grass's works contain a mixture of scurrility, humour, tragedy, satire, and marvellously inventive imagery. He was awarded the Nobel Prize for Literature in 1999.

grasshopper any of several insects with strongly developed hind legs, enabling them to leap into the air. The hind leg in the male usually has a row of protruding joints that produce the characteristic chirping sound when rubbed against the hard wing veins. *Locusts, *crickets, and katydids are related to grasshoppers. (Families Acrididae and Tettigoniidae, order Orthoptera.)

grass of Parnassus plant, unrelated to grasses, found growing in marshes and on wet moors in Europe and Asia. It is low-growing, with a rosette of heart-shaped stalked leaves, and has five-petalled white flowers with conspicuous veins growing singly on stem tips in late summer. (*Parnassia palustris*, family Parnassiaceae.)

Graubünden French **Grisons**, canton in Switzerland, the largest and most sparsely populated canton of the country; area 7,106 sq km/2,743 sq mi; population (2003 est) 183,700. The capital is Chur. The inner valleys are the highest in Europe, and the main sources of the River Rhine rise here. It also includes the resort of Davos and, in the Upper Engadine, St Moritz. Ladin (a form of Romansch) is still spoken by about a quarter of the population. Graubünden entered the Swiss Confederation in 1803.

gravel coarse *sediment consisting of pebbles or small fragments of rock, originating in the beds of lakes and streams or on beaches. Gravel is quarried for use in road building, railway ballast, and for an aggregate in concrete. It is obtained from quarries known as gravel pits, where it is often found mixed with sand or clay.

Graves, Robert (Ranke) (1895–1985) English poet and writer. He was severely wounded on the Somme in World War I, and his frank autobiography *Goodbye to All That* (1929) contains outstanding descriptions of the war. *Collected Poems* (1975) contained those verses he wanted preserved, some of which were influenced by the American poet Laura Riding, with whom he lived for some years. His fiction includes two historical novels of imperial Rome, *I Claudius* and *Claudius the God* (both 1934). His most significant critical work is *The White Goddess: A Historical Grammar of Poetic Myth* (1948, revised edition 1966).

gravitational field region around a body in which other bodies experience a force due to its gravitational attraction. The gravitational field of a massive object such as the Earth is very strong and easily recognized as the force of gravity, whereas that of an object of much smaller mass is very weak and difficult to detect. Gravitational fields produce only attractive forces.

gravitational force *or* **gravity** one of the four fundamental *forces of nature, the other three being the electromagnetic force, the weak nuclear force, and the strong nuclear force. The gravitational force is the weakest of the four forces, but acts over great distances. The particle that is postulated as the carrier of the gravitational force is the graviton.

gravity force of attraction that arises between objects by virtue of their masses. The larger the mass of an object the more strongly it attracts other objects. On Earth, gravity causes objects to have weight; it accelerates objects (at 9.806 metres per second per second/32.174 ft per second per second) towards the centre of the Earth, the ground preventing them falling further.

gravure one of the three main *printing methods, in which printing is done from a plate etched with a pattern of recessed cells in which the ink is held. The greater the depth of a cell, the greater the strength of the printed ink. Gravure plates are expensive to make, but the process is economical for high-volume printing and reproduces illustrations well.

gray symbol Gy, SI unit of absorbed radiation dose. It replaces the rad (1 Gy equals 100 rad), and is defined as the dose absorbed when one kilogram of matter absorbs one joule of ionizing radiation. Different types of radiation cause different amounts of damage for the same absorbed dose; the SI unit of **dose equivalent** is the *sievert.

Gray, Thomas (1716–1771) English poet. His *Elegy Written in a Country Churchyard* (1751), a dignified contemplation of death, was instantly acclaimed and is one of the most quoted poems in the English language. Other poems include *Ode on a Distant Prospect of Eton College* (1747), *The Progress of Poesy*, and *The Bard* (both 1757). He is now seen as a forerunner of *Romanticism.

grayling freshwater fish with a long multirayed dorsal (back) fin and silver to purple body colouring. It is found in northern parts of Europe, Asia, and North America, where it was once common in the Great Lakes. (Species *Thymallus thymallus*, family Salmonidae.)

Great Artesian Basin largest area of artesian water in the world. It underlies much of Queensland, New South Wales, and South Australia, and in prehistoric times formed a sea. It has an area of 1,750,000 sq km/ 675,750 sq mi.

Great Australian Bight broad bay of the Indian Ocean in southern Australia, notorious for storms. It was discovered by a Dutch navigator, Captain Thyssen, in 1627.

Great Barrier Reef chain of *coral reefs and islands about 2,000 km/1,250 mi long, in the Coral Sea, off the east coast of Queensland, Australia, about 16–241 km/ 10–150 mi offshore. The Great Barrier Reef is made up of 3,000 individual reefs, and is believed to be the world's largest living organism. Only ten navigable channels break through the reef. The most valuable products of the reef are pearls, pearl shells, trepangs (edible sea slugs), and sponges. The reef is popular with tourists. In 1976 it became a Marine Park and in 1981 it was declared a World Heritage Site by UNESCO.

Great Bear popular name for the constellation *Ursa Major.

Great Britain official name for *England, *Scotland, and *Wales, and the adjacent islands (except the Channel Islands and the Isle of Man) from 1603, when the English and Scottish crowns were united under James I of England (James VI of Scotland). With *Northern Ireland it forms the United Kingdom.

great circle circle drawn on a sphere such that the diameter of the circle is a diameter of the sphere. On the Earth, all meridians of longitude are half great circles; among the parallels of latitude, only the Equator is a great circle.

Great Dane breed of large, short-haired dog, often fawn or brindle in colour, standing up to 76 cm/30 in tall, and weighing up to 70 kg/154 lb. It has a large head and muzzle, and small, erect ears. It was formerly used in Europe for hunting boar and stags.

Great Dividing Range eastern Australian mountain range, extending 3,700 km/2,300 mi N–S from Cape York Peninsula, Queensland, to Victoria. It includes the Carnarvon Range, Queensland, which has many Aboriginal cave paintings, the Blue Mountains in New South Wales, and the Australian Alps, and ends southwards beyond Bass Strait as the central uplands of Tasmania. In its northern parts in Queensland the Range averages 600–900 m/2,000–3,000 ft in height, while farther south the average is about 900 m/3,000 ft, though the Australian Alps include Mount Kosciusko (2,228 m/7,310 ft), the highest peak in Australia. The Range contains the headwaters of the leading rivers of Australia, with the Darling, Lachlan, Murrumbidgee, and Goulburn flowing westwards to join the Murray, while the Snowy River, a major source of hydroelectricity, flows eastwards to the Pacific. Until exploration by Gregory Blaxland and others in the early 19th century the Range was a formidable barrier to westward migration of European settlers from the eastern coastlands. It is now an area of rich resources for agriculture, lumbering and mining, while its rivers provide water for irrigation in the drier lands to the west as well as power for hydroelectricity and its national parks and ski areas are the basis of a major tourist industry.

Great Exhibition world fair held in Hyde Park, London, UK, in 1851, proclaimed by its originator Prince Albert as 'the Great Exhibition of the Industries of All Nations'. In practice, it glorified British manufacture: over half the 100,000 exhibits were from Britain or the British Empire. Over 6 million people attended the exhibition. The exhibition hall, popularly known as the **Crystal Palace**, was constructed of glass with a cast-iron frame, and designed by Joseph *Paxton.

Great Lake Australia's largest freshwater lake, 1,030 m/ 3,380 ft above sea level, in Tasmania; area 114 sq km/ 44 sq mi. It is used for hydroelectric power and is a tourist attraction.

Great Lakes series of five freshwater lakes along the USA–Canadian border: *Superior, *Michigan, *Huron, *Erie, and *Ontario; total area 245,000 sq km/ 94,600 sq mi. Interconnected by a network of canals and rivers, the lakes are navigable by large ships, and they are connected with the Atlantic Ocean via the *St Lawrence River and by the St Lawrence Seaway (completed in 1959), which is navigable by medium-sized ocean-going ships.

Great Leap Forward change in the economic policy of the People's Republic of China introduced by *Mao Zedong under the second five-year plan of 1958 to 1962. The aim was to achieve rapid and simultaneous agricultural and industrial growth through the creation of large new agro-industrial communes. The inefficient and poorly planned allocation of state resources led to the collapse of the strategy by 1960 and the launch of a 'reactionary programme', involving the use of rural markets and private subsidiary plots. More than 20 million people died in the Great Leap famines of 1959 to 1961.

Great Patriotic War 1941–45, war between the USSR and Germany during *World War II.

Great Plains formerly the **Great American Desert**, semi-arid region of about 3.2 million sq km/1.2 million sq mi in North America, to the east of the Rocky Mountains, stretching as far as the 100th meridian of longitude through Oklahoma, Kansas, Nebraska, and the Dakotas. The Plains, which cover one-fifth of the USA, extend from Texas in the south over 2,400 km/1,500 mi north to Alberta, Saskatchewan, and Manitoba in Canada, where they are known as the **Prairies**. The Great Plains have extensive oil and coal reserves, many of which are actively worked. Ranching and wheat farming have resulted in overuse of the water resources, and the consequent process of erosion has reduced available farmland. Around 15 million people live on the Great Plains.

Great Power any of the major European powers of the 19th century: Russia, Austria (Austria-Hungary), France, Britain, and Prussia.

Great Red Spot prominent oval feature, 14,000 km/8,500 mi wide and some 30,000 km/20,000 mi long, in the atmosphere of the planet *Jupiter, south of its equator. It was first observed in 1664. Space probes show it to be an anticlockwise vortex of cold clouds, coloured possibly by phosphorus.

Great Rift Valley volcanic valley formed 10–20 million years ago owing to rifting of the Earth's crust and running about 8,000 km/5,000 mi from the Jordan Valley through the Red Sea to central Mozambique in southeast Africa. It is marked by a series of lakes, including Lake Turkana (formerly Lake Rudolf), and volcanoes, such as Mount Kilimanjaro. The rift system associated with the Rift Valley extends into northern Botswana, with geological faults controlling the location of the Okavango Delta.

Great Sandy Desert desert in northern Western Australia; 415,000 sq km/160,000 sq mi. It is also the name of an arid region in southern Oregon, USA.

Great Schism in European history, the period 1378–1417 in which rival popes had seats in Rome and in Avignon; it was ended by the election of Martin V during the Council of Constance 1414–17.

Great Slave Lake freshwater lake in the Northwest Territories, Canada; area 28,450 sq km/10,980 sq mi. It is about 480 km/298 mi long and 100 km/62 mi wide, and is the deepest lake (615 m/2,020 ft) in North America. The lake forms two large bays, McLeod's Bay in the north and Christie's Bay in the south. It is connected with Artillery Lake, Clinton-Golden Lake, and Aylmer Lake, and the Mackenzie River flows out from it on the west. The Great Slave Lake contains many fish, including salmon and trout, and has major commercial fisheries.

Great Trek in South African history, the movement of 12,000–14,000 Boer (Dutch) settlers from Cape Colony in 1835 and 1845 to escape British rule. They established republics in Natal and the Transvaal. It is seen by many white South Africans as the main event in the founding of the present republic and was cited as a justification for whites-only rule.

Great Wall of China continuous defensive wall stretching from western Gansu to the Gulf of Liaodong (2,250 km/1,450 mi). It was once even longer. It was built under the Qin dynasty from 214 BC to prevent incursions by the Turkish and Mongol peoples and extended westwards by the Han dynasty. Some 8 m/25 ft high, it consists of a brick-faced wall of earth and stone, has a series of square watchtowers, and sections have been carefully restored.

Great War another name for *World War I.

grebe any of a group of 19 species of water birds. The **great crested grebe** (*Podiceps cristatus*) is the largest of the Old World grebes. It feeds on fish, and lives on ponds and marshes in Europe, Asia, Africa, and Australia. It grows to 50 cm/20 in long and has a white breast, with chestnut and black feathers on its back and head. Dark ear tufts and a prominent collar or crest of feathers around the base of the head appear during the breeding season; these are lost in winter. (Family Podicipedidae, order Podicipediformes.)

Greco, El (1541–1614) born Doménikos Theotokopoulos, Spanish painter called 'the Greek' because he was born in Crete. He studied in Italy, worked in Rome from about 1570, and by 1577 had settled in Toledo. He painted elegant portraits and intensely emotional religious scenes with increasingly distorted figures and unearthly light, such as *The Burial of Count Orgaz* (1586; Church of S Tomé, Toledo).

Greece
National name: *Elliniki Dimokratia/Hellenic Republic*

Area: 131,957 sq km/50,948 sq mi
Capital: Athens
Major towns/cities: Thessaloniki, Peiraias, Patras, Iraklion, Larisa, Peristerio, Kallithéa
Major ports: Peiraias, Thessaloniki, Patras, Iraklion
Physical features: mountainous (Mount Olympus); a large number of islands, notably Crete, Corfu, and Rhodes, and Cyclades and Ionian Islands

Head of state: Konstantinos Stephanopoulos from 1995
Head of government: Kostantinos Karamanlis from 2004
Political system: liberal democracy
Political executive: parliamentary
Political parties: Panhellenic Socialist Movement (PASOK), nationalist, democratic socialist; New Democracy Party (ND), right of centre; Democratic Renewal (DIANA), centrist; Communist Party (KKE), left wing; Political Spring, moderate, left of centre
Currency: euro (drachma until 2002)
GNI per capita (PPP): (US$) 18,240 (2002 est)
Exports: fruit and vegetables, chemicals, clothing, mineral fuels and lubricants, textiles, iron and steel, aluminium and aluminium alloys. Principal market: Germany 12.3% (1999)
Population: 10,976,000 (2003 est)
Language: Greek (official)
Religion: Greek Orthodox, over 96%; about 1% Muslim
Life expectancy: 76 (men); 81 (women) (2000–05)
Chronology
c. 2000–1200 BC: Mycenaean civilization flourished.
c. 1500–1100 BC: Central Greece and Peloponnese invaded by tribes of Achaeans, Aeolians, Ionians, and Dorians.
c. 1000–500 BC: Rise of the Greek city states; Greek colonies established around the shores of the Mediterranean.
c. 490–404 BC: Ancient Greek culture reached its zenith in the democratic city state of Athens.
357–338 BC: Philip II of Macedon won supremacy over Greece; cities fought to regain and preserve independence.
146 BC: Roman Empire defeated Macedon and annexed Greece.
476 AD: Western Roman Empire ended; Eastern Empire continued as Byzantine Empire, based at Constantinople, with essentially Greek culture.
1204: Crusaders partitioned Byzantine Empire; Athens, Achaea, and Thessaloniki came under Frankish rulers.
late 14th century–1461: Ottoman Turks conquered mainland Greece and captured Constantinople in 1453; Greek language and culture preserved by Orthodox Church.
1685: Venetians captured Peloponnese; regained by Turks in 1715.
late 18th century: Beginnings of Greek nationalism among émigrés and merchant class.
1814: *Philike Hetairia* ('Friendly Society') formed by revolutionary Greek nationalists in Odessa.
1821: *Philike Hetairia* raised Peloponnese brigands in revolt against Turks; War of Independence ensued.
1827: Battle of Navarino: Britain, France, and Russia intervened to destroy Turkish fleet; Count Ioannis Kapodistrias elected president of Greece.
1829: Treaty of Adrianople: under Russian pressure, Turkey recognized independence of small Greek state.
1832: Great Powers elected Otto of Bavaria as king of Greece.
1843: Coup forced King Otto to grant a constitution.
1862: Mutiny and rebellion led King Otto to abdicate.
1863: George of Denmark became king of the Hellenes.
1864: Britain transferred Ionian islands to Greece.
1881: Following Treaty of Berlin in 1878, Greece was allowed to annex Thessaly and part of Epirus.

late 19th century: Politics dominated by Kharilaos Trikoupis, who emphasized economic development, and Theodoros Deliyiannis, who emphasized territorial expansion.
1897: Greco-Turkish War ended in Greek defeat.
1908: Cretan Assembly led by Eleutherios Venizelos proclaimed union with Greece.
1910: Venizelos became prime minister and introduced financial, military, and constitutional reforms.
1912–13: Balkan Wars: Greece annexed a large area of Epirus and Macedonia.
1916: 'National Schism': Venizelos formed rebel pro-Allied government while royalists remained neutral.
1917–18: Greek forces fought on Allied side in World War I.
1919–22: Greek invasion of Asia Minor; after Turkish victory, a million refugees came to Greece.
1924: Republic declared amid great political instability.
1935: Greek monarchy restored with George II.
1936: Gen Ioannia Metaxas established right-wing dictatorship.
1940: Greece successfully repelled Italian invasion.
1941–44: German occupation of Greece; rival monarchist and communist resistance groups operated from 1942.
1946–49: Civil war: communists defeated by monarchists with military aid from Britain and USA.
1952: Became a member of NATO.
1967: 'Greek Colonels' seized power under George Papadopoulos; political activity banned; King Constantine II exiled.
1973: Republic proclaimed with Papadopoulos as president.
1974: Cyprus crisis caused downfall of military regime; Constantinos Karamanlis returned from exile to form Government of National Salvation and restore democracy.
1981: Andreas Papandreou was elected Greece's first socialist prime minister; Greece entered the European Community.
1989–93: The election defeat of Panhellenic Socialist Movement (PASOK) was followed by unstable coalition governments.
1993: PASOK returned to power.
1995: Costis Stephanopoulos was elected president.
1996: Costas Simitis succeeded Papandreou as prime minister.
1997: Direct talks with Turkey resulted in an agreement to settle all future disputes peacefully.
2000: Simitis was re-elected as prime minister, and Stephanopoulos was re-elected as president. Greece and Turkey signed a series of agreements aimed at improving relations between the two countries. A passenger ferry was shipwrecked. A general strike in Athens protested against planned labour reforms.
2001: Greece joined the euro.
2003: 15 members of the left-wing 'November 17' terrorist group, responsible for a series of political murders since 1975, were jailed for life.
2004: In March the conservative New Democratic Party came to power under Costas Karamanlis. Later in the year Greece successfully staged the Olympic Games.

Greece, ancient ancient civilization that flourished 2,500 years ago on the shores of the Ionian and Aegean Seas (modern Greece and the west coast of Turkey). Although its population never exceeded 2 million, ancient Greece made great innovations in philosophy, politics, science, architecture, and the arts, and Greek culture forms the basis of western civilization to this day.

Greek architecture the architecture of ancient Greece is the base for virtually all architectural developments in Europe. The Greeks invented the entablature, which allowed roofs to be hipped (inverted V-shape), and perfected the design of arcades with support columns. There were three styles, or orders, of columns: Doric (with no base), Ionic (with scrolled capitals), and Corinthian (with acanthus-leafed capitals).

Greek language member of the Indo-European language family, which has passed through at least five distinct phases since the 2nd millennium BC: ancient Greek 14th–12th centuries BC; Archaic Greek, including Homeric epic language, until 800 BC; classical Greek until 400 BC; hellenistic Greek, the common language of Greece, Asia Minor, West Asia, and Egypt to the 4th century AD, and Byzantine Greek, used until the 15th century and still the ecclesiastical language of the Greek Orthodox Church. Modern Greek is principally divided into the general vernacular (demotic Greek) and the language of education and literature (Katharevousa).

Greek Orthodox Church see *Orthodox Church.

green belt area surrounding a large city, officially designated not to be built on but preserved where possible as open space for agricultural and recreational use. In the UK the first green belts were established from 1938 around conurbations such as London in order to prevent urban sprawl. New towns were set up to take the overspill population.

Greene, (Henry) Graham (1904–1991) English writer. His novels of guilt, despair, and penitence are set in a world of urban seediness or political corruption in many parts of the world. They include *Brighton Rock* (1938), *The Power and the Glory* (1940), *The Heart of the Matter* (1948), *The Third Man* (1949), *The Honorary Consul* (1973), and *Monsignor Quixote* (1982). He was one of the first English novelists both to recognize and to be influenced by the literary potential of the cinema. In 1999 his novel *The End of the Affair* (1951) was made into a film, directed by Neil Jordan. Greene also wrote lighter, comic novels, including *Our Man in Havana* (1958) and *Travels with My Aunt* (1969).

greenfinch olive-green songbird common in Europe and North Africa. It has bright-yellow markings on the outer tail feathers and wings; males are much brighter in colour than females. (Species *Carduelis chloris*, family Fringillidae, order Passeriformes.)

greenfly plant-sucking insect, a type of *aphid.

greenhouse effect phenomenon of the Earth's atmosphere by which solar radiation, trapped by the Earth and re-emitted from the surface as long-wave infrared radiation, is prevented from escaping by various gases (the 'greenhouse gases') in the air. These gases trap heat because they readily absorb infrared radiation. As the energy cannot escape, it warms up the Earth, causing an increase in the Earth's temperature (*global warming). The main greenhouse gases are *carbon dioxide, *methane, and *chlorofluorocarbons (CFCs) as well as water vapour. Fossil-fuel consumption and forest fires are the principal causes of carbon dioxide build-up; methane is a by-product of agriculture (rice, cattle, sheep).

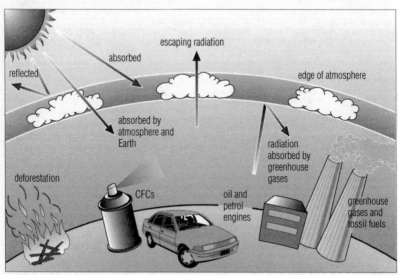

greenhouse effect The warming effect of the Earth's atmosphere is called the greenhouse effect. Radiation from the Sun enters the atmosphere but is prevented from escaping back into space by gases such as carbon dioxide (produced for example, by the burning of fossil fuels), nitrogen oxides (from car exhausts), and CFCs (from aerosols and refrigerators). As these gases build up in the atmosphere, the Earth's average temperature is expected to rise.

Grenada

Greenland Greenlandic **Kalaallit Nunaat**, world's largest island, a dependency of Denmark, lying between the North Atlantic and Arctic Oceans east of North America; area 2,175,600 sq km/840,000 sq mi; population (1993) 55,110, comprising Inuit (Ammassalik Eskimoan), Danish, and other Europeans. The capital is Godthåb (Greenlandic *Nuuk*) on the west coast. The main economic activities are fishing and fish-processing.

Greenland Sea area of the *Arctic Ocean between Spitsbergen and Greenland, to the north of the Norwegian Sea; area 1,200,000 sq km/460,000 sq mi, mainly ice-bound in winter. It consists of two large basins, reaching depths of 4,850 m/15,900 ft, separated by the West Jan Mayen Rise.

Green Man *or* **Jack-in-the-Green** in English folklore, a figure dressed and covered in foliage, associated with festivities celebrating the arrival of spring.

green movement collective term for the individuals and organizations involved in efforts to protect the environment. The movement includes political parties such as the *Green Party and organizations like Friends of the Earth and Greenpeace. See also *environmental issues.

Green Paper publication issued by a British government department setting out various aspects of a matter on which legislation is contemplated, and inviting public discussion and suggestions. In due course it may be followed by a *White Paper, giving details of proposed legislation. The first Green Paper was published in 1967.

Green Party political party aiming to 'preserve the planet and its people', based on the premise that continual economic growth is unsustainable. The leaderless party structure reflects a general commitment to decentralization. Green parties sprang up in Western Europe in the 1970s and in Eastern Europe from 1988. Parties in different countries are linked to one another but unaffiliated with any pressure group.

green revolution in agriculture, the change in methods of arable farming instigated in the 1940s and 1950s in countries of the developing world. The intent was to provide more and better food for their populations, albeit with a heavy reliance on chemicals and machinery. It was abandoned by some countries in the 1980s. Much of the food produced was exported as *cash crops, so that local diet did not always improve.

greenshank greyish shorebird of the sandpiper group. It has long olive-green legs and a long, slightly upturned bill, with white underparts and rump and dark grey wings. It breeds in northern Europe and regularly migrates through the Aleutian Islands, southwest of Alaska. (Species *Tringa nebularia*, family Scolopacidae, order Charadriiformes.)

Greenwich Mean Time (GMT) local time on the zero line of longitude (the **Greenwich meridian**), which passes through the Old Royal Observatory at Greenwich, London. It was replaced in 1986 by coordinated universal time (UTC), but continued to be used to measure longitudes and the world's standard time zones.

Greer, Germaine (1939–) Australian academic and feminist, author of *The Female Eunuch* (1970). The book is a polemical study of how patriarchy – through the nuclear family and capitalism – subordinates women by forcing them to conform to feminine stereotypes that effectively 'castrate' them. With its publication, Greer became identified as a leading figure of the women's movement.

Gregorian chant any of a body of *plainsong choral chants associated with Pope Gregory the Great (540–604), which became standard in the Roman Catholic Church.

Gregory name of 16 popes, including:

Gregory (I) the Great (c. 540–604) also known as **St Gregory**, Pope from 590 who asserted Rome's supremacy and exercised almost imperial powers. In 596 he sent St *Augustine to England. He introduced the choral **Gregorian chant** into the liturgy. His feast day is 12 March.

Gregory VII (c. 1020–1085) born Hildebrand, Pope from 1073 and Catholic saint. He was chief minister to several popes before his election to the papacy, and was one of the great ecclesiastical reformers. He aroused the imperial wrath by prohibiting the abuse of investiture, and was declared deposed by the Holy Roman Emperor Henry IV in 1076. His feast day is 25 May. He was canonized in 1606.

Gregory XIII (1502–1585) Pope from 1572 who introduced the reformed Gregorian calendar, still in use, in which a century year is not a leap year unless it is divisible by 400.

Grenada

Area: (including the southern Grenadine Islands, notably Carriacou and Petit Martinique) 344 sq km/133 sq mi
Capital: St George's
Major towns/cities: Grenville, Sauteurs, Victoria, Gouyave
Physical features: southernmost of the Windward Islands; mountainous; Grand-Anse beach; Annandale Falls; the Great Pool volcanic crater
Head of state: Queen Elizabeth II from 1974, represented by Governor General Daniel Williams from 1996
Head of government: Keith Mitchell from 1995
Political system: liberal democracy
Political executive: parliamentary
Political parties: Grenada United Labour Party (GULP), nationalist, left of centre; National Democratic Congress (NDC), centrist; National Party (TNP), centrist

Currency: East Caribbean dollar
GNI per capita (PPP): (US$) 6,330 (2002 est)
Exports: nutmeg, cocoa, bananas, cocoa, mace, fresh fruit. Principal market: USA 35.8% each (2000)
Population: 80,000 (2003 est)
Language: English (official), some French-African patois
Religion: Roman Catholic 53%, Anglican about 14%, Seventh Day Adventist, Pentecostal, Methodist
Life expectancy: 68 (men); 67 (women) (2000–05)
Chronology
1498: Sighted by the explorer Christopher Columbus; Spanish named it Grenada since its hills were reminiscent of the Andalusian city.
1650: Colonized by French settlers from Martinique, who faced resistance from the local Carib Indian community armed with poison arrows, before the defeated Caribs performed a mass suicide.
1783: Ceded to Britain as a colony by the Treaty of Versailles; black African slaves imported to work cotton, sugar, and tobacco plantations.
1795: Abortive rebellion against British rule led by Julien Fedon, a black planter.
1834: Slavery abolished.
1950: Left-wing Grenada United Labour Party (GULP) founded by trade union leader Eric Gairy.
1951: Universal adult suffrage granted and GULP elected to power in a nonautonomous local assembly.
1958–62: Part of the Federation of the West Indies.
1967: Internal self-government achieved.
1974: Independence achieved within the Commonwealth, with Gairy as prime minister.
1979: Autocratic Gairy was removed in a bloodless coup led by left-wing Maurice Bishop of the New Jewel Movement. The constitution was suspended and a People's Revolutionary Government established.
1982: Relations with the USA and Britain deteriorated as ties with Cuba and the USSR strengthened.
1983: After attempts to improve relations with the USA, Bishop was overthrown by left-wing opponents, precipitating a military coup by Gen Hudson Austin. The USA invaded; there were 250 fatalities. Austin was arrested and the 1974 constitution was reinstated.
1984: Newly formed centre-left New National Party (NNP) won a general election and its leader became prime minister.
1991: Integration of the Windward Islands was proposed.
1995: A general election was won by the NNP, led by Keith Mitchell. A plague of pink mealy bugs caused damage to crops estimated at $60 million.
1999: The ruling NNP gained a sweeping general election victory.
2003: The NNP was re-elected but with a slashed majority.
2004: Hurricane Ivan struck, causing widespread destruction and loss of several lives.

Grenadines chain of about 600 small islands in the Caribbean Sea, part of the group known as the Windward Islands. They are divided between St Vincent and Grenada.

Grenville, George (1712–1770) English Whig politician, prime minister, and chancellor of the Exchequer, whose introduction of the *Stamp Act of 1765 to raise revenue from the colonies was one of the causes of the American Revolution. His government was also responsible for prosecuting the radical John *Wilkes.

Gresham, Thomas (c. 1519–1579) English merchant financier who founded and paid for the Royal Exchange and propounded **Gresham's law**: 'bad money tends to drive out good money from circulation'. He also founded Gresham College in London. The college was provided for by his will, and among the professorships was one for music, which has continued to the present day. Knighted in 1559.

Gretna Green village in Dumfries and Galloway region, Scotland, where runaway marriages were legal after they were banned in England in 1754; all that was necessary was the couple's declaration, before witnesses, of their willingness to marry. From 1856 Scottish law required at least one of the parties to be resident in Scotland for a minimum of 21 days before the marriage, and marriage by declaration was abolished in 1940.

Grey, Charles (1764–1845) 2nd Earl Grey, British Whig politician. He entered Parliament in 1786, and in 1806 became First Lord of the Admiralty, and foreign secretary soon afterwards. As prime minister 1830–34, he carried the Great Reform Bill of 1832 that reshaped the parliamentary representative system and the act abolishing slavery throughout the British Empire in 1833. He succeeded to the earldom in 1807.

Grey, Lady Jane (1537–1554) Queen of England for nine days, 10–19 July 1553, the great-granddaughter of Henry VII. She was married in 1553 to Lord Guildford Dudley (died 1554), son of the Duke of Northumberland. Edward VI was persuaded by Northumberland to set aside the claims to the throne of his sisters Mary and Elizabeth. When Edward died on 6 July 1553, Jane reluctantly accepted the crown and was proclaimed queen four days later. Mary, although a Roman Catholic, had the support of the populace, and the Lord Mayor of London announced that she was queen on 19 July. Grey was executed on Tower Green.

greyhound ancient breed of dog, with a long narrow head, slight build, and long legs. It stands up to 75 cm/30 in tall. It is renowned for its swiftness, and can exceed 60 kph/40 mph. Greyhounds were bred to hunt by sight, their main quarry being hares. Hunting hares with greyhounds is the basis of the ancient sport of *coursing. Track-based greyhound racing is a popular spectator sport.

Grieg, Edvard (Hagerup) (1843–1907) Norwegian nationalist composer. Much of his music is written on a small scale, particularly his songs, dances, sonatas, and piano works, and strongly identifies with Norwegian folk music. Among his orchestral works are the piano concerto in A minor (1869) and the incidental music for Henrik Ibsen's drama *Peer Gynt* (1876), commissioned by Ibsen and the Norwegian government.

griffin mythical monster, the supposed guardian of hidden treasure, with the body, tail, and hind legs of a lion, and the head, forelegs, and wings of an eagle, though in classical times all four legs were those of a lion.

Griffith, D(avid) W(ark) (1875–1948) US film director. He was an influential figure in the development of cinema as an art. He made hundreds of one-reelers 1908–13, in which he pioneered the techniques of masking, fade-out, flashback, crosscut, close-up, and long shot. After much experimentation with photography and new techniques, he directed *The Birth of a Nation* (1915), about the aftermath of the Civil War, later criticized as degrading to African-Americans.

griffon Bruxelloise breed of terrierlike toy dog originally bred in Belgium. It weighs up to 4.5 kg/10 lb and has a harsh and wiry coat that is red or black in colour. The smooth-haired form of the breed is called the **petit Brabançon**.

Grimm brothers Jakob (Ludwig Karl) (1785–1863) and Wilhelm (1786–1859), philologists and collectors of German fairy tales such as 'Hansel and Gretel' and 'Rumpelstiltskin'. Joint compilers of an exhaustive dictionary of German, they saw the study of language and the collecting of folk tales as strands in a single enterprise.

Gris, Juan (1887–1927) adopted name of José Victoriano Gonzalez, Spanish painter, one of the earliest cubists. He developed a distinctive geometrical style, often strongly coloured. He experimented with paper collage and made designs for Serge Diaghilev's Ballets Russes (1922–23).

Gromyko, Andrei Andreyevich (1909–1989) President of the USSR 1985–88. As ambassador to the USA from 1943, he took part in the Tehran, Yalta, and Potsdam conferences; as United Nations representative 1946–49, he exercised the Soviet veto 26 times. He was foreign minister 1957–85. It was Gromyko who formally nominated Mikhail Gorbachev as Communist Party leader in 1985.

Groningen most northerly province of the Netherlands, located on the Ems estuary and also including two of the innermost West Friesian Islands (both uninhabited), bounded to the north by the North Sea, to the south by the province of Drenthe, to the east by Germany, and to the west by Friesland; area 2,350 sq km/907 sq mi; population (2003 est) 574,700. The capital is Groningen; other major towns are Hoogezand-Sappemeer, Stadskanaal, Veendam, Delfzijl, and Winschoten. The chief industries are natural gas, textiles, sugar refining, shipbuilding, and papermaking. Agriculture centres on arable and livestock farming, dairy produce, tobacco, and fishing.

Gropius, Walter Adolf (1883–1969) German architect, in the USA from 1937. He was an early exponent of the *international style, defined by glass curtain walls, cubic blocks, and unsupported corners. A founder director of the *Bauhaus school in Weimar 1919–28, he advocated teamwork in design and artistic standards in industrial production. He was responsible for the new Bauhaus premises in Dessau 1925–26.

Gross, David Jonathon (1941–) US physicist. With US physicists Hugh Politzer and Frank Wilczek, Gross shared the Nobel Prize for Physics in 2004 for his contribution to the theoretical explanation of how the strong nuclear force holds quark subatomic particles together.

gross domestic product (GDP) value of all final goods and services produced within a country within a given time period, usually one year. GDP thus includes the production of foreign-owned firms within the country, but excludes the income from domestically-owned firms located abroad. Intermediate goods, such as plastic and steel, are not included, in order to avoid double counting, because they will be turned into final goods. Household goods are included because they are

intended for consumption or use rather than to be turned into other goods. GDP changes as total output and/or prices change. A rise in total output means that an economy is growing; two consecutive quarters of decline in total output is the technical definition of recession. Optimal economic growth with full employment is considered to be in the range between 2% and 2.5%. GDP needs to be adjusted to account for inflation because it is affected by changes in prices as well as by changes in output. Inflation-adjusted GDP, known as **real GDP**, is calculated by dividing nominal GDP by the appropriate price index. See also *gross national product (GNP).

gross national product (GNP) measure of a country's total economic activity, or the wealth of the country. GNP is usually assessed quarterly or yearly, and is defined as the total value of all goods and services produced by firms owned by the country concerned. It is measured as the *gross domestic product plus income earned by domestic residents from foreign investments, minus income earned during the same period by foreign investors in the country's domestic market. GNP does not allow for inflation or for the overall value of production. It is an important indicator of an economy's strength.

Grosz, George (1893–1959) German-born US expressionist painter and graphic artist. He was a founder of the Berlin Dada group in 1918, and excelled in savage satirical drawings criticizing the government and the military establishment. After numerous prosecutions, he fled his native Berlin in 1932 and went to the USA.

Grotius, Hugo (1583–1645) Dutch **Huig de Groot**, Dutch jurist and politician. His book *De Jure Belli et Pacis/On the Law of War and Peace* (1625) is the foundation of international law.

groundnut another name for *peanut.

groundwater water present underground in porous rock strata and soils; it emerges at the surface as springs and streams. The groundwater's upper level is called the *water table. Rock strata that are filled with groundwater that can be extracted are called **aquifers**. Aquifers must be both porous (filled with holes) and permeable (full of holes that are interconnected so that the water is able to flow).

group in chemistry, a vertical column of elements in the *periodic table. Elements in a group have similar physical and chemical properties; for example, the group I elements (the *alkali metals: lithium, sodium, potassium, rubidium, caesium, and francium) are all highly reactive metals that form univalent ions. There is a gradation of properties down any group: in group I, melting and boiling points decrease, and density and reactivity increase.

grouper any of several species of large sea perch (spiny-finned fish), found in warm waters. Some species grow to 2 m/6.5 ft long, and can weigh 300 kg/660 lbs. (Family Serranidae.)

Group of Eight (G8) formerly Group of Seven (G7) 1975–98, the eight leading industrial nations of the world: the USA, Japan, Germany, France, the UK, Italy, Canada, and Russia, which account for more than three-fifths of global GDP. Founded as the Group of Seven (G7) in 1975, without Russia, the heads of government have met once a year to discuss economic and, increasingly, political matters. Russia attended the annual summits from 1991, and became a full member in 1998, when the name of the organization was changed. Summits are also attended by the president of the European Commission.

grouse plump fowl-like game bird belonging to a subfamily of the pheasant family, which also includes the ptarmigan, capercaillie, and prairie chicken. Grouse are native to North America and northern Europe. They spend most of their time on the ground. During the mating season the males undertake elaborate courtship displays in small individual territories (*leks). (Subfamily Tetraonidae, family Phasianidae, order Galliformes.)

Groznyy or **Grozny** (Russian 'terrible', 'awesome') capital of *Chechnya and of the former Soviet republic of Checheno-Ingush; population (1996) 388,000. Situated on the Sunzha River, a tributary of the Terek, it is the biggest city of the Caucasian foothills. From the late 19th century, it became a major oil centre with pipelines to the Caspian Sea at Makhachkala, the Black Sea at Tuapse, and Trudovaya (near Gorlovka in the Donets Basin). Chemical and engineering industries are also located here.

Grünewald, Matthias (c. 1475–1528) also known as **Mathis Gothardt-Neithardt**, German painter, architect, and engineer. His altarpiece at Isenheim, southern Alsace, (1515, Unterlinden Museum, Colmar, France), with its grotesquely tortured figure of Jesus and its radiant *Resurrection*, is his most important work.

g-scale scale for measuring force by comparing it with the force due to *gravity (g), often called *g-force.

Guadalajara industrial city (textiles, glass, soap, pottery), capital of Jalisco state, western Mexico; population (2000 est) 1,646,200; metropolitan area (2000 est) 3,677,500. The second largest city in Mexico, 535 km/332 mi northwest of Mexico City, Guadalajara is a key communications centre.

Guadalcanal Island largest of the Solomon Islands; area 5,302 sq km/2,047 sq mi; population (1996 est) 59,100. The principal population centres are Honiara, capital of the Solomon Islands, Aola, and Lunga, all on the north coast. Gold, copra, and rubber are produced. The population is Melanesian (or Papuasian). In 1942, during World War II, it was the scene of a battle for control of the area that was won by US forces after six months of fighting.

Guadeloupe group of islands in the Leeward Islands, West Indies (nine of which are inhabited), an overseas *département* of France; area 1,705 sq km/658 sq mi; population (1999 est) 422,500. The main islands are Basse-Terre and Grande-Terre. The chief town and seat of government is Basse-Terre; the largest town is Pointe-à-Pitre on the island of Grande-Terre. Agriculture was long the basis of the economy, though tourism (mostly from the USA) has become the main earner of foreign exchange since the 1980s. Sugar cane and bananas are the major crops, though with the Single European Act of 1987 the export of these crops to European markets became more difficult and resulted in considerable agricultural unemployment on the islands. Industries include cement, rum distilling, and sugar refining.

Guam largest and southernmost of the Mariana Islands in the West Pacific, an unincorporated territory of the USA; it lies between the Philippine Sea and the southwest Pacific Ocean, some 1,540 km/960 mi north of the Equator; length 50 km/30 mi, width 6–19 km/ 4–12 mi; area 549 sq km/212 sq mi; population (2001 est) 158,000. The main towns are Hagåtna (capital), Apra (port), and Tamuning. Tourism is important to the island's economy, as are oil refining, textile manufacture, fishing, and the cultivation of coconuts, sugar cane, and tropical fruits and vegetables, especially sweet potatoes. Guam is the site of major US army, air, and naval bases, and expenditure by the US government on these facilities is also a mainstay of the economy. The land is largely limestone plateau in the north and volcanic in the south, with much jungle.

guanaco hoofed ruminant (cud-chewing) mammal belonging to the camel family, found in South America on the pampas and mountain plateaux. It grows up to 1.2 m/4 ft at the shoulder, with the head and body measuring about 1.5 m/5 ft in length. It is sandy brown in colour, with a blackish face, and has fine wool. It lives in small herds and is the ancestor of the domestic *llama and *alpaca. It is also related to the other wild member of the camel family, the *vicuña. (Species *Lama guanacoe*, family Camelidae.)

Guangdong or **Kwangtung** province of south China, bounded to the north by Hunan and Jiangxi; to the northeast by Fujian; to the south by the South China Sea, Hong Kong (since 1997 an enclave of Guangdong province), Macau, and the island province of Hainan; and to the west by Guangxi Zhuang Autonomous Region; area 197,000 sq km/76,062 sq mi; population (2000 est) 86,420,000. The capital is Guangzhou (previously known as Canton); other major cities are Maoming, Shantou, Shenzhen, and Zhanjiang. The main industries are minerals, electronics, household appliances, and textiles; agriculture is based on rice, sugar, fruit, tobacco, and fish.

Guangxi Zhuang Autonomous Region or **Guangxi** or **Kwangsi Chuang Autonomous Region** autonomous region in south China, bounded to the north by Guizhou, to the northeast by Hunan, to the east by Guangdong, to the south by the Gulf of Tongking, to the southwest by Vietnam, and to the west by Yunnan; area 236,700 sq km/91,400 sq mi; population (2000 est) 44,890,000 (including the Zhuang people, related to the Thai, who form China's largest ethnic minority). The capital is Nanning; other main cities are Guilin, Liuzhou, and Wuzhou. Tourism is an important part of the economy, and the main industries are sugar-refining, metallurgy, fishing (in the Gulf of Tongking), and food- and timber-processing. Because of the tropical climate, the cultivation of crops is possible throughout the year, with rice, maize, barley, millet, sugar cane, tropical fruits, and tea being the main crops.

Guangzhou or **Kwangchow** or English **Canton** capital of Guangdong province, south China; population (1999 est) 3,306,200. On the Zhu River, Guangzhou is one of China's major ports, handling some 15% of the country's foreign trade. Industries include steel, shipbuilding, engineering, and the manufacture of automobiles, electronic goods, chemicals, fertilizers, cement, and textiles.

guano dried excrement of fish-eating birds that builds up under nesting sites. It is a rich source of nitrogen and phosphorus, and is widely collected for use as fertilizer. Some 80% comes from the sea cliffs of Peru.

Guanyin in Chinese Buddhism, the goddess of mercy. In Japan she is **Kannon** or Kwannon, an attendant of the Amida Buddha (Amitabha). Her origins were in India as the male bodhisattva Avalokitesvara.

guarana Brazilian woody climbing plant. A drink with a high caffeine content is made from its roasted seeds, and it is the source of the drug known as zoom in the USA. Starch, gum, and several oils are extracted from it for commercial use. (*Paullinia cupana*, family Sapindaceae.)

Guaraní member of an American Indian people who formerly inhabited the area that is now Paraguay, southern Brazil, and Bolivia. The Guaraní live mainly in reserves; few retain the traditional ways of hunting in the tropical forest, cultivation, and ritual warfare. About 1 million speak Guaraní, a member of the Tupian language group.

Guatemala

National name: *República de Guatemala/ Republic of Guatemala*

Area: 108,889 sq km/42,042 sq mi
Capital: Guatemala City
Major towns/cities: Quezaltenango, Escuintla, Puerto Barrios (naval base), Mixco, Villa Nueva, Chinautla
Physical features: mountainous; narrow coastal plains; limestone tropical plateau in north; frequent earthquakes
Head of state and government: Oscar Berger Perdomo from 2004
Political system: liberal democracy
Political executive: limited presidency
Political parties: Guatemalan Christian Democratic Party (PDCG), Christian, left of centre; Centre Party (UCN), centrist; Revolutionary Party (PR), radical; Movement of National Liberation (MLN), extreme right wing; Democratic Institutional Party (PID), moderate conservative; Solidarity and Action Movement (MAS), right of centre; Guatemalan Republican Front (FRG), right wing; National Advancement Party (PAN), right of centre; Social Democratic Party (PSD), right of centre
Currency: quetzal

GNI per capita (PPP): (US$) 3,880 (2002 est)
Exports: coffee, bananas, sugar, oil, cardamoms, shellfish, tobacco. Principal market: USA 55.3% (2001)
Population: 12,347,000 (2003 est)
Language: Spanish (official), 22 Mayan languages (45%)
Religion: Roman Catholic 70%, Protestant 10%, traditional Mayan
Life expectancy: 63 (men); 69 (women) (2000–05)
Chronology
c. **AD 250–900:** Part of culturally advanced Maya civilization.
1524: Conquered by the Spanish adventurer Pedro de Alvarado and became a Spanish colony.
1821: Independence achieved from Spain, joining Mexico initially.
1823: Became part of United Provinces (Federation) of Central America, also embracing Costa Rica, El Salvador, Honduras, and Nicaragua.
1839: Achieved full independence.
1844–65: Rafael Carrera held power as president.
1873–85: The country was modernized on liberal lines by President Justo Rufino Barrios, the army was built up, and coffee growing introduced.
1944: Juan José Arevalo became president, ending a period of rule by dictators. Socialist programme of reform instituted by Arevalo, including establishing a social security system and redistributing land expropriated from large estates to landless peasants.
1954: Col Carlos Castillo Armas became president in a US-backed coup, after United Fruit Company plantations had been nationalized. Land reform halted.
1966: Civilian rule was restored.
1970s: More than 50,000 died in a spate of political violence as the military regime sought to liquidate left-wing dissidents.
1970: The military were back in power.
1976: An earthquake killed 27,000 and left more than 1 million homeless.
1981: Growth of an antigovernment guerrilla movement. Death squads and soldiers killed an estimated 11,000 civilians during the year.
1985: A new constitution was adopted; PDCG won the congressional elections.
1989: Over 100,000 people were killed, and 40,000 reported missing, since 1980.
1991: Diplomatic relations established with Belize, which Guatemala had long claimed.
1994: Peace talks were held with Guatemalan Revolutionary National Unity (URNG) rebels. Right-wing parties secured a majority in congress after elections.
1995: The government was criticized by USA and United Nations for widespread human-rights abuses. There was a ceasefire by rebels, the first in 30 years.
1996: A peace agreement was signed which ended the 36-year war.
2000: Alfonso Portillo, a right-wing candidate, became president. Guatemala signed a free-trade agreement with Mexico. The US dollar was accepted as a second currency.
2003: Conservative, pro-business candidate Oscar Berger was narrowly elected president in a run-off ballot against Alvaro Colom representing a centre-left coalition.

2004: Former military ruler General Efrain Rios Montt was placed under house arrest based on charges of genocide during the civil war.

Guatemala City capital and largest city of Guatemala, situated in the **Guatemalan Highlands** at an altitude of 1,500 m/4,920 ft on a plateau in the Sierra Madre mountains; population (2002 est) 942,300. A group of volcanoes overlooks the city: Acatenango (3,976 m/13,044 ft), Fuego (3,763 m/12,346 ft), and Agua (3,760 m/12,336 ft). Industries include textiles, tyres, silverware, footwear, and cement. Half of the industrial output of Guatemala emanates from Guatemala City. It was founded in 1776 as Guatemala's third capital after earthquakes destroyed the earlier capitals of Antigua and Cuidad Vieja in 1773 and 1542 respectively. It was itself severely damaged by subsequent earthquakes in 1917–18 and 1976.

guava tropical American tree belonging to the myrtle family; the astringent yellow pear-shaped fruit is used to make guava jelly, or it can be stewed or canned. It has a high vitamin C content. (*Psidium guajava*, family Myrtaceae.)

gudgeon any of an Old World group of freshwater fishes of the carp family, especially the species *G. gobio* found in Europe and northern Asia on the gravel bottoms of streams. It is olive-brown, spotted with black, and up to 20 cm/8 in long, with a distinctive barbel (sensory bristle, or 'whisker') at each side of the mouth. (Genus *Gobio*, family Cyprinidae.)

guelder rose *or* **snowball tree** cultivated shrub or small tree, native to Europe and North Africa, with round clusters of white flowers which are followed by shiny red berries. (*Viburnum opulus*, family Caprifoliaceae.)

Guelph and Ghibelline rival parties in medieval Germany and Italy, which supported the papal party and the Holy Roman emperors respectively.

Guernica large oil painting (3.5 m x 7.8 m/11 ft 5 in x 25 ft 6 in) by Pablo Picasso as a mural for the Spanish pavilion at the Paris Exposition Universelle in 1937 (now in the Museo Nacional Centro de Arte Reina Sofía, Madrid), inspired by the bombing of Guernica, the seat of the Basque parliament during the Spanish Civil War. The painting, executed entirely in black, white, and grey, was the culmination of years of experimentation. It has since become a symbol of the senseless destruction of war.

Guernsey second-largest of the *Channel Islands; area 63 sq km/24.3 sq mi; population (2001 est) 59,800. The capital is St Peter Port. Products include electronics, tomatoes, flowers, and butterflies; and since 1975 it has been a major financial centre. Guernsey cattle, which are a distinctive pale fawn colour and give rich, creamy milk, originated here.

guerrilla (Spanish 'little war') irregular soldier fighting in a small, unofficial unit, typically against an established or occupying power, and engaging in sabotage, ambush, and the like, rather than pitched battles against an opposing army. Guerrilla tactics have been used both by resistance armies in wartime (for example, the Vietnam War) and in peacetime by national liberation groups and militant political extremists (for example, the Tamil Tigers).

Guevara, Che (Ernesto) (1928–1967) Latin American revolutionary. He was born in Resario,

Argentina, and trained there as a doctor, but left his homeland in 1953 because of his opposition to the right-wing president Juan Perón. In effecting the Cuban revolution of 1959 against the Cuban dictator Fulgencio Batista, he was second only to Castro and Castro's brother Raúl. Between 1961 and 1965, he served as Cuba's minister of industry. In 1965 he went to the Congo to fight against white mercenaries, and then to Bolivia, where he was killed in an unsuccessful attempt to lead a peasant rising near Vallegrande. He was an orthodox Marxist and renowned for his guerrilla techniques.

guild *or* **gild** medieval association, particularly of artisans or merchants, formed for mutual aid and protection and the pursuit of a common purpose, whether religious or economic. Guilds became politically powerful in Europe but after the 16th century their position was undermined by the growth of *capitalism.

guillemot any of several diving seabirds belonging to the auk family that breed on rocky North Atlantic and Pacific coasts. The **common guillemot** (*U. aalge*) has a long straight beak and short tail and wings; the feet are three-toed and webbed, the feathers are sooty brown and white. It breeds in large colonies on sea cliffs. The **black guillemot** (*C. grylle*) of northern coasts is much smaller and mostly black in summer, with orange legs when breeding. Guillemots build no nest, but lay one large, almost conical egg. (Genera *Uria* and *Cepphus*, family Alcidae, order Charadriiformes.)

guillotine beheading device consisting of a metal blade that descends between two posts. It was common in the Middle Ages and was introduced to France in 1791 by physician Joseph Ignace Guillotin (1738–1814), who recommended the use of the guillotine for all sentences of death. It was subsequently used for executions during the French Revolution. It is still in use in some countries.

guillotine in politics, a device used by UK governments in which the time allowed for debating a bill in the House of Commons is restricted so as to ensure its speedy passage to receiving the royal assent (that is, to becoming law). The tactic of guillotining was introduced during the 1880s to overcome attempts by Irish members of Parliament to obstruct the passing of legislation. The guillotine is also used as a parliamentary process in France.

Guinea

National name: *République de Guinée/Republic of Guinea*

Area: 245,857 sq km/94,925 sq mi

Capital: Conakry

Major towns/cities: Labé, Nzérékoré, Kankan, Kindia, Mamou, Siguiri

Physical features: flat coastal plain with mountainous interior; sources of rivers Niger, Gambia, and Senegal; forest in southeast; Fouta Djallon, area of sandstone plateaux, cut by deep valleys

Head of state: Lansana Conté from 1984

Head of government: Cellou Dalein Diallo from 2004

Political system: emergent democracy

Political executive: limited presidency

Political parties: Party of Unity and Progress (PUP), centrist; Rally of the Guinean People (RPG), left of centre; Union of the New Republic (UNR), left of centre; Party for Renewal and Progress (PRP), left of centre

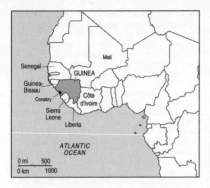

Currency: Guinean franc
GNI per capita (PPP): (US$) 1,980 (2002 est)
Exports: bauxite, aluminium, gold, diamonds, coffee.
Principal market: Belgium 16.4% (2001)
Population: 8,480,000 (2003 est)
Language: French (official), Susu, Pular (Fulfude),
Malinke, and other African languages
Religion: Muslim 85%, Christian 6%, animist
Life expectancy: 49 (men); 50 (women) (2000–05)
Chronology
c. **AD 900:** The Susi people, a community related to the
Malinke, immigrated from the northeast, pushing the
indigenous Baga towards the Atlantic coast.
13th century: Susi kingdoms established, extending
their influence to the coast; northeast Guinea was part
of Muslim Mali Empire, centred to northeast.
mid-15th century: Portuguese traders visited the coast
and later developed trade in slaves and ivory.
1849: French protectorate established over coastal
region around Nunez River, which was administered
with Senegal.
1890: Separate Rivières du Sud colony formed.
1895: Renamed French Guinea, the colony became part
of French West Africa.
1946: French Guinea became an overseas territory of
France.
1958: Full independence from France achieved as
Guinea, after referendum, rejected remaining within
French Community; Sékou Touré of the Democratic
Party of Guinea (PDG) elected president.
1960s and 1970s: Touré established socialist one-party
state, leading to deterioration in economy as 200,000
fled abroad.
1979: Strong opposition to Touré's rigid Marxist
policies forced him to accept a return to mixed
economy and legalize private enterprise.
1984: Touré died. A bloodless military coup brought
Col Lansana Conté to power; the PDG was outlawed
and political prisoners released; and there were market-
centred economic reforms.
1991: Antigovernment general strike and mass protests.
1992: The constitution was amended to allow for
multiparty politics.
1993: Conté was narrowly re-elected in the first direct
presidential election.
1998–99: President Conté was re-elected, and named
his prime minister as Lamine Sidime.

2000–01: From October 2000, civil wars in Liberia and
Sierra Leone began to spill over into Guinea, creating
hundreds of thousands of refugees.
2003: President Conté secured a landslide presidential
election victory with over 95% of the vote in a poll
boycotted by most opposition figures.

Guinea-Bissau

formerly **Portuguese Guinea** (until 1974)
National name: *República da Guiné-Bissau/
Republic of Guinea-Bissau*

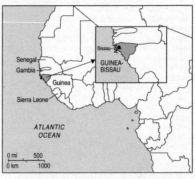

Area: 36,125 sq km/13,947 sq mi
Capital: Bissau (and chief port)
Major towns/cities: Barfatá, Bissorã, Bolama, Gabú,
Bubaque, Cacheu, Catio, Farim
Physical features: flat coastal plain rising to savannah
in east
Head of state: Henrique Rosa from 2004
Head of government: Carlos Gomes, Jr, from 2004
Political system: military
Political executive: military
Political parties: African Party for the Independence
of Portuguese Guinea and Cape Verde (PAIGC),
nationalist socialist; Party for Social Renovation (PRS),
left of centre; Guinea-Bissau Resistance–Barfata
Movement (PRGB-MB), centrist
Currency: Guinean peso
GNI per capita (PPP): (US$) 750 (2002 est)
Exports: cashew nuts, palm kernels, groundnuts, fish and
shrimp, timber. Principal market: Uruguay 40.7% (2001)
Population: 1,493,000 (2003 est)
Language: Portuguese (official), Crioulo (a Cape
Verdean dialect of Portuguese), African languages
Religion: animist 58%, Muslim 40%, Christian 5%
(mainly Roman Catholic)
Life expectancy: 44 (men); 47 (women) (2000–05)
Chronology
10th century: Known as Gabu, became a tributary
kingdom of the Mali Empire to northeast.
1446: Portuguese arrived, establishing nominal control
over coastal areas and capturing slaves to send to Cape
Verde.
1546: Gabu kingdom became independent of Mali and
survived until 1867.
1879: Portugal, which had formerly administered the
area with Cape Verde islands, created the separate
colony of Portuguese Guinea.

by 1915: The interior had been subjugated by the Portuguese.

1956: African Party for the Independence of Portuguese Guinea and Cape Verde (PAIGC) formed to campaign for independence from Portugal.

1961: The PAIGC began to wage a guerrilla campaign against Portuguese rule.

1973: Independence was declared in the two-thirds of the country that had fallen under the control of the PAIGC; heavy losses were sustained by Portuguese troops who tried to put down the uprising.

1974: Independence separately from Cape Verde accepted by Portugal, with Luiz Cabral (PAIGC) president.

1981: PAIGC was confirmed as the only legal party, with João Vieira as its secretary general; Cape Verde decided not to form a union.

1984: A new constitution made Vieira head of both government and state.

1991: Other parties were legalized in response to public pressure.

1994: PAIGC secured a clear assembly majority and Vieira narrowly won the first multiparty presidential elections.

1999: President Vieira was ousted by the army.

2000: Kumba Yalla became president, and Caetano N'Tchama became prime minister.

2001: Former foreign minister Faustino Imbali replaced Caetano N'Tchama as prime minister.

2003: President Yalla was overthrown in a bloodless military coup led by General Verissimo Correia Seabra, who assumed interim control pending elections.

guinea fowl any of a group of chickenlike African birds, including the **helmet guinea fowl** (*Numida meleagris*), which has a horny growth on the head, white-spotted feathers, and fleshy cheek wattles (loose folds of skin). It is the ancestor of the domestic guinea fowl. Guinea fowl are mostly gregarious ground-feeders, eating insects, leaves, and snails; at night they roost in trees. (Family Numididae, order Galliformes.)

guinea pig species of *cavy, a type of rodent.

Guinevere Welsh **Gwenhwyfar**, in British legend, the wife of King Arthur. Her adulterous love affair with the knight *Lancelot of the Lake led ultimately to Arthur's death.

Guinness, Alec (1914–2000) English actor of stage and screen. A versatile performer, he made early appearances in Ealing comedies, notably playing eight parts in *Kind Hearts and Coronets* (1949). In 1957 he played Colonel Nicholson in *The Bridge on the River Kwai*, for which he won awards including an Academy Award, a New York Critics' award, and a Golden Globe. Other films include *The Lavender Hill Mob* (1952), *The Ladykillers* (1955), and *Star Wars* (1977). He was made a CBE in 1955, knighted in 1959, and made a CH (Companion of Honour) in 1994.

guitar plucked, fretted string instrument. It may be called the classical guitar, the Spanish guitar (because of its origins), or the acoustic guitar (to differentiate it from the electric guitar). The fingerboard has frets (strips of metal showing where to place the finger to obtain different notes), and the 6 or 12 strings are plucked or strummed with the fingers or a plectrum. The strings are tuned to E2, A3, D3, G3, B4, and E4.

The Hawaiian guitar is laid across the player's lap, and uses a metal bar to produce a distinctive gliding tone. The solid-bodied electric guitar, was developed in the 1950s by Les Paul and Leo Fender. It mixes and amplifies vibrations from electromagnetic pickups (microphones which 'pick up' the vibration of the strings and convert them to electrical impulses) at different points to produce a range of tone qualities.

Guizhou *or* **Kweichow** province of south China, consisting mainly of high plateaus and bounded to the north by Sichuan, to the east by Hunan, to the south by Guangxi Zhuang Autonomous Region, and to the west by Yunnan; area 174,000 sq km/67,000 sq mi; population (2000 est) 35,250,000 (ethnic minorities comprise about 25% of the population). The capital is Guiyang; other main cities are Zunyi, Anshun, and Duyun. Chief industries include the mining of coal, bauxite, mercury, and manganese, and the manufacture of machinery, foodstuffs, and timber products; agriculture, mainly in the river valleys and terraced slopes, is based on the cultivation of rice, maize, tobacco, tea, and rapeseed.

Gujarat *or* **Gujerat** state of west India, formed from north and west Bombay state in 1960; bordered to the north by Pakistan and Rajasthan, with Madhya Pradesh and Maharashtra to the east and southeast; area 195,984 sq km/75,670 sq mi; population (2001 est) 50,597,000 (70% Hindu). The capital is Gandhinagar (founded in 1961); other major towns are *Ahmadabad and Vadodara; the main port is Kandla. The state is heavily industrialized, with the main industries being petrochemicals, oil (from Kalol, refined at Koyali near Baroda), gas, textiles, coal, limestone, pharmaceuticals, soda ash, electrical engineering, machine tools, cement, fertilizers, and dairy products. Most of the population are dependent on agriculture, which is based on wheat, millet, cotton, rice, maize, tobacco, and groundnuts, but cultivation is limited by the seasonality of rainfall in the south and aridity in the north.

Gujarati inhabitants of Gujarat on the northwest coast of India. The Gujaratis number approximately 30 million and speak their own Indo-European language, Gujarati, which has a long literary tradition. They are predominantly Hindu (90%), with Muslim (8%) and Jain (2%) minorities.

Gujarati language member of the Indo-Iranian branch of the Indo-European language family, spoken in and around the state of Gujarat in western India. It is written in its own script, a variant of the Devanagari script used for Sanskrit and Hindi.

gulag Russian term for the system of prisons and labour camps used to silence dissidents and opponents of the Soviet regime.

Gulf States oil-rich countries sharing the coastline of the *Gulf (Bahrain, Iran, Iraq, Kuwait, Oman, Qatar, Saudi Arabia, and the United Arab Emirates). In the USA, the term refers to those states bordering the Gulf of Mexico (Alabama, Florida, Louisiana, Mississippi, and Texas).

Gulf Stream warm ocean *current that flows north from the warm waters of the Gulf of Mexico along the east coast of America, from which it is separated by a channel of cold water originating in the southerly Labrador current. Off Newfoundland, part of the current is diverted east across the Atlantic, where it is known as the **North Atlantic Drift**, dividing to flow north and south, and warming what would otherwise be a colder climate in the British Isles and northwest Europe.

Gulf, the *or* **Arabian Gulf** *or* **Persian Gulf** large shallow inlet of the Arabian Sea; area 233,000 sq km/90,000 sq mi. It divides the Arabian peninsula from Iran and is linked by the Strait of Hormuz and the Gulf of Oman to the Arabian Sea. Oilfields producing about one-third of the world's oil surround it in the Gulf States of Bahrain, Iran, Iraq, Kuwait, Oman, Qatar, Saudi Arabia, and the United Arab Emirates.

Gulf War war 16 January–28 February 1991 between Iraq and a coalition of 28 nations led by the USA. The invasion and annexation of Kuwait by Iraq on 2 August 1990 provoked a build-up of US troops in Saudi Arabia, eventually totalling over 500,000. The UK subsequently deployed 42,000 troops, France 15,000, Egypt 20,000, and other nations smaller contingents. An air offensive lasting six weeks, in which 'smart' weapons came of age, destroyed about one-third of Iraqi equipment and inflicted massive casualties. A 100-hour ground war followed, which effectively destroyed the remnants of the 500,000-strong Iraqi army in or near Kuwait.

gull any of a group of seabirds that are usually 25–75 cm/10–30 in long, white with grey or black on the back and wings, and have large beaks. Immature birds are normally a mottled brown colour. Gulls are sociable, noisy birds and they breed in colonies. (Genus principally *Larus*, subfamily Larinae, family Laridae, order Charadriiformes.)

gum in botany, complex polysaccharides (carbohydrates) formed by many plants and trees, particularly by those from dry regions. They form four main groups: plant exudates (gum arabic); marine plant extracts (agar); seed extracts; and fruit and vegetable extracts. Some are made synthetically.

gun any kind of firearm or any instrument consisting of a metal tube from which a projectile is discharged; see also *artillery, *machine gun, and *small arms.

gunpowder *or* **black powder** oldest known explosive, a mixture of 75% potassium nitrate (saltpetre), 15% charcoal, and 10% sulphur. Sulphur ignites at a low temperature, charcoal burns readily, and the potassium nitrate provides oxygen for the explosion. As gunpowder produces lots of smoke and burns quite slowly, it has progressively been replaced since the late 19th century by high explosives, although it is still widely used for quarry blasting, fuses, and fireworks. Gunpowder has high *activation energy; a gun based on gunpowder alone requires igniting by a flint or a match.

Gunpowder Plot in British history, the Catholic conspiracy to blow up James I and his parliament on 5 November 1605. It was discovered through an anonymous letter. Guy *Fawkes was found in the cellar beneath the Palace of Westminster, ready to fire a store of explosives. Several of the conspirators were killed as they fled, and Fawkes and seven others were captured and executed.

Guomindang *or* **Kuomintang** Chinese National People's Party formed in 1912 after the overthrow of the Manchu Empire, and led by *Sun Zhong Shan (Sun Yat-sen). The Guomindang was an amalgamation

of small political groups, including Sun's *Hsin Chung Hui* ('New China Party'), founded in 1894. During the *Chinese revolution (1927–49) the right wing, led by *Jiang Jie Shi, was in conflict with the left, led by *Mao Zedong (though the sides united during the Japanese invasion of 1937–45). Zedong emerged victorious in 1949. Guomindang survived as the dominant political party of Taiwan (until 2000), where it is still spelled **Kuomintang**. However, in recent years there have been splits between mainland-born hardliners and moderates, led by *Lee Teng-hui, president of Taiwan 1988–2000 and Kuomintang leader 1988–2001.

Gupta dynasty Indian hereditary rulers that reunified and ruled over much of northern and central India 320–550. The dynasty's stronghold lay in the Magadha region of the middle Ganges valley, with the capital Pataliputra. Gupta influence was extended through military conquest east, west, and south by Chandragupta I, Chandragupta II, and Samudragupta. Hun raids in the northwest from the 6th century undermined the Guptas' decentralized administrative structure.

gurdwara ('the door of the guru' or 'God's house') Sikh place of worship and meeting. As well as a room housing the *Guru Granth Sahib*, the holy book and focus for worship, the gurdwara contains the langar, a kitchen and eating area for the communal meal, where male and female, Sikh and non-Sikh, may eat together as equals.

gurnard any of a group of coastal fish that creep along the sea bottom with the help of three fingerlike appendages detached from the pectoral fins. Gurnards are both tropical and temperate zone fish. (Genus *Trigla*, family Trigilidae.)

guru Hindi **guru**, Hindu or Sikh leader, or religious teacher.

Guru Granth Sahib the holy book of Sikhism, a collection of nearly 6,000 hymns by the first five and the ninth Sikh gurus, but also including the writings of some Hindus and Muslims. It is regarded as a living guru and treated with the respect that this implies.

Gustavus (*or* **Gustaf)** six kings of Sweden, including: **Gustavus Adolphus (1594–1632)** also known as **Gustavus II** or **Gustaf II**, King of Sweden from 1611, when he succeeded his father Charles IX. He waged successful wars with Denmark, Russia, and Poland, and in the *Thirty Years' War became a champion of the Protestant cause. Landing in Germany 1630, he defeated the German general Wallenstein at Lützen, southwest of Leipzig 6 November 1632, but was killed in the battle. He was known as the 'Lion of the North'. **Gustavus Vasa (1496–1560)** also known as **Gustavus I** or **Gustaf I**, King of Sweden from 1523, when he was elected after leading the Swedish revolt against Danish rule. He united and pacified the country and established Lutheranism as the state religion.

gut *or* **alimentary canal** in the *digestive system, the part of an animal responsible for processing food and preparing it for entry into the blood.

Gutenberg, Johannes (c. 1398–1468) born Johann Gensfleisch zur Laden zum Gutenberg, German printer, the inventor of European printing from movable metal type (although Laurens Janszoon Coster has a rival claim).

Guyana
National name: *Cooperative Republic of Guyana*

Area: 214,969 sq km/82,999 sq mi
Capital: Georgetown (and chief port)
Major towns/cities: Linden, New Amsterdam, Bartica, Corriverton
Major ports: New Amsterdam
Physical features: coastal plain rises into rolling highlands with savannah in south; mostly tropical rainforest; Mount Roraima; Kaietur National Park, including Kaietur Falls on the Potaro (tributary of Essequibo) 250 m/821 ft
Head of state: Bharrat Jagdeo from 1999
Head of government: Samuel Hinds from 1999
Political system: liberal democracy
Political executive: limited presidency
Political parties: People's National Congress (PNC), Afro-Guyanan, nationalist socialist; People's Progressive Party (PPP), Indian-based, left wing
Currency: Guyanese dollar
GNI per capita (PPP): (US$) 3,780 (2002 est)
Exports: sugar, gold, bauxite, alumina, rice, rum, timber, molasses, shrimp. Principal market: USA 22.5% (2000)
Population: 765,000 (2003 est)
Language: English (official), Hindi, American Indian languages
Religion: Christian 57%, Hindu 34%, Sunni Muslim 9%
Life expectancy: 60 (men); 66 (women) (2000–05)
Chronology
1498: The explorer Christopher Columbus sighted Guyana, whose name, 'land of many waters', was derived from a local American Indian word.
c. **1620:** Settled by Dutch West India Company, who established armed bases and brought in slaves from Africa.
1814: After a period of French rule, Britain occupied Guyana during the Napoleonic Wars and purchased Demerara, Berbice, and Essequibo.
1831: Became British colony under name of British Guiana.
1834: Slavery was abolished, resulting in an influx of indentured labourers from India and China to work on sugar plantations.

1860: Settlement of the Rupununi Savannah commenced.
1860s: Gold was discovered.
1899: International arbitration tribunal found in favour of British Guiana in a long-running dispute with Venezuela over lands west of Essequibo River.
1953: Assembly elections won by left-wing People's Progressive Party (PPP), drawing most support from the Indian community; Britain suspended constitution and installed interim administration, fearing communist takeover.
1961: Internal self-government granted; Cheddi Jagan (PPP) became prime minister.
1964: Racial violence between the Asian- and African-descended communities.
1966: Independence achieved from Britain as Guyana, with PNC leader Forbes Burnham as prime minister.
1970: Guyana became a republic within the Commonwealth, with Raymond Arthur Chung as president; Burnham remained as prime minister.
1980: Burnham became the first executive president under the new constitution, which ended the three-year boycott of parliament by the PPP.
1992: PPP had a decisive victory in the first completely free assembly elections for 20 years; a privatization programme was launched.
1997: Cheddi Jagan died. His wife, Janet Jagan, was elected president.
1998: Violent antigovernment protests. Government and opposition agreed to an independent audit of elections.
1999: A constitutional reform commission was appointed. Bharrat Jagdeo replaced Janet Jagan as president.
2001: The 1997 elections were declared void, new elections were called, and President Jagdeo was re-elected.

Gwent former county of south Wales, 1974–96, now divided between *Blaenau Gwent, *Caerphilly, *Monmouthshire, *Newport, and *Torfaen unitary authorities.

Gwynedd unitary authority in northwest Wales, created 1996 from part of the former county of Gwynedd.
area: 2,546 sq km/983 sq mi **towns:** Caernarfon (administrative headquarters) **physical:** area includes the highest mountain in Wales, *Snowdon (1,085 m/3,560 ft), and the largest Welsh lake, Llyn Tegid (Bala Lake) **features:** Snowdonia National Park; seaside resorts; Bardsey Island; Portmeirion; 13th-century castles at Harlech, Criccieth, and Caernarfon **population:** (1998 est) 117,500.

Gwynedd, kingdom of Gwynedd was a medieval Welsh kingdom comprising north Wales and Anglesey, whose rulers at times dominated most of Wales. The trouble their leaders caused for the kings of England led to a major offensive against Gwynedd, and the kingdom was ultimately broken up, the royal lands passing to the English Prince of Wales.

gymnastics physical exercises, originally for health and training (so called from the way in which men of ancient Greece trained: *gymnos* 'naked'). The *gymnasia* were schools for training competitors for public games. **Men's gymnastics** includes high bar, parallel bars, horse vault, rings, pommel horse, and floor exercises. **Women's gymnastics** includes asymmetrical bars, horse vault, balance beam, and floor exercises. Also popular are sports acrobatics, performed by gymnasts in pairs, trios, or fours to music, where the emphasis is on dance, balance, and timing, and rhythmic gymnastics, choreographed to music and performed by individuals or six-girl teams, with small hand apparatus such as a ribbon, ball, or hoop.

gymnosperm (Greek 'naked seed') in botany, any plant whose seeds are exposed, as opposed to the structurally more advanced *angiosperms, where they are inside an ovary. The group includes conifers and related plants such as cycads and ginkgos, whose seeds develop in *cones. Fossil gymnosperms have been found in rocks about 350 million years old.

gynaecology medical speciality concerned with disorders of the female reproductive system.

gynoecium *or* **gynaecium** collective term for the female reproductive organs of a flower, consisting of one or more *carpels, either free or fused together.

Gypsy English name for a member of the *Romany people.

gyroscope mechanical instrument, used as a stabilizing device and consisting, in its simplest form, of a heavy wheel mounted on an axis fixed in a ring that can be rotated about another axis, which is also fixed in a ring capable of rotation about a third axis. Applications of the gyroscope principle include the gyrocompass, the gyropilot for automatic steering, and gyro-directed torpedoes.

h

Haakon seven kings of Norway, including:

Haakon IV (1204–1263) King of Norway from 1217, the son of Haakon III. Under his rule, Norway flourished both militarily and culturally; he took control of the Faroe Islands, Greenland in 1261, and Iceland 1262–64. His court was famed throughout northern Europe.

Haakon VII (1872–1957) King of Norway from 1905. Born Prince Charles, the second son of Frederick VIII of Denmark, he was elected king of Norway on the country's separation from Sweden, and in 1906 he took the name Haakon. On the German invasion in 1940 he refused to accept Vidkun *Quisling's collaborationist government, and instead escaped to London and acted as constitutional head of the government-in-exile. He served as a powerful personification of Norwegian nationhood.

habeas corpus (Latin 'you may have the body') in law, a writ directed to someone who has custody of a person, ordering him or her to bring the person before the court issuing the writ and to justify why the person is detained in custody.

Haber, Fritz (1868–1934) German chemist whose conversion of atmospheric nitrogen to ammonia opened the way for the synthetic fertilizer industry. His study of the combustion of hydrocarbons led to the commercial 'cracking' or *fractional distillation of natural oil (petroleum) into its components (for example, diesel fuel, petrol, and paraffin). In electrochemistry, he was the first to demonstrate that oxidation and reduction take place at the electrodes; from this he developed a general electrochemical theory. He was awarded the Nobel Prize for Chemistry in 1918 for his work on the synthesis of ammonia from its elements.

Haber process or **Haber–Bosch process** industrial process by which *ammonia is manufactured by direct combination of its elements, nitrogen and hydrogen. As the method is a *reversible reaction which reaches *chemical equilibrium, the manufacturing conditions have to be chosen carefully in order to achieve the best yield of ammonia. The reaction is carried out at 400–500 °C/752–932 °F and at 200 atmospheres pressure. The two gases, in the proportions of 1:3 by volume, are passed over a *catalyst of finely divided iron. Around 10% of the reactants combine, and the unused gases are recycled. The ammonia is separated either by being dissolved in water or by being cooled to liquid form.

habitat in ecology, the localized environment in which an organism lives, and which provides for all (or almost all) of its needs. The diversity of habitats found within the Earth's ecosystem is enormous, and they are changing all the time. They may vary through the year or over many years. Many can be considered inorganic or physical; for example, the Arctic icecap, a cave, or a cliff face. Others are more complex; for instance, a woodland, or a forest floor. Some habitats are so precise that they are called **microhabitats**, such as the area under a stone where a particular type of insect lives. Most habitats provide a home for many species, which form a community.

Habsburg (or Hapsburg) European royal family, former imperial house of Austria-Hungary. A Habsburg, Rudolf I, became king of Germany in 1273 and began the family's control of Austria and Styria. They acquired a series of lands and titles, including that of Holy Roman Emperor which they held during 1273–91, 1298–1308, 1438–1740, and 1745–1806. The Habsburgs reached the zenith of their power under the emperor Charles V (1519–1556) who divided his lands, creating an Austrian Habsburg line (which ruled until 1918) and a Spanish line (which ruled to 1700).

Hadar or **Beta Centauri** second-brightest star in the constellation of *Centaurus, and the 11th-brightest in the night sky. It is a blue-white giant star of magnitude 0.61, some 320 light years from the Sun. It is a *binary star, comprising two stars of magnitudes 0.7 and 3.9.

haddock marine fish belonging to the cod family and found off the North Atlantic coastline. It is brown with silvery underparts and black markings above the pectoral fins. It can grow up to 1 m/3 ft in length. Haddock are important food fish; about 45 million kg/100 million lb are taken annually off the New England fishing banks alone. (Species *Melanogrammus aeglefinus*, family Gadidae.)

Hades in Greek mythology, the underworld where spirits (shades) went after death, usually depicted as a cavern or pit underneath the Earth, the entrance of which was guarded by the three-headed dog *Cerberus. It was presided over by the god *Pluto, originally also known as Hades (Roman **Dis**). Pluto was the brother of Zeus and married *Persephone, daughter of Demeter and Zeus.

Hadith collection of the teachings of *Muhammad and stories about his life, regarded by Muslims as a guide to living second only to the *Koran.

Hadrian, Publius Aelius Hadrianus (AD 76–138) Roman emperor 117–138. He was adopted by the emperor Trajan, whom he succeeded. He pursued a policy of non-expansion and consolidation after the vast conquests of Trajan's reign. His defensive policy aimed at fixing the boundaries of the empire, which included the building of Hadrian's Wall in Britain. He travelled more widely than any other emperor, and consolidated both the army and Roman administration.

Hadrian's Wall line of fortifications built by the Roman emperor Hadrian across northern Britain from the Cumbrian coast on the west to the North Sea on the east. The wall itself ran from Bowness-on-Windermere on the Solway Firth to Wallsend on the River Tyne, a distance of 110 km/68 mi. It was defended by 16 forts and smaller intermediate fortifications. It was breached by the Picts on several occasions and finally abandoned in about 383.

hadron in physics, a subatomic particle that experiences the strong nuclear force. Each is made up of two or three indivisible particles called *quarks. The hadrons are grouped into the *baryons (protons, neutrons, and hyperons), consisting of three quarks, and the *mesons, consisting of two quarks.

haematite *or* **hematite** principal ore of iron, consisting mainly of iron(III) oxide, Fe_2O_3. It occurs as **specular haematite** (dark, metallic lustre), **kidney ore** (reddish radiating fibres terminating in smooth, rounded surfaces), and a red earthy deposit.

haematology medical speciality concerned with disorders of the blood.

haemoglobin protein used by all vertebrates and some invertebrates for oxygen transport because the two substances combine reversibly. In vertebrates it occurs in red blood cells (erythrocytes), giving them their colour.

haemophilia any of several inherited diseases in which normal blood clotting is impaired. The sufferer experiences prolonged bleeding from the slightest wound, as well as painful internal bleeding without apparent cause.

haemorrhage loss of blood from the circulatory system. It is 'manifest' when the blood can be seen, as when it flows from a wound, and 'occult' when the bleeding is internal, as from an ulcer or internal injury.

haemorrhoids distended blood vessels (*varicose veins) in the area of the anus, popularly called **piles**.

haemostasis natural or surgical stoppage of bleeding. In the natural mechanism, the damaged vessel contracts, restricting the flow, and blood *platelets plug the opening, releasing chemicals essential to clotting.

hafnium chemical symbol Hf, (Latin *Hafnia* 'Copenhagen') silvery, metallic element, atomic number 72, relative atomic mass 178.49. It occurs in nature in ores of zirconium, the properties of which it resembles. Hafnium absorbs neutrons better than most metals, so it is used in the control rods of nuclear reactors; it is also used for light-bulb filaments.

Haggadah *or* **Aggadah** (Hebrew 'to tell') narrative tradition of Judaism, including history, science, folk-history, and legend; also, a prayerbook containing the story of the Exodus from Egypt, used during the Pesach Seder (ceremonial meal of Passover). The Haggadah forms part of the *Talmud, a compilation of Jewish law and tradition. The stories usually have an inspirational, ethical, or theological purpose.

Hague, the Dutch **'s-Gravenhage** or **Den Haag**, legislative and judicial capital of the Netherlands, and capital of South Holland province, 3 km/2 mi from the North Sea; population (2003 est) 465,900. It is linked by canal to Rotterdam and Amsterdam (which is the official capital of the country). Although it has some industries (including the manufacturing of computer software, electrical equipment, petroleum products, and food products), as well as dairying, livestock-raising, and agriculture (flowers, vegetables, fruit), the city's economy revolves around government administration. Banking, insurance, and trade are also economically important.

Haig, Douglas (1861–1928) 1st Earl Haig, Scottish army officer, commander-in-chief in World War I, born in Edinburgh, Scotland. His Somme offensive in France in the summer of 1916 made considerable advances only at enormous cost to human life, and his Passchendaele offensive in Belgium from July to November 1917 achieved little at a similar loss. He was created field marshal in 1917 and, after retiring, became first president of the British Legion in 1921.

haiku 17-syllable Japanese verse *genre, usually divided into three lines of five, seven, and five syllables. Japanese poet *Basho popularized the form in the 17th century. It evolved from the 31-syllable tanka form dominant from the 8th century.

hail precipitation in the form of pellets of ice (hailstones). Water droplets freeze as they are carried upwards. As the circulation continues, layers of ice are deposited around the droplets until they become too heavy to be supported by the air current and they fall as a hailstorm. It is caused by the circulation of moisture in strong convection currents, usually within cumulonimbus *clouds.

Haile Selassie, Ras (Prince) Tafari (1892–1975) called 'the Lion of Judah', Emperor of Ethiopia 1930–74. He pleaded unsuccessfully to the League of Nations against the Italian conquest of his country 1935–36, and was then deposed and fled to the UK. He went to Egypt in 1940 and raised an army, which he led into Ethiopia in January 1941 alongside British forces, and was restored to the throne on 5 May. He was deposed by a military coup in 1974 and died in captivity the following year. Followers of the Rastafarian religion (see *Rastafarianism) believe that he was the Messiah, the incarnation of God (Jah).

Hainan island province of south China, in the South China Sea, off the southwest coast of Guangdong province; area 34,000 sq km/13,000 sq mi; population (2000 est) 7,870,000. The capital is Haikou; major towns are Wenchang, Xincun, Tongzha, and Sanya. Hainan is China's second-largest island. Tourism and food-processing are the main industries, while the most important agricultural activities are the cultivation of rice, sugar cane, rubber, pineapples, and betel nuts, and animal husbandry, including pigs, cattle, and poultry.

Hainaut Flemish **Henegouwen**, industrial province of southwest Belgium, part of the French-speaking community and Walloon region, bounded to the south by France and the Belgian provinces of East and West Flanders, Flemish and Walloon Brabant, and Namur; area 3,800 sq km/1,467 sq mi; population (1997 est) 1,284,300. The capital is Mons, and other major towns include Charleroi, Tournai, and Soignies. The rivers Schelde and Sambre pass through the province.

hair fine filament growing from mammalian skin. Each hair grows from a pit-shaped follicle embedded in the second layer of the skin, the dermis. It consists of dead cells impregnated with the protein *keratin.

hairstreak any of a group of small butterflies, related to blues and coppers. Hairstreaks live in both temperate and tropical regions. Most of them are brownish or greyish-blue with hairlike tips streaked with white at the end of their hind wings. (Genera *Callophrys* and other related genera, family Lycaenidae.)

Haiti

formerly **Hispaniola (with Dominican Republic)** (until 1844)

National name: *République d'Haïti/Republic of Haiti*

Area: 27,750 sq km/10,714 sq mi
Capital: Port-au-Prince
Major towns/cities: Cap-Haïtien, Gonaïves, Les Cayes, St Marc, Carrefour, Delmas, Pétionville
Physical features: mainly mountainous and tropical; occupies western third of Hispaniola Island in Caribbean Sea
Head of state: Boniface Alexandre from 2004
Head of government: Gérard Latortue from 2004
Political system: transitional
Political executive: transitional
Political parties: National Front for Change and Democracy (FNCD), left of centre; Organization of People in Struggle (OPL), populist; Fanmi Lavalas (FL), personalist
Currency: gourde
GNI per capita (PPP): (US$) 1,580 (2002 est)
Exports: manufactured articles, coffee, essential oils, sisal. Principal market: USA 90% (1999)
Population: 8,326,000 (2003 est)
Language: French (20%), Creole (both official)
Religion: Christian 95% (of which 70% are Roman Catholic), voodoo 4%
Life expectancy: 49 (men); 50 (women) (2000–05)
Chronology
14th century: Settled by Carib Indians, who followed an earlier wave of Arawak Indian immigration.
1492: The first landing place of the explorer Christopher Columbus in the New World, who named the island Hispaniola ('Little Spain').
1496: At Santo Domingo, now in the Dominican Republic to the east, the Spanish established the first European settlement in the western hemisphere, which became capital of all Spanish colonies in America.
first half of 16th century: A third of a million Arawaks and Caribs died, as a result of enslavement and exposure to European diseases; black African slaves were consequently brought in to work the island's gold and silver mines, which were swiftly exhausted.
1697: Spain ceded western third of Hispaniola to France, which became known as Haiti, but kept the east, which was known as Santo Domingo (the Dominican Republic).
1804: Independence achieved after uprising against French colonial rule led by the former slave Toussaint

l'Ouverture, who had died in prison in 1803, and Jean-Jacques Dessalines.
1818–43: Ruled by Jean-Pierre Boyer, who excluded the blacks from power.
1821: Santo Domingo fell under the control of Haiti until 1844.
1847–59: Blacks reasserted themselves under President Faustin Soulouque.
1844: Hispaniola was split into Haiti and the Dominican Republic
1915: Haiti invaded by USA as a result of political instability caused by black-mulatto friction; remained under US control until 1934.
1956: Dr François Duvalier (Papa Doc), a voodoo physician, seized power in military coup and was elected president one year later.
1964: Duvalier pronounced himself president for life, establishing a dictatorship based around a personal militia, the Tonton Macoutes.
1971: Duvalier died, succeeded by his son Jean-Claude (Baby Doc); thousands murdered during Duvalier era.
1988: A military coup installed Brig-Gen Prosper Avril as president, with a civilian government under military control.
1990: Left-wing Catholic priest Jean-Bertrand Aristide was elected president.
1991: Aristide was overthrown in a military coup led by Brig-Gen Raoul Cedras. Sanctions were imposed by the Organization of American States (OAS) and the USA.
1993: United Nations (UN) embargo was imposed. Aristide's return was blocked by the military.
1994: The threat of a US invasion led to the regime recognizing Aristide as president.
1995: UN peacekeepers were drafted in to replace US troops. Assembly elections were won by Aristide's supporters. René Préval was elected to replace Aristide as president.
1998: Jacques-Edouard Alexis was nominated prime minister and endorsed by the assembly.
1999: President Préval dissolved parliament. Elections were repeatedly delayed.
2000: Aristide's Fanmi Lavalas Party won parliamentary elections, which were boycotted by the opposition.
2001: Aristide became president for the third time. Jean-Marie Chérestal became prime minister. The opposition set up an internationally unrecognized alternative government.
2004: Violent opposition forced Aristide into exile and a UN peacekeeping force was dispatched to end the bloodshed. Boniface Alexandre became president.

hajj pilgrimage to *Mecca (Arabic Makkah), in Saudi Arabia, that should be undertaken by every Muslim at least once in a lifetime, unless he or she is prevented by financial or health difficulties. A Muslim who has been on hajj may take the additional name **Hajji**. Many of the pilgrims on hajj also visit *Medina, where the prophet Muhammad is buried.

hake any of various marine fishes belonging to the cod family, found in northern European, African, and American waters. They have silvery elongated bodies and grow up to 1 m/3 ft in length. They have two dorsal fins and one long anal fin. The silver hake (*M. bilinearis*) is an important food fish. (Genera *Merluccius* and *Urophycis*, family Gadidae.)

halal (Arabic 'lawful') conforming to the rules laid down by Islam. The term can be applied to all aspects of life, but usually refers to food permissible under Muslim dietary laws, including meat from animals that have been slaughtered in the correct ritual fashion. Unlawful practices are known as haram.

Hale, George Ellery (1868–1938) US astronomer. He made pioneer studies of the Sun and founded three major observatories. In 1889 he invented the spectroheliograph, a device for photographing the Sun at particular wavelengths. In 1917 he established on Mount Wilson, California, a 2.5 m/100 in reflector, the world's largest telescope until superseded in 1948 by the 5 m/200 in reflector on Mount Palomar, which Hale had planned just before he died.

Hale-Bopp C/1995 01, large and exceptionally active comet, which in March 1997 made its closest fly-by to Earth since 2000 BC, coming within 190 million km/118 million mi. It has a nucleus of approximately 40 km/25 mi and an extensive gas coma (when close to the Sun Hale-Bopp released 10 tonnes of gas every second). Unusually, Hale-Bopp has three tails: one consisting of dust particles, one of charged particles, and a third of sodium particles. Hale-Bopp was discovered independently in July 1995 by two US amateur astronomers, Alan Hale and Thomas Bopp.

Haley, Bill (1925–1981) born William John Haley, US musician. A pioneering rock and roll singer, he led country-and-western bands around Philadelphia, Pennsylvania, between 1942 and 1952, when he formed the rhythm and blues-styled Bill Haley and His Comets. In 1954 his recordings of 'Rock Around the Clock' and 'Shake, Rattle and Roll' were among the earliest rock and roll hits. He had his last hit record in 1956, but continued to record and tour in rock and roll revival shows until 1980.

half-life during *radioactive decay, the time in which the activity of a radioactive source decays to half its original value (the time taken for half the atoms to decay). In theory, the decay process is never complete and there is always some residual radioactivity. For this reason, the half-life of a radioactive isotope is measured, rather than the total decay time. It may vary from millionths of a second to billions of years.

halftone process technique used in printing to reproduce the full range of tones in a photograph or other illustration. The intensity of the printed colour is varied from full strength to the lightest shades, even if one colour of ink is used. The picture to be reproduced is photographed through a screen ruled with a rectangular mesh of fine lines, which breaks up the tones of the original into areas of dots that vary in frequency according to the intensity of the tone. In the darker areas the dots run together; in the lighter areas they have more space between them.

halibut any of a group of large flatfishes found in the Atlantic and Pacific oceans. The largest of the flatfishes, they may grow up to 2 m/6 ft in length and weigh 90–135 kg/200–300 lb. They are a very dark mottled brown or green above and pure white on the underside. The Atlantic halibut (*H. hippoglossus*) is caught offshore at depths from 180 m/600 ft to 730 m/2,400 ft. (Genus *Hippoglossus*, family Pleuronectidae.)

Halicarnassus ancient city in Asia Minor (now Bodrum in Turkey), where the tomb of Mausolus, built about 350 BC by widowed Queen Artemisia, was one of the Seven Wonders of the World. The Greek historian Herodotus was born there.

halide any compound produced by the combination of a *halogen, such as chlorine or iodine, with a less electronegative element. Halides may be formed by *ionic bonds or by *covalent bonds. In organic chemistry, alkyl halides consist of a halogen and an alkyl group, such as methyl chloride (chloromethane).

Hall, Radclyffe (1880–1943) pen-name of Marguerite Radclyffe-Hall, English novelist. *The Well of Loneliness* (1928) brought her notoriety because of its lesbian theme. It was successfully prosecuted for obscenity and banned in the UK, but republished in 1949. Her other works include the novel *Adam's Breed* (1926; Femina Vie Heureuse and Tait Black Memorial prizes) and five early volumes of poetry.

Haller, Albrecht von (1708–1777) Swiss physician and scientist, founder of neurology. He studied the muscles and nerves, and concluded that nerves provide the stimulus that triggers muscle contraction. He also showed that it is the nerves, not muscle or skin, that receive sensation.

Halley, Edmond (1656–1742) English astronomer. He not only identified the comet that was later to be known by his name, but also compiled a star catalogue, detected the *proper motion of stars using historical records, and began a line of research that, after his death, resulted in a reasonably accurate calculation of the astronomical unit.

Halley's Comet comet that orbits the Sun roughly every 75 years, named after English astronomer Edmond Halley, who calculated its orbit. It is the brightest and most conspicuous of the periodic comets, and recorded sightings go back over 2,000 years. The comet travels around the Sun in the opposite direction to the planets. Its orbit is inclined at almost 20° to the main plane of the Solar System and ranges between the orbits of Venus and Neptune. It will next reappear in 2061.

hallmark official mark stamped on British gold, silver, and (from 1913) platinum, instituted in 1327 (royal charter of London Goldsmiths) in order to prevent fraud. After 1363 personal marks of identification were added. Now tests of metal content are carried out at authorized assay offices in London, Birmingham, Sheffield, and Edinburgh; each assay office has its distinguishing mark, to which is added a maker's mark, date letter, and mark guaranteeing standard.

hallucinogen any substance that acts on the *central nervous system to produce changes in perception and mood and often hallucinations. Hallucinogens include *LSD, *peyote, and *mescaline. Their effects are unpredictable and they are illegal in most countries.

halogen any of a group of five non-metallic elements with similar chemical bonding properties: *fluorine, *chlorine, *bromine, *iodine, and *astatine. They form a linked group (Group 7) in the *periodic table, descending from fluorine, the most reactive, to astatine, the least reactive. They all have coloured vapours and are poisonous. Melting points and boiling points increase going down the group. They combine directly with most metals to form salts, such as common salt (NaCl). Each halogen has seven electrons in its valence shell, which accounts for the chemical similarities displayed by the group.

halon organic chemical compound containing one or two carbon atoms, together with *bromine and other *halogens. The most commonly used are halon 1211 (bromochlorodifluoromethane) and halon 1301 (bromotrifluoromethane). The halons are gases and are widely used in fire extinguishers. As destroyers of the *ozone layer, they are up to ten times more effective than *chlorofluorocarbons (CFCs), to which they are chemically related.

halophyte plant adapted to live where there is a high concentration of salt in the soil, for example in salt marshes and mud flats.

Hals, Frans (c. 1581–1666) Flemish-born painter. The pioneer in the Dutch school of free, broad brushwork, he painted directly on to the canvas to create portraits that are spontaneous and full of life. His work includes the famous *Laughing Cavalier* (1624; Wallace Collection, London), and group portraits of military companies, governors of charities, and others.

Halton unitary authority in northwest England, created in 1998 from part of Cheshire. **area:** 74 sq km/29 sq mi **towns and cities:** Runcorn, Widnes (administrative headquarters), Ditton **features:** River Mersey divides Runcorn from Widnes and Ditton; Manchester Ship Canal and Bridgewater Canal reach Mersey at Runcorn; Catalyst: the Museum of the Chemical Industry is at Widnes; Norton Priory Museum (Runcorn) is on the site of a 12th-century priory **population:** (2001 est) 118,200.

Hamburg largest inland port of Europe, in Germany, on the Elbe and Alster rivers, 103 km/64 mi from the mouth of the Elbe; population (1995) 1,706,800. Industries include marine engineering, ship-repairing, oil-refining, printing, publishing, and the production of chemicals, electronics, processed foods, and cosmetics. It is the capital of the *Land* (administrative region) of Hamburg, and has been an archbishopric since 834. In alliance with Lübeck, it founded the *Hanseatic League. The city suffered extensive bomb damage during World War II.

Hamburg administrative region (German *Land*) in northern Germany, situated between Schleswig-Holstein and Lower Saxony; area 755 sq km/292 sq mi; population (1999 est) 1,704,700. The capital is *Hamburg. The boundaries of the region coincide with those laid down 1937–38 when the territory of the Free Hanse town was reorganized, the enclave of Cuxhaven being exchanged for three urban districts (Altona, Harburg, and Wandsbek) and 27 rural districts belonging to *Prussia.

Hamilcar Barca (died 229 BC) Carthaginian general, the father of *Hannibal the Great. Hamilcar rose to prominence in 249 BC at the first Battle of Eryx, during the later stages of the First Punic War. He negotiated the peace treaty with the Carthaginians at the end of the war in 241 BC, and suppressed the revolt of Carthage's foreign troops, the Mercenary War (241–237 BC). He then campaigned in Spain until his death, substantially enlarging and enriching the Carthaginian Empire.

Hamilton, Alexander (1757–1804) US politician who influenced the adoption of a constitution with a strong central government and was the first secretary of the Treasury 1789–95. He led the Federalist Party, and incurred the bitter hatred of Aaron Burr when he supported Thomas Jefferson for the presidency in the disputed election of 1800. With his backing, Jefferson

was elected by the House of Representatives in 1801. Hamilton again opposed Burr when he ran for governor of New York in 1804. Challenged to a duel by Burr, Hamilton was wounded and died the next day.

Hamilton, Emma, Lady (c. 1761–1815) born Amy Lyon, English courtesan. In 1782 she became the mistress of Charles Greville and in 1786 of his uncle Sir William Hamilton (1730–1803), the British envoy to the court of Naples, who married her in 1791. After Admiral *Nelson's return from the Nile in 1798 during the Napoleonic Wars, she became his mistress and their daughter, Horatia, was born in 1801.

Hamilton, Richard (1922–) English artist, a pioneer of pop art. His collage *Just What Is It That Makes Today's Homes So Different, So Appealing?* (1956; Kunsthalle, Tübingen, Germany) is often cited as the first pop-art work: its 1950s interior, inhabited by the bodybuilder Charles Atlas and a pin-up, is typically humorous, concerned with popular culture and contemporary kitsch.

Hammarskjöld, Dag (Hjalmar Agne Carl) (1905–1961) Swedish secretary general of the United Nations (UN) 1953–61. His role as a mediator and negotiator, particularly in areas of political conflict, helped to increase the prestige and influence of the UN significantly, and his name is synonymous with the peacekeeping work of the UN today. He was killed in a plane crash while involved in a controversial peacekeeping mission in Congo (now the Democratic Republic of Congo). He was posthumously awarded the Nobel Prize for Peace in 1961 for his peacekeeping work as secretary general of the UN.

hammer throwing event in track and field athletics. The hammer is a spherical weight attached to a wire with a handle. The competitors grip the handle with both hands, spin the hammer in a circular motion about them several times, and throw it as far as they can. The senior men's hammer weighs 7.26 kg/16 lb and may originally have been a blacksmith's hammer. Women and junior men throw lighter weights.

hammerhead any of several species of shark found in tropical seas, characterized by having eyes at the ends of flattened hammerlike extensions of the skull. Hammerheads can grow to 4 m/13 ft in length. (Genus *Sphyrna*, family Sphyrnidae.)

Hammerstein, Oscar, II (1895–1960) US lyricist and librettist. He collaborated with Richard *Rodgers over a period of 16 years on some of the best-known US musicals, including *Oklahoma!* (1943, Pulitzer Prize), *Carousel* (1945), *South Pacific* (1949, Pulitzer Prize), *The King and I* (1951), and *The Sound of Music* (1959).

Hammett, (Samuel) Dashiell (1894–1961) US crime novelist. He introduced the 'hard-boiled' detective character into fiction and attracted a host of imitators, with works including *The Maltese Falcon* (1930, filmed 1941), *The Glass Key* (1931, filmed 1942), and his most successful novel, the light-hearted *The Thin Man* (1932, filmed 1934). His Marxist politics were best expressed in *Red Harvest* (1929), which depicts the corruption of capitalism in 'Poisonville'.

Hammond organ electric *organ invented in the USA by Laurens Hammond in 1934. It is widely used in gospel music. Hammond applied valve technology to miniaturize Thaddeus Cahill's original 'tone-wheel' concept, introduced draw-slide registration to vary timbre, and added a distinctive tremulant using rotating speakers. The *synthesizer was developed from the Hammond organ.

Hampshire county of south England (since April 1997 Portsmouth and Southampton have been separate unitary authorities). **area:** 3,679 sq km/1,420 sq mi **towns and cities:** Winchester (administrative headquarters), Aldershot, Andover, Basingstoke, Eastleigh, Gosport, Romsey, and Lymington **physical:** New Forest (area 373 sq km/144 sq mi), in the southeast of the county, a Saxon royal hunting ground; rivers Avon, Ichen, and Test (which has trout fishing) **features:** Hampshire Basin, where Britain has onshore and offshore oil; Danebury, 2,500-year-old Celtic hill fort; Beaulieu (including Abbey and National Motor Museum); Broadlands (home of Lord Mountbatten); Highclere castle (1842, home of the Earl of Carnarvon, with gardens by English landscape gardener Capability Brown); Hambledon, where the first cricket club was founded in 1750; site of the Roman town of Silchester; Jane Austen's cottage at Chawton (1809–17), now a museum; Twyford Down section of the M3 motorway was completed in 1994 despite protests **population:** (2001 est) 1,240,800.

hamster any of a group of burrowing rodents with a thickset body, short tail, and cheek pouches to carry food. Several genera are found across Asia and in southeastern Europe. Hamsters are often kept as pets. (Genera include *Cricetus* and *Mesocricetus*, family Cricetidae.)

Hamsun, Knut (1859–1952) pseudonym of Knut Pedersen, Norwegian novelist. His first novel *Sult/ Hunger* (1890) was largely autobiographical. Other works include *Pan* (1894) and *Markens grøde/The Growth of the Soil* (1917). He was the first of many European and American writers to attempt to capture 'the unconscious life of the soul'. He was awarded the Nobel Prize for Literature in 1920. His hatred of capitalism made him sympathize with Nazism and he was fined in 1946 for collaboration.

Han the majority ethnic group in China, numbering about 990 million. The Hans speak a wide variety of dialects of the same monosyllabic language, a member of the Sino-Tibetan family. Their religion combines Buddhism, Taoism, Confucianism, and ancestor worship.

Hancock, John (1737–1793) US politician and a leader of the American Revolution. As president of the Continental Congress 1775–77, he was the first to sign the Declaration of Independence of 1776. Because he signed it in a large, bold hand, his name became a colloquial term for a signature in the USA. He was governor of Massachusetts 1780–85 and 1787–93.

hand unit used in measuring the height of a horse from front hoof to shoulder (withers). One hand equals 10.2 cm/4 in.

Handel, George Frideric (1685–1759) born Georg Friedrich Händel, German composer, a British subject from 1726. His first opera, *Almira*, was performed in Hamburg in 1705. In 1710 he was appointed Kapellmeister (director) to the Elector of Hanover (the future George I of England). In 1712 he settled in England, where he established his popularity with such works as the *Water Music* (1717), written for George I.

His great choral works include the *Messiah* (1742) and the later oratorios *Samson* (1743), *Belshazzar* (1745), *Judas Maccabaeus* (1747), and *Jephtha* (1752).

Han dynasty Chinese ruling family from 206 BC to AD 220 established by Liu Bang (256–195 BC) after he overthrew the *Qin dynasty, and named after the Han River. There was territorial expansion to the west, southwest, and north, including the conquest of Korea by Emperor Wudi or Wu-ti (ruling 141–87 BC) and the suppression of the Xiongnu invaders. Under the Han, a Confucianist-educated civil service was established and Buddhism introduced.

hang-gliding technique of unpowered flying using air currents, perfected by US engineer Francis Rogallo in the 1970s. The aeronaut is strapped into a carrier, attached to a sail wing of nylon stretched over an aluminium frame like a paper dart, and jumps into the air from a high place, where updraughts of warm air allow soaring on the thermals. See *gliding.

Hanging Gardens of Babylon in antiquity, gardens at Babylon, the capital of Mesopotamia, considered one of the *Seven Wonders of the World. According to legend, King Nebuchadnezzar constructed the gardens in the 6th century BC for one of his wives, who was homesick for her birthplace in the Iranian mountains. Archaeological excavations at the site of Babylon, 88 km/55 mi south of Baghdad in modern Iraq, have uncovered a huge substructure that may have supported irrigated gardens on terraces.

Hanks, Tom (1956–) US actor. Known for his performances in romantic comedies such as *Sleepless in Seattle* (1993) and *You've Got Mail* (1998), he has also won acclaim for his dramatic roles. His performance as an AIDS-afflicted lawyer in *Philadelphia* (1993) won him a 1994 Academy Award for Best Actor, and he won the same award a year later, for *Forrest Gump* (1994). Hanks received Academy Award nominations in the same category for *Saving Private Ryan* (1998) and *Cast Away* (2000).

Hannibal (247–182 BC) called 'the Great', Carthaginian general from 221 BC, son of Hamilcar Barca. His siege of Saguntum (now Sagunto, near Valencia) precipitated the Second *Punic War with Rome. Following a campaign in Italy (after crossing the Alps in 218), Hannibal was the victor at Trasimene in 217 and Cannae in 216, but he failed to take Rome. In 203 he returned to Carthage to meet a Roman invasion but was defeated at Zama in 202 and exiled in 196 at Rome's insistence.

Hanoi capital of Vietnam, on the Red River, 88 km/ 55 mi upstream from Haiphong; population (1997 est) 3,500,800. The Red River can be navigated by smaller ocean-going vessels, and Hanoi is also linked by rail to the port of Haiphong, to Ho Chi Minh City (Saigon), and to Kunming in the Yunnan province of China. The city is served by Gia Lam international and domestic airport. Industries include electric motors, electric generators, machine tools, textiles, and chemicals, as well as the more traditional tanning, brewing, rice milling, and handicrafts. Central Hanoi has one of the highest population densities in the world: 3,250 people per ha/1,300 per acre.

Hanover, House of German royal dynasty that ruled Great Britain and Ireland from 1714 to 1901. Under the Act of *Settlement of 1701, the succession passed to the ruling family of Hannover, Germany, on the death of Queen Anne. On the death of Queen Victoria, the crown passed to Edward VII of the house of Saxe-Coburg.

Hansard official report of the proceedings of the British Houses of Parliament, named after Luke Hansard (1752–1828), printer of the House of Commons *Journal* from 1774. It is published by Her Majesty's Stationery Office. The name *Hansard* was officially adopted in 1943. Hansard can now be consulted on the Internet.

Hanseatic League (German *Hanse* 'group, society') confederation of northern European trading cities from the 12th century to 1669. At its height in the late 14th century the Hanseatic League included over 160 cities and towns, among them Lübeck, Hamburg, Cologne, Breslau, and Kraków. The basis of the league's power was its monopoly of the Baltic trade and its relations with Flanders and England. The decline of the Hanseatic League from the 15th century was caused by the closing and moving of trade routes and the development of nation states.

Hanukkah *or* **Chanukkah** *or* **'Feast of Lights'** in Judaism, an eight-day festival of dedication and lights that takes place at the beginning of December. It celebrates the recapture of the Temple in Jerusalem from Antiochus IV of Syria in 164 BC by Judas Maccabaeus, and its rededication.

haploid having a single set of *chromosomes in each cell. Most higher organisms are *diploid – that is, they have two sets – but their gametes (sex cells) are haploid. Some plants, such as mosses, liverworts, and many seaweeds, are haploid, and male honey bees are haploid because they develop from eggs that have not been fertilized. See also *meiosis.

Hapsburg alternative form of *Habsburg, former imperial house of Austria-Hungary.

Harare formerly **Salisbury**, capital of Zimbabwe, in Mashonaland East Province, about 1,525 m/5,000 ft above sea level; population (1992) 1,184,200. It is the centre of a rich farming area producing tobacco and maize. The city's industries include milling, textiles, electrical and mechanical engineering, motor assembly, railway rolling stock, chemicals, furniture, consumer goods, and metallurgical and food processing.

hardcore in pop music, of any style, the more extreme and generally less commercial end of the spectrum: hardcore *techno is a minimalist electronic dance music; hardcore *rap is aggressive or offensive; hardcore *punk jettisons form and melody for speed and noise.

hard disk in computing, a storage device usually consisting of a rigid metal disk coated with a magnetic material. Data are read from and written to the disk by means of a disk drive. The hard disk may be permanently fixed into the drive or in the form of a disk pack that can be removed and exchanged with a different pack. Hard disks can have capacities as high as 300 gigabytes, with different versions intended for use with mainframe or personal computers.

Hardicanute (*c.* 1019–1042) King of Denmark from 1028, and of England from 1040; son of Canute. In England he was considered a harsh ruler.

Hardie, (James) Keir (1856–1915) Scottish socialist, the first British Labour politician, member of

Parliament 1892–95 and 1900–15. He worked in the mines as a boy and in 1886 became secretary of the Scottish Miners' Federation. In 1888 he was the first Labour candidate to stand for Parliament; he entered Parliament independently in 1892, as a Labour member in 1892, he became chair of the Labour party 1906–08 and 1909–10, and in 1893 was a chief founder of the Independent Labour Party.

Harding, Warren G(amaliel) (1865–1923) 29th president of the USA 1921–23, a Republican. As president he concluded the peace treaties of 1921 with Germany, Austria, and Hungary, and in the same year called the Washington Naval Conference to resolve conflicting British, Japanese, and US ambitions in the Pacific. He opposed US membership of the *League of Nations. There were charges of corruption among members of his cabinet (the Teapot Dome Scandal), with the secretary of the interior later convicted for taking bribes.

hardness the resistance of a material to indentation by various means, such as scratching, abrasion, wear, and drilling. Methods of heat treatment can increase the hardness of metals. A scale of hardness was devised by German–Austrian mineralogist Friedrich Mohs in the 1800s, based upon the hardness of certain minerals from soft talc (Mohs hardness 1) to diamond (10), the hardest of all materials.

hardware mechanical, electrical, and electronic components of a computer system, as opposed to the various programs, which constitute *software.

hard water water that does not lather easily with soap, and produces a deposit or *scale (limescale) in kettles. It is caused by the presence of certain salts of calcium and magnesium.

Hardy, Thomas (1840–1928) English novelist and poet. His novels, set in rural 'Wessex' (his native West Country), portray intense human relationships played out in a harshly indifferent natural world. They include *Far From the Madding Crowd* (1874), *The Return of the Native* (1878), *The Mayor of Casterbridge* (1886), *The Woodlanders* (1887), *Tess of the d'Urbervilles* (1891), and *Jude the Obscure* (1895). His poetry includes the *Wessex Poems* (1898), the blank-verse epic of the Napoleonic Wars *The Dynasts* (1903–08), and several volumes of lyrics. Many of his books have been successfully dramatized for film and television.

hare mammal closely related to the rabbit, similar in appearance but larger. Hares have very long black-tipped ears, long hind legs, and short upturned tails. (Genus *Lepus*, family Leporidae, order Lagomorpha.)

harebell perennial plant of the *bellflower family, with bell-shaped blue flowers, found on dry grassland and heaths. It is known in Scotland as the bluebell. (*Campanula rotundifolia*, family Campanulaceae.)

Hare Krishna popular name for a member of the *International Society for Krishna Consciousness, derived from their chant.

Hargreaves, James (*c.* 1720–1778) English inventor who co-invented a carding machine for cotton in 1760. In *c.* 1764 he invented his 'spinning jenny' (patented in 1770), which enabled a number of threads to be spun simultaneously by one person.

Haridwar *or* **Hardwar** city in Uttaranchal, India, 170 km/106 mi northeast of Delhi, on the right bank of the River Ganges at the foot of the Shiwalik Hills;

population (1991) 147,300. The name means 'door of Hari' (or Vishnu). In Hindu legend Vishnu's footprint was found on the river bank; it is one of the seven holy cities of the Hindu religion and a pilgrimage centre.

Harijan (Hindi 'children of god') member of the Indian *caste of untouchables. The term was introduced by Mahatma Gandhi during the independence movement.

Harlow, Jean (1911–1937) stage name of Harlean Carpentier, US film actor. She was the original 'platinum blonde' and the wisecracking sex symbol of the 1930s. Her films include *Hell's Angels* (1930), *Red Dust* (1932), *Platinum Blonde* (1932), *Dinner at Eight* (1933), *China Seas* (1935), and *Saratoga* (1937), during the filming of which she died (her part was completed by a double).

harmonica musical instrument, a pocket-sized reed organ blown directly from the mouth, invented by Charles Wheatstone in 1829; see *mouth organ.

harmonics in music, a series (the 'harmonic series') of partial vibrations that combine to form a musical tone. When a stretched string or a column of air in a tube is made to vibrate, it does so as a whole, in two halves, three thirds, four quarters, etc., all at the same time. The easiest vibration to hear is that of the whole. It is the lowest note and is called the **fundamental**. The vibrations of the halves, thirds, quarters, etc., produce a series of fainter, higher pitches at the same time. These are known as the **harmonics**, or **upper partials**, or **overtones**. Instruments vary in their tone colour (or timbre) because of the different number and different intensity of the harmonics. An oboe has many harmonics, while a flute has few.

harmonium small 19th-century organ whose sound was produced by the vibration of free reeds (thin metal tongues). The vibrations were created by air flow from foot-operated bellows, and lever-action knee swells controlled dynamics. It was invented by Alexandre Debain in Paris, France, in about 1842.

harmony in music, the sounding together of notes to produce a chord. Although the term suggests a pleasant or agreeable sound, it is applied to any combination of notes and the chord can therefore be consonant or dissonant. The term also refers to the progression (flow) of chords in a piece of music and the way they relate to each other.

Harold two kings of England:

Harold I (1016–1040) King of England from 1035. The illegitimate son of Canute, known as **Harefoot**, he claimed the crown on the death of his father, when the rightful heir, his half-brother Hardicanute, was in Denmark and unable to ascend the throne. He was elected king in 1037, but died three years later, as Hardicanute was preparing to invade England.

Harold (II) Godwinson (c. 1020–1066) last Anglo-Saxon king of England, January to October 1066. He was defeated and killed by William of Normandy (*William (I) the Conqueror) at the Battle of Hastings.

harp plucked musical string instrument. It consists of a set of strings stretched vertically over a triangle-shaped frame. The strings rise from a sloping soundboard and are tensioned at the opposite end by pegs. The orchestral harp is the largest instrument of its type. It has 47 strings covering the range B0–C7 (seven octaves). At its base there are seven double-action pedals (one for each note of the octave) to alter pitch. Before the pedals are depressed, the strings sound the scale of C flat major, but each note can be raised a semitone or a whole tone by one of the pedals. Thus all the notes of the chromatic scale can be sounded.

Harpers Ferry town in Jefferson County, West Virginia, in the Blue Ridge Mountains, where the Potomac and Shenandoah rivers meet; population (2000 est) 300. First settled in 1732, and incorporated as a town in 1763, it is chiefly significant for its place in the history of the abolitionism. On 16 October 1859 the antislavery leader John *Brown seized the federal government's arsenal here, with the intention of using its store of 100,000 firearms to found a republic for freed slaves. The siege lasted only 36 hours, left ten dead, and was ultimately unsuccessful; Brown was later hanged for treason. The raid signalled a rising trend of violent resistance to slavery and helped precipitate the American *Civil War. In the Civil War Harpers Ferry was captured by Gen Stonewall Jackson. Most of the town has now been reconstructed as the **Harpers Ferry National Historical Park**, established in 1944.

harpsichord largest and grandest of the 18th-century keyboard instruments, used in orchestras and as a solo instrument. The strings are plucked by 'jacks', made of leather or quill, when the keys are pressed. However, unlike the piano, the volume and tone cannot be varied by the player's touch. In the 18th century double-manual (two keyboard) harpsichords were developed (and later three-manuals), which offered greater variation in tone. The revival of the harpsichord repertoire in the 20th century owed much to Wanda Landowska and Ralph Kirkpatrick (1911–84).

Harpy (Greek 'snatcher') in early Greek mythology, a wind spirit; in later legend, such as the story of the *Argonauts, a female monster with a horrific face, pale with hunger, and the body of a vulture. Often associated with the underworld, harpies were believed to abduct those people who disappeared without trace, and were perceived as an instrument of torment used by the gods.

Harrier the only truly successful vertical takeoff and landing fixed-wing aircraft, often called the **jump jet**. It was built in Britain and made its first flight in 1966. It has a single jet engine and a set of swivelling nozzles. These deflect the jet exhaust vertically downwards for takeoff and landing, and to the rear for normal flight. Designed to fly from confined spaces with minimal ground support, it refuels in midair.

harrier any of a group of birds of prey, family Accipitridae, order Falconiformes. Harriers have long wings and legs, a small head with a short beak, an owl-like frill of thickset feathers around the face, and soft plumage. They eat frogs, birds, snakes, and small mammals, and are found mainly in marshy areas throughout the world.

Harris part of the Outer *Hebrides, Western Isles, Scotland; area 500 sq km/193 sq mi; population (1971) 2,900. It is joined to Lewis by a narrow isthmus. Harris tweed cloths are produced here.

Harrison, Benjamin (1833–1901) 23rd president of the USA 1889–93, a Republican. He called the first Pan-American Conference, which led to the establishment of the Pan-American Union, to improve inter-American cooperation and develop commercial ties. In 1948 this became the *Organization of American States.

Harrison, George (1943–2001) English rock and pop guitarist, singer, and songwriter. He played lead guitar and sang in the legendary English rock group the *Beatles, and wrote occasional songs for the group, including 'Something' (1969). After the group split up in 1970, Harrison began a solo career with hit singles including 'My Sweet Lord' (1970).

Harry (1984–) born Henry Charles Albert David, Prince of the UK; second child of the Prince and Princess of Wales.

hartebeest large African antelope with lyre-shaped horns set close on top of the head in both sexes. It can grow to 1.5 m/5 ft tall at the rather humped shoulders and up to 2 m/6 ft long. Although they are clumsy-looking runners, hartebeest can reach speeds of 65 kph/ 40 mph. (Species *Alcelaphus buselaphus*, family Bovidae.)

Hartington, Spencer Compton Cavendish, Marquess of Hartington and 8th Duke of Devonshire (1833–1908) British politician, first leader of the Liberal Unionists 1886–1903. As war minister he opposed devolution for Ireland in cabinet and later led the revolt of the Liberal Unionists that defeated Gladstone's Irish Home Rule Bill of 1886. Hartington refused the premiership three times, in 1880, 1886, and 1887, and led the opposition to the Irish Home Rule Bill in the House of Lords in 1893.

Hartlepool port and administrative centre of Hartlepool unitary authority in northeast England; 40 km/25 mi south of Newcastle upon Tyne; population (2001 est) 88,700. Historically a shipbuilding centre, modern industries include chemicals, metalwork, engineering, oil support services, fishing, and brewing. Hartlepool nuclear power station is located 5 km/3 mi southwest of the town at Seaton Carew.

hart's-tongue fern with straplike undivided fronds, up to 60 cm/24 in long, which have clearly visible brown spore-bearing organs on the undersides. The plant is native to Europe, Asia, and eastern North America, and is found on walls, in shady rocky places, and in woods. (*Phyllitis scolopendrium*, family Polypodiaceae.)

harvestman small animal (an *arachnid) related to spiders with very long, thin legs and a small body. Harvestmen are different from true spiders in that they do not have a waist or narrow part to the oval body. They feed on small insects and spiders, and lay their eggs in autumn, to hatch the following spring or early summer. They are found from the Arctic to the tropics. (Order Opiliones.)

harvest mite another name for the *chigger, a parasitic mite.

Harvey, William (1578–1657) English physician who discovered the circulation of blood. In 1628 he published his book *De motu cordis/On the Motion of the Heart and the Blood in Animals*. He also explored the development of chick and deer embryos. His discovery marked a new epoch in medical science, recognizing that the heart pumps blood in a continuous circulation. Appointed physician to St. Bartholomew's Hospital, London, Harvey attended James I during his last illness and later became physician to his son Charles.

Haryana (Hindi 'God's home') state of northwest India; area 44,222 sq km/17,074 sq mi; population (2001

est) 21,082,000. The capital is Chandigarh (also capital of *Punjab state). The state lies on the Gangetic plain, drained by the Yamuna River. Chief industries are textiles, cement, iron ore, bicycles, farm machinery, and processing of agricultural products, especially cotton and sugar. Agriculture, employing more than three-quarters of the population, is based on wheat, sugar, cotton, oilseed, rice, maize, and pulses, and output increased considerably in the late 20th-century as a result of large-scale investment in irrigation.

hashish drug made from the resin contained in the female flowering tops of hemp (*cannabis).

Hasidism *or* **Hassidism** *or* **Chasidism** *or* **Chassidism** sect of Orthodox Judaism, originating in 18th-century Poland under the leadership of Israel Ba'al Shem Tov (c. 1700–1760), also known as Besht. Hasidic teachings encourage prayer, piety, and 'serving the Lord with joy'. Many of the Hasidic ideas are based on the *Kabbalah, a mystical Jewish tradition.

Hassan II (1929–1999) King of Morocco 1961–99. He succeeded the throne upon the death of his father Mohamed V. Following riots in Casablanca in 1965, he established a royal dictatorship and survived two coup attempts. The occupation of the former Spanish Western Sahara in 1976 enabled him to rally strong popular support and consolidate his power. He returned to constitutional government in 1984, with a civilian prime minister leading a government of national unity. He was succeeded by his 35-year-old son Muhammad.

hassium chemical symbol Hs, synthesized, radioactive element of the *transactinide series, atomic number 108, relative atomic mass 265. It was first synthesized in 1984 by the Laboratory for Heavy-Ion Research in Darmstadt, Germany.

Hastings, Warren (1732–1818) English colonial administrator. A protégé of Lord Clive, who established British rule in India, Hastings carried out major reforms, and became governor general of Bengal in 1774. Impeached for corruption on his return to England in 1785, he was acquitted in 1795.

Hastings, Battle of battle on 14 October 1066 at which William, Duke of Normandy (*William (I) the Conqueror) defeated King *Harold II of England. Harold was killed leaving the throne open for William to complete the *Norman Conquest. The site is 10 km/6 mi inland from Hastings, at Senlac, Sussex; it is marked by Battle Abbey. The story of the battle is told in a sequence of scenes in the *Bayeux Tapestry.

Hatshepsut (c. 1473–c. 1458 BC) Queen (pharaoh) of ancient Egypt during the 18th dynasty. She was the daughter of Thutmose I, and the wife and half-sister of Thutmose II. Throughout his reign real power lay with Hatshepsut, and she continued to rule after his death, as regent for her nephew Thutmose III.

Hattersley, Roy Sydney George (1932–) British Labour politician and author. On the right wing of the Labour Party at that time, he was prices secretary 1976–79, and deputy leader of the party 1983–1992. In 1994 he announced his retirement from active politics, and later expressed disagreement with some of the policies of the new party leadership, which he considered had swung too far to the right in its views on promoting income distribution through the taxation and welfare system.

Hausa member of a people living along the southern edge of the Sahara Desert, especially in northwestern Nigeria, southern Niger, and Dahomey, and numbering 9 million. The Hausa are Muslim farmers and skilled artisans, weavers, leatherworkers, potters, and metalworkers. Their language belongs to the Chadic subfamily of the Hamito-Semitic (Afro-Asiatic) language group.

Haussmann, Georges Eugène (1809–1891) Baron Haussmann, French administrator, financier, and civil servant. In 1853 he was made prefect of the Seine by Louis Napoleon who had vast schemes for the embellishment of Paris. Haussmann replanned medieval Paris 1853–70 to achieve the current city plan, with long wide boulevards and parks. The improvements transformed Paris, but their cost (which amounted to £34,000,000) and his authoritarianism led to considerable opposition, and in 1870 he was forced to resign.

Haute-Normandie English **Upper Normandy**, coastal region of northwest France lying between Basse-Normandie and Picardy and bisected by the River Seine; area 12,317 sq km/4,756 sq mi; population (1999 est) 1,780,200. It comprises the *départements* of Eure and Seine-Maritime; its administrative centre is Rouen. Other chief towns include Évreux, and St-Saëns; ports include Le Havre, Dieppe, and Fécamp. The area is fertile and has many beech forests. Industries include dairy farming, fishing, and petrochemical, paper, and car manufacture.

Havana Spanish **La Habana**, capital and port of Cuba, on the northwest coast of the island; population (1995 est) 2,219,000. Products include cigars and tobacco, sugar, coffee, and fruit. Moved to its present site in 1519, it is one of the oldest cities in the Americas. The old city centre was designated a World Heritage Site in 1981, and the oldest surviving building in the city and in Cuba is La Fuerza, a fortress built in 1538.

Havel, Václav (1936–) Czech dramatist, civil rights activist, and politician, president of Czechoslovakia 1989–92 and of the Czech Republic 1993–2003. A noted playwright, he participated in the 'Prague spring' liberal reforms in 1968, but his plays were banned after the Soviet clampdown later in the year. In 1977 he formed the human rights organization Charter 77, which pressed for democratic reforms, and was subsequently imprisoned 1979–83 and 1989 for dissident activity. He was popularly elected president after the bloodless 'velvet revolution' of November–December 1989, which saw the overthrow of the Communist Party following popular protests, and he became a much respected international statesman.

Hawaii called the **Aloha State**, Pacific state of the USA, the only island state, separate from the North American continent and the world's longest island chain, made up of 8 main islands and 124 islets and reefs; area 16,635 sq km/6,423 sq mi; population (2000) 1,211,500; capital Honolulu on Oahu. It was officially nicknamed the Aloha State in 1959, after the Hawaiian greeting. The island group is surrounded by the Pacific Ocean and the east end is 3,400 km/2,100 mi southwest of *California. The Tropic of Cancer passes through the islands. Tourism is the biggest industry in Hawaii; other important industries are manufacturing and agriculture, with sugar the most important export. Major towns and cities include Hilo, Kailua, Kaneohe, and Waipahu. Settled over a thousand years ago by Polynesian immigrants, the islands remained largely unknown until their discovery by English explorer James *Cook in 1778. King Kamehameha I united the Hawaiian islands into an internationally recognized kingdom in 1793. In the course of the next century, Hawaii evolved from a kingdom, to a republic, to a US territory, and finally a US state, developing a thriving economy from the harvesting of pineapple and sugar cane. Hawaii made world history on 7 December 1941 when Japanese pilots attacked *Pearl Harbor, drawing the USA into World War II. Named after its largest island, Hawaii became the 50th state of the Union in 1959.

hawfinch European *finch, about 18 cm/7 in long. It feeds on berries and seeds, and can crack cherry stones with its large, powerful beak. The male bird has brown plumage, a black throat and black wings with a bold white shoulder stripe, a short white-tipped tail, and a broad band of grey at the back of the neck. (Species *Coccothraustes coccothraustes*, family Fringillidae, order Passeriformes.)

hawk any of a group of small to medium-sized birds of prey, belonging to the same family as eagles, kites, ospreys, and vultures. Hawks have short, rounded wings and a long tail compared with *falcons, and keen eyesight; the *sparrow hawk and *goshawk are examples. (Especially genera *Accipiter* and *Buteo*, family Accipitridae.)

hawk person who believes in the use of military action rather than mediation as a means of solving a political dispute. The term first entered the political language of the USA during the 1960s, when it was applied metaphorically to those advocating continuation and escalation of the Vietnam War. Those with moderate, or even pacifist, views were known as *doves.

Hawke, Bob (Robert James Lee) (1929–) Australian Labor politician, prime minister 1983–91, on the right wing of the party. He was president of the Australian Council of Trade Unions 1970–80. He announced his retirement from politics in 1992.

Hawking, Stephen (William) (1942–) English physicist and cosmologist whose work in general *relativity – particularly gravitational field theory – led to a search for a quantum theory of gravity to explain *black holes and the *Big Bang, singularities that classical relativity theory does not adequately explain. His book *A Brief History of Time* (1988) gives a popular account of cosmology and became an international best-seller. He later co-wrote (with Roger Penrose) *The Nature of Space and Time* (1996), and published *The Universe in a Nutshell* in 2002.

hawk moth any member of a family of *moths with more than 1,000 species distributed throughout the world, but found mainly in tropical regions. Some South American hawk moths closely resemble hummingbirds. (Family Sphingidae.)

Hawks, Howard (Winchester) (1896–1977) US director, screenwriter, and producer. He made a wide range of classic films in virtually every American genre. Swift-moving and immensely accomplished, his films include the gangster movie *Scarface* (1932), the screwball comedy *Bringing Up Baby* (1938), the *film noir The Big Sleep* (1946), the musical comedy *Gentlemen Prefer Blondes* (1953), and the Western *Rio Bravo* (1959).

Hawksmoor, Nicholas (1661–1736) English architect. He was assistant to Christopher *Wren in designing various London churches and St Paul's Cathedral, and joint architect of Castle Howard and Blenheim Palace with John *Vanbrugh. His genius is displayed in a quirky and uncompromising style incorporating elements from both Gothic and classical sources.

hawthorn any of a group of shrubs or trees belonging to the rose family, growing abundantly in eastern North America, and also in Europe and Asia. All have alternate, toothed leaves and bear clusters of showy white, pink, or red flowers. Their small applelike fruits can be red, orange, blue, or black. Hawthorns are popular as ornamentals. (Genus *Crataegus*, family Rosaceae.)

Hawthorne, Nathaniel (1804–1864) US writer. He was the author of American literature's first great classic novel, *The Scarlet Letter* (1850). Set in 17th-century Puritan Boston, it tells the powerful allegorical story of a 'fallen woman' and her daughter who are judged guilty according to men's, not nature's, laws. He wrote three other novels, including *The House of the Seven Gables* (1851), and many short stories, a form he was instrumental in developing, including *Tanglewood Tales* (1853), classic Greek legends retold for children.

Haydn, (Franz) Joseph (1732–1809) Austrian composer. He was instrumental in establishing and perfecting the classical sonata form, and wrote numerous chamber and orchestral works (he produced more than a hundred symphonies). He also composed choral music, including the oratorios *The Creation* (1798) and *The Seasons* (1801). He was the first great master of the string quartet, and was a teacher of Mozart and Beethoven.

Hayes, Rutherford (Birchard) (1822–1893) 19th president of the USA 1877–81, a Republican. He was a major general on the Union side in the Civil War. During his presidency federal troops were withdrawn from the Southern states (after *Reconstruction) and the civil service was reformed.

hay fever allergic reaction to pollen, causing sneezing, with inflammation of the nasal membranes and conjunctiva of the eyes. Symptoms are due to the release of *histamine. Treatment is by antihistamine drugs. An estimated 25% of Britons, 33% of Americans, and 40% of Australians suffer from hayfever.

hazardous waste waste substance, usually generated by industry, that represents a hazard to the environment or to people living or working nearby. Examples include radioactive wastes, acidic resins, arsenic residues, residual hardening salts, lead from car exhausts, mercury, non-ferrous sludges, organic solvents, asbestos, chlorinated solvents, and pesticides. The cumulative effects of toxic waste can take some time to become apparent (anything from a few hours to many years), and pose a serious threat to the ecological stability of the planet; its economic disposal or recycling is the subject of research.

hazel any of a group of shrubs or trees that includes the European common hazel or cob (*C. avellana*), of which the filbert is the cultivated variety. North American species include the American hazel (*C. americana*). (Genus *Corylus*, family Corylaceae.)

Hazlitt, William (1778–1830) English essayist and critic. His work is characterized by invective, scathing irony, an intuitive critical sense, and a gift for epigram.

harmful/irritant

toxic

radioactive

explosive

flammable

corrosive

oxidizing/supports fire

biohazardous/infectious

environmentally dangerous

hazard label The internationally recognized symbols, warning of the potential dangers of handling certain substances.

His essays include 'Characters of Shakespeare's Plays' (1817), 'Lectures on the English Poets' (1818–19), 'English Comic Writers' (1819), and 'Dramatic Literature of the Age of Elizabeth' (1820).

H-bomb abbreviation for *hydrogen bomb.

HDTV abbreviation for *high-definition television.

head louse parasitic insect that lives in human hair (see *louse).

health, world the health of people worldwide is monitored by the *World Health Organization (WHO). Outside the industrialized world in particular, poverty and degraded environmental conditions mean that easily preventable diseases are widespread: WHO estimated in 1990 that 1 billion people, or 20% of the world's population, were diseased, in poor health, or malnourished. In North Africa and the Middle East, 25% of the population were ill.

Heaney, Seamus (Justin) (1939–) Irish poet and critic. He has written powerful verse about the political situation in Northern Ireland and about Ireland's cultural heritage. The technical mastery and linguistic and thematic richness of Heaney's work have gained an international audience, and have exercised a powerful influence on contemporary poetry. He was professor of poetry at Oxford University 1989–94, and was awarded the Nobel Prize for Literature in 1995.

Hearst, William Randolph (1863–1951) US newspaper publisher, famous for his introduction of banner headlines, lavish illustration, and the sensationalist approach known as 'yellow journalism'. A controversialist and a strong isolationist, the film *Citizen Kane* (1941) was based on his life. He was also a Hollywood producer as well as an unsuccessful presidential candidate. He collected art treasures, antiques, zoo animals, and castles – one of which, San Simeon (Hearst Castle), California, became a state museum and zoo.

heart muscular organ that rhythmically contracts to force blood around the body of an animal with a circulatory system. Annelid worms and some other invertebrates have simple hearts consisting of thickened sections of main blood vessels that pulse regularly. An earthworm has ten such hearts. Vertebrates have one heart. A fish heart has two chambers – the thin-walled atrium (once called the auricle) that expands to receive blood, and the thick-walled ventricle that pumps it out. Amphibians and most reptiles have two atria and one ventricle; birds and mammals have two atria and two ventricles. The beating of the heart is controlled by the autonomic nervous system and an internal control centre or pacemaker, the sinoatrial node.

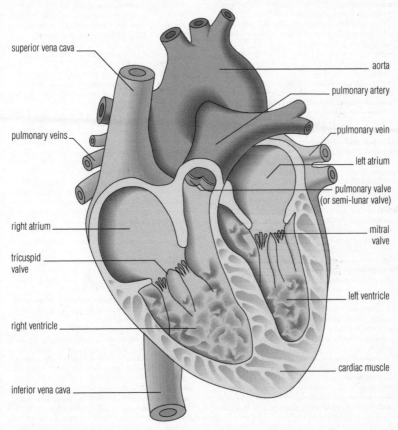

heart The structure of the human heart. During an average lifetime, the human heart beats more than 2,000 million times and pumps 500 million l/110 million gal of blood. The average pulse rate is 70–72 beats per minute at rest for adult males, and 78–82 beats per minute for adult females.

heart attack *or* **myocardial infarction** sudden onset of gripping central chest pain, often accompanied by sweating and vomiting, caused by death of a portion of the heart muscle following obstruction of a coronary artery by thrombosis (formation of a blood clot). Half of all heart attacks result in death within the first two hours, but in the remainder survival has improved following the widespread use of thrombolytic (clot-buster) drugs.

heat form of energy possessed by a substance by virtue of the vibrational movement (kinetic energy) of its molecules or atoms. Heat energy is transferred by conduction, convection, and radiation. It always flows from a region of higher *temperature (heat intensity) to one of lower temperature. Its effect on a substance may be simply to raise its temperature, or to cause it to expand, melt (if a solid), vaporize (if a liquid), or increase its pressure (if a confined gas).

heat capacity in physics, the quantity of heat required to raise the temperature of an object by one degree. The **specific heat capacity** of a substance is the heat capacity per unit of mass, measured in joules per kilogram per kelvin ($J kg^{-1} K^{-1}$).

heath in botany, any of a group of woody, mostly evergreen shrubs, including *heather, many of which have bell-shaped pendant flowers. They are native to Europe, Africa, and North America. (Common Old World genera *Erica* and *Calluna*, family Ericaceae.)

Heath, Edward (Richard George) (1916–) British Conservative politician, party leader 1965–75. As prime minister 1970–74 he took the UK into the European Community (EC) but was brought down by economic and industrial-relations crises at home. He was replaced as party leader by Margaret Thatcher in 1975, and became increasingly critical of her policies and her opposition to the UK's full participation in the EC. During John Major's administration, he continued his attacks on 'Eurosceptics' within the party. He retired from parliament at the 2001 general election.

heather low-growing evergreen shrub of the *heath family, common on sandy or acid soil. The common heather (*Calluna vulgaris*) is a carpet-forming shrub, growing up to 60 cm/24 in high and bearing pale pink-purple flowers. It is found over much of Europe and has been introduced to North America.

heatstroke *or* **sunstroke** rise in body temperature caused by excessive exposure to heat. Mild heatstroke is experienced as feverish lassitude, sometimes with simple fainting; recovery is prompt following rest and replenishment of salt lost in sweat. Severe heatstroke causes collapse akin to that seen in acute *shock, and is potentially lethal without prompt treatment, including cooling the body carefully and giving fluids to relieve dehydration. Death rates increase by 50% during heatwaves; heat stress is responsible for more deaths than any meteorological cause, including cyclones and floods.

heat treatment in industry, the subjection of metals and alloys to controlled heating and cooling after fabrication to relieve internal stresses and improve their physical properties. Methods include *annealing, quenching, and *tempering.

heaven in Christianity and some other religions, the abode of God and the destination of the virtuous after death. In traditional Christian belief, and in Islam, heaven is seen as a paradise of material delights, though such delights are generally accepted as being allegorical. Christians are now more likely to speak of heaven and hell in terms of states of mind, of spiritual happiness and unhappiness.

heavy metal style of rock music characterized by a distorted electric guitar sound and virtuoso guitar solos. Heavy metal developed out of the hard rock of the late 1960s and early 1970s and was performed by such groups as *Led Zeppelin and Deep Purple (formed in 1968), and enjoyed a revival in the late 1980s. Bands included Van Halen (formed 1974), Def Leppard (formed 1977), and Guns n' Roses (formed 1987).

heavy water *or* **deuterium oxide** D_2O, water containing the isotope deuterium instead of hydrogen (relative molecular mass 20 as opposed to 18 for ordinary water).

Hebei *or* **Hopei, Hopeh** *or* **Chihli** province of north China, bounded to the north by Inner Mongolia, to the northeast by Liaoning, to the east by the Bohai Gulf, to the south by Shandong and Henan, and to the west by Shanxi; area 185,900 sq km/71,800 sq mi; population (2000 est) 67,440,000. The capital is Shijiazhuang; other major cities are Baoding, Tangshan, Handan, and Zhangjiakou. The province includes the special municipalities of Beijing and Tianjin. The main industries are coal mining and the manufacture of textiles, iron, steel, machinery, pharmaceuticals, and petroleum products; agricultural production is based on winter wheat, barley, maize, and cotton.

Hebrew member of the Semitic people who lived in Palestine at the time of the Old Testament and who traced their ancestry to *Abraham of Ur, a city of Sumer.

Hebrew Bible *or* **Tenakh** the sacred writings of Judaism (some dating from as early as 1200 BC), called by Christians the *Old Testament. It comprises the *Torah (the first five books, ascribed to Moses), the Nevi'im (books of the prophets), and the Ketuvim (the remaining books and psalms). It was originally written in Hebrew and later translated into Greek (Septuagint) and other languages.

Hebrew language member of the *Afro-Asiatic language family spoken in Southwest Asia by the ancient Hebrews, sustained for many centuries in the *Diaspora as the liturgical language of Judaism, and revived by the late-19th-century Haskalah intellectual movement, which spread modern European culture among Jews. The language developed in the 20th century as Israeli Hebrew, the national language of the state of Israel. It is the original language of the Old Testament of the Bible.

Hebrides group of more than 500 islands (fewer than 100 inhabited) off the west coast of mainland Scotland; total area 2,900 sq km/1,120 sq mi. The Hebrides were settled by Scandinavians during the 6th–9th centuries and passed under Norwegian rule from about 890 to 1266.

Hecate (Greek 'worker from afar') in Greek mythology, the goddess of the underworld and magic arts. Her association with night led to her identification with the goddesses *Selene and *Artemis. She is first mentioned by Hesiod as having universal power to confer wealth and all the blessings of daily life. Ovid depicted her in *Fasti* with three bodies and heads, standing back-to-back to see in three directions.

hectare symbol ha, metric unit of area equal to 100 ares or 10,000 square metres (2.47 acres).

Hector in Greek mythology, a Trojan prince; son of King Priam and Hecuba, husband of *Andromache, and father of Astyanax. He was the foremost warrior in the siege of *Troy until killed by the Greek hero *Achilles.

hedgehog insectivorous mammal native to Europe, Asia, and Africa. The body, including the tail, is 30 cm/ 1 ft long. It is greyish brown in colour, has a piglike snout, and its back and sides are covered with sharp spines. When threatened it rolls itself into a ball bristling with spines. Hedgehogs feed on insects, slugs, mice, frogs, young birds, and carrion. Long-eared hedgehogs and desert hedgehogs are placed in different genera. (Genus *Erinaceus*, family Erinaceidae, order Insectivora.)

hedge sparrow another name for the *dunnock, a small European bird.

hedonism ethical theory that pleasure or happiness is, or should be, the main goal in life. Hedonist sects in ancient Greece were the *Cyrenaics, who held that the pleasure of the moment is the only human good, and the *Epicureans, who advocated the pursuit of pleasure under the direction of reason. Modern hedonistic philosophies, such as those of the British philosophers Jeremy Bentham and J S Mill, regard the happiness of society, rather than that of the individual, as the aim.

Hegel, Georg Wilhelm Friedrich (1770–1831) German philosopher who conceived of mind and nature as two abstractions of one indivisible whole, Spirit. His system, which is a type of *idealism, traces the emergence of Spirit in the logical study of concepts and the process of world history.

hegemony (Greek *hegemonia* 'authority') political dominance of one power over others in a group in which all are supposedly equal. The term was first used for the dominance of Athens over the other Greek city states, later applied to Prussia within Germany, and, in more recent times, to the USA and the USSR with regard to the rest of the world.

Hegira flight of the prophet Muhammad (see *Hijrah).

Heian in Japanese history, the period 794–1185, from the foundation of Kyoto as the new capital to the seizure of power by the Minamoto clan. The cut-off date may also be given as 1186, 1192, or 1200. The Heian period was the golden age of Japanese literature and of a highly refined culture at court; see also *Japanese art.

Heidegger, Martin (1889–1976) German philosopher. He believed that Western philosophy had 'forgotten' the fundamental question of the 'meaning of being' and, in *Sein und Zeit/Being and Time* (1927), analysed the different types of being appropriate to people and to things in general. He lectured and wrote extensively on German and Greek philosophy, and in the later part of his career focussed his attention on the nature of language and technology. His work was an important influence upon the existentialist philosophy of Jean-Paul Sartre.

Heilongjiang or **Heilungkiang** province of northeast China, bordered to the north and east by Russia, to the south by Jilin, and to the northwest by Inner Mongolia; area 463,600 sq km/178,950 sq mi; population (2000 est) 36,890,000. The capital is Harbin; other main cities are Qiqihar, Hegang, and Jiamusi, but much of the province is thinly populated. China's largest oilfield is located in the province, at Daqing, and coal is mined in the east of Heilongjiang; other industries are engineering, including the manufacture of machinery, tools, and building materials, food-processing, timber and wood products, and also ice-skates, of which the province is one of the world's leading producers. Agriculture is based on wheat, maize, sugar beet, soya beans, dairy farming, and sheep rearing.

Heine, Heinrich (Christian Johann) (1797–1856) German Romantic poet and journalist. He wrote *Reisebilder* (1826–31), blending travel writing and satire, and *Das Buch der Lieder/The Book of Songs* (1827). Disillusioned by undercurrents of anti-Semitism and antiliberal censorship, he severed his ties with Germany and from 1831 lived mainly in Paris. His *Neue Gedichte/ New Poems* appeared in 1844. He excelled in both the Romantic lyric and satire. Franz Schubert and Robert Schumann set many of his lyrics to music.

Heisenberg, Werner (Karl) (1901–1976) German physicist who developed *quantum theory and formulated the *uncertainty principle, which places absolute limits on the achievable accuracy of measurement. He was awarded the Nobel Prize for Physics in 1932 for his creation of quantum mechanics, work he carried out when only 24.

Helen in Greek mythology, the most beautiful of women; daughter of *Leda and Zeus (transformed as a swan). She was abducted as a young girl by Theseus, but rescued by her brothers *Castor and Pollux (Greek Polydeuces). Helen married *Menelaus, king of Sparta, and bore him Hermione, but during his absence was seduced by *Paris, prince of Troy; their flight precipitated the Trojan wars.

Helicon mountain in central Greece, on which was situated a spring and a sanctuary sacred to the *Muses.

helicopter powered aircraft that achieves both lift and propulsion by means of a rotary wing, or rotor, on top of the fuselage. It can take off and land vertically, move in any direction, or remain stationary in the air. It can be powered by piston or jet engine. The autogiro was a precursor.

Helios Roman **Sol**, in Greek mythology, the god of the Sun; a *Titan who drove the Sun's chariot across the sky. He was the father of *Phaethon, who almost set the Earth alight. From the 5th century BC, Helios was identified with the god *Apollo.

heliotrope decorative plant belonging to the borage family, with distinctive spikes of blue, lilac, or white flowers, including the Peruvian or cherry pie heliotrope (*H. peruvianum*). (Genus *Heliotropium*, family Boraginaceae.)

helium chemical symbol He, (Greek *helios* 'Sun') colourless, odourless, gaseous, non-metallic element, atomic number 2, relative atomic mass 4.0026. It is grouped with the *noble gases (rare gases) in Group 0 of the *periodic table. Helium is nonreactive because of its full outer shell of *electrons and forms no compounds. It is the second most abundant element (after hydrogen) in the universe, and has the lowest boiling (−268.9 °C/−452 °F) and melting points (−272.2 °C/−458 °F) of all the elements. It is present in small quantities in the Earth's atmosphere from gases issuing from radioactive elements (from alpha decay) in the Earth's crust; after hydrogen it is the second-lightest element.

helix in mathematics, a three-dimensional curve resembling a spring, corkscrew, or screw thread. It is generated by a line that encircles a cylinder or cone at a constant angle.

hell in various religions, a place of punishment after death. In Hinduism, Buddhism, and Jainism, hell is a transitory stage in the progress of the soul, but in Christianity and Islam it is eternal (*purgatory is transitory). Judaism does not postulate such punishment.

hellebore poisonous European herbaceous plant belonging to the buttercup family. The stinking hellebore (*H. foetidus*) has greenish flowers early in the spring. (Genus *Helleborus*, family Ranunculaceae.)

helleborine one of several temperate Old World orchids, including the marsh helleborine (*E. palustris*) and the hellebore orchid (*E. helleborine*) introduced to North America. (Genera *Epipactis* and *Cephalanthera*, family Orchidaceae.)

Hellenic period (from *Hellas*, Greek name for Greece) classical period of ancient Greek civilization, from the first Olympic Games in 776 BC until the death of Alexander the Great in 323 BC.

Hellenistic period period in Greek civilization from the death of Alexander in 323 BC until the accession of the Roman emperor Augustus in 27 BC. Alexandria in Egypt was the centre of culture and commerce during this period, and Greek culture spread throughout the Mediterranean region and the near East.

Heller, Joseph (1923–1999) US novelist. He drew on his experiences in the US air force in World War II to write his best-selling *Catch-22* (1961), satirizing war, the conspiracy of bureaucratic control, and the absurdism of history. A film based on the book appeared in 1970.

Hellespont former name of the *Dardanelles, the strait that separates Europe from Asia.

Héloïse (1101–1164) Abbess of Paraclete in Champagne, France, correspondent and lover of *Abelard. She became deeply interested in intellectual study in her youth and was impressed by the brilliance of Abelard, her teacher, whom she secretly married. After her affair with Abelard, and the birth of a son, Astrolabe, she became a nun in 1129, and with Abelard's assistance, founded a nunnery at Paraclete. Her letters show her strong and pious character and her devotion to Abelard.

Helsinki Swedish **Helsingfors**, capital and port of Finland; population (1994) 516,000. Industries include shipbuilding, engineering, and textiles. The port is kept open by icebreakers in winter.

Helvetia region, corresponding to western Switzerland, occupied by the Celtic Helvetii 1st century BC–5th century AD. In 58 BC Caesar repulsed their invasion of southern Gaul at Bibracte (near Autun) and Helvetia became subject to Rome. Helvetian is another word for Swiss.

Hemingway, Ernest (Miller) (1899–1961) US writer. War, bullfighting, and fishing are used symbolically in his work to represent honour, dignity, and primitivism – prominent themes in his short stories and novels, which include *A Farewell to Arms* (1929), *For Whom the Bell Tolls* (1941), and *The Old Man and the Sea* (1952; Pulitzer Prize). His deceptively simple writing style attracted many imitators. He was awarded the Nobel Prize for Literature in 1954.

hemlock plant belonging to the carrot family, native to Europe, western Asia, and North Africa. It grows up to 2 m/6 ft high and produces delicate clusters of small white flowers. The whole plant, especially the root and fruit, is poisonous, causing paralysis of the nervous system. The name 'hemlock' is also given to some North American and Asiatic conifers (genus *Tsuga*) belonging to the pine family. (*Conium maculatum*, family Umbelliferae.)

hemp annual plant originally from Asia, now cultivated in most temperate countries for the fibres produced in the outer layer of the stem, which are used in ropes, twines, and, occasionally, in a type of linen or lace. The drug *cannabis is obtained from certain varieties of hemp. (*Cannabis sativa*, family Cannabaceae.)

Henan *or* **Honan** province of east central China, bounded to the north by Hebei, to the east by Shandong and Anhui, to the south by Hubei, and to the west by Shaanxi and Shanxi provinces; area 167,000 sq km/64,500 sq mi; population (2000 est) 92,560,000. The province is one of the most densely populated in China. The capital is Zhengzhou; other major cities are Luoyang, Kaifeng, and Anyang. The main industries are coal mining, crude oil production, and the manufacture of iron and steel, heavy machinery, aluminium, textiles, cement, glass, and fertilizers. Agricultural products are cereals (especially wheat), cotton, fruit, tobacco, and peanuts.

henbane poisonous plant belonging to the nightshade family, found on waste ground throughout most of Europe and western Asia. It is a branching plant, up to 80 cm/31 in high, with hairy leaves and a sickening smell. The yellow flowers are bell-shaped. Henbane is used in medicine as a source of the drugs hyoscyamine and scopolamine. (*Hyoscyamus niger*, family Solanaceae.)

Hendrix, Jimi (James Marshall) (1942–1970) US rock guitarist, songwriter, and singer. He was legendary for his virtuoso experimental technique and flamboyance. *Are You Experienced?* (1967) was his first album. His performance at the 1969 *Woodstock festival included a memorable version of *The Star-Spangled Banner* and is recorded in the film *Woodstock* (1970). He greatly expanded the vocabulary of the electric guitar and influenced both rock and jazz musicians.

Hendry, Stephen (1969–) Scottish snooker player. In 1990 he became the youngest ever world champion at the age of 21 years 106 days. He won the title five years in succession, an unprecedented achievement in modern snooker. The world number one from 1990 to 1998, he has won more ranking event tournaments than any other player.

Hengist (died c. 488) Legendary leader, with his brother Horsa, of the Jutes, who originated in Jutland and settled in Kent about 450, the first Anglo-Saxon settlers in Britain.

Henley Royal Regatta UK *rowing festival on the River Thames at Henley, Oxfordshire, inaugurated in 1839. It is as much a social as a sporting occasion. The principal events are the solo *Diamond Challenge Sculls* and the *Grand Challenge Cup*, the leading event for eight-oared shells. The regatta is held in June/July. From 1998 professional rowers were allowed to compete at Henley after the Regatta's stewards had dropped the amateur definition from their rules.

henna small shrub belonging to the loosestrife family, found in Iran, India, Egypt, and North Africa. The leaves and young twigs are ground to a powder, mixed to a paste with hot water, and applied to the fingernails and hair to give an orange-red hue. The colour may then be changed to black by applying a preparation of indigo. (*Lawsonia inermis*, family Lythraceae.)

Henrietta Maria (1609–1669) Queen of England 1625–49. The daughter of Henry IV of France, she married *Charles I of England in 1625. By encouraging him to aid Roman Catholics and make himself an absolute ruler, she became highly unpopular and was exiled 1644–60 during the English Civil War. She returned to England at the Restoration but retired to France in 1665.

henry symbol H, SI unit of *inductance (the reaction of an electric current against the magnetic field that surrounds it). One henry is the inductance of a circuit that produces an opposing voltage of one volt when the current changes at one ampere per second.

Henry born Henry Charles Albert David, prince of the UK (see *Harry).

Henry, Joseph (1797–1878) US physicist, inventor of the electromagnetic motor in 1829 and of a telegraphic apparatus. He also discovered the principle of electromagnetic induction, roughly at the same time as Michael *Faraday, and the phenomenon of self-induction. The unit of inductance, the henry, is named after him.

Henry eight kings of England:

Henry I (1068–1135) King of England from 1100. Youngest son of William the Conqueror, he succeeded his brother William II. He won the support of the Saxons by marrying a Saxon princess, Matilda, daughter of Malcolm III of Scotland. An able administrator, he established a system of travelling judges and a professional bureaucracy, notably the setting up of the Exchequer as a formal government department to deal with the crown's financial matters (the chancellor of the Exchequer is still the government minister in charge of the Treasury in Britain). Henry quarrelled with St *Anselm, the archbishop of Canterbury, who claimed that the king had no right to invest bishops to vacant sees (diocese of a bishop). For a while, Anselm was forced into exile, but in the end Henry had to concede defeat.

Henry II (1133–1189) King of England from 1154. The son of *Matilda and Geoffrey V, Count of Anjou, he succeeded King *Stephen (c. 1097–1154). He brought order to England after the chaos of Stephen's reign, curbing the power of the barons and reforming the legal system. His attempt to bring the church courts under control had to be abandoned after the murder of Thomas à *Becket, archbishop of Canterbury, in 1170. The English conquest of Ireland began during Henry's reign. On several occasions his sons rebelled, notably in 1173–74. Henry was succeeded by his son Richard (I) the Lionheart.

Henry III (1207–1272) King of England from 1216, when he succeeded John, but the royal powers were exercised by a regency until 1232, and by two French nobles, Peter des Roches and Peter des Rivaux, until the barons forced their expulsion in 1234, marking the start of Henry's personal rule. His financial commitments to the papacy and his foreign favourites antagonized the

barons who issued the Provisions of Oxford in 1258, limiting the king's power. Henry's refusal to accept the provisions led to the second Barons' War in 1264, a revolt of nobles led by his brother-in-law Simon de *Montfort. Henry was defeated at Lewes, Sussex, and imprisoned, but restored to the throne after the royalist victory at Evesham in 1265. He was succeeded by his son Edward I.

Henry IV (1367–1413) born Henry Bolingbroke, King of England from 1399, the son of *John of Gaunt. In 1398 he was banished by *Richard II but returned in 1399 to head a revolt and was accepted as king by Parliament. He was succeeded by his son Henry V.

Henry V (1387–1422) King of England from 1413, son of Henry IV. Invading Normandy in 1415 (during the *Hundred Years' War), he captured Harfleur and defeated the French at *Agincourt. He invaded again in 1417–19, capturing Rouen. His military victory forced the French into the Treaty of Troyes in 1420, which gave Henry control of the French government. He married *Catherine of Valois in 1420 and gained recognition as heir to the French throne by his father-in-law Charles VI, but died before him. He was succeeded by his son Henry VI.

Henry VI (1421–1471) King of England from 1422, son of Henry V. He assumed royal power in 1442 and sided with the party opposed to the continuation of the Hundred Years' War with France. After his marriage in 1445, he was dominated by his wife, *Margaret of Anjou. He was deposed in 1461 during the Wars of the *Roses, was captured in 1465, temporarily restored in 1470, but again imprisoned in 1471 and then murdered.

Henry VII (1457–1509) King of England from 1485, when he overthrew Richard III at the Battle of *Bosworth. A descendant of *John of Gaunt, Henry, by his marriage to Elizabeth of York in 1486, united the houses of York and Lancaster. Yorkist revolts continued until 1497, but Henry restored order after the Wars of the Roses by the *Star Chamber and achieved independence from Parliament by amassing a private fortune through confiscations. He was succeeded by his son Henry VIII.

Henry VIII (1491–1547) King of England from 1509, when he succeeded his father Henry VII and married Catherine of Aragón, the widow of his brother. During the period 1513–29 Henry pursued an active foreign policy, largely under the guidance of his lord chancellor, Cardinal Wolsey, who shared Henry's desire to make England stronger. Wolsey was replaced by Thomas More in 1529 after failing to persuade the pope to grant Henry a divorce. After 1532 Henry broke with papal authority, proclaimed himself head of the church in England, dissolved the monasteries, and divorced Catherine. His subsequent wives were Anne Boleyn, Jane Seymour, Anne of Cleves, Catherine Howard, and Catherine Parr. He was succeeded by his son Edward VI.

Henry four kings of France, including:

Henry II (1519–1559) King of France from 1547. He captured the fortresses of Metz and Verdun from the Holy Roman Emperor Charles V and Calais from the English. He was killed in a tournament.

Henry III (1551–1589) King of France from 1574. He fought both the *Huguenots (headed by his successor, Henry of Navarre) and the Catholic League (headed by the third Duke of Guise). Guise expelled Henry from

Paris in 1588 but was assassinated. Henry allied with the Huguenots under Henry of Navarre to besiege the city, but was assassinated by a monk.

Henry IV (1553–1610) King of France from 1589. Son of Antoine de Bourbon and Jeanne, Queen of Navarre, he was brought up as a Protestant and from 1576 led the *Huguenots. On his accession he settled the religious question by adopting Catholicism while tolerating Protestantism. He restored peace and strong government to France and brought back prosperity by measures for the promotion of industry and agriculture and the improvement of communications. He was assassinated by a Catholic extremist.

Henry seven Holy Roman emperors, including:

Henry (III) the Black (1017–1056) King of Germany from 1028, Holy Roman Emperor from 1039 (crowned In 1046). He raised the empire to the height of its power, and extended its authority over Poland, Bohemia, and Hungary.

Henry IV (1050–1106) Holy Roman Emperor from 1056. He was involved from 1075 in a struggle with the papacy. Excommunicated twice (1076 and 1080), Henry deposed *Gregory VII and set up the antipope Clement III (died 1191) by whom he was crowned Holy Roman Emperor 1084.

Henry VI (1165–1197) Holy Roman Emperor 1191–97. He conquered the Norman Kingdom of Sicily in the name of his wife, Constance, aunt and heiress of William II of Sicily, and was crowned at Palermo, Sicily, on Christmas Day, 1194. As part of his plan for making the empire universal, he captured and imprisoned Richard I of England and compelled him to do homage.

Henry the Navigator (1394–1460) Portuguese prince, the fourth son of John I. He is credited with setting up a school for navigators in 1419 and under his patronage Portuguese sailors explored and colonized Madeira, the Cape Verde Islands, and the Azores; they sailed down the African coast almost to Sierra Leone.

Henze, Hans Werner (1926–) German composer. His immense and stylistically restless output is marked by a keen literary sensibility and seductive use of orchestral coloration, as in the opera *Elegy for Young Lovers* (1961) and the cantata *Being Beauteous* (1963). Among later works are the opera *Das Verratene Meer/The Sea Betrayed* (1992), based on Yukio Mishima's novel *The Sailor who Fell from Grace with the Sea*, and *L'Upupa oder Der Triumph der Sohnesliebe/L'Upupa and the Triumph of Filial Love*, an opera commissioned by the 2003 Salzburg Festival and for which Henze also tried his hand for the first time as librettist. He also composed ten symphonies (1947–2002).

hepatitis any inflammatory disease of the liver, usually caused by a virus. Other causes include alcohol, drugs, gallstones, *lupus erythematous, and amoebic *dysentery. Symptoms include weakness, nausea, and jaundice.

Hepburn, Audrey (1929–1993) born Audrey Hepburn-Ruston, English actor. She often played innocent, childlike characters. Slender and doe-eyed, she set a different style from the more ample women stars of the 1950s. After playing minor parts in British films in the early 1950s, she became a Hollywood star in *Roman Holiday* (1951), for which she won an Academy Award, and later starred in such films as *Funny Face* (1957) and *My Fair Lady* (1964).

Hepburn, Katharine (1909–) US actor. An acclaimed actor of the classical Hollywood era, Hepburn has won four Academy Awards and been nominated on 12 separate occasions. Feisty self-assurance was her trademark in both comic and dramatic roles. She was a frequent collaborator with the director George Cukor, and appeared in several films with her off-screen partner Spencer Tracy, including *Woman of the Year* (1942) and *Pat and Mike* (1952).

Hephaestus in Greek mythology, the god of fire and metalcraft (Roman **Vulcan**); the lame son of Zeus and Hera; and in Homer's *Odyssey*, husband of Aphrodite, goddess of love. He created armour for the Greek hero *Achilles, Harmonia's magic necklace, and other objects famed in legend.

Hepplewhite, George (died 1786) English furnituremaker associated with Neo-Classicism. His reputation rests upon his book of designs *The Cabinetmaker and Upholsterer's Guide*, published posthumously in 1788, which contains over 300 designs, characterized by simple elegance and utility. No piece of furniture has been identified as being made by him.

heptathlon multi-event athletics discipline for women consisting of seven events over two days: 100-metre hurdles, high jump, shot-put, 200 metres (day one); long jump, javelin, 800 metres (day two). Points are awarded for performances in each event in the same way as the *decathlon. It replaced the pentathlon (five events) in international competition in 1981.

Hepworth, (Jocelyn) Barbara (1903–1975) English sculptor. She developed a distinctive abstract style, creating slender upright forms reminiscent of standing stones or totems; and round, hollowed forms with spaces bridged by wires or strings, as in *Pelagos* (1946; Tate Gallery, London). Her preferred medium was stone, but she also worked in concrete, wood, and aluminium, and many of her later works were in bronze.

Hera (Greek 'lady') in Greek mythology, the goddess of women and marriage (Roman **Juno**); sister and consort of Zeus; and mother of *Hephaestus, god of fire and metalcraft, the war god Ares, and Hebe, the original cupbearer to the gods. The peacock was sacred to her; the eyes in its tail were transplanted from her servant, the 100-eyed Argus, who had watched over Zeus' lover Io.

Heracles *or* **Alcides** in Greek mythology, an immortalized hero (Roman **Hercules**); son of Zeus and Alcmene; and famed for his strength. While serving Eurystheus, king of Argos, he performed 12 labours, including the cleansing of the *Augean stables. Driven mad by the goddess *Hera, he murdered his children by Megara, his first wife, and was mistakenly poisoned by his second wife Deianira.

heraldry insignia and symbols representing a person, family, or dynasty; the science of armorial bearings. Heraldry originated with simple symbols used on shields and banners for recognition in battle. By the 14th century, it had become a complex pictorial language with its own regulatory bodies (courts of chivalry), used by noble families, corporate bodies, cities, and realms. The world's oldest heraldic court is the English *College of Arms founded in 1484.

herb any plant (usually a flowering plant) tasting sweet, bitter, aromatic, or pungent, used in cooking, medicine, or perfumery; technically, a herb is any plant in which the aerial parts do not remain above ground at the end of the growing season.

herbalism in alternative medicine, the prescription and use of plants and their derivatives for medication. Herbal products are favoured by alternative practitioners as 'natural medicine', as opposed to modern synthesized medicines and drugs, which are regarded with suspicion because of the dangers of side effects and dependence.

Herbert, George (1593–1633) English poet. His volume of religious poems, *The Temple*, appeared in 1633, shortly before his death. His intense though quiet poems embody his religious struggles ('The Temper', 'The Collar') or poignantly contrast mortality and eternal truth ('Vertue', 'Life') in a deceptively simple language.

herbicide any chemical used to destroy plants or check their growth (see *weedkiller).

herbivore animal that feeds on green plants (or photosynthetic single-celled organisms) or their products, including seeds, fruit, and nectar. The most numerous type of herbivore is thought to be the zooplankton, tiny invertebrates in the surface waters of the oceans that feed on small photosynthetic algae. Herbivores are more numerous than other animals because their food is the most abundant. They form a vital link in the food chain between plants and *carnivores.

herb Robert wild *geranium found throughout Europe and central Asia and naturalized in North America. About 30 cm/12 in high, it has hairy leaves and small pinkish to purplish flowers. (*Geranium robertianum*, family Geraniaceae.)

Herculaneum ancient city of Italy between Naples and Pompeii. Along with Pompeii, it was buried when Vesuvius erupted in AD 79. It was excavated from the 18th century onwards.

Hercules fifth-largest constellation, lying in the northern hemisphere. Despite its size it contains no prominent stars. Its most important feature is the best example in the northern hemisphere of a *globular cluster of stars 22,500 light years from the Sun, which lies between Eta and Zeta Herculis.

Hercules in Roman mythology, Roman form of the deified Greek hero *Heracles. Possibly the first foreign cult accepted in Rome, he was popular with merchants due to his legendary travel and ability to ward off evil, and was seen as the personification of strength.

heredity in biology, the transmission of traits from parent to offspring. See also *genetics.

Herefordshire unitary authority in west England, created in 1998 from part of the former county of Hereford and Worcester. **area:** 2,288 sq km/884 sq mi **towns and cities:** Hereford (administrative headquarters), Leominster, Ross-on-Wye, Ledbury **features:** River Wye; Herefordshire Beacon (340 m/ 1,115 ft) Iron Age fort; Hereford Cathedral (11th century) houses the late 13th/early 14th-century Mappa Mundi, and the Chained Library, with over 1,400 chained books and 200 manuscripts dating from the 8th to 12th centuries; Waterworks Museum (Hereford) in restored Victorian pump house; Croft Castle (14th–15th centuries, Leominster); St Mary's Church (1095, Kempley) with medieval wall paintings; The Prospect, a walled clifftop

garden in Ross-on-Wye designed by John Kyrle in the 17th century; Norman Church (Kilpeck) with notable carvings **population:** (2001 est) 174,900.

Hereward the Wake (lived 11th century) legendary Saxon hero of the English resistance to the Normans in 1070. Helped by a Danish army, the rebels attacked and sacked Peterborough Abbey. William bribed the Danes to return home, but Hereward continued the revolt. His stronghold in the Isle of Ely was captured in 1071 by William (I) the Conqueror during the Siege of Ely. Although his actual fate is unkown, legends grew up about him, and he has remained a hero of fiction.

hermaphrodite organism that has both male and female sex organs. Hermaphroditism is the norm in such species as earthworms and snails, and is common in flowering plants. Cross-fertilization is common among hermaphrodites, with the parents functioning as male and female simultaneously, or as one or the other sex at different stages in their development. Human hermaphrodites are extremely rare.

hermeneutics philosophical tradition concerned with the nature of understanding and interpretation of human behaviour and social traditions. From its origins in problems of biblical interpretation, hermeneutics has expanded to cover many fields of enquiry, including aesthetics, literary theory, and science. The German philosophers Wilhelm Dilthey, Martin *Heidegger, and Hans-Georg Gadamer were influential contributors to this tradition.

Hermes in Greek mythology, the messenger of the gods; son of Zeus and *Maia, one of the Pleiades. Homer's *Odyssey* presented the god as the conductor of the dead (shades) to *Hades, in which capacity he became associated with the underworld and dreams. Identified with the Roman *Mercury and ancient Egyptian *Thoth, he protected thieves, travellers, and merchants. As a god of good fortune, he presided over some forms of popular divination, public competitions, and games of dice.

hernia *or* **rupture** protrusion of part of an internal organ through a weakness in the surrounding muscular wall, usually in the groin. The appearance is that of a rounded soft lump or swelling.

Hero and Leander in Greek mythology, a pair of lovers. Hero, virgin priestess of Aphrodite, at Sestos on the Hellespont, fell in love at a festival with Leander on the opposite shore at Abydos. He used to swim to her at night, guided by the light, but during a storm the flame blew out and he was drowned. Seeing his body, Hero threw herself into the sea.

Herod Agrippa I (10 BC–AD 44) Ruler of Palestine from AD 41. His real name was Marcus Julius Agrippa, erroneously called 'Herod' in the Bible. Grandson of Herod the Great, he was made tetrarch (governor) of Palestine by the Roman emperor Caligula and king by Emperor Claudius AD 41. He put the apostle James to death and imprisoned the apostle Peter. His son was Herod Agrippa II.

Herod Agrippa II (c. 40–c. 93 AD) King of Chalcis (now southern Lebanon), son of Herod Agrippa I. He was appointed by the Roman emperor Claudius about AD 50, and in AD 60 tried the apostle Paul. He helped the Roman commander Titus (subsequently emperor) take and sack Jerusalem in AD 70, then went to Rome, where he died.

Herod Antipas (21 BC–AD 39) Tetrarch (governor) of the Roman province of Galilee, northern Palestine, 4 BC–AD 39, son of Herod the Great. He divorced his wife to marry his niece Herodias, and was responsible for the death of John the Baptist. Jesus was brought before him on Pontius Pilate's discovery that he was a Galilean and hence of Herod's jurisdiction, but Herod returned him without giving any verdict. In AD 38 Herod Antipas went to Rome to try to persuade Emperor Caligula to give him the title of king, but was instead banished.

Herodotus (lived 5th century BC) Greek historian, described as the 'Father of History'. He wrote a nine-book account of the Greek-Persian struggle that culminated in the defeat of the Persian invasion attempts in 490 and 480 BC. The work contains lengthy digressions on peoples, places, and earlier history. Herodotus was the first historian to apply critical evaluation to his material while also recording divergent opinions.

Herod the Great (74–4 BC) King of the Roman province of Judaea, southern Palestine, from 40 BC. With the aid of Mark Antony, he established his government in Jerusalem in 37 BC. He rebuilt the Temple in Jerusalem, but his Hellenizing tendencies made him suspect to orthodox Jewry. His last years were a reign of terror, and in the New Testament Matthew alleges that he ordered the slaughter of all the infants in Bethlehem to ensure the death of Jesus, whom he foresaw as a rival. He was the father of Herod Antipas.

heroin or **diamorphine** powerful *opiate analgesic, an acetyl derivative of *morphine. It is more addictive than morphine but causes less nausea.

heron large to medium-sized wading bird belonging to the same family as bitterns, egrets, night herons, and boatbills. Herons have sharp bills, broad wings, long legs, slender bodies, and soft plumage. They are found mostly in tropical and subtropical regions, but also in temperate zones, on lakes, fens, and mudflats, where they wade searching for prey. (Genera include *Ardea*, *Butorides*, and *Nycticorax*; family Ardeidae, order Ciconiiformes.)

herpes any of several infectious diseases caused by viruses of the herpes group. **Herpes simplex I** is the causative agent of a common inflammation, the cold sore. **Herpes simplex II** is responsible for genital herpes, a highly contagious, sexually transmitted disease characterized by painful blisters in the genital area. It can be transmitted in the birth canal from mother to newborn. **Herpes zoster** causes *shingles; another herpes virus causes chickenpox.

Herrick, Robert (1591–1674) English poet and cleric. He published *Hesperides: or the Works both Humane and Divine of Robert Herrick* (1648), a collection of verse admired for its lyric quality, including the well-known poems 'Gather ye rosebuds' and 'Cherry ripe'.

herring any of various marine fishes belonging to the herring family, but especially the important food fish *Clupea harengus*. A silvered greenish blue, it swims close to the surface, and may be 25–40 cm/10–16 in long. Herring travel in schools several kilometres long and wide. They are found in large quantities off the east coast of North America, and the shores of northeastern Europe. Overfishing and pollution have reduced their numbers. (Family Clupeidae.)

Herschel, (Frederick) William (1738–1822) German-born English astronomer. He was a skilled telescopemaker, and pioneered the study of binary stars and nebulae. He discovered the planet Uranus in 1781 and infrared solar rays in 1801. He catalogued over 800 double stars, and found over 2,500 nebulae, catalogued by his sister Caroline Herschel; this work was continued by his son John Herschel. By studying the distribution of stars, William established the basic form of our Galaxy, the Milky Way. He was knighted in 1816.

Hershko, Avram (1937–) Hungarian-born Israeli scientist. With Israeli scientist Aaron Ciechanover and US scientist Irwin Rose shared the Nobel Prize for Chemistry in 2004 for his contributions to the understanding of the process of cell protein degradation.

Hertfordshire county of southeast England, to the north of London. **area:** 1,630 sq km/629 sq mi **towns and cities:** Hertford (administrative headquarters), Bishop's Stortford, Hatfield, Hemel Hempstead, Letchworth (the first *garden city in 1903; followed by Welwyn in 1919), Stevenage (the first *new town, designated in 1946), St Albans, Watford, Hitchin **physical:** rivers Lea, Stort, Colne; part of the Chiltern Hills **features:** Hatfield House; Knebworth House (Tudor house with 19th-century fascia, home of Lord Lytton); Brocket Hall (1760, on 13th-century site, home of Palmerston and Melbourne); home of George Bernard *Shaw at Ayot St Lawrence; Berkhamsted Castle (Norman); Rothamsted agricultural experimental station **population:** (2001 est) 1,034,900.

hertz symbol Hz, SI unit of frequency (the number of repetitions of a regular occurrence in one second). A wave source has a frequency of 1 Hz if it produces one wave each second. Human beings have an audible range from approximately 20 Hz to 20,000 Hz. Radio waves are often measured in megahertz (MHz), millions of hertz, and the *clock rate of a computer is usually measured in megahertz. The unit is named after German physicist Heinrich Hertz.

Hertzsprung-Russell diagram in astronomy, graph on which the surface temperatures of stars are plotted against their luminosities. Most stars, including the Sun, fall into a narrow band called the main sequence. When a star grows old it moves from the main sequence to the upper right part of the graph, into the area of the giants and supergiants. At the end of its life, as the star shrinks to become a white dwarf, it moves again, to the bottom left area. It is named after the Danish astronomer Ejnar Hertzsprung and the US astronomer Henry Russell, who independently devised it in the years 1911–13.

Herzegovina or **Hercegovina** part of Bosnia-Herzegovina (which was formerly, until 1991, a republic of Yugoslavia).

Herzl, Theodor (1860–1904) Austrian founder of the Zionist movement. The *Dreyfus case convinced him that the only solution to the problem of anti-Semitism was the resettlement of the Jews in a state of their own. His book *Der Judenstaad/Jewish State* (1896) launched political *Zionism, and he became the first president of the World Zionist Organization in 1897.

Hess, (Walter Richard) Rudolf (1894–1987) German Nazi leader. Imprisoned with Adolf Hitler 1924–25, he became his private secretary, taking down

Mein Kampf from his dictation. In 1933 he was appointed deputy *Führer* to Hitler, a post he held until replaced by Goering in September 1939. On 10 May 1941 he landed by air in the UK with his own compromise peace proposals and was held a prisoner of war until 1945, when he was tried at Nürnberg as a war criminal and sentenced to life imprisonment. He died in Spandau prison, Berlin.

Hesse German **Hessen**, administrative region (German *Land*) in central Germany, bordered to the west by the state of Rhineland-Palatinate, to the south by Bavaria and Baden-Württemberg, to the east by Thuringia, and to the north by North Rhine-Westphalia and Lower Saxony; area 21,115 sq km/8,153 sq mi; population (1999 est) 6,951,400. The capital is Wiesbaden, and other major cities include Frankfurt-am-Main, Kassel, Darmstadt, Fulda, Giessen, and Offenbach-am-Main. The region includes the valleys of the rivers Rhine, Main, and Fulda; the Taunus Mountains and Vogelsberg Mountains; and the Odenwald Forest.

Hesse, Hermann (1877–1962) German writer, a Swiss citizen from 1923. A conscientious objector in World War I and a pacifist opponent of Hitler, he published short stories, poetry, and novels, including *Peter Camenzind* (1904), *Siddhartha* (1922), and *Steppenwolf* (1927). Later works, such as *Das Glasperlenspiel/The Glass Bead Game* (1943), show the influence of Indian mysticism and Jungian psychoanalysis. Above all, Hesse was the prophet of individualism. He was awarded the Nobel Prize for Literature in 1946.

Heston, Charlton (1924–) stage name of John Charles Carter, US film actor. He often starred in biblical and historical epics; for example, as Moses in *The Ten Commandments* (1956), and in the title role in *Ben Hur* (1959, Academy Award). His other film appearances include *Touch of Evil* (1958), *Major Dundee* (1965), *Earthquake* (1974), *True Lies* (1994), *The Planet of the Apes* and *The Order* (both 2001).

heterosexuality sexual preference for, or attraction mainly to, persons of the opposite sex.

heterotroph any living organism that obtains its energy from organic substances produced by other organisms. All animals and fungi are heterotrophs, and they include *herbivores, *carnivores, and *saprotrophs (those that feed on dead animal and plant material).

heterozygous in a living organism, having two different *alleles for a given trait. In *homozygous organisms, by contrast, both chromosomes carry the same allele. In an outbreeding population an individual organism will generally be heterozygous for some genes but homozygous for others.

Hewish, Antony (1924–) English radio astronomer who, with Martin *Ryle, was awarded the Nobel Prize for Physics in 1974 for his work on the development of radioastronomy, particularly the aperture-synthesis technique, and the discovery of *pulsars, rapidly rotating neutron stars that emit pulses of energy.

hexadecimal number system *or* **hex** number system to the base 16, used in computing. In hex the decimal numbers 0–15 are represented by the characters 0, 1, 2, 3, 4, 5, 6, 7, 8, 9, A, B, C, D, E, F. Hexadecimal numbers are easy to convert to the computer's internal *binary code and are more compact than binary numbers.

Heydrich, Reinhard Tristan Eugen (1904–1942) German Nazi, head of the *Sicherheitsdienst* (SD), the party's security service, and Heinrich *Himmler's deputy. He was instrumental in organizing the *final solution, the policy of genocide used against Jews and others. 'Protector' of Bohemia and Moravia from 1941, he was ambushed and killed the following year by three members of the Czechoslovak forces in Britain, who had landed by parachute. Reprisals followed, including several hundred executions and the massacre in Lidice.

Heyerdahl, Thor (1914–2002) Norwegian ethnologist. He sailed on the ancient-Peruvian-style raft *Kon-Tiki* from Peru to the Tuamotu Archipelago along the Humboldt Current in 1947, and in 1969–70 used ancient-Egyptian-style papyrus-reed boats to cross the Atlantic. His experimental approach to historical reconstruction is not regarded as having made any important scientific contribution.

Hezbollah *or* **Hizbollah** ('Party of God') extremist Muslim organization founded by the Iranian Revolutionary Guards who were sent to Lebanon after the 1979 Iranian revolution. Its aim is to spread the Islamic revolution of Iran among the Shiite population of Lebanon. Hezbollah is believed to be the umbrella movement of the groups that held many of the Western hostages taken from 1984.

hibernation state of dormancy in which certain animals spend the winter. It is associated with a dramatic reduction in all metabolic processes, including body temperature, breathing, and heart rate.

hibiscus any of a group of plants belonging to the mallow family. Hibiscuses range from large herbaceous plants to trees. Popular as ornamental plants because of their brilliantly coloured, red to white, bell-shaped flowers, they include *H. syriacus* and *H. rosa-sinensis* of Asia and the rose mallow (*H. palustris*) of North America. (Genus *Hibiscus*, family Malvaceae.)

hickory tree belonging to the walnut family, native to North America and Asia. It provides a valuable timber, and all species produce nuts, though some are inedible. The pecan (*C. illinoensis*) is widely cultivated in the southern USA, and the shagbark (*C. ovata*) in the northern USA. (Genus *Carya*, family Juglandaceae.)

hieroglyphic (Greek 'sacred carved writing') Egyptian writing system of the mid-4th millennium BC–3rd century AD, which combines picture signs with those indicating letters. The direction of writing is normally from right to left, the signs facing the beginning of the line. It was deciphered in 1822 by the French Egyptologist J F Champollion (1790–1832) with the aid of the *Rosetta Stone, which has the same inscription carved in hieroglyphic, demotic, and Greek. The earliest hieroglyphics were discovered by German archaeologist Gunter Dreyer on clay tablets in southern Egypt in 1998, and record linen and oil deliveries and also taxes paid. From the tomb of King Scorpion I, they are dated to between 3300 BC and 3200 BC and challenge the widely held belief that Sumerians were the first people to write. Hieroglyphics were replaced for everyday use by cursive writing from about 700 BC onwards.

Higgs boson *or* **Higgs particle** postulated *elementary particle whose existence would explain why particles have mass. The current theory of elementary particles, called the standard model, cannot explain how mass arises. To overcome this difficulty, Peter Higgs of the University of Edinburgh and Thomas Kibble of Imperial College, London, proposed in 1964 a new particle that binds to other particles and gives them their mass.

high-definition television (HDTV) type of digital television system offering a significantly greater number of scanning lines, and therefore a clearer picture, than that provided by conventional systems. Typically, HDTV has about twice the horizontal and vertical resolution of current 525-line (such as the American standard, NTSC) or 625-line standards (such as the British standard, PAL); a frame rate of at least 24 Hz; and a picture aspect ratio of 9:16 instead of the current 3:4. HDTV systems have been in development since the mid-1970s.

Higher in Scottish education, a public examination taken at the age of 17, one year after the Scottish O Grade. Highers are usually taken in four or five subjects and qualify students for entry to higher education. Advanced Highers are taken one year later. About 90% of Scottish undergraduates choose to study in Scotland.

high jump field event in athletics in which competitors leap over a horizontal crossbar held between rigid uprights at least 3.66 m/12 ft apart. The bar is placed at increasingly higher levels. Elimination occurs after three consecutive failures to clear the bar.

Highland unitary authority in northern Scotland, created from the region bearing the same name in 1996. **area:** 26,157 sq km/10,100 sq mi (one-third of Scotland) **towns:** Inverness (administrative headquarters), Thurso, Wick, Fort William, Aviemore **physical:** mainland Highland consists of a series of glaciated ancient plateau masses dissected by narrow glens and straths (valleys); in the northeast (Caithness), old red sandstone rocks give a softer, lower topography; Ben Nevis (1,343 m/4,406 ft), Cairngorm Mountains; Loch Ness; Cuillin Hills, Skye; includes many of the Inner Hebridean islands **features:** Caledonian Canal; John O'Groats; Forth Road Bridge to Skye **population:** (2001 est) 208,900 **history:** location of many key historical moments in Scottish history, including the 'massacre' of Glen Coe in 1692 and the Battle of Culloden in 1745–6.

Highland Clearances forced removal of tenants from large estates in Scotland during the early 19th century, as landowners 'improved' their estates by switching from arable to sheep farming. It led ultimately to widespread emigration to North America.

Highlands one of the three geographical divisions of Scotland, lying to the north of a geological fault line that stretches from Stonehaven in the North Sea to Dumbarton on the Clyde. It is a mountainous region of hard rocks, shallow infertile soils, and high rainfall.

high-level language in computing, a programming language designed to suit the requirements of the programmer; it is independent of the internal machine code of any particular computer. High-level languages are used to solve problems and are often described as **problem-oriented languages**; for example, *BASIC was designed to be easily learnt by first-time programmers; *COBOL is used to write programs solving business problems; and *FORTRAN is used for programs solving scientific and mathematical problems. With the increasing popularity of windows-based systems, the next generation of programming languages was designed to facilitate the development of GUI interfaces; for example, Visual Basic wraps the BASIC language in a graphical programming environment. Support for object-oriented programming has also become more common, for example in C++ and Java. In contrast, **low-level languages**, such as *assembly languages, closely reflect the machine codes of specific computers, and are therefore described as **machine-oriented languages**.

highwayman in English history, a thief on horseback who robbed travellers on the highway (those who did so on foot were known as **footpads**).

hijacking illegal seizure or taking control of a vehicle and/or its passengers or goods. The term dates from 1923 and originally referred to the robbing of freight lorries. Subsequently it (and its derivative 'skyjacking') has been applied to the seizure of aircraft, usually in flight, by an individual or group, often with some political aim. International treaties (Tokyo 1963, The Hague 1970, and Montréal 1971) encourage cooperation against hijackers and make severe penalties compulsory.

Hijrah *or* **Hegira** (Arabic 'flight') the flight from Mecca to Medina of the prophet Muhammad, which took place in AD 622 as a result of the persecution of the prophet and his followers. The Muslim calendar dates from this event, and the day of the Hijrah is celebrated as the Muslim New Year.

Hill, (Norman) Graham (1929–1975) English motor-racing driver. He won the Dutch Grand Prix in 1962, progressing to the Formula 1 World Drivers' Champion in 1962 and 1968. In 1972 he became the first Formula 1 World Champion to win the Le Mans Grand Prix d'Endurance (Le Mans 24-Hour Race). He was also the only driver to win the these two competitions and the Indianapolis 500 Race in his career as a driver. Hill started his Formula 1 career with Lotus in 1958, went to BRM 1960–66, returned to Lotus 1967–69, moved to Brabham 1970–72, and formed his own team, Embassy Shadow, 1973–75. He was killed in an air crash. His son **Damon** won his first Grand Prix in 1993, making them the first father and son both to win a Grand Prix.

Hill, Rowland (1795–1879) English Post Office official who reformed the postage system with the introduction of adhesive stamps. His pamphlet *Post Office Reform* (1837) prompted the introduction of the penny prepaid post in 1840 (previously the addressee paid, according to distance, on receipt).

Hill and Adamson David Octavius Hill (1802–1870) and Robert R Adamson (1821–1848), Scottish photographers who worked together 1843–48. They made extensive use of the *calotype process in their portraits of leading members of the Free Church of Scotland and their views of Edinburgh and the Scottish fishing village of Newhaven. They produced some 2,500 calotypes. Their work was rediscovered around 1900.

Hillary, Edmund (Percival) (1919–) New Zealand mountaineer. In 1953, with Nepalese Sherpa mountaineer Tenzing Norgay, he reached the summit of Mount Everest, the first to climb the world's highest peak. As a member of the Commonwealth Transantarctic Expedition 1957–58, he was the first person since R F Scott to reach the South Pole overland, on 3 January 1958. He was knighted in 1953.

hill fort European Iron Age site with massive banks and ditches for defence, used as both a military camp and a permanent settlement. Examples found across Europe, in particular France, central Germany, and the British Isles, include Heuneberg near Sigmaringen, Germany, Spinans Hill in County Wicklow, Ireland, and Maiden Castle, Dorset, England.

Himachal Pradesh state of northwest India, to the south of Kashmir and west of Tibet; area 55,673 sq km/ 21,495 sq mi; population (2001 est) 6,077,248 (mainly Hindu; some Buddhists). The capital is Shimla, which lies at an altitude of 2,213 m/7,200 ft. Himachal Pradesh is a mainly agricultural state, partly forested, producing fruit, grain, rice, and seed potatoes. Timber production is an important industry, and there is small-scale mining of slate, gypsum, and limestone. Manufacturing industries indclude iron founding and the production of agricultural implements, resin, fertilizer, and turpentine at Nahan, television sets at Solan, and electronic goods near Shimla. The mountain scenery attracts increasing numbers of tourists, and Shimla is the leading hill resort in India.

Himalayas vast mountain system of central Asia, extending from the Indian states of Kashmir in the west to Assam in the east, covering the southern part of Tibet, Nepal, Sikkim, and Bhutan. It is the highest mountain range in the world, with more than 100 peaks reaching heights over 7,300 m/24,000 ft; its name means 'abode of snow'. The two highest peaks are Mount *Everest and *K2. Other peaks include *Kanchenjunga, Makalu, Annapurna, and Nanga Parbat, all over 8,000 m/26,000 ft.

Himmler, Heinrich (1900–1945) German Nazi leader, head of the *SS elite corps from 1929, the police and the *Gestapo secret police from 1936, and supervisor of the extermination of the Jews in Eastern Europe. During World War II he replaced Hermann Goering as Hitler's second-in-command. He was captured in May 1945 and committed suicide.

Hindemith, Paul (1895–1963) German composer and teacher. His operas *Cardillac* (1926, revised 1952) and *Mathis der Maler/Mathis the Painter* (1933–35) are theatrically astute and politically aware; as a teacher in Berlin 1927–33 he encouraged the development of a functional modern repertoire ('Gebrauchsmusik'/ 'utility music') for home and school.

Hindenburg, Paul Ludwig Hans Anton von Beneckendorf und Hindenburg (1847–1934) German field marshal and right-wing politician. During World War I he was supreme commander and, with Erich von Ludendorff, practically directed Germany's policy until the end of the war. He was president of Germany 1925–33.

Hindenburg Line German western line of World War I fortifications running from Arras, through Cambrai and St Quentin, to Soissons, built 1916–17. Part of the line was taken by the British in the third battle of Arras, but it generally resisted attack until the British offensive of summer 1918.

Hindi language member of the Indo-Iranian branch of the Indo-European language family, the official language of the Republic of India, although resisted as such by the Dravidian-speaking states of the south. Hindi proper is used by some 30% of Indians, in such northern states as Uttar Pradesh, Uttaranchal, Madhya Pradesh, and Chhattisgarh.

Hinduism (Hindu *sanatana dharma* 'eternal tradition') religion originating in northern India about 4,000 years ago, which is superficially and in some of its forms polytheistic, but has a concept of the supreme spirit, *Brahman, above the many divine manifestations. These include the triad of chief gods (the Trimurti): *Brahma, *Vishnu, and *Shiva (creator, preserver, and destroyer). Central to Hinduism are the beliefs in reincarnation and *karma; the oldest scriptures are the *Vedas. Temple worship is almost universally observed and there are many festivals. There are over 805 million Hindus worldwide. Women are not regarded as the equals of men but should be treated with kindness and respect. Muslim influence in northern India led to the veiling of women and the restriction of their movements from about the end of the 12th century.

Hindu Kush mountain range in central Asia, length 800 km/500 mi, greatest height Tirich Mir, 7,690 m/ 25,239 ft, in Pakistan. The narrow Khyber Pass (53 km/ 33 mi long) connects Pakistan with Afghanistan and was used by *Babur and other invaders of India. The present road was built by the British in the *Afghan Wars (1838–42 and 1878–80).

Hindustan ('land of the Hindus') the whole of India, but more specifically the plain of the *Ganges and Yamuna rivers, or that part of India north of the Deccan.

Hindustani member of the Indo-Iranian branch of the Indo-European language family, closely related to Hindi and Urdu and originating in the bazaars of Delhi. It is a *lingua franca in many parts of the Republic of India.

hip-hop popular music originating in New York in the early 1980s, created with scratching (a percussive effect obtained by manually manipulating a vinyl record backwards and forwards on a turntable) and heavily accented electronic drums (also often produced by a 'human beatbox' – one performer providing the drumbeat with their mouth into a microphone) behind a *rap vocal. Within a decade, *digital sampling had largely replaced scratching. The term 'hip-hop' also includes break-dancing and graffiti.

Hipparchus (c. 190–c. 120 BC) Greek astronomer and mathematician. He invented trigonometry and calculated the lengths of the solar year and the lunar month, discovered the precession of the equinoxes, made a catalogue of 850 fixed stars, and advanced Eratosthenes' method of determining the situation of places on the Earth's surface by lines of latitude and longitude.

hippie member of a youth movement of the late 1960s, also known as **flower power**, which originated in San Francisco, California, and was characterized by nonviolent anarchy, concern for the environment, and rejection of Western materialism. The hippies formed a politically outspoken, anti-war, artistically prolific counterculture in North America and Europe. Their colourful psychedelic style, inspired by drugs such as *LSD, emerged in fashion, graphic art, and music by bands such as Love (1965–71), the Grateful Dead, Jefferson Airplane (1965–74), and *Pink Floyd.

Hippocrates (c. 460–c. 377 BC) Greek physician, often called the founder of medicine. Important Hippocratic ideas include cleanliness (for patients and physicians), moderation in eating and drinking, letting nature take its course, and living where the air is good. He believed that health was the result of the 'humours' of the body being in balance; imbalance caused disease. These ideas were later adopted by *Galen.

Hippolytus in Greek mythology, the charioteer son of *Theseus, loved by his stepmother Phaedra. Enraged by his rejection, she falsely accused him of dishonouring her and committed suicide, turning Theseus against his son. The sea god *Poseidon, who owed Theseus a wish, sent a monster as Hippolytus drove on the shore near Troezen; the frightened chariot horses dragged him to death. His story was dramatized in *Hippolytus* by *Euripides.

hippopotamus (Greek 'river horse') large herbivorous, short-legged, even-toed hoofed mammal. The **common hippopotamus** (*Hippopotamus amphibius*) is found in Africa. It weighs up to 3,200 kg/7,040 lb, stands about 1.6 m/5.25 ft tall, and has a brown or slate-grey skin. It is an endangered species. (Family Hippopotamidae.)

Hirohito (1901–1989) regnal name **Showa**, Emperor of Japan from 1926, when he succeeded his father Taisho (Yoshihito). After the defeat of Japan in World War II in 1945, he was made a figurehead monarch by the US-backed constitution of 1946. He is believed to have played a reluctant role in General *Tojo's prewar expansion plans. He was succeeded by his son *Akihito.

Hiroshige, Ando (1797–1858) Japanese artist. He was one of the leading exponents of *ukiyo-e prints, an art form whose flat, decorative style and choice of everyday subjects influenced such artists as James Whistler and Vincent van Gogh. His landscape prints, often employing snow or rain to create atmosphere, include *Tokaido gojusan tsugi/53 Stations on the Tokaido Highway* (1833).

Hiroshima industrial city and port on the south coast of Honshu Island, Japan; population (1994) 1,077,000. On 6 August 1945 it was destroyed by the first wartime use of an *atomic bomb. The city has been largely rebuilt since then. The main industries include food processing and the manufacture of cars and machinery.

Hispaniola (Spanish 'little Spain') West Indian island, first landing place of Christopher *Columbus in the New World on 6 December 1492. It is now divided into Haiti and the Dominican Republic; total population (2001 est) 15,546,000.

histamine inflammatory substance normally released in damaged tissues, which also accounts for many of the symptoms of *allergy. It is an amine, $C_5H_9N_3$. Substances that neutralize its activity are known as *antihistamines. Histamine was first described in 1911 by British physiologist Henry Dale (1875–1968).

histology in medicine, the laboratory study of cells and tissues.

history record of the events of human societies. The earliest surviving historical records are inscriptions concerning the achievements of Egyptian and Babylonian kings. As a literary form in the Western world, historical writing, or **historiography**, began in the 5th century BC with the Greek Herodotus, who was first to pass beyond the limits of a purely national outlook. Contemporary historians make extensive use of statistics, population figures, and primary records to justify historical arguments.

Hitchcock, Alfred (Joseph) (1899–1980) English film director, a US citizen from 1955. A master of the suspense thriller, he was noted for his meticulously drawn storyboards that determined his camera angles and for cameo walk-ons in his own films. His *Blackmail* (1929) was the first successful British talking film. *The Thirty-Nine Steps* (1935) and *The Lady Vanishes* (1938) are British suspense classics. He went to Hollywood in 1940, and his work there included *Rebecca* (1940; Academy Award), *Notorious* (1946), *Strangers on a Train* (1951), *Rear Window* (1954), *Vertigo* (1958), *North by Northwest* (1959), *Psycho* (1960), and *The Birds* (1963).

Hitler, Adolf (1889–1945) German Nazi dictator, born in Austria. He was *Führer* (leader) of the *Nazi Party from 1921 and wrote *Mein Kampf/My Struggle* (1925–27). As chancellor of Germany from 1933 and head of state from 1934, he created a dictatorship by playing party and state institutions against each other and continually creating new offices and appointments. His position was not seriously challenged until the July Plot of 1944, which failed to assassinate him. In foreign affairs, he reoccupied the Rhineland and formed an alliance with the Italian Fascist Benito *Mussolini in 1936, annexed Austria in 1938, and occupied Sudeten under the *Munich Agreement. The rest of Czechoslovakia was annexed in March 1939. The *Ribbentrop–Molotov pact was followed in September by the invasion of Poland and the declaration of war by Britain and France (see *World War II). He committed suicide as Berlin fell.

Hitler–Stalin pact another name for the *Ribbentrop–Molotov pact.

Hittite member of any of a succession of peoples who inhabited Anatolia and northern Syria from the 3rd millennium to the 1st millennium BC. The city of Hattusas (now Bogazköy in central Turkey) became the capital of a strong kingdom which overthrew the Babylonian Empire. After a period of eclipse the Hittite New Empire became a great power (about 1400–1200 BC), which successfully waged war with Egypt. The Hittite language is an Indo-European language.

HIV abbreviation for human immunodeficiency virus, infectious agent that is believed to cause *AIDS. It was first discovered in 1983 by Luc Montagnier of the Pasteur Institute in Paris, who called it lymphocyte-associated virus (LAV). Independently, US scientist Robert Gallo of the National Cancer Institute in Bethesda, Maryland, claimed its discovery in 1984 and named it human T-lymphocytotrophic virus 3 (HTLV-III).

Hobart capital and principal port of *Tasmania, Australia; population (1996) 126,118. Hobart is situated on the southeast coast of the island, at the mouth of the River Derwent. Hobart is a centre for yachting, fishing, and trading; exports include fruit, textiles, and processed food. The University of Tasmania (founded in 1890) is located here.

Hobbes, Thomas (1588–1679) English political philosopher and the first thinker since Aristotle to attempt to develop a comprehensive theory of nature, including human behaviour. In *Leviathan* (1651), he advocates absolutist government as the only means of ensuring order and security; he saw this as deriving from the social contract.

Hobbs, Jack (1882–1963) born John Berry Hobbs, English cricketer who scored more first-class runs (61,760) and centuries (192) than any other player. An orthodox right-handed opening batsman, he played in 61 Test matches. He retired from first-class cricket in 1934.

hobby small *falcon found across Europe and northern Asia. It is about 30 cm/1 ft long, with a grey-blue back, streaked front, and chestnut thighs. It is found in open woods and heaths, and feeds on insects and small birds. (Species *Falco subbuteo*.)

Ho Chi Minh (1890–1969) adopted name of Nguyen Tat Thanh, North Vietnamese communist politician, prime minister 1954–55, and president 1954–69. Having trained in Moscow shortly after the Russian Revolution, he headed the communist Vietminh from 1941 and fought against the French during the *Indochina War 1946–54, becoming president and prime minister of the republic at the armistice. Aided by the communist bloc, he did much to develop industrial potential. He relinquished the premiership in 1955, but continued as president. In the years before his death, Ho successfully led his country's fight against US-aided South Vietnam in the *Vietnam War 1954–75.

Ho Chi Minh City formerly **Saigon** (until 1976), chief port and industrial city of South Vietnam; population (1997 est) 3,571,000 (the largest city in Vietnam). It lies on the Saigon River, 54 km/34 mi from the South China Sea. Industries include shipbuilding, textiles, rubber, and food products. Since the unification of Vietnam, state-run enterprise in handicraft trades has expanded, producing goods such as carpets, furniture, and lacquerware mostly for export. Saigon was the capital of the Republic of Vietnam (South Vietnam) from 1954 to 1976, when it was renamed, and the city was also the former capital of French Indochina.

hockey game played with hooked sticks and a small, solid ball, the object being to hit the ball into the goal. It is played between two teams, each of not more than 11 players. Hockey has been an Olympic sport since 1908 for men and since 1980 for women. In North America it is known as 'field hockey', to distinguish it from *ice hockey.

Hockney, David (1937–) English painter, printmaker, and designer, resident in California. One of the best-known figures in 20th-century British pop art, he developed a distinctive figurative style, as in his portrait *Mr and Mrs Clark and Percy* (1971; Tate Gallery, London). *A Bigger Splash* (1967) demonstrates his interest in bright flat blocks of colour and distinct line. He has experimented prolifically with technique, and produced drawings; etchings, including *Six Fairy Tales from the Brothers Grimm* (1970); photo collages; and opera sets for Glyndebourne, East Sussex; La Scala, Milan; and the Metropolitan, New York.

Hodgkin, Dorothy Mary Crowfoot (1910–1994) English biochemist who analysed the structure of penicillin, insulin, and vitamin B_{12}. Hodgkin was the first to use a computer to analyse the molecular structure of complex chemicals, and this enabled her to produce three-dimensional models. She was awarded the Nobel Prize for Chemistry in 1964 for her work in the crystallographic determination of the structures of biochemical compounds, notably penicillin and cyanocobalamin (vitamin B_{12}).

Hodgkin's disease *or* **lymphadenoma** rare form of cancer mainly affecting the lymph nodes and spleen. It undermines the immune system, leaving the sufferer susceptible to infection. However, it responds well to radiotherapy and *cytotoxic drugs, and long-term survival is usual.

Hoffman, Dustin (1937–) US actor. He became popular in the 1960s with his unconventional looks, short stature, and versatility. His performance in *The Graduate* (1967) propelled him to stardom, and he subsequently won Academy Awards for his performances in *Kramer vs Kramer* (1979) and *Rain Man* (1988). His other films include *Midnight Cowboy* (1969), *Little Big Man* (1970), *All the President's Men* (1976), *Tootsie* (1982), and *J M Barrie's Neverland* (2004).

Hoffmann, Josef (1870–1956) Austrian architect. Influenced by art nouveau, he was one of the founders of the Wiener Werkstätte/Vienna Workshops (a modern design cooperative of early 20th-century Vienna), and a pupil of Otto *Wagner. One of his best-known works is the Purkersdorf Sanatorium (1903–05).

hog any member of the *pig family. The **river hog** (*Potamochoerus porcus*) lives in Africa, south of the Sahara. Reddish or black, up to 1.3 m/4.2 ft long plus tail, and 90 cm/3 ft at the shoulder, this gregarious animal roots for food in many types of habitat. The **giant forest hog** (*Hylochoerus meinerzthageni*) lives in thick forests of central Africa and grows up to 1.9 m/6 ft long. The **wart hog** is another African wild pig. The **pygmy hog** (*Sus salvanus*), the smallest of the pig family, is about 65 cm long (25 cm at the shoulder) and weighs 8–9 kg.

Hogarth, William (1697–1764) English painter and engraver. He produced portraits and moralizing genre scenes, such as the story series of prints *A Rake's Progress* (1735; Soane Museum, London). His portraits are remarkably direct and full of character, for example *Heads of Six of Hogarth's Servants* (c. 1750–55; Tate Gallery, London) and his oil sketch masterpiece *The Shrimp Girl* (National Gallery, London).

Hogmanay Scottish name for New Year's Eve. A traditional feature is first-footing, visiting the homes of friends and neighbours after midnight to welcome in the new year with salt, bread, whisky, and other gifts. Children may also go from house to house singing carols and receiving oatmeal cakes.

Hohenstaufen German family of princes, several members of which were Holy Roman Emperors 1138–1208 and 1214–54. They were the first German emperors to make use of associations with Roman law and tradition to aggrandize their office, and included Conrad III; Frederick I (Barbarossa), the first to use the title Holy Roman Emperor (previously the title Roman emperor was used); Henry VI; and Frederick II.

Hohenzollern German family, originating in Württemberg, the main branch of which held the titles of *elector of Brandenburg from 1415, king of Prussia from 1701, and German emperor from 1871. The last emperor, Wilhelm II, was dethroned in 1918 after the disastrous course of World War I. Another branch of the family were kings of Romania 1881–1947.

Hokkaido formerly **Yezo** or **Ezo** (until 1868), (Japanese *hoku* 'north'; *kai* 'sea'; *do* 'road') northernmost and second-largest of the four main islands of Japan, separated from Honshu to the south by Tsugaru Strait (20 km/12 mi wide), and from Sakhalin (Russia) to the north by Soya Strait; area 83,500 sq km/32,239 sq mi; population (2000 est) 5,683,000 (including 16,000 *Ainus). The capital is Sapporo; other major cities are Hakodate, Asahikawa, Otaru, and Muroran. The main industries are coal, mercury, manganese, oil, natural gas, and tourism; agriculture centres on rice cultivation, dairying, forestry, and fishing.

Hokusai, Katsushika (1760–1849) Japanese artist. He was the leading printmaker of his time and a major exponent of *ukiyo-e. He published *Fugaku sanju-rokkei/36 Views of Mount Fuji* (c. 1823–29), and produced outstanding pictures of almost every kind of subject – birds, flowers, courtesans, and scenes from legend and everyday life. *Under the Wave at Kanagawa* (British Museum, London) is typical.

Holbein, Hans, the Younger (1497–1543) German painter and woodcut artist who spent much of his career as a portrait artist at the court of Henry VIII of England. One of the finest graphic artists of his age, he executed a woodcut series *Dance of Death* (c. 1525), and designed title pages for Luther's New Testament and Thomas More's *Utopia*.

Holiday, Billie (1915–1959) stage name of Eleanora Fagan, US jazz singer, also known as 'Lady Day'. She made her debut in clubs in Harlem, New York, and became known for her emotionally charged delivery and her unique style of phrasing. Holiday brought a blues feel to her performances with swing bands. Songs she made her own include 'Stormy Weather', 'Strange Fruit', 'I Cover the Waterfront', 'That Ole Devil Called Love', and 'Lover Man (Oh, Where can You Be?)'.

Holinshed (*or* Hollingshead), Raphael (c. 1520–c. 1580) English historian. He published two volumes of the *Chronicles of England, Scotland, and Ireland* (1578), which are a mixture of fact and legend. The *Chronicles* were used as a principal source by Elizabethan dramatists for their plots. Nearly all Shakespeare's English history plays, as well as *Macbeth*, *King Lear*, and *Cymbeline*, are based on Holinshed's work.

holism in philosophy, the concept that the whole is greater than the sum of its parts.

holistic medicine umbrella term for an approach that virtually all alternative therapies profess, which considers the overall health and lifestyle profile of a patient, and treats specific ailments not primarily as conditions to be alleviated but rather as symptoms of more fundamental disease.

Holland popular name for the Netherlands; also two provinces of the Netherlands, see *North Holland and *South Holland.

Hollerith, Herman (1860–1929) US inventor of a mechanical tabulating machine, the first device for high-volume data processing. Hollerith's tabulator was widely publicized after being successfully used in the 1890 census. The firm he established, the Tabulating Machine Company, was later one of the founding companies of IBM.

holly any of a group of trees or shrubs that includes the English Christmas holly (*I. aquifolium*), an evergreen with spiny, glossy leaves, small white flowers, and poisonous scarlet berries on the female tree. Leaves of the Brazilian holly (*I. paraguayensis*) are used to make the tea *yerba maté*. (Genus *Ilex*, family Aquifoliaceae.)

Holly, Buddy (1936–1959) stage name of Charles Hardin Holley, US rock and roll singer, guitarist, and songwriter. He had a distinctive, hiccuping vocal style and was an early experimenter with recording techniques. Many of his hits with his band, the Crickets, such as 'That'll Be the Day' (1957), 'Peggy Sue' (1957), and 'Maybe Baby' (1958), have become classics. His albums include *The Chirping Crickets* (1958) and *Buddy Holly* (1958).

hollyhock tall flowering plant belonging to the mallow family. *A. rosea*, originally a native of Asia, produces spikes of large white, yellow, pink, or red flowers, 3 m/10 ft high when cultivated as a biennial; it is a popular cottage garden plant. (Genus *Althaea*, family Malvaceae.)

Hollywood district in the city of Los Angeles, California; the centre of the US film industry from 1911, when the first film studio was established on Sunset Boulevard. It is the home of film studios such as Twentieth Century Fox, MGM, Paramount, Columbia Pictures, United Artists, Disney, and Warner Bros. Many film stars' homes are situated nearby in Beverly Hills and other communities adjacent to Hollywood.

Holmes, Sherlock fictitious private detective, created by the Scottish writer Arthur Conan *Doyle in *A Study in Scarlet* (1887) and recurring in novels and stories until 1927. Holmes' ability to make inferences from slight clues always astonishes the narrator, Dr Watson.

holmium chemical symbol Ho, (Latin *Holmia* 'Stockholm') silvery, metallic element of the *lanthanide series, atomic number 67, relative atomic mass 164.93. It occurs in combination with other rare-earth metals and in various minerals such as gadolinite. Its compounds are highly magnetic.

Holocaust, the *or* Shoah Hebrew 'whirlwind', the annihilation of an estimated 16 million people by the Nazi regime between 1933 and 1945, principally in the numerous extermination and *concentration camps, most notably *Auschwitz (Oswiecim), Sobibor, Treblinka, and Maidanek in Poland, and Belsen, *Buchenwald, and *Dachau in Germany. Camps were built on railway lines to facilitate transport. Of the victims, around 6 million were Jews (over 67% of European Jews); around 10 million Ukrainian, Polish, and Russian civilians and prisoners of war, Romanies, socialists, homosexuals, and others (labelled 'defectives') were also imprisoned and/or exterminated. Victims were variously starved, tortured, experimented on, and worked to death. Millions were executed in gas chambers, shot, or hanged. It was euphemistically termed the *Final Solution (of the Jewish question). The precise death toll will never be known. Holocaust museums and memorial sites have been established in Israel and in other countries, and many Jews remember those who died by observing Yom Ha-Shoah, or Holocaust Remembrance Day.

Holocene epoch period of geological time that began 10,000 years ago, and continues into the present. During this epoch the climate became warmer, the glaciers retreated, and human civilizations developed significantly.

holography method of producing three-dimensional (3-D) images, called holograms, by means of *laser light. Holography uses a photographic technique (involving the splitting of a laser beam into two beams) to produce a picture, or hologram, that contains 3-D information about the object photographed. Some holograms show meaningless patterns in ordinary light and produce a 3-D image only when laser light is projected through them, but reflection holograms produce images when ordinary light is reflected from them (as found on credit cards).

Holst, Gustav(us Theodore von) (1874–1934) English composer of distant Swedish descent. He wrote operas, including *Sávitri* (1908) and *At the Boar's Head* (1924); ballets; choral works, including *Choral Hymns from the Rig Veda* (1908–12) and *The Hymn of Jesus* (1917); orchestral suites, including *The Planets* (1914–16); and songs. He was a lifelong friend of Ralph *Vaughan Williams, with whom he shared an enthusiasm for English folk music. His musical style, although tonal and drawing on folk song, tends to be severe. He was the father of Imogen Holst (1907–1984), musicologist and his biographer.

Holy Alliance 'Christian Union of Charity, Peace, and Love' initiated by Alexander I of Russia in 1815 and signed by every crowned head in Europe. The alliance became associated with Russian attempts to preserve autocratic monarchies at any price, and served as an excuse to meddle in the internal affairs of other states.

Holy Communion another name for the Eucharist, a Christian sacrament.

Holy Grail in medieval Christian legend, the dish or cup used by Jesus at the Last Supper; credited with supernatural powers and a symbol of Christian grace. In certain stories incorporated in Arthurian legend, it was an object of quest by King Arthur's knights, together with the spear with which Jesus was wounded at the Crucifixion. *Galahad was the only knight to achieve the mission.

Holy Roman Empire empire of Charlemagne and his successors, and the German Empire 962–1806, both being regarded as the Christian (hence 'holy') revival of the Roman Empire. At its height it comprised much of Western and Central Europe. See *Habsburg.

Home, Alec Douglas- British Conservative politician. See *Douglas-Home.

Home Counties those counties in close proximity to London, England: Hertfordshire, Essex, Kent, Surrey, Buckinghamshire, and formerly Berkshire and Middlesex.

Home Guard unpaid force formed in Britain in May 1940 to repel the expected German invasion, and known until July 1940 as the Local Defence Volunteers. It consisted of men aged 17–65 who had not been called up, formed part of the armed forces of the Crown, and was subject to military law. Over 2 million strong in 1944, it was disbanded on 31 December 1945, but revived in 1951, then placed on a reserve basis in 1955. It ceased activity in 1957.

Homelands Policy South Africa's former apartheid policy which set aside *Black National States for black Africans.

homeopathy *or* **homoeopathy** system of alternative medicine based on the principle that symptoms of disease are part of the body's self-healing processes, and on the practice of administering extremely diluted doses of natural substances found to produce in a healthy person the symptoms manifest in the illness being treated. Developed by the German physician Samuel Hahnemann (1755–1843), the system is widely practised today as an alternative to allopathic (orthodox) medicine, and many controlled tests and achieved cures testify its efficacy.

homeostasis maintenance of a constant environment around living cells, particularly with regard to pH, salt concentration, temperature, and blood sugar levels. Stable conditions are important for the efficient functioning of the *enzyme reactions within the cells. In humans, homeostasis in the blood (which provides fluid for all tissues) is ensured by several organs. The *kidneys regulate pH, urea, and water concentration. The lungs regulate oxygen and carbon dioxide (see *breathing). Temperature is regulated by the liver and the skin. Glucose levels in the blood are regulated by the *liver and the pancreas.

Homer According to ancient tradition, the author of the Greek narrative epics, the *Iliad and the *Odyssey (both derived from oral tradition). Little is known about the man, but modern research suggests that both poems should be assigned to the 8th century BC, with the *Odyssey the later of the two.

Homer, Winslow (1836–1910) US painter and lithographer. A leading realist, he is known for his vivid seascapes, in both oil and watercolour, most of which date from the 1880s and 1890s. *The Gulf Stream* (1899; Metropolitan Museum of Art, New York) is an example.

home rule, Irish movement to repeal the Act of *Union of 1801 that joined Ireland to Britain, and to establish an Irish parliament responsible for internal affairs. In 1870 Isaac Butt formed the Home Rule Association and the movement was led in Parliament from 1880 by Charles Stewart *Parnell. After 1918 the demand for an independent Irish republic replaced that for home rule.

Homestead Act in US history, an act of Congress in May 1862 that encouraged settlement of land in the west by offering plots of up to 65-ha/160-acres, cheaply or even free, to citizens aged 21 years and over, or heads of family. In return, they had to promise to stay on the plot for five years, and to cultivate and improve the land, as well as build a house. The law was designed to prevent people from controlling vast amounts of land in order to make a quick fortune. By 1900 about 32 million ha/80 million acres had been distributed. Homestead lands are available to this day.

homicide in law, the killing of a human being. This may be unlawful, lawful, or excusable, depending on the circumstances. Unlawful homicides include *murder, *manslaughter, infanticide, and causing death by dangerous driving. Lawful homicide occurs where, for example, a police officer is justified in killing a criminal in the course of apprehension or when a person is killed in self-defence or defence of others.

homoeopathy variant spelling of *homeopathy.

Homo erectus species of hominid (of the human family) that walked upright and lived more than 1.5 million years ago. Fossil remains have been found in Java, China, Africa, and Europe. See *human species, origins of.

homologous in biology, a term describing an organ or structure possessed by members of different taxonomic groups (for example, species, genera, families, orders) that originally derived from the same structure in a common ancestor. The wing of a bat, the arm of a monkey, and the flipper of a seal are homologous because they all derive from the forelimb of an ancestral mammal.

homologous series in chemistry, any of a number of series of organic compounds with similar chemical properties in which members differ by a constant relative molecular mass.

homophony music comprising a melody lead and accompanying harmony, in contrast to heterophony and *polyphony in which different melody lines of equal importance are combined.

homosexuality sexual preference for, or attraction to, persons of one's own sex; in women it is referred to as *lesbianism. Both sexes use the term 'gay'. Men and women who are attracted to both sexes are referred to as bisexual. The extent to which homosexual behaviour is caused by biological or psychological factors is an area of disagreement among experts.

homozygous in a living organism, having two identical *alleles for a given trait. Individuals homozygous for a trait always breed true; that is, they produce offspring that resemble them in appearance when bred with a genetically similar individual; inbred varieties or species are homozygous for almost all traits. *Recessive alleles are only expressed in the homozygous condition. *Heterozygous organisms have two different alleles for a given trait.

Honduras

National name: *República de Honduras/ Republic of Honduras*

Area: 112,100 sq km/43,281 sq mi
Capital: Tegucigalpa
Major towns/cities: San Pedro Sula, La Ceiba, El Progreso, Choluteca, Juticalpa, Danlí
Major ports: La Ceiba, Puerto Cortés
Physical features: narrow tropical coastal plain with mountainous interior, Bay Islands, Caribbean reefs
Head of state and government: Ricardo Maduro from 2001
Political system: liberal democracy
Political executive: limited presidency
Political parties: Liberal Party of Honduras (PLH), left of centre; National Party (PN), right wing

Currency: lempira
GNI per capita (PPP): (US$) 2,450 (2002 est)
Exports: bananas, lobsters and prawns, coffee, zinc, meat. Principal market: USA 45.7% (2001)
Population: 6,941,000 (2003 est)
Language: Spanish (official), English, American Indian languages
Religion: Roman Catholic 97%
Life expectancy: 67 (men); 71 (women) (2000–05)
Chronology
c. AD 250–900: Part of culturally advanced Maya civilization.
1502: Visited by Christopher Columbus, who named the country Honduras ('depths') after the deep waters off the north coast.
1525: Colonized by Spain, who founded the town of Trujillo, but met with fierce resistance from the American Indian population.
17th century onwards: The northern 'Mosquito Coast' fell under the control of British buccaneers, as the Spanish concentrated on the inland area, with a British protectorate being established over the coast until 1860.
1821: Achieved independence from Spain and became part of Mexico.
1823: Became part of United Provinces (Federation) of Central America, also embracing Costa Rica, El Salvador, Guatemala, and Nicaragua, with the Honduran liberal Gen Francisco Morazan, president of the Federation from 1830.
1838: Achieved full independence when federation dissolved.
1880: Capital transferred from Comayagua to Tegucigalpa.
later 19th–early 20th centuries: The USA's economic involvement significant, with banana production, which provided two-thirds of exports in 1913, being controlled by the United Fruit Company; political instability, with frequent changes of constitution and military coups.
1925: Brief civil war.
1932–49: Under a right-wing National Party (PNH) dictatorship, led by Gen Tiburcio Carias Andino.
1963–74: Following a series of military coups, Gen Oswaldo López Arelano held power, before resigning after allegedly accepting bribes from a US company.
1969: Brief 'Football War' with El Salvador, which attacked Honduras at the time of a football competition between the two states, following evictions of thousands of Salvadoran illegal immigrants from Honduras.
1980: The first civilian government in more than a century was elected, with Dr Roberto Suazo of the centrist Liberal Party (PLH) as president, but the commander in chief of the army, Gen Gustavo Alvárez, retained considerable power.
1983: There was close involvement with the USA in providing naval and air bases and allowing Nicaraguan counter-revolutionaries ('Contras') to operate from Honduras.
1989: The government and opposition declared support for a Central American peace plan to demobilize Nicaraguan Contras (thought to number 55,000 with their dependents) based in Honduras.
1992: A border dispute with El Salvador dating from 1861 was finally resolved.

1997: Carlos Flores (PLH) won the presidential elections, beginning his term of office in January 1998.
2001: Ricardo Maduro headed the government.
2002: Ricardo Maduro (National Party) was elected president.

Honecker, Erich (1912–1994) German communist politician, in power in East Germany 1973–89, elected chair of the council of state (head of state) in 1976. He governed in an outwardly austere and efficient manner and, while favouring East–West détente, was a loyal ally of the USSR. In 1989, following a wave of pro-democracy demonstrations, he was replaced as leader of the Socialist Unity Party (SED) and head of state by Egon *Krenz, and expelled from the Communist Party. He died in exile in Chile.

Honegger, Arthur (1892–1955) Swiss composer. He was one of the group of composers known as *Les Six*. His work was varied in form, for example, the opera *Antigone* (1927), the ballet *Skating Rink* (1922), the dramatic oratorio *Le Roi David/King David* (1921), programme music (*Pacific 231*, 1923), and the *Symphonie liturgique/Liturgical Symphony* (1946). He also composed incidental music for Abel Gance's silent movie classics *La Roue/The Wheel* (1923) and *Napoléon* (1927).

honey sweet syrup produced by honey *bees from the nectar of flowers. It is stored in honeycombs and made in excess of their needs as food for the winter. Honey comprises various sugars, mainly laevulose and dextrose, with enzymes, colouring matter, acids, and pollen grains. It has antibacterial properties and was widely used in ancient Egypt, Greece, and Rome as a wound salve. It is still popular for sore throats, in hot drinks or in lozenges.

honeyeater *or* **honey-sucker** any of a group of small, brightly coloured birds with long, curved beaks and long tails, native to Australia. They have a long tongue divided into four at the end to form a brush for collecting nectar from flowers. (Family Meliphagidae.)

honeysuckle vine or shrub found in temperate regions of the world. The common honeysuckle or woodbine (*L. periclymenum*) of Europe is a climbing plant with sweet-scented flowers, reddish and yellow-tinted outside and creamy white inside; it now grows in the northeastern USA. (Genus *Lonicera*, family Caprifoliaceae.)

Hong Kong special administrative region directly under the central government in the southeast of China, comprising Hong Kong Island, the mainland Kowloon Peninsula and New Territories, and many small islands, of which the largest is Lantau; area 1,070 sq km/413 sq mi; population (2001 est) 6,708,400 (57% Hong Kong Chinese, most of the remainder are refugees from the mainland). A long-established and continuing policy of free trade has helped the rise of Hong Kong as one of the world's major commercial and financial centres. The capital buildings are located in Victoria (Hong Kong City), and other towns and cities include Kowloon and Tsuen Wan (in the New Territories). A former British crown colony, it reverted to Chinese control in July 1997.

Honiara port and capital of the Solomon Islands, on the northwest coast of Guadalcanal Island in the southwest Pacific Ocean; population (1996 est) 43,700. The city, which is on the River Mataniko, grew around a World War II US military base, and replaced Tulagi as the capital of the Solomon Islands in 1952 and is now served by the international airport, Henderson Airfield, which lies 16 km/10 mi to the east. Exports include coconuts, copra , fish, and a little gold from the island's central Gold Ridge.

Honshu principal island of Japan, lying between Hokkaido to the northeast and Kyushu to the southwest. Its land mass comprises approximately four-fifths of the country total area; area 231,100 sq km/89,228 sq mi, including 382 smaller islands; population (2000 est) 102,318,000. The capital is *Tokyo; other major cities are Yokohama, Osaka, Kobe, Nagoya, and Hiroshima. Honshu is linked by bridges and tunnels with the islands of Hokkaido, Kyushu, and Shikoku. A chain of volcanic mountains runs along the island and there are frequent earthquakes. Honshu has both the largest mountain in Japan, Mount Fuji, and the largest lake in the country, Lake Biwa. Agriculture on Honshu is characterized by the intensive cultivation of rice, vegetables and fruit; fish is also a major industry. The Pacific coast is the most densely-populated area of Honshu, especially in the great conurbations of Tokyo-Yokohama and Osaka-Kobe, which are among the world's leading commercial and industrial areas, with a great variety of industry, much of it based on high technology.

hoof horny covering that protects the sensitive parts of the foot of an animal. The possession of hooves is characteristic of the orders Artiodactyla (even-toed ungulates such as deer and cattle), and Perissodactyla (horses, tapirs, and rhinoceroses).

Hooke, Robert (1635–1703) English scientist and inventor, originator of *Hooke's law, and considered the foremost mechanic of his time. His inventions included a telegraph system, the spirit level, marine barometer, and sea gauge. He coined the term 'cell' in biology.

Hooke's law law stating that the deformation of a body is proportional to the magnitude of the deforming force, provided that the body's elastic limit (see *elasticity) is not exceeded. If the elastic limit is not reached, the body will return to its original size once the force is removed. The law was discovered by English physicist Robert Hooke in 1676.

hookworm parasitic roundworm (see *worm) with hooks around its mouth. It lives mainly in tropical and subtropical regions, but also in humid areas in temperate climates. The eggs are hatched in damp soil, and the larvae bore into the host's skin, usually through the soles of the feet. They make their way to the small intestine, where they live by sucking blood. The eggs are expelled with faeces, and the cycle starts again. The human hookworm causes anaemia, weakness, and abdominal pain. It is common in areas where defecation occurs outdoors. (Genus *Necator*.)

hoopoe bird slightly larger than a thrush, with a long, thin, slightly downward-curving bill and a bright pinkish-buff crest tipped with black that expands into a fan shape on top of the head. The wings and tail are banded with black and white, and the rest of the plumage is buff-coloured. The hoopoe is found throughout southern Europe and Asia down to southern Africa, India, Malaya. (Species *Upupa epops*, family Upupidae, order Coraciiformes.)

Hoover, Herbert (Clark) (1874–1964) 31st president of the USA 1929–33, a Republican. He was secretary of commerce 1921–28. Hoover lost public confidence after the stock-market crash of 1929, when he opposed direct government aid for the unemployed in the Depression that followed.

Hoover, J(ohn) Edgar (1895–1972) US lawyer and director of the Federal Bureau of Investigation (FBI) from 1924 until his death. He built up a powerful network for the detection of organized crime, including a national fingerprint collection. His drive against alleged communist activities after World War II and his opposition to the Kennedy administration brought much criticism for abuse of power.

Hopewell member of a prehistoric *American Indian people of the Ohio River Valley and central USA who flourished between 200 BC and AD 500. One of the Moundbuilder cultures, they built cone-shaped burial mounds up to 12 m/40 ft high. The Hopewell were farmers and skilled artisans, known for their silver and copper metalwork, distinctive pottery incised with naturalistic motifs, and exquisite stone ceremonial pipes carved into animal shapes. Artefacts found on Hopewell land, such as alligator teeth from Florida, suggest that they were great traders. The reason for their extinction is unknown, although disease, famine, and war have been suggested.

Hopi (Hopi *hopitue* 'peaceful people') member of an *American Indian people living in southwest USA, especially northeast Arizona, since prehistoric times. They are descendants of the ancient Anasazi, and their language is a branch of the Uto-Aztecan family. A Pueblo Indian people, they live in villages of multi-tiered stone or adobe dwellings perched on rocky plateaus, or mesas, where they farm and herd sheep. Their religious heritage revolves around the Kachinas, or Katsinas (spirits representing the cycle of life, death, and rebirth). Ceremonies include the snake dance, a rain ritual involving live snakes. Hopi culture is regarded as one of the best-preserved in North America. Their population numbers about 11,000 (1995).

Hopkins, (Philip) Anthony (1937–) Welsh actor. Although known for his sympathetic portrayal of emotionally repressed characters in period films such as *84 Charing Cross Road* (1986) and *The Remains of the Day* (1993), he won an Academy Award for his role as a cannibalistic serial killer in *The Silence of the Lambs* (1991). He reprised the role both in the sequel, *Hannibal* (2001), and in the prequel *Red Dragon* (2002). He has also had a successful stage career both in London, England, and on Broadway.

Hopkins, Frederick Gowland (1861–1947) English biochemist who was awarded a Nobel Prize for Physiology or Medicine in 1929 for his discovery of trace substances, now known as vitamins, that stimulate growth. His research into diets revealed the necessity of these vitamins for the maintenance of health. Hopkins shared the prize with Christiaan Eijkman, who had arrived at similar conclusions. He was knighted in 1925.

Hopkins, Gerard Manley (1844–1889) English poet and Jesuit priest. His works are marked by originality of diction and rhythm and include 'The Wreck of the Deutschland' (1876), and 'The Windhover' and 'Pied Beauty' (both 1877). His collected works were published

in 1918 (after the author's death) by his friend, the poet Robert *Bridges. His employment of 'sprung rhythm' (the combination of traditional regularity of stresses with varying numbers of syllables in each line) greatly influenced later 20th-century poetry. His poetry is profoundly religious and records his struggle to gain faith and peace, but also shows freshness of feeling and delight in nature.

Hopper, Edward (1882–1967) US painter, printer, and illustrator. One of the foremost American *realists, and the most famous exponent of New Realism in the 20th century, he is often associated with American Scene painting. His views of New York City and New England in the 1930s and 1940s, painted in rich colours with stark light, convey a brooding sense of emptiness and solitude. Through his use of light, planes of colour, and large angles, verticals, and horizontals, Hopper was able to capture both a moment in time and the inner world of individuals occupying a particular space, as in *Nighthawks* (1942; Art Institute, Chicago).

hops female fruit heads of the hop plant *Humulus lupulus*, family Cannabiaceae; these are dried and used as a tonic and in flavouring beer. In designated areas in Europe, no male hops may be grown, since seedless hops produced by the unpollinated female plant contain a greater proportion of the alpha acid that gives beer its bitter taste.

Horace (65–8 BC) born Quintus Horatius Flaccus, Roman lyric poet and satirist. He became a leading poet under the patronage of Emperor Augustus. His works include *Satires* (35–30 BC); the four books of *Odes* (c. 25–24 BC); *Epistles*, a series of verse letters; and an influential critical work, *Ars poetica*. They are distinguished by their style, wit, discretion, and patriotism.

horehound any of a group of plants belonging to the mint family. The white horehound (*M. vulgare*), found in Europe, North Africa, and western Asia and naturalized in North America, has a thick hairy stem and clusters of dull white flowers; it has medicinal uses. (Genus *Marrubium*, family Labiatae.)

horizon limit to which one can see across the surface of the sea or a level plain, that is, about 5 km/3 mi at 1.5 m/5 ft above sea level, and about 65 km/40 mi at 300 m/1,000 ft.

hormone in biology, a chemical secretion of the ductless *endocrine glands and specialized nerve cells concerned with control of body functions. Hormones act as chemical messengers and are transported to all parts of the body by the bloodstream where they affect target organs. The major glands are the thyroid, parathyroid, pituitary, adrenal, pancreas, ovary, and testis. There are also hormone-secreting cells in the kidney, liver, gastrointestinal tract, thymus (in the neck), pineal (in the brain), and placenta. Hormones bring about changes in the functions of various organs according to the body's requirements. The *hypothalamus, which adjoins the pituitary gland at the base of the brain, is a control centre for overall coordination of hormone secretion; the thyroid hormones determine the rate of general body chemistry; the adrenal hormones prepare the organism during stress for 'fight or flight'; and the sexual hormones such as oestrogen and testosterone govern reproductive functions. Plants produce chemicals that affect growth and development. These chemicals can also be called hormones.

hormone-replacement therapy (HRT) use of *oestrogen and progesterone to help limit the unpleasant effects of the menopause in women. The treatment was first used in the 1970s.

Hormuz *or* **Ormuz** small island in the Strait of Hormuz belonging to Iran; area 41 sq km/16 sq mi; population (1996 est) 2,800. It is strategically important because oil tankers leaving the Gulf for Japan and the West have to pass through the strait to reach the Arabian Sea.

horn member of a family of lip-reed wind instruments used for signalling and ritual, and sharing features of a generally conical bore (although the orchestral horn is of part conical and part straight bore) and curved shape, producing a pitch of rising or variable inflection. The modern keyed horn is built in F and high B flat, with four valves, one of which transposes the instrument from the lower to the higher pitch.

horn broad term for hardened processes on the heads of some members of order Artiodactyla: deer, antelopes, cattle, goats, and sheep; and the rhinoceroses in order Perissodactyla. They are used usually for sparring rather than serious fighting, often between members of the same species rather than against predators.

hornbeam any of a group of trees belonging to the birch family. They have oval leaves with toothed edges and hanging clusters of flowers, each with a nutlike seed attached to the base. The trunk is usually twisted, with smooth grey bark. (Genus *Carpinus*, family Betulaceae.)

hornbill any of a group of omnivorous birds found in Africa, India, and Malaysia. They are about 1 m/3 ft long, and have powerful down-curved beaks, usually surmounted by a bony growth or casque. During the breeding season, the female walls herself into a hole in a tree and does not emerge until the young are hatched. There are about 45 species. (Family Bucerotidae, order Coraciiformes.)

hornblende green or black rock-forming mineral, one of the amphiboles. It is a hydrous *silicate composed mainly of calcium, iron, magnesium, and aluminium in addition to the silicon and oxygen that are common to all silicates. Hornblende is found in both igneous and metamorphic rocks and can be recognized by its colour and prismatic shape.

Horn, Cape Spanish **Cabo de Hornos**, southernmost point of South America, in Magallanes region, Chile; situated on Horn Island to the south of *Tierra del Fuego archipelago. The cape is notorious for gales and heavy seas, and was virtually the only sea route between the Atlantic and the Pacific oceans until the opening of the Panama Canal in 1914. Cape Horn was discovered in 1616 by Dutch explorer Willem Schouten (1580–1625), and named after his birthplace (Hoorn, the Netherlands).

hornet type of *wasp.

hornwort nonvascular plant (with no 'veins' to carry water and food), related to the *liverworts and *mosses. Hornworts are found in warm climates, growing on moist shaded soil. (Class Anthocerotae, order Bryophyta.) The name is also given to a group of aquatic flowering plants which are found in slow-moving water. They have whorls of finely divided leaves and may grow up to 2 m/7 ft long. (Genus *Ceratophyllum*, family Ceratophyllaceae.)

horse hoofed, odd-toed, grazing mammal belonging to the same family as zebras and asses. The many breeds of domestic horse of Euro-Asian origin range in colour from white to grey, brown, and black. The yellow-brown **Mongolian wild horse**, or **Przewalski's horse** (*Equus przewalskii*), named after its Polish 'discoverer' in *c.* 1880, is the only surviving species of wild horse. (Species *Equus caballus*, family Equidae.)

horse chestnut any of a group of trees, especially *A. hippocastanum*, originally from southeastern Europe but widely planted elsewhere. Horse chestnuts have large palmate (five-lobed) leaves, showy upright spikes of white, pink, or red flowers, and large, shiny, inedible seeds (conkers) in prickly green capsules. The horse chestnut is not related to the true chestnut. In North America it is called buckeye. (Genus *Aesculus*, family Hippocastanaceae.)

horsefly any of over 2,500 species of fly. The females suck blood from horses, cattle, and humans; the males live on plants and suck nectar. The larvae are carnivorous. (Family Tabanidae.)

horsepower abbreviation hp, imperial unit of power, now replaced by the *watt. It was first used by the engineer James *Watt, who employed it to compare the power of steam engines with that of horses.

horse racing sport of racing mounted or driven horses. Two forms in Britain are **flat racing**, for thoroughbred horses over a flat course, and **National Hunt racing**, in which the horses have to clear obstacles.

horseradish hardy perennial plant, native to southeastern Europe but naturalized elsewhere. The thick cream-coloured root is strong-tasting and is often made into a savoury sauce to accompany food. (*Armoracia rusticana*, family Cruciferae.)

horsetail plant related to ferns and club mosses; some species are also called **scouring rush**. There are about 35 living species, bearing their spores on cones at the stem tip. The upright stems are ribbed and often have spaced whorls of branches. Today they are of modest size, but hundreds of millions of years ago giant treelike forms existed. (Genus *Equisetum*, order Equisetales.)

horticulture art and science of growing flowers, fruit, and vegetables. Horticulture is practised in gardens and orchards, along with millions of acres of land devoted to vegetable farming. Some areas, like California, have specialized in horticulture because they have the mild climate and light fertile soil most suited to these crops.

Horus called 'the Elder'; or **Haroeris**, in ancient Egyptian mythology, the falcon-headed sky god whose eyes were the Sun and the Moon; adult son of the principal goddess *Isis or Hathor (otherwise his wife), whom she magically conceived by the dead *Osiris, ruler of the underworld. He injured his eye while avenging his father's murder by *Set, the good eye being the Sun and the bad representing the Moon. Every pharaoh was believed to be his incarnation, becoming Osiris on death and ruling the Underworld. The next pharaoh was then thought to be a new incarnation of Horus.

host in biology, an organism that is parasitized by another. In *commensalism, the partner that does not benefit may also be called the host.

hostage person taken prisoner as a means of exerting pressure on a third party, usually with threats of death or injury.

hot spot in earth science, area where a strong current or 'plume' of *magma rises upwards below the Earth's crust. The magma spreads horizontally in all directions, and may break through where the crust is thin. Hot spots occur within, rather than on the edges of, lithospheric *plates. However, the magma usually reaches the surface at plate margins. Examples of hot spots include Hawaii, Iceland, and Yellowstone National Park, Wyoming, USA.

hour period of time comprising 60 minutes; 24 hours make one calendar day.

housefly fly found in and around human dwellings, especially *M. domestica*, a common worldwide species. Houseflies are grey and have mouthparts adapted for drinking liquids and sucking moisture from food and manure. (Genus *Musca*.)

house music dance music of the 1980s originating in the inner-city clubs of Chicago, Illinois. With its origins in disco, it combines funk with European high-tech pop, and uses dub, digital sampling, and cross-fading. **Acid house** has minimal vocals and melody. Instead, a mechanically emphasized 4/4 beat is supported by stripped-down synthesizer riffs and a wandering bass line. Other variants include **hip house**, with rap elements, and **handbag** (mainstream).

House of Commons see *Commons, House of.

House of Lords see *Lords, House of.

House of Representatives lower chamber of the US *Congress, with 435 members elected at regular two-year intervals, every even year, in November. States are represented in proportion to their population. The Speaker of the House is the majority party's leader.

housing provision of residential accommodation. All countries have found some degree of state housing provision or subsidy essential, even in free-enterprise economies such as the USA. In the UK, flats and houses to rent (intended for people with low incomes) are built by local authorities or housing associations under the direction of the Secretary of State for the Environment, but houses in England and Wales would have to last 2,500 years at the rate of replacement being achieved by local authorities in 1991.

Housman, A(lfred) E(dward) (1859–1936) English poet and classical scholar. His *A Shropshire Lad* (1896), a series of deceptively simple, nostalgic, ballad-like poems, has been popular since World War I. This was followed by *Last Poems* (1922), *More Poems* (1936), and *Collected Poems* (1939).

Houston city and port in southeastern Texas, USA; linked by the Houston Ship Canal to the Gulf of Mexico, in the Gulf Coastal Plain; population (2000 est) 1,953,600. A major centre of finance and commerce, Houston is also one of the busiest US ports. Industrial products include refined petroleum, oilfield equipment, and petrochemicals, chief of which are synthetic rubber, plastics, insecticides, and fertilizers. Other products include iron and steel, electrical and electronic machinery, paper products, and milled rice. The Lyndon B Johnson Space Center (1961), the command post for flights by US astronauts, is located here.

hovercraft vehicle that rides on a cushion of high-pressure air, free from all contact with the surface beneath, invented by English engineer Christopher Cockerell in 1959. Hovercraft need a smooth terrain when operating overland and are best adapted to use on waterways. They are useful in places where harbours have not been established.

hoverfly brightly coloured winged insect. Hoverflies usually have spots, stripes, or bands of yellow or brown against a dark-coloured background, sometimes with dense hair covering the body surface. Many resemble bees, bumble bees, and wasps (displaying Batesian *mimicry) and most adults feed on nectar and pollen. (Family Syrphidae (numbering over 2,500 species), suborder Cyclorrhapha, order Diptera, class Insecta, phylum Arthropoda.)

Howard, Catherine (c. 1520–1542) Queen consort of *Henry VIII of England from 1540. In 1541 the archbishop of Canterbury, Thomas Cranmer, accused her of being unchaste before marriage to Henry and she was beheaded in 1542 after Cranmer made further charges of adultery.

Howard, Ebenezer (1850–1928) English town planner. Aiming to halt the unregulated growth of industrial cities, he pioneered the ideal of the *garden city through his book *Tomorrow* (1898; republished as *Garden Cities of Tomorrow* in 1902). He also inspired and took an active part in building the garden cities of Letchworth and Welwyn.

Howard, John (1726–1790) English philanthropist whose work to improve prison conditions is continued today by the **Howard League for Penal Reform** (a charity formed in 1921 by the amalgamation of the Prison Reform League and the Howard Association).

howitzer cannon, in use since the 16th century, with a particularly steep angle of fire. It was much developed in World War I for demolishing the fortresses of the trench system. The multi-national NATO FH70 field howitzer is mobile and fires, under computer control, three 43 kg/95 lb shells at 32 km/20 mi range in 15 seconds.

Hoxha, Enver (1908–1985) Albanian communist politician, the country's leader from 1954. He founded the Albanian Communist Party in 1941, and headed the liberation movement 1939–44. He was prime minister 1944–54, also handling foreign affairs 1946–53, and from 1954 was first secretary of the Albanian Party of Labour. In policy he was a Stalinist and independent of both Chinese and Soviet communism.

Hoyle, Fred(erick) (1915–2001) English astronomer, cosmologist, and writer. His astronomical research dealt mainly with the internal structure and evolution of the stars. In 1948 he developed with Hermann Bondi and Thomas Gold the *steady-state theory of the universe. In 1957, with William Fowler, he showed that chemical elements heavier than hydrogen and helium may be built up by nuclear reactions inside stars. He was knighted in 1972.

Hsuan Tung name adopted by Henry *P'u-i on becoming emperor of China in 1908.

Huang He or **Hwang Ho** English **Yellow River**, river in China; length 5,464 km/3,395 mi. Rising in Qinghai province in the west of the country, it winds eastwards to the Bohai Gulf on the Yellow Sea. The names 'Yellow River' and 'Yellow Sea' derive from the great quantities of fine yellow particles of the soil known as loess (originally wind-blown from central Asia) which the river carries. The deposition of this material helps to explain why the river is sometimes known as 'China's sorrow' because of disastrous floods. Flooding is now largely controlled through hydroelectric works, dykes, and embankments, but the barriers are ceasing to work because loess deposited as silt continues to raise the river bed.

Hubble, Edwin (Powell) (1889–1953) US astronomer. He discovered the existence of *galaxies outside our own, and classified them according to their shape. His theory that the universe is expanding is now generally accepted.

Hubble's law law that relates a galaxy's distance from us to its speed of recession as the universe expands, formulated in 1929 by US astronomer Edwin Hubble. He found that galaxies are moving apart at speeds that increase in direct proportion to their distance apart. The rate of expansion is known as the Hubble constant.

Hubble Space Telescope (HST) space-based astronomical observing facility, orbiting the Earth at an altitude of 610 km/380 mi. It consists of a 2.4 m/94 in telescope and four complimentary scientific instruments, is roughly cylindrical, 13 m/43 ft long, and 4 m/13 ft in diameter, with two large solar panels. HST produces a wealth of scientific data, and allows astronomers to observe the birth of stars, find planets around neighbouring stars, follow the expanding remnants of exploding stars, and search for black holes in the centre of galaxies. HST is a cooperative programme between the European Space Agency (ESA) and the US agency NASA, and is the first spacecraft specifically designed to be serviced in orbit as a permanent space-based observatory. It was launched in 1990.

Hubei *or* **Hupei** *or* **Hupeh** province of central China, bounded to the north by Henan, to the east by Anhui, to the south by Jiangxi and Hunan, and to the west by Sichuan and Shaanxi provinces; area 187,500 sq km/72,375 sq mi; population (2000 est) 60,280,000. The capital is Wuhan; other major cities and towns are Huangshi, Shashi, Yichang, and Xiangfan. The main industries are the mining of copper, gypsum, iron ore, coal, phosphorus, and salt; and the production of steel, machinery, domestic appliances, textiles, food processing, and fibre-optic cables. Agriculture is based on the cultivation of rice, cotton, rapeseed, wheat, beans, and vegetables.

hubris in Greek thought, an act of transgression or overweening pride. In ancient Greek tragedy, hubris was believed to offend the gods, and to lead to retribution.

huckleberry berry-bearing bush closely related to the *blueberry in the USA and bilberry in Britain. Huckleberry bushes have edible dark-blue berries. (Genus *Gaylussacia*, family Ericaceae.)

Hudson river in northeastern USA; length 485 km/300 mi. It rises in the Adirondack Mountains and flows south, emptying into a bay of the Atlantic Ocean at New York City. The Hudson forms the boundary between New Jersey and New York, and the states are linked by bridges and tunnels. The New York Barge Canal system links the Hudson to Lake Champlain, Lake Erie, and the St Lawrence River. It is navigable by small ocean-going vessels as far upstream as Albany and Troy, about 150 mi/240 km from its mouth, and for eight months of the year barge traffic can reach the Great Lakes.

Hudson, Henry (c. 1565–1611) English explorer. Under the auspices of the Muscovy Company

(1607–08), he made two unsuccessful attempts to find the Northeast Passage to China. In September 1609, commissioned by the Dutch East India Company, he reached New York Bay and sailed 240 km/150 mi up the river that now bears his name, establishing Dutch claims to the area. In 1610 he sailed from London in the *Discovery* and entered what is now the Hudson Strait. After an icebound winter, he was turned adrift by a mutinous crew in what is now Hudson Bay.

Hudson Bay inland sea of northeastern Canada, linked with the Atlantic Ocean by Hudson Strait and with the Arctic Ocean by Foxe Channel and the Gulf of Boothia; area 1,233,000 sq km/766,150 sq mi. It is bordered by (clockwise) the provinces of Québec, Ontario, Manitoba, and Nunavut. The Hudson Bay area is sparsely settled, chiefly by trappers, American Indians, and Inuit.

Hudson River School group of US landscape painters working between 1825 and 1870; it was the first US school of landscape painting. Depicting the dramatic, uncultivated regions of the Hudson River Valley and the Catskill Mountains in New York State, their work is characterized by attention to detail and a deep regard for the natural world. Their style, inspired by the New World, was influenced by the Romantic landscapes of J M W *Turner and John Martin. Leading members of the school, which was divided into two periods, were Thomas Cole, who set up a studio at Catskill in 1826, and Albert Bierstadt, from the 1850s.

Hudson's Bay Company chartered company founded by Prince *Rupert in 1670 to trade in furs with North American Indians. In 1783 the rival North West Company was formed, but in 1821 it merged with the Hudson's Bay Company. In 1912 the company planned a chain of department stores in western Canada, and became Canada's leading retail organization, which it remains today. It also has oil and natural gas interests.

Hughes, Ted (Edward James) (1930–1998) English poet. His work is characterized by its harsh portrayal of the crueller aspects of nature, by its reflection of the agonies of personal experience, and by the employment of myths of creation and being, as in *Crow* (1970) and *Gaudete* (1977). His free-verse renderings, *Tales from Ovid* won the 1997 Whitbread Book of the Year Award, and his collection *Birthday Letters* was awarded the 1998 Forward Prize and the 1998 Whitbread Book of the Year Award. His collections include *The Hawk in the Rain* (1957), *Lupercal* (1960), *Wodwo* (1967), *Wolfwatching* (1989), and *Winter Pollen: Occasional Prose* (1994). His novels for children include *The Iron Man* (1968). He was the poet laureate from 1984 until his death, and was awarded the Order of Merit in 1998.

Hughes, Thomas (1822–1896) English writer. He is best known as the author of *Tom Brown's School Days* (1857), a story of Rugby School under Thomas Arnold, with an underlying religious sense, which was the forerunner of the modern school story. It had a sequel, *Tom Brown at Oxford* (1861).

Hugo, Victor (Marie) (1802–1885) French novelist, poet, and dramatist. The verse play *Hernani* (1830) firmly established Hugo as the leader of French Romanticism. This was the first of a series of dramas produced in the 1830s and early 1840s, including *Le Roi s'amuse* (1832) and *Ruy Blas* (1838). His melodramatic novels include *Notre-Dame de Paris* (1831), and *Les Misérables* (1862).

Huguenot French Protestant in the 16th century; the term referred mainly to Calvinists. Persecuted under Francis I and Henry II, the Huguenots survived both an attempt to exterminate them (the Massacre of *St Bartholomew on 24 August 1572) and the religious wars of the next 30 years. In 1598 *Henry IV (himself formerly a Huguenot) granted them toleration under the Edict of Nantes. Louis XIV revoked the edict in 1685, attempting their forcible conversion, and 400,000 emigrated.

Hui one of the largest minority ethnic groups in China, numbering about eight and a half million. Members of the Hui live all over China, but are concentrated in the northern central region. They have been Muslims since the 10th century, for which they have suffered persecution both before and since the communist revolution.

Hull shortened name of *Kingston upon Hull, a city and unitary authority on the north bank of the Humber estuary, northeast England.

Hull, Cordell (1871–1955) US Democratic politician. As F D Roosevelt's secretary of state 1933–44, he was a vigorous champion of free trade, and opposed German and Japanese aggression. He was identified with the Good Neighbor policy of nonintervention in Latin America. An advocate of collective security after World War II, he was called by Roosevelt 'the father of the United Nations'. He was awarded the Nobel Prize for Peace in 1945 for his work in organizing the United Nations (UN).

human body physical structure of the human being. It develops from the single cell of the fertilized ovum, is born at 40 weeks, and usually reaches sexual maturity between 11 and 18 years of age. The bony framework (skeleton) consists of more than 200 bones, over half of which are in the hands and feet. Bones are held together by joints, some of which allow movement. The circulatory system supplies muscles and organs with blood, which provides oxygen and food and removes carbon dioxide and other waste products. Body functions are controlled by the nervous system and hormones. In the upper part of the trunk is the thorax, which contains the lungs and heart. Below this is the abdomen, containing the digestive system (stomach and intestines); the liver, spleen, and pancreas; the urinary system (kidneys, ureters, and bladder); and, in women, the reproductive organs (ovaries, uterus, and vagina). In men, the prostate gland and seminal vesicles only of the reproductive system are situated in the abdomen, the testes being in the scrotum, which, with the penis, is suspended in front of and below the abdomen. The bladder empties through a small channel (urethra); in the female this opens in the upper end of the vulval cleft, which also contains the opening of the vagina, or birth canal; in the male, the urethra is continued into the penis. In both sexes, the lower bowel terminates in the anus, a ring of strong muscle situated between the buttocks.

Human Genome Project (HGP) research scheme to map the complete nucleotide (see *nucleic acid) sequence of human *DNA. It was begun in 1990 and a working draft of the genome (a mapping of 97% of the genome, sequencing of 85%, and completion of 24% of the human genome) was achieved in June 2000, with the results being published in February 2001.

The publicly-funded Human Genome Organization (HUGO) coordinated the US$300 million project (the largest research project ever undertaken in the life sciences), which took place in over 20 centres around the world. Sequencing was also carried out commercially by US biotechnology company Celera Genomics. The completed detailed mapping of the genome is scheduled for 2003.

humanism belief in the high potential of human nature rather than in religious or transcendental values. Humanism culminated as a cultural and literary force in 16th-century Renaissance Europe in line with the period's enthusiasm for classical literature and art, growing individualism, and the ideal of the all-round male who should be statesman and poet, scholar and warrior. *Erasmus is a great exemplar of Renaissance humanism.

human reproduction production of offspring by humans. Human reproduction is an example of *sexual reproduction, where the male produces sperm and the female eggs. These gametes contain only half the normal number of chromosomes, 23 instead of 46, so that on fertilization the resulting cell has the correct genetic complement. Fertilization is internal, which increases the chances of conception; unusually for mammals, pregnancy can occur at any time of the year. Human beings are also remarkable for the length of childhood and for the highly complex systems of parental care found in society. The use of contraception and the development of laboratory methods of insemination and fertilization are issues that make human reproduction more than a merely biological phenomenon.

human rights civil and political rights of the individual in relation to the state; see also *civil rights. Under the terms of the *United Nations Charter human rights violations by countries have become its proper concern, although the implementation of this obligation is hampered by Article 2 (7) of the charter prohibiting interference in domestic affairs. The Universal Declaration of *Human Rights, passed by the General Assembly on 10 December 1948, is based on a belief in the inherent (natural) rights, equality, and freedom of human beings, and sets out in 28 articles the fundamental freedoms – civil, political, economic – to be promoted. The declaration has considerable moral force but is not legally binding on states.

Human Rights, Universal Declaration of charter of civil and political rights drawn up by the United Nations in 1948. They include the right to life, liberty, education, and equality before the law; to freedom of movement, religion, association, and information; and to a nationality. Under the **European Convention of Human Rights** of 1950, the Council of Europe established the **European Commission of Human Rights**, which investigates complaints by states or individuals. Its findings are examined by the **European Court of Human Rights** (established in 1959), whose compulsory jurisdiction (legal power) has been recognized by a number of states, including the UK.

human species, origins of evolution of humans from ancestral *primates. The African apes (gorilla and chimpanzee) are shown by anatomical and molecular comparisons to be the closest living relatives of humans. The oldest known hominids (of the human

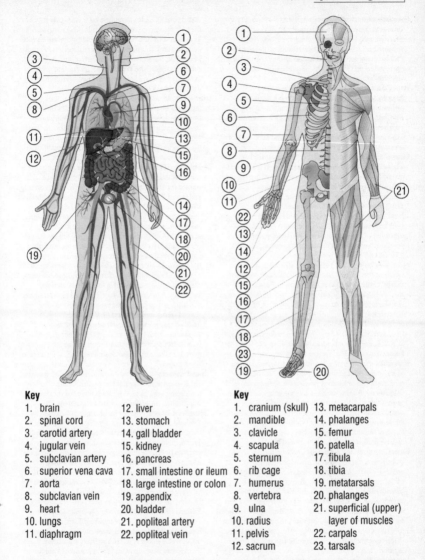

Key

1. brain
2. spinal cord
3. carotid artery
4. jugular vein
5. subclavian artery
6. superior vena cava
7. aorta
8. subclavian vein
9. heart
10. lungs
11. diaphragm
12. liver
13. stomach
14. gall bladder
15. kidney
16. pancreas
17. small intestine or ileum
18. large intestine or colon
19. appendix
20. bladder
21. popliteal artery
22. popliteal vein

Key

1. cranium (skull)
2. mandible
3. clavicle
4. scapula
5. sternum
6. rib cage
7. humerus
8. vertebra
9. ulna
10. radius
11. pelvis
12. sacrum
13. metacarpals
14. phalanges
15. femur
16. patella
17. fibula
18. tibia
19. metatarsals
20. phalanges
21. superficial (upper) layer of muscles
22. carpals
23. tarsals

human body The adult human body has approximately 650 muscles, 100 joints, 100,000 km/60,000 mi of blood vessels and 13,000 nerve cells. There are 206 bones in the adult body, nearly half of them in the hands and feet.

group) had been the australopithecines, found in Africa, dating from 3.5–4.4 million years ago. But in December 2000, scientists unearthed the fossilized remains of a hominid dating back 6 million years. The first hominids to use tools appeared 2 million years ago, and hominids first used fire and moved out of Africa 1.7 million years ago. Modern humans are all believed to descend from one African female of 200,000 years ago, although there is a rival theory that humans evolved in different parts of the world simultaneously.

Humber estuary in northeast England formed by the Ouse and Trent rivers, which meet east of Goole and flow east for 60 km/38 mi to enter the North Sea below Spurn Head. It is an important commercial waterway, and the main ports are *Kingston upon Hull on the north side, and Grimsby on the south side. The Humber Bridge (1981) joins the two banks.

Humboldt, (Friedrich Wilhelm Heinrich) Alexander (1769–1859) Baron von Humboldt, German geophysicist, botanist, geologist, and writer who, with French botanist Aimé Bonpland (1773–1858), explored the regions of the Orinoco and Amazon rivers in South America 1800–04, and gathered 60,000 plant specimens. He was a founder of ecology.

Hume, David (1711–1776) Scottish philosopher whose *Treatise of Human Nature* (1739–40) is a central text of British *empiricism (the theory that experience is the only source of knowledge). Examining meticulously our modes of thinking, he concluded that they are more habitual than rational. Consequently, he not only rejected the possibility of knowlege that goes beyond the bounds of experience (speculative metaphysics), but also arrived at generally sceptical positions about reason, causation, necessity, identity, and the self.

Hume, John (1937–) Northern Ireland politician, leader of the Social Democratic and Labour Party (SDLP) from 1979 to 2001. Hume was a founder member of the Credit Union Party, which later became the SDLP. An MP since 1969, and a member of the European Parliament, he has been one of the chief architects of the peace process in Northern Ireland. He shared the Nobel Prize for Peace in 1998 with David *Trimble for their efforts to further the peace process. Hume announced his resignation in September 2001.

humidity quantity of water vapour in a given volume of the atmosphere (absolute humidity), or the ratio of the amount of water vapour in the atmosphere to the saturation value at the same temperature (relative humidity). At *dew point the relative humidity is 100% and the air is said to be saturated. Condensation (the conversion of vapour to liquid) may then occur. Relative humidity is measured by various types of hygrometer.

hummingbird any of various small, brilliantly coloured birds found in the Americas. The name comes from the sound produced by the rapid vibration of their wings when hovering near flowers to feed. Hummingbirds have long, needlelike bills and tongues to obtain nectar from flowers and capture insects. They are the only birds able to fly backwards. The **Cuban bee hummingbird** (*Mellisuga helenae*), the world's smallest bird, is 5.5 cm/2 in long and weighs less than 2.5 g/0.1 oz. There are over 300 species. (Family Trochilidae, order Apodiformes.)

humours, theory of theory prevalent in the West in classical and medieval times that the human body was composed of four kinds of fluid: phlegm, blood, choler or yellow bile, and melancholy or black bile. Physical and mental characteristics were explained by different proportions of humours in individuals.

Hun member of any of a number of nomad Mongol peoples who were first recorded historically in the 2nd century BC, raiding across the Great Wall into China. They entered Europe about AD 372, settled in the area that is now Hungary, and imposed their supremacy on the Ostrogoths and other Germanic peoples. Under the leadership of Attila they attacked the Byzantine Empire, invaded Gaul, and threatened Rome. After Attila's death in 453 their power was broken by a revolt of their subject peoples. The **White Huns**, or Ephthalites, a kindred people, raided Persia and northern India in the 5th and 6th centuries.

Hunan province of south central China, bounded to the north by Hubei, to the east by Jiangxi, to the south by Guangdong and Guangxi Zhuang Autonomous Region, and to the west by Guizhou and Sichuan; area 210,500 sq km/81,300 sq mi; population (2000 est) 64,400,000. The capital is Changsha; other main cities and towns are Hengyang, Shaoyang, Xiangtan, and Zhuzhou. The main industries are non-ferrous minerals, engineering, chemicals, and electrical goods. Agriculture is the main basis of the province's economy and is based on the cultivation of rice, sweet potatoes, maize, tea, tobacco, and rapeseed.

Although mining and industry have been developed since 1949, Hunan's economy remains mostly agricultural. Hunan ranks first among China's provinces in rice production. Most of Hunan's arable land is farmed using modern techniques, including mechanized irrigation and chemical fertilizers. Most farms are small, however, and mechanization has been confined to the use of simple machines and tools, such as rice transplanters, foot-operated rice-threshing machines, and a tube water raiser that is replacing the old wooden trough and paddles.

hundred days in European history, the period 20 March–28 June 1815, marking the French emperor Napoleon's escape from imprisonment on Elba to his departure from Paris after losing the battle of Waterloo on 18 June.

hundredweight symbol cwt, imperial unit of mass, equal to 112 lb (50.8 kg). It is sometimes called the long hundredweight, to distinguish it from the short hundredweight or **cental**, equal to 100 lb (45.4 kg).

Hundred Years' War series of conflicts between England and France in 1337–1453. Its causes were the French claim (as their fief) to Gascony in southwest France, held by the English kings, and medieval trade rivalries in Flanders. Medieval England and France had a long history of war before 1337, and the Hundred Years' War has sometimes been interpreted as merely an intensification of these struggles. It was caused by fears of French intervention in Scotland, which the English were trying to subdue, and by the claim of England's Edward III (through his mother Isabella, daughter of Philip IV of France) to the crown of France.

Hungarian or **Magyar** the majority population of Hungary or a people of Hungarian descent; also, their culture and language. Hungarian minorities are found in the Slovak Republic, Serbia and Montenegro, and Romania, where the Székely of Transylvania regard themselves as ethnically distinct but speak Hungarian, as do the Csángó of Moldova.

Hungarian language member of the Finno-Ugric language group, spoken principally in Hungary but also in parts of the Slovak Republic, Romania, and Serbia and Montenegro. Hungarian is known as **Magyar** among its speakers. It is written in a form of the Roman alphabet in which *s* corresponds to English *sh*, and *sz* to *s*.

Hungary
  National name: *Magyar Köztársaság/*
  Republic of Hungary

Area: 93,032 sq km/35,919 sq mi
Capital: Budapest
Major towns/cities: Miskolc, Debrecen, Szeged, Pécs, Győr, Nyíregyháza, Székesfehérvár, Kecskemét
Physical features: Great Hungarian Plain covers eastern half of country; Bakony Forest, Lake Balaton, and Transdanubian Highlands in the west; rivers Danube, Tisza, and Raba; more than 500 thermal springs
Head of state: Ferenc Mádl from 2000
Head of government: Ferenc Gyurcsany from 2004
Political system: liberal democracy
Political executive: parliamentary
Political parties: over 50, including Hungarian Socialist Party (HSP), reform-socialist; Alliance of Free Democrats (AFD), centrist, radical free market; Hungarian Democratic Forum (MDF), nationalist, right of centre; Independent Smallholders Party (ISP), right of centre, agrarian; Christian Democratic People's Party (KDNP), right of centre; Federation of Young Democrats, liberal, anticommunist; Fidesz, right of centre
Currency: forint
GNI per capita (PPP): (US$) 12,810 (2002 est)
Exports: raw materials, semi-finished products, industrial consumer goods, food and agricultural products, transport equipment. Principal market: Germany 35.6% (2001)
Population: 9,877,000 (2003 est)
Language: Hungarian (official)
Religion: Roman Catholic 65%, Calvinist 20%, other Christian denominations, Jewish, atheist
Life expectancy: 68 (men); 76 (women) (2000–05)
Chronology
1st century AD: Region formed part of Roman Empire.
4th century: Germanic tribes overran central Europe.
c. 445: Attila the Hun established a short-lived empire, including Hungarian nomads living far to the east.
c. 680: Hungarians settled between the Don and Dniepr rivers under Khazar rule.

9th century: Hungarians invaded central Europe; ten tribes united under Árpád, chief of the Magyar tribe, who conquered the area corresponding to modern Hungary in 896.
10th century: Hungarians colonized Transylvania and raided their neighbours for plunder and slaves.
955: Battle of Lech: Germans led by Otto the Great defeated the Hungarians.
1001: St Stephen founded the Hungarian kingdom to replace tribal organization and converted the Hungarians to Christianity.
12th century: Hungary became a major power when King Béla III won temporary supremacy over the Balkans.
1308–86: Angevin dynasty ruled after the Arpádian line died out.
1456: Battle of Belgrade: János Hunyadi defeated Ottoman Turks and saved Hungary from invasion.
1458–90: Under Mátyás I Corvinus, Hungary enjoyed military success and cultural renaissance.
1526: Battle of Mohács: Turks under Suleiman the Magnificent decisively defeated the Hungarians.
16th century: Partition of Hungary between Turkey, Austria, and the semi-autonomous Transylvania.
1699: Treaty of Karlowitz: Austrians expelled the Turks from Hungary, which was reunified under Habsburg rule.
1707: Prince Ferenc Rákóczi II led an uprising against the Austrians.
1780–90: Joseph II's attempts to impose uniform administration throughout the Austrian Empire provoked nationalist reaction among the Hungarian nobility.
early 19th century: 'National Revival' movement led by Count Stephen Széchenyi and Lajos Kossuth.
1848: Hungarian Revolution: nationalists proclaimed self-government; Croat minority resisted Hungarian rule.
1849: Austrians crushed revolution with Russian support.
1867: Austria conceded equality to Hungary within the dual monarchy of Austria-Hungary.
1918: Austria-Hungary collapsed in military defeat; Count Mihály Károlyi proclaimed Hungarian Republic.
1920: Treaty of Trianon: Hungary lost 72% of its territory to Czechoslovakia, Romania, and Yugoslavia; Admiral Miklós Horthy restored the Kingdom of Hungary with himself as regent.
1938–41: Diplomatic collaboration with Germany allowed Hungary to regain territories lost in 1920; Hungary declared war on USSR in alliance with Germany in 1941.
1944: Germany occupied Hungary and installed a Nazi regime.
1945: USSR 'liberated' Hungary.
1947: Peace treaty restored 1920 frontiers.
1949: Hungary became a Soviet-style dictatorship; communist leader Mátyás Rákosi pursued Stalinist policies.
1956: Hungarian uprising: anti-Soviet demonstrations led the USSR to invade, crush dissent, and install János Kádár as communist leader.
1961: Kádár began to introduce limited liberal reforms.
1988: The Hungarian Democratic Forum was formed by opposition groups.
1989: The communist dictatorship was dismantled, and a transitional constitution restored multi-party

democracy. The opening of the border with Austria destroyed the 'Iron Curtain'.

1990: Elections were won by a centre–right coalition.

1991: The withdrawal of Soviet forces was completed.

1996: A friendship treaty with the Slovak Republic was signed, as was a cooperation treaty with Romania.

1997: Hungary was invited to join NATO and to begin negotiations for membership of the European Union. A referendum showed clear support in favour of joining NATO.

1998: Viktor Orban, leader of right-of-centre Fidesz, became prime minister after the general election.

1999: Hungary became a full member of NATO.

2000: Ferenc Mádl was elected president.

2003: In a referendum 84% of voters endorsed accession to the European Union (EU) in 2004.

2004: Hungary was admitted to the EU.

Hunt, (William) Holman (1827–1910) English painter, one of the founders of the *Pre-Raphaelite Brotherhood in 1848. His paintings, characterized both by a meticulous attention to detail and a clear moral and religious symbolism, include *The Awakening Conscience* (1853; Tate Gallery, London) and *The Light of the World* (1854; Keble College, Oxford).

hunting dog or **painted dog** wild dog (weight 23–35 kg/51–77 lb) that once roamed over virtually the whole of sub-Saharan Africa. A pack might have a range of almost 4,000 km/2,500 mi, hunting zebra, antelope, and other game. Individuals can run at 50 kph/30 mph for up to 5 km/3 mi, with short bursts of even higher speeds. The number of hunting dogs that survive has been reduced to a fraction of the original population. According to a 1997 World Conservation Union report, there were fewer than 3,000 hunting dogs remaining in the wild, with many existing populations too small to be viable. (Species *Lycaon pictus*, family Canidae.)

Huntington's chorea rare hereditary disease of the nervous system that usually begins in middle age. It is characterized by involuntary movements (*chorea), emotional disturbances, and rapid mental degeneration progressing to *dementia. There is no known cure but the genetic mutation giving rise to the disease was located in 1993, making it easier to test individuals for the disease and increasing the chances of developing a cure.

hurling or **hurley** stick-and-ball game played between two teams of 15 players each, popular in Ireland. Its object is to hit the ball, by means of a curved stick, into the opposing team's goal. If the ball passes under the goal's crossbar three points are scored; if it passes above the crossbar one point is scored. First played over 3,000 years ago, the game was at one time outlawed. The rules were standardized in 1884, and are now under the control of the Gaelic Athletic Association. The premier competition, the All-Ireland Championship, was first held in 1887.

Huron, Lake second largest of the *Great Lakes of North America, on the US–Canadian border; area 60,000 sq km/23,160 sq mi. Lake Huron is 331 km/205 mi long, lies at 177 m/581 ft above sea level, and reaches a depth of 230 m/755 ft. It is bounded on the north and east by Ontario, and on the west and south by Michigan. There are several small ports on its shores, and lumbering and fishing are important economic activities in the region.

hurricane or **tropical cyclone** or **typhoon** a severe *depression (region of very low atmospheric pressure) in tropical regions, called **typhoon** in the North Pacific. It is a revolving storm originating at latitudes between 5° and 20° north or south of the Equator, when the surface temperature of the ocean is above 27 °C/80 °F. A central calm area, called the eye, is surrounded by inwardly spiralling winds (anticlockwise in the northern hemisphere and clockwise in the southern hemisphere) of up to 320 kph/200 mph. A hurricane is accompanied by lightning and torrential rain, and can cause extensive damage. In meteorology, a hurricane is a wind of force 12 or more on the *Beaufort scale.

husky any of several breeds of sledge dog used in Arctic regions, growing up to about 60 cm/23 in high, and weighing up to about 27 kg/60 lbs, with pricked ears, thick fur, and a bushy tail. The Siberian husky is the best known.

Hussein, Saddam (1937–) Iraqi leader, in power from 1968, president 1979–2003. He presided over the Iran–Iraq war 1980–88, and harshly repressed Kurdish rebels seeking independence in northern Iraq. He annexed Kuwait in 1990 but was driven out by a US-dominated coalition army in February 1991. Defeat in the Gulf War led to unrest, and both the Kurds in the north and Shiites in the south rebelled. His savage repression of both revolts led to charges of genocide. In 2003 US-led forces invaded Iraq on the grounds that Saddam had weapons of mass destruction (WMD) and was in contravention of UN resolutions requiring Iraqi disarmament. Saddam went into hiding and was captured by coalition forces in December 2003.

Hussein ibn Talal (1935–1999) King of Jordan 1952–99. By 1967 he had lost all his kingdom west of the River Jordan in the Arab-Israeli Wars, and in 1970 suppressed the Palestine Liberation Organization acting as a guerrilla force against his rule on the remaining East Bank territories. Subsequently, he became a moderating force in Middle Eastern politics, and in 1994 signed a peace agreement with Israel, ending a 46-year-old state of war between the two countries.

Husserl, Edmund Gustav Albrecht (1859–1938) German philosopher, regarded as the founder of *phenomenology, the study of mental states as consciously experienced. His early phenomenology resembles linguistic philosophy because he examined the meaning and our understanding of words.

Huston, John (Marcellus) (1906–1987) US film director, screenwriter, and actor. An impulsive and individualistic film-maker, he often dealt with the themes of greed, treachery in human relationships, and the loner. His works as a director include *The Maltese Falcon* (1941), *The Treasure of the Sierra Madre* (1948), *The Asphalt Jungle* (1950), *The African Queen* (1951), and *The Dead* (1987).

Hutton, James (1726–1797) Scottish geologist, known as the 'founder of geology', who formulated the concept of uniformitarianism. In 1785 he developed a theory of the igneous origin of many rocks.

Hutu member of the majority ethnic group of Burundi and Rwanda, numbering around 9.5 million. The Hutu tend to live as peasant farmers. They have been dominated by the *Tutsi minority since the 14th century and there is a long history of violent conflict between the two groups. The Hutu language belongs to the Bantu branch of the Niger-Congo family.

Huxley, Aldous (Leonard) (1894–1963) English writer of novels, essays, and verse. From the disillusionment and satirical eloquence of *Crome Yellow* (1921), *Antic Hay* (1923), and *Point Counter Point* (1928), Huxley developed towards the Utopianism (perfect political and social conditions) exemplified by *Island* (1962). His most popular work, the science fiction novel *Brave New World* (1932) shows human beings mass-produced in laboratories and rendered incapable of freedom by indoctrination and drugs.

Huxley, T(homas) H(enry) (1825–1895) English scientist and humanist. Following the publication of Charles Darwin's *On the Origin of Species* (1859), he became known as 'Darwin's bulldog', and for many years was a prominent champion of evolution. In 1869 he coined the word 'agnostic' to express his own religious attitude, and is considered the founder of scientific humanism.

Huygens (or Huyghens), Christiaan (1629–1695) Dutch mathematical physicist and astronomer. He proposed the wave theory of light, developed the pendulum clock in 1657, discovered polarization, and observed Saturn's rings. He made important advances in pure mathematics, applied mathematics, and mechanics, which he virtually founded. His work in astronomy was an impressive defence of the Copernican view of the Solar System.

hyacinth any of a group of bulb-producing plants belonging to the lily family, native to the eastern Mediterranean and Africa. The cultivated hyacinth (*H. orientalis*) has large, scented, cylindrical heads of pink, white, or blue flowers. (Genus *Hyacinthus*, family Liliaceae.) The *water hyacinth, a floating plant from South America, is unrelated.

hybrid offspring from a cross between individuals of two different species, or two inbred lines within a species. In most cases, hybrids between species are infertile and unable to reproduce sexually. In plants, however, doubling of the chromosomes can restore the fertility of such hybrids.

Hyder Ali (or Haidar Ali) (c. 1722–1782) Indian general, sultan of Mysore in southwestern India from 1759. In command of the army in Mysore from 1749, he became the ruler of the state in 1761, and rivalled British power in the area until his triple defeat by Sir Eyre Coote in 1781 during the Anglo-French wars. He was the father of Tipu Sultan.

Hydra in astronomy, the largest constellation, winding across more than a quarter of the sky between *Cancer and *Libra in the southern hemisphere. Hydra is named after the multi-headed sea serpent slain by Hercules. Despite its size, it is not prominent; its brightest star is second-magnitude Alphard.

Hydra in Greek mythology, a huge monster with nine heads. If one were cut off, two would grow in its place. One of the 12 labours of *Heracles was to kill it.

hydra in zoology, any of a group of freshwater polyps, belonging among the *coelenterates. The body is a double-layered tube (about six to ten hollow tentacles around the mouth), 1.25 cm/0.5 in long when extended, but capable of contracting to a small knob. Usually fixed to waterweed, hydras feed on minute animals that are caught and paralysed by stinging cells on the tentacles. (Genus *Hydra*, family Hydridae, phylum Coelenterata, subphylum Cnidaria.)

hydrangea any of a group of flowering shrubs belonging to the saxifrage family, native to Japan. Cultivated varieties of *H. macrophylla* normally produce round heads of pink flowers, but these may be blue if there are certain chemicals in the soil, such as alum or iron. The name comes from the Greek for 'water vessel', after the cuplike seed capsules. (Genus *Hydrangea*, family Hydrangeaceae.)

hydraulics field of study concerned with utilizing the properties of water and other liquids, in particular the way they flow and transmit pressure, and with the application of these properties in engineering. It applies the principles of *hydrostatics and hydrodynamics. The oldest type of hydraulic machine is the **hydraulic press**, invented by Joseph Bramah in England in 1795. The hydraulic principle of fluid pressure transmitting a small force over a small area in order to produce a larger force over a larger area is commonly used in vehicle braking systems, the forging press, and the hydraulic systems of aircraft and earth-moving machinery.

hydrocarbon any of a class of chemical compounds containing only hydrogen and carbon (for example, the alkanes and alkenes). Hydrocarbons are obtained industrially principally from petroleum and coal tar.

hydrocephalus potentially serious increase in the volume of cerebrospinal fluid (CSF) within the ventricles of the brain. In infants, since their skull plates have not fused, it causes enlargement of the head, and there is a risk of brain damage from CSF pressure on the developing brain.

hydrochloric acid HCl, highly corrosive solution of hydrogen chloride (a colourless, acidic gas) in water. The concentrated acid is about 35% hydrogen chloride. The acid is a typical strong, monobasic acid forming only one series of salts, the chlorides. It has many industrial uses, including recovery of zinc from galvanized scrap iron and the production of chlorine. It is also produced in the stomachs of animals for the purposes of digestion.

hydrocyanic acid or prussic acid solution of hydrogen cyanide gas (HCN) in water. It is a colourless, highly poisonous, volatile liquid, smelling of bitter almonds.

hydrodynamics branch of physics dealing with fluids (liquids and gases) in motion.

hydroelectric power electricity generated by the motion (*kinetic energy) of water. In a typical scheme, the potential energy of water stored in a reservoir, often created by damming a river, is converted into kinetic energy as it is piped into water *turbines. The turbines are coupled to *generators to produce electricity. Hydroelectric power provides about one-fifth of the world's electricity, supplying more than a billion people. Hydroelectricity is a non-polluting, renewable energy resource, produced from water that can be recycled.

hydrofoil wing that develops lift in the water in much the same way that an aeroplane wing develops lift in the air. A hydrofoil boat is one whose hull rises out of the water owing to the lift, and the boat skims along on the hydrofoils. The first hydrofoil was fitted to a boat in 1906. The first commercial hydrofoil went into operation in 1956. One of the most advanced hydrofoil boats is the Boeing *jetfoil. Hydrofoils are now widely used for fast island ferries in calm seas.

hydrogen chemical symbol H, (Greek *hydro* + *gen* 'water generator') colourless, odourless, gaseous, non-metallic element, atomic number 1, relative atomic mass 1.00797. It is the lightest of all the elements and occurs on Earth, chiefly in combination with oxygen, as water. Hydrogen is the most abundant element in the universe, where it accounts for 93% of the total number of atoms and 76% of the total mass. It is a component of most stars, including the Sun, whose heat and light are produced through the nuclear-fusion process that converts hydrogen into helium. When subjected to a pressure 500,000 times greater than that of the Earth's atmosphere, hydrogen becomes a solid with metallic properties, as in one of the inner zones of Jupiter. Hydrogen's common and industrial uses include the hardening of oils and fats by hydrogenation, the creation of high-temperature flames for welding, and as rocket fuel. It has been proposed as a fuel for road vehicles.

hydrogenation addition of hydrogen to an unsaturated organic molecule (one that contains double bonds or triple bonds). It is widely used in the manufacture of margarine and low-fat spreads by the addition of hydrogen to vegetable oils.

hydrogen bomb bomb that works on the principle of nuclear *fusion. Large-scale explosion results from the thermonuclear release of energy when hydrogen nuclei are fused to form helium nuclei. The first hydrogen bomb was exploded at Enewetak Atoll in the Pacific Ocean by the USA in 1952.

hydrogencarbonate *or* **bicarbonate** compound containing the ion HCO_3^-, an acid salt of carbonic acid (solution of carbon dioxide in water). When heated or treated with dilute acids, it gives off carbon dioxide. The most important compounds are sodium hydrogencarbonate (bicarbonate of soda), and calcium hydrogencarbonate.

hydrography study and charting of Earth's surface waters in seas, lakes, and rivers.

hydrological cycle also known as the *water cycle, by which water is circulated between the Earth's surface and its atmosphere.

hydrolysis chemical reaction in which the action of water or its ions breaks down a substance into smaller molecules. Hydrolysis occurs in certain inorganic salts in solution, in nearly all non-metallic chlorides, in esters, and in other organic substances. It is one of the mechanisms for the breakdown of food by the body, as in the conversion of starch to glucose.

hydrophyte plant adapted to live in water, or in waterlogged soil.

hydroplane on a submarine, a movable horizontal fin angled downwards or upwards when the vessel is descending or ascending. It is also a highly manoeuvrable motorboat with its bottom rising in steps to the stern, or a *hydrofoil boat that skims over the surface of the water when driven at high speed.

hydroponics cultivation of plants without soil, using specially prepared solutions of mineral salts. Beginning in the 1930s, large crops were grown by hydroponic methods, at first in California but since then in many other parts of the world.

hydrostatics branch of *statics dealing with fluids in equilibrium – that is, in a static condition. Practical applications include shipbuilding and dam design.

hydroxide any inorganic chemical compound containing one or more hydroxyl (OH) groups and generally combined with a metal. Hydroxides include sodium hydroxide (caustic soda, NaOH), potassium hydroxide (caustic potash, KOH), and calcium hydroxide (slaked lime, $Ca(OH)_2$).

hydroxyl group atom of hydrogen and an atom of oxygen bonded together and covalently bonded to an organic molecule. Common compounds containing hydroxyl groups are alcohols and phenols.

hyena any of three species of carnivorous doglike mammals living in Africa and Asia. Hyenas have extremely powerful jaws. They are scavengers, feeding on the remains of animals killed by predators such as lions, although they will also attack and kill live prey. (Genera *Hyaena* and *Crocuta*, family Hyaenidae, order Carnivora.)

Hymen in Greek mythology, the god of the marriage ceremony; personification of the refrain of a wedding song. In art, he is represented as a boy crowned with flowers, carrying a burning bridal torch.

hyperactivity condition of excessive activity in young children, combined with restlessness, inability to concentrate, and difficulty in learning. There are various causes, ranging from temperamental predisposition to brain disease. In some cases food *additives have come under suspicion; in such instances modification of the diet may help. Mostly there is improvement at puberty, but symptoms may persist in the small proportion diagnosed as having *attention-deficit hyperactivity disorder (ADHD).

hyperbola in geometry, a curve formed by cutting a right circular cone with a plane so that the angle between the plane and the base is greater than the angle between the base and the side of the cone. All hyperbolae are bounded by two asymptotes (straight lines to which the hyperbola moves closer and closer to but never reaches). A hyperbola is a member of the family of curves known as *conic sections.

hypermetropia *or* **long-sightedness** defect of vision in which a person is able to focus on objects in the distance, but not on close objects. It is caused by the failure of the lens to return to its normal rounded shape, or by the eyeball being too short, with the result that the image is focused on a point behind the retina. Hypermetropia is corrected by wearing glasses fitted with converging lenses, each of which acts like a magnifying glass.

hypertension abnormally high *blood pressure due to a variety of causes, leading to excessive contraction of the smooth muscle cells of the walls of the arteries. It increases the risk of kidney disease, stroke, and heart attack.

hypertext in computing, a method of forming connections between different files (including office documents, graphics, and Web pages) so that the user can click a 'link' with the *mouse to jump between them. For example, a software program might display a map of a country; if the user clicks on a particular city the program displays information about that city. The linked files do not need to be on the same computer, or even in the same country, for a hyperlink to be created.

hypnosis artificially induced state of relaxation or altered attention characterized by heightened suggestibility. There is evidence that, with susceptible persons, the sense of pain may be diminished, memory of past events enhanced, and illusions or hallucinations experienced. Posthypnotic amnesia (forgetting what happened during hypnosis) and posthypnotic suggestion (performing an action after hypnosis that had been suggested during it) have also been demonstrated.

hypo in photography, a term for sodium thiosulphate, discovered in 1819 by John Herschel, and used as a fixative for photographic images since 1837.

hypocaust floor raised on tile piers, heated by hot air circulating beneath it. It was first used by the Romans for baths about 100 BC, and was later introduced to private houses.

hypoglycaemia condition of abnormally low level of sugar (glucose) in the blood, which starves the brain. It causes weakness, sweating, and mental confusion, sometimes fainting.

hypotenuse longest side of a right-angled triangle, opposite the right angle. It is of particular application in Pythagoras' theorem (the square of the hypotenuse equals the sum of the squares of the other two sides), and in trigonometry where the ratios *sine and *cosine are defined as the ratios opposite/hypotenuse and adjacent/hypotenuse respectively.

hypothalamus region of the brain below the *cerebrum which regulates rhythmic activity and physiological stability within the body, including water balance and temperature. It regulates the production of the pituitary gland's hormones and controls that part of the *nervous system governing the involuntary muscles.

hypothermia condition in which the deep (core) temperature of the body falls below 35 °C. If it is not discovered coma and death ensue. Most at risk are the aged and babies (particularly if premature).

hypothyroidism *or* **myxoedema** deficient functioning of the thyroid gland, causing slowed mental and physical performance, weight gain, sensitivity to cold, and susceptibility to infection.

hyrax any of a group of small, rodentlike, herbivorous mammals that live among rocks in desert areas, and in forests in Africa, Arabia, and Syria. They are about the size of a rabbit, with a plump body, short legs, short ears, brownish fur, and long, curved front teeth. (Family Procaviidae, order Hyracoidea.)

hyssop aromatic herb belonging to the mint family, found in Asia, southern Europe, and around the Mediterranean. It has blue flowers, oblong leaves, and stems that are woody near the ground but herbaceous (fleshy) above. (*Hyssopus officinalis*, family Labiatae.)

hysterectomy surgical removal of all or part of the uterus (womb). The operation is performed to treat fibroids (benign tumours growing in the uterus) or cancer; also to relieve heavy menstrual bleeding. A woman who has had a hysterectomy will no longer menstruate and cannot bear children.

i

Iasi German **Jassy**, city in northeastern Romania; population (1993) 328,000. It has chemical, machinery, electronic, and textile industries. It was the capital of the principality of Moldavia 1568–1889.

Ibarruri, Dolores (1895–1989) called 'La Pasionaria' (the passion flower), Spanish Basque politician, journalist, and orator; she was first elected to the Cortes (Spanish parliament) in 1936. She helped to establish the Popular Front government and was a Loyalist leader in the Civil War. When Franco came to power in 1939 she left Spain for the USSR, where she was active in the Communist Party. She returned to Spain in 1977 after Franco's death and was re-elected to the Cortes (at the age of 81) in the first parliamentary elections for 40 years.

Iberian Peninsula name given by ancient Greek navigators to the Spanish peninsula, derived from the River Iberus (Ebro). Anthropologists have given the name 'Iberian' to a Neolithic people, traces of whom are found in the Spanish peninsula, southern France, the Canary Isles, Corsica, and part of North Africa.

ibex any of various wild goats found in mountainous areas of Europe, northeastern Africa, and Central Asia. They grow to 100 cm/3.5 ft, and have brown or grey coats and heavy horns. They are herbivorous and live in small groups.

ibid. abbreviation for **ibidem** (Latin 'in the same place'), reference to a book, chapter, or page previously cited.

ibis any of various wading birds, about 60 cm/2 ft tall, belonging to the same family as spoonbills. Ibises have long legs and necks, and long, downward-curved beaks, rather blunt at the end; the upper part is grooved. Their plumage is generally black and white. Various species occur in the warmer regions of the world. (Family Threskiornidae, order Ciconiiformes.)

Ibiza *or* **Eivissa** one of the *Balearic Islands, a popular tourist resort; area 596 sq km/230 sq mi; population (2001 est) 94,300. The capital and port, also called Ibiza, has a cathedral, built sometime between the 14th and 16th centuries. There are Phoenician ruins (necropolises), and the renowned archaeological museum houses Phoenician and Carthaginian remains considered the best of their kind in Spain.

Ibn Battuta (1304–1368) Arab traveller born in Tangier. In 1325, he went on an extraordinary 120,675-km/ 75,000-mi journey via Mecca to Egypt, East Africa, India, and China, returning some 30 years later. During this journey he also visited Spain and crossed the Sahara to Timbuktu. The narrative of his travels, *The Adventures of Ibn Battuta*, was written with an assistant, Ibn Juzayy.

Ibo *or* **Igbo** member of a West African people occupying southeastern Nigeria and numbering about 18 million. Primarily subsistence farmers, they also trade and export palm oil and kernels, and make pottery, woodcarvings, and music. They are divided into five main groups, and their languages belong to the Kwa branch of the Niger-Congo family.

Ibsen, Henrik (Johan) (1828–1906) Norwegian dramatist and poet. His realistic and often controversial plays revolutionized European theatre. Driven into voluntary exile (1864–91) by opposition to the satirical *Kjærlighedens komedie/Love's Comedy* (1862), he wrote the symbolic verse dramas *Brand* (1866) and *Peer Gynt* (1867), followed by realistic plays dealing with social issues, including *Samfundets støtter/Pillars of Society* (1877), *Et dukkehjem/A Doll's House* (1879), *Gengangere/Ghosts* (1881), *En folkefiende/An Enemy of the People* (1882), and *Hedda Gabler* (1890). By the time he returned to Norway, he was recognized as the country's greatest living writer.

IC abbreviation for *integrated circuit.

Icarus in astronomy, *Apollo asteroid 1.5 km/1 mi in diameter, discovered in 1949 by German-born US astronomer Walter Baade. It orbits the Sun every 409 days at a distance of 28–300 million km/18–186 million mi (0.19–2.0 astronomical units). It was the first asteroid known to approach the Sun closer than does the planet Mercury. In 1968 it passed within 6 million km/3.7 million mi of the Earth.

Icarus in Greek mythology, the son of *Daedalus, who with his father escaped from the labyrinth in Crete by making wings of feathers fastened with wax. Icarus plunged to his death when he flew too near the Sun and the wax melted.

ice solid formed by water when it freezes. It is colourless and its crystals are hexagonal. The water molecules are held together by hydrogen bonds.

ice age any period of extensive glaciation (in which icesheets and icecaps expand over the Earth) occurring in the Earth's history, but particularly that in the *Pleistocene epoch (last 2 million years), immediately preceding historic times. On the North American continent, *glaciers reached as far south as the Great Lakes, and an icesheet spread over northern Europe, leaving its remains as far south as Switzerland. In Britain ice reached as far south as Exeter. There were several glacial advances separated by interglacial (warm) stages, during which the ice melted and temperatures were higher than today. We are currently in an interglacial phase of an ice age.

iceberg floating mass of ice, about 80% of which is submerged, rising sometimes to 100 m/300 ft above sea level. Glaciers that reach the coast become extended into a broad foot; as this enters the sea, masses break off and drift towards temperate latitudes, becoming a danger to shipping.

ice hockey game played on ice between two teams of six, developed in Canada from field hockey or bandy. Players, who wear skates and protective clothing, use a curved stick to advance the puck (a rubber disc) and shoot it at the opponents' goal, a netted cage, guarded by the goaltender, or goalie. The other positions are the left and right defencemen and the left wing, centre, and right wing. The latter three are offensive players. The team with the most goals scored at the end of the three 20-minute periods wins; an overtime period may be played if a game ends in a tie.

Iceland
National name: *Lýðveldið Ísland/Republic of Iceland*

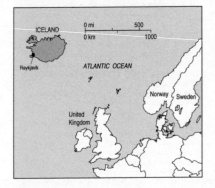

Area: 103,000 sq km/39,768 sq mi
Capital: Reykjavik
Major towns/cities: Akureyri, Kópavogur, Hafnarjördur, Gardhabaer, Keflavik, Reykjanesbaer, Vestmannaeyjar
Physical features: warmed by the Gulf Stream; glaciers and lava fields cover 75% of the country; active volcanoes (Hekla was once thought the gateway to Hell), geysers, hot springs, and new islands created offshore (Surtsey in 1963); subterranean hot water heats 85% of Iceland's homes; Sidujokull glacier moving at 100 metres a day
Head of state: Ólafur Ragnar Grímsson from 1996
Head of government: Halldór Asgrímsson from 2004
Political system: liberal democracy
Political executive: parliamentary
Political parties: Independence Party (IP), right of centre; Progressive Party (PP), radical socialist; People's Alliance (PA), socialist; Social Democratic Party (SDP), moderate, left of centre; Citizens' Party, centrist; Women's Alliance, women- and family-oriented
Currency: krona
GNI per capita (PPP): (US$) 28,590 (2002 est)
Exports: fish and fish products, aluminium, ferrosilicon, diatomite, fertilizer, animal products. Principal market: UK 19.4% (2000)
Population: 290,000 (2003 est)
Language: Icelandic (official)
Religion: Evangelical Lutheran about 90%, other Protestant and Roman Catholic about 4%
Life expectancy: 78 (men); 82 (women) (2000–05)
Chronology
7th century: Iceland discovered by Irish seafarers.
874: First Norse settler, Ingólfr Arnarson, founded a small colony at Reykjavík.
***c.* 900:** Norse settlers came in larger numbers, mainly from Norway.
930: Settlers established an annual parliament, the Althing, to make laws and resolve disputes.

985: Eric the Red left Iceland to found a settlement in Greenland.
1000: Icelanders adopted Christianity.
1263: Icelanders recognized the authority of the king of Norway after a brief civil war.
1397: Norway and Iceland were united with Denmark and Sweden under a single monarch.
15th century: Norway and Iceland were increasingly treated as appendages of Denmark, especially after Sweden seceded in 1449.
1783: Poisonous volcanic eruption caused great loss of life.
1814: Norway passed to the Swedish crown; Iceland remained under Danish rule.
1845: Althing was re-established in modernized form.
1874: New constitution gave Iceland limited autonomy.
1918: Iceland achieved full self-government under the Danish crown.
1940: British forces occupied Iceland after Germany invaded Denmark; US troops took over in 1941.
1944: Iceland became an independent republic under President Sveinn Björnsson.
1949: Iceland became a member of NATO.
1958: The introduction of an exclusive fishing limit led to the first 'Cod War', when Icelandic patrol boats clashed with British fishing boats.
1972–73: Iceland extended its fishing limit, renewing confrontations with Britain.
1975–76: The further extension of the fishing limit caused the third 'Cod War' with the UK.
1985: Iceland declared itself a nuclear-free zone.
1991: Davíd Oddsson was appointed prime minister.
1992: Iceland defied a world ban to resume its whaling industry.
1996: Ólafur Ragnar Grímsson was elected president.
2003: Prime Minister Oddsson's conservative Sjálfstæðisflokkurinn (SSF; Independence Party) and its liberal coalition partner, the Framsóknarflokkurinn (FSF; Progressive Party), retained a slim majority in legislative elections.
2004: Halldor Asgrimsson (FSE; Progressive Party) became coalition prime minister.

Icelandic language member of the northern Germanic branch of the Indo-European language family, spoken only in Iceland, and the most conservative in form of the Scandinavian languages. Despite seven centuries of Danish rule, lasting until 1918, Icelandic has remained virtually unchanged since the 12th century.

Iceni ancient people of eastern England, who revolted against Roman occupation under the chieftainship of *Boudicca.

ice-skating see *skating.

I Ching or *Book of Changes* ancient Chinese book of divination based on 64 hexagrams, or patterns of six lines. The lines may be 'broken' or 'whole' (yin or yang) and are generated by tossing yarrow stalks or coins. The enquirer formulates a question before throwing, and the book gives interpretations of the meaning of the hexagrams.

ichneumon fly any of a large group of parasitic wasps. There are several thousand species in Europe, North America, and other regions. They have slender bodies, and the females have unusually long, curved ovipositors (egg-laying instruments) that can pierce

441

several inches of wood. The eggs are laid in the eggs, larvae, or pupae of other insects, usually butterflies or moths. (Family Ichneumonidae.)

icon in computing, a small picture on the computer screen, or *VDU, representing an object or function that the user may manipulate or otherwise use. It is a feature of *graphical user interface (GUI) systems. Icons make computers easier to use by allowing the user to point to and click with a *mouse on pictures, rather than type commands.

icon in the Greek or Eastern Orthodox Church, a religious picture of *Jesus, Mary, an *angel, or a *saint, in painting, low relief, or mosaic; the full face must always be shown. Painted icons were traditionally made on wood. After the 17th century, and mainly in Russia, a *riza* was often added as protection; this gold and silver covering, that left only the face and hands visible, was sometimes adorned with jewels presented by the faithful in thanksgiving.

iconography in art history, a way to classify works of art with reference to its subject matter, themes, and symbolism, rather than style. Iconographic study can also be used when analysing the style of a work. Attaching significance to symbols can help to identify subject matter (for example, a saint holding keys usually represents St Peter) and makes it possible to place a work of art in its historical context. The pioneer of this approach was the German art historian Erwin Panofsky.

id in Freudian psychology, the mass of motivational and instinctual elements of the human mind, whose activity is largely governed by the arousal of specific needs. It is regarded as the *unconscious element of the human psyche, and is said to be in conflict with the *ego and the *superego.

Idaho called the **Gem State**, state of northwestern USA, bordered to the east by *Montana and *Wyoming, to the south by *Utah and *Nevada, to the west by *Oregon and *Washington, and to the north by *British Columbia, Canada; area 214,314 sq km/ 82,747 sq mi; population (2000) 1,294,000; capital Boise. It is largely mountainous, and its many ranges include the *Rocky Mountains and the Bitterroot Range. The Columbia Plateau in the south has fertile agricultural regions, and crops include wheat and peas. There are large forests, and the state is famous for its waterfalls, such as the 65 m/212 ft high Shoshone Falls on the Snake River. The chief industries are tourism, mining, beef, and agriculture: Idaho is the leading producer of potatoes in the USA. Cities include Nampa, Pocatello, Idaho Falls, Coeur d'Alene, Twin Falls, Caldwell, and Moscow. In 1951, Idaho National Engineering Laboratory (1949) was the first nuclear installation to produce a usable supply of electricity. Idaho was admitted to the Union in 1890 as the 43rd US state.

idealism in philosophy, the theory that states that the external world is fundamentally immaterial and a dimension of the mind. Objects in the world exist but, according to this theory, they lack substance.

Ides in the Roman calendar, the 15th day of March, May, July, and October, and the 13th day of all other months (the word originally indicated the full moon); Julius Caesar was assassinated on the Ides of March 44 BC.

Ife town in western Nigeria, traditionally the oldest of the Yoruba kingdoms in the region. Ife was established in the 6th century and became an important Iron-Age town. It was the cultural and religious, though not political, centre of the region, and reached its peak about 1300. Many sculptures in bronze, brass, clay, and ivory have been excavated in and around the town.

igneous rock rock formed from the cooling and solidification of molten rock called *magma. The acidic nature of this rock type means that areas with underlying igneous rock are particularly susceptible to the effects of acid rain. Igneous rocks that crystallize slowly from magma below the Earth's surface have large crystals. Examples include dolerite and granite.

iguana any of about 700 species of lizard, chiefly found in the Americas. The **common iguana** (*I. iguana*) of Central and South America is a vegetarian and may reach 2 m/6 ft in length. (Especially genus *Iguana*, family Iguanidae.)

iguanodon plant-eating *dinosaur whose remains are found in deposits of the Lower *Cretaceous age, together with the remains of other dinosaurs of the same order (ornithiscians) such as stegosaurus and *triceratops. It was 5–10 m/16–32 ft long and, when standing upright, 4 m/13 ft tall. It walked on its hind legs, using its long tail to balance its body. (Order *Ornithiscia*.)

IJsselmeer lake in the Netherlands, area 1,217 sq km/ 470 sq mi. It was formed in 1932 after the *Zuider Zee was cut off from the North Sea by a dyke 32 km/20 mi long (the *Afsluitdijk*); it has been freshwater since 1944. The rivers Vecht, IJssel, and Zwatewater flow into the lake.

Ile-de-France region of northern France; area 12,012 sq km/ 4,638 sq mi; population (1999 est) 10,952,000. It includes the French capital, *Paris, and the towns of Versailles, Sèvres, and St-Cloud, and comprises the *départements* of Essonne, Val-de-Marne, Val-d'Oise, Ville de Paris, Seine-et-Marne, Hauts-de-Seine, Seine-St-Denis, and Yvelines. From here the early French kings extended their authority over the whole country.

ileum part of the small intestine of the *digestive system, between the duodenum and the colon, that absorbs digested food.

Iliad Greek epic poem, product of an oral tradition; it was possibly written down by 700 BC and is attributed to *Homer. The title is derived from Ilion, the Greek name for Troy. Its subject is the wrath of the Greek hero Achilles at the loss of his concubine Briseis, and at the death of his friend Patroclus, during the Greek siege of Troy. The poems ends with the death of the Trojan hero Hector at the hands of Achilles.

Ilium in classical mythology, an alternative name for the city of *Troy, taken from its founder Ilus.

Illinois called the **Prairie State** and the **Land of Lincoln**, (Algonquian 'warriors') Midwestern state of the USA, bordered to the east by *Indiana, to the southeast by *Kentucky, with the *Ohio River serving as a boundary, to the west by *Missouri and *Iowa, with the *Mississippi River as a boundary, and to the north by *Wisconsin; area 143,962 sq km/55,584 sq mi; population (2000) 12,419,300; capital Springfield. The state is made up of three main physical areas: the Central Plains, the Shawnee Hills, and the Gulf Coastal Plain. In the northeast, Illinois has a shore of 101 km/ 63 mi on Lake Michigan, occupied by *Chicago, the largest city in the state, and its northern suburbs. Illinois is a leading manufacturing state, producing machinery and electronic equipment, and is also a very important agricultural state, with major crops including corn, soybeans, and meat and dairy products. It also has an important mining industry. Other towns and cities include Rockford, Aurora, Naperville, Peoria, Joliet, Elgin, and Waukegan. The state is home to Algonquian Illinois, Kickapoo, Potawatomi, Sac, and Fox, among other indigenous peoples. The growth of the railroads led to Chicago becoming the most important city in the Midwest in the 19th century; after the Civil War the state become a significant producer and there was heavy immigration, and the state experienced labour unrest at the end of the 19th century. After the decline of heavy industry in the 1950s, Chicago remained a major trade centre. Illinois was admitted to the Union in 1818 as the 21st US state.

Illyria ancient name for the eastern coastal region of the Adriatic, north of the Gulf of Corinth. Its three constituent districts were Dalmatia, Iapydia, and Liburnia. It later formed the Roman province of Illyricum. The Albanians are the survivors of its ancient peoples.

image picture or appearance of a real object, formed by light that passes through a lens or is reflected from a mirror. If rays of light actually pass through an image, it is called a **real image**. Real images, such as those produced by a camera or projector lens, can be projected onto a screen. An image that cannot be projected onto a screen, such as that seen in a flat mirror, is known as a **virtual image**.

imaginary number term often used to describe the non-real element of a *complex number. For the complex number $(a + ib)$, ib is the imaginary number where $i = \sqrt{(-1)}$, and b any real number.

Imagism movement in Anglo-American poetry that flourished from 1912 to 1914 and affected much US and British poetry and critical thinking thereafter. A central figure was Ezra *Pound, who asserted the principles of free verse, complex imagery, and poetic impersonation.

imago sexually mature stage of an *insect.

imam (Arabic 'leader') in a mosque, the leader of congregational prayer, but generally any notable Islamic leader.

IMF abbreviation for *International Monetary Fund.

Imhotep (born c. 2630 BC) Egyptian physician, architect, and vizier (chief adviser) of King Zoser (3rd dynasty). He is thought to have designed the step pyramid at Sakkara, the first pyramid ever constructed. Reputedly King Zoser's doctor, Imhotep was raised to the status of god of healing after his death and his tomb (believed to be in the north Sakkara cemetery) became a centre of healing. He was said to be the son of *Ptah, the Egyptian god of the creative force, and was later identified with *Asclepius, the Greek god of medicine.

Immaculate Conception in the Roman Catholic Church, the belief that the Virgin Mary was, by a special act of grace, preserved free from *original sin from the moment she was conceived. This article of the Catholic faith was for centuries the subject of heated controversy, opposed by St Thomas Aquinas and other theologians, but generally accepted from about the 16th century. It became a dogma in 1854 under Pope Pius IX.

immunity protection that organisms have against foreign micro-organisms, such as bacteria and viruses, and against cancerous cells (see *cancer). The cells that provide this protection are called white blood cells, or leucocytes, and make up the immune system. They

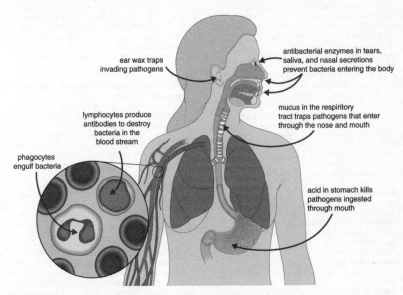

ear wax traps invading pathogens

antibacterial enzymes in tears, saliva, and nasal secretions prevent bacteria entering the body

lymphocytes produce antibodies to destroy bacteria in the blood stream

mucus in the respiratory tract traps pathogens that enter through the nose and mouth

phagocytes engulf bacteria

acid in stomach kills pathogens ingested through mouth

immunity How the body's defence mechanisms keep out invading pathogens or destroy those that succeed in entering the body.

include neutrophils and *macrophages, which can engulf invading organisms and other unwanted material, and natural killer cells that destroy cells infected by viruses and cancerous cells. Some of the most important immune cells are the B cells and T cells. Immune cells coordinate their activities by means of chemical messengers or *lymphokines, including the antiviral messenger *interferon. The lymph nodes play a major role in organizing the immune response.

immunization process of conferring immunity to infectious disease by artificial methods, in other words making someone not liable to catch a disease. The most widely used technique is *vaccination. Immunization is an important public health measure. If most of the population has been immunized against a particular disease, it is impossible for an epidemic to take hold.

immunocompromised lacking a fully effective immune system. The term is most often used in connection with infections such as *AIDS where the virus interferes with the immune response (see *immunity).

immunodeficient lacking one or more elements of a working immune system. Immune deficiency is the term generally used for patients who are born with such a defect, while those who acquire such a deficiency later in life are referred to as *immunocompromised or immunosuppressed.

immunoglobulin human globulin *protein that can be separated from blood and administered to confer immediate immunity to the recipient. It participates in the immune reaction as the antibody for a specific *antigen (disease-causing agent).

impala African *antelope found from Kenya to South Africa in savannahs and open woodland. The body is sandy brown. Males have lyre-shaped horns up to 75 cm/ 2.5 ft long. Impala grow up to 1.5 m/5 ft long and 90 cm/ 3 ft tall. They live in herds and spring high in the air when alarmed. (Species *Aepyceros melampus*, family Bovidae.)

impeachment judicial procedure by which government officials are accused of wrongdoing and brought to trial before a legislative body. In the USA the House of Representatives may impeach offenders to be tried before the Senate, as in the case of President Andrew Johnson in 1868. Richard *Nixon resigned the US presidency in 1974 when threatened by impeachment. President Bill *Clinton's impeachment trial took place in 1999.

impedance symbol Z, total opposition of a circuit to the passage of alternating electric current. It includes the resistance R and the reactance X (caused by *capacitance or *inductance); the impedance can then be found using the equation $Z^2 = R^2 + X^2$.

imperialism policy of extending the power and rule of a government beyond its own boundaries. A country may attempt to dominate others by direct rule and settlement – the establishment of a colony – or by less obvious means such as control of markets for goods or raw materials. These less obvious means are often called *neocolonialism.

imperial system traditional system of units developed in the UK, based largely on the foot, pound, and second (f.p.s.) system.

import product or service that one country purchases from another for domestic consumption, or for processing and re-exporting (Hong Kong, for example,

is heavily dependent on imports for its export business). Imports may be visible (goods) or invisible (services). If an importing country does not have a counterbalancing value of exports, it may experience balance-of-payments difficulties and accordingly consider restricting imports by some form of protectionism (such as an import tariff or import quotas).

Impressionism movement in painting that originated in France in the 1860s and had enormous influence in European and North American painting in the late 19th century. The Impressionists wanted to depict real life, to paint straight from nature, and to capture the changing effects of light. The term was first used abusively to describe Claude *Monet's painting *Impression: Sunrise* (1872). The other leading Impressionists included Paul *Cézanne, Edgar *Degas, Edouard *Manet, Camille *Pissarro, Pierre-Auguste *Renoir, and Alfred *Sisley, but only Monet remained devoted to Impressionist ideas throughout his career.

imprinting in *ethology, the process whereby a young animal learns to recognize both specific individuals (for example, its mother) and its own species.

impromptu in music, a 19th-century character piece in the style of an improvisation. Composers of piano impromptus include Schubert and Chopin.

Inca (Quechua 'king') ancient Peruvian civilization of Quechua-speaking *American Indians that began in the Andean highlands about AD 1200. By the time the Spanish conquered the region in the 1530s, the Inca ruled an empire that stretched from Ecuador in the north to Chile in the south. The word Inca was used for the title of the emperor as well as the people. The empire was based on an agricultural economy, and ruled as a *theocracy (a political system run by priests). Centres such as *Machu Picchu testify to their advanced engineering and architectural ability. Once defeated, the Inca were enslaved by the Spanish, but many *Quechua-speaking Peruvians today are their descendants.

incandescence emission of light from a substance in consequence of its high temperature. The colour of the emitted light from liquids or solids depends on their temperature, and for solids generally the higher the temperature the whiter the light. Gases may become incandescent through *ionizing radiation, as in the glowing vacuum discharge tube.

incarnation assumption of living form (plant, animal, human) by a deity; for example, the gods of Greece and Rome, Hinduism, and Christianity (Jesus as the second person of the Trinity).

incendiary bomb bomb containing inflammable matter. Usually dropped by aircraft, incendiary bombs were used in World War I and incendiary shells were used against Zeppelin aircraft. Incendiary bombs were a major weapon in attacks on cities in World War II, causing widespread destruction. To hinder firefighters, delayed-action high-explosive bombs were usually dropped with them. In the Vietnam War, US forces used *napalm in incendiary bombs.

incest sexual intercourse between persons thought to be too closely related to marry; the exact relationships that fall under the incest taboo vary widely from society to society. A biological explanation for the incest taboo is based on the necessity to avoid inbreeding.

inch imperial unit of linear measure, a twelfth of a foot, equal to 2.54 centimetres.

inclination in astronomy, angle between the *ecliptic and the plane of the orbit of a planet, asteroid, or comet. In the case of satellites orbiting a planet, it is the angle between the plane of orbit of the satellite and the equator of the planet.

income tax direct tax levied on personal income, mainly wages and salaries, but which may include the value of receipts other than in cash. It is one of the main instruments for achieving a government's income redistribution objectives, to make incomes less unequal. In contrast, **indirect taxes** are duties payable whenever a particular product or service is purchased; examples include VAT and customs duties.

incubus in the popular belief of the Middle Ages in Europe, a male demon who had sexual intercourse with women in their sleep. Supposedly the women then gave birth to witches and demons. **Succubus** is the female equivalent.

indemnity in law, an undertaking to compensate another for damage, loss, trouble, or expenses, or the money paid by way of such compensation – for example, under fire-insurance agreements.

indentured labour work under a restrictive contract of employment for a fixed period in a foreign country in exchange for payment of passage, accommodation, and food. Indentured labour was the means by which many British people emigrated to North America during the colonial era, and in the 19th–early 20th centuries it was used to recruit Asian workers for employment elsewhere in European colonial empires.

Independence Day public holiday in the USA commemorating the adoption of the *Declaration of Independence, 4 July 1776.

Independent Television (ITV) Independent television in the UK, formed by a number of regional contractors and paid for by advertising. It began broadcasting in 1955. There are a varying number of regional channels, as well as national channels for news and breakfast programmes. Independent television companies are regulated by the Independent Television Commission (ITC), and are required to provide quality, independent productions, with provision for viewers with disabilities.

indeterminacy principle alternative name for *uncertainty principle.

index plural **indices**, (Latin 'sign', 'indicator') in mathematics, another term for *exponent, the number that indicates the power to which a term should be raised.

India

National name: *Bharat* (Hindi)/*India*; *Bharatiya Janarajya* (unofficial)/*Republic of India*
Area: 3,166,829 sq km/1,222,713 sq mi
Capital: New Delhi
Major towns/cities: Mumbai (formerly Bombay), Kolkata (formerly Calcutta), Chennai (formerly Madras), Bangalore, Hyderabad, Ahmadabad, Kanpur, Pune, Nagpur, Bhopal, Jaipur, Lucknow, Surat
Major ports: Kolkata, Mumbai, Chennai
Physical features: Himalayas on northern border; plains around rivers Ganges, Indus, Brahmaputra; Deccan peninsula south of the Narmada River forms plateau between Western and Eastern Ghats mountain

ranges; desert in west; Andaman and Nicobar Islands, Lakshadweep (Laccadive Islands)
Head of state: Abdul Kalam from 2002
Head of government: Manmohan Singh from 2004
Political system: liberal democracy
Political executive: parliamentary
Political parties: All India Congress Committee, or Congress, cross-caste and cross-religion coalition, left of centre; Janata Dal (People's Party), secular, left of centre; Bharatiya Janata Party (BJP), radical right wing, Hindu-chauvinist; Communist Party of India (CPI), Marxist-Leninist; Communist Party of India–Marxist (CPI–M), West Bengal–based moderate socialist
Currency: rupee
GNI per capita (PPP): (US$) 2,570 (2002 est)
Exports: tea (world's largest producer), coffee, fish, iron and steel, leather, textiles, clothing, polished diamonds, handmade carpets, engineering goods, chemicals. Principal market: USA 20.9% (2000)
Population: 1,065,462,000 (2003 est)
Language: Hindi, English, Assamese, Bengali, Gujarati, Kannada, Kashmiri, Konkani, Malayalam, Manipuri, Marathi, Nepali, Oriya, Punjabi, Sanskrit, Sindhi, Tamil, Telugu, Urdu (all official), more than 1,650 dialects
Religion: Hindu 80%, Sunni Muslim 10%, Christian 2.5%, Sikh 2%, Buddhist, Jewish
Life expectancy: 63 (men); 65 (women) (2000–05)
Chronology
c. **2500–1500 BC:** The earliest Indian civilization evolved in the Indus Valley with the city states of Harappa and Mohenjo Daro.
c. **1500–1200 BC:** Aryan peoples from the northwest overran northern India and the Deccan; Brahmanism (a form of Hinduism) developed.
321 BC: Chandragupta, founder of the Mauryan dynasty, began to unite northern India in a Hindu Empire.
268–232 BC: Mauryan Empire reached its height under Asoka, who ruled two-thirds of India from his capital Pataliputra.
c. **180 BC:** Shunga dynasty replaced the Mauryans; Hindu Empire began to break up into smaller kingdoms.

AD 320–480: Gupta dynasty reunified northern India.

c. 500: Raiding Huns from central Asia destroyed the Gupta dynasty; India reverted to many warring kingdoms.

11th–12th centuries: Rajput princes of northern India faced repeated Muslim invasions by Arabs, Turks, and Afghans, and in 1206 the first Muslim dynasty was established at Delhi.

14th–16th centuries: Muslim rule extended over northern India and the Deccan; south remained independent under the Hindu Vijayanagar dynasty.

1498: Explorer Vasco da Gama reached India, followed by Portuguese, Dutch, French, and English traders.

1526: Last Muslim invasion: Zahir ud-din Muhammad (Babur) defeated the Sultan of Delhi at Battle of Panipat and established the Mogul Empire, which was consolidated by Akbar the Great (1556–1605).

1600: East India Company founded by English merchants, who settled in Madras, Bombay, and Calcutta.

17th century: Mogul Empire reached its zenith under Jahangir (1605–27), Shah Jehan (1628–58), and Aurangzeb (1658–1707).

1739: Persian king Nadir Shah invaded India and destroyed Mogul prestige; the British and French supported rival Indian princes in subsequent internal wars.

1757: Battle of Plassey: Robert Clive defeated Siraj al-Daulah, nawab of Bengal; Bengal came under control of the British East India Company.

1772–85: Warren Hastings, British governor general of Bengal, raised the Indian army and pursued expansionist policies.

early 19th century: British took control (directly or indirectly) throughout India by defeating powerful Indian states in a series of regional wars.

1858: 'Indian Mutiny': mutiny in Bengal army erupted into widespread anti-British revolt; rebels sought to restore powers of Mogul emperor.

1858: British defeated the rebels; East India Company dissolved; India came under the British crown.

1885: Indian National Congress founded in Bombay as a focus for nationalism.

1909: Morley–Minto Reforms: Indians received the right to elect members of Legislative Councils; Hindus and Muslims formed separate electorates.

1919: British forces killed 379 Indian demonstrators at Amritsar; India Act (Montagu–Chelmsford Reforms) conceded a measure of provincial self-government.

1920–22: Mohandas Gandhi won control of the Indian National Congress, which launched a campaign of civil disobedience in support of the demand for complete self-rule.

1935: India Act provided for Indian control of federal legislature, with defence and external affairs remaining the viceroy's responsibility.

1940: Muslim League called for India to be partitioned along religious lines.

1947: British India partitioned into two independent dominions of India (mainly Hindu) and Pakistan (mainly Muslim) amid bloody riots; Jawaharlal Nehru of Congress Party became prime minister.

1950: India became a republic within the Commonwealth.

1962: India lost a brief border war with China; retained Kashmir in war with Pakistan in 1965.

1966: Indira Gandhi, daughter of Nehru, became prime minister.

1971: India defeated Pakistan in a war and helped East Pakistan become independent as Bangladesh.

1975: Found guilty of electoral corruption, Mrs Gandhi declared a state of emergency and arrested opponents.

1977–79: The Janata Party formed a government under Morarji Desai.

1980: Mrs Gandhi, heading a Congress Party splinter group, Congress (I) ('I' for Indira), was returned to power.

1984: Troops cleared Sikh separatists from the Golden Temple, Amritsar; Mrs Gandhi was assassinated by Sikh bodyguards; her son Rajiv Gandhi became prime minister.

1989: After financial scandals, Congress lost elections; V P Singh formed a Janata Dal minority government.

1990: Direct rule was imposed on Jammu and Kashmir after an upsurge in Muslim separatist violence; rising interethnic and religious conflict was seen in the Punjab and elsewhere.

1992: The destruction of a mosque at Ayodhya, northern India, by Hindu extremists resulted in widespread violence.

1995: Bombay was renamed Mumbai.

1996: Madras was renamed Chennai. Direct central rule was imposed on Uttar Pradesh after inconclusive assembly elections.

1997: Kocheril Raman Narayanan became the first 'untouchable' to be elected president.

1998: Atal Behari Vajpayee, leader of the Bharatiya Janata party, was elected prime minister. The creation of three new states was proposed. India carried out five underground nuclear explosions, meeting with international condemnation. There were floods in Uttar Pradesh.

1999: The Indian government renounced further nuclear weapons testing and promised to sign the Comprehensive Test Ban Treaty. India used air power to attack 'infiltrators' in Kashmir. In June Kashmir peace talks were offered to Pakistan.

2000: Relations with Pakistan worsened after India accused Pakistan of involvement (which it denied) of the hijacking of an Indian airliner by Kashmiri militants. Three new states were created: Uttaranchal was carved out of Uttar Pradesh, Jharkhand out of Bihar, and Chhattisgarh out of Madhya Pradesh. Former premier Narasimha Rao was convicted on corruption charges relating to 1993. India declared a unilateral ceasefire in Kashmir in November, renewing it twice over the following months.

2001: Over 30,000 people were killed in an earthquake in Gujarat. A census showed the population to exceed 1 billion. Bribery scandals forced leading ministers to resign.

2002: Hindu–Muslim clashes in the state of Gujarat led to around 800 deaths, and the Indian supreme court barred all religious activity from taking place at a disputed site in Ayodhya that is sacred to both faiths. The longstanding quarrel with Pakistan about the disputed sovereignty over the territory of Kashmir erupted again, prompting international concern.

2003: International tensions between India and Pakistan were re-ignited as a massacre of 24 Hindus by Islamic militants in Indian-administered Kashmir was followed by the test-firing by both countries of missiles capable of delivering nuclear weapons. However India and Pakistan went on to begin their first formal ceasefire in the disputed territory in 20 years. **2004:** The Congress Party won the general election but its leader, Sonia Gandhi, declined the post of prime minister. Her place was taken by Manmohan Singh.

India Acts legislation passed in 1858, 1919, and 1935 which formed the basis of British rule in India until independence in 1947. The 1858 Act abolished the administrative functions of the British *East India Company, replacing them with direct rule from London. The 1919 Act increased Indian participation at local and provincial levels but did not meet nationalist demands for complete internal self-government (Montagu-Chelmsford reforms). The 1935 Act outlined a federal structure but was never implemented.

Indiana called the **Hoosier State,** ('land of the Indians') smallest state of Midwestern USA, bordered by the northeast by *Michigan, to the east by *Ohio, to the south and southeast by *Kentucky, and to the west by *Illinois; area 92,895 sq km/35,867 sq mi; population (2000) 6,080,500; capital Indianapolis. It is situated in the Central Lowlands of the USA, with lakes and low hills in the north and wide expanses of fertile agricultural land in the centre. In the northwest, Indiana has a 72 km-/45 mi-long shoreline on Lake *Michigan, and there are steep hills and limestone caverns in the south. Mining and manufacturing, especially coal and steel production, make significant contributions to the economy of the region, and car manufacture is a particularly important industry. Indiana's agricultural output includes corn (particularly popcorn), soybeans, apples, and hogs. The principal cities are Fort Wayne, Gary, Evansville, and South Bend. Rapid industrial development after the American Civil War led to Indiana becoming one of the leading industrial states at the beginning of the 20th century, a position helped by the state's early association with car and machinery manufacture. Indiana was admitted to the Union in 1816 as the 19th US state.

Indian languages traditionally, the languages of the subcontinent of India; since 1947, the languages of the Republic of India. These number some 200, depending on whether a variety is classified as a language or a dialect. They fall into five main groups, the two most widespread of which are the Indo-European languages (mainly in the north) and the Dravidian languages (mainly in the south).

Indian Mutiny *or* **Sepoy Rebellion** *or* **Mutiny** revolt of Indian soldiers (sepoys) against the British in India from 1857 to 1858. The uprising was confined to the north, from Bengal to the Punjab, and central India. It led to the end of rule by the *British East India Company and its replacement by direct British crown administration.

Indian National Congress (INC) official name for the *Congress Party of India.

Indian Ocean ocean between Africa and Australia, with India to the north, and the southern boundary being an arbitrary line from Cape Agulhas to south Tasmania; area 73,500,000 sq km/28,370,000 sq mi; average depth 3,872 m/12,708 ft. The greatest depth is the Java Trench 7,725 m/25,353 ft. It includes two great bays on either side of the Indian peninsula, the Bay of Bengal to the east, and the Arabian Sea with the gulfs of Aden and Oman to the west.

indicator in chemistry, a compound that changes its structure and colour in response to its environment. The commonest chemical indicators detect changes in *pH (for example, *litmus and universal indicator) or in the oxidation state of a system (redox indicators).

indie abbreviation for independent, in music, a record label that is neither owned nor distributed by one of the large conglomerates ('majors') that dominate the industry. Without a corporate bureaucratic structure, the independent labels are often quicker to respond to new trends and are more idealistic in their aims. What has become loosely known as **indie music** therefore tends to be experimental, amateurish, or at the cutting edge of street fashion.

indigo violet-blue vegetable dye obtained from various tropical plants such as the anil, but now replaced by a synthetic product. It was once a major export crop of India. (Plant genus *Indigofera,* family Leguminosae.)

indium chemical symbol In, (Latin *indicum* 'indigo') soft, ductile, silver-white, metallic element, atomic number 49, relative atomic mass 114.82. It occurs in nature in some zinc ores, is resistant to abrasion, and is used as a coating on metal parts. It was discovered in 1863 by German metallurgists Ferdinand Reich (1799–1882) and Hieronymus Richter (1824–1898), who named it after the two indigo lines of its spectrum.

individualism in politics, a view in which the individual takes precedence over the collective: the opposite of *collectivism. The term **possessive individualism** has been applied to the writings of John *Locke and Jeremy *Bentham, describing society as comprising individuals interacting through market relations.

Indo-Aryan languages another name for the *Indo-European languages.

Indochina, French name given by the French to their colonies in Southeast Asia: Cambodia, Laos, and Vietnam, which became independent after World War II.

Indochina War war of independence 1946–54 between the nationalist forces of what was to become Vietnam and France, the occupying colonial power.

Indo-European languages family of languages that includes some of the world's major classical languages (Sanskrit and Pali in India, Zend Avestan in Iran, Greek and Latin in Europe), as well as several of the most widely spoken languages (English worldwide; Spanish in Iberia, Latin America, and elsewhere; and the Hindi group of languages in northern India). Indo-European languages were once located only along a geographical band from India through Iran into northwestern Asia, Eastern Europe, the northern Mediterranean lands, northern and Western Europe and the British Isles.

Indo-Germanic languages former name for the *Indo-European languages.

Indonesia

formerly **Dutch East Indies** (until 1949)

National name: *Republik Indonesia/Republic of Indonesia*
Area: 1,904,569 sq km/735,354 sq mi
Capital: Jakarta
Major towns/cities: Surabaya, Bandung, Medan, Semarang, Palembang, Tangerang, Bandar Lampung, Ujung Pandang, Malang

447

Indonesia

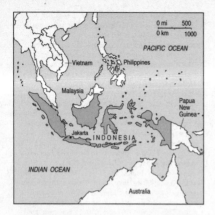

Major ports: Tanjung Priok, Surabaya, Semarang (Java), Ujung Pandang (Sulawesi)

Physical features: comprises 13,677 tropical islands (over 6,000 of them are inhabited): the Greater Sundas (including Java, Madura, Sumatra, Sulawesi, and Kalimantan (part of Borneo)), the Lesser Sunda Islands/Nusa Tenggara (including Bali, Lombok, Sumbawa, Flores, Sumba, Alor, Lomblen, Timor, Roti, and Savu), Maluku/Moluccas (over 1,000 islands including Ambon, Ternate, Tidore, Tanimbar, and Halmahera), and Irian Jaya (part of New Guinea); over half the country is tropical rainforest; it has the largest expanse of peatlands in the tropics

Head of state and government: Susilo Bambang Yudhoyono from 2004

Political system: emergent democracy

Political executive: limited presidency

Political parties: Sekber Golkar, ruling military-bureaucrat-farmers' party; United Development Party (PPP), moderate Islamic; Indonesian Democratic Party (PDI), nationalist Christian

Currency: rupiah

GNI per capita (PPP): (US$) 2,990 (2002 est)

Exports: textiles and garments, petroleum and petroleum products, natural and manufactured gas, rubber, palm oil, wood and wood products, electrical and electronic products, coffee, fishery products, coal, copper, tin, pepper, tea. Principal market: Japan 25.6% (2001)

Population: 219,883,000 (2003 est)

Language: Bahasa Indonesia (closely related to Malay; official), Javanese, Dutch, over 550 regional languages and dialects

Religion: Muslim 87%, Protestant 6%, Roman Catholic 3%, Hindu 2% and Buddhist 1% (the continued spread of Christianity, together with an Islamic revival, have led to greater religious tensions)

Life expectancy: 65 (men); 67 (women) (2000–05)

Chronology

3000–500 BC: Immigrants from southern China displaced original Melanesian population.

6th century AD: Start of Indian cultural influence; small Hindu and Buddhist kingdoms developed.

8th century: Buddhist maritime empire of Srivijaya expanded to include all Sumatra and Malay peninsula.

13th century: Islam introduced to Sumatra by Arab merchants; spread throughout the islands over next 300 years.

14th century: Eastern Javanese kingdom of Majapahit destroyed Srivijaya and dominated the region.

c. 1520: Empire of Majapahit disintegrated; Javanese nobles fled to Bali.

16th century: Portuguese merchants broke the Muslim monopoly on the spice trade.

1602: Dutch East India Company founded; it displaced the Portuguese and monopolized trade with the Spice Islands.

1619: Dutch East India Company captured the port of Jakarta in Java and renamed it Batavia.

17th century: Dutch introduced coffee plants and established informal control over central Java through divide-and-rule policy among local rulers.

1749: After frequent military intervention, the Dutch East India Company obtained formal sovereignty over Mataram.

1799: The Netherlands took over interests of bankrupt Dutch East India Company.

1808: French forces occupied Java; British expelled them in 1811 and returned Java to the Netherlands in 1816.

1824: Anglo-Dutch Treaty: Britain recognized entire Indonesian archipelago as Dutch sphere of influence.

1825–30: Java War: Prince Dipo Negoro led unsuccessful revolt against Dutch rule; further revolt 1894–96.

19th century: Dutch formalized control over Java and conquered other islands; cultivation of coffee and sugar under tight official control made the Netherlands Indies one of the richest colonies in the world.

1908: Dutch completed conquest of Bali.

1927: Communist revolts suppressed; Achmed Sukarno founded Indonesian Nationalist Party (PNI) to unite diverse anti-Dutch elements.

1929: Dutch imprisoned Sukarno and tried to suppress PNI.

1942–45: Japanese occupation; PNI installed as anti-Western puppet government.

1945: When Japan surrendered, President Sukarno declared an independent republic, but the Dutch set about restoring colonial rule by force.

1947: Dutch 'police action': an all-out attack on Java and Sumatra conquered two-thirds of the republic.

1949: Under US pressure, the Dutch agreed to transfer sovereignty of the Netherlands Indies (except Dutch New Guinea or Irian Jaya) to the Republic of the United States of Indonesia.

1950: President Sukarno abolished federalism and proclaimed unitary Republic of Indonesia dominated by Java; revolts in Sumatra and South Moluccas.

1959: To combat severe political instability, Sukarno imposed authoritarian 'guided democracy'.

1963: The Netherlands ceded Irian Jaya to Indonesia.

1963–66: Indonesia tried to break up Malaysia by means of blockade and guerrilla attacks.

1965–66: Clashes between communists and army; Gen Raden Suharto imposed emergency administration and massacred up to 700,000 alleged communists.

1968: Suharto formally replaced Sukarno as president and proclaimed 'New Order' under strict military rule.

1970s: Rising oil exports brought significant agricultural and industrial growth.

1975: Indonesia invaded East Timor when Portuguese rule collapsed; 200,000 died in ensuing war.

1986: After suppressing a revolt on Irian Jaya, Suharto introduced a programme to settle 65,000 Javanese there and on outer islands.

1996: The government initiated a crackdown on its opponents.

1997: Hundreds were killed in ethnic riots in west Kalimantan province. There was a drought and a famine in Irian Jaya. Forest fires in Borneo and Sumatra blighted large areas of SE Asia with heavy smog, and caused catastrophic environmental damage.

1998: Following mass riots, Suharto stepped down as president. There was some withdrawal of troops from East Timor and partial autonomy was offered. The GDP contracted by 15%. Irian Jaya's status as a military occupation zone ended, following a ceasefire agreement with separatist rebels. Troops killed 16 student demonstrators in Jakarta. The repressive legislation of the Suharto era was repealed in a special legislature session and political parties were legalized.

1999: Ethnic violence continued in Borneo, with over 500 people killed in March and April. The government held a referendum on independence for East Timor in August, but after an overwhelming vote in favour, pro-Indonesian militias killed hundreds and displaced thousands of citizens. Intervention by Australian-led United Nations (UN) troops ended the violence. Abdurrahman Wahid became president in October 1999. He agreed to let East Timor become independent, but refused to rule out repression to solve the unrest in Aceh.

2000: A UN transitional government was established in East Timor. Following violence between Muslims and Christians in Maluku in 1999, Indonesian Muslims called for a holy war in Maluku against the Christians. Irian Jaya unilaterally declared independence, while violence continued in Aceh. Corruption charges against ex-president Suharto were dropped on grounds of ill-health, but the high court overruled this judgment and restarted the trial.

2001: Financial scandals involving President Wahid provoked riots. A temporary ceasefire was declared in Aceh, but collapsed when Wahid sent in troops.

2002: A massive car bomb exploded at a nightclub in the tourist centre of Kuta on the island of Bali, killing around 200 people and injuring some 300, mostly Australians. The Indonesian authorities blamed Islamic extremists. Christian and Muslim leaders from the eastern Molucca islands signed a peace accord to end three years of sectarian fighting which had claimed 5,000 lives since 1999 and created 750,000 refugees. The government and separatist rebels in Aceh province signed a peace deal aimed at ending three decades of fighting.

2003: Following the collapse of a ceasefire agreement with Aceh separatists, President Megawati declared martial law and launched a major military operation, involving up to 45,000 troops and paramilitary police, against the Free Aceh Movement.

2004: Almost a quarter of a million Indonesians were among those killed by a powerful tsunami that devastated coastal settlements throughout the region.

Indra Hindu god of the sky, shown as a four-armed man on a white elephant, carrying a thunderbolt. The intoxicating drink soma is associated with him.

inductance in physics, phenomenon in which a changing current in a circuit builds up a magnetic field which induces an *electromotive force either in the same circuit and opposing the current (self-inductance) or in another circuit (mutual inductance). The SI unit of inductance is the henry (symbol H).

induction in obstetrics, deliberate intervention to initiate labour before it starts naturally; then it usually proceeds normally. Induction involves rupture of the fetal membranes (amniotomy) and the use of the hormone oxytocin to stimulate contractions of the womb. In biology, induction is a term used for various processes, including the production of an *enzyme in response to a particular chemical in the cell, and the *differentiation of cells in an *embryo in response to the presence of neighbouring tissues.

indulgence in the Roman Catholic Church, the total or partial remission of temporal punishment for sins for which amendment needs to be made after penitence and confession have secured exemption from eternal punishment. The doctrine of indulgence began as the commutation of church penances in exchange for suitable works of charity or money gifts to the church, and became a great source of church revenue. This trade in indulgences roused Martin Luther to post his 'Ninety-five Theses' on the church door in Wittenberg, and so initiated the Reformation in 1517. The Council of Trent (1545–63) recommended moderate retention of indulgences, and they continue, notably in 'Holy Years'.

Indus river in Asia, rising in Tibet and flowing 3,180 km/1,975 mi to the Arabian Sea. In 1960 the use of its waters, including those of its five tributaries, was divided between India (rivers Ravi, Beas, Sutlej) and Pakistan (rivers Indus, Jhelum, Chenab). In the 3rd and 2nd millennia BC *Indus Valley civilization flourished at centres such as Harappa and Mojenjo Daro.

industrial design branch of artistic activity that came into being as a result of the need to design machine-made products, introduced by the Industrial Revolution in the 18th century. The purpose of industrial design is to ensure that goods satisfy the demands of fashion, style, function, materials, and cost.

industrialization process by which an increasing proportion of a country's economic activity is involved in industry. It is essential for economic development and largely responsible for the growth of cities (*urbanization).

industrial relations relationship between employers and employees, and their dealings with each other. In most industries, wages and conditions are determined by **free collective bargaining** between employers and *trade unions. Some European and American countries have **worker participation** through profit-sharing and industrial democracy. Another solution is **co-ownership**, in which a company is entirely owned by its employees. The aim of good industrial relations is to achieve a motivated, capable workforce that sees its work as creative and fulfilling. A breakdown in industrial relations can lead to an industrial dispute where one party takes industrial action.

Industrial Revolution acceleration of technical and economic development that took place in Britain in the second half of the 18th century. The traditional agricultural economy was replaced by one dominated by machinery and manufacturing, made possible through technical advances such as the steam engine. This transferred the balance of political power from the landowner to the industrial capitalist (for example, a factory owner) and created an urban working class. As the first country to have an industrial revolution, Britain for a while was the 'workshop of the world'. The Industrial Revolution, therefore, became the basis of 19th-century British world power and the British Empire. From 1830 to the early 20th century, the Industrial Revolution spread throughout Europe and the USA, and to Japan and the various colonial empires.

industrial sector any of the different groups into which industries may be divided: primary, secondary, tertiary, and quaternary. **Primary** industries extract or use raw materials; for example, mining and agriculture. **Secondary** industries are manufacturing industries, where raw materials are processed or components are assembled. **Tertiary** industries supply services such as retailing. The **quaternary** sector of industry is concerned with the professions and those services that require a high level of skill, expertise, and specialization. It includes education, research and development, administration, and financial services such as accountancy.

Indus Valley civilization one of the four earliest ancient civilizations of the Old World (the other three being the *Sumerian civilization of 3500 BC; Egypt 3000 BC; and China 2200 BC), developing in the northwest of the Indian subcontinent *c.* 2500 BC.

inert gas alternative name for *noble gas or rare gas.

inertia in physics, the tendency of an object to remain in a state of rest or uniform motion until an external force is applied, as described by Isaac Newton's first law of motion (see *Newton's laws of motion).

infante title given in Spain and Portugal to the sons (infante), other than the heir apparent, and daughters (infanta), respectively, of the sovereign. The heir apparent in Spain bears the title of prince of Asturias.

infant mortality rate measure of the number of infants dying under one year of age, usually expressed as the number of deaths per 1,000 live births. Improved sanitation, nutrition, and medical care have considerably lowered figures throughout much of the world; for example, in the 18th century in the USA and UK infant mortality was about 500/1,000 compared with under 10/1,000 in 1989. The lowest infant mortality rate is in Japan, at 4.5/1,000 live births. In much of the developing world, however, the infant mortality rate remains high.

infection invasion of the body by disease-causing organisms (pathogens, or germs) that become established, multiply, and produce symptoms. Bacteria and viruses cause most diseases, but diseases are also caused by other micro-organisms, protozoans, and other parasites.

inferiority complex in psychology, a *complex or cluster of repressed fears, described by Alfred *Adler, based on physical inferiority. The term is popularly used to describe general feelings of inferiority and the overcompensation that often ensues.

infertility in medicine, inability to reproduce. In women, this may be due to blockage in the Fallopian tubes, failure of ovulation, a deficiency in sex hormones, or general ill health. In men, impotence, an insufficient number of sperm or abnormal sperm may be the cause of infertility. Clinical investigation will reveal the cause of the infertility in about 75% of couples and assisted conception may then be appropriate.

infinity symbol ∞, mathematical quantity that is larger than any fixed assignable quantity. By convention, the result of dividing any number by zero is regarded as infinity.

inflation in economics, a rise in the general level of prices. The many causes include cost-push inflation, which results from rising production costs. Demand-pull inflation occurs when overall demand for goods exceeds the supply. Suppressed inflation occurs in controlled economies and is reflected in rationing, shortages, and black-market prices. Hyperinflation is inflation of more than 50% in one month. Deflation, a fall in the general level of prices, is the reverse of inflation.

influenza any of various viral infections primarily affecting the air passages, accompanied by *systemic effects such as fever, chills, headache, joint and muscle pains, and lassitude. Treatment is with bed rest and analgesic drugs such as aspirin or paracetamol.

information technology (IT) collective term for the various technologies involved in processing and transmitting information. They include computing, telecommunications, and microelectronics. The term became popular in the UK after the Government's 'Information Technology Year' in 1972.

infrared astronomy study of infrared radiation produced by relatively cool gas and dust in space, as in the areas around forming stars. In 1983 the US–Dutch–British Infrared Astronomy Satellite (IRAS) surveyed almost the entire sky at infrared wavelengths. It found five new comets, thousands of galaxies undergoing bursts of star formation, and the possibility of planetary systems forming around several dozen stars.

infrared radiation i.r., electromagnetic *radiation of wavelength between about 700 nanometres and 1 millimetre – that is, between the limit of the red end of the visible spectrum and the shortest microwaves. All bodies above the *absolute zero of temperature absorb and radiate infrared radiation. Infrared radiation is used in medical photography and treatment, and in industry, astronomy, and criminology.

infrastructure relatively permanent facilities that serve an industrial economy. Infrastructure usually includes roads, railways, other communication networks, energy and water supply, and education and training facilities. Some definitions also include sociocultural installations such as health-care and leisure facilities.

Ingres, Jean-Auguste-Dominique (1780–1867) French painter. A leading neoclassicist, he was a student of Jacques Louis *David. He studied and worked in Rome *c.* 1807–20, where he began the *Odalisque* series of sensuous female nudes, then went to Florence, and returned to France in 1824. His portraits painted in the 1840s–50s are meticulously detailed and highly polished.

Ingushetia *or* **Ingushetiya** autonomous republic of the Russian Federation, on the northern slopes of the Caucasus mountains; area 2,000 sq km/770 sq mi; population (1994 est) 250,000 (Ingush 85%). The capital is Nazran. The chief industries are farming and cattle-raising; there is also petroleum drilling. The predominant religion is Islam.

Inkatha Freedom Party (IFP) (from the grass coil worn by Zulu women for carrying head loads; its many strands give it strength) South African political party, representing the nationalist aspirations of the country's largest ethnic group, the *Zulus. It was founded as a paramilitary organization in 1975 by its present leader, Chief Gatsha *Buthelezi, with the avowed aim of creating a non-racial democratic political situation. The party entered South Africa's first multiracial elections in April 1994, after an initial violent boycott, and emerged with 10% of the popular vote.

INLA abbreviation for *Irish National Liberation Army.

Inner Hebrides group of islands that comprise that part of the *Hebrides closest to the west coast of mainland Scotland.

Innocent thirteen popes including:

Innocent III (c. 1161–1216) Pope from 1198. He asserted papal power over secular princes, in particular over the succession of Holy Roman emperors. He also made King *John of England his vassal, compelling him to accept Stephen Langton as archbishop of Canterbury. He promoted the fourth Crusade and crusades against the non-Christian Livonians and Letts, and the Albigensian heretics of southern France.

Inns of Court four private legal societies in London, England: Lincoln's Inn, Gray's Inn, Inner Temple, and Middle Temple. All barristers (advocates in the English legal system) must belong to one of the Inns of Court. The main function of each Inn is the education, government, and protection of its members. Each is under the administration of a body of Benchers (judges and senior barristers).

inoculation injection into the body of dead or weakened disease-carrying organisms or their toxins (*vaccine) to produce immunity by inducing a mild form of a disease.

inorganic chemistry branch of chemistry dealing with the chemical properties of the elements and their compounds, excluding the more complex covalent compounds of carbon, which are considered in *organic chemistry.

input device device for entering information into a computer. Input devices include keyboards, joysticks, mice, light pens, touch-sensitive screens, scanners, graphics tablets, speech-recognition devices, and vision systems. The input into an electronic system is usually through switches or *sensors. Compare with an *output device.

inquest inquiry held by a *coroner into an unexplained death. At an inquest, a coroner is assisted by a jury of between 7 and 11 people. Evidence is on oath, and medical and other witnesses may be summoned.

Inquisition tribunal of the Roman Catholic Church established in 1233 to suppress heresy, originally by excommunication. The Inquisition operated in France, Italy, Spain, and the Holy Roman Empire, and was especially active after the *Reformation; it was later extended to the Americas. Its trials were conducted in secret, under torture, and penalties ranged from fines, through flogging and imprisonment, to death.

insanity in medicine and law, any mental disorder in which the patient cannot be held responsible for their actions. The term is no longer used to refer to psychosis.

insect any of a vast group of small invertebrate animals with hard, segmented bodies, three pairs of jointed legs, and, usually, two pairs of wings; they belong among the *arthropods and are distributed throughout the world. An insect's body is divided into three segments: head, thorax, and abdomen. On the head is a pair of feelers, or antennae. The legs and wings are attached to the thorax, or middle segment of the body. The abdomen,

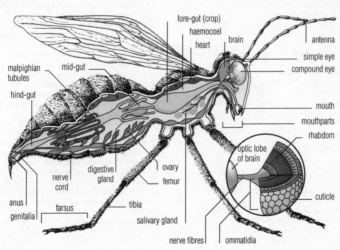

insect Body plan of an insect. The general features of the insect body include a segmented body divided into head, thorax, and abdomen, jointed legs, feelers or antennae, and usually two pairs of wings. Insects often have compound eyes with a large field of vision.

or end segment of the body, is where food is digested and excreted and where the reproductive organs are located. (Class Insecta.) Insects vary in size from 0.02 cm/0.007 in to 35 cm/13.5 in in length. The world's smallest insect is believed to be a 'fairy fly' wasp in the family Mymaridae, with a wingspan of 0.2 mm/0.008 in.

insecticide any chemical pesticide used to kill insects. Among the most effective insecticides are synthetic organic chemicals such as *DDT and dieldrin, which are chlorinated hydrocarbons. These chemicals, however, have proved persistent in the environment and are also poisonous to all animal life, including humans, and are consequently banned in many countries. Other synthetic insecticides include organic phosphorus compounds such as malathion. Insecticides prepared from plants, such as derris and pyrethrum, are safer to use but need to be applied frequently and carefully.

insectivore any animal whose diet is made up largely or exclusively of *insects. In particular, the name is applied to mammals of the order Insectivora, which includes shrews, hedgehogs, moles, and tenrecs.

insectivorous plant plant that can capture and digest live prey (normally insects), to obtain nitrogen compounds that are lacking in its usual marshy habitat. Some are passive traps, for example, the pitcher plants *Nepenthes* and *Sarracenia*. One pitcher-plant species has container-traps holding 1.6 l/3.5 pt of the liquid that 'digests' its food, mostly insects but occasionally even rodents. Others, for example, sundews *Drosera*, butterworts *Pinguicula*, and Venus flytraps *Dionaea muscipula*, have an active trapping mechanism. Insectivorous plants have adapted to grow in poor soil conditions where the number of micro-organisms recycling nitrogen compounds is very much reduced. In these circumstances other plants cannot gain enough nitrates to grow. See also *leaf.

inselberg *or* **kopje** (German 'island mountain') prominent steep-sided hill of resistant solid rock, such as granite, rising out of a plain, usually in a tropical area. Its rounded appearance is caused by so-called onion-skin *weathering (exfoliation), in which the surface is eroded in successive layers.

insemination, artificial see *artificial insemination.

insider trading *or* **insider dealing** illegal use of privileged information in dealing on a stock exchange, for example, when a company takeover bid is imminent. Insider trading is in theory detected by the Securities and Exchange Commission (SEC) in the USA, and by the Securities and Investment Board (SIB) in the UK. Neither agency, however, has any legal powers other than public disclosure and they do not bring prosecutions themselves.

instinct in *ethology, behaviour found in all equivalent members of a given species (for example, all the males, or all the females with young) that is presumed to be genetically determined.

insulator any poor *conductor of heat, sound, or electricity. Most substances lacking free (mobile) *electrons, such as non-metals, are electrical or thermal insulators that resist the flow of electricity or heat through them. Plastics and rubber are good insulators. Usually, devices of glass or porcelain, called insulators, are used for insulating and supporting overhead wires.

insulin protein *hormone, produced by specialized cells in the islets of Langerhans in the pancreas, which regulates the metabolism (rate of activity) of glucose, fats, and proteins. In this way it helps to regulate the concentration of *glucose in the *blood of mammals. If the blood glucose concentration is too high, the pancreas releases insulin into the blood. This causes blood glucose levels to fall. This is partly due to increased uptake of glucose into most body cells (except liver and brain) but also because the liver converts glucose into insoluble glycogen and stores it instead of making glucose. In *diabetes a person's blood glucose may rise to such a high concentration that it can kill. This may be because the pancreas does not make enough insulin, or because the body cells respond less to the insulin.

insurance contract guaranteeing compensation to the payer of a premium against loss by fire, death, accident, and so on, which is known as assurance in the case of a fixed sum and insurance where the payment is proportionate to the loss. Insurance contracts are governed not by the doctrine of *caveat emptor* ('buyer beware') but by the doctrine of *uberrima fides* ('utmost good faith'). This means that all parties to the insurance contract must deal in good faith, making a full declaration of all material facts in the insurance proposal.

intaglio design cut into the surface of gems or seals by etching or engraving; an *engraving technique.

integer any whole number. Integers may be positive or negative; 0 is an integer, and is often considered positive. Formally, integers are members of the set

$$Z = \{\dots -3, -2, -1, 0, 1, 2, 3, \dots \}.$$

This is the integer set of the number line.

integral calculus branch of mathematics using the process of *integration. It is concerned with finding volumes and areas and summing infinitesimally small quantities.

integrated circuit IC *or* **silicon chip** miniaturized electronic circuit produced on a single crystal, or chip, of a semiconducting material – usually silicon. It may contain many millions of components and yet measure only 5 mm/0.2 in square and 1 mm/0.04 in thick. The IC is encapsulated within a plastic or ceramic case, and linked via gold wires to metal pins with which it is connected to a *printed circuit board and the other components that make up such electronic devices as computers and calculators.

Integrated Services Digital Network (ISDN) internationally developed telecommunications network for sending signals in *digital format that offers faster data transfer rates than traditional analogue telephone circuits. It involves converting the 'local loop' – the link between the user's telephone (or private automatic branch exchange) and the digital telephone exchange – from an *analogue system into a digital system, thereby greatly increasing the amount of information that can be carried. The words 'integrated services' refer to the capacity for ISDN to make two connections simultaneously, in any combination of data (voice, video, and fax), over a single line. The data is sent and received in 'digital' format and ISDN is described as a 'network' because it extends from the local telephone exchange to the remote user. The first large-scale use of ISDN began in Japan in 1988.

integration in mathematics, a method in *calculus of determining the solutions of definite or indefinite integrals. An example of a definite integral can be thought of as finding the area under a curve (as represented by an algebraic expression or function) between particular values of the function's variable. In practice, integral calculus provides scientists with a powerful tool for doing calculations that involve a continually varying quantity (such as determining the position at any given instant of a space rocket that is accelerating away from Earth). Its basic principles were discovered in the late 1660s independently by the German philosopher *Leibniz and the British scientist *Newton.

intelligence in military and political affairs, information, often secretly or illegally obtained, about other countries. **Counter-intelligence** is information on the activities of hostile agents. Much intelligence is gained by technical means, such as satellites and the electronic interception of data.

Inter-American Development Bank (IADB) bank founded in 1959, at the instigation of the Organization of American States (OAS), to finance economic and social development, particularly in the less wealthy regions of the Americas. Its membership includes the states of Central and Southern America, the Caribbean, and the USA, as well as Austria, Belgium, Canada, Denmark, Finland, France, Germany, Israel, Italy, Japan, the Netherlands, Norway, Portugal, Spain, Sweden, Switzerland, and the UK. Its headquarters are in Washington DC.

interdict in the Christian church, a punishment that excludes an individual, community, or realm from participation in spiritual activities except for communion. It was usually employed against heretics or realms whose ruler was an excommunicant.

interest in finance, a sum of money paid by a borrower to a lender in return for the loan, usually expressed as a percentage per annum. **Simple interest** is interest calculated as a straight percentage of the amount loaned or invested. In **compound interest**, the interest earned over a period of time (for example, per annum) is added to the investment, so that at the end of the next period interest is paid on that total.

interference in physics, the phenomenon of two or more wave motions interacting and combining to produce a resultant wave of larger or smaller amplitude (depending on whether the combining waves are in or out of *phase with each other).

interferon or **IFN** naturally occurring cellular protein that makes up part of mammalian defences against viral disease. Three types (alpha, beta, and gamma) are produced by infected cells and enter the bloodstream and uninfected cells, making them immune to virus attack.

Intermediate Nuclear Forces Treaty agreement signed 8 December 1987 between the USA and the USSR to eliminate all ground-based nuclear missiles in Europe that were capable of hitting only European targets (including European Russia). It reduced the countries' nuclear arsenals by some 2,000 (4% of the total). The treaty included provisions for each country to inspect the other's bases.

intermediate technology application of machines and other technologies, based on inventions and designs developed in the developed world, but utilizing materials, assembly, and maintenance methods found in less developed regions.

intermediate vector boson member of a group of elementary particles, W^+, W^-, and Z, which mediate the *weak nuclear force. This force is responsible for, among other things, beta decay.

intermezzo in music, initially a one-act comic opera, such as Giovanni Pergolesi's *La serva padrona/The Maid as Mistress* (1732); also a short orchestral interlude played between the acts of an opera to denote the passage of time. By extension, an intermezzo has come to mean a short piece to be played between other more substantial works, such as Brahms's *Three Intermezzos for Piano* (1892).

internal-combustion engine heat engine in which fuel is burned inside the engine, contrasting with an external-combustion engine (such as the steam engine) in which fuel is burned in a separate unit. The *diesel engine and *petrol engine are both internal-combustion engines. Gas *turbines and *jet and *rocket engines are also considered to be internal-combustion engines because they burn their fuel inside their combustion chambers.

International, the coordinating body established by labour and socialist organizations, including: First International or International Working Men's Association (1864–72), formed in London under Karl *Marx; Second International (1889–1940), founded in Paris; Third (Socialist) International or Comintern (1919–43), formed in Moscow by the Soviet leader Lenin, advocating from 1933 a popular front (communist, socialist, liberal) against the German dictator Hitler; Fourth International or Trotskyist International (1938), somewhat indeterminate, anti-Stalinist; Revived Socialist International (1951), formed in Frankfurt, Germany, a largely anticommunist association of social democrats.

International Bank for Reconstruction and Development specialized agency of the United Nations. Its popular name is the *World Bank.

International Court of Justice main judicial organ of the *United Nations, in The Hague, the Netherlands. It hears international law disputes as well as playing an advisory role to UN organs. It was set up by the UN charter in 1945 and superseded the World Court. There are 15 judges, each from a different member state.

International Date Line (IDL) imaginary line that approximately follows the 180° line of longitude. The date is put forward a day when crossing the line going west, and back a day when going east. The IDL was chosen at the International Meridian Conference in 1884.

International Gothic late Gothic style of painting and sculpture flourishing in Europe in the late 14th and 15th centuries. It is characterized by bright colours, a courtly elegance, and a naturalistic rendering of detail. Originally evolving in the court art of France and Burgundy, it spread to many parts of Europe, its leading exponents including the Italian Simone Martini and the Franco-Flemish Limbourg brothers.

International Labour Organization (ILO) specialized agency of the United Nations, originally established in 1919, which formulates standards for labour and social conditions. Its headquarters are in Geneva, Switzerland. It was awarded the Nobel Peace

Prize in 1969. By 1997, the agency was responsible for over 70 international labour conventions.

international law body of rules generally accepted as governing the relations between countries, pioneered by Hugo *Grotius, especially in matters of human rights, territory, and war.

International Monetary Fund (IMF) specialized agency of the United Nations, headquarters Washington, DC, established under the 1944 *Bretton Woods agreement and operational since 1947. It seeks to promote international monetary cooperation and the growth of world trade, and to smooth payment arrangements among member states. IMF standby loans are available to members in balance-of-payments difficulties (the amount being governed by the member's quota), usually on the basis that the country must agree to take certain corrective measures.

International Society for Krishna Consciousness ISKCON *or* **Gaudiya Vaisnavism** Hindu sect based on the demonstration of intense love for Krishna (an incarnation of the god Vishnu), especially by chanting the mantra 'Hare Krishna'. Members wear distinctive yellow robes, and men often have their heads partly shaven. Their holy books are the Hindu scriptures and particularly the *Bhagavad-Gita*, which they study daily.

international style *or* **International Modern** architectural style, an early and influential phase of the *Modern Movement, originating in Western Europe in the 1920s but finding its fullest expression in the 1930s, notably in the USA. It is characterized by a dominance of geometric, especially rectilinear, forms; emphasis on asymmetrical composition; large expanses of glazing; and white rendered walls. Examples are Walter *Gropius's Bauhaus building, Dessau, Germany, (1925–26); *Le Corbusier's Villa Savoye, Poissy, France, (1927–31); Alvar *Aalto's Viipuri Library, Finland (now in Russia), (1927–35); and *Mies van der Rohe's Barcelona Pavilion (1929).

Internet global public computer network that provides the communication infrastructure for applications such as *e-mail, the World Wide Web, and FTP. The Internet is not one individual network, but an interconnected system of smaller networks using common protocols to pass packets of information from one computer to another.

internment detention of suspected criminals without trial. Foreign citizens are often interned during times of war or civil unrest.

Interpol acronym for INTERnational Criminal POLice Organization, agency founded following the Second International Judicial Police Conference (1923) with its headquarters in Vienna, and reconstituted after World War II with its headquarters in Paris. It has an international criminal register, fingerprint file, and methods index.

interval in music, the distance or difference in pitch between two notes. It is written in terms of the major or minor scale. To work out the number of the interval, the letter name of both notes is included. For example, C to D is a second, C to E is a third, C to F is a fourth, and so on. A complete description of an interval includes not only its number, but also its 'quality'. There are five descriptions used: perfect, major, minor, augmented, and diminished; for example, perfect fifth and major second. When the two notes are played

together they form a **harmonic interval**; when one note follows the other, it is a **melodic interval**.

intestine in vertebrates, the digestive tract from the stomach outlet to the anus. The human **small intestine** is 6 m/20 ft long, 4 cm/1.5 in diameter, and consists of the duodenum, jejunum, and ileum; the **large intestine** is 1.5 m/5 ft long, 6 cm/2.5 in diameter, and includes the caecum, colon, and rectum. The contents of the intestine are passed along slowly by *peristalsis (waves of involuntary muscular action). The term intestine is also applied to the lower digestive tract of invertebrates.

Intifada (Arabic 'resurgence' or 'throwing off') Palestinian uprising, specifically between December 1987 and September 1993, during which time a loosely organized group of Palestinians (the **Liberation Army of Palestine**, also called Intifada) rebelled against armed Israeli troops in the occupied territories of the Gaza Strip and the West Bank. Their campaign for self-determination included strikes, demonstrations, stone-throwing, and petrol bombing. It was organized at grass-roots level by the Unified National Command, dominated by the *al-Fatah faction of the *Palestine Liberation Organization (PLO), but the Islamic fundamentalist group Hamas also played a key role, particularly in the Gaza Strip. The September 1993 peace accord between Israel and the PLO provided limited autonomy for Gaza and the town of Jericho and initiated the Israel–Palestine peace process. However, extremist groups that had participated in the Intifada, notably the militant wing of Hamas, opposed the accord and continued a campaign of violence within Israel. A second Intifada began in September 2000, after a visit by right-wing Israeli politician Ariel *Sharon to the holy site of Haram al-Sharif (Temple Mount) in Jerusalem. This Intifada continues, with Hamas again playing a key role and Palestinian public opinion being hardened by Israel's stern counter-measures. In 2003 the USA tried to initiate new moves towards peace.

intrauterine device IUD *or* **coil** a contraceptive device that is inserted into the womb (uterus). It is a tiny plastic object, sometimes containing copper. By causing a mild inflammation of the lining of the uterus it prevents fertilized eggs from becoming implanted.

introversion in psychology, preoccupation with the self, generally coupled with a lack of sociability. The opposite of introversion is *extroversion.

intrusion mass of *igneous rock that has formed by 'injection' of molten rock, or magma, into existing cracks beneath the surface of the Earth, as distinct from a volcanic rock mass which has erupted from the surface. Intrusion features include vertical cylindrical structures such as stocks, pipes, and necks; sheet structures such as dykes that cut across the strata and sills that push between them; laccoliths, which are blisters that push up the overlying rock; and batholiths, which represent chambers of solidified magma and contain vast volumes of rock.

intrusive rock *or* **plutonic rock** *igneous rock formed beneath the Earth's surface. Magma, or molten rock, cools slowly at these depths to form coarse-grained rocks, such as granite, with large crystals. (*Extrusive rocks, which are formed on the surface, are generally fine-grained.) A mass of intrusive rock is called an intrusion.

intuition rapid, unconscious thought process. In philosophy, intuition is that knowledge of a concept which does not derive directly from the senses. Thus, we may be said to have an intuitive idea of God, beauty, or justice. The concept of intuition is similar to Bertrand *Russell's theory of knowledge by acquaintance. In both cases, it is contrasted with empirical knowledge.

Inuit (*inuk* 'a man') member of am *American Indian people inhabiting the Arctic coasts of Alaska, the eastern islands of the Canadian Arctic, Labrador, and the ice-free coasts of Greenland. Originating from Siberia from around 2000 BC, they had populated the region by AD 1000. The Inuit language Inupiaq is spoken in mutually comprehensible dialects from Point Barrow in Alaska to Greenland. Traditionally the Inuit relied on fish, sea mammals, and land animals for food, heat, light, clothing, tools, and shelter. Formerly a nomadic people, most now live in permanent settlements. In 1999 the semi-autonomous Inuit homeland of Nunavut was established as a territory of Canada.

The total number of Inuit (1993 est) is 125,000.

Inverclyde unitary authority in western Scotland, created in 1996 from Inverclyde district in Strathclyde region. **area:** 161 sq km/62 sq mi **towns:** Greenock (administrative headquarters), Port Glasgow, Gourock **physical:** coastal lowland on the Firth of Clyde estuary, rising sharply to an inland plateau of 305 m/1,000 ft **features:** Inverkip Marina **population:** (2000 est) 84,600 **history:** key part in the industrial history of Scotland as a port and a heavy engineering centre.

Invergordon Mutiny incident in the British Atlantic Fleet, Cromarty Firth, Scotland, on 15 September 1931. Ratings refused to prepare the ships for sea following the government's cuts in their pay; the cuts were consequently modified.

invertebrate animal without a backbone. The invertebrates form all of the major divisions of the animal kingdom called phyla, with the exception of vertebrates. Invertebrates include the sponges, coelenterates, flatworms, nematodes, annelids, arthropods, molluscs, and echinoderms.

investment in economics, the purchase of any asset with the potential to yield future financial benefit to the purchaser (such as a house, a work of art, stocks and shares, or even a private education).

in vitro fertilization (IVF) ('fertilization in glass') allowing eggs and sperm to unite in a laboratory to form embryos. The embryos (properly called pre-embryos in their two- to eight-celled state) are stored by cooling to the temperature of liquid air (cryopreservation) until they are implanted into the womb of the otherwise infertile mother (an extension of *artificial insemination). The first baby to be produced by this method was Louise Joy Brown, born in 1978 at Oldham General Hospital, Lancashire, UK. In cases where the Fallopian tubes are blocked, fertilization may be carried out by **intra-vaginal culture**, in which egg and sperm are incubated (in a plastic tube) in the mother's vagina, then transferred surgically into the uterus.

Io in astronomy, third-largest moon of the planet Jupiter, 3,630 km/2,260 mi in diameter, orbiting in 1.77 days at a distance of 422,000 km/262,000 mi. It is the most volcanically active body in the Solar System,

covered by hundreds of vents that erupt sulphur (rather than lava), giving Io an orange-coloured surface. Io and Earth are the only two planetary bodies that are undergoing known high-temperature volcanism.

iodide compound formed between iodine and another element in which the iodine is the more electronegative element (see *halide).

iodine chemical symbol I, (Greek *iodes* 'violet') greyish-black non-metallic element, atomic number 53, relative atomic mass 126.9044. It is a member of the *halogen group (Group 7 of the *periodic table). Its crystals sublime, giving off, when heated, a violet vapour with an irritating odour resembling that of chlorine. It occurs only in combination with other elements. Its salts are known as **iodides** and are found in sea water. As a mineral nutrient it is vital to the proper functioning of the thyroid gland, where it occurs in trace amounts as part of the hormone thyroxine. Absence of iodine from the diet leads to *goitre. Iodine is used in photography, in medicine as an antiseptic, and in making dyes.

ion atom, or group of atoms, that is either positively charged (*cation) or negatively charged (*anion), as a result of the loss or gain of electrons during chemical reactions or exposure to certain forms of radiation. In solution or in the molten state, ionic compounds such as salts, acids, alkalis, and metal oxides conduct electricity. These compounds are known as *electrolytes.

Iona island in the Inner Hebrides; area 850 hectares/2,100 acres. A centre of early Christianity, it is the site of a monastery founded in 563 by St *Columba. It later became a burial ground for Irish, Scottish, and Norwegian kings. It has a 13th-century abbey.

Ionesco, Eugène (1912–1994) Romanian-born French dramatist. He was a leading exponent of the Theatre of the *Absurd. Most of his plays are in one act and concern the futility of language as a means of communication. These include *La Cantatrice chauve/ The Bald Prima Donna* (1950) and *La Leçon/The Lesson* (1951). Later full-length plays include *Le Rhinocéros* (1958) and *Le Roi se meurt/Exit the King* (1961).

Ionia in classical times the east coast of the Aegean Sea and the offshore islands, settled about 1000 BC by the Ionians; it included the cities of Ephesus, Miletus, and later Smyrna, and the islands of Chios and Samos.

Ionian member of a Hellenic people from beyond the Black Sea who crossed the Balkans *c.* 1980 BC and invaded Asia Minor. Driven back by the *Hittites, they settled all over mainland Greece, later being supplanted by the Achaeans.

Ionian Islands Greek **Ionioi Nisoi**, island group off the west coast of Greece; area 860 sq km/332 sq mi; population (1991) 191,000. A British protectorate from 1815 until their cession to Greece in 1864, they include Cephalonia (Greek *Kefallonia*); Corfu (*Kérkyra*), a Venetian possession (1386–1797); Cythera (*Kithira*); Ithaca (*Ithaki*), the traditional home of *Odysseus; Lefkada; Paxos (*Paxoi*); and Zanté (*Zakynthos*).

Ionian Sea part of the Mediterranean Sea that lies between Italy and Greece, to the south of the Adriatic Sea, and containing the Ionian Islands.

ionic bond *or* **electrovalent bond** bond produced when atoms of one element donate electrons to atoms

electronic
arrangement,
2.8.1 of a
sodium atom

electronic
arrangement,
2.8.7 of a
chlorine atom

becomes a
sodium ion, Na⁺,
with an electron
arrangement 2.8

becomes a
chloride ion, Cl⁻,
with an electron
arrangement 2.8.8

ionic bond The formation of an ionic bond between a sodium atom and a chlorine atom to form a molecule of sodium chloride. The sodium atom transfers an electron from its outer electron shell (becoming the positive ion Na⁺) to the chlorine atom (which becomes the negative chloride ion Cl⁻). The opposite charges mean that the ions are strongly attracted to each other. The formation of the bond means that each atom becomes more stable, having a full quota of electrons in its outer shell.

of another element, forming positively and negatively charged *ions respectively. The attraction between the oppositely charged ions constitutes the bond. Sodium chloride (Na⁺Cl⁻) is a typical ionic compound.

ionic compound substance composed of oppositely charged ions. All salts, most bases, and some acids are examples of ionic compounds. They possess the following general properties: they are crystalline solids with a high melting point; are soluble in water and insoluble in organic solvents; and always conduct electricity when molten or in aqueous solution. A typical ionic compound is sodium chloride (Na⁺Cl⁻).

ionizing radiation radiation that removes electrons from atoms during its passage, thereby leaving ions in its path. Alpha and beta particles are far more ionizing in their effect than are neutrons or gamma radiation.

ionosphere ionized layer of Earth's outer *atmosphere (60–1,000 km/38–620 mi) that contains sufficient free electrons to modify the way in which radio waves are propagated, for instance by reflecting them back to Earth. The ionosphere is thought to be produced by absorption of the Sun's ultraviolet radiation. The British Antarctic Survey estimates that the ionosphere is decreasing at a rate of 1 km/0.6 mi every five years, based on an analysis of data from 1960 to 1998. Global warming is the probable cause.

Iowa called the **Corn State** or **Hawkeye State**, state of Midwestern USA, bordered to the south by *Missouri, to the west by *Nebraska and *South Dakota, to the north by *Minnesota, and to the east by *Wisconsin and *Illinois, with the *Mississippi River forming the state boundary; area 144,700 sq km/55,869 sq mi; population (2000) 2,926,300; capital Des Moines. It is nicknamed the Corn State owing to its prodigious yields of the crop, and the Hawkeye State probably in honour of Black Hawk, an American Indian chief. Iowa lies in the Central Lowlands and has large, fertile prairies intersected by tributaries of the Mississippi and *Missouri rivers. There are glaciated plains in the south, and high, rocky lands in the northeast. There are many lakes in the northwest. Iowa is a leading agricultural state in the USA, contributing approximately 7% of the nation's overall food supply. Iowa is a major part of the Corn Belt, and other produce includes soybeans, apples, and livestock, especially hogs. Food processing and service industries, such as finance and healthcare, are also economically significant. Major cities include Cedar Rapids, Davenport, Sioux City, Waterloo, and Iowa City. The *temperance movement was particularly influential in the state, its effects lasting from the 1830s to the 1960s. Iowa was admitted to the Union in 1846 as the 29th US state.

ipecacuanha or **ipecac** South American plant belonging to the madder family, the dried roots of which are used in medicine as an emetic (to cause vomiting) and to treat amoebic dysentery (infection of the intestine with amoebae). (*Psychotria ipecacuanha*, family Rubiaceae.)

IQ abbreviation for intelligence quotient, the ratio between a subject's 'mental' and chronological ages, multiplied by 100. A score of 100 ± 10 in an intelligence test is considered average.

IRA abbreviation for *Irish Republican Army.

Iran
formerly **Persia** (until 1935)
National name: *Jomhúri-ye Eslâmi-ye Írân/ Islamic Republic of Iran*

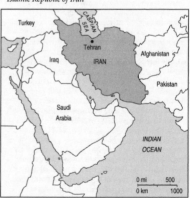

Area: 1,648,000 sq km/636,292 sq mi
Capital: Tehran
Major towns/cities: Esfahan, Mashhad, Tabriz, Shiraz, Ahvaz, Kermanshah, Qom, Karaj

Major ports: Abadan
Physical features: plateau surrounded by mountains, including Elburz and Zagros; Lake Rezayeh; Dasht-e-Kavir desert; occupies islands of Abu Musa, Greater Tunb and Lesser Tunb in the Gulf
Head of state and government: Mohammad Khatami from 1997
Leader of the Islamic Revolution Seyed Ali Khamenei from 1989
Political system: Islamic nationalist
Political executive: unlimited presidency
Political parties: since President Khatami's election (1997), several political parties have been licensed including Executives of Construction, Islamic Iran Solidarity Party, and Islamic Partnership Front
Currency: rial
GNI per capita (PPP): (US$) 6,340 (2002 est)
Exports: crude petroleum and petroleum products, gas, agricultural goods, carpets, metal ores.
Principal market: Japan 19.2% (2001)
Population: 68,920,000 (2003 est)
Language: Farsi (official), Kurdish, Turkish, Arabic, English, French
Religion: Shiite Muslim (official) 91%, Sunni Muslim 8%; Zoroastrian, Christian, Jewish, and Baha'i comprise about 1%
Life expectancy: 69 (men); 72 (women) (2000–05)
Chronology
c. 2000 BC: Migration from southern Russia of Aryans, from whom Persians claim descent.
612 BC: The Medes, from northwest Iran, destroyed Iraq-based Assyrian Empire to the west and established their own empire which extended into central Anatolia (Turkey-in-Asia).
550 BC: Cyrus the Great overthrew Medes' empire and founded the First Persian Empire, the Achaemenid, conquering much of Asia Minor, including Babylonia (Palestine and Syria) in 539 BC. Expansion continued into Afghanistan under Darius I, who ruled 521–486 BC.
499–449 BC: The Persian Wars with Greece ended Persian domination of the ancient world.
330 BC: Collapse of Achaemenid Empire following defeat by Alexander the Great.
AD 224: Sassanian Persian Empire founded by Ardashir, with its capital at Ctesiphon, in the northeast.
637: Sassanian Empire destroyed by Muslim Arabs at battle of Qadisiya; Islam replaced Zoroastrianism.
750–1258: Dominated by the Persianized Abbasid dynasty, who reigned as caliphs (Islamic civil and religious leaders), with a capital in Baghdad (Iraq).
1380s: Conquered by the Mongol leader, Tamerlane.
1501: Emergence of Safavids; the arts and architecture flourished, particularly under Abbas I, 'the Great', who ruled 1588–1629.
1736: The Safavids were deposed by the warrior Nadir Shah Afshar, who ruled until 1747.
1790: Rise of the Qajars, who transferred the capital from Esfahan in central Iran to Tehran, further north.
19th century: Increasing influence in the north of tsarist Russia, which took Georgia and much of Armenia 1801–28. Britain exercised influence in the south and east, and fought Iran 1856–57 over claims to Herat (western Afghanistan).
1906: Parliamentary constitution adopted after a brief revolution.

1925: Qajar dynasty overthrown, with some British official help, in a coup by Col Reza Khan, a nationalist Iranian Cossack military officer, who was crowned shah ('king of kings'), with the title Reza Shah Pahlavi.
1920s onwards: Economic modernization, Westernization, and secularization programme launched, which proved unpopular with traditionalists.
1935: Name changed from Persia to Iran.
1941: Pahlavi Shah was forced to abdicate during World War II by Allied occupation forces and was succeeded by his son Muhammad Reza Pahlavi, who continued the modernization programme.
1946: British, US, and Soviet occupation forces left Iran.
1951: Oilfields nationalized by radical prime minister Muhammad Mossadeq as anti-British and US sentiment increased.
1953: Mossadeq deposed, the nationalization plan changed, and the US-backed shah, Muhammad Reza Shah Pahlavi, took full control of the government.
1963: Hundreds of protesters, who demanded the release of the arrested fundamentalist Shiite Muslim leader Ayatollah Ruhollah Khomeini, were killed by troops.
1970s: Spiralling world oil prices brought rapid economic expansion.
1975: The shah introduced a single-party system.
1977: The mysterious death in An Najaf of Mustafa, eldest son of the exiled Ayatollah Ruhollah Khomeini, sparked demonstrations by students, which were suppressed with the loss of six lives.
1978: Opposition to the shah was organized from France by Ayatollah Ruhollah Khomeini, who demanded a return to the principles of Islam. Hundreds of demonstrators were killed by troops in Jaleh Square, Tehran.
1979: Amid mounting demonstrations by students and clerics, the shah left the country; Khomeini returned to create a nonparty theocratic Islamic state. Revolutionaries seized 66 US hostages at the embassy in Tehran; US economic boycott.
1980: Iraq invaded Iran, provoking a bitter war. The exiled shah died.
1981: US hostages were released.
1985–87: Fighting intensified in the Iran–Iraq War, with heavy loss of life.
1989: Khomeini issued a fatwa (public order) for the death of British writer Salman Rushdie for blasphemy against Islam.
1990: Generous peace terms with Iraq were accepted to close the Iran–Iraq war.
1991: Nearly 1 million Kurds arrived from northwest Iraq, fleeing persecution by Saddam Hussein after the Gulf War between Iraq and UN forces.
1993: Free-market economic reforms were introduced.
1997: Reformist politician Seyyed Muhammad Khatami was elected president.
1998: There were signs of rapprochement with the West. There was increased tension with Afghanistan, after the murder of Iranian civilians by the Taliban.
1999: Diplomatic relations with the UK were to be restored.
2000: Ali Akbar Mohtashami, a former radical, was elected to lead the reforming majority in Iran's parliament. The conservative judiciary closed 15 pro-democracy newspapers, and the minister for culture resigned in the face of strong opposition to his policies.

2001: Eight of Khatami's prominent supporters were convicted of crimes relating to expression and thought.
2002: The government passed the first foreign investment law since the 1950s as part of reforms to open the economy and lessen dependence on oil revenues.
2003: Pressure on the government from the UN International Atomic Energy Agency to address Western concerns over suspected nuclear weapon ambitions ended in an agreement to suspend uranium enrichment, allow spot checks of nuclear installations, and submit a list of present and past nuclear activities. An earthquake measuring 6.7 on the Richter scale devastated the southeastern town of Bam, with a death toll of around 41,000.
2005: Iran was accused by the United States of continuing to carry out uranium enrichment.

Irangate US political scandal in 1987 involving senior members of the Reagan administration (the name echoes the Nixon administration's *Watergate). Congressional hearings 1986–87 revealed that the US government had secretly sold weapons to Iran in 1985 and traded them for hostages held in Lebanon by pro-Iranian militias, and used the profits to supply right-wing Contra guerrillas in Nicaragua with arms. The attempt to get around the law (Boland amendment) specifically prohibiting military assistance to the Contras also broke other laws in the process.

Iranian language the main language of Iran, more commonly known as Persian or *Farsi.

Iran–Iraq War war between Iran and Iraq (1980–88), claimed by the former to have begun with the Iraqi offensive on 21 September 1980, and by the latter with the Iranian shelling of border posts on 4 September 1980. Occasioned by a boundary dispute over the *Shatt-al-Arab waterway, it fundamentally arose because of Saddam Hussein's fear of a weakening of his absolute power base in Iraq by Iran's encouragement of the Shiite majority in Iraq to rise against the Sunni government. An estimated 1 million people died in the war.

Iraq
National name: *al-Jumhuriyya al'Iraqiyya/Republic of Iraq*

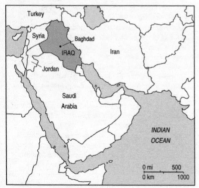

Area: 434,924 sq km/167,924 sq mi
Capital: Baghdad
Major towns/cities: Mosul, Basra, Kirkuk, Hillah, An Najaf, An Nasiriya, As Sulamaniya, Irbil

Major ports: Basra
Physical features: mountains in north, desert in west; wide valley of rivers Tigris and Euphrates running northwest–southeast; canal linking Baghdad and the Gulf opened in 1992
Head of state: Jalal Talabani from 2005
Head of government: Ibrahim Jaafari from 2005
Political system: pending
Political executive: pending
Political party pending
Currency: Iraqi dinar
GNI per capita (PPP): (US$) 1,250 (2002 est)
Exports: crude petroleum (accounting for more than 95% of total foreign-currency earnings in 2000), dates and other dried fruits. Principal market: USA 61.1% (2001)
Population: 25,175,000 (2003 est)
Language: Arabic (80%) (official), Kurdish (15%), Assyrian, Armenian
Religion: Shiite Muslim 60%, Sunni Muslim 37%, Christian 3%
Life expectancy: 60 (men); 62 (women) (2000–05)
Chronology
c. 3400 BC: The world's oldest civilization, the Sumerian, arose in the land between the rivers Euphrates and Tigris, known as lower Mesopotamia, which lies in the heart of modern Iraq. Its cities included Lagash, Eridu, Uruk, Kish, and Ur.
c. 2350 BC: The confederation of Sumerian city-states was forged into an empire by the Akkadian leader Sargon.
7th century BC: In northern Mesopotamia, the Assyrian Empire, based around the River Tigris and formerly dominated by Sumeria and Euphrates-centred Babylonia, created a vast empire covering much of the Middle East.
612 BC: The Assyrian capital of Nineveh was destroyed by Babylon and Mede (in northwest Iran).
c. 550 BC: Mesopotamia came under Persian control.
AD 114: Conquered by the Romans.
266: Came under the rule of the Persian-based Sassanians.
637: Sassanian Empire destroyed by Muslim Arabs at battle of Qadisiya, in southern Iraq; Islam spread.
750–1258: Dominated by Abbasid dynasty, who reigned as caliphs (Islamic civil and religious leaders) in Baghdad.
1258: Baghdad invaded and burned by Tatars.
1401: Baghdad destroyed by Mongol ruler Tamerlane.
1533: Annexed by Suleiman the Magnificent, becoming part of the Ottoman Empire until the 20th century, despite recurrent anti-Ottoman insurrections.
1916: Occupied by Britain during World War I.
1920: Iraq became a British League of Nations protectorate.
1921: Hashemite dynasty established, with Faisal I installed by Britain as king.
1932: Independence achieved from British protectorate status, with Gen Nuri-el Said as prime minister.
1941–45: Occupied by Britain during World War II.
1955: Signed the Baghdad Pact collective security treaty with the UK, Iran, Pakistan, and Turkey.
1958: Monarchy overthrown in military-led revolution, in which King Faisal was assassinated; Iraq became a republic; joined Jordan in an Arab Federation;

withdrew from Baghdad Pact as left-wing military regime assumed power.

1963: Joint socialist-nationalist Ba'athist-military coup headed by Col Salem Aref and backed by US Central Intelligence Agency; reign of terror launched against the left.

1968: Ba'athist military coup put Maj-Gen Ahmed Hassan al-Bakr in power.

1979: Al-Bakr was replaced by Saddam Hussein of the Arab Ba'ath Socialist Party.

1980: The war between Iraq and Iran broke out.

1985–87: Fighting in the Iran–Iraq war intensified, with heavy loss of life.

1988: There was a ceasefire and talks began with Iran. Iraq used chemical weapons against Kurdish rebels seeking greater autonomy in the northwest.

1989: There was an unsuccessful coup against President Hussein; Iraq successfully launched a ballistic test missile.

1990: A peace treaty favouring Iran was agreed. Iraq invaded and annexed Kuwait in August. US forces massed in Saudi Arabia at the request of King Fahd. The United Nations (UN) ordered Iraqi withdrawal and imposed a total trade ban; further UN resolution sanctioned the use of force. All foreign hostages were released.

1991: US-led Allied forces launched an aerial assault on Iraq and destroyed the country's infrastructure; a land–sea–air offensive to free Kuwait was successful. Uprisings of Kurds and Shiites were brutally suppressed by surviving Iraqi troops. Allied troops established 'safe havens' for Kurds in the north prior to the withdrawal, and left a rapid-reaction force near the Turkish border.

1992: The UN imposed a 'no-fly zone' over southern Iraq to protect Shiites.

1993: Iraqi incursions into the 'no-fly zone' prompted US-led alliance aircraft to bomb strategic targets in Iraq. There was continued persecution of Shiites in the south.

1994: Iraq renounced its claim to Kuwait, but failed to fulfil the other conditions required for the lifting of UN sanctions.

1996: Iraqi-backed attacks on Kurds prompted US retaliation; these air strikes destroyed Iraqi military bases in the south.

1997: Iraq continued to resist the US and Allied pressure to allow UN weapons inspections.

1998: Iraq expelled UN weapons inspectors. In April the UN inspectors' report showed that Iraq had failed to meet UN requirements on the destruction of chemical and biological weapons. In December US and UK forces launched Operation Desert Fox which lasted four days; there were further clashes between US–UK forces and Baghdad over the no-fly zone, which continued in to 1999.

1999: In February US–UK air strikes resumed for a short time. The UK suggested the lifting of sanctions if Iraq resumed cooperation with the UN.

2000: The UN head of humanitarian aid efforts in Iraq resigned in protest at continuing sanctions. The Iraq–Syria border was re-opened, and Iraq began pumping oil to Syria in contravention of the UN-approved oil-for-food programme.

2001: Iraq signed free-trade agreements with Egypt and Syria. UK and US aircraft bombed radar sites near Baghdad, aiming to enforce the no-fly zones, despite a lack of unilateral support.

2002: Under increasing threat of military intervention by the USA, the Iraqi government agreed to readmit United Nations (UN) weapons inspectors, expelled in 1998. The UN Security Council agreed unanimously on Resolution 1441, giving Saddam Hussein a final chance to comply with commitments to disarm weapons of mass destruction (WMD) or face 'serious consequences'.

2003: The USA and UK started controversial military action in March, nominally to rid Iraq of weapons of mass destruction (WMD). Following a rapid military advance through Iraq, US ground forces took control of the capital, Baghdad. Saddam Hussein's regime collapsed, his sons Uday and Qusay were killed, and widespread looting by Iraqi civilians followed. A new 25-member Iraqi governing council, appointed by US and UK officials and broadly representing the country's religious and ethnic balance, held its inaugural meeting in July. Iraqi insurgents and suicide bombers maintained almost daily attacks on US and other targets, including the International Red Cross, killing and wounding dozens of people. Saddam Hussein was captured alive and without resistance by US troops near Tikrit in December.

2004: Sovereignty was transferred to a new interim government, despite ongoing terrorist activity by insurgents.

2005: Jalal Talabani was elected as interim president and Ibrahim Jaafari became prime minister.

Irbil or **Arbil** Kurdish capital city, in the governorate of Irbil, in northern Iraq; population (2002 est) 839,600. Its position on the caravan route between Baghdad and Mosul helped it to become, as it still is, an important centre of commerce, particularly for the agricultural produce of the area, including maize, sesame, millet, and fruit. Today Irbil is a rail terminus, as well as a centre for roads to Turkey, Syria, and Iran. In 1974 Irbil became the capital of a Kurdish autonomous region set up by the Iraqi government. It was captured by the Kurdish Democratic Party in 1996 with the help of Saddam Hussein.

Ireland an island lying to the west of Great Britain between the Atlantic Ocean and the Irish Sea. It comprises the provinces of Ulster, Leinster, Munster, and Connacht, and is divided into the Republic of Ireland (which occupies the south, centre, and northwest of the island) and Northern Ireland (which occupies the northeastern corner and forms part of the United Kingdom).

Ireland or **Éire**

National name: *Poblacht Na hÉireann/ Republic of Ireland*

Area: 70,282 sq km/27,135 sq mi

Capital: Dublin

Major towns/cities: Cork, Limerick, Galway, Waterford, Dundalk, Bray

Major ports: Cork, Dun Laoghaire, Limerick, Waterford, Galway

Physical features: central plateau surrounded by hills; rivers Shannon, Liffey, Boyne; Bog of Allen; Macgillicuddy's Reeks, Wicklow Mountains; Lough Corrib, lakes of Killarney; Galway Bay and Aran Islands

Head of state: Mary McAleese from 1997

Head of government: Bertie Ahern from 1997

Political system: liberal democracy

Political executive: parliamentary

Ireland

0 mi 400
0 km 800

Political parties: Fianna Fáil (Soldiers of Destiny), moderate right of centre; Fine Gael (Irish Tribe or United Ireland Party), moderate left of centre; Labour Party, moderate left of centre; Progressive Democrats, radical free-enterprise; Sinn Fein
Currency: euro (Irish pound, or punt Eireannach, until 2002)
GNI per capita (PPP): (US$) 28,040 (2002 est)
Exports: beef and dairy products, live animals, machinery and transport equipment, electronic goods, chemicals. Principal market: UK 21.8% (2000)
Population: 3,956,000 (2003 est)
Language: Irish Gaelic, English (both official)
Religion: Roman Catholic 92%, Church of Ireland, other Protestant denominations 3%
Life expectancy: 74 (men); 80 (women) (2000–05)
Chronology
3rd century BC: The Gaels, a Celtic people, invaded Ireland and formed about 150 small kingdoms.
AD c. 432: St Patrick introduced Christianity.
5th–9th centuries: Irish Church was a centre of culture and scholarship.
9th–11th centuries: The Vikings raided Ireland until defeated by High King Brian Bóruma at Clontarf in 1014.
12th–13th centuries: Anglo-Norman adventurers conquered much of Ireland, but no central government was formed and many became assimilated.
14th–15th centuries: Irish chieftains recovered their lands, restricting English rule to the Pale around Dublin.
1536: Henry VIII of England made ineffectual efforts to impose the Protestant Reformation on Ireland.
1541: Irish parliament recognized Henry VIII as king of Ireland; Henry gave peerages to Irish chieftains.
1579: English suppressed Desmond rebellion, confiscated rebel lands, and tried to 'plant' them with English settlers.
1610: James I established plantation of Ulster with Protestant settlers from England and Scotland.
1641: Catholic Irish rebelled against English rule; Oliver Cromwell brutally reasserted English control (1649–50); Irish landowners evicted and replaced with English landowners.

1689–91: Williamite War: following the 'Glorious Revolution', the Catholic Irish unsuccessfully supported James II against Protestant William III in civil war. Penal laws barred Catholics from obtaining wealth and power.
1720: Act passed declaring British Parliament's right to legislate for Ireland.
1739–41: Famine killed one-third of population of 1.5 million.
1782: Protestant landlords led by Henry Grattan secured end of restrictions on Irish trade and parliament.
1798: British suppressed revolt by Society of United Irishmen (with French support) led by Wolfe Tone.
1800: Act of Union abolished Irish parliament and created United Kingdom of Great Britain and Ireland, effective 1801.
1829: Daniel O'Connell secured Catholic Emancipation Act, which permitted Catholics to enter parliament.
1846–52: Potato famine reduced population by 20% through starvation and emigration.
1870: Land Act increased security for tenants but failed to halt agrarian disorder; Isaac Butt formed political party to campaign for Irish home rule (devolution).
1885: Home-rulers, led by Charles Stewart Parnell, held balance of power in Parliament; first Home Rule Bill rejected in 1886; second Home Rule Bill defeated in 1893.
1905: Arthur Griffith founded the nationalist movement Sinn Fein ('Ourselves Alone').
1914: Ireland came close to civil war as Ulster prepared to resist implementation of Home Rule Act (postponed because of World War I).
1916: Easter Rising: nationalists proclaimed a republic in Dublin; British crushed revolt and executed 15 leaders.
1919: Sinn Fein MPs formed Irish parliament in Dublin in defiance of British government.
1919–21: Irish Republican Army (IRA) waged guerrilla war against British forces.
1921: Anglo-Irish Treaty partitioned Ireland; northern Ireland (Ulster) remained part of the United Kingdom; southern Ireland won full internal self-government with dominion status.
1922: Irish Free State proclaimed; IRA split over Anglo-Irish Treaty led to civil war (1922–23).
1932: Anti-Treaty party, Fianna Fáil, came to power under Éamon de Valera.
1937: New constitution established Eire (Gaelic name for Ireland) as a sovereign state and refused to acknowledge partition.
1949: After remaining neutral in World War II, Eire left the Commonwealth and became the Republic of Ireland.
1973: Ireland joined European Economic Community.
1985: The Anglo-Irish Agreement gave the Republic of Ireland a consultative role, but no powers, in the government of Northern Ireland.
1990: Mary Robinson was elected as the first female president.
1993: The Downing Street Declaration, a joint Anglo-Irish peace proposal for Northern Ireland, was issued.
1997: Mary McAleese was elected president; she appointed Bertie Ahern as her prime minister.
1998: A multiparty agreement (the Good Friday Agreement) was reached on the future of Northern

Ireland. The subsequent referendum showed a large majority in favour of dropping Ireland's claim to Northern Ireland. Strict legislation was passed against terrorism.

1999: The IRA agreed to begin decommissioning discussions and a coalition government was established, with David Trimble as first minister. Powers were devolved to the province by the British government in December.

2000: After it was revealed that there had been no arms handover, the British Secretary of State for Northern Ireland suspended the Northern Ireland Assembly and reintroduced direct rule. Within hours of the suspension of the Assembly, the British government announced a new IRA initiative on arms decommissioning.

2001: Michael Noonan replaced former prime minister John Bruton as leader of the Fine Gael party.

2002: Ireland started using the euro in place of the punt. Bertie Ahern of the Fianna Fáil party was re-elected prime minister. In a second referendum voters reversed their earlier rejection in 2001 of the Treaty of Nice, a European Union (EU) measure to prepare for EU enlargement.

2004: Ireland held the EU presidency.

Ireland, Northern see *Northern Ireland.

Irian Jaya western portion of the island of New Guinea, disputed province of Indonesia; area 420,000 sq km/162,000 sq mi; population (2000 est) 2,220,900. The capital is Jayapura. Most of the population depends on subsistence farming, especially the cultivation of rice and maize. The main industries include copper (with the largest concentration of copper in the world at Tembagapura), palm oil, copra, maize, groundnuts, pepper, tuna, gold, oil, coal, and phosphates. It is mostly a mountainous and forested region, with the Pegunungan Maoke range rising to 5,029 m/16,499 ft at Jaya Peak. The population comprises Melanesians (original settlers of Western New Guinea), Papuans, Negritos, and Europeans. Indigenous animism prevails. The province declared independence from Indonesia, as West Papua, in June 2000. However, the president of Indonesia stated that the declaration was unrepresentative of true feeling in the province.

iridium chemical symbol Ir, (Latin *iridis* 'rainbow') hard, brittle, silver-white, metallic element, atomic number 77, relative atomic mass 192.2. It is resistant to tarnish and corrosion. Iridium is one of the so-called platinum group of metals; it occurs in platinum ores and as a free metal (*native metal) with osmium in osmiridium, a natural alloy that includes platinum, ruthenium, and rhodium.

iris in anatomy, the coloured muscular diaphragm that controls the size of the pupil in the vertebrate eye. It contains radial muscle that increases the pupil diameter and circular muscle that constricts the pupil diameter. Both types of muscle respond involuntarily to light intensity.

iris in botany, any of a group of perennial northern temperate flowering plants belonging to the iris family. The leaves are usually sword-shaped; the purple, white, or yellow flowers have three upright inner petals and three outward- and downward-curving *sepals. The wild yellow iris is called a flag. (Genus *Iris*, family Iridaceae.)

Irish people of Irish culture from Ireland or those of Irish descent. The Irish mainly speak English, though there are approximately 30,000–100,000 speakers of Irish Gaelic (see *Gaelic language), a Celtic language belonging to the Indo-European family.

Irish Gaelic first official language of the Irish Republic, but much less widely used than the second official language, English. See *Gaelic language.

Irish National Liberation Army (INLA) guerrilla organization committed to the end of British rule in Northern Ireland and Irish reunification. The INLA, founded in 1974, is a left-wing offshoot of the *Irish Republican Army (IRA). Among its activities was the killing of British politician Airey Neave in 1979. The INLA initially rejected the IRA's call for a ceasefire in 1994; its assassination in 1997 of loyalist leader Billy Wright threatened to destabilize the peace process and bomb attacks occurred in London in 1998. However, after the Omagh bomb atrocity in 1998 the INLA became the first republican subversive group to state explicitly that the war was over and voice strong support for the peace process.

Irish Republican Armyy (IRA) militant Irish nationalist organization formed in 1919, the paramilitary wing of *Sinn Fein. Its aim is to create a united Irish socialist republic including Ulster. To this end, the IRA has frequently carried out bombings and shootings. Despite its close association with Sinn Fein, it is not certain that the politicians have direct control of the military, the IRA usually speaking as a separate, independent organization. The chief common factor shared by Sinn Fein and the IRA is the aim of a united Ireland.

Irkutsk city in southern Siberian Russia, capital of Irkutsk oblast (region); population (2003 est) 594,400. Irkutsk is situated near Lake Baikal on the River Angara; there is a large hydroelectric station near the city. Coal is mined here, while manufactured goods include iron, steel, aircraft, motor vehicles, textiles, and machine tools. Its industrial development dates from the arrival of the Trans-Siberian railway in 1898.

iron chemical symbol Fe, (Germanic *eis* 'strong') hard, malleable and ductile, silver-grey, metallic element, atomic number 26, relative atomic mass 55.847. It chemical symbol comes from the Latin *ferrum*. It is the fourth most abundant element in the Earth's crust. Iron occurs in concentrated deposits as the ores haematite (Fe_2O_3), spathic ore ($FeCO_3$), and magnetite (Fe_3O_4). It sometimes occurs as a free metal, occasionally as fragments of iron or iron–nickel meteorites.

Iron Age developmental stage of human technology when weapons and tools were made from iron. Preceded by the Stone and Bronze ages, it is the last technological stage in the Three Age System framework for prehistory. Iron was produced in Thailand *c.* 1600 BC, but was considered inferior in strength to bronze until *c.* 1000 BC, when metallurgical techniques improved, and the alloy steel was produced by adding carbon during the smelting process.

Iron Curtain in Europe after World War II, the symbolic boundary between capitalist West and communist East during the *Cold War. The term was popularized by the UK prime minister Winston Churchill from 1946.

iron pyrites *or* **pyrite** FeS_2, common iron ore. Brassy yellow, and occurring in cubic crystals, it is often called

461

'fool's gold', since only those who have never seen gold would mistake it.

Iroquois (Algonquin 'rattlesnakes') member of a confederation of *American Indian peoples of northeastern North America formed about 1570. Known originally as the Five Nations, it included the Cayuga, *Mohawk, Oneida, Onondaga, and Seneca. It became the **Six Nations** after the Tuscarora joined in 1722. From its New York homelands, the confederacy aggressively enlarged its territorial control to include much of Ontario, Québec, Pennsylvania, Ohio, and Michigan. Iroquois also refers to American Indians of the Iroquoian linguistic family, originally from the upper St Lawrence River, such as the *Cherokee and Huron. Iroquois now live in Ontario, Québec, New York, Oklahoma, and Wisconsin, and number about 45,200 (2000).

irradiation subjecting anything to radiation, including cancer tumours (when it is a type of *radiotherapy).

irrational number number that cannot be expressed as an exact *fraction. Irrational numbers include some square roots (for example, $\sqrt{2}$, $\sqrt{3}$, and $\sqrt{5}$ are irrational); numbers such as π (for circles), which is approximately equal to the *decimal 3.14159; and e (the base of *natural logarithms, approximately 2.71828). If an irrational number is expressed as a decimal it would go on for ever without repeating. An irrational number multiplied by itself gives a *rational number.

Irrawaddy Myanmar **Ayeryarwady**, chief river of Myanmar (Burma), flowing roughly north–south for 2,090 km/1,300 mi across the centre of the country into the Bay of Bengal. Its sources are the Mali and N'mai rivers; its chief tributaries are the Chindwin and Shweli.

irrigation artificial water supply for dry agricultural areas by means of dams and channels. Drawbacks are that it tends to concentrate salts at the surface, ultimately causing soil infertility, and that rich river silt is retained at dams, to the impoverishment of the land and fisheries below them.

Irving, Henry (1838–1905) stage name of John Henry Brodribb, English actor. He established his reputation from 1871, chiefly at the Lyceum Theatre in London, where he became manager in 1878. He staged a series of successful Shakespearean productions, including *Romeo and Juliet* (1882), with himself and Ellen Terry playing the leading roles. He was the first actor to be knighted, in 1895.

Isabella (I) the Catholic (1451–1504) Queen of Castile from 1474, after the death of her brother Henry IV. By her marriage with *Ferdinand of Aragon in 1469, the crowns of two of the Christian states in the Spanish peninsula cemented their dynastic link. Her youngest daughter was Catherine of Aragon, first wife of Henry VIII of England. Under Isabella and her husband (the Catholic king), the reconquista was finally fulfilled with the taking of the Moorish city Granada in 1492.

ischaemic heart disease (IHD) disorder caused by reduced perfusion of the coronary arteries due to *atherosclerosis. It is the commonest cause of death in the Western world, leading to more than a million deaths each year in the USA and about 160,000 in the UK. See also *coronary artery disease. Early symptoms of IHD include *angina or palpitations, but sometimes a heart attack is the first indication that a person is affected.

ISDN abbreviation for *Integrated Services Digital Network, a telecommunications system.

Isherwood, Christopher (William Bradshaw) (1904–1986) English-born US novelist. He lived in Germany from 1929–33 just before Hitler's rise to power, a period that inspired *Mr Norris Changes Trains* (1935) and *Goodbye to Berlin* (1939), creating the character of Sally Bowles, the basis of the musical *Cabaret* (1968). Returning to England, he collaborated with W H *Auden in three verse plays.

Ishiguro, Kazuo (1954–) Japanese-born British novelist. His novel *An Artist of the Floating World* won the 1986 Whitbread Prize, and *The Remains of the Day*, about an English butler coming to realize the extent of his self-sacrifice and self-deception, won the 1989 Booker Prize and was made into a successful film in 1993. His works, which are characterized by a sensitive style and subtle structure, also include *The Unconsoled* (1995), and *When We Were Orphans* (2000), which was shortlisted for the 2000 Booker Prize.

Ishtar *or* **Istar** Mesopotamian goddess of fertility, sexual love, wedlock, maternity, and war, worshipped by the Babylonians and Assyrians, and personified as the legendary queen *Semiramis. She was the equivalent of the Canaanite and Syrian Astarte.

Isis (Ancient Egyptian 'seat') principal goddess of ancient Egypt; the daughter of Geb and Nut (Earth and Sky); and the personification of the throne of her brother-husband *Osiris. She searched for the body of Osiris after he was murdered by his brother, Set. Her son, the sky god *Horus, defeated and captured Set, but beheaded his mother because she would not allow Set to be killed. She was later identified with Hathor, and by the Greeks with *Demeter, goddess of agriculture, and Zeus' lover Io.

Islam (Arabic 'submission', that is, to the will of Allah) religion founded in the Arabian peninsula in the early AD 600s. It emphasizes the 'oneness of God' (Arabic tauhid), his omnipotence, beneficence, and inscrutability. Its sacred book is the *Koran, which Muslims believe was divinely revealed to *Muhammad, the prophet or messenger of *Allah (God). There are two main Muslim sects: **Sunni** and **Shiite**. Others include **Sufism**, a mystical movement that originated in the AD 700s. The word Muslim means 'one who makes his peace with God and Man'.

Islamabad capital of Pakistan from 1967 (replacing Karachi), in the Potwar district, at the foot of the Margala Hills, at the head of navigation of the Jhelum River and immediately northwest of Rawalpindi; population (1998 est) 529,200. The city was designed by Constantinos Doxiadis in the 1960s, and its Arabic name means 'city of peace'. The Federal Capital Territory of Islamabad has an area of 907 sq km/ 350 sq mi and a population (1998 est) of 799,100. Islamabad is the centre of an agricultural region in the Vale of Kashmir.

Islamic architecture the architecture of the Muslim world, highly diverse but unified by climate, culture, and a love of geometric and arabesque ornament, as well as by the mobility of ideas, artisans, and architects throughout the region. The central public buildings are *mosques, often with a dome and minaret; domestic houses face an inner courtyard and are grouped together, with vaulted streets linking the blocks.

Islamic art art and design of the Muslim world, dating from the foundation of the Islamic faith in the 7th century AD. Having developed few artistic traditions of their own, the Muslim Arabs who conquered parts of Asia, Europe, and North Africa in the late 7th and early 8th centuries adopted elements of *Byzantine, *Coptic, and *Persian art, fusing them into a distinctive decorative style based on calligraphy. The traditions laid down by Islam created devout, painstaking craftspeople whose creative purpose was the glory of God. Islamic doctrine controlled all artistic endeavour, whether calligraphy, the decorative arts, or representational art. Sculpture was prohibited and carvers turned instead to exquisite inlay and fretwork, notably on doors and screens, in Islamic monuments such as the Alhambra Palace, Granada, Spain, and the Taj Mahal, India. Today, Islamic art is to be found predominantly in Egypt, Iran, Iraq, Turkey, the Indian subcontinent, and the Central Asian republics.

Ismail (1830–1895) Khedive (governor) of Egypt 1866–79. A grandson of Mehmet Ali, he became viceroy of Egypt in 1863, and in 1866 received the title of khedive from the Ottoman sultan. He amassed huge foreign debts and in 1875 Britain, at Prime Minister Disraeli's suggestion, bought the khedive's Suez Canal shares for nearly £4 million, establishing Anglo-French control of Egypt's finances. In 1879 the UK and France persuaded the sultan to appoint Tewfik, his son, khedive in his place.

Ismail I (1486–1524) Shah of Persia from 1501. He was the founder of the **Safavi dynasty**, and established the first national government since the Arab conquest and Shiite Islam as the national religion.

isobar line drawn on maps and weather charts linking all places with the same atmospheric pressure (usually measured in millibars). When used in weather forecasting, the distance between the isobars is an indication of the barometric gradient (the rate of change in pressure).

isolationism in politics, concentration on internal rather than foreign affairs; a foreign policy having no interest in international affairs that do not affect the country's own interests.

Isolde or **Iseult** in Celtic and medieval legend, the wife of King Mark of Cornwall who was brought from Ireland by King Mark's nephew *Tristan. She and Tristan accidentally drank the aphrodisiac given to her by her mother for her marriage, were separated as lovers, and finally died together.

isomer chemical compound having the same *molecular formula but with different molecular structure. For example, the organic compounds butane ($CH_3(CH_2)_2CH_3$) and methyl propane ($CH_3CH(CH_3)CH_3$) are isomers, each possessing four carbon atoms and ten hydrogen atoms but differing in the way that these are arranged with respect to each other.

isostasy condition of gravitational equilibrium of all parts of the Earth's *crust. The crust is in isostatic equilibrium if, below a certain depth, the weight and thus pressure of rocks above is the same everywhere. The idea is that the lithosphere floats on the asthenosphere as a piece of wood floats on water. A thick piece of wood floats lower than a thin piece, and a denser piece of wood floats lower than a less

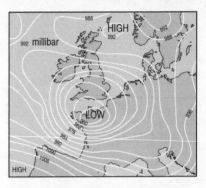

isobar The isobars around a low-pressure area or depression. In the northern hemisphere, winds blow anticlockwise around lows, approximately parallel to the isobars, and clockwise around highs. In the southern hemisphere, the winds blow in the opposite directions.

dense piece. There are two theories of the mechanism of isostasy, the Airy hypothesis and the Pratt hypothesis, both of which have validity. In the **Airy hypothesis** crustal blocks have the same density but different thicknesses: like ice cubes floating in water, higher mountains have deeper roots. In the **Pratt hypothesis**, crustal blocks have different densities allowing the depth of crustal material to be the same. In practice, both mechanisms are at work.

isotope one of two or more atoms that have the same atomic number (same number of protons), but which contain a different number of neutrons, thus differing in their *relative atomic mass. They may be stable or radioactive (as a *radioisotope), naturally occurring, or synthesized. For example, hydrogen has the isotopes ^{2}H (*deuterium) and ^{3}H (*tritium). The term was coined by English chemist Frederick Soddy, a pioneer researcher in atomic disintegration.

Israel ancient kingdom of northern *Palestine, formed after the death of Solomon by Jewish peoples seceding from the rule of his son Rehoboam and electing Jeroboam as their leader.

Israel

National name: *Medinat Israel/State of Israel*
Area: 20,800 sq km/8,030 sq mi (as at 1949 armistice)
Capital: Jerusalem (not recognized by the United Nations)
Major towns/cities: Tel Aviv-Yafo, Haifa, Bat-Yam, Holon, Ramat Gan, Petach Tikva, Rishon Le Ziyyon, Beersheba
Major ports: Tel Aviv-Yafo, Haifa, 'Akko (formerly Acre), Eilat
Physical features: coastal plain of Sharon between Haifa and Tel Aviv noted since ancient times for its fertility; central mountains of Galilee, Samaria, and Judea; Dead Sea, Lake Tiberias, and River Jordan Rift Valley along the east are below sea level; Negev Desert in the south; Israel occupies Golan Heights, West Bank, East Jerusalem, and Gaza Strip (the last was awarded limited autonomy, with West Bank town of Jericho, in 1993)

Israel

Head of state: Moshe Katsav from 2000
Head of government: Ariel Sharon from 2001
Political system: liberal democracy
Political executive: parliamentary
Political parties: Israel Labour Party, moderate, left of centre; Consolidation Party (Likud), right of centre; Meretz (Vitality), left-of-centre alliance
Currency: shekel
GNI per capita (PPP): (US$) 19,920 (2002 est)
Exports: machinery and parts, citrus fruits, worked diamonds, software, food products, chemical products, textiles and clothing. Principal market: USA 38.2% (2001)
Population: 6,433,000 (2003 est)
Language: Hebrew, Arabic (both official), English, Yiddish, other European and west Asian languages
Religion: Israel is a secular state, but the predominant faith is Judaism 80%; also Sunni Muslim (about 15%), Christian, and Druze
Life expectancy: 77 (men); 81 (women) (2000–05)
Chronology
c. **2000 BC:** Abraham, father of the Jewish people, is believed to have come to Palestine from Mesopotamia.
c. **1225 BC:** Moses led the Jews out of slavery in Egypt towards the promised land of Palestine.
11th century BC: Saul established a Jewish kingdom in Palestine; developed by kings David and Solomon.
586 BC: Jews defeated by Babylon and deported; many returned to Palestine in 539 BC.
333 BC: Alexander the Great of Macedonia conquered the entire region.
3rd century BC: Control of Palestine contested by Ptolemies of Egypt and Seleucids of Syria.
142 BC: Jewish independence restored after Maccabean revolt.
63 BC: Palestine fell to Roman Empire.
70 AD: Romans crushed Zealot rebellion and destroyed Jerusalem; start of dispersion of Jews (diaspora).
614: Persians took Jerusalem from Byzantine Empire.
637: Muslim Arabs conquered Palestine.
1099: First Crusade captured Jerusalem; Christian kingdom lasted a century before falling to sultans of Egypt.
1517: Palestine conquered by the Ottoman Turks.
1897: Theodor Herzl organized the First Zionist Congress at Basel to publicize Jewish claims to Palestine.

1917: The Balfour Declaration: Britain expressed support for the creation of a Jewish National Home in Palestine.
1918: British forces expelled the Turks from Palestine, which became a British League of Nations mandate in 1920.
1929: Severe violence around Jerusalem caused by Arab alarm at doubling of Jewish population in ten years.
1933: Jewish riots in protest at British attempts to restrict Jewish immigration.
1937: The Peel Report, recommending partition, accepted by most Jews but rejected by Arabs; open warfare ensued between 1937 and 1938.
1939: Britain postponed independence plans on account of World War II, and increased military presence.
1946: Resumption of terrorist violence; Jewish extremists blew up British headquarters in Jerusalem.
1947: United Nations (UN) voted for partition of Palestine.
1948: Britain withdrew; Independent State of Israel proclaimed with David Ben-Gurion as prime minister; Israel repulsed invasion by Arab nations; many Palestinian Arabs settled in refugee camps in the Gaza Strip and West Bank.
1952: Col Gamal Nasser of Egypt stepped up blockade of Israeli ports and support of Arab guerrillas in Gaza.
1956: War between Israel and Egypt; Israeli invasion of Gaza and Sinai followed by withdrawal in 1957.
1964: Palestine Liberation Organization (PLO) founded to unite Palestinian Arabs with the aim of overthrowing the state of Israel.
1967: Israel defeated Egypt, Syria, and Jordan in the Six-Day War; Gaza, West Bank, east Jerusalem, Sinai, and Golan Heights captured.
1969: Yassir Arafat became chair of the PLO; escalation of terrorism and border raids.
1973: Yom Kippur War: Israel repulsed surprise attack by Egypt and Syria.
1977: President Anwar Sadat of Egypt began peace initiative.
1979: Camp David talks ended with signing of peace treaty between Israel and Egypt; Israel withdrew from Sinai.
1980: United Jerusalem was declared the capital of Israel.
1982: Israeli forces invaded southern Lebanon to drive out PLO guerrillas; occupation continued until 1985.
1988: The Israeli handling of Palestinian uprising (Intifada) in the occupied territories provoked international criticism.
1990: The PLO formally recognized the state of Israel.
1991: Iraq launched missile attacks on Israel during the Gulf War; Middle East peace talks began in Madrid.
1992: A Labour government was elected under Yitzhak Rabin.
1993: Rabin and Arafat signed a peace accord; Israel granted limited autonomy to Gaza Strip and Jericho. Ezer Weizman was elected president.
1994: Arafat became the head of an autonomous Palestinian authority in Gaza and Jericho; a peace agreement was reached between Israel and Jordan.
1995: Rabin was assassinated by a Jewish opponent of the peace accord.
1996: A Likud government was elected under Binyamin Netanyahu, a critic of the peace accord. A revival of

communal violence was seen and the peace process was threatened. The opening of a 2,000-year-old tunnel near the Al-Aqsa mosque in Jerusalem provoked renewed Palestinian–Israeli conflict.

1997: A Jewish settlement in east Jerusalem was widely condemned. There were suicide bombs by Hamas in Jerusalem. There was partial and limited withdrawal from the West Bank.

1998: Violence flared on the West Bank between Palestinians and Israeli troops, again stalling the peace process. The Wye Peace Agreement was signed with the PLO. A land-for-security deal was approved by the Knesset, and the promised Israeli withdrawal from the Lebanon was subsequently placed in doubt. President Clinton attempted to restart the peace process.

1999: The South Lebanon 'security zone' was expanded. Yasser Arafat delayed the declaration of an independent state until after the Israeli elections. Ehud Barak (Labour) was elected prime minister and restarted peace negotiations.

2000: Israel withdrew from the Golan Heights. Moshe Katsav, who opposed Barak's peace initiative, became president. In September, renewed violence between Palestinians and Israeli security forces broke out and quickly escalated, following a visit by right-wing Israeli politican Ariel Sharon to Haram al-Sharif (Temple Mount) in Jerusalem. Repeated efforts to end the violence failed, and Barak announced his resignation in December.

2001: Ariel Sharon was elected prime minister.

2002: After months of violence and military reprisals against the Palestinians, the army besieged Yassir Arafat's Ramallah headquarters for 11 days before withdrawing under US pressure and United Nations (UN) Security Council demands. Prime Minister Sharon's national unity government collapsed when the Labour Party left the 20-month-old administration.

2003: An international blueprint (the so-called 'road map', designed by the USA, European Union, UN, and Russia) for a phased settlement of the Palestinian-Israeli conflict by 2005–06 was released and endorsed by the government under US diplomatic pressure. However, the government authorized the building of a controversial security wall. The Palestine National Authority's new government under Mahmoud Abbas was sworn in, but Abbas was later forced to resign and was replaced by Ahmed Qureia. A peace initiative drafted by unofficial Israeli and Palestinian negotiators and known as the Geneva Accord gained significant international support, but was rejected by the government. Palestinian suicide bombings and Israeli retaliation, including the first direct air attack on Syrian territory since 1973, continued throughout the year.

2004: Yasser Arafat, chairman of the PLO since 1969, died in November.

2005: Mahmoud Abbas, a former prime minister, replaced Arafat as chairman of the PLO and won the presidential election. Ariel Sharon agreed to an Israeli withdrawal from the Gaza Strip and other Jewish settlements in the West Bank, a decision that divided his Likud party. The withdrawal was halted over disarmament of Palestinian militant groups.

Israeli Occupied Territories Arab territories captured by Israel during the 1967 Six-Day War and subsequently occupied. These territories comprised the Gaza Strip and Sinai peninsula (captured from Egypt), the West Bank and East Jerusalem (captured from Jordan), and the Golan Heights (captured from Syria).

Issigonis, Alec (1906–1988) born Alexander Arnold Constantine Issigonis, Turkish-born British engineer who designed the Morris Minor (1948) and the Mini-Minor (1959) cars, comfortable yet cheaper to run than their predecessors. He is credited with adding the word 'mini' to the English language. He was knighted in 1969.

Istanbul city and chief seaport of Turkey; population (1990) urban area 6,407,200; city 6,293,400. It produces textiles, tobacco, cement, glass, and leather. Founded as **Byzantium** in about 660 BC, it was renamed **Constantinople** (AD 330) and was the capital of the *Byzantine Empire until captured by the Turks in 1453. As **Istamboul** it was capital of the Ottoman Empire until 1922.

IT abbreviation for *information technology.

Itagaki, Taisuke (1837–1919) Japanese military and political leader. Involved in the overthrow of the *Tokugawa shogunate and the *Meiji restoration of 1868, Itagaki became leader of the people's rights movement. He was the founder of Japan's first political party, the Jiyuto (Liberal Party), in 1881.

Italian art painting and sculpture of Italy from the early Middle Ages to the present. In the 4th century AD Christian art emerged from Roman art, which was adapted to give expression to religious beliefs and sentiments. Throughout the next 14 centuries Roman art was to be the source of constant reappraisals and renewals in the evolution of the visual arts in Italy, and was fundamental to the major development of the Renaissance. It is from antique art, blended with Byzantine and then Gothic influences, that Italian art emerged.

Italian language member of the Romance branch of the Indo-European language family, the most direct descendant of Latin. Broadcasting and films have standardized the Italian national tongue, but most Italians speak a regional dialect as well as standard Italian.

Italian Somaliland former Italian trust territory on the south Somali coast of Africa extending to 502,300 sq km/193,900 sq mi. Established in 1889–90, it was extended in 1925 with the acquisition of Jubaland from Kenya. It was administered from Mogadishu. In 1936 it was united with Ethiopia to form Italian East Africa. It fell under British rule 1941–50. Thereafter it reverted to Italian authority before uniting with *British Somaliland in 1960 to form the independent state of Somalia.

Italy
National name: *Repubblica Italiana/Italian Republic*
Area: 301,300 sq km/116,331 sq mi
Capital: Rome
Major towns/cities: Milan, Naples, Turin, Palermo, Genoa, Bologna, Florence
Major ports: Naples, Genoa, Palermo, Bari, Catania, Trieste
Physical features: mountainous (Maritime Alps, Dolomites, Apennines) with narrow coastal lowlands; continental Europe's only active volcanoes: Vesuvius, Etna, Stromboli; rivers Po, Adige, Arno, Tiber, Rubicon; islands of Sicily, Sardinia, Elba, Capri, Ischia, Lipari, Pantelleria; lakes Como, Maggiore, Garda
Head of state: Carlo Azeglio Ciampi from 1999

Italy

Head of government: Silvio Berlusconi from 2001

Political system: liberal democracy

Political executive: parliamentary

Political parties: Forza Italia (Go Italy!), free market, right of centre; Northern League (LN), Milan-based, federalist, right of centre; National Alliance (AN), neofascist; Italian Popular Party (PPI), Catholic, centrist; Italian Renewal Party, centrist; Democratic Party of the Left (PDS), Pro-European, moderate left wing (ex-communist); Italian Socialist Party (PSI), moderate socialist; Italian Republican Party (PRI), social democratic, left of centre; Democratic Alliance (AD), moderate left of centre; Christian Democratic Centre (CCD), Christian, centrist; Olive Tree alliance, left of centre; Panella List, radical liberal; Union of the Democratic Centre (UDC), right of centre; Pact for Italy, reformist; Communist Refoundation (RC), Marxist; Verdi, environmentalist; La Rete (the Network), anti-Mafia

Currency: euro (lira until 2002)

GNI per capita (PPP): (US\$) 25,320 (2002 est)

Exports: machinery and transport equipment, textiles, clothing and leather goods, wine (leading producer and exporter), metals and metal products, chemicals, wood, paper and rubber goods. Principal market: Germany 14.5% (2001)

Population: 57,423,000 (2003 est)

Language: Italian (official), German and Ladin (in the north), French (in the Valle d'Aosta region), Greek and Albanian (in the south)

Religion: Roman Catholic 98%

Life expectancy: 76 (men); 82 (women) (2000–05)

Chronology

4th and 3rd centuries BC: Italian peninsula united under Roman rule.

AD 476: End of Western Roman Empire.

568: Invaded by Lombards.

756: Papal States created in central Italy.

800: Charlemagne united Italy and Germany in Holy Roman Empire.

12th and 13th centuries: Papacy and Holy Roman Empire contended for political supremacy; papal power reached its peak under Innocent III (1198–1216).

1183: Cities of Lombard League (founded in 1164) became independent.

14th century: Beginnings of Renaissance in northern Italy.

15th century: Most of Italy ruled by five rival states: the city-states of Milan, Florence, and Venice; the Papal States; and the Kingdom of Naples.

1494: Charles VIII of France invaded Italy.

1529–59: Spanish Habsburgs secured dominance in Italy.

17th century: Italy effectively part of Spanish Empire; economic and cultural decline.

1713: Treaty of Utrecht gave political control of most of Italy to Austrian Habsburgs.

1796–1814: France conquered Italy, setting up satellite states and introducing principles of French Revolution.

1815: Old regimes largely restored; Italy divided between Austria, Papal States, Naples, Sardinia, and four duchies.

1831: Giuseppe Mazzini founded the 'Young Italy' movement with the aim of creating a unified republic.

1848–49: Liberal revolutions occurred throughout Italy; reversed everywhere except Sardinia, which became a centre of nationalism under the leadership of Count Camillo di Cavour.

1859: France and Sardinia forcibly expelled Austrians from Lombardy.

1860: Sardinia annexed duchies and Papal States (except Rome); Giuseppe Garibaldi overthrew Neapolitan monarchy.

1861: Victor Emmanuel II of Sardinia proclaimed King of Italy in Turin.

1866: Italy gained Venetia after defeat of Austria by Prussia.

1870: Italian forces occupied Rome in defiance of Pope, completing unification of Italy.

1882: Italy joined Germany and Austria-Hungary in Triple Alliance.

1896: Attempt to conquer Ethiopia defeated at Battle of Adowa.

1900: King Umberto I assassinated by an anarchist.

1912: Annexation of Libya and Dodecanese after Italo-Turkish War.

1915: Italy entered World War I on side of Allies.

1919: Peace treaties awarded Trentino, South Tyrol, and Trieste to Italy.

1922: Mussolini established fascist dictatorship following period of strikes and agrarian revolts.

1935–36: Conquest of Ethiopia.

1939: Invasion of Albania.

1940: Italy entered World War II as ally of Germany.

1943: Allies invaded southern Italy; Mussolini removed from power; Germans occupied northern and central Italy.

1945: Allies completed liberation.

1946: Monarchy replaced by a republic.

1947: Peace treaty stripped Italy of its colonies.

1948: New constitution adopted; Christian Democrats emerged as main party of government in political system marked by ministerial instability.

1957: Italy became a founder member of European Economic Community (EEC).

1963: Creation of first of long series of fragile centre-left coalition governments.

1976: Communists attempt to join the coalition, the 'historic compromise', rejected by the Christian Democrats.

1978: Christian Democrat Aldo Moro, the architect of historic compromise, was murdered by Red Brigade guerrillas infiltrated by Western intelligence agents.

1983–87: Bettino Craxi, Italy's first Socialist prime minister, led the coalition. The economy improved.

1993: A major political crisis was triggered by the exposure of government corruption and Mafia links, and governing parties were discredited. A new electoral system replaced proportional representation, with 75% majority voting.

1999: Carlo Azeglio Ciampi was elected president. Former prime minister Prodi became president of the new European Commission.

2000: After his centre-left coalition was beaten in regional elections, Massimo d'Alema resigned his position as prime minister, which he had held since 1998, and Giuliano Amato was sworn in as head of Italy's 58th government since 1945. Amato later conceded leadership of the coalition in the next general election to Franceso Rutelli, the mayor of Rome.

2001: Industrialist Silvio Berlusconi, who was prime minister for seven months in 1994 until he was forced to resign after being indicted for tax fraud, was elected prime minister for a second time.

2002: Italy started using the euro in place of the lira.

2003: Berlusconi's trial began but was later halted after parliament passed a law allowing holders of key state posts, including the prime minister, immunity from prosecution. Nineteen Italian servicemen were killed in a suicide bomb attack in Iraq.

2004: The law giving Berlusconi immunity from prosecution was reversed and his trial resumed, eventually clearing him of corruption charges.

2005: Parliament ratified the European Union constitution. Berlusconi resigned when his centre-right coalition government was heavily defeated in regional polls. He formed a new coalition government between his Forza Italia party and the National Alliance, Northern League and Union of Christian Democrats.

Ithaca Greek **Ithaki**, Greek island in the Ionian Sea, area 93 sq km/36 sq mi; population (1996 est) 3,700. Important in pre-classical Greece, Ithaca was (in Homer's poem) the birthplace of *Odysseus, though this is sometimes identified with the island of Lefkada (some archaeologists have equated ancient Ithaca with Lefkada rather than modern Ithaca).

Ito, Hirobumi (1841–1909) Japanese politician, prime minister 1885–88, 1892–96, 1898, and 1900–01. He was a key figure in the modernization of Japan and was involved in the *Meiji restoration of 1868 and in official missions to study forms of government in the USA and Europe in the 1870s and 1880s. He played a major role in drafting the Meiji constitution of 1889.

Ivan six rulers of Russia, including:

Ivan (III) the Great (1440–1505) Grand Duke of Muscovy from 1462. He revolted against Tatar

overlordship by refusing tribute to Grand Khan Ahmed in 1480. He claimed the title of tsar (Caesar), and used the double-headed eagle as the Russian state emblem.

Ivan (IV) the Terrible (1530–1584) Grand Duke of Muscovy from 1533. He assumed power in 1544 and was crowned as first tsar of Russia in 1547. He conquered Kazan in 1552, Astrakhan in 1556, and Siberia in 1581. He reformed the legal code and local administration in 1555 and established trade relations with England. In his last years he alternated between debauchery and religious austerities, executing thousands and, in rage, his own son.

Ives, Charles Edward (1874–1954) US composer. He experimented with *atonality, quarter tones, and clashing time signatures, decades before the avant-garde movement. Most of his music uses (simultaneous) quotations from popular tunes, military marches, patriotic songs, and hymns of the time. He wrote four symphonies, including the *Dvorakian Symphony No. 1* (1895–98); chamber music, including the *Concord Sonata* (piano sonata no. 2, 1909–15); and the orchestral works *Three Places in New England* (1903–14), *New England Holidays* (1904–13), and *The Unanswered Question* (1908).

IVF abbreviation for *in vitro fertilization.

ivory hard white substance of which the teeth and tusks of certain mammals are made. Among the most valuable are elephants' tusks, which are of unusual hardness and density. Ivory is used in carving and other decorative work, and is so valuable that poachers continue to illegally destroy the remaining wild elephant herds in Africa to obtain it.

ivy any of an Old World group of woody climbing, trailing, or creeping evergreen plants. English or European ivy (*H. helix*) has shiny five-lobed leaves and clusters of small, yellowish-green flowers followed by black berries. It climbs by means of rootlike suckers put out from its stem, and causes damage to trees. (Genus *Hedera*, family Araliaceae.)

Iwo Jima or **Iojima** largest of the three Japanese Volcano Islands in the western Pacific Ocean, 1,222 km/760 mi south of Tokyo; area 22 sq km/9 sq mi. Annexed by Japan in 1891, Iwo Jima, also known as Naka Iojima, was captured by the USA in 1945 after fierce fighting. It was returned to Japan in 1968.

Iwo Jima, Battle of intense fighting between Japanese and US forces 19 February–17 March 1945 during World War II. In February 1945, US marines landed on the island of Iwo Jima, a Japanese air base, intending to use it to prepare for a planned final assault on mainland Japan. The 22,000 Japanese troops put up a fanatical resistance but the island was finally secured on 16 March. US casualties came to 6,891 killed and 18,700 wounded, while only 212 of the Japanese garrison survived.

jacamar insect-eating bird related to the woodpeckers, found in dense tropical forest in Central and South America. It has a long, straight, sharply-pointed bill, a long tail, and paired toes. The plumage is golden bronze with a steely lustre. Jacamars are usually seen sitting motionless on trees from which they fly out to catch insects on the wing, then return to crack them on a branch before eating them. The largest species is *Jacamerops aurea*, which is nearly 30 cm/12 in long. (Family Galbulidae, order Piciformes.)

jacana *or* **lily-trotter** wading bird with very long toes and claws enabling it to walk on the floating leaves of water plants. There are seven species. Jacanas are found in Mexico, Central America, South America, Africa, South Asia, and Australia, usually in marshy areas. (Family Jacanidae, order Charadriiformes.)

jacaranda any of a group of tropical American trees belonging to the bignonia family, with fragrant wood and showy blue or violet flowers, commonly cultivated in the southern USA. (Genus *Jacaranda*, family Bignoniaceae.)

jackal any of several wild dogs found in South Asia, southern Europe, and North Africa. Jackals can grow to 80 cm/2.7 ft long, and have greyish-brown fur and a bushy tail. (Genus *Canis*.)

jackdaw bird belonging to the crow family, native to Europe and Asia. It is mainly black, but greyish on the sides and back of the head, and about 33 cm/1.1 ft long. It nests in tree holes or on buildings. Usually it lays five bluish-white eggs, mottled with tiny dark brown spots. Jackdaws feed on a wide range of insects, molluscs, spiders, worms, birds' eggs, fruit, and berries. (Species *Corvus monedula*, family Corvidae, order Passeriformes.)

Jackson largest city and state capital of *Mississippi, USA, on the Pearl River, in the central part of the state, 70 km/43 mi east of Vicksburg; seat of Hinds County; population (2001 est) 185,800. It produces electrical machinery, furniture, cottonseed oil, and iron and steel castings, and owes its prosperity to the discovery of gas fields to the south in the 1930s. Jackson became state capital in 1821.

Jackson, Andrew (1767–1845) nickname 'Old Hickory', 7th president of the USA 1829–37, a Democrat. A major general in the *War of 1812, he defeated a British force in the Battle of New Orleans in 1815 and was involved in the war that led to the purchase of Florida in 1819. The political organization he built as president, with his secretary of state Martin Van Buren (1782–1862), was the basis for the modern *Democratic Party.

Jackson, Glenda (1936–) English actor and politician, Labour member of Parliament from 1992, and parliamentary undersecretary for transport 1997–99. Her many stage appearances for the Royal Shakespeare Company include *Marat/Sade* (1966), *Hedda Gabler* (1975), and *Antony and Cleopatra* (1978). Among her films are the Academy Award-winning *Women in Love* (1969), *Sunday Bloody Sunday* (1971), and *A Touch of Class* (1973). On television she played Queen Elizabeth I in *Elizabeth R* (1971).

Jackson, Michael (Joseph) (1958–) US rock singer and songwriter. His videos and live performances contain precisely choreographed dance routines. His first solo hit was 'Got to Be There' (1971), and his worldwide popularity peaked with the albums *Thriller* (1982), *Bad* (1987), and *Dangerous* (1991). Jackson's career faltered after allegations of child abuse, but he returned with the albums *History* (1995) and *Blood on the Dance Floor* (1997).

Jacobean style in the arts, influential upon architecture and furniture as well as literature, during the reign of James I (1603–25) in England. In the visual arts, Jacobean design follows the general lines of Elizabethan design, but uses classical features with greater complexity and with more extravagant ornamentation, it adopted many motifs from contemporary Italian design. In literature, similarly, the model of Jacobean works was Elizabethan in form, but increasingly complex and ornamented.

Jacobin member of an extremist republican club of the French Revolution founded in Versailles 1789. Helped by *Danton's speeches, they proclaimed the French republic, had the king executed, and overthrew the moderate *Girondins 1792–93. Through the Committee of Public Safety, they began the Reign of Terror, led by *Robespierre. After his execution in 1794, the club was abandoned and the name 'Jacobin' passed into general use for any left-wing extremist.

Jacobite in Britain, a supporter of the royal house of Stuart after the deposition of James II in 1688. They include the Scottish Highlanders, who rose unsuccessfully under *Claverhouse in 1689, despite initial victory at the Battle of *Killiecrankie; and those who rose in Scotland and northern England in 1715 (the Fifteen) under the leadership of *James Edward Stuart, the Old Pretender, and followed his son *Charles Edward Stuart in an invasion of England from 1745 to 1746 (the *Forty-Five) that reached Derby. After the defeat at *Culloden, Jacobitism disappeared as a political force.

Jacquard, Joseph Marie (1752–1834) French textile manufacturer. He invented a punched-card system for programming designs on a silk-weaving loom (the Jacquard loom). In 1801 he constructed looms that used a series of punched cards to control the pattern of longitudinal warp threads depressed before each sideways passage of the shuttle. On later machines the punched cards were joined to form an endless loop that represented the 'program' for the repeating pattern of a carpet.

jade semi-precious stone consisting of either jadeite, $NaAlSi_2O_6$ (a pyroxene), or nephrite, $Ca_2(Mg,Fe)_5Si_8O_{22}(OH,F)_2$ (an amphibole), ranging from colourless through shades of green to black according to the iron content. Jade ranks 5.5–6.5 on the Mohs scale of hardness.

Jade Emperor or **Yu Huang** in Chinese religion, the supreme god of pantheistic Taoism, also known as the August Personage of Jade and Father Heaven, who watches over human actions and is the ruler of life and death. His court inspects the earth annually, making a detailed account from which he apportions praise or blame; the gods could be promoted or lose their rank accordingly.

jaguar largest species of cat in the Americas, formerly ranging from the southwestern USA to southern South America, but now extinct in most of North America. It can grow up to 2.5 m/8 ft long including the tail. Male jaguars weigh up to 150 kg/330 lb; females up to 90 kg/198 lb. The background colour of the fur varies from creamy white to brown or black, and is covered with black spots. The jaguar is usually solitary and lives approximately 11 years in the wild. (Species *Panthera onca*, family Felidae.)

jaguarundi wild cat found in forests in Central and South America. Up to 1.1 m/3.5 ft long, it is very slim with rather short legs and short rounded ears. It is uniformly coloured dark brown or chestnut. A good climber, it feeds on birds and small mammals and, unusually for a cat, has been reported to eat fruit. (Species *Felis yaguarondi*, family Felidae.)

Jahangir (1569–1627) adopted name of Salim, ('Holder of the World') Fourth Mogul emperor of India (1605–27), succeeding his father *Akbar the Great. The first part of his reign was marked by peace, prosperity, and a flowering of the arts, but the latter half by rebellion and succession conflicts.

jai alai another name for the ball game *pelota.

Jainism (Hindi *jaina* 'person who overcomes') ancient Indian religion, sometimes regarded as an offshoot of Hinduism. Jains emphasize the importance of not injuring living beings, and their code of ethics is based on sympathy and compassion for all forms of life. They also believe in *karma but not in any deity. It is a monastic, ascetic religion. There are two main sects: the Digambaras and the Swetambaras. Jainism practises the most extreme form of nonviolence (*ahimsa*) of all Indian sects, and influenced the philosophy of Mahatma Gandhi. Jains number approximately 6 million; there are Jain communities throughout the world but the majority live in India.

Jaipur capital of Rajasthan, India, 240 km/150 mi southeast of Delhi; population (2001 est) 2,324,300. Products include textiles and metal products, as well as distilling and the manufacture of glass, carpets, blankets, and footwear. Founded by Jai Singh II in 1728, it was formerly the capital of the state of Jaipur, which was merged with Rajasthan in 1949.

Jakarta or **Djakarta** formerly **Batavia** (1619–1949), capital of Indonesia on the northwest coast of Java, at the estuary of the River Liwung on Jakarta Bay, designated a special metropolitan district in 1966 with the status of a province; population (2000 est) 8,389,400. Jakarta forms the leading commercial and industrial zone of Indonesia, and industries include textiles, chemicals, plastics, and shipbuilding; a canal links it with its port of Tanjung Priok where timber, rubber, oil, tin, coffee, tea, and palm oil are among its exports. It is also a tourist centre.

Jakeš, Miloš (1922–) Czech communist politician, a member of the Politburo from 1981 and party leader 1987–89. A conservative, he supported the Soviet invasion of Czechoslovakia in 1968. He was forced to resign in November 1989 following a series of pro-democracy mass rallies.

Jalalabad capital of Nangarhar province, east Afghanistan, on the road from Kabul to Peshawar in Pakistan; population (2001 est) 154,200, of which the majority are Pathan (Pashtun). The town stands on the Kabul River, at a height of 590 m/1,940 ft, and lies on the route connecting Kabul and Peshawar via the Khyber Pass. Jalalabad is well-placed to handle much of the trade between Afghanistan to the west and Pakistan and India to the east, and is the commercial centre for the irrigated plain around it. It trades in almonds, rice, grain, and fruit, while industries include sugar refining and handicrafts.

Jamaica

Area: 10,957 sq km/4,230 sq mi
Capital: Kingston
Major towns/cities: Montego Bay, Spanish Town, St Andrew, Portmore, May Pen
Physical features: mountainous tropical island; Blue Mountains (so called because of the haze over them)
Head of state: Queen Elizabeth II from 1962, represented by Governor General Howard Cooke from 1991
Head of government: Percival Patterson from 1992
Political system: liberal democracy
Political executive: parliamentary
Political parties: Jamaica Labour Party (JLP), moderate, centrist; People's National Party (PNP), left of centre; National Democratic Union (NDM), centrist
Currency: Jamaican dollar
GNI per capita (PPP): (US$) 3,550 (2002 est)
Exports: alumina, bauxite, gypsum, sugar, bananas, garments, rum. Principal market: USA 39.3% (2000)
Population: 2,651,000 (2003 est)
Language: English (official), Jamaican Creole
Religion: Protestant 70%, Rastafarian
Life expectancy: 74 (men); 78 (women) (2000–05)
Chronology
c. **AD 900:** Settled by Arawak Indians, who gave the island the name Jamaica ('well watered').

1494: The explorer Christopher Columbus reached Jamaica.

1509: Occupied by Spanish; much of Arawak community died from exposure to European diseases; black African slaves brought in to work sugar plantations.

1655: Captured by Britain and became its most valuable Caribbean colony.

1838: Slavery abolished.

1870: Banana plantations established as sugar cane industry declined in face of competition from European beet sugar.

1938: Serious riots during the economic depression and, as a sign of growing political awareness, the People's National Party (PNP) was formed by Norman Manley.

1944: First constitution adopted.

1958–62: Part of West Indies Federation.

1959: Internal self-government granted.

1962: Independence achieved within the Commonwealth, with Alexander Bustamante of the centre-right Jamaica Labour Party (JLP) as prime minister.

1981: Diplomatic links with Cuba were severed, and a free-market economic programme was pursued.

1988: The island was badly damaged by Hurricane Gilbert.

1992: Percival Patterson of the PNP became prime minister.

1998: Violent crime increased as the economy declined.

2002: Patterson's PNP won the general election again, his third successive victory.

2004: Thousands of homes were destroyed by Hurrican Ivan.

2005: The number of murders increased, giving Jamaica one of the highest murder rates in the world. The increase was blamed on street gang violence.

James, Henry (1843–1916) US novelist, who lived in Europe from 1875 and became a naturalized British subject in 1915. His novels deal with the social, moral, and aesthetic issues arising from the complex relationship between European and American culture. They include *The Portrait of a Lady* (1881), *The Bostonians* (1886), *What Maisie Knew* (1887), *The Ambassadors* (1903), and *The Golden Bowl* (1904). He also wrote more than a hundred shorter works of fiction, notably the novella *The Aspern Papers* (1888) and the supernatural/psychological riddle *The Turn of the Screw* (1898).

James, Jesse Woodson (1847–1882) US bank and train robber. He was a leader, with his brother Frank (1843–1915), of the Quantrill raiders, a Confederate guerrilla band in the Civil War. Jesse was killed by Bob Ford, an accomplice; Frank remained unconvicted and became a farmer.

James, P(hyllis) D(orothy) (1920–) Baroness James of Holland Park, English detective novelist. She created the characters Superintendent Adam Dalgliesh and private investigator Cordelia Gray. She was a tax official, hospital administrator, and civil servant in the Home Office, involved with police matters, before turning to writing full time. Her books include *Death of an Expert Witness* (1977), *The Skull Beneath the Skin* (1982), *A Taste for Death* (1986), *Original Sin* (1994), *Certain Justice* (1997), *Death in Holy Orders* (2001), *The Murder Room* (2003), and her memoirs, *Time to be in Earnest: A Fragment of Autobiography* (1999). She was created a baroness in 1991.

James, William (1842–1910) US psychologist and philosopher. He was among the first to take an approach emphasizing the ends or purposes of behaviour and to advocate a scientific, experimental psychology. His *Varieties of Religious Experience* (1902) is one of the most important works on the psychology of religion.

James two kings of Britain:

James I (1566–1625) King of England from 1603 and Scotland (as **James VI**) from 1567. The son of Mary Queen of Scots and her second husband, Lord Darnley, he succeeded to the Scottish throne on the enforced abdication of his mother and assumed power in 1583. He established a strong centralized authority, and in 1589 married Anne of Denmark (1574–1619). As successor to Elizabeth I in England, he alienated the *Puritans by his High Church views and Parliament by his assertion of *divine right, and was generally unpopular because of his favourites, such as *Buckingham, and his schemes for an alliance with Spain. He was succeeded by his son Charles I.

James II (1633–1701) King of England and Scotland (as **James VII**) from 1685. The second son of Charles I, he succeeded his brother, Charles II. In 1660 James married Anne Hyde (1637–1671; mother of Mary II and Anne) and in 1673 *Mary of Modena (mother of James Edward Stuart). He became a Catholic in 1669, which led first to attempts to exclude him from the succession, then to the rebellions of *Monmouth and Argyll, and finally to the Whig and Tory leaders' invitation to William of Orange to take the throne in 1688. James fled to France, then led an uprising in Ireland in 1689, but after defeat at the Battle of the *Boyne (1690) remained in exile in France.

James seven kings of Scotland:

James I (1394–1437) King of Scotland (1406–37), who assumed power in 1424. He was a cultured and strong monarch whose improvements in the administration of justice brought him popularity among the common people. He was assassinated by a group of conspirators led by the Earl of Atholl.

James II (1430–1460) King of Scotland from 1437, who assumed power in 1449. The only surviving son of James I, he was supported by most of the nobles and parliament. He sympathized with the Lancastrians during the Wars of the *Roses, and attacked English possessions in southern Scotland. He was killed while besieging Roxburgh Castle.

James III (1451–1488) King of Scotland from 1460, who assumed power in 1469. His reign was marked by rebellions by the nobles, including his brother Alexander, Duke of Albany. He was murdered during a rebellion supported by his son, who then ascended the throne as James IV.

James IV (1473–1513) King of Scotland from 1488. He came to the throne after his followers murdered his father, James III, at Sauchieburn. His reign was internally peaceful, but he allied himself with France against England, invaded in 1513, and was defeated and killed at the Battle of *Flodden. James IV was a patron of poets and architects as well as a military leader.

James V (1512–1542) King of Scotland from 1513, who assumed power in 1528. During the long period of his minority, he was caught in a struggle between pro-French and pro-English factions. When he assumed power, he allied himself with France and upheld Catholicism against the Protestants. Following an attack on Scottish territory by Henry VIII's forces, he was defeated near the border at Solway Moss in 1542.

James VI of Scotland. See *James I of England.

James VII of Scotland. See *James II of England.

James Francis Edward Stuart (1688–1766) British prince, known as the **Old Pretender** (for the *Jacobites, he was James III). Son of James II, he was born at St James's Palace and after the *Glorious Revolution of 1688 was taken to France. He landed in Scotland in 1715 to head a Jacobite rebellion (the Fifteen) but withdrew through lack of support. In his later years he settled in Rome.

Jameson, Leander Starr (1853–1917) Scottish colonial administrator, born in Edinburgh, Scotland. In South Africa, early in 1896, he led the **Jameson Raid** from Mafeking into the Transvaal to support the non-Boer colonists there, in an attempt to overthrow the government (for which he served some months in prison). Returning to South Africa, he succeeded Cecil *Rhodes as leader of the Progressive Party of Cape Colony, where he was prime minister 1904–08. He was made 1st baronet in 1911.

James, St several Christian saints, including:
James, St (lived 1st century AD) called 'the Great', New Testament apostle, originally a Galilean fisherman. He was the son of Zebedee and brother of the apostle John. He was put to death by *Herod Agrippa. James is the patron saint of Spain. His feast day is 25 July.

Jammu and Kashmir state of north India; area 222,200 sq km/85,791 sq mi including area occupied by Pakistan and China; population (2001 est) 10,069,900 (Indian-occupied territory). The main cities are Jammu (winter capital), Srinagar (summer capital and the seat of state government), and Leh. The main industries include timber, silk, carpets, and handicrafts. The mountains, lakes, and rivers of the state are attractive to visitors, but the development of tourism has long been hindered by the unsettled political situation. (See *Kashmir.)

Janáček, Leoš (1854–1928) Czech composer. He became director of the Conservatory at Brno in 1919 and professor at the Prague Conservatory in 1920. His music, highly original and influenced by Moravian folk music, includes arrangements of folk songs, operas (*Jenufa*, (1904), *The Cunning Little Vixen* (1924)), and the choral *Glagolitic Mass* (1926).

Janata alliance of political parties in India formed in 1971 to oppose Indira Gandhi's *Congress Party. Victory in the election brought Morarji Desai to power as prime minister but he was unable to control the various groups within the alliance and resigned in 1979. His successors fared little better, and the elections of 1980 overwhelmingly returned Indira Gandhi to office.

Janata Dal or **People's Party** Indian centre-left coalition, formed in October 1988 under the leadership of V P Singh and comprising the Janata, Lok Dal (B), Congress (S), and Jan Morcha parties. In a loose alliance with the Hindu fundamentalist Bharatiya Janata Party and the Communist Party of India, the Janata Dal was victorious in the November 1989 general election, taking power out of the hands of the

Congress (I) Party. Following internal splits, its minority government fell in November 1990. Since 1992, several breakaway Janata Dal factions have been formed. The party has drawn particularly strong support from Hindu lower castes and, with its secular outlook, recently from Muslims. It formed the core of the new government of H D Deve Gowda in June 1996 and that of Inder Kumar Gujral in April 1997. In the 1998 general election the party formed part of the United Front, an alliance with regional parties, which lost much support and finished third in the hung parliament.

janissary (Turkish *yeniçeri* 'new force') bodyguard of the Ottoman sultan, the Turkish standing army from the late 14th century until 1826. Until the 16th century janissaries were Christian boys forcibly converted to Islam; after this time they were allowed to marry and recruit their own children. The bodyguard ceased to exist when it revolted against the decision of the sultan in 1826 to raise a regular force. The remaining janissaries were killed in battle or executed after being taken prisoner.

Jansenism Christian teaching of Cornelius Jansen, which divided the Roman Catholic Church in France in the mid-17th century. Emphasizing the more predestinatory approach of St Augustine of Hippo's teaching, Jansenism was supported by the philosopher Pascal and Antoine Arnauld (a theologian linked with the abbey of Port Royal). Jansenists were excommunicated in 1719.

Janus in Roman mythology, the god of all openings, including doorways and passageways, and the beginning of the day, month, and year. January was dedicated to him. He is represented as having two faces, one looking forwards and one back, (in sculpture, a **herm**), and was associated with wisdom because he knew the past and could foresee the future. In Roman ritual he was invoked first in a list of gods, and at the beginning of any enterprise.

Japan
National name: *Nihon-koku/State of Japan*

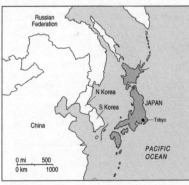

Area: 377,535 sq km/145,766 sq mi
Capital: Tokyo
Major towns/cities: Yokohama, Osaka, Nagoya, Fukuoka, Kitakyushu, Kyoto, Sapporo, Kobe, Kawasaki, Hiroshima
Major ports: Osaka, Nagoya, Yokohama, Kobe

Japan

Physical features: mountainous, volcanic (Mount Fuji, volcanic Mount Aso, Japan Alps); comprises over 1,000 islands, the largest of which are Hokkaido, Honshu, Kyushu, and Shikoku
Head of state: Emperor Akihito from 1989
Head of government: Junichiro Koizumi from 2001
Political system: liberal democracy
Political executive: parliamentary
Political parties: Liberal Democratic Party (LDP), right of centre; Shinshinto (New Frontier Party) opposition coalition, centrist reformist; Social Democratic Party of Japan (SDPJ, former Socialist Party), left of centre but moving towards centre; Shinto Sakigake (New Party Harbinger), right of centre; Japanese Communist Party (JCP), socialist; Democratic Party of Japan (DPJ), Sakigake and SDPJ dissidents; Komeito (Clean Government Party), reformist, pro-democratic
Currency: yen
GNI per capita (PPP): (US$) 26,070 (2002 est)
Exports: electrical machinery, motor vehicles, electronic goods and components, chemicals, iron and steel products, scientific and optical equipment. Principal market: USA 30.1% (2001)
Population: 127,654,000 (2003 est)
Language: Japanese (official), Ainu
Religion: Shinto, Buddhist (often combined), Christian (less than 1%)
Life expectancy: 78 (men); 85 (women) (2000–05)
Chronology
660 BC: According to legend, Jimmu Tenno, descendent of the Sun goddess, became the first emperor of Japan.
c. 400 AD: The Yamato, one of many warring clans, unified central Japan; Yamato chiefs are the likely ancestors of the imperial family.
5th–6th centuries: Writing, Confucianism, and Buddhism spread to Japan from China and Korea.
646: Start of Taika Reform: Emperor Kotoku organized central government on Chinese model.
794: Heian became imperial capital; later called Kyoto.
858: Imperial court fell under control of Fujiwara clan, who reduced the emperor to a figurehead.
11th century: Central government grew ineffectual; real power exercised by great landowners (daimyo) with private armies of samurai.
1185: Minamoto clan seized power under Yoritomo, who established military rule.
1192: Emperor gave Yoritomo the title of shogun (general); the shogun ruled in the name of the emperor.
1274: Mongol conqueror Kublai Khan attempted to invade Japan, making a second attempt in 1281; on both occasions Japan was saved by a typhoon.
1336: Warlord Takauji Ashikaga overthrew Minamoto shogunate; emperor recognized Ashikaga shogunate in 1338.
16th century: Power of Ashikagas declined; constant civil war.
1543: Portuguese sailors were the first Europeans to reach Japan; followed by Spanish, Dutch, and English traders.
1549: Spanish missionary St Francis Xavier began to preach Roman Catholic faith in Japan.
1585–98: Warlord Hideyoshi took power and attempted to conquer Korea in 1592 and 1597.
1603: Ieyasu Tokugawa founded new shogunate at Edo, reformed administration, and suppressed Christianity.

1630s: Japan adopted policy of isolation: all travel forbidden and all foreigners expelled except a small colony of Dutch traders in Nagasaki harbour.
1853: USA sent warships to Edo with demand that Japan open diplomatic and trade relations; Japan conceded in 1854.
1867: Revolt by isolationist nobles overthrew the Tokugawa shogunate.
1868: Emperor Mutsuhito assumed full powers, adopted the title *Meiji* ('enlightened rule'), moved imperial capital from Kyoto to Edo (renamed Tokyo), and launched policy of swift Westernization.
1894–95: Sino-Japanese War: Japan expelled Chinese from Korea.
1902–21: Japan entered a defensive alliance with Britain.
1904–05: Russo-Japanese War: Japan drove Russians from Manchuria and Korea; Korea annexed in 1910.
1914: Japan entered World War I and occupied German possessions in Far East.
1923: Earthquake destroyed much of Tokyo and Yokohama.
1931: Japan invaded Chinese province of Manchuria and created puppet state of Manchukuo; Japanese government came under control of military and extreme nationalists.
1937: Japan resumed invasion of China.
1940: After Germany defeated France, Japan occupied French Indo-China.
1941: Japan attacked US fleet at Pearl Harbor; USA and Britain declared war on Japan.
1942: Japanese conquered Thailand, Burma, Malaya, Dutch East Indies, Philippines, and northern New Guinea.
1945: USA dropped atomic bombs on Hiroshima and Nagasaki; Japan surrendered; US general Douglas MacArthur headed Allied occupation administration.
1947: MacArthur supervised introduction of democratic 'Peace Constitution', accompanied by demilitarization and land reform.
1952: Occupation ended.
1955: Liberal Democratic Party (LDP) founded with support of leading business people.
1956: Japan admitted to United Nations.
1950s–70s: Rapid economic development; growth of manufacturing exports led to great prosperity.
1993: An economic recession and financial scandals brought about the downfall of the LDP government in a general election. A coalition government was formed.
1995: An earthquake devastated Kobe.
1997: A financial crash occurred after bank failures.
1998: Keizo Obuchi, leader of the LDP, became prime minister, with Kiichi Miyazawa as finance minister. The government introduced a new $200 billion economic stimulus package, after GDP contracted 2% in 1998 in the worst recession since World War II.
2000: After Prime Minister Obuchi suffered a stroke, Yoshiro Mori was appointed in his place. The LDP lost its majority in elections in June, but formed a coalition government. The stock market remained weak and three ministers resigned amid a series of scandals.
2001: A US submarine accidentally sank a Japanese fishing trawler, killing nine people. Junichiro Koizumi replaced Yoshiro Mori as prime minister.
2002: Prime Minister Koizumi made a historic visit to communist North Korea, prompting an unprecedented

apology from North Korean leader Kim Jong Il for the abduction of about a dozen Japanese nationals by his country's special forces in the 1970s and 1980s. Koizumi apologized for Japan's occupation of Korea before and during World War II.

2003: The island of Hokkaido was struck by powerful earthquakes measuring up to 8.0 on the Richter scale, some of the strongest tremors in the world during 2003. In parliamentary elections Prime Minister Koizumi's LDP and its coalition partners retained power in the House of Representatives.

2004: Japan sent non-combat soldiers to Iraq, the first deployment of Japanese military since World War II. Japan launched an application for a permanent seat on the United Nations Security Council. An earthquake killed more than 30 people in the north of the country.

2005: Violent anti-Japanese demonstrations took place in China after publication of a Japanese textbook, allegedly minimizing Japan's actions during World War II.

Japanese art early Japanese art was heavily influenced by China and Korea. Like other Far Eastern countries, Japanese art represented nature from a more spiritual perspective rather than pursuing scientific realism; nature was seen as a part of a whole to be projected through the life and experience of the individual artist, a view that became more clearly expressed with the arrival of Buddhism in the 6th century. Painting gradually developed a distinct Japanese character, bolder and more angular, particularly with the spread of Zen Buddhism in the 12th century. Ink painting and calligraphy flourished, followed by book illustration and decorative screens. Japanese prints developed in the 17th century, with multicolour prints invented around 1765. Buddhist sculpture proliferated from 580, and Japanese sculptors excelled at portraits. Japanese pottery stresses simplicity.

Japanese language language of East Asia, spoken almost exclusively in the islands of Japan. Traditionally isolated, but possibly related to Korean, Japanese was influenced by Mandarin Chinese especially in the 6th–9th centuries and is written in Chinese-derived ideograms supplemented by two syllabic systems.

Jaruzelski, Wojciech Witold (1923–) Polish army general, appointed first secretary of the Polish United Workers Party (PUWP) in 1981. He was responsible for the imposition of martial law in Poland in December 1981. He was prime minister 1981–85 and president 1985–90. During martial law he attempted to suppress the *Solidarity trade union, interning its leaders and political dissidents. In 1989 he approved the 'Round Table' talks with the opposition that led to partially free parliamentary elections and to the appointment of a coalition government under a noncommunist prime minister, Tadeusz Mazowiecki.

jasmine any of a group of subtropical plants with white or yellow flowers. The common jasmine (*J. officinale*) has fragrant pure white flowers that yield jasmine oil, used in perfumes; the Chinese winter jasmine (*J. nudiflorum*) has bright yellow flowers that appear before the leaves. (Genus *Jasminum*, family Oleaceae.)

Jason in Greek mythology, the leader of the Argonauts who sailed in the *Argo* to Colchis in search of the *Golden Fleece. He eloped with *Medea, daughter of the king of Colchis, who had helped him achieve his goal, but later deserted her.

Jat an ethnic group living in Pakistan and northern India, and numbering about 11 million; they are the largest group in northern India. The Jat are predominantly farmers. They speak Punjabi, a language belonging to the Iranian branch of the Indo-European family. They are thought to be related to the Romany people.

jaundice yellow discoloration of the skin and whites of the eyes caused by an excess of bile pigment in the bloodstream. Approximately 60% of newborn babies exhibit some degree of jaundice, which is treated by bathing in white, blue, or green light that converts the bile pigment bilirubin into a water-soluble compound that can be excreted in urine. A serious form of jaundice occurs in rhesus disease (see *rhesus factor).

Jaurès, (Auguste Marie Joseph) Jean (Léon) (1859–1914) French socialist politician. He was considered a commanding intellectual presence within the socialist movement in France, through his writings (which included a magisterial social history of the French revolution), his oratory, and his journalism. In the decade leading up to the outbreak of World War I, Jaurès' impassioned opposition to the rising tide of militarism in Europe brought him centre stage within the Second International.

Java *or* **Jawa** *or* **Pulau Djawa** most populated island of Indonesia, situated between Sumatra and Bali; area (with the island of Madura) 132,000 sq km/51,000 sq mi; population (with Madura; 2000 est) 118,230,300. The capital is *Jakarta (which is also the capital of Indonesia). The island is divided into three provinces: Jawa Tengah, Jawa Timur, and Jawa Barat, together with Jakarta Raya (the Jakarta metropolitan district). About half the island is under cultivation, the rest being thickly forested. Mountains and sea breezes keep the temperature down, but humidity is high, with heavy rainfall from December to March. Ports include Surabaya and Semarang.

Javanese the largest ethnic group in the Republic of Indonesia. There are more than 50 million speakers of Javanese, which belongs to the western branch of the Austronesian family. Although the Javanese have a Hindu-Buddhist heritage, they are today predominantly Muslim, practising a branch of Islam known as *Islam Jawa*, which contains many Sufi features.

javelin spear used in athletics events. The men's javelin is about 260 cm/8.5 ft long, weighing 800 g/28 oz; the women's 230 cm/7.5 ft long, weighing 600 g/21 oz. It is thrown from a scratch line at the end of a run-up. The centre of gravity on the men's javelin was altered in 1986 to reduce the vast distances that were being thrown.

jaw one of two bony structures that form the framework of the mouth in all vertebrates except lampreys and hagfishes (the agnathous or jawless vertebrates). They consist of the upper jawbone (maxilla), which is fused to the skull, and the lower jawbone (mandible), which is hinged at each side to the bones of the temple by *ligaments.

jay any of several birds belonging to the crow family, generally brightly coloured and native to Europe, Asia, and the Americas. In the Eurasian **common jay** (*Garrulus glandarius*), the body is fawn with patches of white, blue, and black on the wings and tail. (Family Corvidae, order Passeriformes.)

jazz important type of popular music featuring solo virtuosic improvisation. It developed in the southern USA at the turn of the 20th century. Initially music for dancing, often with a vocalist, it had its roots in African-American and other popular music, especially ragtime. Developing from *blues and spirituals (religious folk songs) in the southern states, it first came to prominence in the early 20th century in New Orleans, St Louis, and Chicago, with a distinctive flavour in each city. Typical features found in all types of jazz are the modified rhythms of West Africa; the emphasis on improvisation; western European harmony emphasizing the dominant seventh and the ambiguity between the major and minor third (the so-called 'blue note'); characteristic textures and *timbres, first illustrated by a singer and rhythm section (consisting of a piano, bass, drums, and guitar, or a combination of these instruments), and later by the addition of the saxophone and various brass instruments, and later still by the adoption of electrically amplified instruments.

Jazz Age the hectic and exciting 1920s in the USA, when 'hot jazz' became fashionable as part of the general rage for spontaneity and social freedom. The phrase is attributed to the novelist F Scott Fitzgerald.

Jefferson, Thomas (1743–1826) 3rd president of the USA 1801–09, founder of the Democratic Republican Party. He published *A Summary View of the Rights of America* (1774) and as a member of the Continental Congresses of 1775–76 was largely responsible for the drafting of the *Declaration of Independence. He was governor of Virginia 1779–81, ambassador to Paris 1785–89, secretary of state 1789–93, and vice-president 1797–1801.

Jehovah or **Jahweh** or **Yahweh** in the Hebrew Bible (Old Testament), the name of God, revealed to Moses; in Hebrew texts it is represented by the letters YHVH (without the vowels 'a o a') because it was regarded as too sacred to be pronounced; other religions say the letters as Yahweh.

Jehovah's Witness member of a religious organization originating in the USA in 1872 under Charles Taze Russell (1852–1916). Jehovah's Witnesses attach great importance to Christ's second coming, which Russell predicted would occur in 1914, and which Witnesses still believe is imminent. All Witnesses are expected to take part in house-to-house preaching; there are no clergy.

Jekyll, Gertrude (1843–1932) English landscape gardener and writer. She created over 300 gardens, many in collaboration with the architect Edwin *Lutyens. In her books, she advocated colour design in garden planning and natural gardens of the cottage type, with plentiful herbaceous borders.

jellyfish marine invertebrate, belonging among the coelenterates (subphylum Cnidaria), with an umbrella-shaped body made of a semi-transparent jellylike substance, often tinted with blue, red, or orange colours, and having stinging tentacles that trail in the water. Most adult jellyfish move freely, but during parts of their life cycle many are polyp-like and attached to rocks, the seabed, or another underwater surface. They use the sense of smell in tracking prey, and feed on small animals that are paralysed by stinging cells in the jellyfish tentacles.

Jenkins, Roy (Harris) (1920–2003) Baron Jenkins of Hillhead, British politician and biographer, born in Monmouthshire, Wales. He became a Labour minister in 1964, was home secretary 1965–67 and 1974–76, and chancellor of the Exchequer 1967–70. He was president of the European Commission 1977–81. In 1981 he became one of the founders of the Social Democratic Party and was elected as an SDP MP in 1982, but lost his seat in 1987. In the same year, he was elected chancellor of Oxford University and made a life peer.

Jenner, Edward (1749–1823) English physician who pioneered vaccination. In Jenner's day, *smallpox was a major killer. His discovery in 1796 that inoculation with cowpox gives immunity to smallpox was a great medical breakthrough.

jerboa any of a group of small nocturnal rodents with long and powerful hind legs developed for leaping. There are about 25 species of jerboa, native to desert areas of North Africa and Southwest Asia. (Family Dipodidae.)

Jeremiah (lived 7th–6th century BC) Old Testament Hebrew prophet, whose ministry continued from 626 to 586 BC. He was imprisoned during *Nebuchadnezzar's siege of Jerusalem on suspicion of intending to desert to the enemy. On the city's fall, he retired to Egypt.

Jerome, St (c. 340–420) one of the early Christian leaders and scholars known as the Fathers of the Church. His Latin versions of the Old and New Testaments form the basis of the Roman Catholic Vulgate. He is usually depicted with a lion. His feast day is 30 September.

Jersey largest of the *Channel Islands; capital St Helier; area 117 sq km/45 sq mi; population (2001 est) 87,200. It is governed by a lieutenant governor, representing the English crown and an assembly. Jersey cattle were originally bred here. Jersey gave its name to a woollen garment.

Jerusalem Arabic **al-Quds**; Hebrew **Yerushalayim**, ancient city of Palestine, 762 m/2,500 ft above sea level, situated in hills 55 km/34 mi from the Mediterranean, divided in 1948 between Jordan and the new republic of Israel; area (pre-1967) 37.5 sq km/14.5 sq mi, (post-1967) 108 sq km/42 sq mi, including areas of the West Bank; population of the city (1997 est) 621,100; district (1997 est) 701,700. In 1950 the western New City was proclaimed as the Israeli capital, and, having captured from Jordan the eastern Old City in 1967, Israel affirmed in 1980 that the united city was the country's capital; the United Nations does not recognize East Jerusalem as part of Israel, and regards Tel Aviv-Yafo as the capital. In order to maintain the historical and religious character of the city, heavy industry has been discouraged and about two-thirds of the working population are employed in the service industry, including government and public services.

Jerusalem artichoke a variety of *artichoke.

Jesuit Society of Jesus the member of the largest and most influential Roman Catholic religious order founded by Ignatius *Loyola in 1534, with the aims of protecting Catholicism against the Reformation and carrying out missionary work. During the 16th and 17th centuries Jesuits took a leading role in the *Counter-Reformation, the defence of Catholicism against Protestantism – many, for instance, came to

England to work to undermine the Elizabethan religious settlement. Others worked as missionaries in Japan, China, Paraguay, and among the North American Indians. The order had (1991) about 29,000 members (15,000 priests plus students and lay members). There are Jesuit schools and universities.

Jesus (c. 6 BC–c. AD 30) *or* **Jesus Christ** Hebrew religious teacher on whose teachings *Christianity was founded. It is difficult to give a historically accurate account of his life. According to the four *Gospels of the *New Testament, Jesus was born in *Bethlehem, Palestine, son of God and the Virgin Mary, and brought up by Mary and her husband Joseph as a carpenter in *Nazareth. After adult *baptism, he gathered 12 *disciples, but his preaching antagonized the Jewish and Roman authorities and he was executed by *crucifixion. Three days later there came reports of his *resurrection and, later, his ascension to heaven.

jet in earth science, hard, black variety of lignite, a type of coal. It is cut and polished for use in jewellery and ornaments. Articles made of jet have been found in Bronze Age tombs.

jetfoil advanced type of *hydrofoil boat built by Boeing, propelled by water jets. It features horizontal, fully submerged hydrofoils fore and aft and has a sophisticated computerized control system to maintain its stability in all waters.

jet propulsion method of propulsion in which an object is propelled in one direction by a jet, or stream of gases, moving in the other. This follows from Isaac *Newton's third law of motion: 'To every action, there is an equal and opposite reaction.' The most widespread application of the jet principle is in the jet (gas turbine) engine, the most common kind of aircraft engine.

jet stream narrow band of very fast wind (velocities of over 150 kph/95 mph) found at altitudes of 10–16 km/ 6–10 mi in the upper troposphere or lower stratosphere. Jet streams usually occur about the latitudes of the Westerlies (35°–60°).

Jew follower of *Judaism, the Jewish religion. The term is also used to refer to those who claim descent from the ancient Hebrews, a Semitic people of the Middle East. Today, some may recognize their ethnic heritage but not practise the religious or cultural traditions. The term came into use in medieval Europe, based on the Latin name for Judeans, the people of Judah. Prejudice against Jews is termed *anti-Semitism.

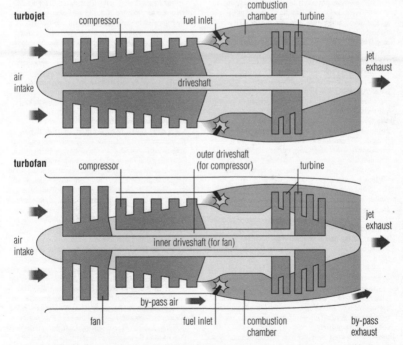

jet propulsion Two forms of jet engine. In the turbojet, air passing into the air intake is compressed by the compressor and fed into the combustion chamber where fuel burns. The hot gases formed are expelled at high speed from the rear of the engine, driving the engine forwards and turning a turbine which drives the compressor. In the turbofan, some air flows around the combustion chamber and mixes with the exhaust gases. This arrangement is more efficient and quieter than the turbojet.

Jew's harp musical instrument consisting of a two-pronged metal frame inserted between the teeth, and a springlike tongue plucked with the finger. The resulting drone excites resonances in the mouth. Changes in the shape of the mouth cavity will vary the pitch of these resonances to produce a melody.

Jharkhand state of northeast India, bordered by Bihar, West Bengal, Orissa, Chhattisgarh, and Uttar Pradesh; area 74,677 sq km/28,833 sq mi; population (2001 est) 26,909,400. It was carved from Bihar and was incorporated in November 2000. The capital is Ranchi. Jharkhand accounts for nearly half of India's mineral wealth, and there is an abundance of bauxite, limestone, mica, coal, iron, and copper ore. Industries include the Tata Iron and Steel Company and the Bokaro Steel Plant. The area is home to 30 tribal groups who are estimated to form one-third of the population. The principal languages spoken are Santali, Kurukh, Mundari, and Nagpuria.

Jiang Jie Shi (*or* Chiang Kai-shek) (1887–1975) Chinese nationalist Kuomintang (*Guomindang) general and politician, president of China 1928–31 and 1943–49, and of Taiwan from 1949, where he set up a US-supported right-wing government on his expulsion from the mainland by the communist forces. Jiang took part in the 1911 revolution that overthrew the Qing dynasty. He collaborated with the communists to fight against the Japanese from 1936, but lost the civil war against the communists in 1949.

Jiang Qing (*or* Chiang Ching) (1914–1991) Chinese communist politician, third wife of the party leader *Mao Zedong. In 1960 she became minister for culture, and played a key role in the 1966–69 *Cultural Revolution as the leading member of the Shanghai-based *Gang of Four, who attempted to seize power in 1976. She was arrested and in 1981 convicted of treason. She died in prison.

Jiang Qing-guo (*or* Chiang Ching-kuo) (1910–1988) Taiwanese politician, eldest son of Jiang Jie Shi (Chiang Kai-shek), prime minister 1972–78, president 1978–88. After Jiang Jie Shi's Kuomintang (*Guomindang, nationalist) forces fled to Taiwan in 1949, in the wake of the communist takeover of the Chinese mainland, Jiang Qing-guo worked to strengthen the security and intelligence forces and established a youth wing for the ruling Kuomintang. He became Taiwan's prime minister in 1972 and, after the death of his father in April 1975, Kuomintang leader and, from 1978, head of state.

Jiangsu *or* Kiangsu province on the coast of east China, bounded to the north by Shandong, to the east by the Yellow Sea, to the southeast by Shanghai, to the south by Zhejiang, and to the west by Anhui; area 102,200 sq km/39,450 sq mi; population (2000 est) 74,380,000, the most densely populated province in China. The capital is Nanjing, which is the province's major centre of industry, manufacturing iron and steel, petrochemicals, machine tools, motor vehicles, textiles, cement, and fertilizers.

Jiangxi *or* Kiangsi province of southeast China, bounded to the north by Hubei and Anhui, to the east by Zhejiang and Fujian, to the south by Guangdong, and to the west by Hunan; area 164,800 sq km/63,600 sq mi; population (2000 est) 41,400,000. The capital is Nanchang; other cities and towns include Ganzhou,

Ji'an, Jingdezhen, Jiujiang, and Pingxiang. The Chang Jiang River and Lake Poyang are found in the province. The main industries are porcelain, coal, tungsten, copper, and uranium; agricultural products include rice, tea, cotton, tobacco, and timber. The province was Mao Zedong's original base in the first phase of the communist struggle against the nationalists.

Jiang Zemin (1926–) Chinese communist politician, leader of the Chinese Communist Party (CCP) 1989–2002 and state president 1993–2003. He succeeded Zhao Ziyang as Communist Party leader after the Tiananmen Square massacre of 1989, and during the next decade he steered a middle course of market-centred economic reform while maintaining the CCP's monopoly of political power. Chinese exports were heavily promoted and foreign investment was attracted, leading to significant economic growth but also growing corruption. Jiang stepped down as party leader in November 2002 and as state president in March 2003, but retained significant power as chairman of the central military commission, overseeing the armed forces.

jihad (Arabic 'conflict') holy war undertaken by Muslims against nonbelievers. In the Mecca Declaration (1981), the Islamic powers pledged a jihad against Israel, though not necessarily military attack.

Jilin *or* Kirin province of northeast China, bounded to the northeast by Heilongjiang, to the southeast by Russia, to the south by North Korea, to the southwest by Liaoning, and to the northwest by Inner Mongolia; area 187,000 sq km/72,000 sq mi; population (2000 est) 27,280,000. The capital is Changchun, and other cities and towns include Jilin, Tonghua, Baicheng, and Liaoyuan. Major industries include coal, iron ore, engineering, food-processing, and chemicals; agricultural products include maize, sorghum, soybeans, and millet.

Jim Crow laws laws designed to enforce racial segregation and deny black Americans their civil rights. These laws originated in the 1880s and were common in the southern USA until the 1960s. The US Supreme Court decision *Plessy* v. *Ferguson* (1896) legitimized these laws by affirming segregation under the 'separate but equal' doctrine. Jim Crow laws were eroded by US Supreme Court decisions during the 1950s and 60s such as *Brown* v. *Board of Education* in 1954 – a landmark ruling which declared that segregation in schools was unconstitutional – and civil-rights legislation such as the Civil Rights Act 1964 and Voting Rights Act 1965. (See also *civil-rights movement.)

Jin dynasty (*or* Chin dynasty) hereditary rulers of northern China, including Manchuria and part of Mongolia, from 1122 to 1234, during the closing part of the *Song era (960–1279). The dynasty was founded by Juchen (Jurchen) nomad hunters, who sacked the northern Song capital Kaifeng in 1126, forcing the Song to retreat south to Hangzhou. The Jin eventually ruled northern China as far south as the Huai River. Over time, the Juchen became Sinicized, but from 1214 they lost much of their territory to the *Mongols led by Genghis Khan.

jingoism blinkered, war-mongering patriotism. The term originated in 1878, when the British prime minister Disraeli developed a pro-Turkish policy, which nearly involved the UK in war with Russia.

His supporters' war song included the line 'We don't want to fight, but by jingo if we do ...'.

Jinnah, Muhammad Ali (1876–1948) Indian politician, Pakistan's first governor general from 1947. He was president of the *Muslim League in 1916 and 1934–48, and by 1940 was advocating the need for a separate state of Pakistan. At the 1946 conferences in London he insisted on the partition of British India into Hindu and Muslim states.

jinni plural **jinn**, in Muslim mythology, a member of a class of spirits able to assume human or animal shape.

Joan of Arc, St (c. 1412–1431) French **Jeanne d'Arc**, French military leader who inspired the French at the Siege of Orléans 1428–29 and at the Battle of Patay, north of Orléans, in 1429. As a young peasant girl, she was the wrong age, class, and gender to engage in warfare, yet her 'heavenly voices' instructed her to expel the English, who had occupied northern France during the Hundred Years' War, and secure the coronation of *Charles VII of France. Because of her strength of character, she achieved both aims. Her subsequent attempt to take Paris was overambitious, however, and she was captured in May 1430 at Compiègne by the Burgundians, who sold her to the English. She was found guilty of witchcraft and heresy by a tribunal of French ecclesiastics who supported the English, and burned to death at the stake in Rouen on 30 May 1431.

Jodrell Bank site in Cheshire, England, of the Nuffield Radio Astronomy Laboratories of the University of Manchester. Its largest instrument is the 76-m/250-ft radio dish (the Lovell Telescope), completed in 1957, modified in 1970, and upgraded in 2001 and 2002, given a new surface and drive system. A 38 × 25-m/125 × 82-ft elliptical radio dish was introduced in 1964, capable of working at shorter wavelengths.

Joffre, Joseph Jacques Césaire (1852–1931) Marshal of France during World War I. He was chief of general staff in 1911. The German invasion of Belgium in 1914 took him by surprise, but his stand at the Battle of the *Marne resulted in his appointment as supreme commander of all the French armies in 1915. His failure to make adequate preparations at Verdun in 1916 and the military disasters on the *Somme led to his replacement by Nivelle in December 1916.

Johannesburg largest city of South Africa, situated on the Witwatersrand in Gauteng Province; population (city area, 1998 est) 849,600 (urban area, 1996 est) 2,200,000. It is the centre of a large gold-mining industry; other industries include engineering works, chemicals, paper, electrical goods, meat-chilling plants, and clothing factories. The city is also an important financial centre, with a stock exchange dating from 1887.

John, Augustus Edwin (1878–1961) Welsh painter. He is known for his vivacious portraits, including *The Smiling Woman* (1910; Tate Gallery, London), portraying his second wife, Dorelia McNeill. His sitters included such literary figures as Thomas Hardy, Dylan Thomas, W B Yeats, T E Lawrence, and James Joyce.

John (I) Lackland (1167–1216) King of England from 1199 and acting king from 1189 during his brother Richard (I) the Lion-Heart's absence on the Third Crusade. Although branded by contemporaries as cruel and power-hungry, he is now recognized as a hardworking, able, reforming monarch, who travelled the country tirelessly. He improved the legal system, was the first king to keep records of government writs, and built a large navy that defeated the French fleet before it could invade. He tried vigorously to extend his kingdom, conducting campaigns in Wales, Ireland, and Normandy, and cowing Scotland into a peace treaty. However, he lost Normandy and nearly all other English possessions in France by 1205. The taxes needed to finance his campaigns brought conflict with his barons, and he was forced to sign the *Magna Carta in 1215. Later repudiation of it led to the first *Barons' War 1215–17, during which he died. He was succeeded by his son Henry III.

John XXIII (1881–1963) born Angelo Giuseppe Roncalli, Pope from 1958. He improved relations with the USSR in line with his encyclical *Pacem in Terris/ Peace on Earth* (1963), established Roman Catholic hierarchies in newly emergent states, and summoned the Second Vatican Council, which reformed church liturgy and backed the ecumenical movement.

John six kings of Portugal, including:

John I (1357–1433) King of Portugal from 1385. An illegitimate son of Pedro I, he was elected by the Cortes (parliament). His claim was supported by an English army against the rival king of Castile, thus establishing the Anglo-Portuguese Alliance in 1386. He married Philippa of Lancaster, daughter of *John of Gaunt.

John Bull imaginary figure who is a personification of England, similar to the American Uncle Sam. He is represented in cartoons and caricatures as a prosperous farmer of the 18th century.

John Dory marine bony fish also called a *dory.

John of Gaunt (1340–1399) English noble and politician, fourth (and third surviving) son of Edward III, Duke of Lancaster from 1362. He distinguished himself during the Hundred Years' War. During Edward's last years, and the years before Richard II attained the age of majority, he acted as head of government, and Parliament protested against his corrupt rule.

John o' Groats village in the northeast of the Highland unitary authority, Scotland, about 3 km/2 mi west of Duncansby Head, the furthest point from *Land's End on the British mainland.

John Paul II (1920–2005) born Karol Jozef Wojtyla, Pope 1978–2005, the first non-Italian to be elected pope since 1522. He was born near Kraków, Poland. He upheld the tradition of papal infallibility and condemned artificial contraception, women priests, married priests, and modern dress for monks and nuns – views that aroused criticism from liberalizing elements in the church.

Johns, Jasper (1930–) US painter, sculptor, and printmaker. He was one of the foremost exponents of *pop art. He rejected abstract art, favouring such mundane subjects as flags, maps, and numbers as a means of exploring the relationship between image and reality. His work employs pigments mixed with wax (encaustic) to create a rich surface with unexpected delicacies of colour.

John, St (lived 1st century AD) New Testament apostle. Traditionally, he wrote the fourth Gospel and the Johannine Epistles (when he was bishop of Ephesus), and the Book of Revelation (while exiled to the Greek island of Patmos). His emblem is an eagle; his feast day is 27 December.

Johnson, Amy (1903–1941) English aviator. She made a solo flight from England to Australia in 1930, in 9½ days, and in 1932 made the fastest ever solo flight from England to Cape Town, South Africa. Her plane disappeared over the English Channel in World War II while she was serving with the Air Transport Auxiliary.

Johnson, Andrew (1808–1875) 17th president of the USA 1865–69, a Democrat. He was a congressman from Tennessee 1843–53, governor of Tennessee 1853–57, senator 1857–62, and vice-president in 1865. He succeeded to the presidency on Abraham Lincoln's assassination (15 April 1865). His conciliatory policy to the defeated South after the Civil War involved him in a feud with the Radical Republicans, culminating in his impeachment in 1868 before the Senate, which failed to convict him by one vote.

Johnson, Lyndon Baines (1908–1973) 36th president of the USA 1963–69, a Democrat. He was a member of Congress 1937–49 and the Senate 1949–60. Born in Texas, he brought critical Southern support as J F Kennedy's vice-presidential running mate in 1960, and became president on Kennedy's assassination.

Johnson, Philip Cortelyou (1906–2005) US architect and architectural historian. Originally designing in the international style of Mies van der Rohe, he later became an exponent of postmodernism. He designed the giant AT&T building in New York City in 1982 – a pink skyscraper with a Chippendale-style cabinet top.

Johnson, Samuel (1709–1784) also known as **Dr Johnson**, English lexicographer (writer of dictionaries), author, and critic. He was also a brilliant conversationalist and dominant figure in 18th-century London literary society. His *Dictionary* (1755) provided the pedigree for subsequent lexicography and remained authoritative for over a century. In 1764 he founded, at the suggestion of the English painter Joshua *Reynolds, a club, known from 1779 as the Literary Club, whose members at various times included also the Irish political philosopher Edmund *Burke, the Irish dramatist Oliver *Goldsmith, the English actor David *Garrick, and Scottish writer James *Boswell, Johnson's biographer.

John the Baptist, St (c. 12 BC–c. AD 27) In the New Testament, an itinerant preacher. After preparation in the wilderness, he proclaimed the coming of the Messiah and baptized Jesus in the River Jordan. He was later executed by *Herod Antipas at the request of Salome, who demanded that his head be brought to her on a platter.

joint point of movement or articulation in any animal with a skeleton. In vertebrates, it is the point where two bones meet. Some joints allow no motion (the sutures between the bones of the skull), others allow a very small motion (the sacroiliac joints in the lower vertebral column), but most allow a relatively free motion. Of these, some allow a gliding motion (one

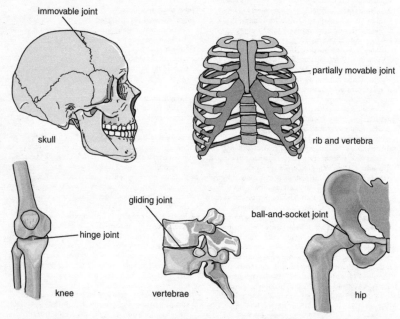

immovable joint

skull

partially movable joint

rib and vertebra

gliding joint

hinge joint

knee

vertebrae

ball-and-socket joint

hip

joint The different types of joint allow varying degrees of movement, for example hinge joints allow movement in only one direction whereas ball-and-socket joints allow almost 360° of movement, and the sutures of the skull allow for no movement at all.

vertebra of the spine on another), some have a hinge action (elbow and knee), and others allow motion in all directions (hip and shoulder joints) by means of a ball-and-socket arrangement.

joint venture in business, an undertaking in which an individual or legal entity of one country forms a company with those of another country, with risks being shared.

Joliot-Curie, Irène (1897–1956) French physicist, daughter of Pierre and Marie *Curie. She and her husband Frédéric Joliot were jointly awarded the Nobel Prize for Chemistry in 1935 for their discovery of artificial radioactivity. She was professor of physics at the Sorbonne from 1937, and director of the Radium Institute 1946–56.

Jolson, Al (1886–1950) stage name of Asa Yoelson, Russian-born US singer and entertainer. Popular in Broadway theatre and vaudeville, he was chosen to star in the first talking picture, *The Jazz Singer* (1927).

Jones, Inigo (1573–1652) English classical architect. He introduced the Palladian style to England. He was employed by James I to design scenery for Ben Jonson's masques and was appointed Surveyor of the King's Works 1615–42. He designed the Queen's House, Greenwich (1616–35), and the Banqueting House in Whitehall, London (1619–22).

jonquil species of small *daffodil, with yellow flowers. It is native to Spain and Portugal, and is cultivated in other countries. (*Narcissus jonquilla*, family Amaryllidaceae.)

Jonson, Ben(jamin) (1572–1637) English dramatist, poet, and critic. *Every Man in his Humour* (1598) established the English 'comedy of humours', in which each character embodies a 'humour', or vice, such as greed, lust, or avarice. This was followed by *Cynthia's Revels* (1600) and *The Poetaster* (1601). His first extant tragedy is *Sejanus* (1603), with Burbage and Shakespeare as members of the original cast. His great comedies are *Volpone, or The Fox* (1606), *The Alchemist* (1610), and *Bartholomew Fair* (1614). He wrote extensively for court entertainment in the form of *masques produced with scenic designer Inigo *Jones.

Joplin, Scott (1868–1917) US *ragtime pianist and composer. He was considered the leading representative of 'classic rag', in which the standard syncopated rhythm was treated with some sophistication. His 'Maple Leaf Rag' (1899) was the first instrumental sheet music to sell a million copies, and 'The Entertainer' (1902), as the Academy Award-winning theme tune of the film *The Sting* (1973), revived his popularity. He was an influence on Jelly Roll Morton and other early jazz musicians.

Jordan Arabic **Nahr al-Urdunn**; Hebrew **Ha-Yarden**, river rising on Mount Hermon, Syria, at 550 m/ 1,800 ft above sea level and flowing south for about 320 km/200 mi via the Lake of Tiberias (the Sea of Galilee) to the Dead Sea, 390 m/1,290 ft below sea level. It is the lowest river in the world. It occupies the northern part of the Great Rift Valley; its upper course forms the boundary of Israel with Syria and the kingdom of Jordan; its lower course runs through Jordan. The West Bank has been occupied by Israel since 1967.

Jordan

National name: *Al-Mamlaka al-Urduniyya al-Hashemiyyah/Hashemite Kingdom of Jordan*

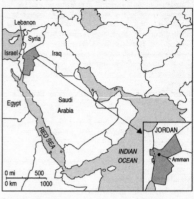

Area: 89,206 sq km/34,442 sq mi (excluding the West Bank 5, 879 sq km/2,269 sq mi)
Capital: Amman
Major towns/cities: Zarqa, Irbid, Saet, Ma'an
Major ports: Aqaba
Physical features: desert plateau in east; Rift Valley separates east and west banks of River Jordan
Head of state: King Abdullah ibn Hussein from 1999
Head of government: Faisal al-Fayez from 2003
Political system: emergent democracy
Political executive: parliamentary
Political parties: independent groups loyal to the king predominate; of the 21 parties registered since 1992, the most significant is the Islamic Action Front (IAF), Islamic fundamentalist
Currency: Jordanian dinar
GNI per capita (PPP): (US$) 4,070 (2002 est)
Exports: phosphate, potash, fertilizers, foodstuffs, pharmaceuticals, fruit and vegetables, cement. Principal market: India 11.7% (2001)
Population: 5,473,000 (2003 est)
Language: Arabic (official), English
Religion: over 90% Sunni Muslim (official religion), small communities of Christians and Shiite Muslims
Life expectancy: 70 (men); 73 (women) (2000–05)
Chronology
13th century BC: Oldest known 'states' of Jordan, including Gideon, Ammon, Moab, and Edom, established.
c. 1000 BC: East Jordan was part of kingdom of Israel, under David and Solomon.
4th century BC: Southeast Jordan occupied by the independent Arabic-speaking Nabataeans.
64 BC: Conquered by the Romans and became part of the province of Arabia.
AD 636: Became largely Muslim after the Byzantine forces of Emperor Heraclius were defeated by Arab armies at battle of Yarmuk, in northern Jordan.
1099–1187: Part of Latin Kingdom established by Crusaders in Jerusalem.
from early 16th century: Part of Turkish Ottoman Empire, administered from Damascus.

1920: Trans-Jordan (the area east of the River Jordan) and Palestine (which includes the West Bank) placed under British administration by League of Nations mandate.

1923: Trans-Jordan separated from Palestine and recognized by Britain as a substantially independent state under the rule of Emir Abdullah ibn Hussein, a member of the Hashemite dynasty of Arabia.

1946: Trans-Jordan achieved independence from Britain, with Abd Allah as king; name changed to Jordan.

1948: British mandate for Palestine expired, leading to fighting between Arabs and Jews, who each claimed the area.

1950: Jordan annexed West Bank; 400,000 Palestinian refugees flooded into Jordan, putting pressure on the economy.

1952: Partially democratic constitution introduced.

1958: Jordan and Iraq formed Arab Federation that ended when Iraqi monarchy was deposed.

1967: Israel defeated Egypt, Syria, and Jordan in Arab–Israeli Six-Day War, and captured and occupied the West Bank, including Arab Jerusalem. Martial law imposed.

1970–71: Jordanians moved against increasingly radicalized Palestine Liberation Organization (PLO), which had launched guerrilla raids on Israel from Jordanian territory, resulting in bloody civil war, before the PLO leadership fled abroad.

1976: Political parties were banned and elections postponed until further notice.

1980: Jordan emerged as an important ally of Iraq in its war against Iran, an ally of Syria, with whom Jordan's relations were tense.

1984: Women voted for the first time; the parliament was recalled.

1985: King Hussein ibn Tal Abdulla el Hashim and PLO leader Yassir Arafat put forward a framework for a Middle East peace settlement. There was a secret meeting between Hussein and the Israeli prime minister.

1988: Hussein announced his willingness to cease administering the West Bank as part of Jordan, passing responsibility to the PLO; parliament was suspended.

1989: There were riots over price increases of up to 50% following a fall in oil revenues. In the first parliamentary elections for 23 years the Muslim Brotherhood won 25 of 80 seats but were exiled from government.

1990: Hussein unsuccessfully tried to mediate after Iraq's invasion of Kuwait. There were huge refugee problems as thousands fled to Jordan from Kuwait and Iraq.

1991: 24 years of martial law ended, the ban on political parties was lifted, and Jordan remained neutral during the Gulf War involving Iraq.

1993: Candidates loyal to Hussein won a majority in the parliamentary elections; several leading Islamic fundamentalists lost their seats.

1994: An economic cooperation pact was signed with the PLO. A peace treaty was signed with Israel, ending the 46-year-old state of war.

1999: King Hussein died and his eldest son, Abdullah, succeeded him. Ali Abu al-Ragheb was appointed prime minister. In May, Abdullah held talks with Yassir Arafat prior to Israeli peace negotiations.

2002: In the first-ever assassination of a Western embassy official in Jordan, US diplomat Lawrence Foley was shot dead by a lone assailant in Amman.

2003: In elections, non-partisan candidates loyal to King Abdullah II won a majority in the lower house of parliament. The fundamentalist Islamic Action Front, together with other Islamist sympathizers, won 24 seats. The king retained the power to veto bills and rule by decree.

2004: King Abdullah II and president of Syria, Bashar al-Assad, launched the Wahdah Dam project. Jordan and Israel agreed to build a science centre on their common border. Al-Qaeda suspects were arrested on suspicion of planning an attack on the intelligence services in Amman.

2005: A new Jordanian ambassador was installed in Israel, the previous ambassador having been recalled in 2000. The government resigned and a new cabinet was installed, led by Prime Minister Adnan Badran.

Josephine, Marie Josèphe Rose Tascher de la Pagerie (1763–1814) as wife of *Napoleon Bonaparte, she was empress of France 1804–09. Born on the island of Martinique, she married in 1779 Alexandre de Beauharnais, who played a part in the French Revolution, and in 1796 Napoleon, who divorced her in 1809 because she had not produced children.

Josephson junction device used in 'superchips' (large and complex integrated circuits) to speed the passage of signals by a phenomenon called 'electron tunnelling'. Although these superchips respond a thousand times faster than the *silicon chip, they have the disadvantage that the components of the Josephson junctions operate only at temperatures close to *absolute zero. They are named after English theoretical physicist Brian Josephson.

Jospin, Lionel (1937–) French socialist politician, first secretary of the Socialist Party (PS) 1981–88 and 1995–97, then prime minister, under President Jacques *Chirac, from June 1997 to April 2002 heading a 'pluralist left' coalition with communist, green, and left radical parties.

Josquin Des Prez (*or* **Josquin des Prés) (1440–1521)** Franco-Flemish composer. His combination of Flemish counterpoint and Italian harmony, learnt while in the service of the Rome papal chapel in 1484–1503, marks a peak in Renaissance vocal music. In addition to Masses on secular as well as sacred themes, including the *Missa 'L'Homme armé'/ Mass on 'The Armed Man'* (1504), he also wrote secular chansons such as 'El grillo'/'The Cricket' using vocal effects that imitate each other.

joule symbol J, SI unit of work and energy (such as *potential energy, *kinetic energy, or electrical energy).

Joule, James Prescott (1818–1889) English physicist. His work on the relations between electrical, mechanical, and chemical effects led to the discovery of the first law of *thermodynamics.

Joyce, James (Augustine Aloysius) (1882–1941) Irish writer. His originality lies in evolving a literary form to express the complexity of the human mind, and he revolutionized the form of the English novel with his linguistic technique which had a far-reaching influence on many modern authors. His works include the short story collection *Dubliners* (1914), *A Portrait of the Artist as a Young Man* (1916), *Ulysses* (1922), and *Finnegans Wake* (1939). *Ulysses*, which records the events of a single day in Dublin, experiments with language and *parody, imitating and sometimes mocking different styles of writing. It combines direct narrative with the unspoken and unconscious reactions of the characters, which is sometimes known as the *stream of consciousness technique. Banned at first for obscenity in the USA and the UK, it made a great impact and is generally regarded as Joyce's masterpiece. He is known as a major figure in the artistic movement of *modernism.

Juan Carlos (1938–) King of Spain. The son of Don Juan, pretender to the Spanish throne, he married Princess Sofia, eldest daughter of King Paul of Greece, in 1962. In 1969 he was nominated by *Franco to succeed on the restoration of the monarchy intended to follow Franco's death; his father was excluded because of his known liberal views. Juan Carlos became king in 1975, and played a vital role in the smooth transition to democratic stability. He was instrumental in the defeat of an attempted military coup in 1981.

Judah or **Judaea** name used in Graeco-Roman times for the southernmost district of Palestine, now divided between Israel and Jordan. After the death of King Solomon in 922 BC, Judah adhered to his son Rehoboam and the Davidic line, whereas the rest of Israel elected Jeroboam as ruler of the northern kingdom. In New Testament times, Judah was the Roman province of Judaea, and in current Israeli usage it refers to the southern area of the West Bank.

Judaism the religion of the ancient Hebrews and their descendants the Jews, based, according to the Old Testament, on a covenant between God and Abraham about 2000 BC, and the renewal of the covenant with Moses about 1200 BC. Judaism is the oldest monotheistic faith, the forebear of Christianity and Islam. It rests on the concept of one eternal invisible God, whose will is revealed in the Torah and who has a special relationship with the Jewish people. The Torah comprises the first five books of the Hebrew Bible (the Pentateuch), which contains the history, laws, and guide to life for correct behaviour. The Jews were dispersed from Palestine (the *diaspora) by the Romans AD 70–135, eventually establishing communities in Europe, North Africa, Asia, and the Middle East. Today, Jewish communities exist throughout the world, including large populations in the USA, the former USSR (mostly Russia, Ukraine, Belarus, and Moldova), the UK and Commonwealth nations. The Jewish state of Israel was proclaimed in 1948. There are approximately 18 million Jews, with about 9 million in the Americas, 5 million in Europe, and 4 million in Asia, Africa, and the Pacific.

Judas Iscariot (lived 1st century AD) in the New Testament, the disciple who betrayed Jesus Christ. Judas was the treasurer of the group. At the last Pesach (Passover) supper, he arranged, for 30 pieces of silver, to point out Jesus to the chief priests so that they could arrest him. Afterward, Judas was overcome with remorse and committed suicide.

Jude, St (lived 1st century AD) supposed half-brother of Jesus and writer of the Epistle of Jude in the New Testament; patron saint of lost causes. Feast day 28 October.

judicial review in English law, action in the High Court to review the decisions of lower courts, tribunals, and administrative bodies. Various court orders can be made: certiorari (which quashes the decision);

mandamus (which commands a duty to be performed); **prohibition** (which commands that an action should not be performed because it is unauthorized); a **declaration** (which sets out the legal rights or obligations); or an injunction.

judiciary in constitutional terms, the system of courts and body of judges in a country. The independence of the judiciary from other branches of the central authority is generally considered to be an essential feature of a democratic political system. This independence is often written into a nation's constitution and protected from abuse by politicians.

Judith in the Old Testament, a Jewish widow who saved her community from a Babylonian siege by pretending to seduce, and then beheading, the enemy general Holofernes. Her story is much represented in Western art.

judo (Japanese *ju do*, 'gentle way') form of wrestling of Japanese origin. The two combatants wear loose-fitting, belted jackets and trousers to facilitate holds, and falls are broken by a square mat; when one has established a painful hold that the other cannot break, the latter signifies surrender by slapping the ground with a free hand. Degrees of proficiency are indicated by the colour of the belt: for novices, white, then yellow, orange (2 degrees), green (2 degrees), blue (2 degrees), brown (2 degrees), then black (Dan grades; 10 degrees, of which 1st to 5th Dan wear black belts, 6th to 9th wear red and white, and 10th wears solid red).

Juggernaut or **Jagannath** a name for Vishnu, the Hindu god, meaning 'Lord of the World'. His temple is in Puri, Orissa, India. A statue of the god, dating from about 318, is annually carried in procession on a large vehicle (hence the word 'juggernaut'). Devotees formerly threw themselves beneath its wheels.

jugular vein one of two veins in the necks of vertebrates; they return blood from the head to the superior (or anterior) *vena cava and thence to the heart.

jujitsu or **jujutsu** traditional Japanese form of self-defence; the modern form is *judo.

jujube any of a group of trees belonging to the buckthorn family, with berrylike fruits. The common jujube (*Z. jujuba*) of Asia, Africa, and Australia, cultivated in southern Europe and California, has fruit the size of small plums, known as Chinese dates when preserved in syrup. See also *lotus. (Genus *Zizyphus*, family Rhamnaceae.)

Julian the Apostate (332–363) Roman emperor. Born in Constantinople, the nephew of Constantine the Great, he was brought up as a Christian but early in life became a convert to paganism. Sent by Constantius to govern Gaul in 355, he was proclaimed emperor by his troops in 360, and in 361 was marching on Constantinople when Constantius' death allowed a peaceful succession. He revived pagan worship and refused to persecute heretics. He was killed in battle against the Persians of the *Sassanian Empire.

Julius II (1443–1513) born Giuliano della Rovere, Pope (1503–13). A politician who wanted to make the Papal States the leading power in Italy, he formed international alliances first against Venice and then against France. He began the building of St Peter's Church in Rome in 1506 and was a patron of the artists Michelangelo and Raphael.

July Revolution revolution 27–29 July 1830 in France that overthrew the restored Bourbon monarchy of Charles X and substituted the constitutional monarchy of Louis Philippe, whose rule (1830–48) is sometimes referred to as the July Monarchy.

jumbo jet popular name for a generation of huge, wide-bodied airliners including the Boeing 747, which is 71 m/232 ft long, has a wingspan of 60 m/196 ft, a maximum takeoff weight of nearly 400 tonnes, and can carry more than 400 passengers.

Jung, Carl Gustav (1875–1961) Swiss psychiatrist. He collaborated with Sigmund *Freud from 1907 until their disagreement in 1914 over the importance of sexuality in causing psychological problems. Jung studied myth, religion, and dream symbolism, saw the unconscious as a source of spiritual insight, and distinguished between introversion and extroversion.

juniper any of a group of aromatic evergreen trees or shrubs of the cypress family, found throughout temperate regions. Junipers produce a valuable wood and their berries are used to flavour gin and in cooking. Some junipers are mistakenly called *cedars. (Genus *Juniperus*, family Cupressaceae.)

junk bond derogatory term for a security officially rated as 'below investment grade'. Junk bonds are fixed interest loans paying above average levels of interest with corresponding above average levels of risk. Junk bonds became popular in the USA during the 1980s economic boom. They are commonly used to raise capital quickly, typically to finance takeovers to be paid for by the sale of assets once the company is acquired. This method of financing takeovers normally beyond a company's reach was invented by US-born bond trader Michael Milken. The problem with this strategy as it was used in the 1980s was that, following the takeover, the resulting company was so highly geared that its debt repayments eroded any potential profits.

Juno in Roman mythology, the principal goddess, identified with the Greek *Hera. The wife of Jupiter and queen of heaven, she was concerned with all aspects of women's lives and also regarded as a patroness of commerce.

junta (Spanish 'council') the military rulers of a country, especially after an army takeover, as in Turkey in 1980. Other examples include Argentina, under Juan Perón and his successors; Chile, under Augusto Pinochet; Paraguay, under Alfredo Stroessner; Peru, under Manuel Odría; Uruguay, under Juan Bordaberry, and Myanmar since 1988. Juntas rarely remain collective bodies, eventually becoming dominated by one member.

Jupiter fifth planet from the Sun and the largest in the Solar System, with a mass equal to 70% of all the other planets combined and 318 larger than that of the Earth. Its main feature is the Great Red Spot, a cloud of rising gases, 14,000 km/8,500 mi wide and 30,000 km/20,000 mi long, revolving anticlockwise. **mean distance from the Sun:** 778 million km/484 million mi **equatorial diameter:** 142,800 km/88,700 mi **rotation period:** 9 hours 51 minutes **year:** 11.86 Earth years **atmosphere:** consists of clouds of white ammonia crystals, drawn out into belts by the planet's high speed of rotation (the fastest of any planet). Darker orange and brown clouds at lower levels may contain sulphur, as well as simple organic compounds. Temperatures range from –140 °C/–220 °F in the upper atmosphere to

as much as 24,000 °C/43,000 °F near the core. This is the result of heat left over from Jupiter's formation, and it is this that drives the turbulent weather patterns of the planet. The Great Red Spot was first observed in 1664. Its top is higher than the surrounding clouds; its colour is thought to be due to red phosphorus. The Southern Equatorial Belt in which the Great Red Spot occurs is subject to unexplained fluctuation. In 1989 it sustained a dramatic and sudden fading. Jupiter's strong magnetic field gives rise to a large surrounding magnetic 'shell', or magnetosphere, from which bursts of radio waves are detected. Jupiter's faint rings are made up of dust from its moons, particularly the four inner moons **surface:** largely composed of hydrogen and helium, which under the high pressure and temperature of the interior behave not as a gas but as a supercritical fluid. Under even more extreme conditions, at a depth of 30,000 km/18,000 mi, hydrogen transforms into a metallic liquid. Jupiter probably has a molten rock core whose mass is 15 to 20 times greater than that of the Earth In 1995, the *Galileo probe revealed Jupiter's atmosphere to consist of 0.2% water, less than previously estimated **satellites:** Jupiter has 28 known moons. The four largest moons, Io, Europa (which is the size of the Moon), Ganymede, and Callisto, are the Galilean satellites, discovered in 1610 by *Galileo Galilei (Ganymede, which is larger than Mercury, is the largest moon in the Solar System). Three small moons were discovered in 1979 by the US *Voyager probes, as was a faint ring of dust around Jupiter's equator 55,000 km/34,000 mi above the cloud tops. One of Jupiter's small inner moons, Almathea (diameter 250 km/155 mi), was shown by pictures from the Galileo probe in April 2000 to have a long, narrow, bright region, as yet unidentified. A new moon was first observed in orbiting Jupiter in October 1999 by US researchers at the Kitt Peak Observatory, Arizona. It was thought to be an asteroid and named S/1999J1, but was confirmed to be a moon in July 2000. The moon is only 5 km/3 mi in diameter and orbits Jupiter once every two years at a distance of 24 million km/15 million mi. Ten previously unobserved moons were discovered orbiting Jupiter in November and December 2000. These moons are all believed to be less than 5 km/3.1 mi in diameter, and were observed by astronomers at the Mauna Kea observatory, Hawaii.

Jupiter *or* **Jove** (Latin *Diovis pater* 'father of heaven') in Roman mythology, the supreme god reigning on Mount Olympus, identified with the Greek *Zeus; son of Saturn and Ops; and husband of Juno, his sister. His titles included Fulgur (thrower of lightning), Tonans (maker of thunder), Invictus (protector in battle), and Triumphator (bestower of victory). His main temple was on the Capitoline Hill in Rome; destination of the solemn triumphal processions of victorious generals. As the particular protector of Rome, he was honoured by consuls taking office.

Jura island of the Inner *Hebrides, Argyll and Bute; area 380 sq km/147 sq mi; population (1991) 196. It is separated from the Scottish mainland by the **Sound of Jura**. The whirlpool Corryvreckan (Gaelic 'Brecan's cauldron') is off the north coast. It has a range of mountains known as the 'Paps of Jura', the highest of which is Beinn an Oir at 784 m/2,572 ft.

Jura Mountains series of parallel mountain ranges running along the French–Swiss frontier between the Rivers Rhône and Rhine, a distance of 250 km/156 mi. The highest peak is Crête de la Neige (1,723 m/5,650 ft). The mountains give their name to the Jura *département* of France, and in 1979 a Jura canton was established in Switzerland, formed from the French-speaking areas of Berne.

Jurassic period period of geological time 208–146 million years ago; the middle period of the Mesozoic era. Climates worldwide were equable, creating forests of conifers and ferns; dinosaurs were abundant, birds evolved, and limestones and iron ores were deposited.

jurisprudence the science of law in the abstract – that is, not the study of any particular laws or legal system, but of the principles upon which legal systems are founded.

jury body of lay people (usually 12) sworn to decide the facts of a case and reach a verdict in a court of law. Juries, used mainly in English-speaking countries, are implemented primarily in criminal cases, but also sometimes in civil cases; for example, inquests and libel trials.

justice of the peace (JP) in England, an unpaid *magistrate. In the USA, where JPs receive fees and are usually elected, their courts are the lowest in the states, and deal only with minor offences, such as traffic violations; they may also conduct marriages.

Justinian (*c.* 483–565) born Flavius Anicianus Justinianus, East Roman emperor 527–565, renowned for overseeing the reconquest of Africa, Italy, and parts of Spain. He ordered the codification of Roman law, which has influenced European jurisprudence; he built the church of Hagia Sophia in Constantinople, and closed the university in Athens in 529. His achievements, however, were short-lived. His reconquests and ambitious building projects overstretched the empire's resources and within a few years of his death much of his newly conquered territory had been lost.

jute fibre obtained from two plants of the linden family: *C. capsularis* and *C. olitorius*. Jute is used for sacks and sacking, upholstery, webbing (woven strips used to support upholstery), string, and stage canvas. (Genus *Corchorus*, family Tiliaceae.)

Jute member of a Germanic people who originated in Jutland but later settled in Frankish territory. They occupied Kent, southeast England, in about 450, according to tradition under Hengist and Horsa, and conquered the Isle of Wight and the opposite coast of Hampshire in the early 6th century.

Jutland Danish **Jylland**, peninsula of northern Europe; area 29,500 sq km/11,400 sq mi. It is separated from Norway by the Skagerrak and from Sweden by the Kattegat strait, with the North Sea to the west. The larger northern part belongs to Denmark, the southern part to Germany.

Jutland, Battle of World War I naval battle between British and German forces on 31 May 1916, off the west coast of Jutland. Its outcome was indecisive, but the German fleet remained in port for the rest of the war.

Juvenal (*c.* AD 60–140) born Decimus Junius Juvenalis, Roman satirical poet. His 16 surviving *Satires* give an explicit and sometimes brutal picture of the corrupt Roman society of his time. Very little is known of his life, but his native place, if not his birthplace, was Aquinum (now Aquino, southern Italy). Juvenal is twice mentioned by *Martial, and he may be the author of a well-known dedication (probably to an altar to Ceres) by one Juvenal who held military rank and some civil offices at Aquinum. This reference to military service agrees with the story of Sidonius Apollinaris (5th century) that Juvenal quarrelled with Paris, a famous ballet dancer in the reign of Domitian, and was sent to the Egyptian frontier as an officer of a local garrison.

K symbol for **kelvin**, a scale of temperature.

K2 *or* **Chogori** second-highest mountain above sea level, 8,611 m/28,251 ft, in the Karakoram range, in a disputed region of Pakistan. It was first climbed in 1954 by an Italian expedition.

Kaaba (Arabic 'chamber') in Mecca, Saudi Arabia, an oblong building in the quadrangle of the Great Mosque, into the northeastern corner of which is built the Black Stone declared by the prophet Muhammad to have been given to Abraham by the archangel Gabriel, and revered by Muslims.

Kabardino-Balkaria *or* **Kabardino-Balkariya** republic in the far southwestern Russian Federation, on the border with Georgia; area 12,500 sq km/4,826 sq mi; population (1996) 790,000 (58% urban) (48% Kabarda, 32% Russians, 9% Balkars). The capital is Nalchik, and other cities include Tyrnyauz and Prokhladnyy. The republic is on the northern slopes and foothills of the main Caucasus mountain range and contains the highest Caucasian peaks (Elbrus and Dykh Tau). It is crossed by the Rivers Terek, the Chegem, the Cherek, and the Baksan. Mineral deposits include wolfram, molybdenum, lead, zinc, and coal.

Kabbalah *or* **Kabbala** *or* **Cabbala** (Hebrew 'tradition') ancient esoteric Jewish mystical tradition of philosophy containing strong elements of pantheism, yet akin to neo-Platonism. Kabbalistic writing reached its peak between the 13th and 16th centuries. It is largely rejected by modern Judaic thought as medieval superstition, but has influenced the ultra-Orthodox *Hasidic and Lubavitch sects.

Kabinda part of Angola; see *Cabinda.

Kabul *or* **Kabol** capital of Afghanistan, capital of Kabul province, and the leading economic and cultural centre of Afghanistan, lying at an altitude of 1,800 m/5,900 ft above sea level, on the River Kabul; population (2001 est) 2,080,000 (the majority Farsi-speaking Tajiks, with a large Pathan (Pashtun) minority). Products include textiles, plastics, leather, and glass. It commands the strategic routes to Pakistan via the *Khyber Pass. The city was captured by the Taliban on 27 September 1996, and recaptured in November 2001 by forces of the Northern Alliance during the US-led War on Terrorism.

Kafka, Franz (1883–1924) Austrian novelist. He wrote in German. His three unfinished allegorical novels *Der Prozess/The Trial* (1925), *Das Schloss/The Castle* (1926), and *Amerika/America* (1927) were

posthumously published despite his instructions that they should be destroyed. His short stories include 'Die Verwandlung/The Metamorphosis' (1915), in which a man turns into a huge insect. His vision of lonely individuals trapped in bureaucratic or legal labyrinths can be seen as a powerful metaphor for modern experience.

Kahlo, Frida (1907–1954) Mexican painter. Using vivid colour and a naive style that was deliberately based on Mexican folk art, she created deeply personal, moving, and emotional paintings. Often referred to as an 'autobiographical' artist, she is known primarily for her surreal self-portraits in which she explored her physical disabilities (she was crippled in a bus accident when 15), her stormy marriage with the artist Diego *Rivera, and her involvement with communism and the Mexican revolution. Her paintings, such as *The Little Deer* (1946; private collection, Houston), are rich in symbolism and personal imagery. Although her work was prized throughout her career, its popularity rose in the 1980s, and she is now considered one of the most exciting and influential artists of the 20th century.

Kahn, Louis Isadore (1901–1974) US architect. A follower of *Mies van der Rohe, he developed a classically romantic style, in which functional 'servant' areas such as stairwells and air ducts feature prominently, often as towerlike structures surrounding the main living and working, or 'served', areas. Kahn's projects are characterized by an imaginative use of concrete and brick and include the Yale Art Gallery 1953, for which he gained instant renown, the Richards Medical Research Building, University of Pennsylvania, 1957–61, and the Centre for British Art and Studies, Yale University 1969–74.

Kaiser title formerly used by the Holy Roman emperors, Austrian emperors 1806–1918, and German emperors 1871–1918. The word, like the Russian 'tsar', is derived from the Latin *Caesar*.

kakapo nocturnal flightless parrot that lives in burrows in New Zealand. It is green, yellow, and brown with a disc of brown feathers round its eyes, like an owl. It weighs up to 3.5 kg/7.5 lb. When in danger, its main defence is to remain perfectly still. Because of the introduction of predators such as dogs, cats, rats, and ferrets, it is in danger of extinction. In 1998 there were only 56 birds left in the wild. (Species *Strigops habroptilus*, order Psittaciformes.)

Kalahari Desert arid to semi-arid desert area forming most of Botswana and extending into Namibia, Zimbabwe, and South Africa; area about 900,000 sq km/347,400 sq mi. The only permanent river, the Okavango, flows into a delta in the northwest forming marshes rich in wildlife.

kale type of *cabbage.

Kalevala ('land of Kaleva') Finnish national epic poem compiled from legends and ballads by Elias Lönnrot 1835–49; its hero is Väinämöinen, god of music and poetry. It inspired the poet Longfellow, who borrowed its metre and some of its incidents for his *Hiawatha*, and the composer Sibelius.

Kali in Hindu mythology, the goddess of destruction and creation. She is the wife of *Shiva. Kali feeds herself on blood, but produces life and destroys ignorance. She shows Hindus that death is an illusion, not to be feared, but another aspect of eternal life.

Kalimantan name given to the Indonesian part of the island of Borneo; area 543,900 sq km/210,000 sq mi. It is divided into four provinces: Kalimantan Barat, population (2000 est) 4,034,200, capital Pontianak; Kalimantan Selatan, population (2000 est) 2,985,200, capital Banjarmasin; Kalimantan Tengah, population (2000 est) 1,857,000, capital Palangkaraya; and Kalimantan Timur, population (2000 est) 2,449,400, capital Samarinda. Other towns include Balikpapan. The land is mostly low-lying, with mountains in the north rising to 2,274 m/7,462 ft at Mount Raya. Industries include petroleum, rubber, coffee, copra, pepper, and timber.

Kali-Yuga in Hinduism, the last of the four **yugas** (ages) that make up one cycle of creation. The Kali-Yuga, in which Hindus believe we are now living, is characterized by wickedness and disaster, and leads up to the destruction of this world in preparation for a new creation and a new cycle of yugas.

Kalki in Hinduism, the last avatar (manifestation) of Vishnu, who will appear at the end of the Kali-Yuga, or final age of the world, to destroy it in readiness for a new creation.

Kalmyk or **Kalmykiya** or **Kalmuck** Kalmyk Khal'mg Tangch, republic in the southwest of the Russian Federation; area 75,900 sq km/29,305 sq mi; population (1996) 319,000 (39% urban) (45% Kalmyks, 38% Russians). The capital is Elista, and Yashkul is another city. The republic is west of the lower Volga and has a short coastline on the northwestern shore of the Caspian Sea. Physical features include dry steppe and semi-desert lowland, and there is a continental climate. Industries include machine building, metalworking, food processing, fish canning. Sheep, pigs, and cattle are reared.

Kaltenbrunner, Ernst (1903–1946) Austrian Nazi leader. After the annexation of Austria in 1938 he joined police chief Himmler's staff, and as head of the Security Police (SD) from 1943 was responsible for the murder of millions of Jews (see the *Holocaust) and Allied soldiers in World War II. After the war, he was tried in Nürnberg for war crimes and hanged in October 1946.

Kamchatka Peninsula mountainous region in the Russian Far East, separating the Sea of Okhotsk from the Pacific Ocean and the Bering Sea. The Kamchatka Peninsula is over 1,200 km/746 mi long, covers an area of 370,000 sq km/142,857 sq mi, and contains a total of over 120 volcanoes (20 of them active), together with many hot springs and geysers. The highest point is Klyuchevskaya Sopka (4,755 m/15,600 ft), itself an active volcano. The region has an extremely severe climate and predominantly tundra vegetation, with forests in sheltered valleys. The Kamchatka Peninsula is home to a huge number of animal and bird species, including the brown bear, sea eagle, and sable. Fishing, sealing, hunting (largely fur trapping), and lumbering are the main occupations. There is some cattle breeding in the south, and farming (potatoes, oats, rye, and vegetables) mainly in the Kamchatka valley; reindeer are also raised. Industries include shipbuilding, fish processing, and woodworking. There are coal, sulphur, gold, mica, and other mineral deposits.

kamikaze (Japanese 'wind of the gods') pilots of the Japanese air force in World War II who deliberately crash-dived their planes, loaded with bombs, usually on to ships of the US Navy.

Kampala capital of Uganda, on Lake Victoria; population (2002 est) 1,208,544. It is linked by rail with Mombasa. Products include tea, coffee, fruit, and vegetables. The varied industries include engineering, chemicals, paint manufacture, textiles, footwear, cement, brewing, distilling, cigarettes, flour- and sugar-milling, and coffee processing.

Kampuchea former name (1975–89) of Cambodia.

Kanchenjunga or **Kangchenjunga** Himalayan mountain on the Nepal–Sikkim border, 8,586 m/28,170 ft high, 120 km/75 mi southeast of Mount Everest. The name means 'five treasure houses of the great snows'. Kanchenjunga was first climbed by a British expedition in 1955.

Kandahar or **Qandahar** or **Candahar** city in Afghanistan, capital of Kandahar province, and the second city in Afghanistan, 450 km/280 mi southwest of Kabul; population (2001 est) 329,000. The city is 1,005 m/3,297 ft above sea level and stands on plateau with an annual rainfall of only 150 mm/6 in, but is irrigated by the Tarnak and other rivers. It is a trading centre, with wool and cotton factories, and other industries which include silk and felt. The city is a market for other agricultural products, including wool, tobacco, grains, fresh and dried fruit, and livestock, especially sheep. The city was severely damaged in the 1980s as a result of hostilities between Soviet-occupying forces and Afghan guerrillas. Further damage occurred in 2001 when the city, as the last major stronghold of the Taliban government, was under attack by the Northern Alliance supported by US and British forces during the War on Terrorism. The Taliban forces in Kandahar surrendered in December 2001.

Kandinsky, Vasily (1866–1944) Russian-born painter. He was a pioneer of abstract art. Between 1910 and 1914 he produced the series *Improvisations* and *Compositions*, the first known examples of purely abstract work in 20th-century art. He was an originator of the expressionist *Blaue Reiter* movement 1911–12, and taught at the *Bauhaus school of design in Germany 1921–33.

Kandy city in central Sri Lanka, on the Mahaweli River; capital of a district of the same name; population (2001 est) 110,000. It lies 116 km/72 mi northeast of Colombo. It is the focus both of a major tea-growing area and of the Sinhalese Buddhist culture. One of the most sacred Buddhist shrines is situated in Kandy. Called the Dalada Maligawa (Temple of the Tooth), it contains an alleged tooth of the Buddha. The temple was bombed by Tamil separatists in 1998 but was subsequently restored.

kangaroo any of a group of marsupials (mammals that carry their young in pouches) found in Australia and Papua New Guinea. Kangaroos are plant-eaters and most live in groups. They are adapted to hopping, the vast majority of species having very large, powerful back legs and feet compared with the small forelimbs. The larger types can jump 9 m/30 ft in a single bound. Most are nocturnal. Species vary from small rat kangaroos, only 30 cm/1 ft long, through the medium-sized wallabies, to the large red and great grey kangaroos, which are the largest living marsupials. These may be 1.8 m/5.9 ft long with 1.1 m/3.5 ft tails. (Family Macropodidae.)

Kannada *or* **Kanarese** language spoken in southern India, the official state language of Karnataka; also spoken in Tamil Nadu and Maharashtra. There are over 20 million speakers of Kannada, which belongs to the Dravidian family. Written records in Kannada date from the 5th century AD.

Kansas called the **Sunflower State**, (from the Kansa, or Kaw, American Indians) state in central USA, bordered to the south by *Oklahoma, to the west by *Colorado, to the north by *Nebraska, and to the east by *Missouri; area 211,900 sq km/81,815 sq mi; population (2000) 2,688,400; capital Topeka. The state's nickname comes from its national flower. Situated in the *Great Plains of the US *Midwest, it contains the geographic centre of the 48 coterminous US states as well as the magnetic centre of the North American land mass, which serves as the reference point for all land surveys of North America and Europe. The state also has one of the country's most precious natural resources – native prairie. Around 90% of the land is used for agriculture, and one-third of the population lives in rural areas. Kansas became more industrial from the mid-19th century, however, and manufacturing is now also an important contributor to the economy, as is the service sector. The state has rich mineral resources. Wichita is the state's largest city; other major cities include Kansas City, Leavenworth (the state's oldest city), Lawrence, Overland Park, Shawnee, and Hutchinson. Originally home to the Kaw and Pawnee American Indians, Kansas was explored by Francisco Vásquez de Coronado for Spain in 1541 and René Robert Cavelier, Sieur de la Salle for France in 1682, and became part of the USA under the *Louisiana Purchase in 1803. Kansas was admitted to the Union in 1861 as the 34th state.

Kant, Immanuel (1724–1804) German philosopher. He believed that knowledge is not merely an aggregate of sense impressions but is dependent on the conceptual apparatus of the human understanding, which is itself not derived from experience. In ethics, Kant argued that right action cannot be based on feelings or inclinations but conforms to a law given by reason, the **categorical imperative**.

kaolin *or* **china clay** group of clay minerals, such as *kaolinite, $Al_2Si_2O_5(OH)_4$, derived from the alteration of aluminium silicate minerals, such as *feldspars and *mica. It is used in medicine to treat digestive upsets, and in poultices.

kaolinite white or greyish *clay mineral, hydrated aluminium silicate, $Al_2Si_2O_5(OH)_4$, formed mainly by the decomposition of feldspar in granite. It is made up of platelike crystals, the atoms of which are bonded together in two-dimensional sheets, between which the bonds are weak, so that they are able to slip over one another, a process made more easy by a layer of water. China clay (kaolin) is derived from it. It is mined in France, the UK, Germany, China, and the USA.

Kapital, Das three-volume work presenting the theories of Karl *Marx on economic production, published 1867–95. It focuses on the exploitation of the worker and appeals for a classless society where the production process and its rewards are shared equally.

kapok silky hairs that surround the seeds of certain trees, particularly the **kapok tree** (*Bombax ceiba*) of India and Malaysia and the **silk-cotton tree** (*Ceiba pentandra*) of tropical America. Kapok is used for stuffing cushions and mattresses and for sound insulation; oil obtained from the seeds is used in food and soap.

Karachay-Cherkessia *or* **Karachay-Cherkess Republic** *or* **Karachayevo-Cherkesiya** republic in the southwestern Russian Federation, part of Stavropol territory; area 14,100 sq km/5,444 sq mi; population (1996) 436,000 (46% urban) (42% Russian, 31% Karachay). Cherkessk is the capital, and Karachayevsk is another city. The republic is located on the northern slopes of the Caucasus Mountains, with lowland steppe in the north and forested foothills in the south. There are rich coal and mineral deposits (lead, zinc, and copper). Industries include mining, production of chemicals, foodstuffs, light industries, and grain and vegetable cultivation. Tourism is increasingly important in the republic.

Karachi largest city and chief port of Pakistan, lying on the Arabian Sea, northwest of the *Indus delta; population (1998 est) 9,269,300; 4 million live in makeshift settlements. It is the capital of *Sind province, and Pakistan's leading centre for commerce, finance, industry, and transport. Its port handles most of the international trade of the country, as well as of the neighbouring landlocked state of Afghanistan. It is also served by a major international airport. Industries include shipbuilding, engineering, chemicals, plastics, and textiles, including the manufacture of cotton and jute. It was the capital of Pakistan 1947–59, when it was replaced by *Islamabad.

Karadzic, Radovan (1945–) Montenegrin-born leader of the Bosnian Serbs' unofficial government 1992–96. He co-founded and became president of the Serbian Democratic Party of Bosnia-Herzegovina (SDS-BH) in 1990 and called for a single country that would unite all ethnic Serbs. In 1992 he launched the siege of Sarajevo, plunging the country into a prolonged and bloody civil war. He pursued a ruthless military campaign that involved ethnic cleansing of tens of thousands of Bosnian Muslims to create 'pure' Serb areas. In 1995 he was charged with genocide and crimes against humanity by the Yugoslav War Crimes Tribunal in The Hague, Netherlands, but he continued to evade arrest.

Karajan, Herbert von (1908–1989) Austrian conductor. He dominated European classical music performance after 1947. He was principal conductor of the Berlin Philharmonic Orchestra 1955–89, and artistic director of the Vienna State Opera 1957–64 and of the Salzburg Festival 1956–60. A perfectionist, he cultivated an orchestral sound of notable smoothness and transparency; he also staged operas and directed his own video recordings. He recorded the complete Beethoven symphonies four times, and had a special affinity with Mozart and Bruckner, although his repertoire extended from Bach to Schoenberg.

Kara-Kalpak *or* **Karakalpakstan** *or* **Qoraqalpoghiston** large autonomous region in northwest Uzbekistan; area 158,000 sq km/61,000 sq mi; population (2001 est) 1,343,000. The capital is Nukus and Munyak is another city in the region. The north of the region consists mainly of lowland around the delta of the *Amu Darya, which formerly flowed into the Aral Sea, the southern half of which is within the region. There are plentiful salt deposits. Industries include heavily irrigated cultivation of cotton, rice, and wheat; there is also some viticulture and manufacture of leather goods.

Karakoram mountain range in central Asia, divided among China, Pakistan, and India. Peaks include *K2, Masharbrum, Gasharbrum, and Mustagh Tower. **Ladakh** subsidiary range is in northeastern Kashmir on the Tibetan border.

Kara-Kum or **Peski Karakumy** (Turkmen **Garagum** 'black sand') sandy desert occupying some 90% of the republic of Turkmenistan; area about 310,800 sq km/ 120,000 sq mi. The Kara-Kum lies to the east of the Caspian Sea, between the Aral Sea to the north and the Iranian border to the south. It is separated from the Kyzyl-Kum desert by the *Amu Darya River. The desert is crossed by the Trans-Caspian railway and the **Kara-Kum Canal**, the largest irrigation canal in the world. The area has rich oil, gas, and sulphur deposits, all of which are being increasingly exploited. Air temperatures of over 50 °C have been recorded here.

Kara Sea Russian **Karskoye More**, part of the Arctic Ocean off the north coast of the Russian Federation, bounded to the northwest by the island of Novaya Zemlya and to the northeast by Severnaya Zemlya; area 880,000 sq km/339,768 sq mi; average depths 30–100 m/98–328 ft, with a maximum of 620 m/2,034 ft. Novy Port on the Gulf of Ob is the chief port. Dikson is also a main port and is located on the mouth of the Yenisey River, which flows into the Kara Sea.

karate (Japanese 'empty hand') one of the *martial arts. Karate is a type of unarmed combat derived from *kempo*, a form of the Chinese Shaolin boxing. It became popular in the West in the 1930s.

Karbala (or **Kerbala**) holy city of the Shiite Muslims and administrative centre of the governorate of the same name, in Iraq, 96 km/60 mi southwest of Baghdad; population (1998 est) 402,500. The city lies on the edge of the Syrian desert and is linked by canal to the Hindiyah branch of the River Euphrates. The chief modern industries are the manufacture of textiles, shoes, and cement.

Karelia or **Kareliya** autonomous republic in the northwest of the Russian Federation, bordering on Finland to the west; area 172,400 sq km/66,550 sq mi; population (1997) 780,000. The capital is Petrozavodsk. The republic is extensively forested with numerous lakes, of which Ladoga and Onega are the largest in Europe. Industries include fishing, timber, chemicals, coal, and mineral and stone quarrying.

Karen member of any of a group of Southeast Asian peoples. Numbering 1.9 million, they live in eastern Myanmar (Burma), Thailand, and the Irrawaddy delta. Traditionally they practised *shifting cultivation. Buddhism and Christianity are their main religions, and their language belongs to the Thai division of the Sino-Tibetan family. In 1984 the Burmese government began a military campaign against the Karen National Liberation Army, the armed wing of the Karen National Union. The Myanmar State Law and Order Council (SLORC) increased the use of Karen civilians as forced labourers 1995–96, especially to build the Ye-Tavoy railway and road. Karen villages were also relocated, crops destroyed and property confiscated, forcing thousands to flee to Thailand.

Kariba Dam concrete dam on the Zambezi River, on the Zambia–Zimbabwe border, about 386 km/240 mi downstream from the Victoria Falls, constructed 1955–60 to supply power to both countries.

Karloff, Boris (1887–1969) stage name of William Henry Pratt, English-born US actor. He achieved Hollywood stardom with his role as the monster in the film *Frankenstein* (1931). Several sequels followed, as well as appearances in such films as *The Mummy* (1932), *Scarface* (1932), *The Lost Patrol* (1934), *The Body Snatcher* (1945), and *The Raven* (1963).

karma or **kamma** (Sanskrit 'action') in Hinduism, Buddhism, and Sikhism, the deeds carried forward from one life to the next through rebirth or *reincarnation. The aim of believers is to free themselves from the cycle of rebirth, attaining union with God or *nirvana.

Karnataka formerly **Mysore** (until 1973), state in southwest India; area 191,773 sq km/74,044 sq mi; population (2001 est) 52,734,000, of which the majority is Hindu. The capital is *Bangalore, and Mangalore is a port. The state has a western coastal plain; inland the forested Western Ghats rise to heights of 1,250 m/4,000 ft. Industries include the mining manganese, chromite, iron ore, bauxite, mica, copper, and India's only sources of gold (from the Kolar fields) and silver. The state is extensively forested, and products include teak and most of the world's supply of sandalwood. The Tungabhadra dam provides hydroelectricity, and irrigates up to 500,000 ha/1.23 million acres in Karnataka and Andrha Pradesh. Agricultural products include rice on the coastal western plain; inland millet, groundnuts, rice with irrigation; cotton in the north; and coffee and tea on the slopes of the Western Ghats. The language is Kannada. Famous people from the state include Haidar Ali and Tipu Sultan.

karst landscape characterized by remarkable surface and underground forms, created as a result of the action of water on permeable limestone. The feature takes its name from the Karst (meaning **dry**) region on the Adriatic coast of Slovenia and Croatia, but the name is applied to landscapes throughout the world, the most dramatic of which is found near the city of Guilin in the Guangxi province of China. Karst landscapes are characterized by underground features such as caves, caverns, stalactites, and stalagmites. On the surface, clints, grikes, gorges, and swallow holes are common features.

karyotype in biology, the set of *chromosomes characteristic of a given species. It is described as the number, shape, and size of the chromosomes in a single cell of an organism. In humans, for example, the karyotype consists of 46 chromosomes, in mice 40, crayfish 200, and in fruit flies 8.

Kashmir disputed area on the border of India and Pakistan in the northwest of the former state of Kashmir, now *Jammu and Kashmir; area 78,900 sq km/ 30,445 sq mi. Physical features include the west Himalayan peak Nanga Parbat (8,126 m/26,660 ft), Karakoram Pass, Indus River, and Baltoro Glacier. Through Kashmir flow the headwaters of the Indus, Jhelum, and Chenab rivers, important sources of water for irrigation of the plains of Pakistan. Azad ('free')

Kashmir in the west has its own legislative assembly based in Muzaffarabad while Gilgit and Baltistan regions to the north and east are governed directly by Pakistan. The Northern Areas are claimed by India and Pakistan. Cities in the region include Gilgit and Skardu.

Kashmiri inhabitants of or natives to the state of Jammu and Kashmir, a disputed territory divided between India and Pakistan. There are approximately 6 million Kashmiris, 4 million of whom live on the Indian side of the ceasefire line.

Kasparov, Garry Kimovich (1963–) born Garry Weinstein, Azerbaijani chess player who has represented Russia in international competition. When he beat his compatriot Anatoly Karpov to win the world title in 1985, he was the youngest ever champion at 22 years 210 days. He held this crown for 15 years until November 2000 when he was beaten by a former Russian pupil, Vladimir Kramnik. During that time Kasparov lost only once – to IBM computer Deep Blue in 1997.

Kathmandu or **Katmandu** capital of Nepal, situated at 1,370 m/4,500 ft in the southern Himalayas, in the Valley of Nepal, at the junction of the Baghmati and Vishnumati rivers; population (2001 est) 696,900. Tourism is an important economic activity and its growth has been aided by the develoment of an international airport at Kathmandu. Manufacturing industries in the Kathmandu area are small-scale and dependent mainly on local raw materials; products include timber, bricks and tiles, milled rice, cigarettes, cement, and beer.

Kattegat strait between Denmark and Sweden. It is about 240 km/150 mi long and 135 km/85 mi wide at its broadest point, and joins the Skagerrak on the north to the Baltic Sea on the south. Its sandbanks are a navigational hazard.

katydid or **bush cricket** or **longhorn grasshopper** one of over 4,000 insect species, most of which are tropical, related to grasshoppers.

Katyn Forest forest near Smolensk, southwest of Moscow, Russia, where 4,500 Polish officer prisoners of war (captured in the German-Soviet partition of Poland 1940) were shot; 10,000 others were killed elsewhere. In 1989 the USSR accepted responsibility for the massacre.

Kaunda, Kenneth David (1924–) Zambian politician, president 1964–91. Imprisoned 1958–60 as founder of the Zambia African National Congress, in 1964 he became the first president of independent Zambia. In 1972 he introduced one-party rule. He supported the nationalist movement in Southern Rhodesia (now Zimbabwe) and survived a coup attempt in 1980. In 1990, widespread anti-government demonstrations forced him to accept a multiparty political system and he was defeated in multiparty elections in 1991 by Frederick Chiluba.

Kazakh or **Kazak** a pastoral Kyrgyz people of Kazakhstan. Kazakhs also live in China (Xinjiang, Gansu, and Qinghai), Mongolia, and Afghanistan. There are 5–7 million speakers of Kazakh, a Turkic language belonging to the Altaic family. They are predominantly Sunni Muslim, although pre-Islamic customs have survived.

Kazakhstan

National name: *Kazak Respublikasy/ Republic of Kazakhstan*

Area: 2,717,300 sq km/1,049,150 sq mi

Capital: Astana (formerly Akmola)

Major towns/cities: Qaraghandy, Pavlodar, Semey, Petropavlosk, Shymkent

Physical features: Caspian and Aral seas, Lake Balkhash; Steppe region; natural gas and oil deposits in the Caspian Sea

Head of state: Nursultan Nazarbayev from 1990

Head of government: Daniyel Akhmetov from 2003

Political system: authoritarian nationalist

Political executive: unlimited presidency

Political parties: Congress of People's Unity of Kazakhstan, moderate, centrist; People's Congress of Kazakhstan, moderate, ethnic; Socialist Party of Kazakhstan (SPK), left wing; Republican Party, right-of-centre coalition

Currency: tenge

GNI per capita (PPP): (US$) 5,480 (2002 est)

Exports: ferrous and non-ferrous metals, mineral products (including petroleum and petroleum products), chemicals. Principal market: Russia 20.2% (2001)

Population: 15,433,000 (2003 est)

Language: Kazakh (related to Turkish; official), Russian

Religion: Sunni Muslim 50–60%, Russian Orthodox 30–35%

Life expectancy: 61 (men); 72 (women) (2000–05)

Chronology

early Christian era: Settled by Mongol and Turkic tribes.

8th century: Spread of Islam.

10th century: Southward migration into east Kazakhstan of Kazakh tribes, displaced from Mongolia by the Mongols.

13th–14th centuries: Part of Mongol Empire.

late 15th century: Kazakhs emerged as distinct ethnic group from Kazakh Orda tribal confederation.

early 17th century: The nomadic, cattle-breeding Kazakhs split into smaller groups, united in the three Large, Middle, and Lesser Hordes (federations), led by khans (chiefs).

1731–42: Faced by attacks from the east by Oirot Mongols, protection was sought from the Russian tsars, and Russian control was gradually established.

1822–48: Conquest by tsarist Russia completed; khans deposed. Large-scale Russian and Ukrainian peasant settlement of the steppes after the abolition of serfdom in Russia in 1861.

1887: Alma-Alta (now Almaty), established in 1854 as a fortified trading centre and captured by the Russians in 1865, destroyed by an earthquake.

1916: 150,000 killed as anti-Russian rebellion brutally repressed.

1917: Bolshevik coup in Russia followed by outbreak of civil war in Kazakhstan.

1920: Autonomous republic in USSR.

early 1930s: More than 1 million died of starvation during the campaign to collectivize agriculture.

1936: Joined USSR and became a full union republic.

early 1940s: Volga Germans deported to the republic by Soviet dictator Joseph Stalin.

1954–56: Part of Soviet leader Nikita Khrushchev's ambitious 'Virgin Lands' agricultural extension programme; large influx of Russian settlers made Kazakhs a minority in their own republic.

1986: There were nationalist riots in Alma-Alta (now Almaty) after the reformist Soviet leader Mikhail Gorbachev ousted the local communist leader and installed an ethnic Russian.

1989: Nursultan Nazarbayev, a reformist and mild nationalist, became leader of the Kazakh Communist Party (KCP) and instituted economic and cultural reform programmes, encouraging foreign inward investment.

1990: Nazarbayev became head of state; economic sovereignty was declared.

1991: Nazarbayev condemned the attempted anti-Gorbachev coup in Moscow; the KCP was abolished. The country joined the new Commonwealth of Independent States (CIS); and independence was recognized by the USA.

1992: Kazakhstan was admitted into the United Nations (UN) and the Conference on Security and Cooperation in Europe (CSCE; now the Organization on Security and Cooperation in Europe, OSCE).

1993: Presidential power was increased by a new constitution. A privatization programme was launched. START-1 (disarmament treaty) and Nuclear Non-Proliferation Treaty were both ratified by Kazakhstan.

1994: There was economic, social, and military union with Kyrgyzstan and Uzbekistan.

1995: An economic and military cooperation pact was signed with Russia. Kazakhstan achieved nuclear-free status.

1997: Astana (formerly known as Akmola) was designated as the new capital. President Nazarbayev appointed Nurlan Balgymbayev, head of the Kazakh Oil state petroleum company, prime minister.

1998: A treaty of 'eternal friendship' and a treaty of deepening economic cooperation was signed with Uzbekistan.

1999: Nazarbayev was re-elected president, though international observers claimed the election was flawed. Kasymzhomart Tokaev was appointed prime minister.

2000: A huge offshore oil field was discovered in the Caspian Sea.

2002: A border agreement and an agreement on eternal friendship was signed with Uzbekistan. Otan and the People's Co-operative Party of Kazakhstan (PCPK), the country's two main political parties, merged.

2003: Parliament passed a land reform bill to allow private ownership of land. President Nazarbayev suspended the death penalty.

2004: Kazakhstan and China agreed on the construction of an oil pipeline across Kazakhstan to the Chinese border. Nazarbayev's Otan party won elections for the lower house of parliament. International observers claimed the elections were flawed.

2005: One of the main opposition parties, Democratic Choice, was ordered to disband, after it was accused of breaching state security by calling for protests against the election results. Opposition groups came together to form the 'For A Just Kazakhstan' movement.

Kazantzakis, Nikos (1885–1957) Greek writer. His works include the poem *I Odysseia/The Odyssey* (1938), which continues Homer's *Odyssey*, and the novels *Zorba the Greek* (1946), *Christ Recrucified* (1948), *The Greek Passion*, and *The Last Temptation of Christ* (both 1951). *Zorba the Greek* was filmed in 1964 and *The Last Temptation of Christ* (controversially) in 1988.

kea hawklike greenish parrot found in New Zealand. It eats insects, fruits, and discarded sheep offal. The Maori name imitates its cry. (Species *Nestor notabilis*, family Psittacidae, order Psittaciformes.) In 2000 there were only about 2,000 keas remaining.

Keating, Paul John (1944–) Australian politician, Labor Party (ALP) leader and prime minister 1991–96. He was treasurer and deputy leader of the ALP 1983–91. In 1993 he announced plans for Australia to become a federal republic by the year 2001, which incited a mixed reaction among Australians. He and his party lost the February 1996 general election to John Howard, leader of the Liberal Party.

Keaton, Buster (Joseph Francis) (1896–1966) called 'Great Stone Face', US comedian, actor, and film director. After being a star in vaudeville, he became one of the great comedians of the silent film era, with an inimitable deadpan expression masking a sophisticated acting ability. At his height he rivalled fellow comic actor Charlie *Chaplin in popularity. He starred in and co-directed *The General* (1927) which, although not a success on its initial release, is widely considered one of the best and most influential US films.

Keats, John (1795–1821) English poet. He produced work of the highest quality and promise, belonging to the artistic school of *Romanticism, before dying at the age of 25. *Poems* (1817), *Endymion* (1818), the great odes (particularly 'Ode to a Nightingale' and 'Ode on a Grecian Urn' written in 1819, published in 1820), and the narratives 'Isabella; or the Pot of Basil' (1818), 'Lamia' (1819), and 'The Eve of St Agnes' (1820), show his lyrical richness and talent for drawing on both classical mythology and medieval lore.

Kedah state in northwestern Peninsular Malaysia; capital Alor Setar; area 9,400 sq km/3,628 sq mi; population (2000 est) 1,572,100. Products include rice, rubber, tapioca, tin, and tungsten. Kedah was transferred by Siam (Thailand) to Britain in 1909, and was one of the Unfederated Malay States until 1948.

Keegan, (Joseph) Kevin (1951–) English footballer and football manager. In February 1999, he was appointed coach of the England team on a part-time basis, while continuing at Fulham, the team he led to the 1998–99 Second Division Championship. In May 1999, he parted company with Fulham after deciding to accept the England manager's job on a full-time basis, and signed a contract to coach England until the end of the 2002 World Cup finals. His first test as a coach in a major international championship ended in failure when England was eliminated from the 2000 European Championships, at the group stage. Keegan's tactics were widely criticized by both the English and the European press. He resigned from the position in October 2000 immediately after losing 1–0 to Germany at home in the first game of England's 2002 World Cup qualifying campaign. His record with England was: played 18, won 7, drawn 7, lost 4. He returned to football in June 2001, when he was appointed manager of Manchester City, and he led the team back to the top division during his first season in charge. As a player, he won nine major European and domestic trophies with Liverpool and Hamburg and represented his country 63 times, scoring 21 goals.

keeshond *or* **Dutch barge dog** sturdily built dog with erect ears and curled tail. It has a long grey top-coat, forming a mane around the neck, and a short, very thick undercoat, with darker 'spectacles' around the eyes. The ideal height is 46 cm/18 in for dogs; 43 cm/17 in for bitches, and the ideal weight is 25–30 kg/55–66 lb.

Keitel, Wilhelm (1882–1946) German field marshal in World War II, chief of the supreme command from 1938 and Hitler's chief military adviser. He dictated the terms of the French armistice in 1940 and was a member of the court that sentenced many officers to death for their part in the July Plot 1944. He signed Germany's unconditional surrender in Berlin on 8 May 1945. Tried at Nürnberg for war crimes, he was hanged.

Kelantan state in northeastern Peninsular Malaysia; capital Kota Bharu; area 14,900 sq km/5,751 sq mi; population (2000 est) 1,289,200. Most of the state lies in the Kalentan river basin, which has a navigable channel leading 130 km/80 mi inland from the port of Tumpat on the South China Sea. The delta of the Kalentan River and the coastal plains are agriculturally rich, producing coconuts, rice, and rubber. Large-scale plantation agriculture has developed in the hill country in the interior of the state, producing rubber and palm oil. Minerals worked in the state include iron ore, manganese, and tin, and industries include sawmilling, boat building, and the manufacture of plywood. Kelantan was transferred by Siam (Thailand) to Britain in 1909, and until 1948 was one of the Unfederated Malay States.

kelim oriental carpet or rug that is flat, pileless, and reversible. Kelims are made by a tapestry-weave technique. Weft thread of one colour is worked to and fro in one area of the pattern; the next colour continues the pattern from the adjacent warp thread, so that no weft thread runs across the full width of the carpet.

Kellogg–Briand Pact agreement negotiated in 1928 between the USA and France to renounce war and seek settlement of disputes by peaceful means. It took its name from the US secretary of state Frank B Kellogg (1856–1937) and the French foreign minister Aristide Briand. Most other nations subsequently signed. Some successes were achieved in settling South American disputes, but the pact made no provision for measures against aggressors and became ineffective in the 1930s, with Japan in Manchuria, Italy in Ethiopia, and Hitler in central Europe.

Kells, Book of 8th-century illuminated manuscript of the Gospels produced at the monastery of Kells in County Meath, Ireland. It is now in Trinity College Library, Dublin.

Kelly, Gene (1912–1996) stage name of Eugene Curran, US film actor, dancer, choreographer, and director. He was a major star of the 1940s and 1950s in a series of MGM musicals, including *On the Town* (1949), *Singin' in the Rain* (1952) (both of which he codirected), and *An American in Paris* (1951). He also directed *Hello Dolly* (1969).

Kelly, Grace (Patricia) (1929–1982) US film actor. She starred in *High Noon* (1952), *The Country Girl* (1954), for which she received an Academy Award, and *High Society* (1955). She also starred in three Hitchcock films – *Dial M for Murder* (1954), *Rear Window* (1954), and *To Catch a Thief* (1955). She retired from acting after marrying Prince Rainier III of Monaco in 1956.

kelp collective name for a group of large brown seaweeds. Kelp is also a term for the powdery ash of burned seaweeds, a source of iodine. (Typical families Fucaceae and Laminariaceae.)

Kelvin, William Thomson (1824–1907) 1st Baron Kelvin, Irish-born physicist who introduced the **Kelvin scale**, the absolute scale of temperature. His work on the conservation of energy in 1851 led to the second law of *thermodynamics. He was knighted in 1866, and made a baron in 1892.

Kelvin scale temperature scale used by scientists. It begins at *absolute zero (-273.15 °C) and increases in kelvins, the same degree intervals as the Celsius scale; that is, 0 °C is the same as 273.15 K and 100 °C is 373.15 K. It is named after the Irish physicist William Thomson, 1st Baron *Kelvin.

Kemal Atatürk, Mustafa Turkish politician; see *Atatürk.

Kempis, Thomas à medieval German monk and religious writer; see *Thomas à Kempis.

Kennedy, Charles Peter (1959–) British politician, leader of the Liberal Democrat party from 1999. He was elected successor to Paddy Ashdown, inheriting a party that had made a huge advance into government through its coalition with the Labour Party in the Scottish Parliament. He led a strong general election campaign in June 2001 and May 2005 promising investment in public services and an honest approach to how increased spending would be financed.

Kennedy, Edward Moore ('Ted') (1932–) US Democratic politician. He aided his brothers John and Robert Kennedy in their presidential campaigns of 1960 and 1968, respectively, and entered politics as a senator for Massachusetts in 1962. He failed to gain the presidential nomination in 1980, largely because of questions about his delay in reporting a car crash at Chappaquiddick Island, near Cape Cod, Massachusetts, in 1969, in which his passenger, Mary Jo Kopechne, was drowned.

Kennedy, John F(itzgerald) ('Jack') (1917–1963) 35th president of the USA 1961–63, a Democrat; the first Roman Catholic and the youngest person to be elected president. In foreign policy he carried through the unsuccessful *Bay of Pigs invasion of Cuba, and secured the withdrawal of Soviet missiles from the island in 1962. His programme for reforms at home, called the **New Frontier**, was posthumously executed by Lyndon Johnson. Kennedy was assassinated while on a visit to Dallas, Texas, on 22 November 1963. Lee Harvey Oswald (1939–1963), who was within a few days shot dead by Jack Ruby (1911–1967), was named as the assassin.

Kennedy, Robert Francis (1925–1968) US Democratic politician and lawyer. He was presidential campaign manager for his brother John F *Kennedy in 1960, and as attorney general 1961–64 pursued a racket-busting policy and worked to enforce federal law in support of civil rights. He was assassinated during his campaign for the 1968 Democratic presidential nomination.

Kennedy Space Center (KSC) NASA launch site on Merritt Island, near Cape Canaveral, Florida, used for *Apollo* project and space shuttle launches. It was established in 1962 and celebrated its 40th anniversary in 2002. The first *Apollo* flight to land on the Moon (1969) and *Skylab*, the first orbiting laboratory (1973), were launched from the site. In 2003, it launched the two spacecraft of the Mars Exploration Rover mission.

Kennelly-Heaviside layer former term for the *E-layer of the ionosphere.

Kenneth two kings of Scotland:

Kenneth I (died 860) called 'MacAlpin', King of Scotland from about 844. Traditionally, he is regarded as the founder of the Scottish kingdom (Alba) by virtue of his final defeat of the Picts about 844. He invaded Northumbria six times, and drove the Angles and the Britons over the River Tweed.

Kenneth II (died 995) King of Scotland from 971, son of Malcolm I. He invaded Northumbria several times, and his chiefs were in constant conflict with Sigurd the Norwegian over the area of Scotland north of the River Spey. He is believed to have been murdered by his subjects.

Kent county of southeast England, known as the 'garden of England' (since April 1998 Medway Towns has been a separate unitary authority). **area:** 3,730 sq km/1,440 sq mi **towns and cities:** Maidstone (administrative headquarters), Ashford, Canterbury, Deal, Dover (ferry terminus), Gravesend, Hythe, New Ash Green (a new town), Sevenoaks, Tunbridge Wells; Folkestone, Margate, Ramsgate, Whitstable (resorts) **physical:** the North Downs; White Cliffs of Dover; rivers: Thames, Darent, Medway (traditionally a 'man of Kent' comes from east of the Medway and a 'Kentish man' from west Kent), Stour; marshes (especially Romney Marsh); the Isles of Grain, Thanet and Sheppey (on which is the resort of Sheerness, formerly a royal dockyard); the Weald (an agricultural area); Dungeness (peninsula and headland) **features:** Leeds Castle (converted to a palace by Henry VIII); Ightham Mote; Hever Castle (where Henry VIII courted Anne Boleyn); Chartwell (Churchill's country home), Knole, Sissinghurst Castle (16th-century) and gardens; Brogdale is home to the national Fruit Collections; the former RAF Manston became Kent International Airport in 1989; Dungeness nuclear power station **population:** (2001 est) 1,331,100.

Kent, William (1685–1748) English architect, landscape gardener, and interior designer. Working closely with Richard *Burlington, he was foremost in introducing the Palladian style to Britain from Italy, excelling in richly carved, sumptuous interiors and furnishings, as at Holkham Hall, Norfolk, begun in 1734. Immensely versatile, he also worked in a neo-Gothic style, and was a pioneer of Romantic landscape gardening, for example, the grounds of Stowe House, Buckinghamshire, and Rousham Park, Oxfordshire (1738–40). Horace Walpole called him 'the father of modern gardening'.

Kentucky called the **Bluegrass State**, (Iroquian/Cherokee *Ken-tah-ten* 'land of tomorrow' or 'meadowland' or 'the dark and bloody ground') state in south-central USA, bounded to the north by the *Ohio River, across which are the states of *Ohio, *Indiana, and *Illinois; to the east, by the Tug Fork and Big Sandy rivers, which separate it from *West Virginia; to the southeast by *Virginia, with the Cumberland Gap at the extreme south; from this point along its southern boundary, as far as the *Mississippi River, it is bordered by *Tennessee; across a small stretch of the Mississippi, on the west, it faces the New Madrid region of *Missouri; area 102,895 sq km/39,728 sq mi; population (2000) 4,041,800; capital Frankfort. Kentucky is nicknamed the Bluegrass State after the blue blossoms on the lush grass of the area around Lexington. The state extends over 640 km/400 mi from east to west, and in the east is part of the Cumberland Plateau of the *Appalachian Mountains; the Bluegrass Region is in the northeast. Kentucky has massive deposits of bituminous coal and is one of the leading US coal producers. Service industries are the leading sources of revenue; other industries include transport equipment, bourbon, and food products. Agricultural output includes tobacco, horses, and dairy products. Major towns are Louisville, Lexington, Owensboro, Bowling Green, Covington, Hopkinsville, Paducah, Henderson, and Jeffersontown. Kentucky was originally home to the Shawnee and *Cherokee American Indians. The state was divided over the slavery question and there were many partisan feuds during the *Civil War. Kentucky was admitted to the Union in 1792 as the 15th US state.

Kenya
National name: *Jamhuri ya Kenya/Republic of Kenya*
Area: 582,600 sq km/224,941 sq mi
Capital: Nairobi

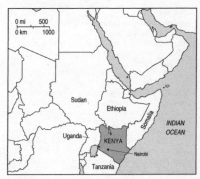

491

Major towns/cities: Mombasa, Kisumu, Nakuru, Eldoret, Nyeri
Major ports: Mombasa
Physical features: mountains and highlands in west and centre; coastal plain in south; arid interior and tropical coast; semi-desert in north; Great Rift Valley, Mount Kenya, Lake Nakuru (salt lake with world's largest colony of flamingos), Lake Turkana (Rudolf)
Head of state and government: Mwai Kibaki from 2002
Political system: authoritarian nationalist
Political executive: unlimited presidency
Political parties: Kenya African National Union (KANU), nationalist, centrist; Forum for the Restoration of Democracy–Kenya (FORD–Kenya), left of centre; Forum for the Restoration of Democracy–Asili (FORD–Asili), left of centre; Democratic Party (DP), centrist; Safina, centrist
Currency: Kenyan shilling
GNI per capita (PPP): (US$) 990 (2002 est)
Exports: coffee, tea, horticultural products, petroleum products, soda ash, cement. Principal market: Uganda 20.4% (2001)
Population: 31,987,000 (2003 est)
Language: English, Kiswahili (both official), many local dialects
Religion: Roman Catholic 28%, Protestant 8%, Muslim 6%, traditional tribal religions
Life expectancy: 44 (men); 46 (women) (2000–05)
Chronology
8th century: Arab traders began to settle along coast of East Africa.
16th century: Portuguese defeated coastal states and exerted spasmodic control over them.
18th century: Sultan of Oman reasserted Arab overlordship of East African coast, making it subordinate to Zanzibar.
19th century: Europeans, closely followed by Christian missionaries, began to explore inland.
1887: British East Africa Company leased area of coastal territory from sultan of Zanzibar.
1895: Britain claimed large inland region as East African Protectorate.
1903: Railway from Mombasa to Uganda built using Indian labourers, many of whom settled in the area; British and South African settlers began to farm highlands.
1920: East African Protectorate became crown colony of Kenya, with legislative council elected by white settlers (and by Indians and Arabs soon afterwards).
1923: Britain rejected demand for internal self-government by white settlers.
1944: First African appointment to legislative council; Kenyan African Union (KAU) founded to campaign for African rights.
1947: Jomo Kenyatta became leader of KAU, which was dominated by Kikuyu tribe.
1952: Mau Mau (Kikuyu secret society) began terrorist campaign to drive white settlers from tribal lands; Mau Mau largely suppressed by 1954 but state of emergency lasted for eight years.
1953: Kenyatta charged with management of Mau Mau activities and imprisoned by the British. He was released in 1959, but exiled to northern Kenya.
1956: Africans allowed to elect members of legislative council on a restricted franchise.

1960: Britain announced plans to prepare Kenya for majority African rule.
1961: Kenyatta allowed to return to help negotiate Kenya's independence.
1963: Kenya achieved independence with Kenyatta as prime minister.
1964: Kenya became a republic with Kenyatta as president.
1969: Kenya became one-party state under Kenyan African National Union (KANU).
1978: President Kenyatta died and was succeeded by Daniel arap Moi.
1984: There were violent clashes between government troops and the ethnic Somali population at Wajir.
1989: Moi announced the release of political prisoners.
1991: A multiparty system was conceded after an opposition group was launched.
1997: There were demonstrations calling for democratic reform. Constitutional reforms were adopted.
1998: A bomb exploded at the US embassy in Nairobi, killing over 230 people and injuring 5,000; an anti-US Islamic group claimed responsibility.
1999: A framework agreement was signed with the leaders of Uganda and Tanzania, intending to reestablish the East African Community (EAC) which had collapsed in 1977, hoping to lead to a Common market and political federation similar to that of the European Union (EU).
2001: Richard Leakey, appointed by President Moi to tackle government corruption, resigned after completing his reform of the civil service.
2002: Tourist hotels bombed by Muslim extremists. Mwai Kibaki replaced Moi as president. In presidential elections, the KANU candidate Uhuru Kenyatta was beaten by the opposition candidate Mwai Kibaki, ending Moi's 24 years as president.
2003: The government announced an anti-corruption commission and the International Monetary Fund resumed lending. Moi was granted immunity from prosecution for corruption.
2004: A new constitution was drafted but the deadline for parliamentary approval was missed. The UN launched an aid appeal after crop failures and drought caused severe food shortages. Wangari Maathai, an ecologist, won the Nobel Peace Prize.

Kenya, Mount or **Kirinyaga** extinct volcano from which Kenya takes its name, height 5,199 m/17,057 ft. It is situated almost exactly on the Equator. The first European to climb it was Halford Mackinder in 1899.

Kenyatta, Jomo (c. **1894–1978**) adopted name of Kamau Ngengi, Kenyan nationalist politician, prime minister from 1963, as well as the first president of Kenya from 1964 until his death. He led the Kenya African Union from 1947 (KANU from 1963) and was active in liberating Kenya from British rule.

Kepler, Johannes (1571–1630) German mathematician and astronomer. He formulated what are now called Kepler's laws of planetary motion. Kepler's laws are the basis of our understanding of the Solar System, and such scientists as Isaac *Newton built on his ideas.

Kerala state of southwest India; area 38,864 sq km/ 15,006 sq mi; population (2001 est) 31,838,600. The capital is Thiruvananthapuram and Kozhikode and

Kochi are other towns. The state extends along the southwest coast from Karnataka almost to the southern tip of India and is bounded on the east by the highlands of the Western Ghats. Industries include textiles, chemicals, electrical goods, and fish. Agricultural products include tea, coffee, rice, coconuts, fruit, and oilseed.

keratin fibrous protein found in the *skin of vertebrates and also in hair, nails, claws, hooves, feathers, and the outer coating of horns.

Kerguelen Islands *or* **Desolation Islands** volcanic archipelago in the Indian Ocean, part of the French Southern and Antarctic Territories; area 7,215 km/2,787 sq mi. They were discovered in 1772 by the Breton navigator Yves de Kerguelen and annexed by France in 1949. Uninhabited except for scientists (centre for joint study of geomagnetism with Russia), the islands support a unique wild cabbage containing a pungent oil.

kernel the inner, softer part of a *nut, or of a seed within a hard shell.

kerosene thin oil obtained from the *fractional distillation of crude oil (unrefined *petroleum; a highly refined form is used in jet aircraft fuel. Kerosene is a mixture of hydrocarbons of the *alkane series, consisting mainly of hydrocarbons with 11 or 12 carbon atoms. Boiling points range from 160 °C/320 °F to 250 °C/480 °F. Crude oil contains approximately 10–15% kerosene.

Kerouac, Jack (Jean Louis) (1922–1969) US novelist. He named and epitomized the *Beat Generation of the 1950s. The first of his autobiographical, myth-making books, *The Town and the City* (1950), was followed by the rhapsodic *On the Road* (1957). Other works written with similar free-wheeling energy and inspired by his interests in jazz and Buddhism include *The Dharma Bums* (1958), *Doctor Sax* (1959), and *Desolation Angels* (1965). His major contribution to poetry was *Mexico City Blues* (1959).

Kerry county of the Republic of Ireland, west of Cork, in the province of Munster; county town Tralee; area 4,700 sq km/1,814 sq mi; population (2002 est) 132,400. Industries include engineering, woollens, fishing, and farming (dairy farming in the north, cattle grazing in the south). Tourism is important. Other towns include Caherciveen, Castleisland, Dingle, Killarney, and Listowel.

Kerry blue terrier compact and sturdy dog, with a soft, full coat of bluish tone. It is 46 cm/18 in high and weighs 15–17 kg/33–37.4 lb. Its ears lie close to the head and it has a thin tail that is held erect.

kestrel *or* **windhover** small hawk that breeds in Europe, Asia, and Africa. About 30 cm/1 ft long, the male has a bluish-grey head and tail and is light chestnut brown back with black spots on the back and pale with black spots underneath. The female is slightly larger and reddish brown above, with bars; she does not have the bluish-grey head. The kestrel hunts mainly by hovering in midair while searching for prey. It feeds on small mammals, insects, frogs, and worms. (Species *Falco tinnunculus*, family Falconidae, order Falconiformes.)

ketone member of the group of organic compounds containing the carbonyl group (C=O) bonded to two atoms of carbon (instead of one carbon and one hydrogen as in *aldehydes). Ketones are liquids or low-melting-point solids, slightly soluble in water. An example is propanone (acetone, CH_3COCH_3), used as a solvent.

key in music, describes any piece where the melodies and harmonies are based on the notes of a major or minor scale. For example, a piece in the key of C major uses mainly the notes of the C major scale, and the harmonies are made up of the notes of that scale. The first note of a scale is known as the *tonic and is the note that tells us the name of the key.

Keynes, John Maynard (1883–1946) 1st Baron Keynes, English economist celebrated for *General Theory of Employment, Interest and Money* (1936), which initiated the so-called Keynesian Revolution. He is also noted for his other writings, especially *A Treatise on Money* (1930), as well as his central role in the Bretton Woods Conference of 1944 which created the International Monetary Fund (IMF) and the International Bank for Reconstruction and Development.

KGB secret police of the USSR, the **Komitet Gosudarstvennoy Bezopasnosti** (Committee of State Security), which was in control of frontier and general security and the forced-labour system. KGB officers held key appointments in all fields of daily life, reporting to administration offices in every major town. On the demise of the USSR in 1991, the KGB was superseded by the Federal Counterintelligence Service, which was renamed the Federal Security Service (FSB) in April 1995, when its powers were expanded to enable it to combat corruption and organized crime, and to undertake foreign-intelligence gathering. Its main successor is the Russian Federal Security Service (FSB), which focuses on 'economic security' and combating foreign espionage.

Khabarovsk large krai (territory) in the Russian Far East; area 824,600 sq km/318,378 sq mi; population (2003) 1,466,500 (about 80% urban). The capital is Khabarovsk, and other towns include Birobidzhan, Okhotsk, Komsomolsk-na-Amure, and Sovetskaya Gavan. The territory extends for over 2,000 km/1,243 mi along the eastern Siberian coast north of the Manchuria and the Amur River, almost entirely enclosing the Sea of Okhotsk. It encompasses the Jewish Autonomous Region (Oblast). It is mountainous and extensively forested, with a cold monsoonal climate. Mineral resources include gold, coal, tin, iron ore, manganese, and molybdenum. Industries include engineering, mining, metallurgy, pulp and paper production; lumbering and fishing.

Khachaturian, Aram Il'yich (1903–1978) Armenian composer. His use of folk themes is shown in the ballets *Gayaneh* (1942), which includes the 'Sabre Dance', and *Spartacus* (1956).

Khaddhafi (or Gaddafi or Qaddafi), Moamer al- (1942–) Libyan revolutionary leader, in power since 1969. Charismatic and unpredictable, he set out to establish himself as leader of the Arab world. His sponsorship of anti-Western terrorist organizations and rebels in Chad the 1980s and 1990s, and attempts at territorial expansion, led to Libya's exclusion from the international community and to the imposition of international sanctions. However, from 1999 Khaddhafi sought to improve relations with the West and in 2003 Libya announced that it was giving up efforts to develop weapons of mass destruction.

Khakass or **Khakasiya** republic of the Russian Federation, in southern Siberia, adjacent to *Krasnoyarsk krai (territory); area 61,900 sq km/23,900 sq mi; population (1996) 586,000 (72% urban) (80% Russians, 11% Khakass). The capital is Abakan and Chernogorsk is another town. The republic is situated between the Kuznetsky Alatau Mountains in the west and the Sayan Mountains in the southeast. It is located in the Minusinsk Basin west of the upper River Yenisey. Coal, iron-ore, and gold deposits are found here. Industries include mining and lumbering; hydroelectric power generation (at Sayanogorsk on the Yenisey); and breeding of sheep, goats, and cattle.

Khalsa or **Pure Ones** the order or community of the Sikhs, created by Guru Gobind Singh at the festival of Baisakhi Mela in 1699. The Khalsa was originally founded as a militant group to defend the Sikh community from persecution. Initiation of both sexes is through the ceremony of Amrit Sanskar, a form of baptism. Membership is a commitment to upholding the Rahit (Sikh code of ethics and rituals) and helping the community.

Khama, Seretse (1921–1980) Botswanan politician, prime minister of Bechuanaland in 1965, and first president of Botswana 1966–80. He founded the Bechuanaland Democratic Party in 1962 and led his country to independence in 1966. Botswana prospered under his leadership, both economically and politically, and he won every post-independence election until his death in July 1980. He was knighted in 1966.

Khan, Imran Niazi (1952–) Pakistani cricketer and politician. In cricket he was an all-rounder, and played in England for both Worcestershire and Sussex, making his Test debut in 1971. He played 88 Test matches for Pakistan, of which 48 were as captain. In 1992 he captained his country to victory in the World Cup. He scored 17,771 first-class runs at an average of 36.79, and took 1,287 wickets at an average of 22.32. He retired from cricket in 1992, and moved into Pakistani politics in 1996, launching the Pakistan Tehreek-e-Insaaf (PTI; in English the Pakistani Justice Movement). However, the party failed to win a single seat in the 1997 election.

Khardung Pass road linking the Indian town of Leh with the high-altitude military outpost on the Siachen Glacier at an altitude of 5,401 m/17,730 ft in the Karakoram range, Kashmir. It is thought to be the highest road in the world.

Khartoum or **El Khartum** capital and trading centre of Sudan, in Khartoum State, at the junction of the Blue and White Nile rivers; population (1998 est) 1,038,600, and of Khartoum North, across the Blue Nile, 890,000. Omdurman is also a suburb of Khartoum, giving the urban area a population of over 3 million. It has long served as a major communications centre between the Arab countries of North Africa and central African countries. The city lies in a rich cotton-growing area and an oil pipeline reached it from Port Sudan on the Red Sea. Industries include tanning, textiles, light engineering, food processing, glassware, and printing.

khedive title granted by the Turkish sultan to his Egyptian viceroy in 1867, retained by succeeding rulers until 1914.

Khmer or **Kmer** the largest ethnic group in Cambodia, numbering about 7 million. Khmer minorities also live in eastern Thailand and South Vietnam. The Khmer language belongs to the Mon-Khmer family of Austro-Asiatic languages.

Khmer Republic former name (1970–76) of Cambodia.

Khmer Rouge communist movement in Cambodia (Kampuchea) formed in the 1960s. Controlling the country 1974–78, it was responsible for mass deportations and executions under the leadership of *Pol Pot. Since then it has conducted guerrilla warfare, and in 1991 gained representation in the governing body.

Khoikhoi formerly **Hottentot**, (*Khoi-khoin* 'men of men') member of any of several peoples living in Namibia and Cape Province of South Africa. They number about 30,000. Their language is related to San (spoken by the Kung) and uses clicks for certain consonants; it belongs to the Khoisan family. The Khoikhoi once inhabited a wider area, but were driven into the Kalahari Desert by invading Bantu peoples and Dutch colonists in the 18th century. They live as nomadic hunter-gatherers, in family groups, and have animist beliefs.

Khomeini, Ayatollah Ruhollah (1900–1989) Iranian Shiite Muslim leader. Exiled from 1964 for his opposition to Shah Pahlavi, he returned when the shah left the country in 1979, and established a fundamentalist Islamic republic. His rule was marked by a protracted war with Iraq, and suppression of opposition within Iran, executing thousands of opponents.

Khrushchev, Nikita Sergeyevich (1894–1971) Soviet politician, secretary general of the Communist Party 1953–64, premier 1958–64. He emerged as leader from the power struggle following Stalin's death and was the first official to denounce Stalin, in 1956. His de-Stalinization programme gave rise to revolts in Poland and Hungary in 1956. Because of problems with the economy and foreign affairs (a breach with China in 1960; conflict with the USA in the *Cuban missile crisis of 1962), he was ousted by Leonid Brezhnev and Alexei Kosygin.

Khuzestan province of southwest Iran, on the northern shores of the Gulf; area 66,560 sq km/25,700 sq mi; population (1996 est) 3,746,800. It has Iran's chief oil resources. Cities include the administrative centre of Ahvaz and the ports of Abadan and Khorramshahr. A large proportion of the population is Arab. The province is often referred to by Arabs as Arabistan.

Khwarizmi, al-, Muhammad ibn-Musa (c. 780– c. 850) Persian mathematician. He wrote a book on algebra, from part of whose title (*al-jabr*) comes the word 'algebra', and a book in which he introduced to the West the Hindu–Arabic decimal number system. The word 'algorithm' is a corruption of his name.

Khyber Pass pass through the mountain range that separates Pakistan from Afghanistan; length 53 km/33 mi; width varies from 140 m/460 ft at its widest to about 15 m/50 ft at its narrowest. On either side are rock faces rising to a height of 915 m/3,000 ft in some places. The highest point, at Landi Kotal, is 520 m/1,700 ft higher than the town of Jamrud at the entrance to the pass. The Khyber Pass was used by invaders of India. The present road was constructed by the British during the *Afghan Wars (1839–42 and 1878–80).

Kiangsi alternative spelling of *Jiangxi, a province of China.

Kiangsu alternative spelling of *Jiangsu, a province of China.

kibbutz Israeli communal collective settlement with collective ownership of all property and earnings, collective organization of work and decision-making, and communal housing for children. A modified version, the *Moshav Shitufi*, is similar to the collective farms that were typical of the USSR. Other Israeli cooperative rural settlements include the *Moshav Ovdim*, which has equal opportunity, and the similar but less strict *Moshav* settlement.

kidney in vertebrates, one of a pair of organs responsible for fluid regulation, excretion of waste products, and maintaining the ionic composition of the blood – in other words the regulation of the concentrations of some chemicals in the blood. The kidneys are situated on the rear wall of the abdomen. Each one consists of a number of long tubules (see *nephron) – the outer parts filter the aqueous components of blood, and the inner parts selectively reabsorb vital salts, leaving waste products in the remaining fluid (urine), which is passed through the ureter to the bladder.

kidney machine medical equipment used in *dialysis.

Kiel Canal German *Nord-Ostsee-Kanal*; formerly **Kaiser Wilhelm Canal**, waterway connecting the Baltic with the North Sea; area 98 km/60 mi long. It provides passage for ocean-going vessels. Built by Germany in the years before World War I, the canal allowed the German navy to move from its Baltic bases to the open sea without travelling through international waters. It was declared an international waterway by the Treaty of Versailles in 1919.

Kierkegaard, Søren Aabye (1813–1855) Danish philosopher and theologian, often considered to be the founder of *existentialism. He argued that no system of thought could explain the unique experience of the individual. He defended Christianity, suggesting that God cannot be known through reason, but only through a 'leap of faith'. His chief works are *Enten-Eller/Either-Or* (1843) and *Begrebet Angest/Concept of Dread* (1844).

Kieslowski, Krzysztof (1941–1996) Polish film director and screenwriter. One of the great European auteurs of the 1980s and 1990s, his films are often personal narratives with broader moral and political implications. His 'Three Colours' trilogy – *Trois couleurs: Bleu/Blue* (1993), *Trois couleurs: Blanc/White* (1993), and *Trois couleurs: Rouge/Red* (1994) – is based on the French flag and the concepts of liberty, equality, and fraternity.

Kiev Ukrainian **Kyyiv**, capital and largest city of Ukraine, situated at the confluence of the Desna and Dnieper rivers; population (2003 est) 2,588,400; urban agglomeration 3,296,100. Kiev was the capital of Russia in the Middle Ages. It is a major industrial centre, producing chemicals, clothing, leather goods, machine tools, electronic, optical, and electrical goods, and is also a market city for the abundant agricultural produce of the western Ukraine.

Kigali capital of Rwanda, 80 km/50 mi east of Lake Kivu, and just south of the Equator; population (2001 est) 327,700. It is an important centre for trade in local produce, including coffee, cattle, cassiterite (tin ore), and tungsten. Manufacturing industries include textiles, chemicals, tin-processing, paints, and cigarettes. Kigali is served by an international airport, and is connected by trunk roads to Uganda to the north and Burundi to the south.

Kikuyu member of the dominant ethnic group in Kenya, numbering about 3 million. The Kikuyu are primarily cultivators of millet, although many have entered the professions. Their language belongs to the Bantu branch of the Niger-Congo family.

Kildare county of the Republic of Ireland, in the province of Leinster; county town Naas; area 1,690 sq km/652 sq mi; population (2002 est) 164,000. The principal rivers are the Barrow, the Boyne, the Lesser Barrow, and the Liffey. Kildare is wet and boggy in the north with extensive grassy plains and rolling hills, and includes part of the Bog of Allen, the highest point being Cupidstown Hill (379 m/1,243 ft). The town of Maynooth houses a constituent part of the National University of Ireland; originally the college was a seminary for Roman Catholic priests. The Curragh, at Tully, is a plain that is the site of the national stud and headquarters of Irish horse racing; steeplechase racing also takes place at Punchestown. Cattle are grazed in the north, and in the south products include wheat, oats, barley, potatoes, beet, and cattle. Other main towns include Athy, Droichead Nua, and Kildare.

Kilimanjaro volcano in Tanzania, the highest mountain in Africa, 5,895 m/19,340 ft. It is situated between Lake Victoria and the coast. It culminates in two peaks, Kibo (5,895 m/19,340 ft) and Mawenzi (5,149 m/16,893 ft), both craters of extinct volcanoes. The first recorded ascent was by the German geographer Hans Meyer and the Austrian mountaineer Ludwig Purtscheller in 1889.

Kilkenny county of the Republic of Ireland, in the province of Leinster; county town Kilkenny; area 2,060 sq km/795 sq mi; population (2002 est) 80,400. It has the rivers Nore, Suir, and Barrow, the highest point being Brandon Hill (516 m/1,693 ft). Industries include clothing, footwear, and brewing, and agricultural activities include cattle rearing and dairy farming. Principal towns include Castlecomer, Callan, Graiguenamanagh, and Thomastown.

killer whale *or* **orca** toothed whale belonging to the dolphin family, found in all seas of the world. It is black on top, white below, and grows up to 9 m/30 ft long. It is the only whale that has been observed to prey on other whales, as well as on seals and seabirds. (Species *Orcinus orca*, family Delphinidae.)

Killiecrankie, Battle of in British history, during the first *Jacobite uprising, defeat on 27 July 1689 of General Mackay (for William of Orange) by John Graham of *Claverhouse, Viscount Dundee, a supporter of James II, at Killiecrankie, Scotland. Despite the victory, Claverhouse was killed by a chance shot and the revolt soon petered out; the remaining forces were routed at Dunkeld on 21 August.

kilo- prefix denoting multiplication by 1,000, as in kilohertz, a unit of frequency equal to 1,000 hertz.

kilobyte K *or* **KB** in computing, a unit of memory equal to 1,024 *bytes. It is sometimes used, less precisely, to mean 1,000 bytes.

kilogram symbol kg, SI unit of mass equal to 1,000 grams (2.24 lb). It is defined as a mass equal to that of the international prototype, a platinum-iridium cylinder held at the International Bureau of Weights and Measures in Sèvres, France.

kilometre symbol km, unit of length equal to 1,000 metres, equivalent to 3,280.89 ft or 0.6214 (about ⅝) of a mile.

kilowatt symbol kW, unit of power equal to 1,000 watts or about 1.34 horsepower. If an electrical appliance has a power rating of 1 kW, it will change 1000 J of electrical energy into other forms of energy every second; for example, a 1 kW electric heater changes 1000 J of electrical energy into 1000 J of heat energy every second it is turned on.

kilowatt-hour symbol kWh, commercial unit of electrical energy, defined as the work done by a power of 1,000 watts in one hour and equal to 3.6 megajoules. It is used to calculate the cost of electrical energy taken from the domestic supply.

kimberlite igneous rock that is ultramafic (containing very little silica); a type of alkaline *peridotite with a porphyritic texture (larger crystals in a fine-grained matrix), containing mica in addition to olivine and other minerals. Kimberlite represents the world's principal source of diamonds.

Kim Il Sung (1912–1994) North Korean communist politician and marshal. He became prime minister in 1948 and led North Korea in the *Korean War 1950–53. He became president in 1972, retaining the presidency of the Communist Workers' party. He liked to be known as the 'Great Leader' and campaigned constantly for the reunification of Korea. His son **Kim Jong Il**, known as the 'Dear Leader', succeeded him.

Kim Jong Il (1942–) North Korean communist politician, national leader from 1994, when he succeeded his father, *Kim Il Sung in what was the first dynastic succession in the communist world. Despite his official designation 'Dear Leader', he lacked his father's charisma and did not automatically inherit the public adulation accorded to him. In October 1997 he formally became general secretary of the ruling communist party amid famine in North Korea.

kimono traditional Japanese costume. Worn in the Heian period (more than 1,000 years ago), it is still used by women for formal wear and informally by men.

kinesis (plural **kineses**) in biology, a nondirectional movement in response to a stimulus; for example, woodlice move faster in drier surroundings. **Taxis** is a similar pattern of behaviour, but there the response is directional.

kinetic energy the energy of a body resulting from motion.

kinetics branch of chemistry that investigates the rates of chemical reactions.

kinetics branch of *dynamics dealing with the action of forces producing or changing the motion of a body; **kinematics** deals with motion without reference to force or mass.

kinetic theory theory describing the physical properties of matter in terms of the behaviour – principally movement – of its component atoms or molecules. It states that all matter is made up of very small particles that are in constant motion, and can be used to explain the properties of solids, liquids, and gases, as well as changes of state. In a solid, the particles are arranged close together in a regular pattern and vibrate on the spot. In a liquid, the particles are still close together but in an irregular arrangement, and the particles are moving a little faster and are able to slide

past one another. In a gas, the particles are far apart and moving rapidly, bouncing off the walls of their container. The temperature of a substance is dependent on the velocity of movement of its constituent particles, increased temperature being accompanied by increased movement.

King, Billie Jean (1943–) born Billie Jean Moffitt, US tennis player. She won a record 20 Wimbledon titles 1961–79 and 39 *Grand Slam titles, and fought for equal treatment and equal pay for women tennis players. In 1973 she formed the Women's Tennis Association and the Players' Union. In 1974, with Olympic swimmer Donna de Varona and others, she created the Women's Sports Foundation to support and promote women in sport. That same year, in front of a worldwide audience, she beat Bobby Riggs, a self-confessed chauvinist and critic of women in sport.

King, Martin Luther, Jr (1929–1968) US civil-rights campaigner, black leader, and Baptist minister. He first came to national attention as leader of the Montgomery, Alabama, bus boycott of 1955–56, and was one of the organizers of the march of 200,000 people on Washington, DC in 1963 to demand racial equality, during which he delivered his famous 'I have a dream' speech. He was awarded the Nobel Prize for Peace in 1964 for his work as a civil-rights leader and an advocate of nonviolence. He was assassinated on 4 April 1968 in Memphis, Tennessee.

King, W(illiam) L(yon) Mackenzie (1874–1950) Canadian Liberal prime minister 1921–26, 1926–30, and 1935–48. He maintained the unity of the English- and French-speaking populations, and was instrumental in establishing equal status for Canada with the UK.

king crab or **horseshoe crab** marine *arthropod found on the Atlantic coast of North America, and the coasts of Asia. The upper side of the body is entirely covered with a dark, rounded shell, and it has a long spinelike tail. It is up to 60 cm/2 ft long. It is unable to swim, and lays its eggs in the sand at the high-water mark. (Class Arachnida, subclass Xiphosura.)

kingdom primary division in biological *classification. At one time, only two kingdoms were recognized: animals and plants. Today most biologists prefer a five-kingdom system, even though it still involves grouping together organisms that are probably unrelated. One widely accepted scheme is as follows: **Kingdom Animalia** (all multicellular animals); **Kingdom Plantae** (all plants, including seaweeds and other algae, except blue-green); **Kingdom Fungi** (all fungi, including the unicellular yeasts, but not slime moulds); **Kingdom Protista** or **Protoctista** (protozoa, diatoms, dinoflagellates, slime moulds, and various other lower organisms with eukaryotic cells); and **Kingdom Monera** (all prokaryotes – the bacteria and cyanobacteria, or *blue-green algae). The first four of these kingdoms make up the eukaryotes.

kingfisher any of a group of heavy-billed birds found near streams, ponds, and coastal areas around the world. The head is exceptionally large, and the long, angular bill is keeled; the tail and wings are relatively short, and the legs very short, with short toes. Kingfishers plunge-dive for fish and aquatic insects. The nest is usually a burrow in a riverbank. (Family Alcedinidae, order Coraciiformes.)

Kingsley, Charles (1819–1875) English author. A rector, he was known as the 'Chartist clergyman' because of such social novels as *Yeast* (1848) and *Alton Locke* (1850). His historical novels include *Westward Ho!* (1855) and *Hereward the Wake* (1866). He also wrote, for children, *The Water Babies* (1863).

Kingston capital, largest city, and principal port of Jamaica, West Indies, on the southeast coast; population (2002 est) 583,900. It is the cultural and commercial centre of the island, and industries include tourism, oil refining, clothing manufacture, and food processing, and there are large exports of sugar, rum, molasses and bananas.

Kingston upon Hull *or* **Hull** port and administrative centre of Kingston upon Hull City unitary authority in northeast England, where the river Hull flows into the north side of the Humber estuary, 90 km/56 mi east of Leeds; population (2001 est) 243,400. Hull has been a flourishing port for 700 years, and there are 11 km/7 mi of modern docks located on the Humber estuary. Industries include fish processing, flour milling, and saw milling – Hull is the largest timber port in the UK. Ferries travel from Hull to Rotterdam, the Netherlands, and Zeebrugge, Belgium.

Kingstown capital and principal port of St Vincent and the Grenadines, West Indies, in the southwest of the island of St Vincent; population (1994 est) 15,900 (town), 26,900 (urban area). The port has a deep-water harbour; exports include bananas, coconuts, and arrowroot.

kinkajou Central and South American carnivorous mammal belonging to the raccoon family. Yellowish-brown, with a rounded face and slim body, the kinkajou grows to 55 cm/1.8 ft with a 50 cm/1.6 ft tail, and has short legs with sharp claws. It spends its time in trees and has a prehensile tail, which it uses as an extra limb when moving from branch to branch. It feeds largely on fruit. (Species *Potos flavus*, family Procyonidae.)

Kinshasa formerly **Léopoldville** (until 1966), capital of the Democratic Republic of Congo on the Congo River, 400 km/250 mi inland from the port of Matadi; population (1994 est) 4,655,300. Industries include ship building and repairing, chemicals, textiles, engineering, food processing, and furniture. It was founded by the explorer Henry Morton Stanley in 1881. The National University of Kinshasa is here.

kinship in anthropology, human relationship based on blood or marriage, and sanctified by law and custom. Kinship forms the basis for most human societies and for such social groupings as the family, clan, or tribe.

Kipling, (Joseph) Rudyard (1865–1936) English writer, born in India. *Plain Tales from the Hills* (1888), about Anglo-Indian society, contains the earliest of his masterly short stories. His books for children, including *The Jungle Book* (1894–95), *Just So Stories* (1902), *Puck of Pook's Hill* (1906), and the picaresque novel *Kim* (1901), reveal his imaginative identification with the exotic. Poems such as 'If–', 'Danny Deever', and 'Gunga Din', express an empathy with common experience, which contributed to his great popularity, together with a vivid sense of 'Englishness' (sometimes belittled as a kind of chauvinistic imperialism). Kipling's work is increasingly valued for its complex characterization and subtle moral viewpoints. He was awarded the Nobel Prize for Literature in 1907.

Kirchner, Ernst Ludwig (1880–1938) German artist. He was a leading member of the expressionist *die Brücke* group in Dresden from 1905 and in Berlin from 1911. In Berlin he painted city scenes and portraits, using lurid colours and bold diagonal paint strokes recalling woodcut technique.

Kirghiz *or* **Kirgiz** member of a pastoral people numbering approximately 1.5 million. The Kirghiz live in Tajikistan, Uzbekistan, Kyrgyzstan, China (Xinjiang), and Afghanistan (Wakhan corridor). They are Sunni Muslims, and their Turkic language belongs to the Altaic family.

Kirghizia alternative form of Kyrgyzstan, a country in central Asia.

Kiribati
formerly **part of the Gilbert and Ellice Islands (until 1979)**

National name: *Ribaberikan Kiribati/Republic of Kiribati*

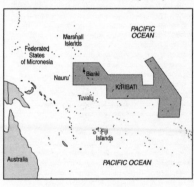

Area: 717 sq km/277 sq mi
Capital: Bairiki (on Tarawa atoll)
Major towns/cities: principal islands are the Gilbert Islands, the Phoenix Islands, the Line Islands, Banaba
Major ports: Bairiki, Betio (on Tarawa)
Physical features: comprises 33 Pacific coral islands: the Kiribati (Gilbert), Rawaki (Phoenix), Banaba (Ocean Island), and three of the Line Islands including Kiritimati (Christmas Island); island groups crossed by Equator and International Date Line
Head of state and government: Anote Tong from 2003
Political system: liberal democracy
Political executive: limited presidency
Political parties: Maneaban Te Mauri (MTM), dominant faction; National Progressive Party (NPP), former governing faction 1979–94
Currency: Australian dollar
GNI per capita (PPP): (US$) 2,070 (2002 est)
Exports: copra, fish, seaweed, bananas, breadfruit, taro. Principal market: Bangladesh 51.4% (1999)
Population: 88,000 (2003 est)
Language: English (official), Gilbertese
Religion: Roman Catholic, Protestant (Congregationalist)
Life expectancy: 58 (men); 63 (women) (2001 est)
Chronology
1st millennium BC: Settled by Austronesian-speaking peoples.

1606: Visited by Spanish explorers.
late 18th century: Visited by British naval officers.
1857: Christian mission established.
1892: Gilbert (Kiribati) and Ellice (Tuvalu) Islands proclaimed a British protectorate.
1916–39: Uninhabited Phoenix Islands, Christmas Island, Ocean Island, and Line Island (Banaba) added to colony.
1942–43: While occupied by Japanese it was the scene of fierce fighting with US troops.
late 1950s: UK tested nuclear weapons on Christmas Island (Kiritimati).
1963: Legislative council established.
1974: Legislative council replaced by an elected House of Assembly.
1975: The mainly Melanesian-populated Ellice Islands separated to become Tuvalu.
1977: The predominantly Micronesian-populated Gilbert Islands was granted internal self-government.
1979: The Gilbert Islands achieved independence within the Commonwealth, as the Republic of Kiribati, with Ieremia Tabai as president.
1985: Kiribati's first political party, the opposition Christian Democrats, was formed.
1994: The government resigned after losing a vote of confidence. Teburoro Tito of the MTM was elected president.
1999: Kiribati was admitted to the UN.
2003: Tito was ousted after a no-confidence vote. Anote Tong was elected president. Kiribati established diplomatic relations with Taiwan. In response to this, China severed diplomatic ties and removed its satellite tracking station, which had been in place since 1997 under a 15-year lease agreement.

Kirkwall administrative headquarters and port of the *Orkney Islands, Scotland, on the north coast of the largest island, Mainland; population (1991) 6,700. The main industry is distilling. The Norse cathedral of St Magnus dates from 1137. The Bishop's Palace is also 12th-century, and the Earl's Palace was completed in 1606.

Kirov, Sergei Mironovich (1886–1934) Russian Bolshevik leader who joined the party in 1904 and played a prominent part in the 1918–20 civil war. As one of *Stalin's closest associates, he became first secretary of the Leningrad Communist Party. His assassination, possibly engineered by Stalin, led to the political trials held during the next four years as part of the purge.

Kissinger, Henry (Alfred) (1923–) German-born US diplomat. After a brilliant academic career at Harvard University, he was appointed national security adviser in 1969 by President Nixon, and was secretary of state 1973–77. His missions to the USSR and China improved US relations with both countries, and he took part in negotiating US withdrawal from Vietnam in 1973 and in Arab-Israeli peace negotiations 1973–75. He shared the Nobel Prize for Peace in 1973 with North Vietnamese diplomat Le Duc Tho for their efforts in securing the peace settlement of the Vietnam War.

kiss of life or **artificial ventilation** in first aid, another name for *artificial respiration.

Kiswahili another name for the *Swahili language.

Kitasato, Shibasaburo (1852–1931) Japanese bacteriologist who discovered the plague bacillus while investigating an outbreak of plague in Hong Kong.

He was the first to grow the tetanus bacillus in pure culture. He and German bacteriologist Emil von *Behring discovered that increasing nonlethal doses of tetanus toxin give immunity to the disease.

Kitchener, Horatio (Herbert) (1850–1916) 1st Earl Kitchener of Khartoum, Irish soldier and administrator. He defeated the Sudanese at the Battle of Omdurman in 1898 and reoccupied Khartoum. In South Africa, he was commander-in-chief 1900–02 during the Boer War, and he commanded the forces in India 1902–09. Appointed war minister on the outbreak of World War I, he was successful in his campaign calling for voluntary recruitment.

kite quadrilateral with two pairs of adjacent equal sides. The geometry of this figure follows from the fact that it has one axis of symmetry.

kite any of a group of birds of prey found in all parts of the world. Kites have long, pointed wings and, usually, a forked tail. There are about 20 species. (Family Accipitridae, order Falconiformes.)

kitsch (German 'trash') in the arts, anything that claims to have an aesthetic purpose but is tawdry and tasteless. It usually applies to cheap sentimental works produced for the mass market, such as those found in souvenir shops and chain stores, but it is also used for any art that is considered in bad taste.

kiwi flightless bird found only in New Zealand. It has long hairlike brown plumage, minute wings and tail, and a very long beak with nostrils at the tip. It is nocturnal and insectivorous. It lays one or two white eggs per year, each weighing up to 450 g/15.75 oz. (Species *Apteryx australis*, family Apterygidae, order Apterygiformes.)

kiwi fruit or **Chinese gooseberry** fruit of a vinelike plant grown commercially on a large scale in New Zealand. Kiwi fruits are egg-sized, oval, and similar in flavour to gooseberries, though much sweeter, with a fuzzy brown skin. (*Actinidithia chinensis*, family Actinidiaceae.)

Klee, Paul (1879–1940) Swiss painter and graphic artist. He was one of the most original and prolific artists of the 20th century. Endlessly inventive and playful, and suggesting a childlike innocence, his works are an exploration of the potential of line, plane, and colour. *Twittering Machine* (1922; Museum of Modern Art, New York) is typical.

kleptomania (Greek *kleptes* 'thief') behavioural disorder characterized by an overpowering desire to possess articles for which one has no need. In kleptomania, as opposed to ordinary theft, there is no obvious need or use for what is stolen and sometimes the sufferer has no memory of the theft.

Klimt, Gustav (1862–1918) Austrian painter. He was influenced by *Jugendstil* (art nouveau) and was a founding member of the Vienna *Sezession group in 1897. His paintings, often sensual and erotic, have a jewelled effect similar to mosaics, for example *The Kiss* (1909; Musée des Beaux-Arts, Strasbourg). His many portraits include *Judith I* (1901; Österreichische Galerie, Vienna).

Klondike former gold-mining area in northwest *Yukon Territory, Canada, near Dawson, where the Klondike and Yukon rivers meet. It is named after the river valley (length 193 km/120 mi) near where gold was found in August 1896. By 1898, at the height of the

'Klondike Gold Rush', over 30,000 people had moved temporarily into the area.

knapweed any of several weedy plants belonging to the daisy family. In the common knapweed (*C. nigra*), also known as a **hardhead**, the hard, dark buds break open at the top into pale purple composite flowers. It is native to Europe and has been introduced to North America. (Genus *Centaurea*, family Compositae.)

Kneller, Godfrey (1646–1723) born Gottfried Kniller, German-born portrait painter who lived in England from 1674. A successful and prolific painter of nearly 6,000 portraits, he dominated English portraiture of the late 17th and early 18th centuries. He was court painter to Charles II, James II, William III, and George I. Kneller was knighted in 1692 and made a baronet in 1715.

Knesset the Israeli parliament, consisting of a single chamber of 120 deputies elected for a period of four years.

knifefish any of a group of fishes in which the body is deep at the front and drawn to a narrow or pointed tail at the rear, the main fin being the well-developed long ventral (stomach) fin that completes the knifelike shape. The ventral fin is rippled for forward or backward movement. Knifefishes produce electrical fields, which they use for navigation. (Genus *Gymnotus* and other allied genera, family Gymnotidae.)

knighthood, orders of fraternity carrying with it the rank of knight, admission to which is granted as a mark of royal favour or as a reward for public services. During the Middle Ages in Europe such fraternities fell into two classes: religious and secular. The first class, including the *Templars and the Knights of *St John, consisted of knights who had taken religious vows and devoted themselves to military service against the Saracens (Arabs) or other non-Christians. The secular orders probably arose from bands of knights engaged in the service of a prince or great noble.

Knock village and parish in County Mayo, Republic of Ireland, 11 km/7 mi northeast of Claremorris; the village has a small population (around 1,000 in 2002) but as an international place of pilgrimage receives a reputed 1.5 million visitors per year. Knock is known as the site of alleged apparitions of the Virgin Mary (the first on 21 August 1879), and for its church shrine, the Basilica of Our Lady, 'Queen of Ireland', which seats 12,000 and was opened in 1976. Horan International Airport, opened in 1986, receives transatlantic flights; it was named after Monsignor James Horan, a parish priest who launched the project to attract pilgrims.

Knossos Middle and Late Bronze Age settlement, 8 km/5 mi south of present-day Iraklion, Crete. Knossos is one of the main cities of what is known as the *Minoan civilization (a modern name derived from the legend of King Minos). The archaeological site, excavated by Arthur Evans in 1899–1935, includes the palace throne room, the remains of frescoes, and construction on more than one level. The Greek myth of Theseus's encounter with the Minotaur in a labyrinth was possibly derived from the ritual 'bull-leaping' by young people depicted in the palace frescoes and from the mazelike layout of the palace.

knot wading bird belonging to the sandpiper family. It is about 25 cm/10 in long, with a short bill, neck, and legs. In the winter, it is grey above and white below, but in the breeding season, it is brick-red on the head and chest and black on the wings and back. It feeds on insects and molluscs. (Species *Calidris canutus*, family Scolopacidae, order Charadriiformes.)

knot in navigation, unit by which a ship's speed is measured, equivalent to one *nautical mile per hour (one knot equals about 1.15 miles per hour). It is also sometimes used in aviation.

knowledge-based system (KBS) computer program that uses an encoding of human knowledge to help solve problems. It was discovered during research into *artificial intelligence that adding heuristics (rules of thumb) enabled programs to tackle problems that were otherwise difficult to solve by the usual techniques of computer science.

Knox, John (c. 1505–1572) Scottish Protestant reformer, founder of the Church of Scotland. He spent several years in exile for his beliefs, including a period in Geneva where he met John *Calvin. He returned to Scotland in 1559 to promote Presbyterianism. His books include *First Blast of the Trumpet Against the Monstrous Regiment of Women* (1558).

koala marsupial (mammal that carries its young in a pouch) found only in eastern Australia. It feeds almost entirely on eucalyptus shoots. It is about 60 cm/2 ft long, and resembles a bear (it is often incorrectly described as a 'koala bear'). The popularity of its greyish fur led to its almost complete extermination by hunters. Under protection since 1936, it rapidly increased in numbers, but recently numbers have fallen from 400,000 in 1985 to 40,000–80,000 in 1995. (Species *Phascolarctos cinereus*, family Phalangeridae.)

Koch, (Heinrich Hermann) Robert (1843–1910) German bacteriologist who was awarded a Nobel Prize for Physiology or Medicine in 1905 for his investigations and discoveries in relation to tuberculosis. Koch and his assistants devised the techniques for culturing bacteria outside the body, and formulated the rules for showing whether or not a bacterium is the cause of a disease.

Kodály, Zoltán (1882–1967) Hungarian composer and educationalist. With Béla Bartók, he recorded and transcribed Magyar folk music, the scales and rhythm of which he incorporated in a deliberately nationalist style. His works include the cantata *Psalmus Hungaricus* (1923), a comic opera *Háry János* (1925–27), and orchestral dances and variations. His 'Kodály method' of school music education is widely practised.

Koestler, Arthur (1905–1983) Hungarian-born British writer. Imprisoned by the Nazis in France 1940, he escaped to England. His novel *Darkness at Noon* (1940), regarded as his masterpiece, is a fictional account of the Stalinist purges, and draws on his experiences as a prisoner under sentence of death during the Spanish Civil War. He also wrote extensively about creativity, science, parapsychology, politics, and culture.

Kohl, Helmut (1930–) German conservative politician, leader of the Christian Democratic Union (CDU) 1976–98, West German chancellor (prime minister) 1982–90, and German chancellor from 1990–98. He oversaw the reunification of East and West Germany 1989–90 and in 1990 won a resounding victory to become the first chancellor of a reunited Germany. His miscalculation of the true costs of reunification and their subsequent effects on the German economy led to a dramatic fall in his popularity, but as the economy recovered, so did his public esteem, enabling him to achieve a historic fourth electoral victory in 1994. He was defeated by Gerhard Schroeder of the Social Democratic Party (SDP) in the elections of September 1998, a year in which unemployment reached record levels. In December 1999, Kohl admitted to receiving secret and therefore illegal payments on behalf of his party when he was chancellor, and he was fined 300,000 marks/US$143,000 in January 2001.

kohlrabi variety of kale, which is itself a variety of *cabbage; it is used for food and resembles a turnip. The leaves of kohlrabi shoot from a round swelling on the main stem. (*Brassica oleracea caulorapa* or *B. oleracea gongylodes*, family Cruciferae.)

Kok, Wim (1938–) Dutch trade unionist and politician, leader of the Partij van der Arbeid (PvdA; Labour Party) (PvdA) and prime minister from 1994. After an inconclusive general election in May 1994, Kok eventually succeeded in forming a broad-based three-party coalition of the PvdA with the People's Party of Freedom and Democracy (VVD) and Democrats 66 (D-66), both centrist parties. In August 2001, Kok announced that he would stand down as PvdA leader after elections in May 2002, and named parliamentary floor leader Ad Melkert as his chosen successor.

Kokoschka, Oskar (1886–1980) Austrian expressionist painter. Initially influenced by the Vienna *Sezession painters, he painted vivid landscapes, and highly charged allegories and portraits, for example *The Bride of the Wind(The Tempest)* (1914; Kunstmuseum, Basel). His writings include expressionist plays and poetry.

kola alternative spelling of *cola, any of a group of tropical trees.

Kola Peninsula Russian **Kolskiy Poluostrov**, peninsula in the far northwestern Russian Federation, between the Barents Sea and the White Sea. Administratively, it forms part of Murmansk oblast (region). Its total area is 129,500 sq km/50,000 sq mi, and it has a population of 1.3 million (of whom 2,000 are Saami). The port of Murmansk and the mining centre of Kirovsk are the chief cities. In the northeast are tundras; the southwest is forested. To the northwest the low-lying granite plateau adjoins Norway's thinly populated county of Finnmark. The peninsula has rich mineral deposits in the Khibiny mountains.

Kollontai, Alexandra Mikhailovna (1872–1952) born Alexandra Mikhailovna Domontovich, Russian revolutionary, politician, and writer. In 1905 she published *On the Question of the Class Struggle*, and, as commissar for public welfare, was the only female member of the first Bolshevik government. She campaigned for domestic reforms such as acceptance of free love, simplification of divorce laws, and collective child care.

Kollwitz, Käthe (1867–1945) born Käthe Schmidt, German graphic artist and sculptor. One of the leading *expressionists, she is noted for her harrowing and often disturbing drawings, etchings, lithographs, and *woodcuts on the themes of social injustice, poverty, and human suffering, as in the woodcut cycle *Never Again War!* (1924). Her woodcut *The Mothers* (1923)

demonstrates her ability to communicate sorrow and political protest through art. She is considered one of the most influential artists of the 20th century.

Komi republic in the northwestern Russian Federation; area 415,900 sq km/160,579 sq mi; population (1996) 1,185,000 (74% urban) (58% Russian, 23% Komi). The capital is Syktyvkar and Vorkuta is another city. The republic is partly in the Arctic Circle and is largely lowland (taiga) with coniferous forests. There are large coal seams (Pechora Basin) and oil deposits, and rich mineral resources (natural gas, oil shale, and bauxite). Industries include coal mining, oil and natural-gas extraction, and lumbering; and grain and dairy farming.

Kong Zi Pinyin form of *Confucius, Chinese philosopher.

Kon-Tiki legendary creator god of Peru and sun king who ruled the country later occupied by the *Incas and was supposed to have migrated out into the Pacific. The name was used by explorer Thor *Heyerdahl in 1947 for his raft.

kookaburra or **laughing jackass** largest of the world's *kingfishers, found in Australia, with an extraordinary laughing call. It feeds on insects and other small creatures. The body and tail measure 45 cm/18 in, the head is greyish with a dark eye stripe, and the back and wings are flecked brown with grey underparts. It nests in shady forest regions, but will also frequent the vicinity of houses, and its cry is one of the most familiar sounds of the bush in eastern Australia. (Species *Dacelo novaeguineae*, family Alcedinidae, order Coraciiformes.)

kora instrument of West African origin, with 21 strings, made from gourds, with a harplike sound. Traditionally played by griots (hereditary troubadours) of the old Mali empire to accompany praise songs and historical ballads, it was first incorporated into an electronically amplified band by Guinean musician Mory Kante.

Koran or **Quran** or **Qur'an** the sacred book of Islam, written in Arabic. It is said to have been divinely revealed through the angel Jibra'el (Gabriel) to the prophet Muhammad between about AD 610 and 632. The Koran is the prime source of all Islamic ethical and legal doctrines. The Koran is divided into 114 **suwar** (chapters, singular sura), some very long, others consisting of only a few words. It includes many events also described in the Hebrew Bible but narrated from a different viewpoint. Other issues are also discussed, giving injunctions relevant to situations that needed alteration or clarification and addressing problems that the Muslims faced at the time it was written.

Korda, Alexander (Laszlo) (1893–1956) Hungarian-born British film producer and director. He was a dominant figure in the British film industry during the 1930s and 1940s. His films as director include *Marius* (1931), in France, and *The Private Life of Henry VIII* (1933), in England. He was the producer of *The Scarlet Pimpernel* (1935), *The Thief of Bagdad* (1940), *The Third Man* (1949), and *Richard III* (1956), among many others.

Korea peninsula in East Asia, divided into north and south; see *North Korea, and *South Korea.

Korean person who is native to or an inhabitant of Korea; also the language and culture. There are approximately 33 million Koreans in South Korea,

15 million in North Korea, and 3 million elsewhere, principally in Japan, China (Manchuria), Russia, Kazakhstan, Uzbekistan, and the USA.

Korean language language of Korea, written from the 5th century AD in Chinese characters until the invention of an alphabet by King Sejong 1443. The linguistic affiliations of Korean are unclear, but it may be distantly related to Japanese.

Korean War war from 1950 to 1953 between North Korea (supported by China) and South Korea, aided by the United Nations (the troops were mainly US). North Korean forces invaded South Korea on 25 June 1950, and the Security Council of the United Nations, owing to a walk-out by the USSR, voted to oppose them. The North Koreans held most of the South when US reinforcements arrived in September 1950 and forced their way through to the North Korean border with China. The Chinese retaliated, pushing them back to the original boundary by October 1950; truce negotiations began in 1951, although the war did not end until 1953. The Korean War established that the USA was prepared to intervene militarily to stop the spread of *communism. After 1953 the Korean peninsula remained a *Cold War battleground.

Kos *or* **Cos** Greek island, one of the Dodecanese, in the Aegean Sea; area 287 sq km/111 sq mi; population (1998 est) 21,300. A partly mountainous island, it is extremely fertile, and lies about 10 km/6 mi off the Turkish coast. The main town is Kos, located in the northeast of the island.

Kosciusko, Mount highest mountain in Australia (2,228 m/7,310 ft), in the Snowy Mountains of the Australian Alps in southeast New South Wales, close to the border with Victoria and 390 km/240 mi to the southwest of Sydney.

Kosciuszko, Tadeusz Andrzej (1746–1817) Polish general and nationalist. He served with George Washington in the American Revolution (1776–83). He returned to Poland in 1784, fought against the Russian invasion that ended in the partition of Poland, and withdrew to Saxony. He returned again in 1794 to lead the revolt against the occupation, but was defeated by combined Russian and Prussian forces and imprisoned until 1796.

kosher (Hebrew 'appropriate') conforming to religious law with regard to the preparation and consumption of food; in Judaism, conforming to the food laws (**kashrut**) of the *Torah (as laid down in Deuteronomy and Leviticus) and the *Mishnah. Forbidden food is called **trefah**. For example, only animals that chew the cud and have cloven (split) hooves may be eaten; cows and sheep are kosher, pigs are trefah. There are rules (**shechitah**) governing their humane slaughter and their preparation (such as complete draining of blood), which also apply to fowl. Only fish with scales and fins may be eaten; not shellfish. Birds listed in Leviticus may not be eaten. Milk products may not be cooked or eaten with meat or poultry, or until four hours after eating them. Utensils for meat must be kept separate from those for milk.

Kosovo *or* **Kossovo** autonomous region 1945–1990 of southern Serbia; capital Priština; area 10,900 sq km/4,207 sq mi; population (2003 est) 2,088,700, of which about 80% are Albanians; Serbs and Muslims are the dominant minorities. A largely mountainous region,

it includes the fertile valleys of Kosovo and Metohija and is drained by the Southern Morava River. Products include wine, nickel, lead, and zinc; the chief occupations are farming, livestock-raising, and mining. In 1990 fighting broke out between ethnic Albanians, who were agitating for unification of Kosovo with Albania, and Kosovo Serbs, who wanted Kosovo to be merged with the rest of Serbia. The Serbian parliament formally annexed Kosovo in September, and Serbian troops were sent to the region in 1998. In 1999, after a three-month bombing campaign against Serbia, NATO forces moved in to Kosovo to keep the peace, and the United Nations (UN) took over the civil administration of the province.

Kosovo Liberation Armm (KLA) Albanian **Ushtria Çlirimtare e Kosovës (UÇK)**, paramilitary force that operated in the predominantly ethnic Albanian province of Kosovo, in the Federal Republic of Yugoslavia (Serbia and Montenegro from 2003), and fought for the independence of Kosovo. The KLA emerged as an organized movement in 1996, and by 1998 found itself in command of an uprising, which quickly spread across parts of the province. Labelled a terrorist organization by the Serb authorities (and Russia), the KLA took large tracts of land 1997–98, but the Serbs began to fight back in the summer of 1998 and by April 1999 – a month into a NATO offensive against the Federal Republic of Yugoslavia – the organization had been decimated. Thousands of new Kosovar recruits from European countries began to arrive. The KLA participated in the February 1999 Rambouillet peace talks and signed the agreement. It cooperated and coordinated its operations with NATO's air forces in its bombing campaign against Yugoslav military targets.

Kossuth, Lajos (1802–1894) Hungarian nationalist and leader of the revolution of 1848. He proclaimed Hungary's independence of Habsburg rule, became governor of a Hungarian republic in 1849, and, when it was defeated by Austria and Russia, fled first to Turkey and then to exile in Britain and Italy.

Kosygin, Alexei Nikolaievich (1904–1980) Soviet politician, prime minister 1964–80. He was elected to the Supreme Soviet in 1938, became a member of the Politburo in 1946, deputy prime minister in 1960, and succeeded Khrushchev as premier (while Brezhnev succeeded him as party secretary). In the late 1960s Kosygin's influence declined.

koto plucked Japanese string instrument; a long *zither of ancient Chinese origin with 13 silk or nylon strings stretched over moveable bridges. It rests on the floor and the strings are plucked with ivory plectrums worn on the thumb and two fingers of the right hand. The left hand presses the strings behind the bridges to alter the tuning, add ornaments, and create effects such as vibrato and slide. The koto produces a brittle sound.

Krajina region on the frontier between Croatia and Bosnia-Herzegovina; the chief town is Knin. Dominated by Serbs, the region proclaimed itself an autonomous Serbian province after Croatia declared its independence from Yugoslavia in 1991. Krajina was the scene of intense inter-ethnic fighting during the civil war in Croatia 1991–92 and, following the ceasefire in January 1992, 10,000 UN troops were deployed here and in eastern and western Slavonia. Krajina and the area around Okucani were reintegrated into Croatia under the 1995 Dayton peace agreement; Eastern Slavonia was reintegrated in early 1998 after two years under UN administration.

Krakatoa Indonesian **Krakatau**, volcanic island in Sunda Strait, Indonesia, that erupted in 1883, causing 36,000 deaths on Java and Sumatra from the tidal waves that followed. The island is now uninhabited.

Krasnodar krai (territory) in the southwestern Russian Federation; area 83,600 sq km/32,278 sq mi; population (1996) 5,044,000 (54% urban). The capital is Krasnodar, and Armavir, Novorossiysk, Maikop, and Sochi are other cities. The territory is in northwestern Caucasia, adjacent to the Black Sea and the Sea of Azov, and crossed by the River Kuban. It is lowland with black earth soil (*chernozem*) in the north, with the heavily forested northwestern part of the main Caucasian range in the south. There are oil, natural gas, and cement-marl deposits. Industries include food processing, engineering, oil extraction and refining, cement production, and manufacture of farm machinery. It is one of the main agricultural regions of the Russian Federation, growing wheat, sunflowers, rice, tobacco, fruit, and wine, and there is extensive livestock rearing.

Krasnoyarsk krai (territory) in the Russian Federation, in central Siberia; area 2,401,600 sq km/927,258 sq mi (including Arctic Ocean Islands); population (1996) 3,106,000 (74% urban). The capital is Krasnoyarsk and Kansk and Norilsk are other cities. The territory stretches some 3,000 km/1,870 mi north–south along the River Yenisey valley from the Arctic Ocean to the Sayan Mountains. There is lowland to the west of the Yenisey, and plateau to the east. The climate is severe, with permafrost in the north, within the Arctic Circle. The area is largely covered with coniferous forests, but with tundra in the north and fertile steppe in the south. There are huge coal, graphite, iron-ore, gold, non-ferrous metals, and uranium deposits.

Krebs, Hans Adolf (1900–1981) German-born British biochemist who was awarded a Nobel Prize for Physiology or Medicine in 1953 for his discovery of the citric acid cycle, also known as the *Krebs cycle, the final pathway by which food molecules are converted into energy in living tissues. He was knighted in 1958.

Krebs cycle or **citric acid cycle** or **tricarboxylic acid cycle** final part of the chain of biochemical reactions by which organisms break down food using oxygen to release energy (respiration). It takes place within structures called *mitochondria in the body's cells, and breaks down food molecules in a series of small steps, producing energy-rich molecules of *ATP.

kremlin citadel or fortress of Russian cities. The Moscow kremlin dates from the 12th century, and the name 'the Kremlin' was once synonymous with the Soviet government.

Krenz, Egon (1937–) East German communist politician. A member of the East German Socialist Unity Party (SED) from 1955, he joined its politburo in 1983 and was a hardline protégé of Erich *Honecker, succeeding him as party leader and head of state in 1989 after widespread pro-democracy demonstrations. Pledging a 'new course', Krenz opened the country's western border and promised more open elections, but his conversion to pluralism proved weak in the face of

popular protest and he resigned in December 1989 after only a few weeks as party general secretary and head of state. In 1997 a Berlin court found Krenz guilty of manslaughter in connection with the deaths of East Germans who had attempted to flee to the West during the period of communist rule, and sentenced him to six and a half years' imprisonment. In 1999 an appeal against his conviction was unsuccessful and his conviction was upheld.

krill any of several Antarctic *crustaceans, the most common species being *Euphausia superba*. Similar to a shrimp, it is up to 5 cm/2 in long, with two antennae, five pairs of legs, seven pairs of light organs along the body, and is coloured orange above and green beneath. It is the most abundant animal, numbering perhaps 600 trillion (million million). (Order Euphausiacea.)

Krishna eighth *avatar (incarnation) of the Hindu god *Vishnu. The devotion of the *bhakti movement is usually directed towards Krishna; an example of this is the *International Society for Krishna Consciousness. Many tales are told of Krishna's mischievous youth; he appears in the epic *Mahabharata and the *Puranas*, and he is the charioteer of Arjuna in the *Bhagavad-Gita.

Kristallnacht ('night of (broken) glass') night of 9–10 November 1938 when the Nazi Sturmabteilung (SA) militia in Germany and Austria mounted a concerted attack on Jews, their synagogues, homes, and shops. It followed the assassination of a German embassy official in Paris by a Polish-Jewish youth. Subsequent measures included German legislation against Jews owning businesses or property, and restrictions on their going to school or leaving Germany. It was part of the *Holocaust.

Kropotkin, Peter Alexeivich, Prince Kropotkin (1842–1921) Russian anarchist. Imprisoned for revolutionary activities in 1874, he escaped to the UK in 1876 and later moved to Switzerland. Expelled from Switzerland in 1881, he went to France, where he was imprisoned 1883–86. He lived in Britain until 1917, when he returned to Moscow. Among his works are *Memoirs of a Revolutionist* (1899), *Mutual Aid* (1902), and *Modern Science and Anarchism* (1903).

Kruger, (Stephanus Johannes) Paul(us) (1825–1904) President of the Transvaal 1883–1900. He refused to remedy the grievances of the uitlanders (English and other non-Boer white residents) and so precipitated the Second *South African War.

krypton chemical symbol Kr, (Greek *kryptos* 'hidden') colourless, odourless, gaseous, non-metallic element, atomic number 36, relative atomic mass 83.80. It is grouped with the *noble gases (rare gases) in Group 0 of the *periodic table, and was long believed not to enter into reactions, but it is now known to combine with fluorine under certain conditions; it remains inert to all other reagents. As with the other noble gases, krypton's lack of reactivity is due to its full outer shell of electrons. It is present in very small quantities in the air (about 114 parts per million). It is used chiefly in fluorescent lamps, lasers, and gas-filled electronic valves.

Kuala Lumpur (Malay 'muddy confluence') capital of the Federation of Malaysia; population (2000 est) 1,297,500. The city lies in a central position on the Malay Peninsula at the confluence of the Kelang and Gombak rivers, 40 km/25 mi from the west coast.

Malaysia's leading commercial and industrial centre, Kuala Lumpur developed after 1873 with the expansion of tin and rubber trading and processing, which remain important. Other industries include iron, cement, food processing, and the manufacture of electrical, electronic, and railway equipment. International trade is conducted through the port at Klang, on the Strait of Malacca, and through the international airport (1998).

Kublai Khan (*or* **Khubilai Khan** *or* **Kubla Khan**) (*c.* **1216–1294**) Mongol emperor of China from 1259. He completed his grandfather *Genghis Khan's conquest of northern China from 1240, and on his brother Mangu's death in 1259 established himself as emperor of China. He moved the capital to Khanbalik or Cambuluc (now the site of Beijing) and founded the Yuan dynasty, successfully expanding his empire into southern China, Tartary, and Tibet. He also conquered Indochina and Burma, and conducted campaigns in other neighbouring countries to secure tribute claims, but was defeated in an attempt to take Japan in 1281.

Kubrick, Stanley (**1928–1999**) US film director, producer, and screenwriter. His work was eclectic in subject matter and ambitious in scale and technique. It includes *Paths of Glory* (1957), *Dr Strangelove* (1964), *2001: A Space Odyssey* (1968), *A Clockwork Orange* (1971), and *Full Metal Jacket* (1987). His last film, *Eyes Wide Shut*, was completed just before his death and was released in 1999.

kudu either of two species of African antelope. The **greater kudu** (*T. strepsiceros*) is fawn-coloured with thin white vertical stripes, and stands 1.3 m/4.2 ft at the shoulder, with head and body 2.4 m/8 ft long. Males have long spiral horns. The greater kudu is found in bush country from Angola to Ethiopia. The similar **lesser kudu** (*T. imberbis*) lives in East Africa and is 1 m/3 ft at the shoulder. (Genus *Tragelaphus*, family Bovidae.)

kudzu Japanese creeper belonging to the *legume family, which helps fix nitrogen (see *nitrogen cycle) and can be used as a feed crop for animals, but became a pest in the southern USA when introduced to check soil erosion. (*Pueraria lobata*, family Leguminosae.)

Ku Klux Klan (KKK) (Greek *kyklos* 'circle') US secret society dedicated to white supremacy. It was founded in 1866 to oppose *Reconstruction in the Southern states after the American Civil War and to deny political rights to the black population. Members wore hooded white robes to hide their identity, and burned crosses at their night-time meetings. In the late 20th century the Klan evolved into a paramilitary extremist group and forged loose ties with other white supremacist groups.

kulak Russian term for a peasant who could afford to hire labour and often acted as village usurer. The kulaks resisted the Soviet government's policy of collectivization, and in 1930 they were 'liquidated as a class', with up to 5 million being either killed or deported to Siberia.

kumquat small orange-yellow fruit of any of several evergreen trees native to East Asia and cultivated throughout the tropics. The trees grow 2.4–3.6 m/8–12 ft high and have dark green shiny leaves and white scented flowers. The fruit is eaten fresh (the skin is edible), preserved, or candied. The oval or Nagami kumquat is the most common variety. (Genus *Fortunella*, family Rutaceae.)

Kun, Béla (**1886–1937**) Hungarian politician. He created a Soviet republic in Hungary in March 1919, which was overthrown in August 1919 by a Western blockade and Romanian military actions. The succeeding regime under Admiral Horthy effectively liquidated both socialism and liberalism in Hungary.

Kundera, Milan (**1929– **) Czech-born French writer. Known for his political and erotic satires, he achieved widespread acclaim with his first novel, *Zert/The Joke* (1967), a satire on Stalinism in Czechoslovakia. Other successful novels include *Kniha smí chu a zapomnení/The Book of Laughter and Forgetting* (1979) and *Nes nesitelná lehkost bytí/The Unbearable Lightness of Being* (1984; filmed 1988).

Kung formerly **Bushman**, member of a small group of hunter-gatherer peoples of the northeastern Kalahari, southern Africa, still living to some extent nomadically. Their language belongs to the Khoisan family.

kung fu Mandarin ch'üan fa, Chinese art of unarmed combat, one of the *martial arts. It is practised in many forms, the most popular being *wing chun*, 'beautiful springtime'. The basic principle is to use attack as a form of defence.

Kuomintang original spelling of the Chinese nationalist party, now known (outside Taiwan) as *Guomindang.

Kurd member of a people living mostly in the Taurus and Sagros mountains of eastern Turkey, western Iran, and northern Iraq in the region called *Kurdistan. The Kurds have suffered repression in several countries, most brutally in Iraq, where in 1991 more than 1 million were forced to flee their homes. They speak an Indo-Iranian language and are predominantly Sunni Muslims, although there are some Shiites in Iran.

Kurdish language language belonging to the Indo-Iranian branch of the Indo-European family, closely related to Farsi (Persian). It is spoken by the Kurds, a geographically divided ethnic group. Its numerous dialects fall into two main groups: northern Kurmanji and southern Kurmanji (also known as Sorani). Around 60% of Kurds speak one of the northern Kurmanji dialects. Related languages include Zaza and Gurani. Three different alphabets are used – Arabic, Latin, and Cyrillic.

Kurdistan *or* **Kordestan** mountain and plateau region in southwest Asia near Mount Ararat, where the borders of Iran, Iraq, Syria, Turkey, Armenia, and Azerbaijan meet; area 193,000 sq km/74,600 sq mi; total population 25–30 million. It is the home of the *Kurds and is the area over which Kurdish nationalists have traditionally fought to win sovereignty. It is also the name of a northwest Iranian province in the Zagros Mountains, covering 25,000 sq km/9,650 sq mi, population (2001 est) 1,465,000. The chief towns of the region are Kermanshah (Iran); Irbil, Sulaymaniyah, and Kirkuk (Iraq); Divarbakir, Erzurum, and Van (Turkey); and Qamishle (Syria).

Kuril Islands *or* **Kuriles** Russian **Kuril'skiye Ostrova**, chain of about 50 small islands belonging to Russia, stretching from the northeast of Hokkaido, Japan, to the south of Kamchatka, Russia, area 14,765 sq km/5,700 sq mi; population (1990 est) 25,000. The islands include many volcanoes, 35 of which are still active; there are also many hot springs. Offshore is the Kuril Trench, one of the deepest ocean areas in the world, which reaches a depth of 10.5 km/6.5 mi. Two of the Kurils (Etorofu and Kunashiri) are claimed by Japan for historical reasons; they are of strategic importance and have mineral deposits. The surrounding waters are rich in salmon and cod.

Kurosawa, Akira (1910–1998) Japanese director. He is known for his adaptation of elements of *No theatre into film, as well as his historical and literary adaptations. His film *Rashomon* (1950), which won an honorary Academy Award in 1952, introduced Western audiences to Japanese cinema. Epics such as *Shichinin no samurai/Seven Samurai* (1954) combined spectacle with intimate human drama, and were hugely influential on Western cinema.

Kuwait Arabic **Al Kuwayt**; formerly **Qurein**, chief port and capital of the state of Kuwait, on the southern shore of Kuwait Bay; population (1995 est) 28,700. The city is also the capital of the governorate of Kuwait; population (2000 est) 382,400. Kuwait is a banking and investment centre which grew rapidly in size and importance as the country's oil industry developed in the second half of the 20th century. The city was heavily damaged during the Gulf War of 1990–91 against the invading forces of Iraq.

Kuwait

National name: *Dowlat al-Kuwayt/State of Kuwait*

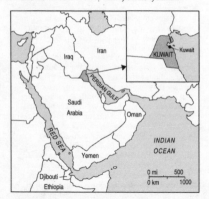

Area: 17,819 sq km/6,879 sq mi
Capital: Kuwait (and chief port)
Major towns/cities: as-Salimiya, Hawalli, Al Farwaaniyah, Abraq Kheetan, Al Jahrah, Al Ahmadi, Al Fuhayhil
Physical features: hot desert; islands of Faylakah, Bubiyan, and Warbah at northeast corner of Arabian Peninsula
Head of state: Sheikh Jabir al-Ahmad al-Jabir al-Sabah from 1977
Head of government: Sabah al-Ahmad al-Jabir al-Sabah from 2003
Political system: absolutist
Political executive: absolute
Political parties: none
Currency: Kuwaiti dinar
GNI per capita (PPP): (US$) 18,800 (2002 est)
Exports: petroleum and petroleum products (accounted for more than 93% of export revenue in 1994), chemical

fertilizer, gas (natural and manufactured), basic manufactures. Principal market: Japan 21.2% (2000)
Population: 2,521,000 (2003 est)
Language: Arabic (78%) (official), English, Kurdish (10%), Farsi (4%)
Religion: Sunni Muslim 45%, Shiite Muslim 40%; Christian, Hindu, and Parsi about 5%
Life expectancy: 75 (men); 79 (women) (2000–05)
Chronology
***c.* 3000 BC:** Archaeological evidence suggests that coastal parts of Kuwait may have been part of a commercial civilization contemporary with the Sumerian, based in Mesopotamia (the Tigris and Euphrates valley area of Iraq).
***c.* 323 BC:** Visited by Greek colonists at the time of Alexander the Great.
7th century AD: Islam introduced.
late 16th century: Fell under nominal control of Turkish Ottoman Empire.
1710: Control was assumed by the Utab, a member of the Anaza tribal confederation in northern Arabia, and Kuwait city was founded, soon developing from a fishing village into an important port.
1756: Autonomous Sheikhdom of Kuwait founded by Abd Rahman of the al-Sabah family, a branch of the Utab.
1776: British East India Company set up a base in the Gulf.
1899: Concerned at the potential threat of growing Ottoman and German influence, Britain signed a treaty with Kuwait, establishing a self-governing protectorate in which the Emir received an annual subsidy from Britain in return for agreeing not to alienate any territory to a foreign power.
1914: Britain recognized Kuwait as an 'independent government under British protection'.
1922–33: Agreement on frontiers with Iraq, to the north, and Nejd (later Saudi Arabia) to the southwest.
1938: Oil discovered; large-scale exploitation after World War II transformed the economy.
1961: Full independence achieved from Britain, with Sheikh Abdullah al-Salem al-Sabah as emir. Attempted Iraqi invasion discouraged by dispatch of British troops to the Gulf.
1962: Constitution introduced, with franchise restricted to 10% of the population.
1977: Crown Prince Jabir Al Ahmad Al Jabir Al Sabah became Emir. The National Assembly was dissolved.
1978: Sheikh Saad al-Abdullah al-Salem al-Sabah was appointed prime minister by the emir.
1981: The National Assembly was reconstituted.
1983: Shiite guerrillas bombed targets in Kuwait; 17 were arrested.
1986: The National Assembly was dissolved.
1987: Kuwaiti oil tankers were reflagged and received US Navy protection; there were missile attacks by Iran.
1988: Aircraft hijacked by pro-Iranian Shiites demanding the release of convicted guerrillas; Kuwait refused.
1989: Two of the convicted guerrillas were released.
1990: Pro-democracy demonstrations were suppressed. Kuwait was annexed by Iraq in August, causing extensive damage to property and environment. The emir set up a government in exile in Saudi Arabia.
1991: US-led coalition forces defeated Iraqi forces in Kuwait in the Gulf War. The new government omitted any opposition representatives.

1992: The reconstituted national assembly was elected, with opposition nominees, including Islamic candidates, winning the majority of seats.

1993: Incursions by Iraq into Kuwait were repelled by US-led air strikes on Iraqi military sites.

1994: The massing of Iraqi troops on the Kuwaiti border prompted a US-led response. Iraqi president Saddam Hussein publicly renounced any claim to Kuwait.

1999: A decree to secure a political voice for women in Kuwait was defeated in parliament, in the belief that female participation in politics would violate the principles of Islam and Kuwaiti traditions.

2000: The high court, and later the constitutional court, upheld parliament's refusal to allow women the vote.

2003: In all-male parliamentary elections, Islamist candidates won 21 seats, supporters of the ruling dynasty 14, and independents 12. Liberals retained only three seats.

2004: Legislation was drafted to allow women to vote and stand for parliament. The government announced that it would be prepared to waive a significant proportion of Iraq's debt and that it was preparing several hundred indictments against Saddam Hussein and his senior officials for war crimes during the Iraqi occuption of Kuwait during 1990 and 1991.

Kwannon *or* **Kannon** in Buddhism, a form, often regarded as female (and known to the West as 'goddess of mercy'), of the bodhisattva *Avalokitesvara. Kwannon is the most important bodhisattva in all main schools of Buddhism, and is an attendant of Amida Buddha. Kwannon is sometimes depicted with many arms extending compassion.

kwashiorkor severe protein deficiency in children under five years, resulting in retarded growth, lethargy, *oedema, diarrhoea, and a swollen abdomen. It is common in developing countries with a high incidence of malnutrition.

KwaZulu-Natal province of the Republic of South Africa, formed from the former province of Natal and the former black homeland of KwaZulu; area 91,481 sq km/35,321 sq mi; population (2000 est) 8,857,600 (75% Zulu). The towns of Ulundi and Pietermaritzburg are joint capital; other towns include Durban and Richards Bay. The province is a narrow plain bounded by the Drakensberg Mountains to the west and the Indian Ocean to the east. Industries include oil refining, coal, iron and steel, engineering, and food processing. Agricultural products include sugar, maize, fruit, black wattle, maize, tobacco, and vegetables. Languages spoken are Zulu (80%), English (15%), and Afrikaans (2%).

Kyd, Thomas (*c.* **1557–1595**) English dramatist. He was the author of a bloody revenge tragedy, *The Spanish Tragedy* (printed about 1590), which anticipated elements present in Shakespeare's *Hamlet*.

Kyoto *or* **Kioto** former capital of Japan 794–1868 (when the capital was changed to Tokyo) on Honshu island, linked by canal with Lake Biwa, 510 km/317 mi west of Tokyo and 40 km/25 mi northeast of Osaka; population (2000 est) 1,468,000. Industries include electrical, chemical, and machinery plants; silk weaving; and the manufacture of porcelain, bronze, lacquerware, dolls, and fans.

Kyoto Protocol international protocol to the United Nations Framework Convention on Climate Change (UNFCCC) that was agreed at Kyoto, Japan, in December 1997. It commits the 186 signatory countries to binding limits on carbon dioxide and other heat-trapping 'greenhouse gases', which many scientists believe contribute to *global warming. For industrialized nations, Kyoto requires cuts in greenhouse gas emissions to an average of 5.2% below 1990 levels by 2012. Developing countries are also committed to emissions targets. The text of the UNFCCC was adopted in 1992 and promoted at the climate summit held in Rio de Janeiro, Brazil, in June 1992. The convention entered into force in 1994, with 166 countries as signatories. The protocol was adopted at the December 1997 Kyoto conference on the UNFCCC. It will come into force on the 90th day after it is ratified by at least 55 parties to the convention which accounted in total for at least 55% of global carbon dioxide emissions in 1990.

Kyrgyzstan

National name: *Kyrgyz Respublikasy/Kyrgyz Republic*

Area: 198,500 sq km/76,640 sq mi

Capital: Bishkek (formerly Frunze)

Major towns/cities: Osh, Karakol, Kyzyl-Kiya, Tokmak, Djalal-Abad

Physical features: mountainous, an extension of the Tien Shan range

Head of state: Kurmanbek Bakiyev (acting) from 2005

Head of government: Kurmanbek Bakiyev (acting) from 2005

Political system: emergent democracy

Political executive: limited presidency

Political parties: Party of Communists of Kyrgyzstan (banned 1991–92); Ata Meken, Kyrgyz-nationalist; Erkin Kyrgyzstan, Kyrgyz-nationalist; Social Democratic Party, nationalist, pro-Akayev; Democratic Movement of Kyrgyzstan, nationalist reformist

Currency: som

GNI per capita (PPP): (US$) 1,520 (2002 est)

Exports: non-ferrous metallurgy, wool, cotton yarn, tobacco, electric power, electronic and engineering

products, food and beverages. Principal market: Germany 28.7% (2001)
Population: 5,138,000 (2003 est)
Language: Kyrgyz (a Turkic language; official), Russian
Religion: Sunni Muslim 70%, Russian Orthodox 20%
Life expectancy: 65 (men); 72 (women) (2000–05)
Chronology
8th century: Spread of Islam.
10th century onwards: Southward migration of Kyrgyz people from upper Yenisey River region to Tien Shan region; accelerated following rise of Mongol Empire in 13th century.
13th–14th centuries: Part of Mongol Empire.
1685: Came under control of Mongol Oirots following centuries of Turkic rule.
1758: Kyrgyz people became nominal subjects of Chinese Empire, following Oirots' defeat by Chinese rulers, the Manchus.
early 19th century: Came under suzerainty of Khanate (chieftaincy) of Kokand, to the west.
1864–76: Incorporated into tsarist Russian Empire.
1916–17: Many Kyrgyz migrated to China after Russian suppression of rebellion in Central Asia and outbreak of civil war following 1917 October Revolution in Russia, with local armed guerrillas (*basmachi*) resisting Bolshevik Red Army.
1917–1924: Part of independent Turkestan republic.
1920s: Land reforms resulted in settlement of many formerly nomadic Kyrgyz; literacy and education improved.
1924: Became autonomous republic within USSR.
1930s: Agricultural collectivization programme provoked *basmachi* resistance and local 'nationalist communists' were purged from Kyrgyz Communist Party (KCP).
1936: Became full union republic within USSR.
1990: A state of emergency was imposed in Bishkek after ethnic clashes.
1991: Askar Akayev, a reform communist, was chosen as president, and condemned the attempted coup in Moscow against the reformist Mikhail Gorbachev; Kyrgyzstan joined the new Commonwealth of Independent States (CIS) and its independence was recognized by the USA.
1992: Kyrgyzstan joined the United Nations and Conference on Security and Cooperation in Europe (CSCE; now the Organization on Security and Cooperation in Europe, OSCE). A market-centred economic reform programme was instituted.
1994: The country joined the Central Asian Union, with Kazakhstan and Uzbekistan.
1996: A constitutional amendment increased the powers of the president. An agreement was made with Kazakhstan and Uzbekistan to create a single economic market.

1997: Private ownership of land was legalized but the privatization programme was suspended. An agreement was made on border controls with Russia.
1998: A referendum approved the private ownership of land.
1999: Amengeldy Muraliyev was appointed prime minister.
2000: Islamist rebels crossed into the country from Afghanistan via Tajikistan, seeking to create an Islamic state in east Uzbekistan. Akayev was re-elected president, despite an economy in crisis, though international observers criticized the conduct of the election. Kurmanbek Bakiyev was appointed prime minister.
2002: Prime Minister Bakiyev resigned after 13 days of anti-government protests and hunger strikes. The civil unrest followed the killing by police of five protesters after the arrest of opposition politician Azimbek Beknazarov. There were also protests against a controversial border treaty agreed with China, in which 95,000 ha/234,750 acres of disputed territory was ceded to China.
2003: Changes to the constitution were approved by referendum. However, international observers reported widespread voting irregularities. A parlamentary bill was passed granting the president and two former Communist Party leaders lifelong immunity from prosecution.
2004: A coalition was formed by opposition parties to challenge the pro-government parties ahead of the 2005 elections.
2005: Demonstrations took place during the parliamentary elections, resulting in President Akayev fleeing the country for Russia. The election results were annulled. The old parliament agreed to dissolve and a newly elected parliament recognized Kurmanbek Bakiev as acting president and prime minister. Akayev resigned as president, remaining in Moscow.

Kyushu *or* **Kiushu** southernmost of the main islands of Japan, separated from Shikoku island by the Bungo Strait, from Honshu island by the Kammon Strait, and from Korea by the Korea Strait; connected to Honshu by bridge and rail tunnel; area 42,150 sq km/16,270 sq mi, including about 370 small islands; population (2000 est) 13,446,000. The capital is *Nagasaki, and Fukuoka, Kumamoto, Kagoshima, and Kitakyushu are other cities. The island is mountainous, with a subtropical climate. It is volcanic and the active volcano Aso-take (1,592 m/5,225 ft) has the world's largest crater. Industries include coal mining and the manufacture of iron and steel, chemicals, tin products, pottery, and semiconductors; there is also a significant tourist trade, for which Beppu, a resort with hot springs, is a noted centre. Cattle and pigs are reared, and agricultural products also include rice, tea, oranges, tobacco, and sweet potatoes.

I

L Roman numeral for 50.

Laâyoune Arabic **El Aaiún**, capital of *Western Sahara; population (1998 est) 139,000. It has expanded from a population of 25,000 in 1970 as a result of Moroccan investment (Morocco lays claim to Western Sahara). Laâyoune is the main urban centre of the country, which was formerly the Spanish Sahara, and lies in an artificial oasis where, through irrigation, cereals and vegetables are grown. To the southwest, especially at Bu Craa, there are large deposits of phosphates, which are linked to the coast by a conveyor belt 29 km/18 mi long, though exploitation has been handicapped by a shortage of water in the area. Since 1976 it has been capital of the (not internationally recognized) Laâyoune province.

labellum lower petal of an orchid flower; it is a different shape from the two lateral petals and gives the orchid its characteristic appearance. The labellum is more elaborate and usually larger than the other petals. It often has distinctive patterning to encourage *pollination by insects; sometimes it is extended backwards to form a hollow spur containing nectar.

Labor Party in Australia, a political party based on socialist principles. It was founded in 1891 and first held office in 1904. It formed governments 1929–31 and 1939–49, but in the intervening periods internal discord provoked splits, and reduced its effectiveness. It returned to power under Gough Whitlam 1972–75, and again under Bob Hawke in 1983; he was succeeded as party leader and prime minister by Paul Keating in 1991, who subsequently lost the 1996 general election.

Labour Party UK political party based on socialist principles, originally formed to represent workers. It was founded in 1900 and first held office in 1924. The first majority Labour government 1945–51 introduced *nationalization and the National Health Service, and expanded *social security. Labour was again in power 1964–70, 1974–79, and from 1997 (winning the 2001 general election). The party leader (Tony *Blair from 1994) is elected by an electoral college, with a weighted representation of the Parliamentary Labour Party (30%), constituency parties (30%), and trade unions (40%). In 2000, the membership of the Labour Party was 361,000.

Labrador area in northeastern Canada, part of the province of *Newfoundland, lying between Ungava Bay on the northwest, the Atlantic Ocean on the east, and the Strait of Belle Isle on the southeast; area

266,060 sq km/102,730 sq mi; population (2001 est) 27,900. The most easterly part of the North American mainland, Labrador consists primarily of a gently sloping plateau with an irregular coastline of numerous bays, fjords, inlets, and cliffs (60–120 m/200–400 ft high). Its industries include fisheries, timber and pulp, and the mining of various minerals, especially iron ore. Hydroelectric resources include Churchill Falls, where one of the world's largest underground power houses is situated (opened in 1971). There is a Canadian Air Force base at Goose Bay on Lake Melville. Many of the small coastal settlements are inhabited primarily by aboriginal groups.

laburnum any of a group of flowering trees or shrubs belonging to the pea family; the seeds develop in pealike pods but are poisonous. *L. anagyroides*, native to the mountainous parts of central Europe, is often grown as an ornamental tree. The flowers, in long drooping clusters, are bright yellow and appear in early spring; some varieties have purple or reddish flowers. (Genus *Laburnum*, family Leguminosae.)

Labyrinth in Greek legend, the maze designed by the Athenian artisan Daedalus at Knossos in Crete for King Minos, as a home for the Minotaur – a monster, half man and half bull. After killing the Minotaur, Theseus, the prince of Athens, was guided out of the Labyrinth by a thread given to him by the king's daughter Ariadne.

labyrinthitis inflammation of the part of the inner ear responsible for the sense of balance (the labyrinth). It results in dizziness, which may then cause nausea and vomiting. It is usually caused by a viral infection of the ear (*otitis), which resolves in a few weeks. The nausea and vomiting may respond to anti-emetic drugs.

lac resinous incrustation produced by the female of the lac insect (*Laccifer lacca*), which eventually covers the twigs of trees in India and the Far East. The gathered twigs are known as **stick lac**, and yield a useful crimson dye; **shellac**, which is used in varnishes, polishes, and leather dressings, is manufactured commercially by melting the separated resin and spreading it into thin layers or flakes.

Laccadive, Minicoy, and Amindivi Islands former name of the Indian island group *Lakshadweep.

lacewing any of a group of insects found throughout the world. Lacewings take their name from the intricate veining of their two pairs of semitransparent wings. They have narrow bodies and long thin antennae. The larvae (called aphid lions) are predators, especially on aphids. (Families Hemerobiidae (brown lacewings) and Chrysopidae (green lacewings), order Neuroptera.)

Laclos, Pierre-Ambroise-François Choderlos de (1741–1803) French author. An army officer, he wrote a single novel in letter form, *Les Liaisons dangereuses/Dangerous Liaisons* (1782), an analysis of moral corruption. A cynical and unscrupulous libertine, the Vicomte de Valmont, encouraged by the Marquise de Merteuil, seduces and destroys two innocent women. A moral twist is given at the end of the book when Valmont is killed in a duel and the Marquise de Merteuil is hideously disfigured by smallpox.

lacquer waterproof resinous varnish obtained from Oriental trees *Toxicodendron verniciflua*, and used for decorating furniture and art objects. It can be applied to wood, fabric, leather, or other materials, with or without added colours. The technique of making and carving small lacquerwork objects was developed in China, probably as early as the 4th century BC, and was later adopted in Japan.

lacrosse Canadian ball game, adopted from the North American Indians, and named after a fancied resemblance of the lacrosse stick (crosse) to a bishop's crosier. Thongs across the curved end of the crosse form a pocket to carry the small rubber ball. The field is approximately 100 m/110 yd long and a minimum of 55 m/60 yd wide in the men's game, which is played with 10 players per side; the women's field is larger, and there are 12 players per side. The goals are just under 2 m/6 ft square, with loose nets. The world championship was first held in 1967 for men, and in 1969 for women.

lactation secretion of milk in mammals, from the mammary glands. In late pregnancy, the cells lining the lobules inside the mammary glands begin extracting substances from the blood to produce milk. The supply of milk starts shortly after birth with the production of colostrum, a clear fluid consisting largely of water, protein, antibodies, and vitamins. The production of milk continues practically as long as the baby continues to suckle.

lactic acid *or* **2-hydroxypropanoic acid**
$CH_3CHOHCOOH$, organic acid, a colourless, almost odourless liquid, produced by certain bacteria during fermentation and by active muscle cells when they are exercised hard and are experiencing oxygen debt. An accumulation of lactic acid in the muscles may cause cramp. It occurs in yogurt, buttermilk, sour cream, poor wine, and certain plant extracts, and is used in food preservation and in the preparation of pharmaceuticals.

lactose white sugar, found in solution in milk; it forms 5% of cow's milk. It is commercially prepared from the whey obtained in cheese-making. Like table sugar (sucrose), it is a disaccharide, consisting of two basic sugar units (monosaccharides), in this case, glucose and galactose. Unlike sucrose, it is tasteless.

Ladoga, Lake Russian **Ladozhskoye Ozero**, largest lake in Europe, and the second largest in the Russian Federation after the Caspian Sea, situated in the far northwest of the Russian Federation, in the Republic of Karelia and Leningrad oblast (region), northeast of the city of St Petersburg. Lake Ladoga covers an area of 17,700 sq km/6,834 sq mi (with its islands, 18,135 sq km/ 7,002 sq mi). The main feeder rivers are the Volkhov, Svir, and Vuoksa, and the lake's outlet is by way of the Neva River into the Gulf of Finland. Its average depth is 51 m/167 ft, and its maximum depth 230 m/755 ft. A valuable commercial fishing industry is based here.

Lady in the UK, the formal title of the daughter of an earl, marquess, or duke, and of any woman whose husband's rank is above that of baronet or knight; the title 'Lady' is prefixed to her first name. The wife of a baronet or a knight is also called 'Lady', but uses the title by courtesy only, and has it prefixed to her surname.

ladybird *or* **ladybug** any of various small beetles, generally red or yellow in colour, with black spots. There are more than 5,200 species worldwide. As larvae and adults, they feed on aphids and scale-insect pests. (Family Coccinellidae, order Coleoptera.)

Lady Day British name for the Christian festival (25 March) of the Annunciation of the Virgin Mary; until 1752 it was the beginning of the legal year in England, and it is still a quarter day (date for the payment of quarterly rates or dues).

Laënnec, René Théophile Hyacinthe (1781–1826) French physician, inventor of the *stethoscope in 1816. He advanced the diagnostic technique of auscultation (listening to the internal organs) with his book *Traité de l'auscultation médiaté* in 1819, which quickly became a medical classic.

Lafayette, Marie Joseph Paul Yves Roch Gilbert de Motier (1757–1834) Marquis de Lafayette, French soldier and politician. He fought against Britain in the American Revolution 1777–79 and 1780–82. During the French Revolution he sat in the National Assembly as a constitutional royalist and in 1789 presented the Declaration of the Rights of Man. After the storming of the *Bastille, he was given command of the National Guard. In 1792 he fled the country after attempting to restore the monarchy and was imprisoned by the Austrians until 1797. He supported Napoleon Bonaparte in 1815, sat in the chamber of deputies as a Liberal from 1818, and played a leading part in the revolution of 1830.

La Fontaine, Jean de (1621–1695) French poet. He was born at Château-Thierry, Champagne, and from 1656 lived largely in Paris, the friend of the playwrights Molière and Racine, and the poet Boileau. His works include *Contes et nouvelles en vers* (1665–74), a series of witty and bawdy tales in verse, and *Fables choisies mises en vers* (1668–94), his universally known verse fables.

Lagerlöf, Selma Ottiliana Lovisa (1858–1940) Swedish novelist. Her first work was the romantic historical novel *Gösta Berling's saga/The Story of Gösta Berling* (1891). The children's fantasy *Nils Holgerssons underbara resa/The Wonderful Voyage of Nils Holgersson* (1906–07) grew from her background as a schoolteacher. She was the first woman to be awarded the Nobel Prize for Literature, in 1909.

lagoon coastal body of shallow salt water, usually with limited access to the sea. The term is normally used to describe the shallow sea area cut off by a *coral reef or barrier islands.

Lagos chief port and former capital of Nigeria, located at the western end of an island in a lagoon and linked by bridges with the mainland via Iddo Island; population (urban area, 1991 est) 5,195,200. Industries include chemicals, metal products, vehicle assembly, textiles, fish, food processing, light engineering, pharmaceuticals, and brewing. Its surrounding waters are heavily polluted. Abuja was designated the new capital in 1982 (officially recognized as such in 1992).

Lagrange, Joseph Louis (1736–1813) born Giuseppe Lodovico Lagrange, Italian-born French mathematician. His *Mécanique analytique* (1788) applied mathematical analysis, using principles established by Isaac *Newton, to such problems as the movements of planets when affected by each other's gravitational force. He presided over the commission that introduced the metric system in 1793.

lahar mudflow formed of a fluid mixture of water and volcanic ash. During a volcanic eruption, melting ice may combine with ash to form a powerful flow capable of causing great destruction. The lahars created by the eruption of Nevado del Ruiz in Colombia, South America, in 1985 buried 22,000 people in 8 m/26 ft of mud.

Lahnda language spoken by 15–20 million people in Pakistan and northern India. It is closely related to Punjabi and Romany, and belongs to the Indo-Iranian branch of the Indo-European language family.

Lahore capital of the province of *Punjab and second largest city of Pakistan, situated on a tributary of the River Ravi, 50 km/30 mi west of Amritsar in India; population (1998 est) 5,063,500. Lahore is a major industrial centre where about one-fifth of Pakistan's industrial capacity is located. The city is also a commercial and banking centre, and industries include textiles, engineering, carpets, iron and steel, rubber, jewellery, and chemicals. Lahore also has the country's leading film studios. It is associated with the Mogul rulers *Akbar, *Jahangir, and *Aurangzeb, whose capital it was in the 16th and 17th centuries.

Lailat ul-Barah the Night of Forgiveness, Muslim festival which takes place two weeks before the beginning of the fast of Ramadan (the ninth month of the Islamic year) and is a time for asking and granting forgiveness.

Lailat ul-Qadr the Night of Power, Muslim festival that celebrates the giving of the Koran to Muhammad. It usually falls at the end of Ramadan.

Laing, R(onald) D(avid) (1927–1989) Scottish psychoanalyst. He was the originator of the social theory of mental illness; for example, that schizophrenia is promoted by family pressure for its members to conform to standards alien to themselves. His books include *The Divided Self* (1960) and *The Politics of the Family* (1971).

laissez faire (French 'let alone') theory that the state should not intervene in economic affairs, except to break up a monopoly. The phrase originated with the Physiocrats, 18th-century French economists whose maxim was *laissez faire et laissez passer* (literally, 'let go and let pass' – that is, leave the individual alone and let commodities circulate freely). The degree to which intervention should take place is still one of the chief problems of economics. The Scottish economist Adam *Smith justified the theory in *The Wealth of Nations* (1776).

lake body of still water lying in depressed ground without direct communication with the sea. Lakes are common in formerly glaciated regions, along the courses of slow rivers, and in low land near the sea. The main classifications are by origin: **glacial lakes**, formed by glacial scouring; **barrier lakes**, formed by *landslides and glacial *moraines; **crater lakes**, found in *volcanoes; and **tectonic lakes**, occurring in natural fissures.

Lake District region in Cumbria, northwest England. It contains the principal English lakes, separated by wild uplands rising to many peaks, including *Scafell Pike (978 m/3,210 ft), the highest peak in England. The area was made a national park in 1951, covering 2,292 sq km/885 sq mi, and is a popular tourist destination.

Lakeland terrier medium-sized wire-haired terrier weighing about 7–8 kg/15.5–17.5 lb with an ideal height of no more than 37 cm/14.5 in. Its skull is moderately broad, with small, V-shaped ears and dark eyes; the body is short and the tail traditionally docked.

Lakshadweep *or* **Laccadive Islands** group of 36 coral islands, 10 inhabited, in the Indian Ocean, 320 km/200 mi off the Malabar coast, forming a Union Territory of India; area 32 sq km/12 sq mi; population (2001 est) 60,600. The administrative headquarters are on Kavaratti Island. Products include coir, copra, and fish. There is a tourist resort on Bangarem, an uninhabited island with a large lagoon. The religion is Islam.

Lakshmi Hindu goddess of wealth, beauty, and good fortune, consort of *Vishnu, and mother of the world; her festival is *Diwali.

Lallans variant of 'lowlands' and a name for Lowland Scots, whether conceived as a language in its own right or as a northern dialect of English. Because of its rustic associations, Lallans has been known since the 18th century as the 'Doric', in contrast with the 'Attic' usage of Edinburgh ('the Athens of the North'). See *Scots language.

Lamaism *or* **Tibetan Buddhism** Buddhism of Tibet, Mongolia, and parts of Nepal and northern India; a form of *Mahayana Buddhism. Buddhism was introduced into Tibet in AD 640, but the real founder of Tibetan Buddhism was the Indian missionary Padma Sambhava, who was active in about 750. Tibetan Buddhism developed several orders, based on lineages of teachings transmitted by reincarnated lamas (teachers). In the 14th–15th centuries Tsong-kha-pa founded the sect of Geluk-Pa ('virtuous'), which became the most powerful order in the country. Its head is the *Dalai Lama, who is considered an incarnation of the bodhisattva Avalokitesvara.

Lamarck, Jean Baptiste Pierre Antoine de Monet (1744–1829) Chevalier de Lamarck, French naturalist. His theory of evolution, known as **Lamarckism**, was based on the idea that acquired characteristics (changes acquired in an individual's lifetime) are inherited by the offspring, and that organisms have an intrinsic urge to evolve into better-adapted forms. *Philosophie zoologique/Zoological Philosophy* (1809) outlined his 'transformist' (evolutionary) ideas.

Lamartine, Alphonse Marie Louis de (1790–1869) French poet. He wrote romantic poems, including *Méditations poétiques/Poetical Meditations* (1820), followed by *Nouvelles méditations/New Meditations* (1823), and *Harmonies poétiques et religieuses/Poetical and Religious Harmonies* (1830). His *Histoire des Girondins/History of the Girondins* (1847) helped to inspire the revolution of 1848. Lamartine was the first to sound a more personal note in his poetry and to establish a direct bond between himself and his public.

Lamb, Charles (1775–1834) English essayist and critic. He collaborated with his sister **Mary Lamb** (1764–1847) on *Tales from Shakespeare* (1807), and his *Specimens of English Dramatic Poets Contemporary with Shakespeare, with Notes* (1808) revealed him as a penetrating critic and helped to revive interest in Elizabethan plays. As 'Elia' he contributed essays to the *London Magazine* from 1820 (collected 1823 and 1833).

Lammas ('loaf-mass') medieval festival of harvest, celebrated 1 August. At one time it was an English quarter day (date for payment of quarterly rates or dues).

lammergeier *or* **bearded vulture** Old World vulture with a wingspan of 2.7 m/9 ft. It ranges over southern

Europe, North Africa, and Asia, in wild mountainous areas. It feeds on offal and carrion and drops bones onto rocks to break them and so get at the marrow. (Species *Gypaetus barbatus*, family Accipitridae.)

lamprey any of various eel-shaped jawless fishes. A lamprey feeds on other fish by fixing itself by its round mouth to its host and boring into the flesh with its toothed tongue. Lampreys breed in fresh water, and the young live as larvae for about five years before migrating to the sea. (Family Petromyzontidae.)

Lancashire county of northwest England (since April 1998 Blackpool and Blackburn have been separate unitary authorities). **area:** 3,040 sq km/1,173 sq mi **towns and cities:** Preston (administrative headquarters), which forms part of Central Lancashire New Town from 1970 (together with Fulwood, Bamber Bridge, Leyland, and Chorley); Lancaster, Accrington, Burnley; ports Fleetwood and Heysham; seaside resorts Morecambe and Southport **features:** the River Ribble; the Pennines; the Forest of Bowland (moors and farming valleys); Pendle Hill **population:** (2001 est) 1,135,800.

Lancaster, Burt (Burton Stephen) (1913–1994) US film actor. A star from his first film, *The Killers* (1946), he proved adept both at action roles and more complex character parts as in *From Here to Eternity* (1953), *Elmer Gantry* (1960; Academy Award), *The Leopard/Il Gattopardo* (1963), *The Swimmer* (1968), and *Atlantic City* (1980).

Lancaster, House of English royal house, a branch of the Plantagenets.

lancelet any of a variety of marine animals about 2.5 cm/1 in long. They have no skull, brain, eyes, heart, vertebral column, centralized brain, or paired limbs, but there is a notochord (a supportive rod) which runs from end to end of the body, a tail, and a number of gill slits. Found in all seas, lancelets burrow in the sand but when disturbed swim freely. (Genus *Amphioxus*, phylum Chordata, subphylum Cephalocordata.)

Lancelot of the Lake in British legend, one of King Arthur's knights of the Round Table. Originally a Celtic folk hero, he was first introduced into the Arthurian cycle of tales in the 12th century. He was designated Queen *Guinevere's lover in the early 13th century by French poet *Chrétien de Troyes, who made him a symbol of fidelity and chivalrous love.

Land plural **Länder**, federal state of Germany or Austria.

Land League Irish peasant-rights organization, formed in 1879 by Michael Davitt and Charles Stewart *Parnell to fight against tenant evictions. Through its skilful use of the boycott against anyone who took a farm from which another had been evicted, it forced Gladstone's government to introduce a law in 1881 restricting rents and granting tenants security of tenure.

Landseer, Edwin Henry (1802–1873) English painter, sculptor, and engraver of animal studies. Much of his work reflects the Victorian taste for sentimental and moralistic pictures, for example *Dignity and Impudence* (1839; Tate Gallery, London). His sculptures include the lions at the base of Nelson's Column in Trafalgar Square, London (1857–67). He was knighted in 1850.

Land's End promontory of southwest Cornwall, 15 km/ 9 mi southwest of Penzance, the westernmost point of mainland England.

landslide sudden downward movement of a mass of soil or rocks from a cliff or steep slope. Landslides happen when a slope becomes unstable, usually because the base has been undercut or because materials within the mass have become wet and slippery.

Landsteiner, Karl (1868–1943) Austrian-born US immunologist who was awarded a Nobel Prize for Physiology or Medicine in 1930 for his discovery of the ABO *blood group system in the period 1900–02. He also aided in the discovery of the Rhesus blood factors in 1940, and discovered the polio virus.

Lanfranc (c. 1010–1089) Italian archbishop of Canterbury from 1070. Following the *Norman Conquest, he was the adviser of *William (I) the Conqueror. As archbishop he rebuilt Canterbury Cathedral, replaced English clergy with Normans, enforced clerical celibacy, and separated the ecclesiastical from the secular courts.

Lang, Fritz (1890–1976) Austrian-born US film director. His films are characterized by a strong sense of fatalism and alienation. His German films include *Metropolis* (1926) and *M* (1931), in which Peter Lorre starred as a child-killer. His US films include *Rancho Notorious* (1952) and *The Big Heat* (1953).

Langland, William (c. 1332–c. 1400) English poet. His alliterative *The Vision of William Concerning Piers the Plowman* (see *Piers Plowman*) was written in three (or possibly four) versions between about 1367 and 1386. The poem forms a series of allegorical visions, in which Piers develops from the typical poor peasant to a symbol of Jesus, and condemns the social and moral evils of 14th-century England. It is a masterpiece in combining the depiction of a spiritual pilgrimage with scenes of contemporary social life for a satirical purpose.

language human communication through speech, writing, or both. Different nationalities or ethnic groups typically have different languages or variations on particular languages; for example, Armenians speaking the Armenian language and British and Americans speaking distinctive varieties of the English language. One language may have various dialects, which may be seen by those who use them as languages in their own right. There are about 6,000 languages spoken worldwide, but 90% of these are in some danger of falling into disuse. More than half the world's population speaks one of just five languages – Chinese, English, Hindi, Russian, and Spanish. The term language is also used for systems of communication with languagelike qualities, such as **animal language** (the way animals communicate), **body language** (gestures and expressions used to communicate ideas), **sign language** (gestures for the deaf or for use as a *lingua franca, as among American Indians), and **computer languages** (such as BASIC and COBOL).

Languedoc former province of southern France, bounded by the River Rhône, the Mediterranean Sea, and the regions of Guienne and Gascony. In 1791 Languedoc was replaced by the eight *départements* of Haute-Loire, Lozère, Ardèche, Aude, Tarn, Hérault, Gard, and Haute-Garonne. Chief cities include Montpellier, Narbonne, Béziers, and Nimes; wine is the chief product. Historic Languedoc's eastern part was united with the former province of Roussillon to form the modern region of *Languedoc-Roussillon.

Languedoc-Roussillon region of southern France, comprising the *départements* of Aude, Gard, Hérault, Lozère, and Pyrénées-Orientales; area 27,376 sq km/10,570 sq mi; population (1999 est) 2,295,600. It was created in the 1980s as part of regionalization laws implemented by the French government, and corresponds approximately with what was historic Lower Languedoc. The administrative centre is Montpellier. Products include fruit, vegetables, and wine.

langur any of various leaf-eating Old World monkeys that live in trees in South Asia. There are about 20 species. Langurs are related to the colobus monkey of Africa. (Genus *Presbytis* and other related genera.)

lanolin sticky, purified wax obtained from sheep's wool and used in cosmetics, soap, and leather preparation.

lanthanide any of a series of 15 metallic elements (also known as rare earths) with atomic numbers 57 (lanthanum) to 71 (lutetium). One of its members, promethium, is radioactive. All occur in nature. Lanthanides are grouped because of their chemical similarities (most are trivalent, but some can be divalent or tetravalent), their properties differing only slightly with atomic number.

lanthanum chemical symbol La, (Greek *lanthanein* 'to be hidden') soft, silvery, ductile and malleable, metallic element, atomic number 57, relative atomic mass 138.91, the first of the lanthanide series. It is used in making alloys. It was named in 1839 by Swedish chemist Carl Mosander (1797–1858).

Lanzarote most easterly of the Spanish Canary Islands; area 795 sq km/307 sq mi; population (1995 est) 76,400; capital and largest town Arrecife. The desertlike volcanic landscape is dominated by the Montañas de Fuego ('Mountains of Fire') with more than 300 volcanic cones. With irrigation, vegetables, grain, and vines can be grown, and fish-canning and tourism are leading industries.

Lao people who live along the Mekong river system in Laos (2 million) and northern Thailand (9 million). The Lao language is a member of the Sino-Tibetan family. The majority of Lao live in rural villages. During the wet season, May–October, they grow rice in irrigated fields, though some shifting or swidden cultivation is practised on hillsides. Vegetables and other crops are grown during drier weather. The Lao are predominantly Buddhist though a belief in spirits, **phi**, is included in Lao devotions. There are some Christians among the minority groups.

Laocoön in classical mythology, a Trojan priest of Apollo and a visionary, brother of Anchises. He and his sons were killed by serpents when he foresaw disaster for Troy in the *Trojan horse left by the Greeks. The scene of their death is the subject of a classical marble group, rediscovered in the Renaissance, and forms an episode in Virgil's *Aeneid*.

Laois *or* **Laoighis** previously spelt **Leix**; also formerly **Queen's County**, county of the Republic of Ireland, in the province of Leinster; county town Portlaoise; area 1,720 sq km/664 sq mi; population (2002 est) 58,700. Other towns are Abbeyleix, Mountmellick, Mountrath, and Portarlington. Laois is flat, except for the Slieve Bloom Mountains in the northwest, the highest point of which is Mount Arderin (529 m/1,734 ft), and there are many bogs. The Barrow and the Nore are the chief

rivers. Agriculture includes dairying, and mixed cattle and arable farming (sugar beet), and industries include peat and agricultural machinery. Part of the Leinster coalfield lies within the county. Limestone is still worked. The Clonsast Bog (1,619 ha/4,000 acres) is an important domestic source of peat.

Laos

National name: *Sathalanalat Praxathipatai Paxaxôn Lao/ Democratic People's Republic of Laos*

Area: 236,790 sq km/91,424 sq mi
Capital: Vientiane
Major towns/cities: Louangphrabang (the former royal capital), Pakse, Savannakhet
Physical features: landlocked state with high mountains in east; Mekong River in west; rainforest covers nearly 60% of land
Head of state: Khamtay Siphandon from 1998
Head of government: Boungnang Volachit from 2001
Political system: communist
Political executive: communist
Political party Lao People's Revolutionary Party (LPRP, the only legal party), socialist
Currency: new kip
GNI per capita (PPP): (US$) 1,610 (2002 est)
Exports: electricity, timber and wood products, textiles and garments, motorcycles, coffee, tin, gypsum. Principal market: Vietnam 41.7% (2001)
Population: 5,657,000 (2003 est)
Language: Lao (official), French, English, ethnic languages
Religion: Theravada Buddhist 85%, animist beliefs among mountain dwellers
Life expectancy: 53 (men); 56 (women) (2000–05)
Chronology
c. **2000–500 BC:** Early Bronze Age civilizations in central Mekong River and Plain of Jars regions.
5th–8th centuries: Occupied by immigrants from southern China.
8th century onwards: Theravada Buddhism spread by Mon monks.
9th–13th centuries: Part of the sophisticated Khmer Empire, centred on Angkor in Cambodia.

12th century: Small independent principalities, notably Louangphrabang, established by Lao invaders from Thailand and Yunnan, southern China; they adopted Buddhism.

14th century: United by King Fa Ngum; the first independent Laotian state, Lan Xang, formed. It was to dominate for four centuries, broken only by a period of Burmese rule 1574–1637.

17th century: First visited by Europeans.

1713: The Lan Xang kingdom split into three separate kingdoms, Louangphrabang, Vientiane, and Champassac, which became tributaries of Siam (Thailand) from the late 18th century.

1893–1945: Laos was a French protectorate, comprising the three principalities of Louangphrabang, Vientiane, and Champassac.

1945: Temporarily occupied by Japan.

1946: Retaken by France, despite opposition by the Chinese-backed Lao Issara (Free Laos) nationalist movement.

1950: Granted semi-autonomy in French Union, as an associated state under the constitutional monarchy of the king of Louangphrabang.

1954: Independence achieved from France under the Geneva Agreements, but civil war broke out between a moderate royalist faction of the Lao Issara, led by Prince Souvanna Phouma, and the communist Chinese-backed Pathet Lao (Land of the Lao) led by Prince Souphanouvong.

1957: A coalition government, headed by Souvanna Phouma, was established by the Vientiane Agreement.

1959: Savang Vatthana became king.

1960: Right-wing pro-Western government seized power, headed by Prince Boun Gum.

1962: Geneva Agreement established a new coalition government, led by Souvanna Phouma, but civil war continued, the Pathet Lao receiving backing from the North Vietnamese, and Souvanna Phouma from the USA.

1973: Vientiane ceasefire agreement divided the country between the communists and the Souvanna Phouma regime and brought the withdrawal of US, Thai, and North Vietnamese forces.

1975: Communists seized power; a republic was proclaimed, with Prince Souphanouvong as head of state and the Communist Party leader Kaysone Phomvihane as the controlling prime minister.

1979: Food shortages and the flight of 250,000 refugees to Thailand led to an easing of the drive towards nationalization and agricultural collectivization.

1985: Greater economic liberalization received encouragement from the Soviet Union's reformist leader Mikhail Gorbachev.

1989: The first assembly elections since communist takeover were held; Vietnamese troops were withdrawn from the country.

1991: A security and cooperation pact was signed with Thailand, and an agreement reached on the phased repatriation of Laotian refugees.

1995: The US lifted its 20-year aid embargo.

1996: The military tightened its grip on political affairs, but inward investment and private enterprise continued to be encouraged, fuelling economic expansion.

1997: Membership of the Association of South East Asian Nations (ASEAN) was announced.

1998: Khamtay Siphandon became president and was replaced as prime minister by Sisavath Keobounphanh.

2001: Boungnang Volachit became prime minister. The International Monetary Fund approved a three-year loan worth $40 million. The United Nations World Food Programme began a three-year operation to feed 70,000 malnourished children in Laos.

2002: In parliamentary elections all but one of the 166 candidates were from the ruling Lao People's Revolutionary Party.

2004: Laos hosted the summit of the Association of South East Nations.

2005: The World Bank approved a loan for the construction of a huge hydroelectric dam project.

Lao Zi (*or* **Lao Tzu**) (*c.* **604–531 BC**) Chinese philosopher. He is commonly regarded as the founder of *Taoism, with its emphasis on the Tao, the inevitable and harmonious way of the universe. Nothing certain is known of his life. The *Tao Te Ching*, the Taoist scripture, is attributed to him but apparently dates from the 3rd century BC.

La Paz capital city of Bolivia and of La Paz department, in Murillo province, 3,800 m/12,400 ft above sea level; population (2001 est) 792,500, metropolitan area (2001 est) 1,487,200). It is in a canyon formed by the La Paz River, and is the world's highest capital city. It is the chief trade centre of the *altiplano plateau, and industries include textiles, copper, glass, and electrical equipment. It has been the seat of government since 1898, but *Sucre is the legal capital and seat of the judiciary.

lapis lazuli rock containing the blue mineral lazurite in a matrix of white calcite with small amounts of other minerals. It occurs in silica-poor igneous rocks and metamorphic limestones found in Afghanistan, Siberia, Iran, and Chile. Lapis lazuli was a valuable pigment of the Middle Ages, also used as a gemstone and in inlaying and ornamental work.

Laplace, Pierre Simon (1749–1827) Marquis de Laplace, French astronomer and mathematician. In 1796 he theorized that the Solar System originated from a cloud of gas (the nebular hypothesis). He studied the motion of the Moon and planets, and published a five-volume survey of *celestial mechanics, *Traité de méchanique céleste* (1799–1825). Among his mathematical achievements was the development of probability theory.

Lapland region of Europe within the Arctic Circle in Norway, Sweden, Finland, and the Kola Peninsula of northwest Russia, without political definition. Its chief resources are chromium, copper, iron, timber, hydroelectric power, and tourism. The indigenous population are the *Saami (formerly known as Lapps), 10% of whom are nomadic, the remainder living mostly in coastal settlements. Lapland has low temperatures, with two months of continuous daylight in summer and two months of continuous darkness in winter. There is summer agriculture.

La Plata capital of Buenos Aires province, Argentina, on the Río de la Plata 48 km/30 mi southeast of the city of Buenos Aires; population (1999 est) 556,300; metropolitan area (1999 est) 693,600. It is 9 km/6 mi from its port, Ensenada, the main outlet for produce from the Pampas. Industries include meat packing and petroleum refining. It has one of the country's best universities. The city was founded in 1882 by Governor Daroo Rocha.

laptop computer portable microcomputer, small enough to be used on the operator's lap. It consists of a single unit, incorporating a keyboard, floppy disk and hard disk drives, and a screen. The screen often forms a lid that folds back in use. It uses a liquid-crystal or gas-plasma display, rather than the bulkier and heavier cathode-ray tubes found in most display terminals. A typical laptop computer measures about 210 x 300 mm/8 x 12 in (about the size of an A4 sheet of paper), is 5 cm/2 in in depth, and weighs less than 3 kg/6 lb 9 oz. In the 1980s there were several types of laptop computer, but in the 1990s designs converged on systems known as notebook computers. The first of these, such as the Epson HX-20 and Tandy 100, became available in the early 1980s, with the first PC-compatible notebook, the Toshiba T1100, following in 1985. In the 1990s, the notebook format became the standard for portable PCs and Apple PowerBooks. Since then, the ability to make smaller and smaller chips and associated hardware has led to hand-held, palm-sized, and pocket PC models. At the end of 2002, manufacturers began to supply a new type of laptop, the tablet PC.

lapwing bird belonging to the plover family, also known as the **green plover** and, from its call, as the **peewit**. Bottle-green above and white below, with a long thin crest and rounded wings, it is about 30 cm/1 ft long. It inhabits moorland in Europe and Asia, making a nest scratched out of the ground, and is also often seen on farmland. (Species *Vanellus vanellus*, family Charadriidae.)

Lara, Brian (1969–) West Indian cricketer. A left-handed batsman who has played cricket for Trinidad and Tobago, and for Warwickshire. In April 1994, he broke the world individual Test batting record with an innings of 375 against England, and 50 days later, he broke the world record for an individual innings in first-class cricket with an unbeaten 501 for Warwickshire against Durham. His Test record, set in St John's, Antigua, beat the previous best of 365 not out by Garfield Sobers in 1958, though it was subsequently beaten by Australia's Matthew Hayden. Lara regained the world record in April 2004 (again in St John's, Antigua), scoring 400 not out v. England in the fourth Test. He was the fourth person in Test history to score over 10,000 runs and has also captained his country in two separate spells.

larch any of a group of trees belonging to the pine family. The common larch (*L. decidua*) grows to 40 m/130 ft. It is one of the few *conifers to shed its leaves annually. The small needlelike leaves are replaced every year by new bright-green foliage, which later darkens. (Genus *Larix*, family Pinaceae.)

La Rioja autonomous community and province of northern Spain; area 5,034 sq km/1,944 sq mi; population (2001 est) 270,400. The River Ebro passes through the region, but it is a tributary of the Río Oja, which gives its name to the region. A fertile region, La Rioja is famous for its fine wines (with a characteristic flavour derived from their storage in oak barrels) which are produced chiefly between Logroño and Haro in the upper Ebro valley. The capital is Logroño; other chief cities are Calahorra, Haro, and Santo Domingo de la Calzada.

lark any of a group of songbirds found mainly in the Old World, but also in North America. Larks are brownish-tan in colour and usually about 18 cm/7 in long; they nest on the ground in the open. The **skylark** (*Alauda arvensis*) sings as it rises almost vertically in the air. It is light brown and 18 cm/7 in long. (Family Alaudidae, order Passeriformes.)

Larkin, Philip Arthur (1922–1985) English poet. His perfectionist, pessimistic verse appeared in *The Less Deceived* (1955), and in the later volumes *The Whitsun Weddings* (1964) and *High Windows* (1974), which confirmed him as one of the most powerful and influential of 20th-century English poets. He edited *The Oxford Book of 20th-Century English Verse* (1973). *Collected Poems* was published in 1988. He also produced two novels, *Jill* (1946, revised 1964), and *A Girl in Winter* (1947), and a collection of his writings on music, *All What Jazz* (1970).

larkspur any of several plants included with the *delphiniums. (Genus *Delphinium*, family Ranunculaceae.)

La Rochefoucauld, François (1613–1680) Duc de, French writer. His 'Réflexions, ou sentences et maximes morales/Reflections, or Moral Maxims', published anonymously in 1665, is a collection of brief, epigrammatic, and cynical observations on life and society, with the epigraph 'Our virtues are mostly our vices in disguise'. The work is remarkable for its literary excellence and its bitter realism in the dissection of basic human motives, making La Rochefoucauld a forerunner of modern 'psychological' writers.

larva stage between hatching and adulthood in those species in which the young have a different appearance and way of life from the adults. Examples include tadpoles (frogs) and caterpillars (butterflies and moths). Larvae are typical of the invertebrates, some of which (for example, shrimps) have two or more distinct larval stages. Among vertebrates, it is only the amphibians and some fishes that have a larval stage.

laryngitis inflammation of the larynx, causing soreness of the throat, a dry cough, and hoarseness. The acute form is due to a virus or other infection, excessive use of the voice, or inhalation of irritating smoke, and may cause the voice to be completely lost. With rest, the inflammation usually subsides in a few days.

larynx in mammals, a cavity at the upper end of the trachea (windpipe) containing the vocal cords. It is stiffened with cartilage and lined with mucous membrane. Amphibians and reptiles have much simpler larynxes, with no vocal cords. Birds have a similar cavity, called the **syrinx**, found lower down the trachea, where it branches to form the bronchi. It is very complex, with well-developed vocal cords.

Lascaux cave system near Montignac-sur-Vezère in the Dordogne, southwestern France, with prehistoric wall art, discovered in 1940. It is richly decorated with realistic and symbolic paintings of aurochs (wild cattle), horses, and red deer of the Upper Palaeolithic period (Old Stone Age, about 15,000 BC), preserved under a glaze of calcite formation.

Lasdun, Denys Louis (1914–2001) English modernist architect. Many of his designs emphasize the horizontal layering of a building, creating the effect of geological strata extending into the surrounding city or landscape. This effect can be seen in his designs for the

University of East Anglia, Norwich (1962–68); and the National Theatre (1967–76) on London's South Bank.

laser acronym for **light amplification by stimulated emission of radiation**, device for producing a narrow beam of light, capable of travelling over vast distances without dispersion, and of being focused to give enormous power densities (10^8 watts per cm^2 for high-energy lasers). The laser operates on a principle similar to that of the *maser (a high-frequency microwave amplifier or oscillator). The uses of lasers include communications (a laser beam can carry much more information than can radio waves), cutting, drilling, welding, satellite tracking, medical and biological research, and surgery. Sound wave vibrations from the window glass of a room can be picked up by a reflected laser beam. Lasers are also used as entertainment in theatres, concerts, and light shows.

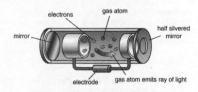

electrons   gas atom

mirror   half silvered mirror

electrode   gas atom emits ray of light

light ray hits another energised atom causing more light to be emitted

laser beam

light rays bounce between the mirrors causing a build up of light

laser In a gas laser, electrons moving between the electrodes pass energy to gas atoms. An energized atom emits a ray of light. The ray hits another energized atom causing it to emit a further light ray. The rays bounce between mirrors at each end causing a build-up of light. Eventually it becomes strong enough to pass through the half-silvered mirror at one end, producing a laser beam.

laser surgery use of intense light sources to cut, coagulate, or vaporize tissue. Less invasive than normal surgery, it destroys diseased tissue gently and allows quicker, more natural healing. It can be used by way of a flexible endoscope to enable the surgeon to view the diseased area at which the laser needs to be aimed.

Lassa fever acute disease caused by an arenavirus, first detected in 1969, and spread by a species of rat found only in West Africa. It is classified as a haemorrhagic fever and characterized by high fever, headache, muscle pain, and internal bleeding. There is no known cure, the survival rate being less than 50%.

Las Vegas (Spanish *las vegas* 'the meadows') city in southeastern Nevada; seat of Clark County; population (2000 est) 478,400. With its many nightclubs and gambling casinos, Las Vegas attracted over 35 million visitors each year. It is also a major convention centre. Founded in 1855 in a ranching area, the modern community developed with the coming of the railroad in 1905 and was incorporated as a city in 1911. The first casino hotel opened here in 1947. Las Vegas is the easiest place to get married in the USA, with numerous chapels along the Strip (main street) and hotel chapels.

latent heat in physics, the heat absorbed or released by a substance as it changes state (for example, from solid to liquid) at constant temperature and pressure.

Lateran Treaties series of agreements that marked the reconciliation of the Italian state with the papacy in 1929. They were hailed as a propaganda victory for the fascist regime. The treaties involved recognition of the sovereignty of the Vatican City State, the payment of an indemnity for papal possessions lost during unification in 1870, and agreement on the role of the Catholic Church within the Italian state in the form of a concordat between Pope Pius XI and the dictator Mussolini.

latex (Latin 'liquid') fluid of some plants (such as the rubber tree and poppy), an emulsion of resins, proteins, and other organic substances. It is used as the basis for making rubber. The name is also applied to a suspension in water of natural or synthetic rubber (or plastic) particles used in rubber goods, paints, and adhesives.

Latimer, Hugh (*c.* 1485–1555) English bishop. After his conversion to Protestantism in 1524 during the *Reformation he was imprisoned several times but was protected by cardinal Thomas *Wolsey and Henry VIII. After the accession of the Catholic *Mary I, he was burned for heresy.

Latin Indo-European language of ancient Italy. Latin has passed through four influential phases: as the language of (1) republican Rome, (2) the Roman Empire, (3) the Roman Catholic Church, and (4) Western European culture, science, philosophy, and law during the Middle Ages and the Renaissance. During the third and fourth phases, much Latin vocabulary entered the English language. It is the parent form of the *Romance languages, noted for its highly inflected grammar and conciseness of expression.

Latin America large territory in the Western hemisphere south of the USA, consisting of Mexico, Central America, South America, and the West Indies. The main languages spoken are Spanish (most widespread), Portuguese (in Brazil), and French (in French Guiana, Haiti, and some West Indian islands including Martinique and Guadeloupe).

Latin American Economic System (LAES) Spanish **Sistema Económico Latino-Americana (SELA)**, international coordinating body for economic, technological, and scientific cooperation in Latin America and the Caribbean, aiming to create and promote multinational enterprises in the region and provide markets. Founded in 1975 as the successor to the Latin American Economic Coordination Commission, its members include Argentina, Barbados, Bolivia, Brazil, Chile, Colombia, Costa Rica, Cuba, Dominican Republic, Ecuador, El Salvador, Grenada, Guatemala, Guyana, Haiti, Honduras, Mexico, Jamaica, Nicaragua, Panama, Paraguay, Peru, Spain (from

1979), Suriname, Trinidad and Tobago, Uruguay, and Venezuela. Its headquarters are in Caracas, Venezuela.

latitude and longitude imaginary lines used to locate position on the globe. Lines of latitude are drawn parallel to the Equator, with 0° at the Equator and 90° at the north and south poles. Lines of longitude are drawn at right-angles to these, with 0° (the Prime Meridian) passing through Greenwich, England.

La Tour, Georges de (1593–1652) French painter. Many of his pictures – which range from religious paintings to domestic genre scenes – are illuminated by a single source of light, with deep contrasts of light and shade, as in *Joseph the Carpenter* about (1645; Louvre, Paris).

Point X lies on longitude 60°W

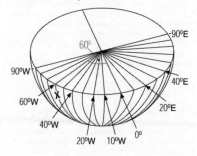

Point X lies on latitude 20°S

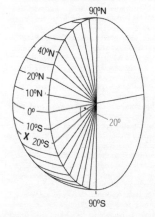

latitude and longitude Locating a point on a globe using latitude and longitude. Longitude is the angle between the terrestrial meridian through a place and the standard meridian 0° passing through Greenwich, England. Latitude is the angular distance of a place from the equator.

Latvia
National name: *Latvijas Republika/Republic of Latvia*

Area: 63,700 sq km/24,594 sq mi
Capital: Riga
Major towns/cities: Daugavpils, Leipaja, Jurmala, Jelgava, Ventspils
Major ports: Ventspils, Leipaja
Physical features: wooded lowland (highest point 312 m/1,024 ft), marshes, lakes; 472 km/293 mi of coastline; mild climate
Head of state: Vaira Vike-Freiberga from 1999
Head of government: Aigars Kalvitis from 2004
Political system: emergent democracy
Political executive: parliamentary
Political parties: Latvian Way (LW), right of centre; Latvian National and Conservative Party (LNNK), right wing, nationalist; Economic-Political Union (formerly known as Harmony for Latvia and Rebirth of the National Economy), centrist; Ravnopravie (Equal Rights), centrist; For the Fatherland and Freedom (FFF), extreme nationalist; Latvian Peasants' Union (LZS), rural based, left of centre; Union of Christian Democrats, right of centre; Democratic Centre Party, centrist; Movement for Latvia, pro-Russian, populist; Master in Your Own Home (Saimnieks), ex-communist, populist; Latvian National Party of Reforms, right-of-centre nationalist coalition
Currency: lat
GNI per capita (PPP): (US$) 8,940 (2002 est)
Exports: timber and timber products, textiles, food and agricultural products, machinery and electrical equipment, metal industry products. Principal market: Germany 16.7% (2001)
Population: 2,307,000 (2003 est)
Language: Latvian (official)
Religion: Lutheran, Roman Catholic, Russian Orthodox
Life expectancy: 66 (men); 76 (women) (2000–05)
Chronology
9th–10th centuries: Invaded by Vikings and Russians.
13th century: Conquered by crusading German Teutonic Knights, who named the area Livonia and converted population to Christianity; Riga joined the Hanseatic League, a northern European union of commercial towns.

515

1520s: Lutheranism established as a result of the Reformation.

16th–17th centuries: Successively under Polish, Lithuanian, and Swedish rule.

1721: Tsarist Russia took control.

1819: Serfdom abolished.

1900s: Emergence of an independence movement.

1914–18: Under partial German occupation during World War I.

1918–19: Independence proclaimed and achieved after Russian Red Army troops expelled by German, Polish, and Latvian forces.

1920s: Land reforms introduced by Farmers' Union government.

1934: Democracy overthrown and, at time of economic depression, an autocratic regime was established; Baltic Entente mutual defence pact made with Estonia and Lithuania.

1940: Incorporated into Soviet Union (USSR) as constituent republic, following secret German–Soviet agreement.

1941–44: Occupied by Germany.

1944: USSR regained control; mass deportations of Latvians to Central Asia, followed by immigration of ethnic Russians; agricultural collectivization.

1960s and 1970s: Extreme repression of Latvian cultural and literary life.

1980s: Nationalist dissent began to grow, influenced by the Polish Solidarity movement and Mikhail Gorbachev's *glasnost* ('openness') initiative in the USSR.

1988: The Latvian Popular Front was established to campaign for independence. The prewar flag was readopted and official status was given to the Latvian language.

1989: The Latvian parliament passed a sovereignty declaration.

1990: The Popular Front secured a majority in local elections and its leader, Ivan Godmanir, became the prime minister. The Latvian Communist Party split into pro-independence and pro-Moscow wings. The country entered a 'transitional period of independence' and the Baltic Council was reformed.

1991: Soviet troops briefly seized key installations in Riga. There was an overwhelming vote for independence in a referendum. Full independence was achieved following the failure of the anti-Gorbachev coup attempt in Moscow; the Communist Party was outlawed. Joined United Nations (UN); a market-centred economic reform programme was instituted.

1992: The curbing of rights of non-citizens prompted Russia to request minority protection by the UN.

1993: The right-of-centre Latvian Way won the general election; a free-trade agreement was reached with Estonia and Lithuania.

1994: The last Russian troops departed.

1995: A trade and cooperation agreement was signed with the European Union (EU). A general election produced a hung parliament in which extremist parties received most support. Applied for EU membership.

1996: Guntis Ulmanis was re-elected president. The finance minister and deputy prime minister resigned from the eight-party coalition.

1997: A new political party was formed, the Latvian National Party of Reforms. Former Communist leader Alfreds Rubiks was released from prison.

1998: The DPS withdrew from the government, leaving the coalition as a minority. Citizenship laws were relaxed to make it easier for ethnic Russians to acquire citizenship.

1999: Andris Skele became prime minister. Vaira Vike-Freiberga was sworn in as president.

2000: Andris Skele resigned as prime minister after a disagreement within his coalition. He was replaced by Andris Berzins, who headed a coalition of the same parties as before, the Union for the Fatherland and Freedom (FF/LNNK), LW, and Skele's People's Party, as well as the additional New Party.

2002: Accepted into membership of EU in 2004.

2003: In a referendum, voters endorsed accession to the European Union in 2004.

2004: Latvia joined NATO and the EU. Indulis Emsis's coalition government resigned when parliament failed to ratify the draft budget. A new government, headed by Aigars Kalvitis, was installed.

2005: US President George Bush visited Latvia.

Latvian language *or* **Lettish** language of Latvia; with Lithuanian it is one of the two surviving members of the Baltic branch of the Indo-European language family.

Laud, William (1573–1645) English priest; archbishop of Canterbury from 1633. Laud's High Church policy, support for Charles I's unparliamentary rule, censorship of the press, and persecution of the Puritans all aroused bitter opposition, while his strict enforcement of the statutes against enclosures and of laws regulating wages and prices alienated the propertied classes. His attempt to impose the use of the Prayer Book on the Scots precipitated the English *Civil War. Impeached by Parliament in 1640, he was imprisoned in the Tower of London. In 1645 he was beheaded.

laudanum alcoholic solution (tincture) of the drug *opium. Used formerly as a narcotic and painkiller, it was available in the 19th century from pharmacists on demand in most of Europe and the USA.

Lauderdale, John Maitland, 1st Duke of Lauderdale (1616–1682) Scottish politician. Formerly a zealous *Covenanter, he joined the Royalists in 1647, and as high commissioner for Scotland 1667–79 persecuted the Covenanters. He was created Duke of Lauderdale in 1672, and was a member of the *Cabal ministry 1667–73.

laughing gas popular name for *nitrous oxide, an anaesthetic.

Laughton, Charles (1899–1962) English actor who became a US citizen in 1950. Initially a classical stage actor, he joined the Old Vic in 1933. His films include such roles as the king in *The Private Life of Henry VIII* (1933; Academy Award), Captain Bligh in *Mutiny on the Bounty* (1935), and Quasimodo in *The Hunchback of Notre Dame* (1939). In 1955 he directed *Night of the Hunter* and in 1962 appeared in *Advise and Consent*.

Laurasia northern landmass formed 200 million years ago by the splitting of the single world continent *Pangaea. (The southern landmass was *Gondwanaland.) It consisted of what was to become North America, Greenland, Europe, and Asia, and is believed to have broken up about 100 million years ago with the separation of North America from Europe.

laurel any of a group of European evergreen trees with glossy aromatic leaves, yellowish flowers, and black berries. The leaves of sweet bay or poet's laurel (*L. nobilis*) are used in cooking. Several species are cultivated worldwide. (Genus *Laurus*, family Lauraceae.)

Laurel and Hardy Stan Laurel (stage name of Arthur Stanley Jefferson) (1890–1965) and Oliver (Norvell) Hardy (1892–1957), US film comedians. They were one of the most successful comedy teams in film history (Laurel was slim, Hardy rotund). Their partnership began in 1927, survived the transition from silent films to sound, and resulted in more than 200 short and feature-length films. Among these are *Pack Up Your Troubles* (1932), *Our Relations* (1936), and *A Chump at Oxford* (1940). *The Music Box* (1932) won an Academy Award as Best Short Film.

lava molten *magma that erupts from a *volcano and cools to form extrusive *igneous rock. Lava types differ in composition, temperature, gas content, and viscosity (resistance to flow).

Laval, Pierre (1883–1945) French extreme-rightwing politician, he gravitated between the wars from socialism through the centre ground (serving as prime minister and foreign secretary 1931–32 and again 1935–36) to the extreme right. As head of the Vichy government and foreign minister 1942–44, he was responsible for the deportation of Jews and for requisitioning French labour to Germany.

lavender sweet-smelling purple-flowering herb belonging to the mint family, native to western Mediterranean countries. The bushy low-growing species *L. angustifolia* has long, narrow, upright leaves of a silver-green colour. The small flowers, borne on spikes, vary in colour from lilac to deep purple and are covered with small fragrant oil glands. Lavender oil is widely used in pharmacy and perfumes. (Genus *Lavandula*, family Labiatae.)

laver any of several edible purplish-red seaweeds, including purple laver (*P. umbilicalis*). Growing on the shore and in the sea, attached to rocks and stones, laver forms thin, roundish sheets of tissue up to 20 cm/8 in across. It becomes almost black when dry. (Genus *Porphyra*, family Rhodophyceae.)

Lavoisier, Antoine Laurent (1743–1794) French chemist. He proved that combustion needs only a part of the air, which he called oxygen, thereby destroying the theory of phlogiston (an imaginary 'fire element' released during combustion). With astronomer and mathematician Pierre de *Laplace, he showed in 1783 that water is a compound of oxygen and hydrogen. In this way he established the basic rules of chemical combination.

law body of rules and principles under which justice is administered or order enforced in a state or nation. In Western Europe there are two main systems: Roman law and English law. US law is a modified form of English law.

Law, Andrew Bonar (1858–1923) British Conservative politician, born in New Brunswick, Canada, of Scottish descent. He succeeded Balfour as leader of the opposition in 1911, became colonial secretary in Asquith's coalition government 1915–16, chancellor of the Exchequer 1916–19, and Lord Privy Seal 1919–21 in Lloyd George's coalition. He formed a Conservative cabinet in 1922, but resigned on health grounds.

law lords in England, the ten Lords of Appeal in Ordinary who, together with the Lord Chancellor and other peers, make up the House of Lords in its judicial capacity. The House of Lords is the final court of appeal in both criminal and civil cases. Law lords rank as life peers.

Lawrence, D(avid) H(erbert) (1885–1930) English writer. His work expresses his belief in emotion and the sexual impulse as creative and true to human nature. However, his ideal of the complete, passionate life is threatened by the advancement of the modern and technological world. His writing first received attention after the publication of the semi-autobiographical *The White Peacock* (1911) and *Sons and Lovers* (1913). Other novels include *The Rainbow* (1915), *Women in Love* (1921), and *Lady Chatterley's Lover*, printed privately in Italy in 1928. Lawrence tried to forge a new kind of novel, with a structure and content so intense that it would reflect emotion and passion more genuinely than ever before. This often led to conflict with official and unofficial prudery, and his interest in sex as a life force and bond was often censured. *The Rainbow* was suppressed for obscenity, and *Lady Chatterley's Lover* could only be published in a censored form in the UK in 1932. Not until 1960, when the obscenity law was successfully challenged, was it published in the original text. Lawrence also wrote short stories (for example, 'The Woman Who Rode Away', written in Mexico from 1922–25) and poetry (*Collected Poems*, 1928).

Lawrence, T(homas) E(dward) (1888–1935) called 'Lawrence of Arabia', British soldier, scholar, and translator. Appointed to the military intelligence department in Cairo, Egypt, during World War I, he took part in negotiations for an Arab revolt against the Ottoman Turks, and in 1916 attached himself to the emir Faisal. He became a guerrilla leader of genius, combining raids on Turkish communications with the organization of a joint Arab revolt, described in his book *The Seven Pillars of Wisdom* (1926).

lawrencium chemical symbol Lr, synthesized, radioactive, metallic element, the last of the actinide series, atomic number 103, relative atomic mass 262. Its only known isotope, Lr-257, has a half-life of 4.3 seconds and was originally synthesized at the University of California at Berkeley in 1961 by bombarding californium with boron nuclei. The original symbol, Lw, was officially changed in 1963.

laxative substance used to relieve constipation (infrequent bowel movement). Current medical opinion discourages regular or prolonged use. Regular exercise and a diet high in vegetable fibre are believed to be the best means of preventing and treating constipation.

LCD abbreviation for *liquid-crystal display.

leaching process by which substances are washed through or out of the soil. Fertilizers leached out of the soil drain into rivers, lakes, and ponds and cause *water pollution. In tropical areas, leaching of the soil after the destruction of forests removes scarce nutrients and can lead to a dramatic loss of soil fertility. The leaching of soluble minerals in soils can lead to the formation of distinct soil horizons as different minerals are deposited at successively lower levels.

lead chemical symbol Pb, heavy, soft, malleable, grey, metallic element, atomic number 82, relative atomic mass 207.19. Its chemical symbol comes from the Latin *plumbum*. Usually found as an ore (most often as the sulphide galena), it occasionally occurs as a free metal (*native metal), and is the final stable product of the decay of uranium. Lead is the softest and weakest of the commonly used metals, with a low melting point; it is a poor conductor of electricity and resists acid corrosion. As a cumulative poison, lead enters the body from lead water pipes, lead-based paints, and leaded petrol. (In humans, exposure to lead shortly after birth is associated with impaired mental health between the ages of two and four.) The metal is an effective shield against radiation and is used in batteries, glass, ceramics, and alloys such as pewter and solder.

lead ore any of several minerals from which lead is extracted. The primary ore is galena or lead sulphite PbS. This is unstable, and on prolonged exposure to the atmosphere it oxidizes into the minerals cerussite $PbCO_3$ and anglesite $PbSO_4$. Lead ores are usually associated with other metals, particularly silver – which can be mined at the same time – and zinc, which can cause problems during smelting.

leaf lateral outgrowth on the stem of a plant, and in most species is the primary organ of *photosynthesis (the process in which the *energy from absorbed sunlight is used to combine *carbon dioxide and *water to form sugars). The chief leaf types are cotyledons (seed leaves), scale leaves (on underground stems), foliage leaves, and bracts (in the axil of which a flower is produced).

leaf-hopper any of numerous species of plant-sucking insects. They feed on the sap of leaves. Each species feeds on a limited range of plants. (Family Cicadellidae, order Homoptera.)

leaf insect any of various insects about 10 cm/4 in long, with a green or brown, flattened body, remarkable for closely resembling the foliage on which they live. They are most common in Southeast Asia. (Genus *Phyllium*, order Phasmida.)

League of Nations international organization formed after World War I to solve international disputes by arbitration. Established in Geneva, Switzerland, in 1920, the League included representatives from states throughout the world, but was severely weakened by the US decision not to become a member, and had no power to enforce its decisions. It was dissolved in 1946. Its subsidiaries included the **International Labour Organization** and the **Permanent Court of International Justice** in The Hague, the Netherlands, both now under the *United Nations (UN).

Lean, David (1908–1991) English film director. His films, painstakingly crafted, include early work co-directed with the playwright Noël *Coward, such as *Brief Encounter* (1946). Among his later films are such accomplished epics as *The Bridge on the River Kwai* (1957; Academy Award), *Lawrence of Arabia* (1962; Academy Award), and *Dr Zhivago* (1965).

Lear, Edward (1812–1888) English artist and humorist. His *Book of Nonsense* (1846) popularized the *limerick (a five-line humorous verse). His *Nonsense Songs, Botany and Alphabets* (1871), includes two of his best-known poems, 'The Owl and the Pussycat' and 'The Jumblies'.

leather material prepared from the hides and skins of animals, by tanning with vegetable tannins and chromium salts. Leather is a durable and water-resistant material, and is used for bags, shoes, clothing, and upholstery. There are three main stages in the process of converting animal skin into leather: cleaning, tanning, and dressing. Tanning is often a highly polluting process.

Lebanon

National name: *Jumhouria al-Lubnaniya/ Republic of Lebanon*

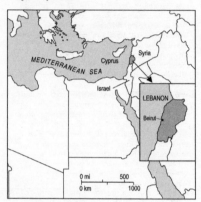

Area: 10,452 sq km/4,035 sq mi
Capital: Beirut (and chief port)
Major towns/cities: Tripoli, Zahlé, Baabda, Baalbek, Jezzine
Major ports: Tripoli, Tyre, Sidon, Jounie
Physical features: narrow coastal plain; fertile Bekka valley running north–south between Lebanon and Anti-Lebanon mountain ranges
Head of state: Emile Lahoud from 1998
Head of government: Oscar Karami from 2004
Political system: emergent democracy
Political executive: dual executive
Political parties: Phalangist Party, Christian, radical, nationalist; Progressive Socialist Party (PSP), Druze, moderate, socialist; National Liberal Party (NLP), Maronite, left of centre; National Bloc, Maronite, moderate; Lebanese Communist Party (PCL), nationalist, communist; Parliamentary Democratic Front, Sunni Muslim, centrist
Currency: Lebanese pound
GNI per capita (PPP): (US$) 4,470 (2002 est)
Exports: paper products, textiles, fruit and vegetables, jewellery. Principal market: Saudi Arabia 9.6% (2001)
Population: 3,653,000 (2003 est)
Language: Arabic (official), French, Armenian, English
Religion: Muslim 70% (Shiite 35%, Sunni 23%, Druze 7%, other 5%); Christian 30% (mainly Maronite 19%), Druze 3%; other Christian denominations including Greek Orthodox, Armenian, and Roman Catholic
Life expectancy: 72 (men); 75 (women) (2000–05)
Chronology
5th century BC–1st century AD: Part of the eastern Mediterranean Phoenician Empire.

1st century: Came under Roman rule; Christianity introduced.

635: Islam introduced by Arab tribes, who settled in southern Lebanon.

11th century: Druze faith developed by local Muslims.

1516: Became part of the Turkish Ottoman Empire.

1860: Massacre of thousands of Christian Maronites by the Muslim Druze led to French intervention.

1920–41: Administered by French under League of Nations mandate.

1943: Independence achieved as a republic, with a constitution that enshrined Christian and Muslim power-sharing.

1945: Joined the Arab League.

1948–49: Lebanon joined the first Arab war against Israel; Palestinian refugees settled in the south.

1958: Revolt by radical Muslims opposed to pro-Western policies of the Christian president, Camille Chamoun.

1964: Palestine Liberation Organization (PLO) founded in Beirut.

1967: More Palestinian refugees settled in Lebanon following the Arab–Israeli war.

1971: PLO expelled from Jordan; established headquarters in Lebanon.

1975: Outbreak of civil war between conservative Christians and leftist Muslims backed by PLO.

1976: Ceasefire agreed; Syrian-dominated Arab deterrent force formed to keep the peace, but considered by Christians as an occupying force.

1978: Israel launched a limited invasion of southern Lebanon in search of PLO guerrillas. An international United Nations peacekeeping force was unable to prevent further fighting.

1979: Part of southern Lebanon declared an 'independent free Lebanon' by a right-wing army officer.

1982: Israel again invaded Lebanon. Palestinians withdrew from Beirut under the supervision of an international peacekeeping force; the PLO moved its headquarters to Tunis.

1983: An agreement was reached for withdrawal of Syrian and Israeli troops but abrogated under Syrian pressure; intense fighting was seen between Christian Phalangists and Muslim Druze militias.

1984: Most of the international peacekeeping force were withdrawn. Radical Muslim militia took control of west Beirut.

1985: Lebanon was in chaos; many foreigners were taken hostage and Israeli troops withdrawn.

1987: Syrian troops were sent into Beirut.

1988: Gen Michel Aoun was appointed to head the caretaker military government; Premier Selim el-Hoss set up a rival government; the threat of partition hung over country.

1989: Gen Aoun declared a 'war of liberation' against Syrian occupation; Arab League-sponsored talks resulted in a ceasefire and a revised constitution recognizing Muslim majority; René Mouhawad was assassinated after 17 days as president; Maronite Christian Elias Hrawi was named as his successor; Aoun occupied the presidential palace, rejecting the constitution.

1990: The release of Western hostages began. Gen Aoun, crushed by Syrians, surrendered and legitimate government was restored.

1991: The government extended its control to the whole country. A treaty of cooperation with Syria was signed.

1992: The remaining Western hostages were released. A pro-Syrian administration led by businessman Rafik al-Hariri was re-elected after many Christians boycotted general election.

1993: Israel launched attacks against Shia fundamentalist Hezbollah strongholds in southern Lebanon before the USA and Syria brokered an agreement to avoid the use of force.

1996: Israel launched a rocket attack on southern Lebanon in response to Hezbollah activity. USA, Israel, Syria, and Lebanon attempted to broker a new ceasefire.

1998: Army chief General Emile Lahoud was elected president. Salim al-Hoss became prime minister.

2000: Israel withdrew its troops from southern Lebanon, and Lebanese troops assumed control in the region from Hezbollah guerillas. Rafik al-Hariri became prime minister for a second time.

2001: Israel objected to Lebanon pumping water from a tributary of the River Jordan.

2002: Israel and Lebanon disagreed on Lebanon's plan to divert water from the River Wazzani, with Israel threatening the use of military force.

2003: Israel was blamed for a car bomb explosion in Beirut which killed a member of Hezbollah.

2004: The United Nations Security Council adopted a resolution calling for all foreign troops to leave Lebanon. Syria, whose troops occupied parts of Lebanon, refused to comply.

2005: The former prime minister Rafiq Hariri was killed by a car bomb. Demonstrations followed, forcing Prime Minister Omar Karami to resign. He was asked and did attempt to form a new government. However, he was replaced by the moderate pro-Syrian MP, Najib Mikati. Syria announced that it had withdrawn all of its troops from Lebanon, to comply with the UN resolution.

Lebensraum (German 'living space') theory developed by Adolf Hitler for the expansion of Germany into Eastern Europe, and in the 1930s used by the Nazis to justify their annexation of neighbouring states on the grounds that Germany was overpopulated.

Le Chatelier's principle *or* **Le Chatelier-Braun principle** principle that if a change in conditions is imposed on a system in equilibrium, the system will react to counteract that change and restore the equilibrium.

lecithin lipid (fat), containing nitrogen and phosphorus, that forms a vital part of the cell membranes of plant and animal cells. The name is from the Greek *lekithos* 'egg yolk', eggs being a major source of lecithin.

Leconte de Lisle, Charles Marie René (1818–1894) French poet. He was born on the Indian Ocean Island of Réunion and settled in Paris in 1846. He played an important part in formulating the aims of the anti-Romantic group *Les Parnassiens* and became their acknowledged leader. His work, characterized by classic regularity and faultlessness of form, drew inspiration from the ancient world; it includes *Poèmes antiques/Antique Poems* (1852), *Poèmes barbares/Barbaric Poems* (1862), and *Poèmes tragiques/Tragic Poems* (1884). Although he advocated impassivity, his poems express a pessimistic awareness of the transitoriness of things.

Le Corbusier (1887–1965) adopted name of Charles-Edouard Jeanneret, Swiss-born French architect. He was an early and influential exponent of the *Modern Movement and one of the most innovative of 20th-century architects. His distinct brand of Functionalism first appears in his town-planning proposals of the early 1920s, which advocate 'vertical garden cities' with zoning of living and working areas and traffic separation as solutions to urban growth and chaos. From the 1940s several of his designs for multistorey villas were realized, notably his Unité d'Habitation, Marseille, (1947–52), using his Modulor system of standard-sized units mathematically calculated according to the proportions of the human figure (see *Fibonacci, *golden section).

LED abbreviation for *light-emitting diode.

Leda in Greek mythology, wife of Tyndareus of Sparta and mother of *Clytemnestra. Zeus, transformed as a swan, was the father of her daughter *Helen of Troy and, in some traditions, the brothers *Castor and Pollux (Greek Polydeuces). In other variants, Castor was fathered by Tyndareus or, according to Homer, both brothers were his sons.

Lederberg, Joshua (1925–) US geneticist who was awarded the Nobel Prize for Physiology or Medicine in 1958 for work on genetic recombination and the organization of bacterial genetic material. He showed that bacteria can reproduce sexually, combining genetic material so that offspring possess characteristics of both parent organisms. He shared the prize with George Beadle and Edward Tatum.

Led Zeppelin UK rock group 1968–80, founders of the *heavy metal genre. Their overblown style, with long instrumental solos, was based on rhythm and blues. Many of their songs, such as 'Stairway to Heaven', 'Rock and Roll', 'Black Dog' (all 1971) and 'Kashmir' (1975), have become classics. Among their most celebrated records were the group's untitled fourth album, popularly known as *Led Zeppelin IV* (1971) and their 1975 album *Physical Graffiti*.

Lee, Laurie (1914–1997) English writer. His autobiographical *Cider with Rosie* (1959) is a classic evocation of childhood; subsequent volumes are *As I Walked Out One Summer Morning* (1969), and *A Moment of War* (1991), in which he describes the horrors of the Spanish Civil War in 1936. His travel writing includes *A Rose for Winter* (1955). *Selected Poems* was published in 1983. One of Lee's great strengths as a writer was his ability to play the inconspicuous observer, always reluctant to identify himself overtly with the characters and events in his work. His evocation of his Gloucestershire childhood conjures up a vanished world that, despite its rigours, seems attractive to people in the modern-day world.

Lee, Robert E(dward) (1807–1870) US military strategist and Confederate general in the *American Civil War. As military adviser to Jefferson *Davis, president of the Confederacy, and as commander of the Army of Northern Virginia, he made several raids into Northern territory, but was defeated at *Gettysburg and surrendered in 1865 at *Appomattox.

leech any of a group of *annelid worms. Leeches live in fresh water, and in tropical countries infest damp forests. As bloodsucking animals they are injurious to people and animals, to whom they attach themselves by means of a strong mouth adapted to sucking. (Class Hirudinea.)

Leeds industrial city and metropolitan borough in West Yorkshire, England, 40 km/25 mi southwest of York, on the River Aire; population (2002 est) 420,300; metropolitan area (1998 est) 727,400. Industries include engineering, printing, chemicals, glass, woollens, clothing, plastics, paper, metal goods, and leather goods. Notable buildings include the Town Hall (1858) designed by Cuthbert Brodrick, the University of Leeds (1904), the Leeds City Art Gallery (1888), Temple Newsam House (early 16th century, altered in about 1630), and the Cistercian Abbey of Kirkstall (1147). It is a centre of communications where road, rail, and canals (to Liverpool and Goole) meet.

leek onionlike plant belonging to the lily family. The cultivated leek is a variety of the wild species *A. ampeloprasum* of the Mediterranean area and Atlantic islands. The lower leaf parts and white bulb are eaten as a vegetable. (Genus *Allium*, family Liliaceae.)

Lee Kuan Yew (1923–) Singaporean politician, prime minister 1959–90. Lee founded the anticommunist Socialist People's Action Party in 1954 and entered the Singapore legislative assembly in 1955. He was elected the country's first prime minister in 1959, and took Singapore out of the Malaysian federation in 1965. He remained in power until his resignation in 1990, and was succeeded by *Goh Chok Tong. Until 1992 he held on to the party leadership.

Lee Teng-hui (1923–) Taiwanese right-wing politician, vice-president 1984–88, president 1988–2000, and Kuomintang (see *Guomindang) party leader 1988–2001. The country's first island-born leader, he was viewed as a reforming technocrat. He was directly elected president in March 1996, defying Chinese opposition to the democratic contest.

Leeuwenhoek, Anton van (1632–1723) Dutch pioneer of microscopic research. He ground his own lenses, some of which magnified up to 300 times. With these he was able to see individual red blood cells, sperm, and bacteria, achievements not repeated for more than a century.

left wing in politics, the socialist parties. The term originated in the French national assembly of 1789, where the nobles sat in the place of honour to the right of the president, and the commons sat to the left. This arrangement has become customary in European parliaments, where the progressives sit on the left and the conservatives on the right. It is also usual to speak of the right, left, and centre, when referring to the different elements composing a single party.

Léger, Fernand (1881–1955) French painter and designer. He was associated with *cubism. From around 1909 he evolved a characteristic style of simplified forms, clear block outlines, and bold colours. Mechanical forms are constant themes in his work, which includes designs for the Swedish Ballet 1921–22, murals, and the abstract film *Ballet mécanique/Mechanical Ballet* (1924).

legionnaires' disease pneumonia-like disease, so called because it was first identified when it broke out at a convention of the American Legion in Philadelphia in 1976. Legionnaires' disease is caused by the bacterium *Legionella pneumophila*, which breeds in warm water (for example, in the cooling towers of air-conditioning systems). It is spread in minute water droplets, which may be inhaled. The disease can be treated successfully with antibiotics, though mortality can be high in elderly patients.

legislature lawmaking body or bodies in a political system. Some legislatures are unicameral (having one chamber), and some bicameral (with two).

legitimacy the justification of a ruling group's right to exercise power. Principles of legitimacy have included divine right, popular approval, and, in the case of communist parties, an insight into the true meaning of history.

legume plant of the family Leguminosae, which has a pod containing dry seeds. The family includes peas, beans, lentils, clover, and alfalfa (lucerne). Legumes are important in agriculture because of their specialized roots, which have nodules containing bacteria capable of fixing nitrogen from the air and increasing the fertility of the soil. The edible seeds of legumes are called **pulses**.

Lehár, Franz (1870–1948) Hungarian composer. He wrote many operettas, among them *The Merry Widow* (1905), *The Count of Luxembourg* (1909), *Gypsy Love* (1910), and *The Land of Smiles* (1929). He also composed songs, marches, and a violin concerto.

Leibniz, Gottfried Wilhelm (1646–1716) German mathematician, philosopher, and diplomat. Independently of, but concurrently with, English scientist Isaac *Newton, he developed the branch of mathematics known as *calculus and was one of the founders of symbolic logic. Free from all concepts of space and number, his logic was the prototype of future abstract mathematics.

Leicester industrial city and administrative centre of Leicester City unitary authority in central England, on the River Soar, 45 km/28 mi northeast of Birmingham; population (2001 est) 279,800. Major industries include engineering, food processing, electronics, chemicals, and clothing manufacture.

Leicester, Robert Dudley, Earl of Leicester (c. 1532–1588) English courtier. Son of the Duke of Northumberland, he was created Earl of Leicester in 1564. He led the disastrous military expedition (1585–87) sent to help the Netherlands against Spain. Despite this failure, he retained the favour of Queen *Elizabeth I, who gave him command of the army prepared to resist the threat of Spanish invasion in 1588.

Leicestershire county of central England (since April 1997 Leicester City and Rutland have been separate unitary authorities). **area:** 2,084 sq km/804 sq mi **towns and cities:** Loughborough, Melton Mowbray, Market Harborough (administrative headquarters at Glenfield, Leicester) **physical:** rivers Soar and Wreake; Charnwood Forest (in the northwest); Vale of Belvoir (under which are large coal deposits) **features:** Belvoir Castle, seat of the dukes of Rutland since the time of Henry VIII, rebuilt by James Wyatt in 1816; Donington Park motor-racing circuit, Castle Donington **population:** (2001 est) 610,300.

Leif Ericsson (lived c. 970) Norse explorer, son of Eric the Red, who sailed west from Greenland to find a country first sighted by Norsemen 986. He visited Baffin Island then sailed along the Labrador coast to Newfoundland, which was named 'Vinland' (Wine Land), because he discovered grape vines growing there.

Leigh, Vivien (1913–1967) stage name of Vivien Mary Hartley, Indian-born English actor. She won Academy Awards for her performances as Scarlett O'Hara in *Gone With the Wind* (1939) and as Blanche du Bois in *A Streetcar Named Desire* (1951). She was married to Laurence *Olivier 1940–60, and starred with him in the play *Antony and Cleopatra* (1951).

Leinster southeastern historic province of the Republic of Ireland, comprising the counties of Carlow, Dublin, Kildare, Kilkenny, Laois, Longford, Louth, Meath, Offaly, Westmeath, Wexford, and Wicklow; area 19,630 sq km/7,580 sq mi; population (2002 est) 2,105,400.

leishmaniasis any of several parasitic diseases caused by microscopic protozoans of the genus *Leishmania*, identified by William Leishman (1865–1926), and transmitted by sandflies. It occurs in two main forms: **visceral** (also called kala-azar), in which various internal organs are affected, and **cutaneous**, where the disease is apparent mainly in the skin. Leishmaniasis occurs in the Mediterranean region, Africa, Asia, and Central and South America. There are 12 million cases of leishmaniasis annually. The disease kills 8,000 people a year in South America and results in hundreds of thousands more suffering permanent disfigurement and disability through skin lesions, joint pain, and swelling of the liver and spleen.

leitmotif German **Leitmotiv**, (German 'leading motive') in music, a recurring theme or motive used to illustrate a character or idea. The term is strongly associated with Richard *Wagner, who frequently employed this technique with great sophistication in his music dramas; it is also strongly prevalent in music for film.

Leitrim county of the Republic of Ireland, in the province of Connacht, bounded on the northwest by Donegal Bay; county town Carrick-on-Shannon; area 1,530 sq km/591 sq mi; population (2002 est) 25,800. Carrick-on-Shannon, Mohill, and Manorhamilton are the most important towns. The rivers Shannon, Bonet, Drowes, and Duff run through Leitrim. There is some coal, and iron and lead in the mountainous areas, though no longer mined. Potatoes and oats are grown, and some cattle and sheep are reared. Tourism is becoming increasingly important. Parke's Castle (17th century) is one of the most popular attractions in the county.

lek in biology, a closely spaced set of very small territories each occupied by a single male during the mating season. Leks are found in the mating systems of several ground-dwelling birds (such as grouse) and a few antelopes, and in some insects.

Lely, Peter (1618–1680) adopted name of Pieter van der Faes, Dutch painter. He was active in England from 1641, painting fashionable portraits in the style of van Dyck. His subjects included Charles I, Cromwell, and Charles II. He painted a series of admirals, *Flagmen* (National Maritime Museum, London), and one of *The Windsor Beauties* (Hampton Court, Richmond), fashionable women of Charles II's court.

Lemaître, Georges Edouard (1894–1966) Belgian cosmologist. He proposed the *Big Bang theory of the origin of the universe in 1933. US astronomer Edwin *Hubble had shown that the universe was expanding, but it was Lemaître who suggested that the expansion had been started by an initial explosion, the Big Bang, a theory that is now generally accepted.

Le Mans industrial city and administrative centre of the Sarthe *département* in western France; population (1990 est) 148,500, conurbation 191,000. It has a motor-racing circuit where the annual endurance 24-hour race (established 1923) for sports cars and their prototypes is held at the Sarthe circuit. It is linked to Paris by a high-speed rail system.

Le Marche English **the Marches**, region of east central Italy, comprising the provinces of Ancona, Ascoli Piceno, Macerata, and Pesaro e Urbino; capital Ancona; area 9,694 sq km/3,743 sq mi; population (1997 est) 1,450,900. Agriculture produces wheat, maize, vines, potatoes, tomatoes, and root crops; and fishing is important.

lemming any of a group of small rodents distributed worldwide in northern latitudes. They are about 12 cm/5 in long, with thick brownish fur, a small head, and a short tail. Periodically, when their population exceeds the available food supply, lemmings undertake mass migrations. (Genus *Lemmus* and other related genera, family Cricetidae.)

Lemmon, Jack (1925–2001) born John Uhler Lemmon III, US actor. He collaborated with Billy Wilder on the comedies *Some Like It Hot* (1959) and *The Apartment* (1960), and teamed up with Walter Matthau on the popular *The Odd Couple* (1968). His performance in *Save the Tiger* (1973) won him an Academy Award.

Lemnos Greek **Limnos**, Greek island in the north of the Aegean Sea; area 476 sq km/184 sq mi; population (1991) 17,600. Towns include Kastron and Mudros. The island is of volcanic origin, rising to 430 m/1,411 ft. Industries include mulberries and other fruit, tobacco, and sheep.

lemon sharp-tasting yellow citrus fruit of the small, evergreen, semitropical lemon tree. It may have originated in northwestern India, and was introduced into Europe by the Spanish Moors in the 12th or 13th century. It is now grown in Italy, Spain, California, Florida, South Africa, and Australia, and is widely used for flavouring and as a garnish. (*Citrus limon*, family Rutaceae.)

lemon balm perennial herb belonging to the mint family, with lemon-scented leaves. It is widely used in teas, liqueurs, and medicines. (*Melissa officinalis*, family Labiatae.)

lemur any of various prosimian primates of the Lemuridae family, found in Madagascar and the Comoros Islands. There are about 16 species, ranging from mouse-sized to dog-sized animals; the pygmy mouse lemur (*Microcebus myoxinus*), weighing 30 g/1 oz, is the smallest primate. The diademed sifaka, weighing 7 kg/15 lb, is the largest species of lemur. Lemurs are arboreal, and some species are nocturnal. They have long, bushy tails, and feed on fruit, insects, and small animals. Many are threatened with extinction owing to loss of their forest habitat and, in some cases, from hunting.

Lena one of the largest rivers of the Russian Federation, in eastern Siberia; length 4,400 km/2,734 mi; total drainage area 490,000 sq km/189,189 sq mi. The Lena rises in the Baikal Mountains, west of Lake Baikal, and flows northeast to Yakutsk, then north into the Laptev Sea (an inlet of the Arctic Ocean), where it forms a large delta 400 km/240 mi wide and covering some 30,000 sq km/11,583 sq mi. The river is navigable almost throughout its course, but is frozen for eight months of the year. Its main tributaries are the Vitim, Olekma, Aldan, and the Vilyui. The main ports on the Lena's course are Osetrovo (since 1954 part of Ust-Kut) and Yakutsk.

Lenin, Vladimir Ilyich (1870–1924) adopted name of Vladimir Ilyich Ulyanov, Russian revolutionary, first leader of the USSR, and communist theoretician. Active in the 1905 Revolution, Lenin had to leave Russia when it failed, settling in Switzerland in 1914. He returned to Russia after the February revolution of 1917 (see *Russian Revolution). He led the Bolshevik revolution of November 1917 and became leader of a Soviet government, concluded peace with Germany, and organized a successful resistance to *White Russian (pro-tsarist) uprisings and foreign intervention during the Russian civil war 1918–21. His modification of traditional Marxist doctrine to fit conditions prevailing in Russia became known as **Marxism-Leninism**, the basis of *communist ideology.

Leninism modification of *Marxism by *Lenin which argues that in a revolutionary situation the industrial proletariat is unable to develop a truly revolutionary consciousness without strong leadership.

Lennon, John Winston (1940–1980) UK rock singer, songwriter, and guitarist; a founder member of the *Beatles. He lived in the USA from 1971. Both before the band's break-up in 1970 and in his solo career, he collaborated intermittently with his wife **Yoko Ono (1933–)**. 'Give Peace a Chance', a hit in 1969, became an anthem of the peace movement. His solo work alternated between the confessional and the political, as on the album *Imagine* (1971). He was shot dead by a crazed fan in 1980.

Le Nôtre, André (1613–1700) French landscape gardener, often considered the greatest designer of formal gardens and parks of the baroque period. He created the gardens at *Versailles 1662–90 and the Tuileries, Paris. His grandiose scheme for Versailles complemented Le Vau's original design for the palace facade, extending its formal symmetry into the surrounding countryside with vast *parterres* (gardens having beds and paths arranged to form a pattern), radiating avenues, and unbroken vistas.

lens in optics, a piece of a transparent material, such as glass, with two polished surfaces – one concave or convex, and the other plane, concave, or convex – that modifies rays of light. A convex lens brings rays of light together; a concave lens makes the rays diverge. Lenses are essential to spectacles, microscopes, telescopes, cameras, and almost all optical instruments.

Lent in the Christian church, the 40-day period of fasting that precedes *Easter, beginning on Ash Wednesday (the day after Shrove Tuesday), but omitting Sundays.

lentil annual Old World plant belonging to the pea family. The plant, which resembles vetch, grows 15–45 cm/6–18 in high and has white, blue, or purplish flowers. The seeds, contained in pods about 1.6 cm/0.6 in long, are widely used as food. (*Lens culinaris*, family Leguminosae.)

Lenya, Lotte (1898–1981) adopted name of Karoline Wilhelmine Blamauer, Austrian actor and singer. She was married five times, twice to the composer Kurt Weill,

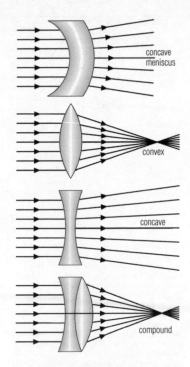

lens The passage of light through lenses. The concave lenses diverges a beam of light from a distant source. The convex and compound lenses focus light from a distant source to a point. The distance between the focus and the lens is called the focal length. The shorter the focus, the more powerful the lens.

first in 1926, with whom she emigrated to the USA in 1935. She appeared in several of the Brecht–Weill operas, notably *Die Dreigroschenoper/The Threepenny Opera* (1928). Her plain looks and untrained singing voice brought added realism to her stage roles.

Lenz's law in physics, a law stating that the direction of an electromagnetically induced current (generated by moving a magnet near a wire or a wire in a magnetic field) will be such as to oppose the motion producing it. It is named after the Russian physicist Heinrich Friedrich Lenz, who announced it in 1833.

Leo zodiacal constellation in the northern hemisphere, represented as a lion. The Sun passes through Leo from mid-August to mid-September. Its brightest star is first-magnitude Regulus at the base of a pattern of stars called the Sickle. In astrology, the dates for Leo are between about 23 July and 22 August (see *precession).

Leo (III) the Isaurian (c. 680–741) Byzantine emperor and soldier. He seized the throne in 717, successfully defended Constantinople against the Saracens 717–18, and attempted to suppress the use of images in church worship.

Leo thirteen popes, including:
Leo (I) the Great, (St Leo) (c. 390–461) Pope from 440. He helped to establish the Christian liturgy. Leo summoned the Chalcedon Council where his Dogmatical Letter was accepted as the voice of St Peter. Acting as ambassador for the emperor Valentian III (425–455), Leo saved Rome from devastation by the Huns by buying off their king, Attila.
Leo X, Giovanni de' Medici (1475–1521) Pope from 1513. The son of Lorenzo the Magnificent of Florence, he was created a cardinal at 13. He bestowed on Henry VIII of England the title of Defender of the Faith. A patron of the arts, he sponsored the rebuilding of St Peter's Church, Rome. He raised funds for this by selling indulgences (remissions of punishment for sin), a sale that led the religious reformer Martin Luther to rebel against papal authority. Leo X condemned Luther in the bull *Exsurge domine* (1520) and excommunicated him in 1521.

Leonardo da Vinci (1452–1519) Italian painter, sculptor, architect, engineer, and scientist. One of the greatest figures of the Italian Renaissance, he was active in Florence, Milan, and, from 1516, France. As state engineer and court painter to the Duke of Milan, he painted the *Last Supper* mural (c. 1495; Sta Maria delle Grazie, Milan), and on his return to Florence painted the *Mona Lisa* (c. 1503–05; Louvre, Paris). His notebooks and drawings show an immensely inventive and enquiring mind, studying aspects of the natural and scientific world from anatomy and botany to aerodynamics and hydraulics.

Leoncavallo, Ruggero (1858–1919) Italian operatic composer. He played in restaurants, composing in his spare time, until the success of *I pagliacci/The Strolling Players* (1892). His other operas include *La Bohème/Bohemian Life* (1897) (contemporary with Puccini's version) and *Zaza* (1900).

Leone, Sergio (1921–1989) Italian film director and screenwriter. One of the pioneers of the 'spaghetti Western', he was largely responsible for making a star of the actor Clint *Eastwood, starting with *Per un pugno di dollari/A Fistful of Dollars* (1964).

leopard or **panther** large wild cat found in Africa and Asia. The background colour of the coat is golden, and the black spots form rosettes that differ according to the variety; **black panthers** are simply a colour variation and retain the patterning as a 'watered-silk' effect. The leopard is 1.5–2.5 m/5–8 ft long, including the tail, which may measure 1 m/3 ft. (Species *Panthera pardus*, family Felidae.)

Leopold three kings of the Belgians, including:
Leopold I (1790–1865) King of the Belgians from 1831. He was elected to the throne on the creation of an independent Belgium. Through his marriage, when prince of Saxe-Coburg, to Princess Charlotte Augusta, he was the uncle of Queen Victoria of Great Britain and had considerable influence over her.
Leopold III (1901–1983) King of the Belgians 1934–51. Against the prime minister's advice he surrendered to the German army in World War II in 1940. Post-war charges against his conduct led to a regency by his brother Charles and his eventual abdication in 1951 in favour of his son Baudouin.

Lepanto, Battle of sea battle on 7 October 1571 between the Ottoman Empire and 'Holy League' forces from Spain, Venice, Genoa, and the Papal States jointly commanded by the Spanish soldier Don John of Austria. The battle took place in the Mediterranean Gulf of Corinth off Lepanto (the Greek port of **Naupaktos**), then in Turkish possession. It was not decisive, but the combined western fleets halted Turkish expansion and broke Muslim sea power.

Le Pen, Jean-Marie (1928–) French extreme-rightwing politician, founder of the National Front (FN) in 1972. His skill as a public speaker, his demagogic mixing of nationalism with law-and-order populism – calling for immigrant repatriation, stricter nationality laws, and the restoration of capital punishment – and his hostility to the European Union attracted a wide swathe of electoral support in the 1980s and 1990s, and in the 2002 presidential election progressed to the run-off round, but was heavily defeated by Jacques Chirac.

leprosy or **Hansen's disease** chronic, progressive disease caused by the bacterium *Mycobacterium leprae*, closely related to that of tuberculosis. The infection attacks the skin and nerves. Leprosy is endemic in 28 countries, and confined almost entirely to the tropics. It is controlled with drugs. Worldwide, there are 700,000 new cases of leprosy a year (2001).

lepton any of a class of *elementary particles that are not affected by the strong nuclear force. The leptons comprise the *electron, *muon, and *tau, and their *neutrinos (the electron neutrino, muon neutrino, and tau neutrino), as well as their six *antiparticles.

Lermontov, Mikhail Yurevich (1814–1841) Russian Romantic poet and novelist. In 1837 he was sent into active military service in the Caucasus for writing a revolutionary poem on the death of Pushkin, which criticized court values, and for participating in a duel. Among his works are the psychological novel *A Hero of Our Time* (1840) and a volume of poems *October* (1840).

Lerner, Alan Jay (1918–1986) US lyricist. He collaborated with Frederick Loewe on musicals including *Brigadoon* (1947), *Paint Your Wagon* (1951), *My Fair Lady* (1956), *Gigi* (1958), and *Camelot* (1960).

lesbianism homosexuality (sexual attraction to one's own sex) between women, so called from the Greek island of Lesbos (now Lesvos), the home of *Sappho the poet and her followers to whom the behaviour was attributed.

lesion any change in a body tissue that is a manifestation of disease or injury.

Lesotho
National name: *Mmuso oa Lesotho/Kingdom of Lesotho*
Area: 30,355 sq km/11,720 sq mi
Capital: Maseru
Major towns/cities: Qacha's Nek, Teyateyaneng, Mafeteng, Hlotse, Roma, Quthing
Physical features: mountainous with plateaux, forming part of South Africa's chief watershed
Head of state: King Letsie III from 1996
Head of government: Bethuel Pakalitha Mosisili from 1998
Political system: emergent democracy
Political executive: parliamentary
Political parties: Basotho National Party (BNP), traditionalist, nationalist, right of centre; Basutoland Congress Party (BCP), left of centre
Currency: loti
GNI per capita (PPP): (US$) 2,710 (2002 est)

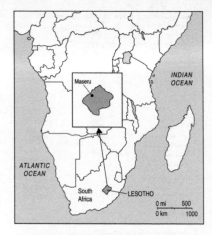

Exports: clothing, footwear, furniture, food and live animals (cattle), hides, wool and mohair, baskets. Principal market: USA and Canada 62.8% (2001)
Population: 1,802,000 (2003 est)
Language: English (official), Sesotho, Zulu, Xhosa
Religion: Protestant 42%, Roman Catholic 38%, indigenous beliefs
Life expectancy: 32 (men); 38 (women) (2000–05)
Chronology
18th century: Formerly inhabited by nomadic hunter-gatherer San, Zulu-speaking Ngunis, and Sotho-speaking peoples settled in the region.
1820s: Under the name of Basutoland, Sotho nation founded by Moshoeshoe I, who united the people to repulse Zulu attacks from south.
1843: Moshoeshoe I negotiated British protection as tension with South African Boers increased.
1868: Became British territory, administered by Cape Colony (in South Africa) from 1871.
1884: Became British crown colony, after revolt against Cape Colony control; Basuto chiefs allowed to govern according to custom and tradition, but rich agricultural land west of the Caledon River was lost to South Africa.
1900s: Served as a migrant labour reserve for South Africa's mines and farms.
1952: Left-of-centre Basutoland African Congress, later Congress Party (BCP), founded by Ntsu Mokhehle to campaign for self rule.
1966: Independence achieved within Commonwealth, as Kingdom of Lesotho, with Moshoeshoe II as king and Chief Leabua Jonathan of the conservative Basotho National Party (BNP) as prime minister.
1970: State of emergency declared; king briefly forced into exile after attempting to increase his authority.
1973: State of emergency lifted; BNP won majority of seats in general election.
1975: Members of ruling party attacked by South African-backed guerrillas, who opposed African National Congress (ANC) guerrillas using Lesotho as a base.
1986: South Africa imposed a border blockade, forcing the deportation of 60 ANC members.

1990: Moshoeshoe II was dethroned and replaced by his son, as King Letsie III.

1993: Free multiparty elections ended the military rule.

1994: Fighting between rival army factions was ended by a peace deal, brokered by the Organization of African Unity (OAU; later African Union).

1995: King Letsie III abdicated to restore King Moshoeshoe II to the throne.

1996: King Moshoeshoe II was killed in car accident; King Letsie III was restored to the throne.

1998: The LCD attained general election victory amidst claims of rigged polls; public demonstrations followed. South Africa sent troops to support the government. An interim political authority was appointed prior to new elections. Bethuel Mosisili became the new prime minister.

2000: King Letsie III married Karabo Montsoeneng.

2002: The LCD won parliamentary elections, held under a new electoral process, and Mosisili was sworn in as prime minister for a second term.

2004: A state of emergency was declared after severe drought caused food shortages. The first phase of the Lesotho Highlands Water Project got underway. The project will supply water to South Africa.

2005: The first local elections were held since independence.

less developed country *or* **least developed country (LDC)** any country late in developing an industrial base, and dependent on cash crops and unprocessed minerals; part of the *developing world. The terms 'less developed', 'least developed', and 'developing' imply that industrial development is desirable or inevitable.

Lesseps, Ferdinand Marie (1805–1894) Vicomte de Lesseps, French engineer. He designed and built the *Suez Canal 1859–69. He began work on the Panama Canal in 1881, but withdrew after failing to construct it without locks.

Lessing, Doris May (1919–) born Doris May Tayler, English novelist and short-story writer. Concerned with social and political themes, particularly the place of women in society, her work includes *The Grass is Singing* (1950), the five-novel series *Children of Violence* (1952–69), *The Golden Notebook* (1962), *The Good Terrorist* (1985), *The Fifth Child* (1988), *London Observed* (1992), and *Love Again* (1996).

Lesvos Greek island in the Aegean Sea, near the coast of Turkey; area 2,154 sq km/831 sq mi; population (1991) 103,700. The capital is Mytilene. Industries include olives, wine, and grain. The island was called Lesbos in ancient times and was an Aeolian settlement, home of the poets Alcaeus and Sappho. It was conquered by the Turks from Genoa in 1462 and was annexed to Greece in 1913.

Lethe (Greek 'oblivion') in Greek mythology, a river of the underworld whose waters when drunk, usually by the shades (dead), brought forgetfulness of the past.

lettuce annual plant whose large edible leaves are commonly used in salads. There are many varieties, including the cabbage lettuce, with round or loose heads, the Cos lettuce, with long, upright heads, and the Iceberg lettuce, with tight heads of crisp leaves. They are all believed to have been derived from the wild species *L. serriola*. (Genus *Lactuca*, especially *L. sativa*, family Compositae.)

leucocyte another name for a *white blood cell.

leucotomy *or* **lobotomy** brain operation to sever the connections between the frontal lobe and underlying structures. It was widely used in the 1940s and 1950s to treat severe psychotic or depressive illness. Though it achieved some success, it left patients dull and apathetic; there was also a considerable risk of epilepsy. It was largely replaced by the use of psychotropic drugs from the late 1950s.

leukaemia any one of a group of cancers of the blood cells, with widespread involvement of the bone marrow and other blood-forming tissue. The central feature of leukaemia is runaway production of white blood cells that are immature or in some way abnormal. These rogue cells, which lack the defensive capacity of healthy white cells, overwhelm the normal ones, leaving the victim vulnerable to infection. Treatment is with radiotherapy and *cytotoxic drugs to suppress replication of abnormal cells, or by bone-marrow transplantation.

levee naturally formed raised bank along the side of a river channel. When a river overflows its banks, the rate of flow is less than that in the channel, and silt is deposited on the banks. With each successive flood the levee increases in height so that eventually the river may be above the surface of the surrounding flood plain. Notable levees are found on the lower reaches of the Mississippi in the USA, and along the Po in Italy. The Hwang Ho in China also has well-developed levees.

Levellers democratic party in the English *Civil War. The Levellers found wide support among *Cromwell's New Model Army and the yeoman farmers, artisans, and small traders, and proved a powerful political force from 1647 to 1649. Their programme included the establishment of a republic, government by a parliament of one house elected by all men over 21, elections every year, freedom of speech, religious toleration, and sweeping social reforms, including education for everyone. They were led by John Lilburne, whose wife Elizabeth campaigned for a 'proportional share in the freedom of this commonwealth' for women.

lever simple machine consisting of a rigid rod pivoted at a fixed point called the fulcrum, used for shifting or raising a heavy load or applying force. Levers are classified into orders according to where the effort is applied, and the load-moving force developed, in relation to the position of the fulcrum. (See diagram, p. ???.)

Levi, Primo (1919–1987) Italian novelist. He joined the antifascist resistance during World War II, was captured, and sent to the concentration camp at Auschwitz. He wrote of these experiences in *Se questo è un uomo/If This Is a Man* (1947). His other books, all based on his experience of the war, include *Period Tables* (1975) and *Moments of Reprieve* (1981).

Levi-Montalcini, Rita (1909–) Italian neurologist who was awarded a Nobel Prize for Physiology or Medicine in 1986 with her co-worker, US biochemist Stanley Cohen, for their discovery of factors that promote the growth of nerve and epidermal cells. This nerve-growth factor controls how many cells make up the adult nervous system.

Lévi-Strauss, Claude (1908–) French anthropologist. He helped to formulate the principles of *structuralism

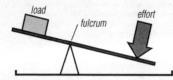

first-order lever

load
fulcrum
effort

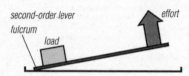

second-order lever

fulcrum
load
effort

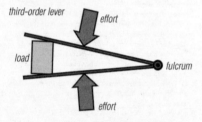

third-order lever

effort
load
fulcrum
effort

lever Types of lever. Practical applications of the first-order lever include the crowbar, seesaw, and scissors. The wheelbarrow is a second-order lever; tweezers or tongs are third-order levers.

by stressing the interdependence of cultural systems and the way they relate to each other, maintaining that social and cultural life can be explained by a postulated unconscious reality concealed behind the reality by which people believe their lives to be ordered.

levitation counteraction of gravitational forces on a body. As claimed by medieval mystics, spiritualist mediums, and practitioners of transcendental meditation, it is unproven. In the laboratory it can be produced scientifically; for example, electrostatic force and acoustical waves have been used to suspend water drops for microscopic study. It is also used in technology; for example, in magnetic levitation as in *maglev trains.

Lewes, Battle of battle in 1264 caused by the baronial opposition to the English King Henry III, led by Simon de Montfort, Earl of Leicester (1208–65). The king was defeated and captured at the battle.

Lewis *or* **Lewis-with-Harris** largest and most northerly island in the Outer *Hebrides, Western Isles; area 2,220 sq km/857 sq mi; population (1991) 21,700. Its main town is Stornoway. It is separated from northwest Scotland by the Minch. The island is 80 km/50 mi long from north to south, and its greatest breadth is 45 km/28 mi. There are many lochs and peat moors. The Callanish standing stones on the west coast are thought to be up to 5,000 years old, second only to Stonehenge (on Salisbury Plain, Wiltshire) in archaeological significance in the UK.

Lewis, (Percy) Wyndham (1882–1957) English writer and artist. He pioneered *Vorticism, which, with its feeling of movement, sought to reflect the age of industry. He had a hard and aggressive style in both his writing and his painting. His literary works include the novel *The Apes of God* (1930); the essay collection *Time and Western Man* (1927); and an autobiography, *Blasting and Bombardiering* (1937). In addition to paintings of a semi-abstract kind, he made a number of portraits; among his sitters were the poets Edith Sitwell, Ezra Pound, and T S Eliot.

Lewis, C(live) S(taples) (1898–1963) English academic and writer, born in Belfast. He became a committed Christian in 1931 and wrote the Chronicles of Narnia, a series of seven novels of Christian allegory for children set in the magic land of Narnia, beginning with *The Lion, the Witch, and the Wardrobe* (1950).

Lewis, Carl (1961–) born Frederick Carlton Lewis, US track and field athlete. He won nine gold medals and one silver in four successive Olympic Games. At the 1984 Olympic Games he equalled the performance of Jesse Owens, winning gold medals in the 100 and 200 metres, 400-metre relay, and long jump. He officially ended his career in 1997 at the age of 36. In November 1999 he was voted 'Sportsman of the Century' by the International Olympic Committee (IOC), and in December 1999 the US magazine *Sports Illustrated* named him the 'Best Olympian of the 20th Century'.

Lewis, Jerry Lee (1935–) US rock-and-roll and country singer and pianist. His trademark was the boogie-woogie-derived 'pumping piano' style in hits such as 'Whole Lotta Shakin' Going On' and 'Great Balls of Fire' (1957); later recordings include 'What Made Milwaukee Famous' (1968).

Lewis, Lennox Claudius (1966–) English boxer. He won the World Boxing Council (WBC) world heavyweight title in 1992, becoming the first British boxer to do so in the 20th century. After defending the title successfully for nearly two years, he lost to Oliver McCall in 1994, but he regained the title in 1997. He became the undisputed heavyweight world champion in November 1999, defeating Evander Holyfield. He lost his WBC, International Boxing Federation (IBF), and International Boxing Organization (IBO) titles in April 2001 when he was surprisingly knocked out in the fifth round by the US challenger Hasim Rahman. He regained his titles later that year, before winning a much-anticipated fight with Mike Tyson in June 2002.

Leyden alternative form of Leiden, a city in the Netherlands.

Lhasa called 'the Forbidden City', capital of the autonomous region of *Tibet, China, at 5,000 m/16,400 ft; population (1999 est) 121,600. Traditional products include handicrafts and light industrial goods. The holy city of *Lamaism, Lhasa was closed to Westerners until 1904, when members of a British expedition led by Col Francis E Young husband visited the city. It was annexed with the rest of Tibet 1950–51 by China, and the spiritual and temporal head of state, the Dalai Lama, fled in 1959 after a popular uprising against Chinese rule. Monasteries have been destroyed and monks killed, and an influx of Chinese settlers has generated resentment. In 1988 and 1989 nationalist demonstrators were shot by Chinese soldiers. In the late 20th century, under Chinese administration, foreign trade was encouraged and the city developed a wider range of industry, including chemicals, electric motors, tractor assembly, pharmaceuticals, fertilizers, and cement.

liana woody, perennial climbing plant with very long stems, which grows around trees right up to the top, where there is more sunlight. Lianas are common in tropical rainforests, where individual stems may grow up to 78 m/255 ft long. They have an unusual stem structure that makes them flexible, despite being woody.

Liao dynasty family that ruled part of northeastern China and Manchuria 945–1125 during the *Song era. It was founded by cavalry-based Qidan (Khidan) people, Mongolian-speakers who gradually became Sinicized. They were later defeated by the nomadic Juchen (Jurchen) who founded the *Jin dynasty.

Liaoning province of northeast China, bounded to the east by Jilin, to the southeast by North Korea, to the south by Korea Bay and the Gulf of Liaodong, to the southwest by Hebei, and to the northwest by Inner Mongolia; area 151,000 sq km/58,300 sq mi; population (2000 est) 42,380,000. The capital is Shenyang, and other cities and towns include Anshan, Fushun, Liaoyang, and Dalian (port). The province includes the Dongbei (Manchurian) Plain and the grasslands of the Mongolian Plateau. Liaoning is the leading province of China for heavy industry, especially coal and iron and steel, while other industries include nonferrous metals, machinery, and chemicals as well as lighter industries such as textiles, paper, and food processing. Agricultural products include cereals. Liaoning was developed by Japan between 1905 and 1945, including the Liaodong Peninsula, whose ports had been conquered from the Russians.

Liaquat Ali Khan, Nawabzada (1895–1951) Indian politician, deputy leader of the *Muslim League 1940–47, first prime minister of Pakistan from 1947. He was assassinated by objectors to his peace policy with India.

libel in law, defamation published in a permanent form, such as in a newspaper, book, or broadcast.

Liberal Democrats UK political party of the centre, led since 1999 by Charles *Kennedy. Britain's third main party, the Liberal Democrats are successors to the *Liberal Party and the *Social Democratic Party, which merged in 1998 to form the Social and Liberal Democrats (SLD). The name Liberal Democrats was adopted in 1989. It is a progressive party, which supports closer integration within the European Union, constitutional reform (including *proportional representation and regional government), and greater investment in state education and the National Health Service, financed by higher direct taxes. The party has strong libertarian and environmentalist wings. It has been in coalition, with Labour, in the Scottish Parliament since 1999, and in the Welsh Assembly 2000–2003. It won 52 seats at the June 2001 general election – the best result for the Liberals and their successors for more than 70 years.

liberalism political and social theory that supports representative government, freedom of the press, speech, and worship, the abolition of class privileges, the use of state resources to protect the welfare of the individual, and international *free trade. It is

historically associated with the Liberal Party in the UK and the Democratic Party in the USA.

Liberal Party British political party, the successor to the *Whig Party, with an ideology of liberalism. In the 19th century it represented the interests of commerce and industry. Its outstanding leaders were Palmerston, Gladstone, and Lloyd George. From 1914 it declined, and the rise of the Labour Party pushed the Liberals into the middle ground. The Liberals joined forces with the Social Democratic Party (SDP) as the Alliance for the 1983 and 1987 elections. In 1988 a majority of the SDP voted to merge with the Liberals to form the Social and Liberal Democrats (SLD), which became known as the *Liberal Democrats from 1989. A minority have retained the name Liberal Party.

Liberal Party, Australian political party established 1944 by Robert Menzies, after a Labor landslide, and derived from the former United Australia Party. After the voters rejected Labor's extensive nationalization plans, the Liberals were in power 1949–72 and 1975–83 and were led in succession by Harold Holt, John Gorton, William McMahon, Billy Snedden, Malcolm Fraser, John Hewson, Alexander Downer, and John Howard. It returned to power in 1996 in a coalition with the National Party.

liberation theology Christian theory of Jesus' prime role as the 'Liberator', a representative of the poor and devoted to freeing them from oppression. Enthusiastically adopted by Christians (mainly Roman Catholic) in Latin America, it embraces the struggle towards a classless society, and has often led to violence. It has been criticized by some Roman Catholic authorities, including Pope John Paul II. The movement has also spread to other nations in the developing world.

Liberia

National name: *Republic of Liberia*

Area: 111,370 sq km/42,999 sq mi
Capital: Monrovia (and chief port)
Major towns/cities: Bensonville, Saniquillie, Gbarnga, Voinjama, Buchanan
Major ports: Buchanan, Greenville
Physical features: forested highlands; swampy tropical coast where six rivers enter the sea
Head of state and government: Charles Gynde Bryant from 2003
Political system: emergent democracy

527

Political executive: limited presidency
Political parties: National Democratic Party of Liberia (NDPL), nationalist, left of centre; National Patriotic Front of Liberia (NPFL), left of centre; United Democratic Movement of Liberia for Democracy (Ulimo), left of centre; National Patriotic Party (NPP), antidemocratic
Currency: Liberian dollar
Exports: rubber, timber, coffee, cocoa, iron ore, palm-kernel oil, diamonds, gold. Principal market: Germany 50% (2001)
Population: 3,367,000 (2003 est)
Language: English (official), over 20 Niger-Congo languages
Religion: animist 70%, Sunni Muslim 20%, Christian 10%
Life expectancy: 41 (men); 42 (women) (2000–05)
Chronology
1821: Purchased by the philanthropic American Colonization Society and turned into settlement for liberated black slaves from southern USA.
1847: Recognized as an independent republic.
1869: The True Whig Party founded, which was to dominate politics for more than a century, providing all presidents.
1926: Large concession sold to Firestone Rubber Company as foreign indebtedness increased.
1980: President Tolbert was assassinated in military coup led by Sgt Samuel Doe, who banned political parties and launched an anticorruption drive.
1984: A new constitution was approved in a referendum. The National Democratic Party (NDPL) was founded by Doe as political parties were relegalized.
1985: Doe and the NDPL won decisive victories in the allegedly rigged elections.
1990: Doe was killed as bloody civil war broke out, involving Charles Taylor and Gen Hezekiah Bowen, who led rival rebel armies, the National Patriotic Front (NPFL) and the Armed Forces of Liberia (AFL). The war left 150,000 dead and 2 million homeless. A West African peacekeeping force was drafted in.
1992: Monrovia was under siege by Taylor's rebel forces.
1995: Ghanaian-backed peace proposals were accepted by rebel factions; an interim Council of State was established, comprising leaders of three main rebel factions.
1996: There was renewed fighting in the capital. A peace plan was reached in talks convened by the Economic Community of West African States (ECOWAS); Ruth Perry became Liberia's first female head of state.
1997: The National Patriotic Party (NPP) won a majority in assembly elections and its leader, Charles Taylor, became head of state.
1998: There was fighting in Monrovia between President Taylor's forces and opposition militias.
1999: Liberia was accused of supporting rebels in Sierra Leone. There were clashes between Liberian troops and rebels on the border with Guinea.
2000: Liberia was accused of buying diamonds from Sierra Leonean rebels, in contravention of an international ban. A massive offensive against rebels in northern Liberia was launched in September.
2001: Fighting worsened, and the UN renewed its arms embargo and the ban on diamond trading.
2003: Despite a ceasefire agreement, hundreds of

people were killed in the ongoing civil war as rebel forces seeking the overthrow of President Taylor launched assaults on Monrovia and Buchanan. West African peacekeeping forces supported by 200 US marines took control of the situation and President Taylor resigned and went into exile. Rebel factions and government representatives signed a power-sharing agreement appointing Gyude Bryant, an industrialist and cleric, to lead a new transitional administration. US forces were replaced by a UN peacekeeping mission, who began to disarm former rebels. Gyde Bryant became head of state.
2004: The UN Security Council voted to freeze the assets of Charles Taylor. Riots in the capital Monrovia were blamed on former rebels.

libido in Freudian psychology, the energy of the sex instinct, which is to be found even in a newborn child. The libido develops through a number of phases, described by Sigmund Freud in his theory of infantile sexuality. The source of the libido is the *id.

Libra faint zodiacal constellation on the celestial equator (see *celestial sphere) adjoining Scorpius, and represented as the scales of justice. The Sun passes through Libra during November. The constellation was once considered to be a part of Scorpius, seen as the scorpion's claws. In astrology, the dates for Libra are between about 23 September and 23 October (see *precession).

libretto (Italian 'little book') the text of an opera or other dramatic vocal work, or the scenario of a ballet.

Libreville (French 'free town') capital and chief port of Gabon, on the northern shore of the Gabon River estuary; population (2002 est) 467,000 (city), 541,000 (urban area). Products include timber, rubber, cacao, palm-oil, cement, and minerals (including uranium and manganese). Libreville was founded in 1849 as a refuge for slaves freed by the French. The city developed rapidly from the 1970s due to the oil trade.

Libya
  National name: *Al-Jamahiriyya al-'Arabiyya al-Libiyya ash-Sha'biyya al-Ishtirakiyya al-'Uzma/Great Libyan Arab Socialist People's State of the Masses*

Area: 1,759,540 sq km/679,358 sq mi
Capital: Tripoli

Major towns/cities: Benghazi, Misurata, Az Zawiyah, Tobruk, Ajdabiya, Darnah

Major ports: Benghazi, Misratah, Az Zawiyah, Tobruk, Ajdabiya, Darnah

Physical features: flat to undulating plains with plateaux and depressions stretch southwards from the Mediterranean coast to an extremely dry desert interior

Head of state: Moamer al-Khaddhafi from 1969

Head of government: Mubarak al-Shamikh from 2000

Political system: nationalistic socialist

Political executive: unlimited presidency

Political party Arab Socialist Union (ASU), radical, left wing

Currency: Libyan dinar

Exports: crude petroleum and natural gas (accounted for 95% of 2000 export earnings), chemicals and related products. Principal market: Italy 42% (2000)

Population: 5,551,000 (2003 est)

Language: Arabic (official), Italian, English

Religion: Sunni Muslim 97%

Life expectancy: 71 (men); 75 (women) (2000–05)

Chronology

7th century BC: Tripolitania, in western Libya, was settled by Phoenicians, who founded Tripoli; it became an eastern province of Carthaginian kingdom, which was centred on Tunis to the west.

4th century BC: Cyrenaica, in eastern Libya, colonized by Greeks, who called it Libya.

74 BC: Became a Roman province, with Tripolitania part of Africa Nova province and Cyrenaica combined with Crete as a province.

19 BC: The desert region of Fezzan (Phazzania), inhabited by Garmante people, was conquered by Rome.

6th century AD: Came under control of Byzantine Empire.

7th century: Conquered by Arabs, who spread Islam: Egypt ruled Cyrenaica and Morrocan Berber Almohads controlled Tripolitania.

mid-16th century: Became part of Turkish Ottoman Empire, who combined the three ancient regions into one regency in Tripoli.

1711: Karamanli (Qaramanli) dynasty established virtual independence from Ottomans.

1835: Ottoman control reasserted.

1911–12: Conquered by Italy.

1920s: Resistance to Italian rule by Sanusi order and Umar al-Mukhtar.

1934: Colony named Libya.

1942: Italians ousted, and area divided into three provinces: Fezzan (under French control), Cyrenaica, and Tripolitania (under British control).

1951: Achieved independence as United Kingdom of Libya, under King Idris, former Amir of Cyrenaica and leader of Sanusi order.

1959: Discovery of oil transformed economy, but also led to unsettling social changes.

1969: King deposed in military coup led by Col Moamer al Khaddhafi. Revolution Command Council set up and Arab Socialist Union (ASU) proclaimed the only legal party in a new puritanical Islamic-socialist republic which sought Pan-Arab unity.

1970s: Economic activity collectivized, oil industry nationalized, opposition suppressed by Khaddhafi's revolutionary regime.

1972: Proposed federation of Libya, Syria, and Egypt abandoned.

1980: A proposed merger with Syria was abandoned. Libyan troops began fighting in northern Chad.

1986: The US bombed Khaddhafi's headquarters, following allegations of his complicity in terrorist activities.

1988: Diplomatic relations with Chad were restored, political prisoners were freed, and the economy was liberalized.

1989: The US navy shot down two Libyan planes. There was a reconciliation with Egypt.

1992: Khaddhafi came under international pressure to extradite the alleged terrorists suspected of planting a bomb on a plane that crashed in Lockerbie in Scotland for trial outside Libya. United Nations sanctions were imposed; several countries severed diplomatic and air links with Libya.

1995: There was an antigovernment campaign of violence by Islamicists. Hundreds of Palestinians and thousands of foreign workers were expelled.

1999: Lockerbie suspects were handed over for trial in the Netherlands, to be tried by Scottish judges, who ruled that the suspects should be tried on every count. Having handed over the suspects, and after Libya paid compensation to the family of PC Yvonne Fletcher who was murdered outside the Libyan embassy in London in 1984, full diplomatic relations with the UK were restored and UN sanctions were suspended.

2000: Khaddhafi installed a new head of government, Prime Minister Mubarak al-Shamikh. He also abolished 12 central government ministries and transferred their powers to provincial bodies.

2001: Libyan national Abdelbaset Ali Mohmed al-Megrahi was found guilty of the Lockerbie bombing.

2002: Libya withdrew from the Arab League.

2003: After negotiations with the USA and the UK, Khaddhafi confirmed that his regime had sought to develop weapons of mass destruction but that he planned to disband all such programmes and open the country's sites to international inspection.

2004: The American Assistant Secretary of State visited Libya and met Khaddhafi, as did Tony Blair, British prime minister, and the French president, Jacques Chirac.

2005: Libya auctioned oil and gas exploration licences.

lichen any organism of a unique group that consists of associations of a specific *fungus and a specific *alga living together in a mutually beneficial relationship. Found as coloured patches or spongelike masses on trees, rocks, and other surfaces, lichens flourish in harsh conditions. (Group Lichenes.)

Lichtenstein, Roy (1923–1997) US pop artist. He is best known for using advertising imagery and comic-strip techniques, often focusing on popular ideals of romance and heroism, as in *Whaam!* (1963; Tate Gallery, London). He has also produced sculptures in brass, plastic, and enamelled metal.

Liebknecht, Karl (1871–1919) German socialist, son of Wilhelm Liebknecht. A founder of the German Communist Party, originally known as the Spartacus League (see *Spartacist), in 1918, he was one of the few socialists who refused to support World War I. He led an unsuccessful revolt with Rosa Luxemburg in Berlin in 1919 and both were murdered by army officers.

Liebknecht, Wilhelm (1826–1900) German socialist. A friend of the communist theoretician

Karl Marx, with whom he took part in the *revolutions of 1848, he was imprisoned for opposition to the Franco-Prussian War 1870–71. He was one of the founders of the Social Democratic Party 1875. He was the father of Karl Liebknecht.

Liechtenstein

National name: *Fürstentum Liechtenstein/ Principality of Liechtenstein*

Area: 160 sq km/62 sq mi
Capital: Vaduz
Major towns/cities: Balzers, Schaan, Ruggell, Triesen, Eschen
Physical features: landlocked Alpine; includes part of Rhine Valley in west
Head of state: Prince Hans Adam II from 1989
Head of government: Otmar Hasler from 2001
Political system: liberal democracy
Political executive: parliamentary
Political parties: Patriotic Union (VU), conservative; Progressive Citizens' Party (FBP), conservative; Free Voters' List (FL)
Currency: Swiss franc
GNI per capita (PPP): (US$) 24,000 (1998 est)
Exports: small machinery, artificial teeth and other material for dentistry, stamps, precision instruments, ceramics. Principal market: Switzerland 14.5% (1996)
Population: 34,000 (2003 est)
Language: German (official), an Alemannic dialect
Religion: Roman Catholic 80%, Protestant 7%
Life expectancy: 79 (men); 84 (women) (2000–05)
Chronology
c. **AD 500:** Settled by Germanic-speaking Alemanni tribe.
1342: Became a sovereign state.
1434: Present boundaries established.
1719: Former independent lordships of Schellenberg and Vaduz were united by Princes of Liechtenstein to form the present state.
1815–66: A member of the German Confederation.
1868: Abolished standing armed forces.
1871: Liechtenstein was the only German principality to stay outside the newly formed German Empire.
1918: Patriotic Union (VU) party founded, drawing most support from the mountainous south.

1919: Switzerland replaced Austria as the foreign representative of Liechtenstein.
1921: Adopted Swiss currency; constitution created a parliament.
1923: United with Switzerland in customs and monetary union.
1938: Prince Franz Josef II came to power.
1970: After 42 years as the main governing party, the northern-based Progressive Citizens' Party (FBP) was defeated by VU which, except for 1974–78, became a dominant force in politics.
1978: Joined the Council of Europe.
1984: The franchise was extended to women in the national elections.
1989: Prince Franz Josef II died; he was succeeded by Hans Adam II.
1990: Joined the United Nations.
1991: Became the seventh member of the European Free Trade Association.
1993: Mario Frick of VU became Europe's youngest head of government, aged 28, after two general elections.
2001: Otmar Hasler was elected prime minister.
2002: The Organization for Economic Cooperation and Development included Liechtenstein on a list of states failing to meet financial transparency and information exchange standards.
2003: A referendum gave new political powers to Crown Prince Hans-Adam.
2004: Crown Prince Hans-Adam remained head of state but transferred the day-to-day running of the country to his son Prince Alois.

lied (German 'song', plural **lieder**) musical dramatization of a poem, usually for solo voice and piano; referring especially to the Romantic songs of Franz Schubert, Robert Schumann, Johannes Brahms, and Hugo Wolf.

lie detector instrument that records graphically certain body activities, such as thoracic and abdominal respiration, blood pressure, pulse rate, and galvanic skin response (changes in electrical resistance of the skin). Marked changes in these activities when a person answers a question may indicate that the person is lying.

liege in the feudal system, the allegiance owed by a vassal to his or her lord (the liege lord).

Liège Flemish **Luik**, province of eastern Belgium, including the French- and German-speaking communities of the Walloon region, bordered by Germany to the east, the Netherlands to the north, and the provinces of Limbourg, Flemish and Walloon Brabant, Namur, and Luxembourg to the west; area 3,900 sq km/1,506 sq mi; population (1997 est) 1,014,900. Its capital is the city of Liège. Other major towns include Verviers, Huy, Eupen, Spa, and Malmédy.

Lifar, Serge (1905–1986) Ukrainian dancer and choreographer. Born in Kiev, he studied under *Nijinsky, joined the Diaghilev company in 1923, and was artistic director and principal dancer of the Paris Opéra 1929–44 and 1947–59. He completely revitalized the company and in so doing, reversed the diminished fortunes of French ballet.

life ability to grow, reproduce, and respond to such stimuli as light, heat, and sound. Life on Earth may have begun about 4 billion years ago when a chemical reaction produced the first organic substance. Over time, life has evolved from primitive single-celled organisms to complex multicellular ones. There are now some 10 million different species of plants and animals living on the Earth. The earliest fossil evidence of life is threadlike chains of cells discovered in 1980 in deposits in northwestern Australia; these 'stromatolites' have been dated as being 3.5 billion years old. *Biology is the study of living organisms – their evolution, structure, functioning, classification, and distribution – while *biochemistry is the study of the chemistry of living organisms. Biochemistry is especially concerned with the function of the chemical components of organisms such as proteins, carbohydrates, lipids, and nucleic acids.

life cycle in biology, the sequence of developmental stages through which members of a given species pass. Most vertebrates have a simple life cycle consisting of *fertilization of sex cells or *gametes, a period of development as an *embryo, a period of juvenile growth after hatching or birth, an adulthood including *sexual reproduction, and finally death. Invertebrate life cycles are generally more complex and may involve major reconstitution of the individual's appearance (*metamorphosis) and completely different styles of life. Plants have a special type of life cycle with two distinct phases, known as *alternation of generations. Many insects such as cicadas, dragonflies, and mayflies have a long larvae or pupae phase and a short adult phase. Dragonflies live an aquatic life as larvae and an aerial life during the adult phase. In many invertebrates and protozoa there is a sequence of stages in the life cycle, and in parasites different stages often occur in different host organisms.

life sciences scientific study of the living world as a whole, a new synthesis of several traditional scientific disciplines including *biology, *zoology, and *botany, and newer, more specialized areas of study such as biophysics and *sociobiology.

Liffey river in the east of the Republic of Ireland; length 129 km/80 mi. The Liffey is formed by two streams that rise in the Wicklow Mountains near Enniskerry. It flows through County Kildare, past Kilcullen and Newbridge, and into Dublin Bay. The **Liffey Plain** is excellent land for pasture, and has the lowest rainfall in the Republic of Ireland.

ligament strong, flexible connective tissue, made of the protein *collagen, which joins bone to bone at moveable joints and sometimes encloses the joints. Ligaments prevent bone dislocation (under normal circumstances) but allow joint flexion. The ligaments around the joints are composed of white fibrous tissue. Other ligaments are composed of yellow elastic tissue, which is adapted to support a continuous but varying stress, as in the ligament connecting the various cartilages of the *larynx (voice box).

Ligeti, György Sándor (1923–) Hungarian-born Austrian composer. He developed a dense, highly chromatic, polyphonic style in which melody and rhythm are sometimes lost in shifting blocks of sound. He achieved international prominence with *Atmosphères* (1961) and *Requiem* (1965), which achieved widespread fame as background music for Stanley Kubrick's film epic *2001: A Space Odyssey* (1968). Other works include an opera *Le Grand Macabre* (1978) and *Poème symphonique* (1962), for 100 metronomes.

light *electromagnetic waves (made up of electric and magnetic components) in the visible range, having a wavelength from about 400 nanometres in the extreme violet to about 700 nanometres in the extreme red. Light is considered to exhibit particle and wave properties, and the fundamental particle, or quantum, of light is called the photon. A light wave comprises two transverse waves of electric and magnetic fields travelling at right angles to each other, and as such is a form of electromagnetic radiation. The speed of light (and of all electromagnetic radiation) in a vacuum is approximately 300,000 km/186,000 mi per second, and is a universal constant denoted by c.

light bulb incandescent filament lamp, first demonstrated by Joseph Swan in the UK in 1878 and Thomas Edison in the USA in 1879. The present-day light bulb is a thin glass bulb filled with an inert mixture of nitrogen and argon gas. It contains a filament made of fine tungsten wire. When electricity is passed through the wire, it glows white hot, producing light.

light-emitting diode (LED) electronic component that converts electrical energy into light or infrared radiation in the range of 550 nm (green light) to 1,300 nm (infrared). They are used for displaying symbols in electronic instruments and devices. An LED is a *diode made of *semiconductor material, such as gallium arsenide phosphide, that glows when electricity is passed through it. The first digital watches and calculators had LED displays, but many later models use *liquid-crystal displays.

lightning high-voltage electrical discharge between two rainclouds or between a cloud and the Earth, caused by the build-up of electrical charges. Air in the path of lightning ionizes (becomes a conductor), and expands; the accompanying noise is heard as thunder. Currents of 20,000 amperes and temperatures of 30,000 °C/54,000 °F are common. Lightning causes nitrogen oxides to form in the atmosphere and approximately 25% of atmospheric nitrogen oxides are formed in this way. (See diagram, p. 532.)

lightning conductor device that protects a tall building from lightning strike, by providing an easier path for current to flow to earth than through the building. It consists of a thick copper strip of very low resistance connected to the ground below. A good connection to the ground is essential and is made by burying a large metal plate deep in the damp earth. In the event of a direct lightning strike, the current in the conductor may be so great as to melt or even vaporize the metal, but the damage to the building will nevertheless be limited.

light year distance travelled by a beam of light in a vacuum in one year. It is equal to approximately 9.4605×10^{12} km/5.9128×10^{12} mi.

lignin naturally occurring substance produced by plants to strengthen their tissues. It is difficult for *enzymes to attack lignin, so living organisms cannot digest wood, with the exception of a few specialized fungi and bacteria. Lignin is the essential ingredient of all wood and is, therefore, of great commercial importance.

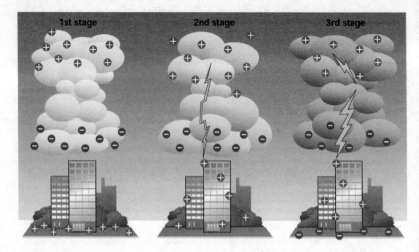

1st stage   2nd stage   3rd stage

lightning The build-up of electrical charge during a thunderstorm that causes lightning. Negative charge builds up at the bottom of a cloud; positive charges rise from the ground and also within the cloud, moving to the top of it. A conducting channel forms through the cloud and a giant spark jumps between opposite charges causing lightning to strike within the cloud and from cloud to ground.

lignite type of *coal that is brown and fibrous, with a relatively low carbon content. As a fuel it is less efficient because more of it must be burned to produce the same amount of energy generated by bituminous coal. Lignite also has a high sulphur content and is more polluting. It is burned to generate power in Scandinavia and some European countries because it is the only fuel resource available without importing.

Liguria region of northwest Italy, lying between the western Alps and the Gulf of Genoa in the Mediterranean, comprising the provinces of Genova, Imperia, La Spezia, and Savona; area 5,421 sq km/2,093 sq mi; population (2001 est) 1,560,800. It is a generally mountainous region, with a steep, narrow coastal strip that includes the Italian Riviera. Genoa is the chief city and port.

Likud (Hebrew 'consolidation' or 'unity') alliance of right-wing Israeli political parties, formed in 1973 by Menachem *Begin, uniting Herut ('freedom'), the Liberal Party of Israel, Laam ('for the nation'), and Ahdut. It defeated the Labour Party coalition in the May 1977 election, bringing Begin to power. Under the leadership of Yitzhak *Shamir 1983–93, Likud became part of an uneasy national coalition with Labour 1984–90, but was defeated by the Labour Party in the 1992 general election. Under the leadership of Binyamin Netanyahu 1993–99 and Ariel *Sharon since 1999, it adopted a much harder line than Labour in the Middle East peace process. In May 1996, Netanyahu became Israel's first directly-elected prime minister, and formed a Likud-led government. He was defeated in May 1999 by Ehud Barak of the Labour party, who was in turn defeated by Sharon in February 2001.

lilac any of a group of flowering Old World shrubs, with clusters (panicles) of small, sweetly scented, white or purple flowers on the main stems. The common lilac

(*S. vulgaris*) is a popular garden ornamental. (Genus *Syringa*, family Oleaceae.)

Lilienthal, Otto (1848–1896) German aviation pioneer who inspired US aviators Orville and Wilbur *Wright. From 1891 he made and successfully flew many gliders, including two biplanes, before he was killed in a glider crash.

Lilongwe capital of Malawi, on the Lilongwe River, lying on a plateau at an altitude of 1,100 m/3,600 ft; population (2001 est) 473,000. It is a commercial and communications centre for a fertile agricultural region, producing ground nuts and tobacco. With hydroelectric power from a dam on the Lilongwe River, it has become a centre for light industry, including engineering, clothes, and the processing of agricultural goods. Tourism is also important, and the city is served by an international airport, and by trunk roads linking it to Zimbabwe, Zambia, and Mozambique.

lily any of a group of plants belonging to the lily family, of which there are about 80 species, most with showy, trumpet-shaped flowers growing from bulbs. The lily family includes hyacinths, tulips, asparagus, and plants of the onion genus. The name 'lily' is also applied to many lilylike plants of related genera and families. (Genus *Lilium*, family Liliaceae.)

lily of the valley plant belonging to the lily family, growing in woods in Europe, northern Asia, and North America. The small bell-shaped white flowers hang downwards from short stalks attached to a central stem; they are strongly scented. The plant is often cultivated. (*Convallaria majalis*, family Liliaceae.)

Lima capital and largest city of Peru, on the River Rímac, 13 km/8 mi from its Pacific port of Callao; population (1998 est) 7,060,600. A rapidly growing metropolitcan area, it comprises about one-third of the country's total population and is the main commercial, manufacturing, and cultural centre of the country. Industries include textiles, motor vehicles, petroleum products, chemicals, glass, and cement.

Limbourg Flemish **Limburg**, province of northeast Belgium, part of the Dutch-speaking Flemish community and region, bordered to the north and east by the Netherlands and the Belgian provinces of Antwerp, Flemish and Walloon Brabant, Namur, and Luxembourg; area 2,422 sq km/935 sq mi; population (1997 est) 780,000. The capital is Hasselt, and other major towns include Genk and Tongeren.

lime or **quicklime** technical name **calcium oxide**; CaO, white powdery substance used in making mortar and cement. It is made commercially by heating calcium carbonate ($CaCO_3$), obtained from limestone or chalk, in a lime kiln. Quicklime readily absorbs water to become calcium hydroxide $Ca(OH)_2$, known as slaked lime, which is used to reduce soil acidity.

lime sharp-tasting green or greenish-yellow citrus fruit of the small thorny lime bush, native to India. The white flowers are followed by the fruits, which resemble lemons but are more round in shape; they are rich in vitamin C. (*Citrus aurantifolia*, family Rutaceae.)

lime or **linden** any of a group of *deciduous trees native to the northern hemisphere. The leaves are heart-shaped and coarsely toothed, and the flowers are cream-coloured and fragrant. (Genus *Tilia*, family Tiliaceae.)

limerick five-line humorous verse, often nonsensical, which first appeared in England in about 1820 and was popularized by English writer Edward *Lear. An example is: 'There was a young lady of Riga, Who rode with a smile on a tiger; They returned from the ride With the lady inside, And the smile on the face of the tiger.'

Limerick county of the Republic of Ireland, in the province of Munster; county town Limerick; area 2,690 sq km/1,038 sq mi; population (1996) 165,000. The principal river is the *Shannon, and towns include Abbeyfeale, Kilmallock, Newcastle West, and Rathkeale. Limerick is hilly in the southwest (Mullaghreirk Mountains) and in the northeast (Galtee Mountains). The low-lying region in the west is very fertile, and is known as the 'Golden Vale'. Dairy cattle, sheep, pigs, and poultry are reared extensively, and corn, sugar-beet, and potatoes are grown. Lace is also produced.

limestone sedimentary rock composed chiefly of calcium carbonate ($CaCO_3$), either derived from the shells of marine organisms or precipitated from solution, mostly in the ocean. Various types of limestone are used as building stone.

Limitation, Statutes of in English law, acts of Parliament limiting the time within which legal action must be inaugurated. Actions for breach of contract and most other civil wrongs must be started within six years. Personal injury claims must usually be brought within three years. In actions in respect of land and of contracts under seal, the period is 12 years.

limited company company for whose debts the members are liable only to a limited extent. The capital of a limited company is divided into small units, and profits are distributed according to shareholding.

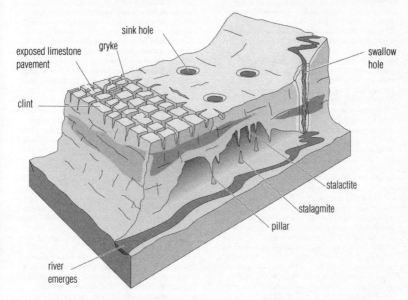

limestone The physical weathering and erosion of a limestone landscape. The freezing and thawing of rain and its mild acidic properties cause cracks and joints to enlarge, forming limestone pavements, potholes, caves, and caverns.

limited liability legal safeguard that allows shareholders to be liable for their company's debts only up to and including the value of their shareholding. For example, if a limited liability company goes bankrupt with debts of £1 million, the shareholders are not liable for any of that debt, although the value of their shares in the company would be worthless.

Limousin modern administrative region and former province of central France; area 16,942 sq km/6,541 sq mi; population (1999 est) 711,000. The modern region consists of the *départements* of Corrèze, Creuse, and Haute-Vienne. The administrative centre is the historic capital, Limoges, famous for its porcelain; Brive-la-Gaillarde, Tulle, and Gueret are the other towns of note. A thinly populated and largely infertile region, it lies west of the Massif Central mountain range. Fruit and vegetables are produced in the more fertile lowlands. Kaolin, which is used in the porcelain industry, is mined here. The cities of Limoges and Tulle are important markets for cattle raised in the region and for their leather products. Limousin has given its name to a type of cloak that used to be worn here, and to the limousine, a large opulent car.

limpet any of various marine *snails belonging to several families and genera, found in the Atlantic and Pacific oceans. A limpet has a conical shell and adheres firmly to rocks by its disclike foot. Limpets leave their fixed positions only to graze on seaweeds, always returning to the same spot. The **common limpet** (*P. vulgata*) can be seen on rocks at low tide (especially genera *Acmaea* and *Patella*).

Limpopo river in southeast Africa, rising in the Magaliesberg to the west of Pretoria in Gauteng Province, South Africa, and flowing through Mozambique and into the Mozambique Channel at Delagoa Bay; length 1,600 km/1,000 mi. It is also known as Crocodile River.

Lin Biao (*or* **Lin Piao**) **(1908–1971)** Chinese communist soldier and politician, deputy leader of the Chinese Communist Party 1969–71. He joined the communists in 1927, became a commander of *Mao Zedong's Red Army, and led the Northeast People's Liberation Army after 1945 during the *Chinese revolution (1927–49). He became the defence minister in 1959, and as vice chair of the party from 1969 he was expected to be Mao's successor. In 1972 the government announced that Lin had been killed in an aeroplane crash in Mongolia on 17 September 1971 while fleeing to the USSR following an abortive coup attempt.

Lincoln, Abraham (1809–1865) 16th president of the USA 1861–65, a Republican. During the American *Civil War, his chief concern was the preservation of the Union from which the Confederate (southern) slave states had seceded on his election. Lincoln strove to reunite the nation, preserve the federal government, and end slavery. In 1863 Lincoln issued the *Emancipation Proclamation, which announced the freedom of Confederate slaves. In 1864, when the Union was close to winning the Civil War, he was re-elected. The Confederate sympathizer John Wilkes Booth assassinated Lincoln the following year.

Lincolnshire county of eastern England. **area:** 5,890 sq km/2,274 sq mi **towns and cities:** Lincoln (administrative headquarters), Skegness, Boston, Stamford **physical:** hills of Lincoln Edge and the Wolds; marshy coastline; the Fens in the southeast; rivers Trent, Welland, Witham **features:** Belton House (1685), a Restoration mansion; Gibraltar Point National Nature Reserve **population:** (2001 est) 647,600.

Lindbergh, Charles A(ugustus) (1902–1974) US aviator. He made the first solo nonstop flight in 33.5 hours across the Atlantic (Roosevelt Field, Long Island, New York, to Le Bourget airport, Paris) in 1927 in the *Spirit of St Louis*, a Ryan monoplane designed by him.

linden another name for the *lime tree.

Lindow Man remains of an Iron Age man discovered in a peat bog at Lindow Marsh, Cheshire, UK, in 1984. The chemicals in the bog had kept the body in an excellent state of preservation.

linear accelerator *or* **linac** in physics, a type of particle *accelerator in which the particles move along a straight tube. Particles pass through a linear accelerator only once – unlike those in a cyclotron or synchrotron (ring-shaped accelerators), which make many revolutions, gaining energy each time.

linear equation in mathematics, a relationship between two variables that, when plotted on Cartesian axes, produces a straight-line graph; the equation has the general form $y = mx + c$, where m is the slope of the line represented by the equation and c is the y-intercept, or the value of y where the line crosses the y-axis in the *Cartesian coordinate system. Sets of linear equations can be used to describe the behaviour of buildings, bridges, trusses, and other static structures.

linear motor type of electric motor, an induction motor in which the fixed stator and moving armature are straight and parallel to each other (rather than being circular and one inside the other as in an ordinary induction motor). Linear motors are used, for example, to power sliding doors. There is a magnetic force between the stator and armature; this force has been used to support a vehicle, as in the experimental *maglev linear motor train.

Lineker, Gary Winston (1960–) English footballer and television presenter. He scored over 250 goals in 550 games for Leicester, Everton, Barcelona, and Tottenham. With 48 goals in 80 internationals he failed by one goal to equal Bobby Charlton's record of 49 goals for England. Lineker was elected Footballer of the Year in 1986 and 1992, and was leading scorer at the 1986 World Cup finals. In 1993 he moved to Japan to play for Nagoya Grampus Eight but retired a year later. Turning to television as a presenter on the football highlights programme *Match of the Day*, for the British Broadcasting Corporation (BBC).

linen yarn spun and the textile woven from the fibres of the stem of the *flax plant. Pieces of linen cloth have been found in the remains of Stone Age settlements and wrapped around mummies from Ancient Egypt. Linen was introduced by the Romans to northern Europe, where production became widespread. Religious refugees from the Low Countries in the 16th century helped to establish the linen industry in England, but it began to decline in competition with cotton in the 18th century. Linen is cool to wear and very resilient, but it is expensive to produce and can crease quite badly unless treated with a crease-resistant finish.

ling any of several deepwater long-bodied fishes of the cod family found in the North Atlantic. (Genus *Molva*, family Gadidae.)

ling another name for common *heather.

lingua franca (Italian 'Frankish tongue') any language that is used as a means of communication by groups who do not themselves normally speak that language; for example, English is a lingua franca used by Japanese doing business in Finland, or by Swedes in Saudi Arabia. The term comes from the mixture of French, Italian, Spanish, Greek, Turkish, and Arabic that was spoken around the Mediterranean from the time of the Crusades until the 18th century.

linguistics scientific study of language. Linguistics has many branches, such as origins (historical linguistics), the changing way language is pronounced (phonetics), derivation of words through various languages (etymology), development of meanings (semantics), and the arrangement and modifications of words to convey a message (grammar).

Linnaeus, Carolus (1707–1778) (Latinized form of Carl von Linné) Swedish naturalist and physician. His botanical work *Systema naturae* (1735) contained his system for classifying plants into groups depending on shared characteristics (such as the number of stamens in flowers), providing a much-needed framework for identification. He also devised the concise and precise system for naming plants and animals, using one Latin (or Latinized) word to represent the genus and a second to distinguish the species.

linnet small seed-eating bird belonging to the finch family, which is very abundant in Europe, Asia, and northwestern Africa. The male has a chestnut back with a pink breast and grey head, and a red breast and forehead during the breeding season; the female is mainly a dull brown. The linnet measures barely 13 cm/5 in in length, begins to breed in April, and generally chooses low-lying bush for its home. The eggs, ranging from four to six in number, are a delicate pale blue streaked with a purplish brown. (Species *Acanthis cannabina*, family Fringillidae, order Passeriformes.)

Lin Piao alternative transliteration of *Lin Biao.

linseed seeds of the *flax plant, from which linseed oil is produced, the residue being used as cattle feed. The oil is used in paint, wood treatments, and varnishes, and in the manufacture of linoleum floor coverings.

lion large wild cat with a tawny coat. The young have darker spot markings to camouflage them; these usually disappear with adulthood. The male has a heavy mane and a tuft at the end of the tail. Head and body measure about 2 m/6 ft, plus 1 m/3 ft of tail; lionesses are slightly smaller. Lions produce litters of two to six cubs, and often live in groups (prides) of several adult males and females with young. They are carnivores and are found only in Africa, south of the Sahara desert, and in the Gir Forest of northwest India.

Lipari Islands or **Aeolian Islands** volcanic group of seven islands off northeastern Sicily, including **Lipari** (on which is the capital of the same name), **Stromboli** (active volcano 926 m/3,038 ft high), and **Vulcano** (also with an active volcano); area 114 sq km/44 sq mi. In Greek mythology, the god Aeolus kept the winds imprisoned in a cave on the Lipari Islands.

lipase enzyme responsible for breaking down fats into fatty acids and glycerol. It is produced by the *pancreas and requires a slightly alkaline environment. The products of fat digestion are absorbed by the intestinal wall.

Li Peng (1928–) Chinese communist politician, a member of the Politburo from 1985, and prime minister 1987–98. A conservative hardliner, during the pro-democracy demonstrations of 1989 he supported the massacre of students by Chinese troops and the subsequent execution of others. He sought improved relations with the USSR and favoured maintaining firm central and party control over the economy. In March 1998 Li stepped down as prime minister, being replaced by the more reformist Zhu Rongji, and was elected chairman of the National People's Congress (China's parliament). He stepped down as NPC chairman in March 2003.

lipid any of a large number of esters of fatty acids, commonly formed by the reaction of a fatty acid with glycerol. They are soluble in alcohol but not in water. Lipids are the chief constituents of plant and animal waxes, fats, and oils.

Li Po (c. 705–762) Taoist Chinese poet of the Tang dynasty (618–907). He used traditional literary forms, but his exuberance, the boldness of his imagination, and the intensity of his feeling have won him recognition as perhaps the greatest of all Chinese poets. Although he was mostly concerned with higher themes, he is also remembered for his celebratory verses on drinking.

Lippershey, Hans (c. 1570–c. 1619) Dutch lensmaker, credited with inventing the telescope in 1608.

Lippi, Filippino (c. 1457–1504) Florentine painter. He was trained by his father Filippo *Lippi and *Botticelli. His most important works are frescoes in the Strozzi Chapel of Sta Maria Novella in Florence, painted in a graceful but also dramatic and at times bizarre style.

Lippi, Fra Filippo (c. 1406–1469) Florentine painter. His most important works include frescoes depicting the lives of St Stephen and St John the Baptist (1452–66; Prato Cathedral), which in their use of perspective and grouping of figures show the influence of *Masaccio. He also painted many altarpieces featuring the Madonna.

Lippmann, Gabriel (1845–1921) French doctor. He invented the direct colour process in photography. He was awarded the Nobel Prize for Physics in 1908 for his photographic reproduction of colours by interference.

liquefaction process of converting a gas to a liquid, normally associated with low temperatures and high pressures (see *condensation).

liquid state of matter between a *solid and a *gas. A liquid forms a level surface and assumes the shape of its container. The way that liquids behave can be explained by the *kinetic theory of matter and particle theory. Its atoms do not occupy fixed positions as in a crystalline solid, nor do they have total freedom of movement as in a gas. Unlike a gas, a liquid is difficult to compress since pressure applied at one point is equally transmitted throughout (Pascal's principle). *Hydraulics makes use of this property.

liquidation in economics, the winding up of a company by converting all its assets into money to pay off its liabilities.

liquid-crystal display (LCD) display of numbers (for example, in a calculator) or pictures (such as on a pocket television screen) produced by molecules of a substance in a semiliquid state with some crystalline properties, so that clusters of molecules align in parallel formations. The display is a blank until the application of an electric field, which 'twists' the molecules so that they reflect or transmit light falling on them. There two main types of LCD are **passive matrix** and **active matrix**.

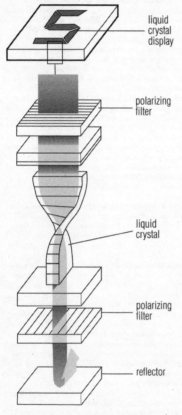

liquid crystal display

polarizing filter

liquid crystal

polarizing filter

reflector

liquid-crystal display A liquid-crystal display consists of a liquid crystal sandwiched between polarizing filters similar to polaroid sunglasses. When a segment of the seven-segment display is electrified, the liquid crystal twists the polarized light from the front filter, allowing the light to bounce off the rear reflector and illuminate the segment.

liquidity in economics, the state of possessing sufficient money and/or assets to be able to pay off all liabilities. **Liquid assets** are those such as shares that may be converted quickly into cash, as opposed to property.

liquorice perennial European herb belonging to the *legume family. The long sweet root yields an extract that is made into a hard black paste and used in confectionery and medicines. (*Glycyrrhiza glabra*, family Leguminosae.)

Lisbon Portuguese **Lisboa**, capital of Portugal, and of the Lisboa district, in the southwest of the country, situated on a tidal lake and estuary formed by the River Tagus; population (1991) 677,800. It is a major commercial and industrial centre, and industries include steel, textiles, chemicals, pottery, shipbuilding, and fishing. Lisbon has been Portugal's capital since 1260 and reached its peak of prosperity in the period of Portugal's empire during the 16th century. In 1755 an earthquake accompanied by a tidal wave killed 30,000–60,000 people (the estimates vary) and destroyed much of the city.

listed building in Britain, a building officially recognized as having historical or architectural interest and therefore legally protected from alteration or demolition. In England the listing is drawn up by the secretary of state for the environment under the advice of the English Heritage organization, which provides various resources for architectural conservation.

Lister, Joseph (1827–1912) 1st Baron Lister, English surgeon. He was the founder of antiseptic surgery, influenced by Louis *Pasteur's work on bacteria. He introduced dressings soaked in carbolic acid and strict rules of hygiene to combat wound sepsis in hospitals. He was made a baronet in 1883, and a baron in 1897.

listeriosis disease of animals that may occasionally infect humans, caused by the bacterium *Listeria monocytogenes*. The bacteria multiply at temperatures close to 0 °C/32 °F, which means they may flourish in precooked frozen meals if the cooking has not been thorough. Listeriosis causes flulike symptoms and inflammation of the brain and its surrounding membranes. It can be treated with penicillin.

Liszt, Franz (1811–1886) Hungarian pianist and composer. An outstanding virtuoso of the piano, he was an established concert artist by the age of 12. His expressive, romantic, and frequently chromatic works include piano music (*Transcendental Studies*, 1851), Masses and oratorios, songs, organ music, and a symphony. Much of his music is programmatic; he also originated the symphonic poem. Liszt was taught by his father, then by Carl Czerny. He travelled widely in Europe, producing an operetta *Don Sanche* in Paris, France, at the age of 14. As musical director and conductor at Weimar, Germany, 1848–59, he championed the music of Hector Berlioz and Richard Wagner.

litchi *or* **lychee** evergreen tree belonging to the soapberry family. The delicately flavoured egg-shaped fruit has a rough brownish outer skin and a hard seed. The litchi is native to southern China, where it has been cultivated for 2,000 years. (*Litchi chinensis*, family Sapindaceae.)

literacy ability to read and write. The level at which functional literacy is set rises as society becomes more complex, and it becomes increasingly difficult for an illiterate person to find work and cope with the other demands of everyday life.

literature words set apart in some way from ordinary everyday communication. In the ancient oral traditions, before stories and poems were written down, literature had a mainly public function – mythic and religious. As literary works came to be preserved in writing, and, eventually, printed, their role became more private, serving as a vehicle for the exploration and expression of emotion and the human situation.

lithium chemical symbol Li, (Greek *lithos* 'stone') soft, ductile, silver-white, metallic element, atomic number 3, relative atomic mass 6.941. It is one of the *alkali metals (being found at the top of Group 1 of the *periodic table). It has a very low density (far less than most woods), and floats on water (relative density 0.57); it is the lightest of all metals. Although in the *reactivity series it is the least reactive of the alkali metals, it reacts readily with water and the oxygen in air, and so has to be kept under oil. Lithium is used to harden alloys, and in batteries; its compounds are used in medicine to treat *manic depression.

lithography printmaking technique invented in 1798 by Aloys Senefelder, based on the mutual repulsion of grease and water. A drawing is made with greasy crayon on an absorbent stone, which is then wetted. The wet stone repels ink (which is greasy) applied to the surface and the crayon absorbs it, so that the drawing can be printed. Lithographic printing is used in book production, posters, and prints, and this basic principle has developed into complex processes.

lithosphere upper rocky layer of the Earth that forms the jigsaw of plates that take part in the movements of *plate tectonics. The lithosphere comprises the *crust and a portion of the upper *mantle. It is regarded as being rigid and brittle and moves about on the more plastic and less brittle *asthenosphere. The lithosphere ranges in thickness from 2–3 km/1–2 mi at mid-ocean ridges to 150 km/93 mi beneath old ocean crust, to 250 km/155 mi under cratons.

Lithuania

National name: *Lietuvos Respublika/ Republic of Lithuania*

Area: 65,200 sq km/25,173 sq mi
Capital: Vilnius
Major towns/cities: Kaunas, Klaipeda, Siauliai, Panevezys
Physical features: central lowlands with gentle hills in west and higher terrain in southeast; 25% forested; some 3,000 small lakes, marshes, and complex sandy coastline; River Nemunas
Head of state: Vladimir Adamkus from 2004
Head of government: Algirdas Brazauskas from 2001
Political system: emergent democracy
Political executive: dual executive
Political parties: Lithuanian Democratic Labour Party (LDLP), reform-socialist (ex-communist); Homeland Union–Lithuanian Conservatives (Tevynes Santara), right of centre, nationalist; Christian Democratic Party of Lithuania, right of centre; Lithuanian Social Democratic Party, left of centre
Currency: litas
GNI per capita (PPP): (US$) 9,880 (2002 est)
Exports: mineral products, textiles, machinery and equipment, non-precious metals, chemicals, animal products, timber and wood products. Principal market: UK 13.8% (2001)
Population: 3,444,000 (2003 est)
Language: Lithuanian (official)
Religion: predominantly Roman Catholic; Evangelical Lutheran, also Russian Orthodox, Evangelical Reformist, and Baptist
Life expectancy: 68 (men); 78 (women) (2000–05)
Chronology
late 12th century: Became a separate nation.
1230: Mindaugas united Lithuanian tribes to resist attempted invasions by German and Livonian Teutonic Knights, and adopted Christianity.
14th century: Strong Grand Duchy formed by Gediminas, founder of Vilnius and Jogaila dynasty, and his son, Algirdas; absorbing Ruthenian territories to east and south, it stretched from the Baltic to the Black Sea and east, nearly reaching Moscow.
1410: Led by Duke Vytautas, and in alliance with Poland, the Teutonic Knights were defeated decisively at the Battle of Tannenberg.
1569: Joined Poland in a confederation, under the Union of Lublin, in which Poland had the upper hand and Lithuanian upper classes were Polonized.
1795: Came under control of Tsarist Russia, following partition of Poland; 'Lithuania Minor' (Kaliningrad) fell to Germany.
1831 and 1863: Failed revolts for independence.
1880s: Development of organized nationalist movement.
1914–18: Occupied by German troops during World War I.
1918–19: Independence declared and, after uprising against attempted imposition of Soviet Union (USSR) control, was achieved as a democracy.
1920–39: Province and city of Vilnius occupied by Poles.
1926: Democracy overthrown in authoritarian coup by Antanas Smetona, who became president.
1934: Baltic Entente mutual-defence pact signed with Estonia and Latvia.
1939–40: Secret German–Soviet agreement brought most of Lithuania under Soviet influence as a constituent republic.
1941: Lithuania revolted and established own government, but during World War II Germany again occupied the country and 210,000, mainly Jews, were killed.
1944: USSR resumed rule.
1944–52: Lithuanian guerrillas fought USSR, which persecuted the Catholic Church, collectivized agriculture, and deported half a million Balts to Siberia.

1972: Demonstrations against Soviet government.

1980s: There was a growth in nationalist dissent, influenced by the Polish Solidarity movement and the glasnost ('openness') initiative of reformist Soviet leader Mikhail Gorbachev.

1988: An independence movement, the Sajudis, was formed to campaign for increased autonomy; the parliament declared Lithuanian the state language and readopted the flag of the interwar republic.

1989: The Communist Party split into pro-Moscow and nationalist wings, and lost the local monopoly of power; over 1 million took part in nationalist demonstrations.

1990: Nationalist Sajudis won elections; their leader, Vytautas Landsbergis, became the president; a unilateral declaration of independence was rejected by the USSR, who imposed an economic blockade.

1991: Soviet paratroopers briefly occupied key buildings in Vilnius, killing 13; the Communist Party was outlawed; Lithuanian independence was recognized by the USSR and Western nations; the country was admitted into the United Nations.

1992: Economic restructuring caused a contraction in GDP.

1993: A free-trade agreement was reached with other Baltic states. The last Russian troops departed.

1994: A friendship and cooperation treaty was signed with Poland.

1994: A trade and cooperation agreement was reached with the European Union.

1997: A border treaty was signed with Russia.

1998: Valdas Adamkus became president.

1999: Andrius Kubelius became prime minister following the resignation of Rolandas Paksas.

2000: Paksas returned to power as prime minister, leading a centre-left coalition.

2003: In presidential elections Paksas won an unexpected victory over Valdas Adamkus in a run-off poll. Impeachment proceedings were begun against Paksas after alleged links to Russian organized crime were deemed a threat to national security. After a referendum, 91% of voters supported accession to the European Union in 2004.

2004: Paksas was impeached and dismissed from parliament. Valdas Adamkus replaced him as president. After general elections, Algirdas Brazauskas continued as prime minister. Lithuania was admitted to NATO and joined the EU.

Lithuanian language Indo-European language spoken by the people of Lithuania, which through its geographical isolation has retained many ancient features of the Indo-European language family. It acquired a written form in the 16th century, using the Latin alphabet, and is currently spoken by some 3–4 million people.

litmus dye obtained from various *lichens and used in chemistry as an indicator to test the acidic or alkaline nature of aqueous solutions; it turns red in the presence of acid, and blue in the presence of alkali.

litotes the use of understatement for effect ('He is no Einstein' = 'He is a bit dim'). It is the opposite of hyperbole.

litre symbol l, metric unit of volume, equal to one cubic decimetre (1.76 imperial pints/2.11 US pints). It was formerly defined as the volume occupied by one kilogram of pure water at 4 °C at standard pressure, but this is slightly larger than one cubic decimetre.

Little Bighorn, Battle of the or **Custer's Last Stand** engagement on a tributary of the Bighorn River in Montana, USA, on 25 June 1876, in which Lt-Col George *Custer suffered a crushing defeat by *Sioux, Cheyenne, and *Arapaho Indians, under chiefs *Sitting Bull, *Crazy Horse, and Gall. The battle was the greatest defeat inflicted on the US Army in the Plains Wars.

Little Red Book book of aphorisms and quotations from the speeches and writings of *Mao Zedong, in which he adapted Marxist theory to Chinese conditions. Published in 1966, the book was printed in huge numbers and read widely at the start of the *Cultural Revolution.

Little Richard (1932–) stage name of Richard Wayne Penniman, US rock singer and pianist. He was one of the creators of rock and roll with his wildly uninhibited renditions of 'Tutti Frutti' (1956), 'Long Tall Sally' (1956), and 'Good Golly Miss Molly' (1957). His subsequent career in soul and rhythm and blues was interrupted by periods as a Seventh-Day Adventist cleric.

Little Rock largest city and capital of *Arkansas, USA, a port of entry on the Arkansas River, 215 km/133 mi west of Memphis, Tennessee; seat of Pulaski County; population (2000 est) 181,100. It is the centre of a rich agricultural, mining, timber, natural gas, and oil region; products include metal goods, oilfield and electronic equipment, valves and pipes, aircraft, ammunition, watches, chemicals, clothing, and processed food.

Liu Shaoqi (or **Liu Shao-chi**) **(1898–1969)** Chinese communist politician, president 1960–65 and the most prominent victim of the 1966–69 leftist *Cultural Revolution. A Moscow-trained labour organizer, he was a firm proponent of the Soviet style of government based around disciplined one-party control, the use of incentive gradings, and priority for industry over agriculture. This was opposed by *Mao Zedong, but began to be implemented by Liu while he was state president 1960–65. Liu was brought down during the *Cultural Revolution.

liver in vertebrates, large organ with many regulatory and storage functions. The human liver is situated in the upper abdomen, and weighs about 2 kg/4.5 lb. It is divided into four lobes. The liver receives the products of digestion (food absorbed from the *gut and carried to the liver by the bloodstream), converts *glucose to glycogen (a long-chain carbohydrate used for storage), and then back to glucose when needed. In this way the liver regulates the level of glucose in the blood (see *homeostasis). This is partly controlled by a *hormone, *insulin. The liver removes excess amino acids from the blood, converting them to urea, which is excreted by the kidneys. The liver also synthesizes vitamins, produces bile and blood-clotting factors, and removes damaged red cells and toxins such as alcohol from the blood.

Liverpool city, seaport, and metropolitan borough in Merseyside, northwest England; population (1998 est) 461,500. Liverpool is the UK's chief Atlantic port. There are ferries to Ireland and the Isle of Man. Traditional industries, such as ship-repairing, have declined. Liverpool's manufacturing sector is dominated by a small number of large firms. Manufacturing has declined in importance, while employment in the service sector in areas such as education, health, insurance, call centres, banking, and tourism has increased. A rail tunnel and Queensway Tunnel (1934) link Liverpool and Birkenhead; Kingsway Tunnel (1971), also known as the Mersey Tunnel, links Liverpool and Wallasey.

Liverpool, Robert Banks Jenkinson, 2nd Earl Liverpool (1770–1828) British Tory politician. He entered Parliament in 1790 and was foreign secretary 1801–03, home secretary 1804–06 and 1807–09, war minister 1809–12, and prime minister 1812–27. His government conducted the Napoleonic Wars to a successful conclusion, but its ruthless suppression of freedom of speech and of the press aroused such opposition that during 1815–20 revolution frequently seemed imminent. He became an earl in 1808.

liverwort nonvascular plant (with no 'veins' to carry water and food), related to *hornworts and *mosses; it is found growing in damp places. (Class Hepaticae, order Bryophyta.)

Livingstone, David (1813–1873) Scottish missionary explorer. In 1841 he went to Africa, reaching Lake Ngami in 1849. He followed the Zambezi to its mouth, saw the Victoria Falls in 1855, and went to East and Central Africa 1858–64, reaching Lakes Shirwa and Nyasa. From 1866, he tried to find the source of the River Nile, and reached Ujiji in Tanganyika in November 1871. British explorer Henry Stanley joined Livingstone in Ujiji.

Livingstone, Ken(neth) (1945–) British Labour politician, mayor of London from 2000. The leader of the Greater London Council (GLC) 1981–86 and member of Parliament for Brent East 1987–2001, he ran as an independent in the London mayoral election in 2000, opposing Frank Dobson, the Labour Party's official candidate. This led to his expulsion from the Labour Party for five years; he was readmitted by the party in January 2004. As mayor, he introduced the pioneering initiative of a 'congestion charge' on vehicles entering central London.

Livonia German Livland, one of the former *Baltic States, divided in 1918 between the modern states of Estonia and Latvia. Livonia belonged to the Teutonic Knights from the 13th to 16th centuries, to Poland from 1561, Sweden from 1629, and Russia from 1721.

Livy (59 BC–AD 17) adopted name of Titus Livius, Roman historian. He was the author of a *History of Rome* from the city's foundation to 9 BC, based partly on legend. It was composed of 142 books, of which 35 survive, covering the periods from the arrival of Aeneas in Italy to 293 BC and from 218 to 167 BC.

lizard reptile generally distinguishable from snakes, which belong to the same order, by having four legs, moveable eyelids, eardrums, and a fleshy tongue, although some lizards are legless and snakelike in appearance. There are over 3,000 species of lizard worldwide. (Suborder Lacertilia, order Squamata.)

Lizard Point southernmost point of mainland England in Cornwall. The coast is broken into small bays, overlooked by two cliff lighthouses. Lizard Point is notable for Cornish heath and other plants similar to those found in southwest Europe.

Ljubljana German Laibach, capital and industrial city of Slovenia, near the confluence of the rivers Ljubljanica and Sava; population (1991) 276,100. Products include textiles, chemicals, paper, and leather goods. It has a nuclear research centre and is linked with southern Austria by the Karawanken road tunnel under the Alps (1979–83).

llama South American even-toed hoofed mammal belonging to the camel family, about 1.2 m/4 ft high at the shoulder. Llamas can be white, brown, or dark, sometimes with spots or patches. They are very hardy, and require little food or water. They spit when annoyed. (Species *Lama glama*, family Camelidae.)

Llewelyn two princes of Wales:

Llewelyn I (1173–1240) Prince of Wales from 1194. He extended his rule to all Wales not in Norman hands, driving the English from northern Wales in 1212, and taking Shrewsbury in 1215. During the early part of Henry III's reign, he was several times attacked by English armies. He was married to Joanna, the illegitimate daughter of King John.

Llewelyn II ap Gruffydd (c. 1225–1282) Prince of Wales from 1246, grandson of Llewelyn I. In 1277 Edward I of England compelled Llewelyn to acknowledge him as overlord and to surrender southern Wales. His death while leading a national uprising ended Welsh independence.

Lloyd George, David, 1st Earl Lloyd-George of Dwyfor (1863–1945) British Liberal politician, prime minister 1916–22. A pioneer of social reform and the *welfare state, as chancellor of the Exchequer 1908–15 he introduced old-age pensions in 1908 and health and unemployment insurance in 1911. High unemployment, intervention in the Russian Civil War, and use of the military police force, the *Black and Tans, in Ireland eroded his support as prime minister. The creation of the Irish Free State in 1921 and his pro-Greek policy against the Turks following the Greek invasion of Anatolia (Asian Turkey) caused the collapse of his coalition government.

Lloyd's Register of Shipping international society for the survey and classification of merchant shipping, which provides rules for the construction and maintenance of ships and their machinery. It was founded in 1760.

Lloyd Webber, Andrew (1948–) English composer and theatre owner. His early musicals, with lyrics by Tim Rice, include *Joseph and the Amazing Technicolor Dreamcoat* (1968), *Jesus Christ Superstar* (1971), and *Evita* (1978). He also wrote the hugely successful *Cats* (1981), based on T S Eliot's *Old Possum's Book of Practical Cats*, *Starlight Express* (1984), *The Phantom of the Opera* (1986), *Aspects of Love* (1989), and *The Beautiful Game* (2000). His company, The Really Useful Group, owns 13 London theatres.

loach carplike freshwater fish with a long narrow body and no teeth in the small downward-pointing mouth, which is surrounded by barbels (sensitive bristles). Loaches are native to Asian and European waters. (Family Cobitidae.)

loam type of fertile soil, a mixture of sand, silt, clay, and organic material. It is porous, which allows for good air circulation and retention of moisture.

lobby individual or pressure group that sets out to influence government action. The lobby is prevalent in the USA, where the term originated in the 1830s from the practice of those wishing to influence state policy waiting for elected representatives in the lobby of the Capitol.

lobelia any of a group of temperate and tropical plants with white to mauve flowers. Lobelias may grow to shrub size but are mostly small annual plants. (Genus *Lobelia*, family Lobeliaceae.)

lobotomy another name for the brain operation *leucotomy.

lobster any of various large marine *crustaceans. Lobsters are grouped with freshwater *crayfish in the suborder Reptantia ('walking'), although both lobsters and crayfish can also swim, using their fanlike tails. Lobsters have eyes on stalks and long antennae, and are mainly nocturnal. They scavenge and eat dead or dying fish. (Family Homaridae, order Decapoda.)

Locarno, Pact of series of diplomatic documents initialled in Locarno, Switzerland, on 16 October 1925 and formally signed in London on 1 December 1925. The pact settled the question of French security, and the signatories – Britain, France, Belgium, Italy, and Germany – guaranteed Germany's existing frontiers with France and Belgium. Following the signing of the pact, Germany was admitted to the League of Nations.

Loch Ness Scottish lake; see *Ness, Loch.

lock construction installed in waterways to allow boats or ships to travel from one level to another. The earliest form, the **flash lock**, was first seen in the East in 1st-century-AD China and in the West in 11th-century Holland. By this method barriers temporarily dammed a river and when removed allowed the flash flood to propel the waiting boat through or over any obstacle. This was followed in 12th-century China and 14th-century Holland by the **pound lock**. In this system the lock has gates at each end. Boats enter through one gate when the levels are the same both outside and inside. Water is then allowed in (or out of) the lock until the level rises (or falls) to the new level outside the other gate. Locks are important to shipping where canals link oceans of differing levels, such as the Panama Canal, or where falls or rapids are replaced by these adjustable water 'steps'.

Locke, John (1632–1704) English philosopher. His *Essay concerning Human Understanding* (1690) maintained that experience is the only source of knowledge (empiricism), and that 'we can have knowledge no farther than we have ideas' prompted by such experience. *Two Treatises on Government* (1690) helped to form contemporary ideas of liberal democracy.

lockjaw former name for *tetanus, a type of bacterial infection.

locomotive engine for hauling railway trains. In 1804 Cornish engineer Richard Trevithick built the first steam engine to run on rails. Locomotive design did not radically improve until English engineer George Stephenson built the *Rocket* in 1829, which featured a multitube boiler and blastpipe, standard in all following **steam locomotives**. Today most locomotives are diesel or electric: **diesel locomotives** have a powerful diesel engine, and **electric locomotives** draw their power from either an overhead cable or a third rail alongside the ordinary track.

locus (Latin 'place') in mathematics, traditionally the path traced out by a moving point, but now defined as the set of all points on a curve satisfying given conditions. The locus of points a fixed distance from a fixed point is a circle. The locus of a point equidistant from two fixed points is a straight line that perpendicularly bisects the line joining them. The locus of points a fixed distance from a line is two parallel lines running either side.

locust swarming grasshopper with short feelers, or antennae, and hearing organs on the abdomen (rear segment of the body). As winged adults, flying in swarms, locusts may be carried by the wind hundreds of miles from their breeding grounds; on landing they devour all vegetation. Locusts occur in nearly every continent. (Family Acrididae, order Orthoptera.)

locust tree another name for the *carob, a small tree of the Mediterranean region. It is also the name of several North American trees of the *legume family (Leguminosae).

lode geological deposit rich in certain minerals, generally consisting of a large vein or set of veins containing ore minerals. A system of veins that can be mined directly forms a lode, for example the mother lode of the California gold rush.

lodestar *or* **loadstar** star used in navigation or astronomy, often *Polaris, the Pole Star.

loess yellow loam, derived from glacial meltwater deposits and accumulated by wind in periglacial regions during the *ice ages. Loess usually attains considerable depths, and the soil derived from it is very fertile. There are large deposits in central Europe (Hungary), China, and North America. It was first described in 1821 in the Rhine area, and takes its name from a village in Alsace.

Loewe, Frederick (1904–1988) German-born US composer. He worked on Broadway from the 1930s and began a collaboration with the lyricist Alan Jay Lerner in 1942. Their joint successes include *Brigadoon* (1947), *Paint Your Wagon* (1951), *My Fair Lady* (1956), *Gigi* (1958), and *Camelot* (1960).

loganberry hybrid between a *blackberry and a *raspberry with large, tart, dull-red fruit. It was developed in 1881 by US judge James H Logan.

logarithm *or* **log** the *exponent or index of a number to a specified base – usually 10. For example, the logarithm to the base 10 of 1,000 is 3 because $10^3 = 1,000$; the logarithm of 2 is 0.3010 because $2 = 10^{0.3010}$. The whole-number part of a logarithm is called the **characteristic**; the fractional part is called the **mantissa**. Before the advent of cheap electronic calculators, multiplication and division could be simplified by being replaced with the addition and subtraction of logarithms.

logic branch of philosophy that studies valid reasoning and argument. It is also the way in which one thing may be said to follow from, or be a consequence of, another (deductive logic). Logic is generally divided into the traditional formal logic of Aristotle and the symbolic logic derived from Friedrich Frege and Bertrand Russell.

logical positivism doctrine that the only meaningful propositions are those that can be verified empirically. Metaphysics, religion, and aesthetics are therefore meaningless. However, the doctrine itself cannot be verified empirically and so is self-refuting.

Loire longest river in France, rising in the Cévennes Mountains in the *département* of Ardèche at 1,350 m/ 4,430 ft near Mont Gerbier de Jonc, and flowing for over 1,000 km/620 mi north through Nevers to Orléans, then west through Tours and Nantes until it reaches the Bay of Biscay at St Nazaire. The Loire drains 116,550 sq km/45,000 sq mi of land, more than a fifth of France, and there are many châteaux and vineyards along its banks. The Loire gives its name to the *départements* of Loire, Haute-Loire, Loire-Atlantique, Indre-et-Loire, Maine-et-Loire, and Saône-et-Loire.

Loki in Norse mythology, the giant-born god and blood-brother of Odin, companion of the Aesir (principal warrior gods), but a source of trickery and evil, and the cause of dissension among the gods. Instrumental in the slaying of *Balder, he hastened the coming of *Ragnarök, the final battle of the gods. His children by the giantess Angrboda were the Midgard serpent Jörmungander, which girdles the Earth; the wolf Fenris; and Hel, goddess of death.

Lollard follower of the English religious reformer John Wycliffe in the 14th century. The Lollards condemned the doctrine of the transubstantiation of the bread and wine of the Eucharist, advocated the diversion of ecclesiastical property to charitable uses, and denounced war and capital punishment. They were active from about 1377; after the passing of the statute *De heretico comburendo* ('The Necessity of Burning Heretics') in 1401 many Lollards were burned, and in 1414 they raised an unsuccessful revolt in London, known as Oldcastle's Rebellion.

Lombard *or* **Langobard** member of a Germanic people who invaded Italy in 568 and occupied Lombardy (named after them) and central Italy. Their capital was Monza. They were conquered by the Frankish ruler Charlemagne in 774.

Lombardy Italian **Lombardia**, region of northern Italy, between the Alps and the River Po, comprising the provinces of Bergamo, Brescia, Como, Cremona, Mantua, Milan, Pavia, Sondrio, and Varese; area 23,861 sq km/9,213 sq mi; population (2001 est) 8,922,500. Its capital is *Milan. It is the country's chief industrial area with chemical, pharmaceutical, textile, and engineering operations, and its most productive agricultural region yielding wheat, maize, wine, meat, and dairy products.

Lombardy League, The Italian regional political party, committed to federalism. It models itself on the 12th–13th century Lombard League. In 1993 it became the core of a new conservative-populist political grouping, the Northern League, led by Umberto Bossi, and fought the 1994 general election as part of the right-wing Freedom Alliance.

Lomé capital, port, largest city, and main administrative and commercial centre of Togo, on the Bight of Benin; population (1997 est) 375,000. It is a centre for gold, silver, and marble crafts. Industries include steel production, oil refining, brewing, plastics, cement, textiles, paper manufacturing, and food processing; tourism is growing in importance. Main exports include cacao, palm nuts, cotton, and coffee. Lomé became capital of the independent Togo in 1960.

Lomond, Loch largest freshwater Scottish lake, 37 km/23 mi long, area 70 sq km/27 sq mi. It is overlooked by the mountain Ben Lomond (973 m/3,192 ft) and is linked to the Clyde estuary by the river Leven.

London capital of England and the United Kingdom, on the River Thames. Since 1965 its metropolitan area has been known as Greater London (see *London, Greater), consisting of the City of London and 32 boroughs; total area 1,580 sq km/610 sq mi; combined population (2000 est) 7,375,100. London is the biggest city in Western Europe at the heart of the most populous region – 15.5 million people live in London and the South East. The **City of London**, known as the 'square mile', is the financial and commercial centre of the UK; area 2.7 sq km/1 sq mi. Over 21 million people visited London in 2001. Popular tourist attractions include the Tower of London, St Paul's Cathedral, Buckingham Palace, and Westminster Abbey.

London, Jack (John Griffith Chaney) (1876–1916) US novelist. He was a prolific author of naturalistic novels, adventure stories, and socialist reportage. His works, which are often based on his own life, typically concern the human struggle for survival against extreme natural forces, as dramatized in such novels as *The Call of the Wild* (1903), *The Sea Wolf* (1904), and *White Fang* (1906). By 1906 he was the most widely read writer in the USA and had been translated into 68 languages.

Londonderry *or* **Derry** historic county of Northern Ireland; area 2,070 sq km/799 sq mi. The principal towns and cities are *Londonderry/Derry, Coleraine, Portstewart, and Limavady. The county is bounded on the north by the Atlantic Ocean, and is dominated by the Sperrin Mountains which run in an arc from southwest to northeast, dividing the lowlands fringing the River Bann in the east from those of the River Foyle in the west. It borders the Republic of Ireland to the west. Administrative responsibility for the county is held by the councils of Londonderry/Derry, Magherafelt, Coleraine, and Limavady.

Londonderry *or* **Derry** formerly **Derry-Calgaich** (until the 10th century), (Irish *derry* 'oak wood'; *Derry-Calgaich* 'the oak wood of Calgaich' (a fierce warrior)) historic city and port on the River Foyle, 35 km/22 mi from Lough Foyle, county town of County *Londonderry, Northern Ireland; population (1991) 95,400. The city was subject to a number of sieges by the Danes between the 9th and 11th centuries, and by the Anglo-Normans in the 12th century; however, these were unsuccessful until James I of England captured the city in 1608. The king granted the borough and surrounding land to the citizens of London. The Irish Society was formed to build and administer the city and a large colony of English Protestants was established. In 1689 the city was unsuccessfully besieged in 1689 by the armies of James II, who had fled England when William of Orange was declared joint sovereign with James's daughter Mary. James's army was led by Richard Talbot, Earl of Tyrconnell, in a conflict known as the **Siege of Derry**, when 13 Derry apprentices and citizens loyal to William of Orange locked the city gates against the Jacobite army. The siege lasted 15 weeks, during which many of the inhabitants died of starvation and disease because of the blockade.

London, Greater metropolitan area of *London, England, comprising the City of London, which forms a self-governing enclave, and 32 surrounding boroughs. Certain powers were exercised over this whole area by the Greater London Council (GLC) 1974–86. **area:** 1,580 sq km/610 sq mi **population:** (1999) 7,285,200.

lone pair in chemistry, a pair of electrons in the outermost shell of an atom that are not used in bonding. In certain circumstances, they will allow the atom to bond with atoms, ions, or molecules (such as boron trifluoride, BF₃) that are deficient in electrons, forming coordinate covalent (dative) bonds in which they provide both of the bonding electrons.

Longfellow, Henry Wadsworth (1807–1882) US poet. He is remembered for his ballads ('Excelsior', 'The Village Blacksmith', 'The Wreck of the Hesperus') and the mythic narrative epics *Evangeline* (1847), *The Song of Hiawatha* (1855), and *The Courtship of Miles Standish* (1858).

Longford county of the Republic of Ireland, in the province of Leinster; county town Longford; area 1,040 sq km/401 sq mi; population (2002 est) 31,100. The county is low-lying (the highest point is Carn Clonhugh 279 m/916 ft), and the western border is formed of the River Shannon and part of Lough Ree, one of several lakes. Other rivers are the Camlin, a tributary of the Shannon, and the Inny, which flows into Lough Ree. Agricultural activities include cattle and sheep rearing, and the production of oats and potatoes.

longhorn beetle beetle with extremely long antennae, usually equalling the length of the entire body, and often twice its length. Their bodies are 2–150 mm/ 0.1–6 in long, usually cylindrical, and often mimic wasps, moss, or lichens. The larvae, white or yellow grubs, are wood-borers, mostly attacking decaying or dead wood, but they may bore into healthy trees causing much damage. (Order Coleoptera, class Insecta, phylum Arthropoda.)

longitude see *latitude and longitude.

long jump field event in athletics in which competitors sprint and jump as far as possible into a sandpit from a takeoff board. The takeoff board is one metre from the landing area, and the sandpit measures nine metres in length. In international competitions, each competitor usually has three attempts, and the leading eight athletes then have a further three jumps; the winner is the one with the longest jump.

Long March in Chinese history, the 10,000 km/6,000 mi trek undertaken from 1934 to 1935 by *Mao Zedong and his communist forces from southeast to northwest China, under harassment from the Guomindang (nationalist) army.

Long Parliament English Parliament 1640–53 and 1659–60, that continued through the English Civil War. After the Royalists withdrew in 1642 and the Presbyterian right was excluded in 1648, the remaining *Rump ruled England until expelled by Oliver *Cromwell in 1653. Reassembled in 1659–60, the Long Parliament initiated the negotiations for the *Restoration of the monarchy.

longship Viking warship, probably developed in the 8th century. Longships were manoeuvrable and fast, well designed for raiding coastal settlements. They could carry 60 or more warriors and travelled under sail or by rowing. There were up to 30 rowing benches in standard longships (the 'great ships' of the late Viking Age had even more). The length-to-breadth ratio of the longship is greater than 6:1 (11.4:1 in one case) enabling them to cut swiftly through the water. Speed was further enhanced by lightness; the timbers of the shell were planed to a width of only 2 cm/0.8 in.

long-sightedness nontechnical term for *hypermetropia, a vision defect.

loom any machine for weaving yarn or thread into cloth. The first looms are thought to have been used to weave sheep's wool in about 5000 BC. A loom is a frame on which a set of lengthwise threads (warp) is strung. A second set of threads (weft), traditionally carried in a shuttle, is inserted at right angles over and under the warp.

Loos, Adolf (1870–1933) Austrian architect. His buildings include private houses on Lake Geneva (1904) and the Steiner House in Vienna (1910). In his article 'Ornament and Crime' (1908) he rejected the ornamentation and curved lines of the Viennese *Jugendstil* movement (see *Art Nouveau).

loosestrife any of several plants belonging to the primrose family, including the yellow loosestrife (*L. vulgaris*), with spikes of yellow flowers, and the low-growing creeping jenny (*L. nummularia*). The striking purple loosestrife (*Lythrum saclicaria*) belongs to a different family. (Genus *Lysimachia*, family Primulaceae; purple loosestrife family Lythraceae.)

Lope de Vega, (Carpio) Felix Spanish poet and dramatist; see *Vega, Lope de.

López, Francisco Solano (1827–1870) Paraguayan dictator in succession to his father Carlos López. He involved the country in a war with Brazil, Uruguay, and Argentina, during which approximately 80% of the population died.

loquat evergreen tree native to China and Japan, also known as the **Japan medlar**. The golden pear-shaped fruit has a delicate sweet-sour taste. (*Eriobotrya japonica*, family Rosaceae.)

Lorca, Federico García (1898–1936) Spanish poet and playwright. His plays include *Bodas de sangre/ Blood Wedding* (1933), *Yerma* (1934), and *La casa de Bernarda Alba/The House of Bernarda Alba* (1936). His poems include the collection *Romancero gitano/ Gypsy Ballad-book* (1928) and the 'Lament' written for the bullfighter Ignacio Sánchez Mejías. Lorca was shot by the Falangists during the Spanish Civil War.

Lord (Old English *hlaford* 'bread keeper') in the UK, prefix used informally as a less formal alternative to the full title of a marquess, earl, or viscount, for example 'Lord Salisbury' instead of 'the Marquess of Salisbury'. Barons are normally referred to as lords, the term baron being used for foreign holders of that rank. 'Lord' is also used as a courtesy title before the forename and surname of younger sons of dukes and marquesses.

Lord Advocate chief law officer of the crown in Scotland who has ultimate responsibility for criminal prosecutions in Scotland. The Lord Advocate does not usually act in inferior courts, where prosecution is carried out by procurators-fiscal acting under the Lord Advocate's instructions.

Lord Chamberlain in the UK, chief officer of the royal household who engages staff and appoints retail suppliers. Until 1968 the Lord Chamberlain licensed and censored plays before their public performance. The office is temporary, and appointments are made by the government.

Lord Chancellor (Latin *cancellarius*) UK state official, originally the royal secretary, today a member of the cabinet, whose office ends with a change of government. The Lord Chancellor acts as Speaker of the House of Lords, may preside over the Court of Appeal, and is head of the judiciary. The reform of the role of Lord Chancellor was announced in 2003.

Lords, House of upper chamber of the UK
*Parliament. Following the House of Lords Act 1999,
the number of hereditary peers (those with an
inherited title) sitting in the upper chamber was
reduced from 750 to a maximum of 92. In October 2001
there were 711 members of the House of Lords:
91 hereditary peers, 620 life peers (with title granted
for the remainder of their lifetime), 2 archbishops,
and 24 bishops. Together the hereditary and life peers
form the Lords Temporal, of whom 26 are 'law lords';
the archbishops and bishops are the Lords Spiritual.
In October 2001 the hereditary peers included
50 Conservative, 4 Labour, and 31 independent
'cross-bench' members. Of the life peers, 172 were
Conservative, 193 Labour, and 145 'cross-benchers'.
There were 117 women peers.

Lorelei in Germanic folklore, a river *nymph of the
Rhine who lures sailors onto the rock where she sits
combing her hair. She features in several poems,
including 'Die Lorelei' by the German Romantic writer
Heinrich Heine. The **Lurlei** rock south of Koblenz is
130 m/430 ft high.

Lorenz, Konrad Zacharias (1903–1989) Austrian
ethologist who was awarded the Nobel Prize for
Physiology or Medicine in 1973 with Nikolaas
*Tinbergen and Karl von Frisch for their work on
animal behaviour patterns. He studied the relationship
between instinct and behaviour, particularly in birds,
and described the phenomenon of *imprinting in 1935.
His books include *King Solomon's Ring* (1952) on
animal behaviour, and *On Aggression* (1966) on human
behaviour.

lorikeet any of various small, brightly coloured parrots
found in Southeast Asia and Australasia.

loris any of a group of small prosimian *primates
native to Southeast Asia. Lorises are slow-moving,
tree-dwelling, and nocturnal. They have very large eyes;
true lorises have no tails. They climb without leaping,
gripping branches tightly and moving on or hanging
below them. (Family Lorisidae.)

Lorrain, Claude French painter; see *Claude Lorrain.

Lorraine German **Lothringen**, region and former
province of northeast France in the upper reaches of
the Meuse and Moselle rivers; bounded in the north
by Belgium, Luxembourg, and Germany, and in the east
by Alsace; area 23,547 sq km/9,092 sq mi; population
(1999 est) 2,310,400. It comprises the *départements* of
Meurthe-et-Moselle, Meuse, Moselle, and Vosges, and
its chief cities are Metz (the administrative capital),
Nancy (the historic capital of the old province),
Luneville, and Epinal. There are deposits of coal, iron
ore, and salt; grain, fruit, and livestock are farmed. In
1871, after the Franco-Prussian War, the northeastern
part of the region was ceded to Germany as part of
*Alsace-Lorraine. The whole area saw heavy fighting
in World War I.

lory any of various small Australasian *parrots. Lories
are very brightly coloured and characterized by a
tongue with a brushlike tip adapted for feeding on
pollen and nectar from flowers. (Subfamily Loriinae,
order Psittaciformes.)

Los Angeles city and port in southwestern California,
USA; population (2000 est) 3,694,800; Los Angeles–
Riverside–Orange County consolidated metropolitan
area (also known as Greater Los Angeles) (1994 est)

15,302,000. In size of population it is the second-largest
city and the second-largest metropolitan area in the
USA. The city occupies 1,204 sq km/465 sq mi.
Industries include aerospace, electronics, motor
vehicles, chemicals, clothing, building materials,
printing, food processing, and films. Los Angeles was
established as a Spanish settlement in 1781.

lost-wax technique method of making sculptures;
see *cire perdue.

Lothair two Holy Roman emperors:

Lothair I (795–855) Holy Roman Emperor from 817
in association with his father Louis I. On Louis's death
in 840, the empire was divided between Lothair and his
brothers; Lothair took northern Italy and the valleys of
the rivers Rhône and Rhine.

Lothair II (c. 1070–1137) Holy Roman Emperor
from 1133 and German king from 1125. His election as
emperor, opposed by the *Hohenstaufen family of
princes, was the start of the feud between the *Guelph
and Ghibelline factions, who supported the papal party
and the Hohenstaufens' claim to the imperial throne
respectively.

Lothian former region of Scotland (1975–96), which
was replaced by East Lothian, Midlothian, West
Lothian, and City of Edinburgh unitary authorities.

Lotto, Lorenzo (c. 1480–1556) Venetian painter
active in Bergamo, Treviso, Venice, Ancona, and Rome.
His early works were influenced by Giovanni Bellini.
He painted religious works but is best known for his
portraits, which often convey a sense of unease or an
air of melancholy.

lotus any of several different plants, especially the **water
lily** (*Nymphaea lotus*), frequent in Egyptian art, and the
pink **Asiatic lotus** (*Nelumbo nucifera*), a sacred symbol
in Hinduism and Buddhism, whose flower head floats
erect above the water.

Lotus Sutra scripture of Mahayana Buddhism. The
original is in Sanskrit (*Saddharmapundarika Sutra*)
and is thought to date from some time after 100 BC.

loudspeaker electromechanical device that converts
electrical signals into sound waves, which are radiated
into the air. The most common type of loudspeaker is
the **moving-coil speaker**. For example, electrical
signals from a radio are fed to a coil of fine wire
wound around the top of a cone. The coil is positioned
between the poles of a permanent magnet. When
signals pass through it, the coil becomes an
electromagnet, experiencing a force at right angles to
the direction of the current and magnetic field, causing
the coil to move. As the signal varies, the coil and the
cone vibrate, setting up sound waves. If the electrical
signals have a frequency of 2,000 hertz (Hz), sound
with a frequency of 2,000 Hz is produced.

Louis, Joe (1914–1981) adopted name of Joseph Louis
Barrow, US boxer, nicknamed 'the Brown Bomber'.
He was world heavyweight champion 1937–49, a record
11 years and 252 days, and successfully defended his title
25 times (a record for any weight). Louis announced his
retirement, undefeated, in 1949, but made a comeback
and lost to US boxer Ezzard Charles in a world title
fight in 1950.

Louis eighteen kings of France, including:

Louis (I) the Pious (788–840) Holy Roman
Emperor from 814, when he succeeded his father
Charlemagne.

Louis III (c. 863–882) King of northern France from 879, while his brother Carloman (866–884) ruled southern France. He was the son of Louis II. Louis countered a revolt of the nobility at the beginning of his reign, and his resistance to the Normans made him a hero of epic poems.

Louis VII (c. 1120–1180) King of France from 1137, who led the Second *Crusade. He annulled his marriage to Eleanor of Aquitaine 1152, whereupon Eleanor married Henry of Anjou, later Henry II of England. Louis was involved in a bitter struggle with Henry 1152–74.

Louis VIII (1187–1226) King of France from 1223, who was invited to become king of England in place of *John by the English barons, and unsuccessfully invaded England 1215–17.

Louis XI (1423–1483) King of France from 1461. He broke the power of the nobility (headed by *Charles the Bold) by intrigue and military power.

Louis XIII (1601–1643) King of France from 1610 (in succession to his father Henry IV), he assumed royal power in 1617. He was under the political control of Cardinal *Richelieu 1624–42.

Louis XIV (1638–1715) called 'the Sun King', King of France from 1643, when he succeeded his father Louis XIII; his mother was Anne of Austria. Until 1661 France was ruled by the chief minister, Jules Mazarin, but later Louis took absolute power, summed up in his saying *L'Etat c'est moi* ('I am the state'). Throughout his reign he was engaged in unsuccessful expansionist wars – 1667–68, 1672–78, 1688–97, and 1701–13 (the War of the *Spanish Succession) – against various European alliances, always including Britain and the Netherlands. He was a patron of the arts.

Louis XV (1710–1774) King of France from 1715, with the Duke of Orléans as regent until 1723. He was the great-grandson of Louis XIV. Indolent and frivolous, Louis left government in the hands of his ministers, the Duke of Bourbon and Cardinal Fleury (1653–1743). On the latter's death he attempted to rule alone but became entirely dominated by his mistresses, Madame de Pompadour and Madame Du Barry. His foreign policy led to French possessions in Canada and India being lost to England.

Louis XVI (1754–1793) King of France from 1774, grandson of Louis XV, and son of Louis the Dauphin. He was dominated by his queen, *Marie Antoinette, and French finances fell into such confusion that in 1789 the *States General (parliament) had to be summoned, and the *French Revolution began. Louis lost his personal popularity in June 1791 when he attempted to flee the country, and in August 1792 the Parisians stormed the Tuileries palace and took the royal family prisoner. Deposed in September 1792, Louis was tried in December, sentenced for treason in January 1793, and guillotined.

Louis XVII (1785–1795) nominal king of France, the son of Louis XVI. During the French Revolution he was imprisoned with his parents in 1792 and probably died in prison.

Louis XVIII (1755–1824) King of France 1814–24, the younger brother of Louis XVI. He assumed the title of king in 1795, having fled into exile in 1791 during the French Revolution, but became king only on the fall of Napoleon I in April 1814. Expelled during Napoleon's brief return (the 'hundred days') in 1815, he resumed power after Napoleon's final defeat at Waterloo, pursuing a policy of calculated liberalism until ultra-royalist pressure became dominant after 1820.

Louisiana called the **Pelican State**, state in southern USA, bordered to the north by *Arkansas, to the west by *Texas, with the Sabine River and Toledo Bend Reservoir forming much of the boundary, and to the east by *Mississippi, with the *Mississippi and Pearl rivers forming much of the boundary; area 112,825 sq km/43,562 sq mi; population (2000 est) 4,469,000; capital Baton Rouge. The state is named after France's King Louis XIV and its nickname is a tribute to the official state bird, the brown pelican, which is native to Louisiana. To the south, the state extends into the Gulf of Mexico, its area expanding continuously through the growth of the delta of the Mississippi River. The Louisiana coast features bayous and marshes, salt domes, islets and channels, and brackish lakes. The economy is based on petroleum products, agriculture, fishing, minerals, and tourism. The state is associated with the development of jazz and blues; the music industry contributes to the economy and is a major tourist attraction. Major cities include *New Orleans (the largest in the state), Shreveport, Lafayette, Lake Charles, and Kenner; other metropolitan areas are Metairie, Marrero, and Chalmette. From the 16th century the state was in the hands of the Spanish and the French, before being bought by the USA in 1803. Its culture has also been influenced by African slaves and Caribbean and French-Canadian immigrants. The state was admitted to the Union in 1812 as the 18th US state.

Louisiana Purchase purchase by the USA from France in 1803 of an area covering 2,144,000 sq km/828,000 sq mi, including the present-day states of Louisiana, Missouri, Arkansas, Iowa, Nebraska, North Dakota, South Dakota, and Oklahoma. The price paid was $15 million (60 million francs), or roughly 4 cents an acre.

Louis Philippe (1773–1850) King of France 1830–48. Son of Louis Philippe Joseph, Duke of Orléans 1747–93; both were known as **Philippe Egalité** from their support of the 1792 Revolution. Louis Philippe fled into exile 1793–1814, but became king after the 1830 revolution with the backing of the rich bourgeoisie. Corruption discredited his regime, and after his overthrow, he escaped to the UK and died there.

Lourdes town in the *département* of Hautes-Pyrénées in the Midi-Pyrénées region of southwest France, on the Gave de Pau River; population (1999 est) 15,600. Its Christian shrine to St *Bernadette has a reputation for miraculous cures from illness, and Lourdes is an important centre for Roman Catholic pilgrimage. In 1858, a young peasant girl, Bernadette Soubirous, claimed to have been shown the healing springs of the Grotte de Massabielle by the Virgin Mary, who visited her on 18 occasions between 11 February and 16 July.

louse parasitic insect that lives on mammals. It has a flat, segmented body without wings, and a tube attached to the head, used for sucking blood from its host. (Order Anoplura.)

Louth smallest county of the Republic of Ireland, in the province of Leinster; county town Dundalk; area 820 sq km/317 sq mi; population (2002 est) 101,800.

It is mainly fertile and low-lying. The chief towns are Dundalk at the north end of Dundalk bay, Drogheda, and Ardee, and the chief rivers are the Fane, Lagan, Glyde, and Dee. There is cattle rearing and fishing; oats and potatoes are grown. Greenore on Carlingford Lough is a container shipping port. Louth is rich in ancient buildings and remains, and was of strategic importance during the 12th–18th centuries. Important monastic sites with extensive remains include Monasterboice (founded in the 5th century), and Mellifont Abbey (founded in the 12th century).

Low Countries region of Europe that consists of Belgium and the Netherlands, and usually includes Luxembourg.

Lower Austria German **Niederösterreich**, largest federal state of Austria, bordered by the Czech Republic to the north, Slovakia to the east, Burgenland to the southeast, Styria to the south, and Upper Austria to the west; area 19,174 sq km/7,403 sq mi; population (2001 est) 1,549,600. Its capital is Sankt Polten. The main towns are Wiener Neustadt and Krems. *Vienna is a provincial enclave within the province.

Lower Saxony German **Niedersachsen**, administrative region (German *Land*) in northern Germany, bordered to the north by Schleswig-Holstein and the city-state of Hamburg, to the northeast by Mecklenburg-West Pomerania, to the south by North Rhine-Westphalia and Hesse, on the east and southeast by Saxony-Anhalt and Thuringia respectively, and on the west by the Netherlands; area 47,613 sq km/18,383 sq mi; population (1999 est) 7,898,800. The capital is Hannover, and other major towns include Braunschweig (Brunswick), Osnabrück, Oldenburg, Göttingen, Wolfsburg, Salzgitter, and Hildesheim. The region includes the Lüneburg Heath, the Harz Mountains, and the Elbe, Weser, Jade, and Ems rivers.

low-level language in computing, a programming language designed for a particular computer and reflecting its internal *machine code; low-level languages are therefore often described as **machine-oriented** languages. They cannot easily be converted to run on a computer with a different central processing unit, and they are relatively difficult to learn because a detailed knowledge of the internal working of the computer is required. Since they must be translated into machine code by an assembler program, low-level languages are also called *assembly languages.

Lowry, L(aurence) S(tephen) (1887–1976) English painter. His works depict life in the industrial towns of the north of England. In the 1920s he developed a naive style characterized by matchstick figures, often in animated groups, and gaunt simplified factories and terraced houses, painted in an almost monochrome palette. *The Pond* (1950; Tate Gallery, London) is an example. The Lowry Arts Centre in Salford, near Manchester, England, opened in 2000 with exhibits of almost 100 Lowry works.

Loyola, St, Ignatius (1491–1556) born Iñigo López de Recalde, Spanish noble who founded the *Jesuit order in 1534, also called the Society of Jesus.

LSD abbreviation for lysergic acid diethylamide, psychedelic drug, a *hallucinogen. Colourless, odourless, and easily synthesized, it is nonaddictive and nontoxic, but its effects are unpredictable. Its use is illegal in most countries.

LSI abbreviation for large-scale integration, technology that enables whole electrical circuits to be etched into a piece of semiconducting material just a few millimetres square.

Luanda formerly **Loanda**, capital, largest city, and main industrial port of Angola; population (1995 est) 2,080,000. Products include cotton, coffee, sugar, tobacco, timber, iron ore, motor vehicles, textiles, paper, fuel oil, and lubricants.

Lubitsch, Ernst (1892–1947) German film director. He worked in the USA from 1921 and became known for the 'Lubitsch touch' – a combination of incisive social critique, witty humour, sophistication, and visual understatement, seen in, for example, *Ninotchka* (1939) and *Heaven Can Wait* (1943).

lubricant substance used between moving surfaces to reduce friction. Carbon-based (organic) lubricants, commonly called grease and oil, are recovered from petroleum distillation.

Lucas, George (1944–) US film director and producer. He wrote and directed *Star Wars* (1977), wrote and produced *The Empire Strikes Back* (1980) and *Return of the Jedi* (1983), and produced a trilogy of adventure films beginning with *Raiders of the Lost Ark* (1981). A second *Star Wars* trilogy, a prequel to the first, followed more than 20 years after the release of the first film. He wrote and directed *Star Wars Episode I: The Phantom Menace* (1999) and *Star Wars Episode II: Attack of the Clones* (2002), and Episode III was due to be released in 2005.

Lucas van Leyden (1494–1533) Dutch painter and engraver. Active in Leiden and Antwerp, he was a pioneer of Netherlandish genre scenes, for example *The Chess Players* (c. 1510; Staatliche Museen, Berlin). His woodcuts and engravings, often more highly regarded than his paintings, were inspired by Albrecht *Dürer.

lucerne another name for the plant *alfalfa.

Lucerne, Lake German **Vierwaldstättersee**, 'lake of the four forest cantons', scenic lake surrounded by mountains in north-central Switzerland; area 114 sq km/44 sq mi. It lies at an altitude of 437 m/1,434 ft and its greatest depth is 215 m/705 ft. It has four main basins, connected by narrow channels. The lake is subject to sudden storms whipped up by the föhn wind.

Lucifer (Latin 'bearer of light') in Christian theology, another name for the *devil, the leader of the angels who rebelled against God. In Greek mythology, Lucifer is another name for the morning star (the planet *Venus).

Lucknow capital of the state of *Uttar Pradesh, India, on the Gumti River, 70 km/46 mi northeast of Kanpur on a railway junction; population (2001 est) 2,266,900. Industries include engineering, chemicals, textiles, and many handicrafts. The city has many beautiful mosques including the Great Mosque and the Pearl Mosque. It was capital of the Nawabs of *Oudh in the 18th century. During the *Indian Mutiny against British rule, the British residency was besieged 2 July–16 November 1857.

Lucretia in Roman legend, the wife of Collatinus, said to have committed suicide after being raped by Sextus, son of *Tarquinius Superbus, the last king of Rome. According to tradition, this incident led to the dethronement of Tarquinius and the establishment of the Roman Republic in 509 BC.

Lucretius

Lucretius (c. 99–55 BC) born Titus Lucretius Carus,
Roman poet and *Epicurean philosopher. His *De
Rerum natura/On the Nature of The Universe*, a didactic
poem in six books, envisaged the whole universe as a
combination of atoms, and had some concept of
evolutionary theory.

Luddite one of a group of people involved in
machine-wrecking riots in northern England 1811–16.
The organizer of the Luddites was referred to as
General Ludd, but may not have existed. Many
Luddites were hanged or transported to penal colonies,
such as Australia.

Ludwig three kings of Bavaria, including:
Ludwig I (1786–1868) King of Bavaria 1825–48,
succeeding his father Maximilian Joseph I. He made
Munich an international cultural centre, but his
association with the dancer Lola Montez, who dictated
his policies for a year, led to his abdication in 1848.
Ludwig II (1845–1886) King of Bavaria from 1864,
when he succeeded his father Maximilian II. He
supported Austria during the Austro-Prussian War of
1866, but brought Bavaria into the Franco-Prussian
War as Prussia's ally and in 1871 offered the German
crown to the king of Prussia. He was the composer
Richard Wagner's patron and built the Bayreuth theatre
for him. Declared insane in 1886, he drowned himself
soon after.

Luftwaffe German air force used both in World War I
and (as reorganized by the Nazi leader Hermann
Goering in 1933) in World War II. The Luftwaffe also
covered anti-aircraft defence and the launching of the
flying bombs V1 and V2.

Lugano, Lake lake partly in Italy, between lakes
Maggiore and Como, and partly in the canton of
Ticino, Switzerland; area 49 sq km/19 sq mi. Noted for
its beautiful scenery, it lies at an altitude of 271 m/890 ft
and its greatest depth is 288 m/945 ft.

lugworm any of a group of marine *annelid worms
that grow up to 10 in/25 cm long. They are common
burrowers between tidemarks and are useful for their
cleansing and powdering of the beach sand, of which
they may annually bring to the surface about 5,000
tonnes per hectare/2,000 tons per acre. (Genus
Arenicola.)

Lukács, Georg (1885–1971) Hungarian philosopher
and literary critic, one of the founders of 'Western'
or 'Hegelian' Marxism, a philosophy opposed to the
Marxism of the official communist movement. He also
wrote on aesthetics and the sociology of literature.

Luke, St (lived 1st century AD) traditionally the
compiler of the third Gospel and of the Acts of the
Apostles in the New Testament. He is the patron saint
of painters; his emblem is a winged ox, and his feast
day 18 October.

Lully, Jean-Baptiste (1632–1687) adopted name of
Giovanni Battista Lulli, French composer of Italian
origin. He was court composer to Louis XIV of France.
He composed music for the ballet and for Molière's
plays, and established French opera with such works
as *Alceste* (1674) and *Armide et Rénaud* (1686). He was
also a ballet dancer.

lumbago pain in the lower region of the back, usually
due to strain or faulty posture. If it occurs with
*sciatica, it may be due to pressure on spinal nerves
from a slipped disc. Treatment includes rest,

application of heat, and skilled manipulation. Surgery
may be needed in rare cases.

lumbar puncture *or* **spinal tap** insertion of a hollow
needle between two lumbar (lower back) vertebrae to
withdraw a sample of cerebrospinal fluid (CSF) for
testing. Normally clear and colourless, the CSF acts as a
fluid buffer around the brain and spinal cord. Changes
in its quantity, colour, or composition may indicate
neurological damage or disease.

lumen symbol lm, SI unit of luminous flux (the
amount of light passing through an area per second).

lumen in biology, the space enclosed by an organ, such
as the bladder, or a tubular structure, such as the
gastrointestinal tract.

Lumière Auguste Marie Louis Nicolas (1862–1954) and
Louis Jean (1864–1948), French brothers who pioneered
cinematography. In February 1895 they patented their
cinematograph, a combined camera and projector
operating at 16 frames per second, screening short films
for the first time on 22 March, and in December
opening the world's first cinema in Paris. Their simple
documentary short *La Sortie des usines Lumière/
Workers Leaving the Lumière Factory* (1895) is
considered the first motion picture.

luminescence emission of light from a body when its
atoms are excited by means other than raising its
temperature. Short-lived luminescence is called
fluorescence; longer-lived luminescence is called
phosphorescence.

luminosity *or* **brightness** in astronomy, amount
of light emitted by a star, measured in *magnitudes.
The apparent brightness of an object decreases in
proportion to the square of its distance from the
observer. The luminosity of a star or other body can
be expressed in relation to that of the Sun.

Lundy Island rocky, granite island at the entrance to
the Bristol Channel; 19 km/12 mi northwest of Hartland
Point, Devon, southwest England; area 9.6 sq km/
3.7 sq mi; population (1981) 52. Formerly used by
pirates and privateers as a lair, it is now the site of a bird
sanctuary and the first British Marine Nature Reserve
(1986). It has Bronze and Iron Age field systems, which
can be traced by their boundaries which stand up above
the surface.

lung in mammals, large cavity of the body, used for gas
exchange. Most tetrapod (four-limbed) vertebrates
have a pair of lungs occupying the thorax. The lungs
are essentially an infolding of the body surface – a sheet
of thin, moist membrane made of a single layer of cells,
which is folded so as to occupy less space while having a
large surface area for the uptake of *oxygen and loss of
*carbon dioxide. The folding creates tiny sacs called
alveoli. Outside the walls of the alveoli there are lots of
blood *capillaries for transporting the products of gas
exchange. The lung tissue, consisting of multitudes of
air sacs and blood vessels, is very light and spongy, and
functions by bringing inhaled air into close contact
with the blood for efficient gas exchange. The efficiency
of lungs is enhanced by *breathing movements, by the
thinness and moistness of their surfaces, and by a
constant supply of circulating blood.

lung cancer in medicine, cancer of the lung.
The main risk factor is smoking, with almost nine out
of ten cases attributed to it. Other risk factors include
workspace exposure to carcinogenic substances such

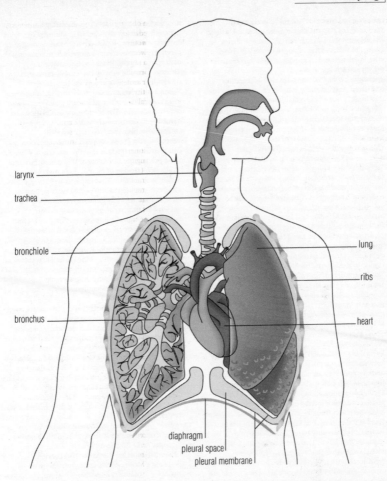

larynx

trachea

bronchiole

bronchus

lung

ribs

heart

diaphragm
pleural space
pleural membrane

lung The human lungs contain 300,000 million tiny blood vessels which would stretch for 2,400 km/1,500 mi if laid end to end. A healthy adult at rest breathes 12 times a minute; a baby breathes at twice this rate. Each breath brings 350 millilitres of fresh air into the lungs, and expels 150 millilitres of stale air from the nose and throat.

as asbestos and radiation. Warning symptoms include a persistent and otherwise unexplained cough, breathing difficulties, and pain in the chest or shoulder. Treatment is with chemotherapy, radiotherapy, and surgery.

lungfish any of a group of fleshy-finned bony fishes found in South America, Australia, and Africa. They have elongated bodies, and grow to about 2 m/6 ft, and in addition to gills have 'lungs' with which they can breathe air during periods of drought conditions. (Genera *Lepidosiren*, *Neoceratodus*, and *Protopterus*, subclass Dipnoi.)

Luo *or* **Lwoo** *or* **Kavirondo** member of the second-largest ethnic group of Kenya, living in the Lake Victoria region and numbering around 2,650,000 (1987). The Luo are a Nilotic people who traditionally lived by farming livestock. Many, however, now work as wage labourers throughout East Africa. Traditionally they had a strong clan system without centralized political authority. Their religion includes beliefs in a supreme creator, Nyasi, and ancestor worship. The Luo language is of the Nilo-Saharan family.

Luoyang *or* **Loyang** city in Henan province, China, south of the Huang He River; population (1999 est)

1,002,200. Industries include oil-refining and the production of glass, machinery, and tractors. Luoyang was the capital of China for nearly eight centuries under the Eastern Zhou (8th–3rd century BC) and other dynasties, and an important Buddhist centre in the 5th and 6th centuries.

Lupercalia annual Roman festival of purification celebrated on 15 February. It has been associated with the Greek Lycaean *Pan, god of flocks and herds (identified with the Roman *Faunus), and the wolf (*lupus*) who supposedly suckled Romulus and Remus, the twin founders of Rome. Goats and dogs were sacrificed at the **Lupercal** at the foot of the Palatine Hill, near the cave of Lupercus, the wolf's lair.

lupin any of a group of leguminous plants (see *legume) that comprises about 300 species. Lupins are native to Mediterranean regions and parts of North and South America, and some species are naturalized in Britain. Their spikes of pealike flowers may be white, yellow, blue, or pink. *L. albus* is cultivated in some places for cattle fodder and for green manuring; other varieties are cultivated in Europe as cottage garden plants. (Genus *Lupinus*, family Leguminosae.)

lupus in medicine, any of various diseases characterized by lesions of the skin. One form (lupus vulgaris) is caused by the tubercle bacillus (see *tuberculosis). The organism produces ulcers that spread and eat away the underlying tissues. Treatment is primarily with standard antituberculous drugs, but ultraviolet light may also be used.

Luria, Salvador Edward (1912–1991) Italian-born US physician who was awarded the Nobel Prize for Physiology or Medicine in 1969 for his work on the replication mechanism and genetic structure of viruses. Luria was a pacifist and was identified with efforts to keep science humanistic.

Lusaka capital of Zambia from 1964 (of Northern Rhodesia 1935–64), 370 km/230 mi northeast of Livingstone; population (1995 est) 1,317,000. With good communications by rail, road, and air, and with hydroelectricity from the Kariba Dam on the Zambezi River, it is Zambia's chief centre of trade, industry, banking, and administration, as well as a manufacturing and agricultural centre. Industries include chemicals (including insecticides and fertilizers), flour mills, tobacco factories, electronic equipment, motor vehicle assembly, plastics, printing, cement, iron and steel, food processing, paints, plastics, furniture, and clothing.

Lusitania ancient area of the Iberian peninsula, roughly equivalent to Portugal. Conquered by Rome in 139 BC, the province of Lusitania rebelled periodically until it was finally conquered by Pompey (73–72 BC).

lute member of a family of plucked stringed musical instruments of the 14th–18th centuries, including the mandore, theorbo, and chitarrone. Lutes are pear-shaped with up to seven courses of strings (single or double), plucked with the fingers. Music for lutes is written in special notation called tablature and chords are played simultaneously, not arpeggiated as for guitar. Modern lutenists include Julian Bream and Anthony Rooley.

luteinizing hormone *hormone produced by the pituitary gland. In males, it stimulates the testes to produce androgens (male sex hormones). In females,

it works together with follicle-stimulating hormone to initiate production of egg cells by the ovary. If fertilization occurs, it plays a part in maintaining the pregnancy by controlling the levels of the hormones oestrogen and progesterone in the body.

lutetium chemical symbol Lu, (Latin *Lutetia* 'Paris') silver-white, metallic element, the last of the *lanthanide series, atomic number 71, relative atomic mass 174.97. It is used in the 'cracking', or breakdown, of petroleum and in other chemical processes. It was named by its discoverer, French chemist Georges Urbain, after his native city.

Luther, Martin (1483–1546) German Christian church reformer, a founder of Protestantism. While he was a priest at the University of Wittenberg, he wrote an attack on the sale of *indulgences (remissions of punishment for sin). The Holy Roman Emperor Charles V summoned him to the Diet (meeting of dignitaries of the Holy Roman Empire) of Worms in Germany, in 1521, where he refused to retract his objections. Originally intending reform, his protest led to schism, with the emergence, following the *Augsburg Confession in 1530 (a statement of the Protestant faith), of a new Protestant Church. Luther is regarded as the instigator of the Protestant revolution, and *Lutheranism is now the predominant religion of many northern European countries, including Germany, Sweden, and Denmark. See also the *Reformation.

Lutheranism form of Protestant Christianity derived from the life and teaching of Martin *Luther; it is sometimes called Evangelical to distinguish it from the other main branch of European Protestantism, the Reformed. The most generally accepted statement of Lutheranism is that of the **Confession of *Augsburg** in 1530 but Luther's Shorter Catechism also carries great weight. It is the largest Protestant body, including some 80 million persons, of whom 40 million are in Germany, 19 million in Scandinavia, 8.5 million in the USA and Canada, with most of the remainder in central Europe.

Luton industrial town and administrative centre of Luton unitary authority situated in south central England, at the northern end of a river gap in the Chiltern hills, 48 km/30 mi north of London; population (2001 est) 184,300. Luton international airport is a secondary airport for London.

Lutyens, Edwin Landseer (1869–1944) English architect. His designs ranged from the picturesque, such as Castle Drogo (1910–30), Devon, to Renaissance-style country houses, and ultimately evolved into a classical style as seen in the Cenotaph, London (1919), and the Viceroy's House, New Delhi, India (1912–31). His complex use of space, interest in tradition, and distorted classical language have proved of great interest to a number of postmodern architects, especially Robert Venturi.

lux symbol lx, SI unit of illuminance or illumination (the light falling on an object). It is equivalent to one *lumen per square metre or to the illuminance of a surface one metre distant from a point source of one *candela.

Luxembourg capital of the country of Luxembourg, on the Alzette and Pétrusse rivers, south of the Ardennes uplands; population (1997) 78,300. The 16th-century

Grand Ducal Palace, European Court of Justice, and European Parliament secretariat are situated here, but plenary sessions of the parliament are now held only in Strasbourg, France. Industries include steel, chemicals, textiles, and processed food.

Luxembourg province of southeastern Belgium, part of the French-speaking community and Walloon region; area 4,400 sq km/1,698 sq mi; population (1995 est) 240,300. The capital is Arlon and other towns and cities include Bastogne, St Hubert, and Bouillon. The province is situated in the southeastern Ardennes and is widely forested. To the south is the Belgian Lorraine, part of the Paris Basin. The rivers Ourthe, Semois, and Lesse run through the province. The province's unpredictable climate and thin soil limit its agricultural production. Cattle and pig raising predominates. Agricultural output includes dairy products and tobacco, and the major industries are iron and steel.

Luxembourg

National name: *Grand-Duché de Luxembourg/ Grand Duchy of Luxembourg*

Area: 2,586 sq km/998 sq mi
Capital: Luxembourg
Major towns/cities: Esch-sur-Alzette, Differdange, Dudelange, Pétange
Physical features: on the River Moselle; part of the Ardennes (Oesling) forest in north
Head of state: Grand Duke Henri from 2000
Head of government: Jean-Claude Juncker from 1995
Political system: liberal democracy
Political executive: parliamentary
Political parties: Christian Social Party (PCS), moderate, left of centre; Luxembourg Socialist Workers' Party (POSL), moderate, socialist; Democratic Party (PD), left of centre; Communist Party of Luxembourg, pro-European left wing
Currency: euro (Luxembourg franc until 2002)
GNI per capita (PPP): (US$) 51,060 (2002 est)
Exports: machinery and transport equipment, base metals and manufactures, mechanical and electrical equipment, rubber and related products, plastics, textiles and clothing. Principal market: Germany 24.6% (2001)

Population: 453,000 (2003 est)
Language: Letzeburgisch (a German-Moselle-Frankish dialect; official), English
Religion: Roman Catholic about 95%, Protestant and Jewish 4%
Life expectancy: 75 (men); 81 (women) (2000–05)
Chronology
963: Luxembourg became autonomous within Holy Roman Empire under Siegfried, Count of Ardennes.
1060: Conrad, descendent of Siegfried, took the title Count of Luxembourg.
1354: Emperor Charles IV promoted Luxembourg to the status of duchy.
1441: Luxembourg ceded to dukes of Burgundy.
1482: Luxembourg came under Habsburg control.
1555: Luxembourg became part of Spanish Netherlands on division of Habsburg domains.
1684–97: Much of Luxembourg occupied by France.
1713: Treaty of Utrecht transferred Spanish Netherlands to Austria.
1797: Conquered by revolutionary France.
1815: Congress of Vienna made Luxembourg a grand duchy, under King William of the Netherlands.
1830: Most of Luxembourg supported Belgian revolt against the Netherlands.
1839: Western part of Luxembourg assigned to Belgium.
1842: Luxembourg entered the Zollverein (German customs union).
1867: Treaty of London confirmed independence and neutrality of Luxembourg to allay French fears about possible inclusion in a unified Germany.
1870s: Development of iron and steel industry.
1890: Link with Dutch crown ended on accession of Queen Wilhelmina, since Luxembourg's law of succession did not permit a woman to rule.
1912: Revised law of succession allowed Marie-Adelaide to become grand duchess.
1914–18: Occupied by Germany.
1919: Plebiscite overwhelmingly favoured continued independence; Marie-Adelaide abdicated after allegations of collaboration with Germany; Charlotte became grand duchess.
1921: Entered into close economic links with Belgium.
1940: Invaded by Germany.
1942–44: Annexed by Germany.
1948: Luxembourg formed Benelux customs union with Belgium and the Netherlands.
1949: Luxembourg became founding member of North Atlantic Treaty Organization (NATO).
1958: Luxembourg became founding member of European Economic Community (EEC).
1964: Grand Duchess Charlotte abdicated in favour of her son Jean.
1994: Former premier Jacques Santer became the president of the European Commission (EC).
1995: Jean-Claude Juncker became prime minister.
2000: Grand Duke Jean abdicated in favour of his son Henri.
2002: Luxembourg started using the Euro.
2004: After an election Jean-Claude Juncker continued as prime minister and formed a coalition government between his Christian Social Party and the Socialist Workers Party.

Luxemburg, Rosa (1870–1919) Polish-born German communist. She helped found the Polish Social Democratic Party in the 1890s, the forerunner of the Polish Communist Party. She was a leader of the left wing of the German Social Democratic Party from 1898 where she collaborated with Karl *Liebknecht in founding the Spartacus League in 1918 (see *Spartacist). Imprisoned during World War I for opposing the continuation of the war, she was also critical of the decision to launch an uprising in November 1918. She disagreed with leading Polish left-wing ideologists on the issue of Polish nationalism. Luxemburg was also the author of a Marxist critique of capitalist imperialism, *The Accumulation of Capital*. She was murdered, together with Liebknecht, in January 1919 by the Frei Corps who put down the Spartacist uprising.

Luxor Arabic **al-Uqsur**, town in Egypt on the east bank of the River Nile; population (1996 est) 360,500. The temple of Luxor, built by Amenhotep III (c. 1411–1375 BC) is found here, and tombs of the pharaohs in the Valley of the Kings can be found on the west side of the Nile, near the ancient city of Thebes.

Lu Xun, pen-name of Chon Shu-jêu (1881–1936) Chinese short-story writer. His three volumes of satirically realistic stories, *Call to Arms, Wandering*, and *Old Tales Retold*, reveal the influence of the Russian writer Nicolai Gogol. He was also an important polemical essayist and literary critic.

Luzon largest island of the Philippines; area 108,130 sq km/41,750 sq mi; capital Quezon City; population (1995 est) 32,558,000. The chief city is Manila, capital of the Philippines. Industries include rice, timber, minerals, sugar cane, and hemp. It has US military bases.

lycanthropy (Greek *lukos* 'wolf' + *anthropos* 'human') in folk belief, the transformation of a human being into a wolf (*werewolf); or, in psychology, a delusion involving this belief.

Lyceum ancient Athenian gymnasium and garden, with covered walks, where the philosopher Aristotle taught. It was southeast of the city and named after the nearby temple of Apollo Lyceus.

lychee alternative spelling of *litchi, a fruit-bearing tree.

Lycurgus Spartan lawgiver. He was believed to have been a member of the royal house of the ancient Greek city-state of Sparta, who, while acting as regent, gave the Spartans their constitution and system of education. Many modern scholars believe him to be at least partly legendary.

Lydia ancient kingdom in Anatolia (7th–6th centuries BC), with its capital at Sardis. The Lydians were the first Western people to use standard coinage. Their last king, Croesus, was defeated by the Persians in 546 BC.

Lyell, Charles (1797–1875) Scottish geologist. In his *Principles of Geology* (1830–33), he opposed the French anatomist Georges Cuvier's theory that the features of the Earth were formed by a series of catastrophes, and expounded the Scottish geologist James *Hutton's view, known as uniformitarianism, that past events were brought about by the same processes that occur today – a view that influenced Charles *Darwin's theory of *evolution. He was knighted in 1848.

lymph fluid found in the lymphatic system of vertebrates.

lymph nodes small masses of lymphatic tissue in the body that occur at various points along the major lymphatic vessels. Tonsils and adenoids are large lymph nodes. As the lymph passes through them it is filtered, and bacteria and other micro-organisms are engulfed by cells known as macrophages.

lymphocyte type of white blood cell with a large nucleus, produced in the bone marrow. Most occur in the *lymph and blood, and around sites of infection. **B lymphocytes** or B cells are responsible for producing *antibodies. **T lymphocytes** or T cells have several roles in the mechanism of *immunity.

lymphokines chemical messengers produced by lymphocytes that carry messages between the cells of the immune system (see *immunity). Examples include interferon, which initiates defensive reactions to viruses, and the interleukins, which activate specific immune cells.

Lynch, Jack (John Mary) (1917–1999) Irish politician, Taoiseach (prime minister) 1966–73 and 1977–79, and leader of Fianna Fáil 1966–79.

lynching killing of an alleged offender by an individual or group having no legal authority. In the USA it originated in 1780 with creation of a 'committee of vigilance' in Virginia; it is named after a member of that committee, Captain William Lynch, to whom is attributed 'Lynch's law'. Later examples occurred mostly in the Southern states after the Civil War, and were racially motivated. During 1882–1900 the annual number of lynchings in the USA varied between 96 and 231, but today it is an exceptional occurrence.

lynx wild cat found in rocky and forested regions of North America and Europe. About 1 m/3 ft in length, it has a short tail, tufted ears, and long, silky fur which is reddish brown or grey with dark spots. The North American **bobcat** or **bay lynx** (*Felix rufus*) looks similar but is smaller. Some zoologists place the lynx, the bobcat, and the *caracal in a separate genus, *Lynx*. (Species *Felis lynx*, family Felidae.)

Lyon French industrial city and administrative centre of Rhône *département* in the Rhône-Alpes region, part of which lies on the long tongue of land between the Rivers Rhône and Saône, 275 km/170 mi north of Marseille; population (2002 est) 444,100, conurbation 1,665,700. Lyon is France's third-largest city, second-largest urban agglomeration, and most important educational centre after Paris; its main industries are textiles, chemicals, machinery, and printing. Formerly a chief fortress of France, it was the ancient **Lugdunum**, taken by the Romans in 43 BC.

Lyra small but prominent constellation of the northern hemisphere, represented as the harp of Orpheus. Its brightest star is *Vega.

lyre stringed musical instrument of great antiquity. It consists of a hollow soundbox with two curved arms extended upwards to a crosspiece to which four to ten strings are attached. It is played with a plectrum or the fingers. It originated in Asia, and was widespread in ancient Greece and Egypt.

lyrebird either of two species of large birds found in southeastern Australia. They have very stout beaks and short, rounded wings; the tail has 16 feathers, and in the males the exterior pair of feathers are curved in the shape of a lyre; the tail of the female is long, broad, and normal in shape. Lyrebirds nest on the ground, and feed on insects, worms, and snails. (Genus *Menura*, family Menuridae, order Passeriformes.)

lyric literary *genre including any short, personal, and passionate form of verse, usually a meditation on a single idea or theme with the goal of evoking emotion. The term does not imply a particular rhythm, rhyme scheme, or technique but an interest in limiting experience to a single, emotional peak; in this way, lyric poetry can be distinguished from narrative verse. A lyric poem often presents a speaker who expresses his or her state of mind or thought processes. *Sonnets, *odes, and elegies are all lyric poems. Originally, a lyric was a song sung to a lyre, and song texts are still called lyrics.

Lysander (died 395 BC) Spartan politician and admiral. He brought the *Peloponnesian War between Athens and Sparta to a successful conclusion by capturing the Athenian fleet at Aegospotami in 405 BC, and by starving Athens into surrender in the following year. He set up puppet governments in Athens and its former allies, and tried to secure for himself the Spartan kingship, but was killed in battle with the Thebans 395 BC.

Lysenko, Trofim Denisovich (1898–1976) Soviet biologist who believed in the inheritance of *acquired characteristics (changes acquired in an individual's lifetime) and used his position under Joseph Stalin officially to exclude Gregor *Mendel's theory of inheritance. He was removed from office after the fall of Nikita Khrushchev in 1964.

lysis in biology, any process that destroys a cell by rupturing its membrane or cell wall (see *lysosome).

lysosome membrane-enclosed structure, or organelle, inside a *cell, principally found in animal cells. Lysosomes contain enzymes that can break down proteins and other biological substances. They play a part in digestion, and in the white blood cells known as phagocytes the lysosome enzymes attack ingested bacteria.

m

M Roman numeral for 1,000.

Maastricht Treaty treaty establishing the *European Union (EU). Agreed in 1991 and signed in 1992, the treaty took effect on 1 November 1993 following ratification by member states. It advanced the commitment of member states to *economic and monetary union (but included an opt-out clause for the United Kingdom); provided for intergovernmental arrangements for a common foreign and security policy; increased cooperation on justice and home affairs policy issues (though the Social Chapter was rejected by the UK until a change of government in 1997); introduced the concept of EU citizenship (as a supplement to national citizenship); established new regional development bodies; increased the powers of the *European Parliament; and accepted the principle of *subsidiarity (a controversial term defining the limits of European Community involvement in national affairs).

Mabuse, Jan (*c.* 1478–*c.* 1533) adopted name of Jan Gossaert, Flemish painter. His visit to Italy in 1508 started a new vogue in Flanders for Italianate ornament and classical detail in painting, including sculptural nude figures, as in his *Neptune and Amphitrite* (*c.* 1516, Staatliche Museen, Berlin).

McAdam, John Loudon (1756–1836) Scottish engineer, inventor of the **macadam** road surface. It originally consisted of broken granite bound together with slag or gravel, raised for drainage. Today, it is bound with tar or asphalt.

macadamia edible nut of a group of trees native to Australia (especially *M. ternifolia*), and cultivated in Hawaii, South Africa, Zimbabwe, and Malawi. The nuts are slow-growing; they are harvested when they drop. (Genus *Macadamia*, family Proteaceae.)

McAleese, Mary Patricia (1951–) Irish lawyer and academic, president from 1997. When President Mary Robinson announced her resignation, McAleese was nominated by the ruling Fianna Fáil and Progressive Democrats as their candidate in preference to former prime minister Albert Reynolds. She asserted her opposition to violence and secured a clear victory over the Fine Gael nominated candidate, Mary Bannotti.

macaque any of a group of medium-sized Old World monkeys. Various species live in forests from the Far East to North Africa. The *rhesus monkey and the *Barbary ape belong to this group. (Genus *Macaca*.)

MacArthur, Douglas (1880–1964) US general in World War II, commander of US forces in the Far East

and, from March 1942, of the Allied forces in the southwestern Pacific. After the surrender of Japan he commanded the Allied occupation forces there. During 1950 he commanded the UN forces in Korea, but in April 1951, after expressing views contrary to US and UN policy, he was relieved of all his commands by President Truman.

Macau *or* **Macao** former Portuguese possession on the south coast of China, about 65 km/40 mi west of Hong Kong, from which it is separated by the estuary of the Pearl River; it consists of a peninsula and the islands of Taipa and Colôane; area 17 sq km/7 sq mi; population (1999 est) 437,300. The capital is Macau, on the peninsula. On 31 December 1999 Portugese rule ended and Macau was reintegrated into China, though, like Hong Kong, with a guarantee of 50 years' non-interference in its political system. Trade is the mainstay of the economy: Macau is a free port and exports include textiles, clothing, fireworks, toys, and electronic goods. Tourism is also important, with many visitors attracted to Macau's numerous casinos, and travelling via the regular hydrofoil services from Hong Kong. The peninsula is linked to Taipa by a bridge and to Colôane by a causeway, both 2 km/1 mi long.

Macaulay, Thomas Babington (1800–1859) 1st Baron Macaulay, British historian, essayist, poet, and politician, secretary of war 1839–41. His *History of England* in five volumes (1849–61) celebrates the Glorious Revolution of 1688 as the crowning achievement of the Whig party. He was made a baron in 1857.

macaw any of a group of large, brilliantly coloured, long-tailed tropical American *parrots, such as the blue and yellow macaw *Ara ararauna*. They can be recognized by the massive beak, about half the size of the head, and by the extremely long tail. (Genera *Ara*, *Aratinga*, and *Anodorhynchus*.)

Macbeth (*c.* 1005–1057) King of Scotland from 1040. The son of Findlaech, hereditary ruler of Moray and Ross, he was commander of the forces of Duncan I, King of Scotland, whom he killed in battle in 1040. His reign was prosperous until Duncan's son Malcolm III led an invasion and killed him at Lumphanan in Aberdeenshire.

McCarthy, Joe (Joseph Raymond) (1908–1957) US right-wing Republican politician. His unsubstantiated claim in 1950 that the State Department had been infiltrated by communists started a wave of anticommunist hysteria, wild accusations, and blacklists, which continued until he was discredited in 1954. He was censured by the Senate for misconduct.

McCartney, (James) Paul (1942–) English rock singer, songwriter, and bass guitarist. He was a founder-member of the *Beatles, and co-wrote most of their songs with fellow band member John *Lennon. After the break-up of the Beatles he had a successful solo career, as well as leading the pop group Wings 1971–81, and released nine UK number one singles 1970–82.

MacDonald, (James) Ramsay (1866–1937) British politician, first Labour prime minister January–October 1924 and 1929–31, born in Morayshire, Scotland. He left the party to form a coalition government in 1931, which was increasingly dominated by Conservatives, until he was replaced by Stanley Baldwin in 1935.

Macdonald, Flora (1722–1790) Scottish heroine. She rescued Prince *Charles Edward Stuart, the Young Pretender, after the *Jacobite defeat at the Battle of *Culloden in 1746. Disguising him as her maid, she escorted him from her home on South Uist in the Hebrides, to France. She was arrested and imprisoned in the Tower of London, but released in 1747.

Macdonald, John Alexander (1815–1891) Canadian Conservative politician, prime minister 1867–73 and 1878–91. He was born in Glasgow, Scotland, but taken to Ontario as a child. In 1857 he became prime minister of Upper Canada. He took the leading part in the movement for federation, and in 1867 became the first prime minister of Canada. He was defeated in 1873 but returned to office in 1878 and retained it until his death. He was knighted in 1867.

Macdonnell Ranges mountain range in Northern Territory, central Australia, running east to west in parallel ridges for 644 km/400 mi. The highest peaks are Mount Liebig (1,524m/5,000 ft) and Mount Zeil (1,510 m/4,955 ft). The town of Alice Springs is situated in the middle of the Macdonnell Ranges. The spectacular scenery, with its deep gorges and red rocks, attracts many tourists.

Macedonia ancient region of Greece, forming parts of modern Greece, Bulgaria, and the Former Yugoslav Republic of Macedonia. Macedonia gained control of Greece after Philip II's victory at Chaeronea in 338 BC. His son, Alexander the Great, conquered a vast empire. Macedonia became a Roman province in 146 BC.

Macedonia Greek **Makedhonia**, mountainous region of northern Greece, part of the ancient country of Macedonia which was divided between Serbia, Bulgaria, and Greece after the Balkan Wars of 1912–13. Greek Macedonia is bounded west and north by Albania and the Former Yugoslav Republic of Macedonia; area 34,177 sq km/13,200 sq mi; population (1991) 2,263,000. There are two regions, Macedonia Central, and Macedonia East and Thrace. The chief city is Thessaloniki. The Former Yugoslav Republic of Macedonia has refused to give up claims to the present Greek province of Macedonia, and has placed the star of Macedonia, symbol of the ancient Greek Kings of Macedonia, on its flag. Fertile valleys produce grain, olives, grapes, tobacco, and livestock. Mount Olympus rises to 2,918 m/9,570 ft on the border with Thessaly.

Macedonia
National name: *Republika Makedonija/ Republic of Macedonia* (official internal name); *Poranesna Jugoslovenska Republika Makedonija/ Former Yugoslav Republic of Macedonia* (official international name:)
Area: 25,700 sq km/9,922 sq mi
Capital: Skopje
Major towns/cities: Bitola, Prilep, Kumanovo, Tetovo
Physical features: mountainous; rivers: Struma, Vardar; lakes: Ohrid, Prespa, Scutari; partly Mediterranean climate with hot summers
Head of state: Branko Crvenkovski from 2004
Head of government: Vlado Buckovski from 2004
Political system: emergent democracy
Political executive: limited presidency
Political parties: Socialist Party (SP); Social Democratic Alliance of Macedonia (SDSM) bloc, former Communist Party; Party for Democratic

Prosperity (PDP), ethnic Albanian, left of centre; Internal Macedonian Revolutionary Organization–Democratic Party for Macedonian National Unity (VMRO–DPMNE), radical nationalist; Democratic Party of Macedonia (DPM), nationalist, free market
Currency: Macedonian denar
GNI per capita (PPP): (US$) 6,210 (2002 est)
Exports: tobacco, manufactured goods, machinery and transport equipment, metals, miscellaneous manufactured articles, sugar beet, vegetables, cheese, lamb. Principal market: Yugoslavia Serbia and Montenegro from 2003) 25.3% (2000)
Population: 2,056,000 (2003 est)
Language: Macedonian (related to Bulgarian; official), Albanian
Religion: Christian, mainly Orthodox 67%; Muslim 30%
Life expectancy: 71 (men); 76 (women) (2000–05)
Chronology
4th century BC: Part of ancient great kingdom of Macedonia, which included northern Greece and southwest Bulgaria and, under Alexander the Great, conquered a vast empire; Thessaloniki founded.
146 BC: Macedonia became a province of the Roman Empire.
395 AD: On the division of the Roman Empire, came under the control of Byzantine Empire, with its capital at Constantinople.
6th century: Settled by Slavs, who later converted to Christianity.
9th–14th centuries: Under successive rule by Bulgars, Byzantium, and Serbia.
1371: Became part of Islamic Ottoman Empire.
late 19th century: The 'Internal Macedonian Revolutionary Organization', through terrorism, sought to provoke Great Power intervention against Turks.
1912–13: After First Balkan War, partitioned between Bulgaria, Greece, and the area that constitutes the current republic of Serbia.
1918: Serbian part included in what was to become Yugoslavia; Serbian imposed as official language.

553

1941–44: Occupied by Bulgaria.

1945: Created a republic within Yugoslav Socialist Federation.

1967: The Orthodox Macedonian archbishopric of Skopje, forcibly abolished 200 years earlier by the Turks, was restored.

1980: The rise of nationalism was seen after the death of Yugoslav leader Tito.

1990: Multiparty elections produced an inconclusive result.

1991: Kiro Gligorov, a pragmatic former communist, became president. A referendum supported independence.

1992: Independence was declared, and accepted by the Federal Republic of Yugoslavia (Serbia and Montenegro), but international recognition was withheld because of Greece's objections to the name.

1993: Sovereignty was recognized by the UK and Albania; United Nations membership was won under the provisional name of the Former Yugoslav Republic of Macedonia; Greece blocked full European Union (EU) recognition.

1994: Independence was recognized by the USA; a trade embargo was imposed by Greece, causing severe economic damage.

1995: Independence was recognized by Greece and the trade embargo lifted. President Gligorov survived a car bomb assassination attempt.

1997: Plans to reduce the strength of the UN Preventive Deployment Force (UNPREDEP) were abandoned. The government announced compensation for the public's losses in failed investment schemes.

1998: The UN extended the mandate of UNPREDEP. A general election resulted in Ljubco Georgievski, the VRMO-DPMNE leader, becoming prime minister. A 1,700-strong NATO force was deployed in Macedonia to safeguard the 2,000 ceasefire verification monitors in neighbouring Kosovo, in the Federal Republic of Yugoslavia.

1999: Boris Trajkovski was elected president.

2001: Heavy fighting broke out between Macedonian security forces and ethnic Albanians.

2002: Albanian was recognized as an official language. Macedonia joined the World Trade Organisation (WTO). Ljubco Georgievski of the VRMO-DPMNE party lost the elections. The Social Democrats, led by Branko Crvenkovski, became the main party.

2003: NATO troops were replaced by European Union (EU) peacekeeping forces.

2004: Boris Trajkovski was killed in a plane crash. Branko Crvenkovski replaced him as president. Hari Kostov was prime minister for six months before resigning. Vlado Buckovski took over leadership of the Social Democratic Union and was installed as prime minister. Parliament approved legislation to redraw local boundaries and give ethnic Albanians greater local autonomy. Later in the year, the nationalists' attempted to repeal this legislation by referendum but failed because of low turnout. Macedonia submitted an application to join the EU.

Macedonian people of Macedonian culture from the Former Yugoslav Republic of Macedonia and the surrounding area, especially Greece, Albania, and Bulgaria. Macedonian, a Slavic language belonging to the Indo-European family, has 1–1.5 million speakers.

The Macedonians are predominantly members of the Greek Orthodox Church and write with a Cyrillic script. They are known for their folk arts.

McEwan, Ian Russell (1948–) English novelist and short-story writer. His works often have sinister or macabre undertones and contain elements of violence and sexuality, as in the short stories in *First Love, Last Rites* (1975). His novel *Amsterdam* was awarded the 1998 Booker Prize for Fiction.

Machel, Samora Moises (1933–1986) Mozambique nationalist leader, president 1975–86. Machel was active in the liberation front Frelimo from its conception in 1962, fighting for independence from Portugal. He became Frelimo leader in 1966, and Mozambique's first president from independence in 1975 until his death in a plane crash near the South African border.

Machiavelli, Niccolò (1469–1527) Italian politician and author. His name is synonymous with cunning and cynical statecraft. In his chief political writings, *Il principe/The Prince* (1513) and *Discorsi/Discourses* (1531), he discussed ways in which rulers can advance the interests of their states (and themselves) through an often amoral and opportunistic manipulation of other people.

machine in mechanics, device that allows a small force (the effort) to overcome a larger one (the load). There are three basic machines: the inclined plane (ramp), the lever, and the wheel and axle. All other machines are combinations of these three basic types. Simple machines derived from the inclined plane include the wedge, the gear, and the screw; the spanner is derived from the lever; the pulley from the wheel.

machine code in computing, a set of instructions that a computer's central processing unit (CPU) can understand and obey directly, without any translation. Each type of CPU has its own machine code. Because machine-code programs consist entirely of binary digits (bits), most programmers write their programs in an easy-to-use *high-level language. A high-level program must be translated into machine code – by means of a *compiler or interpreter program – before it can be executed by a computer.

machine gun rapid-firing automatic gun. The Maxim (named after its inventor, US-born British engineer H S Maxim (1840–1916)) of 1884 was recoil-operated, but some later types have been gas-operated (Bren) or recoil assisted by gas (some versions of the Browning).

Mach number ratio of the speed of a body to the speed of sound in the medium through which the body travels. In the Earth's atmosphere, Mach 1 is reached when a body (such as an aircraft or spacecraft) 'passes the sound barrier', at a velocity of 331 m/1,087 ft per second (1,192 kph/740 mph) at sea level. A *space shuttle reaches Mach 15 (about 17,700 kph/11,000 mph an hour) 6.5 minutes after launch.

Machu Picchu ruined Inca city in the Peruvian Andes, northwest of Cuzco. This settlement and stronghold stands at the top of 300-m/1,000-ft-high cliffs above the Urabamba River and covers an area of 13 sq km/5 sq mi. Built in about AD 1500, the city's remote location saved it from being found and destroyed by the Spanish conquistadors, and the remains of its houses and temples are well preserved. Machu Picchu was discovered in 1911 by the US archaeologist Hiram L Bingham.

Madagascar

Macintosh, Charles (1766–1843) Scottish manufacturing chemist who discovered that rubber could be dissolved in coal-tar naptha, producing a liquid that could be applied to fabric for waterproofing. This waterproof fabric, was used for raincoats – hence **mackintosh**. Other waterproofing processes have now largely superseded this method.

McKellen, Ian Murray (1939–) English actor. He has been acclaimed as the leading Shakespearean player of his generation. His stage roles include Richard II (1968), Macbeth (1977), Max in Martin Sherman's *Bent* (1979), Platonov in Chekhov's *Wild Honey* (1986), Iago in *Othello* (1989), and Richard III (1990). He was knighted in 1991.

Mackenzie River river in the Northwest Territories, northwestern Canada; about 1,705 km/1,060 mi long (from the Great Slave Lake to the Beaufort Sea). It originates as the Athabasca River in British Columbia and flows over 966 km/600 mi to Lake Athabasca; it then flows northwest from the Great Slave Lake until it enters the Beaufort Sea (part of the Arctic Ocean). The Mackenzie River is navigable from June to October, when it eventually freezes over. It is the main channel of the Finlay-Peace-Mackenzie system (4,241 km/2,635 mi long), the second longest system in North America.

mackerel any of various fishes of the mackerel family, especially the **common mackerel** (*Scomber scombrus*) found in the North Atlantic and Mediterranean. It weighs about 0.7 kg/1.5 lb, and is blue with irregular black bands down its sides, the sides and under surface having a metallic sheen. Like all mackerels, it has a deeply forked tail, and a sleek, streamlined body form. (Family Scombroidia.)

McKinley, William (1843–1901) 25th president of the USA 1897–1901, a Republican. His term as president was marked by the USA's adoption of an imperialist foreign policy, as exemplified by the Spanish-American War in 1898 and the annexation of the Philippines. He sat in Congress 1876–91, apart from one term.

McKinley, Mount *or* **Denali** highest peak in North America, situated in the *Rocky Mountains, Alaska; height 6,194 m/20,320 ft. It was named after US president William McKinley in 1896.

Mackintosh, Charles Rennie (1868–1928) Scottish architect, designer, and painter, whose highly original work represents a dramatic break with the late Victorian style. He worked initially in the *Art Nouveau idiom but later developed a unique style, both rational and expressive, that is more angular and stylized than the flowing, full-blown art nouveau style.

Maclean, Donald Duart (1913–1983) English spy who worked for the USSR while in the UK civil service. He defected to the USSR in 1951 together with Guy Burgess.

Macmillan, (Maurice) Harold (1894–1986) 1st Earl of Stockton, British Conservative politician, prime minister 1957–63; foreign secretary 1955 and chancellor of the Exchequer 1955–57. In 1963 he attempted to negotiate British entry into the European Economic Community (EEC), but was blocked by the French president Charles de Gaulle. Much of his career as prime minister was spent defending the UK's retention of a nuclear weapon, and he was responsible for the purchase of US Polaris missiles in 1962.

Macpherson, James (1736–1796) Scottish writer. He published *Fragments of Ancient Poetry Collected in the Highlands of Scotland* in 1760, followed by the epics *Fingal* in 1761 and *Temora* in 1763, which he claimed as the work of the 3rd-century bard *Ossian. After his death they were shown largely, but not entirely, to be forgeries.

Macquarie, Lachlan (1762–1824) Scottish administrator in Australia. He succeeded Admiral *Bligh as governor of New South Wales in 1809, raised the demoralized settlement to prosperity, and did much to rehabilitate ex-convicts. In 1821 he returned to Britain in poor health, exhausted by struggles with his opponents. Lachlan River and Macquarie River and Island are named after him.

McQueen, (Terrence) Steve(n) (1930–1980) US film actor. He was admired for his portrayals of the strong, silent loner, and noted for performing his own stunt work. After television success in the 1950s, he became a film star with *The Magnificent Seven* (1960). His films include *The Great Escape* (1963), *Bullitt* (1968), *Papillon* (1973), and *The Hunter* (1980).

macroeconomics division of economics concerned with the study of whole (aggregate) economies or systems, including such aspects as government income and expenditure, the balance of payments, fiscal policy, investment, inflation, and unemployment. It seeks to understand the influence of all relevant economic factors on each other and thus to quantify and predict aggregate national income.

macrophage type of *white blood cell, or leucocyte, found in all vertebrate animals. Macrophages specialize in the removal of bacteria and other micro-organisms, or of cell debris after injury. Like phagocytes, they engulf foreign matter, but they are larger than phagocytes and have a longer lifespan. They are found throughout the body, but mainly in the lymph and connective tissues, and especially the lungs, where they ingest dust, fibres, and other inhaled particles.

Madagascar

National name: *Republikan'i Madagasikara/ République de Madagascar/Republic of Madagascar*
Area: 587,041 sq km/226,656 sq mi
Capital: Antananarivo

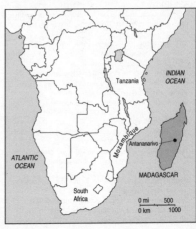

Major towns/cities: Antsirabe, Mahajanga, Fianarantsoa, Toamasina, Ambatondrazaka
Major ports: Toamasina, Antsiranana, Toliara, Mahajanga
Physical features: temperate central highlands; humid valleys and tropical coastal plains; arid in south
Head of state: Marc Ravalomanana from 2002
Head of government: Jacques Sylla from 2002
Political system: emergent democracy
Political executive: limited presidency
Political parties: Association for the Rebirth of Madagascar (AREMA), left of centre; One Should Not Be Judged By One's Works (AVI), left of centre; Rally for Socialism and Democracy (RPSD), left of centre
Currency: Malagasy franc
GNI per capita (PPP): (US$) 720 (2002 est)
Exports: fish, coffee, shrimps and prawns, cloves, vanilla, petroleum products, chromium, cotton fabrics. Principal market: France 39.3% (2000)
Population: 17,404,000 (2003 est)
Language: Malagasy, French (both official), local dialects
Religion: over 50% traditional beliefs, Roman Catholic, Protestant about 40%, Muslim 7%
Life expectancy: 53 (men); 55 (women) (2000–05)
Chronology
***c.* 6th–10th centuries AD:** Settled by migrant Indonesians.
1500: First visited by European navigators.
17th century: Development of Merina and Sakalava kingdoms in the central highlands and west coast.
1642–74: France established a coastal settlement at Fort-Dauphin, which they abandoned after a massacre by local inhabitants.
late 18th–early 19th century: Merinas, united by their ruler Andrianampoinimerina, became dominant kingdom; court converted to Christianity.
1861: Ban on Christianity (imposed in 1828) and entry of Europeans lifted by Merina king, Radama II.
1885: Became French protectorate.
1895: Merina army defeated by French and became a colony; slavery abolished.
1942–43: British troops invaded to overthrow French administration allied to the pro-Nazi Germany Vichy regime and install anti-Nazi Free French government.
1947–48: Nationalist uprising brutally suppressed by French.
1960: Independence achieved from France, with Philibert Tsiranana, the leader of the Social Democratic Party (PSD), as president.
1972: Merina-dominated army overthrew Tsiranana's government, dominated by the cotier (coastal tribes), as the economy deteriorated.
1975: Martial law imposed; new one-party state Marxist constitution adopted, with Lt-Commander Didier Ratsiraka as president.
1978: More than 1,000 people were killed in race riots in Majunga city in the northwest.
1980: Ratsiraka abandoned the Marxist experiment, which had involved nationalization and the severing of ties with France.
1990: Political opposition was legalized and 36 new parties were created.
1991: Antigovernment demonstrations were held. Ratsiraka formed a new unity government, which included opposition members.

1992: Constitutional reform was approved by a referendum.
1995: A referendum backed the appointment of a prime minister by the president, rather than the assembly.
1996: Didier Ratsiraka was elected president again.
1998: ARES largest party following election. Tantely Andrianarivo appointed prime minister.
2000: Around 600,000 people were made homeless when cyclones which had been striking southern Africa swept through the island.
2002: Former president Didier Ratsiraka fled the country, ending a seven-month-long dispute with his rival, Marc Ravalomanana, over the 2001 presidential election and averting the threat of all-out civil war. Ravalomanana had earlier been confirmed as the legitimate president in a court-supervised recount and had been recognized by the USA and France.
2003: A former head of the armed forces was charged with an attempted coup against Ravolomanana. The former president, Didier Ratsiraka, and the former prime minister, Tantely Andrianarivo, were found guilty of embezzlement and abuse of office.
2004: Tropical cyclones Elita and Gafilo hit the island, leaving thousands homeless. The World Bank and the International Monetary Fund agreed to write off almost half of Madagascar's debt.
2005: Madagascar received development aid from the USA under a new scheme to help nations considered to be promoting democracy and market reforms.

mad cow disease common name for *bovine spongiform encephalopathy, an incurable brain condition in cattle.

madder any of a group of plants bearing small funnel-shaped flowers, especially the perennial vine *R. tinctorum* which grows in Europe and Asia, the red root of which yields a red dye called alizarin (now made synthetically from coal tar). (Genus *Rubia*, family Rubiaceae.)

Madeira Islands group of islands forming an autonomous region of Portugal, off the northwest coast of Africa, about 420 km/260 mi north of the Canary Islands; area 796 sq km/308 sq mi; population (1994 est) 256,000. Madeira, the largest, and Porto Santo are the only inhabited islands. The Desertas and Selvagens are uninhabited islets. Their mild climate makes them a popular, year-round tourist destination. The capital is Funchal, on Madeira. Pico Ruivo, also on Madeira, is the highest mountain at 1,861 m/6,106 ft. Industries include Madeira (a fortified wine), sugar cane, fruit, fish, handicrafts, and tourism.

Madhya Bharat state of India 1950–56. It was a union of 24 states of which Gwalior and Indore were the most important. In 1956 Madhya Bharat was absorbed in *Madhya Pradesh.

Madhya Pradesh state of central India, the second largest of the Indian states; area 296,480 sq km/114,472 sq mi; population (2001 est) 60,385,100. The capital is *Bhopal, and other towns and cities are Indore, Jabalpur, Gwalior, and Ujjain. The state is land-locked and mainly upland. The Narmada River originates in the famous holy place, Amarkantaka, in the Shahdol district, and flows westward where it eventually falls into the Arabian sea. Vindhya and Satpura mountain ranges (rising to 600 m/2,000 ft) are found in the state, which is heavily forested. Industries include textiles, engineering, iron ore, steel (at Bhilai complex), coal, bauxite, manganese, paper, aluminium, limestone, diamonds, and cement. Hydroelectric power comes from the Chambal and *Narmada rivers. Main agricultural products include cotton, millet, wheat, oilseed, sugar, groundnuts, and soya.

Madison, James (1751–1836) 4th president of the USA 1809–17. In 1787 he became a member of the Philadelphia Constitutional Convention and took a leading part in drawing up the US Constitution, earning him the title 'Father of the Constitution'. He was determined that the government was to be composed of three divisions: legislative, executive (administrative), and judicial. In the struggle between the more democratic views of Thomas *Jefferson and the aristocratic, upper-class sentiments of Alexander *Hamilton, he allied himself firmly with Jefferson. As secretary of state in Jefferson's government 1801–09, Madison completed the *Louisiana Purchase negotiated by James Monroe. During his period of office the War of 1812 with Britain took place.

Madonna (1958–) stage name of Madonna Louise Veronica Ciccone, US pop singer and actor. Madonna is arguably the most successful female artist in popular music. Her first hit was 'Like a Virgin' (1984); others include 'Material Girl' (1985) and 'Like a Prayer' (1989). Her albums *Ray of Light* (1998) and *Music* (2000), are more influenced by dance and electronic music than her previous releases, and were both immediate commercial and critical successes. Her films include *Desperately Seeking Susan* (1985) and *Evita* (1996).

Madonna Italian name for the Virgin Mary, meaning 'my lady'.

Madras former name, to 1996, of *Chennai, an industrial port and capital of the state of Tamil Nadu, India.

Madras former name of *Tamil Nadu, a state of India.

Madrid autonomous community and province of central Spain; area 7,995 sq km/3,087 sq mi; population (2001 est) 5,372,400. Situated on the countryouths central plateau (meseta), the region is bounded by the Sierra de Guadarrama mountains in the northwest, and by the River Tagus in the southeast. It is crossed by several rivers, including the Jarama, a tributary of the Tagus. Products include cereals, potatoes, fruit and vegetables, grown in the south and southeast; timber from the forests in the northeast, and lime, granite, and gypsum from quarries in the mountains. The Escorial palace lies in the northwest; Aranjuez in the south has had a royal palace since the 15th century and has luxurious gardens. The capital is *Madrid.

Madrid capital city of Spain and of Madrid province, on the Manzanares River; population (2001 est) 2,957,100, conurbation (2003 est) 5,130,000. Built on a vast elevated plateau in the centre of the country, at 655 m/2,183 ft it is the highest capital in Europe and experiences extremes of heat and cold. Industries include the production of food, electronics, pharmaceuticals, leather, chemicals, furniture, tobacco, and paper, and there is engineering and publishing. Madrid is the country's chief transportation and administrative centre, as well as an important commercial and financial centre.

madrigal form of secular song in four or five parts, usually sung without instrumental accompaniment.

It originated in 14th-century Italy. Madrigal composers include Andrea Gabrieli, Monteverdi, Thomas Morley, and Orlando Gibbons.

maenad in Greek mythology, one of the women participants in the orgiastic rites of *Dionysus; maenads were also known as **Bacchae**.

Maeterlinck, Maurice Polydore Marie Bernard (1862–1949) Count Maeterlinck, Belgian poet and dramatist. His plays include *Pelléas et Mélisande* (1892) (on which Debussy based his opera), *L'Oiseau bleu/ The Blue Bird* (1908), and *Le Bourgmestre de Stilmonde/ The Burgomaster of Stilemonde* (1918). This last celebrates Belgian resistance in World War I, a subject that led to his exile in the USA in 1940. His philosophical essays include 'Le Trésor des humbles/The Treasure of the Humble' (1896) and 'La vie des abeilles/The Life of the Bee' (1901). He was awarded the Nobel Prize for Literature in 1911.

Mafia (Italian 'swank') secret society reputed to control organized crime such as gambling, loansharking, drug traffic, prostitution, and protection; connected with the *Camorra of Naples. It originated in Sicily in the late Middle Ages and now operates chiefly there and in countries to which Italians have emigrated, such as the USA and Australia. During the early 1990s many centre and right-wing Italian politicians, such as the former Christian Democrat prime minister Giulio Andreotti, became discredited when it emerged that they had had dealings with the Mafia.

mafic rock plutonic rock composed chiefly of dark-coloured minerals such as olivine and pyroxene that contain abundant magnesium and iron. It is derived from **magnesium** and **ferric** (iron). The term **mafic** also applies to dark-coloured minerals rich in iron and magnesium as a group. 'Mafic rocks' usually refers to dark-coloured igneous rocks such as basalt, but can also refer to their metamorphic counterparts.

Magellan NASA space probe to the planet *Venus, launched from the space shuttle *Atlantis* on 4 May 1989. The probe went into orbit around Venus in August 1990 to make a detailed map by radar of 99% of the planet. It revealed the existence of volcanoes, impact craters, and mountains on the planet's surface.

Magellan, Ferdinand (c. 1480–1521) Portuguese navigator. In 1519 he set sail in the *Victoria* from Seville with the intention of reaching the East Indies by a westerly route. He sailed through the **Strait of Magellan** at the tip of South America, crossed an ocean he named the Pacific, and in 1521 reached the Philippines, where he was killed in a battle with the islanders. His companions returned to Seville in 1522, completing the voyage under del Cano.

Magellanic Clouds two galaxies nearest to our own galaxy. They are irregularly shaped, and appear as detached parts of the *Milky Way, in the southern hemisphere.

Magellan, Strait of Spanish **Estrecho de Magallanes**, channel at the southern tip of Chile; it separates the South American mainland from Tierra del Fuego, and joins the South Pacific and South Atlantic oceans. It is 595 km/370 mi long with a maximum width of 32 km/20 mi. The strait is named after the Portuguese navigator Ferdinand *Magellan who discovered it in 1520. It provided a safer passage than that around Cape Horn, but its importance declined following the opening of the Panama Canal in 1914, an international waterway within Chile's territorial waters.

Maggiore, Lake ancient **Verbanus Lacus**, lake largely in Italy, bounded on the west by Piedmont and on the east by Lombardy; its northern end is in the Swiss canton of Ticino. It is 63 km/39 mi long and up to 9 km/5.5 mi wide, with an area of 212 sq km/82 sq mi.

maggot soft, plump, limbless *larva of flies, a typical example being the larva of the blowfly which is deposited as an egg on flesh.

magi singular **magus**, priests of the Zoroastrian religion of ancient Persia, noted for their knowledge of astrology. The term is used in the New Testament of the Latin Vulgate Bible where the Authorized Version gives 'wise men'. The magi who came to visit the infant Jesus with gifts of gold, frankincense, and myrrh (the **Adoration of the Magi**) were in later tradition described as 'the three kings' – Caspar, Melchior, and Balthazar.

magic art of controlling the forces of nature by supernatural means such as charms and ritual. The central ideas are that like produces like (**sympathetic magic**) and that influence carries by contagion or association; for example, by the former principle an enemy could be destroyed through an effigy, and by the latter principle through personal items such as hair or nail clippings. See also *witchcraft.

magic bullet term sometimes used for a drug that is specifically targeted on certain cells or tissues in the body, such as a small collection of cancerous cells (see *cancer) or cells that have been invaded by a virus. Such drugs can be made in various ways, but *monoclonal antibodies are increasingly being used to direct the drug to a specific target.

magic realism in 20th-century literature, a fantastic situation realistically treated, as in the works of many Latin American writers such as Isabel Allende, Jorge Luis *Borges, and Gabriel *García Márquez.

Maginot Line French fortification system along the German frontier from Switzerland to Luxembourg built 1929–36 under the direction of the war minister, André Maginot. It consisted of semi-underground forts joined by underground passages, and was protected by antitank defences; lighter fortifications continued the line to the sea. In 1940 German forces pierced the Belgian frontier line and outflanked the Maginot Line.

magistrate in English law, a person who presides in a magistrates' court: either a justice of the peace (with no legal qualifications, and unpaid) or a stipendiary magistrate. Stipendiary magistrates are paid, qualified lawyers working mainly in London and major cities.

maglev contraction of magnetic levitation, high-speed surface transport using the repellent force of superconductive magnets (see *superconductivity) to propel and support, for example, a train above a track.

magma molten rock material that originates in the lower part of the Earth's crust, or *mantle, where it reaches temperatures as high as 1,000 °C/1,832 °F. *Igneous rocks are formed from magma. *Lava is magma that has extruded onto the surface.

Magna Carta (Latin 'great charter') in English history, the charter granted by King *John (I) Lackland in 1215, traditionally seen as guaranteeing human rights against the excessive use of royal power. As a reply to the king's demands for feudal dues and attacks on the privileges of the medieval church, Archbishop Stephen Langton proposed to the barons the drawing-up of a binding document in 1213. John was forced to accept this at Runnymede (now in Surrey) on 15 June 1215.

magnesia common name for *magnesium oxide.

magnesium chemical symbol Mg, lightweight, very ductile and malleable, silver-white, metallic element, atomic number 12, relative atomic mass 24.305. It is one of the *alkaline-earth metals, and the lightest of the commonly used metals. Magnesium silicate, carbonate, and chloride are widely distributed in nature. The metal is used in alloys, flares, and flash bulbs. It is a necessary trace element in the human diet, and green plants cannot grow without it since it is an essential constituent of the photosynthetic pigment *chlorophyll ($C_{55}H_{72}MgN_4O_5$).

magnesium oxide or **magnesia** MgO, white powder or colourless crystals, formed when magnesium is burned in air or oxygen; a typical basic oxide. It is used to treat acidity of the stomach, and in some industrial processes; for example, as a lining brick in furnaces, because it is very stable when heated (refractory oxide).

magnet any object that forms a magnetic field (displays *magnetism), either permanently or temporarily through induction, causing it to attract materials such as iron, cobalt, nickel, and alloys of these. It always has two *magnetic poles, called north and south.

magnetic compass device for determining the direction of the horizontal component of the Earth's magnetic field. It consists of a magnetized needle (a small bar magnet) with its north-seeking pole clearly indicated, pivoted so that it can turn freely in a plane parallel to the surface of the Earth (in a horizontal circle). The needle aligns itself with the lines of force of the Earth's magnetic field, turning so that its north-seeking pole points towards the Earth's magnetic north pole. See also *compass.

magnetic field region around a permanent magnet, or around a conductor carrying an electric current, in which a force acts on a moving charge or on a magnet placed in the field. The force cannot be seen; only the effects it produces are visible. The field can be represented by lines of force parallel at each point to the direction of a small compass needle placed on them at that point. These invisible lines of force are called the magnetic field or the flux lines. A magnetic field's magnitude is given by the *magnetic flux density (the number of flux lines per unit area), expressed in *teslas. See also *polar reversal.

magnetic flux measurement of the strength of the magnetic field around electric currents and magnets. Its SI unit is the *weber; one weber per square metre is equal to one tesla.

magnetic pole region of a magnet in which its magnetic properties are strongest. Every magnet has two poles, called north and south. The north (or north-seeking) pole is so named because a freely-suspended magnet will turn so that this pole points towards the Earth's magnetic north pole. The north pole of one magnet will be attracted to the south pole of another, but will be repelled by its north pole. So unlike poles attract, like poles repel.

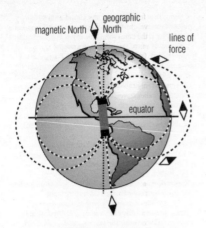

magnetic field A magnet is an object that forms a magnetic field. It has a north pole and a south pole. The Earth acts as a giant magnet.

magnetic resonance imaging (MRI) diagnostic scanning system based on the principles of nuclear magnetic resonance (NMR). MRI yields finely detailed three-dimensional images of structures within the body without exposing the patient to harmful radiation. The technique is invaluable for imaging the soft tissues of the body, in particular the brain and the spinal cord.

magnetic storm in meteorology, a sudden disturbance affecting the Earth's magnetic field, causing anomalies in radio transmissions and magnetic compasses. It is probably caused by *sunspot activity.

magnetic tape narrow plastic ribbon coated with an easily magnetizable material on which data can be recorded. It is used in sound recording, audio-visual systems (videotape), and computing. For mass storage on commercial mainframe computers, large reel-to-reel tapes are still used, but cartridges are becoming popular. Various types of cartridge are now standard on minicomputers and PCs, while audio cassettes were used with early home computers.

magnetism phenomena associated with *magnetic fields. Magnetic fields are produced by moving charged particles. In electromagnets, electrons flow through a coil of wire connected to a battery; in permanent magnets, spinning electrons within the atoms generate the field.

magnetite black, strongly magnetic opaque mineral, Fe_3O_4, of the spinel group, an important ore of iron. Widely distributed, magnetite is found in nearly all igneous and metamorphic rocks. Some deposits, called lodestone, are permanently magnetized. Lodestone has been used as a compass since the first millennium BC. Today the orientations of magnetite grains in rocks are used in the study of the Earth's magnetic field.

magnification measure of the enlargement or reduction of an object in an imaging optical system. **Linear magnification** is the ratio of the size (height) of the image to that of the object. **Angular magnification** is the ratio of the angle subtended at the observer's eye by the image to the angle subtended by the object when viewed directly.

magnitude in astronomy, measure of the brightness of a star or other celestial object. The larger the number denoting the magnitude, the fainter the object. Zero or first magnitude indicates some of the brightest stars. Still brighter are those of negative magnitude, such as Sirius, whose magnitude is –1.46. **Apparent magnitude** is the brightness of an object as seen from the Earth; **absolute magnitude** is the brightness at a standard distance of 10 parsecs (32.616 light years).

magnolia any of a group of trees or shrubs belonging to the magnolia family, native to North America and East Asia, and cultivated as ornamentals. Magnolias vary in height from 60 cm/2 ft to 30 m/150 ft. The large, fragrant flowers are white, pink, or purple. The southern magnolia (*M. grandiflora*) of the USA grows up to 24 m/80 ft tall and has white flowers 23 cm/9 in across. (Genus *Magnolia*, family Magnoliaceae.)

magpie any of various birds belonging to the crow family. They feed on insects, snails, young birds, and carrion, and are found in Europe, Asia, North Africa, and western North America. (Genus *Pica*, family Corvidae, order Passeriformes.)

Magritte, René François Ghislain (1898–1967) Belgian painter, one of the major figures in *surrealism. His work, characteristic of surrealist ideas, focuses on visual paradoxes and everyday objects taken out of context. Recurring motifs include bowler hats, apples, and windows, for example *Golconda* (1953; private collection), in which men in bowler hats are falling from the sky to a street below.

Magyar *or* **Hungarian** member of the largest ethnic group in Hungary, comprising 92% of the population. Most are Roman Catholic. The *Hungarian language belongs to the Uralic group.

Mahabharata (Sanskrit 'great poem of the Bharatas') Sanskrit Hindu epic consisting of 18 books and 90,000 stanzas, originally written in about 900 BC and probably composed in its present form in about 300 BC. It forms with the *Ramayana the two great scriptural epics of the Hindus. It contains the *Bhagavad-Gita, or *Song of the Blessed*, an episode in the sixth book, which is regarded as one of the most sacred of Hindu writings.

Maharashtra state in west central India; area 307,762 sq km/118,828 sq mi; population (2001 est) 96,752,200. The capital is *Mumbai (formerly Bombay), and other towns and cities include Pune, Nagpur, Ulhasnagar, Solapur, Nasik, Thana, Kolhapur, Aurangabad, Sangli, and Amravati. The state is divided by the heavily forested Western *Ghats into the Konkan coastal plain and the Deccan plateau. The plain is subject to the southwest monsoon from June to September. Inland is in a rain shadow receiving only half the coastal rainfall. The Godavari and Krishna rivers rise in the Western Ghats and flow eastwards across the Deccan. The Marathi language is spoken by 50% of the population. 80% of the population are Hindu, with Parsee, Jain, and Sikh minorities. The state was formed in 1960 from the southern part of the former Bombay state.

maharishi (Sanskrit *maha* 'great', *rishi* 'sage') Hindu guru (teacher), or spiritual leader. The Maharishi Mahesh Yogi influenced the Beatles and other Westerners in the 1960s.

Mahayana (Sanskrit 'greater vehicle') one of the two major forms of *Buddhism, found in China, Korea, Japan, and Tibet. Veneration of *bodhisattvas (those who achieve enlightenment but remain on the human plane in order to help other living beings) is a fundamental belief in Mahayana, as is the idea that everyone has within them the seeds of Buddhahood.

Mahdi (Arabic 'he who is guided aright') in Islam, the title of a coming messiah who will establish a reign of justice on earth. The title has been assumed by many Muslim leaders, notably the Sudanese sheikh Muhammad Ahmed (1848–1885), who headed a revolt in 1881 against Egypt and in 1885 captured Khartoum.

Mahfouz, Naguib (1911–) Egyptian novelist and playwright. His novels, which deal with the urban working class, include the semi-autobiographical *Khan al-Kasrain/The Cairo Trilogy* (1956–57). His book *Children of Gebelawi* (1959) was banned in Egypt because of its treatment of religious themes. He was awarded the Nobel Prize for Literature in 1988.

Mahler, Gustav (1860–1911) Austrian composer and conductor. He composed nine large-scale symphonies incorporating folk music and pastoral imagery, with many using voices, including *Symphony No 2, the 'Resurrection'* (1884–86). He revised it in 1893–96, but left a tenth unfinished. He also composed orchestral lieder (songs) including *Das Lied von der Erde/ The Song of the Earth* (1909) and *Kindertotenlieder/ Dead Children's Songs* (1901–04).

Mahmud II (1785–1839) Ottoman sultan from 1808 who attempted to Westernize the declining empire, carrying out a series of far-reaching reforms in the civil service and army. The pressure for Greek independence after 1821 led to conflict with Britain, France, and Russia, and he was forced to recognize Greek independence in 1830.

mahogany timber from any of several trees found in the Americas and Africa. Mahogany is a tropical hardwood obtained chiefly by rainforest logging. It has a warm red colour and can be highly polished. True mahogany comes mainly from *S. mahagoni* and *S. macrophylla*, but other types come from the Spanish and Australian cedars, the Indian redwood, and other trees of the mahogany family, native to Africa and the East Indies. (True mahogany genus *Swietenia*, family Meliaceae.)

Maia in Greek mythology, eldest and most beautiful of the Pleiades, daughters of *Atlas and Pleione, and mother of *Hermes by Zeus. Identified by the Romans with an ancient Italian goddess of spring, also Maia (or **Maiesta**), she was celebrated in May, the month reputedly named after her.

maidenhair any of a group of ferns, especially *A. capillus-veneris*, with delicately hanging hairlike fronds ending in small kidney-shaped spore-bearing lobes. It is widely distributed in the Americas, and is sometimes found in the British Isles. (Genus *Adiantum*, family Polypodiaceae.)

Mailer, Norman Kingsley (1923–) US writer and journalist. One of the most prominent figures of post-war American literature, he gained wide attention with his first, best-selling book *The Naked and the Dead* (1948), a naturalistic war novel. His later works, which use sexual and scatological material, show his personal engagement with history, politics, and psychology.

Always a pugnacious and controversial writer, his polemics on the theory and practice of violence-as-sex brought him into direct conflict with feminist Kate Millett in a series of celebrated debates during the 1970s.

Maimonides, Moses (Ben Maimon) (1135–1204) Spanish-born Jewish rabbi and philosopher, one of the greatest Hebrew scholars. He attempted to reconcile faith and reason. His codification of Jewish law is known as the *Mishneh Torah/Torah Reviewed* (1180); he also formulated the **Thirteen Principles**, which summarize the basic beliefs of Judaism.

mainboard new (and more politically correct) name for a *motherboard.

Maine called the **Pine Tree State**, ('mainland') northeasternmost state of the USA and the largest of the *New England states, bordered to the northwest by *Québec, Canada, to the north and east by *New Brunswick, Canada, to the east and south by the Atlantic Ocean, and to the west by *New Hampshire; area 79,932 sq km/30,862 sq mi; population (2000) 1,274,900; capital Augusta. It is the sole US state to be contiguous with only one other US state, and West Quoddy Head is the easternmost US point; the state is popularly known as 'Down East'. The state divides physically into a Coastal Lowland area, an upland area, and the White Mountains region. Over 80% of the state is forested and it has many offshore islands. The economy is led by the service industry, and manufacturing, lumber, shipbuilding, farming, and fishing are also important. Products include paper and pulp, wood products, textiles, potatoes, blueberries, and apples. The largest city is Portland, and other towns and cities include Lewiston, Bangor, Auburn, and South Portland. Originally home to the Penobscot and Passamaquoddy peoples, Maine was settled by the French in 1604. It was purchased by the Massachusetts Bay Colony in 1677, but intensive settlement did not start until the late 18th century. Maine was admitted to the Union in 1820 as the 23rd US state.

mainframe large computer used for commercial data processing and other large-scale operations. Because of the general increase in computing power, the differences between the mainframe, *supercomputer, *minicomputer, and *microcomputer (personal computer) are becoming less marked.

maize North American **corn**, tall annual *cereal plant, *Zea mays*, that produces spikes of yellow grains that are widely used as an animal feed. Grown extensively in all subtropical and warm temperate regions, its range has been extended to colder zones by hardy varieties developed in the 1960s. It was domesticated by 6,500 BC in Mesoamerica, where it grew wild.

majolica *or* **maiolica** tin-glazed *earthenware and the richly decorated enamel pottery produced in Italy in the 15th to 18th centuries. The name derives from the Italian form of Mallorca, the island from where Moorish lustreware made in Spain was shipped to Italy. During the 19th century the word was used to describe moulded earthenware with relief patterns decorated in coloured glazes.

major in music, one of the two important *scales (the other being minor) of the tonal system. The main characteristic of the major scale is the major third between the first and third degrees (or notes) of the scale. A major key is one based on the major scale.

Major, John (1943–) British Conservative politician, prime minister 1990–97. He was foreign secretary in 1989 and chancellor of the Exchequer 1989–90. As prime minister, his initially positive approach to European Community matters was hindered from 1991 by divisions within the Conservative Party. Despite continuing public dissatisfaction with the poll tax, the decline of the National Health Service, and the recession, Major was returned to power in the April 1992 general election. His subsequent handling of a series of domestic crises called into question his ability to govern the country effectively, but he won backing for his launch of a joint UK–Irish peace initiative on Northern Ireland in 1993, which led to a general ceasefire in 1994. On the domestic front, local and European election defeats and continuing divisions within the Conservative Party led to his dramatic and unexpected resignation of the party leadership in June 1995 in a desperate bid for party unity. He was narrowly re-elected to the post the following month. Criticized for weak leadership of his divided party, he resigned as leader of the Conservative Party after a crushing defeat in the 1997 general election. In March 2000 he announced his retirement from the House of Commons.

Makarios III (1913–1977) born Mikhail Christodoulou Mouskos, Cypriot politician and Greek Orthodox archbishop 1950–77. A leader of the Greek-Cypriot resistance organization EOKA, he was exiled by the British to the Seychelles 1956–57 for supporting armed action to achieve union with Greece (*enosis*). He was president of the republic of Cyprus 1960–77 (briefly deposed by a Greek military coup July–Dec 1974).

Makua a people living to the north of the Zambezi River in Mozambique. With the Lomwe people, they make up the country's largest ethnic group. The Makua are mainly farmers, living in villages ruled by chiefs. The Makua language belongs to the Niger-Congo family, and has about 5 million speakers.

Malabo capital, port, and largest settlement of Equatorial Guinea, on the north coast of the volcanic island of Bioko; population (1994 est) 40,300 (city), 50,000 (urban area). It is the leading commercial centre of the country and trades in cocoa, coffee, copra, and other agricultural products, as well as timber and fish. It was founded in the 1820s by the British as **Port Clarence** (also **Clarencetown**). Under Spanish rule it was known as **Santa Isabel** (until 1973 when it received its present name). It was the capital in colonial times and retained this status at independence in 1968.

Malacca former name of *Melaka, a state of Peninsular Malaysia, and its capital, also called Melaka.

malachite common copper ore, basic copper carbonate, $Cu_2CO_3(OH)_2$. It is a source of green pigment and is used as an antifungal agent in fish farming, as well as being polished for use in jewellery, ornaments, and art objects.

Malagasy inhabitant of the island of Madagascar. The Malagasy language is divided into many dialects and has about 9 million speakers; it belongs to the Austronesian family.

malapropism amusing slip of the tongue, arising from the confusion of similar-sounding words; for example, 'the pineapple [pinnacle] of politeness'. The term derives from the French *mal à propos* (inappropriate); historically, it is associated with Mrs Malaprop, a character in Richard Sheridan's play *The Rivals* (1775).

malaria infectious parasitic disease of the tropics transmitted by mosquitoes, marked by periodic fever and an enlarged spleen. When a female mosquito of the *Anopheles* genus bites a human who has malaria, it takes in with the human blood one of four malaria protozoa of the genus *Plasmodium*. This matures within the insect and is then transferred when the mosquito bites a new victim. Malaria affects around 300–500 million people each year, in 103 countries, and in 1995 around 2.1 million people died of the disease. In sub-Saharan Africa alone between 1.5 and 2 million children die from malaria and its consequences each year. In November 1998, an agreement was reached to establish a multi-agency programme for research and control of the disease. The agencies involved include the World Health Organization (WHO), the World Bank, the United Nations Children's Fund, and the United Nations Development Programme. The Roll Back Malaria campaign aims to halve deaths from malaria by 2010.

Malawi
National name: *Republic of Malawi*

Area: 118,484 sq km/45,735 sq mi
Capital: Lilongwe
Major towns/cities: Blantyre, Mzuzu, Zomba
Physical features: landlocked narrow plateau with rolling plains; mountainous west of Lake Nyasa
Head of state and government: Bingu wa Mutharika from 2004
Political system: emergent democracy
Political executive: limited presidency
Political parties: Malawi Congress Party (MCP), multiracial, right wing; United Democratic Front (UDF), left of centre; Alliance for Democracy (A FORD), left of centre
Currency: Malawi kwacha
GNI per capita (PPP): (US$) 570 (2002 est)
Exports: tobacco, tea, sugar, cotton, coffee, groundnuts. Principal market: South Africa 19.5% (2000)

Population: 12,105,000 (2003 est)
Language: English, Chichewa (both official), other Bantu languages
Religion: Protestant 50%, Roman Catholic 20%, Muslim 2%, animist
Life expectancy: 37 (men); 38 (women) (2000–05)
Chronology
1st–4th centuries AD: Immigration by Bantu-speaking peoples.
1480: Foundation of Maravi (Malawi) Confederacy, which covered much of central and southern Malawi and lasted into the 17th century.
1530: First visited by the Portuguese.
1600: Ngonde kingdom founded in northern Malawi by immigrants from Tanzania.
18th century: Chikulamayembe state founded by immigrants from east of Lake Nyasa; slave trade flourished and Islam introduced in some areas.
mid-19th century: Swahili-speaking Ngoni peoples, from South Africa, and Yao entered the region, dominating settled agriculturists; Christianity introduced by missionaries, such as David Livingstone.
1891: Became British protectorate of Nyasaland; cash crops, particularly coffee, introduced.
1915: Violent uprising, led by Rev John Chilembwe, against white settlers who had moved into the fertile south, taking land from local population.
1953: Became part of white-dominated Central African Federation, which included South Rhodesia (Zimbabwe) and North Rhodesia (Zambia).
1958: Dr Hastings Kamuzu Banda returned to the country after working abroad and became head of the conservative-nationalist Malawi/Malawi Congress Party (MCP), which spearheaded the campaign for independence.
1963: Central African Federation dissolved.
1964: Independence achieved within Commonwealth as Malawi, with Banda as prime minister.
1966: Became one-party republic, with Banda as president.
1967: Banda became pariah of Black Africa by recognizing racist, white-only republic of South Africa.
1971: Banda was made president for life.
1970s: There were reports of human-rights violations and the murder of Banda's opponents.
1980s: The economy began to deteriorate after nearly two decades of expansion.
1986–89: There was an influx of nearly a million refugees from Mozambique.
1992: There were calls for a multiparty political system. Countrywide industrial riots caused many fatalities. Western aid was suspended over human-rights violations.
1993: A referendum overwhelmingly supported the ending of one-party rule.
1994: A new multiparty constitution was adopted. Bakili Muluzi, of the United Democratic Front (UDF), was elected president in the first free elections for 30 years.
1995: Banda and the former minister of state John Tembo were charged with conspiring to murder four political opponents in 1983, but were cleared.
1999: Violent protests followed the announcement that Muluzi had been re-elected as president.
2000: Muluzi sacked his entire cabinet after high-ranking officials were accused of corruption, in a move aimed at placating foreign donors. However, his new government included many of the same people.
2002: Government was accused of worsening severe famine through mismanagement and corruption. The rail link between central Malawi and the port of Nacala in Mozambique was re-opened after nearly 20 years.
2004: The government announced that it would provide anti-viral drugs free of charge to Aids sufferers. Bingu wa Mutharika of the UDF won the presidential elections. Muluzi remained as head of the UDF.
2005: Mutharika resigned from the UDF, citing hostility against his anti-corruption measures as the reason. He remained as president.

Malawi, Lake *or* **Lake Nyasa** lake, bordered by Malawi, Tanzania, and Mozambique, formed in a section of the Great *Rift Valley. It is about 500 m/ 1,650 ft above sea level and 560 km/350 mi long, with an area of 28,749 sq km/11,100 sq mi and a depth of 700 m/2,296 ft, making it the ninth biggest lake in the world. It is intermittently drained to the south by the River Shire into the Zambezi.

Malay member of any of a large group of peoples comprising the majority population of the Malay Peninsula and archipelago, and also found in southern Thailand and coastal Sumatra and Borneo. Their language belongs to the western branch of the Austronesian family.

Malayalam southern Indian language, the official language of the state of Kerala. Malayalam is closely related to Tamil, also a member of the Dravidian language family; it is spoken by about 20 million people. Written records in Malayalam date from the 9th century AD.

Malay language member of the Western or Indonesian branch of the Malayo-Polynesian language family, used in the Malay Peninsula and many of the islands of Malaysia and Indonesia. The Malay language can be written in either Arabic or Roman scripts. The dialect of the southern Malay peninsula is the basis of both Bahasa Malaysia and Bahasa Indonesia, the official languages of Malaysia and Indonesia. Bazaar Malay is a widespread pidgin variety used for trading and shopping.

Malayo-Polynesian family of languages spoken in Malaysia, better known as *Austronesian.

Malay Peninsula southern projection of the continent of Asia, lying between the Strait of Malacca, which divides it from Sumatra, and the China Sea. The northern portion is partly in Myanmar (formerly Burma), partly in Thailand; the south forms part of Malaysia. The island of Singapore lies off its southern extremity.

Malaysia
National name: *Persekutuan Tanah Malaysia/ Federation of Malaysia*
Area: 329,759 sq km/127,319 sq mi
Capital: Kuala Lumpur
Major towns/cities: Johor Bahru, Ipoh, George Town (on Penang island), Kuala Terengganu, Kota Bahru, Petaling Jaya, Kelang, Kuching (on Sarawak), Kota Kinabalu (on Sabah)
Major ports: Kelang
Physical features: comprises peninsular Malaysia (the nine Malay states – Johore, Kedah, Kelantan, Negeri Sembilan, Pahang, Perak, Perlis, Selangor, Terengganu – plus Melaka and Penang); states of Sabah and Sarawak

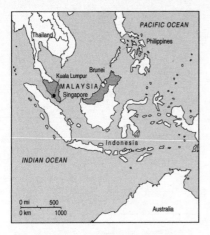

on the island of Borneo; and the federal territory of Kuala Lumpur; 75% tropical rainforest; central mountain range; Mount Kinabalu, the highest peak in southeast Asia, is in Sabah; swamps in east; Niah caves (Sarawak)

Head of state: Syed Sirajuddin bin al-Marhum Syed Putra Jamalullail from 2001

Head of government: Datuk Badawi from 2003

Political system: liberal democracy

Political executive: parliamentary

Political parties: New United Malays' National Organization (UMNO Baru), Malay-oriented nationalist; Malaysian Chinese Association (MCA), Chinese-oriented, conservative; Gerakan Party, Chinese-oriented, socialist; Malaysian Indian Congress (MIC), Indian-oriented; Democratic Action Party (DAP), multiracial but Chinese-dominated, left of centre; Pan-Malayan Islamic Party (PAS), Islamic; Semangat '46 (Spirit of 1946), moderate, multiracial

Currency: ringgit

GNI per capita (PPP): (US$) 8,280 (2002 est)

Exports: electronics and electrical machinery, palm oil, rubber, crude petroleum, machinery and transport equipment, timber, tin, textiles, chemicals. Principal market: USA 20.5% (2001)

Population: 24,425,000 (2003 est)

Language: Bahasa Malaysia (Malay; official), English, Chinese, Tamil, Iban, many local dialects

Religion: Muslim (official) about 53%, Buddhist 19%, Hindu, Christian, local beliefs

Life expectancy: 71 (men); 76 (women) (2000–05)

Chronology

1st century AD: Peoples of Malay peninsula influenced by Indian culture and Buddhism.

8th–13th centuries: Malay peninsula formed part of Buddhist Srivijaya Empire based in Sumatra.

14th century: Siam (Thailand) expanded to include most of Malay peninsula.

1403: Muslim traders founded port of Malacca (now Melaka), which became a great commercial centre, encouraging the spread of Islam.

1511: The Portuguese attacked and captured Malacca.

1641: The Portuguese were ousted from Malacca by the Dutch after a seven-year blockade.

1786: The British East India Company established a trading post on island of Penang.

1795–1815: Britain occupied the Dutch colonies after France conquered the Netherlands.

1819: Stamford Raffles of East India Company obtained Singapore from Sultan of Johore.

1824: Anglo-Dutch Treaty ceded Malacca to Britain in return for territory in Sumatra.

1826: British possessions of Singapore, Penang, and Malacca formed the Straits Settlements, ruled by the governor of Bengal; ports prospered and expanded.

1840: The Sultan of Brunei gave Sarawak to James Brooke, whose family ruled it as an independent state until 1946.

1851: Responsibility for Straits Settlements assumed by the governor general of India.

1858: British government, through India Office, took over administration of Straits Settlements.

1867: Straits Settlements became crown colony of British Empire.

1874: British protectorates established over four Malay states of Perak, Salangor, Pahang, and Negeri Sembilan, which federated in 1896.

1888: Britain declared protectorate over northern Borneo (Sabah).

late 19th century: Millions of Chinese and thousands of Indians migrated to Malaya to work in tin mines and on rubber plantations.

1909–14: Britain assumed indirect rule over five northern Malay states after agreement with Siam (Thailand).

1941–45: Japanese occupation.

1946: United Malay National Organization (UMNO) founded to oppose British plans for centralized Union of Malaya.

1948: Britain federated nine Malay states with Penang and Malacca to form the single colony of the Federation of Malaya.

1948–60: Malayan emergency: British forces suppressed insurrection by communist guerrillas.

1957: Federation of Malaya became independent with Prince Abdul Rahman (leader of UMNO) as prime minister.

1963: Federation of Malaya combined with Singapore, Sarawak, and Sabah to form Federation of Malaysia.

1963–66: 'The Confrontation' – guerrillas supported by Indonesia opposed federation with intermittent warfare.

1965: Singapore withdrew from the Federation of Malaysia.

1968: Philippines claimed sovereignty over Sabah.

1969: Malay resentment of Chinese economic dominance resulted in race riots in Kuala Lumpur.

1971: *Bumiputra* policies which favoured ethnic Malays in education and employment introduced by Tun Abul Razak of UMNO.

1981: Mahathir bin Muhammad (UMNO) became the prime minister; the government became increasingly dominated by Muslim Malays.

1987: Malay–Chinese relations deteriorated; over 100 opposition activists were arrested.

1991: An economic development policy was launched which aimed at 7% annual growth.

1997: The currency was allowed to float. Parts of Borneo and Sumatra were covered by thick smog for several weeks following forest-clearing fires.
1998: The repatriation of foreign workers commenced. Currency controls were introduced as the GDP contracted sharply.
1999: Mahathir bin Muhammad's ruling coalition party was elected to retain power. Tuanku Salehuddin Abdul Aziz Shan bin al-Marhum Hisamuddin Alam Shah was appointed president.
2000: Ex-deputy prime minister Anwar Ibrahim was found guilty of charges of sodomy by the high court and sentenced to nine-years' imprisonment, to be served in addition to the six-year sentence he received in April 1999 for corruption. The International Commission of Jurists condemned the verdict as politically motivated.
2001: Violent clashes between Malays and ethnic Indians.
2002: Harsh laws against illegal immigrants caused many foreign workers to leave.
2003: Prime Minister Muhammad stepped down after 22 years, and was succeeded by his deputy prime minister Abdullah Badawi.
2004: Badawi won the general election. Anwar Ibrahim was released from prison after the courts overturned his conviction for sodomy. Malaysia was spared the full impact of the tsunami, although there was loss of life and damage to infrastructure.
2005: Malaysia and Singapore settled a dispute over land reclamation in their border waters. After a four-month amnesty, extended after the tsunami, illegal immigrants were deported.

Malcolm four Celtic kings of Scotland, including:
Malcolm III (c. 1031–1093) called 'Canmore', King of Scotland from 1058, the son of Duncan I. He fled to England in 1040 when the throne was usurped by *Macbeth, but recovered southern Scotland and killed Macbeth in battle in 1057. In 1070 he married Margaret (c. 1045–1093), sister of Edgar Atheling of England; their daughter Matilda (d. 1118) married Henry I of England. Malcolm was killed at Alnwick while invading Northumberland, England.

Malcolm X (1926–1965) adopted name of Malcolm Little, US black nationalist leader. After converting to Islam, he joined the Nation of Islam sect, became a persuasive speaker about white exploitation of black people, and gained a large popular following, especially among black youth. He opposed the *civil-rights movement and, instead of integration and equality, advocated black separatism and self-dependence, using violent means if necessary for self-defence. His *Autobiography of Malcolm X*, written with Alex Haley, was published in 1965.

Maldives
National name: *Divehi Raajjeyge Jumhuriyya/ Republic of the Maldives*
Area: 298 sq km/115 sq mi
Capital: Malé
Physical features: comprises 1,196 coral islands, grouped into 12 clusters of atolls, largely flat, none bigger than 13 sq km/5 sq mi, average elevation 1.8 m/6 ft; 203 are inhabited
Head of state and government: Maumoon Abd Gayoom from 1978
Political system: authoritarian nationalist

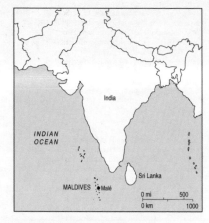

Political executive: unlimited presidency
Political parties: none; candidates elected on basis of personal influence and clan loyalties
Currency: rufiya
GNI per capita (PPP): (US$) 2,740 (2002 est)
Exports: marine products, (tuna bonito ('Maldive Fish')) clothing. Principal market: USA 44.2% (2000)
Population: 318,000 (2003 est)
Language: Divehi (a Sinhalese dialect; official), English, Arabic
Religion: Sunni Muslim
Life expectancy: 68 (men); 67 (women) (2000–05)
Chronology
12th century AD: Islam introduced by seafaring Arabs, who displaced the indigenous Dravidian population.
14th century: Ad-Din sultanate established.
1558–73: Under Portuguese rule.
1645: Became a dependency of Ceylon (Sri Lanka), which was ruled by the Dutch until 1796 and then by the British, with Sinhalese and Indian colonies being established.
1887: Became an internally self-governing British protectorate, which remained a dependency of Sri Lanka until 1948.
1932: The sultanate became an elected position when the Maldives' first constitution was introduced.
1953: Maldive Islands became a republic within the Commonwealth, as the ad-Din sultanate was abolished.
1954: Sultan restored.
1959–60: Secessionist rebellion in Suvadiva (Huvadu) and Addu southern atolls.
1965: Achieved full independence outside Commonwealth.
1968: Sultan deposed after referendum; republic reinstated with Ibrahim Nasir as president.
1975: The closure of a British airforce staging post on the southern island of Gan led to a substantial loss in income.
1978: The autocratic Nasir retired and was replaced by the progressive Maumoon Abd Gayoom.
1980s: Economic growth was boosted by the rapid development of the tourist industry.
1982: Rejoined the Commonwealth.

1985: Became a founder member of the South Asian Association for Regional Cooperation.

1988: A coup attempt by Sri Lankan mercenaries, thought to have the backing of former president Nasir, was foiled by Indian paratroops.

1998: Gayoom was re-elected for a further presidential term.

2003: President Gayoom was re-elected for a record sixth term in office with 90% of the vote in a referendum.

2004: Gayoom annouced planned constitutional change to limit presidential term and to allow the formation of political parties. There were violent pro-democracy demonstrations and a state of emergency was imposed. The Indian Ocean tsunami caused loss of life and severe damage to infrastructure.

Malé capital and chief atoll of the Maldives in the Indian Ocean; population (2000 est) 74,100. It lies 700 km/435 mi southwest of Sri Lanka and has an international airport which has helped the development of the tourist industry in recent decades. It trades in coconuts, copra, breadfruit, fish (especially tuna and bonito), and palm products. It is linked to Sri Lanka and India by regular steamship services.

Mali

National name: *République du Mali/Republic of Mali*

Area: 1,240,142 sq km/478,818 sq mi
Capital: Bamako
Major towns/cities: Mopti, Kayes, Ségou, Tombouctou, Sikasso
Physical features: landlocked state with River Niger and savannah in south; part of the Sahara in north; hills in northeast; Senegal River and its branches irrigate the southwest
Head of state: Amadou Toumani Touré from 2002
Head of government: Ousmane Issoufi Maïga from 2004
Political system: emergent democracy
Political executive: limited presidency
Political parties: Alliance for Democracy in Mali (ADEMA), left of centre; National Committee for Democratic Initiative (CNID), left of centre; Assembly for Democracy and Progress (RDP), left of centre; Civic Society and the Democracy and Progress Party (PDP), left of centre; Malian People's Democratic Union (UDPM), nationalist socialist
Currency: franc CFA

GNI per capita (PPP): (US$) 840 (2002 est)
Exports: gold, cotton, livestock, miscellaneous manufactured articles. Principal market: Thailand 17% (2001)
Population: 13,007,000 (2003 est)
Language: French (official), Bambara, other African languages
Religion: Sunni Muslim 80%, animist, Christian
Life expectancy: 48 (men); 49 (women) (2000–05)
Chronology
5th–13th centuries: Ghana Empire founded by agriculturist Soninke people, based on the Saharan gold trade for which Timbuktu became an important centre. At its height in the 11th century it covered much of the western Sahel, comprising parts of present-day Mali, Senegal, and Mauritania. Wars with Muslim Berber tribes from the north led to its downfall.
13th–15th centuries: Ghana Empire superseded by Muslim Mali Empire of Malinke (Mandingo) people of southwest, from which Mali derives its name. At its peak, under Mansa Musa in the 14th century, it covered parts of Mali, Senegal, Gambia, and southern Mauritania.
15th–16th centuries: Muslim Songhai Empire, centred around Timbuktu and Gao, superseded Mali Empire. It covered Mali, Senegal, Gambia, and parts of Mauritania, Niger, and Nigeria, and included a professional army and civil service.
1591: Songhai Empire destroyed by Moroccan Berbers, under Ahmad al-Mansur, who launched an invasion to take over western Sudanese gold trade and took control over Timbuktu.
18th–19th centuries: Niger valley region was divided between the nomadic Tuareg, in the area around Gao in the northeast, and the Fulani and Bambara kingdoms, around Macina and Bambara in the centre and southwest.
late 18th century: Western Mali visited by Scottish explorer Mungo Park.
mid-19th century: The Islamic Tukolor, as part of a jihad (holy war) conquered much of western Mali, including Fulani and Bambara kingdoms, while in the south, Samori Ture, a Muslim Malinke (Mandingo) warrior, created a small empire.
1880–95: Region conquered by French, who overcame Tukolor and Samori resistance to establish colony of French Sudan.
1904: Became part of the Federation of French West Africa.
1946: French Sudan became an overseas territory within the French Union, with its own territorial assembly and representation in the French parliament; the pro-autonomy Sudanese Union and Sudanese Progressive Parties founded in Bamako.
1959: With Senegal, formed the Federation of Mali.
1960: Separated from Senegal and became independent Republic of Mali, with Modibo Keita, an authoritarian socialist of the Sudanese Union party, as president.
1968: Keita replaced in army coup by Lt Moussa Traore, as economy deteriorated: constitution suspended and political activity banned.
1974: A new constitution made Mali a one-party state, dominated by Traore's nationalistic socialist Malian People's Democratic Union (UDPM), formed in 1976.
1979: More than a dozen were killed after a student strike was crushed.

1985: There was a five-day conflict with Burkina Faso over a long-standing border dispute which was mediated by the International Court of Justice.
late 1980s: Closer ties developed with the West and free-market economic policies were pursued, including privatization, as the Soviet influence waned.
1991: Violent demonstrations and strikes against one-party rule led to 150 deaths; Traore was ousted in a coup.
1992: A referendum endorsed a new democratic constitution. The opposition Alliance for Democracy in Mali (ADEMA) won multiparty elections; Alpha Oumar Konare was elected president. A peace pact was signed with Tuareg rebels fighting in northern Mali for greater autonomy.
1997: President Konare was re-elected.
2000: Mande Sidibe became prime minister.
2002: Amadou Toumani Touré was sworn in as president. It was the first time in Mali history that one constitutionally-elected president handed over to another. The government resigned and a new government of national unity was installed.
2004: The prime minister, Mohamed Ag Amani, resigned and was replaced by Ousmane Issoufi Maiga. A severe locust plague destroyed more than half of the cereal harvest.

Mali Empire Muslim state in northwestern Africa during the 7th–15th centuries. Thriving on its trade in gold, it reached its peak in the 14th century under Mansa Musa (reigned 1312–37), when it occupied an area covering present-day Senegal, the Gambia, Mali, and southern Mauritania. Mali's territory was similar to (though larger than) that of the Ghana Empire (see *Ghana, ancient), and gave way in turn to the *Songhai Empire.

mallard common wild duck from which domestic ducks were bred, found almost worldwide. The male can grow to a length of 60 cm/2 ft and usually has a glossy green head, white collar, and chestnut brown breast with a pale grey body, while the female is mottled brown. Mallards are omnivorous dabbling ducks. (Species *Anas platyrhynchos*, subfamily Anatinae, order Anseriformes.)

Mallarmé, Stéphane (1842–1898) French poet. A leader of the Symbolist school, he became known as a poet's poet for his condensed, hermetic verse and unorthodox syntax, reaching for the ideal world of the intellect. His belief that poetry should be evocative and suggestive was reflected in *L'Après-midi d'un faune/ Afternoon of a Faun* (1876; illustrated by Manet), which inspired the composer Debussy. Later works are *Poésies complètes/Complete Poems* (1887), *Vers et prose/ Verse and Prose* (1893), and the prose *Divagations/ Digressions* (1897).

Malle, Louis (1932–1995) French film director. His early work anticipated the New Wave. Working in both France and the USA, he made such films as *Le Feu follet/A Time to Live and a Time to Die* (1963), *Atlantic City* (1980), and *Damage* (1993).

mallee any of a group of small eucalyptus trees and shrubs with many small stems and thick underground roots that retain water. Before irrigation farming began, dense thickets of mallee characterized most of northwestern Victoria, Australia, known as the mallee region. (Genus *Eucalyptus*, family Myrtaceae.)

Mallorca *or* **Majorca** largest of the *Balearic Islands, belonging to Spain, in the western Mediterranean;

area 3,640 sq km/1,405 sq mi; population (2001 est) 702,100. The capital is Palma. The highest mountain on the island is Puig Mayor (1,445 m/4,741 ft). Industries include olives, figs, oranges, wine, brandy, timber, and sheep farming. Tourism is the mainstay of the economy. The inhabitants speak their own dialect of Catalan.

mallow any flowering plant of the mallow family, including the European common mallow (*M. sylvestris*), the tree mallow (*L. arborea*), marsh mallow (*A. officinalis*), and hollyhock (*A. rosea*). Most mallows have pink or purple flowers. (Genera *Malva*, *Lavatera*, and *Althaea*, family Malvaceae.)

malnutrition condition resulting from a defective diet where certain important food nutrients (such as proteins, vitamins, or carbohydrates) are absent. It can lead to deficiency diseases. A related problem is undernourishment. A high global death rate linked to malnutrition has arisen from famine situations caused by global warming, droughts, and the greenhouse effect, as well as by socio-political factors, such as alcohol and drug abuse, poverty, and war.

Malory, Thomas (*c.* 1410–1471) English author. He is known for the prose romance *Le Morte D'Arthur* (*c.* 1470), printed in 1485, which relates the exploits of King Arthur's knights of the Round Table and the quest for the *Holy Grail. He was knight of the shire from 1445.

Malouf, David George Joseph (1934–) Australian poet, novelist, and short-story writer. He is of Lebanese and English extraction. His poetry collections include *Neighbours in a Thicket* (1974), which won several awards, *Wild Lemons* (1980), and *First Things Last* (1980). Malouf's first novel *Johnno* (1975) deals with his boyhood in Brisbane. It was followed by *An Imaginary Life* (1978) and other novels, including *Fly Away Peter* (1982), *The Great World* (1990), *Remembering Babylon* (1993), and *Dream Stuff* (2000).

Malraux, André (Georges) (1901–1976) French writer, art critic, and politician. An active antifascist, he gained international renown for his novel *La Condition humaine/Man's Estate* (1933), set during the nationalist/ communist revolution in China in the 1920s. *L'Espoir/ Days of Hope* (1937) is set in Civil War Spain, where he was a bomber pilot in the International Brigade. In his revolutionary novels he frequently depicts individuals in situations where they are forced to examine the meaning of their own life. He also made an outstanding contribution to aesthetics with *La Psychologie de l'art* (1947–49), revised as *Les Voix du silence/The Voices of Silence* (1951).

malt in brewing, grain (barley, oats, or wheat) artificially germinated and then dried in a kiln. Malts are fermented to make beers or lagers, or fermented and then distilled to produce spirits such as whisky.

Malta
National name: *Repubblika ta'Malta/Republic of Malta*
Area: 320 sq km/124 sq mi
Capital: Valletta (and chief port)
Major towns/cities: Rabat, Birkirkara, Qormi, Sliema, Zejtun, Zabor
Major ports: Marsaxlokk, Valletta
Physical features: includes islands of Gozo 67 sq km/ 26 sq mi and Comino 3 sq km/1 sq mi
Head of state: Edward Fenech Adami from 2004
Head of government: Lawrence Gonzi from 2004

Political system: liberal democracy
Political executive: parliamentary
Political parties: Malta Labour Party (MLP), moderate, left of centre; Nationalist Party (PN), Christian, centrist, pro-European
Currency: Maltese lira
GNI per capita (PPP): (US$) 16,790 (2002 est)
Exports: machinery and transport equipment, manufactured articles (including clothing), beverages, chemicals, tobacco. Principal market: USA 20.2% (2001)
Population: 394,000 (2003 est)
Language: Maltese, English (both official)
Religion: Roman Catholic 98%
Life expectancy: 76 (men); 81 (women) (2000–05)
Chronology
7th century BC: Invaded and subjugated by Carthaginians from North Africa.
218 BC: Came under Roman control.
AD 60: Converted to Christianity by the apostle Paul.
395: On the division of the Roman Empire, became part of Eastern (Byzantine) portion, dominated by Constantinople.
870: Came under Arab rule.
1091: Arabs defeated by Norman Count Roger I of Sicily; Roman Catholic Church re-established.
1530: Handed over by Holy Roman Emperor Charles V to a religious military order, the Hospitallers (Knights of St John of Jerusalem).
1798–1802: Occupied by French.
1814: Annexed to Britain by the Treaty of Paris on condition that Roman Catholic Church was maintained and Maltese Declaration of Rights honoured.
later 19th century– early 20th century: Became vital British naval base, with famous dockyard that developed as the island's economic mainstay.
1942: Awarded the George Cross for valour in resisting severe Italian aerial attacks during World War II.
1947: Achieved self-government.
1956: Referendum approved MLP's proposal for integration with UK. Plebiscite opposed and boycotted by right-of-centre Nationalist Party (PN).
1958: MLP rejected final British integration proposal.
1964: Independence achieved from Britain, within Commonwealth. A ten-year defence and economic-aid treaty with the UK was signed.

1971: Prime Minister Mintoff adopted a policy of nonalignment and declared the 1964 treaty invalid; negotiations began for leasing NATO base in Malta.
1972: Seven-year NATO agreement signed.
1974: Became a republic.
1979: British military base closed; closer links were established with communist and Arab states, including Libya.
1987: Edward Fenech Adami (PN) was narrowly elected prime minister; he adopted a more pro-European and pro-American policy stance than the preceding administration.
1990: A formal application was made for European Community membership.
1998: The PN was returned to power after a snap election, with Edward Fenech Adami returning as prime minister.
1999: Guido de Marco was elected president.
2003: A referendum resulted in a narrow majority of voters in favour of accession to the European Union (EU) in 2004. The PN won the general election.
2004: Edward Fenech Adami of the PN retired and Lawrence Gonzi replaced him as prime minister. Malta joined the EU.

Maltese dog breed of long-coated lap dog. Its white coat is straight and silky and parted from head to tail and the short tail is doubled into the coat on the back. Maltese dogs have dark eyes, long drooping ears, and small feet. The ideal maximum height is 25 cm/10 in, and the weight is 3–4 kg/6.5–9 lb.

Malthus, Thomas Robert (1766–1834) English economist and social scientist. His fame rested on what was in effect a long pamphlet, *An Essay on the Principle of Population, As It Affects the Future Improvement of Society* (1798), in which he observed that the growth of population is ultimately limited by the food supply. He supported this common thesis with the metaphor that population, when allowed to increase without limit, increases in a *geometrical* ratio, while the food supply can at best increase in an *arithmetical* ratio; so, whatever the plausible rate of increase of the food supply, an unchecked multiplication of human beings could be disastrous.

Maluku *or* **Moluccas** group of Indonesian islands; area 74,500 sq km/28,764 sq mi; population (2000 est) 1,990,600. The capital is Ambon, on the island of Ambon. As the Spice Islands, they were formerly part of the Dutch East Indies; the southern Moluccas have repeatedly attempted secession from the Indonesian republic since 1949, with sectarian fighting continuing in the islands into the 21st century.

mamba either of two venomous snakes belonging to the cobra family, found in Africa south of the Sahara. Unlike cobras, they are not hooded. (Genus *Dendroaspis*, family Elapidae.)

Mameluke member of a powerful political class that dominated Egypt from the 13th century until their massacre in 1811 by Mehmet Ali.

Mamet, David (Alan) (1947–) US dramatist, writer, and director. His plays use vivid, freewheeling language and urban settings. *American Buffalo* (1975), about a gang of hopeless robbers, was his first major success. *Glengarry Glen Ross* (1983) was a dark depiction of US business ethics. He made his film-making debut directing *House of Games* (1987). He also wrote and directed *The Spanish Prisoner* (1997) and *State and Main* (2000). In 2000 he published a collection of essays, *Jafsie and John Henry*, and a novel, *Wilson: A Consideration of the Sources*.

mammal any of a large group of warm-blooded vertebrate animals characterized by having *mammary glands in the female; these are used for suckling the young. Other features of mammals are *hair (very reduced in some species, such as whales); a middle ear formed of three small bones (ossicles); a lower jaw consisting of two bones only; seven vertebrae in the neck; and no nucleus in the red blood cells. (Class Mammalia.) Mammals are divided into three groups: **placental mammals**, where the young develop inside the mother's body, in the *uterus, receiving nourishment from the blood of the mother via the *placenta; **marsupials**, where the young are born at an early stage of development and develop further in a pouch on the mother's body where they are attached to and fed from a nipple; and **monotremes**, where the young hatch from an egg outside the mother's body and are then nourished with milk. The monotremes are the least evolved and have been largely displaced by more sophisticated marsupials and placentals, so that there are only a few types surviving (platypus and echidna). Placentals have spread to all parts of the globe, and where placentals have competed with marsupials, the placentals have in general displaced marsupial types. However, marsupials occupy many specialized niches in South America and, especially, Australasia. According to the Red List of endangered species published by the World Conservation Union for 1996, 25% of mammal species are threatened with extinction.

mammary gland in female mammals, a milk-producing gland derived from epithelial cells underlying the skin, active only after the production of young. In all but monotremes (egg-laying mammals), the mammary glands terminate in teats which aid infant suckling. The number of glands and their position vary between species. In humans there are 2, in cows 4, and in pigs between 10 and 14.

mammography X-ray procedure used to screen for breast cancer. It can detect abnormal growths at an early stage, before they can be seen or felt. It is most effective for screening women over 35, as breast tissue is too dense in younger women.

Mammon evil personification of wealth and greed; originally a Syrian god of riches, cited in the New Testament as opposed to the Christian god.

mammoth extinct elephant, remains of which have been found worldwide. Some were 50% taller than modern elephants; others were much smaller. (Genus *Mammuthus* (or **Elephas**).)

Managua capital, largest city, and chief industrial and commercial centre of Nicaragua, and capital of Managua department, it is situated on the southern shore of Lake Managua, 45km/28 mi from the Pacific coast, on the Pan-American Highway, and 138 km/86 mi from the main port of Corinto; population (2002 est) 1,106,600. One-fifth of the nation's population is resident here. Managua produces around 60% of the nation's goods by value including tobacco, textiles, cement, cotton, drinks, soap, and processed foods. Surrounding lowlands are very fertile, supporting maize, beans, sugar cane, and banana plantations.

manatee any of a group of plant-eating aquatic mammals found in marine bays and sluggish rivers, usually in thick, muddy water. They have flippers as forelimbs, no hindlimbs, and a short rounded and flattened tail used for swimming. The marine manatees can grow up to about 4.5 m/15 ft long and weigh up to 600 kg/1,323 lb. (Genus *Trichechus*, family Trichechidae, order Sirenia.)

Manaus capital of Amazonas federal unit (state), northwest Brazil, on the Río Negro, 16 km/10 mi from its confluence with the River Solimó which forms the River Amazon; population (2000 est) 1,394,700. It is the industrial trading and commercial centre of the state, and its chief port, although 1,600 km/1,000 mi from the Atlantic. Hardwood timber, Brazil nuts, and rubber are the main exports, and there are sawmills and an oil refinery. Manaus is an important free-trade zone (established in 1966) that is a major producer of goods such as television sets, video recorders, and motorcycles, which it distributes nationwide.

Manchester metropolitan district of Greater Manchester, and city in northwest England, on the River Irwell, 50 km/31 mi east of Liverpool; population (1998 est) 429,800. A financial and manufacturing centre, its industries include banking, insurance, and printing; the production of cotton and man-made textiles, petro-chemicals, rubber, paper, machine tools, and processed foods; and heavy, light, and electrical engineering. Tourism has become increasingly important. It is linked to the River Mersey and the Irish Sea by the **Manchester Ship Canal**, opened in 1894, although only one dock remains open.

Manchester, Greater metropolitan county of northwest England, created in 1974; in 1986 most of the functions of the former county council were transferred to metropolitan district councils. **area:** 1,290 sq km/498 sq mi **towns and cities:** Manchester, Bolton, Bury, Oldham, Rochdale, Salford, Stockport, Tameside, Trafford, Wigan **features:** Manchester Ship Canal links it with the River Mersey and the sea; Old Trafford cricket ground near Stretford, and the football ground of Manchester United **population:** (2000 est) 2,585,800.

Manchester terrier breed of smooth-haired black-and-tan terrier. Manchester terriers have a long, wedge-shaped head, small dark eyes, and V-shaped ears, hanging close to the head. The usual weight is 8 kg/17.5 lb and the height 38–41 cm/15–16 in.

Manchu also known as **Qing**, last ruling dynasty in China, from 1644 until its overthrow in 1912; its last emperor was the infant *P'u-i. Originally a nomadic people from Manchuria, they established power through a series of successful invasions from the north, then granted trading rights to the USA and Europeans, which eventually brought strife and the *Boxer Rebellion.

Manchuria European name for the northeastern region of China, comprising the provinces of Heilongjiang, Jilin, and Liaoning. It was united with China by the Manchu dynasty in 1644, but as the Chinese Empire declined, Japan and Russia were rivals for its control. The Russians were expelled after the *Russo-Japanese War 1904–05, and in 1932 Japan consolidated its position by creating a puppet state, **Manchukuo**, nominally led by the Chinese pretender to the throne

Henry P'u-i. At the end of World War II the Soviets occupied Manchuria in a two-week operation in August 1945. Japanese settlers were expelled when the region was returned to Chinese control.

Mandalay chief city of the Mandalay division of Myanmar (formerly Burma) and second city of the county, on the River Irrawaddy, about 495 km/370 mi north of the capital Yangon; population (2001 est) 1,037,000. The city is a major centre of commerce and of transport by road, rail, river, and air. Industries include tourism, tea packing, silk weaving, brewing, and food processing, as well as crafts such as wood carving and the fashioning of gold and silver objects. It is also a leading centre of Buddhist culture.

Mandarin (Sanskrit *mantrin* 'counsellor') standard form of the *Chinese language. Historically it derives from the language spoken by **mandarins**, Chinese imperial officials, from the 7th century onwards. It is used by 70% of the population and taught in schools of the People's Republic of China.

mandate in history, a territory whose administration was entrusted to Allied states by the League of Nations under the Treaty of Versailles after World War I. Mandated territories were former German and Turkish possessions (including Iraq, Syria, Lebanon, and Palestine). When the United Nations replaced the League of Nations in 1945, mandates that had not achieved independence became known as *trust territories.

Mandela, Nelson (Rolihlahla) (1918–) South African politician and lawyer, and the country's first post-apartheid president 1994–99. He was president of the African National Congress (ANC) 1991–97. Imprisoned from 1964, as organizer of the then banned ANC, he became a symbol of unity for the worldwide anti-apartheid movement. In 1990 he was released and, following the first universal-suffrage elections in 1994, was sworn in as South Africa's first post-apartheid president after the ANC won 63% of the vote in universal-suffrage elections. He stepped down as president in 1999 and was succeeded by ANC president, Thabo Mbeki. In 1993 he shared the Nobel Prize for Peace with South African president F W de Klerk for their work towards dismantling apartheid and negotiating the transition to a democracy.

Mandelstam, Osip Emilevich (1891–1938) Russian poet. He was a leader of the Acmeist movement. The son of a Jewish merchant, he was sent to a concentration camp by the communist authorities in the 1930s, and died there. His posthumously published work, with its classic brevity, established his reputation as one of the greatest 20th-century Russian poets.

mandolin plucked string instrument that flourished 1600–1800. It has four to six pairs of strings (courses) and is tuned like a violin. The fingerboard is fretted to regulate intonation. It takes its name from its almond-shaped body (Italian *mandorla* 'almond'). Vivaldi composed two concertos for the mandolin in about 1736.

mandragora *or* **mandrake** any of a group of almost stemless Old World plants with narcotic (pain-killing and sleep-inducing) properties, belonging to the nightshade family. They have large leaves, pale blue or violet flowers, and round berries known as devil's apples. (Genus *Mandragora*, family Solanaceae.)

mandrake another name for the plant *mandragora.

mandrill large West African forest-living baboon, active mainly on the ground. It has large canine teeth like the drill (*M. leucophaeus*), to which it is closely related. The nose is bright red and the cheeks are striped with blue; the thick skin of the buttocks is also red, and the fur is brown, apart from a yellow beard. (Species *Mandrillus sphinx*.)

Manes in ancient Rome, the spirits of the dead, worshipped as divine and sometimes identified with the gods of the underworld (Dis and Proserpine), hence the inscription DMS (*dis manibus sacrum*) on many Roman tombs.

Manet, Edouard (1832–1883) French painter. One of the foremost French artists of the 19th century, he is often regarded as the father of modern painting. Rebelling against the academic tradition, he developed a clear and unaffected realist style that was one of the founding forces of *Impressionism. His subjects were mainly contemporary, such as *A Bar at the Folies-Bergère* (1882; Courtauld Art Gallery, London).

manganese chemical symbol Mn, hard, brittle, grey-white metallic element, atomic number 25, relative atomic mass 54.9380. It resembles iron (and rusts), but it is not magnetic and is softer. It is used chiefly in making steel alloys, also alloys with aluminium and copper. It is used in fertilizers, paints, and industrial chemicals. It is a necessary trace element in human nutrition. The name is old, deriving from the French and Latin forms of Magnesia, a mineral-rich region of Italy.

mango evergreen tree belonging to the cashew family, native to India but now widely cultivated for its large oval fruits in other tropical and subtropical areas, such as the West Indies. (*Mangifera indica*, family Anacardiaceae.)

mangrove any of several shrubs and trees, especially of the mangrove family, found in the muddy swamps of tropical and subtropical coastlines and estuaries. By sending down aerial roots from their branches, they rapidly form close-growing mangrove thickets. Their timber is resistant to water penetration and damage by marine worms. Mangrove swamps are rich breeding grounds for fish and shellfish, but these habitats are being destroyed in many countries. (Genera *Rhizophora* and *Avicennia*, families Rhizophoraceae (mangrove) and Avicenniaceae (related).)

Manhattan island of the city of *New York, USA, forming most of a borough; population (2000 est) 1,537,200. It is 20 km/12.5 mi long and 4 km/2.5 mi wide, and lies between the Hudson and East rivers. The rocks from which it is formed rise to a height of more than 73 m/240 ft in the north of the island. Manhattan Island is bounded on the north and northeast by the Harlem River and Spuyten Duyvil Creek (which separate it from the Bronx); on the south by Upper New York Bay; on the west by the Hudson River (which separates it from New Jersey); and on the east by the East River (which separates it from Queens and Brooklyn). The borough of Manhattan also includes a small port at the Bronx mainland and several islands in the East River. Manhattan is the economic hub of New York City, although there are large residential and industrial areas here also. It includes the Wall Street business centre, Broadway and its theatres, Carnegie Hall (1891), the Empire State Building (1931), the United Nations headquarters (1952), Madison Square Garden, and Central Park. The twin towers of the World Trade Center collapsed on 11 September 2001, minutes after each was struck by hijacked aircraft piloted by terrorists. The death toll was estimated at around 3,000.

Manhattan Project code name for the development of the *atom bomb in the USA in World War II, to which the physicists Enrico Fermi and J Robert Oppenheimer contributed.

manic depression *or* **bipolar disorder** mental disorder characterized by recurring periods of either *depression or mania (inappropriate elation, agitation, and rapid thought and speech) or both. Sufferers may be genetically predisposed to the condition. Some cases have been improved by taking prescribed doses of *lithium.

Manichaeism religion founded by the Persian prophet Mani (Latinized as Manichaeus, *c.* 216–276). Despite persecution, Manichaeism spread and flourished until about the 10th century. Based on the concept of dualism, it held that the material world is evil, an invasion of the spiritual realm of light by the powers of darkness; particles of divine light imprisoned in evil matter were to be rescued by messengers such as Jesus, and finally by Mani himself.

Manila industrial port and capital of the Philippines, in the southwest of the island of Luzon, where the River Pasig enters Manila Bay; population of city (2000 est) 1,581,100; metropolitan area including *Quezon City (2000 est) 9,932,600. Industries include textiles, tobacco, distilling, chemicals, shipbuilding, timber, and food processing.

manioc another name for the plant *cassava.

Manipur state of northeast India; bordered south and east by Myanmar; area 22,356 sq km/8,632 sq mi; population (2001 est) 2,388,600 (30% are hill tribes such as Nagas and Kukis). The capital is Imphal. The state is mostly wooded and mountainous (mainly over 2,000 m/6,500 ft), with a central valley containing Imphal. Features include Loktak Lake, and the state is the original Indian home of polo. Industries include textiles, cement, and handloom weaving. Agricultural products include rice, grain, fruit, vegetables, and sugar. Languages spoken in the state are Manipuri and English. 70% of the population are Hindu.

Man, Isle of Scottish Gaelic **Ellan Vannin**, island in the Irish Sea, a dependency of the British crown, but not part of the UK; area 570 sq km/220 sq mi; population (2001 est) 76,300, almost 50% of which lives in the capital Douglas and nearby Onchan. Other towns and cities include Ramsey, Peel, and Castletown. Industries include light engineering products, agriculture, and fishing. Tourism has declined in importance and has been replaced by financial services as the island's principal industry. The Isle of Man was Norwegian until 1266, when it was ceded to Scotland. It came under UK administration in 1765.

Manitoba (Algonquian *Manitou* 'great spirit') province in central Canada, the easternmost of the Prairie Provinces. Bounded to the south, on the 49th parallel, by the US states of Minnesota (in the east) and North Dakota (in the west); to the west by Saskatchewan; to the north, on the 60th parallel, by the Northwest Territories and Hudson Bay; and to the east by Ontario; area 647,797 sq km/251,000 sq mi; population (2001 est)

1,150,000. The capital is *Winnipeg, and other towns and cities include Brandon, Thompson, St Boniface, Churchill, Flin Flon, Portage La Prairie, and The Pas. Lakes Winnipeg, Winnipegosis, and Manitoba (area 4,700 sq km/1,814 sq mi) are in the province, which is 50% forested. Industries include production of grain and food-processing; manufacture of machinery; fur-trapping; fishing; mining of nickel, zinc, copper, and the world's largest deposits of caesium (a metallic element used in the manufacture of photocells).

Manley, Michael (Norman) (1924–1997) Jamaican trade unionist, centre-left politician, leader of the socialist People's National Party from 1969, and prime minister (1972–80 and 1989–92). A charismatic orator, he was the son of Norman Manley, founder of the socialist People's National Party (PNP), and became leader of the PNP on his father's death in 1969. After a landslide victory in 1972, his 'democratic socialist' programme was beset by economic depression, losing him the election in 1980. He was re-elected on a more moderate manifesto in 1989, but ill health forced his resignation as prime minister in March 1992 and retirement from politics. He was succeeded as premier by Percival Patterson.

Mann, Heinrich (1871–1950) German novelist. He left Nazi Germany in 1937 with his brother Thomas *Mann and went to the USA. His books include *Im Schlaraffenland/In the Land of Cockaigne* (1901) and *Professor Unrat/The Blue Angel* (1904; widely known as a film), depicting the sensual downfall of a schoolteacher. His novels show Germany in its new, vulgar prosperity from the end of the 19th century to the period just before World War I, and his best works were suppressed for a time.

Mann, Thomas (1875–1955) German novelist and critic. A largely subjective artist, he drew his themes from his own experiences and inner thoughts. He was constantly preoccupied with the idea of death in the midst of life and with the position of the artist in relation to society. His first novel was *Buddenbrooks* (1901), a saga of a merchant family which traces through four generations the gradual growth of decay as culture slowly saps virility. *Der Zauberberg/The Magic Mountain* (1924), a vast symbolic work on the subject of disease in sick minds and bodies, and also the sickness of Europe, probes the question of culture in relation to life. Notable among his works of short fiction is 'Der Tod in Venedig/Death in Venice' (1913). He was awarded the Nobel Prize for Literature in 1929.

manna sweetish exudation obtained from many trees such as the ash and larch, and used in medicine. The Old Testament (Exodus ch. 16) relates that God provided manna for the Israelites in the desert when there was no other food. The manna of the Bible is thought to have been from the tamarisk tree, or a form of lichen.

Mannerism in a general sense, any affectation (unnatural imitation or exaggeration) of a style or manner in art, though the term is usually used with reference to Italian painting in the 16th century and represents a distinct phase between the art of the High Renaissance and the rise of baroque. It was largely based on an admiration for *Michelangelo and a consequent exaggeration of the emphasis of his composition and the expressive distortion of his figures.

manometer instrument for measuring the pressure of liquids (including human blood pressure) or gases. In its basic form, it is a U-tube partly filled with coloured liquid. Greater pressure on the liquid surface in one arm will force the level of the liquid in the other arm to rise. A difference between the pressures in the two arms is therefore registered as a difference in the heights of the liquid in the arms.

manor basic economic unit in *feudalism in Europe, established in England under the Norman conquest. It consisted of the lord's house and cultivated land, land rented by free tenants, land held by villagers, common land, woodland, and waste land.

Man Ray US photographer, painter, and sculptor; see Man *Ray.

Mansfield, Katherine (1888–1923) pen-name of Kathleen Beauchamp, New Zealand writer. She lived most of her life in England. Her delicate artistry emerges not only in her volumes of short stories – such as *In a German Pension* (1911), *Bliss* (1920), and *The Garden Party* (1923) – but also in her letters and journal. She developed the technique of the short story in much the same way as Irish writer James Joyce and English writer Virginia Woolf developed the novel; in particular Mansfield recognized that fiction survives if it recreates life, and she was a pioneer of the central character as narrator.

manslaughter in English law, the unlawful killing of a human being in circumstances less culpable than *murder – for example, when the killer suffers extreme provocation, is in some way mentally ill (diminished responsibility), did not intend to kill but did so accidentally in the course of another crime or by behaving with criminal recklessness, or is the survivor of a genuine suicide pact that involved killing the other person.

manta another name for the *devil ray, a large fish.

Mantegna, Andrea (c. 1431–1506) Italian painter and engraver. He painted religious and mythological subjects, his works noted for their *all'antica* style taking elements from Roman antique architecture and sculpture, and for their innovative use of perspective.

mantis any of a group of carnivorous insects related to cockroaches. There are about 2,000 species of mantis, mainly tropical; some can reach a length of 20 cm/8 in. (Family Mantidae, order Dictyoptera.)

mantle intermediate zone of the Earth between the *crust and the *core, accounting for 82% of the Earth's volume. The crust, made up of separate tectonic *plates, floats on the mantle which is made of dark semi-liquid rock that is rich in magnesium and silicon. The temperature of the mantle can be as high as 3,700 °C/6,692 °F. Heat generated in the core causes convection currents in the semi-liquid mantle; rock rises and then slowly sinks again as it cools, causing the movements of the tectonic plates. The boundary (junction) between the mantle and the crust is called the *Mohorovicic discontinuity, which lies at an average depth of 32 km/20 mi. The boundary between the mantle and the core is called the Gutenburg discontinuity, and lies at an average depth of 2,900 km/1,813 mi.

mantra in Hindu and Buddhist belief, a word or phrase repeatedly intoned during meditation to assist concentration and develop spiritual power; for example,

'Om' or 'Aum', which represents the names of Brahma, Vishnu, and Shiva. Followers of a guru may receive their own individual mantra.

Manu in Hindu mythology, the founder of the human race, who was saved by *Brahma from a deluge.

Maoism form of communism based on the ideas and teachings of the Chinese communist leader *Mao Zedong. It involves an adaptation of *Marxism to suit conditions in China and apportions a much greater role to agriculture and the peasantry in the building of socialism, thus effectively bypassing the capitalist (industrial) stage envisaged by Marx. In addition, Maoism stresses ideological, as well as economic, transformation, based on regular contact between party members and the general population.

Maori (New Zealand *Maui* 'native' or 'indigenous') member of the Polynesian people of New Zealand. They number 435,000, about 15% of the total population, and around 89% live in the North Island. Maori civilization had particular strengths in warfare, cultivation, navigation, and wood- and stonework. Speechmaking and oral history, as well as woodcarving, were the main cultural repositories before the European introduction of writing, and Maori mythology and cosmology were highly developed. Their language, Maori, belongs to the eastern branch of the Austronesian family. The Maori Language Act 1987 recognized Maori as an official language of New Zealand.

Mao Tse-tung alternative transcription of *Mao Zedong.

Mao Zedong (or Mao Tse-tung) (1893–1976) Chinese communist politician and theoretician, leader of the Chinese Communist Party (CCP) 1935–76. Mao was a founder of the CCP in 1921, and became its leader in 1935. He organized the *Long March 1934–35 and the war of liberation 1937–49, following which he established a People's Republic and communist rule in China. He was state president until 1959, and headed the CCP until his death. His influence diminished with the failure of his 1958–60 *Great Leap Forward, but he emerged dominant again during the 1966–69 *Cultural Revolution, which he launched in order to promote his own antibureaucratic line and to purge the party of 'revisionism'.

map diagrammatic representation of an area, for example part of the Earth's surface or the distribution of the stars. Modern maps of the Earth are made using satellites in low orbit to take a series of overlapping stereoscopic photographs from which a three-dimensional image can be prepared. The earliest accurate large-scale maps appeared about 1580.

maple any of a group of deciduous trees with lobed leaves and green flowers, followed by two-winged fruits, or samaras. There are over 200 species, chiefly in northern temperate regions. (Genus *Acer*, family Aceraceae.)

map projection way of showing the Earth's spherical surface on a flat piece of paper. The most common approach has been to redraw the Earth's surface within a rectangular boundary. The main weakness of this is that countries in high latitudes are shown disproportionately large. The most famous cylindrical projection is the *Mercator projection, which dates from 1569. Although it gives an exaggerated view of the

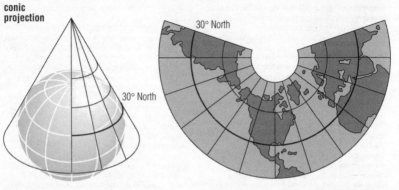

azimuthal projection

North Pole

North Pole

cylindrical projection

Equator

conic projection

30° North

30° North

map projection Three widely used map projections. If a light were placed at the centre of a transparent Earth, the shapes of the countries would be thrown as shadows on a sheet of paper. If the paper is flat, the azimuthal projection results; if it is wrapped around a cylinder or in the form of a cone, the cylindrical or conic projections result.

size of northern continents, it is the best map for navigation because a constant bearing appears as a straight line. In 1973 German historian Arno Peters devised the **Peters projection** in which the countries of the world retain their relative areas. In other projections, lines of longitude and latitude appear distorted, or the Earth's surface is shown as a series of segments joined along the Equator. In 1992 the US physicist Mitchell Feigenbaum devised the **optimal conformal** projection, using a computer program designed to take data about the boundary of a given area and calculate the projection that produces the minimum of inaccuracies.

Maputo formerly **Lourenço Marques** (until 1975), capital of Mozambique, and Africa's second-largest port, on Delagoa Bay; population (2000 est) 1,019,000. Linked by road and rail with Zimbabwe, Swaziland, and South Africa, it is a major outlet for these countries, as well as for Mozambique. Industries include brewing, shipbuilding, and textile and cement manufacture. Minerals, steel, textiles, processed foods, and furniture are exported.

Maquis French *resistance movement that fought against the German occupation during World War II.

marabou African stork, about 120 cm/4 ft tall, with a bald head, long heavy bill, black back and wings and white underparts, and an inflatable throat pouch. It eats snakes, lizards, insects, and carrion. The bald head avoids clogging the plumage when the stork feeds on carcasses left by predators such as lions. (Species *Leptoptilos crumeniferus*, family Ciconiidae, order Ciconiiformes.)

Maradona, Diego Armando (1960–) Argentine footballer. One of the outstanding players of the 1980s, he won 91 international caps, and helped his country to two successive World Cup finals, of which they won the first in 1986. Despite his undoubted talent, his career was dogged by a series of drugs scandals, notably his disqualification from the 1994 World Cup after failing a drugs test.

Marat, Jean Paul (1743–1793) Swiss-born French Revolutionary leader, physician, and journalist. He was elected to the National Convention in 1792, where, as leader of the radical Montagnard faction, he carried on a long struggle with the right-wing *Girondins, which resulted in their overthrow in May 1793. In July he was murdered in his bath by Charlotte Corday, a Girondin supporter.

Maratha *or* **Mahratta** member of a people living mainly in Maharashtra state, western India. There are about 40 million speakers of Marathi, a language belonging to the Indo-European family. The Marathas are mostly farmers, and practise Hinduism. In the 17th and 18th centuries the Marathas formed a powerful military confederacy in rivalry with the Mogul emperors. The latter's Afghan allies defeated the Marathas at Panipat in 1761, and, after a series of wars with the British 1779–1871, most of their territory was annexed. During the *Indian Mutiny and the rise of the movement of independence, the Marathas became a symbol of Hindu revival.

marathon athletics endurance race over 42.195 km/26 mi 385 yd. It was first included in the Olympic Games in Athens in 1896. The distance varied until it was standardized in 1924. More recently, races have been opened to wider participation, including social runners as well as those competing at senior level.

Marathon, Battle of battle fought in September 490 BC at the start of the Persian Wars in which the Athenians and their allies from Plataea resoundingly defeated the Persian king Darius' invasion force. Fought on the Plain of Marathon about 40 km/25 mi northeast of Athens, it is one of the most famous battles of antiquity.

marble rock formed by metamorphosis of sedimentary *limestone. It takes and retains a good polish, and is used in building and sculpture. In its pure form it is white and consists almost entirely of calcite ($CaCO_3$). Mineral impurities give it various colours and patterns. Carrara, Italy, is known for white marble.

Marc, Franz (1880–1916) German expressionist painter. He was associated with Wassily Kandinsky in founding the *Blaue Reiter movement. Animals played an essential part in his view of the world, and bold semi-abstracts of red and blue animals, particularly horses, are characteristic of his work.

Marches boundary areas of England with Wales, and England with Scotland. For several centuries from the time of William the Conqueror, these troubled frontier regions were held by lords of the Marches, those on the Welsh frontier called Marcher Lords, sometimes called *marchiones*, and those on the Scottish border known as earls of March. The first Marcher Lord was Roger de Mortimer (about 1286–1330); the first earl of March, Patrick Dunbar (died in 1285).

Marcian (396–457) Eastern Roman emperor 450–457. He was a general who married Pulcheria, sister of Theodosius II; he became emperor on Theodosius' death. He convened the Council of Chalcedon (the fourth Ecumenical Council of the Christian Church) in 451 and refused to pay tribute to Attila the Hun.

Marconi, Guglielmo (1874–1937) Italian electrical engineer and pioneer in the invention and development of radio. In 1895 he achieved radio communication over more than a mile, and in England in 1896 he conducted successful experiments that led to the formation of the company that became Marconi's Wireless Telegraph Company Ltd. He shared the Nobel Prize for Physics in 1909 for the development of wireless telegraphy.

Marco Polo Venetian traveller and writer; see Marco *Polo.

Marcos, Ferdinand Edralin (1917–1989) Filipino right-wing politician, dictator-president 1965–86, when he was forced into exile in Hawaii by a popular front led by Corazon *Aquino.

Marcus Aurelius (AD 121–180) adopted name of Marcus Annius Verus, Roman emperor from 161 and Stoic philosopher who wrote the philosophical *Meditations*. He fought a series of campaigns against the Germanic tribes on the Rhine–Danube frontier, known collectively as the Marcomannic Wars, and died in Pannonia where he had gone to drive back the invading Marcomanni.

Marengo, Battle of during the Napoleonic Wars, defeat of the Austrians on 14 June 1800 by the French army under Napoleon Bonaparte, as part of his Italian campaign, near the village of Marengo in Piedmont, Italy. It was one of Napoleon's greatest victories which resulted in the Austrians ceding northern Italy to France.

Margaret of Anjou (1430–1482) Queen of England from 1445, wife of *Henry VI of England. After the outbreak of the Wars of the *Roses in 1455, she acted as the leader of the Lancastrians, but was defeated and captured at the battle of Tewkesbury in 1471 by Edward IV.

Margaret, St (c. 1045–1093) Queen of Scotland, the granddaughter of King Edmund Ironside of England. She went to Scotland after the Norman Conquest, and soon after married Malcolm III. The marriage of her daughter Matilda to Henry I united the Norman and English royal houses.

margarine butter substitute made from animal fats and/or vegetable oils. The French chemist Hippolyte Mège-Mouries invented margarine in 1889. Today, margarines are usually made with vegetable oils, such as soya, corn, or sunflower oil, giving a product low in saturated fats (see *polyunsaturate) and fortified with vitamins A and D.

marginal cost pricing in economics, the setting of a price based on the additional cost to a firm of producing one more unit of output (the marginal cost), rather than the actual average cost per unit (total production costs divided by the total number of units produced). In this way, the price of an item is kept to a minimum, reflecting only the extra cost of labour and materials.

marginal theory in economics, the study of the effect of increasing a factor by one more unit (known as the marginal unit). For example, if a firm's production is increased by one unit, its costs will increase also; the increase in costs is called the marginal cost of production. Marginal theory is a central tool of microeconomics.

marginal utility in economics, the measure of additional satisfaction (utility) gained by a consumer who receives one additional unit of a product or service. The concept is used to explain why consumers buy more of a product when the price falls.

margrave German title (equivalent of marquess) for the 'counts of the march', who guarded the frontier regions of the Holy Roman Empire from Charlemagne's time. Later the title was used by other territorial princes. Chief among these were the margraves of Austria and of Brandenburg.

Margrethe II (1940–) Queen of Denmark from 1972, when she succeeded her father Frederick IX. In 1967, she married the French diplomat Count Henri de Laborde de Monpezat, who took the title Prince Hendrik. Her heir is Crown Prince Frederick (1968–).

marguerite European plant belonging to the daisy family. It is a shrubby perennial with white daisylike flowers. Marguerite is also the name of a cultivated variety of *chrysanthemum. (*Leucanthemum vulgare*, family Compositae.)

Mariana Islands *or* **Marianas** archipelago in the northwest Pacific, east of the Philippines, divided politically into *Guam (an unincorporated territory of the USA) and the *Northern Mariana Islands (a commonwealth of the USA).

Mariana Trench lowest region on the Earth's surface; the deepest part of the sea floor. The trench is 2,400 km/ 1,500 mi long and is situated 300 km/200 mi east of the Mariana Islands, in the northwestern Pacific Ocean. Its deepest part is the gorge known as the Challenger Deep, which extends 11,034 m/36,210 ft below sea level.

Maria Theresa (1717–1780) Empress of Austria from 1740, when she succeeded her father, the Holy Roman Emperor Charles VI; her claim to the throne was challenged and she became embroiled, first in the War of the *Austrian Succession 1740–48, then in the *Seven Years' War 1756–63; she remained in possession of Austria but lost Silesia. The rest of her reign was peaceful and, with her son Joseph II, she introduced social reforms.

Marie Antoinette (1755–1793) Queen of France from 1774. She was the fourth daughter of Empress Maria Theresa of Austria and the Holy Roman Emperor Francis I, and married *Louis XVI of France in 1770. Her devotion to the interests of Austria, reputation for extravagance, and supposed connection with the scandal of the Diamond Necklace made her unpopular, and helped to provoke the *French Revolution of 1789. She was tried for treason in October 1793 and guillotined.

Marie de' Medici (1573–1642) Queen of France, wife of Henry IV from 1600, and regent (after his murder) for their son Louis XIII. She left the government to her favourites, the Concinis, until Louis XIII seized power and executed them in 1617. She was banished but, after she led a revolt in 1619, *Richelieu effected her reconciliation with her son. When she attempted to oust him again in 1630, she was exiled.

Mari El *or* **Mariy El** autonomous republic of the Russian Federation; area 23,200 sq km/8,950 sq mi; population (1990) 754,000 (47% Russian, 43% ethnic Mari). The capital is Yoshkar-Ola. The Volga flows through the southwest of the republic, 60% of which is forested. It lies west of the Ural Mountains. Industries include timber, paper, grain, flax, potatoes, fruit; metalworking, food processing, machine tool production, and the manufacture of artificial leather.

marigold any of several plants belonging to the daisy family, including pot marigold (*C. officinalis*) and the tropical American *T. patula*, commonly known as French marigold. (Genera *Calendula* and *Tagetes*, family Compositae.)

marijuana dried leaves and flowers of the hemp plant *cannabis, used as a drug; it is illegal in most countries. It is eaten or inhaled and causes euphoria, distortion of time, and heightened sensations of sight and sound. Mexico is the world's largest producer.

marimba musical instrument with wooden bars like a *xylophone, but much larger and with a larger range and much lower pitch. The instrument has metal tubes under the keys that both amplify and sustain the sound.

Marinetti, (Emilio) Filippo Tommaso (1876–1944) Italian author. In 1909 he published *Manifesto del Futurismo*, the first manifesto of *Futurism, exhorting the youth of Italy to break with tradition in art, poetry, and the novel and face the challenges of a new machine age. He illustrated his theories in *Mafarka le futuriste: Roman africaine/Mafarka the Futurist: African Novel* (1909). His best-known work is the *Manifesto technico della letteratura futuristica/Technical Manifesto of Futurist Literature* (1912; translated 1971). He also wrote plays, a volume on theatrical practice (1916), and a volume of poems *Guerra sola igiene del mondo/ War the Only Hygiene of the World* (1915).

maritime law that part of the law dealing with the sea: in particular, fishing areas, ships, and navigation. Seas are divided into **internal waters** governed by a state's internal laws (such as harbours, inlets); **territorial waters** (the area of sea adjoining the coast over which a state claims rights); the **continental shelf** (the seabed and subsoil that the coastal state is entitled to exploit beyond the territorial waters); and the **high seas**, where international law applies.

Marivaux, Pierre Carlet de Chamblain de (1688–1763) French novelist and dramatist. His sophisticated comedies deal primarily with love and include *Le Jeu de l'amour et du hasard/The Game of Love and Chance* (1730) and *Les Fausses Confidences/False Confidences* (1737). He wrote two novels: *La Vie de Marianne/The Life of Marianne* (1731–41), the study of a young girl written with much psychological insight, which has autobiographical elements; and *Le Paysan parvenu/The Fortunate Villager* (1735–36), which gives a broader picture of French society. Both were left incomplete. Marivaux was a master of brilliant dialogue, full of veiled avowals and subtle indications, and he gave the word *marivaudage* (oversubtle lovers' conversation) to the French language.

marjoram aromatic herb belonging to the mint family. Wild marjoram (*O. vulgare*) is found in both Europe and Asia and has become naturalized in the Americas; the sweet marjoram (*O. majorana*) used in cooking is widely cultivated. (Genus *Origanum* or *Marjorana*, family Labiatae.)

Mark in Celtic legend, king of Cornwall, uncle of *Tristan, and suitor and husband of *Isolde.

Mark Antony (c. 83–30 BC) Latin **Marcus Antonius**, Roman politician and soldier who was the last serious rival to Octavian's (later Augustus) domination of the Roman world. He served under Julius *Caesar in Gaul and during the civil war when he commanded the left wing at the final battle of Pharsalus. He was consul with Caesar in 44 when he tried to secure for him the title of king. After Caesar's assassination, he formed the Second Triumvirate with Octavian and Lepidus. In 42 he defeated Brutus and Cassius at Philippi. He took Egypt as his share of the empire and formed a liaison with the Egyptian queen Cleopatra, but returned to Rome in 40 to marry Octavia, the sister of Octavian. In 32 the Senate declared war on Cleopatra, and Antony, who had combined forces with Cleopatra, was defeated by Octavian at the Battle of Actium in 31. He returned to Egypt and committed suicide.

market capitalization market value of a company, based on the market price of all its issued securities – a price that would be unlikely to apply, however, if a bid were actually made for control of them.

market forces in economics, the forces of demand (a want backed by the ability to pay) and supply (the willingness and ability to supply).

market gardening farming system that specializes in the commercial growing of vegetables, fruit, or flowers. It is an intensive agriculture with crops often being grown inside greenhouses on small farms.

marketing promoting goods and services to consumers. In the modern business world, marketing plays an increasingly larger role in determining company policy, influencing product development, pricing, methods of distribution, advertising, and promotion techniques.

Markievicz, Constance Georgina, Countess Markievicz (1868–1927) born Constance Georgina Gore Booth, Irish socialist, revolutionary, and politician. Founder of Na Fianna, the republican youth organization, in 1909, she joined the Irish Citizen Army and took part in the *Easter Rising of 1916; her resulting death sentence was commuted. In 1918 she was elected to Westminster as a Sinn Fein candidate (technically the first British woman MP), but did not take her seat, instead serving as minister for labour in the first Dáil Éireann (then the illegal republican parliament) 1919–22.

Mark, St (lived 1st century AD) In the New Testament, Christian apostle and evangelist whose name is given to the second Gospel. It was probably written AD 65–70, and used by the authors of the first and third Gospels. He is the patron saint of Venice, and his emblem is a winged lion. His feast day is 25 April.

marl crumbling sedimentary rock, sometimes called **clayey limestone**, including various types of calcareous *clays and fine-grained *limestones. Marls are often laid down in freshwater lakes and are usually soft, earthy, and of a white, grey, or brownish colour. They are used in cement-making and as fertilizer.

Marlborough, John Churchill, 1st Duke of Marlborough (1650–1722) English soldier, created a duke in 1702 by Queen Anne. He was granted the Blenheim mansion in Oxfordshire in recognition of his services, which included defeating the French army outside Vienna in the Battle of Blenheim in 1704, during the War of the *Spanish Succession.

Marley, Bob (1945–1981) born Robert Nesta Marley, Jamaican reggae singer and songwriter. His songs, many of which were topical and political, increased the popularity of reggae worldwide in the 1970s. They include 'Get Up, Stand Up' (1973) and 'No Woman No Cry' (1974); his albums include *Natty Dread* (1975) and *Exodus* (1977).

marlin or **spearfish** any of several open-sea fishes known as billfishes. Some 2.5 m/7 ft long, they are found in warmer waters and have elongated snouts and high-standing dorsal (back) fins. Members of the family include the **sailfish** (*Istiophorus platypterus*), the fastest of all fishes over short distances – reaching speeds of 100 kph/62 mph – and the **blue marlin** (*Makaira nigricans*), highly prized as a 'game' fish. (Family Istiophoridae, order Perciformes.)

Marlowe, Christopher (1564–1593) English poet and dramatist. His work includes the blank-verse (written in unrhymed verse) plays *Tamburlaine the Great* in two parts (1587–88), *The Jew of Malta* (c. 1591), *Edward II* (c. 1592) and *Dr Faustus* (c. 1594), the poem *Hero and Leander* (1598), and a translation of parts of *Ovid's *Amores*. Marlowe transformed the new medium of English blank verse into a powerful, melodic form of expression.

Marmara, Sea of Turkish **Marmara Denizi**; formerly **Prokonessos**, small inland sea in Turkey, connected to the Black Sea by the Bosporus and to the Aegean Sea by the Dardanelles, separating the continents of Europe and Asia; area 11,160 sq km/4,300 sq mi. In parts it reaches depths of over 1,200 m/3,936 ft. There are several islands in the sea that contain white-marble quarries, the largest of which is Marmara.

marmoset any of a group of small tree-dwelling monkeys found in South and Central America;

some reach a body length of only 15 cm/6 in. Most species have characteristic tufted ears, clawlike nails, and a handsome tail, which is not prehensile (it cannot be used to grip branches in the same way as the arms and legs). Some marmosets are known as tamarins. (Genus *Callithrix* and related genera, family Callithricidae.)

marmot any of several large burrowing rodents belonging to the squirrel family. There are about 15 species, distributed throughout Canada and the USA, and from the Alps to the Himalayas. They eat plants and some insects, and live in colonies, make burrows (one to each family), and hibernate in winter (alpine marmots hibernate for six months of the year). In North America they are called **woodchucks** or **groundhogs**. (Genus *Marmota*, family Sciuridae.)

Marne, Battles of the in World War I, two unsuccessful German offensives in northern France. In the **First Battle** 6–9 September 1914, German advance was halted by French and British troops under the overall command of the French general Jospeh Joffre; in the **Second Battle** 15 July–4 August 1918, the German advance was defeated by British, French, and US troops under the French general Henri Pétain, and German morale crumbled.

Maronite member of a Christian sect deriving from refugee Monothelites (Christian heretics) of the 7th century. They were subsequently united with the Roman Catholic Church and number about 400,000 in Lebanon and Syria, with an equal number scattered in southern Europe and the Americas.

Marquesas Islands French **Iles Marquises**, group of mountainous volcanic islands in French Polynesia (a French overseas territory), lying in the southern Pacific Ocean 1,184 km/736 mi northeast of Tahiti; area 1,270 sq km/490 sq mi; population (2002 est) 8,700. The administrative headquarters is Atuona on Hiva Oa. The largest settlement is Taiohae on Hiva Oa; other islands include Kuku Hiva, Ua Pa, Ua Huka, Tahuata, and Fatu Hiva. The islands were annexed by France in 1842. The main products are copra, tobacco, breadfruit, and vanilla.

marquess *or* **marquis** title and rank of a nobleman who in the British peerage ranks below a duke and above an earl. The wife of a marquess is a marchioness.

Márquez, Gabriel García Colombian novelist; see Gabriel *García Márquez*.

marram grass coarse perennial grass that flourishes in sandy areas. Because of its tough, creeping roots, it is widely used to hold coastal dunes in place. (*Ammophila arenaria*, family Gramineae.)

marriage legally or culturally sanctioned union of one man and one woman (monogamy); one man and two or more women (polygamy); one woman and two or more men (polyandry). The basis of marriage varies considerably in different societies (romantic love in the West; arranged marriages in some other societies), but most marriage ceremonies, contracts, or customs involve a set of rights and duties, such as care and protection, and there is generally an expectation that children will be born of the union to continue the family line and maintain the family property. In the 1990s, the concept of marriage was extended in some countries to include the blessing or registration of homosexual relationships.

marrow *or* **vegetable marrow** trailing vine that produces large pulpy fruits, used as vegetables and in preserves; the young fruits of one variety are known as courgettes (US zucchini). (*Cucurbita pepo*, family Cucurbitaceae.)

Mars fourth planet from the Sun. It is much smaller than Venus or Earth, with a mass 0.11 that of Earth. Mars is slightly pear-shaped, with a low, level northern hemisphere, which is comparatively uncratered and geologically 'young', and a heavily cratered 'ancient' southern hemisphere. **mean distance from the Sun:** 227.9 million km/141.6 million mi **equatorial diameter:** 6,780 km/4,210 mi **rotation period:** 24 hours 37 minutes **year:** 687 Earth days **atmosphere:** 95% carbon dioxide, 3% nitrogen, 1.5% argon, and 0.15% oxygen. Red atmospheric dust from the surface whipped up by winds of up to 450 kph/280 mph accounts for the light pink sky. The surface pressure is less than 1% of the Earth's atmospheric pressure at sea level **surface:** the landscape is a dusty, red, eroded lava plain. Mars has white polar caps (water ice and frozen carbon dioxide) that advance and retreat with the seasons **satellites:** two small satellites: Phobos and Deimos.

Mars *or* **Mavors** *or* **Mamers** in Roman mythology, the god of war (**Mars Gradivus**), depicted as a fearless warrior. The month of March is named after him. He was identified with the Greek *Ares*, but achieved greater status.

Marseille chief seaport and second city of France, and administrative centre of the *département* of Bouches-du-Rhône and of the *Provence-Alpes-Côte d'Azur* region, situated on the Golfe du Lion on the Mediterranean Sea; population (2002 est) 815,100, conurbation 1,532,400. Industries include chemicals, metallurgy, shipbuilding, and food processing, as well as oil-refining at the massive industrial complex of Fos-sur-Mer to the west.

marsh low-lying wetland. Freshwater marshes are common wherever groundwater, surface springs, streams, or run-off cause frequent flooding, or more or less permanent shallow water. A marsh is alkaline whereas a *bog* is acid. Marshes develop on inorganic silt or clay soils. Rushes are typical marsh plants. Large marshes dominated by papyrus, cattail, and reeds, with standing water throughout the year, are commonly called *swamps*. Near the sea, *salt marshes* may form.

Marshall, George Catlett (1880–1959) US general and diplomat. He was army chief of staff in World War II, secretary of state 1947–49, and secretary of defence September 1950–September 1951. He was awarded the Nobel Prize for Peace in 1953 for initiating the *Marshall Plan* for European economic recovery in 1947.

Marshall Islands
National name: *Majol/Republic of the Marshall Islands*
Area: 181 sq km/70 sq mi
Capital: Dalap-Uliga-Darrit (on Majuro atoll)
Major towns/cities: Ebeye (the only other town)
Physical features: comprises the Ratak and Ralik island chains in the West Pacific, which together form an archipelago of 31 coral atolls, 5 islands, and 1,152 islets
Head of state and government: Kessai Note from 2000
Political system: liberal democracy
Political executive: limited presidency

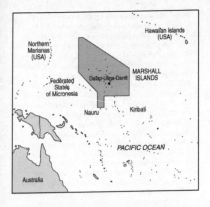

Political parties: no organized party system, but in 1991 an opposition grouping, the Ralik Ratak Democratic Party, was founded to oppose the ruling group
Currency: US dollar
GNI per capita (PPP): (US$) 4,820 (2002 est)
Exports: coconut products, trochus shells, copra, handicrafts, fish, live animals. Principal market: USA 71.2% (2000)
Population: 53,000 (2003 est)
Language: Marshallese, English (both official)
Religion: Christian (mainly Protestant) and Baha'i
Life expectancy: 64 (men); 68 (women) (2001 est)
Chronology
after c. 1000 BC: Micronesians first settled the islands.
1529: Visited by Spanish navigator Miguel de Saavedra and thereafter came under Spanish influence.
1875: Spanish rule formally declared in face of increasing encroachment by German traders.
1885: German protectorate established.
1914: Seized by Japan on the outbreak of World War I.
1920–44: Administered under League of Nations mandate by Japan and vigorously colonized.
1944: Japanese removed after heavy fighting with US troops during World War II.
1946–63: Eniwetok and Bikini atolls used for US atom-bomb tests; islanders later demanded rehabilitation and compensation for the damage.
1947: Became part of United Nations (UN) Pacific Islands Trust Territory, administered by USA.
1979: Amata Kabua was elected president as internal self-government was established.
1986: The Compact of Free Association with the USA granted the islands self-government, with the USA retaining the responsibility for defence and security until 2001.
1990: UN trust status was terminated.
1991: Independence was agreed with Kabua as president; UN membership was granted.
2000: Kessai H Note was elected as president.
2001: A US-funded claims tribunal determined the compensation to be paid for damage caused by nuclear testing.
2003: A new Compact of Free Association was signed with the USA.
2004: Kessai H Note of the United Democratic Party began a second four-year term as president.

Marshall Plan programme of US economic aid to Europe, set up at the end of World War II, totalling $13.3 billion throughout the life of the programme from 1948 to 1952 (equivalent to more than $88 billion late 1990s dollars). Post-war Europe was in a state of economic collapse and physical ruin and the USA, as the world's richest nation, intended to resurrect the European economy and combat the perceived danger of a communist takeover in Europe. Officially known as the European Recovery Program, it was announced by Secretary of State George C *Marshall in a speech at Harvard in June 1947, but it was in fact the work of a State Department group led by Dean Acheson.

marsh gas gas consisting mostly of *methane. It is produced in swamps and marshes by the action of bacteria on dead vegetation.

marsh marigold plant belonging to the buttercup family, known as the kingcup in the UK and as the cowslip in the USA. It grows in moist, sheltered places and has brilliant yellow five-sepalled flowers. (*Caltha palustris*, family Ranunculaceae.)

marsh rose shrub native to South Africa, which grows to 1–4 m/3–13 ft high. It is under threat, partly because its beautiful flowers are frequently picked, but also because of fungi, probably introduced by footwear or equipment, and by changes in management practice that have prevented periodic fires which are necessary for seed germination. Ironically, numbers of the shrub are now so low that uncontrolled fires could wipe out the remaining adult specimens. Although protected, they remain highly threatened. (*Orothamnus zeyheri*.)

Mars Observer NASA space probe launched in 1992 to orbit Mars and survey the planet, its atmosphere, and the polar caps over two years. The probe was also scheduled to communicate information from the robot vehicles delivered by Russia's Mars 94 mission. The US$980 million project miscarried, however, when the probe stopped transmitting in August 1993 after a suspected explosion in its orbital insertion engine.

Marston Moor, Battle of battle fought in the English Civil War on 2 July 1644 on Marston Moor, 11 km/7 mi west of York. The Royalists were conclusively defeated by the Parliamentarians and Scots.

marsupial (Greek *marsupion* 'little purse') mammal in which the female has a pouch where young (born tiny and immature) are carried for a considerable time after birth. Marsupials include omnivorous, herbivorous, and carnivorous species, among them the kangaroo, wombat, opossum, phalanger, bandicoot, dasyure, and wallaby.

Marsyas in Greek mythology, a Phrygian *satyr who found the flute discarded by the goddess *Athena and challenged *Apollo to a musical contest judged by the *Muses. On losing, he was flayed alive, his blood sourcing the River Marsyas.

marten small bushy-tailed carnivorous mammal belonging to the weasel family. Martens live in North America, Europe, and temperate regions of Asia, and are agile tree climbers. (Genus *Martes*, family Mustelidae.)

Martial, (Marcus Valerius Martialis) (c. AD 41–c. 104) Latin poet and epigrammatist. Born in Bilbilis, Spain, Martial settled in Rome in AD 64, where he lived a life of poverty and dependence. His poetry, often obscene, is keenly observant of all classes in contemporary Rome. Of his works the following survive: about 33 poems from *Liber Spectaculorum*, published in AD 80 to commemorate the opening of the Colosseum; two collections of short mottoes entitled *Xenia* and *Apophoreta*, (AD 84–85); and 12 books of *Epigrams*, published in AD 86–102.

martial arts any of several styles of armed and unarmed combat developed in the East from ancient techniques and arts. Common martial arts include aikido, *judo, *jujitsu, *karate, kendo, and *kung fu.

martial law replacement of civilian by military authorities in the maintenance of order.

martin any of several species of birds belonging to the swallow family. (Family Hirundinidae, order Passeriformes.)

Martinique French island in the West Indies (Lesser Antilles); area 1,079 sq km/417 sq mi; population (1999 est) 381,427. The capital is *Fort-de-France. The island features several active volcanoes; a major eruption of the volcano Mont Pelée in 1902 destroyed the city of Saint-Pierre, which was the largest city on the island. Agricultural products include sugar, cocoa, rum, bananas, pineapples, vanilla, and tobacco, although the tourist industry is now more important than agriculture. Petroleum products, cement, and processed foods are also manufactured. The official language is French, with Creole also spoken.

Martinu, Bohuslav Jan (1890–1959) Czech composer. He settled in New York after the Nazi occupation of Czechoslovakia in 1939. His music is voluble, richly expressive, and has great vitality. His works include the operas *Julietta* (1937) and *The Greek Passion* (1959), symphonies, and chamber music.

Marvell, Andrew (1621–1678) English *metaphysical poet and satirist. In 'To His Coy Mistress' (1650–52) and 'An Horatian Ode upon Cromwell's Return from Ireland' (1650) he produced, respectively, the most searching seduction and political poems in the language. He was committed to the Parliamentary cause, and was Member of Parliament for Hull from 1659. He devoted his last years mainly to verse *satire and prose works attacking repressive aspects of the state and government. Today his reputation rests mainly on a small number of skilful and graceful but perplexing and intriguing poems, which were published after his death as *Miscellaneous Poems* (1681).

Marx, Karl Heinrich (1818–1883) German philosopher, economist, and social theorist whose account of class change through conflict, 'the materialist conception of history' is known as historical, or dialectical, materialism (see *Marxism). His *Das *Kapital/Capital* (1867–95) is the fundamental text of Marxist economics, and his systematic theses on class struggle, history, and the importance of economic factors in politics have exercised an enormous influence on later thinkers and political activists.

Marx Brothers Team of US film comedians: the silent Adolph **Harpo** (from the harp he played) (1888–1964); Julius **Groucho** (from his temper) (1890–1977); Leonard **Chico** (from the 'chicks' – women – he chased) (1891–1961); Milton **Gummo** (from his gumshoes, or galoshes) (1892–1977), who left the team before they began making films; and Herbert **Zeppo** (born at the time of the first zeppelins) (1901–1979), part of the team until 1935. They made a total of 13 zany films 1929–49

including *Animal Crackers* (1930), *Monkey Business* (1931), *Duck Soup* (1933), *A Night at the Opera* (1935), *A Day at the Races* (1937), and *Go West* (1940).

Marxism philosophical system, developed by the 19th-century German social theorists *Marx and *Engels, also known as **dialectical materialism**, under which matter gives rise to mind (materialism) and all is subject to change (from dialectic; see *Hegel). As applied to history, it supposes that the succession of feudalism, capitalism, socialism, and finally the classless society is inevitable. The stubborn resistance of any existing system to change necessitates its complete overthrow in the **class struggle** – in the case of capitalism, by the proletariat – rather than gradual modification. See *communism.

Marxism–Leninism term used by the Soviet dictator Stalin and his supporters to define their own views as the orthodox position of *Marxism as a means of refuting criticism. It has subsequently been employed by other communist parties as a yardstick for ideological purity.

Mary Queen of Scots (1542–1587) Queen of Scotland (1542–67). Also known as **Mary Stuart**, she was the daughter of James V. Mary's connection with the English royal line from Henry VII made her a threat to her cousin Elizabeth I, especially as she represented a champion of the Catholic cause. She was married three times. After her forced abdication she was imprisoned but escaped in 1568 to England. Elizabeth I held her prisoner, while the Roman Catholics, who regarded Mary as rightful queen of England, formed many conspiracies to place her on the throne, and for complicity in one of these she was executed. Regarded by some as the pawn of the people who surrounded her, she remains a powerful figure in history and literature. Her life is portrayed in the tragedy *Maria Stuart* (1800) by Schiller and in Walter Scott's popular historical novel *The Abbot* (1820).

Mary two queens of England:

Mary I (1516–1558) called 'Bloody Mary', Queen of England from 1553. She was the eldest daughter of Henry VIII and Catherine of Aragón. When Edward VI died, Mary secured the crown without difficulty in spite of the conspiracy to substitute Lady Jane *Grey. In 1554 Mary married Philip II of Spain, and as a devout Roman Catholic obtained the restoration of papal supremacy and sanctioned the persecution of Protestants (see *Reformation, **England**). She was succeeded by her half-sister Elizabeth I.

Mary II (1662–1694) Queen of England, Scotland, and Ireland from 1688. She was the Protestant elder daughter of the Catholic *James II, and in 1677 was married to her cousin *William of Orange. After the *Glorious Revolution of 1688 she accepted the crown jointly with William.

Maryland called the **Old Line State** or **Free State**, state of eastern USA bordered to the north by *Pennsylvania, along the *Mason–Dixon Line, to the east by *Delaware, to the south by *Virginia, and to the south and west by *West Virginia; area 25,315 sq km/ 9,774 sq mi; population (2000) 5,296,500; capital Annapolis. The Coastal Plain and *Chesapeake Bay dominate the eastern half of the state, while plateaux, valleys, and ridges occupy the west, the two regions being divided by the area known as the Fall Line.

Maryland shares most of the Delmarva Peninsula with West Virginia, and its southern boundary is mainly defined by the *Potomac River. At the point where the Anacostia River joins the Potomac is the *District of Columbia (DC), which was carved out of Maryland and Virginia in 1790. Maryland's most populous city is *Baltimore, 95 km/60 mi to the northeast of Washington, DC. The Baltimore–Washington Consolidated Metropolitan Statistical Area contains 90% of Maryland's population, many of whom live in the major cities of Columbia, Silver Spring, Dundalk, and Bethesda. US federal agencies, defence contractors, and biotechnology, chemical, electronics, and software industries are located here. Other economic activities include tourism, boatbuilding, and the processing of poultry, dairy foods, fish, and shellfish. Maryland was originally home to several Algonquian Indian peoples, including the Piscataway, Accohannock, Assateague, Nanticoke, and Pocomoke. The first European settlement was established on Chesapeake Bay by the English in 1634. One of the original *Thirteen Colonies, Maryland ratified the US Constitution in 1788, becoming the 7th state to join the Union.

Mary of Guise (1515–1560) also known as **Mary of Lorraine**, French-born second wife of James V of Scotland from 1538, and 1554–59 regent of Scotland for her daughter *Mary Queen of Scots. A Catholic, she moved from reconciliation with Scottish Protestants to repression, and died during a Protestant rebellion in Edinburgh.

Mary of Modena (1658–1718) born Marie Beatrice d'Este, Queen consort of England and Scotland. She was the daughter of the Duke of Modena, Italy, and second wife of James, Duke of York, later James II, whom she married in 1673. The birth of their son James Francis Edward Stuart was the signal for the revolution of 1688 that overthrew James II. Mary fled to France.

Masaccio, Tommaso di Giovanni di Simone Guidi (1401–c. 1428) Florentine painter, one of the major figures of the early Italian Renaissance. His frescoes in the Brancacci Chapel of Santa Maria del Carmine, Florence (1425–28) show a decisive break with traditional styles. He was the first painter to apply the scientific laws of perspective, newly discovered by the architect Brunelleschi, and achieved a sense of space and volume that gives his pictures a sculptural quality.

Masada rock fortress 396 m/1,300 ft above the western shore of the Dead Sea, Israel. Site of the Hebrews' final stand in their revolt against the Romans (AD 66–73). After withstanding a year-long siege, the Hebrew population of 953 committed mass suicide rather than be conquered and enslaved.

Masai or **Maasai** member of an East African people whose territory is divided between Tanzania and Kenya. They number about 250,000, and speak a Nilotic language belonging to the Nilo-Saharan family. Traditionally they are warriors and pastoral nomads, but much of their land was taken over by European colonists and today there is considerable pressure on them from the Kenyan government to settle as farmers.

Masaryk, Tomáš Garrigue (1850–1937) Czechoslovak nationalist politician. He directed the revolutionary movement against the Austrian Empire, founding with Edvard *Beneš and Milan Stefanik the Czechoslovak National Council. In 1918 he was elected first president of the newly formed Czechoslovak Republic. Three times re-elected, he resigned in 1935 in favour of Beneš.

Masefield, John (1878–1967) English poet and novelist. His early years in the merchant navy inspired *Salt Water Ballads* (1902) and two further volumes of poetry, and several adventure novels; he also wrote children's books, such as *The Midnight Folk* (1927) and *The Box of Delights* (1935), as well as plays. *The Everlasting Mercy* (1911), characterized by its forcefully colloquial language, and *Reynard the Fox* (1919) are long verse narratives. He was poet laureate from 1930.

maser acronym for **microwave amplification by stimulated emission of radiation**, in physics, a high-frequency microwave amplifier or oscillator in which the signal to be amplified is used to stimulate excited atoms into emitting energy at the same frequency. Atoms or molecules are raised to a higher energy level and then allowed to lose this energy by radiation emitted at a precise frequency. The principle has been extended to other parts of the electromagnetic spectrum as, for example, in the *laser.

Maseru capital of Lesotho, on the Caledon River at the border with Free State in South Africa; population (2002 est) 169,200 (city), 483,100 (urban area). Founded in 1869 by the Basotho chief Mshweshwe I, it is a centre for trade in livestock, wool, hides, and grain, and for light manufacturing and food processing. The city, which retained its position as capital at independence in 1966, is the home of Lesotho Agricultural College (1955), and the National University of Lesotho (1975) is at nearby Roma.

masochism desire to subject oneself to physical or mental pain, humiliation, or punishment, for erotic pleasure, to alleviate guilt, or out of destructive impulses turned inward. The term is derived from Leopold von Sacher-Masoch.

Mason, James (Neville) (1909–1984) English film actor. He portrayed romantic villains in British films of the 1940s. After *Odd Man Out* (1947) he worked in the USA, often playing intelligent but troubled, vulnerable men, notably in *A Star Is Born* (1954). In 1960 he returned to Europe, where he made *Lolita* (1962).

Mason–Dixon Line in the USA, the boundary line between Maryland and Pennsylvania (latitude 39° 43′ 26.3″ N), named after Charles Mason (1730–1787) and Jeremiah Dixon (died 1777), English astronomers and surveyors who surveyed it 1763–67. It is popularly seen as dividing the North from the South.

masque spectacular court entertainment with a fantastic or mythological theme in which music, dance, and extravagant costumes and scenic design figured larger than plot. Originating in Italy, where members of the court actively participated in the performances, the masque reached its height of popularity at the English court between 1600 and 1640, with the collaboration of Ben *Jonson as writer and Inigo *Jones as stage designer. John Milton also wrote masque verses. Composers included Thomas Campion, John Coperario, Henry Lawes, William *Byrd, and Henry Purcell.

Mass in music, a setting of the music for the main service of the Roman Catholic Church. The items of the Mass are sung in Latin and fall into two groups: the **Ordinary** (the items of the Mass are invariable, regardless of day or season) consists of the *Kyrie*,

Gloria, Credo, Sanctus with *Benedictus*, and *Agnus Dei*; the **Proper** (the items of the Mass are 'proper' to the day or season) consists of additional matter namely the Introit, Gradual, Alleluia or Tract, Offertory, and Communion). A notable example of the Ordinary of the Mass is J S Bach's *Mass in B Minor* (about 1748).

mass in physics, quantity of matter in a body as measured by its inertia, including all the particles of which the body is made up. Mass determines the acceleration produced in a body by a given force acting on it, the acceleration being inversely proportional to the mass of the body. The mass also determines the force exerted on a body by *gravity on Earth, although this attraction varies slightly from place to place (the mass itself will remain the same). In the SI system, the base unit of mass is the kilogram.

Massachusetts officially the Commonwealth of Massachusetts; called **Bay State** or **Old Colony State**, (American Indian 'great mountain place') state of northeastern USA, a *New England state and the sixth smallest state in the nation; bounded by the Atlantic Ocean on the east and southeast, *Rhode Island and *Connecticut to the south, *New York to the west, and *Vermont and *New Hampshire to the north; area 20,306 sq km/7,8407,840 sq mi; population (2000) 6,349,100; capital and largest city *Boston. It is nicknamed Bay State because of the early settlement on *Cape Cod Bay, and Old Colony State due to its historical significance. The state includes part of the Taconic Mountains, the valley of the Housatonic River, the Berkshire Massif, known as the Berkshires, and the northeasternmost section of the Atlantic Coastal Plain, including the Cape Cod peninsula. The Massachusetts economy is based on the service industry, and high-tech and electrical industries are also significant. Agricultural products include cranberries, apples, and dairy goods. Towns include Worcester, Springfield, Lowell, Cambridge, Brockton, New Bedford, Fall River, Lynn, and Quincy. One of the *Thirteen Colonies, the state is a region of great significance to US history, being the point of disembarkation for the *Mayflower Pilgrims, as well as the site of key conflicts in the *American Revolution. Massachusetts entered the Union in 1788 as the 6th of the original 13 states.

massage manipulation of the soft tissues of the body, the muscles, ligaments, and tendons, either to encourage the healing of specific injuries or to produce the general beneficial effects of relaxing muscular tension, stimulating blood circulation, and improving the tone and strength of the skin and muscles.

Massawa or **Mesewa** or **Massaua** second biggest town and main port in Eritrea, situated on a small sterile coral island in the Red Sea, 200 m/656 ft from the mainland; population (1995 est) 49,300. It lies 65 km/40 mi northeast of Asmara, the largest town of Eritrea. Activities within the port include salt production, fishing, fish and meat processing, and cement manufacture. Exports include oil seed, coffee, and cattle. It is one of the hottest inhabited places in the world, the temperature reaching 46 °C/115 °F in May.

mass–energy equation German-born US physicist Albert *Einstein's equation $E = mc^2$, denoting the equivalence of mass and energy. In SI units, E is the energy in joules, m is the mass in kilograms, and c, the speed of light in a vacuum, is in metres per second.

Massenet, Jules Emile Frédéric (1842–1912) French composer of operas. His work is characterized by prominent roles for females, sincerity, and sentimentality. Notable works are *Manon* (1884), *Le Cid* (1885), and *Thaïs* (1894); among other works is the orchestral suite *Scènes pittoresques* (1874). He was professor of composition at the Paris Conservatory 1878–96.

mass extinction event that produces the extinction of many species at about the same time. One notable example is the boundary between the Cretaceous and Tertiary periods (known as the K–T boundary) that saw the extinction of the dinosaurs and other large reptiles, and many of the marine invertebrates as well. Mass extinctions have taken place frequently during Earth's history.

Massif Central upland region of south-central France with mountains and plateaux; area 93,000 sq km/36,000 sq mi, highest peak Puy de Sancy, 1,886 m/6,188 ft. It is a source of hydroelectricity. Although the Massif Central covers about one-seventh of France, it is home to only one-fifth of the population. Manufacturing is limited to the cities, such as Clermont-Ferrand and Limoges. Tourism, focused in the area's many health resorts, of which Vichy is the best known, is an important industry.

Massine, Léonide (1895–1979) adopted name of Leonid Fyodorovich Miassin, Russian choreographer and dancer with the Ballets Russes. He was a creator of comedy in ballet and also symphonic ballet using concert music. His works include the first cubist-inspired ballet, *Parade* (1917), *La Boutique fantasque* (1919), and *The Three-Cornered Hat* (1919).

mass number or **nucleon number** symbol A, sum of the numbers of *protons and *neutrons in the nucleus of an atom. It is used along with the *atomic number (the number of protons) in nuclear notation: in symbols that represent nuclear *isotopes, such as $^{14}_{6}$C, the lower number is the atomic number, and the upper number is the mass number. Since the mass of the *electrons in an atom are negligible, the total number of protons is neutrons (mass number) in an atom determines its mass.

Massorah collection of philological notes on the Hebrew text of the Old Testament. It was at first an oral tradition, but was committed to writing in the Aramaic language at Tiberias, Palestine, between the 6th and 9th centuries.

mass production manufacture of goods on a large scale, a technique that aims for low unit cost and high output. In factories mass production is achieved by a variety of means, such as division and specialization of labour and mechanization. These speed up production and allow the manufacture of near-identical, interchangeable parts. Such parts can then be assembled quickly into a finished product on an assembly line. The technique was first implemented by US automobile pioneer Henry *Ford in 1908, for the manufacture of the Model T Ford automobile.

Master of the King's/Queen's Music(k) honorary appointment to the British royal household, the holder composing appropriate music for state occasions. The first was Nicholas Lanier, appointed by Charles I in 1626; later appointments have included Edward Elgar and Arthur Bliss. The present holder, Malcolm Williamson, was appointed in 1975.

Master of the Rolls English judge who is the president of the civil division of the Court of Appeal, besides being responsible for *Chancery records and for the admission of solicitors.

mastiff breed of powerful dog, usually fawn in colour, that was originally bred in Britain for hunting purposes. It has a large head, wide-set eyes, and broad muzzle. It can grow up to 90 cm/36 in at the shoulder, and weigh 100 kg/220 lb.

mastodon any of an extinct family of mammals belonging to the elephant order. They differed from elephants and mammoths in the structure of their grinding teeth. There were numerous species, among which the **American mastodon** (*Mastodon americanum*), about 3 m/10 ft high, of the Pleistocene era, is well known. They were hunted by humans for food. (Family Mastodontidae, order Proboscidae.)

Matabeleland western portion of Zimbabwe between the Zambezi and Limpopo rivers, inhabited by the Ndebele people; population (1992) 1,855,300. It is divided into two provinces (Matabeleland North and Matabeleland South); area 181,605 sq km/70,118 sq mi. Towns and cities include Bulawayo and Hwange. The region features rich plains watered by tributaries of the Zambezi and Limpopo rivers. Industries include gold and other mineral mines, and engineering. Agricultural products include cotton, sugar, maize, and cattle. The language spoken is Ndebele.

Mata Hari (1876–1917) stage name of Margaretha Geertruida Zelle, Dutch courtesan, dancer, and probable spy. In World War I she had affairs with highly placed military and government officials on both sides and told Allied secrets to the Germans. She may have been a double agent, in the pay of both France and Germany. She was shot by the French on espionage charges.

materialism philosophical theory that there is nothing in existence over and above matter and matter in motion. Such a theory excludes the possibility of deities. It also sees mind as an attribute of the physical, denying idealist theories that see mind as something independent of body; for example, Descartes' theory of 'thinking substance'.

mathematics science of relationships between numbers, between spatial configurations, and abstract structures. The main divisions of **pure mathematics** include geometry, arithmetic, algebra, calculus, and trigonometry. Mechanics, statistics, numerical analysis, computing, the mathematical theories of astronomy, electricity, optics, thermodynamics, and atomic studies come under the heading of **applied mathematics**.

Matilda, the Empress Maud (1102–1167) claimant to the throne of England as daughter of Henry I. In 1127 Henry forced the barons to accept Matilda, his only surviving legitimate child since the death of his son, as his successor as monarch of England. However, there had never been a woman ruler in either England or Normandy, and most of the barons, supported by the church, elected her cousin *Stephen to be king on Henry's death in 1135. Matilda invaded England in 1139 and captured Stephen at Lincoln in 1141. She entered London to be crowned, but was driven out when she demanded money from the Londoners. Civil war followed until Stephen acknowledged Matilda's son, the future Henry II, as his successor in 1153.

Matisse, Henri Emile Benoît (1869–1954) French painter, sculptor and illustrator. Matisse was one of the most original creative forces in early 20th-century art. He was a leading figure in *fauvism and later developed a style characterized by strong, sinuous lines, surface pattern, and brilliant colour. *The Dance* (1910; The Hermitage, St Petersburg) is characteristic. Matisse regarded composition as simply the arrangement of elements to express feeling. He was not a believer in heavy theory, but felt that art should be 'restful', natural, joyous, colourful, and above all expressive. Later works include pure abstracts, as in his *collages of coloured paper shapes (*gouaches découpées*).

matriarchy form of society where domestic and political life is dominated by women, where kinship is traced exclusively through the female line, and where religion is centred around the cult of a mother goddess. A society dominated by men is known as a **patriarchy**.

matrix in biology, usually refers to the extracellular matrix.

matrix in mathematics, a square ($n \times n$) or rectangular ($m \times n$) array of elements (numbers or algebraic variables) used to facilitate the study of problems in which the relation between the elements is important. They are a means of condensing information about mathematical systems and can be used for, among other things, solving simultaneous linear equations (see *simultaneous equations and *transformation).

Matsuoka, Yosuke (1880–1946) Japanese politician, foreign minister 1940–41. A fervent nationalist, Matsuoka led Japan out of the League of Nations in 1933 when it condemned Japan for the seizure of Manchuria. As foreign minister, he allied Japan with Germany and Italy. At the end of World War II, he was arrested as a war criminal but died before his trial was concluded.

matter in physics, anything that has mass. All matter is made up of *atoms, which in turn are made up of *elementary particles; it ordinarily exists in one of three physical states: solid, liquid, or gas.

Matterhorn French le Cervin; Italian il Cervino, mountain peak in the Alps on the Swiss-Italian border; 4,478 m/14,690 ft. It was first climbed in 1865 by English mountaineer Edward Whymper (1840–1911); four members of his party of seven were killed when a rope broke during their descent.

Matthews, Stanley (1915–2000) English footballer who played for Stoke City, Blackpool, and England. He played nearly 700 Football League games, and won 54 international caps. He was the first Footballer of the Year in 1948 (and again in 1963), the first European Footballer of the Year in 1956, and the first footballer to be knighted for services to the game in 1965.

Matthew, St (lived 1st century AD) Christian apostle and evangelist, the traditional author of the first listed Gospel of the New Testament. He is usually identified with Levi, who was a tax collector in the service of Herod Antipas, and was called by Jesus to be a disciple as he sat by the Lake of Galilee receiving custom dues. His emblem is a man with wings. His feast day is 21 September.

Maugham, (William) Somerset (1874–1965) English writer. His work includes the novels *Of Human Bondage* (1915), *The Moon and Sixpence* (1919), and *Cakes and Ale* (1930); the short-story collections

Mau Mau

Ashenden (1928) and *Rain and Other Stories* (1933); and the plays *Lady Frederick* (1907) and *Our Betters* (1917). There were new editions of *Collected Stories* in 1900 and *Selected Plays* in 1991. A penetrating observer of human behaviour, his writing is essentially anti-romantic and there is a vein of cynicism running through his work.

Mau Mau Kenyan secret guerrilla movement 1952–60, an offshoot of the Kikuyu Central Association banned in World War II. Its aim was to end British colonial rule. This was achieved in 1960 with the granting of Kenyan independence and the election of Jomo Kenyatta as Kenya's first prime minister.

Mauna Kea astronomical observatory in Hawaii, built on a dormant volcano at 4,200 m/13,784 ft above sea level. Because of its elevation high above clouds, atmospheric moisture, and artificial lighting, Mauna Kea is ideal for infrared astronomy. The first telescope on the site was installed in 1970.

Maupassant, (Henry René Albert) Guy de (1850–1893) French author. He established a reputation with the short story 'Boule de suif/Ball of Fat' (1880) and wrote some 300 short stories in all. His novels include *Une Vie/A Woman's Life* (1883) and *Bel-Ami* (1885). He was encouraged as a writer by Gustave *Flaubert.

Mauriac, François (1885–1970) French novelist. His novels are studies, from a Roman Catholic standpoint, of the psychological and moral problems of the Catholic and provincial middle class, usually set in his native city of Bordeaux and the Landes region of southwestern France. *Le Baiser au lépreux/A Kiss for the Leper* (1922) describes the conflict of an unhappy marriage, while the irreconcilability of Christian practice and human nature is examined in *Fleuve de feu/River of Fire* (1923), *Le Désert de l'amour/The Desert of Love* (1925), and *Thérèse Desqueyroux* (1927). He was awarded the Nobel Prize for Literature in 1952.

Mauritania

National name: *Al-Jumhuriyya al-Islamiyya al-Mawritaniyya/République Islamique Arabe et Africaine de Mauritanie/Islamic Republic of Mauritania*

Area: 1,030,700 sq km/397,953 sq mi
Capital: Nouakchott (and chief port)
Major towns/cities: Nouâdhibou, Kaédi, Zouerate, Kiffa, Rosso, Atar
Major ports: Nouâdhibou

Physical features: valley of River Senegal in south; remainder arid and flat
Head of state: Maaoya Sid'Ahmed Ould Taya from 1984
Head of government: Sghair Ould Mbureck from 2003
Political system: emergent democracy
Political executive: limited presidency
Political parties: Democratic and Social Republican Party (PRDS), left of centre, militarist; Rally for Democracy and National Unity (RDNU), centrist; Mauritanian Renewal Party (MPR), centrist; Umma, Islamic fundamentalist
Currency: ouguiya
GNI per capita (PPP): (US$) 1,740 (2002 est)
Exports: iron ore, fish and fish products. Principal market: Italy 15% (2001)
Population: 2,893,000 (2003 est)
Language: Hasaniya Arabic (official), Pulaar, Soninke, Wolof (all national languages), French (particularly in the south)
Religion: Sunni Muslim (state religion)
Life expectancy: 51 (men); 54 (women) (2000–05)
Chronology
early Christian era: A Roman province with the name Mauritania, after the Mauri, its Berber inhabitants who became active in the long-distance salt trade.
7th–11th centuries: Eastern Mauritania was incorporated in the larger Ghana Empire, centred on Mali to the east, but with its capital at Kumbi in southeast Mauritania. The Berbers were reduced to vassals and converted to Islam in the 8th century.
11th–12th centuries: The area's Sanhadja Berber inhabitants, linked to the Morocco-based Almoravid Empire, destroyed the Ghana Empire and spread Islam among neighbouring peoples.
13th–15th centuries: Southeast Mauritania formed part of the Muslim Mali Empire, which extended to the east and south.
1441: Coast visited by Portuguese, who founded port of Arguin and captured Africans to sell as slaves.
15th–16th centuries: Eastern Mauritania formed part of Muslim Songhai Empire, which spread across western Sahel, and Arab tribes migrated into the area.
1817: Senegal Treaty recognized coastal region (formerly disputed by European nations) as French sphere of influence.
1903: Formally became French protectorate.
1920: Became French colony, within French West Africa.
1960: Independence achieved, with Moktar Ould Daddah, leader of Mauritanian People's Party (PPM), as president. New capital built at Nouakchott.
1968: Underlying tensions between agriculturalist black population of south and economically dominant semi-nomadic Arabo-Berber peoples, or Moors, of desert north became more acute after Arabic was made an official language (with French).
1976: Western Sahara, to the northwest, ceded by Spain to Mauritania and Morocco. Mauritania occupied the southern area and Morocco the mineral-rich north. Polisario Front formed in Sahara to resist this occupation and guerrilla war broke out, with the Polisario receiving backing from Algeria and Libya.
1979: A peace accord was signed with the Polisario Front in Algiers, in which Mauritania renounced its claims to southern Western Sahara and recognized the

582

Polisario regime; diplomatic relations were restored with Algeria.

1981: Diplomatic relations with Morocco were broken after it annexed southern Western Sahara.

1984: Col Maaoya Sid'Ahmed Ould Taya became president.

1985: Relations with Morocco were restored.

1989: There were violent clashes in Mauritania and Senegal between Moors and black Africans, chiefly of Senegalese origins; over 50,000 Senegalese were expelled.

1991: An amnesty was called for political prisoners. Political parties were legalized and a new multiparty constitution was approved in a referendum.

1992: The first multiparty elections were largely boycotted by the opposition; Taya and his Social Democratic Republican Party (DSRP) were re-elected. Diplomatic relations with Senegal resumed.

1998: Cheik el Avia Ould Muhammad Khouna was appointed prime minister.

2002: Black-rights opposition party, Action for Change, was banned.

2003: President Taya was re-elected with 67% of the vote. His main opposition rival, former president Khouna Ould Haidalla, won 19% and rejected the poll as fraudulent. Haidalla was later arrested and accused of plotting to overthrow Taya.

2004: Mauritania was badly hit by a plague of locusts which destroyed crops across Africa, threatening widespread food shortages. The government announced that there had been another attempted coup and President Taya accused Libya and Burkina Faso of financing the attempted coups.

2005: The UN requested food aid for the country. Soldiers accused of plotting coups were given life prison sentences.

Mauritius

National name: *Republic of Mauritius*

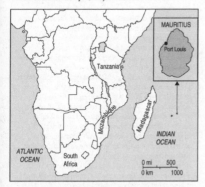

Area: 1,865 sq km/720 sq mi
Capital: Port Louis (and chief port)
Major towns/cities: Beau Bassin-Rose Hill, Curepipe, Quatre Bornes, Vacoas-Phoenix
Physical features: mountainous, volcanic island surrounded by coral reefs; the island of Rodrigues is part of Mauritius; there are several small island dependencies
Head of state: Anerood Jugnauth from 2003

Head of government: Paul Bérenger from 2003
Political system: liberal democracy
Political executive: parliamentary
Political parties: Mauritius Socialist Movement (MSM), moderate socialist-republican; Mauritius Labour Party (MLP), democratic socialist, Hindu-oriented; Mauritius Social Democratic Party (PMSD), conservative, Francophile; Mauritius Militant Movement (MMM), Marxist-republican; Organization of Rodriguan People (OPR), left of centre
Currency: Mauritian rupee
GNI per capita (PPP): (US$) 10,530 (2002 est)
Exports: raw sugar, clothing, tea, molasses, jewellery. Principal market: UK 25.8% (2000)
Population: 1,221,000 (2003 est)
Language: English (official), French, Creole (36%), Bhojpuri (32%), other Indian languages
Religion: Hindu over 50%, Christian (mainly Roman Catholic) about 30%, Muslim 17%
Life expectancy: 68 (men); 76 (women) (2000–05)
Chronology
1598: Previously uninhabited, the island was discovered by the Dutch and named after Prince Morris of Nassau.
1710: Dutch colonists withdrew.
1721: Reoccupied by French East India Company, who renamed it Ile de France, and established sugar cane and tobacco plantations worked by imported African slaves.
1814: Ceded to Britain by the Treaty of Paris.
1835: Slavery abolished; indentured Indian and Chinese labourers imported to work the sugar-cane plantations, which were later hit by competition from beet sugar.
1903: Formerly administered with Seychelles, it became a single colony.
1936: Mauritius Labour Party (MLP) founded, drawing strong support from sugar workers.
1957: Internal self-government granted.
1968: Independence achieved from Britain within Commonwealth, with Seewoosagur Ramgoolam of centrist Indian-dominated MLP as prime minister.
1971: A state of emergency was temporarily imposed as a result of industrial unrest.
1982: Anerood Jugnauth, of the moderate socialist Mauritius Socialist Movement (MSM), became prime minister, pledging a programme of nonalignment, nationalization, and the creation of a republic.
1992: Became a republic within the Commonwealth, with Cassam Uteem elected as president.
1995: The MLP and the cross-community Mauritian Militant Movement (MMM) coalition won election victory; Navin Ramgoolam (MLP) became the prime minister.
2000: General elections in mid-September 2000 were won by an opposition alliance, led by a former prime minister, Anerood Jugnauth.
2003: Prime Minister Jugnauth stepped down and was replaced by deputy prime minister and finance minister Paul Bérenger.

Mauryan dynasty Indian dynasty *c.* 321–*c.* 185 BC, founded by **Chandragupta Maurya** (321–*c.* 297 BC). Under Emperor *Asoka most of India was united for the first time, but after his death in 232 the empire was riven by dynastic disputes. Reliant on a highly organized aristocracy and a centralized administration, it survived until the assassination of Emperor Brihadratha in 185 BC and the creation of the Sunga dynasty.

maxim saying or proverb that gives moral guidance or a piece of advice on the way to live ('First come, first served'; 'Better late than never').

Maximilian I (1459–1519) German king from 1486, Holy Roman Emperor from 1493. He was the son of the emperor Frederick III (1415–93). Through a combination of dynastic marriages and diplomacy backed up by military threats, Maximilian was able to build up the Habsburg inheritance. He married Mary of Burgundy in 1477, and after her death in 1582 held onto Burgundian lands. He married his son, Philip the Handsome, to Joanna, the daughter of *Ferdinand and *Isabella, and undertook long wars with Italy and Hungary in attempts to extend Habsburg power. The eventual legatee of these arrangements was Maximilian's grandson, Charles V.

Maxwell, James Clerk (1831–1879) Scottish physicist. His main achievement was in the understanding of *electromagnetic waves: **Maxwell's equations** bring together electricity, magnetism, and light in one set of relations. He studied gases, optics, and the sensation of colour, and his theoretical work in magnetism prepared the way for wireless telegraphy and telephony.

maya (Sanskrit 'illusion') in Hindu philosophy, mainly in the *Vedanta*, the cosmos that Isvara, the personal expression of Brahman, or the atman, has called into being. This is real, yet also an illusion, since its reality is not everlasting.

Maya member of a prehistoric *American Indian civilization originating in the *Yucatán Peninsula in Central America about 2600 BC, with later sites in Mexico, Guatemala, and Belize. Their language belonged to the Totonac-Mayan family. From AD 325 to 925 (Classical Period) the Maya culture dominated the region, after which it declined under pressure from the Toltec and, from the 16th century, the Spanish. The Maya are known for their ceremonial centres, which included stepped pyramids, ball courts, and astronomical observatories. Today Maya live in Yucatán, Guatemala, Belize, and western Honduras, and number 8–9 million (1994 est). Many speak Maya along with Spanish, but they are now Roman Catholic.

May Day first day of May. In many countries it is a national holiday in honour of labour.

Mayflower ship in which the *Pilgrims sailed in 1620 from Plymouth, England, to found Plymouth plantation and Plymouth colony in present-day Massachusetts.

mayfly any of a group of insects whose adult form lives only very briefly in the spring. The larval stage, which can last a year or more, is passed in water, the adult form developing gradually from the nymph through successive moults. The adult has transparent, net-veined wings. (Order Ephemerida.)

Mayo county of the Republic of Ireland, in the province of Connacht; county town Castlebar; area 5,400 sq km/2,084 sq mi; population (2002 est) 117,400. Its wild Atlantic coastline is about 400 km/249 mi long. The principal towns are Ballina, Ballinrobe, and Westport, and the principal rivers are the Moy, the Robe, and the Owenmore. Loughs Conn and Mask lie within the county. Agriculture includes pig, sheep, and cattle farming, and salmon fishing (particularly in the River Moy). The soil of the central plain is fertile, and crops include potatoes and oats. An excellent marble is found in the northwest district.

mayor title of the head of urban (city or town) administration. In England, Wales, and Northern Ireland, the mayor is the principal officer of a district council that has been given district-borough status under royal charter. The equivalent in Scotland is provost. In the USA a mayor is the elected head of a city or town. In 1996 the Labour Party suggested proposals for directly-elected mayors in Britain, which it confirmed when it came into power in 1997. A referendum in May 1998 approved establishing an elected mayor of London: Ken Livingstone was elected in 2000. A July 1998 government White Paper proposed allowing local authorities to introduce directly-elected mayors, working together with assemblies or executive committees, as a way of reviving local democracy. However, by October 2001, only 13 councils had held referendums, with 7 approving the election of a mayor.

mayweed any of several species of the daisy family native to Europe and Asia and naturalized elsewhere, including the European dog fennel or stinking daisy (*Anthemis cotula*), naturalized in North America, and the pineapple mayweed (*Matricaria matricarioides*), found in Europe and Asia. All have finely divided leaves. (Family Compositae.)

Mazarin, Jules (1602–1661) born Giulio Raimondo Mazzarini, French politician who succeeded Richelieu as chief minister of France in 1642. His attack on the power of the nobility led to the *Fronde and his temporary exile, but his diplomacy achieved a successful conclusion to the Thirty Years' War, and, in alliance with Oliver Cromwell during the British protectorate, he gained victory over Spain.

Mazzini, Giuseppe (1805–1872) Italian nationalist. He was a member of the revolutionary society, the Carbonari, and founded in exile the nationalist movement Giovane Italia (Young Italy) in 1831. Returning to Italy on the outbreak of the 1848 revolution, he headed a republican government established in Rome, but was forced into exile again on its overthrow in 1849. He acted as a focus for the movement for Italian unity (see *Risorgimento).

Mbabane administrative capital of Swaziland, in the northwest of the country, near the South African border; population (2001 est) 74,800. It is situated in the Hhohho District of the Highveld, and is connected by rail to nearby coal mines and to the Indian Ocean port of Maputo, in Mozambique, 160 km/100 mi to the east. The legislative capital, Lobamba, is nearby to the south. In addition to mining and local crafts, industries include cement manufacture, finance, and banking. Aided by the development of a hotel and casino complex in the Ezulwini valley, about 11 km/7 mi from Mbabane, tourism has become a major industry.

Mbeki, Thabo (1942–) South African politician, first executive deputy president from 1994 and president from 1999. As chair of the *African National Congress (ANC) from 1989, he played an important role in the constitutional talks with the de Klerk government that eventually led to the adoption of a nonracial political system. In December 1997 he replaced Nelson Mandela as ANC President, and in June 1999 succeeded him as president.

MDMA (3,4-methylenedio-xymethamphetamine) psychedelic drug, also known as *ecstasy.

ME abbreviation for **myalgic encephalomyelitis**, a popular name for *chronic fatigue syndrome.

meal-worm any larva of the beetle genus *Tenebrio*, especially *T. molitor*. Meal-worms are slender and round, about 2.5 cm/1 in long, and tawny with bright rusty bands. They are pests of stored grain.

mean in mathematics, a measure of the average of a number of terms or quantities. The simple *arithmetic mean is the average value of the quantities, that is, the sum of the quantities divided by their number. The **weighted mean** takes into account the frequency of the terms that are summed; it is calculated by multiplying each term by the number of times it occurs, summing the results and dividing this total by the total number of occurrences. The **geometric mean** of n quantities is the nth root of their product. In statistics, it is a measure of central tendency of a set of data, that is one measure used to express the frequency distribution of a number of recorded events.

meander loop-shaped curve in a *river flowing sinuously across flat country. As a river flows, any curve in its course is accentuated (intensified) by the current. On the outside of the curve the velocity, and therefore the erosion, of the river is greatest. Here the river cuts into the outside bank, producing a **river cliff**. On the inside of the curve the current is slow and so it deposits any transported material, building up a gentle slip-off slope. As each meander migrates in the direction of its outer bank, the river gradually changes its course across the flood plain.

mean deviation in statistics, a measure of the spread of a population from the *mean.

measles also known as **rubeola**, acute virus disease spread by airborne infection. Symptoms are fever, severe catarrh, small spots inside the mouth, and a raised, blotchy red rash appearing for about a week after two weeks' incubation. Prevention is by vaccination.

Meath county of the Republic of Ireland, in the province of Leinster; county town Navan; area 2,340 sq km/ 903 sq mi; population (2002 est) 134,000. The chief river is the Boyne, of which the Blackwater is a tributary. The principal towns are Kells, Trim, Athboy, Bettystown, and Laytown. Cattle and sheep are reared, and oats and potatoes are grown. The largest working lead mine in Europe is located near Navan. Tara Hill, 155 m/509 ft high, was the site of a palace and was the coronation place of many kings of Ireland; St Patrick also preached here. The Book of Kells (now held in Trinity College Library, Dublin) was produced at Kells in the 8th century.

Mecca Arabic **Makkah**, city in Saudi Arabia and, as birthplace of *Muhammad, the holiest city of the Islamic world and a place of annual pilgrimage (the *hajj); population (1992 est) 965,700. Non-Muslims have been forbidden entry to the city since AD 630, when Muhammad made it the centre of the Muslim faith. In the centre of Mecca is the Great Mosque, in the courtyard of which is the *Kaaba, the sacred shrine dating from pre-Islamic times and containing the black stone believed to have been given to Ibrahim (Abraham) by the angel Jibra'el (Gabriel). Because of the predominance of the religious functions of the city,

industrial development is on a small scale, but includes some manufacture of textiles and furniture.

mechanics branch of physics dealing with the motions of bodies and the forces causing these motions, and also with the forces acting on bodies in *equilibrium. It is usually divided into *dynamics and *statics.

Mecklenburg-West Pomerania German **Mecklenburg-Vorpommern**, administrative region (German *Land*) in northern Germany; area 23,170 sq km/ 8,946 sq mi; population (1999 est) 1,789,300; the capital is Schwerin, and other major towns include Rostock, Wismar, Stralsund, and Neubrandenburg. Products of the region include fish, ships, diesel engines, electronics, plastics, and chalk.

Medawar, Peter Brian (1915–1987) Brazilian-born British immunologist who was awarded a Nobel Prize for Physiology or Medicine in 1960 with Macfarlane Burnet for their work on acquired immunological tolerance of transplanted tissues. They discovered that the body's resistance to grafted tissue is undeveloped in the newborn child, and studied the way it is acquired. Medawar was knighted in 1965.

Medea in Greek mythology, the sorceress daughter of the king of Colchis. When *Jason reached Colchis, she fell in love with him, helped him acquire the *Golden Fleece, and they fled together. When Jason later married Creusa, daughter of the king of Corinth, Medea killed his bride with the gift of a poisoned garment, and then killed her own two children by Jason.

Medellín industrial city and capital of Antioquia department, northwest Colombia; situated at 1,538 m/ 5,048 ft above sea level in the Aburrá Valley, Central Cordillera of the Andes; population (1999 est) 1,861,300. It is the second city and a leading industrial centre of Colombia, producing over 80% of the country's total textile output. Other main industries include gold and silver mining, chemicals, coffee-growing, and engineering. Medellín has also had a reputation for cocaine production.

median in mathematics and statistics, the middle number of an ordered group of numbers. If there is no middle number (because there is an even number of terms), the median is the *mean (average) of the two middle numbers. For example, the median of the group 2, 3, 7, 11, 12 is 7; that of 3, 4, 7, 9, 11, 13 is 8 (the mean of 7 and 9). The median together with the *mode and *arithmetic mean make up the *average of a set of *data. In addition it is useful to know the range or spread of the data. In geometry, the term refers to a line from the vertex of a triangle to the midpoint of the opposite side.

medical ethics moral guidelines for doctors governing good professional conduct. The basic aims are considered to be doing good, avoiding harm, preserving the patient's autonomy, telling the truth, and pursuing justice. Ethical issues provoke the most discussion in medicine where these five aims cannot be simultaneously achieved – for example, what is 'good' for a child may clash with his or her autonomy or that of the parents.

Medici, Cosimo de' (1389–1464) Italian politician and banker. Regarded as the model for Machiavelli's *The Prince*, he dominated the government of Florence from 1434 and was a patron of the arts. He was succeeded by his inept son **Piero de' Medici** (1416–1469).

Medici, Cosimo de' (1519–1574) Italian politician, ruler of Florence; duke of Florence from 1537 and 1st grand duke of Tuscany from 1569.

Medici, Lorenzo de', the Magnificent (1449–1492) Italian politician, ruler of Florence from 1469. He was also a poet and a generous patron of the arts.

Medici family noble family that ruled the Italian city-state of Florence from the 15th to the 18th centuries. The Medici arrived in Florence in the 13th century and made their fortune in banking. The first family member to control the city, from 1434 to 1464, was Cosimo de' Medici ('the Elder'); he and his grandson Lorenzo ('the Magnificent'), who ruled from 1469 to 1492, made Florence the foremost city-state in *Renaissance Italy, and were famed as patrons of the arts and *humanist thought. Four Medici were elected pope, and others married into the royal families of Europe.

medicine the practice of preventing, diagnosing, and treating disease, both physical and mental; also any substance used in the treatment of disease. The basis of medicine is anatomy (the structure and form of the body) and physiology (the study of the body's functions).

medicine, alternative forms of medical treatment that do not use synthetic drugs or surgery in response to the symptoms of a disease, but aim to treat the patient as a whole (*holism). The emphasis is on maintaining health (with diet and exercise) and on dealing with the underlying causes rather than just the symptoms of illness. It may involve the use of herbal remedies and techniques like *acupuncture, *homeopathy, and *chiropractic. Some alternative treatments are increasingly accepted by orthodox medicine, but the absence of enforceable standards in some fields has led to the proliferation of eccentric or untrained practitioners.

medieval art painting and sculpture of the Middle Ages in Europe and parts of the Middle East, dating roughly from the 3rd century to the emergence of the Renaissance in Italy in the 1400s. This includes early Christian, Byzantine, Celtic, Anglo-Saxon, and Carolingian art. The Romanesque style was the first truly international style of medieval times, superseded by Gothic in the late 12th century. Religious sculpture, frescoes, and manuscript illumination proliferated; panel painting was introduced only towards the end of the Middle Ages.

Medina Arabic Al Madinah, (Arabic 'the city of the apostle') Saudi Arabian city, about 355 km/220 mi north of Mecca; population (1992 est) 608,300. It is the second holiest city in the Islamic world after Mecca, and contains the tomb of *Muhammad, a focus for Muslim pilgrims during the *hajj (annual pilgrimage).

meditation act of spiritual contemplation, practised by members of many religions or as a secular exercise. It is a central practice in Buddhism and Hinduism (the Sanskrit term is samadhi) and the movement for *transcendental meditation.

Mediterranean Sea inland sea separating Europe from north Africa, with Asia to the east; extreme length 3,860 km/2,400 mi; area 2,966,000 sq km/1,145,000 sq mi. It is linked to the Atlantic Ocean (at the Strait of Gibraltar), Red Sea and Indian Ocean (by the Suez Canal), and the Black Sea (at the Dardanelles and Sea of Marmara). The main subdivisions are the Adriatic, Aegean, Ionian, and Tyrrhenian seas; its coastline extends 46,000 km/28,580 mi, running through 22 countries. It is highly polluted.

medlar small shrub or tree native to southeastern Europe. It is widely cultivated for its fruits, resembling small brown-green pears or quinces. These are palatable when they have begun to decay. (*Mespilus germanica*, family Rosaceae.)

Médoc French district bordering the Gironde in Aquitaine region, north of Bordeaux. It is famed for its claret wines, Margaux and St Julien being two well-known names. Lesparre and Pauillac are the chief towns.

medulla central part of an organ. In the mammalian kidney, the medulla lies beneath the outer cortex and is responsible for the reabsorption of water from the filtrate. In plants, it is a region of packing tissue in the centre of the stem. In the vertebrate brain, the medulla is the posterior region responsible for the coordination of basic activities, such as breathing and temperature control.

medusa free-swimming phase in the life cycle of a coelenterate, such as a *jellyfish or *coral. The other phase is the sedentary polyp.

Medusa in Greek mythology, a mortal woman who was transformed into a snake-haired *Gorgon by Athena for defiling the goddess's temple with the god Poseidon. She was slain by the hero *Perseus who watched her reflection in his shield, as her head was so hideous – even in death – that a direct beholder was turned to stone. The winged horse *Pegasus and warrior Chrysaor were said to have sprung from her blood; offspring of Medusa and Poseidon.

Medway Towns unitary authority in southeast England, created in 1998 by combining the former city council of Rochester upon Medway with Gillingham borough council, both formerly in Kent. **area:** 194 sq km/75 sq mi **towns and cities:** Rochester, Chatham, Gillingham, Strood (administrative headquarters) **features:** River Medway flows through Rochester; River Thames forms northern border of authority; reclaimed estuarine mudflats form the Isle of Grain; Charles Dickens Centre (Rochester) is housed in a 16th-century mansion; Royal Naval Dockyard (Chatham); Royal Engineers Museum (Chatham); Upnor Castle (16th century) at Upper Upnor **population:** (2001 est) 249,700.

meerkat or **suricate** small mammal with long soft grey fur, which is found in southern Africa, and belongs to the mongoose family. A third of its length of 35 cm/14 in is occupied by the tail. It feeds on succulent bulbs, insects, and small vertebrates, and is sociable, living in large extended family groups. Meerkat groups have a dominant breeding pair and up to 23 helpers to assist in the rearing of the babies. The dominant female produces 75% of the young.

meerschaum aggregate of minerals, usually the soft white clay mineral **sepiolite**, hydrous magnesium silicate. It floats on water and is used for making pipe bowls.

mega- prefix denoting multiplication by a million. For example, a megawatt (MW) is equivalent to a million watts.

megabyte (MB) in computing, a unit of memory equal to 1,024 *kilobytes. It is sometimes used, less precisely, to mean 1 million bytes.

megalith (Greek *megas* 'great', *lithos* 'stone') prehistoric stone monument of the late Neolithic (New Stone Age) or early Bronze Age. Most common in Europe, megaliths include single large uprights or *menhirs (for example, the Five Kings, Northumberland, England); rows or **alignments** (for example, Carnac, Brittany, France); stone circles; and the hutlike remains of burial chambers after the covering earth has disappeared, known as *dolmens (for example, Kits Coty, Kent, England, where only the entrance survives).

megamouth deep-sea shark that feeds on plankton. It has a bulbous head with protruding jaws and blubbery lips, is 4.5 m/15 ft long, and weighs 750 kg/1,650 lb. Although first discovered in 1976, the first live specimen was found in 1992 off the coast of Los Angeles. The first female was found in 1994 in Hakata Bay, Kyushu, Japan; she was 4.8 m/16 ft long and weighed 790 kg/1,740 lb. (Species *Megachasma pelagios*.)

megapode *or* **mound-builder** any of a group of chickenlike birds found in the Malay Archipelago and Australia. They pile up large mounds of vegetable matter, earth, and sand 4 m/13 ft across, in which to deposit their eggs, then cover the eggs and leave them to be incubated by the heat produced by the rotting vegetation. There are 19 species, all large birds, 50–70 cm/20–27.5 in in length, with very large feet. They include brush turkeys. (Family Megapodiidae, order Galliformes.)

megaton one million (10^6) tons. Used with reference to the explosive power of a nuclear weapon, it is equivalent to the explosive force of one million tons of trinitrotoluene (TNT).

Meghalaya state of northeast India, bordered to the north by Assam, to the south by Bangladesh; area 22,489 sq km/8,683 sq mi; population (2001 est) 2,306,100, mainly Khasi, Jaintia, and Garo. The capital is Shillong. The state is upland with hills reaching 2,000 m/6,500 ft, rising steeply in the south away from its border with Bangladesh. There is heavy monsoon rainfall. Minerals in the area include coal, limestone, white clay, and corundum, which are mainly unexploited. Industries include mineral extraction, which includes 95% of India's sillimanite, a mineral from which high-grade ceramic clay is derived. Agricultural products include cotton, potatoes, fruit, rice, maize, timber, and jute. 70% of the population are Hindu.

Megiddo site of a fortress town in northern Israel, where Thutmose III defeated the Canaanites; the Old Testament figure Josiah was killed in battle in about 609 BC; and in World War I the British field marshal Allenby broke the Turkish front in 1918. It is identified with *Armageddon.

Mehmet Ali (*or* **Muhammad Ali) (1769–1849)** Pasha (governor) of Egypt from 1805, and founder of the dynasty that ruled until 1953. An Albanian in the Ottoman service, he had originally been sent to Egypt to fight the French. As pasha, he established a European-style army and navy, fought his Turkish overlord in 1831 and 1839, and conquered Sudan.

Meiji, Mutsuhito (1852–1912) Emperor of Japan from 1867, under the regnal era name Meiji ('enlightened'). During his reign Japan became a world industrial and naval power. His ministers abolished the feudal system and discrimination against the lowest caste, established state schools, reformed the civil service, and introduced conscription, the Western calendar, and other measures to modernize Japan, including a constitution in 1889.

Mein Kampf (German 'my struggle') book dictated by the Nazi leader Adolf *Hitler to his deputy Rudolf Hess 1923–24, during their imprisonment in the Bavarian fortress of Landsberg for attempting the 1923 Munich beer-hall putsch. Part autobiography, part political philosophy, the book presents Hitler's ideas of German expansion, anticommunism, and anti-Semitism, and formed the blueprint for the racist ideology of National Socialism. It was published in two volumes, in 1925 and 1927.

meiosis in biology, a process of cell division in which the number of *chromosomes in the cell is halved. It only occurs in *eukaryotic cells, and is part of a life cycle that involves *sexual reproduction because it allows the genes of two parents to be combined without the total number of chromosomes increasing. Cells in reproductive organs – testes and ovaries in humans – divide to form sex cells (gametes) by meiosis.

Meir, Golda (1898–1978) born Golda Mabovitch, later Golda Myerson, Israeli Labour politician; foreign minister 1956–66 and prime minister 1969–74. Criticism of the Israelis' lack of preparation for the 1973 Arab-Israeli War led to election losses for Labour and, unable to form a government, she resigned.

meitnerium chemical symbol Mt, synthesized radioactive element of the *transactinide series, atomic number 109, relative atomic mass 266. It was first produced in 1982 at the Laboratory for Heavy-Ion Research in Darmstadt, Germany, by fusing bismuth and iron nuclei; it took a week to obtain a single new, fused nucleus. It was named in 1997 after the Austrian-born Swedish physicist Lise Meitner.

Mekong river of China, rising as the Za Qu in Qinghai province, flowing through Tibet autonomous region and Yunnan province as the Lancang Jiang, and then through Laos, where part of its course forms the border with Thailand, Cambodia, and Vietnam; length 4,425 km/2,750 mi. The Mekong empties into the South China Sea through a vast delta, covering about 200,000 sq km/77,000 sq mi. It is being developed for irrigation and hydroelectricity by Cambodia, Laos, Thailand, and Vietnam.

Melaka formerly **Malacca**, state of west Peninsular Malaysia; area 1,700 sq km/656 sq mi; population (2000 est) 602,900 (about 70% Chinese). The capital is Melaka. Rubber is the leading export of the state, though the output of coconuts and fruit, especially pineapples, is also commercially significant. Other exports include tin and wire. The town originated in the 13th century as a fishing village frequented by pirates, and later developed into a trading port. Portuguese from 1511, then Dutch from 1641, it was ceded to Britain in 1824, becoming part of the Straits Settlements.

melaleuca tree *or* **paperbark** tropical tree belonging to the myrtle family. The leaves produce **cajuput oil**, which is used in medicine. (*Melaleuca leucadendron*, family Myrtaceae.)

Melanchthon, Philip (1497–1560) adopted name of Philip Schwarzerd, German theologian who helped Martin Luther prepare a German translation of the New Testament. In 1521 he issued the first systematic formulation of Protestant theology, reiterated in the Confession of *Augsburg (1530).

Melanesia islands in the southwestern Pacific between Micronesia to the north and Polynesia to the east, embracing all the islands from the New Britain archipelago to the Fiji Islands.

Melanesian the indigenous inhabitants of Melanesia; any of the Pacific peoples of Melanesia. The Melanesian languages belong to the Austronesian family.

Melanesian languages see *Austronesian languages.

melanin brown pigment that gives colour to the eyes, skin, hair, feathers, and scales of many vertebrates. In humans, melanin helps protect the skin against ultraviolet radiation from sunlight. Both genetic and environmental factors determine the amount of melanin in the skin.

melanoma highly malignant tumour of the melanin-forming cells (melanocytes) of the skin. It develops from an existing mole in up to two-thirds of cases, but can also arise in the eye or mucous membranes. Malignant melanoma is the most dangerous of the skin cancers; it is associated with brief but excessive exposure to sunlight. It is easily treated if caught early but deadly once it has spread. There is a genetic factor in some cases.

Melbourne capital of the state of *Victoria, Australia; population (2001 est) 3,366,500. Australia's second-largest city, Melbourne is situated on the southeast coast of Australia, on Port Philip Bay, at the mouth of the River Yarra. It is separated from Tasmania by the Bass Strait. Industries include engineering, shipbuilding, electronics (including major production of computers), papermaking and printing, oil refining, food processing, brewing, flour-milling, and the manufacture of chemicals, cars, furniture, plastics, textiles, and clothing. The port of Melbourne at the mouth of the Yarra River is the largest handler of general cargo and the largest receiver of container vessels in Australia.

Melbourne, (Henry) William Lamb (1779–1848) 2nd Viscount Melbourne, British Whig politician. Home secretary 1830–34, he was briefly prime minister in 1834 and again in 1835–41. Accused in 1836 of seducing Caroline Norton, he lost the favour of William IV. Viscount 1829.

Méliès, Georges (1861–1938) French film pioneer. From 1896 to 1912 he made over 1,000 films, mostly fantasies (including *Le Voyage dans la lune/A Trip to the Moon*, 1902). He developed trick effects, slow motion, double exposure, and dissolves, and in 1897 built Europe's first film studio in Montreuil, northern France.

melodrama play or film with romantic and sensational plot elements, often concerned with crime, vice, or catastrophe. Originally a melodrama was a play with an accompaniment of music contributing to the dramatic effect. It became popular in the late 18th century, due to works like *Pygmalion* (1770), with pieces written by the French philosopher Jean-Jacques Rousseau. The early melodramas used extravagant theatrical effects to heighten violent emotions and actions artificially. By the end of the 19th century, melodrama had become a popular genre of stage play.

melody (Greek *melos* 'song') in music, a recognizable series of notes of different pitches played or sung one after the other. It could also be described as the tune. Melody is one of the three main elements of music, along with rhythm and *harmony. In Western music a melody is usually formed from the notes of a *scale or mode. A melody, with or without accompaniment, may be a complete piece on its own – such as a simple song. In classical music it is more often used as a theme within a longer piece of music.

melon any of several large, juicy (95% water), thick-skinned fruits of trailing plants of the gourd family. The muskmelon (*Cucumis melo*), of which the honeydew melon is a variety, and the large red *watermelon (*Citrullus vulgaris*) are familiar edible varieties. (Family Cucurbitaceae.)

meltdown the melting of the core of a nuclear reactor, due to overheating. To prevent such accidents all reactors have equipment intended to flood the core with water in an emergency. The reactor is housed in a strong containment vessel, designed to prevent radiation escaping into the atmosphere. The result of a meltdown would be an area radioactively contaminated for 25,000 years or more.

melting point temperature at which a substance melts, or changes from solid to liquid form. A pure substance under standard conditions of pressure (usually one atmosphere) has a definite melting point. If heat is supplied to a solid at its melting point, the temperature does not change until the melting process is complete. The melting point of ice is 0 °C or 32 °F.

Melville, Herman (1819–1891) US writer. His novel *Moby-Dick* (1851) was inspired by his whaling experiences in the South Seas and is considered to be one of the masterpieces of American literature. *Billy Budd, Sailor*, completed just before his death and published in 1924, was the basis of an opera by Benjamin *Britten (1951). Although most of his works were unappreciated during his lifetime, today he is one of the most highly regarded of US authors.

member of Parliament (MP) representative of a section of the UK population who attends the British *parliament. An MP is elected to represent the people who live in a geographical area called a **constituency**, and then attends the *House of Commons, where the activities of the government are considered by the members and legislation is passed. MPs divide their time between their constituencies and the houses of Parliament in London. An MP can ask questions of government ministers, join committees, speak in the House of Commons, and consider and propose new laws.

membrane in living things, a continuous layer, made up principally of fat molecules, that encloses a *cell or *organelles within a cell. Small molecules, such as water and sugars, can pass through the cell membrane by *diffusion. Large molecules, such as proteins, are transported across the membrane via special channels, a process often involving energy input. The Golgi apparatus within the cell is thought to produce certain membranes.

Memling (or Memlinc), Hans (c. 1430–1494) Flemish painter. He was probably a pupil of van der Weyden, but his style is calmer and softer. He painted religious subjects and also portraits, including

Tommaso Portinari and His Wife (about 1480; Metropolitan Museum of Art, New York).

memory in computing, the part of a system used to store data and programs either permanently or temporarily. There are two main types: immediate access memory and backing storage. Memory capacity is measured in *bytes or, more conveniently, in kilobytes (units of 1,024 bytes) or megabytes (units of 1,024 kilobytes).

memory ability to store and recall observations and sensations. Memory does not seem to be based in any particular part of the brain; it may depend on changes to the pathways followed by nerve impulses as they move through the brain. Memory can be improved by regular use as the connections between *nerve cells (neurons) become 'well-worn paths' in the brain. Events stored in **short-term memory** are forgotten quickly, whereas those in **long-term memory** can last for many years, enabling recall of information and recognition of people and places over long periods of time.

Memphis ruined city beside the Nile, 19 km/12 mi southwest of Cairo, Egypt. Once the centre of the worship of Ptah, it was the earliest capital of a united Egypt under King Menes in about 3050 BC, and acted intermittently as capital until around 1300 BC.

Menai Strait Welsh **Afon Menai**, channel of the Irish Sea dividing *Anglesey from the Welsh mainland; about 22 km/14 mi long and up to 3 km/2 mi wide. It is crossed by two bridges. Thomas Telford's suspension bridge (521 m/1,710 ft long) was opened in 1826 but was reconstructed to the original design in 1940, and freed from tolls. Robert Stephenson's tubular rail bridge (420 m/1,378 ft long) was opened in 1850, and is known as the Britannia Bridge.

Mencius (*c. 372–c. 289 BC*) Chinese **Mengzi**, Chinese philosopher and moralist in the tradition of orthodox Confucianism. He considered human nature innately good, although this goodness required cultivation, and based his conception of morality on this conviction. Mencius was born in Shantung (Shandong) province, and founded a Confucian school. After 20 years' unsuccessful search for a ruler to put into practice his enlightened political programme, based on people's innate goodness, he retired. His teachings are preserved in the *Book of Mengzi*.

Mende a West African people living in the rainforests of central east Sierra Leone and western Liberia. They number approximately 1 million. The Mende are farmers as well as hunter-gatherers, and each of their villages is led by a chief and a group of elders. The Mende language belongs to the Niger-Congo family.

Mendel, Gregor Johann (**1822–1884**) Austrian biologist who founded *genetics. His experiments with successive generations of peas gave the basis for his theory of particulate inheritance rather than blending, involving dominant and recessive characters; see *Mendelism. His results, published 1865–69, remained unrecognized until the early 20th century.

mendelevium chemical symbol Md, synthesized, radioactive metallic element of the *actinide series, atomic number 101, relative atomic mass 258. It was first produced by bombardment of Es-253 with helium nuclei. Its longest-lived isotope, Md-258, has a half-life of about two months. The element is chemically similar

to thulium. It was named by the US physicists at the University of California at Berkeley who first synthesized it in 1955 after the Russian chemist Dmitri Mendeleyev, who in 1869 devised the basis for the periodic table of the elements.

Mendeleyev, Dmitri Ivanovich (**1834–1907**) Russian chemist who framed the periodic law in chemistry in 1869, which states that the chemical properties of the elements depend on their relative atomic masses. This law is the basis of the *periodic table of the elements, in which the elements are arranged by atomic number and organized by their related groups.

Mendelism in genetics, the theory of inheritance originally outlined by Austrian biologist Gregor Mendel. He suggested that, in sexually reproducing species, all characteristics are inherited through indivisible 'factors' (now identified with *genes) contributed by each parent to its offspring.

Mendelssohn (-Bartholdy), (Jakob Ludwig) Felix (**1809–1847**) German composer, also a pianist and conductor. His music has the lightness and charm of classical music, applied to Romantic and descriptive subjects. Among his best-known works are *A Midsummer Night's Dream* (1826); the *Fingal's Cave* overture (1830–32); and five symphonies, which include the 'Reformation' (1832), the 'Italian' (1833), and the 'Scottish' (1842). He was involved in promoting the revival of interest in Johann Sebastian Bach's music.

mendicant order religious order dependent on alms. In the Roman Catholic Church there are four orders of mendicant friars: Franciscans, Dominicans, Carmelites, and Augustinians. Buddhism has similar orders.

Mendip Hills *or* **Mendips** range of limestone hills in southern England, stretching nearly 40 km/25 mi southeast–northwest from Wells in Somerset towards the Bristol Channel. There are many cliffs, scars, and caverns, notably Cheddar Gorge. The highest peak is Blackdown (326 m/1,068 ft).

Mendoza, Antonio de (*c. 1490–1552*) First Spanish viceroy of New Spain (Mexico) (1535–51). He attempted to develop agriculture and mining and supported the church in its attempts to convert the Indians. The system he established lasted until the 19th century. He was subsequently viceroy of Peru (1551–52).

Menelaus in Greek mythology, a king of Sparta; son of Atreus; brother of *Agamemnon; husband of *Helen, and father of Hermione. With his brother he ousted Thyestes from the throne of Mycenae and was joint leader of the Greek expedition against *Troy.

Menem (Akil), Carlos (Saul) (**1930– **) Argentine politician, president 1989–99; leader of the populist Perónist Partido Justicialista (PJ; Justicialist Party). Although gaining electoral support from the poor, he introduced sweeping privatization and cuts in public spending to address Argentina's economic crisis of hyperinflation and recession. He pardoned leaders of Argentina's period of military rule (1976–83) who had been imprisoned under his predecessor Raúl Alfonsín for their violation of human rights. He contested for the presidency again in 2003, but withdrew from the run-off race as polls showed he was heading for defeat.

Mengistu, Haile Mariam (**1937– **) Ethiopian soldier and socialist politician, head of state 1977–91 (president 1987–91). He seized power in a coup, and instituted a regime of terror to stamp out any effective opposition. Confronted with severe problems of drought and secessionist uprisings, he survived with help from the USSR and the West until his violent overthrow by rebel forces.

menhir (Breton 'long stone') prehistoric tall, upright stone monument or *megalith. Menhirs may be found singly as *monoliths or in groups. They have a wide geographical distribution in the Americas (mainly as monoliths), and in Europe, Asia, and Africa, and belong to many different periods. Most European examples were erected in the late Neolithic (New Stone Age) or early Bronze Age.

meningitis inflammation of the meninges (membranes) surrounding the brain, caused by bacterial or viral infection. Bacterial meningitis, though treatable by antibiotics, is the more serious threat. Diagnosis is by *lumbar puncture.

meniscus in physics, the curved shape of the surface of a liquid in a thin tube, caused by the cohesive effects of *surface tension (capillary action). When the walls of the container are made wet by the liquid, the meniscus is concave, but with highly viscous liquids (such as mercury) the meniscus is convex. Also, a meniscus lens is a concavo-convex or convexo-concave *lens.

Mennonite member of a Protestant Christian sect, originating as part of the *Anabaptist movement in Zürich, Switzerland in 1523. Members refuse to hold civil office or do military service, and reject infant baptism. They were named Mennonites after Menno Simons (1496–1559), leader of a group in Holland. Persecution drove other groups to Russia and North America.

menopause in women, the cessation of reproductive ability, characterized by menstruation (see *menstrual cycle) becoming irregular and eventually ceasing. The onset is at about the age of 50, but varies greatly. Menopause is usually uneventful, but some women suffer from complications such as flushing, excessive bleeding, and nervous disorders. Since the 1950s, *hormone-replacement therapy (HRT), using *oestrogen alone or with progestogen, a synthetic form of *progesterone, has been developed to counteract such effects.

menorah seven-branched candlestick symbolizing Judaism and the state of Israel. The lowest candle, the *shummash* or 'servant', is used to light the others. A nine-branched version, the hanukkiah, is used during the Jewish festival of *Hanukkah.

Menorca English **Minorca**, second largest of the *Balearic Islands in the Mediterranean; area 689 sq km/ 266 sq mi; population (2001 est) 75,300. The capital and chief port is Mahón; the other main towns are Ciudadela, Alayor, Mercadal, Ferrerias, and Fornells. Leather goods, costume jewellery, and cheese and dairy products are produced on the island, and tourism is also important. Mahón has the finest and largest natural harbour in the Mediterranean. The inhabitants speak their own dialect of Catalan (Menorquin).

Menshevik (Russian *menshinstvo* 'minority') member of the minority of the Russian Social Democratic Party, who split from the *Bolsheviks in 1903. The Mensheviks believed in a large, loosely organized party and that, before socialist revolution could occur in Russia, capitalist society had to develop further. During the

Russian Revolution they had limited power and set up a government in Georgia, but were suppressed in 1922.

menstrual cycle biological cycle occurring in female mammals of reproductive age that prepares the body for pregnancy. At the beginning of the cycle, a Graafian (egg) follicle develops in the ovary, and the inner wall of the uterus forms a soft spongy lining. The egg (*ovum) is released from the ovary, and the *uterus lining (endometrium) becomes vascularized (filled with *blood vessels). At this stage fertilization can take place. If fertilization does not occur, the corpus luteum (remains of the Graafian follicle) degenerates, and the uterine lining breaks down, and is shed. This is what causes the loss of blood that marks menstruation. The cycle then begins again. Human menstruation takes place from puberty to menopause, except during pregnancy, occurring about every 28 days.

mental disability arrested or incomplete development of mental capacities. It can be very mild, but in more severe cases is associated with social problems and difficulties in living independently. A person may be born with a mental disability (for example, *Down's syndrome) or may acquire it through brain damage. Between 90 and 130 million people in the world suffer from such disabilities.

mental illness disordered functioning of the mind. Since normal working cannot easily be defined, the borderline between mild mental illness and normality is a matter of opinion (not to be confused with normative behaviour). It is broadly divided into two categories: *neurosis, in which the patient remains in touch with reality; and *psychosis, in which perception, thought, and belief are disordered.

menthol pungent, waxy, crystalline alcohol $C_{10}H_{19}OH$, derived from oil of peppermint and used in medicines and cosmetics.

Mentor in Homer's *Odyssey*, an old man, adviser to *Telemachus in the absence of his father *Odysseus. His form is often taken by the goddess Athena.

Menzies, Robert Gordon (1894–1978) Australian conservative politician, leader of the United Australia (now Liberal) Party and prime minister 1939–41 and 1949–66.

MEP abbreviation for member of the *European Parliament.

Mephistopheles *or* **Mephisto** another name for the *devil, or an agent of the devil, associated with the *Faust legend.

Mercalli scale qualitative scale describing the intensity of an *earthquake. It differs from the *Richter scale, which indicates earthquake **magnitude** and is quantitative. It is named after the Italian seismologist Giuseppe Mercalli (1850–1914).

mercantilism economic theory, held in the 16th–18th centuries, that a nation's wealth (in the form of bullion or treasure) was the key to its prosperity. To this end, foreign trade should be regulated to create a surplus of exports over imports, and the state should intervene where necessary (for example, subsidizing exports and taxing imports). The bullion theory of wealth was demolished by Adam *Smith in Book IV of *The Wealth of Nations* (1776).

Mercator, Gerardus (1512–1594) Flemish Gerhard Kremer, Flemish mapmaker who devised **Mercator's projection** in which the parallels and meridians on maps are drawn uniformly at 90°. The projection continues to be used, in particular for navigational charts, because compass courses can be drawn as straight lines, but the true area of countries is increasingly distorted the further north or south they are from the Equator. For other types, see *map projection.

mercenary soldier hired by the army of another country or by a private army. Mercenary military service originated in the 14th century, when cash payment on a regular basis was the only means of guaranteeing soldiers' loyalty. In the 20th century mercenaries have been common in wars and guerrilla activity in Asia, Africa, and Latin America.

merchant bank financial institution that specializes in corporate finance and financial and advisory services for business. Originally developed in the UK in the 19th century, merchant banks now offer many of the services provided by the commercial banks.

Merchants Adventurers English trading company founded in 1407, which controlled the export of cloth to continental Europe. It comprised guilds and traders in many northern European ports. In direct opposition to the Hanseatic League, it came to control 75% of English overseas trade by 1550. In 1689 it lost its charter for furthering the traders' own interests at the expense of the English economy. The company was finally dissolved in 1806.

Mercia Anglo-Saxon kingdom that emerged in the 6th century. By the late 8th century it dominated all England south of the Humber, but from about 825 came under the power of Wessex. Mercia eventually came to denote an area bounded by the Welsh border, the River Humber, East Anglia, and the River Thames.

Mercury closest planet to the Sun. Its mass is 0.056 that of Earth. On its sunward side the surface temperature reaches over 400 °C/752 °F, but on the 'night' side it falls to –170 °C/–274 °F. **mean distance from the Sun:** 58 million km/36 million mi **equatorial diameter:** 4,880 km/3,030 mi **rotation period:** 59 Earth days **year:** 88 Earth days **atmosphere:** Mercury's small mass and high daytime temperature mean that it is impossible for an atmosphere to be retained **surface:** composed of silicate rock often in the form of lava flows. In 1974 the US space probe Mariner 10 showed that Mercury's surface is cratered by meteorite impacts **satellites:** none.

mercury chemical symbol Hg; or **quicksilver**, (Latin *mercurius*) heavy, silver-grey, metallic element, atomic number 80, relative atomic mass 200.59. Its symbol comes from the Latin *hydrargyrum*. It is a dense, mobile liquid with a low melting point (–38.87 °C/–37.96 °F). Its chief source is the mineral cinnabar, HgS, but it sometimes occurs in nature as a free metal.

Mercury *or* **Mercurius** (Latin *merx* 'merchandise') in Roman mythology, a god of commerce and gain, and messenger of the gods. He was identified with the Greek *Hermes, and similarly represented with winged sandals and a winged staff entwined with snakes.

Mercury project US project 1961–63 to put a human in space using the one-seat *Mercury* spacecraft.

merganser any of several diving ducks with long, slender, serrated bills for catching fish, widely distributed in the northern hemisphere. Most have crested heads. (Genus *Mergus*, family Anatidae.)

merger the linking of two or more companies, either by creating a new organization by consolidating the original companies or by absorption by one company of the others. Unlike a takeover, which is not always a voluntary fusion of the parties, a merger is the result of an agreement.

meridian half a *great circle drawn on the Earth's surface passing through both poles and thus through all places with the same longitude. Terrestrial longitudes are usually measured from the Greenwich Meridian.

Mérimée, Prosper (1803–1870) French author. Among his works are the short novels *Mateo Falcone* (1829), *Colomba* (1841), *Carmen* (1846) (the basis for Bizet's opera), and the *Lettres à une inconnue/Letters to an Unknown Girl* (1873). Romantically set in foreign countries, his stories nevertheless have a realistic background of local colour and atmosphere.

merino breed of sheep. Its close-set, silky wool is highly valued. Originally from Spain, the merino is now found all over the world, and is the breed on which the Australian wool industry is built.

meristem region of plant tissue containing cells that are actively dividing to produce new tissues (or have the potential to do so). Meristems found in the tip of roots and stems, the apical meristems, are responsible for the growth in length of these organs.

Merit, Order of British order (see *knighthood, order of), instituted in 1902 and limited in number to 24 men and women of eminence. It confers no precedence or knighthood.

merlin small *falcon of Europe, Asia, and North America, where it is also called a **pigeon hawk**. The male, 26 cm/10 in long, has a grey-blue back and reddish-brown barred front; the female, 32 cm/13 in long, has a dark brown back and lighter front with streaks. Merlins fly relatively low over the ground when hunting and 'stoop' quickly onto their prey, which consists mainly of small birds. (Species *Falco columbarius*, order Falconiformes.)

Merlin Welsh **Myrddin**, legendary magician and seer to King *Arthur. Welsh bardic literature has a cycle of poems attributed to him, and he may have been a real person. His legend is related in *Vita Merlini* by the 12th-century chronicler Geoffrey of Monmouth.

mermaid (Old English *mere* 'lake', *maegth* 'maid') mythical sea creature (the male is a **merman**), having a human head and torso, often of great beauty, and a fish's tail. Suggested animals behind the myth include the dugong or manatee and seal.

Merovingian dynasty (lived 5th–8th centuries) Frankish dynasty, named after its founder, **Merovech** (5th century AD). His descendants ruled France from the time of Clovis (481–511) to 751.

Mersey river in northwest England; length 112 km/70 mi. Formed by the confluence of the Goyt and Tame rivers at Stockport, it flows west through the south of Manchester, is joined by the Irwell at Flixton and by the Weaver at Runcorn, and enters the Irish Sea at Liverpool Bay. It drains large areas of the Lancashire and Cheshire plains. The Mersey is linked to the Manchester Ship Canal. Although plans were announced in 1990 to build a 1,800-m/5,907-ft barrage across the Mersey estuary to generate electricity from tides, these were abandoned in 1992 for financial reasons.

Merseyside metropolitan county of northwest England, created in 1974; in 1986, most of the functions of the former county council were transferred to metropolitan borough councils (The Wirral, Sefton, Liverpool, Knowsley, St Helens). **area:** 650 sq km/251 sq mi **towns and cities:** Liverpool, Bootle, Birkenhead, St Helens, Wallasey, Southport **physical:** River Mersey **features:** Merseyside Innovation Centre (MIC), linked with Liverpool and John Moores Universities; Prescot Museum of clock- and watch-making; Speke Hall (Tudor), and Croxteth Hall and Country Park (a working country estate open to the public); Port Sunlight (a garden village for the Lever soap factory workers) **population:** (1996) 1,420,400.

Merthyr Tydfil unitary authority in south Wales, created in 1996 from part of the former county of Mid Glamorgan. **area:** 111 sq km/43 sq mi **towns:** Merthyr Tydfil (administrative headquarters) **physical:** highest point Merthyr Common (530 m/1,739 ft), River Taff **features:** area includes part of Brecon Beacons National Park **population:** (1998 est) 55,800.

mesa (Spanish 'table') flat-topped, steep-sided plateau, consisting of horizontal weak layers of rock topped by a resistant formation; in particular, those found in the desert areas of the USA and Mexico. A small mesa is called a butte.

mescaline psychedelic drug derived from a small, spineless cactus *Lophophora williamsii* of northern Mexico and the southwest USA, known as *peyote. The tops (called mescal buttons), which scarcely appear above ground, are dried and chewed, or added to alcoholic drinks. Mescaline is a crystalline alkaloid $C_{11}H_{17}NO_3$. It is used by some North American Indians in religious rites.

Meskhetian a community of Turkish descent that formerly inhabited Meskhetia, on the then Turkish–Soviet border. They were deported by Stalin in 1944 to Kazakhstan and Uzbekistan, and have campaigned since then for a return to their homeland. In June 1989 at least 70 were killed in pogroms directed against their community in the Fergana Valley of Uzbekistan by the ethnic Uzbeks.

Mesolithic the Middle Stone Age developmental stage of human technology and of *prehistory.

meson in physics, a group of unstable subatomic particles made up of a *quark and an antiquark. It is found in cosmic radiation, and is emitted by nuclei under bombardment by very high-energy particles.

mesophyll tissue between the upper and lower epidermis of a leaf blade (lamina), consisting of parenchyma-like cells containing numerous *chloroplasts.

Mesopotamia the land between the Tigris and Euphrates rivers, now part of Iraq. The civilizations of Sumer and Babylon flourished here. The *Sumerian civilization (3500 BC) may have been the earliest urban civilization. Prior to World War I the area was part of the Turkish Empire, but the British drove the Turks out in October 1918. In 1932 Mesopotamia became part of the newly-established state of Iraq.

Mesopotamian art art of the ancient civilizations that grew up in the area around the Tigris and Euphrates rivers, now in Iraq. Mesopotamian art was largely used to glorify powerful dynasties, and often reflected the belief that kingship and the divine were closely interlocked.

mesosphere layer in the Earth's *atmosphere above the stratosphere and below the thermosphere. It lies between about 50 km/31 mi and 80 km/50 mi above the ground.

Mesozoic era of geological time 245–65 million years ago, consisting of the Triassic, Jurassic, and Cretaceous periods. At the beginning of the era, the continents were joined together as Pangaea; dinosaurs and other giant reptiles dominated the sea and air; and ferns, horsetails, and cycads thrived in a warm climate worldwide. By the end of the Mesozoic era, the continents had begun to assume their present positions, flowering plants were dominant, and many of the large reptiles and marine fauna were becoming extinct.

Messiaen, Olivier Eugène Prosper Charles (1908–1992) French composer, organist, and teacher. His music is mystical in character, vividly coloured, and incorporates transcriptions of birdsong. Among his works are the *Quartet for the End of Time* (1941), the large-scale *Turangalîla Symphony* (1949), and solo organ and piano pieces. As a teacher at the Paris Conservatoire from 1942, he influenced three generations of composers.

Messiah (from Hebrew *mashiach* 'anointed') in Judaism and Christianity, the saviour or deliverer. The prophets of the Hebrew Bible (Old Testament) foretold that a wise and pious man descended from King David would lead and rule over the Messianic age, a time of peace and godliness. Jews from the time of the *Babylonian Captivity (6th century BC), have looked forward to the coming of the Messiah. Christians believe that the Messiah came in the person of *Jesus, and hence called him the *Christ, meaning 'anointed one'.

Messier, Charles (1730–1817) French astronomer. He discovered 15 comets and in 1784 published a list of 103 star clusters and nebulae. Objects on this list are given M (for Messier) numbers, which astronomers still use today, such as M1 (the Crab nebula) and M31 (the Andromeda galaxy).

Messina, Strait of ancient **Siculum Fretum**, channel in the central Mediterranean separating Sicily from mainland Italy, joining the Tyrrhenian and Ionian seas; it is 32 km/20 mi long, and its width varies from 16 km/10 mi in the south to 3 km/2 mi in the north. In Greek legend the monster Scylla devoured sailors from a rock on the Italian shore, while another, Charybdis, created a whirlpool on the Sicilian side which sank ships. The classical hero Odysseus passed safely between them. The currents, whirlpools, and winds of the strait that gave rise to these and other legends in ancient times continue to hamper navigation.

metabolism chemical processes of living organisms enabling them to grow and to function. It involves a constant alternation of building up complex molecules (**anabolism**) and breaking them down (**catabolism**). For example, green plants build up complex organic substances from water, carbon dioxide, and mineral salts (*photosynthesis); by digestion animals partially break down complex organic substances, ingested as food, and subsequently resynthesize them for use in their own bodies (see *digestive system). Within cells, complex molecules are broken down by the process of *respiration. The waste products of metabolism are removed by *excretion.

metal any of a class of chemical elements with specific physical and chemical characteristics. Metallic elements compose about 75% of the 112 elements in the *periodic table of the elements. Physical properties include a sonorous tone when struck; good conduction of heat and electricity; high melting and boiling points; opacity but good reflection of light; malleability, which enables them to be cold-worked and rolled into sheets; and ductility, which permits them to be drawn into thin wires.

metal detector electronic device for detecting metal, usually below ground, developed from the wartime mine detector. In the head of the metal detector is a coil, which is part of an electronic circuit. The presence of metal causes the frequency of the signal in the circuit to change, setting up an audible note in the headphones worn by the user.

metal fatigue condition in which metals fail or fracture under relatively light loads, when these loads are applied repeatedly. Structures that are subject to flexing, such as the airframes of aircraft, are prone to metal fatigue.

metallic bond force of attraction operating in a *metal that holds the atoms together in a metallic structure. In metallic bonding, metal atoms form a close-packed, regular arrangement. The atoms lose their outer-shell electrons to become positive ions. The outer electrons become a 'sea' of mobile electrons surrounding a lattice of positive ions. The lattice is held together by the strong attractive forces between the mobile electrons and the positive ions.

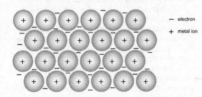

— electron
+ metal ion

metallic bond In metallic bonding, metal ions are tightly packed with their outer shell electrons overlap, so each electron becomes detached from its parent atom (delocalized). The metal is held together by the strong forces of attraction between the positive nuclei and the surrounding sea of delocalized electrons.

metalloid *or* **semimetal** any chemical element having some of but not all the properties of metals; metalloids are thus usually electrically semiconducting. They comprise the elements germanium, arsenic, antimony, and tellurium. Metalloids are found in the *periodic table of the elements between metals and non-metals.

metallurgy the science and technology of producing metals, which includes extraction, alloying, and hardening. **Extractive**, or **process, metallurgy** is concerned with the extraction of metals from their *ores and refining and adapting them for use. **Physical metallurgy** is concerned with their properties and application. **Metallography** establishes the microscopic structures that contribute to hardness, ductility, and strength.

metamorphic rock rock altered in structure, composition, and texture by pressure or heat after its original formation. (Rock that actually melts under heat is called *igneous rock upon cooling.) For example, limestone can be metamorphosed by heat into marble, and shale by pressure into slate. The term was coined in 1833 by Scottish geologist Charles *Lyell. Metamorphism is part of the rock cycle, the gradual formation, change, and re-formation of rocks over millions of years.

metamorphism geological term referring to the changes in rocks of the Earth's crust caused by increasing pressure and temperature. The resulting rocks are metamorphic rocks. All metamorphic changes take place in solid rocks. If the rocks melt and then harden, they are considered *igneous rocks.

metamorphosis period during the life cycle of many invertebrates, most amphibians, and some fish, during which the individual's body changes from one form to another through a major reconstitution of its tissues. For example, adult frogs are produced by metamorphosis from tadpoles, and butterflies are produced from caterpillars following metamorphosis within a pupa. In classical thought and literature, metamorphosis is the transformation of a living being into another shape, either living or inanimate (for example Niobe). The Roman poet *Ovid wrote about this theme.

metaphor (Greek 'transfer') figure of speech using an analogy or close comparison between two things that are not normally treated as if they had anything in common. Metaphor is a common means of extending the uses and references of words. See also *simile.

metaphysical painting (Italian *pittura metafisica*) Italian painting style, developed in 1917 by Giorgio de *Chirico and Carlo Carrà. It tried to create a sense of mystery through the use of dreamlike imagery; human beings were often represented as tailors' dummies, and objects appeared in strange, unfamiliar contexts. Reacting against both *cubism and *Futurism, metaphysical painting paved the way for *surrealism, particularly in its use of familiar, everyday objects in absurd compositions. Though short-lived – only lasting to the early 1920s – its influence was considerable.

metaphysical poets group of early 17th-century English poets whose work is characterized by ingenious, highly intricate wordplay and unlikely or paradoxical imagery. They used rhetoric and literary devices, such as *paradox, hyperbole (exaggeration), and elaborately developed conceits (far-fetched comparisons), in such a way as to engage the reader by their humour, strangeness, or sheer outrageousness. English poets John *Donne and Andrew *Marvell write comic, erotic, and serious poetry in this genre, while English poet George *Herbert concentrated on religious themes.

metaphysics branch of philosophy that deals with first principles, in particular 'being' (ontology) and 'knowing' (*epistemology), and that is concerned with the ultimate nature of reality. It has been maintained that no certain knowledge of metaphysical questions is possible.

Metchnikoff, Elie (1845–1916) Russian Ilya Ilich Mechnikov, Russian zoologist and immunologist who was a pioneer of cellular immunology and shared the

Nobel Prize for Physiology or Medicine in 1908 with Paul *Ehrlich for the discovery of the innate immune response.

meteor flash of light in the sky, popularly known as a **shooting** or **falling star**, caused by a particle of dust, a meteoroid, entering the atmosphere at speeds up to 70 kps/45 mps and burning up by friction at a height of around 100 km/60 mi. On any clear night, several **sporadic meteors** can be seen each hour.

meteorite piece of rock or metal from space that reaches the surface of the Earth, Moon, or other body. Most meteorites are thought to be fragments from asteroids, although some may be pieces from the heads of comets. Most are stony, although some are made of iron and a few have a mixed rock–iron composition.

meteorology scientific observation and study of the *atmosphere, so that *weather can be accurately forecast. Data from meteorological stations and weather satellites are collated by computers at central agencies, and forecast and weather maps based on current readings are issued at regular intervals. Modern analysis, employing some of the most powerful computers, can give useful forecasts for up to six days ahead.

methanal *or* **formaldehyde** HCHO, gas at ordinary temperatures, condensing to a liquid at −21 °C/−5.8 °F. It has a powerful, penetrating smell. Dissolved in water, it is used as a biological preservative. It is used in the manufacture of plastics, dyes, foam (for example, urea-formaldehyde foam, used in insulation), and in medicine.

methane CH_4, simplest *hydrocarbon of the *alkane series. Colourless, odourless, and lighter than air, it burns with a bluish flame and explodes when mixed with air or oxygen. As the chief constituent of natural gas, methane's main use is as a fuel. It also occurs in the explosive firedamp of coal mines. Methane emitted by rotting vegetation forms marsh gas, which may ignite by spontaneous combustion to produce the pale flame seen over marshland and known as *will-o'-the-wisp.

methanoic acid *or* **formic acid** HCOOH, colourless, slightly fuming liquid that freezes at 8 °C/46.4 °F and boils at 101 °C/213.8 °F. It occurs in stinging ants, nettles, sweat, and pine needles, and is used in dyeing, tanning, and electroplating.

methanol common name **methyl alcohol**; CH_3OH, simplest of the alcohols. It can be made by the dry distillation of wood (hence it is also known as wood alcohol), but is usually made from coal or natural gas. When pure, it is a colourless, flammable liquid with a pleasant odour, and is highly poisonous.

Methodism evangelical Protestant Christian movement that was founded by John *Wesley in 1739 within the Church of England, but became a separate body in 1795. The Methodist Episcopal Church was founded in the USA in 1784. In 2001 there were over 50 million Methodists worldwide.

Methodius, St (c. 825–884) Greek Christian bishop, who with his brother *Cyril translated much of the Bible into Slavonic. Feast day 14 February.

Methuselah in the Old Testament, Hebrew patriarch who lived before the Flood; his lifespan of 969 years makes him a byword for longevity.

methylated spirit alcohol that has been rendered undrinkable, and is used for industrial purposes, as a fuel for spirit burners or a solvent.

metre in music, refers to the number and value of the beats in a bar of music. It is also known as **time**. Metre is different from rhythm in that it is regular (although the number can change as in the additive metres of African music and the works of Olivier Messiaen), whereas rhythm is irregular.

metre symbol m, SI unit of length, equivalent to 1.093 yards or 39.37 inches. It is defined by scientists as the length of the path travelled by light in a vacuum during a time interval of 1/299,792,458 of a second.

metric system system of weights and measures developed in France in the 18th century and recognized by other countries in the 19th century. In 1960 an international conference on weights and measures recommended the universal adoption of a revised International System (Système International d'Unités, or SI), with seven prescribed 'base units': the metre (m) for length, kilogram (kg) for mass, second (s) for time, ampere (A) for electric current, kelvin (K) for thermodynamic temperature, candela (cd) for luminous intensity, and mole (mol) for quantity of matter.

Metternich, Klemens Wenzel Nepomuk Lothar, Prince von Metternich (1773–1859) Austrian politician, the leading figure in European diplomacy after the fall of Napoleon. As foreign minister 1809–48 (as well as chancellor from 1821), he tried to maintain the balance of power in Europe, supporting monarchy and repressing liberalism.

Mexican War *or* **Mexican–American War** war between the USA and Mexico 1846–48. The war was ostensibly over disputed boundaries between the two nations, but it was also an excuse for the USA to pursue its 'manifest destiny' to expand westwards. US forces defeated the Mexican army in a series of battles in the disputed regions and Mexico itself, and occupied Mexico City in 1847. Under the Treaty of Guadaloupe Hidalgo that ended the war, the USA acquired what are now California, Nevada, and Utah, and parts of New Mexico, Arizona, Colorado, and Wyoming, all in exchange for $15 million.

Mexico
National name: *Estados Unidos Mexicanos/ United States of Mexico*
Area: 1,958,201 sq km/756,061 sq mi
Capital: Mexico City

Major towns/cities: Guadalajara, Monterrey, Puebla, Netzahualcóyotl, Ciudad Juárez, Tijuana
Major ports: 49 ocean ports
Physical features: partly arid central highlands; Sierra Madre mountain ranges east and west; tropical coastal plains; volcanoes, including Popocatepetl; Rio Grande
Head of state and government: Vicente Fox Quesada from 2000
Political system: liberal democracy
Political executive: limited presidency
Political parties: Institutional Revolutionary Party (PRI), moderate, left wing; National Action Party (PAN), moderate, Christian, right of centre; Party of the Democratic Revolution (PRD), left of centre
Currency: Mexican peso
GNI per capita (PPP): (US$) 8,540 (2002 est)
Exports: petroleum and petroleum products, engines and spare parts for motor vehicles, motor vehicles, electrical and electronic goods, fresh and preserved vegetables, coffee, cotton. Principal market: USA 88.7% (2001)
Population: 103,457,000 (2003 est)
Language: Spanish (official), Nahuatl, Maya, Zapoteco, Mixteco, Otomi
Religion: Roman Catholic about 90%
Life expectancy: 70 (men); 76 (women) (2000–05)
Chronology
c. 2600 BC: Mayan civilization originated in Yucatán peninsula.
1000–500 BC: Zapotec civilization developed around Monte Albán in southern Mexico.
4th–10th centuries AD: Mayan Empire at its height.
10th–12th centuries: Toltecs ruled much of Mexico from their capital at Tula.
12th century: Aztecs migrated south into the valley of Mexico.
c. 1325: Aztecs began building their capital Tenochtitlán on site of present-day Mexico City.
15th century: Montezuma I built up the Aztec Empire in central Mexico.
1519–21: Hernán Cortes conquered Aztec Empire and secured Mexico for Spain.
1520: Montezuma II, last king of the Aztecs, was killed.
1535: Mexico became Spanish viceroyalty of New Spain; plantations and mining developed with Indian labour.
1519–1607: Indigenous population reduced from 21 million to 1 million, due mainly to lack of resistance to diseases transported from Old World.
1810: Father Miguel Hidalgo led unsuccessful revolt against Spanish.
1821: Independence proclaimed by Augustín de Iturbide with support of Church and landowners.
1822: Iturbide overthrew provisional government and proclaimed himself Emperor Augustín I.
1824: Federal republic established amid continuing public disorder.
1824–55: Military rule of Antonio López de Santa Anna, who imposed stability (he became president in 1833).
1846–48: Mexican War: Mexico lost California and New Mexico to USA.
1848: Revolt of Mayan Indians suppressed.
1855: Benito Juárez aided overthrow of Santa Anna's dictatorship.
1857–60: Sweeping liberal reforms and anti-clerical legislation introduced by Juárez led to civil war with conservatives.

1861: Mexico suspended payment on foreign debt leading to French military intervention; Juárez resisted with US support.
1864: Supported by conservatives, France installed Archduke Maximilian of Austria as emperor of Mexico.
1867: Maximilian shot by republicans as French troops withdrew; Juárez resumed presidency.
1872: Death of Juárez.
1876: Gen Porfirio Diaz established dictatorship; Mexican economy modernized through foreign investment.
1911: Revolution overthrew Díaz; liberal president Francisco Madero introduced radical land reform and labour legislation but political disorder increased.
1914 and 1916–17: US military intervened to quell disorder.
1917: New constitution, designed to ensure permanent democracy, adopted with US encouragement.
1924–35: Government dominated by anti-clerical Gen Plutarco Calles, who introduced further social reforms.
1929: Foundation of National Revolutionary Party (PRFN), renamed the Institutional Revolutionary Party (PRI) in 1946.
1938: President Lázaro Cárdenas nationalized all foreign-owned oil wells in face of US opposition.
1942: Mexico declared war on Germany and Japan (and so regained US favour).
1946–52: Miguel Alemán first of succession of authoritarian PRI presidents to seek moderation and stability rather than further radical reform.
1960s: Rapid industrial growth partly financed by borrowing.
1976: Huge oil reserves were discovered in the southeastern state of Chiapas; oil production tripled in six years.
1982: Falling oil prices caused a grave financial crisis; Mexico defaulted on debt.
1985: An earthquake in Mexico City killed thousands.
1994: There was an uprising in Chiapas by the Zapatista National Liberation Army (EZLN), seeking rights for the Mayan Indian population; Mexico formed the North American Free Trade Area (NAFTA) with the USA and Canada. Presidential elections were won by Ernesto Zedillo Ponce de León.
1995: The government agreed to offer greater autonomy to Mayan Indians in Chiapas.
1996: There were short-lived peace talks with the EZLN; and violent attacks against the government by the new leftist Popular Revolutionary Army (EPR) increased.
1997: The PRI lost its assembly majority. A civilian counterpart to the Zapatista rebels, the Zapatista National Liberation Front (EZLN), was formed.
1998: A lapsed peace accord with Zapatist rebels was reactivated, but talks between the government and the rebels broke down.
2000: After 71 years, the PRI lost power, and Vicente Fox of the conservative National Action Party was elected president. He promised national unity, job creation, and an attack on government corruption. He signed a bill on indigenous rights, in response to which the leader of the rebels offered to open peace talks.
2001: The Zapatista leader, Subcomandante Marcos, led a peaceful march from Chiapas to Mexico City to ask Congress to ratify the indigenous rights bill.

2002: Mexico withdrew from the Rio Pact, a mutual-defence treaty for the Americas dating back to the Cold War era.

2003: The PRI beat the National Action Party in mid-term parliamentary elections.

2005: Mexico's top security prisons were put on high alert after increasing tension between the authorities and drug gangs. President Fox stated that drug cartels were trying to infiltrate state institutions.

Mexico City Spanish **Ciudad de México**, capital, industrial, and cultural centre of Mexico, 2,255 m/7,400 ft above sea level on the southern edge of the central plateau; population (2000 est) 8,605,200 (city), 18,327,000 (urban area; the largest urban agglomeration in the world). Over half of the country's manufacturing output originates in the city and its surrounds; industries include iron, steel, chemicals, pharmaceuticals, textiles, and electric and electronic goods. It is one of the world's most polluted cities because of its position in a volcanic basin 2,000 m/7,400 ft above sea level, in which pollutants gather and produce a smog cloud.

Meyerbeer, Giacomo (1791–1864) adopted name of Jakob Liebmann Meyer Beer, German composer. His spectacular operas include *Robert le Diable* (1831) and *Les Huguenots* (1836). From 1826 he lived mainly in Paris, returning to Berlin after 1842 as musical director of the Royal Opera.

mezuzah *or* **mezuza** in Judaism, a small box containing a parchment scroll inscribed with a prayer, the Shema from Deuteronomy (6:4–9; 11:13–21), which is found in the upper third of the right doorpost of every home and every room in a Jewish house, except the bathroom.

Mezzogiorno (Italian 'midday') hot, impoverished area of southern Italy, comprising the regions of Molise, Campania, Apulia, Basilicata, and Calabria, and the islands of Sardinia and Sicily. Agriculture is the chief mainstay of a generally poor economy; the main products are grains, vegetables, grapes, and olives. The region's economic, educational, and income levels are much lower than those of northern Italy.

mezzo-soprano female singing voice with an approximate range of A4–F5, between contralto and soprano. It is commonly abbreviated to just 'mezzo'.

mezzotint (Italian 'half tint') print produced by a method of etching in density of tone rather than line, popular in the 18th and 19th centuries when it was largely used for the reproduction of paintings, especially portraits. A copper or steel plate is roughened with a finely-toothed tool known as a 'rocker' to raise an even, overall burr (rough edge), which will hold ink. At this point the plate would print a rich, even black, so areas of burr are carefully smoothed away with a 'scraper' to produce a range of lighter tones. Primarily a reproductive technique, mezzotint declined rapidly with the invention of photography.

MI5 *or the* **Security Service** abbreviation for **Military Intelligence, section five**, the counter-intelligence agency of the British *intelligence services. Its role is to prevent or investigate espionage, subversion, and sabotage. The headquarters of MI5 are at Thames House, Millbank, London.

MI6 *or the* **Secret Intelligence Service** abbreviation for **Military Intelligence, section six**, the secret intelligence agency of the British *intelligence services which operates largely under Foreign Office control.

Miami industrial city and port in southeastern Florida, on the Atlantic coast of the Florida peninsula about 70 km/43 mi from its southern tip; seat of Dade County; population (2000 est) 362,500. Around 66% of the population is of Hispanic origin, many of whom are Cubans living in the Little Havana area; African Americans comprise 22% of the population, and whites 12%. Miami is the hub of finance, trade, and transport in the region, with air connections to Latin America and the Caribbean; industries include food processing, transportation and electronic equipment, clothing, furniture, and machinery. Major employers are the state and federal governments. With its subtropical climate Miami is also a major tourist resort (tourism is the city's major industry) and a centre for oceanographic research. The city of Miami beach is situated on a barrier island, and is linked to Miami by bridges. The first permanent European settlement dates from the 1870s; Miami was incorporated in 1896.

mica any of a group of silicate minerals that split easily into thin flakes along lines of weakness in their crystal structure (perfect basal cleavage). They are glossy, have a pearly lustre, and are found in many igneous and metamorphic rocks. Their good thermal and electrical insulation qualities make them valuable in industry.

Michael (1921–) King of Romania 1927–30 and 1940–47. The son of Carol II, he succeeded his grandfather as king in 1927 but was displaced when his father returned from exile in 1930. In 1940 he was proclaimed king again on his father's abdication, overthrew in 1944 the fascist dictatorship of Ion Antonescu (1882–1946), and enabled Romania to share in the victory of the Allies at the end of World War II. He abdicated and left Romania in 1947.

Michaelmas daisy popular name for a species of *aster, and also for the sea aster or starwort.

Michaelmas Day in Christian church tradition, the festival of St Michael and all angels, observed 29 September.

Michelangelo (1475–1564) born Michelangelo di Lodovico Buonarroti, Italian sculptor, painter, architect, and poet. Active in his native Florence and in Rome, his giant talent dominated the High Renaissance. The marble *David* (1501–04; Accademia, Florence) set a new standard in nude sculpture. His massive figure style was translated into *fresco on the ceiling (1508–12) and altar wall (1536–41) of the Sistine Chapel in the Vatican. Michelangelo's influence, particularly on the development of *Mannerism, was profound. His architectural works, including the dome of St Peter's basilica, also greatly influenced the emergence of the *baroque style.

Michelson, Albert Abraham (1852–1931) German-born US physicist. With his colleague Edward Morley, he performed in 1887 the **Michelson–Morley experiment** to detect the motion of the Earth through the postulated ether (a medium believed to be necessary for the propagation of light). The failure of the experiment indicated the nonexistence of the ether, and led Albert *Einstein to his theory of *relativity. Michelson was awarded the Nobel Prize for Physics in 1907 for his measurement of the speed of light through the design and application of precise optical instruments such as the interferometer. He was the first American to be awarded a Nobel prize.

Michigan called the **Wolverine State** or the **Great Lakes State**, (Algonquian Indian *Michigama* 'great (or big) lake') state in north-central USA, situated in the *Midwest and *Great Lakes regions, consisting of two peninsular masses separated by the Straits of Mackinac; the mitten-shaped, north–south-oriented Lower Peninsula is bordered to the south by *Ohio and *Indiana, by Lake *Michigan to the west, and to the north and east by lakes *Huron, *Erie, and Saint Clair, and the Detroit and St Clair rivers; the east–west-oriented Upper Peninsula is bordered to the south by *Wisconsin, by Lake *Superior to the north, by *Ontario, Canada, to the northeast, across St Mary's River and by Lake Michigan to the south; area 147,122 sq km/56,804 sq mi; population (2000) 9,938,400; capital Lansing. Michigan's nickname, the Wolverine State, is thought to date back to a land border dispute with Ohio, when Ohioans described Michiganians as 'vicious as wolverines'. It is also called the Great Lakes State, bordering four of the five Great Lakes and home to more than 11,000 inland lakes. During the 20th century Michigan's largest city, *Detroit, became the car capital of the world, known as the Motor City, or Motown. The name *Motown became synonymous with a distinct rhythm and blues music. Steel production and agriculture, particularly corn and fruit, are also important economically. Other major cities include Grand Rapids, Warren, Flint, Sterling Heights, and Ann Arbor. Before pioneer settlement, Michigan was home to the Algonquian-speaking American Indians and Huron peoples. Michigan was admitted to the Union in 1837 as the 26th US state.

Michigan, Lake (Algonquian 'big lake'.) lake in north-central USA, the third largest of the *Great Lakes and the only one lying entirely within the USA, it is bordered by Michigan to the north and east, Indiana to the south, and Wisconsin and Illinois to the west; area 58,000 sq km/22,390 sq mi. The lake is 517 km/321 mi long, 190 km/118 mi at its widest point, has a maximum depth of 282 m/925 ft, and lies 176 m/577 ft above sea level. Lake Michigan is joined to Lake Huron by the Straits of Mackinac in the north. Green Bay is its largest inlet, and Chicago and Milwaukee are its main ports. The first European to see the Lake Michigan was the French explorer Jean Nicolet, in 1634.

micro- symbol μ, prefix denoting a one-millionth part (10^{-6}). For example, a micrometre, μm, is one-millionth of a metre.

microbe another name for *micro-organism.

microbiology study of micro-organisms, mostly viruses and single-celled organisms such as bacteria, protozoa, and yeasts. The practical applications of microbiology are in medicine (since many micro-organisms cause disease); in brewing, baking, and other food and beverage processes, where the micro-organisms carry out fermentation; and in genetic engineering, which is creating increasing interest in the field of microbiology.

microchip popular name for the silicon chip, or *integrated circuit.

microclimate climate of a small area, such as a woodland, lake, or even a hedgerow. Significant differences can exist between the climates of two neighbouring areas – for example, a town is usually

warmer than the surrounding countryside (forming a heat island), and a woodland cooler, darker, and less windy than an area of open land.

microcomputer *or* **micro** *or* **personal computer** small desktop or portable *computer, typically designed to be used by one person at a time, although individual computers can be linked in a network so that users can share data and programs.

microeconomics the division of economics concerned with the study of individual decision-making units within an economy: a consumer, firm, or industry. Unlike macroeconomics, it looks at how individual markets work and how individual producers and consumers make their choices and with what consequences. This is done by analysing how relevant prices of goods are determined and the quantities that will be bought and sold.

micrometre symbol μm, one-millionth of a *metre.

Micronesia, Federated States of *or* **Micronesia**

Area: 700 sq km/270 sq mi
Capital: Palikir (in Pohnpei island state)
Major towns/cities: Kolonia (in Pohnpei), Weno (in Truk), Lelu (in Kosrae)
Major ports: Teketik, Lepukos, Okak
Physical features: an archipelago of 607 equatorial, volcanic islands in the West Pacific
Head of state and government: Joseph Urusemal from 2003
Political system: liberal democracy
Political executive: limited presidency
Political parties: no formally organized political parties
Currency: US dollar
GNI per capita (PPP): (US$) 4,760 (2002 est)
Exports: fish and fish products, copra, pepper. Principal market: Japan 91.9% (1999)
Population: 109,000 (2003 est)
Language: English (official), eight officially recognized local languages (including Trukese, Pohnpeian, Yapese, and Kosrean), a number of other dialects
Religion: Christianity (mainly Roman Catholic in Yap state, Protestant elsewhere)
Life expectancy: 68 (men); 69 (women) (2000–05)

597

Chronology

c. 1000 BC: Micronesians first settled the islands.

1525: Portuguese navigators first visited Yap and Ulithi islands in the Carolines (Micronesia).

later 16th century: Fell under Spanish influence.

1874: Spanish rule formally declared in face of increasing encroachment by German traders.

1885: Yap seized by German naval forces, but was restored to Spain after arbitration by Pope Leo XIII on the condition that Germany was allowed freedom of trade.

1899: Purchased for $4.5 million by Germany from Spain, after the latter's defeat in the Spanish–American War.

1914: Occupied by Japan at the outbreak of World War I.

1919: Administered under League of Nations mandate by Japan, and vigorously colonized.

1944: Occupied by USA after Japanese forces defeated in World War II.

1947: Administered by USA as part of the United Nations (UN) Trust Territory of the Pacific Islands, under the name of the Federated States of Micronesia (FSM).

1979: A constitution was adopted that established a federal system for its four constituent states (Yap, Chuuk, Pohnpei, and Kosrae) and internal self-government.

1986: The Compact of Free Association was entered into with the USA, granting the islands self-government with the USA retaining responsibility for defence and security until 2001.

1990: UN trust status was terminated.

1991: Independence agreed, with Bailey Olter as president. Entered into United Nations (UN) membership.

1997: Jacob Nena was sworn in as president after the existing president, Bailey Olter, was incapacitated by a stroke.

2002: Compact of Free Association was renewed for a further 20 years.

2004: The island of Yap was hit by Typhoon Sudel, destroying much of its infrastructure.

Micronesian any of the indigenous Australoid and Polynesian peoples of Micronesia, including Pacific islands north of the Equator, such as the Caroline, Marshall, Mariana, and Gilbert islands. Their languages belong to the Austronesian family.

micro-organism or **microbe** living organism invisible to the naked eye but visible under a microscope. Micro-organisms include *viruses and single-celled organisms such as bacteria and yeasts. Yeasts are fungi, but other fungi are often big enough to see with the naked eye and so are not micro-organisms. The study of micro-organisms is known as microbiology.

microphone primary component in a sound-reproducing system, whereby the mechanical energy of sound waves is converted into electrical signals by means of a *transducer. A diaphragm is attached to a coil of wire placed between two poles of a permanent magnet. Sound waves cause the diaphragm to vibrate, which in turn causes the coil of wire to move in the magnetic field of the permanent magnet. An induced electrical current, matching the pattern of the sound waves, flows through the coil and is fed to an amplifier. The amplified signals are either stored or sent to a loudspeaker.

microprocessor complete computer *central processing unit contained on a single *integrated circuit, or chip. The appearance of the first microprocessor in 1971 designed by Intel for a pocket calculator manufacturer heralded the introduction of the microcomputer. The microprocessor has led to a dramatic fall in the size and cost of computers, and dedicated computers can now be found in washing machines, cars, and so on. Examples of microprocessors are the Intel Pentium family and the IBM/Motorola PowerPC, used by Apple Computer.

microscope instrument for forming magnified images with high resolution for detail. Optical and electron microscopes are the ones chiefly in use; other types include acoustic, scanning tunnelling, and atomic force microscopes.

microsurgery part or all of an intricate surgical operation – rejoining a severed limb, for example – performed with the aid of a binocular microscope, using miniaturized instruments. Sewing of the nerves and blood vessels is done with a nylon thread so fine that it is only just visible to the naked eye.

microwave heating heating by means of microwaves. Microwave ovens use this form of heating for the rapid cooking or reheating of foods, where heat is generated throughout the interior of the food. If food is not heated completely, there is a danger of bacterial growth that may lead to food poisoning. This method is useful for rapid cooking of frozen and pre-prepared or convenience foods. Industrially, microwave heating is used for destroying insects in grain and enzymes in processed food, pasteurizing and sterilizing liquids, and drying timber and paper.

microwave radiation *electromagnetic wave with a wavelength in the range 0.3 cm to 30 cm/0.1 in to 12 in, or 300–300,000 megahertz (between radio waves and *infrared radiation). Microwaves are used in radar, in radio broadcasting, in satellite communications, and in microwave heating and cooking.

Midas in Greek mythology, a king of Phrygia who was granted the ability to convert all he touched to gold by *Dionysus, god of wine and excess; the gift became a curse when his food and drink also turned to metal. In another story he was given ass's ears by Apollo for preferring the music of Pan in a contest between the two gods.

Middle Ages, the or the **medieval period** term used by Europeans to describe the period between ancient history and the Renaissance. It is not a precise term, but is often taken to cover the time from the fall of the western Roman Empire in AD 476 to the fall of Constantinople (Istanbul) and the end of the Eastern Roman Empire in 1453, or alternatively Columbus's voyage to the Americas in 1492. The term Dark Ages is sometimes used to cover the period from AD 476 to AD 1000, because it was a time when learning and the rule of law were at a low ebb in Europe. During this period Germanic and Scandinavian tribes overran Europe, bringing with them changes in language and culture.

middle C white note, C4, at the centre of the piano keyboard, indicating the division between left- and right-hand regions and between the treble and bass staves of printed music. Middle C is also the pitch indicated by a C clef, for example, for viola.

Middle East indeterminate area now usually taken to include Egypt and the Arab states of the eastern Mediterranean and Arabian Peninsula, sometimes extended to the states of northwest Africa, Turkey, Iran and Afghanistan.

Middlesbrough industrial port and administrative centre of Middlesbrough unitary authority in northeast England, on the estuary of the River Tees, 35 km/22 mi south of Sunderland; population (2001 est) 134,800. The modern town only started to develop in the early 19th century after it was decided to extend the railway to reach deeper anchorage on the river: this allowed the town to become a centre for heavy industry. It diversified in the 1960s into construction, electronics, engineering, and shipbuilding.

Middle Way the path to enlightenment, taught by the Buddha, which avoids the extremes of indulgence and asceticism.

midge common name for many insects resembling *gnats, generally divided into biting midges (family Ceratopogonidae) that suck blood and non-biting midges (family Chironomidae).

Mid Glamorgan Welsh **Morgannwg Ganol**, former county of south Wales, 1974–1996, now divided between Rhondda Cynon Taff, *Merthyr Tydfil, *Bridgend, and Vale of Glamorgan unitary authorities.

MIDI acronym for Musical Instrument Digital Interface, manufacturers' standard allowing different pieces of digital music equipment used in composing and recording to be freely connected.

Midi-Pyrénées region of southwest France, comprising the *départements* of Ariège, Aveyron, Haute-Garonne, Gers, Lot, Hautes-Pyrénées, Tarn, and Tarn-et-Garonne; the capital is Toulouse; area 45,348 sq km/17,509 sq mi; population (1999 est) 2,551,700. The region includes several spa towns (including *Lourdes), winter resorts, and prehistoric caves. It produces fruit, wine, and livestock, and industries include aerospace. There are two large universities. Other notable towns include Montauban, Cahors, and Rodez.

Midlands area of central England corresponding roughly to the Anglo-Saxon kingdom of *Mercia. The **East Midlands** comprises Derbyshire, Leicestershire, Northamptonshire, and Nottinghamshire. The **West Midlands** covers the metropolitan district of *West Midlands created from parts of Staffordshire, Warwickshire, and Worcestershire, and split into the metropolitan boroughs of Dudley, Sandwell, Coventry, Birmingham, Walsall, Solihull, and Wolverhampton; and (often included) the **South Midlands** comprising Bedfordshire, Buckinghamshire, and Oxfordshire.

midnight sun constant appearance of the Sun (within the Arctic and Antarctic circles) above the *horizon during the summer.

Midway Islands two low-lying coral islands in the Pacific Ocean, near the northwestern end of the Hawaiian Islands chain, 1,800 km/1,120 mi northwest of Honolulu; area 6.2 sq km/2 sq mi. They used to be a naval base and had no indigenous population. The islands are individually known as Eastern and Sand; they were annexed by the USA in 1867, and are now administered by the US Department of the Interior (DOI). The naval Battle of Midway (3–6 June 1942), between the USA and Japan, was a turning point in the Pacific in World War II; the US victory marked the end of Japanese expansion in the region.

Midwest or **Middle West** large area of the north-central USA. It is loosely defined geographically, but is generally taken to comprise the states of Illinois, Iowa, Wisconsin, Minnesota, Kansas, Missouri, North Dakota, and South Dakota, and the portions of Montana, Wyoming, and Colorado that lie east of the Rocky Mountains. Ohio, Michigan, and Indiana are often variously included as well. In its broadest sense, the Midwest has an area of 986,800 sq mi/2,556,000 sq km and a population of about 61.5 million – roughly a quarter of the national total. The region is generally flat and well-watered, with good transportation links. Traditionally its economy is divided between agriculture and heavy industry. The main urban Midwest centre is Chicago.

midwifery assistance of women in childbirth. Traditionally, it was undertaken by experienced specialists; in modern medical training it is a nursing speciality for practitioners called midwives.

Mies van der Rohe, Ludwig (1886–1969) German architect. A leading exponent of the *international style, he practised in the USA from 1937. He succeeded Walter *Gropius as director of the *Bauhaus 1929–33. He designed the bronze-and-glass Seagram building in New York City 1956–59 and numerous apartment buildings.

mignonette sweet-scented plant, native to North Africa, with yellowish-green flowers in racemes (along the main stem) and abundant foliage; it is widely cultivated. (*Reseda odorata*, family Resedaceae.)

migraine acute, sometimes incapacitating headache (generally only on one side), accompanied by nausea, that recurs, often with advance symptoms such as flashing lights. No cure has been discovered, but ergotamine normally relieves the symptoms. Some sufferers learn to avoid certain foods, such as chocolate, which suggests an allergic factor.

migrant labour people who move from place to place to work. Economic or political pressures often cause people to leave their homelands to earn wages in this way, but some families live this way for several generations. As economic development has taken place at different rates in different countries, the supplies of and need for labour have been uneven.

migration movement, either seasonal or as part of a single life cycle, of certain animals, chiefly birds and fish, to distant breeding or feeding grounds.

migration movement of population away from the home region, either from one country to another (**international** migration) or from one part of a country to another (**internal** migration). Migrations may be temporary (for example, holidaymakers), seasonal (transhumance), or permanent (people moving to cities to find employment). For people, migration is often a permanent (or long-term) movement, which involves the break-up of a person's residential and social environment. People leave areas due to push factors (negative factors such as overcrowding and lack of employment) and are drawn to areas by pull factors (such as better housing, better jobs, and improved facilities). Barriers such as cost, language, politics, and knowledge also influence migration.

mikado (Japanese 'honourable palace gate') title until 701 of the Japanese emperor, when it was replaced by the term *tenno* ('heavenly sovereign').

Milan Italian **Milano**; Roman **Mediolanum**, second-largest city in Italy, situated in Lombardy, 120 km/75 mi northeast of Genoa; population (1992) 1,358,600. Industries include printing, engineering, and the manufacture of aircraft, cars, locomotives, chemicals, clothing, and textiles. Milan is Italy's chief commercial and industrial centre: the main stock exchange, and the headquarters of banks and insurance companies are here. It is also the country's most important publishing centre.

mildew any *fungus that appears as a destructive growth on plants, paper, leather, or wood when they become damp for a certain length of time; such fungi usually form a thin white coating on the surface.

mile symbol mi, imperial unit of linear measure. A statute mile is equal to 1,760 yards (1.60934 km), and an international nautical mile is equal to 2,026 yards (1,852 m).

milfoil another name for the herb *yarrow. Water milfoils are unrelated; they have whorls of fine leaves and grow underwater. (Genus *Miriophyllum*, family Haloragidaceae.)

Militant Tendency in British politics, left-wing faction originally within the Labour Party, aligned with the publication *Militant*. It became active in the 1970s, with radical socialist policies based on Trotskyism (see *Trotsky), and gained some success in local government, for example in the inner-city area of Liverpool. In the mid-1980s the Labour Party considered it to be a separate organization within the party and banned it.

militia body of civilian soldiers, usually with some military training, who are on call in emergencies, distinct from professional soldiers. In Switzerland, the militia is the national defence force, and every able-bodied man is liable for service in it. In the UK the Territorial Army and in the USA the *National Guard have supplanted earlier voluntary militias.

milk secretion of the *mammary glands of female mammals, with which they suckle their young (during *lactation). Over 85% is water, the remainder comprising protein, fat, lactose (a sugar), calcium, phosphorus, iron, and vitamins. The milk of cows, goats, and sheep is often consumed by humans, but regular drinking of milk after infancy is principally a Western practice.

Milky Way faint band of light crossing the night sky, consisting of stars in the plane of our galaxy. The name Milky Way is often used for the galaxy itself. It is a spiral *galaxy, 100,000 light years in diameter and 2,000 light years thick, containing at least 100 billion stars. The Sun is in one of its spiral arms, about 25,000 light years from the centre, not far from its central plane. An extra arm to the Milky Way was discovered by astronomers in 2004. The arc of hydrogen is a few thousand light years thick and 77,000 light years long, running along the outermost edge of the Milky Way.

Mill, John Stuart (1806–1873) English philosopher and economist who wrote *Principles of Political Economy* (1848), *On Liberty* (1859), and *Utilitarianism* (1863), which promoted a version of the 'greatest happiness for the greatest number' principle in ethics.

Millais, John Everett (1829–1896) English painter, a founder member of the *Pre-Raphaelite Brotherhood in 1848. Among his best known works are *Ophelia* (1852; National Gallery, London) and *Autumn Leaves* (1856; City Art Galleries, Manchester). By the late 1860s he had left the Brotherhood, developing a more fluid and conventional style which appealed strongly to Victorian tastes.

Miller, (Alton) Glenn (1904–1944) US trombonist and bandleader. He was an exponent of the big-band swing sound from 1938. He composed his signature tune 'Moonlight Serenade' in 1935, and it became a major hit upon its release in 1939. Miller became leader of the US Army Air Force Band in Europe in 1942, and made broadcasts to troops throughout the world during World War II. He disappeared without trace on a flight between England and France in 1944.

Miller, Arthur (1915–2005) US dramatist. His plays deal with family relationships and contemporary American values, and include *Death of a Salesman* (1949; Pulitzer Prize), and *The Crucible* (1953), based on the Salem witch trials and reflecting the communist witch-hunts of Senator Joe McCarthy. He was married from 1956 to 1961 to US film star Marilyn Monroe, for whom he wrote the film *The Misfits* (1960).

Miller, Henry (Valentine) (1891–1980) US writer. From 1930 to 1940 he lived a bohemian life in Paris, where he wrote his fictionalized, sexually explicit, autobiographical trilogy *Tropic of Cancer* (1934), *Black Spring* (1936), and *Tropic of Capricorn* (1938). They were banned in the USA and England until the 1960s.

millet any of several grasses of which the grains are used as a cereal food and the stems as animal fodder. Species include *Panicum miliaceum*, extensively cultivated in the warmer parts of Europe, and *Sorghum bicolor*, also known as durra. (Family Gramineae.)

milli- symbol m, prefix denoting a one-thousandth part (10^{-3}). For example, a millimetre, mm, is one thousandth of a metre.

millibar unit of pressure, equal to one-thousandth of a bar.

millimetre of mercury symbol mmHg, unit of pressure, used in medicine for measuring blood pressure defined as the pressure exerted by a column of mercury one millimetre high, under the action of gravity.

millipede any of a group of *arthropods that have segmented bodies, each segment usually bearing two pairs of legs, and a pair of short clubbed antennae on the distinct head. Most millipedes are no more than 2.5 cm/1 in long; a few in the tropics are 30 cm/12 in. (Class Diplopoda.)

Milne, A(lan) A(lexander) (1882–1956) English writer. He is best known as the author of *Winnie-the-Pooh* (1926) and *The House at Pooh Corner* (1928), based on the teddy bear and other toys of his son Christopher Robin, with illustrations by E H Shepard. He also wrote children's verse, including *When We Were Very Young* (1924) and *Now We Are Six* (1927). He was an accomplished dramatist.

Milošević, Slobodan (1941–) Serbian communist-nationalist politician; president of Serbia 1989–97, and president of the Federal Republic of Yugoslavia 1997–2000. Leader of the Socialist Party of Serbia from 1986, he fanned Serbian nationalist sentiment that helped provoke the break-up of Yugoslavia and led to civil war in Bosnia-Herzegovina 1992–94 between Serbs, Croats, and Bosnian Muslims. As president of Yugoslavia, Miloševic faced international condemnation for the brutal treatment of ethnic Albanians by Serbian forces in Kosovo, an autonomous province within Serbia. In March 1999, NATO began a bombing campaign in an attempt to force the Yugoslav government to end the persecution, and in June 1999 Miloševic accepted NATO's peace agreement. He was defeated in presidential elections in 2000 by Vojislav Koštunica. In April 2001 he was extradited to the United Nations (UN) International Criminal Tribunal for the former Yugoslavia in the Hague, Netherlands, on charges of genocide and crimes against humanity. His trial began in 2002.

Milton, John (1608–1674) English poet and prose writer. His epic *Paradise Lost* (1667) is one of the landmarks of English literature. Early poems, including *Comus* (a masque performed in 1634) and *Lycidas* (an elegy, 1638), showed Milton's outstanding lyric gift. He also wrote many pamphlets and prose works, including *Areopagitica* (1644), which opposed press censorship.

Milton Keynes unitary authority in central England, formerly part of Buckinghamshire. **area:** 311 sq km/ 120 sq mi **towns and cities:** Milton Keynes (administrative headquarters), Newport Pagnell, Olney, Bletchley, Stony Stratford, Woburn Sands, Wolverton **features:** Grand Union Canal; River Great Ouse; River Tove; Open University (established in Milton Keynes in 1971); Bletchley Park, government centre of code-breaking during World War II; Milton Keynes' famous concrete cows, constructed in 1978 by a community artist and local schoolchildren **population:** (2001 est) 207,600.

Milwaukee industrial city and port in southeastern Wisconsin, USA, at the mouth of the Milwaukee River, on the western shore of Lake Michigan, 128 km/79 mi north of Chicago; seat of Milwaukee County; population (2000 est) 597,000. It is the centre of a dairying and beef-producing region, and an important port of entry on the Great Lakes–St Lawrence Seaway system; industries include brewing (there are two major breweries, including Millers, the second largest brewery in the USA), engineering, machinery, motorcyles (the Harley-Davidson factory was founded here in 1906), electronic and electrical equipment, and chemicals.

mimicry imitation of one species (or group of species) by another. The most common form is **Batesian mimicry** (named after English naturalist H W *Bates), where the mimic resembles a model that is poisonous or unpleasant to eat, and has aposematic, or warning, coloration; the mimic thus benefits from the fact that predators have learned to avoid the model. Hoverflies that resemble bees or wasps are an example. Appearance is usually the basis for mimicry, but calls, songs, scents, and other signals can also be mimicked.

mimosa any of a group of leguminous trees, shrubs, or herbs belonging to the mimosa family, found in tropical and subtropical regions. They all have small, fluffy, golden, ball-like flowers. A similar but unrelated plant, *Acacia dealbata*, is sold as mimosa by European florists. (True mimosa genus *Mimosa*, family Mimosaceae.)

Mimosa *or* **Becrux** *or* **Beta Crucis** second-brightest star in the southern-hemisphere constellation of Crux,

marking one of the four corners of the Southern Cross, and the 19th-brightest star in the night sky. It is a blue-white giant star of magnitude 0.8 around 460 light years from the Sun.

Minangkabau an Indonesian people of western Sumatra. In addition to approximately 3 million Minangkabau in western Sumatra, there are sizeable communities in the major Indonesian cities. The Minangkabau language belongs to the Austronesian family.

mind in philosophy, the presumed mental or physical being or faculty that enables a person to think, will, and feel; the seat of the intelligence and of memory; sometimes only the cognitive or intellectual powers, as distinguished from the will and the emotions.

Mindanao second-largest island of the Philippines. The indigenous peoples are the Lumad and Moro; area 94,627 sq km/36,536 sq mi; population (1990) 14,298,250. Towns and cities include Davao and Zamboanga. Industries include pineapples, coffee, rice, coconut, rubber, hemp, timber, nickel, gold, steel, chemicals, and fertilizer. The island is mainly mountainous rainforest; the active volcano Apo reaches 2,954 m/9,600 ft, and the island is subject to severe earthquakes. There is a Muslim guerrilla resistance movement, the Moro Islamic Liberation Front.

mineral naturally formed inorganic substance with a particular chemical composition and a regularly repeating internal structure. Either in their perfect crystalline form or otherwise, minerals are the constituents of *rocks. In more general usage, a mineral is any substance economically valuable for mining (including coal and oil, despite their organic origins).

mineral extraction recovery of valuable ores from the Earth's crust. The processes used include open-cast mining, shaft mining, and quarrying, as well as more specialized processes such as those used for sulphur (the Frasch process) and oil.

mineralogy study of minerals. The classification of minerals is based chiefly on their chemical composition and the kind of chemical bonding that holds their atoms together. The mineralogist also studies their crystallographic and physical characters, occurrence, and mode of formation.

Minerva in Roman mythology, the goddess of wisdom and war, and of handicrafts and the arts, equivalent to the Greek *Athena. From the earliest days of ancient Rome, there was a temple to her on the Capitoline Hill, near the Temple of Jupiter.

Ming dynasty (lived 14th–17th centuries) Chinese dynasty 1368–1644, based in Nanjing. During the rule 1402–24 of Yongle (or Yung-lo), there was territorial expansion into Mongolia and Yunnan in the southwest. The administrative system was improved, public works were carried out, and foreign trade was developed. Art and literature flourished and distinctive blue and white porcelain was produced.

miniature painting painting on a very small scale, notably early manuscript illumination, and later miniature portraits, sometimes set in jewelled cases, and Islamic paintings. Hans Holbein the Younger introduced miniature portrait painting into England, the form reaching its height in the works of Hilliard in the 16th century, though continuing well into the 19th century. There was also a very strong tradition of miniature portrait painting in France. Miniatures by Islamic artists flourished in India and Persia, their subjects often bird and flowers, or scenes from history and legend, rather than portraits (see *Islamic art).

minicomputer multiuser computer with a size and processing power between those of a *mainframe and a *microcomputer. Nowadays almost all minicomputers are based on *microprocessors.

minimalism movement in abstract art and music towards extremely simplified composition. Minimal art developed in the USA in the 1950s in reaction to *abstract expressionism, rejecting its emotive approach in favour of impersonality and elemental, usually geometric, shapes. It has found its fullest expression in sculpture, notably in the work of Carl Andre, who employs industrial materials in modular compositions. In music, from the 1960s and 1970s, it manifested itself in large-scale statements, usually tonal or even diatonic, and highly repetitive, based on a few 'minimal' musical ideas. Major minimalist composers are Steve *Reich and Philip *Glass.

minimum lending rate (MLR) in the UK, the rate of interest at which the Bank of England lends to the money market.

minimum wage minimum level of pay for workers, usually set by government. In the UK, minimum pay for many groups of workers has been fixed by wages councils. Minimum wages are set to prevent low-paid workers from being exploited by employers who would otherwise pay them even lower wages. However, minimum wages are argued by some economists to cause unemployment because if wages were allowed to fall below the minimum wage level, some employers would be prepared to take on more workers.

mining extraction of minerals from under the land or sea for industrial or domestic uses. Exhaustion of traditionally accessible resources has led to the development of new mining techniques, for example extraction of oil from offshore deposits and from land shale reserves. Technology is also under development for the exploitation of minerals from entirely new sources such as mud deposits and mineral nodules from the seabed.

mink either of two species of carnivorous mammals belonging to the weasel family, usually found in or near water. They have rich brown fur, and are up to 50 cm/1.6 ft long with bushy tails 20 cm/8 in long. They live in Europe and Asia (*M. lutreola*) and North America (*M. vison*). (Genus *Mustela*.)

Minneapolis (American Indian **minne** 'water', Greek **polis** 'town') city in southeastern Minnesota, USA, 13 km/8 mi from St Paul, with which it forms the 'Twin Cities' area; seat of Hennepin County; population (2000 est) 382,600; metropolitan area (1992) 2,618,000. It is at the head of navigation of the Mississippi River, and is the centre of one of the richest agricultural areas in the USA. Industries include food processing and the manufacture of machinery, electrical and electronic equipment, precision instruments, transport machinery, and metal and paper products. Cray computers – used for long-range weather forecasting, spacecraft design, and code-breaking – are built here.

Minnesota called the **North Star State** or the **Gopher State**, (Dakota Sioux *mnishota* 'land of sky-tinted water') state in north-central USA, situated in the

*Great Lakes region and bordered to the east by Wisconsin and Lake *Superior, to the south by *Iowa, to the west by *North Dakota and *South Dakota, and to the north by the Canadian provinces of Ontario and Manitoba; area 206,189 sq km/79,610 sq mi; population (2000) 4,919,500; capital St Paul. Its nickname the North Star State derives from the French state motto *L'Etoile du Nord* ('star of the north'); the alternative nickname refers to the gophers inhabiting the prairies. Minnesota has more than 15,000 lakes created by receding glaciers following the last ice age. Three major US rivers, the *Mississippi, the Red River of the North, and the *St Lawrence, have their sources in the state. Minnesota's economy has historically been dominated by its timber, mining, and agricultural resources; farming is the most important economic activity, followed by food processing. Other major industries include health care, technology, and tourism. *Minneapolis is the largest city and with St Paul makes up the 'Twin Cities' area, the commercial and cultural centre of the state. Other important cities are Duluth, Rochester, and Bloomington. Originally home to the Dakota *Sioux and Chippewa American Indians, the Chippewa had become dominant by 1862 and remain on seven reservations; the Dakota Sioux retain four communities. Minnesota was made a territory in 1849, and became a major flour-milling centre after the coming of the railway in 1867. Minnesota was admitted to the Union on 11 May 1858 as the 32nd US state.

minnow any of various small freshwater fishes of the carp family, found in streams and ponds worldwide. Most species are small and dull in colour, but some are brightly coloured. They feed on larvae and insects. (Family Cyprinidae.)

Minoan civilization Bronze Age civilization on the Aegean island of Crete. The name is derived from Minos, the legendary king of Crete. The civilization is divided into three main periods: early Minoan, about 3000–2000 BC; middle Minoan, about 2000–1550 BC; and late Minoan, about 1550–1050 BC.

minor legal term for those under the age of majority, which varies from country to country but is usually between 18 and 21. In the USA (from 1971 for voting, and in some states for nearly all other purposes) and certain European countries (in Britain since 1970) the age of majority is 18.

Minos in Greek mythology, a king of Crete, who demanded a yearly tribute of seven youths and seven girls from Athens for the *Minotaur, the offspring of his wife Pasiphaë and a bull. After his death, he became a judge in *Hades.

Minotaur in Greek mythology, a monster with a man's body and bull's head, offspring of Pasiphaë, wife of King Minos of Crete, and a bull sent by Poseidon. It was housed in a Labyrinth designed by *Daedalus at Knossos, and its victims were seven girls and seven youths sent in annual tribute by Athens. The beast was killed by *Theseus with the aid of Ariadne, daughter of Minos.

Minsk Belorussian **Mensk**, industrial city and capital of Belarus (also capital of the Minsk oblast); population (1990) 1,612,800. Motor vehicles, machinery, textiles, leather are produced here; Minsk is also a centre of the computer industry. The city's large pre-war Jewish community, which comprised over half of its inhabitants, was deported and murdered during the Nazi occupation. The headquarters of the Commonwealth of Independent States (CIS) is located here.

mint in botany, any aromatic plant of the mint family, widely distributed in temperate regions. The plants have square stems, creeping roots, and spikes of usually pink or purplish flowers. The family includes garden mint (*M. spicata*) and peppermint (*M. piperita*). (Genus *Mentha*, family Labiatae.)

mint in economics, a place where coins are made under government authority. In Britain, the official mint is the **Royal Mint**; the US equivalent is the **Bureau of the Mint**. The UK Royal Mint also manufactures coinages, official medals, and seals for Commonwealth and foreign countries.

Minton, Thomas (1765–1836) English potter. After an apprenticeship as an engraver for transfer printing at Caughley and working for the potter Josiah Spode, he established himself at Stoke-on-Trent as an engraver of designs in 1789. The Chinese-style blue and white 'willow pattern' was reputedly originated by Minton. In 1796 he founded a pottery, producing a cream-base blue-decorated earthenware and (from 1798) high-quality porcelain and bone china, decorated with flowers and fruit. Chinaware became the chief production under his son Herbert Minton (1792–1858).

minuet French country dance in three time adapted as a European courtly dance of the 17th century. The music was later used as the third movement of a classical four-movement symphony where its gentle rhythm provides a foil to the slow second movement and fast final movement.

minute unit of time consisting of 60 seconds; also a unit of angle equal to one sixtieth of a degree.

Miocene ('middle recent') fourth epoch of the Tertiary period of geological time, 23.5–5.2 million years ago. At this time grasslands spread over the interior of continents, and hoofed mammals rapidly evolved.

mips acronym for Million Instructions Per Second, in computing, a measure of the speed of a processor. It does not equal the computer power in all cases.

Mir (Russian 'peace' or 'world') Russian space station, the core of which was launched on 20 February 1986. It was permanently occupied until 1999, and then purposely brought down on 23 March 2001 to crash into the Pacific Ocean. During its life, *Mir* travelled more than 3 billion km/2 billion mi, and was home to 104 cosmonauts.

Mira *or* **Omicron Ceti** brightest long-period pulsating *variable star, located in the constellation *Cetus. Mira was the first star discovered to vary periodically in brightness.

Mirabeau, Honoré Gabriel Riqueti, comte de (1749–1791) French politician, leader of the National Assembly in the French Revolution. He wanted to establish a parliamentary monarchy on the English model. From May 1790 he secretly acted as political adviser to the king.

Miró, Joan (1893–1983) Spanish painter and sculptor, a major figure in *surrealism. In the mid-1920s he developed an abstract style, lyrical and often witty, with amoeba shapes, some linear, some highly coloured, generally floating on a plain background. *Birth of the World* (1925; Museum of Modern Art, New York) is typical of his more abstract works.

mirror any polished surface that reflects light; often made from 'silvered' glass (in practice, a mercury-alloy coating of glass). A plane (flat) mirror produces a same-size, erect 'virtual' image located behind the mirror at the same distance from it as the object is in front of it. A spherical concave mirror produces a reduced, inverted real image in front or an enlarged, erect virtual image behind it (as in a shaving mirror), depending on how close the object is to the mirror. A spherical convex mirror produces a reduced, erect virtual image behind it (as in a car's rear-view mirror).

miscarriage spontaneous expulsion of a fetus from the womb before it is capable of independent survival. Miscarriage is believed to occur in 15% of pregnancies, often at such an early stage as to go unnoticed. Possible causes include fetal abnormality, abnormality of the uterus or cervix, infection, shock, underactive thyroid, and drug and alcohol use. The risk of miscarriage increases dramatically with age, from 5% for women under 30 to 50% for women in their mid-40s.

mise en scène (French 'stage setting') in cinema, the composition and content of the frame in terms of background scenery, actors, costumes, props, camera movement, and lighting.

Mishima, Yukio (1925–1970) pen-name of Hiraoka Kimitake, Japanese novelist. His work often deals with sexual desire and perversion, as in *Confessions of a Mask* (1949) and *The Temple of the Golden Pavilion* (1956). He committed hara-kiri (ritual suicide) as a protest against what he saw as the corruption of the nation and the loss of the samurai warrior tradition.

Mishnah *or* **Mishna** (Hebrew 'teaching by repetition') collection of commentaries on written Hebrew law, consisting of discussions between rabbis, handed down orally from their inception in AD 70 until about 200 when they were committed to writing. The Mishnah advises Jews how to apply the rules of the Torah, given to Moses by God on Mount Sinai. Together with the Gemara, it forms the *Talmud, a compilation of Jewish law and tradition.

missel thrush bird belonging to the *thrush family.

missile rocket-propelled weapon, which may be nuclear-armed (see *nuclear warfare). Modern missiles are often classified as surface-to-surface missiles (SSM), air-to-air missiles (AAM), surface-to-air missiles (SAM), or air-to-surface missiles (ASM). A **cruise missile** is in effect a pilotless, computer-guided aircraft; it can be sea-launched from submarines or surface ships, or launched from the air or the ground.

Mississippi (American Indian *missi* 'big', *sipi* 'river') river in the USA, the main arm of the great river system draining the USA between the Appalachian and the Rocky mountain ranges. The length of the Mississippi is 3,778 km/2,348 mi; with its tributary the Missouri it totals 6,020 km/3,740 mi. It has the second largest drainage basin in the world and incorporates all or part of 30 US states and two Canadian provinces. The Mississippi rises in the lake region of northern Minnesota in the basin of Lake Itasca, and drops 20 m/65 ft over the St Anthony Falls at Minneapolis. Below the tributaries of the Minnesota, Wisconsin, Des Moines, and Illinois rivers, the confluence of the Missouri and Mississippi occurs at St Louis. Turning at the Ohio junction, it passes Memphis, and takes in the St Francis, Arkansas, Yazoo, and Red tributaries before reaching its delta on the Gulf of Mexico, beyond New Orleans. Altogether the Mississippi has 42 tributary streams and the whole Mississippi river system has a navigable length in excess of 25,900 km/16,100 mi.

Mississippi called **Magnolia State** or **Bayou State**, (Chippewa Indian *mici zibi* 'great river city') state in the south of the USA, bordered to the north by *Tennessee, to the east by *Alabama, to the south by the Gulf of Mexico, *Arkansas, *Louisiana, and to the west the *Mississippi River separates it from Arkansas and Louisiana; area 121,489 sq km/46,907 sq mi; population (2000) 2,844,700; capital and largest city *Jackson. The state lies entirely within the East Gulf Coastal Plain and the Mississippi Alluvial Plain. Along the state's short coastline are many small islands. Traditionally based on agriculture, the economy of Mississippi is now led by manufacturing and service industries; petroleum and natural gas industries are also important to the state economy. Industrial products include furniture, wood products, and transport equipment; cotton is a leading crop and other agricultural products include poultry, cattle, and rice. Major cities include Gulfport, Biloxi, Hattiesburg, Greenville, Meridian, Tupelo, Southaven, Vicksburg, and Pascagoula. Mississippi's original inhabitants were the Choctaw, Chickasaw, and *Natchez American Indian peoples. Part of the Deep South, the state is historically associated with cotton plantations, slavery, and blues music. Mississippi was admitted to the Union in 1817 as the 20th US state.

Mississippian US term for the Lower or Early *Carboniferous period of geological time, 363–323 million years ago. It is named after the state of Mississippi.

Missouri major river in central USA, largest tributary of the *Mississippi, which it joins north of St Louis; length 3,969 km/2,466 mi; drainage area 1,370,000 sq km/ 529,000 sq mi. It rises among the Rocky Mountains in Montana, and passes northwards through a 366 m/ 1,200 ft gorge known as the 'Gate of the Mountains'. The river is formed by the confluence of the Jefferson, Gallatin, and Madison rivers near Gallatin City, southwestern Montana, and flows southeast through the states of Montana, North Dakota, and South Dakota to Sioux City, Iowa. It then turns south to form the borders between Iowa and Nebraska and between Kansas and Missouri, and enters the Mississippi channel 32 km/20 mi north of St Louis. Kansas City, Missouri, is the largest city on its banks.

Missouri called the **Show Me State**, (American Indian 'town of the large canoes') state in the USA, situated in the *Midwest, bordered to the south by *Arkansas, to the west by *Oklahoma, *Kansas, and *Nebraska, to the north by *Iowa, and to the east by *Illinois, *Kentucky, and *Tennessee; area 178,414 sq km/68,886 sq mi; population (2000) 5,595,200; capital Jefferson City. Missouri's nickname refers to its inhabitants' character, which is generally thought to be sturdy and sceptical. In the southeast are the scenic highlands of the Ozark Plateau. The state is a commercial and industrial leader in the region, with a high degree of urbanization and industrial output, particularly in the manufacture of transport and aerospace equipment. The agricultural sector is strong, producing soybeans, livestock, and dairy foods, but has been overtaken by tourism and recreation. There are rich mineral resources, notably lead. The two largest cities are *St Louis and Kansas City. Other important cities and towns are Springfield, Independence, Columbia, St Joseph, St Charles, Florissant, and Lee's Summit. Originally home to the Missouri American Indian people, the region was acquired by the USA under the *Louisiana Purchase in 1803, and became a state in 1820, following the Missouri Compromise. Missouri was the westernmost state of the Union until Texas joined in 1845, and it served for a time as the eastern end of the Santa Fe, Oregon, and California trails. Missouri was admitted to the Union in 1821 as the 24th US state.

mistletoe parasitic evergreen plant, native to Europe. It grows on trees as a small bush with translucent white berries. Used in many Western countries as a Christmas decoration, it also featured in the pagan religion *Druidism. (*Viscum album*, family Loranthaceae.)

mistral cold, dry, northerly wind that occasionally blows during the winter on the Mediterranean coast of France, particularly concentrated along the Rhône valley. It has been known to reach a velocity of 145 kph/ 90 mph.

Mitchum, Robert (Charles Duran) (1917–1997) US film actor. His career spanned more than 50 years of film-making, and embraced more than 100 film and television roles. As one of Hollywood's most enduring stars, he was equally at home as the relaxed modern hero or psychopathic villain. Mitchum's hard-boiled performances in a series of war films, melodramas, *films noirs*, and Westerns of the 1940s and early 1950s established him firmly in the pantheon of Hollywood's leading male performers. His films include *Out of the Past* (1947), *The Night of the Hunter* (1955), and *The Friends of Eddie Coyle* (1973).

mite minute *arachnid related to the *ticks. Some mites are free-living scavengers or predators. Some are parasitic, such as the **itch mite** (*Sarcoptes scabiei*), which burrows in skin causing scabies in humans and mange in dogs, and the **red mite** (*Dermanyssus gallinae*), which sucks blood from poultry and other birds. Others parasitize plants. (Order Acarina.)

Mithras *or* **Mithra** in Persian mythology, the god of light, son of the sublime god, Ahura Mazda. Mithras represented the power of morality and goodness against Ahriman, the personification of evil, and promised his followers compensation for present evil after death. Mithraism was introduced into the Roman Empire in 68 BC and spread rapidly, gaining converts especially among soldiers; by about AD 250, it rivalled Christianity in strength.

Mithridates VI Eupator the Great (c. 120–60 BC) King of Pontus (on the Black Sea coast of modern Turkey), who became the greatest obstacle to Roman expansion in the east. He massacred 80,000 Romans while overrunning Asia Minor and went on to invade Greece. He was defeated by *Sulla during the first Mithridatic War in 88–84 BC, by Lucullus in the second 83–81, and by Pompey the Great in the third 74–64.

mitochondria singular **mitochondrion**, membrane-enclosed organelles within *eukaryotic cells, containing *enzymes responsible for energy production during *aerobic respiration. They are found in both plant and animal cells. Mitochondria absorb oxygen (O_2) and complete the breakdown of glucose to carbon dioxide (CO_2) and water (H_2O) to produce energy in the form of *ATP, which is used in life processes in the cell. These rodlike or spherical bodies are thought to be derived from free-living bacteria that, at a very early stage in the history of life, invaded larger cells and took up a symbiotic way of life inside them. Each still contains its own small loop of DNA called mitochondrial DNA, and new mitochondria arise by division of existing ones. Mitochondria each have 37 genes.

mitosis in biology, the process of cell division by which one parent cell produces two genetically identical 'daughter' cells. The genetic material of *eukaryotic cells is carried on a number of *chromosomes. During mitosis the DNA is duplicated and the chromosome number doubled – identical copies of the chromosomes are separated into the two daughter cells, which contain the same amount of DNA as the original cell. To control movements of chromosomes during cell division so that both new cells get the correct number, a system of protein tubules, known as the spindle, organizes the chromosomes into position in the middle of the cell before they replicate. The spindle then controls the movement of chromosomes as the cell goes through the stages of division: **interphase**, **prophase**, **metaphase**, **anaphase**, and **telophase**. See also *meiosis.

Mitterrand, François (1916–1996) French socialist politician. After a successful ministerial career under the Fourth Republic, holding posts in 11 governments 1947–58, Mitterrand joined the new Parti Socialiste (PS; English Socialist Party) in 1971, establishing it as the most popular party in France before winning two successive terms as president, 1981–88 and 1988–95. From 1982 his administrations reverted from redistributive and reflationary policies to economic orthodoxy and maintenance of the 'strong franc' (linked to the Deutschmark), despite the high levels of unemployment this entailed, and vigorously pursued further European integration.

mixed economy type of economic structure that combines the private enterprise of capitalism with a degree of state monopoly. In mixed economies, governments seek to control the public services, the basic industries, and those industries that cannot raise sufficient capital investment from private sources. Thus a measure of economic planning can be combined with a measure of free enterprise. A notable example was US president Franklin D Roosevelt's *New Deal in the 1930s.

mixed farming farming system where both arable and pastoral farming is carried out. Mixed farming is a lower-risk strategy than *monoculture. If climate, pests, or market prices are unfavourable for one crop or type of livestock, another may be more successful and the risk is shared. Animals provide manure for the fields and help to maintain soil fertility.

Mizoram state of northeast India, lying between Bangladesh and Myanmar; area 21,087 sq km/8,142 sq mi; population (2001 est) 891,100. The capital is Aizawl. The state features north–south ranges in the east that rise to over 2,000 m/6,500 ft. The state is densely forested. Agriculture, including shifting cultivation, is the main economic activity, and products include rice, maize, and hand-loom weaving. Industries are small-

scale, and include sericulture (silk production) and sawmilling. 84% of the population are Christian.

m.k.s. system system of units in which the base units metre, kilogram, and second replace the centimetre, gram, and second of the *c.g.s. system. From it developed the SI system (see *SI units).

Mladic, Ratko (1943–) Bosnian Serb general, leader of the Bosnian Serb army 1992–96. His ruthless conduct in the civil war in Bosnia, including the widespread maltreatment of prisoners and the disappearance of many more, led to his being indicted for war crimes by the United Nations War Crimes Commission in 1995.

mnemonic verbal device to aid memory; often a short sentence or a rhyme (such as 'i before e except after c'). A mnemonic is a form of abbreviation.

moa any of a group of extinct flightless kiwi-like birds, order Dinornithiformes, that lived in New Zealand. There were 19 species; they varied from 0.5 to 3.5 m/2 to 12 ft, with strong limbs, a long neck, and no wings. The largest species was *Dinornis maximus*. The last moa was killed in the 1800s.

Moab ancient country in Jordan, east of the southern part of the River Jordan and the Dead Sea. The inhabitants were closely akin to the Hebrews in culture, language, and religion, but were often at war with them, as recorded in the Old Testament. Moab eventually fell to Arab invaders. The **Moabite Stone**, discovered in 1868 at Dhiban, dates from the 9th century BC and records the rising of Mesha, king of Moab, against Israel.

mobile phone or **cell phone** cordless telephone linked to a cellular radio network. Early cellular networks used analogue technology, but since the late 1990s most services use a digital system. Calls are linked to the public telephone system via a network of connected base stations and exchanges; the area covered by each base station is called a cell. Each cell is about 5 km/3 mi across, and has a separate low-power transmitter. Mobility is possible as calls can be made while moving from one radio cell to another. In Europe, GSM (Global System for Mobile communications) has been adopted by many countries as a digital standard, enabling travellers to use a single phone across different national networks. Tri-band mobile phones are capable of changing frequencies to allow local networks in the USA to be accessed.

Möbius strip structure made by giving a half twist to a flat strip of paper and joining the ends together. It has certain remarkable properties, arising from the fact that it has only one edge and one side. If cut down the centre of the strip, instead of two new strips of paper, only one long strip is produced. It was invented by the German mathematician August Möbius.

mockingbird North American songbird of the mimic thrush family, found in the USA and Mexico. About 25 cm/10 in long, it is brownish grey, with white markings on the black wings and tail. It is remarkable for its ability to mimic the songs of other species. (Species *Mimus polyglottos*, family Mimidae, order Passeriformes.)

mock orange or **syringa** any of a group of deciduous shrubs, including *P. coronarius*, which has white, strongly scented flowers similar to those of the orange tree. (Genus *Philadelphus*, family Philadelphaceae.)

mode in mathematics, the element that appears most frequently in a given set of *data. For example, the mode for the data 0, 0, 0, 9, 9, 9, 12, 87, 87 is 9.

Model Parliament English parliament set up in 1295 by *Edward I; it was the first to include representatives from outside the clergy and aristocracy, and was established because Edward needed the support of the whole country against his opponents: Wales, France, and Scotland. His sole aim was to raise money for military purposes, and the parliament did not pass any legislation.

modem contraction of modulator/demodulator, device for transmitting computer data over telephone lines. Such a device is used to convert *digital signals produced by computers to *analogue signals compatible with the telephone network, and back again.

moderator in a *nuclear reactor, a material such as graphite or heavy water used to reduce the speed of high-energy neutrons. Neutrons produced by nuclear fission are fast-moving and must be slowed to initiate further fission so that nuclear energy continues to be released at a controlled rate.

modern dance 20th-century dance idiom that evolved in opposition to traditional ballet by those seeking a freer and more immediate means of dance expression. Leading exponents include Martha *Graham and Merce Cunningham in the USA, Isadora *Duncan and Mary Wigman in Europe.

modernism in the arts, a general term used to describe the 20th century's conscious attempt to break with the artistic traditions of the 19th century, particularly strong in the period between World War I (1914–18) and World War II (1939–45). Modernism is based on a concern with form and the exploration of technique as opposed to content and narrative. In the **visual arts**, direct representationalism gave way to abstraction (see *abstract art); in **literature**, writers experimented with alternatives to orthodox sequential storytelling, using techniques involving different viewpoints (such as writing as if in the mind of a character in the story; known as the *stream of consciousness technique; in **music**, the traditional concept of key was challenged by atonality; and in **architecture**, *Functionalism ousted decorativeness as a central objective (see *Modern Movement).

Modern Movement the dominant movement in 20th-century architecture, which grew out of the technological innovations of 19th-century Industrial architecture, crystallized in the *international style of the 1920s and 1930s, and has since developed various regional trends, such as *Brutalism. 'Truth to materials' and 'form follows function' are its two most representative dicta, although neither allows for the modernity of large areas of contemporary architecture, concerned with proportion, human scale, and attention to detail. Currently, architectural *postmodernism, a reaction to the movement, is developing alongside such modernist styles as high-tech.

Modigliani, Amedeo (1884–1920) Italian painter and sculptor, active in France from 1906. He is best known for graceful nudes and portraits. His paintings – for example, the portrait of his mistress Jeanne Hébuterne (1919; Guggenheim Museum, New York) – have a distinctive style, the forms elongated and sensual.

modulation in music, movement from one *key to another. In classical dance music, modulation is a guide to phrasing rhythm to the step pattern.

modulation in radio transmission, the variation of frequency, or amplitude, of a radio carrier wave, in accordance with the audio characteristics of the speaking voice, music, or other signal being transmitted.

modulus in mathematics, a number that divides exactly into the difference between two given numbers. Also, the multiplication factor used to convert a logarithm of one base to a logarithm of another base. Also, another name for *absolute value.

Mogadishu or **Muqdisho** capital and chief port of Somalia; population (1995 est) 525,000. The city lies on the Indian Ocean coast of Somalia and is a centre for oil refining, food processing, and chemical production; there are uranium reserves nearby. During the civil war 1991–92, much of the city was devastated and many thousands killed. The population has decreased since the civil war because of famine and the movement of refugees.

Mogul dynasty northern Indian dynasty 1526–1858, established by *Babur, Muslim descendant of Tamerlane, the 14th-century Mongol leader. The Mogul emperors ruled until the last one, *Bahadur Shah II, was dethroned and exiled by the British; they included *Akbar, *Aurangzeb, and *Shah Jahan. The Moguls established a more extensive and centralized empire than their Delhi sultanate forebears, and the Mogul era was one of great artistic achievement as well as urban and commercial development.

Mohács, Battle of comprehensive victory of a combined Austrian and Hungarian army under Charles of Lorraine over a Turkish army under Muhammad IV 12 August 1687; the battle effectively meant the end of Turkish expansion into Europe. Named after the river port of that name on the Danube in Hungary, which is also the site of a Turkish victory in 1526.

mohair (Arabic *mukhayyar* 'goat') yarn made from the long, lustrous hair of the Angora goat or rabbit, loosely woven with cotton, silk, or wool to produce a fuzzy texture. It became popular for jackets, coats, and sweaters in the 1950s. Commercial mohair is now obtained from cross-bred animals, pure-bred supplies being insufficient to satisfy demand.

Mohammed alternative form of *Muhammad, founder of Islam.

Mohave Desert arid region in southern California, USA; see *Mojave Desert.

Mohawk member of an *American Indian people, part of the *Iroquois confederation, who originally inhabited the Mohawk Valley, New York. Their language belongs to the Macro-Siouan group. The Mohawk were maize farmers and hunters, whose traditional aggression towards neighbouring Algonquian peoples was heightened by involvement with the Dutch fur trade in the 17th century, and the acquisition of guns. After fighting with the British during the American Revolution, many Mohawk moved to Canada. They now live on reservations in Ontario, Québec, and New York State, as well as among the general population, and number about 10,000 (1990).

Mohegan member of an *American Indian people who moved from the upper Hudson River Valley to

Connecticut in the 16th century. They were probably originally part of the neighbouring Pequot people, with whom they shared Algonquian linguistic and cultural traditions. The two groups split after the Mohegan allied with English colonists in the 1630s. Traditionally their economy was based on farming maize (corn), and hunting and fishing. Today about 1,400 (1996) Mohegan of mixed ancestry live in Connecticut, Rhode Island, and New York. Efforts are being made to revive the Mohegan language and culture. Current business interests include a large casino in Connecticut.

Mohenjo Daro ('mound of the dead') site of a city about 2500–1600 BC on the lower Indus River, northwestern Pakistan, where excavations from the 1920s have revealed the *Indus Valley civilization, to which the city of Harappa also belongs.

Mohican *or* **Mahican,** *or* **Muh-he-ka-ne-ok** member of an *American Indian people who occupied the upper Hudson River valley in New York State until the mid-17th century. They are closely related to the *Mohegan, and share Algonquian linguistic traditions. The Mohican were divided into five groups, each led by a sachem (hereditary chieftain). Traditionally they lived in stockaded villages of 20–30 houses, and cultivated crops, hunted, and fished. In 1664 they were relocated to Stockbridge, Massachusetts, where they became known as the Stockbridge Indians. They later allied with the Munsee and moved to a reservation in Wisconsin, where most now live.

Moholy-Nagy, Laszlo (1895–1946) Hungarian-born painter, sculptor and photographer. Inspired by *constructivism, he made abstract sculptures from the early 1920s, and from 1923 to 1929 taught at the Bauhaus school in Weimar and later in the USA. He experimented with a wide range of media, materials, and techniques, including the use of photographic techniques to achieve non-naturalistic effects.

Mohorovicic discontinuity *or* **Moho** *or* **M-discontinuity** seismic discontinuity, marked by a rapid increase in the speed of earthquake waves, that is taken to represent the boundary between the Earth's crust and mantle. It follows the variations in the thickness of the crust and is found approximately 35–40 km/22–25 mi below the continents and about 10 km/6 mi below the oceans. It is named after the Croatian geophysicist Andrija Mohorovicic, who suspected its presence after analysing seismic waves from the Kulpa Valley earthquake in 1909. The 'Moho' is as deep as 70 km/45 mi beneath high mountain ranges.

Mohs scale scale of hardness for minerals (in ascending order): 1 talc; 2 gypsum; 3 calcite; 4 fluorite; 5 apatite; 6 orthoclase; 7 quartz; 8 topaz; 9 corundum; 10 diamond.

Moi, Daniel arap (1924–) Kenyan politician, president from 1978 to 2002. Leader of the Kenya African National Union (KANU), he became minister of home affairs in 1964, vice-president in 1967, and succeeded Jomo Kenyatta as president. He enjoyed the support of Western governments but was widely criticized for Kenya's poor human-rights record. His administration, first challenged by a coup attempt in 1982, became increasingly authoritarian. In 1991, in the face of widespread criticism, he promised the eventual introduction of multiparty politics. In 1992 he was elected president in the first free elections amid widespread accusations of vote rigging.

Moirai *or* **Moerae** in Greek mythology, the title of the three *Fates; the name refers to the 'portions' of life they allotted to each human being, a destiny represented by a thread, although they sometimes appeared as goddesses of inevitability. **Lachesis** assigned the length of a life from her distaff, **Clotho** spun its existence, and **Atropos** broke the thread to signify its termination.

Mojave Desert *or* **Mohave Desert** *or* **High Desert** arid region in southern California, USA, part of the Great Basin; average height above sea-level 600 m/ 2,000 ft; area 38,500 sq km/15,000 sq mi. It lies to the northeast of Los Angeles, and to the southeast of the *Sierra Nevada.

mol symbol for *mole, the SI unit of amount of substance, equal to the amount that contains as many elementary entities (such as atoms, ions, or molecules) as there are atoms in 12 grams of carbon.

molar one of the large teeth found towards the back of the mammalian mouth. The structure of the jaw, and the relation of the muscles, allows a massive force to be applied to molars. In herbivores the molars are flat with sharp ridges of enamel and are used for grinding, an adaptation to a diet of tough plant material. Carnivores have sharp powerful molars called carnassials, which are adapted for cutting meat.

Moldavia former principality in southeastern Europe, situated on the River Danube, and occupying an area divided today between the states of Moldova and Romania. Moldavia was independent between the 14th and 16th centuries, when it became part of the Ottoman Empire. In 1861, it was united with its neighbouring principality Wallachia to form the kingdom of Romania. In 1940 the eastern part, *Bessarabia, became part of the USSR (the Moldavian SSR), while the western part remained in Romania.

Moldavian member of the majority ethnic group living in Moldova, comprising almost two-thirds of the population; also, inhabitant of the Romanian province of Moldavia. The Moldavian language is a dialect of Romanian, and belongs to the Romance group of the Indo-European family. They are mostly Orthodox Christians.

Moldova

National name: *Republica Moldova/Republic of Moldova*

Moldova

Area: 33,700 sq km/13,011 sq mi
Capital: Chisinau (Russian Kishinev)
Major towns/cities: Tiraspol, Balti, Tighina
Physical features: hilly land lying largely between the rivers Prut and Dniester; northern Moldova comprises the level plain of the Balti Steppe and uplands; the climate is warm and moderately continental
Head of state: Vladimir Voronin from 2001
Head of government: Vasile Tarlev from 2001
Political system: emergent democracy
Political executive: limited presidency
Political parties: Agrarian Democratic Party (ADP), nationalist, centrist; Socialist Party and Yedinstvo/Unity Movement, reform-socialist; Peasants and Intellectuals, Romanian nationalist; Christian Democratic Popular Front (CDPF), Romanian nationalist; Gagauz-Khalky (GKPM; Gagauz People's Movement), Gagauz separatist; Moldovan Party of Communists (MPC), former Communist Party of Moldova (banned in 1991, revived under new name in 1994)
Currency: leu
GNI per capita (PPP): (US$) 1,560 (2002 est)
Exports: wine, food and agricultural products, machinery and equipment, textiles, clothing. Principal market: Russia 44.5% (2000)
Population: 4,267,000 (2003 est)
Language: Moldovan (official), Russian, Gaganz (a Turkish dialect)
Religion: Eastern Orthodox 98.5%; remainder Jewish
Life expectancy: 66 (men); 72 (women) (2000–05)
Chronology

AD 106: The current area covered by Moldova, which lies chiefly between the Prut River, bordering Romania in the west, and the Dniestr River, with Ukraine in the east, was conquered by the Roman Emperor Trajan and became part of the Roman province of Dacia. It was known in earlier times as Bessarabia.
mid-14th century: Formed part of an independent Moldovan principality, which included areas, such as Bukovina to the west, that are now part of Romania.
late 15th century: Under Stephen IV the Great the principality reached the height of its power.
16th century: Became a tributary of the Ottoman Turks.
1774–75: Moldovan principality, though continuing to recognize Turkish overlordship, was placed under Russian protectorship; Bukovina was lost to Austria.
1812: Bessarabia ceded to tsarist Russia.
1856: Remainder of Moldovan principality became largely independent of Turkish control.
1859: Moldovan Assembly voted to unite with Wallachia, to the southwest, to form the state of Romania, ruled by Prince Alexandru Ion Cuza. The state became fully independent in 1878.
1918: Following the Russian Revolution, Bessarabia was seized and incorporated within Romania.
1924: Moldovan autonomous Soviet Socialist Republic (SSR) created, as part of Soviet Union, comprising territory east of Dniestr River.
1940: Romania returned Bessarabia, east of Prut River, to Soviet Union, which divided it between Moldovan SSR and Ukraine, with Trans-Dniestr region transferred from Ukraine to Moldova.
1941: Moldovan SSR occupied by Romania and its wartime ally Germany.

1944: Red Army reconquered Bessarabia.
1946–47: Widespread famine as agriculture was collectivized; rich farmers and intellectuals were liquidated.
1950: Immigration by settlers from Russia and Ukraine as industries were developed.
late 1980s: There was an upsurge in Moldovan nationalism, encouraged by the *glasnost* initiative of reformist Soviet leader Mikhail Gorbachev.
1988: The Moldovan Movement in Support of Perestroika (economic restructuring) campaigned for accelerated political reform.
1989: There were nationalist demonstrations in Kishinev (now Chisinau). The Moldovan Popular Front (MPF) was founded; Moldovan was made the state language. There were campaigns for autonomy among ethnic Russians, strongest in industrialized Trans-Dniestr region, and Turkish-speaking but Orthodox Christian Gagauz minority in southwest.
1990: The MPF polled strongly in parliamentary elections and Mircea Snegur, a reform-nationalist communist, became president. Economic and political sovereignty was declared.
1991: Independence was declared and the Communist Party outlawed after a conservative coup in Moscow against Gorbachev; joined Commonwealth of Independent States (CIS). There was insurrection in the Trans-Dniestr region.
1992: Admitted into United Nations and the Conference on Security and Cooperation in Europe; a peace agreement was signed with Russia to end the civil war in Trans-Dniestr, giving special status to the region. The MPF-dominated government fell; A 'government of national accord' was formed, headed by Andrei Sangheli and dominated by the ADP.
1993: A new currency, the leu, was introduced. A privatization programme was launched and closer ties were established with Russia.
1994: Parliamentary elections were won by the ADP. Plebiscite rejected nationalist demands for a merger with Romania. Russia agreed to withdraw Trans-Dniestr troops by 1997.
1995: Joined Council of Europe; economic growth resumed.
1996: Petru Lucinschi was elected president.
1997: A cooperation agreement was signed with the Dniestr region. A law was passed that provided for elections using proportional representation.
1999: A new coalition government was formed, headed by Ion Sturza. It fell in November, and Vladimir Voronin, a communist, succeeded as prime minister.
2000: Constitutional changes increased the powers of the Parlamentul (legislature) and the president was now to be elected by the legislature rather than the people. However, the incumbent president Lucinschi refused to stand, and neither of the two presidential candidates in the December contest were able to secure the required majority.
2001: The Communist Party regained power in parliamentary elections. Vladimir Voronin became president, and Vasile Tarlev became prime minister.
2002: Demonstrations were held against plans to make Russian an official language and compulsory in schools. The protests ended when the plans were cancelled. The authorities in Trans-Dniester resumed

the withdrawal of Russian arms and forces, which had been cancelled during 2001. The deadline for completion was extended until 2004.

2003: Anti-communist and nationalist protests were held against the government's ties with Russia. President Voronin did not sign a Russian-proposed deal on the settlement of Trans-Dniester.

2004: Russia stated that it would not complete its withdrawal from Trans-Dniester until a solution to the conflict was reached. There followed disputes over the closure of Moldovan-language schools in Trans-Dniester. Moldova imposed economic sanctions on the area.

2005: The Communist Party won parliamentary elections and Vladimir Voronin was returned as president.

mole symbol mol, unit of the amount of a substance. One mole of a substance is the mass that contains the same number of particles (atoms, molecules, ions, or electrons) as there are atoms in 12 grams of the *isotope carbon-12.

mole small burrowing mammal with typically dark, velvety fur. Moles grow up to 18 cm/7 in long, and have acute senses of hearing, smell, and touch, but poor eyesight. They have short, muscular forelimbs and shovel-like, clawed front feet for burrowing in search of insects, grubs, and worms. Their fur lies without direction so that they can move forwards or backwards in their tunnels without discomfort. Moles are greedy eaters; they cannot live more than a few hours without food. (Family Talpidae, order Insectivora.)

molecular biology study of the molecular basis of life, including the biochemistry of molecules such as DNA, RNA, and proteins, and the molecular structure and function of the various parts of living cells.

molecular formula in chemistry, formula indicating the actual number of atoms of each element present in a single *molecule of a chemical compound. For example, the molecular formula of carbon dioxide is CO_2, indicating that one molecule of carbon dioxide is made up of one atom of carbon and two atoms of oxygen. This is determined by two pieces of information: the empirical *formula and the *relative molecular mass, which is determined experimentally.

molecular mass *or* **relative molecular mass** mass of a molecule, calculated relative to one-twelfth the mass of an atom of carbon-12. It is found by adding the relative atomic masses of the atoms that make up the molecule.

molecular solid in chemistry, solid composed of molecules that are held together by relatively weak intermolecular forces. Such solids are low-melting and tend to dissolve in organic solvents. Examples of molecular solids are sulphur, ice, sucrose, and solid carbon dioxide.

molecular weight see *relative molecular mass.

molecule smallest configuration of an element or compound that can exist independently. One molecule is made up of a group of atoms held together by *covalent or *ionic bonds. Several non-metal elements exist as molecules. For example, hydrogen *atoms, at room temperature, do not exist independently. They are bonded in pairs to form hydrogen molecules. A molecule of a compound consists of two or more different atoms bonded together. For example, carbon dioxide is made up of molecules, each containing one

carbon and two oxygen atoms bonded together. The *molecular formula is made up of the chemical symbols representing each element in the molecule and numbers showing how many atoms of each element are present. For example, the formula for hydrogen is H_2, and for carbon dioxide is CO_2. Molecules vary in size and complexity from the hydrogen molecule to the large macromolecules of proteins. In general, elements and compounds with molecular structures have similar properties. They have low melting and boiling points, so that many molecular substances are gases or liquids at room temperature. They are usually insoluble in water and do not conduct electricity even when melted.

mole rat, naked small underground mammal, almost hairless, with a disproportionately large head. The mole rat is of importance to zoologists as one of the very few mammals that are eusocial, that is, living in colonies with sterile workers and one fertile female. (Species *Heterocephalus glaber*.)

Molière (1622–1673) pen-name of Jean-Baptiste Poquelin, French satirical dramatist and actor. Modern French comedy developed from his work. After the collapse of the Paris-based Illustre Théâtre (of which he was one of the founders), Molière performed in the provinces 1645–58. In 1655 he wrote his first play, *L'Etourdi/The Blunderer*, and on his return to Paris produced *Les Précieuses ridicules/The Affected Ladies* (1659). His satires include *L'Ecole des femmes/The School for Wives* (1662), *Le Misanthrope* (1666), *Le Bourgeois Gentilhomme/The Would-Be Gentleman* (1670), and *Le Malade imaginaire/The Imaginary Invalid* (1673). Other satiric plays include *Tartuffe* (1664) (banned for attacking the hypocrisy of the clergy; revised in 1667; banned again until 1699), *Le Médecin malgré lui/Doctor in Spite of Himself* (1666), and *Les Femmes savantes/The Learned Ladies* (1672).

mollusc any of a group of invertebrate animals, most of which have a body divided into three parts: a head, a central mass containing the main organs, and a foot for movement; the more sophisticated octopuses and related molluscs have arms to capture their prey. The majority of molluscs are marine animals, but some live in fresh water, and a few live on land. They include clams, mussels, and oysters (bivalves), snails and slugs (gastropods), and cuttlefish, squids, and octopuses (cephalopods). The body is soft, without limbs (except for the cephalopods), and cold-blooded. There is no internal skeleton, but many species have a hard shell covering the body. (Phylum Mollusca.)

Moloch *or* **Molech** in the Old Testament, a Phoenician deity worshipped in Jerusalem in the 7th century BC, to whom live children were sacrificed by fire.

Molotov, Vyacheslav Mikhailovich (1890–1986) adopted name of Vyacheslav Mikhailovich Skriabin, Soviet communist politician. He was chair of the Council of People's Commissars (prime minister) 1930–41 and foreign minister 1939–49 and 1953–56. He negotiated the 1939 non-aggression treaty with Germany (the *Ribbentrop–Molotov pact), and, after the German invasion in 1941, the Soviet partnership with the Allies. His post-war stance prolonged the Cold War and in 1957 he was expelled from the government for Stalinist activities.

Molotov cocktail *or* **petrol bomb** home-made weapon consisting of a bottle filled with petrol, plugged with a rag as a wick, ignited, and thrown as a grenade. Resistance groups during World War II named them after the Soviet foreign minister Molotov.

molybdenite molybdenum sulphide, MoS_2, the chief ore mineral of molybdenum. It possesses a hexagonal crystal structure similar to graphite, has a blue metallic lustre, and is very soft (1–1.5 on the *Mohs scale).

molybdenum chemical symbol Mo, (Greek *molybdos* 'lead') heavy, hard, lustrous, silver-white, metallic element, atomic number 42, relative atomic mass 95.94. The chief ore is the mineral sulphide molybdenite. The element is highly resistant to heat and conducts electricity easily. It is used in alloys, often to harden steels. It is a necessary trace element in human nutrition. It was named in 1781 by Swedish chemist Karl Scheele, after its isolation by another Swedish chemist Peter Jacob Hjelm (1746–1813), for its resemblance to lead ore.

Mombasa industrial port and tourist resort in Kenya (the port also serves Uganda and Tanzania); population (2002 est) 707,400. It stands on Mombasa Island and the adjacent mainland (the island of Mombasa is linked to the mainland by the Mukapa causeway). As well as tourism, industries include car assembly, cement manufacture, and oil and sugar refining. Mombasa was founded by Arab traders in the 11th century and was an important centre for ivory and slave trading until the 16th century. One of the oldest buildings, Fort Jesus, was set up by the Portuguese and is now a museum.

moment of a force in physics, measure of the turning effect, or torque, produced by a force acting on a body. It is equal to the product of the force and the perpendicular distance from its line of action to the point, or pivot, about which the body will turn. The turning force around the pivot is called the moment. Its unit is the newton metre.

moment of inertia in physics, the sum of all the point masses of a rotating object multiplied by the squares of their respective distances from the axis of rotation.

momentum product of the mass of a body and its velocity. If the mass of a body is m kilograms and its velocity is v m s^{-1}, then its momentum is given by: momentum = mv. Its unit is the kilogram metre-per-second (kg m s^{-1}) or the newton second. The momentum of a body does not change unless a resultant or unbalanced force acts on that body (see *Newton's laws of motion).

Mon *or* **Talaing** a minority ethnic group living in the Irrawaddy delta region of lower Myanmar (Burma) and Thailand. The Mon founded the city of Bago in 573 and established kingdoms in the area in the 7th century, but much of their culture was absorbed by invaders such as the Toungoo in 1539, and Alaungpaya, founder of the Konbaung dynasty, in 1757.

Monaco

National name: *Principauté de Monaco/ Principality of Monaco*
Area: 1.95 sq km/0.75 sq mi
Physical features: steep and rugged; surrounded landwards by French territory; being expanded by filling in the sea
Head of state: Prince Albert from 2005
Head of government: Patrick Leclercq from 2000
Political system: liberal democracy
Political executive: parliamentary

Political parties: no formal parties, but lists of candidates: Liste Campora, moderate, centrist; Liste Medecin, moderate, centrist
Currency: euro
GNI per capita (PPP): (US$) 27,500 (2001)
Population: 34,000 (2003 est)
Language: French (official), Monégasgne (a mixture of the French Provençal and Italian Ligurian dialects), Italian
Religion: Roman Catholic about 90%
Life expectancy: 75 (men); 83 (women) (2000–05)
Chronology
1191: The Genoese took control of Monaco, which had formerly been part of the Holy Roman Empire.
1297: Came under the rule of the Grimaldi dynasty, the current ruling family, who initially allied themselves to the French.
1524–1641: Came under Spanish protection.
1793: Annexed by France during French Revolutionary Wars. One member of the ruling family was guillotined; the rest imprisoned.
1815: Placed under protection of Sardinia.
1848: The towns of Menton and Roquebrune, which had formed the greater part of the principality, seceded and later became part of France.
1861: Franco-Monegasque treaty restored Monaco's independence under French protection; the first casino was built.
1865: Customs union established with France.
1918: France given veto over succession to throne and established that if a reigning prince dies without a male heir, Monaco is to be incorporated into France.
1941–45: Occupied successively by Italians and Germans during World War II.
1949: Prince Rainier III ascended the throne.
1956: Prince Rainier married US actor Grace Kelly.
1958: Birth of male heir, Prince Albert.
1962: A new, more liberal constitution was adopted.
1982: Princess Grace died in a car accident.
1993: Joined United Nations.
1998: Michel Leveque was appointed head of government.
2000: Patrick Leclercq replaced Michel Leveque as minister of state. France threatened to take punitive measures against Monaco unless it took action against money-laundering and tax-evasion.

2003: In parliamentary elections the opposition Union pour Monaco (UPM; Union for Monaco) defeated the previously dominant Union Nationale et Démocratique (UND; National and Democratic Union), taking 21 of the 24 seats in the National Council.

2005: Prince Rainier died and was succeeded as head of state by his son Prince Albert.

Monaghan Irish Mhuineachain, county of the Republic of Ireland, in the province of Ulster; county town Monaghan; area 1,290 sq km/498 sq mi; population (2002 est) 52,600. The county is low and rolling, with hills in the northwest, the highest point being Slieve Beagh (381 m/1,217 ft). The principal towns are Clones, Carrickmacross, and Castleblayney. Rivers include the Glyde in the south, the Finn in the west, and the Blackwater in the north. Much of the county is fertile. The main form of agriculture is dairy farming, but cattle and pigs are also raised, and cereals and potatoes grown. Industries include leather, linen, knitwear, footwear, furniture, and lacemaking.

Mona Lisa, the or *La Gioconda* oil painting by *Leonardo da Vinci (1503–05; Louvre, Paris), a portrait of the wife of a Florentine official, Francesco del Giocondo, which, according to *Vasari, Leonardo worked on for four years. It was the first Italian portrait to extend below waist level, setting a precedent for composition that was to dominate portraiture until the 19th century. In the *Mona Lisa* Leonardo brought his technique of *sfumato* (avoiding sharp outlines through gentle gradations of colour) to perfection.

monasticism devotion to religious life under vows of poverty, chastity, and obedience, known to Judaism (for example Essenes), Buddhism, and other religions, before Christianity. In Islam, the Sufis formed monastic orders from the 12th century. The first Christian hermits lived alone in the desert, and the first Christian monastery was founded in Egypt by St Pachomius in 346.

Monck, George (1608–1670) 1st Duke of Albemarle; English soldier. During the English Civil War he fought for King Charles I, but after being captured changed sides and took command of the Parliamentary forces in Ireland. Under Oliver *Cromwell he became commander-in-chief in Scotland, and in 1660 he led his army into England and brought about the *Restoration of *Charles II. He became duke in 1660.

Mondrian, Piet (Pieter Cornelis Mondriaan) (1872–1944) Dutch painter. A founder member of the De *Stijl movement, he was the chief exponent of neoplasticism, a rigorous abstract style based on the use of simple geometric forms and pure colours. Typically his works are frameworks of horizontal and vertical lines forming rectangles of white, red, yellow, and blue, as in *Composition in Red, Yellow and Blue* (1920; Stedelijk, Amsterdam).

Monet, Claude (1840–1926) French painter. He was a pioneer of Impressionism and a lifelong exponent of its ideals; his painting *Impression, Sunrise* (1872) gave the movement its name. In the 1870s he began painting the same subjects at different times of day to explore the ever-changing effects of light on colour and form; the *Haystacks* and *Rouen Cathedral* series followed in the 1890s, and from 1899 he painted a series of *Water Lilies* in the garden of his house at Giverny, Normandy (now a museum).

monetarism economic policy that proposes control of a country's money supply to keep it in step with the country's ability to produce goods, with the aim of controlling *inflation. Cutting government spending is advised, and the long-term aim is to return as much of the economy as possible to the private sector, which is said to be in the interests of efficiency. Monetarism was first put forward by the economist Milton Friedman and the Chicago school of economists.

money any common medium of exchange acceptable in payment for goods or services or for the settlement of debts; legal tender. Money is usually coinage (invented by the Chinese in the second millennium BC) and paper notes (used by the Chinese from about AD 800). Developments such as the cheque and credit card fulfil many of the traditional functions of money. In 1994 Mondex electronic money was introduced experimentally in Swindon, Wiltshire, England.

money supply quantity of money in circulation in an economy at any given time. It can include notes, coins, and clearing-bank and other deposits used for everyday payments. Changes in the quantity of lending are a major determinant of changes in the money supply. One of the main principles of *monetarism is that increases in the money supply in excess of the rate of economic growth are the chief cause of inflation.

Mongol member of any of the various Mongol (or Mongolian) ethnic groups of central Asia. Mongols live in Mongolia, Russia, Inner Mongolia (China), Tibet, and Nepal. The Mongol language belongs to the Altaic family, although some groups of Mongol descent speak languages in the Sino-Tibetan family.

Mongol Empire empire established by *Genghis Khan, a loosely constructed federation of tribal groups extending from Russia to northern China; see *Mongol. Genghis became khan of the Mongol tribes in 1206. Divided by his sons at his death in 1227, Ogotai overcame the Jin and Sun dynasties of China in 1234, and another son, Batu, occupied Russia, parts of Hungary, and Georgia and Armenia, establishing the Kipchak Empire and other khanates. The Western Kipchaks, known as the *Golden Horde terrorized Europe from 1237. Genghis's grandson *Kublai Khan conquered China and used foreigners (such as the Venetian traveller Marco Polo) as well as subjects to administer his empire. Another grandson, Hulagu, conquered Baghdad and Syria. The Mongols lost China in 1367 and suffered defeats in the west in 1380; the empire broke up soon afterwards, fragmenting into separate chiefdoms.

Mongolia

formerly **Outer Mongolia** (until 1924), **People's Republic of Mongolia** (1924–91)

National name: *Mongol Uls/State of Mongolia*
Area: 1,565,000 sq km/604,246 sq mi
Capital: Ulaanbaatar
Major towns/cities: Darhan, Choybalsan, Erdenet
Physical features: high plateau with desert and steppe (grasslands); Altai Mountains in southwest; salt lakes; part of Gobi desert in southeast; contains both the world's southernmost permafrost and northernmost desert
Head of state: Natsagiyn Bagabandi from 1997
Head of government: Tsachiagiyn Elbegdorj from 2004

Political system: emergent democracy
Political executive: limited presidency
Political parties: Mongolian People's Revolutionary Party (MPRP), reform-socialist (ex-communist); Mongolian National Democratic Party (MNDP), traditionalist, promarket economy; Union Coalition (UC, comprising the MNPD and the Social Democratic Party (SDP)), democratic, promarket economy
Currency: tugrik
GNI per capita (PPP): (US$) 1,650 (2002 est)
Exports: minerals and metals (primarily copper concentrate), consumer goods, foodstuffs, agricultural products. Principal market: China 58.9% (2000)
Population: 2,594,000 (2003 est)
Language: Khalkha Mongolian (official), Kazakh (in the province of Bagan-Ölgiy), Chinese, Russian, Turkic languages
Religion: there is no state religion, but traditional lamaism (Mahayana Buddhism) is gaining new strength; the Sunni Muslim Kazakhs of Western Mongolia have also begun the renewal of their religious life, and Christian missionary activity has increased
Life expectancy: 62 (men); 66 (women) (2000–05)
Chronology
AD 1206: Nomadic Mongol tribes united by Genghis Khan to form nucleus of vast Mongol Empire which, stretching across central Asia, reached its zenith under Genghis Khan's grandson, Kublai Khan.
late 17th century: Conquered by China to become province of Outer Mongolia.
1911: Independence proclaimed by Mongolian nationalists after Chinese 'republican revolution'; tsarist Russia helped Mongolia to secure autonomy, under a traditionalist Buddhist monarchy in the form of a reincarnated lama.
1915: Chinese sovereignty reasserted.
1921: Chinese rule overthrown with Soviet help.
1924: People's Republic proclaimed on death of king, when the monarchy was abolished; defeudalization programme launched, entailing collectivization of agriculture and suppression of lama Buddhism.
1932: Armed antigovernment uprising suppressed with Soviet assistance; 100,000 killed in political purges.
1946: China recognized Mongolia's independence.

1952: Death of Marshal Horloogiyn Choybalsan, the dominant force in the ruling communist Mongolian People's Revolutionary Party (MPRP) since 1939.
1958: Yumjaagiyn Tsedenbal became the dominant figure in MPRP and country.
1962: Joined Comecon.
1966: 20-year friendship, cooperation, and mutual-assistance pact signed with Soviet Union (USSR). Relations with China deteriorated.
1987: There was a reduction in the number of Soviet troops; Mongolia's external contacts broadened. The tolerance of traditional social customs encouraged a nationalist revival.
1989: Further Soviet troop reductions.
1990: A demonstrations and democratization campaign was launched, influenced by events in Eastern Europe. Ex-communist MPRP elected in the first free multiparty elections; Punsalmaagiyn Ochirbat was indirectly elected president. Mongolian script was readopted.
1991: A privatization programme was launched. GDP declined by 10%.
1992: The MPRP returned to power in assembly elections held under a new, noncommunist constitution. The economic situation worsened; GDP again declined by 10%.
1993: Ochirbat won the first direct presidential elections.
1996: The economy showed signs of revival. The Union Coalition won assembly elections, defeating the MPRP and ending 75 years of communist rule. A defence cooperation agreement was signed with the USA.
1997: The ex-communist Natsagiyn Bagabandi was elected MPRP chairman and then became president. An economic shock therapy programme, supervised by IMF and World Bank, created unemployment and made the government unpopular. All taxes and tariffs on trade were abolished.
1998: The National Democratic Party (DU) government was toppled after losing a no-confidence vote. Attempts to form a new DU-led government, led by Rinchinnyamiyn Amarjargal, failed, and Janlaviyn Narantsatsralt of the MNDP became prime minister.
1999: Rinchinnyamiyn Marajargal became prime minister.
2000: Mongolia's former communists, the MPRP, branding themselves a centre-left party, won a landslide victory in parliamentary elections, led by Nambariin Enkhbayar.
2001: Natsagiyn Bagabandi was re-elected as president. The IMF approved low interest loans of around $40 million to tackle poverty and boost economic growth.
2002: The Dalai Lama visited Mongolia.
2003: Mongolia contributed 200 soldiers to peacekeeping forces in Iraq.
2004: Russia wrote off a significant proportion of Mongolia's debts. Parliamentary elections resulted in political deadlock. Tsakhiagiin Elbegdorj was appointed prime minister following a power sharing deal.
Mongolia, Inner Chinese *Nei Monggol*, autonomous region of north China from 1947; bounded to the north by Mongolia and Russia; to the east by Heilongjiang and Jilin; to the southeast by Liaoning; to the south by Hebei, Shanxi, Shaanxi, and Ningxia Hui Autonomous Region; and to the west by Gansu; area 1,200,00 sq km/ 463,300 sq mi; population (1996) 23,070,000; less than

one-sixth are Mongols. The capital is Hohhot, and Baotou is a town in the region. The region is characterized by grassland and desert. Industries include coal; reserves of iron ore, rare earth oxides europium, and yttrium at Bayan Obo; woollen textiles; dairy-processing; and leather. Agricultural products include cereals under irrigation, animal husbandry, and forestry.

mongoose any of a group of carnivorous tropical mammals. The **Indian mongoose** (*H. mungo*) is greyish in colour and about 50 cm/1.5 ft long, with a long tail. It can be tamed and is often kept for its ability to kill snakes. Like the snakes themselves, the acetylcholine receptors connecting the mongooses' nerves and muscle cells are unaffected by the venom. (Genera *Herpestes*, *Ichneumia*, and other related genera, family Viverridae.)

monitor any of various lizards found in Africa, South Asia, and Australasia. Monitors are generally large and carnivorous, with well-developed legs and claws and a long powerful tail that can be swung in defence. (Family Varanidae.)

monkey any of the various smaller, mainly tree-dwelling anthropoid *primates, excluding humans and the *apes. There are 125 species, living in Africa, Asia, and tropical Central and South America. Monkeys eat mainly leaves and fruit, and also small animals. Several species are endangered due to loss of forest habitat, for example the woolly spider monkey and black saki of the Amazonian forest.

monkey puzzle *or* **Chilean pine** coniferous evergreen tree, native to Chile; its branches, growing in circular arrangements (whorls) around the trunk and larger branches, are covered in prickly, leathery leaves. (*Araucaria araucana*, family Araucariaceae.)

Monmouth, James Scott, 1st Duke of Monmouth (1649–1685) Claimant to the English crown, the illegitimate son of Charles II and Lucy Walter. After James II's accession in 1685, Monmouth landed in England at Lyme Regis, Dorset, claimed the crown, and raised a rebellion, which was crushed at *Sedgemoor in Somerset. He was executed with 320 of his accomplices. He was made duke in 1663.

Monmouthshire Welsh **Trefynwy**, unitary authority in southeast Wales. A former county, between 1974 and 1996 it became (except for a small area on the border with Mid Glamorgan) the county of Gwent.
area: 851 sq km/328 sq mi **towns:** Cwmbran (administrative headquarters), Chepstow, Abergavenny, Caldicot, and Monmouth **physical:** rivers *Wye and Usk; mountainous in north **features:** Chepstow (1067), Raglan (1435), and Caldicot (11th century) castles; Tintern Abbey (1131), salmon and trout fishing; peak of Pen-y-Fal or Sugar Loaf (596 m/1,955 ft), Wye Valley **population:** (2001 est) 84,900.

monocarpic *or* **hapaxanthic** describing plants that flower and produce fruit only once during their life cycle, after which they die. Most *annual plants and *biennial plants are monocarpic, but there are also a small number of monocarpic *perennial plants that flower just once, sometimes often as long as 90 years, dying shortly afterwards, for example century plant *Agave* and some species of bamboo *Bambusa*. The general biological term related to organisms that reproduce only once during their lifetime is semelparity.

monoclonal antibody (MAB) antibody produced by fusing an antibody-producing lymphocyte (white blood cell) with a cancerous myeloma (bone-marrow) cell. The resulting fused cell, called a hybridoma, is immortal and can be used to produce large quantities of a single, specific antibody. By choosing antibodies that are directed against antigens found on cancer cells, and combining them with cytotoxic drugs, it is hoped to make so-called magic bullets that will be able to pick out and kill cancers.

monocotyledon angiosperm (flowering plant) having an embryo with a single cotyledon, or seed leaf (as opposed to *dicotyledons, which have two). Monocotyledons usually have narrow leaves with parallel veins and smooth edges, and hollow or soft stems. Their flower parts are arranged in threes. Most are small plants such as orchids, grasses, and lilies, but some are trees such as palms.

monoculture farming system where only one crop is grown. In developing world countries this is often a *cash crop, grown on plantations, for example sugar and coffee. Cereal crops in the industrialized world are also frequently grown on a monoculture basis, for example wheat in the Canadian prairies.

Monod, Jacques Lucien (1910–1976) French biochemist who was awarded the Nobel Prize for Physiology or Medicine in 1965 with his co-workers André Lwoff and François Jacob for research into the genetic control of enzyme and virus synthesis.

monoecious having separate male and female flowers on the same plant. Maize *Zea mays*, for example, has a tassel of male flowers at the top of the stalk and a group of female flowers (on the ear, or cob) lower down. Monoecism is a way of avoiding self-fertilization. Dioecious plants have male and female flowers on separate plants.

monolith (Greek *monos* 'sole', *lithos* 'stone') single isolated stone or column, usually standing and of great size, used as a form of monument. Some are natural features, such as the Buck Stone in the Forest of Dean, England. Other monoliths may be quarried, resited, finished, or carved; those in Egypt of about 3000 BC take the form of *obelisks. They have a wide distribution including Europe, South America, North Africa, and the Middle East.

monologue one person speaking, though the term is generally understood to mean a virtuoso, highly skilful solo performance. Literary monologues are often set pieces in which a character reveals his or her personality, sometimes unintentionally (as in the dramatic monologue); in drama the soliloquy performs a similar function. A monologue can occur in a dialogue; for example, in a conversation where one person suddenly launches into a lengthy anecdote.

monomer chemical compound composed of simple molecules from which *polymers can be made. Under certain conditions the simple molecules (of the monomer) join together (polymerize) to form a very long chain molecule (macromolecule) called a polymer. For example, the polymerization of *ethene (ethylene) monomers produces the polymer *polythene (polyethylene):

$$2n\text{CH}_2\text{–CH}_2 \rightarrow (\text{CH}_2\text{–CH}_2\text{–CH}_2\text{–CH}_2)_n.$$

monopoly in economics, the domination of a market for a particular product or service by a single company, which can therefore restrict competition and keep prices high. In practice, a company can be said to have a monopoly when it controls a significant proportion of the market (technically an *oligopoly). In a communist country the state itself has the overall monopoly; in capitalist countries some services, such as transport or electricity supply, may be state monopolies.

monorail railway that runs on a single rail; the cars can be balanced on it or suspended from it. It was invented in 1882 to carry light loads, and when run by electricity was called a **telpher**.

monosaccharide *or* **simple sugar** *carbohydrate that cannot be hydrolysed (split) into smaller carbohydrate units. Examples are glucose and fructose, both of which have the molecular formula $C_6H_{12}O_6$.

monosodium glutamate MSG $NaC_5H_8NO_4$, white, crystalline powder, the sodium salt of glutamic acid (an *amino acid found in proteins that plays a role in the metabolism of plants and animals). It has no flavour of its own, but enhances the flavour of foods such as meat and fish. It is used to enhance the flavour of many packaged and 'fast foods', and in Chinese cooking. Ill effects may arise from its overconsumption, and some people are very sensitive to it, even in small amounts. It is commercially derived from vegetable protein. It occurs naturally in soybeans and seaweed.

monotheism (Greek *monos* 'sole', *theos* 'god') belief or doctrine that there is only one God; the opposite of polytheism. Monotheism is also opposed to all systems of moral dualism, asserting the ultimate supremacy of good over evil. The Jewish, Muslim, and Christian religions are strictly monotheistic. Monotheism differs from deism in that it asserts that God is not only the creator of the universe and the source of the laws of nature, but is also constantly active and concerned in the world.

monotreme any of a small group of primitive egg-laying mammals, found in Australasia. They include the *echidnas (spiny anteaters) and the *platypus. (Order Monotremata.)

Monroe, James (1758–1831) 5th president of the USA 1817–25, a Democratic Republican. He served in the American Revolution, was minister to France 1794–96, and in 1803 negotiated the *Louisiana Purchase. He was secretary of state 1811–14 and 1815–17, and secretary of war 1814–15. His name is associated with the *Monroe Doctrine.

Monroe, Marilyn (1926–1962) stage name of Norma Jean Mortenson, US film actor. The voluptuous blonde sex symbol of the 1950s, she made adroit comedies such as *Gentlemen Prefer Blondes* (1953), *How to Marry a Millionaire* (1953), *The Seven Year Itch* (1955), *Bus Stop* (1956), and *Some Like It Hot* (1959).

Monroe Doctrine declaration by US president James *Monroe in 1823 that the USA would not tolerate any European nation trying to establish a colony in the Americas, and that any attempt to do so would be regarded as a threat to US peace and security. At the time, several European countries were proposing to intervene in former Spanish and Portuguese colonies in Latin and South America, and Russia was attempting to extend its Alaskan territories into Oregon country. In return for the cessation of such European ambitions, the USA would not interfere in European affairs. The doctrine, subsequently broadened, has been a recurrent theme in US foreign policy, although it has no basis in US or international law.

Monrovia capital and port of Liberia, at the mouth of the St Paul River; population (2002 est) 543,000 (city), 1,407,700 (urban area). Iron ore and rubber are leading exports, and industries include oil refining and the manufacture of cement, chemicals, pharmaceuticals, and processed foods.

monsoon wind pattern that brings seasonally heavy rain to South Asia; it blows towards the sea in winter and towards the land in summer. The monsoon may cause destructive flooding all over India and Southeast Asia from April to September, leaving thousands of people homeless each year.

monstera *or* **Swiss cheese plant** evergreen climbing plant belonging to the arum family, native to tropical America. *M. deliciosa* is grown as a house plant. Areas between the veins of the leaves dry up, forming deep notches and eventually holes. (Genus *Monstera*, family Araceae.)

Montaigne, Michel Eyquem de (1533–1592) French writer. He is regarded as the creator of the essay form. In 1580 he published the first two volumes of his *Essais*; the third volume appeared in 1588, and the definitive edition was issued posthumously in 1595. In his writings Montaigne considers all aspects of life from an urbanely sceptical viewpoint. He is critical of human pride and suspicious of philosophy and religion, seeking his own independent path to self-knowledge. Francis *Bacon was among the thinkers who have been challenged and stimulated by his work, and through the translation by John Florio in 1603, he influenced Shakespeare and other English writers.

Montana called the **Treasure State**, (Spanish *montaña* 'mountainous area') state in northwestern USA, the most northerly Rocky Mountain state and the fourth largest state in the USA, bordered to the north by the Canadian provinces of *British Columbia, *Alberta, and *Saskatchewan; to the east by *North Dakota and *South Dakota; to the south by *Wyoming; and to the southwest and west by *Idaho; area 376,981 sq km/145,553 sq mi; population (2000) 902,200; capital Helena. Montana is known as the Treasure State owing to its abundant mineral resources. The state is divided into the *Rocky Mountain region, which has peaks with elevations of between 2,400 m/8,000 ft and 3,000 m/10,000 ft, and the eastern *Great Plains. It is subject to climatic extremes, with cold winters and summer hailstorms in the Rockies and summer droughts on the Great Plains. Montana's economy is traditionally based on mining, lumber, and cattle ranches. Oil and gas were major resources during the 1970s, but tourism and the service industries have since become increasingly important. Farming has been greatly helped by irrigation programmes and soil improvements. The chief crop is wheat, but barley and alfalfa yields are also significant. Billings is the largest city; other cities include Missoula, Great Falls, Butte, Bozeman, Kalispell, Havre, Anaconda, and Miles City. Montana joined the Union in 1889 as the 41st state.

Montanism movement within the early Christian church that strove to return to the purity of primitive Christianity. It originated in Phrygia in about 156 with the teaching of a prophet named Montanus, and spread to Anatolia, Rome, Carthage, and Gaul. The theologian Tertullian was a Montanist.

Mont Blanc Italian **Monte Bianco**, the highest mountain in the *Alps, on the border between France and Italy, and one of the highest points in Europe at 4,807 m/15,772 ft. Lying 10 km/6 mi south of Chamonix, it forms part of the Mont Blanc range. The peak was first climbed in 1786 by Jacques Balmat and Michel Paccard of Chamonix. In 1965 the longest road tunnel in the world (12 km/7.5 mi) was opened under the mountain, linking Chamonix to Courmayeur in Italy. There are many resorts along the base of the mountain which attract both summer and winter tourists and sportspeople; the main resorts on the French side are Argentière, Chamonix, Saint-Gervais-les-Bains, and Megève.

montbretia plant belonging to the iris family, native to South Africa, with orange or reddish flowers on long stems. They are grown as ornamental pot plants. (*Tritonia crocosmiflora*, family Iridaceae.)

Montcalm-Gozon, Louis-Joseph de (1712–1759) Marquis de Montcalm, French general, appointed military commander in Canada in 1756. He won a succession of victories over the British during the French and Indian War, but was defeated in 1759 by James *Wolfe at Québec on the Plains of Abraham, where both he and Wolfe were killed; this battle marked the end of French rule in Canada.

Montenegrin Slavic inhabitants of Montenegro, a constituent republic of Serbia and Montenegro, whose culture has much in common with the Serbs.

Montessori, Maria (1870–1952) Italian educationist. Working with mentally disabled children, she developed the **Montessori method**, an educational system for all children based on an informal approach, incorporating instructive play and allowing children to develop at their own pace.

Monteverdi, Claudio Giovanni Antonio (1567–1643) Italian composer. He contributed to the development of the opera with *La favola d'Orfeo/The Legend of Orpheus* (1607) and *L'incoronazione di Poppea/The Coronation of Poppea* (1642). He also wrote madrigals, motets, and sacred music, notably the *Vespers* (1610).

Montevideo capital and chief port of Uruguay, situated on the northen shore of the Río de la Plata estuary; 210 km/130 mi east of Buenos Aires; population (1996 est) 1,303,200. It is Uruguay's chief industrial and commercial centre, and handles almost 90% of the country's imports and exports. Industries include meat packing, tanning, footwear, flour milling, and textiles. The main exports are grain, meat products, and hides. All Uruguay's railways converge on the city, and a large fishing fleet is based here. Montevideo is also a tourist resort with extensive beaches.

Montezuma II (1466–1520) Aztec emperor of Mexico. He succeeded his uncle in 1502. Although he was a great warrior and legislator, heavy centralized taxation provoked resentment in outlying areas. When the Spanish conquistador Hernán *Cortés landed at Veracruz in 1519 and attempted to march on Tenochtitlán, he was well received by the inhabitants and made Montezuma his prisoner. The emperor was restored to his throne as a vassal of Spain, but dissident groups among his subjects rebelled and killed him.

Montfort, Simon de (c. 1208–1265) called 'the Younger', English politician and soldier. From 1258 he led the baronial opposition to Henry III's misrule during the second *Barons' War, and in 1264 defeated and captured the king at Lewes, Sussex. In 1265, as head of government, he summoned the first parliament in which the towns were represented; he was killed at the Battle of Evesham during the last of the Barons' Wars.

Montgolfier Joseph Michel (1740–1810) and Jacques Etienne (1745–1799), French brothers whose hot-air balloon was used for the first successful human flight 21 November 1783.

Montgomery state capital of *Alabama, in Montgomery County, on the Alabama River; population (2000 est) 201,600. Linked to the port of Mobile by river, it is a long-established administrative and commercial centre with diverse light industries. Two major air force bases are located nearby. Montgomery was incorporated in 1819; it became state capital in 1846.

Montgomery, Bernard Law (1887–1976) 1st Viscount Montgomery of Alamein; called 'Monty', English field marshal. In World War II he commanded the 8th Army in North Africa in the Second Battle of El *Alamein in 1942. As commander of British troops in northern Europe from 1944, he received the German surrender in 1945.

month unit of time based on the motion of the *Moon around the Earth. The time taken for the Moon to orbit the Earth (from one new or full Moon to the next) is known as a **synodic** or **lunar month** and is 29.53 days. The Western calendar is not based on the lunar month, but rather on the **calendar month**, a human invention devised to fit the calendar year. However, the Islamic calendar is based on the lunar month, and therefore each year a fixed date goes back by about ten days.

Montmartre district of *Paris, France, dominated by the basilica of Sacré-Coeur, completed in 1919. It is situated in the north of the city on a hill 120 m/400 ft high. It is known for its night-life and artistic associations and is a popular tourist site.

Montréal inland port and commercial centre of Québec, Canada, on Montréal Island at the junction of the Ottawa and St Lawrence rivers; population (2001 est) 1,039,500; metropolitan area (2001 est) 3,426,400. It is the second-largest port on the North American east coast, the chief port of the St Lawrence–Great Lakes waterway system, and the world's farthest inland port, situated 1,600 km/1,000 mi from the Atlantic. Industries include oil-refining, engineering, food-processing, distilling, brewing, and the manufacture of steel, aircraft, ships, petrochemicals, tobacco products, clothing, pulp, and paper. Founded by the French in 1642, Montréal became a British possession in 1763. The city was badly affected by the great ice storm of January 1998 which coated electricity pylons with ice and the weight brought many of them down, blacking out parts of Montréal and Québec.

Montrose, James Graham, 1st Marquess and 5th Earl of Montrose (1612–1650) Scottish soldier, son of the 4th Earl of Montrose. He supported the *Covenanters against Charles I, but after 1640 changed sides. As lieutenant general in 1644, he rallied the loyalist Highland clans to Charles, defeating the Covenanters' forces at Tipeprmuir and Aberdeen, but his subsequent attempt to raise the Royalist standard in the Lowlands ended in failure at Philiphaugh in 1645, and he escaped to Holland. Returning in 1650 to raise a revolt, he survived shipwreck only to have his weakened forces defeated, and (having been betrayed to the Covenanters) was hanged in Edinburgh.

Montserrat volcanic island in the West Indies, one of the Leeward group, a British crown colony; capital Plymouth; area 110 sq km/42 sq mi; population (1995 est) 13,000. Montserrat produces cotton, cotton-seed, coconuts, citrus and other fruits, and vegetables. The island's population has suffered from repeated eruptions of the Soufriere volcano; the eruption in July 1997 buried the capital, Plymouth, under rock and ashes, and around 7,000 islanders were evacuated. Practically all buildings were destroyed by Hurricane Hugo in September 1989.

Moon natural satellite of Earth, 3,476 km/2,160 mi in diameter, with a mass 0.012 (approximately one-eightieth) that of Earth. Its surface gravity is only 0.16 (one-sixth) that of Earth. Its average distance from Earth is 384,400 km/238,855 mi, and it orbits in a west-to-east direction every 27.32 days (the **sidereal month**).

It spins on its axis with one side permanently turned towards Earth. The Moon has no atmosphere and was thought to have no water until ice was discovered on its surface in 1998.

moon in astronomy, any natural *satellite that orbits a planet. Mercury and Venus are the only planets in the Solar System that do not have moons.

Moor any of the northwestern African Muslims, of mixed Arab and Berber origin, who conquered Spain and ruled its southern part from 711 to 1492, when they were forced to renounce their faith and became Christian (they were then known as *Moriscos*). The name (English form of Latin *Maurus*) was originally applied to an inhabitant of the Roman province of Mauritania, in northwestern Africa.

moor in earth science, a stretch of land, usually at a height, which is characterized by a vegetation of heather, coarse grass, and bracken. A moor may be poorly drained and contain boggy hollows.

Moore, Bobby (Robert Frederick) (1941–1993) English footballer who led the England team to victory against West Germany in the 1966 World Cup final. A superb defender, he played 107 games for England

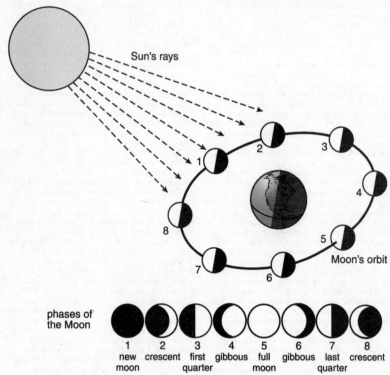

Sun's rays

Moon's orbit

phases of the Moon

| 1 | 2 | 3 | 4 | 5 | 6 | 7 | 8 |
| new moon | crescent | first quarter | gibbous | full moon | gibbous | last quarter | crescent |

Moon The phases of the Moon as viewed from the Earth. The Moon takes a lunar month (about 29 days) to orbit the Earth. When the Earth is between the Sun and the Moon, the Moon appears to be 'full' because we can see all the light from the Sun reflected by the Moon.

1962–73 (until 1978, a world-record number of international appearances) and was captain 90 times. His Football League career, spent at West Ham 1968–74 and Fulham 1974–77, spanned 19 years and 668 matches.

Moore, Henry (Spencer) (1898–1986) English sculptor. Considered one of the leading artists of the 20th century, he is known for his monumental semi-abstracts of the human form, such as *Reclining Figure* (1957–58; outside the UNESCO building in Paris). Influenced by primitive art and nature, his subjects include the nude, mother-and-child groups, the warrior, and interlocking abstract forms. Many of his post-1945 works are in bronze or marble, and are often designed to be placed in open urban or landscape settings.

moorhen marsh bird belonging to the rail family, common in swamps, lakes, and ponds throughout Europe, Asia, Africa, and North and South America. It is about 33 cm/13 in long, brown above and dark grey below, with a red bill and forehead, a white stripe along the edge of the folded wings, a vivid white underside to the tail, and green legs. Its big feet are not webbed or lobed, but the moorhen can swim well. The nest is built by the waterside, and the eggs are buff-coloured with orange-brown spots. (Species *Gallinula chloropus*, family Rallidae, order Gruiformes.)

moose North American name for the *elk.

moraine rocky debris or *till carried along and deposited by a *glacier. Material eroded from the side of a glaciated valley and carried along the glacier's edge is called a **lateral moraine**; that worn from the valley floor and carried along the base of the glacier is called a **ground moraine**. Rubble dropped at the snout (front end) of a melting glacier is called a **terminal moraine**.

morality play didactic medieval European verse drama, in part a development of the *mystery play (or miracle play), in which human characters are replaced by personified virtues and vices, the limited humorous elements being provided by the Devil. In England, morality plays, such as *Everyman*, flourished in the 15th century. They exerted an influence on the development of Elizabethan drama and comedy.

Moravia Czech **Morava**, area of central Europe, forming two regions of the Czech Republic: **South Moravia** (Czech Jihomoravský) and **North Moravia** (Czech Severomoravský). South Moravia has an area of 15,030 sq km/5,800 sq mi and a population (1991) of 2,048,900. Its capital is Brno. North Moravia has an area of 11,070 sq km/4,273 sq mi and a population (1991) of 1,961,500. Its capital is Ostrava. The River Morava is found in the region. 25% of the region is forested. Products include maize, grapes, and wine in the south; wheat, barley, rye, flax, and sugar beet in the north; and coal and iron.

Moravian member of a Christian Protestant sect, the **Moravian Brethren**. An episcopal church that grew out of the earlier Bohemian Brethren, it was established by the Lutheran Count Zinzendorf in Saxony in 1722.

Mordred in Arthurian legend, nephew and final opponent of King Arthur. What may be an early version of his name (Medraut) appears with Arthur in annals from the 10th century, listed under the year AD 537.

Mordvin or **Mordovian** member of a Finnish people inhabiting the middle Volga Valley in western Asia. They are agriculturalists, known to have lived in the

region since the 1st century AD. Although nominally Christian, their faith also includes non-Christian divinities. There are 1 million speakers of Mordvin scattered throughout western Russia, about one-third of whom live in the Mordvinian republic. Mordvin is a Finno-Ugric language belonging to the Uralic family.

Mordvinia or **Mordoviya** autonomous republic of central Russian Federation; area 26,200 sq km/10,100 sq mi; population (1990) 964,000 (60% Russian, 35% Mordvinians). The capital is Saransk. The republic is about 350 km/217 mi southeast of Moscow. The River Sura is in the east, and there are forests in the west. Industries include sugar beet, grains, hemp, and potatoes; sheep and dairy farming; commercial vehicles, timber, furniture, and textiles. Languages spoken are Russian and Mordvin.

More, (St) Thomas (1478–1535) English politician and author. From 1509 he was favoured by *Henry VIII and employed on foreign embassies. He was a member of the privy council from 1518 and Lord Chancellor from 1529 but resigned over Henry's break with the pope. For refusing to accept the king as head of the church, he was executed. The title of his political book *Utopia* (1516) has come to mean any supposedly perfect society.

morel any of a group of edible *mushrooms. The common morel (*M. esculenta*) grows in Europe and North America. The yellowish-brown cap is pitted with holes like a sponge and is about 2.5 cm/1 in long. It is used for seasoning gravies, soups, and sauces and is second only to the *truffle as the world's most sought-after mushroom. (Genus *Morchella*, order Pezizales.)

Morgan le Fay in the romance and legend of the English king Arthur, an enchantress and healer, ruler of *Avalon and sister of the king, whom she tended after his final battle. In *Le Morte d'Arthur* (completed in 1470) she revealed the intrigue between *Guinevere and *Lancelot to her brother.

Morisot, Berthe Marie Pauline (1841–1895) French painter, the first woman to join the Impressionist movement. Taught by *Corot, she was also much influenced by *Manet and, in the 1880s, *Renoir. She specialized in sensitive pictures of women and children, as in *The Cradle* (1872; Impressionist Museum, Paris).

Mormon or **Latter-day Saint** member of a Christian sect, the **Church of Jesus Christ of Latter-day Saints**, founded at Fayette, New York, in 1830 by Joseph Smith. According to Smith, who had received visions and divine revelations during the 1820s, Mormon was an ancient prophet in North America whose hidden writings, the *Book of Mormon*, were shown to him in 1827. The book is accepted by Mormons as part of the Christian scriptures. Originally persecuted, the Mormons migrated west to *Salt Lake City, Utah, under Brigham *Young's leadership and prospered; their headquarters are here. The Mormon Church is a missionary church with a worldwide membership of about 6 million.

morning glory any of a group of twining or creeping plants native to tropical America, especially *I. purpurea*, with dazzling blue flowers. Small quantities of substances similar to the hallucinogenic drug LSD are found in the seeds of some species. (Genus *Ipomoea*, family Convolvulaceae.)

Moro, Aldo (1916–1978) Italian Christian Democrat politician. Prime minister 1963–68 and 1974–76, he was expected to become Italy's president, but he was kidnapped and shot by Red Brigade urban guerrillas.

Moroccan Crises two periods of international tension in 1905 and 1911 following German objections to French expansion in Morocco. Their wider purpose was to break up the Anglo-French entente of 1904, but both crises served to reinforce the entente and isolate Germany. The first was resolved at the Algeciras Conference. The second brought Europe to the brink of war and is known as the Agadir Incident.

Morocco

National name: *Al-Mamlaka al-Maghribyya/ Kingdom of Morocco*

Area: 458,730 sq km/177,115 sq mi (excluding Western Sahara)
Capital: Rabat
Major towns/cities: Casablanca, Marrakesh, Fès, Oujda, Kenitra, Tétouan, Meknès
Major ports: Casablanca, Tangier, Agadir
Physical features: mountain ranges, including the Atlas Mountains northeast–southwest; fertile coastal plains in west
Head of state: Sayyid Muhammad VI ibn-Hassan from 1999
Head of government: Driss Jettou from 2002
Political system: emergent democracy
Political executive: dual executive
Political parties: Constitutional Union (UC), right wing; National Rally of Independents (RNI), royalist; Popular Movement (MP), moderate, centrist; Istiqlal, nationalist, centrist; Socialist Union of Popular Forces (USFP), progressive socialist; National Democratic Party (PND), moderate, nationalist
Currency: dirham
GNI per capita (PPP): (US$) 3,690 (2002 est)
Exports: phosphates and phosphoric acid, mineral products, seafoods and seafood products, citrus fruit, tobacco, clothing, hosiery. Principal market: France 33.6% (2000)
Population: 30,566,000 (2003 est)
Language: Arabic (75%) (official), Berber dialects (25%), French, Spanish

Religion: Sunni Muslim; Christian and Jewish minorities
Life expectancy: 67 (men); 71 (women) (2000–05)
Chronology
10th–3rd centuries BC: Phoenicians from Tyre settled along north coast.
1st century AD: Northwest Africa became Roman province of Mauritania.
5th–6th centuries: Invaded by Vandals and Visigoths.
682: Start of Arab conquest, followed by spread of Islam.
8th century: King Idris I established small Arab kingdom.
1056–1146: The Almoravids, a Berber dynasty based at Marrakesh, built an empire embracing Morocco and parts of Algeria and Spain.
1122–1268: After a civil war, the Almohads, a rival Berber dynasty, overthrew the Almoravids; Almohads extended empire but later lost most of Spain.
1258–1358: Beni Merin dynasty supplanted Almohads.
14th century: Moroccan Empire fragmented into separate kingdoms, based in Fès and Marrakesh.
15th century: Spain and Portugal occupied Moroccan ports; expulsion of Muslims from Spain in 1492.
16th century: Saadian dynasty restored unity of Morocco and resisted Turkish invasion.
1649: Foundation of current Alaouite dynasty of sultans; Morocco remained an independent and isolated kingdom.
1856: Under British pressure, the sultan opened Morocco to European commerce.
1860: Spain invaded Morocco, which was forced to cede the southwestern region of Ifni.
1905: A major international crisis was caused by German objections to increasing French influence in Morocco.
1911: Agadir Crisis: further German objections to French imperialism in Morocco were overcome by territorial compensation in central Africa.
1912: Morocco was divided into French and Spanish protectorates; the sultan was reduced to puppet ruler.
1921: Moroccan rebels, the Riffs, led by Abd el-Krim, defeated a large Spanish force at Anual.
1923: The city of Tangier was separated from Spanish Morocco and made a neutral international zone.
1926: French forces crushed Riff revolt.
1944: A nationalist party, Istiqlal, was founded to campaign for full independence.
1948: Consultative assemblies introduced.
1953–55: Serious anti-French riots.
1956: French and Spanish forces withdrew; Morocco regained effective independence under Sultan Muhammad V, who took title of king in 1957.
1961: Muhammad V succeeded by Hassan II.
1962: First constitution adopted; replaced in 1970 and 1972.
1965–77: King Hassan suspended the constitution and ruled by decree.
1969: Spanish overseas province of Ifni returned to Morocco.
1975: Spain withdrew from Western Sahara, leaving Morocco and Mauritania to divide it between themselves.
1976: Polisario Front, supported by Algeria, began guerrilla war in Western Sahara with the aim of securing its independence as the Sahrahwi Arab Democratic Republic.

1979: Mauritania withdrew from its portion of Western Sahara, which Morocco annexed after major battles with Polisario.

1984: Morocco signed mutual defence with Libya, which had previously supported Polisario.

1991: A UN-sponsored ceasefire came into effect in the Western Sahara.

1992: The constitution was amended in an attempt to increase the influence of parliament.

1996: A new two-chamber assembly was approved.

1998: Prime Minister Abderrahmane Youssoufi formed a centre–left coalition.

1999: King Hassan II died and was succeeded by his son, Muhammad VI.

2000: King Muhammad VI embarked on a programme of social and political reform, including strengthening the rights of women.

2002: Driss Jettou became prime minister.

2003: In Casablanca, 12 suicide bombers thought to be Islamic fundamentalists linked to the al-Qaeda international terrorist network killed about 30 other people and injured many more in five coordinated explosions at a hotel, a nightclub, a Jewish community centre and cemetery, and the Belgian consulate.

2004: A major earthquake killed more than 500 people in the north of the country. Morocco signed a free trade deal with the USA.

2005: King Juan Carlos of Spain made a state visit to Morocco.

Moroni capital of the Comoros Republic, on Njazidja (Grand Comore); population (1992) 22,000. It has a small natural harbour from which coffee, cacao, and vanilla are exported. Local agricultural markets trade in coconuts, cassava, bananas, and rice.

Morpheus in Greek and Roman mythology, the god of dreams, son of Hypnos or Somnus, god of sleep.

morphine narcotic alkaloid, $C_{17}H_{19}NO_3$, derived from *opium and prescribed only to alleviate severe pain. Its use produces serious side effects, including nausea, constipation, tolerance, and addiction, but it is highly valued for the relief of the terminally ill.

morphogen in medicine, one of a class of substances believed to be present in the growing embryo, controlling its growth pattern. It is thought that variations in the concentration of morphogens in different parts of the embryo cause them to grow at different rates.

morphology in biology, the study of the physical structure and form of organisms, in particular their soft tissues.

morphology in the study of language, the analysis of the formation of words, the breaking-down of a language into morphemes.

Morris, William (1834–1896) English designer, socialist, and writer. A founder of the *Arts and Crafts Movement, he condemned 19th-century mechanization and sought a revival of traditional crafts, such as furnituremaking, book illustration, fabric design, and so on. He linked this to a renewal of society based on Socialist principles.

morris dance English folk dance. The dances take different forms and various theories about the origin of morris dancing have been put forward. These include the claim that it originated in pagan fertility rites, that it was imported to England in the 15th century as a European court entertainment, and that it was a staple of springtime church and village festivals. Shakespeare refers to it as a dance for festivals, as well as referring to the dancers as 'Moriscos', which may indicate a moorish influence via Spain. Today morris dancers still appear at public and local festivals, and may have bells, handkerchiefs, or sticks as their props.

Morrison, Herbert Stanley (1888–1965) Baron Morrison of Lambeth, British Labour politician. He was a founder member and later secretary of the London Labour Party 1915–45, and a member of the London County Council 1922–45. He entered Parliament in 1923, representing South Hackney in 1923, 1929–31, and 1935–45, and East Lewisham 1945–59. He organized the Labour Party's general election victory in 1945. He was twice defeated in the contest for leadership of the party, once by Clement Attlee in 1932, and then by Hugh Gaitskell in 1955. A skilful organizer, he lacked the ability to unite the party. He was created baron in 1959.

Morrison, Toni (1931–) born Chloe Anthony Wofford, US novelist. Her fiction records African-American life in the South. *Beloved*, based on a true story of infanticide in Kentucky, won the 1988 Pulitzer Prize and was filmed in 1998. Her other novels include *Song of Solomon* (1978), *Tar Baby* (1981), *Jazz* (1992), *Paradise* (1998), and *Love* (2003). She was awarded the Nobel Prize for Literature in 1993, the first African-American woman to receive it.

Morse code international code for transmitting messages by wire or radio using signals of short (dots) and long (dashes) duration, originated by US inventor Samuel Morse for use on his invention, the telegraph (see *telegraphy).

mortar method of projecting a bomb via a high trajectory at a target up to 6–7 km/3–4 mi away. A mortar bomb is stabilized in flight by means of tail fins. The high trajectory results in a high angle of attack and makes mortars more suitable than artillery for use in built-up areas or mountains; mortars are not as accurate, however. Artillery also differs in firing a projectile through a rifled barrel, thus creating greater muzzle velocity.

mortgage transfer of property, usually a house, as a security for repayment of a loan. The loan is normally repaid to a bank or building society over a period of years.

Mortimer, Roger de (c. 1287–1330) 8th Baron of Wigmore and 1st Earl of March, English politician and adventurer. He opposed Edward II and with Edward's queen, Isabella, led a rebellion against him in 1326, bringing about his abdication. From 1327 Mortimer ruled England as the queen's lover, until Edward III had him executed. Knighted 1306, Earl 1328.

mosaic design or picture, usually for a floor or wall, produced by setting small pieces (*tesserae*) of marble, glass, or other materials in a cement ground. The ancient Greeks were the first to use large-scale mosaic (in the Macedonian royal palace at Pella, for example). Mosaic was commonly used by the Romans for their baths and villas (a well-known example being at Hadrian's Villa in Tivoli) and reached its highest development in the early Byzantine period (for example, in the church of San Vitale, Ravenna).

Moscow Russian **Moskva**, industrial and commercial city, capital of the Russian Federation and of the

Moscow region, and formerly (1922–91) of the USSR; population (1990) 8,801,000. Moscow lies on the Moskva River 640 km/400 mi southeast of St Petersburg, and covers an area of some 880 sq km/340 sq mi. It is the main political, economic, and cultural centre of Russia. A major manufacturing city, its industries include aerospace technology and vehicle assembly, machine and precision tool manufacture, and the production of such diverse goods as electrical equipment, chemicals, and many food products. Moscow's State University was founded in 1755; other cultural institutions include the extensive Russian State Library and the Academy of Sciences. The city is home to the renowned Bolshoi Theatre of Opera and Ballet, the Pushkin Fine Arts Museum, the Tretyakov Gallery, and the Exhibition of Economic Achievements.

Moselle German **Mosel**, river in Western Europe, some 515 km/320 mi long. It rises in the Vosges Mountains, France, in two headwaters uniting near St-Maurice. It flows north past Metz and is canalized from Thionville to its confluence with the Rhine at Koblenz in Germany. It gives its name to the *départements* of Moselle and Meurthe-et-Moselle in France. Vineyards along the Moselle in Germany produce popular white wines.

Moses (lived *c.* 13th century BC) Hebrew lawgiver and judge who led the Israelites out of Egypt to the promised land of Canaan. On Mount Sinai he claimed to have received from Jehovah the oral and written Law, including the **Ten Commandments** engraved on tablets of stone. The first five books of the Old Testament – in Judaism, the *Torah* – are ascribed to him.

Moslem alternative spelling of **Muslim**, a follower of *Islam.

Mosley, Oswald (Ernald) (1896–1980) British politician, founder of the British Union of Fascists (BUF) in 1932. He was a member of Parliament 1918–31. A Conservative MP for Harrow 1918–22, he joined the Labour party in 1924 and represented Shetwick 1926–31. He resigned in 1931 and founded the New Party. He then led the BUF until his internment 1940–43 during World War II. In 1946 Mosley was denounced when it became known that Italy had funded his prewar efforts to establish *fascism in the UK, but in 1948 he resumed fascist propaganda with his Union Movement, the revived BUF.

mosque (Arabic *mesjid*) in Islam, a place of worship. Chief features are: the dome; the minaret, a balconied turret from which the faithful are called to prayer; the mihrab, or prayer niche, in one of the interior walls, showing the direction of the holy city of *Mecca; and an open court surrounded by porticoes.

mosquito any of a group of flies in which the female has needlelike mouthparts and sucks blood before laying eggs. The males feed on plant juices. Some mosquitoes carry diseases such as *malaria. (Family Culicidae, order Diptera.)

Mosquito Coast Spanish **Costa de Mosquitos**, Caribbean coast of Honduras and Nicaragua, characterized by swamp, lagoons, and tropical rainforest. The territory is inhabited by Miskito Indians, Garifunas, and Zambos, many of whom speak English. Between 1823 and 1860 Britain maintained a protectorate over the Mosquito Coast which was ruled by a succession of 'Mosquito Kings'.

Moss, Stirling (1929–) English racing-car driver. Despite being one of the best-known names in British motor racing, Moss never won the world championship. He was runner-up on four occasions, losing to Juan Manuel Fangio in 1955, 1956, and 1957, and to fellow Briton Mike Hawthorn in 1958. He received a knighthood in 2000.

moss small nonflowering plant of the class Musci (10,000 species), forming with the *liverworts and the *hornworts the order Bryophyta. The stem of each plant bears rhizoids that anchor it; there are no true roots. Leaves spirally arranged on its lower portion have sexual organs at their tips. Most mosses flourish best in damp conditions where other vegetation is thin. There are 1,000 British species of moss and more than 1,200 North American species.

Mossi member of the majority ethnic group living in Burkina Faso. Their social structure, based on a monarchy, aristocracy, commoners, and slaves, was established in the 13th–14th centuries. There are about 4 million speakers of Mossi, a language belonging to the Gur branch of the Niger–Congo family.

motet sacred, polyphonic music for unaccompanied voices in a form that originated in 13th-century Europe.

moth any of a large number of mainly night-flying insects closely related to butterflies. Their wings are covered with microscopic scales. Most moths have a long sucking mouthpart (proboscis) for feeding on the nectar of flowers, but some have no functional mouthparts and rely instead upon stores of fat and other reserves built up during the caterpillar stage. At least 100,000 different species of moth are known. (Order Lepidoptera.)

motherboard *printed circuit board that contains the main components of a microcomputer. The power, memory capacity, and capability of the microcomputer may be enhanced by adding expansion boards to the motherboard, now more commonly called a mainboard.

mother-of-pearl *or* **nacre** the smooth lustrous lining in the shells of certain molluscs – for example pearl oysters, abalones, and mussels. When this layer is especially thick it is used commercially for jewellery and decorations. Mother-of-pearl consists of calcium carbonate. See *pearl.

motor anything that produces or imparts motion; a machine that provides mechanical power – for example, an electric motor. Machines that burn fuel (petrol, diesel) are usually called engines, but the internal-combustion engine that propels vehicles has long been called a motor, hence 'motoring' and 'motor car'. Actually the motor is a part of the car engine.

motorcycle *or* **motorbike** two-wheeled vehicle propelled by a *petrol engine. The first successful motorized bicycle was built in France in 1901, and British and US manufacturers first produced motorbikes in 1903.

motorcycle racing speed contests on motorcycles. It has many different forms: **road racing** over open roads; **circuit racing** over purpose-built tracks; **speedway** over oval-shaped dirt tracks; **motocross** over natural terrain, incorporating hill climbs; and **trials**, also over natural terrain, but with the addition of artificial hazards.

motor nerve in anatomy, any nerve that transmits impulses from the central nervous system to muscles or organs. Motor nerves cause voluntary and involuntary muscle contractions, and stimulate glands to secrete hormones.

motor neuron disease MND *or* **amyotrophic lateral sclerosis** chronic disease in which there is progressive degeneration of the nerve cells which instigate movement. It leads to weakness, wasting, and loss of muscle function and usually proves fatal within two to three years of onset. Motor neuron disease occurs in both familial and sporadic forms but its causes remain unclear. A gene believed to be implicated in familial cases was discovered in 1993.

motor racing competitive racing of motor vehicles. It has forms as diverse as hill-climbing, stock-car racing, rallying, sports-car racing, and *Formula 1 Grand Prix racing. The first organized race was from Paris to Rouen, France, in 1894.

Motown first black-owned US record company, founded in Detroit (Mo[tor] Town) in 1959 by Berry Gordy, Jr (1929–). Its distinctive, upbeat sound (for example, the Four Tops and the Supremes) was a major element in 1960s pop music.

mouflon wild sheep found in mountain areas of Cyprus, Corsica, and Sardinia. It has woolly underfur in winter, but this is covered by heavy guard hairs. The coat is brown with a white belly and rump. Males have strong, curving horns. (Species *Ovis ammon*, family Bovidae.)

mould furlike growth caused by any of a group of fungi (see *fungus) living on foodstuffs and other organic matter; a few are parasitic on plants, animals, or each other. Many moulds are of medical or industrial importance; for example, the antibiotic penicillin comes from a type of mould.

moulting periodic shedding of the hair or fur of mammals, feathers of birds, or skin of reptiles. In mammals and birds, moulting is usually seasonal and is triggered by changes of day length.

mountain natural upward projection of the Earth's surface, higher and steeper than a hill. Mountains are at least 330 m/1,000 ft above the surrounding topography. The existing rock below a high mountain may be subjected to high temperatures and pressures, causing metamorphism. Plutonic activity also can accompany mountain building.

mountain ash *or* **rowan** European flowering tree. It grows to 15 m/50 ft and has pinnate leaves (leaflets growing either side of the stem) and large clusters of whitish flowers, followed by scarlet berries in autumn. (*Sorbus aucuparia*, family Rosaceae.)

mountain biking recreational sport that enjoyed increasing popularity in the 1990s. Mountain bikes were developed from the rugged 'clunkers' ridden by a small group of off-road riders on the steep, rocky hillsides of Marin County, California, in the mid-70s. The fashion spread and the first mass-produced model appeared in the USA in 1981, and in the UK in 1984.

mountaineering art and practice of mountain climbing. For major peaks of the Himalayas it was formerly thought necessary to have elaborate support from the native Sherpas, fixed ropes, and oxygen at high altitudes (**siege-style** climbing). In the 1980s the **Alpine style** was introduced. This dispenses with these aids, and relies on human ability to adapt to high altitude.

mountain gorilla highly endangered ape found in bamboo and rainforest on the Rwanda, Democratic Republic of Congo (formerly Zaire), and Uganda borders in central Africa, with a total population of around 600 (1995). It is threatened by deforestation and illegal hunting for skins and the zoo trade. (Subspecies *Gorilla gorilla beringei*.)

mountain lion another name for the *puma.

Mountbatten, Louis Francis Albert Victor Nicholas (1900–1979) 1st Earl Mountbatten of Burma, English admiral and administrator, a great-grandson of Queen Victoria. In World War II he became chief of combined operations in 1942 and commander-in-chief in southeast Asia in 1943. As last viceroy and governor general of India 1947–48, he oversaw that country's transition to independence. He was killed by an Irish Republican Army (IRA) bomb aboard his yacht at Mullaghmore, County Sligo, in the Republic of Ireland. He was knighted in 1922, became a viscount in 1945, and an earl in 1947.

Mounties popular name for the Royal Canadian Mounted Police.

Mount Wilson site near Los Angeles, California, of the 2.5 m/100 in Hooker telescope, opened in 1917, with which US astronomer Edwin Hubble discovered the expansion of the universe. Two solar telescopes in towers 18.3 m/60 ft and 45.7 m/150 ft tall, and a 1.5 m/60 in reflector opened in 1908, also operate there.

mouse in computing, an input device used to control a pointer on a computer screen. It is a feature of *graphical user interface (GUI) systems. The mouse is about the size of a pack of playing cards, is connected to the computer by a wire or infrared link, and incorporates one or more buttons that can be pressed. Moving the mouse across a flat surface causes a corresponding movement of the pointer. In this way, the operator can manipulate objects on the screen and make menu selections.

mouse in zoology, one of a number of small rodents with small ears and a long, thin tail. The **house mouse** (*Mus musculus*) is distributed worldwide. It is 75 mm/3 in long, with a naked tail of the same length, and has a grey-brown body. (Family Muridae.)

mousebird any of a family of small crested birds found only in Africa. They have hairlike feathers, long tails, and move with a mouselike agility. The largest is the **blue-naped mousebird** (*Colius macrourus*), about 35 cm/14 in long. (Family Coliidae, order Coliiformes.)

mouth cavity forming the entrance to the digestive tract (gut or alimentary canal). In land vertebrates, air from the nostrils enters the mouth cavity to pass down the trachea. The mouth in mammals is enclosed by the jaws, cheeks, and palate. It contains teeth that may have a variety of functions depending on the way of life of the mammal. They may be used to hold things, to kill other organisms, or to cut food.

mouth organ any of a family of small portable free-reed wind instruments originating in Eastern and South Asia. The compact **harmonica**, or European mouth organ, developed by Charles Wheatstone in 1829, has tuned metal free reeds of variable length contained in a narrow rectangular box and is played by blowing and sucking air while moving the instrument from side to side through the lips.

movement in music, a self-contained composition of specific character, usually a constituent piece of a *suite, *symphony, or similar work, with its own tempo, distinct from that of the other movements.

Mozambique

National name: *República de Moçambique/ Republic of Mozambique*

INDIAN OCEAN

Tanzania

Malawi
Zambia

Zimbabwe

Madagascar

ATLANTIC OCEAN

Swaziland

MOZAMBIQUE
Maputo

South Africa

0 mi   500
0 km   1000

Area: 799,380 sq km/308,640 sq mi
Capital: Maputo (and chief port)
Major towns/cities: Beira, Nampula, Nacala, Chimoio
Major ports: Beira, Nacala, Quelimane
Physical features: mostly flat tropical lowland; mountains in west; rivers Zambezi and Limpopo
Head of state: Joaquim Alberto Chissano from 1986
Head of government: Luisa Diogo from 2004
Political system: emergent democracy
Political executive: limited presidency
Political parties: National Front for the Liberation of Mozambique (Frelimo), free market; Renamo, or Mozambique National Resistance (MNR), former rebel movement, right of centre
Currency: metical
GNI per capita (PPP): (US$) 1,180 (2002 est)
Exports: alumimium, shrimps, lobsters, and other crustaceans, cashew nuts, raw cotton, coal, sugar, sisal, copra. Principal market: Spain 15.3% (2001)
Population: 18,863,000 (2003 est)
Language: Portuguese (official), 16 African languages
Religion: animist 48%, Muslim 20%, Roman Catholic 16%, Protestant 16%
Life expectancy: 37 (men); 40 (women) (2000–05)

Chronology

1st–4th centuries AD: Bantu-speaking peoples settled in Mozambique.

8th–15th century: Arab gold traders established independent city-states on the coast.

1498: Portuguese navigator Vasco da Gama was the first European visitor; at this time the most important local power was the Maravi kingdom of the Mwene Matapa peoples, who controlled much of the Zambezi basin.

1626: The Mwene Matapa formally recognized Portuguese sovereignty. Portuguese soldiers set up private agricultural estates and used slave labour to exploit gold and ivory resources.

late 17th century: Portuguese temporarily pushed south of Zambezi by the ascendant Rozwi kingdom.

1752: First Portuguese colonial governor appointed; slave trade outlawed.

late 19th century: Concessions given by Portugal to private companies to develop and administer parts of Mozambique.

1930: Colonial Act established more centralized Portuguese rule, ending concessions to monopolistic companies and forging closer integration with Lisbon.

1951: Became an overseas province of Portugal and, economically, a cheap labour reserve for South Africa's mines.

1962: Frelimo (National Front for the Liberation of Mozambique) established in exile in Tanzania by Marxist guerrillas, including Samora Machel, to fight for independence.

1964: Fighting broke out between Frelimo forces and Portuguese troops, starting a ten-year liberation war; Portugal despatched 70,000 troops to Mozambique.

1969: Eduardo Mondlane, leader of Frelimo, was assassinated.

1975: Following revolution in Portugal, independence was achieved as a socialist republic, with Machel as president, Joaquim Chissano as prime minister, and Frelimo as the sole legal party; Portuguese settlers left the country. Lourenço Marques renamed Maputo. Key enterprises were nationalized.

1977: Renamo resistance group formed, with covert backing of South Africa.

1979: Machel encouraged Patriotic Front guerrillas in Rhodesia to accept Lancaster House Agreement, creating Zimbabwe.

1983: Good relations were restored with Western powers.

1984: The Nkomati Accord of nonaggression was signed with South Africa.

1986: Machel was killed in air crash near the South African border and was succeeded by Chissano.

1988: Tanzanian troops withdrawn from Mozambique.

1989: Renamo continued attacks on government facilities and civilians.

1990: One-party rule officially ended, and Frelimo abandoned Marxism–Leninism and embraced market economy.

1992: A peace accord was signed with Renamo.

1993: There were price riots in Maputo as a result of the implementation of IMF-promoted reforms to restructure the economy, which was devastated by war and drought.

1994: The demobilization of contending armies was completed. Chissano and Frelimo were re-elected in the first multiparty elections; Renamo (now a political party) agreed to cooperate with the government. Pascoal Mocumbi was appointed prime minister by President Chissano.

1995: Mozambique was admitted to the Commonwealth.

2000: Severe flooding was estimated to involve the loss of 10,000 lives and 1 million homes. The Paris Club of rich countries agreed to suspend Mozambique's repayment of foreign debts.

2001: Further flooding made over 80,000 people homeless.

2002: Severe drought hit central and southern areas of the country.

2003: Brazil pledged to build a factory for production of anti-retroviral drugs for HIV-Aids sufferers in Mozambique. **2004:** Armando Guebuza of Frelimo won the presidential elections.

Mozart, (Johann Chrysostom) Wolfgang Amadeus (1756–1791) Austrian composer and performer who was a child prodigy and an adult virtuoso. He was trained by his father, **Leopold Mozart** (1719–1787). From an early age he composed prolifically, and his works include 27 piano concertos, 23 string quartets, 35 violin sonatas, and 41 symphonies including the E^b K543, G minor K550, and C major K551 ('Jupiter') symphonies, all three being composed in 1788. His operas include *Idomeneo* (1780), *Entführung aus dem Serail/ The Abduction from the Seraglio* (1782), *Le nozze di Figaro/ The Marriage of Figaro* (1786), *Don Giovanni* (1787), *Così fan tutte/Thus Do All Women* (1790), and *Die Zauberflöte/The Magic Flute* (1791). Together with the work of Joseph Haydn, Mozart's music marks the height of the classical age in its purity of melody and form.

MP abbreviation for *member of Parliament.

Mpumalanga formerly **Eastern Transvaal**, province of the Republic of South Africa from 1994, formerly part of Transvaal province; area 81,816 sq km/31,589 sq mi; population (2000 est) 3,004,900. The capital is Nelspruit. Features of the province include Limpopo River, Vaal River, Blyde River Canyon Nature Reserve, and Mpumalanga Drakensberg Mountains. Mineral resources include asbestos, copper, iron ore, manganese, platinum, chromium, and coal and attractions such as the Kruger National Park and other game reserves have helped the development of a major tourist industry. However, the economy is mainly based on agriculture, with the focus on beef cattle and wool production from merino sheep in the drier western plateaux and on the cultivation of maize, wheat, groundnuts, cotton, and potatoes in the wetter east. Fruit production, including oranges and mangoes, is important in the subtropical Lowveld area bordering Mozambique, and forestry is significant in the Drakensberg mountains. Languages spoken in the province are Siswati, Zulu, and Afrikaans.

Mubarak, (Muhammad) Hosni (Said) (1928–) Egyptian soldier and politician, president from 1981. Vice-president to Anwar Sadat from 1975, Mubarak succeeded him on Sadat's assassination. He continued to pursue Sadat's moderate policies, including support for a peace treaty with Israel, and introduced economic reforms, including a privatization programme, and increased the freedom of the press and of political association, while trying to repress the growing Islamic fundamentalist movement led by the Muslim Brotherhood and Islamic Jihad. He was re-elected in 1987, 1993, and 1999. He survived assassination attempts in 1995 and 1999.

Mucha, Alphonse Maria (1860–1939) Czech painter and designer, one of the leading figures of *art nouveau. His posters and decorative panels brought him international fame, presenting idealized images of young women with long, flowing hair, within a patterned flowered border. His early theatre posters were done for the actor Sarah Bernhardt, notably the lithograph *Gismonda* (1894).

mucous membrane thin skin lining all animal body cavities and canals that come into contact with the air (for example, eyelids, breathing and digestive passages,

genital tract). It contains goblet cells that secrete mucus, a moistening, lubricating, and protective fluid. In the air passages mucus captures dust and bacteria. In the gut it helps food slip along, and protects the epithelial cells from being damaged by digestive enzymes. Mucous membranes line the air passages from the *mouth to the *lungs and to the *gut. The layer of cells next to the space in the tubes is an epithelium. In the air passages many of these cells have hair-like projections called cilia and the epithelium is then called a ciliated epithelium.

mucus lubricating and protective fluid, secreted by mucous membranes in many different parts of the body. In the gut, mucus smooths the passage of food and keeps potentially damaging digestive enzymes away from the gut lining. In the lungs, it traps airborne particles so that they can be expelled.

mudnester any of an Australian group of birds that make their nests from mud, including the **apostle bird** (*Struthidea cinerea*) (so called from its appearance in little flocks of about 12), the **white-winged chough** (*Corcorax melanorhamphos*), and the **magpie lark** (*Grallina cyanoleuca*).

mudpuppy any of five species of brownish *salamanders, living in fresh water in North America. They all breathe in water using external gills. The species *N. maculatus* is about 20 cm/8 in long. Mudpuppies eat fish, snails, and other invertebrates. (Genus *Necturus*, family Proteidae.)

mudskipper any of a group of fishes belonging to the goby family, found in brackish water and shores in the tropics, except for the Americas. It can walk or climb over mudflats, using its strong pectoral (chest) fins as legs, and has eyes set close together on top of the head. It grows up to 30 cm/12 in long. (Genus *Periophthalmus*, family Gobiidae.)

muezzin (Arabic) a person whose job is to perform the call to prayer five times a day from the minaret of a Muslim mosque.

mufti Muslim legal expert who guides the courts in their interpretation. In Turkey the **grand mufti** had supreme spiritual authority until the establishment of the republic in 1924.

Mugabe, Robert (Gabriel) (1924–) Zimbabwean politician, prime minister from 1980 and executive president from 1987. He was detained and imprisoned in Rhodesia (as Zimbabwe was then known) for nationalist activities 1964–74, then carried on guerrilla warfare from Mozambique as leader of ZANU (Zimbabwe African National Union). He became the first prime minister of an independent Zimbabwe. Mugabe came under increasing criticism from the 1990s as Zimbabwe suffered economic decline and growing political violence. The deterioration in political and human rights in Zimbabwe led to the European Union (EU) and USA imposing targeted sanctions on the Zimbabwean government in 2002, and in 2003 Zimbabwe withdrew from the Commonwealth in protest against its earlier and continuing suspension.

Muhammad (*or* Mohammed *or* Mahomet) (c. 570–632) (Arabic 'praised') Founder of Islam, born in *Mecca on the Arabian peninsula. In about 616 he began to preach the worship of one God, who allegedly revealed to him the words of the *Koran (it was later written down by his followers) through the angel Jibra'el (Gabriel). Muhammad fled from persecution to the town now known as *Medina in 622: the flight, **Hijrah** or **Hegira**, marks the beginning of the Islamic era.

Mujahedin (Arabic *mujahid* 'fighters', from *jihad* 'holy war') Islamic fundamentalist guerrillas of contemporary Afghanistan and Iran.

mulberry any of a group of trees consisting of a dozen species, including the black mulberry (*M. nigra*). It is native to western Asia and has heart-shaped, toothed leaves and spikes of whitish flowers. It is widely cultivated for its compound fruits, which resemble raspberries. The leaves of the Asiatic white mulberry (*M. alba*) are those used in feeding silkworms. (Genus *Morus*, family Moraceae.)

mule hybrid animal, usually the offspring of a male ass and a female horse.

Mull second-largest island of the Inner *Hebrides, Argyll and Bute, Scotland; area 950 sq km/367 sq mi; population (1991) 2,700. It is mountainous, and is separated from the mainland by the **Sound of Mull** and the Firth of Lorne; it lies 11 km/7 mi west of Oban. The main town is Tobermory, from which there are ferry connections to Oban; Craignure is also connected by ferry to Oban.

mullein any of a group of herbaceous plants belonging to the figwort family. The great mullein (*V. thapsus*) has lance-shaped leaves 30 cm/12 in or more in length, covered in woolly down, and a large spike of yellow flowers. It is found in Europe and Asia and is naturalized in North America. (Genus *Verbascum*, family Scrophulariaceae.)

mullet either of two species of fish. The **red mullet** (*Mullus surmuletus*) is found in the Mediterranean and warm Atlantic as far north as the English Channel. It is about 40 cm/16 in long, red with yellow stripes, and has long barbels (sensitive bristles) round the mouth. (Family Mullidae.) The **grey mullet** (*Crenimugil labrosus*) lives in ponds and estuaries. It is greyish above, with horizontal dark stripes, and grows to 60 cm/24 in. (Family Mugilidae.)

Mulroney, Brian (1939–) Canadian politician, Progressive Conservative Party leader 1983–93, prime minister 1984–93. He achieved a landslide victory in the 1984 election, and won the 1988 election on a platform of free trade with the USA, but with a reduced majority. Opposition within Canada to the 1987 Meech Lake agreement, a prerequisite to signing the 1982 Constitution, continued to plague Mulroney in his second term. A revised reform package in October 1992 failed to gain voters' approval, and in February 1993 he was forced to resign the leadership of the Conservative Party, though he remained prime minister until Kim Campbell was appointed his successor in June.

multimedia computerized method of presenting information by combining audio and video components using text, sound, and graphics (still, animated, and video sequences). For example, a multimedia database of musical instruments may allow a user not only to search and retrieve text about a particular instrument but also to see pictures of it and hear it play a piece of music. Multimedia applications emphasize interactivity between the computer and the user.

multinational corporation company or enterprise operating in several countries, usually defined as one that has 25% or more of its output capacity located outside its country of origin.

multiple birth in humans, the production of more than two babies from one pregnancy. Multiple births can be caused by more than two eggs being produced and fertilized (often as the result of hormone therapy to assist pregnancy), or by a single fertilized egg dividing more than once before implantation. See also *twin.

multiple sclerosis MS *or* **disseminated sclerosis** incurable chronic disease of the central nervous system, occurring in young or middle adulthood. Most prevalent in temperate zones, it affects more women than men. It is characterized by degeneration of the myelin sheath that surrounds nerves in the brain and spinal cord.

multiplier in economics, the theoretical concept, formulated by John Maynard Keynes, of the effect on national income or employment by an adjustment in overall demand. For example, investment by a company in a new plant will stimulate new income and expenditure, which will in turn generate new investment, and so on, so that the actual increase in national income may be several times greater than the original investment.

multitasking *or* **multiprogramming** in computing, a system in which one processor appears to run several different programs (or different parts of the same program) at the same time. All the programs are held in memory together and each is allowed to run for a certain period.

Mumbai formerly **Bombay** (until 1995), Indian city, industrial port, and commercial centre; population (2001 est) 11,914,400; metropolitan area (2001 est) 16,368,100. Previously known as Bombay, the city was once the capital of Bombay Presidency and Bombay State and in 1960 became the capital of *Maharashtra, a newly created state. By a decision of the Maharashtra government implemented in 1995, the city was renamed Mumbai. Long-established industries include textiles (especially cotton), engineering, pharmaceuticals, and diamonds. The city is the centre of the Hindi film industry, and the newer industries also include chemicals, motor vehicles, electronics, and papermaking.

mummers' play *or* **St George play** British folk drama enacted in dumb show by a masked cast, performed on Christmas Day to celebrate the death of the old year and its rebirth as the new year. The plot usually consists of a duel between St George and an infidel knight, in which one of them is killed but later revived by a doctor. Mummers' plays are still performed in some parts of Britain, often by Morris dance teams.

mummy any dead body, human or animal, that has been naturally or artificially preserved. Natural mummification can occur through freezing (for example, mammoths in glacial ice from 25,000 years ago), drying, or preservation in bogs or oil seeps. Artificial mummification may be achieved by embalming (for example, the mummies of ancient Egypt) or by freeze-drying.

mumps *or* **infectious parotitis** virus infection marked by fever, pain, and swelling of one or both parotid salivary glands (situated in front of the ears). It is usually short-lived in children, although meningitis is a possible complication. In adults the symptoms are more serious and it may cause sterility in men.

Munch, Edvard (1863–1944) Norwegian painter and graphic artist, a major influence on *expressionism. His highly charged paintings, characterized by strong colours and distorted forms, often focus on intense emotional states, as in one of his best-known works *The Scream* (1893). His works brought a new urgency and power to the two themes that dominated late 19th-century decadence, death and sexuality.

Münchhausen's syndrome emotional disorder in which a patient feigns or invents symptoms to secure medical treatment. It is the chronic form of factitious disorder, which is more common, and probably underdiagnosed. In some cases the patient will secretly ingest substances to produce real symptoms. It was named after the exaggerated tales of Baron Münchhausen. Some patients invent symptoms for their children, a phenomenon known as Münchhausen's by proxy.

Munda any one of several groups living in northeastern and central India, numbering above 5 million (1983). Their most widely spoken languages are Santali and Mundari, languages of the Munda group, an isolated branch of the Austro-Asiatic family. The Mundas were formerly nomadic hunter-gatherers, but now practise shifting cultivation. They are Hindus but retain animist beliefs.

Munich German **München**, capital of Bavaria, Germany, on the River Isar, about 520 m/1,706 ft above sea level, some 45 km/28 mi from the edge of the Alps; population (1995) 1,240,600. The main industries are brewing, printing, precision instruments, machinery, electrical goods, computers, telecommunications, fashion, and food processing.

Munich Agreement pact signed on 29 September 1938 by the leaders of the UK (Neville *Chamberlain), France (Edouard *Daladier), Germany (Adolf *Hitler), and Italy (Benito *Mussolini), under which Czechoslovakia was compelled to surrender its Sudeten-German districts (the **Sudeten**) to Germany. Chamberlain claimed it would guarantee 'peace in our time', but it did not prevent Hitler from seizing the rest of Czechoslovakia in March 1939.

Munster historic southern province of the Republic of Ireland, comprising the counties of Clare, Cork, Kerry, Limerick, North and South Tipperary, and Waterford; area 24,140 sq km/9,320 sq mi; population (2002 est) 1,100,600.

muntjac any of about nine species of small deer found in Southeast Asia. They live mostly in dense vegetation and do not form herds. The males have short spiked antlers and two sharp canine teeth forming tusks. They are sometimes called 'barking deer' because of their voices. (Genus *Muntiacus*.)

muon *elementary particle similar to the electron except for its mass which is 207 times greater than that of the electron. It has a half-life of 2 millionths of a second, decaying into electrons and *neutrinos. The muon was originally thought to be a *meson but is now classified as a *lepton. See also *tau.

mural painting (Latin *murus* 'wall') decoration of the wall designed for a specific site and incorporated into the architecture; unlike an easel painting, a mural's composition is influenced by its surroundings. Traditionally painted directly onto the wall surface, murals may also be created with mosaic, collage, and photographs, or painted onto a canvas and later fixed into position, a method more frequently used in modern times. *Fresco (painting onto wet plaster) is the principal technique of traditional murals, although

other media include tempera, encaustic, and oil. Murals have been popular for centuries, but as they are distinct from decorative, domestic easel paintings, they are more usually found in palaces, churches, or the interiors of important public buildings; the earliest appear in ancient Egyptian tombs of the 3rd century BC.

Murasaki, Shikibu (c. 978–c. 1015) Japanese writer. She was a lady at the court. Her masterpiece of fiction, *The Tale of Genji* (c. 1010), is one of the classic works of Japanese literature, and may be the world's first novel.

Murcia autonomous community and province of southeast Spain, with a coastline on the Mediterranean Sea; area 11,317 sq km/4,370 sq mi; population (2001 est) 1,190,400. The River Segura and its tributaries (the Sangonera and the Quipar) flow through the region, which is very mountainous in the south and east. It is one of the hottest and driest regions of Europe, resembling North Africa in its vegetation and climate. The irrigated area, the huerta of Murcia, is one of the most intensively farmed areas in Spain and is especially important for citrus fruits. Products include esparto grass (for weaving into simple items such as sandals), iron, olives, and fruit. There are large deposits of salt and minerals, especially lead and zinc. The main port is Cartagena and the capital is Murcia. It became an independent region in 1982.

murder unlawful killing of one person by another. In the USA, first-degree murder requires proof of premeditation; second-degree murder falls between first-degree murder and *manslaughter.

Murdoch, (Jean) Iris (1919–1999) English novelist, born in Dublin. Her novels combine philosophical speculation with often outrageous situations and tangled human relationships. They include *The Sandcastle* (1957), *The Bell* (1958), *The Sea, The Sea* (1978; Booker Prize), *Nuns and Soldiers* (1980), *The Message to the Planet* (1989), *The Green Knight* (1993), and *Jackson's Dilemma* (1995).

Murillo, Bartolomé Esteban (c. 1618–1682) Spanish painter. Active mainly in Seville, he painted sentimental pictures of the Immaculate Conception, and also specialized in studies of street urchins. His *Self-Portrait* (c. 1672; National Gallery, London) is generally considered to be one of his finest works.

Murmansk seaport and capital of the Murmansk oblast (region) located 1000 km/624 mi north of St Petersburg on the Kola Peninsula in the northwest of the Russian Federation; population (1990) 472,000. Situated on an estuary 50 km/31 mi inland from the Barents Sea, it is the largest city in the Arctic, Russia's principal fishing port, and a base for icebreakers that keep the *Northeast Passage open. Shipbuilding is a major industry, and polar research institutes are located here.

Murray principal river of Australia, which rises in the Snowy Mountains of the Australian Alps near Mount Kosciusko, in New South Wales; length 2,540 km/1,578 mi. The Murray flows west and northwest, for most of its length forming the boundary between New South Wales and Victoria, then turns south to reach the Southern Ocean at Encounter Bay, southeast of Adelaide in South Australia. The River Murray is an important source of hydroelectric power and irrigation. With its main tributary, the *Darling, it is 3,750 km/2,330 mi long. Together they produce 40% of the country's agricultural wealth.

Murray, James Stuart (1531–1570) 1st Earl of Murray; or **Moray**, Regent of Scotland from 1567, an illegitimate son of James V by Lady Margaret Erskine, daughter of the 4th Earl of Mar. He became chief adviser to his half-sister *Mary Queen of Scots on her return to Scotland in 1561, but lost her favour when he opposed her marriage in 1565 to Henry, Lord Darnley. He was one of the leaders of the Scottish Reformation, and after the deposition of Mary he became regent. He was assassinated by one of her supporters.

Murray cod Australian freshwater fish that grows to about 2 m/6 ft. It is is named after the river in which it is found. (Species *Maccullochella macquariensis*.)

Murrumbidgee river in New South Wales, Australia; length 1,609 km/1,000 mi. The Murrumbidgee rises in the Australian Alps, then flows north and west to meet the River *Murray on the Victoria border. It is a major tributary of the Murray. The Murrumbidgee is navigable for 807 km/501 mi to Wagga Wagga during the winter months. The Murrumbidgee Irrigation Area is a large, fertile region irrigated by the waters of the Murrumbidgee.

Muscat or **Masqat** capital and port of Oman, lying on the Gulf of Oman; population (2001 est) 57,600. The Muscat region has a population of 635,300 (1999 est). With the advantage of a deepwater harbour at Matrah, in the western part of the city, Muscat handles the bulk of the country's foreign trade, especially the export of crude oil and the import of food. Port Qabus, a modern deepwater port built in the 1970s and named after the sultan, is an extension of Matrah and Mina, with a terminal for loading supertankers, and Riyam, which handles incoming refined petroleum products, are both nearby. Natural gas and chemical industries are also important. Muscat is served by an international airport, As-Sib, and the city is linked to Salalah, a former capital, by a 1,000 km/625 mi trunk road completed in 1984.

muscle contractile animal tissue that produces locomotion and power and maintains the movement of body substances. Muscle contains very specialized animal cells – long cells – that can contract to between one-half and one-third of their relaxed length.

muscular dystrophy any of a group of inherited chronic muscle disorders marked by weakening and wasting of muscle. Muscle fibres degenerate, to be replaced by fatty tissue, although the nerve supply remains unimpaired. Death occurs in early adult life.

Muse in Greek mythology, one of the nine inspiring deities of the creative arts: Clio, Euterpe, Thalia, Melpomene, Terpsichore, Erato, Polyhymnia, Urania, and Calliope; daughters of Zeus and Mnemosyne, goddess of memory. Reputedly born in Pieria, at the foot of Mount Olympus, they were originally only three in number, but became nine from the time of Hesiod.

Museveni, Yoweri Kaguta (1945–) Ugandan soldier and politician, president from 1986. He led the opposition to Idi Amin's brutal and autocratic regime 1971–79, and became minister of defence 1979–80. As president, Museveni sought national reconciliation and developed a 'no-party' state, in which political party activity and political gatherings were banned. The economy expanded through an economic liberalization programme, with International Monetary Fund (IMF)

backing and involving privatizing state enterprises. There have also been successes in improving education, reducing poverty, and slowing rates of HIV infection through a successful campaign against AIDS. Museveni was popularly re-elected in 2001 for a second and final presidential term (to 2006).

Musgrave Ranges Australian mountain ranges on the border between South Australia and the Northern Territory; the highest peak is Mount Woodruffe at 1,525 m/5,000 ft. The area is an Aboriginal reserve.

mushroom fruiting body of certain fungi (see *fungus), consisting of an upright stem and a spore-producing cap with radiating gills on the undersurface. There are many edible species belonging to the genus *Agaricus*, including the field mushroom (*A. campestris*). See also *toadstool.

music art of combining sounds into a structured form, usually according to conventional patterns and for an aesthetic (artistic) purpose. Music is generally divided into different genres or styles such as classical music, *jazz, *pop music, *country, and so on.

musical 20th-century form of dramatic musical performance, combining elements of song, dance, and the spoken word, often characterized by lavish staging and large casts. It developed from the operettas and musical comedies of the 19th century.

music hall British light theatrical entertainment, in which singers, dancers, comedians, and acrobats perform in 'turns'. The music hall's heyday was at the beginning of the 20th century, with such artistes as Marie Lloyd, Harry Lauder, and George Formby. The US equivalent is vaudeville.

musique concrète (French 'concrete music') music created by reworking natural sounds recorded on disk or tape. It was developed in 1948 by Pierre Schaeffer and Pierre Henry in the drama studios of Paris Radio. The term was used to differentiate the process from *electronic music, which used synthesized tones and sounds. From the mid-1950s the two techniques were usually combined, and the term is now purely historic.

musk in botany, perennial plant whose small oblong leaves give off the musky scent from which it takes its name; it is also called **monkey flower**. The name 'musk' is also given to several other plants with a similar scent, including the musk mallow (*Malva moschata*) and the musk rose (*Rosa moschata*). (*Mimulus moschatus*, family Scrophulariaceae.)

musk deer any of three species of small deer native to the mountains of central and northeastern Asia. A solitary animal, the musk deer is about 80–100 cm/30–40 in, sure-footed, and has large ears and no antlers. Males have long tusklike upper canine teeth. They are hunted and farmed for their musk (a waxy substance secreted by the male from a gland in the stomach area), which is used as medicine or perfume. (Genus *Moschus*.)

musk ox ruminant (cud-chewing) mammal native to the Arctic regions of North America. It has characteristics of both sheep and oxen, is about the size of a small domestic cow, and has long brown hair. At certain seasons it has a musky smell. (Species *Ovibos moschatus*, family Bovidae.)

muskrat North American rodent, about 30 cm/12 in long, that lives beside streams, rivers, and lakes. It has webbed hind feet, a side-to-side flattened tail, and shiny, light-brown fur. It builds up a store of food, plastering it over with mud, for winter consumption. It is hunted for its fur. (Species *Ondatra zibethicus*, family Cricetidae.)

Muslim *or* **Moslem** a follower of the religion of *Islam.

Muslim League Indian political organization. The All India Muslim League was founded in 1906 under the leadership of the Aga Khan. In 1940 the league, led by Muhammad Ali *Jinnah, demanded an independent Muslim state. The *Congress Party and the Muslim League won most seats in the 1945 elections for an Indian central legislative assembly. In 1946 the Indian constituent assembly was boycotted by the Muslim League. It was partly the activities of the League that led to the establishment of Pakistan.

mussel any of a group of shellfish, some of which are edible, such as the **common mussel** (*Mytilus edulis*) which has a blue-black hinged shell and is found in clusters attached to rocks around the North Atlantic and American coasts. Mussels are bivalve *molluscs. (Class Bivalvia, phylum Mollusca.)

Mussolini, Benito Amilcare Andrea (1883–1945) Italian dictator 1925–43. As founder of the Fascist Movement (see *fascism) in 1919 and prime minister from 1922, he became known as *Il Duce* ('the leader'). He invaded Ethiopia 1935–36, intervened in the Spanish Civil War 1936–39 in support of Franco, and conquered Albania in 1939. In June 1940 Italy entered World War II supporting Hitler. Forced by military and domestic setbacks to resign in 1943, Mussolini established a breakaway government in northern Italy 1944–45, but was killed trying to flee the country.

Mussorgsky, Modest Petrovich (1839–1881) Russian composer. He was a member of the group of five composers ('The Five'). His opera masterpiece *Boris Godunov* (1869, revised 1871–72), touched a political nerve and employed realistic transcriptions of speech patterns. Many of his works, including *Pictures at an Exhibition* (1874) for piano, were 'revised' and orchestrated by others, including Rimsky-Korsakov, Ravel, and Shostakovich, and some have only recently been restored to their original harsh beauty.

Mustafa Kemal Pasha Turkish leader who assumed the name *Atatürk.

mustard any of several annual plants belonging to the cress family, with seed-bearing pods and sweet-smelling yellow flowers. Brown and white mustard are cultivated as an accompaniment to food in Europe and North America. The seeds of brown mustard (*B. juncea*) and white mustard (*Sinapis alba*) are used in the preparation of table mustard. (Genus mainly *Brassica*, family Cruciferae.)

mutagen any substance that increases the rate of gene *mutation. A mutagen may also act as a *carcinogen.

mutation in biology, a change in the *genes produced by a change in the *DNA that makes up the hereditary material of all living organisms. It can be a change in a single gene or a change that affects sections of *chromosomes. In the process of DNA replication, which takes place before any cell divides, the two halves of DNA separate and new halves are made. Because of specific base pairing, the inherited information is copied exactly. Despite this, rarely, a mistake occurs and the sequence of bases is altered. This changes the sequence of amino acids in a protein. This is mutation,

the raw material of evolution. The consequences of mutation are varied. Due to the redundancy built into genetic code many mutations have no effect upon DNA functions. Genes describe how to make *proteins. As a result of mutation a protein may not be produced, may be produced but act abnormally, or remain fully functional. Only a few mutations improve the organism's performance and are therefore favoured by *natural selection. Mutation rates are increased by certain chemicals and by ionizing radiation.

mute in music, any device used to dampen the vibration of an instrument and so affect the tone. Orchestral strings apply a form of clamp to the bridge – the change is used to dramatic effect by Bartók in the opening bars of *Music for Strings, Percussion, and Celesta* (1936). Brass instruments use the hand or a plug of metal or cardboard inserted in the bell.

mutiny organized act of disobedience or defiance by two or more members of the armed services. In naval and military law, mutiny has always been regarded as one of the most serious of crimes, punishable in wartime by death.

mutton bird any of various shearwaters and petrels that breed in burrows on Australasian islands. Each parent feeds the chick for 2–3 days and then leaves for up to three weeks in search of food. These foraging trips can cover a distance of 15,000 km/9,300 mi and mean the chick may be left unattended for over a week. By the time the chicks have reached independence they weigh around 900 g/32 lb, twice as heavy as their parents. The young are killed for food and oil.

Muybridge, Eadweard (1830–1904) adopted name of Edward James Muggeridge, English-born US photographer. He made a series of animal locomotion photographs in the USA in the 1870s and proved that, when a horse trots, there are times when all its feet are off the ground. He also explored motion in birds and humans.

Myanmar

formerly **Burma** (until 1989)

National name: *Pyedawngsu Myanma Naingngan/ Union of Myanmar*

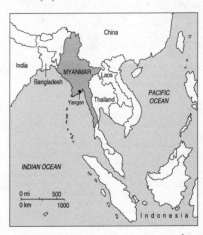

Myanmar

Area: 676,577 sq km/261,226 sq mi
Capital: Yangon (formerly Rangoon) (and chief port)
Major towns/cities: Mandalay, Mawlamyine, Bago, Pathein, Taunggyi, Sittwe, Manywa
Physical features: over half is rainforest; rivers Irrawaddy and Chindwin in central lowlands ringed by mountains in north, west, and east
Head of state: Than Shwe from 1992
Head of government: Soe Win from 2004
Political system: military
Political executive: military
Political parties: National Unity Party (NUP), military-socialist ruling party; National League for Democracy (NLD), pluralist opposition grouping
Currency: kyat
GNI per capita (PPP): (US$) 1,570 (2002 est)
Exports: gas, teak, rice, pulses and beans, rubber, hardwood, prawns, fish and fish products, base metals, gems, cement. Principal market: Thailand 31.2% (2001)
Population: 49,485,000 (2003 est)
Language: Burmese (official), English, tribal dialects
Religion: Hinayana Buddhist 89%, Christian 5%, Muslim 4%, animist 1.5%
Life expectancy: 55 (men); 60 (women) (2000–05)
Chronology
3rd century BC: Sittoung valley settled by Mons; Buddhism introduced by missionaries from India.
3rd century AD: Arrival of Burmans from Tibet.
1057: First Burmese Empire established by King Anawrahta, who conquered Thaton, established capital inland at Pagan, and adopted Theravada Buddhism.
1287: Pagan sacked by Mongols.
1531: Founding of Toungoo dynasty, which survived until mid-18th century.
1755: Nation reunited by Alaungpaya, with port of Rangoon as capital.
1824–26: First Anglo-Burmese war resulted in Arakan coastal strip, between Chittagong and Cape Negrais, being ceded to British India.
1852: Following defeat in second Anglo-Burmese war, Lower Burma, including Rangoon, was annexed by British.
1886: Upper Burma ceded to British after defeat of Thibaw in third Anglo-Burmese war; British united Burma, which was administered as a province of British India.
1886–96: Guerrilla warfare waged against British in northern Burma.
early 20th century: Burma developed as a major rice, teak and, later, oil exporter, drawing in immigrant labourers and traders from India and China.
1937: Became British crown colony in Commonwealth, with a degree of internal self-government.
1942: Invaded and occupied by Japan, who installed anti-British nationalist puppet government headed by Ba Maw.
1945: Liberated from Japanese control by British, assisted by nationalists Aung San and U Nu, formerly ministers in puppet government, who had formed the socialist Anti Fascist People's Freedom League (AFPFL).
1947: Assassination of Aung San and six members of interim government by political opponents.
1948: Independence achieved from Britain as Burma, with U Nu as prime minister. Left Commonwealth. Quasi-federal state established.

1958–60: Administered by emergency government, formed by army chief of staff Gen Ne Win.
1962: Gen Ne Win reassumed power in left-wing army coup; he proceeded to abolish federal system and follow the 'Burmese way to socialism', involving sweeping nationalization and international isolation, which crippled the economy.
1973–74: Adopted presidential-style 'civilian' constitution.
1975: The opposition National Democratic Front was formed by regionally-based minority groups, who mounted guerrilla insurgencies.
1987: There were student demonstrations in Rangoon as food shortages worsened.
1988: The government resigned after violent student demonstrations and workers' riots. Gen Saw Maung seized power in a military coup; over 2,000 were killed.
1989: Martial law was declared; thousands were arrested including advocates of democracy and human rights. The country was renamed Myanmar, and its capital Yangon.
1990: The landslide general election victory for opposition National League for Democracy (NLD) was ignored by the military junta; NLD leaders U Nu and Suu Kyi, the daughter of Aung San, were placed under house arrest.
1991: Martial law and human-rights abuses continued. Suu Kyi, still imprisoned, was awarded the Nobel Peace Prize. There was a pogrom against the Muslim community in the Arakan province in southwest Myanmar. Western countries imposed sanctions.
1992: Saw Maung was replaced as head of state by Than Shwe. Several political prisoners were liberated. Martial law was lifted, but restrictions on political freedom remained.
1993: A ceasefire was agreed with Kachin rebels in the northeast.
1995: Suu Kyi was released from house arrest, but her appointment as NLD leader was declared illegal. NLD boycotted the constitutional convention.
1996: Suu Kyi held the first party congress since her release; 200 supporters were detained by the government. There were major demonstrations in support of Suu Kyi.
1997: Admission to Association of South East Asian Nations (ASEAN) granted, despite US sanctions for human-rights abuses.
1998: Japan resumed a flow of aid, which had been stopped in 1988. The military junta ignored pro-democracy roadside protests by Aung San Suu Kyi and broke up student demonstrations. 300 members of the opposition NLD were released from detention.
2000: Aung San Suu Kyi was forced to give up a pro-democracy roadside protest after nine days and placed under house arrest for two weeks.
2001: The government began talks with Suu Kyi and released 84 members of the NLD from prison.
2002: The government released Aung San Suu Kyi from almost 20 months of house arrest. Her release was widely seen as a move to get US and European Union (EU) sanctions against the regime eased.
2003: Aung San Suu Kyi was again put under house arrest. Khin Nyunt became prime minister. Senior NLD leaders were released from house arrest following a visit by a UN human rights envoy.
2004: The government and the Karen National Union, the most significant anti-government ethnic group,

agreed to a ceasefire. A constitutional convention was boycotted by the NLD because Aung San Suu Kyi was still under house arrest. Khin Nyunt was replaced as prime minister and placed under house arrest. The country was hit by the Indian Ocean tsunami, leaving more than 50 people dead and several thousand people homeless.

2005: The constitutional convention, adjourned in 2004, was resumed, with the participation of the main opposition and ethnic groups.

Mycenae ancient Greek city in the eastern Peloponnese, which gave its name to the Mycenaean (Bronze Age) civilization. Its peak was 1400–1200 BC, when the Cyclopean walls (using close-fitting stones) were erected. The city ceased to be inhabited after about 1120 BC.

Mycenaean civilization Bronze Age civilization that flourished in Crete, Cyprus, Greece, the Aegean Islands, and western Anatolia about 3000–1000 BC. During this period, magnificent architecture and sophisticated artefacts were produced.

mycorrhiza mutually beneficial (mutualistic) association occurring between plant roots and a soil fungus. Mycorrhizal roots take up nutrients more efficiently than non-mycorrhizal roots, and the fungus benefits by obtaining carbohydrates from the plant or tree.

myelin sheath insulating layer that surrounds nerve cells in vertebrate animals. It serves to speed up the passage of nerve impulses.

My Lai massacre killing of 109 civilians in My Lai, a village in South Vietnam, by US troops in March 1968. An investigation in 1969 produced enough evidence to charge 30 soldiers with war crimes, but the only soldier convicted was Lt William Calley, commander of the platoon.

mynah any of various tropical starlings found in Southeast Asia. The glossy black **hill mynah** (*Gracula religiosa*) of India can realistically mimic sounds and human speech. It is up to 40 cm/16 in long with yellow wattles (loose folds of skin) on the head, and a yellow bill and legs. (Family Sturnidae, order Passeriformes.)

myoglobin globular protein, closely related to *haemoglobin and located in vertebrate muscle. Oxygen binds to myoglobin and is released only when the haemoglobin can no longer supply adequate oxygen to muscle cells.

myopia *or* **short-sightedness** defect of the eye in which a person can see clearly only those objects that are close up. It is caused either by the eyeball being too long or by the cornea and lens system of the eye being too powerful, both of which cause the images of distant objects to be formed in front of the retina instead of on it. Nearby objects are sharply perceived. Myopia can be corrected by suitable glasses or contact lenses.

myopia, low-luminance poor night vision. About 20% of people have poor vision in twilight and nearly 50% in the dark. Low-luminance myopia does not show up in normal optical tests, but in 1989 a method was developed of measuring the degree of blurring by projecting images on a screen using a weak laser beam.

Myrmidon in Greek mythology, a member of a legendary race, subjects of the Greek warrior *Achilles, whom he commanded at the siege of Troy in Homer's *Iliad*. Originally from Aegina, many Myrmidones followed Achille's father Peleus to Phthiotis in Thessaly,

northern Greece.

Myron (c. 500–440 BC) Greek sculptor. A late contemporary of *Phidias, he is known to have made statues of the athletes Timanthes (456 BC) and Lycinus (448 BC), excelling in the representation of movement. His bronze *Discobolus/Discus-Thrower* and *Athene and Marsyas*, much admired in his time, are known through Roman copies, which confirm his ancient reputation for brilliant composition and naturalism.

myrrh gum *resin produced by several small trees belonging to the bursera family, especially *C. myrrha*, found in Ethiopia and Arabia. In ancient times it was used for incense and perfume and in embalming dead bodies. (Genus *Commiphora*, family Burseraceae.)

myrtle any of a group of Old World evergreen shrubs belonging to the myrtle family. The commonly cultivated Mediterranean myrtle (*M. communis*) has oval opposite leaves and white flowers followed by purple berries, all of which are fragrant. (Genus *Myrtus*, family Myrtaceae.)

mystery play *or* **miracle play** medieval religious drama based on stories from the Bible. Mystery plays were performed around the time of church festivals, reaching their height in Europe during the 15th and 16th centuries. A whole cycle running from the Creation to the Last Judgement was performed in separate scenes on mobile wagons by various town guilds, usually on the festival of Corpus Christi in midsummer.

mystery religion any of various cults of the ancient world that were open only to the initiated; for example, the cults of Demeter, Dionysus, Cybele, Isis, and Mithras. Underlying some of them is a fertility ritual, in which a deity undergoes death and resurrection and the initiates feed on the flesh and blood to attain communion with the divine and ensure their own life beyond the grave. The influence of mystery religions on early Christianity was considerable.

mysticism religious belief or spiritual experience based on direct, intuitive communion with the divine or apprehension of truths beyond the understanding. It does not always involve an orthodox deity, though it is found in all the main religions – for example, Kabbalism in Judaism, Sufism in Islam, and the bhakti movement in Hinduism.

mythology (Greek *mythos, logos* 'story-telling' or a 'rationale of stories') *genre of traditional stories symbolically underlying a given culture. These stories describe gods and other supernatural beings with whom humans may have relationships, and are often intended to explain the workings of the universe, nature, or human history. Mythology is sometimes distinguished from legend as being entirely fictitious and imaginary, legend being woven around an historical figure or nucleus such as the tale of Troy, but such division is difficult as myth and legend are often closely interwoven.

myxoedema thyroid-deficiency disease developing in adult life, most commonly in middle-aged women. The symptoms include loss of energy and appetite, weight gain, inability to keep warm, mental dullness, and dry, puffy skin. It is reversed by giving the thyroid hormone thyroxine.

myxomatosis contagious, usually fatal, virus infection of rabbits which causes much suffering. It has been deliberately introduced in the UK and Australia since the 1950s to reduce the rabbit population.

n

Nabis, les (Hebrew 'prophets') group of French painters formed towards the end of the 19th century in an effort to clarify modern purpose in painting. Paul Sérusier, a follower of Gauguin, brought them together and invented the name for them from the Hebrew Nabiim ('the divinely inspired'). He was joined by Maurice Denis, who became the theoretician of the movement, Paul Ranson, K X Roussel, Pierre Bonnard, Edouard Vuillard, and Félix Vallotton. The subtitle of Denis's book *Théories*, 'From Symbolism and Gauguin towards a new Classic Order', sums up their aim. Reacting against Impressionism, they sought to give ideas aesthetic form (see *Symbolism). The adherence of Bonnard and Vuillard seems fortuitous and it became necessary to invent a special term for their absence of theory. The movement is of note as part of the ferment of ideas that preceded fauvism and cubism.

Nabokov, Vladimir Vladimirovich (1899–1977) US writer. He left his native Russia in 1917 and began writing in English in the 1940s. His most widely known book is *Lolita* (1955), the story of the middle-aged Humbert Humbert's infatuation with a precocious girl of 12. His other books, remarkable for their word play and ingenious plots, include *Laughter in the Dark* (1938), *The Real Life of Sebastian Knight* (1945), *Pnin* (1957), and his memoirs *Speak, Memory* (1947).

nadir point on the celestial sphere vertically below the observer and hence diametrically opposite the **zenith**.

naevus mole, or patch of discoloration on the skin which has been present from birth. There are many different types of naevi, including those composed of a cluster of small blood vessels, such as the 'strawberry mark' (which usually disappears early in life) and the 'port-wine stain'.

NAFTA acronym for *North American Free Trade Agreement.

Naga member of any of the various peoples who inhabit the highland region near the Indian-Myanmar (Burma) border; they number approximately 800,000. These peoples do not possess a common name; some of the main groups are Ao, Konyak, Sangtam, Lhota, Sema, Rengma, Chang, and Angami. They live by farming, hunting, and fishing, with rice as the staple diet. Some peoples are egalitarian, others are stratified into aristocrats and commoners. Their languages belong to the Sino-Tibetan family.

Nagaland state of northeast India, bordering Myanmar on the east, and the Indian states of Manipur to the south, and Assam to the north and west; area 16,527 sq km/6,381 sq mi; population (2001 est) 1,988,600, which is made up of many different tribal groups. The capital is Kohima. The state is mainly upland, averaging over 1,500 m/4,900 ft, and densely forested. Wildlife includes tigers and elephants. Agriculture occupies 90% of the population, and produce includes tea, sugar, coffee, rice, millet, maize, and vegetables. Industries in the state include timber and paper, and petroleum at Dikhu. Dimapur, with a sugar mill, distillery, brick factory, and television assembly works, is the main industrial centre. The population is mainly Christian.

Nagasaki industrial port (coal, iron, shipbuilding) on Nagasaki Bay, Kyushu Island, Japan, capital of Nagasaki prefecture; population (2000 est) 438,600. Industries include the manufacture of steel and electrical equipment. Nagasaki was the only Japanese port open to European trade from the 16th century until 1859. The first modern Japanese shipyard opened here 1855–61. On 9 August 1945, an *atomic bomb was dropped on Nagasaki by the USA.

Nagorno-Karabakh (Russian 'mountainous Qarabagh') autonomous region of Azerbaijan; area 4,400 sq km/1,700 sq mi; population (1997 est) 204,800 (77% Armenian, 23% Azeri), the Christian Armenians forming an enclave within the predominantly Shiite Muslim Azerbaijan. The capital is Xankändi. The region lies on the eastern slopes of the Lesser *Caucasus Mountains, partly covered with oak and beech forests. Main agricultural products include cotton, grapes, wheat, silk, and livestock (sheep, cattle, pigs, and horses). Since 1989 the region has experienced conflict between local Armenian troops and Azeri forces. By 1998, Nagorno-Karabakh was effectively an independent state.

Nagy, Imre (1895–1958) Hungarian politician, prime minister 1953–55 and 1956. He led the Hungarian revolt against Soviet domination in 1956, for which he was executed.

Nahuatl any of a group of Mesoamerican Indian peoples (Mexico and Central America), of which the best-known group were the Aztecs. The Nahuatl are the largest ethnic group in Mexico, and their languages, which belong to the Uto-Aztecan (Aztec-Tanoan) family, are spoken by over a million people today.

naiad in classical mythology, a water nymph. Naiads lived in rivers and streams; *nereids in the sea.

nail in biology, a hard, flat, flexible outgrowth of the digits of primates (humans, monkeys, and apes). Nails are composed of *keratin.

Naipaul, V(idiadhar) S(urajprasad) (1932–) Trinidadian novelist and travel writer living in Britain. His novels include *A House for Mr Biswas* (1961), *The Mimic Men* (1967), *In a Free State* (1971; for which he won the Booker Prize), *A Bend in the River* (1979), *Finding the Centre* (1984), *A Way in the World* (1994), and *Letters Between a Father and Son* (1999) – letters between him and his family in India while he was in Oxford, England. In 2001 he published *Half a Life*. In the same year he was awarded a Nobel Prize for Literature.

Nairobi capital and chief commercial and industrial centre of Kenya, in the central highlands at 1,660 m/5,450 ft; population (2002 est) 3,043,100 (urban area). Industries include engineering, paints, brewing, textiles, clothing, and food processing. It is the headquarters of the United Nations Environment Programme (UNEP), and has the UN Centre for Human Settlements. It is one of Africa's largest and fastest-growing cities.

naive art *or* **primitive painting** fresh, childlike style of painting, employing bright colours and strong, rhythmic designs. It is usually the work of self-taught artists with no formal training, and is less technical in approach. Outstanding naive artists include Henri *Rousseau and Camille Bombois (1883–1970) in France, and Alfred Wallis in England. The term is also used to describe the work of trained artists who employ naive techniques and effects, for example, L S *Lowry.

Najibullah, Ahmadzai (1947–1996) Afghan communist politician, leader of the People's Democratic Party of Afghanistan (PDPA) from 1986, and state president 1986–92. Although his government initially survived the withdrawal of Soviet troops in February 1989, continuing pressure from the Mujahedin forces resulted in his eventual overthrow. He was executed in September 1996 by the Taliban (Islamic student army), who had seized control of most of Afghanistan.

Nakhichevan autonomous region of Azerbaijan, an enclave within the neighbouring state of Armenia, located on the Iranian frontier and separated from the rest of Azerbaijan by a narrow strip of Armenian territory; area 5,500 sq km/2,124 sq mi; population (1997 est) 333,200. The capital is *Nakhichevan, and Paragachay is another city in the enclave. The region is extremely arid, a mountainous country with large salt deposits. With irrigation, agriculture produces cotton, tobacco, grain, and market garden produce, and in the drier areas sheep farming is significant. Minerals are produced, including salt, molybdenum, and lead, while industries include cotton ginning, silk spinning, fruit canning, meat packing, and tobacco products.

Namib Desert coastal desert region between the Kalahari Desert and the Atlantic Ocean, extending some 2,800 km/1,740 mi from Luanda in Angola to St Helena Bay in South Africa. Its aridity is caused by the descent of dry air cooled by the cold Benguela current along the coast. The sand dunes of the Namib Desert are among the tallest in the world, reaching heights of 370 m/1,200 ft. In the most arid parts rainfall can be as little as 23 mm/0.9 in per year.

Namibia

formerly **South West Africa** (until 1968)
National name: *Republic of Namibia*
Area: 824,300 sq km/318,262 sq mi
Capital: Windhoek
Major towns/cities: Swakopmund, Rehoboth, Rundu
Major ports: Walvis Bay
Physical features: mainly desert (Namib and Kalahari); Orange River; Caprivi Strip links Namibia to Zambezi River; includes the enclave of Walvis Bay (area 1,120 sq km/432 sq mi)
Head of state: Samuel Nujoma from 1990
Head of government: Theo-Ben Gurirab from 2002
Political system: emergent democracy
Political executive: limited presidency
Political parties: South West Africa People's Organization (SWAPO), socialist Ovambo-oriented; Democratic Turnhalle Alliance (DTA), moderate,

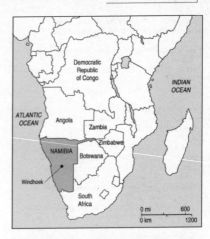

multiracial coalition; United Democratic Front (UDF), disaffected ex-SWAPO members; National Christian Action (ACN), white conservative
Currency: Namibian dollar
GNI per capita (PPP): (US$) 6,650 (2002 est)
Exports: diamonds, fish and fish products, live animals and meat, uranium, copper, karakul pelts. Principal market: UK 43% (2000)
Population: 1,987,000 (2003 est)
Language: English (official), Afrikaans, German, Ovambo (51%), Nama (12%), Kavango (10%), other indigenous languages
Religion: about 90% Christian (Lutheran, Roman Catholic, Dutch Reformed Church, Anglican)
Life expectancy: 43 (men); 46 (women) (2000–05)
Chronology
1480s: Coast visited by European explorers.
16th century: Bantu-speaking Herero migrated into northwest and Ovambo settled in northernmost areas.
1840s: Rhenish Missionary Society began to spread German influence; Jonkar Afrikaner conquest state dominant in southern Namibia.
1884: Germany annexed most of the area, calling it South West Africa, with Britain incorporating a small enclave around Walvis Bay in the Cape Colony of South Africa.
1892: German farmers arrived to settle in the region.
1903–04: Uprisings by the long-settled Nama (Khoikhoi) and Herero peoples brutally repressed by Germans, with over half the local communities slaughtered.
1908: Discovery of diamonds led to a larger influx of Europeans.
1915: German colony invaded and seized by South Africa during World War I and the Ovambo, in the north, were conquered.
1920: Administered by South Africa, under League of Nations mandate.
1946: Full incorporation in South Africa refused by United Nations (UN).
1949: White voters in South West Africa given representation in the South African parliament.

631

1958: South West Africa People's Organization (SWAPO) formed to campaign for racial equality and full independence.

1960: Radical wing of SWAPO, led by Sam Nujoma, forced into exile.

1964: UN voted to end South Africa's mandate, but South Africa refused to relinquish control or soften its policies towards the economically disenfranchised black majority.

1966: South Africa's apartheid laws extended to the country; 60% of land was allocated to whites, who formed 10% of the population.

1968: South West Africa redesignated Namibia by UN; SWAPO, drawing strong support from the Ovambo people of the north, began armed guerrilla struggle against South African rule, establishing People's Liberation Army of Namibia (PLAN).

1971: Prolonged general strike by black Namibian contract workers.

1973: The UN recognized SWAPO as the 'authentic representative of the Namibian people'.

1975–76: The establishment of a new Marxist regime in independent Angola strengthened the position of SWAPO guerrilla movement, but also led to the increased military involvement of South Africa in the region.

1978: UN Security Council Resolution 435 for the granting of full independence was accepted by South Africa, and then rescinded.

1983: Direct rule was reimposed by Pretoria after the resignation of the Democratic Turnhalle Alliance (DTA), a conservative administration dominated by whites.

1985: South Africa installed a new puppet administration, the Transitional Government of National Unity (TGNU), which tried to reform the apartheid system, but was not recognized by the UN.

1988: Peace talks between South Africa, Angola, and Cuba led to an agreement on troop withdrawals and full independence for Namibia.

1989: UN peacekeeping force were stationed to oversee free elections to the assembly to draft a new constitution; SWAPO won the elections.

1990: A liberal multiparty constitution was adopted and independence was achieved. Sam Nujoma, SWAPO's former guerrilla leader, was elected president. Joined the Commonwealth. Hage Geingob was appointed prime minister.

1993: South Africa, with its new multiracial government, relinquished its claim to Walvis Bay sovereignty. Namibia dollar was launched with South African rand parity.

1994: SWAPO won assembly elections; Nujoma re-elected president.

2002: Theo-Ben Gurirab became prime minister.

2003: The government announced that illegal land occupation by black farmworkers would not be allowed. The union representing the farmworkers cancelled their planned occupation of white-owned farms.

2004: A road bridge was opened betweem Namibia and Zambia across the River Zambezi. Hifikepunye Pohamba, nominated by President Nujoma, won the presidential elections.

Nanak (1469–c. 1539) Indian guru and founder of Sikhism, a religion based on the unity of God and the equality of all human beings. He was strongly opposed to caste divisions.

nano- prefix used in *SI units of measurement, equivalent to a one-billionth part (10^{-9}). For example, a nanosecond is one-billionth of a second.

nanotechnology experimental technology using individual atoms or molecules as the components of minute machines, measured by the nanometre, or millionth of a millimetre. Nanotechnology research in the 1990s focused on testing molecular structures and refining ways to manipulate atoms using a scanning tunnelling microscope. The ultimate aim is to create very small computers and molecular machines which could perform vital engineering or medical tasks.

Nansen, Fridtjof (1861–1930) Norwegian explorer and scientist. In 1893 he sailed to the Arctic in the *Fram*, which was deliberately allowed to drift north with an iceflow. Nansen, accompanied by F Hjalmar Johansen (1867–1923), continued north on foot and reached 86° 14′ N, the highest latitude then attained. After World War I, Nansen became League of Nations high commissioner for refugees. He was awarded the Nobel Prize for Peace in 1922 for his relief work after World War I.

napalm fuel used in flamethrowers and incendiary bombs. Produced from jellied petrol, it is a mixture of **na**phthenic and **pal**mitic acids. Napalm causes extensive burns because it sticks to the skin even when aflame. It was widely used by the US Army during the Vietnam War, and by Serb forces in the civil war in Bosnia-Herzegovina.

naphtha mixtures of hydrocarbons obtained by destructive distillation of petroleum, coal tar, and shale oil. It is a raw material for the petrochemical and plastics industries. The term was originally applied to naturally occurring liquid hydrocarbons.

Napier, John (1550–1617) 8th Laird of Merchiston, Scottish mathematician who invented *logarithms in 1614 and in 1617 he published his description of what was arguably the first mechanical calculator – a set of numbered rods, usually made of bone or ivory and therefore known as Napier's bones. Using them, multiplication became merely a process of reading off the appropriate figures and making simple additions.

Naples Italian **Napoli**, (Greek *Neapolis* 'new city') industrial port and capital of Campania, Italy, on the Tyrrhenian Sea; population (2001 est) 993,400. Industries include shipbuilding, food-processing, and the manufacture of cars, textiles, and paper. An important commercial and tourist centre, to the south is the Isle of Capri, and behind the city is Mount Vesuvius, with the ruins of Pompeii at its foot.

Naples, Kingdom of the southern part of Italy, alternately independent and united with *Sicily in the Kingdom of the Two Sicilies.

Napoleon I (1769–1821) also known as **Napoleon Bonaparte**, Emperor of the French 1804–14 and 1814–15. A general from 1795 in the *Revolutionary Wars, in 1799 he overthrew the ruling Directory (see *French Revolution) and made himself dictator. From 1803 he conquered most of Europe (the *Napoleonic Wars) and installed his brothers as puppet kings (see *Bonaparte). After the Peninsular War and retreat from Moscow in 1812, he was forced to abdicate in 1814 and was banished to the island of Elba. In March 1815 he reassumed power but was defeated by British and Prussian forces at the Battle of *Waterloo and exiled to the island of St Helena, 1,900 km/1,200 mi west of Africa, where he died. His internal administrative reforms and laws are still evident in France.

Napoleon II (1811–1832) born François Charles Joseph Bonaparte. Title given by the Bonapartists to the son of Napoleon I and Marie Louise; until 1814 he was known as the king of Rome and after 1818 as the duke of Reichstadt. After his father's abdication in 1814 he was taken to the Austrian court, where he spent the rest of his life.

Napoleon III (1808–1873) born Charles Louis Napoleon Bonaparte, Emperor of the French 1852–70, known as **Louis-Napoleon**. After two attempted coups (1836 and 1840) he was jailed, then went into exile, returning for the revolution of 1848, when he became president of the Second Republic but proclaimed himself emperor in 1852. In 1870 he was manoeuvred by the German chancellor Bismarck into war with Prussia (see *Franco-Prussian war); he was forced to surrender at Sedan, northeastern France, and the empire collapsed.

Napoleonic Wars series of European wars (1803–15) conducted by *Napoleon I of France against an alliance of Britain, the German states, Spain, Portugal, and Russia, following the *Revolutionary Wars, and aiming for French conquest of Europe. At one time nearly all of Europe was under Napoleon's domination. He was finally defeated at the Battle of *Waterloo in 1815.

Narayanan, Kocheril Raman (1920–) Indian politician and public servant, president from 1997. A *dalit* ('untouchable') from the southern state of Kerala, after a career chiefly as a diplomat, he became vice-president in 1992 and, in July 1997, was indirectly elected, with cross-party support, as the country's first ever *dalit* president.

narcissism in psychology, an exaggeration of normal self-respect and self-involvement which may amount to mental disorder when it precludes relationships with other people.

narcissus any of a group of bulbous plants belonging to the amaryllis family. Species include the daffodil, jonquil, and narcissus. All have flowers with a cup or trumpet projecting from the centre. (Genus *Narcissus*, family Amaryllidaceae.)

Narcissus in late Greek mythology, a beautiful youth who rejected the love of the nymph *Echo and was condemned by Nemesis, goddess of retribution, to fall in love with his reflection in a pool. He pined away, and a flower which appeared at the spot was named after him.

narcotic pain-relieving and sleep-inducing drug. The term is usually applied to heroin, morphine, and other opium derivatives, but may also be used for other drugs which depress brain activity, including anaesthetic agents and hypnotics.

Narmada river that rises in the Maikala range in Madhya Pradesh state, central India, and flows 1,245 km/778 mi west and southwest to the Gulf of Khambat, an inlet of the Arabian Sea. Forming the traditional boundary between Hindustan and Deccan, the Narmada is a holy river of the Hindus. The Narmada Valley Project involves the building of over 3,000 dams, many of them multi-purpose for water supply, flood control, and the generation of hydroelectricity, along the length of the Narmada River.

narwhal toothed whale found only in the Arctic Ocean. It grows to 5 m/16 ft long, has a grey and black body, a small head, and short flippers. The male has a single spiral tusk growing straight out in front of its upper lip that can measure up to 2.7 m/9 ft long. (Species *Monodon monoceros*, family Monodontidae.)

NASA acronym for **National Aeronautics and Space Administration**, US government agency for space flight and aeronautical research, founded in 1958 by the National Aeronautics and Space Act. Its headquarters are in Washington, DC, and its main installations include the Kennedy Space Center on Merritt Island in Florida, the Johnson Space Center in Houston, Texas, the Jet Propulsion Laboratory in Pasadena, California, the Goddard Space Flight Center in Beltsville, Maryland, and the Marshall Space Flight Center in Huntsville, Alabama. NASA's early planetary and lunar programmes included the Pioneer probes, from 1958, which gathered data for the later crewed missions, and the *Apollo* project, which took the first astronauts to the Moon in *Apollo 11* on 16–24 July 1969.

Naseby, Battle of decisive battle of the English Civil War on 14 June 1645, when the Royalists, led by Prince Rupert, were defeated by the Parliamentarians ('Roundheads') under Oliver *Cromwell and General *Fairfax. It is named after the nearby village of Naseby, 32 km/20 mi south of Leicester.

Nash, John (1752–1835) English architect. His large country-house practice, established about 1796 with the landscape gardener Humphry Repton, used a wide variety of styles, and by 1798 he was enjoying the patronage of the Prince of Wales (afterwards George IV). Later he laid out Regent's Park, London, and its approaches, as well as Trafalgar Square and St James's Park. Between 1811 and 1821 he planned Regent Street (later rebuilt), repaired and enlarged Buckingham Palace (for which he designed Marble Arch), and rebuilt the Royal Pavilion, Brighton, in flamboyant oriental style.

Nash, Paul (1889–1946) English painter. He was an official war artist in World Wars I and II. In the 1930s he was one of a group of artists promoting avant-garde style, and was deeply influenced by surrealism. Two works which illustrate the visionary quality of his paintings are *Totes Meer/Dead Sea* (1940–41; Tate Gallery, London) and *Solstice of the Sunflower* (1945; National Gallery of Canada, Ottawa). 'Structural purpose' was an aim which led him into many forms of design, for textiles, ceramics, the stage and the book, but the surrealist trend of the 1930s and the exhibition of 1936 brought out an imaginative and poetic feeling already apparent in his oils and watercolours.

Nassau capital and port of the Bahamas, on New Providence Island; population (1998 est) 205,400. It is a popular tourist resort, especially in winter, and was the scene in 1994 of an international conference on biological diversity.

Nasser, Gamal Abdel (1918–1970) Egyptian politician, prime minister 1954–56 and from 1956 president of Egypt (the United Arab Republic 1958–71). In 1952 he was the driving power behind the Neguib coup, which ended the monarchy. His nationalization of the Suez Canal in 1956 led to an Anglo-French invasion and the *Suez Crisis, and his ambitions for an Egyptian-led union of Arab states led to disquiet in the

Middle East (and in the West). Nasser was also an early and influential leader of the non-aligned movement.

nastic movement plant movement that is caused by an external stimulus, such as light or temperature, but is directionally independent of its source, unlike *tropisms. Nastic movements occur as a result of changes in water pressure within specialized cells or differing rates of growth in parts of the plant. Examples include the opening and closing of crocus flowers following an increase or decrease in temperature (**thermonasty**), and the opening and closing of evening primrose *Oenothera* flowers on exposure to dark and light (**photonasty**).

nasturtium any of a group of plants that includes watercress (*N. officinale*), a perennial aquatic plant of Europe and Asia, grown as a salad crop. Belonging to a different family altogether, the South American trailing nasturtiums include the cultivated species *T. majus*, with orange, scarlet, or yellow flowers, and *T. minus*, which has smaller flowers. (Genus *Nasturtium*, family Cruciferae; South American genus *Tropaeolum*, family Tropaeolaceae.)

Natal former province of South Africa to 1994, bounded on the east by the Indian Ocean. The capital was Pietermaritzburg. In 1994 the province became part of *KwaZulu-Natal Province. It was called Natal ('of [Christ's] birth') because the Portuguese navigator Vasco da Gama reached it on Christmas Day in 1497.

Natchez (Choctaw *nakni sakti chaha* 'warriors of the high bluff') member of an *American Indian people who lived along the Gulf of Mexico and the lower Mississippi river valley from AD 700 to the 1730s. Their Muskogean language is extinct. One of the Moundbuilder cultures, they had a highly developed caste or ranking system and were ruled by a chief priest called the Great Sun. In 1700 the Natchez numbered about 6,000, but conflict with French settlers brought them close to extinction by 1730. The surviving Natchez took refuge with the Chickasaw, *Cherokee, and Creek and accompanied them to Oklahoma in the 1830s. They now live in the southern Appalachians and Oklahoma.

National Assembly for Wales devolved parliamentary body for Wales, comprising 60 members and based in Cardiff. The Assembly was created by the July 1998 Government of Wales Act, which was passed following the Welsh electorate's narrow approval of government proposals in an 18 September 1997 referendum on devolution. Its temporary base is the Cardiff University Council Chamber and Crickhowell House on Cardiff Bay. A new building is being built at Cardiff Bay to house the assembly.

National Curriculum in England and Wales from 1988, a course of study in ten subjects common to all primary and secondary state schools. The National Curriculum is divided into three core subjects – English, maths, and science – and seven foundation subjects: geography, history, technology, a foreign language (for secondary school pupils), art, music, and physical education (plus Welsh in Wales). There are four key stages, on completion of which the pupil's work is assessed. The stages are for ages 5–7, 7–11, 11–14, and 14–16. Its content is under review.

national debt debt incurred by the central government of a country to its own people and institutions and also to overseas creditors. A government can borrow from the public by means of selling interest-bearing bonds, for example, or from abroad. Traditionally, a major cause of national debt was the cost of war but in recent decades governments have borrowed heavily in order to finance development or nationalization, to support an ailing currency, or to avoid raising taxes.

National Front in the UK, extreme right-wing political party founded in 1967. In 1991 the party claimed 3,000 members. Some of its members had links with the National Socialist Movement of the 1960s (see *Nazism). It attracted attention during the 1970s through the violence associated with its demonstrations in areas with large black and Asian populations and, in response, the left-wing Anti Nazi League was formed to mount counter protests.

National Guard *militia force recruited by each state of the USA. The volunteer National Guard units are under federal orders in emergencies, and under the control of the governor in peacetime, and are now an integral part of the US Army. The National Guard has been used against demonstrators; in May 1970 at Kent State University, Ohio, they killed four students who were protesting against the bombing of Cambodia by the USA.

national income the total income of a state in one year, including both the wages of individuals and the profits of companies. It is equal to the value of the output of all goods and services during the same period. National income is equal to gross national product (the value of a country's total output) minus an allowance for replacement of ageing capital stock.

nationalism in music, the development by 19th-century composers of a musical style that would express the characteristics of their own country. They did this by including tunes from their nation's folk music, and taking scenes from their country's history, legends, and folk tales, as a basis for their compositions. Nationalism was encouraged by governments in the early 20th century for propaganda purposes in times of war and political tension. Composers of nationalist music include Bedrich *Smetana, Jean *Sibelius, Edvard *Grieg, Antonín *Dvořák, Carl *Nielsen, Zoltán *Kodály, Aaron *Copland, Edward *Elgar, Dmitri *Shostakovich, and Stephen Foster.

nationalism in politics, a movement that consciously aims to unify a nation, create a state, or free it from foreign or imperialistic rule. Nationalist movements became an important factor in European politics during the 19th century; since 1900 nationalism has become a strong force in Asia and Africa and in the late 1980s revived strongly in Eastern Europe.

nationalization policy of bringing a country's essential services and industries under public ownership. It was pursued, for example, by the UK Labour government 1945–51. Assets in the hands of foreign governments or companies may also be nationalized; for example, Iran's oil industry, the *Suez Canal, and US-owned fruit plantations in Guatemala, all in the 1950s.

National Missile Defense (NMD) US programme to create a system to defend the USA against a limited strategic ballistic missile attack. NMD is a much reduced version of the *Strategic Defense Initiative (SDI). It involves launching interceptor missiles from the ground, using land-based radars and space-based infrared sensors to guide them to destroy incoming long-range missiles. The NMD initiative is overseen by the **Ballistic Missile Defense Organization** (BMDO), set up in 1993.

National Party of Australia Australian political party, favouring free enterprise and seeking to promote the interests of people outside the major metropolitan areas. It holds the balance of power between Liberals and Labor. It was formed in 1916 as the **Country Party of Australia** and adopted its present name in 1982. It gained strength following the introduction of proportional representation in 1918 and was in coalition with the Liberals 1949–83. In 1996 it entered into a coalition with the Liberal Party led by Prime Minister John Howard.

National Security Agency (NSA) largest and most secret of US intelligence agencies. Established in 1952 to intercept foreign communications as well as to safeguard US transmissions, the NSA collects and analyses computer communications, telephone signals, and other electronic data, and gathers intelligence. Known as the Puzzle Palace, its headquarters are at Fort Meade, Maryland (with a major facility at Menwith Hill, England).

national service *conscription into the armed services in peacetime.

national socialism official name for the *Nazi movement in Germany; see also *fascism.

Native American alternative term for *American Indian.

native metal *or* **free metal** any of the metallic elements that occur in nature in the chemically uncombined or elemental form (in addition to any combined form). They include bismuth, cobalt, copper, gold, iridium, iron, lead, mercury, nickel, osmium, palladium, platinum, ruthenium, rhodium, tin, and silver. Some are commonly found in the free state, such as gold; others occur almost exclusively in the combined state, but under unusual conditions do occur as native metals, such as mercury. Examples of native non-metals are carbon and sulphur.

natural symbol [natural], in music, a sign placed in front of a note, cancelling a previous sharp or flat. A **natural trumpet** or **horn** is an instrument without valves, and can therefore only play natural harmonics.

natural gas mixture of flammable gases found in the Earth's crust (often in association with petroleum). It is one of the world's three main fossil fuels (with coal and oil).

naturalism in the arts generally, an approach that advocates the factual and realistic representation of the subject of a painting or novel with no stylization. Specifically, **naturalism** refers to a movement in literature and drama that developed as a reaction to the mannered, conventional and heavily stylized approach to all the arts favoured in the 18th century.

natural justice the concept that there is an inherent quality in law that compares favourably with arbitrary action by a government. It is largely associated with the idea of the rule of law. For natural justice to be present, it is generally argued that no one should be a judge in his or her own case, and that each party in a dispute has an unalienable right to be heard and to prepare their case thoroughly (the rule of *audi alterem partem*).

natural logarithm in mathematics, the *exponent of a number expressed to base e, where e represents the *irrational number 2.71828... . Natural *logarithms are also called Napierian logarithms, after their inventor, the Scottish mathematician John Napier.

natural radioactivity radioactivity generated by those radioactive elements that exist in the Earth's crust. All the elements from polonium (atomic number 84) to uranium (atomic number 92) are radioactive. *Radioisotopes of some lighter elements are also found in nature (for example potassium-40). See *background radiation.

natural selection process by which gene frequencies in a population change through certain individuals producing more descendants than others because they are better able to survive and reproduce in their environment. The accumulated effect of natural selection is to produce *adaptations such as the insulating coat of a polar bear or the spadelike forelimbs of a mole. The process is slow, relying firstly on random variation in the genes of an organism being produced by *mutation and secondly on the genetic *recombination of sexual reproduction. It was recognized by Charles *Darwin and English naturalist Alfred Russel Wallace as the main process driving *evolution.

nature–nurture controversy *or* **environment– heredity controversy** long-standing dispute among philosophers and psychologists over the relative importance of environment, that is, upbringing, experience, and learning ('nurture'), and heredity, that is, genetic inheritance ('nature'), in determining the make-up of an organism, as related to human personality and intelligence.

Nauru

National name: *Republic of Nauru*

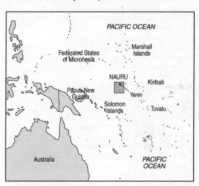

Area: 21 sq km/8.1 sq mi
Capital: Yaren District (seat of government)
Physical features: tropical coral island in southwest Pacific; plateau encircled by coral cliffs and sandy beaches
Head of state and government: Ludwig Scotty from 2004
Political system: liberal democracy
Political executive: limited presidency
Political parties: candidates are traditionally elected as independents, grouped into pro- and antigovernment factions; Democratic Party of Nauru (DPN), only formal political party, antigovernment

Currency: Australian dollar
GNI per capita (PPP): (US$) 5,120 (2002 est)
Exports: phosphates. Principal market: Australia
Population: 13,000 (2003 est)
Language: Nauruan, English (both official)
Religion: majority Protestant, Roman Catholic
Life expectancy: 59 (men); 66 (women) (2000–05)
Chronology
1798: British whaler Capt John Fearn first visited Nauru and named it Pleasant Island.
1830s–80s: The island was a haven for white runaway convicts and deserters.
1888: Annexed by Germany at the request of German settlers who sought protection from local clan unrest.
1899: Phosphate deposits discovered; mining began eight years later, with indentured Chinese labourers brought in to work British Australian-owned mines.
1914: Occupied by Australia on the outbreak of World War I.
1920: Administered by Australia on behalf of itself, New Zealand, and the UK until independence, except 1942–43, when occupied by Japan, and two-thirds of the population were deported briefly to Micronesia.
1951: Local Government Council set up to replace Council of Chiefs.
1956: Hammer DeRoburt became head chief of Nauru.
1968: Independence achieved, with 'special member' British Commonwealth status. Hammer DeRoburt elected president.
1976: Bernard Dowiyogo was elected president for the first time.
1987: Kennan Adeang established the Democratic Party of Nauru.
1994: Australia agreed to an out-of-court settlement of A$107 million, payable over 20 years, for environmental damage caused by phosphate mining which had left 80% of land agriculturally barren.
2000: Bernard Dowiyogo was elected president for the sixth time. General elections saw Rene Harris win the popular vote, but he resigned and Dowiyogo was installed.
2001: Dowiyogo was ousted in a parliamentary vote, and Harris was re-elected president.
2003: Dowiyogo was re-installed as president and agreed to close Nauru's offshore banking facilities after US allegations of money-laundering. Dowiyogo died during the year, after heart surgery. Ludwig Scotty won the presidential elections but was ousted in a vote of no confidence. Harris was re-elected as president.
2004: The country's assets were placed in receivership in Australia after it defaulted on loan payments. Australian officials took charge of the state finances. Harris lost a vote of no confidence and was replaced as president by Scotty, who later sacked parliament after it failed to pass his reform budget. Scotty later won the general election.
2005: Naura agreed to re-establish diplomatic relations with Taiwan.

nautical mile unit of distance used in navigation, an internationally agreed standard (since 1959) equalling the average length of one minute of arc on a great circle of the Earth, or 1,852 m/6,076 ft. The term formerly applied to various units of distance used in navigation.

nautilus sea animal related to octopuses and squids, with many short, grasping tentacles surrounding a sharp beak, but different in that it has an outer shell. It is a *cephalopod, a type of *mollusc, and is found in the Indian and Pacific oceans. The well-known **pearly nautilus** (*N. pompilius*) has a chambered spiral shell about 20 cm/8 in in diameter. Its body occupies the outer chamber. (Genus *Nautilus*, class Cephalopoda.)

Navajo *or* **Navaho** *or* **Dine** (Tena *Navahu* 'large planted field') member of an *American Indian people, who migrated from Canada to southwest USA (Arizona, New Mexico, and Utah) in about AD 1000. They are related to the *Apache, and speak an Athabaskan language, belonging to the Na-Dene family. During World War II, Navajo code talkers in the US Marine Corps transmitted radio messages directly in their native language, which the enemy could not translate. The Navajo were traditionally cultivators, although many now herd sheep, which they acquired from the Spanish. Renowned for their artistry, their painted pottery, woven rugs and blankets, and silver and turquoise jewellery are sold internationally; tourism also generates income. They are the second-largest group of American Indians, numbering about 269,200 (2000).

Navarino, Battle of during the Greek war of liberation, destruction on 20 October 1827 of a joint Turkish–Egyptian fleet by the combined fleets of the British, French, and Russians under Vice-Admiral Edward Codrington (1770–1851). The destruction of their fleet left the Turks highly vulnerable in Greece as they had no protection to their rear and no supply line, and this proved to be the decisive battle of the war. Navarino is the Italian and historic name of Pylos Bay, Greece, on the southwest coast of the Peloponnese.

Navarre Spanish **Navarra**, autonomous community and province of northern Spain, bordered by France on the north; area 10,421 sq km/4,024 sq mi; population (1996 est) 520,600. The region is mountainous, containing spurs of the Pyrenees, and includes Monte Adi (1,503 m/4,933 ft high); the rivers Arga, Aragón, and Ebro flow through the area. Cereals and wine are produced in the lowlands. The capital is Pamplona.

Navarre, Kingdom of former kingdom comprising the Spanish province of Navarre and part of what is now the French *département* of Basses-Pyrénées. It resisted the conquest of the *Moors and was independent until it became French in 1284 on the marriage of Philip IV to the heiress of Navarre. In 1479 Ferdinand of Aragón annexed Spanish Navarre, with French Navarre going to Catherine of Foix (1483–1512), who kept the royal title. Her grandson became Henry IV of France, and Navarre was absorbed in the French crown lands in 1620.

nave (Latin *navis* 'a ship') in architecture, the central area of a church extending from the entrance to the crossing, if any; otherwise, up to the altar. It was developed by the early Christian builders out of the Roman hall of justice. The central space became flanked by side aisles and the early flat timber roofs gave way to stone vaulting. It is the section of the building used by the laity.

navel *or* **umbilicus** small indentation in the centre of the abdomen of mammals, marking the site of attachment of the *umbilical cord, which connects the fetus to the *placenta.

navigation the science and technology of finding the position, course, and distance travelled by a ship, plane, or other craft. Traditional methods include the magnetic *compass and *sextant. Today the gyrocompass is usually used, together with highly sophisticated electronic methods, employing beacons of radio signals, such as Decca, Loran, and Omega. Satellite navigation uses satellites that broadcast time and position signals.

Navratilova, Martina (1956–) Czech tennis player who became a naturalized US citizen in 1981. The most outstanding woman player of the 1980s, she won 56 Grand Slam victories, including 18 singles titles. She won the Wimbledon singles title a record nine times, including six in succession 1982–87.

Nazareth city in Galilee, northern Israel, 30 km/19 mi southeast of Haifa; population (1997 est) 55,500. According to the New Testament it was the boyhood home of Jesus. In modern times Nazareth is a commercial centre for the Galilee area and a centre of local government in the Northern District of Israel, as well having a significant tourist industry. Since the late 20th century industries such as vehicle assembly, textiles, and food-processing, have developed in the newer eastern suburbs.

Nazi member of the *Nationalsozialistische Deutsche Arbeiterpartei*, usually abbreviated to the **Nazi Party**. The party was based on the ideology of *Nazism.

Nazism ideology based on racism, nationalism, and the supremacy of the state over the individual. The German Nazi party, the *Nationalsozialistische Deutsche Arbeiterpartei* (National Socialist German Workers' Party), was formed from the German Workers' Party (founded in 1919) and led by Adolf *Hitler from 1921 to 1945.

Nazi–Soviet pact another name for the *Ribbentrop–Molotov pact.

Ndjamena formerly **Fort Lamy** (until 1973), capital of Chad, in the southwest of the country, at the confluence of the Chari and Logone rivers, on the Cameroon border; population (1993) 531,000. Industries include cotton, textiles, and meat packing. The city's agricultural markets trade in livestock, salt, dates, and grain. The Great Mosque built 1974–78 is an important landmark. It is a staging point for many pilgrims from West Africa to Mecca.

Neagh, Lough lake in Northern Ireland, 25 km/15 mi west of Belfast; area 396 sq km/153 sq mi. It is the largest lake in the British Isles, being 27 km/17 mi long, 16 km/10 mi wide, with an average depth of 12 m/39 ft. The shores are mostly flat and marshy; there are a few islands of which Ram's Island is the largest, on which is an early round tower. The lake is famous for trout and eel fishing, and breeding waterbirds.

Neanderthal hominid of the Mid-Late Palaeolithic, named after the Neander Tal (valley) near Düsseldorf, Germany, where a skeleton was found in 1856. *Homo sapiens neanderthalensis* lived from about 150,000 to 35,000 years ago and was similar in build to present-day people, but slightly smaller, stockier, and heavier-featured with a strong jaw and prominent brow ridges on a sloping forehead. The condition of the Neanderthal teeth that have been found suggests that they were used as clamps for holding objects with the hands.

Neath Port Talbot unitary authority in south Wales, created in 1996 from part of the former county of West Glamorgan. **area:** 442 sq km/171 sq mi **towns:** Port Talbot (administrative headquarters), Neath, Pontardarwe **physical:** the terrain is dominated by the alternation of river valleys and high moorland interfluves **features:** Roman fort of Nidum is near Neath; 19th-century Margam House and county park **population:** (2001 est) 134,500.

Nebraska called the **Cornhusker State** or the **Blackwater State**, (Oto Indian *nebrathka* 'flat water') state in central USA, bordered to the west by *Wyoming, to the north by *South Dakota, to the east by *Iowa and *Missouri, to the south by *Kansas, and to the southwest by *Colorado; area 199,098 sq km/76,872 sq mi; population (2000) 1,711,300; capital Lincoln. Part of the *Midwest, Nebraska's landscape rises gradually from the east to the High Plains of the west. The state is a leading crop producer, including corn and wheat, and has an important cattle and hog industry. Food processing is also significant economically. Major towns and cities include Omaha, Bellevue, Grand Island, Kearney, Fremont, North Platte, Hastings, Norfolk, and Columbus. Originally home to *Plains Indians, including the Cheyenne, *Arapaho, Omaha, *Sioux, Oto, and Pawnee people, Nebraska was acquired by the USA as part of the *Louisiana Purchase in 1803. Nebraska was organized as a territory in 1854 and was admitted to the Union in 1867 as the 37th US state.

Nebuchadnezzar (or Nebuchadrezzar II) (c. 630–c. 562 BC) King of Babylonia from 605 BC. Shortly before his accession he defeated the Egyptians at Carchemish and brought Palestine and Syria into his empire. Judah revolted, with Egyptian assistance, in 596 and 587–586 BC; on both occasions he captured Jerusalem and took many Hebrews into captivity. He largely rebuilt Babylon and constructed the hanging gardens.

nebula cloud of gas and dust in space. Nebulae are the birthplaces of stars, but some nebulae are produced by gas thrown off from dying stars (see *planetary nebula; *supernova). Nebulae are classified depending on whether they emit, reflect, or absorb light.

neck structure between the head and the trunk in animals. In the back of the neck are the upper seven vertebrae of the spinal column, and there are many powerful muscles that support and move the head. In front, the neck region contains the pharynx and *trachea, and behind these the oesophagus. The large arteries (carotid, temporal, maxillary) and veins (jugular) that supply the brain and head are also located in the neck. The *larynx (voice box) occupies a position where the trachea connects with the pharynx, and one of its cartilages produces the projection known as Adam's apple. The *thyroid gland lies just below the larynx and in front of the upper part of the trachea.

nectar sugary liquid secreted by some plants from a nectary, a specialized gland usually situated near the base of the flower. Nectar often accumulates in special pouches or spurs, not always in the same location as the nectary. Nectar attracts insects, birds, bats, and other animals to the flower for *pollination and is the raw material used by bees in the production of honey.

nectarine smooth, shiny-skinned variety of *peach, usually smaller than other peaches and with firmer flesh. It arose from a natural variation of the original form.

needlefish any of a group of bony marine fishes with an elongated body and long jaws lined with many sharp teeth. They live in warm, tropical seas. (Family Belonidae.)

Nefertiti (*or* **Nofretete**) Queen of Egypt and wife of the pharaoh *Akhenaton.

negative number number less than zero. On a number line, any number to the left of zero is negative. Negative numbers are always written with a minus sign in front, for example, −6 is negative, 6 is positive. Scales often display negative numbers. On a temperature scale, 5 °C below freezing is −5 °C.

negative/positive in photography, a reverse image, which when printed is again reversed, restoring the original scene. It was invented by Fox *Talbot in about 1834.

Negev triangular desert region in southern Israel that tapers to the port of Elat, 120 km/75 mi wide at Beersheba, 13 km/8 mi at Elat; area 12,215 sq km/4,716 sq mi. It is fertile under irrigation, and minerals include oil and copper.

Nehru, Jawaharlal (1889–1964) Indian nationalist politician, prime minister from 1947 until his death. Before the partition (the division of British India into India and Pakistan), he led the socialist wing of the nationalist *Congress Party, and was second in influence only to Mahatma Gandhi. He was imprisoned nine times by the British 1921–45 for political activities. As prime minister from the creation of the dominion (later republic) of India in August 1947, he originated the idea of non-alignment (neutrality towards major powers). His daughter was Prime Minister Indira Gandhi. His sister, Vijaya Lakshmi Pandit was the UN General Assembly's first female president 1953–54.

Nelson, Horatio (1758–1805) 1st Viscount Nelson, English admiral. He joined the navy in 1770 at the age of 12. During the Revolutionary Wars against France he lost the sight in his right eye in 1794, and lost his right arm in 1797. He became a rear admiral and a national hero after the victory off Cape St Vincent, Portugal. In 1798 he tracked the French fleet to the Egyptian seaport of Aboukir Bay where he almost entirely destroyed it at the Battle of *Aboukir Bay (also known as the Battle of the Nile). In 1801 he won a decisive victory over Denmark at the Battle of *Copenhagen, and in 1805, after two years of blockading Toulon, he defeated the Franco-Spanish fleet at the Battle of *Trafalgar, near Gibraltar. He was knighted in 1797, made a baron in 1798, and a viscount in 1801.

nematode any of a group of unsegmented *worms that are pointed at both ends, with a tough, smooth outer skin. They include many free-living species found in soil and water, including the sea, but a large number are parasites, such as the roundworms and pinworms that live in humans, or the eelworms that attack plant roots. They differ from *flatworms in that they have two openings to the gut (a mouth and an anus). The group includes *Caenorhabditis elegans* which is a model genetic organism and the first multicellular animal to have its complete genome sequenced. (Phylum Nematoda.)

Nemesis in late Greek mythology, the goddess of retribution, who especially punished hubris (Greek *hybris*), violent acts carried through in defiance of the gods and human custom.

neo- (Greek *neos* 'new') prefix used to indicate a revival or development of an older form, often in a different spirit. Examples include **neo-Marxism** and **neo-Darwinism**.

neoclassicism movement in art, architecture, and design in Europe and North America about 1750–1850, characterized by a revival of classical Greek and Roman styles. Leading figures of the movement were the architects Claude-Nicolas Ledoux and Robert *Adam; the painters Jacques-Louis *David, Jean *Ingres, and Anton Mengs; the sculptors Antonio Canova, John Flaxman, Bertel Thorvaldsen, and Johann Sergel; and the designers Josiah Wedgwood, George Hepplewhite, and Thomas Sheraton.

neocolonialism disguised form of *imperialism, by which a country may grant independence to another country but continue to dominate it by control of markets for goods or raw materials. Examples of countries that have used economic pressure to secure and protect their interests internationally are the USA and Japan.

neo-Darwinism modern theory of *evolution, built up since the 1930s by integrating the 19th-century English scientist Charles *Darwin's theory of evolution through natural selection with the theory of genetic inheritance founded on the work of the Austrian biologist Gregor *Mendel.

neodymium chemical symbol Nd, yellowish metallic element of the *lanthanide series, atomic number 60, relative atomic mass 144.24. Its rose-coloured salts are used in colouring glass, and neodymium is used in lasers.

neo-expressionism style of modern painting in which the artist handles the materials in a rough and raw way, typically expressing violent emotion. It developed in the late 1970s as a reaction against *conceptual art and *minimalism, and became a dominant force in avant-garde art during the 1980s, especially in the USA, Germany, and Italy. Pablo *Picasso's late paintings, which are often aggressively sexual in subject and almost frenzied in brushwork, were a major influence, although neo-expressionists also borrowed heavily from a wide range of sources and styles, from newspapers and novel covers to classical mythology. Neo-expressionist paintings often feature the human figure, but they are sometimes virtually abstract; what characterized the work was a return to traditional formats such as easel painting. In Italy neo-expressionism is sometimes known as the *Transavantgarde* ('beyond the avant-garde'), and German neo-expressionists are sometimes called *Neue Wilden* ('new wild ones'). Various alternative names have been used in the USA, including new fauvism, punk art, and bad painting (the latter because, in spite of the commercial success enjoyed by several exponents, many critics find the work crude and ugly, flaunting a lack of conventional skills).

Neo-Impressionism movement in French painting that developed from *Impressionism in the 1880s and flourished until the early years of the 20th century. The name was coined in 1886 in a review of the eighth and last Impressionist exhibition, held in Paris that year. Among the artists who exhibited there was Georges Seurat, who was the chief creator and outstanding exponent of Neo-Impressionism.

Neolithic literally 'New Stone', the last period of the *Stone Age. It was characterized by settled agricultural communities who kept domesticated animals, and made pottery and sophisticated, finely finished stone tools. The Neolithic period began and ended at different times in different parts of the world. For example, the earliest Neolithic communities appeared about 9000 BC in the Middle East, and were followed by those in Egypt, India, and China. In Europe farming began in about 6500 BC in the Balkans and Aegean Sea areas, spreading north and east by 1000 BC. The Neolithic period ended with the start of the *Bronze Age, when people began using metals. Some Stone Age cultures persisted into the 20th century, notably in remote parts of New Guinea.

neon chemical symbol Ne, (Greek *neos* 'new') colourless, odourless, non-metallic, gaseous element, atomic number 10, relative atomic mass 20.183. It is grouped with the *noble gases (rare gases) in Group 0 of the *periodic table. Neon is nonreactive, and forms no compounds. It occurs in small quantities in the Earth's atmosphere.

neo-Nazism the upsurge in racial and political intolerance in Eastern and Western Europe of the early 1990s. In Austria, Belgium, France, Germany, Russia, and Italy, the growth of extreme right-wing political groupings, coupled with racial violence, particularly in Germany, has revived memories of the Nazi period in Hitler's Germany. Ironically, the liberalization of politics in the post-Cold War world has unleashed anti-liberal forces hitherto checked by authoritarian regimes. The most significant parties in Western Europe described by the media as 'neo-nazi' were the National Front in France, led by Jean-Marie *Le Pen, and the National Alliance in Italy (although, by 1998, the National Alliance claimed to be a mainstream conservative party).

neoplasm (Greek 'new growth') any lump or tumour, which may be benign or malignant (cancerous).

neoplatonism school of philosophy that flourished during the declining centuries of the Roman Empire (3rd–6th centuries AD). Neoplatonists argued that the highest stage of philosophy is attained not through reason and experience, but through a mystical ecstasy. Many later philosophers, including Nicholas of Cusa, were influenced by neoplatonism.

Neo-Rationalism in architecture, a movement originating in Italy in the 1960s which rejected the functionalist and technological preoccupations of mainstream Modernism, advocating a rationalist approach to design based on an awareness of formal properties. It developed in the light of a re-evaluation of the work of Giuseppe Terragni led by Aldo Rossi, and gained momentum through the work of Giorgio Grassi (1935–). Characterized by elemental forms and an absence of detail, the style has adherents throughout Europe and the USA.

neo-realism movement in Italian cinema that emerged in the 1940s. It is characterized by its naturalism, social themes, frequent use of nonprofessional actors, and the visual authenticity achieved through location filming. Exponents include the directors Vittorio de Sica, Luchino Visconti, and Roberto Rossellini.

Nepal
National name: *Nepál Adhirajya/Kingdom of Nepal*

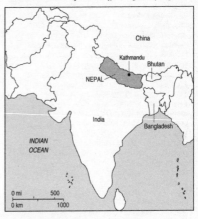

Area: 147,181 sq km/56,826 sq mi
Capital: Kathmandu
Major towns/cities: Moráng, Biratnagar, Lalitpur, Bhaktapur, Pokhara, Birganj
Physical features: descends from the Himalayas in the north through foothills to the River Ganges plain in the south; Mount Everest, Mount Kanchenjunga
Head of state: King Gyanendra Bir Bikram Shah Dev from 2001
Head of government: King Gyanendra Bir Bikram Shah Dev from 2005
Political system: emergent democracy
Political executive: parliamentary
Political parties: Nepali Congress Party (NCP), left of centre; United Nepal Communist Party (UNCP; Unified Marxist–Leninist), left wing; Rashtriya Prajatantra Party (RPP), monarchist
Currency: Nepalese rupee
GNI per capita (PPP): (US$) 1,350 (2002 est)
Exports: clothing, woollen carpets, hides and skins, food grains, jute goods, timber, toothpaste, oil seeds, ghee, potatoes, medicinal herbs, cattle. Principal market: India 47.7% (2001)
Population: 25,164,000 (2003 est)
Language: Nepali (official), Tibetan, numerous local languages
Religion: Hindu 90%; Buddhist 5%, Muslim 3%, Christian
Life expectancy: 60 (men); 60 (women) (2000–05)
Chronology
8th century BC: Kathmandu Valley occupied by Ahirs (shepherd kings), Tibeto-Burman migrants from northern India.
***c.* 563 BC:** In Lumbini in far south, Prince Siddhartha Gautama, the historic Buddha, was born.
AD 300: Licchavis dynasty immigrated from India and introduced caste system.
13th–16th centuries: Dominated by Malla dynasty, great patrons of the arts.
1768: Nepal emerged as a unified kingdom after the ruler of the principality of the Gurkhas in the west, King Prithwi Narayan Shah, conquered Kathmandu Valley.

1792: Nepal's expansion halted by defeat at the hands of Chinese in Tibet; commercial treaty signed with Britain.

1815–16: Anglo-Nepali 'Gurkha War'; Nepal became British-dependent buffer state with British resident stationed in Kathmandu.

1846: Fell under sway of Rana family, who became hereditary chief ministers, dominating powerless monarchy and isolating Nepal from outside world.

1923: Full independence formally recognized by Britain.

1951: Monarchy restored to power and Ranas overthrown in 'palace revolution' supported by Nepali Congress Party (NCP).

1959: Constitution created an elected legislature.

1960–61: Parliament dissolved by King Mahendra; political parties banned after NCP's pro-India socialist leader B P Koirala became prime minister.

1962: New constitution provided for tiered, traditional system of indirectly elected local councils (*panchayats*) and an appointed prime minister.

1972: King Mahendra died; succeeded by his son, King Birendra Bikram Shah Dev.

1980: A constitutional referendum was held, following popular agitation led by B P Koirala, resulted in the introduction of direct, but nonparty, elections to the National Assembly.

1983: The monarch-supported prime minister was overthrown by directly elected deputies to the National Assembly.

1986: New assembly elections returned a majority opposed to the *panchayat* system of partyless government.

1988: Strict curbs were placed on opposition activity; over 100 supporters of the banned NCP were arrested, and censorship was imposed.

1989: A border blockade was imposed by India during a treaty dispute.

1990: The *panchayat* system collapsed after mass NCP-led violent pro-democracy demonstrations; a new democratic constitution was introduced, and the ban on political parties lifted.

1991: The Nepali Congress Party, led by Girija Prasad Koirala, won the general election.

1992: Communists led antigovernment demonstrations in Kathmandu and Pátan.

1994: Koirala's government was defeated on a no-confidence motion; parliament was dissolved. A minority communist government was formed under Man Mohan Adhikari.

1995: Parliament was dissolved by King Birendra at Prime Minister Adhikari's request; fresh elections were called but the Supreme Court ruled the move unconstitutional.

1996: Maoist guerillas began a violent insurgency aimed at overthrowing the government.

1998: Krishna Prasad Bhattarai became prime minister and formed a new coalition government. A declared priority was to end the Maoist insurgency.

2000: A vote of no confidence in Bhattarai led to his replacement by Girija Prasad Koirala. Secret unofficial talks with the Maoist guerillas began, but were broken off.

2001: King Birendra and eight other members of the royal family were shot dead by Crown Prince Dipendra. However, Dipendra, who was briefly named the new king, died in hospital three days later from self-inflicted wounds. Gyanendra, Birendra's brother, was subsequently crowned.

2002: In the ongoing Maoist rebellion against the constitutional monarchy, more than 150 people were killed in Mangelsen in the far west of the country. In response a government offensive targetted rebel bases, killing more than 150 insurgents.

2003: Maoist insurgents and the government agreed a ceasefire designed to lead to peace talks. The talks ended in political stalemate, with a resurgence of violence.

2004: Nepal joined the World Trade Organization. The royalist prime minister, Surya Bahadur Thapa, resigned and King Gyanendra reappointed Sher Bahadur Deuba as prime minister. Maoist rebels staged several blockades of Kathmandu, stopping supplies from reaching the city.

2005: The king dismissed the prime minister and his government, assumed direct power and called a three month state of emergency.

nephritis *or* **Bright's disease** general term used to describe inflammation of the kidney. The degree of illness varies, and it may be acute (often following a recent streptococcal infection), or chronic, requiring a range of treatments from antibiotics to *dialysis or transplant.

nephron microscopic unit in vertebrate kidneys that forms urine. A human kidney is composed of over a million nephrons. Each nephron consists of a knot of blood capillaries called a glomerulus, contained in the Bowman's capsule, and a long narrow tubule enmeshed with yet more capillaries. Waste materials and water pass from the bloodstream into the tubule, and essential minerals and some water are reabsorbed from the tubule back into the bloodstream. The remaining filtrate (urine) is passed out from the body.

Neptune eighth planet in average distance from the Sun. It is a giant gas (hydrogen, helium, methane) planet, with a mass 17.2 times that of Earth. It has the fastest winds in the Solar System. **mean distance from the Sun:** 4.4 billion km/2.794 billion mi **equatorial diameter:** 48,600 km/30,200 mi **rotation period:** 16 hours 7 minutes **year:** 164.8 Earth years **atmosphere:** methane in its atmosphere absorbs red light and gives the planet a blue colouring. Consists primarily of hydrogen (85%) with helium (13%) and methane (1–2%) **surface:** hydrogen, helium, and methane. Its interior is believed to have a central rocky core covered by a layer of ice **satellites:** of Neptune's eight moons, two (*Triton and Nereid) are visible from Earth. Six more were discovered by the Voyager 2 probe in 1989, of which Proteus (diameter 415 km/260 mi) is larger than Nereid (300 km/200 mi) **rings:** there are four faint rings: Galle, Le Verrier, Arago, and Adams (in order from Neptune). Galle is the widest at 1,700 km/1,060 mi. Le Verrier and Arago are divided by a wide diffuse particle band called the plateau.

Neptune in Roman mythology, god of water, who became god of the sea only after his identification with the Greek *Poseidon.

neptunium chemical symbol Np, silvery, radioactive metallic element of the *actinide series, atomic number 93, relative atomic mass 237.048. It occurs in nature in minute amounts in *pitchblende and other uranium ores, where it is produced from the decay of neutron-bombarded uranium in these ores. The longest-lived isotope, Np-237, has a half-life of 2.2 million years. The element can be produced by bombardment of U-238 with neutrons and is chemically highly reactive.

Nereid in Greek mythology, any of 50 sea goddesses, or *nymphs, who sometimes mated with mortals. Their father was Nereus, a sea god, and their mother was Doris.

Nero (AD 37–68) adopted name of Lucius Domitius Ahenobarbus, Roman emperor from 54. In 59 he had his mother Agrippina and his wife Octavia put to death. The great fire at Rome in 64 was blamed on the Christians, whom he subsequently persecuted. In 65 a plot against Nero was discovered. Further revolts followed in 68, and he committed suicide.

Neruda, Pablo (1904–1973) pen-name of Neftalí Ricardo Reyes y Basoalto, Chilean poet and diplomat. His work includes lyrics and the epic poem of the American continent *Canto General* (1950). He was awarded the Nobel Prize for Literature in 1971. He served as consul and ambassador to many countries during the period 1927–44.

Nerva, Marcus Cocceius (AD c. 30–98) Roman emperor. He was proclaimed emperor on Domitian's death in AD 96, and introduced state loans for farmers, family allowances, and allotments of land to poor citizens in his sixteen-month reign.

nerve bundle of nerve cells enclosed in a sheath of connective tissue and transmitting nerve impulses to and from the brain and spinal cord. A single nerve may contain both *motor and sensory nerve cells, but they function independently.

nerve cell *or* **neuron** elongated cell that transmits information rapidly between different parts of the body, the basic functional unit of the *nervous system. Each nerve cell has a cell body, containing the nucleus, from which trail processes called dendrites, responsible for receiving incoming signals. The unit of information is the nerve impulse, a travelling wave of chemical and electrical changes involving the membrane of the nerve cell. The cell's longest process, the *axon, carries impulses away from the cell body. The *brain contains many nerve cells.

nervous breakdown popular term for a reaction to overwhelming psychological stress. There is no

equivalent medical term. People said to be suffering from a nervous breakdown may be suffering from a neurotic illness, such as depression or anxiety, or a psychotic illness, such as schizophrenia.

nervous system system of interconnected *nerve cells of most invertebrates and all vertebrates. It is composed of the *central and *autonomic nervous systems. It may be as simple as the nerve net of coelenterates (for example, jellyfishes) or as complex as the mammalian nervous system, with a central nervous system comprising *brain and *spinal cord and a peripheral nervous system connecting up with sensory organs, muscles, and glands.

Ness, Loch lake in the Highland unitary authority, Scotland, extending northeast to southwest. Forming part of the Caledonian Canal, it is 36 km/22.5 mi long, 2 km/1 mi wide (on average), 229 m/754 ft deep, and is the greatest expanse of fresh water in Europe. There have been unconfirmed reports of a Loch Ness monster since the 6th century.

nest place chosen or constructed by a bird or other animal for incubation of eggs, hibernation, and shelter. Nests vary enormously, from saucerlike hollows in the ground, such as the scrapes of hares, to large and elaborate structures, such as the 4 m/13 ft diameter mounds of the *megapode birds.

Nestorianism Christian doctrine held by the Syrian ecclesiastic Nestorius (died c. 451), patriarch of Constantinople 428–431. He asserted that Jesus had two natures, human and divine. He was banished for maintaining that Mary was the mother of the man Jesus only, and therefore should not be called the mother of God. Today the Nestorian Church is found in small communities in Syria, Iraq, Iran, and India.

netball game developed from basketball, played by two teams of seven players each on a hard court 30.5 m/100 ft long and 15.25 m/50 ft wide. At each end is a goal, consisting of a post 3.05 m/10 ft high, at the top of which is attached a circular hoop and net. The object of the game is to pass an inflated spherical ball through the opposing team's net. The ball is thrown from player to player; no contact is allowed between players, who must not run with the ball.

Netherlands Antilles two groups of Caribbean islands, overseas territories of the Netherlands with full

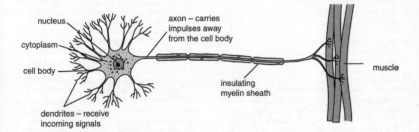

nerve cell The anatomy of a nerve cell. The nerve cell or neuron consists of a cell body with the nucleus and projections called dendrites which pick up messages. An extension of the cell, the axon, connects one cell to the dendrites of the next. When a nerve cell is stimulated, waves of sodium (Na^+) and potassium (K^+) ions carry an electrical impulse down the axon.

internal autonomy, comprising Curaçao and Bonaire off the coast of Venezuela (Aruba is considered separately), and St Eustatius, Saba, and the southern part of St Maarten in the Leeward Islands, 800 km/500 mi to the northeast; area 797 sq km/308 sq mi; population (2001 est) 212,200. The capital is Willemstad on Curaçao. Oil from Venezuela is refined here. The leading industry is the refining of oil from Venezuela; other industries include the production of rum, petrochemicals, textiles, and electronic goods, while tourism is also important. Dutch is the official language, and Papiamento and English are also spoken.

Netherlands, The or Holland

National name: *Koninkrijk der Nederlanden/ Kingdom of the Netherlands*

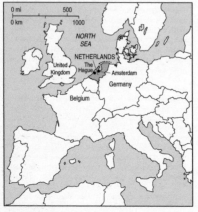

Area: 41,863 sq km/16,163 sq mi
Capital: Amsterdam (official), the Hague (legislative and judicial)
Major towns/cities: Rotterdam, Utrecht, Eindhoven, Groningen, Tilburg, Maastricht, Apeldoorn, Nijmegen, Breda
Major ports: Rotterdam
Physical features: flat coastal lowland; rivers Rhine, Schelde, Maas; Frisian Islands
Territories: Aruba, Netherlands Antilles (Caribbean)
Head of state: Queen Beatrix Wilhelmina Armgard from 1980
Head of government: Jan Peter Balkenende from 2002
Political system: liberal democracy
Political executive: parliamentary
Political parties: Christian Democratic Appeal (CDA), Christian, right of centre; Labour Party (PvdA), democratic socialist, left of centre; People's Party for Freedom and Democracy (VVD), liberal, free enterprise; Democrats 66 (D66), ecologist, centrist; Political Reformed Party (SGP), moderate Calvinist; Evangelical Political Federation (RPF), radical Calvinist; Reformed Political Association (GPV), fundamentalist Calvinist; Green Left, ecologist; General League of the Elderly (AOV), pensioner-oriented
Currency: euro (guilder until 2002)
GNI per capita (PPP): (US$) 27,470 (2002 est)

Exports: machinery and transport equipment, foodstuffs, live animals, petroleum and petroleum products, natural gas, chemicals, plants and cut flowers, plant-derived products. Principal market: Germany 26% (2001)
Population: 16,149,000 (2003 est)
Language: Dutch (official)
Religion: atheist 39%, Roman Catholic 31%, Dutch Reformed Church 14%, Calvinist 8%
Life expectancy: 76 (men); 81 (women) (2000–05)
Chronology
55 BC: Julius Caesar brought lands south of River Rhine under Roman rule.
4th century AD: Region overrun by Franks and Saxons.
7th–8th centuries: Franks subdued Saxons north of Rhine and imposed Christianity.
843–12th centuries: Division of Holy Roman Empire: the Netherlands repeatedly partitioned, not falling clearly into either French or German kingdoms.
12th–14th centuries: Local feudal lords, led by count of Holland and bishop of Utrecht, became practically independent; Dutch towns became prosperous trading centres, usually ruled by small groups of merchants.
15th century: Low Countries (Holland, Belgium, and Flanders) came under rule of dukes of Burgundy.
1477: Low Countries passed by marriage to Habsburgs.
1555: The Netherlands passed to Spain upon division of Habsburg domains.
1568: Dutch rebelled under leadership of William the Silent, Prince of Orange, and fought a long war of independence.
1579: Union of Utrecht: seven northern rebel provinces formed United Provinces.
17th century: 'Golden Age': Dutch led world in trade, art, and science, and founded colonies in East and West Indies, primarily through Dutch East India Company, founded in 1602.
1648: Treaty of Westphalia: United Provinces finally recognized as independent Dutch Republic.
1652–54: Commercial and colonial rivalries led to naval war with England.
1652–72: Johann de Witt ruled Dutch Republic as premier after conflict between republicans and House of Orange.
1665–67: Second Anglo-Dutch war.
1672–74: Third Anglo-Dutch war.
1672: William of Orange became stadholder (ruling as chief magistrate) of the Dutch Republic, an office which became hereditary in the Orange family.
1672–78: The Netherlands fought to prevent domination by King Louis XIV of France.
1688–97 and 1701–13: War with France resumed.
18th century: Exhausted by war, the Netherlands ceased to be a Great Power.
1795: Revolutionary France conquered the Netherlands and established Batavian Republic.
1806: Napoleon made his brother Louis king of Holland.
1810: France annexed the Netherlands.
1815: Northern and southern Netherlands (Holland and Belgium) unified as Kingdom of the Netherlands under King William I of Orange, who also became grand duke of Luxembourg.
1830: Southern Netherlands rebelled and declared independence as Belgium.
1848: Liberal constitution adopted.

1890: Queen Wilhelmina succeeded to throne; dynastic link with Luxembourg broken.

1894–96: Dutch suppressed colonial revolt in Java.

1914–18: The Netherlands neutral during World War I.

1940–45: Occupied by Germany during World War II.

1948: The Netherlands formed Benelux customs union with Belgium and Luxembourg; Queen Wilhelmina abdicated in favour of her daughter Juliana.

1949: Became a founding member of the North Atlantic Treaty Organization (NATO); most of Dutch East Indies became independent as Indonesia after four years of war.

1953: Dykes breached by storm; nearly two thousand people and tens of thousands of cattle died in flood.

1954: Remaining Dutch colonies achieved internal self-government.

1958: The Netherlands became a founding member of the European Economic Community (EEC).

1963: The Dutch colony of Western New Guinea was ceded to Indonesia.

1975: Dutch Guiana became independent as Suriname.

1980: Queen Juliana abdicated in favour of her daughter Beatrix.

1994: Following an inconclusive general election, a three-party coalition was formed under PvdA leader Wim Kok.

1999: The coalition government resigned in May after the smallest party, Democrats 66 (D-66), withdrew.

2000: The Netherlands became the first country to legalize euthanasia.

2001: The country became the first to legalize homosexual marriages.

2002: The government resigned in response to a critical report on the inaction of Dutch peacekeeping troops in the Bosnian town of Srebrenica where a massacre of Muslims took place during the Balkan war in 1995. Pim Fortuyn, a far-right populist Dutch politician, was assassinated in Hilversum. His party, List Pim Fortuyn (LPF; Pim Fortuyn List) came second in general elections, but the subsequent ruling coalition collapsed after only four months.

2003: The governing centre-right Christen-Democratisch Appèl (CDA; Christian Democratic Appeal) narrowly defeated a revived PvdA in parliamentary elections. The far-right LPF slumped from 26 to eight seats. The International Criminal Court was formally inaugurated in The Hague.

2004: Queen Mother Juliana died, aged 94. Large protests were held against public spending cuts and welfare reforms.

nettle any of a group of weedy plants with stinging hairs on oval, tooth-edged leaves; the hairs contain nerve poisons that penetrate the skin and cause a rash. The flowers are small and greenish, carried on spikes emerging at the same point where the leaves join the stem. The common nettle (*U. dioica*) grows on waste ground in Europe and North America, where it was introduced. (Genus *Urtica*, family Urticaceae.)

network in computing, a method of connecting computers so that they can share data and peripheral devices, such as printers. The main types are classified by the pattern of the connections – star or ring network, for example – or by the degree of geographical spread allowed; for example, local area networks (LANs) for communication within a room or building, and wide area networks (WANs) for more remote systems. The Internet is the linking of computer networks of institutions throughout the world: by 2004, there were about 650 million users.

neuralgia sharp or burning pain originating in a nerve and spreading over its area of distribution. Trigeminal neuralgia, a common form, is a severe pain on one side of the face.

neurology medical speciality concerned with the study and treatment of disorders of the brain, spinal cord, and peripheral nerves.

neuron another name for a *nerve cell.

neurosis in psychology, a general term referring to emotional disorders, such as anxiety, depression, and phobias. The main disturbance tends to be one of mood; contact with reality is relatively unaffected, in contrast to *psychosis.

neurotransmitter chemical that diffuses across a *synapse, and thus transmits impulses between *nerve cells, or between nerve cells and effector organs (for example, muscles). Common neurotransmitters are noradrenaline (which also acts as a hormone) and acetylcholine, the latter being most frequent at junctions between nerve and muscle. Nearly 50 different neurotransmitters have been identified.

neutrality the legal status of a country that decides not to choose sides in a war. Certain states, notably Switzerland and Austria, have opted for permanent neutrality. Neutrality always has a legal connotation. In peacetime, neutrality towards the big power alliances is called **non-alignment** (see *non-alignedmovement).

neutralization in chemistry, a process occurring when the excess acid (or excess base) in a substance is reacted with added base (or added acid) so that the resulting substance is neither acidic nor basic.

neutrino in physics, any of three uncharged *elementary particles (and their antiparticles) of the *lepton class, having a mass that is very small (possibly zero). The most familiar type, the antiparticle of the electron neutrino, is emitted in the beta decay of a nucleus. The other two are the muon and tau neutrinos.

neutron one of the three main subatomic particles, the others being the *proton and the *electron. Neutrons have about the same mass as protons but no electric charge, and occur in the nuclei of all atoms except hydrogen. They contribute to the mass of atoms but do not affect their chemistry.

neutron bomb *or* **enhanced radiation weapon** small hydrogen bomb for battlefield use that kills by radiation, with minimal damage to buildings and other structures. See *nuclear warfare.

neutron star very small, 'superdense' star composed mostly of *neutrons. They are thought to form when massive stars explode as *supernovae, during which the protons and electrons of the star's atoms merge, owing to intense gravitational collapse, to make neutrons. A neutron star has a mass two to three times that of the Sun, compressed into a globe only 20 km/ 12 mi in diameter.

Nevada called the **Sagebrush State** or the **Silver State**, (Spanish *nevada* 'snow-capped') state in southwestern USA, one of the Rocky Mountain states, bordered to the east by *Utah and *Arizona, to the south and west by *California, and to the north by *Oregon and *Idaho; area 284,448 sq km/109,826 sq mi; population

(2000) 1,998,300; capital Carson City. Physically stark, mountainous, and arid, its nicknames derive from the abundance of sagebrush shrubs and silver mines. Most of Nevada lies in the Great Basin between the Wasatch Mountains to the east and the *Sierra Nevada mountains, for which the state is named, to the west. The *Mojave Desert lies to the south. Nevada is a famous gambling and entertainment centre, and is also known historically as the state where marriages and divorces can be quickly obtained. The discovery of gold and silver in the 19th century created Nevada's first boom period, and mining and cattle ranching dominated the state's economy until 1931 when gambling was legalized; tourism and related industries now generate more than half of the state's income. Over 80% of the land is owned by the US government, much of it being given over to wilderness areas and weapons testing sites. *Las Vegas is Nevada's largest city. Other major towns and cities include Reno, Sparks, and Henderson. Nevada's indigenous peoples include the Shoshone, Washoe, and Paiute. The region was claimed by Spain in the mix-16th century and ceded to the USA after the *Mexican War (1846–48). Nevada was admitted to the Union in 1864 as the 36th US state.

new age movement of the late 1980s characterized by an emphasis on the holistic view of body and mind, alternative (or complementary) medicines, personal growth therapies, and a loose mix of theosophy, ecology, oriental mysticism, and a belief in the dawning of an astrological age of peace and harmony.

New Britain largest island in the *Bismarck Archipelago, part of Papua New Guinea; capital Rabaul; population (1995 est) 285,000. It has an area of 37,800 sq km/14,600 sq mi, an average width of 80 km/50 mi and is 482 km/300 mi long. The highest mountain is Mount Sinewit, 2,438 m/7,999 ft. Copra is the chief product; coffee, cocoa, palm oil, timber, and iron ore also produced. Gold, copper, and coal are mined. The population is Melanesian.

New Brunswick largest of the three Maritime Provinces of eastern Canada; area 73,400 sq km/28,332 sq mi; population (2001 est) 787,100; 33% French-speaking; 52% rural inhabitants. It is bounded on the north by Québec, with the Matapédia and Restigouche rivers forming part of the border; in the northeast Chaleur Bay separates New Brunswick's north shore from Québec's Gaspé Peninsula. Off its eastern coast is the Gulf of St Lawrence and in the southeast the Northumberland Strait, on the far side of which lies Prince Edward Island. Nova Scotia province is situated to its south and southeast, across the Bay of Fundy and the narrow land bridge known as the Chignecto Isthmus. To the southwest lies the US state of Maine, with the Saint John and Saint Croix rivers forming parts of the boundary. The capital of the province is Fredericton, and Saint John and Moncton are other towns.

New Caledonia French **Nouvelle Calédonie**, island group in the South Pacific, a French overseas territory between Australia and the Fiji Islands; area 18,576 sq km/7,170 sq mi; population (2001 est) 204,900. The capital, largest city and chief port is Nouméa. The islands are surrounded by a barrier reef, and are the world's third-largest producer of nickel. Other industries include chrome, iron, chlorine, oxygen, and cement works; agricultural products include beef, pork, coffee, and maize; tourism is also an important industry. The currency used is the CFP franc. French is the official language, although English is widely spoken. 60% of the population are Roman Catholic, and 30% are Protestant.

Newcastle industrial city and port in New South Wales, Australia, on the Hunter River, 157 km/98 mi north of Sydney; population (1996) 270,324. Newcastle is the second-largest city in the state after Sydney, and is dependent mainly on coalmining and alumina production. Other industries include shipbuilding and the manufacture of electronic equipment, textiles, chemicals, fertilizers, and wine products. Newcastle has a university (1965).

Newcastle, Thomas Pelham-Holles, 1st Duke of Newcastle (1693–1768) British Whig politician, prime minster 1754–56 and 1757–62. He served as secretary of state for 30 years from 1724, then succeeded his younger brother, Henry *Pelham, as prime minister in 1754. In 1756 he resigned as a result of setbacks in the Seven Years' War, but returned to office in 1757 with *Pitt the Elder (1st Earl of Chatham) taking responsibility for the conduct of the war. He was made an earl in 1714, and a duke in 1715.

Newcastle upon Tyne city and metropolitan borough in Tyne and Wear in northeast England on the River Tyne opposite Gateshead, 17 km/10 mi from the North Sea; population (1999 est) 273,000. It is the administrative centre of Tyne and Wear and a centre for retail, commerce, communications, and the arts. Newcastle first began to trade in coal in the 13th century, and was an important centre for coal and ship-building until the 1980s. Other industries include engineering (including offshore technology), food processing, brewing, and the manufacture of electronics. Only 1% of the workforce is now in heavy industry, 80% are in the public or service sectors.

New Deal in US history, the programme introduced by President Franklin D Roosevelt in 1933 to tackle the Great Depression, including employment on public works, farm loans at low rates, and social reforms such as old-age and unemployment insurance, prevention of child labour, protection of employees against unfair practices by employers, and loans to local authorities for slum clearance.

New Delhi capital of India, situated in the north of the country on the Yamuna River in the Union Territory of *Delhi; population (2001 est) 294,800. It lies near the old city of *Delhi, some 5 km/3 mi south of the Red Fort. Predominantly an administrative centre, it also produces chemicals, textiles, machine tools, electrical goods, and footwear.

New Democratic Party (NDP) Canadian political party, moderately socialist, formed in 1961 by a merger of the Labour Congress and the Cooperative Commonwealth Federation. Its leader is Alexa McDonough.

New Economic Policy (NEP) economic policy of the USSR 1921–29 devised by the Soviet leader Vladimir Ilyich *Lenin. Rather than requisitioning all agricultural produce above a stated subsistence allowance, the state requisitioned only a fixed proportion of the surplus; the rest could be traded freely by the peasant. The NEP thus reinstated a limited form of free-market trading, although the state retained complete control of major industries.

New England region of northeast USA, comprising the states of Maine, New Hampshire, Vermont, Massachusetts, Rhode Island, and Connecticut; population (2000 est) 13,922,500. It is a geographic region rather than a political entity, with an area of 172,681 sq km/66,672 sq mi. Boston is the principal urban centre of the region, and Harvard and Yale are its major universities. First inhabited by the American Indian Algonquin peoples, New England was named by the explorer John Smith in 1614, and settled by Pilgrims and Puritans from England in the 17th century.

New Forest ancient forest in southwest Hampshire, southern England, and the largest stretch of semi-natural vegetation in lowland Britain. Lying between the River Avon on the west and Southampton Water on the east, its legal boundary encloses 38,000 ha/93,898 acres (1995). Of this area 8,400 ha/20,756 acres is enclosed plantation, and 20,000 ha/49,420 acres is common land, including ancient woodland, heath, grassland, and bog. The remainder is privately owned land and villages. More than six million tourists visit annually.

Newfoundland breed of large, gentle dog said to have originated in Newfoundland, Canada. Males can grow to 70 cm/27.5 in tall, and weigh 65 kg/145 lb; the females are slightly smaller. They have a dense, flat coat, usually dull black, and an oily, water-repellent undercoat, and they are excellent swimmers.

Newfoundland officially **Newfoundland and Labrador**, Canadian province on the Atlantic Ocean, the country's most easterly administrative region, comprising the island of *Newfoundland and mainland *Labrador, separated by the Strait of Belle Isle; area 405,700 sq km/156,600 sq mi; population (2001 est) 533,800. It is bounded on the west by Québec, while to the southwest lie the Gulf of St Lawrence and the provinces of Nova Scotia and Prince Edward Island. The capital is St John's, and other towns and cities are Corner Brook, Gander, and Goose Bay (Labrador). Industries include offshore oil extraction; fishing and fish-processing; mining (iron, copper, zinc, and uranium); wood-processing and paper manufacture; and hydroelectric power generation. The information technology industry is increasingly important in the St John's area.

New Guinea island in the southwest Pacific, north of Australia, comprising Papua New Guinea and the Indonesian province of *Irian Jaya; total area about 885,780 sq km/342,000 sq mi. Part of the Dutch East Indies from 1828, West Irian was ceded by the United Nations to Indonesia in 1963 and renamed Irian Jaya ('victorious Irian') in 1973.

New Hampshire called the **Granite State**, state in the USA, one of the *New England states, one of the original *Thirteen Colonies, and one of the smallest US states; bordered to the north by the Canadian province of *Québec, to the east by *Maine and the Atlantic Ocean, to the south by *Massachusetts, and to the west by *Vermont; area 23,227 sq km/8,968 sq mi; population (2000) 1,235,800; capital Concord. New Hampshire is known as the Granite State owing to its high concentration of granite deposits. Other nicknames include Mother of Rivers, after the many New England rivers that originate in New Hampshire's mountains; the White Mountain State, after the White Mountain range; and the Switzerland of America, after the state's mountain scenery. The state is named after the county of Hampshire in England. The White Mountains in the north of the state are rugged and heavily forested, with picturesque gorges and ravines. The central rolling uplands are characterized by a large number of lakes and streams, and there is a short, rocky length of Atlantic coastline in the southeast. The economy is based on service industries and tourism, with the manufacture of industrial machinery and computer equipment also providing significant income. Agricultural produce includes greenhouse products, hay, and apples. Manchester is the largest city, and other major cities include Nashua, Derry, Rochester, Salem, Dover, Merrimack, Londonderry, and Hudson. New Hampshire was admitted to the Union in 1788 as the ninth US state.

New Hebrides former name (to 1980) of Vanuatu, a country in the South Pacific.

New Jersey called the **Garden State**, state in the Middle Atlantic region of the USA, bordered to the east by the Atlantic Ocean, with the *Hudson River forming a natural boundary to the northeast and north, beyond which lies *New York State; the Delaware River borders to the south, and Delaware Bay and the state of *Delaware lie beyond it; bordered to the west by *Pennsylvania; area 19,210 sq km/7,417 sq mi; population (2000) 8,414,400; capital Trenton. It is named after an early landowner's birthplace, the English Channel Island of Jersey. Its nickname derives from its historical role as an important agricultural region serving New York. The fifth smallest US state, New Jersey lies largely in the Atlantic Coastal Plain, a region of rich soil. The Atlantic coastline is sandy and the Jersey shore extends for about 200 km/125 mi. Formerly a manufacturing and agricultural state, the New Jersey economy is dominated by tourism, finance, insurance, and construction. It is the leading US producer of chemicals; other important manufactured products are printed materials, photographic equipment, electronic and electrical equipment, cars, and aircraft parts. Agricultural products include vegetables, eggs, peaches, and blueberries. The largest city is Newark. Other cities and metropolitan areas include Jersey City, Paterson, Elizabeth, Edison Township, Woodbridge Township, Dover Township, Hamilton, and Camden. The region was originally home to the Delaware American Indians; it was colonized by the Dutch and then ceded to England before becoming one of the original *Thirteen Colonies. The state saw much fighting during the *American Revolution. New Jersey entered the Union in 1787 as the third US state.

newly industrialized country (NIC) country formerly classified as less developed, but which is becoming rapidly industrialized. The first wave of countries to be identified as newly industrializing included Hong Kong, South Korea, Singapore, and Taiwan. These countries underwent rapid industrial growth in the 1970s and 1980s, attracting significant financial investment, and are now associated with high-technology industries. More recently, Thailand,

645

China, and Malaysia have been classified as newly industrializing countries.

Newman, John Henry (1801–1890) English Roman Catholic theologian. While still an Anglican, he wrote a series of *Tracts for the Times*, which gave their name to the Tractarian Movement (subsequently called the *Oxford Movement) for the revival of Catholicism. He became a Catholic in 1845 and was made a cardinal in 1879. In 1864 his autobiography, *Apologia pro vita sua*, was published.

Newman, Paul (1925–) US actor and director. He was one of Hollywood's leading male stars of the 1960s and 1970s, in such films as *The Hustler* (1961), *Sweet Bird of Youth* (1962), *Hud* (1963), *Butch Cassidy and the Sundance Kid* (1969), and *The Sting* (1973). He won an Academy Award for *The Color of Money* (1986).

New Mexico called the **Land of Enchantment**, (Spanish/Aztec *nuevo* 'new', *mexitli* 'place of Mexitli', an Aztec god) state in southwestern USA, bordered in the north by *Colorado, to the east by *Oklahoma, to the east and south by *Texas, to the south by Mexico, and to the west by *Arizona; its northwest corner borders Arizona, Utah, and Colorado at the 'Four Corners'; area 314,311 sq km/121,356 sq mi; population (2000) 1,819,000; capital *Santa Fe, the oldest capital city in the USA. New Mexico is known for its rich heritage and stunningly diverse landscapes – all the major biomes of the world, with the exception of the tropical rainforest, are found in the state. The state's most important river is the Rio Grande. The service industry and tourism are important elements in the economy of New Mexico, as are agriculture, mining, and the manufacture of electronic equipment. Major towns and cities include Albuquerque, Las Cruces, Rio Rancho, and Roswell. The upper region of the Rio Grande was called Nuevo Mexico as early as 1561, becoming New Mexico after it was ceded to the USA following the *Mexican War (1846–48). Home to the Pueblo Indians, *Apache, and *Navajo peoples, the state still has many traces of its early history, from prehistoric artefacts and adobe dwellings (made of sun-dried earth bricks), to remnants of pre-Columbian and Spanish architecture, making it a major tourist destination. New Mexico was admitted to the Union in 1912 as the 47th US state.

New Model Army army created in 1645 by Oliver *Cromwell to support the cause of Parliament during the English *Civil War. It was characterized by organization and discipline. Thomas *Fairfax was its first commander.

New Orleans called 'the Big Easy', city and river port in southeast Louisiana, USA, on the Mississippi River, and the Gulf of Mexico; population (2000 est) 484,700. It is a commercial and manufacturing centre with shipbuilding, oil-refining, and petrochemical industries. Tourism is a major activity. New Orleans is regarded as the traditional birthplace of jazz, believed to have developed from the singing and voodoo rhythms of the weekly slave gatherings in Congo Square, during the 18th and 19th centuries. The city was founded by the French in 1718.

Newport unitary authority in south Wales, created in 1996 from part of the former county of Gwent. **area:** 190 sq km/73 sq mi **towns:** Newport (administrative headquarters) **physical:** rivers Usk Ebbw, Afon Llwyd, Wentwood Hills (309 m/1,014 ft) **features:** Legionary

Museum, fortress baths and Roman amphitheatre at Caerleon, Tregdegar House (17th century) and Park, Penhow Castle (12th century) **population:** (2001 est) 137,000.

New South Wales state of southeast Australia, including the dependency of Lord Howe Island; area 801,600 sq km/309,500 sq mi; population (2001 est) 6,609,300 (over half in the capital, *Sydney). It is the most populous of the Australian states, the population having more than doubled, especially in coastal areas, in the second half of the 20th century as immigration from South America, the Middle East and Asia, as well as Europe, increased substantially. At the same time, the hydroelectricity and irrigation waters of the Snowy Mountains Scheme fostered economic development, and coastal industries such as the iron and steel works of Newcastle and Wollongong expanded. The state is bounded by Queensland on the north, the Tasman Sea on the east, Victoria on the south, and South Australia on the west. Products include cereals, fruit, wine, sugar, tobacco, dairy products, meat, wool, gold, silver, copper, zinc, lead, coal, iron and steel, machinery, electrical appliances, cars, furniture, textiles and textile goods, hides and leather, tobacco, chemicals, paint, oil, paper, hydroelectric power from the Snowy River, mineral sands, glassware, timber, poultry, opals, fish and other seafood. Other towns and cities in the state are Newcastle, Wollongong, Wagga Wagga, Broken Hill, Goulburn, Bathurst, Armidale, Coffs Harbour, Albury, and Tamworth.

newspaper daily or weekly publication in the form of folded sheets containing news and comment. Newssheets became commercial undertakings after the invention of printing and were introduced in 1609 in Germany and 1616 in the Netherlands. In 1622 the first newspaper appeared in English, the *Weekly News*, edited by Nicholas Bourne and Thomas Archer. Improved *printing (steam printing in 1814, the rotary press in 1846 in the USA and in 1857 in the UK), newsprint (paper made from wood pulp), and a higher literacy rate (those able to read) led to the growth of newspapers. In the 20th century production costs fell with the introduction of new technology. The oldest national newspaper currently printed in the UK is *The Observer* (1791). The world's most widely-read newspaper is Japan's *Yomiuri Shimbun*, with a daily circulation of 10 million.

newt small *salamander found in Europe, Asia, northwestern Africa, and North America. (Family Salamandridae, order Urodela.)

New Testament the second part of the *Bible, recognized by the Christian church from the 4th century as sacred doctrine. Biblical scholars have credited the individual sections to various authors, whose main aim was to proclaim the message of Christian salvation. The New Testament consists of 27 books, containing Christian history, letters, and prophecies. It includes the *Gospels, which tell of the life and teachings of Jesus, the Acts of the Apostles, and the book of Revelation.

newton symbol N, SI unit of *force. A newton is defined as the amount of force needed to move an object of 1 kg so that it accelerates at 1 metre per second per second. It is also used as a unit of weight. The weight of a medium size (100 g/3 oz) apple is one newton.

Newton, Isaac (1642–1727) English physicist and mathematician who laid the foundations of physics as a modern discipline. During 1665–66, he discovered the binomial theorem, differential and integral *calculus, and that white light is composed of many colours. He developed the three standard laws of motion (*Newton's laws of motion) and the universal law of gravitation, set out in *Philosophiae naturalis principia mathematica* (1687), usually referred to as the *Principia*. He was knighted for his work in 1705.

Newton's laws of motion in physics, three laws that form the basis of Newtonian mechanics, describing the motion of objects. (1) Unless acted upon by an unbalanced force, a body at rest stays at rest, and a moving body continues moving at the same speed in the same straight line. (2) An unbalanced force applied to a body gives it an acceleration proportional to the force (and in the direction of the force) and inversely proportional to the mass of the body. (3) When a body A exerts a force on a body B, B exerts an equal and opposite force on A; that is, to every action there is an equal and opposite reaction.

Newton's rings in optics, an *interference phenomenon seen (using white light) as concentric rings of spectral colours where light passes through a thin film of transparent medium, such as the wedge of air between a large-radius convex lens and a flat glass plate. With monochromatic light (light of a single wavelength), the rings take the form of alternate light and dark bands. They are caused by interference (interaction) between light rays reflected from the plate and those reflected from the curved surface of the lens.

new town in the UK, centrally planned urban area. New towns such as Milton Keynes and Stevenage were built after World War II to accommodate the overspill from cities and large towns, notably London, at a time when the population was rapidly expanding and inner-city centres had either decayed or been destroyed. In 1976 the policy, which had been criticized for disrupting family groupings and local communities, destroying small shops and specialist industries, and furthering the decay of city centres, was abandoned.

New Wave French *nouvelle vague*, the work of certain French film-makers – Jean-Luc Godard and François Truffaut among them – who in the late 1950s and 1960s rebelled against conventionality, seeking instead a vital spontaneity. Their early modernist films proved to be hugely influential throughout Europe.

New World the Americas, so called by the first Europeans who reached them. The term also describes animals and plants of the Western hemisphere.

New York the most populous city in the USA, located on an inlet of the Atlantic Ocean in the far southeastern corner of *New York State; population (2000 est, excluding suburban metropolitan areas under separate administration) 8,008,300. New York is composed of five city boroughs that are also counties of New York State: *Manhattan (New York County); the Bronx (Bronx County); Queens (Queens County); Brooklyn (Kings County); and Staten Island (Richmond County). As well as being the main port in North America, New York is one of the world's principal commercial and cultural centres. The many industries and services operating here include banking and other financial activities, publishing and printing, the electronic media, advertising, clothing manufacture and the fashion industry, and the production of food, chemicals, machinery, and textiles. With its great diversity of cultural institutions, places of entertainment, and sightseeing opportunities, the city also attracts a large number of tourists each year. New York is also known as the 'Big Apple'.

New York called the **Empire State**, state in northeast USA, in the mid-Atlantic region, bordered by the Canadian states of *Ontario and *Québec to the north, by Lake *Ontario and Lake *Erie to the northwest and west, and by *Pennsylvania to the west and south; the east is bordered by *Connecticut, *Massachusetts, and *Vermont; in the southeast it faces *New Jersey across the lower *Hudson River; Long Island extends east from New York Bay into the Atlantic Ocean, with *Connecticut lying to the north across the Long Island Sound; area 122,284 sq km/47,214 sq mi; population (2000) 18,976,500; capital Albany. New York is named after England's Duke of York, and the state's nickname is a tribute to its vast wealth and wide range of resources. Physically, the state is varied, with many mountain ranges, including the *Adirondacks, *Catskills, and Taconic, and many lakes and rivers, including the Niagara River which flows into *Niagara Falls. Service industries, retail and wholesale trade, and tourism are important to New York's economy. The state ranks fourth in manufacturing; products include electrical equipment, chemicals, and clothing. Agriculturally, the dairy industry is important, and poultry, fruit, and vegetables are leading products. The largest city is *New York; other major cities and urban areas include Buffalo, Rochester, Yonkers, Syracuse, New Rochelle, Schenectady, Utica, and the New York City-northeastern New Jersey area east of Long Island and north along the Hudson Valley. The Algonquian and the Iroquoian peoples were the earliest inhabitants of the New York region. The area was explored by the French, English, and Dutch, with the first permanent settlement at Albany. New York City's harbour became the focus of the *Thirteen Colonies and saw some fighting during the *American Revolution. The harbour later became a gateway for many European immigrants; *Ellis Island, once the main immigration reception centre in the USA, and Liberty Island, where the Statue of Liberty is situated, both lie in the harbour. After the American *Civil War the state became an industrial giant. New York joined the Union in 1788 as the 11th state.

New Zealand

National name: *Aotearoa/New Zealand*
Area: 268,680 sq km/103,737 sq mi
Capital: Wellington
Major towns/cities: Auckland, Hamilton, Christchurch, Manukau, North Shore, Waitakere
Major ports: Auckland, Wellington
Physical features: comprises North Island, South Island, Stewart Island, Chatham Islands, and minor islands; mainly mountainous; Ruapehu in North Island, 2,797 m/9,180 ft, highest of three active volcanoes; geysers and hot springs of Rotorua district; Lake Taupo (616 sq km/238 sq mi), source of Waikato River; Kaingaroa state forest. In South Island are the Southern Alps and Canterbury Plains

New Zealand

Territories: Tokelau (three atolls transferred in 1926 from former Gilbert and Ellice Islands colony); Niue Island (one of the Cook Islands, separately administered from 1903: chief town Alafi); Cook Islands are internally self-governing but share common citizenship with New Zealand; Ross Dependency in Antarctica
Head of state: Queen Elizabeth II from 1952, represented by Governor General Silvia Cartwright from 2001
Head of government: Helen Clark from 1999
Political system: liberal democracy
Political executive: parliamentary
Political parties: Labour Party, moderate, left of centre; New Zealand National Party, free enterprise, right of centre; Alliance Party bloc, left of centre, ecologists; New Zealand First Party (NZFP), centrist; United New Zealand Party (UNZ), centrist
Currency: New Zealand dollar
GNI per capita (PPP): (US$) 20,020 (2002 est)
Exports: meat, dairy products, wool, fish, timber and wood products, fruit and vegetables, aluminium, machinery. Principal market: Australia 19% (2001)
Population: 3,875,000 (2003 est)
Language: English (official), Maori
Religion: Christian (Anglican 18%, Roman Catholic 14%, Presbyterian 13%)
Life expectancy: 76 (men); 81 (women) (2000–05)
Chronology
1642: Dutch explorer Abel Tasman reached New Zealand but indigenous Maori prevented him from going ashore.
1769: English explorer James Cook surveyed coastline of islands.
1773 and 1777: Cook again explored coast.
1815: First British missionaries arrived in New Zealand.
1826: New Zealand Company founded in London to establish settlement.
1839: New Zealand Company relaunched, after initial failure, by Edward Gibbon Wakefield.
1840: Treaty of Waitangi: Maori accepted British sovereignty; colonization began and large-scale sheep farming developed.
1845–47: Maori revolt against loss of land.
1851: Became separate colony (was originally part of the Australian colony of New South Wales).

1852: Colony procured constitution after dissolution of New Zealand Company; self-government fully implemented in 1856.
1860–72: Second Maori revolt led to concessions, including representation in parliament.
1891: New Zealand took part in Australasian Federal Convention in Sydney but rejected the idea of joining the Australian Commonwealth.
1893: Became the first country to give women the right to vote in parliamentary elections.
1898: Liberal government under Richard Seddon introduced pioneering old-age pension scheme.
1899–1902: Volunteers from New Zealand fought alongside imperial forces in Boer War.
1907: New Zealand achieved dominion status within British Empire.
1912–25: Government of Reform Party, led by William Massey, reflected interests of North Island farmers and strongly supported imperial unity.
1914–18: 130,000 New Zealanders fought for the British Empire in World War I.
1916: Labour Party of New Zealand established.
1931: Statute of Westminster affirmed equality of status between Britain and dominions, effectively granting independence to New Zealand.
1935–49: Labour governments of Michael Savage and Peter Fraser introduced social reforms and encouraged state intervention in industry.
1936: Liberal Party merged with Reform Party to create National Party.
1939–45: New Zealand troops fought in World War II, notably in Crete, North Africa, and Italy.
1947: Parliament confirmed independence of New Zealand within British Commonwealth.
1951: New Zealand joined Australia and USA in ANZUS Pacific security treaty.
1965–72: New Zealand contingent took part in Vietnam War.
1973: British entry into European Economic Community (EEC) forced New Zealand to seek closer trading relations with Australia.
1985: Non-nuclear military policy led to disagreements with France and USA.
1986: The USA suspended defence obligations to New Zealand after it banned the entry of US warships.
1988: A free-trade agreement was signed with Australia.
1991: The Alliance Party was formed to challenge the two-party system.
1998: The government was ordered to return more than £2 million worth of land confiscated from its Maori owners more than 30 years earlier.
1999: The conservative government was replaced by a centre-left coalition of the Labour Party and New Zealand Alliance, with Helen Clark, leader of the Labour Party, as the new prime minister.
2000: Dame Silvia Cartwright was named as next governor-general, to take office in April 2001, at which point all top political offices would be held by women.
2002: Helen Clark was re-elected prime minister, following the National Party's worst election result in 70 years.
2004: A proposal to nationalize the sea bed provoked intense debate and Maori protests. The government survived a vote of no confidence. New Zealand suspended high level contact with Israel, after two

Israelis jailed for trying to illegally obtain New Zealand passports were revealed as suspected Mossad agents. New Zealand and China began talks on a free trade agreement.

Ney, Michel (1769–1815) Duke of Elchingen, Prince of Ney, Marshal of France under *Napoleon I, who commanded the rearguard of the French army during the retreat from Moscow, and for his personal courage was called 'the bravest of the brave'. When Napoleon returned from Elba, Ney was sent to arrest him, but instead deserted to him and fought at Waterloo. He was subsequently shot for treason.

niacin one of the 'B group' vitamins; see *nicotinic acid.

Niagara Falls two waterfalls on the Niagara River, on the Canada–USA border, between lakes Erie and Ontario and separated by Goat Island. The **American Falls** are 56 m/183 ft high, 328 m/1,076 ft wide; the more spectacular **Horseshoe Falls**, in Canada, are 52 m/ 170 ft high, 675 m/2,215 ft across.

Niamey port, capital, and administrative centre of Niger, in the southwest of the country, on the northeast bank of the Niger River; population (1995 est) 495,000. It produces textiles, chemicals, pharmaceuticals, ceramics, plastics, and foodstuffs. It replaced Zinder as the capital in 1926. It has an international airport and railway terminus.

Nibelungenlied *Song of the Nibelung*, anonymous 12th-century German epic poem, derived from older sources. The composer Richard Wagner made use of the legends in his *Ring* cycle.

Nicaragua
National name: *República de Nicaragua/ Republic of Nicaragua*

Area: 127,849 sq km/49,362 sq mi
Capital: Managua
Major towns/cities: León, Chinandega, Masaya, Granada, Estelí
Major ports: Corinto, Puerto Cabezas, El Bluff
Physical features: narrow Pacific coastal plain separated from broad Atlantic coastal plain by volcanic mountains and lakes Managua and Nicaragua; one of the world's most active earthquake regions
Head of state and government: Enrique Bolaños Geyer from 2002

Political system: emergent democracy
Political executive: limited presidency
Political parties: Sandinista National Liberation Front (FSLN), Marxist–Leninist; Opposition Political Alliance (APO, formerly National Opposition Union: UNO), loose US-backed coalition
Currency: cordoba
GNI per capita (PPP): (US$) 1,970 (2002 est)
Exports: coffee, meat, cotton, sugar, seafood, bananas, chemical products. Principal market: USA 28.2% (2001)
Population: 5,466,000 (2003 est)
Language: Spanish (official), English, American Indian languages
Religion: Roman Catholic 95%
Life expectancy: 67 (men); 72 (women) (2000–05)
Chronology
10th century: Indians from Mexico and Mesoamerica migrated to Nicaragua's Pacific lowlands.
1522: Visited by Spanish explorer Gil Gonzalez de Avila, who named the area Nicaragua after local Indian chief, Nicarao.
1523–24: Colonized by the Spanish, under Francisco Hernandez de Cordoba, who was attracted by local gold deposits and founded the cities of Granada and León.
17th–18th centuries: Britain was the dominant force on the Caribbean side of Nicaragua, while Spain controlled the Pacific lowlands.
1821: Independence achieved from Spain; Nicaragua was initially part of Mexican Empire.
1823: Became part of United Provinces (Federation) of Central America, also embracing Costa Rica, El Salvador, Guatemala, and Honduras.
1838: Became fully independent when it seceded from the Federation.
1857–93: Ruled by succession of Conservative Party governments.
1860: The British ceded control over the Caribbean ('Mosquito') Coast to Nicaragua.
1893: Liberal Party leader, José Santos Zelaya, deposed the Conservative president and established a dictatorship which lasted until overthrown by US marines in 1909.
1912–25: At the Nicaraguan government's request, with the political situation deteriorating, the USA established military bases and stationed marines.
1927–33: Re-stationed US marines faced opposition from the anti-American guerrilla group led by Augusto César Sandino, who was assassinated in 1934 on the orders of the commander of the US-trained National Guard, Gen Anastasio Somoza Garcia.
1937: Gen Somoza was elected president; start of near-dictatorial rule by the Somoza family, which amassed a huge personal fortune.
1961: Left-wing Sandinista National Liberation Front (FSLN) formed to fight the Somoza regime.
1978: The Nicaraguan Revolution: Pedro Joaquin Chamorro, a popular publisher and leader of the anti-Somoza Democratic Liberation Union (UDEL), was assassinated, sparking a general strike and mass movement in which moderates joined with the FSLN to overthrow the Somoza regime.
1979: The Somoza government was ousted by the FSLN after a military offensive.
1980: A FSLN junta took power in Managua, headed by Daniel Ortega Saavedra; lands held by Somozas were nationalized and farming cooperatives established.

1982: There was subversive activity against the government by right-wing Contra guerrillas, promoted by the USA, attacking from bases in Honduras. A state of emergency was declared.

1984: US troops mined Nicaraguan harbours. The action was condemned by the World Court in 1986 and $17 billion in reparations ordered. FSLN won the assembly elections.

1985: The US president Ronald Reagan denounced the Sandinista government, vowing to 'remove it', and imposed a US trade embargo.

1987: A Central American peace agreement was cosigned by Nicaraguan leaders.

1988: The peace agreement failed. Nicaragua held talks with the Contra rebel leaders. A hurricane left 180,000 people homeless.

1989: Demobilization of rebels and release of former Somozan supporters; the ceasefire ended but the economy was in ruins after the Contra war; there was 60% unemployment.

1990: The FSLN was defeated by right-of-centre National Opposition Union (UNO), a US-backed coalition; Violeta Barrios de Chamorro, widow of the murdered Pedro Joaquin Chamorro, was elected president. There were antigovernment riots.

1992: Around 16,000 people were made homeless by an earthquake.

1994: A peace accord was made with the remaining Contra rebels.

1996: Right-wing candidate Arnoldo Aleman won the presidential elections.

1998: Daniel Ortega was re-elected FSLN leader.

2002: Enrique Bolaños became president.

2003: Nicaragua, together with Guatemala, Honduras and El Salvador, signed a free trade agreement with the US.

2004: The World Bank and Russia wrote off a large proportion of Nicaragua's debt.

2005: The US suspended some military aid after a dispute over the destruction of Nicaraguan missiles. Rises in the cost of living and fuel prices led to street protests.

Nicaragua, Lake lake in southwest Nicaragua, the largest in Central America; area 8,250 sq km/3,185 sq mi. It is 24 km/15 mi from the Pacific Ocean and drains into the Caribbean at San Juan del Norte via the Río San Juan. It is a freshwater lake inhabited by a variety of salt-water fish including shark and swordfish. The lake contains about 310 small islands, most of which are inhabited. The largest island, Ometepe, has two volcanoes: Concepción (1,610 m/5,282 ft), and Madera (1,394 m/4,573 ft). Lake Managua to the north drains into Lake Nicaragua via the River Tipitapa. The area is ecologically important for many rare and colourful birds.

Nicaraguan Revolution the revolt 1978–79 in Nicaragua, led by the socialist **Sandinistas** against the US-supported right-wing dictatorship established by Anastasio Somoza. His son, President Anastasio (Debayle) Somoza (1925–1980), was forced into exile in 1979 and assassinated in Paraguay. The Sandinista National Liberation Front (FSLN) was named after Augusto César Sandino, a guerrilla leader killed by the US-trained National Guard in 1934.

Nicene Creed one of the fundamental *creeds of Christianity, drawn up by the Council of Nicaea, a meeting of bishops in AD 325.

niche in ecology, the 'place' occupied by a species in its habitat, including all chemical, physical, and biological components, such as what it eats, the time of day at which the species feeds, temperature, moisture, the parts of the habitat that it uses (for example, trees or open grassland), the way it reproduces, and how it behaves.

Nicholas two tsars of Russia:

Nicholas I (1796–1855) tsar of Russia from 1825. His Balkan ambitions led to war with Turkey 1827–29 and the Crimean War 1853–56.

Nicholas II (1868–1918) tsar of Russia 1894–1917. He was dominated by his wife, Tsarina Alexandra, who was under the influence of the religious charlatan *Rasputin. His mismanagement of the Russo-Japanese War and of internal affairs led to the revolution of 1905, which he suppressed, although he was forced to grant limited constitutional reforms. He took Russia into World War I in 1914, was forced to abdicate in 1917 after the *Russian Revolution, and was executed with his family.

Nicholas, St (lived 4th century) also known as **Santa Claus**, In the Christian church, patron saint of Russia, children, merchants, sailors, and pawnbrokers; bishop of Myra (now in Turkey). His legendary gifts of dowries to poor girls led to the custom of giving gifts to children on the eve of his feast day, 6 December, still retained in some countries, such as the Netherlands; elsewhere the custom has been transferred to Christmas Day. His emblem is three balls.

Nicholson, Ben(jamin Lauder) (1894–1982) English abstract artist. After early experiments influenced by *cubism and the Dutch *De Stijl group, Nicholson developed an elegant style of geometrical reliefs, notably a series of white reliefs (1933–38). He won the first Guggenheim Award in 1957.

Nicholson, Jack (1937–) US film actor and director. He is known for his darkly comic portrayals of social outcasts. Films in which he has appeared include *One Flew Over the Cuckoo's Nest* (Academy Award, 1975), *The Shining* (1979), *Terms of Endearment* (Academy Award, 1983), *Batman* (1989), and *As Good As It Gets* (Academy Award, 1998). In 1994 Nicholson received the American Film Institute's life achievement award.

nickel chemical symbol Ni, hard, malleable and ductile, silver-white, metallic element, atomic number 28, relative atomic mass 58.71. It occurs in igneous rocks and as a free metal (*native metal), occasionally occurring in fragments of iron–nickel meteorites. It is a component of the Earth's core, which is held to consist principally of iron with some nickel. It has a high melting point, low electrical and thermal conductivity, and can be magnetized. It does not tarnish and therefore is much used for alloys, electroplating, and for coinage.

Nicklaus, Jack William (1940–) US golfer, nicknamed 'the Golden Bear' and widely regarded as the game's greatest ever player. He won a record 20 major titles, including 18 professional majors between 1962 and 1986. In 1999, the US magazine *Sports Illustrated* named him 'Best Individual Male Athlete of the 20th Century'. He played his last major championship in 2000.

Nicolle, Charles Jules Henri (1866–1936) French bacteriologist who was awarded a Nobel Prize for Physiology or Medicine in 1928 for his work on the role of the body louse in transmitting typhus. In 1909 he discovered that typhus is transmitted by the body louse and delousing was made a compulsory part of the military routine for the armies of World War I.

Nicosia Greek **Lefkosia**; Turkish **Lefkosha**, capital of Cyprus, with leather, textile, and pottery industries; population (1993) 177,000. Nicosia was the residence of Lusignan kings of Cyprus 1192–1475. The Venetians, who took Cyprus in 1489, surrounded Nicosia with a high wall, which still exists; the city fell to the Turks in 1571. It was again partly taken by the Turks in the invasion in 1974.

nicotine $C_{10}H_{14}N_2$, *alkaloid (nitrogenous compound) obtained from the dried leaves of the tobacco plant *Nicotiana tabacum*. A colourless oil, soluble in water, it turns brown on exposure to the air. Nicotine is found in tobacco smoke. It can be described as a recreational *drug. It stimulates the human body and produces feelings that cause people to carry on *smoking. However, nicotine is usually addictive (see *addiction). Regular smokers find that it is very difficult or impossible to give up smoking even though they may try to. This is a problem, in that other chemicals in the smoke cause a wide range of diseases and increase the risk of dying early. Nicotine has also been used as an insecticide.

nicotinic acid *or* **niacin** water-soluble *vitamin ($C_5H_5N.COOH$) of the B complex, found in meat, fish, and cereals; it can also be formed in small amounts in the body from the essential *amino acid tryptophan. Absence of nicotinic acid from the diet leads to the disease *pellagra.

Nielsen, Carl August (1865–1931) Danish composer. His works combine an outward formal strictness with an inner waywardness of tonality and structure, best exemplified by his six programmatic symphonies 1892–1925.

Niemeyer, (Soares Filho) Oscar (1907–) Brazilian architect. He was joint designer of the United Nations headquarters in New York in 1947 and from 1957 architect of many public buildings in the capital, Brasília. His idiosyncratic interpretation of the modernist idiom uses symbolic form to express the function of a building; for example, the Catholic cathedral in Brasília.

Nietzsche, Friedrich Wilhelm (1844–1900) German philosopher who rejected the accepted absolute moral values and the 'slave morality' of Christianity. He argued that 'God is dead' and therefore people were free to create their own values. His ideal was the *Übermensch*, or 'Superman', who would impose his will on the weak and worthless. Nietzsche claimed that knowledge is never objective but always serves some interest or unconscious purpose.

Niger Semitic **Nihal**, third-longest river in Africa, 4,185 km/2,600 mi. It rises in the highlands bordering Sierra Leone and Guinea, flows northeast through Mali, then southeast through Niger and Nigeria to an inland delta on the Gulf of Guinea. Its total catchment area is 1.5 million sq km/579,150 sq mi. The flow is sluggish and the river frequently floods its banks. It was navigated by the Scottish explorer Mungo Park 1795–1806, who was drowned in the river near Bussa.

Niger
National name: *République du Niger/Republic of Niger*

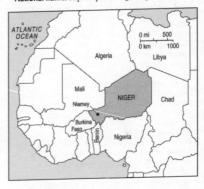

Area: 1,186,408 sq km/458,072 sq mi
Capital: Niamey
Major towns/cities: Zinder, Maradi, Tahoua, Agadez, Birnin Konni, Arlit
Physical features: desert plains between hills in north and savannah in south; River Niger in southwest, Lake Chad in southeast
Head of state: Mamadou Tandja from 1999
Head of government: Hama Amadou from 2000
Political system: military
Political executive: military
Political parties: National Movement for a Development Society (MNSD–Nassara), left of centre; Alliance of the Forces for Change (AFC), left-of-centre coalition; Party for Democracy and Socialism–Tarayya (PNDS–Tarayya), left of centre
Currency: franc CFA
GNI per capita (PPP): (US$) 770 (2002 est)
Exports: uranium ore, live animals, hides and skins, cow-peas, cotton. Principal market: France 33.5% (2000)
Population: 11,972,000 (2003 est)
Language: French (official), Hausa (70%), Djerma, other ethnic languages
Religion: Sunni Muslim 95%; also Christian, and traditional animist beliefs
Life expectancy: 46 (men); 47 (women) (2000–05)
Chronology
10th–13th centuries: Kanem-Bornu Empire flourished in southeast, near Lake Chad, spreading Islam from the 11th century.
15th century: Tuareg sultanate of Agades dominant in the north.
17th century: Songhai-speaking Djerma established an empire on Niger River.
18th century: Powerful Gobir kingdom founded by Hausa people, who had migrated from the south in the 14th century.
late 18th–early 19th centuries: Visited by European explorers, including the Scottish explorer, Mungo Park; Sultanate of Sokoto formed by Islamic revivalist Fulani, who had defeated the Hausa in a jihad (holy war).
1890s: French conquered the region and ended the local slave trade.

1904: Became part of French West Africa, although Tuareg resistance continued until 1922.

1946: Became French overseas territory, with its own territorial assembly and representation in the French parliament.

1958: Became an autonomous republic within the French community.

1960: Achieved full independence; Hamani Diori of Niger Progressive Party (NPP) elected president, but maintained close ties with France.

1971: Uranium production commenced.

1974: Diori was ousted in an army coup; the military government launched a drive against corruption.

1977: A cooperation agreement was signed with France.

1984: There was a partial privatization of state firms due to further drought and increased government indebtedness as world uranium prices slumped.

1989: Ali Saibu was elected president without opposition.

1991: Saibu was stripped of executive powers, and a transitional government was formed amid student and industrial unrest.

1992: The transitional government collapsed amid economic problems and ethnic unrest among secessionist Tuareg in the north. A referendum approved of a new multiparty constitution.

1993: The Alliance of the Forces for Change (AFC), a left-of-centre coalition, won an absolute majority in assembly elections. Mahamane Ousmane, a Muslim Hausa, was elected president in the first free presidential election.

1994: A peace agreement was signed with northern Tuareg.

1996: President Ousmane was ousted in a military coup led by Ibrahim Barre Mainassara. Civilian government was restored with Boukary Adji as premier; Mainassara was formally elected president.

1997: Ibrahim Hassane Mayaki was appointed prime minister.

1999: President Mainassara was assassinated in a coup; Major Daouda Mallam Wanke, the commander of Niger's presidential guard, assumed power. In the elections which followed, Tandja Mamadou was elected president, and Hama Amadou was appointed prime minister.

2001: Niger outlawed hunting in order to protect its wildlife.

2003: A claim that Iraq tried to acquire uranium from Niger was disproved.

2004: In local elections, parties backing the president won most of the seats. President Tandja Mamadou was re-elected for a second term with 65.5% of the vote.

2005: A planned ceremony to free around 7,000 slaves was cancelled when the government stated that slavery did not exist in Niger.

Niger-Congo languages the largest group of languages in Africa. It includes about 1,000 languages and covers a vast area south of the Sahara desert, from the west coast to the east, and down the east coast as far as South Africa. It is divided into groups and subgroups; the most widely spoken Niger-Congo languages are Swahili (spoken on the east coast), the members of the Bantu group (southern Africa), and Yoruba (Nigeria).

Nigeria
   National name: *Federal Republic of Nigeria*

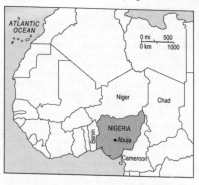

Area: 923,773 sq km/356,668 sq mi
Capital: Abuja
Major towns/cities: Ibadan, Lagos, Ogbomosho, Kano, Oshogbo, Ilorin, Abeokuta, Zaria, Port Harcourt
Major ports: Lagos, Port Harcourt, Warri, Calabar
Physical features: arid savannah in north; tropical rainforest in south, with mangrove swamps along coast; River Niger forms wide delta; mountains in southeast
Head of state and government: Olusegun Obasanjo from 1999
Political system: emergent democracy
Political executive: limited presidency
Political parties: political parties, suppressed by the military government, were allowed to form in July 1998. Three parties were registered: All People's Party (APP), right of centre; People's Democratic Party (PDP), left of centre; Alliance for Democracy (AD), left of centre
Currency: naira
GNI per capita (PPP): (US$) 780 (2002 est)
Exports: petroleum, cocoa beans, rubber, palm products, cotton and yarn, urea and ammonia, fish and shrimps. Principal market: USA 40.1% (2001)
Population: 124,009,000 (2003 est)
Language: English (official), Hausa, Ibo, Yoruba
Religion: Sunni Muslim 50% (in north), Christian 35% (in south), local religions 15%
Life expectancy: 51 (men); 52 (women) (2000–05)
Chronology
4th century BC–2nd century AD: Highly organized Nok culture flourished in northern Nigeria.
9th century: Northeast Nigeria became part of empire of Kanem-Bornu, based around Lake Chad.
11th century: Creation of Hausa states, including Kano and Katsina.
13th century: Arab merchants introduced Islam in the north.
15th century: Empire of Benin at its height in south; first contact with European traders.
17th century: Oyo Empire dominant in southwest; development of slave trade in Niger delta.
1804–17: Islamic Fulani (or Sokoto) Empire established in north.
1861: British traders procured Lagos; spread of Christian missionary activity in south.

1884–1904: Britain occupied most of Nigeria by stages.

1914: North and south protectorates united; growth of railway network and trade.

1946: Nigerians allowed a limited role in decision-making in three regional councils.

1951: The introduction of elected representation led to the formation of three regional political parties.

1954: New constitution increased powers of the regions.

1958: Oil discovered in the southeast.

1960: Achieved independence from Britain, within the Commonwealth.

1963: Became a republic, with Nnamdi Azikiwe as president.

1966: Gen Aguiyi-Ironsi of Ibo tribe seized power and imposed unitary government; massacre of Ibo by Hausa in north; Gen Gowon seized power and restored federalism.

1967: Conflict over oil revenues led to secession of eastern region as independent Ibo state of Biafra; ensuing civil war claimed up to a million lives.

1970: Surrender of Biafra and end of civil war; development of the oil industry financed more effective central government.

1975: Gowon ousted in military coup; second coup put Gen Olusegun Obasanjo in power.

1979: Civilian rule restored under President Shehu Shagari.

1983: A bloodless coup was staged by Maj-Gen Muhammadu Buhari.

1985: Buhari was replaced by Maj-Gen Ibrahim Babangida; Islamic northerners were dominant in the regime.

1992: Multiparty elections were won by Babangida's SDP.

1993: Moshood Abiola (SDP) won the first free presidential election; the results were suspended. Gen Sani Abacha restored military rule and dissolved political parties.

1995: Commonwealth membership was suspended in protest at human-rights abuses by the military regime.

1998: General Abdulsalam Abubakar took over as president. Nigeria's most prominent political prisoner, Moshood Abiola, died suddenly on the eve of his expected release. There were moves towards political liberalization, with the formation of new political parties and the release of some dissidents.

1999: The People's Democratic Party won a Senate majority. Olusegun Obasanjo was elected president. Nigeria rejoined the Commonwealth.

2000: Throughout the year, violent clashes between Christians and Muslims accompanied the adoption of Islamic law (sharia) in a number of states throughout Nigeria. Ethnic violence erupted between the militant Yoruba separatists' group Odua People's Congress (OPC) and the Hausas in October. The OPC was outlawed.

2002: Muslim-Christian violence in Lagos amid claims clashes were caused deliberately to bring about restoration of military rule. Miss World beauty contest was moved from Nigeria following Muslim rioting and 200 deaths.

2003: President Obasanjo, a Christian from the southwest of the country, was re-elected with 62% of the vote. His victory over Muhammadu Buhari, a former coup leader from the Muslim north, threatened to aggravate ethnic and religious tensions. Nigeria's first satellite was launched by Russian rocket.

2004: Further violent clashes occurred between Muslim and Christian militia and troops were called in to stop the fighting. A four-day strike was called to protest at fuel prices.

2005: The opposition boycotted a national political conference designed to discuss constitutional reform.

nightingale songbird belonging to the thrush family; it sings with remarkable beauty by night as well as during the day. About 16.5 cm/6.5 in long, it is dull brown with a reddish-brown rounded tail; the breast is dull greyish-white, tinting to brown. It migrates in summer to Europe and winters in Africa. It feeds on insects, small animals, and occasionally fruit. It has a huge musical repertoire, built from about 900 melodic elements. (Species *Luscinia megarhyncos*, family Muscicapidae.)

Nightingale, Florence (1820–1910) English nurse, the founder of nursing as a profession. She took a team of nurses to Scutari (now Üsküdar, Turkey) in 1854 and reduced the *Crimean War hospital death rate from 42% to 2%. In 1860 she founded the Nightingale School and Home for Nurses in London, attached to St Thomas's Hospital, London.

nightjar any of about 65 species of night-hunting birds. They have wide, bristly mouths for catching flying insects. Their distinctive calls have earned them such names as 'whippoorwill' and 'church-will's-widow'. Some US species are called nighthawks. (Family Caprimulgidae, order Caprimulgiformes.)

Night Journey Arabic al-Miraj, 'the ascent', in Islam, the journey of the prophet Muhammad, guided by the archangel Gabriel, from Mecca to Jerusalem, where he met the earlier prophets, including Adam, Moses, and Jesus; he then ascended to paradise, where he experienced the majesty of Allah, and was also shown hell.

nightshade any of several plants in the nightshade family. They include the annual herbaceous black nightshade (*S. nigrum*), with white flowers similar to those of the potato plant and black berries; the perennial shrubby bittersweet or woody nightshade (*S. dulcamara*), with purple, potatolike flowers and scarlet berries; and, belonging to a different genus, deadly nightshade or *belladonna (A. belladonna)*. (Genera *Solanum* and *Atropa*, family Solanaceae.)

nihilism the rejection of all traditional values, authority, and institutions. The term was coined 1862 by Ivan Turgenev in his novel *Fathers and Sons*, and was adopted by the *Nihilists, the Russian radicals of the period. Despairing of reform, they saw change as possible only through the destruction of morality, justice, marriage, property, and the idea of God. Since then nihilism has come to mean a generally negative and destructive outlook.

Nihilist member of a group of Russian revolutionaries in the reign of Alexander II 1855–81. Despairing of reform, they saw change as possible only through the destruction of morality, justice, marriage, property, and the idea of God. In 1878 the Nihilists launched a guerrilla campaign leading to the murder of the tsar in 1881.

Nijinksa, Bronislava (1891–1972) Russian choreographer and dancer. Nijinksa was the first major female choreographer to work in classical ballet, creating several dances for Diaghilev's Ballets Russes, including *Les Noces* (1923), a landmark in 20th-century modernist dance. She was the sister of Vaslav *Nijinsky,

Nijinsky, Vaslav Fomich

continuing his revolutionary ideas of kinetic movement in dance. Other pieces include *Les Biches* (1924).

Nijinsky, Vaslav Fomich (1890–1950) Russian dancer and choreographer. Noted for his powerful but graceful technique, he was a legendary member of *Diaghilev's Ballets Russes, for whom he choreographed Debussy's *Prélude à l'après-midi d'un faune* (1912) and *Jeux* (1913), and Stravinsky's *Le Sacre du printemps/The Rite of Spring* (1913).

Nile Arabic (Egypt) **Nahr en Nil**; Arabic (Sudan) **Bahr el Nil**, (Semitic *nihal* 'river') river in Africa, the world's longest, 6,695 km/4,160 mi. The **Blue Nile** rises in Lake Tana, Ethiopia, the **White Nile** at Lake Victoria, and they join at Khartoum, Sudan. The river enters the Mediterranean Sea at a vast delta in northern Egypt.

Nile, Battle of the alternative name for the Battle of *Aboukir Bay.

Nineveh capital of the Assyrian Empire from the 8th century BC until its destruction by the Medes under King Cyaxares in 612 BC. It was situated on the River Tigris (opposite the present city of Mosul, Iraq) and was adorned with palaces.

Ningxia Hui Autonomous Region or **Ningxia** formerly **Ninghsia**, administrative area of northwest China, bounded to the north by Inner Mongolia, to the east by Shaanxi, and to the south by Gansu; area 66,400 sq km/25,600 sq mi; population (2000 est) 5,620,000; one-third are Hui (Chinese Muslims) and there is a large Mongolian population in the north. The capital is Yinchuan. It is a desert plateau, and the Huang He River is in the area. Industries include coal and chemicals, and agricultural products include cereals and rice under irrigation, and animal herding.

niobium chemical symbol Nb, soft, grey-white, somewhat ductile and malleable, metallic element, atomic number 41, relative atomic mass 92.906. It occurs in nature with tantalum, which it resembles in chemical properties. It is used in making stainless steel and other alloys for jet engines and rockets and for making superconductor magnets.

Nippon or **Nihon** English transliteration of the Japanese name for *Japan.

nirvana (Sanskrit 'a blowing out') in Buddhism, and other Indian religions, the ultimate religious goal characterized by the attainment of perfect serenity, compassion, and wisdom by the eradication of all desires. When nirvana is attained, the cycle of life and death, known as samsara, is broken and a state of liberty, free from pain and desire, is reached.

Nirvana US rock group 1986–94. They made popular a hard-driving, dirty sound, a tuneful grunge, as heard on their second album, *Nevermind* (1991), and its hit single 'Smells Like Teen Spirit'.

nitrate salt or ester of nitric acid, containing the NO_3^- ion. Nitrates are used in explosives, in the chemical and pharmaceutical industries, in curing meat (as *nitre), and as fertilizers. They are the most water-soluble salts known and play a major part in the nitrogen cycle. Nitrates in the soil, whether naturally occurring or from inorganic or organic fertilizers, can be used by plants to make proteins and nucleic acids. However, run-off from fields can result in *nitrate pollution.

nitrate pollution contamination of water by nitrates. Increased use of artificial fertilizers and land cultivation means that higher levels of nitrates are being washed

from the soil into rivers, lakes, and aquifers. There they cause an excessive enrichment of the water (*eutrophication), leading to a rapid growth of algae, which in turn darkens the water and reduces its oxygen content. The water is expensive to purify and many plants and animals die. High levels are now found in drinking water in arable areas. These may be harmful to newborn babies, and it is possible that they contribute to stomach cancer, although the evidence for this is unproven.

nitre or **saltpetre** potassium nitrate, KNO_3, a mineral found on and just under the ground in desert regions; used in explosives. Nitre occurs in Bihar, India, Iran, and Cape Province, South Africa. The salt was formerly used for the manufacture of gunpowder, but the supply of nitre for explosives is today largely met by making the salt from nitratine (also called Chile saltpetre, $NaNO_3$). Saltpetre is a *preservative and is widely used for curing meats.

nitric acid or **aqua fortis** HNO_3, fuming acid obtained by the oxidation of ammonia or the action of sulphuric acid on potassium nitrate. It is a highly corrosive acid, dissolving most metals, and a strong oxidizing agent. It is used in the nitration and esterification of organic substances, and in the making of sulphuric acid, nitrates, explosives, plastics, and dyes.

nitrification process that takes place in soil when bacteria oxidize ammonia, turning it into nitrates. Nitrates can be absorbed by the roots of plants, so this is a vital stage in the *nitrogen cycle.

nitrite salt or ester of nitrous acid, containing the nitrite ion (NO_2^-). Nitrites are used as preservatives (for example, to prevent the growth of botulism spores) and as colouring agents in cured meats such as bacon and sausages.

nitrogen chemical symbol N, (Greek *nitron* 'native soda', sodium or potassium nitrate) colourless, odourless, tasteless, gaseous, non-metallic element, atomic number 7, relative atomic mass 14.0067. It forms almost 80% of the Earth's atmosphere by volume and is a constituent of all plant and animal tissues (in proteins and nucleic acids). Nitrogen is obtained for industrial use by the liquefaction and *fractional distillation of air. Its compounds are used in the manufacture of foods, drugs, fertilizers, dyes, and explosives.

nitrogen cycle process of nitrogen passing through the ecosystem. Nitrogen, in the form of inorganic compounds (such as nitrates) in the soil, is absorbed by plants and turned into organic compounds (such as proteins) in plant tissue. A proportion of this nitrogen is eaten by *herbivores, with some of this in turn being passed on to the carnivores, which feed on the herbivores. The nitrogen is ultimately returned to the soil as excrement and when organisms die, and is converted back to inorganic forms by *decomposers.

nitrogen fixation process by which nitrogen in the atmosphere is converted into nitrogenous compounds by the action of micro-organisms, such as cyanobacteria (see *blue-green algae) and bacteria, in conjunction with certain legumes. Several chemical processes duplicate nitrogen fixation to produce fertilizers; see *nitrogen cycle.

nitrogen oxide any chemical compound that contains only nitrogen and oxygen. All nitrogen oxides are gases. Nitrogen monoxide and nitrogen dioxide contribute to air pollution. See also *nitrous oxide.

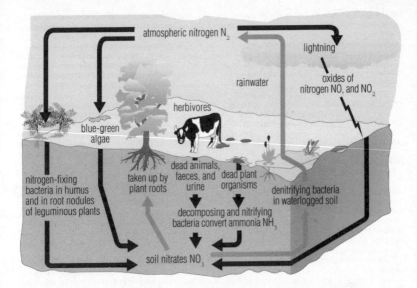

nitrogen cycle The nitrogen cycle is one of a number of cycles during which the chemicals necessary for life are recycled. The carbon, sulphur, and phosphorus cycles are others. Since there is only a limited amount of these chemicals in the Earth and its atmosphere, the chemicals must be continuously recycled if life is to go on.

nitroglycerine *or* **glycerol trinitrate** $C_3H_5(ONO_2)_3$, flammable, explosive oil produced by the action of nitric and sulphuric acids on glycerol. Although poisonous, it is used in cardiac medicine. It explodes with great violence if heated in a confined space and is used in the preparation of dynamite, cordite, and other high explosives.

nitrous oxide *or* **dinitrogen oxide** N_2O, colourless, nonflammable gas that, used in conjunction with oxygen, reduces sensitivity to pain. In higher doses it is an anaesthetic. Well tolerated, it is often combined with other anaesthetic gases to enable them to be used in lower doses. It may be self-administered; for example, in childbirth. It is a greenhouse gas; about 10% of nitrous oxide released into the atmosphere comes from the manufacture of nylon. It used to be known as 'laughing gas'.

Nixon, Richard M(ilhous) (1913–1994) 37th president of the USA 1969–74, a Republican. He attracted attention as a member of the House Un-American Activities Committee in 1948, and was vice-president to Eisenhower 1953–61. As president he was responsible for US withdrawal from Vietnam, and the normalization of relations with communist China, but at home his culpability in the cover-up of the *Watergate scandal and the existence of a 'slush fund' for political machinations during his re-election campaign of 1972 led him to resign in 1974 when threatened with *impeachment.

Nkomo, Joshua (1917–1999) Zimbabwean trade unionist and politician, vice president 1990–99. As president of ZAPU (Zimbabwe African People's Union)

from 1961, he was a leader of the black nationalist movement against the white Rhodesian regime. He was a member of Robert *Mugabe's cabinet 1980–82 and from 1987.

Nkrumah, Kwame (1909–1972) Ghanaian nationalist politician, prime minister of the Gold Coast (Ghana's former name) 1952–57 and of newly independent Ghana 1957–60. He became Ghana's first president in 1960 but was overthrown in a coup in 1966. His policy of 'African socialism' led to links with the communist bloc.

No *or* **Noh** classical, aristocratic Japanese drama which developed from the 14th to the 16th centuries and is still performed. There is a repertoire of some 250 pieces, of which five, one from each of the several classes devoted to different subjects, may be put on in a performance lasting a whole day. Dance, mime, music, and chanting develop the mythical or historical themes. All the actors are men, some of whom wear masks and elaborate costumes; scenery is limited. No influenced kabuki drama.

Nobel, Alfred Bernhard (1833–1896) Swedish chemist and engineer. He invented *dynamite in 1867, gelignite in 1875, and ballistite, a smokeless gunpowder, in 1887. Having amassed a large fortune from the manufacture of explosives and the exploitation of the Baku oilfields in Azerbaijan, near the Caspian Sea, he left this in trust for the endowment of five *Nobel prizes.

nobelium chemical symbol No, synthesized, radioactive, metallic element of the *actinide series, atomic number 102, relative atomic mass 259. It is synthesized by bombarding curium with carbon nuclei.

Nobel Prize annual international prize, first awarded in 1901 under the will of Alfred Nobel, Swedish chemist, who invented dynamite. The interest on the Nobel endowment fund is divided annually among the persons who have made the greatest contributions in the fields of physics, chemistry, medicine, literature, and world peace. The first four are awarded by academic committees based in Sweden, while the Nobel Prize for Peace is awarded by a committee of the Norwegian parliament. A sixth prize, for economics, financed by the Swedish National Bank, was first awarded in 1969. The prizes have a large cash award and are given to organizations – such as the United Nations peacekeeping forces, which received the Nobel Prize for Peace in 1988 – as well as individuals.

noble gas or **rare gas** or **inert gas** any of a group of six elements (*helium, *neon, *argon, *krypton, *xenon, and *radon), originally named 'inert' because they were thought not to enter into any chemical reactions. This is now known to be incorrect: in 1962, xenon was made to combine with fluorine, and since then, compounds of argon, krypton, and radon with fluorine and/or oxygen have been described.

nocturne in music, a reflective character piece, often for piano, introduced by John Field (1782–1837) and adopted by Frédéric *Chopin.

nodule in geology, a lump of mineral or other matter found within rocks or formed on the seabed surface; *mining technology is being developed to exploit them.

Nolan, Sidney Robert (1917–1992) Australian artist. Largely self-taught, he created atmospheric paintings of the outback, exploring themes from Australian history such as the life of the outlaw Ned Kelly. His work, along with that of Drysdale and others, marked the beginning of modernism in Australian art. He was knighted in 1981.

nomadic pastoralism farming system where animals (cattle, goats, camels) are taken to different locations in order to find fresh pastures. It is practised in the developing world; out of an estimated 30–40 million (1990) nomadic pastoralists worldwide, most are in central Asia and the Sahel region of West Africa. Increasing numbers of cattle may lead to overgrazing of the area and to *desertification.

non-aligned movement countries with a strategic and political position of neutrality ('non-alignment') towards major powers, specifically the USA and former USSR. The movement emerged in the 1960s during the *Cold War between East and West 1949–89. Although originally used by poorer states, the non-aligned position was later adopted by oil-producing nations. Its 113 members hold more than half the world's population and 85% of oil resources, but only 7% of global GDP (1995).

Nonconformist in religion, originally a member of the Puritan section of the Church of England clergy who, in the Elizabethan age, refused to conform to certain practices, for example the wearing of the surplice and kneeling to receive Holy Communion.

noncooperation movement or **satyagraha** in India, a large-scale civil disobedience campaign orchestrated by Mahatma *Gandhi in 1920 following the *Amritsar Massacre in April 1919. Based on a policy of peaceful non-cooperation, the strategy was to bring the British administrative machine to a halt by the total withdrawal of Indian support. British-made goods were boycotted, as were schools, courts of law, and elective offices. The campaign made little impression on the British government, since they could ignore it when it was peaceful; when it became violent, Gandhi felt obliged to call off further demonstrations. Its most successful aspect was that it increased political awareness among the Indian people.

non-metal one of a set of elements (around 20 in total) with certain physical and chemical properties opposite to those of *metal elements. The division between metal and non-metal elements forms the simplest division of the *periodic table of the elements. Common physical properties are that non-metals have low electrical conductivity, are brittle when solid, or are gases or liquids. Exceptions include *graphite, a form of carbon, which is a good electrical conductor.

Nono, Luigi (1924–1990) Italian composer. He wrote attenuated pointillist works such as *Il canto sospeso/ Suspended Song* (1955–56) for soloists, chorus, and orchestra, in which influences of Webern and Gabrieli are applied to issues of social conscience. After the opera *Intolleranza/Intolerance* (1960) his style became more richly expressionist, and his causes more overtly polemical.

non-renewable resource natural resource, such as coal, oil, or natural gas, that takes millions of years to form naturally and therefore cannot be replaced once it is consumed; it will eventually be used up. The main energy sources used by humans are non-renewable; *renewable resources, such as solar, tidal, wind, and geothermal power, have so far been less exploited.

noradrenaline in the body, a *hormone that acts directly on specific receptors to stimulate the sympathetic nervous system. Released by nerve stimulation or by drugs, it slows the heart rate mainly by constricting arterioles (small arteries) and so raising blood pressure. It is used therapeutically to treat *shock.

Nord-Pas-de-Calais region of northern France, bounded by the English Channel to the northwest; area 12,414 sq km/4,793 sq mi; population (1999 est) 3,996,600. Its administrative centre is Lille, and it consists of the *départements* of Nord and Pas-de-Calais. The land is predominantly flat and well-drained, with northern sections below sea level. The coasts are dotted with high chalk cliffs.

Norfolk county of eastern England. **area:** 5,360 sq km/ 2,069 sq mi **towns and cities:** Norwich (administrative headquarters), King's Lynn, Great Yarmouth (ports); Cromer, Hunstanton (resorts) **physical:** low-lying with the Fens in the west and the *Norfolk Broads in the east; rivers Bure, Ouse, Waveney, Yare **features:** the Broads (a series of lakes famous for fishing and water fowl, and for boating); Halvergate Marshes wildlife area; traditional reed thatching; Grime's Graves (Neolithic flint mines); shrine of Our Lady of Walsingham, a medieval and present-day centre of pilgrimage; Blickling Hall (Jacobean, built 1619–24, situated 14 km/7 mi south of Cromer); residence of Elizabeth II at Sandringham (built 1869–71) **population:** (1996) 777,000.

Norfolk Broads area of interlinked shallow freshwater lakes in Norfolk, eastern England, between Norwich, Sea Palling, and Lowestoft. The area has about 200 km/

125 mi of navigable waterways, and the region is a popular tourist destination for boating and fishing.

Norfolk terrier breed of dog identical to the *Norwich terrier except that the ears drop forward rather than being pricked.

Noriega Morena, Manuel (Antonio) (1940–) Panamanian soldier and politician, effective ruler and dictator of Panama from 1983, as head of the National Guard, until deposed by the USA in 1989. An informer for the US Central Intelligence Agency (CIA) from the late 1960s, he was known to be involved in drug trafficking as early as 1972, but enjoyed US support until 1987. In the 1989 US invasion of Panama, he was forcibly taken to the USA, where in 1992 he was tried and convicted of cocaine trafficking, racketeering, and money laundering. He was the first foreign head of state to be convicted on criminal charges by a US jury.

Norman any of the descendants of the Norsemen (to whose chief, Rollo, Normandy was granted by Charles III of France in 911) who adopted French language and culture. During the 11th and 12th centuries they conquered England in 1066 (under William the Conqueror), Scotland in 1072, parts of Wales and Ireland, southern Italy, Sicily, and Malta, and took a prominent part in the Crusades.

Norman architecture style of architecture used in England in the 11th and 12th centuries, also known as *Romanesque. Norman buildings are massive, with round arches (although trefoil arches are sometimes used for small openings). Buttresses are of slight projection, and vaults are barrel-roofed. Examples in England include the Keep of the Tower of London and parts of the cathedrals of Chichester, Gloucester, and Ely.

Norman Conquest invasion and settlement of England by the *Normans, following the victory of William (I) the Conqueror at the Battle of *Hastings in 1066. The story of the conquest from the Norman point of view is told in the *Bayeux Tapestry.

Normandy French **Normandie**, former duchy of northwest France now divided into two regions: *Haute-Normandie and *Basse-Normandie; area 29,900 sq km/11,544 sq mi; population (both parts, 1999 est) 3,202,400. Normandy was named after the Viking Norsemen (Normans) who conquered and settled in the area in the 9th century. As a French duchy it reached its peak under William the Conqueror and was renowned for its centres of learning established by Lanfranc and St Anselm. Normandy was united with England from 1100 to 1135. England and France fought over it during the Hundred Years' War, England finally losing it in 1449 to Charles VII. In World War II the Normandy beaches were the site of the Allied invasion on D-day, 6 June 1944.

Normandy landings alternative name for *D-day.

Norman French form of French used by the Normans in Normandy from the 10th century, and by the Norman ruling class in England after the Conquest in 1066. It remained the language of the English court until the 15th century, and the official language of the law courts until the 17th century.

Norse early inhabitant of Norway or *Scandinavia; also referring to their language and culture.

Norsemen early inhabitants of Norway. The term Norsemen is also applied to Scandinavian *Vikings who traded, explored, and raided far afield from their homelands during the 8th–11th centuries, settling in Iceland, Greenland, Russia, the British Isles, and northern France. The term is sometimes used to refer specifically to western Scandinavians or just to Norwegians.

North America third largest of the continents (including Greenland and Central America), and over twice the size of Europe. **area:** 24,000,000 sq km/9,400,000 sq mi **largest cities:** (population over 1 million) Mexico City, New York, Chicago, Toronto, Los Angeles, Montréal, Guadalajara, Monterrey, Philadelphia, Houston, Guatemala City, Vancouver, Detroit, San Diego, Dallas **physical:** occupying the northern part of the landmass of the Western hemisphere between the Arctic Ocean and the tropical southeast tip of the isthmus that joins Central America to South America; the northernmost point on the mainland is the tip of Boothia Peninsula in the Canadian Arctic; the northernmost point on adjacent islands is Cape Morris Jesup on Greenland; the most westerly point on the mainland is Cape Prince of Wales, Alaska; the most westerly point on adjacent islands is Attu Island in the Aleutians; the most easterly point on the mainland lies on the southeast coast of Labrador; the highest point is Mount McKinley, Alaska, 6,194 m/20,320 ft; the lowest point is Badwater in Death Valley –86 m/–282 ft. Perhaps the most dominating characteristic is the western cordillera running parallel to the coast from Alaska to Panama; it is called the *Rocky Mountains in the USA and Canada and its continuation into Mexico is called the *Sierra Madre. The cordillera is a series of ranges divided by intermontane plateaus and takes up about one-third of the continental area. To the east of the cordillera lie the Great Plains, the agricultural heartland of North America, which descend in a series of steps to the depressions occupied by the *Great Lakes in the east and the Gulf of Mexico coastal lowlands in the southeast. The Plains are characterized by treeless expanses crossed by broad, shallow river valleys. To the north and east of the region lie the Canadian Highlands, an ancient plateau or shield area. Glaciation has deeply affected its landscape. In the east are the Appalachian Mountains, flanked by the narrow coastal plain which widens further south. Erosion here has created a line of planed crests, or terraces, at altitudes between 300–1,200 m/985–3,935 ft. This has also formed a ridge-and-valley topography which was an early barrier to continental penetration. The Fall Line is the abrupt junction of plateau and coastal plain in the east **features:** Lake Superior (the largest body of fresh water in the world); Grand Canyon on the Colorado River; Redwood National Park, California, has some of the world's tallest trees; San Andreas Fault, California; deserts: Death Valley, Mojave, Sonoran; rivers (over 1,600 km/1,000 mi) include Mississippi, Missouri, Mackenzie, Rio Grande, Yukon, Arkansas, Colorado, Saskatchewan-Bow, Columbia, Red, Peace, Snake **population:** (2000 est) 450 million; annual growth rate from 1980 to 1985: Canada 1.08%, USA 0.88%, Mexico 2.59%, Honduras 3.39%; the American Indian, Inuit, and Aleut peoples are now a minority within a population predominantly of European immigrant origin. Many Africans were brought in as part of the slave trade **language:** English predominates in Canada, the USA, and Belize; Spanish is the chief language of the countries of Latin America and a sizeable minority in the USA; French is spoken by about 25% of the population of Canada, and by people of the French possession of St Pierre and Miquelon; indigenous non-European minorities, including the Inuit of Arctic Canada, the Aleuts of Alaska, North American Indians, and the Maya of Central America, have their own languages and dialects **religion:** Christian and Jewish religions predominate; 97% of Latin Americans, 47% of Canadians, and 21% of those living in the USA are Roman Catholic.

North American Free Trade Agreement (NAFTA) trade agreement between the USA, Canada, and Mexico, intended to promote trade and investment between the signatories, agreed in August 1992, and effective from January 1994. The first trade pact of its kind to link two highly-industrialized countries to a developing one, it created a free market of 375 million people, with a total GDP of $6.8 trillion (equivalent to 30% of the world's GDP). Tariffs were to be progressively eliminated over a 10–15 year period (tariffs on trade in originating goods from Mexico and Canada are to be eliminated by 2008) and investment into low-wage Mexico by Canada and the USA progressively increased. Another aim of the agreement was to make provisions on transacting business in the free trade area. The NAFTA Centre is located in Dallas, Texas.

Northamptonshire county of central England. **area:** 2,370 sq km/915 sq mi **towns and cities:** Northampton (administrative headquarters), Kettering, Corby, Daventry, Wellingborough **physical:** rivers Avon, Cherwell, Leam, Nene, Ouse, and Welland **features:** Althorp Park, Spencer family home and burial place of Diana, Princess of Wales; Canons Ashby, Tudor house, home of the Drydens for 400 years; churches with broached spires (an octagonal spire on a square tower) **population:** (1996) 604,300.

North Atlantic Drift warm *ocean current in the North Atlantic Ocean; an extension of the *Gulf Stream. It flows east across the Atlantic and has a mellowing effect on the climate of northwestern Europe, particularly the British Isles and Scandinavia.

North Atlantic Treaty agreement signed on 4 April 1949 by Belgium, Canada, Denmark, France, Iceland, Italy, Luxembourg, the Netherlands, Norway, Portugal, the UK, and the USA, in response to the Soviet blockade of Berlin June 1948–May 1949. They agreed that 'an armed attack against one or more of them in Europe or North America shall be considered an attack against them all'. The *North Atlantic Treaty Organization (NATO), which other countries have joined since, is based on this agreement.

North Atlantic Treaty Organization (NATO) military association of major Western European and North American states set up under the* North Atlantic Treaty of 4 April 1949. The original signatories were Belgium, Canada, Denmark, France, Iceland, Italy, Luxembourg, Netherlands, Norway, Portugal, the UK, and the USA. Greece and Turkey were admitted to NATO in 1952, West Germany in 1955, Spain in 1982, Poland, Hungary, and the Czech Republic in 1999, and Bulgaria, Estonia, Latvia, Lithuania, Romania, Slovenia, and the Slovak Republic in 2004. NATO has been the

basis of the defence of the Western world since 1949. During the Cold War (1945–89), NATO stood in opposition to the perceived threat of communist Eastern Europe, led by the USSR and later allied under the military Warsaw Pact (1955–91). Having outlasted the *Warsaw Pact, NATO has increasingly redefined itself as an agent of international peace-keeping and enforcement.

North Ayrshire unitary authority in western Scotland, created in 1996 from Cunninghame district in Strathclyde region. **area:** 889 sq km/343 sq mi **towns:** Irvine (administrative headquarters), Kilwinning, Saltcoats, Largs, Kilbirnie **physical:** low-lying coastal plain on the mainland, rising inland to a plateau of over 305 m/1,000 ft; the islands of the Firth of Clyde are Arran, Holy Isle, and the Cumbraes; the rivers Irvine and Garnock reach the sea at Irvine; Goat Fell (874 m/2,867 ft) **features:** Pencil Monument, Largs; Scottish Maritime Museum, Irvine; Hunterston nuclear power station; the Cathedral of the Isles at Great Cumbrae (1851, the UK's smallest cathedral); the Big Idea Inventor Centre celebrating the work of Nobel prizewinners is linked by the Bridge of Scottish Invention to Irvine Harbourside **population:** (2001 est) 135,800 **history:** Eglinton Tournament (19th century); Battle of Largs (1263), when the Scots captured the Hebrides from the Norwegians.

North Brabant Dutch **Noord Brabant**, largest province of the Netherlands, located in the south of the country, lying between the Maas River (Meuse) and Belgium; area 4,940 sq km/1,907 sq mi; population (1997) 2,304,100. The capital is 's-Hertogenbosch. Industries include brewing, tobacco, engineering, microelectronics, and textiles. There is cattle farming, and wheat and sugar beet are grown.

North Cape Norwegian **Nord Kapp**, cape in the Norwegian county of Finnmark; the most northerly point of Europe.

North Carolina called the **Old North State** or the **Tar Heel State**, state in southeastern USA, bordered to the north by *Virginia, to the west and northwest by *Tennessee, to the south by *Georgia and *South Carolina, and to the east by the Atlantic Ocean; area 126,161 sq km/48,711 52,650 sq mi; population 8,049,300 (2000); capital Raleigh. Named after Charles I of England, its nickname the Old North State refers to the division of Carolina into north and south in 1712; the Tar Heel State comes from a remark made by troops during the *Civil War that tar – one of North Carolina's first products – should be put on the heels of deserters to make them 'stick better in the next fight'. North Carolina varies from flat-lying coastal plain with marshes, bogs, and barrier islands, to the rugged Great Smoky Mountains in the west, and the state is heavily forested. The natural setting, along with growing technology industries and thriving financial centres such as Charlotte, have made the state one of the USA's most desirable places to live. It also supports a strong manufacturing sector, producing textiles, furniture, chemicals, and machinery. Other cities include Greensboro, Winston-Salem, and Durham. North Carolina was home to many American Indian peoples, including the *Cherokee, *Algonquin, and Siouan-speaking tribes. Explored by Italian navigator Giovanni da Verrazano in 1524 and settled by immigrants from

Virginia in the 1650s, North Carolina was one of the original *Thirteen Colonies. During the Civil War it joined the *Confederacy. North Carolina ratified the US Constitution in 1789 to become the 12th state to join the Union.

Northcliffe, Alfred Charles William Harmsworth, 1st Viscount Northcliffe (1865–1922) British newspaper proprietor, born in Dublin. Founding the *Daily Mail* in 1896, he revolutionized popular journalism, and with the *Daily Mirror* in 1903 originated the picture paper. In 1908 he also obtained control of *The Times*.

North Dakota called the **Peace Garden State**, (Sioux *dakota* 'allies') state in west north-central USA, one of the *Great Plains states, bordered to the south by *South Dakota, to the west by *Montana, to the north by the Canadian states of Saskatchewan and Manitoba, and to the east by *Minnesota; area 178,647 sq km/68,976 sq mi; population (2000) 642,200; capital Bismarck. Located at the geographical centre of the North American continent, North Dakota is a sparsely populated rural state, characterized by plains and black-soiled prairies. It ranks among the top states in the USA for its number of national wildlife refuges, most of which are managed for waterfowl production. Crops and livestock are the most important industries in the state, as well as energy and tourism. Products include barley, sunflower seeds, and flaxseed. Oil has been important to the economy since it was discovered in the state in the 1950s. The largest city is Fargo and other major towns and cities are Grand Forks and Minot. One of the last US frontier states to be settled, it is known for its Old *West legacy. North Dakota was admitted to the Union in 1889 as the 39th US state.

North-East India or **North-East Hill States** area of India (Meghalaya, Assam, Mizoram, Tripura, Manipur, Nagaland, and Arunachal Pradesh) linked with the rest of India only by a narrow corridor, and bounded by Myanmar (Burma), China, Bhutan, and Bangladesh. There is opposition to immigration from Bangladesh and the rest of India, and demand for secession.

North East Lincolnshire unitary authority in eastern England created in 1996 from part of the former county of Humberside. **area:** 192 sq km/74 sq mi **towns and cities:** Grimsby (administrative headquarters), Immingham, Cleethorpes **features:** Humber Estuary forms east border of authority; Immingham Museum; National Fishing Heritage Centre (Grimsby) **population:** (1996) 164,000.

Northeast Passage sea route from the North Atlantic, around Asia, to the North Pacific, pioneered by the Swedish explorer Nils Nordenskjöld 1878–79 and developed by the USSR in settling Northern Siberia from 1935.

Northern Cape province of the Republic of South Africa from 1994, formerly part of Cape Province; area 363,389 sq km/140,305 sq mi; population (2000 est) 869,200. The capital is Kimberley. The province is situated in the northwest of the republic, and is bordered to the west by the Atlantic Ocean and to the north by Namibia and Botswana. It is sparsely populated, consisting mainly of a dry plateau with little vegetation. In the wetter areas to the south and east, with the aid of irrigation, more wine is produced than in any other province and is a major export, while other

agricultural products include citrus fruits, cotton, groundnuts, cereals, and wool. Kimberley has the largest diamond mine in the world and other minerals worked in the province include asbestos, copper, tungsten, zinc, iron, manganese, and tin. Tourism is of growing importance.

Northern Ireland or **Ulster** constituent part of the United Kingdom, in the northeast of the island of Ireland; area 13,460 sq km/5,196 sq mi; population (2001 est) 1,727,900. It is comprised of six of the nine counties that form Ireland's northernmost province of *Ulster (Antrim, Armagh, Down, Fermanagh, Londonderry, and Tyrone) which are divided into 26 regional districts for administrative purposes. The capital is *Belfast, and other major towns and cities include Londonderry, Enniskillen, Omagh, Newry, Armagh, and Coleraine. Geographical features are the Mourne Mountains, Belfast Lough, Lough Neagh, and the Giant's Causeway. Major industries include engineering, shipbuilding, aircraft components, textiles, processed foods (especially dairy and poultry products), rubber products, and chemicals.

Northern Ireland Assembly power-sharing assembly based in Belfast, Northern Ireland. The Assembly came into being as a result of the 10 April 1998 Good Friday peace agreement between the contending Unionist and Irish Nationalist communities in Northern Ireland. The agreement negotiated the devolution (handing over) of a range of executive (administrative) and legislative (law-making) powers – in areas including agriculture, economic development, education, the environment, finance, health, and social security – from the secretary of state for Northern Ireland to an elected assembly. Elections were first held on 25 June 1998. The Assembly met for the first time on 1 July 1998, but following disagreements over the creation of a power-sharing executive, did not become fully operational until December 1999. The assembly was suspended in 2002.

northern lights common name for the *aurora borealis.

Northern Mariana Islands archipelago in the northwestern Pacific, with *Guam known collectively as the Mariana Islands; area 471 sq km/182 sq mi; population (1995 est) 47,200. The Northern Marianas are a commonwealth in union with the USA. The capital is Garapan on Saipan. The archipelago consists of 16 islands and atolls extending 560 km/350 mi north of Guam. The main language is English, and the principal religion is Roman Catholicism.

Northern Province formerly **Northern Transvaal**, province of the Republic of South Africa from 1994, formerly part of Transvaal; area 119,606 sq km/46,180 sq mi; population (2000 est) 5,495,700. The capital is Pietersburg. The province consists mostly of tropical and subtropical savannah grassland with scattered trees, while higher areas such as the Soutpansberg are forested. Much of the agriculture, including much cattle farming and rearing of goats and sheep, is on a subsistence basis. Wheat, maize, tobacco, and groundnuts are grown. Minerals worked include chromium, coal, and platinum. Diamonds are mined, and there are copper, asbestos, and iron industries. Tourism is important, and the Kruger National Park is being developed as a major tourist attraction.

Northern Rhodesia former name (to 1964) of Zambia, a country in Africa.

Northern Territory territory of north-central Australia, bounded on the north by the Timor and Arafura seas, on the east by Queensland, on the south by South Australia, and on the west by Western Australia; area 1,346,200 sq km/519,770 sq mi; population (2001 est) 200,000. The capital is Darwin. The main products are beef, bauxite, gold, copper, uranium, manganese, tropical fruits, and fish. Tourism is important.

North Holland Dutch *Noord Holland*, low-lying coastal province of the Netherlands occupying the peninsula jutting northward between the North Sea and the IJsselmeer, bounded on the south by the provinces of South Holland and Utrecht, and includes the island of Texel to the north; area 2,670 sq km/1,031 sq mi; population (1997) 2,474,800. The capital is Haarlem. There are iron and steel works in the province, and agriculture includes dairying and the growing of flower bulbs, grain, and vegetables.

North Island smaller of the two main islands of New Zealand.

North Korea

National name: *Chosun Minchu-chui Inmin Konghwa-guk/Democratic People's Republic of Korea*

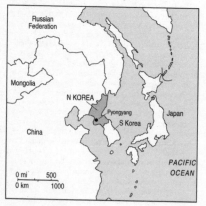

Area: 120,538 sq km/46,539 sq mi
Capital: Pyongyang
Major towns/cities: Hamhung, Chongjin, Nampo, Wonsan, Sinuiji
Physical features: wide coastal plain in west rising to mountains cut by deep valleys in interior
Head of state: Kim Jong Il from 1994
Head of government: Pak Pong Ju from 2003
Political system: communist
Political executive: communist
Political parties: Korean Workers' Party (KWP), Marxist-Leninist (leads Democratic Front for the Reunification of the Fatherland, including Korean Social Democratic Party and Chondoist Chongu Party)
Currency: won
GNI per capita (PPP): (US$) 820 (2001)
Exports: textiles, base metals, vegetable products, machinery and electronic goods. Principal market: Japan 36.3% (2000)

Population: 22,664,000 (2003 est)
Language: Korean (official)
Religion: Buddhist (predominant religion), Chondoist, Christian, traditional beliefs
Life expectancy: 61 (men); 66 (women) (2000–05)
Chronology
2333 BC: Legendary founding of Korean state by Tangun dynasty.
1122 BC–4th century AD: Period of Chinese Kija dynasty.
668–1000: Peninsula unified by Buddhist Shilla kingdom, with capital at Kyongju.
1392–1910: Period of Chosun, or Yi, dynasty, during which Korea became a vassal of China and Confucianism became the dominant intellectual force.
1910: Korea formally annexed by Japan.
1920s and 1930s: Heavy industries developed in the coal-rich north, with Koreans forcibly conscripted as low-paid labourers; suppression of Korean culture led to the development of a resistance movement.
1945: Russian and US troops entered Korea at the end of World War II, forced surrender of Japanese, and divided the country in two at the 38th parallel. Soviet troops occupied North Korea.
1946: Soviet-backed provisional government installed, dominated by Moscow-trained Korean communists, including Kim Il Sung; radical programme of land reform and nationalization launched.
1948: Democratic People's Republic of Korea declared after pro-USA Republic of Korea founded in the south; Soviet troops withdrew.
1950: North Korea invaded South Korea to unite the nation, beginning the Korean War.
1953: Armistice agreed to end the Korean War, which had involved US participation on the side of South Korea, and Chinese on that of North Korea. The war ended in stalemate, at a cost of 2 million lives.
1961: Friendship and mutual assistance treaty signed with China.
1972: A new constitution, with an executive president, was adopted. Talks were held with South Korea about possible reunification.
1983: Four South Korean cabinet ministers were assassinated in Rangoon, Burma (Myanmar), by North Korean army officers.
1985: Relations improved with the Soviet Union.
1990: Diplomatic contacts with South Korea and Japan suggested a thaw in North Korea's relations with the rest of the world.
1991: North Korea became a member of the United Nations (UN). A nonaggression agreement with South Korea was signed.
1992: The Nuclear Safeguards Agreement was signed, allowing international inspection of nuclear facilities. A pact was also signed with South Korea for mutual inspection of nuclear facilities.
1994: Kim Il Sung died and was succeeded by his son, Kim Jong Il. An agreement was made to halt the nuclear-development programme in return for US aid, resulting in the easing of a 44-year-old US trade embargo.
1996: US aid was sought in the face of a severe famine caused by floods; rice was imported from South Korea and food aid provided by the UN.
1997: Kang Song San was replaced as prime minister by Hong Song Nam. Grave food shortages were revealed.
1998: A UN food-aid operation was instituted in an

effort to avert widespread famine. A ballistic missile test was fired over Japan. Deceased former leader Kim Il Sung was declared 'president for perpetuity'. Relations with the USA deteriorated when the USA demanded access to an underground site in Kumchangri suspected of being part of nuclear-weapons program.

1999: Japan lifted sanctions, and the USA eased sanctions, against North Korea.

2000: North Korea forged diplomatic links with Japan, the USA, Italy, and the UK. At a first summit meeting between Kim Jong Il and Kim Dae Jung of South Korea, the two leaders agreed to South Korean economic investment in North Korea, and rail links between the two countries.

2002: In the worst clash between North and South Korea in three years naval vessels fired on each other in disputed coastal waters in the Yellow Sea. The government admitted that it had been pursuing a secret nuclear weapons development programme in contravention of a 1994 agreement with the US government.

2003: The 687 candidates nominated by the Democratic Front for the Reunification of the Fatherland for the Supreme People's Assembly all stood unopposed, reportedly winning 100% of the votes in a 99.9% turnout. North Korea withdrew from the Nuclear Non-Proliferation Treaty and delegations from North Korea, China and the US began discussions on North Korea's nuclear ambitions. Further talks later in the year ended in stalemate.

2004: A third round of talks on the nuclear crisis ended and North Korea pulled out of further talks planned for later in the year.

2005: North Korea suspended talks on its nuclear programme.

North Lanarkshire unitary authority in central Scotland, created in 1996 from three districts of Strathclyde region. **area:** 475 sq km/183 sq mi **towns:** Airdrie, Coatbridge, Cumbernauld, Motherwell (administrative headquarters) **physical:** low-lying, heavily urbanized area; River Clyde **population:** (2000 est) 327,460 **history:** former industrial region of central Scotland.

North Lincolnshire unitary authority in eastern England created in 1996 from part of the former county of Humberside. **area:** 850 sq km/328 sq mi **towns and cities:** Scunthorpe (administrative headquarters), Brigg **features:** Humber Estuary forms north border; River Trent; Isle of Axholme; Humber Bridge southern landfall at Barton upon Humber; Julian's Bower (near Alkborough) – medieval maze cut in turf; Old Rectory (Epworth) where John Wesley, founder of Methodism, was born **population:** (1996) 153,000.

North, Oliver (1943–) US Marine lieutenant colonel. In 1981 he joined the staff of the National Security Council (NSC), where he supervised the mining of Nicaraguan harbours in 1983, an air-force bombing raid on Libya in 1986, and an arms-for-hostages deal with Iran in 1985, which, when uncovered in 1986 (*Irangate), forced his dismissal and trial.

North Pole the northern point where an imaginary line penetrates the Earth's surface by the axis about which it revolves; see also *pole, *Arctic.

North Rhine-Westphalia German **Nordrhein-Westfalen**, administrative region (German *Land*) in northwestern Germany, bordered to the north and northeast by Lower Saxony, to the east by Hesse, to the

south by the Rhineland-Palatinate, and to the west by Belgium and the Netherlands; area 34,079 sq km/13,158 sq mi; population (1999 est) 18,000,000. The capital is Düsseldorf, and other major towns include Cologne, Essen, Dortmund, Gelsenkirchen, Münster, and Mönchengladbach.

North Sea sea to the east of Britain and bounded by the coasts of Belgium, The Netherlands, Germany, Denmark, and Norway; part of the Atlantic Ocean; area 523,000 sq km/202,000 sq mi; average depth 55 m/180 ft, greatest depth 660 m/2,165 ft. The Dogger Bank extends east to west with shallows of as little as 11 m/36 ft, forming a traditionally well-stocked fishing ground. A deep channel follows the coast of Scandinavia reaching as far as the Skagerrak arm. In the northeast the North Sea joins the Norwegian Sea, and in the south it meets the Strait of Dover. It has 300 oil platforms, 10,000 km/6,200 mi of gas pipeline (gas was discovered in 1965), and fisheries (especially mackerel and herring).

North Somerset unitary authority in southwest England created in 1996 from part of the former county of Avon. **area:** 372 sq km/144 sq mi **towns and cities:** Weston-Super-Mare (administrative headquarters), Clevedon, Portishead, Yatton, Congresbury **features:** Severn Estuary forms northwest border of authority; River Yea; River Avon forms northeast border; west end of the Mendips including Bleadon Hill (134 m/440 ft); Clevedon Court – 14th/15th century manor house owned by Elton family; Weston Woods and Worlebury Hill iron age sites (Weston-Super-Mare); International Helicopter Museum (Weston-Super-Mare) **population:** (1996) 177,000.

North–South divide geographical division of the world that theoretically demarcates the rich from the poor. The South includes all of Asia except Japan, Australia, New Zealand, Brunei, and the East and South East Asian 'dragons' of Hong Kong, South Korea, Malaysia, Singapore, Taiwan, and Thailand; all of Africa; the Middle East, except the oil-rich UAE, Qatar, Saudi Arabia, and Bahrain; and Central and South America. The North includes Europe; the USA, except Bermuda and the Bahamas; Canada; and the European republics of the former Soviet Union. Newly industrialized countries such as South Korea and Taiwan now have more in common with the industrialized North and fast-developing Argentina, Mexico, Brazil, Peru, and Chile than with other countries in the *developing world.

Northumberland county of northern England. **area:** 5,030 sq km/1,942 sq mi **towns and cities:** Morpeth (administrative headquarters), Berwick-upon-Tweed, Hexham **physical:** Cheviot Hills; rivers Aln, Coquet, Rede, Till, Tweed, upper Tyne; Northumberland National Park in the west **features:** Holy Island (Lindisfarne); the Farne island group 8 km/5 mi east of Bamburgh, home to seal and bird colonies; part of Hadrian's Wall (a World Heritage site), including Housesteads Fort; Alnwick and Bamburgh castles; Thomas Bewick museum; Hexham Abbey; the walls of Berwick-upon-Tweed; large moorland areas used for military manoeuvres; Longstone Lighthouse from which Grace Darling rowed to rescue the crew of the *Forfarshire*; wild white cattle of Chillingham; Kielder Water (1982), the largest artificial lake in northern Europe **population:** (1996) 307,400.

Northumbria Anglo-Saxon kingdom that covered northeast England and southeast Scotland. Comprising the 6th-century kingdoms of Bernicia (Forth–Tees) and Deira (Tees–Humber), united in the 7th century, it accepted the supremacy of Wessex in 827 and was conquered by the Danes in the late 9th century. It was not until the reign of William the Conqueror that Northumbria became an integral part of England.

North West province of the Republic of South Africa from 1994; area 118,710 sq km/45,834 sq mi; population (2000 est) 3,532,800. The capital is Mmabatho. The terrain consists of part of the plateau known as the Highveld, with savannah grassland and thorn scrub. The mining industry employs about a quarter of the working population and Merensky Reef, near Rustenburg, has the largest platinum mines in the world, while other minerals worked here include gold, rhodium and palladium. Klerksdorp is the centre of a gold-mining area. In agriculture, the drier northern and western areas concentrate on sheep and cattle farming, while the wetter southern and eastern areas produce tobacco, wheat, maize, groundnuts, vegetables, and fruit. There are platinum, chrome, and iron industries; groundnuts are grown.

North-West Frontier Province province of Pakistan; capital *Peshawar; area 74,500 sq km/28,800 sq mi; population (1993 est) 20,090,000. It was a province of British India 1901–47. It includes the strategic Khyber Pass, the site of constant struggle between the British Raj and the *Pathan warriors. In the 1980s it had to accommodate a stream of refugees from neighbouring Afghanistan.

Northwest Ordinances three US Congressional acts 1784–87 setting out procedures for the sale and settlement of lands still occupied by American Indians. The lands, making up the Northwest Territory, lay between the Great Lakes and the Mississippi and Ohio rivers. They were to be formed into townships and sold at a minimum of $1 per acre. The sales revenue was the first significant source of income for the new federal government. The most important act was the Ordinance of 1787, which guaranteed freedom of religion for settlers, and prohibited slavery in the territory.

Northwest Passage Atlantic–Pacific sea route around the north of Canada. Canada, which owns offshore islands, claims it as an internal waterway; the USA insists that it is an international waterway and sent an icebreaker through without permission in 1985.

Northwest rebellion revolt against the Canadian government March–May 1885 by the métis (people of mixed French-Canadian and American Indian descent). Led by their political leader Louis Riel and his military lieutenant Gabriel Dumont (1838–1906), the métis population of what is now Saskatchewan rebelled after a number of economic and political grievances were ignored by the government.

Northwest Territories large administrative area of Canada, extending into the *Arctic Circle. Covering one-eighth of the total area of the country, it comprises the mainland lying north of the 60th parallel (latitude 60° north) and some islands between the Canadian mainland and the North Pole. It is bounded by Yukon Territory to the west, Nunavut to the east, the Beaufort Sea and the Arctic Ocean to the north, and the provinces of British Columbia, Alberta, and Saskatchewan to the south; area 1,299,070 sq km/501,441 sq mi; population (2001 est) 40,900 (with substantial numbers of indigenous peoples: Inuvialuit, Slavey, Dene, Métis, Inuit; about half the population is aboriginal). The capital is Yellowknife. Industries include oil and natural gas extraction and mining of zinc, lead, and gold; other activities are fur-trapping and fishing.

North Yorkshire county of northeast England, created in 1974 from most of the North Riding and parts of the East and West Ridings of Yorkshire (since April 1996 York has been a separate unitary authority). **area:** 8,037 sq km/3,103 sq mi **towns and cities:** Northallerton (administrative headquarters); resorts: Harrogate, Scarborough, Whitby **physical:** England's largest county; rivers Derwent, Esk, Ouse; includes part of the Pennines; the Vale of York (a vast plain); the Cleveland Hills; North Yorkshire Moors, which form a national park (within which is Fylingdales radar station to give early warning – 4 minutes – of nuclear attack) **features:** Rievaulx Abbey (1132); Yorkshire Dales National Park (including Swaledale, Wensleydale, and Bolton Abbey (1170) in Wharfedale); Fountains Abbey (1113) near Ripon, with Studley Royal Gardens (a World Heritage site); Castle Howard (1699), designed by Vanbrugh, has Britain's largest collection of 18th–20th-century costume; Battlefield Chamber at Ingleton, the largest accessible cavern in Britain **population:** (2000 est) 576,000.

Norway

National name: *Kongeriket Norge/Kingdom of Norway*

Area: 387,000 sq km/149,420 sq mi (including Svalbard and Jan Mayen)
Capital: Oslo
Major towns/cities: Bergen, Trondheim, Stavanger, Kristiansand, Drammen
Physical features: mountainous with fertile valleys and deeply indented coast; forests cover 25%; extends north of Arctic Circle
Territories: dependencies in the Arctic (Svalbard and Jan Mayen) and in Antarctica (Bouvet and Peter I Island, and Queen Maud Land)
Head of state: King Harald V from 1991
Head of government: Kjell Magne Bondevik from 2001
Political system: liberal democracy
Political executive: parliamentary

Political parties: Norwegian Labour Party (DNA), moderate left of centre; Conservative Party, progressive, right of centre; Christian People's Party (KrF), Christian, centre left; Centre Party (Sp), left of centre, rural-oriented; Progress Party (FrP), right wing, populist
Currency: Norwegian krone
GNI per capita (PPP): (US$) 35,840 (2002 est)
Exports: petroleum, natural gas, fish products, non-ferrous metals, wood pulp and paper. Principal market: UK 19.8% (2001)
Population: 4,533,000 (2003 est)
Language: Norwegian (official), Saami (Lapp), Finnish
Religion: Evangelical Lutheran (endowed by state) 88%; other Protestant and Roman Catholic 4%
Life expectancy: 76 (men); 82 (women) (2000–05)
Chronology
5th century: First small kingdoms established by Goths.
c. 900: Harald Fairhair created united Norwegian kingdom; it dissolved after his death.
8th–11th centuries: Vikings from Norway raided and settled in many parts of Europe.
c. 1016–28: Olav II (St Olav) reunited the kingdom and introduced Christianity.
1217–63: Haakon VI established royal authority over nobles and church and made the monarchy hereditary.
1263: Iceland submitted to the authority of the king of Norway.
1397: Union of Kalmar: Norway, Denmark, and Sweden united under a single monarch.
15th century: Norway, the weakest of the three kingdoms, was increasingly treated as an appendage of Denmark.
1523: Secession of Sweden further undermined Norway's status.
16th century: Introduction of the sawmill precipitated the development of the timber industry and the growth of export trade.
1661: Denmark restored formal equality of status to Norway as a twin kingdom.
18th century: Norwegian merchants profited from foreign wars which increased demand for naval supplies.
1814: Treaty of Kiel: Denmark ceded Norway (minus Iceland) to Sweden; Norway retained its own parliament but cabinet appointed by the king of Sweden.
19th century: Economic decline followed slump in timber trade due to Canadian competition; expansion of merchant navy and whaling industry.
1837: Democratic local government introduced.
1884: Achieved internal self-government when the king of Sweden made the Norwegian cabinet accountable to the Norwegian parliament.
1895: Start of constitutional dispute over control of foreign policy: Norway's demand for a separate consular service refused by Sweden.
1905: Union with Sweden dissolved; Norway achieved independence under King Haakon VII.
1907: Norway became first the European country to grant women the right to vote in parliamentary elections.
early 20th century: Development of industry based on hydroelectric power; long period of Liberal government committed to neutrality and moderate social reform.
1940–45: German occupation with Vidkun Quisling as puppet leader.
1945–65: Labour governments introduced economic planning and permanent price controls.

1949: Became a founding member of the North Atlantic Treaty Organization (NATO).
1952: Joined the Nordic Council.
1957: Olaf V succeeded his father King Haakon VII.
1960: Joined European Free Trade Association (EFTA).
1972: A national referendum rejected membership of European Economic Community (EEC).
1975: The export of North Sea oil began.
1981: Gro Harlem Brundtland (Labour) became Norway's first woman prime minister.
1986: Falling oil prices caused a recession.
1991: Olaf V was succeeded by his son Harald V.
1994: A national referendum rejected membership of European Union (EU).
1997: Kjell Magne Bondevik (KrF) became prime minister.
1998: There was a decline in the state of the economy.
2000: Bondevik resigned as prime minister and was succeeded by Jens Stoltenberg.
2001: The Labour government was defeated in a general election. No single party gained sufficient votes to form a majority government and a coalition was formed, with Kjell Magne Bondevik as prime minister.
2003: Plans to explore for oil in the Barents Sea were criticized by environmentalists and the fishing industry.
2004: The government intervened to end a week-long oil workers strike.

Norwegian people of Norwegian culture. There are 4–4.5 million speakers of Norwegian (including some in the USA), a Germanic language belonging to the Indo-European family. The seafaring culture of the Norwegians can be traced back to the Viking age from about AD 800–1050, when people of Norwegian descent settled Iceland and Greenland, and voyaged to Vinland (coast of Newfoundland).

Norwich terrier small compact breed of terrier. It has a hard and wiry coat, that is close-lying and straight, and is coloured red, black, and tan; red grizzle; or grizzle and tan. Its head is rather foxlike, the muzzle being rather short and the skull wide between the erect ears. The legs are short, straight, and strong; the tail is traditionally docked. The height is usually 25 cm/10 in and the weight 5–6 kg/11–13 lb.

nose in humans, the upper entrance of the respiratory tract; the organ of the sense of smell. The external part is divided down the middle by a septum of *cartilage. The nostrils contain plates of cartilage that can be moved by muscles and have a growth of stiff hairs at the margin to prevent foreign objects from entering. The whole nasal cavity is lined with a *mucous membrane that warms and moistens the air as it enters and ejects dirt. In the upper parts of the cavity the membrane contains 50 million olfactory receptor cells (cells sensitive to smell).

Nostradamus, Michael (1503–1566) French Michel de Nôtredame, French physician and astrologer who was consulted by Catherine de' Medici and Charles IX of France. His book of prophecies in verse, *Centuries* (1555), makes cryptic predictions about world events up to the year 3797.

nostril in vertebrates, the opening of the nasal cavity, in which cells sensitive to smell are located. (In fish, these cells detect water-borne chemicals, so they are effectively organs of taste.) In vertebrates with lungs, the nostrils also take in air. In humans, and most other mammals, the nostrils are located on the *nose.

notary public legal practitioner who attests or certifies deeds and other documents. British diplomatic and consular officials may exercise notarial functions outside the UK.

notation system of signs and symbols for writing music, either for performers to read from, or to make a permanent record. Early systems of music notation were developed by the ancient Sumerians, by the Chinese in the 3rd century BC, and later by the ancient Greeks and Romans for their music dramas. The Greeks were the first to name the notes of the *scale with letters of the alphabet.

note in music, the written symbol indicating pitch and duration, the sound of which is a tone.

Nottingham city and administrative centre of Nottingham City unitary authority in central England, on the River Trent, 38 km/24 mi north of Leicester; population (1999 est) 282,000; metropolitan area (1999 est) 620,000. The city's prosperity was based on the expansion of the lace and hosiery industries in the 18th century. The pharmacy chain Boots was started here in 1892, and the economy has diversified into industries including tourism and engineering.

Nottinghamshire county of central England, which has contained the unitary authority Nottingham City since April 1998. **area:** 2,160 sq km/834 sq mi **towns and cities:** West Bridgford (administrative headquarters), Mansfield, Newark, Worksop **physical:** rivers: Erewash Idle, Soar, Trent **features:** the remaining areas of Sherwood Forest (home of *Robin Hood) are included in the Dukeries, an area of estates; originally 32 km/20 mi long and 12 km/7 mi wide, the forest was formerly a royal hunting ground; Cresswell Crags (remains of prehistoric humans); D H Lawrence commemorative walk from Eastwood (where he lived) to Old Brinsley Colliery **population:** (2000 est) 748,300.

Nouméa port and capital on the southwest coast of *New Caledonia; population (1992) 65,000.

nouvelle cuisine (French 'new cooking') contemporary French cooking style that avoids traditional rich sauces, emphasizing fresh ingredients and attractive presentation. The phrase was coined in the British magazine *Harpers & Queen* in June 1975.

nova plural **novae**, faint star that suddenly erupts in brightness by 10,000 times or more, remains bright for a few days, and then fades away and is not seen again for very many years, if at all. Novae are believed to occur in close *binary star systems, where gas from one star flows to a companion *white dwarf. The gas ignites and is thrown off in an explosion at speeds of 1,500 kps/930 mps or more. Unlike a *supernova, the star is not completely disrupted by the outburst. After a few weeks or months it subsides to its previous state; it may erupt many more times.

Nova Scotia one of the three Maritime Provinces of eastern Canada, comprising the peninsula of Nova Scotia, extending southeast from New Brunswick into the Atlantic Ocean, and Cape Breton Island, which is separated from the northeastern end of the mainland by the Canso Strait; area 55,500 sq km/21,400 sq mi; population (2001 est) 942,700. The capital (and chief port) is Halifax. Industries include mineral extraction (coal, baryte, gypsum), lumbering, paper-milling, and fishing. Agricultural products include dairy produce, poultry, eggs, vegetables, and fruit. Tourism is important.

novel extended fictional *prose narrative, usually between 30,000 and 100,000 words in length, that deals imaginatively with human experience through the psychological development of the central characters and their relationship with a broader world. The modern novel took its name and inspiration from the Italian *novella*, the short tale of varied character which became popular in the late 13th century. As the main form of narrative fiction in the 20th century, the novel is frequently classified according to *genres and subgenres such as the historical novel, detective fiction, fantasy, and science fiction.

Nu, U (Thakin) (1907–1995) Myanmar politician, prime minister of Burma (now Myanmar) for most of the period from 1947 to the military coup of 1962. He was the country's first democratically elected prime minister. Exiled from 1966, U Nu returned to the country in 1980 and, in 1988, helped found the National League for Democracy opposition movement.

Nuba member of a minority ethnic group forming many small autonomous groups in southern Sudan, and numbering about 1 million (1991). They are primarily agriculturalists, and go in for elaborate body painting. They speak related dialects of Nubian, which belongs to the Chari-Nile family. Forced Islamization threatens their cultural identity, and thousands were killed in the Sudan civil war.

nuclear energy or **atomic energy** energy released from the inner core, or *nucleus, of the atom. Energy produced by nuclear *fission (the splitting of certain atomic nuclei) has been harnessed since the 1950s to generate electricity, and research continues into the possible controlled use of *nuclear fusion (the fusing, or combining, of atomic nuclei).

nuclear fusion process whereby two atomic nuclei are fused, with the release of a large amount of energy. Very high temperatures and pressures are required for the process. Under these conditions the atoms involved are stripped of all their electrons so that the remaining particles, which together make up a **plasma**, can come close together at very high speeds and overcome the mutual repulsion of the positive charges on the atomic nuclei. At very close range the strong nuclear force will come into play, fusing the particles to form a larger nucleus. As fusion is accompanied by the release of large amounts of energy, the process might one day be harnessed to form the basis of commercial energy production. Methods of achieving controlled fusion are therefore the subject of research around the world.

nuclear physics study of the properties of the nucleus of the *atom, including the structure of nuclei; nuclear forces; the interactions between particles and nuclei; and the study of radioactive decay. The study of elementary particles is *particle physics.

nuclear reactor device for producing *nuclear energy in a controlled manner. There are various types of reactor in use, all using nuclear *fission. In a **gas-cooled reactor**, a circulating gas under pressure (such as carbon dioxide) removes heat from the core of the reactor, which usually contains natural uranium. The efficiency of the fission process is increased by slowing neutrons in the core by using a *moderator such as carbon. The reaction is controlled with neutron-absorbing rods made of boron. An **advanced gas-cooled reactor** (AGR) generally has enriched uranium as its fuel. A **water-cooled reactor**, such as the steam-

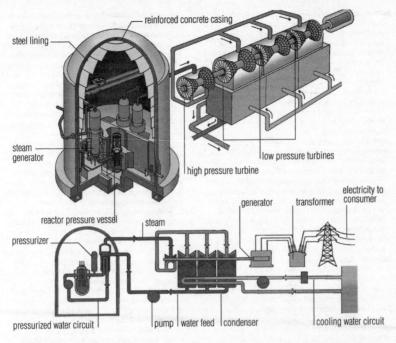

nuclear energy A pressurized water nuclear power station. Water at high pressure is circulated around the reactor vessel where it is heated. The hot water is pumped to the steam generator where it boils in a separate circuit; the steam drives the turbines coupled to the electricity generator. This is the most widely used type of reactor. More than 20 countries have pressurized water reactors.

generating heavy water (deuterium oxide) reactor, has water circulating through the hot core. The water is converted to steam, which drives turbo-alternators for generating electricity. The most widely used reactor is the **pressurized-water reactor** (PWR), which contains a sealed system of pressurized water that is heated to form steam in heat exchangers in an external circuit. The **fast reactor** has no moderator and uses fast neutrons to bring about fission. It uses a mixture of plutonium and uranium oxide as fuel. When operating, uranium is converted to plutonium, which can be extracted and used later as fuel. It is also called the fast breeder or breeder reactor because it produces more plutonium than it consumes. Heat is removed from the reactor by a coolant of liquid sodium.

nuclear warfare war involving the use of nuclear weapons. Nuclear-weapons research began in Britain in 1940, but was transferred to the USA after it entered World War II. The research programme, known as the *Manhattan Project, was directed by J Robert Oppenheimer. The development of technology that could destroy the Earth by the two major superpowers, the USA and USSR, as well as by Britain, France, and China, has since become a source of contention and heated debate. The worldwide total of nuclear weapons in 1990 was estimated to be about 50,000, and the number of countries possessing nuclear weapons stood officially at five – USA, USSR, UK, France, and China; South Africa developed nuclear weapons in the 1980s but gave them up voluntarily in 1991. India and Pakistan exploded nuclear devices in 1998. Countries suspected of possessing or developing nuclear capability include Israel, North Korea, and Iran.

nuclear waste the radioactive and toxic by-products of the nuclear energy and nuclear weapons industries. Nuclear waste may have an active life of several thousand years. Reactor waste is of three types: **high-level** spent fuel, or the residue when nuclear fuel has been removed from a reactor and reprocessed; **intermediate**, which may be long- or short-lived; and **low-level**, but bulky, waste from reactors, which has only short-lived radioactivity. Disposal, by burial on land or at sea, has raised problems of safety, environmental pollution, and security.

nuclear winter possible long-term effect of a widespread nuclear war. In the wake of the destruction caused by nuclear blasts and the subsequent radiation, it has been suggested that atmospheric pollution by dust, smoke, soot, and ash could prevent the Sun's rays from penetrating for a period of time sufficient to eradicate most plant life on which other life depends, and create a new Ice Age.

nucleic acid complex organic acid made up of a long chain of nucleotides, present in the nucleus and sometimes the cytoplasm of the living cell. The two types, known as *DNA (deoxyribonucleic acid) and *RNA (ribonucleic acid), form the basis of heredity. The nucleotides are made up of a sugar (deoxyribose or ribose), a phosphate group, and one of four purine or pyrimidine bases. The order of the bases along the nucleic acid strand contains the genetic code.

nucleon in particle physics, either a *proton or a *neutron, when present in the atomic nucleus. **Nucleon number** is an alternative name for the *mass number of an atom.

nucleus in biology, the central, membrane-enclosed part of a eukaryotic cell, containing threads of *DNA. It is found in both plant and animal cells. During cell division the threads of DNA coil up to form *chromosomes. The nucleus controls the function of the cell by determining which proteins are produced within it. It is where inherited information is stored as *genes. Because proteins are the chief structural molecules of living matter and, as enzymes, regulate all aspects of metabolism, it may be seen that the genetic code within the nucleus is effectively responsible for building and controlling the whole organism.

nucleus plural **nuclei**, in physics, the positively-charged central part of an *atom, which constitutes almost all its mass. Except for hydrogen nuclei, which have only one proton, nuclei are composed of both protons and neutrons. Surrounding the nucleus are electrons, of equal and opposite charge to that of the protons, thus giving the atom a neutral charge. Nuclei that are unstable may undergo *radioactive decay or nuclear *fission. In all stars, including our Sun, small nuclei join together to make more stable, larger nuclei. This process is called nuclear *fusion.

nuclide in physics, a species of atomic nucleus characterized by the number of protons (*Z*) and the number of neutrons (*N*). Nuclides with identical *proton number but differing neutron number are called *isotopes.

nuée ardente rapidly flowing, glowing white-hot cloud of ash and gas emitted by a volcano during a violent eruption. The ash and other pyroclastics in the lower part of the cloud behave like an ash flow. In 1902 a *nuée ardente* produced by the eruption of Mount Pelee in Martinique swept down the volcano in a matter of seconds and killed 28,000 people in the nearby town of St Pierre.

Nuku'alofa capital and port of Tonga on Tongatapu Island; population (1998 est) 30,400.

number symbol used in counting or measuring. In mathematics, there are various kinds of number. The everyday number system is the decimal ('proceeding by tens') system, using the base ten. ***Real numbers** include all rational numbers (*integers, or whole numbers, and *fractions) and *irrational numbers (those not expressible as fractions). ***Complex numbers** include the real and imaginary numbers (real-number multiples of the *square root of −1). The ***binary number system**, used in computers, has two as its base. The **natural numbers**, 0, 1, 2, 3, 4, 5, 6, 7, 8, and 9, give a counting system that, in the ***decimal number system**, continues 10, 11, 12, 13, and so on. These are whole numbers

(integers), with fractions represented as, for example, $\frac{1}{4}$, $\frac{1}{2}$, $\frac{3}{4}$, or as decimal fractions (0.25, 0.5, 0.75). They are also **rational numbers**. **Irrational numbers** cannot be represented in this way and require symbols, such as $\sqrt{2}$, π, and e. They can be expressed numerically only as the (inexact) approximations 1.414, 3.142, and 2.718 (to three places of decimals), respectively. The symbols π and e are also examples of **transcendental numbers**, because they (unlike $\sqrt{2}$) cannot be derived by solving a *polynomial equation (an equation with one *variable quantity) with rational *coefficients (multiplying *factors). Complex numbers, which include the real numbers as well as imaginary numbers, take the general form $a + bi$, where $i = \sqrt{-1}$ (that is, $i^2 = -1$), and a is the real part and bi the imaginary part.

Nuremberg rallies annual meetings 1933–38 of the German *Nazi Party. They were characterized by extensive torchlight parades, marches in party formations, and mass rallies addressed by Nazi leaders such as Hitler and Goebbels.

Nuremberg trials after World War II, the trials of the 24 chief *Nazi war criminals November 1945–October 1946 by an international military tribunal consisting of four judges and four prosecutors: one of each from the USA, UK, USSR, and France. An appendix accused the German cabinet, general staff, high command, Nazi leadership corps, *SS, *Sturmabteilung, and *Gestapo of criminal behaviour.

Nureyev, Rudolf Hametovich (1938–1993) Russian dancer and choreographer. A soloist with the Kirov Ballet, he defected to the West during a visit to Paris in 1961. Mainly associated with the Royal Ballet (London) and as Margot *Fonteyn's principal partner, he was one of the most brilliant dancers of the 1960s and 1970s. Nureyev danced in such roles as Prince Siegfried in *Swan Lake* and Armand in *Marguerite and Armand*, which was created especially for Fonteyn and Nureyev. He also danced and acted in films and on television and choreographed several ballets. It was due to his enormous impact on the ballet world that the male dancer's role was elevated to the equivalent of the ballerina's.

nursing care of the sick, the very young, the very old, and the disabled. Organized training originated in 1836 in Germany, and was developed in Britain by the work of Florence *Nightingale, who, during the Crimean War, established standards of scientific, humanitarian care in military hospitals. Nurses give day-to-day care and carry out routine medical and surgical duties under the supervision of doctors.

nut any dry, single-seeded fruit that does not split open to release the seed, such as the chestnut. A nut is formed from more than one carpel, but only one seed becomes fully formed, the remainder aborting. The wall of the fruit, the pericarp, becomes hard and woody, forming the outer shell.

nutcracker either of two species of bird similar to a jay, belonging to the crow family. One species is found in the Old World and the other in the New World. (Genus *Nucifraga*, family Corvidae, order Passeriformes.)

nuthatch any of a group of small birds with short tails and pointed beaks. Nuthatches climb head first up, down, and around tree trunks and branches, foraging for insects and their larvae. (Family Sittidae, order Passeriformes.)

nutmeg kernel of the hard aromatic seed of the evergreen nutmeg tree, native to the Maluku Islands, Indonesia. Both the nutmeg and its secondary covering, known as **mace**, are used as spices in cookery. (*Myristica fragrans*, family Myristicaceae.)

nutrition strategy adopted by an organism to obtain the chemicals it needs to live, grow, and reproduce. These chemicals are nutrients that are absorbed from the environment, such as mineral salts, or chemicals made inside the body of a plant or animal. Nutrition is a term also used to describe the science of food, and its effect on human and animal life, health, and disease. Nutrition involves the study of the basic nutrients required to sustain life, their bioavailability in foods and overall diet, and the effects upon them of cooking and storage. It is also concerned with dietary deficiency diseases.

Nyanja a central African people living mainly in Malawi, and numbering about 400,000 (1984). The Nyanja are predominantly farmers, living in villages under a hereditary monarchy. They speak a Bantu language belonging to the Niger-Congo family.

Nyasa, Lake alternative name for Lake *Malawi.

Nyasaland former name (to 1964) for Malawi.

Nyerere, Julius Kambarage (1922–1999) Tanzanian socialist politician, president 1964–85. He devoted himself from 1954 to the formation of the Tanganyika African National Union and subsequent campaigning for independence. He became chief minister in 1960, was prime minister of Tanganyika 1961–62, president of the newly formed Tanganyika Republic 1962–64, and first president of Tanzania 1964–85.

nylon synthetic long-chain polymer similar in chemical structure to protein. Nylon was the first fully *synthetic fibre. Made from petroleum, natural gas, air, and water, nylon was developed in 1935 by the US chemist W H Carothers and his associates, who worked for Du Pont. It is used in the manufacture of moulded articles, textiles, and medical sutures. Nylon fibres are stronger and more elastic than silk and are relatively insensitive to moisture and mildew. Nylon is used for a wide range of different textiles including carpets, and can be used in knitting or weaving. It is also used for simulating other fabrics such as silks and furs.

nymph in entomology, the immature form of insects that do not have a pupal stage; for example, grasshoppers and dragonflies. Nymphs generally resemble the adult (unlike larvae), but do not have fully formed reproductive organs or wings.

nymph in Greek mythology, a guardian spirit of nature. *Dryads or **hamadryads** guarded trees; **naiads**, springs and pools; **oreads**, hills and rocks; **oceanids**, the open sea; and *Nereids, the Aegean.

O

oak any of a group of trees or shrubs belonging to the beech family, with over 300 known species widely distributed in temperate zones. Oaks are valuable for timber, the wood being durable and straight-grained. Their fruits are called acorns. (Genus *Quercus*, family Fagaceae.)

oarfish any of a group of deep-sea bony fishes, found in warm parts of the Atlantic, Pacific, and Indian oceans. Oarfish are large, up to 9 m/30 ft long, elongated, and compressed, with a fin along the back and a manelike crest behind the head. They have a small mouth, no teeth or scales, and large eyes. They are often described as sea serpents. (Genus *Regalecidae*.)

OAS abbreviation for *Organization of American States.

oasis area of land made fertile by the presence of water near the surface in an otherwise arid region. The occurrence of oases affects the distribution of plants, animals, and people in the desert regions of the world.

oat type of annual grass, a *cereal crop. The plant has long narrow leaves and a stiff straw stem; the panicles of flowers (clusters around the main stem), and later of grain, hang downwards. The cultivated oat (*A. sativa*) is produced for human and animal food. (Genus *Avena*.)

Oates, Titus (1648–1705) English conspirator. A priest, he entered the Jesuit colleges at Valladolid, Spain, and St Omer, France, as a spy in 1677–78, and on his return to England announced he had discovered a 'Popish Plot' to murder Charles II and re-establish Catholicism. Although this story was almost entirely false, many innocent Roman Catholics were executed during 1678–80 on Oates's evidence.

oath solemn promise to tell the truth or perform some duty, combined with a declaration naming a deity or something held sacred. In English courts, witnesses normally swear to tell the truth holding a *New Testament in their right hand. In the USA, witnesses raise their right hand in taking the oath. People who object to the taking of oaths, such as Quakers (members of the Society of *Friends) and atheists, give a solemn promise (affirmation) to tell the truth. Jews swear holding the Torah (Pentateuch), with their heads covered. Muslims and Hindus swear by their respective sacred books.

OAU abbreviation for Organization of African Unity, the former name (until 2001) of the African Union.

Oaxaca capital of a state of the same name in the Sierra Madre del Sur mountain range, central Mexico; population (1990) 212,900. Industries include food processing, textiles, and handicrafts.

Ob major river in Asian Russia, flowing 3,380 km/2,100 mi from the Altai Mountains through the western Siberian Plain to the Gulf of Ob in the Kara Sea (an inlet of the Arctic Ocean). With its main tributary, the **Irtysh**, the Ob is 5,600 km/3,480 mi long, and drains a total area of 2,990,000 sq km/1,150,000 sq mi.

obelisk tall, tapering column of stone, much used in ancient Egyptian and Roman architecture. Examples are Cleopatra's Needles (1475 BC), one of which is in London, another in New York. Ancient Egyptian obelisks were originally placed in pairs at the entrance to temples. They were carved from a single piece of stone, usually red granite; an inscription from the base of an obelisk at Karnak reveals that it took seven months to cut that particular stone out of the quarry. All four sides of an obelisk are decorated with hieroglyphs that typically commemorate the lives of rulers or make dedications to the gods.

Oberon in folklore, king of the elves or fairies and, according to the 13th-century French romance *Huon of Bordeaux*, an illegitimate son of Julius Caesar. Shakespeare used the character in *A Midsummer Night's Dream*. Oberon's name was taken as the title of a masque by Ben Jonson in 1616, an epic by Christoph Wieland in 1780, and an opera by Weber in 1826.

obesity condition of being overweight (generally, 20% or more above the medically recommended weight for one's sex, build, and height). Obesity increases susceptibility to disease, strains the vital organs, and reduces life expectancy; it is usually remedied by controlled weight loss, healthy diet, and exercise.

oboe double-reed woodwind instrument with a conical bore and moderately flared bell, descended from the shawm. It is one of the four instruments that make up the woodwind section of the orchestra. The oboe was developed by the Hotteterre family of instrument makers in about 1700 and was played in the court ensemble of Louis XIV of France. Pitched in C, with a normal range of about 2 and a half octaves, it has a reedy and penetrating tone. This is why it is used at the beginning of concerts to sound the note A for the other players to tune their instruments. Oboe concertos have been composed by Antonio Vivaldi, Tomaso Albinoni, Richard Strauss, Bohuslav Martinu, and others. Heinz Holliger is a modern virtuoso oboist and important composer.

Obote, (Apollo) Milton (1924–) Ugandan politician, prime minister 1962–66, and president 1966–71 and 1980–85. After forming the Uganda People's Congress (UPC) in 1959, he led the independence movement from 1961. As prime minister, his rule became increasingly authoritarian, and in 1966 he suspended the constitution and declared himself president. He was ousted by Idi *Amin in 1971, fleeing to exile in Tanzania. Returning in 1979 after the collapse of the Amin regime, he was re-elected president in 1980 but failed to restore order and was deposed by Lieutenant General Tito Okello in 1985.

obscenity law law established by the Obscene Publications Act 1959 prohibiting the publishing of any material that tends to deprave or corrupt. In Britain, obscene material can be, for example, pornographic or violent, or can encourage drug taking. Publishing includes distribution, sale, and hiring of the material. There is a defence in support of the public good if the defendant can produce expert evidence to show that publication was in the interest of, for example, art, science, or literature.

observatory site or facility for observing astronomical or meteorological phenomena. The modern observatory dates from the invention of the telescope. Observatories may be ground-based, carried on aircraft, or sent into orbit as satellites, in space stations, and on the space shuttle.

obsession persistently intruding thought, emotion, or impulse, often recognized by the sufferer as irrational, but nevertheless causing distress. It may be a brooding on destiny or death, or chronic doubts interfering with everyday life (such as fearing the gas is not turned off and repeatedly checking), or an impulse leading to repetitive action, such as continually washing one's hands.

obsessive-compulsive disorder (OCD) in psychiatry, anxiety disorder that manifests itself in the need to check constantly that certain acts have been performed 'correctly'. Sufferers may, for example, feel compelled to wash themselves repeatedly or return home again and again to check that doors have been locked and appliances switched off. They may also hoard certain objects and insist in these being arranged in a precise way, or be troubled by intrusive and unpleasant thoughts. In extreme cases, normal life is disrupted through the hours devoted to compulsive actions. Treatment involves *cognitive therapy and drug therapy with serotonin-blocking drugs such as Prozac.

obsidian black or dark-coloured glassy volcanic rock, chemically similar to *granite, but formed by cooling rapidly on the Earth's surface at low pressure.

obstetrics medical speciality concerned with the management of pregnancy, childbirth, and the immediate postnatal period.

O'Casey, Seán (1884–1964) adopted name of John Casey, Irish dramatist. His early plays are tragicomedies, blending realism with symbolism and poetry with vernacular (commonly spoken dialect) speech. They include *The Shadow of a Gunman* (1923), *Juno and the Paycock* (1924), and *The Plough and the Stars* (1926). Later plays include *Red Roses for Me* (1946) and *The Drums of Father Ned* (1959). His six-volume *Autobiographies* (1939–54) evokes his early impressions and memories of his childhood and dramatic career.

Occam (or Ockham), William of (c. 1300–1349) English philosopher and scholastic logician who revived the fundamentals of nominalism. As a Franciscan monk he defended evangelical poverty against Pope John XXII, becoming known as the Invincible Doctor. He was imprisoned in Avignon, France, on charges of heresy in 1328 but escaped to Munich, Germany, where he died. The principle of reducing assumptions to the absolute minimum is known as **Occam's razor**.

occult (Latin 'hidden from general view') vague term describing a wide range of activities connected with the supernatural, from seances to black magic. The term has come to have largely sinister overtones and an association with Satanism and witchcraft.

ocean great mass of salt water. Geographically speaking three oceans exist – the Atlantic, Indian, and Pacific – to which the Arctic is often added. They cover approximately 70% or 363,000,000 sq km/140,000,000

sq mi of the total surface area of the Earth. According to figures released in August 2001, the total volume of the world's oceans is 1,370 million cubic km/329 million cubic mi. Water levels recorded in the world's oceans have shown an increase of 10–15 cm/4–6 in over the past 100 years.

ocean current fast-flowing body of seawater forced by the wind or by variations in water density (as a result of temperature or salinity variations) between two areas. Ocean currents are partly responsible for transferring heat from the Equator to the poles and thereby evening out the global heat imbalance.

Oceania the groups of islands in the southern and central Pacific Ocean, comprising all those intervening between the southeastern shores of Asia and the western shores of America.

Oceanic art art of the native peoples of Australia and the South Pacific islands, including New Guinea and New Zealand. Covering a wide geographical area, Oceanic art is extremely diverse in style and technique. Artefacts were not considered 'art' by their creators, but were an integral part of the religious and social ceremony of everyday island life. Art objects include ancestor figures, canoe-prow ornaments, ceremonial shields, masks, stone carvings, decorated human skulls, pottery, and stools. Fertility is a recurrent theme, along with occasional references to headhunting and ritual cannibalism. Most Oceanic arts are considered primitive in that until recently the indigenous cultures possessed no metal, and cutting tools were of stone or shell. Although Oceanic art is considered to have little historic depth, an outstanding example of prehistoric art is found in the sculpture of *Easter Island, huge standing carved-stone figures up to 18 m/60 ft high, possibly representing ancestors.

oceanography study of the oceans. Its subdivisions deal with each ocean's extent and depth, the water's evolution and composition, its physics and chemistry, the bottom topography, currents and wind, tidal ranges, biology, and the various aspects of human use. Computer simulations are widely used in oceanography to plot the possible movements of the waters, and many studies are carried out by remote sensing.

ocean trench submarine valley. Ocean trenches are characterized by the presence of a volcanic arc on the concave side of the trench. Trenches are now known to be related to subduction zones, places where a plate of oceanic *lithosphere dives beneath another plate of either oceanic or continental lithosphere. Ocean trenches are found around the edge of the Pacific Ocean and the northeastern Indian Ocean; minor ones occur in the Caribbean and near the Falkland Islands.

ocelot wild cat of the southwestern USA, Mexico, and Central and South America. It is up to 1 m/3 ft long, with a 45 cm/1.5 ft tail, weighs about 18 kg/40 lb, and has a pale yellowish coat marked with horizontal stripes and blotches. As a result of being hunted for its fur, it is close to extinction. (Species *Felis pardalis*, family Felidae.)

O'Connell, Daniel (1775–1847) Irish lawyer and politician, known as 'the Liberator'. In 1823 he formed the Catholic Association, to campaign for Catholic emancipation and the repeal of the 1801 Act of Union between Britain and Ireland. He achieved the first objective in 1829, but failed in the second.

octane rating numerical classification of petroleum fuels indicating their combustion characteristics.

octave in music, a span of eight notes as measured on the white notes of a piano keyboard. It corresponds to the consonance of first and second harmonics.

Octavian original name of *Augustus, the first Roman emperor.

October Revolution second stage of the *Russian Revolution 1917, when, on the night of 24 October (6 November in the Western calendar), the Bolshevik forces under Trotsky, and on orders from Lenin, seized the Winter Palace and arrested members of the Provisional Government. The following day the Second All-Russian Congress of Soviets handed power over to the Bolsheviks.

octopus soft-bodied sea animal with a round or oval body and eight slender arms (tentacles) in a ring surrounding its mouth. They are solitary creatures, living alone in rocky dens. They feed on crabs and other small animals. There are about 50 different species of octopus living in all the oceans of the world. Some are small, having bodies only 8 cm/3 in long, but the largest deep-sea species can grow to lengths of 20 m/64 ft.

ode *lyric poem with complex rules of structure. Odes originated in ancient Greece, where they were chanted to a musical accompaniment. Classical writers of odes include Sappho, Pindar, Horace, and Catullus. English poets who adopted the form include Edmund *Spenser, John *Milton, John *Dryden, and John *Keats.

Oder Polish **Odra**, European river flowing north from the Czech Republic to the Baltic Sea (the Neisse River is a tributary); length 885 km/550 mi.

Odin German **Woden** or **Wotan**, ('the raging one') chief god of Norse mythology, god of war, and the source of wisdom. A sky god, he lived in Asgard at the top of the world-tree *Yggdrasil. From the *Valkyries, his divine maidens, he received the souls of half those heroes slain in battle, feasting with them in his great hall Valhalla; the remainder were feasted by *Freya. His son was *Thor, god of thunder. Wednesday or Woden's day is named after him.

Odysseus Latin **Ulysses**, ('son of wrath') chief character of Homer's *Odyssey*, king of the island of Ithaca (modern Thiaki or Levkas); he is also mentioned in the *Iliad* as one of the leaders of the Greek forces at the siege of Troy. Odysseus was distinguished among Greek leaders for his cleverness and cunning. He appears in other later tragedies, but his ten years' odyssey by sea after the fall of Troy is the most commonly known tradition.

Odyssey Greek epic poem; the product of an oral tradition, it was probably written before 700 BC and is attributed to *Homer. It describes the voyage home of Odysseus after the fall of Troy, and the vengeance he takes with his son Telemachus on the suitors of his wife Penelope on his return. During his ten-year wanderings, he encounters the Cyclops, the enchantress Circe, Scylla and Charybdis, and the Sirens.

OECD abbreviation for *Organization for Economic Cooperation and Development.

oedema any abnormal accumulation of fluid in tissues or cavities of the body; waterlogging of the tissues due to excessive loss of *plasma through the capillary walls. It may be generalized (the condition once known as

dropsy) or confined to one area, such as the ankles.

Oedipus in Greek mythology, king of Thebes who unwittingly killed his father, Laius, and married his mother, Jocasta, in fulfilment of a prophecy. When he learned what he had done, he put out his eyes. His story was dramatized by the Greek tragedian *Sophocles.

Oedipus complex in psychology, the unconscious antagonism of a son to his father, whom he sees as a rival for his mother's affection. For a girl antagonistic to her mother as a rival for her father's affection, the term is **Electra complex**. The terms were coined by Sigmund *Freud.

oesophagus muscular tube through which food travels from the mouth to the stomach. The human oesophagus is about 23 cm/9 in long. It extends downwards from the pharynx, immediately behind the windpipe. It is lined with a mucous membrane made of epithelial cells, which secretes lubricant fluid to assist the downward movement of food. In its wall is *muscle, which contracts to squeeze the food towards the stomach (*peristalsis).

oestrogen any of a group of *hormones produced by the *ovaries of vertebrates; the term is also used for various synthetic hormones that mimic their effects. The principal oestrogen in mammals is oestradiol. Oestrogens control female sexual development, promote the growth of female *secondary sexual characteristics at puberty, stimulate egg (*ovum) production, and, in mammals, prepare the lining of the uterus for pregnancy. In other words, together with another hormone, progesterone, they regulate the growth and functioning of sex organs for *sexual reproduction. Oestrogens are also used in female oral contraceptives, to inhibit the production of ova.

oestrus in mammals, the period during a female's reproductive cycle (also known as the oestrus cycle or *menstrual cycle) when mating is most likely to occur. It usually coincides with ovulation.

oeuvre (French 'work') in the arts, the entire body of work produced by an artist. It can also mean a single work.

Offa (died c. 796) King of the Anglo-Saxon kingdom of Mercia (west-central England) 757–97. He conquered Essex, Kent, Sussex, and Surrey; defeated the Welsh and the West Saxons; and established Mercian supremacy over all England south of the River Humber. He built the earthwork known as Offa's Dyke along the Welsh border to defend his frontier in the west.

Offaly county of the Republic of Ireland, in the province of Leinster, between Galway and Roscommon in the west and Kildare in the east; county town Tullamore; area 2,000 sq km/772 sq mi; population (2002 est) 63,700. It is low-lying, with part of the Bog of Allen to the north. It shares its highest point, Arderin (527 m/729 ft), with Co. Laois.

Offa's Dyke defensive earthwork dyke along the English–Welsh border, of which there are remains from the mouth of the River Dee to that of the River *Severn. It was built about AD 785 by King *Offa of Mercia, England, and represents the boundary secured by his wars with Wales.

Offenbach, Jacques (1819–1880) adopted name of Jakob Levy Eberst, French composer. He wrote light opera, initially for presentation at the Bouffes Parisiens. Among his works are *Orphée aux enfers/Orpheus in the*

Underworld (1858, revised 1874), *La belle Hélène* (1864), and *Les contes d'Hoffmann/The Tales of Hoffmann* (1881).

Official Secrets Act UK act of Parliament 1989, prohibiting the disclosure of confidential material from government sources by employees; it remains an absolute offence for a member or former member of the security and intelligence services (or those working closely with them) to disclose information about their work. There is no public-interest defence, and disclosure of information already in the public domain is still a crime. Journalists who repeat disclosures may also be prosecuted.

offset printing the most common method of *printing, which works on the principle of *lithography: that is, that grease and water repel one another.

Ogaden desert region in southeastern Ethiopia, between the Ethiopian Highlands and the border with Somalia. It is a desert plateau, rising to 1,000 m/3,280 ft, inhabited mainly by Somali nomads practising arid farming.

Ogoni an ethnic minority of about 500,000 (1990) occupying an impoverished area of about 350 sq mi in the Niger river delta of Nigeria. The Ogoni speak Khana, Gokama, and Eleme languages that form a distinct branch of the Benue-Congo language family. They are fishermen and farmers, yams being the principal crop. In 1958 oil was discovered under their land. In protest at the pollution from the oil wells and their lack of any benefit from oil revenues, the Movement for the Survival of the Ogoni People (MOSOP) was founded in 1990 to seek both political autonomy and compensation for the destruction of their environment from the Nigerian government.

O'Higgins, Bernardo (1778–1842) Chilean revolutionary, known as 'the Liberator of Chile'. He was a leader of the struggle for independence from Spanish rule 1810–17 and head of the first permanent national government 1817–23.

Ohio river in east-central USA, 1,580 km/980 mi long and 365–1,220 m/1,200–4,005 ft wide; the second-largest tributary of the Mississippi; navigable throughout its length. It is formed by the union of the Allegheny and Monongahela rivers at Pittsburgh, Pennsylvania, and flows southwest to join the Mississippi at Cairo, Illinois.

Ohio called the **Buckeye State,** (Iroquoian 'great river') state in northern central USA, bordered to the west by *Indiana, to the north by *Michigan's Lower Peninsula and Lake *Erie, to the east by *Pennsylvania, to the east and southeast by *West Virginia, to the southwest by *Kentucky, the southeastern and southern borders being formed by the *Ohio River; area 106,055 sq km/40,948 sq mi; population (2000) 11,353,100; capital Columbus. It is called the Buckeye State after the region's native tree. Ohio is part of the *Midwest and comprises the eastern section of the Corn Belt. Western Ohio's level, verdant topography and thick fertile soils contrast with the southeast quarter of the state, which retains the more rugged hills and valleys of the Appalachian Plateau, along with its deposits of coal and oil. Ohio's economy is sustained by manufacturing, principally of steel, rubber, plastics, motor vehicles and parts, and industrial machinery, along with service-based industries. Cereals, livestock, and dairy foods are the main products of farmland in the west. The

*Cleveland-Akron consolidated area is the state's most populous metropolitan region; other major towns and cities include *Cincinnati, Dayton, Toledo, Youngstown, and Canton. Originally, Ohio was home to the Miami, Shawnee, Ottawa, and Huron peoples. It was explored for France by René Robert Cavelier, Sieur de la Salle in 1669. Ceded to Britain by France in 1763, and to the USA after the *American Revolution, the state was settled extensively in 1787 following the *Northwest Ordinance. Ohio was admitted to the Union in 1803 as the 17th US state.

ohm symbol Ω, SI unit of electrical *resistance (the property of a conductor that restricts the flow of electrons through it).

Ohm's law law that states that, for many materials over a wide range of conditions, the current flowing in a conductor maintained at constant temperature is directly proportional to the potential difference (voltage) between its ends. The law was discovered by German physicist Georg Ohm in 1827. He found that if the voltage across a conducting material is changed, the current flow through the material is changed proportionally (for example, if the voltage is doubled then the current also doubles).

oil flammable substance, usually insoluble in water, and composed chiefly of carbon and hydrogen. Oils may be solids (fats and waxes) or liquids. Various plants produce vegetable oils; mineral oils are based on petroleum.

oil crop plant from whose seeds vegetable oils are pressed. Cool temperate areas grow rapeseed and linseed; warm temperate regions produce sunflowers, olives, and soybeans; tropical regions produce groundnuts (peanuts), palm oil, and coconuts.

oil paint painting medium in which ground pigment (colour) is bound with oil, usually linseed. It has the advantage of being slow to dry and therefore reworkable. Oil paint can be applied with a brush or a palette knife to a prepared ground, usually stretched canvas.

oil palm African *palm tree, the fruit of which yields valuable oils, used as food or processed into margarine, soaps, and livestock feeds. (*Elaeis guineensis*.)

okapi ruminant (cud-chewing) mammal related to the giraffe, although with a much shorter neck and legs, found in the tropical rainforests of central Africa. Its purplish brown body, creamy face, and black and white stripes on the legs and hindquarters provide excellent camouflage. Okapis have remained virtually unchanged for millions of years. (Species *Okapia johnstoni*, family Giraffidae.)

Okavango Delta marshy area in northwest Botswana covering about 20,000 km/7,722 sq mi, fed by the Okavango River, which rises in Angola and flows southeast about 1,600 km/1,000 mi. It is an important area for wildlife as it provides the main area of permanently available water in the Kalahari Desert.

O'Keeffe, Georgia (1887–1986) US painter. One of the best known US painters of the 20th century, O'Keefe is known chiefly for her large, semi-abstract studies of flowers, bones, and other imagery, such as *Black Iris* (1926; Metropolitan Museum of Art, New York). Although painting representational subjects, her strong lines, geometric forms, and flat planes sometimes verge on abstraction, as in *Jack-in-the-Pulpit* (1930; collection of Georgia O'Keeffe).

Okhotsk, Sea of arm of the North Pacific Ocean between the Kamchatka Peninsula and Sakhalin, and bordered to the south by the Kuril Islands, and the northern Japanese island of Hokkaido; area 937,000 sq km/361,700 sq mi, average depth 777 m/2,550 ft, maximum depth 3,372 m/11,062 ft. It is free of ice only in summer, and is often fog-bound. Magadan is the chief port, and the River Amur flows into it.

Okinawa group of islands, 520 km/323 mi from the Japanese mainland, forming part of the Japanese *Ryukyu Islands in the west Pacific; Okinawa is also the name of the largest island, and of a city on Okinawa; area 2,250 sq km/869 sq mi; population (1995 est) 1,318,000. The capital is Naha.

Oklahoma called the **Sooner State**, (Choctaw *okla* 'people', *homma* 'red') state in southern central USA, bordered to the south by *Texas, to the west, at the extreme of the Oklahoma panhandle, by *New Mexico, to the north by *Colorado and *Kansas, and to the east by *Missouri and *Arkansas; area 177,847 sq km/68,667 sq mi; population (2000) 3,450,700; capital Oklahoma City. It is nicknamed the Sooner State because during the Oklahoma Land Run in 1889, when the land was opened up to white settlers, many took land before it was officially allowed. The state has a number of land regions, including the Ozark Plateau, the Prairie Plains, and the Ouachita Mountains. Oklahoma ranks among the leading states in petroleum and natural gas production, and it is the only US state that produces iodine. Beef cattle are the major source of agricultural income and cowhands still ride the range, although ranching has been thoroughly modernized. Other towns and cities are Tulsa, Norman, Lawton, Broken Arrow, Edmond, Midwest City, and Enid. Oklahoma is the US state most associated with *American Indians, and has the largest American Indian population of any of the states, most of whom are descended from the 67 tribes who inhabited the Indian Territory. Oklahoma was admitted to the Union in 1907 as the 46th US state.

okra plant belonging to the Old World hibiscus family. Its red-and-yellow flowers are followed by long, sticky, green fruits known as **ladies' fingers** or **bhindi**. The fruits are cooked in soups and stews. (*Hibiscus esculentus*, family Malvaceae.)

Old English general name for the range of dialects spoken by Germanic settlers in England between the 5th and 12th centuries AD, also known as Anglo-Saxon. The literature of the period includes *Beowulf*, an epic in West Saxon dialect. See also *English language.

Old Pretender nickname of *James Edward Stuart, the son of James II of England.

Old Testament Christian term for the Hebrew *Bible, a collection of Jewish scriptures that form the first part of the Christian Bible. Gathered over many centuries, it contains 39 (according to Christianity) or 24 (according to Judaism) books, which include an account of beliefs about God's creation of the world, the history of the ancient Hebrews and their covenant with God, prophetical writings, and religious poetry. The first five books (Genesis, Exodus, Leviticus, Numbers, and Deuteronomy) are traditionally ascribed to *Moses and known as the *Pentateuch (by Christians) or the *Torah (by Jews). They contain the basic principles for living in a relationship with God, and include the *Ten Commandments.

Olduvai Gorge deep cleft in the Serengeti steppe, Tanzania, where Louis and Mary Leakey found prehistoric stone tools in the 1930s. They discovered Pleistocene remains of prehumans and gigantic animals 1958–59. The gorge has given its name to the **Olduvai culture**, a simple stone-tool culture of prehistoric hominids, dating from 2–0.5 million years ago.

Old World the continents of the eastern hemisphere, so called because they were familiar to Europeans before the Americas. The term is used as an adjective to describe animals and plants that live in the eastern hemisphere.

oleander *or* **rose bay** evergreen Mediterranean shrub belonging to the dogbane family, with pink or white flowers and aromatic leaves that produce and release the poison oleandrin. (*Nerium oleander*, family Apocynaceae.)

oligarchy (Greek *oligarchia* 'government of the few') rule of the few, in their own interests. It was first identified as a form of government by the Greek philosopher Aristotle. In modern times there have been a number of oligarchies, sometimes posing as democracies; the paramilitary rule of the *Duvalier family in Haiti, 1957–86, is an example.

Oligocene epoch third epoch of the Tertiary period of geological time, 35.5–3.25 million years ago. The name, from Greek, means 'a little recent', referring to the presence of the remains of some modern types of animals existing at that time.

oligopoly in economics, a situation in which a few companies control the major part of a particular market. For example, in the UK the two largest soap-powder companies, Procter & Gamble and Unilever, control over 85% of the market. In an oligopolistic market, firms may well join together in a *cartel, colluding to fix high prices. This collusion, an example of a *restrictive trade practice, is illegal in the UK and the European Union (EU).

olive evergreen tree belonging to the olive family. Native to Asia but widely cultivated in Mediterranean and subtropical areas, it grows up to 15 m/50 ft high and has twisted branches and lance-shaped silvery leaves that grow opposite each other. The white flowers are followed by small green oval fruits that turn bluish-black when ripe. They are preserved in brine or oil, dried; or pressed to make olive oil. (*Olea europaea*, family Oleaceae.)

olive branch ancient symbol of peace; in the Bible (Genesis 9), an olive branch is brought back by the dove to Noah to show that the flood has abated.

Olives, Mount of range of hills east of Jerusalem, associated with the Christian religion: a former chapel (now a mosque) marks the traditional site of Jesus' ascension to heaven, with the Garden of Gethsemane at its foot.

Olivier, Laurence (Kerr) (1907–1989) English actor and director. For many years associated with the Old Vic Theatre, he was director of the National Theatre company 1962–73. His stage roles include Henry V, Hamlet, Richard III, and Archie Rice in John Osborne's *The Entertainer* (1957; filmed 1960). He directed and starred in filmed versions of Shakespeare's plays; for example, *Henry V* (1944) and *Hamlet* (1948) (Academy Award). He was knighted in 1947 and created a baron in 1970.

olm cave-dwelling aquatic *salamander. Olms are found in underground caves along the Adriatic seaboard in Italy, Croatia, and Serbia and Montenegro. The adult is permanently larval in form, about 25 cm/10 in long, almost blind, with external gills and underdeveloped limbs. (Species *Proteus anguinus*, family Proteidae.)

Olmec first civilization of Mesoamerica and thought to be the mother culture of the Mayans. It developed in the coastal zone south of Vera Cruz and in adjacent Tabasco 1200–400 BC. The Olmecs built a large clay pyramid and several smaller mounds on the island of La Venta. Some gigantic stone heads, vestiges of their religion, also remain. The naturalistic Olmec art had a distinctive and influential style, often using the 'were-jaguar' motif of a sexless figure with fangs.

Olympia ancient sanctuary in the western Peloponnese, Greece, with a temple of Zeus, stadium (for foot races, boxing, and wrestling) and hippodrome (for chariot and horse races), where the original Olympic Games, held 776 BC, were held every four years. The gold and ivory statue of Zeus that stood here, made by *Phidias, was one of the *Seven Wonders of the World. It was removed to Constantinople, where it was destroyed in a fire. The face of Zeus may have served as a model for the face of Christ Pantocrator in the dome of St Sophia.

Olympic Games sporting contests originally held in Olympia, ancient Greece, every four years during a sacred truce; records were kept from 776 BC. Women were forbidden to be present, and the male contestants were naked. The ancient Games were abolished in AD 394. The present-day games have been held every four years since 1896. Since 1924 there has been a separate winter Games programme; since 1994 the winter and summer Games have been held two years apart.

Olympus or **Olympos** Greek **Olimbos**, any of several mountains in Greece and elsewhere, one of which is **Mount Olympus** in northern Thessaly, Greece, which is 2,918 m/9,577 ft high. In ancient Greece it was considered the home of the gods.

Om or **Aum** sacred word in Hinduism, used to begin prayers and placed at the beginning and end of books. It is composed of three syllables, symbolic of the Hindu Trimurti, or trinity of gods.

Oman
National name: *Saltanat `Uman/Sultanate of Oman*

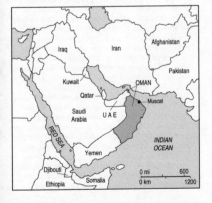

Area: 272,000 sq km/105,019 sq mi
Capital: Muscat
Major towns/cities: Salalah, Ibri, Sohar, Al-Buraimi, Nizwa, Sur, Matrah
Major ports: Mina Qaboos, Mina Raysut
Physical features: mountains to the north and south of a high arid plateau; fertile coastal strip; Jebel Akhdar highlands; Kuria Muria Islands
Head of state and government: Qaboos bin Said from 1970
Political system: absolutist
Political executive: absolute
Political parties: none
Currency: Omani rial
GNI per capita (PPP): (US$) 12,910 (2002 est)
Exports: petroleum and gas, metals and metal goods, textiles, animals and products. Principal market: China 22.3% (2001)
Population: 2,851,000 (2003 est)
Language: Arabic (official), English, Urdu, other Indian languages
Religion: Muslim 75% (predominantly Ibadhi Muslim), about 25% Hindu
Life expectancy: 71 (men); 74 (women) (2000–05)
Chronology
***c.* 3000 BC:** Archaeological evidence suggests Oman may have been the semilegendary Magan, a thriving seafaring state at the time of the Sumerian Civilization of Mesopotamia (the Tigris and Euphrates region of Iraq).
9th century BC: Migration of Arab clans to Oman, notably the Qahtan family from southwest Arabia and the Nizar from northwest Arabia, between whom rivalry has continued.
4th century BC–AD 800: North Oman under Persian control.
AD 630: Converted to Islam.
751: Julanda ibn Masud was elected imam (spiritual leader); Oman remained under imam rule until 1154.
1151: Dynasty established by Banu Nabhan.
1428: Dynastic rule came under challenge from the imams.
1507: Coastal area, including port city of Muscat, fell under Portuguese control.
1650: Portuguese ousted by Sultan ibn Sayf, a powerful Ya'ariba leader.
early 18th century: Civil war between the Hinawis (descendents of the Qahtan) and the Ghafiris (descendents of the Nizar).
1749: Independent Sultanate of Muscat and Oman established by Ahmad ibn Said, founder of the Al Bu Said dynasty that still rules Oman.
first half of 19th century: Muscat and Oman was the most powerful state in Arabia, ruling Zanzibar until 1861, and coastal parts of Persia, Kenya, and Pakistan; came under British protection.
1951: The Sultanate of Muscat and Oman achieved full independence from Britain. Treaty of Friendship with Britain signed.
1964: Discovery of oil led to the transformation of the undeveloped kingdom into a modern state.
1970: After 38 years' rule, Sultan Said bin Taimur was replaced in a bloodless coup by his son Qaboos bin Said. Name was changed to the Sultanate of Oman and a modernization programme was launched.

1975: Left-wing rebels in Dhofar in the south, who had been supported by South Yemen, defeated with UK military assistance, ending a ten-year insurrection.

1981: The Consultative Council was set up; Oman played a key role in the establishment of a six-member Gulf Cooperation Council.

1982: The Memorandum of Understanding with the UK was signed, providing for regular consultation on international issues.

1991: Joined the US-led coalition opposing Iraq's occupation of Kuwait.

1999: Oman and the United Arab Emirates agreed on the definition of their borders.

2002: Sultan Qaboos bin Said extended voting rights to all citizens over 21.

2003: The Sultan permitted the first free elections to the lower chamber of the advisory council.

Omar alternative spelling of *Umar, 2nd caliph of Islam.

Omar Khayyám (c. 1050–c. 1123) Persian astronomer, mathematician, and poet. In the West, he is chiefly known as a poet through Edward Fitzgerald's version of 'The Rubaiyat of Omar Khayyám' (1859).

Omayyad dynasty alternative spelling of *Umayyad dynasty.

ombudsman (Swedish 'commissioner') official who acts on behalf of the private citizen in investigating complaints against the government. The post is of Scandinavian origin; it was introduced in Sweden in 1809, Denmark in 1954, and Norway in 1962, and spread to other countries from the 1960s.

omnivore animal that feeds on both plant and animal material. Omnivores have digestive adaptations intermediate between those of *herbivores and *carnivores, with relatively unspecialized digestive systems and gut micro-organisms that can digest a variety of foodstuffs. Omnivores include humans, the chimpanzee, the cockroach, and the ant.

onager wild ass found in western Asia. Onagers are sandy brown, lighter underneath, and about the size of a small horse. (Species *Equus hemionus*.)

onchocerciasis *or* **river blindness** disease found in tropical Africa and Central America. It is transmitted by bloodsucking black flies, which infect the victim with parasitic filarial worms (genus *Onchocerca*), producing skin disorders and intense itching; some invade the eyes and may cause blindness.

oncogene gene carried by a virus that induces a cell to divide abnormally, giving rise to a cancer. Oncogenes arise from mutations in genes (proto-oncogenes) found in all normal cells. They are usually also found in viruses that are capable of transforming normal cells to tumour cells. Such viruses are able to insert their oncogenes into the host cell's DNA, causing it to divide uncontrollably. More than one oncogene may be necessary to transform a cell in this way.

oncology medical speciality concerned with the diagnosis and treatment of *neoplasms, especially cancer.

Onega, Lake Russian **Onezhskoye Ozero**, lake in the far northwestern Russian Federation, near the Finnish border. With an area of some 9,600 sq km/3,700 sq mi (excluding islands), it is the second-largest lake in Europe. Lake Onega is connected by the River Svir with Lake Ladoga (the largest lake in Europe) and the Baltic Sea, and by artificial waterways with the White Sea and the Volga (the 'Mariinsk' system).

O'Neill, Eugene Gladstone (1888–1953) US playwright. He is widely regarded as the greatest US dramatist. His plays, although tragic, are characterized by a down-to-earth quality and are often experimental in form, influenced by German expressionism, Strindberg, and Freud. They were a radical departure from the romantic and melodramatic American theatre entertainments. They include *Beyond the Horizon* (1920) and *Anna Christie* (1921), both of which won a Pulitzer Prize, as well as *The Emperor Jones* (1920), *The Hairy Ape* (1922), *Desire Under the Elms* (1924), *The Iceman Cometh* (1946), and the posthumously produced autobiographical drama *A Long Day's Journey into Night* (1956; written 1941), also a Pulitzer prizewinner. He was awarded the Nobel Prize for Literature in 1936.

one-party state state in which one political party dominates, constitutionally or unofficially, to the point where there is no effective opposition. There may be no legal alternative parties, as, for example, in Cuba. In other instances, a few token members of an opposition party may be tolerated, or one party may be permanently in power, with no elections. The one-party state differs from the 'dominant-party' state, where one party controls government for an extended period, as the Liberal Democrats did in Japan 1955–93, but where there are openly-democratic competitive elections.

onion plant belonging to the lily family, whose bulb has a strong, distinctive smell and taste. Cultivated from ancient times, it may have originated in Asia. The bulb is edible; its pale concentric layers of leaf bases contain an oil that is released into the air when the onion is cut open, causing the eyes to water. Onions are used extensively in cooking. (*Allium cepa*, family Liliaceae.)

online system in computing, originally a system that allows the computer to work interactively with its users, responding to each instruction as it is given and prompting users for information when necessary. As almost all the computers used now work this way, 'online system' is now used to refer to large database, e-mail, and conferencing systems accessed via a dial-up modem. These often have tens or hundreds of users from different places – sometimes from different countries – 'online' at the same time.

onomatopoeia (Greek 'name-making') figure of speech that copies natural sounds. For example, the word 'cuckoo' imitates the sound that the cuckoo makes.

Ontario province of southeastern–central Canada, in area the country's second-largest province, and its most populous. It is bounded to the north and northeast by Hudson Bay and James Bay, to the east by Québec (with the Ottawa River forming most of the boundary), and by Manitoba to the west. On the south, it borders on, and extends into, all of the Great Lakes except Lake Michigan. From west to east along Ontario's southern boundary lie the US states of Minnesota, Wisconsin, Michigan, Ohio, Pennsylvania, and New York; area 1,068,600 sq km/412,600 sq mi; population (2001 est) 11,874,400. The capital is Toronto (Canada's largest city). Industries include mining (nickel, iron, gold, copper, uranium) and the production of cars, aircraft, iron, steel, high-tech goods, pulp, paper, oil, and chemicals; agriculture includes livestock rearing, and cultivation of fruit, vegetables, and cereals.

Ontario, Lake smallest and easternmost of the *Great Lakes, on the US–Canadian border; area 19,200 sq km/7,400 sq mi. Extending for 310 km/194 mi, it has an average width of about 80 km/50 mi, average depth of 86 m/283 ft, and maximum depth of 244 m/800 ft. It is connected to Lake Erie in the southeast by the Welland Ship Canal and the Niagara River, and drains into the *St Lawrence River to the northeast. The opening of the St Lawrence Seaway in 1959 made the lake accessible to large ocean-going vessels. Its main port is Toronto, Canada.

ontogeny process of development of a living organism, including the part of development that takes place after hatching or birth. The idea that 'ontogeny recapitulates phylogeny' (the development of an organism goes through the same stages as its evolutionary history), proposed by the German scientist Ernst Heinrich Haeckel, is now discredited.

onyx semi-precious variety of chalcedonic *silica (SiO_2) in which the crystals are too fine to be detected under a microscope, a state known as cryptocrystalline. It has straight parallel bands of different colours: milk-white, black, and red.

oolite limestone made up of tiny spherical carbonate particles, called **ooliths**, cemented together. Ooliths have a concentric structure with a diameter up to 2 mm/0.08 in. They were formed by chemical precipitation and accumulation on ancient sea floors.

Oort, Jan Hendrik (1900–1992) Dutch astronomer. In 1927 he calculated the mass and size of our Galaxy, the *Milky Way, and the Sun's distance from its centre, from the observed movements of stars around the Galaxy's centre. In 1950 Oort proposed that comets exist in a vast swarm, now called the *Oort cloud, at the edge of the Solar System.

Oort cloud spherical cloud of comets beyond Pluto, extending out to about 100,000 astronomical units (approximately one light year) from the Sun. The gravitational effect of passing stars and the rest of our Galaxy disturbs comets from the cloud so that they fall in towards the Sun on highly elongated orbits, becoming visible from Earth. As many as 10 trillion comets may reside in the Oort cloud, named after Dutch astronomer Jan Oort who postulated its existence in 1950.

opal form of hydrous *silica ($SiO_2.nH_2O$), often occurring as stalactites and found in many types of rock. The common opal is translucent, milk-white, yellow, red, blue, or green, and lustrous. Precious opal is opalescent, the characteristic play of colours being caused by close-packed silica spheres diffracting light rays within the stone.

op art *or* **optical art**, *or* **retinal art**, *or* **perceptual abstraction** type of abstract art, mainly painting, in which patterns are used to create the impression that the image is flickering or vibrating. Often pictures are a mass of lines, small shapes, or vivid, clashing colours that seem to shift under the eye. Op art emerged in 1960 although its roots lie in the colour theories and optical experimentation of Joseph Alber in Germany in the 1920s. Its name, first used in 1964, is a pun on *pop art, which was popular at the time.

OPEC acronym for *Organization of Petroleum-Exporting Countries.

open-hearth furnace method of steelmaking, now largely superseded by the *basic–oxygen process. It was developed in 1864 in England by German-born William and Friedrich Siemens, and improved by Pierre and Emile Martin in France in the same year. In the furnace, which has a wide, saucer-shaped hearth and a low roof, molten pig iron and scrap are packed into the shallow hearth and heated by overhead gas burners using preheated air.

Open University institution established in the UK in 1969 to enable mature students without qualifications to study to degree level without regular attendance. Open University teaching is based on a mixture of correspondence courses, television and radio lectures and demonstrations, personal tuition organized on a regional basis, and summer schools.

opera dramatic musical work in which singing takes the place of speech. In opera, the music accompanying the action is the main element, although dancing and spectacular staging may also play their parts. Opera originated in late 16th-century Florence when the musical declamation, lyrical monologues, and choruses of classical Greek drama, were reproduced in the style of that time.

operating system (OS) in computing, a program that controls the basic operation of a computer. A typical OS controls the peripheral devices such as printers, organizes the filing system, provides a means of communicating with the operator, and runs other programs.

operetta light form of opera, with music, dance, and spoken dialogue. The story line is romantic and sentimental, often employing farce and parody. Its origins lie in the 19th-century *opéra comique* and it is intended to amuse. Examples of operetta are Jacques Offenbach's *Orphée aux enfers/Orpheus in the Underworld* (1858), Johann Strauss' *Die Fledermaus/The Flittermouse* (1874), and Gilbert and Sullivan's *The Pirates of Penzance* (1879) and *The Mikado* (1885).

ophthalmology medical speciality concerned with diseases of the eye and its surrounding tissues.

opiate, endogenous naturally produced chemical in the body which has effects similar to morphine and other opiate drugs; a type of neurotransmitter. Examples include *endorphins and encephalins.

opinion poll attempt to measure public opinion by taking a survey of the views of a representative sample of the electorate; the science of opinion sampling is called **psephology**. Most standard polls take random samples of around a thousand voters, which give results that should be accurate to within three percentage points, 95% of the time. The first accurately sampled opinion poll was carried out by George Gallup during the US presidential election in 1936.

opium drug extracted from the unripe seeds of the opium poppy (*Papaver somniferum*) of southwestern Asia. An addictive *narcotic, it contains several alkaloids, including **morphine**, one of the most powerful natural painkillers and addictive narcotics known, and **codeine**, a milder painkiller.

Opium Wars two wars, the First Opium War (1839–42) and the Second Opium War (1856–60), waged by Britain against China to enforce the opening of Chinese ports to trade in *opium. Opium from British India paid for Britain's imports from China, such as porcelain, silk, and, above all, tea.

opossum any of a family of marsupials (mammals that carry their young in a pouch) native to North and South America. Most opossums are tree-living, nocturnal animals, with prehensile tails that can be used as an additional limb, and hands and feet well adapted for grasping. They range from 10 cm/4 in to 50 cm/ 20 in in length and are insectivorous, carnivorous, or, more commonly, omnivorous. (Family Didelphidae.)

Oppenheimer, J(ulius) Robert (1904–1967)
US physicist. As director of the Los Alamos Science Laboratory 1943–45, he was in charge of the development of the atom bomb (the Manhattan Project). He objected to the development of the hydrogen bomb, and was alleged to be a security risk in 1953 by the US Atomic Energy Commission (AEC).

opposition in astronomy, moment at which a body in the Solar System lies opposite the Sun in the sky as seen from the Earth and crosses the *meridian at about midnight.

Opposition, Leader of His/Her Majesty's in UK politics, official title (from 1937) of the leader of the largest opposition party in the House of Commons. Since 1989 the post has received a government salary. Ian *Duncan Smith has been Leader of the Opposition since 2001.

optical character recognition (OCR) in computing, a technique for inputting text to a computer by means of a document reader. First, a *scanner produces a digital image of the text; then character-recognition software makes use of stored knowledge about the shapes of individual characters to convert the digital image to a set of internal codes that can be stored and processed by a computer.

optical disc in computing, a storage medium in which laser technology is used to record and read large volumes of digital data. Types include *CD-ROM, *WORM, and DVD.

optical fibre very fine, optically-pure glass fibre through which light can be reflected to transmit images or data from one end to the other. Although expensive to produce and install, optical fibres can carry more data than traditional cables, and are less susceptible to interference. Standard optical fibre transmitters can send up to 10 billion bits of information per second by switching a laser beam on and off.

optical illusion scene or picture that fools the eye. An example of a natural optical illusion is that the Moon appears bigger when it is on the horizon than when it is high in the sky, owing to the *refraction of light rays by the Earth's atmosphere.

optical mark recognition (OMR) in computing, a technique that enables marks made in predetermined positions on computer-input forms to be detected optically and input to a computer. An **optical mark reader** shines a light beam onto the input document and is able to detect the marks because less light is reflected back from them than from the paler, unmarked paper.

optic nerve large nerve passing from the eye to the brain, carrying visual information. In mammals, it may contain up to a million nerve fibres, connecting the sensory cells of the retina to the optical centres in the brain. Embryologically, the optic nerve develops as an outgrowth of the brain.

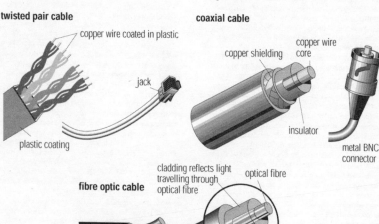

twisted pair cable

copper wire coated in plastic

jack

plastic coating

coaxial cable

copper shielding

copper wire core

insulator

metal BNC connector

fibre optic cable

cladding reflects light travelling through optical fibre

optical fibre

plastic coating

metal wire strengthens cable

plastic coating

glass fibres

optical fibre The major differences in construction between twisted pair (telephone), coaxial, and fibre optic cable.

optics branch of physics that deals with the study of *light and vision – for example, shadows and mirror images, lenses, microscopes, telescopes, and cameras. On striking a surface, light rays are reflected or refracted with some absorption of energy, and the study of this is known as geometrical optics.

option in business, a contract giving the owner the right (as opposed to the obligation, as with futures contracts; see *futures trading) to buy or sell a specific quantity of a particular commodity or currency at a future date and at an agreed price, in return for a premium. A right to purchase is known as a call, and a right to sell is known as a put. The price to be paid is called the strike, or the exercise price, and the date by which the option must be used is called the expiry date. The buyer can decide not to exercise the option if it would prove disadvantageous, but in this case would lose the premium paid. Equities and commodities, such as gold, are common assets for which options are issued.

optoelectronics branch of electronics concerned with the development of devices (based on the *semiconductor gallium arsenide) that respond not only to the *electrons of electronic data transmission, but also to *photons ('particles' of light).

opuntia any *cactus belonging to the same group of plants as the *prickly pear. They all have showy flowers and fleshy, jointed stems. (Genus *Opuntia*, family Cactaceae.)

Opus *or* **Op.** (Latin 'work') in music, a prefix, used with a figure, to indicate the numbering of a composer's works, usually in chronological order.

oracle (Latin *orare* 'to speak') sacred site where a deity gives answers or oracles, through the mouth of its priest, to a supplicant's questions about personal affairs or state policy. These were often ambivalent. There were more than 250 oracular seats in the Greek world. The earliest example was probably at Dodona (in Epirus), where priests interpreted the sounds made by the sacred oaks of *Zeus, but the most celebrated was that of *Apollo, god of prophecy, at *Delphi.

oral literature stories that are or have been transmitted in spoken form, such as public recitation, rather than through writing or printing. Most pre-literate societies have had a tradition of oral literature, including short folk tales, legends, myths, proverbs, and riddles, as well as longer narrative works; and most of the ancient epics – such as the Greek *Odyssey* and the Mesopotamian *Gilgamesh* – seem to have been composed and added to over many centuries before they were committed to writing.

orange round orange-coloured juicy citrus fruit of several species of evergreen trees, which bear white blossom and fruits at the same time. Thought to have originated in Southeast Asia, orange trees are commercially cultivated in Spain, Israel, the USA, Brazil, South Africa, and elsewhere. The sweet orange (*C. sinensis*) is commonly eaten fresh; the Jaffa, blood, and navel orange are varieties of this species. (Genus *Citrus*, family Rutaceae.)

Orange river in South Africa, rising at the Mont-aux-Sources in the Maluti Mountains in Lesotho and flowing west to the Atlantic Ocean; length 2,100 km/1,300 mi. It runs along the southern boundary of the Free State Province. Water from the Orange is diverted via the Orange-Fish River Tunnel (1975) to irrigate the semi-arid Eastern Cape Province. It was named in 1779 after William of Orange.

Orange, House of royal family of the Netherlands. The title is derived from the small principality of Orange in southern France, held by the family from the 8th century to 1713. They held considerable possessions in the Netherlands, to which, after 1530, was added the German county of Nassau.

Orange Order in Northern Ireland, solely Protestant organization founded in County Armagh in 1795 in opposition to the Defenders, a Catholic secret society. It was a revival of the **Orange Institution** founded in 1688 to support *William (III) of Orange, whose victory over the Catholic James II at the Battle of the *Boyne in 1690 has been commemorated annually by Protestants in parades since 1796. The new order was organized into **Orange Societies** in a similar way to freemasonry, with a system of lodges. It has institutional ties with the Ulster Unionist Party.

orang-utan large ape found only in Borneo and Sumatra. Up to 1.65 m/5.5 ft in height, it is covered with long, red-brown hair and lives a largely solitary life in the trees, feeding mainly on fruit. Now an endangered species, it is officially protected because its habitat is being systematically destroyed by *deforestation. In 1998 there were fewer than 27,000 orang-utans in the wild, with an estimated 5,000–7,000 in Sumatra, 3,000–5,000 in Sabah (northeast Borneo), and 12,000–15,000 in Kalimantan (Indonesia). (Species *Pongo pygmaeus*.)

oratorio dramatic, musical setting of religious texts, scored for orchestra, chorus, and solo voices. Originally it was acted out with scenery and costumes, but gradually it became more commonly performed as a concert. Its origins lie in the *Laude spirituali* performed by St Philip Neri's Oratory in Rome in the 16th century, followed by the first definitive oratorio in the 17th century by Cavalieri. The form reached perfection in such works as Johann Sebastian Bach's *Christmas Oratorio* (performed 1734–35), and George Handel's *Messiah* (1742).

orbit path of one body in space around another, such as the orbit of the Earth around the Sun or of the Moon around the Earth. When the two bodies are similar in mass, as in a *binary star, both bodies move around their common centre of mass. The movement of objects in orbit follows Kepler's laws, which apply to artificial satellites as well as to natural bodies.

orchestra large group of musicians playing together on different instruments. In Western music, an orchestra is usually based on the bowed, stringed instruments of the violin family, to which is usually added the woodwind, brass, and percussion sections. The number of players per section and the instruments used may vary according to the needs of the composer.

orchestration scoring of a composition for orchestra; the choice of instruments of a score expanded for orchestra (often by another hand). A work may be written for piano, then transferred to an orchestral score.

orchid any plant of a large family that contains at least 15,000 species and 700 genera, distributed throughout the world except in the coldest areas, and most numerous in damp equatorial regions. The flowers are the most highly evolved of the plant kingdom; they have three *sepals and three petals and sometimes grow singly, but more usually appear with other flowers on spikes, growing up one side of the main stem, or all around the main stem, which may be upright or drooping. (Family Orchidaceae.)

ordeal, trial by in tribal societies and in Europe in medieval times, a method of testing the guilt of an accused person based on the belief in heaven's protection of the innocent. Examples of such ordeals include walking barefoot over heated iron, dipping the hand into boiling water, and swallowing consecrated bread (causing the guilty to choke).

order in classical architecture, the *column (including capital, shaft, and base) and the entablature, considered as an architectural whole. The five orders are Doric, Ionic, Corinthian, Tuscan, and Composite.

order in biological classification, a group of related *families. For example, the horse, rhinoceros, and tapir families are grouped in the order Perissodactyla, the odd-toed ungulates, because they all have either one or three toes on each foot. The names of orders are not shown in italic (unlike genus and species names) and by convention they have the ending '-formes' in birds and fish; '-a' in mammals, amphibians, reptiles, and other animals; and '-ales' in fungi and plants. Related orders are grouped together in a *class.

order in council in the UK, an order issued by the sovereign with the advice of the *Privy Council; in practice it is issued only on the advice of the cabinet. Acts of Parliament often provide for the issue of orders in council to regulate the detailed administration of their provisions.

ordinal number in mathematics, one of the series first, second, third, fourth, ... Ordinal numbers relate to order, whereas *cardinal numbers (1, 2, 3, 4, ...) relate to quantity, or count.

Ordovician period period of geological time 510–439 million years ago; the second period of the *Palaeozoic era. Animal life was confined to the sea: reef-building algae and the first jawless fish are characteristic.

ore body of rock, a vein within it, or a deposit of sediment, worth mining for the economically valuable mineral it contains. The term is usually applied to sources of metals. Occasionally metals are found uncombined (native metals), but more often they occur as compounds such as carbonates, sulphides, or oxides. The ores often contain unwanted impurities that must be removed when the metal is extracted.

oregano any of several perennial herbs belonging to the mint family, especially the aromatic *O. vulgare*, also known as wild marjoram. It is native to Mediterranean countries and western Asia and naturalized in the Americas. Oregano is extensively used to season Mediterranean cooking. (Genus *Origanum*, family Labiatae.)

Oregon called the **Beaver State**, (possibly French *ouragan* 'hurricane') state in northwestern USA, bordered to the east by *Idaho, to the north by *Washington, to the south by *California and *Nevada, and to the west by the *Pacific Ocean; area 248,631 sq km/ 95,997 sq mi; population 3,421,400; capital Salem. Oregon's nickname was coined because of the large beaver population that roamed the region in the early 19th century, when fur traders flocked there to seek their fortunes. The state features mountains, including the Cascade Range, including the state's highest point,

Mount Hood, and the Klamath Mountains. More than half of the state is forested. After the fashion for fur faded, Oregon developed a timber industry, which sustained the area's economic growth until the early 1990s. The state's economy was then bolstered by a thriving high-tech industry, particularly in the Willamette Valley, home to Oregon's three largest cities, Portland, Eugene, and Salem. Other major cities include Gresham and Beaverton. Originally home to the Chinook and Tillamook in the northwest, the Bannock and Nez Percé in the northeast, and the Klamath in the southwest, the state saw heavy settlement by US pioneers heading west via the Oregon Trail. The introduction of a transcontinental railway link in 1833 increased industrialization and development. Oregon was admitted to the Union in 1859 as the 33rd US state.

Orestes in Greek mythology, the son of *Agamemnon and *Clytemnestra, who killed his mother on the instructions of Apollo because she and her lover Aegisthus had murdered his father. He was subsequently hounded by the *Furies until he was purified, and acquitted of the crime of matricide.

Øresund strait leading from the *Kattegat strait to the Baltic Sea, between Sweden on the east and the Danish island of Sjaelland on the west. Its length is 113 km/ 70 mi; its narrowest point, between Helsingor and Hälsingborg, is 5 km/3 mi; its widest point is 60 km/ 37 mi; and its deepest part is about 25 m/80 ft. In English it is called the Sound.

orfe freshwater fish belonging to the carp family. It grows up to 50 cm/1.7 ft in length, and feeds on small aquatic animals. The species is generally greyish-black, but an ornamental variety is orange. It lives in rivers and lakes of Europe and northwestern Asia. (Species *Leuciscus idus*, family Cyprinidae.)

Orff, Carl (1895–1982) German composer. An individual stylist, his work is characterized by sharp dissonances and percussion. Among his compositions are the cantata *Carmina Burana* (1937) and the opera *Antigone* (1949).

organ in biology, a part of a living body that has a distinctive function or set of functions. Examples include the *oesophagus, *liver, or *brain in animals, or a *leaf in plants. An organ is composed of a group of coordinated *tissues. A group of organs working together to perform a function is called an organ system, for example, the *digestive system comprises a number of organs including the oesophagus, stomach, the small *intestine, the pancreas, and the liver. The tissues of a leaf include the epidermis, palisade mesophyll, and spongy mesophyll. The tissues of the oesophagus include *muscle, and epithelium.

organ oldest of the keyboard instruments, in which sound is produced when a depressed key opens a valve, allowing compressed air to pass through a single pipe or a series of pipes. The number of pipes may vary according to the size of the instrument. Apart from its continued use in serious compositions and for church music, the organ has been adapted for light entertainment.

organelle discrete and specialized structure in a living cell; organelles include mitochondria, chloroplasts, lysosomes, ribosomes, and the nucleus.

organic chemistry branch of chemistry that deals with carbon compounds. Organic compounds form the chemical basis of life and are more abundant than inorganic compounds. In a typical organic compound, each carbon atom forms bonds covalently with each of its neighbouring carbon atoms in a chain or ring, and additionally with other atoms, commonly hydrogen, oxygen, nitrogen, or sulphur.

Formula	Name	Atomic bonding
CH_3	methyl	
CH_2CH_3	ethyl	
CC	double bond	
CHO	aldehyde	
CH_2OH	alcohol	
CO	ketone	
$COOH$	acid	
CH_2NH_2	amine	
C_6H_6	benzene ring	

organic chemistry Common organic molecule groupings. Organic chemistry is the study of carbon compounds, which make up over 90% of all chemical compounds. This diversity arises because carbon atoms can combine in many different ways with other atoms, forming a wide variety of rings and chains.

organic farming farming without the use of synthetic fertilizers (such as nitrates and phosphates) or pesticides (herbicides, insecticides, and fungicides) or other agrochemicals (such as hormones, growth stimulants, or fruit regulators). Food produced by genetic engineering cannot be described as organic.

Organization for Economic Cooperation and Development (OECD) international organization of 29 industrialized countries that provides a forum for discussion and coordination of member states' economic and social policies. Founded in 1961, with its headquarters in Paris, the OECD replaced the Organization for European Economic Cooperation (OEEC), which had been established in 1948 to implement the *Marshall Plan. The Commission of the European Union also takes part in the OECD's work.

Organization of American States (OAS) association founded in 1948 at Bogotá, Colombia by a charter signed by representatives of North, Central, and South American states. It aims to maintain peace and solidarity within the hemisphere, and is also concerned with the social and economic development of Latin America.

Organization of Arab Petroleum Exporting Countries (OAPEC) body established in 1968 to safeguard the interests of its members and encourage economic cooperation within the petroleum industry. Its members are Algeria, Bahrain, Egypt, Iraq, Kuwait, Libya, Qatar, Saudi Arabia, Syria, and the United Arab Emirates; together they account for more than 25% of the world's oil output. The organization's headquarters are in Kuwait.

Organization of Petroleum-Exporting Countries (OPEC) body established in 1960 to coordinate price and supply policies of oil-producing states, protecting its members' interests by manipulating oil production and the price of crude oil. Its concerted action in raising prices in the 1970s triggered worldwide recession but also lessened demand so that its influence was reduced by the mid-1980s. However, continued reliance on oil re-strengthened its influence in the late 1990s. OPEC members are: Algeria, Gabon, Indonesia, Iran, Iraq, Kuwait, Libya, Nigeria, Qatar, Saudi Arabia, the United Arab Emirates, and Venezuela. Ecuador, formerly a member, withdrew in 1993.

Organization of the Islamic Conference (OIC) association of 44 states in the Middle East, Africa, and Asia, established in 1971 in Rabat, Morocco, to promote Islamic solidarity between member countries, and to consolidate economic, social, cultural, and scientific cooperation. Its headquarters are in Jeddah, Saudi Arabia.

orienteering sport of cross-country running and route-finding. Competitors set off at one-minute intervals and have to find their way, using map and compass, to various checkpoints (approximately 0.8 km/ 0.5 mi apart), where their control cards are marked. World championships have been held since 1966.

original sin Christian doctrine that the *Fall of Man rendered humanity predisposed to sin and unable to achieve salvation except through divine grace and the redemptive power of Jesus.

Orinoco river in northern South America; it rises in the Sierra Parima range, part of the Guiana Highlands, in southern Venezuela near the Brazilian border and flows north for about 2,400 km/1,500 mi through Venezuela, forming the boundary with Colombia for about 320 km/200 mi; tributaries include the Guaviare, Meta, Apure, Ventuari, Caura, Arauca, and Caroní rivers. It is navigable by ocean-going ships for about 420 km/260 mi, and by large steamers for 1,125 km/700 mi from its Atlantic delta; rapids obstruct the upper river. The Orinoco is South America's third-largest river; its drainage basin area is 962,000 sq km/371,500 sq mi.

oriole any of several brightly coloured songbirds belonging to two families: New World orioles belong to the family Icteridae, and Old World orioles are members of the family Oriolidae. They eat insects, seeds, and fruit.

Orion very prominent constellation in the equatorial region of the sky (see *celestial sphere), identified with the hunter of Greek mythology.

Orion nebula luminous cloud of gas and dust 1,500 light years away, in the constellation Orion, from which stars are forming. It is about 15 light years in diameter, and contains enough gas to make a cluster of thousands of stars.

Orissa state of northeast India; area 155,782 sq km/60,148 sq mi; population (2001 est) 36,706,900. The capital is Bhubaneshwar. Industries include chemicals, paper, steel, aluminium smelting, and mineral extraction. Over 80% of the population make their living from agriculture, with rice as the dominant crop. Wheat, oilseed, jute, coconuts, and sugarcane are also grown. Oriya is the official language, and 90% of the population are Hindu.

Orkney Islands island group and unitary authority off the northeast coast of Scotland. **area:** 1,014 sq km/391 sq mi **towns:** *Kirkwall (administrative headquarters), Stromness, both on Mainland (Pomona) **physical:** there are 90 islands and inlets in the group. Next to Mainland, the most important of the islands are North and South Ronaldsay, Hoy, Rousay, Stronsay, Flotta, Shapinsay, Eday, Sanday, and Westray. The highest peak is Ward Hill in Hoy, which has an elevation of 479 m/1,572 ft. The Old Man of Hoy is an isolated stack of red sandstone 137 m/450 ft high, off Hoy's northwest coast **features:** Skara Brae Neolithic village, Stones of Steness, and Maes Howe burial chamber; Scapa Flow; oil terminal on Flotta **population:** (1996 est) 19,500 **history:** population of Scandinavian descent; Harald I (Fairhair) of Norway conquered the islands in 876; pledged to James III of Scotland in 1468 for the dowry of Margaret of Denmark; Scapa Flow, between Mainland and Hoy, was a naval base in both world wars, the German fleet scuttled itself here on 21 June 1919.

Ormuzd another name for **Ahura Mazda**, the good god of *Zoroastrianism.

ornithology study of birds. It covers scientific aspects relating to their structure and classification, and their habits, song, flight, and value to agriculture as destroyers of insect pests. Worldwide scientific banding (or the fitting of coded rings to captured specimens) has resulted in accurate information on bird movements and distribution. There is an International Council for Bird Preservation with its headquarters at the Natural History Museum, London.

ornithophily *pollination of flowers by birds. Ornithophilous flowers are typically brightly coloured, often red or orange. They produce large quantities of thin, watery nectar, and are scentless because most birds do not respond well to smell. They are found mostly in tropical areas, with hummingbirds being important pollinators in North and South America, and the sunbirds in Africa and Asia.

orogenesis in its original, literal sense, orogenesis means 'mountain building', but today it more specifically refers to the tectonics of mountain building (as opposed to mountain building by erosion).

Orpheus mythical Greek poet and musician of Thrace; the son of *Apollo and the Muse Calliope. Orpheus ventured into Hades, the underworld, to bring back his wife Eurydice, who had died from a snakebite. His lyre playing was so charming that Pluto granted her return to life, but on condition that Orpheus walked ahead without looking back. He turned at the entrance and Eurydice was irretrievably lost. In his grief, he offended the *maenad women of Thrace, and they tore him to pieces.

Orphism type of abstract or semi-abstract painting practised by a group of artists in Paris between 1911 and 1914. Orphism owed much to the fragmented forms of *cubism (indeed it is sometimes called Orphic cubism). However, while cubism at this time was coolly intellectual and almost colourless, Orphism used lush and exciting colour. The name Orphism was first used in 1913 by the poet and art critic Guillaume Apollinaire, alluding to Orpheus, the poet and singer in Greek mythology; it indicated that the Orphists wanted to introduce a feeling of poetry to the serious and strict approach to cubism, as practised by Georges Braque and Pablo Picasso. The central figure of Orphism was Robert *Delaunay, and other artists in his circle included Marcel *Duchamp, Fernand *Léger, Francis Picabia, and the Czech-born Franz Kupka. Initially the Orphists based their pictures on the external world (Delaunay, for example, did a series of paintings featuring the Eiffel Tower), but by 1912 both Delaunay and Kupka (whose work was very similar at this time) were painting pure abstracts. These were the first abstracts painted by French artists.

orris root underground stem of a species of *iris grown in southern Europe. It is violet-scented and is used in perfumery and herbal medicine.

Ortega Saavedra, Daniel (1945–) Nicaraguan guerrilla leader and socialist politician, head of state 1979–90. He headed a moderate faction of the Marxist Sandinista National Liberation Front (FSLN), which in 1989 overthrew the regime of Anastasio Somoza Debayle, Latin America's longest dictatorship. His government's efforts at economic reconstruction became deflected by the military campaign waged against it from 1982 by Contra guerrillas backed by the USA.

orthodontics branch of *dentistry concerned with *dentition, and with treatment of any irregularities, such as correction of malocclusion (faulty position of teeth).

Orthodox Church *or* **Eastern Orthodox Church** *or* **Greek Orthodox Church** (Greek 'true thinking' or 'right thinking') federation of national and regional self-governing Christian churches, mainly found in Eastern Europe and parts of Asia. The final schism between the Orthodox Church and the Roman Catholic Church occurred in 1054. The centre of worship is the Eucharist. Clergy, other than the bishops, may marry, and the *Immaculate Conception is not accepted. The highest rank in the church is that of ecumenical patriarch, or bishop of Istanbul. There are (1990) about 130 million adherents.

Orthodox Judaism branch of Judaism that asserts the supreme authority of the Torah and the Talmud, including the Halachah (oral legal tradition). Orthodox Jews form the majority in Judaism. Ultra-Orthodox sects include *Hasidism, which developed in 18th-century Poland, and Lubavitch, which originated in Russia; both are influenced by the *Kabbalah, a mystical Jewish tradition.

orthopaedics (Greek *orthos* 'straight'; *pais* 'child') medical speciality concerned with the correction of disease or damage in bones and joints.

Orton, Joe (John Kingsley) (1933–1967) English dramatist. In his black comedies, surreal and violent action takes place in genteel and unlikely settings. Plays include *Entertaining Mr Sloane* (1964), *Loot* (1966), and *What the Butler Saw* (1968). His diaries deal frankly with his personal life. He was murdered by his lover Kenneth Halliwell.

Orwell, George (1903–1950) pen-name of Eric Arthur Blair, English writer. His books include the satirical fable *Animal Farm* (1945), an attack on the Soviet Union and its leader, Stalin, which includes such slogans as 'All animals are equal, but some are more equal than others'; and the prophetic *Nineteen Eighty-Four* (1949), targeting Cold War politics, which portrays the catastrophic excesses of state control over the individual. He also wrote numerous essays. Orwell was distrustful of all political parties and ideologies, and a deep sense of social conscience and antipathy towards political dictatorship characterizes his work.

oryx any of a group of large antelopes native to Africa and Asia. The **Arabian oryx** (*O. leucoryx*), at one time extinct in the wild, was successfully reintroduced into its natural habitat using stocks bred in captivity in 1982. By 1998 the oryx reintroduction project was seriously reduced through poaching. The population fell to 138, and 40 animals were returned to captivity as the population was believed to be no longer viable. By January 1999 there were fewer than 100 oryx remaining in the wild and only 11 of these were female. (Genus *Oryx*, family Bovidae.)

Osborne, John James (1929–1994) English dramatist. He became one of the first *Angry Young Men (anti-establishment writers of the 1950s) of British theatre with his debut play, *Look Back in Anger* (1956). Other plays include *The Entertainer* (1957), *Luther* (1960), *Inadmissible Evidence* (1964), and *A Patriot for Me* (1965).

oscillating universe in astronomy, theory stating that the gravitational attraction of the mass within the universe will eventually slow down and stop the expansion of the universe. The outward motions of the galaxies will then be reversed, eventually resulting in a 'Big Crunch' where all the matter in the universe will be contracted into a small volume of high density. This could undergo a further *Big Bang, thereby creating another expansion phase. The theory suggests that the universe would alternately expand and collapse through alternate Big Bangs and Big Crunches.

oscillation one complete to-and-fro movement of a vibrating object or system. For any particular vibration,

the time for one oscillation is called its period and the number of oscillations in one second is called its *frequency. The maximum displacement of the vibrating object from its rest position is called the *amplitude of the oscillation.

oscilloscope another name for *cathode-ray oscilloscope.

osier any of several willow trees and shrubs, cultivated for their supple branches which are used in basket making; in particular, *S. viminalis*. (Genus *Salix*.)

Osiris ancient Egyptian god, the embodiment of goodness, who ruled the underworld after being killed by *Set. The pharaohs were believed to be his incarnation. The sister-wife of Osiris was *Isis or Hathor; she miraculously conceived their son *Horus after the death of Osiris, and he eventually captured his father's murderer.

Oslo industrial port and capital of Norway; population (1996) 731,600. The main industries are shipbuilding, textiles, electrical equipment, engineering, machine tools, timber, and food processing. The first recorded settlement was made in the 11th century by Harald III Hardrada, but after a fire in 1624, it was entirely replanned by the Danish king Christian IV and renamed **Christiania** from 1624 to 1924. Following Norway's separation from Denmark (1814) and then Sweden (1905), the city reverted in 1925 to its original Norwegian name of Oslo.

Osman I (or Uthman I) (1259–1326) Turkish ruler from 1299. He began his career in the service of the Seljuk Turks, but in 1299 he set up a kingdom of his own in Bithynia, northwestern Asia, and assumed the title of sultan. He conquered a great part of Anatolia, so founding a Turkish empire. His successors were known as 'sons of Osman', from which the term *Ottoman Empire is derived.

osmium chemical symbol Os, (Greek *osme* 'odour') hard, heavy, bluish-white, metallic element, atomic number 76, relative atomic mass 190.2. It is the densest of the elements, and is resistant to tarnish and corrosion. It occurs in platinum ores and as a free metal (see *native metal) with iridium in a natural alloy called osmiridium, containing traces of platinum, ruthenium, and rhodium. Its uses include pen points and light-bulb filaments; like platinum, it is a useful catalyst.

osmosis movement of *water through a partially (selectively) permeable membrane separating solutions of different concentrations. Water passes by *diffusion from a **weak solution** (high water concentration) to a **strong solution** (low water concentration) until the two concentrations are equal. A membrane is partially permeable if it lets water through but not the molecules or ions dissolved in the water (the solute; for example, sugar molecules). Many cell membranes behave in this way, and osmosis is a vital mechanism in the transport of fluids in living organisms. One example is in the transport of water from soil (weak solution) into the roots of plants (stronger solution of cell sap) via the root hair cells. Another is the uptake of water by the epithelium lining the *gut in animals. There are also membranes that humans can manufacture that are partially permeable.

osprey bird of prey, sometimes called 'fish hawk' because it plunges feet first into the water to catch fish. It is dark brown above and a striking white below, and measures 60 cm/2 ft with a 2 m/6 ft wingspan. The nest is often built in trees near the seashore or lakeside, and two or three white eggs, blotched with crimson, are laid. Ospreys occur on all continents except Antarctica and have faced extinction in several areas. (Species *Pandion haliaetus*, family Pandionidae, order Falconiformes.)

Ossian Irish **Oisin**, Legendary Gaelic hero and bard, claimed by both Ireland and Scotland. He is sometimes represented as the son of *Finn Mac Cumhaill, in about AD 250, and as having lived to tell the tales of Finn and the Ulster heroes to St Patrick, in about 400. The publication in 1760 of James *Macpherson's poems, attributed to Ossian, made Ossian's name familiar throughout Europe.

osteomyelitis infection of bone, with spread of pus along the marrow cavity. Now quite rare, it may follow from a compound fracture (where broken bone protrudes through the skin), or from infectious disease elsewhere in the body. It is more common in children whose bones are not yet fully grown.

osteopathy system of alternative medical practice that relies on physical manipulation to treat mechanical stress. It was developed over a century ago by US physician Andrew Taylor Still, who maintained that most ailments can be prevented or cured by techniques of spinal manipulation.

osteoporosis disease in which the bone substance becomes porous and brittle. It is common in older people, affecting more women than men. It may be treated with calcium supplements and etidronate. Approximately 1.7 million people worldwide, mostly women, suffer hip fractures, mainly due to osteoporosis. A single gene was discovered in 1993 to have a major influence on bone thinning.

ostinato (Italian 'obstinate') musical pattern that is continuously repeated during a section or throughout a complete piece of music. The repeating idea may be a rhythmic pattern, part of a tune, or a complete melody.

ostrich large flightless bird. There is only one species, found in Africa. The male may be about 2.5 m/8 ft tall and weigh 135 kg/300 lb, and is the largest living bird. It has exceptionally strong legs and feet (two-toed) that enable it to run at high speed, and are also used in defence. It lives in family groups of one cock with several hens, each of which lays about 14 eggs. (Species *Struthio camelus*, order Struthioniformes.)

Ostrogoth member of a branch of the eastern Germanic people, the *Goths.

Oswald, St (c. 605–642) King of Northumbria from 634, after killing the Welsh king Cadwallon. He became a Christian convert during exile on the Scottish island of Iona. With the help of St *Aidan he furthered the spread of Christianity in northern England. Feast day 9 August.

Othman alternative spelling of *Uthman, third caliph of Islam.

Othman I another name for the Turkish sultan *Osman I.

Otis, Elisha Graves (1811–1861) US engineer who developed a lift that incorporated a safety device, making it acceptable for passenger use in the first skyscrapers. The device, invented in 1852, consisted of vertical ratchets on the sides of the lift shaft into which spring-loaded catches would engage and lock the lift in position in the event of cable failure.

otitis inflammation of the ear. *Otitis externa*, occurring in the outer ear canal, is easily treated with antibiotics. Inflamed conditions of the middle ear (*otitis media*) or inner ear (*otitis interna*) are more serious, carrying the risk of deafness and infection of the brain. Treatment is with antibiotics or, more rarely, surgery. A 1999 US survey of children's middle-ear problems indicated that the risk is, to a large extent, hereditary.

Ottawa capital of Canada, in eastern Ontario, on the hills overlooking the Ottawa River, and divided by the Rideau Canal (1832) into the Upper (western) and Lower (eastern) towns; population (2001 est) 774,100, in a metropolitan area (with adjoining Hull, Québec) of 1,063,700. Industries include engineering, hi-tech and information technology, telecommunications, biotechnology, food-processing, publishing, lumber, and the manufacture of pulp, paper, textiles, and leather products. Government, and community and health services employ a large section of the workforce. Ottawa was founded 1826–32 as Bytown, in honour of John By (1781–1836), whose army engineers were building the Rideau Canal. In 1854 it was renamed after the Ottawa River, the name deriving from the Outaouac, native Canadian Algonquin people of the area.

otter any of various aquatic carnivores belonging to the weasel family, found on all continents except Australia. Otters have thick brown fur, short limbs, webbed toes, and long, compressed tails. They are social, playful, and agile.

Otto four Holy Roman emperors, including:

Otto I (912–973) Holy Roman Emperor from 962. He restored the power of the empire and asserted his authority over the pope and the nobles. His son, Liudolf, led a German rebellion allied with the Magyars, but Otto drew them from the siege of Augsburg (Bavaria) and ended the Magyar menace by his victory at Lechfeld in 955. He refounded the East Mark, or Austria, as a barrier against them.

Otto IV (c. 1174–1218) Holy Roman Emperor, elected in 1198. He was the son of Henry the Lion (1129–95), and was made Count of Poitou by his uncle, Richard (I) the Lionheart (1157–99). He clashed with Philip, Duke of Swabia, in rivalry for the empire. He engaged in controversy with Pope Innocent III (*c.* 1160–1216), and was defeated by the pope's ally Philip (II) Augustus of France at Bouvines in 1214. Otto lost the throne to Holy Roman Emperor *Frederick II, and retired to Brunswick (Germany).

Otto cycle alternative name for the *four-stroke cycle, introduced by the German engineer Nikolaus Otto (1832–1891) in 1876.

Ottoman Empire Muslim empire of the Turks from 1300 to 1920, the successor of the *Seljuk Empire. It was founded by *Osman I and reached its height with *Suleiman in the 16th century. From 1453 its capital city was Istamboul (*Istanbul; formerly *Constantinople).

Ouagadougou *or* **Wagadugu** capital and industrial centre of Burkina Faso, and of Kadiogo Province; population (2002 est) 839,800. Industries include textiles, beverages, and the manufacture of vegetable oil products, especially soap. Its pre-eminence as a commercial centre is challenged by Bobo-Dioulasso. It was the capital of the Mossi empire from the 15th century.

Oudh region of north India, now part of *Uttar Pradesh state. An independent kingdom before it fell under Mogul rule, Oudh regained independence 1732–1856, when it was annexed by Britain. Its capital was Lucknow, centre of the *Indian Mutiny 1857–58. In 1877 it was joined with Agra, from 1902 as the United Provinces of Agra and Oudh, renamed Uttar Pradesh in 1950.

ounce unit of mass, one-sixteenth of a pound *avoirdupois, equal to 437.5 grains (28.35 g); also one-twelfth of a pound troy, equal to 480 grains.

Ouse, Great (Celtic 'water') river that rises near Brackley in Northamptonshire, central England, and flows eastwards through Buckinghamshire, Bedfordshire, Cambridgeshire, and Norfolk, before entering the Wash north of King's Lynn; length 250 km/160 mi. A large sluice across the Great Ouse, near King's Lynn, was built as part of extensive flood-control works in 1959.

outback the inland region of Australia. Its main inhabitants are Aborigines, miners (including opal miners), and cattle ranchers. Its harsh beauty has been recorded by such artists as Sidney Nolan.

Outer Hebrides group of islands that comprise that part of the *Hebrides further from the west coast of mainland Scotland.

outlawry in medieval England, a declaration that a criminal was outside the protection of the law, with his or her lands and goods forfeited to the crown, and all civil rights being set aside. It was a lucrative royal 'privilege'; *Magna Carta restricted its use, and under Edward III it was further modified. Some outlaws, such as *Robin Hood, became popular heroes.

output device any device for displaying, in a form intelligible to the user, the results of processing carried out by a computer.

ouzel or **ousel** ancient name for the blackbird. The **ring ouzel** (*Turdus torquatus*) is similar to a blackbird, but has a white band across the breast. It is found in Europe in mountainous and rocky country. **Water ouzel** is another name for the *dipper.

ovary in female animals, the organ that generates the ovum. In humans, the ovaries are two whitish rounded bodies about 25 mm/1 in by 35 mm/1.5 in, located in the lower abdomen on either side of the uterus. Every month, from puberty to the onset of the menopause, an ovum is released from the ovary. This is called ovulation, and forms part of the menstrual cycle. In botany, an ovary is the expanded basal portion of the carpel of flowering plants, containing one or more ovules. It is hollow with a thick wall to protect the ovules. Following fertilization of the ovum, it develops into the fruit wall or pericarp.

Overijssel province of the east central Netherlands, extending from the IJsselmeer to the German border; area 3,340 sq km/1,290 sq mi; population (1997) 1,057,900. The capital is Zwolle. Industries include textile production (cotton-spinning in the district of Twente). Other activities are livestock rearing, dairying, and fishing.

overlander one of the Australian drovers in the 19th century who opened up new territory by driving their cattle through remote areas to new stations, or to market, before the establishment of regular stock routes.

overpopulation too many people for the resources available in an area (such as food, land, and water). The consequences were first set out by English economist Thomas *Malthus at the start of the population explosion.

overture in music, the opening piece of a concert or opera. It has two roles: settling the audience before the main music starts, and allowing the conductor and musicians to become acquainted with the acoustics of a concert auditorium. See also *prelude.

Ovid (43 BC–AD 17) born Publius Ovidius Naso, Latin poet. His poetry deals mainly with the themes of love (*Amores* (20 BC), *Ars amatoria/The Art of Love* (1 BC)), mythology (*Metamorphoses* (AD 2)), and exile (*Tristia* (AD 9–12)). Born at Sulmo, Ovid studied rhetoric in Rome in preparation for a legal career, but soon turned to literature. In AD 9 he was banished by Augustus to Tomis, on the Black Sea, where he died. Sophisticated, ironical, and self-pitying, his work was highly influential during the Middle Ages and Renaissance.

oviparous method of animal reproduction in which eggs are laid by the female and develop outside the body, in contrast to *ovoviviparous and *viviparous. It is the most common form of reproduction.

ovoviviparous method of animal reproduction in which fertilized eggs develop within the female (unlike *oviparous), and the embryo gains no nutritional substances from the female (unlike *viviparous). It occurs in some invertebrates, fishes, and reptiles.

ovulation in female animals, the process of releasing egg cells (ova) from the *ovary. In mammals it occurs as part of the *menstrual cycle.

ovum plural **ova**, female gamete (sex cell) before fertilization. In mammals it is called an egg, and is produced by a special cell division called *meiosis in the ovaries during the *menstrual cycle. In plants, where it is also known as an egg cell or oosphere, the ovum is produced in an ovule. The ovum does not move by itself. It must be fertilized by a male gamete before it can develop further, except in cases of *parthenogenesis.

Owen, Robert (1771–1858) British socialist, born in Wales. In 1800 he became manager of a mill at New Lanark in Scotland, where, by improving working and housing conditions and providing schools, he created a model community. His ideas stimulated the *cooperative movement (the pooling of resources for joint economic benefit).

Owen, Wilfred Edward Salter (1893–1918) English poet. His verse, owing much to the encouragement of English poet Siegfried *Sassoon, is among the most moving of World War I poetry; it shatters the illusion of the glory of war, revealing its hollowness and the cruel destruction of beauty. Only four poems were published during his lifetime; he was killed in action a week before the Armistice. After Owen's death, Sassoon collected and edited his *Poems* (1920). Among the best known are 'Dulce et Decorum Est' and 'Anthem for Doomed Youth', published in 1921. English composer Benjamin *Britten used several of the poems in his *War Requiem* (1962). In technique Owen's work is distinguished by the extensive use of *assonance in place of rhyme, anticipating the later school of the poets W H *Auden and Stephen *Spender.

Owens, Jesse (1913–1980) born James Cleveland Owens, US track and field athlete who excelled in sprints, hurdles, and the long jump. At the 1936 Berlin Olympics he won four gold medals.

owl any of a group of mainly nocturnal birds of prey found worldwide. They have hooked beaks, heads that can turn quickly and far round on their very short necks, and forward-facing immobile eyes, surrounded by 'facial discs' of rayed feathers; they fly silently and have an acute sense of hearing. Owls comprise two families: typical owls (family Strigidae), of which there are about 120 species, and barn owls (family Tytonidae), of which there are 10 species. (Order Strigiformes.)

ox castrated male of domestic cattle, used in developing countries for ploughing and other agricultural work. Also the extinct wild ox or *aurochs of Europe, and surviving wild species such as buffaloes and yaks.

oxalic acid *or* **ethamedioic acid** (COOH)₂.2H₂O, white, poisonous solid, soluble in water, alcohol, and ether. Oxalic acid is found in rhubarb leaves, and its salts (oxalates) occur in wood sorrel (genus *Oxalis*, family Oxalidaceae) and other plants. It also occurs naturally in human body cells. It is used in the leather and textile industries, in dyeing and bleaching, ink manufacture, metal polishes, and for removing rust and ink stains.

oxbow lake curved lake found on the flood plain of a river. Oxbows are caused by the loops of *meanders that are cut off at times of flood and the river subsequently adopts a shorter course. In the USA, the term bayou is often used.

Oxford university city and administrative centre of *Oxfordshire in south central England, at the confluence of the rivers Thames (called the Isis around Oxford) and Cherwell, 84 km/52 mi northwest of London; population (1994 est) 121,000. Oxford University has 36 colleges, the oldest being University College (1249). Industries include steel products, car production, publishing and English language schools. Tourism is important.

Oxford Movement *or* **Tractarian Movement** *or* **Catholic Revival** movement that attempted to revive Catholic religion in the Church of England. Cardinal Newman dated the movement from Keble's sermon in Oxford in 1833. The Oxford Movement by the turn of the century had transformed the Anglican communion, and survives today as Anglo-Catholicism.

Oxfordshire county of south central England. **area:** 2,610 sq km/1,007 sq mi **towns and cities:** *Oxford (administrative headquarters), Abingdon, Banbury, Goring, Henley-on-Thames, Wallingford, Witney, Woodstock, Wantage, Chipping Norton, Thame **physical:** River Thames and tributaries (the Cherwell, Evenlode, Ock, Thame, and Windrush); Cotswold Hills (in the north) and Chiltern Hills (in the southeast) **features:** Vale of the White Horse (with a chalk hill figure 114 m/374 ft, below the hill camp known as Uffington Castle); Oxford University; Blenheim Palace (a World Heritage site), Woodstock, started in 1705 by Vanbrugh with help from Nicholas Hawksmoor, completed in 1722, with landscaped grounds by Capability *Brown; early 14th-century Broughton Castle; Rousham Park (1635), remodelled by William *Kent (1738–40), with landscaped garden; Ditchley Park, designed by James Gibbs in 1720; Europe's major fusion project JET (Joint European Torus) at the UK Atomic Energy Authority's fusion laboratories at Culham; the Manor House, Kelmscott (country house of William Morris, leader of the Arts and Crafts Movement); Henley Regatta **population:** (1996) 603,100.

oxidation in chemistry, the loss of *electrons, gain of oxygen, or loss of hydrogen by an atom, ion, or molecule during a chemical reaction.

oxide compound of oxygen and another element, frequently produced by burning the element or a compound of it in air or oxygen.

oxlip plant closely related to the *cowslip.

oxpecker *or* **tick-bird** either of two species of African birds belonging to the starling family. They were thought to climb around on the bodies of large mammals, feeding on ticks and other parasites and on cattle earwax, but in a British study, published in April 2000, of red-billed oxpeckers on oxen in Zimbabwe, researchers found that the oxpeckers were not eating the oxen ticks, but were feeding on blood by pecking at existing wounds. Oxpeckers are usually seen in groups of seven or eight, attending a herd of buffaloes or antelopes, and may help to warn the host of approaching dangers.

oxygen chemical symbol O, (Greek *oxys* 'acid'; *genes* 'forming') colourless, odourless, tasteless, *non-metallic, gaseous element, atomic number 8, relative atomic mass 15.9994. It is the most abundant element in the Earth's crust (almost 50% by mass), forms about 21% by volume of the atmosphere, and is present in combined form in water and many other substances. Oxygen is a by-product of *photosynthesis and the basis for *respiration in plants and animals.

oxymoron (Greek 'sharply dull' or 'pointedly foolish') figure of speech involving the combination of two or more words that are normally opposites, in order to startle. *Bittersweet* is an oxymoron, as are *cruel to be kind* and *beloved enemy*.

oyster edible shellfish with a rough, irregular hinged shell, found on the sea bottom in coastal areas. Oysters are bivalve *molluscs; the upper valve (shell) is flat, the lower hollow, like a bowl, and the two are hinged by an elastic ligament. The mantle, a protective layer of skin, lies against the shell, shielding the inner body, which includes the organs for breathing, digesting food, and reproduction. Oysters commonly change their sex once a year, sometimes more often; females can release up to one million eggs during a spawning period. (Family Ostreidae.)

oyster catcher any of several quite large, chunky shorebirds, with a long, heavy bill which is flattened at the sides and used to prise open the shells of oysters, mussels, and other shellfish. (Family Haematopodidae, order Charadriiformes.)

ozone gas consisting of three atoms of oxygen (O₃), which is therefore an allotrope of oxygen. It is formed when the molecule of the stable form of oxygen (O₂) is split by ultraviolet radiation or electrical discharge. It forms the *ozone layer in the upper atmosphere, which protects life on Earth from ultraviolet rays, a cause of skin cancer.

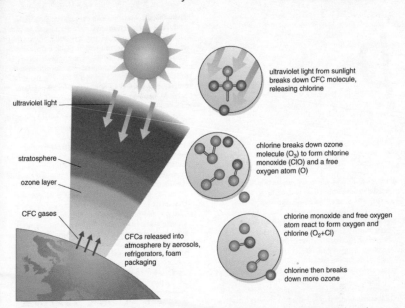

ultraviolet light from sunlight breaks down CFC molecule, releasing chlorine

chlorine breaks down ozone molecule (O_3) to form chlorine monoxide (ClO) and a free oxygen atom (O)

chlorine monoxide and free oxygen atom react to form oxygen and chlorine (O_2+Cl)

chlorine then breaks down more ozone

ultraviolet light

stratosphere

ozone layer

CFC gases

CFCs released into atmosphere by aerosols, refrigerators, foam packaging

ozone layer The destruction of the ozone layer by chlorofluorocarbons (CFCs). CFCs discharged into the atmosphere break down in sunlight releasing chlorine, which breaks down the ozone to form chlorine monoxide and a free oxygen atom. These products react together to form oxygen and chlorine, leaving the chlorine to break down another ozone molecule, and so on.

ozone depleter any chemical that destroys the ozone in the stratosphere. Most ozone depleters are chemically stable compounds containing chlorine or bromine, which remain unchanged for long enough to drift up to the upper atmosphere. The best known are *chlorofluorocarbons (CFCs).

ozone layer thin layer of the gas *ozone in the upper atmosphere which shields the Earth from harmful ultraviolet rays. A continent-sized hole has formed over Antarctica as a result of damage to the ozone layer. This has been caused in part by *chlorofluorocarbons

(CFCs), but many reactions destroy ozone in the stratosphere: nitric oxide, chlorine, and bromine atoms are implicated.

Ozu, Yasujiro (1903–1963) Japanese film director. He made silent films until 1936, by which time his basic style and themes were clear: an absorption in family life, in the interrelationships of its characters, and the use of comedy to reveal character. His *Tokyo monogatari/Tokyo Story* (1953) is one of the great classics of world cinema.

paca large, tailless, nocturnal, burrowing *rodent, related to the agoutis. The paca, about 60 cm/2 ft long, is native to Central and South America. (Genus *Cuniculus*, family Dasyproctidae.)

pacemaker *or* **sinoatrial node (SA node)** in vertebrates, a group of muscle cells in the wall of the heart that contracts spontaneously and rhythmically, setting the pace for the contractions of the rest of the heart. The pacemaker's intrinsic rate of contraction is increased or decreased, according to the needs of the body, by stimulation from the *autonomic nervous system. The term also refers to a medical device implanted under the skin of a patient whose heart beats inefficiently. It delivers minute electric shocks to stimulate the heart muscles at regular intervals and restores normal heartbeat.

Pacific Community (PC) formerly **South Pacific Commission** until 1998, organization to promote economic and social cooperation in the region, including dialogue between Pacific countries and those, such as France and the UK, that have dependencies in the region. It was established in February 1947. Its members include American Samoa, Australia, Cook Islands, Federated States of Micronesia, Fiji Islands, France, French Polynesia, Guam, Kiribati, Marshall Islands, Nauru, New Caledonia, New Zealand, Niue, Northern Marianas, Palau, Papua New Guinea, Pitcairn Islands, Samoa, Solomon Islands, Tokelau, Tonga, Tuvalu, United Kingdom, United States of America, Vanuatu, and Wallis and Futuna; headquarters are in Nouméa, New Caledonia.

Pacific Islands former (1947–1990) United Nations (UN) *trust territory in the western Pacific captured from Japan during World War II. The territory comprised over 2,000 islands and atolls and was assigned to the USA in 1947. The islands were divided into four governmental units: the **Northern Mariana Islands** (except Guam) which became a self-governing commonwealth in union with the USA in 1975 (inhabitants granted US citizenship 1986); the Marshall Islands, the Federated States of Micronesia, and the Republic of Palau (formerly also known as Belau) became self-governing 1979–80, signing agreements of free association with the USA in 1986. In December 1990 the UN Security Council voted to dissolve its trusteeship over the islands with the exception of Palau. The Marshall Islands and the Federated States of Micronesia were granted UN membership in 1991.

Pacific Ocean world's largest ocean, extending from Antarctica to the Bering Strait; area 166,242,500 sq km/ 64,186,500 sq mi; greatest breadth 16,000 km/9,942 mi; length 11,000 km/6,835 mi; average depth 4,188 m/ 13,749 ft; greatest depth of any ocean is the found in the Mariana Trench, in the northwest Pacific, with a depth of 11,034 m/36,201 ft.

Pacific Security Treaty military alliance agreement between Australia, New Zealand, and the USA, signed in 1951. Military cooperation between the USA and New Zealand has been restricted by the latter's policy of banning ships that might be carrying nuclear weapons or nuclear power sources.

Pacific War war 1879–83 fought by an alliance of Bolivia and Peru against Chile. Chile seized Antofagasta and the coast between the mouths of the rivers Loa and Paposo, rendering Bolivia landlocked, and also annexed the south Peruvian coastline from Arica to the mouth of the Loa, including the nitrate fields of the Atacama Desert.

pacifism belief that violence, even in self-defence, is unjustifiable under any conditions and that arbitration is preferable to war as a means of solving disputes. In the East, pacifism has roots in Buddhism, and non-violent action was used by Mahatma *Gandhi in the struggle for Indian independence.

Pacino, Al(fredo James) (1940–) US film actor. He has played powerful, introverted but violent roles in such films as *The Godfather* (1972), *Serpico* (1973), and *Scarface* (1983). *Dick Tracy* (1990) added comedy to his range. He won an Academy Award for his role in *Scent of a Woman* (1992).

paediatrics medical speciality concerned with the care of children. Paediatricians treat childhood diseases such as measles, chicken pox, and mumps, and immunize children against more serious infections such as diphtheria. Their role also includes treating and identifying disorders caused by lack of proper nutrition or child abuse.

Pagan archaeological site in Myanmar, on the Irrawaddy River, with the ruins of the former capital (founded 847, taken by the Mongol leader Kublai Khan 1287). These include Buddhist pagodas, shrines, and temples with wall paintings of the great period of Burmese art (11th–13th centuries), during which the Pagan state controlled much of Burma (now Myanmar).

pagan (Latin *paganus* 'a person from the countryside') usually, a member of one of the pre-Christian cultures of northern Europe, primarily Celtic or Norse, linked to the stone circles and to an agricultural calendar of which the main festivals are the summer and winter solstices and Beltane, the spring festival.

Paganini, Niccolò (1782–1840) Italian violinist and composer. He was a concert soloist from the age of nine. A prodigious technician, he drew on folk and gypsy idioms to create the modern repertoire of virtuoso techniques. His dissolute appearance, wild love life, and amazing powers of expression, even on a single string, fostered rumours of his being in league with the devil. His compositions include six concertos and various sonatas and variations for violin and orchestra, sonatas for violin and guitar, and guitar quartets.

Pahang state on the South China Sea coast of eastern Peninsular Malaysia; area 36,000 sq km/14,000 sq mi;

population (2000 est) 1,231,200. The capital is Kuantan. Much of the state is situated in the Pahang river basin, an area of dense jungle dependent on river transport. Plantation agriculture, mainly producing rubber, is important along the Pahang River, and other commercial crops include palm oil, coconuts, tobacco, rattan, and hemp. Mineral exploitation is important to the economy, including gold mining at Raub, tin mining at Sungai Lembing, and the working of substantial offshore reserves of oil and natural gas. There is a port at Tanjung Gelang. Pahang is ruled by a sultan.

Pahlavi dynasty Iranian dynasty founded by Reza Khan (1877–1944), an army officer who seized control of the government in 1921 and was proclaimed shah in 1925. During World War II, Britain and the USSR were nervous about his German sympathies and occupied Iran 1941–46. They compelled him to abdicate in 1941 in favour of his son Muhammad Reza Shah Pahlavi who was deposed in the Islamic revolution of 1979.

pain sense that gives an awareness of harmful effects on or in the body. It may be triggered by stimuli such as trauma, inflammation, and heat. Pain is transmitted by specialized nerves and also has psychological components controlled by higher centres in the brain. Drugs that control pain are known as painkillers or *analgesics.

Paine, Thomas (1737–1809) English left-wing political writer. He was active in the American and French revolutions. His pamphlet *Common Sense* (1776) ignited passions in the American Revolution; others include *The Rights of Man* (1791) and *The Age of Reason* (1793). He advocated republicanism, deism, the abolition of slavery, and the emancipation of women.

paint any of various materials used to give a protective and decorative finish to surfaces or for making pictures. A paint consists of a pigment suspended in a vehicle, or binder, usually with added solvents. It is the vehicle that dries and hardens to form an adhesive film of paint. Among the most common kinds are cellulose paints (or lacquers), oil-based paints, emulsion (water-based) paints, and special types such as enamels and primers.

painting application of coloured pigment to a surface. The chief methods of painting are: **tempera** emulsion painting, with a gelatinous (for example, egg yolk) rather than oil base – known in ancient Egypt; **fresco** watercolour painting on plaster walls – the palace of Knossos, Crete, contains examples from about 2000 BC; **ink** developed in China for calligraphy in the Sung period and highly popular in Japan from the 15th century; **oil** ground pigments in linseed, walnut, or other oil, it spread from northern to southern Europe in the 15th century; **watercolour** pigments combined with gum arabic and glycerol, which are diluted with water – the method was developed in the 15th–17th centuries for wash drawings; **acrylic** synthetic pigments developed after World War II, the colours are very hard and brilliant.

Paisley, Ian (Richard Kyle) (1926–) Northern Ireland politician, cleric, and leader of the Democratic Unionist Party (DUP) from 1971. An imposing and deeply influential member of the Protestant community, he remains staunchly committed to the union with Britain and fiercely opposed to a re-unified

Ireland or closer cooperation with the Republic of Ireland. His political career has been one of high drama, marked by protests, resignations, fervent oratory, and a pugnacious and forthright manner.

Pakistan

National name: *Islami Jamhuriyya e Pakistan/ Islamic Republic of Pakistan*

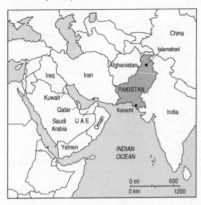

Area: 803,940 sq km/310,321 sq mi
Capital: Islamabad
Major towns/cities: Lahore, Rawalpindi, Faisalabad, Karachi, Hyderabad, Multan, Peshawar, Gujranwala, Quetta
Major ports: Karachi, Port Qasim
Physical features: fertile Indus plain in east, Baluchistan plateau in west, mountains in north and northwest; the 'five rivers' (Indus, Jhelum, Chenab, Ravi, and Sutlej) feed the world's largest irrigation system; K2 mountain; Khyber Pass
Head of state: Pervez Musharraf from 2001
Head of government: Shaukat Aziz from 2004
Political system: military
Political executive: military
Political parties: Islamic Democratic Alliance (IDA), conservative; Pakistan People's Party (PPP), moderate, Islamic, socialist; Pakistan Muslim League (PML), Islamic conservative (contains pro- and anti-government factions); Pakistan Islamic Front (PIF), Islamic fundamentalist, right wing; Awami National Party (ANP), left wing; National Democratic Alliance (NDA) bloc, left of centre; Mohajir National Movement (MQM), Sind-based *mohajir* settlers (Muslims previously living in India); Movement for Justice, reformative, anti-corruption
Currency: Pakistan rupee
GNI per capita (PPP): (US$) 1,940 (2002 est)
Exports: garments and hosiery, cotton, textiles, leather, rice, food and live animals. Principal market: USA 24.4% (2001)
Population: 153,578,000 (2003 est)
Language: Urdu (official), English, Punjabi, Sindhi, Pashto, Baluchi, other local dialects
Religion: Sunni Muslim 90%, Shiite Muslim 5%; also Hindu, Christian, Parsee, Buddhist
Life expectancy: 61 (men); 61 (women) (2000–05)

Chronology

2500–1600 BC: The area was the site of the Indus Valley civilization, a sophisticated, city-based ancient culture.

327 BC: Invaded by Alexander the Great of Macedonia.

1st–2nd centuries: North Pakistan was the heartland of the Kusana Empire, formed by invaders from Central Asia.

8th century: First Muslim conquests, in Baluchistan and Sind, followed by increasing immigration to Muslims from the west, from the 10th century.

1206: Establishment of Delhi Sultanate, stretching from northwest Pakistan and across northern India.

16th century: Sikh religion developed in Punjab.

16th–17th centuries: Lahore served intermittently as a capital city for the Mogul Empire, which stretched across the northern half of the Indian subcontinent.

1843–49: Sind and Punjab annexed by British and incorporated within empire of 'British India'.

late 19th century: Major canal irrigation projects in West Punjab and the northern Indus Valley drew in settlers from the east, as wheat and cotton production expanded.

1933: The name 'Pakistan' (Urdu for 'Pure Nation') invented by Choudhary Rahmat Ali, as Muslims within British India began to campaign for the establishment of an independent Muslim territory that would embrace the four provinces of Sind, Baluchistan, Punjab, and the Northwest Frontier.

1940: The All-India Muslim League (established in 1906), led by Karachi-born Muhammad Ali Jinnah, endorsed the concept of a separate nation for Muslims in the Lahore Resolution.

1947: Independence achieved from Britain, as a dominion within the Commonwealth. Pakistan, which included East Bengal, a Muslim-dominated province more than 1,600 km/1,000 mi from Punjab, was formed following the partition of British India. Large-scale and violent cross-border migrations of Muslims, Hindus, and Sikhs followed, and a brief border war with India over disputed Kashmir.

1956: Proclaimed a republic.

1958: Military rule imposed by Gen Ayub Khan.

1965: Border war with India over disputed territory of Kashmir.

1969: Power transferred to Gen Yahya Khan following strikes and riots.

1970: A general election produced a clear majority in East Pakistan for the pro-autonomy Awami League, led by Sheikh Mujibur Rahman, and in West Pakistan for Islamic socialist Pakistan People's Party (PPP), led by Zulfiqar Ali Bhutto.

1971: East Pakistan secured independence, as Bangladesh, following a civil war in which it received decisive military support from India. Power was transferred from the military to the populist Bhutto in Pakistan.

1977: Bhutto overthrown in military coup by Gen Zia ul-Haq following months of civil unrest; martial law imposed.

1979: Bhutto executed for alleged murder; tight political restrictions imposed by Zia regime.

1980: 3 million refugees fled to the Northwest Frontier Province and Baluchistan as a result of the Soviet invasion of Afghanistan.

1981: The broad-based Opposition Movement for the Restoration of Democracy was formed. The

Islamization process was pushed forward by the government.

1985: Martial law and the ban on political parties was lifted.

1986: Agitation for free elections was launched by Benazir Bhutto, the daughter of Zulfiqar Ali Bhutto.

1988: An Islamic legal code, the Shari'a, was introduced; Zia was killed in a military plane crash. Benazir Bhutto became prime minister after the (now centrist) PPP won the general election.

1989: Tension with India was increased by outbreaks of civil war in Kashmir. Pakistan rejoined the Commonwealth, which it had left in 1972.

1990: Bhutto was dismissed as prime minister by President Ghulam Ishaq Khan on charges of incompetence and corruption. The conservative Islamic Democratic Alliance (IDA), led by Nawaz Sharif, won the general election and launched a privatization and economic deregulation programme.

1993: Khan and Sharif resigned. Benazir Bhutto and PPP were re-elected. Farooq Leghari (PPP) was elected president.

1994: There was regional sectarian violence between Shia and Sunni Muslims, centred in Karachi.

1996: Benazir Bhutto was dismissed amid allegations of corruption.

1997: The right-of-centre Pakistan Muslim League won the general election, returning Nawaz Sharif to power as prime minister. President Leghari resigned.

1998: Rafiq Tarar became president. Pakistan conducted its first ever nuclear tests, provoking international condemnation and sanctions by the USA. Benazir Bhutto and her husband were charged with corruption. Federal rule was imposed on Sindh as a result of escalating violence. A $5.5 billion economic bailout package was agreed with the IMF and World Bank.

1999: Benazir Bhutto and her husband were found guilty of corruption, sentenced to five years in prison, and fined £5.3 million. India agreed to enter peace talks on Kashmir. Pakistan's army overthrew the government after Sharif tried to sack Gen Pervez Musharraf from the top military job. Musharraf, who appointed himself the country's chief executive, declared a state of emergency, and assumed all power, although he maintained Tarar as president.

2000: Relations with India worsened as India accused Pakistan of involvement in the hijacking of an Indian airliner by Kashmiri militants. Pakistan denied any involvement. Sharif was given two life sentences for hijacking and terrorism, and was also sentenced for corruption. He was later freed and fled to Saudi Arabia. Musharraf announced local elections from December, but decreed that anyone convicted of a criminal offence or of corruption would be disqualified from standing.

2001: All bank transactions came under Sharia (Islamic) law, forbidding the charging of interest.

2002: President Musharraf claimed endorsement in a referendum for an extension of his presidency for a further five years. The longstanding quarrel with India about disputed sovereignty over the territory of Kashmir erupted again, prompting international concern.

2003: Pakistan and India began their first formal ceasefire in the disputed territory of Kashmir in 20 years. President Musharraf narrowly survived a second assassination attempt in less than two weeks as two car bombs exploded near his motorcade at Rawalpindi.

2004: Shaukat Aziz was elected as prime minister, but with the parliamentary opposition abstaining from the vote. Pakistan was readmitted to the Commonwealth, from which it had been suspended after the military coup of 1999.

Pala dynasty (lived 8th–13th centuries)
northeastern Indian hereditary rulers, influential between the 8th and 13th centuries. Based in the agriculturally rich region of Bihar and Bengal, the dynasty was founded by Gopala, who had been elected king, and reached its peak under his son Dharmapala (reigned *c.* 770–810).

Palaeocene epoch (Greek 'old' + 'recent') first epoch of the Tertiary period of geological time, 65–56.5 million years ago. Many types of mammals spread rapidly after the disappearance of the great reptiles of the Mesozoic. Flying mammals replaced the flying reptiles, swimming mammals replaced the swimming reptiles, and all the ecological niches vacated by the reptiles were adopted by mammals.

Palaeolithic the Old Stone Age period, the earliest stage of human technology; see *prehistory.

palaeontology the study of ancient life, encompassing the structure of ancient organisms and their environment, evolution, and ecology, as revealed by their *fossils and the rocks in which those fossils are found. The practical aspects of palaeontology are based on using the presence of different fossils to date particular rock strata and to identify rocks that were laid down under particular conditions; for instance, giving rise to the formation of oil.

Palaeozoic era era of geological time 570–245 million years ago. It comprises the Cambrian, Ordovician, Silurian, Devonian, Carboniferous, and Permian periods. The Cambrian, Ordovician, and Silurian constitute the Lower or Early Palaeozoic; the Devonian, Carboniferous, and Permian make up the Upper or Late Palaeozoic. The era includes the evolution of hard-shelled multicellular life forms in the sea; the invasion of land by plants and animals; and the evolution of fish, amphibians, and early reptiles.

Palatinate German **Pfalz**, historic division of Germany, dating from before the 8th century. It was ruled by a **count palatine** (a count with royal prerogatives) and varied in size.

Palau *or* **Belau**
National name: *Belu'u era Belau/Republic of Palau*
Area: 508 sq km/196 sq mi
Capital: Koror (on Koror island)
Physical features: more than 350 (mostly uninhabited) islands, islets, and atolls in the west Pacific; warm, humid climate, susceptible to typhoons
Head of state and government: Tommy Remengesau from 2001
Political system: liberal democracy
Political executive: limited presidency
Political parties: Palau Nationalist Party (PVP); Ta Belau Party
Currency: US dollar
GNI per capita (PPP): (US$) 7,460 (2002 est)
Exports: copra, coconut oil, handicrafts, trochus, tuna
Population: 20,000 (2003 est)

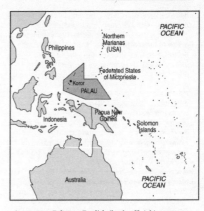

Language: Palauan, English (both official in most states)
Religion: Christian, principally Roman Catholic; Modekngei (indigenous religion)
Life expectancy: 65 (men); 69 (women) (2000–05)
Chronology
c. **1000 BC:** Micronesians first settled the islands.
AD 1543: First visited by Spanish navigator Ruy Lopez de Villalobos.
16th century: Colonized by Spain.
1899: Purchased from Spain by Germany.
1914: Occupied by Japan at the outbreak of World War I.
1920: Administered by Japan under League of Nations mandate.
1944: Occupied by USA after Japanese removed during World War II.
1947: Became part of United Nations (UN) Pacific Islands Trust Territory, administered by USA.
1981: Acquired autonomy as the Republic of Belau (Palau) under a constitution which prohibited the entry, storage, or disposal of nuclear or biological weapons.
1982: The Compact of Free Association signed with the USA, providing for the right to maintain US military facilities in return for economic aid. The compact could not come into force since it contradicted the constitution, which could only be amended by a 75% vote in favour.
1992: Kuniwo Nakamura was elected president, taking office in 1993.
1993: A referendum approved a constitutional amendment allowing the implementation of the Compact of Free Association with the USA.
1994: Independence was achieved and UN membership granted.
2001: Tommy Remengesau became president.
2004: President Remengesau was re-elected for a further term.

Palestine (Arabic *Falastin*, 'Philistine') historic geographical area at the eastern end of the Mediterranean sea, also known as the Holy Land because of its historic and symbolic importance for Jews, Christians, and Muslims. Early settlers included the Canaanites, Hebrews, and Philistines. Over the centuries it became part of the Egyptian, Assyrian,

689

Babylonian, Macedonian, Ptolemaic, Seleucid, Roman, Byzantine, Arab, Ottoman, and British empires. Today it comprises parts of modern Israel and Jordan.

Palestine Liberation Organization (PLO) Arab organization founded in 1964 to bring about an independent state in Palestine. It consists of several distinct groupings, the chief of which is al-*Fatah, led by Yassir *Arafat, the president of the PLO from 1969. Another major faction is the Popular Front for the Liberation of Palestine, a Marxist party formed in 1967, which is more hard line, opposing negotiations with Israel and the 1993 peace accord. Recognized in 1973 by Arab nations as the 'sole representative of the Palestinian people', and given observer status by the United Nations in 1974, the PLO has played a central role in the Israel–Palestine peace process.

Palestine Wars another name for the *Arab-Israeli Wars.

Palestrina, Giovanni Pierluigi da (c. 1525–1594) Italian composer. He wrote secular and sacred choral music, and is regarded as the outstanding exponent of Renaissance *counterpoint. Apart from motets and madrigals, he also wrote 105 Masses, including *Missa Papae Marcelli*.

Pali ancient Indo-European language of northern India, related to Sanskrit, and a classical language of Buddhism.

Palikir capital of the Federated States of Micronesia, on the island of Pohnpei; population (1998 est) 9,885.

palindrome word, sentence, or *verse that reads the same backwards as forwards (ignoring word breaks and *punctuation). 'Madam, in Eden, I'm Adam.' 'Ten animals I slam in a net.'

palisade cell cylindrical cell lying immediately beneath the upper epidermis of a leaf. Palisade cells normally exist as one closely packed row and contain many *chloroplasts. During the hours of daylight palisade cells are photosynthetic, using the energy of the sun to create carbohydrates from water and carbon dioxide.

Palladio, Andrea (1508–1580) Italian architect who created harmonious and balanced classical structures. He designed numerous palaces and country houses in and around Vicenza, making use of Roman classical forms, symmetry, and proportion. The Villa Malcontenta and the Villa Rotonda are examples of houses designed from 1540 for patrician families of the Venetian Republic. He also designed churches in Venice and published his studies of classical form in several illustrated books.

palladium chemical symbol Pd, lightweight, ductile and malleable, silver-white, metallic element, atomic number 46, relative atomic mass 106.4. It is one of the so-called platinum group of metals, and is resistant to tarnish and corrosion. It often occurs in nature as a free metal (see *native metal) in a natural alloy with platinum. Palladium is used as a catalyst, in alloys of gold (to make white gold) and silver, in electroplating, and in dentistry.

Pallas in Greek mythology, a title of the goddess *Athena, possibly meaning virgin.

Pallava dynasty (lived 4th–9th centuries) hereditary Hindu rulers who dominated south-eastern India between the 4th and 9th centuries. The dynasty's greatest kings were Simhavisnu (ruled c. 575–600) and Narasimhavarman I (ruled 630–668). Their capital was Kanchi, southwest of Madras (now Chennai).

palliative in medicine, any treatment given to relieve symptoms rather than to cure the underlying cause. In conditions that will resolve of their own accord (for instance, the common cold) or that are incurable, the entire treatment may be palliative.

palm any of a group of large treelike plants with a single tall stem that has a thick cluster of large palmate (five-lobed) leaves or pinnate leaves (leaflets either side of the stem) at the top. Most of the numerous species are tropical or subtropical. Some, such as the coconut, date, sago, and oil palms, are important economically. (Family Palmae.)

Palma de Mallorca chief port, commercial centre, and capital of the *Balearic Islands, an autonomous community of Spain, situated on a wide bay on the southwest coast of the island of *Mallorca, population (2001 est) 346,700. It is one of Europe's most renowned resorts. Palma was founded as a Roman colony in 276 BC. It has a Gothic cathedral, begun in 1229; the 14th-century Almudaina palace, a former royal residence; and the 13th-century church of St Francis of Assisi, which contains the tomb of the Mallorcan scholar Ramon Llull. During the Spanish civil war (1936–39), Palma was an important naval and air base of the Nationalists.

Palmer, Arnold Daniel (1929–) US golfer who helped to popularize the professional sport in the USA in the 1950s and 1960s. He won the Masters in 1958, 1960, 1962, and 1964, the US Open in 1960, and the British Open in 1961 and 1962. He won the Ryder Cup seven times, including once as playing captain and once as non-playing captain.

Palmer, Samuel (1805–1881) English landscape painter and etcher. His early works, small pastoral scenes mostly painted in watercolour and sepia, have an intense, visionary quality, greatly influenced by a meeting with the aged William Blake, and the latter's engravings for Thornton's *Virgil*. From 1826 to 1835 he lived in Shoreham, Kent, with a group of artists who followed Blake, styling themselves 'the Ancients'.

Palmerston, Henry John Temple, 3rd Viscount Palmerston (1784–1865) British politician. He was prime minister 1855–58 (when he rectified Aberdeen's mismanagement of the Crimean War, suppressed the *Indian Mutiny, and carried through the Second Opium War) and 1859–65 (when he almost involved Britain in the American Civil War on the side of the South). Initially a Tory, in Parliament from 1807, he was secretary-at-war 1809–28. He broke with the Tories in 1830 and sat in the Whig cabinets of 1830–34, 1835–41, and 1846–51 as foreign secretary. He became viscount in 1802.

Pamir central Asian plateau mainly in Tajikistan, but extending into China and Afghanistan, traversed by mountain ranges. Its highest peak is Kommunizma Pik (Communism Peak, 7,495 m/24,590 ft) in the Akademiya Nauk range.

pampas grass any of a group of large grasses native to South America, especially *C. argentea*, which is grown in gardens and has tall leaves and large clusters of feathery white flowers growing around the tips of the flower-bearing stems. (Genus *Cortaderia*.)

Pan (Greek 'all') in Greek mythology, the god of flocks and herds. He is depicted as a man with the horns, ears, and hoofed legs of a goat, and plays a shepherd's syrinx or **panpipes**; an instrument he reputedly invented. Later he was regarded as the personification of nature, the existing order of things. The Romans identified him with *Faunus and Silvanus.

Pan-Africanist Congress (PAC) South African political party, formed as a militant black nationalist group in 1959, when it broke away from the African National Congress (ANC), promoting a black-only policy for Africa. PAC was outlawed 1960–90; its military wing was called Poqo ('we alone'). It suspended its armed struggle in 1994, and transformed itself into a political party to contest the first multiracial elections. It is more radical than the ANC, advocating a radical redistribution of land and a state-run economy.

Panama

National name: *República de Panamá/Republic of Panama*

Area: 77,100 sq km/29,768 sq mi
Capital: Panamá
Major towns/cities: San Miguelito, Colón, David, La Chorrera, Santiago, Chitré, Changuinola
Major ports: Colón, Cristóbal, Balboa
Physical features: coastal plains and mountainous interior; tropical rainforest in east and northwest; Archipelago de las Perlas in Gulf of Panama; Panama Canal
Head of state and government: Martín Torrijos from 2004
Political system: liberal democracy
Political executive: limited presidency
Political parties: Democratic Revolutionary Party (PRD), right wing; Arnulfista Party (PA), left of centre; Authentic Liberal Party (PLA), left of centre; Nationalist Liberal Republican Movement (MOLIRENA), right of centre; Papa Ego Movement (MPE), moderate, left of centre
Currency: balboa
GNI per capita (PPP): (US$) 5,870 (2002 est)
Exports: bananas, shrimps and lobsters, sugar, clothing, coffee. Principal market: USA 49.6% (2001)
Population: 3,120,000 (2003 est)
Language: Spanish (official), English
Religion: Roman Catholic 93%
Life expectancy: 72 (men); 77 (women) (2000–05)

Chronology
1502: Visited by Spanish explorer Rodrigo de Bastidas, at which time it was inhabited by Cuna, Choco, Guaymi, and other Indian groups.
1513: Spanish conquistador Vasco Núñez de Balboa explored Pacific Ocean from Darien isthmus; he was made governor of Panama (meaning 'abundance of fish').
1519: Spanish city established at Panama, which became part of the Spanish viceroyalty of New Andalucia (later New Granada).
1572–95 and 1668–71: Spanish settlements sacked by British buccaneers Francis Drake and Henry Morgan.
1821: Achieved independence from Spain; joined confederacy of Gran Colombia, which included Colombia, Venezuela, Ecuador, Peru, and Bolivia.
1830: Gran Colombia split up and Panama became part of Colombia.
1846: Treaty signed with USA, allowing it to construct a railway across the isthmus.
1880s: French attempt to build a Panama canal connecting the Atlantic and Pacific Oceans failed as a result of financial difficulties and the death of 22,000 workers from yellow fever and malaria.
1903: Full independence achieved with US help on separation from Colombia; USA bought rights to build Panama Canal, and were given control of a 10-mile strip, the Canal Zone, in perpetuity.
1914: Panama Canal opened.
1939: Panama's status as a US protectorate was terminated by mutual agreement.
1968–81: Military rule of Gen Omar Torrijos Herrera, leader of the National Guard, who deposed the elected president and launched a costly programme of economic modernization.
1977: USA–Panama treaties transferred the canal to Panama (effective from 2000), with the USA guaranteeing protection and annual payment.
1987: Gen Manuel Noriega (head of the National Guard and effective ruler since 1983) resisted calls for his removal, despite suspension of US military and economic aid.
1988: Noriega, charged with drug smuggling by the USA, declared a state of emergency after a coup against him failed.
1989: 'State of war' with USA announced, and US invasion (codenamed 'Operation Just Cause') deposed Noriega; 4,000 Panamanians died in the fighting. Guillermo Endara, who had won earlier elections, was installed as president in December.
1991: Constitutional reforms were approved by the assembly, including the abolition of the standing army; a privatization programme was introduced.
1992: Noriega was found guilty of drug offences and given a 40-year prison sentence in USA. A referendum rejected the proposed constitutional reforms.
1994: The constitution was amended by assembly; the army was formally abolished.
1998: Voters rejected a proposed constitutional change to allow the president to run for a second term.
1999: Mireya Moscoso, widow of former president Arnulfo Arias, became Panama's first female head of state. Panama formally took control of its canal.
2000: A commission was formed to determine the fate of 150 people who disappeared under military regimes 1968–89.

691

2004: Martin Torrijos, leader of the Democratic Revolutionary Party and son of the military dictator Omar Torrijos Herrera, was elected as president.

Panamá capital of the Republic of Panama, on the east bank of the Pacific entrance to the Panama Canal, with its port at Balboa in the Canal Zone; population (2000 est) 463,100. It became capital in 1903 following independence from Colombia. The city developed rapidly following the completion of the Canal. Its good communications by air and rail, as well as by the Pan-American Highway, have enabled the city to become the main transport and industrial centre of Panama. Products include oil, plastics, leather, food, and drink.

Panama Canal canal across the Panama isthmus in Central America, connecting the Pacific and Atlantic oceans. Built by the USA 1904–14, it is one of the world's most strategic waterways. The Panama Canal and the **Panama Canal Zone**, comprising land extending about 5 km/3 mi on either side of the canal, were controlled by the USA from 1903. Under the terms of the Panama Canal treaty of 1977, Panama took control of the zone in 1979 and complete control of the canal on 1 January 2000.

pancreas in vertebrates, a gland of the digestive system located close to the duodenum. When stimulated by the hormone secretin, it releases enzymes into the duodenum that digest starches, proteins, and fats. In humans, it is about 18 cm/7 in long, and lies behind and below the stomach. It contains groups of cells called the **islets of Langerhans**, which secrete the hormones insulin and glucagon that regulate the blood sugar level.

panda one of two carnivores of different families, native to northwestern China and Tibet. The **giant panda** *Ailuropoda melanoleuca* has black-and-white fur with black eye patches and feeds mainly on bamboo shoots, consuming about 8 kg/17.5 lb of bamboo per day. It can grow up to 1.5 m/4.5 ft long, and weigh up to 140 kg/300 lb. It is an endangered species. In 2000 there were only 1,000 remaining in the wild, and a further 120 in zoos. The **lesser**, or **red, panda** *Ailurus fulgens*, of the raccoon family, is about 50 cm/1.5 ft long, and is black and chestnut, with a long tail.

Pandora (Greek 'all gifts') in Greek mythology, the first mortal woman. Zeus sent her to Earth with a box containing every human woe to counteract the blessings brought to mortals by *Prometheus, whose gift of fire was stolen from the gods. In the most common tradition, she opened the box, and the evils flew out; only hope was left inside as a consolation.

Pandya dynasty (lived 3rd century BC–16th century AD) southern Indian hereditary rulers based in the region around Madurai (its capital). The dynasty extended its power into Kerala (southwestern India) and Sri Lanka during the reigns of kings Kadungon (ruled 590–620), Arikesar Maravarman (670–700), Varagunamaharaja I (765–815), and Srimara Srivallabha (815–862). Pandya influence peaked in Jatavarman Sundara's reign 1251–1268. After Madurai was invaded by forces from the Delhi sultanate in 1311, the Pandyas declined into merely local rulers.

Pangaea or **Pangea** (Greek 'all-land') single land mass, made up of all the present continents, believed to have existed between 300 and 200 million years ago; the rest of the Earth was covered by the Panthalassa ocean.

Pangaea split into two land masses – *Laurasia in the north and *Gondwanaland in the south – which subsequently broke up into several continents. These then moved slowly to their present positions (see *plate tectonics).

pangolin or **scaly anteater** toothless mammal of tropical Africa and Southeast Asia. They are long-tailed and covered with large, overlapping scales, except on the muzzle, sides of the head, throat, chest, and belly. They have an elongated skull and a long, extensible tongue. Pangolins measure 30–100 cm/12–39 in long, exclusive of the prehensile tail, which is about twice as long as the body. Some are arboreal and others terrestrial. All live on ants and termites. Pangolins comprise the order Pholidota. There is only one genus (*Manis*) and family Manidae, with seven species.

Pankhurst, Emmeline (1858–1928) born Emmeline Goulden, English *suffragette. Founder of the Women's Social and Political Union (WSPU) in 1903, she launched the militant suffragette campaign in 1905 and was arrested several times for her sometimes violent campaigning, undertaking hunger strikes and enduring forcible feeding. During World War I, she abandoned her militancy and encouraged the industrial recruitment of women. In 1926 she joined the Conservative Party and was a prospective Parliamentary candidate for Whitechapel.

pansy cultivated plant derived from the European wild pansy (*Viola tricolor*) and including many different varieties and strains. The flowers are usually purple, yellow, or cream, or a mixture of these colours, and there are many highly developed varieties bred for size, colour, or special markings. Several of the 400 different species are scented. (Family Violaceae.)

Panthalassa ocean that covered the surface of the Earth not occupied by the world continent *Pangaea between 300 and 200 million years ago.

pantheism (Greek *pan* 'all'; *theos* 'God') doctrine that regards all of reality as divine, and God as present in all of nature and the universe. It is expressed in Egyptian religion and Brahmanism; Stoicism, neo-Platonism, Judaism, Christianity, and Islam can be interpreted in pantheistic terms. Pantheistic philosophers include Giordano Bruno, Baruch Spinoza, J G Fichte, F W J Schelling, and G W F Hegel.

pantheon originally a temple for worshipping all the gods, such as that in ancient Rome, rebuilt by the emperor Hadrian between AD 118 and about 128, and still used as a church. In more recent times, the name has been used for a building where famous people are buried (as in the Panthéon, Paris).

panther another name for the *leopard.

pantomime in British theatre, a traditional Christmas entertainment. It has its origins in the harlequinade of the 18th century and *burlesque of the 19th century, which gave rise to the tradition of the principal boy being played by a woman and the dame by a man. The harlequin's role diminished altogether as themes developed on folk tales such as 'The Sleeping Beauty' and 'Cinderella', and with the introduction of additional material such as popular songs, topical comedy, and audience participation. Popular television stars regularly feature in modern pantomime.

papal infallibility doctrine formulated by the Roman Catholic Vatican Council in 1870, which stated that the pope, when speaking officially on certain doctrinal or moral matters, was protected from error by God, and therefore such rulings could not be challenged.

Papal States area of central Italy in which the pope was temporal ruler from 756 until the unification of Italy in 1870.

papaya tropical evergreen tree, native from Florida to South America. Varieties are grown throughout the tropics. The edible fruits are like melons, with orange-coloured flesh and large numbers of blackish seeds in the centre; they can weigh up to 9 kg/20 lb. (*Carica papaya*, family Caricaceae.)

Papeete capital and port of French Polynesia on the northwest coast of Tahiti; population (1992) 24,200. Products include vanilla, copra, and mother-of-pearl.

paper thin, flexible material made in sheets from vegetable fibres (such as wood pulp) or rags and used for writing, drawing, printing, packaging, and various household needs. The name comes from papyrus, a form of writing material made from water reed, used in ancient Egypt. The invention of true paper, originally made of pulped fishing nets and rags, is credited to Tsai Lun, Chinese minister of agriculture, in AD 105.

papier mâché (French 'chewed paper') craft technique using paper pulp or shredded paper mixed with resin or a water-based glue, such as PVA. The pasted paper can then be moulded, modelled, or built up in layers to form the required shape. Once dry the material hardens, and may be painted and lacquered; mother-of-pearl is a traditional decoration. As papier mâché is light, versatile, and cheap to make, it has many decorative uses, including trays, bowls, and even furniture.

Papineau, Louis Joseph (1786–1871) Canadian politician. He led a mission to England to protest against the planned union of Lower Canada (Québec) and Upper Canada (Ontario), and demanded economic reform and an elected provincial legislature. In 1835 he gained the cooperation of William Lyon Mackenzie in Upper Canada, and in 1837 organized an unsuccessful rebellion of the French against British rule in Lower Canada. He fled the country, but returned in 1847 to sit in the United Canadian legislature until 1854.

Pap test *or* **Pap smear** common name for *cervical smear.

Papuan native to or inhabitant of Papua New Guinea; speaker of any of various Papuan languages, used mainly on the island of New Guinea, although some 500 are used in New Britain, the Solomon Islands, and the islands of the southwest Pacific. The Papuan languages belong to the Indo-Pacific family.

Papua New Guinea

National name: *Gau Hedinarai ai Papua-Matamata Guinea/Independent State of Papua New Guinea*

Area: 462,840 sq km/178,702 sq mi

Capital: Port Moresby (on East New Guinea)

Major towns/cities: Lae, Madang, Arawa, Wewak, Goroka, Rabaul

Major ports: Port Moresby, Rabaul

Physical features: mountainous; swamps and plains; monsoon climate; tropical islands of New Ireland, New Britain, and Bougainville; Admiralty Islands, D'Entrecasteaux Islands, and Louisiade Archipelago; active volcanoes Vulcan and Tavurvur

Head of state: Queen Elizabeth II from 1975, represented by Governor General Paulias Matane from 2004

Head of government: Michael Somare from 2002

Political system: liberal democracy

Political executive: parliamentary

Political parties: Papua New Guinea Party (Pangu Pati: PP), urban- and coastal-oriented nationalist; People's Democratic Movement (PDM), 1985 breakaway from the PP; National Party (NP), highlands-based, conservative; Melanesian Alliance (MA), Bougainville-based, pro-autonomy, left of centre; People's Progress Party (PPP), conservative; People's Action Party (PAP), right of centre

Currency: kina

GNI per capita (PPP): (US$) 2,080 (2002 est)

Exports: gold, copper ore and concentrates, crude petroleum, timber, coffee beans, coconut and copra products. Principal market: Australia 23.9% (2001)

Population: 5,711,000 (2003 est)

Language: English (official), pidgin English, over 700 local languages

Religion: Christian 97%, of which 3% Roman Catholic; local pantheistic beliefs

Life expectancy: 57 (men); 59 (women) (2000–05)

Chronology

c. **3000 BC:** New settlement of Austronesian (Melanesian) immigrants.

AD 1526: Visited by Portuguese navigator Jorge de Menezes, who named the main island the Ilhos dos Papua.

1545: Spanish navigator Ynigo Ortis de Retez gave the island the name of New Guinea, as a result of a supposed resemblance of the peoples with those of the Guinea coast of Africa.

17th century: Regularly visited by Dutch merchants.

1828: Dutch East India Company incorporated the western part of New Guinea into Netherlands East Indies (becoming Irian Jaya, in Indonesia).

1884: Northeast New Guinea annexed by Germany; the southeast was claimed by Britain.

1870s: Visits by Western missionaries and traders increased.

1890s: Copra plantations developed in German New Guinea.

1906: Britain transferred its rights to Australia, which renamed the lands Papua.

1914: German New Guinea occupied by Australia at the outbreak of World War I; from the merged territories Papua New Guinea was formed.

1920–42: Held as League of Nations mandate by Australia.

1942–45: Occupied by Japan, who lost 150,000 troops resisting Allied counterattack.

1947: Held as United Nations Trust Territory by Australia.

1951: Legislative Council established.

1964: Elected House of Assembly formed.

1967: Pangu Party (Pangu Pati; PP) formed to campaign for home rule.

1975: Independence achieved from Australia, within Commonwealth, with Michael Somare (PP) as prime minister.

1985: Somare challenged by deputy prime minister Paias Wingti, who later left the PP and formed the People's Democratic Movement (PDM); he became head of a five-party coalition government.

1988: Joined Solomon Islands and Vanuatu to form the Spearhead Group, aiming to preserve Melanesian cultural traditions.

1989: State of emergency imposed on copper-rich Bougainville in response to separatist violence.

1990: The Bougainville Revolutionary Army (BRA) issued a unilateral declaration of independence.

1991: There was an economic boom as gold production doubled.

1994: There was a short-lived peace agreement with the BRA.

1996: The prime minister of Bougainville was murdered, jeopardizing the peace process. Gerard Sinato was elected president of the transitional Bougainville government.

1997: The army and police mutinied following the government's use of mercenaries against secessionist rebels. Silas Atopare was appointed governor general.

1998: There was a truce with Bougainville secessionists. At least 1,500 people died and thousands were left homeless when tidal waves destroyed villages on the north coast.

1999: A coalition of parties headed by Mekere Morauta won a parliamentary majority to form a new government. Bougainville Transitional Government (BTG) was replaced by the new interim Bougainville Reconciliation Government (BRG), headed by former rebel leader Joseph Kabui and BTG leader Gerard Sinato.

2001: Economic reforms and proposed military cuts sparked demonstrations.

2002: Sir Michael Somare (National Alliance Party) was again elected as prime minister.

papyrus type of paper made by the ancient Egyptians. Typically papyrus was made by gluing together some 20 sheets of the pith of the papyrus or paper reed plant *Cyperus papyrus*, family Cyperaceae. These sheets were arranged in alternating layers aligned vertically, followed by horizontally. The strips were then covered with linen and beaten with a mallet. Finally, the papyrus was polished with a stone. Papyrus was in use before the First Dynasty.

parabola in mathematics, a curve formed by cutting a right circular cone with a plane parallel to the sloping side of the cone. A parabola is one of the family of curves known as *conic sections. The graph of $y = x^2$ is a parabola.

paracetamol analgesic, particularly effective for musculoskeletal pain. It is as effective as aspirin in reducing fever, and less irritating to the stomach, but has little anti-inflammatory action. An overdose can cause severe, often irreversible or even fatal, liver and kidney damage.

parachute any canopied fabric device strapped to a person or a package, used to slow down descent from a high altitude, or returning spent missiles or parts to a safe speed for landing, or sometimes to aid (through braking) the landing of a plane or missile. Modern designs enable the parachutist to exercise considerable control of direction, as in skydiving.

Paradise Lost epic poem in 12 books, by John *Milton, first published in 1667. The poem describes the Fall of Man and the battle between God and Satan, as enacted through the story of Adam and Eve in the Garden of Eden. A sequel, *Paradise Regained*, was published in 1671 and relates the temptation of Christ in the wilderness.

paradox literary device or device of rhetoric which is a statement that seems opposing or contradictory but contains an element of truth. The truth is emphasized by the unexpected form of expression. The Bible is a rich source of paradox: 'Love your enemies'; 'The first shallbe last and the last shall be first.'

paraffin common name for *alkane, any member of the series of hydrocarbons with the general formula C_nH_{2n+2}. The lower members are gases, such as methane (marsh or natural gas). The middle ones (mainly liquid) form the basis of petrol, kerosene, and lubricating oils, while the higher ones (paraffin waxes) are used in ointment and cosmetic bases.

Paraguay

National name: *República del Paraguay/ Republic of Paraguay*

Area: 406,752 sq km/157,046 sq mi

Capital: Asunción (and chief port)

Major towns/cities: Ciudad del Este, Pedro Juan Caballero, San Lorenzo, Fernando de la Mora, Lambare, Luque, Capiatá

Major ports: Concepción

Physical features: low marshy plain and marshlands; divided by Paraguay River; Paraná River forms southeast boundary

Head of state and government: Oscar Duarte Frutos from 2003
Political system: emergent democracy
Political executive: limited presidency
Political parties: National Republican Association (Colorado Party), right of centre; Authentic Radical Liberal Party (PLRA), centrist; National Encounter, right of centre; Radical Liberal Party (PLR), centrist; Liberal Party (PL), centrist
Currency: guaraní
GNI per capita (PPP): (US$) 4,450 (2002 est)
Exports: soybeans (and other oil seeds), cotton, timber and wood manufactures, hides and skins, meat. Principal market: Brazil 28.1% (2001)
Population: 5,878,000 (2003 est)
Language: Spanish (official), Guaraní (an indigenous Indian language)
Religion: Roman Catholic (official religion) 85%; Mennonite, Anglican
Life expectancy: 69 (men); 73 (women) (2000–05)
Chronology
1526: Visited by Italian navigator Sebastian Cabot, who travelled up the Paraná River; at this time the east of the country had long been inhabited by Guaraní-speaking Amerindians, who gave the country its name, which means 'land with an important river'.
1537: Spanish made an alliance with Guaraní Indians against hostile Chaco Indians, enabling them to colonize interior plains; Asunción founded by Spanish.
1609: Jesuits arrived from Spain to convert local population to Roman Catholicism and administer the country.
1767: Jesuit missionaries expelled.
1776: Formerly part of Spanish Viceroyalty of Peru, which covered much of South America, became part of Viceroyalty of La Plata, with capital at Buenos Aires (Argentina).
1808: With Spanish monarchy overthrown by Napoleon Bonaparte, La Plata Viceroyalty became autonomous, but Paraguayans revolted against rule from Buenos Aires.
1811: Independence achieved from Spain.
1814: Under dictator Gen José Gaspar Rodriguez Francia ('El Supremo'), Paraguay became an isolated state.
1840: Francia was succeeded by his nephew, Carlos Antonio Lopez, who opened country to foreign trade and whose son, Francisco Solano Lopez, as president from 1862, built up a powerful army.
1865–70: War with Argentina, Brazil, and Uruguay over access to sea; more than half the population died and 150,000 sq km/58,000 sq mi of territory lost.
late 1880s: Conservative Colorado Party and Liberal Party founded.
1912: Liberal leader Edvard Schaerer came to power, ending decades of political instability.
1932–35: Territory in west won from Bolivia during Chaco War (settled by arbitration in 1938).
1940–48: Presidency of autocratic Gen Higinio Morínigo.
1948–54: Political instability; six different presidents.
1954: Gen Alfredo Stroessner seized power in a coup. He ruled as a ruthless autocrat, suppressing civil liberties; the country received initial US backing as the economy expanded.

1989: Stroessner was ousted in a coup led by Gen Andrés Rodríguez. Rodríguez was elected president; the right-of-centre military-backed Colorado Party won assembly elections.
1992: A new democratic constitution was adopted.
1993: The Colorado Party won the most seats in the first free multiparty elections, but no overall majority; its candidate, Juan Carlos Wasmosy, won the first free presidential elections.
1999: Senate leader Luis Gonzalez Macchi became president.
2000: An attempted anti-government coup, led by supporters of the ex-army chief Lino Oviedo, failed after the USA and Brazil put pressure on the army's commanders. The opposition candidate, Julio César Franco, of the Authentic Liberal Radical Party, won the vice-presidential elections, the first national defeat for the Colorado Party. Congress approved the start of a programme of privatization.
2003: Oscar Duarte Frutos of the authoritarian Colorado Party won the presidential election, but with only 38% of the vote.

parakeet any of various small long-tailed *parrots, order Psittaciformes, with a moderate beak. They include the **ring-necked parakeets**, genus *Psittacula*, which are very common in India and Africa, and *cockatiels, and *budgerigars, natives of Australia. The **king parakeet** is about the size of a magpie and has a red head and breast and green wings.

parallax change in the apparent position of an object against its background when viewed from two different positions. In astronomy, nearby stars show a shift owing to parallax when viewed from different positions on the Earth's orbit around the Sun. A star's parallax is used to deduce its distance from the Earth.

parallel lines and parallel planes straight lines or planes that always remain a constant distance from one another no matter how far they are extended.

parallelogram a quadrilateral (a shape with four sides) with opposite pairs of sides equal in length and parallel, and opposite angles equal. The diagonals of a parallelogram bisect each other. Its area is the product of the length (l) of one side and the perpendicular distance (height h) between this and the opposite side; the formula is $A = l \times h$. In the special case when all four sides are equal in length, the parallelogram is known as a rhombus, and when the internal angles are right angles, it is a rectangle or square.

parallelogram of forces in physics and applied mathematics, a method of calculating the resultant (combined effect) of two different forces acting together on an object. Because a force has both magnitude and direction it is a vector quantity and can be represented by a straight line. A second force acting at the same point in a different direction can be represented by another line drawn at an angle to the first. By completing the parallelogram (of which the two lines are sides) a diagonal may be drawn from the original angle to the opposite corner to represent the resultant force vector.

parallel processing emerging computer technology that allows more than one computation at the same time. Although in the 1990s this technology enabled only a small number of computer processor units to work in parallel, in theory thousands or millions of processors could be used at the same time.

695

paralysis loss of voluntary movement due to failure of nerve impulses to reach the muscles involved. It may result from almost any disorder of the nervous system, including brain or spinal cord injury, poliomyelitis, stroke, and progressive conditions such as a tumour or multiple sclerosis. Paralysis may also involve loss of sensation due to sensory nerve disturbance.

Paramaribo chief port and capital of Suriname, on the west bank of the Suriname River 24 km/15 mi inland from the Atlantic coast; population (1996 est) 150,000; metropolitan area (1996 est) 205,000. Products include coffee, fruit, timber, and bauxite, and tourism is a significant source of revenue.

paramilitary uniformed, armed force found in many countries, occupying a position between the police and the military. In France such a force is called the Gendarmerie and in Germany the Federal Border Guard. In recent years the term has been extended to include illegal organizations of a terrorist or guerrilla nature.

paranoia mental disorder marked by delusions of grandeur or persecution. In popular usage, paranoia means baseless or exaggerated fear and suspicion.

paraplegia paralysis of the lower limbs, involving loss of both movement and sensation; it is usually due to spinal injury.

parapsychology (Greek *para* 'beyond') study of paranormal phenomena, which are generally subdivided into two types: *extrasensory perception (ESP), or the paracognitive; and psychokinesis (PK), telekinesis, or the paraphysical – movement of an object without the use of physical force or energy.

parasite organism that lives on or in another organism (called the host) and depends on it for nutrition, often at the expense of the host's welfare. Parasites that live inside the host, such as liver flukes and tapeworms, are called **endoparasites**; those that live on the exterior, such as fleas and lice, are called **ectoparasites**.

Pareto, Vilfredo (1848–1923) Italian economist and political philosopher who began his career as a liberal but ended it as an early fascist. His two important books on economics were the *Cours d'économie politique* (1906) and *The Manual of Political Economy* (1906).

Paris capital of France, on the River Seine; *département* (Ville de Paris) in the Île-de-France region; area of the *agglomération parisienne* (comprising the Ville de Paris, which is divided into 20 *arrondissements* and surrounding suburbs) 105 sq km/40.5 sq mi; population Ville de Paris (2002 est) 2,113,000; *agglomération parisienne* (2002 est) 11,293,200. The city is the core of a highly centralized national administration, a focus of European transport networks, and France's leading centre for education, research, finance, and industry. Manufactured products include metal, electrical and luxury goods, chemicals, glass, and tobacco. As one of the world's principal historic and cultural centres, Paris attracts enormous numbers of tourists throughout the year.

Paris in Greek mythology, a Trojan prince whose abduction of *Helen, wife of *Menelaus, caused the Trojan wars. Helen had been promised to him by the goddess Aphrodite as a bribe, during his judgement between her beauty and that of the goddesses, Hera and Athena. During the wars, he killed the Greek hero *Achilles by shooting an arrow into his heel, but was later mortally wounded by the archer Philoctetes.

Paris Commune name given to two separate periods in the history of Paris: **The Paris municipal government of 1789–94** was established after the storming of the *Bastille and remained powerful in the French Revolution until the fall of Robespierre in 1794. **The provisional national government of 18 March–May 1871** was formed while Paris was besieged by the German troops during the Franco-Prussian War. It consisted of socialists and left-wing republicans, and is often considered the first socialist government in history. Elected after the right-wing National Assembly at Versailles tried to disarm the National Guard, it fell when the Versailles troops captured Paris and massacred 20,000–30,000 people during 21–28 May.

parish council lowest neighbourhood unit of local government in England and Wales, based on church parishes. They developed as units for local government with the introduction of the Poor Law in the 17th century. In Wales and Scotland they are commonly called **community councils**. In England approximately 8,200 out of the 10,000 parishes have elected councils. There are 730 community councils in Wales and about 1,000 in Scotland, which, unlike their English and Welsh counterparts, do not have statutory powers.

Paris, Treaty of any of various peace treaties signed in Paris, including: **1763** ending the *Seven Years' War; **1783** (also known as the Peace of Versailles) recognizing American independence; **1814** and **1815** following the abdication and final defeat of *Napoleon I; **1856** ending the *Crimean War; **1898** ending the *Spanish-American War; **1919–20** the conference preparing the Treaty of *Versailles at the end of World War I was held in Paris; **1947** after World War II, the peace treaties between the *Allies and Italy, Romania, Hungary, Bulgaria, and Finland; **1951** treaty signed by France, West Germany, Italy, Belgium, Netherlands, and Luxembourg, embodying the Schuman Plan to set up a single coal and steel authority; **1973** ending US participation in the *Vietnam War.

parity of a number, the state of being either even or odd. In computing, the term refers to the number of 1s in the binary codes used to represent data. A binary representation has **even parity** if it contains an even number of 1s and **odd parity** if it contains an odd number of 1s.

parity in economics, equality of price, rate of exchange, wages, and buying power. Parity ratios may be used in the setting of wages to establish similar status to different work groups. Parity in international exchange rates means that those on a par with each other share similar buying power. In the USA, agricultural output prices are regulated by a parity system.

Park, Mungo (1771–1806) Scottish explorer who traced the course of the Niger River 1795–97. He disappeared and probably drowned during a second African expedition 1805–06. He published *Travels in the Interior of Africa* (1799).

Parker, Charlie (Charles Christopher) (1920–1955) also called 'Bird' or 'Yardbird', US alto saxophonist and jazz composer. He was associated with the trumpeter Dizzy *Gillespie in developing the *bebop style. His skilful improvisations inspired performers on all jazz instruments.

Parker, Dorothy (1893–1967) born Dorothy Rothschild, US writer and wit. She was a leading member of the literary circle known as the Algonquin Round Table. She reviewed for the magazines *Vanity Fair* and the *New Yorker*, and wrote wittily ironic verses, collected in several volumes including *Enough Rope* (1927), and *Not So Deep as a Well* (1936). Her short stories include the collections 'Laments for Living' (1930), and 'Here Lies' (1939). She also wrote screenplays in Hollywood, having moved there from New York City along with other members of her circle.

Parkinson's disease *or* **parkinsonism** *or* **paralysis agitans** degenerative disease of the brain characterized by a progressive loss of mobility, muscular rigidity, tremor, and speech difficulties. The condition is mainly seen in people over the age of 50.

Parkinson's law formula invented by the English political analyst Cyril Northcote Parkinson, which states that 'work expands so as to fill the time available for its completion'.

parliament (French 'speaking') legislative (law-making) body of a country. The world's oldest parliament is the Icelandic Althing, which dates from about 930. The UK Parliament is usually dated from 1265. The legislature of the USA is called *Congress and comprises the *House of Representatives and the *Senate.

Parliament, European governing body of the European Union (formerly the European Community); see *European Parliament.

Parnassos Greek name for *Parnassus, a mountain in central Greece.

Parnassus Greek **Parnassos**, mountain in central Greece, height 2,457 m/8,200 ft, revered by the ancient Greeks as the abode of Apollo and the Muses. The sacred site of Delphi lies on its southern flank.

Parnell, Charles Stewart (1846–1891) Irish nationalist politician. He supported a policy of obstruction and violence to attain *home rule, and became the president of the Nationalist Party in 1877. In 1879 he approved the *Land League, and his attitude led to his imprisonment in 1881. His career was ruined in 1890 when he was cited as co-respondent in a divorce case. Because of his great influence over his followers, he was called 'the uncrowned king of Ireland'.

parody in literature and the other arts, a *genre of work that imitates the style of another work, usually with mocking or comic intent; it is similar to *satire and distinguished from pastiche (in which the intent is homage rather than mockery).

parole conditional release of a prisoner from jail. The prisoner remains on licence until the date release would have been granted, and may be recalled if the authorities deem it necessary.

Parr, Catherine (1512–1548) Sixth wife of Henry VIII of England. She had already lost two husbands when in 1543 she married Henry. She survived him, and in 1547 married the Lord High Admiral Thomas Seymour of Sudeley (1508–1549).

parrot tropical bird found mainly in Australia and South America. These colourful birds have been valued as pets in the Western world for many centuries. Parrots have the ability to imitate human speech. They are mainly vegetarian, and range in size from the 8.5 cm/3.5 in pygmy parrot to the 100 cm/40 in Macaw. The smaller species are commonly referred to as *parakeets. The plumage is often very colourful, and the call is usually a harsh screech. In most species the sexes are indistinguishable. Several species are endangered. Parrots are members of the family Psittacidae, of the order Psittaciformes.

parsec symbol pc, unit used for distances to stars and galaxies. One parsec is equal to 3.2616 *light years, 2.063×10^5 *astronomical units, and 3.857×10^{13} km.

Parsee *or* **Parsi** (Persian *parsi* 'Persian') follower of the religion *Zoroastrianism. The Parsees fled from Persia after its conquest by the Arabs, and settled in India in the 8th century AD. About 100,000 Parsees now live mainly in the former Bombay State.

Parsifal in Germanic mythology, one of the knights who sought the *Holy Grail; the father of Lohengrin.

parsley herb belonging to the carrot family, cultivated for flavouring and garnishing in cookery and for its nutrient value, being rich in vitamin C and minerals. It can grow up to 45 cm/1.5 ft high and has aromatic, curled or flat pinnate leaves (leaflets either side of the stem) and delicate open clusters of yellow flowers. It is a biennial plant. (*Petroselinum crispum*, family Umbelliferae.)

parsnip temperate biennial plant belonging to the carrot family, found in Europe and Asia, and cultivated for its tapering, creamy-white, aromatic root, which is much used as a winter vegetable. (*Pastinaca sativa*, family Umbelliferae.)

parthenogenesis development of an ovum (egg) without any genetic contribution from a male. Parthenogenesis is the normal means of reproduction in a few plants (for example, dandelions) and animals (for example, certain fish). Some sexually reproducing species, such as aphids, show parthenogenesis at some stage in their life cycle to accelerate reproduction to take advantage of good conditions.

Parthenon temple of Athena Parthenos ('the Virgin') on the Acropolis at Athens; built 447–438 BC by Callicrates and Ictinus under the supervision of the sculptor *Phidias, and the most perfect example of Doric architecture. In turn a Christian church and a Turkish mosque, it was then used as a gunpowder store, and reduced to ruins when the Venetians bombarded the Acropolis in 1687. The *Elgin marbles were removed from the Parthenon in the early 19th century and are now in the British Museum, London.

Parthia ancient country in western Asia in what is now northeastern Iran, capital Ctesiphon. Parthian ascendancy began with the Arsacid dynasty in 248 BC, and reached the peak of its power under Mithridates I in the 2nd century BC; the region was annexed to Persia under the Sassanians AD 226.

particle detector one of a number of instruments designed to detect subatomic particles and track their paths; they include the *cloud chamber, *bubble chamber, spark chamber, and multiwire chamber.

particle physics study of the particles that make up all atoms, and of their interactions. More than 300 subatomic particles have now been identified by physicists, categorized into several classes according to their mass, electric charge, spin, magnetic moment, and interaction. Subatomic particles include the *elementary particles (*quarks, *leptons, and *gauge bosons), which are indivisible, so far as is known, and so may be considered the fundamental units of matter; and the *hadrons (baryons, such as the proton and neutron, and mesons), which are composite particles, made up of two or three quarks. Quarks, protons, electrons, and neutrinos are the only stable particles (the neutron being stable only when in the atomic nucleus). The unstable particles decay rapidly into other particles, and are known from experiments with particle accelerators and cosmic radiation. See *atomic structure.

particle, subatomic a particle that is smaller than an atom; see *particle physics.

partisan member of an armed group that operates behind enemy lines or in occupied territories during wars. The name 'partisans' was first given to armed bands of Russians who operated against Napoleon's army in Russia during 1812, but has since been used to describe Russian, Yugoslav, Italian, Greek, and Polish Resistance groups against the Germans during World War II. In Yugoslavia the communist partisans under their leader, Tito, played a major role in defeating the Germans.

part of speech grammatical function of a word, described in the grammatical tradition of the Western world, based on Greek and Latin. The four major parts of speech are: noun, verb, adjective, and adverb; the minor parts of speech vary according to schools of grammatical theory, but include: conjunction, preposition, pronoun, and interjection.

partridge any of various medium-sized ground-dwelling fowl of the family Phasianidae, order Galliformes, that also includes pheasants, quail, and chickens. Partridges are Old World birds, some of which have become naturalized in North America.

Pascal acronym for **Program Appliqué à la Selection et la Compilation Automatique de la Littérature**, high-level computer-programming language. Designed by Niklaus Wirth in the 1960s as an aid to teaching programming, it is still widely used as such in universities, and as a good general-purpose programming language. Most professional programmers, however, now use *C or C++. Pascal was named after the 17th-century French mathematician Blaise *Pascal.

pascal symbol Pa, SI unit of pressure, equal to one newton per square metre. It replaces bars and millibars (10^5 Pa equals one bar). It is named after the French mathematician Blaise Pascal.

Pascal, Blaise (1623–1662) French philosopher and mathematician. He contributed to the development of hydraulics, *calculus, and the mathematical theory of *probability.

Pashto language or **Pushto** or **Pushtu** Indo-European language, the official language of Afghanistan, also spoken in northern Pakistan.

Passchendaele, Battle of in World War I, successful but costly British operation to capture the Passchendaele ridge in western Flanders, part of the third Battle of *Ypres October–November 1917; British casualties numbered nearly 310,000. The name is often erroneously applied to the whole of the battle of Ypres, but Passchendaele was in fact just part of that battle.

passion flower any of a group of tropical American climbing plants. They have distinctive flowers consisting of a saucer-shaped petal base, a fringelike corona or circle of leafy outgrowths inside the ring of petals, and a central stalk bearing five pollen-producing *stamens and three pollen-receiving *stigmas. The flowers can be yellow, greenish, purple, or red. Some

species produce edible fruit. (Genus *Passiflora*, family Passifloraceae.)

passion play play representing the death and resurrection of Jesus, performed on Good Friday throughout medieval Europe. It has its origins in medieval *mystery plays. Traditionally, a passion play takes place every ten years at Oberammergau, Germany.

pass laws South African laws that required the black population to carry passbooks (identity documents) at all times and severely restricted freedom of movement. The laws, a major cause of discontent, formed a central part of the policies of *apartheid. They were repealed in 1986.

Passover alternative term for the Jewish festival of Pesach.

pastel in art, chalky material consisting of ground pigment bound with gum. Pastel is a form of painting in dry colours and produces a powdery surface, which is delicate and difficult to conserve. Artists renowned for their use of pastel include Rosalba Carriera (1675–1785), La Tour, *Chardin, *Degas, and Mary Cassatt.

Pasternak, Boris Leonidovich (1890–1960) Russian poet and novelist. His novel *Dr Zhivago* (1957) was banned in the USSR as a 'hostile act', and was awarded the Nobel Prize for Literature in 1957 (which Pasternak declined). The ban on *Dr Zhivago* has since been lifted and Pasternak's reputation as a writer has been revived since his death.

Pasteur, Louis (1822–1895) French chemist and microbiologist who discovered that fermentation is caused by micro-organisms and developed the germ theory of disease. He also created a vaccine for *rabies, which led to the foundation of the Pasteur Institute in Paris in 1888.

pasteurization treatment of food to reduce the number of micro-organisms it contains and so protect consumers from disease. Harmful bacteria are killed and the development of others is delayed. For milk, the method involves heating it to 72 °C/161 °F for 15 seconds followed by rapid cooling to 10 °C/50 °F or lower. The process also kills beneficial bacteria and reduces the nutritive property of milk.

Patagonia geographic region of South America, in southern Argentina and Chile; area 780,000 sq km/ 301,000 sq mi. A thinly populated vast plateau area, it stretches from the Río Colorado in central Argentina to eastern part of the Tierra del Fuego archipelago in the south, and slopes eastwards from the Andes to the Atlantic coast. It consists of the provinces of Neuquén, Rio Negro, Chubut, and Santa Cruz. The main towns are the port of Comodoro Rivadavia (Argentina) and Punta Arenas (Chile).

patchouli soft-wooded eastern Indian shrub belonging to the mint family; the leaves are the source of the perfume patchouli. (*Pogostemon heyneanus*, family Labiateae.)

patella or **kneecap** flat bone embedded in the knee tendon of birds and mammals, which protects the joint from injury.

Pathan or **Pathkun** or **Pashtun** member of a people of northwestern Pakistan and Afghanistan, numbering about 14 million (1984). The majority are Sunni Muslims. The Pathans speak Pashto, a member of the Indo-Iranian branch of the Indo-European family.

pathogen (Greek 'disease producing') any micro-organism that causes disease. Most pathogens are *parasites, and the diseases they cause are incidental to their search for food or shelter inside the host. Nonparasitic organisms, such as soil bacteria or those living in the human gut and feeding on waste foodstuffs, can also become pathogenic to a person whose immune system or liver is damaged. The larger parasites that can cause disease, such as nematode worms, are not usually described as pathogens.

pathology medical speciality concerned with the study of disease processes and how these provoke structural and functional changes in the body.

patina effect produced on bronze by oxidation, which turns the surface green, and by extension any lacquering or finishing technique, other than gilding, applied to bronze objects. Patina can also mean the surface texture of old furniture, silver, and antique objects.

Patmos Greek island in the Aegean Sea, one of the Dodecanese; the chief town is Hora. St John is said to have written the New Testament Book of Revelation while in exile here.

patriarch (Greek 'ruler of a family') in the Old Testament, one of the ancestors of the human race, and especially those of the ancient Hebrews, from Adam to Abraham, Isaac, Jacob, and his sons (who became patriarchs of the Hebrew tribes). In the Eastern Orthodox Church, the term refers to the leader of a national church.

patriarchy (Greek 'rule of the father') form of social organization in which a man heads and controls the family unit. By extension, in a patriarchal society men also control larger social and working groups as well as government. The definition has been broadened by feminists to describe the dominance of male values throughout society.

patrician member of a privileged class in ancient Rome, which originally dominated the *Senate. During the 5th and 4th centuries BC many of the rights formerly exercised by the patricians alone were extended to the plebeians, and patrician descent became a matter of prestige.

Patrick, St (c. 389–c. 461) Patron saint of Ireland. Born in Britain, probably in South Wales, he was carried off by pirates to six years' slavery in Antrim, Ireland, before escaping either to Britain or Gaul to train as a missionary. He is variously said to have landed again in Ireland in 432 or 456, and his work was a vital factor in the spread of Christian influence there. His symbols are snakes and shamrocks; his feast day is 17 March.

patronage power to give a favoured appointment to an office or position in politics, business, or the church; or sponsorship of the arts. Patronage was for centuries bestowed mainly by individuals (in Europe often royal or noble) or by the church. In the 20th century, patrons have tended to be political parties, the state, and – in the arts – private industry and foundations.

Patten, Chris(topher Francis) (1944–) British Conservative politician, governor of Hong Kong 1992–97. He was MP for Bath 1979–1992 and Conservative Party chair 1990–92, orchestrating the party's campaign for the 1992 general election, in which he lost his parliamentary seat. He accepted the governorship of Hong Kong for the crucial five years prior to its transfer to China in 1997. He went on to propose reform of the Royal Ulster Constabulary. In 1999 he became an EU Commissioner.

Patton, George Smith (1885–1945) US general in World War II, known as 'Old Blood and Guts'. During World War I, he formed the first US tank force and led it in action in 1918. He was appointed to command the 2nd Armored Division in 1940 and became commanding general of the 1st Armored Corps in 1941. In 1942 he led the Western Task Force that landed at Casablanca, Morocco. After commanding the 7th Army in the invasion of Sicily, he led the 3rd Army across France and into Germany, reaching the Czech frontier.

Paul six popes, including:

Paul VI, Giovanni Battista Montini (1897–1978) Pope from 1963. His encyclical *Humanae Vitae/Of Human Life* (1968) reaffirmed the church's traditional teaching on birth control, thus following the minority report of the commission originally appointed by Pope John rather than the majority view.

Pauling, Linus Carl (1901–1994) US theoretical chemist and biologist. He was awarded the Nobel Prize for Chemistry in 1954 for his study of the nature of chemical bonds, especially in complex substances. His ideas are fundamental to modern theories of molecular structure. He also investigated the properties and uses of vitamin C as related to human health. He was awarded the Nobel Prize for Peace in 1962 for having campaigned for the control of nuclear weapons and nuclear testing.

Paul, St (c. AD 3–c. AD 68) Christian missionary and martyr; in the New Testament, one of the apostles and author of 13 *Epistles. Originally known as Saul, he was opposed to Christianity, and took part in the stoning of St *Stephen. Acts of the Apostles (Chapter 9) tells how he was converted by a vision on the road to *Damascus while on the way to persecute Christians. After his conversion he journeyed on great missions, for example to Philippi and Ephesus, becoming known as the Apostle of the Gentiles (non-Jews). His emblems are a sword and a book; his feast day is 29 June.

Pavlov, Ivan Petrovich (1849–1936) Russian physiologist who was awarded a Nobel Prize for Physiology or Medicine in 1904 for his discovery of the physiology of digestion. Pavlov studied conditioned reflexes in animals (see *conditioning). His work had a great impact on behavioural theory (see *behaviourism) and learning theory.

Pavlova, Anna (1881–1931) Russian dancer. Prima ballerina of the Imperial Ballet from 1906, she left Russia in 1913, and went on to become one of the world's most celebrated exponents of classical ballet. With London as her home, she toured extensively with her own company, influencing dancers worldwide with roles such as Mikhail *Fokine's *The Dying Swan* solo (1907). She was opposed to the modern reforms of Diaghilev's Ballets Russes, adhering strictly to conservative aesthetics.

pawpaw *or* **papaw** small tree belonging to the custard-apple family, native to the eastern USA. It produces oblong fruits 13 cm/5 in long with yellowish edible flesh. The name 'pawpaw' is also used for the *papaya. (*Asimina triloba*, family Annonaceae.)

Paxton, Joseph (1801–1865) English architect. He was also garden superintendent to the Duke of

Devonshire from 1826. He designed the Great
Exhibition building 1851 (the Crystal Palace), which
was revolutionary in its structural use of glass and iron.
Knighted 1851.

Pays de la Loire agricultural region of western France,
comprising the *départements* of Loire-Atlantique,
Maine-et-Loire, Mayenne, Sarthe, and La Vendée;
area 32,082 sq km/12,387 sq mi; population (1999 est)
3,222,100. The administrative centre is Nantes.
Industries include shipbuilding and wine production.

Paz, Octavio (1914–1998) Mexican poet, essayist,
and political thinker. His works reflect many
influences, including Marxism, surrealism, and Aztec
mythology. *El laberinto de la soledad/The Labyrinth of
Solitude* (1950), the book which brought him to world
attention, explores Mexico's heritage. His long poem
Piedra del sol/Sun Stone (1957) uses contrasting images,
centring on the Aztec Calendar Stone (representing
the Aztec universe), to symbolize the loneliness of
individuals and their search for union with others.
He was awarded the Nobel Prize for Literature in 1990.

PC abbreviation for **personal computer; politically
correct; police constable; Privy Councillor.**

pea climbing leguminous plant (see *legume) with
pods of round green edible seeds, grown since
prehistoric times for food. The pea is a popular
vegetable and is eaten fresh, canned, frozen, or dried.
The **sweet pea** (*Lathyrus odoratus*) of the same family
is grown for its scented red, purple, pink, and white
butterfly-shaped flowers; it is a popular cottage garden
plant. (Edible pea *Pisum sativum*, family Leguminosae.)

peace movement collective opposition to war. The
Western peace movements of the late 20th century can
trace their origins to the *pacifists of the 19th century
and conscientious objectors during World War I.
The campaigns after World War II have tended
to concentrate on nuclear weapons, but there are
numerous organizations devoted to peace, some
wholly pacifist, some merely opposed to escalation.

peach yellow-reddish round edible fruit of the peach
tree, which is cultivated for its fruit in temperate
regions and has oval leaves and small, usually pink,
flowers. The fruits have thick velvety skins; nectarines
are a smooth-skinned variety. (*Prunus persica*, family
Rosaceae.)

peacock technically, the male of any of various large
*pheasants, order Galliformes. The name is most often
used for the common peacock *Pavo cristatus*, a bird of
the pheasant family, native to South Asia. It is rather
larger than a pheasant. The male has a large fan-shaped
tail, brightly coloured with blue, green, and purple
'eyes' on a chestnut background, that is raised during
courtship displays. The female (peahen) is brown with
a small tail.

Peak District elevated plateau of the south
*Pennines in northwest Derbyshire, central England;
area 1,438 sq km/555 sq mi. It is a tourist region and
part of it forms a national park. The highest point
is Kinder Scout (636 m/2,087 ft), part of High Peak.
In the surrounding area the main cities are Manchester,
Sheffield, and Derby, and the town of Bakewell is
located within the Peak District.

peanut *or* **groundnut** *or* **monkey nut** South American
vinelike annual plant. After flowering, the flower stalks
bend and force the pods into the earth to ripen

underground. The nuts are a staple food in many
tropical countries and are widely grown in the southern
USA. They provide a valuable edible oil and are the
basis for a large number of processed foods. (*Arachis
hypogaea*, family Leguminosae.)

pear succulent, gritty-textured edible fruit of the pear
tree, native to temperate regions of Europe and Asia.
White flowers precede the fruits, which have a
greenish-yellow and brown skin and taper towards the
stalk. Pear trees are cultivated for their fruit which are
eaten fresh or canned; a wine known as perry is made
from pear juice. (*Pyrus communis*, family Rosaceae.)

pearl shiny, hard, rounded abnormal growth composed
of nacre (or mother-of-pearl), a chalky substance.
Nacre is secreted by many molluscs, and deposited in
thin layers on the inside of the shell around a parasite,
a grain of sand, or some other irritant body. After
several years of the mantle (the layer of tissue between
the shell and the body mass) secreting this nacre, a
pearl is formed.

Pearl Harbor US Pacific naval base on Oahu island,
Hawaii, USA, the scene of a Japanese aerial attack on
7 December 1941, which brought the USA into World
War II. The attack took place while Japanese envoys
were holding so-called peace talks in Washington.
More than 2,000 members of the US armed forces
were killed, and a large part of the US Pacific fleet was
destroyed or damaged.

Pearse, Patrick Henry (1879–1916) Irish writer,
educationalist and revolutionary. He was prominent
in the Gaelic revival, and a leader of the *Easter Rising
in 1916. Proclaimed president of the provisional
government, he was court-martialled and shot after
its suppression.

Pearson, Lester Bowles (1897–1972) Canadian
politician, leader of the Liberal Party from 1958, prime
minister 1963–68. He was awarded the Nobel Prize for
Peace in 1957 for playing a key role in settling the *Suez
Crisis of 1956 when as foreign minister 1948–57, he
represented Canada at the United Nations (UN).

Peary, Robert Edwin (1856–1920) US polar explorer
who, after several unsuccessful attempts, became the
first person to reach the North Pole on 6 April 1909.
In 1988 an astronomer claimed Peary's measurements
were incorrect.

Peasants' Revolt the rising of the English peasantry
in June 1381, the result of economic, social, and political
discontent. It was sparked off by the attempt to levy
a new poll tax in the village of Fobbing, Essex, three
times the rates of those imposed in 1377 and 1379. The
poll tax was a common tax, paid by all, which badly
affected those least able to pay. Led by Wat *Tyler and
John *Ball, rebels from southeast England marched
on London and demanded reforms. The authorities
put down the revolt by pretending to make concessions
and then using force.

peat organic matter found in bogs and formed by the
incomplete decomposition of plants such as sphagnum
moss. Northern Asia, Canada, Finland, Ireland, and
other places have large deposits, which have been dried
and used as fuel from ancient times. Peat can also be
used as a soil additive.

pecan nut-producing *hickory tree (*C. illinoensis* or
C. pecan), native to the central USA and northern
Mexico and now widely cultivated. The trees grow to

700

over 45 m/150 ft, and the edible nuts are smooth-shelled, the kernel resembling a smooth, oval walnut. (Genus *Carya*, family Juglandaceae.)

peccary one of two species of the New World genus *Tayassu* of piglike hoofed mammals. A peccary has a gland in the middle of its back which secretes a strong-smelling substance. Peccaries are blackish in colour, covered with bristles, and have tusks that point downwards. Adults reach a height of 40 cm/16 in, and a weight of 25 kg/60 lb.

Peck, (Eldred) Gregory (1916–2003) US film actor. He specialized in strong, upright characters, but also had a gift for light comedy. His films include *Spellbound* (1945), *Duel in the Sun* (1946), *Gentleman's Agreement* (1947), *Roman Holiday* (1953), *To Kill a Mockingbird* (1962), for which he won an Academy Award, and (cast against type as a Nazi doctor) *The Boys from Brazil* (1978).

pectoral relating to the upper area of the thorax associated with the muscles and bones used in moving the arms or forelimbs, in vertebrates. In birds, the *pectoralis major* is the very large muscle used to produce a powerful downbeat of the wing during flight.

pediment in architecture, the triangular structure crowning the portico of a classical building. The pediment was a distinctive feature of Greek temples.

Peel, Robert (1788–1850) British Conservative politician. As home secretary 1822–27 and 1828–30, he founded the modern police force and in 1829 introduced Roman Catholic emancipation. He was prime minister 1834–35 and 1841–46, when his repeal of the *Corn Laws caused him and his followers to break with the party. During his second term as conservative prime minister, poor harvests in England and the failure of the Irish potato crop in 1845 led Peel to repeal the *Corn Laws in 1846, contrary to his election pledge. The move split the party and Peel resigned.

peepul another name for the *bo tree.

peerage the high nobility; in the UK, holders, in descending order, of the titles of duke, marquess, earl, viscount, and baron. In the late 19th century the peerage was augmented by the Lords of Appeal in Ordinary (the nonhereditary life peers) and, from 1958, by a number of specially created life peers of either sex (usually long-standing members of the House of Commons). Since 1963 peers have been able to disclaim their titles, usually to enable them to take a seat in the Commons (where peers are disqualified from membership).

peer group in the social sciences, people who have a common identity based on such characteristics as similar social status, interests, age, or ethnic group. The concept has proved useful in analysing the power and influence of co-workers, school friends, and ethnic and religious groups in socialization and social behaviour.

Pegasus a constellation of the northern hemisphere, near Cygnus, and represented as the winged horse of Greek mythology.

Pegasus in Greek mythology, the winged horse that sprang from the blood of the *Gorgon Medusa when she was decapitated by the hero Perseus. He carried Bellerophon in his fight with the *chimera, and was later transformed into a constellation.

pekan *or* **fisher marten** North American marten (carnivorous mammal) *Martes penanti* about 1.2 m/4 ft long, with a doglike face, and brown fur with white patches on the chest. It eats porcupines.

Peking alternative transcription of *Beijing, the capital of China.

pekingese breed of small long-haired dog first bred at the Chinese court as the 'imperial lion dog'. It has a flat skull and flat face, is typically less than 25 cm/10 in tall, and weighs less than 5 kg/11 lb.

Peking man Chinese representative of an early species of human, found as fossils, 500,000–750,000 years old, in the cave of Choukoutien in 1927 near Beijing (Peking). Peking man used chipped stone tools, hunted game, and used fire. Similar varieties of early human have been found in Java and East Africa. Their classification is disputed: some anthropologists classify them as *Homo erectus*, others as *Homo sapiens pithecanthropus*.

pelargonium *or* **geranium** any of a group of shrubby, tender flowering plants belonging to the geranium family, grown extensively for their colourful white, pink, scarlet, and black-purple flowers. They are the familiar summer bedding and pot 'geraniums'. Ancestors of the garden hybrids came from southern Africa. (Genus *Pelargonium*, family Geraniaceae.)

Pelé (1940–) adopted name of Edson Arantes do Nascimento, Brazilian footballer, and one of the sport's most famous players. A prolific goal scorer, he appeared in four World Cup competitions 1958–70 and led Brazil to three championships (1958, 1962, 1970).

Pelham, Henry (1696–1754) English Whig politician. He held a succession of offices in Robert Walpole's cabinet 1721–42, and was prime minister 1743–54. His influence in the House of Commons was based on systematic corruption rather than ability. He concluded the War of the Austrian Succession and was an able financier.

pelican large water bird of family Pelecanidae, order Pelecaniformes, remarkable for the pouch beneath the bill, which is used as a fishing net and temporary store for catches of fish. Some species grow up to 1.8 m/6 ft and have wingspans of 3 m/10 ft.

Pelion mountain in Thessaly, Greece, near Mount Ossa; height 1,548 m/5,079 ft. In Greek mythology it was the home of the centaurs, creatures half-human and half-horse.

pellagra chronic disease mostly seen in subtropical countries in which the staple food is maize. It is caused by deficiency of *nicotinic acid (one of the B vitamins), which is contained in protein foods, beans and peas, and yeast. Symptoms include diarrhoea, skin eruptions, and mental disturbances.

Peloponnese Greek **Peloponnisos**, mainly mountainous peninsula forming the southern part of Greece; area 21,549 sq km/8,320 sq mi; population (2003 est) 1,166,000. It is joined to the mainland by the narrow isthmus of Corinth and is divided into the nomes (administrative areas) of Argolis, Arcadia, Achaea, Elis, Corinth, Lakonia, and Messenia, representing its seven ancient states. It is divided into two departments; Western Greece (including Achaea and Elis), and Peloponnese (including Argolis, Arcadia, Corinth, Lakonia, and Messenia). Tourism is important; the port cities of Patras, Corinth, Kalamata, and Návplion are the principal modern centres.

Peloponnesian War war fought 431–404 BC between Athens and Sparta and their respective allies, involving most of the Greek world from Asia Minor to Sicily and from Byzantium (present-day Istanbul, Turkey) to Crete. Sparked by Spartan fears about the growth of Athenian power, it continued until the Spartan general Lysander captured the Athenian fleet in 405 BC at Aegospotami and starved the Athenians into surrender in 404 BC. As a result of this victory, Athens' political power collapsed.

pelota or **jai alai** ('merry festival') very fast ball game of Basque derivation, popular in Latin American countries and in the USA where it is a betting sport. It is played by two, four, or six players, in a walled court, or *cancha*, and somewhat resembles squash, but each player uses a long, curved, wickerwork basket, or *cesta*, strapped to the hand, to hurl the ball, or pelota, against the walls.

Peltier effect in physics, a change in temperature at the junction of two different metals produced when an electric current flows through them. The extent of the change depends on what the conducting metals are, and the nature of change (rise or fall in temperature) depends on the direction of current flow. It is the reverse of the *Seebeck effect. It is named after the French physicist Jean Charles Peltier (1785–1845) who discovered it in 1834.

pelvis in vertebrates, the lower area of the abdomen featuring the bones and muscles used to move the legs or hindlimbs. The **pelvic girdle** is a set of bones that allows movement of the legs in relation to the rest of the body and provides sites for the attachment of relevant muscles.

Pembrokeshire Welsh **Sir Benfro**, unitary authority in southwest Wales; a former county, from 1974 to 1996 it was part of the county of Dyfed. **area:** 1,588 sq km/613 sq mi **towns:** Haverfordwest (administrative headquarters), Milford Haven **physical:** bounded on the south by the Bristol Channel; valleys and hills inland; rivers East and West Cleddau **features:** Pembrokeshire Coast National Park, Castell Henllys (reconstructed Iron Age fort near Crymych), beaches, walled town and castle ruins (13th century) at Tenby, Pembroke Castle (1093), Manorbier Castle (12th century), near Havorfordwest, Carew Castle (13th century), Tidal Mill, Preseli Hills, Neolithic burial grounds at St Davids **population:** (2001 est) 112,900.

Penang Malay **Pulau Pinang**, state in western Peninsular Malaysia, formed of **Penang Island**, Province Wellesley, and the Dindings on the mainland, total area 1,030 sq km/398 sq mi; population (2000 est) 1,225,500. The capital is George Town. The island and the mainland are linked by the 8.4 km/5.2 mi-long Penang Bridge (1985). Rubber, produced on large-scale plantations, is the leading crop of the state, but rice, coffee, spices, and coconuts are also produced. George Town has a large, sheltered harbour and is the leading seaport of Malaysia. During the late 20th century Penang Island, served by an international airport at Bayan Lepas, became the chief tourist resort of Malaysia, with the largest development of beach hotels at Batu Feringgi on the north coast.

Penda (c. 577–654) King of Mercia, an Anglo-Saxon kingdom in England, from about 632. He raised Mercia to a powerful kingdom, and defeated and killed two Northumbrian kings, Edwin in 632 and *Oswald in 642. He was killed in battle by Oswy, king of Northumbria.

Penelope in Greek mythology, the wife of *Odysseus, king of Ithaca; their son was *Telemachus. She represented wifely faithfulness. While Odysseus was absent at the siege of Troy, she kept her many suitors at bay by asking them to wait while she completed a shroud for Laertes, her father-in-law; every night she unravelled her weaving. When Odysseus returned after 20 years, he and Telemachus killed her suitors.

penguin marine flightless bird, family Spheniscidae, order Sphenisciformes, mostly black and white, found in the southern hemisphere. They comprise 18 species in six genera. Males are usually larger than the females. Penguins range in size from 40 cm/1.6 ft to 1.2 m/4 ft tall, and have thick feathers to protect them from the intense cold. They are awkward on land (except on snow slopes down which they propel themselves at a rapid pace), but their wings have evolved into flippers, making them excellent swimmers. Penguins congregate to breed in 'rookeries', and often spend many months incubating their eggs while their mates are out at sea feeding. They feed on a mixture of fish, squid, and krill.

penicillin any of a group of *antibiotic (bacteria killing) compounds obtained from filtrates of moulds of the genus *Penicillium* (especially *P. notatum*) or produced synthetically. Penicillin was the first antibiotic to be discovered (by Alexander *Fleming); it kills a broad spectrum of bacteria, many of which cause disease in humans.

Peninsular War war of 1808–14 caused by the French emperor Napoleon's invasion of Portugal and Spain. British expeditionary forces under Sir Arthur Wellesley (Duke of *Wellington), combined with Spanish and Portuguese resistance, succeeded in defeating the French at Vimeiro in 1808, Talavera in 1809, Salamanca in 1812, and Vittoria in 1813. The results were inconclusive, and the war was ended by Napoleon's forced abdication in 1814.

penis male reproductive organ containing the *urethra, the channel through which urine and semen are voided. It transfers sperm to the female reproductive tract to fertilize the ovum. In mammals, the penis is made erect by vessels that fill with blood, and in most mammals (but not humans) is stiffened by a bone.

Penn, William (1644–1718) English member of the Society of Friends (Quakers) and founder of the American colony of *Pennsylvania. Born in London, he joined the Society in 1667 and was imprisoned several times for his beliefs. In 1681 he obtained a grant of land in America (in settlement of a debt owed by King Charles II to his father) on which he established Pennsylvania as a refuge for persecuted Quakers.

Pennines, the range of hills in northern England, known as the 'the backbone of England'; length (from the Scottish border to the Peaks in Derbyshire) 400 km/250 mi. The highest peak in the Pennines (which are sometimes referred to as mountains rather than hills) is Cross Fell (893 m/2,930 ft). It is the watershed for the main rivers of northeast England. The rocks are carboniferous limestone and millstone grit, the land high moorland and fell.

Pennsylvania called the **Keystone State**, (named after William Penn, and Latin *sylvania*, 'woodland') state in northeastern USA bordered to the north by *New York, with a coastal strip on Lake *Erie, to the west by *Ohio and the *West Virginia panhandle, to the south, on the *Mason–Dixon Line, by West Virginia, *Maryland, and *Delaware, and to the east by *New Jersey, across the Delaware River; area 116,075 sq km/44,817 sq mi; population (2000) 12,281,100; capital Harrisburg. It is nicknamed the Keystone State due to its geographical position between the northeast and south of the USA. The Appalachian Plateau dominates over half of Pennsylvania, defined on its eastern border by the Allegheny Front, a spine of mountains running diagonally southwest–northeast across the centre of the state. The Susquehanna and the Juniata rivers cut east–southeast across the front. One of the original *Thirteen Colonies, Pennsylvania is a leader in both agriculture and industry, producing hay, cereals, dairy products, coal, steel, petroleum products, and textiles. *Philadelphia is the state's most populous city; other major cities include *Pittsburgh, Erie, Allentown, and Scranton. Pennsylvania was home to several Iroquoian and Algonquian tribes, including the Delaware, Shawnee, Susquehannock, and Seneca. First explored by the English and the Dutch, and fought over by early Swedish and Dutch settlers, Pennsylvania became an English colony in 1681. Pennsylvania played a key role in the *American Revolution and in the founding of the new American government: the *Declaration of Independence, the Articles of *Confederation, and the US Constitution were written in Philadelphia. The state became the second to join the Union, in 1787.

pension organized form of saving for retirement. Pension schemes, which may be government-run or privately administered, involve regular payment for a qualifying period; when the person retires, a payment is made each week or month from the invested pension fund. Pension funds have become influential investors in major industries. The decline in share value and the ageing population in many countries has led to increasing concerns over the payment of pensions in the future.

pentadactyl limb typical limb of the mammals, birds, reptiles, and amphibians. These vertebrates (animals with backbone) are all descended from primitive amphibians whose immediate ancestors were fleshy-finned fish. The limb which evolved in those amphibians had three parts: a 'hand/foot' with five digits (fingers/toes), a lower limb containing two bones, and an upper limb containing one bone.

Pentagon the headquarters of the US Department of Defense, Arlington, Virginia from 1947, situated on the Potomac River opposite Washington, DC. One of the world's largest office buildings (five storeys high and five-sided, with a pentagonal central court), it houses the administrative and command headquarters for the US armed forces and has become synonymous with the military establishment bureaucracy. In September 2001, as part of a coordinated terrorist attack on the USA, the Pentagon was severely damaged when a hijacked aircraft was crashed into its northwest wall, bringing part of the structure down and killing 126 people.

pentagon five-sided plane figure. A regular pentagon has all five sides of equal length and all five angles of equal size, 108°. It has *golden section proportions between its sides and diagonals. The five-pointed star

formed by drawing all the diagonals of a regular pentagon is called a **pentagram**. This star has further golden sections.

Pentateuch Greek (and Christian) name for the first five books of the Bible, ascribed to Moses, and called the *Torah by Jews.

pentathlon five-sport competition. Pentathlon consists of former military training pursuits: swimming, fencing, running, horsemanship, and shooting. It has been an Olympic event for men since 1912, but the Sydney 2000 Games were the first Olympics to include a women's event. The first modern pentathlon world championships for men took place in 1949, and for women in 1981.

Pentecost or **Whit Sunday** Christian festival that celebrates the gift of the Holy Spirit. It is celebrated seven weeks after Easter, and is regarded as the birthday of the Christian church. Traditionally a time of *baptism, the name Whit Sunday, or White Sunday, derives from the custom of wearing white while being baptized.

Pentecost another name for the Jewish festival of Shavuot.

Pentecostal movement Christian revivalist movement inspired by the experience of the apostles after the resurrection of Jesus, when they were baptized in the Holy Spirit and able to speak in tongues. The Pentecostal movement represents a reaction against the rigid theology and formal worship of traditional churches. It originated in the USA in 1906.

peony any of a group of perennial plants native to Europe, Asia, and North America, remarkable for their large, round, brilliant white, pink, or red flowers. Most popular in gardens are the common peony (*P. officinalis*), the white peony (*P. lactiflora*), and the taller tree peony (*P. suffruticosa*). (Genus *Paeonia*, family Paeoniaceae.)

Pepin the Short (*c.* 714–*c.* 768) King of the Franks from 751. The son of Charles Martel, he acted as Mayor of the Palace to the last Merovingian king, Childeric III, deposed him and assumed the royal title himself, founding the *Carolingian dynasty. He was *Charlemagne's father.

pepper climbing plant native to the East Indies. When gathered green, the berries are crushed to release the seeds for the spice called black pepper. When the berries are ripe, the seeds are removed and their outer skin is discarded, to produce white pepper. Chilli pepper, cayenne or red pepper, and the sweet peppers used as a vegetable come from *capsicums native to the New World. (*Piper nigrum*, family Piperaceae.)

peppermint perennial herb of the mint family, native to Europe, with oval aromatic leaves and purple flowers. Oil of peppermint is used in medicine and confectionery. (*Mentha piperita*, family Labiatae.)

pepsin *enzyme that breaks down proteins during digestion. It is produced by the walls of the *stomach. It requires a strongly acidic environment such as that present in the stomach. It digests large protein molecules into smaller protein molecules (smaller polypeptides) and is therefore a protease – an enzyme that breaks down a protein.

peptide molecule comprising two or more *amino acid molecules (not necessarily different) joined by **peptide bonds**, whereby the acid group of one acid is linked to the amino group of the other (–CO.NH). The number of amino acid molecules in the peptide is indicated by referring to it as a di-, tri-, or polypeptide (two, three, or many amino acids).

Pepys, Samuel (1633–1703) English naval administrator and diarist. His *Diary* (1660–69) is a unique record of the daily life of the period, the historical events of the Restoration, the manners and scandals of the court, naval administration, and Pepys's own interests, weaknesses, and intimate feelings. Written in shorthand, it was not deciphered until 1825. Highlights include his accounts of the Great Plague of London in 1665, the Fire of London in 1666, and the sailing up the Thames of the Dutch fleet in 1667.

Perak (Malay *perak* 'tin') state of western Peninsular Malaysia; area 21,000 sq km/8,000 sq mi; population (2000 est) 2,030,400. The capital is Ipoh. The state consists largely of coastal plains, through which the Perak River flows. Tin mining has been important since the 18th century and remains an important industry, especially in the Kinta Valley. Plantation agriculture, concentrating on rubber and coconut production, is important to the state's economy, and there is some mining of iron ore.

percentage way of representing a number as a *fraction of 100. For example, 45 percent (45%) equals $^{45}/100$, and 45% of 20 is $^{45}/100 \times 20 = 9$.

perch any of the largest order of spiny-finned bony fishes, the Perciformes, with some 8,000 species. This order includes the sea basses, cichlids, damselfishes, mullets, barracudas, wrasses, and gobies. Perches of the freshwater genus *Perca* are found in Europe, Asia, and North America. They have varied shapes and are usually a greenish colour. They are very prolific, spawning when about three years old, and have voracious appetites.

percussion instrument musical instrument played by being struck with the hand or a beater, crashed, shaken, or scraped. Percussion instruments can be divided into those that can be tuned to produce a sound of definite pitch, such as the timpani, tubular bells, glockenspiel, xylophone, and piano, and those of indefinite pitch, including the bass drum, tambourine, triangle, cymbals, castanets, and gong.

perennating organ in plants, that part of a *biennial plant or herbaceous perennial that allows it to survive the winter; usually a root, tuber, rhizome, bulb, or corm.

perennial plant plant that lives for more than two years. Herbaceous perennials have aerial stems and leaves that die each autumn. They survive the winter by means of an underground storage (perennating) organ, such as a bulb or rhizome. Trees and shrubs or woody perennials have stems that persist above ground throughout the year, and may be either *deciduous or *evergreen. See also *annual plant, *biennial plant.

Peres, Shimon (1923–) Israeli Labour politician, prime minister 1984–86 and 1995–96. He was prime minister, then foreign minister, under a power-sharing agreement with the leader of the Likud Party, Yitzhak *Shamir. From 1989 to 1990 he was foreign minister in a Labour–Likud coalition. As foreign minister in Yitzhak Rabin's Labour government from 1992, he negotiated the 1993 peace agreement with the *Palestine Liberation Organization (PLO). He shared the Nobel Prize for Peace in 1994 with Yitzhak Rabin and PLO leader Yassir

*Arafat for their agreement of an accord on Palestinian self-rule. Following the assassination of Rabin in November 1995, Peres succeeded him as prime minister, and pledged to continue the peace process in which they had both been so closely involved, but in May 1996 he was defeated in Israel's first direct elections for prime minister.

perestroika (Russian 'restructuring') in Soviet politics, the wide-ranging economic and political reforms initiated from 1985 by Mikhail Gorbachev, finally leading to the demise of the Soviet Union. Originally, in the economic sphere, *perestroika* was conceived as involving 'intensive development' concentrating on automation and improved labour efficiency. It evolved to attend increasingly to market indicators and incentives ('market socialism') and the gradual dismantling of the Stalinist central-planning system, with decision-taking being devolved to self-financing enterprises.

Pérez de Cuéllar, Javier (1920–) Peruvian politician and diplomat, fifth secretary general of the United Nations 1982–91, prime minister of Peru from 2000. He raised the standing of the UN by his successful diplomatic efforts to end the Iran–Iraq War in 1988 and secure the independence of Namibia in 1989. He was a candidate in the Peruvian presidential elections of 1995, but was defeated by his opponent Alberto Fujimori. After Fujimori's resignation in 2000, Pérez de Cuéllar was appointed prime minister by President Valentin Paniagua until 2002.

performance art type of modern art activity presented before a live audience, and combining elements of the visual arts and the theatrical arts, such as music, video, theatre, and poetry reading. Performance art developed in the 1910s, but flourished in the late 1960s and early 1970s. It often overlaps with other avant-garde forms of expression, particularly body art, happenings, and fluxus art. The term happening is sometimes used synonymously with performance art, but happenings are often more informal and improvised than performance art, which is usually carefully planned.

Pergamum ancient Greek city in Mysia in western Asia Minor, which became the capital of an independent kingdom in 283 BC under the Attalid dynasty. As the ally of Rome it achieved great political importance in the 2nd century BC, and became a centre of art and culture. It had a famous library, the contents of which were transported to Alexandria when they were given by *Mark Antony to Cleopatra, queen of Egypt. Pergamum was the birthplace of the physician *Galen. Most of its territory became the Roman province of Asia in 133 BC, when the childless King Attalus III bequeathed it to Rome. Close to its site is the modern Turkish town of Bergama.

Pergau Dam hydroelectric dam on the Pergau River in Malaysia, near the Thai border. Building work began in 1991 with money from the UK foreign aid budget. Concurrently, the Malaysian government bought around £1 billion worth of arms from the UK. The suggested linkage of arms deals to aid became the subject of a UK government enquiry from March 1994. In November 1994 a High Court ruled as illegal British foreign secretary Douglas Hurd's allocation of £234 million towards the funding of the dam, on the grounds that it was not of economic or humanitarian benefit to the Malaysian people.

Peri, Jacopo (1561–1633) Italian composer who lived in Florence in the service of the Medici. His experimental melodic opera *Euridice* (1600) established the opera form and influenced Monteverdi. His first opera, *Dafne* (1597), believed to be the earliest opera, is now lost.

pericarp wall of a *fruit. It encloses the seeds and is derived from the *ovary wall. In fruits such as the acorn, the pericarp becomes dry and hard, forming a shell around the seed. In fleshy fruits the pericarp is typically made up of three distinct layers. The **epicarp**, or **exocarp**, forms the tough outer skin of the fruit, while the **mesocarp** is often fleshy and forms the middle layers. The innermost layer or **endocarp**, which surrounds the seeds, may be membranous or thick and hard, as in the *drupe (stone) of cherries, plums, and apricots.

Pericles (c. 495–429 BC) Athenian politician under whom Athens reached the height of power. He persuaded the Athenians to reject Sparta's ultimata in 432 BC, and was responsible for Athenian strategy in the opening years of the Peloponnesian War. His policies helped to transform the Delian League into an empire, but the disasters of the *Peloponnesian War led to his removal from office in 430 BC. Although quickly reinstated, he died soon after.

peridotite rock consisting largely of the mineral olivine; pyroxene and other minerals may also be present. Peridotite is an ultramafic rock containing less than 45% silica by weight. It is believed to be one of the rock types making up the Earth's upper mantle, and is sometimes brought from the depths to the surface by major movements, or as inclusions in lavas.

perigee in astronomy, the point at which an object, travelling around in an elliptical orbit around the Earth, is at its closest to the Earth. The point at which it is furthest from the Earth is the *apogee.

perihelion in astronomy, the point at which an object, travelling in an elliptical orbit around the Sun, is at its closest to the Sun. The point at which it is furthest from the Sun is the *aphelion.

periodic table of the elements a table in which the *elements are arranged in order of their atomic number. There are eight groups of elements, plus a block of *transition metals in the centre. Group I contains the *alkali metals; Group II the alkaline-earth *metals; Group VII the *halogens; and Group 0 the *noble gases (rare gases). A zigzag line through the groups separates the metals on the left-hand side of the table from the non-metals on the right. The horizontal rows in the table are called **periods**. The table summarizes the major properties of the elements and enables predictions to be made about their behaviour. (See diagram, p. 706.)

periodontal disease formerly **pyorrhoea**, disease of the gums and bone supporting the teeth, caused by the accumulation of plaque and micro-organisms; the gums recede, and the teeth eventually become loose and may drop out unless treatment is sought. Bacteria can eventually erode the bone that supports the teeth, so that surgery becomes necessary.

peripheral device in computing, any item connected to a computer's *central processing unit (CPU). Typical peripherals include keyboard, mouse, monitor, and printer. Users who enjoy playing games might add a joystick or a trackball; others might connect a

*modem, *scanner, or *integrated services digital network (ISDN) terminal to their machines.

peristalsis wavelike contractions, produced by the contraction of smooth muscle, that pass along tubular organs, such as the intestines. The same term describes the wavelike motion of earthworms and other invertebrates, in which part of the body contracts as another part elongates.

periwinkle in botany, any of several trailing blue-flowered evergreen plants of the dogbane family, native to Europe and Asia. They range in length from 20 cm/8 in to 1 m/3 ft. (Genus *Vinca*, family Apocynaceae.)

periwinkle in zoology, any marine snail of the family Littorinidae, found on the shores of Europe and eastern North America. Periwinkles have a conical spiral shell, and feed on algae.

perjury the offence of deliberately making a false statement on *oath (or affirmation) when appearing as a witness in legal proceedings, on a point material to the question at issue. In Britain and the USA it is punishable by a fine, imprisonment, or both.

Perlis border state of northwestern Peninsular Malaysia, area 800 sq km/309 sq mi; population (2000 est) 198,300. The capital is Kangar, which is situated on the Perlis river. It produces rice, coconuts, and tin. Industries include sawmilling, rubber processing, and the manufacture of cement and paper.

permafrost condition in which a deep layer of soil does not thaw out during the summer. Permafrost occurs under periglacial conditions. It is claimed that 26% of the world's land surface is permafrost.

Permian period of geological time 290–245 million years ago, the last period of the Palaeozoic era. Its end was marked by a dramatic change in marine life – the greatest mass extinction in geological history – including the extinction of many corals and trilobites. Deserts were widespread, terrestrial amphibians and mammal-like reptiles flourished, and cone-bearing plants (gymnosperms) came to prominence. In the oceans, 49% of families and 72% of genera vanished in the late Permian. On land, 78% of reptile families and 67% of amphibian families disappeared.

Perón, Eva ('Evita') Duarte de (1919–1952) born María Eva Duarte, Argentine populist leader. A successful radio actor, she became the second wife of Juan *Perón in 1945. When he became president the following year, she became his chief adviser and virtually ran the health and labour ministries, devoting herself to helping the poor, improving education, and achieving women's suffrage. She founded a social welfare organization called the Eva Perón Foundation. She was politically astute and sought the vice-presidency in 1951, but was opposed by the army and withdrew. After her death from cancer in 1952, Juan Perón's political strength began to decline.

Perón, Juan Domingo (1895–1974) Argentine politician, dictator 1946–55 and from 1973 until his death. His populist appeal to the poor was enhanced by the charisma and political work of his second wife Eva ('Evita') Perón. After her death in 1952 his popularity waned and, with increasing economic difficulties and labour unrest, he was deposed in a military coup in 1955. He fled to Paraguay and, in 1960, to Spain. He returned from exile to the presidency in 1973, but died in office in 1974, and was succeeded by his third wife, Isabel Perón.

periodic table of elements

Legend:

atomic number — 1
name — Hydrogen
symbol — H
relative atomic mass — 1.00794
element

nonmetals
metals

I	II	III	IV	V	VI	VII	0
1 Hydrogen H 1.00794							2 Helium He 4002.60
3 Lithium Li 6.941	4 Beryllium Be 9.012	5 Boron B 10.81	6 Carbon C 12.011	7 Nitrogen N 14.0067	8 Oxygen O 15.9994	9 Fluorine F 18.9984	10 Neon Ne 20.179
11 Sodium Na 22.989977	12 Magnesium Mg 24.305	13 Aluminium Al 26.98154	14 Silicon Si 28.086	15 Phosphorus P 30.9738	16 Sulphur S 32.06	17 Chlorine Cl 35.453	18 Argon Ar 39.948
19 Potassium K 39.098	20 Calcium Ca 40.08	31 Gallium Ga 69.72	32 Germanium Ge 72.59	33 Arsenic As 74.9216	34 Selenium Se 78.96	35 Bromine Br 79.904	36 Krypton Kr 83.80
37 Rubidium Rb 85.4678	38 Strontium Sr 87.62	49 Indium In 114.82	50 Tin Sn 118.69	51 Antimony Sb 121.75	52 Tellurium Te 127.26	53 Iodine I 126.9045	54 Xenon Xe 131.30
55 Caesium Cs 132.9054	56 Barium Ba 137.34	81 Thallium Tl 204.37	82 Lead Pb 207.37	83 Bismuth Bi 207.2	84 Polonium Po 210	85 Astatine At 211	86 Radon Rn 222.0176
87 Francium Fr 223.0197	88 Radium Ra 226.0254						

Transition elements (periods 4–7):

21 Scandium Sc 44.9559	22 Titanium Ti 47.90	23 Vanadium V 50.9414	24 Chromium Cr 51.996	25 Manganese Mn 54.9380	26 Iron Fe 55.847	27 Cobalt Co 58.9332	28 Nickel Ni 58.70	29 Copper Cu 63.546	30 Zinc Zn 65.38
39 Yttrium Y 88.9059	40 Zirconium Zr 91.22	41 Niobium Nb 92.9064	42 Molybdenum Mo 95.94	43 Technetium Tc 97.9072	44 Ruthenium Ru 101.07	45 Rhodium Rh 102.9055	46 Palladium Pd 106.4	47 Silver Ag 107.868	48 Cadmium Cd 112.40
57 Lanthanum La 138.9055	72 Hafnium Hf 178.49	73 Tantalum Ta 180.9479	74 Tungsten W 183.85	75 Rhenium Re 186.207	76 Osmium Os 190.2	77 Iridium Ir 192.22	78 Platinum Pt 195.09	79 Gold Au 196.9665	80 Mercury Hg 200.59
89 Actinium Ac 227.0278	104 Rutherfordium Rf 261.109	105 Dubnium Db 262.114	106 Seaborgium Sg 263.120	107 Bohrium Bh 262	108 Hassium Hs 265	109 Meitnerium Mt 266	110 Ununnilium Uun 269	111 Unununium Uuu 272	112 Ununbium Uub 277

Lanthanide series:

58 Cerium Ce 140.12	59 Praseodymium Pr	60 Neodymium Nd 144.24	61 Promethium Pm 144.9128	62 Samarium Sm 150.36	63 Europium Eu 151.96	64 Gadolinium Gd 157.25	65 Terbium Tb 158.9254	66 Dysprosium Dy 162.50	67 Holmium Ho 164.9304	68 Erbium Er 167.26	69 Thulium Tm 168.9342	70 Ytterbium Yb 173.04	71 Lutetium Lu 174.97

Actinide series:

90 Thorium Th 232.0381	91 Protactinium Pa 231.0359	92 Uranium U 238.029	93 Neptunium Np 237.0482	94 Plutonium Pu 244.0642	95 Americium Am 243.0614	96 Curium Cm 247.0703	97 Berkelium Bk 247	98 Californium Cf 251.0796	99 Einsteinium Es 252.0828	100 Fermium Fm 257.0951	101 Mendelevium Md 258.0986	102 Nobelium No 259.1009	103 Lawrencium Lr 260.1054

periodic table of the elements The periodic table of the elements arranges the elements into horizontal rows (called periods) and vertical columns (called groups) according to their atomic numbers. The elements in a group or column all have similar properties – for example, all the elements in the far right-hand column are noble gases.

Perpendicular period of English Gothic architecture lasting from the end of the 14th century to the mid-16th century. It is characterized by window tracery consisting chiefly of vertical members, two or four arc arches, lavishly decorated vaults, and the use of traceried panels. Examples include the choir, transepts, and cloister of Gloucester Cathedral (about 1331–1412); and King's College Chapel, Cambridge, built in three phases: 1446–61, 1477–85, and 1508–15.

perpendicular at a right angle; also, a line at right angles to another line or to a plane. Everyday examples include lamp posts, which are perpendicular to the road, and walls, which are perpendicular to the ground.

perpetual motion idea that a machine can be designed and constructed in such a way that, once started, it will do work indefinitely without requiring any further input of energy (motive power). Such a device would contradict at least one of the two laws of thermodynamics that state that (1) energy can neither be created nor destroyed (the law of conservation of energy) and (2) heat cannot by itself flow from a cooler to a hotter object. As a result, all practical (real) machines require a continuous supply of energy, and no heat engine is able to convert all the heat into useful work.

Perrault, Charles (1628–1703) French writer who published a collection of fairy tales, *Contes de ma mère l'oye/Mother Goose's Fairy Tales* (1697). These are based on traditional stories and include 'The Sleeping Beauty', 'Little Red Riding Hood', 'Blue Beard', 'Puss in Boots', and 'Cinderella'.

Perry, Fred (Frederick John) (1909–1995) English lawn-tennis player, the last Briton to win the men's singles at Wimbledon, in 1936. He also won the world table-tennis title in 1929. Perry later became a television commentator and a sports-goods manufacturer.

Persephone Roman **Proserpina**, in Greek mythology, the goddess and queen of the underworld; the daughter of Zeus and *Demeter, goddess of agriculture. She was carried off to the underworld by *Pluto, also known as Hades, although Zeus later ordered that she should spend six months of the year above ground with her mother. The myth symbolizes the growth and decay of vegetation and the changing seasons.

Perseus a bright constellation of the northern hemisphere, near *Cassiopeia. It is represented as the mythological hero; the head of the decapitated Gorgon, Medusa, is marked by *Algol (Beta Persei), the best known of the eclipsing binary stars.

Perseus in Greek mythology, the son of Zeus and Danaë. He beheaded the *Gorgon Medusa, watching the reflection in his shield to avoid being turned to stone. Having rescued and married Andromeda, he later became king of Tiryns. He used the Gorgon's head, set on his shield, to turn the tyrant Polydectes and, in some traditions, the Titan *Atlas, to stone.

Persia, ancient kingdom in southwestern Asia. The early Persians were a nomadic Aryan people who migrated through the Caucasus to the Iranian plateau. Cyrus organized the empire into provinces which were each ruled by Satraps. The royal house is known as the Achaemenids after the founder of the line. The administrative centre was Susa, with the royal palace at Persepolis. Expansion led the Persians into conflicts with Greek cities, notably in the Ionian Revolt, Darius I's campaign that ended at the Athenian victory

of Marathon (490 BC), and Xerxes I's full-blown invasion of the Greek mainland in 480.

Persian inhabitant or native to Persia, now Iran, and referring to the culture and the language (see also *Farsi). The Persians claim descent from central Asians of southern Russia (Aryans) who are thought to have migrated south into the region around 2000 BC.

Persian art the arts of Persia (now Iran) from the 6th century BC. Subject to invasions from both east and west, Persia has over the centuries blended many influences to create a rich diversity of arts, styles, and techniques. Persian art is particularly noted for its architecture and production of exquisite miniatures, although perhaps best known today for ornate carpets. Although the wide diversity of outside influences make it difficult to pin down distinct characteristics, Persian art is generally characterized by its firm lines, extensive detail, and bold use of colour.

Persian Gulf alternative name for the *Gulf, a large inlet of the Arabian Sea.

Persian language language belonging to the Indo-Iranian branch of the Indo-European family; see *Farsi.

Persian Wars series of conflicts between Greece and Persia in 499–479 BC. Greek involvement with Persia began when *Cyrus (II) the Great (reigned 559–530 BC) conquered the Greek cities of western Asia Minor and ended with *Alexander (III) the Great's conquest of Persia, but the term 'Persian Wars' usually refers to the two Persian invasions of mainland Greece in 490 BC and 480–79 BC. The Greek victory marked the end of Persian domination of the ancient world and the beginning of Greek supremacy.

persimmon any of a group of tropical trees belonging to the ebony family, especially the common persimmon (*D. virginiana*) of the southeastern USA. Growing up to 19 m/60 ft high, the persimmon has alternate oval leaves and yellow-green flowers. The small, sweet, orange fruits are edible. (Genus *Diospyros*, family Ebenaceae.)

personification figure of speech or literary device in which animals, plants, objects, and ideas are treated as if they were human or alive ('Clouds chased each other across the face of the Moon'; 'Nature smiled on their work and gave it her blessing'; 'The future beckoned eagerly to them'). See also *anthropomorphism.

perspective realistic representation of a three-dimensional object in two dimensions. **One-point linear perspective** is an effective way to give a picture depth and a sense of distance and space. It is based on three key principles: that the horizon line is always at eye-level; that the vanishing point is the point to which all lines parallel to the viewer recede; and that convergence lines meet at the vanishing point (all diagonal lines recede to the vanishing point). All horizontal and vertical lines remain parallel to one another to avoid objects becoming distorted. **Two-point linear perspective** follows the same principles, but uses two sets of converging lines and no horizontal lines; as a result there are two vanishing points.

perspiration excretion of water and dissolved substances from the *sweat glands of the skin of mammals. Perspiration has two main functions: body cooling by the evaporation of water from the skin surface, and excretion of waste products such as salts.

Perth capital of the state of *Western Australia; population (1996) 1,096,829. Perth is situated on the southwest coast of Australia, on the River Swan, 19 km/12 mi inland. Its port is at Fremantle, to the southwest at the mouth of the Swan. Industries include oil refining, electronics, food processing, shipbuilding, banking and finance, and tourism; products include textiles, nickel, alumina, fertilizers, cement, furniture, and motor vehicles. Perth is an important centre for the export of primary products: refined oil, minerals, wool, wheat, meat, fruit, timber, and dairy produce. Perth has four universities: the University of Western Australia (founded 1911); Murdoch University (1975); Curtin University of Technology (1987); Edith Cowan University (1990).

Perth and Kinross unitary authority in central Scotland, created in 1996 from the district bearing the same name in Tayside region. **area:** 5,388 sq km/ 2,080 sq mi **towns:** Blairgowrie, Crieff, Kinross, Perth (administrative headquarters), Pitlochry, Aberfeldy **physical:** the geological fault that gives the distinctive character to lowland and highland Scotland passes southwest–northeast through the area. The population is largely centred in the lowlands, along wide fertile valleys such as Strathearn, and the Carse of Gowrie. To the north and west are the Grampians intersected by narrow glens with lochs in their valley floors. Among the highest elevations in the Grampians are Ben Lawers (1,214 m/3,984 ft) and Schiehallion (1,083 m/3,554 ft); in the south are the lower Ochil and Sidlaw Hills **features:** Highland Games at Pitlochry; Dunkeld Cathedral; Scone Palace; Glenshee Ski Development **population:** (2000 est) 133,600.

Peru
   National name: *República del Perú/Republic of Peru*

Area: 1,285,200 sq km/496,216 sq mi
Capital: Lima
Major towns/cities: Arequipa, Iquitos, Chiclayo, Trujillo, Huancayo, Piura, Chimbote
Major ports: Callao, Chimbote, Salaverry

Physical features: Andes mountains running northwest–southeast cover 27% of Peru, separating Amazon river-basin jungle in northeast from coastal plain in west; desert along coast north–south (Atacama Desert); Lake Titicaca
Head of state: Alejandro Toledo Manrique from 2001
Head of government: Carlos Ferrero Costa from 2003
Political system: liberal democracy
Political executive: limited presidency
Political parties: American Popular Revolutionary Alliance (APRA), moderate, left wing; United Left (IU), left wing; Change 90 (Cambio 90), centrist; New Majority (Nueva Mayoria), centrist; Popular Christian Party (PPC), right of centre; Liberal Party (PL), right wing
Currency: nuevo sol
GNI per capita (PPP): (US$) 4,800 (2002 est)
Exports: gold, copper, fishmeal, zinc, refined petroleum products. Principal market: USA 27.2% (2001)
Population: 27,167,000 (2003 est)
Language: Spanish, Quechua (both official), Aymara, many indigenous dialects
Religion: Roman Catholic (state religion) 95%
Life expectancy: 67 (men); 72 (women) (2000–05)
Chronology
4000 BC: Evidence of early settled agriculture in Chicama Valley.
AD 700–1100: Period of Wari Empire, first expansionist militarized empire in Andes.
1200: Manco Capac became the first emperor of South American Indian Quechua-speaking Incas, who established a growing and sophisticated empire centred on the Andean city of Cuzco, and believed their ruler was descended from the Sun.
late 15th century: At its zenith, the Inca Empire stretched from Quito in Ecuador to beyond Santiago in southern Chile. It superseded the Chimu civilization, which had flourished in Peru 1250–1470.
1532–33: Incas defeated by Spanish conquistadores, led by Francisco Pizarro. Empire came under Spanish rule, as part of the Viceroyalty of Peru, with capital in Lima, founded in 1535.
1780: Tupac Amaru, who claimed to be descended from the last Inca chieftain, led a failed native revolt against Spanish.
1810: Peru became the headquarters for the Spanish government as European settlers rebelled elsewhere in Spanish America.
1820–22: Fight for liberation from Spanish rule led by Gen José de San Martín and Army of Andes which, after freeing Argentina and Chile, invaded southern Peru.
1824: Became last colony in Central and South America to achieve independence from Spain after attacks from north by Field Marshal Sucre, acting for freedom fighter Simón Bolívar.
1836–39: Failed attempts at union with Bolivia.
1849–74: Around 80,000–100,000 Chinese labourers arrived in Peru to fill menial jobs such as collecting guano.
1866: Victorious naval war fought with Spain.
1879–83: Pacific War fought in alliance with Bolivia and Chile over nitrate fields of the Atacama Desert in the south; three provinces along coastal south lost to Chile.
1902: Boundary dispute with Bolivia settled.

mid–1920s: After several decades of civilian government, a series of right-wing dictatorships held power.

1927: Boundary dispute with Colombia settled.

1929: Tacna province, lost to Chile in 1880, was returned.

1941: A brief war with Ecuador secured Amazonian territory.

1945: Civilian government, dominated by left-of-centre American Popular Revolutionary Alliance (APRA, formed 1924), came to power after free elections.

1948: Army coup installed military government led by Gen Manuel Odría, who remained in power until 1956.

1963: Return to civilian rule, with centrist Fernando Belaúnde Terry as president.

1968: Return of military government in bloodless coup by Gen Juan Velasco Alvarado, following industrial unrest. Populist land reform programme introduced.

1980: Return to civilian rule, with Fernando Belaúnde as president; agrarian and industrial reforms pursued. Sendero Luminoso ('Shining Path') Maoist guerrilla group active.

1981: Boundary dispute with Ecuador renewed.

1985: Belaúnde succeeded by Social Democrat Alan García Pérez, who launched campaign to remove military and police 'old guard'.

1988: García was pressured to seek help from International Monetary Fund (IMF) as the economy deteriorated. Sendero Luminoso increased its campaign of violence.

1990: Right-of-centre Alberto Fujimori defeated ex-communist writer Vargas Llosa in presidential elections. Inflation rose to 400%; a privatization programme was launched.

1992: Fujimori allied himself with the army and suspended the constitution, provoking international criticism. The Sendero Luminoso leader was arrested and sentenced to life imprisonment. A new single-chamber legislature was elected.

1993: A new constitution was adopted.

1994: 6,000 Sendero Luminoso guerrillas surrendered to the authorities.

1995: A border dispute with Ecuador was resolved after armed clashes. Fujimori was re-elected. A controversial amnesty was granted to those previously convicted of human-rights abuses.

1996: Hostages were held in the Japanese embassy by Marxist Tupac Amaru Revolutionary Movement (MRTA) guerrillas.

1997: The hostage siege ended.

1998: A border dispute that had lasted for 157 years was settled with Ecuador.

1999: Alberto Bustamante was made prime minister.

2000: Fujimori was re-elected as president for a third term in July. In September, the head of the national intelligence service, Vladimiro Montesinos, was proved to have bribed a member of congress. Fujimori sent his resignation from Japan, from where he could not be extradited, and Valentín Paniagua became president. He appointed former United Nations (UN) secretary general Javier Pérez de Cuéllar as prime minister.

2001: President Paniagua set up a commission to investigate the disappearance of 4,000 people during the fighting in the 1980s and 1990s. Alejandro Toledo was elected president.

2002: Luis Solari became prime minister.

2003: A wave of strikes led President Toledo to declare a state of emergency and impose order.

Peru Current formerly **Humboldt Current**, cold ocean *current flowing north from the Antarctic along the west coast of South America to southern Ecuador, then west. It reduces the coastal temperature, making the western slopes of the Andes arid because winds are already chilled and dry when they meet the coast.

Peshawar capital of *North-West Frontier Province, Pakistan, 18 km/11 mi east of the Khyber Pass and 72 km/107 mi west of Islamabad, on the Bara River; population (1998 est) 988,100. The Khyber Pass provides the easiest route between the Indian subcontinent and Afghanistan, and the city grew to importance as the long-established terminus, first for camel caravan trade and later for paved motor road trade, from Kabul in Afghanistan. Industries include textiles, sugar milling, fruit canning, leatherwork, pottery, and handicrafts such as copper goods, carpets, embroidery, and ornamental woodwork.

pessary medical device designed to be inserted into the vagina either to support a displaced womb or as a contraceptive. The word is also used for a vaginal suppository used for administering drugs locally, made from glycerol or oil of theobromine, which melts within the vagina to release the contained substance – for example, a contraceptive, antibiotic, antifungal agent, or *prostaglandin (to induce labour).

pest in biology, any insect, fungus, rodent, or other living organism that has a harmful effect on human beings, other than those that directly cause human diseases. Most pests damage crops or livestock, but the term also covers those that damage buildings, destroy food stores, and spread disease.

pesticide any chemical used in farming, gardening, or in the home, to combat pests. Pesticides are of three main types: **insecticides** (to kill insects), **fungicides** (to kill fungal diseases), and **herbicides** (to kill plants, mainly those considered weeds). Pesticides cause a number of pollution problems through spray drift onto surrounding areas, direct contamination of users or the public, and as residues on food. The World Health Organization (WHO) estimates that thousands of people die annually worldwide from pesticide poisoning.

petal part of a flower whose function is to attract pollinators such as insects or birds. Petals are frequently large and brightly coloured and may also be scented. Some have a nectary at the base and markings on the petal surface, known as honey guides, to direct pollinators to the source of the nectar. In wind-pollinated plants, however, the petals are usually small and insignificant, and sometimes absent altogether. Petals are derived from modified leaves, and are known collectively as a corolla.

Peter three tsars of Russia, including:

Peter (I) the Great (1672–1725) Tsar of Russia from 1682 on the death of his half-brother Tsar Feodor III; he took full control of the government in 1689. He attempted to reorganize the country on Western lines. He modernized the army, had a modern fleet built, remodelled the administrative and legal systems, encouraged education, and brought the Russian Orthodox Church under state control. On the Baltic coast, where he had conquered territory from Sweden, Peter built a new city, *St Petersburg, and moved the capital there from Moscow.

Peterborough unitary authority in eastern England, created in 1998 from part of Cambridgeshire. **area:** 334 sq km/129 sq mi **towns and cities:** Peterborough (administrative headquarters), Wittering, Old Fletton, Thorney, Glinton, Northborough, Peakirk **features:** River Nene; western margins of the Fens; St Peter's Cathedral (Peterborough), 12th century, containing Catherine of Aragon's tomb; Wildfowl and Wetlands Centre at Peakirk **population:** (1996) 156,900.

Peterloo massacre the events in St Peter's Fields in Manchester, England, on 16 August 1819, when an open-air meeting in support of parliamentary reform was charged by yeomanry (voluntary cavalry soldiers) and hussars (regular cavalry soldiers). Eleven people were killed and 500 wounded. The name was given in analogy with the Battle of Waterloo.

Peter, St (lived 1st century) Christian martyr, the author of two *Epistles in the New Testament and leader of the apostles. Peter is regarded as the first bishop of *Rome, whose position the *pope inherits directly through *apostolic succession. His real name was Simon, but he was renamed Peter (from the Greek *petros* 'rock') after Jesus nicknamed him Kephas, the rock upon which he would build his church. His emblem is two keys, as he is said to hold the keys to *heaven. His feast day is 29 June.

Petipa, Marius (1822–1910) French choreographer. He created some of the most important ballets in the classical repertory. For the Imperial Ballet in Russia he created masterpieces such as *Don Quixote* (1869), *La Bayadère* (1877), *The Sleeping Beauty* (1890), *Swan Lake* (1895) (with Ivanov), and *Raymonda* (1898).

Petra Arabic **Wadi Musa**, ancient city carved out of the red rock at a site in Jordan, on the eastern slopes of the Wadi el Araba, 90 km/56 mi south of the Dead Sea. An Edomite stronghold and capital of the Nabataeans in the 2nd century, it was captured by the Roman emperor Trajan in 106 and destroyed by the Arabs in the 7th century. It was forgotten in Europe until 1812 when the Swiss traveller Johann Ludwig Burckhardt (1784–1817) came across it.

Petrarch (1304–1374) born Francesco Petrarca, Italian poet, humanist, and leader of the revival of classical learning. His *Il canzoniere/Songbook* (also known as *Rime Sparse/Scattered Lyrics*) contains madrigals, songs, and *sonnets in praise of his idealized love, 'Laura', whom he first saw in 1327 (she was a married woman and refused to become his mistress). These were Petrarch's greatest contributions to Italian literature; they shaped the lyric poetry of the Renaissance and greatly influenced French and English love poetry. Although he did not invent the sonnet form, he was its finest early practitioner and the 'Petrarchan sonnet' was admired as an ideal model by later poets.

petrel any of various families of seabirds in the order Procellariiforme, including the worldwide **storm petrels** (family Hydrobatidae), which include the smallest seabirds (some only 13 cm/5 in long), and the **diving petrels** (family Pelecanoididae) of the southern hemisphere. All have a hooked bill, rudimentary hind toes, tubular nostrils, and feed by diving underwater. They include *fulmars and *shearwaters.

petrochemical chemical derived from the processing of petroleum (crude oil). **Petrochemical industries** are those that obtain their raw materials from the processing of petroleum and natural gas. Polymers, detergents, solvents, and nitrogen fertilizers are all major products of the petrochemical industries. Inorganic chemical products include carbon black, sulphur, ammonia, and hydrogen peroxide.

Petrograd former name (1914–24) of *St Petersburg, a city in Russia. It adopted this Russian-style name as a patriotic gesture at the outbreak of World War I, but was renamed Leningrad on the death of the USSR's first leader.

petrol mixture of hydrocarbons derived from *petroleum, mainly used as a fuel for internal-combustion engines. It is colourless and highly volatile. **Leaded petrol** contains antiknock (a mixture of tetra ethyl lead and dibromoethane), which improves the combustion of petrol and the performance of a car engine. The lead from the exhaust fumes enters the atmosphere, mostly as simple lead compounds. There is strong evidence that it can act as a nerve poison on young children and cause mental impairment. This prompted a gradual switch to the use of **unleaded petrol** in the UK.

petrol engine the most commonly used source of power for motor vehicles, introduced by the German engineers Gottlieb Daimler and Karl Benz in 1885. The petrol engine is a complex piece of machinery made up of about 150 moving parts. It is a reciprocating piston engine, in which a number of pistons move up and down in cylinders. A mixture of petrol and air is introduced to the space above the pistons and ignited. The gases produced force the pistons down, generating power. The engine-operating cycle is repeated every four strokes (upward or downward movement) of the piston, this being known as the *four-stroke cycle. The motion of the pistons rotate a crankshaft, at the end of which is a heavy flywheel. From the flywheel the power is transferred to the car's driving wheels via the transmission system of clutch, gearbox, and final drive.

petroleum *or* **crude oil** natural mineral oil, a thick greenish-brown flammable liquid found underground in permeable rocks. Petroleum consists of hydrocarbons mixed with oxygen, sulphur, nitrogen, and other elements in varying proportions. It is thought to be derived from ancient organic material that has been converted by, first, bacterial action, then heat, and pressure (but its origin may be chemical also). From crude petroleum, various products are made by *fractional distillation and other processes; for example, fuel oil, petrol, kerosene, diesel, and lubricating oil. Petroleum products and chemicals are used in large quantities in the manufacture of detergents, artificial fibres, plastics, insecticides, fertilizers, pharmaceuticals, toiletries, and synthetic rubber.

petrology branch of geology that deals with the study of rocks, their mineral compositions, their textures, and their origins.

pewter any of various alloys of mostly tin with varying amounts of lead, copper, or antimony. Pewter has been known for centuries and was once widely used for domestic utensils but is now used mainly for ornamental ware.

peyote spineless cactus of northern Mexico and the southwestern USA. It has white or pink flowers. Its

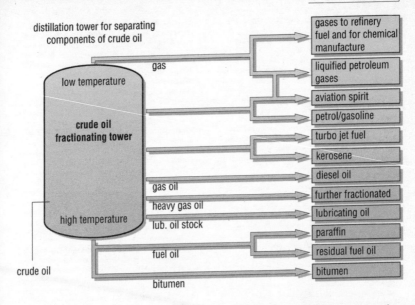

distillation tower for separating components of crude oil

low temperature

crude oil fractionating tower

gas

high temperature

gas oil

heavy gas oil

lub. oil stock

fuel oil

crude oil

bitumen

gases to refinery fuel and for chemical manufacture

liquified petroleum gases

aviation spirit

petrol/gasoline

turbo jet fuel

kerosene

diesel oil

further fractionated

lubricating oil

paraffin

residual fuel oil

bitumen

petroleum Refining petroleum using a distillation column. The crude petroleum is fed in at the bottom of the column where the temperature is high. The gases produced rise up the column, cooling as they travel. At different heights up the column, different gases condense to liquids called fractions, and are drawn off.

buttonlike tops contain **mescaline**, which causes hallucinations and is used by American Indians in religious ceremonies. (*Lophopora williamsii*, family Cactaceae.)

pH scale from 0 to 14 for measuring acidity or alkalinity. A pH of 7 indicates neutrality, below 7 is *acid, while above 7 is alkaline. Strong acids, such as those used in car batteries, have a pH of about 2; strong *alkalis such as sodium hydroxide have a pH of about 13.

Phaethon (Greek 'shining one') in Greek mythology, the son of *Helios, god of the Sun, and Clymene. He was allowed to drive his father's chariot for one day, but lost control of the horses and almost set the Earth on fire, whereupon he was killed by Zeus with a thunderbolt and hurled into the River Eridanos.

phage another name for a *bacteriophage, a virus that attacks bacteria.

phagocyte type of *white blood cell, or leucocyte, that can engulf a bacterium or other invading micro-organism. Phagocytes are found in blood, lymph, and other body tissues, where they also ingest foreign matter and dead tissue. A *macrophage differs in size and lifespan.

Phalangist member of a Phalange, specifically the Lebanese military organization (**Phalanges Libanaises**), since 1958 the political and military force of the *Maronite Church in Lebanon. The Phalangists' unbending right-wing policies and resistance to the introduction of democratic institutions were among the contributing factors to the civil war in Lebanon.

phalanx in ancient Greece and Macedonia, a battle formation using up to 16 lines of infantry with pikes about 4 m/13 ft long, protected to the sides and rear by cavalry. It was used by Philip II and Alexander the Great of Macedonia, and though more successful than the conventional hoplite formation, it proved inferior to the Roman legion.

phalarope any of a genus *Phalaropus* of small, elegant shorebirds in the sandpiper family (Scolopacidae). They have the habit of spinning in the water to stir up insect larvae. They are native to North America, the UK, and the polar regions of Europe.

Phanerozoic eon (Greek *phanero* 'visible') eon in Earth history, consisting of the most recent 570 million years. It comprises the Palaeozoic, Mesozoic, and Cenozoic eras. The vast majority of fossils come from this eon, owing to the evolution of hard shells and internal skeletons. The name means 'interval of well-displayed life'.

Pharaoh Hebrew form of the Egyptian royal title Per-'o. This term, meaning 'great house', was originally applied to the royal household, and after about 950 BC to the king.

Pharisee (Hebrew 'separatist') member of a conservative Jewish sect that arose in Roman-occupied Palestine in the 2nd century BC in protest against all movements favouring compromise with Hellenistic culture. The Pharisees were devout adherents of the law, both as found in the Torah and in the oral tradition known as the Mishnah.

pharmacology study of the properties of drugs and their effects on the human body.

phase in astronomy, apparent shape of the Moon or a planet when all or part of its illuminated hemisphere is facing the Earth. As the Moon orbits the Earth its appearance from Earth changes as different amounts of its surface are illuminated by the Sun. During one orbit of the Earth (29.5 days – a lunar *month*) the Moon undergoes a full cycle of phases from new, to first quarter, to full, to last quarter.

phase in physics, a stage in an oscillatory motion, such as a wave motion: two waves are in phase when their peaks and their troughs coincide. Otherwise, there is a **phase difference**, which has consequences in *interference phenomena and *alternating current electricity.

pheasant any of various large, colourful Asiatic fowls of the family Phasianidae, order Galliformes, which also includes grouse, quail, and turkey. The typical pheasants are in the genus *Phasianus*, which has two species: the Japanese pheasant, *P. versicolor*, found in Japan, and the Eurasian ring-necked or common pheasant, *P. colchicus*, also introduced to North America. The genus is distinguished by the very long wedge-shaped tail and the absence of a crest. The plumage of the male common pheasant is richly tinted with brownish-green, yellow, and red markings, but the female is a camouflaged brownish colour. The nest is made on the ground. The male is polygamous.

phenol member of a group of aromatic chemical compounds with weakly acidic properties, which are characterized by a hydroxyl (OH) group attached directly to an aromatic ring. The simplest of the phenols, derived from benzene, is also known as phenol and has the formula C_6H_5OH. It is sometimes called **carbolic acid** and can be extracted from coal tar.

phenomenalism philosophical position that argues that statements about objects can be reduced to statements about what is perceived or perceivable. Thus English philosopher John Stuart Mill defined material objects as 'permanent possibilities of sensation'. Phenomenalism is closely connected with certain forms of *empiricism.

phenomenology the philosophical perspective, founded by the German philosopher Edmund *Husserl, that concentrates on phenomena as objects of perception (rather than as facts or occurrences that exist independently) in attempting to examine the ways people think about and interpret the world around them. It has been practised by the philosophers Martin Heidegger, Jean-Paul Sartre, and Maurice Merleau-Ponty.

phenotype in genetics, visible traits, those actually displayed by an organism. The phenotype is not a direct reflection of the *genotype because some alleles are masked by the presence of other, dominant alleles (see *dominance). The phenotype is further modified by the effects of the environment (for example, poor nutrition stunts growth).

pheromone chemical signal (such as an odour) that is emitted by one animal and affects the behaviour of others. Pheromones are used by many animal species to attract mates.

Phidias (*or* **Pheidias**) (**lived mid-5th century BC**) Greek sculptor. Active in Athens, he supervised the sculptural programme for the Parthenon (most of it is preserved in the British Museum, London, and known as the *Elgin marbles). He also executed the colossal statue of Zeus at Olympia, one of the *Seven Wonders of the World. No surviving sculptures can be credited to him with certainty.

Philadelphia (Greek 'the city of brotherly love') river port and chief city in Pennsylvania, USA, on the Delaware River at the junction with the Schuykill River; population (2000 est) 1,517,600. It is the world's largest freshwater port, the fifth largest city in the USA, and a financial, business, and research centre. Industries include oil-refining, food-processing, electronics, printing, publishing, and the production of iron, steel, chemicals, textiles, carpets, and transportation equipment, although manufacturing is less important than it was. Philadelphia was originally settled by Swedish settlers in 1682, and was the capital of the USA 1790–1800.

philanthropy love felt by an individual towards humankind. It is expressed through acts of generosity and charity and seeks to promote the greater happiness and prosperity of humanity.

Philby, Kim (Harold Adrian Russell) (1912–1988) British intelligence officer from 1940 and Soviet agent from 1933. He was liaison officer in Washington 1949–51, when he was confirmed to be a double agent and asked to resign. Named in 1963 as having warned Guy Burgess and Donald Maclean (also double agents) that their activities were known, he fled to the USSR and became a Soviet citizen and a general in the KGB. A fourth member of the ring was Anthony Blunt.

Philip, Duke of Edinburgh (1921–) Prince of the UK, husband of Elizabeth II, a grandson of George I of Greece and a great-great-grandson of Queen Victoria. He was born in Corfu, Greece, but brought up in England.

Philip French Philippe, six kings of France, including:
Philip II (1165–1223) also known as **Philip Augustus**, King of France from 1180. As part of his efforts to establish a strong monarchy and evict the English from their French possessions, he waged war in turn against the English kings *Henry II, Richard (I) the Lionheart (with whom he also went on the Third Crusade), and John (1167–1216).

Philip IV the Fair (1268–1314) King of France from 1285. He engaged in a feud with Pope Boniface VIII and made him a prisoner 1303. Clement V (1264–1314), elected pope through Philip's influence in 1305, moved the papal seat to Avignon in 1309 and collaborated with Philip to suppress the *Templars, a powerful order of knights. Philip allied with the Scots against England and invaded Flanders.

Philip VI (1293–1350) King of France from 1328, first of the house of Valois, elected by the barons on the death of his cousin, Charles IV. His claim was challenged by Edward III of England, who defeated him at Crécy in 1346.

Philip Spanish Felipe, five kings of Spain, including:
Philip II (1527–1598) King of Spain from 1556. He was born at Valladolid, the son of the Habsburg emperor Charles V, and in 1554 married Queen *Mary I of England. In 1559, after Mary's death, he pursued his ambitions on England by offering to marry her half-sister *Elizabeth I, who had succeeded to the English

throne. On his father's abdication in 1556 he inherited
Spain, the Netherlands, and the Spanish possessions in
Italy and the Americas, and in 1580 he took control of
Portugal. His intolerance and lack of understanding of
the Netherlanders drove them into revolt. He tried to
conquer England in 1588, sending the unsuccessful
*Spanish Armada, and in 1589 he claimed the throne
of France for his daughter Isabella.

Philip II of Macedon (382–336 BC) King of
*Macedonia from 359 BC. He seized the throne from
his nephew, for whom he was regent, defeated the
Greek city states at the battle of Chaeronea (in central
Greece) in 338 and formed them into a league whose
forces could be united against Persia. He was
assassinated while he was planning this expedition,
and was succeeded by his son Alexander the Great.

Philippines

National name: *Republika Ñg Pilipinas/
Republic of the Philippines*

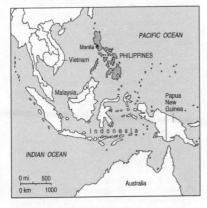

Area: 300,000 sq km/115,830 sq mi
Capital: Manila (on Luzon island) (and chief port)
Major towns/cities: Quezon City, Davao, Cebu,
Bacolod, Cagayan de Oro, Iloilo City
Major ports: Cebu, Davao (on Mindanao), Iloilo City,
Zamboanga (on Mindanao)
Physical features: comprises over 7,000 islands;
volcanic mountain ranges traverse main chain
north–south; 50% still forested. The largest islands
are Luzon 108,172 sq km/41,754 sq mi and Mindanao
94,227 sq km/36,372 sq mi; others include Samar,
Negros, Palawan, Panay, Mindoro, Leyte, Cebu, and
the Sulu group; Pinatubo volcano (1,759 m/5,770 ft);
Mindanao has active volcano Apo (2,954 m/9,690 ft)
and mountainous rainforest
Head of state and government: Gloria Macapagal
Arroyo from 2001
Political system: liberal democracy
Political executive: limited presidency
Political parties: Laban ng Demokratikong Pilipino
(Democratic Filipino Struggle Party; LDP–DFSP),
centrist, liberal-democrat coalition; Lakas ng Edsa
(National Union of Christian Democrats; LNE–NUCD),
centrist; Liberal Party, centrist; Nationalist Party
(Nacionalista), right wing; New Society Movement

(NSM; Kilusan Bagong Lipunan), conservative, pro-
Marcos; National Democratic Front, left-wing umbrella
grouping, including the Communist Party of the
Philippines (CPP); Mindanao Alliance, island-based
decentralist body
Currency: peso
GNI per capita (PPP): (US$) 4,280 (2002 est)
Exports: electrical and electronic products (notably
semiconductors and microcircuits), machinery and
transport equipment, garments, agricultural products
(particularly fruit and seafood), woodcraft and
furniture, lumber, chemicals, coconut oil. Principal
market: USA 30.4% (2001)
Population: 79,999,000 (2003 est)
Language: Filipino, English (both official), Spanish,
Cebuano, Ilocano, more than 70 other indigenous
languages
Religion: Christian 94%, mainly Roman Catholic
(84%), Protestant; Muslim 4%, local religions
Life expectancy: 68 (men); 72 (women) (2000–05)
Chronology
14th century: Traders from Malay peninsula
introduced Islam and created Muslim principalities
of Manila and Jolo.
1521: Portuguese navigator Ferdinand Magellan
reached the islands, but was killed in battle with
islanders.
1536: Philippines named after Charles V's son (later
Philip II of Spain) by Spanish navigator Ruy López de
Villalobos.
1565: Philippines conquered by Spanish army led by
Miguel López de Lagazpi.
1571: Manila was made capital of the colony, which
was part of the Viceroyalty of Mexico.
17th century: Spanish missionaries converted much
of the lowland population to Roman Catholicism.
1762–63: British occupied Manila.
1834: End of Spanish monopoly on trade; British and
American merchants bought sugar and tobacco.
1896–97: Emilio Aguinaldo led a revolt against Spanish
rule.
1898: Spanish-American War: US navy destroyed
Spanish fleet in Manila Bay; Aguinaldo declared
independence, but Spain ceded Philippines to USA.
1898–1901: Nationalist uprising suppressed by US troops;
200,000 Filipinos killed.
1907: Americans set up elected legislative assembly.
1916: Bicameral legislature introduced based on the
US model.
1935: Philippines gained internal self-government with
Manuel Quezon as president.
1942–45: Occupied by Japan.
1946: Philippines achieved independence from USA
under President Manuel Roxas; USA retained military
bases and supplied economic aid.
1957–61: 'Filipino First' policy introduced by President
Carlos García to reduce economic power of Americans
and Chinese; official corruption increased.
1972: President Ferdinand Marcos declared martial law
and ended the freedom of the press; economic
development financed by foreign loans, of which large
sums were diverted by Marcos for personal use.
1981: Martial law officially ended but Marcos retained
sweeping emergency powers, ostensibly needed to combat
long-running Muslim and communist insurgencies.

1983: Opposition leader Benigno Aquino was murdered at Manila airport while surrounded by government troops.

1986: Corazon Aquino (widow of Benigno Aquino) used 'people's power' to force Marcos to flee the country.

1987: A 'Freedom constitution' was adopted; Aquino's People's Power won congressional elections.

1989: A state of emergency was declared after the sixth coup attempt was suppressed with US aid.

1991: The Philippine senate called for the withdrawal of US forces; US renewal of Subic Bay naval base lease was rejected.

1992: Fidel Ramos was elected to succeed Aquino; a 'Rainbow Coalition' government was formed.

1995: Imelda Marcos (the widow of Ferdinand Marcos) was elected to the House of Representatives while on bail from prison on a sentence for corruption.

1996: The LDP withdrew from the LDP–DFSP coalition. A peace agreement was made between the government and the Moro National Liberation Front (MNLF) after 25 years of civil unrest on Mindanao.

1997: Preliminary peace talks took place between the government and the Moro Islamic Liberation Front (MILF), fighting for an independent Muslim state on Mindanao. The Supreme Court rejected a proposal to allow a second presidential term.

1998: Joseph Estrada was inaugurated as president and Gloria Macapagal Arroyo as vice-president. Imelda Marcos was acquitted of corruption charges. A dispute with China over the mineral-rich Spratly Islands was resolved with an agreement on the joint use of the resources.

2000: The worst fighting since 1996 erupted between government troops and the MILF. In April, another Islamic separatist group, Abu Sayyaf, took 21 foreign hostages from holiday resorts in Malaysia. They were slowly released, the last few in September when Libya paid US$4 million/£2.8 million to the captors. However, further hostages continued to be taken throughout the year. Some were rescued by the Philippine army in September. In November, President Estrada was impeached on corruption charges.

2001: Estrada's trial was suspended after senators blocked the presentation of vital evidence. This caused mass public demonstrations, and Estrada left office. Former vice-president Gloria Macapagal Arroyo, who had led the call for Estrada's impeachment, became president.

2003: A military coup was attempted against President Arroyo but it was unsuccessful.

2004: President Arroyo was re-elected for a further six-year term.

Philip, St (lived 1st century AD) In the New Testament, one of the 12 apostles. He was an inhabitant of Bethsaida (northern Israel), and is said to have worked as a missionary in Anatolia. Feast day 3 May.

Philistine member of a seafaring people of non-Semitic origin who founded city-states on the Palestinian coastal plain in the 12th century BC, adopting a Semitic language and religion.

philology (Greek 'love of language') in historical *linguistics, the study of the development of languages. It is also an obsolete term for the study of literature.

philosophy (Greek 'love of wisdom') systematic analysis and critical examination of fundamental problems such as the nature of reality, mind, perception, self, free will, causation, time and space, and moral judgements. Traditionally, philosophy has three branches: metaphysics (the nature of being), epistemology (theory of knowledge), and logic (study of valid inference). Modern philosophy also includes ethics, aesthetics, political theory, the philosophy of science, and the philosophy of religion.

phloem tissue found in vascular plants. Its main function is to transport *sugars and other food materials such as amino acids (see *protein) from the leaves, where they are produced, to all other parts of the plant. This could be from the leaves to the roots to provide the chemicals needed for growth. However, it could be from a leaf and up to a developing fruit that is rich in sugars. The sugars are made by *photosynthesis, which occurs in green parts of plants, such as leaves (see *leaf). The amino acids are made from sugars and *minerals, such as nitrate absorbed from the soil. Phloem tissue is usually found close to the other transport tissue in plants, *xylem, which transports *water and minerals. In non-woody plants phloem and xylem are found in bundles, such as the veins of a leaf.

phlox any of a group of plants native to North America and Siberia. Phloxes are small with alternate leaves and clusters of showy white, pink, red, or purple flowers. (Genus *Phlox*, family Polemoniaceae.)

Phnom Penh or **Phnum Penh** capital of Cambodia, lying in the south of the country, at the confluence of the Mekong and Tonle Sap rivers, 210 km/130 mi northwest of Ho Chi Minh City, Vietnam; population (1994 est) 920,000. Industries include textiles, food processing, footwear, paper, tyres, and glassware.

phobia excessive irrational fear of an object or situation – for example, agoraphobia (fear of open spaces and crowded places), acrophobia (fear of heights), and claustrophobia (fear of enclosed places). *Behaviour therapy is one form of treatment.

Phoenicia ancient Greek name for northern *Canaan on the east coast of the Mediterranean. The Phoenician civilization flourished from about 1200 until the capture of Tyre by Alexander the Great in 332 BC. Seafaring traders and artisans, they are said to have circumnavigated Africa and established colonies in Cyprus, North Africa (for example, Carthage), Malta, Sicily, and Spain. Their cities (Tyre, Sidon, and Byblos were the main ones) were independent states ruled by hereditary kings but dominated by merchant ruling classes.

phoenix in Egyptian and Oriental mythology, a sacred bird born from the sun. The Egyptians believed it was also connected with the soul and the obelisk. In China the phoenix signified good and its appearance prosperity; its departure boded calamity. According to the Greek historian Herodotus, the creature visited the temple of the sun at Heliopolis every 500 years to bury its dead father, embalmed in a ball of myrrh. In another version, the phoenix placed itself on the city's burning altar or built a nest as a funeral pyre, and rose rejuvenated from the ashes. Only one phoenix existed at a time.

phonetics the identification, description, and classification of sounds used in articulate speech. These sounds are codified in the International Phonetic Alphabet (IPA), a highly modified version of the Roman alphabet.

phosphate salt or ester of phosphoric acid. Incomplete neutralization of phosphoric acid gives rise to acid phosphates. Phosphates are used as fertilizers, and are required for the development of healthy root systems. They are involved in many biochemical processes, often as part of complex molecules, such as *ATP.

phosphor any substance that is phosphorescent, that is, gives out visible light when it is illuminated by a beam of electrons or ultraviolet light. The television screen is coated on the inside with phosphors that glow when beams of electrons strike them. Fluorescent lamp tubes are also phosphor-coated. Phosphors are also used in Day-Glo paints, and as optical brighteners in detergents.

phosphorescence emission of light by certain substances after they have absorbed energy, whether from visible light, other electromagnetic radiation such as ultraviolet rays or X-rays, or cathode rays (a beam of electrons). When the stimulating energy is removed phosphorescence persists for more than 0.1 nanoseconds before ceasing (unlike *fluorescence, which stops immediately). See also *luminescence.

phosphorus chemical symbol P, (Greek *phosphoros* 'bearer of light') highly reactive, non-metallic element, atomic number 15, relative atomic mass 30.9738. It occurs in nature as phosphates (commonly in the form of the mineral apatite), and is essential to plant and animal life. Compounds of phosphorus are used in fertilizers, various organic chemicals, for matches and fireworks, and in plant and steel.

photocell or **photoelectric cell** device for measuring or detecting light or other electromagnetic radiation, since its electrical state is altered by the effect of light. In a **photoemissive** cell, the radiation causes electrons to be emitted and a current to flow (*photoelectric effect); a **photovoltaic** cell causes an *electromotive force to be generated in the presence of light across the boundary of two substances. A **photoconductive** cell, which contains a semiconductor, increases its conductivity when exposed to electromagnetic radiation.

photochemical reaction any chemical reaction in which light is produced or light initiates the reaction. Light can initiate reactions by exciting atoms or molecules and making them more reactive: the light energy becomes converted to chemical energy. Many photochemical reactions set up a *chain reaction and produce *free radicals.

photoelectric effect process by which electromagnetic radiation, including visible light, incident on a material releases an electric charge. It is commonly thought of as the emission of *electrons from a substance (usually a metallic surface) when it is struck by *photons (quanta of electromagnetic radiation), usually those of visible light or ultraviolet radiation.

photography process for reproducing permanent images on light-sensitive materials by various forms of radiant energy, including visible light, ultraviolet, infrared, X-rays, atomic radiations, and electron beams. Photography was developed in the 19th century; among the pioneers were Louis *Daguerre in France and William Henry *Fox Talbot in the UK. Colour photography dates from the early 20th century.

photogravure *printing process that uses a plate prepared photographically, covered with a pattern of recessed cells in which the ink is held. See *gravure.

photon in physics, the *elementary particle or 'package' (quantum) of energy in which light and other forms of electromagnetic radiation are emitted. The photon has both particle and wave properties; it has no charge, is considered massless but possesses momentum and energy. It is one of the *gauge bosons, and is the carrier of the *electromagnetic force, one of the fundamental forces of nature.

Photorealism or **Superrealism** or **Hyperrealism** style of painting and sculpture popular in the late 1960s and 1970s, especially in the USA, characterized by intense, photographic realism and attention to minute detail. The Photorealists' aim was to create a purely descriptive and objective record of peoples, places, and objects that was dispassionate to the extent of being almost surreal. Favoured subjects included scenes of American life, including shiny cars and motorcycles, diners, and neon lights. Leading exponents were US painters Chuck Close, Richard Estes, Audrey Flack, and Don Eddy.

photosynthesis process by which green plants trap light energy from sunlight in order to combine *carbon dioxide and *water to make high-energy chemicals – *glucose and other *carbohydrates. The simple sugar glucose provides the basic food for both plants and animals. For photosynthesis to occur, the plant must possess *chlorophyll (the green chemical that absorbs the energy from the sunlight) and must have a supply of carbon dioxide and water. Photosynthesis takes place inside *chloroplasts, which contain the enzymes and chlorophyll necessary for the process. They are found mainly in the leaf cells of plants. The by-product of photosynthesis, oxygen, is of great importance to all living organisms, and virtually all atmospheric oxygen has originated from photosynthesis. (See diagram, p. 716.)

phototropism movement of part of a plant toward or away from a source of light. Leaves are positively phototropic, detecting the source of light and orientating themselves to receive the maximum amount.

Phrygia former kingdom of western Asia covering the Anatolian plateau. It was inhabited in ancient times by an Indo-European people and achieved great prosperity in the 8th century BC under a line of kings bearing in turn the names Gordius and Midas, but then fell under Lydian rule. From Phrygia the cult of the Earth goddess Cybele was introduced into Greece and Rome.

phylloxera plant-eating insect of the family Phylloxeridae, closely related to the aphids.

phylogeny historical sequence of changes that occurs in a given species during the course of its evolution. It was once erroneously associated with ontogeny (the process of development of a living organism).

phylum plural **phyla**, major grouping in biological classification. Mammals, birds, reptiles, amphibians, fishes, and tunicates belong to the phylum Chordata; the phylum Mollusca consists of snails, slugs, mussels, clams, squid, and octopuses; the phylum Porifera contains sponges; and the phylum Echinodermata includes starfish, sea urchins, and sea cucumbers. In classifying plants (where the term 'division' often takes the place of 'phylum'), there are between four and nine phyla depending on the criteria used; all flowering

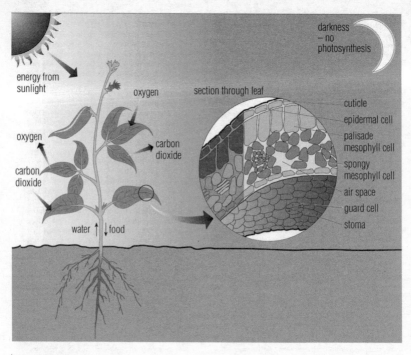

photosynthesis Process by which green plants and some bacteria manufacture carbohydrates from water and atmospheric carbon dioxide, using the energy of sunlight. Photosynthesis depends on the ability of chlorophyll molecules within plant cells to trap the energy of light, in order to split water molecules, giving off oxygen as a by-product. The hydrogen of the water molecules is then used to reduce carbon dioxide to simple carbohydrates.

plants belong to a single phylum, Angiospermata, and all conifers to another, Gymnospermata. Related phyla are grouped together in a *kingdom; phyla are subdivided into *classes.

physical chemistry branch of chemistry concerned with examining the relationships between the chemical compositions of substances and the physical properties that they display. Most chemical reactions exhibit some physical phenomenon (change of state, temperature, pressure, or volume, or the use or production of electricity), and the measurement and study of such phenomena has led to many chemical theories and laws.

physics branch of science concerned with the laws that govern the structure of the universe, and the investigation of the properties of matter and energy and their interactions. Before the 19th century, physics was known as **natural philosophy**.

physiology branch of biology that deals with the functioning of living organisms, as opposed to anatomy, which studies their structures.

physiotherapy treatment of injury and disease by physical means such as exercise, heat, manipulation, massage, and electrical stimulation.

phytomenadione one form of vitamin K, a fat-soluble chemical found in green vegetables. It is involved in the production of prothrombin, which is essential in blood clotting. It is given to newborns to prevent potentially fatal brain haemorrhages.

pi symbol π, ratio of the circumference of a circle to its diameter. Pi is an irrational number: it cannot be expressed as the ratio of two integers, and its expression as a decimal never terminates and never starts recurring. The value of pi is 3.1415926, correct to seven decimal places. Common approximations to pi are $^{22}/_7$ and 3.14, although the value 3 can be used as a rough estimation.

piano *or* **pianoforte** keyboard instrument. The sound is produced when a depressed key strikes the strings with a felt-covered hammer, causing them to vibrate. It is therefore a form of mechanized *dulcimer, a percussion instrument. It is different from the earlier *harpsichord, a mechanized harp, where the strings are plucked. The piano is capable of a wide range of dynamics from soft (Italian *piano*) to loud (Italian *forte*), hence its name. The first piano was built in 1704 and introduced in 1709 by Bartolommeo Cristofori, a harpsichord maker from Padua. It uses a clever mechanism to make the keyboard touch-sensitive. Extensively developed during the 18th century, the piano became popular among many composers, although it was not until 1768 that Johann Christian *Bach gave one of the first public recitals on the instrument.

Picardy French **Picardie**, region of northern France, bordered by the English Channel to the west and Champagne to the south, including the Aisne, Oise, and Somme *départements*; area 19,399 sq km/7,490 sq mi; population (1999 est) 1,857,500. Most of Picardy is occupied by a chalky limestone plateau, while its central Somme River valley is marshy in many areas. Industries include chemicals and metals. Principal towns include Abbeville and Amiens; the latter is the administrative centre and was capital of the old province. Boulogne-sur-Mer and Calais are major fishing and commercial seaports; Le Touquet and Le Crotoy are tourist resorts, particularly for the British.

Picasso, Pablo Ruiz y (1881–1973) Spanish artist, chiefly active in France. Picasso was one of the most inventive and prolific talents in 20th-century art. His Blue Period 1901–04 and Rose Period 1904–06 preceded the revolutionary *Les Demoiselles d'Avignon* (1907; Museum of Modern Art, New York), which paved the way for *cubism. In the early 1920s he was considered a leader of the surrealist movement. From the 1930s his work included sculpture, ceramics, and graphic works in a wide variety of media; in his life he created over 20,000 works of art. Among his best-known paintings is *Guernica* (1937; Museo Nacional Centro de Arte Reina Sofía, Madrid), a comment on the bombing of civilians in the Spanish Civil War.

piccolo woodwind instrument, the smallest member of the *flute family, with a brilliant and penetrating tone. It sounds an octave higher than the flute, and for this reason is sometimes known as the *ottavino* (Italian, 'octave'). Antonio Vivaldi composed three concertos for the piccolo, and it can also be heard in the first movement of Sergey Prokofiev's *Lieutenant Kijé* (1934).

Pickford, Mary (1893–1979) stage name of Gladys Mary Smith, Canadian-born US actor. The first star of the silent screen, she was known as 'America's Sweetheart,' and played innocent ingenue roles into her thirties. She and her second husband (from 1920), Douglas *Fairbanks Sr, were known as 'the world's sweethearts'. With her husband, Charlie *Chaplin, and D W *Griffith she founded United Artists studio in 1919. For many years she was the wealthiest and most influential woman in Hollywood.

Pict Roman term for a member of the peoples of northern Scotland, possibly meaning 'painted' (tattooed). Of pre-Celtic origin, and speaking a Celtic language which died out in about the 10th century, the Picts are thought to have inhabited much of England before the arrival of the Celtic Britons. They were united with the Celtic Scots under the rule of Kenneth MacAlpin in 844. Their greatest monument is a series of carved stones, whose symbols remain undeciphered.

pidgin language any of various trade jargons, contact languages, or *lingua francas arising in ports and markets where people of different linguistic backgrounds meet for commercial and other purposes. Usually a pidgin language is a rough blend of the vocabulary of one (often dominant) language with the syntax or grammar of one or more other (often dependent) groups. Pidgin English in various parts of the world, *français petit negre*, and Bazaar Hindi or Hindustani are examples of pidgins that have served long-term purposes to the extent of being acquired by children as one of their everyday languages. At this point they become *creole languages.

Piedmont Italian **Piemonte**, region of northern Italy, comprising the provinces of Alessandria, Asti, Biella, Cuneo, Novara, Turin, Verbania, and Vercelli; area 25,399 sq km/9,807 sq mi; population (2001 est) 4,166,500. One of the richest regions in Italy, it borders Switzerland to the north and France to the west, and is surrounded, except to the east, by the Alps and the Apennines. The regional capital is Turin. Piedmont also includes the fertile Po valley. Products include rice, fruit, grain, wine, cattle, cars, and textiles. The movement for the unification of Italy started in the 19th century in Piedmont, under the House of Savoy.

Piero della Francesca (c. 1420–1492) Painter from Borgo San Sepulcro in Umbria. Active in Arezzo and Urbino, he was one of the major artists of the 15th century. His work has a solemn stillness and unusually solid figures, luminous colour, and carefully calculated compositional harmonies. It includes several important fresco series and panel paintings such as the *Flagellation of Christ* (c. 1455; Ducal Palace, Urbino), which is remarkable for its use of perspective.

Pietro da Cortona (1596–1669) born Pietro Berrettini, Italian painter and architect. He was a major influence in the development of the high baroque. His enormous fresco *Allegory of Divine Providence* (1633–39; Barberini Palace, Rome) glorifies his patron the pope and the Barberini family, and gives a convincing illusion of reality.

piezoelectric effect property of some crystals (for example, quartz) to develop an electromotive force or voltage across opposite faces when subjected to tension or compression, and, conversely, to expand or contract in size when subjected to an electromotive force. Piezoelectric crystal oscillators are used as frequency standards (for example, replacing balance wheels in watches), and for producing ultrasound. Crystalline quartz is a good example of a piezoelectric material.

pig any even-toed hoofed mammal of the family Suidae. They are omnivorous, and have simple, non-ruminating stomachs and thick hides. The Middle Eastern **wild boar** *Sus scrofa* is the ancestor of domesticated breeds; it is 1.5 m/4.5 ft long and 1 m/3 ft high, with formidable tusks, but not naturally aggressive. The smallest member of the pig family is the **pygmy hog** *Sus salvanus*. Males are 65 cm long (25 cm at the shoulder) and weigh 8–9 kg.

pigeon *or* **dove** bird of the family Columbidae, order Columbiformes, distinguished by its large crop, which becomes glandular in the breeding season and secretes a milky fluid ('pigeon's milk') that aids digestion of food for the young. There are many species and they are found worldwide.

Piggott, Lester Keith (1935–) English jockey. He adopted a unique high riding style and is renowned as a brilliant tactician. A champion jockey 11 times between 1960 and 1982, he rode a record nine *Derby winners. Piggott retired from riding in 1985 and took up training. In 1987 he was imprisoned for tax evasion.

He returned to racing in 1990 and has ridden over 5,300 winners in 28 countries, including a record 30 English classics. He retired as a jockey for the second time in September 1995.

pig iron or **cast iron** iron produced in a *blast furnace. It contains around 4% carbon plus some other impurities.

Pigs, Bay of inlet on the south coast of Cuba about 145 km/90 mi southwest of Havana. It was the site of an unsuccessful invasion attempt to overthrow the government of Fidel *Castro by some 1,500 US-sponsored Cuban exiles 17–20 April 1961; 1,173 were taken prisoner. The failure of the invasion strengthened Castro's power in Cuba and his links to the USSR. It also sparked the *Cuban missile crisis of 1962.

pika or **mouse-hare** any small mammal of the family Ochotonidae, belonging to the order Lagomorpha (rabbits and hares). The single genus *Ochotona* contains about 15 species, most of which live in mountainous regions of Asia, although two species are native to North America.

pike any of a family Esocidae in the order Salmoniformes, of slender, freshwater bony fishes with narrow pointed heads and sharp, pointed teeth. The northern pike *Esox lucius*, of North America and Eurasia, may reach a length of 2.2 m/7 ft and a weight of 9 kg/20 lb.

pikeperch any of various freshwater members of the perch family, resembling pikes, especially the walleye *Stizostedion vitreum*, common in Europe, western Asia, and North America. It reaches over 1 m/3 ft.

Pilate, Pontius (died *c.* AD 36) Roman procurator of Judea AD 26–36. The New Testament Gospels describe his reluctant ordering of Jesus' crucifixion, but there has been considerable debate about his actual role in it.

pilchard any of various small, oily members of the herring family, Clupeidae, especially the commercial sardine of Europe *Sardina pilchardus*, and the California sardine *Sardinops sagax*.

pilgrimage journey to sacred places inspired by religious devotion. For Hindus, the holy places include *Varanasi and the purifying River *Ganges; for Buddhists, the places connected with the crises of *Buddha's career; for the ancient Greeks, shrines such as those at Delphi and Ephesus; for Jews, the Western Wall or *Wailing Wall in Jerusalem; for Muslims, *Mecca and *Medina; and for Roman Catholics, *Lourdes in France, among others. Pilgrimages are usually undertaken as opportunities to reflect upon and deepen one's religious faith, or to earn religious merit.

Pilgrimage of Grace rebellion against *Henry VIII of England 1536–37, originating in Yorkshire and Lincolnshire. The uprising was directed against the policies of the monarch (such as the Dissolution of the Monasteries during the *Reformation and the effects of the *enclosure of common land).

Pilgrim Fathers or **Pilgrims** emigrants who sailed from Plymouth, Devon, England, in the *Mayflower* on 16 September 1620 to found the first colony in New England, North America, at New Plymouth, Massachusetts. Of the 102 passengers about a third were Puritan refugees.

Pilgrim's Progress allegory by John Bunyan, published in 1678–84, that describes the journey through life to the Celestial City of a man called Christian. On his way through the Slough of Despond, the House Beautiful, Vanity Fair, Doubting Castle, and other landmarks, he meets a number of allegorical figures.

Pill, the commonly used term for the contraceptive pill, based on female hormones. The combined pill, which contains synthetic hormones similar to oestrogen and progesterone, stops the release of eggs, and makes the mucus produced by the cervix hostile to sperm. It is the most effective form of contraception apart from sterilization, being more than 99% effective.

pilotfish small marine fish *Naucrates ductor* of the family Carangidae, which also includes pompanos. It hides below sharks, turtles, or boats, using the shade as a base from which to prey on smaller fish. It is found in all warm oceans and grows to about 36 cm/1.2 ft.

pimento or **allspice** any of several evergreen trees belonging to the myrtle family, found in tropical parts of the New World. The dried berries of the species *P. dioica* are used as a spice (see *allspice). Also, a sweet variety of *capsicum pepper (more correctly spelled pimiento). (Pimento genus *Pimenta*, family Myrtaceae.)

pimpernel any of a group of plants belonging to the primrose family, comprising about 30 species mostly native to Western Europe. The European scarlet pimpernel (*A. arvensis*) grows in cornfields, the small star-shaped flowers opening only in full sunshine. It is naturalized in North America. (Genus *Anagallis*, family Primulaceae.)

pine any of a group of coniferous, *resin-producing trees with evergreen needle-shaped leaves; there are about 70–100 species of pines, making them the largest family of *conifers. (Genus *Pinus*, family Pinaceae.)

pineal body or **pineal gland** cone-shaped outgrowth of the vertebrate brain. In some lower vertebrates, it develops a rudimentary lens and retina, which show it to be derived from an eye, or pair of eyes, situated on the top of the head in ancestral vertebrates. In fishes that can change colour to match their background, the pineal perceives the light level and controls the colour change. In birds, the pineal detects changes in daylight and stimulates breeding behaviour as spring approaches. Mammals also have a pineal gland, but it is located deeper within the brain. It secretes a hormone, melatonin, thought to influence rhythms of activity. In humans, it is a small piece of tissue attached by a stalk to the rear wall of the third ventricle of the brain.

pineapple large, juicy fruit of the pineapple plant, which belongs to the bromeliad family and is native to South and Central America but now cultivated in many other tropical areas, such as Hawaii and Queensland, Australia. The plant's mauvish flowers are produced in the second year, and afterwards join with their bracts (specialized leaves protecting the buds) to form the fleshy fruit, which looks like a giant cone. (Genus *Ananas comosus*, family Bromeliaceae.)

Pinero, Arthur Wing (1855–1934) English dramatist. A leading exponent of the 'well-made' play, he enjoyed great contemporary success with his farces, beginning with *The Magistrate* (1885). More substantial social drama followed with *The Second Mrs Tanqueray* (1893), and comedies including *Trelawny of the 'Wells'* (1898). He was knighted in 1909.

pink any of a group of annual or perennial plants that have stems with characteristic swellings (nodes) and scented flowers ranging in colour from white through pink to purple. Members of the pink family include carnations, sweet williams, and baby's breath (*Gypsophila paniculata*). (Genus *Dianthus*, family Carophyllaceae.)

Pink Floyd British psychedelic rock group, formed in 1965. The original members were Syd Barrett (1946–), Roger Waters (1944–), Richard Wright (1945–), and Nick Mason (1945–). Dave Gilmour (1944–) joined the band in 1968. Their albums include *The Dark Side of the Moon* (1973) and *The Wall* (1979).

pinnate leaf leaf that is divided up into many small leaflets, arranged in rows along either side of a midrib, as in ash trees (*Fraxinus*). It is a type of compound leaf. Each leaflet is known as a **pinna**, and where the pinnae are themselves divided, the secondary divisions are known as pinnules.

Pinochet (Ugarte), Augusto (1915–) Chilean military dictator 1973–89. He came to power when a coup backed by the US Central Intelligence Agency (CIA) ousted and killed President Salvador Allende. He governed ruthlessly, crushing all political opposition (including more than 3,000 people who 'vanished' or were killed), but also presiding over the country's economic expansion in the 1980s, stimulated further by free-market reforms. He was voted out of power when general elections were held in December 1989, but remained head of the armed forces until March 1998 when he became senator-for-life. In January 2001, he was arrested on the charge of organizing the killings of 77 left-wing activists and union leaders. However, in July 2001, Chile's appeal court ruled that he was mentally unfit to stand trial, ending lengthy efforts to prosecute him for human rights abuses.

pint symbol pt, imperial dry or liquid measure of capacity equal to 20 fluid ounces, half a quart, one-eighth of a gallon, or 0.568 litre. In the USA, a liquid pint is equal to 0.473 litre, while a dry pint is equal to 0.550 litre.

Pinter, Harold (1930–) English dramatist and poet. He specializes in the tragicomedy of the breakdown of communication, broadly in the tradition of the Theatre of the Absurd (see *Absurd, Theatre of the* – for example, *The Birthday Party* (1958; filmed 1968) and *The Caretaker* (1960). Later plays include *The Homecoming* (1965), *Old Times* (1971), *Betrayal* (1978), *Moonlight* (1993), and *Celebration* (2000). His anthology *Various Voices: Prose, Poetry, Politics, 1948–1998* was published in 1998.

pinworm *nematode worm Enterobius vermicularis*, an intestinal parasite of humans.

Pinyin Chinese phonetic alphabet approved in 1956 by the People's Republic of China, and used since 1979 in transcribing all names of people and places from Chinese ideograms into other languages using the English/Roman alphabet. For example, the former transcription Chou En-lai becomes Zhou Enlai, Hua Kuo-feng became Hua Guofeng, Teng Hsiao-ping became Deng Xiaoping, and Peking became Beijing.

pion *or* **pi meson** in physics, a subatomic particle with a neutral form (mass 135 MeV) and a charged form (mass 139 MeV). The charged pion decays into muons and neutrinos and the neutral form decays into gamma-ray photons. They belong to the *hadron class of *elementary particles.

pipefish any of various long-snouted, thin, pipelike marine fishes in the same family (Syngnathidae) as seahorses. The great pipefish *Syngnathus acus* grows up to 50 cm/1.6 ft. The male has a brood pouch for eggs and developing young, in which he carries the eggs from three to four different females. The eggs hatch in five to six weeks as tiny versions of the adults; there is no larval stage.

pipit any of various sparrow-sized ground-dwelling songbirds of the genus *Anthus* of the family Motacillidae, order Passeriformes.

piracy the taking of a ship, aircraft, or any of its contents, from lawful ownership, punishable under international law by the court of any country where the pirate may be found or taken. When the craft is taken over to alter its destination, or its passengers held to ransom, the term is *hijacking. Piracy is also used to describe infringement of *copyright.

Pirandello, Luigi (1867–1936) Italian dramatist, novelist, and short-story writer. His plays, which often deal with the themes of illusion and reality, and the tragicomic absurdity of life, include *Sei personaggi in cerca d'autore/Six Characters in Search of an Author* (1921), and *Enrico IV/Henry IV* (1922). Among his novels are *L'esclusa/The Outcast* (1901), *Il fu Mattia Pascal/The Late Mattia Pascal* (1904), and *I vecchi e i giovani/The Old and the Young* (1909). He was awarded the Nobel Prize for Literature in 1934.

Piranesi, Giambattista (Giovanni Battista) (1720–1778) Italian architect and graphic artist. He made powerful etchings of Roman antiquities and was an influential theorist of architecture, advocating imaginative use of Roman models. His series of etchings *Carceri d'Invenzione/Prisons of Invention* (*c.* 1745–61) depicts imaginary prisons, vast and gloomy.

piranha any South American freshwater fish of the genus *Serrusalmus*, in the same order as cichlids. They can grow to 60 cm/2 ft long, and have razor-sharp teeth; some species may rapidly devour animals, especially if attracted by blood.

Pisces inconspicuous zodiac constellation, mainly in the northern hemisphere between *Aries and *Aquarius, near *Pegasus. It is represented as two fish tied together by their tails. The Circlet, a delicate ring of stars, marks the head of the western fish in Pisces. The constellation contains the **vernal equinox**, the point at which the Sun's path around the sky (the **ecliptic**) crosses the celestial equator (see *celestial sphere). The Sun reaches this point around 21 March each year as it passes through Pisces from mid-March to late April. In astrology, the dates for Pisces are between about 19 February and 20 March (see *precession).

Piscis Austrinus *or* **Southern Fish** constellation of the southern hemisphere near *Capricornus. Its brightest star is the first-magnitude *Fomalhaut.

Pisistratus (*or* Peisistratos) (*c.* 605–527 BC) Athenian tyrant. Although of noble family, he became the leader of the anti-aristocratic party, and seized power in 561 BC. He was twice expelled, but recovered power securely from 546 BC until his death. Ruling as a tyrant under constitutional forms (the historians Herodotus and Thucydides both attest that he left the rules and regulations of *Solon as he found them), Pisistratus was a patron of the arts and literature and the first to have the poems of *Homer written down.

He introduced the Dionysiac rural festivals into Athens. He was succeeded by his sons Hippias and Hipparchus.

Pissarro, Camille (1830–1903) French painter. A leading member of the Impressionists, he experimented with various styles, including *pointillism, in the 1880s. Though he is closely linked with pictures of the French countryside and peasant life, he also painted notable street scenes, as in *Boulevard Montmartre* (1897; Hermitage, St Petersburg).

pistachio deciduous tree of the cashew family, native to Europe and Asia, whose green nuts are eaten salted or used to enhance and flavour food, especially ice cream. (Genus *Pistacia vera*, family Anacardiaceae.)

pistil general term for the female part of a flower, either referring to one single *carpel or a group of several fused carpels.

piston any disc or cyclinder, circular in cross-section, used in reciprocating engines (steam, petrol, diesel oil) to harness power. Pistons are driven up and down in cylinders by expanding steam or hot gases. They pass on their motion via a connecting rod and crank to a crankshaft, which turns the driving wheels. In a pump or compressor, the role of the piston is reversed, being used to move gases and liquids. See also *internal-combustion engine.

pit bull terrier *or* **American pit bull terrier** variety of dog that was developed in the USA solely as a fighting dog. It usually measures about 50 cm/20 in at the shoulder and weighs roughly 23 kg/50 lb, but there are no established criteria since it is not recognized as a breed by either the American or British Kennel Clubs. Selective breeding for physical strength and aggression has created a dog unsuitable for life in the modern community.

Pitcairn Islands British colony in Polynesia, 5,300 km/3,300 mi northeast of New Zealand; area 47 sq km/18 sq mi; population (1996) 58. The capital is Adamstown. Products are coconuts, bananas, breadfruit, yams, pineapples, tomatoes, oranges, and pineapples; souvenirs are sold to passing ships.

pitch in chemistry, a black, sticky substance, hard when cold, but liquid when hot, used for waterproofing, roofing, and paving. It is made by the destructive distillation of wood or coal tar, and has been used since antiquity for caulking wooden ships.

pitch in mechanics, the distance between the adjacent threads of a screw or bolt. When a screw is turned through one full turn it moves a distance equal to the pitch of its thread. A screw thread is a simple type of machine, acting like a rolled-up inclined plane, or ramp (as may be illustrated by rolling a long paper triangle around a pencil). A screw has a mechanical advantage greater than one.

pitch in music, the technical term used to describe how high or low a note is. It depends on the frequency (number of vibrations per second) of the sound, which is measured in hertz (Hz). Pitch also refers to the standard to which instruments are tuned. Nowadays the internationally agreed-upon pitch is the A above middle C (A4 or a'), which has a frequency of 440 Hz (vibrations per second). This is often known as concert pitch. Pitch can now be measured accurately by electronic tuning devices. These are beginning to replace the traditional tuning fork, but it is still normal practice for orchestras to tune to an oboe playing A4.

pitchblende *or* **uraninite** brownish-black mineral, the major uranium ore, consisting mainly of uranium oxide (UO_2). It also contains some lead (the final, stable product of uranium decay) and variable amounts of most of the naturally occurring radioactive elements, which are products of either the decay or the fissioning of uranium isotopes. The uranium yield is 50–80%; it is also a source of radium, polonium, and actinium. Pitchblende was first studied by Pierre and Marie *Curie, who found radium and polonium in its residues in 1898.

pitcher plant any of various *insectivorous plants, the leaves of which are shaped like a pitcher and filled with a fluid that traps and digests insects. (Genera especially *Nepenthes* and *Sarracenia*, family Sarraceniaceae.)

Pitman, Isaac (1813–1897) English teacher and inventor of Pitman's shorthand. He studied Samuel Taylor's scheme for shorthand writing, and in 1837 published his own system, *Stenographic Soundhand*, fast, accurate, and adapted for use in many languages. He was knighted in 1894.

pitot tube instrument that measures fluid (gas or liquid) flow. It is used to measure the speed of aircraft, and works by sensing pressure differences in different directions in the airstream. It was invented in the 1730s by the French scientist Henri Pitot (1695–1771).

Pitt, William, the Elder (1708–1778) 1st Earl of Chatham, British Whig politician, 'the Great Commoner'. As paymaster of the forces 1746–55, he broke with tradition by refusing to enrich himself; he was dismissed for attacking the Duke of Newcastle, the prime minister. He served effectively as prime minister in coalition governments 1756–61 (successfully conducting the Seven Years' War) and 1766–68. He was created an earl in 1766.

Pitt, William, the Younger (1759–1806) British Tory prime minister 1783–1801 and 1804–06. He raised the importance of the House of Commons, clamped down on corruption, carried out fiscal reforms, and effected the union with Ireland. He attempted to keep Britain at peace but underestimated the importance of the French Revolution and became embroiled in wars with France from 1793; he died on hearing of Napoleon's victory at Austerlitz.

Pittsburgh called 'City of Bridges', second-largest city in Pennsylvania, USA, in Allegheny County at the confluence of the Allegheny and Monongahela rivers, forming the Ohio River; population (2000 est) 334,600. It is a business and financial centre with one of the largest river ports in the world (it is the 11th-largest port in the USA overall and the largest inland port). High-technology and healthcare services dominate an economy formerly based on iron, steel, heavy engineering, and glass industries.

pituitary gland major *endocrine gland of vertebrates, situated in the centre of the brain. It is attached to the *hypothalamus by a stalk. The pituitary consists of two lobes. The posterior lobe is an extension of the hypothalamus, and is in effect nervous tissue. It stores two hormones synthesized in the hypothalamus: ADH and oxytocin. The anterior lobe secretes six hormones, some of which control the activities of other glands (thyroid, gonads, and adrenal cortex); others are direct-acting hormones affecting milk secretion and controlling growth.

Pius 12 popes, including:

Pius V, Antonio Etrislieri (1504–1572) Pope from 1566. His early career was in the Inquisition, a role which brought him the support of Paul IV who made him a cardinal in 1558. From the beginning of his own pontificate, he stressed his determination to carry out the reforms of the Council of Trent. He also excommunicated Elizabeth I of England, and organized the expedition against the Turks that won the victory of *Lepanto.

Pius IX (1792–1878) Pope from 1846. He never accepted the incorporation of the papal states and of Rome in the kingdom of Italy. He proclaimed the dogmas of the Immaculate Conception of the Virgin in 1854 and papal infallibility in 1870; his pontificate was the longest in history.

Pius XII (1876–1958) born Eugenio Pacelli, Pope from 1939. He was conservative in doctrine and politics, and condemned modernism. In 1950 he proclaimed the dogma of the bodily assumption of the Virgin Mary, and in 1951 restated the doctrine (strongly criticized by many) that the life of an infant must not be sacrificed to save a mother in labour. He was criticized for failing to speak out against atrocities committed by the Germans during World War II and has been accused of collusion with the Nazis.

pixel derived from picture element, single dot on a computer screen. All screen images are made up of a collection of pixels, with each pixel being either off (dark) or on (illuminated, possibly in colour). The number of pixels available determines the screen's resolution. Typical resolutions of microcomputer screens vary from 320 × 200 pixels to 800 × 600 pixels, but screens with 1,024 × 768 pixels or more are now common for high-quality graphic (pictorial) displays.

Pizarro, Francisco (1475–1541) Spanish conquistador. He took part in the expeditions of Vasco Núñez de *Balboa and others. He began exploring the northwest coast of South America in 1524, and, with the permission of the king of Spain, conquered Peru in 1531 with 180 followers. The Inca king Atahualpa was seized and murdered. In 1535 Pizarro founded the Peruvian city of Lima. Internal feuding led to his assassination.

pizzicato (Italian 'pinched') in music, an instruction to string players to pluck the strings with the fingers instead of using the bow. It is frequently abbreviated to 'pizz'.

PKK abbreviation for Workers' Party of Kurdistan, a Kurdish guerrilla organization.

placebo (Latin 'I will please') any harmless substance, often called a 'sugar pill', that has no active ingredient, but may nevertheless bring about improvement in the patient's condition.

placenta organ that attaches the developing *embryo or *fetus to the *uterus (womb) in placental mammals (mammals other than marsupials, platypuses, and echidnas). Composed of maternal and embryonic tissue, it links the blood supply of the embryo to the blood supply of the mother, allowing the exchange of oxygen, nutrients, and waste products. The two blood systems are not in direct contact, but are separated by thin membranes, with materials diffusing across from one system to the other. The placenta also produces hormones that maintain and regulate pregnancy. It is shed as part of the afterbirth.

plague term applied to any epidemic disease with a high mortality rate, but it usually refers to bubonic plague. This is a disease transmitted by fleas (carried by the black rat), which infect the sufferer with the bacillus *Yersinia pestis*. An early symptom is swelling of lymph nodes, usually in the armpit and groin; such swellings are called 'buboes'. It causes virulent blood poisoning and the death rate is high. The European epidemics in the years from 1600 to 1750 were among the most devastating in human history. The waves of the plague which struck northern Italy and Tuscany in 1630 were believed to have killed up to 70% of the population.

plaice fish *Pleuronectes platessa* belonging to the flatfish group, abundant in the North Atlantic. It is white beneath and brownish with orange spots on the 'eyed' side. It can grow to 75 cm/2.5 ft long and weigh about 2 kg/4.5 lb. Plaice feed on molluscs, crustaceans, and worms, and may live for up to 30 years.

Plaid Cymru (Welsh 'Party of Wales') Welsh nationalist political party established in 1925. Its aim is separation from and independence of the UK, in order to safeguard the culture, language, and economic life of Wales. In 2001 it had about 15,000 members. In 1966 the first Plaid Cymru member of Parliament was elected. Four Plaid Cymru MPs were returned in both the 1997 and 2001 general elections. At Westminster, the Plaid Cymru MP's form a single parliamentary grouping with the Scottish National Party, following a formal pact signed in 1986. The party has 17 seats in the Welsh Assembly, and two members in the European Parliament (2001).

plain *or* **grassland** land, usually flat, upon which grass predominates. The plains cover large areas of the Earth's surface, especially between the *deserts of the tropics and the *rainforests of the Equator, and have rain in one season only. In such regions the *climate belts move north and south during the year, bringing rainforest conditions at one time and desert conditions at another. Temperate plains include the North European Plain, the High Plains of the USA and Canada, and the Russian Plain (also known as the *steppe).

plainchant type of medieval church music; see *plainsong.

Plains Indian member of any of the *American Indian peoples of the *Great Plains, a region of North America extending over 3,000 km/2,000 mi from Alberta, Canada, to Texas, USA. The Plains Indians were drawn from diverse linguistic stocks fringing the Plains. They shared many cultural traits, especially the nomadic hunting of the North American buffalo (bison) herds after horses became available early in the 18th century. The Plains Indians provide the traditional image of American Indians as war-painted warrior-horseriders, living in conical tepees, and dressing in buffalo robes and eagle-feather bonnets. The various peoples include the Blackfeet, Cheyenne, Comanche, Pawnee, and the *Sioux or Lakota.

plainsong *or* **plainchant** traditional single-line chant melodies used for singing the texts of the Christian church. Plainsong was first adopted by Ambrose, Bishop of Milan, and then by Pope Gregory in the 6th century, the latter being referred to as *Gregorian chant. It is properly sung in unison, without harmony and with no definitely measured rhythms. Its groupings of notes have, however, a strongly rhythmic character, but it resembles the free rhythm of prose, whereas that of measured music is comparable to the rhythm of verse. The old *notation on a stave of four lines, with square or diamond-shaped notes and ligatures, is still used for plainsong.

Planck, Max Karl Ernst Ludwig (1858–1947)

German physicist who was awarded the Nobel Prize for Physics in 1918 for his formulation of the *quantum theory in 1900. His research into the manner in which heated bodies radiate energy led him to report that energy is emitted only in indivisible amounts, called 'quanta', the magnitudes of which are proportional to the frequency of the radiation. His discovery ran counter to classical physics and is held to have marked the commencement of modern science.

Planck's constant symbol h, fundamental constant that relates the energy (E) of one quantum of electromagnetic radiation (a 'packet' of energy; see *quantum theory) to the frequency (f) of its radiation by $E = hf$. Its value is 6.6262×10^{-34} joule seconds.

plane in botany, any of several trees belonging to the plane family. Species include the oriental plane (*P. orientalis*), a favourite plantation tree of the Greeks and Romans, and the American plane or buttonwood (*P. occidentalis*). A hybrid of these two is the London plane (*P. x acerifolia*), with palmate, usually five-lobed leaves, which is widely planted in cities for its resistance to air pollution. (Genus *Platanus*, family Platanaceae.)

planet (Greek 'wanderer') large celestial body in orbit around a star, composed of rock, metal, or gas. There are nine planets in the *Solar System orbiting the *Sun: Mercury, Venus, Earth, Mars, Jupiter, Saturn, Neptune, Uranus, and Pluto. The inner four, called the **terrestrial planets**, are small and rocky, and have few natural *satellites. The outer planets, with the exception of Pluto, are called the **major planets**, and have denser atmospheres consisting mainly of hydrogen and helium gases, and many natural satellites. The largest planet in the Solar System is Jupiter (about 780 million km/490 million mi from the Sun) with a diameter of 140,000 km/ 87,500 mi, which contains a mass greater than all the other planets combined. The smallest (and furthest from the Sun at about 5,900 million km/3,600 million mi) is Pluto with a diameter of 2,300 km/1,400 mi.

planetary nebula shell of gas thrown off by a star at the end of its life. Planetary nebulae have nothing to do with planets. They were named by German-born English astronomer William Herschel, who thought their rounded shape resembled the disc of a planet. After a star such as the Sun has expanded to become a *red giant, its outer layers are ejected into space to form a planetary nebula, leaving the core as a *white dwarf at the centre.

plankton small, often microscopic, forms of plant and animal life that live in the upper layers of fresh and salt water, and are an important source of food for larger animals. Marine plankton is concentrated in areas where rising currents bring mineral salts to the surface.

plant organism that carries out *photosynthesis, has cellulose cell walls and complex cells, and is immobile. A few parasitic plants have lost the ability to photosynthesize but are still considered to be plants. Plants are *autotrophs, that is, they make carbohydrates from water and carbon dioxide, and

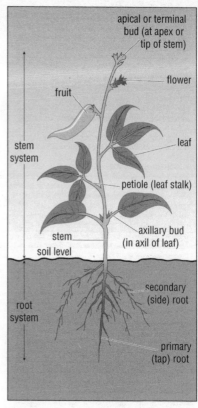

plant The external anatomy of a typical flowering plant.

are the primary producers in all food chains, so that all animal life is dependent on them. They play a vital part in the carbon cycle, removing carbon dioxide from the atmosphere and generating oxygen. The study of plants is known as *botany.

Plantagenet English royal house, which reigned from 1154 to 1399, and whose name comes from the nickname of Geoffrey, Count of Anjou (1113–1151), father of Henry II, who often wore in his hat a sprig of broom, *planta genista*. In the 1450s, Richard, Duke of York, took 'Plantagenet' as a surname to emphasize his superior claim to the throne over that of Henry VI.

plantain any of a group of northern temperate plants. The great plantain (*P. major*) is low-growing with large oval leaves close to the ground, grooved stalks, and spikes of green flowers with purple anthers (in which the pollen matures) followed by seeds, which are used in bird food. (Genus *Plantago*, family Plantaginaceae.)

plant classification taxonomy or *classification of plants. Originally the plant kingdom included bacteria, diatoms, dinoflagellates, fungi, and slime moulds, but these are not now thought of as plants. The groups that are always classified as plants are the bryophytes (mosses and liverworts), pteridophytes (ferns, horsetails, and club mosses), gymnosperms (conifers, yews, cycads, and ginkgos), and angiosperms (flowering plants). The angiosperms are split into monocotyledons (for example, orchids, grasses, lilies) and dicotyledons (for example, oak, buttercup, geranium, and daisy).

plaque any abnormal deposit on a body surface, especially the thin, transparent film of sticky protein (called mucin) and bacteria on tooth surfaces. If not removed, this film forms tartar (calculus), promotes tooth decay, and leads to gum disease. Another form of plaque is a deposit of fatty or fibrous material in the walls of blood vessels causing atheroma.

plasma in biology, the liquid component of the *blood. It is a straw-coloured fluid, largely composed of water (around 90%), in which a number of substances are dissolved. These include a variety of proteins (around 7%) such as fibrinogen (important in *blood clotting), inorganic mineral salts such as sodium and calcium, waste products such as *urea, traces of *hormones, and *antibodies to defend against infection.

plasma in physics, ionized gas produced at extremely high temperatures, as in the Sun and other stars. It contains positive and negative charges in equal numbers. It is a good electrical conductor. In thermonuclear reactions the plasma produced is confined through the use of magnetic fields.

plasmid small, mobile piece of *DNA found in bacteria that, for example, confers antibiotic resistance, used in *genetic engineering. Plasmids are separate from the bacterial chromosome but still multiply during cell growth. Their size ranges from 3% to 20% of the size of the chromosome. Some plasmids carry 'fertility genes' that enable them to move from one bacterium to another and transfer genetic information between strains. Plasmid genes determine a wide variety of bacterial properties including resistance to antibiotics and the ability to produce toxins.

plastic any of the stable synthetic materials that are fluid at some stage in their manufacture, when they can be shaped, and that later set to rigid or semi-rigid solids. Plastics today are chiefly derived from petroleum. Most are polymers, made up of long chains of identical molecules.

plate *or* **tectonic plate** *or* **lithospheric plate** one of several relatively distinct sections of the *lithosphere, approximately 100 km/60 mi thick, which together comprise the outermost layer of the Earth (like the pieces of the cracked shell of a hard-boiled egg).

plateau elevated area of fairly flat land, or a mountainous region in which the peaks are at the same height. An **intermontane plateau** is one surrounded by mountains. A **piedmont plateau** is one that lies between the mountains and low-lying land. A **continental plateau** rises abruptly from low-lying lands or the sea. Examples are the Tibetan Plateau and the Massif Central in France.

platelet tiny disc-shaped structure found in the blood, which helps it to clot. Platelets are not true cells, but membrane-bound cell fragments without nuclei that bud off from large cells in the bone marrow.

plate tectonics theory formulated in the 1960s to explain the phenomena of *continental drift and sea-

floor spreading, and the formation of the major physical features of the Earth's surface. The Earth's outermost layer, the *lithosphere, is seen as a jigsaw puzzle of rigid major and minor plates that move relative to each other, probably under the influence of convection currents in the *mantle beneath. At the margins of the plates, where they collide or move apart or slide past one another, major landforms such as *mountains, *rift valleys, *volcanoes, *ocean trenches, and **mid-ocean ridges** are created. The rate of plate movement is on average 2–3 cm/1 in per year and at most 15 cm/6 in per year. (See diagram, p. 724.)

Plath, Sylvia (1932–1963) US poet and novelist. Her powerful, highly personal poems, often expressing a sense of desolation, are distinguished by their intensity and sharp imagery. Her *Collected Poems* (1981) was awarded a Pulitzer Prize. Her autobiographical novel *The Bell Jar* (1961) deals with the events surrounding a young woman's emotional breakdown.

platinum chemical symbol Pt, (Spanish *platina* 'little silver') heavy, soft, silver-white, malleable and ductile, metallic element, atomic number 78, relative atomic mass 195.09. It is the first of a group of six metallic elements (platinum, osmium, iridium, rhodium, ruthenium, and palladium) that possess similar properties, such as resistance to tarnish, corrosion, and attack by acid, and that often occur as free metals (*native metals). They often occur in natural alloys with each other, the commonest of which is osmiridium. Both pure and as an alloy, platinum is used in dentistry, jewellery, and as a catalyst.

Plato (c. 427–347 BC) Greek philosopher. He was a pupil of Socrates, teacher of Aristotle, and founder of the Academy school of philosophy. He was the author of philosophical dialogues on such topics as metaphysics, ethics, and politics. Central to his teachings is the notion of Forms, which are located outside the everyday world – timeless, motionless, and absolutely real.

platypus monotreme, or egg-laying, mammal *Ornithorhynchus anatinus*, found in Tasmania and eastern Australia. Semiaquatic, it has small eyes and no external ears, and jaws resembling a duck's beak. It lives in long burrows along river banks, where it lays two eggs in a rough nest. It feeds on water worms and insects, and when full-grown is 60 cm/2 ft long.

plc abbreviation for *public limited company.

plebeian Roman citizen who did not belong to the privileged class of the *patricians. During the 5th–4th centuries BC, plebeians waged a long struggle to win political and social equality with the patricians, eventually securing admission to the offices formerly reserved for patricians.

plebiscite (Latin *plebiscitium* 'ordinance, decree') *referendum or direct vote by all the electors of a country or district on a specific question. Since the 18th century plebiscites have been employed on many occasions to decide to what country a particular area should belong; for example, in Upper Silesia and elsewhere after World War I, and in the Saar in 1935. The term fell into disuse during the 1930s, after the widespread abuse by the Nazis in Germany to legitimize their regime.

Pleiades in astronomy, an open star cluster about 400 light years away from Earth in the constellation Taurus,

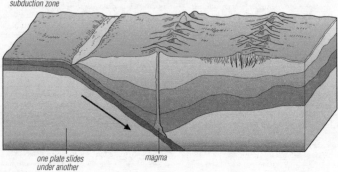

seafloor spreading

plates move outwards from ridge | ridge | pillow lava | accumulating sediment

rising magma

subduction zone

one plate slides under another | magma

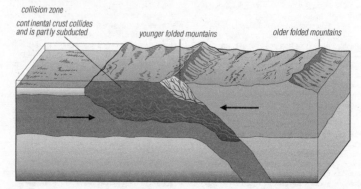

collision zone

continental crust collides and is partly subducted | younger folded mountains | older folded mountains

plate tectonics Constructive and destructive action in plate tectonics. (top) Seafloor spreading. The upwelling of magma forces apart the crust plates, producing new crust at the joint. Rapid extrusion of magma produces a domed ridge; more gentle spreading produces a central valley. (middle) The drawing downwards of an oceanic plate beneath a continent produces a range of volcanic fold mountains parallel to the plate edge. (bottom) Collision of continental plates produces immense fold mountains, such as the Himalayas. Younger mountains are found near the coast with older ranges inland. The plates of the Earth's lithosphere are always changing in size and shape of as material is added at constructive margins and removed at destructive margins. The process is extremely slow, but it means that the tectonic history of the Earth cannot be traced back further than about 200 million years.

represented as the Seven Sisters of Greek mythology. Its brightest stars (highly luminous, blue-white giants only a few million years old) are visible to the naked eye, but there are many fainter ones.

Pleistocene epoch first part of the Quaternary period of geological time, beginning 1.64 million years ago and ending 10,000 years ago. The polar ice caps were extensive and glaciers were abundant during the ice age of this period, and humans evolved into modern *Homo sapiens sapiens* about 100,000 years ago.

plesiosaur prehistoric carnivorous marine reptile of the Jurassic and Cretaceous periods, which reached a length of 12 m/36 ft, and had a long neck and paddlelike limbs. The pliosaurs evolved from the plesiosaurs.

pleurisy inflammation of the pleura, the thin, secretory membrane that covers the lungs and lines the space in which they rest. Pleurisy is nearly always due to bacterial or viral infection, but may also be a complication of other diseases.

Plimsoll line loading mark painted on the hull of merchant ships, first suggested by the 19th-century English politician Samuel Plimsoll. It shows the depth to which a vessel may be safely (and legally) loaded.

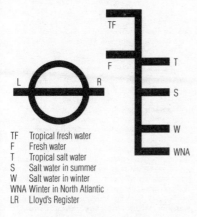

TF	Tropical fresh water
F	Fresh water
T	Tropical salt water
S	Salt water in summer
W	Salt water in winter
WNA	Winter in North Atlantic
LR	Lloyd's Register

Plimsoll line The Plimsoll line on the hull of a ship indicates the maximum safe loading levels for sea or fresh water, winter or summer, in tropical or temperate waters.

Pliny the Elder (c. AD 23–79) born Gaius Plinius Secundus, Roman scientific encyclopedist and historian. Many of his works have been lost, but in *Historia naturalis/Natural History*, probably completed AD 77, Pliny surveys all the known sciences of his day, notably astronomy, meteorology, geography, mineralogy, zoology, and botany.

Pliny the Younger (c. AD 61–113) born Gaius Plinius Caecilius Secundus, Roman administrator. He was the nephew of Pliny the Elder. His correspondence is of great interest; among his surviving letters are those describing the eruption of Vesuvius, his uncle's death, and his correspondence with the emperor *Trajan.

Pliocene Epoch ('almost recent') fifth and last epoch of the Tertiary period of geological time, 5.2–1.64 million years ago. The earliest hominid, the humanlike ape *Australopithecines*, evolved in Africa.

pliosaur prehistoric carnivorous marine reptile, descended from the plesiosaurs, but with a shorter neck, and longer head and jaws. It was approximately 5 m/15 ft long. In 1989 the skeleton of one of a previously unknown species was discovered in northern Queensland, Australia. A hundred million years ago, it lived in the sea that once covered the Great Artesian Basin.

PLO abbreviation for *Palestine Liberation Organization, founded in 1964 to bring about an independent state of Palestine.

Plough, the popular name for the most prominent part of the constellation *Ursa Major.

plough agricultural implement used for tilling the soil. The plough dates from about 3500 BC, when oxen were used to pull a simple wooden blade, or ard. In about 500 BC the iron ploughshare came into use. By about AD 1000 horses as well as oxen were being used to pull wheeled ploughs, equipped with a ploughshare for cutting a furrow, a blade for forming the walls of the furrow (called a coulter), and a mouldboard to turn the furrow.

plover any shore bird of the family Charadriidae, order Charadriiformes, found worldwide. Plovers are usually black or brown above and white below, and have short bills. The European **golden plover** *Pluviatilis apricaria*, of heathland and sea coast, is about 28 cm/11 in long. In winter the upper parts are a sooty black with large yellow spots, and white throat and underparts, changing to black in the spring. It nests on the ground, laying four yellowish eggs blotched with brown.

plum smooth-skinned, oval, reddish-purple or green edible fruit of the plum tree. There are many varieties, including the Victoria, czar, egg-plum, greengage, and damson; the wild sloe (*P. spinosa*), which is the fruit of the *blackthorn, is closely related. Dried plums are known as prunes. (Genus *Prunus domestica*, family Rosaceae.)

pluralism in political science, the view that decision-making in current liberal democracies is the outcome of competition among several interest groups in a political system characterized by free elections, representative institutions, and open access to the organs of power. This concept is opposed by corporatism and other approaches that view power as centralized in the state and its principal elites (the Establishment).

Plutarch (c. AD 46–c. 120) Greek biographer and essayist. He is best remembered for his *Lives*, a collection of short biographies of famous figures from Greek and Roman history arranged in contrasting pairs (for example, Alexander the Great and Julius Caesar are paired). He also wrote *Moralia*, a collection of essays on moral and social themes.

Pluto smallest and, usually, outermost planet of the Solar System. The existence of Pluto was predicted by calculation by US astronomer Percival Lowell and the planet was located by US astronomer Clyde Tombaugh in 1930. Its highly elliptical orbit occasionally takes it within the orbit of Neptune, as in 1979–99. Pluto has a mass about 0.002 of that of Earth. **mean distance from the Sun:** 5.8 billion km/3.6 billion mi

725

equatorial diameter: 2,300 km/1,438 mi **rotation period:** 6.39 Earth days **year:** 248.5 Earth years **atmosphere:** thin atmosphere with small amounts of methane gas **surface:** low density, composed of rock and ice, primarily frozen methane; there is an ice cap at Pluto's north pole **satellites:** one moon, Charon.

Pluto or **Hades** in Greek mythology, lord of *Hades, the underworld and also his original name. His Roman counterpart was **Dis** (also Orcus). He was the son of the Titans *Kronos and Rhea; and brother of Zeus, Poseidon, Hera, Hestia, and Demeter. He abducted and married *Persephone, daughter of the goddess of agriculture *Demeter, causing winter on Earth; Persephone was eventually allotted six months of each year in Hades, and six with her mother.

plutonic rock igneous rock derived from magma that has cooled and solidified deep in the crust of the Earth; granites and gabbros are examples of plutonic rocks.

plutonium chemical symbol Pu, silvery-white, radioactive, metallic element of the *actinide series, atomic number 94, relative atomic mass 239.13. It occurs in nature in minute quantities in *pitchblende and other ores, but is produced in quantity only synthetically. It has six allotropic forms (see *allotropy) and is one of three fissile elements (elements capable of splitting into other elements – the others are thorium and uranium). Plutonium dioxide, PuO_2, a yellow crystalline solid, is the compound most widely used in the nuclear industry. It was believed to be inert until US researchers discovered in 1999 that it reacts very slowly with oxygen and water to form a previously unknown green crystalline compound that is soluble in water.

Plymouth seaport and administrative centre of Plymouth City unitary authority in southwest England, at the mouth of the river Plym, 179 km/112 mi southwest of Bristol; population (1999 est) 253,200. The city's prosperity is based around its three harbours, and industries include marine and machine tool manufacture and servicing, food processing, and the production of clothing and radio equipment.

Plymouth Brethren fundamentalist Christian Protestant sect characterized by extreme simplicity of belief, founded in Dublin in about 1827 by the Reverend John Nelson Darby (1800–1882). The Plymouth Brethren have no ordained priesthood, affirming the ministry of all believers, and maintain no church buildings. They hold prayer meetings and Bible study in members' houses.

pneumoconiosis disease of the lungs caused by an accumulation of dust, especially from coal, asbestos, or silica. Inhaled particles make the lungs gradually fibrous and the victim has difficulty breathing. Over many years the condition causes severe disability.

pneumonia inflammation of the lungs, generally due to bacterial or viral infection but also to particulate matter or gases. It is characterized by a build-up of fluid in the alveoli, the clustered air sacs (at the ends of the air passages) where oxygen exchange takes place.

Po Greek *Eridanos*; Latin *Padus*, longest river in Italy, flowing from the Cottian Alps to the Adriatic Sea; length 668 km/415 mi. Its valley is fertile and contains natural gas. It winds generally eastward in a wide valley, passing Turin, Pavia, Piacenza, Cremona, and Ferrara before entering the Adriatic. The river is heavily polluted with nitrates, phosphates, and arsenic.

pochard any of various diving ducks found in Europe and North America, especially the genus *Aythya*. They feed largely on water plants. Their nest is made in long grass on the borders of lakes and pools.

pocket borough a borough in the UK before the *Reform Act of 1832, where all the houses were owned by one man, whose vote returned two members of Parliament. An example was Gatton in Surrey. See also *rotten borough.

pod in botany, a type of fruit that is characteristic of legumes (plants belonging to the Leguminosae family), such as peas and beans. It develops from a single *carpel and splits down both sides when ripe to release the seeds.

Podgorica formerly **Titograd** (1946–92), capital of Montenegro, in Serbia and Montenegro; population (1993 est) 135,000. Industries include metalworking, furniture-making, and tobacco. It was damaged in World War II and after rebuilding was renamed in honour of Marshal Tito; it reverted to its original name with the collapse of communism. It was the birthplace of the Roman emperor Diocletian.

Poe, Edgar Allan (1809–1849) US writer and poet. His short stories are renowned for their horrific atmosphere, as in 'The Fall of the House of Usher' (1839) and 'The Masque of the Red Death' (1842), and for their acute reasoning (ratiocination), as in 'The Gold Bug' (1843) and 'The Murders in the Rue Morgue' (1841, in which the investigators Legrand and Dupin anticipate the character of Sherlock Holmes by Scottish writer Arthur Conan *Doyle). His poems include 'The Raven' (1845). His novel *The Narrative of Arthur Gordon Pym of Nantucket* (1838) has attracted critical attention.

poet laureate poet of the British royal household or of the USA, so called because of the laurel wreath awarded to eminent poets in the Greco-Roman world. Early UK poets with unofficial status were John Skelton, Samuel Daniel, Ben *Jonson, and William Davenant. John *Dryden was the first to receive the title by letters-patent in 1668 and from then on the post became a regular institution. Andrew Motion was appointed UK poet laureate in 1999. His was the first appointment to the post to be made for ten years, rather than for life.

poetry imaginative literary form, particularly suitable for describing emotions and thoughts. Poetry is highly 'compressed' writing, often using figures of speech to talk about one thing in terms of another, such as *metaphor and *simile, that allows the reader to 'unpack' the poem's meaning for itself. This leads to people interpreting poems differently in different times and places, which is part of the fascination of the medium. Poetry does not have to follow the strict grammatical rules of *prose (ordinary written language) – although the writer may choose to do so – and often uses richer language to appeal to the reader's senses and intellect. The use of comparative language and elevated or uncommon word choice or diction contributes to poetry's ability to make a familiar world seem strange and new again.

pogrom (Russian 'destruction') unprovoked violent attack on an ethnic group, particularly Jews, carried out with official sanction. The Russian pogroms against Jews began in 1881, after the assassination of Tsar Alexander II, and again in 1903–06; persecution of the

Jews remained constant until the Russian Revolution. Later there were pogroms in Eastern Europe, especially in Poland after 1918, and in Germany under Hitler (see *Holocaust).

poikilothermy condition in which an animal's body temperature is largely dependent on the temperature of the air or water in which it lives. It is characteristic of all animals except birds and mammals, which maintain their body temperatures by homeothermy (they are 'warm-blooded').

poinsettia *or* **Christmas flower** winter-flowering shrub with large red leaves encircling small greenish-yellow flowers. It is native to Mexico and tropical America and is a popular houseplant in North America and Europe. (Genus *Euphorbia pulcherrima*, family Euphorbiaceae.)

pointer any of several breeds of gun dog, bred especially to scent the position of game and indicate it by standing, nose pointed towards it, often with one forefoot raised, in silence. English pointers have smooth coats, mainly white mixed with black, tan, or dark brown. They stand about 60 cm/24 in tall and weigh 28 kg/62 lb.

pointillism *or* **divisionism** *or* **confetti-ism** method of oil painting developed in the 1880s by the French neo-Impressionist Georges *Seurat. He used small dabs of pure colour laid side by side that, when viewed from a distance, blend together to make other colours, forms, and outlines, and give an impression of shimmering light.

poison *or* **toxin** any chemical substance that, when introduced into or applied to the body, is capable of injuring health or destroying life. The liver removes some poisons from the blood. The majority of poisons may be divided into **corrosives**, such as sulphuric, nitric, and hydrochloric acids; **irritants**, including arsenic and copper sulphate; **narcotics**, such as opium and carbon monoxide; and **narcotico-irritants** from any substances of plant origin including phenol acid and tobacco.

Poitier, Sidney (1924–) US actor and film director. He was a major black star in Hollywood. His won acclaim in *No Way Out* (1950), and later films include *Something of Value* (1957), *Lilies of the Field* (1963), *In the Heat of the Night* (1967), *Sneakers* (1992), and *The Jackal* (1997). He has directed *Stir Crazy* (1980) and *Ghost Dad* (1990).

Poitou-Charentes region of west-central France, comprising the *départements* of Charente, Charente-Maritime, Deux-Sèvres, and Vienne; area 25,809 sq km/9,965 sq mi; population (2001 est) 1,640,100. It is situated between the Armorican and Central mountain ranges, between the Paris and Aquitaine basins, and on the edge of the Atlantic Ocean. The River Charente flows through the region. Its administrative centre is Poitiers. The area contains cereal plains, wooded valleys, wine-growing areas, and coastal and marsh areas. The majority of the population live in the region's valleys. Industries include dairy products, wheat, maize, chemicals, and metal goods; brandy is made at Cognac. The Côte de Beauté attracts tourists throughout the year and the Port des Minimes, is the first nautical port in Europe. The area is also well known for goats cheese, sunflower crops, and pedigree cattle rearing.

poker card game of US origin, in which two to eight people play (usually for stakes), and try to obtain a 'hand' of five cards ranking higher than those of their opponents. The one with the highest scoring hand wins the 'pot' (the central pool).

Poland

National name: *Rzeczpospolita Polska/Republic of Poland*

Area: 312,683 sq km/120,726 sq mi
Capital: Warsaw
Major towns/cities: Lódz, Kraków, Wroclaw, Poznan, Gdansk, Szczecin, Katowice, Bydgoszcz, Lublin
Major ports: Gdansk (Danzig), Szczecin (Stettin), Gdynia (Gdingen)
Physical features: part of the great plain of Europe; Vistula, Oder, and Neisse rivers; Sudeten, Tatra, and Carpathian mountains on southern frontier
Head of state: Aleksander Kwasniewski from 1995
Head of government: Marek Belka from 2004
Political system: liberal democracy
Political executive: limited presidency
Political parties: Democratic Left Alliance (SLD), reform socialist (ex-communist); Polish Peasant Party (PSL), moderate, agrarian; Freedom Union (UW), moderate, centrist; Labour Union (UP), left wing; Non-Party Bloc in support of Reforms (BBWR), Christian Democrat, right of centre, pro-Walesa; Confederation for an Independent Poland (KPN), right wing; Solidarity Electoral Action (AWS), Christian, right wing
Currency: zloty
GNI per capita (PPP): (US$) 10,130 (2002 est)
Exports: machinery and transport equipment, textiles, chemicals, coal, coke, copper, sulphur, steel, food and agricultural products, clothing and leather products, wood and paper products. Principal market: Germany 34.3% (2001)
Population: 38,587,000 (2003 est)
Language: Polish (official)
Religion: Roman Catholic 95%
Life expectancy: 70 (men); 78 (women) (2000–05)
Chronology
966: Polish Slavic tribes under Mieszko I, leader of Piast dynasty, adopted Christianity and united region around Poznan to form first Polish state.

727

1241: Devastated by Mongols.

13th–14th centuries: German and Jewish refugees settled among Slav population.

1386: Jagellonian dynasty came to power: golden age for Polish culture.

1569: Poland united with Lithuania to become the largest state in Europe.

1572: Jagellonian dynasty became extinct; future kings were elected by nobility and gentry, who formed 10% of the population.

mid-17th century: Defeat in war against Russia, Sweden, and Brandenburg (in Germany) set in a process of irreversible decline.

1772–95: Partitioned between Russia, which ruled the northeast; Prussia, the west, including Pomerania; and Austria in the south-centre, including Galicia, where there was greatest autonomy.

1815: After Congress of Vienna, Russian eastern portion of Poland re-established as kingdom within Russian Empire.

1830 and 1863: Uprisings against repressive Russian rule.

1892: Nationalist Polish Socialist Party (PPS) founded.

1918: Independent Polish republic established after World War I, with Marshal Józef Pilsudski, founder of the PPS, elected president.

1919–21: Abortive advance into Lithuania and Ukraine.

1926: Pilsudski seized full power in coup and established an autocratic regime.

1935: On Pilsudski's death, a military regime held power under Marshal Smigly-Rydz.

1939: Invaded by Germany; western Poland incorporated into Nazi Reich (state) and the rest became a German colony; 6 million Poles – half of them Jews – were slaughtered in the next five years.

1944–45: Liberated from Nazi rule by Soviet Union's Red Army; boundaries redrawn westwards at the Potsdam Conference. One half of 'old Poland', 180,000 sq km/70,000 sq mi in the east, was lost to the USSR; 100,000 sq km/40,000 sq mi of ex-German territory in Silesia, along the Oder and Neisse rivers, was added, shifting the state 240 km/150 mi westwards; millions of Germans were expelled.

1947: Communist people's republic proclaimed after manipulated election.

1949: Joined Comecon.

early 1950s: Harsh Stalinist rule under communist leader Boleslaw Bierut: nationalization; rural collectivization; persecution of Catholic Church members.

1955: Joined Warsaw Pact defence organization.

1956: Poznan strikes and riots. The moderate Wladyslaw Gomulka installed as Polish United Workers' Party (PUWP) leader.

1960s: Private farming reintroduced and Catholicism tolerated.

1970: Gomulka replaced by Edward Gierek after Gdansk riots against food price rises.

1970s: Poland heavily indebted to foreign creditors after a failed attempt to boost economic growth.

1980: Solidarity, led by Lech Walesa, emerged as free trade union following Gdansk disturbances.

1981: Martial law imposed by General Wojciech Jaruzelski, trade-union activity banned, and Solidarity leaders and supporters arrested.

1983: Martial law ended.

1984: Amnesty for 35,000 political prisoners.

1988: Solidarity-led strikes and demonstrations for pay increases. Reform-communist Mieczyslaw Rakowski became prime minister.

1989: Agreement to relegalize Solidarity, allow opposition parties, and adopt a more democratic constitution, after round-table talks involving Solidarity, the Communist Party, and the Catholic Church. Widespread success for Solidarity in first open elections for 40 years; noncommunist 'grand coalition' government was formed, headed by Tadeusz Mazowiecki of Solidarity; an economic austerity and free-market restructuring programme began.

1990: The PUWP was dissolved and re-formed as the Democratic Left Alliance (SLD). Walesa was elected president and Jan Bielecki became prime minister.

1991: A shock-therapy economic restructuring programme, including large-scale privatization, produced a sharp fall in living standards and a rise in the unemployment rate to 11%. The unpopular Bielecki resigned and, after inconclusive elections, Jan Olszewski formed a fragile centre–right coalition government.

1992: The political instability continued.

1993: The economy became the first in Central Europe to grow since the collapse of communism.

1994: Poland joined the NATO 'partnership for peace' programme; the last Russian troops left the country.

1995: Aleksander Kwasniewski, leader of the SLD, was elected president.

1997: Further structural reform and privatization took place and a new constitution was approved. Poland was invited to join NATO and begin negotiations to join the European Union (EU). A general election was won by Solidarity Electoral Action (AWS). A coalition government was formed, led by Jerzy Buzek.

1998: Full EU membership negotiations commenced. The government was weakened by defections to the opposition. The number of provinces was reduced from 49 to 16.

1999: Poland became a full member of NATO.

2000: Alexander Kwasniewski was elected for a further five years as president at a time when Poland's economy was progressing well.

2001: The newly-formed Citizens's Platform party attracted considerable public support.

2002: The first direct local elections since the fall of communism were held.

2003: In a referendum, 77.5% of voters backed accession to the European Union in 2004. Poland sent troops to Iraq.

2004: Poland joined the European Union. Marek Belka (Democratic Left Alliance) became prime minister.

polar bear large white-coated bear that lives in the Arctic. Polar bears are normally solitary, except for females when rearing cubs. They feed mainly on seals but will eat berries and scavenge when food is scarce. Males weigh 400–800 kg/880–1,760 lb and are up to 2.5 m/8.25 ft in length (twice as large as females, 200–400 kg). The estimated world population in 1997 was 20,000–30,000 bears.

polar coordinates in mathematics, a way of defining the position of a point in terms of its distance r from a fixed point (the origin) and its angle θ to a fixed line or axis. The coordinates of the point are (r, θ).

Polaris or **Pole Star** or **North Star** bright star closest to the north celestial pole, and the brightest star in the constellation *Ursa Minor. Its position is indicated by the 'pointers' in *Ursa Major. Polaris is a yellow *supergiant about 500 light years away from the Sun. It is also known as **Alpha Ursae Minoris**.

polarized light light in which the electromagnetic vibrations take place in one particular plane. In ordinary (unpolarized) light, the electric fields vibrate in all planes perpendicular to the direction of propagation. After reflection from a polished surface or transmission through certain materials (such as Polaroid), the electric fields are confined to one direction, and the light is said to be **linearly polarized**. In **circularly polarized** and **elliptically polarized** light, the electric fields are confined to one direction, but the direction rotates as the light propagates. Polarized light is used to test the strength of sugar solutions and to measure stresses in transparent materials.

Polaroid camera instant-picture camera, invented by Edwin Land in the USA in 1947. The original camera produced black-and-white prints in about one minute. Modern cameras can produce black-and-white prints in a few seconds, and colour prints in less than a minute. An advanced model has automatic focusing and exposure. It ejects a piece of film on paper immediately after the picture has been taken.

polar reversal or **magnetic reversal** change in polarity of Earth's magnetic field. Like all magnets, Earth's magnetic field has two opposing regions, or poles, positioned approximately near geographical North and South Poles. During a period of normal polarity the region of attraction corresponds with the North Pole. Today, a compass needle, like other magnetic materials, aligns itself parallel to the magnetizing field and points to the North Pole. During a period of reversed polarity, the region of attraction would change to the South Pole and the needle of a compass would point south. Studies of the magnetism retained in rocks at the time of their formation (like small compasses frozen in time) have shown that the polarity of the magnetic field has reversed repeatedly throughout geological time.

polder area of flat reclaimed land that used to be covered by a river, lake, or the sea. Polders have been artificially drained and protected from flooding by building dykes. They are common in the Netherlands, where the total land area has been increased by nearly one-fifth since AD 1200. Such schemes as the Zuider Zee project have provided some of the best agricultural land in the country.

pole either of the geographic north and south points of the axis about which the Earth rotates. The geographic poles differ from the magnetic poles, which are the points towards which a freely suspended magnetic needle will point.

Pole people of Polish culture from Poland and the surrounding area. There are 37–40 million speakers of Polish (including some in the USA), a Slavic language belonging to the Indo-European family. The Poles are predominantly Roman Catholic, though there is an Orthodox Church minority. They are known for their distinctive cooking, folk festivals, and folk arts.

polecat Old World weasel *Mustela putorius* with a brown back and dark belly and two yellow face patches.

The body is about 50 cm/20 in long and it has a strong smell from anal gland secretions. It is native to Asia, Europe, and North Africa. In North America, *skunks are sometimes called polecats. A ferret is a domesticated polecat.

Pole Star another name for *Polaris, the northern pole star. There is no bright star near the southern celestial pole.

pole vault athletics field event in which the athlete attempts to clear a high cross bar by means of a long flexible pole. Competitive pole vaulting, for height as opposed to distance, began in the mid-19th century. It has been an Olympic sport for men since the first modern games in 1896; however, women's pole vaulting was not treated seriously by the athletics authorities until the 1990s, and the Sydney 2000 Games was the first Olympics to include a women's as well as a men's pole vault event.

police civil law-and-order force. In the UK, it is responsible to the Home Office, with 56 separate police forces, generally organized on a county basis; mutual aid is given between forces in circumstances such as mass picketing in the 1984–85 miners' strike, but there is no national police force or police riot unit (such as the French CRS riot squad). The forerunners of these forces were the ineffective medieval watch and London's Bow Street runners, introduced in 1749 by Henry *Fielding, which formed a model for the London police force established by Robert *Peel's government in 1829 (hence 'peelers' or 'bobbies'); the system was introduced throughout the country from 1856.

polio or **poliomyelitis** viral infection of the central nervous system affecting nerves that activate muscles. The disease used to be known as infantile paralysis since children were most often affected. Two kinds of vaccine are available, one injected (see *Salk) and one given by mouth. The Americas were declared to be polio-free by the Pan American Health Organization in 1994. In 1997 the World Health Organization (WHO) reported that causes of polio had dropped by nearly 90% since 1988 when the organization began its programme to eradicate the disease by the year 2000. Most remaining cases were in Africa and southeast Asia in early 2000.

Polish language member of the Slavonic branch of the Indo-European language family, spoken mainly in Poland. Polish is written in the Roman and not the Cyrillic alphabet and its standard form is based on the dialect of Poznan in western Poland.

Politburo contraction of 'political bureau', the executive committee (known as the Presidium 1952–66) of the Supreme Soviet in the USSR, which laid down party policy. It consisted of about 12 voting and 6 candidate (nonvoting) members.

political correctness or **PC** shorthand term for a set of liberal attitudes about education and society, and the terminology associated with them. To be politically correct is to be sensitive to unconscious racism and sexism and to display environmental awareness. However, the real or alleged enforcement of PC speech codes ('people of colour' instead of 'coloured people', 'differently abled' instead of 'disabled', and so on) at more than 130 US universities by 1991 attracted derision and was criticized as a form of thought-policing.

politics ruling by the consent of the governed; an activity whereby solutions to social and economic problems are arrived at and different aspirations are met by the process of discussion and compromise rather than by the application of decree or force.

Politzer, Hugh David (1949–) US physicist. With the US physicists David Gross and Frank Wilczek he shared the Nobel Prize for Physics in 2004 for his contributions to the development of a theory to explain how quark subatomic particles are held together by the strong nuclear force.

Polk, James Knox (1795–1849) 11th president of the USA 1845–49, a Democrat. Presiding over a period of westward expansion, he allowed Texas admission to the Union, and forced the war on Mexico that resulted in the annexation of California and New Mexico.

polka Bohemian dance in quick duple time (2/4). Originating in the 19th century, it became popular throughout Europe. The basic step is a hop followed by three short steps. The polka spread with German immigrants to the USA, becoming a style of Texas country music. It was also used by European composers, including Bedrich Smetana in *The Bartered Bride* (1866) and *Bohemian Dances* (1878), Antonín Dvořák, and others.

pollack marine fish *Pollachius virens* of the cod family, growing to 75 cm/2.5 ft, and found close to the shore on both sides of the North Atlantic.

Pollack, Sydney (1934–) US director, actor, and producer. His work includes a variety of genres, including period pieces, action films, and comedies. He directed *Out of Africa* (1985), which won Academy Awards for best picture and best director.

pollen grains of *seed plants that contain the male gametes. In *angiosperms (flowering plants) pollen is produced within *anthers; in most *gymnosperms (cone-bearing plants) it is produced in male cones. A pollen grain is typically yellow and, when mature, has a hard outer wall. Pollen of insect-pollinated plants (see *pollination) is often sticky and spiny and larger than the smooth, light grains produced by wind-pollinated species.

pollen tube outgrowth from a pollen grain that grows towards the ovule, following germination of the grain on the *stigma. In *angiosperms (flowering plants) the pollen tube reaches the ovule by growing down through the *style, carrying the male gametes inside. The gametes are discharged into the ovule and one fertilizes the egg cell.

pollination process by which pollen is transferred from one plant to another. The male *gametes are contained in pollen grains, which must be transferred from the anther to the stigma in *angiosperms (flowering plants), and from the male cone to the female cone in *gymnosperms (cone-bearing plants). Fertilization (not the same as pollination) occurs after the growth of the pollen tube to the ovary. Self-pollination occurs when pollen is transferred to a stigma of the same flower, or to another flower on the same plant; cross-pollination occurs when pollen is transferred to another plant. This involves external pollen-carrying agents, such as wind, water, insects, birds (see *ornithophily), bats, and other small mammals.

Pollock, (Paul) Jackson (1912–1956) US painter. He was a pioneer of abstract expressionism and one of the foremost exponents of *action painting. His style is characterized by complex networks of swirling, interwoven lines of great delicacy and rhythmic subtlety.

poll tax tax levied on every individual, without reference to income or property. Being simple to administer, it was among the earliest sorts of tax (introduced in England in 1379), but because of its indiscriminate nature (it is a regressive tax, in that it falls proportionately more heavily on poorer people) it has often proved unpopular.

pollution harmful effect on the environment of by-products of human activity, principally industrial and agricultural processes – for example, noise, smoke, car emissions, pesticides, radiation, sewage disposal, household waste, and chemical and radioactive effluents in air, seas, and rivers. *Air pollution contributes to the *greenhouse effect.

Pollux *or* **Beta Geminorum** brightest star in the constellation *Gemini and the 17th-brightest star in the night sky. Pollux is a yellow star with a true luminosity 45 times that of the Sun. It is 36 light years away from the Sun.

polo stick-and-ball game played between two teams of four on horseback. It originated in Iran, spread to India, and was first played in England in 1869. Polo is played on the largest field of any game, measuring up to 274 m/300 yd by 182 m/200 yd. A small solid ball is struck with the side of a long-handled mallet through goals at each end of the field. A typical match lasts about an hour, and is divided into 'chukkas' of 7½ minutes each. No pony is expected to play more than two chukkas in the course of a day.

Polo, Marco (1254–1324) Venetian traveller and writer. He joined his father (Niccolo) and uncle (Maffeo), who had travelled to China as merchants (1260–69), when they began a journey overland back to China (1271). Once there, he learned Mongolian and served the emperor Kubla Khan until he returned to Europe by sea 1292–95.

polonaise Polish dance in stately 3/4 time that was common in 18th-century Europe. The composer Frédéric *Chopin developed the polonaise as a pianistic form.

polonium chemical symbol Po, radioactive, metallic element, atomic number 84, relative atomic mass 210. Polonium occurs in nature in small amounts and was isolated from *pitchblende. It is the element having the largest number of isotopes (27) and is 5,000 times as radioactive as radium, liberating considerable amounts of heat. It was the first element to have its radioactive properties recognized and investigated.

Pol Pot (c. 1925–1998) also known as **Saloth Sar**, **Tol Saut**, or **Pol Porth**, Cambodian politician and leader of the Khmer Rouge communist movement that overthrew the government in 1975. After widespread atrocities against the civilian population, his regime was deposed by a Vietnamese invasion in 1979. Pol Pot continued to help lead the Khmer Rouge despite officially resigning from all positions in 1989. He was captured in 1997 but escaped from Cambodia, reportedly to Thailand, in January 1998 to avoid facing an international court for his crimes against humanity. The Cambodian government announced mid-April 1998 that he had been captured inside Thailand. However, a few days later reports of Pol Pot's death were confirmed. He died following a heart attack, in a Cambodian village two miles from the Thai border.

polyandry system whereby a woman has more than one husband at the same time. It is found in various parts of the world, for example, in Madagascar, Malaysia, and certain Pacific isles, and among certain Inuit and American Indian groups. In Tibet and parts of India, polyandry takes the form of the marriage of one woman to several brothers, as a means of keeping intact a family's heritage and property.

polyanthus cultivated variety of *primrose, with several flowers on one stalk, bred in a variety of colours. (Family Primulaceae, *Primula polyantha*.)

polychlorinated biphenyl (PCB) any of a group of chlorinated isomers of biphenyl (C_6H_5)$_2$. They are dangerous industrial chemicals, valuable for their fire-resistant qualities. They constitute an environmental hazard because of their persistent toxicity. Since 1973 their use had been limited by international agreement. In December 2000, 122 nations agreed a treaty to ban the toxic chemicals known as persistent organic polluters (POPs), which include PCBs, although they are unlikely to be totally eliminated until about 2025.

polyester synthetic resin formed by the condensation of polyhydric alcohols (alcohols containing more than one hydroxyl group) with dibasic acids (acids containing two replaceable hydrogen atoms). Polyesters are thermosetting *plastics, used for constructional plastics and, with glass fibre added as reinforcement, they are used in car bodies and boat hulls. Polyester is also a major *synthetic fibre used for knitting or weaving fabrics which are strong but lightweight, and resist creasing but can be heat-set into pleats. Polyester is often mixed with other fibres and can be found in a wide range of different textiles.

polyethylene alternative term for *polythene.

polygamy the practice of having more than one spouse at the same time. It is found among many peoples. Normally it has been confined to the wealthy and to chiefs and nobles who can support several women and their offspring, as among ancient Egyptians, Teutons, Irish, and Slavs. Islam limits the number of legal wives a man may have to four. Certain Christian sects – for example, the Anabaptists of Münster, Germany, and the Mormons – have practised polygamy because it was the norm in the Old Testament.

polygon in geometry, a plane (two-dimensional) figure with three or more straight-line sides. **Regular polygons** have sides of the same length, and all the exterior angles are equal. Common polygons have names that define the number of sides (for example, *triangle (3),

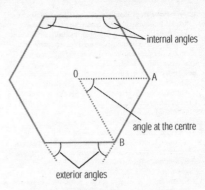

polygon The types of angles in a regular polygon are shown here. These are the angles in a regular hexagon.

*quadrilateral (4), *pentagon (5), hexagon (6), heptagon (7), octagon (8), and so on). These are all convex polygons, having no interior angle greater than 180°.

polyhedron in geometry, a solid figure with four or more plane faces. The more faces there are on a polyhedron, the more closely it approximates to a sphere. Knowledge of the properties of polyhedra is needed in crystallography and stereochemistry to determine the shapes of crystals and molecules.

polymer very long-chain molecule made up of many repeated simple units (*monomers) linked together by *polymerization. There are many polymers, both natural (cellulose, chitin, lignin, rubber) and synthetic (polyethylene and nylon, types of plastic). Synthetic polymers belong to two groups: thermosoftening and thermosetting (see *plastic).

polymerization chemical union of two or more (usually small) molecules of the same kind to form a new compound. **Addition polymerization** produces simple multiples of the same compound. **Condensation polymerization** joins molecules together with the elimination of water or another small molecule. In polymerization, small molecules (monomers) join together to make large molecules (polymers). In the polymerization of ethene to polyethene (polythene), electrons are transferred from the carbon–carbon double bond of the ethene molecule, allowing the molecules to join together as a long chain of carbon–carbon single bonds.

dodecahedron

icosahedron

tetrahedron

cube

octahedron

polyhedron The five regular polyhedra or Platonic solids.

polymorphism in genetics, the coexistence of several distinctly different types in a population (groups of animals of one species). Examples include the different blood groups in humans, different colour forms in some butterflies, and snail shell size, length, shape, colour, and stripiness.

polymorphism in mineralogy, the ability of a substance to adopt different internal structures and external forms, in response to different conditions of temperature and/or pressure. For example, diamond and graphite are both forms of the element carbon, but they have very different properties and appearance.

Polynesia islands of Oceania east of 170° E latitude, including Hawaii, Kiribati, Tuvalu, Fiji Islands, Tonga, Tokelau, Samoa, Cook Islands, and French Polynesia.

Polynesian languages see *Malayo-Polynesian languages.

polynomial in mathematics, an algebraic expression that has one or more *variables (denoted by letters). A polynomial equation has the form:

$$f(x) = a_n x^n + a_{n-1} x^{n-1} + \ldots + a_2 x^2 + a_1 x + a_0$$

where $a_n, a_{n-1}, \ldots, a_0$ are all constants, n is a positive integer, and $a_n \neq 0$. Examples of polynomials are:

$$f(x) = 3x^4 + 2x^2 + 1 \text{ or}$$
$$f(x) = x^5 - 18x + 71 \text{ or}$$
$$f(x) = 2x + 3.$$

A polynomial of degree one, that is, whose highest *power of x is 1, is called a linear polynomial; $3x^2 + 2x + 1$ is quadratic; $4x^3 + 3x^2 + 2x + 1$ is cubic.

polyp or **polypus** small 'stalked' benign tumour, usually found on mucous membrane of the nose or bowels. Intestinal polyps are usually removed, since some have been found to be precursors of cancer.

polyphony in music, when two or more lines of melody combine so that they fit well together. *Counterpoint is another word that has a similar meaning.

polysaccharide long-chain *carbohydrate made up of hundreds or thousands of linked simple sugars (monosaccharides) such as glucose and closely related molecules. A typical polysaccharide molecule, glycogen (animal starch), is formed from linked glucose ($C_6H_{12}O_6$) molecules. A glycogen molecule has 100–1,000 linked glucose units.

polystyrene type of *plastic used in kitchen utensils or, in an expanded form, in insulation and ceiling tiles. CFCs (*chlorofluorocarbons) are used to produce expanded polystyrene so alternatives are being sought.

polytetrafluoroethene (PTFE) polymer made from the monomer tetrafluoroethene (CF_2CF_2). It is a thermosetting plastic with a high melting point that is used to produce 'nonstick' surfaces on pans and to coat bearings. Its trade name is Teflon.

polytheism (Greek *polus* 'many', *theos* 'god') the worship of many gods, as opposed to monotheism (belief in one god). Examples are the religions of ancient Egypt, Babylon, Greece, Rome, and Mexico. Modern Hinduism, while worshipping God in many forms, teaches an underlying unity of the godhead.

polythene or **polyethylene** or **polyethene** *polymer of the gas *ethene (C_2H_4). It is a tough, white, translucent, waxy thermoplastic (which means it can be repeatedly softened by heating). It is used for packaging, bottles, toys, wood preservation, electric cable, pipes, and tubing.

polyunsaturate type of *fat or oil containing a high proportion of triglyceride molecules whose *fatty acid chains contain several double bonds. By contrast, the fatty-acid chains of the triglycerides in saturated fats (such as lard) contain only single bonds. Medical evidence suggests that polyunsaturated fats, used widely in margarines and cooking fats, are less likely to contribute to cardiovascular disease than saturated fats, but there is also some evidence that they may have adverse effects on health.

polyvinyl chloride PVC type of *plastic used for drainpipes, floor tiles, audio discs, shoes, and handbags. It is derived from vinyl chloride (CH_2=CHCl).

pomegranate round, leathery, reddish-yellow fruit of the pomegranate tree, a deciduous shrub or small tree native to southwestern Asia but cultivated widely in tropical and subtropical areas. The fruit contains a large number of seeds that can be eaten fresh or made into wine. (Genus *Punica granatum*, family Punicaceae.)

Pomerania Polish **Pomorze**; German **Pommern**, region along the southern shore of the Baltic Sea, including the island of Rügen, divided between Poland and (west of the Oder–Neisse line) East Germany 1945–90, and the Federal Republic of Germany after reunification in 1990. The chief port is Gdansk. It was formerly a province of Germany.

pomeranian breed of toy dog, about 15 cm/6 in high, weighing about 3 kg/6.5 lb. It has long straight hair with a neck frill, and the tail is carried over the back.

Pompadour, Jeanne Antoinette Poisson, Marquise de Pompadour (1721–1764) also known as **Madame de Pompadour**, Mistress of *Louis XV of France from 1744, born in Paris. She largely dictated the government's ill-fated policy of reversing France's anti-Austrian policy for an anti-Prussian one. She acted as the patron of the Enlightenment philosophers Voltaire and Diderot.

Pompeii ancient city in Italy, near the volcano *Vesuvius, 21 km/13 mi southeast of Naples. In AD 63 an earthquake destroyed much of the city, which had been a Roman port and pleasure resort; it was completely buried beneath volcanic ash when Vesuvius, a composite – and therefore explosive – *volcano erupted in AD 79. Over 2,000 people were killed. Pompeii was rediscovered in 1748 and the systematic excavation begun in 1763 still continues.

Pompey the Great (106–48 BC) born Gnaeus Pompeius Magnus, Roman soldier and politician. From 60 BC to 53 BC, he was a member of the First Triumvirate with Julius Caesar and Marcus Livius Crassus. Originally a supporter of Sulla, Pompey became consul with Crassus in 70 BC. He defeated *Mithridates VI Eupator of Pontus, and annexed Syria and Palestine. He married Caesar's daughter Julia (died 54 BC) in 59 BC. When the Triumvirate broke down after 53 BC, Pompey was drawn into leadership of the senatorial faction. On the outbreak of civil war in 49 BC he withdrew to Greece, was defeated by Caesar at Pharsalus in 48 BC, and was murdered in Egypt.

Pompidou, Georges Jean Raymond (1911–1974)
French Gaullist politician and head of state, President
*de Gaulle's second prime minister 1962–68 and his
successor as president 1969–74. As prime minister he
played a key role in managing the Gaullist party but his
moderate and pragmatic conservativism brought a rift
with de Gaulle in May–June 1968, when he negotiated
the Grenelle Agreement with employers and unions to
end the strike movement. Their political divergences
were confirmed when, during his own presidency, he
authorized a devaluation of the franc (which de Gaulle
had vetoed in 1968), agreed to British entry into the
European Community (which de Gaulle had twice
vetoed in the 1960s), and approved initial steps towards
a European Monetary System. Pompidou diedin office
before completing his full seven-year presidential term.

Ponce de León, Juan (c. 1460–1521) Spanish soldier
and explorer. He is believed to have sailed to the
Americas with Christopher Columbus in 1493, and
served in Hispaniola 1502–04. He conquered Puerto Rico
in 1508, and was made governor in 1509. In 1513 he was
the first European to reach Florida.

Pondicherry Union Territory of southeast India;
area 492 sq km/190 sq mi; population (2001 est) 973,800.
Its capital is Pondicherry which lies on the Coromandel
Coast, 196 km/122 mi south of Chennai (formerly
Madras). Its products include rice, millet, groundnuts,
cotton, and sugar; industries include textiles, food
processing, electrical appliances, and paper, while the
tourist industry is important throughout the area.

pond-skater water *bug (insect of the Hemiptera
order with piercing mouth parts) that rows itself across
the surface by using its middle legs. It feeds on smaller
insects. As pond-skaters do not hunt in packs, it is
likely that their prey fell dead, or dying, on to the
water surface.

pondweed any of a group of aquatic plants that either
float on the surface of the water or are submerged.
The leaves of floating pondweeds are broad and
leathery, whereas leaves of the submerged forms are
narrower and translucent; the flowers grow in green
spikes. (Genus *Potamogeton*, family Potamogetonaceae.)

pony small *horse under 1.47 m/4.5 ft (14.2 hands)
shoulder height. Although of Celtic origin, all the pony
breeds have been crossed with thoroughbred and Arab
stock, except for the smallest – the hardy Shetland,
which is less than 105 cm/42 in shoulder height.

poodle breed of gun dog, including standard (above
38 cm/15 in at shoulder), miniature (below 38 cm/
15 in), and toy (below 28 cm/11 in) varieties. The dense
curly coat, usually cut into an elaborate style, is often
either black or white, although greys and browns are
also bred.

Poole unitary authority in southwest England, created
in 1997 from part of Dorset. **area:** 64 sq km/25 sq mi
towns and cities: Poole (administrative headquarters),
Broadstone, Hillbournes, Sandbanks **features:** River
Stour formers northern border of authority; Poole
Harbour; Holes Bay; Pergins Island; Maritime Museum
(Poole); Compton Acres themed gardens (including
water, rock, heather, Japanese, Roman, Italian);
Canford Heath, tumuli field; Sandbanks spit guarding
entrance to harbour; ferry from Poole to Brownsea
Island and the Channel Islands **population:** (1996)
138,100.

poor law English system for relief for the poor,
established by the Poor Relief Act of 1601. Each parish
was responsible for its own poor, paid for by a parish
tax. The care of the poor was transferred to the
Ministry of Health in 1919, but the poor law remained
in force until 1929.

pop art abbreviation for popular art, movement in
modern art that took its imagery from the glossy world
of advertising and from popular culture such as comic
strips, films, and television; it developed in the 1950s
and flourished in the 1960s, notably in Britain and the
USA. Pop art reflected the new wealth, consumerism,
and light-hearted attitudes that followed the austerity
of the post-war period. It was also a reaction against
*abstract expressionism, the dominant art movement
of the 1950s, which was serious and inward-looking –
pop art was playful and ironic, and ignored the rules
of the traditional art world. The movement helped
to prepare the way for *postmodernism, a feature
of Western culture since the 1970s. Leading US pop
artists include Andy *Warhol, Jasper *Johns, and
Roy *Lichtenstein; UK exponents include Richard
*Hamilton and Allen Jones. Andy Warhol's famous
Twenty Marilyns (1962; Paris, private collection),
depicting Marilyn Monroe, is a typical example of
pop art.

pope the bishop of Rome, head of the Roman Catholic
Church, which claims that he is the spiritual
descendant of St Peter. Elected by the Sacred College
of Cardinals, a pope dates his pontificate from his
coronation with the tiara, or triple crown, at St Peter's
Basilica, Rome. The pope had great political power
in Europe from the early Middle Ages until the
Reformation.

Pope, Alexander (1688–1744) English poet and
satirist. He established his poetic reputation with the
precocious *Pastorals* (1709) and *An Essay on Criticism*
(1711), which were followed by a parody of the heroic
*epic form, *The Rape of the Lock* (1712–14), as well as
The Temple of Fame (1715), and 'Eloisa to Abelard'
(1717). Pope's highly neoclassical translations from the
Greek, of *Homer's *Iliad* and *Odyssey* (1715–26) were
very successful but his edition of Shakespeare (1725)
attracted scholarly ridicule, which led Pope to write
a satire on scholarly dullness, *The Dunciad* (1728).
His finest mature works are his *Imitations of the Satires
of Horace* (1733–38) and his personal letters.

poplar any of a group of deciduous trees with
characteristically broad leaves. The white poplar
(*P. alba*) has a smooth grey trunk and leaves with
white undersides. (Genus *Populus*, family Salicaceae.)

pop music any contemporary music not
categorizable as jazz or classical. Pop music contains
strong rhythms of African origin, simple harmonic
structures often repeated to strophic melodies, and
the use of electrically amplified instruments. Pop
music generically includes the areas of rock, country
and western, rhythm and blues, soul, and others.
Pop became distinct from folk music with the
development of sound-recording techniques;
electronic amplification and other technological
innovations have played a large part in the creation
of new styles. The traditional format is a song of
roughly three minutes with verse, chorus, and middle
eight bars.

Popper, Karl Raimund (1902–1994) British philosopher of science, who was born in Austria and became a naturalized British subject in 1945. His theory of falsificationism states that although scientific generalizations cannot be conclusively verified, they can be conclusively falsified by a counterinstance; therefore, science is not certain knowledge but a series of 'conjectures and refutations', approaching, though never reaching, a definitive truth. For Popper, psychoanalysis and Marxism are unfalsifiable and therefore unscientific.

poppy any of a group of plants belonging to the poppy family. They have brightly coloured mainly red and orange flowers, often with dark centres, and yield a milky sap. Species include the crimson European field poppy (*P. rhoeas*) and the Asian opium poppy (*P. somniferum*), source of the drug *opium. Closely related are the California poppy (*Eschscholtzia californica*) and the yellow horned or sea poppy (*Glaucium flavum*). (Poppy genus *Papaver*, family Papaveraceae.)

popular front political alliance of liberals, socialists, communists, and other centre and left-wing parties. This policy was propounded by the Communist International in 1935 against fascism and was adopted in France and Spain, where popular-front governments were elected in 1936; that in France was overthrown in 1938 and the one in Spain fell with the defeat of the Republic in the Spanish Civil War in 1939.

population the number of people living in a specific area or region, such as a town or country, at any one time. The study of populations, their distribution and structure, resources, and patterns of *migration, is called *demography. Information on population is obtained in a number of ways, such as through the registration of births and deaths. These figures are known as 'vital statistics'. However, more detailed information on population distribution, population density, and change is necessary to enable governments to plan for education, health, housing, and transport on local and national levels. This information is usually obtained from *censuses (population counts), which provide data on sex, age, occupation, and nationality.

population control measures taken by some governments to limit the growth of their countries' populations by trying to reduce *birth rates. Propaganda, freely available contraception, and tax disincentives for large families are some of the measures that have been tried.

population cycle in biology, regular fluctuations in the size of a population, as seen in lemmings, for example. Such cycles are often caused by density-dependent mortality: high mortality due to overcrowding causes a sudden decline in the population, which then gradually builds up again. Population cycles may also result from an interaction between a predator and its prey.

population explosion the rapid and dramatic rise in world population that has occurred over the last few hundred years. Between 1950 and 2000, the world's population increased from 2.5 billion to 6.1 billion people. According to United Nations projections, the world population will be between 7.9 billion and 10.9 billion by 2050.

porcelain *or* **hardpaste** translucent ceramic material with a shining finish, see *pottery and porcelain.

porcupine any *rodent with quills on its body, belonging to either of two families: Old World porcupines (family Hystricidae), terrestrial in habit and having long black-and-white quills; or New World porcupines (family Erethizontidae), tree-dwelling, with prehensile tails and much shorter quills.

porphyria group of rare genetic disorders caused by an enzyme defect. Porphyria affects the digestive tract, causing abdominal distress; the nervous system, causing psychotic disorder, epilepsy, and weakness; the circulatory system, causing high blood pressure; and the skin, causing extreme sensitivity to light. No specific treatments exist.

porpoise any small whale of the family Delphinidae that, unlike dolphins, have blunt snouts without beaks. Common porpoises of the genus *Phocaena* can grow to 1.8 m/6 ft long; they feed on fish and crustaceans.

Port-au-Prince capital and chief port of Haiti, on the west coast of the island of Hispaniola; population (2001 est) 1,047,600. The port is able to berth 10,000-tonne ships, and handles half of the country's foreign trade, with coffee and sugar as the major exports. Manufacturing industries include sugar, rum, textiles, tobacco, cement, and plastics. An international airport supports the significant tourist industry.

Port Elizabeth industrial port in Eastern Cape Province, South Africa, about 710 km/440 mi east of Cape Town, on Algoa Bay; population (urban area, 1991) 853,200. Local industries include motor assembly plants, shoemaking, foundries, sawmills, flour mills, canning factories, engineering, food processing, and the production of soap, tyres, furniture, chemicals, safety glass, electrical goods, cable, steel, textiles, plastics, and paints. The port also exports manganese ore and has large pre-cooling plants for fruit.

Porter, Cole (Albert) (1892–1964) US composer and lyricist. He wrote mainly musical comedies. His witty, sophisticated songs like 'Let's Do It' (1928), 'I Get a Kick Out of You' (1934), and 'Don't Fence Me In' (1944) have been widely recorded and admired. His shows, many of which were made into films, include *The Gay Divorce* (1932, filmed 1934 as *The Gay Divorcee*) and *Kiss Me Kate* (1948, filmed 1953). He also wrote movie musicals, such as *Born to Dance* (1936) and *High Society* (1956).

Portland, William Henry Cavendish Bentinck (1738–1809) 3rd Duke of Portland, English Whig politician. He was prime minister in 1783 and 1807–09, each time as titular leader of a government dominated by stronger characters. He served as home secretary in William Pitt's Tory administration 1794–1801.

Port Louis capital of Mauritius since independence in 1968, on the island's northwest coast; population (2000 est) 144,300. Exports include sugar, textiles, and electronic goods. Industries include chemicals, plastics, fertilizers, printed fabrics, and sugar and food processing. It was founded by the French in 1735 and became, until the opening of the Suez Canal in 1869, important as a port-of-call on voyages from Europe to Asia.

Port Moresby capital and port of Papua New Guinea, on the south coast of New Guinea; population (1995 est) 215,000. The port trades in coffee, copper, gold, copra, palm oil, and timber. There is an airport; the town is the country's centre for national broadcasting and for overseas telecommunications.

Port-of-Spain port and capital of Trinidad and Tobago, on the island of Trinidad; population (1990) 58,400. It has a cathedral (1813–28) and the San Andres Fort (1785).

Porto-Novo port and capital of Benin, on Porto-Novo lagoon; population (1994) 179,000. It trades in palm oil, palm kernels, and cotton. A former Portuguese centre for the slave and tobacco trade with Brazil, it became a French protectorate in 1863. The National Museum of Ethnography is here.

Portsmouth port and administrative centre of Portsmouth City unitary authority in south England, on the peninsula of Portsea Island opposite the Isle of Wight, 118 km/73 mi southwest of London; population (2001 est) 188,800. Famed for its naval history, some naval facilities remain despite the closure of the dockyard in 1981. It is also a ferry port, with links to the Channel Islands, France, and the Isle of Wight. Industries are based around high technology and manufacturing, including aircraft engineering, electronics, and shipbuilding and maintenance.

Portugal

National name: *República Portuguesa/ Republic of Portugal*

Area: 92,000 sq km/35,521 sq mi (including the Azores and Madeira)
Capital: Lisbon
Major towns/cities: Porto, Coimbra, Amadora, Setúbal, Funchal, Braga, Vila Nova de Gaia
Major ports: Porto, Setúbal
Physical features: mountainous in the north (Serra da Estrêla mountains); plains in the south; rivers Minho, Douro, Tagus (Tejo), Guadiana
Head of state: Jorge Branco de Sampaio from 1996
Head of government: Pedro Santana Lopes from 2004
Political system: liberal democracy
Political executive: dual executive
Political parties: Social Democratic Party (PSD), moderate left of centre; Socialist Party (PS), left of centre; People's Party (PP), right wing, anti-European integration
Currency: euro (escudo until 2002)
GNI per capita (PPP): (US$) 17,350 (2002 est)

Exports: textiles, clothing, footwear, pulp and waste paper, wood and cork manufactures, tinned fish, electrical equipment, wine, refined petroleum. Principal market: Germany 19.2% (2001)
Population: 10,062,000 (2003 est)
Language: Portuguese (official)
Religion: Roman Catholic 97%
Life expectancy: 73 (men); 80 (women) (2000–05)
Chronology
2nd century BC: Romans conquered Iberian peninsula.
5th century AD: Iberia overrun by Vandals and Visigoths after fall of Roman Empire.
711: Visigoth kingdom overthrown by Muslims invading from North Africa.
997–1064: Christians resettled northern area, which came under rule of Léon and Castile.
1139: Afonso I, son of Henry of Burgundy, defeated Muslims; the area became an independent kingdom.
1340: Final Muslim invasion defeated.
15th century: Age of exploration: Portuguese mariners surveyed coast of Africa, opened sea route to India (Vasco da Gama), and reached Brazil (Pedro Cabral).
16th century: 'Golden Age': Portugal flourished as commercial and colonial power.
1580: Philip II of Spain took throne of Portugal.
1640: Spanish rule overthrown in bloodless coup; Duke of Braganza proclaimed as King John IV.
1668: Spain recognized Portuguese independence.
1755: Lisbon devastated by earthquake.
1807: Napoleonic France invaded Portugal; Portuguese court fled to Brazil.
1807–11: In the Peninsular War British forces played a leading part in liberating Portugal from the French.
1820: Liberal revolution forced King John VI to return from Brazil and accept constitutional government.
1822: First Portuguese constitution adopted.
1828: Dom Miguel blocked the succession of his niece, Queen Maria, and declared himself absolute monarch; civil war ensued between liberals and conservatives.
1834: Queen Maria regained the throne with British, French, and Brazilian help; constitutional government restored.
1840s: Severe disputes between supporters of radical 1822 constitution and more conservative 1826 constitution.
late 19th century: Government faced severe financial difficulties; rise of socialist, anarchist, and republican parties.
1908: Assassination of King Carlos I.
1910: Portugal became republic after a three-day insurrection forced King Manuel II to flee.
1911: New regime adopted liberal constitution, but republic proved unstable, violent, and corrupt.
1916–18: Portugal fought in World War I on Allied side.
1926–51: Popular military coup installed Gen António de Fragoso Carmona as president.
1933: Authoritarian 'Estado Novo' ('New State') constitution adopted.
1949: Portugal became founding member of North Atlantic Treaty Organization (NATO).
1974: Army seized power to end stalemate situation in African colonial wars.
1975: Portuguese colonies achieved independence.
1976: First free elections in 50 years.
1986: Soares became the first civilian president in 60 years; Portugal joined the European Community (EC).

1989: The Social Democrat government started to dismantle the socialist economy and privatize major industries.

1995: Antonio Gutteres was elected prime minister in the legislative elections.

1996: Jorge Sampaio was elected president.

2001: Sampaio was re-elected president. A cattle slaughter programme was instituted to combat the growing threat of mad cow disease (BSE). A bridge over the River Douro collapsed, killing 70 and prompting the resignation of the public works minister.

2005: The Socialist Party won the general election and its leader, Jose Socrates, became prime minister.

Portuguese inhabitants of Portugal. The Portuguese have a mixed cultural heritage that can be traced back to the Lusitanian Celts who were defeated by the Romans in about 140 BC. In the 5th century AD the Suebi, a Germanic group, overran the Iberian peninsula, and were later subdued by the Visigoths. In the 8th century AD southern Portugal was invaded by the Moors. The Portuguese are predominantly Roman Catholic.

Portuguese language member of the Romance branch of the Indo-European language family; spoken by 120–135 million people worldwide, it is the national language of Portugal, closely related to Spanish and strongly influenced by Arabic. Portuguese is also spoken in Brazil, Angola, Mozambique, Cape Verde, and other former Portuguese colonies.

Portuguese man-of-war any of a genus *Physalia* of phylum *Coelenterata* (see *coelenterate). They live in the sea, in colonies, and have a large air-filled bladder (or 'float') on top and numerous hanging tentacles made up of feeding, stinging, and reproductive individuals. The float can be 30 cm/1 ft long.

Port-Vila port and capital of Vanuatu, on the southwest of Efate Island; population (1996 est) 31,800. Local industries include meat canning.

Poseidon Roman Neptune, in Greek mythology, the chief god of the sea, brother of Zeus and Pluto. The brothers dethroned their father, *Kronos, and divided his realm, Poseidon taking the sea. Husband of Amphitrite, his sons were the merman sea god *Triton and the Cyclops Polyphemus.

positivism theory that confines genuine knowledge within the bounds of science and observation. The theory is associated with the French philosopher Auguste Comte and *empiricism. **Logical positivism** developed in the 1920s. It rejected any metaphysical world beyond everyday science and common sense, and confined statements to those of formal logic or mathematics.

positron antiparticle of the electron; an *elementary particle having the same mass as an electron but exhibiting a positive charge. The positron was discovered in 1932 by US physicist Carl Anderson at the California Institute of Technology, USA, its existence having been predicted by the British physicist Paul Dirac in 1928.

positron emission tomography (PET) imaging technique that enables doctors to observe the metabolic activity of the human body by following the progress of a radioactive chemical that has been inhaled or injected, detecting *gamma radiation given out when *positrons emitted by the chemical are annihilated.

The technique has been used to study a wide range of conditions, including schizophrenia, Alzheimer's disease, and Parkinson's disease.

possum another name for the *opossum, a marsupial animal with a prehensile tail found in North, Central and South America. The name is also used for many of the smaller marsupials found in Australia.

poster public notice used for advertising or propaganda, often illustrated. Ancestors of the modern poster were **handbills** with woodcut illustrations, which were posted up in public places. The French artist Jules Chéret pioneered the medium of colour lithography in his posters of the early 1860s, but the 1890s were the classic age of the poster, notable producers being *Toulouse-Lautrec, Aubrey *Beardsley, and the 'Beggarstaff Brothers' (William Nicholson and James Pryde). Poster design flourished again in the 1960s with the arrival of psychedelic art, and artists such as Rick Griffin (1944–1991) and Stanley Mouse (1921–) in the USA, and Michael English (1942–) in the UK.

post-Impressionism broad term covering various developments in French painting that developed out of *Impressionism in the period from about 1880 to about 1905. Some of these developments built on the achievements of Impressionism, but others were reactions against its concentration on surface appearances, seeking to reintroduce a concern with emotional and symbolic values.

postmodernism late-20th-century movement in architecture and the arts that rejected the preoccupation of post-war *modernism with purity of form and technique, and sought to dissolve the divisions between art, popular culture, and the media. Postmodernists use a combination of style elements from the past, such as the classical and the baroque, and apply them to spare modern forms, often with ironic effect. Their slightly off-key familiarity creates a more immediate appeal than the strict severity of modernism. Among a diverse number of groups and individuals who emerged in the 1970s and 1980s are the architects Robert Venturi and Michael Graves (both US), the novelists David Lodge (English) and Thomas Pynchon (US), and the artists Gerhard Richter and Sherrie Levine.

postmortem *or* **autopsy** (Latin 'after death') dissection of a dead body to determine the cause of death.

postnatal depression mood change occurring in many mothers a few days after the birth of a baby, also known as 'baby blues'. It is usually a short-lived condition but can sometimes persist; one in five women suffer a lasting depression after giving birth. The most severe form of post-natal depressive illness, **puerperal psychosis**, requires hospital treatment.

potash general name for any potassium-containing mineral, most often applied to potassium carbonate (K_2CO_3) or potassium hydroxide (KOH). Potassium carbonate, originally made by roasting plants to ashes in earthenware pots, is commercially produced from the mineral sylvite (potassium chloride, KCl) and is used mainly in making artificial fertilizers, glass, and soap.

potassium chemical symbol K, (Dutch *potassa* 'potash') soft, waxlike, silver-white, metallic element, atomic number 19, relative atomic mass 39.0983. Its chemical symbol comes from the Latin *kalium*. It is one of the *alkali metals (in Group 1 of the *periodic table of the elements), and has a very low density – it floats on water, and is the second lightest metal (after lithium). It is one of the most reactive in the *reactivity series of metals, oxidizing rapidly when exposed to air and reacting violently with water. Of great abundance in the Earth's crust, it is widely distributed. It is found in salt and mineral deposits in the form of potassium aluminium silicates and potassium nitrate (saltpetre). Potassium has to be extracted from its compounds by *electrolysis because of its high reactivity.

potato perennial plant with edible tuberous roots that are rich in starch and are extensively eaten as a vegetable. Used by the Andean Indians for at least 2,000 years before the Spanish Conquest, the potato was introduced to Europe by the mid-16th century, and reputedly to England by the explorer Walter Raleigh. (Genus *Solanum tuberosum*, family Solanaceae.)

potato blight disease of the potato caused by a parasitic fungus *Phytophthora infestans*. It was the cause of the 1845 potato famine in Ireland. New strains of *P. infestans* continue to arise. The most virulent version so far is *P. infestans US-8*, which arose in Mexico in 1992, spreading to North America in 1994.

potential difference (PD) difference in the electrical potential (see *potential, electric) of two points, being equal to the electrical energy converted by a unit electric charge moving from one point to the other. Electrons flow in a conducting material towards the part that is relatively more positive (fewer negative charges). The SI unit of potential difference is the volt (V). The potential difference between two points in a circuit is commonly referred to as voltage (and can be measured with a voltmeter). See also *Ohm's law.

potential, electric energy required to bring a unit electric charge from infinity to the point at which potential is defined. The SI unit of potential is the volt (V). Positive electric charges will flow 'downhill' from a region of high potential to a region of low potential.

potential energy (PE) *energy possessed by an object by virtue of its relative position or state (for example, as in a compressed spring or a muscle). It can be thought of as 'stored' energy. An object that has been raised up has energy stored due to its height. It is described as having gravitational potential energy.

potentiometer electrical *resistor that can be divided so as to compare, measure, or control voltages. In radio circuits, any rotary variable resistance (such as volume control) is referred to as a potentiometer.

Potomac river of the eastern USA, forming the boundaries between West Virginia, Virginia, and Maryland states. Rising in the Allegheny Mountains, it flows 459 km/285 mi southeast into Chesapeake Bay. It is created by the confluence of the North Potomac, 153 km/95 mi long, and South Potomac, 209 km/130 mi long, and its chief tributaries are the Shenandoah and the Monocacy. At *Washington, DC, 185 km/116 mi from its mouth, the Potomac becomes tidal and navigable for large ships.

Potsdam Conference conference held in Potsdam, Germany, 17 July–2 August 1945, between representatives of the USA, the UK, and the USSR. They established the political and economic principles governing the treatment of Germany in the initial period of Allied control at the end of World War II, and sent an ultimatum to Japan demanding unconditional surrender on pain of utter destruction.

Potter, (Helen) Beatrix (1866–1943) English writer and illustrator of children's books. Her first book was *The Tale of Peter Rabbit* (1900), followed by *The Tailor of Gloucester* (1902), based on her observation of family pets and wildlife. Other books in the series include *The Tale of Mrs Tiggy-Winkle* (1904), *The Tale of Jeremy Fisher* (1906), and a sequel to Peter Rabbit, *The Tale of the Flopsy Bunnies* (1909). Her tales are told with a childlike wonder, devoid of sentimentality, and accompanied by delicate illustrations.

pottery and porcelain ceramics in domestic and ornamental use, including *earthenware, stoneware, and **bone china** (or softpaste porcelain). Made of 5% bone ash and china clay, bone china was first made in the West in imitation of Chinese porcelain. The standard British bone china was developed about 1800, with a body of clay mixed with ox bones; a harder version, called **parian**, was developed in the 19th century and was used for figurine ornaments. Hardpaste **porcelain** is characterized by its hardness, ringing sound when struck, translucence, and shining finish, like that of a cowrie shell (Italian *porcellana*). It is made of kaolin and petuntse (fusible feldspar consisting chiefly of silicates reduced to a fine white powder); it is high-fired at 1,400 °C/2,552 °F. Porcelain first evolved from stoneware in China in about the 6th century AD. A formula for making porcelain was developed in the 18th century in Germany, also in France, Italy, and Britain. It was first produced in the USA in the early 19th century.

potto arboreal, nocturnal, African prosimian primate *Perodicticus potto* belonging to the *loris family. It has a thick body, strong limbs, and grasping feet and hands, and grows to 40 cm/16 in long, with horny spines along its backbone, which it uses in self-defence. It climbs slowly, and eats insects, snails, fruit, and leaves.

Poulenc, Francis Jean Marcel (1899–1963) French composer and pianist. A self-taught composer of witty and irreverent music, he was a member of the group of French composers known as *Les Six*. Among his many works are the operas *Les Mamelles de Tirésias/The Breasts of Tiresias* (1947) and *Dialogues des Carmélites/Dialogues of the Carmelites* (1957), and the ballet *Les Biches/The Little Darlings* (1923).

poultry domestic birds such as chickens, turkeys, ducks, and geese. They were domesticated for meat and eggs by early farmers in China, Europe, Egypt, and the Americas. Chickens were domesticated from the Southeast Asian jungle fowl *Gallus gallus* and then raised in the East as well as the West. Turkeys are New World birds, domesticated in ancient Mexico. Geese and ducks were domesticated in Egypt, China, and Europe.

pound abbreviation lb, imperial unit of mass. The commonly used avoirdupois pound, also called the **imperial standard pound** (7,000 grains/0.45 kg), differs from the **pound troy** (5,760 grains/0.37 kg), which is used for weighing precious metals. It derives from the Roman *libra*, which weighed 0.327 kg.

pound British standard monetary unit, issued as a gold sovereign before 1914, as a note 1914–83, and as a

737

circular yellow metal-alloy coin from 1983. The pound is also the name given to the unit of currency in Egypt, Lebanon, Malta, Sudan, and Syria.

Pound, Ezra Loomis (1885–1972) US poet and cultural critic. He is regarded as one of the most important figures of 20th-century literature, and his work revolutionized modern poetry. His *Personae* and *Exultations* (1909) established and promoted the principles of *Imagism, and influenced numerous poets, including T S *Eliot. His largest work was his series of *Cantos* (1925–69), a highly complex, eclectic collage that sought to create a unifying, modern cultural tradition.

Poussin, Nicolas (1594–1665) French painter. Active chiefly in Rome, he was the foremost exponent of 17th-century baroque classicism. He painted several major religious works, but is best known for his mythological and literary scenes executed in an austere classical style, for example, *Et in Arcadia Ego* (1638–39; Louvre, Paris). His style had a profound effect on the development of French art.

poverty condition in which the basic needs of human beings (shelter, food, and clothing) are not being met. Over one-fifth of the world's population was living in extreme poverty in 1995, of which around 70% were women. Nearly 13.5 million children under five die each year from poverty-related illness (measles, diarrhoea, malaria, pneumonia, and *malnutrition). In its annual report, the UN Children's Fund (UNICEF) said that 600 million children continue to live in poverty. There are different definitions of the standard of living considered to be the minimum adequate level (known as the **poverty level**). The European Union (EU) definition of poverty is an income of less than half the EU average (£150 a week in 1993). By this definition, there were 50 million poor in the EU in 1993.

poverty cycle set of factors or events by which poverty, once started, is likely to continue unless there is outside intervention. Once an area or a person has become poor, this tends to lead to other disadvantages, which may in turn result in further poverty. The situation is often found in inner city areas and shanty towns. Applied to countries, the poverty cycle is often called the **development trap**.

Powell, Michael (Latham) (1905–1990) English film director and producer. In collaboration with the Hungarian-born screenwriter Emeric *Pressburger, he produced a succession of ambitious and richly imaginative films, including *I Know Where I'm Going!* (1945), *A Matter of Life and Death* (1946), and *The Red Shoes* (1948).

power in mathematics, that which is represented by an *exponent or index, denoted by a superior numeral. A number or symbol raised to the power of 2 – that is, multiplied by itself – is said to be squared (for example, 3^2, x^2), and when raised to the power of 3, it is said to be cubed (for example, 2^3, y^3). Any number to the power zero always equals 1.

power in physics, the rate of doing work or transferring energy from one form to another. It is measured in watts (joules per second) or other units of work per unit time.

Powys unitary authority in central Wales, created in 1996 from the former county of Powys. **area:** 5,179 sq km/ 1,999 sq mi **towns:** Llandrindod Wells (administrative headquarters), Brecon, Builth Wells, Newtown, Welshpool **physical:** mountainous to the north, Black Mountains, rivers *Wye and *Severn, which both rise on the eastern slopes of Plynlimon **features:** the Brecon Beacons National Park, Lake Vyrnwy (an artificial reservoir supplying Liverpool and Birmingham), alternative-technology centre near Machynlleth **population:** (2001 est) 126,300.

pragmatism philosophical tradition that interprets truth in terms of the practical effects of what is believed and, in particular, the usefulness of these effects. The US philosopher Charles Peirce is often accounted the founder of pragmatism; it was further advanced by William James.

Prague Czech **Praha**, city and capital of the Czech Republic on the River Vltava; population (1993) 1,217,300. Industries include cars, aircraft, chemicals, paper and printing, clothing, brewing, and food processing. It was the capital of Czechoslovakia 1918–93.

Prague Spring the 1968 programme of liberalization, begun under a new Communist Party leader in Czechoslovakia. In August 1968 Soviet tanks invaded Czechoslovakia and entered the capital Prague to put down the liberalization movement initiated by the prime minister Alexander Dubcek, who had earlier sought to assure the Soviets that his planned reforms would not threaten socialism. Dubcek was arrested but released soon afterwards. Most of the Prague Spring reforms were reversed.

prairie central North American plain, formerly grass-covered, extending over most of the region between the Rocky Mountains to the west, and the Great Lakes and Ohio River to the east.

prairie dog any of the North American genus *Cynomys* of burrowing rodents in the squirrel family (Sciuridae). They grow to 30 cm/12 in, plus a short 8 cm/3 in tail. Their 'towns' can contain up to several thousand individuals. Their barking cry has given them their name. Persecution by ranchers has brought most of the five species close to extinction.

Prakrit general name for the ancient Indo-European dialects of northern India, contrasted with the sacred classical language Sanskrit. The word is itself Sanskrit, meaning 'natural', as opposed to *Sanskrit*, which means 'perfected'. The Prakrits are considered to be the ancestors of such modern northern Indian languages as Hindi, Punjabi, and Bengali.

Prasad, Rajendra (1884–1963) Indian politician. He was president of the Indian National Congress several times between 1934 and 1948 and India's first president after independence 1950–62.

praseodymium chemical symbol Pr, (Greek *prasios* 'leek-green' + *didymos* 'twin') silver-white, malleable, metallic element of the *lanthanide series, atomic number 59, relative atomic mass 140.907. It occurs in nature in the minerals monzanite and bastnaesite, and its green salts are used to colour glass and ceramics. It was named in 1885 by Austrian chemist Carl von Welsbach.

prawn any of various *shrimps of the suborder Natantia ('swimming'), of the crustacean order Decapoda, as contrasted with lobsters and crayfishes, which are able to 'walk'. Species called prawns are generally larger than species called shrimps.

Praxiteles (lived mid-4th century BC) Greek sculptor. His *Aphrodite of Cnidus* of about 350 BC is thought to have initiated the tradition of life-size free-standing female nudes in Greek sculpture. It was destroyed by fire in AD 475, but a Roman copy exists in the Vatican.

prayer address to divine power, ranging from a ritual formula to attain a desired end, to selfless communication in meditation. Within Christianity, the Catholic and Orthodox churches sanction prayer to the Virgin Mary, angels, and saints as intercessors, whereas Protestantism limits prayer to God alone.

praying mantis another name for *mantis.

Precambrian era in geology, the time from the formation of the Earth (4.6 billion years ago) up to 570 million years ago. Its boundary with the succeeding Cambrian period marks the time when animals first developed hard outer parts (exoskeletons) and so left abundant fossil remains. It comprises about 85% of geological time and is divided into two eons: the Archaean and the Proterozoic.

precession slow wobble of the Earth on its axis, like that of a spinning top. The gravitational pulls of the Sun and Moon on the Earth's equatorial bulge cause the Earth's axis to trace out a circle on the sky every 25,800 years. The position of the celestial poles (see *celestial sphere) is constantly changing owing to precession, as are the positions of the equinoxes (the points at which the celestial equator intersects the Sun's path around the sky). The **precession of the equinoxes** means that there is a gradual westward drift in the ecliptic – the path that the Sun appears to follow – and in the coordinates of objects on the celestial sphere.

precipitation in chemistry, the formation of an insoluble solid in a liquid as a result of a reaction within the liquid between two or more soluble substances. For example, if solutions of lead nitrate and potassium iodide are added together, bright yellow, insoluble lead iodide appears as a precipitate in the solution, making it cloudy. The **precipitation reaction** is: lead nitrate + potassium iodide → lead iodide + potassium nitrate. If the newly formed solid settles, it forms a **precipitate**; if the particles of solid are very small, they will remain in suspension, forming a *colloidal precipitate.

precipitation in meteorology, water that falls to the Earth from the atmosphere. It is part of the *water (hydrological) cycle. Forms of precipitation include *rain, snow, sleet, *hail, *dew, and *frost.

pre-Columbian art art of the Central and South American civilizations that existed prior to the arrival of European colonizers in the 16th century. Pre-Columbian art thrived over a wide timescale, from 1800 BC to AD 1500. However, despite the great range and variety of artwork, certain characteristics were repeated throughout the region, namely a preference for angular, linear patterns, and three-dimensional ceramics.

predestination in Christian theology, the doctrine asserting that God has determined all events beforehand, including the ultimate salvation or damnation of the individual human soul. Today Christianity in general accepts that humanity has free will, though some forms, such as Calvinism, believe that salvation can only be attained by the gift of God. The concept of predestination is also found in Islam.

pre-eclampsia *or* **toxaemia of pregnancy** potentially serious condition developing in the third trimester and marked by high blood pressure and fluid retention. Arising from unknown causes, it disappears when pregnancy is over. It may progress to eclampsia if untreated. Pre-eclampsia affects 5–10% of pregant women globally.

pregnancy in humans, the process during which a developing embryo grows within the woman's womb. It begins at conception and ends at birth, and the normal length is 40 weeks, or around nine months. The division of the fertilized egg, or ovum, begins within hours of conception. Within a week a ball of cells – a blastocyst – has developed. After the third week, the embryo has changed from a mass of cells into a recognizable shape. At four weeks, the embryo is 3 mm/0.1 in long, with a large bulge for the heart and small pits for the ears. At six weeks, the embryo is 1.5 cm/0.6 in, with a pulsating heart and ear flaps. At the eighth week, the embryo is 2.5 cm/1 in long and recognizably human, with eyelids, small fingers, and toes. From the end of the second month, the embryo is almost fully formed and further development is mainly by growth. After this stage, the embryo is termed a fetus.

prehistoric art art that predates written records. The history of the fine arts – painting, engraving, and sculpture – begins around 40000 BC in the Palaeolithic period (Old Stone Age). The oldest known rock engravings are in Australia, but within the next 30000 years art occurs on every continent. The earliest surviving artefacts in Europe date from approximately 30000–10000 BC, a period of hunter-gatherer cultures. Small sculptures are generally of fecund female nudes and relate to the cult of the Mother Goddess; for example, the stone *Willendorf Venus* (Kunsthistorisches Museum, Vienna) about 21000 BC. The murals of the caves of *Lascaux, France, and *Altamira, Spain, depict mostly animals. During the Neolithic period (New Stone Age) 10000–2000 BC, settled communities were established, which led to a greater technical and aesthetic sophistication in tools, ceramic vessels, jewellery, and human and animal figures. Human figures appear more often in wall paintings, and are skilfully composed into groups. The period 4000–2000 BC saw the erection of the great *megalith monuments, such as those at Carnac, France, and Stonehenge, England, and the production of ceramic pots and figurines with decorative elements that were later to be developed in *Celtic art.

prehistoric life diverse organisms that inhabited Earth from the origin of life about 3.5 billion years ago to the time when humans began to keep written records, about 3500 BC. During the course of evolution, new forms of life developed and many other forms, such as the dinosaurs, became extinct. Prehistoric life evolved over this vast timespan from simple bacteria-like cells in the oceans to algae and protozoans and complex multicellular forms such as worms, molluscs, crustaceans, fishes, insects, land plants, amphibians, reptiles, birds, and mammals. On a geological timescale humans evolved relatively recently, about 4 million years ago, although the exact dating is a matter of some debate. See also *geological time.

prehistory human cultures before the use of writing. The study of prehistory is mainly dependent on archaeology. General chronological dividing lines between prehistoric eras, or history and prehistory, are difficult to determine because communities have developed at differing rates. The Three Age System of classification (published in 1836 by the Danish archaeologist Christian Thomsen) is based on the predominant materials used by early humans for tools and weapons: *Stone Age, *Bronze Age, and *Iron Age.

prelude in music, a composition intended as the preface to further music, especially preceding a *fugue, forming the opening piece of a *suite, or setting the mood for a stage work, as in Richard Wagner's *Lohengrin*. As used by Frédéric Chopin, a prelude is a short self-contained piano work.

prematurity condition of an infant born before the full term. In obstetrics, an infant born before 37 weeks' gestation is described as premature.

premenstrual tension (PMT) or **premenstrual syndrome** medical condition caused by hormone changes and comprising a number of physical and emotional features that occur cyclically before menstruation and disappear with its onset. Symptoms include mood changes, breast tenderness, a feeling of bloatedness, and headache.

Pre-Raphaelite Brotherhood (PRB) group of British painters (1848–53); Dante Gabriel *Rossetti, John Everett *Millais, and Holman *Hunt – at this time young students at the Royal Academy – were the leading figures among the seven founders. They aimed to paint serious subjects, to study nature closely, and to return to the sincerity of spirit of painters before the time of *Raphael Sanzio (1483–1520). Their subjects were mainly biblical and literary, painted with obsessive naturalism and attention to detail. The group was short-lived but added a new realism to the art of the 1850s, and influenced many painters.

Presbyterianism system of Christian Protestant church government, expounded during the Reformation by John Calvin in Geneva, Switzerland, which gives its name to the established Church of Scotland, and is also practised in England, Wales, Ireland, Switzerland, North America, and elsewhere. There is no compulsory form of worship and each congregation is governed by presbyters or elders (clerical or lay), who are of equal rank. Congregations are grouped in presbyteries, synods, and general assemblies.

Prescott, John Leslie (1938–) British Labour politician, deputy leader from 1994, deputy prime minister from 1997. He was minister for the department of environment, transport, and the regions 1997–2001. In 2001, after a second Labour election victory, he took on a newly created post in the Cabinet Office to oversee the implementation of manifesto pledges, keeping responsibility for policy on housing, devolution, regional and local government, and the Government Offices for the Regions, under what, from May 2002, was named the Office of the Deputy Prime Minister.

preservative substance (*additive) added to a food in order to inhibit the growth of bacteria, yeasts, moulds, and other micro-organisms, and therefore extend its shelf life. The term sometimes refers to *anti-oxidants (substances added to oils and fats to prevent their becoming rancid) as well. All preservatives are potentially damaging to health if eaten in sufficient quantity. Both the amount used, and the foods in which they can be used, are restricted by law.

president in government, the usual title of the head of state in a republic; the power of the office may range from the equivalent of a constitutional monarch to the actual head of the government.

Presley, Elvis (Aron) (1935–1977) US singer and guitarist, the most influential performer of the rock-and-roll era. With his recordings for Sun Records in Memphis, Tennessee in 1954–55, and early hits such as 'Heartbreak Hotel', 'Hound Dog', and 'Love Me Tender' (all 1956), he created an individual vocal style, influenced by southern blues, gospel music, country music, and rhythm and blues. His records continue to sell in their millions.

Pressburger, Emeric (1902–1988) adopted name of Imre József Pressburger, Hungarian-born film producer, screenwriter, and novelist. He worked on films in Germany, France, and Britain. Together with Michael *Powell, he made 14 films between 1942 and 1956, including such classics of the British cinema as *The Life and Death of Colonel Blimp* (1943), *A Canterbury Tale* (1944), and *The Red Shoes* (1948).

press gang method used to recruit soldiers and sailors into the British armed forces in the 18th and early 19th centuries. In effect it was a form of kidnapping carried out by the services or their agents, often with the aid of armed men. This was similar to the practice of 'shanghaiing' sailors for duty in the merchant marine, especially in the Far East.

pressure in a fluid, the force exerted normally (at right angles) on the surface of a body immersed in the fluid. The SI unit of pressure is the pascal (Pa), equal to a pressure of one newton per square metre. In the atmosphere, the pressure declines with increasing height from about 100 kPa at sea level to zero where the atmosphere fades into space. Pressure is commonly measured with a *barometer, *manometer, or *Bourdon gauge. Other common units of pressure are the bar and the torr.

pressurized water reactor (PWR) *nuclear reactor design used in nuclear power stations in many countries, and in nuclear-powered submarines. In the PWR, water under pressure is used in a closed system, as a coolant, passing through the reactor to the generator. Boric acid is added as a *moderator. It circulates through a steam generator, where its heat boils water to provide steam to drive power *turbines.

Pretoria city in Gauteng Province, South Africa, and the country's administrative capital; population (1991) 1,080,200. Industries include engineering, chemicals, iron, steel, cement, diamonds, granite quarrying, chemicals, and food processing. Founded in 1855, it was named after Boer leader Andries Pretorius (1799–1853). It was the administrative capital of the Union of South Africa from 1910 and capital of Transvaal Province 1860–1994.

Priapus in Greek mythology, the god of fertility, son of Dionysus and Aphrodite, represented as grotesquely ugly, with an exaggerated phallus. He was later a Roman god of gardens, where his image was frequently used as a scarecrow.

prickly pear any of several cacti (see *cactus) native to Central and South America, mainly Mexico and Chile, but naturalized in southern Europe, North Africa, and

Australia, where it is a pest. The common prickly pear (*O. vulgaris*) is low-growing, with flat, oval stem joints, bright yellow flowers, and prickly, oval fruit; the flesh and seeds of the peeled fruit have a pleasant taste. (Genus *Opuntia*, family Cactaceae.)

Priestley, J(ohn) B(oynton) (1894–1984) English novelist and dramatist. His best-known plays are the mysterious and puzzling *An Inspector Calls* (1945) and *The Linden Tree* (1948), a study of post-war social issues. Priestley had a gift for family comedy, which is seen in *When We Are Married* (1938). He was also known for his wartime BBC broadcasts and literary criticism, such as *Literature and Western Man* (1960). He was a stern critic of the social effects of 20th-century modernization, and in his work he fondly reflects his youth in Edwardian Yorkshire.

Primakov, Yevgeny Maksimovich (1928–) Russian politician, prime minister 1998–99. He was appointed foreign minister in 1995 in order to give President Boris *Yeltsin some credibility with those who supported the communists and nationalists. His championing of Russia's interests and his willingness to use anti-Western rhetoric restored some of the damage done to injured pride. As prime minister, Primakov saw the achievement of consensus as more important than reform, and refused to adopt an economic programme that could attract the support of the IMF. Political peace was preserved, at the cost of a disastrously declining economy. Primakov was sacked by Yeltsin in a surprise move in May 1999.

primary in presidential election campaigns in the USA, a statewide ballot in which voters indicate their candidate preferences for the two main parties. Held in 41 states, primaries begin with New Hampshire in February and continue until June; they operate under varying complex rules. primaries are also held to choose candidates for other posts, such as Congressional seats.

primate in zoology, any member of the order of mammals that includes monkeys, apes, and humans (together called **anthropoids**), as well as lemurs, bushbabies, lorises, and tarsiers (together called **prosimians**). Generally, they have forward-directed eyes, gripping hands and feet, opposable thumbs, and big toes. They tend to have nails rather than claws, with gripping pads on the ends of the digits, all adaptations to the arboreal, climbing mode of life.

prime minister *or* **premier** head of a parliamentary government, usually the leader of the largest party. In countries with an executive president, the prime minister is of lesser standing, whereas in those with dual executives, such as France, power is shared with the president. In federal countries, such as Australia, the head of the federal government has the title prime minister, while the heads of government of the states are called premiers. In Germany, the equivalent of the prime minister is known as the chancellor.

prime number number that can be divided only by 1 and itself, that is, having no other factors. There is an infinite number of primes, the first ten of which are 2, 3, 5, 7, 11, 13, 17, 19, 23, and 29 (by definition, the number 1 is excluded from the set of prime numbers). The number 2 is the only even prime because all other even numbers have 2 as a factor. Numbers other than primes can be expressed as a product of their prime factors.

Primitivism influence on modern art (Ernst *Kirchner, Amedeo *Modigliani, Pablo *Picasso, Paul *Gauguin, and others) of **primitive art**: *prehistoric art; the indigenous arts of Africa, Oceania, and the Americas; and Western folk art.

primrose any of a group of plants belonging to the primrose family, with showy five-lobed flowers. The common primrose (*P. vulgaris*) is a woodland plant, native to Europe, with abundant pale yellow flowers in spring. Related to it is the *cowslip. (Genus *Primula*, family Primulaceae.)

Prince Edward Island smallest province of Canada, situated in the Gulf of St Lawrence, separated from Nova Scotia (to the south and east) and New Brunswick (to the west) by the Northumberland Strait; area 5,700 sq km/2,200 sq mi; population (2001 est) 138,500. The capital is Charlottetown. Industries include fishing, food processing, and information technology. Potatoes are cultivated and there is also dairying.

printed circuit board (PCB) electrical circuit created by laying (printing) 'tracks' of a conductor such as copper on one or both sides of an insulating board. The PCB was invented in 1936 by Austrian scientist Paul Eisler, and was first used on a large scale in 1948.

printer in computing, an output device for producing printed copies of text or graphics. Types include the daisywheel printer, which produces good-quality text but no graphics; the dot matrix printer, which produces text and graphics by printing a pattern of small dots; the ink-jet printer, which creates text and graphics by spraying a fine jet of quick-drying ink onto the paper; and the laser printer, which uses electrostatic technology very similar to that used by a photocopier to produce high-quality text and graphics.

printing reproduction of multiple copies of text or illustrative material on paper, as in books or newspapers, or on an increasing variety of materials; for example, on plastic containers or on fabrics. The first printing used woodblocks, followed by carved wood type or moulded metal type and hand-operated presses. Modern printing is effected by electronically controlled machinery. Current printing processes include electronic phototypesetting with *offset printing, and *gravure print.

printmaking creating a picture or design by printing from a plate (woodblock, stone, or metal sheet) that holds ink or colour. The oldest form of print is the *woodcut, common in medieval Europe, followed by line *engraving (from the 15th century), and *etching (from the 17th century); in Japanese printmaking, the production of *ukiyo-e ('pictures of the floating world') using coloured woodcuts, flourished from the 17th century. *Lithography was invented in 1796.

prion acronym, by rearrangement, for PROteinaceous INfectious particle, infectious agent, a hundred times smaller than a virus. Composed of protein, and without any detectable nucleic acid (genetic material), it is strongly linked to a number of fatal degenerative brain diseases in mammals, such as bovine spongiform encephalopathy (BSE) in cattle, scrapie in sheep, and Creutzfeldt–Jakob disease (CJD) and kuru in humans.

prism in mathematics, a solid figure whose cross-section is the same along its length. When a slice is cut through a prism, the size and shape of the cross-section is always the same. A cube, for example, is a rectangular prism with all faces (bases and sides) the same shape and size. A cylinder is a prism with a circular cross section. The name of a prism is often derived from the shape of its prism, such as a triangular prism and a cuboid.

prism in optics, a triangular block of transparent material (plastic, glass, or silica) commonly used to 'bend' a ray of light or split a light beam (for example, white light) into its component colours. Prisms are used as mirrors to define the optical path in binoculars, camera viewfinders, and periscopes. The dispersive property of prisms is used in the *spectroscope.

prisoner of war (POW) person captured in war, who has fallen into the hands of, or surrendered to, an opponent. Such captives may be held in prisoner-of-war camps. The treatment of POWs is governed by the *Geneva Convention.

private finance initiative (PFI) an idea suggested by the UK Labour Party when in opposition before 1997, and particularly by the deputy leader, John *Prescott, who argued that the country's infrastructure (services) could be improved by combining public expenditure with private finance. Since assuming office in May 1997 the Labour government has kept the initiative alive by gaining the support of major companies for its investment plans and inviting industrialists to work in or with the administration.

private limited company *or* **ltd** registered company which has limited liability (the shareholders cannot lose more than their original shareholdings), and a minimum of two shareholders and a maximum of fifty. It cannot offer its shares or debentures to the public and their transfer is restricted. A private limited company is treated as a legal entity.

private sector the part of the economy that is owned and controlled by private individuals and business organizations such as private and public limited companies. In a free enterprise economy, the private sector is responsible for allocating most of the resources within the economy. This contrasts with the *public sector, where economic resources are owned and controlled by the state.

privatization policy or process of selling or transferring state-owned or public assets and services (notably nationalized industries) to private investors. Privatization of services involves the government giving contracts to private firms to supply services previously supplied by public authorities.

privet any of a group of evergreen shrubs with dark green leaves, belonging to the olive family. They include the European common privet (*L. vulgare*) with white flowers and black berries, naturalized in North America, and the native North American California privet (*L. ovalifolium*), also known as hedge privet. (Genus *Ligustrum*, family Oleaceae.)

Privy Council council composed originally of the chief royal officials of the Norman kings in Britain; under the Tudors and early Stuarts it became the chief governing body. It was replaced in 1688 by the cabinet, originally a committee of the council, and the council itself now retains only formal powers in issuing royal proclamations and orders in council. In 2003 there were over 500 privy counsellors. Cabinet ministers are automatically members, and it is presided

over by the lord president of the council (Baroness Amos from 2003).

privy purse personal expenditure of the British sovereign, which derives from his/her own resources (as distinct from the *civil list, which now finances only expenses incurred in pursuance of official functions and duties). The office that deals with this expenditure is also known as the Privy Purse.

probability likelihood, or chance, that an event will occur, often expressed as odds, or in mathematics, numerically as a fraction or decimal. In general, the probability that n particular events will happen out of a total of m possible events is n/m. A certainty has a probability of 1; an impossibility has a probability of 0.

probate formal proof of a will. In the UK, if a will's validity is unquestioned, it is proven in 'common form'; the executor, in the absence of other interested parties, obtains at a probate registry a grant upon his or her own oath. Otherwise, it must be proved in 'solemn form': its validity established at a probate court (in the Chancery Division of the High Court), those concerned being made parties to the action.

processor in computing, another name for the *central processing unit or *microprocessor of a computer.

Procrustes *or* **Damastes** *or* **Polypemon** (Greek 'the stretcher') in Greek mythology, a robber of Attica who tied his victims to a bed and adjusted them to its length by amputating their legs or racking (stretching) their bodies. He was killed by the hero *Theseus.

procurator fiscal officer of a Scottish sheriff's court who (combining the role of public prosecutor and coroner) inquires into suspicious deaths and carries out the preliminary questioning of witnesses to crime.

Procyon *or* **Alpha Canis Minoris** brightest star in the constellation *Canis Minor and the eighth-brightest star in the night sky. Procyon is a white star 11.4 light years from the Sun, with a mass 1.7 times that of the Sun. It has a *white dwarf companion that orbits it every 40 years.

productivity in economics, the output produced by a given quantity of labour, usually measured as output per person employed in the firm, industry, sector, or economy concerned. Productivity is determined by the quality and quantity of the fixed *capital used by labour, and the effort of the workers concerned.

profit difference between the selling price and the production cost. This means production cost in its wide sense, that is not only the cost of manufacturing a product, but all the fixed and variable costs incurred in the process of producing and delivering the product or service. A more refined definition of profit is that of net profit. This is the income remaining after all costs have been subtracted. The net profit figure may be stated as being before or after tax. Operating profit is a term used to define profit (or loss) arising from the principal trading activity of a company. Operating profit is calculated by deducting operating expenses – expenses vital to core activity – from trading profit – profit before deduction of items such as auditors fees, interest etc.

progesterone *steroid hormone that occurs in vertebrates. In mammals, it regulates the menstrual cycle and pregnancy. Progesterone is secreted by the corpus luteum (the ruptured Graafian follicle of a discharged ovum).

program in computing, a set of instructions that controls the operation of a computer. There are two main kinds: *applications programs, which carry out tasks for the benefit of the user – for example, word processing; and systems programs, which control the internal workings of the computer. A utility program is a systems program that carries out specific tasks for the user. Programs can be written in any of a number of *programming languages but are always translated into machine code before they can be executed by the computer.

programme music instrumental music that interprets a story, depicts a scene or painting, or illustrates a literary or philosophical idea. The term was first used by Franz *Liszt in the 19th century, when programme music was especially popular with composers of Romantic music (see *Romanticism), but there had been a great deal of descriptive music before then. Examples include Antonio Vivaldi's *Four Seasons* concertos (1725), Ludwig van Beethoven's *Eroica* and *Pastoral* symphonies (1803 and 1808), Felix Mendelssohn's *Hebrides Overture* ('Fingal's Cave', 1830), and the *symphonic poems of Liszt and Richard Strauss.

programming writing instructions in a programming language for the control of a computer. **Applications programming** is for end-user programs, such as accounts programs or word-processing packages. **Systems programming** is for operating systems and the like, which are concerned more with the internal workings of the computer.

programming language in computing, a special notation in which instructions for controlling a computer are written. Programming languages are designed to be easy for people to write and read, but must be capable of being mechanically translated (by a *compiler or an interpreter) into the *machine code that the computer can execute. Programming languages may be classified as *high-level languages or *low-level languages.

progression sequence of numbers each occurring in a specific relationship to its predecessor. An **arithmetic progression** has numbers that increase or decrease by a common sum or difference (for example, 2, 4, 6, 8); a **geometric progression** has numbers each bearing a fixed ratio to its predecessor (for example, 3, 6, 12, 24); and a **harmonic progression** has numbers whose *reciprocals are in arithmetical progression, for example 1, $\frac{1}{2}$, $\frac{1}{3}$, $\frac{1}{4}$.

Prohibition in US history, the period 1920–33 when the Eighteenth Amendment to the US Constitution was in force, and the manufacture, transportation, and sale of alcohol was illegal. This led to *bootlegging (the illegal distribution of liquor, often illicitly distilled), to the financial advantage of organized crime.

prokaryote in biology, an organism whose cells lack organelles (specialized segregated structures such as nuclei, mitochondria, and chloroplasts). Prokaryote DNA is not arranged in chromosomes but forms a coiled structure called a **nucleoid**. The prokaryotes comprise only the **bacteria** and **cyanobacteria** (see *blue-green algae); all other organisms are eukaryotes.

Prokofiev, Sergey Sergeyevich (1891–1953) Russian composer. His music includes operas such as *The Love for Three Oranges* (after Carlo Gozzi, 1921);

ballets for Sergei Diaghilev, including *Romeo and Juliet* (1935); seven symphonies including the *Classical Symphony* (1916–17); music for film, including Sergei Eisenstein's *Alexander Nevsky* (1938); piano and violin concertos; songs and cantatas (for example, that composed for the 30th anniversary of the October Revolution); and *Peter and the Wolf* (1936) for children, to his own libretto after a Russian folk tale.

proletariat (Latin *proletarii* 'the class possessing no property') in Marxist theory, those classes in society that possess no property, and therefore depend on the sale of their labour or expertise (as opposed to the capitalists or bourgeoisie, who own the means of production, and the petty bourgeoisie, or working small-property owners). They are usually divided into the industrial, agricultural, and intellectual proletariat.

PROM acronym for Programmable Read-Only Memory, in computing, a memory device in the form of an integrated circuit (chip) that can be programmed after manufacture to hold information permanently. PROM chips are empty of information when manufactured, unlike ROM (read-only memory) chips, which have information built into them. Other memory devices are EPROM (erasable programmable read-only memory) and *RAM (random-access memory).

Prometheus (Greek 'forethought') in Greek mythology, a *Titan who stole fire from heaven for the human race. In revenge, Zeus chained him to a rock and sent an eagle to gnaw at his liver by day; the organ grew back each night. *Heracles rescued him from the torture.

promethium chemical symbol Pm, radioactive, metallic element of the *lanthanide series, atomic number 61, relative atomic mass 145. It occurs in nature only in minute amounts, produced as a fission product/by-product of uranium in *pitchblende and other uranium ores; for a long time it was considered not to occur in nature. The longest-lived isotope has a half-life of slightly more than 20 years.

prominence bright cloud of gas projecting from the Sun into space 100,000 km/60,000 mi or more. **Quiescent prominences** last for months, and are held in place by magnetic fields in the Sun's corona. **Surge prominences** shoot gas into space at speeds of 1,000 kps/600 mps. **Loop prominences** are gases falling back to the Sun's surface after a solar *flare.

pronghorn ruminant mammal *Antilocapra americana* constituting the family Antilocapridae, native to the western USA. It is not a true antelope. It is light brown and about 1 m/3 ft high. It sheds its horns annually and can reach speeds of 100 kph/60 mph. The loss of prairies to agriculture, combined with excessive hunting, has brought this unique animal close to extinction.

propaganda systematic spreading (propagation) of information or disinformation (misleading information), usually to promote a religious or political doctrine with the intention of instilling particular attitudes or responses. As a system of spreading information it was considered a legitimate instrument of government, but became notorious through the deliberate distortion of facts or the publication of falsehoods by totalitarian regimes, notably Nazi Germany.

propane C_3H_8, gaseous hydrocarbon of the *alkane series, found in petroleum and used as a fuel and as a refrigerant.

propanol or **propyl alcohol** third member of the homologous series of *alcohols. Propanol is usually a mixture of two isomeric compounds (see *isomer): propan-1-ol ($CH_3CH_2CH_2OH$) and propan-2-ol ($CH_3CHOHCH_3$). Both are colourless liquids that can be mixed with water and are used in perfumery.

propanone common name **acetone**; CH_3COCH_3, colourless flammable liquid used extensively as a solvent, as in nail-varnish remover, and for making acrylic plastics. It boils at 56.5 °C/133.7 °F, mixes with water in all proportions, and has a characteristic odour.

propellant substance burned in a rocket for propulsion. With **bipropellant**, two propellants are used: oxidizer and fuel are stored in separate tanks and pumped independently into the combustion chamber. Liquid oxygen (oxidizer) and liquid hydrogen (fuel) are common propellants, used, for example, in the space shuttle main engines. The explosive charge that propels a projectile from a gun is also called a propellant.

propeller screwlike device used to propel some ships and aeroplanes. A propeller has a number of curved blades that describe a helical path as they rotate with the hub, and accelerate fluid (liquid or gas) backwards during rotation. Reaction to this backward movement of fluid sets up a propulsive thrust forwards. The marine screw propeller was developed by Francis Pettit Smith in the UK and Swedish-born John Ericson in the USA and was first used in 1839.

propene common name **propylene**; $CH_3CH=CH_2$, second member of the alkene series of hydrocarbons. A colourless, flammable gas, it is widely used by industry to make organic chemicals, including polypropylene plastics.

proper motion gradual change in the position of a star that results from its motion in orbit around our Galaxy, the Milky Way. Proper motions are slight and undetectable to the naked eye, but can be accurately measured on telescopic photographs taken many years apart. Barnard's Star is the star with the largest proper motion, 10.3 arc seconds per year.

property the right to control the use of a thing (such as land, a building, a work of art, or a computer program). In English law, a distinction is made between **real property**, which involves a degree of geographical fixity, and **personal property**, which does not. Property is never absolute, since any society places limits on an individual's property (such as the right to transfer that property to another). Different societies have held widely varying interpretations of the nature of property and the extent of the rights of the owner of that property.

prophylaxis any measure taken to prevent disease, including exercise and *vaccination. Prophylactic (preventive) medicine is an aspect of public-health provision that is receiving increasing attention.

proportional representation (PR) electoral system in which share of party seats corresponds to their proportion of the total votes cast, and minority votes are not wasted (as opposed to a simple majority, or 'first past the post', system).

propylene common name for *propene.

prose spoken or written language without regular metre; in literature, prose corresponds more closely to the patterns of everyday speech than *poetry, and often uses standard grammar and syntax and traditional rhetoric to achieve its ends.

prosecution in law, the party instituting legal proceedings. In the UK, the prosecution of a criminal case is begun by bringing the accused (defendant) before a magistrate, either by warrant or summons, or by arrest without warrant. Most criminal prosecutions are conducted by the *Crown Prosecution Service, although other government departments may also prosecute some cases; for example, the Department of Inland Revenue. An individual may bring a private prosecution, usually for assault.

Proserpina in Roman mythology, the goddess of the underworld. Her Greek equivalent is *Persephone.

prostaglandin any of a group of complex fatty acids present in the body that act as messenger substances between cells. Effects include stimulating the contraction of smooth muscle (for example, of the womb during birth), regulating the production of stomach acid, and modifying hormonal activity. In excess, prostaglandins may produce inflammatory disorders such as arthritis. Synthetic prostaglandins are used to induce labour in humans and domestic animals.

prostate cancer *cancer of the *prostate gland. It is a slow progressing cancer, and about 60% of cases are detected before metastasis (spreading), so it can be successfully treated by surgical removal of the gland and radiotherapy. It is, however, the second commonest cancer-induced death in males (after lung cancer). It kills 32,000 men a year in the USA alone.

prostate gland gland surrounding and opening into the *urethra at the base of the *bladder in male mammals.

prosthesis artificial device used to substitute for a body part which is defective or missing. Prostheses include artificial limbs, hearing aids, false teeth and eyes, heart *pacemakers and plastic heart valves and blood vessels.

protactinium chemical symbol Pa, (Latin protos 'before' + aktis 'first ray') silver-grey, radioactive, metallic element of the *actinide series, atomic number 91, relative atomic mass 231.036. It occurs in nature in very small quantities in *pitchblende and other uranium ores. It has 14 known isotopes; the longest-lived, Pa-231, has a half-life of 32,480 years.

protectionism in economics, the imposition of heavy duties or import quotas by a government as a means of discouraging the import of foreign goods likely to compete with domestic products. Price controls, quota systems, and the reduction of surpluses are among the measures taken for agricultural products in the European Union. The opposite practice is *free trade.

protectorate formerly in international law, a small state under the direct or indirect control of a larger one. The 20th-century equivalent was a *trust territory. In English history the rule of Oliver and Richard *Cromwell 1653–59 is referred to as the Protectorate.

protein large, complex, biologically-important molecules composed of amino acids joined by *peptide bonds. The number of amino acids used can be many hundreds. There are 20 different amino acids and they can be joined in any order. Proteins are essential to all living organisms. As *enzymes they regulate all aspects of metabolism. Structural proteins such as keratin and collagen make up skin, claws, bones, tendons, and ligaments; muscle proteins produce movement; haemoglobin transports oxygen; and membrane proteins regulate the movement of substances into and out of cells. For humans, protein is an essential part of the diet, and is found in greatest quantity in soy beans and other grain legumes, meat, eggs, and cheese. During digestion protein molecules are broken down into amino acids which are then easily absorbed into the body.

protein engineering creation of synthetic proteins designed to carry out specific tasks. For example, an enzyme may be designed to remove grease from soiled clothes and remain stable at the high temperatures in a washing machine.

Proterozoic Eon eon of geological time, 3.5 billion to 570 million years ago, the second division of the Precambrian. It is defined as the time of simple life, since many rocks dating from this eon show traces of biological activity, and some contain the fossils of bacteria and algae.

Protestantism one of the main divisions of Christianity, which emerged from Roman Catholicism at the *Reformation, a movement that questioned and 'protested' against the teachings and authority of the Roman Catholic Church. Denominations include some groups within the *Anglican communion, *Baptists, *Congregationalists (United Church of Christ), *Lutherans, *Methodists, and *Presbyterians, with a total membership of about 300 million.

Proteus in Greek mythology, the warden of the sea beasts of *Poseidon; his flocks were usually said to comprise of seals. He possessed the gift of prophecy but could transform himself into many forms to evade questioning.

protist single-celled organism which has a eukaryotic cell, but which is not a member of the plant, fungal, or animal kingdoms. The main protists are *protozoa.

proton (Greek 'first') in physics, a positively charged subatomic particle, a constituent of the nucleus of all *atoms. It carries a unit positive charge equal to the negative charge of an *electron. Its mass is almost 1,836 times that of an electron, or 1.673×10^{-24} g. The number of protons in the atom of an *element is equal to the *atomic number of that element.

proton number alternative name for *atomic number.

protoplasm contents of a living cell. Strictly speaking it includes all the discrete structures (organelles) in a cell, but it is often used simply to mean the jellylike material in which these float. The contents of a cell outside the nucleus are called *cytoplasm.

protozoa group of single-celled organisms without rigid cell walls. Some, such as amoeba, ingest other cells, but most are *saprotrophs or parasites. The group is polyphyletic (containing organisms which have different evolutionary origins).

Proudhon, Pierre Joseph (1809–1865) French anarchist, born in Besançon. He sat in the Constituent Assembly of 1848, was imprisoned for three years, and had to go into exile in Brussels. He published *Qu'est-ce que la propriété/What is Property?* (1840) and *Philosophie de la misère/Philosophy of Poverty* (1846).

Proust, Marcel (1871–1922) French novelist and critic. His immense autobiographical work *A la Recherche du temps perdu/Remembrance of Things Past* (1913–27), consisting of a series of novels, is the expression of his childhood memories coaxed from his subconscious; it is also a precise reflection of life in France at the end of the 19th century.

Provence-Alpes-Côte d'Azur region of southeast France, comprising the *départements* of Alpes-de-Haute-Provence, Hautes-Alpes, Alpes-Maritimes, Bouches-du-Rhône, Var, and Vaucluse; area 31,400 sq km/12,123 sq mi; the administrative centre is *Marseille; population (1999 est) 4,506,200. The Côte d'Azur, on the Mediterranean, is a tourist centre. Provence was an independent kingdom in the 10th century, and the area still has its own traditional language, Provençal.

Proxima Centauri closest star to the Sun, 4.2 light years away from the Sun. It is a faint *red dwarf, visible only with a telescope, and is a member of the Alpha Centauri triple-star system.

Prussia northern German state 1618–1945 on the Baltic coast. It was an independent kingdom until 1867, when it became, under Otto von *Bismarck, the military power of the North German Confederation and part of the German Empire in 1871 under the Prussian king Wilhelm I. West Prussia became part of Poland under the Treaty of *Versailles, and East Prussia was largely incorporated into the USSR after 1945.

prussic acid former name for *hydrocyanic acid.

Prut *or* **Pruc** *or* **Prutul** river in eastern Europe; length 900 km/565 mi. The Prut rises in the Carpathian Mountains in southwestern Ukraine, and flows south to meet the Danube at Reni. For most of its course it forms the frontier between Romania and Moldova.

psalm sacred poem or song of praise. The Book of Psalms in the Old Testament is divided into five books containing 150 psalms, traditionally ascribed to David, the second king of Israel. In the Christian church they may be sung antiphonally in *plainsong or set by individual composers to music in a great variety of styles, from Josquin Desprez's *De profundis* to Igor Stravinsky's *Symphony of Psalms* (1930).

PSBR abbreviation for *public sector borrowing requirement.

pseudocarp fruitlike structure that incorporates tissue that is not derived from the ovary wall. The additional tissues may be derived from floral parts such as the *receptacle and *calyx. For example, the coloured, fleshy part of a strawberry develops from the receptacle and the true fruits are small achenes – the 'pips' embedded in its outer surface. Rose hips are a type of pseudocarp that consists of a hollow, fleshy receptacle containing a number of achenes within. Different types of pseudocarp include pineapples, figs, apples, and pears.

pseudocopulation attempted copulation by a male insect with a flower. It results in *pollination of the flower and is common in the orchid family, where the flowers of many species resemble a particular species of female bee. When a male bee attempts to mate with a flower, the pollinia (groups of pollen grains) stick to its body. They are transferred to the stigma of another flower when the insect attempts copulation again.

psi in parapsychology, a hypothetical faculty common to humans and other animals, said to be responsible for *extrasensory perception, telekinesis, and other paranormal phenomena.

psoriasis chronic, recurring skin disease characterized by raised, red, scaly patches, on the scalp, elbows, knees, and elsewhere. Tar preparations, steroid creams, and ultraviolet light are used to treat it, and sometimes it disappears spontaneously. Psoriasis may be accompanied by a form of arthritis (inflammation of the joints). It affects 100 million people worldwide.

Psyche late Greek personification of the soul as a winged girl or young woman. In Greek mythology, she was the youngest and most beautiful of three princesses. Incensed by her beauty, Aphrodite ordered her son Eros, the god of love, to inspire Psyche with desire for the vilest creatures. Instead, he fell in love with her, in some traditions by accidently grazing himself with his arrow.

psychedelic drug any drug that produces hallucinations or altered states of consciousness. Such sensory experiences may be in the auditory, visual, tactile, olfactory, or gustatory fields or in any combination. Among drugs known to have psychedelic effects are LSD (lysergic acid diethylamide), mescaline, and, to a mild degree, marijuana, along with a number of other plant-derived or synthetically prepared substances.

psychiatry branch of medicine dealing with the diagnosis and treatment of mental disorder, normally divided into the areas of **neurotic conditions**, including anxiety, depression, and hysteria, and **psychotic disorders**, such as schizophrenia. Psychiatric treatment consists of drugs, analysis, or electroconvulsive therapy.

psychoanalysis theory and treatment method for neuroses, developed by Sigmund *Freud in the 1890s. Psychoanalysis asserts that the impact of early childhood sexuality and experiences, stored in the *unconscious, can lead to the development of adult emotional problems. The main treatment method involves the free association of ideas, and their interpretation by patient and analyst, in order to discover these long-buried events and to grasp their significance to the patient, linking aspects of the patient's historical past with the present relationship to the analyst. Psychoanalytic treatment aims to free the patient from specific symptoms and from irrational inhibitions and anxieties.

psychology systematic study of human and animal behaviour. The first psychology laboratory was founded in 1879 by Wilhelm Wundt at Leipzig, Germany. The subject includes diverse areas of study and application, among them the roles of instinct, heredity, environment, and culture; the processes of sensation, perception, learning, and memory; the bases of motivation and emotion; and the functioning of thought, intelligence, and language. Significant psychologists have included Gustav Fechner, founder of psychophysics; Wolfgang Köhler, one of the *Gestalt or 'whole' psychologists; Sigmund Freud and his associates Carl Jung and Alfred Adler; William James; Jean Piaget; Carl Rogers; Hans Eysenck; J B Watson; and B F Skinner.

psychometrics measurement of mental processes. This includes intelligence and aptitude testing to help in job selection and in the clinical assessment of cognitive deficiencies resulting from brain damage.

psychopathy personality disorder characterized by chronic antisocial behaviour (violating the rights of others, often violently) and an absence of feelings of guilt about the behaviour.

psychosis *or* **psychotic disorder** general term for a serious mental disorder in which the individual commonly loses contact with reality and may experience hallucinations (seeing or hearing things that do not exist) or delusions (fixed false beliefs). For example, in a paranoid psychosis, an individual may believe that others are plotting against him or her. A major type of psychosis is *schizophrenia.

psychosomatic of a physical symptom or disease thought to arise from emotional or mental factors.

psychotherapy any treatment for psychological problems that involves talking rather than surgery or drugs. Examples include *cognitive therapy and *psychoanalysis.

Ptah Egyptian god, the divine potter, a personification of the creative force. Worshipped at *Memphis, he was portrayed as a primitive human statue or mummy holding an ankh, symbol of life. He was said to be the father of *Imhotep, the physician and architect.

ptarmigan hardy, northern ground-dwelling bird of genus *Lagopus*, family Phasianidae (which also includes *grouse), with feathered legs and feet.

pteridophyte simple type of *vascular plant. The pteridophytes comprise four classes: the Psilosida, including the most primitive vascular plants, found mainly in the tropics; the Lycopsida, including the club mosses; the Sphenopsida, including the horsetails; and the Pteropsida, including the ferns. They do not produce seeds.

pterodactyl genus of *pterosaur.

pterosaur extinct flying reptile of the order Pterosauria, existing in the Mesozoic age. They ranged from the size of a starling to the 12 m/39 ft wingspan of *Arambourgiania philadelphiae*; the largest of the pterosaurs discovered so far. Some had horns on their heads that, when in flight, made a whistling to roaring sound.

Ptolemy (c. AD 100–c. AD 170) born Claudius Ptolemaeus, Egyptian astronomer and geographer. His *Almagest* developed the theory that Earth is the centre of the universe, with the Sun, Moon, and stars revolving around it. In 1543 the Polish astronomer *Copernicus proposed an alternative to the **Ptolemaic system**. Ptolemy's *Geography* was a standard source of information until the 16th century.

Ptolemy dynasty of kings of Macedonian origin who ruled Egypt over a period of 300 years; they included:
Ptolemy I (c. 367–283 BC) called 'Soter' (Saviour), Ruler of Egypt from 323 BC, king from 304 BC. One of Alexander the Great's most valued generals, he was given Egypt as his share of Alexander's conquests. His capital, *Alexandria, became a centre of trade and learning; here, the mathematician Euclid worked under his patronage, and construction of the great library and museum began. Ptolemy's rule established a dynasty of Macedonian kings that governed Egypt until 30 BC.
Ptolemy II (308–246 BC) Ruler of Egypt 283–246 BC. He consolidated Greek control and administration, constructing a canal from the Red Sea to the Nile as well as the museum, library, and the Pharos (lighthouse) at Alexandria, one of the *Seven Wonders of the World. He was the son of Ptolemy I.

Ptolemy XIII (63–47 BC) Joint ruler of Egypt with his sister-wife *Cleopatra in the period preceding the Roman annexation of Egypt. He was killed fighting against Julius Caesar.

puberty stage in human development when the individual becomes sexually mature. It may occur from the age of ten upwards, but each person is individual. The sexual organs take on their adult form and pubic hair grows. In girls, menstruation begins, and the breasts develop; in boys, the voice breaks and becomes deeper, and facial hair develops. Both boys and girls will experience emotional as well as physical changes.

public corporation company structure that is similar in organization to a public limited company but with no shareholder rights. Such corporations are established to carry out state-owned activities, but are financially independent of the state and are run by a board. The first public corporation to be formed in the UK was the Central Electricity Board in the 1920s.

public limited company (plc) company registered as a plc under the provisions of the Companies Act 1980. The company's name must carry the words 'public limited company' or initials 'plc' and must have authorized share capital over £50,000, with £12,500 paid up – paid to the company by the shareholders. Plcs may offer shares to the public and are more tightly regulated than limited companies. Converting a private limited company into a public one has advantages, such as the ability to raise share capital. However, it does have potential disadvantages, such as being subject to the scrutiny of the financial media and city analysts (the company's financial records must be available for any member of the public to scrutinize). If the founder of a plc perceives the company share price to undervalue the company they may take the company private once more, as Richard Branson did with Virgin in 1989.

public school in England and Wales, a prestigious fee-paying independent school. In Scotland, the USA, and many other English-speaking countries, a 'public' school is a state-maintained school, and independent schools are generally known as 'private' schools.

public sector the part of the economy that is owned and controlled by the state, namely central government, local government, and government enterprises. In a *command economy, the public sector provides most of the resources in the economy. The opposite of the public sector is the *private sector, where resources are provided by private individuals and business organizations.

public sector borrowing requirement (PSBR) amount of money needed by a government to cover any deficit in financing its own activities.

public spending expenditure by government, covering the military, health, education, infrastructure, development projects, and the cost of servicing (paying off the interest on) overseas borrowing.

Puccini, Giacomo (Antonio Domenico Michele Secondo Maria) (1858–1924) Italian opera composer. His music shows a strong gift for melody and dramatic effect and his operas combine exotic plots with elements of *verismo* (realism). They include *Manon Lescaut* (1893), *La Bohème* (1896), *Tosca* (1900), *Madama Butterfly* (1904), and the unfinished *Turandot* (1926).

puddle clay clay, with sand or gravel, that has had water added and mixed thoroughly so that it becomes watertight. The term was coined in 1762 by the canal builder James Brindley, although the use of such clay in dams goes back to Roman times.

pueblo (Spanish 'village') settlement of flat-roofed stone or adobe houses that are the communal dwelling houses of the Hopi, Zuni, and other American Indians of Arizona and New Mexico. The word has also come to refer to the pueblo-dwelling American Indians of the southwest Americas.

Puerto Rico in full the **Commonwealth of Puerto Rico**, easternmost island of the Greater Antilles, situated between the US Virgin Islands and the Dominican Republic; area 9,000 sq km/3,475 sq mi; population (2000 est) 3,808,600. The capital is *San Juan. Exports include sugar, tobacco, rum, pineapples, textiles, plastics, chemicals, processed foods, vegetables, and coffee. It is a self-governing territory of the United States.

puffball ball-shaped fruiting body of certain fungi (see *fungus) that cracks open when it ripens, releasing the enclosed spores in the form of a brown powder; for example, the common puffball (*L. perlatum*). (Genera *Lycoperdon* and *Calvatia*.)

puffer fish fish of the family Tetraodontidae. As a means of defence it inflates its body with water until it becomes spherical and the skin spines become erect. Puffer fish are mainly found in warm waters, where they feed on molluscs, crustaceans, and coral.

puffin any of various sea birds of the genus *Fratercula* of the *auk family, found in the northern Atlantic and Pacific. The puffin is about 35 cm/14 in long, with a white face and front, red legs, and a large deep bill, very brightly coloured in summer. Having short wings and webbed feet, puffins are poor fliers but excellent swimmers. They nest in rock crevices, or make burrows, and lay a single egg.

pug breed of small dog with short wrinkled face, hanging ears, chunky body, and tail curled over the hip. It weighs 6–8 kg/13–18 lb. Its short coat may be black, beige or grey; the beige or grey dogs have black on the face and ears.

Puget Sound inlet of the Pacific Ocean on the west coast of Washington State, USA, extending southwards for about 160 km/100 mi, from the eastern end of the Strait of Juan de Fuca to Olympia, the state capital. It covers an area of about 5,180 sq km/1,990 sq mi, and contains a number of islands; Whidbey, Vashon, and Bainbridge are the largest. The major port of *Seattle lies on its eastern shore, and a government naval yard, Puget Sound Naval Shipyard, is situated at Bremerton. The sound contains two main branches, Admiralty Inlet and Hood Canal, and receives rivers from the Cascade Range. Its waterways serve a rich industrial and agricultural area, and timber is rafted from its well-wooded shores to lumber and paper mills along the coast.

Pugin, Augustus Welby Northmore (1812–1852) English architect and designer. He collaborated with Charles *Barry in the detailed design of the New Palace of Westminster (Houses of Parliament). He did much to instigate the *Gothic Revival in England, largely through his books *Contrasts: or a Parallel between the Architecture of the 15th and 19th Centuries* (1836) and

747

Gothic Ornaments from Ancient Buildings in England and France (1828–31).

P'u-i (*or* **Pu-Yi**), **Henry** (1906–1967) Last Manchu Qing emperor of China (as Hsuan Tung) from 1908 until he was deposed in the republican revolution of 1912; he was restored for a week in 1917. After his deposition he chose to be called Henry. He was president 1932–34 and emperor 1934–45 of the Japanese puppet state of Manchukuo (see *Manchuria).

pulley simple machine consisting of a fixed, grooved wheel, sometimes in a block, around which a rope or chain can be run. A simple pulley serves only to change the direction of the applied effort (as in a simple hoist for raising loads). The use of more than one pulley results in a mechanical advantage, so that a given effort can raise a heavier load.

pulsar celestial source that emits pulses of energy at regular intervals, ranging from a few seconds to a few thousandths of a second. Pulsars are thought to be rapidly rotating *neutron stars, which flash at radio and other wavelengths as they spin. They were discovered in 1967 by Jocelyn Bell Burnell and Antony *Hewish at the Mullard Radio Astronomy Observatory, Cambridge, England. By 1998, 1,000 pulsars had been discovered since the initial identification in 1967.

pulse in biology, impulse transmitted by the heartbeat throughout the arterial systems of vertebrates. When the heart muscle contracts, it forces blood into the *aorta (the chief artery). Because the arteries are elastic, the sudden rise of pressure causes a throb or sudden swelling through them. The actual flow of the blood is about 60 cm/2 ft a second in humans. The average adult pulse rate is generally about 70 per minute. The pulse can be felt where an artery is near the surface, for example in the wrist or the neck.

pulse crop such as peas and beans. Pulses are grown primarily for their seeds, which provide a concentrated source of vegetable protein, and make a vital contribution to human diets in poor countries where meat is scarce, and among vegetarians. Soybeans are the major temperate protein crop in the West; most are used for oil production or for animal feed. In Asia, most are processed into soymilk and beancurd. Peanuts dominate pulse production in the tropical world and are generally consumed as human food.

puma *or* **cougar** *or* **mountain lion** large wild cat *Felis concolor* found in North and South America. Tawny-coated, it is 1.5 m/4.5 ft long with a 1-m/3-ft tail. Pumas live alone, with each male occupying a distinct territory; they eat deer, rodents, and cattle. Pumas need large territories, with females maintaining up to 100 sq km and males even more. Two to four cubs are born and will remain with the mother till they are 18–24 months old (they are completely weaned at six months).

pumice light volcanic rock produced by the frothing action of expanding gases during the solidification of lava. It has the texture of a hard sponge and is used as an abrasive.

pump any device for moving liquids and gases, or compressing gases. Some pumps, such as the traditional **lift pump** used to raise water from wells, work by a reciprocating (up-and-down) action. Movement of a piston in a cylinder with a one-way valve creates a partial vacuum in the cylinder, thereby sucking water into it.

pumpkin creeping plant whose large round fruit has a thick orange rind, pulpy flesh, and many seeds. Pumpkins are used in cookery (especially pies and soups) and are hollowed out to form candle lanterns at Halloween. (Genus *Cucurbita pepo*, family Cucurbitaceae.)

pun figure of speech, a play on words, or double meaning that is technically known as **paronomasia** (Greek 'adapted meaning'). Double meaning can be accidental, often resulting from homonymy, or the multiple meaning of words; puns, however, are deliberate, intended as jokes or as clever and compact remarks.

punctuated equilibrium model evolutionary theory developed by Niles Eldredge and US palaeontologist Stephen Jay Gould in 1972 to explain discontinuities in the fossil record. It claims that evolution continues through periods of rapid change alternating with periods of relative stability (stasis), and that the appearance of new lineages is a separate process from the gradual evolution of adaptive changes within a species.

punctuation system of conventional signs (punctuation marks) and spaces employed to organize written and printed language in order to make it as readable, clear, and logical as possible.

Punic (Latin *Punicus* 'a Phoenician') relating to *Carthage, ancient city in North Africa founded by the Phoenicians.

Punic Wars three wars between *Rome and *Carthage:
First Punic War 264–241 BC, resulted in the defeat of the Carthaginians under *Hamilcar Barca and the cession of Sicily to Rome.
Second Punic War 218–201 BC, Hannibal invaded Italy, defeated the Romans at Trebia, Trasimene, and at Cannae (under Fabius Maximus), but was finally defeated himself by Scipio Africanus Major at Zama (now in Algeria).
Third Punic War 149–146 BC, ended in the destruction of Carthage, and its possessions becoming the Roman province of Africa.

Punjab (Sanskrit 'five rivers': the Indus tributaries Jhelum, Chenab, Ravi, Beas, and Sutlej) former state of British India, now divided between India and Pakistan. Punjab was annexed by Britain in 1849 after the Sikh Wars (1845–46 and 1848–49), and formed into a province with its capital at Lahore. Under the British, West Punjab was extensively irrigated, and land was granted to Indians who had served in the British army.

Punjab *or* **Punjub** state of northwest India, bordering Pakistan; area 50,362 sq km/19,445 sq mi; population (2001 est) 24,289,300. The capital is Chandigarh, which is also the capital of Hindi-speaking state of Haryana. Both industry and agriculture are very productive and support a population which has the highest standard of living and longest life expectancy in India. Textiles, hosiery, bicycles, and sewing machines are produced; wheat, rice, sugar, maize, millet, barley, and cotton are grown.

Punjab state of northeast Pakistan; area 205,344 sq km/79,263 sq mi; population (1998 est) 72,585,400. The capital is *Lahore. Wheat is cultivated (by irrigation). The state contains a semi-arid alluvial plain, drained by the *Indus River and its tributaries, the Jhelum, Chenab, Ravi and Sutlej rivers. To the north are the

Himalayan foothills, and the Salt Range mountains (containing oil) are between the Indus and Jhelum valleys. There are ruins from the *Indus Valley civilization (2500 to 1600 BC). The main languages are Punjabi and Urdu; the principal religion is Islam. The state was formed as West Punjab in 1947 upon partition of India and the formation of Pakistan.

Punjabi the majority ethnic group living in the Punjab. Approximately 37 million live in the Pakistan half of Punjab, while another 14 million live on the Indian side of the border. In addition to Sikhs, there are Rajputs in Punjab, some of whom have adopted Islam. The Punjabi language belongs to the Indo-Iranian branch of the Indo-European family. It is considered by some to be a variety of Hindi, by others to be a distinct language.

Punjab massacres in the violence occurring after the partition of India in 1947, more than a million people died while relocating in the Punjab. The eastern section became an Indian state, while the western area, dominated by the Muslims, went to Pakistan. Violence occurred as Muslims fled from eastern Punjab, and Hindus and Sikhs moved from Pakistan to India.

punk or **punk rock** musical movement of disaffected youth in the late 1970s. It combined simple melodies and harmonies with strong lyrics (often crude and deliberately offensive) about youth rebellion. Image was important to punk and consisted of bizarre and outlandish fashions, spiked hair, and scowling expressions. Punk music stressed an aggressive performance designed to shock or intimidate within a three-chord, three-minute format, as demonstrated by the *Sex Pistols.

pupa nonfeeding, largely immobile stage of some insect life cycles, in which larval tissues are broken down, and adult tissues and structures are formed.

Purcell, Henry (c. 1659–1695) English baroque composer. His works include the opera *Dido and Aeneas* (1689) and music for John Dryden's *King Arthur* (1691) and *The Fairy Queen* (1692). He wrote more than 500 works, ranging from secular operas and incidental music for plays to cantatas and church music.

purdah (Persian and Hindu 'curtain') seclusion of women practised by some Islamic and Hindu peoples. It had begun to disappear with the adoption of Western culture, but the fundamentalism of the 1980s revived it; for example, the wearing of the chador (an all-enveloping black mantle) in Iran.

Pure Land Buddhism dominant form of Buddhism in China and Japan. It emphasizes faith in and love of Amida Buddha (Sanskrit Amitabha; Amituofo in China), the ideal 'Buddha of boundless light', who has vowed that all believers who call on his name will be reborn in his Pure Land, or Western Paradise, Sukhavati. There are over 16 million Pure Land Buddhists in Japan.

purgatory in Roman Catholic belief, a purificatory state or place where the souls of those who have died in a state of grace can expiate their venial sins, with a limited amount of suffering, before going to heaven.

Purim Jewish festival celebrated in February or March (the 14th of Adar in the Jewish calendar), commemorating Esther, who saved the Jews from extermination by the Persian king's vizier (executive officer) in 473 BC during the Persian occupation.

Puritan from 1564, a member of the Church of England who wished to eliminate Roman Catholic survivals in church ritual, or substitute a presbyterian for an episcopal form of church government. Activities included the Marprelate controversy, a pamphleteering attack carried out under the pseudonym 'Martin Marprelate'. The term also covers the separatists who withdrew from the church altogether. The Puritans were characterized by a strong conviction of human sinfulness and the wrath of God and by a devotion to plain living and hard work.

pus yellowish fluid that forms in the body as a result of bacterial infection; it includes white blood cells (leucocytes), living and dead bacteria, dead tissue, and serum. An enclosed collection of pus is called an abscess.

Pushkin, Aleksandr Sergeyevich (1799–1837) Russian poet and writer. His works include the novel in verse *Eugene Onegin* (1823–31) and the tragic drama *Boris Godunov* (1825). Pushkin's range was wide, and his willingness to experiment freed later Russian writers from many of the archaic conventions of the literature of his time.

Pushtu another name for the *Pashto language of Afghanistan and northern Pakistan.

Pu-Yi alternative transliteration of the name of the last Chinese emperor, Henry *P'u-i.

Pygmalion in Greek mythology, a king of Cyprus who fell in love with an ivory statue he had carved. When Aphrodite breathed life into it, he married the woman and named her Galatea. Their children were Paphos and Metharme.

Pygmy or **Negrillo** member of any of several groups of small-statured, dark-skinned peoples living in the equatorial jungles of Africa. The most important groups are the Twa, Aka, Mbuti, Binga, Baka, Gelli Efé; their combined population is less than 200,000. They were probably the aboriginal inhabitants of the region, before the arrival of farming peoples from elsewhere. They live nomadically in small groups, as hunter-gatherers; they also trade with other, settled people in the area.

pylon in modern usage, a steel lattice tower that supports high-tension electrical cables. In ancient Egyptian architecture, a pylon is one of a pair of inward-sloping towers that flank an entrance.

Pym, John (1584–1643) English Parliamentarian, largely responsible for the Petition of Right in 1628. As leader of the Puritan opposition in the *Long Parliament from 1640, he moved the impeachment of Charles I's advisers the Earl of Strafford and William Laud, drew up the *Grand Remonstrance, and was the chief of five members of Parliament Charles I wanted arrested in 1642. The five hid themselves and then emerged triumphant when the king left London.

Pyongyang or **P'yongyang** or **Pingyang** capital and largest city of North Korea, lying in the west of the country on the Taedong River, 50 km/30 mi inland from the Yellow Sea; population (2002 est) 2,724,700, conurbation 3,171,800. It is the leading commercial, transport, and manufacturing centre of North Korea, and industries include aircraft, tractors and electrical vehicles, iron and steel, armaments, textiles, chemicals, machinery, ceramics, and rubber products.

pyramid four-sided building with triangular sides. Pyramids were used in ancient Egypt to enclose a royal tomb; for example, the Great Pyramid of Khufu/Cheops at El Gīza, near Cairo, 230 m/755 ft square and 147 m/481 ft high. The three pyramids at El Gīza were considered one of the *Seven Wonders of the World. In Babylon and Assyria, broadly stepped pyramids (*ziggurats) were used as the base for a shrine to a god: the Tower of *Babel was probably one of these.

pyramid in geometry, a solid shape with triangular side-faces meeting at a common vertex (point) and with a *polygon as its base. The volume V of a pyramid is given by $V = \frac{1}{3}Bh$, where B is the area of the base and h is the perpendicular height.

Pyrenees French **Pyrénées**; Spanish **Pirineos**, mountain range in southwest Europe between France and Spain, extending from the Atlantic Ocean (Bay of Biscay) to the Mediterranean Sea (Golfe du Lion); length about 435 km/270 mi; highest peak Aneto (French Néthon) 3,404 m/11,172 ft. Andorra lies entirely within the range. Hydroelectric power has encouraged industrial development in the foothills.

pyrethrum popular name for several cultivated chrysanthemums. The ornamental species *C. coccineum*, and hybrids derived from it, are commonly grown in gardens. Pyrethrum powder, made from the dried flower heads of some species, is a powerful pesticide for aphids and mosquitoes. (Genus *Chrysanthemum*, family Compositae.)

pyridoxine *or* **vitamin B₆** $C_8H_{11}NO_3$, water-soluble *vitamin of the B complex. There is no clearly identifiable disease associated with deficiency but its absence from the diet can give rise to malfunction of the central nervous system and general skin disorders. Good sources are liver, meat, milk, and cereal grains. Related compounds may also show vitamin B_6 activity.

pyrite *or* **fool's gold** iron sulphide FeS_2. It has a yellow metallic lustre and a hardness of 6–6.5 on the Mohs scale. It is used in the production of sulphuric acid.

Pyrrho (c. 360–c. 270 BC) Greek philosopher, founder of *Scepticism, who maintained that since certainty was impossible, peace of mind lay in renouncing all claims to knowledge.

Pyrrhus (319–272 BC) King of Epirus (an area of northwestern Greece and southern Albania) from 307 BC. In the early years of his reign he struggled to maintain his throne and retain independence from Macedonian control. In 280 BC he invaded Italy as an ally of the Tarentines against Rome. He twice defeated the Romans, but with such heavy losses that a 'Pyrrhic victory' has come to mean a victory not worth winning. He returned to Epirus in 275 after his defeat at Beneventum and was killed in street fighting at Argos.

Pythagoras (c. 580–500 BC) Greek mathematician and philosopher who formulated *Pythagoras' theorem.

Pythagoras' theorem in geometry, a theorem stating that in a right-angled triangle, the square of the *hypotenuse (the longest side) is equal to the sum of the squares of the other two sides. If the hypotenuse is h units long and the lengths of the other sides are a and b, then $h^2 = a^2 + b^2$.

python any constricting snake of the Old World subfamily Pythoninae of the family Boidae, which also includes *boas and the *anaconda. Pythons are found in the tropics of Africa, Asia, and Australia. Unlike boas, they lay eggs rather than produce living young. Some species are small, but the reticulated python *Python reticulatus* of Southeast Asia can grow to 10 m/33 ft.

q

Qaboos bin Said (1940–) Sultan of Oman, the
14th descendant of the Albusaid family. Opposed to
the conservative views of his father, he overthrew him
in 1970 in a bloodless coup and assumed the sultanship.
Since then he has followed more liberal and
expansionist policies, while maintaining his country's
position of international non-alignment.

Qaddafi alternative form of *Khaddhafi, Libyan leader.

qat *or* **kat** *or* **khat** evergreen shrub with white flowers
belonging to the staff-tree family, native to Africa and
Asia. The leaves are chewed as a mild narcotic drug in
some Arab countries. Its use was banned in Somalia
1983. (Genus *Catha edulis*, family Celastraceae.)

Qatar

National name: *Dawlat Qatar/State of Qatar*

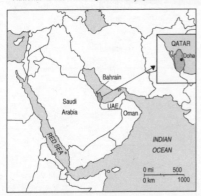

Area: 11,400 sq km/4,401 sq mi
Capital: Doha (and chief port)
Major towns/cities: Dukhan, Wakra, ad-Dawhah,
ar-Rayyan, Umm Salal, Musay'id, Ash Shahaaniyah
Physical features: mostly flat desert with salt flats in south
Head of state: Sheikh Hamad bin Khalifa al-Thani
from 1995
Head of government: Sheikh 'Abd Allah ibn Khalifah
al-Thani from 1996
Political system: absolutist
Political executive: absolute
Political parties: none
Currency: Qatari riyal

Exports: petroleum, liquefied natural gas, petrochemicals.
Principal market: Japan 43.5% (2001)
Population: 610,000 (2003 est)
Language: Arabic (official), English
Religion: Sunni Muslim 95%
Life expectancy: 71 (men); 75 (women) (2000–05)
Chronology
7th century AD: Islam introduced.
8th century: Developed into important trading centre
during time of Abbasid Empire.
1783: The al-Khalifa family, who had migrated to
northeast Qatar from west and north of the Arabian
Peninsula, foiled Persian invasion and moved their
headquarters to Bahrain Island, while continuing to
rule the area of Qatar.
1867–68: After the Bahrain-based al-Khalifa had
suppressed a revolt by their Qatari subjects, destroying
the town of Doha, Britain intervened and installed
Muhammad ibn Thani al-Thani, from the leading
family of Qatar, as the ruling sheikh (or emir). A British
Resident was given power to arbitrate disputes with
Qatar's neighbours.
1871–1914: Nominally part of Turkish Ottoman Empire,
although in 1893 sheik's forces inflicted a defeat on
Ottomans.
1916: Qatar became British protectorate after treaty
signed with Sheikh Adbullah al-Thani.
1949: Oil production began at onshore Dukhan field
in west.
1960: Sheikh Ahmad al-Thani became new emir.
1968: Britain's announcement that it would remove
its forces from the Gulf by 1971 led Qatar to make an
abortive attempt to arrange a federation of Gulf states.
1970: Constitution adopted, confirming emirate as
absolute monarchy.
1971: Independence achieved from Britain.
1991: Qatar forces joined the United Nations (UN)
coalition in the Gulf War against Iraq.
1995: Sheikh Khalifa was ousted by his son,
Crown Prince Sheikh Hamad bin Khalifa al-Thani.
1996: The announcement of plans to introduce
democracy were followed by an assassination attempt
on Sheikh Hamad. Sheikh 'Abd Allah ibn Khalifah Al
Thani was appointed prime minister.
2001: The ruling of the International Court of Justice
on a long-standing territorial dispute with Bahrain
was accepted.
2003: A permanent constitution was approved by a
referendum.

Qin dynasty China's first imperial dynasty 221–206 BC.
It was established by *Shi Huangdi, ruler of the Qin,
the most powerful of the Zhou era warring states.
The power of the feudal nobility was curbed and
greater central authority exerted over north central
China, which was unified through a bureaucratic
administrative system.

Qinghai *or* **Tsinghai** Mongolian **Koko Nor**; Tibetan
Amdo, province of northwest China, bounded to the
north by Gansu, to the south by Sichuan, to the west
by Tibet, and to the northwest by Xinjiang Uygur
Autonomous Region; area 721,000 sq km/278,400 sq mi;
population (2000 est) 5,180,000. The capital is Xining
and Golmud is another major town. Industries include
minerals, chemicals, livestock, oil, and medical
products. There is animal rearing and bee-keeping.

quadratic equation in mathematics, a polynomial *equation of second degree (that is, an equation containing as its highest power the square of a variable, such as x^2). The general *formula of such equations is

$$ax^2 + bx + c = 0$$

in which a, b, and c are real numbers, and only the *coefficient a cannot equal 0. In *coordinate geometry, a quadratic function represents a *parabola.

quadrilateral plane (two-dimensional) figure with four straight sides. The sum of all interior angles is 360°. The following are all quadrilaterals, each with distinguishing properties: **square** with four equal angles and sides, and four axes of *symmetry; **rectangle** with four equal angles, opposite sides equal, and two axes of symmetry; **rhombus** with four equal sides, and two axes of symmetry; **parallelogram** with two pairs of parallel sides, and rotational symmetry; **kite** with two pairs of adjacent equal sides, and one axis of symmetry; and **trapezium** with one pair of parallel sides.

Quadruple Alliance in European history, three military alliances of four nations:

the Quadruple Alliance 1718 Austria, Britain, France, and the United Provinces (Netherlands) joined forces to prevent Spain from annexing Sardinia and Sicily.

the Quadruple Alliance 1813 Austria, Britain, Prussia, and Russia allied to defeat the French emperor Napoleon; renewed in 1815 and 1818. See Congress of *Vienna.

the Quadruple Alliance 1834 Britain, France, Portugal, and Spain guaranteed the constitutional monarchies of Spain and Portugal against rebels in the Carlist War.

quaestor junior Roman magistrate whose primary role was to oversee the finances of individual provinces under the Republic. Quaestors originated as assistants to the consuls. They often commanded units in the army when the governor of the province fought a campaign.

quail any of several genera of small ground-dwelling birds of the family Phasianidae, which also includes grouse, pheasants, bobwhites, and prairie chickens. Species are found in Africa, India, Australia, North America, and Europe.

Quaker popular name, originally derogatory, for a member of the Society of *Friends.

qualitative analysis in chemistry, a procedure for determining the identity of the component(s) of a single substance or mixture. A series of simple reactions and tests can be carried out on a compound to determine the elements present.

quango acronym for QUasi-Autonomous NonGovernmental Organization, any administrative body that is nominally independent but relies on government funding; for example, the British Council (1935), the Equal Opportunities Commission (1975) in the UK, and the Environmental Protection Agency (1970) in the USA.

quantitative analysis in chemistry, a procedure for determining the precise amount of a known component present in a single substance or mixture. A known amount of the substance is subjected to particular procedures. **Gravimetric analysis** determines the mass of each constituent present; **volumetric analysis** determines the concentration of a solution by *titration against a solution of known concentration.

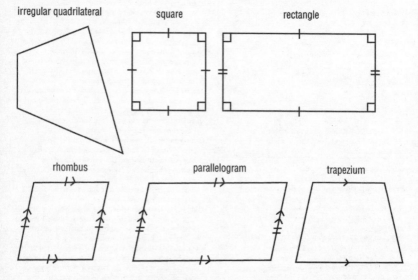

quadrilateral Different types of quadrilateral.

quantum mechanics branch of physics dealing with the interaction of *matter and *radiation, the structure of the *atom, the motion of atomic particles, and with related phenomena (see *elementary particle and *quantum theory).

quantum number in physics, one of a set of four numbers that uniquely characterize an *electron and its state in an *atom. The **principal quantum number** n defines the electron's main energy level. The **orbital quantum number** l relates to its angular momentum. The **magnetic quantum number** m describes the energies of electrons in a magnetic field. The **spin quantum number** m_s gives the spin direction of the electron.

quantum theory or **quantum mechanics** in physics, the theory that *energy does not have a continuous range of values, but is, instead, absorbed or radiated discontinuously, in multiples of definite, indivisible units called quanta. Just as earlier theory showed how light, generally seen as a wave motion, could also in some ways be seen as composed of discrete particles (*photons), quantum theory shows how atomic particles such as electrons may also be seen as having wavelike properties. Quantum theory is the basis of particle physics, modern theoretical chemistry, and the solid-state physics that describes the behaviour of the silicon chips used in computers.

quarantine (from French *quarantine* '40 days') any period for which people, animals, plants, or vessels may be detained in isolation to prevent the spread of contagious disease.

quark in physics, the *elementary particle that is the fundamental constituent of all *hadrons (subatomic particles that experience the strong nuclear force and divided into baryons, such as neutrons and protons, and mesons). Quarks have electric charges that are fractions of the electronic charge ($+\frac{2}{3}$ or $-\frac{1}{3}$ of the electronic charge). There are six types, or 'flavours': up, down, top, bottom, strange, and charmed, each of which has three varieties, or 'colours': red, green, and blue (visual colour is not meant, although the analogy is useful in many ways). To each quark there is an antiparticle, called an antiquark.

quart imperial liquid or dry measure, equal to two pints or 1.136 litres. In the USA, a liquid quart is equal to 0.946 litre, while a dry quart is equal to 1.101 litres.

quarter day in the financial year, any of the four dates on which such payments as ground rents become due: in England 25 March (Lady Day), 24 June (Midsummer Day), 29 September (Michaelmas), and 25 December (Christmas Day).

quartz crystalline form of *silica SiO_2, one of the most abundant minerals of the Earth's crust (12% by volume). Quartz occurs in many different kinds of rock, including sandstone and granite. It ranks 7 on the Mohs scale of hardness and is resistant to chemical or mechanical breakdown. Quartzes vary according to the size and purity of their crystals. Crystals of pure quartz are coarse, colourless, transparent, show no cleavage, and fracture unevenly; this form is usually called rock crystal. Impure coloured varieties, often used as gemstones, include *agate, citrine quartz, and *amethyst. Quartz is also used as a general name for the cryptocrystalline and noncrystalline varieties of silica, such as chalcedony, chert, and opal. Quartz is used in

ornamental work and industry, where its reaction to electricity makes it valuable in electronic instruments (see *piezoelectric effect). Quartz can also be made synthetically.

quasar contraction of quasi-stellar object; or QSO, one of the most distant extragalactic objects known, discovered in 1963. Quasars appear starlike, but each emits more energy than 100 giant galaxies. They are thought to be at the centre of galaxies, their brilliance emanating from the stars and gas falling towards an immense *black hole at their nucleus. The *Hubble Space Telescope revealed in 1994 that quasars exist in a remarkable variety of galaxies.

quassia any of a group of tropical American trees with bitter bark and wood. The heartwood of *Q. amara* is a source of quassiin, an infusion of which was formerly used as a tonic; it is now used in insecticides. (Genus *Quassia*, family Simaroubaceae.)

Quaternary Period period of geological time from 1.64 million years ago through to the present. It is divided into the *Pleistocene (1.64 million to 10,000 years ago) and *Holocene (last 10,000 years) epochs.

Quatre Bras, Battle of battle fought on 16 June 1815 during the Napoleonic Wars, in which the British commander Wellington defeated French forces under Marshal Ney. It is named after a hamlet in Brabant, Belgium, 32 km/20 mi southeast of Brussels.

Québec (Iroquois *Kebec*, 'a place where waters narrow') capital and port of Québec province, Canada, at the junction of the Saint-Charles and St Lawrence rivers, Canada; population (2001 est) 169,100, metropolitan area (2001 est) 682,800. It is a major inland seaport, and a commercial, financial, and administrative centre. Industries include printing and publishing, and the production of paper, pulp, wood products, electronic goods, textiles, and leather. Lumber and wheat are exported. It is a centre of French culture, and most of its inhabitants are French-speaking.

Québec province of eastern Canada; the largest province, second only in area among the nation's administrative subdivisions to the Northwest Territories. Québec is bordered on the northeast by Labrador, on the east by Newfoundland, on the southeast by New Brunswick and Nova Scotia, and on the west and southwest by Ontario. On its southern border lie (west–east) the US states of New York, Vermont, New Hampshire, and Maine; area 1,540,700 sq km/594,900 sq mi; population (1991) 6,811,800. The capital is *Québec. Industries include mining (iron, copper, gold, zinc), fishing, and the production of paper, textiles, and maple syrup (70% of world output). Cereals and potatoes are grown.

Québec Conference two conferences of Allied leaders in the city of Québec, Canada, during World War II. The **first conference** in 1943 approved British admiral Mountbatten as supreme Allied commander in Southeast Asia and made plans for the invasion of France, for which US general Eisenhower was to be supreme commander. The **second conference** in September 1944 adopted plans for intensified air attacks on Germany, created a unified strategy against Japan, and established a post-war policy for a defeated Germany.

quebracho any of several South American trees belonging to the cashew family, with very hard, tannin-rich wood; chiefly the red quebracho (*S. lorentzii*), used in the tanning of leather. (Genus *Schinopsis*, family Anacardiaceae.)

Quechua *or* **Quichua** *or* **Kechua** the largest group of American Indians living in South America. The Quechua live in the Andean region. Their ancestors included the Inca, who established the Quechua language in the region, now the second official language of Peru and widely spoken as a lingua franca in Ecuador, Bolivia, Colombia, Argentina, and Chile; it belongs to the Andean-Equatorial family.

Queen British glam-rock group 1971–91 credited with making the first successful pop video, for their hit 'Bohemian Rhapsody' (1975). The operatic flamboyance of lead singer Freddie Mercury (1946–1991) was the cornerstone of their popularity; other members of the band were Brian May (1947–), John Deacon (1951–), and Roger Taylor (1949–). Among their other hits were 'We Will Rock You' (1977) and the rockabilly pastiche 'Crazy Little Thing Called Love' (1980).

Queen Anne style decorative art style in England (1700–20), characterized by plain, simple lines, mainly in silver and furniture.

Queensberry, John Sholto Douglas, 8th Marquess of Queensberry (1844–1900) British patron of boxing. In 1867 he gave his name to a new set of boxing rules. Devised by the pioneering British sports administrator John Chambers (1841–1883), the **Queensberry Rules**, form the basis of today's boxing rules.

Queen's Counsel (QC) in England, a barrister appointed to senior rank by the Lord Chancellor. When the monarch is a king the term is **King's Counsel** (KC). A QC wears a silk gown and takes precedence over a junior member of the Bar.

Queensland state in northeast Australia, including the adjacent islands in the Pacific Ocean and in the Gulf of *Carpentaria; bordered on the west by Northern Territory, on the southwest by South Australia, on the south by New South Wales, on the east by the Pacific Ocean, and on the extreme northwest by the Gulf of Carpentaria; area 1,727,200 sq km/666,900 sq mi; population (2001 est) 3,635,100, concentrated in the southeast. The capital is *Brisbane. Products include sugar, wheat, pineapples, beef, cotton, wool, tobacco, copper, gold, silver, lead, zinc, coal, nickel, bauxite, uranium, natural gas, oil, and fish.

quetzal long-tailed Central American bird *Pharomachus mocinno* of the *trogon family, order Trogoniformes. The male is brightly coloured, with green, red, blue, and white feathers. It has a train of blue-green plumes (tail coverts) that hang far beyond the true tail feathers. There is a crest on the head and decorative drooping feathers on the wings. It is about 1.3 m/4.3 ft long including tail. The female is smaller and lacks the tail and plumage.

Quetzalcoatl in pre-Columbian cultures of Central America, a feathered serpent god of air and water. In his human form, he was said to have been fair-skinned and bearded and to have reigned on Earth during a golden age. He disappeared across the eastern sea, with a promise to return; the Spanish conquistador Hernán *Cortés exploited the myth in his own favour when he invaded. Ruins of Quetzalcoatl's temples survive in various ancient Mesoamerican ceremonial centres,

including the one at Teotihuacán in Mexico. (See also *Aztec, *Mayan, and *Toltec civilizations).

Quezon City former capital of the Philippines 1948–76, northeastern part of metropolitan *Manila (the present capital), on Luzon Island; population (2000 est) 2,173,800. It was named after the Philippines' first president, Manuel Luis Quezon.

quince small tree native to western Asia but widely cultivated elsewhere. The bitter, yellow, pear-shaped fruit is used in preserves. Flowering quinces are cultivated mainly for their attractive flowers. (*Cydonia oblonga*; flowering quince; genus *Chaenomeles*; family Rosaceae.)

quinine antimalarial drug extracted from the bark of the cinchona tree. Peruvian Indians taught French missionaries how to use the bark in 1630, but quinine was not isolated until 1820. It is a bitter alkaloid, with the formula $C_{20}H_{24}N_2O_2$.

Quinn, Anthony (Rudolph Oaxaca) (1915–2001) Mexican-born US actor who starred in over 159 films. His roles frequently displayed great machismo and he often played larger-than-life characters, such as the title role in *Zorba the Greek* (1964). In *Viva Zapata!* (1952), for which Quinn won the Academy Award for Best Supporting Actor, he played the brother of the Mexican rebel Pancho Villa. His other films include *Lust for Life* (1956), for which he won a second Academy Award for Best Supporting Actor, Federico Fellini's *La strada* (1954), *The Guns of Navarone* (1962), and *Lawrence of Arabia* (1962).

Quirinal one of the seven hills on which ancient Rome was built. Its summit is occupied by a palace built in 1574 as a summer residence for the pope and occupied 1870–1946 by the kings of Italy. The name Quirinal is derived from that of Quirinus, local god of the *Sabines.

Quisling, Vidkun Abraham Lauritz Jonsson (1887–1945) Norwegian politician. Leader from 1933 of the Norwegian Fascist Party, he aided the Nazi invasion of Norway in 1940 by delaying mobilization and urging nonresistance. He was made premier by Hitler in 1942, and was arrested and shot as a traitor by the Norwegians in 1945. His name became a generic term for a traitor who aids an occupying force.

Quito industrial city, capital of Ecuador and of Pichincha province; situated on a plateau in the Andes, 22 km/14 mi south of the Equator, at an altitude of 2,850 m/9,350 ft; population (1997 est) 1,487,513. Industries include textiles, chemicals, leather, gold, silver, pharmaceuticals, and motor vehicles. Quito lies at the foot of the volcano Pichincha (4,794 m/15,728 ft), which last erupted in 1666, in an area prone to earthquakes. It has a temperate climate all year round. The city, which is the oldest capital in South America, was declared a World Cultural Heritage Site by UNESCO in 1978.

Qumran *or* **Khirbet Qumran** archaeological site in Jordan, excavated from 1951, in the foothills northwest of the Dead Sea. Originally an Iron Age fort (6th century BC), it was occupied in the late 2nd century BC by a monastic community, the Essenes, until the buildings were burned by Romans in AD 68. The monastery library once contained the *Dead Sea Scrolls, which had been hidden in caves for safekeeping and were discovered in 1947.

Quorn mycoprotein, a tiny relative of mushrooms, that feeds on carbohydrates and grows prolifically in culture using a form of liquid fermentation. It is moist, looks like meat, and is used in cooking. It is rich in protein (12.3 g/100 g) and fibre (3.6 g/100 g) and low in fat (0.49 g/100 g).

QwaQwa former black homeland for South Sotho people in Orange Free State (now Free State), South Africa.

r

Rabat capital and industrial port of Morocco, on the Atlantic coast, 177 km/110 mi west of Fès; population (city, 1994 est) 787,700; Rabat-Salé (urban area, 1998 est) 1,453,400. It is situated on the Bou Regreg River, opposite Salé. Industries include textiles, asbestos, carpets, pottery, leather goods, fishing; carpets, blankets, and leather handicrafts are also important, and other exports include skins, wax, cork, slippers, and beans. Founded in 1190, it is named after its original *ribat* or fortified monastery. From 1912 Rabat was the capital of the French protectorate of Morocco and became the capital of the newly-independent state of Morocco in 1956.

rabbi in Judaism, the chief religious leader of a synagogue or the spiritual leader (not a hereditary high priest) of a Jewish congregation; also, a scholar of Judaic law and ritual from the 1st century AD.

rabbit any of several genera of hopping mammals of the order Lagomorpha, which together with *hares constitute the family Leporidae. Rabbits differ from hares in bearing naked, helpless young and in occupying burrows.

Rabelais, François (c. 1495–1553) French satirist, monk, and physician. His name has become synonymous with bawdy humour. He was educated in the humanist tradition and was the author of satirical allegories, including a cycle known as Gargantua and Pantagruel which included *La Vie estimable du grand Gargantua, père de Pantagruel/The Inestimable Life of the Great Gargantua, Father of Pantagruel*, the first to be written, but published in 1534, two years after *Les Horribles et Épouvantables Faits et prouesses du très renommé Pantagruel/The Horrible and Dreadful Deeds and Prowess of the Very Renowned Pantagruel* (1532).

rabies *or* **hydrophobia** (Greek 'fear of water') viral disease of the central nervous system that can afflict all warm-blooded creatures. It is caused by a lyssavirus. It is almost invariably fatal once symptoms have developed. Its transmission to humans is generally by a bite from an infected animal. Rabies continues to kill hundreds of thousands of people every year; almost all these deaths occur in Asia, Africa, and South America.

raccoon any of several New World species of carnivorous mammals of the genus *Procyon*, in the family Procyonidae. The common raccoon *P. lotor* is about 60 cm/2 ft long, with a grey-brown body, a black-and-white ringed tail, and a black 'mask' around its eyes. The crab-eating raccoon *P. cancrivorus* of South America is slightly smaller and has shorter fur.

race term sometimes applied to a physically distinctive group of people, on the basis of their difference from other groups in skin colour, head shape, hair type, and physique. Formerly, anthropologists divided the human race into three hypothetical racial groups: Caucasoid, Mongoloid, and Negroid. Others postulated from 6 to 30 races. Scientific studies, however, have produced no proof of definite genetic racial divisions. Race is a cultural, political, and economic concept, not a biological one. Genetic differences do exist between populations but they do not define historical lineages, and are minimal compared to the genetic variation between individuals. Most anthropologists today, therefore, completely reject the concept of race, and social scientists tend to prefer the term 'ethnic group'.

Rachmaninov, Sergei Vasilevich (1873–1943) Russian composer, conductor, and pianist. After the 1917 Revolution he emigrated to the USA. His music is melodious and emotional and includes operas, such as *Francesca da Rimini* (1906), three symphonies, four piano concertos, piano pieces, and songs. Among his other works are the *Prelude in C-Sharp Minor* (1892) and *Rhapsody on a Theme of Paganini* (1934) for piano and orchestra.

Racine, Jean Baptiste (1639–1699) French dramatist. He was an exponent of the classical tragedy in French drama, taking his subjects from Greek mythology and observing the rules of classical Greek drama. Most of his tragedies have women in the title role, for example *Andromaque* (1667), *Iphigénie* (1674), and *Phèdre* (1677).

racism belief in, or set of implicit assumptions about, the superiority of one's own *race or ethnic group, often accompanied by prejudice against members of an ethnic group different from one's own. Racism may be used to justify *discrimination, verbal or physical abuse, or even *genocide, as in Nazi Germany, or as practised by European settlers against American Indians in both North and South America.

rackets *or* **racquets** indoor game played on an enclosed court. Although first played in the Middle Ages, rackets developed in the 18th century and was played against the walls of London buildings. It is considered the forerunner of many racket and ball games, particularly *squash.

rad unit of absorbed radiation dose, now replaced in the SI system by the *gray (one rad equals 0.01 gray). It is defined as the dose when one kilogram of matter absorbs 0.01 joule of radiation energy.

radar acronym for **radio direction and ranging**, device for locating objects in space, direction finding, and navigation by means of transmitted and reflected high-frequency radio waves.

radar astronomy bouncing of radio waves off objects in the Solar System, with reception and analysis of the 'echoes'. Radar contact with the Moon was first made in 1945 and with Venus in 1961. The travel time for radio reflections allows the distances of objects to be determined accurately. Analysis of the reflected beam reveals the rotation period and allows the object's surface to be mapped topographically. The rotation periods of Venus and Mercury were first determined by radar. Radar maps of Venus were obtained first by Earth-based radar and subsequently by orbiting space probes.

radian symbol rad, SI unit of plane angles, an alternative unit to the *degree. It is the angle at the centre of a circle when the centre is joined to the two ends of an arc (part of the circumference) equal in length to the radius of the circle. There are 2π (approximately 6.284) radians in a full circle (360°).

radiation emission of radiant *energy as particles or waves – for example, heat, light, alpha particles, and beta particles (see *electromagnetic waves and *radioactivity). See also *atomic radiation.

radiation sickness sickness resulting from exposure to radiation, including X-rays, gamma rays, neutrons, and other nuclear radiation, as from weapons and fallout. Such radiation ionizes atoms in the body and causes nausea, vomiting, diarrhoea, and other symptoms. The body cells themselves may be damaged even by very small doses, causing leukaemia and other cancers.

radiation units units of measurement for radioactivity and radiation doses. In SI units, the activity of a radioactive source is measured in becquerels (symbol Bq), where one becquerel is equal to one nuclear disintegration per second (an older unit is the curie). The exposure is measured in coulombs per kilogram ($C\,kg^{-1}$); the amount of ionizing radiation (X-rays or gamma rays) that produces one coulomb of charge in one kilogram of dry air (replacing the roentgen). The absorbed dose of ionizing radiation is measured in grays (symbol Gy) where one gray is equal to one joule of energy being imparted to one kilogram of matter (the rad is the previously used unit). The dose equivalent, which is a measure of the effects of radiation on living organisms, is the absorbed dose multiplied by a suitable factor that depends upon the type of radiation. It is measured in sieverts (symbol Sv), where one sievert is a dose equivalent of one joule per kilogram (an older unit is the rem).

Radical in Britain, supporter of parliamentary reform before the Reform Bill of 1832. As a group the Radicals later became the progressive wing of the Liberal Party. During the 1860s (led by Cobden, Bright, and J S Mill) they campaigned for extension of the franchise, free trade, and *laissez-faire*, but after 1870, under the leadership of Joseph Chamberlain and Charles Dilke, they adopted a republican and semi-socialist programme. With the growth of *socialism in the later 19th century, Radicalism ceased to exist as an organized movement.

radical in chemistry, a group of atoms forming part of a molecule, which acts as a unit and takes part in chemical reactions without disintegration, yet often cannot exist alone for any length of time; for example, the methyl radical $-CH_3$, or the carboxyl radical $-COOH$.

radical in politics, anyone with opinions more extreme than the main current of a country's major political party or parties. It is more often applied to those with left-wing opinions, although the radical right also exists.

radicle part of a plant embryo that develops into the primary root. Usually it emerges from the seed before the embryonic shoot, or plumule, its tip protected by a root cap, or calyptra, as it pushes through the soil. The radicle may form the basis of the entire root system, or it may be replaced by adventitious roots (positioned on the stem).

radio transmission and reception of radio waves. In radio transmission a microphone converts sound waves (pressure variations in the air) into a varying electric

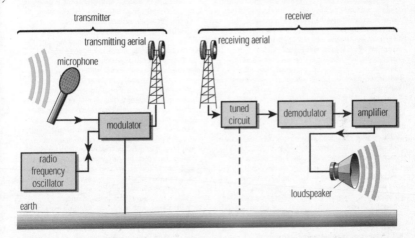

radio Radio transmission and reception. The radio frequency oscillator generates rapidly varying electrical signals, which are sent to the transmitting aerial. In the aerial, the signals produce radio waves (the carrier wave), which spread out at the speed of light. The sound signal is added to the carrier wave by the modulator. When the radio waves fall on the receiving aerial, they induce an electrical current in the aerial. The electrical current is sent to the tuning circuit, which picks out the signal from the particular transmitting station desired. The demodulator separates the sound signal from the carrier wave and sends it, after amplification, to the loudspeaker.

current, which is amplified and used to modulate a carrier wave which is transmitted as *electromagnetic waves, which are then picked up by a receiving aerial, amplified, and fed to a loudspeaker, which converts them back into sound waves.

radioactive decay process of disintegration undergone by the nuclei of radioactive elements, such as radium and various isotopes of uranium and the transuranic elements, in order to produce a more stable nucleus. The three most common forms of radioactive decay are alpha, beta, and gamma decay.

radioactive tracer any of various radioactive *isotopes added to fluids in order to monitor their flow and therefore identify leaks or blockages.

radioactive waste any waste that emits radiation in excess of the background level. See *nuclear waste.

radioactivity spontaneous change of the nuclei of atoms, accompanied by the emission of radiation. Such atoms are called radioactive. It is the property exhibited by the radioactive *isotopes of stable elements and all isotopes of radioactive elements, and can be either natural or induced. See *radioactive decay.

radio astronomy study of radio waves emitted naturally by objects in space, by means of a *radio telescope. Radio emission comes from hot gases (**thermal radiation**); electrons spiralling in magnetic fields (**synchrotron radiation**); and specific wavelengths (**lines**) emitted by atoms and molecules in space, such as the 21 cm/8.3 in line emitted by hydrogen gas.

radiocarbon dating or **carbon dating** method of dating organic materials (for example, bone or wood), used in archaeology. Plants take up carbon dioxide gas from the atmosphere and incorporate it into their tissues, and some of that carbon dioxide contains the radioactive isotope carbon-14. As this decays at a known rate (half of it decays every 5,730 years), the time elapsed since the plant died can be measured in a laboratory. Animals take carbon-14 into their bodies from eating plant tissues and their remains can be similarly dated. After 120,000 years so little carbon-14 is left that no measure is possible (see *half-life).

radiochemistry chemical study of radioactive isotopes and their compounds (whether produced from naturally radioactive or irradiated materials) and their use in the study of other chemical processes.

radio frequencies and wavelengths see *electromagnetic waves.

radiography branch of science concerned with the use of radiation (particularly *X-rays) to produce images on photographic film or fluorescent screens. X-rays penetrate matter according to its nature, density, and thickness. In doing so they can cast shadows on photographic film, producing a radiograph. Radiography is widely used in medicine for examining bones and tissues and in industry for examining solid materials; for example, to check welded seams in pipelines.

radioisotope or **radioactive isotope** naturally occurring or synthetic radioactive form of an element. Most radioisotopes are made by bombarding a stable element with neutrons in the core of a nuclear reactor (see *fission). The radiations given off by radioisotopes are easy to detect (hence their use as tracers), can in some instances penetrate substantial thicknesses of

materials, and have profound effects (such as genetic *mutation) on living matter.

radiology medical speciality concerned with the use of radiation, including X-rays, and radioactive materials in the diagnosis and treatment of injury and disease.

radiometric dating method of dating rock by assessing the amount of *radioactive decay of naturally occurring *isotopes. The dating of rocks may be based on the gradual decay of uranium into lead. The ratio of the amounts of 'parent' to 'daughter' isotopes in a sample gives a measure of the time it has been decaying, that is, of its age. Different elements and isotopes are used depending on the isotopes present and the age of the rocks to be dated. Once-living matter can often be dated by *radiocarbon dating, employing the half-life of the isotope carbon-14, which is naturally present in organic tissue. Radiometric methods have been applied to the decay of long-lived isotopes, such as potassium-40, rubidium-87, thorium-232, and uranium-238, which are found in rocks. These isotopes decay very slowly and this has enabled rocks as old as 3,800 million years to be dated accurately. Carbon dating can be used for material between 1,000 and 100,000 years old. **Potassium** dating is used for material more than 100,000 years old, **rubidium** for rocks more than 10 million years old, and **uranium** and **thorium** dating is suitable for rocks older than 20 million years.

radio telescope instrument for detecting radio waves from the universe in *radio astronomy. Radio telescopes usually consist of a metal bowl that collects and focuses radio waves the way a concave mirror collects and focuses light waves. Radio telescopes are much larger than optical telescopes, because the wavelengths they are detecting are much longer than the wavelength of light. The largest single dish is at Arecibo Observatory, Puerto Rico.

radiotherapy treatment of disease by *radiation from X-ray machines or radioactive sources. Radiation in the correct dosage can be used to kill cancerous cells and prevent their spreading.

radio wave electromagnetic wave possessing a long wavelength (ranging from about 10^{-3} to 10^4 m) and a low frequency (from about 10^5 to 10^{11} Hz) that travels at the speed of light. Included in the radio wave part of the spectrum are: *microwaves, used for both communications and for cooking; ultra high- and very high-frequency waves, used for television and FM (*frequency modulation) radio communications; and short, medium, and long waves, used for AM (*amplitude modulation) radio communications. Radio waves that are used for communications have all been modulated (see *modulation) to carry information. Certain astronomical objects emit radio waves, which may be detected and studied using *radio telescopes.

radish annual herb native to Europe and Asia, and cultivated for its fleshy, pungent, edible root, which is usually reddish but sometimes white or black; it is eaten raw in salads. (Genus *Raphanus sativus*, family Cruciferae.)

radium chemical symbol Ra, (Latin *radius* 'ray') white, radioactive, metallic element, atomic number 88, relative atomic mass 226.02. It is one of the *alkaline-earth metals, found in nature in *pitchblende and other uranium ores. Of the 16 isotopes, the commonest, Ra-226, has a half-life of 1,620 years. The element was discovered and named in 1898 by Pierre and Marie *Curie, who were investigating the residues of pitchblende.

radius straight line from the centre of a circle to its circumference, or from the centre to the surface of a sphere.

radon chemical symbol Rn, colourless, odourless, gaseous, radioactive, non-metallic element, atomic number 86, relative atomic mass 222. It is grouped with the *noble gases (rare gases) and was formerly considered nonreactive, but is now known to form some compounds with fluorine. Of the 20 known isotopes, only three occur in nature; the longest half-life is 3.82 days (Rn-222).

Raffles, (Thomas) Stamford (1781–1826) British colonial administrator, born in Jamaica. He served in the British *East India Company, took part in the capture of Java from the Dutch in 1811, and while governor of Sumatra 1818–23 was responsible for the acquisition and founding of Singapore in 1819. He was knighted in 1817.

rafflesia or **stinking corpse lily** any of a group of parasitic plants without stems, native to Malaysia, Indonesia, and Thailand. There are 14 species, several of which are endangered by the destruction of the forests where they grow. The fruit is used locally for medicine. The largest flowers in the world are produced by *R. arnoldiana*. About 1 m/3 ft across and weighing 7 kg/15 lb, they exude a smell of rotting flesh, which attracts flies to pollinate them. (Genus *Rafflesia*, family Rafflesiaceae.)

Rafsanjani, Hojatoleslam Ali Akbar Hashemi (1934–) Iranian politician and cleric, president 1989–97. When his former teacher Ayatollah *Khomeini returned after the revolution of 1979–80, Rafsanjani became the speaker of the Iranian parliament and, after Khomeini's death, state president and effective political leader. He was succeeded in 1997 by Seyyed Muhammad Khatami. In parliamentary elections in late February 2000 Rafsanjani failed to win a seat, while supporters of President Khatami and their reformist allies won a convincing majority. Following the pro-reformist election, it was disclosed that Rafsanjani was allegedly linked to government officials who had committed human rights abuses and executions of dissidents, intellectuals, and criminals during his presidency.

raga (Sanskrit *raga* 'tone' or 'colour') in Indian music, a scale of notes and style of ornament for music associated with a particular mood or time of day; the equivalent term in rhythm is tala. A choice of raga and tala forms the basis of improvised music; however, a written composition may also be based on (and called) a raga.

Ragnarök in Norse mythology, the ultimate cataclysmic battle that would be fought between the gods and forces of evil, and from which a new order would come. In Germanic mythology, this is known as Götterdämmerung.

ragtime syncopated music ('ragged time') in 2/4 rhythm, usually played on piano. It developed in the USA among black musicians in the late 19th century; it was influenced by folk tradition, minstrel shows, and marching bands, and was later incorporated into jazz.

Scott *Joplin was a leading writer of ragtime pieces, called 'rags'.

ragwort any of several European perennial plants, usually with yellow flower heads; some are poisonous. (Genus *Senecio*, family Compositae.)

Rahman, Tunku (Prince) Abdul (1903–1990) Malaysian politician, first prime minister of independent Malaya 1957–63 and of Malaysia 1963–70.

rail any wading bird of the family Rallidae, including the rails proper (genus *Rallus*), coots, moorhens, and gallinules. Rails have dark plumage, a short neck and wings, and long legs. They are 10–45 cm/4–18 in long.

railway method of transport in which trains convey passengers and goods along a twin rail track. Following the work of British steam pioneers such as the Scottish engineer James *Watt, English engineers, such as George *Stephenson, developed the steam locomotive and built the first railways; Stephenson built the first public steam railway, from Stockton to Darlington, England, in 1825. This heralded extensive railway building in Britain, continental Europe, and North America, providing a fast and economical means of transport and communication. After World War II, steam engines were replaced by electric and diesel engines. At the same time, the growth of road building, air services, and car ownership brought an end to the supremacy of the railways.

rain form of *precipitation in which separate drops of water fall to the Earth's surface from clouds. The drops are formed by the accumulation of fine droplets that condense from water vapour in the air. The *condensation is usually brought about by rising and subsequent cooling of air. Frontal (or cyclonic) rain is caused by warm air rising over cold air in a low pressure area. Relief (or orthographic) rainfall occurs when warm, moist air cools as it is forced to rise over hills or mountains. Convectional rainfall is caused when the surface of the Earth has been warmed by the Sun and the air in contact with it rises and meets colder layers. It is usually accompanied by a thunderstorm and is common in tropical regions.

rainbow arch in the sky displaying the colours of he *spectrum formed by the refraction and reflection of the Sun's rays through rain or mist. Its cause was discovered by Theodoric of Freiburg in the 14th century.

rainforest dense forest usually found on or near the *Equator where the climate is hot and wet. Moist air brought by the converging trade winds rises because of the heat and produces heavy rainfall. More than half the tropical rainforests are in Central and South America, primarily the lower Amazon and the coasts of Ecuador and Columbia. The rest are in Southeast Asia (Malaysia, Indonesia, and New Guinea) and in West Africa and the Congo. Tropical rainforests once covered 14% of the Earth's land surface, but are now being destroyed at an increasing rate as their valuable timber is harvested and the land cleared for agriculture, causing problems of *deforestation. Although by 1991 over 50% of the world's rainforests had been removed, they still comprise about 50% of all growing wood on the planet, and harbour at least 40% of the Earth's species (plants and animals).

Raj, the the period of British rule in India before independence in 1947.

Rajasthan state of northwest India; area 342,214 sq km/ 132,130 sq mi; population (2001 est) 56,473,100. The capital is *Jaipur. Kota is the leading industrial centre, with nylon and precision-instrument factories, while other industries include textiles, cement, glass, asbestos, chemicals, and the mining of silver, lead, and zinc. Millet, wheat, and barley are grown; oilseed, cotton, and sugar are produced; and cattle, sheep, and camels are raised.

Rajneesh meditation meditation based on the teachings of the Indian Shree Rajneesh (born Chaadra Mohan Jain), established in the early 1970s. Until 1989 he called himself **Bhagwan** (Hindi 'God'). His followers, who number about 0.5 million worldwide, regard themselves as *sannyasin, or Hindu ascetics; they wear orange robes and carry a string of prayer beads. They are not expected to observe any specific prohibitions but to be guided by their instincts.

Raleigh (*or* **Ralegh**), **Walter** (*c.* 1552–1618) English adventurer, writer, and courtier to Queen Elizabeth I. He organized expeditions to colonize North America 1584–87, all unsuccessful, and made exploratory voyages to South America in 1595 and 1616. His aggressive actions against Spanish interests, including attacks on Spanish ports, brought him into conflict with the pacific James I. He was imprisoned for treason 1603–16 and executed on his return from an unsuccessful final expedition to South America. He is traditionally credited with introducing the potato to Europe and popularizing the use of tobacco.

RAM acronym for **random-access memory**, in computing, a memory device in the form of a collection of integrated circuits (chips), frequently used in microcomputers. Unlike *ROM (read-only memory) chips, RAM chips can be both read from and written to by the computer, but their contents are lost when the power is switched off.

Rama seventh *avatar (incarnation) of *Vishnu, whose purpose was to ensure that justice and peace (*dharma) ruled. He is the hero of the epic *Ramayana*, and he is regarded as an example of morality and virtue.

Ramadan in the Muslim calendar, the ninth month of the year. Ramadan follows a lunar year and occurs 11 days earlier each solar year. Throughout Ramadan a strict fast (sawm) is observed during the hours of daylight. On the Night of Power (Lailat al-Qadr), which falls during the last ten days of the month, the Koran states that a Muslim who prays throughout the night will receive the benefits of praying for a thousand nights. For Muslims, this prayer vigil commemorates the night when Muhammad first received his revelations from the angel Jibra'el (Gabriel).

Ramayana Sanskrit Hindu epic of about 300 BC, in which *Rama (an incarnation of the god Vishnu), his half-brother Lakshmana, and his friend Hanuman (the monkey chieftain) strive to recover Rama's wife, *Sita, abducted by the demon Ravana, king of Lanka (Sri Lanka).

Rambert, Marie (1888–1982) adopted name of Cyvia Myriam Rambam, Polish-born British ballet dancer and teacher. One of the major innovative and influential figures in modern ballet, she worked with Vaslav Nijinsky on *The Rite of Spring* for the Diaghilev Ballet in Paris 1912–13, opened the Rambert School in London in 1920, and in 1926 founded the Ballet Rambert which she directed. It became a modern-dance company from 1966 and was renamed the Rambert Dance Company in 1987. Rambert became a British citizen in 1918. She was created a DBE in 1962.

Rameau, Jean-Philippe (1683–1764) French organist and composer. His *Traité de l'harmonie/ Treatise on Harmony* (1722) established academic rules for harmonic progression, and his varied works include keyboard and vocal music and many operas, such as *Castor and Pollux* (1737).

Rameses alternative spelling of *Ramses, name of kings of ancient Egypt.

Ramsay, William (1852–1916) Scottish chemist who, with Lord Rayleigh, discovered argon in 1894. In 1895 Ramsay produced helium and in 1898, in cooperation with Morris Travers, identified neon, krypton, and xenon. In 1903, with Frederick *Soddy, he noted the transmutation of radium into helium, which led to the discovery of the density and relative atomic mass of radium. He was awarded the Nobel Prize for Chemistry in 1904 for his discovery of noble gases (rare gases) in air and their locations in the periodic table. He was made a KCB in 1902.

Ramses (*or* **Rameses**) 11 kings (pharaohs) of ancient Egypt, including:

Ramses II (*or* **Rameses II**) called 'Ramses the Great', King (pharaoh) of ancient Egypt about 1279–1213 BC, the son of Seti I. He campaigned successfully against the Hittites, and built two rock temples at *Abu Simbel in southern Egypt.

Ramses III (*or* **Rameses III**) King (pharaoh) of ancient Egypt about 1187–1156 BC. He won victories over the Libyans and the *Sea Peoples and asserted his control over Palestine.

Ramsey, Alf(red) Ernest (1920–1999) English football player and manager. England's most successful manager ever, he won the 1966 World Cup. Of the 113 matches in which he was in charge of the national side between 1963 and 1974, England had 69 victories, 27 draws, and only 17 defeats. Shrewd, pragmatic, and single-minded, he was not afraid to go against traditional football wisdom, most notably in 1966 when he decided to play without wingers; a step which was greeted with widespread scepticism, but subsequently was hailed as a masterstroke when England won the World Cup. He led England to the quarter-finals of the 1970 World Cup, but was sacked four years later after the team failed to qualify for the 1974 finals.

random number one of a series of numbers having no detectable pattern. Random numbers are used in computer simulation and computer games. It is impossible for an ordinary computer to generate true random numbers, but various techniques are available for obtaining pseudo-random numbers – close enough to true randomness for most purposes.

Rangoon former name (to 1989) of *Yangon, the capital of Myanmar (Burma).

Ranjit Singh (1780–1839) Indian maharajah. He succeeded his father as a minor Sikh leader in 1792, and created a Sikh army that conquered Kashmir and the Punjab. In alliance with the British, he established himself as 'Lion of the Punjab', ruler of the strongest of the independent Indian states.

Rao, P(amulaparti) V(enkata) Narasimha (1921–) Indian politician, prime minister 1991–96 and Congress leader 1991–96. He governed the state of Andhra

Pradesh as chief minister 1971–73, and served in the cabinets of Indira and Rajiv Gandhi as minister of external affairs 1980–85 and 1988–90 and of human resources 1985–88. He took over the Congress party leadership after the assassination of Rajiv Gandhi. Elected prime minister the following month, he instituted a market-centred and outward-looking reform of the economy. He survived a vote of no confidence in 1993. After Congress was defeated in national elections in May 1996, Rao resigned as prime minister and dissolved parliament. He resigned as Congress leader in December 1996 as allegations mounted over his alleged involvement in political bribery. Along with his home minister, Buta Singha, he was sentenced in October 2000 to three years imprisonment, having been found guilty of bribing opposition MPs to swing a vote the government's way in a crucial confidence vote in 1993.

rap rapid, rhythmic chant over a pre-recorded repetitive backing track. Rap emerged in New York in 1979 as part of the *hip-hop culture, although the macho, swaggering lyrics with which it started have their roots in ritual boasts and insults. During the 1990s rap became increasingly commercial, and even its more extreme offshoots, such as gangsta rap, were represented in the pop charts.

rape in botany, either of two plant species of the mustard family grown for their seeds, which yield a pungent edible oil. The common turnip is a variety of *B. rapa* and the swede turnip is a variety of *B. napus*. (Genus *Brassica rapa* and *B. napus*, family Cruciferae.)

Raphael Sanzio (1483–1520) born Raffaello Sanzio, Painter and architect born in Urbino and eventually settled in Rome. He painted portraits and mythological and religious works, noted for their harmony of colour and composition. He was active in Perugia, Florence, and (from 1508) Rome, where he painted frescoes in the Vatican. Among his best-known works are *The Marriage of the Virgin* (1504; Brera, Milan) and the fresco *The School of Athens* (1509–11; Vatican, Rome).

rare-earth element alternative name for *lanthanide.

raspberry any of a group of prickly cane plants native to Europe, Asia, and North America, and widely cultivated. They have white flowers followed by hollow red composite fruits, which are eaten fresh as a delicacy and used for making jam and wine. (Genus *Rubus*, family Rosaceae.)

Rasputin (1871–1916) born Grigory Efimovich Novykh, (Russian 'dissolute') Siberian Eastern Orthodox mystic. He acquired influence over the Tsarina Alexandra, wife of *Nicholas II, and was able to make political and ecclesiastical appointments. His abuse of power and notorious debauchery (reputedly including the tsarina) led to his murder by a group of nobles.

Rastafarianism religion originating in the West Indies, based on the ideas of Marcus *Garvey, who called on black people to return to Africa and set up a black-governed country there. When Haile Selassie (**Ras Tafari**, 'Lion of Judah') was crowned emperor of Ethiopia in 1930, this was seen as a fulfilment of prophecy and some Rastafarians acknowledged him as an incarnation of God (**Jah**), others as a prophet. The use of ganja (marijuana) is a sacrament. There are no churches. In 2000 it was estimated that there were 700,000 Rastafarians worldwide.

rat any of numerous long-tailed *rodents (especially of the families Muridae and Cricetidae) larger than mice and usually with scaly, naked tails. The genus *Rattus* in the family Muridae includes the rats found in human housing.

rate of reaction speed at which a chemical reaction proceeds. It is usually expressed in terms of the concentration (usually in *moles per litre) of a reactant consumed, or product formed, in unit time; so the units would be moles per litre per second (mol l^{-1} s^{-1}). The rate of a reaction may be affected by the concentration of the reactants, the temperature of the reactants (or the amount of light in the case of a photochemical reaction), and the presence of a *catalyst. If the reaction is entirely in the gas state, the rate is affected by pressure, and, where one of the reactants is a solid, it is affected by the particle size.

rates in the UK, a local government tax levied on industrial and commercial property (business rates) and, until the introduction of the community charge (see *poll tax) 1989–90, also on residential property to pay for local amenities such as roads, footpaths, refuse collection and disposal, and community and welfare activities. The water companies also use a rating system to charge most householders for water supply.

ratio measure of the relative size of two quantities or of two measurements (in similar units), expressed as a proportion. For example, the ratio of vowels to consonants in the alphabet is 5:21. As a *fraction $^5/_{26}$ of the letters are vowels. The ratio of 500 m to 2 km is 500:2,000, or in its simplest integer form 1:4 (dividing both sides of the ratio by 500). Ratios are normally expressed as whole numbers, so 2:3.5 would become 4:7 (the ratio remains the same provided both parts of the ratio are multiplied or divided by the same number).

rationalism in theology, the belief that human reason rather than divine revelation is the correct means of ascertaining truth and regulating behaviour. In philosophy, rationalism takes the view that self-evident a priori propositions (deduced by reason alone) are the sole basis of all knowledge. It is usually contrasted with *empiricism, which argues that all knowledge must ultimately be derived from the senses.

rational number in mathematics, any number that can be expressed as an exact fraction (with a denominator not equal to 0), that is, as a/b where a and b are integers; or an exact decimal. For example, $^2/_1$, $^1/_4$, $1^5/_4$, $-^3/_5$ are all rational numbers, whereas π (which represents the constant 3.141592 ...) is not. Numbers such as π are called *irrational numbers.

rat-tail *or* **grenadier** any fish of the family Macrouridae of deep-sea bony fishes. They have stout heads and bodies, and long tapering tails. They are common in deep waters on the continental slopes. Some species have a light-emitting organ in front of the anus.

Rattle, Simon (1955–) English conductor, principal conductor of the City of Birmingham Symphony Orchestra (CBSO) 1979–98. He built the CBSO into a world-class orchestra, with a core repertoire of early 20th-century music; he also commissioned new works. A popular and dynamic conductor, he achieves a characteristically clear and precise sound. In 2002 he was appointed artistic director of the Berlin

Philharmonic Orchestra; one of the most prestigious posts in the classical music world.

rattlesnake any of various New World pit *vipers of the genera *Crotalus* and *Sistrurus* (the massasaugas and pygmy rattlers), distinguished by horny flat segments of the tail, which rattle when vibrated as a warning to attackers. They can grow to 2.5 m/8 ft long. The venom injected by some rattlesnakes can be fatal.

Rauschenberg, Robert (1925–) born Milton Rauschenberg, US pop artist. He has created happenings and multimedia works, called 'combined painting', such as *Monogram* (1959; Moderna Museet, Stockholm), a stuffed goat daubed with paint and wearing a car tyre around its body. In the 1960s he returned to painting and used the silk-screen printing process to transfer images to canvas.

Ravel, (Joseph) Maurice (1875–1937) French composer and pianist. His work is characterized by its sensuousness, exotic harmonics, and dazzling orchestral effects. His opera *L'enfant et les sortilèges* (1924) illustrates most of the various styles that influenced him at different times. Other works include the piano pieces *Pavane pour une infante défunte/Pavane for a Dead Infanta* (1899) and *Jeux d'eau/Waterfall* (1901), and the ballets *Daphnis et Chloë* (1912) and *Boléro* (1928).

raven any of several large *crows, genus *Corvus*, of the Corvidae family, order Passeriformes. The common raven *C. corax* is about 60 cm/2 ft long with a wingspan of nearly 1 m/3 ft, and has black, lustrous plumage; the beak and mouth, tongue, legs, and feet are also black. It is a scavenger and is found only in the northern hemisphere.

ray any of several orders (especially Ragiformes) of cartilaginous fishes with a flattened body, winglike pectoral fins, and a whiplike tail.

Ray, Man (1890–1976) adopted name of Emmanuel Rabinovich Rudnitsky, US photographer, painter, and sculptor. He was active mainly in France and was associated with the *Dada movement and then *surrealism. One of his best-known sculptures is *Gift* (1921), a surrealist ready-made consisting of an iron on to which a row of nails has been glued.

Ray, Satyajit (1921–1992) Indian film director. He became internationally known with his trilogy of life in his native Bengal: *Pather Panchali*, *Unvanquished*, and *The World of Apu* (1955–59). Later films include *The Music Room* (1963), *Charulata* (1964), *The Chess Players* (1977), and *The Home and the World* (1984).

rayon *synthetic fibre derived from *cellulose that has been regenerated, by treating wood pulp and/or cotton linters (very short fibres) with chemicals to produce a syrupy, yellowish solution. The solution is then pressed through very small holes and the resulting filaments (long fibres) are solidified. There are many different types of rayon and these include *viscose and cuprammonium. They all have different characteristics, but because they are derived from cellulose (like *cotton), many of these are similar to those of natural fibres. Rayon can be given properties which make it look similar to silk, cotton, or wool. It absorbs moisture, does not shrink, is cool to wear, can be mixed other fibres, and is cheaper to produce than natural fibres.

razorbill North Atlantic sea bird *Alca torda* of the auk family, order Charadriiformes, which breeds on cliffs and migrates south in winter. It is about 40 cm/16 in long, has a large curved beak, and is black above and white below. It uses its wings as paddles when diving. Razorbills make no nest; the female lays a single egg, which is white with brown markings. They are common off Newfoundland.

razor-shell or **razor-fish** US name **razor clam**, any bivalve mollusc in two genera *Ensis* and *Solen* with narrow, elongated shells, resembling an old-fashioned razor handle and delicately coloured. They can burrow rapidly into sand and are good swimmers.

reaction in chemistry, the coming together, or interaction, of two or more atoms, ions, or molecules with the result that a chemical change takes place and a new substance is formed, with a different chemical composition. The nature of the reaction is described by a *chemical equation. For example, in the chemical reaction that occurs when magnesium burns in oxygen, a new substance, magnesium oxide is made:

$$2Mg_{(s)} + O_{2(g)} \rightarrow 2MgO_{(s)}.$$

reactivity series chemical series produced by arranging the metals in order of their ease of reaction with reagents such as oxygen, water, and acids. An example of such an arrangement, starting with the most reactive, is: potassium, sodium, calcium, magnesium, aluminium, zinc, iron, tin, lead, copper, silver, gold. This arrangement aids the understanding of the properties of metals, helps to explain differences between them, and enables predictions to be made about a metal's behaviour, based on a knowledge of its position or properties. It also allows prediction of the relative stability of the compounds formed by an element: the more reactive the metal, the more stable its compounds are likely to be.

Reading industrial town and administrative centre of Reading unitary authority, in south England, at the confluence of the rivers Thames and Kennet, 61 km/38 mi west of London; population (2001 est) 210,000. It has a large number of high-technology industries.

realism in the arts and literature generally, a 'true-to-life' approach to subject matter; also described as naturalism. Taken to its extreme, *trompe l'oeil paintings trick the eye into believing objects are real. More specifically, **realism** refers to a movement in mid-19th-century European art and literature, that was a reaction against Romantic and classical idealization and a rejection of conventional academic themes, such as mythology, history, and sublime landscapes. Realism favoured themes of everyday life and carefully observed social settings. The movement was particularly important in France, where it had political overtones; the painters Gustave *Courbet and Honoré *Daumier, two leading realists, both used their art to expose social injustice.

realism in philosophy, the theory that universals (properties such as 'redness') have an existence independent of the human mind. Realists hold that the essence of things is objectively given in nature, and that our classifications are not arbitrary. As such, realism is contrasted with nominalism, the theory that universals are merely names or general terms.

real number in mathematics, any of the *rational numbers (which include the integers) or *irrational numbers. Real numbers exclude *imaginary numbers, found in *complex numbers of the general form $a + bi$ where $i = \sqrt{-1}$, although these do include a real component a.

realpolitik (German *Realpolitik* 'politics of realism') belief that the pragmatic pursuit of self-interest and power, backed up by force when convenient, is the only realistic option for a great state. The term was coined in 1859 to describe the German chancellor *Bismarck's policies.

real tennis racket and ball game played in France, from about the 12th century, over a central net in an indoor court, but with a sloping roof let into each end and one side of the court, against which the ball may be hit. The term 'real' here means 'royal', not 'genuine'. Basic scoring is as for lawn *tennis, but with various modifications.

real-time system in computing, a program that responds to events in the world as they happen. For example, an automatic-pilot program in an aircraft must respond instantly in order to correct deviations from its course. Process control, robotics, games, and many military applications are examples of real-time systems.

receiver in law, a person appointed by a court to collect and manage the assets of an individual, company, or partnership in serious financial difficulties. In the case of bankruptcy, the assets may be sold and distributed by a receiver to creditors.

receptacle the enlarged end of a flower stalk to which the floral parts are attached. Normally the receptacle is rounded, but in some plants it is flattened or cup-shaped. The term is also used for the region on that part of some seaweeds which becomes swollen at certain times of the year and bears the reproductive organs.

recession in economics, a fall in business activity lasting more than a few months, causing stagnation in a country's output.

recessive gene *allele (alternative form of a gene) that will show in the (*phenotype observed characteristics of an organism) only if its partner allele on the paired chromosome is similarly recessive. Such an allele will not show if its partner is dominant, that is if the organism is *heterozygous for a particular characteristic. Alleles for blue eyes in humans and for shortness in pea plants are recessive. Most mutant alleles are recessive and therefore are only rarely expressed (see *haemophilia).

reciprocal result of dividing a given quantity into 1. Thus the reciprocal of 2 is ½; the reciprocal of ⅔ is ³⁄₂; and the reciprocal of x^2 is $\frac{1}{x^2}$ or x^{-2}. Reciprocals are used to replace division by multiplication, since multiplying by the reciprocal of a number is the same as dividing by that number.

recitative declamatory, speechlike style of singing used in opera and oratorio. It rises and falls according to the meaning of the text and follows the rhythms and inflections of natural speech. A form of sung narration, it is used to carry the plot of the work forward. It is usually sparingly accompanied by harpsichord or organ.

recombination in genetics, any process that recombines, or 'shuffles', the genetic material, thus increasing genetic variation in the offspring. The two main processes of recombination both occur during meiosis (reduction division of cells). One is **crossing over**, in which chromosome pairs exchange segments;

the other is the random reassortment of chromosomes that occurs when each gamete (sperm or egg) receives only one of each chromosome pair.

Reconquista (Spanish 'reconquest') Christian defeat of the *Moors 9th–15th centuries, and their expulsion from Spain.

Reconstruction in US history, the period 1865–77 after the *Civil War during which the nation was reunited under the federal government after the defeat of the Southern *Confederacy and Union troops were stationed in Southern states.

rectangle quadrilateral (four-sided plane figure) with opposite sides equal and parallel and with each interior angle a right angle (90°). Its area A is the product of the length l and height h; that is, $A = l \times h$. A rectangle with all four sides equal is a *square.

rectifier device for obtaining one-directional current (DC) from an alternating source of supply (AC). (The process is necessary because almost all electrical power is generated, transmitted, and supplied as alternating current, but many devices, from television sets to electric motors, require direct current.) Types include plate rectifiers, thermionic *diodes, and *semiconductor diodes.

rectum lowest part of the large intestine of animals, which stores faeces prior to elimination (defecation).

recycling processing of industrial and household waste (such as paper, glass, and some metals and plastics) so that the materials can be reused. This saves expenditure on scarce raw materials, slows down the depletion of *non-renewable resources, and helps to reduce pollution. Aluminium is frequently recycled because of its value and special properties that allow it to be melted down and re-pressed without loss of quality, unlike paper and glass, which deteriorate when recycled.

Red Army the army of the USSR until 1946; it later became known as the Soviet Army. Founded by the revolutionary Leon *Trotsky, it developed from the Red Guards, volunteers who were in the vanguard of the Bolshevik revolution. The force took its name from its rallying banner, the red flag. At its peak, during World War II, it reached a strength of around 12 million men and women. The revolutionary army that helped the communists under *Mao Zedong win power in China in 1949 was also popularly known as the Red Army.

red blood cell *or* **erythrocyte** most common type of blood cell, and responsible for transporting *oxygen around the body. They contain haemoglobin, a red protein, which combines with oxygen from the lungs to form oxyhaemoglobin. When transported to the tissues the oxyhaemoglobin splits into its original constituents, and the cells are able to release the oxygen. There are about 6 million red cells in every cubic centimetre of blood.

Red Brigades Italian **Brigate rosse**, extreme left-wing guerrilla groups active in Italy during the 1970s and early 1980s. They were implicated in many kidnappings and killings, some later attributed to right-wing *agents provocateurs*, including that of Christian Democrat leader Aldo Moro in 1978.

Redcar and Cleveland unitary authority in northeast England created in 1996 from part of the former county of Cleveland. **area:** 240 sq km/93 sq mi **towns and cities:** Redcar (administrative headquarters),

Skelton, Guisborough, Marske-by-the-Sea, Saltburn-by-the-Sea, Brotton, Loftus **features:** North Sea coast; River Tees forms northwest border; Boulby Cliffs are highest cliffs on England's east coast (203 m/666 ft); 12th-century Priory at Guisborough; Cleveland Way long-distance path reaches coast at Saltburn; RNLI Zetland Lifeboat Museum (Redcar); Ironstone Mining Museum (Saltburn-by-the-Sea) **population:** (1996) 144,000.

Red Cross or **International Federation of the Red Cross** international relief agency founded by the Geneva Convention in 1863, having been proposed by the Swiss doctor Henri Dunant, to assist the wounded and prisoners in war. Its symbol is a symmetrical red cross on a white ground. In addition to dealing with associated problems of war, such as refugees and the care of the disabled, the Red Cross is concerned with victims of natural disasters – floods, earthquakes, epidemics, and accidents. It was awarded the Nobel Prize for Peace in 1917, 1944, and 1963.

red deer large deer widely distributed throughout Europe, Asia and North Africa. A full-grown male (stag or hart) stands 1.2 m/4 ft at the withers, and typical antlers measure about 80 cm/31 in in length with a spread of about the same. During the breeding season the colour is a rich brown, turning grey at the approach of winter. The young are spotted with white.

red dwarf any star that is cool, faint, and small (about one-tenth the mass and diameter of the Sun). Red dwarfs burn slowly, and have estimated lifetimes of 100 billion years. They may be the most abundant type of star, but are difficult to see because they are so faint. Two of the closest stars to the Sun, *Proxima Centauri and *Barnard's Star, are red dwarfs.

Redford, (Charles) Robert (1937–) US actor and film director. His boyish good looks and versatility earned him his first starring role in *Barefoot in the Park* (1967), followed by *Butch Cassidy and the Sundance Kid* (1969) and *The Sting* (1973), both with Paul *Newman.

red giant any large bright star with a cool surface. It is thought to represent a late stage in the evolution of a star like the Sun, as it runs out of hydrogen fuel at its centre and begins to burn heavier elements, such as helium, carbon, and silicon. Because of more complex nuclear reactions that then occur in the red giant's interior, it eventually becomes gravitationally unstable and begins to collapse and heat up. The result is either explosion of the star as a *supernova, leaving behind a *neutron star, or loss of mass by more gradual means to produce a *white dwarf.

Redgrave, Michael (Scudamore) (1908–1985) English actor. His stage roles included Hamlet and Lear (Shakespeare), Uncle Vanya (Chekhov), and the schoolmaster in Terence Rattigan's *The Browning Version* (filmed 1951). On screen he appeared in *The Lady Vanishes* (1938), *The Importance of Being Earnest* (1952), and *Goodbye Mr Chips* (1969). He was knighted in 1959.

Redgrave, Steve(n) Geoffrey (1962–) English rower and gold medallist at five successive Olympic Games 1984–2000. He also won nine gold medals at the World Championships 1986–99, was world indoor rowing champion in 1990, and was a member of the winning four-man bobsleigh team at the National Bobsleigh Championships in 1989. He announced his retirement from rowing in November 2000. In December 2000, he received the British Broadcasting Corporation (BBC) Sports Personality of the Year award, and was elected vice-president of the British Olympic Association (BOA).

Redgrave, Vanessa (1937–) English actor. She has played Shakespeare's Lady Macbeth and Cleopatra on the stage, Ellida in Ibsen's *Lady From the Sea* (1976 and 1979), and Olga in Chekhov's *Three Sisters* (1990). She won an Academy Award for Best Supporting Actress for the title role in the film *Julia* (1977).

Red Guard one of the militant school and college students, wearing red armbands, who were the shock-troops of the *Cultural Revolution in China from 1966 to 1969. After killing many party officials and plunging the country into chaos, the Red Guards were outlawed and suppressed by the Chinese leader *Mao Zedong.

red-hot poker any of a group of perennial plants native to Africa, in particular *K. uvaria*, with a flame-coloured spike of flowers. (Genus *Kniphofia*, family Liliaceae.)

Redmond, John Edward (1856–1918) Irish nationalist politician, leader of the Irish Parliamentary Party (IPP) 1900–18. He rallied his party after Charles Stewart *Parnell's imprisonment in 1881, and came close to achieving home rule for all Ireland in 1914. However, the pressure of World War I, Unionist intransigence, and the fallout of the 1916 *Easter Rising destroyed both his career and his party.

Redon, Odilon (1840–1916) French painter and graphic artist. One of the major figures of *Symbolism, he is famous for his fantastic and dreamlike images. From 1890 onwards he produced oil paintings and pastels, brilliant in colour, including numerous flower pieces. His works anticipated *surrealism.

redox reaction chemical change where one reactant is reduced and the other reactant oxidized. The reaction can only occur if both reactants are present and each changes simultaneously. For example, hydrogen reduces copper(II) oxide to copper while it is itself oxidized to water. The corrosion of iron and the reactions taking place in electric and electrolytic cells are just a few examples of redox reactions.

Red River or **Red River of the South** western tributary of the *Mississippi River, USA, 1,638 km/1,018 mi long; so called because of the reddish soil sediment it carries. Formed in Oklahoma by the confluence of the North Fork and the Prairie Dog Town Fork, it flows through Texas, Arkansas, and Louisiana, before entering the Mississippi near Baton Rouge, about 500 km/310 mi above the Gulf of Mexico. The stretch that forms the Texas–Oklahoma border is called Tornado Alley because of the storms caused by the collision in spring of warm air from the Gulf of Mexico with cold fronts from the north. The largest city on its course is Shreveport, Louisiana.

Red River Vietnamese **Song Hông**, river in north Vietnam, 500 km/310 mi long, that flows into the Gulf of Tonkin. Its extensive delta is a main centre of population.

Red Sea branch of the Indian Ocean, formed from a submerged (and still gradually widening) section of the Great *Rift Valley, extending northwest from the Gulf of Aden. It is 2,000 km/1,200 mi long and up to 320 km/200 mi wide, reaching depths of over 2,300 m/7,545 ft. Egypt, Sudan, Ethiopia, and Eritrea (in Africa) and Saudi Arabia (Asia) are on its shores. At its northern end, it divides into the gulfs of Suez and Aqaba, separated by the Sinai peninsula. No rivers flow into the Red Sea; in addition to high temperatures, this results in very high levels of salinity and other dissolved salts.

red setter breed of dog. See *setter.

red shift in astronomy, lengthening of the wavelengths of light from an object as a result of the object's motion away from us. It is an example of the *Doppler effect. The red shift causes lines in the spectra of galaxies to be shifted towards he red end of the spectrum. More distant galaxies have greater red shifts than closer galaxies. The red shift indicates that distant galaxies are moving apart rapidly, as the universe expands.

redstart any bird of the genus *Phoenicurus*, a member of the thrush family Muscicapidae, order Passeriformes. It winters in Africa and spends the summer in Eurasia. The **American redstart** *Setophaga ruticulla* belongs to the family Parulidae.

reduction in chemistry, the gain of electrons, loss of oxygen, or gain of hydrogen by an atom, ion, or molecule during a chemical reaction.

redwood giant coniferous tree, one of the two types of *sequoia.

reed any of various perennial tall, slender grasses found growing in wet or marshy environments; also the hollow, jointed stalks of any of these plants. The common reed (*P. australis*) reaches a height of 3 m/10 ft, having stiff, upright leaves and straight stems with a plume of purplish flowers at the top. (Especially species of the genera *Phragmites* and *Arundo*, family Gramineae.)

Reed, Lou(is Firbank) (1942–) US rock singer, songwriter, and guitarist. He was a member (1965–70 and 1993) of the New York avant-garde group the Velvet Underground, one of the most influential bands of the period. His solo work deals largely with urban alienation and angst, and includes the albums *Berlin* (1973), *Street Hassle* (1978), and *New York* (1989). His best-known recording is 'Walk on the Wild Side' from the album *Transformer* (1972).

referendum procedure whereby a decision on proposed legislation is referred to the electorate for settlement by direct vote of all the people. It is most frequently employed in Switzerland, the first country to use it, but has become increasingly widespread.

refining any process that purifies or converts something into a more useful form. Metals usually need refining after they have been extracted from their ores by such processes as *smelting. Petroleum, or crude oil, needs refining before it can be used; the process involves *fractional distillation, the separation of the substance into separate components or 'fractions'.

reflection throwing back or deflection of waves, such as *light or sound waves, when they hit a surface. Reflection occurs whenever light falls on an object. The **law of reflection** states that the angle of incidence (the angle between the ray and a perpendicular line drawn to the surface) is equal to the angle of reflection (the angle between the reflected ray and a perpendicular to the surface). Looking at an image on the surface of the water in a lake is an example of light rays reflecting towards the observer. Reflection of light takes place from all materials. Some materials absorb a small amount of light and reflect most of it back; for example, a shiny, silvery surface. Other materials absorb most of the light and reflect only a small amount back; for example, a dark, dull surface. Reflected light gives objects their visible texture and colour.

reflex in animals, a very rapid involuntary response to a particular stimulus. It is controlled by the *nervous system. A reflex involves only a few nerve cells, unlike the slower but more complex responses produced by the many processing nerve cells of the brain.

reflex camera the single-lens relfex (SLR) camera uses a mirror and prisms to reflect light passing through the lens into the viewfinder, showing the photographer the exact scene that is being shot. When the shutter button is released the mirror springs out of the way, allowing light to reach the film. The twin-lens reflex (TLR) camera has two lenses: one has a mirror for viewing, the other is used for exposing the film.

reflexology in alternative medicine, manipulation and massage of the feet to ascertain and treat disease or dysfunction elsewhere in the body.

Reform Acts in the UK, acts of Parliament in 1832, 1867, and 1884 that extended voting rights and redistributed parliamentary seats; also known as *Representation of the People Acts.

Reformation religious and political movement in 16th-century Europe to reform the Roman Catholic Church,

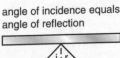

angle of incidence equals
angle of reflection

ray box

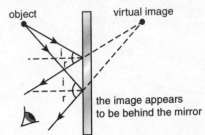

object

virtual image

the image appears
to be behind the mirror

reflection Light rays reflected from a regular (plane) mirror. The angle of incidence is the angle between the ray and a perpendicular line drawn to the surface and the angle of reflection is the angle between the reflected ray and a perpendicular to the surface. The image of an object in a plane mirror is described as virtual or imaginary because it appears to be the position from which the rays are formed.

which led to the establishment of the Protestant churches. Anticipated by medieval movements such as the Waldenses, *Lollards, and Hussites, it was started by the German priest Martin *Luther in 1517, and became effective when local princes gave it support by challenging the political power of the papacy and confiscating church wealth.

refraction bending of a wave when it passes from one medium into another. It is the effect of the different speeds of wave propagation in two substances that have different densities. For example, when light passes from air (less dense) into glass (more dense) it slows down (from 300 million to 200 million metres per second) and is refracted. The amount of refraction depends on the densities of the media, the angle at which the wave strikes the surface of the second medium, and the amount of bending and change of velocity corresponding to the wave's frequency (dispersion). Refraction occurs with all types of progressive waves – *electromagnetic waves, sound waves, and water waves – and differs from *reflection, which involves no change in velocity.

refractory (of a material) able to resist high temperature, for example *ceramics made from clay, minerals, or other earthy materials. Furnaces are lined with refractory materials such as silica and dolomite.

refrigeration use of technology to transfer heat from cold to warm, against the normal temperature gradient, so that an object can remain substantially colder than its surroundings. Refrigeration equipment is used for the chilling and deep-freezing of food in food technology, and in air conditioners and industrial processes.

refugee according to international law, a person fleeing from oppressive or dangerous conditions (such as political, religious, or military persecution) and seeking refuge in a foreign country. In 1995 there were an estimated 27 million refugees worldwide; their resettlement and welfare is the responsibility of the United Nations High Commission for Refugees (UNHCR). An estimated average of 10,000 people a day become refugees. Women and children make up 75% of all refugees and displaced persons. Many more millions are 'economic' or 'environmental' refugees, forced to emigrate because of economic circumstances, lack of access to land, or environmental disasters.

Regency in Britain, the years 1811–20 during which *George IV (then Prince of Wales) acted as regent for his father *George III, who was finally declared insane and unfit to govern in December 1810. The Regency was marked by the Prince Regent's turbulent private life, his dissolute public image, and the fashionable society he patronized.

Regency style style of architecture and interior furnishings popular in England during the late 18th and early 19th centuries. It is characterized by restrained simplicity and the imitation of ancient classical elements, often Greek.

regeneration in biology, regrowth of a new organ or tissue after the loss or removal of the original. It is

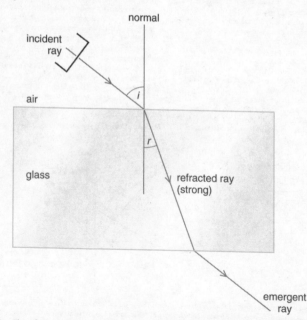

refraction The refraction of light through glass. When the light ray strikes the glass (a denser medium than the air) it is bent towards the normal. When it leaves the glass and re-enters the less dense medium it is bent away from the normal.

common in plants, where a new individual can often
be produced from a 'cutting' of the original. In animals,
regeneration of major structures is limited to lower
organisms; certain lizards can regrow their tails if these
are lost, and new flatworms can grow from a tiny
fragment of an old one. In mammals, regeneration is
limited to the repair of tissue in wound healing and the
regrowth of peripheral nerves following damage.

regent person who carries out the duties of a sovereign
during the sovereign's minority, incapacity, or lengthy
absence from the country. In England since the time of
Henry VIII, Parliament has always appointed a regent
or council of regency when necessary.

reggae major form of West Indian popular music of
the 1970s and 1980s, characterized by a heavily accented
offbeat and a thick bass line. The lyrics often refer to
*Rastafarianism. Musicians include Bob *Marley, Lee
'Scratch' Perry (performer and producer), and the
group Black Uhuru. Reggae is also popular in the UK,
USA, South Africa, and elsewhere.

regressive tax tax such that the higher the income of
the taxpayer the smaller the proportion or percentage
paid in that tax. This contrasts with progressive taxes
where the proportion paid rises as income increases,
and proportional taxes where the proportion paid
remains the same at all levels of income. Examples
of regressive taxes in the UK are the *council tax and
*excise duties.

Rehoboam King of Judah about 932–915 BC, son of
Solomon. Under his rule the Jewish nation split into
the two kingdoms of **Israel** and **Judah**. Ten of the tribes
revolted against him and took Jeroboam as their ruler,
leaving Rehoboam only the tribes of Judah and Benjamin.

Reich (German 'empire') three periods in European
history. The First Reich was the Holy Roman Empire
(962–1806), the Second Reich the German Empire
(1871–1918), and the *Third Reich Nazi Germany
(1933–45).

Reich, Steve (1936–) US composer. His minimalist
music employs simple patterns carefully superimposed
and modified to highlight constantly changing
melodies and rhythms; examples are *Phase Patterns*
for four electronic organs (1970), *Music for Mallet
Instruments, Voices, and Organ* (1973), and *Music for
Percussion and Keyboards* (1984).

Reichstag Fire burning of the German parliament
building in Berlin 27 February 1933, less than a month
after the Nazi leader Hitler became chancellor. The fire
was used as a justification for the suspension of many
constitutional guarantees and also as an excuse to
attack the communists. There is still debate over
whether the Nazis were involved in this crime, of
which they were the main beneficiaries.

reincarnation *or* **transmigration** *or* **metempsychosis**
belief that after death the human soul or the spirit of
a plant or animal may live again in another human or
animal. It is part of the teachings of many religions and
philosophies; for example, ancient Egyptian and Greek
(the philosophies of Pythagoras and Plato), Buddhism,
Hinduism, Jainism, Sikhism, certain Christian heresies
(such as the Cathars), and theosophy.

reindeer *or* **caribou** deer *Rangifer tarandus* of Arctic
and subarctic regions, common to North America and
Eurasia. About 1.2 m/4 ft at the shoulder, it has a thick,
brownish coat and broad hooves well adapted to travel

over snow. It is the only deer in which both sexes have
antlers; these can grow to 1.5 m/5 ft long, and are shed
in winter.

relative atomic mass mass of an atom relative to one-
twelfth the mass of an atom of carbon-12. It depends
primarily on the number of protons and neutrons in
the atom, the electrons having negligible mass. If more
than one *isotope of the element is present, the relative
atomic mass is calculated by taking an average that
takes account of the relative proportions of each
isotope, resulting in values that are not whole numbers.
The term **atomic weight**, although commonly used,
is strictly speaking incorrect.

relative molecular mass mass of a molecule,
calculated relative to one-twelfth the mass of an atom
of carbon-12. It is found by adding the relative atomic
masses of the atoms that make up the molecule.
The term **molecular weight**, although commonly used,
is strictly speaking incorrect.

relativism philosophical position that denies the
possibility of objective truth independent of some
specific social or historical context or conceptual
framework.

relativity in physics, theory of the relative rather than
absolute character of mass, time, and space, and their
interdependence, as developed by German-born US
physicist Albert *Einstein in two phases: **Special theory
of relativity** (1905) Starting with the premises that
(1) the laws of nature are the same for all observers
in unaccelerated motion and (2) the speed of light
is independent of the motion of its source, Einstein
arrived at some rather unexpected consequences.
Intuitively familiar concepts, like mass, length, and
time, had to be modified. For example, an object
moving rapidly past the observer will appear to be both
shorter and more massive than when it is at rest (that
is, at rest relative to the observer), and a clock moving
rapidly past the observer will appear to be running
slower than when it is at rest. These predictions of
relativity theory seem to be foreign to everyday
experience merely because the changes are quite
negligible at speeds less than about 1,500 kps/930 mps
and only become appreciable at speeds approaching
the speed of light. **General theory of relativity** (1915)
The geometrical properties of space-time were to be
conceived as modified locally by the presence of a body
with mass. A planet's orbit around the Sun (as observed
in three-dimensional space) arises from its natural
trajectory in modified space-time. Einstein's general
theory accounts for a peculiarity in the behaviour of
the motion of the perihelion of the orbit of the planet
Mercury that cannot be explained in Newton's theory.
The new theory also said that light rays would bend
when they pass by a massive object. The predicted
bending of starlight was observed during the eclipse
of the Sun in 1919. A third corroboration is found in
the shift towards the red in the spectra of the Sun and,
in particular, of stars of great density – white dwarfs
such as the companion of Sirius.

relay in electrical engineering, an electromagnetic
switch that allows a small amount of electrical current
to control a large amount of current. A small current
passing through a coil of wire wound around an iron
core attracts an *armature whose movement closes a
pair of sprung contacts to complete a secondary circuit,

which may carry a large current or activate other devices. A car starter motor uses a relay to solve the problem that a car has in needing a large amount of current to start the engine. A starter relay is installed in series between the battery and the starter. The solid-state equivalent is a thyristor switching device.

relief in sculpture, particularly architectural sculpture, carved figures and other forms that project from the background. The Italian terms *basso-rilievo* (low relief), *mezzo-rilievo* (middle relief), and *alto-rilievo* (high relief) are used according to the extent to which the sculpture projects. The French term *bas-relief* is commonly used to mean low relief.

religion (Latin *religare* 'to bind'; bond of humans to God) code of belief or philosophy that often involves the worship of a *God or gods. Belief in a supernatural power is not essential (absent in, for example, Buddhism and Confucianism), but faithful adherence is usually considered to be rewarded; for example, by escape from human existence (Buddhism), by a future existence (Christianity, Islam), or by worldly benefit (Soka Gakkai Buddhism). Religions include: **ancient and pantheist** religions of Babylonia, Assyria, Egypt, Greece, and Rome **animist or polytheistic** traditional central African religions, voodoo and related beliefs in Latin America and the Caribbean, traditional faiths of American Indians, Maoris, Australian Aborigines, and Javanese **oriental** Hinduism, Buddhism, Jainism, Zoroastrianism, Confucianism, Taoism, and Shinto **'religions of a book'** Judaism, Christianity (the principal divisions are Roman Catholic, Eastern Orthodox, and Protestant), and Islam (the principal divisions are Sunni and Shiite) **combined derivation** these include Baha'ism, the Unification church, and Mormonism.

rem acronym for **roentgen equivalent man**, unit of radiation dose equivalent.

Remarque, Erich Maria (1898–1970) German novelist. He was a soldier in World War I. His *All Quiet on the Western Front* (1929), one of the first anti-war novels, led to his being deprived of German nationality. He lived in Switzerland 1929–39, and then in the USA.

Rembrandt, Harmensz van Rijn (1606–1669) Dutch painter, etcher, and teacher. Rembrandt was one of the most prolific and significant artists in Europe of the 17th century. Between 1629 and 1669 he painted about 60 penetrating self-portraits, many of them used as studies for later paintings. He also painted religious subjects, and produced about 300 etchings and over 1,000 drawings. His major group portraits include *The Anatomy Lesson of Dr Tulp* (1632; Mauritshuis, The Hague) and *The Night Watch* (1642; Rijksmuseum, Amsterdam). Known for his mastery of the *chiaroscuro effect and the *baroque style, his later work is passionate, psychologically charged, and atmospherically moody.

remora any of a family of warm-water fishes that have an adhesive disc on the head, by which they attach themselves to whales, sharks, and turtles. These provide the remora with shelter and transport, as well as food in the form of parasites on the host's skin.

remote sensing gathering and recording information from a distance. Aircraft and satellites can observe a planetary surface or atmosphere, and space probes have sent back photographs and data about planets as distant as Neptune. Remote sensing usually refers to gathering data of the electromagnetic spectrum (such as visible light, ultraviolet light, and infrared light). In archaeology, surface survey techniques provide information without disturbing subsurface deposits.

REM sleep acronym for **rapid-eye-movement sleep**, phase of sleep that recurs several times nightly in humans and is associated with dreaming. The eyes flicker quickly beneath closed lids.

Renaissance or Revival of Learning period in European cultural history that began in Italy around 1400 and lasted there until the end of the 1500s. Elsewhere in Europe it began later, and lasted until the 1600s. One characteristic of the Renaissance was the rediscovery of ancient Greek and Roman literature, led by the writers Giovanni *Boccaccio and Francesco *Petrarch who translated and studied the works of the classical civilizations. A central theme of the Renaissance was *humanism, a belief in actively searching for knowledge rather than accepting what already exists, and a faith in the *republican ideal. The greatest expression of the Renaissance was in the arts and learning. The term 'Renaissance' (French for 'rebirth') to describe this period of cultural history was invented by historians in the 1800s.

renewable energy power from any source that can be replenished. Most renewable systems rely on solar energy directly or through the weather cycle as wave power, hydroelectric power, wind power via wind turbines, or solar energy collected by plants (alcohol fuels, for example). In addition, the gravitational force of the Moon can be harnessed through tidal power stations, and the heat trapped in the centre of the Earth is used via geothermal energy systems. Other examples are energy from biofuel and fuel cells. Renewable energy resources have the advantage of being non-polluting. However, some (such as wind energy) can be unreliable and therefore lose their effectiveness in providing a constant supply of energy.

renewable resource natural resource that is replaced by natural processes in a reasonable amount of time. Soil, water, forests, plants, and animals are all renewable resources as long as they are properly conserved. Solar, wind, wave, and geothermal energies are based on renewable resources.

rennet extract, traditionally obtained from a calf's stomach, that contains the enzyme rennin, used to coagulate milk in the cheesemaking process. The enzyme can now be chemically produced.

Renoir, Jean (1894–1979) French film director. His films, characterized by their humanism and naturalistic technique, include *Boudu sauvé des eaux/Boudu Saved from Drowning* (1932), *Le Crime de Monsieur Lange/ The Crime of Monsieur Lange* (1936), *La Grande Illusion* (1937), and *La Règle du jeu/The Rules of the Game* (1939).

Renoir, Pierre-Auguste (1841–1919) French Impressionist painter. He met Claude *Monet and Alfred *Sisley in the early 1860s, and together they formed the nucleus of *Impressionism. He developed a lively, colourful painting style with feathery brushwork (known as his 'rainbow style') and painted many scenes of everyday life, such as *The Luncheon of the Boating Party* (1881; Phillips Collection, Washington, DC), and also female nudes, such as *The Bathers* (about 1884–87; Philadelphia Museum of Art).

repetitive strain injury (RSI) generic term for various kinds of work-related musculoskeletal injuries, such as carpal tunnel syndrome and tendonitis. Symptoms of RSI include inflammation of tendon sheaths, mainly in the hands and wrists, which may be disabling. It is found predominantly in factory workers involved in constant repetitive movements, and in those who work with computer keyboards. The symptoms include aching muscles, weak wrists, tingling fingers, and in severe cases, pain and paralysis. Some victims have successfully sued their employers for damages.

replication in biology, production of copies of the genetic material DNA; it occurs during cell division (*mitosis and *meiosis). Most mutations are caused by mistakes during replication.

representational art *or* **figurative art** in the visual arts, images that can be recognized from the real world, even if they are distorted or appear in unusual combinations, as in surrealism. The English artist David *Hockney's portraits and swimming-pool paintings are contemporary examples of representational art. The opposite is *abstract, or non-figurative, art.

Representation of the People Acts series of UK acts of Parliament from 1867 that extended voting rights, creating universal suffrage in 1928. The 1867 and 1884 acts are known as the second and third *Reform Acts.

repression in psychology, a mental process that ejects and excludes from consciousness ideas, impulses, or memories that would otherwise threaten emotional stability.

reproduction in biology, the process by which a living organism produces other organisms more or less similar to itself. The ways in which species reproduce differ, but the two main methods are by *asexual reproduction and *sexual reproduction. Asexual reproduction involves only one parent without the formation of *gametes: the parent's cells divide by *mitosis to produce new cells with the same number and kind of *chromosomes as its own. Thus offspring produced asexually are clones of the parent and there is no variation. Sexual reproduction involves two parents, one male and one female. The parents' sex cells divide by *meiosis producing gametes, which contain only half the number of chromosomes of the parent cell. In this way, when two sets of chromosomes combine during *fertilization, a new combination of genes is produced. Hence the new organism will differ from both parents, and variation is introduced. The ability to reproduce is considered one of the fundamental attributes of living things.

reptile any member of a class (Reptilia) of vertebrates. Unlike amphibians, reptiles have hard-shelled, yolk-filled eggs that are laid on land and from which fully formed young are born. Some snakes and lizards retain their eggs and give birth to live young. Reptiles are cold-blooded, and their skin is usually covered with scales. The metabolism is slow, and in some cases (certain large snakes) intervals between meals may be months. Reptiles date back over 300 million years.

republic (Latin *res publica* 'the state'; from *res* 'affair', and *publica* 'public') country where the head of state is not a monarch, either hereditary or elected, but usually a president, whose role may or may not include political functions.

Republican Party younger of the two main political parties of the USA, formed in 1854. It is more right-wing than the Democratic Party, favouring capital and big business and opposing state financial assistance and federal controls. In the late 20th century most presidents have come from the Republican Party, but in Congress Republicans have generally been outnumbered. In 1992 Republican George Bush lost the presidency to Democrat Bill Clinton, who in 1996 was re-elected for a second term, although the Republicans retained control of Congress and had governors in 32 of the country's 50 states. The Republicans took the presidency in 2000, with George W *Bush slimly beating the Democrat Al Gore in a conflict-ridden election.

requiem (from Latin *Requiem aeternam dona eis, Domine,* 'Give them eternal rest, O Lord') in the Roman Catholic Church, a Mass for the dead. Musical settings include those by Palestrina, Mozart, Berlioz, Verdi, Fauré, and Britten.

resin substance exuded from pines, firs, and other trees in gummy drops that harden in air. Varnishes are common products of the hard resins, and ointments come from the soft resins.

resistance in physics, that property of a conductor that restricts the flow of electricity through it, associated with the conversion of electrical energy to heat; also the magnitude of this property.

resistance movement opposition movement in a country occupied by an enemy or colonial power, especially in the 20th century; for example, the resistance to Nazism and *Nazi occupation in Europe during *World War II.

resistivity in physics, a measure of the ability of a material to resist the flow of an electric current. It is numerically equal to the *resistance of a sample of unit length and unit cross-sectional area, and its unit is the ohm metre (symbol Ωm). A good conductor has a low resistivity (1.7×10^{-8} Ωm for copper); an insulator has a very high resistivity (10^{15} Ωm for polyethane).

resistor in physics, any component in an electrical circuit used to introduce *resistance to a current by restricting the flow of electrons. Resistors are often made from wire-wound coils (higher resistance) or pieces of carbon (lower resistance). Rheostats and *potentiometers are variable resistors.

resonance rapid amplification of a vibration when the vibrating object is subject to a force varying at its natural frequency. In a trombone, for example, the length of the air column in the instrument is adjusted until it resonates with the note being sounded. Resonance effects are also produced by many electrical circuits. Tuning a radio, for example, is done by adjusting the natural frequency of the receiver circuit until it coincides with the frequency of the radio waves falling on the aerial.

respiration process that occurs inside cells in which carbohydrate, particularly glucose, is broken down to release *energy that the cell can use. This energy is used for many different processes, but in all of them energy transfer occurs. The processes range from muscle contraction to the manufacture of protein for new cells. Respiration is a key feature of life and is carried out by all living *cells. There are two kinds of respiration in

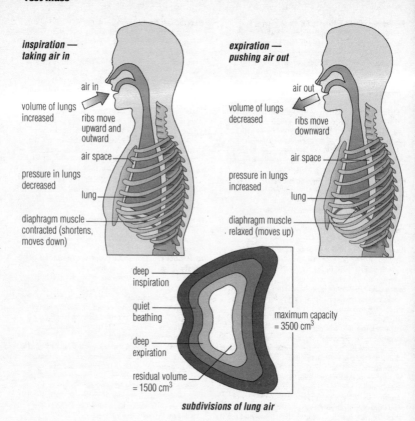

*inspiration —
taking air in*

volume of lungs
increased

air in

ribs move
upward and
outward

air space

pressure in lungs
decreased

lung

diaphragm muscle
contracted (shortens,
moves down)

*expiration —
pushing air out*

volume of lungs
decreased

air out

ribs move
downward

air space

pressure in lungs
increased

lung

diaphragm muscle
relaxed (moves up)

deep
inspiration

quiet
beathing

deep
expiration

residual volume
= 1500 cm^3

maximum capacity
= 3500 cm^3

subdivisions of lung air

respiration The two phases of the process of aerobic respiration in humans. Gas exchange occurs in the alveoli, tiny air tubes in the lungs.

organisms – aerobic and anaerobic respiration. Aerobic respiration is a complex process of chemical reactions in which oxygen is used to break down glucose into *carbon dioxide and *water. This releases energy in the form of energy-carrying molecules (*ATP). Respiration sometimes occurs without oxygen, and this is called anaerobic respiration. In this case, glucose is only partially broken down, and the end products are energy and either lactic acid or ethanol (alcohol) and carbon dioxide; this process is termed *fermentation.

rest mass in physics, the mass of a body when its velocity is zero or considerably below that of light. According to the theory of *relativity, at very high velocities, there is a relativistic effect that increases the mass of the particle.

Restoration in English history, the period when the monarchy, in the person of *Charles II, was re-established after the English *Civil War and the fall of the Protectorate in 1660.

Restoration comedy style of English theatre, dating from the *Restoration period. The genre placed much emphasis on wit and sexual intrigues. It also witnessed the first appearance of women on the English stage, most notably in the 'breeches part', specially created in order to costume the actress in male attire, thus revealing her figure to its best advantage. Examples of Restoration comedy include English dramatists William *Wycherley (whose works include *The Country Wife*, 1675) and William *Congreve (whose works include *The Way of the World*, 1700), and Irish dramatist George *Farquhar (whose works include *The Beaux Stratagem*, 1707).

restrictive trade practice any agreement between people in a particular trade or business that restricts free trade in a market. For example, several producers may join together to form a *cartel and fix prices; or a manufacturer may refuse to supply goods to a retailer if the retailer stocks the products of a rival company.

resurrection in Christian, Jewish, and Muslim belief, the rising from the dead that all souls will experience at the Last Judgement. The Resurrection also refers to Jesus rising from the dead on the third day after his crucifixion, a belief central to Christianity and celebrated at *Easter.

resuscitation steps taken to revive anyone on the brink of death. The most successful technique for life-threatening emergencies, such as electrocution, near-drowning, or heart attack, is mouth-to-mouth resuscitation. Medical and paramedical staff are trained in cardiopulmonary resuscitation (CPR): the use of specialized equipment and techniques to attempt to restart the breathing and/or heartbeat and stabilize the patient long enough for more definitive treatment. CPR has a success rate of less than 30%.

retail sale of goods and services to a consumer. The retailer is the last link in the distribution chain. A retailer's purchases are usually made from a wholesaler, who in turn buys from a manufacturer. The lack of space and high cost of land in city centres forced retail developers to look outside urban areas for locations to develop. Rising car ownership and new road developments have meant that out-of-town sites are now often more accessible and attractive than the centres of cities, especially since car parking tends to be free.

retail-price index (RPI) UK index, compiled by the Office for National Statistics, to reflect the cost of living at any particular time. The Retail Price Index was introduced in 1947, superseding the Cost of Living Index, which had been published monthly from April 1914. Today, in order to avoid confusion, the Cost of Living Index for the years 1914 to 1947 is also referred to as the RPI, and the dates given for the RPI start from 1914. The US equivalent to the RPI is the consumer price index (CPI), compiled on a monthly basis by the Bureau of Labor Statistics (BLS). The CPI was introduced in 1919 and was calculated retrospectively starting from the year 1913.

retina light-sensitive area at the back of the *eye connected to the brain by the optic nerve. It has several layers and in humans contains over a million rods and cones, sensory cells capable of converting light into nervous messages that pass down the optic nerve to the brain.

retinol or **vitamin A** fat-soluble chemical derived from β-carotene and found in milk, butter, cheese, egg yolk, and liver. Lack of retinol in the diet leads to the eye disease **xerophthalmia**.

retriever any of several breeds of hunting dogs, often used as guide dogs for the blind. The commonest breeds are the **Labrador retriever**, large, smooth-coated, and usually black or yellow; and the **golden retriever**, with either flat or wavy coat. They can grow to 60 cm/2 ft high and weigh 40 kg/90 lb.

retrovirus any of a family of *viruses (Retroviridae) containing the genetic material *RNA rather than the more usual *DNA.

Réunion French tropical island of the Mascarenes group, in the Indian Ocean, 650 km/400 mi east of Madagascar and 180 km/110 mi southwest of Mauritius; area 2,512 sq km/970 sq mi; population (1995 est) 653,400. The capital is St Denis. Produce includes sugar, maize, vanilla, tobacco, and rum.

reverberation in acoustics, the multiple reflections, or echoes, of sounds inside a building that merge and persist a short time (up to a few seconds) before fading away. At each reflection some of the sound energy is absorbed, causing the amplitude of the sound wave and the intensity of the sound to reduce a little.

Revere, Paul (1735–1818) American revolutionary, a Boston silversmith, who carried the news of the approach of British troops to Lexington and Concord (see *American Revolution) on the night of 18 April 1775. On the next morning the first shots of the Revolution were fired at Lexington. Henry Wadsworth Longfellow's poem 'Paul Revere's Ride' (1863) commemorates the event.

reversible reaction chemical reaction that proceeds in both directions at the same time, as the product decomposes back into reactants as it is being produced. Such reactions do not run to completion, provided that no substance leaves the system. Examples include the manufacture of ammonia from hydrogen and nitrogen, and the oxidation of sulphur dioxide to sulphur trioxide.

revisionism political theory derived from Marxism that moderates one or more of the basic tenets of Karl Marx, and is hence condemned by orthodox Marxists.

revolution any rapid, far-reaching, or violent change in the political, social, or economic structure of society. It is usually applied to political change: examples include the American Revolution, where the colonists broke free from their colonial ties and established a sovereign, independent nation; the *French Revolution, where an absolute monarchy was overthrown by opposition from inside the country and a popular uprising; and the *Russian Revolution, where a repressive monarchy was overthrown by those seeking to institute widespread social and economic changes based on a socialist model. In 1989–90 the Eastern Bloc nations demonstrated against and voted out the Communist Party, in many cases creating a pro-democracy revolution.

Revolutionary Wars series of wars from 1791 to 1802 between France and the combined armies of England, Austria, Prussia, and others, during the period of the *French Revolution and *Napoleon's campaign to conquer Europe.

revolutions of 1848 series of revolts in various parts of Europe against monarchical rule. Although some of the revolutionaries had republican ideas, many more were motivated by economic grievances. The revolution began in France with the overthrow of Louis Philippe and then spread to Italy, the Austrian Empire, and Germany, where the short-lived Frankfurt Parliament put forward ideas about political unity in Germany. None of the revolutions enjoyed any lasting success, and most were violently suppressed within a few months.

revolutions of 1989 popular uprisings in many countries of Eastern Europe against communist rule, prompted by internal reforms in the USSR that permitted dissent within its sphere of influence. By 1990 nearly all the Warsaw Pact countries had moved from one-party to pluralist political systems, in most cases peacefully but with growing hostility between various nationalist and ethnic groups.

revue stage presentation involving short satirical and topical items in the form of songs, sketches, and monologues; it originated in the late 19th century.

Reykjavik chief port and capital (from 1918) of Iceland, on the southwest coast on Faxa Bay; population (1994) 103,000. Fish processing is the main industry. Most of the city is heated by an underground water mains system, built in 1945, the source of the hot water being volcanic springs and geysers. It was a seat of Danish administration from 1801 to 1918, and has been the seat of the Parliament since 1843. Reykjavik is the world's most northerly capital.

Reynolds, Albert (1932–) Irish Fianna Fáil politician, Taoiseach (prime minister) 1992–94. He was minister for industry and commerce 1987–88 and minister of finance 1988–92. In December 1993 Reynolds and UK prime minister John Major issued a joint peace initiative for Northern Ireland, the Downing Street Declaration, which led to a ceasefire by both the Irish Republican Army (IRA) and the loyalist paramilitaries the following year.

Reynolds, Joshua (1723–1792) English painter. One of the greatest portraitists of the 18th century, he displayed a facility for striking and characterful compositions in the 'Grand Manner', a style based on classical and Renaissance art. He often borrowed classical poses, for example *Mrs Siddons as the Tragic Muse* (1784; San Marino, California). His elegant portraits are mostly of wealthy patrons, though he also painted such figures as the writers Laurence Sterne and Dr Johnson, and the actor David Garrick. Active in London from 1752, he became the first president of the Royal Academy in 1768 and founded the Royal Academy schools. He was knighted in 1769.

rhea one of two flightless birds of the family Rheidae, order Rheiformes. The common rhea *Rhea americana* is 1.5 m/5 ft high and is distributed widely in South America. The smaller Darwin's rhea *Pterocnemia pennata* occurs only in the south of South America and has shorter, feathered legs, and mottled plumage. Rheas differ from the ostrich in their smaller size and in having a feathered neck and head, three-toed feet, and no plumelike tail feathers.

rhenium chemical symbol Re, (Latin *Rhenus* 'Rhine') heavy, silver-white, metallic element, atomic number 75, relative atomic mass 186.2. It has chemical properties similar to those of manganese and a very high melting point (3,180 °C/5,756 °F), which makes it valuable as an ingredient in alloys.

rhesus factor group of *antigens on the surface of red blood cells of humans which characterize the rhesus blood group system. Most individuals possess the main rhesus factor (Rh+), but those without this factor (Rh–) produce *antibodies if they come into contact with it. The name comes from rhesus monkeys, in whose blood rhesus factors were first found.

rhesus monkey macaque monkey *Macaca mulatta* found in northern India and Southeast Asia. It has a pinkish face, red buttocks, and long, straight, brown-grey hair. It can grow up to 60 cm/2 ft long, with a 20 cm/8 in tail.

rheumatic fever *or* **acute rheumatism** acute or chronic illness characterized by fever and painful swelling of joints. Some victims also experience involuntary movements of the limbs and head, a form of *chorea. It is now rare in the developed world.

rheumatism nontechnical term for a variety of ailments associated with inflammation and stiffness of the joints and muscles.

rheumatoid arthritis inflammation of the joints; a chronic progressive disease, it begins with pain and stiffness in the small joints of the hands and feet and spreads to involve other joints, often with severe disability and disfigurement. There may also be damage to the eyes, nervous system, and other organs. The disease is treated with a range of drugs and with surgery, possibly including replacement of major joints.

Rhineland province of Prussia from 1815. Its unchallenged annexation by Nazi Germany in 1936 was a harbinger of World War II.

Rhineland-Palatinate German **Rheinland-Pfalz**, administrative region (German *Land*) in southwest Germany, bordered to the north by North Rhine-Westphalia, to the east by Hesse and Baden-Württemberg, to the south by France, to the southwest by the Saarland, and to the west by Luxembourg and Belgium; area 19,847 sq km/7,663 sq mi; population (1999 est) 4,030,800. The capital is Mainz, and other major towns include Ludwigshafen, Koblenz, Trier, Worms, and Kaiserslautern.

rhinoceros large grazing mammal with one or more horns on its snout. Rhinoceroses have thick, loose skin with little hair, stumpy, powerful legs with three toes on each foot. The largest species (the one-horned Indian rhinoceros) can grow up to 2 m/6 ft high at the shoulder and weigh 2,300–4,000 kg/5,060–8,800 lb. Rhinoceroses eat grass, leafy twigs, and shrubs, and are solitary. They have poor eyesight but excellent hearing and smell. Although they look clumsy, rhinos can reach speeds of 56 kph/35 mph. In the wild they are thought to live for about 25 years, and up to 47 in captivity. There are five species: three Asian and two African, all in danger of extinction.

rhizome *or* **rootstock** horizontal underground plant stem. It is a *perennating organ in some species, where it is generally thick and fleshy, while in other species it is mainly a means of *vegetative reproduction, and is therefore long and slender, with buds all along it that send up new plants. The potato is a rhizome that has two distinct parts, the tuber being the swollen end of a long, cordlike rhizome.

Rhode Island officially Rhode Island and Providence Plantations; called the **Ocean State**, smallest state of the USA, located in *New England, bordered to the north and east by *Massachusetts, to the west by *Connecticut, and to the south by the Atlantic Ocean; area 2,707 sq km/1,045 sq mi; population (2000) 1,048,300; capital Providence. Eastern Rhode Island lies on Narragansett Bay, a sound in the Atlantic, and consists of coastal lowlands, estuaries, and islands. The state has 640 km/400 mi of coastline. The northwestern portion of the state, behind the coast, is part of the Eastern New England Upland. The state economy is reliant on the service sector, and tourism is significant. The most important industry is the manufacture of jewellery and silverware; other products include textiles, metals, greenhouse plants, shrubs, and potatoes. Rhode Island Red hens were first bred here in the 19th century. Other major towns and cities in Rhode Island include Warwick, Cranston, Newport, and Woonsocket. Rhode Island was originally home to the Narragansett, Niantic, Nipmuck, Pequot, and Wampanoag American Indian peoples. The Rhode

Island colony was founded in 1636 by Roger Williams, and was one of the original *Thirteen Colonies. Rhode Island ratified the US Constitution in 1790, becoming the 13th state to join the Union.

Rhodes Greek *Rodos*, Greek island, largest of the Dodecanese, in the eastern Aegean Sea; area 1,412 sq km/545 sq mi; population (2003 est) 55,600. The island has a central mountain range, the Attaviros Mountains. Rhodes town is the capital of the island, and is located at the most northerly point on the island. Wheat, tobacco, cotton, wine grapes, oranges, vegetables, and olives are grown. Tourism is the most important industry; fishing and wine production are also sources of income.

Rhodes, Cecil John (1853–1902) South African politician, born in the UK, prime minister of Cape Colony 1890–96. Aiming at the formation of a South African federation and the creation of a block of British territory from the Cape to Cairo, he was responsible for the annexation of Bechuanaland (now Botswana) in 1885. He formed the British South Africa Company in 1889, which occupied Mashonaland and Matabeleland, thus forming **Rhodesia** (now Zambia and Zimbabwe).

Rhodesia former name of *Zambia (Northern Rhodesia) and *Zimbabwe (Southern Rhodesia), in southern Africa.

rhodium chemical symbol Rh, (Greek *rhodon* 'rose') hard, silver-white, metallic element, atomic number 45, relative atomic mass 102.905. It is one of the so-called platinum group of metals and is resistant to tarnish, corrosion, and acid. It occurs as a free metal in the natural alloy osmiridium and is used in jewellery, electroplating, and thermocouples.

rhododendron any of numerous, mostly evergreen shrubs belonging to the heath family. The leaves are usually dark and leathery, and the large funnel-shaped flowers, which grow in tight clusters, occur in all colours except blue. They thrive on acid soils. *Azaleas belong to the same genus. (Genus *Rhododendron*, family Ericaceae.)

rhombus equilateral (all sides equal) *parallelogram. As with a parallelogram, the rhombus has diagonally opposed angles of equal size. Its diagonals bisect each other at right angles, and its area is half the product of the lengths of the two diagonals. The shape is sometimes called a diamond. A rhombus whose internal angles are 90° is called a *square.

Rhône river of southern Europe; length 810 km/500 mi. It rises at the Rhône Glacier (altitude 1,825 m/5,987 ft) in the canton of Valais in Switzerland and flows through Lake Geneva to Lyon into France, where, at its confluence with the *Saône, the upper limit of navigation is reached. The river then turns due south and passes Vienne and Avignon. Near Arles it divides into the **Grand** and **Petit Rhône**, flowing respectively southeast and southwest into the Mediterranean west of Marseille. Here it forms a two-armed delta; the area between the tributaries is the marshy region known as the *Camargue.

Rhône-Alpes region of eastern France in the upper reaches of the *Rhône; area 43,698 sq km/16,872 sq mi; population (1999 est) 5,645,400. It consists of the *départements* of Ain, Ardèche, Drôme, Isère, Loire, Rhône, Savoie, and Haute-Savoie. The capital is *Lyon. There are several wine-producing areas, including

Chenas, Fleurie, and Beaujolais. Industrial products include chemicals, textiles, and motor vehicles.

rhubarb perennial plant grown for its pink edible leaf stalks. The large leaves contain *oxalic acid, and are poisonous. There are also wild rhubarbs native to Europe and Asia. (Genus *Rheum rhaponticum*, family Polygonaceae.)

rhyme correspondence of sound, usually in the final syllable or group of syllables in lines of *verse, as in 'There was once an old man with a *beard*/Who said, 'It is just as I *feared*.'' The rhyme depends on the vowel sounds and all the consonants *except* the first.

rhythm and blues (R & B) style of popular music developed in the USA during the 1940s–60s. It drew on swing and jazz rhythms and blues vocals, and was an important influence on rock and roll. It diversified into soul, funk, and other styles. R & B artists include Bo Diddley, Jackie Wilson, and Etta James.

rhythm method method of natural contraception that relies on refraining from intercourse during *ovulation. The time of ovulation can be worked out by the calendar (counting days from the last period), by temperature change, or by inspection of the cervical mucus. All these methods are unreliable because it is possible for ovulation to occur at any stage of the menstrual cycle.

rib long, usually curved bone that extends laterally from the *spine in vertebrates. Most fishes and many reptiles have ribs along most of the spine, but in mammals they are found only in the chest area. In humans, there are 12 pairs of ribs. The ribs protect the lungs and heart, and allow the chest to expand and contract easily.

Ribbentrop, Joachim von (1893–1946) German Nazi politician and diplomat. As foreign minister 1938–45, he negotiated the nonaggression pact between Germany and the USSR (the Ribbentrop–Molotov pact of 1939). He was tried at Nürnberg as a war criminal in 1946 and hanged.

Ribbentrop–Molotov pact *or* **Nazi–Soviet pact** non-aggression treaty signed by Germany and the USSR on 23 August 1939. The pact is named after the German foreign minister Joachim von *Ribbentrop and Russian foreign minister Vyacheslav *Molotov, working under German Nazi dictator Adolf Hitler and Soviet dictator Joseph Stalin respectively. Under the terms of the treaty both countries agreed to remain neutral and to refrain from acts of aggression against each other if either went to war. Secret clauses allowed for the partition of Poland – Hitler was to acquire western Poland, Stalin the eastern part. On 1 September 1939 Hitler invaded Poland. The pact ended when Hitler invaded Russia on 22 June 1941 during *World War II.

riboflavin *or* **vitamin B₂** *vitamin of the B complex important in cell respiration. It is obtained from eggs, liver, and milk. A deficiency in the diet causes stunted growth.

ribonucleic acid full name of *RNA.

ribosome protein-making machinery of the cell. Ribosomes are located on the endoplasmic reticulum (ER) of eukaryotic cells, and are made of proteins and a special type of *RNA, ribosomal RNA. They receive messenger RNA (copied from the *DNA) and *amino acids, and 'translate' the messenger RNA by using its chemically coded instructions to link amino acids in a specific order, to make a strand of a particular protein.

Ricardo, David (1772–1823) English economist. With the possible exception of German philosopher and economist Karl *Marx, no great economist of the past has received so many divergent and even contradictory interpretations as David Ricardo. No sooner had his *Principles of Political Economy and Taxation* (1817) appeared, but he attracted a number of ardent disciples who hailed him as the founder of a new rigorous science of political economy. However, these were soon followed by an even larger number of detractors, who struggled to escape from the grip of Ricardo's overwhelming influence on the economic thinking of his times.

rice principal cereal (*Oryza sativa*) of the wet regions of the tropics, derived from wild grasses probably native to India and Southeast Asia. Rice is unique among cereal crops in that it is grown standing in water. The yield is very large, and rice is the staple food of one-third of the world's population.

Richard, Cliff (1940–) stage name of Harry Roger Webb, English pop singer. Initially influenced by Elvis Presley, he soon became a Christian family entertainer. One of his best-selling early records was 'Livin' Doll' (1959); it was followed by a string of other successful singles. His original backing group was the Shadows (1958–68 and later re-formed). During the 1960s he starred in a number of musical films including *The Young Ones* (1962) and *Summer Holiday* (1963). Fulfilling a personal ambition, he produced the musical *Heathcliff* (1997) in which he played the title role.

Richard three kings of England:

Richard (I) the Lion-Heart (1157–1199) French **Coeur-de-Lion**, King of England 1189–99. He spent all but six months of his reign abroad. He was the third son of Henry II, against whom he twice rebelled. In the Third *Crusade 1191–92 he won victories at Cyprus, Acre, and Arsuf (against *Saladin), but failed to recover Jerusalem. While returning overland he was captured by the Duke of Austria, who handed him over to the emperor Henry VI, and he was held prisoner until a large ransom was raised. He then returned briefly to England, where his brother John had been ruling in his stead. His later years were spent in warfare in France, where he was killed by a crossbow bolt while besieging Châlus-Chabrol in 1199. He left no heir.

Richard II (1367–1400) also known as **Richard of Bordeaux**, King of England from 1377 (effectively from 1389), son of Edward the Black Prince. He reigned in conflict with Parliament; they executed some of his associates in 1388, and he executed a number of the opposing barons in 1397, whereupon he made himself absolute. Two years later, forced to abdicate in favour of *Henry IV, he was jailed and probably assassinated.

Richard III (1452–1485) King of England from 1483. The son of Richard, Duke of York, he was created Duke of Gloucester by his brother Edward IV, and distinguished himself in the Wars of the *Roses. On Edward's death in 1483 he became protector to his nephew Edward V, and soon secured the crown for himself on the plea that Edward IV's sons were illegitimate. He proved a capable ruler, but the suspicion that he had murdered Edward V and his brother made him unpopular. In 1485 Henry, Earl of Richmond (later *Henry VII), raised a rebellion, and Richard III was defeated and killed at *Bosworth.

Richards, Gordon (1904–1986) English jockey and trainer who was champion on the flat a record 26 times between 1925 and 1953.

Richardson, Samuel (1689–1761) English novelist. He was one of the founders of the modern novel. *Pamela* (1740–41), written in the form of a series of letters and containing much dramatic conversation, was sensationally popular all across Europe, and was followed by *Clarissa* (1747–48) and *Sir Charles Grandison* (1753–54).

Richelieu, Armand Jean du Plessis de (1585–1642) French cardinal and politician, chief minister from 1624. He aimed to make the monarchy absolute; he ruthlessly crushed opposition by the nobility and destroyed the political power of the *Huguenots, while leaving them religious freedom. Abroad, he sought to establish French supremacy by breaking the power of the Habsburgs; he therefore supported the Swedish king Gustavus Adolphus and the German Protestant princes against Austria and in 1635 brought France into the Thirty Years' War.

Richter scale quantitative scale of earthquake magnitude based on the measurement of seismic waves, used to indicate the magnitude of an *earthquake at its epicentre. The Richter scale is logarithmic, so an earthquake of 6.0 is ten times greater than one of 5.0. The magnitude of an earthquake differs from its intensity, measured by the *Mercalli scale, which is qualitative and varies from place to place for the same earthquake. The scale is named after US seismologist Charles Richter.

ricin extremely poisonous extract from the seeds of the castor-oil plant. When incorporated into *monoclonal antibodies, ricin can attack cancer cells, particularly in the treatment of lymphoma and leukaemia.

rickets defective growth of bone in children due to an insufficiency of calcium deposits. The bones, which do not harden adequately, are bent out of shape. It is usually caused by a lack of vitamin D and insufficient exposure to sunlight. Renal rickets, also a condition of malformed bone, is associated with kidney disease.

Ridley, Nicholas (c. 1500–1555) English Protestant bishop. He became chaplain to Henry VIII in 1541, and bishop of London in 1550. He took an active part in the *Reformation and supported Lady Jane Grey's claim to the throne. After *Mary I's accession he was arrested and burned as a heretic.

rifle *firearm that has spiral grooves (rifling) in its barrel. When a bullet is fired, the rifling makes it spin, thereby improving accuracy. Rifles were first introduced in the late 18th century.

rift valley valley formed by the subsidence of a block of the Earth's *crust between two or more parallel *faults. Rift valleys are steep-sided and form where the crust is being pulled apart, as at mid-ocean ridges, or in the Great Rift Valley of East Africa. In cross-section they can appear like a widened gorge with steep sides and a wide floor.

Rift Valley, Great longest 'split' in the Earth's surface; see *Great Rift Valley.

Riga capital and port of Latvia; population (1995) 840,000. Industries include engineering, brewing, food processing, and the manufacture of textiles and chipboard.

Rigel *or* **Beta Orionis** brightest star in the constellation Orion. It is a blue-white supergiant, with an estimated diameter 50 times that of the Sun. It is 910 light years from Earth, and is intrinsically the brightest of the first-magnitude stars, its true luminosity being about 100,000 times that of the Sun. It is the seventh-brightest star in the night sky.

rights issue in finance, new shares offered to existing shareholders to raise new capital. Shareholders receive a discount on the market price while the company benefits from not having the costs of a relaunch of the new issue.

Rights of Man and the Citizen, Declaration of the historic French document. According to the statement of the French National Assembly in 1789, these rights include representation in the legislature; equality before the law; equality of opportunity; freedom from arbitrary imprisonment; freedom of speech and religion; taxation in proportion to ability to pay; and security of property. In 1946 were added equal rights for women; right to work, join a union, and strike; leisure, social security, and support in old age; and free education.

right wing the more conservative or reactionary section of a political party or spectrum. It originated in the French national assembly in 1789, where the nobles sat in the place of honour on the president's right, whereas the commons were on his left (hence *left wing).

Rigil Kent *or* **Alpha Centauri** brightest star in the constellation Centaurus and the third-brightest star in the night sky. It is actually a triple star (see *binary star); the two brighter stars orbit each other every 80 years, and the third, Proxima Centauri, is the closest star to the Sun, 4.2 light years away, 0.1 light years closer than the other two.

Rig-Veda oldest of the *Vedas*, the chief sacred writings of Hinduism. It consists of hymns to the Aryan gods, such as Indra, and to nature gods.

Riley, Bridget Louise (1931–) English painter. She is known primarily as a pioneer of *op art. After brief experimentation with pointillism and colour-field painting, she developed her characteristic style in the early 1960s, arranging hard-edged black lines in regular patterns to create disturbing effects of scintillating light and movement. *Current* (1964; Museum of Modern Art, New York) is a fine example of her style.

Rilke, Rainer Maria (1875–1926) Austrian writer. His prose works include the semi-autobiographical *Die Aufzeichnungen des Malte Laurids Brigge/The Notebook of Malte Laurids Brigge* (1910). His verse is characterized by a form of mystic pantheism that seeks to achieve a state of ecstasy in which existence can be apprehended as a whole.

Rimbaud, (Jean Nicolas) Arthur (1854–1891) French Symbolist poet. His verse was chiefly written before the age of 20, notably *Les Illuminations* (published 1886). From 1871 he lived with the poet Paul *Verlaine.

Rimsky-Korsakov, Nikolai Andreievich (1844–1908) Russian composer. He composed many operas and works for orchestra; he also wrote an influential text on orchestration. His opera *The Golden Cockerel* (1907) was a satirical attack on tyranny that was banned until 1909. He also completed works by other composers, for example, Modest Mussorgsky's *Boris Godunov* (1868–69).

ringworm any of various contagious skin infections due to related kinds of fungus, usually resulting in circular, itchy, discoloured patches covered with scales or blisters. The scalp and feet (athlete's foot) are generally involved. Treatment is with antifungal preparations.

Rio de Janeiro (Portuguese 'river of January') port and resort in southeast Brazil; capital of Rio de Janeiro federal unit (state), and former national capital (1763–1960); population (2000 est) 5,850,500; metropolitan area (2000 est) 10,389,400. It is situated on the southwest shore of Guanabara Bay, an inlet of the Atlantic Ocean; Sugar Loaf Mountain (a 395 m/ 1,296 ft-high cone-shaped rock outcrop, composed of granite, quartz and feldspar) stands at the entrance to the harbour, and the city is dominated by the 40 m/ 131 ft-high figure of Christ on the top of Corcovado, a jagged peak 690 m/2,264 ft high. Industries include ship-repair, sugar refining, textiles, and the manufacture of foodstuffs.

ripple tank in physics, shallow water-filled tray used to demonstrate various properties of waves, such as reflection, refraction, diffraction, and interference.

RISC acronym for Reduced Instruction-Set Computer, in computing, a microprocessor (processor on a single chip) that carries out fewer instructions than other (CISC) microprocessors in common use in the 1990s. Because of the low number and the regularity of *machine code instructions, the processor carries out those instructions very quickly.

Risorgimento 19th-century movement for Italian national unity and independence, begun 1815. Leading figures in the movement included *Cavour, *Mazzini, and *Garibaldi. Uprisings 1848–49 failed, but with help from France in a war against Austria – to oust it from Italian provinces in the north – an Italian kingdom was founded in 1861. Unification was finally completed with the addition of Venetia in 1866 and the Papal States in 1870.

rite of passage ritual that accompanies any of the most significant moments or transitions (birth, puberty, marriage, and so on) in an individual's life.

ritualization in ethology, a stereotype that occurs in certain behaviour patterns when these are incorporated into displays. For example, the exaggerated and stylized head toss of the goldeneye drake during courtship is a ritualization of the bathing movement used to wet the feathers; its duration and form have become fixed. Ritualization may make displays clearly recognizable, so ensuring that individuals mate only with members of their own species.

river large body of water that flows down a slope along a channel restricted by adjacent banks and *levees. A river starts at a point called its **source**, and enters a sea or lake at its **mouth**. Along its length it may be joined by smaller rivers called **tributaries**; a river and its tributaries are contained within a drainage basin. The point at which two rivers join is called the confluence. (See diagram, p. 776.)

Rivera, Diego (1886–1957) Mexican painter. He was one of the most important muralists of the 20th century. An exponent of social realism, he received many public commissions for murals depicting the Mexican revolution, his vivid style influenced by Mexican folk art. A vast cycle on historical themes (National Palace, Mexico City) was begun in 1929.

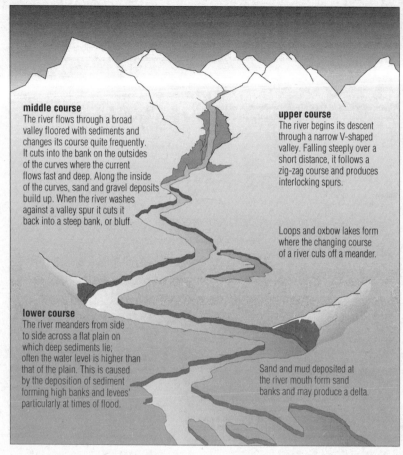

middle course
The river flows through a broad valley floored with sediments and changes its course quite frequently. It cuts into the bank on the outsides of the curves where the current flows fast and deep. Along the inside of the curves, sand and gravel deposits build up. When the river washes against a valley spur it cuts it back into a steep bank, or bluff.

upper course
The river begins its descent through a narrow V-shaped valley. Falling steeply over a short distance, it follows a zig-zag course and produces interlocking spurs.

Loops and oxbow lakes form where the changing course of a river cuts off a meander.

lower course
The river meanders from side to side across a flat plain on which deep sediments lie; often the water level is higher than that of the plain. This is caused by the deposition of sediment forming high banks and levees' particularly at times of flood.

Sand and mud deposited at the river mouth form sand banks and may produce a delta.

river The course of a river from its source of a spring or melting glacier, through to maturity where it flows into the sea.

Riviera the Mediterranean coast of France and Italy from Hyères to La Spezia. The most exclusive stretch of the Riviera, with the finest climate, is the *Côte d'Azur, from Menton to St-Tropez, which includes Monaco.

Riyadh Arabic **Ar Riyad**, capital of Saudi Arabia and of the Riyadh region, situated in an oasis and connected by road and rail with Dammam 450 km/280 mi away on the Gulf; population (1992 est) 2,776,100. Exploitation of the country's huge oil deposits since the 1930s greatly increased the prosperity of the city, which has a modern airport and industries which include an oil refinery.

RNA abbreviation for ribonucleic acid, nucleic acid involved in the process of translating the genetic material *DNA into proteins. It is usually single-stranded, unlike the double-stranded DNA, and consists of a large number of nucleotides strung together, each of which comprises the sugar ribose, a phosphate group, and one of four bases (uracil, cytosine, adenine, or guanine). RNA is copied from DNA by the formation of *base pairs, with uracil taking the place of thymine.

roach any freshwater fish of the Eurasian genus *Rutilus*, of the carp family, especially *R. rutilus* of northern Europe. It is dark green above, whitish below, with reddish lower fins; it grows to 35 cm/1.2 ft.

roadrunner crested North American ground-dwelling bird *Geococcyx californianus* of the *cuckoo family, found in the southwestern USA and Mexico. It can run at a speed of 25 kph/15 mph.

Robben Island island in Table Bay, Cape Town, South Africa. It was used by the South African government to house political prisoners. Nelson *Mandela was imprisoned here 1964–82.

Robbia, della Italian family of sculptors and architects. They were active in Florence. **Luca della Robbia** (1400–1482) created a number of major works in Florence, notably the marble *cantoria* (singing gallery) in the cathedral 1431–38 (Museo del Duomo), with lively groups of choristers. Luca also developed a characteristic style of glazed terracotta work.

Robbins, Jerome (1918–1998) US dancer and choreographer. He was co-director of the New York City Ballet 1969–83 (with George *Balanchine). His ballets were internationally known and he was considered the greatest US-born ballet choreographer. He also choreographed the musicals *The King and I* (1951), *West Side Story* (1957), and *Fiddler on the Roof* (1964).

Robert two dukes of Normandy:

Robert (I) the Devil Duke of Normandy from 1027. Also known as **the Magnificent**, he was the father of William the Conqueror, and was legendary for his cruelty. He became duke after the death of his brother Richard III, in which he may have been implicated.

Robert (II) Curthose (c. 1054–1134) Duke of Normandy 1087–1106. He was the son of William the Conqueror, and a noted crusader 1096–1100. When the English throne passed to his younger brother William II in 1087, Robert was unable to recover it by war. In 1106 Robert again attempted to recover England from Henry I, but was defeated at Tinchebrai and imprisoned until his death.

Robert three kings of Scotland:

Robert (I) the Bruce (1274–1329) King of Scots from 1306, successful guerrilla fighter, and grandson of Robert de Bruce. In 1307 he displayed his tactical skill in the Battle of Loudun Hill against the English under Edward I, and defeated the English again under Edward II at Bannockburn in 1314. In 1328 the Treaty of Northampton recognized Scotland's independence and Robert the Bruce as king.

Robert II (1316–1390) King of Scotland from 1371. He was the son of Walter (1293–1326), steward of Scotland, and Marjory, daughter of Robert the Bruce. He acted as regent during the exile and captivity of his uncle David II, whom he eventually succeeded. He was the first king of the house of Stuart.

Robert III (c. 1340–1406) King of Scotland from 1390, son of Robert II. He was unable to control the nobles, and the government fell largely into the hands of his brother, Robert, Duke of Albany (c. 1340–1420).

Robeson, Paul Bustill (1898–1976) US singer, actor, lawyer, and activist. From the 1930s he was a staunch fighter against anti-semitism and racism against black people, and he was a supporter of the various national liberation movements that came to prominence in Africa after World War II. Robeson appeared in Eugene O'Neill's play *The Emperor Jones* (1924) and the Jerome Kern musical *Show Boat* (1927), in which he sang 'Ol' Man River', and took the title role in *Othello* in 1930.

Robespierre, Maximilien François Marie Isidore de (1758–1794) French politician in the *French Revolution. As leader of the *Jacobins in the National Convention (1792), he supported the execution of Louis XVI and the overthrow of the right-wing republican Girondins, and in July 1793 was elected to the Committee of Public Safety. A year later he was guillotined; many believe that he was a scapegoat for the Reign of *Terror since he ordered only 72 executions personally.

robin migratory songbird *Erithacus rubecula* of the thrush family Muscicapidae, order Passeriformes, found in Europe, West Asia, Africa, and the Azores. About 13 cm/5 in long, both sexes are olive brown with a red breast. Two or three nests are constructed during the year in sheltered places, and from five to seven white freckled eggs are laid.

Robin Hood in English legend, an outlaw and champion of the poor against the rich, said to have lived in Sherwood Forest, Nottinghamshire, during the reign of Richard I (1189–99). He feuded with the sheriff of Nottingham, accompanied by Maid Marian and a band of followers known as his 'merry men'. He appears in many popular ballads from the 13th century, but his first datable appearance is in William Langland's *Piers Plowman* in the late 14th century. He became popular in the 15th century.

Robinson, Mary (1944–) Irish Labour politician, president 1990–97. She became a professor of law at the age of 25. A strong supporter of women's rights, she campaigned for the liberalization of Ireland's laws prohibiting divorce and abortion. From 1997 to 2002 she was United Nations (UN) high commissioner for human rights.

Robinson, Sugar Ray (1921–1989) adopted name of Walker Smith, US boxer. He was world welterweight champion 1945–51; he defended his title five times. Defeating Jake LaMotta in 1951, he took the middleweight title. He lost the title six times and won it seven times. He retired at the age of 45.

Robinson, W(illiam) Heath (1872–1944) English cartoonist and illustrator. He made humorous drawings of bizarre machinery for performing simple tasks, such as raising one's hat. A clumsily designed apparatus is often described as a 'Heath Robinson' contraption.

robot any computer-controlled machine that can be programmed to move or carry out work. Robots are often used in industry to transport materials or to perform repetitive tasks. For instance, robotic arms, fixed to a floor or workbench, may be used to paint machine parts or assemble electronic circuits. Other robots are designed to work in situations that would be dangerous to humans – for example, in defusing bombs or in space and deep-sea exploration.

rock constituent of the Earth's crust composed of *minerals or materials of organic origin that have consolidated into hard masses. There are three basic types of rock: *igneous, *sedimentary, and *metamorphic. Rocks are composed of a combination (or aggregate) of minerals, and the property of a rock will depend on its components. Where deposits of economically valuable minerals occur they are termed *ores. As a result of *weathering, rock breaks down into very small particles that combine with organic materials from plants and animals to form *soil. In *geology the term 'rock' can also include unconsolidated materials such as *sand, mud, *clay, and *peat. (See diagram, p. 778.)

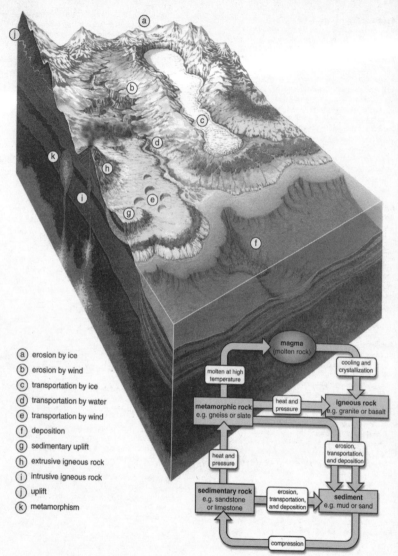

(a) erosion by ice

(b) erosion by wind

(c) transportation by ice

(d) transportation by water

(e) transportation by wind

(f) deposition

(g) sedimentary uplift

(h) extrusive igneous rock

(i) intrusive igneous rock

(j) uplift

(k) metamorphism

rock The rock cycle. Rocks are not as permanent as they seem but are being constantly destroyed and renewed. When a rock becomes exposed on the Earth's surface, it starts to break down through weathering and erosion. The resulting debris is washed or blown away and deposited, for example in sea or river beds, or in deserts, where it eventually becomes buried by yet more debris. Over time, this debris is compressed and compacted to form sedimentary rock, which may in time become exposed and eroded once more. Alternatively the sedimentary rock may be pushed further towards the Earth's centre where it melts and solidifies to form igneous rock or is heated and crushed to such a degree that its mineral content alters and it becomes metamorphic rock. Igneous and metamorphic rock may also become exposed and eroded by the same processes as sedimentary rock, and the cycle continues.

rock and roll pop music born of a fusion of rhythm and blues, and country and western, and based on electric guitar and drums. Its sound usually features an energetic driving rhythm and heavy insistent beat. The music is usually in four-beat time (often 4/4) with a strong accent on the second and fourth beats. In the mid-1950s, with the rise to fame of Elvis *Presley, it became the heartbeat of teenage rebellion in the West and also had considerable impact on other parts of the world. It found perhaps its purest form in late-1950s rockabilly, the style of white Southerners in the USA. The blanket term 'rock' later lost any specific meaning.

rock climbing sport originally an integral part of mountaineering. It began as a form of training for Alpine expeditions and is now divided into three categories: the **outcrop climb** for climbs of up to 30 m/100 ft; the **crag climb** on cliffs of 30–300 m/100–1,000 ft, and the **big wall climb**, which is the nearest thing to Alpine climbing, but without the hazards of snow and ice.

Rockefeller, John D(avison) (1839–1937) US millionaire industrialist and philanthropist. He was the founder of Standard Oil in 1870, from which were descended four of the world's largest oil companies – Amoco, Chevron, Exxon, and Mobil. He also founded the philanthropic Rockefeller Foundation in 1913, to which his son John D(avison) Rockefeller Jr devoted his life. Rockefeller created the first great corporate trust, Standard Oil Trust, which achieved control of 90% of US refineries by 1882. Its activities led to an outcry against monopolies and the passing of the Sherman Anti-Trust Act of 1890. Standard Oil was finally broken up in 1911.

rocket projectile driven by the reaction of gases produced by a fast-burning fuel. Unlike jet engines, which are also reaction engines, rockets carry their own oxygen supply to burn their fuel and do not require any surrounding atmosphere. For warfare, rocket heads carry an explosive device.

Rocky Mountains *or* **Rockies** largest North American mountain system, extending for 4,800 km/3,000 mi from the Mexican plateau near Sante Fe, north through the west-central states of the USA, and through Canada to the Alaskan border. It forms part of the Continental Divide, which separates rivers draining into the Atlantic or Arctic oceans from those flowing toward the Pacific Ocean. To the east lie the Great Plains, and to the west, the plateaux separating the Rocky Mountains from parallel Pacific coast ranges. Mount Elbert is the highest peak, 4,400 m/14,433 ft. Some geographers consider the Yukon and Alaskan ranges as part of the system, making the highest point Mount McKinley (Denali) 6,194 m/20,320 ft, and its total length 5,150 km/3,219 mi.

rococo movement in the arts and architecture in 18th-century Europe, particularly in France, that tended towards lightness, elegance, delicacy, and decorative charm. The term 'rococo' is derived from the French *rocaille* (rock- or shell-work), a soft style of interior decoration, based on S-curves and scroll-like forms, that developed as a reaction against the formal, heavy atmosphere of Louis XIV's court. Painting developed its own rococo style, as in the work of Jean-Antoine *Watteau and François Boucher. Sèvres porcelain also belongs to the French rococo fashion. In the 1730s the

movement became widespread in Europe, notably in the churches and palaces of southern Germany and Austria. Chippendale furniture is an English example of the French rococo style.

rodent any mammal of the worldwide order Rodentia, making up nearly half of all mammal species. Besides ordinary 'cheek teeth', they have a single front pair of incisor teeth in both upper and lower jaw, which continue to grow as they are worn down.

rodeo originally a practical means of rounding up cattle in North America. It is now a professional sport in the USA and Canada. Ranching skills such as bronco busting, bull riding, steer wrestling, and calf roping are all rodeo events. Because rodeo livestock is valuable, rules for its handling are laid out by the American Humane Association, yet criticism has been levelled at rodeos for cruel treatment of their animals.

Rodgers, Richard Charles (1902–1979) US composer. He collaborated with librettist Lorenz Hart (1895–1943) on songs like 'Blue Moon' (1934) and musicals like *On Your Toes* (1936). With Oscar Hammerstein II, he wrote many musicals, including *Oklahoma!* (1943), *South Pacific* (1949), *The King and I* (1951), and *The Sound of Music* (1959).

Rodin, (René François) Auguste (1840–1917) French sculptor. He is considered by many the greatest of his day. Rodin freed sculpture from the idealizing conventions of the time by his realistic treatment of the human form and his emphasis on style and expression over subject. Many of his figures are characterized by an unfinished look, emerging from a block of marble. His works show extraordinary technical ability and a deep understanding of human anatomy. Examples are *Le Penseur/The Thinker* (1904; Musée Rodin, Paris), *Le Baiser/The Kiss* (1886; marble version in the Louvre, Paris), and *The Burghers of Calais* (1884–86; copy in Embankment Gardens, Westminster, London).

roebuck male of the Eurasian roe *deer.

roentgen *or* **röntgen** symbol R, unit of radiation exposure, used for X-rays and gamma rays. It is defined in terms of the number of ions produced in one cubic centimetre of air by the radiation. Exposure to 1,000 roentgens gives rise to an absorbed dose of about 870 rads (8.7 grays), which is a dose equivalent of 870 rems (8.7 sieverts).

Rogers, Ginger (1911–1995) stage name of Virginia Katherine McMath, US actor, dancer, and singer. She worked from the 1930s to the 1950s, often starring with Fred *Astaire in such films as *Top Hat* (1935) and *Swing Time* (1936). Her other film work includes *Bachelor Mother* (1939) and *Kitty Foyle* (1940; Academy Award). She later appeared in stage musicals.

Rogers, Richard George (1933–) English high-tech architect. His works include the Pompidou Centre in Paris (1972–76), with Renzo Piano; the Lloyd's of London building in London (1979–84); the Reuters building at Blackwall Yard, London (1992), which won him a RIBA award, and the Millennium Dome, London (1999).

Roland (died c. 778) French hero. His real and legendary deeds of valour and chivalry inspired many medieval and later romances, including the 11th-century *Chanson de Roland* and Ariosto's *Orlando furioso*. A knight of *Charlemagne, Roland was killed in 778 with his friend Oliver and the 12 peers of France at Roncesvalles (in the Pyrenees) by Basques. He headed the rearguard during Charlemagne's retreat from his invasion of Spain.

roller any brightly coloured bird of the Old World family Coraciidae, resembling crows but in the same order as kingfishers and hornbills. Rollers grow up to 32 cm/13 in long. The name is derived from the habit of some species of rolling over in flight.

rolling common method of shaping metal. Rolling is carried out by giant mangles, consisting of several sets, or stands, of heavy rollers positioned one above the other. Red-hot metal slabs are rolled into sheet and also (using shaped rollers) girders and rails. Metal sheets are often cold-rolled finally to impart a harder surface.

Rolling Stones, the British band formed in 1962, once notorious as the 'bad boys' of rock. Original members were Mick Jagger (1943–), Keith Richards (1943–), Brian Jones (1942–1969), Bill Wyman (1936–), Charlie Watts (1941–), and Ian Stewart (1938–1985). A rock-and-roll institution, the Rolling Stones were still performing and recording in the 1990s.

ROM acronym for **read-only memory**, in computing, a memory device in the form of a collection of integrated circuits (chips), frequently used in microcomputers. ROM chips are loaded with data and programs during manufacture and, unlike *RAM (random-access memory) chips, can subsequently only be read, not written to, by a computer. However, the contents of the chips are not lost when the power is switched off, as happens in RAM.

Roman art sculpture and painting of ancient Rome, from the 4th century BC to the fall of the Western Empire in the 5th century AD. Much Roman art was intended for public education, notably the sculpted triumphal arches and giant columns, such as Trajan's Column AD 106–113, and portrait sculptures of soldiers, politicians, and emperors. Surviving mural paintings (in Pompeii, Rome, and Ostia) and mosaic decorations show Greek influence. Roman art was to prove of lasting inspiration in the West.

Roman Britain period in British history from the two expeditions by Julius Caesar in 55 and 54 BC to the early 5th century AD. Roman relations with Britain began with Caesar's expeditions, but the actual conquest was not begun until AD 43. During the reign of the emperor Domitian, the governor of the province, Agricola, campaigned in Scotland. After several unsuccessful attempts to conquer Scotland, the northern frontier was fixed between the Solway and the Tyne at *Hadrian's Wall.

Roman Catholicism (Greek *katholikos* 'universal') one of the main divisions of the *Christian religion, separate from the Eastern Orthodox Church from 1054. It is headed by the *pope, who traces his authority back through St *Peter (the first bishop of Rome) to Jesus, through *apostolic succession. Its headquarters are in the Vatican City State, in Rome. Membership is concentrated in southern Europe, Latin America, and the Philippines. In February 2000 Rome reported the number of baptized Roman Catholics to be 1.045 billion, an increase of 40 million since 1998, and more than half the Christians in the world.

Romance languages branch of Indo-European languages descended from the Latin of the Roman Empire ('popular' or 'vulgar' as opposed to 'classical'

Latin). The present-day Romance languages with national status are French, Italian, Portuguese, Romanian, and Spanish.

Roman Empire from 27 BC to the 5th century AD; see *Rome, ancient.

Romanesque architecture style of Western European *architecture of the 10th to 12th centuries, marked by rounded arches, solid volumes, and an emphasis on perpendicular elements such as arcades. The ribbed groin vault developed in this period, which was to become central to *Gothic architecture. In England Romanesque style is also known as *Norman architecture.

Romanesque art European art of the 10th to 12th centuries; see *medieval art.

Romania

National name: *România/Romania*

Area: 237,500 sq km/91,698 sq mi
Capital: Bucharest
Major towns/cities: Brasov, Timisoara, Cluj-Napoca, IasI, Constanta, Galati, Craiova
Major ports: Galati, Constanta, Braila
Physical features: mountains surrounding a plateau, with river plains in south and east. Carpathian Mountains, Transylvanian Alps; River Danube; Black Sea coast; mineral springs
Head of state: Traian Basescu from 2004
Head of government: Calin Tariceanu from 2004
Political system: liberal democracy
Political executive: limited presidency
Political parties: Democratic Convention of Romania (DCR), centre-right coalition; Social Democratic Union (SDU), reformist; Social Democracy Party of Romania (PSDR), social democrat; Romanian National Unity Party (RNUP), Romanian nationalist, right wing, anti-Hungarian; Greater Romania Party (Romania Mare), far right, ultranationalist, anti-Semitic; Democratic Party–National Salvation Front (DP–NSF), promarket; National Salvation Front (NSF), left of centre; Hungarian Democratic Union of Romania (HDUR), ethnic Hungarian; Christian Democratic–National Peasants' Party (CD–PNC),

right of centre, promarket; Socialist Labour Party (SLP), ex-communist

Currency: leu

GNI per capita (PPP): (US$) 6,290 (2002 est)

Exports: base metals and metallic articles, textiles and clothing, machinery and equipment, mineral products, foodstuffs. Principal market: Italy 24.9% (2001)

Population: 22,334,000 (2003 est)

Language: Romanian (official), Hungarian, German

Religion: Romanian Orthodox 87%; Roman Catholic and Uniate 5%, Reformed/Lutheran 3%, Unitarian 1%

Life expectancy: 67 (men); 74 (women) (2000–05)

Chronology

106: Formed heartland of ancient region of Dacia, which was conquered by Roman Emperor Trajan and became a province of Roman Empire; Christianity introduced.

275: Taken from Rome by invading Goths, a Germanic people.

4th–10th centuries: Invaded by successive waves of Huns, Avars, Bulgars, Magyars, and Mongols.

c. 1000: Transylvania, in north, became an autonomous province under Hungarian crown.

mid-14th century: Two Romanian principalities emerged, Wallachia in south, around Bucharest, and Moldova in northeast.

15th–16th centuries: The formerly autonomous principalities of Wallachia, Moldova, and Transylvania became tributaries to Ottoman Turks, despite peasant uprisings and resistance from Vlad Tepes ('the Impaler'), ruling prince of Wallachia.

late 17th century: Transylvania conquered by Austrian Habsburgs.

1829: Wallachia and Moldova brought under tsarist Russian suzerainty.

1859: Under Prince Alexandru Ion Cuza, Moldova and Wallachia united to form Romanian state.

1878: Romania's independence recognized by Great Powers in Congress of Berlin.

1881: Became kingdom under Carol I.

1916–18: Fought on Triple Entente side (Britain, France, and Russia) during World War I; acquired Transylvania and Bukovina, in north, from dismembered Austro-Hungarian Empire, and Bessarabia, in east, from Russia. This made it the largest state in Balkans.

1930: King Carol II abolished democratic institutions and established dictatorship.

1940: Forced to surrender Bessarabia and northern Bukovina, adjoining Black Sea, to Soviet Union, and northern Transylvania to Hungary; King Carol II abdicated, handing over effective power to Gen Ion Antonescu, who signed Axis Pact with Germany.

1941–44: Fought on Germany's side against Soviet Union; thousands of Jews massacred.

1944: Romania joined war against Germany.

1945: Occupied by Soviet Union; communist-dominated government installed.

1947: Paris Peace Treaty reclaimed Transylvania for Romania, but lost southern Dobruja to Bulgaria and northern Bukovina and Bessarabia to Soviet Union; King Michael, son of Carol II, abdicated and People's Republic proclaimed.

1955: Romania joined Warsaw Pact.

1958: Soviet occupation forces removed.

1965: Nicolae Ceausescu became Romanian Communist

Party leader, and pursued foreign policy autonomous of Moscow.

1975: Ceausescu made president.

1985–87: Winter of austerity and power cuts as Ceausescu refused to liberalize the economy. Workers' demonstrations against austerity programme are brutally crushed at Brasov.

1989: Bloody overthrow of Ceausescu regime in 'Christmas Revolution'; Ceausescu and wife tried and executed; estimated 10,000 dead in civil war. Power assumed by NSF, headed by Ion Iliescu.

1990: Securitate secret police was replaced by new Romanian Intelligence Service; Eastern Orthodox Church and private farming were re-legalized.

1994: A military cooperation pact was made with Bulgaria. Far-right parties were brought into the governing coalition.

1996: There were signs of economic growth; parliamentary elections were won by the DCR, who formed a coalition government with the SDU.

1997: An economic reform programme and drive against corruption were announced; there was a sharp increase in inflation. Former King Michael returned from exile.

1998: The Social Democrats withdrew support from ruling coalition, criticizing the slow pace of reform. Full EU membership negotiations commenced. The economy deteriorated sharply.

1999: Roadblocks were imposed by tanks north of Bucharest to prevent 10,000 striking miners entering Bucharest. Mugur Isarescu became prime minister.

2000: Former communist president Ion Iliescu was elected president, and his Social Democrats won the largest share of the vote in parliamentary elections.

2004: Romania joined NATO.

2005: Traian Basescu was elected president. A European Union accession treaty was signed, giving Romania the possibility of membership in 2007, subject to carrying out reforms.

Romanian people of Romanian culture from Romania, Serbia and Montenegro, Moldova, and the surrounding area. There are 20–25 million speakers of the Romanian language.

Romanian language member of the Romance branch of the Indo-European language family, spoken in Romania, Macedonia, Albania, and parts of northern Greece. It has been strongly influenced by the Slavonic languages and by Greek. The Cyrillic alphabet was used until the 19th century, when a variant of the Roman alphabet was adopted.

Roman law legal system of ancient Rome that is now the basis of *civil law, one of the main European legal systems.

Roman numerals ancient European number system using symbols different from Arabic numerals (the ordinary numbers 1, 2, 3, 4, 5, and so on). The seven key symbols in Roman numerals, as represented today, are I (1), V (5), X (10), L (50), C (100), D (500), and M (1,000). There is no zero, and therefore no place-value as is fundamental to the Arabic system. The first ten Roman numerals are I, II, III, IV (or IIII), V, VI, VII, VIII, IX, and X. When a Roman symbol is preceded by a symbol of equal or greater value, the values of the symbols are added (XVI = 16). When a symbol is preceded by a symbol of less value, the values are subtracted (XL = 40). A horizontal bar over a symbol indicates a multiple of 1,000. Although addition and subtraction are fairly straightforward using Roman numerals, the absence of a zero makes other arithmetic calculations (such as multiplication) clumsy and difficult.

Romanov dynasty rulers of Russia from 1613 to the *Russian Revolution in 1917. Under the Romanovs, Russia developed into an absolutist empire.

Roman religion religious system that retained early elements of animism (with reverence for stones and trees) and totemism (see *Romulus and Remus), and had a strong domestic base in the lares and penates, the cult of Janus and Vesta. It also had a main pantheon of gods derivative from the Greek one, which included Jupiter and Juno, Mars and Venus, Minerva, Diana, Ceres, and many lesser deities.

Romansch member of the Romance branch of the Indo-European language family, spoken by some 50,000 people in the eastern cantons of Switzerland. It was accorded official status in 1937 alongside French, German, and Italian. It is also known among scholars as **Rhaeto-Romanic**.

Romanticism in literature and the visual arts, a style that emphasizes the imagination, emotions, and creativity of the individual artist. Romanticism also refers specifically to late-18th- and early-19th-century European culture, as contrasted with 18th-century *classicism.

Romanticism in music, the period from about 1810 to around 1910 – that is, after the classical period. Classical composers had tried to create a balance between expression and formal structure; Romantic composers altered this balance by applying more freedom to the form and structure of their music, and using deeper, more intense expressions of moods, feelings, and emotions. An increased interest in literature, nature, the supernatural, and love, along with nationalistic feelings and the idea of the musician as visionary artist and hero (virtuoso) all added to the development of Romanticism. The movement reached its height in the late 19th century, as in the works of Robert *Schumann and Richard *Wagner.

Romany *or* **Gypsy** member of a nomadic people believed to have originated in northwestern India and now living throughout the world. They used to be thought of as originating in Egypt, hence the name Gypsy (a corruption of 'Egyptian'). The Romany language, spoken in several different dialects, belongs to the Indic branch of the Indo-European family.

Rome Italian **Roma**, capital of Italy and of Lazio region, on the River Tiber, 27 km/17 mi from the Tyrrhenian Sea; population (2001 est) 2,459,800. Rome is an important transport hub and cultural centre. A large section of the population finds employment in government and other offices: the headquarters of the Roman Catholic Church (the Vatican City State, a separate sovereign area within Rome) and other international bodies, such as the Food and Agriculture Organization (FAO), are here. It is also a destination for many tourists and pilgrims. Industries include engineering, printing, food processing, electronics, and the manufacture of chemicals, pharmaceuticals, plastics, and clothes. The city is a centre for the film and fashion industries. Called the Eternal City, Rome is one of the world's richest cities in history and art; among the remains of the ancient city (see *Rome, ancient) are the Forum, *Colosseum, and Pantheon.

Rome, ancient history Ancient Rome was a civilization based on the city of *Rome. It lasted for about 800 years. Rome is traditionally said to have been founded as a kingdom in 753 BC. Following the expulsion of its last king, Tarquinius Superbus, the monarchy became a *republic (traditionally in 509 BC). From then, its history is one of almost continual expansion until the murder of Julius Caesar and the foundation of the Roman Empire in 27 BC under *Augustus and his successors. At its peak under *Trajan, the empire stretched from *Roman Britain to *Mesopotamia and the Caspian Sea. A long line of emperors ruling by virtue of military, rather than civil, power marked the beginning of Rome's long decline; under Diocletian the empire was divided into two parts – East and West – although it was temporarily reunited under *Constantine, the first emperor to formally adopt Christianity. The end of the Roman Empire is generally dated by the removal of the last emperor in the West in AD 476. The Eastern or Byzantine Empire continued until 1453 with its capital at Constantinople (modern Istanbul).

Rome, Treaties of two international agreements signed 25 March 1957 by Belgium, France, West Germany, Italy, Luxembourg, and the Netherlands, which established the European Economic Community and the European Atomic Energy Commission (Euratom).

Rommel, Erwin Johannes Eugen (1891–1944) German field marshal. He served in World War I, and in World War II he played an important part in the invasions of central Europe and France. He was commander of the North African offensive from 1941 (when he was nick-named 'Desert Fox') until defeated in the Battles of El *Alamein and he was expelled from Africa in March 1943.

Romney, George (1734–1802) English painter. Active in London from 1762, he became, with Thomas Gainsborough and Joshua Reynolds, one of the most successful portrait painters of the late 18th century. His best work is to be found in the straightforward realism of *The Beaumont Family* (1777–79; National Gallery, London) or the simple charm of *The Parson's Daughter* (c. 1785; Tate Gallery, London).

Romulus in Roman legend, the founder and first king of Rome; the son of Mars and Rhea Silvia, daughter of Numitor, king of Alba Longa. Romulus and his twin brother Remus were thrown into the Tiber by their great-uncle Amulius, who had deposed Numitor, but the infants were saved and suckled by a she-wolf, and later protected by the shepherd Faustulus. On reaching adulthood they killed Amulius, restored Numitor, and founded the city of Rome on the River Tiber.

Romulus Augustulus (born c. AD 461) Last Roman emperor in the western Roman empire. He was made emperor, while still a child, by his father the patrician Orestes about 475. He was compelled to abdicate 476 by Odoacer, leader of the barbarian mercenaries, who nicknamed him Augustulus (meaning 'little Augustus'). Orestes was executed and Romulus Augustulus was sent to live on a pension in Campania. His subsequent fate and the date of his death are unknown.

rondo *or* **rondeau** musical form where the main theme keeps recurring with contrasting sections in between (ABACADA). The A section is always in the tonic key, while the contrasting section (or episode) is in a related key. The rondo is often lively in character and is a popular final movement of a sonata, concerto, or symphony.

röntgen alternative spelling for *roentgen, unit of X- and gamma-ray exposure.

Röntgen (or Roentgen), Wilhelm Konrad (1845–1923) German physicist. He was awarded the Nobel Prize for Physics in 1901 for his discovery of *X-rays in 1895. While investigating the passage of electricity through gases, he noticed the *fluorescence of a barium platinocyanide screen. This radiation passed through some substances opaque to light, and affected photographic plates. Developments from this discovery revolutionized medical diagnosis.

rook gregarious European *crow *Corvus frugilegus.* The plumage is black and lustrous and the face bare; the legs, toes, and claws are also black. A rook can grow to 45 cm/18 in long. Rooks nest in colonies (rookeries) at the tops of trees. They feed mainly on invertebrates found just below the soil surface. The last 5 mm/0.2 in of beak tip is mostly cartilage containing lots of nerve endings to enable the rook to feel for hidden food.

Roosevelt, Franklin D(elano) (1882–1945) 32nd president of the USA 1933–45, a Democrat. He served as governor of New York 1928–33. Becoming president during the Great Depression, he launched the *New Deal economic and social reform programme, which made him popular with the people. After the outbreak of World War II he introduced lend-lease for the supply of war materials and services to the Allies and drew up the Atlantic Charter of solidarity.

Roosevelt, Theodore (1858–1919) 26th president of the USA 1901–09, a Republican. After serving as governor of New York 1898–1901 he became vice president to *McKinley, whom he succeeded as president on McKinley's assassination in 1901. He campaigned against the great trusts (associations of enterprises that reduce competition), while carrying on a jingoist foreign policy designed to enforce US supremacy over Latin America. He was awarded the Nobel Prize for Peace in 1906 for his mediation at the end of the Russo-Japanese War in 1904.

root the part of a plant that is usually underground, and whose primary functions are anchorage and the absorption of water and dissolved mineral salts. Roots usually grow downwards and towards water (that is, they are positively geotropic and hydrotropic; see *tropism). Plants such as epiphytic orchids, which grow above ground, produce aerial roots that absorb moisture from the atmosphere. Others, such as ivy, have climbing roots arising from the stems, which serve to attach the plant to trees and walls.

root of an equation, a value that satisfies the equality. For example, $x = 0$ and $x = 5$ are roots of the equation $x^2 - 5x = 0$.

root in language, the basic element from which a word is derived. The root is a morpheme, a unit that cannot be subdivided. The Latin word *dominus* ('master'), for example, is a root from which many English words are derived, such as 'dominate', 'dominion', and 'domino'.

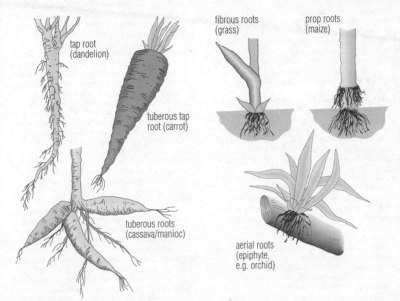

fibrous roots (grass)

prop roots (maize)

tap root (dandelion)

tuberous tap root (carrot)

tuberous roots (cassava/manioc)

aerial roots (epiphyte, e.g. orchid)

root Types of root. Many flowers (dandelion) and vegetables (carrot) have swollen tap roots with smaller lateral roots. The tuberous roots of the cassava are swollen parts of an underground stem modified to store food. The fibrous roots of the grasses are all of equal size. Prop roots grow out from the stem and then grow down into the ground to support a heavy plant. Aerial roots grow from stems but do not grow into the ground; many absorb moisture from the air.

root crop plant cultivated for its swollen edible root (which may or may not be a true root). Potatoes are the major temperate root crop; the major tropical root crops are cassava, yams, and sweet potatoes. Root crops are second in importance only to cereals as human food. Roots have a high carbohydrate content, but their protein content rarely exceeds 2%. Consequently, communities relying almost exclusively upon roots may suffer from protein deficiency. Food production for a given area from roots is greater than from cereals.

rootstock another name for *rhizome, an underground plant organ.

Rorschach test in psychology, a method of diagnosis involving the use of inkblot patterns that subjects are asked to interpret, to help indicate personality type, degree of intelligence, and emotional stability. It was invented by the Swiss psychiatrist Hermann Rorschach.

Roscommon formerly Ros-Comain, ('wood around a monastery') county of the Republic of Ireland, in the province of Connacht; county town **Roscommon**; area 2,460 sq km/950 sq mi; population (2002 est) 53,800. It has rich pastures and is bounded on the east by the River Shannon, with bogs and lakes, including Lough Key and Lough Gara. The three largest lakes (loughs Allen, Boderg, and Ree) lie only partly within the county. There is agriculture, especially cattle rearing. Roscommon was established as a county in about 1580. Other important towns are Castlerea, Elphin, and Boyle.

rose any shrub or climbing plant belonging to the rose family, with prickly stems and fragrant flowers in many different colours. Numerous cultivated forms have been derived from the sweetbrier or eglantine (*R. rubiginosa*) and dogrose (*R. canina*) native to Europe and Asia. There are many climbing varieties, but the forms most commonly grown in gardens are bush roses and standards (cultivated roses grafted on to a brier stem). (Genus *Rosa*, family Rosaceae.)

rosebay willowherb common perennial weed. See *willowherb.

Rosebery, Archibald Philip Primrose, 5th Earl of Rosebery (1847–1929) British Liberal politician. He was foreign secretary in 1886 and 1892–94, when he succeeded Gladstone as prime minister, but his government survived less than a year. After 1896 his imperialist views gradually placed him further from the mainstream of the Liberal Party. He was made an Earl in 1868.

Rose, Irwin (1926–) US scientist. With Israeli scientist Aaron Ciechanover and Hungarian-born Israeli scientist Avram Hershko, Rose shared the Nobel Prize for Chemistry in 2004 for his contributions to the discovery of how cells use selection and degradation processes to regulate protein levels.

rosemary evergreen shrub belonging to the mint family, native to the Mediterranean and western Asia, with small, narrow, scented leaves and clusters of pale blue or purple flowers. It is widely cultivated as a herb for use in cooking and for its aromatic oil, used in perfumery and pharmaceuticals. Rosemary is a traditional symbol of remembrance. (*Rosmarinus officinalis*, family Labiatae.)

Roses, Wars of the civil wars in England 1455–85 between the houses of *Lancaster (badge: red rose) and *York (badge: white rose), both of which claimed the throne through descent from the sons of Edward III.

As a result of *Henry VI's lapse into insanity in 1453, Richard, Duke of York, was installed as protector of the realm. Upon his recovery, Henry forced York to take up arms in self-defence.

Rosetta Stone slab of basalt with inscriptions from 197 BC, found near the town of Rosetta, Egypt, 1799. Giving the same text in three versions – Greek, hieroglyphic, and demotic script – it became the key to deciphering other Egyptian inscriptions.

Rosh Hashanah or **Rosh Hashana** (Hebrew 'head of the year') two-day religious observance that marks the start of the Jewish New Year (first new moon after the autumn equinox, beginning the month of Tishri). It is traditionally announced by blowing a shofar, a ram's-horn trumpet. It is the first of the high holy days, or 'days of awe', and celebrates the creation of the world, the repentance of sins, and the renewal of God's relationship with the Jewish people.

Rosicrucians group of early 17th-century philosophers who claimed occult powers and employed the terminology of *alchemy to expound their mystical doctrines (said to derive from Paracelsus). The name comes from books published in 1614 and 1615, attributed to Christian Rosenkreutz ('rosy cross'), most probably a pen-name but allegedly a writer living around 1460. Several societies have been founded in Britain and the USA that claim to be their successors, such as the Rosicrucian Fraternity (1614 in Germany, 1861 in the USA).

Ross, James Clark (1800–1862) English explorer. He discovered the north magnetic pole in 1831. He also went to the Antarctic 1839; Ross Island, Ross Sea, and Ross Dependency are named after him. He was knighted in 1843.

Ross, Ronald (1857–1932) Indian-born British physician and bacteriologist who was awarded a Nobel Prize for Physiology or Medicine in 1902 for his work on the role of the *Anopheles* mosquito in transmitting malaria. From 1881 to 1899 he served in the Indian Medical Service, and during 1895–98 identified mosquitoes of the genus *Anopheles* as being responsible for the spread of malaria. He was knighted in 1911.

Ross Dependency all the Antarctic islands and territories between 160° east and 150° west longitude, and situated south of 60° south latitude; it includes Edward VII Land, the Ross Sea and its islands (including the Balleny Isles), and parts of Victoria Land. It is claimed by New Zealand; area 450,000 sq km/173,745 sq mi.

Rossellini, Roberto (1906–1977) Italian film director. His World War II trilogy, *Roma città aperta/Rome, Open City* (1945), *Paisà/Paisan* (1946), and *Germania anno zero/Germany Year Zero* (1947), reflects his humanism and is considered a landmark of European cinema.

Rossetti, Christina Georgina (1830–1894) English poet and a devout High Anglican (see *Oxford movement). Her best-known work is *Goblin Market and Other Poems* (1862); among others are *The Prince's Progress* (1866), *Annus Domini* (1874), and *A Pageant* (1881). She was the sister of Dante Gabriel *Rossetti and William Michael Rossetti. Her verse expresses unfulfilled spiritual yearning and frustrated love. She was a skilful technician and made use of irregular rhyme and line length.

Rossetti, Dante Gabriel (1828–1882) English painter and poet. He was a founding member of the *Pre-Raphaelite Brotherhood (PRB) in 1848. As well as romantic medieval scenes, he produced many idealized portraits of women, including the *Beata Beatrix* (1864). His verse includes 'The Blessed Damozel' (1850). His sister was the poet Christina *Rossetti.

Rossini, Gioacchino Antonio (1792–1868) Italian composer. His first success was the opera *Tancredi* in 1813. In 1816 his opera buffa (comic opera) *Il barbiere di Siviglia/The Barber of Seville* was produced in Rome. He was the most successful opera composer of his time, producing 20 operas in the period 1815–23. He also created (with Gaetano Donizetti and Vincenzo Bellini) the 19th-century Italian operatic style.

Rostand, Edmond (1868–1918) French poetic dramatist. He wrote *Cyrano de Bergerac* (1898) and *L'Aiglon* (1900) (based on the life of Napoleon III), in which Sarah Bernhardt played the leading role.

Roth, Philip (Milton) (1933–) US novelist. His witty, sharply satirical, and increasingly fantastic novels depict the moral and sexual anxieties of 20th-century Jewish-American life, most notably in *Goodbye Columbus* (1959) and *Portnoy's Complaint* (1969). He was awarded the Pulitzer Prize for his novel *American Pastoral* (1997) and the National Medal of Arts in 1998.

Rothermere, Vere Harold Esmond Harmsworth, 3rd Viscount Rothermere (1925–1998) British newspaper proprietor. He became chair of Associated Newspapers in 1971, controlling the right-wing *Daily Mail* (founded by his great-uncle Lord *Northcliffe) and *Mail on Sunday* (launched in 1982), the London *Evening Standard*, and a string of regional newspapers.

Rothko, Mark (1903–1970) adopted name of Marcus Rothkovich, Russian-born US painter. He was a leading exponent of *abstract expressionism and a pioneer, towards the end of his life, of colour-field painting. Typically, his works are canvases covered in large hazy rectangles of thin paint, the colours subtly modulated, as in *Light Red over Black* (1957; Tate Gallery, London).

rotifer any of the tiny invertebrates, also called 'wheel animalcules', of the phylum Rotifera. Mainly freshwater, some marine, rotifers have a ring of *cilia that carries food to the mouth and also provides propulsion. They are the smallest of multicellular animals – few reach 0.05 cm/0.02 in.

rotten borough English parliamentary constituency, before the Great Reform Act of 1832, that returned members to Parliament in spite of having small numbers of electors. Such a borough could easily be manipulated by those with sufficient money or influence.

Rotterdam industrial city and port in South Holland province, the Netherlands, in the Rhine-Maas delta, 90 km/56 mi southwest of Amsterdam; population (1997) 590,000. The Rotterdam-Europoort complex is the biggest oil refining centre in the world, and one of its foremost ocean cargo ports. Other industries include brewing, distilling, shipbuilding, sugar and petroleum refining, margarine, and tobacco. A canal, the New Waterway (*Nieuwe Waterweg*), links Rotterdam with the North Sea.

Rottweiler breed of dog originally developed in Rottweil, Germany, as a herding and guard dog, and subsequently used as a police dog. Powerfully built,

the dog is about 63–66 cm/25–27 in high at the shoulder, black with tan markings. It has a short coat and docked tail.

Rouault, Georges Henri (1871–1958) French painter, etcher, illustrator, and designer. He was one of the major religious artists of the 20th century. Early in his career he was associated with the *Fauves, but created his own highly distinctive style using rich, dark colours and heavy outlines. His subjects include clowns, prostitutes, lawyers, and religious figures, as in *Christ Mocked* (1932; Museum of Modern Art, New York).

Roubiliac (*or* Roubillac), Louis François (*c*. 1705–1762) French sculptor. A Huguenot, he fled religious persecution to settle in England in 1732. He became a leading sculptor of the day, creating a statue of German composer Georg Handel for Vauxhall Gardens, London, in 1737.

rounders bat-and-ball game similar to *baseball but played on a much smaller pitch. The first reference to rounders was in 1744.

Roundhead member of the Parliamentary party during the English Civil War 1640–60, opposing the Royalist Cavaliers. The term referred to the short hair then worn only by men of the lower classes.

Rousseau, Henri Julien Félix (1844–1910) called 'Le Douanier', French painter. A self-taught naive artist, he painted scenes of the Parisian suburbs, portraits, and exotic scenes with painstaking detail, as in *Tropical Storm with a Tiger* (1891; National Gallery, London). He was much admired by artists such as Gauguin and Picasso, and writers such as the poet Apollinaire.

Rousseau, Jean-Jacques (1712–1778) French social philosopher and writer. His book *Du Contrat social/ Social Contract* (1762), emphasizing the rights of the people over those of the government, was a significant influence on the French Revolution. In the novel *Emile* (1762), he outlined a new theory of education.

rowan another name for the European *mountain ash tree.

rowing propulsion of a boat by oars, either by one or two rowers with two oars each (**sculling**) or by crews (two, four, or eight persons) with one oar each, often with a coxswain (the non-rowing member who steers and determines rowing speed). Major events include the world championships, first held in 1962 for men and 1974 for women, and the *Boat Race (between Oxford and Cambridge universities in the UK), first held in 1829.

Rowlandson, Thomas (1757–1827) English painter and illustrator. One of the greatest caricaturists of 18th-century England, his fame rests on his humorous, often bawdy, depictions of the vanities and vices of Georgian social life. He illustrated many books, including *Tour of Dr Syntax in Search of the Picturesque* (1809), which was followed by two sequels between 1812 and 1821.

Rowntree, B(enjamin) Seebohm (1871–1954) English entrepreneur and philanthropist. He used much of the money he acquired as chair (1925–41) of the family firm of confectioners, H I Rowntree, to fund investigations into social conditions. His writings include *Poverty, A Study of Town Life* (1901), a landmark in empirical sociology (study supported by observed evidence). The three **Rowntree Trusts**, which were founded by his father **Joseph Rowntree** (1836–1925) in 1904, fund research into housing, social care, and social policy, support projects relating to social justice, and give grants to pressure groups working in these areas.

royal assent in the UK, formal consent given by a British sovereign to the passage of a bill through Parliament, after which it becomes an *act of Parliament. The last instance of a royal refusal was the rejection of the Scottish Militia Bill of 1702 by Queen Anne.

royal commission in the UK and Canada, a group of people appointed by the government (nominally by the sovereign) to investigate a matter of public concern and make recommendations on any actions to be taken in connection with it, including changes in the law. In cases where agreement on recommendations cannot be reached, a minority report can be submitted by dissenters.

Royal Greenwich Observatory originally one of the two UK national astronomical observatories run by the Particle Physics and Astronomy Research Council (PPARC). It was founded in 1675 at Greenwich, East London, to provide navigational information to sailors. After World War II it moved to Herstmonceux Castle in Sussex, where the 2.5 m/8.2 ft Isaac Newton Telescope (INT) was constructed in 1967. Following the relocation of the INT to the island of La Palma, in the Canary Islands, RGO was relocated to Cambridge in 1988–90. In 1998 the Cambridge site was closed and the RGO merged with the Royal Observatory Edinburgh to form a new Astronomy Technology Centre on the Edinburgh site.

Royalist term often used to describe monarchist factions. In England, it is used especially for those who supported Charles I during the English *Civil War. They are also known as 'Cavaliers', and their opponents as 'Parliamentarians' or * Roundheads.

royal prerogative powers, immunities, and privileges recognized in common law as belonging to the crown. Most prerogative acts in the UK are now performed by the government on behalf of the crown. The royal prerogative belongs to the Queen as a person as well as to the institution called the crown, and the award of some honours and dignities remain her personal choice. As by prerogative 'the king can do no wrong', the monarch is immune from prosecution.

royalty in law, payment to the owner for rights to use or exploit literary or artistic copyrights and patent rights in new inventions of all kinds.

Rozwi empire *or* **Changamire** highly advanced empire in southeastern Africa, located south of the Zambezi River and centred on the stone city of Great Zimbabwe. It replaced the gold-trading empire of Mwene Mutapa from the 15th century. The Rozwi empire survived until the Mfecane of the 1830s, when overpopulation to the south drove the Nguni and Ndebele people northwards into Rozwi territory in search of more land.

RPI abbreviation for *retail price index.

RSFSR abbreviation for ***Russian Soviet Federal Socialist Republic**, a republic of the former Soviet Union.

RSI abbreviation for *repetitive strain injury, a condition that can affect people who repeatedly perform certain movements with their hands and wrists for long periods of time, such as typists, musicians, or players of computer games.

Rt Hon abbreviation for **Right Honourable**, title of members of the Privy Council (including all present and former UK Cabinet members).

Ruanda part of the former Belgian territory of Ruanda-Urundi until it achieved independence as Rwanda, a country in central Africa.

rubato (from Italian *tempo rubato*, 'rubbed time') in music, a pushing or dragging against the beat for expressive effect.

rubber coagulated *latex of a variety of plants, mainly from the New World. Most important is Para rubber, which comes from the tree *Hevea brasiliensis*, belonging to the spurge family. It was introduced from Brazil to Southeast Asia, where most of the world supply is now produced, the chief exporters being Peninsular Malaysia, Indonesia, Sri Lanka, Cambodia, Thailand, Sarawak, and Brunei. At about seven years the tree, which may grow to 20 m/60 ft, is ready for tapping. Small cuts are made in the trunk and the latex drips into collecting cups. In pure form, rubber is white and has the formula $(C_5H_8)_n$.

rubber plant Asiatic tree belonging to the mulberry family, native to Asia and North Africa, which produces *latex in its stem. It has shiny, leathery, oval leaves, and young specimens are grown as house plants. (*Ficus elastica*, family Moraceae.)

rubella technical term for *German measles.

Rubens, Peter Paul (1577–1640) Flemish painter. He was one of the greatest figures of the *baroque period. Bringing the exuberance of Italian baroque to northern Europe, he created innumerable religious and allegorical paintings for churches and palaces. These show mastery of drama and movement in large compositions, and a love of rich colour and texture. He also painted portraits and, in his last years, landscapes. *The Rape of the Daughters of Leucippus* (1617; Alte Pinakothek, Munich) is typical.

Rubicon ancient name of the small river flowing into the Adriatic that, under the Roman Republic, marked the boundary between Italy proper and Cisalpine Gaul. When Caesar led his army across it 49 BC, he therefore declared war on the Republic; hence to 'cross the Rubicon' means to take an irrevocable step.

rubidium chemical symbol Rb, (Latin *rubidus* 'red') soft, silver-white, metallic element, atomic number 37, relative atomic mass 85.47. It is one of the *alkali metals in Group 1 of the *periodic table. Reactivity of the alkali metals increases down the group and so rubidium is more reactive than lithium, sodium, and potassium. Rubidium ignites spontaneously in air and reacts violently with water. It is used in photocells and vacuum-tube filaments.

ruby red transparent gem variety of the mineral *corundum Al_2O_3, aluminium oxide. Small amounts of chromium oxide, Cr_2O_3, substituting for aluminium oxide, give ruby its colour. Natural rubies are found mainly in Myanmar (Burma), but rubies can also be produced artificially and such synthetic stones are used in *lasers.

rudd *or* **red eye** freshwater bony fish allied to the *roach. It is tinged with bronze, and has reddish fins, the dorsal being farther back than that of the roach. It is found in British and European lakes and sluggish streams. The largest weigh over 1 kg/2.2 lb and may be as much as 45 cm/18 in long. The rudd *Scardinius *erythropthalmus* belongs to the order Cypriniformes, class Osteichthyes.

Rudolf, Lake former name (to 1979) of Lake *Turkana in eastern Africa.

Rudolph two Holy Roman Emperors:

Rudolph I (1218–1291) Holy Roman Emperor from 1273. Originally count of Habsburg, he was the first Habsburg emperor and expanded his dynasty by investing his sons with the duchies of Austria and Styria.

Rudolph II (1552–1612) Holy Roman Emperor from 1576, when he succeeded his father Maximilian II. His policies led to unrest in Hungary and Bohemia, which led to the surrender of Hungary to his brother Matthias in 1608 and religious freedom for Bohemia.

rue shrubby perennial herb native to southern Europe and temperate Asia. It bears clusters of yellow flowers. An oil extracted from the strongly scented blue-green leaves is used in perfumery. (*Ruta graveolens*, family Rutaceae.)

ruff bird *Philomachus pugnax* of the sandpiper family Scolopacidae. The name is taken from the frill of erectile purple-black feathers developed in the breeding season around the neck of the male. The females (reeves) have no ruff; they lay four spotted green eggs in a nest of coarse grass made amongst reeds or rushes. The ruff is found across northern Europe and Asia, and migrates south in winter. It is a casual migrant throughout North America.

Rugby League form of rugby football founded in England in 1895 as the Northern Union when a dispute about pay caused northern clubs to break away from the Rugby Football Union. The game is similar to *Rugby Union, but the number of players was reduced from 15 to 13 in 1906, and other rule changes have made the game more open and fast-moving. There are also differences in the scoring.

Rugby Union form of rugby in which there are 15 players on each side. Points are scored by 'tries', scored by 'touching down' the ball beyond the goal line or by kicking goals from penalties. The Rugby Football Union was formed in 1871 and has its headquarters in England (Twickenham, Middlesex). Formerly an amateur game, the game's status was revoked in August 1995 by the International Rugby Football Board, which lifted restrictions on players moving between Rugby Union and Rugby League.

Ruhr river in Germany, length 235 km/146 mi. It rises in the Rothaargebirge Mountains at the eastern boundary of North Rhine-Westphalia, and flows west to join the Rhine at Duisburg. The **Ruhr Valley**, a metropolitan industrial area, produces petrochemicals, cars, iron, and steel at Duisburg and Dortmund; it is also a coal-mining area.

Ruisdael (*or* Ruysdael), Jacob Isaakszoon van (*c.* 1628–1682) Dutch artist. He is widely considered the greatest of the Dutch landscape painters. He painted scenes near his native town of Haarlem and in Germany, his works often concentrating on the dramatic aspects of nature. A notable example of his atmospheric style is *The Jewish Cemetery* (*c.* 1660; Gemäldegalerie, Dresden).

rule of law doctrine that no individual, however powerful, is above the law. The principle had a significant influence on attempts to restrain the arbitrary use of power by rulers and on the growth of legally enforceable human rights in many Western countries. It is often used as a justification for separating legislative from judicial power.

rum spirit fermented and distilled from sugar cane. Scummings from the sugar pans produce the best rum, molasses the lowest grade. Puerto Rico and Jamaica are the main producing countries.

ruminant any even-toed hoofed mammal with a rumen, the 'first stomach' of its complex digestive system. Plant food is stored and fermented before being brought back to the mouth for chewing (chewing the cud) and then is swallowed to the next stomach. Ruminants include cattle, antelopes, goats, deer, and giraffes, all with a four-chambered stomach. Camels are also ruminants, but they have a three-chambered stomach.

Rump, the English parliament formed between December 1648 and November 1653 after Pride's purge of the *Long Parliament to ensure a majority in favour of trying Charles I. It was dismissed in 1653 by Cromwell, who replaced it with the *Barebones Parliament.

Rumsfeld, Donald (1932–) US Republican politician, defense secretary from 2001. A veteran of the Richard Nixon and Gerald Ford Republican administrations of the 1970s, he formulated an aggressive US defence doctrine that supports the use of pre-emptive strikes against countries that are perceived as risks to the USA, particularly those supporting international terrorism. In 2003, as part of the George W Bush administration, Rumsfeld oversaw the US-led Iraq War to overthrow Iraqi president Saddam Hussein, based on the assertion that Iraq was developing weapons of mass destruction (a claim subsequently unproven). He has also given support to the building of a US National Missile Defense system, to provide protection against ballistic missiles.

Rundstedt, (Karl Rudolf) Gerd von (1875–1953) German field marshal in World War II. Largely responsible for the German breakthrough in France in 1940, he was defeated on the Ukrainian front in 1941. As commander-in-chief in France from 1942, he resisted the Allied invasion in 1944 and in December launched the temporarily successful Ardennes offensive.

runner *or* **stolon** in botany, aerial stem that produces new plants that grows horizontally near the base of some plants, such as the strawberry. It produces roots along its length and new plants grow at these points.

Rupert, Prince (1619–1682) called 'Rupert of the Rhine', English Royalist general and admiral, born in Prague, son of the Elector Palatine Frederick V and James I's daughter Elizabeth. Defeated by Cromwell at *Marston Moor and *Naseby in the Civil War, he commanded a privateering fleet 1649–52, until routed by Admiral Robert Blake and, returning after the Restoration, was a distinguished admiral in the Dutch Wars. He founded the *Hudson's Bay Company. He was created Duke of Cumberland and Earl of Holderness in 1644.

rush any of a group of grasslike plants found in wet places in cold and temperate regions. The round stems and flexible leaves of some species have been used for making mats and baskets since ancient times. (Genus *Juncus*, family Juncaceae.)

Rushdie, (Ahmed) Salman (1947–) British writer. He was born in India of a Muslim family. His book *Midnight's Children* (1981) deals with India from the date of independence and won the Booker Prize. His novel *The Satanic Verses* (1988) (the title refers to verses deleted from the Koran) offended many Muslims with alleged blasphemy. In 1989 the Ayatollah Khomeini of Iran placed a religious *fatwa* on Rushdie, calling for him and his publishers to be killed.

Ruskin, John (1819–1900) English art and social critic. Much of his finest art criticism appeared in two widely influential works, *Modern Painters* (1843–60) and *The Seven Lamps of Architecture* (1849). He was a keen advocate of painters considered unorthodox at the time, such as J M W *Turner and members of the *Pre-Raphaelite Brotherhood. His later writings were concerned with social and economic problems.

Russell, Bertrand Arthur William (1872–1970) 3rd Earl Russell, English philosopher, mathematician, and peace campaigner. He contributed to the development of modern mathematical logic and wrote about social issues. His works include *Principia Mathematica* (1910–13; with A N Whitehead), in which he attempted to show that mathematics could be reduced to a branch of logic; *The Problems of Philosophy* (1912); and *A History of Western Philosophy* (1946). He was an outspoken liberal pacifist. He was awarded the Nobel Prize for Literature in 1950. He was made an Earl in 1931.

Russell, John (1792–1878) 1st Earl Russell; known until 1861 as Lord John Russell, British Liberal politician, son of the 6th Duke of Bedford. He entered the House of Commons in 1813 and supported Catholic emancipation and the Reform Bill. He held cabinet posts 1830–41, became prime minister 1846–52, and was again a cabinet minister until becoming prime minister again 1865–66. He retired after the defeat of his Reform Bill in 1866.

Russian Federation *or* **Russia;**
formerly **Russian Soviet Federal Socialist Republic (RSFSR; within the Soviet Union USSR) (until 1991)**
National name: *Rossiiskaya Federatsiya/ Russian Federation*
Area: 17,075,400 sq km/6,592,811 sq mi

Capital: Moscow
Major towns/cities: St Petersburg, Nizhniy Novgorod, Samara, Yekaterinburg, Novosibirsk, Chelyabinsk, Kazan, Omsk, Perm, Ufa
Physical features: fertile Black Earth district; extensive forests; the Ural Mountains with large mineral resources; Lake Baikal, world's deepest lake
Head of state: Vladimir Putin from 2000
Head of government: Mikhail Fradkov from 2004
Political system: emergent democracy
Political executive: limited presidency
Political parties: Russia is Our Home, centrist; Party of Unity and Accord (PRUA), moderate reformist; Communist Party of the Russian Federation (CPRF), left wing, conservative (ex-communist); Agrarian Party, rural-based, centrist; Liberal Democratic Party, far right, ultranationalist; Congress of Russian Communities, populist, nationalist; Russia's Choice, reformist, right of centre; Yabloko, gradualist free market; Russian Social Democratic People's Party (Derzhava), communist-nationalist; Patriotic Popular Union of Russia (PPUR), communist-led; Russian People's Republican Party (RPRP)
Currency: rouble
GNI per capita (PPP): (US$) 7,820 (2002 est)
Exports: mineral fuels, ferrous and non-ferrous metals and derivatives, precious stones, chemical products, machinery and transport equipment, weapons, timber and paper products. Principal market: Germany 9.2% (2001)
Population: 143,246,000 (2003 est)
Language: Russian (official) and many East Slavic, Altaic, Uralic, Caucasian languages
Religion: traditionally Russian Orthodox; significant Muslim and Buddhist communities
Life expectancy: 61 (men); 73 (women) (2000–05)
Chronology
9th–10th centuries: Viking chieftains established own rule in Novgorod, Kiev, and other cities.
10th–12th centuries: Kiev temporarily united Russian peoples into its empire. Christianity introduced from Constantinople 988.
13th century: Mongols (Golden Horde) overran the southern steppes in 1223, compelling Russian princes to pay tribute.
14th century: Byelorussia and Ukraine came under Polish rule.
1462–1505: Ivan the Great, grand duke of Muscovy, threw off Mongol yoke and united lands in the northwest.
1547–84: Ivan the Terrible assumed title of tsar and conquered Kazan and Astrakhan; colonization of Siberia began.
1613: First Romanov tsar, Michael, elected after period of chaos.
1667: Following Cossack revolt, eastern Ukraine reunited with Russia.
1682–1725: Peter the Great modernized the bureaucracy and army; he founded a navy and a new capital, St Petersburg, introduced Western education, and wrested the Baltic seaboard from Sweden. By 1700 colonization of Siberia had reached the Pacific.
1762–96: Catherine the Great annexed the Crimea and part of Poland and recovered western Ukraine and Byelorussia.

1798–1814: Russia intervened in Revolutionary and Napoleonic Wars (1798–1801, 1805–07); repelled Napoleon, and took part in his overthrow (1812–14).

1827–29: Russian attempts to dominate the Balkans led to a war with Turkey.

1853–56: Crimean War.

1856–64: Caucasian War of conquest completed the annexation of northern Caucasus, causing more than a million people to emigrate.

1858–60: Treaties of Aigun (1858) and Peking (1860) imposed on China, annexing territories north of the Amur and east of the Ussuri rivers; Vladivostok founded on Pacific coast.

1861: Serfdom abolished. Rapid growth of industry followed, a working-class movement developed, and revolutionary ideas spread, culminating in the assassination of Alexander IIin 1881.

1877–78: Russo-Turkish War

1898: Social Democratic Party founded by Russian Marxists; split into Bolshevik and Menshevik factions in 1903.

1904–05: Russo-Japanese War caused by Russian expansion in Manchuria.

1905: A revolution, though suppressed, forced tsar to accept parliament (Duma) with limited powers.

1914: Russo-Austrian rivalry in Balkans was a major cause of outbreak of World War I; Russia fought in alliance with France and Britain.

1917: Russian Revolution: tsar abdicated, provisional government established; Bolsheviks seized power under Vladimir Lenin.

1918: Treaty of Brest-Litovsk ended war with Germany; murder of former tsar; Russian Empire collapsed; Finland, Poland, and Baltic States seceded.

1918–22: Civil War between Red Army, led by Leon Trotsky, and White Russian forces with foreign support; Red Army ultimately victorious; control regained over Ukraine, Caucasus, and Central Asia.

1922: Former Russian Empire renamed Union of Soviet Socialist Republics.

1924: Death of Lenin.

1928: Joseph Stalin emerged as absolute ruler after ousting Trotsky.

1928–33: First five-year plan collectivized agriculture by force; millions died in famine.

1936–38: The Great Purge: Stalin executed his critics and imprisoned millions of people on false charges of treason and sabotage.

1939: Nazi-Soviet nonaggression pact; USSR invaded eastern Poland and attacked Finland.

1940: USSR annexed Baltic States.

1941–45: 'Great Patriotic War' against Germany ended with Soviet domination of eastern Europe and led to 'Cold War' with USA and its allies.

1949: Council for Mutual Economic Assistance (Comecon) created to supervise trade in Soviet bloc.

1953: Stalin died; 'collective leadership' in power.

1955: Warsaw Pact created.

1956: Nikita Khrushchev made 'secret speech' criticizing Stalin; USSR invaded Hungary.

1957–58: Khrushchev ousted his rivals and became effective leader, introducing limited reforms.

1960: Rift between USSR and Communist China.

1962: Cuban missile crisis: Soviet nuclear missiles installed in Cuba but removed after ultimatum from USA.

1964: Khrushchev ousted by new 'collective leadership' headed by Leonid Brezhnev and Alexei Kosygin.

1968: USSR and allies invaded Czechoslovakia.

1970s: 'Détente' with USA and Western Europe.

1979: USSR invaded Afghanistan; fighting continued until Soviet withdrawal ten years later.

1985: Mikhail Gorbachev became leader and announced wide-ranging reform programme (*perestroika*).

1986: Chernobyl nuclear disaster.

1988: Special All-Union Party Congress approved radical constitutional changes and market reforms; start of open nationalist unrest in Caucasus and Baltic republics.

1989: Multi-candidate elections held in move towards 'socialist democracy'; collapse of Soviet satellite regimes in eastern Europe; end of Cold War.

1990: Baltic and Caucasian republics defied central government; Boris Yeltsin became president of Russian Federation and left the Communist Party.

1991: There was an unsuccessful coup by hardline communists; republics declared independence; communist rule dissolved in the Russian Federation; the USSR was replaced by a loose Commonwealth of Independent States (CIS). Mikhail Gorbachev, president of the USSR, resigned, leaving power to Yeltsin.

1992: Russia assumed former USSR seat on the United Nations (UN) Security Council; a new constitution was devised; end of price controls.

1993: There was a power struggle between Yeltsin and the Congress of People's Deputies; congress was dissolved; an attempted coup was foiled; a new parliament was elected.

1994: Russia joined NATO 'Partnership for Peace'; Russian forces invaded the breakaway republic of Chechnya.

1997: A peace treaty was signed with Chechnya. Yeltsin signed an agreement on cooperation with NATO. Russia gained effective admission to the G-7 group.

1998: President Yeltsin sacked the government and appointed Sergei Kiriyenko as prime minister. The rouble was heavily devalued. Yevgeny Primakov replaced Kiriyenko as prime minister and market-centred reform was abandoned. The USA pledged aid of over 3 million tonnes of grain and meat, after a 5% contraction in GDP in 1998.

1999: Yeltsin dismissed first Primakov's government, and then in August, Stepashin's government, appointing Vladimir Putin as prime minister. Troubles with Chechnya continued and Russian forces claimed to have surrounded the capital, Groznyy, and issued an ultimatum to civilians that they must leave or die. After Western protests the Russian ultimatum was deferred by a week. President Yeltsin resigned on 31 December, and Putin took over as acting president.

2000: Vladimir Putin was elected president, and sought to reassert central control. Mikhail Kasyanov was appointed prime minister. The Russian army in Chechnya declared it had secured control of the region, despite continuing rebel activity. In August a nuclear-powered submarine, the Kursk, sank after an explosion caused by the misfire of a torpedo. Putin was slow to request Western help in the abortive rescue mission, and all 118 crew died. In December the Duma voted to restore the old Soviet national anthem, though with different words, and re-instate the tsarist flag and double-eagle crest as national emblems.

2001: Putin announced that control of the war in Chechnya would be transferred to the secret police.

2002: The 1972 Anti-Ballistic Missile (ABM) Treaty between the USA and the then Soviet Union lapsed when the US withdrew. US President George Bush visited Moscow to sign a Strategic Offensive Reduction Treaty (SORT), to reduce US and Russian strategic nuclear arsenals by two-thirds by the end of 2012.

2003: Parliamentary elections resulted in a landslide victory for parties that supported President Putin. Mikhail Khodorkovsky, the billionaire head of Russia's biggest oil company Yukos and an open critic of Putin, was arrested for alleged fraud and tax evasion, which was widely viewed as a political manoeuvre. Akhmad Kadyrov, the Moscow-appointed head of the Chechen administration for the last three years, officially won 81% of the vote. However, the validity of the election was widely questioned by observers and human rights groups.

2004: President Putin was re-elected with another landslide majority. He soon faced criticism of his government's handling of the Beslan hostage crisis, in which militants, many identified as Chechens, took over a school and held its staff and pupils hostage. Over 300 died in the military storming of the school.

2005: US President George W. Bush visited Russia and took part in the ceremonies to mark the 60th anniversary of the end of World War II in Europe.

Russian or **Great Russian** member of the majority ethnic group living in Russia. Russians are also often the largest minority in neighbouring republics. The Russian language is a member of the East Slavonic branch of the Indo-European language family and was the official language of the USSR. It has 130–150 million speakers and is written in the Cyrillic alphabet. The ancestors of the Russians migrated from central Europe in the 6th–8th centuries AD.

Russian art painting and sculpture of Russia, including art from the USSR 1917–91. For centuries Russian art was dominated by an unchanging tradition of church art inherited from Byzantium, responding slowly and hesitantly to Western influences. Briefly, in the early 20th century, it assumed a leading and influential role in European avant-garde art. However, official Soviet disapproval of this trend resulted in its suppression in favour of art geared to the glorification of workers.

Russian Orthodox Church another name for the *Orthodox Church.

Russian Revolution two revolutions of February and October 1917 (Julian *calendar) that began with the overthrow of the Romanov dynasty and ended with the establishment of a communist soviet (council) state, the Union of Soviet Socialist Republics (USSR). In October Bolshevik workers and sailors, led by Vladimir Ilyich *Lenin, seized government buildings and took over power.

Russian revolution, 1905 political upheaval centred in and around St Petersburg, Russia (1905–06), leading up to the February and October revolutions of 1917. On 22 January 1905 thousands of striking unarmed workers marched to Tsar Nicholas II's Winter Palace in St Petersburg to ask for reforms. Government troops fired on the crowd, killing many people. After this 'Bloody Sunday' slaughter the revolution gained

strength, culminating in a general strike which paralysed the whole country in October 1905. Revolutionaries in St Petersburg formed a 'soviet' (council) called the Soviet of Workers' Deputies. Nicholas II then granted the Duma (parliament) the power to pass or reject proposed laws. Although these measures satisfied the liberal element, the revolution continued to gain ground and came to a head when the army crushed a serious uprising in December 1905.

Russian Soviet Federal Socialist Republic (RSFSR) the largest republic of the former Soviet Union; it became independent as the Russian Federation in 1991.

Russo-Japanese War war between Russia and Japan 1904–05, which arose from conflicting ambitions in Korea and *Manchuria, specifically, the Russian occupation of Port Arthur (modern Lüshun) in 1897 and of the Amur province in 1900. Japan successfully besieged Port Arthur May 1904–January 1905, took Mukden (modern Shenyang) on 29 February–10 March, and on 27 May defeated the Russian Baltic fleet, which had sailed halfway around the world to Tsushima Strait. A peace treaty was signed on 23 August 1905. Russia surrendered its lease on Port Arthur, ceded southern Sakhalin to Japan, evacuated Manchuria, and recognized Japan's interests in Korea.

russula any of a large group of fungi (see *fungus), containing many species. They are medium-to-large mushrooms with flattened caps and many are brightly coloured. (Genus *Russula*.)

rust in botany, common name for a group of minute parasitic fungi (see *fungus) that appear on the leaves of their hosts as orange-red spots, later becoming darker. The commonest is the wheat rust *Puccinia graminis*, order Uredinales.

rust reddish-brown oxide of iron formed by the action of moisture and oxygen on the metal. It consists mainly of hydrated iron(III) oxide ($Fe_2O_3.H_2O$) and iron(III) hydroxide ($Fe(OH)_3$). Rusting is the commonest form of *corrosion. Sacrificial metal is used to protect pipes and other exposed metal on oil rigs from corrosion by rust. A more reactive metal than iron, such as zinc or magnesium, is attached in large lumps by conducting wires, at intervals along the pipes. Electrons released during the reaction travel along the conducting wires to the pipes, preventing rust from occurring. It is cheaper to replace the sacrificial metal than it is to replace the pipes.

Ruthenia or **Carpathian Ukraine** region in western Ukraine, central Europe, on the southern slopes of the Carpathian Mountains, home of the Ruthenes or Russniaks. Dominated by Hungary from the 10th century, it was part of Austria-Hungary until World War I. In 1918 it was divided between Czechoslovakia, Poland, and Romania; independent for a single day in 1938, it was immediately occupied by Hungary, captured by the USSR in 1944 and incorporated 1945–47 (as the Transcarpathian Region) into Ukraine Republic, which became independent as Ukraine in 1991.

ruthenium chemical symbol Ru, hard, brittle, silver-white, metallic element, atomic number 44, relative atomic mass 101.07. It is one of the so-called platinum group of metals; it occurs in platinum ores as a free metal and in the natural alloy osmiridium. It is used as a hardener in alloys and as a catalyst; its compounds are used as colouring agents in glass and ceramics.

Rutherford, Ernest (1871–1937) 1st Baron
Rutherford of Nelson, New Zealand-born British
physicist. He was a pioneer of modern atomic science.
His main research was in the field of *radioactivity, and
he discovered alpha, beta, and gamma rays. He was the
first to recognize the nuclear nature of the atom in 1911.
He was awarded the Nobel Prize for Chemistry in 1908
for his work in atomic disintegration and the chemistry
of radioactive substances.

rutherfordium chemical symbol Rf, synthesized,
radioactive, metallic element. It is the first of the
*transactinide series, atomic number 104, relative atomic
mass 262. It is produced by bombarding californium
with carbon nuclei and has ten isotopes, the longest-
lived of which, Rf-262, has a half-life of 70 seconds.

Ruysdael, Jacob van Dutch painter; see Jacob van
*Ruisdael.

Rwanda
formerly **Ruanda (until 1962)**
   National name: *Republika y'u Rwanda/*
   Republic of Rwanda

Area: 26,338 sq km/10,169 sq mi
Capital: Kigali
Major towns/cities: Butare, Ruhengeri, Gisenyi,
Kibungo, Cyangugu
Physical features: high savannah and hills, with volcanic
mountains in northwest; part of lake Kivu; highest peak
Mount Karisimbi 4,507 m/14,792 ft; Kagera River
(whose headwaters are the source of the Nile)
Head of state: Paul Kagame from 2000
Head of government: Bernard Makuza from 2000
Political system: authoritarian nationalist
Political executive: unlimited presidency
Political parties: National Revolutionary Development
Movement (MRND), nationalist-socialist, Hutu-
oriented; Social Democratic Party (PSD), left of centre;
Christian Democratic Party (PDC), Christian, centrist;
Republican Democratic Movement (MDR), Hutu
nationalist; Liberal Party (PL), moderate centrist;
Rwanda Patriotic Front (FPR), Tutsi-led but claims to
be multi-ethnic
Currency: Rwandan franc
GNI per capita (PPP): (US$) 1,210 (2002 est)
Exports: coffee, tea, tin ores and concentrates,
pyrethrum, quinquina, hides. Principal market:
Germany 39.4% (2001)

Population: 8,387,000 (2003 est)
Language: Kinyarwanda, French (both official),
Kiswahili
Religion: about 50% animist; about 40% Christian,
mainly Roman Catholic; 9% Muslim
Life expectancy: 39 (men); 40 (women) (2000–05)
Chronology
10th century onwards: Hutu peoples settled in region
formerly inhabited by hunter-gatherer Twa Pygmies,
becoming peasant farmers.
14th century onwards: Majority Hutu community
came under dominance of cattle-owning Tutsi peoples,
immigrants from the east, who became a semi-
aristocracy and established control through land and
cattle contracts.
15th century: Ruganzu Bwimba, a Tutsi leader,
founded kingdom near Kigali.
17th century: Central Rwanda and outlying Hutu
communities subdued by Tutsi mwami (king)
Ruganzu Ndori.
late 19th century: Under the great Tutsi king, Kigeri
Rwabugiri, a unified state with a centralized military
structure was established.
1890: Known as Ruandi, the Tutsi kingdom, along with
neighbouring Burundi, came under nominal German
control, as Ruanda-Urundi.
1916: Occupied by Belgium during World War I.
1923: Belgium granted League of Nations mandate to
administer Ruanda-Urundi; they were to rule
'indirectly' through Tutsi chiefs.
1959: Inter-ethnic warfare between Hutu and Tutsi,
forcing mwami Kigeri V into exile.
1961: Republic proclaimed after mwami deposed.
1962: Independence from Belgium achieved as
Rwanda, with Hutu Grégoire Kayibanda as president;
many Tutsis left the country.
1963: 20,000 killed in inter-ethnic clashes, after Tutsis
exiled in Burundi had launched a raid.
1973: Kayibanda ousted in military coup led by Hutu
Maj-Gen Juvenal Habyarimana; this was caused by
resentment of Tutsis, who held some key government
posts.
1981: Elections created civilian legislation, but
dominated by Hutu socialist National Revolutionary
Development Movement (MRND), in a one-party state.
1988: Hutu refugees from Burundi massacres streamed
into Rwanda.
1990: The government was attacked by the Rwanda
Patriotic Front (FPR), a Tutsi refugee military-political
organization based in Uganda, which controlled parts
of northern Rwanda.
1993: A United Nations (UN) mission was sent to
monitor the peace agreement made with the FPR in 1992.
1994: President Habyarimana and Burundian Hutu
president Ntaryamira were killed in an air crash;
involvement of FPR was suspected. Half a million
people were killed in the ensuing civil war, with many
Tutsi massacred by Hutu death squads and the exodus
of 2 million refugees to neighbouring countries. The
government fled as FPR forces closed in. An interim
coalition government was installed, with moderate
Hutu and FPR leader, Pasteur Bizimungu, as president.
1995: A war-crimes tribunal opened and government
human-rights abuses were reported. Pierre Rwigema
was appointed prime minister by President Bizimungu.

1996–97: Rwanda and Zaire (Democratic Republic of Congo) were on the brink of war after Tutsi killings of Hutu in Zaire. A massive Hutu refugee crisis was narrowly averted as thousands were allowed to return to Rwanda.

1998: 378 rebels were killed by the Rwandan army.

2000: President Bizimungu resigned after disagreeing with his party, the Rwanda Patriotic Front. Paul Kagame, the vice-president, was installed as interim president in March, and inaugurated as president the following month. Bernard Makuza became prime minister of a new cabinet.

2002: A peace deal was struck with the Democratic Republic of Congo. Rwanda promised to withdraw its troops from the east of the country if the Congolese government disarmed or expelled the Hutu militias who had been hiding there since the early 1990s.

2003: In the first multiparty presidential elections since the genocide of 1994, President Kagame won with 95% of the vote. The main challenger, former prime minister Faustin Twagiramungu, won just 3.7% and claimed that voters were intimidated.

Ryder Cup golf tournament for professional men's teams from the USA and Europe. It is played every two years, and the match is made up of a series of singles, foursomes, and fourballs played over three days. A women's version of the Ryder Cup, the **Solheim Cup**, was introduced in 1990.

rye tall annual *cereal grass grown extensively in northern Europe and other temperate regions. The flour is used to make dark-coloured ('black') breads. Rye is grown mainly as a food crop for animals, but the grain is also used to make whisky and breakfast cereals. (*Secale cereale.*)

Ryle, Martin (1918–1984) English radio astronomer. At the Mullard Radio Astronomy Observatory, Cambridge, he developed the technique of sky-mapping using 'aperture synthesis', combining smaller dish aerials to give the characteristics of one large one. His work on the distribution of radio sources in the universe brought confirmation of the *Big Bang theory. He was awarded with his co-worker, the English radio astronomer Antony *Hewish, the Nobel Prize for Physics in 1974 for his work on the development of radio astronomy, particularly the aperture-synthesis technique, and the discovery of *pulsars, rapidly rotating neutron stars that emit pulses of energy. He was knighted in 1966.

Ryukyu Islands *or* **Riukiu** *or* **Nansei** southernmost island group of Japan, stretching towards Taiwan and including *Okinawa, Miyako, and Ishigaki; area 2,254 sq km/870 sq mi; population (2000 est) 1,318,000. Most of the larger islands are composed of volcanic rock, while the smaller islands are formed from coral. The capital is Naha (on Okinawa). Produce includes sugar, pineapples, and fish.

S

Saami or **Lapp** an indigenous people numbering over 60,000 (1996) and living in northern Finland (7,000), Norway (36,000), Sweden (17,000) and Russia (2,000). Traditionally fishermen, hunter-gatherers, and nomadic reindeer herders, the Saami have lost large areas of pasture since 1965 due to forestry, mining and other economic activities. Today many are settled and have entered the professions. Their religion was originally animist, but most Saami now belong either to the Russian Orthodox or Lutheran churches. Their language belongs to the Finno-Ugric group.

Saarinen, Eero (1910–1961) Finnish-born US architect. He was renowned for his wide range of innovative modernist designs, experimenting with different structures and shapes. His works include the US embassy, London (1955–61); the TWA terminal at John F Kennedy Airport, New York City (1956–62); and Dulles Airport, Washington, DC (1958–63). He collaborated on a number of projects with his father, Eliel *Saarinen.

Saarinen, (Gottlieb) Eliel (1873–1950) Finnish-born US architect and town planner. He founded the Finnish Romantic school. His best-known European project is the Helsinki railway station (1905–14). In 1923 he emigrated to the USA, where he is remembered for his designs for the Cranbrook Academy of Art in Bloomfield Hills, Michigan (1926–43), and Christ Church, Minneapolis (1949).

Saarland French **Sarre**, administrative region (German *Land*) in southwest Germany, bordered by Rhineland-Palatinate and the French *département* of Moselle; area 2,570 sq km/992 sq mi; population (1997) 1,083,000. The capital is Saarbrücken, and other major towns include Neunkirchen, Völklingen, and Saarlouis. The region is one-third forest, and crossed northwest–south by the River Saar.

Sabah formerly **North Borneo**, self-governing state of the federation of Malaysia, occupying northeast Borneo, forming (with Sarawak) East Malaysia; area 73,613 sq km/28,415 sq mi; population (2000 est) 2,449,400. The capital is Kota Kinabalu. The state has considerable mineral wealth, including tin, antimony, diamonds, iron, and sulphur, but development has been hindered by the lack of an effective transport system. In many areas navigable rivers, such as the rivers Labuk, Padas, and Kinabatangan, offer the only means of transport. Of these the Kinabatangan, along which shallow-draft vessels are able to navigate 300 km/

186 mi inland, is the most important. Since the early 20th century plantation agriculture has produced commercial crops of tobacco, coconuts, palm oil, and rubber. Industries include sawmilling and rubber processing.

Sabah, Sheikh Jabir al-Ahmad al-Jabir al- (1928–) Emir of Kuwait from 1977. He suspended the national assembly in 1986, after mounting parliamentary criticism, ruling in a feudal, paternalistic manner. On the invasion of Kuwait by Iraq in 1990 he fled to Saudi Arabia, returning to Kuwait in March 1991. In 1992 a reconstituted national assembly was elected.

Sabbath or **Shabbat** (Hebrew *shabath*, 'to rest') the seventh day of the week, commanded by God in the Old Testament as a sacred day of rest after his creation of the world; in Judaism, from sunset Friday to sunset Saturday; in Christianity, Sunday (or, in some sects, Saturday). Keeping the Sabbath is one of the Ten Commandments.

Sabin, Albert Bruce (1906–1993) Russian-born US microbiologist who developed a highly effective, live vaccine against polio. The earlier vaccine, developed by physicist Jonas *Salk, was based on heat-killed viruses. Sabin was convinced that a live form would be longer-lasting and more effective, and in 1957 he succeeded in weakening the virus so that it lost its virulence. The vaccine can be given by mouth.

Sabine member of an ancient people of central Italy, conquered by the Romans and amalgamated with them in the 3rd century BC. The so-called **rape of the Sabine women** – a mythical attempt by *Romulus in the early days of Rome to carry off the Sabine women to colonize the new city – is frequently depicted in art.

sable marten *Martes zibellina*, about 50 cm/20 in long and usually brown. It is native to northern Eurasian forests, but now found mainly in eastern Siberia. The sable has diminished in numbers because of its valuable fur, which has long attracted hunters. Conservation measures and sable farming have been introduced to save it from extinction.

saccharide another name for a *sugar.

saccharin or **ortho-sulpho benzimide** $C_7H_5NO_3S$, sweet, white, crystalline solid derived from coal tar and substituted for sugar. Since 1977 it has been regarded as potentially carcinogenic. Its use is not universally permitted and it has been largely replaced by other sweetening agents.

sacred cow any person, institution, or custom that is considered above criticism. The term comes from the Hindu belief that cows are sacred and must not be killed. This animal is historically associated with certain Hindu deities, and is also symbolic of the sanctity of all life.

Sadat, (Muhammad) Anwar (1918–1981) Egyptian politician, president 1970–81. Succeeding *Nasser as president in 1970, he restored morale by his handling of the Egyptian campaign in the 1973 war against Israel. In 1974 his plan for economic, social, and political reform to transform Egypt was unanimously adopted in a referendum. In 1977 he visited Israel to reconcile the two countries, and he shared the Nobel Prize for Peace in 1978 with Israeli prime minister Menachem *Begin for their efforts towards the Israel-Egypt peace treaty of 1979. Although feted by the West for pursuing peace with Israel, Sadat was denounced by the Arab world. He was assassinated by Islamic fundamentalists and succeeded by Hosni Mubarak.

Sade, Donatien Alphonse François, comte de (1740–1814) also known as **the Marquis de Sade**, French writer. He was imprisoned for sexual offences and finally committed to an asylum. He wrote plays and novels dealing explicitly with a variety of sexual practices, including sadism, deriving pleasure or sexual excitement from inflicting pain on others.

sadism tendency to derive pleasure (usually sexual) from inflicting physical or mental pain on others. The term is derived from the Marquis de *Sade.

sadomasochism sexual behaviour that combines *sadism and *masochism. The term was coined in 1907 by sexologist Richard von Krafft-Ebing.

safety lamp portable lamp designed for use in places where flammable gases such as methane may be encountered; for example, in coal mines. The electric head lamp used as a miner's working light has the bulb and contacts in protected enclosures. The flame safety lamp, now used primarily for gas detection, has the wick enclosed within a strong glass cylinder surmounted by wire gauzes. English chemist Humphrey *Davy (1815) and English engineer George *Stephenson each invented flame safety lamps.

safflower thistlelike Asian plant with large orange-yellow flowers. It is widely grown for the oil from its seeds, which is used in cooking, margarine, and paints and varnishes; the leftovers are used as cattle feed. (*Carthamus tinctorius*, family Compositae.)

saffron crocus plant belonging to the iris family, probably native to southwestern Asia, and formerly widely cultivated in Europe; also the dried orange-yellow *stigmas of its purple flowers, used for colouring and flavouring in cookery. (*Crocus sativus*, family Iridaceae.)

saga prose narrative written down in the 11th–13th centuries in Norway and Iceland. The sagas range from family chronicles, such as the *Landnamabok* of Ari (1067–1148), to legendary and anonymous works such as *Njal's Saga* (c. 1280). The term 'saga' is generally applied to any long (often heroic) story.

sage perennial herb belonging to the mint family, with grey-green aromatic leaves used for flavouring in cookery. It grows up to 50 cm/20 in high and has bluish-lilac or pink flowers. (*Salvia officinalis*, family Labiatae.)

Sagittarius bright zodiac constellation in the southern hemisphere, represented as an archer aiming a bow and arrow at neighbouring Scorpius. The Sun passes through Sagittarius from mid-December to mid-January, including the winter solstice, when it is farthest south of the Equator. The constellation contains many nebulae and *globular clusters, and open star clusters. Kaus Australis and Nunki are its brightest stars. The centre of our Galaxy, the *Milky Way, is marked by the radio source Sagittarius A. In astrology, the dates for Sagittarius are about 22 November–21 December (see *precession).

sago starchy material obtained from the pith of the sago palm *Metroxylon sagu*. It forms a nutritious food and is used for manufacturing glucose and sizing textiles.

Sahara (Arabic *Sahra*, 'wilderness') largest desert in the world, occupying around 9,065,000 sq km/ 3,500,000 sq mi of north Africa from the Atlantic to the Nile, covering: west Egypt; part of west Sudan; large parts of Mauritania, Mali, Niger, and Chad; and southern parts of Morocco, Algeria, Tunisia, and Libya. Small areas in Algeria and Tunisia are below sea level, but it is mainly a plateau with a central mountain system, including the Ahaggar Mountains in Algeria, the Aïr Massif in Niger, and the Tibesti Massif in Chad, of which the highest peak is Emi Koussi, 3,415 m/11,208 ft.

Sahel (Arabic *sahil* 'coast') marginal area to the south of the Sahara, from Senegal to Somalia, which experiences desert-like conditions during periods of low rainfall. The *desertification is partly due to climatic fluctuations but has also been caused by the pressures of a rapidly expanding population, which has led to overgrazing and the destruction of trees and scrub for fuelwood. In recent years many famines have taken place in the area.

saiga antelope *Saiga tartarica* of eastern European and western Asian steppes and deserts. Buff-coloured, whitish in winter, it stands 75 cm/30 in at the shoulder, with a body about 1.5 m/5 ft long. Its nose is unusually large and swollen, an adaptation which may help warm and moisten the air inhaled, and keep out the desert dust. The saiga can run at 80 kph/50 mph.

Saigon former name (to 1976) of *Ho Chi Minh City, Vietnam.

Saigon, Battle of during the Vietnam War, battle 29 January–23 February 1968, when 5,000 Vietcong were expelled by South Vietnamese and US forces. The city was finally taken by North Vietnamese forces 30 April 1975, after South Vietnamese withdrawal from the central highlands.

saint holy man or woman respected for his or her wisdom, spirituality, and dedication to their faith. Within the *Roman Catholic Church the *pope officially recognizes a saint through *canonization. Many saints are associated with miracles, and canonization usually occurs after a thorough investigation of their lives and the miracles attributed to them. A **patron saint** is regarded as the patron of a particular group or country. For individual saints, see under forename; for example, *Paul, St.

St Bartholomew's Day Massacre slaughter of *Huguenots (Protestants) in Paris, 24 August–17 September 1572, and until 3 October in the provinces. About 25,000 people are believed to have been killed. When *Catherine de' Medici's plot to have Admiral Coligny assassinated failed, she resolved to have all the Huguenot leaders killed, persuading her son Charles IX it was in the interest of public safety.

St Bernard breed of large, heavily built dog, named after the monks of Grand St Bernard Hospice, Switzerland, who kept them for finding lost travellers in the Alps and to act as guides. They are 70 cm/30 in high at the shoulder, and weigh about 70 kg/154 lb. They have pendulous ears and lips, large feet, and drooping lower eyelids. They are usually orange and white.

St Elmo's fire bluish, flamelike electrical discharge that sometimes occurs above ships' masts and other pointed objects or about aircraft in stormy weather. Although of high voltage, it is of low current and therefore harmless. St Elmo (or St Erasmus) is the patron saint of sailors.

Saint-Exupéry, Antoine Marie Roger de (1900–1944) French author and pilot. He wrote the autobiographical *Vol de nuit/Night Flight* (1931) and *Terre des hommes/Wind, Sand, and Stars* (1939). His children's book *Le Petit Prince/The Little Prince* (1943) is also an adult allegory.

St George's port and capital of Grenada, on the southwest coast; population (1994 est) 30,000. The port has a well-sheltered harbour, exporting nutmeg, bananas, and rum, and is also an administrative and commercial centre. Refined sugar and alcoholic drinks are leading products and there is an established tourist industry. It was founded in 1650 by the French, and was the capital of the Windward Islands 1885–1958 (at that time a British dependency).

St Helena British island in the south Atlantic, 1,900 km/1,200 mi west of Africa, area 122 sq km/47 sq mi; population (1997) 5,644. Its capital is Jamestown, and it exports fish and timber. *Napoleon, after his defeat at the battle of Waterloo, was sent into exile here until his death in 1821. Ascension and Tristan da Cunha are dependencies.

St Helens, Mount volcanic mountain in Skamania County, Washington. It is located on the western flank of the Cascade Range, 56 km/35 mi east of Kelso, in the Gifford Pinchot National Forest. Dormant since 1857, it erupted on 18 May 1980, devastating an area of 600 sq km/230 sq mi, and killing 57 people; its height was reduced from 2,950 m/9,682 ft to 2,560 m/8,402 ft. The Mount St Helens National Volcanic Monument now surrounds the peak.

St John, Order of or **Knights Hospitallers of St John of Jerusalem** oldest order of Christian chivalry, named after the hospital at Jerusalem founded about 1048 by merchants of Amalfi for pilgrims, whose travel routes the knights defended from the Muslims. Today there are about 8,000 knights (male and female), and the Grand Master is the world's highest-ranking Roman Catholic lay person.

St John's port and capital of Antigua and Barbuda, on the northwest coast of Antigua; population (1992) 38,000. It exports rum, cotton, and sugar.

St Kitts and Nevis or **St Christopher and Nevis,** formerly part of Leeward Islands Federation (until 1956)

National name: *Federation of St Christopher and St Nevis*

Area: 262 sq km/101 sq mi (St Kitts 168 sq km/65 sq mi, Nevis 93 sq km/36 sq mi)
Capital: Basseterre (on St Kitts) (and chief port)
Major towns/cities: Charlestown (Nevis), Newcastle, Sandy Point Town, Dieppe Bay Town, Saint Paul
Physical features: both islands are volcanic; fertile plains on coast; black beaches
Head of state: Queen Elizabeth II from 1983, represented by Governor General Dr Cuthbert Montraville Sebastian from 1996
Head of government: Denzil Douglas from 1995
Political system: liberal democracy
Political executive: parliamentary
Political parties: People's Action Movement (PAM), right of centre; Nevis Reformation Party (NRP), Nevis-separatist, centrist; Labour Party (SKLP), moderate left of centre
Currency: East Caribbean dollar
GNI per capita (PPP): (US$) 9,780 (2002 est)
Exports: sugar, manufactures, postage stamps; sugar and sugar products accounted for approximately 20% of export earnings in 2000. Principal market: USA 72.4% (2001)
Population: 42,000 (2003 est)
Language: English (official)
Religion: Anglican 36%, Methodist 32%, other Protestant 8%, Roman Catholic 10%
Life expectancy: 68 (men); 72 (women) (2000–05)
Chronology
1493: Visited by the explorer Christopher Columbus, after whom the main island is named, but for next two centuries the islands were left in the possession of indigenous Caribs.
1623 and 1628: St Kitts and Nevis islands successively settled by British as their first Caribbean colony, with 2,000 Caribs brutally massacred in 1626.
1783: In the Treaty of Versailles France, which had long disputed British possession, rescinded its claims to the islands, on which sugar cane plantations developed, worked by imported African slaves.
1816: Anguilla was joined politically to the two islands.
1834: Abolition of slavery.
1871–1956: Part of the Leeward Islands Federation.
1937: Internal self-government granted.
1952: Universal adult suffrage granted.
1958–62: Part of the Federation of the West Indies.
1967: St Kitts, Nevis, and Anguilla achieved internal self-government, within the British Commonwealth, with Robert Bradshaw, Labour Party leader, as prime minister.
1970: NRP formed, calling for separation for Nevis.
1971: Anguilla returned to being a British dependency after rebelling against domination by St Kitts.
1980: People's Action Movement (PAM) and NRP centrist coalition government, led by Kennedy Simmonds, formed after inconclusive general election.
1983: Full independence was achieved within the Commonwealth.
1994: A three-week state of emergency was imposed after violent antigovernment riots by Labour Party supporters in Basseterre.
1995: Labour Party won a general election; Denzil Douglas became prime minister.
1997: Nevis withdrew from the federation.

795

1998: Nevis referendum on secession failed to secure support.

2000: Denzil Douglas was re-elected as prime minister.

2004: Denzil Douglas won his third consecutive term as prime minister.

Saint-Laurent, Yves Henri Donat Mathieu (1936–) French fashion designer. He has had an exceptional influence on fashion in the second half of the 20th century. He began working for Christian *Dior 1955 and succeeded him as designer on Dior's death 1957. He went on to create the first 'power-dressing' looks for men and women: classic, stylish city clothes. He established his own label in 1962 and

St Lawrence river in eastern North America. With the *Great Lakes and linking canals such as the Welland Ship Canal, it forms the St Lawrence Seaway, an inland route for small ocean-going ships from the Gulf of St Lawrence, an arm of the Atlantic Ocean, to Thunder Bay at the head of Lake Superior; larger vessels stop at *Montréal. The river is 1,200 km/745 mi long and icebound for four months each year. Enormous quantities of hydroelectric power are generated along its course.

St Louis city and riverport in Missouri, on the Mississippi River; population (2000 est) 348,200. Occupying a central US location, it is a warehousing and distribution hub, and a major market for livestock, grain, wool, and lumber. The port handles oil, coal, sulphur, cement, and agricultural and manufactured goods. Products include aerospace and transport equipment, pharmaceuticals, refined oil, rubber, printed materials, and processed metals, tobacco, and food.

St Lucia

formerly **part of Windward Islands Federation (until 1960)**

Area: 617 sq km/238 sq mi

Capital: Castries

Major towns/cities: Soufrière, Vieux Fort, Choiseul, Gros Islet

Major ports: Vieux-Fort

Physical features: mountainous island with fertile valleys; mainly tropical forest; volcanic peaks; Gros and Petit Pitons

Head of state: Queen Elizabeth II from 1979, represented by Governor General Dr Perlette Louisy from 1997

Head of government: Kenny Anthony from 1997

Political system: liberal democracy

Political executive: parliamentary

Political parties: United Workers' Party (UWP), moderate left of centre; St Lucia Labour Party (SLP), moderate left of centre; Progressive Labour Party (PLP), moderate left of centre

Currency: East Caribbean dollar

GNI per capita (PPP): (US$) 5,000 (2002 est)

Exports: bananas, coconut oil, cocoa beans, copra, beverages, tobacco, miscellaneous articles. Principal market: UK 55.7% (2000)

Population: 149,000 (2003 est)

Language: English (official), French patois

Religion: Roman Catholic 85%; Anglican, Protestant

Life expectancy: 71 (men); 74 (women) (2000–05)

Chronology

1502: Sighted by the explorer Christopher Columbus on St Lucia's day but not settled for more than a century due to hostility of the island's Carib Indian inhabitants.

1635: Settled by French, who brought in slaves to work sugar cane plantations as the Carib community was annihilated.

1814: Ceded to Britain as a crown colony, following Treaty of Paris; African slaves brought in to work sugar cane plantations.

1834: Slavery abolished.

1860s: A major coal warehousing centre until the switch to oil and diesel fuels in 1930s.

1871–1960: Part of Windward Islands Federation.

1951: Universal adult suffrage granted.

1967: Acquired internal self-government as a West Indies associated state.

1979: Independence achieved within Commonwealth with John Compton, leader of United Workers' Party (UWP), as prime minister.

1979–82: St Lucia Party (SLP) was in power under Allan Louisy then Winston Cenac.

1982: John Compton was returned to power.

1991: Integration with other Windward Islands (Dominica, Grenada, and St Vincent) was proposed.

1993: Unrest and strikes by farmers and agricultural workers arose as a result of depressed prices for the chief cash crop, bananas.

1996: John Compton resigned and was succeeded by Vaughan Lewis.

1997: Kenny Anthony (St Lucia Labour Party) became prime minister.

2001: Kenny Anthony was re-elected as prime minister.

2002: Tropical Storm Lili destroyed half the banana crop.

St Petersburg Russian **Sankt-Peterburg**, capital of the St Petersburg region, Russian Federation, at the head of the Gulf of Finland; population (1994) 4,883,000. Industries include shipbuilding, machinery, chemicals, and textiles. It was renamed **Petrograd** 1914 and was called **Leningrad** 1924–91, when its original name was restored. Built on a low and swampy site, St Petersburg is split up by the mouths of the River Neva, which connects it with Lake Ladoga. The climate is severe. The city became a seaport when it was linked with the

Baltic by a ship canal built 1875–93. It is also linked by canal and river with the Caspian and Black seas, and in 1975 a seaway connection was completed via lakes Onega and Ladoga with the White Sea near Belomorsk, allowing naval forces to reach the Barents Sea free of NATO surveillance.

St-Pierre and Miquelon territorial collectivity of France, comprising eight small islands off the south coast of Newfoundland, Canada; area St-Pierre group 26 sq km/10 sq mi; Miquelon-Langlade group 216 sq km/ 83 sq mi; population (1998 est) 6,900. The capital is St-Pierre. Industries include fishing and farming. Cattle are raised and there is some light farming.

Saint-Saëns, (Charles) Camille (1835–1921) French composer, pianist, and organist. Saint-Saëns was a master of technique and a prolific composer. He wrote many lyrical Romantic pieces and symphonic poems. He is well known for the opera *Samson et Dalila* (1877), which was prohibited on the French stage until 1892, and the uncharacteristic orchestral piece *Le carnaval des animaux/The Carnival of the Animals* (1886), his most popular work.

St Vincent and the Grenadines

Area: 388 sq km/150 sq mi (including islets of the Northern Grenadines 43 sq km/17 sq mi)
Capital: Kingstown
Major towns/cities: Georgetown, Châteaubelair, Layon, Dovers
Physical features: volcanic mountains, thickly forested; La Soufrière volcano
Head of state: Queen Elizabeth II from 1979, represented by Governor General Frederick Ballantyne from 2002
Head of government: Ralph Gonsalves from 2001
Political system: liberal democracy
Political executive: parliamentary
Political parties: New Democratic Party (NDP), right of centre; St Vincent Labour Party (SVLP), moderate left of centre
Currency: East Caribbean dollar
GNI per capita (PPP): (US$) 5,100 (2002 est)
Exports: bananas, rice, eddoes, dasheen, sweet potatoes, flour, ginger, tannias, plantains. Principal market: UK 37.4% (2001)

Population: 120,000 (2003 est)
Language: English (official), French patois
Religion: Anglican, Methodist, Roman Catholic
Life expectancy: 73 (men); 76 (women) (2000–05)
Chronology
1498: Main island visited by the explorer Christopher Columbus on St Vincent's day.
17th–18th centuries: Possession disputed by France and Britain, with fierce resistance from the indigenous Carib community.
1783: Recognized as British crown colony by Treaty of Versailles.
1795–97: Carib uprising, with French support, resulted in deportation of 5,000 to Belize and Honduras.
1834: Slavery abolished.
1902: Over 2,000 killed by the eruption of La Soufrière volcano.
1951: Universal adult suffrage granted.
1958–62: Part of West Indies Federation.
1969: Achieved internal self-government.
1979: Achieved full independence within Commonwealth.
1981: General strike against new industrial-relations legislation at a time of economic recession.
1984: James Mitchell, of the centre-right New Democratic Party (NDP) became prime minister.
2000: Prime Minister James Mitchell gave up his presidency of the ruling New Democratic Party (NDP), and was later replaced as prime minister by Arnhim Eustace.
2001: Ralph Gonsalves replaced Eustace as prime minister.

Sakha formerly **Yakutia; Yakutsk Autonomous Soviet Socialist Republic,** autonomous republic of the Russian Federation, in eastern Siberia; area 3,103,000 sq km/1,198,100 sq mi; population (1997) 1,032,000 (50% Russians, 33% Yakuts). The capital is Yakutsk. Industries include fur trapping, gold and natural gas extraction, and lumbering; there is some agriculture in the south.

Sakhalin formerly Japanese **Karafuto** (1855–75; 1905–45), island in the Russian Far East between the Sea of Okhotsk and the Sea of Japan, separated from the mainland of the Russian Federation by the Tatar Strait and from the northernmost island of Japan, Hokkaido, by La Pérouse Strait. Sakhalin is some 965 km/ 600 mi long and covers an area of 76,400 sq km/29,498 sq mi. The main town is Yuzhno-Sakhalinsk. Coal, oil, natural gas, iron ore, and gold deposits, together with extensive coniferous and mixed forests, provide the basis for mining, oil extraction, and industries producing timber, cellulose, and paper (the latter established by the Japanese). The oil that is extracted on Sakhalin is piped across the Tatar Strait to Komsomolsk-na-Amure. Fishing is also an important economic activity. Sakhalin supports limited arable (potatoes and vegetables) and dairy farming.

Sakharov, Andrei Dmitrievich (1921–1989) Soviet physicist. He was an outspoken human-rights campaigner, who with Igor Tamm developed the hydrogen bomb. He later protested against Soviet nuclear tests and was a founder of the Soviet Human Rights Committee in 1970. In 1975 he was awarded the Nobel Prize for Peace for his advocacy of human rights and disarmament. For criticizing Soviet action in Afghanistan, he was sent into internal exile 1980–86.

Saladin (c. 1138–1193) Arabic in full **Salah ad-Din Yusuf ibn Ayyub**, (Arabic *Salah ad-Din*, 'righteousness of the faith') Kurdish conqueror of the Kingdom of Jerusalem. Saladin believed in *jihad (holy war) – the Muslim equivalent of the crusades. He conquered Syria 1174–87, and recovered Jerusalem from the Christians in 1187, sparking the Third *Crusade (1191–92). The Christian army, headed by Philip II of France and Richard (I) the Lion-heart of England retook Acre in 1191, but Saladin was a brilliant general and the Third Crusade, although inflicting some defeats, achieved little. In 1192 he made peace with Richard (I) the Lionheart, left fighting alone after quarrels with his allies.

salamander tailed amphibian of the order Urodela. They are sometimes confused with *lizards, but unlike lizards they have no scales or claws. Salamanders have smooth or warty moist skin. The order includes some 300 species, arranged in nine families, found mainly in the northern hemisphere. Salamanders include hellbenders, *mudpuppies, *olms, waterdogs, sirens, mole salamanders, *newts, and lungless salamanders (dusky, woodland, and spring salamanders).

Salamis ancient city on the east coast of Cyprus, the capital under the early Ptolemies until its harbour silted up about 200 BC, when it was succeeded by Paphos in the southwest.

Salamis, Battle of in the Persian Wars, sea battle fought in the Strait of Salamis west of Athens, Greece, in 480 BC between the Greeks and the invading Persians. Despite being heavily outnumbered, the Greeks inflicted a crushing defeat on the invading Persians which effectively destroyed their fleet.

Salazar, António de Oliveira (1889–1970) Portuguese prime minister 1932–68 who exercised a virtual dictatorship. During World War II he maintained Portuguese neutrality but fought long colonial wars in Africa (Angola and Mozambique) that impeded his country's economic development as well as that of the colonies.

salicylic acid HOC_6H_4COOH, active chemical constituent of aspirin, an analgesic drug. The acid and its salts (salicylates) occur naturally in many plants; concentrated sources include willow bark and oil of wintergreen.

Salinger, J(erome) D(avid) (1919–) US writer. He wrote the classic novel of mid-20th-century adolescence *The Catcher in the Rye* (1951). He developed his lyrical Zen themes in *Franny and Zooey* (1961), *Raise High the Roof Beam, Carpenters*, and *Seymour: An Introduction* (1963). Some of his best short stories, such as 'For Esmé – With Love and Squalor', are collected in *Nine Stories* (1953).

Salisbury, Robert Arthur Talbot Gascoyne-Cecil, 3rd Marquess of Salisbury (1830–1903) British Conservative politician. He entered the Commons in 1853 and succeeded to his title in 1868. As foreign secretary 1878–80, he took part in the Congress of Berlin, and as prime minister 1885–86, 1886–92, and 1895–1902 gave his main attention to foreign policy, remaining also as foreign secretary for most of this time.

Salisbury Plain undulating plateau between Salisbury and Devizes in Wiltshire, southwest England; area 775 sq km/300 sq mi. It rises to 235 m/770 ft in Westbury Down. Since the mid-19th century it has been a military training area. *Stonehenge stands on Salisbury Plain.

saliva in vertebrates, an alkaline secretion from the salivary glands that aids the swallowing and digestion of food in the mouth. In mammals, it contains the enzyme amylase, which converts starch to sugar. The salivary glands of mosquitoes and other blood-sucking insects produce *anticoagulants.

Salk, Jonas Edward (1914–1995) US physician and microbiologist. In 1954 he developed the original vaccine that led to virtual eradication of paralytic *polio in industrialized countries. He was director of the Salk Institute for Biological Studies, University of California, San Diego, 1963–75.

salmon any of the various bony fishes of the family Salmonidae. More specifically the name is applied to several species of game fishes of the genera Salmo and Oncorhynchus of North America and Eurasia that mature in the ocean but, to spawn, return to the freshwater streams where they were born. Their normal colour is silvery with a few dark spots, but the colour changes at the spawning season.

salmonella any of a very varied group of bacteria, genus *Salmonella*, that colonize the intestines of humans and some animals. Some strains cause typhoid and paratyphoid fevers, while others cause salmonella *food poisoning, which is characterized by stomach pains, vomiting, diarrhoea, and headache. It can be fatal in elderly people, but others usually recover in a few days without antibiotics. Most cases are caused by contaminated animal products, especially poultry meat.

salsify *or* **vegetable oyster** hardy biennial plant native to the Mediterranean region. Its white fleshy roots and spring shoots are cooked and eaten; the roots are said to taste like oysters. (*Tragopogon porrifolius*, family Compositae.)

salt in chemistry, any compound formed from an acid and a base through the replacement of all or part of the hydrogen in the acid by a metal or electropositive radical. **Common *salt** is sodium chloride.

salt, common *or* **sodium chloride** NaCl, white crystalline solid, found dissolved in seawater and as rock salt (the mineral halite) in large deposits and salt domes. Common salt is used extensively in the food industry as a preservative and for flavouring, and in the chemical industry in the making of chlorine and sodium.

Salt Lake City capital of *Utah, seat of Salt Lake County, on the River Jordan, 605 km/378 mi northwest of Denver, Colorado; population (2000 est) 181,700. It is the commercial centre and world capital of the Church of Jesus Christ of the Latter-day Saints (the *Mormon Church). Industries include service, government, and trade. Copper, silver, lead, zinc, coal, and iron mines are worked nearby. In 1995 Salt Lake City was chosen as the site for the 2002 Winter Olympic, and Paralympic, Games. It was incorporated in 1851 and became state capital in 1896, when Utah became a state.

salt marsh wetland with halophytic vegetation (tolerant to seawater). Salt marshes develop around estuaries and on the sheltered side of sand and shingle *spits. They are formed by the deposition of mud around salt-tolerant vegetation. This vegetation must tolerate being covered by seawater as well as being exposed to the air. It also traps mud as the tide comes in and out. This helps build up the salt marsh. Salt marshes usually have a network of creeks and drainage channels by which tidal waters enter and leave the marsh.

saltpetre *or* **potassium nitrate** KNO₃, compound used in making gunpowder (from about 1500). It occurs naturally, being deposited during dry periods in places with warm climates, such as India.

saluki ancient breed of hunting dog resembling the greyhound. It is about 65 cm/26 in high and has a silky coat, which is usually fawn, cream, or white.

Salvation Army Christian evangelical, social-service, and social-reform organization, originating in 1865 in London with the work of William *Booth. Originally called the Christian Revival Association, it was renamed the East London Christian Mission in 1870 and from 1878 has been known as the Salvation Army, now a worldwide organization. It has military titles for its officials, with a general in an overall command. It is well known for its brass bands and its weekly journal, the *War Cry*.

Salyut (Russian 'salute') series of seven space stations launched by the USSR 1971–86. *Salyut* was cylindrical in shape, 15 m/50 ft long, and weighed 19 tonnes. It housed two or three cosmonauts at a time, for missions lasting up to eight months.

Salzburg federal state of Austria, bounded by Bavaria to the northwest, Upper Austria to the north, Styria to the east, Carinthia to the south, and Tyrol to the southwest; area 7,154 sq km/2,762 sq mi; population (2001 est) 518,600. It lies mainly in the Salzburg Alps. Its capital is Salzburg. The main cities are Hallein, Badgastein, and Saalfelden.

Samara formerly **Kuibyshev** (1935–91), capital city and river port of Samara oblast (region), west-central Russian Federation; population (1996 est) 1,175,000. Samara is located on the River Volga and the main Trans-Siberian Railway, 820 km/510 mi southeast of Moscow. It is a major industrial centre, with large heavy-engineering industries (producing road vehicles and railway rolling stock), as well as chemical, oil-processing, wood-processing, and light industries.

Samaria region of ancient Israel. The town of Samaria (now **Sebastiyeh**) on the west bank of the River Jordan was the capital of Israel in the 10th–8th centuries BC. It was renamed **Sebarte** in the 1st century BC by the Roman administrator Herod the Great. Extensive remains have been excavated.

Samaritan members or descendants of the colonists forced to settle in Samaria (now northern Israel) by the Assyrians after their occupation of the ancient kingdom of Israel 722 BC. Samaritans adopted a form of Judaism, but adopted only the Pentateuch, the five books of Moses of the Old Testament, and regarded their temple on Mount Gerizim as the true sanctuary.

samarium chemical symbol Sm, hard, brittle, grey-white, metallic element of the *lanthanide series, atomic number 62, relative atomic mass 150.4. It is widely distributed in nature and is obtained commercially from the minerals monzanite and bastnaesite. It is used only occasionally in industry, mainly as a catalyst in organic reactions. Samarium was discovered by spectroscopic analysis of the mineral samarskite and named in 1879 by French chemist Paul Lecoq de Boisbaudran (1838–1912) after its source.

Samarkand Uzbek **Samarqand**, city in eastern Uzbekistan, capital of Samarkand wiloyat (region), near the River Zerafshan, 217 km/135 mi east of Bukhara; population (1999 est) 362,300. Industries include cotton-ginning, silk manufacture, production of foodstuffs, and engineering, especially the manufacture of tractor and motor car components. Samarkand is one of the oldest cities in Central Asia, dating from the 3rd or 4th millennium BC. The Registan – a collection of mosques, courtyards and former Muslim theological seminaries ('madrasahs') – forms the centrepiece of the historic town. A university, established in 1933, is situated here and there are also colleges specializing in agriculture, medicine, architecture and commerce.

samba Latin American ballroom dance; the music for this. Samba originated in Brazil and became popular in the West in the 1940s. There are several different samba rhythms; the *bossa nova is a samba-jazz fusion.

samizdat (Russian 'self-published') in the USSR and eastern Europe before the 1989 uprisings, written material circulated underground to evade state censorship; for example, reviews of Solzhenitzyn's banned novel *August 1914* (1972).

Samoa volcanic island chain in the southwestern Pacific. It is divided into Samoa and American Samoa.

Samoa
formerly **Western Samoa (until 1997)**
National name: *'O la Malo Tu To'atasi o Samoa/ Independent State of Samoa*

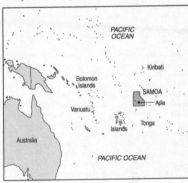

Area: 2,830 sq km/1,092 sq mi
Capital: Apia (on Upolu island) (and chief port)
Major towns/cities: Lalomanu, Tuasivi, Falealupo, Falelatai, Salotulafai, Taga
Physical features: comprises South Pacific islands of Savai'i and Upolu, with two smaller tropical islands and uninhabited islets; mountain ranges on main islands; coral reefs; over half forested
Head of state: King Malietoa Tanumafili II from 1962
Head of government: Tuila'epa Sa'ilele Malielegaoi from 1998
Political system: liberal democracy
Political executive: parliamentary
Political parties: Human Rights Protection Party (HRPP), led by Tofilau Eti Alesana, centrist; Samoa Democratic Party (SDP), led by Le Tagaloa Pita;

Samoa National Development Party (SNDP), led by Tupuola Taisi Efi and Va'ai Kolone, conservative. All 'parties' are personality-based groupings
Currency: tala, or Samoan dollar
GNI per capita (PPP): (US$) 5,350 (2002 est)
Exports: fresh fish, coconut oil and cream, beer, cigarettes, taro, copra, cocoa, bananas, timber. Principal market: Australia 64.7% (2001)
Population: 178,000 (2003 est)
Language: English, Samoan (both official)
Religion: Congregationalist; also Roman Catholic, Methodist
Life expectancy: 67 (men); 74 (women) (2000–05)
Chronology
c. 1000 BC: Settled by Polynesians from Tonga.
AD 950–1250: Ruled by Tongan invaders; the Matai (chiefly) system was developed.
15th century: United under the Samoan Queen Salamasina.
1722: Visited by Dutch traders.
1768: Visited by the French navigator Louis Antoine de Bougainville.
1830: Christian mission established and islanders were soon converted to Christianity.
1887–89: Samoan rebellion against German attempt to depose paramount ruler and install its own puppet regime.
1889: Under the terms of the Act of Berlin, Germany took control of the nine islands of Western Samoa, while the USA was granted American Samoa, and Britain Tonga and the Solomon Islands.
1900s: More than 2,000 Chinese brought in to work coconut plantations.
1914: Occupied by New Zealand on the outbreak of World War I.
1918: Nearly a quarter of the population died in an influenza epidemic.
1920s: Development of nationalist movement, the Mau, which resorted to civil disobedience.
1920–61: Administered by New Zealand under League of Nations and, later, United Nations mandate.
1959: Local government established, headed by chief minister Fiame Mata'afa Mulinu'u.
1961: Referendum favoured independence.
1962: King Malietoa Tanumafili succeeded to the throne.
1962: Independence achieved within Commonwealth, with Mata'afa as prime minister, a position he retained (apart from a short break 1970–73) until his death in 1975.
1990: Universal adult suffrage was introduced and the power of Matai (elected clan leaders) reduced.
1991: Major damage was caused by 'Cyclone Val'.
1997: Name was changed officially from Western Samoa to Samoa, despite protests from American Samoa that it would undermine American Samoa's identity.
1998: Tuila'epa Sa'ilele Malielegaoi, of the HRPP, became the new prime minister.
2001: Malielegaoi was re-elected.
Samoa, American group of islands 4,200 km/2,610 mi south of Hawaii, administered by the USA; area 200 sq km/77 sq mi; population (2000 est) 57,300. The capital is Pago Pago. Exports include canned tuna (over 90% of exports), handicrafts, and copra. The main languages are Samoan and English; the principal religion is Christianity.

samphire *or* **glasswort** *or* **sea asparagus** perennial plant found on sea cliffs and coastlines in Europe. The aromatic, salty leaves are fleshy and sharply pointed; the flowers grow in yellow-green open clusters. Samphire is used in salads, or pickled. (*Crithmum maritimum*, family Umbelliferae.)

Sampras, Pete (1971–) US tennis player. At the age of 19 years and 28 days, he became the youngest winner of the US Open in 1990. A fine serve-and-volleyer, Sampras also won the inaugural Grand Slam Cup in Munich in 1990. In 1998 he finished at the top of the ATP men's world rankings for an unprecedented sixth consecutive year. In 2000 he won his 7th Wimbledon men's singles title, equalling the record established by English player William Renshaw between 1881 and 1889. It was Sampras's 13th Grand Slam singles title, an unprecedented achievement in the men's game. He didn't win another tournament until September 2002, when he triumphed in the US Open for the fifth time and claimed his 14th Grand Slam.

samurai *or* **bushi** (Japanese 'one who serves') Japanese term for the warrior class which became the ruling military elite for almost 700 years. A samurai was an armed retainer of a *daimyo* (large landowner) with specific duties and privileges and a strict code of honour. The system was abolished in 1869 and all samurai were pensioned off by the government.

San'a *or* **Sana'a** capital of Yemen, southwest Arabia, 320 km/200 mi north of Aden on the central plateau, 2,210 m/7,250 ft above sea level; population (1995) 972,000. A walled city, with fine mosques and traditional architecture, it is rapidly being modernized. Weaving and jewellery are local handicrafts.

San Andreas Fault geological fault stretching for 1,125 km/700 mi northwest–southeast through the state of California, USA. It marks a conservative plate margin, where two plates slide past each other (see *plate tectonics).

San Marino
National name: *Serenissima Repubblica di San Marino/ Most Serene Republic of San Marino*

Area: 61 sq km/24 sq mi
Capital: San Marino

Major towns/cities: Serravalle, Faetano, Fiorentino, Borgo Maggiore, Domagnano

Physical features: the slope of Mount Titano

Heads of state and government: Guiseppe Arzilli and Roberto Raschi from 2004

Political system: liberal democracy

Political executive: parliamentary

Political parties: San Marino Christian Democrat Party (PDCS), Christian centrist; Progressive Democratic Party (PDP) (formerly the Communist Party: PCS), moderate left wing; Socialist Party (PS), left of centre

Currency: euro

GNI per capita (PPP): (US$) 26,960 (2001)

Exports: wood machinery, chemicals, wine, olive oil, textiles, tiles, ceramics, varnishes, building stone, lime, chestnuts, hides. Principal market: Italy

Population: 28,000 (2003 est)

Language: Italian (official)

Religion: Roman Catholic 95%

Life expectancy: 78 (men); 85 (women) (2001 est)

Chronology

c. **AD 301:** Founded as a republic (the world's oldest surviving) by St Marinus and a group of Christians who settled there to escape persecution.

12th century: Self-governing commune.

1600: Statutes (constitution) provided for a parliamentary form of government, based around the Great and General Council.

1815: Independent status of the republic recognized by the Congress of Vienna.

1862: Treaty with Italy signed; independence recognized under Italy's protection.

1945–57: Communist–Socialist administration in power, eventually ousted in a bloodless 'revolution'.

1957–86: Governed by a series of left-wing and centre-left coalitions.

1971: Treaty with Italy renewed.

1992: San Marino joined the United Nations (UN).

1998: The ruling PDCS–PSS coalition remained in power after a general election.

2000: Gian Franco Terenzi and Enzo Colombini were appointed as captains regent.

sanction economic or military measure taken by a state or number of states to enforce international law. The first use of sanctions, as a trade embargo, was the attempted economic boycott of Italy 1935–36 during the Abyssinian War by the League of Nations.

sand loose grains of rock, 0.0625–2.00 mm/0.0025–0.08 in in diameter, consisting most commonly of *quartz, but owing their varying colour to mixtures of other minerals. Sand is used in cement-making, as an abrasive, in glass-making, and for other purposes.

Sand, George (1804–1876) pen-name of Amandine Aurore Lucie Dupin, French author. Her prolific literary output was often autobiographical. In 1831 she left her husband after nine years of marriage and, while living in Paris as a writer, had love affairs with Alfred de Musset, Chopin, and others. Her first novel *Indiana* (1832) was a plea for women's right to independence.

sandalwood fragrant heartwood of any of several Asiatic and Australian trees, used for ornamental carving, in perfume, and burned as incense. (Genus *Santalum*, family Santalaceae.)

sandbar ridge of sand built up by the currents across the mouth of a river or bay. A sandbar may be entirely

underwater or it may form an elongated island that breaks the surface. A sandbar stretching out from a headland is a **sand spit**.

sandgrouse any bird of the family Pteroclidae, order Columbiformes. They look like long-tailed grouse, but are actually closely related to pigeons. They live in warm, dry areas of Europe, Asia, and Africa and have long wings, short legs and bills, a wedge-shaped tail, and thick skin. They are sandy coloured and feed on vegetable matter and insects.

sand hopper *or* **beachflea** any of various small crustaceans belonging to the order Amphipeda, with laterally compressed bodies, that live in beach sand and jump like fleas. The eastern sand hopper *Orchestia agilis* of North America is about 1.3 cm/0.5 in long.

San Diego city and US naval air station, on the Pacific Ocean, and on the border of Mexico, in California, USA; population (2000 est) 1,223,400. San Diego is linked to Tijuana, Mexico, by a 26 km/16 mi transit line (1981) popular with tourists. It is an important fishing port. Manufacturing includes aerospace and electronic equipment, metal fabrication, printing and publishing, seafood-canning, and shipbuilding. San Diego is the oldest Spanish settlement in California; a Spanish mission and fort were established here in 1769.

Sandinista member of a Nicaraguan left-wing organization (Sandinist National Liberation Front, FSLN) named after Augusto César Sandino, a guerrilla leader killed in 1934. It was formed in 1962 and obtained widespread support from the trade unions, the church, and the middle classes, which enabled it to overthrow the regime of General Anastasio Somoza in July 1979. The FSLN dominated the Nicaraguan government and fought a civil war against US-backed Contra guerrillas until 1988. The FSLN was defeated in elections of 1990 by a US-backed coalition, but remained the party with the largest number of seats.

sandpiper shorebird with a long, slender bill, which is compressed and grooved at the tip. They belong to the family Scolopacidae, which includes godwits, *curlews, and *snipes, order Charadriiformes.

sandstone *sedimentary rocks formed from the consolidation of sand, with sand-sized grains (0.0625–2 mm/0.0025–0.08 in) in a matrix or cement. Their principal component is quartz. Sandstones are commonly permeable and porous, and may form freshwater *aquifers. They are mainly used as building materials.

San Francisco chief Pacific port in California, USA, on the tip of a peninsula in San Francisco Bay; population (1996 est) 735,300. The entrance channel from the Pacific to San Francisco Bay was named the Golden Gate in 1846; its strait was crossed in 1937 by the world's second-longest single-span bridge, 1,280 m/4,200 ft in length. Manufactured goods include textiles, machinery and metalware, electrical equipment, petroleum products, and pharmaceuticals. San Francisco is also a financial, trade, corporate, and diversified service centre. Tourism is a major industry. A Spanish fort (the Presidio) and the San Francisco de Asis Mission were established here in 1776. San Francisco has the largest Chinese community outside Asia.

Sanger, Frederick (1918–) English biochemist. He was awarded the Nobel Prize for Chemistry in 1958 for determining the structure of *insulin, and again in

801

1980 for work on the chemical structure of *genes. He was the first person to be awarded the chemistry prize twice.

Sangha in Buddhism, the monastic orders, one of the Three Treasures, or Three Refuges, of Buddhism (the other two are Buddha and the teaching, or dharma). The term Sangha is sometimes used more generally by Mahayana Buddhists to include all followers, including the Buddhist laity.

San José capital of Costa Rica, and of San José province; population (1999 est) 341,700. It is situated in the broad fertile valley of the central plateau. Products include coffee, cocoa, sugar cane, textiles, and pharmaceuticals. There is a cathedral, and the University of Costa Rica, which was founded in 1843. San José was founded in 1737 and became capital in 1823, replacing the former capital Cartago because it had a better all-year-round climate.

San José city in Santa Clara County, California, at the head of the southern arm of San Francisco Bay; population (2000 est) 894,900. It is situated at one end of 'Silicon Valley', the site of many high-technology electronic firms turning out semiconductors and other computer components. There are also electrical, aerospace, missile, rubber, metal, and machine industries, and it is a commercial and transportation centre for orchard crops and wines produced in the area.

San Juan industrial city and capital of Puerto Rico; population (2000 est) 422,000; metropolitan area (1998 est) 2,004,100. It is a major port, exporting sugar, tobacco, coffee, and tropical fruits, mostly to the US mainland, and provides the world's busiest cruise-ship base. It stands on an island joined by a bridge to the north coast of Puerto Rico. Industries include tourism, banking, metalworking, publishing, cigars, sugar, and clothing. Products include chemicals, pharmaceuticals, machine tools, electronic equipment, textiles, cement, metals, plastics, and rum.

San Marino capital of the republic of San Marino; population (1996) 4,372. It is on the western slope of Monte Titano, 19 km/12 mi southwest of Rimini. Its economy relies on tourism. It is encircled by triple walls, with three fortresses, the 13th-century Rocca Guaita, Rocca Cesta, and Rocca Montale, and the 14th-century Church of San Francesco.

sannyasin in Hinduism, a person who has renounced worldly goods to live a life of asceticism and seek *moksha*, or liberation from reincarnation, through meditation and prayer.

San Salvador capital of El Salvador and of San Salvador department; situated at the foot of San Salvador volcano (2,548 m/8,360 ft) on the River Acelhuate, 48 km/30 mi from the Pacific Ocean; population (1992) 422,600. Industries include coffee, food-processing, pharmaceuticals, and textiles. One-third of the country's industrial output comes from the city. Founded in 1525, it was destroyed by an earthquake in 1854 and rebuilt on the present site. It is now a modern city with architecture conditioned to seismic activity, to which the region is prone, although many buildings collapsed during a further earthquake in 1986.

sans-culotte (French 'without knee breeches') in the French Revolution, a member of the working classes, who wore trousers, as opposed to the aristocracy and

bourgeoisie, who wore knee breeches. In Paris, the sans-culottes, who drew their support predominantly from apprentices, small shopkeepers, craftspeople, and the unemployed, comprised a large armed force that could be mobilized by radical politicians, for example in the *Jacobin seizure of power from the *Girondins in June 1793. Their fate was sealed by the fall of the Jacobins between 1794 and 1795.

Sanskrit the dominant classical language of the Indian subcontinent, a member of the Indo-Iranian group of the Indo-European language family, and the sacred language of Hinduism. The oldest form of Sanskrit is **Vedic**, the variety used in the *Vedas* and *Upanishads* (about 1500–700 BC).

Santa Anna, Antonio López de (*c.* 1795–1876) Mexican revolutionary. He became general and dictator of Mexico for most of the years between 1824 and 1855. He led the attack on the *Alamo fort in Texas in 1836.

Santa Fe capital of *New Mexico, in Santa Fe County, on the Santa Fe River, 65 km/40 mi west of Las Vegas; population (2000 est) 62,200. It is situated in the Rio Grande Valley, over 2,000 m/6,500 ft above sea level, on the western slopes of the Sangre de Cristo Mountains. Santa Fe is the cultural and tourist capital of the southwest, home to many artists, theatre, and opera. Precision instruments, pottery, and American Indian jewellery and textiles are produced.

Santiago capital of Chile, on the Mapocho River; population (1999 est) 4,735,000; metropolitan area (1999 est) 6,013,200). It is the fifth largest city in South America and the country's cultural, commercial, and manufacturing centre. Industries include textiles, chemicals, and food processing. It has three universities, and several theatres, libraries, and museums.

Santiago second-largest city in the Dominican Republic; population (1991 est) 375,000. It is a processing and trading centre for sugar, coffee, and cacao.

Santiago de Compostela capital of *Galicia autonomous community, in the province of La Coruña, northwest Spain; population (1991) 87,500. Textiles, chocolate, and soap are manufactured here, and there is a trade in agricultural produce. The 11th-century cathedral was reputedly built over the grave of Sant Iago el Mayor (St *James the Great), patron saint of Spain, and was a world-famous centre for medieval pilgrims. Santiago is the seat of an archbishop, and there is also a university, founded in 1532.

Santo Domingo capital and chief sea port of the Dominican Republic; population (1993 est) 1,609,700; metropolitan area (1993 est) 2,138,300. Industries include food processing, distilling, and tanning. Founded in 1496 by Bartolomeo, brother of the Italian explorer Christopher Columbus, it is the oldest colonial city in the Americas. Its cathedral was built 1515–40, and contains the tomb of Christopher Columbus.

Saône river in eastern France, rising in the Vosges Mountains and flowing 480 km/300 mi to join the *Rhône at Lyon. After rising in the Faucilles Mountains of the Vosges, it flows south past Gray, Chalon-sur-Saône, and Mâçon. The chief tributaries are the Doubs and the Ognon. It is connected by canal with the rivers Loire, Seine, Meuse, Moselle, and Rhine.

São Paulo industrial city and capital of São Paulo state, southeast Brazil, 72 km/45 mi northwest of its port Santos, and 400 km/249 mi southwest of Rio de Janeiro; population (2001 est) 9,785,600; metropolitan area (2001 est) 17,833,800. It is Latin America's second-largest city after Mexico City and is 900 m/3,000 ft above sea level and 2° south of the Tropic of Capricorn. São Paulo is also South America's leading industrial city, producing electronic equipment, steel, motor vehicles, chemicals, and packed meat. It is Brazil's chief financial centre as well as the centre of the country's coffee trade.

São Tomé port and capital of São Tomé e Príncipe, on the northeast coast of São Tomé island, Gulf of Guinea; population (1991) 43,400. It exports sugar, cocoa, and coffee.

São Tomé and Príncipe

National name: *República Democrática de São Tomé e Príncipe/Democratic Republic of São Tomé and Príncipe*

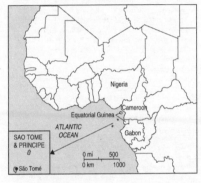

Area: 1,000 sq km/386 sq mi
Capital: São Tomé
Major towns/cities: Santo António, Santana, Porto-Alegre, Trinidade, Neves, Santo Amaro
Physical features: comprises two main islands and several smaller ones, all volcanic; thickly forested and fertile
Head of state: Fradique de Menezes from 2001
Head of government: Damião Vaz d'Almeida from 2004
Political system: emergent democracy
Political executive: limited presidency
Political parties: Movement for the Liberation of São Tomé e Príncipe–Social Democratic Party (MLSTP–PSD), nationalist socialist; Democratic Convergence Party–Reflection Group (PCD–GR), moderate left of centre; Independent Democratic Action (ADI), centrist
Currency: dobra
GNI per capita (PPP): (US$) 1,310 (2002 est)
Exports: cocoa, copra, coffee, bananas, palm oil. Principal market: the Netherlands 27.3% (2001)
Population: 161,000 (2003 est)
Language: Portuguese (official), Fang (a Bantu language), Lungwa São Tomé (a Portuguese Creole)
Religion: Roman Catholic 80%, animist
Life expectancy: 67 (men); 73 (women) (2000–05)

Chronology
1471: First visited by the Portuguese, who imported convicts and slaves to work on sugar plantations in the formerly uninhabited islands.
1522: Became a province of Portugal.
1530: Slaves successfully revolted, forcing plantation owners to flee to Brazil; thereafter became a key staging post for Congo-Americas slave trade.
19th century: Forced contract labour used to work coffee and cocoa plantations.
1953: More than 1,000 striking plantation workers gunned down by Portuguese troops.
1960: First political party formed, the forerunner of the socialist-nationalist Movement for the Liberation of São Tomé e Príncipe (MLSTP).
1974: Military coup in Portugal led to strikes, demonstrations, and army mutiny in São Tomé; thousands of Portuguese settlers fled the country.
1975: Independence achieved, with Manuel Pinto da Costa (MLSTP) as president; close links developed with communist bloc, and plantations nationalized.
1984: Formally declared a nonaligned state as economy deteriorated.
1988: Coup attempt against da Costa foiled by Angolan and East European troops.
1990: Influenced by collapse of communism in Eastern Europe, MLSTP abandoned Marxism; a new pluralist constitution was approved in a referendum.
1991: First multiparty elections.
1994: MLSTP returned to power with Carlos da Graca as prime minister.
1998: MLSTP–PSD won an absolute majority in the assembly.
2000: Guilherme Posser de Costa became prime minister.
2003: A coup by the armed forces led by Fernando Pereira against the elected government ended peacefully as President Menezes, backed by Nigeria, agreed to an amnesty for the mutineers and to the replacement of ministers. The political turmoil was linked to control of the country's abundant potential offshore oil resources.

sap fluids that circulate through *vascular plants, especially woody ones. Sap carries water and food to plant tissues. Sap contains alkaloids, protein, and starch; it can be milky (as in rubber trees), resinous (as in pines), or syrupy (as in maples).

saponification in chemistry, the *hydrolysis (splitting) of an *ester by treatment with a strong alkali, resulting in the liberation of the alcohol from which the ester had been derived and a salt of the constituent fatty acid. The process is used in the manufacture of soap.

sapphire deep-blue, transparent gem variety of the mineral *corundum Al_2O_3, aluminium oxide. Small amounts of iron and titanium give it its colour. A corundum gem of any colour except red (which is a ruby) can be called a sapphire; for example, yellow sapphire.

Sappho (*c.* 610–*c.* 580 BC) Greek lyric poet. A native of Lesbos and contemporary of the poet Alcaeus, she was famed for her female eroticism (hence lesbianism). The surviving fragments of her poems express a keen sense of loss, and delight in the worship of the goddess *Aphrodite.

saprotroph formerly **saprophyte**, organism that feeds on the excrement or the dead bodies or tissues of others. They include most fungi (the rest being parasites); many bacteria and protozoa; animals such as dung beetles and vultures; and a few unusual plants, including several orchids. Saprotrophs cannot make food for themselves, so they are a type of *heterotroph. They are useful scavengers, and in sewage farms and refuse dumps break down organic matter into nutrients easily assimilable by green plants.

Saracen ancient Greek and Roman term for an Arab, used in the Middle Ages by Europeans for all Muslims. The equivalent term used in Spain was *Moor.

Sarajevo capital of Bosnia-Herzegovina; population (1991) 526,000. Industries include engineering, brewing, chemicals, carpets, and ceramics. A Bosnian, Gavrilo Princip, assassinated Archduke *Franz Ferdinand here in 1914, thereby precipitating World War I. From April 1992 the city was the target of a siege by Bosnian Serb forces in their fight to carve up the newly independent republic. A United Nations ultimatum and the threat of NATO bombing led to a ceasefire February 1994 and the effective end of the siege as Serbian heavy weaponry was withdrawn from the high points surrounding the city.

Sarawak state of Malaysia, in the northwest of the island of Borneo; area 124,400 sq km/48,018 sq mi; population (2000 est) 2,012,600 (24 ethnic groups make up almost half this number). The capital is Kuching. The economy is based mainly on agriculture, and commercial crops include rubber, pepper, and sago. Rice is grown widely as a subsistence crop. Industries include the processing of these crops, as well as sawmilling of tropical hardwoods, oil refining, and the manufacture of textiles, soap, and tiles. Navigable rivers form an important means of communication.

sarcoma malignant *tumour arising from the fat, muscles, bones, cartilage, or blood and lymph vessels and connective tissues. Sarcomas are much less common than *carcinomas.

sardine common name for various small fishes (*pilchards) in the herring family.

Sardinia Italian **Sardegna**, mountainous island and special autonomous region of Italy, about 240 km/150 mi southwest of the Orbetello promontory in Tuscany; area 24,090 sq km/9,301 sq mi; population (2001 est) 1,599,500. It is the second-largest Mediterranean island and comprises the provinces of Cagliari, Nuoro, Oristano, and Sassari; its capital is Cagliari. Cork, fruit, grain, tobacco, minerals (lead, zinc, manganese), and petrochemicals are exported. Features include the Costa Smeralda (Emerald Coast) tourist area in the northeast, and thousands of *nuraghi*, fortified Bronze Age dwellings unique to the island. After centuries of foreign rule, Sardinia became linked with Piedmont in 1720, and this dual kingdom became the basis of a united Italy in 1861.

Sargent, John Singer (1856–1925) US portrait painter. Born in Florence, Italy, of American parents, he studied there and in Paris, and settled in England in 1885. He quickly became a fashionable and prolific painter, though not in the sense that he flattered: he brilliantly depicted affluent late Victorian and Edwardian society, British and American. His portrait of Mme Gautreau, *Madame X* (1884; Metropolitan Museum of Art, New York), criticized for its impropriety when first shown in Paris, is one of his best-known works.

SARS acronym for *severe acute respiratory syndrome* highly infectious disease with symptoms similar to influenza, notably chills, headaches, muscle pains, a sore throat, and a high fever. Pneumonia develops as the disease progresses, and can result in death – the mortality rate is estimated by the World Health Organization (WHO) at around 15%. First identified in 2003, there is no known cure or vaccine for the disease. SARS is caused by a type of coronavirus, which usually produces colds in humans but severe conditions such as pneumonia and diarrhoea in animals. The SARS virus was thought to have mutated to allow it to jump the species barrier from animals to humans. The disease spreads by victims being in close proximity to an infected person. The incubation period of SARS varies but is on average between two and ten days. The risk of death increases with age and the mortality rate is as high as 50% in those over 60 years of age. The first outbreak of SARS is thought to have been near Foshan in the southern Chinese province of Guangdong in November 2002, but the disease only came to public attention in February 2003 as it rapidly spread worldwide due to the use of air travel. By the end of the 2003 outbreak, over 8,000 victims of SARS had been reported globally, of whom over 700 died since the outbreak began.

Sartre, Jean-Paul (1905–1980) French author and philosopher. He was a leading proponent of *existentialism. He published his first novel, *La Nausée/ Nausea* (1937), followed by the trilogy *Les Chemins de la liberté/Roads to Freedom* (1944–45) and many plays, including *Les Mouches/The Flies* (1943), *Huis clos/ In Camera* (1944), and *Les Séquestrés d'Altona/ The Condemned of Altona* (1960). *L'Etre et le néant/ Being and Nothingness* (1943), his first major philosophical work, sets out a radical doctrine of human freedom. In the later work *Critique de la raison dialectique/Critique of Dialectical Reason* (1960) he tried to produce a fusion of existentialism and Marxism. He was awarded the Nobel Prize for Literature in 1964, which he declined.

Saskatchewan called 'Canada's breadbasket' and 'Land of the Living Skies', (Cree *Kis-is-ska-tche-wan* 'swift flowing') province of west-central Canada, the middle Prairie Province, bordered to the west by Alberta and to the east by Manitoba. To the north of Saskatchewan (above the 60th parallel) are the Northwest Territories, while to the south (below the 49th parallel) lie the US states of North Dakota and Montana; area 652,300 sq km/251,854 sq mi; population (2001 est) 1,011,800. The capital is Regina. Towns and cities include Saskatoon (the largest city), Moose Jaw, Prince Albert, Yorkton, and Swift Current. Industries include extraction of oil, natural gas, uranium, zinc, potash, copper, and helium; and manufacture of cement, chemicals, fertilizers, and wood products. Wheat, oats, barley, rye, and flax are grown, and there is cattle-rearing and dairying.

Sassanian Empire Persian empire founded AD 224 by Ardashir, a chieftain in the area of what is now Fars, in Iran, who had taken over *Parthia; it was named after his grandfather, Sasan. The capital was Ctesiphon, near modern *Baghdad, Iraq. After a rapid period of expansion, when it contested supremacy with Rome, it was destroyed in 637 by Muslim Arabs at the Battle of Qadisiya.

Sassoon, Siegfried Loraine (1886–1967) English poet. His anti-war poems which appeared in *The Old Huntsman* (1917), *Counter-Attack* (1918), and later volumes, were begun in the trenches during World War I and express the disillusionment of his generation. His later poetry tended towards the reflective and the spiritual. His three fictionalized autobiographical studies, including *Memoirs of a Fox-Hunting Man* (1928), *Memoirs of an Infantry Officer* (1930), and *Sherston's Progress* (1936), were published together as *The Complete Memoirs of George Sherston* (1937).

Satan a name for the *Devil.

satellite any small body that orbits a larger one. Natural satellites that orbit planets are called **moons**. The first **artificial satellite**, Sputnik 1, was launched into orbit around the Earth by the USSR in 1957. Artificial satellites can transmit data from one place on Earth to another, or from space to Earth. Satellite applications include science, communications, weather forecasting, and military use.

satellite television transmission of broadcast signals through artificial communications satellites. Mainly positioned in *geostationary orbit, satellites have been used since the 1960s to relay television pictures around the world. Higher-power satellites have more recently been developed to broadcast signals to cable systems or directly to people's homes.

Satie, Erik (Alfred Leslie) (1866–1925) French composer. His piano pieces, such as the three *Gymnopédies* (1888), are precise and tinged with melancholy, and parody romantic expression with surreal commentary. His aesthetic of ironic simplicity, as in the *Messe des pauvres/Poor People's Mass* (1895), acted as a nationalist antidote to the perceived excesses of German Romanticism.

satire *genre of literary or dramatic work that ridicules human pretensions or exposes social evils. Satire is related to *parody in its intention to mock, but satire tends to be more subtle and to mock an attitude or a belief, whereas parody tends to mock a particular work (such as a poem) by imitating its style, often with purely comic intent.

satrap title of a provincial governor in ancient Persia. Under Darius I, the Persian Empire was divided between some 20 satraps, each owing allegiance only to the king.

saturated fatty acid *fatty acid in which there are no double bonds in the hydrocarbon chain.

saturated solution in physics and chemistry, a solution obtained when a solvent (liquid) can dissolve no more of a solute (usually a solid) at a particular temperature. Normally, a slight fall in temperature causes some of the solute to crystallize out of solution. If this does not happen the phenomenon is called supercooling, and the solution is said to be supersaturated.

Saturn sixth planet from the Sun, and the second-largest in the Solar System, encircled by bright and easily visible equatorial rings. Viewed through a telescope it is ochre. Its polar diameter is 12,000 km/7,450 mi smaller than its equatorial diameter, a result of its fast rotation and low density, the lowest of any planet. Its mass is 95 times that of the Earth and its magnetic field 1,000 times stronger. **mean distance from the Sun:** 1.427 billion km/0.886 billion mi

equatorial diameter: 120,000 km/75,000 mi **rotational period:** 10 hours 14 minutes at equator, 10 hours 40 minutes at higher latitudes **year:** 29.46 Earth years **atmosphere:** visible surface consists of swirling clouds, probably made of frozen ammonia at a temperature of –170 °C/–274 °F, although the markings in the clouds are not as prominent as Jupiter's. The *Voyager probes, visiting in 1980 and 1981, found winds reaching 1,800 kph/1,100 mph **surface:** Saturn is believed to have a small core of rock and iron, encased in ice and topped by a deep layer of liquid hydrogen **satellites:** 22 known moons, more than for any other planet. The largest moon, *Titan, has a dense atmosphere. Other satellites include Epimetheus, Janus, Pandora, and Prometheus **rings:** The rings visible from Earth begin about 14,000 km/9,000 mi from the planet's cloudtops and extend out to about 76,000 km/47,000 mi. Made of small chunks of ice and rock (averaging 1 m/3.3 ft across), they are 275,000 km/170,000 mi rim to rim, but only 100 m/300 ft thick. The Voyager probes showed that the rings actually consist of thousands of closely spaced ringlets, looking like the grooves in a gramophone record.

Saturn or Saturnus in Roman mythology, the god of agriculture, identified by the Romans with the Greek god *Kronos. His period of rule was the ancient Golden Age, when he introduced social order and the arts of civilization. Saturn was dethroned by his sons Jupiter, Neptune, and Dis. At the **Saturnalia**, his festival in December, gifts were exchanged, and slaves were briefly treated as their masters' equals.

satyagraha (Sanskrit 'insistence on truth') nonviolent resistance to British rule in India, as employed by Mahatma *Gandhi from 1918 to press for political reform; the idea owes much to the Russian writer Leo *Tolstoy.

satyr in Greek mythology, a lustful, drunken woodland creature, half man and half beast, characterized by pointed ears, two horns on the forehead, and a tail. Satyrs attended the god of wine, *Dionysus. They represented the vital powers of nature. Roman writers confused the satyr with their goat-footed Italian *Faunus.

Saudi Arabia

National name: *Al-Mamlaka al-'Arabiyya as-Sa'udiyya/ Kingdom of Saudi Arabia*

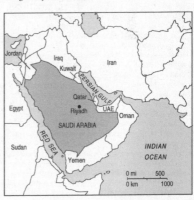

805

Area: 2,200,518 sq km/849,620 sq mi
Capital: Riyadh
Major towns/cities: Jiddah, Mecca, Medina, Ta'if, Dammam, Hofuf, Tabuk, Buraida
Major ports: Jiddah, Dammam, Jubail, Jizan, Yanbu
Physical features: desert, sloping to the Gulf from a height of 2,750 m/9,000 ft in the west
Head of state and government: King Fahd Ibn Abdul Aziz from 1982
Political system: absolutist
Political executive: absolute
Political parties: none
Currency: riyal
GNI per capita (PPP): (US$) 11,480 (2002 est)
Exports: crude and refined petroleum, petrochemicals, wheat. Principal market: USA 17.3% (2000)
Population: 24,217,000 (2003 est)
Language: Arabic (official), English
Religion: Sunni Muslim 85%; there is a Shiite minority
Life expectancy: 71 (men); 74 (women) (2000–05)
Chronology
622: Muhammad began to unite Arabs in Muslim faith.
7th–8th centuries: Muslim Empire expanded, ultimately stretching from India to Spain, with Arabia itself being relegated to a subordinate part.
12th century: Decline of Muslim Empire; Arabia grew isolated and internal divisions multiplied.
13th century: Mameluke sultans of Egypt became nominal overlords of Hejaz in western Arabia.
1517: Hejaz became a nominal part of the Ottoman Empire after the Turks conquered Egypt.
18th century: Al Saud family united tribes of Nejd in central Arabia in support of the Wahhabi religious movement.
c. 1830: The Al Saud established Riyadh as the Wahhabi capital.
c. 1870: Turks took effective control of Hejaz and also Hasa on the Gulf.
late 19th century: Rival Wahhabi dynasty of Ibn Rashid became leaders of Nejd.
1902: Ibn Saud organized Bedouin revolt and regained Riyadh.
1913: Ibn Saud completed the reconquest of Hasa from Turks.
1915: Britain recognized Ibn Saud as emir of Nejd and Hasa.
1916–18: British-backed revolt, under aegis of Sharif Hussein of Mecca, expelled Turks from Arabia.
1919–25: Ibn Saud fought and defeated Sharif Hussein and took control of Hejaz.
1926: Proclamation of Ibn Saud as king of Hejaz and Nejd.
1932: Hejaz and Nejd renamed the United Kingdom of Saudi Arabia.
1933: Saudi Arabia allowed US-owned Standard Oil Company to prospect for oil, which was discovered in Hasa in 1938.
1939–45: Although officially neutral in World War II, Saudi Arabia received subsidies from USA and Britain.
1940s: Commercial exploitation of oil began, bringing great prosperity.
1987: Rioting by Iranian pilgrims caused 400 deaths in Mecca and a breach in diplomatic relations with Iran.
1990: Iraqi troops invaded Kuwait and massed on the Saudi Arabian border, prompting King Fahd to call for assistance from US and UK forces.

1991: Saudi Arabia fought on the Allied side against Iraq in the Gulf War.
1992: Under international pressure to move towards democracy, King Fahd formed a 'consultative council' to assist in the government of the kingdom.
1995: King Fahd had a stroke and Crown Prince Abdullah had effective power.
2003: Residential compounds in Riyadh were attacked by suicide bombers linked to the al-Qaeda international Islamic terrorist network, killing over 50 people.

Saul (lived 11th century BC) In the Old Testament, the first king of Israel. He was anointed by Samuel and warred successfully against the neighbouring Ammonites and Philistines, but fell from God's favour in his battle against the Amalekites. He became jealous and suspicious of *David and turned against him and Samuel. After being wounded in battle with the Philistines, in which his three sons died, he committed suicide.

savannah *or* **savanna** extensive open tropical grasslands, with scattered trees and shrubs. Savannahs cover large areas of Africa, North and South America, and northern Australia. The soil is acidic and sandy and generally considered suitable only as pasture for low-density grazing.

Savimbi, Jonas Malheiro (1934–2002) Angolan soldier and right-wing revolutionary, founder and leader of the National Union for the Total Independence of Angola (UNITA). From 1975 UNITA, under Savimbi's leadership, tried to overthrow the government. A peace agreement was signed in 1994. Savimbi rejected the offer of vice presidency in a coalition government in 1996; however, in 1998, UNITA was demilitarized and accepted as a national political party.

Savonarola, Girolamo (1452–1498) Italian reformer, a Dominican friar and an eloquent preacher. His crusade against political and religious corruption won him popular support, and in 1494 he led a revolt in Florence that expelled the ruling Medici family and established a democratic republic. His denunciations of Pope *Alexander VI led to his excommunication 1497, and in 1498 he was arrested, tortured, hanged, and burned for heresy.

Savoy area of France between the Alps, Lake Geneva, and the River Rhône. A medieval duchy, it was made into the *départements* of Savoie and Haute-Savoie, in the Rhône-Alpes region.

sawfish any fish of the order Pristiformes of large, sharklike *rays, characterized by a flat, sawlike snout edged with teeth. The common sawfish *Pristis pectinatus*, also called the smalltooth, is more than 6 m/19 ft long. It has some 24 teeth along an elongated snout (2 m/6 ft) that can be used as a weapon.

sawfly any of several families of insects of the order Hymenoptera, related to bees, wasps, and ants, but lacking a 'waist' on the body. The egg-laying tube (ovipositor) of the female is surrounded by a pair of sawlike organs, which it uses to make a slit in a plant stem to lay its eggs. Horntails are closely related.

Saw Maung (1929–) Myanmar (Burmese) soldier and politician. Appointed head of the armed forces in 1985 by Ne Win, he led a coup to remove Ne Win's successor, Maung Maung, in 1988 and became leader of a totalitarian 'emergency government', which remained in office despite being defeated in the May 1990 election. In April 1992 he was replaced as chair of the ruling military junta, prime minister, and commander of the armed forces by Than Shwe.

Saxe-Coburg-Gotha Saxon duchy. Albert, the Prince Consort of Britain's Queen Victoria, was a son of the 1st Duke, Ernest I (1784–1844), who was succeeded by Albert's elder brother, Ernest II (1818–1893). It remained the name of the British royal house until 1917, when it was changed to Windsor.

saxifrage any of a group of plants belonging to the saxifrage family, found growing in rocky, mountainous, and alpine areas in the northern hemisphere. They are low plants with groups of small white, pink, or yellow flowers. (Genus *Saxifraga*, family Saxifragaceae.)

Saxon member of a Germanic tribe once inhabiting the Danish peninsula and northern Germany. The Saxons migrated from their homelands in the early Middle Ages, under pressure from the Franks, and spread into various parts of Europe, including Britain (see *Anglo-Saxon). They also undertook piracy in the North Sea and the English Channel.

Saxony German **Sachsen**, administrative region (German *Land*) in eastern Germany; area 18,412 sq km/ 7,109 sq mi; population (1999 est) 4,459,700. The capital is *Dresden, and other major towns include Leipzig, Chemnitz, and Zwickau. The region is on the plain of the River Elbe north of the Erzgebirge mountain range. Industries include electronics, textiles, vehicles, machinery, chemicals, and coal.

Saxony-Anhalt German **Sachsen-Anhalt**, administrative region (German *Land*) in eastern central Germany; area 20,450 sq km/7,895 sq mi; population (1999 est) 2,648,700. The capital is Magdeburg, and other major towns include Halle and Dessau. Industries include chemicals, electronics, rolling stock, and footwear. Cereals and vegetables are grown.

saxophone member of a hybrid brass instrument family of conical bore, with a single-reed woodwind mouthpiece and keyworks, invented about 1840 by Belgian instrument-maker Adolphe Sax (1814–1894). Soprano, alto, tenor, and baritone forms remain current. The soprano saxophone is usually straight; the others are characteristically curved back at the mouthpiece and have an upturned bell. Initially a concert instrument of suave tone, the saxophone was incorporated into dance bands of the 1930s and 1940s, and assumed its modern guise as a solo jazz instrument after 1945. It has a voicelike ability to bend a note.

Sayers, Dorothy L(eigh) (1893–1957) English writer of detective fiction, playwright, and translator. Her books, which feature the detective Lord Peter Wimsey and the heroine Harriet Vane, include classics of the detective fiction genre such as *Strong Poison* (1930), *Murder Must Advertise* (1933), *The Nine Tailors* (1934), and *Gaudy Night* (1935).

Say's law in economics, the 'law of markets' formulated by Jean-Baptiste Say (1767–1832) to the effect that supply creates its own demand and that resources can never be underused.

scabies contagious infection of the skin caused by the parasitic itch mite *Sarcoptes scabiei*, which burrows under the skin to deposit eggs. Treatment is by antiparasitic creams and lotions.

scabious any of a group of plants belonging to the teasel family, native to Europe and Asia, with many small, usually purplish-blue flowers borne in a single head on a tall stalk. The small scabious (*S. columbaria*) and the Mediterranean sweet scabious (*S. atropurpurea*) are often cultivated. (Genus *Scabiosa*, family Dipsacaceae.)

Scafell Pike highest mountain in England, in the *Lake District, Cumbria, northwest England; height 978 m/3,210 ft. It is separated from Scafell (964 m/3,164 ft) by a ridge called Mickledore.

scale *or* **limescale** in chemistry, *calcium carbonate precipitates that form on the inside of a kettle or boiler as a result of boiling *hard water (water containing concentrations of soluble calcium and magnesium salts). The salts present in hard water also precipitate out by reacting with soap molecules.

scale in music, a progression of single notes upwards or downwards in 'steps' (scale originally meant 'ladder'). For example, the most common scale is that of C major, which can be found by playing all the white notes on the keyboard from any C to the next C above or below. A scale is defined by its starting note and may be *major or minor depending on its arrangement of tones and semitones. A *chromatic scale is made up entirely of semitones. It includes all the notes (black and white) on the keyboard and has no key because there is no fixed starting point. (See diagram, p. 808.)

scale insect any small plant-sucking insect, order Homoptera, of the superfamily Coccoidea. Some species are major pests – for example, the citrus mealy bug (genus *Pseudococcus*), which attacks citrus fruits in North America. The female is often wingless and legless, attached to a plant by the head and with the body covered with a waxy scale. The rare males are winged.

scallop any marine bivalve *mollusc of the family Pectinidae, with a fan-shaped shell. There are two 'ears' extending from the socketlike hinge. Scallops use water-jet propulsion to move through the water to escape predators such as starfish. The giant Pacific scallop found from Alaska to California can reach 20 cm/8 in width.

scaly anteater another name for the *pangolin.

Scandinavia peninsula in northwestern Europe, comprising Norway and Sweden; politically and culturally it also includes Denmark, Iceland, the *Faroe Islands, and Finland.

scandium chemical symbol Sc, silver-white, metallic element of the *lanthanide series, atomic number 21, relative atomic mass 44.956. Its compounds are found widely distributed in nature, but only in minute amounts. The metal has little industrial importance.

scanner in computing, a device that can produce a digital image file of a document for input and storage in a computer. It uses technology similar to that of a photocopier. Small scanners can be passed over the document surface by hand; larger versions have a flat bed, like that of a photocopier, on which the input document is placed and scanned.

scanning in medicine, the noninvasive examination of body organs to detect abnormalities of structure or function. Detectable waves – for example, *ultrasound, gamma, or *X-rays – are passed through the part to be scanned. Their absorption pattern is recorded, analysed by computer, and displayed pictorially on a screen.

807

Pentatonic

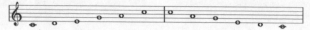

Major

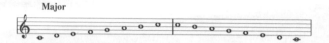

Minor (melodic)

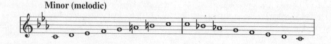

Minor (harmonic)

Whole-tone

scale Pentatonic, major, minor, and whole-tone scales on C.

scapula *or* **shoulder blade** large, flat, triangular bone which lies over the second to seventh ribs on the back, forming part of the pectoral girdle, and assisting in the articulation of the arm with the chest region. Its flattened shape allows a large region for the attachment of muscles.

scarab any of a family Scarabaeidae of beetles, often brilliantly coloured, and including *cockchafers, June beetles, and dung beetles. Many scarabs collect and bury dung on which to rear their larvae. The *Scarabeus sacer* was revered by the ancient Egyptians as the symbol of resurrection.

Scargill, Arthur (1938–) British trade-union leader. Elected president of the National Union of Miners (NUM) in 1981, he embarked on a collision course with the Conservative government of Margaret Thatcher. The damaging strike of 1984–85 split the miners' movement. By 1997 membership of the NUM had fallen to 10,000.

Scarlatti, (Giuseppe) Domenico (1685–1757) Italian composer. The eldest son of Alessandro *Scarlatti, he lived most of his life in Portugal and Spain in the service of the Queen of Spain. He wrote over 500 sonatas for harpsichord, short pieces in binary form demonstrating the new freedoms of keyboard composition and inspired by Spanish musical styles. Scarlatti was the most famous harpsichordist of his time, and his music provided the foundation for modern piano technique.

Scarlatti, (Pietro) Alessandro (Gaspare) (1660–1725) Italian baroque composer. He was maestro di capella at the court of Naples and developed the opera form. He composed more than 100 operas, including *Tigrane* (1715), as well as church music and oratorios.

scarlet fever *or* **scarlatina** acute infectious disease, especially of children, caused by the bacteria in the *Streptococcus pyogenes* group. It is marked by fever, vomiting, sore throat, and a bright red rash spreading from the upper to the lower part of the body. The rash is followed by the skin peeling in flakes. It is treated with antibiotics.

scarp and dip in geology, the two slopes that comprise an escarpment. The scarp is the steep slope and the dip is the gentle slope. Such a feature is common when sedimentary rocks are uplifted, folded, or eroded, the scarp slope cuts across the bedding planes of the sedimentary rock while the dip slope follows the direction of the strata. An example is Salisbury Crags in Edinburgh, Scotland.

scepticism ancient philosophical view that absolute knowledge of things is ultimately unobtainable, hence the only proper attitude is to suspend judgement. Its origins lay in the teachings of the Greek philosopher Pyrrho, who maintained that peace of mind lay in renouncing all claims to knowledge.

Scheherazade the storyteller in the *Arabian Nights*.

Schengen Group association of states in Europe that in theory adhere to the ideals of the Schengen Convention, notably the abolition of passport controls at common internal borders and the strengthening of external borders. The Convention, which first came into effect in March 1995, was signed by Belgium, France, Germany, Luxembourg, and the Netherlands in 1985; Italy in November 1990; Portugal and Spain in 1991; Greece in 1992; Austria in 1995; and Denmark, Sweden, Finland, and the first two non-European Union (EU) countries, Iceland and Norway in 2001.

scherzo (Italian 'joke') in music, a lively piece, usually in rapid triple (3/4) time; often used for the third movement of a symphony, sonata, or quartet as a substitute for the statelier *minuet and trio.

Schiele, Egon (1890–1918) Austrian artist. Strongly influenced by *art nouveau, and in particular Gustav *Klimt, he developed an angular, contorted style, employing garish colours, that made him an important pioneer of *expressionism. His subject matter includes portraits and openly erotic nudes.

Schiller, Johann Christoph Friedrich von (1759–1805) German dramatist, poet, and historian. He wrote *Sturm und Drang ('storm and stress') verse and plays, including the dramatic trilogy *Wallenstein* (1798–99). He was an idealist, and much of his work concerns the aspiration for political freedom and the avoidance of mediocrity.

schist *metamorphic rock containing *mica; its crystals are arranged in parallel layers or bands. Schist may contain additional minerals such as *garnet.

schizophrenia mental disorder, a psychosis of unknown origin, which can lead to profound changes in personality, behaviour, and perception, including delusions and hallucinations. It is more common in males and the early-onset form is more severe than when the illness develops in later life. Modern treatment approaches include drugs, family therapy, stress reduction, and rehabilitation.

Schleswig-Holstein administrative region (German *Land*) in north Germany, bounded to the north by Denmark, to the east by the Baltic Sea and Mecklenberg-West Pomerania, to the south by Lower Saxony and Hamburg, and to the west by the North Sea and the Heligoland Bight; area 15,770 sq km/6,089 sq mi; population (2003 est) 2,814,100. The capital is Kiel, and other major towns include Lübeck, Flensburg, Schleswig, Neumünster, and Rendsburg.

Schliemann, Heinrich (1822–1890) German archaeologist. In 1870 he began excavating at Hissarlik, Turkey, the traditional site of *Troy, and uncovered its ruins and those of other cities on the site. His later excavations were at Mycenae, Greece, 1874–76, where he discovered the ruins of the *Mycenaean civilization.

Schmidt, Helmut Heinrich Waldemar (1918–) German socialist politician, member of the Social Democratic Party (SPD), chancellor of West Germany 1974–83. As chancellor, Schmidt introduced social reforms and continued Brandt's policy of Ostpolitik. With the French president Giscard d'Estaing, he instigated annual world and European economic summits. He was a firm supporter of NATO and of the deployment of US nuclear missiles in West Germany during the early 1980s.

Schoenberg, Arnold Franz Walter (1874–1951) born Arnold Franz Walter Schönberg, Austro-Hungarian composer, a US citizen from 1941. After late Romantic early works such as *Verklärte Nacht/Transfigured Night* (1899) and the *Gurrelieder/Songs of Gurra* (1900–11), he was one of the first composers to use *atonality (absence of key), producing works such as *Pierrot lunaire/Moonstruck Pierrot* (1912) for chamber ensemble and voice, before developing the *twelve-tone system of musical composition.

scholasticism the theological and philosophical systems and methods taught in the schools of medieval Europe, especially in the 12th–14th centuries. Scholasticism tried to integrate orthodox Christian teaching with Aristotelian and some Platonic philosophy. The scholastic method involved surveying different opinions and the reasons given for them, and then attempting solutions of the problems raised, using logic and dialectic.

Schopenhauer, Arthur (1788–1860) German philosopher. His *The World as Will and Idea* (1818), inspired by Immanuel Kant and ancient Hindu philosophy, expounded an atheistic and pessimistic world view: an irrational will is considered as the inner principle of the world, producing an ever-frustrated cycle of desire, of which the only escape is aesthetic contemplation or absorption into nothingness.

Schrödinger, Erwin (1887–1961) Austrian physicist. He advanced the study of wave mechanics to describe the behaviour of electrons in atoms. In 1926 he produced a solid mathematical explanation of the *quantum theory and the structure of the atom. He shared the Nobel Prize for Physics in 1933 for his work in the development of quantum mechanics.

Schubert, Franz Peter (1797–1828) Austrian composer. His ten symphonies include the incomplete eighth in B minor (the 'Unfinished') (1822) and the 'Great' in C major (1825). He wrote chamber and piano music, including the *Trout Quintet*, and over 600 lieder (songs) combining the Romantic expression of emotion with pure melody. They include the cycles *Die schöne Müllerin/The Beautiful Maid of the Mill* (1823) and *Die Winterreise/The Winter Journey* (1827).

Schumacher, Fritz (1911–1977) born Ernst Friedrich Schumacher, German-born economist and conservationist. He studied in England and the USA before becoming an economic adviser first to the British Control Commission (1946–50) and then to the National Coal Board (1950–70). He founded the Intermediate Technology Group in 1966 as a non-governmental organization to work in developing countries.

Schumacher, Michael (1969–) German racing driver. He has won a record number of drivers' titles. He began his career in the Mercedes-Benz junior team; he joined the Jordan Formula 1 team in 1991, but moved to Benetton almost immediately. He won his first Grand Prix in Belgium in 1992. Hailed by many as a gifted 'natural' driver, he joined Ferrari at the end of the 1995 season. In October 2000, he won the first Drivers' Championship for Ferrari since 1979. On 2 September 2001, he won the Belgium Grand Prix for a fifth time, thereby overtaking Alain Prost's record of 51 Grand Prix wins. He won the World Drivers' Championship for a sixth time in 2003, breaking Juan Manuel Fangio's record, and won his seventh title the following year. In October 2004 he won a record 13th race in a single season. His 2004 season points total of 148 was also a new record.

Schuman, Robert Jean-Baptiste Nicolas (1886–1963) French Christian-Democrat politician, prime minister 1947–48 and foreign minister 1948–55. He was a member of the post-war Mouvement Républicain Populaire (MRP). His Schuman Declaration of May 1950, drafted by Jean Monnet, outlines a scheme for pooling coal and iron-ore resources. The resultant European Coal and Steel Community, established by France, Belgium, Germany, the Netherlands, Italy and Luxembourg under the 1951 Paris Treaty, was the forerunner of the European Community (now the European Union).

Schumann, Robert Alexander (1810–1856) German composer and writer. His songs and short piano pieces portray states of emotion with great economy. Among his compositions are four symphonies, a violin concerto, a piano concerto, sonatas, and song cycles, such as *Dichterliebe/Poet's Love* (1840). Mendelssohn championed many of his works.

Schwarzkopf, Norman (1934–) called 'Stormin' Norman', US general. He was supreme commander of the Allied forces in the *Gulf War 1991. He planned and executed a blitzkrieg campaign, 'Desert Storm', sustaining remarkably few Allied casualties in the liberation of Kuwait. He was a battalion commander in the Vietnam War and deputy commander of the US invasion of Grenada in 1983.

Schweitzer, Albert (1875–1965) Protestant theologian, organist, and missionary surgeon. He founded the hospital at Lambaréné in Gabon in 1913, giving organ recitals to support his work there. He wrote a life of German composer J S Bach and *Von reimarus zu Wrede/The Quest for the Historical Jesus* (1906). He was awarded the Nobel Prize for Peace in 1952 for his teaching of 'reverence for life' and for his medical and other work in Africa.

sciatica persistent pain in the back and down the outside of one leg, along the sciatic nerve and its branches. Causes of sciatica include inflammation of the nerve or pressure of a displaced disc on a nerve root leading out of the lower spine.

science (Latin *scientia* 'knowledge') any systematic field of study or body of knowledge that aims, through experiment, observation, and deduction, to produce reliable explanations of phenomena, with reference to the material and physical world.

Scientology (Latin *scire* 'to know' and Greek *logos* 'branch of learning') 'applied religious philosophy' based on dianetics, founded in California 1952 by L Ron Hubbard as the **Church of Scientology**, and claiming to 'increase man's spiritual awareness'. Its headquarters from 1984 have been in Los Angeles.

scilla any of a group of bulbous plants belonging to the lily family, with blue, pink, or white flowers; they include the spring *squill (S. verna). (Genus *Scilla*, family Liliaceae.)

Scilly, Isles of or **Scilly Isles/Islands** or **Scillies** group of 140 islands and islets lying 40 km/25 mi southwest of Land's End, England; administered by the Duchy of Cornwall; area 16 sq km/6.3 sq mi; population (2001 est) 2,050. The five inhabited islands are **St Mary's**, the largest, on which Hugh Town, capital of the Scillies is situated; **Tresco**, the second largest, with subtropical gardens; **St Martin's**, noted for its beautiful shells; **St Agnes**; and **Bryher**. The islands are designated areas of outstanding natural beauty, heritage coasts, and conservation areas; under the European Union

Habitats directive they are also a Marine Special Area of Conservation (SAC). Produce includes vegetables and early spring flowers. Tourism is important and the islands are a famous birdwatching centre.

Scipio, Publius Cornelius (236–c. 183 BC) also known as **Scipio Africanus Major**, Roman general whose tactical and strategic abilities turned the tide of the Second Punic War in 208–201 BC and established his reputation as one of Rome's greatest commanders. He defeated the Carthaginians in Spain in 210–206 BC and invaded Africa in 204 BC. At Zama in 202 BC he defeated the Carthaginian general *Hannibal to win the war for Rome. He adopted the name 'Africanus' in recognition of the place of his greatest victory, but he felt that his achievements had not been sufficiently rewarded and retired to his villa embittered.

Scipio Aemilianus, Publius Cornelius (c. 185–129 BC) also known as **Scipio Africanus Minor**, Roman general, the adopted grandson of Scipio Africanus Major. He destroyed Carthage in 146, and subdued Spain in 133. He was opposed to his brothers-in-law, the Gracchi (see *Gracchus).

sclerenchyma plant tissue whose function is to strengthen and support, composed of thick-walled cells that are heavily lignified (toughened). On maturity the cell inside dies, and only the cell walls remain.

sclerosis any abnormal hardening of body tissues, especially the nervous system or walls of the arteries. See *multiple sclerosis and *atherosclerosis.

scorched earth in warfare, the policy of burning and destroying everything that might be of use to an invading army, especially the crops in the fields. It was used to great effect in Russia in 1812 against the invasion of the French emperor Napoleon and again during World War II to hinder the advance of German forces in 1941.

scorpion any arachnid of the order Scorpiones, common in the tropics and subtropics. Scorpions have four pairs of walking legs, large pincers, and long tails ending in upcurved poisonous stings, though the venom is not usually fatal to a healthy adult human. Some species reach 25 cm/10 in. The scorpion belongs to an ancient group of animals. Scorpions were perhaps the first arachnids to adapt to life on land, some 400 million years ago. There are about 600 different species.

Scorpius bright zodiacal constellation in the southern hemisphere between *Libra and *Sagittarius, represented as a scorpion. The Sun passes briefly through Scorpius in the last week of November. The heart of the scorpion is marked by the bright red supergiant star *Antares. Scorpius contains rich *Milky Way star fields, plus the strongest *X-ray source in the sky, Scorpius X-1. The whole area is rich in clusters and nebulae. In astrology, the dates for Scorpius are about 24 October–21 November (see *precession).

Scot inhabitant of Scotland, part of Britain; or a person of Scottish descent. Originally the Scots were a Celtic (Gaelic) people of Northern Ireland who migrated to Scotland in the 5th century.

Scotland Roman **Caledonia**, constituent part of the United Kingdom, the northernmost part of Britain, formerly an independent country; area 78,470 sq km/30,297 sq mi; population (2000 est) 5,114,600. The capital is *Edinburgh, and other major towns and cities include Glasgow, Dundee, and Aberdeen. Geographical features include the Highlands in the north (with the *Grampian Mountains), the central Lowlands, including valleys of the Clyde and Forth, the Southern Uplands (including the Lammermuir Hills), and islands of the Orkneys, Shetlands, and Western Isles. Industries include marine and aircraft engines, oil, natural gas, chemicals, textiles, clothing, printing, paper, food processing, tourism, whisky, coal (in decline), financial services and insurance, forestry, quarrying, electronics, and computers (Scotland's 'Silicon Glen' produces over 35% of Europe's personal computers).

Scots language the form of the English language as traditionally spoken and written in Scotland, regarded by some scholars as a distinct language. Scots derives from the Northumbrian dialect of Anglo-Saxon or Old English, and has been a literary language since the 14th century.

Scott, (George) Gilbert (1811–1878) English architect. As the leading practical architect of the mid-19th-century *Gothic Revival in England, Scott was responsible for the building or restoration of many public buildings and monuments, including the Albert Memorial (1863–72), the Foreign Office in Whitehall (1862–73), and the St Pancras Station Hotel (1868–74), all in London.

Scott, Giles Gilbert (1880–1960) English architect. He was the grandson of Gilbert *Scott. He designed Liverpool Anglican Cathedral (begun 1903; completed 1978), Cambridge University Library (1931–34), Battersea Power Station (1932–34), and Waterloo Bridge, London (1939–45). He also designed and supervised the rebuilding of the House of Commons chamber at the Palace of Westminster in a modern Gothic style after World War II.

Scott, Robert Falcon (1868–1912) called 'Scott of the Antarctic', English explorer who commanded two Antarctic expeditions, 1901–04 and 1910–12. On 18 January 1912 he reached the South Pole, shortly after the Norwegian Roald *Amundsen, but on the return journey he and his companions died in a blizzard only a few miles from their base camp. His journal was recovered and published in 1913.

Scott, Walter (1771–1832) Scottish novelist and poet. His first works were translations of German ballads and collections of Scottish ballads, which he followed with narrative poems of his own, such as *The Lay of the Last Minstrel* (1805), *Marmion* (1808), and *The Lady of the Lake* (1810). He gained a European reputation for his historical novels such as *Waverley* (1814), *Rob Roy* (1817), *The Heart of Midlothian* (1818), and *Ivanhoe* (1819), all published anonymously.

Scottish Borders unitary authority in southeast Scotland, created in 1996 to replace the former Borders region. **area:** 4,733 sq km/1,827 sq mi **towns:** Galashiels, Hawick, Jedburgh, Kelso, Newtown St Boswells (administrative headquarters), Peebles, Selkirk **physical:** much of the west part of the area is upland (Lammermuir, Moorfoot and Pentland Hills); Broad Law (840 m/2,756 ft), near Tweedsmuir, is the highest point. The principal river, the Tweed, traverses the region west–east; its tributaries include the River Teviot. The largest loch is St Mary's, and the only substantial area of low-lying agricultural land is the Merse in the southeast, near the English border. The coast is generally precipitous **features:** Walter Scott's home at Abbotsford; Field Marshal Haig and Walter Scott buried at Dryburgh Abbey; Melrose Abbey (12th century) **population:** (2000 est) 106,900.

Scottish Executive the government of Scotland for devolved matters. The Executive comprises a First Minister and a team of Scottish ministers, including law officers, supported by civil servants. The ministers are politicians drawn from the Scottish Parliament – from the party or coalition with a majority of seats – to whom they are accountable. The Executive comprised six main functional departments: justice; health; rural affairs; development; education; and enterprise and lifelong learning. The Executive also overseas nine agencies, which include the Scottish Courts, Scottish Prison Service, Historic Scotland, and the National Archives of Scotland.

Scottish law the legal system of Scotland. Owing to its separate development, Scotland has a system differing from the rest of the UK, being based on *civil law. Its continued separate existence was guaranteed by the Act of Union with England in 1707.

Scottish Parliament devolved legislative (law-making) body of Scotland. It comprises 129 members and was created by the November 1998 Scotland Act, which was passed following the Scottish electorate's overwhelming approval of government proposals in a referendum on devolution held on 11 September 1997. The first elections to the Parliament were held on 6 May 1999 and the Parliament opened on 1 July 1999.

Scouts worldwide youth organization that emphasizes character, citizenship, and outdoor life. It was founded (as the Boy Scouts) in England in 1908 by Robert *Baden-Powell. His book *Scouting for Boys* (1908) led to the incorporation in the UK of the Boy Scout Association by royal charter in 1912. There are some 25 million members of the World Organization of the Scout Movement (1998).

scrapie fatal disease of sheep and goats that attacks the central nervous system, causing deterioration of the brain cells, and leading to the characteristic staggering gait and other behavioural abnormalities, before death. It is caused by the presence of an abnormal version of the brain protein PrP and is related to *bovine spongiform encephalopathy, the disease of cattle known as 'mad cow disease', and Creutzfeldt–Jakob disease in humans. It is a transmissible spongiform encephalopathy.

screamer any South American marsh-dwelling bird of the family Anhimidae, order Anseriformes; there are only three species, all in the genus *Anhima*. They are about 80 cm/30 in long, with short curved beaks, long toes, dark plumage, spurs on the fronts of the wings, and a crest or horn on the head.

scree pile of rubble and sediment that collects at the foot of a mountain range or cliff. The rock fragments that form scree are usually broken off by the action of frost (*freeze–thaw weathering).

scuba acronym for Self-Contained Underwater Breathing Apparatus, another name for *aqualung.

sculpture artistic shaping of materials such as wood, stone, clay, metal, and, more recently, plastic and other synthetics. Since ancient times, the human form has been the principal subject of sculpture around the world; the earliest prehistoric human artefacts include sculpted stone figurines. Many indigenous cultures have maintained rich traditions of sculpture. Those of Africa (see *African art), South America, and the Caribbean in particular have been influential in the development of contemporary Western sculpture.

scurvy disease caused by deficiency of vitamin C (ascorbic acid), which is contained in fresh vegetables and fruit. The signs are weakness and aching joints and muscles, progressing to bleeding of the gums and other spontaneous haemorrhage, and drying-up of the skin and hair. It is reversed by giving the vitamin.

Scylla and Charybdis in Greek mythology, a sea monster and a whirlpool, between which *Odysseus had to sail. Later writers located them at the northern end of the Straits of Messina, between Sicily and Italy.

Scythia region north of the Black Sea between the Carpathian Mountains and the River Don, inhabited by the Scythians 7th–1st centuries BC. From the middle of the 4th century, they were slowly superseded by the Sarmatians. The Scythians produced ornaments and vases in gold and electrum with animal decoration. Although there is no surviving written work, there are spectacular archaeological remains, including vast royal burial mounds which often contain horse skeletons.

SDLP abbreviation for *Social Democratic and Labour Party, a Northern Ireland political party.

SDP abbreviation for *Social Democratic Party, former British political party.

sea anemone invertebrate marine animal of the phylum Cnidaria with a tubelike body attached by the base to a rock or shell. The other end has an open 'mouth' surrounded by stinging tentacles, which capture crustaceans and other small organisms. Many sea anemones are beautifully coloured, especially those in tropical waters.

seaborgium chemical symbol Sg, synthesized radioactive element of the *transactinide series, atomic number 106, relative atomic mass 263. It was first synthesized in 1974 in the USA and given the temporary name unnilhexium. The discovery was not confirmed until 1993. It was officially named in 1997 after US nuclear chemist Glenn Seaborg.

sea cucumber any echinoderm of the class Holothuroidea with a cylindrical body that is tough-skinned, knobbed, or spiny. The size ranges from 3 cm/ 1.2 in to 2 m/6.6 ft. There are around 900 species, which are mostly black, brown, or olive green in colour. Sea cucumbers are sometimes called 'cotton-spinners' because of the sticky filaments they eject from the anus in self-defence.

seafloor spreading growth of the ocean *crust outwards (sideways) from ocean ridges. The concept of seafloor spreading has been combined with that of continental drift and incorporated into *plate tectonics.

seagull see *gull.

sea horse any marine fish of several related genera, especially *Hippocampus*, of the family Syngnathidae, which includes the *pipefishes. The body is small and compressed and covered with bony plates raised into tubercles or spines. The tail is prehensile, and the tubular mouth sucks in small shellfish and larvae as food. The head and foreparts, usually carried upright, resemble those of a horse. They swim vertically and beat their fins up to 70 times a second.

seakale perennial European coastal plant with broad, fleshy leaves and white flowers; it is cultivated in Europe and the young shoots are eaten as a vegetable. (*Crambe maritima*, family Cruciferae.)

seal aquatic carnivorous mammal of the families Otariidae and Phocidae (sometimes placed in a separate order, the Pinnipedia). The eared seals or sea lions (Otariidae) have small external ears, unlike the true seals (Phocidae). Seals have a streamlined body with thick blubber for insulation, and front and hind flippers. They are able to close their nostrils as they dive, and obtain oxygen from their blood supply while under water. They feed on fish, squid, or crustaceans, and are commonly found in Arctic and Antarctic seas, but also in Mediterranean, Caribbean, and Hawaiian waters.

sea lily any *echinoderm of the class Crinoidea. In most, the rayed, cuplike body is borne on a sessile stalk (permanently attached to a rock) and has feathery arms in multiples of five encircling the mouth. However, some sea lilies are free-swimming and unattached.

sea lion any of several genera of *seals of the family Otariidae (eared seals), which also includes the fur seals. These streamlined animals have large fore flippers which they use to row themselves through the water. The hind flippers can be turned beneath the body to walk on land.

Sea Peoples unidentified seafaring warriors who may have been Achaeans, Etruscans, or *Philistines, who ravaged and settled the Mediterranean coasts in the 12th–13th centuries BC. They were defeated by Ramses III of Egypt 1191 BC.

search engine in computing, online program to help users find information on the Internet. Commercial search engines such as Google and Lycos comprise databases of documents, Usenet articles, images, and news stories, which can be searched by keying in a key word or phrase. The databases are compiled by a mixture of automated agents (spiders) and webmasters registering their sites.

sea slug any of an order (Nudibranchia) of marine gastropod molluscs in which the shell is reduced or absent. The order includes some very colourful forms, especially in the tropics. They are largely carnivorous, feeding on hydroids and *sponges.

season period of the year having a characteristic climate. The change in seasons is mainly due to the Earth's axis being tilted in relation to the Sun, and hence the position of the Sun in the sky at a particular place changes as the Earth orbits the Sun. As the Earth orbits the Sun, its axis of rotation always points in the same direction. This means that, during the northern hemisphere summer solstice (usually 21 June), the Sun is overhead in the northern hemisphere. At the northern hemisphere winter solstice (usually 22 December), the Sun is overhead in the southern hemisphere.

seasonal affective disorder (SAD) form of depression that occurs in winter and is relieved by the coming of spring. Its incidence decreases closer to the Equator. One type of SAD is associated with increased sleeping and appetite.

sea squirt or **tunicate** any solitary or colonial-dwelling saclike *chordate of the class Ascidiacea. A pouch-shaped animal attached to a rock or other base, it draws in food-carrying water through one siphon and expels it through another after straining it through numerous gill slits. The young are free-swimming tadpole-shaped organisms, which, unlike the adults, have a notochord.

Seattle called 'the Emerald City', port on Lake Washington in King County, *Washington, USA, and the largest city in the Pacific Northwest; population (2000 est) 563,400, Greater Seattle (King, Snohomish, Pierce, and Kitsap counties) 3,275,800. It is the fifth-largest container port in the USA and the main transit point for supplies to Alaska; trade with Japan is important. Industries include aerospace (the manufacturing plants of the Boeing Corporation are here), timber, tourism, banking and insurance, paper industries, electronics, computing (Microsoft, based in adjoining Redmond, is one of several thousand software firms), biotechnology, ocean science, shipbuilding and repair, and fishing. Coffee has been an important commodity since the development of the Starbucks Company in the 1970s.

sea urchin any of various orders of the class Echinoidea among the *echinoderms. They all have a globular body enclosed with plates of lime and covered with spines. Sometimes the spines are anchoring organs, and they also assist in locomotion. Sea urchins feed on seaweed and the animals frequenting them, and some are edible, as is their roe.

seaweed any of a vast group of simple multicellular plant forms belonging to the *algae group, and found growing in the sea, brackish estuaries, and salt marshes, from near the high-tide mark to depths of 100–200 m/ 300–600 ft. Many seaweeds have holdfasts (attaching them to rocks or other surfaces), stalks, and fronds, sometimes with air bladders to keep them afloat, and are green, blue-green, red, or brown. The purple laver, dulse, brown gulfweed, and the green laver (or sea lettuce) are among the seaweeds harvested for food. Other varieties such as kelp are used in fertilizers, while *Gelidium* is used to make agar (a thickening agent used in the food industry).

Sebastiano del Piombo (c. 1485–1547) adopted name of Sebastiano Luciani, Venetian painter, he was a pupil of *Giorgione and developed a similar style. In 1511 he moved to Rome, where his friendship with Michelangelo (and rivalry with Raphael) inspired his finest works, such as *The Raising of Lazarus* (1517–19; National Gallery, London).

Sebastian, St (died c. 258) Roman soldier. He was traditionally a member of Emperor Diocletian's bodyguard until his Christian faith was discovered. He was condemned to be killed by arrows. Feast day 20 January.

secession Latin *secessio*, in politics, the withdrawal from a federation of states by one or more of its members, as in the secession of the Confederate states from the Union in the USA 1860, Singapore from the Federation of Malaysia 1965, and Croatia and Slovenia from the Yugoslav Federation 1991.

second symbol sec or s, basic SI unit of time, one-sixtieth of a minute. It is defined as the duration of 9,192,631,770 cycles of regulation (periods of the radiation corresponding to the transition between two hyperfine levels of the ground state) of the caesium-133 isotope. In mathematics, the second is a unit (symbol ″) of angular measurement, equalling one-sixtieth of a minute, which in turn is one-sixtieth of a degree.

secondary growth *or* **secondary thickening** increase in diameter of the roots and stems of certain plants (notably shrubs and trees) that results from the production of new cells by the *cambium. It provides the plant with additional mechanical support and new conducting cells, the secondary *xylem and *phloem. Secondary growth is generally confined to *gymnosperms and, among the *angiosperms, to the dicotyledons. With just a few exceptions, the monocotyledons (grasses, lilies) exhibit only primary growth, resulting from cell division at the apical *meristems.

secondary sexual characteristic external feature of an organism that is indicative of its gender (male or female), but not the reproductive organs themselves. They include facial hair in men and breasts in women, combs in cockerels, brightly coloured plumage in many male birds, and manes in male lions. In many cases, they are involved in displays and contests for mates and have evolved by *sexual selection. Their development is stimulated by sex *hormones – in humans the change in concentrations of these hormones at puberty results not only in the development of the physical secondary sexual characteristics, but also emotional changes.

Second World former term for the industrialized *communist countries of the Soviet Union and Eastern bloc, used by the West during the *Cold War, alongside the terms First World (industrialized free-market countries of the West) and Third World (non-aligned, developing nations). Originally denoting political alignment, the classifications later took on economic connotations. The terms have now lost their political meaning, and are considered derogatory.

Second World War alternative name for *World War II, 1939–45.

secretary bird ground-hunting, long-legged, mainly grey-plumaged bird of prey *Sagittarius serpentarius*. It is about 1.2 m/4 ft tall, with an erectile head crest tipped with black. It is protected in southern Africa because it eats poisonous snakes.

secretary of state in the UK, a title held by a number of ministers; for example, the secretary of state for foreign and commonwealth affairs.

secretin *hormone produced by the small intestine of vertebrates that stimulates the production of digestive secretions by the pancreas and liver.

secretion in biology, any substance (normally a fluid) produced by a cell or specialized gland, for example, sweat, saliva, enzymes, and hormones. The process whereby the substance is discharged from the cell is also known as secretion.

sect small ideological group, usually religious in nature, that may have moved away from a main group, often claiming a monopoly of access to truth or salvation. Sects are usually highly exclusive. They demand strict conformity, total commitment to their code of behaviour, and complete personal involvement, sometimes to the point of rejecting mainstream society altogether in terms of attachments, names, possessions, and family.

sector in geometry, part of a circle enclosed by two radii and the arc that joins them. A **minor sector** has an angle at the centre of the circle of less than 180°. A **major sector** has an angle at the centre of the circle of more than 180°.

secularization the process through which religious thinking, practice, and institutions lose their religious and/or social significance. The concept is based on the theory, held by some sociologists, that as societies become industrialized their religious morals, values, and institutions give way to secular ones and some religious traits become common secular practices.

Security Council the most important body of the United Nations; see *United Nations.

sedative any drug that has a calming effect, reducing anxiety and tension. Sedatives will induce sleep in larger doses. Examples are *barbiturates, *narcotics, and *benzodiazepines.

sedge any of a group of perennial grasslike plants, usually with three-cornered solid stems, common in low water or on wet and marshy ground. (Genus *Carex*, family Cyperaceae.)

Sedgemoor, Battle of in English history, a battle on 6 July 1685 in which *Monmouth's rebellion was crushed by the forces of James II, on a tract of marshy land 5 km/3 mi southeast of Bridgwater, Somerset.

sediment any loose material that has 'settled' after deposition from suspension in water, ice, or air, generally as the water current or wind speed decreases. Typical sediments are, in order of increasing coarseness: clay, mud, silt, sand, gravel, pebbles, cobbles, and boulders.

sedimentary rock rock formed by the accumulation and cementation of deposits that have been laid down by water, wind, ice, or gravity. Sedimentary rocks cover more than two-thirds of the Earth's surface and comprise three major categories: clastic, chemically precipitated, and organic (or biogenic). Clastic sediments are the largest group and are composed of fragments of pre-existing rocks; they include clays, sands, and gravels. Chemical precipitates include some limestones and evaporated deposits such as gypsum and halite (rock salt). Coal, oil shale, and limestone made of fossil material are examples of organic sedimentary rocks.

sedition in the UK, the offence of inciting unlawful opposition to the crown and government. Unlike *treason, sedition does not carry the death penalty.

Seebeck effect generation of a voltage in a circuit containing two different metals, or semiconductors, by keeping the junctions between them at different temperatures. Discovered by the German physicist Thomas Seebeck (1770–1831), it is also called the thermoelectric effect, and is the basis of the *thermocouple. It is the opposite of the *Peltier effect (in which current flow causes a temperature difference between the junctions of different metals).

seed reproductive structure of higher plants (*angiosperms and *gymnosperms). It develops from a fertilized ovule and consists of an embryo and a food store, surrounded and protected by an outer seed coat, called the testa. The food store is contained either in a specialized nutritive tissue, the endosperm, or in the *cotyledons of the embryo itself. In angiosperms the seed is enclosed within a *fruit, whereas in gymnosperms it is usually naked and unprotected, once shed from the female cone. Following *germination the seed develops into a new plant.

seed drill machine for sowing cereals and other seeds, developed by Jethro *Tull in England in 1701, although simple seeding devices were known in Babylon in 2000 BC. The sowing of seeds in uniform rows allowed weeding between the rows of seedlings during growth, so improving the yield. Previously seeds had been broadcast by hand across the land.

seed plant any seed-bearing plant; also known as a spermatophyte. The seed plants are subdivided into two classes: the *angiosperms, or flowering plants, and the *gymnosperms, principally the cycads and conifers. Together, they comprise the major types of vegetation found on land.

Seikan Tunnel the world's longest underwater tunnel, opened 1988, linking the Japanese islands of Hokkaido and Honshu, which are separated by the Tsungaru Strait; length 51.7 km/32.3 mi.

Seine French river rising on the Langres plateau in the *département* of Côte d'Or, 30 km/19 mi northwest of Dijon, and flowing 774 km/472 mi northwest through *Paris and Rouen to join the English Channel at Le Havre. It is the third-longest, but economically the most important, river in the country.

seismic wave energy wave generated by an *earthquake or an artificial explosion. There are two types of seismic waves: **body waves** that travel through the Earth's interior; and **surface waves** that travel through the surface layers of the crust and can be felt as the shaking of the ground, as in an earthquake.

seismology study of *earthquakes, the seismic waves they produce, the processes that cause them, and the effects they have. By examining the global pattern of waves produced by an earthquake, seismologists can deduce the nature of the materials through which they have passed. This leads to an understanding of the Earth's internal structure.

Selangor state of the Federation of Malaysia; area 7,956 sq km/3,071 sq mi; population (2000 est) 3,947,500. The state consists mainly of a coastal plain of alluvial soils bordering the Strait of Malacca on the western side of the Malay Peninsula. Selangor is agriculturally rich, producing coconuts, palm oil, pineapples, rice, coffee, and tea, but the state has especially prospered since the rise of the rubber plantations and tin mines in the late 19th century. With coal mining in Batu Arang, a major industrial and commercial area has developed between the cities of Kuala Lumpur (part of Selangor until 1974), Petaling Jaya, and Klang.

select committee any of several long-standing committees of the UK House of Commons, such as the Environment Committee and the Treasury and Civil Service Committee. These were intended to restore parliamentary control of the executive, improve the quality of legislation, and scrutinize public spending and the work of government departments. Select committees represent the major parliamentary reform of the 20th century, and a possible means – through their all-party membership – of avoiding the automatic repeal of one government's measures by its successor.

Selene in Greek mythology, the goddess of the Moon; daughter of the Titan Hyperion; and sister of the Sun god *Helios and *Eos, goddess of the dawn. In later times she was identified with *Artemis.

selenium chemical symbol Se, (Greek *Selene* 'Moon') grey, non-metallic element, atomic number 34, relative atomic mass 78.96. It belongs to the sulphur group and occurs in several allotropic forms that differ in their physical and chemical properties. It is an essential trace element in human nutrition. Obtained from many sulphide ores and selenides, it is used as a red colouring for glass and enamel.

Seleucus (I) Nicator (*c.* 358–281 BC) Macedonian general under *Alexander (III) the Great and founder of the Seleucid dynasty of Syria. After Alexander's death in 323 BC, Seleucus became governor and then, in 312 BC, ruler of Babylonia, founding the city of Seleucia on the River Tigris. He conquered Syria and had himself crowned king in 306 BC, but his expansionist policies brought him into conflict with the Ptolemies of Egypt and he was assassinated. He was succeeded by his son Antiochus I.

Seljuk Empire empire of the Turkish people (converted to Islam during the 7th century) under the leadership of the invading Tatars or Seljuk Turks. The Seljuk Empire (1055–1243) included Iran, Iraq, and most of Anatolia. It was a loose confederation whose centre was in Iran, jointly ruled by members of the family and led by a great sultan exercising varying degrees of effective power. It was succeeded by the *Ottoman Empire.

Sellers, Peter (1925–1980) stage name of Richard Henry Sellers, English comedian and film actor. He was particularly skilled at mimicry. He made his name in the innovative British radio programme *The Goon Show* (1949–60). His films include *The Ladykillers* (1955), *I'm All Right Jack* (1960), *Lolita* (1962), *Dr Strangelove* (1964), *The Pink Panther* and its sequels (1964–78), and *Being There* (1979).

Selznick, David O(liver) (1902–1965) US film producer. His early work includes *King Kong*, *Dinner at Eight*, and *Little Women*, all 1933. His independent company, Selznick International (1936–40), made such lavish films as *A Star is Born* (1937) and *Gone With the Wind* (1939). He produced English director Alfred Hitchcock's first US film, *Rebecca* (1940), and worked with him again on *Spellbound* (1945). His last film was *A Farewell to Arms* (1957).

semantics branch of linguistics dealing with the meaning of words and sentences. Semantics asks how we can use language to express things about the real world and how the meanings of linguistic expressions can reflect people's thoughts. Semantic knowledge is **compositional**; the meaning of a sentence is based on the meanings of the words it contains and the order they appear in. For example, the sentences 'Teachers love children' and 'Children love teachers' both involve people loving other people but because of the different order of words they mean different things.

semaphore visual signalling code in which the relative positions of two movable pointers or hand-held flags stand for different letters or numbers. The system is used by ships at sea and for railway signals.

Semele in Greek mythology, the daughter of Cadmus of Thebes and mother of Dionysus by Zeus. At Hera's suggestion she demanded that Zeus should appear to her in all his glory, but when he did so she was consumed by lightning.

semiconductor material with electrical conductivity intermediate between metals and insulators and used in a wide range of electronic devices. Certain crystalline materials, most notably silicon and germanium, have a small number of free electrons that have escaped from the bonds between the atoms. The atoms from which they have escaped possess vacancies, called holes, which are similarly able to move from atom to atom and can be regarded as positive charges. Current can be carried by both electrons (negative carriers) and holes (positive carriers). Such materials are known as **intrinsic semiconductors**.

semiology *or* **semiotics** the study of the function of signs and symbols in human communication, both in language and by various nonlinguistic means. Beginning with the notion of the Swiss linguist Ferdinand de Saussure that no word or other sign (**signifier**) is intrinsically linked with its meaning (**signified**), it was developed as a scientific discipline, especially by Claude *Lévi-Strauss and Roland *Barthes. Signs and symbols can also be used in design drawings such as electrical circuits or computer flowcharts.

Semiramis in Greek legend, founder of *Nineveh (Ninua) with her husband Ninus. The legends probably originated in the deeds of two vigorous queen-mothers: **Sammuramat**, who ruled Assyria for her son Adad-nirari III from 810 to 806 BC; and **Naqi'a**, wife of Sennacherib (d. 681 BC) and mother of Esarhaddon, who administered Babylonia. Semiramis was later identified with the chief Assyrian goddess *Ishtar.

Semite any of the peoples of the Middle East originally speaking a Semitic language, and traditionally said to be descended from Shem, a son of Noah in the Bible. Ancient Semitic peoples include the Hebrews, Ammonites, Moabites, Edomites, Babylonians, Assyrians, Chaldaeans, Phoenicians, and Canaanites. The Semitic peoples founded the monotheistic religions of Judaism, Christianity, and Islam.

Semitic languages branch of the Hamito-Semitic language; see *Afro-Asiatic language.

Senate in ancient Rome, the 'council of elders'. Originally consisting of the heads of patrician families, it was recruited from ex-magistrates and persons who had rendered notable public service, but was periodically purged by the censors. Although nominally advisory, it controlled finance and foreign policy. Sulla doubled its size to 600.

Sendak, Maurice Bernard (1928–) US writer and book illustrator. His children's books with their deliberately arch illustrations include *Where the Wild Things Are* (1963), *In the Night Kitchen* (1970), and *Outside Over There* (1981).

Sendero Luminoso *or* **Shining Path** Maoist guerrilla group active in Peru, formed 1980 to overthrow the government; until 1988 its activity was confined to rural areas. From 1992 its attacks intensified in response to a government crackdown. By 1997 the 17-year war had caused 30,000 deaths. In 1999 the movement was believed to have fewer than 1,000 fighters.

Seneca, Lucius Annaeus (*c.* 4 BC–AD *c.* 65) Roman Stoic playwright, author of essays and nine tragedies. He was tutor to the future emperor Nero but lost favour after Nero's accession to the throne and was ordered to commit suicide. His tragedies were accepted as classical models by 16th-century dramatists.

Senefelder, (Johann Nepomuk Franz) Alois (1771–1834) Austrian engraver and playwright, born in Prague. Working as an actor and playwright, he is thought to have invented the printing technique of *lithography about 1796, possibly as a way of reproducing his own plays.

Senegal river in West Africa, formed by the confluence of the Bafing and Bakhoy rivers and flowing 1,125 km/700 mi northwest and west to join the Atlantic Ocean near Saint-Louis, Senegal. In 1968 the Organization of Riparian States of the River Senegal (Guinea, Mali, Mauritania, and Senegal) was formed to develop the river valley, including a dam for hydroelectric power and irrigation at Joina Falls in Mali; its headquarters is in Dakar. The river gives its name to the Republic of Senegal.

Senegal

National name: *République du Sénégal/ Republic of Senegal*

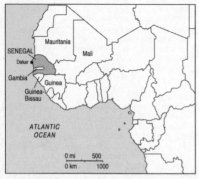

Area: 196,200 sq km/75,752 sq mi
Capital: Dakar (and chief port)
Major towns/cities: Thiès, Kaolack, Saint-Louis, Ziguinchor, Diourbel, Mbour
Physical features: plains rising to hills in southeast; swamp and tropical forest in southwest; River Senegal; The Gambia forms an enclave within Senegal
Head of state: Abdoulaye Wade from 2000
Head of government: Macky Sall from 2004
Political system: nationalistic socialist
Political executive: unlimited presidency
Political parties: Senegalese Socialist Party (PS), democratic socialist; Senegalese Democratic Party (PDS), centrist
Currency: franc CFA
GNI per capita (PPP): (US$) 1,510 (2002 est)
Exports: fresh and processed fish, phosphate products, refined petroleum products, cotton, chemicals, groundnuts and related products. Principal market: India 18.1% (2000)
Population: 10,095,000 (2003 est)
Language: French (official), Wolof, other ethnic languages
Religion: mainly Sunni Muslim; Christian 4%, animist 1%
Life expectancy: 51 (men); 55 (women) (2000–05)
Chronology
10th–11th centuries: Links established with North Africa; the Tukolor community was converted to Islam.

1445: First visited by Portuguese explorers.
1659: French founded Saint-Louis as a colony.
17th–18th centuries: Export trades in slaves, gums, ivory, and gold developed by European traders.
1854–65: Interior occupied by French who checked the expansion of the Islamic Tukulor Empire; Dakar founded.
1902: Became territory of French West Africa.
1946: Became French overseas territory, with own territorial assembly and representation in French parliament.
1948: Leopold Sedar Senghor founded the Senegalese Democratic Bloc to campaign for independence.
1959: Formed Federation of Mali with French Sudan.
1960: Achieved independence and withdrew from federation. Senghor, leader of socialist Senegalese Progressive Union (UPS), became president.
1966: UPS declared only legal party.
1974: Pluralist system re-established.
1976: UPS reconstituted as Socialist Party (PS).
1980: Troops sent to defend The Gambia against suspected Libyan invasion.
1981: Military help again sent to The Gambia to thwart coup attempt. Abdou Diouf was appointed president.
1982: Confederation of Senegambia came into effect.
1988: Mamadou Lamine Loum was appointed prime minister.
1989: Diplomatic links with Mauritania severed after 450 died in violent clashes; over 50,000 people repatriated from both countries. Senegambia federation abandoned.
1992: Diplomatic links with Mauritania were re-established.
1993: Assembly and presidential elections were won by the ruling PS.
1998: PS won the general election despite claims of fraud. Abdou Diouf became 'president for life'.
1999: A new 60-member Senate was created as Senegal's second legislative chamber.
2000: In presidential elections, Abdou Diouf lost to Abdoulaye Wade, who appointed Mustafa Niasse as his prime minister. Diouf later announced his withdrawal from politics.
2001: A new constitution was approved by voters in a national referendum. Madior Boye replaced Niasse as prime minister.
2004: A peace settlement was reached with southern separatist Dioula rebels.

Senghor, Léopold Sédar (1906–2001) Senegalese politician and writer, the first president of independent Senegal 1960–80. Previously he was Senegalese deputy to the French national assembly 1946–58, and founder of the Senegalese Progressive Union. He was also a well-known poet and a founder of *négritude*, a black literary and philosophical movement.

senile dementia *dementia associated with old age, often caused by *Alzheimer's disease.

Sennacherib (died 681 BC) King of Assyria from 705 BC. Son of Sargon II, he rebuilt the city of Nineveh on a grand scale, sacked Babylon 689, and defeated Hezekiah, King of Judah, but failed to take Jerusalem. He was assassinated by his sons, and one of them, Esarhaddon, succeeded him.

sense organ any organ that an animal uses to gain information about its surroundings. All sense organs have specialized receptors (such as light receptors in the eye) and some means of translating their response into a nerve impulse that travels to the brain. The main human sense organs are the eye, which detects light and colour (different wavelengths of light); the ear, which detects sound (vibrations of the air) and gravity; the nose, which detects some of the chemical molecules in the air; and the tongue, which detects some of the chemicals in food, giving a sense of taste. There are also many small sense organs in the skin, including pain, temperature, and pressure sensors, contributing to our sense of touch.

sensitivity in biology, the ability of an organism, or part of an organism, to detect changes in the environment. All living things are capable of some sensitivity, and any change detected by an organism is called a stimulus. Plant response to stimuli (for example, light, heat, moisture) is by directional growth (*tropism). In animals, the body cells that detect the stimuli are called receptors, and these are often contained within a *sense organ. For example, the eye is a sense organ, within which the retina contains rod and cone cells which are receptors. The part of the body that responds to a stimulus, such as a muscle, is called an effector, and the communication of stimuli from receptors to effectors is termed 'coordination'; messages are passed from receptors to effectors either via the *nerves or by means of chemicals called *hormones. Rapid communication and response to stimuli, such as light, sound, and scent, can be essential to an animal's well-being and survival, and evolution has led to the development of highly complex mechanisms for this purpose.

sensor in computing, a device designed to detect a physical state or measure a physical quantity, and produce an input signal for a computer. For example, a sensor may detect the fact that a printer has run out of paper or may measure the temperature in a kiln.

sentence in law, the judgement of a court stating the punishment to be imposed following a plea of guilty or a finding of guilt by a jury. Before a sentence is imposed, the antecedents (criminal record) and any relevant reports on the defendant are made known to the judge and the defence may make a plea in mitigation of the sentence.

Seoul *or* **Soul** capital and largest city of South Korea, in the northwest of the country, 32 km/20 mi inland on the Han River, and with its chief port at Inchon on the Yellow Sea; population (2002 est) 11,153,200. The metropolitan area, in which about a quarter of the total population of South Korea live, has grown rapidly since the mid-19th century and is now one of the ten largest in the world. Industries, which provide about half the industrial employment in the country, include engineering, textiles, food processing, electrical and electronic equipment, chemicals, and machinery.

sepal part of a flower, usually green, that surrounds and protects the flower in bud. The sepals are derived from modified leaves, and are collectively known as the *calyx.

separation of powers limiting the powers of government by separating governmental functions into the executive, legislative, and judiciary. The concept has its fullest practical expression in the US constitution (see *federalism). Articles I, II, and III establish the three branches of government, and specify powers entrusted to each as a means of ensuring that no one branch can exert unlimited power.

Sephardi plural **Sephardim**, Jews descended from those expelled from Spain and Portugal in the 15th century, or from those forcibly converted during the Inquisition to Christianity (Marranos). Many settled in North Africa and in the Mediterranean countries, as well as in the Netherlands, England, and Dutch colonies in the New World. Sephardim speak Ladino, a 15th-century Romance dialect, as well as the language of their nation.

sepia brown pigment produced from the black fluid of cuttlefish. After 1870 it replaced the use of bistre (made from charred wood) in wash drawings due to its warmer range of colours. Sepia fades rapidly in bright light.

Sepoy Rebellion alternative name for the *Indian Mutiny, a revolt of Indian soldiers against the British in India 1857–58.

sepsis general term for infectious change in the body caused by bacteria or their toxins.

septicaemia general term for any form of *blood poisoning.

sequencing in biochemistry, determining the sequence of chemical subunits within a large molecule. Techniques for sequencing amino acids in proteins were established in the 1950s, insulin being the first for which the sequence was completed. The Human Genome Project was set up to determine the sequence of the 3 billion base pairs within human DNA. On 14 April 2003, scientists announced the completion of the mapping of the whole human genome.

sequoia either of two species of *conifer tree belonging to the redwood family, native to the western USA. The **redwood** (*Sequoia sempervirens*) is a long-living timber tree, and one specimen, the Howard Libbey Redwood, is the world's tallest tree at 110 m/361 ft, with a trunk circumference of 13.4 m/44 ft. The **giant sequoia** (*Sequoiadendron giganteum*) reaches up to 30 m/100 ft in circumference at the base of the trunk, and grows almost as tall as the redwood. It is also (except for the bristlecone pine) the oldest living tree, some specimens being estimated at over 3,500 years of age. (Family Taxodiaceae.)

Serapis *or* **Sarapis** ancient Graeco-Egyptian god, a combination of *Apis, the bull of Memphis who carried the dead, and *Osiris, ruler of the underworld. Invented by Ptolemy I to unify his Greek and Egyptian subjects, he became the official deity of the kingdom replacing Osiris. He was worshipped in Greek at the **Serapeum**, a Greek-style temple and statue in Alexandria, and was mainly regarded as a healer of the sick.

Serb largest ethnic group in the former Yugoslavia, found mainly in Serbia and Montenegro, but also in the neighbouring independent republics of Bosnia-Herzegovina and Croatia. Their language is generally recognized to be the same as Croat and is hence known as *Serbo-Croat.

Serbia Serbo-Croat **Srbija**, constituent republic, together with Montenegro, of Serbia and Montenegro, which includes *Kosovo and *Vojvodina; area 88,400 sq km/34,100 sq mi; population (1991 est) 9,791,400. The capital is *Belgrade.

Serbia and Montenegro

formerly **the Federal Republic of Yugoslavia (1992–2003)**
National name: *Srbija i Crna Gora/Serbia and Montenegro*

Area: 102,173 sq km/39,449 sq mi
Capital: Belgrade
Major towns/cities: Priština, Novi Sad, Niš, Kragujevac, Podgorica (formerly Titograd), Subotica
Physical features: federation of republics of Serbia and Montenegro and two former autonomous provinces, Kosovo and Vojvodina
Head of state: Svetozar Marovic from 2003
Head of government: Vojislav Koštunica (Serbia) from 2004 and Milo Djukanovic (Montenegro) from 2003
Political system: emergent democracy
Political executive: limited presidency
Political parties: Socialist Party of Serbia (SPS), Serb nationalist, reform socialist (ex-communist); Montenegrin Social Democratic Party (SDPCG), federalist, reform socialist (ex-communist); Serbian Radical Party (SRS), Serb nationalist, extreme right wing; People's Assembly Party, Christian democrat, centrist; Democratic Party (DS), moderate nationalist; Democratic Party of Serbia (DSS), moderate nationalist; Democratic Community of Vojvodina Hungarians (DZVM), ethnic Hungarian; Democratic Party of Albanians/Party of Democratic Action (DPA/PDA), ethnic Albanian; New Socialist Party of Montenegro (NSPM), left of centre
Currency: new Yugoslav dinar
GNI per capita (PPP): (US$) 2,500 (2002 est)
Exports: basic manufactures, machinery and transport equipment, clothing, miscellaneous manufactured articles, food and live animals. Principal market: Italy 16.3% (2001)
Population: 10,527,000 (2003 est)
Language: Serbian, as well as ethnic minority languages (including Albanian)
Religion: Serbian and Montenegrin Orthodox; Muslim in southern Serbia
Life expectancy: 71 (men); 76 (women) (2000–05)

Chronology

3rd century BC: Serbia (then known as Moesia Superior) conquered by Romans; empire was extended to Belgrade centuries later by Emperor Augustus.
6th century AD: Slavic tribes, including Serbs, Croats, and Slovenes, crossed River Danube and settled in Balkan Peninsula.
879: Serbs converted to Orthodox Church by St Cyril and St Methodius.
mid-10th–11th centuries: Serbia broke free briefly from Byzantine Empire to establish independent state.
1217: Independent Serbian kingdom re-established, reaching its height in mid-14th century under Stefan Dushan, when it controlled much of Albania and northern Greece.
1389: Serbian army defeated by Ottoman Turks at Battle of Kosovo; area became Turkish *pashalik* (province). Montenegro in southwest survived as sovereign principality. Croatia and Slovenia in northwest became part of Habsburg Empire.
18th century: Vojvodina enjoyed protection from the Austrian Habsburgs.
1815: Uprisings against Turkish rule secured autonomy for Serbia.
1878: Independence achieved as Kingdom of Serbia, after Turks defeated by Russians in war over Bulgaria.
1912–13: During Balkan Wars, Serbia expanded its territory at expense of Turkey and Bulgaria.
1918: Joined Croatia and Slovenia, formerly under Austrian Habsburg control, to form Kingdom of Serbs, Croats, and Slovenes under Serbian Peter Karageorgevic (Peter I); Montenegro's citizens voted to depose their ruler, King Nicholas, and join the union.
1929: New name of Yugoslavia ('Land of the Southern Slavs') adopted; Serbian-dominated military dictatorship established by King Alexander I as opposition mounted from Croatian federalists.
1934: Alexander I assassinated by a Macedonian with Croatian terrorist links; his young son Peter II succeeded, with Paul, his uncle, as regent; Nazi Germany and fascist Italy increased their influence.
1941: Following a coup by pro-Allied air-force officers, Nazi Germany invaded. Peter II fled to England. Armed resistance to German rule began, spearheaded by pro-royalist, Serbian-based Chetniks ('Army of the Fatherland'), led by Gen Draza Mihailovic, and communist Partisans ('National Liberation Army'), led by Marshal Tito. An estimated 900,000 Yugoslavs died in the war, including more than 400,000 Serbs and 200,000 Croats.
1943: Provisional government formed by Tito at liberated Jajce in Bosnia.
1945: Yugoslav Federal People's Republic formed under leadership of Tito; communist constitution introduced.
1948: Split with Soviet Union after Tito objected to Soviet 'hegemonism'; expelled from Cominform.
1953: Workers' self-management principle enshrined in constitution and private farming supported; Tito became president.
1961: Nonaligned movement formed under Yugoslavia's leadership.
1971: In response to mounting separatist demands in Croatia, new system of collective and rotating leadership introduced.
1980: Tito died; collective leadership assumed power.

serenade

1981–82: Armed forces suppressed demonstrations in Kosovo province, southern Serbia, by Albanians demanding full republic status.

1986: Slobodan Milošević, a populist-nationalist hardliner who had the ambition of creating a 'Greater Serbia', became leader of communist party in the Serbian republic.

1988: Economic difficulties: 1,800 strikes, 250% inflation, 20% unemployment. Ethnic unrest in Montenegro and Vojvodina, and separatist demands in rich northwestern republics of Croatia and Slovenia; 'market socialist' reform package, encouraging private sector, inward investment, and liberalizing prices combined with austerity wage freeze.

1989: Reformist Croatian Ante Markovic became prime minister. Ethnic riots in Kosovo province against Serbian attempt to end autonomous status of Kosovo and Vojvodina; at least 30 were killed and a state of emergency imposed.

1990: Multiparty systems were established in the republics; Kosovo and Vojvodina were stripped of autonomy. In Croatia, Slovenia, Bosnia, and Macedonia elections brought to power new noncommunist governments seeking a looser confederation.

1991: Demonstrations against Serbian president Slobodan Milošević in Belgrade were crushed by riot police and tanks. Slovenia and Croatia declared their independence, resulting in clashes between federal and republican armies; Slovenia accepted a peace pact sponsored by the European Community (EC), but fighting intensified in Croatia, where Serb militias controlled over a third of the republic; Federal President Stipe Mesic and Prime Minister Markovic resigned.

1992: There was an EC-brokered ceasefire in Croatia; the EC and the USA recognized Slovenia's and Croatia's independence. Bosnia-Herzegovina and Macedonia then declared their independence, and Bosnia-Herzegovina's independence was recognized by the EC and the USA. A New Federal Republic of Yugoslavia (FRY) was proclaimed by Serbia and Montenegro but not internationally recognized; international sanctions were imposed and UN membership was suspended. Ethnic Albanians proclaimed a new 'Republic of Kosovo', but it was not recognized.

1993: Pro-Milošević Zoran Lilic became Yugoslav president. There was antigovernment rioting in Belgrade. Macedonia was recognized as independent under the name of the Former Yugoslav Republic of Macedonia. The economy was severely damaged by international sanctions.

1994: A border blockade was imposed by Yugoslavia against Bosnian Serbs; sanctions were eased as a result.

1995: Serbia played a key role in the US-brokered Dayton peace accord for Bosnia-Herzegovina and accepted the separate existence of Bosnia and Croatia.

1996: Diplomatic relations were restored between Serbia and Croatia, and UN sanctions against Serbia were lifted. Allies of Milošević were successful in parliamentary elections. Diplomatic relations were established with Bosnia-Herzegovina. There was mounting opposition to Milošević's government following its refusal to accept opposition victories in municipal elections.

1997: Milošević was elected president and the pro-democracy mayor of Belgrade was ousted. The validity of Serbian presidential elections continued to be questioned. The anti-Milošević candidate was elected president of Montenegro.

1998: A Serb military offensive against ethnic Albanian separatists in Kosovo led to a refugee and humanitarian crisis. The offensive against the Kosovo Liberation Army (KLA) was condemned by the international community and NATO military intervention was threatened. President Milošević appointed Momir Bulatovic as prime minister.

1999: Fighting continued between Serbians and Albanian separatists in Kosovo. In March, following the failure of efforts to reach a negotiated settlement, NATO began a bombing campaign against the Serbs; the ethnic cleansing of Kosovars by Serbs intensified and the refugee crisis in neighbouring countries worsened as hundreds of thousands of ethnic Albanians fled Kosovo. In May President Milošević was indicted for crimes against humanity by the International War Crimes Tribunal in The Hague. A peace was agreed on NATO terms in June. Refugees began returning to Kosovo.

2000: Presidential elections were held in September in which opposition candidate Vojislav Koštunica claimed outright victory against President Slobodan Milošević, but the federal election commission ordered a second round of voting to be held. The opposition claimed ballot-rigging and organized mass demonstrations throughout Yugoslavia, in the face of which Milošević conceded defeat. Zoran Djindjic was appointed prime minister. The UN reinstated Yugoslavia's membership, which had been suspended in 1992, in October. There were clashes with Albanian guerillas on the border between Serbia and Kosovo in November. Fresh parliamentary elections held in December gave a majority to Koštunica's party.

2001: Former president Milošević was arrested and charged with abuse of power, corruption, and fraud.

2002: The most significant war crimes trial since World War II – that of former president Slobodan Milošević – began in the Hague, the Netherlands. The constituent republics of Serbia and Montenegro agreed to stay together in a looser federation. Both republics were given equal powers and would have common foreign and defence policies.

2003: The Federal Republic of Yugoslavia ceased to exist as the two remaining republics of the former Yugoslav federation officially became a new constitutional entity called Serbia and Montenegro. Prime Minister Zoran Djindjic was assassinated in Belgrade. Serbia and Montenegro became the 45th member of the Council of Europe.

2005: Montenegro sought to end the union on grounds of cost and inefficiency but this was rejected by Serbia.

Serbo-Croat *or* **Serbo-Croatian** the most widely spoken language in the former constituent republics of Yugoslavia – especially Serbia and Montenegro, Croatia, and Bosnia-Herzegovina – it is a member of the South Slavonic branch of the Indo-European family, and has over 17 million speakers. The different dialects of Serbo-Croat tend to be written by the Greek Orthodox Serbs in the Cyrillic script, and by the Roman Catholic Croats in the Latin script.

serenade musical piece for chamber orchestra or wind instruments in several movements, originally intended for informal evening entertainment, such as Mozart's *Eine kleine Nachtmusik/A Little Night Music*.

serfdom the legal and economic status of peasants under *feudalism. Serfs could not be sold like slaves, but they were not free to leave their master's estate without his permission. They had to work the lord's land without pay for a number of days every week and pay a percentage of their produce to the lord every year. They also served as soldiers in the event of conflict. Serfs also had to perform extra labour at harvest time and other busy seasons; in return they were allowed to cultivate a portion of the estate for their own benefit.

Sergius, St, of Radonezh (1314–1392) born Barfolomay Kirillovich, Patron saint of Russia, who founded the Eastern Orthodox monastery of the Blessed Trinity near Moscow 1334. Mediator among Russian feudal princes, he inspired the victory of Dmitri, Grand Duke of Moscow, over the Tatar khan Mamai at Kulikovo, on the upper Don, in 1380.

serialism in music, a later form of the *twelve-tone system of composition, invented by Arnold *Schoenberg, and hinted at in the later works of Max Reger.

series circuit electrical circuit in which the components are connected end to end, so that the current flows through them all one after the other.

Serpens constellation on the celestial equator (see *celestial sphere), represented as a serpent coiled around the body of Ophiuchus. It is the only constellation divided into two halves: **Serpens Caput**, the head (on one side of Ophiuchus), and **Serpens Cauda**, the tail (on the other side). Its main feature is the Eagle nebula.

serpentine member of a group of minerals, hydrous magnesium silicate, $Mg_3Si_2O_5(OH)_4$, occurring in soft *metamorphic rocks and usually dark green. The fibrous form **chrysotile** is a source of *asbestos; other forms are **antigorite** and **lizardite**. Serpentine minerals are formed by hydration of ultramafic rocks during metamorphism. Rare snake-patterned forms are used in ornamental carving.

serum clear fluid that separates out from clotted blood. It is blood plasma with the anticoagulant proteins removed, and contains *antibodies and other proteins, as well as the fats and sugars of the blood. It can be produced synthetically, and is used to protect against disease.

serval African wild cat *Felis serval*. It is a slender, long-limbed cat, about 1 m/3 ft long, with a yellowish-brown, black-spotted coat. It has large, sensitive ears, with which it locates its prey, mainly birds and rodents.

service industry or **tertiary industry** sector of the economy that supplies services such as retailing, banking, and education.

service tree deciduous tree (*S. domestica*) with alternate pinnate leaves (leaflets growing either side of the stem), creamy white flowers, and small, brown, edible, oval fruits, native to Europe and Asia. The European wild service tree (*S. torminalis*) has oblong rather than pointed leaflets. It is related to the *mountain ash. (Genus *Sorbus*, family Rosaceae.)

servomechanism automatic control system used in aircraft, motor cars, and other complex machines. A specific input, such as moving a lever or joystick, causes a specific output, such as feeding current to an electric motor that moves, for example, the rudder of the aircraft. At the same time, the position of the

rudder is detected and fed back to the central control, so that small adjustments can continually be made to maintain the desired course.

sesame annual herbaceous plant, probably native to Southeast Asia, and widely cultivated in India. It produces oily seeds used in cooking and soap making. (*Sesamum indicum*, family Pedaliaceae.)

sessile in botany, describing a leaf, flower, or fruit that lacks a stalk and sits directly on the stem, as with the sessile acorns of certain *oaks. In zoology, it is an animal that normally stays in the same place, such as a barnacle or mussel. The term is also applied to the eyes of *crustaceans when these lack stalks and sit directly on the head.

set or **class** in mathematics, any collection of defined things (elements), provided the elements are distinct and that there is a rule to decide whether an element is a member of a set. It is usually denoted by a capital letter and indicated by curly brackets.

Set or **Seth** or **Setekh** in Egyptian mythology, the god of night, the desert, and of all evils. Portrayed as a grotesque animal with long ears and a tail, Set was the murderer of his brother *Osiris, later ruler of the underworld.

setter any of various breeds of gun dog, called 'setters' because they were trained to crouch or 'set' on the sight of game to be pursued. They stand about 66 cm/26 in high and weigh about 25 kg/55 lb. They have a long, smooth coat, feathered tails, and spaniel-like faces.

Settlement, Act of in Britain following the *Glorious Revolution of 1688, a law passed in 1701 during the reign of King William III, designed to ensure a Protestant succession tothe throne by excluding the Roman Catholic descendants of *James II in favour of the Protestant House of Hanover. Elizabeth II still reigns under this act.

Seurat, Georges Pierre (1859–1891) French artist. One of the major post-Impressionists, he originated, with Paul Signac, the technique of *pointillism (painting with small dabs rather than long brushstrokes). One of his best-known works is *A Sunday Afternoon on the Island of La Grande Jatte* 1886 (Art Institute of Chicago).

seven deadly sins in Christian theology, anger, avarice, envy, gluttony, lust, pride, and sloth (or dejection). These vices are considered fundamental to all other sins.

Seventh-Day Adventist or **Adventist** member of the Protestant religious sect of the same name. It originated in the USA in the fervent expectation of Christ's Second Coming, or advent, that swept across New York State following William Miller's prophecy that Christ would return on 22 October 1844. When this failed to come to pass, a number of Millerites, as his followers were called, reinterpreted his prophetic speculations and continued to maintain that the millennium was imminent. Adventists observe Saturday as the Sabbath and emphasize healing and diet; many are vegetarians. The sect has 36,920 organized churches and almost 8 million members in 210 countries and territories (1995).

Seven Weeks' War war 1866 between Austria and Prussia, engineered by the German chancellor *Bismarck. It was nominally over the possession of *Schleswig-Holstein, but it was actually to confirm Prussia's superseding Austria as the leading German state. The Prussian victory at the Battle of Sadowa was the culmination of General von Moltke's victories.

Seven Wonders of the World in antiquity, the *pyramids of Egypt, the *Hanging Gardens of Babylon, the temple of Artemis at *Ephesus, the Greek sculptor Phidias' chryselephantine statue of Zeus at *Olympia, the Mausoleum at *Halicarnassus, the *Colossus of Rhodes, and the lighthouse on the island of Pharos in the Bay of Alexandria.

Seven Years' War war in North America 1756–63 arising from the conflict between Austria and Prussia, and between France and Britain over colonial supremacy. Britain and Prussia defeated France, Austria, Spain, and Russia; Britain gained control of India and many of France's colonies, including Canada. The fighting between France and Britain in North American was known as the French and Indian War.

Severn Welsh Hafren, river in Britain, which rises on the slopes of Plynlimon, in Ceredigion, west Wales, and flows east and then south, finally forming a long estuary leading into the Bristol Channel; length 336 km/208 mi. The Severn is navigable for 290 km/180 mi, up to Welshpool (Trallwng) on the Welsh border. The principal towns on its course are Shrewsbury, Worcester, and Gloucester. England and South Wales are linked by two road bridges and a railway tunnel crossing the Severn. A remarkable feature of the river is a tidal wave known as the 'Severn Bore' that flows for some miles upstream and can reach a height of 2 m/6 ft.

Severus, Lucius Septimius (AD 146–211) Roman emperor 193–211. After holding various commands under the emperors *Marcus Aurelius and *Commodus, Severus was appointed commander-in-chief of the army on the Danube, in the Roman provinces, Pannonia and Illyria. After the murder of Pertinax (Roman emperor 193), he was proclaimed emperor by his troops. Severus was an able administrator. He was born in North Africa at Leptis Magna, and was the only native of Africa to become emperor. He died at York.

sewing machine apparatus for the mechanical sewing of cloth, leather, and other materials by a needle, powered by hand, treadle, or electric motor. The lockstitch machine, in common use, which uses a double thread, was invented independently in the USA by both Walter Hunt (in 1834) and Elias Howe, who patented his machine in 1846. Howe's machine was the basis of the machine patented in 1851 by US inventor Isaac *Singer. His first machine was developed for factory use, but he went on to produce sewing machines for the domestic market. His name became associated with the sewing machine.

sex determination process by which the sex of an organism is determined. In many species, the sex of an individual is dictated by the two sex chromosomes (X and Y) it receives from its parents. In mammals, some plants, and a few insects, males are XY, and females XX; in birds, reptiles, some amphibians, and butterflies the reverse is the case. In bees and wasps, males are produced from unfertilized eggs, females from fertilized eggs. In 1991 it was shown that maleness is caused by a single gene, 14 base pairs long, on the Y chromosome. Environmental factors can affect

some fish and reptiles, such as turtles, where sex is influenced by the temperature at which the eggs develop. (See diagram, p. 822.)

sex hormone steroid hormone produced and secreted by the gonads (testes and ovaries). Sex hormones control development and reproductive functions and influence sexual and other behaviour.

sexism belief in (or set of implicit assumptions about) the superiority of one's own sex, often accompanied by a *stereotype or preconceived idea about the opposite sex. Sexism may also be accompanied by *discrimination on the basis of sex, generally as practised by men against women.

sex linkage in genetics, the tendency for certain characteristics to occur exclusively, or predominantly, in one sex only. Human examples include red-green colour blindness and haemophilia, both found predominantly in males. In both cases, these characteristics are *recessive and are determined by genes on the *X chromosome.

Sex Pistols, the UK punk-rock group (1975–78) that became notorious under the guidance of their manager Malcolm McLaren (1946–). Their first singles, 'Anarchy in the UK' (1976) and 'God Save the Queen' (1977), unrestrained attacks on contemporary Britain, made the Pistols into figures the media loved to hate.

sextant navigational instrument for determining latitude by measuring the angle between some heavenly body and the horizon. It was invented in 1730 by John Hadley (1682–1744) and can be used only in clear weather.

sexually transmitted disease (STD) any disease transmitted by sexual contact, involving transfer of body fluids. STDs include not only traditional *venereal disease, but also a growing list of conditions, such as *AIDS and scabies, which are known to be spread primarily by sexual contact. Other diseases that are transmitted sexually include viral *hepatitis. The World Health Organization (WHO) estimates that there are 356,000 new cases of STDs daily worldwide (1995).

sexual reproduction reproductive process in organisms that requires the union, or *fertilization, of gametes (such as eggs and sperm). These are usually produced by two different individuals, although self-fertilization occurs in a few *hermaphrodites such as tapeworms. Most organisms other than bacteria and cyanobacteria (*blue-green algae) show some sort of sexual process. Except in some lower organisms, the gametes are of two distinct types called the egg (*ovum) and the *sperm. The organisms producing the eggs are called females, and those producing the sperm, males. The fusion of a male and female gamete produces a zygote, from which a new individual develops. See *reproduction.

sexual selection process similar to *natural selection but relating exclusively to success in finding a mate for the purpose of sexual reproduction and producing offspring. Sexual selection occurs when one sex (usually but not always the female) invests more effort in producing young than the other. Members of the other sex compete for access to this limited resource (usually males competing for the chance to mate with females).

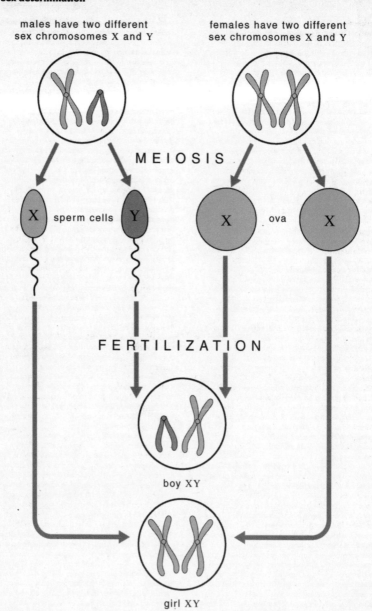

males have two different
sex chromosomes X and Y

females have two different
sex chromosomes X and Y

MEIOSIS

X   sperm cells   Y

X   ova   X

FERTILIZATION

boy XY

girl XY

sex determination In humans, sex is determined by the male. Sperm cells contain an X or a Y chromosome but egg cells contain only X chromosomes. If a sperm cell carrying an X chromosome fertilizes the egg the resulting baby will be female; if the sperm cell is carrying a Y chromosome then the baby will be male.

Seychelles
National name: *Republic of Seychelles*

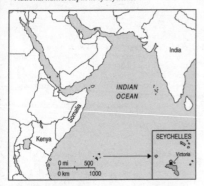

Area: 453 sq km/174 sq mi
Capital: Victoria (on Mahé island) (and chief port)
Major towns/cities: Cascade, Port Glaud, Misere, Anse Boileau, Takamaka
Physical features: comprises two distinct island groups: one, the Granitic group, concentrated, the other, the Outer or Coralline group, widely scattered; totals over 100 islands and islets
Head of state and government: James Michel from 2004
Political system: emergent democracy
Political executive: limited presidency
Political parties: Seychelles People's Progressive Front (SPPF), nationalist socialist; Democratic Party (DP), left of centre
Currency: Seychelles rupee
GNI per capita (PPP): (US$) 11,150 (2001)
Exports: canned tuna, frozen prawns, fresh and frozen fish, shark fins, cinnamon bark, refined petroleum products. Principal market: UK 30.7% (2000)
Population: 81,000 (2003 est)
Language: Creole (an Asian, African, European mixture) (95%), English, French (all official)
Religion: Roman Catholic 90%
Life expectancy: 68 (men); 78 (women) (2000–05)
Chronology
Early 16th century: First sighted by European navigators.
1744: Became French colony.
1756: Claimed as French possession and named after an influential French family.
1770s: French colonists brought African slaves to settle the previously uninhabited islands; plantations established.
1794: Captured by British during French Revolutionary Wars.
1814: Ceded by France to Britain; incorporated as dependency of Mauritius.
1835: Slavery abolished by British, leading to influx of liberated slaves from Mauritius and Chinese and Indian immigrants.
1903: Became British crown colony, separate from Mauritius.
1963–64: First political parties formed.

1976: Independence achieved from Britain as republic within Commonwealth, with a moderate, James Mancham, of the centre-right Seychelles Democratic Party (SDP) as president.
1977: More radical France-Albert René ousted Mancham in armed bloodless coup and took over presidency; white settlers emigrated.
1979: Nationalistic socialist Seychelles People's Progressive Front (SPPF) became sole legal party under new constitution; became nonaligned state.
1981: An attempted coup by South African mercenaries was thwarted.
1993: A new multiparty constitution was adopted. René defeated Mancham, who had returned from exile, in competitive presidential elections; SPPF won parliamentary elections.
1998: President René was re-elected. SPUP won assembly elections.
2004: President René resigned from office and was replaced by the vice-president James Michel.

Seyfert galaxy galaxy in which a small, bright centre is caused by hot gas moving at high speed around a massive central object, possibly a *black hole. Almost all Seyferts are spiral galaxies. They seem to be closely related to *quasars, but are about 100 times fainter. They are named after their discoverer, US astronomer Carl Seyfert.

Seymour, Jane (c. 1509–1537) English noble, third wife of Henry VIII, whom she married 1536. She died soon after the birth of her son Edward VI.

Sezession (German 'secession') name given to various groups of German and Austrian artists in the 1890s who 'seceded' from official academic art institutions in order to found new schools of painting. The first was in Munich in 1892; the next, linked with the paintings of Gustav *Klimt and the art nouveau movement, was the Vienna Sezession in 1897; the Berlin Sezession, led by the Impressionist Max Liebermann (1847–1935), followed in 1899.

Shaanxi *or* **Shensi** province of northwest China, bounded to the north by Inner Mongolia, to the east by Shanxi and Henan, to the south by Hubei and Sichuan, and to the west by Gansu and Ningxia Hui Autonomous Region; area 195,800 sq km/75,600 sq mi; population (2000 est) 36,050,000. The capital is *Xi'an. There are coalmining, iron, steel, textile, and aerospace industries. Wheat, maize, rice, fruit, and tea are grown.

Shackleton, Ernest Henry (1874–1922) Irish Antarctic explorer. In 1908–09, he commanded the British Antarctic expedition that reached 88° 23′ S latitude, located the magnetic South Pole, and climbed Mount *Erebus. He was knighted in 1909. On his second Antarctic expedition (1914–16) his ship *Endurance* left South Georgia in December 1914 for the transantarctic crossing but was crushed by the ice. Shackleton and his crew eventually reached Elephant Island, from where he and five others set out in an open boat to get help. They finally landed in South Georgia in May 1916.

shad any of several marine fishes, especially the genus *Alosa*, the largest (60 cm/2 ft long and 2.7 kg/6 lb in weight) of the herring family (Clupeidae). They migrate in shoals to breed in rivers.

shadow area of darkness behind an opaque object that cannot be reached by some or all of the light coming

823

from a light source in front. Its presence may be explained in terms of light rays travelling in straight lines and being unable to bend around obstacles. The light in front of the object is blocked. A point source of light produces an umbra, a completely black shadow with sharp edges. An extended source of light produces both a central umbra and a penumbra, a region of semidarkness with blurred edges where darkness gives way to light.

shadow cabinet the chief members of the British parliamentary opposition, each of whom is responsible for commenting on the policies and performance of a government ministry.

Shaftesbury or **Shaston** market town and agricultural centre in Dorset, southwest England, 30 km/19 mi southwest of Salisbury; population (1991) 6,200. Industries include tourism. King Alfred is said to have founded an abbey on the site in 880 (consecrated in 888); King Canute died at Shaftesbury in 1035.

Shaftesbury, Anthony Ashley Cooper, 1st Earl of Shaftesbury (1621–1683) English politician, a supporter of the Restoration of the monarchy. He became Lord Chancellor in 1672, but went into opposition in 1673 and began to organize the *Whig Party. He headed the Whigs' demand for the exclusion of the future James II from the succession, secured the passing of the Habeas Corpus Act of 1679, then, when accused of treason in 1681, fled to Holland. He became baronet in 1631, baron in 1661, and was created earl in 1672.

shag waterbird *Phalacrocorax aristoclis*, order Pelecaniformes, related to the *cormorant. It is smaller than the cormorant, with a green tinge to its plumage and in the breeding season has a crest. Its food consists mainly of sand eels for which it dives, staying underwater for up to 54 seconds. It breeds on deeply fissured cliffs, and on rocky parts of isolated islands.

shah (more formally, **shahanshah** 'king of kings') traditional title of ancient Persian rulers, and also of those of the recent *Pahlavi dynasty in Iran.

Shah Jahan (1592–1666) Mogul emperor of India from 1628, under whom the dynasty reached its zenith. Succeeding his father *Jahangir, he extended Mogul authority into the Deccan plateau (eastern India), subjugating Ahmadnagar, Bijapur, and Golconda 1636, but lost Kandahar in the northwest to the Persians 1653. His reign marked the high point of Indo-Muslim architecture, with Delhi being rebuilt as Shahjahanabad, while the Taj Mahal and Pearl Mosque were constructed at Agra. On falling seriously ill 1658 he was dethroned and imprisoned by his son *Aurangzeb.

Shaka (or **Chaka) (c. 1787–1828)** Zulu chief who formed a Zulu empire in southeastern Africa. He seized power from his half-brother 1816 and then embarked on a bloody military campaign to unite the Zulu clans. He was assassinated by his two half-brothers.

Shaker member of the Christian sect of the **United Society of Believers in Christ's Second Appearing**, called Shakers because of their ecstatic trembling and shaking during worship. The movement was founded by James and Jane Wardley in England about 1747, and taken to North America in 1774 by Ann Lee (1736–1784).

Shakespeare, William (1564–1616) English dramatist and poet. He is considered the greatest English dramatist. His plays, written in blank verse with some prose, can be broadly divided into *comedies,

including *A Midsummer Night's Dream, The Comedy of Errors, As You Like It, Much Ado About Nothing,* and *Measure For Measure*; historical plays, such as *Henry VI* (in three parts), *Richard III,* and *Henry IV* (in two parts), which often show cynical political wisdom; and tragedies, including *Romeo and Juliet, Hamlet, Othello, King Lear,* and *Macbeth.* He also wrote numerous *sonnets and longer poetry, often for wealthy patrons.

shale fine-grained and finely layered *sedimentary rock composed of silt and clay. It is a weak rock, splitting easily along bedding planes to form thin, even slabs (by contrast, mudstone splits into irregular flakes). Oil shale contains kerogen, a solid bituminous material that yields *petroleum when heated.

shallot small onion in which bulbs are clustered like garlic; it is used for cooking and in pickles. (*Allium ascalonicum,* family Liliaceae.)

shaman (Tungu *samân*) ritual leader who acts as intermediary between society and the supernatural world in many indigenous cultures of Asia, Africa, and the Americas. Also known as a **medicine man, seer,** or **sorcerer,** the shaman is expected to use special powers to cure illness and control good and evil spirits.

Shamir, Yitzhak Yernitsky (1915–) Polish-born Israeli right-wing politician; prime minister 1983–84 and 1986–92; leader of the Likud (Consolidation Party) until 1993. He was foreign minister under Menachem Begin 1980–83, and again foreign minister in Shimon *Peres's unity government 1984–86.

shamrock any of several leguminous plants (see *legume) whose leaves are divided into three leaflets, including *clovers. St Patrick is said to have used one to illustrate the doctrine of the Holy Trinity, and it was made the national badge of Ireland. (Family Leguminosae.)

Shan member of a people of the mountainous borderlands separating Thailand, Laos, Myanmar (Burma), and China. They are related to the Laos and *Thais, and their language belongs to the Sino-Tibetan family.

Shandong or **Shantung** province of east China, bounded to the north by the Bohai Gulf, to the east by the Yellow Sea, to the south by Jiangsu and Anhui, and to the west by Henan and Hebei provinces; area 153,300 sq km/59,200 sq mi; population (2000 est) 90,790,000. It is one of the most densely populated provinces of China. The capital is Jinan. There are coal, oil, petrochemical, engineering, and textile industries. Cereals, cotton, peanuts, wild silk, and wine are produced.

Shang dynasty also known as **Yin dynasty,** China's first fully authenticated dynasty, *c.* 1500–*c.* 1066 BC, which saw the start of the Bronze Age. Shang rulers dominated the Huang He (Yellow River) plain of northern China, developing a complex agricultural civilization which used a written language.

Shanghai largest urban settlement and mainland port in China, on the East China Sea in Jiangsu province, on the Huangpu and Wusong rivers, 24 km/15 mi from the Chang Jiang estuary; population (1999 est) 8,937,200. The municipality of Shanghai, which has the status of a province, answering directly to the central government, has an area of 5,800 sq km/2,239 sq mi; population (2000 est) 16,740,000. Shanghai is one of the largest seaports in the world and is China's principal commercial and financial centre, as well as being a major centre of industry. Textiles, paper, chemicals, steel, vehicles, agricultural machinery, precision instruments, and flour are produced; other industries include vegetable-oil milling, shipbuilding, and oil refining.

Shankar, Ravi (1920–) Indian composer and virtuoso of the sitar. He has been influential in making Indian music more popular in the West. He has composed two concertos for sitar and orchestra (1971 and 1981), and film music, including scores for Satyajit Ray's *Pather Panchali* (1955) and Richard Attenborough's *Gandhi* (1982). He also founded music schools in Bombay (now Mumbai), India (1962), and Los Angeles, California (1967).

Shannon longest river in Ireland, rising 105 m/344 ft above sea level in the Cuilcagh Mountains in County Cavan, and flowing 386 km/240 mi to the Atlantic Ocean past Athlone, and through loughs Allen, Boderg, Forbes, Ree, and Derg. The estuary, which is 110 km/68 mi long and 3–16 km/2–10 mi wide, forms the northern boundary of County Limerick. The river is navigable as far as Limerick city, above which are the rapids of Doonas and Castletroy. The river is known for its salmon farms, Castleconnell being an important centre. It also has the first and largest hydroelectric scheme in the Republic of Ireland (constructed 1925–29), with hydroelectric installations at and above Ardnacrusha, 5 km/3 mi north of Limerick.

Shanxi or **Shansi** province of north China, bounded to the north by Inner Mongolia, to the east by Hebei, to the south by Henan, and to the west by Shaanxi; area 157,100 sq km/60,700 sq mi; population (2000 est) 32,970,000. The capital is Taiyuan. There are coal, iron and steel, heavy machinery, mining equipment, and chemical industries, while cement, paper, and textiles are also manufactured. Fruit and cereals are grown, and meat is produced.

share in finance, that part of the *capital of a company held by a member (shareholder). Shares may be numbered and are issued as units of definite face value; shareholders are not always called on to pay the full face value of their shares, though they bind themselves to do so.

sharecropping farming someone else's land, where the farmer gives the landowner a proportion of the crop instead of money. This system of rent payment was common in the USA, especially the South, until after World War II. It is still common in parts of the developing world; for example, in India. Often the farmer is left with such a small share of the crop that he or she is doomed to poverty.

Shari'a or **Shari'ah** the law of *Islam believed by Muslims to be based on divine revelation. It consists of the *Koran (or Quran or Qur'an), with the Sunna, the *Hadith, and the Sirah as written secondary sources. Other sources include the usual custom of the Muslim community, and the agreement of Muslim lawyers or the opinion of one pious Muslim lawyer. Under the Shari'a, *qisas*, or retribution, allows a family to exact equal punishment on an accused; *diyat*, or blood money, is payable to a dead person's family as compensation.

shark any member of various orders of cartilaginous fishes (class Chondrichthyes), found throughout the oceans of the world. There are about 400 known species of shark. They have tough, usually grey skin covered in denticles (small toothlike scales). A shark's streamlined body has side pectoral fins, a high dorsal fin, and a forked tail with a large upper lobe. Five open gill slits are visible on each side of the generally pointed head. They shed and replace their teeth continually, even before birth. Teeth may be replaced as frequently as every week. Most sharks are fish-eaters, and a few will attack humans. They range from several feet in length to the **great white shark** *Carcharodon carcharias*, 9 m/30 ft long, and the harmless plankton-feeding **whale shark** *Rhincodon typus*, over 15 m/50 ft in length.

Sharman, Helen (1963–) English astronaut and the first Briton to fly in space, chosen from 13,000 applicants for a 1991 joint UK–Russian space flight. A research chemist, she was launched on 18 May 1991 in *Soyuz* TM-12 and spent six days with Russian cosmonauts conducting scientific experiments aboard the *Mir space station.

Sharon, Ariel (1928–) Israeli right-wing Likud politician, prime minister from 2001. Initially a soldier, he left the army in 1973 to help found the Likud party with Menachem *Begin. He was elected to the Knesset (Israeli parliament) in 1977, and held a succession of influential posts. A leading member of the staunchly nationalist new right, he took over Likud's leadership from Binyamin Netanyahu after the party's defeat in the 1999 general election. His electoral victory over Labour's Ehud Barak in February 2001 endangered the Israel–Palestine peace process, as it was his controversial visit to Jerusalem's Haram al-Sharif (Temple Mount) in September 2000 that precipitated a second Palestinian intifada (uprising) against Israeli forces that claimed hundreds of lives.

sharp symbol #, in music, a sign that tells a player to raise the pitch of a note by one semitone. It can also describe the inaccurate intonation of players when they are playing higher in pitch than they should be.

Sharpeville black township in South Africa, 65 km/40 mi south of Johannesburg and north of Vereeniging; 69 people were killed here when police fired on a crowd of anti-apartheid demonstrators 21 March 1960.

Shatt-al-Arab ('river of Arabia') waterway formed by the confluence of the rivers *Euphrates and *Tigris; length 190 km/120 mi to the Gulf. Basra, Khorramshahr, and Abadan stand on it. Its main tributary is the Karun River.

Shaw, George Bernard (1856–1950) Irish dramatist, critic, and novelist, and an early member of the socialist *Fabian Society, although he resigned in 1911. His plays combine comedy with political, philosophical, and controversial aspects, aiming to make an impact on his audience's social conscience as well as their emotions. They include *Arms and the Man* (1894), *The Devil's Disciple* (1897), *Man and Superman* (1903), *Pygmalion* (1913), and *St Joan* (1923). He was awarded the Nobel Prize for Literature in 1925.

shearwater any sea bird of the genus *Puffinus*. All the species are oceanic, and either dark above and white below or all dark. Shearwaters are members of the same family (Procellariidae) as the diving *petrels, order Procellariiformes. They get their name from their habit of skimming low over the sea on still wings.

Sheba ancient name for southern Yemen (Sha'abijah). It was once renowned for gold and spices. According to the Old Testament, its queen visited Solomon; until 1975 the Ethiopian royal house traced its descent from their union.

sheep any of several ruminant, even-toed, hoofed mammals of the family Bovidae. Wild species survive in the uplands of central and eastern Asia, North Africa, southern Europe and North America. The domesticated breeds are all classified as *Ovis aries*. Various breeds of sheep are reared worldwide for meat, wool, milk, and cheese, and for rotation on arable land to maintain its fertility.

sheepdog any of several breeds of dog, bred originally for herding sheep. The dog now most commonly used by shepherds and farmers in Britain to tend sheep is the border collie. Non-pedigree dogs of the border collie type, though more variable in size and colour, are referred to as working sheepdogs. Other recognized British breeds are the *Old English and Shetland sheepdogs. Many countries have their own breeds of sheepdog, such as the Belgian sheepdog, Australian kelpie, and Hungarian puli.

Sheffield industrial city and metropolitan borough on the River Don, South Yorkshire, England; population of metropolitan district (1995) 528,500. From the 12th century, iron smelting was the chief industry, and by the 14th century, Sheffield cutlery, silverware, and plate were being made. During the Industrial Revolution the iron and steel industries developed rapidly. It now produces alloys and special steels, cutlery of all kinds, permanent magnets, drills, and precision tools. Other industries include electroplating, type-founding, and the manufacture of optical glass. It is an important conference centre.

sheikh leader or chief of an Arab family or village; also Muslim title meaning 'religious scholar'.

Shelburne, William Petty, 2nd Earl of Shelburne (1737–1805) British Whig politician. He was an opponent of George III's American policy, and, as prime minister in 1783, he concluded peace with the USA.

shelduck duck *Tadorna tadorna* of family Anatidae, order Anseriformes. It has a dark-green head and red bill, with the rest of the plumage strikingly marked in black, white, and chestnut. The drake is about 60 cm/ 24 in long. Widely distributed in Europe and Asia, it lays 10–12 white eggs in rabbit burrows on sandy coasts, and is usually seen on estuary mudflats.

shell in zoology, hard outer covering of a wide variety of invertebrates. The covering is usually mineralized, normally with large amounts of calcium. The shell of birds' eggs is also largely made of calcium.

shellac resin derived from secretions of the *lac insect.

Shelley, Mary Wollstonecraft (1797–1851) born Mary Godwin, English writer. She is best known as the author of the *gothic novel *Frankenstein* (1818), which is considered to be the origin of modern science fiction, and her other novels include *The Last Man* (1826) and *Valperga* (1823).

Shelley, Percy Bysshe (1792–1822) English lyric poet and critic. He was a commanding figure in the artistic movement of *Romanticism. His skill in poetic form and metre and his intellectual capacity and searching mind were clouded by his rebellious nature and his notorious moral nonconformity. He fought against religion and for political freedom. This is reflected in his early poems such as *Queen Mab* (1813). He later wrote tragedies including *The Cenci* (1818), lyric dramas such as *Prometheus Unbound* (1820), and *lyric poems such as 'Ode to the West Wind'.

shellfish popular name for molluscs and crustaceans, including the whelk and periwinkle, mussel, oyster, lobster, crab, and shrimp.

shell shock *or* **combat neurosis** *or* **battle fatigue** any of the various forms of mental disorder that affect soldiers exposed to heavy explosions or extreme *stress. Shell shock was first diagnosed during World War I.

Shenzhen city and special economic zone on the coast of Guangdong province, south China, established in 1980 opposite Hong Kong; population of the city (1999 est) 899,100. A poor rural area in 1979, with a population of 20,000, it grew spectacularly with the relocation of toy, textiles, and electronics factories from Hong Kong. Diverse light industries have subsequently been introduced, particularly the manufacture of chemicals and electrical goods. It is also an international financial centre, housing one of China's two stock exchanges. The zone is fenced off, and immigration strictly controlled.

Sheraton, Thomas (1751–1806) English designer of elegant inlaid neoclassical furniture. He was influenced by his predecessors *Hepplewhite and *Chippendale.

Sheridan, Philip Henry (1831–1888) Union general in the American *Civil War. Recognizing Sheridan's aggressive spirit, General Ulysses S *Grant gave him command of his cavalry 1864, and soon after of the Army of the Shenandoah Valley, Virginia. Sheridan laid waste to the valley, cutting off grain supplies to the Confederate armies. In the final stage of the war, Sheridan forced General Robert E *Lee to retreat to Appomattox Court House and surrender.

Sheridan, Richard Brinsley (1751–1816) Irish dramatist and politician. His social comedies include *The Rivals* (1775), celebrated for the character of Mrs Malaprop, whose unintentional misuse of words gave the English language the word 'malapropism', and his best-known piece, *The School for Scandal* (1777). He also wrote a burlesque (mockingly imitative) play, *The Critic* (1779), on the staging of inferior dramatic work. In 1776 he became lessee of the Drury Lane Theatre, London.

sheriff (Old English *scir* 'shire', *gerefa* 'reeve') in England and Wales, the crown's chief executive officer in a county for ceremonial purposes; in Scotland, the equivalent of the English county-court judge, but also dealing with criminal cases; and in the USA the popularly elected head law-enforcement officer of a county, combining judicial authority with administrative duties.

Sherman, William Tecumseh (1820–1891) Union general in the American *Civil War. In 1864 he captured and burned Atlanta; continued his march eastward, to the sea, laying Georgia waste; and then drove the Confederates northward. He was US Army Chief of Staff 1869–83.

Sherpa member of a Mongolian people who originally migrated from Tibet and now live in northeastern Nepal. They are related to the Tibetans. Skilled mountaineers, they frequently work as support staff and guides for climbing expeditions.

Sherwood Forest hilly stretch of parkland in west Nottinghamshire, central England; area about 520 sq km/ 200 sq mi. Formerly an ancient royal forest extending from Nottingham to Worksop, it is associated with the

826

legendary outlaw *Robin Hood. According to the Forestry Commission, Sherwood Forest is over 1,000 years old.

Shetland Islands (Old Norse **Hjaltland** 'high land' or 'Hjalte's land') islands and unitary authority off the north coast of Scotland, 80 km/50 mi northeast of the Orkney Islands, an important centre of the North Sea oil industry, and the most northerly part of the UK. **area:** 1,452 sq km/560 sq mi **towns:** Lerwick (administrative headquarters), on Mainland, largest of 12 inhabited islands **physical:** the 100 islands are mostly bleak, hilly, and clad in moorland. The climate is moist, cool, and windy; in summer there is almost perpetual daylight, whilst winter days are very short. On clear winter nights, the aurora borealis ('northern lights') can frequently be seen in the sky **population:** (2000 est) 22,400 **history:** dialect derived from Norse, the islands having been a Norse dependency from the 9th century until 1472 when they were annexed by Scotland.

Shevardnadze, Edvard Amvrosievich (1928–) Georgian politician, Soviet foreign minister 1985–91, head of the state of Georgia from 1992. A supporter of Mikhail *Gorbachev, he was first secretary of the Georgian Communist Party from 1972 and an advocate of economic reform. In 1985 he became a member of the Politburo, working for détente and disarmament. In July 1991 he resigned from the Soviet Communist Party (CPSU) and, along with other reformers and leading democrats, established the Democratic Reform Movement. In March 1992 he was chosen as chair of Georgia's ruling military council, and in October was elected speaker of parliament (equivalent to president). He survived assassination attempts in 1995 and in 1998, and was re-elected to a second term as president in 2000.

shiatsu in alternative medicine, Japanese method of massage derived from *acupuncture and sometimes referred to as 'acupressure', which treats organic or physiological dysfunctions by applying finger or palm pressure to parts of the body remote from the affected part.

shifting cultivation farming system where farmers move on from one place to another when the land becomes exhausted. The most common form is **slash-and-burn** agriculture: land is cleared by burning, so that crops can be grown. After a few years, soil fertility is reduced and the land is abandoned. A new area is cleared while the old land recovers its fertility.

Shi Huangdi (or Shih Huang Ti) (c. 259–c. 210 BC) Emperor of China. He succeeded to the throne of the state of Qin 246 BC and had reunited China as an empire by 228 BC. He burned almost all existing books in 213 to destroy ties with the past; rebuilt the *Great Wall of China; and was buried in Xi'an, Shaanxi province, in a tomb complex guarded by 10,000 life-size terracotta warriors (excavated in the 1980s).

Shiite or Shiah member of a sect of *Islam that believes that *Ali, a cousin of the prophet *Muhammad, was his first true successor. The Shiites are doctrinally opposed to the Sunni Muslims. They developed their own version of the Sunna (traditional law of Islam), with only minor differences, such as inheritance and the status of women. In Shiism, the clergy are empowered to intervene between God and humans, whereas among the Sunni, the relationship with God is direct and the clergy serve as advisers. The Shiites

are prominent in Iran, the Lebanon, and Indo-Pakistan, and are also found in Iraq and Bahrain.

Shikoku smallest of the four main islands of Japan, south of Honshu, east of Kyushu; area 18,800 sq km/7,250 sq mi; population (2000 est) 4,154,000. This mountainous island consists of four prefectures, Kagawa, Tokushima, Ehime, and Kochi. The chief towns are Matsuyama and Takamatsu. The population is largely concentrated in the small coastal plains which front the Inland Sea. Agricultural products include rice, wheat, soybeans, sugar cane, and orchard fruits. Mineral products include salt and copper, while manufactured goods include petroleum products, textiles, wood pulp, and paper.

shingles common name for *herpes zoster, a disease characterized by infection of sensory nerves, with pain and eruption of blisters along the course of the affected nerves.

Shinto (Chinese *shin tao* 'way of the gods') the indigenous religion of Japan. It combines an empathetic oneness with natural forces and loyalty to the reigning dynasty as descendants of the Sun goddess, Amaterasu-Omikami. An aggressive nationalistic form of Shinto, known as State Shinto, was developed under the Emperor Meiji (1868–1912) and remained official until 1945, when it was discarded.

shinty Scottish Gaelic **camanachd**, stick-and-ball game resembling hurling, popular in the Scottish Highlands. It is played between teams of 12 players each, on a field 132–183 m/144–200 yd long and 64–91 m/70–99 yd wide. A curved stick ('camán') is used to propel a leather-covered cork and worsted ball into the opposing team's goal ('hail'). The premier tournament, the Camanachd Cup, was instituted in 1896.

ship large seagoing vessel. The Greeks, Phoenicians, Romans, and Vikings used ships extensively for trade, exploration, and warfare. European voyages of exploration began in the 14th century, greatly aided by the invention of the compass; most of the great European voyages of discovery were made between 1450 and 1550. In the 15th century Britain's Royal Navy was first formed, but in the 16th to 19th centuries Spanish and Dutch fleets dominated the shipping lanes of both the Atlantic and Pacific. The ultimate sailing ships, the fast US and British tea clippers, were built in the 19th century. Also in the 19th century, iron was first used for some shipbuilding instead of wood. Steam-propelled ships of the late 19th century were followed by compound engine and turbine-propelled vessels from the early 20th century.

Shiraz ancient walled city of southern Iran, the capital of Fars province, on the highway from Tehran to Bushire; population (1991) 965,000. Grain, rice, pulses, tobacco, gum tragacanth, clarified butter, wine, wool, skins, and carpets are the main products, as well as cotton goods, glass, attar of roses, and inlaid craftwork. There are many mosques. The tombs of the poets Sa'di and Hafiz are on the outskirts of the city.

shire administrative area formed in Britain for the purpose of raising taxes in Anglo-Saxon times. By AD 1000 most of southern England had been divided into shires with fortified strongholds at their centres. The Midland counties of England are still known as **the Shires**; for example Derbyshire, Nottinghamshire, and Staffordshire.

Shiva or **Siva** (Sanskrit 'propitious') in Hinduism, the third chief god (with *Brahma and *Vishnu) making up the *Trimurti. As Mahadeva (great lord), he is the creator, symbolized by the phallic lingam, who restores what as Mahakala he destroys. He is often sculpted as Nataraja, performing his fruitful cosmic dance. His consort or shakti (female principle) is Parvati, otherwise known as *Kali or Durga.

shock in medicine, circulatory failure marked by a sudden fall of blood pressure and resulting in pallor, sweating, fast (but weak) pulse, and sometimes complete collapse. Causes include disease, injury, and psychological trauma.

shoebill or **whale-headed stork** large, grey, long-legged, swamp-dwelling African bird *Balaeniceps rex*. Up to 1.5 m/5 ft tall, it has a large wide beak 20 cm/8 in long and more than 10 cm/4 in wide, with which it scoops fish, molluscs, reptiles, and carrion out of the mud. Shoebills occupy largish territories of several square kilometres and build their nests on floating mats of vegetation, approximately 1.5 m in diameter. In 1998 there were approximately 10,000–15,000 shoebills in Africa. They are the only species in the family Balaenicipitidae of the order Ciconiiformes.

shogun Japanese term for military dictator and abbreviation for 'seii tai shogun' – 'great barbarian-conquering general'. Technically an imperial appointment, the office was treated as hereditary and was held by a series of clans, the Minamoto 1192–1219, the Ashikaga 1336–1573, and the *Tokugawa 1603–1868. The shogun held legislative, judicial, and executive power.

Sholes, Christopher Latham (1819–1890) American printer and newspaper editor who, in 1867, invented the first practicable typewriter in association with Carlos Glidden and Samuel Soulé. In 1873, they sold their patents to Remington & Sons, a firm of gunsmiths in New York, who developed and sold the machine commercially. In 1878 Sholes developed a shift-key mechanism that made it possible to touch-type.

Shona a Bantu-speaking people of South Africa, comprising approximately 80% of the population of Zimbabwe. They also occupy the land between the Save and Pungure rivers in Mozambique, and smaller groups are found in South Africa, Botswana, and Zambia. The Shona are mainly farmers, living in scattered villages. The Shona language belongs to the Niger-Congo family.

short circuit unintended direct connection between two points in an electrical circuit. *Resistance is proportional to the length of wire through which current flows. By bypassing the rest of the circuit, the short circuit has low resistance and a large current flows through it. This may cause the circuit to overheat dangerously.

shorthand any system of rapid writing, such as the abbreviations practised by the Greeks and Romans. The first perfecter of an entirely phonetic system was Isaac *Pitman, by which system speeds of about 300 words a minute are said to be attainable.

Short Parliament English Parliament summoned by *Charles I on 13 April 1640 to raise funds for his war against the Scots. It was succeeded later in the year by the *Long Parliament.

short-sightedness nontechnical term for *myopia.

Shostakovich, Dmitri Dmitrievich (1906–1975) Russian composer. His music is chromatically tonal/modal, expressive, and sometimes highly dramatic; it was not always to official Soviet taste. He wrote 15 symphonies, chamber and film music, ballets, and operas, the latter including *Lady Macbeth of the Mtsensk District* (first performed in 1934), which was suppressed as being 'too divorced from the proletariat', but revived as *Katerina Izmaylova* in 1963. His symphonies are very highly regarded.

shot put or **putting the shot** in athletics, the sport of throwing (or putting) overhand from the shoulder a metal ball (or shot). Standard shot weights are 7.26 kg/16 lb for men and 4 kg/8.8 lb for women.

shoveler fresh-water duck *Anas clypeata*, family Anatidae, order Anseriformes, so named after its long and broad flattened beak used for filtering out small organisms from sand and mud. The male has a green head, white and brown body plumage, black and white wings, greyish bill, orange feet, and can grow up to 50 cm/20 in long. The female is speckled brown. Spending the summer in northern Europe and North America, it winters further south.

Shrapnel, Henry (1761–1842) British army officer who invented shells containing bullets, to increase the spread of casualties, first used in 1804; hence the word **shrapnel** to describe shell fragments.

shrew insectivorous mammal of the family Soricidae, order Insectivora, found in the Americas and Eurasia. It is mouselike, but with a long nose and pointed teeth. Its high metabolic rate means that it must eat almost constantly. Elephant shrews, which are found only in Africa, typically have a highly mobile and flexible elephantlike snout which is used for seeking out termites, the main food of many species.

shrike or **butcher-bird** bird of the family Laniidae, of which there are over 70 species, living mostly in Africa, but also in Eurasia and North America. They often impale insects and small vertebrates on thorns. They can grow to 35 cm/14 in long, have grey, black, or brown plumage, sharply clawed feet, and hooked beaks.

shrimp crustacean related to the *prawn. It has a cylindrical, semi-transparent body, with ten jointed legs. Some shrimps grow as large as 25 cm/10 in long.

Shropshire county of western England, which has contained the unitary authority of Telford and Wrekin since April 1998. Sometimes abbreviated to **Salop**, Shropshire was officially known by this name from 1974 until local protest reversed the decision in 1980.
area: 3,490 sq km/1,347 sq mi **towns:** Shrewsbury (administrative headquarters), Ludlow, Oswestry
physical: Shropshire is bisected, on the Welsh border, northwest–southeast by the River Severn; River Teme; Ellesmere (47 ha/116 acres), the largest of several lakes; the Clee Hills rise to about 610 m/1,800 ft (Brown Clee) in the southwest **features:** Ironbridge Gorge open-air museum of industrial archaeology, with the Iron Bridge (1779), the world's first cast-iron bridge; Market Drayton is famous for its gingerbread, and Wem for its sweet peas **population:** (1996) 421,200.

siamang the largest *gibbon *Symphalangus syndactylus*, native to Malaysia and Sumatra. Siamangs have a large throat pouch to amplify the voice, making the territorial 'song' extremely loud.

Sibelius, Jean Julius Christian (1865–1957) Finnish composer. His works include nationalistic symphonic poems such as *En saga* (1893) and *Finlandia* (1900), a violin concerto (1904), and seven symphonies. In 1940 he suddenly ceased composing and spent the rest of his life as a recluse. Restoration of many works to their original state has helped to remove his conservative image and reveal unexpectedly revolutionary features.

Siberia Russian **Sibir**, Asian region of Russia, extending from the Ural Mountains to the Pacific Ocean; area 12,050,000 sq km/4,650,000 sq mi. Hydroelectric power is generated from the rivers Lena, Ob, and Yenisey; forestry and agriculture are practised. There are vast mineral resources, including coal (in the Kuznetsk Basin), gold, diamonds, oil, natural gas, iron, copper, nickel, and cobalt.

Sibyl in Roman mythology, one of many priestesses who prophesied under a deity's direct inspiration; most notably the Sibyl of Cumae, near Naples. A priestess of *Apollo, she guided *Aeneas to Hades, and offered to sell nine collections of prophecies, the **Sibylline Books**, to the legendary king of Rome, *Tarquinius Superbus. The price was too high, but after she had destroyed all but three, he bought those surviving for the initial sum. They were kept in the Capitol for consultation in emergency by order of the Senate.

Sichuan or **Szechwan** ('four rivers') province of central China, bounded to the north by Qinghai, Gansu, and Shaanxi; to the east by Hubei and Hunan; to the south by Guizhou and Yunnan; and to the west by Tibet; area 539,000 sq km/208,000 sq mi; population (2000 est) 83,290,000. The capital is *Chengdu. There are coal, natural gas, iron ore, salt brine, textile, engineering, and electronics industries. Rice, wheat, and maize are grown.

Sicily Italian **Sicilia**, the largest Mediterranean island and an autonomous region of Italy, divided from the Italian mainland by the Strait of Messina; area 25,708 sq km/9,926 sq mi; population (2001 est) 4,866,200. It consists of nine provinces: Agrigento, Caltanissetta, Catania, Enna, Messina, Palermo, Ragusa, Syracuse, and Trapani; its capital is Palermo. Exports include Marsala wine, olives, citrus, refined oil and petrochemicals, pharmaceuticals, potash, asphalt, and marble. The region also incorporates the Lipari Islands, the Egadi Islands, the Pelagie Islands, Ustica island, and Pantelleria island. Etna, 3,323 m/10,906 ft high, is the highest volcano in Europe; its last major eruption was in 1993.

sick building syndrome malaise diagnosed in the early 1980s among office workers and thought to be caused by such pollutants as formaldehyde (from furniture and insulating materials), benzene (from paint), and the solvent trichloroethene, concentrated in air-conditioned buildings. Symptoms include headache, sore throat, tiredness, colds, and flu. Studies have found that it can cause a 40% drop in productivity and a 30% rise in absenteeism.

Sickert, Walter Richard (1860–1942) English artist. His works, broadly Impressionist in style, capture subtleties of tone and light, often with a melancholic atmosphere, their most familiar subjects being the rather shabby cityscapes and domestic and music-hall interiors of late Victorian and Edwardian London. *Ennui* (c. 1913; Tate Gallery, London) is a typical interior painting. His work inspired the *Camden Town Group.

sickle-cell disease or **sickle-cell anaemia** hereditary chronic blood disorder common among people of black African descent; also found in the eastern Mediterranean, parts of the Gulf, and in northeastern India. It is characterized by distortion and fragility of the red blood cells, which are lost too rapidly from the circulation. This often results in *anaemia.

sidewinder rattlesnake *Crotalus cerastes* that lives in the deserts of the southwestern USA and Mexico, and moves by throwing its coils into a sideways 'jump' across the sand. It can grow up to 75 cm/30 in long.

Sidney, Philip (1554–1586) English poet and incompetent soldier. He wrote the sonnet sequence *Astrophel and Stella* (1591), *Arcadia* (1590), a prose romance, and *Apologie for Poetrie* (1595). Politically, Sidney became a charismatic, but hardly powerful, figure supporting a 'forward' foreign policy that would help the Protestant Netherlands against the Spanish.

SIDS acronym for **sudden infant death syndrome**, the medical name for *cot death.

Siegfried legendary Germanic and Norse hero. His story, which may contain some historical elements, occurs in the German *Nibelungenlied/Song of the Nibelung* and in the Norse *Elder* or *Poetic* *Edda* and the prose *Völsunga Saga* (in the last two works, the hero is known as Sigurd). Siegfried wins Brunhild for his liege lord and marries his sister, but is eventually killed in the intrigues that follow. He is the hero of the last two operas in Wagner's *The Ring of the Nibelung* cycle.

Siegfried Line in World War I, a defensive line established in 1917 by the Germans in France, really a subdivision of the main *Hindenburg Line; in World War II, the Allies' name for the West Wall, a German defensive line established along its western frontier, from the Netherlands to Switzerland.

siemens symbol S, SI unit of electrical conductance, the reciprocal of the *resistance of an electrical circuit. One siemens equals one ampere per volt. It was formerly called the mho or reciprocal ohm.

Sierra Leone
National name: *Republic of Sierra Leone*

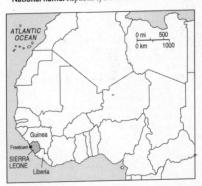

Area: 71,740 sq km/27,698 sq mi
Capital: Freetown
Major towns/cities: Koidu, Bo, Kenema, Makeni, Marampa
Major ports: Bonthe-Sherbro

Sierra Madre

Physical features: mountains in east; hills and forest; coastal mangrove swamps

Head of state and government: Ahmad Tejan Kabbah from 1996

Political system: transitional

Political executive: transitional

Political parties: All People's Congress (APC), moderate socialist; United Front of Political Movements (UNIFORM), left of centre. Party political activity suspended from 1992

Currency: leone

GNI per capita (PPP): (US$) 490 (2002 est)

Exports: diamonds, rutile, bauxite, gold, coffee, cocoa beans. Principal market: Greece 32.1% (2001)

Population: 4,971,000 (2003 est)

Language: English (official), Krio (a Creole language), Mende, Limba, Temne

Religion: animist 45%, Muslim 44%, Protestant 8%, Roman Catholic 3%

Life expectancy: 33 (men); 36 (women) (2000–05)

Chronology

15th century: Mende, Temne, and Fulani peoples moved from Senegal into region formerly populated by Bulom, Krim, and Gola peoples. The Portuguese, who named the area Serra Lyoa, established a coastal fort, trading manufactured goods for slaves and ivory.

17th century: English trading posts established on Bund and York islands.

1787–92: English abolitionists and philanthropists bought land to establish settlement for liberated and runaway African slaves (including 1,000 rescued from Canada), known as Freetown.

1808: Became a British colony and Freetown a base for British naval operations against slave trade, after Parliament declared it illegal.

1896: Hinterland conquered and declared British protectorate.

1951: First political party, Sierra Leone People's Party (SLPP), formed by Dr Milton Margai, who became 'leader of government business', in 1953.

1961: Independence achieved within Commonwealth, with Margai as prime minister.

1965: Free-trade area pact signed with Guinea, Liberia, and the Côte d'Ivoire.

1967: Election won by All People's Congress (APC), led by Siaka Stevens, but disputed by army, who set up National Reformation Council and forced governor general to leave the country.

1968: Army revolt brought back Stevens as prime minister.

1971: New constitution made Sierra Leone a republic, with Stevens as president.

1978: New constitution made APC the only legal party.

1985: Stevens retired and was succeeded as president and APC leader by Maj-Gen Joseph Momoh.

1991: A referendum endorsed multiparty politics and new constitution. A Liberian-based rebel group began guerrilla activities.

1992: President Momoh was overthrown by the military, and party politics were suspended as the National Provisional Ruling Council was established under Capt Valentine Strasser; 500,000 Liberians fled to Sierra Leone as a result of the civil war.

1995: The ban on political parties was lifted.

1996: Ahmad Tejan Kabbah became president after multiparty elections.

1997: President Kabbah's civilian government was ousted in a bloody coup. Maj Johnny Paul Koroma seized the presidency and the Revolutionary Council was formed.

1998: A Nigerian-led peacekeeping force drove out Maj Koroma's junta; President Kabbah returned from exile. Former members of military government were executed for treason.

1999: Fighting between government and rebel forces continued. Diplomatic efforts were spearheaded by the Organization of African Unity (OAU; later African Union); a ceasefire and peace agreement were reached with rebels, and in November the first unit of what would become a 6,000-strong United Nations (UN) peacekeeping force arrived in Sierra Leone.

2000: As rebel activity continued, the UN force was increased to 11,000, the largest UN force in current operation. Some UN peacekeepers were besieged by rebels but most were released by July and the remainder freed by UN troops. In August, 11 British soldiers were captured. Five were later released and the remaining six rescued in September. In November, the government and rebels signed a 30-day truce at a meeting in Nigeria.

2001: Fighting between the Guinean army and Sierra Leonean rebels left 170,000 refugees trapped in southern Guinea.

2002: Peaceful presidential and parliamentary elections were held after a decade of civil war. Kabbah was returned to power after ongoing armed conflict between the deposed government (with British military backing) and the rebel Revolutionary United Front (RUF).

Sierra Madre chief mountain system of Mexico, consisting of three ranges, the Sierra Madre Oriental, the Sierra Madre del Sur, and the Sierra Madre Occidental, enclosing the central plateau of the country; the highest peak is Citlaltepetl at 5,700 m/ 18,700 ft. The Sierra Madre del Sur ('of the south') runs along the southwest Pacific coast.

Sierra Nevada mountain range of southern Spain, mainly in the province of Granada, but also extending east into Almería. The highest point is Mulhacén (3,481 m/11,425 ft high). It has several winter sports resorts; the main centre is Sol y Nieve.

Sierra Nevada mountain range in eastern California, USA, extending for about 640 km/400 mi, with a general ridge line at over 2,500 m/8,202 ft. Its highest point is Mount Whitney, which rises to 4,418 m/14,500ft. The Sierra Nevada includes the King's Canyon, *Yosemite, and Sequoia national parks.

sievert symbol Sv, SI unit of radiation dose equivalent. It replaces the rem (1 Sv equals 100 rem). Some types of radiation do more damage than others for the same absorbed dose – for example, an absorbed dose of alpha radiation causes 20 times as much biological damage as the same dose of beta radiation. The equivalent dose in sieverts is equal to the absorbed dose of radiation in grays multiplied by the relative biological effectiveness. Humans can absorb up to 0.25 Sv without immediate ill effects; 1 Sv may produce radiation sickness; and more than 8 Sv causes death.

Sigismund (1368–1437) Holy Roman Emperor from 1411, king of Hungary 1387–1437, and king of Bohemia 1419–37. Sigismund's reign was overshadowed by two religious issues: the Great Schism and the agitation of the reformer John Huss. Sigismund demonstrated his ability as a European leader in working to end the schism by arranging the Council of Constance in 1414–18; his weakness was manifest in his continual failure to suppress the Hussites.

Sihanouk, Norodom (1922–) Cambodian politician, king 1941–55 and from 1993. He was prime minister 1955–70, when his government was overthrown in a military coup led by Lon Nol. With *Pol Pot's resistance front, he overthrew Lon Nol in 1975 and again became prime minister 1975–76, when he was forced to resign by the *Khmer Rouge. He returned from exile in November 1991 under the auspices of a United Nations-brokered peace settlement to head a coalition intended to comprise all Cambodia's warring factions (the Khmer Rouge, however, continued fighting). He was re-elected king after the 1993 elections, in which the royalist party won a majority; in 1996, however, it was announced that he was suffering from a brain tumour and might abdicate. In October 1997, three months after a successful coup by communists, he left for China and his return was uncertain. In March 1998 he pardoned his son, prince Norodom Ranariddh, who had been sentenced to 30 years' imprisonment for smuggling arms and colluding with the Khmer Rouge.

Sikhism religion professed by 14 million Indians, living mainly in the Punjab. Sikhism was founded by Guru *Nanak. Sikhs believe in a single God (monotheism) who is the immortal creator of the universe and who has never been incarnate in any form, and in the equality of all human beings; Sikhism is strongly opposed to caste divisions. Their holy book is the *Guru Granth Sahib*. Guru *Gobind Singh instituted the *Khanda-di-Pahul*, the baptism of the sword, and established the *Khalsa ('pure'), the company of the faithful. The Khalsa wear the Panj Kakas (five Ks): kesh, long hair; kangha, a comb; kirpan, a sword; kachha, short trousers; and kara, a steel bracelet. Sikh men take the last name 'Singh' ('lion') and women 'Kaur' ('princess').

Sikh Wars two wars in India between the Sikhs and the British: The **First Sikh War 1845–46** followed an invasion of British India by Punjabi Sikhs. The Sikhs were defeated and part of their territory annexed. The **Second Sikh War 1848–49** arose from a Sikh revolt in Multan. They were defeated, and the British annexed the Punjab.

Sikkim *or* **Denjong** upland state of northeast India, bounded by Nepal to the west, Bhutan to the east, Tibet (China) to the north and West Bengal state to the south; area 7,299 sq km/2,818 sq mi; population (2001 est) 540,500. The capital is Gangtok. Industries include carpets, textiles, cigarettes, and food processing, but the state is largely dependent on agriculture. Cardamom, tea, maize, rice, wheat, fruit, ginger, and soybeans are grown, and the livestock raised includes cattle and buffalo in the humid subtropical area, and yaks and sheep on the plateaus and lower slopes of the Himalayas.

Sikorski, Wladyslaw Eugeniusz (1881–1943) Polish general and politician; prime minister 1922–23, and 1939–43 in the Polish government in exile in London during World War II. He was killed in an aeroplane crash near Gibraltar in controversial circumstances.

Sikorsky, Igor Ivan (1889–1972) Ukrainian-born US engineer. He built the first successful Helicopter in 1939 (commercially produced from 1943). His first biplane flew in 1910, and in 1929 he began to construct multi-engined flying boats.

silage fodder preserved through controlled fermentation in a silo, an airtight structure that presses green crops. It is used as a winter feed for livestock. The term also refers to stacked crops that may be preserved indefinitely.

Silbury Hill artificial mound of the Neolithic (New Stone Age) period, around 2800 BC, situated just south of *Avebury in Wiltshire, England. Steep and rounded, it towers 40 m/130 ft high with a surrounding ditch approximately 6 m/20 ft deep, made when quarrying for the structure. It is the largest ancient artificial mound in Europe.

Silesia region of Europe that has long been disputed because of its geographical position, mineral resources, and industrial potential; now in Poland and the Czech Republic with metallurgical industries and a coalfield in Polish Silesia. Dispute began in the 17th century with claims on the area by both Austria and Prussia. It was seized by Prussia's Frederick the Great, which started the War of the *Austrian Succession; this was finally recognized by Austria in 1763, after the Seven Years' War. After World War I, it was divided in 1919 among newly formed Czechoslovakia, revived Poland, and Germany, which retained the largest part. In 1945, after World War II, all German Silesia east of the Oder-Neisse line was transferred to Polish administration; about 10 million inhabitants of German origin, both there and in Czechoslovak Silesia, were expelled.

silica silicon dioxide, SiO_2, the composition of the most common mineral group, of which the most familiar form is quartz. Other silica forms are *chalcedony, chert, opal, tridymite, and cristobalite. Common sand consists largely of silica in the form of quartz.

silicate one of a group of minerals containing silicon and oxygen in tetrahedral units of SiO_4, bound together in various ways to form specific structural types. Silicates are the chief rock-forming minerals. Most rocks are composed, wholly or in part, of silicates (the main exception being limestones). Glass is a manufactured complex polysilicate material in which other elements (boron in borosilicate glass) have been incorporated.

silicon chemical symbol Si, (Latin *silex* 'flint') brittle, non-metallic element, atomic number 14, relative atomic mass 28.086. It is the second-most abundant element (after oxygen) in the Earth's crust and occurs in amorphous and crystalline forms. In nature is is found only in combination with other elements, chiefly with oxygen in silica (silicon dioxide, SiO_2) and the silicates. These form the mineral *quartz, which makes up most sands, gravels, and beaches.

silicon chip *integrated circuit with microscopically small electrical components on a piece of silicon crystal only a few millimetres square.

Silicon Valley nickname given to a region of southern California, USA, approximately 32 km/20 mi long, between Palo Alto and San Jose. It is the site of many high-technology electronic firms, whose prosperity is based on the silicon chip. Silicon Valley faces increasing competition from computer companies in Asia.

silicosis chronic disease of miners and stone cutters who inhale *silica dust, which makes the lung tissues fibrous and less capable of aerating the blood. It is a form of *pneumoconiosis.

silk natural fibre made from fine soft thread produced by the larva of the *silkworm moth when making its cocoon. It is soaked, carefully unwrapped, and used in the manufacture of textiles. The introduction of *synthetic fibre originally harmed the silk industry, but rising standards of living have produced an increased demand for real silk. Silk is produced in China, India, Japan, and Thailand.

Silk Road ancient and medieval overland route of about 6,400 km/4,000 mi by which silk was brought from China to Europe in return for trade goods; it ran west via the Gobi Desert, Samarkand, and Antioch to Mediterranean ports in Greece, Italy, the Middle East, and Egypt. Buddhism came to China via this route, which was superseded from the 16th century by sea trade.

silk-screen printing or **serigraphy** method of *printing based on stencilling. It can be used to print on most surfaces, including paper, plastic, fabric, and wood. A fine mesh (originally silk) is stretched across a wooden frame to form the screen. An impermeable stencil (either paper or a photosensitized coating) is applied to it, so that the ink passes through to the area beneath only where an image is required. The design can also be painted directly on to the screen with varnish. Once the stencil is attached, the screen is placed on top of fabric. Printing ink or dye is then drawn across, transferring the design to the fabric. A series of screens can be used to add successive layers of colour to the design.

silkworm usually the larva of the **common silkworm** moth *Bombyx mori*. After hatching from the egg and maturing on the leaves of white mulberry trees (or a synthetic substitute), it spins a protective cocoon of fine silk thread 275 m/900 ft long. To keep the thread intact, the moth is killed before emerging from the cocoon, and several threads are combined to form the commercial silk thread woven into textiles.

Silurian Period period of geological time 439–409 million years ago, the third period of the Palaeozoic era. Silurian sediments are mostly marine and consist of shales and limestone. Luxuriant reefs were built by coral-like organisms. The first land plants began to evolve during this period, and there were many ostracoderms (armoured jawless fishes). The first jawed fishes (called acanthodians) also appeared.

silver chemical symbol Ag, white, lustrous, extremely malleable and ductile, metallic element, atomic number 47, relative atomic mass 107.868. Its chemical symbol comes from the Latin *argentum*. It occurs in nature in ores and as a free metal; the chief ores are sulphides, from which the metal is extracted by smelting with lead. It is the best metallic conductor of both heat and electricity; its most useful compounds are the chloride and bromide, which darken on exposure to light and are the basis of photographic emulsions.

silverfish wingless insect, a type of *bristletail.

Simenon, Georges Joseph Christian (1903–1989) Belgian crime writer. Initially a pulp fiction writer, in 1931 he created Inspector Maigret of the Paris Sûreté who appeared in a series of detective novels.

simile (Latin 'likeness') figure of speech that in English uses the conjunctions *like* and *as* to express the comparison between two different things ('run like the devil'; 'as deaf as a post'). It is sometimes confused with *metaphor. The simile makes an explicit comparison (suggesting that something is *like* something else), while a metaphor's comparison is implicit (suggesting that something *is* something else).

Simon, Paul (1942–) US pop singer and songwriter. In a folk-rock duo with Art Garfunkel, he had such hits as 'The Sound of Silence' (1965), 'Mrs Robinson' (1968) and 'Bridge Over Troubled Water' (1970). Simon's solo work includes the critically acclaimed album *Graceland* (1986), for which he drew on Cajun and African music. Other solo albums include *Hearts and Bones* (1983), *The Rhythm of the Saints* (1990), and *You're the One* (2000).

Simpson, Wallis Warfield, Duchess of Windsor (1896–1986) US socialite, twice divorced. She married *Edward VIII 1937, who abdicated in order to marry her. He was given the title Duke of Windsor by his brother, George VI, who succeeded him.

Simpson Desert desert area in Australia, chiefly in Northern Territory; area 145,000 sq km/56,000 sq mi. The desert was named after a president of the South Australian Geographical Society who financed its exploration.

simultaneous equations two or more algebraic equations that contain two or more unknown quantities that may have a unique solution. For example, in the case of two linear equations with two unknown variables, such as: (i) $x + 3y = 6$ and (ii) $3y - 2x = 4$ the solution will be those unique values of x and y that are valid for both equations. Linear simultaneous equations canbe solved by using algebraic manipulation to eliminate one of the variables, *coordinate geometry, or matrices (see *matrix).

Sinai Egyptian peninsula, largely desert, at the head of the Red Sea; area 65,000 sq km/25,000 sq mi. Resources include oil, natural gas, manganese, and coal; irrigation water from the River Nile is carried under the Suez Canal. The main towns are Al-Arish (the capital of South Sinai governorate) and Al-Tur (capital of North Sinai governorate). It is the ancient source of turquoise. Tourism is of increasing importance. Among the highest peaks are Mount Catherine (2,642 m/8,668 ft), Umm Shawmar (2,585 m/8,482 ft), and *Mount Sinai (2,285 m/7,500 ft).

Sinai, Battle of battle 6–24 October 1973 during the Yom Kippur War between Israel and Egypt. It was one of the longest tank battles in history. Israeli troops crossed the Suez Canal 16 October, cutting off the Egyptian 3rd Army.

Sinai, Mount or **Horeb** mountain near the tip of the Sinai Peninsula; height 2,285 m/7,500 ft. According to the Old Testament this is where *Moses received the Ten Commandments from God. Its identity is not absolutely certain, but it is traditionally thought to be Jebel Musa ('Mountain of Moses').

Sinan (1489–1588) Ottoman architect. He was chief architect to Suleiman the Magnificent from 1538. Among the hundreds of buildings he designed are the Suleimaniye mosque complex in Istanbul 1551–58 and the Selimiye mosque in Adrinople (now Edirne) 1569–74.

Sinatra, Frank (Francis Albert) (1915–1998) US singer and film actor. Celebrated for his phrasing and emotion, especially on love ballads, he was particularly associated with the song 'My Way'. His films included *From Here to Eternity* (1953), for which he won an Academy Award, *The Man with the Golden Arm* (1955), *Some Came Running* (1959), and the political thriller *The Manchurian Candidate* (1962).

Sind province of southeast Pakistan, mainly in the Indus delta; area 140,914 sq km/54,393 sq mi; population (1993 est) 28,930,000. The capital and chief port is *Karachi. Industries include shipbuilding, cement, textiles, and foundries; salt is mined. Wheat, rice, cotton, barley, oilseeds, and vegetables are grown; red Sindhi cattle, buffaloes, and camels are raised.

Sindhi the majority ethnic group living in the Pakistani province of Sind. The Sindhi language is spoken by about 15 million people. Since the partition of India and Pakistan 1947, large numbers of Urdu-speaking refugees have moved into the region from India, especially into the capital, Karachi.

sine *sin*, in trigonometry, a function of an angle in a right-angled *triangle that is defined as the ratio of the length of the side opposite the angle to the length of the hypotenuse (the longest side). This function can be used to find either angles or sides in a right-angled triangle.

sine rule in trigonometry, a rule that relates the sides and angles of a triangle, stating that the ratio of the length of each side and the sine of the angle opposite is constant (twice the radius of the circumscribing circle). If the sides of a triangle are a, b, and c, and the angles opposite are A, B, and C, respectively, then the sine rule may be expressed as

$$\frac{a}{\sin A} = \frac{b}{\sin B} = \frac{c}{\sin C}.$$

sinfonietta orchestral work that is of a shorter, lighter nature than a *symphony, for example Leoš *Janáček's *Sinfonietta* (1926). It is also the name for a small-scale orchestra specializing in such works, for example the London Sinfonietta.

Singapore

formerly **part of Straits Settlement (1826–1942)**, **part of the Federation of Malaysia (1963–65)**

National name: *Republik Singapura/ Republic of Singapore*

Area: 622 sq km/240 sq mi

Capital: Singapore City

Physical features: comprises Singapore Island, low and flat, and 57 small islands; Singapore Island is joined to the mainland by causeway across Strait of Johore

Head of state: Sellapan Rama Nathan from 1999

Head of government: Lee Hsien Loong from 2004

Political system: liberal democracy

Political executive: parliamentary

Political parties: People's Action Party (PAP), conservative, free market, multi-ethnic; Workers' Party (WP), socialist; Singapore Democratic Party (SDP), liberal pluralist

Currency: Singapore dollar

GNI per capita (PPP): (US$) 23,090 (2002 est)

Exports: electrical and nonelectrical machinery, transport equipment, petroleum products, chemicals, rubber, foodstuffs, clothing, metal products, iron

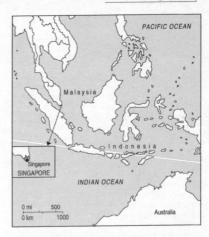

and steel, orchids and other plants, aquarium fish. Principal market: Malaysia 17.3% (2001)

Population: 4,253,000 (2003 est)

Language: Malay, Mandarin Chinese, Tamil, English (all official), other Indian languages, Chinese dialects

Religion: Buddhist, Taoist, Muslim, Hindu, Christian

Life expectancy: 76 (men); 80 (women) (2000–05)

Chronology

12th century: First trading settlement established on Singapore Island.

14th century: Settlement destroyed, probably by Javanese Empire of Mahapahit.

1819: Stamford Raffles of British East India Company obtained Singapore from sultan of Johore.

1826: Straits Settlements formed from British possessions of Singapore, Penang, and Malacca (now Melaka) ruled by governor of Bengal.

1832: Singapore became capital of Straits Settlements; the port prospered, attracting Chinese and Indian immigrants.

1851: Responsibility for Straits Settlements fell to governor general of India.

1858: British government, through the India Office, took over administration of Straits Settlements.

1867: Straits Settlements became crown colony of British Empire.

1922: Singapore chosen as principal British military base in Far East.

1942: Japan captured Singapore, taking 70,000 British and Australian prisoners.

1945: British rule restored after defeat of Japan.

1946: Singapore became separate crown colony.

1959: Internal self-government achieved as State of Singapore with Lee Kuan Yew (PAP) as prime minister.

1960s: Rapid development as leading commercial and financial centre.

1963: Singapore combined with Federation of Malaya, Sabah, and Sarawak to form Federation of Malaysia.

1965: Became independent republic after withdrawing from Federation of Malaysia in protest at alleged discrimination against ethnic Chinese.

1971: Last remaining British military bases closed.

1984: Two opposition members elected to national assembly for first time.

1988: Ruling PAP won all but one of available assembly seats; increasingly authoritarian rule.

1990: Lee Kuan Yew retired from the premiership after 31 years and was succeeded by Goh Chok Tong.

1996: Constitutional change was introduced, allowing better representation of minority races.

1997: The PAP, led by Prime Minister Goh Chok Tong, won a general election.

1998: Pay cuts were introduced as Singapore slipped into recession for the first time in 13 years.

1999: After all other candidates were screened out of the election, Sellapan Ramanathan Nathan, the government's candidate, became the new president.

2001: Hundreds joined the first legally sanctioned political demonstration outside a general election in support of opposition leader J B Jeyaretnam.

2002: Governing People's Action Party secured a landslide election win.

2004: Lee Hsien Loong (son of Lee Kuan Yew) became prime minister.

Singapore City capital of Singapore, on the southeast coast of the island of Singapore; population (2000 est) 3,151,300. Its deepwater harbour, its free port status, and its position between the Indian Ocean and the South China Sea have helped the city to become the largest port of Southeast Asia and a commercial centre of world class. Major industries include trade, shipping, banking, electronics, shipbuilding, tin-smelting, rubber processing, fruit canning, and oil refining. Formerly a British colonial town, it was occupied by Japanese forces during World War II.

Singer, Isaac Bashevis (1904–1991) Polish-born US novelist and short-story writer. He lived in the USA from 1935. His works, written in Yiddish, often portray traditional Jewish life in Poland and the USA, and the loneliness of old age. They include *The Family Moskat* (1950) and *Gimpel the Fool and Other Stories* (1957). He was awarded the Nobel Prize for Literature in 1978.

Singer, Isaac Merrit (1811–1875) US inventor of domestic and industrial sewing machines. Within a few years of opening his first factory in 1851, he became the world's largest sewing-machine manufacturer (despite infringing the patent of Elias Howe), and by the late 1860s more than 100,000 Singer sewing machines were in use in the USA alone.

Single European Act act signed in 1986 (and in force from July 1987) to establish a *single European market, defined as an area without frontiers in which free movement of goods, services, people, and capital is ensured.

single European currency former name for the *euro.

single European market single market within the *European Union. Established under the *Single European Act, it was the core of the process of European economic integration, involving the removal of obstacles to the free movement of goods, services, people, and capital between member states of the EU. It covers, among other benefits, the elimination of customs barriers, the liberalization of capital movements, the opening of public procurement markets, and the mutual recognition of professional qualifications. It came into effect on 1 January 1993.

singularity in astrophysics, point in *space-time at which the known laws of physics break down.

Singularity is predicted to exist at the centre of a black hole, where infinite gravitational forces compress the infalling mass of a collapsing star to infinite density. It is also thought, according to the Big Bang model of the origin of the universe, to be the point from which the expansion of the universe began.

Sinn Fein (Irish 'we ourselves') Irish political party founded in 1905, whose aim is the creation of a united republican Ireland. The driving political force behind Irish nationalism between 1916 and 1921, Sinn Fein returned to prominence with the outbreak of violence ('the Troubles') in *Northern Ireland in the late 1960s, when it split into 'Provisional' and 'Official' wings at the same time as the *Irish Republican Army (IRA), with which it is closely associated. From the late 1970s 'Provisional' Sinn Fein took on a more active political role, putting up candidates to stand in local and national elections. Sinn Fein won two seats in the 1997 UK general election and one seat in the 1997 Irish general election. In the 2001 UK general election, it increased its number of seats to four. Gerry *Adams became party president in 1978. Sinn Fein took part in the multiparty negotiations (known as the Stormont Talks) and became a signatory of the agreement reached on Good Friday, 10 April 1998. The party gained 17.6% of votes in the June 1998 elections to the 108-seat Belfast assembly. In September a historic meeting between Gerry Adams and the Ulster Unionist leader, David Trimble, took place at Stormont; Sinn Fein also agreed to appoint a contact with the international body overseeing the decommissioning of arms – the party's chief negotiator, Martin McGuinness. In October 2001 Gerry Adams made an unprecedented plea to the Irish Republican Army (IRA) to proceed with decommissioning in order to save the peace process and the devolved power-sharing administration of Northern Ireland from collapse; on 22 October it was verified that the IRA had put some arms beyond use.

Sino-Japanese Wars two wars waged by Japan against China 1894–95 and 1931–45 to expand to the mainland. Territory gained in the First Sino-Japanese War (Korea) and in the 1930s (Manchuria, Shanghai) was returned at the end of World War II.

Sino-Tibetan languages group of languages spoken in Southeast Asia. This group covers a large area, and includes Chinese and Burmese, both of which have numerous dialects. Some classifications include the Tai group of languages (including Thai and Lao) in the Sino-Tibetan family.

sinusitis painful inflammation of one of the sinuses, or air spaces, that surround the nasal passages. Most cases clear with antibiotics and nasal decongestants, but some require surgical drainage.

Sioux *or* **Lakots, Dakota** *or* **Nakota** (Chippewa *nadowessioux* 'snake' or 'enemy') member of an *American Indian people who inhabit the Great Plains region; the largest group of *Plains Indians. Their language belongs to the Siouan family, and they are divided into three groups: Dakota, Nakota, and Lakota. Originally hunter-gatherers living around Lake Superior, Michigan, they were forced into North and South Dakota by the Cree and Chippewa around 1650, and took up a nomadic, buffalo-hunting lifestyle. They developed a warrior culture in which status was achieved by bravery in warfare. With reservations in the Dakotas, and other parts of the USA and Canada, they now number about 108,200 (2000) in the USA and 60,000 in Canada (1991).

Siraj-ud-Daula (1728–1757) Nawab of Bengal, India, from April 1756. He captured Calcutta (now Kolkata) from the British in June 1756 and imprisoned some of the British in the *Black Hole of Calcutta (a small room in which a number of them died), but was defeated in 1757 by Robert *Clive, and lost Bengal to the British at the Battle of Plassey. He was killed in his capital, Murshidabad.

siren in Greek mythology, a sea *nymph, half woman and half bird, who lured sailors to shipwreck along rocky coasts with her irresistible singing, before devouring them. *Odysseus, on the advice of the enchantress *Circe, tied himself to the mast of his ship in order to hear the sirens safely, and plugged his crew's ears with wax.

Sirius *or* **the Dog Star** *or* **Alpha Canis Majoris** brightest star in the night sky, 8.6 light years from the Sun in the constellation *Canis Major. Sirius is a double star: Sirius A is a white star with a mass 2.3 times that of the Sun, a diameter 1.8 times that of the Sun, and a true luminosity of 23 Suns. It is orbited every 50 years by a *white dwarf, Sirius B, also known as the Pup.

sirocco hot, normally dry and dust-laden wind that blows from the deserts of North Africa across the Mediterranean into southern Europe. It occurs mainly in the spring. The name 'sirocco' is also applied to any hot oppressive wind.

sisal strong fibre made from various species of *agave, such as *Agave sisalina*.

siskin North American finch *Carduelis pinus* with yellow markings or greenish-yellow bird *Carduelis spinus* about 12 cm/5 in long, found in Eurasia. They are members of the finch family Fringillidae, order Passeriformes.

Sisley, Alfred (1839–1899) French Impressionist painter, born in Paris of English parents. Lyrical and harmonious, his landscapes are distinctive for their lightness of touch and subtlety of tone. Among his works are *The Square at Argenteuil* (1872) and *The Canal* (1872) (both in the Louvre, Paris).

Sisulu, Walter Max Ulyate (1912–2003) South African civil-rights activist, deputy president of the African National Congress (ANC). In 1964 he became, with Nelson Mandela, one of the first full-time secretaries general of the ANC. He was imprisoned following the 1964 Rivonia Trial for opposition to the apartheid system and released in 1989, at the age of 77, as a gesture of reform by President F W de Klerk. In 1991, when Mandela became ANC president, Sisulu became his deputy.

Sisyphus in Greek mythology, a king of Corinth who was condemned to Tartarus, a region of the underworld for the wicked. As punishment for his evil life, he was forced to roll a huge stone uphill for eternity; it always fell back before he could reach the top.

Sita in Hinduism, the wife of Rama, an avatar (manifestation) of the god Vishnu; a character in the *Ramayana* epic, characterized by chastity and kindness.

sitatunga herbivorous antelope *Tragelaphus spekei* found in several swamp regions in Central Africa.

Its hooves are long and splayed to help progress on soft surfaces. It grows to about 1.2 m/4 ft high at the shoulder; the male has thick horns up to 90 cm/3 ft long.

Sitting Bull (c. 1834–1890) Sioux **Tatanka Iyotake**, 'Sitting Buffalo Bull', American Indian chief of the Hunkpapa Sioux during the Plains Wars of 1865–90, the struggle between the *Plains Indians and the USA. In 1868 Sitting Bull agreed to *Sioux resettlement in North and South Dakota, but when gold was discovered in the Black Hills region, miners and the US army invaded Sioux territory. With the treaty broken, Sitting Bull led the Sioux against Lt-Col *Custer at the Battle of the *Little Bighorn, Montana, in 1876.

situationism in ethics, the doctrine that any action may be good or bad depending on its context or situation. Situationists argue that no moral rule can apply in all situations and that what may be wrong in most cases may be right if the end is sufficiently good. In general, situationists believe moral attitudes are more important than moral rules.

SI units French **Système International d'Unités**, standard system of scientific units used by scientists worldwide. Originally proposed in 1960, it replaces the *m.k.s., *c.g.s., and *f.p.s. systems. It is based on seven basic units: the metre (m) for length, kilogram (kg) for mass, second (s) for time, ampere (A) for electrical current, kelvin (K) for temperature, mole (mol) for amount of substance, and candela (cd) for luminosity.

Siva alternative spelling of *Shiva, Hindu god.

Six Counties the six counties that form Northern Ireland: *Antrim, *Armagh, *Down, *Fermanagh, *Londonderry/Derry, and *Tyrone. Administrative responsibilities are held by 26 district councils.

Six-Day War another name for the third *Arab-Israeli War.

Sjælland *or* **Zealand** main island of Denmark, on which Copenhagen is situated; area 7,000 sq km/ 2,700 sq mi; population (1995) 2,157,700. It is low-lying with an irregular coastline. The chief industry is dairy farming.

skate any of several species of flatfish of the ray group. The common skate *Raja batis* is up to 1.8 m/6 ft long and greyish, with black specks. Its egg cases ('mermaids' purses') are often washed ashore by the tide.

skateboard single flexible board mounted on wheels and steerable by weight positioning. As a land alternative to surfing, skateboards developed in California in the 1960s and became a worldwide craze in the 1970s. Skateboarding is practised in urban environments and has enjoyed a revival since the late 1980s.

skating self-propulsion on ice by means of bladed skates, or on other surfaces by skates with small rollers (wheels of wood, metal, or plastic). The chief competitive ice-skating events are figure skating, for singles or pairs, ice-dancing, and speed skating. The first world ice-skating championships were held in 1896. In pairs figure skating competitors perform compulsory movements and free routines to music that they have selected. Marks are given for both technical merit, and artistic impression. In men's short track speed skating,. the competitors race around a track over distances of 500–3000 m/1650–9,800 ft in individual races, relays, or pursuit races.

skeleton framework of bones that supports and gives form to the body, protects its internal organs, and provides anchorage points for its *muscles. It is composed of about 200 bones. Each bone is made of a *mineral, calcium phosphate, and *protein. Bones of the skeleton are joined to each other by ligaments. In the human body, walking, running, arm and leg movements, hand actions, and even just standing, are all achieved by the operation of muscles attached to bones of the skeleton. Movement of the body is brought about by the moveable *joints of the body. The elbow joint is a good example. Muscles are attached to bones by tendons, and contractions of the muscle bring about movement.

skiing self-propulsion on snow by means of elongated runners (skis) for the feet, slightly bent upward at the tip. It is a popular recreational sport, as cross-country ski touring or as downhill runs on mountain trails; events include downhill; slalom, in which a series of turns between flags have to be negotiated; cross-country racing; and ski jumping, when jumps of over 150 m/490 ft are achieved from ramps up to 90 m/295 ft high. Speed-skiing uses skis approximately one-third longer and wider than normal with which speeds of up to 200 kph/125 mph have been recorded. Recently, **snowboarding**, the use of a single, very broad ski, similar to a small surf board, has become increasingly popular. **Monoskiing**, where both feet face the front, side-by-side, on a single ski, is also practised.

skin covering of the body of a vertebrate. In mammals, the outer layer (epidermis) is dead and its cells are constantly being rubbed away and replaced from below; it helps to protect the body from infection and to prevent dehydration. The lower layer (dermis) contains blood vessels, *nerves, hair roots, and sweat and sebaceous glands (producing oil), and is supported by a network of fibrous and elastic cells. The medical speciality concerned with skin diseases is called dermatology.

skink lizard of the family Scincidae, a large family of about 700 species found throughout the tropics and subtropics. The body is usually long and the legs are reduced. Some skinks are legless and rather snakelike. Many are good burrowers, or can 'swim' through sand, like the **sandfish** genus *Scincus* of North Africa. Some skinks lay eggs, others bear live young.

Skinner, B(urrhus) F(rederic) (1904–1990)
US psychologist. He was a radical behaviourist who rejected mental concepts, seeing the organism as a 'black box' where internal processes are not significant in predicting behaviour. He studied operant conditioning (influencing behaviour patterns by reward or punishment) and held that behaviour is shaped and maintained by its consequences.

Skopje capital and industrial city of Macedonia; population (1991 est) 563,300. Industries include iron, steel, chromium mining, and food processing.

Skriabin (*or* Scriabin), Aleksandr Nikolaievich (1872–1915) Russian composer and pianist. His visionary tone poems such as *Prometheus* (1911), and symphonies such as *Divine Poem* (1903), employed unusual scales and harmonies.

skua dark-coloured gull-like seabird, living in Arctic and Antarctic waters. Skuas can grow up to 60 cm/2 ft long, with long, well-developed wings and short, stout

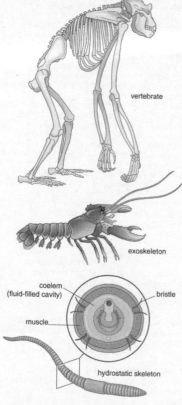

vertebrate

exoskeleton

coelem (fluid-filled cavity)

bristle

muscle

hydrostatic skeleton

skeleton Different types of skeleton. Vertebrate skeletons (top) are made of bone and cartilage and provide a scaffold for the flesh. Only in certain parts (for example the skull and the rib cage) are organs encased totally. A gorilla is shown here. Invertebrates may have an exoskeleton, made of chitin, as in insects and crustacea, such as the lobster (middle). The exoskeleton totally encases the animal and is periodically moulted to allow growth. Molluscs, worms, and other 'soft' invertebrates have a hydrostatic 'skeleton' that supports the body and facilitates locomotion. A cross-section of the fluid-filled cavity of an earthworm is shown below.

legs; in colour they are greyish above and white below. They are aggressive scavengers, and seldom fish for themselves but force gulls to disgorge their catch, and also eat chicks of other birds. Skuas are in the family Stercorariidae, order Charadriiformes.

skull in vertebrates, the collection of flat and irregularly shaped bones (or cartilage) that enclose the brain and the organs of sight, hearing, and smell, and provide support for the jaws. In most mammals, the skull consists of 22 bones joined by fibrous immobile joints called sutures. The floor of the skull is pierced by a large hole (*foramen magnum*) for the spinal cord and a number of smaller apertures through which other nerves and blood vessels pass.

skunk North American mammal of the weasel family. The common skunk *Mephitis mephitis* has a long, arched body, short legs, a bushy tail, and black fur with white streaks on the back. In self-defence, it discharges a foul-smelling fluid.

Skye largest island of the Inner *Hebrides, Highland region, off the west coast of Scotland; area 1,740 sq km/ 672 sq mi; population (2000 est) 12,000. It is separated from the mainland to the southeast by the Sound of Sleat and by the islands of Raasay and Scalpay to the northeast. The Cuillin Hills, which range from Sgurr Alasdair in the south to Sgurr nan Gillean ('Peak of the Young Men'), which reaches an altitude of 965 m/ 3,166 ft, in the north, provide some of the most difficult climbs in the Highlands of Scotland. The chief port and town is Portree. The economy is based on crofting, craft industries, tourism, and livestock. The **Skye Bridge**, a privately financed toll bridge to Kyleakin on the island from the Kyle of Lochalsh, was completed in 1995.

Skylab US space station, launched on 14 May 1973, made from the adapted upper stage of a Saturn V rocket. At 75 tonnes, it was the heaviest object ever put into space and had a length of 25.6 m/84 ft. *Skylab* contained a workshop for carrying out experiments in weightlessness, an observatory for monitoring the Sun, and cameras for photographing the Earth's surface.

skylark a type of *lark.

skyscraper building so tall that it appears to 'scrape the sky', developed 1868 in New York, USA, where land prices were high and the geology allowed such methods of construction. Skyscrapers are now found in cities throughout the world. The world's tallest free-standing structure is the CN (Canadian National) Tower, Toronto, at 553 m/1,815 ft.

slander spoken defamatory statement; if written, or broadcast on radio or television, it constitutes *libel.

slash and burn *or* **shifting cultivation** simple agricultural method whereby natural vegetation is cut and burned, and the clearing then farmed for a few years until the soil loses its fertility, whereupon farmers move on and leave the area to regrow. Although this is possible with a small, widely dispersed population, as in the Amazon rainforest for example, it becomes unsustainable with more people and is now a cause of *deforestation.

slate fine-grained, usually grey metamorphic rock that splits readily into thin slabs along its cleavage planes. It is the metamorphic equivalent of *shale. Slate tiles are a traditional roof covering in many parts of the UK.

Slav *or* **Slavonian** member of an Indo-European people in central and Eastern Europe, the Balkans, and parts of northern Asia, speaking closely related *Slavonic or Slavic languages, some written in the Cyrillic and some in the Roman alphabet. The ancestors of the Slavs are believed to have included the Sarmatians and *Scythians. Moving west from central Asia, they settled in eastern and southeastern Europe during the 2nd and 3rd millennia BC.

slavery the enforced servitude of one person (a slave) to another or one group to another. A slave has no

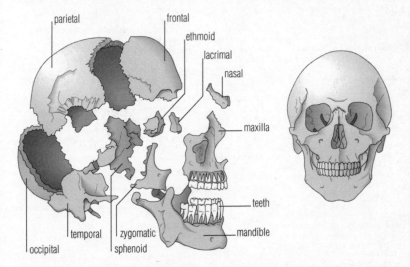

skull The skull is a protective box for the brain, eyes, and hearing organs. It is also a framework for the teeth and flesh of the face. The cranium has eight bones: occipital, two temporal, two parietal, frontal, sphenoid, and ethmoid. The face has 14 bones, the main ones being two maxillae, two nasal, two zygoma, two lacrimal, and the mandible.

personal rights and is considered the property of another person through birth, purchase, or capture. Slavery goes back to prehistoric times; it flourished in classical times, but declined in Europe after the fall of the Roman Empire. During the imperialistic eras of Spain, Portugal, and Britain in the 16th to 18th centuries, and in the American South in the 17th to 19th centuries, slavery became a mainstay of an agricultural labour-intensive economy, with millions of Africans sold to work on plantations in North and South America. Millions more died during transportation, but the profits from this trade were enormous. Slavery was abolished in the *British Empire in 1833 and in the USA at the end of the Civil War (1863–65); however, it continues illegally in some countries today.

Slavonia region of eastern Croatia bounded by the Sava, Drava, and Danube rivers; Osijek is the largest town. Eastern and western Slavonia declared themselves autonomous provinces of Serbia following Croatia's declaration of independence from Yugoslavia 1991, and the region was the scene of fierce fighting between Croatian forces and Serb-dominated Yugoslav federal troops 1991–92. After the ceasefire 1992, 10,000 UN troops were deployed in eastern and western Slavonia and contested Krajina. Rebel Serbs in Croatia agreed November 1995 to return the region of eastern Slavonia to Croatian control.

Slavonic languages or **Slavic languages** branch of the Indo-European language family spoken in central and Eastern Europe, the Balkans, and parts of northern Asia. The family comprises the **southern group** (Slovene, Serbo-Croat, Macedonian, and Bulgarian); the **western group** (Czech and Slovak, Sorbian in Germany, and Polish and its related dialects); and the **eastern group** (Russian, Ukrainian, and Belorussian).

sleep state of natural unconsciousness and activity that occurs at regular intervals in most mammals and birds, though there is considerable variation in the amount of time spent sleeping. Sleep differs from hibernation in that it occurs daily rather than seasonally, and involves less drastic reductions in metabolism. The function of sleep is unclear. People deprived of sleep become irritable, uncoordinated, forgetful, hallucinatory, and even psychotic.

sleeping pill any *sedative that induces sleep; in small doses, such drugs may relieve anxiety.

sleeping sickness infectious disease of tropical Africa, a form of *trypanosomiasis. Early symptoms include fever, headache, and chills, followed by *anaemia and joint pains. Later, the disease attacks the central nervous system, causing drowsiness, lethargy, and, if left untreated, death. Sleeping sickness is caused by either of two trypanosomes, *Trypanosoma gambiense* or *T. rhodesiense*. Control is by eradication of the tsetse fly, which transmits the disease to humans. Out of the 1 million people in Africa who become infected with the sleeping sickness, 100,000 people die each year from the disease, it was reported in August 2000.

slide rule mathematical instrument with pairs of logarithmic sliding scales, used for rapid calculations, including multiplication, division, and the extraction of square roots. It has been largely superseded by the electronic calculator.

Sligo county of the Republic of Ireland, in the province of Connacht, situated on the Atlantic coast of northwest Ireland; county town Sligo; area 1,800 sq km/ 695 sq mi; population (2002 est) 58,200. Limestone mountains rise behind a boggy coastal plain. There is some mineral wealth, including barytes, coal, lead, and copper. Agricultural activity includes cattle farming and dairy farming. The other principal town is Ballymote.

Slim, William Joseph, 1st Viscount Slim (1891–1970) British field marshal in World War II. He served in the North Africa campaign 1941 then commanded the 1st Burma Corps 1942–45, stemming the Japanese invasion of India, and then forcing them out of Burma (now Myanmar) in 1945. He was governor general of Australia 1953–60. He was created a KCB in 1944 and a Viscount in 1960.

slime mould or **myxomycete** extraordinary organism that shows some features of *fungus and some of *protozoa. Slime moulds are not closely related to any other group, although they are often classed, for convenience, with the fungi. There are two kinds, cellular slime moulds and plasmodial slime moulds, differing in their complex life cycles.

sloe fruit of the *blackthorn bush. The blueish bloom on the fruit of the blackthorn is characteristic although eventually washed off by the rain. The sloe is a drupe (a fleshy fruit having a single stone containing the seed), and has an exceptionally sour taste. Sloes are used to flavour and colour the traditional liquor, sloe gin.

sloth slow-moving South American mammal, about 70 cm/2.5 ft long, family Bradypodidae, order Edentata. Sloths are greyish brown and have small rounded heads, almost invisible tails, and prolonged forelimbs. Each foot has long curved claws adapted to clinging upside down from trees. On the ground the animals cannot walk, but drag themselves along. They are vegetarian.

Slough industrial town and administrative centre of Slough unitary authority in southern England, 32 km/20 mi west of London; population (2001 est) 111,000. Industries include pharmaceuticals, electronics, engineering, aviation support services, and the manufacture of chocolate, paint, and power tools.

Slovakia one of the two republics that formed the Federative Republic of Czechoslovakia. Settled in the 5th–6th centuries by Slavs; it was occupied by the Magyars in the 10th century, and was part of the kingdom of Hungary until 1918, when it became a province of Czechoslovakia. Slovakia was a puppet state under German domination 1939–45, and was abolished as an administrative division in 1949. Its capital and chief town was Bratislava. It was re-established as a sovereign state, the Slovak Republic, after the break-up of Czechoslovakia in 1993.

Slovak Republic
formerly **Czechoslovakia** (with the Czech Republic) (1918–93)
National name: *Slovenská Republika/Slovak Republic*
Area: 49,035 sq km/18,932 sq mi
Capital: Bratislava
Major towns/cities: Košice, Nitra, Prešov, Banská Bystrica, Zilina, Trnava, Martin

Physical features: Western range of Carpathian Mountains, including Tatra and Beskids in north; Danube plain in south; numerous lakes and mineral springs
Head of state: Ivan Gasparovic from 2004
Head of government: Mikulas Dzurinda from 1998
Political system: emergent democracy
Political executive: parliamentary
Political parties: Movement for a Democratic Slovakia (MDS), left of centre, nationalist-populist; Democratic Union of Slovakia (DUS), centrist; Christian Democratic Movement (KSDH), right of centre; Slovak National Party (SNP), nationalist; Party of the Democratic Left (PDL), reform socialist, (ex-communist); Association of Workers of Slovakia, left wing; Hungarian Coalition, ethnic Hungarian
Currency: Slovak koruna (based on Czechoslovak koruna)
GNI per capita (PPP): (US$) 12,190 (2002 est)
Exports: basic manufactures, machinery and transport equipment, miscellaneous manufactured articles. Principal market: Germany 26.8% (2000)
Population: 5,402,000 (2003 est)
Language: Slovak (official), Hungarian, Czech, other ethnic languages
Religion: Roman Catholic (over 50%), Lutheran, Reformist, Orthodox, atheist 10%
Life expectancy: 70 (men); 78 (women) (2000–05)
Chronology
9th century: Part of kingdom of Greater Moravia, in Czech lands to west, founded by Slavic Prince Sviatopluk; Christianity adopted.
906: Came under Magyar (Hungarian) domination and adopted Roman Catholicism.
1526: Came under Austrian Habsburg rule.
1867: With creation of dual Austro-Hungarian monarchy, came under separate Hungarian rule; policy of forced Magyarization stimulated a revival of Slovak national consciousness.
1918: Austro-Hungarian Empire dismembered; Slovaks joined Czechs to form independent state of Czechoslovakia. Slovak-born Tomas Masaryk remained president until 1935, but political and economic power became concentrated in Czech lands.

1939: Germany annexed Czechoslovakia, which became Axis puppet state under the Slovak autonomist leader Monsignor Jozef Tiso; Jews persecuted.
1944: Popular revolt against German rule ('Slovak Uprising').
1945: Liberated from German rule by Soviet troops; Czechoslovakia re-established.
1948: Communists assumed power in Czechoslovakia.
1950s: Heavy industry introduced into previously rural Slovakia; Slovak nationalism and Catholic Church forcibly suppressed.
1968–69: 'Prague Spring' political reforms introduced by Slovak-born Communist Party leader Alexander Dubcek; Warsaw Pact forces invaded Czechoslovakia to stamp out reforms; Slovak Socialist Republic, with autonomy over local affairs, created under new federal constitution.
1989: Pro-democracy demonstrations in Bratislava; new political parties, including centre-left People Against Violence (PAV), formed and legalized; Communist Party stripped of powers; new government formed, with ex-dissident playwright Václav Havel as president.
1990: Slovak nationalists polled strongly in multiparty elections, with Vladimir Meciar (PAV) becoming prime minister.
1991: There was increasing Slovak separatism as the economy deteriorated. Meciar formed a PAV splinter group, Movement for a Democratic Slovakia (HZDS), pledging greater autonomy for Slovakia. Pro-Meciar rallies in Bratislava followed his dismissal.
1992: Meciar returned to power following an electoral victory for the HZDS. Slovak parliament's declaration of sovereignty led to Havel's resignation.
1993: The Slovak Republic joined the United Nations (UN) and Council of Europe as a sovereign state, with Meciar as prime minister and Michal Kovac, formerly of HZDS, as president.
1994: The Slovak Republic joined NATO's 'Partnership for Peace' programme.
1995: Slovak was made the sole official language; a Treaty of Friendship and Cooperation was signed with Hungary.
1996: An anti-Meciar coalition, the Slovak Democratic Coalition, was formed, comprising five opposition parties.
1997: A referendum on NATO membership and presidential elections was declared invalid after confusion over voting papers.
1998: Presidential powers were assumed by Meciar after failure to elect new president. The national council chair, Ivan Gasparovic, became acting head of state. Meciar stepped down as prime minister after the opposition Slovak Democratic Coalition (SDC) polled strongly in a general election. A new SDC-led coalition was formed under Mikulas Dzurinda. The koruna was devalued by 6%.
1999: Rudolf Schuster was elected president.
2000: Dzurinda formed a new coalition. The death penalty was abolished. Meciar was arrested on charges of corruption.
2003: In a referendum, 92.5% of voters supported accession to the European Union in 2004.
2004: In March the Slovak Republic joined NATO, and in May was admitted to the European Union.

Slovene

Slovene member of the southern *Slav people of Slovenia and parts of the Alpine provinces of Styria and Carinthia in Austria, and Gorizia and Carniola in Italy. Formerly under *Habsburg rule, they united with the Serbs and Croats to form the state of Yugoslavia after World War II. There are 1.5–2 million speakers of Slovene, a language belonging to the South Slavonic branch of the Indo-European family. The Slovenes use the Roman alphabet and the majority belong to the Roman Catholic Church.

Slovenia

National name: *Republika Slovenija/ Republic of Slovenia*

Area: 20,251 sq km/7,818 sq mi
Capital: Ljubljana
Major towns/cities: Maribor, Kranj, Celje, Velenje, Koper, Novo Mesto
Major ports: Koper
Physical features: mountainous; Sava and Drava rivers
Head of state: Janez Drnovšek from 2002
Head of government: Janez Jansa from 2004
Political system: emergent democracy
Political executive: dual executive
Political parties: Slovenian Christian Democrats (SKD), right of centre; Slovenian People's Party (SPP), conservative; Liberal Democratic Party of Slovenia (LDS), centrist; Slovenian Nationalist Party (SNS), right-wing nationalist; Democratic Party of Slovenia (LDP), left of centre; United List of Social Democrats (ZLSD) left of centre, ex-communist
Currency: tolar
GNI per capita (PPP): (US$) 17,690 (2002 est)
Exports: raw materials, semi-finished goods, machinery, electric motors, transport equipment, foodstuffs, clothing, pharmaceuticals, cosmetics. Principal market: Germany 26.2% (2001)
Population: 1,984,000 (2003 est)
Language: Slovene (related to Serbo-Croat; official), Hungarian, Italian
Religion: Roman Catholic 70%; Eastern Orthodox, Lutheran, Muslim
Life expectancy: 73 (men); 80 (women) (2000–05)

Chronology

1st century BC: Came under Roman rule.
AD 395: In the division of the Roman Empire, stayed in the west, along with Croatia and Bosnia.
6th century: Settled by the Slovene South Slavs.
7th century: Adopted Christianity as Roman Catholics.
8th–9th centuries: Under successive rule of Franks and dukes of Bavaria.
907–55: Came under Hungarian domination.
1335: Absorbed in Austro-Hungarian Habsburg Empire, as part of Austrian crownlands of Carniola, Styria, and Carinthia.
1848: Slovene struggle for independence began.
1918: On collapse of Habsburg Empire, Slovenia united with Serbia, Croatia, and Montenegro to form the 'Kingdom of Serbs, Croats and Slovenes', under Serbian Karageorgevic dynasty.
1929: Kingdom became known as Yugoslavia.
1941–45: Occupied by Nazi Germany and Italy during World War II; anti-Nazi Slovene Liberation Front formed and became allies of Marshal Tito's communist-led Partisans.
1945: Slovenia became a constituent republic of the Yugoslav Socialist Federal Republic.
mid-1980s: The Slovenian Communist Party liberalized itself and agreed to free elections. Yugoslav counterintelligence (KOV) began repression.
1989: The constitution was changed to allow secession from the federation.
1990: A Nationalist Democratic Opposition of Slovenia (DEMOS) coalition secured victory in the first multiparty parliamentary elections; Milan Kucan, a reform communist, became president. Sovereignty was declared. Independence was overwhelmingly approved in a referendum.
1991: Slovenia seceded from the Yugoslav federation, along with Croatia; 100 people were killed after the Yugoslav federal army intervened; a ceasefire brokered by the European Community (EC) brought the withdrawal of the Yugoslav army.
1992: Janez Drnovšek, a centrist Liberal Democrat, was appointed prime minister; independence was recognized by the EC and the USA. Slovenia was admitted into the United Nations (UN).
1997: A new government was formed by the ruling LDS, led by Prime Minister Janez Drnovšek. President Kucan was re-elected. The European Union (EU) agreed to open membership talks with Slovenia.
2000: A right-wing coalition government, led by Andrej Bajuk, briefly took office, but broke down over whether to move away from the system of election by proportional representation. New elections were won by a centre-left coalition led by former prime minister, Janez Drnovšek.
2003: In referenda, 90% of voters supported accession to the European Union in 2004 and 66% agreed to accession to the North Atlantic Treaty Organization (NATO) military alliance.
2004: Slovenia joined both NATO and the European Union.

slow-worm harmless species of lizard *Anguis fragilis*, once common in Europe, now a protected species in Britain. Superficially resembling a snake, it is distinguished by its small mouth and movable eyelids. It is about 30 cm/1 ft long, and eats worms and slugs.

slug soft-bodied land-living gastropod (type of *mollusc) related to the snails, but without a shell, or with a much reduced shell. All slugs have a protective coat of slime and a distinctive head with protruding tentacles. The eyes are at the end of the tentacles, which are also used to smell and locate food. Slugs eat dead animal matter and plants; some species are carnivorous and eat other slugs, snails, and earthworms. Slugs are hermaphrodite (having both male and female organs). They can fertilize themselves, but usually mate with another. Slugs can live for up to three years, and are invertebrates (animals without backbones).

small arms one of the two main divisions of firearms: guns that can be carried by hand. The first small arms were portable handguns in use in the late 14th century, supported on the ground and ignited by hand. Today's small arms range from breech-loading single-shot rifles and shotguns to sophisticated automatic and semiautomatic weapons.

smallpox acute, highly contagious viral disease, marked by aches, fever, vomiting, and skin eruptions leaving pitted scars. Widespread vaccination programmes have wiped out this often fatal disease.

smart drug any drug or combination of nutrients (vitamins, amino acids, minerals, and sometimes herbs) said to enhance the functioning of the brain, increase mental energy, lengthen the span of attention, and improve the memory. As yet there is no scientific evidence to suggest that these drugs have any significant effect on healthy people.

smart weapon programmable bomb or missile that can be guided to its target by laser technology, TV homing technology, or terrain-contour matching (TERCOM). A smart weapon relies on its pinpoint accuracy to destroy a target rather than on the size of its warhead.

smell sense that responds to chemical molecules in the air. It works by having receptors for particular chemical groups, into which the airborne chemicals must fit to trigger a message to the brain.

smelt small fish, usually marine, although some species are freshwater. They occur in Europe and North America. The most common European smelt is the sparling *Osmerus eperlanus*.

smelting processing a metallic ore in a furnace to produce the metal. Oxide ores such as iron ore are smelted with coke (carbon), which reduces the ore into metal and also provides fuel for the process.

Smetana, Bedrich (1824–1884) Bohemian composer. He established a Czech nationalist style in, for example, the operas *Prodaná Nevesta/The Bartered Bride* (1866) and *Dalibor* (1868), and the symphonic suite *Má Vlast/My Country* (1875–80). He conducted at the National Theatre of Prague in 1866–74.

Smith, Adam (1723–1790) Scottish economist. Until comparatively recently, Adam Smith was known only as the author of a single book, *An Inquiry into the Nature and Causes of the Wealth of Nations* (1776), published in the same year as the American Revolution. This book is said to have established economics as an autonomous subject and, at the same time, to have launched the doctrine of free enterprise upon an unsuspecting world. It is true that he also published another major treatise, *The Theory of Moral Sentiments* (1759), a work about those standards of ethical conduct that hold

society together, but this was a book that economists generally left unread. However, the recent publication of his many essays on philosophical and literary subjects suggests that he may have been working towards a complete system of social science, which he never lived to complete.

Smith, Ian (Douglas) (1919–   ) Rhodesian politician. He was a founder of the Rhodesian Front in 1962 and prime minister 1964–79. In 1965 he made a unilateral declaration of Rhodesia's independence and, despite UN sanctions, maintained his regime with tenacity. In 1979 he was succeeded as prime minister by Bishop Abel Muzorewa, when the country was renamed Zimbabwe. He was suspended from the Zimbabwe parliament in April 1987 and resigned in May as head of the white opposition party. In 1992 he helped found a new opposition party, the United Front.

Smith, William (1769–1839) English geologist. He produced the first geological maps of England and Wales, setting the pattern for geological cartography. Often called the founder of stratigraphical geology, he determined the succession of English strata across the whole country, from the Carboniferous up to the Cretaceous. He also established their fossil specimens.

smokeless fuel fuel that does not give off any smoke when burned, because all the carbon is fully oxidized to carbon dioxide (CO_2). Natural gas, oil, and coke are smokeless fuels.

smoking inhalation (breathing in) of the fumes from burning substances, generally *tobacco in the form of cigarettes. The practice is habit-forming and dangerous to health, since carbon monoxide and other toxic materials result from the combustion process. Smoking is addictive (see *addiction) because of the presence of the drug *nicotine in the smoke. A direct link between lung cancer and tobacco smoking was established in 1950; the habit is also linked to respiratory and coronary heart diseases. In the West, smoking is now forbidden in many public places because even **passive smoking** – breathing in fumes from other people's cigarettes – can be harmful. Some illegal drugs, such as *crack and *opium, are also smoked. In 2001, it was estimated that there were 1.1 billion smokers worldwide.

Smollett, Tobias George (1721–1771) Scottish novelist. He wrote the picaresque novels *Roderick Random* (1748), *Peregrine Pickle* (1751), *Ferdinand Count Fathom* (1753), *Sir Launcelot Greaves* (1760–62), and *Humphrey Clinker* (1771). His novels are full of gusto and vivid characterization.

smuggling illegal import or export of prohibited goods or the evasion of customs duties on dutiable goods. Smuggling has a long tradition in most border and coastal regions; goods smuggled commonly include tobacco, spirits, diamonds, gold, and illegal drugs.

smut in botany, any of a group of parasitic fungi (see *fungus) that infect flowering plants, particularly cereal grasses. (Order Ustilaginales.)

Smuts, Jan Christian (1870–1950) South African politician and soldier; prime minister 1919–24 and 1939–48. He supported the Allies in both world wars and was a member of the British imperial war cabinet 1917–18.

Smyrna ancient city near the modern Turkish port of Izmir. The earliest remains date from the 3rd millennium BC, and excavations have revealed that by the 8th century BC the city had a circuit of defensive walls. This is one of the earliest signs of the revival of Greek culture after the collapse of the *Mycenaean civilization.

snail air-breathing gastropod mollusc with a spiral shell. There are thousands of species, on land and in water. The typical snails of the genus *Helix* have two species in Europe. The common garden snail *H. aspersa* is very destructive to plants.

snake reptile of the suborder Serpentes of the order Squamata, which also includes lizards. Snakes are characterized by an elongated limbless body, possibly evolved because of subterranean ancestors. However, a team of US and Israeli palaeontologists rediscovered a fossil collection in 1996 which suggested that snakes evolved from sea-dwelling predators. One of the striking internal modifications is the absence or greatly reduced size of the left lung. The skin is covered in scales, which are markedly wider underneath where they form. There are 3,000 species found in the tropical and temperate zones, but none in New Zealand, Ireland, Iceland, and near the poles. Only three species are found in Britain: the adder, smooth snake, and grass snake.

snapdragon perennial herbaceous plant belonging to the figwort family, with spikes of brightly coloured two-lipped flowers. (*Antirrhinum majus*, family Scrophulariaceae.)

Snel's law of refraction in optics, the rule that when a ray of light passes from one medium to another, the sine of the angle of incidence divided by the sine of the angle of refraction is equal to the ratio of the indices of refraction in the two media. For a ray passing from medium 1 to medium 2: $n_2/n_1 = \sin i/\sin r$ where n_1 and n_2 are the refractive indices of the two media. The law was devised by the Dutch physicist, Willebrord Snel.

snipe marsh bird of the family Scolopacidae, order Charadriiformes closely related to the *woodcock. Snipes use their long, straight bills to probe marshy ground for worms, insects, and molluscs. Their nests are made on the grass, and they lay four eggs.

snooker indoor game derived from *billiards (via pool). It is played with 22 balls: 15 red, one each of yellow, green, brown, blue, pink, and black, and one white cueball. A tapered pole (cue) is used to propel the balls around the table. Red balls are worth one point when sunk (or 'potted'), while the coloured balls have ascending values from two points for the yellow to seven points for the black. The world professional championship was first held in 1927. The world amateur championship was first held in 1963. A snooker World Cup team event was inaugurated at Bangkok, Thailand, in 1996. The International Olympic Committee recognized snooker as an Olympic sport in 1998.

Snowdon Welsh **Eryri**, highest mountain in Wales, 1,085 m/3,560 ft above sea level. Situated 16 km/10 mi southeast of the Menai Strait, it consists of a cluster of five peaks. At the foot of Snowdon are the Llanberis, Aberglaslyn, and Rhyd-ddu passes. A rack railway ascends to the summit from Llanberis. Snowdonia, the surrounding mountain range, was made a national park in 1951. It covers 2,188 sq km/845 sq mi of mountain, lakes, and forest land.

snowdrop small bulbous European plant; its white bell-shaped hanging flowers, tinged with green, are among the first to appear in early spring. (*Galanthus nivalis*, family Amaryllidaceae.)

snow leopard a type of *leopard.

Snowy Mountains range in the Australian Alps, chiefly in New South Wales, near which the **Snowy River** rises; both river and mountains are known for a hydroelectric and irrigation system.

Soane, John (1753–1837) English architect. His refined neoclassical designs anticipated contemporary taste. Soane was a master of the established conventions of classical architecture, he also developed a highly individual style based on an elegantly mannered interpretation of neoclassicism. He designed his own house in Lincoln's Inn Fields, London (1812–13), now **Sir John Soane's Museum**, which he bequeathed to the nation in 1835, together with his collection of antiques, architectural elements and casts, papers, and drawings. Little remains of his extensive work at the Bank of England, London (rebuilt 1930–40).

soap mixture of the sodium salts of various *fatty acids: palmitic, stearic, and oleic acid. It is made by the action of sodium hydroxide (caustic soda) or potassium hydroxide (caustic potash) on fats of animal or vegetable origin. Soap makes grease and dirt disperse in water in a similar manner to a *detergent.

Soares, Mario Alberto Nobre Lopes (1924–) Portuguese socialist politician, president 1986–96. Exiled in 1970, he returned to Portugal in 1974 and, as leader of the Portuguese Socialist Party, was prime minister 1976–78. He resigned as party leader in 1980, but in 1986 he was elected Portugal's first socialist president.

Sobers, Garry (Garfield St Auburn) (1936–) West Indian Test cricketer, arguably the world's finest ever all-rounder. He held the world individual record for the highest Test innings with 365 not out, until beaten by Brian Lara in 1994. He played county cricket for Nottinghamshire and, in a match against Glamorgan at Swansea in 1968, he became the first cricketer to score six sixes in an over in first-class cricket. He played for the West Indies on 93 occasions, and was captain 39 times. He was knighted for services to cricket in 1975.

Social and Liberal Democrats (SLD) original name for the British political party formed in 1988 from the former Liberal Party and most of the Social Democratic Party. Since 1989 the party has been called the *Liberal Democrats.

social costs and benefits in economics, the costs and benefits to society as a whole that result from economic decisions. These include private costs (the financial cost of production incurred by firms) and benefits (the profits made by firms and the value to people of consuming goods and services) and external costs and benefits (affecting those not directly involved in production or consumption); pollution is one of the external costs.

social democracy political ideology or belief in the gradual evolution of a democratic *socialism within existing political structures. The earliest was the German Sozialdemokratische Partei (SPD), now one of the two main German parties, which had been created in 1875 by the amalgamation of other groups including August Bebel's earlier German Social Democratic

Workers' Party, founded in 1869. Parties along the lines of the German model were founded in the last two decades of the 19th century in a number of countries, including Austria, Belgium, the Netherlands, Hungary, Poland, and Russia. The British Labour Party is in the social democratic tradition.

Social Democratic and Labour Party (SDLP) Northern Ireland left-of-centre political party, formed in 1970. It aims ultimately at Irish unification, but has distanced itself from violent tactics, adopting a constitutional, conciliatory role. Its leader, John Hume, played a key role in the negotiations which ended in the 1998 Good Friday Agreement on power-sharing. It secured 24 of the 108 seats in the new Northern Ireland Assembly, elected in June 1998; the party's deputy leader, Seamus Mallon, was voted deputy first minister (to Ulster Unionist David Trimble) by the first meeting of the Assembly. Mallon resigned with Trimble in July 2001, following the failure of the IRA to proceed with decommissioning. In October 2001, after it was confirmed that the IRA had put some arms beyond use, the SDLP nominated their leader elect, Mark Durkan, to the post of deputy first minister.

Social Democratic Party (SDP) British centrist political party 1981–90, formed by members of Parliament who resigned from the Labour Party. The 1983 and 1987 general elections were fought in alliance with the Liberal Party as the Liberal/SDP Alliance. A merger of the two parties was voted for by the SDP in 1987, and the new party became the Social and Liberal Democrats, which became the *Liberal Democrats, leaving a rump SDP that folded in 1990.

social history branch of history that documents the living and working conditions of people rather than affairs of state. In recent years, television programmes, books, and museums have helped to give social history a wide appeal.

socialism movement aiming to establish a classless society by substituting public for private ownership of the means of production, distribution, and exchange. The term has been used to describe positions as widely apart as anarchism and social democracy. Socialist ideas appeared in classical times, in early Christianity, among later Christian sects such as the *Anabaptists and *Diggers, and, in the 18th and early 19th centuries, when they were put forward as systematic political aims by Jean-Jacques Rousseau, Claude Saint-Simon, François Fourier, and Robert Owen, among others. Socialist theories were also promoted by the German social and political philosophers Karl *Marx and Friedrich *Engels.

socialist realism officially approved type of art in the former USSR and other communist countries. The creation of artworks came under the communist doctrine that all material goods, and the means of producing them, were the collective property of the community. Art was to be produced solely for the education and inspiration of the people. Optimistic images of work and the heroic worker celebrated the virtues of *communism and patriotism, and glorified the state. In Soviet Russia, as in other totalitarian countries (run by one party), the government controlled all artistic organizations. All forms of artistic experimentation were condemned as a sign of decadent Western influence and, therefore, anticommunist

principles. Although the term is used mainly with reference to painting, it can apply to literature and music.

social mobility movement of groups and individuals up and down the social scale in a classed society. The extent or range of social mobility varies in different societies. Individual social mobility may occur through education, marriage, talent, and so on; group mobility usually occurs through change in the occupational structure caused by new technological or economic developments.

social realism *or* **urban realism** *or* **social protest painting** in painting, art that realistically depicts the life, struggles, and urban environment of the lower classes in the 20th century, and focuses on subjects of social and political concern, such as poverty and deprivation. Those described as Social Realists include: in the USA, members of the Ashcan School, Ben Shahn, Jacob Lawrence, and Romare Bearden; in the UK, the kitchen-sink painters, for example John Bratby; and in Mexico, the Muralists José Orozco and Diego *Rivera.

social science the group of academic disciplines that investigate how and why people behave the way they do, as individuals and in groups. The term originated with the 19th-century French thinker Auguste *Comte. The academic social sciences are generally listed as sociology, economics, anthropology, political science, and psychology.

social security state provision of financial aid to reduce poverty. The term 'social security' was first applied officially in the USA, in the Social Security Act of 1935. In Britain it was first used officially in 1944, and following the *Beveridge Report of 1942 a series of acts was passed from 1945 to widen the scope of social security. Basic entitlements of those paying National Insurance contributions in Britain include an old-age pension, unemployment benefit (known as jobseeker's allowance from October 1996), widow's pension, incapacity benefit, and payment during a period of sickness in one's working life (Statutory Sick Pay). Other benefits, which are non-contributory, include family credit, income support, child benefit, and attendance allowance for those looking after sick or disabled people. It was announced in the March 1998 budget that family credit and the disabled working allowance would be replaced from October 1999 by a working families tax credit and disabled persons tax credit, to be administered by the Inland Revenue.

Society Islands French Archipel de la Société, archipelago in *French Polynesia, divided into the Windward Islands and the Leeward Islands; area 1,685 sq km/650 sq mi; population (1995 est) 178,000. The administrative headquarters is Papeete on *Tahiti. The **Windward Islands** (French Iles du Vent) have an area of 1,200 sq km/460 sq mi and a population (1995 est) of 151,000. They comprise Tahiti, Moorea (area 132 sq km/51 sq mi), Maio (or Tubuai Manu; 9 sq km/3.5 sq mi), and the smaller Tetiaroa and Mehetia. The **Leeward Islands** (French Iles sous le Vent) have an area of 404 sq km/156 sq mi and a population of 27,000 (1995 est). They comprise the volcanic islands of Raiatea (including the main town of Uturoa), Huahine, Bora-Bora, Maupiti, Tahaa, and four small atolls. The islands were named after the Royal Society by Captain Cook, who visited them in 1769. Claimed by France in 1768, the group became a French protectorate in 1843, and a colony in 1880. Products include copra, phosphates, mother-of-pearl, and vanilla.

sociobiology study of the biological basis of all social behaviour, including the application of population genetics to the evolution of behaviour. It builds on the concept of inclusive fitness, contained in the notion of the 'selfish gene'. Contrary to some popular interpretations, it does not assume that all behaviour is genetically determined.

sociology systematic study of the origin and constitution of human society, in particular of social order and social change, social conflict and social problems. It studies institutions such as the family, law, and the church, as well as concepts such as norm, role, and culture. Sociology attempts to study people in their social environment according to certain underlying moral, philosophical, and political codes of behaviour.

Socrates (c. 469–399 BC) Athenian philosopher. He wrote nothing but was immortalized in the dialogues of his pupil Plato. In his desire to combat the scepticism of the *sophists, Socrates asserted the possibility of genuine knowledge. In ethics, he put forward the view that the good person never knowingly does wrong. True knowledge emerges through dialogue and systematic questioning and an abandoning of uncritical claims to knowledge.

Socratic method method of teaching used by Socrates, in which he aimed to guide pupils to clear thinking on ethics and politics by asking questions and then exposing their inconsistencies in cross-examination. This method was effective against the *sophists.

Soddy, Frederick (1877–1956) English physical chemist who pioneered research into atomic disintegration and coined the term *isotope. He was awarded the Nobel Prize for Chemistry in 1921 for investigating the origin and nature of isotopes.

sodium chemical symbol Na, soft, waxlike, silver-white, metallic element, atomic number 11, relative atomic mass 22.989. Its chemical symbol comes from the Latin *natrium*. It is one of the *alkali metals (in Group 1 of the *periodic table) and has a very low density, being light enough to float on water. It is the sixth-most abundant element (the fourth-most abundant metal) in the Earth's crust. Sodium is highly reactive, oxidizing rapidly when exposed to air and reacting violently with water. It is one of the most reactive metals in the *reactivity series of metals. Its most familiar compound is sodium chloride (common salt), which occurs naturally in the oceans and in salt deposits left by dried-up ancient seas.

sodium chloride *or* **common salt** *or* **table salt** NaCl, white, crystalline compound found widely in nature. The crystals are cubic in shape. It is a typical ionic solid with a high melting point (801 °C/1,474 °F); it is soluble in water, insoluble in organic solvents, and is a strong electrolyte when molten or in aqueous solution. Found in concentrated deposits as the mineral halite, it is widely used in the food industry as a flavouring and preservative, and in the chemical industry in the manufacture of sodium, chlorine, and sodium carbonate.

sodium hydroxide *or* **caustic soda** NaOH, commonest alkali. The solid and the solution are

corrosive. It is used to neutralize acids, in the manufacture of soap, and in drain and oven cleaners. It is prepared industrially from sodium chloride by the *electrolysis of concentrated brine.

Sodom and Gomorrah two ancient cities in the Dead Sea area of the Middle East, recorded in the Old Testament (Genesis) as being destroyed by fire and brimstone for their wickedness.

softball bat and ball game, a form of *baseball played with similar equipment. The two main differences are the distances between the bases (18.3 m/60 ft) and that the ball is pitched underhand in softball. There are two forms of the game, **fast pitch** and **slow pitch**; in the latter the ball must be delivered to home plate in an arc that must not be less than 2.4 m/8 ft at its height. The fast-pitch world championship was instituted in 1965 for women and 1966 for men; it is now contested every four years.

software in computing, a collection of programs and procedures for making a computer perform a specific task, as opposed to *hardware, the physical components of a computer system. Software is created by programmers and is either distributed on a suitable medium, such as *CD-ROM, or built into the computer in the form of firmware. Examples of software include *operating systems, *compilers, and applications such as payroll or word processing programs. No computer can function without some form of software.

soft water water that contains very few dissolved metal ions such as calcium (Ca^{2+}) or magnesium (Mg^{2+}). It lathers easily with soap, and no *scale is formed inside kettles or boilers. It has been found that the incidence of heart disease is higher in soft-water areas.

soil loose covering of broken rocky material and decaying organic matter overlying the bedrock of the Earth's surface. It is composed of minerals (formed from physical weathering and chemical weathering of rocks), organic matter (called humus) derived from decomposed plants and organisms, living organisms, air, and water. Soils differ according to climate, parent material, rainfall, relief of the bedrock, and the proportion of organic material. The study of soils is **pedology**.

soil erosion wearing away and redistribution of the Earth's soil layer. It is caused by the action of water, wind, and ice, and also by improper methods of *agriculture. If unchecked, soil erosion results in the formation of deserts (*desertification). It has been estimated that 20% of the world's cultivated topsoil was lost between 1950 and 1990.

solar energy energy derived from the light and heat from the Sun. The amount of energy falling on just 1 sq km/0.4 sq mi is about 4,000 megawatts, enough to heat and light a small town. In one second the Sun gives off 13 million times more energy than all the electricity used in the USA in one year. **Solar heaters** usually consist of concave mirrors or reflective parabolic surfaces that concentrate the Sun's rays onto a black (heat-absorbing) panel containing pipes through which air or water is circulated, either by thermal *convection or by a pump. The heat energy of the air or water is converted into electrical energy via a *turbine and a *generator. Hot water for industrial and domestic use can be produced by circulating water through panels, the water absorbing heat from the Sun as it passes through the panels. Solar energy may also be harnessed indirectly using **solar cells** (photovoltaic cells) made of panels of *semiconductor material (usually silicon), which generate electricity when illuminated by sunlight. Although it is difficult to generate a high output from solar energy compared to sources such as nuclear or fossil fuels, it is a major nonpolluting and renewable energy source used as far north as Scandinavia as well as in the southwestern USA and in Mediterranean countries.

solar flare brilliant eruption on the Sun above a *sunspot, thought to be caused by release of magnetic energy. Flares reach maximum brightness within a few minutes, then fade away over about an hour. They eject a burst of atomic particles into space at up to 1,000 kps/600 mps. When these particles reach Earth they can cause radio blackouts, disruptions of the Earth's magnetic field, and *auroras.

solar pond natural or artificial 'pond', such as the Dead Sea, in which salt becomes more soluble in the Sun's heat. Water at the bottom becomes saltier and hotter, and is insulated by the less salty water layer at the top. Temperatures at the bottom reach about 100 °C/212 °F and can be used to generate electricity.

solar radiation radiation given off by the Sun, consisting mainly of visible light, *ultraviolet radiation, and *infrared radiation, although the whole spectrum of *electromagnetic waves is present, from radio waves to X-rays. High-energy charged particles, such as electrons, are also emitted, especially from solar *flares. When these reach the Earth, they cause magnetic storms (disruptions of the Earth's magnetic field), which interfere with radio communications.

Solar System *Sun (a star) and all the bodies orbiting it: the nine *planets (Mercury, Venus, Earth, Mars, Jupiter, Saturn, Uranus, Neptune, and Pluto), their moons, and smaller objects such as *asteroids and *comets. The Sun contains 99.86% of the mass of the Solar System. The planets orbit the Sun in elliptical paths, and in the same direction as the Sun itself rotates. The planets nearer the Sun have shorter orbital times than those further away since the distance they travel in each orbit is less. Most of the objects in the Solar System lie close to the plane of the ecliptic. The planets are tiny compared to the Sun. If the Sun were the size of a basketball, the planet closest to the Sun, Mercury, would be the size of a mustard seed 15 m/48 ft from the Sun. The most distant planet, Pluto, would be a pinhead 1.6 km/1 mi away from the Sun. The Earth, which is the third planet out from the Sun, would be the size of a pea 32 m/100 ft from the Sun. To remember the order of planets moving away from the Sun, the mnemonic 'My very educated mother just served us nine pies' may be useful.

solar wind stream of atomic particles, mostly protons and electrons, from the Sun's corona, flowing outwards at speeds of between 300 kps/200 mps and 1,000 kps/600 mps.

solder any of various *alloys used when melted for joining metals such as copper, its common alloys (brass and bronze), and tin-plated steel, as used for making food cans.

soldier beetle reddish beetle with soft, black elytra (wing cases) and a black patch and black legs. It reaches a length of 15 mm/0.5 in and can be found in the daytime during the months of April to July on field, garden, and forest plants. It feeds particularly on aphids. Its larvae are black, and are to be found in the soil or among moss. The soldier beetle is in family Cantharidae, order Coleoptera, class Insecta, phylum Arthropoda.

sole flatfish found in temperate and tropical waters. The **common sole** *Solea solea*, also called **Dover sole**, is found in the southern seas of northwestern Europe. Up to 50 cm/20 in long, it is a prized food fish, as is the **sand** or **French sole** *Pegusa lascaris* further south.

solenodon rare insectivorous shrewlike mammal, genus *Solenodon*. There are two species, one each on Cuba and Hispaniola. They are about 30 cm/12 in long with a 25 cm/10 in naked tail, shaggy hair, long, pointed snouts, and strong claws, and they produce venomous saliva. They are slow-moving, come out mostly at night, and eat insects, worms, and other invertebrate animals. They are threatened with extinction owing to introduced predators.

solenoid coil of wire, usually cylindrical, in which a magnetic field is created by passing an electric current through it (see *electromagnet). This field can be used to temporarily magnetize, and so move, an iron rod placed on its axis. Mechanical valves attached to the rod can be operated by switching the current on or off, so converting electrical energy into mechanical energy. Solenoids are used to relay energy from the battery of a car to the starter motor by means of the ignition switch.

Solent, the channel between the coast of Hampshire, southern England, and the Isle of *Wight. It is a yachting centre.

sole trader *or* **sole proprietor** one person who runs a business, receiving all profits and responsible for all liabilities. Many small businesses are sole traders.

sol-fa in music, abbreviation for tonic sol-fa, a method of teaching music, usually singing, systematized by John Curwen (1816–1880).

solicitor in the UK, a member of one of the two branches of the English legal profession, the other being a *barrister. A solicitor is a lawyer who provides all-round legal services (making wills, winding up estates, conveyancing, divorce, and litigation). A solicitor cannot appear at High Court level, but must brief a barrister on behalf of his or her client. Solicitors may become circuit judges and recorders.

solid in physics, a state of matter that holds its own shape (as opposed to a liquid, which takes up the shape of its container, or a gas, which totally fills its container). According to the *kinetic theory of matter, the atoms or molecules in a solid are packed closely together in a regular arrangement, and are not free to move but merely vibrate about fixed positions, such as those in crystal lattices.

Solidarity Polish **Solidarnosc**, national confederation of independent trade unions in Poland, formed under the leadership of Lech *Walesa September 1980. An illegal organization from 1981 to 1989, it was then elected to head the Polish government. Divisions soon emerged in the leadership and in 1990 its political wing began to fragment (Walesa resigned as chairman in December of that year). In the September 1993 elections Solidarity gained less than 5% of the popular vote but, in September 1997, under the leadership of Marian Krzaklewski, Solidarity Electoral Action (AWS) won 34% of the vote and led the subsequent coalition government with Jerzy Buzek as prime minister.

solid-state circuit electronic circuit in which all the components (resistors, capacitors, transistors, and diodes) and interconnections are made at the same time, and by the same processes, in or on one piece of single-crystal silicon. The small size of this construction accounts for its use in electronics for space vehicles and aircraft.

solipsism in philosophy, a view that maintains that the self is the only thing that can be known to exist. It is an extreme form of *scepticism. The solipsist sees himself or herself as the only individual in existence, assuming other people to be a reflection of his or her own consciousness.

Solomon (c. 974–c. 922 BC) In the Old Testament, third king of Israel, son of David by Bathsheba. During a peaceful reign, he was famed for his wisdom and his alliances with Egypt and Phoenicia. The much later biblical Proverbs, Ecclesiastes, and Song of Songs are attributed to him. He built the temple in Jerusalem with the aid of heavy taxation and forced labour, resulting in the revolt of northern Israel.

Solomon Islands

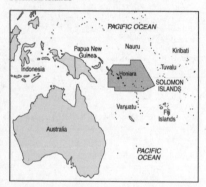

Area: 27,600 sq km/10,656 sq mi
Capital: Honiara (on Guadalcanal island) (and chief port)
Major towns/cities: Gizo, Auki, Kirakira, Buala
Major ports: Yandina
Physical features: comprises all but the northernmost islands (which belong to Papua New Guinea) of a Melanesian archipelago stretching nearly 1,500 km/900 mi. The largest is Guadalcanal (area 6,500 sq km/2,510 sq mi); others are Malaita, San Cristobal, New Georgia, Santa Isabel, Choiseul; mainly mountainous and forested
Head of state: Queen Elizabeth II from 1978, represented by Governor General Nathaniel Waena from 2004
Head of government: Allan Kemakeza from 2001
Political system: emergent democracy
Political executive: parliamentary
Political parties: Group for National Unity and Reconciliation (GNUR), centrist coalition;

National Coalition Partners (NCP), broad-based coalition; People's Progressive Party (PPP); People's Alliance Party (PAP), socialist
Currency: Solomon Island dollar
GNI per capita (PPP): (US$) 1,520 (2002 est)
Exports: timber, fish products, oil palm products, copra, cocoa, coconut oil. Principal market: Japan 19.8% (2001)
Population: 477,000 (2003 est)
Language: English (official), pidgin English, more than 80 Melanesian dialects (85%), Papuan and Polynesian languages
Religion: more than 80% Christian; Anglican 34%, Roman Catholic 19%, South Sea Evangelical, other Protestant, animist 5%
Life expectancy: 68 (men); 71 (women) (2000–05)
Chronology
1568: The islands, rumoured in South America to be the legendary gold-rich 'Islands of Solomon', were first sighted by Spanish navigator Alvaro de Mendana, journeying from Peru.
1595 and 1606: Unsuccessful Spanish efforts to settle the islands, which had long been peopled by Melanesians.
later 18th century: Visited again by Europeans.
1840s: Christian missions established.
1870s: Development of copra export trade and shipment of islanders to work on sugar cane plantations in Australia and Fiji Islands.
1886: Northern Solomon Islands became German protectorate.
1893: Southern Solomon Islands placed under British protection.
1899: Germany ceded Solomon Islands possessions to Britain in return for British recognition of its claims to Western Samoa.
1900: Unified British Solomon Islands Protectorate formed and placed under jurisdiction of Western Pacific High Commission (WPHC), with its headquarters in Fiji Islands.
1942–43: Occupied by Japan. Site of fierce fighting, especially on Guadalcanal, which was recaptured by US forces, with the loss of 21,000 Japanese and 5,000 US troops.
1943–50: Development of Marching Rule (Ma'asina Ruru) cargo cult populist movement on Malaita island, campaigning for self-rule.
1945: Headquarters of WPHC moved to Honiara.
1960: Legislative and executive councils established by constitution.
1974: Became substantially self-governing, with Solomon Mamaloni of centre-left People's Progressive Party (PPP) as chief minister.
1976: Became fully self-governing, with Peter Kenilorea of right-of-centre Solomon Islands United Party (SIUPA) as chief minister.
1978: Independence achieved from Britain within Commonwealth, with Kenilorea as prime minister.
1988: The Solomon Islands joined Vanuatu and Papua New Guinea to form the Spearhead Group, aiming to preserve Melanesian cultural traditions.
1997: Bartholomew Ulufa'alu was elected prime minister.
1998: Ulufa'alu's Alliance for Change government narrowly survived a no-confidence vote.

2000: A military coup, led by rebel leader, Andrew Nori, in June forced the resignation of Prime Minister Ulufa'alu. The former opposition leader, Mannesseh Sogavare, was elected to become the new prime minister. A peace treaty was signed by rival ethnic militias in October and fighting ceased.

2001: The Central Bank warned that the country was on the verge of economic collapse.

2003: A 2,300-strong Australian-led international peacekeeping force arrived to restore order and government authority.

Solomon's seal any of a group of perennial plants belonging to the lily family, native to Europe and found growing in moist, shady woodland areas. They have drooping bell-like white or greenish-white flowers which appear just above the point where the leaves join the arching stems, followed by blue or black berries. (Genus *Polygonatum*, family Liliaceae.)

Solon (*c.* 638–*c.* 558 BC) Athenian statesman. As one of the chief magistrates about 594 BC, he carried out the cancellation of all debts from which land or liberty was the security and the revision of the constitution that laid the foundations of Athenian democracy. He was one of the Seven Sages of Greece.

solstice either of the days on which the Sun is farthest north or south of the celestial equator each year. In the northern hemisphere, the **summer solstice**, when the Sun is farthest north, occurs around 21 June and the **winter solstice** around 22 December.

solubility measure of the amount of solute (usually a solid or gas) that will dissolve in a given amount of solvent (usually a liquid) at a particular temperature. Solubility may be expressed as grams of solute per 100 grams of solvent or, for a gas, in parts per million (ppm) of solvent.

solute substance that is dissolved in another substance (see *solution).

solution two or more substances mixed to form a single, homogenous phase. One of the substances is the **solvent** and the others (**solutes**) are said to be dissolved in it.

solution *or* **dissolution** in earth science, process by which the minerals in a rock are dissolved in water. Solution is one of the processes of *erosion as well as *weathering (in which the breakdown of rock occurs without transport of the dissolved material). An example of this is when weakly acidic rainfall dissolves calcite.

solvent substance, usually a liquid, that will dissolve another substance (see *solution). Although the commonest solvent is water, in popular use the term refers to low-boiling-point organic liquids, which are harmful if vapour from them is breathed in as a result of their use in a confined space, or from skin contact with the liquid. They can give rise to respiratory problems, liver damage, and neurological complaints.

Solway Firth inlet of the Irish Sea, formed by the estuaries of the rivers Eden and Esk, at the western end of the border between England and Scotland, separating Cumbria in England from Dumfries and Galloway in Scotland. Solway Firth is in part the estuary of the River Esk, and in part an inlet of the Irish Sea.

Solyman I alternative spelling of *Suleiman, Ottoman sultan.

Solzhenitsyn, Alexander Isayevich (1918–) Russian novelist. He became a US citizen in 1974. He was in prison and exile 1945–57 for anti-Stalinist comments. Much of his writing is semi-autobiographical and highly critical of the system of Russian dictator Joseph *Stalin, including *One Day in the Life of Ivan Denisovich* (1962), which deals with the labour camps under Stalin, and *The Gulag Archipelago* (1973), an exposé of the whole Soviet labour-camp network. The latter work led to his expulsion from the USSR in 1974. He was awarded the Nobel Prize for Literature in 1970.

Somali member of a group of East African peoples from the Horn of Africa. Although the majority of Somalis live in the Somali Republic, there are minorities in Ethiopia and Kenya. Primarily nomadic pastoralists and traders, they live in families, grouped in clans, under an elective or hereditary chieftain. They are mainly Sunni Muslims. Their Cushitic language belongs to the Hamitic branch of the Afro-Asiatic family.

Somalia

National name: *Jamhuuriyadda Soomaaliya/ Republic of Somalia*

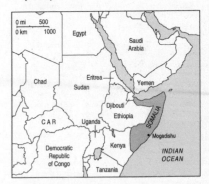

Area: 637,700 sq km/246,215 sq mi
Capital: Mogadishu (and chief port)
Major towns/cities: Hargeysa, Berbera, Kismaayo, Marka
Major ports: Berbera, Marka, Kismaayo
Physical features: mainly flat, with hills in north
Head of state: Abdiqasim Salad Hassan from 2000
Head of government: Hasan Abshir Farah from 2001
Political system: military
Political executive: military
Political parties: parties are mainly clan-based and include the United Somali Congress (USC), Hawiye clan; Somali Patriotic Movement (SPM), Darod clan; Somali Southern Democratic Front (SSDF), Majertein clan; Somali Democratic Alliance (SDA), Gadabursi clan; United Somali Front (USF), Issa clan; Somali National Movement (SNM) based in self-proclaimed Somaliland Republic
Currency: Somali shilling
Exports: livestock, skins and hides, bananas, fish and fish products, myrrh. Principal market: Saudi Arabia 32% (2001)

Population: 9,890,000 (2003 est)
Language: Somali, Arabic (both official), Italian, English
Religion: Sunni Muslim; small Christian community, mainly Roman Catholic
Life expectancy: 46 (men); 50 (women) (2000–05)
Chronology
8th–10th centuries: Arab ancestors of Somali clan families migrated to the region and introduced Sunni Islam; coastal trading cities, including Mogadishu, were formed by Arabian immigrants and developed into sultanates.
11th–14th century: Southward and westward movement of Somalis and Islamization of Christian Ethiopian interior.
early 16th century: Portuguese contacts with coastal region.
1820s: First British contacts with northern Somalia.
1884–87: British protectorate of Somaliland established in north.
1889: Italian protectorate of Somalia established in south.
1927: Italian Somalia became a colony and part of Italian East Africa from 1936.
1941: Italian Somalia occupied by Britain during World War II.
1943: Somali Youth League (SYL) formed as nationalist party.
1950: Italy resumed control over Italian Somalia under UN trusteeship.
1960: Independence achieved from Italy and Britain as Somalia, with Aden Abdullah Osman as president.
1963: Border dispute with Kenya; diplomatic relations broken with Britain for five years.
1969: President Ibrahim Egal assassinated in army coup led by Maj-Gen Muhammad Siad Barre; constitution suspended, political parties banned, Supreme Revolutionary Council set up, and socialist-Islamic state formed.
1972: 20,000 died in severe drought.
1978: Defeated in eight-month war with Ethiopia fought on behalf of Somali guerrillas in Ogaden to the southwest. Armed insurrection began in north and hundreds of thousands became refugees.
1979: New constitution for socialist one-party state dominated by Somali Revolutionary Socialist Party (SRSP).
1982: The antigovernment Ethiopian-backed Somali National Movement (SNM) was formed in the north, followed by oppressive countermeasures by the government.
late 1980s: Guerrilla activity increased in the north as the civil war intensified.
1991: Mogadishu was captured by rebels; Ali Mahdi Muhammad took control of the north of the town, and General Aidid took control of the south; free elections were promised. The secession of northeast Somalia, as the Somaliland Republic, was announced but not recognized internationally.
1992: There was widespread famine. Western food-aid convoys were hijacked by 'warlords'. United Nations (UN) peacekeeping troops, led by US Marines, were sent in to protect relief operations.
1993: Leaders of armed factions (except the Somaliland-based faction) agreed to a federal system

of government. US-led UN forces destroyed the headquarters of warlord General Aidid after the killing of Pakistani peacekeepers.
1994: Ali Mahdi Muhammad and Aidid signed a truce. Most Western peacekeeping troops were withdrawn, but clan-based fighting continued.
1996: Aidid was killed in renewed faction fighting; his son Hussein Aidid succeeded him as interim president.
1998: A peace plan was agreed.
1999: In June the Ethiopian army, supporting opponents of Aidid, invaded Somalia.
2000: The four-month Somali reconciliation conference in Djibouti ended in August after the new transitional parliament elected Abdulkassim Salat Hassan as Somalia's first civilian president since civil war broke out nine years earlier. In October, Ali Khalifa Galad became prime minister.
2001: Ethiopia-backed warlords threatened to form a breakaway national government. Heavy fighting took place in Mogadishu, and Kismayo was seized.
2002: Six districts unilaterally declared autonomy as a 'Southwestern Regional Government'. Dahir Riyale Kahin became president of breakaway Somaliland and pledged to preserve its sovereignty. The transitional government and 21 warring factions signed a ceasefire.
2003: Dahir Riyale Kahin won the first Somaliland presidential elections.
2004: Although little progress had been made towards political unity, politicians and clan leaders agreed to set up a further parliament.

Somaliland region of Somali-speaking peoples situated in eastern Africa between the Gulf of Aden to the north, and the Indian Ocean to the southeast. It includes the former regions of *British Somaliland (established 1887), *Italian Somaliland (established 1889–90), and French Somaliland (established 1888). British and Italian Somaliland became independent as Somalia in 1960. French Somaliland became independent as Djibouti in 1977. Part of Somaliland unilaterally declared independence from Somalia in 1991.

Somerset county of southwest England. **area:** 3,460 sq km/1,336 sq mi **towns:** Taunton (administrative headquarters); Bridgwater, Frome, Glastonbury, Wells, Yeovil; Burnham-on-Sea, Minehead (coastal resorts) **physical:** rivers Avon, Axe, Brue, Exe, Parret (the principal river), and Yeo; marshy coastline on the Bristol Channel; Mendip Hills; Quantock Hills; Exmoor; Blackdown Hills **features:** Cheddar Gorge and Wookey Hole, a series of limestone caves where Stone Age flint implements and bones of extinct animals have been found; Glastonbury Tor **population:** (1996) 482,600.

Somerset, Edward Seymour, 1st Duke of Somerset (c. 1506–1552) English politician. Created Earl of Hertford after Henry VIII's marriage to his sister Jane, he became Duke of Somerset and protector (regent) for Edward VI in 1547. His attempt to check *enclosure (the transfer of land from common to private ownership) offended landowners and his moderation in religion upset the Protestants. Knighted in 1523, viscount in 1536, earl in 1537, he was eventually beheaded on a treason charge in 1552.

Somme river in northern France, on which Amiens and Abbeville stand; length 245 km/152 mi. It rises in Aisne *département* near St Quentin and flows west through

Somme *département* to the English Channel near St Valéry-sur-Somme. It is connected by canal with the Oise and the Schelde (French Escaut). Its tributaries include the rivers Ancre and Avre. Some of the heaviest fighting of World War I took place on the banks of the Somme, especially in July–November 1916 (see *Somme, Battle of the).

Somme, Battle of the Allied offensive in World War I July–November 1916 on the River Somme in northern France, during which severe losses were suffered by both sides. It was planned by the Marshal of France, Joseph Joffre, and UK commander-in-chief Douglas Haig; the Allies lost over 600,000 soldiers and advanced approximately 8 km/5 mi (13 km/8 mi at its furthest point). It was the first battle in which tanks were used. The German offensive around St Quentin March–April 1918 is sometimes called the Second Battle of the Somme.

sonar acronym for SOund Navigation And Ranging, method of locating underwater objects by the reflection of ultrasonic waves. The time taken for an acoustic beam to travel to the object and back to the source enables the distance to be found since the velocity of sound in water is known. Sonar devices, or **echo sounders**, were developed in 1920, and are the commonest means of underwater navigation.

sonata (Italian 'sounded') in music, an important type of instrumental composition. Although it can be a piece for a solo player or a small ensemble, it is now commonly used to describe a work for solo piano (piano sonata), or piano and one other instrument (violin sonata – violin and piano; flute sonata – flute and piano). It usually consists of three or four contrasting movements with one or more being in sonata form. The name means that the work is not beholden to a text or existing dance form, but is self-sufficient.

sonata form in music, one of the most important forms. The structure divides into three main sections: exposition, development, and recapitulation. It introduced great dramatic possibilities and increased freedom for 18th-century music, which had previously been limited to closed dance routines. It developed initially in the instrumental *sonata, from which it took its name, but it is used in many other works besides sonatas. The form does not apply to a whole work but only to one movement of it. It is often associated with the first movement of a work, hence its alternative name of **first movement form**, but this is a misleading term as it can also be found in the second and last movements.

song a setting of words to music for one or more singers, with or without instrumental accompaniment. Song may be sacred, for example a psalm, motet, or cantata, or secular, for example a folk song or ballad. In verse song, the text changes in mood while the music remains the same; in *lied and other forms of art song, the music changes in response to the emotional development of the text.

song cycle sequence of songs related in mood and sung as a group, used by romantic composers such as Franz Schubert, Robert Schumann, and Hugo Wolf.

Song dynasty (*or* **Sung dynasty**) **(lived 10th–13th centuries)** Chinese imperial family ruling from 960 to 1279, founded by northern general Taizu or Zhao Kuangyin (928–76). A distinction is conventionally made between the Northern Song period (960–1126), when the capital was at Kaifeng, and Southern Song (1127–1279), when it was at Hangzhou (Hangchow). A stable government was supported by a thoroughly centralized administration. The dynasty was eventually ended by Mongol invasion.

Songhai Empire former kingdom of northwestern Africa, founded in the 8th century, which developed into a powerful Muslim empire under the rule of Sonni Ali (reigned 1464–92). It superseded the *Mali Empire and extended its territory, occupying an area that included parts of present-day Guinea, Burkina Faso, Senegal, Gambia, Mali, Mauritania, Niger, and Nigeria. In 1591 it was invaded and overthrown by Morocco.

sonic boom noise like a thunderclap that occurs when an aircraft passes through the *sound barrier, or begins to travel faster than the speed of sound. It happens when the cone-shaped shock wave caused by the plane touches the ground.

sonnet *genre of 14-line poem of Italian origin introduced to England by English poet Thomas Wyatt in the form used by Italian poet *Petrarch and followed by English poets John *Milton and William *Wordsworth; English playwright and poet William *Shakespeare wrote 14-line sonnets consisting of three groups of four lines (quatrains) and two final rhyming lines (a couplet), following] the rhyme scheme *abab cdcd efef gg*.

Sophia, Electress of Hanover (1630–1714) Twelfth child of Frederick V, elector palatine of the Rhine and king of Bohemia, and Elizabeth, daughter of James I of England. She married the elector of Hannover in 1658. Widowed in 1698, she was recognized in the succession to the English throne in 1701, and when Queen Anne died without issue in 1714, her son George I founded the Hanoverian dynasty.

sophist (Greek *sophistes* 'wise man') in ancient Greece, one of a group of 5th-century BC itinerant lecturers on culture, rhetoric, and politics. Sceptical about the possibility of achieving genuine knowledge, they applied bogus reasoning and were concerned with winning arguments rather than establishing the truth. *Plato regarded them as dishonest and **sophistry** came to mean fallacious reasoning. In the 2nd century AD the term was linked to the art of public speaking.

Sophocles (c. 496–406 BC) Athenian dramatist. He is credited with having developed tragedy by introducing a third actor and scene-painting, and ranked with *Aeschylus and *Euripides as one of the three great tragedians. He wrote some 120 plays, of which seven tragedies survive. These are *Antigone* (443 BC), *Oedipus the King* (429), *Electra* (410), *Ajax*, *Trachiniae*, *Philoctetes* (409 BC), and *Oedipus at Colonus* (401; produced after his death).

soprano highest range of the female voice, from around D4 (the D above middle C) to A6. Some operatic roles require the extended upper range of a *coloratura soprano, reaching to around F6, for example Kiri Te Kanawa. It is also used before the name of an instrument that sounds in the same range as the soprano voice.

sorbic acid $CH_3CH=CHCH=CHCOOH$, tasteless acid found in the fruit of the mountain ash (genus *Sorbus*) and prepared synthetically. It is widely used in the preservation of food – for example, cider, wine, soft drinks, animal feeds, bread, and cheese. .

sorghum *or* **great millet** *or* **Guinea corn** any of a group of *cereal grasses native to Africa but cultivated widely in India, China, the USA, and southern Europe. The seeds are used for making bread. *Durra is a member of the genus. (Genus *Sorghum*.)

sorrel (Old French *sur* 'sour') any of several plants belonging to the buckwheat family. *R. acetosa* is grown for its bitter salad leaves. *Dock plants are of the same genus. (Genus *Rumex*, family Polygonaceae.)

SOS internationally recognized distress signal, using letters of the *Morse code (... – – – ...).

Sotho a large ethnic group in southern Africa, numbering about 7 million (1987) and living mainly in Botswana, Lesotho, and South Africa. The Sotho are predominantly farmers, living in small village groups. They speak a variety of closely related languages belonging to the Bantu branch of the Niger-Congo family. With English, Sotho is the official language of Lesotho.

soul music style of vocal popular music developed in the 1960s by African Americans. It is an emotionally intense style of *rhythm and blues that combines blues, gospel music, and jazz. Among its main singers are James Brown, Sam Cooke, Aretha Franklin, Al Green, and Otis Redding.

sound physiological sensation received by the ear, originating in a vibration causing sound waves. The sound waves are pressure variations in the air and travel in every direction, spreading out as an expanding sphere. Sound energy cannot travel in a vacuum.

sound barrier concept that the speed of sound, or sonic speed (about 1,220 kph/760 mph at sea level), constitutes a speed limit to flight through the atmosphere, since a badly designed aircraft suffers severe buffeting at near sonic speed owing to the formation of shock waves. US test pilot Chuck Yeager first flew through the 'barrier' in 1947 in a Bell X-1 rocket plane. Now, by careful design, such aircraft as Concorde can fly at supersonic speed with ease, though they create in their wake a *sonic boom.

sound synthesis the generation of sound (usually music) by electronic *synthesizer.

soundtrack band at one side of a cine film on which the accompanying sound is recorded. Usually it takes the form of an optical track (a pattern of light and shade). The pattern is produced on the film when signals from the recording microphone are made to vary the intensity of a light beam. During playback, a light is shone through the track on to a photocell, which converts the pattern of light falling on it into appropriate electrical signals. These signals are then fed to loudspeakers to recreate the original sounds.

sousaphone large bass *tuba designed to wrap round the player in a circle and having a forward-facing bell. The form was suggested by US bandmaster John Sousa. Today sousaphones are largely fabricated in lightweight fibreglass.

South Africa

National name: *Republiek van Suid-Afrika/ Republic of South Africa*
Area: 1,222,081 sq km/471,845 sq mi
Capital: Cape Town (legislative), Pretoria (administrative), Bloemfontein (judicial)
Major towns/cities: Johannesburg, Durban, Port Elizabeth, Vereeniging, Pietermaritzburg, Kimberley, Soweto, Tembisa

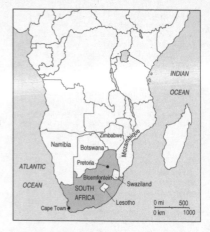

Major ports: Cape Town, Durban, Port Elizabeth, East London
Physical features: southern end of large plateau, fringed by mountains and lowland coastal margin; Drakensberg Mountains, Table Mountain; Limpopo and Orange rivers
Territories: Marion Island and Prince Edward Island in the Antarctic
Head of state and government: Thabo Mbeki from 1999
Political system: emergent democracy
Political executive: limited presidency
Political parties: African National Congress (ANC), left of centre; National Party (NP), right of centre; Inkatha Freedom Party (IFP), centrist, multiracial (formerly Zulu nationalist); Freedom Front (FF), right wing; Democratic Party (DP), moderate, left of centre, multiracial; Pan-Africanist Congress (PAC), black, left wing; African Christian Democratic Party (ACDP), Christian, right of centre
Currency: rand
GNI per capita (PPP): (US$) 9,870 (2002 est)
Exports: metals and metal products, gold, precious and semiprecious stones, mineral products and chemicals, natural cultured pearls, machinery and mechanical appliances, wool, maize, fruit, sugar. Principal market: USA 10.6% (2001)
Population: 45,026,000 (2003 est)
Language: English, Afrikaans, Xhosa, Zulu, Sesotho (all official), other African languages
Religion: Dutch Reformed Church and other Christian denominations 77%, Hindu 2%, Muslim 1%
Life expectancy: 45 (men); 51 (women) (2000–05)
Chronology
1652: Dutch East India Company established colony at Cape Town as a port of call.
1795: Britain occupied Cape after France conquered the Netherlands.
1814: Britain bought Cape Town and hinterland from the Netherlands for £6 million.
1820s: Zulu people established military kingdom under Shaka.

1836–38: The Great Trek: 10,000 Dutch settlers (known as Boers, meaning 'farmers') migrated north to escape British rule.

1843: Britain established colony of Natal on east coast.

1852–54: Britain recognized Boer republics of Transvaal and Orange Free State.

1872: The Cape became self-governing colony within British Empire.

1877: Britain annexed Transvaal.

1879: Zulu War: Britain destroyed power of Zulus.

1881: First Boer War: Transvaal Boers defeated British at Majuba Hill and regained independence.

1886: Discovery of gold on Witwatersrand attracted many migrant miners (uitlanders) to Transvaal, which denied them full citizenship.

1895: Jameson Raid: uitlanders, backed by Cecil Rhodes, tried to overthrow President Paul Kruger of Transvaal.

1899–1902: Second South African War (also known as Boer War): dispute over rights of uitlanders led to conflict which ended with British annexation of Boer republics.

1907: Britain granted internal self-government to Transvaal and Orange Free State on a whites-only franchise.

1910: Cape Colony, Natal, Transvaal, and Orange Free State formed Union of South Africa, with Louis Botha as prime minister.

1912: Gen Barry Hertzog founded (Boer) Nationalist Party; ANC formed to campaign for rights of black majority.

1914: Boer revolt in Orange Free State suppressed; South African troops fought for British Empire in World War I.

1919: Jan Smuts succeeded Botha as premier; South West Africa (Namibia) became South African mandate.

1924: Hertzog became prime minister, aiming to sharpen racial segregation and loosen ties with British Empire.

1939–45: Smuts led South Africa into World War II despite neutralism of Hertzog; South African troops fought with Allies in Middle East, East Africa, and Italy.

1948: Policy of apartheid ('separateness') adopted when National Party (NP) took power under Daniel Malan; continued by his successors Johannes Strijdom 1954–58, Hendrik Verwoerd 1958–66, B J Vorster 1966–78, and P J Botha 1978–89.

1950: Entire population classified by race; Group Areas Act segregated blacks and whites; ANC responded with campaign of civil disobedience.

1960: 70 black demonstrators killed at Sharpville; ANC banned.

1961: South Africa left Commonwealth and became republic.

1964: ANC leader Nelson Mandela sentenced to life imprisonment.

1967: Terrorism Act introduced indefinite detention without trial.

1970s: Over 3 million people forcibly resettled in black 'homelands'.

1976: Over 600 killed in clashes between black protesters and security forces in Soweto.

1984: New constitution gave segregated representation to coloureds and Asians, but continued to exclude blacks.

1985: Growth of violence in black townships led to proclamation of a state of emergency.

1986: USA and Commonwealth imposed limited economic sanctions against South Africa.

1989: F W de Klerk succeeded P W Botha as president; public facilities were desegregated; many ANC activists were released.

1990: The ban on the ANC was lifted; Mandela was released; talks began between the government and the ANC; there was a daily average of 35 murders.

1991: De Klerk repealed the remaining apartheid laws; sanctions were lifted; however, there was severe fighting between the ANC and the Zulu Inkatha movement.

1993: An interim majority rule constitution was adopted; de Klerk and Mandela agreed to form a government of national unity after free elections.

1994: The ANC were victorious in the first nonracial elections; Mandela became president; Commonwealth membership was restored.

1996: De Klerk withdrew the NP from the coalition after the new constitution failed to provide for power-sharing after 1999.

1997: A new constitution was signed by President Mandela. De Klerk announced his retirement from politics.

1999: Mandela retired as state president; he was succeeded by Thabo Mbeki. ANC won an assembly majority in election.

2001: Pharmaceutical companies dropped their case to stop the country importing generic Aids drugs. The high court ruled pregnant women must have Aids drugs to prevent transmission of the virus to their babies.

2002: The government was forced to provide an anti-Aids drug at public hospitals, despite the high cost.

2004: President Mbeki was re-elected for a further term.

South African Wars *or* **Boer Wars** two wars between the Boers (settlers of Dutch origin) and the British; essentially fought for the gold and diamonds of the Transvaal. The **War of 1881** was triggered by the attempt of the Boers of the *Transvaal to reassert the independence surrendered in 1877 in return for British aid against African peoples. The British were defeated at Majuba, and the Transvaal again became independent. The **War of 1899–1902**, also known as the **Boer War**, was preceded by the armed Jameson Raid into the Boer Transvaal in 1895 – a failed attempt, inspired by the Cape Colony prime minister Cecil Rhodes, to precipitate a revolt against Paul Kruger, the Transvaal president. The *uitlanders* (non-Boer immigrants) were still not given the vote by the Boers, negotiations failed, and the Boers invaded British territory, besieging Ladysmith, Mafeking (now Mafikeng), and Kimberley. The war ended with the Peace of Vereeniging following the Boer defeat.

South America fourth largest of the continents, nearly twice as large as Europe (13% of the world's land surface), extending south from *Central America. **area:** 17,864,000 sq km/6,897,000 sq mi **largest cities:** (population over 3.5 million) Buenos Aires, São Paulo, Rio de Janeiro, Bogotá, Santiago, Lima, Belo Horizonte **features:** Lake Titicaca (the world's highest navigable lake); La Paz (highest capital city in the world); Atacama Desert; Inca ruins at Machu Picchu; rivers

851

include the Amazon (world's largest and second longest), Paraná, Madeira, São Francisco, Purús, Paraguay, Orinoco, Araguaia, Negro, Uruguay **physical:** occupying the southern part of the landmass of the Western hemisphere, the South American continent stretches from Point Gallinas on the Caribbean coast of Colombia to Cape Horn at the southern tip of Horn Island, which lies adjacent to Tierra del Fuego; the most southerly point on the mainland is Cape Froward on the Brunswick peninsula, southern Chile; at its maximum width (5,120 km/ 3,200 mi) the continent stretches from Point Pariñas, Peru, in the extreme west to Point Coqueiros, just north of Recife, Brazil, in the east; five-sixths of the continent lies in the southern hemisphere and two-thirds within the tropics **population:** (2001 est) 350 million. Because of rapid, but now declining, population growth rates, about a third of the population are under 15 years of age. The urban population has increased rapidly since 1950, as millions of poor people left the countryside in the hope of a better standard of living in the cities. By 1998 over 75% of the population was living in cities **language:** Spanish, Portuguese (chief language in Brazil), Dutch (Suriname), French (French Guiana), American Indian languages; Hindi, Javanese, and Chinese spoken by descendants of Asian immigrants to Suriname and Guyana; a variety of Creole dialects spoken by those of African descent **religion:** 90–95% Roman Catholic; local animist beliefs among Amerindians; Hindu and Muslim religions predominate among the descendants of Asian immigrants in Suriname and Guyana.

Southampton industrial seaport and administrative centre of Southampton City unitary authority in southern England, at the head of Southampton Water, 128 km/80 mi southwest of London; population (1999 est) 215,300. Industries include marine engineering, chemicals, plastics, flour milling, and tobacco. It is a major passenger and container port.

South Australia state of south-central Australia, including Kangaroo Island and other islands in the Indian Ocean; bounded on the northeast by Queensland, on the east by New South Wales, on the southeast by Victoria, on the south by the Indian Ocean, and on the west by Western Australia; area 984,381 sq km/380,071 sq mi; population (1996) 1,428,000. The capital (and chief port) is *Adelaide. Products are meat, wool, wine, wheat, barley, almonds, oranges and other citrus fruits, and dried and canned fruit, coal, copper, uranium, silver, zinc, gold, steel, jade, slate, opals, marble, granite, household and electrical goods, vehicles, oil, and natural gas.

South Ayrshire unitary authority in southwest Scotland, created in 1996 from Kyle and Carrick district (1975–96), Strathclyde region. **area:** 1,245 sq km/ 480 sq mi **towns:** Ayr (administrative headquarters), Prestwick, Girvan, Troon, Maybole **physical:** coastal plain which rises to higher ground inland (500 m/ 1,640 ft); rivers Ayr, Stinchar, Water of Girvan; Brown Carrick Hill (287 m/942 ft); Ailsa Craig; many beaches interspersed with cliffs and caves **features:** Glasgow Prestwick Airport; Culzean Castle; Crossraguel Abbey; Royal Troon and Turnberry championship golf courses; Ayr racecourse **population:** (2000 est) 113,920 **history:** birthplace of Robert Burns.

South Carolina called the **Palmetto State**, state in eastern USA, bordered to the north and northeast by *North Carolina, to the south and west by *Georgia, and to the southeast by the Atlantic Ocean; area 77,982 sq km/30,109 sq mi; population (2000) 4,012,012; capital and largest city Columbia. South Carolina is the smallest state of the Deep South region, and is roughly triangular in shape, with the Savannah River forming much of the state boundary with Georgia. The *Blue Ridge Mountains rise in the northwest, and there are numerous sea islands along the subtropical coastline. Service industries, particularly tourism, form the basis of South Carolina's economy, but farming, fishing, wood processing, and the manufacture of chemicals and textiles are also important. The state is a leading producer of tobacco in the USA. Columbia is situated in the central industrial heartland. Other major cities include the seaport of Charleston, and the former textile centres of Greenville and Spartanburg in the Blue Ridge Mountains. Settled as an English colony from 1670, the name Carolina derives from the Latin for Charles, after King Charles I; South was added when the colony was divided into north and south in 1712. One of the original *Thirteen Colonies, South Carolina was also one of the original US plantation states, associated with *slavery. South Carolina's first constitution was drafted in 1776, and it was admitted to the Union in 1788, becoming the 8th state.

South China Sea see *China Sea.

South Dakota called the **Mount Rushmore State** or the **Coyote State**, (Sioux *dakota* 'allies') state in north-central USA, a *Great Plains state, bordered to the north by *North Dakota, to the west by *Montana and *Wyoming, to the south by *Nebraska, to the east by *Minnesota and *Iowa; area 196,541 sq km/ 75,885 sq mi; population (2000) 754,800; capital Pierre. South Dakota was formerly known as the Coyote State due to the abundance of coyotes that roam the prairies, but its official nickname is now the Mount Rushmore State because of the famous mountain sculpture, Mount Rushmore, which is the state's biggest tourist attraction. South Dakota is primarily a rural state, bisected by the *Missouri River, with rolling hills and flat plains to the east and rocky uplifts to the west. Thousands of buffalo once roamed the prairies and grassland of the state. Tourism is key to the state economy, second only to livestock and grain production in terms of economic importance. Other towns and cities include Sioux Falls, Rapid City, and Aberdeen. The influence of the *Sioux tribe, both historically and culturally, is important to South Dakota. Colourful historical figures such as Wild Bill Hickok, Calamity Jane, *Sitting Bull, and George *Custer contribute to South Dakota's legendary Wild West status. South Dakota was admitted to the Union in 1889 as the 40th US state.

Southend seaside resort and administrative centre of Southend unitary authority in southeastern England, on the Thames estuary, 60 km/37 mi east of London; population (1999 est) 176,600. Southend is the closest seaside resort to London and as such attracts nearly 3 million visitors a year; its major industry is tourism.

Southern Alps range of mountains running the entire length of South Island, New Zealand. They are forested to the west, with scanty scrub to the east. The highest peaks are Aoraki, 3,764 m/12,349 ft, and Mount Tasman 3,498m/11,476 ft. Scenic features include gorges, glaciers, lakes, and waterfalls. Among its lakes are those at the southern end of the range: Manapouri, Te Anau, and the largest, Wakatipu, 83 km/52 mi long, which lies about 300 m/1,000 ft above sea level and has a depth of 378 m/1,242 ft. The Fiordland National Park also lies in the south of the range.

Southern Cross popular name for the constellation Crux.

southern lights common name for the *aurora australis, coloured light in southern skies.

Southern Uplands one of the three geographical divisions of Scotland, being most of the hilly Scottish borderland to the south of a geological fault line that stretches from Dunbar, East Lothian, on the North Sea to Girvan, South Ayrshire, on the Firth of Clyde. The Southern Uplands, largely formed by rocks of the Silurian and Ordovician age, are intersected by the broad valleys of the Nith and Tweed rivers.

South Georgia island in the South Atlantic, a British crown colony administered, with the South Sandwich Islands, from the Falkland Islands by a commissioner; area 3,757 sq km/1,450 sq mi. The average temperature on the island is −2 °C/28.4 °F. There has been no permanent population since the whaling station was abandoned in 1966. South Georgia lies 1,300 km/800 mi southeast of the Falkland Islands, of which it was a dependency until 1985. The British Antarctic Survey has a station on nearby Bird Island.

South Glamorgan Welsh **De Morgannwg**, former county of south Wales, 1974–96, now divided between *Cardiff and *Vale of Glamorgan unitary authorities.

South Gloucestershire unitary authority in southwest England created in 1996 from part of the former county of Avon. **area:** 497 sq km/192 sq mi **towns and cities:** Thornbury (administrative headquarters), Patchway, Yate, Chipping Sodbury **features:** River Severn borders northwest; Vale of Berkeley; Severn Road Bridge; Marshfield has one of Britain's longest village streets with 17th-century almshouses; 13th-century church of St Peter (Dyrham); late 17th century Dyrham Park Mansion **population:** (1996) 220,000.

South Holland Dutch **Zuid Holland**, low-lying coastal province of the Netherlands, bounded to the north by North Holland, to the east by Utrecht and North Brabant, to the south by Zeeland, and to the west by the North Sea; area 2,910 sq km/1,124 sq mi; population (1997) 3,344,700. The capital is the *Hague. There are chemical, textile, distilling, and petroleum refining industries. Bulbs are grown, and there is horticulture, livestock raising, and dairying.

South Korea
National name: *Daehan Minguk/Republic of Korea*
Area: 98,799 sq km/38,146 sq mi
Capital: Seoul
Major towns/cities: Pusan, Taegu, Inchon, Kwangju, Taejon, Songnam
Major ports: Pusan, Inchon
Physical features: southern end of a mountainous peninsula separating the Sea of Japan from the Yellow Sea
Head of state: Roh Moo Hyun from 2004
Head of government: Lee Hai Chan from 2004
Political system: liberal democracy

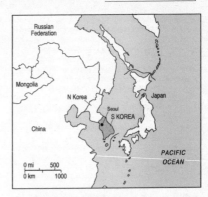

Political executive: limited presidency
Political parties: New Korea Party (NKP, formerly Democratic Liberal Party (DLP)), right of centre; National Congress for New Politics (NCNP), left of centre; Democratic Party (DP), left of centre; New Democratic Party (NDP), centrist, pro-private enterprise; United Liberal Democratic Party (ULD), ultra-conservative, pro-private enterprise
Currency: won
GNI per capita (PPP): (US$) 16,480 (2002 est)
Exports: electrical machinery, textiles, clothing, footwear, telecommunications and sound equipment, chemical products, ships ('invisible export' – overseas construction work). Principal market: USA 20.7% (2001)
Population: 47,700,000 (2003 est)
Language: Korean (official)
Religion: Buddhist 48%, Confucian 3%, Christian 47%, mainly Protestant; Chund Kyo (peculiar to Korea, combining elements of Shaman, Buddhist, and Christian doctrines)
Life expectancy: 72 (men); 79 (women) (2000–05)
Chronology
2333 BC: Traditional date of founding of Korean state by Tangun (mythical son from union of bear-woman and god).
1122 BC: Ancient texts record founding of kingdom in Korea by Chinese nobleman Kija.
194 BC: Northwest Korea united under warlord, Wiman.
108 BC: Korea conquered by Chinese.
1st–7th centuries AD: Three Korean kingdoms – Koguryo, Paekche, and Silla – competed for supremacy.
668: Korean peninsula unified by Buddhist Silla kingdom; culture combining Chinese and Korean elements flourished.
935: Silla dynasty overthrown by Wang Kon of Koguryo, who founded Koryo dynasty in its place.
1258: Korea accepted overlordship of Mongol Yüan Empire.
1392: Yi dynasty founded by Gen Yi Song-gye, vassal of Chinese Ming Empire; Confucianism replaced Buddhism as official creed; extreme conservatism characterized Korean society.
1592 and 1597: Japanese invasions repulsed by Korea.
1636: Manchu invasion forced Korea to sever ties with Ming dynasty.

853

18th–19th centuries: Korea resisted change in political and economic life and rejected contact with Europeans.
1864: Attempts to reform government and strengthen army by Taewongun (who ruled in name of his son, King Kojong); converts to Christianity persecuted.
1873: Taewongun forced to cede power to Queen Min; reforms reversed; government authority collapsed.
1882: Chinese occupied Seoul and installed governor.
1894–95: Sino-Japanese War: Japan forced China to recognize independence of Korea; Korea fell to Japanese influence.
1904–05: Russo-Japanese War: Japan ended Russian influence in Korea.
1910: Korea formally annexed by Japan; Japanese settlers introduced modern industry and agriculture; Korean language banned.
1919: 'Samil' nationalist movement suppressed by Japanese.
1945: After defeat of Japan in World War II, Russia occupied regions of Korea north of 38th parallel (demarcation line agreed at Yalta Conference) and USA occupied regions south of it.
1948: The USSR refused to permit United Nations (UN) supervision of elections in the northern zone; the southern zone became independent as the Republic of Korea, with Syngman Rhee as president.
1950: North Korea invaded South Korea; UN forces (mainly from the USA) intervened to defend South Korea; China intervened in support of North Korea.
1953: The Korean War ended with an armistice which restored the 38th parallel; no peace treaty was agreed and US troops remained in South Korea.
1961: Military coup placed Gen Park Chung Hee in power; a major programme of industrial development began.
1972: Martial law was imposed and presidential powers increased.
1979: The government of President Choi Kyu-Hah introduced liberalizing reforms.
1979: Gen Chun Doo Hwan assumed power after anti-government riots; Korea emerged as a leading shipbuilding nation and exporter of electronic goods.
1987: The constitution was made more democratic as a result of Liberal pressure; ruling Democratic Justice Party (DJP) candidate Roh Tae Woo Was elected president amid allegations of fraud.
1988: The Olympic Games were held in Seoul.
1991: Large-scale antigovernment protests were forcibly suppressed; South Korea joined the UN.
1992: South Korea established diplomatic relations with China.
1994: The US military presence was stepped up in response to the perceived threat from North Korea.
1997: South Korea was admitted to the OECD. Kim Dae Jung, former dissident and political prisoner, became the first opposition politician to lead South Korea.
1998: Kim Dae Jung was sworn in as president, with Kim Jong Pil as prime minister. New labour laws ended lifetime employment and the financial system was opened up. More than 2,000 prisoners were released, including 74 political prisoners. There was continuing labour unrest as GDP contracted by 5%.
1999: Talks on possible reunification with North Korea were suspended.
2000: Kim Jong Pil resigned as prime minister and was replaced by Park Tae Joon, who in turn resigned after

the opposition Grand National Party won a majority in elections. He was replaced by Lee Han Dong. At the first summit meeting between the divided countries, Kim Dae Jung was welcomed by the leader of North Korea, Kim Jong Il, in Pyongyang, North Korea. The two leaders agreed to further economic investment by South Korea investment in North Korea, and to open rail links between the two countries. Kim Dae Jung was awarded the Nobel Peace Prize.
2002: In the worst clash between North and South Korea in three years naval vessels fired on each other in disputed coastal waters in the Yellow Sea. The incident threatened to derail President Kim Dae Jung's policy of engagement with North Korea.
2004: In March parliament attempted to impeach President Roh Moo-hyun but this was blocked by the Constitutional Court. The President's Uri party won a parliamentary majority in April.

South Lanarkshire unitary authority in south central Scotland, created in 1996 from three districts of Strathclyde region. **area:** 1,772 sq km/684 sq mi **towns:** Hamilton (administrative headquarters), Lanark, Rutherglen, East Kilbride, Carluke, Cambuslang **physical:** area of stark contrast: predominantly rural to the south and urban to the north. The River Clyde flows through the area. Tinto (707 m/2,320 ft) is a key landmark to the south **features:** Craignethan Castle; Carstairs State Hospital, New Lanark **population:** (2000 est) 307,400 **history:** New Lanark village is a World Heritage Site, significant for the attempt to improve living conditions for workers and their families in the 19th and early 20th centuries.

South Ossetia autonomous region of the Georgian republic, part of the region of Ossetia; population (1990 est) 99,800. It lies on the southern slopes of the Greater Caucasus mountains, mostly above 1,000 m/3,300 ft above sea level. Its capital is Tskinvali. Its rivers are used to produce hydroelectric power, and less than 10% of the land is cultivated. Cereals, vines, and fruit are grown, while the higher land is used for forestry and rearing sheep, goats, and cattle. Traditional industries produce leather goods, fur clothing, and metal objects.

South Pole the southern point where an imaginary line penetrates the Earth's surface by the axis about which it revolves; see also *pole and *Antarctica.

South Sea Bubble financial crisis in Britain in 1720. The South Sea Company, founded in 1711, which had a monopoly of trade with South America, offered in 1719 to take over more than half the national debt in return for further concessions. Its 100 shares rapidly rose to 1,000, and an orgy of speculation followed. When the 'bubble' burst, thousands were ruined. The discovery that cabinet ministers had been guilty of corruption led to a political crisis.

South, the historically, the states of the USA bounded on the north by the *Mason–Dixon Line, the Ohio River, and the eastern and northern borders of Missouri, with an agrarian economy based on plantations worked by slaves, and which, as the *Confederacy, seceded from the Union in 1861, beginning the American Civil War. The term is now loosely applied in a geographical and cultural sense, with Texas often regarded as part of the Southwest rather than the South.

South Yorkshire metropolitan county of northeast England, created in 1974; in 1986, most of the functions of the former county council were transferred to the metropolitan borough councils. **area:** 1,560 sq km/ 602 sq mi **towns:** Barnsley, Doncaster, Rotherham, Sheffield (all administrative centres for the districts of the same name) **physical:** River Don; part of Peak District National Park; the county contains a rich diversity of rural landscapes between the barren Pennine moors in the southwest and the very low, flat carr-lands (a mixture of marsh and copses) in the east **features:** the Earth Centre for Environmental Research **population:** (2000 est) 1,302,000.

Soutine, Chaïm (1893–1943) Lithuanian-born French painter. The greatest of the French expressionists, he used brilliant colours and thick, energetically applied paint to create intense, emotionally charged works, mostly landscapes and portraits. *Page Boy* (1927; Albright-Knox Art Gallery, Buffalo, New York) is typical.

sovereignty absolute authority within a given territory. The possession of sovereignty is taken to be the distinguishing feature of the state, as against other forms of community. The term has an internal aspect, in that it refers to the ultimate source of authority within a state, such as a parliament or monarch, and an external aspect, where it denotes the independence of the state from any outside authority.

soviet (Russian 'council') originally a strike committee elected by Russian workers in the 1905 revolution; in 1917 these were set up by peasants, soldiers, and factory workers. The soviets sent delegates to the All-Russian Congress of Soviets to represent their opinions to a future government. They were later taken over by the *Bolsheviks.

Soviet Central Asia former name (to 1991) of the *Central Asian Republics.

Soviet Union alternative name for the former Union of Soviet Socialist Republics (USSR).

Soweto acronym for SOuth WEst TOwnship, urban settlement in South Africa, southwest of Johannesburg; population (1991) 597,000. It experienced civil unrest during the *apartheid regime. Industries include wood pulp and paper manufacturing.

soybean leguminous plant (see *legume), native to East Asia, in particular Japan and China. Originally grown as a food crop for animals, it is increasingly used for human consumption in cooking oils and margarine, as a flour, soya milk, soy sauce, or processed into *tofu, miso, or textured vegetable protein (*TVP). (*Glycine max*)

Soyinka, Wole (1934–) pen-name of Akinwande Oluwole Soyinka, Nigerian author and dramatist who founded a national theatre in Nigeria. His plays explore Yoruba myth, ritual, and culture, and later challenged his country's government. He was the first African to be awarded the Nobel Prize for Literature, in 1986.

Soyuz (Russian 'union') Soviet (later Russian) series of spacecraft, capable of carrying up to three cosmonauts. It is the longest serving crewed spacecraft in the world. *Soyuz* spacecraft consist of three parts: a rear section containing engines; the central crew compartment; and a forward compartment for working and living space. Although the craft were originally used for independent space flight, from 1998 the *Soyuz* ferried crews and components to the *International Space Station* (*ISS*), scheduled for completion in 2006. When NASA grounded its space shuttles after the 2003 *Columbia* space shuttle disaster, the *Soyuz* craft assumed all of the flights to the *ISS* until the shuttles' projected return in 2005.

space *or* **outer space** void that exists beyond Earth's atmosphere. Above 120 km/75 mi, very little atmosphere remains, so objects can continue to move quickly without extra energy. The space between the planets is not entirely empty, but filled with the tenuous gas of the *solar wind as well as dust.

Spacelab small space station built by the European Space Agency (ESA), carried in the cargo bay of the US space shuttle, in which it remains throughout each flight, returning to Earth with the shuttle. *Spacelab* consists of a pressurized module in which astronauts can work, and a series of pallets, open to the vacuum of space, on which equipment is mounted. *Spacelab* is used for astronomy, Earth observation, and experiments utilizing the conditions of weightlessness and vacuum in orbit.

space probe any instrumented object sent beyond Earth to collect data from other parts of the Solar System and from deep space. The first probe was the Soviet Lunik 1, which flew past the Moon in 1959. The first successful planetary probe was the US Mariner 2, which flew past Venus in 1962, using a transfer orbit. The first space probe to leave the Solar System was Pioneer 10 in 1983. Space probes include Galileo, Giotto, Magellan, Mars Observer, Ulysses, the Moon probes, and the Mariner, Pioneer, Viking, and Voyager series.

space shuttle in full **space shuttle orbiter**, reusable crewed spacecraft developed by NASA to reduce the cost of using space for commercial, scientific, and military purposes. The orbiter, the part that goes into space, is 37.2 m/122 ft long and weighs 68 tonnes. The first, *Columbia*, was launched on 12 April 1981. After leaving its payload in space, the space shuttle can be flown back to Earth to land on a special runway 4.5 km/ 2.8 mi long and 91 m/100 yd wide. Unlike previous spacecraft, the shuttle can be used again and again because the orbiter has a protective outer shell to prevent it from burning up during re-entry into the Earth's atmosphere. Following the break-up of a shuttle craft on re-entry in 2003, however, the shuttle programme was grounded.

space station any large structure designed for human occupation in space for extended periods of time. Space stations are used for carrying out astronomical observations and surveys of Earth, as well as for biological studies and the processing of materials in weightlessness. The first space station was the Soviet *Salyut 1* (1971). In 1973, NASA launched *Skylab*. The core of the Soviet space station *Mir* was launched in 1986. In 1998 the first component of the *International Space Station*, being constructed by the USA, Russia, and 14 other nations, was launched.

space-time in physics, combination of space and time used in the theory of *relativity. When developing relativity, Albert Einstein showed that time was in many respects like an extra dimension (or direction) to space. Space and time can thus be considered as entwined into a single entity, rather than two separate things.

Spain
National name: *España/Spain*

Area: 504,750 sq km/194,883 sq mi (including the Balearic and Canary islands)
Capital: Madrid
Major towns/cities: Barcelona, Valencia, Zaragoza, Seville, Málaga, Bilbao, Las Palmas (on Gran Canarias island), Murcia, Palma (on Mallorca)
Major ports: Barcelona, Valencia, Cartagena, Málaga, Cádiz, Vigo, Santander, Bilbao
Physical features: central plateau with mountain ranges, lowlands in south; rivers Ebro, Douro, Tagus, Guadiana, Guadalquivir; Iberian Plateau (Meseta); Pyrenees, Cantabrian Mountains, Andalusian Mountains, Sierra Nevada
Territories: Balearic and Canary islands; in North Africa: Ceuta, Melilla, Peña d'Alhucemas, Islas Chafarinas, Peñón de Vélez de la Gomera
Head of state: King Juan Carlos I from 1975
Head of government: José Luis Rodríguez Zapatero from 2004
Political system: liberal democracy
Political executive: parliamentary
Political parties: Socialist Workers' Party (PSOE), democratic socialist; Popular Party (PP), right of centre
Currency: euro (peseta until 2002)
GNI per capita (PPP): (US$) 20,460 (2002 est)
Exports: motor vehicles, machinery and electrical equipment, vegetable products, metals and their manufactures, foodstuffs, wine. Principal market: France 19.5% (2001)
Population: 41,060,000 (2003 est)
Language: Spanish (Castilian; official), Basque, Catalan, Galician
Religion: Roman Catholic 98%
Life expectancy: 76 (men); 83 (women) (2000–05)
Chronology
2nd century BC: Roman conquest of the Iberian peninsula, which became the province of Hispania.
5th century AD: After the fall of the Roman Empire, Iberia was overrun by Vandals and Visigoths.
711: Muslims invaded from North Africa and overthrew Visigoth kingdom.

9th century: Christians in northern Spain formed kingdoms of Asturias, Aragón, Navarre, and Léon, and county of Castile.
10th century: Abd-al-Rahman III established caliphate of Córdoba; Muslim culture at its height in Spain.
1230: León and Castile united under Ferdinand III, who drove the Muslims from most of southern Spain.
14th century: Spain consisted of Christian kingdoms of Castile, Aragón, and Navarre, and the Muslim emirate of Granada.
1469: Marriage of Ferdinand of Aragón and Isabella of Castile; kingdoms united on their accession in 1479.
1492: Conquest of Granada ended Muslim rule in Spain.
1494: Treaty of Tordesillas; Spain and Portugal divided newly discovered America; Spain became a world power.
1519–56: Emperor Charles V was both King of Spain and Archduke of Austria; he also ruled Naples, Sicily, and the Low Countries; Habsburgs dominant in Europe.
1555: Charles V divided his domains between Spain and Austria before retiring; Spain retained the Low Countries and southern Italy as well as South American colonies.
1568: Dutch rebelled against Spanish rule; Spain recognized independence of Dutch Republic in 1648.
1580: Philip II of Spain inherited the throne of Portugal, where Spanish rule lasted until 1640.
1588: Spanish Armada: attempt to invade England defeated.
17th century: Spanish power declined amid wars, corruption, inflation, and loss of civil and religious freedom.
1701–14: War of the Spanish Succession: allied powers fought France to prevent Philip of Bourbon inheriting throne of Spain.
1713–14: Treaties of Utrecht and Rastat: Bourbon dynasty recognized, but Spain lost Gibraltar, southern Italy, and Spanish Netherlands.
1793: Spain declared war on revolutionary France; reduced to a French client state in 1795.
1808: Napoleon installed his brother Joseph as King of Spain.
1808–14: Peninsular War: British forces played a large part in liberating Spain and restoring Bourbon dynasty.
1810–30: Spain lost control of its South American colonies.
1833–39: Carlist civil war: Don Carlos (backed by conservatives) unsuccessfully contested the succession of his niece Isabella II (backed by liberals).
1870: Offer of Spanish throne to Leopold of Hohenzollern-Sigmaringen sparked Franco-Prussian War.
1873–74: First republic ended by military coup which restored Bourbon dynasty with Alfonso XII.
1898: Spanish-American War: Spain lost Cuba and Philippines.
1923–30: Dictatorship of Gen Primo de Rivera with support of Alfonso XIII.
1931: Proclamation of Second Republic, initially dominated by anticlerical radicals and socialists.
1933: Moderates and Catholics won elections; insurrection by socialists and Catalans in 1934.
1936: Left-wing Popular Front narrowly won fresh elections; General Francisco Franco launched military rebellion.

1936–39: Spanish Civil War: Nationalists (with significant Italian and German support) defeated Republicans (with limited Soviet support); Franco became dictator of nationalist-fascist regime.
1941: Though officially neutral in World War II, Spain sent 40,000 troops to fight USSR.
1955: Spain admitted to the United Nations (UN).
1975: Death of Franco; he was succeeded by King Juan Carlos.
1978: A referendum endorsed democratic constitution.
1982: Socialists took office under Felipe González; Spain joined the North Atlantic Treaty Organization (NATO); Basque separatist organization ETA stepped up its terrorist campaign.
1986: Spain joined the European Economic Community (EEC).
1997: 23 Basque nationalist leaders were jailed for terrorist activities.
1998: ETA announced an indefinite ceasefire. The government announced that it would begin peace talks.
2000: Prime Minister Aznar was re-elected. ETA ended its ceasefire with a bombing in Madrid, and assassinations and bombing continued throughout the year. 37 suspected ETA terrorists, including its commander, were arrested in September, but the violence continued.
2002: Herri Batasuna, a Basque nationalist party, was outlawed on the grounds that it was the political wing of ETA. In the worst oil spill since the *Exxon Valdez* broke up off the coast of Alaska in 1989, over 300 km/186 mi of the Galician coast was polluted by an oil spill from the tanker *Prestige*, which eventually sank.
2004: Over 200 people were killed in one day by terrorist bombs on Madrid trains. Basque separatists were initially blamed but suspicion later fell on al-Qaeda. José Luis Rodriguez Zapatero (Socialist Workers' Party) became prime minister.

spaniel any of several breeds of small and medium-sized gundog, characterized by large, drooping ears and a wavy, long, silky coat. Spaniels are divided into two groups: those that are still working gundogs – Clumber, cocker, Irish water, springer, and Sussex – and the toy breeds that are kept as pets – including the Japanese, King Charles, papillon, and Tibetan.

Spanish-American War brief war in 1898 between Spain and the USA over Spanish rule in Cuba and the Philippines; the complete defeat of Spain made the USA a colonial power. The Treaty of Paris ceded the Philippines, Guam, and Puerto Rico to the USA; Cuba became independent. The USA paid $20 million to Spain. This ended Spain's colonial presence in the Americas.

Spanish Armada fleet sent by Philip II of Spain against England in 1588. Consisting of 130 ships, it sailed from Lisbon and carried on a running fight up the Channel with the English fleet of 197 small ships under Howard of Effingham and Francis *Drake – although only three Spanish ships were lost to the English attack. The Armada anchored off Calais but the Duke of Parma, the leader of the Spanish army, was unwilling to embark until the English fleet was defeated. The English forced the Armada to put to sea by sending in fire ships, and a general action followed off Gravelines, although only four Spanish ships were lost in the battle. What remained of the Armada escaped around the north of Scotland and west of Ireland, losing an estimated 55 ships to storm and shipwreck on the way. Only about half the original fleet returned to Spain.

Spanish art painting and sculpture of Spain. Spanish art has been fashioned by both European and Islamic traditions, with notable regional adaptations. Whatever the source of its influences, Spanish art has always transformed styles and given them a distinctively Spanish character.

Spanish Civil War 1936–39 See *Civil War, Spanish.

Spanish language member of the Romance branch of the Indo-European language family, also known as Castilian. As the language of the court, it has been the standard and literary language of the Spanish state since the 13th century. It is now a world language, spoken in Mexico and all South and Central American countries (except Brazil, Guyana, Suriname, and French Guiana) as well as in the Philippines, Cuba, Puerto Rico, and much of the USA.

Spanish Main common term for the Caribbean Sea in the 16th–17th centuries, but more properly the South American mainland between the River Orinoco and Panama.

Spanish Succession, War of the war 1701–14 of Britain, Austria, the Netherlands, Portugal, and Denmark (the Allies) against France, Spain, and Bavaria. It was caused by Louis XIV's acceptance of the Spanish throne on behalf of his grandson, Philip, in defiance of the Partition Treaty of 1700, under which it would have passed to Archduke Charles of Austria (later Holy Roman Emperor Charles VI).

Spark, Muriel (1918–) born Muriel Sarah Camberg, Scottish-born novelist. Her novels focus on social misfits, such as feature in *The Comforters* (1957) (her first novel), *The Prime of Miss Jean Brodie* (1961), and *A Far Cry from Kensington* (1988). Blacker satire is in *Memento Mori* (1959), *Symposium* (1990), and *Realities and Dreams* (1996). *Collected Poems* appeared in 1967 and *The Collected Stories* was published in 1994. The novel *Aiding and Abetting* was published in 2000.

spark plug plug that produces an electric spark in the cylinder of a petrol engine to ignite the fuel mixture. It consists essentially of two electrodes insulated from one another. High-voltage (18,000 V) electricity is fed to a central-electrode via the distributor. At the base of the electrode, inside the cylinder, the electricity jumps to another electrode earthed to the engine body, creating a spark.

sparrow any of a family (Passeridae) of small Old World birds of the order Passeriformes with short, thick bills, but applied particularly to the different members of the genus *Passer* in the family Ploceidae, order Passeriformes. Many members of the New World family Emberizidae, which includes *warblers, orioles, and buntings, are also called sparrows; for example, the North American song sparrow *Melospize melodia*.

sparrow hawk small woodland *hawk *Accipiter nisus*, of the family Falconidae, order Falconiformes, found in Eurasia and North Africa. It is bluish-grey, with brown and white markings, and has a long tail and short wings. The male grows to 28 cm/11 in long, and the female to 38 cm/15 in. It hunts small birds and mice.

Sparta ancient Greek city-state in the southern Peloponnese (near Sparte), developed from Dorian settlements in the 10th century BC. The Spartans, known for their military discipline and austerity, took part in the *Persian and *Peloponnesian Wars.

Spartacist member of a group of left-wing radicals in Germany at the end of World War I, founders of the **Spartacus League**, which became the German Communist Party in 1919. The league participated in the Berlin workers' revolt of January 1919, which was suppressed by the Freikorps on the orders of the socialist government. The agitation ended with the murder of Spartacist leaders Karl *Liebknecht and Rosa *Luxemburg.

Spartacus (died 71 BC) Thracian gladiator. In 73 BC he led a revolt of gladiators and slaves in Capua, near Naples, and swept through southern Italy and Cisalpine Gaul. He was eventually caught by Roman general Crassus 71 BC. The fate of Spartacus is not known, although his followers were executed in mass crucifixions.

spastic term applied generally to limbs with impaired movement, stiffness, and resistance to passive movement, and to any body part (such as the colon) affected with spasm.

speakeasy bar that illegally sold alcoholic beverages during the *Prohibition period (1920–33) in the USA. The term is probably derived from the need to speak quickly or quietly to the doorkeeper in order to gain admission.

Speaker presiding officer charged with the preservation of order in the legislatures of various countries. In the UK the equivalent of the Speaker in the House of Lords is the *Lord Chancellor; in the House of Commons the Speaker is elected for each parliament, usually on an agreed basis among the parties, but often holds the office for many years. The original appointment dates from 1377. The chair of the US House of Representatives also has the title of Speaker.

spearmint perennial herb belonging to the mint family, with aromatic leaves and spikes of purple flowers; the leaves are used for flavouring in cookery. (*Mentha spicata*, family Labiatae.)

Special Air Service (SAS) specialist British regiment recruited from regiments throughout the army. It has served in Malaysia, Oman, Yemen, the Falklands, Northern Ireland, and during the 1991 Gulf War, as well as against international urban guerrillas, as in the siege of the Iranian embassy in London in 1980.

speciation emergence of a new species during evolutionary history. One cause of speciation is the geographical separation of populations of the parent species, followed by reproductive isolation and selection for different environments so that they no longer produce viable offspring when they interbreed. Other causes are *assortative mating and the establishment of a polyploid population.

species in biology, a distinguishable group of organisms that resemble each other or consist of a few distinctive types (as in *polymorphism), and that can all interbreed to produce fertile offspring. Species are the lowest level in the system of biological classification.

specific gravity alternative term for relative density.

specific heat capacity quantity of heat required to raise unit mass (1 kg) of a substance by one *kelvin (1 K). The unit of specific heat capacity in the SI system is the *joule per kilogram per kelvin ($J\ kg^{-1}\ K^{-1}$).

specific latent heat heat that changes the physical state of a unit mass (one kilogram) of a substance without causing any temperature change.

Spector, Phil (1940–) US record producer. He is known for the 'wall of sound', created using a large orchestra, which distinguished his work in the early 1960s with vocal groups such as the Crystals and the Ronettes. He withdrew into semi-retirement 1966 but his influence can still be heard.

spectroscopy study of spectra (see *spectrum) associated with atoms or molecules in the solid, liquid, or gaseous phase. Spectroscopy can be used to identify unknown compounds and is an invaluable tool in science, medicine, and industry (for example, in checking the purity of drugs).

spectrum plural **spectra**, in physics, the pattern of frequencies or wavelengths obtained when electromagnetic radiations are separated into their constituent parts. Visible light is part of the *electromagnetic spectrum and most sources emit waves over a range of wavelengths that can be broken up or 'dispersed'; white light can be separated (for example, using a triangular prism) into red, orange, yellow, green, blue, indigo, and violet. The visible spectrum was first studied by English physicist Isaac *Newton, who showed in 1666 how white light could be broken up into different colours.

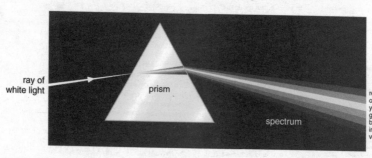

spectrum A prism (a triangular block of transparent material such as plastic, glass, or silica) is used to split a ray of white light into its spectral colours.

speech recognition or **voice input** in computing, any technique by which a computer can understand ordinary speech. Spoken words are divided into 'frames', each lasting about one-thirtieth of a second, which are converted to a wave form. These are then compared with a series of stored frames to determine the most likely word. Research into speech recognition started in 1938, but the technology did not become sufficiently developed for commercial applications until the late 1980s.

speech synthesis or **voice output** computer-based technology for generating speech. A speech synthesizer is controlled by a computer, which supplies strings of codes representing basic speech sounds (phonemes); together these make up words. Speech-synthesis applications include children's toys, car and aircraft warning systems, and talking books for the blind.

speed rate at which an object moves, or how fast an object moves. The average speed v of an object may be calculated by dividing the distance s it has travelled by the time t taken to do so, and may be expressed as:

$$v = \frac{s}{t}.$$

The usual units of speed are metres per second or kilometres per hour.

speed of light speed at which light and other *electromagnetic waves travel in a vacuum. Its value is 299,792,458 m per second/186,282 mi per second but for most calculations 3×10^8 m s^{-1} (300 million metres per second) suffices. In glass the speed of light is two-thirds of its speed in air, about 200 million metres per second. The speed of light is the highest speed possible, according to the theory of *relativity, and its value is independent of the motion of its source and of the observer. It is impossible to accelerate any material body to this speed because it would require an infinite amount of energy.

speed of sound speed at which sound travels through a medium, such as air or water. In air at a temperature of 0 °C/32 °F, the speed of sound is 331 m/1,087 ft per second. At higher temperatures, the speed of sound is greater; at 18 °C/64 °F it is 342 m/1,123 ft per second. It is also affected by the humidity of the air. It is greater in liquids and solids; for example, in water it is about 1,440 m/4,724 ft per second, depending on the temperature.

speedway sport of motorcycle racing on a dirt track. Four riders compete in each heat over four laps. A series of heats make up a match or competition. In Britain there are two main leagues, the Elite League and the Premier League. World championships exist for individuals, pairs (first held in 1970), four-rider teams (first held in 1960), long-track racing, and ice speedway.

speedwell any of a group of flowering plants belonging to the snapdragon family. Of the many wild species, most are low-growing with small bluish flowers. (Genus *Veronica*, family Scrophulariaceae.)

Speer, Albert (1905–1981) German architect and minister in the Nazi government during World War II. He was appointed Hitler's architect and, like his counterparts in Fascist Italy, chose an overblown classicism to glorify the state, for example, his plan for the Berlin and Nürnberg Party Congress Grounds in 1934.

He built the New Reich Chancellery, Berlin, 1938–39 (now demolished), but his designs for an increasingly megalomaniac series of buildings in a stark classical style were never realized.

speleology scientific study of caves, their origin, development, physical structure, flora, fauna, folklore, exploration, mapping, photography, cave-diving, and rescue work. **Potholing**, which involves following the course of underground rivers or streams, has become a popular sport.

Spence, Basil Urwin (1907–1976) Scottish architect. For nearly 20 years his work comprised houses, factories, theatres, and the Scottish Pavilion at the Empire Exhibition in 1938. In 1951 he won the competition for Coventry Cathedral, and in 1952 began the Nuclear Physics Building at Glasgow University. He was professor of architecture at the Royal Academy, London, from 1961 to 1968.

Spencer, Stanley (1891–1959) English painter. He was born and lived in Cookham-on-Thames, and recreated the Christian story in a Cookham setting. Typically his dreamlike compositions combine a dry, meticulously detailed, and often humorous depiction of everyday life with an elaborate religious symbolism, as in *The Resurrection, Cookham* (1924–26; Tate Gallery, London).

Spender, Stephen (Harold) (1909–1995) English poet and critic. His early poetry has a left-wing political content. With Cyril Connolly he founded the magazine *Horizon* (of which he was co-editor 1939–41), and Spender was co-editor of *Encounter* 1953–66. His *Journals 1939–83* and *Collected Poems 1928–1985* were published in 1985. He was knighted in 1983.

Spengler, Oswald (1880–1936) German philosopher whose *Decline of the West* (1918) argued that civilizations go through natural cycles of growth and decay. He was admired by the Nazis.

Spenser, Edmund (c. 1552–1599) English poet. His major work is the allegorical epic *The Faerie Queene*, of which six books survive (three published in 1590 and three in 1596). Other books include *The Shepheard's Calendar* (1579), *Astrophel* (1586), the love sonnets *Amoretti*, and the marriage poem *Epithalamion* (1595).

sperm or **spermatozoon** in biology, the male *gamete of animals before fertilization in *sexual reproduction. Each sperm cell has a head capsule containing a nucleus, a middle portion containing *mitochondria (which provide energy), and a long tail (flagellum). In mammals sperm cells are produced in the testes of a male. They are produced by a special kind of cell division called *meiosis, which halves the number of *chromosomes present. Only a single sperm is needed to fertilize an egg, or ovum. Yet up to 500 million may start the journey towards the egg. Once a sperm has fertilized an egg, the egg's wall cannot be penetrated by other sperm. The unsuccessful sperm die after about three days.

spermatophore small capsule containing *sperm and other nutrients produced in invertebrates, newts, and cephalopods. For example, the male bush cricket *Eupholidoptera chabrieri* produces the spermatophore and deposits it in the female's cloaca during their courtship ritual. Internal fertilization can then take place.

spermatophyte another name for a *seed plant.

spermicide any cream, jelly, pessary, or other preparation that kills the *sperm cells in semen. Spermicides are used for contraceptive purposes, usually in combination with a *condom or *diaphragm. Sponges impregnated with spermicide have been developed but are not yet in widespread use. Spermicide used alone is only 75% effective in preventing pregnancy.

sphere perfectly round object with all points on its surface the same distance from the centre. This distance is the radius of the sphere. For a sphere of radius r, the volume $V = \frac{4}{3}\pi r^3$ and the surface area $A = 4\pi r^2$. When a sphere is cut along a great circle (a circle on the sphere that has the same diameter as the sphere), two hemispheres are produced.

Sphinx mythological creature, depicted in Egyptian, Assyrian, and Greek art as a lion with a human head. The Greek Sphinx of Thebes was winged with a woman's breasts, and was adopted as an emblem of wisdom. She killed all those who failed to answer her riddle about which animal went on four, then two, and finally three legs: the answer being humanity (baby, adult, and old person with stick). When *Oedipus gave the right reply, she committed suicide. The Great Sphinx at Gîza, Egypt, dating to the 3rd millennium BC, is carved from the bedrock of the Giza plateau and stands 58 m/189 ft in height. The monument has been buried by sand over the centuries and repeatedly dug out.

Spica or **Alpha Virginis** brightest star in the constellation Virgo and the 16th-brightest star in the night sky. Spica has a true luminosity of over 1,500 times that of the Sun and is 260 light years from the Sun. It is a spectroscopic binary star, the components of which orbit each other every four days.

spice any aromatic vegetable substance used as a condiment and for flavouring food. Spices are mostly obtained from tropical plants, and include pepper, nutmeg, ginger, and cinnamon. They have little food value but increase the appetite and may help digestion.

spider any arachnid (eight-legged animal) of the order Araneae. There are about 30,000 known species, mostly a few centimetres in size, although a few tropical forms attain great size, for example, some bird-eating spiders attain a body length of 9 cm/3.5 in. Spiders produce silk, and many spin webs to trap their prey. They are found everywhere in the world except Antarctica. Many species are found in woods and dry commons; a few are aquatic. Spiders are predators; they bite their prey, releasing a powerful toxin from poison glands which causes paralysis, together with digestive juices. They then suck out the juices and soft parts.

spider plant African plant belonging to the lily family. Two species (*C. comosum* and *C. elatum*) are popular house plants. They have long, narrow, variegated leaves and produce flowering shoots from which the new plants grow, hanging below the main plant. The flowers are small and white. Spider plants absorb toxins from the air and therefore help to purify the atmosphere around them. (Genus *Chlorophytum*, family Liliaceae.)

Spielberg, Steven (1947–) US film director, writer, and producer. One of the most commercially successful film-makers in the history of US cinema, Spielberg began his career in television, most famously directing *Duel* (1971). His credits include the box-office successes *Jaws* (1975), *Close Encounters of the Third Kind* (1977), *Raiders of the Lost Ark* (1981), *ET The Extraterrestrial* (1982), *Jurassic Park* (1992), the multi-award-winning *Schindler's List* (1993), and *Saving Private Ryan* (1998). In 1994 he formed a partnership with David Geffen and Jeffrey Katzenberg to create a new Hollywood studio called DreamWorks SKG, although he remains an independent contractor.

spikelet in botany, one of the units of a grass inflorescence. It comprises a slender axis on which one or more flowers are borne.

spin in physics, the intrinsic angular momentum of a subatomic particle, nucleus, atom, or molecule, which continues to exist even when the particle comes to rest. A particle in a specific energy state has a particular spin, just as it has a particular electric charge and mass. According to *quantum theory, this is restricted to discrete and indivisible values, specified by a spin *quantum number. Because of its spin, a charged particle acts as a small magnet and is affected by magnetic fields.

spina bifida congenital defect in which part of the spinal cord and its membranes are exposed, due to incomplete development of the spine (vertebral column). It is a neural tube defect.

spinach annual plant belonging to the goosefoot family. It is native to Asia and widely cultivated for its leaves, which are eaten as a vegetable. (*Spinacia oleracea*, family Chenopodiaceae.)

spinal cord major component of the *central nervous system in vertebrates. It consists of bundles of nerves enveloped in three layers of membrane (the meninges) and is bathed in cerebrospinal fluid. The spinal cord is encased and protected by the vertebral column, lying within the vertebral canal formed by the posterior arches of successive vertebrae.

spinal tap another term for *lumbar puncture, a medical test.

spine backbone of vertebrates. In most mammals, it contains 26 small bones called **vertebrae**, which enclose and protect the **spinal cord** (which links the peripheral nervous system to the brain). The spine articulates with the skull, ribs, and hip bones, and provides attachment for the back muscles.

spinet 17th-century domestic keyboard instrument. It has a laterally tapered case with a single manual (keyboard) of up to a three-and-a-half octave range, having a plucking action and single strings. It was the precursor of the *harpsichord.

spinifex spiny grass chiefly found in Australia, growing on the coastal sand dunes. It is often planted to bind sand along the seashore. The term also refers to porcupine grass, any of a group of spiny-leaved, tussock-forming grasses of inland Australia. (Genus *Spinifex*; porcupine grass genus *Triodia*.)

spinning art of drawing out and twisting fibres (originally wool or linen) into a long thread, or yarn, by hand or machine. Synthetic fibres are spun when the liquid is forced through the holes of a spinneret (a piece of metal with very fine holes in it). Once through the spinneret the filaments (strands or fibres) go through a solidifying process. Spinning was originally done by hand, then with the spinning wheel, and in about 1764 in England James *Hargreaves built the **spinning jenny**, a machine that could spin 8, then 16, bobbins at once. Later, Samuel *Crompton's **spinning mule**, introduced in 1779, had a moving carriage carrying the spindles; this is still in use today. Also used is the ring-spinning frame, introduced in the USA in 1828, where sets of rollers moving at various speeds draw out finer and finer thread, which is twisted and wound onto rotating bobbins. Once spun, the thread or yarn is then ready to be made into fabric, usually by *weaving or knitting.

Spinoza, Benedict (or Baruch) (1632–1677) Dutch philosopher. He believed in a rationalistic pantheism that owed much to René *Descartes's mathematical appreciation of the universe. Mind and matter are two modes of an infinite substance that he called God or Nature, good and evil being relative. He was a determinist, believing that human action was motivated by self-preservation.

spiny anteater alternative name for *echidna.

spiracle in insects, the opening of a *trachea, through which oxygen enters the body and carbon dioxide is expelled. In cartilaginous fishes (sharks and rays), the same name is given to a circular opening that marks the remains of the first gill slit.

spiraea any of a group of herbaceous plants or shrubs, which includes many cultivated species with ornamental sprays of white or pink flowers; their delicate appearance has given rise to the popular name bridal wreath. (Genus *Spiraea*, family Rosaceae.)

spiritualism belief in the survival of the human personality and in communication between the living and those who have died. The spiritualist movement originated in the USA in 1848. Adherents practise **mediumship**, which claims to allow clairvoyant knowledge of distant events and spirit healing. The writer Arthur Conan *Doyle and the Victorian prime minister William *Gladstone were converts.

spit ridge of sand or shingle projecting from the land into a body of water. It is formed by a combination of longshore drift, tides, river currents, and/or a bend in the coastline. The decrease in wave energy causes more material to be deposited than is transported down the coast, building up a finger of sand that points in the direction of the longshore drift. Deposition in the brackish water behind a spit may result in the formation of a *salt marsh.

Spitsbergen mountainous island with a deeply indented coastline, situated in the Arctic Ocean between Franz Josef Land and Greenland. It is the main island in the Norwegian archipelago of *Svalbard, 657 km/408 mi north of Norway, and now owned by that country; area 39,043 sq km/15,075 sq mi. Fishing, hunting, and coal mining are the chief economic activities. The Norwegian Polar Research Institute operates an all-year scientific station on the west coast. The highest point is Newtontoppen, which rises to 1,713 m/5,620 ft. The island was formerly called West Spitsbergen when part of the Svalbard archipeligo was named Spitsbergen.

Spitz, Mark Andrew (1950–) US swimmer. He won a record seven gold medals at the 1972 Olympic Games, all in world record times.

spleen organ in vertebrates, part of the reticuloendothelial system, which helps to process *lymphocytes. It also regulates the number of red blood cells in circulation by destroying old cells, and stores iron. It is situated on the left side of the body, behind the stomach.

Spock, Benjamin (McLane) (1903–1998) US paediatrician and writer on child care. His *Common Sense Book of Baby and Child Care* (1946) urged less rigidity in bringing up children than had been advised by previous generations of writers on the subject, but this was misunderstood as advocating permissiveness. He was also active in the peace movement, especially during the Vietnam War.

Spode, Josiah (1754–1827) English potter. Around 1800, he developed bone porcelain (made from bone ash, china stone, and china clay), which was produced at all English factories in the 19th century. He became potter to King George III in 1806.

sponge any saclike simple invertebrate of the phylum Porifera, usually marine. A sponge has a hollow body, its cavity lined by cells bearing flagellae, whose whiplike movements keep water circulating, bringing in a stream of food particles. The body walls are strengthened with protein (as in the bath sponge) or small spikes of silica, or a framework of calcium carbonate.

spontaneous combustion burning that is not initiated by the direct application of an external source of heat. A number of materials and chemicals, such as hay and sodium chlorate, can react with their surroundings, usually by oxidation, to produce so much internal heat that combustion results.

spoonbill any of several large wading birds of the ibis family Threskiornithidae, order Ciconiiformes, characterized by a long, flat bill, dilated at the tip in the shape of a spoon. Spoonbills are white or pink, and up to 90 cm/3 ft tall. Their feet are adapted for wading, and the birds obtain their food, consisting chiefly of fish, frogs, molluscs, and crustaceans, from shallow water.

spoonerism exchange of elements in a flow of words. Usually a slip of the tongue, a spoonerism can also be contrived for comic effect (for example 'a troop of Boy Scouts' becoming 'a scoop of Boy Trouts'). William Spooner gave his name to the phenomenon.

spore small reproductive or resting body, usually consisting of just one cell. Unlike a *gamete, it does not need to fuse with another cell in order to develop into a new organism. Spores are produced by the lower plants, most fungi, some bacteria, and certain protozoa. They are generally light and easily dispersed by wind movements. Plant spores are haploid and are produced by the sporophyte, following *meiosis; see *alternation of generations.

Spratly Islands Chinese **Nanshan Islands**, disputed group of small islands, coral reefs, and sandbars dispersed over a distance of 965 km/600 mi in the South China Sea. The islands are of strategic importance, commanding the sea passage from Japan to Singapore, and in 1976 oil was discovered.

spring device, usually a metal coil, that returns to its original shape after being stretched or compressed. Springs are used in some machines (such as clocks) to store energy, which can be released at a controlled rate. In other machines (such as engines) they are used to close valves.

spring in geology, a natural flow of water from the ground, formed at the point of intersection of the water table and the ground's surface. The source of water is rain that has percolated through the overlying rocks.

During its underground passage, the water may have dissolved mineral substances that may then be precipitated at the spring (hence, a mineral spring).

springbok South African antelope *Antidorcas marsupialis* about 80 cm/30 in at the shoulder, with head and body 1.3 m/4 ft long. It may leap 3 m/10 ft or more in the air when startled or playing, and has a fold of skin along the middle of the back which is raised to a crest in alarm. Springboks once migrated in herds of over a million, but are now found only in small numbers where protected.

Springsteen, Bruce (1949–) US rock singer, songwriter, and guitarist. His music combines melodies in traditional rock idiom and reflective lyrics about working-class life and the pursuit of the American dream on such albums as *Born to Run* (1975), *Born in the USA* (1984), *Human Touch* (1992), and *The Rising* (2002).

springtail small wingless insect. The maximum size is 6 mm/0.2 in in length. Springtails are extremely widespread and can be found in soil, decaying vegetable matter, under the bark of trees, in ant and termite nests, and on the surface of fresh water. There are about 1,500 species of springtail and some species are, unusually for insects, marine.

spruce coniferous tree belonging to the pine family, found over much of the northern hemisphere. Pyramidal in shape, spruces have rigid, prickly needles and drooping, leathery cones. Some are important forestry trees, such as the sitka spruce (*P. sitchensis*), native to western North America, and the Norway spruce (*P. abies*), now planted widely in North America. (Genus *Picea*, family Pinaceae.)

Sputnik (Russian 'fellow traveller') series of ten Soviet Earth-orbiting satellites launched from 1957 by R-7 rockets. Sputnik 1 was the first artificial satellite, launched on 4 October 1957. It weighed 84 kg/184 lb, with a 58 cm/23 in diameter, and carried only a simple radio transmitter, which allowed scientists to track the spacecraft as it orbited Earth. It burned up in the atmosphere 92 days later. The Sputnik research team was headed by Sergei Korolev. Sputniks were superseded in the early 1960s by the Cosmos series.

square in geometry, a quadrilateral (four-sided) plane figure with all sides equal and each angle a right angle. Its diagonals bisect each other at right angles. The area A of a square is the length l of one side multiplied by itself ($A = l \times l$). Also, any quantity multiplied by itself is termed a square, represented by an *exponent of power 2; for example, $4 \times 4 = 4^2 = 16$ and $6.8 \times 6.8 = 6.8^2 = 46.24$.

square root number that when it is *squared (multiplied by itself) equals a given number. For example, the square root of 25 (written as $\sqrt{25}$) is +5 or –5. This is because $+5 \times +5 = 25$, and $-5 \times -5 = 25$. A square root can be written as $\sqrt{}$.
For example, $16^{1/2} = +4$. This is called an *exponent.

squash *or* **squash rackets** racket-and-ball game usually played by two people on an enclosed court, derived from *rackets. Squash became a popular sport in the 1970s and later gained competitive status. There are two forms of squash: the American form, which is played in North and some South American countries, and the English, which is played mainly in Europe and Commonwealth countries such as Pakistan, Australia, and New Zealand.

squill bulb-forming perennial plant belonging to the lily family, found growing in dry places near the sea in Western Europe. Cultivated species usually bear blue flowers, either singly or in clusters, at the top of the stem. (Genus *Scilla*, family Liliaceae.)

squint *or* **strabismus** common condition in which one eye deviates in any direction. A squint may be convergent (with the bad eye turned inwards), divergent (outwards), or, in rare cases, vertical. A convergent squint is also called **cross-eye**.

squirrel rodent of the family Sciuridae. Squirrels are found worldwide except for Australia, Madagascar, and polar regions. Some are tree dwellers; these generally have bushy tails, and some, with membranes between their legs, are called *flying squirrels. Others are terrestrial, generally burrowing forms called ground squirrels; these include chipmunks, gophers, marmots, and prairie dogs.

Sri Lanka
formerly **Ceylon (until 1972)**
National name: *Sri Lanka Prajatantrika Samajavadi Janarajaya/Democratic Socialist Republic of Sri Lanka*

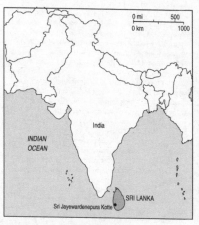

Area: 65,610 sq km/25,332 sq mi
Capital: Sri Jayewardenapura Kotte
Major towns/cities: Colombo, Kandy, Dehiwala-Mount Lavinia, Moratuwa, Jaffna, Kotte, Galle
Major ports: Colombo, Jaffna, Galle, Negombo, Trincomalee
Physical features: flat in north and around coast; hills and mountains in south and central interior
Head of state: Chandrika Bandaranaike Kumaratunga from 1994
Head of government: Mahinda Rajapakse from 2004
Political system: liberal democracy
Political executive: dual executive
Political parties: United National Party (UNP), right of centre; Sri Lanka Freedom Party (SLFP), left of centre; Democratic United National Front (DUNF), left of centre; Tamil United Liberation Front (TULF), Tamil autonomy (banned from 1983); Eelam People's Revolutionary Liberation Front (EPRLF), Indian-backed Tamil-secessionist 'Tamil

Tigers'; People's Liberation Front (JVP), Sinhalese-chauvinist, left wing (banned 1971–77 and 1983–88)
Currency: Sri Lankan rupee
GNI per capita (PPP): (US$) 3,390 (2002 est)
Exports: clothing and textiles, tea (world's largest exporter and third-largest producer), precious and semi-precious stones, coconuts and coconut products, rubber. Principal market: USA 40% (2001)
Population: 19,065,000 (2003 est)
Language: Sinhala, Tamil (both official), English
Religion: Buddhist 69%, Hindu 15%, Muslim 8%, Christian 8%
Life expectancy: 70 (men); 76 (women) (2000–05)
Chronology
c. 550 BC: Arrival of the Sinhalese, led by Vijaya, from northern India, displacing long-settled Veddas.
5th century BC: Sinhalese kingdom of Anuradhapura founded by King Pandukabaya.
c. 250–210 BC: Buddhism, brought from India, became established in Sri Lanka.
AD 992: Downfall of Anuradhapura kingdom, defeated by South Indian Colas.
1070: Overthrow of Colas by Vijayabahu I and establishment of the Sinhalese kingdom of Polonnaruva, which survived for more than two centuries before a number of regional states arose.
late 15th century: Kingdom of Kandy established in central highlands.
1505: Arrival of Portuguese navigator Lorenço de Almeida, attracted by spice trade developed by Arab merchants who had called the island Serendip.
1597–1618: Portuguese controlled most of Sri Lanka, with the exception of Kandy.
1658: Dutch conquest of Portuguese territories.
1795–98: British conquest of Dutch territories.
1802: Treaty of Amiens recognized island as British colony of Ceylon.
1815: British won control of Kandy, becoming the first European power to rule whole island.
1830s: Immigration of south Indian Hindu Tamil labourers to work central coffee plantations.
1880s: Tea and rubber become chief cash crops after blight ended production of coffee.
1919: Formation of the Ceylon National Congress to campaign for self rule; increasing conflicts between Sinhalese majority community and Tamil minority.
1931: Universal adult suffrage introduced for elected legislature and executive council in which power was shared with British.
1948: Ceylon achieved independence from Britain within Commonwealth, with Don Senanayake of conservative United National Party (UNP) as prime minister.
1949: Indian Tamils disenfranchised.
1956: Sinhala established as official language.
1960: Sirimavo Bandaranaike, the widow of assassinated prime minister Solomon Bandaranaike, won general election and formed an SLFP government, which nationalized oil industry.
1971: Sinhalese Marxist uprising, led by students and People's Liberation Army (JVP).
1972: Socialist Republic of Sri Lanka proclaimed; Buddhism given 'foremost place' in new state, antagonizing Tamils.

1976: Tamil United Liberation Front formed to fight for independent Tamil state ('Eelam') in north and east Sri Lanka.
1978: Presidential constitution adopted by new free-market government headed by Junius Jayawardene of UNP.
1982: Sri Jayewardenepura Kotte was designated the new national capital, replacing Colombo.
1983: Ethnic riots as Tamil guerrilla violence escalated; state of emergency imposed; more than 1,000 Tamils killed by Sinhalese mobs.
1987: President Jayawardene and Indian prime minister Rajiv Gandhi signed Colombo Accord aimed at creating new provincial councils, disarming Tamil militants ('Tamil Tigers'), and stationing 7,000-strong Indian Peace Keeping Force. Violence continued despite ceasefire policed by Indian troops.
1988: Left-wing JVP guerrillas campaigned against Indo-Sri Lankan peace pact. Prime Minister Ranasinghe Premadasa elected president.
1989: Dingiri Banda Wijetunga became prime minister. Leaders of Tamil Tigers and banned Sinhala extremist JVP assassinated.
1990: The Indian peacekeeping force was withdrawn. Violence continued, with a death toll of over a thousand a month.
1991: The Sri Lankan army killed 2,552 Tamil Tigers at Elephant Pass in the northern Jaffna region. A new party, the Democratic National United Front (DUNF), was formed by former members of UNP.
1992: Several hundred Tamil Tiger rebels were killed in an army offensive, code-named 'Strike Force Two'.
1993: President Premadasa was assassinated by Tamil Tiger terrorists; he was succeeded by Dingiri Banda Wijetunge.
1994: The UNP were narrowly defeated in a general election; Chandrika Kumaratunga became prime minister in an SLFP-led left-of-centre coalition (People's Alliance). Peace talks opened with the Tamil Tigers. Kumaratunga was elected the first female president; her mother, Sirimavo Bandaranaike, became prime minister.
1995: Renewed bombing campaign by Tamil Tigers. A major offensive drove out Tamil Tigers from Jaffna city.
1996: A state of emergency was extended nationwide after Tamils bombed the capital.
1998: The Tamil Tigers were outlawed after the bombing of Sri Lanka's holiest Buddhist site. In September over 1,300 Sri Lankan soldiers and Tamil Tiger rebels died in renewed fighting in the north. In October the Tamil Tigers captured the strategic northern town of Kilinochchi, killing more than 600 government troops.
1999: In late 1999, the government lost a large amount of territory, including military bases, to Tamil guerrillas. In the late December presidential elections, President Kumaratunga was re-elected, just days after she survived an attack by a Tamil suicide bomber.
2000: Terrorist activity continued, and government forces suffered their worst setback in the 17-year civil war in April when they were forced to surrender Pallai, a key military base, to Tamil guerrillas. Prime Minister Bandaranaike died two months after resigning her position because of poor health. She was replaced by Ratnasiri Wickremanayake. An election in October re-established the president, prime minister, and ruling

party. The Tamil Tigers announced a month-long ceasefire, but the government did not reciprocate.

2002: In an indefinite ceasefire between the government and the Tamil Tigers, mediated by the Norwegian government, the guerrilla group conceded to autonomy rather than a separate state for minority Tamils.

2003: President Kumaratunga suspended parliament, sacked three government ministers, and declared a brief state of emergency after accusing Prime Minister Wickremesinghe of making too many concessions in peace negotiations with the Tamil Tiger separatist forces.

2004: Sri Lanka suffered heavily in the tsunami that struck the region, with over 30,000 lives lost and extensive damage to coastal areas.

SS (German *Schutz-Staffel*, 'protective squadron') Nazi elite corps established 1925. Under *Himmler its 500,000 membership included the full-time **Waffen-SS** (armed SS), which fought in World War II, and spare-time members. The SS performed state police duties and was brutal in its treatment of the Jews and others in the concentration camps and occupied territories. It was condemned as an illegal organization at the Nuremberg Trials of war criminals.

stadholder *or* **stadtholder** leader of the United Provinces of the Netherlands from the 15th to the 18th century.

Staffordshire county of west central England (since April 1997 Stoke-on-Trent has been a separate unitary authority). **area:** 2,720 sq km/1,050 sq mi **towns:** Stafford (administrative headquarters), Newcastle-under-Lyme, Lichfield, Tamworth, Leek, Uttoxeter **physical:** largely flat, with hilly regions in the north (part of the Peak district) and southwest; River Trent and its tributaries (the Churnet, Dove, Penk, Sow, and Tame); Cannock Chase (a large open area in the middle of the county) **features:** castles at Chartley, Tamworth, and Tutbury; Lichfield Cathedral; Keele University (1962); Shugborough Hall (17th century), seat of the earls of Lichfield; Staffordshire bull terriers **population:** (1996) 555,700.

stained glass pieces of coloured glass held in place by thin strips of metal (usually lead) to form pictures in a window. One of the great medieval arts, it developed with the increase of window space in the Gothic church, and to some extent serves the same purpose as a wall-painting, with the added richness given by translucence and the variations of light piercing through from outside.

stainless steel widely used *alloy, in which chromium is dominant with traces of nickel, that resists rusting. Its chromium content also gives it a high tensile strength. It is used for cutlery and kitchen fittings, and in surgical instruments. Stainless steel was first produced in the UK in 1913 and in Germany in 1914.

stalactite and stalagmite cave structures formed by the deposition of calcite dissolved in ground water. **Stalactites** grow downwards from the roofs or walls and can be icicle-shaped, straw-shaped, curtain-shaped, or formed as terraces. **Stalagmites** grow upwards from the cave floor and can be conical, fir-cone-shaped, or resemble a stack of saucers. Growing stalactites and stalagmites may meet to form a continuous column from floor to ceiling.

Stalin, Joseph (1879–1953) adopted name of Joseph Vissarionovich Djugashvili, (Russian 'steel') Soviet politician. A member of the October Revolution committee of 1917, Stalin became general secretary of the Communist Party in 1922. After *Lenin's death in 1924, Stalin sought to create 'socialism in one country' and clashed with *Trotsky, who denied the possibility of socialism inside Russia until revolution had occurred in Western Europe. Stalin won this ideological struggle by 1927, and a series of five-year plans was launched to collectivize industry and agriculture from 1928. All opposition was eliminated in the Great Purge 1936–38. During World War II, Stalin intervened in the military direction of the campaigns against Nazi Germany. He managed not only to bring the USSR through the war but to help it emerge as a superpower, although only at an immense cost in human suffering to his own people. After the war, Stalin quickly turned Eastern Europe into a series of Soviet satellites and maintained an autocratic rule domestically. His role was denounced after his death by Khrushchev and other members of the Soviet regime.

Stalingrad former name (1925–61) of the Russian city of Volgograd.

stamen male reproductive organ of a flower. The stamens are collectively referred to as the *androecium. A typical stamen consists of a stalk, or filament, with an anther, the pollen-bearing organ, at its apex, but in some primitive plants, such as *Magnolia*, the stamen may not be markedly differentiated.

Stamp Act UK act of Parliament in 1765 that sought to raise enough money from the American colonies to cover the cost of their defence. The act taxed (by requiring an official stamp) all publications and legal documents published in British colonies. The colonists' refusal to use the required tax stamps, and their blockade of British merchant shipping in the American colonies, forced repeal of the act the following year. It helped to precipitate the *American Revolution.

standard atmosphere alternative term for *atmosphere, a unit of pressure.

standard deviation in statistics, a measure (symbol σ or s) of the spread of data. The deviation (difference) of each of the data items from the mean is found, and their values squared. The mean value of these squares is then calculated. The standard deviation is the square root of this mean.

Standard English form of English that in its *grammar, *syntax, vocabulary, and spelling system is the accepted form in speaking and writing. It is the form of English recognized as most appropriate for formal situations and is used widely in public and professional life. It does not identify the speaker or writer with a particular geographical area or social grouping. In Britain, the accent associated with Standard English is received pronunciation, but these are not the same thing. All forms of slang, dialect, and grammatical deviation are non-Standard. In multi-cultural society, non-Standard accents and word forms are increasingly accepted and promoted in the mass media, and the concepts of Standard English and received pronunciation as standards of correctness have become less important, and are possibly seen as elitist.

standard form *or* **scientific notation** method of writing numbers often used by scientists, particularly for very large or very small numbers. The numbers are written with one digit before the decimal point and multiplied by a power of 10. The number of digits given after the decimal point depends on the accuracy required. For example, the *speed of light is 2.9979×10^8 m/1.8628×10^5 mi per second.

standard gravity acceleration due to gravity, generally taken as 9.81274 m/32.38204 ft per second per second. See also *g scale.

standard illuminant any of three standard light intensities, A, B, and C, used for illumination when phenomena involving colour are measured. A is the light from a filament at 2,848 K (2,575 °C/4,667 °F), B is noon sunlight, and C is normal daylight. B and C are defined with respect to A. Standardization is necessary because colours appear different when viewed in different lights.

standard of living in economics, the measure of consumption and welfare of a country, community, class, or person. Individual standard-of-living expectations are heavily influenced by the income and consumption of other people in similar jobs.

standard temperature and pressure (STP) in chemistry, a standard set of conditions for experimental measurements, to enable comparisons to be made between sets of results. Standard temperature is 0 °C/32 °F (273 K) and standard pressure 1 atmosphere (101,325 Pa).

standard volume in physics, the volume occupied by one kilogram molecule (the molecular mass in kilograms) of any gas at standard temperature and pressure. Its value is approximately 22.414 cubic metres.

standing committee committee of the UK House of Commons that examines parliamentary bills (proposed acts of Parliament) for detailed correction and amendment. The committee comprises members of Parliament from the main political parties, with a majority usually held by the government. Several standing committees may be in existence at any time, each usually created for a particular bill.

Stanislavsky, Konstantin Sergeivich Alekseyev (1863–1938) Russian actor, director, and teacher of acting. He rejected the declamatory style of acting in favour of a more realistic approach, concentrating on the psychological basis for the development of character. The Actors Studio is based on his methods. As a director, he is acclaimed for his productions of the great plays of *Chekhov.

Stanley, Henry Morton (1841–1904) adopted name of John Rowlands, Welsh-born US explorer and journalist who made four expeditions to Africa. He and David *Livingstone met at Ujiji in 1871 and explored Lake Tanganyika. He traced the course of the Congo River to the sea 1874–77, established the Congo Free State (Democratic Republic of Congo) 1879–84, and charted much of the interior 1887–89. GCB 1899.

Stanton, Elizabeth Cady (1815–1902) born Elizabeth Cady, US women's rights and antislavery leader. She organized the Seneca Falls Convention with Lucretia Coffin Mott in 1848, and drafted the Declaration of Sentiments, which advocated equal rights for women in a variety of areas, including suffrage. With Susan B Anthony, she founded the National Woman Suffrage Association in 1869, the first women's movement in the USA, and was its first president.

stanza (Italian 'resting or stopping place') group of lines in a poem. A stanza serves the same function in poetry as a paragraph in prose. Stanzas are often of uniform length and separated by a blank line.

star luminous globe of gas, mainly hydrogen and helium, which produces its own heat and light by nuclear reactions. Although stars shine for a very long time – many billions of years – they change in appearance at different stages in their lives (they are said to have a 'life cycle'). Stars seen at night belong to our *galaxy, the Milky Way. The Sun is the nearest star to Earth; other stars in the Milky Way are large distances away (to get to the nearest would take about 4 years travelling at the speed of light). New stars are being formed all the time when nebulae (giant clouds of dust and gas) contract due to the action of gravity. As the star contracts and heats up eventually nuclear reactions begin and the star becomes a main sequence star. If the star is less than 1.2 times the mass of the Sun, it eventually forms a white dwarf that finally fades to a dark body. If it is a massive star, then the main sequence star expands to become a red supergiant that eventually explodes as a supernova. It leaves part of the core as a neutron star (pulsar), or as a black hole if the mass of the collapsing supernova core is three times greater than the Sun.

starch widely distributed, high-molecular-mass *carbohydrate, produced by plants as a food store; main dietary sources are cereals, legumes, and tubers, including potatoes. It consists of varying proportions of two *glucose polymers (*polysaccharides): straight-chain (amylose) and branched (amylopectin) molecules.

Star Chamber in English history, a civil and criminal court, named after the star-shaped ceiling decoration of the room in the Palace of Westminster, London, where its first meetings were held. Created in 1487 by *Henry VII, the Star Chamber comprised some 20 or 30 judges. It was abolished in 1641 by the *Long Parliament.

starfish or **sea star** any *echinoderm of the subclass Asteroidea with arms radiating from a central body. Usually there are five arms, but some species have more. They are covered with spines and small pincerlike organs. There are also a number of small tubular processes on the skin surface that assist in locomotion and respiration. Starfish are predators, and vary in size from 1.2 cm/0.5 in to 90 cm/3 ft.

star fruit fruit of the *carambola tree.

starling any member of a large widespread Old World family (Sturnidae) of chunky, dark, generally gregarious birds of the order Passeriformes. The European starling *Sturnus vulgaris*, common in northern Eurasia, has been naturalized in North America from the late 19th century. The black, speckled plumage is glossed with green and purple. The feathers on the upper parts are tipped with buff, and the wings are greyish-black, with a reddish-brown fringe. The female is less glossy and lustrous than the male. Its own call is a bright whistle, but it is a mimic of the songs of other birds. It is about 20 cm/8 in long.

Star of David or **Magen David** (Hebrew 'shield of David') six-pointed star (made with two equilateral triangles), a symbol of Judaism since the 17th century. It is the central motif on the flag of Israel, and, since 1897, the emblem of Zionism.

Starr, Ringo (1940–) born Richard Starkey, English rock and pop drummer with the legendary English rock group the *Beatles. Starr replaced original Beatles' drummer Pete Best in 1962. He occasionally sang vocals for the group, including on 'Yellow Submarine' (1966). After the group split up in 1970, he pursued a solo musical career. He has also appeared in films and as a broadcaster on children's television, including narrating the series *Thomas the Tank Engine* 1984–96.

state territory that forms its own domestic and foreign policy, acting through laws that are typically decided by a government and carried out, by force if necessary, by agents of that government. It can be argued that the growth of regional international bodies such as the European Union (formerly the European Community) means that states no longer enjoy absolute *sovereignty.

State, Department of US government department responsible for foreign relations, headed by the secretary of state, the senior cabinet officer of the executive branch.

States General former French parliament that consisted of three estates: nobility, clergy, and commons. First summoned in 1302, it declined in importance as the power of the crown grew. It was not called at all between 1614 and 1789 when the crown needed to institute fiscal reforms to avoid financial collapse. Once called, the demands made by the States General formed the first phase in the *French Revolution. States General is also the name of the Dutch parliament.

states of matter forms (solid, liquid, or gas) in which material can exist. Whether a material is solid, liquid, or gaseous depends on its temperature and pressure. The transition between states takes place at definite temperatures, called the melting point and boiling point.

static electricity *electric charge that is stationary, usually acquired by a body by means of electrostatic induction or friction. Rubbing different materials can produce static electricity, as seen in the sparks produced on combing one's hair or removing a nylon shirt. The frictional force causes electrons to move out of their orbits. The electrons are then transferred to another material. The material that gains electrons becomes negatively charged and the material that loses electrons becomes positively charged. In some processes static electricity is useful, as in paint spraying where the parts to be sprayed are charged with electricity of opposite polarity to that on the paint droplets, and in xerography.

statics branch of mechanics concerned with the behaviour of bodies at rest and forces in equilibrium, and distinguished from *dynamics.

statistics branch of mathematics concerned with the collection and interpretation of data. For example, to determine the *mean age of the children in a school, a statistically acceptable answer might be obtained by calculating an average based on the ages of a representative sample, consisting, for example, of a random tenth of the pupils from each class. *Probability is the branch of statistics dealing with predictions of events.

status in the social sciences, an individual's social position, or the esteem in which he or she is held by others in society. Both within and between most occupations or social positions there is a status hierarchy. **Status symbols**, such as insignia of office or an expensive car, often accompany high status.

Statute of Westminster in the history of the British Empire, legislation enacted in 1931 which gave the dominions of the British Empire complete autonomy in their conduct of external affairs. It made them self-governing states whose only allegiance was to the British crown.

Stauffenberg, Claus von (1907–1944) German colonel in World War II who, in a conspiracy to assassinate Hitler (the July Plot), planted a bomb in the dictator's headquarters conference room in the Wolf's Lair at Rastenburg, East Prussia, on 20 July 1944. Hitler was merely injured, and Stauffenberg and 200 others were later executed by the Nazi regime.

STD abbreviation for *sexually transmitted disease.

steady-state theory in astronomy, rival theory to that of the *Big Bang, which claims that the universe has no origin but is expanding because new matter is being created continuously throughout the universe. The theory was proposed in 1948 by Austrian-born British cosmologist Hermann Bondi, Austrian-born US astronomer Thomas Gold, and English astronomer, cosmologist, and writer Fred *Hoyle, but it was dealt a severe blow in 1965 by the discovery of *cosmic background radiation (radiation left over from the Big Bang and the formation of the universe) and is now largely rejected.

stealth technology methods used to make an aircraft as invisible as possible, primarily to radar detection but also to detection by visual means and heat sensors. This is achieved by a combination of aircraft-design elements: smoothing off all radar-reflecting sharp edges; covering the aircraft with radar-absorbent materials; fitting engine coverings that hide the exhaust and heat signatures of the aircraft; and other, secret technologies.

steam dry, invisible gas formed by vaporizing water. The visible cloud that normally forms in the air when water is vaporized is due to minute suspended water particles. Steam is widely used in chemical and other industrial processes and for the generation of power.

steam engine engine that uses the power of steam to produce useful work. The first successful steam engine was built in 1712 by English inventor Thomas Newcomen at Dudley, West Midlands; it was developed further by Scottish instrument maker James *Watt from 1769 and by English mining engineer Richard *Trevithick, whose high-pressure steam engine of 1802 led to the development of the steam locomotive.

stearic acid $CH_3(CH_2)_{16}COOH$, saturated long-chain *fatty acid, soluble in alcohol and ether but not in water. It is found in many fats and oils, and is used to make soap and candles and as a lubricant. The salts of stearic acid are called stearates.

steel alloy or mixture of iron and up to 1.7% carbon, sometimes with other elements, such as manganese, phosphorus, sulphur, and silicon. The USA, Russia, Ukraine, and Japan are the main steel producers. Steel has innumerable uses, including ship and car manufacture, skyscraper frames, and machinery of all kinds.

Steele, Richard (1672–1729) Irish essayist, playwright, and politician. Born in Dublin, he entered the Life Guards, and then settled in London. He founded the journal *The Tatler* (1709–11), in which Joseph *Addison collaborated. They continued their joint work in the *Spectator* (1711–12), also founded by Steele, and *The Guardian* (1713). He also wrote plays, such as *The Conscious Lovers* (1722). In 1713 Steele was elected to Parliament. He was knighted in 1715.

Stefan–Boltzmann law in physics, a law that relates the energy, E, radiated away from a perfect emitter (a black body), to the temperature, T, of that body. It has the form $E = \sigma T^4$, where E is the energy radiated per unit area per second, T is the temperature, and σ is the **Stefan–Boltzmann constant**. Its value is 5.6697 $\times 10^{-8}$ W m^{-2} K^{-4}. The law was derived by the Austrian physicists Josef Stefan and Ludwig Boltzmann.

Stegosaurus genus of late Jurassic North American dinosaurs of the order Ornithischia. They were ungainly herbivores, with very small heads, a double row of triangular plates along the back, and spikes on the tail.

Stein, Gertrude (1874–1946) US writer. She influenced authors Ernest *Hemingway, Sherwood Anderson, and F Scott *Fitzgerald with her radical prose style. Drawing on the stream-of-consciousness psychology of William James and on the geometry of Cézanne and the cubist painters in Paris, she evolved a 'continuous present' style made up of constant repetition and variation of simple phrases. Her work includes the self-portrait *The Autobiography of Alice B Toklas* (1933).

Steinbeck, John Ernst (1902–1968) US novelist. His realist novels, such as *In Dubious Battle* (1936), *Of Mice and Men* (1937), and *The Grapes of Wrath* (1939; Pulitzer Prize; filmed 1940), portray agricultural life in his native California, where migrant farm labourers from the Oklahoma dust bowl struggled to survive. He was awarded the Nobel Prize for Literature in 1962.

Steinem, Gloria (1934–) US journalist and liberal feminist. She emerged as a leading figure in the US women's movement in the late 1960s. She was also involved in radical protest campaigns against racism and the Vietnam War. She cofounded the Women's Action Alliance in 1970 and *Ms* magazine. In 1983 a collection of her articles was published as *Outrageous Acts and Everyday Rebellions*.

Steiner, Rudolf (1861–1925) Austrian philosopher, occultist, and educationalist. He formulated his own mystic and spiritual teaching, which he called anthroposophy. This rejected materialism and aimed to develop the whole human being, intellectually, socially, and, above all, spiritually. A number of Steiner schools follow a curriculum laid down by him with a strong emphasis on the arts.

stem main supporting axis of a plant that bears the leaves, buds, and reproductive structures; it may be simple or branched. The plant stem usually grows above ground, although some grow underground, including *rhizomes, *corms, *rootstocks, and *tubers. Stems contain a continuous vascular system that conducts water and food to and from all parts of the plant.

Stendhal (1783–1842) pen-name of Marie Henri Beyle, French novelist. His novels *Le Rouge et le Noir/ The Red and the Black* (1830) and *La Chartreuse de Parme/ The Charterhouse of Parma* (1839) were pioneering

works in their treatment of disguise and hypocrisy and outstanding for their psychological analysis; a review of the latter by fellow novelist *Balzac (1840) furthered Stendhal's reputation, but he was not fully understood during his lifetime.

Stephen (c. 1097–1154) King of England from 1135. A grandson of William the Conqueror, he was elected king in 1135, although he had previously recognized Henry I's daughter *Matilda as heiress to the throne. Matilda landed in England in 1139, and civil war disrupted the country until 1153, when Stephen acknowledged Matilda's son, Henry II, as his own heir.

Stephen, St (lived c. AD 35) The first Christian martyr; he was stoned to death. Feast day 26 December.

Stephenson, George (1781–1848) English engineer. He built the first successful steam locomotive. He also invented a safety lamp independently of Humphrey *Davy in 1815. He was appointed engineer of the Stockton and Darlington Railway, the world's first public railway, in 1821, and of the Liverpool and Manchester Railway in 1826. In 1829 he won a prize with his locomotive *Rocket*.

Stephenson, Robert (1803–1859) English civil engineer. He constructed railway bridges such as the high-level bridge at Newcastle-upon-Tyne, England, and the Menai and Conway tubular bridges in Wales. He was the son of George *Stephenson.

steppe temperate grasslands of Europe and Asia. The term is sometimes used to refer to other temperate grasslands and semi-arid desert edges.

steradian symbol sr, SI unit of measure of solid (three-dimensional) angles, the three-dimensional equivalent of the *radian. One steradian is the angle at the centre of a sphere when an area on the surface of the sphere equal to the square of the sphere's radius is joined to the centre.

stereotype (Greek 'fixed impression') in sociology, a fixed, exaggerated, and preconceived description about a certain type of person, group, or society. It is based on prejudice rather than fact, but by repetition and with time, stereotypes become fixed in people's minds, resistant to change and ignoring factual evidence to the contrary.

sterilization killing or removal of living organisms such as bacteria and fungi. A sterile environment is necessary in medicine, food processing, and some scientific experiments. Methods include heat treatment (such as boiling), the use of chemicals (such as disinfectants), irradiation with gamma rays, and filtration. See also *asepsis.

sterilization in medicine, any surgical operation to terminate the possibility of reproduction. In women, this is normally achieved by sealing or tying off the *Fallopian tubes (tubal ligation) so that fertilization can no longer take place. In men, the transmission of sperm is blocked by *vasectomy.

sterling silver *alloy containing 925 parts of silver and 75 parts of copper. The copper hardens the silver, making it more useful.

Sterne, Laurence (1713–1768) Irish writer. Sterne was born in Clonmel, County Tipperary, and ordained in 1737. He created the comic anti-hero Tristram Shandy in *The Life and Opinions of Tristram Shandy, Gent* (1759–67). An eccentrically whimsical and bawdy novel, its associations of ideas on the philosophic principles of John Locke, and other devices, foreshadow in part some of the techniques associated with the 20th-century novel, such as stream-of-consciousness. His other works include *A Sentimental Journey through France and Italy* (1768).

steroid any of a group of cyclic, unsaturated alcohols (lipids without fatty acid components), which, like sterols, have a complex molecular structure consisting of four carbon rings. Steroids include the sex hormones, such as *testosterone, the corticosteroid hormones produced by the *adrenal gland, bile acids, and *cholesterol. The term is commonly used to refer to *anabolic steroid. In medicine, synthetic steroids are used to treat a wide range of conditions.

sterol any of a group of solid, cyclic, unsaturated alcohols, with a complex structure that includes four carbon rings; cholesterol is an example. Steroids are derived from sterols.

stethoscope instrument used to ascertain the condition of the heart and lungs by listening to their action. It consists of two earpieces connected by flexible tubes to a small plate that is placed against the body. It was invented in 1819 in France by René Théophile Hyacinthe *Laënnec.

Stevenson, Robert Louis Balfour (1850–1894) Scottish novelist and poet. He wrote the adventure stories *Treasure Island* (1883), *Kidnapped* (1886), and *The Master of Ballantrae* (1889), notable for their characterization as well as their action. He was a master also of shorter fiction such as *The Strange Case of Dr Jekyll and Mr Hyde* (1886), and of stories of the supernatural such as *Thrawn Janet* (1881). *A Child's Garden of Verses* (1885) is a collection of nostalgic poetry reflecting childhood.

Stewart, James (Maitland) (1908–1997) US film actor. He was noted for his awkward, almost bemused screen presence, his hesitant, drawling delivery, and, in many of his film roles, his embodiment of traditional American values and ideals. His films included *Mr Smith Goes to Washington* (1939), *The Philadelphia Story* (1940), for which he won an Academy Award, and *It's a Wonderful Life* (1946).

stick insect insect of the order Phasmida, closely resembling a stick or twig. The eggs mimic plant seeds. Many species are wingless. The longest reach a length of 30 cm/1 ft.

stickleback any fish of the family Gasterosteidae, found in marine and fresh waters of the northern hemisphere. It has a long body that can grow to 18 cm/ 7 in. The spines along a stickleback's back take the place of the first dorsal fin, and can be raised to make the fish difficult to eat for predators. After the eggs have been laid the female takes no part in rearing the young: the male builds a nest for the eggs, which he then guards and rears for the first two weeks.

stigma in a flower, the surface at the tip of a *carpel that receives the *pollen. It often has short outgrowths, flaps, or hairs to trap pollen and may produce a sticky secretion to which the grains adhere.

Stijl, De (Dutch 'the style') influential movement in art, architecture, and design founded in 1917 in the Netherlands. The focus of the movement was an attempt to simplify art to pure abstraction; form was reduced to rectangles and other geometric shapes, while colour was limited to the primary colours and black and white. The De Stijl group wanted to bring art and design together in a single coherent, simplified system. Its best-known member was the abstract painter Piet *Mondrian. The group's main theorist and publicist was Theo van Doesburg (1883–1931), and his death in 1931 effectively marked its end.

still life in painting and other visual arts, a depiction of inanimate objects, such as flowers, fruit, or tableware. Still-life painting was popular among the ancient Greeks and Romans (who also made still-life mosaics), but thereafter it was sidelined in European art for centuries, as art was overwhelmingly devoted to religious subjects during the Middle Ages. It reappeared during the Renaissance and became established as a distinctive branch of painting in the 17th century, flourishing first in the Netherlands, where the Reformation had discouraged religious imagery and artists were seeking new subjects. Pictures of dead animals are also covered by the term.

stimulant any substance that acts on the brain to increase alertness and activity; for example, *amphetamine. When given to children, stimulants may have a paradoxical, calming effect. Stimulants cause liver damage, are habit-forming, have limited therapeutic value, and are now prescribed only to treat narcolepsy and severe obesity.

stinkwood any of various trees with unpleasant-smelling wood. The South African tree *O. bullata* has offensive-smelling wood when newly felled, but fine, durable timber used for furniture. Another stinkwood is *G. augusta* from tropical America. (Genera *Ocotea*, family Lauraceae; *Gustavia*.)

Stirling unitary authority in central Scotland, created in 1996 from Stirling district, Central region. **area:** 2,196 sq km/848 sq mi **towns:** Dunblane, Stirling (administrative headquarters) **physical:** mountainous to the north, including the forested Trossachs, and the open moorland north and west of Breadalbane, flatter within the flood plain of the River Forth to the south around Stirling (the Carse of Stirling). The area contains many famous lochs (Tay, Katrine, Lomond) and Scotland's only lake (Lake of Menteith). Peaks include Ben More (1,174 m/3,852 ft) and Ben Venue (727 m/2,385 ft) **features:** Bannockburn Heritage Centre; Stirling Castle (most visited paid attraction in Scotland outside Edinburgh), Dunblane Cathedral, Doune Castle, Loch Lomond and Trossachs National Park **population:** (2000 est) 85,200 **history:** William Wallace won battle of Stirling Bridge in 1297; English defeated at Bannockburn by Robert the Bruce in 1314; battle at Sheriffmuir in 1715 between Jacobites and Hanoverians.

Stirling, James Frazer (1926–1992) Scottish architect. He was possibly the most influential of his generation. While in partnership with James Gowan (1924–), he designed an influential housing estate at Ham Common, Richmond (1958), and the Leicester University Engineering Building (1959–63) in a constructivist vein. He later adopted a more eclectic approach, exemplified in his considered masterpiece, the Staatsgalerie, Stuttgart, Germany (1977–83), which blended constructivism, modernism, and several strands of classicism. He also designed the Clore Gallery (1980–86) extension to the Tate Gallery, London. He was knighted in 1983.

stoat carnivorous mammal *Mustela erminea* of the northern hemisphere, in the weasel family, about 37 cm/15 in long including the black-tipped tail. It has a long body and a flattened head. The upper parts and tail are red-brown, and the underparts are white. In the colder regions, the coat turns white (ermine) in winter. Its young are called kits.

stock in botany, any of a group of herbaceous plants commonly grown as garden ornamentals. Many cultivated varieties, including simple-stemmed, queen's, and ten-week stocks, have been derived from the wild stock (*M. incana*); night-scented (or evening) stock (*M. bicornis*) becomes aromatic at night. (Genus *Matthiola*, family Cruciferae.)

stock in finance, the UK term for the fully paid-up capital of a company. It is bought and sold by subscribers not in units or shares, but in terms of its current cash value. In US usage the term stock generally means an ordinary share. See also *stocks and shares.

stock exchange institution for the buying and selling of stocks and shares (securities). The world's largest stock exchanges are London, New York (Wall Street), and Tokyo. The oldest stock exchanges are Antwerp (1460), Hamburg (1558), Amsterdam (1602), New York (1790), and London (1801). The former division on the London Stock Exchange between brokers (who bought shares from jobbers to sell to the public) and jobbers (who sold them only to brokers on commission, the 'jobbers' turn') was abolished in 1986.

Stockhausen, Karlheinz (1928–) German composer of avant-garde music. He has continued to explore new musical sounds and compositional techniques since the 1950s. His major works include *Gesang der Jünglinge/Song of the Youths* (1956), *Kontakte* (1960) (electronic music), and *Sirius* (1977).

Stockholm capital and industrial port of Sweden; population (1994 est) 703,600. Gamla Stan, Stockholm's first settlement, has many medieval buildings and merchant's houses. Founded in the mid-13th century, Stockholm grew as an important trading centre, and became the capital of Sweden in 1436. It is built on a group of some 14 islands and the nearby mainland where Lake Mälar joins the Baltic Sea. In the 17th century it became an important trading centre of the Hanseatic League, a confederation of North European trading cities. Industries include engineering, brewing, electrical goods, paper, textiles, and pottery.

stocks and shares investment holdings (securities) in private or public undertakings. Although distinctions have become blurred, in the UK stock usually means fixed-interest securities – for example, those issued by central and local government – while *shares represent a stake in the ownership of a trading company which, if they are ordinary shares, yield to the owner dividends reflecting the success of the company. In the USA the term stock generally signifies what in the UK is an ordinary share.

Stockton-on-Tees unitary authority in northeast England created in 1996 from part of the former county of Cleveland. **area:** 200 sq km/77 sq mi **towns and cities:** Stockton-on-Tees (administrative headquarters), Billingham, Yarm, Longnewton **features:** River Tees forms east border; Tees Barrage; Yarm viaduct; Preston Hall Museum and Park (Stockton); Castlegate Quay (Stockton) includes full-scale replica of HMS *Endeavour*

population: (1996) 176,600.

Stoicism (Greek *stoa* 'porch') Greek school of philosophy, founded about 300 BC by Zeno of Citium. The Stoics were pantheistic materialists who believed that happiness lay in accepting the law of the universe. They emphasized human brotherhood, denounced slavery, and were internationalist. The name is derived from the porch on which Zeno taught.

Stoke-on-Trent city and administrative centre of Stoke-on-Trent City unitary authority in central England, on the River Trent, 48 km/30 mi north of Wolverhampton; population (1999 est) 252,500. The city is situated in the heart of the Potteries, a major ceramic centre, and is the largest clayware producer in the world. Other industries include the manufacture of steel, chemicals, and engineering machinery, and the Michelin tyre company has its headquarters in the town.

STOL (acronym for **short takeoff and landing**) aircraft fitted with special devices on the wings (such as sucking flaps) that increase aerodynamic lift at low speeds. Small passenger and freight STOL craft may become common with the demand for small airports, especially in difficult terrain.

stoma plural **stomata**, in botany, a pore (tiny hole) in the epidermis (outer layer of tissue) of a plant. There are lots of these holes, usually in the lower surface of the *leaf. A leaf contains several layers of *tissue. The outer layer is the epidermis and is only one cell thick. Stomata occur in the lower epidermis. Each stoma is surrounded by a pair of guard cells that are crescent-shaped when the stoma is open but can collapse to an oval shape, thus closing off the opening between them. Stomata allow the exchange of carbon dioxide and oxygen (needed for *photosynthesis and *respiration) between the internal tissues of the plant and the outside atmosphere. They are also the main route by which water is lost from the plant, and they can be closed to conserve water, the movements being controlled by changes in turgidity of the guard cells.

stomach organ that forms the first cavity in the digestive system of animals. In mammals it is a bag of *muscle situated just below the diaphragm. Food enters it from the *oesophagus, is digested by the acid and *enzymes secreted by the stomach lining. The wall of the stomach contracts to mix the food with the digestive juice to help digestion of *protein. After a while, partly digested food is then passed into the small *intestine (duodenum). Some plant-eating mammals have multi-chambered stomachs that harbour bacteria in one of the chambers to assist in the digestion of *cellulose. The human stomach can hold about 1.5 l/2.6 pt of liquid. The digestive juices are acidic enough to dissolve metal. To avoid damage, the cells of the stomach lining are replaced quickly – 500,000 cells are replaced every minute, and the whole stomach lining every three days.

stone plural **stone**; abbreviation st, imperial unit of mass. One stone is 14 pounds (6.35 kg).

Stone Age the developmental stage of humans in *prehistory before the use of metals, when tools and weapons were made chiefly of stone, especially flint. The Stone Age is subdivided into the Old or **Palaeolithic**, when flint implements were simply chipped into shape; the Middle or **Mesolithic**;

and the New or **Neolithic**, when implements were ground and polished. Palaeolithic people were hunters and gatherers; by the Neolithic period people were taking the first steps in agriculture, the domestication of animals, weaving, and pottery.

stonecrop any of a group of plants belonging to the orpine family, succulent herbs with fleshy leaves and clusters of red, yellow, or white starlike flowers. Stonecrops are characteristic of dry, rocky places and some grow on walls. (Genus *Sedum*, family Crassulaceae.)

stonefish any of a family (Synanceiidae) of tropical marine bony fishes with venomous spines and bodies resembling encrusted rocks.

Stonehenge (Old English 'hanging stones') megalithic monument on Salisbury Plain, 3 km/1.9 mi west of Amesbury in Wiltshire, England. The site developed over various periods from a simple henge (earthwork circle and ditch), dating from about 3000 BC, to a complex stone structure, from about 2100 BC, which included a circle of 30 upright stones, their tops linked by lintel stones to form a continuous circle about 30 m/ 100 ft across.

Stopes, Marie Charlotte Carmichael (1880–1958) Scottish birth-control campaigner. With her second husband H V Roe (1878–1949), an aircraft manufacturer, she founded Britain's first birth-control clinic in London in 1921. In her best-selling manual *Married Love* (1918) she urged women to enjoy sexual intercourse within their marriage, a revolutionary view for the time. She also wrote plays and verse.

Stoppard, Tom (1937–) born Thomas Straussler, Czech-born British dramatist. His works use wit and wordplay to explore logical and philosophical ideas. The successful *Rosencrantz and Guildenstern are Dead* (1967) was followed by many other highly acclaimed plays including *Travesties* (1974), *The Real Thing* (1982), *Hapgood* (1988), *Arcadia* (1993), and *The Invention of Love* (1997). He has also written for radio, television, and the cinema, sharing the 1999 Academy Award for Best Original Screenplay (with Marc Norman) for *Shakespeare in Love* (1998).

stork any of the 17 species of the Ciconiidae, a family of long-legged, long-necked wading birds with long, powerful wings, and long conical bills used for spearing prey. Some species grow up to 1.5 m/5 ft tall.

Stormont suburb 8 km/5 mi east of Belfast, Northern Ireland. It is the site of the new Northern Ireland Assembly, elected as a result of the Good Friday agreement in 1998 and functioning from 1999 when some powers were transferred back to Northern Ireland from Westminster. It was previously the seat of the government of Northern Ireland 1921–72.

Stowe, Harriet Elizabeth Beecher (1811–1896) US writer, abolitionist, and suffragist. She is best known for her antislavery novel *Uncle Tom's Cabin*, first published serially in 1851–52, which is considered one of the most important books in US literature. Her Christian and abolitionist ideals, combined with the death of her infant son in 1849, provided the context and inspiration for the novel, which when published in book form was an immediate success.

Strachey, (Giles) Lytton (1880–1932) English critic and biographer. He was a member of the *Bloomsbury Group of writers and artists. His *Landmarks in French Literature* was written in 1912. The mocking and witty treatment of Cardinal Manning, Florence Nightingale, Thomas Arnold, and General Gordon in *Eminent Victorians* (1918) won him recognition. His biography of *Queen Victoria* (1921) was more affectionate.

Stradivari, Antonio (c. 1644–1737) Latin **Stradivarius**, Italian stringed instrument maker, generally considered the greatest of all violin makers. He produced more than 1,100 instruments from his family workshops, over 600 of which survive; they have achieved the status (and sale-room prices) of works of art.

Strafford, Thomas Wentworth, 1st Earl of Strafford (1593–1641) English politician. He was originally an opponent of *Charles I, but from 1628 he was on the Royalist side. He ruled despotically as Lord Deputy of Ireland 1632–39, when he returned to England as Charles's chief adviser and received an earldom. He was impeached in 1640 by Parliament, abandoned by Charles as a scapegoat, and beheaded. He was knighted in 1611, became Baron in 1628, and created Earl in 1640.

Straits Settlements former province of the *East India Company 1826–58, a British crown colony 1867–1946; it comprised Singapore, Malacca (now Melaka), Penang, Cocos Islands, Christmas Island, and Labuan.

Strasberg, Lee (1901–1982) born Israel Strassberg, US actor and artistic director of the Actors Studio from 1948. He developed Method acting from *Stanislavsky's system; pupils have included Marlon Brando, Paul Newman, Julie Harris, Kim Hunter, Geraldine Page, Al Pacino, and Robert De Niro.

Strasbourg German **Strassburg**, administrative centre of the Bas-Rhin *département* and of *Alsace region, northeast France, situated near the German border on the River Ill, 3 km/1.9 mi west of the Rhine near its confluence with the Rhine–Rhône and Rhine and Marne canals; population (1999 est) 264,000; Strasbourg-Kehl agglomeration (2002 est) 652,300. Industries include car manufacture, tobacco, printing and publishing, and preserves. The town was selected as the headquarters for the *Council of Europe in 1949, and sessions of the European Parliament alternate between here and Luxembourg. Its majestic Gothic cathedral of Notre Dame, begun in 1015 and completed in 1439, has a famed astronomical clock that was installed in its tower in 1574.

Strategic Arms Limitation Talks (SALT) series of US-Soviet discussions 1969–79 aimed at reducing the rate of nuclear-arms build-up (as opposed to *disarmament, which would reduce the number of weapons, as discussed in *Strategic Arms Reduction Talks [START]). The accords of the 1970s sought primarily to prevent the growth of nuclear arsenals.

Strategic Arms Reduction Talks (START) phase in peace discussions dealing with *disarmament, initially involving the USA and the Soviet Union, from 1992 the USA and Russia, and from 1993 Belarus and the Ukraine. It began with talks in Geneva, Switzerland, in 1983, leading to the signing of the *Intermediate Nuclear Forces Treaty in 1987. In 1989 proposals for reductions in conventional weapons were added to the agenda. As the Cold War drew to a close from 1989, negotiations moved rapidly. Reductions of about 30% in strategic nuclear weapons systems were agreed in Moscow in July 1991 (START) and more significant cuts were agreed in January 1993 (START II); the latter treaty was ratified by the US Senate in January 1996. Russia's Duma ratified START II in April 2000. just following the inauguration of Russian President Vladimir Putin. Under the treaty, which applies to inter-continental rockets, the USA and Russia will both halve their stocks of atomic warheads to between 3,000 and 3,500 each by 2007. A START III treaty, currently being negotiated, would increase arms reduction even further.

Strategic Defense Initiative (SDI) or **Star Wars** US programme (1983–93) to explore the technical feasibility of developing a comprehensive defence system against incoming nuclear missiles, based in part outside the Earth's atmosphere. The programme was started by President Ronald Reagan in March 1983, and was overseen by the Strategic Defense Initiative Organization (SDIO). In May 1993, the SDIO changed its name to the Ballistic Missile Defense Organization (BMDO), to reflect its focus on defence against short-range rather than long-range missiles. SDI lives on today in the less ambitious *National Missile Defense (NMD) programme.

Stratford-upon-Avon market town on the River Avon, in Warwickshire, England, 35 km/22 mi southeast of Birmingham; population (1991) 22,200. It is the birthplace of William *Shakespeare and has the Royal Shakespeare Theatre (1932), the Swan Theatre, and The Other Place. Stratford receives over 2 million tourists a year. Industries include canning, aluminium ware, and boat building.

stratosphere that part of the atmosphere 10–40 km/ 6–25 mi from the Earth's surface, where the temperature slowly rises from a low of −55 °C/−67 °F to around 0 °C/32 °F. The air is rarefied and at around 25 km/15 mi much *ozone is concentrated.

Strauss, Richard (Georg) (1864–1949) German composer and conductor. He followed the German Romantic tradition but had a strongly personal style, characterized by his bold, colourful orchestration. He first wrote tone poems such as *Don Juan* (1889), *Till Eulenspiegel's Merry Pranks* (1895), and *Also sprach Zarathustra/Thus Spake Zarathustra* (1896). He then moved on to opera with *Salome* (1905) and *Elektra* (1909), both of which have elements of polytonality. He reverted to a more traditional style with *Der Rosenkavalier/The Knight of the Rose* (1909–10).

Stravinsky, Igor Fyodorovich (1882–1971) Russian composer, later of French (1934) and US (1945) nationality. He studied under Nikolai *Rimsky-Korsakov and wrote the music for the Diaghilev ballets *The Firebird* (1910), *Petrushka* (1911), and *The Rite of Spring* (1913), which were highly controversial at the time for their use of driving rhythms and bi-tonal harmonies. At the first performance of *The Rite of Spring* the audience's reaction caused a riot. His works also include symphonies, concertos (for violin and piano), chamber music, and operas; for example, *The Rake's Progress* (1951) and *The Flood* (1962).

Straw, Jack (1946–) British Labour lawyer and politician, foreign secretary from 2001. Situated on the right wing of the Labour party, Straw was home secretary during the Labour government's first term 1997–2001 and introduced crime reduction programmes, while also facing a rising level of political asylum applications. As foreign secretary, he backed Prime Minister Tony Blair during the US-led Iraq War in 2003, although he had reservations about proceeding without broader United Nations support.

strawberry low-growing perennial plant widely cultivated for its red, fleshy fruits, which are rich in vitamin C. Commercial cultivated forms bear one crop of fruit in summer, with the berries resting on a bed of straw to protect them from the damp soil, and multiply by runners. The flowers are normally white, although pink-flowering varieties are cultivated as ornamentals. (Genus *Fragaria*, family Rosaceae.)

stream of consciousness narrative technique in which a writer presents directly the uninterrupted flow of a character's thoughts, impressions, and feelings, without the conventional devices of dialogue and description. It first came to be widely used in the early 20th century. Leading exponents have included the novelists Virginia Woolf, James Joyce, and William Faulkner.

Streep, Meryl (Mary Louise) (1949–) US actor. She has played strong character roles, portrayed with emotionally dramatic intensity, in such films as *The Deer Hunter* (1978), *Kramer vs Kramer* (1979, Academy Award for Best Supporting Actress), *The French Lieutenant's Woman* (1981), *Sophie's Choice* (1982, Academy Award), and *Out of Africa* (1985).

stress in psychology, any event or situation that makes heightened demands on a person's mental or emotional resources. Stress can be caused by overwork, anxiety about exams, money, job security, unemployment, bereavement, poor relationships, marriage breakdown, sexual difficulties, poor living or working conditions, and constant exposure to loud noise.

stridulatory organs in insects, organs that produce sound when rubbed together. Crickets rub their wings together, but grasshoppers rub a hind leg against a wing. Stridulation is thought to be used for attracting mates, but may also serve to mark territory.

Strindberg, (Johan) August (1849–1912) Swedish dramatist and novelist. His plays are in a variety of styles including historical dramas, symbolic dramas (the two-part *Dödsdansen/The Dance of Death* (1901)), and 'chamber plays' such as *Spöksonaten/The Ghost [Spook] Sonata* (1907). *Fadren/The Father* (1887) and *Fröken Julie/Miss Julie* (1888) are among his best-known works.

string quartet *chamber music written for two violins, viola, and cello. The term also refers to the group that performs such a composition. It has always been the most popular of all the types of chamber works and is considered to be the most pure and abstract genre. Important composers for the string quartet include Haydn (more than 80 string quartets), Mozart (27), Schubert (20), Beethoven (17), Bartók (6), and Shostakovich (15). Recent important composers for the string quartet include US composer Elliott Carter (5 quartets) and English composer Brian Ferneyhough (4).

stroke or **cerebrovascular accident** or **apoplexy** interruption of the blood supply to part of the brain due to a sudden bleed in the brain (cerebral haemorrhage) or *embolism or *thrombosis. Strokes vary in severity from producing almost no symptoms to proving rapidly fatal. In between are those (often recurring) that leave a wide range of impaired function, depending on the size and location of the event.

stromatolite mound produced in shallow water by mats of algae that trap mud particles. Another mat grows on the trapped mud layer and this traps another layer of mud and so on. The stromatolite grows to heights of a metre or so. They are uncommon today but their fossils are among the earliest evidence for living things – over 2,000 million years old.

Stromboli Italian island in the Tyrrhenian Sea, one of the *Lipari Islands; area 12 sq km/5 sq mi. It has an active volcano, 926 m/3,039 ft high. The island produces Malmsey wine and capers, partly as a result of the fertile soil the lava has produced.

strong nuclear force one of the four fundamental *forces of nature, the other three being the gravitational force or gravity, the electromagnetic force, and the weak nuclear force. The strong nuclear force was first described by the Japanese physicist Hideki Yukawa in 1935. It is the strongest of all the forces, acts only over very small distances within the nucleus of the atom (10^{-13} cm), and is responsible for binding together *quarks to form *hadrons, and for binding together protons and neutrons in the atomic nucleus. The particle that is the carrier of the strong nuclear force is the *gluon, of which there are eight kinds, each with zero mass and zero charge.

strontium chemical symbol Sr, soft, ductile, pale-yellow, metallic element, atomic number 38, relative atomic mass 87.62. It is one of the *alkaline-earth metals, widely distributed in small quantities only as a sulphate or carbonate. Strontium salts burn with a red flame and are used in fireworks and signal flares.

structuralism 20th-century philosophical movement that has influenced such areas as linguistics, anthropology, and literary criticism. Inspired by the work of the Swiss linguist Ferdinand de Saussure, structuralists believe that objects should be analysed as systems of relations, rather than as positive entities.

strychnine $C_{21}H_{22}O_2N_2$, bitter-tasting, poisonous alkaloid. It is a poison that causes violent muscular spasms, and is usually obtained by powdering the seeds of plants of the genus *Strychnos* (for example *S. nux vomica*). Curare is a related drug.

Stuart (or Stewart) royal family that inherited the Scottish throne in 1371 and the English throne in 1603, holding it until 1714, when Queen Anne died without heirs; the house of Stuart was succeeded by the house of *Hanover. The claimants to the British throne James Francis Edward Stuart (the 'Old Pretender', son of the deposed James VII of Scotland and II of England) and his son Charles Edward Stuart (the 'Young Pretender') both attempted unsuccessful invasions of England in support of their claims, in 1715 and 1745 (see *Jacobites).

Stubbs, George (1724–1806) English artist. He is renowned for his paintings of horses, such as *Mares and Foals* (about 1763; Tate Gallery, London). After the publication of his book of engravings *The Anatomy of the Horse* (1766), he was widely commissioned as an animal painter. The dramatic *Lion Attacking a Horse* (1770; Yale University Art Gallery, New Haven, Connecticut) and the peaceful *Reapers* (1786; Tate Gallery, London) show the variety of mood in his painting.

sturgeon large, primitive, bony fish with five rows of bony plates and chin barbels used for exploring the bottom of the water for prey.

Sturmabteilung (SA) (German 'storm section') German militia, also known as **Brownshirts**, of the *Nazi Party, established in 1921 under the leadership of Ernst Röhm, in charge of physical training and political indoctrination.

Sturm und Drang (German 'storm and stress') German early Romantic *genres in literature and music, from about 1775, concerned with the depiction of extravagant passions. Writers associated with the movement include Johann Gottfried von Herder, Johann Wolfgang von Goethe, and Friedrich von Schiller. The name is taken from a play by Friedrich von Klinger in 1776.

style in flowers, the part of the *carpel bearing the *stigma at its tip. In some flowers it is very short or completely lacking, while in others it may be long and slender, positioning the stigma in the most effective place to receive the pollen.

Styria German **Steiermark**, Alpine state of southeast Austria, bordered to the east by Hungary and to the south by Slovenia; area 16,388 sq km/6,327 sq mi; population (2001 est) 1,185,900. Its capital is Graz.

Styx (Greek 'hateful') in Greek mythology, the river surrounding *Hades, the underworld. When an oath was sworn by Styx, its waters were taken to seal the promise. Gods who broke such a vow suffered a year's unconsciousness and nine years' exile, while to mortal transgressors its waters were deadly poison. The tradition may have derived from some form of trial by ordeal.

subatomic particle in physics, a particle that is smaller than an atom. Such particles may be indivisible *elementary particles, such as the *electron and *quark, or they may be composites, such as the *proton, *neutron, and *alpha particle. See also *particle physics.

subduction zone in *plate tectonics, a region where two plates of the Earth's rigid *lithosphere collide, and one plate descends below the other into the weaker *asthenosphere. Subduction results in the formation of ocean trenches, most of which encircle the Pacific Ocean.

sub judice (Latin 'under a judge') of judicial proceedings, not yet decided by a court of law or judge. As long as a matter is sub judice all discussion is prohibited elsewhere.

sublimation conversion of a solid to vapour without passing through the liquid phase. It is one of the *changes of state of matter. Very few chemicals sublimate; those that do include iodine, arsenic, and zinc chloride.

submarine underwater warship. The first underwater boat was constructed in 1620 for James I of England by the Dutch scientist Cornelius van Drebbel (1572–1633). A naval submarine, or submersible torpedo boat, the *Gymnote*, was launched by France in 1888. The conventional submarine of World War I was driven by diesel engine on the surface and by battery-powered electric motors underwater. The diesel engine also drove a generator that produced electricity to charge the batteries.

submersible vessel designed to operate under water, especially a small submarine used by engineers and research scientists as a ferry craft to support diving operations. The most advanced submersibles are the so-called lock-out type, which have two compartments:

one for the pilot, the other to carry divers. The diving compartment is pressurized and provides access to the sea.

subpoena (Latin 'under penalty') in law, an order requiring someone who might not otherwise come forward of his or her own volition to give evidence before a court or judicial official at a specific time and place. A witness who fails to comply with a subpoena is in *contempt of court.

subsidiarity devolution of decision-making within the European Union from the centre to the lowest level possible. Since the signing of the *Maastricht Treaty on European union 1991, which affirms that, wherever possible, decisions should be 'taken as closely as possible to the citizens', subsidiarity has been widely debated as a means of countering trends towards excessive centralization.

substitution reaction in chemistry, the replacement of one atom or *functional group in an organic molecule by another.

succession in ecology, a series of changes that occur in the structure and composition of the vegetation in a given area from the time it is first colonized by plants (**primary succession**), or after it has been disturbed by fire, flood, or clearing (**secondary succession**). The succession of plant types along a lake. As the lake gradually fills in, a mature climax community of trees forms inland from the shore. Extending out from the shore, a series of plant communities can be discerned with small, rapidly growing species closest to the shore.

Succoth or **Sukkot,** or **Feast of Boothd,** or **Feast of Tabernacles** in Judaism, a festival celebrated in September/October, which commemorates the time when the Israelites lived in the wilderness during the Exodus from Egypt. As a reminder of the shelters used in the wilderness, huts (*sukkah*) are built and used for eating and sleeping during the seven-day celebration. Succoth occurs at harvest time, and has elements of a harvest festival.

succulent plant thick, fleshy plant that stores water in its tissues; for example, cacti and stonecrops *Sedum*. Succulents live either in areas where water is very scarce, such as deserts, or in places where it is not easily obtainable because of the high concentrations of salts in the soil, as in salt marshes. Many desert plants are *xerophytes.

suckering in plants, reproduction by new shoots (suckers) arising from an existing root system rather than from seed. Plants that produce suckers include elm, dandelion, and members of the rose family.

Sucre legal capital and seat of the judiciary of Bolivia, also capital of Chuquisaca department; population (2001 est) 194,900. It stands on the central plateau in the Andes at an altitude of 2,840 m/9,320 ft. It is the commercial centre for the surrounding agricultural area, and has an oil refinery and cement works.

sucrose or **cane sugar** or **beet sugar** $C_{12}H_{22}O_{11}$, sugar found in the stem of sugar cane and in sugar beet. It is popularly known as *sugar.

Sudan

National name: *Al-Jumhuryyat es-Sudan/ Republic of Sudan*
Area: 2,505,800 sq km/967,489 sq mi
Capital: Khartoum

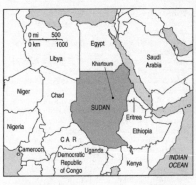

Major towns/cities: Omdurman, Port Sudan, Juba, Wad Medani, El Obeid, Kassala, al-Qadarif, Nyala
Major ports: Port Sudan
Physical features: fertile Nile valley separates Libyan Desert in west from high rocky Nubian Desert in east
Head of state and government: Gen Omar Hassan Ahmed al-Bashir from 1989
Political system: military
Political executive: military
Political parties: officially banned from 1989, but an influential grouping is the fundamentalist National Islamic Front
Currency: Sudanese dinar
GNI per capita (PPP): (US$) 1,690 (2002 est)
Exports: cotton, sesame seed, gum arabic, sorghum, livestock, hides and skins. Principal market: China 49.3% (2001)
Population: 33,610,000 (2003 est)
Language: Arabic (51%) (official), 100 local languages
Religion: Sunni Muslim 70%; also animist 25%, and Christian 5%
Life expectancy: 54 (men); 57 (women) (2000–05)
Chronology
c. **600 BC–AD 350:** Meroë, near Khartoum, was capital of the Nubian Empire, which covered southern Egypt and northern Sudan.
6th century: Converted to Coptic Christianity.
7th century: Islam first introduced by Arab invaders, but did not spread widely until the 15th century.
16th–18th centuries: Arab-African Fur and Fung Empires established in central and northern Sudan.
1820: Invaded by Muhammad Ali and brought under Egyptian control.
1881–85: Revolt led to capture of Khartoum by Sheik Muhammad Ahmed, a self-proclaimed Mahdi ('messiah'), and the killing of British general Charles Gordon.
1898: Anglo-Egyptian offensive led by Lord Kitchener subdued Mahdi revolt at Battle of Omdurman in which 20,000 Sudanese died.
1899: Sudan administered as Anglo-Egyptian condominium.
1923: White Flag League formed by Sudanese nationalists in north; British instituted policy of reducing contact between northern and southern Sudan, with the aim that the south would eventually become part of federation of eastern African states.

1955: Civil war between the dominant Arab Muslim north and black African Christian and animist south broke out.

1956: Sudan achieved independence from Britain and Egypt as a republic.

1958: Military coup replaced civilian government with Supreme Council of the Armed Forces.

1964: Civilian rule reinstated after October Revolution of student demonstrations.

1969: Coup led by Col Gaafar Mohammed al-Nimeri abolished political institutions and concentrated power in a leftist Revolutionary Command Council.

1971: Nimeri confirmed as president and the Sudanese Socialist Union (SSU) declared the only legal party by a new constitution.

1972: Plans to form Federation of Arab Republics, comprising Sudan, Egypt, and Syria, abandoned due to internal opposition. To end 17-year-long civil war, Nimeri agreed to give south greater autonomy.

1974: National assembly established.

1980: Country reorganized into six regions, each with own assembly and effective autonomy.

1983: Shari'a (Islamic law) imposed. Sudan People's Liberation Movement (SPLM) formed in south as civil war broke out again.

1985: Nimeri deposed in a bloodless coup led by Gen Swar al-Dahab following industrial unrest in north.

1986: Coalition government formed after general election, with Sadiq al-Mahdi, great-grandson of the Mahdi, as prime minister.

1987: Civil war with Sudan People's Liberation Army (SPLA); drought and famine in south and refugee influx from Ethiopa and Chad.

1988: A peace pact was signed with SPLA, but fighting continued.

1989: Al-Mahdi was overthrown in a coup led by Islamic fundamentalist Gen Omar Hassan Ahmed el-Bashir. All political activity was suspended.

1991: A federal system was introduced, with division of the country into nine states as the civil war continued.

1998: Civil war continued between the SPLA and the Islamist government. There was famine in the south, where millions faced starvation. The USA launched a missile attack on a suspected chemical weapons-producing site in retaliation for bombings of US embassies in Nairobi and Dar es Salaam. There was a temporary ceasefire by the SPLA.

1999: Multiparty politics were reintroduced. Steps to restore diplomatic ties with Uganda were taken when in December an agreement was signed to attempt to end rebel wars across the mutual border by ceasing to support rebel factions in the other's country. In late December, the president declared a state of emergency and dissolved parliament.

2000: President Bashir dismissed his entire cabinet in January, but then reappointed key ministers. In Khartoum, women were banned from working in public places where they might meet men. Elections re-established a parliament and confirmed Bashir in power, but were boycotted by opposition parties. Famine threatened the lives of 3 million people.

2001: The state of emergency was extended for a further year by President Bashir.

2002: The Islamic government and the SPLA agreed a framework for ending the ongoing civil war. The agreement envisaged power sharing for a six-year transitional period, after which a referendum on self-determination would be held, and non-Muslims in the south would be exempted from Islamic law.

2003: Rebellion broke out in Darfur region. Arab pro-government militias were accused of ethnic cleansing of non-Arab peoples.

2005: A peace agreement was signed, ending the long-running civil war.

sudden infant death syndrome (SIDS) in medicine, the technical term for *cot death.

Sudeten mountainous region in northeast Bohemia, Czech Republic, extending eastwards along the border with Poland. Sudeten was annexed by Germany under the *Munich Agreement 1938; it was returned to Czechoslovakia in 1945. Germany and the Czech Republic sought to bury decades of mutual antagonism in January 1997 by signing a joint declaration aimed at drawing a line under the vexed issue of the Sudetenland. Germany apologized for the suffering caused during the Nazi occupation. For their part, the Czechs expressed regret over the 'injustices' that took place during the expulsion of more than 2.5 million Sudetenland Germans after World War II. It took over two years to reach agreement.

Suetonius, Gaius Suetonius Tranquillus (c. AD 69–c. 140) Roman historian. He was the author of *Lives of the Caesars* (Julius Caesar to Domitian).

Suez Arabic El Suweis, port at the Red Sea terminus of the Suez Canal, 120 km/75 mi east of Cairo, Egypt; population (1994) 458,000. Industries include oil refining and the manufacture of fertilizers. Port Ibrahim, 3 km/1.8 mi south of Suez, lies at the entrance to the canal. It was reconstructed in 1979 after the *Arab-Israeli Wars.

Suez Canal artificial waterway from Port Said to Suez, linking the Mediterranean and Red Seas; 160 km/100 mi long. It separates Africa from Asia and provides the shortest eastwards sea route from Europe. It was opened in 1869, nationalized in 1956, blocked by Egypt during the Arab-Israeli War in 1967, and not reopened until 1975.

Suez Crisis military confrontation from October to December 1956 following the nationalization of the Suez Canal by President Nasser of Egypt. In an attempt to reassert international control of the canal, Israel launched an attack, after which British and French troops landed. Widespread international censure forced the withdrawal of the British and French. The crisis resulted in the resignation of British prime minister Anthony *Eden.

Suffolk county of eastern England. **area:** 3,800 sq km/1,467 sq mi **towns:** Ipswich (administrative headquarters), Aldeburgh, Beccles, Bury St Edmunds, Felixstowe, Lowestoft, Sudbury, Southwold **physical:** undulating lowlands in the south and west; flat coastline; rivers Waveney (the boundary with Norfolk), Alde, Deben, Orwell, Stour (the boundary with Essex), Little Ouse; part of the Norfolk Broads **features:** Minsmere marshland bird reserve, near Aldeburgh; the Sandlings (heathlands and birds); bloodstock rearing and horse racing at Newmarket; *Sutton Hoo (7th-century ship burial); Sizewell B, Britain's first pressurized-water nuclear reactor plant; Aldeburgh Festival, held every June at Snape Maltings **population:** (1996) 661,600.

suffragette woman fighting for the right to vote. In the UK, the repeated defeat in Parliament of women's suffrage bills, introduced by supporters of the *women's movement between 1886 and 1911, led to the launch of a militant campaign in 1906 by Emmeline *Pankhurst and her daughters, founders of the Women's Social and Political Union (WSPU). In 1918 women were granted limited franchise; in 1928 it was extended to all women over 21.

Sufism mystical movement of *Islam that originated in the 8th century. Sufis emphasize the development of spiritual knowledge of God, and believe that deep intuition is the only real guide to knowledge. They follow the *Shari'a (law of Islam), but are also trained through meditation and other spiritual practices to concentrate on a direct experience of God. The movement has a strong strain of asceticism (severe self-discipline), rejects material values, and emphasizes humility and kindness. Sufi leaders are called shaikhs. There are a number of groups or brotherhoods within Sufism, each with its own method of meditative practice, one of which is the whirling dance of the *dervishes.

sugar or **sucrose** sweet, soluble, crystalline carbohydrate found in the pith of sugar cane and in sugar beet. It is a **disaccharide** sugar, each of its molecules being made up of two simple-sugar (**monosaccharide**) units: glucose and fructose. Sugar is easily digested and forms a major source of energy in humans, being used in cooking and in the food industry as a sweetener and, in high concentrations, as a preservative. A high consumption is associated with obesity and tooth decay. In the UK, sucrose may not be used in baby foods.

Suharto, Thojib I (1921–) Indonesian politician and general, president 1967–98. His authoritarian rule met with domestic opposition from the left, but the Indonesian economy enjoyed significant growth until 1997. He was re-elected in 1973, 1978, 1983, 1988, 1993, and, unopposed, in March 1998. This was despite his deteriorating health and the country's economy being weakened by a sharp decline in value of the Indonesian currency (the rupiah), which had provoked student unrest and food riots. After mounting civil unrest reached a critical point, on 21 May 1998 he handed over the presidency to the vice-president, Bacharuddin Jusuf Habibie.

Sui dynasty Chinese ruling family 581–618 which reunited China after the strife of the *Three Kingdoms era. There were two Sui emperors: Yang Qien (Yang Chien, 541–604), and Yangdi (Yang-ti, ruled 605–17). Though short-lived, the Sui re-established strong centralized government, rebuilding the *Great Wall and digging canals which later formed part of the Grand Canal system. The Sui capital was Chang'an.

suite in baroque music, a set of contrasting instrumental pieces based on dance forms, known by their French names as allemande, bourrée, courante, gavotte, gigue, minuet, musette, passepied, rigaudon, sarabande, and so on. The term refers in more recent usage to a concert arrangement of set pieces from an extended ballet or stage composition, such as Tchaikovsky's *Nutcracker Suite* (1891–92). Igor Stravinsky's suite from *The Soldier's Tale* (1920) incorporates a tango, waltz, and ragtime.

Sukarno, Achmed (1901–1970) Indonesian nationalist, president 1945–67. During World War II he cooperated in the local administration set up by the Japanese, replacing Dutch rule. After the war he became the first president of the new Indonesian republic, becoming president-for-life in 1966; he was ousted by *Suharto.

Sulawesi formerly **Celebes**, island in eastern Indonesia, one of the Sunda Islands; area (with dependent islands) 190,000 sq km/73,000 sq mi. It includes the provinces of Sulawesi Selatan, population (2000 est) 8,059,627, capital Ujung Pandang; Sulawesi Tengah, population (2000 est) 2,218,435, capital Palu; Sulawesi Tenggara, population (2000 est), capital Kendari; and Sulawesi Utara, population (2000 est) 2,847,142, capital Manado. A mountainous and forested island, it lies off the coast of eastern Borneo. Maize, rice, yams, copra, coffee, and tobacco are the leading crops, and minerals worked include sulphur, iron, nickel, gold, and diamonds.

Suleiman (or **Solyman**) (c. 1494–1566) Ottoman sultan from 1520, known as **the Magnificent** and **the Lawgiver**. Under his rule, the Ottoman Empire flourished and reached its largest extent. He made conquests in the Balkans, the Mediterranean, Persia, and North Africa, but was defeated at Vienna in 1529 and Valletta (on Malta) in 1565. He was a patron of the arts, a poet, and an administrator.

Sulla, Lucius Cornelius (138 BC–78 BC) Roman general and dictator. He was elected consul in 88 BC after defeating the Samnites several times during the Italian Social War. In the same year, Marius tried to deprive him of the command against the king of Pontus, Mithridates (VI) Eupator (120–60 BC). Sulla's unprecedented response was to march on Rome, executing or putting to flight his rivals. His campaign against Mithridates ended successfully in 85 BC, and Sulla returned to Italy in 83 where his opponents had raised armies against him. Sulla defeated them in 82 and massacred all his opponents. After holding supreme power as dictator and carrying out a series of political reforms, he retired to private life in 80 BC.

Sullivan, Arthur Seymour (1842–1900) English composer. He wrote operettas in collaboration with William Gilbert, including *HMS Pinafore* (1878), *The Pirates of Penzance* (1879), and *The Mikado* (1885). Their partnership broke down in 1896. Sullivan also composed serious instrumental, choral, and operatic works – for example, the opera *Ivanhoe* (1890) – which he valued more highly than the operettas.

sulphate SO_4^{2-}, salt or ester derived from sulphuric acid. Most sulphates are water soluble (the chief exceptions are lead, calcium, strontium, and barium sulphates) and require a very high temperature to decompose them.

sulphide compound of sulphur and another element in which sulphur is the more electronegative element. Sulphides occur in many minerals. Some of the more volatile sulphides have extremely unpleasant odours (hydrogen sulphide smells of bad eggs).

sulphite SO_3^{2-}, salt or ester derived from sulphurous acid.

sulphonamide any of a group of compounds containing the chemical group sulphonamide (SO_2NH_2) or its derivatives, which were, and still are in some cases, used to treat bacterial diseases. Sulphadiazine ($C_{10}H_{10}N_4O_2S$) is an example.

sulphur chemical symbol S, brittle, pale-yellow, non-metallic element, atomic number 16, relative atomic mass 32.064. It occurs in three allotropic forms: two crystalline (called rhombic and monoclinic, following the arrangements of the atoms within the crystals) and one amorphous. It burns in air with a blue flame and a stifling odour. Insoluble in water but soluble in carbon disulphide, it is a good electrical insulator. Sulphur is widely used in the manufacture of sulphuric acid (used to treat phosphate rock to make fertilizers) and in making paper, matches, gunpowder and fireworks, in vulcanizing rubber, and in medicines and insecticides.

sulphur dioxide SO_2, pungent gas produced by burning sulphur or sulphide ores in air or oxygen. It is widely used for making sulphuric acid and for disinfecting food vessels and equipment for bleaching paper, and as a preservative in some food products. It occurs in industrial flue gases and is a major cause of *acid rain.

sulphuric acid *or* **oil of vitriol** H_2SO_4, dense, viscous, colourless liquid that is extremely corrosive. It gives out heat when added to water and can cause severe burns. Sulphuric acid is used extensively in the chemical industry, in the refining of petrol, and in the manufacture of fertilizers, detergents, explosives, and dyes. It forms the acid component of car batteries.

sulphurous acid H_2SO_3, solution of sulphur dioxide (SO_2) in water. It is a weak acid.

Sulu Archipelago group of about 870 islands off southwest Mindanao in the Philippines, between the Sulawesi and Sulu seas; area 2,700 sq km/1,042 sq mi; population (1990 est) 698,200. The capital is Jolo, on the island (the largest) of the same name. Until 1940 the islands were an autonomous sultanate.

Sumatra *or* **Sumatera** second-largest island of Indonesia, one of the Sunda Islands; area 473,600 sq km/182,800 sq mi, length 1,760 km/1,094 mi, width 400 km/250 mi; population (2000 est) 39,460,100. About a third of the area, mainly in the southeast, is permanently waterlogged. The highest part is in the west where, at Gunung Kerinci, the Bukit Barisan volcanic mountain range reaches a height of 3,805 m/12,483 ft. East of the range is a wide plain; both are heavily forested. Products include rubber, rice, tobacco, tea, timber, tin, petroleum, bauxite, gold, natural gas, coffee, and pepper.

Sumerian civilization the world's earliest civilization, dating from about 3500 BC and located at the confluence of the Tigris and Euphrates rivers in lower Mesopotamia (present-day Iraq). It was a city-state with priests as secular rulers. After 2300 BC, Sumer declined.

summer time practice introduced in the UK in 1916 whereby legal time from spring to autumn is an hour in advance of Greenwich Mean Time. Continental Europe 'puts the clock back' a month earlier than the UK in autumn. British summer time was permanently in force February 1940–October 1945 and February 1968–October 1971. Double summer time (2 hours in advance) was in force during the summers of 1941–45 and 1947. In North America the practice is known as **daylight saving time**.

sumo wrestling national sport of Japan. Fighters of larger than average size (rarely less than 130 kg/21 st or 285 lb) try to push, pull, or throw each other out of a circular ring.

Sun *star at the centre of our Solar System. It is about 5 billion years old, with a predicted lifetime of 10 billion years; its diameter is 1.4 million km/865,000 mi; its temperature at the surface (the photosphere) is about 5,800 K/5,530 °C/9,986 °F, and at the centre 15 million K/about 15 million °C/about 27 million °F. It is composed of about 70% hydrogen and 30% helium, with other elements making up less than 1%. The Sun's energy is generated by nuclear fusion reactions that turn hydrogen into helium, producing large amounts of light and heat that sustain life on Earth.

Sunda Islands islands west of Maluku (Moluccas), in the Malay Archipelago, the greater number belonging to Indonesia. They are so named because they lie largely on the Indonesian extension of the Sunda continental shelf. The **Greater Sundas** include Borneo, Java (including the small island of Madura), Sumatra, Sulawesi, and Belitung. The **Lesser Sundas** (Indonesian *Nusa Tenggara*) are all Indonesian and include Bali, Lombok, Flores, Sumba, Sumbawa, and Timor.

Sundanese the second-largest ethnic group in the Republic of Indonesia. There are more than 20 million speakers of Sundanese, a member of the western branch of the Austronesian family. Like their neighbours, the Javanese, the Sundanese are predominantly Muslim. They are known for their performing arts, especially *jaipongan* dance traditions, and distinctive batik fabrics.

Sunderland city and port in Tyne and Wear, northeast England, at the mouth of the River Wear; population (1991) 183,200. A former coalmining and shipbuilding centre, Sunderland now has electronics, engineering, and brewing industries, and manufactures glass, pottery, chemicals, paper, furniture, and cars. It also has some tourism.

sundew any of a group of insectivorous plants found growing in bogs; sticky hairs on the leaves catch and digest insects that land on them. (Genus *Drosera*, family Droseraceae.)

sunfish marine fish *Mola mola* with a disc-shaped body 3 m/10 ft long found in all temperate and tropical oceans. The term also applies to fish of the North American freshwater Centrarchidae family, which have compressed, almost circular bodies, up to 80 cm/30 in long, and are nestbuilders and avid predators.

sunflower tall, thick-stemmed plant with a large, single, yellow-petalled flower, belonging to the daisy family. The common or giant sunflower (*H. annuus*), probably native to Mexico, can grow up to 4.5 m/15 ft high. It is commercially cultivated in central Europe, the USA, Russia, Ukraine, and Australia for the oil-bearing seeds that ripen in the central disc of the flower head; sunflower oil is widely used as a cooking oil and in margarine. (Genus *Helianthus*, family Compositae.)

Sunni member of the larger of the two main sects of *Islam, with about 680 million adherents. Sunni Muslims believe that the caliph *Abu Bakr, adviser to the prophet Muhammad, was his true successor. They believe that guidance on belief and life should come from the *Koran (or Quran or Qur'an), the Sunna, the *Hadith, and the *Shari'a, not from a human authority or spiritual leader. *Imams in Sunni Islam are educated lay teachers of the faith and prayer leaders.

sunspot dark patch on the surface of the Sun, actually an area of cooler gas, thought to be caused by strong magnetic fields that block the outward flow of heat to

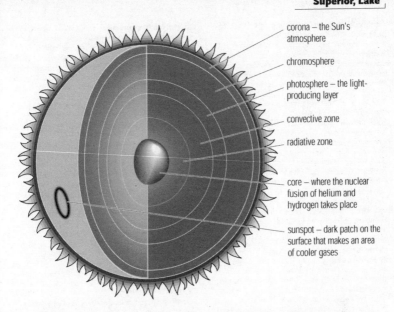

corona – the Sun's atmosphere

chromosphere

photosphere – the light-producing layer

convective zone

radiative zone

core – where the nuclear fusion of helium and hydrogen takes place

sunspot – dark patch on the surface that makes an area of cooler gases

Sun The structure of the Sun. Nuclear reactions at the core release vast amounts of energy in the form of light and heat that radiate out to the photosphere and corona. Surges of glowing gas rise as prominences from the surface of the Sun and cooler areas, known as sunspots, appear as dark patches on the star's surface.

the Sun's surface. Sunspots consist of a dark central **umbra**, about 4,000 K (3,700 °C/6,700 °F), and a lighter surrounding **penumbra**, about 5,500 K (5,200 °C/9,400 °F). They last from several days to over a month, ranging in size from 2,000 km/1,250 mi to groups stretching for over 100,000 km/62,000 mi.

Sun Yat-sen Wade-Giles transliteration of *Sun Zhong Shan.

Sun Zhong Shan (*or* **Sun Yat-sen**) (**1867–1925**) Chinese revolutionary leader. He founded the *Hsin Chung Hui* ('New China Party') in 1894, one of the political groups that merged to form the Kuomintang (*Guomindang, nationalist party) in 1912 after the overthrow of the Manchu Empire. He was elected provisional president of the Republic of China in December 1911 and played a vital part in deposing the emperor, who abdicated in February 1912. He was president of a breakaway government from 1921.

supercomputer fastest, most powerful type of computer, with speeds measured in gigaflops (billions of floating-point calculations per second) or, at the high end, in teraflops (trillions of floating-point calculations per second).

superconductivity increase in electrical conductivity at low temperatures. The resistance of some metals and metallic compounds decreases uniformly with decreasing temperature until at a critical temperature (the superconducting point), within a few degrees of absolute zero (0 K/–273.15 °C/–459.67 °F), the resistance suddenly falls to zero. The phenomenon was discovered by Dutch scientist Heike Kamerlingh Onnes in 1911.

supercooling cooling of a liquid below its freezing point without freezing taking place; or the cooling of a *saturated solution without crystallization taking place, to form a supersaturated solution. In both cases supercooling is possible because of the lack of solid particles around which crystals can form. Crystallization rapidly follows the introduction of a small crystal (seed) or agitation of the supercooled solution.

superego in Freudian psychology, the element of the human mind concerned with the ideal, responsible for ethics and self-imposed standards of behaviour. It is characterized as a form of conscience, restraining the *ego, and responsible for feelings of guilt when the moral code is broken.

superfluid fluid that flows without viscosity or friction and has a very high thermal conductivity. Liquid helium at temperatures below 2 K (–271 °C/–456 °F) is a superfluid: it shows unexpected behaviour. For instance, it flows uphill in apparent defiance of gravity and, if placed in a container, will flow up the sides and escape.

supergiant largest and most luminous type of star known, with a diameter of up to 1,000 times that of the Sun and an apparent magnitude of between 0.4 and 1.3. Supergiants are likely to become *supernovae.

Superior, Lake largest and deepest of the *Great Lakes and the largest freshwater lake in the world; area 82,100 sq km/31,700 sq mi. Extending east–west for 616 km/385 mi, it reaches a maximum width of 260 km/163 mi and depth of 407 m/1,335 ft. The lake is bordered by the

Canadian province of Ontario and the US states of Minnesota, Wisconsin, and Michigan. As the westernmost of the Great Lakes, Superior is at the western end of the St Lawrence Seaway.

supernova explosive death of a star, which temporarily attains a brightness of 100 million Suns or more, so that it can shine as brilliantly as a small galaxy for a few days or weeks. Very approximately, it is thought that a supernova explodes in a large galaxy about once every 100 years. Many supernovae – astronomers estimate some 50% – remain undetected because of obscuring by interstellar dust.

superpower state that through disproportionate military or economic strength can dominate smaller nations. The term was used to describe the USA and the USSR from the end of World War II, when they emerged as significantly stronger than all other countries. With the collapse of the Soviet Union in 1991, the USA is, arguably, now the world's sole superpower.

supersonic speed speed greater than that at which sound travels, measured in *Mach numbers. In dry air at 0 °C/32 °F, sound travels at about 1,170 kph/727 mph, but decreases its speed with altitude until, at 12,000 m/ 39,000 ft, it is only 1,060 kph/658 mph.

superstring theory in physics and cosmology, a mathematical theory developed in the 1980s to explain the properties of *elementary particles and the forces between them (in particular, gravity and the nuclear forces) in a way that combines *relativity and *quantum theory. In string theory, the fundamental objects in the universe are not pointlike particles but extremely small stringlike objects. These objects exist in a universe of ten dimensions, but since the earliest moments of the Big Bang six of these have been compacted or 'rolled up', so that now, only three space dimensions and one dimension of time are discernible.

supersymmetry in physics, a theory that relates the two classes of elementary particle, the *fermions and the *bosons. According to supersymmetry, each fermion particle has a boson partner particle, and vice versa. It has not been possible to marry up all the known fermions with the known bosons, and so the theory postulates the existence of other, as yet undiscovered fermions, such as the photinos (partners of the photons), gluinos (partners of the gluons), and gravitinos (partners of the gravitons). Using these ideas, it has become possible to develop a theory of gravity – called **supergravity** – that extends Einstein's work and considers the gravitational, nuclear, and electromagnetic forces to be manifestations of an underlying superforce. Supersymmetry has been incorporated into the *superstring theory, and appears to be a crucial ingredient in the 'theory of everything' sought by scientists.

supply and demand one of the fundamental approaches to economics, which examines and compares the supply of a good with its demand (usually in the form of a graph of supply and demand curves plotted against price). For a typical good, the supply curve is upward-sloping (the higher the price, the more the manufacturer is willing to sell), while the demand curve is downward-sloping (the cheaper the good, the more demand there is for it). The point where the curves intersect is the equilibrium price at which supply equals demand.

supply-side economics school of economic thought advocating government policies that allow market forces to operate freely, such as privatization, cuts in public spending and income tax, reductions in trade-union power, and cuts in the ratio of unemployment benefits to wages. Supply-side economics developed as part of the monetarist (see *monetarism) critique of Keynesian economics.

Supremacy, Acts of two UK acts of Parliament 1534 and 1559, which established Henry VIII and Elizabeth I respectively as head of the English church in place of the pope.

Supreme Court highest US judicial tribunal, composed since 1869 of a chief justice and eight associate justices. Appointments are made for life by the president, with the advice and consent of the Senate, and justices can be removed only by impeachment. Supreme Court decisions set precedents that lower courts are expected to follow.

surface tension property that causes the surface of a liquid to behave as if it were covered with a weak elastic skin; this is why a needle can float on water. It is caused by the exposed surface's tendency to contract to the smallest possible area because of cohesive forces between *molecules at the surface. Allied phenomena include the formation of droplets, the concave profile of a meniscus, and the capillary action by which water soaks into a sponge.

surfing sport of riding on the crest of large waves while standing on a narrow, keeled surfboard, usually of light synthetic material such as fibreglass, about 1.8 m/6 ft long (or about 2.4–7 m/8–9 ft known as the Malibu), as first developed in Hawaii and Australia. Windsurfing is a recent development.

surgeon fish any fish of the tropical marine family Acanthuridae. It has a flat body up to 50 cm/20 in long, is brightly coloured, and has a movable spine on each side of the tail that can be used as a weapon.

surgery branch of medicine concerned with the treatment of disease, abnormality, or injury by operation. Traditionally it has been performed by means of cutting instruments, but today a number of technologies are used to treat or remove lesions, including ultrasonic waves and laser surgery.

surgical spirit *ethanol to which has been added a small amount of methanol to render it unfit to drink. It is used to sterilize surfaces and to cleanse skin abrasions and sores.

Suriname

formerly **Dutch Guiana** (1954–75)

National name: *Republiek Suriname/ Republic of Suriname*

Area: 163,820 sq km/63,250 sq mi

Capital: Paramaribo

Major towns/cities: Nieuw Nickerie, Moengo, Brokopondo, Nieuw Amsterdam, Albina, Groningen

Physical features: hilly and forested, with flat and narrow coastal plain; Suriname River

Head of state: Ronald Venetiaan from 2000

Head of government: Jules Ajodhia from 2000

Political system: emergent democracy

Political executive: limited presidency

Political parties: New Front (NF), alliance of four left-of-centre parties: Party for National Unity and Solidarity (KTPI), Suriname National Party (NPS),

after opposition leaders, charged with plotting a coup, were executed.

1985: Ban on political activities lifted.

1989: Bouterse rejected a peace accord reached by President Shankar with guerrilla insurgents, the Bush Negro (descendants of escaped slaves) maroons, and vowed to continue fighting.

1991: A New Front opposition alliance won an assembly majority.

1992: A peace accord was reached with guerrilla groups.

2000: Ronald Venetiaan was chosen as president in August. He had previously been president 1991–96. Jules Ajodhia was elected prime minister.

surrealism movement in art, literature, and film that developed out of *Dada around 1922. Led by André *Breton, who produced the *Surrealist Manifesto* (1924), the surrealists were inspired by the thoughts and visions of the subconscious mind. They explored varied styles and techniques, and the movement became the dominant force in Western art between World Wars I and II.

Surrey county of southern England. **area:** 1,660 sq km/641 sq mi **towns:** Kingston upon Thames (administrative headquarters), Farnham, Guildford, Leatherhead, Reigate, Woking, Epsom, Dorking **physical:** rivers Mole, Thames, and Wey; Box Hill (183 m/600 ft), Gibbet Hill (277 m/909 ft), and Leith Hill (299 m/981 ft, 5 km/3 mi south of Dorking, the highest hill in southeast England); North Downs **features:** Kew Palace and Royal Botanic Gardens, Kew; Yehudi Menuhin School (one of four specialist music schools in England) **population:** (1996) 1,047,100.

surrogacy practice whereby a woman is sought, and usually paid, to bear a child for an infertile couple or a single parent.

surveying accurate measuring of the Earth's crust, or of land features or buildings. It is used to establish boundaries, and to evaluate the topography for engineering work. The measurements used are both linear and angular, and geometry and trigonometry are applied in the calculations.

suspension mixture consisting of small solid particles dispersed in a liquid or gas, which will settle on standing. An example is milk of magnesia, which is a suspension of magnesium hydroxide in water.

Sussex former county of England, on the south coast, now divided into *East Sussex and *West Sussex.

Sutherland, Graham Vivian (1903–1980) English painter, graphic artist, and designer. He was active mainly in France from the 1940s. A leading figure of the neo-Romantic movement (1935–55), which revived the spirit of 19th-century Romanticism in a more modern idiom, he executed portraits, landscapes, and religious subjects, often using a semi-abstract style. In the late 1940s he turned increasingly to portraiture. His portrait of Winston Churchill (1954) was disliked by its subject and eventually burned on the instructions of Lady Churchill (studies survive). He was awarded the OM in 1960.

suttee Hindu custom whereby a widow committed suicide by joining her husband's funeral pyre, often under public and family pressure. Banned in the 17th century by the Mogul emperors, the custom continued even after it was made illegal under British rule in 1829. There continue to be sporadic revivals.

Progressive Reform Party (VHP), Suriname Labour Party (SPA); National Democratic Party (NDP), left of centre; Democratic Alternative 1991 (DA '91), alliance of three left-of-centre parties

Currency: Suriname guilder

GNI per capita (PPP): (US$) 3,420 (2002 est)

Exports: alumina, aluminium, shrimps, bananas, plantains, rice, wood and wood products. Principal market: USA 30.9% (2001)

Population: 436,000 (2003 est)

Language: Dutch (official), Spanish, Sranan (Creole), English, Hindi, Javanese, Chinese, various tribal languages

Religion: Christian 47%, Hindu 28%, Muslim 20%

Life expectancy: 69 (men); 74 (women) (2000–05)

Chronology

AD 1593: Visited and claimed by Spanish explorers; the name Suriname derived from the country's earliest inhabitants, the Surinen, who were driven out by other Amerindians in the 16th century.

1602: Dutch settlements established.

1651: British colony founded by settlers sent from Barbados.

1667: Became a Dutch colony, received in exchange for New Amsterdam (New York) by Treaty of Breda.

1682: Coffee and sugar cane plantations introduced, worked by imported African slaves.

1795–1802 and 1804–16: Under British rule.

1863: Slavery abolished and indentured labourers brought in from China, India, and Java.

1915: Bauxite discovered and gradually became main export.

1954: Achieved internal self-government as Dutch Guiana.

1958–69: Politics dominated by Johan Pengel, charismatic leader of the mainly Creole Suriname National Party (NPS).

1975: Independence achieved, with Dr Johan Ferrier as president and Henck Arron (NPS) as prime minister; 40% of population emigrated to the Netherlands.

1980: Arron's government overthrown in an army coup. The army replaced Ferrier with Dr Chin A Sen.

1982: The army, led by Lt Col Desi Bouterse, seized power, setting up a Revolutionary People's Front; economic aid from the Netherlands and US was cut off

Sutton Hoo archaeological site in Suffolk, England, where in 1939 a Saxon ship burial was excavated. It may be the funeral monument of Raedwald, King of the East Angles, who died about 624 or 625. The jewellery, armour, and weapons discovered were placed in the British Museum, London.

Suu Kyi, Aung San (1945–) Myanmar (Burmese) politician and human-rights campaigner, leader of the National League for Democracy (NLD), the main opposition to the military junta. She is the daughter of former Burmese premier *Aung San, who fought for the country's independence. Despite Suu Kyi being placed under house arrest in 1989, the NLD won the 1990 elections, although the junta refused to surrender power. She was awarded the Nobel Prize for Peace in 1991 in recognition of her 'nonviolent struggle for democracy and human rights' in Myanmar. Although officially released from house arrest in 1995, she was banned from resuming any leadership post within the NLD by the junta.

Suzman, Helen Gavronsky (1917–) South African politician and human-rights activist. A university lecturer concerned about the inhumanity of the *apartheid system, she joined the white opposition to the ruling National Party and became a strong advocate of racial equality, respected by black communities inside and outside South Africa. In 1978 she received the United Nations Human Rights Award. She retired from active politics in 1989.

Svalbard Norwegian archipelago in the Arctic Ocean; population (1995) 2,900 (41% being Norwegian). The main island is *Spitsbergen, which includes the largest town, Longyearbyen; other islands include Edgeøya, Barentsøya, Svenskøya, Nordaustlandet, Prins Karls Foreland, Wilhelmøya, Lågøya, Storøya, Danskøya, and Sørkappøya. The other main centres of population are the Russian mining settlements of Barentsburg and Grumantbyen. The total land area is 62,000 sq km/ 23,938 sq mi.

Svengali person who moulds another into a performer and masterminds his or her career. The original Svengali was a character in the novel *Trilby* (1894) by George Du Maurier.

Swabia German Schwaben, historic region of southwestern Germany, an independent duchy in the Middle Ages. It includes Augsburg and Ulm and forms part of the *Länder* (states) of Baden-Württemberg, Bavaria, and Hessen.

Swahili or **Kiswahili** (Arabic *sawahil* 'language of the coast') language belonging to the Bantu branch of the Niger-Congo family, widely used in east and central Africa. Swahili originated on the East African coast as a *lingua franca* used among traders, and contains many Arabic loan words. It is an official language in Kenya and Tanzania.

swallow any bird of the family Hirundinidae of small, insect-eating birds in the order Passeriformes, with long, narrow wings, and deeply forked tails. Swallows feed while flying, capturing winged insects in the mouth, which is lined with bristles made viscid (sticky) by a salivary secretion.

swamp region of low-lying land that is permanently saturated with water and usually overgrown with vegetation; for example, the everglades of Florida, USA. A swamp often occurs where a lake has filled up with

sediment and plant material. The flat surface so formed means that run-off is slow, and the water table is always close to the surface. The high humus content of swamp soil means that good agricultural soil can be obtained by draining.

Swan, Joseph Wilson (1828–1914) English physicist and chemist who produced the incandescent-filament electric lamp and invented bromide paper for use in developing photographs. He was knighted in 1904.

Swansea unitary authority in south Wales, created in 1996 from part of the former county of West Glamorgan. **area:** 377 sq km/146 sq mi **towns:** Swansea (administrative headquarters) **physical:** River Tawe; highest point Penlle'r Castle (374 m/1,215 ft) **features:** Gower Peninsula (an area of outstanding natural beauty), with Mumbles village and beach. University of Wales, Swansea, at Singleton Park west of Swansea City; birthplace of Dylan Thomas **population:** (2001 est) 223,300.

SWAPO acronym for South West Africa People's Organization, organization formed 1959 in South West Africa (now Namibia) to oppose South African rule. SWAPO guerrillas, led by Sam Nujoma, began attacking with support from Angola. In 1966 SWAPO was recognized by the United Nations as the legitimate government of Namibia, and won the first independent election in 1989.

swastika (Sanskrit *svasti* 'prosperity') cross in which the bars are extended at right angles in the same clockwise or anticlockwise direction. Its origin is uncertain, but it appears frequently as an ancient good luck and religious symbol in both the Old World and the New. In Hinduism it is a symbol of good luck and goodness. In this religion it originates from a symbol for the sun, and takes the form of a cross in which the bars are extended at right angles, usually pointing in a clockwise direction. A swastika with clockwise bars was adopted as the emblem of the Nazi Party and incorporated into the German national flag 1935–45.

Swazi member of the majority Bantu group of people in Swaziland. The Swazi are primarily engaged in cultivating and raising livestock, but many work in industries in South Africa. The Swazi language belongs to the Bantu branch of the Niger-Congo family.

Swazi kingdom South African kingdom, established by Sobhuza I (died 1839), and named after his successor Mswati (ruled 1840–68), who did much to unify the country.

Swaziland

National name: *Umbuso wakaNgwane/ Kingdom of Swaziland*
Area: 17,400 sq km/6,718 sq mi
Capital: Mbabane (administrative), Lobamba (legislative)
Major towns/cities: Manzini, Big Bend, Mhlume, Havelock Mine, Nhlangano
Physical features: central valley; mountains in west (Highveld); plateau in east (Lowveld and Lubombo plateau)
Head of state: King Mswati III from 1986
Head of government: Themba Dlamini from 1996
Political system: absolutist
Political executive: absolute
Political parties: Imbokodvo National Movement (INM), nationalist monarchist; Swaziland United Front (SUF), left of centre; Swaziland Progressive Party (SPP),

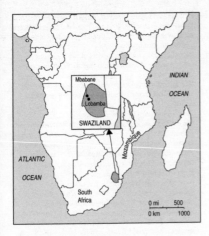

1983: Queen Dzeliwe ousted by a younger wife, Queen Ntombi, as real power passed to the prime minister, Prince Bhekimpi Dlamini.

1986: The crown prince was formally invested as King Mswati III.

1990: Following demands for greater freedom, King Mswati called for the creation of an *indaba* (popular parliament).

1992: King Mswati approved further democratic constitutional amendments.

1993: Direct elections of *tinkhundla* candidates were held for the first time.

1996: Barnabas Sibusiso Dlamini was appointed prime minister.

2000: There was further agitation for democratic reform. When the leader of the opposition party Mario Masuku called for an end to the 27-year-old state of emergency, he was arrested for allegedly making seditious comments.

sweat gland *gland within the skin of mammals that produces surface perspiration. In primates, sweat glands are distributed over the whole body, but in most other mammals they are more localized; for example, in cats and dogs they are restricted to the feet and around the face.

swede annual or biennial plant widely cultivated for its edible root, which is purple, white, or yellow. It is similar in taste to the turnip but is of greater food value, firmer fleshed, and can be stored for a longer time. (*Brassica napus*, family Cruciferae.)

Sweden

National name: *Konungariket Sverige/Kingdom of Sweden*

left of centre; People's United Democratic Movement, left of centre

Currency: lilangeni

GNI per capita (PPP): (US$) 4,530 (2002 est)

Exports: sugar, wood pulp, cotton yarn, canned fruits, asbestos, coal, diamonds, gold. Principal market: South Africa 59.7% (2000)

Population: 1,077,000 (2003 est)

Language: Swazi, English (both official)

Religion: about 60% Christian, animist

Life expectancy: 33 (men); 35 (women) (2000–05)

Chronology

Late 16th century: King Ngwane II crossed Lubombo mountains from the east and settled in southeast Swaziland; his successors established a strong centralized Swazi kingdom, dominating the long-settled Nguni and Sothi peoples.

mid-19th century: Swazi nation was ruled by the warrior King Mswati who, at the height of his power, controlled an area three times the size of the present-day state.

1882: Gold was discovered in the northwest, attracting European fortune hunters, who coerced Swazi rulers into granting land concessions.

1894: Came under joint rule of Britain and the Boer republic of Transvaal.

1903: Following the South African War, Swaziland became a special British protectorate, or High Commission territory, against South Africa's wishes.

1922: King Sobhuza II succeeded to the Swazi throne.

1968: Independence achieved within the Commonwealth, as the Kingdom of Swaziland, with King (or Ngwenyama) Sobhuza II as head of state.

1973: The king suspended the constitution, banned political activity, and assumed absolute powers after the opposition deputies had been elected to parliament.

1977: The king announced substitution of traditional tribal communities (*tinkhundla*) for the parliamentary system, arguing it was more suited to Swazi values.

1982: King Sobhuza died; his place was taken by one of his wives, Queen Dzeliwe, until his son, Prince Makhosetive, was old enough to become king.

Area: 450,000 sq km/173,745 sq mi

Capital: Stockholm

Major towns/cities: Göteborg, Malmö, Uppsala, Norrköping, Västerås, Linköping, Orebro, Helsingborg

Major ports: Helsingborg, Malmö, Göteborg, Stockholm

Physical features: mountains in west; plains in south; thickly forested; more than 20,000 islands off the Stockholm coast; lakes, including Vänern, Vättern, Mälaren, and Hjälmaren

Head of state: King Carl XVI Gustaf from 1973

Head of government: Göran Persson from 1996

Political system: liberal democracy

Political executive: parliamentary

Political parties: Christian Democratic Community Party (KdS), Christian, centrist; Left Party (Vp), European, Marxist; Social Democratic Party (SAP), moderate, left of centre; Moderate Party (M), right of centre; Liberal Party (Fp), left of centre; Centre Party (C), centrist; Ecology Party (MpG), ecological; New Democracy (NG), right wing, populist

Currency: Swedish krona

GNI per capita (PPP): (US$) 25,080 (2002 est)

Exports: machinery and transport equipment, forestry products (wood, pulp, and paper), motor vehicles, power-generating non-electrical machinery, chemicals, iron and steel. Principal market: Germany 10.6% (2001)

Population: 8,876,000 (2003 est)

Language: Swedish (official), Finnish, Saami (Lapp)

Religion: Evangelical Lutheran, Church of Sweden (established national church) 90%; Muslim, Jewish

Life expectancy: 78 (men); 83 (women) (2000–05)

Chronology

8th century: Kingdom of the Svear, based near Uppsala, extended its rule across much of southern Sweden.

9th–11th centuries: Swedish Vikings raided and settled along the rivers of Russia.

c. 1000: Olaf Skötkonung, king of the Svear, adopted Christianity and united much of Sweden (except south and west coasts, which remained Danish until 17th century).

11th–13th centuries: Sweden existed as isolated kingdom under the Stenkil, Sverker, and Folkung dynasties; series of crusades incorporated Finland.

1397: Union of Kalmar: Sweden, Denmark, and Norway united under a single monarch; Sweden effectively ruled by succession of regents.

1448: Breach with Denmark: Sweden alone elected Charles VIII as king.

1523: Gustavus Vasa, leader of insurgents, became king of a fully independent Sweden.

1527: Swedish Reformation: Gustavus confiscated Church property and encouraged Lutherans.

1544: Swedish crown became hereditary in House of Vasa.

1592–1604: Sigismund Vasa, a Catholic, was king of both Sweden and Poland until ousted from Swedish throne by his Lutheran uncle Charles IX.

17th century: Sweden, a great military power under Gustavus Adolphus 1611–32, Charles X 1654–60, and Charles XI 1660–97, fought lengthy wars with Denmark, Russia, Poland, and Holy Roman Empire.

1720: Limited monarchy established; political power passed to *Riksdag* (parliament) dominated by nobles.

1721: Great Northern War ended with Sweden losing nearly all its conquests of the previous century.

1741–43: Sweden defeated in disastrous war with Russia; further conflict 1788–90.

1771–92: Gustavus III increased royal power and introduced wide-ranging reforms.

1809: Russian invaders annexed Finland; Swedish nobles staged coup and restored powers of *Riksdag*.

1810: Napoleonic marshal, Jean-Baptiste Bernadotte, elected crown prince of Sweden, as Charles XIII had no heir.

1812: Bernadotte allied Sweden with Russia against France.

1814: Treaty of Kiel: Sweden obtained Norway from Denmark.

1818–44: Bernadotte reigned in Sweden as Charles XIV John.

1846: Free enterprise established by abolition of trade guilds and monopolies.

1866: Series of liberal reforms culminated in new two-chambered *Riksdag* dominated by bureaucrats and farmers.

late 19th century: Development of large-scale forestry and iron-ore industry; neutrality adopted in foreign affairs.

1905: Union with Norway dissolved.

1907: Adoption of proportional representation and universal suffrage.

1920s: Economic boom transformed Sweden from an agricultural to an industrial economy.

1932: Social Democrat government of Per Halbin Hansson introduced radical public-works programme to combat trade slump.

1940–43: Under duress, neutral Sweden permitted limited transit of German forces through its territory.

1946–69: Social Democrat government of Tage Erlander developed comprehensive welfare state.

1959: Sweden joined European Free Trade Association.

1971: Constitution amended to create single-chamber *Riksdag*.

1975: Remaining constitutional powers of monarch removed.

1976–82: Centre–right coalition government under Prime Minister Thorbjörn Fälldin ended 44 years of Social Democrat dominance.

1991: The leader of the Moderate Party, Carl Bildt, headed up a coalition of the Moderate, Centre, Liberal, and Christian Democratic parties.

1995: Sweden became a member of the European Union.

1996: Göran Persson (SAP) became prime minister.

1998: The SAP were narrowly re-elected in a general election.

2000: Sweden was linked to Denmark by the Oresund bridge.

2002: Göran Persson gained a third term as prime minister.

2003: Voters rejected a proposal to adopt the European Union single currency, the euro, by 56% to 42% in a referendum, despite widespread support for the move among Sweden's political establishment and industrial sector.

Swedish language member of the Germanic branch of the Indo-European language family, spoken in Sweden and Finland and closely related to Danish and Norwegian.

sweet pea plant belonging to the *pea family.

sweet potato tropical American plant belonging to the morning-glory family; the white-orange tuberous root is used as a source of starch and alcohol and eaten as a vegetable. (*Ipomoea batatas*, family Convolvulaceae.)

sweet william biennial to perennial plant belonging to the pink family, native to southern Europe. It is grown for its fragrant red, white, and pink flowers. (*Dianthus barbatus*, family Caryophyllaceae.)

swift fast-flying, short-legged bird of the family Apodidae, order Apodiformes, of which there are about 75 species, found largely in the tropics. They are 9–23 cm/4–11 in long, with brown or grey plumage, long, pointed wings, and usually a forked tail. They are capable of flying at 110 kph/70 mph.

Swift, Jonathan (1667–1745) Irish satirist and
Anglican cleric,dean of St Patrick's Cathedral, Dublin.
His best-known work is *Gulliver's Travels* (1726),
an allegory (symbolic story with meaning beyond
its literal sense) describing travel to lands inhabited
by giants, miniature people, and intelligent horses.
His satirical talents are evident in the pamphlet
A Modest Proposal (1729), which he wrote in protest
of the on-going famine in Ireland; it suggested that
children of the poor should be eaten. His other works
include *The Tale of a Tub* (1704), attacking corruption
in religion and learning. His lucid prose style is simple
and controlled and he imparted his views with fierce
indignation and wit.

swim bladder thin-walled, air-filled sac found between
the gut and the spine in bony fishes. Air enters the
bladder from the gut or from surrounding capillaries
(see *capillary), and changes of air pressure within the
bladder maintain buoyancy whatever the water depth.

swimming self-propulsion of the body through water.
There are four strokes in competitive swimming:
freestyle, breaststroke, backstroke, and butterfly. Distances
of races vary between 50 and 1,500 metres. Olympic-
size pools are 50 m/55 yd long and have eight lanes.

swimming, synchronized aquatic sport that demands
artistry as opposed to speed. Competitors, either
individual (solo) or in pairs, perform rhythmic routines
to music. Points are awarded for interpretation and
style. It was introduced into the Olympic swimming
programme in 1984.

Swinburne, Algernon Charles (1837–1909)
English poet. He attracted attention with the choruses
of his Greek-style tragedy *Atalanta in Calydon* (1865),
but he and *Rossetti were attacked in 1871 as leaders
of 'the fleshly school of poetry', and the revolutionary
politics of *Songs before Sunrise* (1871) alienated others.
His verse is notable for its emotion and opulent
language.

Swindon unitary authority in southwest England,
created in 1997 from the former district council of
Thamesdown. **area:** 230 sq km/89 sq mi **towns and
cities:** Swindon (administrative headquarters);
villages of Stanton, Fitzwarren, Highworth
features: River Thames forms northern border of
authority; Barbury Castle, Iron Age hill fort on
Marlborough Downs; Great Western Railway Museum
and National Monuments Records Centre (Swindon)
population: (1996) 170,000.

Swiss cheese plant common name for *monstera,
a plant belonging to the arum family.

Switzerland

National name: *Schweizerische Eidgenossenschaft*
(German)/*Confédération Suisse* (French)/
Confederazione Svizzera (Italian)/*Confederaziun Svizra*
(Romansch)/*Swiss Confederation*

Area: 41,300 sq km/15,945 sq mi

Capital: Bern

Major towns/cities: Zürich, Geneva, Basel, Lausanne,
Lucerne, St Gallen, Winterthur

Major ports: river port Basel (on the Rhine)

Physical features: most mountainous country in Europe
(Alps and Jura mountains); highest peak Dufourspitze
4,634 m/15,203 ft in Apennines

Head of state and government: Samuel Schmid
from 2005

Government liberal democracy

Political executive: limited presidency

Political parties: Radical Democratic Party
(FDP/PRD), radical, left of centre; Social Democratic
Party (SP/PS), moderate, left of centre; Christian
Democratic People's Party (CVP/PDC), Christian,
moderate, centrist; Swiss People's Party (SVP/UDC),
left of centre; Liberal Party (LPS/PLS), federalist,
right of centre; Green Party (GPS/PES), ecological

Currency: Swiss franc

GNI per capita (PPP): (US$) 31,250 (2002 est)

Exports: pharmaceutical and chemical products,
machinery and equipment, foodstuffs, precision
instruments, clocks and watches, metal products.
Principal market: Germany 22.2% (2001)

Population: 7,169,000 (2003 est)

Language: German (65%), French (18%), Italian (10%),
Romansch (1%) (all official)

Religion: Roman Catholic 46%, Protestant 40%

Life expectancy: 76 (men); 82 (women) (2000–05)

Chronology

58 BC: Celtic Helvetii tribe submitted to Roman
authority after defeat by Julius Caesar.

4th century AD: Region overrun by Germanic tribes,
Burgundians, and Alemannians.

7th century: Formed part of Frankish kingdom and
embraced Christianity.

9th century: Included in Charlemagne's Holy Roman
Empire.

12th century: Many autonomous feudal holdings
developed as power of Holy Roman Empire declined.

13th century: Habsburgs became dominant as
overlords of eastern Switzerland.

1291: Cantons of Schwyz, Uri, and Lower Unterwalden
formed Everlasting League, a loose confederation to
resist Habsburg control.

1315: Battle of Morgarten: Swiss Confederation
defeated Habsburgs.

14th century: Lucerne, Zürich, Basel, and other
cantons joined Swiss Confederation, which became
independent of Habsburgs.

1523–29: Zürich, Bern, and Basel accepted Reformation
but rural cantons remained Roman Catholic.

1648: Treaty of Westphalia recognized Swiss independence from Holy Roman Empire.
1798: French invasion established Helvetic Republic, a puppet state with centralized government.
1803: Napoleon's Act of Mediation restored considerable autonomy to cantons.
1814: End of French domination; Switzerland reverted to loose confederation of sovereign cantons with a weak federal parliament.
1815: Great Powers recognized 'Perpetual Neutrality' of Switzerland.
1845: Seven Catholic cantons founded Sonderbund league to resist any strengthening of central government by Liberals.
1847: Federal troops defeated Sonderbund in brief civil war.
1848: New constitution introduced greater centralization; Bern chosen as capital.
1874: Powers of federal government increased; principle of referendum introduced.
late 19th century: Development of industry, railways, and tourism led to growing prosperity.
1920: League of Nations selected Geneva as its headquarters.
1960: Joined European Free Trade Association (EFTA).
1971: Women gained right to vote in federal elections.
1986: A proposal for membership of the United Nations (UN) was rejected in a referendum.
1992: Closer ties with the European Community (EC) were rejected in a national referendum.
2000: Adolf Ogi was elected president.
2001: Moritz Leuenberger replaced Ogi as president. A proposal for European Union (EU) membership was rejected in a national referendum.
2002: Switzerland became the 190th member of the United Nations (UN) after a public referendum. It maintained its traditional neutrality.
2003: Following the success of the far-right, nationalist Schweizerische Volkspartei (SVP; Swiss People's Party) in general elections, party leader Christoph Blocher was elected by parliament to the seven-member ruling cabinet.

swordfish marine bony fish *Xiphias gladius*, the only member of its family (Xiphiidae), characterized by a long swordlike beak protruding from the upper jaw. It may reach 4.5 m/15 ft in length and weigh 450 kg/1,000 lb.

sycamore deciduous tree native to Europe. The leaves are five-lobed, and the hanging clusters of flowers are followed by winged fruits. The timber is used for furniture making. (*Acer pseudoplatanus.*)

Sydney principal port of Australia and capital of the state of *New South Wales; population (1996) 3,276,500. Founded in 1788, Sydney is situated on Port Jackson inlet on the southeast coast of Australia, and is built around a number of bays and inlets that form an impressive natural harbour. Industries include financial services, oil refining, engineering, electronics, and the manufacture of scientific equipment, chemicals, clothing, and furniture. Notable architectural landmarks are the Harbour Bridge, the nearby Sydney Opera House, and Centre Point Tower. There are many parks, as well as coastal beaches ideal for surfing, such as Bondi and Manly. Sydney hosted the Olympic Games in the year 2000.

syllable unit of pronunciation within a word, or as a monosyllabic word, made by a vowel or a combination of vowels and consonants. For example, the word 'competition' contains four syllables: 'com/pe/ti/tion'.

syllogism set of philosophical statements devised by Aristotle in his work on logic. It establishes the conditions under which a valid conclusion follows or does not follow by deduction from given premises. The following is an example of a valid syllogism: 'All men are mortal, Socrates is a man, therefore Socrates is mortal.'

symbiosis any close relationship between two organisms of different species, and one where both partners benefit from the association. A well-known example is the pollination relationship between insects and flowers, where the insects feed on nectar and carry pollen from one flower to another. This is sometimes known as mutualism.

Symbolism in the arts, the use of symbols to concentrate or intensify meaning, making the work more subjective than objective. In the visual arts, symbols have been used in works throughout the ages to transmit a message or idea, for example, the religious symbolism of ancient *Egyptian art, *Gothic art, and Renaissance art. Symbolism also refers to the **Symbolist movement** in art and literature, which flourished between 1885 and 1910. Symbolist painters rejected *realism and *Impressionism. They felt that art should not simply depict, but should suggest ideas, moods, and psychological states through colour, line, and form. Their subjects were often mythological, mystical, or fantastic. Gustave Moreau was a leading Symbolist painter. Others included Pierre Puvis de Chavannes and Odilon *Redon in France, Arnold Böcklin in Switzerland, Edward *Burne-Jones in Britain, and Jan Theodoor Toorop in the Netherlands.

Symbolism late 19th-century movement in French poetry, which inspired a similar trend in French painting. The Symbolist poets used words for their symbolic rather than concrete meaning. Leading exponents were Paul Verlaine, Stéphane Mallarmé, and Arthur Rimbaud.

symmetry exact likeness in shape about a given line (axis), point, or plane. A figure has symmetry if one half can be rotated and/or reflected onto the other. (Symmetry preserves length, angle, but not necessarily orientation.) In a wider sense, symmetry exists if a change in the system leaves the essential features of the system unchanged; for example, reversing the sign of electric charges does not change the electrical behaviour of an arrangement of charges.

symphonic poem in music, a term originated by Franz *Liszt for his 13 one-movement orchestral works that interpret a story from literature or history, also used by many other composers. Richard Strauss preferred the term 'tone poem'.

symphony most important form of composition for the orchestra. It usually consists of four separate but closely related movements, although early works often have three. It developed from the smaller *sonata form, the Italian *overture, and the concerto grosso.

symptom any change or manifestation in the body suggestive of disease as perceived by the sufferer. Symptoms are subjective phenomena. In strict usage, **symptoms** are events or changes reported

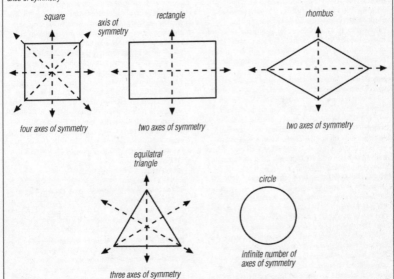

plane symmetry

plane of
symmetry

cuboid has three planes of symmetry

square-based pyramid has four planes of symmetry

sphere has infinite number of planes of symmetry

axes of symmetry

square

axis of
symmetry

rectangle

rhombus

four axes of symmetry

two axes of symmetry

two axes of symmetry

equilatral
triangle

circle

*infinite number of
axes of symmetry*

three axes of symmetry

symmetry

by the patient; **signs** are noted by the doctor during the patient's examination.

synaesthesia the experience of one sense as a result of the stimulation of a different sense; for example, an experience of colour may result from hearing a sound. Approximately 1 in 2,000 have the condition, and the majority are female. The commonest form of synaesthesia is experiencing words as colours. Some synaesthesics experience sounds as colours or shapes, and tastes as shapes. A 1995 UK study produced evidence that it is genetically controlled, possibly X-linked.

synagogue *or* **bet ha-knesset** *or* **bet ha-tefillah** *or* **bet midrash** Yiddish **shul**, (Hebrew 'gathering') in Judaism, a place of worship, study, and gathering; in the USA a synagogue is also called a temple by the non-Orthodox. As an institution it dates from the destruction of the *Temple in Jerusalem in AD 70, though it had been developing from the time of the *Babylonian exile as a substitute for the Temple. In antiquity it was a public meeting hall where the Torah was also read, but today it is used primarily for prayer and services. A service requires a quorum (minyan) of ten adult Jewish men.

synapse junction between two *nerve cells, or between a nerve cell and a muscle (a neuromuscular junction), across which a nerve impulse is transmitted. The two cells are separated by a narrow gap called the **synaptic cleft**. The gap is bridged by a chemical *neurotransmitter, released by the nerve impulse.

synchronized swimming see *swimming, synchronized.

syncopation in music, the rhythmic effect of moving the accent on to a beat that is normally unaccented.

syndicalism (French *syndicat* 'trade union') political movement in 19th-century Europe that rejected parliamentary activity in favour of direct action, culminating in a revolutionary general strike to secure worker ownership and control of industry. After 1918 syndicalism was absorbed in communism, although it continued to have an independent existence in Spain until the late 1930s.

synecdoche (Greek 'accepted together') figure of speech that uses either the part to represent the whole ('There were some *new faces* at the meeting', rather than *new people*), or the whole to stand for the part ('The West Indies beat England at cricket', using the country to stand for the national teams in question).

synergy in medicine, the 'cooperative' action of two or more drugs, muscles, or organs; applied especially to drugs whose combined action is more powerful than their simple effects added together.

Synge, J(ohn) M(illington) (1871–1909) Irish dramatist and leading figure in the Irish literary revival of the early 20th century, born in Rathfarnham, County Dublin. His six plays, which include *In the Shadow of the Glen* (1903), *Riders to the Sea* (1904), and *The Playboy of the Western World* (1907), reflect the speech patterns of the Aran Islands and western Ireland. *The Playboy of the Western World*, Synge's best-known work, caused violent disturbances at the Abbey Theatre, Dublin, when it was first performed.

Synge, Richard Laurence Millington (1914–1994) British biochemist who improved paper *chromatography (a means of separating mixtures)

to the point where individual amino acids could be identified. He shared the Nobel Prize for Chemistry in 1952 with his colleague Archer Martin for the development in 1944 of the technique known as partition chromatography.

synovial fluid viscous colourless fluid that bathes movable joints between the bones of vertebrates. It nourishes and lubricates the *cartilage at the end of each bone.

syntax structure of language; the ways in which words are ordered and combined to convey meaning. Syntax applies principally to *grammar, and a grammatically correct sentence is also syntactically correct, but syntax also involves the order of the words in the sentence.

synthesis in chemistry, the formation of a substance or compound from more elementary components. The synthesis of a drug can involve several stages from the initial material to the final product; the complexity of these stages is a major factor in the cost of production.

synthesizer electronic musical device for the simulation of vocal or instrumental *timbre (tone quality).

synthetic any material made from chemicals. Since the 1900s, more and more of the materials used in everyday life are synthetics, including plastics (polythene, polystyrene), *synthetic fibres (nylon, acrylics, polyesters), synthetic resins, and synthetic rubber. Most naturally occurring organic substances can now be made synthetically, especially pharmaceuticals.

synthetic fibre fibre made by chemical processes, unknown in nature. There are two kinds. One, a regenerated synthetic fibre, is made from natural materials that have been chemically processed in some way; *rayon, for example, is made by processing the cellulose in wood pulp. The other type is the true synthetic fibre, made entirely from chemicals. *Nylon was the original true synthetic fibre, made from chemicals obtained from petroleum (crude oil).

syphilis sexually transmitted disease caused by the spiral-shaped bacterium (spirochete) *Treponema pallidum*. Untreated, it runs its course in three stages over many years, often starting with a painless hard sore, or chancre, developing within a month on the area of infection (usually the genitals). The second stage, months later, is a rash with arthritis, hepatitis, and/or meningitis. The third stage, years later, leads eventually to paralysis, blindness, insanity, and death. The Wassermann test is a diagnostic blood test for syphilis.

Syria

National name: *al-Jumhuriyya al-Arabiyya as-Suriyya/ Syrian Arab Republic*

Area: 185,200 sq km/71,505 sq mi

Capital: Damascus

Major towns/cities: Aleppo, Homs, Latakia, Hama, Ar Raqqah, Deir-es-Zor

Major ports: Latakia

Physical features: mountains alternate with fertile plains and desert areas; Euphrates River

Head of state: Bashar al-Assad from 2000

Head of government: Naji al-Otari from 2003

Political system: nationalistic socialist

Political executive: unlimited presidency

Political parties: National Progressive Front (NPF), pro-Arab, socialist coalition, including the Communist Party of Syria, the Arab Socialist Party, the Arab Socialist

Unionist Party, the Syrian Arab Socialist Union Party, the Ba'ath Arab Socialist Party
Currency: Syrian pound
GNI per capita (PPP): (US$) 3,250 (2002 est)
Exports: crude petroleum, textiles, vegetables, fruit, raw cotton, natural phosphate. Principal market: France 20.6% (2001)
Population: 17,800,000 (2003 est)
Language: Arabic (89%) (official), Kurdish (6%), Armenian (3%), French, English, Aramaic, Circassian
Religion: Sunni Muslim 74%; other Islamic sects 16%, Christian 10%
Life expectancy: 71 (men); 73 (women) (2000–05)
Chronology
c. **1750 BC:** Syria became part of Babylonian Empire; during the next millennium it was successively conquered by Hittites, Assyrians, Chaldeans, and Persians.
333 BC: Alexander the Great of Macedonia conquered Persia and Syria.
301 BC: Seleucus I, one of the generals of Alexander the Great, founded the kingdom of Syria, which the Seleucid dynasty ruled for over 200 years.
64 BC: Syria became part of Roman Empire.
4th century AD: After division of Roman Empire, Syria came under Byzantine rule.
634: Arabs conquered most of Syria and introduced Islam.
661–750: Damascus was the capital of Muslim Empire.
1055: Seljuk Turks overran Syria.
1095–99: First Crusade established Latin states on Syrian coast.
13th century: Mameluke sultans of Egypt took control.
1516: Ottoman Turks conquered Syria.
1831: Egyptians led by Mehemet Ali drove out Turks.
1840: Turkish rule restored; Syria opened up to European trade.
late 19th century: French firms built ports, roads, and railways in Syria.
1916: Sykes-Picot Agreement: secret Anglo-French deal to partition Turkish Empire allotted Syria to France.
1918: British expelled Turks with help of Arab revolt.
1919: Syrian national congress called for independence under Emir Faisal and opposed transfer to French rule.

1920: Syria became League of Nations protectorate, administered by France.
1925: People's Party founded to campaign for independence and national unity; insurrection by Druze religious sect against French control.
1936: France promised independence within three years, but martial law imposed in 1939.
1941: British forces ousted Vichy French regime in Damascus and occupied Syria in conjunction with Free French.
1944: Syrian independence proclaimed but French military resisted transfer of power.
1946: Syria achieved effective independence when French forces withdrew.
1948–49: Arab–Israeli War: Syria joined unsuccessful invasion of newly independent Israel.
1958: Syria and Egypt merged to form United Arab Republic (UAR).
1959: USSR agreed to give financial and technical aid to Syria.
1961: Syria seceded from UAR.
1964: Ba'ath Socialist Party established military dictatorship.
1967: Six-Day War: Syria lost Golan Heights to Israel.
1970–71: Syria invaded Jordan in support of Palestinian guerrillas.
1971: Hafez al-Assad was elected president.
1973: Yom Kippur War: Syrian attack on Israel repulsed.
1976: Start of Syrian military intervention in Lebanese civil war.
1978: Syria opposed peace deal between Egypt and Israel.
1986: Britain broke off diplomatic relations, accusing Syria of involvement in international terrorism.
1990: Diplomatic links with Britain were restored.
1991: Syria contributed troops to a US-led coalition in the Gulf War against Iraq. A US Middle East peace plan was approved by Assad.
1994: Israel offered a partial withdrawal from the Golan Heights in return for peace, but Syria remained sceptical.
1995: A security framework agreement was made with Israel. 1,200 political prisoners, including members of the banned Muslim Brotherhood, were released to commemorate the 25th anniversary of President Assad's seizure of power.
1996: Syria re-deployed armed forces in southern Lebanon.
1997: Three border points with Iraq, closed since 1980, were re-opened.
1998: Relations with Israel deteriorated after Israeli forces seized land cultivated by Arab farmers in the Golan heights.
1999: Amnesty International charged Syrian authorities with human rights abuses and called for the release of over 300 political prisoners. Peace talks with Israel over Lebanon and the Golan Heights resumed after a break of three years. Relations with Iraq were normalized.
2000: Further peace talks were held with Israel, and Israel withdrew from the Golan Heights. President Assad appointed Muhammad Mustafa Miro as prime minister. President Assad died in June, and his son Bashar became president. The Iraq–Syria border was reopened.
2001: Syria signed a free-trade accord with Iraq.

2003: In parliamentary elections the ruling National Progressive Front retained its constitutionally mandated majority.

2004: Syria was accused of supporting insurgents in Iraq.

Syriac language ancient Semitic language, originally the Aramaic dialect spoken in and around Edessa (now in Turkey) and widely used in western Asia from about 700 BC to AD 700. From the 3rd to 7th centuries it was a Christian liturgical and literary language.

Système International d'Unités official French name for *SI units.

systemic in medicine, relating to or affecting the body as a whole. A systemic disease is one where the effects are present throughout the body, as opposed to local disease, such as *conjunctivitis, which is confined to one part.

systems analysis in computing, the investigation of a business activity or clerical procedure, with a view to deciding if and how it can be computerized. The analyst discusses the existing procedures with the people involved, observes the flow of data through the business, and draws up an outline specification of the required computer system. The next step is *systems design. A recent system is Unified Modeling Language (UML), which is specifically designed for the analysis and design of object-oriented programming systems.

systems design in computing, the detailed design of an applications package. The designer breaks the system down into component programs, and designs the required input forms, screen layouts, and printouts. Systems design forms a link between systems analysis and *programming.

Szechwan alternative spelling for the central Chinese province of *Sichuan.

t

table tennis *or* **ping pong** indoor game played on a rectangular table by two or four players. It was developed in Britain in about 1880 and derived from lawn tennis. World championships were first held in 1926.

taboo (Polynesian *tabu*, 'that contact would profane') prohibition applied to magical and religious objects. In psychology and the social sciences the term refers to practices that are generally prohibited because of religious or social pressures; for example, *incest is forbidden in most societies.

Tachisme (French 'blotting, staining') French style of abstract painting current in the 1940s and 1950s, the European equivalent to *abstract expressionism. Breaking free from the restraints of *cubism, the Tachistes adopted a novel, spontaneous approach to brushwork, typified by all-over blotches of impastoed colour and dribbled paint, or swirling calligraphy applied straight from the tube, as in the work of Georges Mathieu. The terms **L'Art Informel**, meaning gestural or *action painting, and **abstraction lyrique** ('lyrical abstraction') are also used to describe the style.

tachograph combined speedometer and clock that records a vehicle's speed and the length of time the vehicle is moving or stationary. It is used to monitor a lorry driver's working hours.

Tacitus, Publius Cornelius (AD 55–c. 120) Roman historian. A public orator in Rome, he was consul under Nerva 97–98 and proconsul of Asia 112–113. He wrote histories of the Roman empire, *Annales* and *Historiae*, covering the years 14–68 and 69–97 respectively. He also wrote a *Life of Agricola* in 97 (he married Agricola's daughter in 77) and a description of the Germanic tribes, *Germania* in 98.

tae kwon do Korean *martial art, similar to *karate, that includes punching and kicking. It was included in the 1988 Olympic Games as a demonstration sport, and became a full medal discipline at the Sydney 2000 Olympic Games.

Taft, William Howard (1857–1930) 27th president of the USA 1909–13, a Republican. He was secretary of war 1904–08 in Theodore Roosevelt's administration, but as president his conservatism provoked Roosevelt to stand against him in the 1912 election. Taft served as chief justice of the Supreme Court 1921–30.

Tagalog the majority ethnic group living around Manila on the island of Luzon, in the Philippines, who number about 10 million (1988). The Tagalog live by fishing and trading. In its standardized form, known as Pilipino, Tagalog is the official language of the Philippines, and belongs to the Western branch of the Austronesian family. The Tagalog religion is a mixture of animism, Christianity, and Islam.

tagging, electronic long-distance monitoring of the movements of people charged with or convicted of a crime, thus enabling them to be detained in their homes rather than in prison.

Tagore, Rabindranath (1861–1941) Bengali Indian writer. He translated into English his own verse *Gitanjali/Song Offerings* (1912) and his verse play *Chitra* (1896). He was awarded the Nobel Prize for Literature in 1913.

Tagus Spanish **Tajo**, Portuguese **Tejo**, river in Spain and Portugal; length 1,007 km/626 mi. It rises in the Sierra de Albarracín, Spain, on the border between the provinces of Cuenca and Teruel. It flows west past Toledo and Alcántara, then follows the Spanish-Portuguese frontier for 50 km/31 mi, and crosses Portugal to the Atlantic Ocean at Lisbon.

Tahiti largest of the Society Islands, in *French Polynesia; area 1,042 sq km/402 sq mi; population (1996) 150,700. Its capital is Papeete. The volcano, Orohena, reaches 2,237 m/7,339 ft, and much of the soil is volcanic, producing coconuts, sugar cane, and vanilla. Tourism is increasingly important as a source of revenue. English explorer Captain James *Cook observed the transit of Venus across the sun during a visit to Tahiti in 1769. It came under French control in 1843 and became a colony in 1880. Paul *Gauguin, French painter, lived here 1891–93, painting many pictures of local people.

Tai member of any of the groups of Southeast Asian peoples who speak Tai languages, all of which belong to the Sino-Tibetan language family. There are over 60 million speakers, the majority of whom live in Thailand. Tai peoples are also found in southwestern China, northwestern Myanmar (Burma), Laos, and North Vietnam.

T'ai Chi series of 108 complex, slow-motion movements, each named (for example, the White Crane Spreads Its Wings) and designed to ensure effective circulation of the **chi**, or intrinsic energy of the universe, through the mind and body. It derives partly from the Shaolin *martial arts of China and partly from *Taoism.

taiga *or* **boreal forest** Russian name for the forest zone south of the *tundra, found across the northern hemisphere. Here, dense forests of conifers (spruces and hemlocks), birches, and poplars occupy glaciated regions punctuated with cold lakes, streams, bogs, and marshes. Winters are prolonged and very cold, but the summer is warm enough to promote dense growth.

taipan species of small-headed cobra *Oxyuranus scutellatus*, found in northeastern Australia and New Guinea. It is about 3 m/10 ft long, and has a brown back and yellow belly. Its venom is fatal within minutes.

Taipei *or* **Taibei** capital and commercial centre of Taiwan; population (1998 est) 2,639,900. It is the leading industrial area of Taiwan, and industries include electronics, plastics, textiles, machinery, and shipbuilding. The National Palace Museum (1965) houses the world's greatest collection of Chinese art, brought here from the mainland in 1948.

889

Taiping Rebellion popular revolt 1851–64 that undermined China's Qing dynasty (see *Manchu). By 1853 the rebels had secured control over much of the central and lower Chang Jiang valley region, instituting radical, populist land reforms. Civil war continued until 1864, when the Taipings, weakened by internal dissension, were overcome by the provincial Hunan army of Zeng Guofan and the Ever-Victorious Army, led by American F T Ward and British soldier Charles *Gordon.

Taiwan
formerly **Formosa** (until 1949)
National name: *Chung-hua Min-kuo/Republic of China*

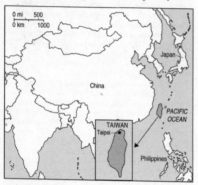

Area: 36,179 sq km/13,968 sq mi
Capital: Taipei
Major towns/cities: Kaohsiung, Taichung, Tainan, Panchiao, Chungho, Sanchung
Major ports: Kaohsiung, Keelung
Physical features: island (formerly Formosa) off People's Republic of China; mountainous, with lowlands in west; Penghu (Pescadores), Jinmen (Quemoy), Mazu (Matsu) islands
Head of state: Chen Shui-bian from 2000
Head of government: Yu Shyi-kun from 2002
Political system: emergent democracy
Political executive: limited presidency
Political parties: Nationalist Party of China (Kuomintang: KMT; known as Guomindang outside Taiwan), anticommunist, Chinese nationalist; Democratic Progressive Party (DPP), centrist-pluralist, proself-determination grouping; Workers' Party (Kuntang), left of centre
Currency: New Taiwan dollar
GNI per capita (PPP): (US$) 22,650 (2002 est)
Exports: electronic products, base metals and metal articles, textiles and clothing, machinery, information and communication products, plastic and rubber products, vehicles and transport equipment, footwear, headwear, umbrellas, toys, games, sports equipment. Principal market: USA 22.5% (2001)
Population: 22,500,000 (2002 est)
Language: Chinese (dialects include Mandarin (official), Min, and Hakka)
Religion: officially atheist; Buddhist 23%, Taoist 18%, I-Kuan Tao 4%, Christian 3%, Confucian and other 3%
Life expectancy: 74 (men); 80 (women) (2001 est)

Chronology
7th century AD: Island occupied by aboriginal community of Malayan descent; immigration of Chinese from mainland began, but remained limited before 15th century.
1517: Sighted by Portuguese vessels en route to Japan and named Ilha Formosa ('beautiful island').
1624: Occupied and controlled by Dutch.
1662: Dutch defeated by Chinese Ming general, Cheng Ch'eng-kung (Koxinga), whose family came to rule Formosa for a short period.
1683: Annexed by China's rulers, the Manchu Qing.
1786: Major rebellion against Chinese rule.
1860: Ports opened to Western trade.
1895: Ceded 'in perpetuity' to Japan under Treaty of Shominoseki at end of Sino-Japanese war.
1945: Recovered by China's Nationalist Guomindang government at end of World War II.
1947: Rebellion against Chinese rule brutally suppressed.
1949: Flight of Nationalist government, led by Generalissimo Jiang Jie Shi (Chiang Kai-shek), to Taiwan after Chinese communist revolution. They retained the designation of Republic of China (ROC), claiming to be the legitimate government for all China, and were recognized by USA and United Nations (UN). Taiwan replaced Formosa as the name of the country.
1950s onwards: Rapid economic growth as Taiwan became a successful export-orientated Newly Industrializing Country (NIC).
1954: US–Taiwanese mutual defence treaty.
1971: Expulsion from UN as USA adopted new policy of détente towards communist China.
1972: Commencement of legislature elections as a programme of gradual democratization and Taiwanization was launched by the mainlander-dominated Guomindang.
1975: President Jiang Jie Shi died; replaced as Guomindang leader by his son, Jiang Ching-kuo.
1979: USA severed diplomatic relations and annulled the 1954 security pact.
1986: Centrist Democratic Progressive Party (DPP) formed as opposition to nationalist Guomindang.
1987: Martial law lifted; opposition parties legalized; press restrictions lifted.
1988: President Jiang Ching-kuo died; replaced by Taiwanese-born Lee Teng-hui.
1990: Chinese-born Guomindang members became a minority in parliament.
1991: President Lee Teng-hui declared an end to the civil war with China. The constitution was amended. Guomindang won a landslide victory in elections to the new National Assembly, the 'superparliament'.
1993: A cooperation pact was signed with China.
1996: Lee Teng-hui was elected president in the first ever Chinese democratic elections.
1997: The government narrowly survived a no-confidence motion. Vincent Siew became prime minister.
1998: President Lee Teng-hui announced that reunion with mainland China was impossible until Beijing adopted democracy. The ruling Guomindang increased its majority in parliamentary and local elections.
2000: Despite threats of invasion from China if Taiwan made moves towards independence, a pro-independence president, Chen Shui-bian, was elected,

who appointed a member of the former government, Tang Fei, as prime minister. Tang Fei was replaced by Chang Chun-hsiung after he resigned in October.

2001: Taiwan partially lifted its 52-year ban on direct trade and communications with China.

2004: Chen Shui-bian was re-elected as president, but an opposition alliance in favour of further rapprochement with China won a parliamentary majority.

Tajik *or* **Tadzhik**   member of the majority ethnic group in Tajikistan. Tajiks also live in Afghanistan and parts of Pakistan and western China. The Tajiki language belongs to the West Iranian sub-branch of the Indo-European family, and is similar to Farsi; it is written in the Cyrillic script. The Tajiks have long been associated with neighbouring Turkic peoples and their language contains Altaic loan words. The majority of the Tajik people are Sunni Muslims; there is a Shiite minority in Afghanistan.

Tajikistan

National name: *Jumhurii Tojikston/ Republic of Tajikistan*

Area: 143,100 sq km/55,250 sq mi
Capital: Dushanbe
Major towns/cities: Khojand, Qurghonteppa, Kulob, Uroteppa, Kofarnihon
Physical features: mountainous, more than half of its territory lying above 3,000 m/10,000 ft; huge mountain glaciers, which are the source of many rapid rivers
Head of state: Imamali Rakhmanov from 1994
Head of government: Akil Akilov from 1999
Political system: authoritarian nationalist
Political executive: unlimited presidency
Political parties: Communist Party of Tajikistan (CPT), pro-Rakhmanov; Democratic Party of Tajikistan (DP), anticommunist (banned from 1993); Party of Popular Unity and Justice, anticommunist
Currency: Tajik rouble
GNI per capita (PPP): (US$) 900 (2002 est)
Exports: aluminium, electricity, cotton lint. Principal market: Russia 30% (2000)

Population: 6,245,000 (2003 est)
Language: Tajik (related to Farsi; official), Russian
Religion: Sunni Muslim; small Russian Orthodox and Jewish communities
Life expectancy: 66 (men); 71 (women) (2000–05)
Chronology
c. 330: Formed an eastern part of empire of Alexander the Great of Macedonia.
8th century: Tajiks established as distinct ethnic group, with semi-independent territories under the tutelage of the Uzbeks, to the west; spread of Islam.
13th century: Conquered by Genghis Khan and became part of Mongol Empire.
1860–1900: Northern Tajikistan came under tsarist Russian rule, while the south was annexed by Emirate of Bukhara, to the west.
1917–18: Attempts to establish Soviet control after Bolshevik revolution in Russia resisted initially by armed guerrillas (basmachi).
1921: Became part of Turkestan Soviet Socialist Autonomous Republic.
1924: Tajik Autonomous Soviet Socialist Republic formed.
1929: Became constituent republic of Soviet Union (USSR).
1930s: Stalinist era of collectivization led to widespread repression of Tajiks.
1978: 13,000 participated in anti-Russian riots.
late 1980s: Resurgence in Tajik consciousness, stimulated by the *glasnost* initiative of Soviet leader Mikhail Gorbachev.
1989: Rastokhez ('Revival') Popular Front established and Tajik declared state language. New mosques constructed.
1990: Violent interethnic Tajik–Armenian clashes in Dushanbe; a state of emergency was imposed.
1991: President Kakhar Makhkamov, local communist leader since 1985, was forced to resign after supporting the failed anti-Gorbachev coup in Moscow. Independence was declared. Rakhman Nabiyev, communist leader 1982–85, was elected president. Joined new Commonwealth of Independent States (CIS).
1992: Joined Muslim Economic Cooperation Organization, the Conference on Security and Cooperation in Europe (CSCE; now the Organization on Security and Cooperation in Europe, OSCE), and the United Nations (UN). Violent demonstrations by Islamic and pro-democracy groups forced Nabiyev to resign. Civil war between pro- and anti-Nabiyev forces claimed 20,000 lives, made 600,000 refugees, and wrecked the economy. Imamali Rakhmanov, a communist sympathetic to Nabiyev, took over as head of state.
1993: Government forces regained control of most of the country. CIS peacekeeping forces were drafted in to patrol the border with Afghanistan, the base of the pro-Islamic rebels.
1994: A ceasefire was agreed. Rakhmanov was popularly elected president under a new constitution.
1995: Parliamentary elections were won by Rakhmanov's supporters. There was renewed fighting on the Afghan border.
1996: Pro-Islamic rebels captured towns in the southwest. There was a UN-sponsored ceasefire between government and pro-Islamic rebels.

1997: A four-stage peace plan was signed. There was a peace accord with the Islamic rebel group the United Tajik Opposition (UTO).

1998: Members of UTO were appointed to the government as part of a peace plan. The UN military observer mission (UNMOT) suspended its operations, following the killing of four UN workers. More than 200 people were killed in clashes in Leninabad between the army and rebel forces loyal to the renegade Tajik army commander Col Makhmud Khudoberdiyev; the deputy leader of the Islamic-led UTO, Ali Akbar Turadzhonzada, was appointed first deputy prime minister.

1999: Constitutional changes approved the creation of a two-chamber legislature. President Rakhmanov was popularly re-elected and appointed Akil Akilov as his prime minister.

2000: A new national currency, the somoni, was introduced.

2001: Tajikistan joined the post-11 September US-led anti-terror coalition.

2002: Borders were tightened to prevent al-Qaeda members leaving neighbouring Afghanistan.

2003: A referendum granted president Rakhmanov the right to run for further terms.

2004: Russia established a military base at Dushanbe.

2005: The People's Democratic Party won a landslide majority in parliamentary elections.

Taj Mahal white marble mausoleum built 1632–48 on the River Yamuna near Agra, India. Erected by Shah Jahan to the memory of Mumtaz Mahal, his favourite wife, it is a celebrated example of Indo-Islamic architecture, the fusion of Muslim and Hindu styles. The white marble walls are inlaid with semiprecious stones, and it is now considered one of the architectural wonders of the world.

takahe flightless bird *Porphyrio mantelli* of the rail family, order Gruiformes, native to New Zealand. It is about 60 cm/2 ft tall and weighs just over 2 kg/4.4 lb, with blue and green plumage and a red bill. The takahe was thought to have become extinct at the end of the 19th century, but in 1948 small numbers were rediscovered in the tussock grass of a mountain valley on South Island.

Talbot, William Henry Fox (1800–1877) English pioneer of photography. He invented the paper-based *calotype process, patented in 1841, which was the first negative/positive method. Talbot made photograms several years before Louis Daguerre's invention was announced.

talc $Mg_3Si_4O_{10}(OH)_2$, mineral, hydrous magnesium silicate. It occurs in tabular crystals, but the massive impure form, known as **steatite** or **soapstone**, is more common. It is formed by the alteration of magnesium compounds and is usually found in metamorphic rocks. Talc is very soft, ranked 1 on the Mohs scale of hardness. It is used in powdered form in cosmetics, lubricants, and as an additive in paper manufacture.

Talgai skull cranium of a pre-adult male, dating from 10,000–20,000 years ago, found at Talgai station, southern Queensland, Australia. It was one of the earliest human archaeological finds in Australia, having been made in 1886. Its significance was not realized, however, until the work of Edgeworth David and others after 1914. The skull is large with heavy eyebrow ridges and cheekbones.

Taliesin (lived c. 550) Legendary Welsh poet, a bard at the court of the king of Rheged in Scotland. Taliesin allegedly died at Taliesin (named after him) in Dyfed, Wales.

Talleyrand-Périgord, Charles Maurice de (1754–1838) French politician and diplomat. As bishop of Autun 1789–91 he supported moderate reform during the *French Revolution, was excommunicated by the pope, and fled to the USA during the Reign of Terror (persecution of anti-revolutionaries). He returned and became foreign minister under the Directory 1797–99 and under Napoleon 1799–1807. He represented France at the Congress of *Vienna 1814–15.

Tallinn German **Reval**; Russian **Revel**, naval port and capital of Estonia, 300 km/186 mi west of St Petersburg on the Gulf of Finland; population (1990) 505,100. Industries include the manufacture of electrical and oil-drilling machinery, textiles, and paper production. It is a major cultural centre, containing the Estonian Academy of Sciences and a number of polytechnic, arts, and other institutes. Founded as a Danish fortress in 1219, Tallinn was a member of the *Hanseatic League throughout the Middle Ages; it came under the control of the *Teutonic Knights in 1346, Sweden in 1561, and Russia in 1750. It was occupied by German forces in both world wars, and suffered widespread damage.

Tallis, Thomas (c. 1505–1585) English composer. He was a master of *counterpoint, and has become best known for his elaborate and ingenious 40-part motet *Spem in alium* (c. 1573). His works also include *Tallis's Canon* ('Glory to thee my God this night') (1567), and a collection of 34 motets, *Cantiones sacrae* (1575), of which 16 are by Tallis and 18 by William Byrd.

Talmud the two most important works of post-biblical Jewish literature. The Babylonian (Bavli) Talmud, compiled around AD 600, and the Jerusalem (Yerushalmi) Talmud, compiled around AD 500, provide a compilation of ancient Jewish law and tradition. The Babylonian Talmud is the more authoritative version for later Judaism; both Talmuds are written in a mix of Hebrew and Aramaic. They contain the rabbinical commentary (the Gemara) on the *Mishnah (early rabbinical commentaries committed to writing in about AD 200). The Talmud can be generally divided into Halachah (or Halakhah), consisting of legal and ritual matters, and *Haggadah (or Aggadah), concerned with ethical, theological, and folklorist matters.

tamandua tree-living toothless anteater *Tamandua tetradactyla* found in tropical forests and tree savannah from southern Mexico to Brazil. About 56 cm/1.8 ft long with a prehensile tail of equal length, it uses its strong foreclaws to break into nests of tree ants and termites, which it licks up with its narrow tongue.

tamarind evergreen tropical tree native to the Old World, with pinnate leaves (leaflets either side of the stem) and reddish-yellow flowers, followed by pods. The pulp surrounding the seeds is used in medicine and as a flavouring. (*Tamarindus indica*, family Leguminosae.)

tamarisk any of a group of small trees or shrubs that flourish in warm, salty, desert regions of Europe and Asia where no other vegetation is found. The common tamarisk *T. gallica*, which grows in European coastal areas, has small, scalelike leaves on feathery branches and produces spikes of small pink flowers. (Genus *Tamarix*, family Tamaricaceae.)

tambourine musical percussion instrument of ancient origin, almost unchanged since Roman times, consisting of a shallow frame drum with a single skin and loosely set jingles in the rim which add their noise when the drum skin is struck or rubbed, or sound separately when the instrument is shaken.

Tamerlane (*or* **Timur Leng** *or* **Timur the Lame**) **(1335–1405)** Turco-Mongol ruler of Samarkand, in Uzbekistan, from 1369 who conquered Persia, Azerbaijan, Armenia, and Georgia. He defeated the *Golden Horde in 1395, sacked Delhi in 1398, invaded Syria and Anatolia, and captured the Ottoman sultan Bayezid I (*c.* 1360–1403) in Ankara in 1402; he died invading China.

Tamil the majority ethnic group living in the Indian state of Tamil Nadu (formerly Madras). Tamils also live in southern India, northern Sri Lanka, Malaysia, Singapore, and South Africa, totalling 35–55 million worldwide. Tamil belongs to the Dravidian family of languages; written records in Tamil date from the 3rd century BC. The 3 million Tamils in Sri Lanka are predominantly Hindu, unlike the Sinhalese, the majority group there, who are mainly Buddhist. The **Tamil Tigers**, the most prominent of the various Tamil groups, are attempting to create a separate homeland in northern Sri Lanka through both political and military means.

Tamil Nadu formerly **Madras State** (until 1968), state of southeast India, bounded on the north by Karnataka and Andhra Pradesh, on the west by Kerala, and on the east and south by the Bay of Bengal and the Indian Ocean; area 130,069 sq km/50,220 sq mi; population (2001 est) 62,110,800. The capital is *Chennai (formerly Madras). There are cotton, leather, sugar-refining, oil-refining, and road and railway vehicle manufacturing industries. Tea, coffee, spices, sugar cane, and coconuts are grown, and there is a major fishing industry.

Tammany Hall Democratic Party organization in New York. It originated in 1789 as the Society of St Tammany, named after the building in which they met. It was dominant from 1800 until the 1930s and gained a reputation for corruption and rule by bosses; its domination was broken by Mayor La Guardia in the 1930s and Mayor Koch in the 1970s.

Tanabata (Japanese 'star festival') festival celebrated annually on 7 July, introduced to Japan from China in the 8th century. It is dedicated to Altair and Vega, two stars in the constellations Aquila and Lyra respectively, separated by the Milky Way. According to legend they represent two star-crossed lovers allowed by the gods to meet on that night.

tanager New World bird of the family Emberizidae, order Passeriformes. There are about 230 species in forests of Central and South America, all brilliantly coloured. They are 10–20 cm/4–8 in long, with plump bodies and conical beaks. The tanagers of North America all belong to the genus *Piranga*.

Tanganyika, Lake lake 772 m/2,534 ft above sea level in the Great Rift Valley, East Africa, with the Democratic Republic of Congo to the west, Zambia to the south, and Tanzania and Burundi to the east. It is about 645 km/400 mi long, with an area of about 31,000 sq km/12,000 sq mi, and is the deepest lake (1,435 m/4,710 ft) in

Africa, and the second-deepest freshwater lake in the world. The mountains around its shores rise to about 2,700 m/8,860 ft. The chief ports on the lake are Bujumbura (Burundi), Kigoma (Tanzania), and Kalémié (Democratic Republic of Congo).

Tang dynasty the greatest of China's imperial dynasties, which ruled from 618 to 907. Founded by the *Sui official Li Yuan (566–635), it extended Chinese authority into central Asia, Tibet, Korea, and Annam, establishing what was then the world's largest empire. The dynasty's peak was reached during the reign of Emperor Minghuang or Hsuan-tsung (712–56).

tangent line that touches a *circle at only one point. A tangent is at right angles to the radius at the point of contact. From any point outside a circle, the lines of two tangents drawn to the circle will be of equal length.

tangent tan, in trigonometry, a function of an acute angle in a right-angled *triangle, defined as the ratio of the length of the side opposite the angle to the length of the side adjacent to it; a way of expressing the gradient of a line. This function can be used to find either sides or angles in a right-angled triangle.

tangerine small type of *orange.

tango dance for couples, the music for which was developed in Argentina during the early 20th century. The dance consists of two long steps followed by two short steps then one long step, using stylized body positions. The music is in moderately slow duple time (2/4) and employs syncopated rhythms. Similar to the habanera, from which it evolved, the tango consists of two balanced sections, the second usually in the *dominant key or the relative minor of the first section. William Walton uses in his suite *Façade* (1923).

tangram puzzle made by cutting up a square into seven pieces.

tank armoured fighting vehicle that runs on tracks and is fitted with weapons systems capable of defeating other tanks and destroying life and property. The term was originally a code name for the first effective tracked and armoured fighting vehicle, invented by the British soldier and scholar Ernest Swinton, and first used in the Battle of the Somme in 1916.

tanning treating animal skins to preserve them and make them into leather. In vegetable tanning, the prepared skins are soaked in tannic acid. Chrome tanning, which is much quicker, uses solutions of chromium salts.

tansy perennial herb belonging to the daisy family, native to Europe. The yellow flower heads grow in clusters on stalks up to 120 cm/4 ft tall, and the aromatic leaves are used in cookery. (*Tanacetum vulgare*, family Compositae.)

tantalum symbol Ta, hard, ductile, lustrous, grey-white, metallic element, atomic number 73, relative atomic mass 180.948. It occurs with niobium in tantalite and other minerals. It can be drawn into wire with a very high melting point and great tenacity, useful for lamp filaments subject to vibration. It is also used in alloys, for corrosion-resistant laboratory apparatus and chemical equipment, as a catalyst in manufacturing synthetic rubber, in tools and instruments, and in rectifiers and capacitors.

Tantalus in Greek mythology, a king of Lydia, son of Zeus, and father of Pelops and Niobe. He offended the gods by divulging their secrets and serving them

893

human flesh at a banquet. His crimes were punished in Tartarus (a part of the underworld for the wicked) by the provision of food and drink he could not reach. The word 'tantalize' derives from his torment.

Tantrism forms of Hinduism and Buddhism that emphasize the division of the universe into male and female forces which maintain its unity by their interaction. Tantric Hinduism is associated with magical and sexual yoga practices that imitate the union of Shiva and Sakti, as described in scriptures known as the *Tantras*. In Buddhism, the *Tantras* are texts attributed to the Buddha, describing magical ritual methods of attaining enlightenment.

Tanzania

formerly **Tanganyika (until 1964)**

National name: *Jamhuri ya Muungano wa Tanzania/ United Republic of Tanzania*

Area: 945,000 sq km/364,864 sq mi
Capital: Dodoma (official), Dar es Salaam (administrative)
Major towns/cities: Zanzibar, Mwanza, Mbeya, Tanga, Morogoro
Major ports: Dar es Salaam
Physical features: central plateau; lakes in north and west; coastal plains; lakes Victoria, Tanganyika, and Nyasa; half the country is forested; comprises islands of Zanzibar and Pemba; Mount Kilimanjaro, 5,895 m/19,340 ft, the highest peak in Africa; Olduvai Gorge; Ngorongoro Crater, 14.5 km/9 mi across, 762 m/2,500 ft deep
Head of state: Benjamin Mkapa from 1995
Head of government: Frederick Sumaye from 1995
Political system: emergent democracy
Political executive: limited presidency
Political parties: Revolutionary Party of Tanzania (CCM), African, socialist; Civic Party (Chama Cha Wananchi), left of centre; Tanzania People's Party (TPP), left of centre; Democratic Party (DP), left of centre; Justice and Development Party, left of centre; Zanzibar United Front (Kamahuru), Zanzibar-based, centrist

Currency: Tanzanian shilling
GNI per capita (PPP): (US$) 550 (2002 est)
Exports: minerals, coffee beans, raw cotton, tobacco, tea, cloves, cashew nuts, petroleum products. Principal market: India 15.4% (2001)
Population: 36,977,000 (2003 est)
Language: Kiswahili, English (both official), Arabic (in Zanzibar), many local languages
Religion: Muslim, Christian, traditional religions
Life expectancy: 43 (men); 44 (women) (2000–05)
Chronology
8th century: Growth of city states along coast after settlement by Arabs from Oman.
1499: Portuguese navigator Vasco da Gama visited island of Zanzibar.
16th century: Portuguese occupied Zanzibar, defeated coastal states, and exerted spasmodic control over them.
1699: Portuguese ousted from Zanzibar by Arabs of Oman.
18th century: Sultan of Oman reasserted Arab overlordship of East African coast, which became subordinate to Zanzibar.
1744–1837: Revolt of ruler of Mombasa against Oman spanned 93 years until final victory of Oman.
1822: Moresby Treaty: Britain recognized regional dominance of Zanzibar, but protested against the slave trade.
1840: Sultan Seyyid bin Sultan moved his capital from Oman to Zanzibar; trade in slaves and ivory flourished.
1861: Sultanates of Zanzibar and Oman separated on death of Seyyid.
19th century: Europeans started to explore inland, closely followed by Christian missionaries.
1884: German Colonization Society began to acquire territory on mainland in defiance of Zanzibar.
1890: Britain obtained protectorate over Zanzibar, abolished slave trade, and recognized German claims to mainland.
1897: German East Africa formally established as colony.
1905–06: Maji Maji revolt suppressed by German troops.
1916: Conquest of German East Africa by British and South African forces, led by Gen Jan Smuts.
1919: Most of German East Africa became British League of Nations mandate of Tanganyika.
1946: Britain continued to govern Tanganyika as United Nations (UN) trusteeship.
1954: Julius Nyerere organized the Tanganyikan African National Union (TANU) to campaign for independence.
1961–62: Tanganyika achieved independence from Britain with Nyerere as prime minister, and became a republic in 1962 with Nyerere as president.
1963: Zanzibar achieved independence.
1964: Arab-dominated sultanate of Zanzibar overthrown by Afro-Shirazi Party in violent revolution; Zanzibar merged with Tanganyika to form United Republic of Tanzania.
1967: East African Community (EAC) formed by Tanzania, Kenya, and Uganda; Nyerere pledged to build socialist state.
1974: Dodoma was designated the new national capital, replacing Dar es Salaam. However, Dar es Salaam continued as the administrative capital into the next century, as the move to Dodoma takes many years.

1977: Revolutionary Party of Tanzania (CCM) proclaimed as only legal party; EAC dissolved.

1979: Tanzanian troops intervened in Uganda to help overthrow President Idi Amin.

1992: Multiparty politics were permitted.

1995: Benjamin Mkapa of CCM was elected president.

1998: A bomb exploded at the US embassy in Dar es Salaam, killing 6 people and injuring 60; an anti-American Islamic group claimed responsibility.

1999: Tanzania withdrew from Africa's largest trading block, the Common Market for Eastern and Southern Africa. In October, the country's founder, Julius Nyerere, died.

2000: President Mkapa and the CCM, who had improved the economy over the preceding five years, were re-elected.

2001: Violence broke out between opposition supporters and troops on Zanzibar after the elections had been partially rerun following claims of corruption.

Taoiseach plural **Taoisigh**, Irish title for the prime minister of the Republic of Ireland. The Taoiseach has broadly similar powers to the UK prime minister.

Taoism Chinese philosophical system, traditionally founded by the Chinese philosopher Lao Zi in the 6th century BC. He is also attributed authorship of the scriptures, *Tao Te Ching*, although these were apparently compiled in the 3rd century BC. The 'tao' or 'way' denotes the hidden principle of the universe, and less stress is laid on good deeds than on harmonious interaction with the environment, which automatically ensures right behaviour. The magical side of Taoism is illustrated by the **I Ching* or *Book of Changes*, a book of divination.

tap dancing rapid step dance, derived from clog dancing. Its main characteristic is the tapping of toes and heels accentuated by metal segments, known as taps, affixed to the shoes. It was popularized in vaudeville and in 1930s films by such dancers as Fred Astaire and Bill 'Bojangles' Robinson.

tape recording, magnetic method of recording electric signals on a layer of iron oxide, or other magnetic material, coating a thin plastic tape. The electrical signals from the microphone are fed to the electromagnetic recording head, which magnetizes the tape in accordance with the frequency and amplitude of the original signal. The impulses may be audio (for sound recording), video (for television), or data (for computer). For playback, the tape is passed over the same, or another, head to convert magnetic into electrical signals, which are then amplified for reproduction. Tapes are easily demagnetized (erased) for reuse, and come in cassette, cartridge, or reel form.

tapeworm any of various parasitic flatworms of the class Cestoda. They lack digestive and sense organs, can reach 15 m/50 ft in length, and attach themselves to the host's intestines by means of hooks and suckers. Tapeworms are made up of hundreds of individual segments, each of which develops into a functional hermaphroditic reproductive unit capable of producing numerous eggs. The larvae of tapeworms usually reach humans in imperfectly cooked meat or fish, causing anaemia and intestinal disorders. If a person eats pork from an infected pig that has not been properly cooked, the cysticercus attaches to the intestine and develops into an adult tapeworm.

The tapeworm is a hermaphrodite and fertilizes itself, releasing proglottis, each of which may contain as many as 40,000 embryos encased in separate capsules. If the embryos are eaten by a pig, they bore from the pig's intestine into the bloodstream which carries them to the muscles, where they may be eaten by a human and the cycle continues.

tapioca granular starch used in cooking, produced from the **cassava root.

tapir any of the odd-toed hoofed mammals (perissodactyls) of the single genus *Tapirus*, now constituting the family Tapiridae. There are four species living in the American and Malaysian tropics. They reach 1 m/3 ft at the shoulder and weigh up to 350 kg/770 lb. Their survival is in danger because of destruction of the forests. Tapirs have thick, hairy, black skin, short tails, and short trunks. They are vegetarian, harmless, and shy. They are related to the **rhinoceros, and slightly more distantly to the horse.

taproot in botany, a single, robust, main **root that is derived from the embryonic root, or **radicle, and grows vertically downwards, often to considerable depth. Taproots are often modified for food storage and are common in biennial plants such as the carrot *Daucus carota*, where they act as **perennating organs.

tar dark brown or black viscous liquid obtained by the destructive distillation of coal, shale, and wood. Tars consist of a mixture of hydrocarbons, acids, and bases. Creosote and **paraffin oil are produced from wood tar.

Tara Hill *or* **Hill of Tara** ancient religious and political centre in County Meath, Republic of Ireland. A national monument, and depicted in a 7th-century *Life of St Patrick* as the 'capital of the Irish', Tara Hill was the site of a palace and was the coronation place of many Irish kings. Its heyday was in the 3rd century AD, and the site was still in use in the 10th century. St **Patrick, patron saint of Ireland, preached here. Some tumuli and earthworks remain, and the pillar stone, reputed to be the coronation stone, can still be seen on the summit. In 1843 it was the venue for a meeting held by Daniel O'Connell, 'the Liberator', following the launch of his campaign for the repeal of the Act of Union (1801) in 1841.

tarantella southern Italian dance in very fast compound time (6/8); also a piece of music composed for, or in the rhythm of, this dance. It is commonly believed to be named after the tarantula spider which was (incorrectly) thought to cause tarantism (hysterical ailment), at one time epidemic in the southern Italian town of Taranto, the cure for which was thought to involve wild dancing. The dance became popular during the 19th century, several composers writing tarantellas employing a perpetuum mobile in order to generate intense energy. Examples include those by Chopin, Liszt, and Weber.

tarantula wolf spider *Lycosa tarantula* (family Lycosidae) with a 2.5 cm/1 in body. It spins no web, relying on its speed in hunting to catch its prey. The name 'tarantula' is also used for any of the numerous large, hairy spiders of the family Theraphosidae, with large poison fangs, native to the southwestern USA and tropical America.

Tarkovsky, Andrei Arsenyevich (1932–1986) Soviet film director. His work is characterized by an epic style combined with intense personal spirituality.

His films include *Solaris* (1972), *Zerkalo/Mirror* (1975), *Stalker* (1979), and *Offret/The Sacrifice* (1986).

taro *or* **eddo** plant belonging to the arum family, native to tropical Asia; the tubers (underground stems) are edible and are the source of Polynesian poi (a fermented food). (*Colocasia esculenta*, family Araceae.)

tarot cards fortune-telling aid consisting of 78 cards: the 56 **minor arcana** in four suits (resembling playing cards) and the **major arcana**, 22 cards with densely symbolic illustrations that have links with astrology and the *Kabbalah.

tarpon large silver-sided fish *Tarpon atlanticus* of the family Megalopidae. It reaches 2 m/6 ft and may weigh 135 kg/300 lb. It lives in warm western Atlantic waters.

Tarquinius Superbus (lived 6th century BC) called 'Tarquin the Proud', Last king of Rome 534–509 BC. He abolished certain rights of Romans, and made the city powerful. According to legend, he was deposed when his son Sextus raped *Lucretia.

tarragon perennial bushy herb belonging to the daisy family, native to the Old World. It grows up to 1.5 m/ 5 ft tall and has narrow leaves and small green-white flower heads arranged in groups. Tarragon contains an aromatic oil; its leaves are used to flavour salads, pickles, and tartar sauce. It is closely related to wormwood. (*Artemisia dracunculus*, family Compositae.)

tarsier any of three species of the prosimian primates, genus *Tarsius*, of the East Indies and the Philippines. These survivors of early primates are about the size of a rat with thick, light-brown fur, very large eyes, and long feet and hands. They are nocturnal, arboreal, and eat insects and lizards.

tartan woollen cloth woven in specific chequered patterns individual to Scottish clans, with stripes of different widths and colours crisscrossing on a coloured background; it is used in making skirts, kilts, trousers, and other articles of clothing.

Tartar variant spelling of *Tatar, member of a Turkic people now living mainly in the autonomous region of Tatarstan, Russia.

tartaric acid HOOC(CHOH)$_2$COOH, organic acid present in vegetable tissues and fruit juices in the form of salts of potassium, calcium, and magnesium. It is used in carbonated drinks and baking powders.

tartrazine E102, yellow food colouring produced synthetically from petroleum. Many people are allergic to foods containing it. Typical effects are skin disorders and respiratory problems. It has been shown to have an adverse effect on hyperactive children.

Tashkent Uzbek **Toshkent**, capital of Uzbekistan and of Tashkent wiloyat (region), located in the western foothills of the Tien Shan mountain range and in the valley of the River Chirchiq. With a population (1999 est) of 2,142,700, it is the largest city in Central Asia. It is an important transit centre for the region; there is an international airport terminal here. The Tashkent region is the major industrial centre of Uzbekistan, and industries include the manufacture of mining and textile machinery, chemicals, textiles, food processing, and leather goods. The city is also a major educational and cultural centre, home to the University of Tashkent (1920), the Uzbek Academy of Sciences (1943), and a number of museums and theatres, including the Navoi Theatre of Opera and Ballet. Tashkent suffered severe damage in an earthquake in 1966, but was rapidly rebuilt.

Tasman, Abel Janszoon (1603–1659) Dutch navigator. In 1642, he was the first European to see the island now named Tasmania. He also made the first European sightings of New Zealand, Tonga, and the Fiji Islands.

Tasmania formerly **Van Diemen's Land** (1642–1856), island in the Indian Ocean, southeast of Australia, separated from the mainland by Bass Strait; state of Australia; area about 68,000 sq km/26,000 sq mi; population (1996 est) 459,700. The capital is *Hobart. Products include wool, dairy products, apples and other fruit, processed foods, timber, paper, iron, tungsten, copper, silver, coal, and cement.

Tasmanian devil carnivorous marsupial *Sarcophilus harrisii*, in the same family (Dasyuridae) as native 'cats'. It is about 65 cm/2.1 ft long with a 25 cm/10 in bushy tail. It has a large head, strong teeth, and is blackish with white patches on the chest and hind parts. It is nocturnal, carnivorous, and can be ferocious when cornered. It has recently become extinct in Australia and survives only in remote parts of Tasmania.

Tasmanian wolf *or* **Tasmanian tiger** *or* **thylacine** carnivorous marsupial *Thylacinus cynocephalus*, in the family Dasyuridae. It is doglike in appearance with a long tail, characteristic dark stripes on back and hindquarters, and measures nearly 2 m/6 ft from nose to tail tip. It was hunted to probable extinction in the 1930s, the last known Tasmanian wolf dying in Hobart Zoo, Tasmania, in 1936, but there are still occasional unconfirmed reports of sightings, both on the Australian mainland and in the Tasmanian mountains, its last known habitat.

Tasman Sea part of the *Pacific Ocean between southeast Australia and northwest New Zealand. It is named after the Dutch explorer Abel Tasman.

Tasso, Torquato (1544–1595) Italian poet. He was the author of the romantic epic poem of the First Crusade *Gerusalemme liberata/Jerusalem Delivered* completed by 1575 and first published in 1581, which he revised as *Gerusalemme conquistata/Jerusalem Conquered*, published in 1593.

taste sense that detects some of the chemical constituents of food. The human *tongue can distinguish four basic tastes (sweet, sour, bitter, and salty) but it is supplemented by the sense of smell. What we refer to as taste is really a composite sense made up of both taste and smell. In 2000 US researchers confirmed the existence of the fifth taste, 'umami', which was first proposed in the early 19th century by Japanese researcher Kikunae Ikeda. Umami is now called L-glutamate and a specific molecule receptor for it has been identified in taste buds.

Tatar *or* **Tartar** member of a Turkic people, the descendants of the mixed Mongol and Turkic followers of *Genghis Khan. The Tatars now live mainly in the Russian autonomous republic of Tatarstan, western Siberia, Turkmenistan, and Uzbekistan (where they were deported from the Crimea in 1944). There are over 5 million speakers of the Tatar language, which belongs to the Turkic branch of the Altaic family.

Tatarstan formerly **Tatar Autonomous Republic**, autonomous republic in the eastern Russian Federation; area 68,000 sq km/26,255 sq mi; population (1990) 3,658,000 (48% Tatars, 43% Russian). The capital is Kazan. There are oil, natural gas, chemical, textile, and timber industries; and there is arable and dairy farming.

Tate, Nahum (1652–1715) Irish poet. Tate was born in Dublin, and educated there at Trinity College before moving to London. He wrote an adaptation of Shakespeare's *King Lear* with a happy ending, entitled *The History of King Lear* (1681). He wrote the libretto for Purcell's *Dido and Aeneas*; he also produced *A New Version of the Psalms* (1696); his hymn 'While Shepherds Watched Their Flocks by Night' appeared in the *Supplement* (1703). He became British poet laureate in 1692.

Tatlin, Vladimir (Yevgrapovich) (1885–1953) Russian artist. He was a cofounder of *constructivism. After encountering cubism in Paris in 1913, he evolved his first constructivist works, using such materials as glass, metal, plaster, and wood to create totally abstract sculptures, some of which were meant to be suspended in the air. He worked as a stage designer 1933–52.

Tatra Mountains range in central Europe, extending for about 65 km/40 mi along the Polish-Slovakian border; the highest part of the central *Carpathian Mountains.

Tatum, Art(hur) (1910–1956) US jazz pianist. He is considered among the most technically brilliant of jazz pianists and is highly rated by classical pianists. His technique and chromatic harmonies influenced many musicians, such as Oscar Peterson. He worked mainly as a soloist in the 1930s and improvised with the guitarist Tiny Grimes in a trio from 1943.

tau *elementary particle with the same electric charge as the electron but a mass nearly double that of a proton. It has a lifetime of around 3×10^{-13} seconds and belongs to the *lepton family of particles – those which interact via the electromagnetic, weak nuclear, and gravitational forces, but not the strong nuclear force.

Taupo, Lake largest lake in New Zealand, in central North Island; area 620 sq km/239 sq mi. It is 357 m/1,170 ft above sea level, maximum depth 159 m/522 ft. The lake is in a volcanic area of hot springs and is the source of the Waikato River. The lake and its tributary rivers attract tourists and anglers.

Taurus conspicuous zodiacal constellation in the northern hemisphere near *Orion, represented as a bull. The Sun passes through Taurus from mid-May to late June. In astrology, the dates for Taurus are between about 20 April and 20 May (see *precession).

Tavener, John Kenneth (1944–) English composer. He has written austere vocal works, including the dramatic cantata *The Whale* (1968) and the opera *Thérèse* (1979). *The Protecting Veil*, composed in 1987 for cello and strings alone, became a best-selling classical recording. Recent works include *Vlepondas* for soprano, bass and cello, and *Feast of Feasts* for chorus, both 1996. His *Song for Athene* was played at the funeral of Diana, Princess of Wales.

taxation raising of money from individuals and organizations by the state in order to pay for the goods and services it provides. Taxation can be **direct** (a deduction from income) or **indirect** (added to the purchase price of goods or services, that is, a tax on consumption). The proportions of direct and indirect taxation in the total tax revenue vary widely from country to country. In the UK, taxation is below average by comparison with other members of the

*Organization for Economic Cooperation and Development (OECD).

tax avoidance conducting of financial affairs in such a way as to keep tax liability to a minimum within the law.

tax evasion failure to meet tax liabilities by illegal action, such as not declaring income. Tax evasion is a criminal offence.

taxis plural **taxes**; or **tactic movement**, in botany, the movement of a single cell, such as a bacterium, protozoan, single-celled alga, or gamete, in response to an external stimulus. A movement directed towards the stimulus is described as positive taxis, and away from it as negative taxis. The alga *Chlamydomonas*, for example, demonstrates positive **phototaxis** by swimming towards a light source to increase the rate of photosynthesis. **Chemotaxis** is a response to a chemical stimulus, as seen in many bacteria that move towards higher concentrations of nutrients.

taxonomy another name for the *classification of living organisms.

Tay longest river in Scotland; length 193 km/120 mi, it flows northeast through **Loch Tay**, then east and southeast past Perth to the **Firth of Tay**, crossed at Dundee by the **Tay Bridge**, before joining the North Sea. The Tay has salmon fisheries; its main tributaries are the Tummel, Isla, and Earn, Braan, and Almond.

Taylor, Elizabeth (Rosemond) (1932–) English-born US actor. She graduated from juvenile leads to dramatic roles, becoming one of the most glamorous stars of the 1950s and 1960s. Her films include *National Velvet* (1944), *Cat on a Hot Tin Roof* (1958), *Butterfield 8* (1960; Academy Award), *Cleopatra* (1963), and *Who's Afraid of Virginia Woolf?* (1966; Academy Award).

TB abbreviation for the infectious disease *tuberculosis.

Tbilisi formerly **Tiflis**, capital and cultural centre of Georgia, located on the Kura River in the *Caucasus Mountains; population (1996) 1,200,000. It is a major economic, transportation, and industrial centre. Engineering industries, including electric locomotives and equipment, machine tools, and agricultural machinery, are of leading importance; other industries include the manufacture of textiles, leather goods, ceramics, foodstuffs, and tobacco. In the lead-up to the collapse of the USSR in 1989 and Georgian independence, the city was the scene of bloody clashes between Russian security forces and nationalist demonstrators.

Tchaikovsky, Pyotr Il'yich (1840–1893) Russian composer. He successfully united Western European influences with native Russian musical material and tradition, and was the first Russian composer to establish a reputation with Western audiences. His strong sense of melody, personal expression, and brilliant orchestration are clear throughout his many Romantic works, which include six symphonies, three piano concertos, a violin concerto, operas (including *Eugene Onegin* (1879)), ballets (including *The Nutcracker* (1892)), orchestral fantasies (including *Romeo and Juliet* (1869)), and chamber and vocal music.

tea evergreen shrub or small tree whose fermented, dried leaves are soaked in hot water to make a refreshing drink, also called tea. Known in China as early as 2737 BC, tea was first brought to Europe AD 1610 and rapidly became a popular drink. In 1823 the shrub was found growing wild in northern India, and plantations were later established in Assam and Sri Lanka; producers today include Africa, South America, Georgia, Azerbaijan, Indonesia, and Iran. (*Camellia sinensis*, family Theaceae.)

teak tropical Asian timber tree with yellowish wood used in furniture and shipbuilding. (*Tectona grandis*, family Verbenaceae.)

teal any of various small, short-necked dabbling ducks of the genus *Anas*, order Anseriformes, but particularly *A. crecca*. The male is dusky grey; its tail feathers ashy grey; the crown of its head deep cinnamon or chestnut; its eye is surrounded by a black band, glossed with green or purple, which unites on the nape; its wing markings are black and white; and its bill is black. The female is mottled brown. The total length is about 35cm/14 in.

tear gas any of various volatile gases that produce irritation and watering of the eyes, used by police against crowds and used in chemical warfare. The gas is delivered in pressurized, liquid-filled canisters or grenades, thrown by hand or launched from a specially adapted rifle. Gases (such as Mace) cause violent coughing and blinding tears, which pass when the victim breathes fresh air, but there are no lasting effects.

teasel upright prickly biennial herb, native to Europe and Asia. It grows up to 1.5 m/5 ft tall, has prickly stems and leaves, and a large prickly head of purple flowers. The dry, spiny seed heads were once used industrially to tease or fluff up the surface fibres of cloth. (*Dipsacus fullonum*, family Dipsacaceae.)

tea tree shrub or small tree native to Australia and New Zealand. It is thought that some species of tea tree were used by the explorer Captain Cook to brew tea; it was used in the first years of settlement for this purpose. (Genus *Leptospermum*, family Myrtaceae.)

technetium chemical symbol Tc, (Greek *technetos* 'artificial') silver-grey, radioactive, metallic element, atomic number 43, relative atomic mass 98.906. It occurs in nature only in extremely minute amounts, produced as a fission product from uranium in *pitchblende and other uranium ores. Its longest-lived isotope, Tc-99, has a half-life of 216,000 years. It is a superconductor and is used as a hardener in steel alloys and as a medical tracer.

techno dance music in minimalist style played on electronic instruments. It is created with extensive use of studio technology for a futuristic, machine-made sound, sometimes with sampled soul vocals. The German band Kraftwerk (formed in 1970) is an early example, and Germany continued to produce some of the best techno records in the 1990s.

technology the use of tools, power, and materials, generally for the purposes of production. Almost every human process for getting food and shelter depends on complex technological systems, which have been developed over a 3-million-year period. Significant milestones include the advent of the *steam engine in 1712, the introduction of *electricity and the *internal combustion engine in the mid-1870s, and recent developments in communications, *electronics, and the nuclear and space industries. The **advanced technology** (highly automated and specialized) on which modern industrialized society depends is frequently contrasted with the **low technology** (labour-intensive and unspecialized) that characterizes some developing countries. ***Intermediate technology** is an attempt to adapt scientifically advanced inventions to less developed areas by using local materials and methods of manufacture. **Appropriate technology** refers to simple and small-scale tools and machinery of use to developing countries.

tectonics in geology, the study of the movements of rocks on the Earth's surface. On a small scale tectonics involves the formation of *folds and *faults, but on a large scale *plate tectonics deals with the movement of the Earth's surface as a whole.

Tecumseh (1768–1813) American Indian chief of the Shawnee. He attempted to unite the Indian peoples from Canada to Florida against the encroachment of white settlers, but the defeat of his brother Tenskwatawa, 'the Prophet', at the battle of Tippecanoe in November 1811 by W H Harrison, governor of the Indiana Territory, largely destroyed the confederacy built up by Tecumseh.

Tedder, Arthur William (1890–1967) 1st Baron Tedder, UK marshal of the Royal Air Force in World War II. As deputy supreme commander under US general Eisenhower 1943–45, he was largely responsible for the initial success of the 1944 Normandy landings. He was made a KCB in 1942, and became a baron in 1946.

Tees river flowing from the Pennines in Cumbria, northwest England, to the North Sea via Tees Bay, Middlesbrough unitary authority, in northeast England; length 130 km/80 mi. Its port, Teesport, handles in excess of 42 million tonnes per annum, with port trade mainly chemical-related.

Teesside industrial area at the mouth of the River Tees, northeast England; population (1994 est) 323,000. It includes the towns of Stockton-on-Tees, *Middlesbrough, Billingham, and Thornaby. There are high-technology industries, as well as petrochemicals, electronics, steelmaking, and plastics. The area includes an oil-fuel terminal and the main North Sea natural gas terminal.

tefillin *or* **phylacteries** in Judaism, two small leather boxes containing scrolls from the Torah, that are strapped to the left arm and the forehead by Jewish men for daily prayer. The tefillin on the arm points to the heart, while that on the forehead to the mind and thoughts.

Tegucigalpa capital of Honduras; situated at an altitude of 975 m/3,199 ft in the highlands of south-central Honduras, on the River Choluteca at the foot of the extinct El Picacho volcano; population (1999 est) 968,400. Industries include textiles, chemicals, and food-processing, mostly for domestic consumption. It was founded by the Spanish in the 16th century as a gold- and silver-mining centre, and replaced Comayagua as capital in 1880.

Tehran (*or* **Tehran** *or* **Teheran)** capital of Iran; population (1996 est) 6,758,800. The city produces over half of the country's manufactured goods, and industries include textiles, chemicals, pottery, electrical equipment, oil refining, vehicle assembly, engineering, and tobacco and sugar processing. It is built at an average altitude of 1,220 m/3,937 ft on a slope running south from the Elburz Mountains.

Teilhard de Chardin, Pierre (1881–1955) French Jesuit theologian, palaeontologist, and philosopher. He developed a creative synthesis of nature and religion, based on his fieldwork and fossil studies. Publication of his *Le Phénomène humain/The Phenomenon of Man*, written 1938–40, was delayed (owing to his unorthodox views) until after his death by the embargo of his superiors. He saw humanity as being in a constant process of evolution, moving towards a perfect spiritual state.

tektite (from Greek *tektos* 'molten') small, rounded glassy stone, found in certain regions of the Earth, such as Australasia. Tektites are probably the scattered drops of molten rock thrown out by the impact of a large *meteorite.

Tel Aviv-Yafo *or* **Tel Aviv-Jaffa** city in Israel, situated on the coast of Sharon Plain, 77 km/48 mi northwest of Jerusalem; population (2002 est) 347,800. Industries include textiles, chemicals, sugar, printing, publishing, and tourism. Tel Aviv was founded in 1909 as a Jewish residential area in the Arab town of Jaffa (or Yafo), with which it was combined in 1950; their ports were superseded in 1965 by Ashdod to the south. It is regarded by the United Nations (UN) as the capital of Israel. The combined city is a major tourist centre and the home of Israel's only stock exchange; other industries include textiles, engineering, motor vehicles, diamond polishing, publishing, and electronic equipment.

telecommunications communications over a distance, generally by electronic means. Long-distance voice communication was pioneered in 1876 by Scottish scientist Alexander Graham Bell when he invented the telephone. The telegraph, radio, and television followed. Today it is possible to communicate internationally by telephone cable or by satellite or microwave link, with over 100,000 simultaneous conversations and several television channels being carried by the latest satellites. Cable links are increasingly made of optical fibres. The capacity of these links is enormous. The TDRS-C (tracking and data-relay satellite communications) satellite, the world's largest and most complex satellite, can transmit in a single second the contents of a 20-volume encyclopedia, with each volume containing 1,200 pages of 2,000 words. A bundle of optical fibres, no thicker than a finger, can carry 10,000 phone calls – more than a copper wire as thick as an arm.

telegraphy transmission of messages along wires by means of electrical signals. The first modern form of telecommunication, it now uses printers for the transmission and receipt of messages. Telex is an international telegraphy network.

Telemachus in Greek mythology, son of *Odysseus and *Penelope. He was a child when his father set out for the Trojan wars. In Homer's *Odyssey*, he attempted to control his mother's suitors while his father was believed dead, but on Odysseus' return after 20 years, he helped him to kill them, with the support of the goddess *Athena.

Telemann, Georg Philipp (1681–1767) German baroque composer, organist, and conductor. He was the best-known German composer of his time with a contemporary reputation much greater than Johann Sebastian Bach's. His prolific output of concertos for both new and old instruments, including violin, viola da gamba, recorder, flute, oboe, trumpet, horn, and bassoon, represents a methodical and fastidious investigation into the tonal resonances and structure of the new baroque orchestra, research which was noted by Bach. Other works include 25 operas, numerous sacred cantatas, and instrumental fantasias.

telepathy 'the communication of impressions of any kind from one mind to another, independently of the recognized channels of sense', as defined by the English essayist F W H Myers (1843–1901), cofounder in 1882 of the Psychical Research Society, who coined the term. It is a form of *extrasensory perception.

telephone instrument for communicating by voice along wires, developed by Scottish-US inventor Alexander Graham *Bell in 1876, consisting of an earpiece that receives electrical signals and a mouthpiece that sends electrical signals. The transmitter (mouthpiece) consists of a carbon microphone, with a diaphragm that is vibrated by sound waves when a person speaks into it. The diaphragm vibrations compress grains of carbon to a greater or lesser extent, altering their resistance to an electric current passing through them. This sets up variable electrical signals, which travel along the telephone lines to the receiver of the person being called. The earpiece contains an electromagnet attached to a diaphragm. As the incoming electrical signal varies, the strength of the electromagnet also varies, resulting in a variable movement of an armature of the electromagnet. These movements cause the diaphragm to vibrate, producing the pattern of sound waves that originally entered the mouthpiece.

telescope optical instrument that magnifies images of faint and distant objects; any device for collecting and focusing light and other forms of electromagnetic radiation. A telescope with a large aperture, or opening, can distinguish finer detail and fainter objects than one with a small aperture. The refracting telescope uses a large objective lens to gather light and form an image which the smaller eyepiece lens magnifies. A reflecting

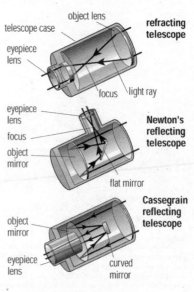

telescope Three kinds of telescope.

telescope uses a mirror to gather light. The Schmidt telescope uses a corrective lens to achieve a wide field of view. It is one of the most widely used tools of astronomy. See also *radio telescope.

television (TV) reproduction of visual images at a distance using radio waves. For transmission, a television camera converts the pattern of light it takes in into a pattern of electrical charges. This is scanned line by line by a beam of electrons from an electron gun, resulting in variable electrical signals that represent the picture. These signals are combined with a radio carrier wave and broadcast as electromagnetic waves. The TV aerial picks up the wave and feeds it to the receiver (TV set). This separates out the vision signals, which pass to a cathode-ray tube where a beam of electrons is made to scan across the screen line by line, mirroring the action of the electron gun in the TV camera. The result is a recreation of the pattern of light that entered the camera.

Telford, Thomas (1757–1834) Scottish civil engineer. He opened up northern Scotland by building roads and waterways. He constructed many aqueducts and *canals, including the *Caledonian Canal (1802–23),

and erected the Menai road suspension bridge between Wales and Anglesey (1819–26), a type of structure scarcely tried previously in the UK. In Scotland he constructed over 1,600 km/1,000 mi of road and 1,200 bridges, churches, and harbours.

Telford and Wrekin unitary authority in west England, created in 1998 from part of Shropshire. **area:** 291 sq km/112 sq mi **towns and cities:** Telford (administrative headquarters), Newport **features:** The Wrekin, isolated hill (407 m/1,334 ft); Ironbridge Gorge (World Heritage Site) includes world's first iron bridge, built across the River Severn in 1779 by Abraham Darby, and Ironbridge Gorge Museum Trust (seven industrial history museums including Museum of the River, Museum of Iron, Blists Hill Open Air Museum, Coalport China Museum) **population:** (1996) 144,600.

Tell, William (German **Wilhelm**) legendary 14th-century Swiss archer, said to have refused to salute the Habsburg badge at Altdorf on Lake Lucerne. Sentenced to shoot an apple from his son's head, he did so, then shot the tyrannical Austrian ruler Gessler, symbolizing his people's refusal to submit to external authority.

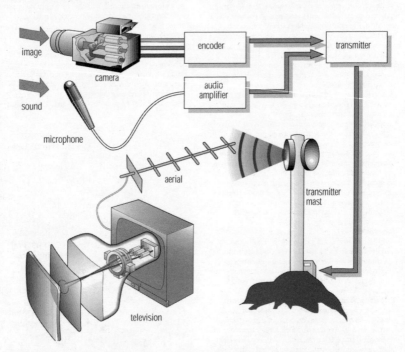

television Simplified block diagram of a complete colour television system – transmitting and receiving. The camera separates the picture into three colours – red, blue, green – by using filters and different camera tubes for each colour. The audio signal is produced separately from the video signal. Both signals are transmitted from the same aerial using a special coupling device called a diplexer. There are four sections in the receiver: the aerial, the tuners, the decoders, and the display. As in the transmitter, the audio and video signals are processed separately. The signals are amplified at various points.

tellurium chemical symbol Te, (Latin *Tellus* 'Earth') silver-white, semi-metallic (*metalloid) element, atomic number 52, relative atomic mass 127.60. Chemically it is similar to sulphur and selenium, and it is considered one of the sulphur group. It occurs naturally in telluride minerals, and is used in colouring glass blue-brown, in the electrolytic refining of zinc, in electronics, and as a catalyst in refining petroleum.

Telstar US communications satellite, launched on 10 July 1962, which relayed the first live television transmissions between the USA and Europe. Telstar orbited the Earth every 2.63 hours, and unlike later geostationary satellites was only usable when in line-of-sight of two tracking stations.

Telugu language spoken in southeastern India. It is the official language of Andhra Pradesh, and is also spoken in Malaysia, giving a total number of speakers of around 50 million. Written records in Telugu date from the 7th century AD. Telugu belongs to the Dravidian family.

tempera painting medium in which powdered pigments are mixed with a water-soluble binding agent such as egg yolk removed from its sac. It is noted for its strong, translucent colours, and can be thinned with water. In use before the introduction of oils, a form of tempera was used in ancient Egypt, and egg tempera was the foremost medium for panel painting in late medieval and early Renaissance Europe. It was gradually replaced in popularity by oils from the late 15th century onwards.

temperance movement societies dedicated to curtailing the consumption of alcohol by total prohibition, local restriction, or encouragement of declarations of personal abstinence ('the pledge'). Temperance movements were first set up in the USA, Ireland, and Scotland, then in northern England in the 1830s.

temperature measure of how hot an object is. It is temperature difference that determines whether heat transfer will take place between two objects and in which direction it will flow, that is from warmer object to cooler object. The temperature of an object is a measure of the average kinetic energy possessed by the atoms or molecules of which it is composed. The SI unit of temperature is the kelvin (symbol K) used with the Kelvin scale. Other measures of temperature in common use are the Celsius scale and the Fahrenheit scale. The Kelvin scale starts at absolute zero (0 K = −273 °C). The Celsius scale starts at the freezing point of water (0 °C = 273 K). 1 K is the same temperature interval as 1 °C.

tempering heat treatment for improving the properties of metals, often used for steel alloys. The metal is heated to a certain temperature and then quenched (cooled suddenly) in a water or oil bath to fix its state.

Templars or **Knights Templar** or **Order of Poor Knights of Christ and of the Temple of Solomon** military religious order founded in Jerusalem 1119–20 to protect pilgrims travelling to the Holy Land. They played an important part in the *Crusades of the 12th and 13th centuries. Innocent II placed them under direct papal authority in 1139, and their international links allowed them to adapt to the 13th-century decline of the Crusader states by becoming Europe's bankers. The Templars' independence, power, and wealth, rather than their alleged heresy, probably motivated *Philip IV

of France, helped by the Avignon pope Clement V, to suppress the order in 1307–14.

Temple of Jerusalem centre of Jewish national worship in Jerusalem, in both ancient and modern times, sited on Mount Moriah (or Temple Mount), one of the hills of Mount Zion. The **Wailing Wall** is the surviving part of the western wall of the enclosure of Herod's Temple. Since the destruction of the Temple in AD 70, Jews have gone there to pray and to mourn their dispersion and the loss of their homeland.

tempo (Italian 'time') in music, the speed at which a piece should be played. One way of indicating the tempo of a piece of music is to give a metronome marking, which states the number of beats per minute; for example, 'crotchet = 60' means that there should be 60 crotchet beats to the minute, that is, one per second. Modern electronic metronomes measure tempo very accurately. Performers sometimes change or even ignore metronome markings, playing at a tempo that suits their interpretation of the music. However, the knowledge of performance practice gained by academic investigation into early music has encouraged performers to pay more attention to original tempo markings.

tench European freshwater bony fish *Tinca tinca*, a member of the carp family, now established in North America. It is about 45 cm/18 in long, weighs 2 kg/4.5 lb, and is coloured olive-green above and grey beneath. The scales are small and there is a barbel at each side of the mouth.

Ten Commandments or the **Law of Moses** or the **Decalogue** in the Old Testament, the laws given by God to the Hebrew leader Moses on Mount Sinai, engraved on two tablets of stone. They are: 1. to have no other gods besides Jehovah (the One God); 2. to make no images of anything in heaven or on earth, or in the water under the earth, and not to worship idols; 3. not to use the name of God for evil purposes; 4. to observe the Sabbath and keep it holy; 5. to honour (respect) one's father and mother; 6. not to commit murder; 7. not to commit adultery; 8. not to commit theft; 9. not to give false evidence; and 10. not to be covetous – do not desire another man's house; do not desire his wife, his slaves, his cattle, his donkeys, or anything else that he owns. The commandments form the basis of Jewish and Christian moral codes; the 'tablets of the Law' given to Moses are also mentioned in the Koran. The giving of the Ten Commandments is celebrated in the Jewish festival of Shavuot.

tendon or **sinew** in vertebrates, a cord of very strong, fibrous connective tissue that joins muscle to bone. Tendons are largely composed of bundles of fibres made of the protein collagen, and because of their inelasticity are very efficient at transforming muscle power into movement.

tendril in botany, a slender, threadlike structure that supports a climbing plant by coiling around suitable supports, such as the stems and branches of other plants. It may be a modified stem, leaf, leaflet, flower, leaf stalk, or stipule (a small appendage on either side of the leaf stalk), and may be simple or branched. The tendrils of Virginia creeper *Parthenocissus quinquefolia* are modified flower heads with suckerlike pads at the end that stick to walls, while those of the grapevine *Vitis* grow away from the light and thus enter dark crevices where they expand to anchor the plant firmly.

Tenerife largest of the *Canary Islands, in the province of Santa Cruz de Tenerife, Spain; area 2,060 sq km/795 sq mi; population (1991) 706,900. Fruit and vegetables are produced, especially bananas and tomatoes, and the island is a popular tourist resort. Santa Cruz is the main town here, and Pico de Teide, an active volcano, is the highest peak in Spain (3,713 m/12,186 ft high).

Teng Hsiao-ping alternative spelling of *Deng Xiaoping, Chinese politician.

Tennessee called the **Volunteer State** or the **Big Bend State**, (Yuhi *Tana-see* 'meeting place') state in east-central USA, bordered to the east by *North Carolina, to the south by *Georgia, *Alabama, and *Mississippi, to the west by *Arkansas and *Missouri, across the *Mississippi River, and to the north by *Kentucky and *Virginia; area 106,752 sq km/41,217 sq mi; population (2000) 5,689,300; capital Nashville. The Tennessee River flows through the state twice, giving rise to its nickname the Big Bend State; its more common nickname, the Volunteer State, refers to Tennessee's military traditions. The terrain drops from east to west, with wooded mountains, including part of the Great Smoky Mountains, giving way to a central area of hills, and then plains and swamps. Tennessee is one of the states that link the North and South of the USA; the lifestyle of west and central Tennessee resembles that of the Deep South, while eastern Tennessee is closer to the North. Service industries and manufacturing make the greatest contribution to the state economy; products include chemicals, processed foods, machinery, and metals. Mining is also important. Agricultural produce includes beef, milk, and cotton. Memphis is the largest city. Other major towns and cities are Knoxville, Chattanooga, Clarksville, Murfreesboro, Jackson, Johnson City, Kingsport, Franklin, and Hendersonville. Historically, Tennessee was a plantation state, associated with *slavery, and cotton remains one of its leading crops. Culturally, it is one of the centres of country music in the USA. Tennessee was admitted to the Union in 1796 as the 16th US state.

Tenniel, John (1820–1914) English illustrator and cartoonist. He is known for his cartoons for *Punch* magazine and for his illustrations for Lewis Carroll's *Alice's Adventures in Wonderland* (1865) and *Through the Looking-Glass* (1872). He was knighted in 1893.

tennis racket-and-ball game invented towards the end of the 19th century. Although played on different surfaces (grass, wood, shale, clay, concrete), it is also called 'lawn tennis'. The aim of the two or four players (in singles or doubles matches) is to strike the ball into the prescribed area of the court, with oval-headed rackets (strung with gut or nylon), in such a way that it cannot be returned. The game is won by those first winning four points (called 15, 30, 40, game), unless both sides reach 40 (deuce), when two consecutive points are needed to win. A set is won by winning six games with a margin of two over opponents, although a tie-break system operates at six games to each side (or in some cases eight) except in the final set. A match lasts a maximum of five sets for men, three for women.

Tennyson, Alfred (1809–1892) 1st Baron Tennyson, English poet. He was poet laureate 1850–92. His verse has a majestic, musical quality, and few poets have surpassed his precision and delicacy of language.

His works include 'The Lady of Shalott' (1833), 'The Lotus Eaters' (1833), 'Ulysses' (1842), 'Break, Break, Break' (1842), and 'The Charge of the Light Brigade' (1854); the longer narratives *Locksley Hall* (1832) and *Maud* (1855); the elegy *In Memoriam* (1850); and a long series of poems on the Arthurian legends, *The Idylls of the King* (1859–89). Tennyson's poetry is characterized by a wide range of interests; an intense sympathy with the deepest feelings and aspirations of humanity; an exquisite sense of beauty; and a marvellous power of vivid and minute description, often achieved by a single phrase, and heightened by the perfect matching of sense and sound.

Tenochtitlán capital of the Mexican *Aztecs. It was founded *c.* 1325 on an island among the lakes that occupied much of the Valley of Mexico, on the site of modern Mexico City. Its population reached about 150,000. Spanish conquistador Hernán *Cortés met Aztec ruler *Montezuma here in November 1519. Welcomed as guests, the Spaniards captured Montezuma and forced him to recognize the sovereignty of *Charles V. Cortés destroyed Tenochtitlán in 1521 and rebuilt it as a Spanish colonial city.

tenor highest range of the adult male singing voice when not using falsetto, approximately C3–A5. It is the preferred voice for operatic heroic roles. Well-known tenors include Luciano Pavarotti and Placido *Domingo. It is also used before the name of an instrument that sounds in the same range as the tenor voice, for example tenor saxophone.

Teotihuacán huge ancient city in central Mexico, founded about 300 BC, about 32 km/20 mi north of modern Mexico City. Known as the 'metropolis of the gods', it reached its zenith in the 5th–6th centuries AD. As a religious centre of Mesoamerica, it contained two great pyramids and the temple of *Quetzalcoatl. It is one of the best-excavated archaeological sites in Mexico.

terbium chemical symbol Tb, soft, silver-grey, metallic element of the *lanthanide series, atomic number 65, relative atomic mass 158.925. It occurs in gadolinite and other ores, with yttrium and ytterbium, and is used in lasers, semiconductors, and television tubes. It was named in 1843 by Swedish chemist Carl Mosander (1797–1858) after the town of Ytterby, Sweden, where it was first found.

Terence (c. 190–c. 159 BC) born Publius Terentius Afer, Roman dramatist. Born in Carthage, he was taken as a slave to Rome where he was freed and came under the patronage of the Roman general Scipio Africanus Minor. His surviving six comedies (including *The Eunuch* (161 BC)) are subtly characterized and based on Greek models. They were widely read and performed during the Middle Ages and the Renaissance.

Teresa, Mother (1910–1997) born Agnes Gonxha Bojaxhiu, Roman Catholic nun who devoted her life to working among the sick and poor of Calcutta (now Kolkata), India. She established the Missionaries of Charity, now a multinational organization with 517 centres around the world. More than 4,000 nuns staff the Missionaries of Charity orphanages, Aids hospices, mental homes and basic medical clinics, alongside numerous volunteers. Mother Teresa was awarded the Nobel Prize for Peace in 1979 for her work with the destitute in India.

Teresa, St (1515–1582) Spanish mystic who founded an order of nuns in 1562. She was subject to fainting fits, during which she saw visions. She wrote *The Way to Perfection* (1583) and an autobiography, *Life of the Mother Teresa of Jesus* (1611). In 1622 she was canonized, and in 1970 was made the first female Doctor of the Church. She was born in Avila.

terminal in computing, a device consisting of a keyboard and display screen (*VDU) to enable the operator to communicate with the computer. The terminal may be physically attached to the computer or linked to it by a telephone line (remote terminal). A dumb terminal has no processor of its own, whereas an intelligent terminal has its own processor and takes some of the processing load away from the main computer.

terminal moraine linear, slightly curved ridge of rocky debris deposited at the front end, or snout, of a glacier. It represents the furthest point of advance of a glacier, being formed when deposited material (till), which was pushed ahead of the snout as it advanced, became left behind as the glacier retreated.

termite any member of the insect order Isoptera. Termites are soft-bodied social insects living in large colonies which include one or more queens (of relatively enormous size and producing an egg every two seconds), much smaller kings, and still smaller soldiers, workers, and immature forms. Termites build galleried nests of soil particles that may be 6 m/20 ft high.

tern any of various lightly built seabirds in the gull family Laridae, order Charadriiformes, with pointed wings and bill, and usually a forked tail. Terns plunge-dive after aquatic prey. They are 20–50 cm/8–20 in long, and usually coloured in combinations of white and black. They are extensively distributed, especially in temperate climates.

terracotta (Italian 'baked earth') brownish-red baked clay, usually unglazed, used in building, sculpture, and pottery. The term is specifically applied to small figures or figurines, such as those found at Tanagra in central Greece. Excavations at Xi'an, China, have revealed life-size terracotta figures of the army of the Emperor Shi Huangdi dating from the 3rd century BC.

terrapin member of some species of the order Chelonia (*turtles and *tortoises). Terrapins are small to medium-sized, aquatic or semi-aquatic, and are found widely in temperate zones. They are omnivorous, but generally eat aquatic animals. Some species are in danger of extinction owing to collection for the pet trade; most of the animals collected die in transit.

terrier any of various breeds of highly intelligent, active dogs. They are usually small. Types include the bull, cairn, fox, Irish, Scottish, Sealyham, Skye, and Yorkshire terriers. They were originally bred for hunting rabbits and following quarry such as foxes down into burrows.

terrorism systematic violence in the furtherance of political aims, often by small *guerrilla groups.

Terror, Reign of phase of the *French Revolution when the *Jacobins were in power (October 1793 to July 1794) under *Robespierre and began systematically to murder their political opponents. The Terror was at its height in the early months of 1794. Across France, it is thought that between 17,000 and 40,000 people were executed, mainly by guillotine, until public indignation rose and Robespierre was overthrown and guillotined in July 1794.

Tertiary period period of geological time 65 to 1.64 million years ago, divided into five epochs: Palaeocene, Eocene, Oligocene, Miocene, and Pliocene. During the Tertiary period, mammals took over all the ecological niches left vacant by the extinction of the dinosaurs, and became the prevalent land animals. The continents took on their present positions, and climatic and vegetation zones as we know them became established. Within the geological time column the Tertiary follows the Cretaceous period and is succeeded by the Quaternary period.

tesla symbol T, SI unit of *magnetic flux density. One tesla represents a flux density of one *weber per square metre, or 10^4 *gauss. It is named after the Croatian-born US physicist Nikola Tesla.

Test Ban Treaty agreement signed by the USA, the USSR, and the UK on 5 August 1963 contracting to test nuclear weapons only underground. All nuclear weapons testing in the atmosphere, in outer space, and under water was banned. In the following two years 90 other nations signed the treaty, the only major nonsignatories being France and China, which continued underwater and ground-level tests. In January 1996 France announced the ending of its test programme, and supported the implementation of a universal test ban. The treaty did not restrict or regulate underground testing, or the possession or use of nuclear weapons during wartime.

testis plural **testes**, organ that produces *sperm in male (and hermaphrodite) animals. In vertebrates it is one of a pair of oval structures that are usually internal, but in mammals (other than elephants and marine mammals), the paired testes (or testicles) descend from the body cavity during development, to hang outside the abdomen in a scrotal sac. The testes also secrete the male sex hormone *androgen.

Test match sporting contest between two nations, the most familiar being those played between the ten nations that play Test cricket (England, Australia, West Indies, India, New Zealand, Pakistan, South Africa, Sri Lanka, Zimbabwe, and Bangladesh). Test matches are also played in Rugby League and Rugby Union. A cricket Test match lasts a maximum of five days and a Test series usually consists of three to five matches. The first cricket Test match was between Australia and England in Melbourne, Australia, in 1877.

testosterone *hormone secreted chiefly by the testes, but also by the ovaries and the cortex of the adrenal glands. It promotes the development of *secondary sexual characteristics in males at puberty. It is also needed for the development of the male sex organs and for male fertility. The hormone is partly responsible for the difference in behaviour that may be seen between males and females. In animals with a breeding season, the onset of breeding behaviour is accompanied by a rise in the level of testosterone in the blood.

tetanus *or* **lockjaw** acute disease caused by the toxin of the bacillus *Clostridium tetani*, which usually enters the body through a wound. The bacterium is chiefly found in richly manured soil. Untreated, in seven to ten days tetanus produces muscular spasm and rigidity of the jaw spreading to other parts of the body, convulsions, and death. There is a vaccine, and the disease may be treatable with tetanus antitoxin and antibiotics.

Tethys in Greek mythology, one of the *Titans; a daughter of Uranus and Gaia; and the wife of the sea god Oceanus, by whom she was the mother of over three thousand children: the river gods, oceanids (*nymphs of the open sea), and the waves.

Tethys Sea sea that in the Mesozoic era separated *Laurasia from *Gondwanaland. The formation of the Alpine fold mountains caused the sea to separate into the Mediterranean, the Black, the Caspian, and the Aral seas.

tetra any of various brightly coloured tropical freshwater bony fishes of the family Characidae, formerly placed in the genus *Tetragonopterus*. Tetras are found mainly in tropical South America, and also in Africa.

tetrachloromethane *or* **carbon tetrachloride** CCl₄, chlorinated organic compound that is a very efficient solvent for fats and greases, and was at one time the main constituent of household dry-cleaning fluids and of fire extinguishers used with electrical and petrol fires. Its use became restricted after it was discovered to be carcinogenic and it has now been largely removed from educational and industrial laboratories.

tetracycline one of a group of antibiotic compounds having in common the four-ring structure of chlortetracycline, the first member of the group to be isolated. They are prepared synthetically or obtained from certain bacteria of the genus *Streptomyces*. They are broad-spectrum antibiotics, effective against a wide range of disease-causing bacteria.

tetrahedron plural **tetrahedra**, in geometry, a solid figure (*polyhedron) with four triangular faces; that is, a *pyramid on a triangular base. A regular tetrahedron has equilateral triangles as its faces.

tetrapod (Greek 'four-legged') type of *vertebrate. The group includes mammals, birds, reptiles, and amphibians. Birds are included because they evolved from four-legged ancestors, the forelimbs having become modified to form wings. Even snakes are tetrapods, because they are descended from four-legged reptiles.

Teutonic Knight member of a German Christian military order, the **Knights of the Teutonic Order**, founded in 1190 by Hermann of Salza in Palestine. They crusaded against the pagan Prussians and Lithuanians from 1228 and controlled Prussia until the 16th century. Their capital was Marienburg (now Malbork, Poland).

Texas called the **Lone Star State**, (Caddo Indian *tejas* 'friends') state in southwestern USA, one of the *Great Plains states, bordered to the east by *Louisiana (partly along the Sabine River), to the northeast by *Arkansas, to the north by *Oklahoma (part of this boundary being along the *Red River), to the west by *New Mexico, to the southwest by the Rio Grande River and Mexico, and to the southeast by the Gulf of Mexico; area 678,051 sq km/261,797 sq mi; population (2000) 20,851,800; capital Austin. Texas's nickname derives from the state flag's single star. The landscape of Texas varies, with the Great Plains in the north, the Basin and Range region in the west, and the Coastal Plain region and the Gulf of Mexico in the south. Huge inland seas created much of the bedrock of present-day Texas, and the state's sedimentary rocks contain many fossils and are rich in oil reserves. Texas produces nearly one-third of US petroleum. Chemicals, petrochemicals, cotton, sorghum, wheat, and livestock are among the state's chief economic products. Despite the vast rural landscape, over 80% of the Texas population resides in urban areas. The *Dallas-Forth Worth Consolidated Metropolitan Area is the state's most populous; other cities include *Houston, San Antonio, and *El Paso. Originally home to the *Apache, Comanche, and Karankawa peoples, Texas was settled by the Spanish in the 16th and 17th centuries. Texas was part of Mexico 1821–36, after which it became an independent republic. Texas was admitted to the Union in 1845 as the 28th US state. The annexation of Texas was one of the causes of the *Mexican War (1846–48).

Thackeray, William Makepeace (1811–1863) English novelist and essayist. He was a regular contributor to *Fraser's Magazine* and *Punch*. His first novel was *Vanity Fair* (1847–48), significant for the breadth of its canvas as well as for the depth of the characterization. This was followed by *Pendennis* (1848), *Henry Esmond* (1852) (and its sequel *The Virginians* (1857–59)), and *The Newcomes* (1853–55), in which Thackeray's tendency to sentimentality is most marked.

Thai the majority ethnic group living in Thailand and northern Myanmar (Burma). Thai peoples also live in southwestern China, Laos, and North Vietnam. They speak Tai languages, all of which belong to the Sino-Tibetan language family. There are over 60 million speakers, the majority of whom live in Thailand. Most Thais are Buddhists, but the traditional belief in spirits, **phi**, remains.

Thailand
formerly **Siam** (until 1939 and 1945–49)
National name: *Ratcha Anachak Thai/ Kingdom of Thailand*

Area: 513,115 sq km/198,113 sq mi
Capital: Bangkok (and chief port)
Major towns/cities: Chiang Mai, Hat Yai, Khon Kaen, Songkhla, Nakhon Ratchasima, Nonthaburi, Udon Thani
Major ports: Nakhon Sawan
Physical features: mountainous, semi-arid plateau in northeast, fertile central region, tropical isthmus in south; rivers Chao Phraya, Mekong, and Salween

Head of state: King Bhumibol Adulyadej from 1946
Head of government: Thaksin Shinawatra from 2001
Political system: emergent democracy
Political executive: parliamentary
Political parties: Democrat Party (DP), left of centre; Thai Nation (Chart Thai), right wing, pro-private enterprise; New Aspiration Party (NAP), centrist; Palang Dharma Party (PDP), anti-corruption, Buddhist; Social Action Party (SAP), moderate, conservative; Chart Pattana (National Development), conservative
Currency: baht
GNI per capita (PPP): (US$) 6,680 (2002 est)
Exports: machinery and mechanical appliances, textiles and clothing, electronic goods, rice, rubber, gemstones, sugar, cassava (tapioca), fish (especially prawns), chemicals. Principal market: USA 22.2% (2001)
Population: 62,833,000 (2003 est)
Language: Thai, Chinese (both official), English, Lao, Malay, Khmer
Religion: Buddhist 95%; Muslim 5%
Life expectancy: 65 (men); 74 (women) (2000–05)
Chronology
13th century: Siamese (Thai) people migrated south and settled in valley of Chao Phraya River in Khmer Empire.
1238: Siamese ousted Khmer governors and formed new kingdom based at Sukhothai.
14th and 15th centuries: Siamese expanded at expense of declining Khmer Empire.
1350: Siamese capital moved to Ayatthaya (which also became name of kingdom).
1511: Portuguese traders first reached Siam.
1569: Conquest of Ayatthaya by Burmese ended years of rivalry and conflict.
1589: Siamese regained independence under King Naresuan.
17th century: Foreign trade under royal monopoly developed with Chinese, Japanese, and Europeans.
1690s: Siam expelled European military advisers and missionaries and adopted policy of isolation.
1767: Burmese invaders destroyed city of Ayatthaya, massacred ruling families, and withdrew, leaving Siam in a state of anarchy.
1782: Reunification of Siam after civil war under Gen Phraya Chakri, who founded new capital at Bangkok and proclaimed himself King Rama I.
1824–51: King Rama III reopened Siam to European diplomats and missionaries.
1851–68: King Mongkut employed European advisers to help modernize the government, legal system, and army.
1856: Royal monopoly on foreign trade ended.
1868–1910: King Chulalongkorn continued modernization and developed railway network using Chinese immigrant labour; Siam became major exporter of rice.
1896: Anglo-French agreement recognized Siam as independent buffer state between British Burma and French Indo-China.
1932: Bloodless coup forced King Rama VII to grant a constitution with a mixed civilian-military government.
1939: Siam changed its name to Thailand (briefly reverting to Siam 1945–49).

1941: Japanese invaded; Thailand became puppet ally of Japan under Field Marshal Phibun Songkhram.
1945: Japanese withdrawal; Thailand compelled to return territory taken from Laos, Cambodia, and Malaya.
1947: Phibun regained power in military coup, reducing monarch to figurehead; Thailand adopted strongly pro-American foreign policy.
1955: Political parties and free speech introduced.
1957: State of emergency declared; Phibun deposed in bloodless coup; military dictatorship continued under Gen Sarit Thanarat (1957–63) and Gen Thanom Kittikachorn (1963–73).
1967–72: Thai troops fought in alliance with USA in Vietnam War.
1973: Military government overthrown by student riots.
1974: Adoption of democratic constitution, followed by civilian coalition government.
1976: Military reassumed control in response to mounting strikes and political violence.
1978: Gen Kriangsak Chomanan introduced constitution with mixed civilian–military government.
1980: Gen Prem Tinsulanonda assumed power.
1983: Prem relinquished army office to head civilian government; martial law maintained.
1988: Chatichai Choonhavan succeeded Prem as prime minister.
1991: A military coup imposed a new military-oriented constitution despite mass protests.
1992: A general election produced a five-party coalition; riots forced Prime Minister Suchinda Kraprayoon to flee; Chuan Leekpai formed a new coalition government.
1995–96: The ruling coalition collapsed. A general election in 1996 resulted in a new six-party coalition led by Chavalit Yongchaiyudh.
1997: A major financial crisis led to the floating of currency. An austerity rescue plan was agreed with the International Monetary Fund (IMF). Chuan Leekpai was re-elected prime minister.
1998: Repatriation of foreign workers commenced, as the economy contracted sharply due to the rescue plan. The opposition Chart Patthana party was brought into the coalition government of Chuan Leekpai, increasing its majority to push through economic reforms.
2001: The Thai Rak Thai party won general elections, but failed to achieve an absolute majority. Thaksin Shinawatra became prime minister.
2004: The tsunami that struck the region caused over 5000 deaths, many of them foreign tourists.
2005: Prime minister Thaksin retained power, with his Thai Rak Thai party winning a landslide election victory.

thalassaemia or **Cooley's anaemia** any of a group of chronic hereditary blood disorders that are widespread in the Mediterranean countries, Africa, the Far East, and the Middle East. They are characterized by an abnormality of the red blood cells and bone marrow, with enlargement of the spleen. The genes responsible are carried by about 100 million people worldwide. The diseases can be diagnosed prenatally.

thallium chemical symbol Tl, (Greek *thallos* 'young green shoot') soft, bluish-white, malleable, metallic element, atomic number 81, relative atomic mass 204.38. It is a poor conductor of electricity. Its compounds are poisonous and are used as insecticides and rodent poisons; some are used in the optical-glass and infrared-glass industries and in photocells.

Thames river in south England, flowing through London; length 338 km/210 mi. The longest river in England, it rises in the Cotswold Hills above Cirencester and is tidal as far as Teddington. Below London there is protection from flooding by means of the **Thames Barrier** (1982). The headstreams unite at Lechlade.

Thanksgiving *or* **Thanksgiving Day** national holiday in the USA (fourth Thursday in November) and Canada (second Monday in October), first celebrated by the Pilgrim settlers in Massachusetts after their first harvest in 1621.

Thant, U (1909–1974) Burmese diplomat, secretary general of the United Nations 1962–71. He helped to resolve the US–Soviet crisis over the Soviet installation of missiles in Cuba, and he made the controversial decision to withdraw the UN peacekeeping force from the Egypt–Israel border in 1967 (see *Arab-Israeli Wars).

Thatcher, Margaret Hilda (1925–) Baroness Thatcher; born Margaret Hilda Roberts, British Conservative politician, prime minister 1979–90. She was education minister 1970–74 and Conservative Party leader 1975–90. In 1982 she sent British troops to recapture the Falkland Islands from Argentina. She confronted trade-union power during the miners' strike 1984–85, sold off majority stakes in many public utilities to the private sector, and reduced the influence of local government through such measures as the abolition of metropolitan councils, the control of expenditure through 'rate-capping', and the introduction of the community charge, or *poll tax, in 1989. In 1990, splits in the cabinet over the issues of Europe and consensus government forced her resignation. An astute parliamentary tactician, she tolerated little disagreement, either from the opposition or from within her own party.

Thatcherism political outlook comprising a belief in the efficacy of market forces, the need for strong central government, and a conviction that self-help is preferable to reliance on the state, combined with a strong element of *nationalism. The ideology is associated with the former UK premier Margaret *Thatcher, but stems from an individualist view found in Britain's 19th-century Liberal and 20th-century Conservative parties, and is no longer confined to Britain.

theatre place or building in which dramatic performances for an audience take place; these include *drama, dancing, music, mime, *opera, *ballet, and puppet performances. Theatre history can be traced to Egyptian religious ritualistic drama as long ago as 3200 BC. The first known European theatres were in Greece from about 600 BC.

Thebes Greek name of an ancient city (**Niut-Amen**) in Upper Egypt, on the Nile. Probably founded under the first dynasty, it was the centre of the worship of Amen, and the Egyptian capital under the New Kingdom from about 1550 BC. Temple ruins survive near the villages of Karnak and Luxor, and in the nearby **Valley of the Kings** are buried the 18th to 20th dynasty kings, including Tutankhamen and Amenhotep III.

Thebes capital of Boeotia in ancient Greece. In the Peloponnesian War it was allied with Sparta against Athens. For a short time after 371 BC when Thebes defeated Sparta at Leuctra, it was the most powerful state in Greece. Alexander the Great destroyed it in 336 BC and although it was restored, it never regained its former power.

theism belief in the existence of gods, but more specifically in that of a single personal God, at once immanent (active) in the created world and transcendent (separate) from it.

Themis in Greek mythology, one of the *Titans, the daughter of Uranus and Gaia. She was the personification of law and order.

Themistocles (c. 524–c. 460 BC) Athenian admiral and politician. His success in persuading the Athenians to build a navy is credited with saving Greece from Persian conquest. During the Persian War, he fought with distinction in the battles of Artemisium and *Salamis in 480 BC. After the war he pursued an anti-Spartan line which got him ostracized, possibly in 471. Some years later he fled to Asia Minor where he died.

theocracy political system run by priests, as was once found in Tibet. In practical terms it means a system where religious values determine political decisions. The closest modern examples have been Iran during the period when Ayatollah Khomeini was its religious leader, 1979–89, and Afghanistan under the Islamic fundamentalist Taliban regime, 1996–2001. The term was coined by the historian Josephus in the 1st century AD.

theodolite instrument for the measurement of horizontal and vertical angles, used in surveying. It consists of a small telescope mounted so as to move on two graduated circles, one horizontal and the other vertical, while its axes pass through the centre of the circles.

Theodora (c. 508–548) Byzantine empress from 527. She was originally the mistress of Emperor Justinian before marrying him in 525. She earned a reputation for charity, courage, and championing the rights of women.

Theodoric the Great (c. 455–526) King of the Ostrogoths 471–526. He led the Ostrogoths from the Danube frontier regions of the Roman Empire to conquer Italy, where he established a peaceful and prosperous kingdom. Although remembered for his benevolent rule in later years, Theodoric was ruthless in his efforts to attain power. He had no strong successor and his kingdom eventually became part of the Byzantine Empire of Justinian.

Theodosius (I) the Great (c. AD 346–395) Roman emperor. Appointed emperor of the East in 379, he fought against the *Goths successfully, and established Christianity throughout the region. He invaded Italy in 393, restoring unity to the empire, and died in Milan. He was buried in Constantinople.

theology study of God or gods, either by reasoned deduction from the natural world (natural theology) or through divine revelation (revealed theology), as in the scriptures of Christianity, Islam, or other religions.

theorbo musical instrument, a bass *lute or archlute developed around 1500 and incorporating dual sets of strings, a set of freely vibrating bass strings for plucking with the thumb in addition to five to seven courses over a fretted fingerboard. It survived to form part of the Italian baroque orchestra from about 1700.

theorem mathematical proposition that can be deduced by logic from a set of axioms (basic facts that are taken to be true without proof). Advanced mathematics consists almost entirely of theorems and proofs, but even at a simple level theorems are important.

theory in science, a set of ideas, concepts, principles, or methods used to explain a wide set of observed facts. Among the major theories of science are *relativity, *quantum theory, *evolution, and *plate tectonics.

theosophy any religious or philosophical system based on intuitive insight into the nature of the divine, but especially that of the Theosophical Society, founded in New York in 1875 by Madame Blavatsky and H S Olcott. It was based on Hindu ideas of *karma and *reincarnation, with *nirvana as the eventual aim.

Theravada *or* **Hinayana** one of the two major forms of *Buddhism, common in Southeast Asia (Sri Lanka, Thailand, Cambodia, and Myanmar); the other is the later Mahayana.

Thérèse of Lisieux, St (1873–1897) born Thérèse Martin, French saint. She was born in Alençon, and entered a Carmelite convent in Lisieux at 15, where her holy life induced her superior to ask her to write her spiritual autobiography. She advocated the 'Little Way of Goodness' in small things in everyday life, and became known as the 'Little Flower of Jesus'. She died of tuberculosis and was canonized in 1925.

thermal conductivity ability of a substance to conduct heat. Good thermal conductors, like good electrical conductors, are generally materials with many free electrons, such as *metals. A poor conductor, called an *insulator, has low conductivity.

thermal reactor nuclear reactor in which the neutrons released by fission of uranium-235 nuclei are slowed down in order to increase their chances of being captured by other uranium-235 nuclei, and so induce further fission. The material (commonly graphite or heavy water) responsible for doing so is called a **moderator**. When the fast newly emitted neutrons collide with the nuclei of the moderator's atoms, some of their kinetic energy is lost and their speed is reduced. Those that have been slowed down to a speed that matches the thermal (heat) energy of the surrounding material are called **thermal neutrons**, and it is these that are most likely to induce fission and ensure the continuation of the chain reaction. See *nuclear reactor and *nuclear energy.

thermocouple electric temperature measuring device consisting of a circuit having two wires made of different metals welded together at their ends. A current flows in the circuit when the two junctions are maintained at different temperatures (*Seebeck effect). The electromotive force generated – measured by a millivoltmeter – is proportional to the temperature difference.

thermodynamics branch of physics dealing with the transformation of heat into and from other forms of energy. It is the basis of the study of the efficient working of engines, such as the steam and internal combustion engines. The three laws of thermodynamics are: (1) energy can be neither created nor destroyed, heat and mechanical work being mutually convertible; (2) it is impossible for an unaided self-acting machine to convey heat from one body to

another at a higher temperature; and (3) it is impossible by any procedure, no matter how idealized, to reduce any system to the *absolute zero of temperature (0 K/–273.15 °C/–459.67 °F) in a finite number of operations. Put into mathematical form, these laws have widespread applications in physics and chemistry.

thermography photographic recording of heat patterns. It is used medically as an imaging technique to identify 'hot spots' in the body – for example, tumours, where cells are more active than usual. Thermography was developed in the 1970s and 1980s by the military to assist night vision by detecting the body heat of an enemy or the hot engine of a tank. It uses detectors sensitive to infrared (heat) radiation.

thermometer instrument for measuring temperature. There are many types, designed to measure different temperature ranges to varying degrees of accuracy. Each makes use of a different physical effect of temperature. Expansion of a liquid is employed in common **liquid-in-glass thermometers**, such as those containing mercury or alcohol. The more accurate **gas thermometer** uses the effect of temperature on the pressure of a gas held at constant volume. A **resistance thermometer** takes advantage of the change in resistance of a conductor (such as a platinum wire) with variation in temperature. Another electrical thermometer is the *thermocouple. Mechanically, temperature change can be indicated by the change in curvature of a **bimetallic strip** (as commonly used in a *thermostat).

Thermopylae, Battle of battle between the Greeks under the Spartan king Leonidas and the invading Persians under Xerxes I. They clashed at the narrow mountain pass of Thermopylae, leading from Thessaly to Locrish in central Greece. Although the Greeks were defeated, the heroism of those who fought to the last against the Persians boosted Greek morale.

thermosphere layer in the Earth's *atmosphere above the mesosphere and below the exosphere. Its lower level is about 80 km/50 mi above the ground, but its upper level is undefined. The ionosphere is located in the thermosphere. In the thermosphere the temperature rises with increasing height to several thousand degrees Celsius. However, because of the thinness of the air, very little heat is actually present.

thermostat temperature-controlling device that makes use of feedback. It employs a temperature sensor (often a bimetallic strip) to operate a switch or valve to control electricity or fuel supply. Thermostats are used in central heating, ovens, and engine cooling systems.

thesaurus (Greek 'treasure') extensive collection of synonyms or words with related meaning. Thesaurus compilers include Francis *Bacon, Comenius (see Jan Amos Komensky), and Peter Mark Roget, whose work was published in 1852.

Theseus in Greek mythology, a hero of *Attica, who was believed to have united the states of the area under a constitutional government in Athens. He killed the monstrous *Minotaur with the aid of *Ariadne, fought the *Amazons, and took part in the expedition of the *Argonauts.

Thessaloníki English **Salonika**; also known as **Thessalonica** and **Saloniki**, port in Macedonia, northeastern Greece, at the head of the Gulf of

Thessaloníki; the second-largest city in Greece; population (2003 est) 361,200, urban agglomeration 802,200. A major modern port (opened in 1901), and an industrial and commercial centre, its exports include grain, food products, manganese and chrome ores, tobacco, and hides. Industries include textiles, shipbuilding, oil refining, petrochemicals, steel, brewing, machinery, and tanning.

Thessaly Greek **Thessalia**, region of eastern central Greece, on the Aegean; area 13,904 sq km/5,368 sq mi; population (1991) 731,200. It is a major area of cereal production. It was an independent state in ancient Greece and later formed part of the Roman province of *Macedonia. It was Turkish from the 14th century until incorporated in Greece in 1881.

Thetis in Greek mythology, the most beautiful *Nereid (a sea goddess), and mother of *Achilles. She dipped the baby in the *Styx, rendering him invulnerable except for the heel which she held. In Homer's *Iliad* she also gave Achilles armour forged by Hephaestus. Fated to have a son more powerful than his father, she was married by the gods against her will to a mortal, Peleus.

thiamine or **vitamin B₁** a water-soluble vitamin of the B complex. It is found in seeds and grain. Its absence from the diet causes the disease *beriberi.

Thimphu or **Thimbu, Thimpu,** or **Thimpago** capital of Bhutan, lying on the River Raidak at an altitude of 2,000 m/7,000 ft; population (2001 est) 48,300. It is also the capital of Thimphu District, with a population (1995 est) of 116,000, and is the main marketing centre for agricultural goods produced in the surrounding valley and on terraced hill slopes, including rice, maize, and wheat. Power is supplied by a hydroelectric station (1966), and industries include sawmilling, wood products, and food processing. The Indo-Bhutan Highway (1968) is the main route from Thimphu into India via Phuntsholing.

Third Reich or **Third Empire** Germany during the years of Adolf *Hitler's dictatorship after 1933. Hitler and the *Nazis wanted to place their government into the history of Germany for both historical precedent and legitimacy. The idea of the Third Reich was based on the existence of two previous German empires: the medieval *Holy Roman Empire, and the second empire of 1871 to 1918.

Third World former term used to describe countries of the *developing world, now considered derogatory. The classifications First (western industrialized free-market), Second (eastern Communist bloc), and Third (developing or non-aligned) worlds arose during the *Cold War, but began to lose their political meaning as the Cold War came to an end in the late 1980s.

Thirteen Colonies original North American colonies that signed the *Declaration of Independence from Britain in 1776. After the Continental Army (the first regular US fighting force, organized in 1775 to supplement local militias) defeated the British army in the *American Revolution 1776–81, the 13 colonies became the original 13 United States of America: Connecticut, Delaware, Georgia, Maryland, Massachusetts, New Hampshire, New Jersey, New York, North Carolina, Pennsylvania, Rhode Island, South Carolina, and Virginia. They were united first under the Articles of *Confederation and from 1789, the US Constitution.

38th parallel demarcation line between North (People's Democratic Republic of) and South (Republic of) Korea, agreed at the Yalta Conference in 1945 and largely unaltered by the Korean War 1950–53.

35 mm width of photographic film, the most popular format for the camera today. The 35-mm camera falls into two categories, the SLR and the rangefinder.

Thirty-Nine Articles set of articles of faith defining the doctrine of the Anglican Church; see under *Anglican communion.

Thirty Years' War major war 1618–48 in central Europe. Beginning as a German conflict between Protestants and Catholics, it was gradually transformed into a struggle to determine whether the ruling Austrian Habsburg family could gain control of all Germany. The war caused serious economic and demographic problems in central Europe. Under the **Peace of Westphalia** the German states were granted their sovereignty and the emperor retained only nominal control.

thistle any of a group of prickly plants with spiny stems, soft cottony purple flower heads, and deeply indented leaves with prickly edges. The thistle is the national emblem of Scotland. (Genera include *Carduus, Carlina, Onopordum,* and *Cirsium*; family Compositae.)

Thomas, Dylan Marlais (1914–1953) Welsh poet. His poems, characterized by complex imagery and a strong musicality, include the celebration of his 30th birthday 'Poem in October' and the evocation of his youth 'Fern Hill' (1946). His 'play for voices' *Under Milk Wood* (1954) describes with humour and compassion a day in the life of the residents of a small Welsh fishing village, Llareggub. The short stories of *Portrait of the Artist as a Young Dog* (1940) are autobiographical.

Thomas à Kempis (c. 1380–1471) adopted name of Thomas Hämmerken, German Augustinian monk, author of *De Imitatio Christi/Imitation of Christ* (1441), a devotional handbook of the *devotio moderna*. The work proved quickly popular, being translated into Dutch and French.

Thomas, St (died AD 53) In the New Testament, one of the 12 Apostles, said to have preached in southern India, hence the ancient churches there were referred to as the 'Christians of St Thomas'. He is not the author of the Gospel of St Thomas, the Gnostic collection of Jesus' sayings.

Thomson, George Paget (1892–1975) English physicist who shared the Nobel Prize for Physics in 1937 for his work on *interference phenomena in the scattering of electrons by crystals which helped to confirm the wavelike nature of particles. He was knighted in 1943.

Thomson, J(oseph) J(ohn) (1856–1940) English physicist. He discovered the *electron in 1897. His work inaugurated the electrical theory of the atom, and his elucidation of positive rays and their application to an analysis of neon led to the discovery of *isotopes. He was awarded the Nobel Prize for Physics in 1906 for his theoretical and experimental work on the conduction of electricity by gases. He was knighted in 1908.

Thor in Norse and Teutonic mythology, the god of thunder (his hammer), represented as a man of enormous strength defending humanity against demons and the frost giants. He was the son of Odin and Freya, and one of the Aesir (warrior gods). Thursday is named after him.

thorax part of the body in four-limbed vertebrates containing the *heart and *lungs, and protected by the ribcage. It is separated from the abdomen by the diaphragm. During *breathing (ventilation) the volume inside the thorax is changed. This then causes air to move in or out of the air passages that lead to the lungs. The volume of the thorax is altered by the contraction of *muscles in the diaphragm and the contraction of muscles between the ribs – the intercostal muscles.

Thoreau, Henry David (1817–1862) US author. One of the most influential figures of 19th-century US literature, he is best known for his vigorous defence of individualism and the simple life. His work *Walden, or Life in the Woods* (1854) stimulated the back-to-nature movement, and he completed some 30 volumes based on his daily nature walks. His essay 'Civil Disobedience' (1849), prompted by his refusal to pay taxes, advocated peaceful resistance to unjust laws and had a wide impact, even in the 20th century.

thorium chemical symbol Th, dark-grey, radioactive, metallic element of the *actinide series, atomic number 90, relative atomic mass 232.038. It occurs throughout the world in small quantities in minerals such as thorite and is widely distributed in monazite beach sands. It is one of three fissile elements (the others are uranium and plutonium) and its longest-lived isotope has a half-life of 1.39×10^{10} years. Thorium is used to strengthen alloys. It was discovered by Jöns Berzelius in 1828 and was named by him after the Norse god Thor.

thorn apple or **jimson weed** annual plant belonging to the nightshade family, native to America and naturalized worldwide. It grows to 2 m/6 ft in northern temperate and subtropical areas and has white or violet trumpet-shaped flowers followed by capsulelike fruits that split to release black seeds. All parts of the plant are poisonous. (*Datura stramonium*, family Solanaceae.)

thoroughbred horse bred for racing purposes. All racehorses are thoroughbreds, and all are direct descendants of one of three stallions imported into Britain during the 17th and 18th centuries: the Darley Arabian, Byerley Turk, and Godolphin Barb.

Thoth in Egyptian mythology, the god of wisdom, learning, and magic. Inventor of *hieroglyphic writing, he was the patron of scribes, and associated with the Moon, whose phases were used for reckoning. He was represented as a dog-faced baboon or as a scribe with the head of an ibis; the bird was sacred to him. He was identified by the Greeks with Hermes Trismegistos.

Thrace Greek **Thráki**, ancient region of the Balkans, southeastern Europe, formed by parts of modern Greece and Bulgaria. It was held successively by the Greeks, Persians, Macedonians, and Romans.

threadworm or **pinworm** parasitic *nematode that may infest the human gut. Threadworms are relatively harmless and found mainly in children.

Three Kingdoms period in Chinese history from 220 to 581, an era of disruptive, intermittent warfare between three powers. Sometimes the term is used to cover only the period 220 to 280 following the end of the *Han dynasty when the Wei, Shu, and Wu fought for supremacy.

Three Mile Island island in the Susquehana River near Harrisburg, Pennsylvania. It is the site of a nuclear power station which was put out of action following a serious accident in March 1979. Opposition to nuclear power in the USA was reinforced after this accident and safety standards reassessed. Only part of the plant was affected and the other reactor re-opened in 1985. The clean-up took 12 years and cost nearly $1 billion.

thrift or **sea pink** any of several perennial low-growing coastal plants. The common sea pink *A. maritima* occurs in clumps on seashores and cliffs throughout Europe. The leaves are small and linear and the dense round heads of pink flowers rise on straight stems. (Genus *Armeria*, family Plumbaginaceae.)

thrips any of a number of tiny insects of the order Thysanoptera, usually with feathery wings. Many of the 3,000 species live in flowers and suck their juices, causing damage and spreading disease. Others eat fungi, decaying matter, or smaller insects.

throat in human anatomy, the passage that leads from the back of the nose and mouth to the *trachea and *oesophagus. It includes the pharynx and the *larynx, the latter being at the top of the trachea. The word 'throat' is also used to mean the front part of the neck, both in humans and other vertebrates; for example, in describing the plumage of birds. In engineering, it is any narrowing entry, such as the throat of a carburettor.

thrombosis condition in which a blood clot forms in a vein or artery, causing loss of circulation to the area served by the vessel. If it breaks away, it often travels to the lungs, causing pulmonary embolism.

thrush any bird of the large family Turdidae, order Passeriformes, found worldwide and known for their song. Thrushes are usually brown with speckles of other colours. They are 12–30 cm/5–12 in long.

thrush infection usually of the mouth (particularly in infants), but also sometimes of the vagina, caused by a yeastlike fungus (*Candida*). It is seen as white patches on the mucous membranes.

Thucydides (c. 455 BC–c. 400 BC) Athenian historian. He was briefly a general during the *Peloponnesian War with Sparta, but as a result of his failure to save Amphipolis from the Spartan general Brasidas, he was banished from Athens in 424. His *History of the Peloponnesian War* gives a detailed account of the conflict to 411.

thug originally a member of a Hindu sect who strangled travellers as sacrifices to *Kali, the goddess of destruction. The sect was suppressed in about 1830.

Thule Greek and Roman name for the most northerly land known, originally used by the explorer Pytheas to refer to land he discovered six days after leaving the northern coast of Britain. It has been identified with the Shetlands, the Orkneys, Iceland, and Scandinavia.

thulium chemical symbol Tm, soft, silver-white, malleable and ductile, metallic element of the *lanthanide series, atomic number 69, relative atomic mass 168.94. It is the least abundant of the rare earth metals, and was first found in gadolinite and various other minerals. It is used in arc lighting.

Thunderbird legendary bird of the North American Indians, the creator of storms. It is said to produce thunder by flapping its wings and lightning by opening and closing its eyes.

thunderstorm severe storm of very heavy rain, thunder, and lightning. Thunderstorms are usually caused by the intense heating of the ground surface during summer. The warm air rises rapidly to form tall cumulonimbus clouds with a characteristic anvil-shaped top. Electrical charges accumulate in the clouds and are discharged to the ground as flashes of lightning. Air in the path of lightning becomes heated and expands rapidly, creating shock waves that are heard as a crash or rumble of thunder.

Thuringia German **Thüringen**, administrative region (German *Land*) in central Germany, bounded to the north by Saxony-Anhalt and Lower Saxony, to the east by Saxony, to the south by Bavaria, and to the west by Hesse; area 16,172 sq km/6,244 sq mi; population (1999 est) 2,449,100. The capital is Erfurt, and other major towns include Weimar, Gera, Jena, and Eisenach.

thyme any of several herbs belonging to the mint family. Garden thyme *T. vulgaris*, native to the Mediterranean, grows to 30 cm/1 ft high and has small leaves and pinkish flowers. Its aromatic leaves are used for seasoning in cookery. (Genus *Thymus*, family Labiatae.)

thymus organ in vertebrates, situated in the upper chest cavity in humans. The thymus processes *lymphocyte cells to produce T-lymphocytes (T denotes 'thymus-derived'), which are responsible for binding to specific invading organisms and killing them or rendering them harmless.

thyroid *endocrine gland of vertebrates, situated in the neck in front of the trachea. It secretes several hormones, principally thyroxine, an iodine-containing hormone that stimulates growth, metabolism, and other functions of the body. The thyroid gland may be thought of as the regulator gland of the body's metabolic rate.If it is overactive, as in hyperthyroidism, the sufferer feels hot and sweaty, has an increased heart rate, diarrhoea, and weight loss. Conversely, an underactive thyroid leads to myxoedema, a condition characterized by sensitivity to the cold, constipation, and weight gain. In infants, an underactive thyroid leads to cretinism, a form of mental retardation.

Tiananmen Square (Chinese 'Square of Heavenly Peace') paved open space in central Beijing (Peking), China, the largest public square in the world (area 0.4 sq km/0.14 sq mi). On 3–4 June 1989 more than 1,000 unarmed protesters were killed by government troops in a massacre that crushed China's emerging pro-democracy movement.

Tiber Italian **Tevere**; Latin **Tiberis**, river in Italy that flows through Rome; its length from its source in the Apennines to the Tyrrhenian Sea is 400 km/250 mi. It is Italy's third longest river.

Tiberias, Lake *or* **Sea of Galilee** *or* **Lake of Gennesaret** Hebrew **Yam Kinneret**, lake in north Israel, 210 m/689 ft below sea level, into which the River *Jordan flows; area 170 sq km/66 sq mi. The first Israeli *kibbutz (cooperative settlement) was founded nearby in 1909.

Tiberius (42 BC–AD 37) born Tiberius Claudius Nero, Roman emperor, the stepson, adopted son, and successor of Augustus from AD 14. He was a cautious ruler whose reign was marred by the heavy incident of trials for treason or conspiracy. Tiberius fell under the influence of Sejanus who encouraged the emperor's fear of assassination and was instrumental in Tiberius' departure from Rome to Caprae (Capri). He never returned to Rome.

Tibet Chinese **Xizang**, autonomous region of southwestern China; area 1,221,600 sq km/471,700 sq mi; population (2000 est) 2,620,000 (many Chinese have settled in Tibet; 2 million Tibetans live in China outside Tibet). The capital is *Lhasa. Although Tibet has its own People's Government and People's Congress, Tibetan nationalists regard the province as being under colonial rule. The controlling force in Tibet is the Communist Party of China, represented locally by First Secretary Wu Jinghua from 1985. There is a government-in-exile in Dharmsala, Himachal Pradesh, India, where the *Dalai Lama lives. The religion in the region is traditionally *Lamaism (a form of Mahayana Buddhism).

Tibetan a Mongolian people inhabiting Tibet who practise a form of Mahayana Buddhism, introduced in the 7th century. Since China's Cultural Revolution 1966–68, refugee communities have formed in India and Nepal. The Tibetan language belongs to the Sino-Tibetan language family.

Tibetan mastiff large breed of dog regarded as the ancestor of many present breeds. It is a very powerful animal with a long black or black and tan coat. It is about 71 cm/28 in in height and 60 kg/132 lb in weight.

tibia anterior of the pair of bones in the leg between the ankle and the knee. In humans, the tibia is the shinbone. It articulates with the *femur above to form the knee joint, the *fibula externally at its upper and lower ends, and with the talus below, forming the ankle joint.

tick any of the arachnid family Ixodoidae, order Acarina, of large bloodsucking mites. They have flat bodies protected by horny shields. Many carry and transmit diseases to mammals (including humans) and birds.

tidal energy energy derived from the tides. The tides mainly gain their potential energy from the gravitational forces acting between the Earth and the Moon. If water is trapped at a high level during high tide, perhaps by means of a barrage across an estuary, it may then be gradually released and its associated gravitational potential energy exploited to drive *turbines and generate electricity. Several schemes have been proposed for the Bristol Channel, in southwestern England, but environmental concerns as well as construction costs have so far prevented any decision from being taken.

tidal wave common name for a *tsunami.

tide rhythmic rise and fall of the sea level in the Earth's oceans and their inlets and estuaries due to the gravitational attraction of the Moon and, to a lesser extent, the Sun, affecting regions of the Earth unequally as it rotates. Water on the side of the Earth nearest to the Moon feels the Moon's pull and accumulates directly below the Moon, producing a high tide.

Tiepolo, Giovanni Battista (Giambattista) (1696–1770) Italian painter. He was one of the first exponents of Italian rococo and created monumental decorative schemes in palaces and churches in northeastern Italy, southwestern Germany, and Madrid. His style is light-hearted, his colours light and warm, and he made great play with illusion.

Tierra del Fuego island group separated from the southern extremity of South America by the Strait of Magellan; Cape Horn is at the southernmost point.

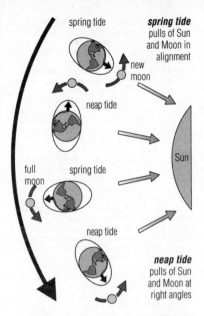

spring tide

spring tide
pulls of Sun
and Moon in
alignment

new
moon

neap tide

Sun

full
moon

spring tide

neap tide

neap tide
pulls of Sun
and Moon at
right angles

tide The gravitational pull of the Moon is the main cause of the tides. Water on the side of the Earth nearest the Moon feels the Moon's pull and accumulates directly under the Moon. When the Sun and the Moon are in line, at new and full Moon, the gravitational pull of Sun and Moon are in line and produce a high spring tide. When the Sun and Moon are at right angles, lower neap tides occur.

The islands are all mountainous and cool, with a mean annual temperature of 6 °C/43 °F. There are oil, natural gas, and sheep farming industries. Tourism is also important. The largest island is Tierra del Fuego, or **Isla Grande**, with an area of 48,100 sq km/18,571 sq mi; half of this island, and the islands west of it, belong to Chile, and form part of the Magallanes region, the capital and chief town of which is Punta Arenas. The eastern part of the archipelago belongs to Argentina, forming the federal district of Tierra del Fuego; its capital, Ushuaia, is the world's most southerly town.

Tiffany, Louis Comfort (1848–1933) US artist and glassmaker. He was the son of Charles Louis Tiffany, who founded Tiffany and Company, the New York City jewellers. He produced stained-glass windows, iridescent Favrile (from Latin *faber* 'craftsman') glass, and lampshades in the art nouveau style. He used glass that contained oxides of iron and other elements to produce rich colours.

tiger largest of the great cats, *Panthera tigris* (family Felidae, order Carnivora), formerly found in much of central and South Asia, from Siberia south to Sumatra, but nearing extinction (5,000 in 1997) because of hunting and the high prices paid for the pelt, as well as the destruction of its natural habitat. The male tiger

can grow to 3.6 m/12 ft long, while the female averages about 2.6 m/8.5 ft. It weighs up to 300 kg/660 lb, and has a yellow-orange coat with black stripes. Tigers are solitary, and largely nocturnal. They will eat carrion, but generally kill for themselves. Their food consists mainly of deer, antelopes, and smaller animals, but they sometimes kill wild boar. Human-eating tigers are rare and are the result of weakened powers or shortage of game.

Tigré a people of northern Ethiopia. The Tigré language is spoken by about 2.5 million people; it belongs to the southeastern Semitic branch of the Afro-Asiatic (Hamito-Semitic) family. **Tigrinya** is a closely related language spoken slightly to the south.

Tigré *or* **Tigray** region in the northern highlands of Ethiopia; area 65,900 sq km/25,444 sq mi; population (1999 est) 3,593,000. The chief town is Mek'ele. In the mountainous region in the west the highest point is Mokada, rising to 2,295 m/7,529 ft. The east of the region is much lower; some of the Danakil Depression is below sea level. Most of the population live by cultivation in the south and by nomadic herding in the north, but the area suffers from periodic severe droughts. Tigré is a major source of hides and skins for export and also an important producer of grain, beeswax, and wool. Potash and sulphur deposits occur in significant quantities.

Tigris Arabic Dijla, river flowing through Turkey and Iraq (see also *Mesopotamia), joining the *Euphrates 80 km/50 mi northwest of Basra, where it forms the *Shatt-al-Arab; length 1,600 km/1,000 mi.

Tijuana city and resort in northwestern Mexico, on the Pacific coast, in the state of Baja California; population (2000 est) 1,210,800. The border with the USA at Tijuana and *San Diego is believed to be the busiest frontier in the world and there is a considerable tourist trade, for which local horse and dog racing, bullfighting and casinos are attractions. Local industries include electronic equipment, textiles, and processed food.

till *or* **boulder clay** deposit of clay, mud, gravel, and boulders left by a *glacier. It is unsorted, with all sizes of fragments mixed up together, and shows no stratification; that is, it does not form clear layers or *beds.

timber wood used in construction, furniture, and paper pulp. **Hardwoods** include tropical mahogany, teak, ebony, rosewood, temperate oak, elm, beech, and eucalyptus. All except eucalyptus are slow-growing, and world supplies are limited. **Softwoods** comprise the *conifers (pine, fir, spruce, and larch), which are quick to grow and easy to work but inferior in quality of grain. **White woods** include ash, birch, and sycamore; all have light-coloured timber, are fast-growing, and can be used as veneers on cheaper timber.

timbre (French 'tone') in music, the tone colour, or quality of tone, of a particular *sound. Different instruments playing a note at the same *pitch have different sound qualities, and it is the timbre that enables the listener to distinguish the sound of, for example, a trumpet from that of a violin. The tone quality of a sound depends on several things, including its waveform, the strength of its *harmonics, and its attack and decay – the 'shape' of the sound. The study of the elements of sound quality is part of the science of acoustics.

time continuous passage of existence, recorded by division into hours, minutes, and seconds. Formerly the measurement of time was based on the Earth's rotation on its axis, but this was found to be irregular. Therefore the second, the standard *SI unit of time, was redefined in 1956 in terms of the Earth's annual orbit of the Sun, and in 1967 in terms of a radiation pattern of the element caesium.

Timișoara capital of Timiș county, western Romania; population (1993) 325,000. Industries include electrical engineering, chemicals, pharmaceuticals, textiles, food processing, metal, and footwear. The revolt against the Ceaușescu regime began here in December 1989 when demonstrators prevented the arrest and deportation of a popular Protestant minister who was promoting the rights of ethnic Hungarians. This soon led to large pro-democracy rallies.

Timon Athenian of the age of *Pericles notorious for his misanthropy, which was reported and elaborated by classical authors, and became the subject of the play by *Shakespeare.

Timor largest and most easterly of the Lesser Sunda Islands, in the Malay Archipelago; area 33,610 sq km/ 12,973 sq mi. It is divided into **West Timor**, under Indonesian rule, and the country of ***East Timor**. Its indigenous people were the Atoni; successive migrants have included Malaysians, Melanesians, Chinese, Arabs, and Gujerati. Produce includes coffee, maize, rice, and coconuts.

tin chemical symbol Sn, soft, silver-white, malleable and somewhat ductile, metallic element, symbol Sn, atomic number 50, relative atomic mass 118.69. Its chemical symbol comes from the Latin *stannum*. Tin exhibits *allotropy, having three forms: the familiar lustrous metallic form above 13.2 °C/55.8 °F, a brittle form above 161 °C/321.8 °F, and a grey powder form below 13.2 °C/55.8 °F (commonly called tin pest or tin disease). The metal is quite soft (slightly harder than lead) and can be rolled, pressed, or hammered into extremely thin sheets; it has a low melting point. In nature it occurs rarely as a free metal. It resists corrosion and is therefore used for coating and plating other metals.

Tinbergen, Niko(laas) (1907–1988) Dutch-born British zoologist who was awarded a Nobel Prize for Physiology or Medicine in 1973 for his work in animal behaviour patterns. He specialized in the study of instinctive behaviour in animals, and was one of the founders of *ethology, the scientific study of animal behaviour in natural surroundings. He shared the prize with Konrad *Lorenz (with whom he worked on several projects) and Karl von Frisch.

tinnitus in medicine, constant buzzing or ringing in the ears. The phenomenon may originate from prolonged exposure to noisy conditions (drilling, machinery, or loud music) or from damage to or disease of the middle or inner ear. The victim may become overwhelmed by the relentless noise in the head.

Tintagel village resort on the coast of north Cornwall, southwest England; population (1991) 1,800. There are castle ruins, and legend has it that King Arthur was born and held court here.

Tintoretto (1518–1594) adopted name of Jacopo Robusti, Venetian painter who produced portraits and religious works of great intensity. Outstanding among his many works is a series of religious works in the

Scuola di S Rocco in Venice (1564–88), the dramatic figures lit by a flickering, unearthly light, the space around them distorted into long perspectives. Among his best-known works is *St George and the Dragon* (c.1570; National Gallery, London).

Tipperary county of the Republic of Ireland, in the province of Munster, divided into the administrative areas of North and South Ridings; county town Clonmel; area 4,255 sq km/1,643 sq mi; population (2002 est) 61,000. It includes part of the Golden Vale, a fertile dairy-farming region. Agriculture is the chief industry; barley and oats are the main crops, but potatoes and turnips are also grown. Cattle are reared in large numbers, and there are flour mills and butter factories. There is also horse and greyhound breeding. Other main towns are Cahir, Carrick-on-Suir, Cashel, Templemore, Tipperary, Thurles, Nenagh, and Roscrea. Major tourist attractions in the county include the Rock of Cashel (a group of medieval buildings including a 12th-century round tower and 13th-century cathedral) and Cahir Castle (15th century).

Tippett, Michael (Kemp) (1905–1998) English composer. With Benjamin Britten, he became the foremost English composer of his generation. His works include the operas *The Midsummer Marriage* (1952), *The Knot Garden* (1970), and *New Year* (1989); four symphonies; *Songs for Ariel* (1962); and choral music, including *The Mask of Time* (1982).

Tipu Sultan (c. 1750–1799) Sultan of Mysore (now Karnataka) in southwestern India from the death of his father, *Hyder Ali in 1782. He died of wounds when his capital, Seringapatam, was captured by the British. His rocket brigade led Sir William Congreve (1772–1828) to develop the weapon for use in the *Napoleonic Wars.

Tirana (or Tiranë) capital (since 1920) of Albania; population (1991) 251,000. Industries include metallurgy, cotton textiles, soap, and cigarettes. It was founded in the early 17th century by Turks when part of the Ottoman Empire. Although the city is now largely composed of recent buildings, some older districts and mosques have been preserved.

Tiresias or Teiresias in Greek mythology, a man of Thebes blinded by the gods and given the ability to predict the future.

Tirol federal state of Austria, bounded to the north by Bavaria and to the south by Italy; area 12,648 sq km/ 4,883 sq mi; population (2001 est) 675,100. Its capital is Innsbruck. East Tirol, the part south of the Hohe Tauern, is detached from the rest of the province.

tissue in biology, any kind of cellular fabric that occurs in an organism's body. It is a group of similar *cells that are carrying out a function in a plant or animal. Several kinds of tissue can usually be distinguished, each consisting of cells of a particular kind bound together by cell walls (in plants) or extracellular matrix (in animals). Thus, nerve and muscle are different kinds of tissue in animals, as are parenchyma and *sclerenchyma in plants. Tissues of different kinds may be found in a distinct structure, which is then called an *organ. The leaf of a plant or the heart of a mammal is an organ.

tissue culture process by which cells from a plant or animal are removed from the organism and grown under controlled conditions in a sterile medium containing all the necessary nutrients. Tissue culture can provide information on cell growth and differentiation, and is also used in plant propagation and drug production.

tit *or* **titmouse** any of 65 species of insectivorous, acrobatic bird of the family Paridae, order Passeriformes. Tits are 8–20 cm/3–8 in long and have grey or black plumage, often with blue or yellow markings. They are found in Eurasia and Africa, and also in North America, where they are called **chickadees.**

Titan in astronomy, largest moon of the planet Saturn, with a diameter of 5,150 km/3,200 miand a mean distance from Saturn of 1,222,000 km/759,000 mi. It was discovered in 1655 by Dutch mathematician and astronomer Christiaan *Huygens, and is the second-largest moon in the Solar System (only Ganymede, of Jupiter, is larger).

Titan in Greek mythology, any of the giant children of *Uranus, the primeval sky god, and *Gaia, goddess of the Earth, whose six sons and six daughters included *Kronos, Rhea, *Themis, and Oceanus. Kronos and Rhea were in turn the parents of Zeus, who ousted his father as ruler of the world.

Titanic British passenger liner, supposedly unsinkable, that struck an iceberg and sank off the Grand Banks of Newfoundland on its first voyage on 14–15 April 1912; estimates of the number of lives lost, largely due to inadequate provision of lifeboats, vary between 1,503 and 1,517. In 1985 it was located by robot submarine 4 km/2.5 mi down in an ocean canyon, preserved by the cold environment, and in 1987 salvage operations began.

titanium chemical symbol Ti, strong, lightweight, silver-grey, metallic element, atomic number 22, relative atomic mass 47.90. The ninth most abundant element in the Earth's crust, its compounds occur in practically all igneous rocks and their sedimentary deposits. It is very strong and resistant to corrosion, so it is used in building high-speed aircraft and spacecraft; it is also widely used in making alloys, as it unites with almost every metal except copper and aluminium. Titanium oxide is used in high-grade white pigments.

titanium ore any mineral from which titanium is extracted, principally ilmenite ($FeTiO_3$) and rutile (TiO_2). Brazil, India, and Canada are major producers. Both these ore minerals are found either in rock formations or concentrated in heavy mineral sands.

tithe formerly, payment exacted from the inhabitants of a parish for the maintenance of the church and its incumbent; some religious groups continue the practice by giving 10% of members' incomes to charity.

Titian (c. 1487–1576) Italian Tiziano Vecellio, Italian painter. He was one of the greatest artists of the High Renaissance. During his long career he was court painter to Charles V, Holy Roman Emperor, and to his son, Philip II of Spain. He produced a vast number of portraits, religious paintings, and mythological scenes, including *Bacchus and Ariadne* (1520–23; National Gallery, London) and *Venus and Adonis* (1554; Prado, Madrid).

Titicaca, Lake lake in the Andes, 3,810 m/12,500 ft above sea level and 1,220 m/4,000 ft above the treeline; area 8,300 sq km/3,200 sq mi, the largest lake in South America, and the world's highest navigable body of water. It is divided between Bolivia (port at Guaqui) and Peru (ports at Puno (principal port) and Huancane). The lake is fed by several streams which originate in the snow-capped surrounding mountains. It has a maximum depth of 280 m/920 ft and a mean annual temperature of 11 °C/51 °F, and moderates the climate of the surrounding area so that crops such as maize, barley, and potatoes can be grown. The lake contains enormous frogs, which are farmed, the legs being an edible delicacy, and there is some trout farming. The herding of alpacas and llamas is also common. It is one of the few places in the world where balsas (reed boats) are still made, and here the craft is practised by the Uru indigenous people. The lake is also used for irrigation.

Tito (1892–1980) adopted name of Josip Broz, Yugoslav communist politician, in effective control of Yugoslavia from 1943. In World War II he organized the National Liberation Army to carry on guerrilla warfare against the German invasion in 1941, and was created marshal in 1943. As prime minister 1945–53 and president from 1953 until his death, he followed a foreign policy of 'positive neutralism'.

titration in analytical chemistry, a technique to find the concentration of one compound in a solution by determining how much of it will react with a known amount of another compound in solution. Typically a burette is filled with an acid of unknown concentration which is slowly (drop by drop) added to a known volume of an alkali of a known concentration, mixed with an indicator (such as phenolphthalein). The volume of acid need to neutralize the alkali in the flask can be used to calculate the concentration of the acid.

Titus (AD 39–81) born Titus Flavius Vespasianus, Roman emperor from AD 79. Eldest son of *Vespasian, he captured Jerusalem in 70 to end the Jewish revolt in Roman Palestine. He completed the Colosseum, and helped to mitigate the suffering from the eruption of Vesuvius in 79, which destroyed Pompeii and Herculaneum.

Tlingit member of an *American Indian people living on the coasts of southwest Alaska and northern British Columbia for thousands of years. Their language belongs to the Na-Dene family, but is rarely spoken. Like other Northwest Indians, they are known for their dugout canoes, potlatch ceremonies (gift-giving to gain status), and carved wooden 'totem' poles representing family crests. Pacific salmon provided their main staple food. Most Tlingit are now Christian, with traditional ceremonies performed mainly for tourists. In Alaska they share tribal government with the Haida, and have a joint population of 14,800 (2000). Tlingit lands and resources are managed by their Sealaska corporation.

TNT abbreviation for **trinitrotoluene**, $CH_3C_6H_2(NO_2)_3$, a powerful high explosive. It is a yellow solid, prepared in several isomeric forms from *toluene by using sulphuric and nitric acids.

toad any of the more terrestrial warty-skinned members of the tailless amphibians (order Anura). The name commonly refers to members of the genus *Bufo*, family Bufonidae, which are found worldwide, except for Australia (where the marine or *cane toad *B. marinus* has been introduced), Madagascar, and Antarctica. They differ from *frogs chiefly by the total absence of teeth, and in certain other anatomical features.

toadflax any of a group of small plants belonging to the snapdragon family, native to Western Europe and Asia.

913

Toadflaxes have spurred, two-lipped flowers, commonly purple or yellow, and grow 20–80 cm/8–32 in tall. (Genus *Linaria*, family Scrophulariaceae.)

toadstool common name for many umbrella-shaped fruiting bodies of fungi (see *fungus). The term is normally applied to those that are inedible or poisonous.

tobacco any of a group of large-leaved plants belonging to the nightshade family, native to tropical parts of the Americas. The species *Nicotiana tabacum* is widely cultivated in warm, dry climates for use in cigars and cigarettes, and in powdered form as snuff. (Genus *Nicotiana*, family Solanaceae.) When it is smoked, it burns and the smoke is inhaled. Smoking tobacco causes lung cancer.

Tobago island in the West Indies; part of the republic of Trinidad and Tobago.

toccata (from Italian *toccare*, 'to touch') in music, a composition for keyboard instruments, such as the organ, in which the performer's finger technique is emphasized. This is often done by including passages using features such as arpeggios and elaborate fast runs.

tocopherol *or* **vitamin E** fat-soluble chemical found in vegetable oils. Deficiency of tocopherol leads to multiple adverse effects on health. In rats, vitamin E deficiency has been shown to cause sterility.

Tocqueville, Alexis Charles Henri Clérel de (1805–1859) French politician, sociologist, and historian. He was the author of the first analytical study of the strengths and weaknesses of US society, *De la Démocratie en Amérique/Democracy in America* (1835). He also wrote a penetrating description of France before the Revolution, *L'Ancien Régime et la Révolution/ The Old Regime and the Revolution* (1856).

tofu pressed *soybean curd derived from soymilk. It is a good source of protein and naturally low in fat.

Togo
formerly **Togoland** (until 1956)
National name: *République Togolaise/Togolese Republic*

Area: 56,800 sq km/21,930 sq mi
Capital: Lomé
Major towns/cities: Sokodé, Palimé, Kara, Atakpamé, Bassar, Tsévié
Physical features: two savannah plains, divided by range of hills northeast–southwest; coastal lagoons and marsh; Mono Tableland, Oti Plateau, Oti River
Head of state: Fauré Gnassingbé Eyadéma from 2005

Head of government: Koffi Sama from 2002
Political system: emergent democracy
Political executive: limited presidency
Political parties: Rally of the Togolese People (RPT), nationalist, centrist; Action Committee for Renewal (CAR), left of centre; Togolese Union for Democracy (UTD), left of centre
Currency: franc CFA
GNI per capita (PPP): (US$) 1,430 (2002 est)
Exports: re-exports, phosphates (mainly calcium phosphates), ginned cotton, green coffee, cocoa beans. Principal market: Benin 13% (2001)
Population: 4,909,000 (2003 est)
Language: French (official), Ewe, Kabre, Gurma, other local languages
Religion: animist about 50%, Catholic and Protestant 35%, Muslim 15%
Life expectancy: 48 (men); 51 (women) (2000–05)
Chronology
15th–17th centuries: Formerly dominated by Kwa peoples in southwest and Gur-speaking Voltaic peoples in north, Ewe clans immigrated from Nigeria and the Ane (Mina) from Ghana and the Côte d'Ivoire.
18th century: Coastal area held by Danes.
1847: Arrival of German missionaries.
1884–1914: Togoland was a German protectorate until captured by Anglo-French forces; cocoa and cotton plantations developed, using forced labour.
1922: Divided between Britain and France under League of Nations mandate.
1946: Continued under United Nations trusteeship.
1957: British Togoland, comprising one-third of the area and situated in the west, integrated with Ghana, following a referendum.
1956: French Togoland voted to become an autonomous republic within the French union. The new Togolese Republic achieved internal self-government
1960: French Togoland, situated in the east, achieved full independence from France as the Republic of Togo with Sylvanus Olympio, leader of the United Togolese (UP) party, as head of state.
1967: Lt-Gen Etienne Gnassingbé Eyadéma became president in a bloodless coup; political parties were banned.
1969: Assembly of the Togolese People (RPT) formed by Eyadéma as the sole legal political party.
1975: EEC Lomé convention signed in Lomé, establishing trade links with developing countries.
1977: An assassination plot against Eyadéma, allegedly involving the Olympio family, was thwarted.
1979: Eyadéma returned in election. Further EEC Lomé convention signed.
1986: Attempted coup failed and situation stabilized with help of French troops.
1990: There were casualties as violent antigovernment demonstrations in Lomé were suppressed; Eyadéma relegalized political parties.
1991: Eyadéma was forced to call a national conference that limited the president's powers, and elected Joseph Kokou Koffigoh head of an interim government. Three attempts by Eyadéma's troops to unseat the government failed.
1992: There were strikes in southern Togo. A referendum showed overwhelming support for multiparty politics. A new constitution was adopted.

1993: Eyadéma won the first multiparty presidential elections amid widespread opposition.

1994: An antigovernment coup was foiled. The opposition CAR polled strongly in assembly elections. Eyadéma appointed Edem Kodjo of the minority UTD prime minister.

1998: President Eyadéma was re-elected.

2000: Agbeyome Messan Kodjo was appointed prime minister.

2002: Koffi Sama became prime minister.

2003: President Eyadéma extended his 36-year term of office in Togo with a presidential election victory in which he controversially claimed 57% of the vote.

2005: President Eyadéma died and the military attempted to install his son, Faure Gnassingbé as president. Popular unrest and international pressure led to the calling of a presidential election, which was won by Faure Gnassingbé.

Tojo, Hideki (1884–1948) Japanese general and premier 1941–44 during World War II. Promoted to chief of staff of Japan's Guangdong army in Manchuria in 1937, he served as minister for war 1940–41 where he was responsible for negotiating the tripartite Axis alliance with Germany and Italy in 1940. He was held responsible for defeats in the Pacific in 1944 and forced to resign. After Japan's defeat, he was hanged as a war criminal.

Tokugawa military family which controlled Japan as *shoguns from 1603 to 1868. **Tokugawa Ieyasu** (1542–1616) was the Japanese general and politician who established the Tokugawa shogunate. The Tokugawa were feudal lords who ruled about one-quarter of Japan. Undermined by increasing foreign incursions, they were overthrown by an attack of provincial forces from Choshu, Satsuma, and Tosa, who restored the *Meiji emperor to power.

Tokyo capital of Japan, on Honshu island; population (2000 est) 8,130,000. It is Japan's main cultural, commercial, financial and industrial centre (engineering, chemicals, textiles, electrical goods). Founded in the 16th century as Yedo (or Edo), it was renamed when the emperor moved his court here from Kyoto in 1868. By the end of the 18th century, Yedo, with 1 million people, was the largest city in the world. An earthquake in 1923 killed 58,000 people and destroyed much of the city, which was again severely damaged by Allied bombing in World War II when 60% of Tokyo's housing was destroyed; US firebomb raids of 1945 were particularly destructive with over 100,000 people killed in just one night of bombing on 9 March. The subsequent rebuilding has made it into one of the world's most modern cities.

Tokyo trials war-crimes trials 1946–48 of Japan's wartime leaders, held during the Allied occupation after World War II. Former prime minister Tojo was among the seven sentenced to death by an international tribunal, while 16 were given life imprisonment. Political considerations allowed Emperor *Hirohito (Showa) to escape trial.

Tolkien, J(ohn) R(onald) R(euel) (1892–1973) English writer and scholar. To express his theological and philosophical beliefs, and as a vehicle for his linguistic scholarship, he created a complete mythological world of 'Middle Earth', on which he drew for his children's fantasy *The Hobbit* (1937), and the trilogy *The Lord of the Rings* (1954–55), nominated in a UK bookselling chain's survey in 1997 as the 'greatest book of the 20th century'. His work developed a cult following in the 1960s and had many imitators. At Oxford University he was professor of Anglo-Saxon from 1925–45 and Merton professor of English from 1945–59.

Tolpuddle Martyrs six farm labourers of Tolpuddle, a village in Dorset, England, who were transported to Australia in 1834. The labourers had formed a union on the advice of the Grand National Consolidated Trades Union (GNCTU) to try to prevent their wages being reduced. Entry into their 'union' involved a payment of a shilling (5p), and swearing before a picture of a skeleton never to tell anyone the union's secrets. Local magistrates used an old law to convict the men for 'administering unlawful oaths'. The severity of the punishment destroyed the GNCTU. After nationwide agitation, the labourers were pardoned two years later. They returned to England and all but one migrated to Canada.

Tolstoy, Leo Nikolaievich (1828–1910) Russian novelist. He wrote *War and Peace* (1863–69) and *Anna Karenina* (1873–77). He was offended by the materialism of Western Europe and in the 1860s and 1870s became a pioneer of 'free education'. From 1880 he underwent a profound spiritual crisis and took up various moral positions, including passive resistance to evil, rejection of authority (religious or civil) and private ownership, and a return to basic mystical Christianity. He was excommunicated by the Orthodox Church, and his later works were banned.

Toltec ('builder') member of an ancient American Indian people who ruled much of Mexico and Central America in the 10th–12th centuries, with their capital and religious centre at Tula or Tollán, northeast of Mexico City. They also occupied and extended the ancient Maya city of Chichen Itzá in Yucatán. After the fall of the Toltecs the Aztecs took over much of their former territory, except for the regions regained by the Maya.

toluene *or* **methyl benzene** $C_6H_5CH_3$, colourless, inflammable liquid, insoluble in water, derived from petroleum. It is used as a solvent, in aircraft fuels, in preparing phenol (carbolic acid, used in making resins for adhesives, pharmaceuticals, and as a disinfectant), and the powerful high explosive *TNT.

tomato annual plant belonging to the nightshade family, native to South America. It is widely cultivated for its shiny, round, red fruit containing many seeds (technically a berry), which is widely used in salads and cooking. (*Lycopersicon esculentum*, family Solanaceae.)

Tombouctou *or* **Timbuktu** town in Mali, near the most northerly point on the Niger River; population (1996) 20,500 (town); (1987) 453,000 (region). It was a Tuareg camel caravan centre on the fringe of the Sahara from the 11th century. Since 1960 the area surrounding the town has become increasingly arid, and the former canal link with the River Niger is dry. Products include salt.

tomography technique of using X-rays or ultrasound waves to procure images of structures deep within the body for diagnostic purposes. In modern medical imaging there are several techniques, such as the *CAT scan (computerized axial tomography).

ton

ton symbol t, imperial unit of mass. The **long ton**, used in the UK, is 1,016 kg/2,240 lb; the **short ton**, used in the USA, is 907 kg/2,000 lb. The **metric ton** or **tonne** is 1,000 kg/2,205 lb.

ton in shipping, unit of volume equal to 2.83 cubic metres/100 cubic feet. **Gross tonnage** is the total internal volume of a ship in tons; **net register tonnage** is the volume used for carrying cargo or passengers. **Displacement tonnage** is the weight of the vessel, in terms of the number of imperial tons of seawater displaced when the ship is loaded to its load line; it is used to describe warships.

tonality in music, refers to the major-minor key system. It is also used as the opposite of *atonality.

Tone, (Theobald) Wolfe (1763–1798) Irish nationalist, prominent in the revolutionary society of the *United Irishmen. In 1798 he accompanied the French invasion of Ireland and was captured and condemned to death, but slit his own throat in prison.

tone poem in music, an alternative name for *symphonic poem, or a similar piece for smaller forces.

Tonga
or **Friendly Islands**
  National name: *Pule'anga Fakatu'i 'o Tonga/ Kingdom of Tonga*

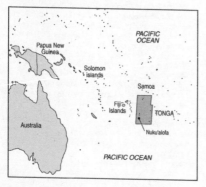

Area: 750 sq km/290 sq mi
Capital: Nuku'alofa (on Tongatapu island)
Major towns/cities: Neiafu, Haveloloto, Vaini, Tofoa-Koloua
Physical features: three groups of islands in southwest Pacific, mostly coral formations, but actively volcanic in west; of the 170 islands in the Tonga group, 36 are inhabited
Head of state: King Taufa'ahau Tupou IV from 1965
Head of government: Prince Lavaka Ata Ulukalala from 2000
Political system: absolutist
Political executive: absolute
Political parties: legally none, but one pro-democracy grouping, the People's Party
Currency: pa'anga, or Tongan dollar
GNI per capita (PPP): (US$) 6,340 (2002 est)
Exports: fish, vanilla beans, pumpkins, coconut oil and other coconut products, watermelons, knitted clothes, cassava, yams, sweet potatoes, footwear. Principal market: Japan 42.3% (2001)

Population: 104,000 (2003 est)
Language: Tongan (official), English
Religion: mainly Free Wesleyan Church; Roman Catholic, Anglican
Life expectancy: 68 (men); 69 (women) (2000–05)
Chronology
c. **1000 BC:** Settled by Polynesian immigrants from the Fiji Islands.
c. **AD 950:** The legendary Aho'eitu became the first hereditary Tongan king (Tu'i Tonga).
13th–14th centuries: Tu'i Tonga kingdom at the height of its power.
1643: Visited by the Dutch navigator, Abel Tasman.
1773: Islands visited by British navigator Capt James Cook, who named them the 'Friendly Islands'.
1826: Methodist mission established.
1831: Tongan dynasty founded by a Christian convert and chief of Ha'apai, Prince Taufa'ahau Tupou, who became king 14 years later.
1845–93: Reign of King George Tupou I, during which the country was reunited after half a century of civil war; Christianity was spread and a modern constitution adopted in 1875.
1900: Friendship ('Protectorate') treaty signed between King George Tupou II and Britain, establishing British control over defence and foreign affairs, but leaving internal political affairs under Tongan control.
1918: Queen Salote Tupou III ascended the throne.
1965: Queen Salote died; she was succeeded by her son, King Taufa'ahau Tupou IV, who had been prime minister since 1949.
1970: Tonga achieved independence from Britain, but remained within the Commonwealth.
1991: Baron Vaea was appointed prime minister.
1993: Six pro-democracy candidates were elected. There were calls for reform of absolutist power.
1996: A pro-democracy movement led by the People's Party won a majority of the 'commoner' seats in the legislative assembly. Pro-democracy campaigner Akilisis Pohiva was released after a month's imprisonment.
2000: Upon the retirement of Prime Minister Baron Vaea, he was replaced by Prince Ulakalala Lavaka Ata.
2005: For the first time, elected members of parliament were admitted to the cabinet, which had always been composed of royal appointees.

tongue in tetrapod vertebrates, a muscular organ usually attached to the floor of the mouth. It has a thick root attached to a U-shaped bone (hyoid), and is covered with a *mucous membrane containing nerves and taste buds. It is the main organ of taste. The tongue directs food to the teeth and into the throat for chewing and swallowing. In humans, it is crucial for speech; in other animals, for lapping up water and for grooming, among other functions. In some animals, such as frogs, it can be flipped forwards to catch insects; in others, such as anteaters, it serves to reach for food found in deep holes.

tonic in music, the key note of a *scale (for example, the note C in the scale of C major), or the 'home key' in a composition (for example, the chord of C major in a composition in the same key).

Tonkin Gulf Incident clash that triggered US entry into the Vietnam War in August 1964. Two US destroyers (USS *C Turner Joy* and USS *Maddox*)

916

reported that they were fired on by North Vietnamese torpedo boats. It is unclear whether hostile shots were actually fired, but the reported attack was taken as a pretext for making air raids against North Vietnam. On 7 August the US Congress passed the **Tonkin Gulf Resolution**, which formed the basis for the considerable increase in US military involvement in the Vietnam War.

tonne symbol t, metric ton of 1,000 kg/2,204.6 lb; equivalent to 0.9842 of an imperial *ton.

tonsillitis inflammation of the *tonsils.

tonsils in higher vertebrates, masses of lymphoid tissue situated at the back of the mouth and throat (palatine tonsils), and on the rear surface of the tongue (lingual tonsils). The tonsils contain many *lymphocytes and are part of the body's defence system against infection.

Tonton Macoute member of a private army of death squads on Haiti. The Tontons Macoutes were initially organized by François ('Papa Doc') *Duvalier, president of Haiti 1957–71, and continued to terrorize the population under his successor J C ('Baby Doc') Duvalier. It is alleged that the organization continued to operate after J C Duvalier's exile to France.

tooth in vertebrates, one of a set of hard, bonelike structures in the mouth, used for biting and chewing food, and in defence and aggression. In humans, the first set (20 milk teeth) appear from age six months to two and a half years. The permanent *dentition replaces these from the sixth year onwards, the wisdom teeth (third molars) sometimes not appearing until the age of 25 or 30. Adults have 32 teeth: two incisors, one canine (eye tooth), two premolars, and three molars on each side of each jaw. Each tooth consists of an enamel coat (hardened calcium deposits), dentine (a thick, bonelike layer), and an inner pulp cavity, housing nerves and blood vessels. Mammalian teeth have roots surrounded by cementum, which fuses them into their sockets in the jawbones. The neck of the tooth is covered by the gum, while the enamel-covered crown protrudes above the gum line.

topaz mineral, aluminium fluorosilicate, $Al_2(F_2SiO_4)$. It is usually yellow, but pink if it has been heated, and is used as a gemstone when transparent. It ranks 8 on the Mohs scale of hardness.

tope slender shark *Galeorhinus galeus* ranging through temperate and tropical seas. Dark grey above and white beneath, it reaches 2 m/6 ft in length. The young are born well-formed, sometimes 40 at a time.

topography surface shape and composition of the landscape, comprising both natural and artificial features, and its study. Topographical features include the relief and contours of the land; the distribution of mountains, valleys, and human settlements; and the patterns of rivers, roads, and railways.

topology branch of geometry that deals with those properties of a figure that remain unchanged even when the figure is transformed (bent, stretched) – for example, when a square painted on a rubber sheet is deformed by distorting the sheet. Topology has scientific applications, as in the study of turbulence in flowing fluids.

Torah *or* **Pentateuch** *or* **Five Books of Moses** in Judaism, the first five books of the Tenakh, or *Hebrew Bible (Christian Old Testament): Genesis, Exodus, Leviticus, Numbers, and Deuteronomy. It contains a traditional history of the world from the Creation to the death of Moses; it also includes the Hebrew people's covenant with their one God (through the prophets *Abraham and *Moses), and the 613 mitzvot (commandments, or laws) that Jews should follow, beginning with the *Ten Commandments. The mitzvot include rules for religious observance and guidelines for social conduct.

Torfaen unitary authority in south Wales, created in 1996 from part of the former county of Gwent. **area:** 98 sq km/38 sq mi **towns:** Pontypool (administrative headquarters), Cwmbran (the first new town in Wales) **physical:** Cefn Coch (571 m/1,873 ft), River Afon Llwyd **features:** Big Pit colliery museum at Blaenafon **population:** (2001 est) 91,000.

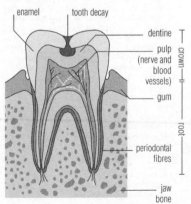

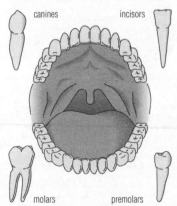

tooth Adults have 32 teeth: two incisors, one canine, two premolars, and three molars on each side of each jaw. The crown consists of a dense layer of mineral, the enamel, surrounding hard dentine with a soft centre, the pulp.

tornado extremely violent revolving storm with swirling, funnel-shaped clouds, caused by a rising column of warm air propelled by strong wind. A tornado can rise to a great height, but with a diameter of only a few hundred metres or less. Tornadoes move with wind speeds of 160–480 kph/100–300 mph, destroying everything in their path. They are common in the central USA and Australia.

Toronto (Huron 'place of meeting') port and capital of *Ontario, Canada, at the mouths of the Humber and Don rivers on Lake Ontario; population (1999 est) 2,529,300, metropolitan area (2001 est) 4,881,400. In 1998 the former area of Metropolitan Toronto merged with York, East York, Etebicoke, Scarborough, North York, and Toronto to form the City of Toronto. It is a major shipping point on the St Lawrence Seaway, and Canada's main financial, business, commercial, and manufacturing centre. Industries include shipbuilding, food-processing, publishing, biotechnology, information technology, and the production of fabricated metals, aircraft, farm machinery, cars, chemicals, and clothing. It is also a tourist and cultural centre, with a thriving film industry.

torpedo *or* **electric ray** any species of the order Torpediniformes of mainly tropical rays (cartilaginous fishes), whose electric organs between the pectoral fin and the head can give a powerful shock. They can grow to 180 cm/6 ft in length.

torpedo self-propelled underwater missile, invented 1866 by English engineer Robert Whitehead. Modern torpedoes are homing missiles; some resemble mines in that they lie on the seabed until activated by the acoustic signal of a passing ship. A television camera enables them to be remotely controlled, and in the final stage of attack they lock on to the radar or sonar signals of the target ship.

torque turning effect of force on an object. A turbine produces a torque that turns an electricity generator in a power station. Torque is measured by multiplying the force by its perpendicular distance from the turning point.

Torquemada, Tomás de (1420–1498) Spanish Dominican monk, confessor to Queen Isabella I. In 1483 he revived the *Inquisition on her behalf, and at least 2,000 'heretics' were burned; Torquemada also expelled the Jews from Spain 1492, with a resultant decline of the economy.

torr unit of pressure equal to 1/760 of an *atmosphere, used mainly in high-vacuum technology.

Torricelli, Evangelista (1608–1647) Italian physicist who established the existence of atmospheric pressure and devised the mercury *barometer in 1644.

torsion in physics, the state of strain set up in a twisted material; for example, when a thread, wire, or rod is twisted, the torsion set up in the material tends to return the material to its original state. The **torsion balance**, a sensitive device for measuring small gravitational or magnetic forces, or electric charges, balances these against the restoring force set up by them in a torsion suspension.

tort in law, a wrongful act for which someone can be sued for damages in a civil court. It includes such acts as libel, trespass, injury done to someone (whether intentionally or by negligence), and inducement to break a contract (although breach of contract itself is not a tort).

tortoise reptile of the order Chelonia, family Testudinidae, with the body enclosed in a hard shell. Tortoises are related to the *terrapins and *turtles, and range in length from 10 cm/4 in to 150 cm/5 ft. The shell consists of a curved upper carapace and flattened lower plastron joined at the sides; it is generally more domed than that of turtles. The head and limbs are withdrawn into it when the tortoise is in danger. Most land tortoises are herbivorous, feeding on plant material, and have no teeth. The mouth forms a sharp-edged beak. They occur in the warmer regions of all continents except Australia. Tortoises have been known to live for 150 years.

Tory Party the forerunner of the British *Conservative Party from about 1680 to 1830. It was the party of the squire and parson, as opposed to the Whigs (which was supported by the trading classes and Nonconformists). The name is still applied colloquially to the Conservative Party. In the USA a Tory was an opponent of the break with Britain in the American Revolution 1775–83.

totalitarianism government control of all activities within a country, openly political or otherwise, as in fascist or communist dictatorships. Examples of totalitarian regimes are Italy under Benito *Mussolini 1922–45; Germany under Adolf *Hitler 1933–45; the USSR under Joseph *Stalin from the 1930s until his death in 1953; and more recently Romania under Nicolae *Ceausescu 1974–89.

totemism (Algonquin Indian 'mark of my family') the belief in individual or clan kinship with an animal, plant, or object. This totem is sacred to those concerned, and they are forbidden to eat or desecrate it; marriage within the clan is usually forbidden. Totemism occurs among Pacific Islanders and Australian Aborigines, and was formerly prevalent throughout Europe, Africa, and Asia. Most American Indian societies had totems as well.

toucan any South and Central American forest-dwelling bird of the genus *Ramphastos*, family Ramphastidae, order Piciformes. Toucans have very large, brilliantly coloured beaks and often handsome plumage. They live in small flocks and eat fruits, seeds, and insects. They nest in holes in trees, where the female lays 2–4 eggs; both parents care for the eggs and young. There are 37 species, ranging from 30 cm/1 ft to 60 cm/2ft in size.

touch sensation produced by specialized nerve endings in the skin. Some respond to light pressure, others to heavy pressure. Temperature detection may also contribute to the overall sensation of touch. Many animals, such as nocturnal ones, rely on touch more than humans do. Some have specialized organs of touch that project from the body, such as whiskers or antennae.

Toulouse-Lautrec, Henri (Marie Raymond de) (1864–1901) French artist. He was active in Paris, where he painted entertainers and prostitutes in a style characterized by strong colours, bold design, and brilliant technical skill. From 1891 his lithographic posters were a great success, skilfully executed and yet retaining the spontaneous character of sketches. His later work was to prove vital to the development of *poster art.

touraco *or* **turaco** any fruit-eating African bird of the family Musophagidae, order Cuculiformes. They have a small high bill, notched and serrated mandibles, a long tail, erectile crest, and short, rounded wings. The largest are 70 cm/28 in long.

Tour de France French road race for professional cyclists held annually over approximately 4,800 km/ 3,000 mi of primarily French roads. The race takes about three weeks to complete and the route varies each year, often taking in adjoining countries, but always ending in Paris. A separate stage is held every day, and the overall leader at the end of each stage wears the coveted 'yellow jersey' (French *maillot jaune*).

Toussaint L'Ouverture, Pierre Dominique (c. 1743–1803) Haitian revolutionary leader, born a slave. He joined the insurrection of 1791 against the French colonizers and was made governor by the revolutionary French government. He expelled the Spanish and British, but when the French emperor Napoleon reimposed slavery he revolted, was captured, and died in prison in France. In 1983 his remains were returned to Haiti.

toxaemia another term for *blood poisoning; **toxaemia of pregnancy** is another term for *pre-eclampsia.

toxic shock syndrome rare condition marked by rapid onset of fever, vomiting, and low blood pressure, sometimes leading to death. It is caused by a toxin of the bacterium *Staphylococcus aureus*, normally harmlessly present in the body. It is seen most often in young women using tampons during menstruation.

toxic waste *hazardous waste, especially when it has been dumped.

toxin any poison produced by another living organism (usually a bacterium) that can damage the living body. In vertebrates, toxins are broken down by *enzyme action, mainly in the liver.

toxoplasmosis disease transmitted to humans by animals, often in pigeon or cat excrement, or in undercooked meat. It causes flulike symptoms and damages the central nervous system, eyes, and visceral organs. It is caused by a protozoan, *Toxoplasma gondii*. Congenital toxoplasmosis, transmitted from an infected mother to her unborn child, can lead to blindness and retardation.

trace element chemical element necessary in minute quantities for the health of a plant or animal. For example, magnesium, which occurs in chlorophyll, is essential to photosynthesis, and iodine is needed by the thyroid gland of mammals for making hormones that control growth and body chemistry.

trachea tube that forms an airway in air-breathing animals. In land-living *vertebrates, including humans, it is also known as the **windpipe** and runs from the larynx to the upper part of the chest. Its diameter is about 1.5 cm/0.6 in and its length 10 cm/4 in. It is strong and flexible, and reinforced by rings of *cartilage. In the upper chest, the trachea branches into two tubes: the left and right bronchi, which enter the lungs. Insects have a branching network of tubes called tracheae, which conduct air from holes (*spiracles) in the body surface to all the body tissues. The finest branches of the tracheae are called tracheoles.

tracheotomy *or* **tracheostomy** surgical opening in the windpipe (trachea), usually created for the insertion of a tube to enable the patient to breathe. It is done either to bypass an airway impaired by disease or injury, or to safeguard it during surgery or a prolonged period of mechanical ventilation.

trachoma chronic eye infection, resembling severe *conjunctivitis. The conjunctiva becomes inflamed, with scarring and formation of pus, and there may be damage to the cornea. It is caused by a viruslike organism (*chlamydia), and is a disease of dry tropical regions. Although it responds well to antibiotics, numerically it remains the biggest single cause of blindness worldwide. In 2001 alone, 6 million people worldwide went blind through trachoma and a further 540 million were at risk.

Tractarianism another name for the *Oxford Movement, 19th-century movement for Catholic revival within the Church of England.

tradescantia any of a group of plants native to North and Central America, with variegated or striped leaves. The spiderwort *T. virginiana* is a cultivated garden plant; the wandering jew *T. albiflora* is a common house plant, with green oval leaves tinged with pink, purple or silver-striped. They are named after English botanist John Tradescant the Younger. (Genus *Tradescantia*, family Commelinaceae.)

Trades Union Congress (TUC) voluntary organization of trade unions, founded in the UK in 1868, in which delegates of affiliated unions meet annually to consider matters affecting their members. In 1997 there were 67 affiliated unions, with an aggregate membership of 6 million.

trade union organization of workers that exists to promote and defend the interests of its members, to achieve improved working conditions, and to undertake collective bargaining (negotiating on behalf of its members) with employers. Attitudes of government to unions and of unions to management vary greatly from country to country. Probably the most effective trade union system is that of Sweden, and the most internationally known is the Polish confederation of trade unions, *Solidarity. The largest union in the world is 'Verdi', in Germany, which in 2001 had 3 million members across 1,000 trades and professions. Trade unions are particularly concerned with pay, working conditions, job security, and redundancy. Four types of trade union are often distinguished: general unions (covering all skilled and semi-skilled workers), craft unions (for those performing a specific type of work, for example electricians or printers), industrial unions (covering workers in one industry or sector, for example steel or car workers), and white-collar unions (covering those in clerical and administrative jobs). Unions may also be affiliated to a larger organization that negotiates with the government, for example the *Trades Union Congress (TUC) in the UK and the American Federation of Labor and Congress of Industrial Organizations (AFL-CIO) in the USA.

trade wind prevailing wind that blows towards the Equator from the northeast and southeast. Trade winds are caused by hot air rising at the Equator and the consequent movement of air from north and south to take its place. The winds are deflected towards the west because of the Earth's west-to-east rotation. The unpredictable calms known as the *doldrums lie at their convergence.

Trafalgar, Battle of during the *Napoleonic Wars, victory of the British fleet, commanded by Admiral Horatio *Nelson, over a combined French and Spanish fleet on 21 October 1805. Nelson was mortally wounded during the action. The victory laid the foundation for British naval supremacy throughout the 19th century. It is named after Cape Trafalgar, a low headland in southwest Spain, near the western entrance to the Straits of Gibraltar.

tragopan any of several species of bird of the genus *Tragopan*, a short-tailed pheasant living in wet forests along the southern Himalayas. Tragopans are brilliantly coloured with arrays of spots, long crown feathers and two blue erectile crests. All have been reduced in numbers by destruction of their habitat. The western tragopan is the rarest, as a result of extensive deforestation.

Trajan (AD 52–117) born Marcus Ulpius Trajanus, Roman emperor from AD 98. He conquered Dacia (Romania) in 101–07 and much of *Parthia in 113–17, bringing the empire to its greatest extent.

tranquillizer common name for any drug for reducing anxiety or tension (anxiolytic), such as *benzodiazepines, barbiturates, antidepressants, and beta-blockers. The use of drugs to control anxiety is becoming much less popular, because most of the drugs available are capable of inducing dependence.

transactinide element any of a series of eight radioactive, metallic elements with atomic numbers that extend beyond the *actinide series, those from 104 (rutherfordium) upwards. They are grouped because of their expected chemical similarities (they are all bivalent), the properties differing only slightly with atomic number. All have *half-lives of less than two minutes.

Transcaucasia geographical region south of the Caucasus Mountains, encompassing the independent states of Armenia, Azerbaijan, and Georgia; it is bounded by the Caucasus Mountains in the north, the frontier with Turkey and Iran in the south, and the Black and Caspian Seas in the west and east respectively. Transcaucasia covers a total area of 186,100 sq km/71,853 sq mi.

transcendentalism philosophy inaugurated in the 18th century by the German philosopher Immanuel Kant. As opposed to metaphysics in the traditional sense, transcendental philosophy is concerned with the conditions of possibility of experience, rather than the nature of being. It seeks to show the necessary structure of our 'point of view' on the world.

transcendental meditation (TM) technique of focusing the mind, based in part on Hindu meditation. Meditators are given a mantra (a special word or phrase) to repeat over and over in the mind; such meditation is believed to benefit the practitioner by relieving stress and inducing a feeling of well-being and relaxation. It was introduced to the West by Maharishi Mahesh Yogi and popularized by the *Beatles in the late 1960s.

Trans-Dniester region of northeastern Moldova, lying between the River Dniester and the Ukraine, and largely inhabited by ethnic Slavs (Russians and Ukrainians). The main city in the region is Tiraspol. In the early 1990s, Trans-Dniester was the scene of violent agitation for a separate state; it was granted special autonomous status in the new Moldovan constitution of 1994.

transducer device that converts one form of energy into another. For example, a thermistor is a transducer that converts heat into an electrical voltage, and an electric motor is a transducer that converts an electrical voltage into mechanical energy. Transducers are

important components in many types of *sensor, converting the physical quantity to be measured into a proportional voltage signal.

transformation in mathematics, a mapping or *function, especially one which causes a change of shape or position in a geometric figure. Reflection, rotation, enlargement, and translation are the main geometrical transformations.

transformer device in which, by electromagnetic induction, an alternating current (AC) of one voltage is transformed to another voltage, without change of *frequency. Transformers are widely used in electrical apparatus of all kinds, and in particular in power transmission where high voltages and low currents are utilized. A step-up transformer increases voltage and has more turns on the secondary coil than on the primary. A step-down transformer decreases voltage and has more turns on the primary coil than on the secondary.

transfusion intravenous delivery of blood or blood products (plasma, red cells) into a patient's circulation to make up for deficiencies due to disease, injury, or surgical intervention. Cross-matching is carried out to ensure the patient receives the right blood group. Because of worries about blood-borne disease, there is a growing interest in autologous transfusion with units of the patient's own blood 'donated' over the weeks before an operation.

transistor solid-state electronic component, made of *semiconductor material, with three or more electrical contacts that can regulate a current passing through it. A transistor can act as an amplifier, oscillator, *photocell, or switch, and (unlike earlier thermionic valves) usually operates on a very small amount of power. Transistors commonly consist of a tiny sandwich of *germanium or *silicon, alternate layers having different electrical properties because they are impregnated with minute amounts of different impurities.

transition metal any of a group of metallic *elements that have incomplete inner electron shells and exhibit variable valency – for example, cobalt, copper, iron, and molybdenum. They form a long block in the middle of the *periodic table of the elements, between groups 2 and 3. They are excellent conductors of electricity, and generally form highly coloured compounds.

Transkei former independent homeland *Black National State within South Africa, part of Eastern Cape Province from 1994; area 43,808 sq km/16,914 sq mi. Its capital was Umtata. It became self-governing in 1963, and achieved full independence in 1976, but this was not recognized outside South Africa. The largest of South Africa's homelands, it extended northwest from the Great Kei River, on the coast of Cape Province, to the border of Natal.

transpiration loss of water from a plant by evaporation. Most water is lost by *diffusion of water vapour from the leaves through pores known as *stomata to the outside air. The primary function of stomata is to allow gas exchange between the plant's internal tissues and the atmosphere. Transpiration from the leaf surfaces causes a continuous upward flow of water from the roots via the *xylem, which is known as the transpiration stream. This replaces the water that is lost, and allows minerals absorbed from the soil to be transported through the xylem to the leaves. This is

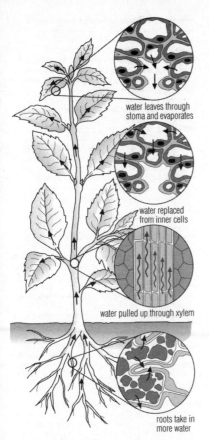

water leaves through stoma and evaporates

water replaced from inner cells

water pulled up through xylem

roots take in more water

transpiration The loss of water from a plant by evaporation is known as transpiration. Most of the water is lost through the surface openings, or stomata, on the leaves. The evaporation produces what is known as the transpiration stream, a tension that draws water up from the roots through the xylem, water-carrying vessels in the stem.

important because many plant cells need the minerals as nutrients.

transplant in medicine, the transfer of a tissue or organ from one human being to another or from one part of the body to another (skin grafting). In most organ transplants, the operation is for life-saving purposes. The immune system tends to reject foreign tissue, so careful matching and immunosuppressive drugs must be used, though these are not always successful.

Transport and General Workers' Union (TGWU)
UK trade union founded in 1921 by the amalgamation of a number of dockers' and road-transport workers' unions, previously associated in the Transport Workers'

Federation. With more than 900,000 members, it ranks behind the public employers' union, UNISON, as the second-largest trade union in Britain.

transportation punishment of sending convicted persons to overseas territories to serve their sentences. It was introduced in England towards the end of the 17th century and although it was abolished in 1857 after many thousands had been transported, mostly to Australia, sentences of penal servitude continued to be partly carried out in Western Australia up until 1867. Transportation was used for punishment of criminals by France until 1938.

transsexual person who identifies himself or herself completely with the opposite sex, believing that the wrong sex was assigned at birth. Unlike **transvestites**, who desire to dress in clothes traditionally worn by the opposite sex, transsexuals think and feel emotionally in a way typically considered appropriate to members of the opposite sex, and may undergo surgery to modify external sexual characteristics.

Trans-Siberian Railway the world's longest single-service railway, connecting the cities of European Russia with Omsk, Novosibirsk, Irkutsk, and Khabarovsk, and terminating at Nakhodka on the Pacific coast east of Vladivostok. The line was built between 1891 and 1915, and has a total length of 9,289 km/5,772 mi, from Moscow to Vladivostok.

transubstantiation in Christian theology, the doctrine that the whole substance of the bread and wine, while retaining its outward appearance, changes into the substance of the body and blood of Jesus when consecrated in the Eucharist.

transuranic element *or* **transuranium element** chemical element with an atomic number of 93 or more – that is, with a greater number of protons in the nucleus than has uranium. All transuranic elements are radioactive. Neptunium and plutonium are found in nature; the others are synthesized in nuclear reactions.

Transvaal former province of northeast South Africa to 1994, when it was divided into Mpumalanga, Northern, and Gauteng provinces. It bordered Zimbabwe to the north, Botswana to the northwest, and Swaziland and Mozambique to the east. It was settled by *Voortrekkers*, Boers who left Cape Colony in the Great Trek from 1831. Independence was recognized by Britain in 1852, until the settlers' difficulties with the conquered Zulus led to British annexation in 1877. It was made a British colony after the South African War 1899–1902, and in 1910 became a province of the Union of South Africa.

Transylvania mountainous area of central and northwestern Romania, bounded to the south by the Transylvanian Alps (an extension of the *Carpathian Mountains). Formerly a principality, with its capital at Cluj-Napoca, it was part of Hungary from about 1000 until its people voted to unite with Romania 1918. In a 1996 treaty Hungary renounced its claims on Transylvania.

trapezium US **trapezoid**, in geometry, a quadrilateral (a shape with four sides) with two of its sides parallel. If the parallel sides have lengths a and b and the perpendicular distance between them is h (the height of the trapezium), its area $A = \frac{1}{2} h(a + b)$.

Trappist member of a Roman Catholic order of monks and nuns, renowned for the strictness of their rule, which includes the maintenance of silence, manual labour, and a vegetarian diet. The order was founded 1664 at La Trappe, in Normandy, France, by Armand de Rancé (1626–1700) as a reformed version of the *Cistercian order.

treason act of betrayal, in particular against the sovereign or the state to which the offender owes allegiance.

Treasury UK government department, established in 1612, which oversees monetary policy; tax policy; planning and control of public spending; government accounting; and the regime for supervision of financial services, management of central government debt, and the supply of notes and coins. Technically, the prime minister is the first lord of the Treasury, but the chancellor of the Exchequer is the acting financial head.

treaty port port in Asia where the Western powers had special commercial privileges in the 19th century. As a result of the enforced unequal treaties, treaty ports were established mainly in China, from 1842; and Japan, from 1854 to 1899. Foreigners living in 'concessions' in the ports were not subject to local taxes or laws.

tree perennial plant with a woody stem, usually a single stem (trunk), made up of *wood and protected by an outer layer of *bark. It absorbs water through a *root system. There is no clear dividing line between shrubs and trees, but sometimes a minimum achievable height of 6 m/20 ft is used to define a tree.

tree creeper small, short-legged bird of the family Certhiidae, which spirals with a mouselike movement up tree trunks searching for food with its thin down-curved beak.

trefoil any of several *clover plants of a group belonging to the pea family, the leaves of which are divided into three leaflets. The name is also used for other plants with leaves divided into three lobes. (Genus *Trifolium*, family Leguminosae.)

trematode parasitic flatworm with an oval non-segmented body, of the class Trematoda, including the *fluke.

Trent third longest river of England; length 275 km/ 170 mi. Rising in the south Pennines (at Norton in the Moors) by the Staffordshire–Cheshire border, it flows south and then northeast through Derbyshire, along the county boundary of Leicestershire, and through Nottinghamshire and Lincolnshire, joining the Ouse east of Goole to form the Humber estuary, and entering the North Sea below Spurn Head. Its drainage basin covers more than 10,000 sq km/4,000 sq mi. Main tributaries are the Churnet, Dove, and Derwent.

Trent, Council of conference held 1545–63 by the Roman Catholic Church at Trento, northern Italy, initiating the so-called *Counter-Reformation; see also *Reformation.

Trentino-Alto Adige formerly **Venezia Tridentina**, province and special autonomous region of northern Italy, comprising the provinces of Bolzano and Trento; area 13,607 sq km/5,254 sq mi; population (1998 est) 929,600. Its chief towns are Trento (the capital) in the Italian-speaking southern area, and Bolzano (Bozen) in the northern German-speaking area of South Tirol (the region was Austrian until ceded to Italy in 1919 in the settlement following World War I). Wine, fruit, dairy products, and timber are produced. Paper, chemical, and metal industries use hydroelectric power.

Trevithick, Richard (1771–1833) English engineer, constructor of a steam road locomotive in 1801, the first to carry passengers, and probably the first steam engine to run on rails in 1804.

Triad secret society, founded in China as a Buddhist cult AD 36. It became known as the Triad because the triangle played a significant part in the initiation ceremony. Today it is reputed to be involved in organized crime (drugs, gambling, prostitution) among overseas Chinese. Its headquarters are alleged to be in Hong Kong.

trial in law, the determination of an accused person's innocence or guilt by means of the judicial examination of the issues of the case in accordance with the law of the land. The two parties in a trial, the defendant and plaintiff, or their counsels, put forward their cases and question the witnesses; on the basis of this evidence the jury or other tribunal body decides on the innocence or guilt of the defendant.

trial by ordeal in the Middle Ages, a test of guilt or innocence; see *ordeal, trial by.

triangle in geometry, a three-sided plane figure, the sum of whose interior angles is 180°. Triangles can be classified by the relative lengths of their sides. A **scalene triangle** has three sides of unequal length. An **isosceles triangle** has at least two equal sides; it has one line of *symmetry. An **equilateral triangle** has three equal sides (and three equal angles of 60°); it has three lines of symmetry.

Triassic Period period of geological time 245–208 million years ago, the first period of the Mesozoic era. The present continents were fused together in the form of the world continent *Pangaea. Triassic sediments contain remains of early dinosaurs and other animals now extinct. By late Triassic times, the first mammals had evolved. There was a mass extinction of 95% of plants at the end of the Triassic possibly caused by rising temperatures.

triathlon test of stamina involving three sports: swimming, cycling, and running, each one immediately following the last. The Olympic distances are a 1,500 m/ 1 mi swim, a 40 km/24.9 mi cycle, and a 10 km/6.2 mi run.

tribune Roman magistrate of *plebeian family, elected annually to defend the interests of the common people; only two were originally chosen in the early 5th century BC, but there were later ten. They could veto the decisions of any other magistrate.

triceratops any of a genus *Triceratops* of massive, horned dinosaurs of the order Ornithischia. They had three horns and a neck frill and were up to 8 m/25 ft long; they lived in the Cretaceous period.

trichloromethane technical name for *chloroform.

triggerfish any marine bony fish of the family Balistidae, with a laterally compressed body, up to 60 cm/2 ft long, and a deep belly. They have small mouths but strong jaws and teeth. The first spine on the dorsal fin locks into an erect position, allowing them to fasten themselves securely in crevices for protection; it can only be moved by depressing the smaller third ('trigger') spine.

triglyceride chemical name for *fat comprising three fatty acids reacted with the three hydroxyl groups in glycerol.

trigonometry branch of mathematics that concerns finding lengths and angles in *triangles. In a right-angled triangle the sides and angles are related by three trigonometric ratios: *sine, *cosine, and *tangent. Trigonometry is used frequently in navigation, surveying, and simple harmonic motion in physics.

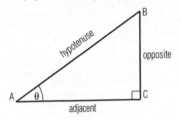

for any right-angled triangle with angle θ as shown the trigonometrical ratios are

$$\sin(e)\ \theta = \frac{BC}{AB} = \frac{opposite}{hypotenuse}$$

$$\cos \theta = \frac{AC}{AB} = \frac{adjacent}{hypotenuse}$$

$$\tan \theta = \frac{BC}{AC} = \frac{opposite}{adjacent}$$

trigonometry At its simplest level, trigonometry deals with the relationships between the sides and angles of triangles. Unknown angles or lengths are calculated by using trigonometrical ratios such as sine, cosine, and tangent. The earliest applications of trigonometry were in the fields of navigation, surveying, and astronomy, and usually involved working out an inaccessible distance such as the distance of the Earth from the Moon.

trilobite any of a large class (Trilobita) of extinct, marine, invertebrate arthropods of the Palaeozoic era, with a flattened, oval body, 1–65 cm/0.4–26 in long. The hard-shelled body was divided by two deep furrows into three lobes. Some were burrowers, others were swimming and floating forms. Their worldwide distribution, many species, and the immense quantities of their remains make them useful in geological dating.

Trimble, David (1944–) Northern Ireland politician, leader of the *Ulster Unionist party (or Official Unionist Party, OUP) from 1995 and Northern Ireland's first minister from 1998. Representing the Upper Bann constituency in the House of Commons from 1990, he won the leadership of the OUP in August 1995, when James Molyneaux decided to retire at the age of 75. Trimble shared the Nobel Prize for Peace in 1998 with John *Hume for their efforts to find a peaceful solution to the conflict in Northern Ireland, and was one of the leading negotiators in the creation of a cross-community government in Belfast which met for the first time in December 1999 as powers were devolved to the province by the British government.

Trimurti the Hindu triad of gods, representing *Brahman, the Absolute Spirit, in its three aspects: *Brahma, personifying creation; *Vishnu, preservation; and *Shiva, destruction. Brahma has four heads, carries the sacred Vedas, and holds beads and other objects used in worship. Vishnu holds a discus and a club to destroy evil, and a lotus to bless his followers. Shiva carries a trident, representing his three aspects as creator, preserver, and destroyer, and holds a snake, depicting his power over deadly animals.

Trinidad and Tobago

National name: *Republic of Trinidad and Tobago*

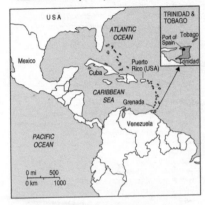

Area: 5,130 sq km/1,980 sq mi (Trinidad 4,828 sq km/1,864 sq mi and Tobago 300 sq km/115 sq mi)
Capital: Port-of-Spain (and chief port)
Major towns/cities: San Fernando, Arima, Point Fortin
Major ports: Scarborough, Point Lisas
Physical features: comprises two main islands and some smaller ones in Caribbean Sea; coastal swamps and hills east–west
Head of state: George Maxwell Richards from 2003
Head of government: Patrick Manning from 2001
Political system: liberal democracy
Political executive: parliamentary
Political parties: National Alliance for Reconstruction (NAR), nationalist, left of centre; People's National Movement (PNM), nationalist, moderate, centrist; United National Congress (UNC), left of centre; Movement for Social Transformation (Motion), left of centre
Currency: Trinidad and Tobago dollar
GNI per capita (PPP): (US$) 8,680 (2002 est)
Exports: mineral fuels and lubricants, chemicals, basic manufactures, food. Principal market: USA 38.8% (2000)
Population: 1,303,000 (2003 est)
Language: English (official), Hindi, French, Spanish
Religion: Roman Catholic 33%, Hindu 25%, Anglican 15%, Muslim 6%, Presbyterian 4%
Life expectancy: 68 (men); 74 (women) (2000–05)
Chronology
1498: Visited by the explorer Christopher Columbus, who named Trinidad after the three peaks at its southeastern tip and Tobago after the local form of

tobacco pipe. Carib and Arawak Indians comprised the indigenous community.

1532: Trinidad colonized by Spain.

1630s: Tobago settled by Dutch, who introduced sugar-cane growing.

1797: Trinidad captured by Britain and ceded by Spain five years later under Treaty of Amiens.

1814: Tobago ceded to Britain by France.

1834: Abolition of slavery resulted in indentured labourers being brought in from India, rather than Africa, to work sugar plantations.

1889: Trinidad and Tobago amalgamated as a British colony.

1956: The People's National Movement (PNM) founded by Eric Williams, a moderate nationalist.

1958–62: Part of West Indies Federation.

1959: Achieved internal self-government, with Williams as chief minister.

1962: Independence achieved within Commonwealth, with Williams as prime minister.

1970: Army mutiny and violent Black Power riots directed against minority East Indian population; state of emergency imposed for two years.

1976: Became a republic, with former Governor General Ellis Clarke as president and Williams as prime minister.

1986: Tobago-based National Alliance for Reconstruction (NAR), headed by A N R Robinson, won the general election.

1990: An attempted antigovernment coup by Islamic fundamentalists was foiled.

1991: A general election resulted in victory for PNM, with Patrick Manning as prime minister.

1995: The UNC and PNM tied in general election; a UNC–NAR coalition was formed, led by Basdeo Panday.

1997: Former Prime Minister Robinson was elected president.

2000: The UNC won an absolute majority in parliamentary elections.

2001: Patrick Manning became prime minister again.

2002: Patrick Manning again became prime minister.

Trinity in Christianity, the union of three persons – God the Father, God the Son, and God the Holy Spirit/Holy Ghost – in one Godhead. The precise meaning of the doctrine has been the cause of unending dispute, and was the chief cause of the split between the Eastern *Orthodox and *Roman Catholic churches. **Trinity Sunday** occurs on the Sunday after Pentecost.

Tripitaka or **Pali Canon** ('three baskets') the canonical texts of Theravada Buddhism, divided into three parts: the *Vinaya-pitaka*, containing the rules governing the monastic community; the *Sutra-pitaka*, a collection of scriptures recording the teachings of the Buddha; and *Abhidharma-pitaka*, a collection of Buddhist philosophical writings.

Triple Alliance pact from 1882 between Germany, Austria-Hungary, and Italy to offset the power of Russia and France. It was last renewed in 1912, but during World War I Italy's initial neutrality gradually changed and it denounced the alliance in 1915. The term also refers to other alliances: in 1668 – England, Holland, and Sweden; in 1717 – Britain, Holland, and France (joined in 1718 by Austria); in 1788 – Britain, Prussia, and Holland; in 1805 – Britain, Russia, and Austria (also known as the Third Coalition).

Triple Entente alliance of Britain, France, and Russia 1907–17. In 1911 this became a military alliance and formed the basis of the Allied powers in World War I against the Central Powers, Germany and Austria-Hungary.

triple jump track and field event in athletics comprising a hop, step, and jump sequence from a takeoff board into a sandpit landing area measuring 8 m/26.25 ft (minimum) in length. The takeoff board is usually 13 m/42.65 ft from the landing area. Each competitor has six trials and the winner is the one who covers the longest distance.

triple nose-leaf bat one of many threatened bats in Africa, *Triaenops persicus* is found scattered along much of the coastal regions of East Africa and faces threats from disturbance of the caves in which it breeds. Tourism development, resulting in disturbance to coral caves which the bats inhabit, is a particular problem.

Tripoli Arabic **Tarabulus**, capital and chief port of Libya, on the Mediterranean coast, 600 km/373 mi west of Benghazi; population (1996 est) 990,000. Products include olive oil, fruit, fish, and textiles; industries include oil refining and food processing. Tripoli was founded about the 7th century BC by Phoenicians from Oea (now Tripoli in Lebanon). It was a base for the Axis powers during World War II. In 1986 it was bombed by the US Air Force in retaliation for international guerrilla activity.

Tripura hill state of northeast India since 1972, formerly a princely state, between Bangladesh and Assam; area 10,477 sq km/4,045 sq mi; population (2001 est) 3,191,200. The capital is Agartala. The economy is largely dependent on agriculture: rice is the most widely grown crop, while cash crops include jute, cotton, tea, and sugarcane. Industries are mostly concerned with processing agricultural products, but there are also factories producing bricks, steel, pharmaceuticals and plywood.

trireme (Anglicized Latin 'three-oared') ancient Greek warship with three banks of oars. They were used at the Battle of *Salamis and by the Romans until the 4th century AD.

Tristan or **Tristram** legendary Celtic hero of a tragic romance. He fell in love with Isolde, the bride he was sent to win for his uncle King Mark of Cornwall. The story became part of the Arthurian cycle and is the subject of Richard Wagner's opera *Tristan und Isolde* (1865).

tritium radioactive isotope of hydrogen, three times as heavy as ordinary hydrogen, consisting of one proton and two neutrons. It has a half-life of 12.5 years.

Triton in astronomy, largest of Neptune's moons. It has a diameter of 2,700 km/1,680 mi, and orbits Neptune every 5.88 days in a retrograde (east to west) direction at a distance of 354,000 km/220,000 mi. It takes the same time to rotate about its own axis as it does to make one revolution of Neptune.

Triton in Greek mythology, a merman sea god with the lower body of a dolphin; the son of *Poseidon and the sea goddess Amphitrite. Traditionally, he is shown blowing on a conch shell to raise or calm a storm.

triumvir one of a group of three administrators sharing power in ancient Rome, as in the **First Triumvirate** 60 BC: Caesar, Pompey, Crassus; and **Second Triumvirate** 43 BC: Augustus, Antony, and Lepidus.

trogon (Greek *trogein* 'to gnaw') any species of the family Trogonidae, order Trogoniformes, of tropical birds, up to 50 cm/1.7 ft long, with resplendent plumage, living in the Americas, Africa, and Asia. They are primarily birds of forest or woodland, living in trees. Their diet consists mainly of insects and other arthropods, and sometimes berries and other fruit. Most striking is the *quetzal.

Trojan horse seemingly innocuous but treacherous gift from an enemy. In Greek mythology, during the siege of Troy, an enormous wooden horse was left by the Greek army outside the gates of the city. The Greeks had sailed away as if they had retreated. The Trojans, believing the horse to be a religious offering, brought it into the city. Greek soldiers then emerged from their hiding place within the hollow horse and opened the city gates to enable the rest of the Greek army to enter and capture the city.

Trollope, Anthony (1815–1882) English novelist. He described provincial English middle-class society in a series of novels set in or around the imaginary cathedral city of Barchester. *The Warden* (1855) began the series, which includes *Barchester Towers* (1857), *Doctor Thorne* (1858), and *The Last Chronicle of Barset* (1867). His political novels include *Can You Forgive Her?* (1864), *Phineas Finn* (1867–69), and *The Prime Minister* (1875–76).

trombone brass instrument with a deep cup-shaped mouthpiece and a mainly cylindrical bore that expands into a moderately flared bell. Instead of valves, the trombone has a movable slide: a U-shaped piece of tubing that can be pushed towards or pulled towards the player. This lengthens or shortens the sounding length of the tube to create lower or higher-pitched notes. All the notes of the chromatic scale are available by placing the slide in any of seven basic positions, and blowing a harmonic series of notes built upon each basic note. The slide mechanism also makes possible a continuous glissando (slide) in pitch over a span of half an octave.

trompe l'oeil (French 'deceives the eye') painting that gives a convincing illusion of three-dimensional reality. As an artistic technique, it has been in common use in most stylistic periods in the West, originating in classical Greek art.

tropical cyclone another term for *hurricane.

tropics area between the tropics of Cancer and Capricorn, defined by the parallels of latitude approximately 23° 30´ north and south of the Equator. They are the limits of the area of Earth's surface in which the Sun can be directly overhead. The mean monthly temperature is over 20 °C/68 °F.

tropism *or* **tropic movement** directional growth of a plant, or part of a plant, in response to an external stimulus such as gravity or light. If the movement is directed towards the stimulus it is described as positive; if away from it, it is negative. Geotropism for example, the response of plants to gravity, causes the root (positively geotropic) to grow downwards, and the stem (negatively geotropic) to grow upwards. Most plants exhibit positive phototropism and grow towards light. Thigmotropism is found in most climbing plants.

troposphere lower part of the Earth's *atmosphere extending about 10.5 km/6.5 mi from the Earth's surface, in which temperature decreases with height to about −60 °C/−76 °F except in local layers of temperature inversion. The **tropopause** is the upper boundary of the troposphere, above which the temperature increases slowly with height within the atmosphere. All of the Earth's weather takes place within the troposphere.

Trotsky, Leon (1879–1940) adopted name of Lev Davidovitch Bronstein, Russian revolutionary. He joined the Bolshevik party and took a leading part in the seizure of power in 1917 and in raising the Red Army that fought the Civil War 1918–20. In the struggle for power that followed *Lenin's death in 1924, *Stalin defeated Trotsky, and this and other differences with the Communist Party led to his exile in 1929. He settled in Mexico, where he was assassinated at Stalin's instigation. Trotsky believed in world revolution and in permanent revolution (see *Trotskyism), and was an uncompromising, if liberal, idealist.

Trotskyism form of Marxism advocated by Leon Trotsky. Its central concept is that of **permanent revolution**. In his view a proletarian revolution, leading to a socialist society, could not be achieved in isolation, so it would be necessary to spark off further revolutions throughout Europe and ultimately worldwide. This was in direct opposition to the Stalinist view that socialism should be built and consolidated within individual countries.

troubadour (French, from Provençal *trobador* [from Latin *tropus*]) poet-musician of Provence and southern France in the 12th–13th centuries. The troubadours originated a type of lyric poetry devoted to themes of courtly love and the idealization of women and to glorifying the chivalric ideals of the period. Little is known of their music, which was passed down orally.

trout any of various bony fishes in the salmon family, popular for sport and food, usually speckled and found mainly in fresh water. They are native to the northern hemisphere. Trout have thick bodies and blunt heads, and vary in colour. The common trout *Salmo trutta* is widely distributed in Europe, occurring in British fresh and coastal waters. Sea trout are generally silvery and river trout olive-brown, both with spotted fins and sides.

Troy *or* **Ilium** ancient city in Asia Minor (modern Hissarlik in Turkey), just south of the Dardanelles. It has a long and complex history dating from about 3000 BC to AD 1200. In 1820 the city was identified as Troy, the site of the legendary ten-year Trojan War described in Homer's epic *Iliad*, but its actual name is unknown.

troy system system of units used for precious metals and gems. The pound troy (0.37 kg) consists of 12 ounces (each of 120 carats) or 5,760 grains (each equal to 65 mg).

Trudeau, Pierre Elliott (1919–2000) Canadian Liberal politician. He was prime minister 1968–79 and 1980–84. In 1980, he was re-elected by a landslide on a platform opposing Québec separatism, and the Québec independence movement was later defeated in a referendum. He repatriated the constitution from the UK in 1982, but by 1984 had so lost support that he resigned.

Truffaut, François (1932–1984) French *New Wave film director and actor. A romantic and intensely humane film-maker, he wrote and directed a series of semi-autobiographical films starring Jean-Pierre Léaud, beginning with *Les Quatre Cent Coups/The 400*

Blows (1959). His other films include *Jules et Jim* (1961), *Fahrenheit 451* (1966), *L'Enfant sauvage/The Wild Child* (1970), and *La Nuit américaine/Day for Night* (1973) (Academy Award).

truffle any of a group of underground fungi (see *fungus), certain of which are highly valued as edible delicacies; in particular, the species *Tuber melanosporum*, generally found growing under oak trees. It is native to the Périgord region of France but is cultivated in other areas as well. It is rounded, blackish-brown, externally covered with warts, and has blackish flesh. (Order Tuberales.)

Truman, Harry S (1884–1972) 33rd president of the USA 1945–53, a Democrat. In January 1945 he became vice-president to Franklin D Roosevelt, and president when Roosevelt died in April that year. He used the atomic bomb against Japan to end World War II, launched the *Marshall Plan to restore Western Europe's post-war economy, and nurtured the European Community (now the European Union) and NATO (including the rearmament of West Germany).

Truman Doctrine US president Harry *Truman's 1947 dictum that the USA would 'support free peoples who are resisting attempted subjugation by armed minorities or by outside pressures'. It was used to justify sending a counter-insurgency military mission to Greece after World War II, and evolved into the policy of containment of Soviet expansion.

trumpet brass instrument with a long history. It exists worldwide in a variety of forms and materials. It has a shallow, cup-shaped mouthpiece and a generally cylindrical bore that expands into a moderately flared bell. The sound can be brilliant, penetrating, and of stable pitch, making it useful for signalling and ceremonies. In Medieval times, the trumpet was a 'natural' instrument, consisting of a simple tube with no extra mechanisms. It was therefore only able to produce the 'natural' notes of the harmonic series, depending on the length of its tube. In the early 17th century, valves were introduced, giving access to the full range of notes.

trumpeter any South American bird of the genus *Psophia*, family Psophiidae, order Gruiformes, up to 50 cm/20 in tall, related to the cranes. Trumpeters have long legs, a short bill, and dark plumage. The trumpeter swan is unrelated.

trust territory country or area placed within the United Nations trusteeship system and, as such, administered by a UN member state on the UN's behalf. A trust territory could be one of three types: one administered under a mandate given by the UN, or its predecessor, the League of Nations; a territory which was removed from an enemy state, namely Germany, Italy, or Japan, at the end of World War II; or a territory which had been placed voluntarily within the trusteeship system by a member state responsible for its administration. The last territory remaining under the UN trusteeship system, the Republic of Palau, became independent in 1994.

trypanosomiasis any of several debilitating long-term diseases caused by a trypanosome (protozoan of the genus *Trypanosoma*). They include sleeping sickness in Africa, transmitted by the bites of *tsetse flies, and *Chagas's disease in Central and South America, spread by assassin bugs.

tsar Russian imperial title in use from 1547 to 1721, derived from the Latin *caesar*, the title of the Roman emperors.

tsetse fly any of a number of blood-feeding African flies of the genus *Glossina*, some of which transmit the disease nagana to cattle and sleeping sickness to human beings. Tsetse flies may grow up to 1.5 cm/0.6 in long.

tsunami (Japanese 'harbour wave') ocean wave generated by vertical movements of the sea floor resulting from *earthquakes or volcanic activity or large submarine landslides. Unlike waves generated by surface winds, the entire depth of water is involved in the wave motion of a tsunami. In the open ocean the tsunami takes the form of several successive waves, rarely in excess of 1 m/3 ft in height but travelling at speeds of 650–800 kph/400–500 mph. In the coastal shallows tsunamis slow down and build up producing huge swells over 15 m/45 ft high in some cases and over 30 m/90 ft in rare instances. The waves sweep inland causing great loss of life and damage to property.

Tswana member of the majority ethnic group living in Botswana. The Tswana are divided into four subgroups: the Bakwena, Bamangwato, Bangwaketse, and Batawana. The Tswana language belongs to the Bantu branch of the Niger-Congo family.

Tuamotu Archipelago French **Archipel des Tuamotu**, two parallel ranges of 78 atolls, part of *French Polynesia; area 690 sq km/266 sq mi; population (1996) 15,370, including the Gambier Islands to the east. The atolls stretch 2,100 km/1,300 mi north and east of the Society Islands. The administrative headquarters is Apataki. This archipelago is made up of the largest group of coral atolls in the world. The largest atoll is Rangiroa, the most significant is Hao; they produce pearl shell and copra. Spanish explorers landed 1606, and the islands were annexed by France in 1881. France conducted nuclear test explosions at the Mururoa and Fangataufa atolls between 1966 and 1996 (46 above ground and 147 below).

Tuareg plural **Tuareg**, (Arabic *tawarek* 'God-forsaken') member of one of a group of eight nomadic peoples, mainly stock breeders, from west and central Sahara and Sahel (Algeria, Libya, Mali, Niger, and Burkina Faso). Their language, Tamashek, belongs to the Berber branch of the Hamito-Semitic family and is spoken by 500,000–850,000 people. Many are Muslims.

tuatara lizardlike reptile of the genus *Sphenodon*. It grows up to 70 cm/2.3 ft long, is greenish black, and has a spiny crest down its back. On the top of its head is the *pineal body, or so-called 'third eye', linked to the brain, which probably acts as a kind of light meter. It has remained unchanged for 220 million years, and is the sole survivor of the reptilian order Rhynchocephalia. It has an average lifespan of 60 years. It lays eggs in burrows that it shares with seabirds, and has the longest incubation period of all reptiles (up to 15 months).

tuba member of a family of large brass instruments with a conical bore, deep cup-shaped mouthpiece, widely flaring bell, and three to six valves, producing a deep, mellow tone. Tubas were introduced around 1830 as the bass members of the orchestra brass section and the brass band. Despite their size and pitch, they can be surprisingly agile. These qualities have been exploited by composers such as Hector Berlioz, Maurice Ravel, and Vaughan Williams.

tuber swollen region of an underground stem or root, usually modified for storing food. The potato is a **stem tuber**, as shown by the presence of terminal and lateral buds, the 'eyes' of the potato. **Root tubers**, for example dahlias, developed from adventitious roots (growing from the stem, not from other roots) lack these. Both types of tuber can give rise to new individuals and so provide a means of *vegetative reproduction.

tuberculosis (TB) formerly known as **consumption** or **phthisis**, infectious disease caused by the bacillus *Mycobacterium tuberculosis*. It takes several forms, of which pulmonary tuberculosis is by far the most common. A vaccine, *BCG, was developed around 1920 and the first anti-tuberculosis drug, streptomycin, in 1944. The bacterium is mostly kept in check by the body's immune system; about 5% of those infected develop the disease. Treatment of patients with a combination of anti-TB medicines for 6–8 months produces a cure rate of 80%. In 1999 there were 8 million new cases of TB and 2 million deaths. Only 5% of cases are in developed countries. Worldwide there are 16 million people with TB and 2 billion (a third of the global population) are infected with *Mycobacterium tuberculosis*.

tuberose Mexican flowering plant belonging to the *agave family, grown as a sweet-smelling greenhouse plant. It has spikes of scented white flowers like lilies. (*Polianthes tuberosa*, family Agavaceae.)

TUC abbreviation for *Trades Union Congress.

tucu-tuco any member of the genus *Ctenomys*, a burrowing South American rodent about 20 cm/8 in long with a 7 cm/3 in tail. It has a large head, sensitive ears, and enormous incisor teeth.

Tudjman, Franjo (1922–1999) Croatian nationalist leader and historian, president from 1990. As leader of the centre-right Croatian Democratic Union (CDU), he led the fight for Croatian independence. During the 1991–92 civil war, his troops were hampered by lack of arms and the military superiority of the Serb-dominated federal army, but Croatia's independence was recognized following a successful United Nations-negotiated ceasefire in January 1992. Tudjman was re-elected in August 1992 and again in October 1995. Despite suffering from stomach cancer, he was re-elected president in June 1997. He died in December 1999 while still president.

Tudor dynasty English dynasty 1485–1603, founded by Henry VII, who became king by overthrowing Richard III (the last of the York dynasty) at the Battle of Bosworth. Henry VII reigned from 1485 to 1509, and was succeeded by Henry VIII (reigned 1509–47); Edward VI (reigned 1547–53); Mary I (reigned 1553–58); and Elizabeth I (reigned 1558–1603). Elizabeth died childless and the throne of England passed to her cousin James VI of Scotland, who thus became James I of England and the first of the Stuart line.

tufa *or* **travertine** soft, porous, *limestone rock, white in colour, deposited from solution from carbonate-saturated ground water around hot springs and in caves.

tulip any of a group of spring-flowering bulbous plants belonging to the lily family, usually with single goblet-shaped flowers on the end of an upright stem and narrow oval leaves with pointed ends. Tulips come in a large range of shapes, sizes, and colours and are widely cultivated as a garden flower. (Genus *Tulipa*, family Liliaceae.) The tulip was introduced into Europe in 1572. Dutch growers developed many new varieties, resulting in tulip mania in the 1630s, when vast sums were paid for bulbs of rare colours.

Tull, Jethro (1674–1741) English agriculturist who in about 1701 developed a drill that enabled seeds to be sown mechanically and spaced so that cultivation between rows was possible in the growth period. His chief work, *Horse-Hoeing Husbandry*, was published in 1733.

tumour overproduction of cells in a specific area of the body, often leading to a swelling or lump. Tumours are classified as **benign** or **malignant** (see *cancer). Benign tumours grow more slowly, do not invade surrounding tissues, do not spread to other parts of the body, and do not usually recur after removal. However, benign tumours can be dangerous in areas such as the brain. The most familiar types of benign tumour are warts on the skin. In some cases, there is no sharp dividing line between benign and malignant tumours.

tuna any of various large marine bony fishes of the mackerel family, especially the genus *Thunnus*, popular as food and game. Albacore *T. alalunga*, bluefin tuna *T. thynnus*, and yellowfin tuna *T. albacares* are commercially important.

tundra region in high latitudes with almost no trees – they cannot grow because the ground is permanently frozen (*permafrost). The vegetation consists mostly of grasses, sedges, heather, mosses, and lichens. Tundra stretches in a continuous belt across northern North America and Eurasia. Tundra is also used to describe similar conditions at high altitudes.

tungsten chemical symbol W, (Swedish *tung sten* 'heavy stone') hard, heavy, grey-white, metallic element, atomic number 74, relative atomic mass 183.85. Its chemical symbol comes from the German *Wolfram*. It occurs in the minerals wolframite, scheelite, and hubertite. It has the highest melting point of any metal (3,410 °C/6,170 °F) and is added to steel to make it harder, stronger, and more elastic; its other uses include high-speed cutting tools, electrical elements, and thermionic couplings. Its salts are used in the paint and tanning industries.

Tunguska Event explosion at Tunguska, central Siberia, Russia, in June 1908, which devastated around 6,500 sq km/2,500 sq mi of forest. It is thought to have been caused by either a cometary nucleus or a fragment of *Encke's Comet about 200 m/660 ft across, or possibly an asteroid. The magnitude of the explosion was equivalent to an atom bomb (10–20 megatons) and produced a colossal shock wave; a bright falling object was seen 600 km/375 mi away and was heard up to 1,000 km/625 mi away.

Tunis capital and chief port of Tunisia; population (1994) 674,100. Industries include chemicals, textiles, engineering, lead smelting, and distilling. Velvets, silks, linen, and fez caps are also manufactured. Exports include phosphates, iron ore, fruit, and vegetables. Founded by the Arabs, it was captured by the Turks in 1533, then occupied by the French in 1881 and by the Axis powers 1942–43. The ruins of ancient *Carthage are to the northeast.

Tunisia

Tunisia
National name: *Al-Jumhuriyya at-Tunisiyya/ Tunisian Republic*

Area: 164,150 sq km/63,378 sq mi
Capital: Tunis (and chief port)
Major towns/cities: Sfax, L'Ariana, Bizerte, Gabès, Sousse, Kairouan, Ettadhamen
Major ports: Sfax, Sousse, Bizerte
Physical features: arable and forested land in north graduates towards desert in south; fertile island of Jerba, linked to mainland by causeway (identified with island of lotus-eaters); Shott el Jerid salt lakes
Head of state: Zine el-Abidine Ben Ali from 1987
Head of government: Muhammad Ghannouchi from 1999
Political system: nationalistic socialist
Political executive: unlimited presidency
Political parties: Constitutional Democratic Rally (RCD), nationalist, moderate, socialist; Popular Unity Movement (MUP), radical, left of centre; Democratic Socialists Movement (MDS), left of centre; Renovation Movement (MR), reformed communists
Currency: Tunisian dinar
GNI per capita (PPP): (US$) 6,280 (2002 est)
Exports: textiles and clothing, electrical equipment, crude petroleum, phosphates and fertilizers, electricity, gas, water, olive oil, fruit, leather and shoes, fishery products. Principal market: France 28.8% (2001)
Population: 9,832,000 (2003 est)
Language: Arabic (official), French
Religion: Sunni Muslim (state religion); Jewish and Christian minorities
Life expectancy: 68 (men); 73 (women) (2000–05)
Chronology
814 BC: Phoenician emigrants from Tyre, in Lebanon, founded Carthage, near modern Tunis, as a trading post. By 6th century BC Carthaginian kingdom dominated western Mediterranean.
146 BC: Carthage destroyed by Punic Wars with Rome, which began in 264 BC; Carthage became part of Rome's African province.
AD 533: Came under control of Byzantine Empire.
7th century: Invaded by Arabs, who introduced Islam. Succession of Islamic dynasties followed, including

Aghlabids (9th century), Fatimids (10th century), and Almohads (12th century).
1574: Became part of Islamic Turkish Ottoman Empire and a base for 'Barbary Pirates' who operated against European shipping until 19th century.
1705: Husayn Bey founded local dynasty, which held power under rule of Ottomans.
early 19th century: Ahmad Bey launched programme of economic modernization, which nearly bankrupted the country.
1881: Became French protectorate, with bey retaining local power.
1920: Destour (Constitution) Party, named after the original Tunisian constitution of 1861, founded to campaign for equal Tunisian participation in French-dominated government.
1934: Habib Bourguiba founded a radical splinter party, the Neo-Destour Party, to spearhead the nationalist movement.
1942–43: Brief German occupation during World War II.
1956: Independence achieved as monarchy under bey, with Bourguiba as prime minister.
1957: Bey deposed; Tunisia became one-party republic with Bourguiba as president.
1975: Bourguiba made president for life.
1979: Headquarters for Arab League moved to Tunis after Egypt signed Camp David Accords with Israel.
1981: Multiparty elections held, as a sign of political liberalization, but were won by Bourguiba's Destourian Socialist Party (DSP).
1982: Allowed Palestine Liberation Organization (PLO) to use Tunis for its headquarters.
1985: Diplomatic relations with Libya severed; Israel attacked PLO headquarters.
1987: Zine el-Abidine Ben Ali, the new prime minister, declared Bourguiba (now aged 84) incompetent for government and seized power as president.
1988: 2,000 political prisoners freed; privatization initiative. Diplomatic relations with Libya restored. DSP renamed RCD.
1990: The Arab League's headquarters returned to Cairo, Egypt.
1991: There was opposition to US actions during the Gulf War, and a crackdown on religious fundamentalists.
1992: Human-rights transgressions provoked Western criticism.
1994: Ben Ali and the RCD were re-elected. The PLO transferred its headquarters to Gaza City in Palestine.
1999: In the country's first ever 'competitive' presidential elections, Ben Ali was re-elected president. Muhammad Ghannouchi was elected prime minister.
2002: Al-Qaeda was blamed for a synagogue bomb in Djerba that killed 19, 11 of them German tourists.
2004: Ben Ali was re-elected for his fourth term as president.

turbine engine in which steam, water, gas, or air is made to spin a rotating shaft by pushing on angled blades, like a fan. There are two sets of blades, the stator (does not rotate) and the rotor (does rotate). The rotating turbine shaft can be connected to an electricity generator. Turbines are among the most powerful machines.

turbocharger turbine-driven device fitted to engines to force more air into the cylinders, producing extra power. The turbocharger consists of a 'blower', or compressor, driven by a turbine, which in most units is driven by the exhaust gases leaving the engine.

turbofan jet engine of the type used by most airliners, so called because of its huge front fan. The fan sends air not only into the engine for combustion but also around the engine for additional thrust. This results in a faster and more fuel-efficient propulsive jet (see *jet propulsion).

turbojet jet engine that derives its thrust from a jet of hot exhaust gases. Pure turbojets can be very powerful but use a lot of fuel.

turbot any of various flatfishes of the flounder group prized as food, especially *Scophthalmus maximus* found in European waters. It grows up to 1 m/3 ft long and weighs up to 14 kg/30 lb. It is brownish above and whitish underneath.

Turgenev, Ivan Sergeievich (1818–1883) Russian writer. He is notable for poetic realism, pessimism, and skill in characterization. His works include the play *A Month in the Country* (1849), and the novels *A Nest of Gentlefolk* (1858), *Fathers and Sons* (1862), and *Virgin Soil* (1877). His series *A Sportsman's Sketches* (1852) criticized serfdom.

Turing, Alan Mathison (1912–1954) English mathematician and logician. In 1936 he described a 'universal computing machine' that could theoretically be programmed to solve any problem capable of solution by a specially designed machine. This concept, now called the Turing machine, foreshadowed the digital computer.

Turin shroud ancient piece of linen bearing the image of a body, claimed to be that of Jesus. Independent tests carried out in 1988 by scientists in Switzerland, the USA, and the UK showed that the cloth of the shroud dated from between 1260 and 1390. The shroud, property of the pope, is kept in Turin Cathedral, Italy. A more detailed 20-year study published in 1997 revealed that the shroud was made, around 1325, by daubing a man in red ochre paint and then wrapping him tightly in the linen sheet. Vermillion paint was then splashed on the head and wrists to suggest blood stains. Why it was made, and by whom, remains a mystery.

Turk *or* **Turkic** member of any of the Turkic-speaking peoples of Asia and Europe, especially the principal ethnic group of Turkey. Turkic languages belong to the Altaic family and include Uzbek, Ottoman, Turkish, Azeri, Turkoman, Tatar, Kirghiz, and Yakut. The ancestors of the Turks were pastoral nomads in central Asia. Islam was introduced during the 7th century.

Turkana, Lake formerly **Lake Rudolf** (until 1979), lake in the Great Rift Valley, 375 m/1,230 ft above sea level, with its northernmost end in Ethiopia and the rest in Kenya; area 8,000 sq km/3,100 sq mi. It is saline, and shrinking by evaporation. Its shores were an early human hunting ground, and valuable remains have been found that are accurately datable because of undisturbed stratification.

Turkestan historical area of Central Asia extending from the Caspian Sea in the west to the Gobi desert in the east. It is now divided among Kazakhstan, Kyrgyzstan, Tajikistan, Turkmenistan, Uzbekistan, Afghanistan (Northeast province), and China (part of Xinjiang Uygur province). It formerly covered an area of some 2,600,000 sq km/1,003,680 sq mi; its principal cities were *Tashkent, *Samarkand, and *Bukhara.

Turkey

National name: *Türkiye Cumhuriyeti/ Republic of Turkey*

Area: 779,500 sq km/300,964 sq mi
Capital: Ankara
Major towns/cities: Istanbul, Izmir, Adana, Bursa, Gaziantep, Konya, Mersin, Antalya
Major ports: Istanbul and Izmir
Physical features: central plateau surrounded by mountains, partly in Europe (Thrace) and partly in Asia (Anatolia); Bosporus and Dardanelles; Mount Ararat (highest peak Great Ararat, 5,137 m/16,854 ft); Taurus Mountains in southwest (highest peak Kaldi Dag, 3,734 m/ 12,255 ft); sources of rivers Euphrates and Tigris in east
Head of state: Ahmet Necdet Sezer from 2000
Head of government: Recep Erdogan from 2003
Political system: liberal democracy
Political executive: parliamentary
Political parties: Motherland Party (ANAP), Islamic, nationalist, right of centre; Republican People's Party (CHP), left of centre; True Path Party (DYP), right of centre, pro-Western; Virtue Party (FP), Islamic fundamentalist
Currency: Turkish lira
GNI per capita (PPP): (US$) 6,120 (2002 est)
Exports: textiles and clothing, metals, motor vehicles and parts, agricultural products and foodstuffs (including figs, nuts, and dried fruit), tobacco, beverages, leather, glass, refined petroleum and petroleum products. Principal market: Germany 17.2% (2001)
Population: 71,325,000 (2003 est)
Language: Turkish (official), Kurdish, Arabic
Religion: Sunni Muslim 99%; Orthodox, Armenian churches
Life expectancy: 68 (men); 73 (women) (2000–05)
Chronology
1st century BC: Asia Minor became part of Roman Empire, later passing to Byzantine Empire.
6th century AD: Turkic peoples spread from Mongolia into Turkestan, where they adopted Islam.
1055: Seljuk Turks captured Baghdad; their leader Tughrul took the title of sultan.
1071: Battle of Manzikert: Seljuk Turks defeated Byzantines and conquered Asia Minor.

929

13th century: Ottoman Turks, driven west by Mongols, became vassals of Seljuk Turks.

c. 1299: Osman I founded small Ottoman kingdom, which quickly displaced Seljuks to include all Asia Minor.

1354: Ottoman Turks captured Gallipoli and began their conquests in Europe.

1389: Battle of Kossovo: Turks defeated Serbs to take control of most of Balkan peninsula.

1453: Constantinople, capital of Byzantine Empire, fell to the Turks; became capital of Ottoman Empire as Istanbul.

16th century: Ottoman Empire reached its zenith under Suleiman the Magnificent 1520–66; Turks conquered Egypt, Syria, Arabia, Mesopotamia, Tripoli, Cyprus, and most of Hungary.

1683: Failure of Siege of Vienna marked the start of the decline of the Ottoman Empire.

1699: Treaty of Karlowitz: Turks forced out of Hungary by Austrians.

1774: Treaty of Kuchuk Kainarji: Russia drove Turks from Crimea and won the right to intervene on behalf of Christian subjects of the sultan.

19th century: 'The Eastern Question': Ottoman weakness caused intense rivalry between powers to shape future of Near East.

1821–29: Greek war of independence: Greeks defeated Turks with help of Russia, Britain, and France.

1854–56: Crimean War: Britain and France fought to defend Ottoman Empire from further pressure by Russians.

1877–78: Russo-Turkish War ended with Treaty of Berlin and withdrawal of Turks from Bulgaria.

1908: Young Turk revolution forced sultan to grant constitution; start of political modernization.

1911–12: Italo-Turkish War: Turkey lost Tripoli (Libya).

1912–13: Balkan War: Greece, Serbia, and Bulgaria expelled Turks from Macedonia and Albania.

1914: Ottoman Empire entered World War I on German side.

1919: Following Turkish defeat, Mustapha Kemal launched nationalist revolt to resist foreign encroachments.

1920: Treaty of Sèvres partitioned Ottoman Empire, leaving no part of Turkey fully independent.

1922: Kemal, having defied Allies, expelled Greeks, French, and Italians from Asia Minor; sultanate abolished.

1923: Treaty of Lausanne recognized Turkish independence; secular republic established by Kemal, who imposed rapid Westernization.

1935: Kemal adopted surname Atatürk ('Father of the Turks').

1938: Death of Kemal Atatürk; succeeded as president by Ismet Inönü.

1950: First free elections won by opposition Democratic Party; Adnan Menderes became prime minister.

1952: Turkey became a member of NATO.

1960: Military coup led by Gen Cemal Gürsel deposed Menderes, who was executed in 1961.

1961: Inönü returned as prime minister; politics dominated by the issue of Cyprus.

1965: Justice Party came to power under Suleyman Demirel.

1971–73: Prompted by strikes and student unrest, the army imposed military rule.

1974: Turkey invaded northern Cyprus.

1980–83: Political violence led to further military rule.

1984: Kurds began guerrilla war in a quest for greater autonomy.

1989: Application to join European Community rejected.

1990–91: Turkey joined the UN coalition against Iraq in the Gulf War.

1995: Turkish offensives against Kurdish bases in northern Iraq; the Islamicist Welfare Party won the largest number of seats in general election.

1997: Plans were agreed for the curbing of Muslim fundamentalism. Mesut Yilmaz was appointed prime minister. An agreement was reached with Greece on the peaceful resolution of disputes.

1998: The Islamic Welfare Party (RP) was banned by Constitutional Court, and regrouped as the Virtue Party (FP).

1999: Bülent Ecevit became prime minister. Ecevit's ruling centre-left party won the majority of seats in the general election. Turkey suffered two devastating earthquakes, causing extensive loss of life and structural damage. At a European Union (EU) summit, Turkey was at last declared an EU candidate, but to become a full member would first have to settle its territorial dispute with Greece and satisfy EU human rights regulations.

2000: Ahmet Necdet Sezer was inaugurated as president. He urged reform to push Turkey closer to EU membership and overruled a decree that had allowed the government to dismiss bureaucrats deemed to be too pro-Kurdish or insufficiently secular.

2001: A stock market crash significantly devalued the lira.

2002: EU delayed membership application.

2003: Suicide bombings at two synagogues in Istanbul, Turkey, killed at least 25 people and injured over 300. Suicide bombers also targeted the British consulate and the local headquarters of the UK-based bank HSBC, killing 30 people including the British consul Roger Short and injuring over 450. Islamic extremists with links to the al-Qaeda international terrorist network were thought responsible.

2004: The European Union granted Turkey accession talks, to begin in late 2005, after Turkey agreed to recognize Cyprus as an EU member.

turkey any of several large game birds of the pheasant family, Meleagrididae, order Galliformes, native to the Americas. The wild turkey *Meleagris galloparvo* reaches a length of 1.3 m/4.3 ft, and is native to North and Central American woodlands. The domesticated turkey derives from the wild species. Turkeys in the wild lay a single clutch of 12 eggs every spring, whereas domestic turkeys lay 120 over 27 weeks. Wild turkeys weigh up to 10 kg/22 lb; domestic turkeys up to 30 kg/66 lb. The ocellated turkey *Agriocharis ocellata* is found in Central America; it has eyespots on the tail.

Turkish language language of central and West Asia, the national language of Turkey. It belongs to the Altaic language family. Varieties of Turkish are spoken in northwestern Iran and several of the Central Asian Republics, and all have been influenced by Arabic and Persian. Originally written in Arabic script, it has been written within Turkey in a variant of the Roman alphabet since 1928.

Turkmenistan
National name: *Türkmenistan/Turkmenistan*

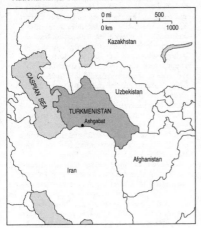

Area: 488,100 sq km/188,455 sq mi
Capital: Ashgabat
Major towns/cities: Chärjew, Mary, Nebitdag, Dashhowuz, Turkmenbashi
Major ports: Turkmenbashi
Physical about 90% of land is desert including the Kara Kum 'Black Sands' desert (area 310,800 sq km/120,000 sq mi)
Head of state and government: Saparmurad Niyazov from 1990
Political system: authoritarian nationalist
Political executive: unlimited presidency
Political parties: Democratic Party of Turkmenistan, ex-communist, pro-Niyazov; Turkmen Popular Front (Agzybirlik), nationalist
Currency: manat
GNI per capita (PPP): (US$) 4,570 (2002 est)
Exports: natural gas, cotton yarn, electric energy, petroleum and petroleum products. Principal market: Ukraine 46% (2001)
Population: 4,867,000 (2003 est)
Language: Turkmen (a Turkic language; official), Russian, Uzbek, other regional languages
Religion: Sunni Muslim
Life expectancy: 64 (men); 70 (women) (2000–05)
Chronology
6th century BC: Part of the Persian Empire of Cyrus the Great.
4th century BC: Part of the empire of Alexander the Great of Macedonia.
7th century: Spread of Islam into Transcaspian region, followed by Arab rule from 8th century.
10th–13th centuries: Immigration from northeast by nomadic Oghuz Seljuk and Mongol tribes, whose Turkic-speaking descendants now dominate the country; conquest by Genghis Khan.
16th century: Came under dominance of Persia, to the south.
1869–81: Fell under control of tsarist Russia after 150,000 Turkmen were killed in Battle of Gok Tepe in 1881;

became part of Russia's Turkestan Governor-Generalship.
1916: Turkmen revolted violently against Russian rule; autonomous Transcaspian government formed after Russian Revolution of 1917.
1919: Brought back under Russian control following invasion by the Soviet Red Army.
1921: Part of Turkestan Soviet Socialist Autonomous Republic.
1925: Became constituent republic of USSR.
1920s–30s: Soviet programme of agricultural collectivization and secularization provoked sporadic guerrilla resistance and popular uprisings.
1960–67: Lenin Kara-Kum Canal built, leading to dramatic expansion in cotton production in previously semidesert region.
1985: Saparmurad Niyazov replaced Muhammad Gapusov, local communist leader since 1971, whose regime had been viewed as corrupt.
1989: Stimulated by the *glasnost* initiative of reformist Soviet leader Mikhail Gorbachev, Agzybirlik 'popular front' formed by Turkmen intellectuals.
1990: Economic and political sovereignty was declared. Niyazov was elected state president.
1991: Niyazov initially supported an attempted anti-Gorbachev coup in Moscow. Independence was later declared; Turkmenistan joined the new Commonwealth of Independent States (CIS).
1992: Joined the Muslim Economic Cooperation Organization and the United Nations; a new constitution was adopted.
1993: A new currency, the manat, was introduced and a programme of cautious economic reform introduced, with foreign investment in the country's huge oil and gas reserves encouraged. The economy continued to contract.
1994: A nationwide referendum overwhelmingly backed Niyazov's presidency. Ex-communists won most seats in parliamentary elections.
1997: Private land ownership was legalized.
2002: President Saparmurad Niyazov survived an assassination attempt. It was alleged that four former government ministers and officials were behind the attack.
2005: President Niyazov declared that a democratic presidential election could be held in 2009.
Turkoman *or* **Turkman** plural **Turkomen**, member of the majority ethnic group in Turkmenistan. They live to the east of the Caspian Sea, around the Kara Kum Desert, and along the borders of Afghanistan, Iraq, Syria, Turkey, and Iran. Their language belongs to the Turkic branch of the Altaic family and is closely related to the language of Turkey.
Turks and Caicos Islands British crown colony in the West Indies, the southeastern archipelago of the Bahamas; area 430 sq km/166 sq mi; population (1997 est) 14,600 (90% of African descent). The capital is Cockburn Town on Grand Turk, which is the site of a US tracking station for guided missiles. Exports include crayfish and conch (flesh and shell); financial services and tourism are important to the economy, and the main tourist island is Providenciales.
turmeric perennial plant belonging to the ginger family, native to India and the East Indies; also the ground powder from its tuberous rhizomes (underground stems), used in curries to give a yellow colour and as a dyestuff. (*Curcuma longa*, family Zingiberaceae.)

Turner, Joseph Mallord William (1775–1851)
English painter. He was one of the most original artists
of his day. He travelled widely in Europe, and his
landscapes became increasingly Romantic, with the
subject often transformed in scale and flooded with
brilliant, hazy light. His innovative use of emotive
colour, as in *The Slave Ship* (1840; Museum of Fine Arts,
Boston, Massachusetts); and his passionate depiction of
feeling as it exists in the natural environment, had a
tremendous influence on modern art. Many later works
anticipate Impressionism, for example *Rain, Steam and
Speed* (1844; National Gallery, London).

turnip biennial plant widely cultivated in temperate
regions for its edible white- or yellow-fleshed root
and young leaves, which are used as a green vegetable.
Closely allied to it is the *swede (*B. napus*). (*Brassica rapa*,
family Cruciferae.)

turnover in finance, the value of sales of a business
organization over a period of time. For example, if
a shop sells 10,000 items in a week at an average price
of £2 each, then its weekly turnover is £20,000. The
*profit of a company is not only affected by the total
turnover but also by the rate of turnover.

turnpike road road with a gate or barrier preventing
access until a toll had been paid, common from the
mid-16th–19th centuries. The first turnpike road to be
built in the UK since the 18th century is the privately
funded Birmingham northern relief road, 50 km/31 mi
long, opened in 2003.

turnstone any small wading shorebirds of the genus
Arenaria, order Charadriiformes, especially the ruddy
turnstone *A. interpres*, which breeds in the Arctic and
migrates to the southern hemisphere. It is seen on
rocky beaches, turning over stones for small crustaceans
and insects. It is about 23 cm/9 in long and has a
summer plumage of black and chestnut above, white
below; it is duller in winter.

turpentine solution of resins distilled from the sap of
conifers, used in varnish and as a paint solvent but now
largely replaced by white spirit.

Turpin, Dick (Richard) (1705–1739) English
highwayman. The son of an innkeeper, he turned to
highway robbery, cattle-thieving, and smuggling, and
was hanged at York, England.

turquoise mineral, hydrous basic copper aluminium
phosphate, $CuAl_6(PO_4)_4(OH)_8 \cdot 5H_2O$. Blue-green, blue,
or green, it is a gemstone. Turquoise is found in Australia,
Egypt, Ethiopia, France, Germany, Iran, Turkestan,
Mexico, and southwestern USA. It was originally
introduced into Europe through Turkey, from which
its name is derived.

turtle freshwater or marine reptile whose body is
protected by a shell. Turtles are related to tortoises, and
some species can grow to a length of up to 2.5 m/8 ft.
Turtles often travel long distances to lay their eggs on the
beaches where they were born. Many species have suffered
through destruction of their breeding sites as well as
being hunted for food and their shells. Unlike tortoises,
turtles cannot retract their heads into their shells.

Tuscany Italian *Toscana*; Roman *Etruria*, region of
north central Italy, on the west coast, comprising the
provinces of Massa e Carrara, Arezzo, Florence,
Grosseto, Livorno, Lucca, Pisa, Pistoia, Prato, and Siena;
area 22,997 sq km/8,879 sq mi; population (2001 est)
3,460,800. Its capital is Florence, and cities include Pisa,
Livorno, and Siena. The area is mainly agricultural,
producing cereals, wine (Chianti hills), olives (Lucca)
and tobacco (plain of Arno); lignite (upper Arno)
and iron (Elba) are also mined, and marble quarried
(Carrara, Apuan Alps). During the 14th and 15th
centuries, Italy's classical literary language became
based on the Tuscan dialect, after it was used by
Dante Alighieri, Petrarch, and Bocaccio.

Tutankhamen King (pharaoh) of ancient Egypt of the
18th dynasty, about 1333–1323 BC. A son of Akhenaton
(also called Amenhotep IV), he was about 11 at his
accession. In 1922 his tomb was discovered by the
British archaeologists Lord Carnarvon and Howard
Carter in the Valley of the Kings at Luxor, almost
untouched by tomb robbers. The contents included
many works of art and his solid-gold coffin, which are
now displayed in a Cairo museum.

Tutsi member of a minority ethnic group living in
Rwanda and Burundi. They have politically dominated
the *Hutu majority and the Twa (or *Pygmies) since
their arrival in the area in the 14th century. In Burundi,
positions of power were monopolized by the Tutsis, who
carried out massacres in response to Hutu rebellions,
notably 1972 and 1988. In Rwanda, where the balance
of power is more even, Tutsis were massacred in their
thousands by Hutu militia during the 1994 civil war.

Tutu, Desmond Mpilo (1931–) South African priest,
Anglican archbishop of Cape Town 1986–96 and
secretary general of the South African Council of
Churches 1979–84. One of the leading figures in the
struggle against *apartheid in the Republic of South
Africa, he was awarded the Nobel Prize for Peace in
1984 for encouraging peaceful reconciliation between
the black and white communities.

Tuva *or* **Tyva** republic in the southern Russian
Federation; area 170,500 sq km/65,830 sq mi;
population (1996) 309,000 (49% urban) (64% Tyvans).
The capital is Kyzyl. There are coal and mineral mining,
woodworking, and food-processing industries; sheep,
goats, and cattle are raised.

Tuvalu
formerly **Ellice Islands (until 1978)**
  National name: *Fakavae Aliki-Malo i Tuvalu/
Constitutional Monarchy of Tuvalu*

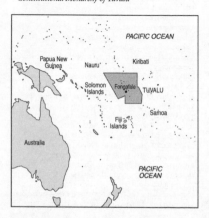

Area: 25 sq km/9.6 sq mi
Capital: Fongafale (on Funafuti atoll)
Physical features: nine low coral atolls forming a chain of 579 km/650 mi in the Southwest Pacific
Head of state: Queen Elizabeth II from 1978, represented by Governor General Faimalaga Luka from 2003
Head of government: Maatia Toafa from 2004
Political system: liberal democracy
Political executive: parliamentary
Political parties: none; members are elected to parliament as independents
Currency: Australian dollar
GNI per capita (PPP): (US$) 1,300 (2001)
Exports: copra, handicrafts, garments, stamps, fisheries licences. Principal market: Belgium 22.8% (2000)
Population: 11,000 (2003 est)
Language: Tuvaluan, English (both official), a Gilbertese dialect (on Nui)
Religion: Protestant 96% (Church of Tuvalu)
Life expectancy: 65 (men); 69 (women) (2001 est)
Chronology
c. **300 BC:** First settled by Polynesian peoples.
16th century: Invaded and occupied by Samoans.
1765: Islands first reached by Europeans.
1850–75: Population decimated by European slave traders capturing Tuvaluans to work in South America and by exposure to European diseases.
1856: The four southern islands, including Funafuti, claimed by USA.
1865: Christian mission established.
1877: Came under control of British Western Pacific High Commission (WPHC), with its headquarters in the Fiji Islands.
1892: Known as the Ellice Islands, they were joined with Gilbert Islands (now Kiribati) to form a British protectorate.
1916: Gilbert and Ellice Islands colony formed.
1942–43: Became a base for US airforce operations when Japan occupied the Gilbert Islands during World War II.
1975: Following a referendum, the predominantly Melanesian-peopled Ellice Islands, fearing domination by Micronesian-peopled Gilbert Islands in an independent state, were granted separate status.
1978: Independence achieved within Commonwealth, with Toaripi Lauti as prime minister; reverted to former name Tuvalu ('eight standing together').
1979: The USA signed a friendship treaty, relinquishing its claim to the four southern atolls in return for continued access to military bases.
1986: Islanders rejected proposal for republican status.
1999: Ionatana Ionatana became prime minister.
2000: Tuvalu entered the United Nations. Ionatana died and was replaced by Lagitupu Tuilimu.
2001: Faimalaga Luka was elected prime minister.
2002: Saufatu Sopoangu headed the government.
2004: Maatia Toafa was elected prime minister, promising a referendum the following year on whether or not to replace the British monarch as head of state.

TVP abbreviation for texturized vegetable protein, meat substitute usually made from soybeans. In manufacture, the soybean solids (what remains after oil has been removed) are ground finely and mixed with a binder to form a sticky mixture. This is forced through a spinneret and extruded into fibres, which are treated with salts and flavourings, wound into hanks, and then chopped up to resemble meat chunks.

Twain, Mark (1835–1910) pen-name of Samuel Langhorne Clemens, US writer. He established his reputation with the comic masterpiece *The Innocents Abroad* (1869) and two classic American novels, in dialect, *The Adventures of Tom Sawyer* (1876) and *The Adventures of Huckleberry Finn* (1885). Twain's use of the vernacular (commonly spoken dialect), vivid characterization and descriptions, and the theme of *The Adventures of Huckleberry Finn*, underlying the humour, of man's inhumanity to man, has given it universal appeal. He also wrote satire, as in *A Connecticut Yankee at King Arthur's Court* (1889). He is recognized as one of America's finest and most characteristic writers.

Tweed river rising in the Tweedsmuir Hills, 10 km/6 mi north of Moffat, southwest Scottish Borders, Scotland, and entering the North Sea at Berwick-upon-Tweed, Northumberland; length 156 km/97 mi. It flows in a northeasterly direction, and from Coldstream until near Berwick-upon-Tweed it forms the border between England and Scotland.

Twelve Tables in ancient Rome, the earliest law code, drawn from religious and secular custom. It was published on tablets of bronze or wood at the Roman *forum *c.* 450 BC*, and though these were destroyed in the sack of Rome by Celts 387 BC, the code survived to have influence into the later Republic.

twelve-tone system *or* **twelve-note system** method of musical composition invented by Arnold *Schoenberg about 1921 in which all 12 notes of the *chromatic scale are arranged in a particular order of the composer's choice, without repeating any of the notes. Such an arrangement is called a 'series' or 'tone row'. The initial series may be transposed, divided, and otherwise mutated to provide a complete resource for all melodic and harmonic material in a work.

twin one of two young produced from a single pregnancy. Human twins may be genetically identical (monozygotic), having been formed from a single fertilized egg that splits into two cells, both of which became implanted. Nonidentical (fraternal or dizygotic) twins are formed when two eggs are fertilized at the same time.

two-stroke cycle operating cycle for internal combustion piston engines. The engine cycle is completed after just two strokes (up or down) of the piston, which distinguishes it from the more common *four-stroke cycle. Some power mowers and lightweight motorcycles use two-stroke petrol engines, which are cheaper and simpler than four-strokes.

Tyche personification of Chance in classical Greek thought, whose cult developed in the Hellenistic and Roman periods, when it was identified with that of the Roman Fortuna.

Tyler, Wat (died 1381) English leader of the *Peasants' Revolt of 1381. He was probably born in Kent or Essex, and may have served in the French wars. After taking Canterbury, he led the peasant army to Blackheath, outside London, and went on to invade the city. King Richard II met the rebels at Mile End and promised to redress their grievances, which included the imposition of a poll tax. At a further conference at Smithfield, London, Tyler was murdered.

Tyndale, William (c. 1492–1536) English translator of the Bible. The printing of his New Testament was begun in Cologne in 1525 and, after he had been forced to flee, completed in Worms. Tyndale introduced some of the most familiar phrases to the English language, such as 'filthy lucre', and 'God forbid'. He was strangled and burned as a heretic at Vilvorde in Belgium.

Tyne river of northeast England formed by the union of the North Tyne (rising in the Cheviot Hills) and South Tyne (rising near Cross Fell in Cumbria) near Hexham, Northumberland, and reaching the North Sea at Tynemouth; length 72 km/45 mi. Kielder Water (1980) in the North Tyne Valley is Europe's largest artificial lake, 12 km/7.5 mi long and 0.8 km/0.5 mi wide, and supplies the industries of Tyneside, Wearside, and Teesside. As well as functioning as a reservoir, it is a major resource for recreational use.

Tyne and Wear metropolitan county of northeast England, created in 1974; in 1986, most of the functions of the former county council were transferred to the metropolitan borough councils. **area:** 540 sq km/208 sq mi **towns and cities:** Newcastle upon Tyne, Gateshead, Sunderland (administrative centres for the districts of the same name), South Shields (administrative centre of South Tyneside district), North Shields (administrative centre of North Tyneside district) **physical:** rivers: Tyne and Wear **features:** part of *Hadrian's Wall; Newcastle and Gateshead, linked with each other and with the coast on both sides by the Tyne and Wear Metro (a light railway using existing suburban lines, extending 54 km/34 mi); Tyneside International Film Festival **population:** (1996) 1,127,300.

typesetting means by which text, or copy, is prepared for *printing, now usually carried out by using specialized computer programs. Text is keyed on a typesetting machine in a similar way to typing. Laser or light impulses are projected on to light-sensitive film that, when developed, can be used to make plates for printing.

typewriter keyboard machine that produces characters on paper. The earliest known typewriter design was patented by Henry Mill in England in 1714. However, the first practical typewriter was built in 1867 in Milwaukee, Wisconsin, USA, by Christopher Sholes, Carlos Glidden, and Samuel Soulé. By 1873 Remington and Sons, US gunmakers, had produced under contract the first typing machines for sale and in 1878 they patented the first with lower-case as well as upper-case (capital) letters. Typewriters are being superseded by word processors.

typhoid fever acute infectious disease of the digestive tract, caused by the bacterium *Salmonella typhi*, and usually contracted through a contaminated water supply. It is characterized by bowel haemorrhage and damage to the spleen. Treatment is with antibiotics.

typhoon violent revolving storm, a *hurricane in the western Pacific Ocean.

typhus any one of a group of infectious diseases caused by bacteria transmitted by lice, fleas, mites, and ticks. Symptoms include fever, headache, and rash. The most serious form is epidemic typhus, which also affects the brain, heart, lungs, and kidneys and is associated with insanitary overcrowded conditions. Treatment is by antibiotics.

typography design and layout of the printed word. Typography began with the invention of writing and developed as printing spread throughout Europe after the invention of metal moveable type by Johann *Gutenberg about 1440. Hundreds of variations have followed since, but the basic design of the Frenchman Nicholas Jensen (about 1420–1480), with a few modifications, is still the ordinary ('roman') type used in printing. Typography, for centuries the domain of engravers and printers, is now a computerized process, carried out by using specialist software.

Tyr in Norse and Teutonic mythology, the god of battles, whom the Anglo-Saxons called Ty'w, from where 'Tuesday' is derived. He was a member of the Aesir (principal warrior gods).

tyrannosaurus any of a genus *Tyrannosaurus* of gigantic flesh-eating *dinosaurs, order Saurischia, that lived in North America and Asia about 70 million years ago. They had two feet, were up to 15 m/50 ft long, 6.5 m/20 ft tall, weighed 10 tonnes, and had teeth 15 cm/6 in long.

Tyrol variant spelling of *Tirol, a state of Austria.

Tyrone historic county of Northern Ireland; area 3,160 sq km/1,220 sq mi. The county is largely rural, and still contains evidence of the once-flourishing linen industry. The principal towns and cities are Omagh, Dungannon, Strabane, and Cookstown. Lough Neagh is in the east and the Sperrin Mountains in the north. The main rivers are the Derg, Blackwater, and Foyle. Administrative responsibility for the county is held by the councils of Omagh, Dungannon, Strabane, and Cookstown.

Tyrrhenian Sea Italian **Tirreno**, arm of the Mediterranean Sea (c.760 km/475 mi long and 97 km/60 mi wide) surrounded by mainland Italy, Sicily, Sardinia, Corsica, and the Ligurian Sea. It is connected to the Ionian Sea through the Straits of Messina. Islands include Elba, Ustica, Capri, Stromboli, and the Lipari Islands. Naples and Palermo are its chief ports. It has a deep seabed plain reaching a maximum depth of 3,620 m/11,876 ft.

Tzu-Hsi alternative transliteration of *Zi Xi, dowager empress of China.

U

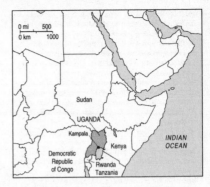

U2 Irish rock group formed in Dublin, Ireland, in 1977. U2 became one of the most popular and successful rock bands of the 1980s and 1990s, managing to sustain their fan base throughout two decades by clever reinvention. The group are known for combining their music with political messages, for example in 'Sunday, Bloody Sunday' (1983) about the conflict in Northern Ireland. The album *The Joshua Tree* (1987) took the band to super-stardom, and the band continued to release highly successful and critically acclaimed albums, including *Achtung Baby* (1992), *Pop* (1997), *All That You Can't Leave Behind* (2001), and *How to Dismantle an Atomic Bomb* (2004).

uakari any of several rare South American monkeys of the genus *Cacajao*. There are three species, all with bald faces and long fur. About 55 cm/1.8 ft long in head and body, and with a comparatively short 15 cm/6 in tail, they rarely leap, but are good climbers, remaining in the tops of the trees in swampy forests and feeding largely on fruit. The black uakari is in danger of extinction because it is found in such small numbers already, and the forests where it lives are fast being destroyed.

Uccello, Paolo (1397–1475) adopted name of Paolo di Dono, Florentine painter. He was one of the first to experiment with perspective, though his love of detail, decorative colour, and graceful line remains traditional. His works include *St George and the Dragon* (*c.* 1460, National Gallery, London) and *A Hunt* (*c.* 1460, Ashmolean Museum, Oxford).

Udmurt or **Udmurtiya** Russian **Udmurtskaya**, autonomous republic in central Russian Federation, north of Tatarstan and northwest of Bashkortostan; area 42,100 sq km/16,200 sq mi; population (1990) 1,619,000 (59% Russian, 31% Udmurt, 7% Tatar). The capital is Izhevsk. There are timber, peat, quartz, tool and machine manufacturing, oil, and hydroelectric power generation industries. Flax and potatoes are grown.

UFO acronym for *unidentified flying object.

Uganda
National name: *Republic of Uganda*
Area: 236,600 sq km/91,351 sq mi
Capital: Kampala
Major towns/cities: Jinja, Mbale, Entebbe, Masaka, Mbarara, Soroti
Physical features: plateau with mountains in west (Ruwenzori Range, with Mount Margherita, 5,110 m/ 16,765 ft); forest and grassland; 18% is lakes, rivers, and wetlands (Owen Falls on White Nile where it leaves Lake Victoria; Lake Albert in west); arid in northwest
Head of state: Yoweri Museveni from 1986
Head of government: Apolo Nsibambi from 1999
Political system: authoritarian nationalist
Political executive: unlimited presidency
Political parties: National Resistance Movement (NRM), left of centre; Democratic Party (DP), left of centre; Conservative Party (CP), right of centre; Uganda People's Congress (UPC), left of centre; Uganda Freedom Movement (UFM), left of centre. From 1986, political parties were forced to suspend activities
Currency: Ugandan new shilling
GNI per capita (PPP): (US$) 1,320 (2002 est)
Exports: coffee, cotton, tea, gold, tobacco, oil seeds and oleaginous fruit; fish and fish products, textiles. Principal market: Germany 12% (2000)
Population: 25,827,000 (2003 est)
Language: English (official), Kiswahili, other Bantu and Nilotic languages
Religion: Christian 65%, animist 20%, Muslim 15%
Life expectancy: 45 (men); 47 (women) (2000–05)
Chronology
16th century: Bunyoro kingdom founded by immigrants from southeastern Sudan.
17th century: Rise of kingdom of Buganda people, which became particularly powerful from 17th century.
mid-19th century: Arabs, trading ivory and slaves, reached Uganda; first visits by European explorers and Christian missionaries.
1885–87: Uganda Martyrs: Christians persecuted by Buganda ruler, Mwanga.
1890: Royal Charter granted to British East African Company, a trading company whose agent, Frederick Lugard, concluded treaties with local rulers, including the Buganda and the western states of Ankole and Toro.
1894: British protectorate established, with Buganda retaining some autonomy under its traditional prince (Kabaka) and other resistance being crushed.
1904: Cotton growing introduced by Buganda peasants.
1958: Internal self-government granted.
1962: Independence achieved from Britain, within Commonwealth, with Milton Obote of Uganda People's Congress (UPC) as prime minister.

935

1963: Proclaimed federal republic with King Mutesa II (of Buganda) as president and Obote as prime minister.
1966: King Mutesa, who opposed creation of a one-party state, ousted in coup led by Obote, who ended federal status and became executive president.
1969: All opposition parties banned after assassination attempt on Obote; key enterprises nationalized.
1971: Obote overthrown in army coup led by Maj-Gen Idi Amin Dada; constitution suspended and ruthlessly dictatorial regime established; nearly 49,000 Ugandan Asians expelled; over 300,000 opponents of regime killed.
1976: Relations with Kenya strained by Amin's claims to parts of Kenya.
1979: After annexing part of Tanzania, Amin forced to leave the country by opponents backed by Tanzanian troops. Provisional government set up.
1978–79: Fighting broke out against Tanzanian troops.
1980: Provisional government overthrown by army. Elections held and Milton Obote returned to power.
1985: After opposition by pro-Lule National Resistance Army (NRA), and indiscipline in army, Obote ousted by Gen Tito Okello; constitution suspended; power-sharing agreement entered into with NRA leader Yoweri Museveni.
1986: Museveni became president, heading broad-based coalition government.
1993: The King of Buganda was reinstated as formal monarch, in the person of Ronald Muwenda Mutebi II.
1996: A landslide victory was won by Museveni in the first direct presidential elections.
1997: Allied Democratic Forces (ADF) led uprisings by rebels.
1999: The leaders of Uganda and Sudan signed an agreement to bring an end to rebel wars across their mutual border by ceasing to support rebel factions in the other's country. President Museveni appointed Apolo Nsibambi as prime minister.
2000: Rebels attacked towns in northern Uganda and fought the Ugandan army along the border with Congo. A fire at the headquarters of the Restoration of the Ten Commandments of God cult in western Uganda killed up to 500 people. It was later discovered the cult leaders had engaged in mass murder. An outbreak of the ebola virus killed 160 people between September and December.
2001: President Museveni was re-elected, despite allegations of electoral fraud.

UHF abbreviation for ultra high frequency, referring to radio waves of very short wavelength, used, for example, for television broadcasting.

UHT abbreviation for **ultra-heat treated** or *ultra-heat treatment.

Uigur *or* **Uygur** member of a Turkic people living in northwestern China, Uzbekistan, Kazakhstan, and Kyrgyzstan; they form about 80% of the population of the Chinese province of Xinjiang Uygur. There are about 5 million speakers of Uigur, a language belonging to the Turkic branch of the Altaic family; it is the official language of the province.

ukiyo-e (Japanese 'pictures of the floating world') Japanese picture or print depicting the pleasures of everyday life; mainly produced by the technique of *woodcut, or woodblock. Beginning in the 17th century, ukiyo-e became the dominant art form in 18th- and 19th-century Japan. Originally made in black and white, advances in woodcut printing in the late 18th century enabled the production of multicoloured works. Aiming to satisfy the tastes of the increasingly affluent merchant classes, ukiyo-e artists employed bright colours and strong images, and featured actors, women, and landscapes among their favoured subjects; over a quarter of ukiyo-e were erotic works.
*Hiroshige, Utamaro, *Hokusai, and Suzuki were leading exponents. The flat decorative colour and lively designs of ukiyo-e prints were later to influence many prominent French avant-garde artists.

Ukraine
National name: *Ukrayina/Ukraine*

Area: 603,700 sq km/233,088 sq mi
Capital: Kiev
Major towns/cities: Kharkov, Donetsk, Dnipropetrovs'k, Lviv, Krivoy Rog, Zaporizhzhya, Odessa
Physical features: Russian plain; Carpathian and Crimean Mountains; rivers: Dnieper (with the Dnieper dam 1932), Donetz, Bug
Head of state: Viktor Yushchenko from 2004
Head of government: Yulia Tymoshenko from 2004
Political system: emergent democracy
Political executive: limited presidency
Political parties: Ukrainian Communist Party (UCP), left wing, anti-nationalist (banned 1991–93); Peasants' Party of the Ukraine (PPU), conservative agrarian; Ukrainian Socialist Party (SPU), left wing, anti-nationalist; Ukrainian People's Movement (Rukh); Ukrainian Republican Party (URP), moderate nationalist; Congress of Ukrainian Nationalists (CUN), moderate nationalist; Democratic Party of Ukraine (DPU), moderate nationalist; Social Democratic Party of Ukraine (SDPU), federalist
Currency: hryvna
GNI per capita (PPP): (US$) 4,650 (2002 est)
Exports: non-precious metals, machinery and equipment, food, beverages, agriculture products, coal, oil, various minerals. Principal market: Russia 21.5% (2001)
Population: 48,523,000 (2003 est)
Language: Ukrainian (a Slavonic language; official), Russian (also official in Crimea), other regional languages

Religion: traditionally Ukrainian Orthodox; also Ukrainian Catholic; small Protestant, Jewish, and Muslim communities

Life expectancy: 65 (men); 75 (women) (2000–05)

Chronology

9th century: Rus' people established state centred on Kiev and adopted Eastern Orthodox Christianity 988.

1199: Reunification of southern Rus' lands, after period of fragmentation, under Prince Daniel of Galicia-Volhynia.

13th century: Mongol-Tatar Golden Horde sacked Kiev and destroyed Rus' state.

14th century: Poland annexed Galicia; Lithuania absorbed Volhynia and expelled Tatars; Ukraine peasants became serfs of Polish and Lithuanian nobles.

1569: Poland and Lithuania formed single state; clergy of Ukraine formed Uniate Church, which recognized papal authority but retained Orthodox rites, to avoid Catholic persecution.

16th and 17th centuries: Runaway serfs known as Cossacks ('outlaws') formed autonomous community in eastern borderlands.

1648: Cossack revolt led by Gen Bogdan Khmelnitsky drove out Poles from central Ukraine; Khmelnitsky accepted Russian protectorate in 1654.

1660–90: 'Epoch of Ruins': Ukraine devastated by civil war and invasions by Russians, Poles, and Turks; Poland regained western Ukraine.

1687: Gen Ivan Mazepa entered into alliance with Sweden in effort to regain Cossack autonomy from Russia.

1709: Battle of Poltava: Russian victory over Swedes ended hopes of Cossack independence.

1772–95: Partition of Poland: Austria annexed Galicia, Russian annexations included Volhynia.

1846–47: Attempt to promote Ukrainian national culture through formation of Cyril and Methodius Society.

1899: Revolutionary Ukrainian Party founded.

1917: Revolutionary parliament (Rada), proclaimed Ukrainian autonomy within a federal Russia.

1918: Ukraine declared full independence; civil war ensued between Rada (backed by Germans) and Reds (backed by Russian Bolsheviks).

1919: Galicia united with Ukraine; conflict escalated between Ukrainian nationalists, Bolsheviks, anarchists, White Russians, and Poles.

1921: Treaty of Riga: Russia and Poland partitioned Ukraine.

1921–22: Several million people perished in famine.

1922: Ukrainian Soviet Socialist Republic (Ukrainian SSR) became part of Union of Soviet Socialist Republics (USSR).

1932–33: Enforced collectivization of agriculture caused another catastrophic famine with more than 7.5 million deaths.

1939: USSR annexed eastern Poland and added Galicia-Volhynia to Ukrainian SSR.

1940: USSR seized northern Bukhovina from Romania and added it to Ukrainian SSR.

1941–44: Germany occupied Ukraine; many Ukrainians collaborated; millions of Ukrainians and Ukrainian Jews were enslaved and exterminated by Nazis.

1945: USSR annexed Ruthenia from Czechoslovakia and added it to Ukrainian SSR, which became a nominal member of the United Nations (UN).

1946: Uniate Church forcibly merged with Russian Orthodox Church.

1954: Crimea transferred from Russian Federation to Ukrainian SSR.

1986: Major environmental disaster caused by explosion of nuclear reactor at Chernobyl, north of Kiev.

1989: Rukh (nationalist movement) established as political party; ban on Uniate Church lifted.

1990: Ukraine declared its sovereignty under President Leonid Kravchuk, leader of the CP.

1991: Ukraine declared its independence from USSR; President Kravchuk left the CP; Ukraine joined the newly formed Commonwealth of Independent States (CIS).

1992: Crimean sovereignty was declared but then rescinded.

1994: Election gains were made by radical nationalists in western Ukraine and by Russian unionists in eastern Ukraine; Leonid Kuchma succeeded Kravchuk as president.

1996: A new constitution replaced the Soviet system, making the presidency stronger; remaining nuclear warheads were returned to Russia for destruction; a new currency was introduced.

1997: New government appointments were made to speed economic reform. A treaty of friendship was signed with Russia, solving the issue of the Russian Black Sea fleet. A loan of $750 million from the International Monetary Fund (IMF) was approved.

1998: The communists won the largest number of seats in parliamentary elections, but fell short of an absolute majority. The value of the hryvnya fell by over 50% against the US dollar after the neighbouring Russian currency crisis. The government survived a no-confidence vote tabled by left-wing factions that opposed the government's economic program.

1999: Kuchma was re-elected as president; Viktor Yushchenko became prime minister.

2000: The death penalty was abolished. The Chernobyl nuclear power station was closed permanently.

2001: Protests in Kiev called for Kuchma's resignation on grounds of corruption and mismanagement.

2004: Viktor Yanukovych claimed victory in the presidential election, but accusations of electoral fraud and mass protests by supporters of the pro-Western Viktor Yushchenko led to a re-run of the election, which was won by Yushchenko.

Ukrainian the majority ethnic group living in Ukraine; there are minorities in Siberian Russia, Kazakhstan, Poland, Slovakia, and Romania. There are 40–45 million speakers of Ukrainian, a member of the East Slavonic branch of the Indo-European family, closely related to Russian. Ukrainian-speaking communities are also found in Canada and the USA.

ukulele musical instrument, a small four-stringed Hawaiian guitar, of Portuguese origin. It is easy to play; music for ukulele is written in a form of tablature showing finger positions on a chart of the fingerboard.

Ulaanbaatar or **Ulan Bator** formerly **Urga** (until 1924), (Mongolian 'Red Warrior/Hero') capital and largest city of Mongolia, lying to the north in the valley of the River Tuul in the Khenti Mountains; population (2000 est) 760,100. Industries include machine tools, cement, bricks, pharmaceuticals, carpets, textiles, footwear, meat packing, brewing, and distilling, especially of vodka. It is the centre of Mongolia's road and rail network, and connected to the Trans-Siberian and Chinese railways. The city is also served by an international airport.

ulcer any persistent breach in a body surface (skin or mucous membrane). It may be caused by infection, irritation, or tumour and is often inflamed. Common ulcers include aphthous (mouth), gastric (stomach), duodenal, decubitus ulcers (pressure sores), and those complicating varicose veins.

ulna one of the two bones found in the lower limb of the tetrapod (four-limbed) vertebrate. It articulates with the shorter radius and humerus (upper arm bone) at one end and with the radius and wrist bones at the other.

Ulster a former kingdom and province in the north of Ireland, annexed by England in 1461. From Jacobean times it was a centre of English, and later Scottish, settlement and was confiscated from its owners; divided in 1921 into Northern Ireland (counties Antrim, Armagh, Down, Fermanagh, Londonderry, and Tyrone) and the Republic of Ireland (counties Cavan, Donegal, and Monaghan).

Ulster Defence Association (UDA) Northern Ireland Protestant paramilitary organization responsible for a number of sectarian killings. Fanatically loyalist, it established a paramilitary wing (the Ulster Freedom Fighters) to combat the *Irish Republican Army (IRA) on its own terms and by its own methods. No political party has acknowledged any links with the UDA. In 1994, following a cessation of military activities by the IRA, the UDA, along with other Protestant paramilitary organizations, declared a ceasefire.

Ulster Freedom Fighters (UFF) paramilitary wing of the *Ulster Defence Association.

Ulster Unionist Party *or* **Official Unionist Party (OUP)** the largest political party in *Northern Ireland. Right-of-centre in orientation, its aim is equality for Northern Ireland within the UK, and it opposes union with the Republic of Ireland. The party has the broadest support of any Ulster party, and has consistently won a large proportion of parliamentary and local seats. Its central organization, dating from 1905, is formally called the Ulster Unionist Council. Its leader from 1995 is David *Trimble. It secured 28 of the 108 seats in the new Northern Ireland Assembly, elected in June 1998, and Trimble was elected Northern Ireland's first minister at the Assembly's first meeting on 1 July (he resigned in June 2001, but agreed to stand for re-election in October 2001).

ultra-heat treatment (UHT) preservation of milk by raising its temperature to 132 °C/269 °F or more. It uses higher temperatures than pasteurization, and kills all bacteria present, giving the milk a long shelf life but altering the flavour.

ultrasonics branch of physics dealing with the theory and application of ultrasound: sound waves occurring at frequencies too high to be heard by the human ear (that is, above about 20 kHz).

ultrasound scanning *or* **ultrasonography** in medicine, the use of ultrasonic pressure waves to create a diagnostic image. It is a safe, noninvasive technique that often eliminates the need for exploratory surgery.

ultraviolet astronomy study of cosmic ultraviolet emissions using artificial satellites. The USA launched a series of satellites for this purpose, receiving the first

useful data in 1968. Only a tiny percentage of solar ultraviolet radiation penetrates the atmosphere, this being the less dangerous longer-wavelength ultraviolet radiation. The dangerous shorter-wavelength radiation is absorbed by gases in the ozone layer high in the Earth's upper atmosphere.

ultraviolet radiation electromagnetic radiation of wavelengths from about 400 to 10 nanometres (where the *X-ray range begins). Physiologically, ultraviolet radiation is extremely powerful, producing sunburn and causing the formation of vitamin D in the skin. Ultraviolet radiation is invisible to the human eye, but its effects can be demonstrated.

Ulysses Roman name for *Odysseus, the Greek mythological hero.

Ulysses space probe to study the Sun's poles, launched in 1990 by a US space shuttle. It is a joint project by NASA and the European Space Agency. In February 1992, the gravity of Jupiter swung Ulysses on to a path that looped it first under the Sun's south pole in 1994 and then over its north pole in 1995 to study the Sun and solar wind at latitudes not observable from the Earth.

Umar (c. 581–644) Muslim caliph (civic and religious leader of Islam) in 634–44, succeeding Abu Bakr. He laid the foundations of a regular, organized Muslim army, employing the brilliant Khalid ibn al-Walid to lead his armies in battle, and conquered Syria, Palestine, Egypt, and Persia. He was murdered by a Persian slave. The Mosque of Omar in Jerusalem is attributed to him.

Umayyad dynasty Arabian dynasty of the Islamic Empire who reigned as caliphs (civic and religious leaders of Islam) from 661 to 750, when they were overthrown by Abbasids. A member of the family, Abd al-Rahmam, escaped to Spain and in 756 assumed the title of Emir of Córdoba. His dynasty, which took the title of caliph in 929, ruled in Córdoba until the early 11th century.

Umberto II (1904–1983) King of Italy May–June 1946. When his father *Victor Emmanuel III abdicated in May 1946, he was proclaimed king, and ruled 9 May–13 June 1946. He was forced to abdicate as the monarchy's collusion in the rise of fascism made him highly unpopular, and a referendum decided in favour of a republic. He retired to Portugal, where he died.

umbilical cord connection between the *embryo (or fetus) and the *placenta inside the *uterus of placental mammals. It has one vein and two arteries, transporting *oxygen and nutrients to the developing young, and removing waste products. *Blood is carried from the fetus along the umbilical cord and into the placenta. Here it is brought close to the mother's blood. Oxygen, nutrients, and antibodies from the mother diffuse (see *diffusion) into the fetal blood. Waste materials from the fetus pass into the mother's blood. The fetal blood, which has been enriched with nutrients, oxygenated, and cleaned of waste, is carried back to the fetus by another blood vessel in the umbilical cord. At birth, the connection between the young and the placenta is no longer necessary. The umbilical cord drops off or is severed, leaving a scar called the navel.

umbrella bird any of three species of bird of tropical South and Central America, family Cotingidae, order Passeriformes, about 45 cm/18 in long. The Amazonian species *Cephalopterus ornatus*, the **ornate umbrella bird**, has an inflatable wattle at the neck to amplify its humming call, and in display elevates a long crest (12 cm/4 in) lying above the bill so that it rises umbrella-like above the head. These features are less noticeable in the female, which is brownish, while the male is blue-black.

Umbria mountainous or hilly landlocked region of Italy in the central Apennines, including the provinces of Perugia and Terni; area 8,456 sq km/3,265 sq mi; population (2001 est) 815,600. Its capital is Perugia, and the River Tiber rises in the region; it is on the Nera, the region's other principal river, at Terni that several hydroelectric plants supply power for local industries. Manufacturing includes textiles and clothing, chemicals, processed food, and metalworking. Wine is produced (Orvieto), and tobacco, grain, grapes, and olives (Lake Trasimeno) are grown. This is the home of the Umbrian school of artists (15th-16th centuries), including Pinturicchio, Perugino, and the latter's pupil, Raphael.

UN abbreviation for *United Nations.

uncertainty principle *or* **indeterminacy principle** in quantum mechanics, the principle that it is impossible to know with unlimited accuracy the position and momentum of a particle. The principle arises because in order to locate a particle exactly, an observer must bounce light (in the form of a *photon) off the particle, which must alter its position in an unpredictable way.

unconscious in psychoanalysis, a part of the personality of which the individual is unaware, and which contains impulses or urges that are held back, or repressed, from conscious awareness.

Underground Railroad US abolitionist network established in the North before the American *Civil War to provide sanctuary and assistance for escaped African-American slaves. The informal system, established by abolitionists in defiance of the Fugitive Slave Act of 1850, used safe houses, transport facilities, and volunteers to lead the slaves to safety in the North and Canada.

UNESCO acronym for United Nations Educational, Scientific, and Cultural Organization, specialized agency of the United Nations, established in 1946, to promote international cooperation in education, science, and culture, with its headquarters in Paris.

ungulate general name for any hoofed mammal. Included are the odd-toed ungulates (perissodactyls) and the even-toed ungulates (artiodactyls), along with subungulates such as elephants.

UNHCR abbreviation for **United Nations High Commission for Refugees**.

UNICEF acronym for **United Nations International Children's Emergency Fund**, a specialized agency of the *United Nations.

unicellular organism animal or plant consisting of a single cell. Most are invisible without a microscope but a few, such as the giant *amoeba, may be visible to the naked eye. The main groups of unicellular organisms are bacteria, protozoa, unicellular algae, and unicellular fungi or yeasts. Some become disease-causing agents (*pathogens).

unicorn mythical animal referred to by classical writers, said to live in India and resembling a horse, but with one spiralled horn growing from the forehead.

unidentified flying object (UFO) any light or object seen in the sky of which the immediate identity is not apparent. Despite unsubstantiated claims, there is no evidence that UFOs are alien spacecraft. On investigation, the vast majority of sightings turn out to have been of natural or identifiable objects, notably bright stars and planets, meteors, aircraft, and satellites, or to have been perpetrated by pranksters. The term **flying saucer** was coined in 1947.

Unification Church church founded in Korea 1954 by the Reverend Sun Myung Moon. The number of members (often called 'Moonies') is about 200,000 worldwide. The theology unites Christian and Taoist ideas and is based on Moon's book *Divine Principle*, which teaches that the original purpose of creation was to set up a perfect family, in a perfect relationship with God.

unified field theory in physics, the theory that attempts to explain the four fundamental forces (strong nuclear, weak nuclear, electromagnetic, and gravity) in terms of a single unified force (see *particle physics).

unilateralism in politics, support for **unilateral nuclear disarmament**: scrapping a country's nuclear weapons without waiting for other countries to agree to do so at the same time.

Union, Acts of act of Parliament of 1707 that brought about the union of England and Scotland; that of 1801 united England and Ireland.

Union flag British national flag. It is popularly called the **Union jack**, although, strictly speaking, this applies only when it is flown on the jackstaff of a warship.

Union Movement British political group. Founded as the **New Party** by Oswald *Mosley and a number of Labour members of Parliament in 1931, it developed into the **British Union of Fascists** in 1932. In 1940 the organization was declared illegal and its leaders interned, but it was revived as the Union Movement in 1948, characterized by racist doctrines including anti-Semitism.

Union of Soviet Socialist Republics (USSR) former country in northern Asia and Eastern Europe that revested to independent states in 1991; see *Armenia, *Azerbaijan, *Belarus, *Estonia, *Georgia, *Kazakhstan, *Kyrgyzstan, *Latvia, *Lithuania, *Moldova, *Russia, *Tajikistan, *Turkmenistan, *Ukraine and *Uzbekistan. See also *Commonwealth of Independent States.

Unitarianism a Christian denomination that rejects the orthodox doctrine of the Trinity, asserts the fatherhood of God and the brotherhood of humanity, and gives a pre-eminent position to Jesus as a religious teacher, while denying his divinity.

unitary authority administrative unit of Great Britain. Since 1996 the two-tier structure of local government has ceased to exist in Scotland and Wales, and in some parts of England, and has been replaced by unitary authorities, responsible for all local government services.

United Arab Emirates

formerly **Trucial States** (until 1968), **Federation of Arab Emirates** (with Bahrain and Qatar) (1968–71)

National name: *Dawlat Imarat al-'Arabiyya al Muttahida/ State of the Arab Emirates* (UAE)

Area: 83,657 sq km/32,299 sq mi

Capital: Abu Dhabi

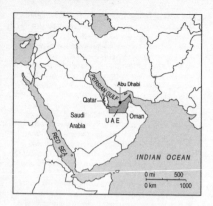

Major towns/cities: Dubai, Sharjah, Ras al Khaimah, Ajman, Al 'Ayn
Major ports: Dubai
Physical features: desert and flat coastal plain; mountains in east
Head of state: Sheikh Zayed bin Sultan al-Nahayan of Abu Dhabi from 1971
Head of government: Sheikh Maktum bin Rashid al-Maktum from 1990
Political system: absolutist
Political executive: absolute
Political parties: none
Currency: UAE dirham
GNI per capita (PPP): (US$) 20,620 (2001)
Exports: crude petroleum, natural gas, re-exports (mainly machinery and transport equipment). Principal market: Japan 31.1% (2001)
Population: 2,995,000 (2003 est)
Language: Arabic (official), Farsi, Hindi, Urdu, English
Religion: Muslim 96% (of which 80% Sunni); Christian, Hindu
Life expectancy: 73 (men); 77 (women) (2000–05)
Chronology
7th century AD: Islam introduced.
early 16th century: Portuguese established trading contacts with Gulf states.
18th century: Rise of trade and seafaring among Qawasim and Bani Yas, respectively in Ras al Khaimah and Sharjah in north and Abu Dhabi and Dubai in desert of south. Emirates' current ruling families are descended from these peoples.
early 19th century: Britain signed treaties ('truces') with local rulers, ensuring that British shipping through the Gulf was free from 'pirate' attacks and bringing Emirates under British protection.
1892: Trucial Sheiks signed Exclusive Agreements with Britain, agreeing not to cede, sell, or mortgage territory to another power.
1952: Trucial Council established by seven sheikdoms of Abu Dhabi, Ajman, Dubai, Fujairah, Ras al Khaimah, Sharjah, and Umm al Qawain, with a view to later forming a federation.
1958: Large-scale exploitation of oil reserves led to rapid economic progress.

1968: Britain's announcement that it would remove its forces from the Gulf by 1971 led to an abortive attempt to arrange federation between seven Trucial States and Bahrain and Qatar.
1971: Bahrain and Qatar ceded from the Federation of Arab Emirates, which was dissolved. Six Trucial States formed the United Arab Emirates, with the ruler of Abu Dhabi, Sheikh Zayed, as president. A provisional constitution was adopted. The UAE joined the Arab League and the United Nations (UN).
1972: Seventh state, Ras al Khaimah, joined the federation.
1976: Sheikh Zayed threatened to relinquish presidency unless progress towards centralization became more rapid.
1985: Diplomatic and economic links with the Soviet Union and China were established.
1987: Diplomatic relations with Egypt were restored.
1990: Sheikh Maktum bin Rashid al-Maktum of Dubai was appointed prime minister.
1990–91: UAE opposed the Iraqi invasion of Kuwait, and UAE troops fought as part of the UN coalition.
1991: The Bank of Commerce and Credit International (BCCI), partly owned and controlled by Abu Dhabi's ruler Zayed bin Sultan al-Nahayan, collapsed at a cost to the UAE of $10 billion.
1992: There was a border dispute with Iran.
1994: Abu Dhabi agreed to pay BCCI creditors $1.8 billion.
2001: Financial institutions were ordered to freeze the assets of suspected terrorist-funding organizations.
2004: After the death of Zayed bin Sultan al-Nahayan, his son, Khalifa bin Zayed, became president and ruler.

United Arab Republic union formed in 1958, broken in 1961, between Egypt and Syria. Egypt continued to use the name after the break up until 1971.

United Irishmen society formed in 1791 by Wolfe *Tone to campaign for parliamentary reform in Ireland. It later became a secret revolutionary group.

United Kingdom

National name: *United Kingdom of Great Britain and Northern Ireland* (UK)
Area: 244,100 sq km/94,247 sq mi
Capital: London

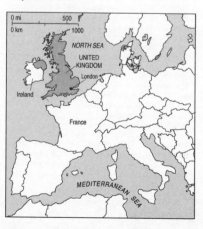

Major towns/cities: Birmingham, Glasgow, Leeds, Sheffield, Liverpool, Manchester, Edinburgh, Bradford, Bristol, Coventry, Belfast, Cardiff

Major ports: London, Grimsby, Southampton, Liverpool

Physical features: became separated from European continent in about 6000 BC; rolling landscape, increasingly mountainous towards the north, with Grampian Mountains in Scotland, Pennines in northern England, Cambrian Mountains in Wales; rivers include Thames, Severn, and Spey

Territories: Anguilla, Bermuda, British Antarctic Territory, British Indian Ocean Territory, British Virgin Islands, Cayman Islands, Falkland Islands, Gibraltar, Montserrat, Pitcairn Islands, St Helena and Dependencies (Ascension, Tristan da Cunha), South Georgia, South Sandwich Islands, Turks and Caicos Islands; the Channel Islands and the Isle of Man are not part of the UK but are direct dependencies of the crown

Head of state: Queen Elizabeth II from 1952

Head of government: Tony Blair from 1997

Political system: liberal democracy

Political executive: parliamentary

Political parties: Conservative and Unionist Party, right of centre; Labour Party, moderate left of centre; Social and Liberal Democrats, left of centre; Scottish National Party (SNP), Scottish nationalist; Plaid Cymru (Welsh Nationalist Party), Welsh nationalist; Official Ulster Unionist Party (OUP), Democratic Unionist Party (DUP), Ulster People's Unionist Party (UPUP), all Northern Ireland right of centre, in favour of remaining part of UK; Social Democratic Labour Party (SDLP), Northern Ireland, moderate left of centre; Green Party, ecological; Sinn Fein, Irish nationalist

Currency: pound sterling

GNI per capita (PPP): (US$) 25,870 (2002 est)

Exports: industrial and electrical machinery, automatic data-processing equipment, motor vehicles, petroleum, chemicals, finished and semi-finished manufactured products, agricultural products and foodstuffs. Principal market: USA 15.4% (2001)

Population: 59,251,000 (2003 est)

Language: English (official), Welsh (also official in Wales), Gaelic

Religion: about 46% Church of England (established church); other Protestant denominations, Roman Catholic, Muslim, Jewish, Hindu, Sikh

Life expectancy: 76 (men); 81 (women) (2000–05)

Chronology

c. 400–200 BC: British Isles conquered by Celts.

55–54 BC: Romans led by Julius Caesar raided Britain.

AD 43–60: Romans conquered England and Wales, which formed the province of Britannia; Picts stopped them penetrating further north.

5th–7th centuries: After Romans withdrew, Anglo-Saxons overran most of England and formed kingdoms, including Wessex, Northumbria, and Mercia; Wales was stronghold of Celts.

500: The Scots, a Gaelic-speaking tribe from Ireland, settled in the kingdom of Dalriada (Argyll).

5th–6th centuries: British Isles converted to Christianity.

829: King Egbert of Wessex accepted as overlord of all England.

c. 843: Kenneth McAlpin unified Scots and Picts to become the first king of Scotland.

9th–11th centuries: Vikings raided the British Isles, conquering north and east England and northern Scotland.

1066: Normans led by William I defeated Anglo-Saxons at Battle of Hastings and conquered England.

12th–13th centuries: Anglo-Norman adventurers conquered much of Ireland, but effective English rule remained limited to area around Dublin.

1215: King John of England forced to sign Magna Carta, which placed limits on royal powers.

1265: Simon de Montfort summoned the first English parliament in which the towns were represented.

1284: Edward I of England invaded Scotland; Scots defeated English at Battle of Stirling Bridge in 1297.

1314: Robert the Bruce led Scots to victory over English at Battle of Bannockburn; England recognized Scottish independence in 1328.

1455–85: Wars of the Roses: House of York and House of Lancaster disputed English throne.

1513: Battle of Flodden: Scots defeated by English; James IV of Scotland killed.

1529: Henry VIII founded Church of England after break with Rome; Reformation effective in England and Wales, but not in Ireland.

1536–43: Acts of Union united Wales with England, with one law, one parliament, and one official language.

1541: Irish parliament recognized Henry VIII of England as king of Ireland.

1557: First Covenant established Protestant faith in Scotland.

1603: Union of crowns: James VI of Scotland became James I of England also.

1607: First successful English colony in Virginia marked the start of three centuries of overseas expansion.

1610: James I established plantation of Ulster in Northern Ireland with Protestant settlers from England and Scotland.

1642–52: English Civil War between king and Parliament, with Scottish intervention and Irish rebellion, resulted in victory for Parliament.

1649: Execution of Charles I; Oliver Cromwell appointed Lord Protector in 1653; monarchy restored in 1660.

1689: 'Glorious Revolution' confirmed power of Parliament; replacement of James II by William III resisted by Scottish Highlanders and Catholic Irish.

1707: Act of Union between England and Scotland created United Kingdom of Great Britain, governed by a single parliament.

1721–42: Cabinet government developed under Robert Walpole, in effect the first prime minister.

1745: 'The Forty-Five': rebellion of Scottish Highlanders in support of Jacobite pretender to throne; defeated 1746.

c. 1760–1850: Industrial Revolution: Britain became the first industrial nation in the world.

1775–83: American Revolution: Britain lost 13 American colonies; empire continued to expand in Canada, India, and Australia.

1793–1815: Britain at war with revolutionary France, except for 1802–03.

1800: Act of Union created United Kingdom of Great Britain and Ireland, governed by a single parliament; effective 1801.

1832: Great Reform Act extended franchise; further extensions in 1867, 1884, 1918, and 1928.

1846: Repeal of Corn Laws reflected shift of power from landowners to industrialists.

1870: Home Rule Party formed to campaign for restoration of separate Irish parliament.

1880–90s: Rapid expansion of British Empire in Africa.

1906–14: Liberal governments introduced social reforms and curbed the power of the House of Lords.

1914–18: The UK played a leading part in World War I; the British Empire expanded in Middle East.

1919–21: The Anglo-Irish war ended with the secession of southern Ireland as the Irish Free State; Ulster remained within the United Kingdom of Great Britain and Northern Ireland with some powers devolved to a Northern Irish parliament.

1924: The first Labour government was led by Ramsay MacDonald.

1926: A general strike arose from a coal dispute. Equality of status was recognized between the UK and Dominions of the British Commonwealth.

1931: A National Government coalition was formed to face a growing economic crisis; unemployment reached 3 million.

1939–45: The UK played a leading part in World War II.

1945–51: The Labour government of Clement Attlee created the welfare state and nationalized major industries.

1947–71: Decolonization brought about the end of the British Empire.

1969: Start of the Troubles in Northern Ireland; the Northern Irish Parliament was suspended in 1972.

1973: The UK joined the European Economic Community.

1979–90: The Conservative government of Margaret Thatcher pursued radical free-market economic policies.

1982: Unemployment reached over 3 million. The Falklands War with Argentina over the disputed sovereignty of the Falkland Islands cost more than a thousand lives but ended with the UK retaining control of the islands.

1983: Coal pits were closed by the Conservative government and the miners went on strike.

1991: British troops took part in a US-led war against Iraq under a United Nations (UN) umbrella. Following the economic successes of the 1980s there was a period of severe economic recession and unemployment.

1993: A peace proposal for Northern Ireland, the Downing Street Declaration, was issued jointly with the Irish government.

1994: The IRA and Protestant paramilitary declared a ceasefire in Northern Ireland.

1996: The IRA renewed its bombing campaign in London.

1997: The Labour Party won a landslide victory in a general election; Tony Blair became prime minister. Blair launched a new Anglo-Irish peace initiative. Blair met with Sinn Fein leader Gerry Adams; all-party peace talks began in Northern Ireland. Scotland and Wales voted in favour of devolution. Princess Diana was killed in a car crash.

1998: A historic multiparty agreement (the 'Good Friday Agreement') was reached on the future of Northern Ireland; a peace plan was approved by referenda in Northern Ireland and the Irish Republic. The UUP leader, David Trimble, was elected first minister.

1999: The Scottish Parliament and the Welsh Assembly opened, with Labour the largest party in both. The IRA agreed to begin decommissioning discussions and a coalition government was established. In December, the British government announced that it would write off the debts of low-income countries in the developing world.

2000: After it was revealed that there had been no arms handover by the IRA, the Secretary of State for Northern Ireland suspended the Northern Ireland Assembly. After the IRA agreed to allow independent inspectors access to its arms, and to put its weapons out of use, Northern Ireland's power sharing executive resumed work in May. Feuding between loyalist paramilitary groups broke out in Belfast, Northern Ireland. Protesters against the high price of fuel blockaded refineries in September, causing a shortage of petrol throughout the country.

2001: Peter Mandelson, the Secretary of State for Northern Ireland, was forced to resign from the cabinet for the second time over allegations of corruption. An outbreak of foot-and-mouth disease spread rapidly, resulting in the slaughter of over 2 million animals.

2002: Queen Elizabeth II completed 50 years as monarch, and the Queen Mother died. The devolved administration in Northern Ireland was suspended and direct rule imposed by the British government. A warning by Prime Minister Blair to the IRA to disband was rejected, and the IRA subsequently broke off contact with the international body overseeing terrorist arms decommissioning.

2003: In a parliamentary debate, Prime Minister Blair's support for a military response to disarm the Iraqi regime was rejected by more than 120 members of his own Labour Party – the biggest rebellion within a governing party in over a century. The UK launched military action in Iraq with the USA in March despite widespread public opposition. The government was damaged by allegations by the BBC (British Broadcasting Corporation) that it exaggerated intelligence information about Iraq's weapons programmes to justify going to war. Elections to the Northern Ireland Assembly were held despite the continuing suspension of the devolved administration – the hardline Democratic Unionist Party and Sinn Fein made gains at the expense of more moderate parties.

2005: The Labour Party won the general election, making Tony Blair the first Labour prime minister to achieve a third term in office. The government's reduced majority was partly blamed on the unpopularity of its policy on Iraq.

United Nations (UN) association of states for international peace, security, and cooperation, with its headquarters in New York City. The UN was established on 24 October 1945 by 51 states as a successor to the *League of Nations. Its Charter, whose obligations member states agree to accept, sets out four purposes for the UN: to maintain international peace and security; to develop friendly relations among nations; to cooperate in solving international problems and in promoting respect for human rights; and to be a centre for the harmonizing the actions of nations. The UN has played a role in development assistance, disaster relief, cultural cooperation, aiding refugees, and peacekeeping. Its membership in 2001 stood at 189 states, and the total proposed budget for 2000–01 (raised by the member states) was US$2.5 billion, supporting more than 50,000 staff. The UN has six principal institutions. Five are based in New York: the General Assembly, the Security Council, the Economic and Social Council, the Trusteeship Council, and the Secretariat. The sixth, the International Court of Justice, is located at the Peace Palace in the Hague, Netherlands. Kofi Annan, from Ghana, became secretary general in 1997, and was re-elected for a second term in 2001. In January 1998, Louise Fréchette, a Canadian, was elected its first deputy secretary general. In October 2001, Annan and the UN itself were awarded the 2001 Nobel Prize for Peace. There are six official working languages: English, French, Russian, Spanish, Chinese, and Arabic. The name 'United Nations' was coined by US president Franklin D Roosevelt.

United States of America

National name: *United States of America* (USA)

Area: 9,826,632 sq km/3,794,084 sq mi
Capital: Washington, DC
Major towns/cities: New York, Los Angeles, Chicago, Philadelphia, Detroit, San Francisco, Dallas, San Diego, San Antonio, Houston, Boston, Phoenix, Indianapolis, Honolulu, San José
Physical features: topography and vegetation from tropical (Hawaii) to arctic (Alaska); mountain ranges parallel with east and west coasts; the Rocky Mountains separate rivers emptying into the Pacific from those flowing into the Gulf of Mexico; Great Lakes in north; rivers include Hudson, Mississippi, Missouri, Colorado, Columbia, Snake, Rio Grande, Ohio
Territories: the commonwealths of Puerto Rico and Northern Marianas; Guam, the US Virgin Islands, American Samoa, Wake Island, Midway Islands, Johnston Atoll, Baker Island, Howland Island, Jarvis Island, Kingman Reef, Navassa Island, Palmyra Island
Head of state and government: George W Bush from 2001
Political system: liberal democracy
Political executive: limited presidency

Political parties: Democratic Party, liberal centre; Republican Party, right of centre; Reform Party, prodemocratic
Currency: US dollar
GNI per capita (PPP): (US$) 35,060 (2002 est)
Exports: machinery, motor vehicles, agricultural products and foodstuffs, aircraft, weapons, chemicals, electronics. Principal market: Canada 22.7% (2001)
Population: 294,043,000 (2003 est)
Language: English, Spanish
Religion: Protestant 58%; Roman Catholic 28%; atheist 10%; Jewish 2%; other 4% (1998)
Life expectancy: 74 (men); 80 (women) (2000–05)
Chronology

c. 15,000 BC: First evidence of human occupation in North America.
1513: Ponce de León of Spain explored Florida in search of the Fountain of Youth; Francisco Coronado explored southwest region of North America 1540–42.
1565: Spanish founded St Augustine (Florida), the first permanent European settlement in North America.
1585: Sir Walter Raleigh tried to establish an English colony on Roanoke Island in what he called Virginia.
1607: English colonists founded Jamestown, Virginia, and began growing tobacco.
1620: The Pilgrim Fathers founded Plymouth Colony (near Cape Cod); other English Puritans followed them to New England.
1624: Dutch formed colony of New Netherlands; Swedes formed New Sweden in 1638; both taken by England in 1664.
17th–18th centuries: Millions of Africans were sold into slavery on American cotton and tobacco plantations.
1733: Georgia became thirteenth British colony on east coast.
1763: British victory over France in Seven Years' War secured territory as far west as Mississippi River.
1765: British first attempted to levy tax in American colonies with Stamp Act; protest forced repeal in 1767.
1773: 'Boston Tea Party': colonists boarded ships and threw cargoes of tea into sea in protest at import duty.
1774: British closed Boston harbour and billeted troops in Massachusetts; colonists formed First Continental Congress.
1775: American Revolution: colonies raised Continental Army led by George Washington to fight against British rule.
1776: American colonies declared independence; France and Spain supported them in a war with Britain.
1781: Americans defeated British at Battle of Yorktown; rebel states formed loose confederation, codified in Articles of Confederation.
1783: Treaty of Paris: Britain accepted loss of colonies.
1787: 'Founding Fathers' devised new constitution for United States of America.
1789: Washington elected first president of USA.
1791: Bill of Rights guaranteed individual freedom.
1803: Louisiana Purchase: France sold former Spanish lands between Mississippi River and Rocky Mountains to USA.
1812–14: War with Britain arose from dispute over blockade rights during Napoleonic Wars.
1819: USA bought Florida from Spain.
19th century: Mass immigration from Europe; settlers moved westwards, crushing Indian resistance and

claiming 'manifest destiny' of USA to control North America. By end of century, the number of states in the Union had increased from 17 to 45.

1846–48: Mexican War: Mexico ceded vast territory to USA.

1854: Kansas–Nebraska Act heightened controversy over slavery in southern states; abolitionists formed Republican Party.

1860: Abraham Lincoln (Republican) elected president.

1861: Civil war broke out after 11 southern states, wishing to retain slavery, seceded from USA and formed the Confederate States of America under Jefferson Davis.

1865: USA defeated Confederacy; slavery abolished; President Lincoln assassinated.

1867: Alaska bought from Russia.

1869: Railway linked east and west coasts; rapid growth of industry and agriculture 1870–1920 made USA very rich.

1876: Sioux Indians defeated US troops at Little Big Horn; Indians finally defeated at Wounded Knee in 1890.

1898: Spanish–American War: USA gained Puerto Rico and Guam; also Philippines (until 1946) and Cuba (until 1901); USA annexed Hawaii.

1917–18: USA intervened in World War I; President Woodrow Wilson took leading part in peace negotiations in 1919, but USA rejected membership of League of Nations.

1920: Women received right to vote; sale of alcohol prohibited, until 1933.

1924: American Indians made citizens of USA by Congress.

1929: 'Wall Street Crash': stock market collapse led to Great Depression with 13 million unemployed by 1933.

1933: President Franklin Roosevelt launched the 'New Deal' with public works to rescue the economy.

1941: Japanese attacked US fleet at Pearl Harbor, Hawaii; USA declared war on Japan; Germany declared war on USA, which henceforth played a leading part in World War II.

1945: USA ended war in Pacific by dropping two atomic bombs on Hiroshima and Nagasaki, Japan.

1947: 'Truman Doctrine' pledged US aid for nations threatened by communism; start of Cold War between USA and USSR.

1950–53: US forces engaged in Korean War.

1954: Racial segregation in schools deemed unconstitutional; start of campaign to secure civil rights for black Americans.

1962: Cuban missile crisis: USA forced USSR to withdraw nuclear weapons from Cuba.

1963: President Kennedy assassinated.

1964–68: President Lyndon Johnson introduced the 'Great Society' programme of civil-rights and welfare measures.

1961–75: USA involved in Vietnam War.

1969: US astronaut Neil Armstrong was first person on the Moon.

1974: 'Watergate' scandal: evidence of domestic political espionage compelled President Richard Nixon to resign.

1979–80: Iran held US diplomats hostage, humiliating President Jimmy Carter.

1981–89: Tax-cutting policies of President Ronald Reagan led to large federal budget deficit.

1986: 'Irangate' scandal: secret US arms sales to Iran illegally funded Contra guerrillas in Nicaragua.

1990: President George Bush declared an end to the Cold War.

1991: USA played leading part in expelling Iraqi forces from Kuwait in the Gulf War.

1992: Democrat Bill Clinton won presidential elections, beginning his term of office in 1993.

1996: US launched missile attacks on Iraq in response to Hussein's incursions into Kurdish safe havens.

1998: The House of Representatives voted to impeach Clinton on the grounds of perjury and obstruction of justice, due to his misleading the public about his relationship with a White House intern. Clinton's national approval rating remained high, and he was acquitted in 1999. In response to bombings of US embassies in Tanzania and Kenya by an Islamic group, the USA bombed suspected sites in Afghanistan and Sudan. The USA also led air strikes against Iraq following the expulsion of UN weapons inspectors by Saddam Hussein.

1999: US forces led NATO air strikes against the Federal Republic of Yugoslavia in protest against Serb violence against ethnic Albanians in Kosovo. Three million people fled inland in the largest evacuation in US history as Hurricane Floyd hit the east coast in September.

2000: In August, the worst wildfires in 30 years consumed 4.4 million acres/6,875 sq mi of land in the west. The presidential elections in November were the closest ever, the result being decided by a few hundred votes in Florida.

2001: Republican George W Bush, son of former president George Bush, was inaugurated as president. California experienced an electricity crisis, leading to mandatory blackouts in January. A mid-air collision between a US spy plane and a Chinese fighter jet provoked diplomatic tensions.

2001: The world's worst terrorist atrocity occurred in the USA on 11 September, when Islamic extremists hijacked civil airliners and flew them into US landmarks. Two planes were flown into the twin towers of the World Trade Center, which later collapsed, and another hit the Pentagon in Washington, DC. Around 6,000 people were killed as a result of the atrocity. The US government declared the attack an 'act of war' and pledged military retaliation against the terrorists and any government sponsoring them. US forces began to congregate around Afghanistan, where the Taliban government were thought to be hiding Osama bin Laden, the chief suspect. The already ailing world economy suffered a large setback as a result of the terrorist acts, and the airline industries announced huge job losses.

2002: The financial collapse of the US corporations Enron and WorldCom and the subsequent accusations of corporate fraud sparked turmoil in stock markets around the world. The US government adopted an increasingly threatening stance towards the regime of Iraqi president Saddam Hussein over the latter's alleged development of weapons of mass destruction and its continuing exclusion of United Nations (UN) weapons inspectors. The threat of war prompted international concern, and an estimated 100,000 people attended an anti-war demonstration in Washington, DC – the largest such demonstration in the USA since the Vietnam War. A wave of seemingly random sniper shootings in Washington, DC, resulted in ten deaths and three serious woundings before the two assailants were apprehended.

2003: President Bush unveiled a US$670 billion package of tax cuts over ten years to revitalize the economy. The USA, with the UK, launched military action to disarm Iraq, despite widespread international opposition. The World Trade Organization (WTO) ruled that US tariffs on imported steel imposed in 2002 were illegal; they were subsequently lifted. The first US case of bovine spongiform encephalopathy (BSE or mad cow disease) was confirmed.

2004: President Bush defeated challenger John Kerry to win a second term in the White House.

2005: Condoleeza Rice was installed as Secretary of State, the first African-American woman to hold the office. The USA declared that the fruitless search in Iraq for weapons of mass destruction was over. American forces continued to battle Iraqi insurgents, and the number of US military deaths in the campaign rose beyond 1600.

universe all of space and its contents, the study of which is called cosmology. The universe is thought to be between 10 billion and 20 billion years old, and is mostly empty space, dotted with galaxies for as far as telescopes can see. These galaxies are moving further apart as the universe expands. Several theories attempt to explain how the universe came into being and evolved; for example, the Big Bang theory of an expanding universe originating in a single explosive event (creating hydrogen and helium gases), and the contradictory steady-state theory.

unleaded petrol petrol manufactured without the addition of antiknock. It has a slightly lower octane rating than leaded petrol, but has the advantage of not polluting the atmosphere with lead compounds. Many cars can be converted to run on unleaded petrol by altering the timing of the engine, and most new cars are designed to do so. Cars fitted with a *catalytic converter must use unleaded fuel.

unnilennium temporary name assigned to the element *meitnerium, atomic number 109.

unnilhexium temporary name assigned to the element *seaborgium 1974–97.

unniloctium temporary name assigned to the element *hassium, atomic number 108.

unnilpentium temporary name assigned to the element *dubnium.

unnilquadium temporary name assigned to the element *rutherfordium 1964–97.

unnilseptium temporary name assigned to the element *bohrium 1964–97.

unsaturated compound chemical compound in which two adjacent atoms are linked by a double or triple covalent bond. Alkenes, such as *ethene, are unsaturated *hydrocarbons that contain a carbon to carbon double bond.

untouchable or **harijan** member of the lowest Indian *caste, formerly forbidden to be touched by members of the other castes.

unununilium symbol Uun, temporary name for a synthesized radioactive element of the *transactinide series, atomic number 110, relative atomic mass 269. It was discovered in October 1994, detected for a millisecond, at the GSI heavy-ion cyclotron, Darmstadt, Germany, while lead atoms were bombarded with nickel atoms.

unununium symbol Uuu, temporary name for a synthesized radioactive element of the *transactinide series, atomic number 111, relative atomic mass 272. It was detected at the GSI heavy-ion cyclotron, Darmstadt, Germany, in December 1994, when bismuth-209 was bombarded with nickel.

Upanishad one of a collection of Hindu sacred treatises, written in Sanskrit, connected with the *Vedas but composed later, about 800–200 BC. Metaphysical and ethical, their doctrine equated the atman (self) with the Brahman (supreme spirit) – 'Tat tvam asi' ('Thou art that') – and developed the theory of the transmigration of souls.

Updike, John Hoyer (1932–) US writer. Associated with the *New Yorker* magazine from 1955, he soon established a reputation for polished prose, poetry, and criticism. His novels include *The Poorhouse Fair* (1959), *The Centaur* (1963), *Couples* (1968), *The Witches of Eastwick* (1984), *Roger's Version* (1986), and *S.* (1988), and deal with the tensions and frustrations of contemporary US middle-class life and their effects on love and marriage.

Upper Austria German **Oberösterreich**, mountainous federal state of Austria, drained by the Danube, and bordered to the north by the Czech Republic and to the west by Bavaria; area 11,980 sq km/4,625 sq mi; population (2001 est) 1,382,000. Its capital is Linz and the main towns are Steyr and Wels.

Upper Volta former name (to 1984) of Burkina Faso.

Ur ancient city of the *Sumerian civilization, in modern Iraq. Excavations by the British archaeologist Leonard Woolley show that it was inhabited from about 3500 BC. He discovered evidence of a flood that may have inspired the *Epic of *Gilgamesh* as well as the biblical account, and remains of ziggurats, or step pyramids.

Ural Mountains Russian **Ural'skiy Khrebet**, mountain system extending for over 2,000 km/1,242 mi from the Arctic Ocean to the Caspian Sea, and traditionally regarded as separating Europe from Asia. The highest peak is Naradnaya, 1,894 m/6,214 ft. The mountains hold vast mineral wealth.

uranium chemical symbol U, hard, lustrous, silver-white, malleable and ductile, radioactive, metallic element of the *actinide series, atomic number 92, relative atomic mass 238.029. It is the most abundant radioactive element in the Earth's crust, its decay giving rise to essentially all radioactive elements in nature; its final decay product is the stable element lead. Uranium combines readily with most elements to form compounds that are extremely poisonous. The chief ore is *pitchblende, in which the element was discovered by German chemist Martin Klaproth in 1789; he named it after the planet Uranus, which had been discovered in 1781.

Uranus seventh planet from the Sun, discovered by German-born British astronomer William *Herschel in 1781. It is twice as far out as the sixth planet, Saturn. Uranus has a mass 14.5 times that of Earth. The spin axis of Uranus is tilted at 98°, so that one pole points towards the Sun, giving extreme seasons.
mean distance from the Sun: 2.9 billion km/1.8 billion mi **equatorial diameter:** 50,800 km/31,600 mi **rotation period:** 17 hours 12 minutes **year:** 84 Earth years **atmosphere:** deep atmosphere composed mainly of hydrogen and helium **surface:** composed primarily

of rock and various ices with only about 15% hydrogen and helium, but may also contain heavier elements, which might account for Uranus's mean density being higher than that of Saturn. **satellites:** 18 moons (two discovered in 1997, one in 1999) **rings:** 11 rings, composed of rock and dust, around the planet's equator, were detected by the US space probe Voyager 2 in 1977. The rings are charcoal black and may be debris of former 'moonlets' that have broken up. The ring furthest from the planet centre (51,000 km/31,800 mi), Epsilon, is 100 km/62 mi at its widest point. In 1995, US astronomers determined that the ring particles contained long-chain hydrocarbons. Looking at the brightest region of Epsilon, they were also able to calculate the precession of Uranus as 264 days, the fastest known precession in the Solar System.

Uranus in Greek mythology, the primeval sky god, whose name means 'Heaven'. He was responsible for both the sunshine and the rain, and was the son and husband of *Gaia, the goddess of the Earth. Uranus and Gaia were the parents of *Kronos and his fellow *Titans, the one-eyed giant Cyclops, and the 100-handed **Hecatoncheires**.

Urban six popes, including:

Urban II (c. 1042–1099) Pope 1088–99. He launched the First *Crusade at the Council of Clermont in France in 1095.

Urban VIII, Maffeo Barberini (1568–1644) Pope 1623–44. His policies during the *Thirty Years' War were designed more to maintain the balance of forces in Europe and prevent one side from dominating the papacy than to further the *Counter-Reformation. He extended the papal dominions and improved their defences. During his papacy, *Galileo was summoned in 1633 to recant the theories that the Vatican condemned as heretical.

urbanization process by which the proportion of a population living in or around towns and cities increases through migration and natural increase. The growth of urban concentrations in the USA and Europe is a relatively recent phenomenon, dating back only about 150 years to the beginning of the *Industrial Revolution (although the world's first cities were built more than 5,000 years ago). The UN Population Fund reported in 1996 that within ten years the majority of the world's population would be living in urban conglomerations. Almost all urban growth will occur in the developing world, creating ten large cities a year.

Urdu language member of the Indo-Iranian branch of the Indo-European language family, related to Hindi and written not in Devanagari but in Arabic script. Urdu is strongly influenced by Farsi (Persian) and Arabic. It is the official language of Pakistan and is used by Muslims in India.

urea $CO(NH_2)_2$, waste product formed in the mammalian liver when nitrogen compounds are broken down. It is filtered from the blood by the kidneys, and stored in the bladder as urine prior to release. When purified, it is a white, crystalline solid. In industry it is used to make urea-formaldehyde plastics (or resins), pharmaceuticals, and fertilizers.

ureter tube connecting the kidney to the bladder. Its wall contains fibres of smooth muscle whose contractions aid the movement of urine out of the kidney.

urethra in mammals, a tube connecting the bladder to the exterior. It carries urine and, in males, semen.

Urey, Harold Clayton (1893–1981) US chemist. In 1932 he isolated *heavy water and was awarded the Nobel Prize for Chemistry in 1934 for his discovery of *deuterium (heavy hydrogen).

uric acid $C_5H_4N_4O_3$, nitrogen-containing waste substance, formed from the breakdown of food and body protein. It is only slightly soluble in water. Uric acid is the normal means by which most land animals that develop in a shell (birds, reptiles, insects, and land gastropods) deposit their waste products. The young are unable to get rid of their excretory products while in the shell and therefore store them in this insoluble form.

urinary system system of organs that removes nitrogenous waste products and excess water from the bodies of animals. In vertebrates, it consists of a pair of kidneys, which produce urine; ureters, which drain the kidneys; and (in bony fishes, amphibians, some reptiles, and mammals) a bladder that stores the urine before its discharge. In mammals, the urine is expelled through the urethra; in other vertebrates, the urine drains into a common excretory chamber called a *cloaca, and the urine is not discharged separately.

urine amber-coloured fluid filtered out by the kidneys from the blood. It contains excess water, salts, proteins, waste products in the form of urea, a pigment, and some acid. It is stored in the bladder until it can be expelled from the body via the urethra. Analysing the composition of an individual's urine can reveal a number of medical conditions, such as poorly functioning kidneys, kidney stones, and diabetes.

Ursa Major (Latin 'Great Bear') third-largest constellation in the sky, in the north polar region. Its seven brightest stars make up the familiar shape or asterism of the **Big Dipper** or **Plough**. The second star of the handle of the dipper, called Mizar, has a companion star, Alcor. Two stars forming the far side of the dipper bowl act as pointers to the north pole star, *Polaris. Dubhe, one of them, is the constellation's brightest star.

Ursa Minor (Latin 'Little Bear') small constellation of the northern hemisphere, popularly known as the Little Dipper. It is shaped like a dipper, with the bright north pole star *Polaris at the end of the handle.

urticaria *or* **nettle rash** *or* **hives** irritant skin condition characterized by itching, burning, stinging, and the spontaneous appearance of raised patches of skin. Treatment is usually by *antihistamines or steroids taken orally or applied as lotions. Its causes are varied and include allergy and stress.

Uruguay
National name: *República Oriental del Uruguay/ Eastern Republic of Uruguay*
Area: 176,200 sq km/68,030 sq mi
Capital: Montevideo
Major towns/cities: Salto, Paysandú, Las Piedras, Rivera, Tacuarembó
Physical features: grassy plains (pampas) and low hills; rivers Negro, Uruguay, Río de la Plata
Head of state and government: Jorge Batlle Ibáñez from 2000
Political system: liberal democracy
Political executive: limited presidency

Brazil

PACIFIC
OCEAN

ATLANTIC
OCEAN

URUGUAY
Montevideo

Argentina

0 mi   500
0 km   1000

Political parties: Colorado Party (PC), progressive, left of centre; National (Blanco) Party (PN), traditionalist, right of centre; New Space (NE), moderate, left wing; Progressive Encounter (EP), left wing
Currency: Uruguayan peso
GNI per capita (PPP): (US$) 12,010 (2002 est)
Exports: textiles, meat (chiefly beef), live animals and by-products (mainly hides and leather products), rice, food and beverages, mineral products.
Principal market: Brazil 23.8% (2001)
Population: 3,415,000 (2003 est)
Language: Spanish (official), Brazilero (a mixture of Spanish and Portuguese)
Religion: mainly Roman Catholic
Life expectancy: 72 (men); 79 (women) (2000–05)
Chronology
1516: Río de la Plata visited by Spanish navigator Juan Diaz de Solis, who was killed by native Charrua Amerindians. This discouraged European settlement for more than a century.
1680: Portuguese from Brazil founded Nova Colonia do Sacramento on Río de la Plata estuary.
1726: Spanish established fortress at Montevideo and wrested control over Uruguay from Portugal, with much of the Amerindian population being killed.
1776: Became part of Viceroyalty of La Plata, with capital at Buenos Aires.
1808: With Spanish monarchy overthrown by Napoleon Bonaparte, La Plata Viceroyalty became autonomous, but Montevideo remained loyal to Spanish Crown and rebelled against Buenos Aires control.
1815: Dictator José Gervasio Artigas overthrew Spanish and Buenos Aires control.
1820: Artigas ousted by Brazil, which disputed control of Uruguay with Argentina.
1825: Independence declared after fight led by Juan Antonio Lavalleja.
1828: Independence recognized by country's neighbours.
1836: Civil war between Reds and Whites, after which Colorado and Blanco parties were named.

1840: Merino sheep introduced by British traders, who later established meat processing factories for export trade.
1865–70: Fought successfully alongside Argentina and Brazil in war against Paraguay.
1903: After period of military rule, José Battle y Ordonez, a progressive from centre-left Colorado Party, became president. As president 1903–07 and 1911–15, he gave women the franchise and created an advanced welfare state as a successful ranching economy developed.
1930: First constitution adopted, but period of military dictatorship followed during Depression period.
1958: After 93 years out of power, the right-of-centre Blanco Party returned to power.
1967: The Colorado Party were in power, with Jorge Pacheco Areco as president. A period of labour unrest and urban guerrilla activity by left-wing Tupamaros.
1972: Juan María Bordaberry Arocena of the Colorado Party became president.
1973: Parliament dissolved and Bordaberry shared power with military dictatorship, which crushed Tupamaros and banned left-wing groups.
1976: Bordaberry deposed by army; Dr Aparicio Méndez Manfredini became president.
1981: Gen Grigorio Alvárez Armellino became new military ruler.
1984: Violent antigovernment protests after ten years of repressive rule and deteriorating economy.
1985: Agreement reached between army and political leaders for return to constitutional government and freeing of political prisoners.
1986: Government of national accord established under President Sanguinetti.
1992: The public voted against privatization in a national referendum.
2000: Jorge Batlle Ibáñez, of the Colorado Party, was elected president.
2004: Tabare Vasquez (Broad Front coalition) became Uruguay's first left-wing president.

user interface in computing, the procedures and methods through which the user operates a program. These might include menus, input forms, error messages, and keyboard procedures. A *graphical user interface (GUI or WIMP) is one that makes use of icons (small pictures) and allows the user to make menu selections with a mouse.

USSR See *Union of Soviet Socialist Republics.

Ustaše Croatian nationalist terrorist organization founded 1929 and led by Ante Pavelic against the Yugoslav state. During World War II, it collaborated with the Nazis and killed thousands of Serbs, Romanies, and Jews. It also carried out deportations and forced conversions to Roman Catholicism in its attempt to create a 'unified' Croatian state.

usury former term for charging interest on a loan of money. In medieval times, usury was held to be a sin, and Christians were forbidden to lend (although not to borrow).

Utah called the **Beehive State**, state in western USA, one of the Mountain States, bordered to the east by *Colorado, to the south by *Arizona, to the west by *Nevada, and to the north by *Wyoming; at the Four Corners in the southeast, it also touches *New Mexico; area 212,752 sq km/82,144 sq mi; population (2000)

2,233,200; capital and largest city *Salt Lake City. The name Utah derives from the American Indian Ute, meaning 'high land'; its nickname symbolizes thrift and industry. Utah has a spectacular landscape of canyons, *Rocky Mountain peaks, and vast deserts. It is an important transport hub for the western USA, and service industries and tourism are the state's largest employers. Products include transport equipment, processed foods, and scientific materials. Beef, milk, and hay are the main agricultural products. Salt Lake City is the headquarters of the Church of Jesus Christ of the Latter-Day Saints, or *Mormons; 70% of Utah's population are Mormon. Other important towns and cities include West Valley City, Provo, Sandy, Orem, and Ogden. Originally home to the Ute, Paiute, and Goshiute, the region was first claimed by Spain and, after 1821, by Mexico. From the 1840s US explorers surveyed Utah, and settlement began in 1847 when the Mormons under Brigham *Young arrived in Salt Lake City. The region was ceded to the USA in 1848, and the extension of the Union Pacific Railroad in 1869 opened the state to further settlement. Utah was admitted to the Union in 1896 as the 45th US state.

uterus hollow muscular organ of female mammals, located between the bladder and rectum, and connected to the Fallopian tubes above and the vagina below. The embryo develops within the uterus, and in placental mammals is attached to it after implantation via the *placenta and umbilical cord. The lining of the uterus changes during the *menstrual cycle to prepare it for pregnancy. In humans and other higher primates, it is a single structure, but in other mammals it is paired.

Uthman (c. 574–656) Third caliph (leader of the Islamic Empire) from 644, a son-in-law of the prophet Muhammad. Under his rule, the Arabs became a naval power and extended their rule to North Africa and Cyprus, but Uthman's personal weaknesses led to his assassination. He was responsible for the compilation of the authoritative version of the Koran, the sacred book of Islam.

Uthman I another name for the Turkish sultan *Osman I.

utilitarianism philosophical theory of ethics outlined by the philosopher Jeremy *Bentham and developed by John Stuart Mill. According to utilitarianism, an action is morally right if it has consequences that lead to happiness, and wrong if it brings about the reverse. Thus society should aim for the greatest happiness of the greatest number.

Utrecht province of the Netherlands, lying southeast of Amsterdam, and south of the IJsselmeer, on the Kromme Rijn (Crooked Rhine); area 1,330 sq km/ 514 sq mi; population (1997) 1,079,400. The capital is Utrecht. Industries include petrochemicals, textiles, electrical goods, engineering, steelworks, railway workshops, and furniture. Fruit, vegetables, and cereals are grown, and there is livestock raising and dairying.

Utrecht, Union of in 1579, the union of seven provinces of the northern Netherlands – Holland, Zeeland, Friesland, Groningen, Utrecht, Gelderland, and Overijssel – that, as the United Provinces, became the basis of opposition to the Spanish crown and the foundation of the present-day Dutch state.

Utrillo, Maurice (1883–1955) French artist. A self-taught painter, he was first influenced by the Impressionists, but soon developed a distinctive, almost naive style characterized by his subtle use of pale tones and muted colours. He painted views of his native Paris, many depicting Montmartre.

Uttaranchal or **Dev Bhoomi** state of north India, situated at the foot of the Himalayas and bordered by Himachal Pradesh and Uttar Pradesh; area 51,125 sq km/ 19,739 sq mi; population (2001 est) 8,479,600. It was carved from Uttar Pradesh and was incorporated as a state in November 2000. The capital is Dehra Dun. Uttaranchal shares international borders with Nepal and China. Nanda Devi, one of the highest peaks in India at 7,817m/25,645 ft, is located in the Region; many rivers originate in Uttaranchal including the Ganges and Yamuna. The state's principal industry is tourism – an average of 83 million tourists visit the area every year, and Dehra Dun and Mussoorie, with the advantage of a cooler summer climate because of their high altitude, are leading hill resorts. Other industries include forest production, a developing herbal pharmaceutical industry, and hydroelectric power. Grains and horticultural crops such as apple, orange, pear, grapes, peach, plum, apricot, mango, and guava are also produced.

Uttar Pradesh state of north India, bordered by Nepal and Uttaranchal to the northeast, with Madhya Pradesh to the south, Haryana, Delhi, and Rajasthan to the west, and Bihar in the east; area 243,288 sq km/93,934 sq mi; population (2001 est) 166,052,900. The capital is *Lucknow. Economically the state is one of the least developed in India, with three-quarters of the population dependent on agriculture, much of it on a subsistence basis in very small holdings. Wheat, rice, millet, barley, sugar cane, groundnuts, peas, cotton, oilseed, potatoes and fruit are grown, and there is livestock raising and dairy farming. Silica, limestone, and coal are mined and industries, mostly on a small scale in centres such as Varanasi and Lucknow and based on the mineral and agricultural outputs, include the production of sugar, vegetable oil, textiles, leatherwork, cement, chemicals and handicrafts. As part of the Uttar Pradesh Reorganization Act, the region was split in November 2000 to form the new state of *Uttaranchal, carved out of its northwest section.

Uzbek member of the majority ethnic group (almost 70%) living in Uzbekistan. Minorities live in Turkmenistan, Tajikistan, Kazakhstan, and Afghanistan and include *Turkomen, *Tatars, *Armenians, Kazakhs, and Kirghiz. There are 10–14 million speakers of the Uzbek language, which belongs to the Turkic branch of the Altaic family. Uzbeks are predominantly Sunni Muslims but retain aspects of shamanism.

Uzbekistan
National name: *Özbekiston Respublikasi/ Republic of Uzbekistan*
Area: 447,400 sq km/172,741 sq mi
Capital: Tashkent
Major towns/cities: Samarkand, Bukhara, Namangan, Andijon, Nukus, Qarshi
Physical features: oases in deserts; rivers: Amu Darya, Syr Darya; Fergana Valley; rich in mineral deposits
Head of state: Islam Karimov from 1990
Head of government: Shavkat Mirziyayev from 2003
Political system: authoritarian nationalist
Political executive: unlimited presidency

Political parties: People's Democratic Party of Uzbekistan (PDP), reform socialist (ex-communist); Fatherland Progress Party (FP; Vatan Taraqioti), pro-private enterprise; Erk (Freedom Democratic Party), mixed economy; Social Democratic Party of Uzbekistan, pro-Islamic; National Revival Democratic Party, centrist, intelligentsia-led
Currency: som
GNI per capita (PPP): (US$) 1,590 (2002 est)
Exports: cotton fibre, textiles, machinery, food and energy products, gold. Principal market: Russia 16.7% (2000)
Population: 26,093,000 (2003 est)
Language: Uzbek (a Turkic language; official), Russian, Tajik
Religion: predominantly Sunni Muslim; small Wahhabi, Sufi, and Orthodox Christian communities
Life expectancy: 67 (men); 73 (women) (2000–05)
Chronology
6th century BC: Part of the Persian Empire of Cyrus the Great.
4th century BC: Part of the empire of Alexander the Great of Macedonia.
1st century BC: Samarkand (Maracanda) developed as transit point on strategic Silk Road trading route between China and Europe.
7th century: City of Tashkent founded; spread of Islam.
12th century: Tashkent taken by Turks; Khorezem (Khiva), in northwest, became centre of large Central Asian polity, stretching from Caspian Sea to Samarkand in the east.
13th–14th centuries: Conquered by Genghis Khan and became part of Mongol Empire, with Samarkand serving as capital for Tamerlane.
18th–19th centuries: Dominated by independent emirates and khanates (chiefdoms) of Bukhara in southwest, Kokand in east, and Samarkand in centre.
1865–67: Tashkent was taken by Russia and made capital of Governor-Generalship of Turkestan.

1868–76: Tsarist Russia annexed emirate of Bukhara (1868); and khanates of Samarkand (1868), Khiva (1873), and Kokand (1876).
1917: Following Bolshevik revolution in Russia, Tashkent soviet ('people's council') established, which deposed the emir of Bukhara and other khans in 1920.
1918–22: Mosques closed and Muslim clergy persecuted as part of secularization drive by new communist rulers, despite nationalist guerrilla (basmachi) resistance.
1921: Part of Turkestan Soviet Socialist Autonomous Republic.
1925: Became constituent republic of USSR.
1930s: Skilled ethnic Russians immigrated into urban centres as industries developed.
1944: About 160,000 Meskhetian Turks forcibly transported from their native Georgia to Uzbekistan by Soviet dictator Joseph Stalin.
1950s–80s: Major irrigation projects stimulated cotton production, but led to desiccation of Aral Sea.
late 1980s: Upsurge in Islamic consciousness stimulated by *glasnost* initiative of Soviet Union's reformist leader Mikhail Gorbachev.
1989: Birlik ('Unity'), nationalist movement, formed. Violent attacks on Meskhetian and other minority communities in Fergana Valley.
1990: Economic and political sovereignty was declared by the increasingly nationalist UCP, led by Islam Karimov, who became president.
1991: An attempted anti-Gorbachev coup by conservatives in Moscow was initially supported by President Karimov. Independence was declared. Uzbekistan joined the new Commonwealth of Independent States (CIS); Karimov was re-elected president.
1992: There were violent food riots in Tashkent. Uzbekistan joined the Economic Cooperation Organization and the United Nations (UN). A new constitution was adopted.
1993: There was a crackdown on Islamic fundamentalists as the economy deteriorated.
1994: Economic, military, and social union was forged with Kazakhstan and Kyrgyzstan, and an economic integration treaty was signed with Russia. Links with Turkey were strengthened and foreign inward investment encouraged.
1995: The ruling PDP (formerly UCP) won a general election, from which the opposition was banned from participating, and Otkir Sultonov was appointed prime minister. Karimov's tenure as president was extended for a further five-year term by national referendum.
1996: An agreement was made with Kazakhstan and Kyrgyzstan to create a single economic market.
1998: A treaty of eternal friendship and deepening economic cooperation was signed with Kazakhstan.
1999: Uzbekistan threatened to end participation in a regional security treaty, accusing Russia of seeking to integrate the former Soviet republics into a superstate.
2000: President Islam Karimov was re-elected. Islamist rebels crossed into the country from Afghanistan via Tajikistan, reportedly seeking to create an Islamic state in east Uzbekistan.
2005: Several hundred anti-government protesters were shot dead by troops in the town of Andijan.

V

v in physics, symbol for *velocity.

Vaal river in South Africa, the chief tributary of the Orange River. It rises in the Drakensberg mountain range, on the border of Swaziland, and is 805 km/500 mi long.

vaccine any preparation of modified pathogens (viruses or bacteria) that is introduced into the body, usually either orally or by a hypodermic syringe, to induce the specific *antibody reaction that produces *immunity against a particular disease.

vacuole in biology, a fluid-filled, membrane-bound cavity inside a cell. It may be a reservoir for fluids that the cell will secrete to the outside, or may be filled with excretory products or essential nutrients that the cell needs to store.

vacuum in general, a region completely empty of matter; in physics, any enclosure in which the gas pressure is considerably less than atmospheric pressure (101,325 pascals).

vacuum cleaner cleaning device invented in 1901 by the Scot Hubert Cecil Booth. Having seen an ineffective dust-blowing machine, he reversed the process so that his machine (originally on wheels, and operated from the street by means of tubes running into the house) operated by suction.

vacuum flask *or* **Dewar flask** *or* **Thermos flask** container for keeping things either hot or cold. It has two silvered glass walls with a vacuum between them, in a metal or plastic outer case. This design reduces the three forms of heat transfer: radiation (prevented by the silvering), conduction, and convection (both prevented by the vacuum). A vacuum flask is therefore equally efficient at keeping cold liquids cold or hot liquids hot. It was invented by the British scientist James Dewar in about 1872, to store liquefied gases.

Vaduz capital of the European principality of Liechtenstein; population (1995) 5,100. The economic base is now tourism and financial services. It trades in wine, fruit, and vegetables. Above the town stands the castle of the ruling prince.

vagina lower part of the reproductive tract in female mammals, linking the uterus to the exterior. It admits the penis during sexual intercourse, and is the birth canal down which the baby passes during delivery.

valence in chemistry, the measure of an element's ability to combine with other elements, expressed as the number of atoms of hydrogen (or any other standard univalent element) capable of uniting with

(or replacing) its atoms. The number of electrons in the outermost shell of the atom dictates the combining ability of an element.

Valencian Community Spanish **Comunidad Valenciana**, autonomous community of western Spain, comprising the provinces of Alicante, Castellón de la Plana, and Valencia; area 23,305 sq km/8,998 sq mi; population (2001 est) 4,202,600. The region is chiefly mountainous, with a rich agricultural area on the coastal plain, producing citrus and other fruits, vegetables, rice, olive oil, and wine. Valencia is called the 'garden of Spain' for its intensive cultivation under irrigation that was started by the Moors. Industries include iron and steel production and car manufacture, while manufacturing includes processed foods, ceramics, furniture, textiles, and metal products. Tourism, especially to seaside resorts has become increasingly important. The capital is Valencia.

Valentino, Rudolph (1895–1926) adopted name of Rodolfo Alfonso Guglielmi di Valentina d'Antonguolla, Italian-born US film actor and dancer. He was the archetypal romantic lover of the Hollywood silent era. His screen debut was in 1919, but his first starring role was in *The Four Horsemen of the Apocalypse* (1921). His subsequent films include *The Sheik* (1921) and *Blood and Sand* (1922).

Vale of Glamorgan unitary authority in south Wales, created in 1996 from parts of the former counties of Mid Glamorgan and South Glamorgan. **area:** 337 sq km/130 sq mi **towns:** Barry (administrative headquarters), Penarth **physical:** lowland area **features:** Cosmeston Lake and Medieval Village, Fonmon castle (17th century), Beaupre Castle (12th and 16th centuries), Dyffryn Gardens, Penarth Pier, Barry Island and Waterfront, Glamorgan Heritage Coast Conservation Area **population:** (2001 est) 119,300.

valerian any of a group of perennial plants native to the northern hemisphere, with clustered heads of fragrant tubular flowers in red, white, or pink. The root of the common valerian or garden heliotrope *V. officinalis* is used in medicine to relieve wind and to soothe or calm patients. (Genera *Valeriana* and *Centranthus*, family Valerianaceae.)

Valhalla in Norse mythology, the golden hall in *Odin's palace in Asgard, where he feasted with the souls of half those heroes killed in battle (*valr*) chosen by his female attendants, the *Valkyries; the remainder celebrated in Sessrumnir with *Freya, goddess of love and war.

Valkyrie (Old Norse *valr* 'slain', *kjosa* 'choose') in Norse mythology, any of the female attendants of *Odin. They directed the course of battles and selected the most valiant warriors to die; half being escorted to *Valhalla, and the remainder to Sessrumnir, the hall of *Freya.

Valle d'Aosta province and special autonomous region of northwest Italy, in the Alps; area 3,263 sq km/1,260 sq mi; population (1998 est) 120,000, many of whom are French-speaking. Its capital is Aosta. Wine and livestock are produced, and industries include the manufacture of special steels and textiles, and the production of hydroelectricity; tourism is also important.

Valletta capital and port of Malta; population (1995) 9,129 (inner harbour area 102,600).

valley a long, linear depression sloping downwards towards the sea or an inland drainage basin. Types of valleys include the V-shaped valley, U-shaped valley, hanging valley, dry valley, misfit valley, asymmetric valley, and *rift valley.

Valley Forge site in Pennsylvania 32 km/20 mi northwest of Philadelphia, USA, where George *Washington's army spent the winter of 1777–78 in great hardship during the *American Revolution. Of the 10,000 men there, 2,500 died of disease and the rest suffered from lack of rations and other supplies; many deserted.

Valley of the Kings burial place of ancient kings opposite *Thebes, Egypt, on the left bank of the Nile. It was established as a royal cemetery during the reign of Thotmes I (c. 1500 BC) and abandoned during the reign of Ramses XI (c. 1100 BC).

Valois branch of the Capetian dynasty, originally counts of Valois (see Hugh *Capet) in France, members of which occupied the French throne from Philip VI (1328) to Henry III (1589).

value-added tax (VAT) general consumption tax assessed on the value of goods and services, applied at each stage of the production of a commodity, and charged only on the value added at that stage. It is a general tax because the tax applies to all commercial activities that involve the production and distribution of goods and the provision of services; and a consumption tax because the burden falls on the consumer. VAT is charged as a percentage of price. In the USA the individual states impose their own sales taxes. A 2001 initiative that has broad state approval, the Streamlined Sales Tax Project, aims to simplify and modernize sales and use tax collection and administration.

valve in animals, a structure for controlling the direction of the blood flow. In humans and other vertebrates, the contractions of the beating heart cause the correct blood flow into the arteries because a series of valves prevents back flow. Diseased valves, detected as 'heart murmurs', have decreased efficiency. The tendency for low-pressure venous blood to collect at the base of limbs under the influence of gravity is counteracted by a series of small valves within the veins. It was the existence of these valves that prompted the 17th-century physician William Harvey to suggest that the blood circulated around the body.

valvular heart disease damage to the heart valves, leading to either narrowing of the valve orifice when it is open (stenosis) or leaking through the valve when it is closed (regurgitation).

vampire (Hungarian *vampir* (and similar forms in other Slavonic languages) in Hungarian and Slavonic folklore, an 'undead' corpse that sleeps in its coffin by day and sucks the blood of the living by night, often in the form of a bat. *Dracula is a vampire in popular fiction, based on the creation of Bram Stoker.

vampire bat South and Central American bat of the family Desmodontidae, of which there are three species. The **common vampire** *Desmodus rotundus* is found from northern Mexico to central Argentina; its head and body grow to 9 cm/3.5 in. Vampire bats feed on the blood of birds and mammals; they slice a piece of skin from a sleeping animal with their sharp incisor teeth and lap up the flowing blood. They chiefly approach their prey by flying low then crawling and leaping.

vanadium chemical symbol V, silver-white, malleable and ductile, metallic element, atomic number 23, relative atomic mass 50.942. It occurs in certain iron, lead, and uranium ores and is widely distributed in small quantities in igneous and sedimentary rocks. It is used to make steel alloys, to which it adds tensile strength.

Van Allen radiation belts two zones of charged particles around the Earth's magnetosphere, discovered in 1958 by US physicist James Van Allen. The atomic particles come from the Earth's upper atmosphere and the *solar wind, and are trapped by the Earth's magnetic field. The inner belt lies 1,000–5,000 km/620–3,100 mi above the Equator, and contains *protons and *electrons. The outer belt lies 15,000–25,000 km/9,300–15,500 mi above the Equator, but is lower around the magnetic poles. It contains mostly electrons from the solar wind. The Van Allen belts are a hazard to spacecraft, affecting on-board electronics and computer systems. Similar belts have been discovered around the planets Mercury, Jupiter, Saturn, Uranus, and Neptune.

Vanbrugh, John (1664–1726) English baroque architect, dramatist, and soldier. Although entirely untrained as an architect, he designed the huge mansions of Castle Howard (1699–1726), Blenheim (1705–16; completed by Nicholas Hawksmoor 1722–25), Seaton Delaval (1720–29), and many others, as well as much of Greenwich Hospital (1718 onwards). He also wrote the comic dramas *The Relapse* (1696) and *The Provok'd Wife* (1697).

Vancouver chief Pacific seaport of Canada, on the mainland of British Columbia; population (2001 est) 582,000, metropolitan area. (2001 est) 2,078,800. A major commercial, distribution, and tourist centre, it is the terminus of transcontinental rail and road routes, and a 1,144-km/715-mi pipeline from the Alberta oilfields. It is Canada's third-largest metropolitan area. Industries include oil-refining, engineering, shipbuilding, fishing and fish-canning, brewing, timber-milling, and the manufacture of aircraft, pulp and paper, and textiles.

Vancouver Island island off the west coast of Canada, part of British Columbia, separated from the mainland by the straits of Juan de Fuca, Haro, Georgia, Johnstone, and Queen Charlotte Sound; area 32,136 sq km/12,404 sq mi. Industries include coal, timber, fish, and tourism. Fruit is grown, and there is dairying.

Vandal member of a Germanic people related to the *Goths. In the 5th century AD the Vandals invaded Roman *Gaul and Spain, many settling in Andalusia (formerly Vandalitia) and others reaching North Africa 429. They sacked Rome 455 but were defeated by Belisarius, general of the emperor Justinian, in the 6th century.

van de Graaff generator electrostatic generator capable of producing a voltage of over a million volts. It consists of a continuous vertical conveyor belt that carries electrostatic charges (resulting from friction) up to a large hollow sphere supported on an insulated stand. The lower end of the belt is earthed, so that charge accumulates on the sphere. The size of the voltage built up in air depends on the radius of the sphere, but can be increased by enclosing the generator in an inert atmosphere, such as nitrogen.

van der Waals' law modified form of the *gas laws that includes corrections for the non-ideal behaviour of real gases (the molecules of ideal gases occupy no space and exert no forces on each other). It is named after Dutch physicist J D van der Waals (1837–1923).

van Dyck, Anthony Flemish painter; see *Dyck, Anthony van.

van Eyck, Jan Flemish painter; see *Eyck, Jan van.

van Gogh, Vincent Dutch painter; see *Gogh, Vincent van.

vanilla any of a group of climbing orchids native to tropical America but cultivated elsewhere, with large, fragrant white or yellow flowers. The dried and fermented fruit, or podlike capsules, of the species *V. planifolia* are the source of the vanilla flavouring used in cookery and baking. (Genus *Vanilla*.)

Vanuatu

formerly **New Hebrides** (until 1980)

National name: *Ripablik blong Vanuatu/ République de Vanuatu/Republic of Vanuatu*

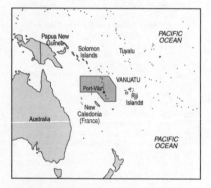

Area: 14,800 sq km/5,714 sq mi
Capital: Port-Vila (on Efate island) (and chief port)
Major towns/cities: Luganville (on Espíritu Santo)
Major ports: Santo
Physical features: comprises around 70 inhabited islands, including Espíritu Santo, Malekula, and Efate; densely forested, mountainous; three active volcanoes; cyclones on average twice a year
Head of state: Kalkot Mataskelekele from 2004
Head of government: Ham Lini from 2004
Political system: liberal democracy
Political executive: parliamentary
Political parties: Union of Moderate Parties (UMP), Francophone centrist; National United Party (NUP), formed by Walter Lini; Vanua'aku Pati (VP), Anglophone centrist; Melanesian Progressive Party (MPP), Melanesian centrist; Fren Melanesian Party,
Currency: vatu
GNI per capita (PPP): (US$) 2,770 (2002 est)
Exports: timber, copra, beef, cocoa, shells. Principal market: Indonesia 34.8% (2001)
Population: 212,000 (2003 est)
Language: Bislama (82%), English, French (all official)
Religion: Christian 80%, animist about 8%
Life expectancy: 68 (men); 71 (women) (2000–05)

Chronology
1606: First visited by Portuguese navigator Pedro Fernandez de Queiras, who named the islands Espíritu Santo.
1774: Visited by British navigator Capt James Cook, who named them the New Hebrides, after the Scottish islands.
1830s: European merchants attracted to islands by sandalwood trade. Christian missionaries arrived, but many were attacked by the indigenous Melanesians who, in turn, were ravaged by exposure to European diseases.
later 19th century: Britain and France disputed control; islanders were shipped to Australia, the Fiji Islands, Samoa, and New Caledonia to work as plantation labourers.
1906: The islands were jointly administered by France and Britain as the Condominium of the New Hebrides.
1963: Indigenous Na-Griamel (NG) political grouping formed on Espíritu Santo to campaign against European acquisition of more than a third of the land area.
1975: A representative assembly was established following pressure from the VP, formed in 1972 by English-speaking Melanesian Protestants.
1978: A government of national unity was formed, with Father Gerard Leymang as chief minister.
1980: A revolt on the island of Espíritu Santo by French settlers and pro-NG plantation workers delayed independence but it was achieved within the Commonwealth, with George Kalkoa (adopted name Sokomanu) as president and left-of-centre Father Walter Lini (VP) as prime minister.
1988: The dismissal of Lini by Sokomanu led to Sokomanu's arrest for treason. Lini was later reinstated.
1991: Lini was voted out by party members and replaced by Donald Kalpokas. A general election produced a coalition government of the Francophone Union of Moderate Parties (UMP) and Lini's new National United Party (NUP) under Maxime Carlot Korman.
1993: A cyclone caused extensive damage.
1995: The governing UMP–NUP coalition won a general election, but Serge Vohor of the VP-dominated Unity Front became prime minister in place of Carlot Korman.
1996: The VP, led by Donald Kalpokas, joined the governing coalition.
1997: Prime Minister Vohor formed a new coalition. The legislature was dissolved and new elections called after a no-confidence motion against Vohor.
1998: A two-week state of emergency followed rioting in the capital.
1999: John Bernard Bani was elected president, and Barak Sope was elected prime minister.
2001: Edward Natapei became prime minister.
2002: Barak Sope was jailed for 3 years for abuse of office – he had forged government guarantees – but was released after 3 months, apparently suffering from diabetes.
2004: Ham Lini became prime minister.

vapour one of the three states of matter (see also *solid and *liquid). The molecules in a vapour move randomly and are far apart, the distance between them, and therefore the volume of the vapour, being limited only by the walls of any vessel in which they might be contained. A vapour differs from a *gas only in that a vapour can be liquefied by increased pressure, whereas a gas cannot unless its temperature is lowered below its critical temperature; it then becomes a vapour and may be liquefied.

vapour density density of a gas, expressed as the *mass of a given volume of the gas divided by the mass of an equal volume of a reference gas (such as hydrogen or air) at the same temperature and pressure. If the reference gas is hydrogen, it is equal to half the relative molecular weight (mass) of the gas.

vapour pressure pressure of a vapour given off by (evaporated from) a liquid or solid, caused by atoms or molecules continuously escaping from its surface. In an enclosed space, a maximum value is reached when the number of particles leaving the surface is in equilibrium with those returning to it; this is known as the **saturated vapour pressure** or **equilibrium vapour pressure**.

Varanasi or **Benares** or **Banaras** city in Uttar Pradesh, India, one of the seven holy cities of Hinduism, on the River Ganges; population (2001 est) 1,211,700. There are 1,500 golden shrines, and a 5 km/3 mi frontage to the Ganges with sacred stairways (ghats) for purification by bathing. Varanasi is also a sacred centre of *Jainism, *Sikhism, and *Buddhism: Buddha came to Varanasi from Gaya and is believed to have preached in the Deer Park. One-third of its inhabitants are Muslim. Varanasi has long been a major centre of education, with three universities including the Banaras Hindu University (1915), and many colleges and schools, including religious schools. The city is noted for the manufacture of silks and brocades, and its handicrafts include brassware, ivory goods, glass bangles and wooden toys.

variable in mathematics, a changing quantity (one that can take various values), as opposed to a *constant. For example, in the algebraic expression $y = 4x^3 + 2$, the variables are x and y, whereas 4 and 2 are constants.

variable star star whose brightness changes, either regularly or irregularly, over a period ranging from a few hours to months or years. The *Cepheid variables regularly expand and contract in size every few days or weeks.

variation one of the earliest musical forms. A theme or melody is first presented in a straightforward manner and then repeated as often as the composer wishes but each time it is varied in one or more ways. The theme is usually easily recognizable; it may be a popular tune or – as a gesture of respect – the work of a fellow composer; for example, Johannes Brahms's *Variations on a Theme by Haydn* (1873), based on a theme known as the *St Antony Chorale*, although it may also be an original composition. The principle of variations has been used in larger-scale and orchestral works by modern composers, for example Arnold Schoenberg's *Variations for Orchestra* (1928).

varicose veins or **varicosis** condition in which the veins become swollen and twisted. The veins of the legs are most often affected; other vulnerable sites include the rectum (*haemorrhoids) and testes.

variegation description of plant leaves or stems that exhibit patches of different colours. The term is usually applied to plants that show white, cream, or yellow on their leaves, caused by areas of tissue that lack the green pigment *chlorophyll. Variegated plants are bred for their decorative value, but they are often considerably weaker than the normal, uniformly green plant. Many will not breed true and require *vegetative reproduction.

Vasa dynasty Swedish royal house founded by *Gustavus Vasa. He liberated his country from Danish rule 1520–23 and put down local uprisings of nobles and peasants. By 1544 he was secure enough to make his title hereditary. His grandson, *Gustavus Adolphus, became king 1611 and led the armies of the Protestant princes in the *Thirty Years' War until his death. The dynasty ended 1809 when Gustavus IV was deposed by a revolution and replaced by his uncle Charles XIII. With no heir to the throne, the crown was offered 1810 to one of Napoleon's generals, Bernadotte, who became King Charles John until his death in 1844.

Vasarely, Victor (1908–1997) Hungarian **Viktor Vásárhelyi**, Hungarian-born French artist. He was one of the leading exponents of *op art. In the 1940s he developed precise geometric compositions, full of visual puzzles and effects of movement, which he created with complex arrangements of hard-edged geometric shapes and subtle variations in colours.

Vasari, Giorgio (1511–1574) Italian art historian, architect, and painter. He is best known for *Le vite de' più eccelenti architetti, pittori, et sculteri italiani/ The Lives of the Most Excellent Italian Architects, Painters, and Sculptors* (1550; enlarged 1568), which provides an invaluable source of information on Italian Renaissance artists. His most important architectural work was the Uffizi Palace, Florence (now an art gallery).

vascular bundle in botany, strand of primary conducting tissue (a 'vein') in vascular plants, consisting mainly of water-conducting tissues, metaxylem and protoxylem, which together make up the primary *xylem, and nutrient-conducting tissue, *phloem. It extends from the roots to the stems and leaves. Typically the phloem is situated nearest to the epidermis and the xylem towards the centre of the bundle. In plants exhibiting *secondary growth, the xylem and phloem are separated by a thin layer of vascular *cambium, which gives rise to new conducting tissues.

vascular plant plant containing vascular bundles. *Pteridophytes (ferns, horsetails, and club mosses), *gymnosperms (conifers and cycads), and *angiosperms (flowering plants) are all vascular plants.

vas deferens in male vertebrates, a tube conducting sperm from the testis to the urethra. The sperm is carried in a fluid secreted by various glands, and can be transported very rapidly when the smooth muscle in the wall of the vas deferens undergoes rhythmic contraction, as in sexual intercourse.

vasectomy male sterilization; an operation to cut and tie the ducts (see *vas deferens) that carry sperm from the testes to the penis. Vasectomy does not affect sexual performance, but the semen produced at ejaculation no longer contains sperm.

vassal in medieval Europe, a person who paid feudal homage to a superior lord (see *feudalism), and who promised military service and advice in return for a grant of land. The term was used from the 9th century.

VAT abbreviation for *value-added tax.

Vatican City State
National name: *Stato della Città del Vaticano/ Vatican City State*

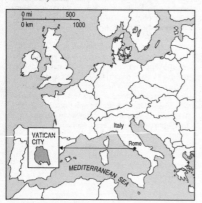

Area: 0.4 sq km/0.2 sq mi
Physical features: forms an enclave in the heart of Rome, Italy
Head of state: pending as of 2005
Head of government: Cardinal Angelo Sodano from 1990
Political system: theocratic
Political executive: theocratic
Currency: euro
GNI per capita (PPP): see Italy
Population: 1,000 (2003 est)
Language: Latin (official), Italian
Religion: Roman Catholic
Life expectancy: see Italy
Chronology
AD 64: Death of St Peter, a Christian martyr who, by legend, was killed in Rome and became regarded as the first bishop of Rome. The Pope, as head of the Roman Catholic Church, is viewed as the spiritual descendent of St Peter.
756: The Pope became temporal ruler of the Papal States, which stretched across central Italy, centred around Rome.
11th–13th centuries: Under Gregory VII and Innocent III the papacy enjoyed its greatest temporal power.
1377: After seven decades in which the papacy was based in Avignon (France), Rome once again became the headquarters for the Pope, with the Vatican Palace becoming the official residence.
1860: Umbria, Marche, and much of Emilia Romagna which, along with Lazio formed the Papal States, were annexed by the new unified Italian state.
1870: First Vatican Council defined as a matter of faith the absolute primacy of the Pope and the infallibility of his pronouncements on 'matters of faith and morals'.
1870–71: French forces, which had been protecting the Pope, were withdrawn, allowing Italian nationalist forces to capture Rome, which became the capital of Italy; Pope Pius IX retreated into the Vatican Palace, from which no Pope was to emerge until 1929.

1929: The Lateran Agreement, signed by the Italian fascist leader Benito Mussolini and Pope Pius XI, restored full sovereign jurisdiction over the Vatican City State to the bishopric of Rome (Holy See) and declared the new state to be a neutral and inviolable territory.
1947: A new Italian constitution confirmed the sovereignty of the Vatican City State.
1962: The Second Vatican Council was called by Pope John XXIII.
1978: John Paul II became the first non-Italian pope for more than 400 years.
1985: A new concordat was signed under which Roman Catholicism ceased to be Italy's state religion.
1992: Relations with East European states were restored.
2005: John Paul II died and was succeeded by Cardinal Joseph Ratzinger, who took the title of Benedict XVI.

Vaucluse mountain range in southeast France, part of the Provence Alps east of Avignon, rising to 1,242 m/4,075 ft. It gives its name to the *département* of Vaucluse. The Italian poet Petrarch lived in the Vale of Vaucluse from 1337 to 1353.

Vaughan Williams, Ralph (1872–1958) English composer. His style was late-Romantic tonal/modal, and his works contain many references to the English countryside through the use of folk themes. Among his works are the orchestral *Fantasia on a Theme by Thomas Tallis* (1910); the opera *Sir John in Love* (1929), featuring the Elizabethan song 'Greensleeves'; and nine symphonies (1909–57).

vault in architecture, a continuous arch of brick, stone, or concrete, forming a self-supporting roof over a building or part of a building; also a vaulted structure, for example under a street pavement.

VDU abbreviation for *visual display unit.

Veda (Sanskrit 'divine knowledge') the most sacred of the Hindu scriptures, hymns written in an old form of Sanskrit; the oldest may date from 1500 or 2000 BC. The four main collections are: the *Rig Veda* (hymns and praises); *Yajur Veda* (prayers and sacrificial formulae); *Sâma Veda* (tunes and chants); and *Atharva Veda*, or Veda of the Atharvans, the officiating priests at the sacrifices.

Vedda (Sinhalese 'hunter') member of any of the aboriginal peoples of Sri Lanka, who occupiedthe island before the arrival of the Aryans about 550 BC. Formerly cave-dwelling hunter-gatherers, they have now almost died out or merged with the dominant Sinhalese and Tamil populations. They speak a Sinhalese language, belonging to the Indo-European family.

Vega *or* **Alpha Lyrae** brightest star in the constellation *Lyra and the fifth-brightest star in the night sky. It is a blue-white star, 25 light years from the Sun, with a true luminosity 50 times that of the Sun.

Vega, Lope Felix de (Carpio) (1562–1635) Spanish poet and dramatist. He was one of the founders of modern Spanish drama. He wrote epics, pastorals, odes, sonnets, novels, and over 500 plays (of which 426 are still in existence), mostly tragicomedies. He set out his views on drama in *Arte nuevo de hacer comedias/ The New Art of Writing Plays* (1609), in which he defended his innovations while reaffirming the classical forms. *Fuenteovejuna* (c. 1614) has been acclaimed as the first proletarian drama.

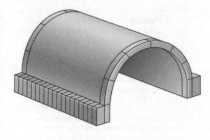

barrel vault (Romanesque)

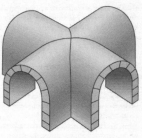

groin vault (late Romanesque)

rib vault (late Romanesque and early Gothic)

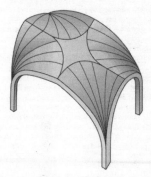

fan vault (Gothic)

vault Some of the many different types of vault.

vegan vegetarian who eats no foods of animal origin whatever, including fish, eggs, and milk.

vegetarian person who eats only foods obtained without slaughter, for humanitarian, aesthetic, political, or health reasons. There are many types of vegetarians. Lacto-ovo-vegetarians will eat eggs and dairy products; lacto-vegetarians will eat dairy products but not eggs; and pesco-vegetarians will eat fish as well as dairy products. *Vegans abstain from all foods of animal origin.

vegetative reproduction type of *asexual reproduction in plants that relies not on spores, but on multicellular structures formed by the parent plant. Some of the main types are stolons and runners, gemmae, bulbils, sucker shoots produced from roots (such as in the creeping thistle *Cirsium arvense*), *tubers, *bulbs, *corms, and *rhizomes. Vegetative reproduction has long been exploited in horticulture and agriculture, with various methods employed to multiply stocks of plants.

vein vessel that carries *blood from the body to the *heart in animals with a circulatory system. Veins contain valves that prevent the blood from running back when moving against gravity. They carry blood

at low pressure, so their walls are thinner than those of arteries. They always carry deoxygenated blood, with the exception of the pulmonary vein, leading from the lungs to the heart in birds and mammals, which carries newly oxygenated blood.

Vela bright constellation of the southern hemisphere near Carina, represented as the sails of a ship. It contains large wisps of gas – called the Gum nebula after its discoverer, the Australian astronomer Colin Gum (1924–1960) – believed to be the remains of one or more *supernovae. Vela also contains the second optical *pulsar (a pulsar that flashes at a visible wavelength) to be discovered.

Velázquez, Diego Rodríguez de Silva y (1599–1660) Spanish painter. One of the outstanding artists of the 17th century, he was court painter to Philip IV in Madrid, where he produced many portraits of the royal family as well as occasional religious paintings, genre scenes, and other works. Notable among his portraits is *Las Meninas/The Maids of Honour* (1656; Prado, Madrid), while *Women Frying Eggs* (1618; National Gallery of Scotland, Edinburgh) is a typical genre scene.

veldt subtropical grassland in South Africa, equivalent to the Pampas of South America.

velocity symbol *v*, speed of an object in a given direction, or how fast an object changes its position in a given direction. Velocity is a vector quantity, since its direction is important as well as its magnitude (or speed). For example, a car could have a speed of 48 kph/30 mph and a velocity of 48 kph/30 mph northwards. Velocity = change in position/time taken.

vena cava either of the two great veins of the trunk, returning deoxygenated blood to the right atrium of the *heart. The **superior vena cava**, beginning where the arches of the two innominate veins join high in the chest, receives blood from the head, neck, chest, and arms; the **inferior vena cava**, arising from the junction of the right and left common iliac veins, receives blood from all parts of the body below the diaphragm.

Vendée, La river in western France, rising near the village of La Châtaigneraie and flowing 72 km/45 mi to join the Sèvre Niortaise 11 km/7 mi east of the Bay of Biscay.

venereal disease (VD) any disease mainly transmitted by sexual contact, although commonly the term is used specifically for gonorrhoea and syphilis, both occurring worldwide, and chancroid ('soft sore') and lymphogranuloma venerum, seen mostly in the tropics. The term *sexually transmitted disease (STD) is more often used to encompass a growing list of conditions passed on primarily, but not exclusively, by sexual contact.

Veneto also Venetia, region of northeast Italy, comprising the provinces of Belluno, Padua, Treviso, Rovigo, Venice, Verona, and Vicenza; area 18,392 sq km/7,101 sq mi; population (2001 est) 4,490,600. Its capital is *Venice, and major towns include Padua, Verona, and Vicenza. Veneto forms part of the north Italian plain, with the delta of the River Po; it includes part of the Alps and Dolomites, and Lake Garda. Products include cereals, fruit, vegetables, wine, tobacco, chemicals, ships, and textiles.

Venezuela

National name: *República de Venezuela/ Republic of Venezuela*

Area: 912,100 sq km/352,161 sq mi
Capital: Caracas
Major towns/cities: Maracaibo, Maracay, Barquisimeto, Valencia, Ciudad Guayana, Petare

Major ports: Maracaibo
Physical features: Andes Mountains and Lake Maracaibo in northwest; central plains (llanos); delta of River Orinoco in east; Guiana Highlands in southeast
Head of state and government: Hugo Chávez Frías from 1999
Political system: liberal democracy
Political executive: limited presidency
Political parties: Democratic Action Party (AD), moderate left of centre; Christian Social Party (COPEI), Christian, right of centre; National Convergence (CN), broad coalition grouping; Movement towards Socialism (MAS), left of centre; Radical Cause (LCR), left wing
Currency: bolívar
GNI per capita (PPP): (US$) 5,080 (2002 est)
Exports: petroleum and petroleum products, metals (mainly aluminium, gold, and iron ore), natural gas, chemicals, cement, plastics, fish, shellfish, processed fish. Principal market: USA 50% (2001)
Population: 25,699,000 (2003 est)
Language: Spanish (official), Indian languages (2%)
Religion: Roman Catholic 92%
Life expectancy: 71 (men); 77 (women) (2000–05)
Chronology
1st millennium BC: Beginnings of settled agriculture.
AD 1498–99: Visited by explorers Christopher Columbus and Alonso de Ojeda, at which time the principal indigenous Indian communities were the Caribs, Arawaks, and Chibchas; it was named Venezuela ('little Venice') since the coastal Indians lived in stilted thatched houses.
1521: Spanish settlement established on the northeast coast and was ruled by Spain from Santo Domingo (Dominican Republic).
1567: Caracas founded by Diego de Losada.
1739: Became part of newly created Spanish Viceroyalty of New Granada, with capital at Bogotá (Colombia), but, lacking gold mines, retained great autonomy.
1749: First rebellion against Spanish colonial rule.
1806: Rebellion against Spain, led by Francisco Miranda.
1811–12: First Venezuelan Republic declared by patriots, taking advantage of Napoleon Bonaparte's invasion of Spain, but Spanish Royalist forces re-established their authority.
1813–14: The Venezuelan, Simón Bolívar, 'El Libertador' (the Liberator), created another briefly independent republic, before being forced to withdraw to Colombia.
1821: After the battle of Carabobo, Venezuelan independence achieved within Republic of Gran Colombia (which also comprised Colombia, Ecuador, and Panama).
1829: Became separate state of Venezuela after leaving Republic of Gran Colombia.
1830–48: Gen José Antonio Páez, the first of a series of caudillos (military leaders), established political stability.
1870–88: Antonio Guzmán Blanco ruled as benevolent liberal–conservative dictator, modernizing infrastructure and developing agriculture (notably coffee) and education.
1899: International arbitration tribunal found in favour of British Guiana (Guyana) in long-running dispute over border with Venezuela.

1902: Ports blockaded by British, Italian, and German navies as a result of Venezuela's failure to repay loans.

1908–35: Harsh rule of dictator Juan Vicente Gómez, during which period Venezuela became world's largest exporter of oil, which had been discovered in 1910.

1947: First truly democratic elections held, but the new president, Rómulo Gallegos, was removed within eight months by the military in the person of Col Marcos Pérez Jimenez.

1958: Overthrow of Pérez and establishment of an enduring civilian democracy, headed by left-wing Romulo Betancourt of Democratic Action Party (AD).

1964: Dr Raúl Leoni (AD) became president in first-ever constitutional handover of civilian power.

1974: Carlos Andrés Pérez (AD) became president, with economy remaining buoyant through oil revenues. Oil and iron industries nationalized.

1984: Social pact established between government, trade unions, and business; national debt rescheduled as oil revenues plummetted.

1987: Widespread social unrest triggered by inflation; student demonstrators shot by police.

1989: An economic austerity programme was instigated. Price increases triggered riots known as 'Caracazo'; 300 people were killed. Martial law was declared and a general strike followed. Elections were boycotted by opposition groups.

1992: An attempted antigovernment coup failed, at a cost of 120 lives.

1996: Former President Carlos Andrés Pérez was found guilty on corruption charges and imprisoned.

1999: Hugo Chávez was inaugurated as president. Flooding and mudslides swamped Venezuela's Caribbean coast in late December, resulting in death tolls as high as 30,000, at least 150,000 homeless civilians from 23,000 destroyed homes, 70,000 evacuees, and 96,000 damaged homes.

2000: Despite a shrinking economy, Hugo Chávez was re-elected as president, pledging to redistribute oil wealth from the rich to the poor. He later took a leading role in persuading the Organization of Petroleum-Exporting Countries (OPEC) to restrict world oil production to force up prices. In November, Chávez was given powers to legislate on certain issues by decree.

2002: President Chávez resigned from office under military pressure following street violence. Pedro Carmona Estanga, leader of the conservative business lobby, headed a transitional government; the National Assembly and Supreme Court were closed by decree, the recent constitution annulled, and the country renamed 'Republic of Venezuela'. However, within a day he was forced to resign as Chávez returned to power with the support of paratroops and the presidential guard.

2003: A two-month opposition-led strike against the government of left-wing President Hugo Chavez crumbled as private-sector workers returned to work. However, the country's political and economic situation remained unstable.

2004: In the face of mounting protests, President Chavez conceded a referendum on his rule and was announced as winner.

Venice Italian **Venezia**, city, port, and naval base on the northeast coast of Italy; population (2001 est) 266,200.

It is the capital of the *Veneto region. The old city is built on piles on low-lying islands in a salt-water lagoon, sheltered from the Adriatic Sea by the Lido and other small strips of land. There are about 150 canals crossed by some 400 bridges. Apart from tourism, industries include glass, jewellery, textiles, and lace.

veni, vidi, vici (Latin 'I came, I saw, I conquered') Julius Caesar's description of his victory over King Pharnaces II (63–47 BC) at Zela in 47 BC.

Venn diagram in mathematics, a diagram representing a *set or sets and the logical relationships between them. The sets are drawn as circles. An area of overlap between two circles (sets) contains elements that are common to both sets, and thus represents a third set. Circles that do not overlap represent sets with no elements in common (disjoint sets). The method is named after the English logician John Venn.

ventral surface front of an animal. In vertebrates, the side furthest from the backbone; in invertebrates, the side closest to the ground. The positioning of the main nerve pathways on the ventral side is a characteristic of invertebrates.

ventricle in zoology, either of the two lower chambers of the heart that force blood to circulate by contraction of their muscular walls. The term also refers to any of four cavities within the brain in which cerebrospinal fluid is produced.

Venus in Roman mythology, the goddess of love and beauty, equivalent to the Greek *Aphrodite. The patricians of Rome claimed descendance from her son, the Trojan prince *Aeneas, and she was consequently venerated as the guardian of the Roman people. Venus was also worshipped as a goddess of military victory and patroness of spring.

Venus second planet from the Sun. It can approach Earth to within 38 million km/24 million mi, closer than any other planet. Its mass is 0.82 that of Earth. Venus rotates on its axis more slowly than any other planet, from east to west, the opposite direction to the other planets (except Uranus and possibly Pluto).
mean distance from the Sun: 108.2 million km/67.2 million mi **equatorial diameter:** 12,100 km/7,500 mi **rotation period:** 243 Earth days **year:** 225 Earth days **atmosphere:** Venus is shrouded by clouds of sulphuric acid droplets that sweep across the planet from east to west every four days. The atmosphere is almost entirely carbon dioxide, which traps the Sun's heat by the *greenhouse effect and raises the planet's surface temperature to 480 °C/900 °F, with an atmospheric pressure of 90 times that at the surface of the Earth **surface:** consists mainly of silicate rock and may have an interior structure similar to that of Earth: an iron-nickel core, a *mantle composed of more mafic rocks (rocks made of one or more ferromagnesian, dark-coloured minerals), and a thin siliceous outer *crust. The surface is dotted with deep impact craters. Some of Venus's volcanoes may still be active **satellites:** no moons.

Venus flytrap insectivorous plant belonging to the sundew family, native to the southeastern USA. Its leaves have two hinged surfaces that rapidly close together to trap any insect which brushes against the sensitive leaf hairs; digestive juices then break down the insect body so that it can be absorbed by the plant. (*Dionaea muscipula*, family Droseraceae.)

verbena any of a group of plants containing about 100 species, mostly found in the American tropics. The leaves are fragrant and the tubular flowers are arranged in close spikes in colours ranging from white to rose, violet, and purple. The garden verbena is a hybrid annual. (Genus *Verbena*, family Verbenaceae.)

Vercingetorix (died 46 BC) Gallic chieftain. Leader of a revolt of all the tribes of Gaul against the Romans 52 BC; he lost, was captured, displayed in Julius Caesar's triumph 46 BC, and later executed. This ended the Gallic resistance to Roman rule.

Verdi, Giuseppe Fortunino Francesco (1813–1901) Italian opera composer of the Romantic period. He took his native operatic style to new heights of dramatic expression. In 1842 he wrote the opera *Nabucco*, followed by *Ernani* in 1844 and *Rigoletto* in 1851. Other works include *Il trovatore/The Troubadour* and *La traviata/The Fallen Woman* (both 1853), *Aïda* (1871), and the masterpieces of his old age, *Otello* (1887) and *Falstaff* (1893). His *Requiem* (1874) honoured the poet and novelist Alessandro Manzoni.

Verdun fortress town in northeast France in the *département* of the Meuse, 280 km/174 mi east of Paris. During World War I it became a symbol of French resistance and was the centre of a series of bitterly fought actions between French and German forces, finally being recaptured September 1918.

Verlaine, Paul Marie (1844–1896) French lyric poet. He was acknowledged as the leader of the Symbolist poets (see *Symbolism). His volumes of verse, strongly influenced by the poets Charles *Baudelaire and Arthur *Rimbaud, include *Poèmes saturniens/Saturnine Poems* (1866), *Fêtes galantes/Amorous Entertainments* (1869), and *Romances sans paroles/Songs without Words* (1874). In 1873 he was imprisoned for shooting and wounding Rimbaud. His later works reflect his attempts to lead a reformed life.

Vermeer, Jan (1632–1675) Dutch painter, active in Delft. He painted quiet, everyday scenes that are characterized by an almost abstract simplicity, subtle colour harmonies, and a remarkable ability to suggest the fall of light on objects. Examples are *The Lacemaker* (*c.* 1655; Louvre, Paris) and *Maidservant Pouring Milk* (*c.* 1658; Rijksmuseum, Amsterdam).

Vermont called the **Green Mountain State**, (French *les monts verts* 'the green mountains') state in northeastern USA, one of the *New England states, bordered to the north by *Québec, Canada, to the east by *New Hampshire along the Connecticut River, to the south by *Massachusetts, and to the west by *New York, two-thirds of this border running down the centre of Lake *Champlain; area 23,957 sq km/9,250 sq mi; population (2000) 608,800; capital Montpelier. Physically, the state varies between mountainous, in particular the Green Mountains running north–south through the centre of the state, and fertile lowland river valleys, such as the Champlain Valley in the northwest and the Connecticut Valley in the east. The Green Mountain National Forest, with its brilliant autumn foliage, is one of many attractions for Vermont's tourist industry, along with skiing and hiking. The river valleys support a thriving dairy industry. Other agricultural products include apples and maple syrup. Mining of granite, marble, slate, and talc has been economically important throughout the state's history. Burlington is the state's most populous city; other notable towns and cities include Rutland, Brattleboro, Barre, Woodstock, Bennington, and Waterbury. The region was home to the Abnaki American Indian people. Explored by Samuel de *Champlain, Vermont was settled first by the French and then the English. Vermont was admitted to the Union in 1791 as the 14th US state, the first to join after the original *Thirteen Colonies.

Verne, Jules (1828–1905) French author. He wrote tales of adventure that anticipated future scientific developments: *Five Weeks in a Balloon* (1862), *Journey to the Centre of the Earth* (1864), *Twenty Thousand Leagues under the Sea* (1870), and *Around the World in Eighty Days* (1873).

Verona town in Veneto, Italy, on the Adige River, 100 km/62 west of Venice; population (2001 est) 243,500. It is the capital of Verona province and an important industrial and agricultural centre, lying at the junction of the Brenner Pass road with the Venice–Milan motorway. Industries include printing, engineering, and the manufacture of paper, plastics, furniture, and pasta. Noted for its annual agricultural fairs, Verona is one of Italy's main marketing centres for fruit and vegetables. Wine production and hand-crafted metal and marble items are also important industries.

verruca growth on the skin; see *wart.

Versailles administrative centre of the *département* of Yvelines in northern France, situated 18 km/11 mi southwest of Paris; population (2001 est) 83,900. From 1678 Versailles was the principal residence of the kings of France until 1793, and the seat of government from 1682 to 1789. The baroque palace was built 1661–87 for Louis XIV (on the site of a hunting lodge) to a design by the architect Louis Le Vau, with later enlargements and alterations by Hardouin-Mansart.

Versailles, Treaty of peace treaty after World War I between the Allies (except the USA and China) and Germany, signed on 28 June 1919. It established the *League of Nations, an international organization intended to solve disputes by arbitration. Germany surrendered Alsace-Lorraine to France, and large areas in the east to Poland, and made smaller cessions to Czechoslovakia, Lithuania, Belgium, and Denmark. The Rhineland was demilitarized, German rearmament was restricted, and Germany agreed to pay reparations for war damage. The treaty was never ratified by the USA, which signed separate treaties with Germany and Austria in 1921. The terms of Versailles and its reshaping of Europe contributed to the outbreak of *World War II.

verse arrangement of words in a rhythmic pattern, which may depend on the length of syllables (as in Greek or Latin verse), or on stress, as in English. Classical Greek verse depended upon quantity, a long syllable being regarded as occupying twice the time taken up by a short syllable.

vertebral column backbone, giving support to an animal and protecting its spinal cord. It is made up of a series of bones or vertebrae running from the skull to the tail, with a central canal containing the nerve fibres of the spinal cord.

vertebrate any animal with a backbone. The 41,000 species of vertebrates include mammals, birds, reptiles, amphibians, and fishes. They include most of the larger animals, but in terms of numbers of species are only a tiny proportion of the world's animals. The zoological taxonomic group Vertebrata is a subgroup of the *phylum Chordata.

vertigo dizziness; a whirling sensation accompanied by a loss of any feeling of contact with the ground. It may be due to temporary disturbance of the sense of balance (as in spinning for too long on one spot), psychological reasons, disease such as *labyrinthitis, or intoxication.

Verulamium Romano-British town near St Albans, Hertfordshire, occupied until about AD 450. Verulamium superseded a nearby Belgic settlement and was first occupied by the Romans in 44–43 BC. The earliest English martyr, St Alban, was martyred here, perhaps during the reign of Septimus *Severus. A fragmentary inscription from the site of the forum records the name of the Roman governor *Agricola. The site became deserted in the late 5th or 6th century.

Vesalius, Andreas (1514–1564) Belgian physician who revolutionized anatomy by performing postmortem dissections and making use of illustrations to teach anatomy. Vesalius upset the authority of *Galen, and his book – the first real textbook of anatomy – marked the beginning of biology as a science.

Vespasian (9–79) also known as **Titus Flavius Vespasianus**, Roman emperor from AD 69. Proclaimed emperor by his soldiers while he was campaigning in Palestine, he reorganized the eastern provinces, and was a capable administrator. He was responsible for the construction of the Colosseum in Rome, which was completed by his son *Titus.

Vespucci, Amerigo (1454–1512) Florentine merchant. The Americas were named after him as a result of the widespread circulation of his accounts of his explorations. His accounts of the voyage from 1499 to 1501 include descriptions of places he could not possibly have reached (the Pacific Ocean, British Columbia, Antarctica).

Vesta in Roman mythology, the goddess of the hearth, equivalent with the Greek Hestia. In Rome, the sacred flame in her shrine at the Forum represented the spirit of the community, and was kept constantly alight by the six **Vestal Virgins**.

Vestmannaeyjar English **Westman Islands**, small group of islands off the south coast of Iceland. The volcanic island of Surtsey emerged from the ocean in 1963, and in 1973 the volcano Helgafell erupted, causing the population of 5,200 to be temporarily evacuated and adding 2.5 sq km/1 sq mi to the islands' area. The eruption created the volcanic cone of Eldfell. Heimaey, the largest of the islands, is one of Iceland's chief fishing ports.

Vesuvius Italian **Vesuvio**, active volcano in Campania, Italy, 15 km/9 mi southeast of Naples, Italy; height 1,277 m/4,190 ft (1969; the height of the main cone changes with each eruption). In AD 79 it destroyed the cities of Pompeii, Herculaneum, and Stabiae. It is the only active volcano on the European mainland.

veto (Latin 'I forbid') exercise by a sovereign, branch of legislature, or other political power, of the right to prevent the enactment or operation of a law, or the taking of some course of action.

VHF abbreviation for very high frequency, referring to radio waves that have very short wavelengths (10 m to 1 m). They are used for interference-free FM transmissions (see *frequency modulation).

VHF transmitters have a relatively short range, producing frequencies in the 30–300 MHz band.

vibraphone electrophonic percussion instrument resembling a *xylophone but with metal keys. Electrically driven discs spin within resonating tubes under each key to add a tremulant effect that can be controlled in length with a foot pedal.

vibrato in music, a tiny and rapid fluctuation of pitch for dynamic and expressive effect, used mostly by string players and singers. It is different from a tremolo, which is a rapid fluctuation in intensity (rapid repeating) of the same note.

viburnum any of a group of small trees or shrubs belonging to the honeysuckle family, found in temperate and subtropical regions, including the wayfaring tree, the laurustinus, and the guelder rose of Europe and Asia, and the North American blackhaws and arrowwoods. (Genus *Viburnum*, family Caprifoliaceae.)

Vichy government in World War II, the right-wing government of unoccupied France after the country's defeat by the Germans in June 1940, named after the spa town of Vichy, France, where the national assembly was based under Prime Minister Pétain until the liberation in 1944. **Vichy France** was that part of France not occupied by German troops until November 1942. Authoritarian and collaborationist, the Vichy regime cooperated with the Germans even after they had moved to the unoccupied zone in November 1942. It imprisoned some 135,000 people, interned another 70,000, deported some 76,000 Jews, and sent 650,000 French workers to Germany.

Victor Emmanuel three kings of Italy, including:
Victor Emmanuel II (1820–1878) First king of united Italy from 1861. He became king of Sardinia on the abdication of his father Charles Albert 1849. In 1855 he allied Sardinia with France and the UK in the Crimean War. In 1859 in alliance with the French he defeated the Austrians and annexed Lombardy. By 1860 most of Italy had come under his rule, and in 1861 he was proclaimed king of Italy. In 1870 he made Rome his capital.

Victor Emmanuel III (1869–1947) King of Italy from the assassination of his father, Umberto I, in 1900. He acquiesced in the Fascist regime of Mussolini from 1922 and, after the dictator's fall in 1943, relinquished power to his son Umberto II, who cooperated with the Allies. Victor Emmanuel formally abdicated in 1946.

Victoria state of southeast Australia; bounded on the north and northeast by New South Wales, from which it is separated by the River Murray; on the west by South Australia; and on the south and southeast by the Southern Ocean, Bass Strait, and the Pacific Ocean; area 227,600 sq km/87,876 sq mi; population (1996) 4,373,500. The capital is *Melbourne. Produce includes wool, beef, dairy products, tobacco, wheat, wine, dried fruit, orchard fruits, and vegetables. Gold, brown coal, gypsum, kaolin, and bauxite are mined, and there are oil, natural gas, electronics, food processing, chemical, pharmaceutical, machinery, car, textile, wine, aquaculture, wool, and building material industries.

Victoria port and capital of *British Columbia, Canada, on the southeastern tip of Vancouver Island, overlooking the Strait of Juan de Fuca, 132 km/83 mi west of mainland Vancouver; population (1996 est) 73,500. It is a manufacturing, tourist, and retirement centre, and has a naval base. Industries include shipbuilding, food-processing, sawmilling, fishing, and the manufacture of chemicals, clothing, and furniture.

Victoria (1819–1901) Queen of the UK from 1837, when she succeeded her uncle *William IV, and Empress of India from 1877. In 1840 she married Prince *Albert of Saxe-Coburg and Gotha. Her relations with her prime ministers ranged from the affectionate (Melbourne and Disraeli) to the occasionally stormy (Peel, Palmerston, and Gladstone). Her Golden Jubilee in 1887 and Diamond Jubilee in 1897 marked a waning of republican sentiment, which had developed with her withdrawal from public life on Albert's death in 1861.

Victoria Cross British decoration for conspicuous bravery in wartime, instituted by Queen Victoria in 1856.

Victoria Falls or **Mosi-oa-tunya** 'smoke that thunders', waterfall on the River Zambezi, on the Zambia–Zimbabwe border. The river is 1,700 m/5,580 ft wide and drops 120 m/400 ft to flow through a gorge 30 m/100 ft wide. During the rainy season approximately 20,000 cu m/706,292 cu ft of water pours over the brink. The falls were named after Queen Victoria by the Scottish explorer David Livingstone in 1855.

Victoria, Lake or **Victoria Nyanza** largest lake in Africa and third-largest freshwater lake in the world; area over 68,800 sq km/26,560 sq mi; length 410 km/255 mi; average depth 80 m/260 ft. It lies on the Equator at an altitude of 1,136 m/3,728 ft, bounded by Uganda, Kenya, and Tanzania. It is a source of the River Nile.

Victorian style of architecture, furnituremaking, and decorative art covering the reign of Queen Victoria, from 1837 to 1901. The era was influenced by significant industrial and urban development, and the massive expansion of the British Empire. Victorian style was often very ornate, markedly so in architecture, where there was more than one 'revival' of earlier styles, beginning with a lengthy competition between the **classic** and **Gothic** schools. Gothic Revival drew on the original Gothic architecture of medieval times. The Gothic boom had begun in 1818, when Parliament voted a million pounds for building 214 new Anglican churches. No fewer than 174 of them were constructed in a Gothic or near-Gothic style, and for nearly a century, most churches in England were Gothic in design. Despite the popularity of extravagant decoration, Renaissance or classic styles were also favoured for public buildings, examples being St George's Hall, Liverpool (1815), and Birmingham Town Hall (1832–50).

vicuña *ruminant mammal *Lama vicugna* of the camel family that lives in herds on the Andean plateau. It can run at speeds of 50 kph/30 mph. It has good eyesight, fair hearing, and a poor sense of smell. Hunted close to extinction for its meat and soft brown fur, which was used in textile manufacture, the vicuña is now a protected species. Its populations are increasing thanks to strict conservation measures; by 1996 they had reached 100,000–200,000. The vicuña is listed on CITES Appendix 2 (vulnerable). It is related to the *alpaca, the *guanaco, and the *llama.

video camera or **camcorder** portable television camera that records moving pictures electronically on magnetic tape. It produces an electrical output signal corresponding to rapid line-by-line scanning of the field of view. The output is recorded on video cassette and is played back on a television screen via a video

cassette recorder. From the mid 1990s, these machines began to be replaced by digital versions which store images on memory cards that can be downloaded onto computers or played directly via DVD players.

videotape recorder (VTR) device for recording pictures and sound on cassettes or spools of magnetic tape. The first commercial VTR was launched in 1956 for the television broadcasting industry, but from the late 1970s cheaper models developed for home use, to record broadcast programmes for future viewing and to view rented or owned video cassettes of commercial films.

Vienna German **Wien**, capital city and autonomous region of Austria, on the River Danube at the foot of the Wiener Wald (Vienna Woods); population (2001 est) 1,562,700, area 415 sq km/160 sq mi. Although contained within the territory of Lower Austria, it is a separate province.

Vienna, Congress of international conference held from 1814 to 1815 which agreed the settlement of Europe after the Napoleonic Wars. National representatives included the Austrian foreign minister Metternich, Alexander I of Russia, the British foreign secretary Castlereagh and military commander Wellington, and the French politician Talleyrand.

Vientiane Lao **Viangchan**, ('City of the Moon') capital, largest city, and chief port of Laos, lying in the north on the Mekong River, on the border with Thailand; population (2002 est) 189,600, conurbation 528,100. Though the Mekong is navigable only by small vessels, Vientiane's strategic position on one of the main waterways of southeast Asia has helped it to become a centre for government, commerce, and religion for over a millennium. Noted for its pagodas, canals, and houses on stilts, it is situated in a rich agricultural area and is a trading centre for forest products and textiles.

Vietnam

formerly **part of French Indo-China (1884–1945), communist Democratic Republic of Vietnam (in north) (1945–75), non-communist Republic of Vietnam (in south) (1949–75)**

National name: *Công-hòa xã-hôi chu-nghia Viêt Nam/ Socialist Republic of Vietnam*

Area: 329,600 sq km/127,258 sq mi

Capital: Hanoi

Major towns/cities: Ho Chi Minh City (formerly Saigon), Haiphong, Da Nang, Can Tho, Nha Trang, Bien Hoa, Hué

Major ports: Ho Chi Minh City (formerly Saigon), Da Nang, Haiphong

Physical features: Red River and Mekong deltas, centre of cultivation and population; tropical rainforest; mountainous in north and northwest

Head of state: Tran Duc Luong from 1997

Head of government: Phan Van Khai from 1997

Political system: communist

Political executive: communist

Political party Communist Party

Currency: dong

GNI per capita (PPP): (US$) 2,240 (2002 est)

Exports: crude petroleum, rice (leading exporter), textiles and garments, footwear, coal, coffee, marine products, handicrafts, light industrial goods, rubber, nuts, tea, tin. Principal market: Japan 17.1% (2001)

Population: 81,377,000 (2003 est)

Language: Vietnamese (official), French, English, Khmer, Chinese, local languages

Religion: mainly Buddhist; Christian, mainly Roman Catholic (8–10%); Taoist, Confucian, Hos Hoa, and Cao Dai sects

Life expectancy: 67 (men); 72 (women) (2000–05)

Chronology

300 BC: Rise of Dong Son culture.

111 BC: Came under Chinese rule.

1st–6th centuries AD: Southern Mekong delta region controlled by independent Indianized Funan kingdom.

939: Chinese overthrown by Ngo Quyen at battle of Bach Dang River; first Vietnamese dynasty founded.

11th century: Theravada Buddhism promoted.

15th century: North and South Vietnam united, as kingdom of Champa in the south was destroyed in 1471.

16th century: Contacts with French missionaries and European traders as political power became decentralized.

early 19th century: Under Emperor Nguyen Anh authority was briefly recentralized.

1858–84: Conquered by France and divided into protectorates of Tonkin (North Vietnam) and Annam (South Vietnam).

1887: Became part of French Indo-China Union, which included Cambodia and Laos.

late 19th–early 20th century: Development of colonial economy based in south on rubber and rice, drawing migrant labourers from north.

1930: Indo-Chinese Communist Party (ICP) formed by Ho Chi Minh to fight for independence.

1941: Occupied by Japanese during World War II; ICP formed Vietminh as guerrilla resistance force designed to overthrow Japanese-installed puppet regime headed by Bao Dai, Emperor of Annam.

1945: Japanese removed from Vietnam at end of World War II; Vietminh, led by Ho Chi Minh, in control of much of the country, declared independence.

1946: Vietminh war began against French, who tried to reassert colonial control and set up noncommunist state in south in 1949.

1954: France decisively defeated at Dien Bien Phu. Vietnam divided along 17th parallel between communist-controlled north and US-backed south.

1963: Ngo Dinh Diem, leader of South Vietnam, overthrown in military coup by Lt-Gen Nguyen Van Thieu.

1964: US combat troops entered Vietnam War as North Vietnamese army began to attack South and allegedly attacked US destroyers in the Tonkin Gulf.

1969: Death of Ho Chi Minh, who was succeeded as Communist Party leader by Le Duan. US forces, which numbered 545,000 at their peak, gradually began to be withdrawn from Vietnam as a result of domestic opposition to the rising casualty toll.

1973: Paris ceasefire agreement provided for the withdrawal of US troops and release of US prisoners of war.

1975: Saigon captured by North Vietnam, violating Paris Agreements.

1976: Socialist Republic of Vietnam proclaimed. Hundreds of thousands of southerners became political prisoners; many more fled abroad. Collectivization extended to south.

1978: Diplomatic relations severed with China. Admission into Comecon. Vietnamese invasion of Cambodia.

1979: Sino-Vietnamese 17-day border war; 700,000 Chinese and middle-class Vietnamese fled abroad as refugee 'boat people'.

1986: Death of Le Duan and retirement of 'old guard' leaders; pragmatic Nguyen Van Linh became Communist Party leader.

1987–88: Over 10,000 political prisoners were released.

1989: Troops were fully withdrawn from Cambodia.

1991: A Cambodia peace agreement was signed. Relations with China were normalized.

1992: A new constitution was adopted, guaranteeing economic freedoms. Relations with South Korea were normalized.

1994: The US 30-year trade embargo was removed.

1995: Full diplomatic relations were re-established with the USA. Vietnam became a full member of ASEAN.

1997: Diplomatic relations with the USA were restored. Tran Duc Luong and Phan Van Khai were elected president and prime minister respectively. The size of the standing army was reduced.

1998: The Vietnamese currency was devalued. A new emphasis was placed on agricultural development after export and GDP growth slumped to 3%.

1999: Vietnam signed a trade agreement with the USA, encouraging foreign investment.

2000: US president Clinton visited Vietnam.

2001: Nong Duc Manh was elected as Communist Party leader, one of his policies being the increased industrialization of Vietnam.

2002: Seizure of unauthorised books by leading dissidents.

2003: The National Assembly appointed Tran Duc Luong and Phan Van Khai for second terms.

Vietnam War 1954–75, war from 1954 to 1975 between communist North Vietnam and US-backed South Vietnam, in which North Vietnam aimed to conquer South Vietnam and unite the country as a communist state. North Vietnam was supported by communist rebels from South Vietnam, the Vietcong. The USA, in supporting the South against the North, aimed to prevent the spread of communism in Southeast Asia, but at the end of the war North and South Vietnam were reunited as a socialist republic.

Vijayanagar the capital of the last extensive Hindu empire in India between the 14th and 17th centuries, situated on the River Tungabhadra, southern India. The empire attained its peak under the warrior Krishna Deva Raya (reigned 1509–65), when the city had an estimated population of 500,000. Thereafter it came under repeated attack by the Deccani Muslim kingdoms of Ahmadnagar, Bijapur, and Golconda.

Viking either of two US space probes to the planet Mars, each one consisting of an orbiter and a lander. They were launched on 20 August and 9 September 1975, and transmitted colour pictures and analysed the planet's soil.

Viking or **Norseman** one of the inhabitants of Scandinavia in the period 800–1100. They traded with, and raided, much of Europe, and often settled there. In their narrow, shallow-draught, highly manoeuvrable longships, the Vikings penetrated far inland along rivers. They plundered for gold and land, and were equally energetic as colonists – with colonies stretching from North America to central Russia – and as traders, with main trading posts at Birka (near Stockholm) and Hedeby (near Schleswig). The Vikings had a sophisticated literary culture, with *sagas and runic inscriptions, and an organized system of government with an assembly ('thing'). Their kings and chieftains were buried with their ships, together with their possessions.

Viking art sculpture and design of the Vikings, dating from the 8th to 11th century. Viking artists are known for woodcarving and finely wrought personal ornaments in gold and silver, and for an intricate interlacing decorative style similar to that found in *Celtic art. A dragonlike creature, known as the 'Great Beast', is a recurring motif.

villus plural **villi**, small fingerlike projection extending into the interior of the small intestine and increasing the absorptive area of the intestinal wall. Digested nutrients, including sugars and amino acids, pass into the villi and are carried away by the circulating blood.

Vilnius German Wilna; Russian Vilna; Polish **Wilno**, capital of Lithuania, situated on the River Neris; population (1991) 593,000. Vilnius is an important railway crossroads and commercial centre. Its industries include electrical engineering, woodworking, and the manufacture of textiles, chemicals, and foodstuffs.

Vimy Ridge hill in northern France, taken in World War I by Canadian troops during the battle of Arras, April 1917, at the cost of 11,285 lives. It is a spur of the ridge of Notre Dame de Lorette, 8 km/5 mi northeast of Arras.

vincristine *alkaloid extracted from the blue periwinkle plant *Vinca rosea*. Developed as an anticancer agent, it has revolutionized the treatment of childhood acute leukaemias; it is also included in *chemotherapy regimens for some lymphomas (cancers arising in the lymph tissues) and lung and breast cancers. Side effects, such as nerve damage and loss of hair, are severe but usually reversible.

vine or **grapevine** any of a group of climbing woody plants, especially *V. vinifera*, native to Asia Minor and cultivated from antiquity. The fruits (grapes) are eaten or made into wine or other fermented drinks; dried fruits of certain varieties are known as raisins and currants. Many other species of climbing plant are also called vines. (Genus *Vitis*, family Vitaceae.)

Vinland Norse name for the area of North America, probably the coast of Nova Scotia or New England, which the Norse adventurer and explorer Leif Ericsson visited about 1000. It was named after the wild grapes that grew there and is celebrated in an important Norse saga.

Vinson Massif highest point in *Antarctica, rising to 5,140 m/16,863 ft in the Ellsworth Mountains.

viol member of a Renaissance family of bowed six-stringed musical instruments with flat backs, fretted fingerboards, and narrow shoulders that flourished particularly in England about 1540–1700, before their role was taken by the violins. Normally performing as an ensemble or consort, their repertoire is a development of *madrigal style with idiomatic decoration.

viola bowed, string instrument, the second largest member of the violin family. It is also one of the instruments that form the string quartet, where its traditional role is to provide harmonies. It is played tucked under the chin, like the violin, and its four strings are tuned to C3, G3, D4, and A5. With its dark, vibrant tone, it is often used for music of a reflective character, as in Igor Stravinsky's *Elegy* (1944) or Benjamin Britten's *Lachrymae* (1950). Concertos have been written for the viola by composers such as George Telemann, Hector Berlioz, William Walton, Paul Hindemith, and Béla Bartók.

violet any of a group of perennial herbaceous plants found in temperate regions; they have heart-shaped leaves and mauve, blue, or white five-petalled flowers, for example the dog violet *V. canina*, found on sandy heaths, and the fragrant sweet violet *V. odorata*. A *pansy is a kind of violet. (Genus *Viola*, family Violaceae.)

violin bowed, string instrument, the smallest and highest pitched (treble) of the violin family. Its four strings are tuned in fifths to G3, D4, A5, and E5. It is usually played tucked between the shoulder and left side of the chin. The right hand draws the bow across a string causing it to vibrate and produce a note.

VIP abbreviation for **very important person**.

viper any front-fanged venomous snake of the family Viperidae. Vipers range in size from 30 cm/1 ft to 3 m/10 ft, and often have diamond or jagged markings. Most give birth to live young.

Virgil (70–19 BC) born Publius Vergilius Maro, Roman poet. He wrote the *Eclogues* (37 BC), a series of pastoral poems; the *Georgics* (30 BC), four books on the art of farming; and his epic masterpiece, the *Aeneid* (30–19 BC). He was patronized by Maecenas on behalf of Octavian (later the emperor Augustus).

virginal plucked stringed keyboard instrument of the 16th and 17th centuries, often called 'virginals' or 'a pair of virginals' in England, where the term was applied to any quilled keyboard instrument well into the 17th century. The virginal is rectangular or polygonal in shape and is distinguished from the *harpsichord and *spinet by its strings being set at right angles to the keys, rather than parallel with them.

Virgin Birth orthodox Christian belief in the virginal (or immaculate) conception of Jesus through the power of the Holy Spirit at work in the Virgin Mary.

Roman Catholic dogma also asserts the perpetual virginity of Mary, teaching that she bore Jesus in a miraculous way so that she remained a virgin and subsequently had no other children; the brothers and sisters of Jesus, mentioned in the Gospels, are assumed to be Joseph's by a previous marriage.

Virginia officially the Commonwealth of Virginia; called **Old Dominion**, state in eastern USA, bordered to the north by *Maryland and the *District of Columbia, to the west by *Kentucky and *West Virginia, to the south by *North Carolina and *Tennessee; area 102,548 sq km/39,594 sq mi; population (2000) 7,078,500; capital Richmond. It was named after Queen Elizabeth I of England, the virgin queen. In the east it occupies the southern tip of the Delamarva Peninsula and is bordered by the *Atlantic Ocean. The state includes *Chesapeake Bay and the Shenandoah Valley. The most important industries are the service and tourist industries. Virginia's industrial output includes textiles, chemicals, cars, and electrical equipment; agricultural products include tobacco, soybeans, peanuts, and apples. Coal is the most important mineral. Major towns and cities include Virginia Beach, Norfolk, Chesapeake, Newport News, Arlington, Hampton, Alexandria, Portsmouth, and Roanoke. One of the *Thirteen Colonies, the first permanent English settlement was made at Jamestown in 1607, and in 1619 the colonists established the first representative legislature in America. During the American *Civil War, Virginia was the northeastern-most state of the Confederacy. Virginia ratified the US Constitution in 1788, becoming the 10th US state.

Virginia creeper *or* **woodbine** eastern North American climbing vine belonging to the grape family, having tendrils, palmately compound leaves (made up of leaflets arranged like an open hand), green flower clusters, and blue berries eaten by many birds but inedible to humans. (*Parthenocissus quinquefolia*, family Vitaceae.)

Virgin Islands group of about 100 small islands, northernmost of the Leeward Islands in the Antilles, West Indies. Tourism is the main industry. They comprise the **US Virgin Islands** St Thomas (with the capital, Charlotte Amalie), St Croix, St John, and about 50 small islets; area 350 sq km/135 sq mi; total population (2001 est) 122,200; and the **British Virgin Islands** Tortola (with the capital, Road Town), Virgin Gorda, Anegada, and Jost van Dykes, and about 40 islets (11 islands are inhabited); area 150 sq km/58 sq mi; total population (1997 est) 13,400.

Virgo zodiacal constellation of the northern hemisphere, the second-largest in the sky. It is represented as a maiden holding an ear of wheat, marked by first-magnitude *Spica, Virgo's brightest star. The Sun passes through Virgo from late September to the end of October. In astrology, the dates for Virgo are between about 23 August and 22 September (see *precession).

virtual memory in computing, a technique whereby a portion of the computer backing storage, or external, *memory is used as an extension of its immediate-access, or internal, memory. The contents of an area of the immediate-access memory are stored on, say, a hard disk while they are not needed, and brought back into main memory when required.

virtual reality advanced form of computer simulation, in which a participant has the illusion of being part of an artificial environment. The participant views the environment through two tiny television screens (one for each eye) built into a visor. Sensors detect movements of the participant's head or body, causing the apparent viewing position to change. Gloves (datagloves) fitted with sensors may be worn, which allow the participant seemingly to pick up and move objects in the environment.

virus in computing, a piece of software that can replicate and transfer itself from one computer to another, without the user being aware of it. Some viruses are relatively harmless, but others can damage or destroy data. The earliest was the Brain virus, written in Pakistan in 1986.

virus infectious particle consisting of a core of nucleic acid (*DNA or RNA) enclosed in a protein shell. They are extremely small and cause disease. They differ from all other forms of life in that they are not cells – they are acellular. They are able to function and reproduce only if they can invade a living cell to use the cell's system to replicate themselves. In the process they may disrupt or alter the host cell's own DNA. They use the cell they invade to make more virus particles that are then released. This usually kills the cell. The healthy human body reacts by producing an antiviral protein, *interferon, which prevents the infection spreading to adjacent cells. There are around 5,000 species of virus known to science (1998), although there may be as many as half a million actually in existence. (See diagram, p. 964.)

viscacha Argentine Pampas and scrubland-dwelling rodent *Lagostomus maximus* of the chinchilla family. It is up to 70 cm/2.2 ft long with a 20 cm/8 in tail, and weighs 7 kg/15 lb. It is grey and black and has a large head and small ears. Viscachas live in warrens of up to 30 individuals. They are usually nocturnal and feed on grasses, roots, and seeds.

viscose yellowish, syrupy solution made by treating cellulose with sodium hydroxide and carbon disulphide or with cuprammonium liquor and sodium hydroxide. The solution is then regenerated as continuous filament (*rayon) by forcing it through very small holes and solidifying it (in a process known as *spinning). Forcing viscose through a slit instead of small holes produces *cellophane.

viscosity the resistance of a fluid to flow, caused by its internal friction, which makes it resist flowing past a solid surface or other layers of the fluid. Treacle and other thick, sticky liquids are highly viscous liquids. Water and petrol are runny liquids and have low viscosity.

viscount (medieval Latin *vicecomes* 'in place of a count/earl') in the UK *peerage, the fourth degree of nobility, between earl and baron.

Vishnu in Hinduism, the second in the triad of gods (with *Brahma and *Shiva) representing three aspects of *Brahman, the supreme spirit. Vishnu is the **Preserver**, and is believed to have assumed human appearance in nine avatars, or incarnations, in such forms as *Rama and *Krishna. His worshippers are the Vaishnavas.

Visigoth member of the western branch of the *Goths, an East Germanic people.

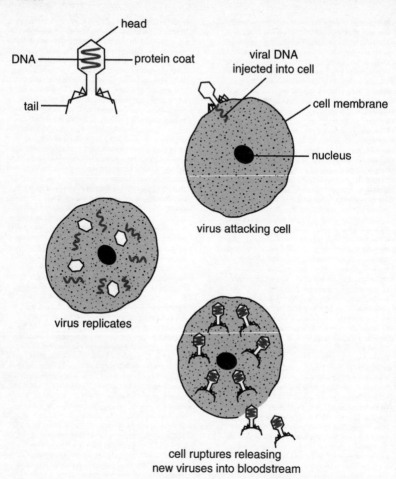

head

DNA — protein coat

tail

viral DNA
injected into cell

cell membrane

nucleus

virus attacking cell

virus replicates

cell ruptures releasing
new viruses into bloodstream

virus How a virus replicates itself to spread infection through the body.

vision ability or act of seeing. Light that enters the *eye
is focused by the eye lens, creating a sharp image on the
*retina. Electrical signals from the retina travel down
the optic nerve where they are interpreted by the brain.

vision defect any abnormality of the eye that causes
less-than-perfect sight. Common defects are short-
sightedness or *myopia; long-sightedness or
*hypermetropia; lack of *accommodation or
presbyopia; and *astigmatism. Other eye defects
include colour blindness.

Vistula Polish Wisła, river in Poland that rises in the
Carpathian Mountains and runs northwest to the

Baltic Sea at Gdansk; length 1,090 km/677 mi. It is
heavily polluted, carrying into the Baltic every year
large quantities of industrial and agricultural waste,
including phosphorus, oil, nitrogen, mercury,
cadmium, and zinc.

visual display unit (VDU) computer terminal
consisting of a keyboard for input data and a screen for
displaying output. The screen and its housing are now
more usually termed a monitor.

vitamin any of various chemically-unrelated organic
(carbon-containing) compounds that are necessary in
small quantities for the normal functioning of the

mammalian body. Many act as coenzymes, small molecules that enable *enzymes to function effectively. Vitamins must be supplied by the diet because the body generally cannot make them. Deficiency of a vitamin may lead to a metabolic disorder ('deficiency disease'), which can be remedied by sufficient intake of the vitamin. Vitamins are generally classified as **water-soluble** (B and C) or **fat-soluble** (A, D, E, and K).

vitamin A another name for *retinol.

vitamin B₁ another name for *thiamine.

vitamin B₆ another name for *pyridoxine.

vitamin B₁₂ another name for *cyanocobalamin.

vitamin B₂ another name for *riboflavin.

vitamin C another name for *ascorbic acid.

vitamin D another name for *cholecalciferol.

vitamin E another name for *tocopherol.

vitamin H another name for *biotin.

vitamin K another name for *phytomenadione.

vitreous humour transparent jellylike substance behind the lens of the vertebrate *eye. It gives rigidity to the spherical form of the eye and allows light to pass through to the retina.

vitriol former name for any of a number of sulphate salts. Blue, green, and white vitriols are copper, ferrous, and zinc sulphate, respectively. **Oil of vitriol** is a former name for sulphuric acid.

Vivaldi, Antonio Lucio (1678–1741) Italian Baroque composer, violinist, and conductor. One of the most prolific composers of his day, he was particularly influential through his concertos, several of which were transcribed by Johann Sebastian Bach. He wrote 23 symphonies; 75 sonatas; over 400 concertos, including *The Four Seasons* (1725) for violin and orchestra; over 40 operas; and much sacred music. His work was largely neglected until the 1930s.

viviparous in animals, a method of reproduction in which the embryo develops inside the body of the female from which it gains nourishment (in contrast to *oviparous and *ovoviviparous). Vivipary is best developed in placental mammals, but also occurs in some arthropods, fishes, amphibians, and reptiles that have placentalike structures. In plants, it is the formation of young plantlets or bulbils instead of flowers. The term also describes seeds that germinate prematurely, before falling from the parent plant.

vivisection literally, cutting into a living animal. Used originally to mean experimental surgery or dissection practised on a live subject, the term is often used by *antivivisection campaigners to include any experiment on animals, surgical or otherwise.

Vladivostok city on the western shore of the Sea of Japan, on a peninsula extending into Peter the Great Bay; population (1996 est) 627,000. It is the capital of the Primorski (Maritime) Krai of the Russian Federation, and one of the most important economic and cultural centres of the Russian Far East, where it is the largest city. Vladivostok is a terminus of the Trans-Siberian Railway (9,224 km/mi from Moscow) and the Northern Sea Route, centre of communications for the Pacific territories, the largest Russian port on the Pacific, and the chief base of the Pacific Fleet. The port is kept open by icebreakers during winter.

vocal cords paired folds, ridges, or cords of tissue within a mammal's larynx, and a bird's syrinx. Air expelled from the lungs passes between these folds or membranes and makes them vibrate, producing sounds. Muscles in the larynx change the pitch of the sounds produced, by adjusting the tension of the vocal cords.

vodka strong colourless alcoholic beverage distilled from rye, potatoes, or barley.

Vojvodina autonomous province in northern Serbia and Montenegro, area 21,500 sq km/8,299 sq mi; population (1991 est) 2,012,500, including 1,110,000 Serbs and 390,000 Hungarians, as well as Croat, Slovak, Romanian, and Ukrainian minorities. Its capital is Novi Sad. In September 1990 Serbia effectively stripped Vojvodina of its autonomous status, causing antigovernment and anticommunist riots in early 1991.

volatile describing a substance that readily passes from the liquid to the vapour phase. Volatile substances have a high *vapour pressure.

volcanic rock another name for *extrusive rock, igneous rock formed on the Earth's surface.

volcano crack in the Earth's crust through which hot *magma (molten rock) and gases well up. The magma is termed **lava** when it reaches the surface. A volcanic mountain, usually cone-shaped with a crater on top, is formed around the opening, or vent, by the build-up of solidified lava and ash (rock fragments). Most volcanoes occur on plate margins (see *plate tectonics), where the movements of plates generate magma or allow it to rise from the mantle beneath. However, a number are found far from plate-margin activity, on *hot spots where the Earth's crust is thin, for example in Hawaii. There are two main types of volcano: composite volcanoes and shield volcanoes. (See diagram, p. 966.)

vole any of various rodents of the family Cricetidae, subfamily Microtinae, distributed over Europe, Asia, and North America, and related to hamsters and lemmings. They are characterized by stout bodies and short tails. They have brown or grey fur, and blunt noses, and some species reach a length of 30 cm/12 in. They feed on grasses, seeds, aquatic plants, and insects. Many show remarkable fluctuations in numbers over 3–4 year cycles.

Volga ancient **Rha**, longest river in Europe, entirely within the territory of the Russian Federation. The Volga has a total length 3,685 km/2,290 mi, 3,540 km/2,200 mi of which are navigable. It rises in the Valdai plateau northwest of Moscow, and flows into the Caspian Sea 88 km/55 mi below the city of Astrakhan. The Volga basin drains most of the central and eastern parts of European Russia, its total drainage area being 1,360,000 sq km/525,100 sq mi.

volleyball indoor and outdoor team game played on a court between two teams of six players each. A net is placed across the centre of the court, and players hit the ball with their hands over it, the aim being to ground it in the opponents' court.

volt symbol V, SI unit of electromotive force or electric potential (see *potential, electric). A small battery has a potential of 1.5 volts, while a high-tension transmission line may carry up to 765,000 volts. The domestic electricity supply in the UK is 230 volts (lowered from 240 volts in 1995); it is 110 volts in the USA.

Volta main river in Ghana, about 1,600 km/1,000 mi long, with two main upper branches, the **Black Volta** and **White Volta**. It has been dammed at Akosombo to provide power.

composite
volcano

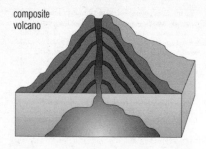

cinder
cone

shield volcano

volcano There are two main types of volcano, but three distinctive cone shapes. Composite volcanoes emit a stiff, rapidly solidifying lava which forms high, steep-sided cones. Volcanoes that regularly throw out ash build up flatter domes known as cinder cones. The lava from a shield volcano is not ejected violently, flowing over the crater rim forming a broad low profile.

**Volta, Alessandro Giuseppe Antonio Anastasio
(1745–1827)** Count Volta, Italian physicist who invented the first electric cell (the voltaic pile, in 1800), the electrophorus (an early electrostatic generator, in 1775), and an *electroscope.

voltage commonly used term for *potential difference (PD).

Voltaire (1694–1778) pen-name of François-Marie Arouet, French writer. He is the embodiment of the 18th-century *Enlightenment. He wrote histories, books of political analysis and philosophy, essays on science and literature, plays, poetry, and the satirical fable *Candide* (1759), his best-known work. A trenchant satirist of social and political evils, he was often forced to flee from his enemies and was twice imprisoned. His works include *Lettres philosophiques sur les Anglais/*

Philosophical Letters on the English (1733) (essays in favour of English ways, thought, and political practice), *Le Siècle de Louis XIV/The Age of Louis XIV* (1751), and *Dictionnaire philosophique/Philosophical Dictionary* (1764).

volume in geometry, the space occupied by a three-dimensional (3D) solid object. A *prism such as a *cube, cuboid, or a *cylinder has a volume equal to the *area of the base multiplied by the height. For a *pyramid or *cone, the volume is equal to one-third of the area of the base multiplied by the perpendicular height. The volume of a *sphere is equal to $\frac{4}{3} \times \pi r^3$, where r is the radius. Volumes of irregular solids may be calculated by the technique of *integration.

**von Braun, Wernher Magnus Maximilian
(1912–1977)** German rocket engineer responsible for Germany's rocket development programme in World War II (V1 and V2), who later worked for the space agency *NASA in the USA. He also invented the Saturn rocket (Saturn V) that sent the *Apollo* project spacecraft to the Moon in 1969.

voodoo set of magical beliefs and practices, followed in some parts of Africa, South America, and the West Indies, especially Haiti. It arose in the 17th century on slave plantations as a combination of Roman Catholicism and West African religious traditions; believers retain membership in the Roman Catholic Church. It was once practiced in New Orleans and other areas of southern USA by African-Americans. Beliefs include the existence of **loa**, spirits who closely involve themselves in human affairs, and some of whose identities mesh with those of Christian saints. The loa are invoked by the priest (*houngan*) or priestess (*manbo*) at ceremonies, during which members of the congregation become possessed by the spirits and go into a trance.

Vorarlberg (German 'in front of the Arlberg') Alpine federal state of Austria, bounded to the north by Bavaria, to the west by Lake Constance, the Rhine, and Liechtenstein, to the east by north Tirol, and to the south by Switzerland; area 2,601 sq km/1,004 sq mi; population (2001 est) 351,400. Its capital is Bregenz.

Vorticism short-lived British literary and artistic movement (1912–15), influenced by cubism and Futurism and led by Wyndham *Lewis. Lewis believed that painting should reflect the complexity and rapid change of the modern world; he painted in a harsh, angular, semi-abstract style. The last Vorticist exhibition was held in 1915.

Vosges mountain range in eastern France near the Franco-German frontier between the *départements* of Haut-Rhin and Vosges, 250 km/155 mi in length and rising to its highest point at the Ballon de Guebwiller (1,422 m/4,667 ft). The Vosges forms the western edge of the Rhine rift valley. It gives its name to the *département* of Vosges. The Vosges is separated from the Jura Mountains to the south by the Belfort Gap.

Voskhod (Russian 'ascent') either of two Soviet spacecraft launched in October 1964 and March 1965. *Voskhod* was modified from the single-seat *Vostok*, and was the first spacecraft capable of carrying two or three cosmonauts. During *Voskhod* 2's flight in 1965, Aleksi Leonov made the first space walk.

Vostok (Russian 'east') first Soviet spacecraft, used 1961–63. *Vostok* was a metal sphere 2.3 m/7.5 ft in

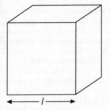

volume of a **cube**
= length³
= l^3

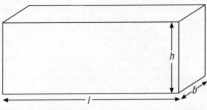

volume of a **cuboid**
= length × breadth × height
= $l \times b \times h$

volume of a **cylinder**
= π × (radius of cross section)² × height
= $\pi r^2 h$

volume of a **cone**
= ⅓ π × (radius of cross section)² × height
= $\frac{1}{3}\pi r^2 h$

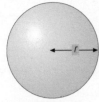

volume of a **sphere**
= ⅘ π radius³
= $\frac{4}{3}\pi r^3$

volume Volume of common three-dimensional shapes.

diameter, capable of carrying one cosmonaut. It made flights lasting up to five days. *Vostok 1* carried the first person into space, Yuri *Gagarin.

vote expression of opinion by *ballot, show of hands, or other means. In systems that use direct vote, the *plebiscite and *referendum are fundamental mechanisms. In parliamentary elections the results can be calculated in a number of ways. The main electoral systems are: **simple plurality** or **first past the post**, with single-member constituencies (USA, UK, India, Canada); **absolute majority**, achieved for example by the **alternative vote**, where the voter, in single-member constituencies, chooses a candidate by marking preferences (Australia), or by the **second ballot**, where, if a clear decision is not reached immediately, a second ballot is held (France, Egypt); **proportional representation**, achieved for example by the **party list** system (Israel, most countries of Western Europe, and several in South America), the **additional member** system or AMS (Germany), the **single transferable vote** (Ireland and Malta), and the **limited vote** Japan's upper house and Liechtenstein). Revised voting systems were adopted by Italy and New Zealand in 1993, in which both houses were elected by a combination of simple majority voting and proportional representation on the AMS model. In Japan AMS was adopted for the lower house in 1994.

Voyager either of two US space probes. Voyager 1, launched on 5 September 1977, passed the planet Jupiter in March 1979, and reached Saturn in November 1980. Voyager 2 was launched earlier, on 20 August 1977, on a slower trajectory that took it past Jupiter in July 1979, Saturn in August 1981, Uranus in January 1986, and Neptune in August 1989. Like the Pioneer probes, the Voyagers are on their way out of the Solar System; by March 2001, Voyager 1 had travelled 13.8 billion km/ 8.6 billion mi from Earth, and Voyager 2 had covered 13 billion km/8 billion mi.

Vulcan or **Vulcanus** in Roman mythology, the god of fire and destruction, later identified with the Greek god *Hephaestus.

vulcanization technique for hardening rubber by heating and chemically combining it with sulphur. The process also makes the rubber stronger and more elastic. If the sulphur content is increased to as much as 30%, the product is the inelastic solid known as ebonite. More expensive alternatives to sulphur, such as selenium and tellurium, are used to vulcanize rubber for specialized products such as vehicle tyres. The process was discovered by US inventor Charles *Goodyear in 1839 and patented in 1844.

vulture any of various carrion-eating birds of prey in the order Falconiformes, with naked heads and necks, strong hooked bills, and keen senses of sight and smell. Vultures are up to 1 m/3.3 ft long, with wingspans of up to 3.7 m/12 ft. The plumage is usually dark, and the head brightly coloured.

wadi in arid regions of the Middle East, a steep-sided valley containing an intermittent stream that flows in the wet season.

Wagner, (Wilhelm) Richard (1813–1883) German opera composer. He revolutionized the 19th-century idea of opera, seeing it as a wholly new art form in which musical, poetic, and scenic elements should come together through such devices as the *leitmotif. His operas include *Tannhäuser* (1845) *Lohengrin* (1850), and *Tristan und Isolde* (1865). In 1872 he founded the Festival Theatre in Bayreuth; his masterpiece *Der Ring des Nibelungen/The Ring of the Nibelung*, a sequence of four operas, was first performed there in 1876. His last work, *Parsifal*, was produced in 1882.

Wagner, Otto (1841–1918) Viennese architect. Initially working in the art nouveau style, for example the Vienna Stadtbahn 1894–97, he later rejected ornament for rationalism, as in the Post Office Savings Bank, Vienna, 1904–06. He influenced such Viennese architects as Josef Hoffmann, Adolf Loos, and Joseph Olbrich.

wagtail slim, narrow-billed bird of the genus *Motacilla*, in the family Motacillidae, order Passeriformes, about 18 cm/7 in long, with a characteristic flicking movement of the tail. There are about 30 species, found mostly in Eurasia and Africa.

Wahabi puritanical Saudi Islamic sect founded by Muhammad ibn-Abd-al-Wahab (1703–1792), which regards all other sects as heretical. By the early 20th century it had spread throughout the Arabian peninsula; it still remains the official ideology of the Saudi Arabian kingdom.

Wailing Wall or (in Judaism) **Western Wall** the remaining part of the *Temple in Jerusalem, a sacred site of pilgrimage and prayer for Jews. Midrash tradition holds that this portion of wall avoided destruction in AD 70 because the Holy Spirit (Shekinah) resided there. For this reason, people will pray there aloud ('wailing'), slip prayers on pieces of paper in between the stones, and sometimes hold ceremonies such as *bar mitzvahs.

Walcott, Derek Walton (1930–) St Lucian writer, poet, and playwright. His work fuses Caribbean and European, classical and contemporary elements, and deals with the divisions within colonial society and his own search for cultural identity. His works include the long poem *Omeros* (1990), and his adaptation for the stage of Homer's *Odyssey* (1992); his *Collected Poems*

were published in 1986. He was awarded the Nobel Prize for Literature in 1992. His biography of French impressionist painter Pissarro, *Tiepolo's Hound*, was published in 2000.

Wales Welsh **Cymru**, constituent part of the United Kingdom, in the west between the British Channel and the Irish Sea; area 20,780 sq km/8,020 sq mi; population (2001 est) 2,903,100. The capital is *Cardiff, and other major towns and cities include Swansea, Wrexham, Newport, and Carmarthen. Geographical features include the Snowdonia Mountains (Snowdon, at 1,085 m/3,560 ft, is the highest point in England and Wales), the Black Mountains, the Brecon Beacons, the Black Forest ranges, and the rivers Severn, Wye, Usk, and Dee. There are oil refineries and open-cast coal mines, but traditional industries have declined, and the last deep coal mine in north Wales closed in 1996. Varied modern and high-technology ventures are being developed, and Wales has the largest concentration of Japanese-owned plants in the UK. In 1999 the Welsh Assembly was established, with some powers devolved from London.

Walesa, Lech (1943–) Polish trade union leader, president of Poland 1990–95. One of the founding members of the *Solidarity free-trade-union movement, which emerged to challenge the communist government during strikes in the Gdansk shipyards in August 1980. Walesa led the movement to become a national force. He was awarded the Nobel Prize for Peace in 1983 for his work with the Solidarity movement. After his election as president, he gradually became estranged from Solidarity. In 1997 he formed a Christian Democratic party, which was, however, unlikely to make a significant impact on Polish political life.

Wales, Church in the Welsh Anglican Church, independent from the *Church of England.

Wales, Prince of title conferred on the eldest son of the UK's sovereign. Prince *Charles was invested as 21st prince of Wales at Caernarfon in 1969 by his mother, Elizabeth II.

walkabout Australian Aboriginal term for a nomadic ritual return into the bush by an urbanized Aboriginal; also used more casually for any official public excursion.

Walker, Alice Malsenior (1944–) US poet, novelist, critic, and essay writer. She has been active in the US civil-rights movement since the 1960s and, as a black woman, wrote about the double burden of racist and sexist oppression, about colonialism, and the quest for political and spiritual recovery. Her novel *The Color Purple* (1982; filmed 1985), told in the form of letters, won a Pulitzer Prize. Her other works include *Possessing the Secret of Joy* (1992), which deals passionately with female circumcision; *By the Light of My Father's Smile* (1998); and *The Way Forward is with a Broken Heart* (2001).

Wallace, Alfred Russel (1823–1913) Welsh naturalist who collected animal and plant specimens in South America and Southeast Asia, and independently arrived at a theory of evolution by natural selection similar to that proposed by Charles *Darwin.

Wallace, William (1272–1305) Scottish nationalist who led a revolt against English rule in 1297, won a victory at Stirling, and assumed the title 'governor of Scotland'. *Edward I defeated him at Falkirk in 1298, and Wallace was captured and executed. He was styled Knight in a charter of 1298.

Wallace line imaginary line running down the Lombok Strait in Southeast Asia, between the island of Bali and the islands of Lombok and Sulawesi. It was identified by English naturalist Alfred Russel Wallace as separating the South Asian (Oriental) and Australian biogeographical regions, each of which has its own distinctive animals.

Wallachia independent medieval principality, founded in 1290, with allegiance to Hungary until 1330 and under Turkish rule 1387–1861, when it was united with the neighbouring principality of Moldavia to form Romania.

wallflower European perennial cottage garden plant with fragrant spikes of red, orange, yellow, brown, or purple flowers in spring. (Genus *Cheiranthus cheiri*, family Cruciferae.)

Wallis and Futuna two island groups in the southwestern Pacific Ocean, an overseas territory of France; area 367 sq km/143 sq mi; population (1997 est) 14,800. The people live mostly by subsistence agriculture and farming of livestock, especially pigs and goats. Much food is imported, mainly rice, sugar and beef, as are virtually all manufactured goods. The export trade is very small, chiefly copra and handicrafts. Because of deforestation, through cutting down timber for fuel, soil erosion is a problem, especially in Futuna.

Walloon a French-speaking people of southeastern Belgium and adjacent areas of France. The name 'Walloon' is etymologically linked to 'Welsh'.

Walloon Brabant Flemish **Wallon-Brabant**, province of Belgium, part of the French-speaking Walloon community and region, bordered by Flemish Brabant to the north and Liége, Namur, and Hainaut to the south; area 1,091 sq km/421 sq mi; population (1997 est) 341,600. The province was created in 1995 when the province of Brabant was divided into three autonomous administrative divisions: Flemish Brabant, Walloon Brabant, and Brussels-Capital Region. Its capital is Wavre. The Battle of Waterloo was fought in the northwestern part of the region.

Wall Street the financial centre of the USA, a street on lower Manhattan Island, New York City, on which the New York Stock Exchange is situated; also a synonym for stock dealing in the USA. Office skyscrapers house many of the major banks, trust companies, insurance corporations, and financial institutions of the city; coffee, cotton, metal, produce, and corn exchanges are sited here. Its narrow course follows the line of a stockade wall erected by the Dutch to protect New Amsterdam in 1653.

Wall Street Crash, 1929 panic selling on the New York Stock Exchange following an artificial boom from 1927 to 1929 fed by speculation. On 24 October 1929, 13 million shares changed hands, with further heavy selling on 28 October and the disposal of 16 million shares on 29 October. Many shareholders were ruined, banks and businesses failed, and in the *depression that followed, unemployment rose to approximately 17 million.

walnut deciduous tree, probably originating in southeastern Europe and now widely cultivated elsewhere. It can grow up to 30 m/100 ft high, and produces a full crop of edible nuts about 12 years after planting; the timber is used in furniture and the oil is used in cooking. (Genus *Juglans regia*, family Juglandaceae.)

Walpole, Horace (1717–1797) 4th Earl of Orford, English novelist, letter writer and politician, the son of Robert Walpole. He was a Whig member of Parliament 1741–67. He converted his house at Strawberry Hill, Twickenham (then a separate town southwest of London), into a Gothic castle; his *The Castle of Otranto* (1764) established the genre of the Gothic, or 'romance of terror', novel. More than 4,000 of his letters have been published. He became Earl in 1791.

Walpole, Robert (1676–1745) 1st Earl of Orford, British Whig politician, the first 'prime minister'. As First Lord of the Treasury and chancellor of the Exchequer (1715–17 and 1721–42) he encouraged trade and tried to avoid foreign disputes (until forced into the War of Jenkins' Ear with Spain in 1739).

Walpurga, St (c. 710–c. 779) English abbess who preached Christianity in Germany. **Walpurgis Night**, the eve of 1 May (one of her feast days), became associated with witches' sabbaths and other superstitions. Her feast day is 25 February.

walrus Arctic marine carnivorous mammal *Odobenus rosmarus* of the same family (Otariidae) as the eared *seals. It can reach 4 m/13 ft in length, and weigh up to 1,400 kg/3,000 lb. It has webbed flippers, a bristly moustache, and large tusks. It is gregarious except at breeding time and feeds mainly on molluscs. It has been hunted for its ivory tusks, hide, and blubber; the Alaskan walrus is close to extinction.

Walsingham, Francis (c. 1530–1590) English politician and principal secretary of state to *Elizabeth I from 1573 until his death. A staunch Puritan, he advocated a strong anti-Spanish foreign policy and controlled an efficient government spy network to identify and forestall Roman Catholic conspiracies against the queen. Walsingham's spies uncovered planned assassinations by Francis Throckmorton (1584) and Antony Babington (1586). His exposure of the involvement of *Mary Queen of Scots in the latter plot persuaded Elizabeth to order her execution. Walsingham was knighted for his services in 1577.

Walton, Izaak (1593–1683) English writer. He is known for his classic fishing compendium *The Compleat Angler, or the Contemplative Man's Recreation* (1653). He also wrote lives of the poets John Donne (1658) and George Herbert (1670), and the theologian Richard Hooker (1665).

Walton, William Turner (1902–1983) English composer. Among his works are *Façade* (1923), a series of instrumental pieces designed to be played in conjunction with the recitation of surrealist poems by Edith Sitwell; the oratorio *Belshazzar's Feast* (1931); and *Variations on a Theme by Hindemith* (1963).

waltz ballroom dance in moderate triple time (3/4) that developed in Germany and Austria during the late 18th century from the Austrian *Ländler* (traditional peasants' country dance). Associated particularly with Vienna and the Strauss family, whose works include *The Blue Danube* and *The Emperor Waltz*, and has remained popular up to the present day. Well-known composers of waltzes who use the waltz as a base for works include Frédéric Chopin, Johannes Brahms, and Maurice Ravel.

wampum cylindrical beads ground from sea shells of white and purple, woven into articles of personal adornment and also used as money by American Indians of the northeastern woodlands.

Wandering Jew in medieval legend, a Jew named Ahasuerus, said to have insulted Jesus on his way to Calvary and to have been condemned to wander the world until the Second Coming.

WAP acronym for Wireless Application Protocol, initiative started in the 1990s by Unwired Planet and mobile phone manufacturers Motorola, Nokia, and Ericsson to develop a standard for delivering Web-like applications on *mobile phones and other wireless devices. In theory WAP phones can be used for e-mail and messaging, reading Web pages, shopping, booking tickets, and making other financial transactions, as well as for phone calls. WAP as been superseded to some extent by 3G (third generation) mobile phone technology.

wapiti *or* **elk** species of deer *Cervus canadensis*, native to North America, Europe, and Asia, including New Zealand. It is reddish-brown in colour, about 1.5 m/5 ft at the shoulder, weighs up to 450 kg/1,000 lb, and has antlers up to 1.2 m/4 ft long. It is becoming increasingly rare, although the wapiti population in Yellowstone National Park, USA, was a thriving 25,000 in 1998. In North America, the wapiti is also called an elk.

war act of force, usually on behalf of the state, intended to compel a declared enemy to obey the will of the other. The aim is to render the opponent incapable of further resistance by destroying its capability and will to bear arms in pursuit of its own aims. War can therefore be seen as a continuation of politics carried on with violent and destructive means, as an instrument of policy. Conversely, politics and diplomacy can be seen as attempts to avoid war.

Warbeck, Perkin (c. 1474–1499) Flemish pretender to the English throne. Claiming to be Richard, brother of Edward V, he led a rising against Henry VII in 1497, and was hanged after attempting to escape from the Tower of London.

War between the States another (usually Southern) name for the American *Civil War.

warble fly large, brownish, hairy flies, with mouthparts that are reduced or vestigial. The larva is a large maggot covered with spines. They cause myiasis (invasion of the tissues by fly larvae) in animals.

warbler any of two families of songbirds, order Passeriformes. The Old World warblers are in the family Sylviidae, while the New World warblers are members of the Parulidae.

war crime offence (such as murder of a civilian or a prisoner of war) that contravenes the internationally accepted laws governing the conduct of wars, particularly the Hague Convention of 1907 and the Geneva Convention of 1949. A key principle of the law relating to such crimes is that obedience to the orders of a superior is no defence. In practice, prosecutions are generally brought by the victorious side.

Warhol, Andy (1928–1987) adopted name of Andrew Warhola, US artist and film-maker. Known as the 'Pope of Pop', Warhol was a leader of the *pop art movement. He achieved renown in 1962 when he exhibited works based on popular objects, images, and celebrities, for example his Campbell's soup cans,

Green Coca-Cola Bottles (1962; Leo Castelli Gallery, New York City), and *The Twenty Marilyns* (1962; Private Collection, Paris). In his New York studio, the Factory, he and his assistants reproduced the images in series of garishly-coloured silk-screen prints on canvas. Inspired by popular culture and mass media, Warhol changed the face of 20th-century art. His films include *Chelsea Girls* (1966) and *Trash* (1970).

warlord in China, any of the provincial leaders who took advantage of central government weakness, after the death of the first president of republican China in 1912, to organize their own private armies and fiefdoms. They engaged in civil wars until the nationalist leader Jiang Jie Shi's (Chiang Kai-shek's) Northern Expedition against them in 1926, and they exerted power until the communists seized control under Mao Zedong in 1949.

War of 1812 war between the USA and Britain caused by British interference with US shipping trade as part of Britain's economic warfare against Napoleonic France. A treaty signed in Ghent, Belgium, in December 1814 ended the conflict, with neither side victorious.

Warrington unitary authority in northwest England, created in 1998 from part of Cheshire. **area:** 176 sq km/ 68 sq mi **towns and cities:** Warrington (administrative headquarters), Lymm, Great Sankey **features:** River Mersey; Manchester Ship Canal; Warrington Museum and Art Gallery includes over 1,000 paintings; Risley Moss bog and woodland with nature trails and visitors' centre **population:** (1996) 151,000.

Warsaw Polish **Warszawa**, capital of Poland, on the River Vistula; population (1993) 1,653,300. Industries include engineering, food processing, printing, clothing, and pharmaceuticals. The old city of Warsaw, Poland, was reduced to rubble during its invasion, and subsequent occupation, by Germany in World War II.

Warsaw Pact *or* **Eastern European Mutual Assistance Pact** military defensive alliance 1955–91 between the USSR and East European communist states, originally established as a response to the admission of West Germany into NATO. Its military structures and agreements were dismantled early in 1991; a political organization remained until the alliance was officially dissolved in July 1991.

wart protuberance composed of a local overgrowth of skin. The common wart (*Verruca vulgaris*) is due to a virus infection. It usually disappears spontaneously within two years, but can be treated with peeling applications, burning away (cautery), freezing (cryosurgery), or laser treatment.

wart hog African wild *pig *Phacochoerus aethiopicus*, which has a large head with a bristly mane, fleshy pads beneath the eyes, and four large tusks. It has short legs and can grow to 80 cm/2.5 ft at the shoulder.

Warwickshire county of central England. **area:** 1,980 sq km/764 sq mi **towns and cities:** Warwick (administrative headquarters), Nuneaton, Royal Leamington Spa, Rugby, Stratford-upon-Avon (birthplace of the English dramatist Shakespeare) **physical:** rivers Avon, Stour, and Tame; remains of the 'Forest of Arden' (portrayed by Shakespeare in *As You Like It*) **features:** Kenilworth and Warwick castles; Edgehill, site of the Battle of Edgehill in 1642, during the English Civil War; annual Royal Agricultural Show held at Stoneleigh **population:** (1996) 500,600.

Wash, the bay of the North Sea between Norfolk and Lincolnshire, eastern England; 24 km/15 mi long, 40 km/25 mi wide. The rivers Nene, Ouse, Welland, and Witham drain into the Wash. In 1992, 10,120 ha/25,000 acres of the mudflats, marshes, and sand banks on its shores were designated a national nature reserve.

washing soda chemical name **sodium carbonate decahydrate**; $Na_2CO_3.10H_2O$, substance added to washing water to 'soften' *hard water. The calcium and magnesium ions in hard water react with the carbonate ions from the sodium carbonate and a precipitate of calcium carbonate results.

Washington called the **Evergreen State**, state in northwestern USA, bordered to the east by *Idaho, to the south by *Oregon, to the north by *British Columbia, Canada, and to the west by the Pacific Ocean; area 172,348 sq km/66,544 sq mi; population (2000) 5,894,100; capital Olympia. Mountainous and lushly forested, the aptly nicknamed 'Evergreen State' has a mild temperate climate and plentiful rainfall. *Puget Sound, a natural harbour covering some 5,180 sq km/1,990 sq mi, has made Washington a gateway for shipping and travel to Asia. Service industries lead the economy. The creation of computer software and other high-tech products has become a dominant industry, with Microsoft based in Seattle; aircraft manufacturing and timber and food processing are also important. With the exception of Spokane in the east, Washington's major cities are ports on Puget Sound: *Seattle, which has the largest urban population in the state, Tacoma, Bellevue, and Everett. Washington Territory, named for George Washington, was separated from the Oregon Territory in 1853. Washington was admitted to the Union in 1889 as the 42nd state and is governed under its original constitution, adopted in 1889.

Washington, George (1732–1799) commander of the American forces during the *American Revolution and 1st president of the USA 1789–97; known as 'the father of his country'. An experienced soldier, he had fought in campaigns against the French during the French and Indian War. He was elected to the Virginia House of Burgesses in 1759 and was a leader of the Virginia militia, gaining valuable exposure to wilderness fighting. As a strong opponent of the British government's policy, he sat in the Continental Congresses of 1774 and 1775, and on the outbreak of the *American Revolution was chosen commander-in-chief of the Continental Army. After many setbacks, he accepted the surrender of British general Cornwallis at Yorktown in 1781. After the war Washington retired to his Virginia estate, Mount Vernon, but in 1787 he re-entered politics as president of the Constitutional Convention in Philadelphia, and was elected US president in 1789. He attempted to draw his ministers from all factions, but his aristocratic outlook and acceptance of the fiscal policy championed by Alexander *Hamilton alienated his secretary of state, Thomas Jefferson, who resigned in 1793, thus creating the two-party system. Washington was re-elected president in 1792 but refused to serve a third term, setting a precedent that stood until 1940. He died and was buried at his home in Mount Vernon, Virginia.

Washington, DC in full **Washington, District of Columbia**, capital of the USA, on the Potomac River; the world's first planned national capital. It was named Washington, DC, to distinguish it from Washington state, and because it is coextensive with the *District of Columbia, hence DC; population (2000 est) 572,100; metropolitan area extending outside the District of Columbia (2000 est) 7,608,100. The District of Columbia, the federal district of the USA, is an area of 158 sq km/61 sq mi. Its site was chosen by President George *Washington, and the first structures date from 1793. It became the seat of government in 1800, taking over from Philadelphia, and houses the national executive, legislative, and judicial government of the USA; it is also a centre for international diplomacy and finance. Federal and district government are key employers. Public, trade, business, and social organizations maintain a presence, as well as law and other service agencies. Tourism is a major industry.

wasp any of several families of winged stinging insects of the order Hymenoptera, characterized by a thin stalk between the thorax and the abdomen. Wasps can be social or solitary. Among social wasps, the queens devote themselves to egg laying, the fertilized eggs producing female workers; the males come from unfertilized eggs and have no sting. The larvae are fed on insects, but the mature wasps feed mainly on fruit and sugar. In winter, the fertilized queens hibernate, but the other wasps die.

waste materials that are no longer needed and are discarded. Examples are household waste, industrial waste (which often contains toxic chemicals), medical waste (which may contain organisms that cause disease), and *nuclear waste (which is radioactive). By *recycling, some materials in waste can be reclaimed for further use. In 1990 the industrialized nations generated 2 billion tonnes of waste. In the USA, 40 tonnes of solid waste are generated annually per person, roughly twice as much as in Europe or Japan.

water chemical compound of hydrogen and oxygen elements – H_2O. It can exist as a solid (ice), liquid (water), or gas (water vapour). Water is the most common compound on Earth and vital to all living organisms. It covers 70% of the Earth's surface, and provides a habitat for large numbers of aquatic organisms. It is the largest constituent of all living organisms – the human body consists of about 65% water. It is found in all cells and many chemicals involved in processes such as respiration and photosynthesis need to be in solution in water in order to react. Pure water is a colourless, odourless, tasteless liquid which freezes at 0 °C/32 °F, and boils at 100 °C/212 °F. Natural water in the environment is never pure and always contains a variety of dissolved substances. Some 97% of the Earth's water is in the oceans; a further 2% is in the form of snow or ice, leaving only 1% available as freshwater for plants and animals. The recycling and circulation of water through the *biosphere is termed the **water cycle**, or 'hydrological cycle'; regulation of the water balance in organisms is termed osmoregulation. Water becomes more dense when it cools but reaches maximum density at 4 °C/39 °F. When cooled below this temperature the cooler water floats on the surface, as does ice formed from it. Animals and plants can survive under the ice.

water beetle aquatic beetle with an oval, flattened, streamlined shape. The head is sunk into the thorax and the hindlegs are flattened into flippers for swimming; there is a wide variation in size within the species; they are usually dark or black in colour and the entire body has a resplendent sheen. Both the adults and larvae are entirely aquatic, and are common in still, fresh waters such as ponds and lakes. Water beetles are in family Dytiscidae, order Coleoptera, class Insecta, phylum Arthropoda.

water boatman any water *bug of the family Corixidae that feeds on plant debris and algae. It has a flattened body 1.5 cm/0.6 in long, with oarlike legs.

water-borne disease disease associated with poor water supply. In developing world countries four-fifths of all illness is caused by water-borne diseases, with diarrhoea being the leading cause of childhood death. Malaria, carried by mosquitoes that are dependent on stagnant water for breeding, affects 400 million people every year and kills 5 million. Polluted water is also a problem in industrialized nations, where industrial dumping of chemical, hazardous, and radioactive wastes causes a range of medical conditions from headache to cancer.

waterbuck any of several African *antelopes of the genus *Kobus* which usually inhabit swampy tracts and reedbeds. They vary in size from about 1.8m/6 ft to 2.1 m/7.25 ft long, are up to 1.4 m/4.5 ft tall at the shoulder, and have long brown fur. The large curved horns, normally carried only by the males, have corrugated surfaces. Some species have white patches on the buttocks. Lechwe, kor, and defassa are alternative names for some of the species.

watercolour painting method of painting with pigments mixed with water, known in China as early as the 3rd century. Watercolour is usually diluted to the point where it is translucent and applied to paper in broad areas known as washes. White paper is often left exposed to create highlights, and washes are applied over one another to achieve gradations of tone. The use of watercolour requires great skill since its transparency rules out overpainting. A fast-drying and portable medium, watercolours have become popular for sketching out-of-doors. The use of watercolour in Western art began in England in the 18th century with the work of Paul Sandby and was initially developed by Thomas Girtin, John Sell Cotman, and J M W *Turner.

watercress perennial aquatic plant found in Europe and Asia and cultivated for its pungent leaves which are used in salads. (Genus *Nasturtium officinale*, family Cruciferae.)

water cycle or **hydrological cycle** natural circulation of water through the upper part of the Earth. It is a complex system involving a number of physical and chemical processes (such as *evaporation, *precipitation, and infiltration) and stores (such as rivers, oceans, and soil).

waterfall cascade of water in a river or stream. It occurs when a river flows over a bed of rock that resists erosion; weaker rocks downstream are worn away, creating a steep, vertical drop and a plunge pool into which the water falls. Over time, continuing erosion causes the waterfall to retreat upstream forming a deep valley, or gorge. Good examples of waterfalls include Victoria Falls (Zimbabwe/Zambia), Niagara Falls (USA/Canada), and Angel Falls (Venezuela).

water flea any aquatic crustacean in the order Cladocera, of which there are over 400 species. The commonest species is *Daphnia pulex*, used in the pet trade to feed tropical fish.

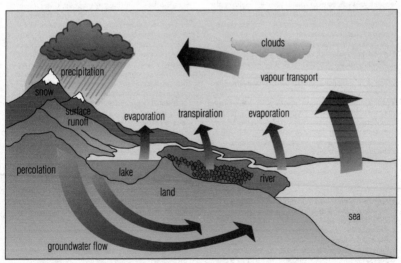

water cycle About one-third of the solar energy reaching the Earth is used in evaporating water. About 380,000 cubic km/95,000 cubic mi is evaporated each year. The entire contents of the oceans would take about one million years to pass through the water cycle.

Waterford county of the Republic of Ireland, in the province of Munster; county town Waterford; area 1,840 sq km/710 sq mi; population (2002 est) 56,600. Other towns include Dungarvon, Lismore, and Tramore. The chief rivers are the Suir and the Blackwater; the Comeragh and Monavallagh mountain ranges lie in the north and centre of the county. Agriculture and dairy farming are important; wheat, barley, and vegetables are also grown. Industries include glassware, pharmaceuticals, and electronics, and there are tanneries, bacon factories, and flour mills.

waterfowl any water bird, but especially any member of the family Anatidae, which consists of ducks, geese, and swans.

Watergate US political scandal, named after the building in Washington, DC, which housed the headquarters of the Democratic National Committee in the 1972 presidential election. Five men, hired by the Republican Committee for the Re-election of the President (popularly known as CREEP), were caught after breaking into the Watergate with complex electronic surveillance equipment. Investigations revealed that the White House was implicated in the break-in, and that there was a 'slush fund' used to finance unethical activities, including using the CIA and the Internal Revenue Service (IRS) for political ends, setting up paramilitary operations against opponents, altering and destroying evidence, and bribing defendants to lie or remain silent. In August 1974, President *Nixon was forced by the Supreme Court to surrender to Congress tape recordings of conversations he had held with administration officials, which indicated his complicity in a cover-up. Nixon resigned rather than face impeachment for obstruction of justice and other crimes.

water hyacinth tropical aquatic plant belonging to the pickerelweed family. In one growing season 25 plants can produce 2 million new plants. It is liable to choke waterways, removing nutrients from the water and blocking out the sunlight, but it can be used to purify sewage-polluted water as well as in making methane gas, compost, concentrated protein, paper, and baskets. Originating in South America, it now grows in more than 50 countries. (Genus *Eichhornia crassipes*, family Pontederiaceae.)

water lily any of a group of aquatic plants belonging to the water lily family. The fleshy roots are embedded in mud and the large round leaves float on the surface of the water. The cup-shaped flowers may be white, pink, yellow, or blue. (Genera *Nymphaea* and *Nuphar*, family Nymphaeaceae.)

Waterloo, Battle of final battle of the Napoleonic Wars on 18 June 1815 in which a coalition force of British, Prussian, and Dutch troops under the Duke of Wellington defeated Napoleon near the village of Waterloo, 13 km/8 mi south of Brussels, Belgium. Napoleon found Wellington's army isolated from his allies and began a direct offensive to smash them, but the British held on until joined by the Prussians under Marshal Gebhard von Blücher. Four days later Napoleon abdicated for the second and final time.

water meadow irrigated meadow. By flooding the land for part of each year, increased yields of hay are obtained. Water meadows were common in Italy, Switzerland, and England (from 1523) but have now largely disappeared.

watermelon large *melon belonging to the gourd family, native to tropical Africa, with a dark green rind and reddish juicy flesh studded with a large number of black seeds. It is widely cultivated in subtropical regions. (Genus *Citrullus vulgaris*, family Cucurbitaceae.)

water pollution any addition to fresh or seawater that interferes with biological processes or causes a health or environmental hazard. Common pollutants include nitrates, pesticides, and sewage (resulting from poor sewage disposal methods), although a huge range of industrial contaminants, such as chemical by-products and residues created in the manufacture of various goods, also enter water – legally, accidentally, and through illegal dumping.

water polo water sport developed in England in 1869, originally called 'soccer-in-water'. The aim is to score goals, as in soccer, at each end of a swimming pool. It is played by teams of seven on each side (from squads of 13).

water skiing water sport in which a person is towed across water on a ski or skis (wider than those used for skiing on snow), or barefoot, by means of a rope attached to a speedboat. Competitions are held for overall performances, slalom, tricks, jumping, and racing.

water softener any substance or unit that removes the hardness from water. Hardness is caused by the presence of calcium and magnesium ions, which combine with soap to form an insoluble scum, prevent lathering, and cause deposits to build up in pipes and cookware (kettle fur). A water softener replaces these ions with sodium ions, which are fully soluble and cause no scum.

water supply distribution of water for domestic, municipal, or industrial consumption. Water supply in sparsely populated regions usually comes from underground water rising to the surface in natural springs, supplemented by pumps and wells. Urban sources are deep artesian wells, rivers, and reservoirs, usually formed from enlarged lakes or dammed and flooded valleys, from which water is conveyed by pipes, conduits, and aqueducts to filter beds. As water seeps through layers of shingle, gravel, and sand, harmful organisms are removed and the water is then distributed by pumping or gravitation through mains and pipes.

water treatment Often other substances are added to the water, such as chlorine and fluoride; aluminium sulphate, a clarifying agent, is the most widely used chemical in water treatment. In towns, domestic and municipal (road washing, sewage) needs account for about 135 l/30 gal per head each day. In coastal desert areas, such as the Arabian peninsula, desalination plants remove salt from sea water. The Earth's waters, both fresh and saline, have been polluted by industrial and domestic chemicals, some of which are toxic and others radioactive (see *water pollution).

water table upper level of *groundwater (water collected underground in porous rocks). Water that is above the water table will drain downwards; a spring forms where the water table meets the surface of the ground. The water table rises and falls in response to rainfall and the rate at which water is extracted, for example for irrigation and industry.

Watson, James Dewey (1928–) US biologist who was awarded a Nobel Prize for Physiology or Medicine in 1962 for the discovery of the double-helical structure of DNA and determining the significance of this structure in the replication and transfer of genetic information. He shared the prize with his co-worker Francis *Crick.

watt symbol W, SI unit of power (the rate of expenditure or transformation of energy from one form to another) defined as one joule per second. A light bulb, for example, may use 40, 60, 100, or 150 watts of power; an electric heater will use several kilowatts (thousands of watts). The watt is named after the Scottish engineer James *Watt.

Watt, James (1736–1819) Scottish engineer who developed the *steam engine in the 1760s, making Thomas Newcomen's engine vastly more efficient by cooling steam in a condenser separate from the main cylinder. He eventually made a double-acting machine that supplied power with both directions of the piston and developed rotary motion. He also invented devices associated with the steam engine, artistic instruments and a copying process, and devised the horsepower as a description of an engine's rate of working. The modern unit of power, the **watt**, is named after him.

Watteau, (Jean-)Antoine (1684–1721) French rococo painter. He developed a new category of genre painting known as the *fête galante* – fanciful scenes depicting elegantly dressed young people engaged in outdoor entertainment. One of the best-known examples is *The Embarkation for Cythera* (1717; Louvre, Paris).

wattle any of certain species of *acacia in Australia, where their fluffy golden flowers are the national emblem. The leathery leaves are adapted to drought conditions and avoid loss of water through *transpiration by turning their edges to the direct rays of the sun. Wattles are used for tanning leather and in fencing.

wattle and daub method of constructing walls consisting of upright stakes bound together with withes (strong flexible shoots or twigs, usually of willow), and covered in mud or plaster. This was the usual way of building houses in medieval Europe; it was also the traditional method used in Australia, Africa, the Middle East, and the Far East.

Watts, George Frederick (1817–1904) English painter and sculptor. Influenced by the Venetian masters, he painted biblical and classical subjects, but his fame was based largely on his moralizing allegories, such as *Hope* (1886; Tate Gallery, London). He was also a portrait painter, his works including *Gladstone* and *Tennyson* (National Portrait Gallery, London). As a sculptor he executed *Physical Energy* (1904) for Cecil Rhodes's memorial in Cape Town, South Africa; a replica is in Kensington Gardens, London. He was a forerunner of Symbolism.

Waugh, Evelyn (Arthur St John) (1903–1966) English novelist. His humorous social satires include *Decline and Fall* (1928), *Vile Bodies* (1930), *Scoop* (1938), and *The Loved One* (1948). He developed a serious concern with religious issues in *Brideshead Revisited* (1945) (successfully dramatized for television in the 1980s). *The Ordeal of Gilbert Pinfold* (1957) is largely autobiographical.

wave in the oceans, a ridge or swell formed by wind or other causes. The power of a wave is determined by the strength of the wind and the distance of open water over which the wind blows (the fetch). Waves are the main agents of *coastal erosion and deposition: sweeping away or building up beaches, creating *spits and berms, and wearing down cliffs by their hydraulic action and by the *corrosion of the sand and shingle that they carry. A *tsunami (misleadingly called a 'tidal wave') is formed after a submarine earthquake.

wave in physics, oscillation that is propagated from a source. Mechanical waves require a medium through which to travel. Electromagnetic waves do not; they can travel through a vacuum. Waves carry energy but they do not transfer matter. The medium (for example the Earth, for seismic waves) is not permanently displaced by the passage of a wave. The model of waves as a pattern is used to help understand the properties of light and sound. Experiments conducted in a ripple tank with water waves can explain how waves slow down as water becomes shallower, how waves change direction when travelling through another medium, and how waves are reflected from different surfaces.

wavelength distance between successive crests or troughs of a *wave. The wavelength of a light wave determines its colour; red light has a wavelength of about 700 nanometres, for example. The complete range of wavelengths of electromagnetic waves is called the electromagnetic *spectrum.

Wavell, Archibald Percival, 1st Earl Wavell (1883–1950) British field marshal in World War II. As commander-in-chief in the Middle East, he successfully defended Egypt against Italy in July 1939 and successfully conducted the North African war against Italy 1940–41. He was transferred as commander-in-chief in India in July 1941, and became Allied Supreme Commander after Japan entered the war. He was unable to prevent Japanese advances in Malaya and Burma (now Myanmar), and Churchill became disillusioned with him. He was made viceroy of India 1943–47. He was honoured as a KCB in 1939, created Viscount in 1943, and Earl in 1947.

wave power power obtained by harnessing the energy of water waves. Various schemes have been advanced since 1973 when oil prices rose dramatically and an energy shortage threatened. In 1974 the British engineer Stephen Salter developed the 'duck' – a floating boom, the segments of which nod up and down with the waves. The nodding motion can be used to drive pumps and spin generators. Another device, developed in Japan, uses an oscillating water column to harness wave power. A major technological breakthrough will be required if wave power is ever to contribute significantly to the world's energy needs, although several ideas have reached prototype stage.

wax solid fatty substance of animal, vegetable, or mineral origin. Waxes are composed variously of *esters, *fatty acids, free *alcohols, and solid hydrocarbons.

waxbill any of a group of small, mainly African, seed-eating birds in the family Estrildidae, order Passeriformes, which also includes the grass finches of Australia. Waxbills grow to 15 cm/6 in long, are brown and grey with yellow, red, or brown markings, and have waxy-looking red or pink beaks.

waxwing any of several fruit-eating birds of the family Bombycillidae, order Passeriformes. They are found in the northern hemisphere. The Bohemian waxwing *Bombycilla garrulus* of North America and Eurasia is about 18 cm/7 in long, and is greyish-brown above with a reddish-chestnut crest, black streak at the eye, and variegated wings. It undertakes mass migrations in some years.

wayfaring tree European shrub belonging to the honeysuckle family, with clusters of fragrant white flowers, found on limy soils; it is naturalized in the northeastern USA. (Genus *Viburnum lantana*, family Caprifoliaceae.)

Wayne, John (1907–1979) called 'Duke'; stage name of Marion Michael Morrison, US actor. He played the archetypal Western hero: plain-speaking, brave, and solitary. His films include *Stagecoach* (1939), *Red River* (1948), *She Wore a Yellow Ribbon* (1949), *The Searchers* (1956), *Rio Bravo* (1959), *The Man Who Shot Liberty Valance* (1962), and *True Grit* (1969; Academy Award).

weak nuclear force *or* **weak interaction** one of the four fundamental *forces of nature, the other three being the gravitational force or gravity, the electromagnetic force, and the strong nuclear force. It causes radioactive beta decay and other subatomic reactions. The particles that carry the weak force are called *weakons (or intermediate vector bosons) and comprise the positively and negatively charged W particles and the neutral Z particle.

weakon *or* **intermediate vector boson** member of a group of elementary particles, see * intermediate vector boson.

Weald, the *or* **the Kent Weald** (Old English 'forest') area between the North and South Downs, England, a raised tract of forest 64 km/40 mi wide. It forms part of Kent, Sussex, Surrey, and Hampshire. Once thickly wooded, it is now an agricultural area producing fruit, hops, and vegetables. Crowborough and Wadhurst are the largest villages in the area. In the Middle Ages its timber and iron ore made it the industrial heart of England.

weapon any implement used for attack and defence, from simple clubs, spears, and bows and arrows in prehistoric times to machine guns and nuclear bombs in modern times. The first revolution in warfare came with the invention of *gunpowder and the development of cannons and shoulder-held guns. Many other weapons now exist, such as grenades, shells, torpedoes, rockets, and guided missiles. The ultimate in explosive weapons are the atomic (fission) and hydrogen (fusion) bombs. They release the enormous energy produced when atoms split or fuse together (see *nuclear warfare). There are also chemical and bacteriological weapons, which release poisons or disease.

Wear river in northeast England; length 107 km/67 mi. From its source near Wearhead in the Pennines in County Durham, it flows eastwards along a narrow valley, Weardale, to Bishop Auckland and then northeast past Durham and Chester-le-Street, to meet the North Sea at Sunderland.

weasel any of various small, short-legged, lithe carnivorous mammals with bushy tails, especially the genus *Mustela*, found worldwide except Australia. They feed mainly on small rodents although some, like the mink *M. vison*, hunt aquatic prey. Most are 12–25 cm/5–10 in long, excluding the tail.

weather variation of atmospheric conditions at any one place over a short period of time. Such conditions include humidity, precipitation, temperature, cloud cover, visibility, and wind. Weather differs from *climate in that the latter is a composite of the average weather conditions of a locality or region over a long period of time (at least 30 years). *Meteorology is the study of short-term weather patterns and data within a particular area; climatology is the study of weather over longer timescales on a zonal or global basis. Weather forecasts are based on current meterological data, and predict likely weather for a particular area.

weathering process by which exposed rocks are broken down on the spot (in situ) by the action of rain, frost, wind, and other elements of the weather. It differs from *erosion in that no movement or transportion of the broken-down material takes place. Two types of weathering are recognized: physical (or mechanical) weathering and chemical weathering. They usually occur together, and are an important part of the development of landforms.

weaver any small bird of the family Ploceidae, order Passeriformes; they are mostly about 15 cm/6 in long. The majority of weavers are African, a few Asian. The males use grasses to weave elaborate globular nests in bushes and trees. The nests are entered from beneath, and the male hangs from it calling and flapping his wings to attract a female. Their bodies are somewhat elongated and the tails long, and the prominent conical bill is very powerful. They eat insects and may eat cultivated grain. Males are often more brightly coloured than females.

weaving the production of textile fabric by means of a *loom. The basic process involves the interlacing at right angles of vertical threads (the warp) and horizontal threads (the weft). The weft is traditionally carried across from one side of the loom to the other by a type of bobbin called a shuttle, and weaves in and out of the warp, creating the fabric.

Webb, Philip Speakman (1831–1915) English architect and designer. He was a leading figure (along with Richard Norman Shaw and Charles Voysey) of the Arts and Crafts Movement, which was instrumental in the revival of English domestic architecture in the late 19th century. He mostly designed private houses, notably the Red House, Bexleyheath, Kent (1859), for William *Morris.

weber symbol Wb, SI unit of *magnetic flux (the magnetic field strength multiplied by the area through which the field passes). It is named after German chemist Wilhelm Weber. One weber equals 10^8 maxwells.

Weber, Carl Maria Friedrich Ernst von (1786–1826) German composer. He established the German Romantic school of opera with *Der Freischütz/ The Marksman* (1821) and *Euryanthe* (1823). He was Kapellmeister (chief conductor) at Breslau in 1804–06, Prague in 1813–16, and Dresden in 1816. He died during a visit to London, where he produced his opera *Oberon* (1826), written for the Covent Garden Theatre.

Webern, Anton (Friedrich Wilhelm von) (1883–1945) Austrian composer. He wrote spare, enigmatic miniatures combining a pastoral poetic with severe structural rigour. A Renaissance musical scholar, he became a pupil of Arnold *Schoenberg, whose

12-tone system he reinterpreted as abstract design in works such as the *Concerto for Nine Instruments* (1931–34) and the *Second Cantata* (1941–43). His constructivist aesthetic influenced the post-war generation of advanced composers.

Webster, John (*c.* 1580–*c.* 1625) English dramatist. His reputation rests on two tragedies, *The White Devil* (1612) and *The Duchess of Malfi* (*c.* 1613). Though both show the preoccupation with melodramatic violence and horror typical of the Jacobean revenge tragedy, they are also remarkable for their poetry and psychological insight. He collaborated with a number of other dramatists, notably with Thomas Dekker on the comedy *Westward Ho* (*c.* 1606).

Weddell Sea arm of the Southern Atlantic Ocean that cuts into the Antarctic continent southeast of Cape Horn; area 8,000,000 sq km/3,088,800 sq mi. Much of it is covered with thick pack ice for most of the year.

Wedgwood, Josiah (1730–1795) English pottery manufacturer. He set up business in Staffordshire in the early 1760s to produce his agateware as well as unglazed blue or green stoneware (jasper) decorated with white neo-classical designs, using pigments of his own invention.

weedkiller *or* herbicide chemical that kills some or all plants. Selective herbicides are effective with cereal crops because they kill all broad-leaved plants without affecting grasslike leaves. Those that kill all plants include sodium chlorate and paraquat; see also *Agent Orange. The widespread use of weedkillers in agriculture has led to an increase in crop yield but also to pollution of soil and water supplies and killing of birds and small animals, as well as creating a health hazard for humans.

weever fish any of a family (Trachinidae) of marine bony fishes of the perch family, especially the genus *Trachinus*, with poison glands on the dorsal fin and gill cover that can give a painful sting. It grows up to 5 cm/2 in long, has eyes near the top of the head, and lives on sandy seabeds.

weevil any of a superfamily (Curculionoidea) of *beetles, usually less than 6 mm/0.25 in in length, and with a head prolonged into a downward beak, which is used for boring into plant stems and trees for feeding.

Wei, Jingsheng (1951–) Chinese pro-democracy activist and essayist, imprisoned 1979–97 for attacking the Chinese communist system. He is regarded as one of China's most important political dissidents.

weight force exerted on an object by *gravity. The weight of an object depends on its mass – the amount of material in it – and the strength of the Earth's gravitational pull (the acceleration due to gravity), which decreases with height. Consequently, an object weighs less at the top of a mountain than at sea level. On the surface of the Moon, an object has only one-sixth of its weight on Earth (although its mass is unchanged), because the Moon's surface gravity is one-sixth that of the Earth's.

weightlessness apparent loss in weight of a body in free fall. Astronauts in an orbiting spacecraft do not feel any weight because they are falling freely in the Earth's gravitational field (not because they are beyond the influence of Earth's gravity). The same phenomenon can be experienced in a falling lift or in an aircraft imitating the path of a freely falling object.

weightlifting sport of lifting the heaviest possible weight above one's head to the satisfaction of judges. In international competitions there are two standard lifts: **snatch** and **jerk**.

weights and measures see under *c.g.s. system, *f.p.s. system, *m.k.s. system, *SI units.

Weil's disease *or* leptospirosis infectious disease of animals that is occasionally transmitted to human beings, usually by contact with water contaminated with rat urine. It is characterized by acute fever, and infection may spread to the brain, liver, kidneys, and heart. It has a 10% mortality rate.

Weimar Republic constitutional republic in Germany from 1919 to 1933, which was crippled by the election of antidemocratic parties to the Reichstag (parliament), and then subverted by the Nazi leader Hitler after his appointment as chancellor in 1933. It took its name from the city where in February 1919 a constituent assembly met to draw up a democratic constitution.

Weismann, August Friedrich Leopold (1834–1914) German biologist, one of the founders of *genetics. He postulated that every living organism contains a special hereditary substance, the 'germ plasm', and in 1892 he proposed that changes to the body do not in turn cause an alteration of the genetic material.

Weizmann, Chaim Azriel (1874–1952) Zionist leader, the first president of Israel 1948–52. He conducted the negotiations leading up to the Balfour Declaration, by which the UK declared its support for an independent Jewish state.

welding joining pieces of metal (or non-metal) at faces rendered plastic or liquid by heat or pressure (or both). The principal processes today are gas and arc welding, in which the heat from a gas flame or an electric arc melts the faces to be joined. Additional 'filler metal' is usually added to the joint.

welfare state political system under which the state (rather than the individual or the private sector) has responsibility for the welfare of its citizens, providing a guaranteed minimum standard of life, and insurance against the hazards of poverty, illness, and social deprivation. Welfare services include *social security, which makes provision against interruption of earnings through sickness, injury, old age, or unemployment. They take the forms of unemployment and sickness benefits, family allowances, and income supplements, provided and typically financed through state insurance schemes. The services also include health and education, financed typically through taxation, and the provision of subsidized 'social housing'. Subsidized public transport, leisure facilities, and public libraries, with special discounts for the elderly, unemployed, and disabled, are other noncore elements of a welfare state.

Welles, (George) Orson (1915–1985) US actor, director, screenwriter, and producer. His first and greatest film was *Citizen Kane* (1941), which he produced, directed, and starred in. Later work includes the *films noirs The Lady from Shanghai* (1948) and *Touch of Evil* (1958). As an actor, he created the character of Harry Lime in the film *The Third Man* (1949).

Wellington capital and industrial port of New Zealand, in the province of the same name on North Island, on the Cook Strait; population (2001 est) 163,800. Wellington's harbour at Port Nicholson is one of

New Zealand's principal ports for the shipment of wool, frozen meat, dairy produce, and apples, and a large proportion of the country's imports arrive there. After Auckland it is the second-largest manufacturing centre of New Zealand, and industries in the city include woollen textiles, chemicals, engineering, food processing, and electrical goods. The harbour was sighted by Captain James Cook in 1773.

Wellington, Arthur Wellesley, 1st Duke of Wellington (1769–1852) Irish-born British soldier and Tory politician. As commander in the *Peninsular War, he expelled the French from Spain in 1814. He defeated Napoleon Bonaparte at Quatre-Bras and Waterloo in 1815, and was a member of the Congress of Vienna. As prime minister 1828–30, he was forced to concede Roman Catholic emancipation. He was made Viscount in 1809, Earl in 1812, Marquess in 1812, and Duke in 1814.

Wells, H(erbert) G(eorge) (1866–1946) English writer. He was a pioneer of science fiction with such novels as *The Time Machine* (1895) and *The War of the Worlds* (1898) (describing a Martian invasion of Earth), which brought him nationwide recognition. His later novels had an anti-establishment, anticonventional humour remarkable in its day, for example *Kipps* (1905) and *Tono-Bungay* (1909). He was originally a Fabian (member of a socialist organization that sought reform), and later he became a Labour party supporter. He was a Labour candidate for London University in 1921 and 1922.

Welsh people of *Wales; see also *Celt. The term is thought to be derived from an old Germanic term for 'foreigner', and so linked to Walloon (Belgium) and Wallachian (Romania). It may also derive from the Latin *Volcae*, the name of a Celtic people of France.

Welsh Assembly devolved governmental body based in Cardiff; see *National Assembly for Wales.

Welsh corgi breed of dog with a foxlike head and pricked ears, originally bred for cattle herding. The coat is dense, with several varieties of colouring. Corgis are about 30 cm/12 in at the shoulder, and weigh up to 12 kg/27 lb.

Welsh language Welsh **Cymraeg**, member of the Celtic branch of the Indo-European language family, spoken chiefly in the rural north and west of Wales. Spoken by approximately 20% of the Welsh population, it is the strongest of the surviving *Celtic languages.

welwitschia woody plant found in the deserts of southwestern Africa. It has a long, water-absorbent taproot and can live for up to 100 years. (Genus *Welwitschia mirabilis*, order Gnetales.). It is a gymnosperm like conifers and cycads but it is quite different from them.

Wenceslas, St (c. 907–929) Duke of Bohemia. He attempted to Christianize his people and was murdered by his brother. He is patron saint of the Czech Republic and the 'good King Wenceslas' of a popular carol. Feast day 28 September.

werewolf in folk belief, a human being either turned into a wolf by a spell or having the ability to assume a wolf form. The symptoms of *porphyria may have fostered the legends.

Wesley, John (1703–1791) English founder of *Methodism. When the pulpits of the Church of England were closed to him and his followers, he took the gospel to the people. For 50 years he travelled the country on horseback, preaching daily, largely in the open air. His sermons became the doctrinal standard of the Wesleyan Methodist Church. With his brother Charles, and George Whitefield, John Wesley formed the Methodist Church in reaction to the rationalism and social apathy of the Anglican Church. He is said to have preached 40,000 open-air sermons to the poor throughout Britain.

West, American *or* **the West** western frontier of the USA. Specifically the term refers to the period 1840–90, when the Pacific West and Great Plains to the west of the Mississippi were settled. This was the era of the gold rush, the homesteader, the cowboy, and the Plains Wars. Despite the resistance of the indigenous Plains Indians, by 1890 they were confined to Indian reservations, and US citizens had achieved their self-proclaimed manifest destiny to expand westwards. The legends of the Wild West began during this period. Many of the figures of Western novels and films were real people, such as lawmen 'Wild Bill' Hickok and Wyatt Earp, and criminals such as Jesse James and Billy the Kid, although stories about them have on the whole been greatly exaggerated.

West, Mae (1892–1980) US vaudeville, stage, and film actor. She wrote her own dialogue, setting herself up as a provocative sex symbol and the mistress of verbal innuendo. She appeared on Broadway in *Sex* (1926), *Drag* (1927), and *Diamond Lil* (1928), which was the basis of the film (with Cary Grant) *She Done Him Wrong* (1933).

West Bank area (5,879 sq km/2,270 sq mi) on the west bank of the River Jordan; population (1997 est) 1,873,500. Its main cities are Jenin, Tulkarm, and Nablus in the north; Jerusalem, Jericho, and Ramallah in the centre; and Bethlehem and Hebron in the south. The area was captured by Israel from Jordan in 1967; Jordan finally renounced any claim to it in 1988. Israel refers to the area as Judaea and *Samaria, and in 2001 75% of the area of the West Bank remained under Israeli military control, protecting the 180,000 Israeli settlers.

West Bengal state of northeast India; area 87,853 sq km/33,920 sq mi; population (2001 est) 80,221,200. The capital is Kolkata (formerly Calcutta). In spite of its relatively small size, the state is economically very productive. Often with the help of extensive irrigation and through intensive cultivation there are high yields of agricultural products, including rice, jute, tea (in Darjeeling and Jalpaiguri), oilseed, sugar, pulses, and tobacco, and there is a substantial fishing industry. Manufacturing industries include jute (particularly at Hooghly industrial complex), iron and steel (at Durgapur, Asansol, based on the Raniganj coalfield), cars, locomotives, aluminium, fertilizers, chemicals, cotton textiles, oil-refining, shipbuilding, and printing.

West Berkshire unitary authority in southeast England, created in 1998 from part of the former county of Berkshire. **area:** 705 sq km/272 sq mi **towns and cities:** Newbury (administrative headquarters), Hungerford, Lambourn **features:** River Kennet; River Cambourn; Kennet and Avon Canal; Snelsmore Common Country Park covers 59 ha/146 acres including wetland habitats; Inkpen Hill (291 m/854 ft) with Stone Age tomb and Walbury Hill (297 m/974 ft) with Iron Age fort are the highest chalk hills in England; Thatcham Moors reedbeds are designated Sites of Special Scientific Interest (SSSI); Greenham Common Women's Peace Camp has been the site of campaigning against nuclear weapons development at Greenham, Burghfield, and Aldermaston since 1981 **population:** (1996) 142,600.

West Dunbartonshire unitary authority in west central Scotland, created in 1996 from parts of two districts of Strathclyde region. **area:** 177 sq km/68 sq mi **towns:** Dumbarton (administrative headquarters), Clydebank, Alexandria **physical:** Leven valley and coastal land of Firth of Clyde rise toward the upland plateau of the Kilpatrick Hills **features:** Dumbarton Castle (14th century) **population:** (2000 est) 96,400 **history:** industrial area of west central Scotland, targeted by Germans and bombed in World War II; heart of ancient kingdom of Strathclyde.

Western Australia state of Australia, bounded on the north and west by the Indian Ocean, on the east by Northern Territory and South Australia, on the south by the Southern Ocean; area 2,525,500 sq km/975,100 sq mi; population (1996) 1,726,100. The capital is *Perth. Products include wheat, fresh and dried fruit, beef, dairy products, wool, wine, natural gas, oil, iron, gold, nickel, diamonds, bauxite, cultured and freshwater pearls, timber, and fish. Tourism is important to the state.

Western Cape province of the Republic of South Africa from 1994, formerly part of Cape Province; area 129,386 sq km/49,956 sq mi; population (2000 est) 4,178,600. The capital is *Cape Town, which is also the legislative capital of the republic. Industries in the province include textiles, footwear, motor vehicles, tyres, oil refining, pharmaceuticals, fertilisers, pesticides, and marine engineering. Agriculture is, however, the leading economic activity of Western Cape. The coastal lowlands, with the advantage of a Mediterranean-type climate, yield large quantities of fruit, including oranges, grapefruit, peaches and apricots, as well as most of the grapes and wine produced in the republic. Separated from the coastal lowlands by mountain ranges, the dry interior plateaus, including the Great Karoo, have sparse natural vegetation, though there is some cattle farming and cultivation of fodder crops, are used mainly for sheep rearing, with a concentration on wool production. There is also a substantial tourist industry.

Western Front battle zone in World War I between Germany and its enemies France and Britain, extending as lines of trenches from Nieuport on the Belgian coast through Ypres, Arras, Albert, Soissons, and Rheims to Verdun, constructed by both Germany and the Allies.

Western Isles island administrative unitary authority area in Scotland, also known as the Outer Hebrides, including the major islands of Lewis-with-Harris, North and South Uist, Benbecula, and Barra. **area:** 3,057 sq km/1,180 sq mi **towns:** Stornoway on Lewis (administrative headquarters), Castlebay, Lochboisdale, Lochmaddy, Tarbert **physical:** open to the Atlantic Ocean on the west and the stormy Minch to the east, the islands are almost treeless and have extensive peat bogs. There are areas of hills and mountains on all the islands. The only fertile land is the sandy Machair on the west coast. The islands are

mainly composed of the oldest rock in Britain, the Lewisian gneiss. Lewis is divided from the mainland by the Minch channel. The islands south of Lewis are divided from the Inner Hebrides by the Little Minch and the Sea of the Hebrides; uninhabited islands include St Kilda and Rockall **features:** Callanish monolithic Stone Age circles on Lewis **population:** (2000 est) 27,200.

Western Sahara formerly **Spanish Sahara**, disputed territory in northwest Africa, bounded to the north by Morocco, to the east and south by Mauritania, and to the west by the Atlantic Ocean; area 266,800 sq km/103,000 sq mi; population (1993 est) 214,000, including indigenous Sawrawis (traditionally nomadic herders). The capital is *Laâyoune (Arabic *El Aaiún*). Exports include phosphates and iron ore.

West Glamorgan Welsh **Gorllewin Morgannwg**, former county of southwest Wales, 1974–96, now divided into *Neath Port Talbot and *Swansea unitary authorities.

West Indian inhabitant of or native to the West Indies, or person of West Indian descent. The West Indies are culturally heterogeneous; in addition to the indigenous Carib and Arawak Indians, there are peoples of African, European, and Asian descent, as well as peoples of mixed descent.

West Indies archipelago of about 1,200 islands, dividing the Atlantic Ocean from the Gulf of Mexico and the Caribbean Sea. The archipelago is divided into: **Bahamas; Greater Antilles:** Cuba, Hispaniola (Haiti, Dominican Republic), Jamaica, and Puerto Rico; **Lesser Antilles:** Aruba, Netherlands Antilles, Trinidad and Tobago, the Windward Islands (Grenada, Barbados, St Vincent, St Lucia, Martinique, Dominica, Guadeloupe), the Leeward Islands (Montserrat, Antigua, St Kitts and Nevis, Barbuda, Anguilla, St Martin, British and US Virgin Islands), and many smaller islands.

West Irian former name of *Irian Jaya, a province of Indonesia.

Westmeath county of the Republic of Ireland, in the province of Leinster; county town Mullingar; area 1,760 sq km/679 sq mi; population (2002 est) 71,600. The rivers Brosna, Inny, and Shannon flow through the county, and its principal lakes are loughs Ree (the largest, and an extension of the River Shannon), Ennell, Owel, and Sheelin. The Royal Canal cuts through the county but is now disused. The land is low-lying, about 76 m/249 ft above sea-level, with much pasture. The main agricultural activity is cattle and dairy farming. Fishing for trout is popular. Other principal towns are Athlone and Moate.

West Midlands metropolitan county of central England, created in 1974; in 1986, most of the functions of the former county council were transferred to the metropolitan borough councils. **area:** 900 sq km/347 sq mi **towns and cities:** Birmingham, Coventry, Dudley, Solihull, Walsall, Wolverhampton (all administrative centres for districts of the same name), Oldbury (administrative centre for Sandwell) **population:** (1996) 2,642,500.

Westminster, City of inner borough of central Greater London, on the north bank of the River Thames between Kensington and the City of London. It encompasses Bayswater, Belgravia, Mayfair,

Paddington, Pimlico, Soho, St John's Wood, and Westminster. Population (1991) 174,800.

Westphalia independent medieval duchy, incorporated in Prussia by the Congress of Vienna in 1815, and made a province in 1816 with Münster as its capital. Since 1946 it has been part of the German *Land* (region) of *North Rhine-Westphalia.

Westphalia, Treaty of agreement in 1648 ending the *Thirty Years' War. The peace marked the end of the supremacy of the Holy Roman Empire and the emergence of France as a dominant power. It recognized the sovereignty of the German states, Switzerland, and the Netherlands; Lutherans, Calvinists, and Roman Catholics were given equal rights.

West Sussex county of southern England, created in 1974, formerly part of Sussex. **area:** 1,990 sq km/768 sq mi **towns and cities:** Chichester (administrative headquarters), Crawley, Horsham, Haywards Heath, Shoreham (port); Bognor Regis, Littlehampton, Worthing (resorts) **physical:** the Weald; South Downs; rivers Adur, Arun, and West Rother **features:** Arundel and Bramber castles; Chichester cathedral; Goodwood House and racecourse; Petworth House (17th century); Uppark House (1685–90); Fishbourne villa (important Roman site near Chichester); Selsey (reputed landing place of the South Saxons in 447); Gatwick Airport **population:** (1996) 737,300.

West Virginia called the **Mountain State**, state in eastern central USA, bordered to the south and east by *Virginia, to the north by *Ohio, *Pennsylvania, and *Maryland, and to the west by Ohio and *Kentucky; area 62,350 sq km/24,078 sq mi; population (2000) 1,808,300; capital Charleston. West Virginia is hilly and rugged, hence its nickname, and has a mean altitude of 460 m/1,500 ft, the highest average altitude east of the *Mississippi River. The service industry is the most significant contributor to the economy, and the state's industrial base is mining. Industrial products include coal, chemicals, and glass. Agricultural output includes dairy and meat products. Other major towns and cities include Huntington, Wheeling, Parkersburg, Morgantown, Weirton, Fairmont, Beckley, Clarksburg, and Martinsburg. West Virginia was composed from those Virginia counties that, unsympathetic to the plantation South, refused to join Virginia in its 1861 secession from the Union at the start of the American *Civil War. West Virginia was admitted to the Union in 1863 as the 35th US state.

West Yorkshire metropolitan county of northeast England, created in 1974; in 1986, most of the functions of the former county council were transferred to the metropolitan borough councils. **area:** 2,040 sq km/787 sq mi **towns and cities:** Bradford, Leeds, Wakefield (administrative centres for districts of the same name), Halifax (administrative centre of Calderdale district), Huddersfield (administrative centre of Kirklees district) **physical:** Ilkley Moor, Haworth Moor; high Pennine moorlands in the west, Vale of York to the east; rivers Aire, Calder, Colne, Wharfe **features:** Haworth Parsonage; part of the Peak District National Park; British Library, Boston Spa Document Supply Centre (part of the British Library) **population:** (2000 est) 2,115,000.

wetland permanently wet land area or habitat. Wetlands include areas of *marsh, fen, *bog, flood

plain, and shallow coastal areas. Wetlands are extremely fertile. They provide warm, sheltered waters for fisheries, lush vegetation for grazing livestock, and an abundance of wildlife. Estuaries and seaweed beds are more than 16 times as productive as the open ocean.

Wexford county of the Republic of Ireland, in the province of Leinster; county town Wexford; area 2,350 sq km/907 sq mi; population (2002 est) 116,600. Wexford is one of the most intensively cultivated areas in Ireland. The main crops are wheat, barley, beet, and potatoes. Fishing is important, the main fishing port being Kilmore Quay in the south; sheep and cattle rearing are also significant, as is dairy farming. Industries include agricultural machinery and food processing. Wexford was the first part of Ireland to be colonized from England; Normans arrived in 1169. The John F Kennedy Arboretum is one of the most popular visitor attractions in the county.

whale any marine mammal of the order Cetacea. The only mammals to have adapted to living entirely in water, they have front limbs modified into flippers and no externally visible traces of hind limbs. They have horizontal tail flukes. When they surface to breathe, the hot air they breathe out condenses to form a 'spout' through the blowhole (single or double nostrils) in the top of the head. Whales are intelligent and have a complex communication system, known as 'songs'. They occur in all seas of the world. The order is divided into two groups: the toothed whales (Odontoceti) and the baleen whales (Mysticeti). Toothed whales are predators, feeding on fish and squid. They include *dolphins and *porpoises, along with large forms such as sperm whales. The largest whales are the baleen whales, with plates of modified mucous membrane called baleen (whalebone) in the mouth; these strain the food, mainly microscopic plankton, from the water. Baleen whales include the finback and right whales, and the blue whale, the largest animal that has ever lived, of length up to 30 m/100 ft. Whales have been hunted for hundreds of years (see *whaling); today they are close to extinction. Of the 11 great whale species, 7 were listed as either endangered or vulnerable in 1996. Whale-watching, as an economic alternative to whaling, generated US$121 million worldwide in 1994.

whaling the hunting of whales. Whales have been killed by humans since at least the middle ages. There were hundreds of thousands of whales at the beginning of the 20th century, but the invention of the harpoon in 1870 and improvements in ships and mechanization have led to the near-extinction of several species of whale. Commercial whaling was largely discontinued in 1986, although Norway and Japan have continued commercial whaling.

Wharton, Edith Newbold (1862–1937) born Edith Newbold Jones, US novelist. Her work, known for its subtlety and form and influenced by her friend Henry *James, was mostly set in New York society. It includes *The House of Mirth* (1905), which made her reputation; the grim, uncharacteristic novel of New England *Ethan Frome* (1911); *The Custom of the Country* (1913); and *The Age of Innocence* (1920; Pulitzer Prize), which was made into a film in 1993.

wheat cereal plant derived from the wild *Triticum*, a grass native to the Middle East. It is the chief cereal used in breadmaking and is widely cultivated in temperate climates suited to its growth. Wheat is killed by frost, and damp makes the grains soft, so warm, dry regions produce the most valuable grain.

wheatear small (15 cm/6 in long) migratory bird *Oenanthe oenanthe* of the family Muscicapidae, order Passeriformes (which includes thrushes). Wheatears are found throughout the Old World and also breed in far northern parts of North America. The plumage is light grey above and white below with a buff tinge on the breast, a black face-patch, and black and white wings and tail. In flight a white patch on the lower back and tail is conspicuous. The wheatear's food consists chiefly of insects.

whelk any of various families of large marine snails with a thick spiral shell, especially the family Buccinidae. Whelks are scavengers, and also eat other shellfish. The largest grow to 40 cm/16 in long. Tropical species, such as the conches, can be very colourful.

whey watery by-product of the cheesemaking process, which is drained off after the milk has been heated and *rennet (a curdling agent) added to induce its coagulation.

Whig Party in the UK, predecessor of the Liberal Party. The name was first used of rebel *Covenanters and then of those who wished to exclude James II from the English succession (as a Roman Catholic). They were in power continuously from 1714 to 1760 and pressed for industrial and commercial development, a vigorous foreign policy, and religious toleration. During the French Revolution, the Whigs demanded parliamentary reform in Britain, and from the passing of the Reform Bill in 1832 became increasingly known as Liberals.

whimbrel wading bird *Numenius phaeopus*, order Charadriiformes, with a medium-sized down-curved bill, streaked brown plumage, and striped head. About 40 cm/1.3 ft long, it breeds in the Arctic, and winters in Africa, southern North America, South America, and South Asia. It is related to the *curlew.

whip (the whipper-in of hounds at a foxhunt) in UK politics, the member of Parliament who ensures the presence of colleagues in the party when there is to be a vote in Parliament at the end of a debate. The written appeal sent by the whips to MPs is also called a whip; this letter is underlined once, twice, or three times to indicate its importance. A **three-line whip** is the most important, and every MP is expected to attend and vote with their party. An MP who fails to attend may be temporarily suspended from the party, a penalty known as 'having the whip withdrawn'.

whippet breed of dog resembling a small greyhound. It grows to 56 cm/22 in at the shoulder, and 9 kg/20 lb in weight.

whippoorwill North American *nightjar *Caprimulgus vociferus*, order Caprimulgiformes, so called from its cry during the nights of its breeding season. It is about 25 cm/10 in long, mottled tawny brown in colour, with a white collar on the throat, and long, stiff bristles at the base of the bill.

whip snake or **coachwhip** any of the various species of nonpoisonous slender-bodied tree-dwelling snakes of the New World genus *Masticophis*, family Colubridae. They are closely allied to members of the genus *Coluber* of southwestern North America, Eurasia, Australasia, and North Africa, some of which are called whip snakes in the Old World, but racers in North America.

whirlwind rapidly rotating column of air, often synonymous with a *tornado. On a smaller scale it produces the dust-devils seen in deserts.

whisky or **whiskey** (Scottish Gaelic *uisge beatha* 'water of life') distilled spirit made from cereals: Scotch whisky from malted barley, Irish whiskey usually from barley, and North American whiskey and bourbon from maize and rye. Scotch is usually blended; pure malt whisky is more expensive. Whisky is generally aged in wooden casks for 4–12 years.

Whistler, James Abbott McNeill (1834–1903) US painter and etcher. Active in London from 1859, he was a leading figure in the *Aesthetic Movement. Influenced by Japanese prints, he painted riverscapes and portraits that show subtle composition and colour harmonies, for example *Arrangement in Grey and Black: Portrait of the Painter's Mother* (1871; Musée d'Orsay, Paris).

Whitby, Synod of council summoned by King Oswy of Northumbria in 664, which decided to adopt the Roman rather than the Celtic form of Christianity for Britain.

White term denoting a counter-revolutionary, especially a member of the anticommunist forces in the Russian Civil War of 1918 to 1821. In this conflict, the Whites were led by former tsarist officers and supported by troops from foreign countries, but were eventually defeated by the Bolshevik *Red Army. They were named after the royalist opponents of the French Revolution, who took the white lily of the French Bourbon monarchy as their emblem.

White, Gilbert (1720–1793) English naturalist and cleric. He was the author of *The Natural History and Antiquities of Selborne* (1789), which records the flora and fauna of an area of Hampshire.

White, Patrick Victor Martindale (1912–1990) Australian writer. He did more than any other to put Australian literature on the international map. His partly allegorical novels explore the lives of early settlers in Australia and often deal with misfits or inarticulate people. They include *The Aunt's Story* (1948), written during his voyage back to Australia, *The Tree of Man* (1955), *Voss* (1957), based on the ill-fated 19th-century explorer Ludwig Leichhardt, and *Riders in the Chariot* (1961), exploring suburban life. He was awarded the Nobel Prize for Literature in 1973. White became a fervent republican after the dismissal of the Gough *Whitlam government in 1975, returning his Order of Australia in 1976, and supported conservation causes in his later years.

whitebait any of the fry (young) of various silvery fishes, especially *herring. It is also the name for a Pacific smelt *Osmerus mordax*.

whitebeam tree native to southern Europe, usually found growing on chalk or limestone. It can reach 20 m/60 ft in height. It takes its name from the dense coat of short white hairs on the underside of the leaves. (Genus *Sorbus aria*, family Rosaceae.)

white blood cell or **leucocyte** one of a number of different cells that play a part in the body's defences and give immunity against disease. Some (neutrophils and *macrophages) engulf invading micro-organisms, others kill infected cells, while *lymphocytes produce more specific immune responses. White blood cells are colourless, with clear or granulated cytoplasm, and are capable of independent amoeboid movement. They occur in the blood, *lymph, and elsewhere in the body's tissues. Unlike mature red blood cells they contain a nucleus.

white dwarf small, hot *star, the last stage in the life of a star such as the Sun. White dwarfs make up 10% of the stars in the Galaxy; most have a mass 60% of that of the Sun, but only 1% of the Sun's diameter, similar in size to the Earth. Most have surface temperatures of 8,000 °C/14,400 °F or more, hotter than the Sun. However, being so small, their overall luminosities may be less than 1% of that of the Sun. The Milky Way contains an estimated 50 billion white dwarfs.

whitefish any of various freshwater fishes, genera *Coregonus* and *Prosopium*, of the salmon family, found in lakes and rivers of North America and Eurasia. They include the whitefish *C. clupeaformis* and cisco *C. artedi*.

White House official residence of the president of the USA, in Washington, DC. It is a plain three-storeyed edifice of grey sandstone, built in Italian Renaissance style 1792–99 to the designs of Philadelphia architect James Hoban, who also restored the house after it was burned by the British in 1814; it was then painted white to hide the scorches.

White Paper in the UK and some other countries, an official document that expresses government policy on an issue. It is usually preparatory to the introduction of a parliamentary bill (a proposed act of Parliament). Its name derives from its having fewer pages than a government blue book, and therefore needing no blue paper cover.

White Sea Russian **Beloye More**, gulf of the Arctic Ocean on the northwest coast of Russia, on which the port of Arkhangelsk stands; area 90,000 sq km/ 34,750 sq mi; average depth 60 m/200 ft, maximum depth 330 m/1,082 ft. There isa warship construction base, including nuclear submarines, at Severodvinsk. The North Dvina, Mezen, and Onega rivers flow into it, and there are canal links with the Baltic, Black, and Caspian seas. In winter the bays are often ice-bound, with drifting ice offshore.

White terror general term used by socialists and Marxists to describe a right-wing counterrevolution: for example, the attempts by the Chinese Guomindang to massacre the communists 1927–31; see *White.

whitethroat any of several Old World warblers of the genus *Sylvia* in the family Muscicapidae, order Passeriformes. They are found in scrub, hedges, and wood clearings of Eurasia in summer, migrating to Africa in winter. They are about 14 cm/5.5 in long.

White Volta one of the two main upper branches of the River *Volta, running through Burkina Faso and Ghana.

whiting predatory fish *Merlangius merlangus* common in shallow sandy northern European waters. It grows to 70 cm/2.3 ft.

Whitlam, (Edward) Gough (1916–) Australian politician, leader of the Labor Party 1967–78 and prime minister 1972–75. He ended conscription and Australia's military commitment in Vietnam, introduced the Medibank national health service, abolished university fees, expanded Aboriginal rights, attempted redistribution of wealth, raised loans to increase national ownership of industry and resources, and recognized mainland China.

Whitman, Walt(er) (1819–1892) US poet. He published *Leaves of Grass* (1855), which contains the symbolic 'Song of Myself'. It used unconventional free verse (with no rhyme or regular rhythm) and scandalized the public by its frank celebration of sexuality. His poems were often set by composers such as Hindemith, Vaughan Williams, Henze, and Delius.

Whitney, Eli (1765–1825) US inventor who in 1794 patented the cotton gin, a device for separating cotton fibre from its seeds. Also a manufacturer of firearms, he created a standardization system that was the precursor of the assembly line.

Whittle, Frank (1907–1996) English engineer. He patented the basic design for the turbojet engine in 1930. In the Royal Air Force he worked on jet propulsion 1937–46. In May 1941 the Gloster E 28/39 aircraft first flew with the Whittle jet engine. Both the German (first operational jet planes) and the US jet aircraft were built using his principles. He was knighted in 1948.

WHO acronym for *World Health Organization, an agency of the United Nations established to prevent the spread of diseases.

wholesale the business of selling merchandise to anyone other than the final customer. Most manufacturers or producers sell in bulk to a wholesale organization which distributes the smaller quantities required by retail outlets.

whooping cough *or* **pertussis** acute infectious disease, seen mainly in children, caused by colonization of the air passages by the bacterium *Bordetella pertussis*. There may be catarrh, mild fever, and loss of appetite, but the main symptom is violent coughing, associated with the sharp intake of breath that is the characteristic 'whoop', and often followed by vomiting and severe nose bleeds. The cough may persist for weeks.

whortleberry a form of *bilberry.

whydah any of various African birds of the genus *Vidua*, order Passeriformes, of the weaver family. They lay their eggs in the nests of *waxbills, which rear the young. Young birds resemble young waxbills, but the adults do not resemble adult waxbills. Males have long tail feathers used in courtship displays.

Whymper, Edward (1840–1911) English mountaineer. He made the first ascent of many Alpine peaks, including the Matterhorn 1865, and in the Andes scaled Chimborazo and other mountains.

Wicklow county of the Republic of Ireland, in the province of Leinster; county town Wicklow; area 2,030 sq km/784 sq mi; population (2002 est) 114,700. It includes the **Wicklow Mountains**, the rivers Slaney, Avoca, Vartry, and Liffey, and the coastal resort of Bray. Other towns include Arklow, Greystones, and Baltinglass. The village of Shillelagh gave its name to rough cudgels of oak or blackthorn made there. Agriculture is important; there is livestock rearing (in particular a special breed of mountain sheep), and dairy farming. Wheat and oats are grown, and seed potatoes and bulbs are produced.

Wiesel, Elie(zer) (1928–) US academic and human-rights campaigner, born in Romania. He was held in Buchenwald concentration camp during World War II, and assiduously documented wartime atrocities against the Jews in an effort to alert the world to the dangers of racism and violence. His novel *La Nuit/Night* (1956) was based on his experiences in the camps. A leading figure in human-rights campaigns, he was awarded the Nobel Prize for Peace in 1986 for his work as a writer and human-rights activist.

wigeon either of two species of dabbling duck of genus *Anas*, order Anseriformes. The **American wigeon** *A. americana*, about 48 cm/19 in long, is found along both coasts in winter and breeds inland. Males have a white-capped head and a green eye stripe.

Wight, Isle of island and unitary authority of southern England. **area:** 380 sq km/147 sq mi **towns:** Newport (the administrative headquarters); Ryde, Sandown, Shanklin, Ventnor (all resorts) **physical:** chalk cliffs and downs, and deep ravines, known locally as 'chines'; the highest point is St Boniface Down (240 m/787 ft); the Needles, a group of pointed chalk rocks up to 30 m/100 ft high in the sea to the west; the Solent, the sea channel between Hampshire and the island **features:** Benedictine monastery at Quarr Abbey; Parkhurst Prison, just outside Newport; Cowes, venue of Regatta Week and headquarters of the Royal Yacht Squadron; Osborne House, built for Queen Victoria in 1845, sawmills, tourism **population:** (1996) 130,000 **history:** conquered by the Romans in AD 43; there are Roman villas at Newport and Brading. Charles I was imprisoned (1647–48) in Carisbrooke Castle, now ruined.

Wightman Cup annual tennis competition between international women's teams from the USA and the UK. The trophy, first contested in 1923, was donated by Hazel Hotchkiss Wightman (1886–1974), a former US tennis player who won singles, doubles, and mixed-doubles titles in the US Championships 1909–1911. Because of US domination of the contest it was abandoned in 1990.

Wilberforce, William (1759–1833) English reformer. He was instrumental in abolishing *slavery in the British Empire. He entered Parliament in 1780. In 1807 his bill banning the trade in slaves from the West Indies was passed, and by 1833 further acts had eradicated slavery throughout the empire. He died shortly before the Slavery Abolition Act was passed.

Wilczek, Frank (1951–) US physicist. With US physicists David Gross and Hugh Politzer he shared the Nobel prize in Physics in 2004 for his contribution to the theoretical explanation of how the strong nuclear force holds quark subatomic particles together.

Wilde, Oscar (Fingal O'Flahertie Wills) (1854–1900) Irish writer. With his flamboyant style and quotable conversation, he dazzled London society and, on his lecture tour in 1882, the USA. He published his only novel, The Picture of Dorian Gray, in 1891, followed by a series of sharp dramatic comedies, including A Woman of No Importance (1893). Two of his most famous satirical social dramas, The Ideal Husband and The Importance of Being Earnest, were published in 1895. This was the same year in which Wilde was imprisoned for homosexual offences, as a result of legal action taken by the Marquess of Queensbury, father of Wilde's intimate, Lord Alfred Douglas. Wilde left prison two years later and settled in Paris, a broken man.

wildebeest *or* **gnu** either of two species of African *antelope, with a cowlike face, a beard and mane, and heavy curved horns in both sexes. The body is up to 1.3 m/4.2 ft high at the shoulder and slopes away to the hindquarters. (Genus *Connochaetes*.)

wilderness area of uninhabited land that has never been disturbed by humans, usually located some distance from towns and cities. According to estimates by US group Conservation International, 52% (90 million sq km/35 million sq mi) of the Earth's total land area was still undisturbed in 1994.

wildlife trade international trade in live plants and animals, and in wildlife products such as skins, horns, shells, and feathers. The trade has made some species virtually extinct, and whole ecosystems (for example, coral reefs) are threatened. Wildlife trade is to some extent regulated by CITES (Convention on International Trade in Endangered Species).

wild type in genetics, the naturally occurring gene for a particular character that is typical of most individuals of a given species, as distinct from new genes that arise by mutation.

Wilkes, John (1727–1797) British Radical politician, imprisoned for his political views; member of Parliament 1757–64 and from 1774. He championed parliamentary reform, religious tolerance, and US independence.

Wilkins, Maurice Hugh Frederick (1916–2004) New Zealand-born British molecular biologist who was awarded the Nobel Prize for Physiology or Medicine in 1962 with Francis Crick and James Watson for the discovery of the double-helical structure of DNA and of the significance of this structure in the replication and transfer of genetic information.

Wilkins, William (1778–1839) English architect. He pioneered the Greek Revival in England with his design for Downing College, Cambridge (1807–20). His other works include Haileybury College (1806–09); and in London, the main block of University College (1827–28), the National Gallery (1834–38), and St George's Hospital (1828–29). All these buildings are classical in style, but in his extensions of Corpus, King's, and Trinity colleges at Cambridge he adopted the Gothic style.

William (1982–) born William Arthur Philip Louis, Prince of the UK, first child of the Prince and Princess of Wales.

William four kings of England:

William (I) the Conqueror (1028–1087) King of England from 25 December 1066. He was the illegitimate son of Duke Robert the Devil whom he succeeded as Duke of Normandy in 1035. Claiming that his relative King Edward the Confessor had bequeathed him the English throne, William invaded England in 1066, defeating *Harold (II) Godwinson at the Battle of Hastings on 14 October 1066, and was crowned King of England.

William (II) Rufus (c. 1056–1100) called 'William the Red', King of England from 1087, the third son of William (I) the Conqueror. He spent most of his reign attempting to capture Normandy from his brother *Robert (II) Curthose, Duke of Normandy. His extortion of money led his barons to revolt and caused confrontation with Bishop Anselm. He was killed while hunting in the New Forest, Hampshire, and was succeeded by his brother Henry I.

William (III) of Orange (1650–1702) King of Great Britain and Ireland from 1688, the son of William II of Orange and Mary, daughter of Charles I. He was offered the English crown by the parliamentary opposition to James II. He invaded England in 1688 and in 1689 became joint sovereign with his wife, *Mary II, daughter of the deposed James II. He spent much of his reign campaigning, first in Ireland, where he defeated James II at the Battle of the *Boyne in 1690, and later against the French in Flanders. He died childless and was succeeded by Mary's sister, Anne.

William IV (1765–1837) King of Great Britain and Ireland from 1830, when he succeeded his brother George IV. Third son of George III, he was created Duke of Clarence in 1789, and married Adelaide of Saxe-Meiningen (1792–1849) in 1818. During the Reform Bill crisis he secured its passage by agreeing to create new peers to overcome the hostile majority in the House of Lords. He was succeeded by his niece Victoria.

William (German **Wilhelm**) two emperors of Germany:

William I (1797–1888) King of Prussia from 1861 and Emperor of Germany from 1871; the son of Friedrich Wilhelm III. He served in the Napoleonic Wars 1814–15 and helped to crush the 1848 revolution. After he succeeded his brother Friedrich Wilhelm IV to the throne of Prussia, his policy was largely dictated by his chancellor *Bismarck, who secured his proclamation as emperor.

William II (1859–1941) Emperor of Germany from 1888, the son of Frederick III and Victoria, daughter of Queen Victoria of Britain. In 1890 he forced Chancellor Bismarck to resign in an attempt to assert his own political authority. The result was an exacerbation of domestic and international political instability, although his personal influence declined in the 1900s. He was an enthusiastic supporter of Admiral Tirpitz's plans for naval expansion. In 1914 he first approved Austria's ultimatum to Serbia and then, when he realized war was inevitable, tried in vain to prevent it. In 1918 he fled to Doorn in the Netherlands after Germany's defeat and his abdication.

William (Dutch **Willem**) three kings of the Netherlands, including:

William I (1772–1844) King of the Netherlands 1815–40. He lived in exile during the French occupation 1795–1813 and fought against the emperor Napoleon at Jena and Wagram. The Austrian Netherlands were added to his kingdom by the Allies in 1815, but secured independence (recognized by the major European states in 1839) by the revolution of 1830. William's unpopularity led to his abdication in 1840.

William the Lion (1143–1214) King of Scotland from 1165. He was captured by Henry II while invading England in 1174, and forced to do homage, but Richard I abandoned the English claim to suzerainty for a money payment in 1189. In 1209 William was forced by King John to renounce his claim to Northumberland.

William the Silent (1533–1584) Prince of Orange from 1544. Leading a revolt against Spanish rule in the Netherlands from 1573, he briefly succeeded in uniting the Catholic south and Protestant northern provinces, but the former provinces submitted to Spain while the latter formed a federation in 1579 (Union of Utrecht) which repudiated Spanish suzerainty in 1581.

Williams, Tennessee (1911–1983) born Thomas Lanier Williams, US dramatist. His work is characterized by fluent dialogue and searching analysis

of the psychological deficiencies of his characters. His plays, usually set in the US Deep South against a background of decadence and degradation, include *The Glass Menagerie* (1945), *A Streetcar Named Desire* (1947), and *Cat on a Hot Tin Roof* (1955), the last two of which earned Pulitzer Prizes.

Williams, William Carlos (1883–1963) US poet, essayist, and theoretician. He was associated with *Imagism and Objectivism. One of the most original and influential of modern poets, he is noted for advancing poetics of visual images and colloquial American rhythms, conceiving the poem as a 'field of action'. His epic, five-book poem *Patterson* (1946–58) is written in a form of free verse that combines historical documents, newspaper material, and letters, to celebrate his home town in New Jersey. *Pictures from Brueghel* (1963) won him, posthumously, a Pulitzer Prize. His vast body of prose work includes novels, short stories, essays, and the play *A Dream of Love* (1948).

William the Marshall (c. 1146–1219) 1st Earl of Pembroke, English knight, regent of England from 1216. After supporting the dying Henry II against Richard (later Richard I), he went on a crusade to Palestine, was pardoned by Richard, and was granted an earldom in 1189. On King John's death he was appointed guardian of the future Henry III, and defeated the French under Louis VIII to enable Henry to gain the throne.

will-o'-the-wisp light sometimes seen over marshy ground, believed to be burning gas containing methane from decaying organic matter.

willow any of a group of trees or shrubs containing over 350 species, found mostly in the northern hemisphere, flourishing in damp places. The leaves are often lance-shaped, and the male and female catkins are borne on separate trees. (Genus *Salix*, family Salicaceae.)

willowherb any of a group of perennial flowering plants belonging to the evening primrose family. The **rosebay willowherb** or **fireweed** *C. angustifolium* is common in woods and wasteland. It grows to 1.2 m/ 4 ft with tall upright spikes of red or purplish flowers. (Genera *Epilobium* and *Chamaenerion*, family Onagraceae.)

willow warbler bird *Phylloscopus trochilus*, family Muscicapidae, order Passeriformes. It is about 11 cm/4 in long, similar in appearance to the chiffchaff, but with a distinctive song. It is found in woods and shrubberies, and migrates from northern Eurasia to Africa.

Wilson, (James) Harold (1916–1995) Baron Wilson of Rievaulx, British Labour politician, party leader from 1963, prime minister 1964–70 and 1974–76. His premiership was dominated by the issue of UK admission to membership of the European Community (now the European Union), the social contract (unofficial agreement with the trade unions), and economic difficulties.

Wilson, (Thomas) Woodrow (1856–1924) 28th president of the USA 1913–21, a Democrat. One of the USA's most successful presidents and world's most respected statesmen, he was known for his humanity, honesty, and integrity. He kept the USA out of *World War I until 1917, and in January 1918 issued his Fourteen Points as a basis for a just peace settlement, which included the formation of a *League of Nations. He was awarded the Nobel Peace Prize in 1919. Congress later refused to commit the USA to the League.

Wiltshire county of southwest England (since April 1997 Swindon has been a separate unitary authority). **area:** 3,480 sq km/1,343 sq mi **towns and cities:** Trowbridge (administrative headquarters), Salisbury, Wilton, Devizes, Chippenham, Warminster **physical:** Marlborough Downs; Savernake Forest; rivers Kennet, Wylye, Avons (Salisbury and Bristol); Salisbury Plain (32 km/20 mi by 25 km/16 mi, lying at about 120 m/394 ft above sea-level), a military training area used since Napoleonic times **features:** Longleat House; Wilton House; Stourhead, with 18th-century gardens; Neolithic Stonehenge, Avebury, Silbury Hill, West Kennet Long Barrow; Stonehenge, Avebury, and associated sites are a World Heritage site; Salisbury Cathedral, which has the tallest spire in Britain (123 m/404 ft) **population:** (1996) 593,300.

Wimbledon English lawn tennis centre used for international championship matches, situated in south London. There are currently 18 courts.

WIMP acronym for **Windows, icons, menus, pointing device**, in computing, another name for *graphical user interface (GUI).

wind lateral movement of the Earth's atmosphere from high-pressure areas (anticyclones) to low-pressure areas (depressions). Its speed is measured using an *anemometer or by studying its effects on, for example, trees by using the *Beaufort scale. Although modified by features such as land and water, there is a basic worldwide system of *trade winds, westerlies, and polar easterlies.

wind-chill factor *or* **wind-chill index** estimate of how much colder it feels when a wind is blowing. It is arrived at by combining the actual temperature and wind speed and is given as a different temperature.

Windermere largest lake in England, in the *Lake District, Cumbria, northwest England; length 17 km/10.5 mi; width 1.6 km/1 mi. Windermere is the principal centre of tourism in the Lake District. The town of the same name extends towards Bowness-on-Windermere on the eastern shore of the lake.

wind farm array of windmills or *wind turbines used for generating electrical power. The world's largest wind farm at Altamont Pass, California, USA, consists of 6,000 wind turbines generating 1 TWh of electricity per year. Wind farms supply about 1.5% of California's electricity needs. To produce 1,200 megawatts of electricity (an output comparable with that of a nuclear power station), a wind farm would need to occupy around 370 sq km/140 sq mi.

Windhoek capital of Namibia, and administrative centre of Khomas region; population (1997 est) 169,000. It is just north of the Tropic of Capricorn, in the Khomas Highlands, 290 km/180 mi from the west coast. It is the world centre of the karakul (breed of sheep) industry and there is a considerable trade in fleece and skins; other industries include engineering, clothing manufacture, and food processing.

wind instrument any musical instrument where a column of air (created by the player's breath) vibrates in a tube (the body of the instrument), producing a sound. There are two main types of wind instrument: *woodwind instruments, including flute, piccolo, clarinet, and oboe; *brass instruments, including trumpet, horns, and trombone.

Windows in computing, originally Microsoft's graphical user interface (GUI) for IBM PCs and clones running MS-DOS. Windows has developed into a family of operating systems that run on a wide variety of computers from pen-operated palmtop personal digital assistants (PDAs) to large, multiprocessor computers in corporate data centres.

wind power power produced from the harnessing of wind energy. The wind has long been used as a source of energy: sailing ships and windmills are ancient inventions. After the energy crisis of the 1970s *wind turbines began to be used to produce electricity on a large scale. The wind turbine is the modern counterpart of the windmill. The rotor blades are huge – up to 100 m/330 ft across – in order to extract as much energy as possible from the wind. Inside the turbine head, gears are used to increase the speed of the turning shaft so that the electricity generation is as efficient as possible.

Windsor and Maidenhead unitary authority in southeast England, created in 1998 from part of the former county of Berkshire. **area:** 198 sq km/76 sq mi **towns and cities:** Windsor, Maidenhead (administrative headquarters) **features:** River Thames; Windsor Castle, royal residence originally built by William the Conqueror; Eton College, founded by Henry VI in 1440; Household Cavalry Museum (Windsor); Stanley Spencer (1891–1959) Gallery (Cookham on Thames); Ascot Racecourse **population:** (1996) 140,200.

Windsor, House of official name of the British royal family since 1917, adopted in place of Saxe-Coburg-Gotha. Since 1960 those descendants of Elizabeth II not entitled to the prefix HRH (His/Her Royal Highness) have borne the surname Mountbatten-Windsor.

wind turbine windmill of advanced aerodynamic design connected to a generator producing electrical energy and used in wind-power installations. Wind is a form of *renewable energy that is used to turn the *turbine blades of the windmill. Wind turbines can be either large propeller-type rotors mounted on a tall tower, or flexible metal strips fixed to a vertical axle at top and bottom.

Windward Islands group of islands in the West Indies, forming part of the lesser *Antilles.

wine alcoholic beverage, usually made from fermented grape pulp, although wines have also traditionally been made from many other fruits such as damsons and elderberries. **Red wine** is the product of the grape with the skin; **white wine** of the inner pulp of the grape. The sugar content is converted to ethyl alcohol by the yeast *Saccharomyces ellipsoideus*, which lives on the skin of the grape. For **dry wine** the fermentation is allowed to go on longer than for **sweet** or **medium**; *champagne (sparkling wine from the Champagne region of France) is bottled while still fermenting, but other sparkling wines are artificially carbonated. Some wines are fortified with additional alcohol obtained from various sources, and with preservatives. Some of the latter may cause dangerous side effects (see *additive). For this reason, organic wines, containing no preservatives, have recently become popular. The largest wine-producing countries are Italy, France, Russia, Georgia, Moldova, Armenia, and Spain; others include almost all European countries, Australia, South Africa, the USA, and Chile.

wine, fortified wine that has extra alcohol added to raise its alcohol content to about 20%. Fortified wines keep well because the alcohol kills the micro-organisms that spoil natural wines. Port, which originates from Oporto in Portugal, is made by adding brandy to wine before fermentation is complete; sherry, originally made in Jerez in Spain, is a dry wine fortified after fermentation and later blended with sugar for sweet sherry; vermouth is flavoured with bitter herbs. Marsala, from Sicily, is fortified after fermentation and then heated gradually.

wing in biology, the modified forelimb of birds and bats, or the membranous outgrowths of the *exoskeleton of insects, which give the power of flight. Birds and bats have two wings. Bird wings have feathers attached to the fused digits ('fingers') and forearm bones, while bat wings consist of skin stretched between the digits. Most insects have four wings, which are strengthened by wing veins. Birds can fly because of the specialized shape of their wings: a rounded leading edge, flattened underneath and round on top. This aerofoil shape produces lift in the same way that an aircraft wing does. The outline of the wing is related to the speed of flight. Fast birds of prey have a streamlined shape. Larger birds, such as the eagle, have large wings with separated tip feathers which reduce drag and allow slow flight. Insect wings are not aerofoils. They push downwards to produce lift, in the same way that oars are used to push through water.

Winnipeg called 'Gateway to the West', (Cree *win-nipuy* 'muddy water') capital of Manitoba, Canada, at the confluence of the Red and Assiniboine rivers, 65 km/ 40 mi south of Lake Winnipeg, 30 km/20 mi north of the US border; population (2001 est) 709,400. It is a focus for trans-Canada and Canada–US traffic, and a market and transhipment point for wheat and other produce from the Prairie Provinces: Manitoba, Alberta, and Saskatchewan. Processed foods, textiles, farming machinery, and transport equipment are manufactured. Established as Winnipeg in 1870 on the site of earlier forts, the city expanded with the arrival of the Canadian Pacific Railway in 1881.

wintergreen any of a group of plants belonging to the heath family, especially the species *G. procumbens* of northeastern North America, which creeps underground and sends up tiny shoots. Oil of wintergreen, used in treating rheumatism, is extracted from its leaves. Wintergreen is also the name for various plants belonging to the wintergreen family Pyrolaceae, including the green pipsissewa *C. maculata* of northern North America, Europe, and Asia. (Genus *Gaultheria*, family Ericaceae; also genera *Pyrola*, *Chimaphila*, *Orthilia*, and *Moneses*, family Pyrolaceae.)

wireless original name for a radio receiver. In early experiments with transmission by radio waves, notably by Italian inventor Guglielmo *Marconi in Britain, signals were sent in Morse code, as in telegraphy. Radio, unlike the telegraph, used no wires for transmission, and the means of communication was termed 'wireless telegraphy'.

wireworm larva of some species of *click beetle. Wireworms are considered agricultural pests as they attack the seeds of many crops.

Wisconsin called the **Badger State**, (American Indian *Ouisconsin* 'gathering of waters' or 'grassy place') state in north-central USA, one of the *Great Lakes states, bordered to the south by *Illinois, to the west by *Iowa and *Minnesota, to the north by Lake *Superior and the Upper Peninsula of *Michigan, and to the east by Lake *Michigan; area 140,662 sq km/54,310 sq mi; population (2000) 5,363,700; capital Madison. Wisconsin's nickname is derived from the underground living habits of early miners, who dug their homes out of hillsides or lived inside the mines. The state contains many lakes. Features include the Apostle Islands, Door Peninsula, and the Wisconsin Dells, a scenic gorge. Wisconsin's most important industries are manufacturing and food processing, and the state is the nation's leader in the production of paper and dairy products. The brewing of beer is one of the state's oldest industries. Other towns and cities include *Milwaukee, Green Bay, Kenosha, and Racine. The earliest inhabitants of Wisconsin were the *Sioux and Chippewa American Indians. Prior to the influx of pioneers, the Chippewa had pushed the Sioux westward towards the plains. Originally settled by the French, and then the British, Wisconsin became part of the USA in 1783, as part of the Northwest Territory, but Britain did not fully remove control until after the *War of 1812. Wisconsin's state motto is 'Forward', and it is one of the most progressive states in the USA. Wisconsin was admitted to the Union in 1858 as the 32nd US state.

wisent another name for the European *bison.

wisteria any of a group of climbing leguminous shrubs (see *legume), including *W. sinensis*, native to the eastern USA and East Asia. Wisterias have hanging clusters of bluish, white, or pale mauve flowers, and pinnate leaves (leaflets on either side of the stem). They are grown against walls as ornamental plants. (Genus *Wisteria*, family Leguminosae.)

witchcraft the alleged possession and exercise of magical powers – **black magic** if used with evil intent, and **white magic** if benign. Its origins lie in traditional beliefs and religions. Supposed practitioners of witchcraft have often had considerable skill in, for example, herbal medicine and traditional remedies; this prompted the World Health Organization in 1976 to recommend the integration of traditional healers into the health teams of African states.

witch doctor alternative name for a *shaman.

witch hazel any of a group of flowering shrubs or small trees belonging to the witch hazel family, native to North America and East Asia, especially *H. virginiana*. An astringent extract prepared from the bark or leaves is used in medicine as an eye lotion and a liniment to relieve pain or stiffness. (Genus *Hamamelis*, family Hamamelidaceae.)

witch-hunt persecution of minority political opponents or socially nonconformist groups without any regard for their guilt or innocence. Witch-hunts are often accompanied by a degree of public hysteria; for example, the *McCarthy anticommunist hearings during the 1950s in the USA.

Wittgenstein, Ludwig Josef Johann (1889–1951) Austrian philosopher. *Tractatus Logico-Philosophicus* (1922) postulated the 'picture theory' of language: that words represent things according to social agreement. He subsequently rejected this idea, and developed the idea that usage was more important than convention.

woad biennial plant native to Europe, with arrow-shaped leaves and clusters of small yellow flowers. It was formerly cultivated for a blue dye extracted from its leaves. Ancient Britons used the blue dye as a body paint in battle. (Genus *Isatis tinctoria*, family Cruciferae.)

Wodehouse, P(elham) G(renville) (1881–1975) English novelist. He became a US citizen in 1955. His humorous novels and stories portray the accident-prone world of such characters as the socialite Bertie Wooster and his invaluable and impeccable manservant Jeeves, and Lord Emsworth of Blandings Castle with his prize pig, the Empress of Blandings.

Woden or **Wodan** the foremost Anglo-Saxon god, whose Norse counterpart is *Odin.

Wokingham unitary authority in southeast England, created in 1998 from part of the former county of Berkshire. **area:** 179 sq km/69 sq mi **towns and cities:** Wokingham (administrative headquarters), Twyford **features:** River Thames forms northern border of authority; Henley Regatta course; large areas of mixed woodland including remnants of old Royal Chase of Windsor Forest and tree-lined avenues; Finchampstead Ridges **population:** (1996) 142,000.

wolf any of two species of large wild dogs of the genus *Canis*. The **grey** or **timber wolf** *C. lupus*, of North America and Eurasia, is highly social, measures up to 90 cm/3 ft at the shoulder, and weighs up to 45 kg/100 lb. It has been greatly reduced in numbers except for isolated wilderness regions. The **red wolf** *C. rufus*, generally more slender and smaller (average weight about 15 kg/35 lb) and tawnier in colour, may not be a separate species, but a grey wolf–coyote hybrid. It used to be restricted to southern central USA, but is now thought to be extinct in the wild.

Wolf, Hugo (Filipp Jakob) (1860–1903) Austrian composer. He wrote more than 250 *lieder* (songs), including the *Mörike-Lieder/Mörike Songs* (1888) and the two-volume *Italienisches Liederbuch/Italian Songbook* (1892, 1896).

Wolfe, James (1727–1759) English soldier. He served in Canada and commanded a victorious expedition against the French general Montcalm in Québec on the Plains of *Abraham, during which both commanders were killed. The British victory established their supremacy over Canada.

wolfram alternative name for *tungsten.

Wollongong (Aboriginal 'sound of the sea') industrial city on the coast of New South Wales, Australia, 80 km/50 mi south of Sydney; population (1996, with Port Kembla) 219,761. Wollongong, the third-largest city in New South Wales, is the main residential and business centre of the Illawarra district. Its chief industries are steel production, tourism, fishing, dairying, and the manufacture of textiles and clothing. Wollongong is situated on Australia's southern coalfield, and exports coal from its port at Port Kembla. Greater Wollongong includes Port Kembla.

Wollstonecraft, Mary (1759–1797) British feminist and writer. She was a member of a group of radical intellectuals called the English Jacobins. Her book *A Vindication of the Rights of Women* (1792) demanded equal educational opportunities for women. She married William Godwin in 1797 and died giving birth to a daughter, Mary (later Mary *Shelley).

Wolof the majority ethnic group living in Senegal. There is also a Wolof minority in Gambia. There are about 2 million speakers of Wolof, a language belonging to the Niger-Congo family. The Wolof are Muslims.

Wolsey, Thomas (c. 1475–1530) English cleric and politician. In Henry VIII's service from 1509, he became archbishop of York in 1514, cardinal and lord chancellor in 1515, and began the dissolution of the monasteries. His reluctance to further Henry's divorce from Catherine of Aragon led to his downfall in 1529. He was charged with high treason in 1530 but died before being tried.

wolverine *Gulo gulo*, largest land member of the weasel family (Mustelidae), found in Europe, Asia, and North America. It is stocky in build, and about 1 m/3.3 ft long. Its long, thick fur is dark brown on the back and belly and lighter on the sides. It covers food that it cannot eat with an unpleasant secretion. Destruction of habitat and trapping for its fur have greatly reduced its numbers.

womb common name for the *uterus.

wombat any of a family (Vombatidae) of burrowing, herbivorous marsupials, native to Tasmania and southern Australia. They are about 1 m/3.3 ft long, heavy, with a big head, short legs and tail, and coarse fur. In some ways, they resemble badgers, being large burrowing animals, building burrows up to 30 m/100 ft long with a nest chamber at the end.

women's movement campaign for the rights and *emancipation (freedom) of women, including social, political, and economic equality with men. Early campaigners of the 17th–19th centuries fought for women's rights to own property, to have access to higher education, and to vote. The suffragists campaigned for women's voting rights; in the UK they formed two groups, the suffragists, who pursued reform by purely peaceful means, and the *suffragettes, who were willing to take militant action. Once women's suffrage (the right to vote) was achieved in the 20th century, the emphasis of the movement shifted to the goals of equal social and economic opportunities for women, including employment. A continuing area of concern in industrialized countries is the contradiction between the now generally accepted principle of equality and the actual inequalities that remain between the sexes in state policies and in everyday life.

wood hard tissue beneath the bark of many perennial plants; it is composed of water-conducting cells, or secondary *xylem, and gains its hardness and strength from deposits of *lignin. **Hardwoods**, such as oak, and **softwoods**, such as pine, have commercial value as structural material and for furniture.

Wood, Henry Joseph (1869–1944) English conductor. From 1895 until his death, he conducted the London Promenade Concerts, now named after him. He promoted a national interest in music and encouraged many young composers. As a composer he is remembered for the *Fantasia on British Sea Songs* (1905), which ends each Promenade season.

woodcock either of two species of wading birds, genus *Scolopax*, of the family Scolopacidae, which have barred plumage and long bills, and live in wet woodland areas. They belong to the long-billed section of the snipes, order Charadriiformes.

woodcut print made by a woodblock in which a picture or design has been cut in relief. Areas that are intended to be white are cut away leaving the raised remainder to catch and transfer the ink, which is usually black. The woodcut is the oldest method of *printing, invented in China in the th century AD. In the Middle Ages woodcuts became popular in Europe, initially for printing playing cards and block books, and later for more artistic applications, as in the work of German artist Albrecht *Dürer.

woodland area in which trees grow more or less thickly; generally smaller than a forest. Temperate climates, with four distinct seasons a year, tend to support a mixed woodland habitat, with some conifers but mostly broad-leaved and deciduous trees, shedding their leaves in autumn and regrowing them in spring. In the Mediterranean region and parts of the southern hemisphere, the trees are mostly evergreen.

woodlouse crustacean of the order Isopoda. Woodlice have segmented bodies, flattened undersides, and 14 legs. The eggs are carried by the female in a pouch beneath the thorax. They often live in high densities: up to as many as 8,900 per square metre.

woodmouse or **long-tailed field mouse** *Apodemus sylvaticus*, rodent that lives in woodlands, hedgerows, and sometimes open fields in Britain and Europe. About 9 cm/3.5 in long, with a similar length of tail, it is yellow-brown above, white below, and has long oval ears. It is nocturnal and feeds largely on seeds, but eats a range of foods, including some insects.

woodpecker bird of the family Picidae, order Piciformes. They are adapted for climbing up the bark of trees, and picking out insects to eat from the crevices. The feet, though very short, are usually strong; the nails are broad and crooked and the toes placed in pairs, two forward and two backward. As an additional support their tail feathers terminate in points, and are uncommonly hard. Woodpeckers have a long extensile tongue, which has muscles enabling the bird to dart it forth and to retract it again quickly. There are about 200 species worldwide.

Woods, Tiger (1976–) born Eldrick Woods, US golfer. In 1994 he became the youngest player, at the age of 18, to win the US Amateur Championship, the first of an unprecedented three successive titles. He turned professional in 1996, immediately becoming one of the wealthiest people in US sport as a result of endorsement deals worth US$64 million. In his first six months as a professional he won four tournaments on the US PGA circuit, and in 1997 he won the Masters. In February 2000, he became the first player to win six successive tournaments on the US PGA Tour since Ben Hogan in 1948. With his victory at the Masters in 2001, he became the first professional golfer to hold all four major titles at the same time.

Woodstock the first free rock festival, held near Bethel, New York State, USA, over three days in August 1969. It was attended by 400,000 people, and performers included the Band, Country Joe and the Fish, the Grateful Dead, Jimi Hendrix, Jefferson Airplane, and the Who. The festival was a landmark in the youth culture of the 1960s (see *hippie) and was recorded in the film *Woodstock* (1970).

woodwind musical instrument from which sound is produced by blowing into a tube, causing the air within

to vibrate. These instruments were originally made of wood but are now more commonly made of metal. The saxophone, made of metal, is an honorary woodwind instrument because it is related to the clarinet. The flute, clarinet, oboe, and bassoon make up the normal woodwind section of an orchestra.

woodworm common name for the larval stage of certain wood-boring beetles. Dead or injured trees are their natural target, but they also attack structural timber and furniture.

wool natural hair covering of the sheep, and also of the llama, angora goat, and some other *mammals. The domestic sheep *Ovis aries* provides the great bulk of the fibres used in textile production. A by-product of wool production is *lanolin.

Woolf, (Adeline) Virginia (1882–1941) born (Adeline) Virginia Stephen, English novelist and critic. In novels such as *Mrs Dalloway* (1925), *To the Lighthouse* (1927), and *The Waves* (1931), she used a 'stream of consciousness' technique to render inner experience. In *A Room of One's Own* (1929) (non-fiction), *Orlando* (1928), and *The Years* (1937), she examines the importance of economic independence for women and other feminist principles.

Worcestershire two-tier county of west central England. Herefordshire and Worcestershire existed as counties until 1974, when they were amalgamated to form the county of Hereford and Worcester; in 1998 this county was divided back into Worcestershire and Herefordshire, which regained their pre-1974 boundaries. **area:** 1,735 sq km/670 sq mi **towns and cities:** Worcester (administrative headquarters), Bewdley, Bromsgrove, Evesham, Kidderminster, Pershore, Stourport, Tenbury Wells **physical:** Malvern Hills in the southwest (highest point Worcester Beacon 425 m/1,394 ft); rivers Severn with tributaries Stour, Teme, and Avon (running through the fertile Vale of Evesham) **features:** Droitwich, once a Victorian spa, reopened its baths in 1985 (the town lies over a subterranean brine reservoir); Three Choirs Festival at Great Malvern **population:** (1996) 535,700.

word processing input, amendment, manipulation, storage, and retrieval of text. A computer system that runs such software is known as a **word processor**. Since word-processing programs became available to microcomputers, the method has largely replaced the typewriter for producing letters or other text. Typical facilities include insert, delete, cut and paste, reformat, search and replace, copy, print, mail merge, and spelling check.

Wordsworth, William (1770–1850) English poet. A leader of *Romanticism, Wordsworth is best known as the poet who reawakened his readers to the beauty of nature, describing the emotions and perceptive insights which natural beauty arouses in the sensitive observer. He advocated a poetry of simple feeling and the use of the language of ordinary speech, demonstrated in the unadorned simplicity of lyrics such as 'To the cuckoo' and 'I wandered lonely as a cloud'. He collaborated with English poet Samuel Taylor *Coleridge on *Lyrical Ballads* (1798) (which included 'Tintern Abbey', a meditation on his response to nature). His most notable individual poems were published in *Poems* (1807) (including 'Intimations of Immortality'). At intervals between then and 1839 he revised *The Prelude* (posthumously published in 1850), the first part of his uncompleted philosophical, creative, and spiritual autobiography in verse. He was appointed poet laureate in 1843.

work in physics, a measure of the result of transferring energy from one system to another to cause an object to move. Work should not be confused with *energy (the capacity to do work, which is also measured in joules) or with *power (the rate of doing work, measured in joules per second).

workhouse in the UK, a former institution to house and maintain people unable to earn their own living, established under the *poor law. Groups of parishes in England combined to build workhouses for the poor, the aged, the disabled, and orphaned children from about 1815 until about 1930.

World Bank officially the **International Bank for Reconstruction and Development**, specialized agency of the United Nations that borrows in the commercial market and lends on commercial terms. It was established in 1945 under the 1944 Bretton Woods agreement, which also created the International Monetary Fund (IMF). The **International Development Association** is an arm of the World Bank.

World Cup the most prestigious competition in international soccer, organized by the sport's world governing body, Fédération Internationale de Football Association (FIFA). Similar international competitions are also held in rugby union, cricket, athletics, and other sports.

World Health Organization (WHO) specialized agency of the United Nations established in 1946 to prevent the spread of diseases and to eradicate them. From 1996 to 1997 it had a budget of US$842.654 million. Its headquarters are in Geneva, Switzerland. The WHO's greatest achievement to date has been the eradication of smallpox.

World Intellectual Property Organization (WIPO) specialist agency of the United Nations established in 1974 to coordinate the international protection (initiated by the Paris convention in 1883) of inventions, trademarks, and industrial designs, and also literary and artistic works (as initiated by the Berne convention in 1886).

world music *or* **roots music** popular music that has its roots in *folk music, especially non-European folk music. It is usually performed by artists from the country it comes from, and has a distinct regional character. Examples are West African mbalax, East African soukous, South African mbaqanga, French Antillean zouk, Latin American salsa and lambada, and *Cajun music, as well as combinations of these with European folk music or rural *blues. The term is used primarily by the music industry and media. It is sometimes used to include non-Western classical music, such as the Javanese gamelan and Spanish flamenco, or simply to describe any music other than Western classical music or *pop music.

World Series annual *baseball competition between the winning teams of the National League (NL) and American League (AL). It is a best-of-seven series played each October. The first World Series was played in 1903 (as a best-of-nine series) and the AL's Boston Pilgrims defeated the NL's Pittsburgh Pirates in eight games.

World Trade Organization (WTO) specialized, rules-based, member-driven agency of the United Nations, world trade monitoring body established in January 1995, on approval of the Final Act of the Uruguay round of the *General Agreement on Tariffs and Trade (GATT). Under the Final Act, the WTO, a permanent trading body with a status comparable with that of the International Monetary Fund or the World Bank, effectively replaced GATT. The WTO oversees and administers agreements to reduce barriers to trade, such as tariffs, subsidies, quotas, and regulations which discriminate against imported products. Other functions of the WTO include: handling trade disputes, offering a forum for trade negotiations, technical assistance and training for developing countries, and monitoring national trade policies.

World War I 1914–18, war between the Central European Powers (Germany, Austria-Hungary, and allies) on one side and the *Triple Entente (Britain and the British Empire, France, and Russia) and their allies, including the USA (which entered in 1917), on the other side. Described as the war to end all wars, an estimated 10 million lives were lost and twice that number were wounded. It was fought on the eastern and western fronts, in the Middle East, in Africa, and at sea. By the end of the war Germany had mobilized around 11 million men. The trench system on the Western Front consisted of frontline trenches, support and reserve trenches (used to transport soldiers, equipment, and food supplies), and communication trenches, dug at an angle to the trenches facing the enemy. Soldiers were rotated so they only spent short periods at the front, where most casualties occurred, although as the war progressed and men became in shorter supply, the time at the front was often much longer. Conditions in the trenches were often appalling and, apart from the onslaught of enemy shot and shell, soldiers suffered numerous diseases as a result of their conditions, such as trench foot (foot rot caused by the continual damp), and trench fever and typhus (spread by body lice). The Russians took Poland against German forces in 1914, but were driven out by a combined Austro-German offensive in 1915. They suffered such heavy losses of men and supplies on the Eastern Front that they were unable to make a significant contribution to the remainder of the war.

World War II 1939–45, war between Germany, Italy, and Japan (the *Axis powers) on one side, and Britain, the Commonwealth, France, the USA, the USSR, and China (the *Allies) on the other. An estimated 55 million lives were lost (20 million of them citizens of the USSR), and 60 million people in Europe were displaced because of bombing raids. The war was fought in the Atlantic theatre (Europe, North Africa, and the Atlantic Ocean) and the Pacific theatre (Far East and the Pacific). It is estimated that, during the course of the war, for every tonne of bombs dropped on the UK, 315 tonnes fell on Germany. In 1945 Germany surrendered (May), but Japan fought on until the USA dropped atomic bombs on Hiroshima and Nagasaki (August).

worm any of various elongated, limbless invertebrates belonging to several phyla. Worms include the *flatworms, such as *flukes and *tapeworms; the roundworms or *nematodes, such as the eelworm

989

WORM

and the hookworm; the marine ribbon worms or nemerteans; and the segmented worms or *annelids.

WORM acronym for **write once read many times**, in computing, a storage device, similar to a *CD-ROM. The computer can write to the disk directly, but cannot later erase or overwrite the same area. WORMs are mainly used for archiving and back-up copies.

wormwood any of a group of plants belonging to the daisy family and mainly found in northern temperate regions, especially the aromatic herb *A. absinthium*, the leaves of which are used in the alcoholic drink absinthe. Tarragon is closely related to wormwood. (Genus *Artemisia*, family Compositae.)

Wounded Knee site on the Oglala Sioux Reservation, South Dakota, USA, of a confrontation between the US Army and American Indians on 29 December 1890; the last 'battle' of the Plains Wars. On 15 December the Hunkpapa Sioux chief *Sitting Bull had been killed, supposedly resisting arrest for involvement in the Ghost Dance movement. The remaining Hunkpapa fled with a group of Miniconjou Sioux led by Big Foot, but were captured by the 7th Cavalry. A shot fired during their disarmament led to the gunning down of Big Foot and over 150 Sioux, half of whom were women and children.

W particle *elementary particle, one of the *intermediate vector bosons responsible for transmitting the *weak nuclear force. The W particle exists as both W⁺ and W⁻.

wrack any of the large brown *seaweeds characteristic of rocky shores. The bladder wrack *F. vesiculosus* has narrow, branched fronds up to 1 m/3.3 ft long, with oval air bladders, usually in pairs on either side of the midrib or central vein. (Genus *Fucus*.)

wrasse any bony fish of the family Labridae, found in temperate and tropical seas. They are slender and often brightly coloured, with a single long dorsal fin. They have elaborate courtship rituals, and some species can change their colouring and sex. Species vary in size from 5 cm/2 in to 2 m/6.5 ft.

wren any of the family Troglodytidae of small birds of the order Passeriformes, with slender, slightly curved bills, and uptilted tails.

Wren, Christopher (1632–1723) English architect. His ingenious use of a refined and sober *baroque style can be seen in his best-known work, St Paul's Cathedral, London (1675–1711), and in the many churches he built in London including St Mary-le-Bow, Cheapside (1670–77), and St Bride's, Fleet Street (1671–78). His other works include the Sheldonian Theatre, Oxford (1664–69), Greenwich Hospital, London (begun 1694), and Marlborough House, London (1709–10; now much altered).

wrestling sport popular in ancient Egypt, Greece, and Rome, and included in the Olympics from 704 BC. The two main modern international styles are **Greco-Roman**, concentrating on above-waist holds, and **freestyle**, which allows the legs to be used to hold or trip; in both the aim is to throw the opponent to the ground.

Wrexham unitary authority in northeast Wales, created in 1996 from part of the former county of Clwyd. **area:** 500 sq km/193 sq mi **towns:** Wrexham (administrative headquarters), Holt, Ruabon **physical:** western side is mountainous, including

Ruabon Mountain; highest point Craig Berwy (790 m/2,592 ft); River Dee: Clywedog Valley, with notable countryside and industrial archaeology **population:** (2001 est) 128,500.

Wright Orville (1871–1948) and Wilbur (1867–1912), US inventors; brothers who pioneered powered, powered flight. Inspired by Otto *Lilienthal's gliding, they perfected their piloted glider in 1902. In 1903 they built a powered machine, a 12-hp 341-kg/750-lb plane, and became the first to make a successful powered flight, near Kitty Hawk, North Carolina. Orville flew 36.6 m/120 ft in 12 seconds; Wilbur, 260 m/852 ft in 59 seconds.

Wright, Frank Lloyd (1869–1959) US architect. He is known for 'organic architecture', in which buildings reflect their natural surroundings. From the 1890s, he developed his celebrated **prairie house** style, a series of low, spreading houses with projecting roofs. He later diversified, employing reinforced concrete to explore a variety of geometric forms. Among his buildings are his Wisconsin home, Taliesin East (1925), in prairie-house style; Falling Water, near Pittsburgh, Pennsylvania (1936), a house of cantilevered terraces straddling a waterfall; and the Guggenheim Museum, New York (1959), a spiral ramp rising from a circular plan.

Wright, Joseph (1734–1797) English painter. He was known as **Wright of Derby**, from his birthplace. He painted portraits, landscapes, and groups performing scientific experiments. His work is often dramatically lit – by fire, candlelight, or even volcanic explosion.

written communication form of *communication using a set of symbols. Written English has its own techniques and conventions. The content, structure, and style of a piece of writing are guided by its purpose. Where a piece of writing is narration and is intended to entertain it will often take the form of a story, make use of direct speech, and build up to a climax. Traditionally, narrative is carefully structured and there is likely to be a clearly defined beginning, middle, and end. An explanation or an analysis in writing is factual and straightforward. Headings and subdivisions may be used for the sake of clarity. Writing intended as persuasion to move the reader to a point of view will often use an emotive style, present lists of points, and include devices of rhetoric (or figures of speech).

wrought iron fairly pure iron containing some beads of slag, widely used for construction work before the days of cheap steel. It is strong, tough, and easy to machine. It is made in a puddling furnace, invented by Henry Colt in England in 1784. Pig iron is remelted and heated strongly in air with iron ore, burning out the carbon in the metal, leaving relatively pure iron and a slag containing impurities. The resulting pasty metal is then hammered to remove as much of the remaining slag as possible. It is still used in fences and gratings.

Wuhan river port and capital of *Hubei province, central China, at the confluence of the Han and Chang Jiang rivers; population (1999 est) 3,911,800. It was formed in 1950 as one of China's greatest industrial areas by the amalgamation of Hankou, Hanyang, and Wuchang, and by the late 20th century, with the advantage of large nearby reserves of coal and iron ore, it had become, after Anshan, the second

990

largest metallurgical centre in China. Iron, steel, heavy machine tools, railway rolling stock, lorries, agricultural machinery, electrical equipment, including fibre optic cables, textiles, cement, fertilizers, and consumer goods including food and drinks, bicycles, watches, and radios are manufactured.

Wycherley, William (1640–c. 1716) English Restoration dramatist. His first comedy, *Love in a Wood*, won him court favour in 1671, and later bawdy works include *The Country Wife* (1675) and *The Plain Dealer* (1676).

Wycliffe (or Wyclif), John (c. 1320–1384) English religious reformer. Allying himself with the party of John of Gaunt, which was opposed to ecclesiastical influence at court, he attacked abuses in the medieval church, maintaining that the Bible rather than the church was the supreme authority. He criticized such fundamental doctrines as priestly absolution, confession, and indulgences, and set disciples to work on the first translation of the Bible into English.

Wye Welsh **Gwy**, river in Wales and England; length 208 km/130 mi. It rises on Plynlimon in northeast Ceredigion, flows southeast and east through Powys and Hereford and Worcester, and follows the Gwent–Gloucestershire border before joining the River *Severn 4 km/2.5 mi south of Chepstow. It has salmon fisheries and is noted for its scenery.

Wyndham, John (1903–1969) pen-name of John Wyndham Parkes Lucas Beynon Harris, English science fiction writer. He wrote *The Day of the Triffids* (1951), describing the invasion of Earth by a strange plant mutation; *The Chrysalids* (1955); and *The Midwich Cuckoos* (1957). A recurrent theme in his work is people's response to disaster, whether caused by nature, aliens, or human error.

Wyoming called the **Equality State**, (Delaware Indian 'upon the great plain') state in western USA, one of the Mountain States, bordered to the east by *Nebraska and *South Dakota, to the north by *Montana, to the west by Montana, *Idaho, and *Utah, and to the south by Utah and *Colorado; area 251,488 sq km/97,100 sq mi; population (2000) 493,800; capital Cheyenne. Wyoming's nickname stems from its reputation for firsts in granting rights to women, including voting, jury service, and the holding of public office. The state is famous for the towering peaks of the *Rocky Mountains which dominate the landscape and are the setting of *Yellowstone National Park. It is the most sparsely populated state in the USA. The state's most important products are petroleum, coal, and natural gas. Cattle ranching is the most significant agricultural activity, and products include wool, sugar beet, and dairy produce. Other major towns and cities are Casper, Laramie, Rock Springs, Gillette, and Sheridan. Wyoming was home to indigenous people, including the Crow, Cheyenne, *Sioux, *Arapaho, and Shoshone, and was not visited by whites until the early 19th century, when it was explored by John Colter. It was acquired by the USA in 1803 as part of the *Louisiana Purchase. Fort Laramie, a trading post, was settled in 1834. Wyoming became a territory after the Union Pacific Railroad arrived in 1867–68. Wyoming was admitted to the Union in 1890 as the 44th US state.

WYSIWYG acronym for **what you see is what you get**, in computing, a program that attempts to display on the screen a faithful representation of the final printed output is said to use a WYSIWYG display. For example, a WYSIWYG *word processor would show actual page layout – line widths, page breaks, and the sizes and styles of type.

X

X Roman numeral **ten**; a person or thing unknown.

Xavier, St Francis (1506–1552) Spanish Jesuit missionary. He went to the Portuguese colonies in the East Indies, arriving at Goa in 1542. He was in Japan 1549–51, establishing a Christian mission that lasted for 100 years. He returned to Goa in 1552, and sailed for China, but died of fever there. He was canonized in 1622.

X chromosome larger of the two sex chromosomes, the smaller being the *Y chromosome. These two chromosomes are involved in sex determination. In humans, whether a person is male or female is determined by the particular combination of the two sex chromosomes in the body cells. In females both the sex chromosomes are the same – two X chromosomes (XX). In males the two are different – one X chromosome and one Y chromosome (XY). The Y chromosome is shorter than the X. *Genes on these chromosomes determine a person's sex. Genes carried on the X chromosome produce the phenomenon of *sex linkage.

xenon chemical symbol Xe, (Greek *xenos* 'stranger') colourless, odourless, gaseous, non-metallic element, atomic number 54, relative atomic mass 131.30. It is grouped with the *noble gases (rare gases) and was long believed not to enter into reactions, but is now known to form some compounds, mostly with fluorine. It is a heavy gas present in very small quantities in the air (about one part in 20 million).

Xenophon (c. 430–c. 350 BC) Greek soldier and writer who was a disciple of *Socrates (described in Xenophon's *Symposium*). He joined the Persian prince Cyrus the Younger against his brother Artaxerxes II in 401 BC, and after the Battle of Cunaxa the same year took command. His book *Anabasis* describes how he led 10,000 Greek mercenaries on a 1,600-km/1,000-mile march home across enemy territory.

xerophyte plant adapted to live in dry conditions. Common adaptations to reduce the rate of *transpiration include a reduction of leaf size, sometimes to spines or scales; a dense covering of hairs over the leaf to trap a layer of moist air (as in edelweiss); water storage cells; sunken stomata; and permanently rolled leaves or leaves that roll up in dry weather (as in marram grass). Many desert cacti are xerophytes.

Xerxes I (c. 519–465 BC) Achaemenid king of Persia 486–465 BC, the son and successor of Darius (I) the Great. He suppressed Babylonian revolts in 484 and 482, then in 480, at the head of a great army supported by a fleet, he crossed the Hellespont (Dardanelles) on bridges of boats and marched through Thrace into Greece. He occupied Athens, but the Persian fleet was defeated at Salamis and Xerxes was forced to retreat. His general Mardonius remained behind, but was defeated by the Greeks at Plataea in 479 BC.

Xhosa plural **Xhosa**, member of a Bantu people of South Africa, living mainly in the Eastern Cape province. Traditionally, the Xhosa were farmers and cattle herders, cattle having great social and religious importance to them. Their social structure is based on a monarchy. Their Bantu language belongs to the Niger-Congo family.

Xia dynasty (or Hsia dynasty) China's first legendary ruling family, *c.* 2200–*c.* 1500 BC, reputedly founded by the model emperor Yu the Great. He is believed to have controlled floods by constructing dykes. Archaeological evidence suggests that the Xia dynasty really did exist, as a Bronze Age civilization where writing was being developed, with its capital at Erlidou (Erh-li-t'ou) in Henan (Honan).

Xi'an ('western peace') industrial city and capital of *Shaanxi province, China, on the Wei He River; population (1999 est) 2,295,000. It produces chemicals, including fertilizers and plastics, machinery, electrical and electronic equipment, aircraft, and textiles. Close to Xi'an is the tomb of the emperor Shi Huangdi who ruled in the 3rd century BC, guarded by the Terracotta Army, full-scale pottery models of some seven thousand warriors. The collection is considered by many to be the eighth wonder of the world.

Xi Jiang or Si-Kiang ('west river') river in China, which rises in Yunnan province and flows into the South China Sea; length 1,900 km/1,200 mi. Guangzhou lies on the northern arm of its delta and the island of Hong Kong at its mouth. It is the longest river in south China.

Xinjiang Uygur Autonomous Region or Xinjiang or Sinkiang Uighur Autonomous Region autonomous region of northwest China, bounded to the north by Kyrgyzstan, Kazakhstan, and Russia; to the east by Mongolia and Gansu; to the south by Qinghai and Tibet; and to the west by Jammu and Kashmir, Afghanistan, and Tajikistan; area 1,646,800 sq km/635,800 sq mi (the largest political unit of China); population (2000 est) 19,250,000. The capital is Urumqi. Industries include oil, chemicals, iron, textiles, coal, copper, and tourism. Cereals, cotton, and fruit are grown, and there is animal husbandry.

Xiongnu or Hsiung-nu nomadic confederacy, possibly of Turkish origin, that fought against the Chinese states in the 3rd century BC. Their power began in Mongolia in about 200 BC, but they were forced back to the Gobi Desert in 119 BC by China's Han-dynasty emperor Wudi (Wu-ti) (reigned 141–87 BC) and Qin Shi Huangdi built the Great Wall of China against them. They were eventually conquered and the survivors were employed as frontier troops.

X-ray band of electromagnetic radiation in the wavelength range 10^{-12} to 10^{-8} m (between gamma rays and ultraviolet radiation; see *electromagnetic waves). Applications of X-rays make use of their short wavelength (as in *X-ray diffraction) or their penetrating power (as in medical X-rays of internal body tissues). X-rays are dangerous and can cause cancer.

X-ray astronomy detection of X-rays from intensely hot gas in the universe. Such X-rays are prevented from reaching the Earth's surface by the atmosphere, so detectors must be placed in rockets and satellites. The first celestial X-ray source, Scorpius X-1, was discovered by a rocket flight in 1962.

X-ray diffraction method of studying the atomic and molecular structure of crystalline substances by using *X-rays. X-rays directed at such substances spread out as they pass through the crystals owing to *diffraction (the slight spreading of waves around the edge of an opaque object) of the rays around the atoms. By using measurements of the position and intensity of the diffracted waves, it is possible to calculate the shape and size of the atoms in the crystal. The method has been used to study substances such as *DNA that are found in living material.

xylem transport tissue found in *vascular plants, whose main function is to conduct water and dissolved mineral nutrients from the roots to other parts of the plant. The water is ultimately lost by *transpiration from the leaves (see *leaf). Xylem is composed of a number of different types of cell, and may include long, thin, usually dead cells known as tracheids; fibres (schlerenchyma); thin-walled parenchyma cells; and conducting vessels.

xylophone musical *percussion instrument of African and Indonesian origin. It consists of a series of hardwood bars of varying lengths, each with its own distinct pitch, arranged in a similar way to a piano. Beneath each bar is a metal tube resonator that helps to enrich and sustain the sound. It is usually played with hard beaters to produce a hard, bright, penetrating sound, or soft beaters for a mellower sound. It first appeared as an orchestral instrument in Charles Camille Saint-Saëns's *Danse macabre* in 1874, illustrating dancing skeletons, and can also be heard in 'Fossils' from *The Carnival of Animals* (1887).

y

yak species of cattle *Bos grunniens*, family Bovidae, which lives in wild herds at high altitudes in Tibet. It stands about 2 m/6 ft at the shoulder and has long shaggy hair on the underparts. It has large, upward-curving horns and humped shoulders. It is in danger of becoming extinct. The yak is a mainstay of the Tibetan economy, providing meat, milk, and leather, and serving as a pack and saddle animal. Their dried dung also serves as fuel on the treeless plateaus. Wild yaks have been greatly reduced in number and are now an endangered species.

yakuza (Japanese 'good for nothing') Japanese gangster. Organized crime in Japan is highly structured, and the various syndicates between them employed some 110,000 people 1989, with a turnover of an estimated 1.5 trillion yen. The *yakuza* have been unofficially tolerated and are very powerful.

Yalta Conference strategic conference held 4–11 February 1945 in Yalta (a Soviet holiday resort in the Crimea) by the main Allied leaders in World War II. At this, the second of three key meetings between the 'Big Three' – Winston Churchill (UK), Franklin D Roosevelt (USA), and Joseph Stalin (USSR) – plans were drawn up for the final defeat and disarmament of Nazi Germany, the post-war partition of Europe (see *Cold War), and the foundation of the *United Nations.

yam any of a group of climbing plants cultivated in tropical regions; the starchy tubers (underground stems) are eaten as a vegetable. The Mexican yam (*D. composita*) contains a chemical that is used in the contraceptive pill. (Genus *Dioscorea*, family Dioscoreaceae.)

Yamato ancient name of Japan and particularly the province of western Honshu where Japanese civilization began and where the early capitals were located; also the clan from which all emperors of Japan are descended, claiming the sun-goddess as ancestor. The Yamato period is often taken as AD 539–710 (followed by the Nara period).

Yamoussoukro capital since 1983 of Côte d'Ivoire; population (1995 est) 174,000. The city is in Bouaké department and lies northwest of Abidjan. The economy is based on tourism, fishing, agricultural trade and production, and petroleum distribution to the surrounding region. Other industries include forestry and perfume manufacture.

Yanamamo *or* **Yanomamo** plural **Yanamami**, a semi-nomadic Native South American people, numbering approximately 22,000 (9,500 in northern Brazil and the rest in Venezuela), where most continue to follow their traditional way of life. The Yanamamo language belongs to the Macro-Chibcha family. In November 1991 Brazil granted the Yanamami possession of their original land, 58,395 km/36,293 sq mi on its northern border.

Yangon formerly **Rangoon** (until 1989), capital and chief port of Myanmar (Burma) on the Yangon River, 32 km/20 mi from the Indian Ocean; population (2001 est) 3,938,900. Yangon is a centre of communications by road, rail, and air, as well as by river transport, and is one of the greatest rice markets in the world. Over three-quarters of Myanmar's international trade goes through Yangon, with rice, teak, and metal ores being the leading exports. Major industries, all state-owned, in the city include soap, rubber, and aluminium manufacturing. There is also some shipbuilding, oil refining, and textile and pottery manufacture. The population includes many Indians and Chinese.

Yao a people living in southern China, North Vietnam, northern Laos, Thailand, and Myanmar (Burma), and numbering about 4 million (1984). The Yao language may belong to either the Sino-Tibetan or the Thai language family. The Yao incorporate elements of ancestor worship in their animist religion.

Yaoundé capital of Cameroon, 210 km/130 mi east of the port of Douala; population (1991) 750,000. Industries include tourism, oil refining, food production, and textile manufacturing. It is linked by the Transcameroon railway to Douala and to Ngaoundere in the north.

yapok nocturnal *opossum *Chironectes minimus* found in tropical South and Central America. It is about 33 cm/1.1 ft long, with a 40 cm/1.3 ft tail. It has webbed hind feet and thick fur, and is the only aquatic marsupial. The female has a watertight pouch.

yard symbol yd, unit of length, equivalent to 3 feet (0.9144 m).

yarrow *or* **milfoil** perennial herb belonging to the daisy family, with feathery, scented leaves and flat-topped clusters of white or pink flowers. It is native to Europe and Asia. (*Achillea millefolium*, family Compositae.)

yaws contagious tropical disease common in the West Indies, West Africa, and some Pacific islands, characterized by red, raspberrylike eruptions on the face, toes, and other parts of the body, sometimes followed by lesions of the bones; these may progress to cause gross disfigurement. It is caused by a spirochete (*Treponema pertenue*), a bacterium related to the one that causes *syphilis. Treatment is by antibiotics.

Y chromosome smaller of the two sex chromosomes. In male mammals it occurs paired with the other type of sex chromosome (X), which carries far more genes. The Y chromosome is the smallest of all the mammalian chromosomes and is considered to be largely inert (that is, without direct effect on the physical body), apart from containing the genes that control the development of the testes. There are only 20 genes discovered so far on the human Y chromosome, far fewer than on all other human chromosomes. In humans, whether a person is male or female is determined by the particular combination of the two sex chromosomes in the body cells. In females both the sex chromosomes are the same – two X chromosomes (XX). In males the two are different – one X chromosome and one Y chromosome (XY). The Y chromosome is shorter than the X. *Genes on these chromosomes determine a person's sex (*sex determination).

year unit of time measurement, based on the orbital period of the Earth around the Sun. The **tropical year** (also called equinoctial and solar year), from one spring *equinox to the next, lasts 365.2422 days (nearly 365¼ days). It governs the occurrence of the seasons, and is the period on which the calendar year is based. Every four years is a leap year, when the four quarters of a day are added as one extra day. A year on Mercury is only 88 days; a year on Mars is 23 months.

yeast one of various single-celled fungi (see *fungus) that form masses of tiny round or oval cells by budding. When placed in a sugar solution the cells multiply and convert the sugar into alcohol and carbon dioxide. Yeasts are used as fermenting agents in baking, brewing, and the making of wine and spirits. Brewer's yeast (*S. cerevisiae*) is a rich source of vitamin B. (Especially genus *Saccharomyces*; also other related genera.)

Yeats, W(illiam) B(utler) (1865–1939) Irish poet, dramatist, and scholar. He was a leader of the Irish literary revival and a founder of the *Abbey Theatre in Dublin. His early work was romantic and lyrical, as in the poem 'The Lake Isle of Innisfree' and the plays *The Countess Cathleen* (1892) and *The Land of Heart's Desire* (1894). His later poetry, which includes *The Wild Swans at Coole* (1917) and *The Winding Stair* (1929), was much influenced by European and Eastern thought. Throughout his career Yeats's poetic style underwent an extraordinary process of reinvention and modernization, and shaped itself around an array of personal, mythological, and political concerns. His deep influence on both Irish literature and on poetry in English in general, and his stature as an imaginative artist, can hardly be exaggerated. He was a senator of the Irish Free State 1922–28, and was awarded the Nobel Prize for Literature in 1923.

yeheb nut small tree found in Ethiopia and Somalia, formerly much valued for its nuts as a food source. Although cultivated as a food crop in Kenya and Sudan, it is now critically endangered in the wild and is only known to survive at three sites. Overgrazing by cattle and goats has prevented regrowth, and the taking of nuts for consumption prevents reseeding. Although reintroduction would be possible from cultivated trees, the continuing grazing pressure would make establishment unlikely without proper management. (Genus *Cordeauxia adulis*.)

yellow archangel flowering plant belonging to the mint family, found over much of Europe. It grows up to 60 cm/2 ft tall and has nettlelike leaves and rings, or whorls, of yellow flowers growing around the main stem; the lower lips of the flowers are streaked with red in early summer. (Genus *Lamiastrum galeobdolon*, family Labiatae.)

yellow fever or **yellow jack** acute tropical viral disease, prevalent in the Caribbean area, Brazil, and on the west coast of Africa. The yellow fever virus is an arbovirus transmitted by mosquitoes. Its symptoms include a high fever, headache, joint and muscle pains, vomiting, and yellowish skin (jaundice, possibly leading to liver failure); the heart and kidneys may also be affected. The mortality rate is 25%, with 91% of all cases occurring in Africa.

yellowhammer Eurasian bird *Emberiza citrinella* of the bunting family Emberizidae, order Passeriformes. About 16.5 cm/6.5 in long, the male has a yellow head and underside, a chestnut rump, and a brown-streaked back. The female is duller.

Yellow River English name for the *Huang He River, China.

Yellow Sea Chinese **Huang Hai**, gulf of the Pacific Ocean between China and Korea; length approximately 1,000 km/620 mi, greatest width 700 km/435 mi; area 466,200 sq km/180,000 sq mi. To the north are the gulfs of Korea, Chihli, and Liaotung. There are many small islands to the east near the Korean coast. It receives the Huang He (Yellow River) and Chang Jiang (Yangtze Kiang), which transport yellow mud (derived from the soil known as loess, which was originally wind-blown from central Asia) down into the shallow waters (average depth 44 m/144 ft).

Yellowstone National Park oldest US nature reserve, and largest in the lower 48 states, situated on a broad plateau in the *Rocky Mountains, chiefly in northwest Wyoming, but also projecting about 3 km/2 mi into southwest Montana and eastern Idaho; area 8,987 sq km/3,469 sq mi. The world's first national park, Yellowstone contains more than 10,000 geothermal features with more than 200 active geysers, including Old Faithful, which erupts about every 80 minutes. Established in 1872, the park is now a World Heritage Site and one of the world's greatest wildlife refuges, with around 50 animal species. In 1988 naturally occurring forest fires burned 36% of the park.

Yeltsin, Boris Nikolayevich (1931–) Russian politician, president of the Russian Soviet Federative Socialist Republic (RSFSR) 1990–91, and president of the newly independent Russian Federation 1991–99. He directed the Federation's secession from the USSR and the formation of a new, decentralized confederation, the *Commonwealth of Independent States (CIS), with himself as the most powerful leader. A referendum in 1993 supported his policies of price deregulation and accelerated privatization, despite severe economic problems and civil unrest. He survived a coup attempt later the same year, but was subsequently forced to compromise on the pace of his reforms after far-right electoral gains, and lost considerable public support. He suffered two heart attacks in October and November 1995, yet still contested the June 1996 presidential elections, in which he secured re-election by defeating Communist Party leader Gennady Zyuganov in the second round run-off. Yeltsin resigned as president on 31 December 1999. Announcing that he was bowing out to give a younger generation a chance, he apologized to his country for failing to fulfil their hopes. He relinquished his power six months early to his chosen successor, Vladimir Putin, in return for receiving guarantees of immunity from any future prosecution for any of his actions in the Kremlin.

Yemen

Yemen
**divided into North Yemen (Yemen Arab Republic)
and South Yemen until 1990**
 National name: *Al-Jumhuriyya al Yamaniyya/
 Republic of Yemen*

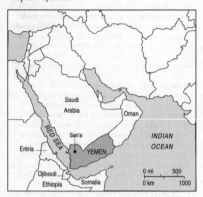

Area: 531,900 sq km/205,366 sq mi
Capital: San'a
Major towns/cities: Aden, Ta'izz, Al Mukalla,
Hodeidah, Ibb, Dhamar
Major ports: Aden
Physical features: hot, moist coastal plain, rising to
plateau and desert
Head of state: Ali Abdullah Saleh from 1990
Head of government: Abdel Qadir Bajamal from 2001
Political system: emergent democracy
Political executive: limited presidency
Political parties: General People's Congress (GPC),
left of centre; Yemen Socialist Party (YSP), left wing;
Yemen Reform Group (al-Islah), Islamic, right of
centre; National Opposition Front, left of centre
Currency: riyal
GNI per capita (PPP): (US$) 750 (2002 est)
Exports: petroleum and petroleum products, cotton,
basic manufactures, clothing, live animals, hides and
skins, fish, rice, coffee. Principal market: China 19%
(2000)
Population: 20,010,000 (2003 est)
Language: Arabic (official)
Religion: Sunni Muslim 63%, Shiite Muslim 37%
Life expectancy: 59 (men); 61 (women) (2000–05)
Chronology
1st millennium BC: South Yemen (Aden) divided
between economically advanced Qataban and
Hadramawt kingdoms.
***c.* 5th century BC:** Qataban fell to the Sabaeans
(Shebans) of North Yemen (Sana).
***c.* 100 BC–AD 525:** All of Yemen became part of the
Himyarite kingdom.
AD 628: Islam introduced.
1174–1229: Under control of Egyptian Ayyubids.
1229–1451: 'Golden age' for arts and sciences under the
Rasulids, who had served as governors of Yemen under
the Ayyubids.
1538: North Yemen came under control of Turkish
Ottoman Empire.

1636: Ottomans left North Yemen and power fell into
hands of Yemeni Imams, based on local Zaydi tribes,
who also held South Yemen until 1735.
1839: Aden became a British territory. Port developed
into an important ship refuelling station after opening
of Suez Canal in 1869; protectorate was gradually
established over 23 Sultanates inland.
1870s: The Ottomans re-established control over
North Yemen.
1918: North Yemen became independent, with Imam
Yahya from the Hamid al-Din family as king.
1937: Aden became a British crown colony.
1948: Imam Yahya assassinated by exiled Free Yemenis
nationalist movement, but the uprising was crushed
by his son, Imam Ahmad.
1959: Federation of South Arabia formed by Britain
between city of Aden and feudal Sultanates (Aden
Protectorate).
1962: Military coup on death of Imam Ahmad;
North Yemen declared Yemen Arab Republic (YAR),
with Abdullah al-Sallal as president. Civil war broke
out between royalists (supported by Saudi Arabia)
and republicans (supported by Egypt).
1963: Armed rebellion by National Liberation Front
(NLF) began against British rule in Aden.
1967: Civil war ended with republicans victorious.
Sallal deposed and replaced by Republican Council.
The Independent People's Republic of South Yemen
was formed after the British withdrawal from Aden.
Many fled to the north as the repressive communist
NLF regime took over in south.
1970: People's Republic of South Yemen renamed
People's Democratic Republic of Yemen.
1971–72: War between South Yemen and YAR; union
agreement brokered by Arab League signed but not kept.
1974: The pro-Saudi Col Ibrahim al-Hamadi seized
power in North Yemen; Military Command Council
set up.
1977: Hamadi assassinated; replaced by Col Ahmed ibn
Hussein al-Ghashmi.
1978: Constituent people's assembly appointed in
North Yemen and Military Command Council
dissolved. Ghashmi killed by envoy from South Yemen;
succeeded by Ali Abdullah Saleh. War broke out again
between the two Yemens. The South Yemen president
was deposed and executed; the Yemen Socialist Party
(YSP) was formed in the south by communists.
1979: A ceasefire was agreed with a commitment to
future union.
1986: There was civil war in South Yemen; the
autocratic head of state Ali Nasser was dismissed.
A new administration was formed under the more
moderate Haydar Abu Bakr al-Attas, who was
committed to negotiating union with the north
because of the deteriorating economy in the south.
1989: A draft multiparty constitution for a single
Yemen state was published.
1990: The border between the two Yemens was opened;
the countries were formally united on 22 May as the
Republic of Yemen. Ali Abdullah Saleh, president of
North Yemen since 1978, was appointed president of
the new unified Yemen.
1991: The new constitution was approved; Yemen
opposed US-led operations against Iraq in the Gulf War.
1992: There were antigovernment riots.

1993: Saleh's General People's Congress (GPC) won most seats in a general election but no overall majority; a five-member presidential council was elected, including Saleh as president, YSP leader Ali Salim al-Baidh as vice-president, and Bakr al-Attas as prime minister.

1994: Fighting erupted between northern forces, led by President Saleh, and southern forces, led by Vice-president al-Baidh, as southern Yemen announced its secession. Saleh inflicted crushing defeat on al-Baidh and a new GPC coalition was appointed.

1998: A new government was headed by Abdul Ali al-Rahman al-Iryani.

1999: In the first ever popular elections for the presidency, Ali Abdullah Saleh, the president for 21 years, was successful.

2000: A terrorist suicide bomb attack on a US destroyer, USS *Cole*, killed 17 crew members.

2001: Abdel Qadir Bajamal replaced al-Iryani as prime minister.

2002: A French supertanker, the *Limburg*, suffered extensive damage in an explosion while off the south-east coast of Yemen, which killed one crew member. The blast was widely believed to be the result of a terrorist attack.

2003: In parliamentary elections the General People Congress, led by President Saleh, retained power with over two-thirds of the seats in the 301-member Assembly of Representatives.

yeoman in England, a small landowner who farmed his own fields – a system that formed a bridge between the break-up of feudalism and the agrarian revolution of the 18th–19th centuries.

Yerevan capital city, economic, and cultural centre of the independent Republic of Armenia, situated in the southern Caucasus 25 km/16 mi north of the Turkish border; population (1996) 1,200,000. Yerevan stands on the Razdan River, and is a major industrial city, manufacturing machine tools, agricultural equipment, chemicals, bricks, bicycles, and wine. Other industries include the production of aluminium, plastics, and textiles, fruit canning, and distilling.

Yevtushenko, Yevgeny Aleksandrovich (1933–) Russian poet. He aroused controversy with his anti-Stalinist 'Stalin's Heirs' (1956), published with Khrushchev's support, and 'Babi Yar' (1961), which attacked Russian as well as Nazi anti-Semitism. His other works include the long poem *Zima Junction* (1956), the novel *Berries* (1981), and *Precocious Autobiography* (1963).

yew any of a group of evergreen coniferous trees native to the northern hemisphere. The dark green flat needlelike leaves and bright red berrylike seeds are poisonous; the wood is hard and close-grained. (Genus *Taxus*, family Taxaceae.)

Yggdrasil in Norse mythology, the world tree, a sacred ash which spanned heaven and hell. It was evergreen and tended by the Norns, goddesses of past, present, and future.

Yi plural **Yi**, member of a people living in the mountainous regions of southwestern China, northern Vietnam, Laos, Thailand, and Myanmar, totalling about 5.5 million (1987). The Yi are farmers, producing both crops and livestock, and opium as a cash crop. Traditionally they were stratified into princes, aristocrats, commoners, and debt slaves. Their language belongs to the Sino-Tibetan family; their religion is animist.

Yiddish language member of the west Germanic branch of the Indo-European language family, deriving from 13th–14th-century Rhineland German and spoken by northern, central, and eastern European Jews, who have carried it to Israel, the USA, and many other parts of the world. It is written in the Hebrew alphabet and has many dialects reflecting European areas of residence, as well as many borrowed words from Polish, Russian, Lithuanian, and other languages encountered.

yin and yang (Chinese 'dark' and 'bright') the passive (characterized as feminine, negative, intuitive) and active (characterized as masculine, positive, intellectual) principles of nature. Their interaction is believed to maintain equilibrium and harmony in the universe and to be present in all things. In Taoism and Confucianism they are represented by two interlocked curved shapes within a circle, one white, one black, with a spot of the contrasting colour within the head of each.

Ymir in Norse mythology, the first living being, a giant who grew from melting frost; father of the Jotuns, a race of evil giants. He was nurtured by four streams of milk from the cow Audhumla, mother of Buri, the grandfather of Odin. After Ymir was killed by Odin and his brothers, Vili and Ve, heaven and earth were created from parts of his body.

yoga (Sanskrit 'union') Hindu philosophical system attributed to Patanjali, who lived about 150 BC at Gonda, Uttar Pradesh, India. He preached mystical union with a personal deity through the practice of self-hypnosis and a rising above the senses by abstract meditation, adoption of special postures, and ascetic practices. As practised in the West, yoga is more a system of mental and physical exercise, and of induced relaxation as a means of relieving stress.

yogurt *or* **yoghurt** *or* **yoghourt** semisolid curdlike dairy product made from milk fermented with bacteria. It was originally made by nomadic tribes of Central Asia, from mare's milk in leather pouches attached to their saddles. It is drunk plain throughout the Asian and Mediterranean region, to which it spread, but honey, sugar, and fruit were added in Europe and the USA, and the product was made solid and creamy, to be eaten by spoon.

yolk store of food, mostly in the form of fats and proteins, found in the *eggs of many animals. It provides nourishment for the growing embryo.

Yom Kippur *or* **Day of Atonement** Jewish high holy day, or 'day of awe', held on the tenth day of Tishri (September–October), the first month of the Jewish year. It is a day of fasting, penitence, and cleansing from sin, ending the ten days of penitence that follow *Rosh Hashanah, the Jewish New Year.

Yom Kippur War the surprise attack on Israel in October 1973 by Egypt and Syria; see *Arab-Israeli Wars. It is named after the Jewish national holiday on which it began, the holiest day of the Jewish year.

York cathedral and industrial city and administrative headquarters of *York unitary authority in northern England, on the River Ouse; population (1998 est) 177,400. It was the administrative headquarters of the county of North Yorkshire until 1996. Industries include tourism and the manufacture of scientific instruments, sugar, chocolate, and glass. Founded in AD 71 as the Roman provincial capital **Eboracum**, York retains many of its medieval streets and buildings and much of its 14th-century city wall; the Gothic York Minster, England's largest medieval cathedral, includes fine 15th-century stained glass. The city is visited by some 3 million tourists a year.

York English dynasty founded by Richard, Duke of York (1411–60). He claimed the throne through his descent from Lionel, Duke of Clarence (1338–68), third son of Edward III, whereas the reigning monarch, Henry VI of the rival house of Lancaster, was descended from the fourth son, John of Gaunt. The argument was fought out in the Wars of the *Roses. York was killed at the Battle of Wakefield in 1460, but the following year his son became King Edward IV. Edward was succeeded by his son Edward V and then by his brother Richard III, with whose death the line ended. The Lancastrian victor in that battle was crowned Henry VII, and consolidated his claim by marrying Edward IV's eldest daughter, Elizabeth, thus founding the House of Tudor.

York unitary authority in northeast England created in 1996 from part of the county of North Yorkshire. **area:** 271 sq km/105 sq mi **towns:** *York (administrative headquarters) **features:** River Ouse; River Fosse; York Minster – largest medieval cathedral in England, with 15th-century stained glass; York Castle and Museum; National Railway Museum; city walls built by Henry III in 13th century with 4 gates and 39 towers; Jorvik Viking Centre; the Shambles medieval streets **population:** (1998 est) 177,400.

Yorkshire former county in northeast England on the North Sea divided administratively into North, East, and West Ridings (thirds), but reorganized to form a number of new counties in 1974: the major part of **Cleveland** and **Humberside**, **North Yorkshire**, **South Yorkshire**, and **West Yorkshire**. Small outlying areas also went to Durham, Cumbria, Lancashire, and Greater Manchester. In 1996 Cleveland and Humberside were abolished, and a number of unitary authorities were created to replace them.

Yorkshire Dales series of river valleys in northern England, see *Dales.

Yoruba the majority ethnic group living in southwestern Nigeria; there is a Yoruba minority in eastern Benin. They number approximately 20 million in all, and their language belongs to the Kwa branch of the Niger-Congo family. The Yoruba established powerful city states in the 15th century, known for their advanced culture which includes sculpture, art, and music.

Yosemite region in the Sierra Nevada, eastern California, USA, a national park from 1890; area 3,079 sq km/1,189 sq mi. Embracing 12 km/8 mi of the Yosemite Valley, its main features are Yosemite Gorge, cut by the Merced River; Yosemite Falls, the highest waterfall in the USA, plunging 739 m/2,425 ft in three leaps; Half Dome Mountain, a 2 km-/1 mi-high sheer cliff on El Capitan, the largest body of exposed granite in the world; Mount Lyell, rising to 3,997 m/ 13,114 ft; and groves of giant sequoia trees. It is a World Heritage Site.

Yoshida, Shigeru (1878–1967) Japanese diplomat and conservative Liberal politician who served as prime minister for most of the period 1946–54, including much of the US occupation 1945–52. Under Yoshida, Japan signed the San Francisco Peace Treaty with the USA and its allies in 1951.

Young, Brigham (1801–1877) US *Mormon religious leader, born in Vermont. He joined the Mormon Church, or Church of Jesus Christ of Latter-day Saints, in 1832, and three years later was appointed an apostle. After a successful recruiting mission in Liverpool, England, he returned to the USA and, as successor of Joseph Smith (who had been murdered), led the Mormon migration to the Great Salt Lake in Utah in 1846, founded *Salt Lake City, and headed the colony until his death.

Young Pretender nickname of *Charles Edward Stuart, claimant to the Scottish and English thrones.

Young Turk member of a reformist movement of young army officers in the Ottoman Empire founded 1889. The movement was instrumental in the constitutional changes of 1908 and the abdication of Sultan Abd al-Hamid II 1909. It gained prestige during the Balkan Wars 1912–13 and encouraged Turkish links with the German empire. Its influence diminished after 1918. The term is now used for a member of any radical or rebellious faction within a party or organization.

Ypres, Battles of Flemish Ieper, in World War I, three major battles 1914–17 between German and Allied forces near Ypres, a Belgian town in western Flanders, 40 km/25 mi south of Ostend. Neither side made much progress in any of the battles, despite heavy casualties, but the third battle in particular (also known as Passchendaele) July–November 1917 stands out as an enormous waste of life for little return. The Menin Gate (1927) is a memorial to British soldiers lost in these battles.

ytterbium chemical symbol Yb, soft, lustrous, silvery, malleable, and ductile metallic element of the *lanthanide series, symbol Yb, atomic number 70, relative atomic mass 173.04. It occurs with (and resembles) yttrium in gadolinite and other minerals, and is used in making steel and other alloys.

yttrium chemical symbol Y, silver-grey, metallic element, atomic number 39, relative atomic mass 88.905. It is associated with and resembles the rare-earth elements (*lanthanides), occurring in gadolinite, xenotime, and other minerals. It is used in colour-television tubes and to reduce steel corrosion.

Yuan dynasty *Mongol rulers of China 1279–1368 after *Kublai Khan defeated the Song dynasty. Much of Song China's administrative infrastructure survived and internal and foreign trade expanded. The Silk Road to the west was re-established and the Grand Canal extended north to Beijing to supply the court with grain.

Yüan Shikai (1859–1916) Chinese soldier and politician, leader of Republican China 1911–16. He assumed dictatorial powers in 1912, dissolving parliament and suppressing Sun Zhong Shan's (Sun Yat-sen's) Kuomintang (*Guomindang). He died soon after proclaiming himself emperor.

Yucatán peninsula in Central America, divided among Mexico, Belize, and Guatemala; area 180,000 sq km/ 70,000 sq mi. Tropical crops are grown. It is inhabited by Maya Indians and contains the remains of their civilization.

yucca any of a group of plants belonging to the lily family, with over 40 species found in Latin America and the southwestern USA. The leaves are stiff and sword-shaped and the flowers, which grow on upright central spikes, are white and bell-shaped. (Genus *Yucca*, family Liliaceae.)

Yugoslavia A former country in the Balkans, its name meaning 'the land of the Southern Slavs'. It came into existence in 1918 and took the name Yugoslavia in 1929. From 1945 until his death in 1980, the country was ruled by *Tito, an authoritarian communist who kept ethnic tensions under control. In the 1990s, however, the country began to split up, sometimes with great violence, and in 2003 the Federal Republic of Yugoslavia formally ceased to exist. See *Bosnia–Herzegovina, *Croatia, *Macedonia, *Serbia and Montenegro, and *Slovenia. *Kosovo is legally part of Serbia but de facto currently an international protectorate.

Yukon Territory (Dené *you-kon* 'great water') most northwesterly administrative division of Canada, bordered by the Beaufort Sea to the north, the Northwest Territories to the east, British Columbia to the south (below the 60th Parallel), and Alaska, USA, to the west; area 483,500 sq km/186,631 sq mi; population (2002 est) 29,900 (including 5,530 American Indians). The capital is Whitehorse. Gold, silver, lead, coal, and zinc are mined, and oil and natural gas extracted. There is lumbering, fur-trapping, and fishing.

Yunnan province of southwest China, bounded to the north by Tibet and Sichuan, to the east by Guizhou and Guangxi Zhuang Autonomous Region, to the south by Vietnam and Laos, and to the west by Myanmar (formerly Burma); area 436,200 sq km/168,373 sq mi; population (2000 est) 42,880,000. The capital is Kunming. There are tin, copper, lead, gold, zinc, coal, salt, and cigarette industries. Rice, tea, timber, wheat, cotton, and tobacco are grown, and rubber is produced.

Z

Zagreb industrial city (leather, linen, carpets, paper, and electrical goods) and capital of Croatia, on the Sava River; population (1991) 726,800. Zagreb was a Roman city (**Aemona**) and has a Gothic cathedral. Its university was founded in 1874. The city was damaged by bombing in October 1991 during the Croatian civil war.

Zahir ud-Din Muhammad first Mogul emperor of India; see *Babur.

Zambezi *or* **Zambesi** river in central and southeast Africa; length 2,650 km/1,650 mi from northwest Zambia through Mozambique to the Indian Ocean, with a wide delta near Chinde. Major tributaries include the Kafue in Zambia. It is interrupted by rapids, and includes on the Zimbabwe–Zambia border the Victoria Falls (Mosi-oa-tunya) and Kariba Dam, which forms the reservoir of Lake Kariba with large fisheries. Its drainage area is about 1,347,000 sq km/520,000 sq mi.

Zambia

formerly **Northern Rhodesia** (until 1964)
National name: *Republic of Zambia*

Area: 752,600 sq km/290,578 sq mi
Capital: Lusaka
Major towns/cities: Kitwe, Ndola, Kabwe, Mufulira, Chingola, Luanshya, Livingstone

Physical features: forested plateau cut through by rivers; Zambezi River, Victoria Falls, Kariba Dam
Head of state and government: Levy Mwanawasa from 2002
Political system: emergent democracy
Political executive: limited presidency
Political parties: United National Independence Party (UNIP), African socialist; Movement for Multiparty Democracy (MMD), moderate, left of centre; Multiracial Party (MRP), moderate, left of centre, multiracial; National Democratic Alliance (NADA), left of centre; Democratic Party (DP), left of centre
Currency: Zambian kwacha
GNI per capita (PPP): (US$) 770 (2002 est)
Exports: copper, zinc, lead, cobalt, tobacco. Principal market: South Africa 24.5% (2001)
Population: 10,812,000 (2003 est)
Language: English (official), Bantu languages
Religion: about 64% Christian, animist, Hindu, Muslim
Life expectancy: 33 (men); 32 (women) (2000–05)
Chronology
16th century: Immigration of peoples from Luba and Lunda Empires of Zaire, to the northwest, who set up small kingdoms.
late 18th century: Visited by Portuguese explorers.
19th century: Instability with immigration of Ngoni from east, Kololo from west, establishment of Bemba kingdom in north, and slave-trading activities of Portuguese and Arabs from East Africa.
1851: Visited by British missionary and explorer David Livingstone.
1889: As Northern Rhodesia, came under administration of British South Africa Company of Cecil Rhodes, and became involved in copper mining, especially from 1920s.
1924: Became a British protectorate.
1948: Northern Rhodesia African Congress (NRAC) formed by black Africans to campaign for self-rule.
1953: Became part of Central African Federation, which included South Rhodesia (Zimbabwe) and Nyasaland (Malawi).
1960: UNIP was formed by Kenneth Kaunda as a breakaway from NRAC, as African socialist body to campaign for independence and dissolution of federation dominated by South Rhodesia's white minority.
1963: The federation was dissolved and internal self-government achieved.
1964: Independence was achieved within the Commonwealth as the Republic of Zambia, with Kaunda of the UNIP as president.
later 1960s: Key enterprises were brought under state control.
1972: UNIP was declared the only legal party.
1975: The opening of the Tan-Zam railway from the Zambian copperbelt, 322 mi/200 km north of Lusaka, to port of Dar es Salaam in Tanzania, reduced Zambia's dependence on the rail route via Rhodesia (Zimbabwe) for its exports.
1976: Zambia declared its support for Patriotic Front (PF) guerrillas fighting to topple the white-dominated regime in Rhodesia (Zimbabwe).
1980: There was an unsuccessful South African-promoted coup against President Kaunda; relations with Zimbabwe improved when the PF came to power.

1985: Kaunda was elected chair of African Front Line States.

1991: A new multiparty constitution was adopted. The MMD won a landslide election victory, and its leader Frederick Chiluba became president in what was the first democratic change of government in English-speaking black Africa.

1993: A state of emergency was declared after rumours of a planned antigovernment coup. A privatization programme was launched.

1996: Kaunda was effectively barred from future elections by an amendment to the constitution.

1997: There was an abortive antigovernment coup.

1998: Former president Kaunda was placed under house arrest after alleged involvement in the antigovernment coup. Kaunda was charged but the charges were subsequently dropped.

2001: Levy Mwanawasa was elected president and sought to combat government corruption.

2002: Ballot-rigging allegations clouded Levy Mwanawasa's election as president. Parliament voted to remove Chiluba's immunity from prosecution.

2003: Chiluba was arrested and charged on 59 counts, including abuse of office.

Zanzibar island region of Tanzania, 40 km/25 mi from the mainland, separated by the Zanzibar Channel; area 1,658 sq km/640 sq mi (80 km/50 mi long); population (2002 est) 622,500. Fishing is an important industry and cloves, tobacco, and copra are produced. The main town is Zanzibar.

Zapata, Emiliano (1879–1919) Mexican Indian revolutionary leader. He led a revolt against dictator Porfirio Díaz from 1910 under the slogan 'Land and Liberty', to repossess for the indigenous Mexicans the land taken by the Spanish. By 1915 he was driven into retreat, and was assassinated in his stronghold, Morelos, by an agent of Venustiano Carranza.

Zapotec an American Indian people of southern Mexico, now numbering approximately 250,000, living mainly in Oaxaca. The Zapotec language, which belongs to the Oto-Mangean family, has nine dialects. The ancient Zapotec built the ceremonial centre of Monte Albán 1000–500 BC. They developed one of the classic Mesoamerican civilizations by AD 300, but declined under pressure from the Mixtecs from 900 until the Spanish Conquest in the 1530s.

Zappa, Frank (Francis Vincent) (1940–1993) US rock musician, bandleader, and composer. His crudely satirical songs, as in *Joe's Garage* (1980), deliberately bad taste, and complex orchestral and electronic compositions make his work hard to categorize. His group the Mothers of Invention 1965–73 was part of the 1960s avant-garde, and the Mothers' hippie parody *We're Only in It for the Money* (1967) was popular with its target.

Zarathustra another name for the Persian religious leader *Zoroaster.

zebra black and white striped member of the horse genus *Equus* found in Africa; the stripes serve as camouflage or dazzle and confuse predators. It is about 1.5 m/5 ft high at the shoulder, with a stout body and a short, thick mane. Zebras live in family groups and herds on mountains and plains, and can run at up to 60 kph/40 mph. Males are usually solitary.

zebu any of a species of *cattle *Bos indicus* found domesticated in East Asia, India, and Africa. It is usually light-coloured, with large horns and a large fatty hump near the shoulders. It is used for pulling loads and is held by some Hindus to be sacred. There are about 30 breeds.

Zeeland province of southwest Netherlands, consisting of five islands lying in the Schelde river estuary, and the region north of the Belgian province of East Flanders; area 1,790 sq km/691 sq mi; population (1997) 368,400. The capital is Middelburg. There are shipbuilding, engineering, and petrochemical industries. There is livestock raising, dairying, and cereals and potatoes are grown.

Zeffirelli, Franco (Corsi) (1923–) Italian theatre, opera and film director, and stage designer. He is associated with stylish designs and lavish productions. His films include *Romeo and Juliet* (1968), *La Traviata* (1983), *Otello* (1986), and *Hamlet* (1990).

Zeitgeist (German 'time spirit') spirit of the age. The term was used as the title of an exhibition of neo-expressionist paintings held in Berlin in 1982.

Zen (abbreviation of Japanese *zenna* 'quiet mind concentration') form of *Buddhism introduced from India to Japan via China from the 12th century. **Rinzai Zen** (founded 1191) features koan (paradoxical questions), intense meditation, and sudden enlightenment (satori). **Soto Zen** (founded 1227) was spread by the priest Dogen (1200–1253), who emphasized work, practise, discipline, and philosophical questions to discover one's Buddha-nature in the 'realization of self'. Simplicity in art forms and the writing of *haiku verses are the products of Japanese Zen Buddhist thought.

Zend-Avesta sacred scriptures of *Zoroastrianism, today practised by the Parsees. They comprise the **Avesta** (liturgical books for the priests); the **Gathas** (the discourses and revelations of Zoroaster); and the **Zend** (commentary upon them).

zenith uppermost point of the celestial horizon, immediately above the observer; the *nadir is below, diametrically opposite. See *celestial sphere.

Zeno of Elea (c. 490–c. 430 BC) Greek philosopher. He pointed out several paradoxes that raised 'modern' problems of space and time. For example, motion is an illusion, since an arrow in flight must occupy a determinate space at each instant, and therefore must be at rest.

Zephyrus in Greek mythology, the god of the west wind, husband of Iris, and father of the horses of *Achilles in Homer's *Iliad*.

Zeppelin, Ferdinand Adolf August Heinrich, Count von Zeppelin (1838–1917) German *airship pioneer. His first airship was built and tested in 1900. During World War I a number of **zeppelins** bombed England. They were also used for luxury passenger transport but the construction of hydrogen-filled airships with rigid keels was abandoned after several disasters in the 1920s and 1930s. Zeppelin also helped to pioneer large multi-engine bomber planes.

Zeus in Greek mythology, the chief of the Olympian gods (Roman *Jupiter). He was the son of *Kronos, whom he overthrew; his brothers included Pluto and Poseidon, his sisters Demeter, Hestia, and Hera. As the supreme god he dispensed good and evil and was the father and ruler of all humankind, the fount of kingly power and law and order. His emblems were the thunderbolt and aegis (shield), representing the thundercloud. The colossal ivory and gold statue of the seated god, made by Phidias for the temple of Zeus in the Peloponnese, was one of the *Seven Wonders of the World.

Zhao Ziyang (1919–2005) Chinese politician, prime minister 1980–87 and leader of the Chinese Communist Party 1987–89. His reforms included self-management and incentives for workers and factories. He lost his secretaryship and other posts after the Tiananmen Square massacre in Beijing in June 1989.

Zhejiang *or* **Chekiang** coastal province of southeast China, bounded to the north by Jiangsu, to the east by the East China Sea, to the south by Fujian, and to the west by Jiangxi and Anhui; area 101,800 sq km/ 39,300 sq mi; population (2000 est) 46,770,000. The capital is Hangzhou. There are silk, chemical fibre, canning, tea-processing, and handicrafts industries. Rice, cotton, sugar, jute, maize, and timber are grown; silkworms are farmed and there is fishing. Zhejiang is the second smallest of the Chinese provinces, and densely populated.

Zhirinovsky, Vladimir (1946–) Russian politician, leader of the far-right Liberal Democratic Party of Russia (LDPR) from 1991. His strong, sometimes bizarre views, advocating the use of nuclear weapons and the restoration of the Russian empire, initially cast him as a lightweight politician. However, his ability to win third place out of six candidates in Russia's first free presidential elections in 1991, and the success of his party in winning nearly 23% of the vote and 15% of the seats in the December 1993 federal assembly elections, forced a reassessment. However, in the June 1996 presidential elections his support fell to below 6%.

Zhou dynasty (*or* **Chou dynasty)** Chinese succession of rulers *c.* 1066–256 BC, during which cities emerged and philosophy flourished. The dynasty was established by the Zhou, a semi-nomadic people from the Wei Valley region, west of the great bend in the Huang He (Yellow River). Zhou influence waned from 403 BC, as the Warring States era began.

Zhou Enlai (*or* **Chou En-lai) (1898–1976)** Chinese communist politician. Zhou, a member of the Chinese Communist Party (CCP) from the 1920s, was prime minister 1949–76 and foreign minister 1949–58. He was a moderate Maoist and weathered the *Cultural Revolution. He played a key role in foreign affairs.

Zhu De (*or* **Chu The) (1886–1976)** Chinese communist military leader, 'father' and commander of the Chinese Red Army 1931–54. He devised the tactic of mobile guerrilla warfare and organized the *Long March to Shaanxi 1934–36. He was made a marshal in 1955.

Zhukov, Georgi Konstantinovich (1896–1974) Marshal of the USSR in World War II and minister of defence 1955–57. As chief of staff from 1941, he defended Moscow in 1941, counter-attacked at Stalingrad (now Volgograd) in 1942, organized the relief of Leningrad (now St Petersburg) in 1943, and led the offensive from the Ukraine March in 1944 which ended in the fall of Berlin.

Zia ul-Haq, Muhammad (1924–1988) Pakistani general, in power from 1977 until his death, probably an assassination, in an aircraft explosion. He became army chief of staff in 1976, led the military coup against Zulfikar Ali Bhutto in 1977, and became president in 1978. Zia introduced a fundamentalist Islamic regime and restricted political activity.

zidovudine formerly **AZT**, antiviral drug used in the treatment of *AIDS. It is not a cure for AIDS but is effective in prolonging life; it does not, however, delay the onset of AIDS in people carrying the virus.

ziggurat in ancient Babylonia and Assyria, a step pyramid of sun-baked brick faced with glazed bricks or tiles on which stood a shrine. The Tower of Babel as described in the Bible may have been a ziggurat.

Zimbabwe
formerly **Southern Rhodesia** (until 1980)
National name: *Republic of Zimbabwe*

Area: 390,300 sq km/150,694 sq mi
Capital: Harare
Major towns/cities: Bulawayo, Gweru, Kwe Kwe, Mutare, Kadoma, Chitungwiza
Physical features: high plateau with central high veld and mountains in east; rivers Zambezi, Limpopo; Victoria Falls
Head of state and government: Robert Mugabe from 1987
Political system: nationalistic socialist
Political executive: unlimited presidency
Political parties: Zimbabwe African National Union–Patriotic Front (ZANU–PF), African socialist; opposition parties exist but none have mounted serious challenge to ruling party
Currency: Zimbabwe dollar
GNI per capita (PPP): (US$) 2,120 (2002 est)
Exports: tobacco, gold, nickel, ferro-alloys, textiles and clothing, sugar, cotton lint. Principal market: South Africa 15% (2000)
Population: 12,891,000 (2003 est)
Language: English, Shona, Ndebele (all official)
Religion: 50% follow a syncretic (part Christian, part indigenous beliefs) type of religion, Christian 25%, animist 24%, small Muslim minority
Life expectancy: 34 (men); 33 (women) (2000–05)

Chronology

13th century: Shona people settled Mashonaland (eastern Zimbabwe), erecting stone buildings (hence name Zimbabwe, 'stone house').

15th century: Shona Empire reached its greatest extent.

16th–17th centuries: Portuguese settlers developed trade with Shona states and achieved influence over the kingdom of Mwanamutapa in northern Zimbabwe in 1629.

1837: Ndebele (or Matabele) people settled in southwest Zimbabwe after being driven north from Transvaal by Boers; Shona defeated by Ndebele led by King Mzilikazi who formed military empire based at Bulawayo.

1870: King Lobengula succeeded King Mzilikazi.

1889: Cecil Rhodes's British South Africa Company (SA Co) obtained exclusive rights to exploit mineral resources in Lobengula's domains.

1890: Creation of white colony in Mashonaland and founding of Salisbury (Harare) by Leander Starr Jameson, associate of Rhodes.

1893: Matabele War: Jameson defeated Lobengula; white settlers took control of country.

1895: Matabeleland, Mashonaland, and Zambia named Rhodesia after Cecil Rhodes.

1896: Matabele revolt suppressed.

1898: Southern Rhodesia (Zimbabwe) became British protectorate administered by BSA Co; farming, mining, and railways developed.

1922: Union with South Africa rejected by referendum among white settlers.

1923: Southern Rhodesia became self-governing colony; Africans progressively disenfranchised.

1933–53: Prime Minister Godfrey Huggins (later Lord Malvern) pursued 'White Rhodesia' policy of racial segregation.

1950s: Immigration doubled white population to around 250,000, while indigenous African population stood at around 6 million.

1953: Southern Rhodesia formed part of Federation of Rhodesia and Nyasaland.

1961: Zimbabwe African People's Union (ZAPU) formed with Joshua Nkomo as leader; declared illegal a year later.

1962: Rhodesia Front party of Winston Field took power in Southern Rhodesia, pledging to preserve white rule.

1963: Federation of Rhodesia and Nyasaland dissolved as Zambia and Malawi moved towards independence; Zimbabwe African National Union (ZANU) formed, with Robert Mugabe as secretary; declared illegal a year later.

1964: Ian Smith became prime minister; he rejected British terms for independence which required moves towards black majority rule; Nkomo and Mugabe imprisoned.

1965: Smith made unilateral declaration of independence (UDI); Britain broke off all relations.

1966–68: United Nations (UN) imposed economic sanctions on Rhodesia, which still received help from South Africa and Portugal.

1969: Rhodesia declared itself a republic.

1972: Britain rejected draft independence agreement as unacceptable to African population.

1974: Nkomo and Mugabe released and jointly formed Patriotic Front to fight Smith regime in mounting civil war.

1975: Geneva Conference between British, Smith regime, and African nationalists failed to reach agreement.

1978: At height of civil war, whites were leaving Rhodesia at rate of 1,000 per month.

1979: Rhodesia became Zimbabwe-Rhodesia with new 'majority' constitution which nevertheless retained special rights for whites; Bishop Abel Muzorewa became premier; Mugabe and Nkomo rejected settlement; Lancaster House Agreement temporarily restored Rhodesia to British rule.

1980: Zimbabwe achieved independence from Britain with full transition to African majority rule; Mugabe became prime minister with Rev. Canaan Banana as president.

1984: A ZANU–PF party congress agreed to the principle of a one-party state.

1987: Mugabe combined the posts of head of state and prime minister as executive president; Nkomo became vice-president.

1989: ZANU–PF and ZAPU formally merged; the Zimbabwe Unity Movement was founded by Edgar Tekere to oppose the one-party state.

1992: The United Party was formed to oppose ZANU–PF. Mugabe declared drought and famine a national disaster.

1996: Mugabe was re-elected president.

1998: Mugabe issued new rules banning strikes and restricting political and public gatherings. The government's radical land distribution plans were watered down after pressure from aid donors. There were violent antigovernment demonstrations.

1999: Further violent antigovernment protests took place. In June the human rights group African Rights produced a scathing report on Mugabe's government.

2000: Veterans of the war of independence, supported by the government, began to invade and claim white-owned farms. To international and internal opposition, the government invoked special powers to seize the farms without compensation. Elections in June, which returned Mugabe's government, were condemned by international observers. In October rioters protested at soaring food and transport costs. In November the high court ruled Mugabe's land acquisition program illegal.

2001: Mugabe's government agreed to remove all white judges from Zimbabwe's judiciary and decided to replace the five members of the Supreme Court.

2002: The European Union (EU) imposed sanctions on President Mugabe and his government following the expulsion of the leader of the EU's team of observers planning to monitor the general elections. Mugabe claimed re-election as president after a campaign marred by alleged ballot rigging and intimidation of opponents of the ruling ZANU-PF regime. International condemnation of the result was reinforced by Zimbabwe's suspension from the Commonwealth for a year. The government ordered 2,900 white commercial farmers, whose farms had been targeted for seizure and redistribution to poor black workers, to stop work with immediate effect under threat of imprisonment. Zimbabwe faced its worst food shortage in 60 years, due to drought and violent land-reform policies.

2003: Zimbabwe withdrew from the Commonwealth.
2005: Mugabe's government claimed victory in the general elections, by a majority large enough to allow him to change the constitution. The opposition party, Movement for Democratic Change, alleged that large-scale ballot-rigging had taken place.

zinc chemical symbol Zn, (Germanic *Zinke* 'point') hard, brittle, bluish-white, metallic element, atomic number 30, relative atomic mass 65.37. The principal ore is sphalerite or zinc blende (zinc sulphide, ZnS). Zinc is hardly affected by air or moisture at ordinary temperatures; its chief uses are in alloys such as brass, in coating metals (for example, galvanized iron), and in making batteries. Its compounds include zinc oxide, used in ointments (as an astringent) and cosmetics, paints, glass, and printing ink. Zinc is an essential trace element in most animals; adult humans have 2–3 g/0.07–0.1 oz of zinc in their bodies. There are more than 300 known enzymes that contain zinc.

zinc oxide ZnO, white powder, yellow when hot, that occurs in nature as the mineral zincite. It is used in paints and as an antiseptic in zinc ointment; it is the main ingredient of calamine lotion.

zinc sulphide ZnS, yellow-white solid that occurs in nature as the mineral sphalerite (also called zinc blende). It is the principal ore of zinc, and is used in the manufacture of fluorescent paints.

zinnia any of a group of annual plants belonging to the daisy family, native to Mexico and South America; notably the cultivated hybrids of *Z. elegans* with brightly coloured daisylike flowers. (Genus *Zinnia*, family Compositae.)

Zinovyev (*or* **Zinoviev**), **Grigory Yevseyevich** (**1883–1936**) Russian communist politician whose name was attached to a forgery, the *Zinovyev letter*, inciting Britain's communists to rise, which helped to topple the Labour government in 1924.

Zion Jebusite (Amorites of Canaan) stronghold in Jerusalem captured by King David, and the hill on which he built the Temple, symbol of Jerusalem and of Jewish national life.

Zionism national liberation movement advocating the re-establishment of a Jewish homeland (the *Eretz Israel*) in Palestine. Here, in the 'Promised Land' of the Bible, its adherents called for the Jewish people to be granted a sovereign state with its capital at Jerusalem, the 'city of Zion'. The movement was founded by the Hungarian writer Theodor *Herzl, who in 1897 convened the First Zionist Congress in the Swiss city of Basel. Zionism was the driving force behind the creation of the state of Israel in 1948.

zip fastener fastening device used in clothing, patented in the USA by Whitcomb Judson in 1893, originally for doing up shoes. It has two sets of interlocking teeth, meshed by means of a slide that moves up and down. It became widely used in the clothing industry in the 1930s.

zircon zirconium silicate, $ZrSiO_4$, a mineral that occurs in small quantities in a wide range of igneous, sedimentary, and metamorphic rocks. It is very durable and is resistant to erosion and weathering. It is usually coloured brown, but can be other colours, and when transparent may be used as a gemstone.

zirconium chemical symbol Zr, (Germanic *zircon*, from Persian *zargun* 'golden') lustrous, greyish-white,

strong, ductile, metallic element, atomic number 40, relative atomic mass 91.22. It occurs in nature as the mineral zircon (zirconium silicate), from which it is obtained commercially. It is used in some ceramics, alloys for wire and filaments, steel manufacture, and nuclear reactors, where its low neutron absorption is advantageous.

zither member of a family of musical instruments consisting of one or more strings stretched over a resonating frame or soundbox, played horizontally. The modern concert zither has up to 45 strings of which five, passing over frets, are plucked with a plectrum for melody, and the remainder are plucked with the fingers for harmonic accompaniment.

Zi Xi (*or* **Tz'u-shi**) (**c. 1834–1908**) Empress dowager of China. She was presented as a concubine to the emperor Xianfeng. On his death in 1861 she became regent for her young son Tongzhi (1856–1875) until 1873 and, after his death, for her nephew Guangxu (1871–1908) until 1889. A ruthless conservative, she blocked the Hundred Days' Reform launched in 1898 and assumed power again, having Guangxu imprisoned. Her policies helped deny China a peaceful transition to political and economic reform.

zodiac zone of the heavens containing the paths of the Sun, Moon, and planets. When this was devised by the ancient Greeks, only five planets were known, making the zodiac about 16° wide. In astrology, the zodiac is divided into 12 signs, each 30° in extent: Aries, Taurus, Gemini, Cancer, Leo, Virgo, Libra, Scorpio, Sagittarius, Capricorn, Aquarius, and Pisces. These do not cover the same areas of sky as the astronomical constellations.

zodiacal light cone-shaped light sometimes seen extending from the Sun along the *ecliptic (that is, the path that the Sun appears to follow each year as it is orbited by Earth), visible after sunset or before sunrise. It is due to thinly spread dust particles in the central plane of the Solar System. It is very faint, and requires a dark, clear sky to be seen.

Zoë (**c. 978–1050**) Byzantine empress who ruled from 1028 until 1050. She gained the title by marriage to the heir apparent Romanus III Argyrus, but was reputed to have poisoned him (1034) in order to marry her lover Michael. He died in 1041 and Zoë and her sister Theodora were proclaimed joint empresses. Rivalry led to Zoë marrying Constantine IX Monomachus with whom she reigned until her death.

Zola, Émile Edouard Charles Antoine (**1840–1902**) French novelist and social reformer. He made his name with *Thérèse Raquin* (1867), a grim, powerful story of remorse. With *La Fortune des Rougon/The Fortune of the Rougons* (1867) he began a series of some 20 naturalistic novels collectively known as *Le Rougon-Macquart*, portraying the fortunes of a French family under the Second Empire. They include *Le Ventre de Paris/The Underbelly of Paris* (1873), *Nana* (1880), and *La Débâcle/The Debacle* (1892). In 1898 he published *J'accuse/I Accuse*, a pamphlet indicting the persecutors of Alfred *Dreyfus, for which he was prosecuted for libel but later pardoned.

zombie corpse believed to be reanimated by a spirit and enslaved. The idea, widespread in Haiti, possibly arose from voodoo priests using the nerve poison tetrodotoxin (from the puffer fish) to produce a semblance of death from which the victim afterwards physically recovers. Those eating incorrectly prepared puffer fish in Japan have been similarly affected.

zoo abbreviation for ZOOlogical gardens, place where animals are kept in captivity. Originally created purely for visitor entertainment and education, zoos have become major centres for the breeding of endangered species of animals; a 1984 report identified 2,000 vertebrate species in need of such maintenance.

zoology branch of biology concerned with the study of animals. It includes any aspect of the study of animal form and function – description of present-day animals, the study of evolution of animal forms, *anatomy, *physiology, *embryology, behaviour, and geographical distribution.

zoonosis any infectious disease that can be transmitted to humans by other vertebrate animals. Probably the most feared example is *rabies. The transmitted micro-organism sometimes causes disease only in the human host, leaving the animal host unaffected.

Zoroaster (*or* **Zarathustra**) (*c.* **638–c. 553 BC**) Persian prophet and religious teacher, founder of Zoroastrianism. Zoroaster believed that he had seen God, Ahura Mazda, in a vision. His first vision came at the age of 30 and, after initial rejection and violent attack, he converted King Vishtaspa. Subsequently, his teachings spread rapidly, becoming the official religion of the kingdom.

Zoroastrianism pre-Islamic Persian religion founded by the Persian prophet Zoroaster in the 6th century BC, and still practised by the *Parsees in India. The *Zend-Avesta are the sacred scriptures of the faith. The theology is dualistic, **Ahura Mazda** or **Ormuzd** (the good God) being perpetually in conflict with **Ahriman** (the evil God), but the former is assured of eventual victory. There are approximately 100,000 (1991) Zoroastrians worldwide; membership is restricted to those with both parents belonging to the faith.

Z particle in physics, an *elementary particle, one of the *intermediate vector bosons responsible for carrying the *weak nuclear force. The Z particle is neutral.

Zsigmondy, Richard Adolf (1865–1929) Austrian-born German chemist who devised and built an ultramicroscope in 1903. The microscope's illumination was placed at right angles to the axis. (In a conventional microscope the light source is placed parallel to the instrument's axis.) Zsigmondy's arrangement made it possible to observe particles with a diameter of one 10-millionth of a millimetre. He was awarded the Nobel Prize for Chemistry in 1925 for the elucidation of heterogeneity of colloids.

zucchini another name for the courgette, a type of *marrow.

Zuider Zee former sea inlet in the northwestern Netherlands, closed off from the North Sea by a 32-km/20-mi dyke in 1932; much of it has been reclaimed as land. The remaining lake is called the *IJsselmeer.

Zulu member of a group of southern African peoples mainly from Kwa Zulu-Natal, South Africa. They are traditionally agriculturalists. The Zulu language, closely related to Xhosa, belongs to the Bantu branch of the Niger-Congo family. Many Zulus are supporters of the political organization *Inkatha, founded by Chief *Buthelezi in 1975.

Zululand region in KwaZulu-Natal, South Africa, largely corresponding to the former Black National State KwaZulu. The Zulus formed a powerful kingdom in the early 19th century under Shaka (died 1828) and built up an empire in Natal, displacing other peoples of southern Africa. They were defeated by the British army at Ulundi in 1879. Zululand became part of the British colony of Natal in 1897.

Zürich city and capital of **Switzerland**, situated at the exit of the Limmat River from Lake Zürich; population (1995) 422,700. Lying at the foot of the Alps, it is the capital of Zürich canton, the principal financial and business centre of Switzerland, and one of the world's leading international banking and insurance centres (the 'Gnomes of Zürich'). Manufactured goods include machinery, electrical goods, textiles, and printed works. It is the largest city in Switzerland.

Zwingli, Ulrich (1484–1531) Swiss Protestant reformer. He was ordained a Roman Catholic priest in 1506, but by 1519 was a Reformer and led the Reformation in Switzerland with his insistence on the sole authority of the Scriptures. He was killed in a skirmish at Kappel during a war against the cantons that had not accepted the Reformation.

zwitterion ion that has both a positive and a negative charge, such as an *amino acid in neutral solution. For example, glycine contains both a basic amino group (NH_2) and an acidic carboxyl group (COOH); when these are both ionized in aqueous solution, the acid group loses a proton to the amino group, and the molecule is positively charged at one end and negatively charged at the other.

APPENDIX

IMPERIAL AND METRIC CONVERSION FACTORS

To convert from Imperial	Multiply by	To convert from Metric	Multiply by
Length			
inches to millimetres	25.4	millimetres to inches	0.0393701
feet to metres	0.3048	metres to feet	3.28084
yards to metres	0.9144	metres to yards	1.09361
furlongs to kilometres	0.201168	kilometres to furlongs	4.97097
miles to kilometres	1.609344	kilometres to miles	0.621371
Area			
square inches to square centimetres	6.4516	square centimetres to square inches	0.1550
square feet to square metres	0.092903	square metres to square feet	10.7639
square yards to square metres	0.836127	square metres to square yards	1.19599
square miles to square kilometres	2.589988	square kilometres to square miles	0.386102
acres to square metres	4,046.856422	square metres to acres	0.000247
acres to hectares	0.404685	hectares to acres	2.471054
Volume/capacity			
cubic inches to cubic centimetres	16.387064	cubic centimetres to cubic inches	0.061024
cubic feet to cubic metres	0.028317	cubic metres to cubic feet	35.3147
cubic yards to cubic metres	0.764555	cubic metres to cubic yards	1.30795
cubic miles to cubic kilometres	4.1682	cubic kilometres to cubic miles	0.239912
fluid ounces (imperial) to millilitres	28.413063	millilitres to fluid ounces (imperial)	0.035195
fluid ounces (US) to millilitres	29.5735	millilitres to fluid ounces (US)	0.033814
pints (imperial) to litres	0.568261	litres to pints (imperial)	1.759754
pints (US) to litres	0.473176	litres to pints (US)	2.113377
quarts (imperial) to litres	1.136523	litres to quarts (imperial)	0.879877
quarts (US) to litres	0.946353	litres to quarts (US)	1.056688
gallons (imperial) to litres	4.54609	litres to gallons (imperial)	0.219969
gallons (US) to litres	3.785412	litres to gallons (US)	0.364172
Mass/weight			
ounces to grams	28.349523	grams to ounces	0.035274
pounds to kilograms	0.453592	kilograms to pounds	2.20462
stones (14 lb) to kilograms	6.350293	kilograms to stones (14 lb)	0.157473
tons (imperial) to kilograms	1,016.046909	kilograms to tons (imperial)	0.000984
tons (US) to kilograms	907.18474	kilograms to tons (US)	0.001102
tons (imperial) to metric tonnes	1.016047	metric tonnes to tons (imperial)	0.984207
tons (US) to metric tonnes	0.907185	metric tonnes to tons (US)	1.10231
Speed			
miles per hour to kilometres per hour	1.609344	kilometres per hour to miles per hour	0.621371
feet per second to metres per second	0.3048	metres per second to feet per second	3.28084
Force			
pounds-force to newtons	4.44822	newtons to pounds-force	0.224809
		newtons to kilograms-force	0.101972
		kilograms-force to newtons	9.80665
Pressure			
pounds-force per square inch to kilopascals	6.89476	kilopascals to pounds-force per square inch	0.145038
tons-force per square inch (imperial) to megapascals	15.4443	megapascals to tons-force per square inch (imperial)	0.064779
atmospheres to newtons per square centimetre	10.1325	newtons per square centimetre to atmospheres	0.098692
pounds-force per square inch to atmospheres	0.068948		

Appendix

To convert from Imperial	Multiply by	To convert from Metric	Multiply by
Energy			
British thermal units to joules	1055	joules to calories	0.238846
		calories to joules	4.1868
Power			
horsepower to kilowatts	0.7457	kilowatts to horsepower	1.34102
Fuel consumption			
miles per gallon (imperial) to kilometres per litre	0.3540	kilometres per litre to miles per gallon (imperial)	2.824859
miles per gallon (US) to kilometres per litre	0.4251	kilometres per litre to miles per gallon (US)	2.3521
gallons per mile (imperial) to litres per kilometre	2.824859	litres per kilometre to gallons per mile (imperial)	0.3540
gallons per mile (US) to litres per kilometre	2.3521	litres per kilometre to gallons per mile (US)	0.4251

SI UNITS

Quantity	SI unit	Symbol
Base units		
length	metre	m
mass	kilogram	kg
time	second	s
electric current	ampere	A
temperature, thermodynamic	kelvin	K
amount of substance	mole	mol
luminous intensity	candela	cd
Derived units		
absorbed radiation dose	gray	Gy
electric capacitance	farad	F
electric charge	coulomb	C
electric conductance	siemens	S
energy or work	joule	J
force	newton	N
frequency	hertz	Hz
illuminance	lux	lx
inductance	henry	H
luminous flux	lumen	lm
magnetic flux	weber	Wb
magnetic flux density	tesla	T
plane angle	radian	rad
potential difference	volt	V
power	watt	W
pressure	pascal	Pa
radiation dose equivalent	sievert	Sv
radiation exposure	roentgen	R
radioactivity	becquerel	Bq
resistance	ohm	Ω
solid angle	steradian	sr
sound intensity	decibel	dB
temperature	degree Celsius	°C

PHYSICAL CONSTANTS

Physical constants, or fundamental constants, are physical quantities that are constant in all circumstances throughout the whole universe.

Constant	Symbol	Value in SI units
acceleration of free fall	g	9.80665 m s^{-2}
Avogadro's constant	N_A	6.0221367×10^{23} mol^{-1}
Boltzmann's constant	k	1.380658×10^{-23} J K^{-1}
elementary charge	e	$1.60217733 \times 10^{-19}$ C
electronic rest mass	m_e	$9.1093897 \times 10^{-31}$ kg
Faraday's constant	F	9.6485309×104 C mol^{-1}
gas constant	R	8.314510 J K^{-1} mol^{-1}
gravitational constant	G	6.672×10^{-11} N m2 kg^{-2}
Loschmidt's number	N_L	2.686763×1025 m^{-3}
neutron rest mass	m_n	$1.6749286 \times 10^{-27}$ kg
Planck's constant	h	$6.6260755 \times 10^{-34}$ J s
proton rest mass	m_p	$1.6726231 \times 10^{-27}$ kg
speed of light in a vacuum	c	2.99792458×108 m s^{-1}
standard atmosphere	atm	1.01325×105 Pa
Stefan–Boltzmann constant	σ	5.67051×10^{-8} W m^{-2} K^{-4}

MISCELLANEOUS UNITS

Unit	Definition
acoustic ohm	cgs unit of acoustic impedance (the ratio of sound pressure on a surface to sound flux through the surface)
acre	traditional English land measure; 1 acre = 4,480 sq yd (4,047 sq m or 0.4047 ha)
acre-foot	unit sometimes used to measure large volumes of water such as reservoirs; 1 acre-foot = 1,233.5 cu m/43,560 cu ft
astronomical unit	unit (symbol AU) equal to the mean distance of the Earth from the Sun: 149,597,870 km/ 92,955,808 mi
atmosphere	unit of pressure (abbreviation atm); 1 standard atmosphere = 101,325 Pa
barn	unit of area, especially the cross-sectional area of an atomic nucleus; 1 barn = 10^{-28} sq m
barrel	unit of liquid capacity; the volume of a barrel depends on the liquid being measured and the country and state laws. In the USA, 1 barrel of oil = 42 gal (159 l/34.97 imperial gal), but for federal taxing of fermented liquor (such as beer), 1 barrel = 31 gal (117.35 l/25.81 imperial gal). Many states fix a 36-gallon barrel for cistern measurement and federal law uses a 40-gallon barrel to measure 'proof spirits'. 1 barrel of beer in the UK = 163.66 l (43.23 US gal/36 imperial gal)
base box	imperial unit of area used in metal plating; 1 base box = 20.232 sq m/31,360 sq in
baud	unit of electrical signalling speed equal to 1 pulse per second
brewster	unit (symbol B) for measuring reaction of optical materials to stress
British thermal unit	imperial unit of heat (symbol Btu); 1 Btu = approximately 1,055 J
bushel	measure of dry and (in the UK) liquid volume. 1 bushel (struck measure) = 8 dry US gallons (64 dry US pt/35.239 l/2,150.42 cu in). 1 heaped US bushel = 1,278 bushels, struck measure (81.78 dry pt/45.027 l/2,747.715 cu in), often referred to a 11/4 bushels, struck measure. In the UK, 1 bushel = 8 imperial gallons (64 imperial pt); 1 UK bushel = 1.03 US bushels
cable	unit of length used on ships, taken as $^1/10$ of a nautical mile (185.2 m/607.6 ft)
calorie	cgs unit of heat, now replaced by the joule; 1 calorie = 4.1868 J
carat	unit for measuring mass of precious stones; 1 carat = 0.2 g/0.00705 oz
carat	unit of purity in gold; pure gold is 24-carat
carcel	obsolete unit of luminous intensity

Appendix

Unit	Definition
cental	name for the short hundredweight; 1 cental = 45.36 kg/100 lb
chaldron	obsolete unit measuring capacity; 1 chaldron = 1.309 cu m/46.237 cu ft
clausius	in engineering, a unit of entropy; defined as the ratio of energy to temperature above absolute zero
cleanliness unit	unit for measuring air pollution; equal to the number of particles greater than 0.5 mm in diameter per cu ft of air
clo	unit of thermal insulation of clothing; standard clothes have insulation of about 1 clo, the warmest have about 4 clo per 2.5 cm/1 in of thickness
clusec	unit for measuring the power of a vacuum pump
condensation number	in physics, the ratio of the number of molecules condensing on a surface to the number of molecules touching that surface
cord	unit for measuring the volume of wood cut for fuel; 1 cord = 3.62 cu m/128 cu ft, or a stack 2.4 m/8 ft long, 1.2 m/4 ft wide and 1.2 m/4 ft high
crith	unit of mass for weighing gases; 1 crith = the mass of 1 litre of hydrogen gas at standard temperature and pressure
cubit	earliest known unit of length; 1 cubit = approximately 45.7 cm/18 in, the length of the human forearm from the tip of the middle finger to the elbow
curie	former unit of radioactivity (symbol Ci); 1 curie = 3.7×10^{10} becquerels
dalton	international atomic mass unit, equivalent to $^{1}/_{12}$ of the mass of a neutral carbon-12 atom
darcy	cgs unit (symbol D) of permeability, used mainly in geology to describe the permeability of rock
darwin	unit of measurement of evolutionary rate of change
decontamination factor	unit measuring the effectiveness of radiological decontamination; the ratio of original contamination to the radiation remaining
demal	unit measuring concentration; 1 demal = 1 gram-equivalent of solute in 1 cu dm of solvent
denier	unit used to measure the fineness of yarns; 9,000 m of 15 denier nylon weighs 15 g/0.5 oz
dioptre	optical unit measuring the power of a lens; the reciprocal of the focal length in metres
dram	unit of apothecaries' measure; 1 dram = 60 grains/3.888 g
dyne	cgs unit of force; 10^5 dynes = 1 N
einstein unit	unit for measuring photoenergy in atomic physics
eotvos unit	unit (symbol E) for measuring small changes in the intensity of the Earth's gravity with horizontal distance
erg	cgs unit of work; equal to the work done by a force of 1 dyne moving through 1 cm
erlang	unit for measuring telephone traffic intensity; for example, 90 minutes of carried traffic measured over 60 minutes = 1.5 erlangs ('carried traffic' refers to the total duration of completed calls made within a specified period)
fathom	unit of depth measurement in mining and seafaring; 1 fathom = 1.83 m/6 ft
finsen unit	unit (symbol FU) for measuring intensity of ultraviolet light
fluid ounce	measure of capacity; equivalent in the USA to $^{1}/_{16}$ of a pint ($^{1}/_{20}$ of a pint in the UK and Canada)
foot	imperial unit of length (symbol ft), equivalent to 0.3048 m
foot-candle	unit of illuminance, replaced by the lux; 1 foot-candle = 10.76391 lux
foot-pound	imperial unit of energy (symbol ft-lb); 1 ft-lb = 1.356 joule
frigorie	unit (symbol fg) used in refrigeration engineering to measure heat energy, equal to a rate of heat extraction of 1 kilocalorie per hour
furlong	unit of measurement, originating in Anglo-Saxon England, equivalent to 201.168 m/220 yd
galileo	unit (symbol Gal) of acceleration; 1 galileo = 10^{-2} m s^{-2}
gallon	imperial liquid or dry measure subdivided into 4 quarts or 8 pints; 1 US gal = 3.785 l; 1 imperial gal = 4.546 l
gauss	cgs unit (symbol Gs) of magnetic flux density, replaced by the tesla; 1 gauss = 1×10^{-4} tesla

Unit	Definition
gill	imperial unit of volume for liquid measure; equal to $^1/_4$ of a pint (in the USA, 4 fl oz/0.118 l; in the UK, 5 fl oz/0.142 l)
grain	smallest unit of mass in the three English systems of measurement (avoirdupois, troy, apothecaries' weights) used in the UK and USA; 1 grain = 0.0648 g
hand	unit used in measuring the height of a horse from front hoof to shoulder (withers); 1 hand = 10.2 cm/4 in
hardness number	unit measuring hardness of materials. There are many different hardness scales: Brinell, Rockwell, and Vickers scales measure the degree of indentation or impression of materials; Mohs' scale measures resistance to scratching against a standard set of minerals
hartree	atomic unit of energy, equivalent to atomic unit of charge divided by atomic unit of length; 1 hartree = 4.850×10^{-18} J
haze factor	unit of visibility in mist or fog; the ratio of brightness of mist compared with that of the object
Hehner number	unit measuring concentration of fatty acids in oils; a Hehner number of 1 = 1 kg of fatty acid in 100 kg of oil or fat
hide	unit of measurement used in the 12th century to measure land; 1 hide = 60–120 acres/25–50 ha
horsepower	imperial unit (abbreviation hp) of power; 1 horsepower = 746 W
hundredweight	imperial unit (abbreviation cwt) of mass; 1 cwt = 45.36 kg/100 lb in the USA and 50.80 kg/112 lb in the UK
inch	imperial unit (abbreviation in) of linear measure, $^1/_{12}$ of a ft; 1 in = 2.54 cm
inferno	unit used in astrophysics for describing the temperature inside a star; 1 inferno = 1 billion K (kelvin)
iodine number	unit measuring the percentage of iodine absorbed in a substance, expressed as grams of iodine absorbed by 100 grams of material
jansky	unit used in radio astronomy to measure radio emissions or flux densities from space; 1 jansky = 10^{-26} W m^{-2} Hz^{-1}. Flux density is the energy in a beam of radiation which passes through an area normal to the beam in a single unit of time. A jansky is a measurement of the energy received from a cosmic radio source per unit area of detector in a single time unit
kayser	unit used in spectroscopy to measure wave number (number of waves in a unit length); a wavelength of 1 cm has a wave number of 1 kayser
knot	unit used in navigation to measure a ship's speed; 1 knot = 1 nautical mile per hour, or about 1.15 miles per hour
league	obsolete imperial unit of length; 1 league = 3 nautical mi/5.56 km or 3 statute mi/4.83 km
light year	unit used in astronomy to measure distance; the distance travelled by light in one year, approximately 9.46×10^{12} km/5.88×10^{12} mi
mache	obsolete unit of radioactive concentration; 1 mache = 3.7×10^{-7} curies of radioactive material per cu m of a medium
maxwell	cgs unit (symbol Mx) of magnetic flux, the strength of a magnetic field in an area multiplied by the area; 1 maxwell = 10^8 weber
megaton	measurement of the explosive power of a nuclear weapon; 1 megaton = 1 million tons of trinitrotoluene (TNT)
mil	(a) one-thousandth of a litre; contraction of the word millilitre; (b) imperial measure of length, equal to one-thousandth of an inch; also known as the thou
mile	imperial unit of linear measure; 1 statute mile = 1.60934 km/5,280 ft; 1 international nautical mile = 1.852 km/6,076 ft
millimetre of mercury	unit of pressure (symbol mmHg) used in medicine for measuring blood pressure
morgan	arbitrary unit used in genetics; 1 morgan is the distance along the chromosome in a gene that gives a recombination frequency of 1%
nautical mile	unit of distance used in navigation, equal to the average length of 1 minute of arc on a great circle of the Earth; 1 international nautical mile = 1.852 km/6,076 ft
neper	unit used in telecommunications; gives the attenuation of amplitudes of currents or powersas the natural logarithm of the ratio of the voltage between two points or the current between two points

Unit	Definition
oersted	cgs unit (symbol Oe) of magnetic field strength, now replaced by amperes per metre (1 Oe = 79.58 amp per m)
ounce	unit of mass, $^1/16$ of a pound avoirdupois, equal to 437.5 grains/28.35 g; or 14.6 pound troy, equal to 480 grains/31.10 g
parsec	unit (symbol pc) used in astronomy for distances to stars and galaxies; 1 pc = 3.262 light years, 2.063×10^5 astronomical units, or 3.086×10^{13} km
peck	obsolete unit of dry measure, equal to 8 imperial quarts or 1 quarter bushel (8.1 l in the USA or 9.1 l in the UK)
pennyweight	imperial unit of mass; 1 pennyweight = 24 grains = 1.555×10^{-3} kg
perch	obsolete imperial unit of length; 1 perch = $5^1/2$ yards = 5.029 m, also called the rod or pole
pint	imperial unit of liquid or dry measure; in the USA, 1 liquid pint = 16 fl oz/0.473 l, while 1 dry pint = 0.551 l; in the UK, 1 pt = 20 fl oz, $^1/2$ quart, $^1/8$ gal, or 0.568 l
point	metric unit of mass used in relation to gemstones; 1 point = 0.01 metric carat = 2×10^{-3} g
poise	cgs unit of dynamic viscosity; 1 poise = 1 dyne-second per sq cm
pound	imperial unit (abbreviation lb) of mass; the avoirdupois pound or imperial standard pound = 0.45 kg/7,000 grains, while the pound troy (used for weighing precious metals) = 0.37 kg/5,760 grains
poundal	imperial unit (abbreviation pdl) of force; 1 poundal = 0.1383 newton
quart	imperial liquid or dry measure; in the USA, 1 liquid quart = 0.946 l, while 1 dry quart = 1.101 l; in the UK, 1 quart = 2 pt/1.137 l
rad	unit of absorbed radiation dose, replaced in the SI system by the gray; 1 rad = 0.01 joule of radiation absorbed by 1 kg of matter
relative biological effectiveness	relative damage caused to living tissue by different types of radiation
roentgen	unit (symbol R) of radiation exposure, used for X- and gamma rays
rood	imperial unit of area; 1 rood = $^1/4$ acre = 1,011.7 sq m
rydberg	atomic unit of energy; 1 rydberg = 2.425×10^{-18} J
sabin	unit of sound absorption, used in acoustical engineering; 1 sabin = absorption of 1 sq ft (0.093 sq m) of a perfectly absorbing surface
scruple	imperial unit of apothecaries' measure; 1 scruple = 20 grains = 1.3×10^{-3} kg
shackle	unit of length used at sea for measuring cable or chain; 1 shackle = 15 fathoms (90 ft/27 m)
slug	obsolete imperial unit of mass; 1 slug = 14.59 kg/32.17 lb
snellen	unit expressing the visual power of the eye
sone	unit of subjective loudness
standard volume	in physics, the volume occupied by 1 kilogram molecule (molecular mass in kilograms) of any gas at standard temperature and pressure; approximately 22.414 cu m
stokes	cgs unit (symbol St) of kinematic viscosity; 1 stokes = 10^{-4} m^2 s^{-1}
stone	imperial unit (abbreviation st) of mass; 1 stone = 6.35 kg/14 lb
strontium unit	measures concentration of strontium-90 in an organic medium relative to the concentration of calcium
tex	metric unit of line density; 1 tex is the line density of a thread with a mass of 1 gram and a length of 1 kilometre
tog	measure of thermal insulation of a fabric, garment, or quilt; the tog value is equivalent to 10 times the temperature difference (in °C) between the two faces of the article, when the flow of heat across it is equal to 1 W per sq m
ton	unit of mass; the long ton (UK) = 1,016 kg/2,240 lb; 1 short ton (USA) = 907 kg/2,000 lb; 1 metric tonne = 1000 kg/2205 lb
yard	imperial unit (symbol yd) of length, equivalent to 0.9144 m/3 ft

TABLE OF EQUIVALENT TEMPERATURES

Celsius and Fahrenheit temperatures can be interconverted as follows: $C = (F - 32) \times 100/180$; $F = (C \times 180/100) + 32$.

°C	°F	°C	°F	°C	°F	°C	°F
100	212.0	70	158.0	40	104.0	10	50.0
99	210.2	69	156.2	39	102.2	9	48.2
98	208.4	68	154.4	38	100.4	8	46.4
97	206.6	67	152.6	37	98.6	7	44.6
96	204.8	66	150.8	36	96.8	6	42.8
95	203.0	65	149.0	35	95.0	5	41.0
94	201.2	64	147.2	34	93.2	4	39.2
93	199.4	63	145.4	33	91.4	3	37.4
92	197.6	62	143.6	32	89.6	2	35.6
91	195.8	61	141.8	31	87.8	1	33.8
90	194.0	60	140.0	30	86.0	0	32.0
89	192.2	59	138.2	29	84.2	−1	30.2
88	190.4	58	136.4	28	82.4	−2	28.4
87	188.6	57	134.6	27	80.6	−3	26.6
86	186.8	56	132.8	26	78.8	−4	24.8
85	185.0	55	131.0	25	77.0	−5	23.0
84	183.2	54	129.2	24	75.2	−6	21.2
83	181.4	53	127.4	23	73.4	−7	19.4
82	179.6	52	125.6	22	71.6	−8	17.6
81	177.8	51	123.8	21	69.8	−9	15.8
80	176.0	50	122.0	20	68.0	−10	14.0
79	174.2	49	120.2	19	66.2	−11	12.2
78	172.4	48	118.4	18	64.4	−12	10.4
77	170.6	47	116.6	17	62.6	−13	8.6
76	168.8	46	114.8	16	60.8	−14	6.8
75	167.0	45	113.0	15	59.0	−15	5.0
74	165.2	44	111.2	14	57.2	−16	3.2
73	163.4	43	109.4	13	55.4	−17	1.4
72	161.6	42	107.6	12	53.6	−18	−0.4
71	159.8	41	105.8	11	51.8	−19	−2.2

Appendix

RELATIVE TIMES IN CITIES THROUGHOUT THE WORLD

The time indicated in the table below is fixed by law and is called standard time. At 12:00 noon, GMT, the standard time elsewhere around the world is as follows:

City	Time	City	Time
Abu Dhabi, United Arab Emirates	16:00	Frankfurt am Main, Germany	13:00
Accra, Ghana	12:00	Gdansk, Poland	13:00
Addis Ababa, Ethiopia	15:00	Geneva, Switzerland	13:00
Adelaide, Australia	21:30	Hague, The, Netherlands	13:00
Alexandria, Egypt	14:00	Harare, Zimbabwe	14:00
Algiers, Algeria	13:00	Havana, Cuba	07:00
Al Manamah (also called Bahrain), Bahrain	15:00	Helsinki, Finland	14:00
Amman, Jordan	14:00	Hobart, Australia	22:00
Amsterdam, Netherlands	13:00	Ho Chi Minh City, Vietnam	19:00
Anchorage (AK), USA	03:00	Hong Kong, China	20:00
Ankara, Turkey	14:00	Istanbul, Turkey	14:00
Athens, Greece	14:00	Jakarta, Indonesia	19:00
Auckland, New Zealand	24:00	Jerusalem, Israel	14:00
Baghdad, Iraq	15:00	Johannesburg, South Africa	14:00
Bahrain (also called Al Manamah), Bahrain	15:00	Karachi, Pakistan	17:00
Bangkok, Thailand	19:00	Kiev, Ukraine	14:00
Barcelona, Spain	13:00	Kolkata (formerly Calcutta), India	17:30
Beijing, China	20:00	Kuala Lumpur, Malaysia	20:00
Beirut, Lebanon	14:00	Kuwait City, Kuwait	15:00
Belgrade, Yugoslavia	13:00	Kyoto, Japan	21:00
Berlin, Germany	13:00	Lagos, Nigeria	13:00
Bern, Switzerland	13:00	Le Havre, France	13:00
Bogotá, Colombia	07:00	Lima, Peru	07:00
Bonn, Germany	13:00	Lisbon, Portugal	12:00
Brazzaville, Republic of the Congo	13:00	London, England	12:00
Brisbane, Australia	22:00	Luanda, Angola	13:00
Brussels, Belgium	13:00	Luxembourg, Luxembourg	13:00
Bucharest, Romania	14:00	Lyon, France	13:00
Budapest, Hungary	13:00	Madrid, Spain	13:00
Buenos Aires, Argentina	09:00	Manila, Philippines	20:00
Cairo, Egypt	14:00	Marseille, France	13:00
Canberra, Australia	22:00	Mecca, Saudi Arabia	15:00
Cape Town, South Africa	14:00	Melbourne, Australia	22:00
Caracas, Venezuela	08:00	Mexico City, Mexico	06:00
Casablanca, Morocco	12:00	Milan, Italy	13:00
Chennai (formerly Madras), India	17:30	Minsk, Belarus	14:00
Chicago (IL), USA	06:00	Monrovia, Liberia	12:00
Cologne, Germany	13:00	Montevideo, Uruguay	09:00
Colombo, Sri Lanka	18:00	Montreal, Canada	07:00
Copenhagen, Denmark	13:00	Moscow, Russian Federation	15:00
Damascus, Syria	14:00	Mumbai (formerly Bombay), India	17:30
Dar es Salaam, Tanzania	15:00	Munich, Germany	13:00
Darwin, Australia	21:30	Nairobi, Kenya	15:00
Delhi, India	17:30	New Orleans (LA), USA	06:00
Denver (CO), USA	05:00	New York (NY), USA	07:00
Dhaka, Bangladesh	18:00	Nicosia, Cyprus	14:00
Dubai, United Arab Emirates	16:00	Oslo, Norway	13:00
Dublin, Republic of Ireland	12:00	Ottawa, Canada	07:00
Florence, Italy	13:00	Panamá, Panama	07:00

City	Time	City	Time
Paris, France	13:00	Tehran, Iran	15:30
Perth, Australia	20:00	Tel Aviv-Yafo, Israel	14:00
Port Said, Egypt	14:00	Tenerife, Canary Islands	12:00
Prague, Czech Republic	13:00	Tokyo, Japan	21:00
Rawalpindi, Pakistan	17:00	Toronto, Canada	07:00
Reykjavík, Iceland	12:00	Tripoli, Libya	13:00
Rio de Janeiro, Brazil	09:00	Tunis, Tunisia	13:00
Riyadh, Saudi Arabia	15:00	Valparaiso, Chile	08:00
Rome, Italy	13:00	Vancouver, Canada	04:00
San Francisco (CA), USA	04:00	Vatican City	13:00
Santiago, Chile	08:00	Venice, Italy	13:00
Seoul, South Korea	21:00	Vienna, Austria	13:00
Shanghai, China	20:00	Vladivostok, Russian Federation	22:00
Singapore City, Singapore	20:00	Volgograd, Russian Federation	16:00
Sofia, Bulgaria	14:00	Warsaw, Poland	13:00
St Petersburg, Russian Federation	15:00	Wellington, New Zealand	24:00
Stockholm, Sweden	13:00	Yangon (formerly Rangoon), Myanmar	18:30
Sydney, Australia	22:00	Yokohama, Japan	21:00
Taipei, Taiwan	20:00	Zagreb, Croatia	13:00
Tashkent, Uzbekistan	17:00	Zürich, Switzerland	13:00

Appendix

LARGEST COUNTRIES BY POPULATION SIZE

Source: *State of the World Population 1999*; Population Division and Statistics Division of the United Nations Secretariat

Countries with a population of over 100 million, 2000 and 2050.

Rank	Country	Population (millions)	% of world population
2000			
1	China	1,278	21.11
2	India	1,014	16.75
3	United States	278	4.59
4	Indonesia	212	3.50
5	Brazil	170	2.81
6	Pakistan	156	2.58
7	Russian Federation	147	2.43
8	Bangladesh	129	2.13
9	Japan	127	2.10
10	Nigeria	112	1.85
	World total	6,055	
2050 (projected)			
1	India	1,529	17.16
2	China	1,478	16.58
3	United States	349	3.91
4	Pakistan	346	3.88
5	Indonesia	312	3.50
6	Nigeria	244	2.73
7	Brazil	244	2.73
8	Bangladesh	213	2.39
9	Ethiopia	170	1.90
10	Congo, Democratic Republic of	160	1.79
11	Mexico	147	1.65
12	Philippines	131	1.47
13	Vietnam	127	1.42
14	Russian Federation	122	1.42
15	Iran	115	1.29
16	Egypt	115	1.29
17	Japan	105	1.17
18	Turkey	101	1.13
	World total	8,909	

RELIGION: FESTIVALS

Date	Festival	Religion	Event commemorated
6 Jan	Epiphany	Western Christian	coming of the Magi
6–7 Jan	Christmas	Orthodox Christian	birth of Jesus
18–19 Jan	Epiphany	Orthodox Christian	coming of the Magi
Jan–Feb	New Year	Chinese	Return of kitchen god to heaven
Feb–March	Shrove Tuesday	Christian	day before Lent
	Ash Wednesday	Christian	first day of Lent
	Purim	Jewish	story of Esther
	Mahashivaratri	Hindu	Shiva
March–April	Palm Sunday	Western Christian	Jesus' entry into Jerusalem
	Good Friday	Western Christian	crucifixion of Jesus
	Easter Sunday	Western Christian	resurrection of Jesus
	Passover	Jewish	escape from slavery in Egypt
	Holi	Hindu	Krishna
	Holi Mohalla	Sikh	(coincides with Holi)
	Rama Naumi	Hindu	birth of Rama
	Ching Ming	Chinese	remembrance of the dead
13 April	Baisakhi	Sikh	founding of the Khalsa
April–May	Easter	Orthodox Christian	death and resurrection of Jesus
May–June	Shavuot	Jewish	giving of Ten Commandments to Moses
	Pentecost (Whitsun)	Western Christian	Jesus' followers receiving the Holy Spirit
	Wesak	Buddhist	day of the Buddha's birth, enlighenment and death
	Martyrdom of Guru Arjan	Sikh	death of fifth guru of Sikhism
June	Dragon Boat Festival	Chinese	Chinese martyr
	Pentecost	Orthodox Christian	Jesus' followers receiving the Holy Spirit
July	Dhammacakka	Buddhist	preaching of Buddha's first sermon
Aug	Raksha Bandhan	Hindu	family
Aug–Sept	Janmashtami	Hindu	birthday of Krishna
Sept	Moon Festival	Chinese	Chinese hero
Sept–Oct	Rosh Hashana	Jewish	start of Jewish New Year
	Yom Kippur	Jewish	day of atonement
	Succoth	Jewish	Israelites' time in the wilderness
Oct	Dusshera	Hindu	goddess Devi
Oct–Nov	Divali	Hindu	goddess Lakshmi
	Divali	Sikh	release of Guru Hargobind from prison
Nov	Guru Nanak's birthday	Sikh	founder of Sikhism
Nov–Dec	Bodhi Day	Buddhist (Mahayana)	Buddha's enlightenment
Dec	Hanukkah	Jewish	recapture of Temple of Jerusalem
	Winter Festival	Chinese	time of feasting
25 Dec	Christmas	Western Christian	birth of Christ
Dec–Jan	Birthday of Guru Gobind Sind	Sikh	last (tenth) human guru of Sikhism
	Martyrdom of Guru Tegh Bahadur	Sikh	ninth guru of Sikhism

Appendix

LARGEST DESERTS IN THE WORLD

Desert	Location	Area[1] sq km	Area[1] sq mi
Sahara	northern Africa	9,065,000	3,500,000
Gobi	Mongolia/northeastern China	1,295,000	500,000
Patagonian	Argentina	673,000	260,000
Rub al-Khali	southern Arabian peninsula	647,500	250,000
Kalahari	southwestern Africa	582,800	225,000
Chihuahuan	Mexico/southwestern USA	362,600	140,000
Taklimakan	northern China	362,600	140,000
Great Sandy	northwestern Australia	338,500	130,000
Great Victoria	southwestern Australia	338,500	130,000
Kyzyl Kum	Uzbekistan/Kazakhstan	259,000	100,000
Thar	India/Pakistan	219,000	84,556
Sonoran	Mexico/southwestern USA	181,300	70,000
Simpson	Australia	103,600	40,000
Mojave	southwestern USA	65,000	25,000

[1] Desert areas are very approximate because clear physical boundaries may not occur.

LARGEST LAKES IN THE WORLD

Lake	Location	Area sq km	Area sq mi
Caspian Sea	Azerbaijan/Russian Federation/Kazakhstan/Turkmenistan/Iran	370,990	143,239
Superior	USA/Canada	82,071	31,688
Victoria	Tanzania/Kenya/Uganda	69,463	26,820
Aral Sea	Kazakhstan/Uzbekistan	64,500	24,903
Huron	USA/Canada	59,547	22,991
Michigan	USA	57,735	22,291
Tanganyika	Tanzania/Democratic Republic of Congo/Zambia/Burundi	32,880	12,695
Baikal	Russian Federation	31,499	12,162
Great Bear	Canada	31,316	12,091
Malawi (or Nyasa)	Malawi/Tanzania/Mozambique	28,867	11,146
Great Slave	Canada	28,560	11,027
Erie	USA/Canada	25,657	9,906
Winnipeg	Canada	25,380	9,799
Ontario	USA/Canada	19,010	7,340
Balkhash	Kazakhstan	18,421	7,112
Ladoga	Russian Federation	17,695	6,832
Chad	Chad/Cameroon/Nigeria	16,310	6,297
Maracaibo	Venezuela	13,507	5,215

HIGHEST MOUNTAINS IN THE WORLD AND FIRST ASCENTS

Mountain	Location	Height		Year of first ascent	Expedition nationality (leader)
		m	**ft**		
Everest	China/Nepal	8,848	29,028	1953	British/New Zealander (J Hunt)
K2	Kashmir/Jammu	8,611	28,251	1954	Italian (A Desio)
Kangchenjunga	India/Nepal	8,598	28,208	1955	British (C Evans; by the southwest face)
Lhotse	China/Nepal	8,511	27,923	1956	Swiss (E Reiss)
Yalung Kang (formerly Kangchenjunga West Peak)	India/Nepal	8,502	27,893	1973	Japanese (Y Ageta)
Kangchenjunga South Peak	India/Nepal	8,488	27,847	1978	Polish (W Wróz)
Makalu I	China/Nepal	8,481	27,824	1955	French (J Couzy)
Kangchenjunga Middle Peak	India/Nepal	8,475	27,805	1973	Polish (W Wróz)
Lhotse Shar	China/Nepal	8,383	27,503	1970	Austrian (S Mayerl)
Dhaulagiri	Nepal	8,172	26,811	1960	Swiss/Austrian (K Diemberger)
Manaslu	Nepal	8,156	26,759	1956	Japanese (T Imanishi)
Cho Oyu	China/Nepal	8,153	26,748	1954	Austrian (H Tichy)
Nanga Parbat	Kashmir/Jammu	8,126	26,660	1953	German (K M Herrligkoffer)
Annapurna I	Nepal	8,078	26,502	1950	French (M Herzog)
Gasherbrum I	Kashmir/Jammu	8,068	26,469	1958	US (P K Schoening; by the southwest ridge)
Broad Peak	Kashmir/Jammu	8,047	26,401	1957	Austrian (M Schmuck)
Gasherbrum II	Kashmir/Jammu	8,034	26,358	1956	Austrian (S Larch; by the southwest spur)
Gosainthan	China	8,012	26,286	1964	Chinese (195-strong team; accounts are inconclusive)
Broad Peak (Middle)	Kashmir/Jammu	8,000	26,246	1975	Polish (K Glazek)
Gasherbrum III	Kashmir/Jammu	7,952	26,089	1975	Polish (J Onyszkiewicz)
Annapurna II	Nepal	7,937	26,040	1960	British (C Bonington)
Gasherbrum IV	Kashmir/Jammu	7,923	25,994	1958	Italian (W Bonatti, C Mouri)
Gyachung Kang	Nepal	7,921	25,987	1964	Japanese (Y Kato, K Sakaizqwa)
Disteghil Shar	Kashmir	7,884	25,866	1960	Austrian (G Stärker, D Marchart)
Himalchuli	Nepal	7,864	25,800	1960	Japanese (M Harada, H Tanabe)
Nuptse	Nepal	7,841	25,725	1961	British (D Davis, C Bonington, L Brown)
Manaslu II	Nepal	7,835	25,705	1970	Japanese (H Watanabe, Lhakpa Tsering)
Masherbrum East	Kashmir	7,821	25,659	1960	Pakistani/US (G Bell, W Unsoeld)
Nanda Devi	India	7,817	25,646	1936	British (H W Tilman)
Chomo Lonzo	Nepal	7,815	25,639	1954	French (J Couzy, L Terry)

Appendix

MAJOR OCEANS AND SEAS OF THE WORLD

Ocean/sea	Area[1]		Average depth	
	sq km	sq mi	m	ft
Pacific Ocean	166,242,000	64,186,000	3,939	12,925
Atlantic Ocean	86,557,000	33,420,000	3,575	11,730
Indian Ocean	73,429,000	28,351,000	3,840	12,598
Arctic Ocean	13,224,000	5,106,000	1,038	3,407
South China Sea	2,975,000	1,149,000	1,464	4,802
Caribbean Sea	2,754,000	1,063,000	2,575	8,448
Mediterranean Sea	2,510,000	969,000	1,501	4,926
Bering Sea	2,261,000	873,000	1,491	4,893
Sea of Okhotsk	1,580,000	610,000	973	3,192
Gulf of Mexico	1,544,000	596,000	1,614	5,297
Sea of Japan	1,013,000	391,000	1,667	5,468
Hudson Bay	730,000	282,000	93	305
East China Sea	665,000	257,000	189	620
Andaman Sea	565,000	218,000	1,118	3,667
Black Sea	461,000	178,000	1,190	3,906
Red Sea	453,000	175,000	538	1,764
North Sea	427,000	165,000	94	308
Baltic Sea	422,000	163,000	55	180
Yellow Sea	294,000	114,000	37	121
Gulf	230,000	89,000	100	328
Gulf of California	153,000	59,000	724	2,375
English Channel	90,000	35,000	54	177
Irish Sea	89,000	34,000	60	197

[1] All figures are approximate as boundaries of oceans and seas cannot be exactly determined.

LONGEST RIVERS IN THE WORLD

River	Location	Approximate Length	
		km	mi
Nile	Africa	6,695	4,160
Amazon	South America	6,570	4,083
Chang Jiang (Yangtze)	China	6,300	3,915
Mississippi–Missouri–Red Rock	USA	6,020	3,741
Huang He (Yellow River)	China	5,464	3,395
Ob–Irtysh	China/Kazakhstan/Russian Federation	5,410	3,362
Amur–Shilka	Asia	4,416	2,744
Lena	Russian Federation	4,400	2,734
Congo	Africa	4,374	2,718
Mackenzie–Peace–Finlay	Canada	4,241	2,635
Mekong	Asia	4,180	2,597
Niger	Africa	4,100	2,548
Yenisei	Russian Federation	4,100	2,548
Paraná	Brazil	3,943	2,450
Mississippi	USA	3,779	2,348
Murray–Darling	Australia	3,751	2,331
Missouri	USA	3,726	2,315
Volga	Russian Federation	3,685	2,290
Madeira	Brazil	3,241	2,014
Purus	Brazil	3,211	1,995
São Francisco	Brazil	3,199	1,988
Yukon	USA/Canada	3,185	1,979
Rio Grande	USA/Mexico	3,058	1,900
Indus	Tibet/Pakistan	2,897	1,800
Danube	central and eastern Europe	2,858	1,776
Japura	Brazil	2,816	1,750
Salween	Myanmar/China	2,800	1,740
Brahmaputra	Asia	2,736	1,700
Euphrates	Iraq	2,736	1,700
Tocantins	Brazil	2,699	1,677
Zambezi	Africa	2,650	1,647
Orinoco	Venezuela	2,559	1,590
Paraguay	Paraguay	2,549	1,584
Amu Darya	Tajikistan/Turkmenistan/Uzbekistan	2,540	1,578
Ural	Russian Federation/Kazakhstan	2,535	1,575
Kolyma	Russian Federation	2,513	1,562
Ganges	India/Bangladesh	2,510	1,560
Arkansas	USA	2,344	1,459
Colorado	USA	2,333	1,450
Dnieper	Russian Federation/Belarus/Ukraine	2,285	1,420
Syr Darya	Asia	2,205	1,370
Irrawaddy	Myanmar	2,152	1,337
Orange	South Africa	2,092	1,300

Appendix

MAJOR VOLCANOES ACTIVE IN THE 20TH CENTURY

As of 22 February 2001.

Volcano	Height		Location	Date of last eruption or activity
	m	**ft**		
Africa				
Cameroon	4,096	13,353	isolated mountain, Cameroon	2000
Nyiragongo	3,470	11,385	Virunga, Democratic Republic of Congo	1994
Nyamuragira	3,056	10,028	Democratic Republic of Congo	2001
Ol Doinyo Lengai	2,886	9,469	Tanzania	1993
Lake Nyos	918	3,011	Cameroon	1986
Erta-Ale	503	1,650	Ethiopia	1995
Antarctica				
Erebus	4,023	13,200	Ross Island, McMurdo Sound	1995
Deception Island	576	1,890	South Shetland Island	1970
Asia				
Kliuchevskoi	4,750	15,584	Kamchatka Peninsula, Russia	2000
Kerinci	3,800	12,467	Sumatra, Indonesia	1987
Rindjani	3,726	12,224	Lombok, Indonesia	1966
Semeru	3,676	12,060	Java, Indonesia	2000
Koryakskaya	3,456	11,339	Kamchatka Peninsula, Russia	1957
Slamet	3,428	11,247	Java, Indonesia	1989
Raung	3,322	10,932	Java, Indonesia	1993
Sheveluch	3,283	10,771	Kamchatka Peninsula, Russia	2000
Agung	3,142	10,308	Bali, Indonesia	1964
On-Taka	3,063	10,049	Honshu, Japan	1991
Merapi	2,911	9,551	Java, Indonesia	2001
Marapi	2,891	9,485	Sumatra, Indonesia	1993
Bezymianny	2,882	9,455	Kamchatka Peninsula, Russia	2000
Asama	2,530	8,300	Honshu, Japan	1990
Nigata Yake-yama	2,475	8,111	Honshu, Japan	1989
Mayon	2,462	8,084	Luzon, Philippines	2001
Canlaon	2,459	8,070	Negros, Philippines	1993
Alaid	2,335	7,662	Kuril Islands, Russia	1986
Chokai	2,225	7,300	Honshu, Japan	1974
Galunggung	2,168	7,113	Java, Indonesia	1984
Azuma	2,042	6,700	Honshu, Japan	1977
Sangeang Api	1,935	6,351	Lesser Sunda Island, Indonesia	1988
Tiatia	1,833	6,013	Kuril Islands, Russia	1981
Pinatubo	1,759	5,770	Luzon, Philippines	1995
Kelut	1,730	5,679	Java, Indonesia	2001
Sarychev Peak	1,512	4,960	Kuril Islands, Russia	1989
Unzen	1,360	4,462	Japan	1996
Krakatoa	818	2,685	Sumatra, Indonesia	2000
Taal	300	984	Philippines	1999
Atlantic Ocean				
Pico de Teide	3,716	12,192	Tenerife, Canary Islands, Spain	1909
Fogo	2,835	9,300	Cape Verde Islands	1995
Beerenberg	2,277	7,470	Jan Mayen Island, Norway	1985
Hekla	1,491	4,920	Iceland	2000
Krafla	654	2,145	Iceland	1984
Helgafell	215	706	Iceland	1973
Surtsey	174	570	Iceland	1967

Volcano	Height		Location	Date of last eruption or activity
	m	**ft**		
Caribbean				
La Grande Soufrière	1,467	4,813	Basse-Terre, Guadeloupe	1977
Pelée	1,397	4,584	Martinique	1932
La Soufrière St Vincent	1,234	4,048	St Vincent and the Grenadines	1979
Soufrière Hills/ 2000Chances Peak	968	3,176	Montserrat	
Central America				
Acatenango	3,960	12,992	Sierra Madre, Guatemala	1972
Fuego	3,835	12,582	Sierra Madre, Guatemala	2000
Tacana	3,780	12,400	Sierra Madre, Guatemala	1988
Santa Maria	3,768	12,362	Sierra Madre, Guatemala	1993
Irazú	3,452	11,325	Cordillera Central, Costa Rica	1992
Turrialba	3,246	10,650	Cordillera Central, Costa Rica	1992
Póas	2,721	8,930	Cordillera Central, Costa Rica	1994
Pacaya	2,543	8,346	Sierra Madre, Guatemala	2000
San Miguel	2,131	6,994	El Salvador	1986
Arenal	1,552	5,092	Costa Rica	2000
Europe				
Etna	3,236	10,625	Sicily, Italy	2000
Vesuvius	1,289	4,203	Italy	1944
Stromboli	931	3,055	Lipari Islands, Italy	1998
Santorini (Thera)	584	1,960	Cyclades, Greece	1950
Indian Ocean				
Karthala	2,440	8,000	Comoros	1991
Piton de la Fournaise (Volcan)	1,823	5,981	Réunion Island, France	2000(Le
Mid-Pacific				
Mauna Loa	4,170	13,681	Hawaii, USA	1984
Kilauea	1,247	4,100	Hawaii, USA	2000
North America				
Popocatépetl	5,452	17,887	Altiplano de México, Mexico	2001
Colima	4,268	14,003	Altiplano de México, Mexico	2000
Spurr	3,374	11,070	Alaska Range (AK), USA	1953
Lassen Peak	3,186	10,453	California, USA	1921
Redoubt	3,108	10,197	Alaska Range (AK), USA	1991
Iliamna	3,052	10,016	Alaska Range (AK), USA	1978
Shishaldin	2,861	9,387	Aleutian Islands (AK), USA	2000
St Helens	2,549	8,364	Skamania County (WA), USA	1998
Pavlof	2,517	8,261	Alaska Range (AK), USA	1997
Veniaminof	2,507	8,225	Alaska Range (AK), USA	1995
Novarupta (Katmai)	2,298	7,540	Alaska Range (AK), USA	1931
El Chichon	2,225	7,300	Altiplano de México, Mexico	1982
Makushin	2,036	6,680	Aleutian Islands (AK), USA	1987

Appendix

Volcano	Height		Location	Date of last eruption or activity
	m	**ft**		
Oceania				
Ruapehu	2,796	9,175	New Zealand	1999
Ulawun	2,296	7,532	Papua New Guinea	2000
Ngauruhoe	2,290	7,515	New Zealand	1977
Bagana	1,998	6,558	Papua New Guinea	1993
Manam	1,829	6,000	Papua New Guinea	1998
Lamington	1,780	5,844	Papua New Guinea	1956
Karkar	1,499	4,920	Papua New Guinea	1979
Lopevi	1,450	4,755	Vanuatu	1982
Ambrym	1,340	4,376	Vanuatu	1991
Tarawera	1,149	3,770	New Zealand	1973
Langila	1,093	3,586	Papua New Guinea	1996
Rabaul	688	2,257	Papua New Guinea	1997
Pagan	570	1,870	Mariana Islands	1993
White Island	328	1,075	New Zealand	2000
South America				
San Pedro	6,199	20,325	Andes, Chile	1960
Guallatiri	6,060	19,882	Andes, Chile	1993
Lascar	5,990	19,652	Andes, Chile	2000
San José	5,919	19,405	Andes, Chile	1931
Cotopaxi	5,897	19,347	Andes, Ecuador	1975
Tutupaca	5,844	19,160	Andes, Ecuador	1902
Ubinas	5,710	18,720	Andes, Peru	1969
Tupungatito	5,640	18,504	Andes, Chile	1986
Islunga	5,566	18,250	Andes, Chile	1960
Nevado del Ruiz	5,435	17,820	Andes, Colombia	1992
Tolima	5,249	17,210	Andes, Colombia	1943
Sangay	5,230	17,179	Andes, Ecuador	1996

SOVEREIGNS OF ENGLAND AND THE UNITED KINGDOM FROM 899

Edward the Elder made the first major advances towards the unification of England under one sovereign and established the ascendancy of his dynasty.

Reign	Name	Relationship
West Saxon Kings		
899–924	Edward the Elder	son of Alfred the Great
924–39	Athelstan	son of Edward the Elder
939–46	Edmund	half-brother of Athelstan
946–55	Edred	brother of Edmund
955–59	Edwy	son of Edmund
959–75	Edgar	brother of Edwy
975–78	Edward the Martyr	son of Edgar
978–1016	Ethelred (II) the Unready	son of Edgar
1016	Edmund Ironside	son of Ethelred (II) the Unready
Danish Kings		
1016–35	Canute	son of Sweyn I of Denmark who conquered England in 1013
1035–40	Harold I	son of Canute
1040–42	Hardicanute	son of Canute
West Saxon Kings (restored)		
1042–66	Edward the Confessor	son of Ethelred (II) the Unready
1066	Harold II	son of Godwin
Norman Kings		
1066–87	William I	illegitimate son of Duke Robert the Devil
1087–1100	William II	son of William I
1100–35	Henry I	son of William I
1135–54	Stephen	grandson of William II
House of Plantagenet		
1154–89	Henry II	son of Matilda (daughter of Henry I)
1189–99	Richard I	son of Henry II
1199–1216	John	son of Henry II
1216–72	Henry III	son of John
1272–1307	Edward I	son of Henry III
1307–27	Edward II	son of Edward I
1327–77	Edward III	son of Edward II
1377–99	Richard II	son of the Black Prince
House of Lancaster		
1399–1413	Henry IV	son of John of Gaunt
1413–22	Henry V	son of Henry IV
1422–61, 1470–71	Henry VI	son of Henry V
House of York		
1461–70, 1471–83	Edward IV	son of Richard, Duke of York
1483	Edward V	son of Edward IV
1483–85	Richard III	brother of Edward IV
House of Tudor		
1485–1509	Henry VII	son of Edmund Tudor, Earl of Richmond
1509–47	Henry VIII	son of Henry VII
1547–53	Edward VI	son of Henry VIII
1553–58	Mary I	daughter of Henry VIII
1558–1603	Elizabeth I	daughter of Henry VIII

Reign	Name	Relationship
House of Stuart		
1603–25	James I	great-grandson of Margaret (daughter of Henry VII)
1625–49	Charles I	son of James I
1649–60	the Commonwealth	
House of Stuart (restored)		
1660–85	Charles II	son of Charles I
1685–88	James II	son of Charles I
1689–1702	William III and Mary	son of Mary (daughter of Charles I); daughter of James II
1702–14	Anne	daughter of James II
House of Hanover		
1714–27	George I	son of Sophia (granddaughter of James I)
1727–60	George II	son of George I
1760–1820	George III	son of Frederick (son of George II)
1820–30	George IV (regent 1811–20)	son of George III
1830–37	William IV	son of George III
1837–1901	Victoria	daughter of Edward (son of George III)
House of Saxe-Coburg		
1901–10	Edward VII	son of Victoria
House of Windsor		
1910–36	George V	son of Edward VII
1936	Edward VIII	son of George V
1936–52	George VI	son of George V
1952–	Elizabeth II	daughter of George VI

SCOTTISH MONARCHS 1005–1603

This table covers the period from the unification of Scotland to the union of the crowns of Scotland and England.

Reign	Name	Reign	Name
Celtic Kings		**English Domination**	
1005–34	Malcolm II	1292–96	John Baliol
1034–40	Duncan I	1296–1306	annexed to England
1040–57	Macbeth		
1057–93	Malcolm III Canmore	**House of Bruce**	
1093–94	Donald III Donalbane	1306–29	Robert I the Bruce
1094	Duncan II	1329–71	David II
1094–97	Donald III (restored)		
1097–1107	Edgar	**House of Stuart**	
1107–24	Alexander I	1371–90	Robert II
1124–53	David I	1390–1406	Robert III
1153–65	Malcolm IV	1406–37	James I
1165–1214	William the Lion	1437–60	James II
1214–49	Alexander II	1460–88	James III
1249–86	Alexander III	1488–1513	James IV
1286–90	Margaret of Norway	1513–42	James V
		1542–67	Mary
		1567–1625	James VI[1]

[1] After the union of crowns in 1603, he became James I of England.

PRIME MINISTERS OF GREAT BRITAIN AND THE UK

Term	Name	Party
1721–42	Robert Walpole[1]	Whig
1742–43	Spencer Compton, Earl of Wilmington	Whig
1743–54	Henry Pelham	Whig
1754–56	Thomas Pelham-Holles, 1st Duke of Newcastle	Whig
1756–57	William Cavendish, 4th Duke of Devonshire	Whig
1757–62	Thomas Pelham-Holles, 1st Duke of Newcastle	Whig
1762–63	John Stuart, 3rd Earl of Bute	Tory
1763–65	George Grenville	Whig
1765–66	Charles Watson Wentworth, 2nd Marquess of Rockingham	Whig
1766–68	William Pitt, 1st Earl of Chatham	Tory
1768–70	Augustus Henry Fitzroy, 3rd Duke of Grafton	Whig
1770–82	Frederick North, Lord North[2]	Tory
1782	Charles Watson Wentworth, 2nd Marquess of Rockingham	Whig
1782–83	William Petty-Fitzmaurice, 2nd Earl of Shelburne[3]	Whig
1783	William Henry Cavendish-Bentinck, 3rd Duke of Portland	Whig
1783–1801	William Pitt, The Younger	Tory
1801–04	Henry Addington	Tory
1804–06	William Pitt, The Younger	Tory
1806–07	William Wyndham Grenville, 1st Baron Grenville	Whig
1807–09	William Henry Cavendish-Bentinck, 3rd Duke of Portland	Whig
1809–12	Spencer Perceval	Tory
1812–27	Robert Banks Jenkinson, 2nd Earl of Liverpool	Tory
1827	George Canning	Tory
1827–28	Frederick John Robinson, 1st Viscount Goderich	Tory
1828–30	Arthur Wellesley, 1st Duke of Wellington	Tory
1830–34	Charles Grey, 2nd Earl Grey	Whig

Appendix

Term	Name	Party
1834	William Lamb, 2nd Viscount Melbourne	Whig
1834	Arthur Wellesley, 1st Duke of Wellington	Tory
1834–35	Sir Robert Peel, 2nd Baronet	Tory
1835–41	William Lamb, 2nd Viscount Melbourne	Whig
1841–46	Sir Robert Peel, 2nd Baronet	Conservative
1846–52	John Russell, Lord Russell	Whig-Liberal
1852	Edward Geoffrey Stanley, 14th Earl of Derby	Conservative
1852–55	George Hamilton-Gordon, 4th Earl of Aberdeen	Peelite
1855–58	Henry John Temple, 3rd Viscount Palmerston	Liberal
1858–59	Edward Geoffrey Stanley, 14th Earl of Derby	Conservative
1859–65	Henry John Temple, 3rd Viscount Palmerston	Liberal
1865–66	John Russell, 1st Earl Russell	Liberal
1866–68	Edward Geoffrey Stanley, 14th Earl of Derby	Conservative
1868	Benjamin Disraeli	Conservative
1868–74	William Ewart Gladstone	Liberal
1874–80	Benjamin Disraeli[4]	Conservative
1880–85	William Ewart Gladstone	Liberal
1885–86	Robert Cecil, 3rd Marquess of Salisbury	Conservative
1886	William Ewart Gladstone	Liberal
1886–92	Robert Cecil, 3rd Marquess of Salisbury	Conservative
1892–94	William Ewart Gladstone	Liberal
1894–95	Archibald Philip Primrose, 5th Earl of Rosebery	Liberal
1895–1902	Robert Cecil, 3rd Marquess of Salisbury	Conservative
1902–05	Arthur James Balfour	Conservative
1905–08	Sir Henry Campbell-Bannerman	Liberal
1908–16	Herbert Henry Asquith	Liberal
1916–22	David Lloyd George	Liberal
1922–23	Bonar Law	Conservative
1923–24	Stanley Baldwin	Conservative
1924	Ramsay Macdonald	Labour
1924–29	Stanley Baldwin	Conservative
1929–35	Ramsay Macdonald	Labour
1935–37	Stanley Baldwin	Conservative
1937–40	Neville Chamberlain	Conservative
1940–45	Winston Churchill	Conservative
1945–51	Clement Attlee	Labour
1951–55	Winston Churchill[5]	Conservative
1955–57	Sir Anthony Eden	Conservative
1957–63	Harold Macmillan	Conservative
1963–64	Sir Alec Douglas-Home	Conservative
1964–70	Harold Wilson	Labour
1970–74	Edward Heath	Conservative
1974–76	Harold Wilson	Labour
1976–79	James Callaghan	Labour
1979–90	Margaret Thatcher	Conservative
1990–97	John Major	Conservative
1997–	Tony Blair	Labour

[1] From 1725, Sir Robert Walpole.
[2] From 1790, 2nd Earl of Guilford.
[3] From 1784, 1st Marquess of Lansdowne.
[4] From 1876, Earl of Beaconsfield.
[5] From 1953, Sir Winston Churchill.

AUSTRALIAN PRIME MINISTERS FROM 1901

The Commonwealth of Australia was created in 1901 when the six colonies of New South Wales, Victoria, Queensland, South Australia, Western Australia, and Tasmania federated as sovereign states.

Term	Name	Party
1901–03	Edmund Barton	Protectionist
1903–04	Alfred Deakin	Protectionist
1904	John Watson	Labor
1904–05	George Reid	Free Trade–Protectionist coalition
1905–08	Alfred Deakin	Protectionist
1908–09	Andrew Fisher	Labor
1909–10	Alfred Deakin	Fusion
1910–13	Andrew Fisher	Labor
1913–14	Joseph Cook	Liberal
1914–15	Andrew Fisher	Labor
1915–23	William Hughes	Labor (National Labor from 1917)
1923–29	Stanley Bruce	National–Country Coalition
1929–32	James Scullin	Labor
1932–39	Joseph Lyons	United Australia–Country coalition
1939	Earle Page	United Australia–Country coalition
1939–41	Robert Menzies	United Australia
1941	Arthur Fadden	Country–United Australia coalition
1941–45	John Curtin	Labor
1945	Francis Forde	Labor
1945–49	Joseph Chifley	Labor
1949–66	Robert Menzies	Liberal–Country coalition
1966–67	Harold Holt	Liberal–Country coalition
1967–68	John McEwen	Liberal–Country coalition
1968–71	John Gorton	Liberal–Country coalition
1971–72	William McMahon	Liberal–Country coalition
1972–75	Gough Whitlam	Labor
1975–83	Malcolm Fraser	Liberal–National coalition
1983–91	Robert Hawke	Labor
1991–96	Paul Keating	Labor
1996–	John Howard	Liberal–National coalition

CANADIAN PRIME MINISTERS FROM 1867

In 1867 the British North America Act established the Dominion of Canada.

Term	Name	Party
1867–73	John A Macdonald	Conservative
1873–78	Alexander Mackenzie	Liberal
1878–91	John A Macdonald	Conservative
1891–92	John J Abbott	Conservative
1892–94	John S D Thompson	Conservative
1894–96	Mackenzie Bowell	Conservative
1896	Charles Tupper	Conservative
1896–1911	Wilfred Laurier	Liberal
1911–20	Robert L Borden	Conservative
1920–21	Arthur Meighen	Conservative
1921–26	William L M King	Liberal
1926	Arthur Meighen	Conservative
1926–30	William L M King	Liberal
1930–35	Richard B Bennett	Conservative
1935–48	William L M King	Liberal
1948–57	Louis S St Laurent	Liberal
1957–63	John G Diefenbaker	Conservative
1963–68	Lester B Pearson	Liberal
1968–79	Pierre E Trudeau	Liberal
1979–80	Joseph Clark	Progressive Conservative
1980–84	Pierre E Trudeau	Liberal
1984	John Turner	Liberal
1984–93	Brian Mulroney	Progressive Conservative
1993	Kim Campbell	Progressive Conservative
1993–2003	Jean Chrétien	Liberal
2003–	Paul Martin	Liberal

NEW ZEALAND PRIME MINISTERS FROM 1906

New Zealand has been self-governing from 1856. It gained dominion status within the British Empire under Joseph Ward in 1907; the country was granted autonomy by the 1931 Statute of Westminster, formally accepted in 1947.

Term	Name	Party
1906–12	Joseph Ward	Liberal
1912	Thomas MacKenzie	Liberal
1912–25	William Massey	Reform
1925–28	Joseph Coates	Reform
1925	Francis Bell	Reform
1928–30	Joseph Ward	United
1930–35	George Forbes	United
1935–40	Michael Savage	Labour
1940–49	Peter Fraser	Labour
1949–57	Sidney Holland	National
1957	Keith Holyoake	National
1957–60	Walter Nash	Labour
1960–72	Keith Holyoake	National
1972	John Marshall	National
1972–74	Norman Kirk	Labour
1974–75	Wallace Rowling	Labour
1975–84	Robert Muldoon	National
1984–89	David Lange	Labour
1989–90	Geoffrey Palmer	Labour
1990	Michael Moore	Labour
1990–97	Jim Bolger	National
1997–99	Jenny Shipley	National
1999–	Helen Clark	Labour

US PRESIDENTS

After having beaten the British at Yorktown in 1783, George Washington took part in drafting a new constitution for the US and was elected its first president in 1789.

Year elected/ took office	President	Party	Losing candidate(s)	Party
1789	1 George Washington	Federalist	no opponent	
1792	George Washington[1]	Federalist	no opponent	
1796	2 John Adams	Federalist	Thomas Jefferson	Democrat–Republican
1800	3 Thomas Jefferson	Democrat–Republican	Aaron Burr	Democrat–Republican
1804	Thomas Jefferson[1]	Democrat–Republican	Charles Pinckney	Federalist
1808	4 James Madison	Democrat–Republican	Charles Pinckney	Federalist
1812	James Madison[1]	Democrat–Republican	DeWitt Clinton	Federalist
1816	5 James Monroe	Democrat–Republican	Rufus King	Federalist
1820	James Monroe	Democrat–Republican	John Quincy Adams	Democrat–Republican
1824	6 John Quincy Adams	Democrat–Republican	Andrew Jackson	Democrat–Republican
			Henry Clay	Democrat–Republican
			William H Crawford	Democrat–Republican
1828	7 Andrew Jackson	Democrat	John Quincy Adams	National Republican
1832	Andrew Jackson[1]	Democrat	Henry Clay	National Republican
1836	8 Martin Van Buren	Democrat	William Henry Harrison	Whig
1840	9 William Henry Harrison	Whig	Martin Van Buren	Democrat
1841	10 John Tyler[2]	Whig		
1844	11 James K Polk	Democrat	Henry Clay	Whig
1848	12 Zachary Taylor	Whig	Lewis Cass	Democrat
1850	13 Millard Fillmore[3]	Whig		
1852	14 Franklin Pierce	Democrat	Winfield Scott	Whig
1856	15 James Buchanan	Democrat	John C Fremont	Republican
1860	16 Abraham Lincoln	Republican	Stephen Douglas	Democrat
			John Breckinridge	Democrat
			John Bell	Constitutional Union
1864	Abraham Lincoln[1]	Republican	George McClellan	Democrat
1865	17 Andrew Johnson[4]	Democrat		
1868	18 Ulysses S Grant	Republican	Horatio Seymour	Democrat
1872	Ulysses S Grant[1]	Republican	Horace Greeley	Democrat–Liberal Republican
1876	19 Rutherford B Hayes	Republican	Samuel Tilden	Democrat
1880	20 James A Garfield	Republican	Winfield Hancock	Democrat
1881	21 Chester A Arthur[5]	Republican		
1884	22 Grover Cleveland	Democrat	James Blaine	Republican
1888	23 Benjamin Harrison	Republican	Grover Cleveland	Democrat
1892	24 Grover Cleveland	Democrat	Benjamin Harrison	Republican
		James Weaver	People's	
1896	25 William McKinley	Republican	William J Bryan	Democrat–People's
1900	William McKinley[1]	Republican	William J Bryan	Democrat
1901	26 Theodore Roosevelt[6]	Republican		
1904	Theodore Roosevelt[1]	Republican	Alton B Parker	Democrat
1908	27 William Howard Taft	Republican	William J Bryan	Democrat
1912	28 Woodrow Wilson	Democrat	Theodore Roosevelt	Progressive
		William Howard Taft	Republican	
1916	Woodrow Wilson[1]	Democrat	Charles E Hughes	Republican
1920	29 Warren G Harding	Republican	James M Cox	Democrat
1923	30 Calvin Coolidge[7]	Republican		
1924	Calvin Coolidge[1]	Republican	John W Davis	Democrat
		Robert M LaFollette	Progressive	
1928	31 Herbert Hoover	Republican	Alfred E Smith	Democrat
1932	32 Franklin D Roosevelt	Democrat	Herbert C Hoover	Republican
		Norman Thomas	Socialist	

Appendix

Year elected/ took office		President	Party	Losing candidate(s)	Party
1936		Franklin D Roosevelt[1]	Democrat	Alfred Landon	Republican
1940		Franklin D Roosevelt[1]	Democrat	Wendell Willkie	Republican
1944		Franklin D Roosevelt[1]	Democrat	Thomas E Dewey	Republican
1945	33	Harry S Truman[8]	Democrat		
1948		Harry S Truman[1]	Democrat	Thomas E Dewey	Republican
			J Strom Thurmond	States' Rights	
			Henry A Wallace	Progressive	
1952	34	Dwight D Eisenhower	Republican	Adlai E Stevenson	Democrat
1956		Dwight D Eisenhower[1]	Republican	Adlai E Stevenson	Democrat
1960	35	John F Kennedy	Democrat	Richard M Nixon	Republican
1963	36	Lyndon B Johnson[9]	Democrat		
1964		Lyndon B Johnson[1]	Democrat	Barry M Goldwater	Republican
1968	37	Richard M Nixon	Republican	Hubert H Humphrey	Democrat
				George C Wallace	American Independent
1972		Richard M Nixon[1]	Republican	George S McGovern	Democrat
1974	38	Gerald R Ford[10]	Republican		
1976	39	James Earl Carter	Democrat	Gerald R Ford	Republican
1980	40	Ronald Reagan	Republican	James Earl Carter	Democrat
				John B Anderson	Independent
1984		Ronald Reagan[1]	Republican	Walter Mondale	Democrat
1988	41	George Bush	Republican	Michael Dukakis	Democrat
				Ross Perot	Independent
1992	42	Bill Clinton	Democrat	George Bush	Republican
1996		Bill Clinton[1]	Democrat	Bob Dole	Republican
				Ross Perot	Reform
2000	43	George W Bush	Republican	Al Gore	Democrat
				Ralph Nader	Green Party
2004		George W Bush	Republican	John Kerry	Democrat
				Ralph Nader	Independent

[1] Re-elected.
[2] Became president on death of Harrison.
[3] Became president on death of Taylor.
[4] Became president on assassination of Lincoln.
[5] Became president on assassination of Garfield.
[6] Became president on assassination of McKinley.
[7] Became president on death of Harding.
[8] Became president on death of F D Roosevelt.
[9] Became president on assassination of Kennedy.
[10] Became president on resignation of Nixon and Agnew.

Finding further information on the internet

The internet has a vast amount of information available to academics, students and the general reader. Finding reliable data should not be difficult although a few points need to ibe borne in mind. The material should be up to date. Small organizations and departments within academic institutions sometimes encounter funding difficulties and are unable to continue with their researches. Make sure to look at the 'Last updated' section of the main website page before using any data. Try clicking on the links to make sure that they have been maintained properly and do not result in error messages. Ideally information should be obtained from websites run by universities, research institutes, and other reputable organizations. Websites maintained by individuals may not be up to date and comprehensive. It is also possible that the prejudices of those maintaining the websites will be reflected in the content and list of links. There are a number of encyclopedias available on the internet, although some only give small amounts of information on each topic. One of the most interesting sites to visit is www.wikipedia.org.

abstract expressionism
www.artlex.com/ArtLex/a/abstractexpr.htm
http://wwar.com/categories/Artists/Masters

addiction
www.addictionsearch.com
www.adpana.com
www.alcoholicsanonymous.org

aeronautics
www.sae.org/technology/aerospace.htm
www.aeronautics.ru/links.htm

aeroplane
www.aerospaceweb.org/aircraft/index.shtml
www.airliners.net/info

Afghanistan
www.afghanistan.org

African National Congress
www.anc.org.za

African Union
www.africa-union.org

agriculture
www.vlib.org/Agriculture.html
www.agnic.org
www.fao.org

AIDS
www.aids.org
www.amfar.org

Albania
www.instat.gov.al

Alberta
www.gov.ab.ca
www.discoveralberta.com

alcohol
www.ias.org.uk
www.alcoholconcern.org.uk

Algeria
www.gouvernement.dz

allergy
www.aafa.org

alphabet
www.omniglot.com/writing/atoz.htm

Alzheimer's disease
www.zarcrom.com/users/yeartorem
www.alz.org

American football
www.nfl.com

Andorra
www.andorra.ad

angling
www.cips-fips.org

Angola
www.angola.org

animal
www.biosis.org.uk/free_resources/classifn/
    classifn.html
http://animaldiversity.ummz.umich.edu/
    index.html

anthropology
http://vlib.anthrotech.com/
www.sosig.ac.uk/anthropology/
www.rai.anthropology.org.uk

Antigua and Barbuda
www.antiguagov.com
www.antigua-barbuda.org

Anzac
www.anzacs.net
www.awm.gov.au

apartheid
www.apartheidmuseum.org
http://racerelations.about.com/cs/apartheid

archaeology
www.britac.ac.uk/portal/
    bysection.asp?section=H7

archery
www.archery.org

architecture
www.architecture.com
www.architectureweek.com
http://architecture.about.com

Argentina
www.nic.ar
www.turismo.gov.ar

Armenia
www.armenia.com

art deco
www.art-deco.com

art nouveau
www.artchive.com/artchive/art_nouveau.htm

Association of South East Asian Nations
www.aseansec.org

Assyria
www.allempires.com/empires/assyria

astronomy
www.astronomy.net
www.astronomytoday.com
www.astronomynow.com
www.popastro.com/home.htm
www.bbc.co.uk/science/space
www.rog.nmm.ac.uk

athletics
www.iaaf.org

Auckland
www.aucklandcity.govt.nz
www.aucklandnz.com

Australia
www.gov.au
www.australia.com

Austria
www.austria.org
www.austria-tourism.at

Azerbaijan
www.president.az

Aztec
www.aztecempire.com
www.indians.org/welker/aztec.html

Babylonia
http://ragz-international.com/babylonia.htm
www.bible-history.com/babylonia

backgammon
www.worldbackgammonfederation.com

badminton
www.intbadfed.org

Bahamas
www.bahamas.com
www.bahamas.gv.bs

Bahrain
www.bahrain.gov.bh
www.bahraintourism.com

ballet
www.ballet.co.uk
www.culturekiosque.com/dance

balloon
www.fai.org/ballooning

Bangladesh
www.bangladeshgov.org
www.bangladesh.com

Bank of England
www.bankofengland.co.uk

Barbados
www.barbados.gov.bb
www.barbados.org

baroque
http://witcombe.sbc.edu/ARTHbaroque.html
www.artlex.com/ArtLex/b/baroque.html
www.baroquemusic.org
www.baroque-music.co.uk

baseball
www.majorleaguebaseball.com
www.baseball-links.com

basketball
www.basketball.com
www.nba.com

batik
www.batikguild.org.uk

Bauhaus
www.cs.umb.edu/~alilley/bauhaus.html

Bayeaux
http://hastings1066.com/baythumb.shtml
www.historylearningsite.co.uk/
  bayeaux_tapestry.htm

BBC (British Broadcasting Corporation)
www.bbc.co.uk

beer
www.realbeer.com
www.howstuffworks.com/beer.htm

Belarus
www.president.gov.by
www.belarustourist.minsk.by

Belgium
www.belgium.be
www.visitbelgium.com

Belize
www.belize.gov.bz
www.travelbelize.org

Benin
www.benintourisme.com

Bhutan
www.bhutan.gov.bt
www.tourism.gov.bt

bicycle
www.ibike.org

billiards
http://moveto/wbfsuperstars

biochemistry
http://restools.sdsc.edu/
www.geocities.com/peterroberts.geo/
  biology.htm#bioch

biodiversity
www.biosis.org.uk/zrdocs/zoolinfo/biodiv.htm
www.eti.uva.nl
www.biodiv.org

biological warfare
www.howstuffworks.com/biochem_war.htm

biology
http://mcb.harvard.edu/BioLinks
http://biology-online.org/
http://cellbiol.com/
www.webref.org/biology/biology.htm

biotechnology
www.cato.com/biotech
www.academicinfo.net/biotechmeta.html
www.bio.com

blindness
www.eyecarefoundation.org

blues
http://members.lycos.nl/bluesmanharry
www.allmusic.com
www.jazzinamerica.org

Boer War
www.wikipedia.org/wiki/Boer_War
www.nationmaster.com/encyclopedia/Boer-War

Bolivia
www.bolivia.gov.bo
www.bolivia-tourism.com

Bolshevik
www.imternationalist.org/
stalinism&bolshevism.html
www.1upinfo.com/encyclopedia/B/
Bolshevism.html

bomb
www.fas.org/man/dod-101/sys/dumb

boogie-woogie
www.jazzinamerica.org

Bosnia-Herzogovina
www.fbihvlada.gov.ba
www.bhtourism.ba

botany
www.ou.edu/cas/botany-micro/www-vl
www.botany.net/IDB
www.academicinfo.net/bot.html

Botswana
www.gov.bw
www,gov.bw/tourism

boules
http://boules.dsnsports.com/accueil_fib

bowls
www.wbc.org.uk
www.lawnbowls.com

boxing
www.ibf-usba-boxing.com
www.wbaonline.com
www.wbcboxing.com

www.ibuboxing.com
www.aiba.net
www.wibf.org

Braille
www.braille.org

Brazil
www.brazil.gov.br

brewing
www.beerinfo.com/vlib/index.html

British Columbia
www.gov.bc.ca
www.bc-tourism.com

British Empire
www.britishempire.co.uk
www.empiremuseum.co.uk

Brunei
www.brunei.gov.bn

Bulgaria
www.government.bg/English
www.tourism-bulgaria.com

Burkina-Faso
www.primature.gov.bf

Burundi
http://burundi.gov.bi

Byzantine
www.archaeolink.com/
byzantine_civilization.htm
www.metmuseum.org/explore/
Byzantium/art.html
http://historymedren.about.com/cs/
byzantinestudies

Byzantine Empire
http://chaos1.hypermart.net/byz/tbe.html
www.gogreece.com/learn/history/
Byzantine_empire.html

calligraphy
www.chinapage.com/callig1.htm
www.sakkal.com/ArtArabicCalligraphy.htm
www.islamicart.com/main/calligraphy

Cambodia
www.camnet.com.kh/ocm

Cameroon
www.spm.gov.cm
www.camnet.cm/mintour/tourisme

Canada
http://canada.gc.ca
www.travelcanada.org

cancer
www.jasperweb.com/texascanceronline
www.cancercare.org

Cape Verde
www.governo.cv

car
www.planet-cars.net

CARICOM
www.caricom.org

caviar
www.foodsubs.com/Caviar.html

Celt
www.ibiblio.org/gaelic/celts.html
http://celt.net/Celtic/celtopedia/indices/
encyintro.html

census
www.census.gov/ipc/www/idbnew.html

Central African Republic
http://segegob.cl

ceramic
www.acers.org
www.ceramicsmonthly.org
www.ceramicstoday.com

Chad
www.tit.td

champagne
www.champagne.com

cheese
www.cheese.com
www.cheesesociety.org

chemical warfare
www.howstuffworks.com/biochem_war.htm

chemistry
www.chemweb.com
www.psigate.ac.uk/newsite

chess
www.fide.com

Chile
www.gov.cl

China
www.china.org.cn/english
www.cnto.org.au

choreography
www.instchordance.com
www.culturekiosque.com/dance

cinema
www.cinema.com
www.sensesofcinema.com
www.learner.org/exhibits/cinema
www.scoot.co.uk/cinemafinder/default.asp

civil engineering
www.ce.gatech.edu/WWW-CE/

Civil War, American
http://americancivilwar.com
www.civilwar.com

Civil War, English
www.open2.net/civilwar
http://easyweb.easynet.co.uk/~crossby/ECW

coffee
www.coffeeresearch.org
www.ico.org
www.nationalgeographic.com/coffee

cold war
www.coldwar.org
www.fas.harvard.edu/~hpcws

Colombia
www.gobiernoenlinea.gov.co
www.idct.gov.co

Commonwealth
www.thecommonwealth.org

Comoros
www.presidence-uniondescomores.com/v3/us/

computer
www.vlib.org/Computing.html

Congo
www.rdcongo.org
www.congo-site.cg

conquistador
www.bbc.co.uk/history/discovery/
exploration/conquistadors
www.incaconquest.com

constant
http://physics.nist.gov/cuu/Constants/
index.html

constitution
www.psa.ac.uk/www/constitutions.htm
www.kmtspace.com/constructivism.htm

cosmology
www.damtp.cam.ac.uk/user/gr/public/
cos_home.html

Costa Rica
www.casapres.go.cr
www.visitcostarica.com

Côte d'Ivoire
www.presidence.gov.ci
www.encodivoire.com/En/tourisme.php

Covenanter
www.tartans.com/articles/covmain.html
www.sorbie.net/covenanters.htm

cricket
www.cricket.org

Croatia
www.vlada.hr
www.croatia.hr

croquet
www.croquet.org.uk
www.croquetamerica.com

crusade
www.medievalcrusades.com
www.fordham.edu/halsall/sbook.1k.html

Cuba
www.cubagob.cu/ingles
www.cubatravel.cu

cubism
www.artlex.com/ArtLex/c/cubism.html
http://wwar.com/categories/Artists/Masters/
Cubism
http://abstractart.20m.com/cubism.htm

curling
http://icing.org

Cyprus
www.pio.gov.cy
www.cyprustourism.org

Czech Republic
www.czech.cz
www.visitczech.cz

Dada
www.peak.org/~dadaist/English/Graphics

Dark Ages
http://cfcc.net/dutch/DarkAges.htm
www.fernweb.pwp.blueyonder.co.uk/mf

darts
www.dartswdf.com

D-day
www.dday.co.uk
www.ddaymuseum.org

deafness
www.drf.org

Decorated style
www.britainexpress.com/architecture/
    decorated.htm

demography
www.un.org/popin/data.html
http://unstats.un.org/unsd/demographic/
    social/default.htm

Denmark
www.denmark.dk
www.visitdenmark.com

dentistry
www.dental—health.com

dermatology
www.aad.org

diabetes
www.insulinchoice.org
www.diabetes.org.uk

diamond
www.adiamondisforever.com
www.amnh.org/exhibitions/diamonds

Dixieland jazz
www.jazzinamerica.org

Djibouti
www.republique-djibouti.com/
    gouvernement.htm

Domesday Book
www.domesdaybook.co.uk
www.pro.gov.uk/virtualmuseum/
    millennium/domesday/book

Dominica
www.ndcdominica.dm

Dominican Republic
www.presidencia.gov.do
www.dominicanrepublic.com/Tourism

drama
http://vl-theatre.com

draughts
www.fmjd.nl

druid
www.crystalinks.com/druids.html
http://celt.net/Celtic/History/druidsintro.html

dyeing
www.straw.com/sig/dyehist.html
www.ritdye.com

Early English
www.britainexpress.com/architecture/
    early-english.htm

Earth
http://earthobservatory.nasa.gov
www.earth.nasa.gov
www.itc.nl

earth science
www.psigate.ac.uk/newsite/earth-gateway.html

East Timor
www.gov.east-timor.org
www.econometricsociety.org

economics
www.sosig.ac.uk/economics/
www.res.org.uk

ECOWAS
www.ecowas.int

Ecuador
www.ec-gov.net
www.vivecuador.com/html2/eng/
    tourism_news.htm

EFTA
www.efta.int

Egypt
www.sis.gov.eg
www.egypttourism.org

Egypt, ancient
www.ancientegypt.co.uk
www.ancient-egypt.org

election
www.electionworld.org/

electronic publishing
www.elpub.org

electronics
www.eetuk.com

El Salvador
www.el-salvador.org.il
www.elsalvadorturismo.gob.sv

engineering
www.er-online.co.uk/others.htm
www.eevl.ac.uk
www.e4engineering.com

England
www.visitengland.com

environment
www.conservation.org
www.doc.mmu.ac.uk/aric/eae/english.html

epilepsy
www.apa.org/science/efa.html

Equatorial Guinea
www.ceiba-equatorial-guinea.org

Eritrea
www.shabait.com

Estonia
www.riik.ee/en/valitsus
http://visitestonia.com

Ethiopia
www.ethiopar.net/English/contents.htm
www.tourismethiopia.org

ethnography
www.sosig.ac.uk/roads/subject-listing/
    World-cat/ethnostud.html

Etruscan
www.mysteriousetruscans.com
www.crystalinks.com/etruscians.html

European Commission
http://europa.eu.int/comm/index_en.htm

European Council
http://ue.eu.int/en/summ.htm

European Parliament
www.europarl.eu.int/home/default_en.htm

European Union
www.europa.eu.int/index_en.htm
www.eia.org.uk/websites.htm

expressionism
www.artlex.com/ArtLex/e/Expressionism.html
www.ibiblio.org/wm/paint/tl/20th/
    expressionism.html

family planning
www.icea.org

Fascism
www.fordham.edu/halshall/mod/
    modsbook42.html
www.remember.org/hist.root.what.html

Fauvism
www.ibiblio.org/wm/paint/glo/fauvism
www.artlex.com/ArtLex/f/fauvism.html

FBI
www.fbi.gov

fencing
www.fencing.net
www.foilcommittee.pwp.blueyonder.co.uk

Fiji
www.fiji.gov.fj

film noir
www.filmsite.org/filmnoir.html
www.nyfavideo.com

Finland
www.valtioneuvosto.fi/vn/liston/base.lsp?k=en
www.finland-tourism.com

football
www.fifa.com

football, Australian Rules
www.afl.com.au

forestry
www.metla.fi/info/vlib/Forestry
www.forestry.gov.uk

Formula 1
www.formula1.com
www.fia.com

France
www.assemblee-nationale.com/
    english/index.asp
www.francetourism.com

French Foreign Legion
www.foreignlegionlife.com

fungus
www.agarics.org/Index.jsp
www.fungaljungal.org
www.botanical.com
www.ucmp.berkeley.edu/fungi/fungi.html
http://elib.cs.berkeley.edu/photos/fungi

Futurism
www.futurism.org.uk/futurism.htm

Gabon
www.tourisme-gabon.com

Gambia
www.gambia.com

gem
www.min.uni-bremen.de/sgmcol

genetics
www.geneticalliance.org
www.genetics.org

geography
www.sosig.ac.uk/geography

geology
www.psigate.ac.uk/newsite/
    earth-gateway.html
www.earthquakes.bgs.ac.uk

Georgia
www.parliament.ge

Germany
www.bundesregierung.de
www.visits-to-germany.com

Ghana
www.ghana.gov.gh

golf
www.pga.com
www.randa.org

gospel music
www.gospelmusic.org

Gothic
www.greatbuildings.com/types/styles/gothic.html

Gothic Revival
www.britainexpress.com/architecture

Greece
www.parliament.gr/english/default.asp
www.gnto.gr

Greece, ancient
www.ancientgreece.com
www.historylink101.com/ancient_greece.htm

Grenada
http://grenadagrenadines.com

Guatemala
www.congreso.gob.gt
www.terra.com.gt/turismogt

Guinea
www.guinee.gov.gn

Gulf War
www.ngwrc.org

gymnastics
www.fig-gymnastics.com

haemophilia
www.hemophilia.org

Haiti
www.port-haiti.com
www.haititourisme.org

heart
www.americanheart.org

helicopter
www.helicoptermuseum.org/museum/links.htm
www.helikopter.li

heraldry
www.college-of-arms.gov.uk
www.heraldica.org

hip-hop
www.hiphop-elements.com

Hiroshima
www.lclark.edu/~history/HIROSHIMA

hockey
www.fihockey.org

Holocaust
www.holocaust-history.org
www.nizkor.org

Holy Roman Empire
www.heraldica.org/topics/national/hre.htm

homeopathy
www.homeopathy.org

Honduras
www.congreso.gob.hn

Hubble Space Telescope
http://hubblesite.org
www.gsfc.nasa.gov

human rights
www.unhchr.ch
www.echr.coe.int

Hungary
www.mkogy.hu
www.gotohungary.com

hurling
www.gaa.ie/sports/hurling

hydrography
www.imo.org/home.asp

ice hockey
www.iihf.com
www.nhl.com

Iceland
http://government.is
www.icetourist.is

impressionism
www.artcyclopedia.com/history/
    impressionism.html
www.artlex.com/ArtLex/ij/impressionism.html

Inca
www.wsu.edu/~dee/CIVAMRCA/INCAS.HTM
www.incaconquest.com

India
http://goidirectory.nic.in
http://goidirectory.nic.in/tourism.htm

Indonesia
www.indonesia.go.id
www.indonesiatourism.com

Industrial Revolution
http://members.aol.com/TeacherNet/
    Industrial.html
www.bergen.org/technology/industrial

Inquisition
www.fordham.edu/halsall/source/
    inquisition1.html
www.catholic.com/library/inquisition.asp

International Court of Justice
www.icj-cij.org

Interpol
www.interpol.int

Iran
www.president.ir
www.itto.org

Iraq
www.iraq.net

Ireland
www.irlgov.ie
www.ireland.travel.ie

Israel
www.mfa.gov.il
www.goisrael.com

Italy
www.italiantourism.com
www.governo.it

Jacobean
www.building-history.pwp.blueyonder.co.uk
www.probertencyclopaedia.com/T8.HTM

Jamaica
www.cabinet.gov.jm
www.conferencejamaica.com/
  tourist-board.htm

Japan
http://jin.jcic.or.jp
www.jnto.go.jp

jazz
www.apassion4jazz.net
www.jazzreview.com
www.allmusic.com
www.jazzonln.com
www.jazzinamerica.org

Jodrell Bank
www.jb.man.ac.uk

Jordan
www.kinghussein.gov.jo/government.html
www.see-jordan.com

judo
www.ijf.org
worldjudo.org

Jupiter
www.solarviews.com/eng/jupiter.htm

karate
www.wkf.net
www.itkf.org

Kazakhstan
www.president.kz
www.kazconsul.ca

Kenya
http://kenya.go.ke
www.magicalkenya.com

kidney
www.kidney.org

Kiribati
www.tskl.net.ki/Kiribati
www.tskl.net.ki/Kiribati/tourism/index.htm

Kuwait
www.kems.net
www.kuwaitiah.net/tourism.html

Kyrgyzstan
www.gov.kg

lacrosse
www.lacrosse.ca

language
www.britac.ac.uk/portal/
www.ilovelanguages.com
http://babel.uoregon.edu/yamada/guides.html
www.languagelearn.co.uk
www.languages-on-the-web.com

Laos
www.global.lao.net/laovl/gov.htm
www.visit-mekong.com/laos

Latvia
www.saeima.lv/index_eng.html
www.latviatourism.com

law
www.worldlii.org
www.llrx.com
www.law.gla.ac.uk/scot_guide/guide.html

Lebanon
www.presidency.gov.lib
www.lebanon-tourism.gov.lb

Lesotho
www.lesotho.gov.ls
www.lesotho.gov.ls/mnsports.htm

Liberia
www.liberiaemb.org

Libya
www.libya-un.org

Liechtenstein
www.liechtenstein.li
www.tourismus.li

life science
www.vlib.org/Biosciences.html
www.sciencekomm.at/
www.biologybrowser.org
http://biotech.icmb.utexas.edu

linen
www.irishlinen.co.uk
www.ulsterlinen.com/2.htm

linguistics
www.britac.ac.uk/portal/
http://linguistlist.org/sp/LangAnalysis.html
www-nlp.stanford.edu/links/
  linguistics.html
www.phil.uni-passau.de/linguistik/
  linguistik_urls

literature
www.britac.ac.uk/portal/
http://etext.lib.virginia.edu/modeng/
  modeng0.browse.html
www.lib.virginia.edu/wess/etexts.html
www.themodernword.com/themodword.cfm

Lithuania
www.lrv.lt/main_en.php
www.tourism.lt

liver
www.liverfoundation.org

Luxembourg
www.ont.lu
www.luxembourg.co.uk

Macedonia
www.gov.mk

macroeconomics
www.stern.nyu.edu/globalmacro

Madagascar
www.embassy.org/madagascar

Magna Carta
www.bl.uk/collections/treasures/magna.html

Malawi
www.malawi.gov.mv

Maldives
www.maldivesinfo.gov.mv
www.visitmaldives.com

Mali
www.maliendsdelexterieur.gov.ml

Malta
www.malta.co.uk/malta/geninfo.htm
www.visitmalta.com

Manitoba
www.gov.mb.ca
www.travelmanitoba.com

mannerism
www.artcyclopedia.com/history/
  mannerism.html
www.artlex.com/ArtLex/m/mannerism.html
www.tigtail.org/TVM/M_View/X1/
  c.Mannerism

Mars
mars.jpl.nasa.gov
www.solarviews.com/eng/mars.htm

Marshall Islands
www.miembassyus.org
www.visitmarshallislands.com

martial art
www.martialinfo.com
martialarts.about.com

mathematics
www.martindalecenter.com/GradMath.html
www.math.psu.edu/MathLists/Contents.html
http://carbon.cudenver.edu/~hgreenbe/
  glossary/index.php

Mauritania
www.mauritania.mr

Mauritius
www.gov.mu
www.mauritius.net

Maya
www.indians.org/welker/mayamenu.htm
www.wsu.edu:8080/~dee/CIVAMRCA/
  MAYAS.HTM

MCC
www.lords.org/mcc

medicine
www.medhelp.org
www.medbioworld.com/home/lists/
  med-db.html
www.ipl.org/div/subject/browse/hea00.00.00/

Mercury
http://pds.jpl.nasa.gov/planets/choices/
  mercury1.htm

Mesopotamia
www.mesopotamia.co.uk/menu.html
www.fordham.edu/halsall/ancient/
  asbook03.html

metallurgy
www.psigate.ac.uk/newsite/materials-
  gateway.html

meteorology
http://sciencepolicy.colorado.edu/socasp/
  toc_img.html
http://webs.cmich.edu/resgi/
www.wmo.ch
www.worldweather.org

Mexico
www.presidencia.gob.mx
www.visitmexico.com
www.travelguidemexico.com

microbiology
www.microbiol.org/vl_micro
www.microbes.inf
www.virology.net

microeconomics
www.helsinki.fi/WebEc/webecd.html

Micronesia
www.fsmgov.org
visit-fsm.org

Middle Ages
www.mnsu.edu/emuseum/history/middleages
http://radiantworks.com/middleages

mineral
www.psigate.ac.uk/newsite/earth-gateway.html
www.minerals.net/glossary/glossary.htm

minimalism
www.artlex.com/ArtLex/m/minimalism.html
www.nortexinfo.net/McDaniel/
  minimalist_music.htm

mining
http://dir.yahoo.com/Science/Engineering/
  Mining

Minoan
www.historywiz.com/minoans-mm.htm
www.dragonridge.com/greece/minoan1.htm

missile
http://jmr.janes.com
www.fas.org/man/dod-101/sys/missile

modernism
www.artsmia.org/modernism
www.bc.edu/bc_org/avp/cas/fnart/HP/
  20th_mod.html

Mogul
www.wikipedia.org/wiki/Mogul_Empire
www.nationmaster.com/encyclopedia/
  Mogul-Empire

Moldova
www.moldova.md
www.turism.md

Monaco
www.monaco.gouv.mc/PortGb
www.visitmonaco.com

monetarism
www.econlib.org/library/Enc/Monetarism.html

Mongolia
www.pmis.gov.mn/indexeng.php
www.mongoliatourism.gov.mn
www.asianinfo.org

Morocco
www.mincom.gov.ma

Motown
www.motown.com

Mozambique
www.mozambique.mz

music
www.allmusic.com
www.musicsearch.com
www.dotmusic.com
www.music.ucc.ie/wrrm
www.classical.net
www.essentialsofmusic.com/glossary/n.html
www.nme.com

musical
www.musicals101.com

music hall
www.rfwilmut.clara.net
www.theatrelinks.com

Myanmar
www.myanmar.com
www.myanmar-tourism.com/
about_myanmar.htm

Mycenaean
www.archaeonia.com/history/mycenaean.htm

Namibia
www.grnnet.gov.na
www.met.gov.na

nanotechnology
www.nano.org.uk/links.htm
www.nano.gov

NASA
www.nasa.gov

National Curriculum
www.nc.uk.net/index.html

NATO
www.nato.int

Nauru
www.un.int/nauru

navigation
www.navcen.uscg.gov
www.rin.org.uk

Nazi
www.phoenixpress.co.uk/articles/
institution/national-socialism-pp.asp
www.tiscali.co.uk/reference/encyclopaedia/
hutchinson/M0010979.html
http://en.wikipedia.org/wiki/Nazism

neoclassicism
www.comcen.com.au/~carowley/neoclass.htm
www.hypermusic.ca/hist/twentieth3.html

Nepal
www.nepalhmg.gov.np
www.welcomenepal.com

Neptune
http://solarsystem.nasa.gov/features/planets

netball
www.netball.org

Netherlands
www.overheid.nl/guest
www.visitholland.com

New Brunswick
www.gnb.ca
www.tourismenouveau-brunswick.ca/
Cultures/en-CA/welcome.htm

Newfoundland
www.gov.nf.ca
www.gov.nf.ca/tourism

New South Wales
www.nsw.gov.au
www.tourism.nsw.gov.au

New Zealand
www.govt.nz/en/aboutnz
www.purenz.com

Nicaragua
www.asamblea.gob.ni
www.visit-nicaragua.com

Niger
www.delgi.ne/presidence

Nigeria
www.nigeria.gov.ng
www.nigeriatourism.net

No
www.jinjapan.org/access/noh
www.iijnet.or.jp/NOH-KYOGEN/english/
english.html

Nobel prize
www.nobel.se

Norman
www.bbc.co.uk/history/war/normans
/index.shtml
www.spartacus.schoolnet.co.uk/Normans.htm

Northern Ireland
www.nio.gov.uk
www.discovernorthernireland.com

Northern Territory
www.nt.gov.au
www.nttc.com.au

North Korea
www.korea-dpr.com

Northland
www.nrc.govt.nz
www.northland-nz.worldweb.com

Northwest Territories
www.gov.nt.com
www.nwttravel.nt.ca

Norway
http://odin.dep.no/smk/engelsk/
regjeringen/index-b-n-a.html
www.visitnorway.com

Nova Scotia
www.gov.ns.ca
www.gov.ns.ca/tourism.htm

nuclear bomb
http://science.howstuffworks.com/
nuclear-bomb.htm

nuclear physics
http://ie.lbl.gov/education/glossary/
glossaryf.htm
www.atomicarchive.com
www.visionlearning.com/library/
module_viewer.php?mid=59
www.iaea.org/inis/ws/

nutrition
www.crnusa.org

OECD
www.oecd.org

Olmec
www.beautyworlds.com/olmecs.htm
www.bbc.co.uk/dna/h2g2/A414109

Olympic Games
www.olympics.org

Oman
www.omanet.com
www.omantourism.gov.om

Ontario
www.gov.on.ca
www.tourism.gov.on.ca/english

op art
www.artcyclopedia.com/history/optical.html
www.artlex.com/ArtLex/o/opart.html

OPEC
www.opec.org

opera
www.aria-database.com/index2.html
http://theoperacritic.com
www.teatroallascala.org

operetta
www.operetta.org

Ottoman Empire
www.wsu.edu:8080/~dee/OTTOMAN/
CONTENTS.HTM
http://campus.northpark.edu/history/
WebChron/MiddleEast/Ottoman.html

pain
www.painconsultant.com
www.theacpa.org

Pakistan
www.pak.org
www.tourism.gov.pk

palaeontology
www.ucmp.berkeley.edu/index.html
www.dinosauria.com

Palladian
www.britainexpress.com/architecture

Panama
www.pa
www.visitpanama.com

papacy
www.wayoflife.org/papacy

Papua New Guinea
www.pngonline.gov.pg

Paraguay
www.presidencia.gov.py
www.senataur.gov.py

Paris
www.paris.org

Paris Commune
www.wikipedia.org/wiki/Paris_Commune
www.library.northwestern.edu/spec/siege

parliament
www.ipu.org/english/parlweb.htm

pathology
www.medbioworld.com/home/lists/
diseases.html
www.cdc.gov/health

Pearl Harbor
www.history.navy.mil/faqs/faq66-1.htm
www.ibiscom.com/pearl.htm

periodic table
www.psigate.ac.uk/newsite/reference/
periodic-table.html
www.colorado.edu/physics/2000/applets/
a2.html

Perpendicular
www.britainexpress.com/architecture

Persian Empire
www.wikipedia.org/wiki/Persian_Empire
http://ancienthistory.about.com/cs/
persianempir1

Peru
www.peru.org.pe/defaulteng.htm
www.peruonline.net

pharmacology
www.pharmacy.org
www.pharmweb.net
www.medbioworld.com/home/lists/
medications.html

Philippines
www.gov.ph
www.tourism.gov.ph

Phoenician
www.fordham.edu/halsall/ancient/
430phoenicia.html

phonetics
www2.arts.gla.ac.uk/IPA/ipa.html
http://faculty.washington.edu/dillon/
PhonResources

photography
www.photolinks.net
www.nyip.com

physics
www.physlink.com
www.physicsweb.org
www.vlib.org/Physics.html

physiology
www.physoc.org/links/

Pilgrim Fathers
www.usahistory.info/New-England/
Pilgrims.html
www.mayflowersteps.co.uk

plainsong
www.1upinfo.com/encyclopedia/P/
plainson.html

Plantagenet
www.royal.gov.uk/output/Page58.asp
www.wikipedia.org/wiki/Plantagenet

Pluto
http://solarsystem.nasa.gov/features/planets
www.solarviews.com/eng/pluto.htm

poetry
www.bartleby.com/verse
www.bbc.co.uk/bbcfour/audiointerviews/
professions

pointillism
www.artcyclopedia.com/history/
pointillism.html

poker
www.pokerfederation.com

Poland
www.poland.pl
www.nto-poland.gov.pl/wyd_dwlnd.asp

police
www.police.uk
www.ipa-iac.org/index2.htm

politics
www.political-theory.org/
www.sosig.ac.uk/politics

polo
www.fippolo.com

pop art
www.artchive.com/ftp_site_reg.htm
www.artcyclopedia.com/history/pop.html

pop music
www.dotmusic.com
www.musicsearch.com

www.nme.com
www.popmusic.com

porcelain
www.gotheborg.com
www.porcelainpainters.com

Portugal
www.portugal.gov.pt
www.portugalinsite.pt

postimpressionism
www.artchive.com/ftp_site_reg.htm
www.artcyclopedia.com/history

postmodernism
www.haberarts.com

pottery
www.potterymaking.org/pmionline.html
www.ceramicstoday.com
www.studiopottery.com

Pre-Raphaelite
www.artchive.com/ftp_site_reg.htm

Prince Edward Island
www.gov.pe.ca
www.gov.pe.ca/visitorsguide/index.php3

printing
www.gain.net
www.bpif.org.uk

psychiatry
www.nmha.org
www.psycline.org/journals/psycline.html

psychoanalysis
http://aapsa.org/
www.freudfile.org/psychoanalysis

psychology
www.psych.neu.edu/facllinks
www.sosig.ac.uk/psychology
www.clas.ufl.edu/users/gthursby/psi

punk rock
www.punkrock.org
www.punk77.co.uk

Qatar
www.english.mofa.gov.qa
www.qatartourism.org
www.experienceqatar.com

Quebec
www.gouv.qc.ca/index_en.html
www.tourisme.gouv.qc.ca/anglais

Queensland
www.qld.gov.au
www.qttc.com.au

ragtime
www.wikipedia.org/wiki/Ragtime
www.dropbears.com/r/ragtime
www.jazzinamerica.org

rally
www.worldrally.net
www.ukmotorsport.com

realism
www.artlex.com/ArtLex/r/realism.html
www.artcyclopedia.com/history/realism.html

real tennis
www.real-tennis.com

reformation
http://history.hanover.edu/early/prot.htm
www.wikipedia.org/wiki/
Protestant_Reformation

reggae
http://niceup.com
www.allmusic.com

Renaissance
www.learner.org/exhibits/renaissance
www.ibiblio.org/wm/paint/glo/renaissance

respiration
www.osrc.org

restoration
www.bbc.co.uk/history/timelines/britain/
stu_charles_ii.shtml
www.britainexpress.com/History/
Cromwell_and_Restoration.htm

rhythm and blues
www.rhythm-n-blues.org

rice
www.riceweb.org

rock and roll
www.reasontorock.com
www.allmusic.com
www.dotmusic.com

rococo
www.artchive.com/ftp_site_reg.htm
www.artlex.com/ArtLex/r/rococo.htmlm

Roman Empire
www.roman-empire.net

Romanesque
www.britainexpress.com/architecture

Romania
www.guv.ro
www.romaniatourism.com

romanticism
www.artchive.com/ftp_site_reg.htm
www.artcyclopedia.com/history/
romanticism.html
www.artlex.com/ArtLex/r/romanticism.html

Rome
www.comune.roma.it/eng/index.asp

rowing
www.worldrowing.com

rugby league
http://world.rleague.com

rugby union
www.irfu.com
www.irfb.com

Russia
www.gov.ru
www.russiatourism.ru

Rwanda
www.rwanda1.com
www.rwandatourism.com

Saint Kitts and Nevis
www.stkittsnevis.net
www.stkitts-tourism.com

Saint Lucia
www.stlucia.gov.lc
www.stlucia.org

Saint Vincent and the Grenadines
www.svgtourism.com

Samoa
www.govt.ws
www.visitsamoa.ws

samurai
www.samurai-archives.com

San Marino
www.sanmarinosite.com
www.interni.segreteria.sm

São Tomé and Príncipe
www.uns.st
www.sao-tome.com/english.html

Saskatchewan
www.gov.sk.ca
www.sasktourism.com

Saturn
www.solarviews.com/eng/saturn.htm
http://nssdc.gsfc.nasa.gov/planetary/planets

Saudi Arabia
www.saudinf.com

Saxon
www.anglo-saxons.net
www.bbc.co.uk/history/ancient/
anglo_saxons/index.shtml

science
www.scicentral.com
www.100TopScienceSites.com
www.sciencedaily.com
www.treasure-troves.com
www.science.gov
www.scitechresources.gov
www.howstuffworks.com
http://vlib.org/Science.html
http://gill.stanford.edu/collect/science
www.getscience.co.uk
www.eurekalert.org

Scotland
www.scotland.gov.uk
www.visitscotland.com

sculpture
www.sculptor.org
www.bluffton.edu/~sullivanm/index

Senegal
www.gouv.sn
www.senegal-tourism.com

Serbia
www.serbia.sr.gov.yu
www.montenegro.yu/english
www.visit-montenegro.com

Seven Wonders of the World
www.unmuseum.org/wonders.htm

Seven Years' War
www.militaryheritage.com/7yrswar.htm
www.usahistory.com/wars/sevenyrs.htm

Seychelles
www.seychelles.com

ship
www.janes.com/transport/digests/ship.shtml

SI
www.bipm.fr/en/si

Sierra Leone
www.sierraleone.gov.sl

Singapore
www.gov.sg
www.visitsingapore.com

skiing
www.fis-ski.com

slave trade
www.spartacus.schoolnet.co.uk/slavery.htm
http://webworld.unesco.org/slave_quest/en

sleep
www.sleepfoundation.org
www.stanford.edu/~dement

Slovakia
www.government.gov.sk
www.slovakia.org

Slovenia
www.sigov.si
www.slovenia-tourism.si

snooker
www.worldsnooker.com

social science
www.sosig.ac.uk/social_science_general

sociology
www.sosig.ac.uk/sociology

solar system
www.solarviews.com
www.the-solar-system.net

Solomon Islands
www.solomons.com
www.commerce.gov.sb/Tourism

soul
www.jazzinamerica.org
www.bluesandsoul.co.uk

South Africa
www.gov.za
www.southafrica.net

South Australia
www.sa.gov.au
www.tourism.sa.gov.au

South Korea
www.korea.net
http://english.tour2korea.com

South Sea Bubble
www.dal.ca/~dmcneil/sketch.html
www.historyhouse.com/in_history/south_sea

Spain
www.la-moncloa.es
www.spain.info

Sparta
www.sikyon.com/Sparta/history_eg.html

spinal cord
www.spinalcord.uab.edu
www.spinalcord.org

squash
www.worldsquash.org

Sri Lanka
www.priu.gov.lk
www.lanka.net/ctb

statistics
www.sosig.ac.uk/statistics

stroke
www.neuro.wustl.edu/stroke

Stuart
www.royal.gov.uk/output/Page74.asp
www.wsu.edu:8080/~dee/GREECE/
    SPARTA.HTM

submarine
www.howstuffworks.com/submarine.htm

Sudan
www.sudan.gov.sd
www.sudan.net

suffragette
www.cjbooks.demon.co.uk/suffrage.htm
www.san.beck.org/GPJ19-Suffragettes.html

Sumerian
www.crystalinks.com/sumerlanguage.html
www.islandnet.com/~edonon/Sumer.htm

Sun
www.solarviews.com/eng/sun.htm
www.michielb.nl/sun/kaft.htm
www.hao.ucar.edu/public/education/
    education.html

Surinam
www.kabinet.sr.org
www.mintct.sr

surrealism
www.artchive.com/ftp_site_reg.htm

Swaziland
www.gov.sz
www.mintour.gov.sz

Sweden
www.sweden.gov.se
www.visit-sweden.com

swimming
www.fina.org

Switzerland
www.admin.ch
www.switzerlandtourism.ch

Syria
www.moi-syria.com
www.syriatourism.org

table tennis
www.ittf.com
www.ettu.org
www.usatt.org

Taiwan
www.gov.tw
www.tbroc.gov.tw

Tajikistan
www.tjvs.org
www.tajiktour.tajnet.com

Tanzania
www.tanzania.go.tz
www.tanzania-web.com

Tasmania
www.parliament.tas.gov.au
www.discovertasmania.com.au

tea
www.teacouncil.co.uk
www.tea.co.uk

telecommunications
www.analysys.com
www.itu.int/home

television
www.emmys.com

tennis
www.lta.org.uk
www.atptennis.com

terrorism
www.ict.org.il/default.htm
www.un.org/terrorism

textile
www.textilemuseum.org

Thailand
www.thaigov.go.th
www.tourismthailand.org

theatre
http://vl-theatre.com
www.theatrelinks.com
www.uktw.co.uk
www.artslynx.org/theatre

Togo
www.republicoftogo.com

Toltec
www.mnsu.edu/emuseum/prehistory/
latinamerica/meso/cultures/toltec.html
http://members.aol.com/xiuhcoatl/toltec.htm

Tonga
www.pmo.gov.to
www.vacations.tvb.gov.to

trade union
www.tuc.org.uk
www.actu.asn.au
www.union.org.nz
www.clc-ctc.ca
www.cosatu.org.za

Trafalgar
www.nelsonsnavy.co.uk/battle-of-trafalgar.html
www.napoleonguide.com/battle_trafalgar.htm

Trinidad and Tobago
www.gov.tt
www.visittnt.com
www.discover-tt.com

Tudor
www.artchive.com/ftp_site_reg.htm
www.britainexpress.com/architecture/tudor.htm
www.bbc.co.uk/history/timelines/wales/
tudor.shtml
www.2hwy.com/eg/d/dynt.htm

Tunisia
www.tunisiaonline.com
www.tourismtunisia.com

Turkey
www.turkey.org
www.turizm.gov.tr

Turkmenistan
www.turkmenistanembassy.org

Uganda
www.government.go.ug
www.visituganda.com

Ukraine
www.kmu.gov.ua/control/en

UNCTAD
www.unctad.org

UNESCO
www.unesco.org

UNICEF
www.unicef.org

unit
www.psigate.ac.uk/newsite/reference/
units.html
www.ex.ac.uk/cimt/dictunit/dictunit.htm
www.unc.edu/~rowlett/units/index.html

United Arab Emirates
www.uaeinteract.com
www.uae.org.ae/tourist/index.htm

United Kingdom
www.ukonline.gov.uk
www.visitbritain.com

United Nations
www.unsystem.org

United States of America
www.whitehouse.gov/government
www.usatourism.com

Uranus
www.solarviews.com/eng/uranus.htm
http://nssdc.gsfc.nasa.gov/planetary/planets

Uruguay
www.presidencia.gub.uy
www.turismo.gub.uy

Uzbekistan
www.gov.uz
www.uzbekistanembassy.uk.net

Vanuatu
www.vanuatugovernment.gov.vu
www.vanuatutourism.com

Vatican City
www.vatican.va

Venezuela
www.embavenez-us.org
www.turismo-venezuela.com

Venus
http://nssdc.gsfc.nasa.gov/planetary/planets
www.solarviews.com/eng/venus.htm

Victoria
www.vic.gov.au
www.victoria-australia.worldweb.com

Vietnam
www.cpv.org.vn
www.vietnamtourism.com

Viking
http://viking.no/e/
www.pbs.org/wgbh/nova/vikings

virus
www.tulane.edu/~dmsander/garryfavweb.html

volleyball
www.volleyball.org/iva

Wales
www.wales.gov.uk
www.visitwales.com

Warsaw Pact
www.fordham.edu/halsall/mod/
1955warsawpact.html
www.nationmaster.com/encyclopedia/
Warsaw-Pact

Watergate
http://watergate.info
www.wikipedia.org/wiki/Watergate_scandal

water polo
www.fina.org

weather
http://sciencepolicy.colorado.edu/socasp/
toc_img.html

www.wmo.ch
www.worldweather.org

Western Australia
www.wa.gov.au
www.westernaustralia.net

whisky
www.scotchwhisky.net

WHO
www.who.int/en

wine
www.intowine.com

World Bank
www.worldbank.org

world music
www.africanmusic.org
www.ceolas.org/ceolas.html
www.sbgmusic.com/html/teacher/reference/
cultures.html
www.rootsworld.com/rw

World War I
www.worldwar1.com
www.firstworldwar.com

World War II
www.ibiblio.org/pha

wrestling
www.fila-wrestling.com

Yemen
www.nic.gov.ye
www.yementourism.com

yoga
www.yoga.com

Yukon
www.gov.yk.ca
www.yukonweb.com/tourism

Zambia
www.state.gov.zm
www.zambiatourism.com

Zimbabwe
www.zim.gov.zw
www.zimbabwetourism.co.zw

zoology
www.biosis.org.uk/zrdocs/zoolinfo/info_gen.htm
www.academicinfo.net/zoo.html